Baker Encyclopedia of Christian Apologetics

Baker Reference Library

Evangelical Dictionary of Theology
Edited by Walter A. Elwell

Baker Encyclopedia of Psychology
Edited by David G. Benner

Evangelical Commentary on the Bible
Edited by Walter A. Elwell

Topical Analysis of the Bible
Edited by Walter A. Elwell

New Twentieth-Century Encyclopedia of Religious Knowledge
Edited by J. D. Douglas

Handbook of Evangelical Theologians
Edited by Walter A. Elwell

Baker Encyclopedia of Christian Apologetics

Norman L. Geisler

A Division of Baker Book House Co
Grand Rapids, Michigan 49516

Published by Baker Books
a division of Baker Book House Company
P.O. Box 6287, Grand Rapids, MI 49516-6287

Sixth printing, August 2002

Printed in the United States of America

Library of Congress Cataloging-in-Publication Data

Geisler, Norman L.
Baker encyclopedia of Christian apologetics / Norman L. Geisler.
p. cm.
Includes bibliographical references and index.
ISBN 0-8010-2151-0
1. Apologetics—Encyclopedias. I. Title.
BT1102.G42 1998
239'.03—dc 21 98-8735

For information about academic books, resources for Christian leaders, and all new releases available from Baker Book House, visit our web site:
http://www.bakerbooks.com

Acknowledgments

I wish to thank those who gave valuable help in the preparation of this manuscript. This includes Larry Blythe, Steve Bright, Mac Craig, Mark Dorsett, Jeff Drauden, Scott Henderson, Holly Hood, Kenny Hood, David Johnson, Eric LaRock, Trevor Mander, Doug Potter, Steve Puryear, Jeff Spencer, and Frank Turek.

I am especially grateful to Joan Cattell for the untold sacrificial hours of her valuable editing of the complete manuscript. Special thanks are also due to my son, David Geisler, who put together the vast bibliography and for my faithful secretary, Laurel Maugel, who carefully typed and proofed it.

Most of all, I would like to thank my devoted wife, Barbara, for her love, support, and sacrifice that made this volume possible.

Abbreviations

ATR *Anglican Theological Review*
BA *The Biblical Archaeologist*
BAR *Biblical Archaeology Review*
Bib. Sac. *Bibliotheca Sacra*
BJRL *Bulletin of the John Rylands Library*
Bk. Book
BR *Bible Review*
ca. circa
CRJ *Christian Research Journal*
CT *Christianity Today*
EB *Encyclopaedia Biblica*
Eng. English
ERE *Encyclopedia of Religion and Ethics*
Fr. French
Gk. Greek
GOTR *Greek Orthodox Theological Review*
IEJ *Israel Exploration Journal*
ISBE *International Standard Bible Encyclopedia*
JAMA *Journal of the American Medical Association*
JASA *Journal of the American Scientific Affiliation*
JETS *Journal of the Evangelical Theological Society*
KJV King James Version
Lat. Latin
LXX Septuagint
NASB New American Standard Bible
NIV New International Version
NKJV New King James Version
NTCERK *New Twentieth Century Encylcopedia of Religious Knowledge*
RSV Revised Standard Version
SE *Studia Evangelica*
WTJ *Westminster Theological Journal*

Absolute Truth. *See* **Truth, Nature of.**

Absolutes, Moral. *See* **Morality, Absolute Nature of.**

Accommodation Theory. In apologetics, *accommodation theory* can refer to either of two views, one acceptable and one objectionable to evangelical Christians. It can refer to God's accommodation of his revelation to our finite circumstances to communicate with us, as in Scripture or the incarnation of Christ (*see* Bible, Evidence for; Calvin, John; Christ, Deity of). Both of these are forms of divine self-limiting accommodation in order to communicate with finite creatures.

Negative critics of the Bible (*see* Bible Criticism) believe that Jesus accommodated himself to the erroneous views of the Jews of his day in their view of Scripture as inspired and infallible (*see* Bible, Jesus' View of). Orthodox scholars reject this form of accommodation.

Two Kinds of Accommodation. Legitimate accommodation can be more accurately called "adaptation." God, because of infinitude, *adapts* himself to our finite understanding in order to reveal himself. However, the God who is truth never accommodates himself to human error. The vital differences are easily seen when these concepts are compared:

Adaptation	**Accommodation**
Adaptation to finite understanding	Accommodation to finite error
Finitude	Sinfulness
Partial truths	Actual errors
Disclosed truth in human language	Disguised truth in human language
Condescension with truth	Compromise with truth
Anthropomorphisms necessary	Myths necessary
God's nature revealed	God's activity revealed
What really is	What seems to be

The Bible teaches the transcendence of God. His ways and thoughts are far beyond ours (Isa. 55:9; Rom. 11:33). Human beings are infinitesimal in view of God's infinity. God must "stoop down" in order to speak to us. However, this divine act of adaptation to our finitude never involves accommodation to our error. For God cannot err (Heb. 6:18). God uses anthropomorphisms (a true expression of who God is that is couched in human terms) to speak to us, but he does not use myths. He sometimes gives us only part of the truth but that partial truth is never error (1 Cor. 13:12). He reveals himself progressively, but never erroneously (*see* Progressive Revelation). He does not always tells us *all*, but all that he tells us is true.

Jesus and Accommodation. It is well known that Jesus expressed a high view of Scripture in the New Testament (*see* Bible, Jesus' View of). He accepted the divine authority (Matt. 4:4, 7, 10), imperishability (Matt. 5:17–18), divine inspiration (Matt. 22:43), unbreakability (John 10:35), supremacy (Matt. 15:3, 6), inerrancy (Matt. 22:29; John 17:17), historical reliability (Matt. 12:40; 24:37–38), and scientific accuracy (Matt. 19:4–5). To avoid the conclusion that Jesus was actually affirming all this to be true, some critics insist that he was merely accommodating himself to the accepted Jewish belief of the day without attempting to debunk their views. These erroneous views were a starting point for what he wanted to teach about more important matters of morality and theology.

Accommodation Contrary to Jesus' Life. Everything that is known about Jesus' life and teaching reveals that he never accommodated to the false teaching of the day. On the contrary, Jesus rebuked those who accepted Jewish teaching that contradicted the Bible, declaring: "And why do you break the command of God for the sake of your tradition? . . . Thus you nullify the word of God for the sake of your tradition" (Matt. 15:3, 6b).

Jesus corrected false views about the Bible. For instance, in his famous Sermon on the Mount,

Jesus affirmed emphatically: "You have heard that it was said to the people long ago, 'Do not murder, and anyone who murders will be subject to judgment.' But I tell you that anyone who is angry with his brother will be subject to judgment" (Matt. 5:21–22). This or the similar formula of "It has been said. . . . But I say unto you . . ." is repeated in following verses (cf. Matt. 5:23–43).

He rebuked the famous Jewish teacher Nicodemus: "You are Israel's teacher," said Jesus, "and do you not understand these things?" (John 3:10). This is far from accommodating his false views. He even rebuked Nicodemus for not understanding empirical things, saying, "I have spoken to you of earthly things and you do not believe; how then will you believe if I speak of heavenly things?" (John 3:12). Speaking specifically about their erroneous view of Scripture Jesus told the Sadducees bluntly, "You are in error because you do not know the Scriptures or the power of God" (Matt. 22:29).

Jesus' denunciations of the Pharisees were scarcely accommodating. "Woe to you, blind guides! . . . Woe to you, teachers of the law and Pharisees, you hypocrites! . . . You blind guides! You strain out a gnat but swallow a camel. Woe to you, teachers of the law and Pharisees, you hypocrites! . . . You snakes! You brood of vipers! How will you escape being condemned to hell?" (Matt. 23:16–33).

Jesus went so far from accommodating to the false beliefs and practices in the temple that "he made a whip out of cords, and drove all from the temple area, both sheep and cattle; he scattered the coins of the money-changers and overturned their tables. To those who sold doves he said, 'Get these out of here! How dare you turn my Father's house into a market!'" (John 2:15–16).

Even Jesus' enemies recognized that he would not compromise. The Pharisees said: "Teacher, we know you are a man of integrity and that you teach the way of God in accordance with the truth. You aren't swayed by men, because you pay no attention to who they are" (Matt. 22:16). Nothing in the Gospel record indicates that Jesus accommodated to accepted error on any topic.

Accommodation Contrary to Jesus' Character. From a purely human standpoint, Jesus was known as a man of high moral character. His closest friends found him impeccable (1 John 3:3; 4:17; 1 Peter 1:19). The crowds were amazed at his teaching "because he taught as one who had authority, and not as their teachers of the law" (Matt. 7:29).

Pilate examined Jesus and declared, "I find no basis for a charge against this man" (Luke 23:4). The Roman soldier crucifying Jesus exclaimed, "Surely, this was a righteous man" (Luke 23:47). Even unbelievers have paid high tribute to Christ. Ernest Renan, the French atheist, declared about Jesus: "his perfect idealism is the highest rule of the unblemished and virtuous life" (Renan, 383). Renan also wrote, "Let us place, then, the person of Jesus at the highest summit of human greatness" (ibid., 386) and "Jesus remains an inexhaustible principle of moral regeneration for humanity" (ibid., 388).

From a biblical point of view, Jesus was the Son of God and as such could not deceive. For God "does not lie" (Titus 1:2). Indeed, "It is impossible for God to lie" (Heb. 6:18). His "word is truth" (John 17:17). "Let God be true and every man a liar" (Rom. 3:4). Whatever divine self-limitation is necessary in order to communicate with human beings, there is no error, for God cannot err. It is contrary to his very nature.

An Objection Answered. Admittedly, God adapts to human limitations to communicate with us. Indeed, Jesus, who was God, was also a human being. As a human being he was limited in his knowledge. This is borne out by several passages of Scripture. First, as a child "he grew in wisdom" (Luke 2:52). Even as an adult he had certain limitations on his knowledge. According to Matthew, Jesus did not know what was on the fig tree before he got to it (Matt. 21:19). Jesus said he did not know the time of his second coming: "No one knows about that day or hour, not even the angels in heaven, *nor the Son*, but only the Father" (Matt. 24:36, emphasis added).

However, despite the limitations on Jesus' human knowledge, limits on understanding differ from misunderstanding. The fact that he did not know some things as man does not mean he was wrong in what he did know. It is one thing to say Jesus did not know as a man the J-E-P-D theory of the authorship of the Law. But it is quite another to say Jesus was wrong when he affirmed that David wrote Psalm 110 (Matt. 22:43), that Moses wrote the Law (Luke 24:27; John 7:19, 23), or that Daniel wrote a prophecy (Matt. 24:15; *see* BIBLE, JESUS' VIEW OF). Jesus' limitations on things he did not know as a man did not hinder him from affirming truly the things he did know (*see* PENTATEUCH, MOSAIC AUTHORSHIP OF; PROPHECY, AS PROOF OF THE BIBLE).

What Jesus did know he taught with divine authority. He said to his disciples: "All authority in heaven and on earth has been given to me. Therefore go and make disciples of all nations, baptizing them in the name of the Father and of the Son and of the Holy Spirit, and teaching them to obey everything I have commanded you. And surely I am with you always, to the very end of the age" (Matt. 28:18–20). He taught with emphasis. In the Gospel of John, Jesus said twenty-five times "Truly, truly . . ." (John 3:3, 5, 11). Indeed, he claimed his words were on the level of God's, declaring, "Heaven and earth will pass away, but my words will never pass away" (Matt. 24:35). What is more, Jesus taught only what the

Father told him to teach. He said, "I do nothing on my own but speak just what the Father has taught me" (John 8:28b). He added, "By myself I can do nothing; I judge only as I hear, and my judgment is just, for I seek not to please myself but him who sent me" (John 5:30). So to charge Jesus with error is to charge God the Father with error, since he spoke only what the Father told him.

Summary. There is no evidence that Jesus ever accommodated himself to human error in anything he taught. Nor is there any indication that his self-limitation in the incarnation resulted in error. He never taught anything in the areas in which the incarnation limited him as a man. And what he did teach, he affirmed with the authority of the Father, having all authority in heaven and earth.

Sources

"Accommodation," *ISBE*

N. L. Geisler, *Christian Apologetics*, chapter 18

E. Renan, *The Life of Jesus*

J. W. Wenham, *Christ and the Bible*

Acognosticism. Acognosticism should not be confused with *agnosticism*. Agnosticism claims that we cannot *know* God; acognosticism asserts that we cannot *speak meaningfully* (cognitively) about God. The view is also called "non-cognitivism" or "semantical atheism."

*The Acognosticism of A. J. *Ayer.* Following Hume's distinction between definition and empirical statements, A. J. Ayer offered the principle of empirical verifiability. This affirmed that, in order for statements to be meaningful, they must be either analytic (David Hume's [1711–1776]) "relation of ideas" or synthetic (Hume's "matter of fact"); that is, definitional or empirical (Ayer, chap. 1). Definition statements are devoid of content and say nothing about the world; empirical statements have content but tell us nothing about any alleged reality beyond the empirical world. They are only probable in nature and are never philosophically certain (*see* CERTAINTY/CERTITUDE). Definitional statements are useful in empirical and practical matters but not at all informative about reality in any metaphysical sense.

The Nonsense of God-talk. The result of Ayer's logical positivism is as devastating to theism as is traditional agnosticism. God is unknowable and inexpressible. In fact, the term *God* is meaningless. Hence, even traditional agnosticism is untenable, since the agnostic assumes that it is meaningful to ask the question whether God exists. For Ayer, however, the word *God* or any transcendent equivalent, has no meaning. Hence, it is impossible to be an agnostic. The term *God* is neither analytic nor synthetic. It is neither offered by theists as an empty, contentless definition corresponding to nothing in reality, nor is it a term filled with empirical content, since "God" is allegedly a supra-empirical being. Hence, it is literally nonsense to talk about God.

Ayer came to revise his principle of verifiability (see ibid., 10f.). This form admitted the possibility that some empirical experiences are certain, such as those of a single sensory experience, and that there is a third kind of statement with some analytic or definitional verifiability. He did not come to allow for the meaningfulness of God-talk. The verifiable experiences would be neither true nor false nor factual, but simply meaningfully definitional. Ayer acknowledged that an effective elimination of metaphysics needs to be supported by detailed analysis of metaphysical arguments (Ayer, 16). Even a revised principle of empirical verifiability would make it impossible to utter meaningfully true statements about a transempirical reality such as a God. There is no cognitive knowledge of God; we must remain "a-cog-nostic."

Inexpressible or Mystical. Following the lead of Ludwig Wittgenstein's (1889–1951) *Tractatus*, Ayer held that, while God might be experienced, such an experience could never be meaningfully expressed. Wittgenstein believed that "how things are in the world is a matter of complete indifference for what is higher. God does not reveal himself in the world." For "there are indeed, things that cannot be put in words . . . They are what is mystical," and "what we cannot speak about we must consign to silence." If God could express himself in our words, it would indeed be "a book to explode all books," but such is impossible. Hence, there not only is no propositional revelation, but there is no cognitively transcendent being. Hence, whether one take the more strict logical positivist's principle of verifiability or the broader Wittgensteinian linguistic limitations, God-talk is metaphysically meaningless.

Wittgenstein believed that language games are possible, even religious language games. God-talk can and does occur, but it is not metaphysical; it tells us nothing about the existence and nature of God.

It is disastrous to the theist, whether God cannot be known (as in Immanuel Kant) or whether he cannot be spoken of (as in Ayer). Both traditional agnosticism and contemporary acognosticism leave us in the same dilemma philosophically: There are no bases for truth statements about God.

Unfalsifiability of Religious Beliefs. The other side of the principle of verifiability is that of falsifiability. Taking his cue from John Wisdom's parable of the invisible gardener, Antony Flew posed a challenge to believers as follows: "What would have to have occurred to constitute for you a disproof of the love of, or of the existence of, God?" (Flew, 99). For one cannot allow anything to count for his belief in God unless he is willing to allow something to count against it. Whatever is meaningful is also falsifiable. There is no difference between an invisible, undetectable gardener and no gardener at all. Likewise, a God who does not make a verifiable or falsifiable difference is no God at all. Unless the believer can show how the world would be different if there were no God, conditions in the world cannot be used as evidence. It matters little whether theism rests on a parable or a myth, the believer has no meaningful or verifiable knowledge of God. This is little or no improvement over Kant's traditional agnosticism.

Evaluation. Like its cousin agnosticism, acognosticism is vulnerable to serious criticism.

Reply to Ayer's Acognosticism. As already noted, the principle of empirical verifiability set fourth by Ayer is self-defeating. It is neither purely definition nor strictly fact. Hence, on its own grounds it would fall into the third category of non-sense statements. Ayer recognized this problem and engaged a third category for which he claimed no truth value. Verifiability, he contended, is analytic and definitional, but not arbitrary or true. It is *metacognitive*, that is, beyond verification as true or false. It is simply useful as a guide to meaning. This is an ill-fated move for two reasons. First, it no longer eliminates the possibility of making metaphysical statements. Rather, it admits that one cannot arbitrarily legislate meaning, but must consider the meaning of alleged metaphysical statements. But that means it is possible to make meaningful statements about reality, a denial of complete agnosticism and acognosticism. Second, to restrict what is meaningful is to limit what could be true, since only the meaningful can be true. Hence, the attempt to limit meaning to the definitional or the verifiable is to make a truth claim that must itself be subject to some test. If it cannot be tested, then it is itself unfalsifiable and a meaningless belief by its own standards.

Reply to Wittgensteinian Mysticism. Ludwig Wittgenstein engages in a self-stultifying acognosticism. He attempts to define the limits of language in such a way that it is impossible to speak cognitively about God. God is literally inexpressible. And that whereof one cannot speak, he should not attempt to speak. But Wittgenstein can be no more successful in drawing the lines of linguistic limitation than was Kant in delimiting the realm of phenomena or appearance. The very attempt to deny all expressions about God is an expression about God.

One cannot draw the limits of language and thought without transcending those very limits. It is self-defeating to express the contention that the inexpressible cannot be expressed. In like manner even to think the thought that the unthinkable cannot be thought is self-destructive. Language (thought) and reality cannot be mutually exclusive, for every attempt to completely separate them implies some interaction between them. If the ladder was used to get on top of the house, one cannot stand up there to deny the ability of the ladder to get one there (*see* TRUTH, NATURE OF).

Reply to Flew's Falsifiability. Two things must be said about Flew's principle of falsifiability. First, in the narrow sense of empirical falsifiability, it is too restrictive. Not everything need be empirically falsifiable. Indeed that very principle is not empirically falsifiable. But in the broader sense of testable or arguable, surely the principle is alive and helpful. For unless there are criteria for truth and falsity, then no truth claims can be supported. Everything, including opposing views, could be true.

Second, not everything that is verifiable need be falsifiable in the same manner. As John Hick pointed out, there is an asymmetrical relation between verifiability and falsifiability. One can verify personal immortality by consciously observing his own funeral. But one cannot falsify personal immortality. One who does not survive death is not there to falsify anything. Nor could another person falsify one's immortality without being omniscient. But if it is necessary to posit an omniscient mind or God, then it would be eminently self-defeating to use falsification to disprove God. So we may conclude that every truth claim must be testable or arguable, but not all truth claims need be falsifiable. A total state of nonexistence of anything would be unfalsifiable, for example, since there would be no one and no way to falsify it. On the other hand, the existence of something is testable by experience or inference.

Sources

A. J. Ayer, *Language, Truth and Logic*

H. Feigel, "Logical Positivism after Thirty-Five Years," *PT*, Winter 1964

A. Flew, "Theology and Falsification," in *New Essays in Philosophical Theology*

N. L. Geisler, *Christian Apologetics*, chapter 1

———, *Philosophy of Religion*

J. Hick, *The Existence of God*

I. Ramsay, *Religious Language*

J. Wisdom, "Gods," A. Flew, ed., *Logic and Language I*

L. Wittgenstein, *Tractatus Logico-Philosophicus*

Acts, Historicity of. The date and authenticity of the Acts of the Apostles is crucial to the historicity of early Christianity (*see* NEW TESTAMENT, HISTORICITY OF) and, thus, to apologetics in general (*see* APOLOGETICS, ARGUMENT OF; NEW TESTAMENT APOLOGETIC CONCERNS).

- If Acts was written before A.D. 70 while the eyewitnesses were still alive (*see* NEW TESTAMENT DOCUMENTS, DATING OF), then it has great historical value in informing us of the earliest Christian beliefs.

- If Acts was written by Luke, the companion of the apostle Paul, it brings us right to the apostolic circle, those who participated in the events reported.
- If Acts was written by A.D. 62 (the traditional date), then it was written by a contemporary of Jesus, who died in 33 (*see* NEW TESTAMENT, DATING OF).
- If Acts is shown to be accurate history, then it brings credibility to its reports about the most basic Christian beliefs of miracles (Acts 2:22; *see* MIRACLES, APOLOGETIC VALUE OF; MIRACLES IN THE BIBLE), the death (Acts 2:23), resurrection (Acts 2:23, 29–32), and ascension of Christ (Acts 1:9–10).
- If Luke wrote Acts, then his "former treatise" (Acts 1:1), the Gospel of Luke, should be extended the same early date (within the lifetime of apostles and eye-witnesses) and credibility.

The Testimony of a Roman Historian. While New Testament scholarship, long dominated by higher criticism (*see* BIBLE CRITICISM) has been skeptical of the historicity of the Gospels and Acts, this has not been true of Roman historians of the same period. Sherwin-White is a case in point (e.g., Sherwin-White).

Another historian added the weight of his scholarship to the question of the historicity of the book of Acts. Colin J. Hemer lists seventeen reasons to accept the traditional early date that would place the research and writing of Acts during the lifetime of many participants. These strongly support the historicity of Acts and, indirectly, the Gospel of Luke (cf. Luke 1:1–4; Acts 1:1):

1. There is no mention in Acts of the fall of Jerusalem in A.D. 70, an unlikely omission, given the content, if it had already occurred.
2. There is no hint of the outbreak of the Jewish War in A.D. 66, or of any drastic or specific deterioration of relations between Romans and Jews, which implies it was written before that time.
3. There is no hint of the deterioration of Christian relations with Rome involved in the Neronian persecution of the late 60s.
4. The author betrays no knowledge of Paul's letters. If Acts were written later, why would Luke, who shows himself so careful of incidental detail, not attempt to inform his narrative by relevant sections of the Epistles. The Epistles evidently circulated and must have become available sources. This question is beset with uncertainties, but an early date is suggested by the silence.
5. There is no hint of the death of James at the hands of the Sanhedrin in ca. 62 recorded by Josephus (*Antiquities* 20.9.1.200).
6. The significance of Gallio's judgment in Acts 18:14–17 may be seen as setting a precedent to legitimize Christian teaching under the umbrella of tolerance to Judaism.
7. The prominence and authority of the Sadducees in Acts belongs to the pre-70 era, before the collapse of their political cooperation with Rome.
8. Conversely, the relatively sympathetic attitude in Acts to Pharisees (unlike that in Luke's Gospel) does not fit well in the period of Pharisaic revival after scholars of Jamnia met, ca. 90. As a result of that meeting, a phase of escalated conflict with Christianity was led by the Pharisees.
9. Some have argued that the book antedates the coming of Peter to Rome, and also that it uses language which implies that Peter and John, as well as Paul himself, were still alive.
10. The prominence of "God-fearers" in the synagogues in Acts would seem to point to the pre–Jewish War situation.
11. The insignificant cultural details are difficult to place with precision, but may best represent the cultural milieu of the Julio–Claudian Roman era.
12. Areas of controversy within Acts presuppose the relevance of the Jewish setting during the temple period.
13. Adolf Harnack argued that the prophecy placed in Paul's mouth at Acts 20:25 (cf. 20:38) may have been contradicted by later events. If so it presumably was penned before those events occurred.
14. Primitive formulation of Christian terminology is used in Acts which fits an early period. Harnack lists christological titles, such as *Insous* and *ho kurios*, that are used freely, whereas *ho Christos* always designates "the Messiah," rather than a proper name, and *Christos* is otherwise used only in formalized combinations.
15. Rackham draws attention to the optimistic tone of Acts, which would not have been natural after Judaism was destroyed and Christians martyred in the Neronian persecutions of the late 60s. [Hemer, 376–82]
16. The ending of the book of Acts. Luke does not continue Paul's story at the end of the two years of Acts 28:30. "The mention of this defined period implies a terminal point, at least impending" (Hemer, 383). He adds, "It may be argued simply that Luke had brought the narrative up to date at the time of writing, the final note being added

at the conclusion of the two years" (ibid., 387).

17. The "immediacy" of Acts 27–28:

> This is what we have called the "immediacy" of the latter chapters of the book, which are marked in a special degree by the apparently unreflective reproduction of insignificant details, a feature which reaches its apogee in the voyage narrative of Acts 27–28. . . . The vivid "immediacy" of this passage in particular may be strongly contrasted with the "indirectness" of the earlier part of Acts, where we assume that Luke relied on sources or the reminiscences of others, and could not control the context of his narrative. [ibid., 388–89]

Other Support for Historicity. The traditional argument for historical veracity based on "undesigned coincidences" is a debatable concept. However, the following may be seen as a more refined development of that approach. The book of Acts contains:

1. *Geographical details* that are assumed to be generally known. It remains difficult to estimate the range of general knowledge that should be expected of an ancient writer or reader.
2. *More specialized details* that are assumed to be widely known: titles of governors, army units, and major routes. This information would have been accessible to those who traveled or were involved in administration, but perhaps not to others.
3. *Local specifics* of routes, boundaries, and titles of city magistrates that are unlikely to have been known except to a writer who had visited the districts.
4. *Correlation of dates* of known kings and governors with the ostensible chronology of the Acts framework.
5. *Details appropriate to the date* of Paul or Luke in the early church, but not appropriate to conditions earlier or later.
6. *"Undesigned coincidences"* or connective details that connect Acts with the Pauline Epistles.
7. *Latent internal correlations* within Acts.
8. *Independently attested details* which agree with the Alexandrian against the Western texts. Since there are differences between textual families, independent corroboration can help determine when changes were imported into the textual tradition of Acts. A secondary reading may refer to conditions of a later period, and so indirectly help discriminate time periods.
9. *Matters of common geographic knowledge*, mentioned perhaps informally or allusively, with an unstudied accuracy which bespeaks familiarity.
10. *Textual stylistic differences* that indicate Luke's use of different sources.
11. *Peculiarities in the selection of detail*, such as the inclusion of details that are theologically unimportant but that may bear on historical concerns.
12. *Peculiarities in details from "immediacy"* that suggest the author's reference to recent experience. Such details are not so readily explained as the product of longer-term reflective editing and shaping.
13. *Cultural or idiomatic references* that suggest a first-century atmosphere.
14. *Interrelated complexes* combining two or more kinds of correlation. Such a range of connections makes it possible to accurately reconstruct a fragment of history from the jigsaw of interlocking bits of information.
15. Instances where new discoveries and expanded knowledge shed more light on the background information. These are of use to the commentator, but do not bear significantly on historicity.
16. Precise details which lie within the range of contemporary possibilities, but whose accuracy cannot be verified.

Knowledgeable Author. Some examples of the first three categories illustrate how such connections help place Luke's writing and analyze its accuracy. Acts reflects a thorough understanding of what was generally known in A.D. 60, what might be called specialized knowledge of the world in which Paul and Luke traveled, and accurate knowledge of the locales they visited.

Common Knowledge. The emperor's *title* "Augustus" is rendered formally *ho Sebastos* in words attributed to a Roman official (Acts 25:21, 25), whereas "Augustus," as the *name* bestowed on the first emperor, is transliterated *Augoustos* in Luke 2:1. This distinction may be illustrated *from other texts as well.*

General facts of navigation and a knowledge of the empire's corn supply are part of the narrative of the voyage of an Alexandrian ship to the Italian port of Puteoli. The state system of supply was instituted by Claudius. These are samples of a large body of trivia. Luke appears in general to be careful in his rendering of common places, and numerous small points of terminology could be illustrated from the inscriptions reproduced. Luke thinks it necessary to explain some terms to his reader but not others. Points of Judean topography or Semitic nomenclature are glossed or explained (Acts 1:12, 19), whereas basic Jewish institutions are not (1:12; 2:1; 4:1).

Specialized Knowledge. Knowledge of the topography of Jerusalem is shown in 1:12, 19, and 3:2, 11.

In 4:6 Annas is pictured as continuing to have great prestige and to bear the title high priest after his formal deposition by the Romans and the appointment of Caiaphas (cf. Luke 3:2; *Antiquities* 18.2.2.34–35; 20.9.1.198).

Among Roman terms, 12:4 gives detail on the organization of a military guard (cf. Vegetius, *de Re Milit.* 3.8); 13:7 correctly identifies Cyprus as a proconsular (senatorial) province, with the proconsul resident at Paphos.

The part played by Troas in the system of communication is acknowledged in 16:8 (cf. Section C, pp. 112f., 16:11). Amphipolis and Apollonia are known as stations (and presumably overnight stops) on the Egnatian Way from Philippi to Thessalonica, as in 17:1. Chapters 27–28 contain geographic and navigational details of the voyage to Rome.

These examples illustrate the range of places and contexts in the narrative of which Luke possesses information. The author of Acts was well traveled in the areas mentioned in the narrative or had access to special sources of information.

Specific Local Knowledge. In addition, Luke manifests an incredible array of knowledge of local places, names, conditions, customs, and circumstances that befits an eyewitness contemporary recording the time and events. Acts 13–28, covering Paul's travels, particularly shows intimate knowledge of local circumstances. The evidence is strongly represented in the "we-passages," when Luke was accompanying Paul, but extends beyond them. In some cases, specific local knowledge must be discounted because evidence is not available. Some scholars also find Luke's remarks occasionally to be at odds with existing knowledge (for example, in the case of Theudas). Numerous things are confirmed by historical and archaeological research.

1. A natural crossing between correctly named ports (13:4–5). Mount Casius, south of Seleucia, stands within sight of Cyprus. The *name* of the proconsul in 13:7 cannot be confirmed, but the *family* of the Sergii Pauli is attested.
2. The proper river port, Perga, for a ship crossing from Cyprus (13:13).
3. The proper location of Lycaonia (14:6).
4. The unusual but correct declension of the name *Lystra* and the correct language spoken in Lystra. Correct identification of the two gods associated with the city, Zeus and Hermes (14:12).
5. The proper port, Attalia, for returning travelers (14:25).
6. The correct route from the Cilician Gates (16:1).
7. The proper form of the name *Troas* (16:8).
8. A conspicuous sailors' landmark at Samothrace (16:11).
9. The proper identification of Philippi as a Roman colony. The right location for the river Gangites near Philippi (16:13).
10. Association of Thyatira with cloth dyeing (16:14). Correct designations of the titles for the colony magistrates (16:20, 35, 36, 38).
11. The proper locations where travelers would spend successive nights on this journey (17:1).
12. The presence of a synagogue in Thessalonica (17:1), and the proper title of *politarch* for the magistrates (17:6).
13. The correct explanation that sea travel is the most convenient way to reach Athens in summer with favoring east winds (17:14).
14. The abundance of images in Athens (17:16), and reference to the synagogue there (17:17).
15. Depiction of philosophical debate in the agora (17:17). Use in 17:18–19 of the correct Athenian slang epithet for Paul, *spermologos*, and the correct name of the court (*areios pagos*); accurate depiction of Athenian character (17:21). Correct identification of altar to "an unknown god" (17:23). Logical reaction of philosophers who denied bodily resurrection. Areopogites the correct title for a member of the court (17:34).
16. Correct identification of the Corinthian synagogue (18:4). Correct designation of Gallio as proconsul (18:12). The *bema* (judgment seat) can still be seen in Corinth's forum (18:16).
17. The name *Tyrannus*, attested on a first-century inscription (19:9).
18. The cult of Artemis of the Ephesians (19:24, 27). The cult is well attested, and the Ephesian theater was the city meeting-place (19:29).
19. Correct title *grammateus* for the chief executive magistrate and the proper title of honor, *Neokoros* (19:35). Correct name to identify the goddess (19:37). Correct designation for those holding court (19:38). Use of plural *anthupatoi* in 19:38 is probably a remarkably exact reference to the fact that two men jointly exercised the functions of proconsul at this time.
20. Use of precise ethnic designation *beroiaios* and the ethnic term *Asianos* (20:4).
21. Implied recognition of the strategic importance assigned to Troas (20:7–13).
22. Implication of the danger of the coastal trip in this area that caused Paul to travel by land (20:13). Correct sequence of places visited and correct neuter plural of the city name Patara (21:1).
23. The appropriate route passing across the open sea south of Cyprus favored by persistent northwest winds (21:3). The proper

distance between Ptolemais and Caesarea (21:8).
24. Purification rite characteristic of pious Jewish (21:24).
25. Accurate representation of the Jewish law regarding Gentile use of the temple area (21:28).
26. The permanent stationing of a Roman cohort in the Fortress Antonia to suppress disturbances at festival times (21:31). The flight of steps used by guards (21:31, 35).
27. The two common ways of obtaining Roman citizenship (22:28). The tribune is impressed with Paul's Roman rather than Tarsian citizenship (22:29).
28. The correct identifications of Ananias as high priest (23:2) and Felix as governor (23:34).
29. Identification of a common stopping point on the road to Caesarea (23:31).
30. Note of the proper jurisdiction of Cilicia (23:34).
31. Explanation of the provincial penal procedure (24:1–9).
32. Agreement with Josephus of the name *Porcius Festus* (24:27).
33. Note of the right of appeal by a Roman citizen (25:11). The legal formula of *de quibus cognoscere volebam* (25:18). The characteristic form of reference to the emperor (25:26).
34. Correct identification of the best shipping lanes at the time (27:4).
35. Use of the commonly joined names of Cilicia and Pamphylia to describe the coast (27:4). Reference to the principal port at which to find a ship sailing to Italy (27:5). Note of the typically slow passage to Cnidus in the face of a northwest wind (27:7). The locations of Fair Havens and neighboring Lasea (27:8) and correct description of Fair Havens as poorly sheltered for wintering (27:12).
36. Description of the tendency in these climes for a south wind to suddenly become a violent northeaster, the *gregale* (27:13). The nature of a square-rigged ship to have no option but be driven before a gale correctly stated (27:15).
37. Precise name and place given for the island of Clauda (27:16). Appropriate sailors' maneuvers at the time for a storm (27:16–19). The fourteenth night judged by experienced Mediterranean navigators, to be an appropriate time for this journey in a storm (27:27). The proper term for this section of the Adriatic Sea at this time (27:27). The precise term, *bolisantes*, for taking soundings. The position of probable approach of a ship running aground before an easterly wind (27:39).
38. Correct description of the severe liability on guards who permitted a prisoner to escape (27:42).
39. Accurate description of the local people and superstitions of the day (28:4–6).
40. The proper title *protos* (*tes nesou*) for a man in Publius's position of leadership on the islands.
41. Correct identification of Rhegium as a refuge to await a southerly wind to carry a ship through the strait (28:13).
42. Appii Forum and Tres Tabernae as stopping-places along the Appian Way (28:15).
43. Common practice of custody with a Roman soldier (28:16) and conditions of imprisonment at one's own expense (28:30–31).

Conclusion. The historicity of the book of Acts is confirmed by overwhelming evidence. Nothing like this amount of detailed confirmation exists for another book from antiquity. This is not only a direct confirmation of the earliest Christian belief in the death and resurrection of Christ, but also, indirectly, of the Gospel record, since the author of Acts (Luke) also wrote a detailed Gospel. This Gospel directly parallels the other two Synoptic Gospels. The best evidence is that this material was composed by A.D. 60, only twenty-seven years after the death of Jesus. This places the writing during the lifetime of eyewitnesses to the events recorded (cf. Luke 1:1–4). This does not allow time for an alleged mythological development by persons living generations after the events. The Roman historian Sherwin-White has noted that the writings of Herodotus enable us to determine the rate at which legends develop. He concluded that "the tests suggest that even two generations are too short a span to allow the mythical tendency to prevail over the hard historic core of the oral tradition" (Sherwin-White, 190). Julius Müller (1801–1878) challenged the scholars of his day to produce even one example in which an historical event developed many mythological elements within one generation (Müller, 29). None exist.

Sources

W. L. Craig, *The Son Rises*
J. Müller, *The Theory of Myths, in Its Application to the Gospel History, Examined and Confuted*
C. J. Hemer, *The Book of Acts in the Setting of Hellenistic History*, C. H. Gempf, ed.
A. N. Sherwin-White, *Roman Society and Roman Law in the New Testament*

Adam, Historicity of. Critical scholars generally consider the first chapters of Genesis to be myth (*see* ARCHAEOLOGY, OLD TESTAMENT; FLOOD, NOAH'S; MIRACLES, MYTH AND), not history. They point to the poetic nature of the text, the parallel of the early chapters of Genesis to other ancient myths, the alleged contradiction of the text with evolution (*see* EVOLUTION, BIOLOGICAL; EVOLUTION

HUMAN), and the late date for Adam in the Bible (ca. 4000 B.C.) which is opposed to scientific dating that places the first humans much earlier. All of this they consider as evidence that the story of Adam and Eve is mythical. However, the Bible presents Adam and Eve as literal people, who had real children from whom the rest of the human race descended (cf. Gen. 5:1f.).

Historical Adam and Eve. There is good evidence to believe that Adam and Eve were historical persons. First, Genesis 1–2 presents them as actual persons and even narrates the important events in their lives. Second, they gave birth to literal children who did the same (Genesis 4–5). Third, the same phrase ("this is the history of"), used to record later history in Genesis (for example, 6:9; 10:1; 11:10, 27; 25:12, 19), is used of the creation account (2:4) and of Adam and Eve and their descendants (Gen. 5:1; *see* PENTATEUCH, MOSAIC AUTHORSHIP OF). Fourth, later Old Testament chronologies place Adam at the top of the list (Gen. 5:1; 1 Chron. 1:1). Fifth, the New Testament places Adam at the beginning of Jesus' literal ancestors (Luke 3:38). Sixth, Jesus referred to Adam and Eve as the first literal "male and female," making their physical union the basis of marriage (Matt. 19:4). Seventh, the book of Romans declares that literal death was brought into the world by a literal "one man"—Adam (Rom. 5:12, 14). Eighth, the comparison of Adam (the "first Adam") with Christ (the "last Adam") in 1 Corinthians 15:45 manifests that Adam was understood as a literal, historical person. Ninth, Paul's declaration that "Adam was first formed, then Eve" (1 Tim 2:13-14) reveals that he speaks of real persons. Tenth, logically there had to be a first real set of human beings, male and female, or else the race would have had no way to get going. The Bible calls this literal couple "Adam and Eve," and there is no reason to doubt their real existence.

Objections to Historicity. *The Poetic Nature of Genesis 1.* Despite the common assumption to the contrary and the beautiful language of Genesis 1 and 2, the creation record is not poetry. Although there is possible parallelism of ideas between the first three and last three days, this is not in the typical form of Hebrew poetry, which involves couplets in parallel form. A comparison with the Psalms or Proverbs readily shows the difference. Genesis 2 has no poetical parallelism at all. Rather, the creation account is like any other historical narrative in the Old Testament. The account is introduced like other historical accounts in Genesis with the phrase, "This is the history of . . ." (Gen. 2:4; 5:1). Jesus and New Testament writers refer to the creation events as historical (cf. Matt. 19:4; Rom. 5:14; 1 Cor. 15:45; 1 Tim. 2:13–14). The Ebla tablets have added an early nonbiblical witness of a monotheistic *ex nihilo* creation (*see* CREATION, VIEWS OF).

Contradiction with Evolution. The Genesis creation account contradicts macro-evolution. Genesis speaks of the creation of Adam from the dust of the ground, not his evolution from other animals (Gen. 2:7). It speaks of direct immediate creation at God's command, not long natural processes (cf. Gen. 1:1, 3, 6, 9, 21, 27). Eve was created from Adam; she did not evolve separately. Adam was an intelligent being who could speak a language, study and name animals, and engage in life-sustaining activity. He was not an ignorant half-ape (*see* EVOLUTION, THEISTIC).

However, granted that the Genesis record conflicts with macro-evolution, it begs the question to affirm Genesis is wrong and evolution is right. In fact, there is substantial scientific evidence to critique macro-evolution on its own merits. See articles under Evolution.

The Late-Date Objection. The traditional biblical date for the creation of Adam (ca. 4000 B.C.) is much too late to fit the fossil evidence for early human beings, which ranges from tens of thousands to hundreds of thousands of years. The early date for humankind is based on scientific dating and analysis of bone fragments.

However, there are false or challengeable assumptions in this objection. First, it is assumed that one can simply add all the genealogical records of Genesis 5 and 11 and arrive at an approximate date of 4000 B.C. for Adam's creation. But this is based on the false assumption that there are no gaps in these tables, which there are (*see* GENEALOGIES, OPEN OR CLOSED).

This objection also assumes that the dating method for early human-like fossil finds is accurate. Yet these dating methods are subject to many variables including the change in atmospheric conditions, contamination of the sample, and changes of rates of decay (*see* SCIENCE AND THE BIBLE and SCIENTIFIC DATING).

It assumes that early human-like fossil finds were really human beings created in the image of God. But this is a questionable assumption. Many of these finds are so fragmentary that reconstruction is highly speculative. The so-called "Nebraska Man" was actually an extinct pig's tooth! Identification had been based on a tooth. "Piltdown Man" was a fraud. Identifying a creature from bones, especially bone fragments, is extremely speculative.

There may have been human-like creatures that were morphologically similar to human beings but were not created in the image of God. Bone structure cannot prove there was an immortal soul made in God's image inside the body. Evidence for simple tool making proves nothing. Animals (apes, seals, and birds) are known to use simple tools.

This objection also assumes that the "days" of Genesis were twenty-four-hour solar days. This is not certain, since *day* in Genesis is used of all six days (cf. Gen. 2:4). And "day seven," on which God rested, is still going on, thousands of years later (cf. Heb. 4:4–6; *see* GENESIS, DAYS OF).

It is impossible to affirm that Genesis is not historical. In fact, given the unproven assumptions, the history of misinterpretation of early fossils, and the mistaken assumption that there are no gaps in the biblical genealogies of Genesis 5 and 11, the arguments against the historicity of Adam and Eve fail.

Sources

G. L. Archer, Jr., *An Encyclopedia of Biblical Difficulties*
A. Custance, *Genesis and Early Man*
N. L. Geisler and T. Howe, *When Critics Ask*
R. C. Newman, *Genesis and the Origin of the Earth*
B. Ramm, *The Christian View of Science and Scripture*

Age of Accountability. *See* INFANTS, SALVATION OF.

Age of the Earth. *See* Genealogies, Open or Closed

Agnosticism. *Agnosticism* comes from two Greek words (*a*, "no"; *gnosis*, "knowledge"). The term *agnosticism* was coined by T. H. Huxley. It literally means "no-knowledge," the opposite of a Gnostic (Huxley, vol. 5; *see* GNOSTICISM). Thus, an agnostic is someone who claims not to know. As applied to knowledge of God, there are two basic kinds of agnostics, those who claim that the existence and nature of God are not known, and those who hold God to be unknowable (*see* ANALOGY, PRINCIPLE OF; GOD, EVIDENCE FOR). Since the first type does not eliminate all religious knowledge, attention here will center on the second.

Over 100 years before Huxley (1825–1895), the writings of David *Hume (1711–1776) and Immanuel *Kant (1724–1804) laid down the philosophical basis of agnosticism. Much of modern philosophy takes for granted the general validity of the types of arguments they set forth.

Skepticism of Hume. Even Kant was a rationalist (*see* RATIONALISM) until he was "awakened from his dogmatic slumbers" by reading Hume. Technically Hume's views are skeptical but they serve agnostic aims. Hume's reasoning is based in his claim that there are only two kinds of meaningful statements.

"If we take into our hands any volume, of divinity or school metaphysics for instance, does it contain any abstract reasoning concerning quantity or number? No. Does it contain any experimental reasoning concerning matter of fact and existence? No. Commit it then to the flames, for it can contain nothing but sophistry and illusion" (*Enquiry Concerning Human Understanding*).

Any statement that is neither purely a relation of ideas (definitional or mathematical) on the one hand or a matter of fact (empirical or factual) on the other is meaningless. Of course all statements about God fall outside these categories, hence knowledge of God becomes impossible (*see* ACOGNOSTICISM).

Empirical Atomism. Furthermore, all sensations are experienced as "entirely loose and separate." Causal connections are made by the mind only after one has observed a constant conjunction of things in experience. All one really experiences is a series of unconnected and separate sensations. Indeed, there is no direct knowledge even of one's "self," for all we know of ourselves is a disconnected bundle of sense impressions. It does make sense to speak of connections made only in the mind *a priori* or independent of experience. Hence, from experience there are no known and certainly no necessary connections. All matters of experience imply a possible contrary state of affairs.

Causality Based on Custom. According to Hume "all reasoning concerning matters of fact seems to be founded on the relation of *cause and effect*. . . . By means of that relation alone can we go beyond the evidence of our memory and senses" (Hume IV, 2; *see* CAUSALITY, PRINCIPLE OF; FIRST PRINCIPLES). And knowledge of the relation of cause and effect is not *a priori* but arises entirely from experience. There is always the possibility of the *post hoc* fallacy—namely, that things happen after other events (even regularly) but are not really caused by them. For example, the sun rises regularly *after* the rooster crows but certainly not *because* the rooster crows. One can never know causal connections. And without a knowledge of the Cause of this world, for example, one is left in agnosticism about such a supposed God.

Knowledge by Analogy. Even if one grants that every event has a cause, we cannot be sure what the cause is like. Hence, in his famous *Dialogues Concerning Natural Religion*, Hume contends that the cause of the universe may be (1) different from human intelligence since human inventions differ from those of nature; (2) finite, since the effect is finite and one only need infer a cause adequate for the effect; (3) imperfect, since there are imperfections in nature; (4) multiple, for the creation of the world looks more like a long-range trial and error product of many cooperating deities; (5) male and female, since this is how humans generate; and (6) anthropomorphic, with hands, nose, eyes, and other body parts such as his creatures have. Hence, analogy leaves us in skepticism about the nature of any supposed Cause of the world.

Agnosticism of Kant. The writings of Hume had a profound influence on the thinking of Kant. Before reading them, *Kant held a form of rationalism in the tradition of Gottfried Leibniz (1646–1716). Leibniz, and Christian Freiherr von Wolff (1679–1754) following him, believed reality was rationally knowable and that theism was demonstrable. It was the pen of Kant that put an abrupt end to this sort of thinking in the philosophical world.

The Impossibility of Knowing Reality. Kant granted to the rational tradition of Leibniz a rational, *a priori* dimension to knowledge, namely, the form of all knowledge is independent of experience. On the other hand, Kant agreed with Hume and the empiricists that the content of all knowledge came via the senses. The "stuff" of knowledge is provided by the senses but the structure of knowledge is attained eventually in the mind. This creative synthesis solved the problem of rationalism and empiricism. However, the unhappy result of this synthesis is agnosticism, for if one cannot know anything until after it is structured by sensation (time and space) and the categories of understanding (such as unity and causality), then there is no way to get outside one's own being and know what it really was before he so formed it. That is, one can know what something is to him but never what it is in itself. Only the phenomenal, but not the noumenal, can be known. We must remain agnostic about reality. We know only that it is there but can never know what it is (Kant, 173f.).

The Antinomies of Human Reason. Not only is there an unbridgeable gulf between knowing and being, between the categories of our understanding and the nature of reality, but inevitable contradictions also result once we begin to trespass the boundary line (Kant, 393f.). For example, there is the antinomy of causality. If everything has a cause, then there cannot be a beginning cause and the causal series must stretch back infinitely. But it is impossible that the series be both infinite and also have a beginning. Such is the impossible paradox resulting from the application of the category of causality to reality.

These arguments do not exhaust the agnostic's arsenal, but they do lie at the heart of the contention that God cannot be known. However, even some who are unwilling to admit to the validity of these arguments opt for a more subtle agnosticism. Such is the case with the school of thought called logical positivism.

Logical Positivism. Logical positivism or logical empiricism is a philosophy of logic and language that seeks to describe all reality in terms of the senses or experience. Its foundational ideas were developed by the nineteenth-century philosopher Auguste *Comte (1798–1857). Its theological implications were described by A. J. *Ayer (1910–1989) in his principle of empirical verifiability. Ayer alleged that human beings cannot analyze or define the infinite God, so it is impossible to speak more than gibberish about God. The idea of knowing or speaking of a noumenal being is preposterous. One may not even use the term *God*. Hence, even traditional agnosticism is untenable. The agnostic asks the question of whether God exists. For the positivist, even the question is meaningless. Hence, it is impossible to be an agnostic.

Oddly, Ayer's acognosticism does not automatically negate the possibility of religious experience, as does agnosticism. Someone might experience God, but such a touching of infinitude could never be meaningfully expressed, so it is worthless to anyone except the recipient of its wonder. The logical positivist Ludwig *Wittgenstein (1889–1951) was perhaps more consistent in placing a deist type of restriction on positivistic thought (*see* DEISM). If it is meaningless for us to speak of a God or even to use the term, then any infinite being would have the same problem regarding the physical. Wittgenstein denied that God could be concerned about, or revelatory within, the world. Between the noumenal and phenomenal spheres there can be only silence. In summary, for religious noncognitivists Ayer and Wittgenstein, metaphysical acognosticism is the net result of language analysis (*see* ANALOGY, PRINCIPLE OF).

Unfalsifiability. Antony *Flew develops an agnostic philosophy by taking another angle on the limitations of language and awareness of the divine. There may or may not be a God; one cannot prove either thesis empirically. Therefore, one may not legitimately believe either thesis. To be verifiable, an argument must be falsifiable. God must be shown, one way or the other, to make a difference. Unless the theist can answer the challenge head-on, it would appear that he must have what R. M. Hare called a "blik" (Flew, 100). That is to say, he has an unfalsifiable belief in God despite all facts or states of affairs.

Logic of Agnosticism. There are two forms of agnosticism: The weak form simply holds that God is unknown. This of course leaves the door open that one may know God and indeed that some possibly do know God. As such, this agnosticism does not threaten Christian theism. The stronger form of agnosticism is mutually exclusive with Christianity. It claims that God is unknowable, that God cannot be known.

Another distinction must be made: There is unlimited and limited agnosticism. The former claims that God and all reality is completely unknowable. The latter claims only that God is partially unknowable because of the limitations of human finitude and sinfulness. The latter form of agnosticism may be granted by Christians as both possible and desirable.

This leaves three basic alternatives with respect to knowledge about God.

1. We can know nothing about God; he is unknowable.
2. We can know everything about God; he can be exhaustively known.
3. We can know something, but not everything; God is partially knowable.

The first position is agnosticism; the second, dogmatism, and the last, realism. The dogmatic position is untenable. One would have to be infinite in order to know an infinite being exhaustively. Few if any informed theists have seriously held this kind of dogmatism.

However, theists (*see* THEISM) sometimes argue as though partial agnosticism is also wrong. The form this argument takes is that agnosticism is wrong simply because one cannot know something is unknowable about reality without having knowledge about that something. But this is faulty reasoning. There is no contradiction in saying, "I know enough about reality to affirm that there are some things about reality that I cannot know." For example, we can know enough about observation and reporting techniques to say that it is impossible for us to know the exact population of the world at a given instant (unknowability in practice). Likewise, one may know enough about the nature of finitude to say that it is impossible for finite beings to know exhaustively an infinite being. Thus, the Christian holds a controversy only against the complete agnostic who rules out in theory and practice all knowledge of God.

Self-defeating Agnosticism. Complete agnosticism reduces to the self-destructing (*see* SELF-REFUTING STATEMENTS) assertion that "one knows enough about reality to affirm that nothing can be known about reality" (*see* LOGIC). This statement is self-falsifying. One who knows something about reality cannot affirm in the same breath that all of reality is unknowable. And one who knows nothing whatsoever about reality has no basis for making a statement about reality. It will not suffice to say that knowledge of reality can only be purely and completely negative, that is, knowledge can only say what reality is not. For every negative presupposes a positive; one cannot meaningfully affirm that something is not and be totally devoid of a knowledge of the "something." It follows that total agnosticism is self-defeating. It assumes knowledge of reality in order to deny all knowledge of reality.

Some have attempted to avoid this critique by forming their skepticism as a question: "What do I know about reality?" However, this merely delays the dilemma. Both agnostic and Christian should ask this question, but the answer separates the agnostic from the realist. "I can know something about God" differs significantly from "I can know nothing about God." Once the answer is given in the latter form, a self-defeating assertion has been unavoidably made.

Neither will it help to take the mutist alternative by saying nothing. Thoughts can be as self-stultifying as assertions. The mutist cannot even think he or she knows absolutely nothing about reality without implying knowledge about reality.

Someone may be willing to grant that knowledge about finite reality is possible but not knowledge about infinite reality, the sort of knowledge at issue in Christian theism. If so, the position is no longer complete agnosticism, for it holds that something can be known about reality. This leaves the door open to discuss whether this reality is finite or infinite, personal or impersonal. Such discussion ventures beyond the question of agnosticism to debate finite godism and theism.

Kant's Self-defeating Agnosticism. Kant's argument that the categories of thought (such as unity and causality) do not apply to reality is just as unsuccessful. Unless categories of reality corresponded to categories of the mind, no statements can be made about reality, including the statement Kant made. Unless the real world were intelligible, no statement about it would apply. A preformation of the mind to reality is necessary whether one says anything about it—positive or negative. Otherwise, we think of an unthinkable reality.

The argument may be pressed that the agnostic need not be making any statement at all about reality but simply defining the limits of what we can know. Even this approach is self-defeating, however. To say that one cannot know any more than the limits of the phenomena or appearance is to draw a line in the sand while straddling it. To set such firm limits is to surpass them. It is not possible to contend that appearance ends here and reality begins there unless one can see at least some distance on the other side. How can one know the difference between appearance and reality who has not seen enough of appearance and reality to make the comparison?

Another self-defeating dimension is implied within Kant's admission *that* he knows that the noumena is there but not *what* it is. Is it possible to know that something is without knowing something about what it is? Can pure "that-ness" be known? Does not all knowledge imply some knowledge of characteristics? Even a strange creature one had never seen before could not be observed to exist unless it had some recognizable characteristics as size, color, or movement. Even something invisible must leave some effect or trace in order to be observed. One need not know the origin or function of a thing or phenomenon. But it has been observed or the observer could not know that it is. It is not possible to affirm *that* something is without simultaneously declaring something about *what* it is. Even to describe it as the "in-itself" or the "real" is to say something. Further, Kant acknowledged the noumenal to be the unknowable "source" of the appearance we are receiving. All of this is informative about the real; there is a real, in-itself source of impressions. This is something less than complete agnosticism.

Other Forms of Skepticism. Hume's Skepticism. The overall skeptical attempt to suspend all judgment about reality is self-defeating, since it implies a judgment about reality. How else could one know that suspending all judgment about reality is the wisest course, unless he knows indeed that realty is unknowable? Skepticism implies agnosticism; as shown above, agnosticism implies knowledge about reality. Unlimited skepticism that commends the suspension of all judgments about reality implies a most sweeping judgment about the knowability of reality. Why discourage all truth attempts, unless one knows in advance that they are futile? And how can one be in possession of this advance information without already knowing something about reality?

Hume's contention that all meaningful statements are either a relation of ideas or else about matters of fact breaks its own rules. The statement fits neither category. Hence, on its own grounds it would be meaningless. It could not be purely a relation of ideas, for in that case it would not be informative about reality, as it purports to be. It is not purely a matter-of-fact statement since it claims to cover more than empirical matters. In short, Hume's distinction is the basis for Ayer's empirical verifiability principle, and the verifiability principle is itself not empirically verifiable (*see* AYER, A. J.).

Hume's radical empirical atomism that all events are "entirely loose and separate" and that even the self is only a bundle of sense impressions is unfeasible. If everything were unconnected, there would be no way of even making that particular statement, since some unity and connection are implied in the affirmation that everything is disconnected. To affirm "I am nothing but the impressions about myself" is self-defeating, for there is always the assumed unity of the "I (self)" making the assertion. But one cannot assume a unified self in order to deny it.

For replies to acognosticism, Wittgenstein's mystic form of it, and Flew's principle of falsifiability, *see* ACOGNOSTICISM.

Some Specific Agnostic Claims. Hume denied the traditional uses of both causality and analogy as means of knowing the theistic God. Causality is based on custom and analogy would lead to either a finite, human god or to a God totally different than the alleged analog.

The Justification of Causality. Hume never denied the principle of causality. He admitted it would be absurd to maintain that things arise without a cause (Hume, I.187). What he did attempt was to deny that there is any philosophical way of *establishing* the principle of causality. If the causal principle is not a mere analytic relation of ideas, but is belief based on customary conjunction of matter-of-fact events, then there is no necessity in it. One cannot use it with philosophical justification. But we have already seen that dividing all content statements into these two classes is self-defeating. Hence, it is possible that the causal principle is both contentful and necessary.

The very denial of causal necessity implies a causal necessity. Unless there is a necessary ground (or cause) for the denial, then the denial does not necessarily stand. And if there is a necessary ground or cause for the denial, then the denial is self-defeating; in that event it is using a necessary causal connection to deny that there are necessary causal connections.

Some have attempted to avoid this objection by limiting necessity to the reality of logic and propositions but denying that necessity applies to reality. This does not succeed; in order for this statement to exclude necessity from the realm of reality, it must be a necessary statement about reality. It must claim that it is necessarily true about reality that no necessary statements can be made about reality. This actually does what it claims cannot be done.

A Foundation for Analogy. Likewise, Hume cannot deny all similarity between the world and God, for this would imply that the creation must be totally dissimilar from the Creator. It would mean that effects must be entirely different from their cause. This statement too is self-destructive; unless there is some knowledge of the cause, there can be no basis for denying all similarity between cause and its effect. Even a negative comparison implies positive knowledge of the terms being compared. Hence, either there is no basis for the affirmation that God must be totally dissimilar, or else there can be some knowledge of God in terms of our experience, in which case God is not necessarily totally dissimilar to what we know in our experience.

One should be cautioned here about overdrawing the conclusion of these arguments. Once it has been shown that total agnosticism is self-defeating, it does not *ipso facto* follow that God exists or that one has knowledge of God. These arguments show only that, if there is a God, one cannot maintain that he *cannot* be known. From this it follows only that God *can* be known, not that we *do* know anything about God. The disproof of agnosticism is not thereby the proof of realism or theism. Agnosticism only destroys itself and makes it *possible* to build Christian theism. The positive case for Christian knowledge of God must then be built (*see* GOD, EVIDENCE FOR).

Kant's Antinomies. In each of Kant's alleged antinomies there is a fallacy. One does not end in inevitable contradictions by speaking about reality in terms of the necessary conditions of human thought. For instance, it is a mistake to view everything as needing a cause, for in this case there would be an infinity of causes, and even God would need a cause. Only limited, changing, contingent things need causes. Once one arrives at an unlimited, unchanging, Necessary Being, there no longer is a need for a cause. The finite must be caused, but the infinite being would be uncaused. Kant's other antinomies are likewise invalid (*see* KANT, IMMANUEL).

Conclusion. There are two kinds of agnosticism: limited and unlimited. The former is compatible with Christian claims of finite knowledge of an infinite God. Unlimited agnosticism, however, is self-destructive; it implies knowledge about reality in order to deny the possibility of any knowledge of reality. Both skepticism and noncognitivisms (acognosticism) are reducible to agnosticism. Unless it is impossible to know the real, it is unnecessary to disclaim the possibility of all cognitive knowledge of it or to dissuade men from making any judgments about it.

Unlimited agnosticism is a subtle form of dogmatism. In completely disclaiming the possibility of all knowledge of the real, it stands at the opposite pole from the position that claims all knowledge about reality. Either extreme is dogmatic. Both are *must* positions regarding knowledge as opposed to the position that we *can* or *do* know something about reality. And there is simply no process short of omniscience by which one can make such sweeping and categorical statements. Agnosticism is negative dogmatism, and every negative presupposes a positive. Hence, total agnosticism is not only self-defeating; it is self-deifying. Only an omniscient mind could be totally agnostic, and finite men confessedly do not possess omniscience. Hence, the door remains open for some knowledge of reality. Reality is not unknowable.

Sources

J. Collins, *God in Modern Philosophy*, chapters 4 and 6

A. Flew, "Theology and Falsification," A. Flew, et al., eds., *New Essays in Philosophical Theology*

R. Flint, *Agnosticism*

R. Garrigou-Lagrange, *God: His Existence and His Nature*

S. Hackett, *The Resurrection of Theism*. Part 1

D. Hume, "A Letter from a Gentleman to his Friend in Edinburgh," in E. C. Mossner, et al., eds., *The Letters of David Hume*

———, *An Enquiry Concerning Human Understanding*

———, *Dialogues Concerning Natural Religion*

T. H. Huxley, *Collected Essays*, Vol. 5

I. Kant, *Critique of Pure Reason*

L. Stephen, *An Agnostic's Apology*

J. Ward, *Naturalism and Agnosticism*

Albright, William F. William Foxwell Albright (1891–1971) was called the dean of American biblical archaeologists. Born in Chili to Methodist missionaries, he received his Ph.D. from Johns Hopkins University in 1916. Among major works are *From Stone Age to Christianity*, *Archaeology and the Religion of Israel*, *The Archaeology of Palestine and the Bible*, *Yahweh and the Gods of Canaan*, *The Excavation at Tell Beit Mirsim*, and *Archaeology of Palestine*. He wrote numerous articles and extended his influence as editor of the *Bulletin of the American School of Oriental Research* from 1931 to 1968. He was a leader in the American School of Oriental Research (ASOR) for some forty years.

Apologetic Importance. Albright's influence on biblical apologetics was enormous and reflected his own theological movement from liberal Protestant to conservative. His work destroyed many old liberal critical views (*see* BIBLE CRITICISM), which now may be called pre-archaeological. Through his discoveries and research, Albright determined several vital affirmations:

Mosaic Authorship of the Pentateuch. "The contents of our Pentateuch are, in general, very much older than the date at which they were finally edited; new discoveries continue to confirm the historical accuracy of the literary antiquity of detail after detail in it. Even when it is necessary to assume later additions to the original nucleus of Mosaic tradition, these additions reflect the normal growth of ancient institutions and practices, or the effort made by later scribes to save as much as possible of extant traditions about Moses. It is, accordingly, sheer hypercriticism to deny the substantially Mosaic character of the Pentateuchal tradition" (*Archaeology of Palestine*, 225).

Historicity of the Patriarchs. "The narratives of the patriarchs, of Moses and the exodus, of the conquest of Canaan, of the judges, the monarchy, exile and restoration, have all been confirmed and illustrated to an extent that I should have thought impossible forty years ago" (*Christian Century*, 1329).

"Aside from a few die-hards among older scholars, there is scarcely a single biblical historian who has not been impressed by the rapid accumulation of data supporting the substantial historicity of patriarchal tradition" (*Biblical Period*, 1).

"Abraham, Isaac, and Jacob no longer seem isolated figures, much less reflections of later Israelite history; they now appear as true children of their age, bearing the same names, moving about over the same territory, visiting the same towns (especially Harran and Nahor), practicing the same customs as their contemporaries. In other words, the patriarchal narratives have a historical nucleus throughout, though it is likely that long oral transmission of the original poems and later prose sagas which underlie the present text of Genesis has considerably refracted the original events" (*Archaeology of Palestine*, 236).

Support for the Old Testament. "There can be no doubt that archaeology has confirmed the substantial historicity of the Old Testament tradition" (*Archaeology and the Religion of Israel*, 176).

"As critical study of the Bible is more and more influenced by the rich new material from the ancient Near East we shall see a steady rise in respect for the historical significance of now neglected or despised passages and details in the Old and New Testaments" (*From Stone Age to Christianity*, 81).

The Dead Sea Scrolls prove "conclusively that we must treat the consonantal text of the Hebrew Bible with the utmost respect and that the free emending of difficult passages in which modern critical scholars have indulged cannot be tolerated any longer" (*Recent Discoveries in Bible Lands*, 128).

"Thanks to the Qumran discoveries, the New Testament proves to be in fact what it was formerly believed to be: the teaching of Christ and his immediate followers between cir. 25 and cir. 80 A.D." (*From Stone Age to Christianity*, 23).

"Biblical historical data are accurate to an extent far surpassing the ideas of any modern critical students, who have consistently tended to err on the side of hypercriticism" (*Archaeology of Palestine*, 229).

Unity of Isaiah. Of the long-popular theory that there were two writers of Isaiah (*see* ISAIAH, DEUTERO), Albright demurred in an interview:

Question: "Many passages in Isaiah 40–66 denounce idolatry as a current evil in Israel (for example 44:9–20; 51:4–7; 65:2, 3; 66:17). How can these be reconciled with a theory of post-Exilic authorship, since idolatry admittedly was never reintroduced into Judah after the restoration . . . ?"

Answer: "I do not believe that anything in Isaiah 40–66 is later than the sixth century" (*Toward a More Conservative View*, 360).

Dating the New Testament. "In my opinion, every book of the New Testament was written by a baptized Jew between the forties and the eighties of the first century A.D. (very probably between about 50 and 75 A.D." (ibid., 359).

"We can already say emphatically that there is no longer any solid basis for dating any book of the New Testament after about A.D. 80, two full generations before the date between 130 and 150 given by the more radical New Testament critics of today" (*Recent Discoveries in Bible Lands*, 136).

In the article "Recent Discoveries in Palestine and the Gospel of St. John," Albright argued throughout that the evidence at Qumran shows that the concepts, terminology, and mindset of the Gospel of John, probably belonged to the early first century (*see* NEW TESTAMENT, DATING OF).

Conclusion. From an apologetic standpoint, the eminent and respected archaeologist strongly supports the pillars of historical apologetics. With some uncertainty about transmission of the oral record of the Pentateuch, Albright believes that both evidence to date and anticipated findings will show both testaments to be historically reliable. The dates of these books are early. Both the predictive prophecy of the Old Testament and the historicity of the story of Christ and the early church in the New Testament are validated by modern archaeology (*see* ACTS, HISTORICITY OF; BIBLE, EVIDENCE FOR; NEW TESTAMENT DOCUMENTS, RELIABILITY OF; NEW TESTAMENT, HISTORICITY OF).

Sources

W. F. Albright, *Archaeology and the Religion of Israel*

———, "Recent Discoveries in Palestine and the Gospel of St. John," in W. D. Davies and D. Daube, eds., *The Background of the New Testament and Its Eschatology*

———, "William Albright: Toward a More Conservative View," in *CT* (18 January 1963)

———, Interview, *Christian Century* (19 November 1958)

———, *Recent Discoveries in Bible Lands*

———, *The Biblical Period*

———, *The Archaeology of Palestine*

———, *From Stone Age to Christianity*

H. H. Vos, "Albright, William Foxwell," in W. Elwell, ed., *The Dictionary of Evangelical Theology*

Alfarabi. Alfarabi or Al Farabi (870?–950) was an Arabian philosopher of Turkish descent who lived in Aleppo. He was one of the first monist or pantheist philosophers to introduce the Middle Ages to Aristotle and Plato. He influenced both Avicenna (Ibn Sinâ, 980–1037) and Averroes (1126–1198), whose views dominated the discussion in later Medieval times.

Alfarabi's thought was highly influential on later Christian forms of the cosmological argument (*see* GOD, EVIDENCE FOR; *KALAM* COSMOLOGICAL ARGUMENT). He provided the heart of later scholastic arguments by his distinction between *what* a thing is and *that* it is. Alfarabi took this as a sign of the real distinction between a creature's essence and its existence—a concept later championed by *Thomas Aquinas.

Alfarabi's Cosmological Argument. Implied in this real distinction is an argument for God's existence that takes this form:

1. Things exist whose essence is distinct from their existence. Called "possible beings," they can be conceived as not existing even though they do exist.
2. These beings have existence only accidentally, that is, it is not part of their very essence to exist. It is logically possible that they might never exist.
3. Anything that has existence accidentally (and not essentially).must receive its existence from another. Since existence is not essential to it, there must be some explanation as to why it exists.
4. There cannot be an infinite regression of causes for existence. Since the existence of all possible beings is received from another, there must ultimately be a cause from which existence is received.
5. Therefore, there must be a First Cause of existence whose essence and existence are identical. This is a *Necessary*, and not a mere possible, Being. The First Cause cannot be a mere possible being (whose essence is not to

exist), since no possible beings explain their own existence.

Evaluation of Alfarabi's Argument. Many criticisms of the cosmological argument have been leveled by atheists, agnostics, and skeptics. Most of these emanate from David Hume and Immanuel Kant and have been answered by theists (*see* GOD, OBJECTIONS TO PROOFS FOR).

Conclusion. If there are beings whose essence is not to exist, there must be a Being whose essence is to exist, for the possible beings are not possible unless there is a Necessary Being. No beings are given existence unless some Being gives this existence. Since a being cannot give existence to another when it is dependent for its own existence on another, there must be a first Being whose existence was not given to it by another, but who gives existence to all others. This is basically the same argument as that beneath the first three of Aquinas's "five ways" to prove God's existence (*see* THOMAS AQUINAS).

Sources

F. Copleston, *History of Philosophy*
E. Gilson, "Al Farabi," *EP*
———, *History of Christian Philosophy in the Middle Ages*

Altizer, Thomas J. J. G. W. F. Hegel (1770–1831) wrote that "God is dead" (Hegel, 506) and Friedrich Nietzsche (1844–1900) took the concept seriously. He wrote: "God is dead! God remains dead! And we have killed him" (Nietzsche, no. 125). In the 1960s Thomas J. J. Altizer drew out the radial implications of this form of atheism in his "Death of God" theology.

The Meaning of the Death of God. There are several kinds of atheism. The *traditional* atheist believes that there is not now, nor ever was, a God (*see* FEUERBACH, LUDWIG; FREUD, SIGMUND; SARTRE, JEAN-PAUL). The *semantical* atheists assert that the term God is dead, that religious language has no meaning (*see* AYER, A. J.; ACOGNOSTICISM). The *mythological* atheists, of whom Nietzsche is representative, affirm that the myth God was once alive but died in the twentieth century. *Conceptual* atheists believe that there is a God but that he is hidden from our view, being obscured by our conceptual constructions (*see* BUBER, MARTIN). The *practical* atheists contend that God exists, but we should live *as if* he does not, not using God as a crutch for our failure to act in a spiritual and responsible way. Altizer was a *dialectical* atheist. These held that God actually once lived, but then died in our century.

Stages of the Death. Altizer called Nietzsche the first radical Christian (Altizer, *The Gospel of Christian Atheism,* 25). Altizer believed that "only the Christian knows that God is dead, that the death of God is a final and irrevocable event" (ibid., 111). God is not merely hidden from our view, as Martin Buber believed. He actually died in three stages:

Death at the Incarnation. First, God died when he became incarnated in Christ. "To know that God is Jesus, is to know that God himself has become flesh; no longer does God exist as transcendent Spirit or sovereign Lord." As Spirit becomes Word, it empties itself. That is, "if Spirit truly empties itself in entering the world, then its own essential or original Being must be left behind in an empty and lifeless form" (ibid., 67–68). In brief, when God came to earth, heaven was emptied (*see* CHRIST OF FAITH VS. JESUS OF HISTORY; JESUS, QUEST FOR HISTORICAL).

Death on the Cross. Further, God not only died in general in the incarnation, but he died in particular on the cross when Christ was crucified (and never rose from the grave). "Yes, God died in the Crucifixion: therein he fulfills the movement of the Incarnation by totally emptying himself of his primordial sacrality." In fact, only in the crucifixion, in the death of the Word on the Cross, does the Word actually and wholly become flesh. And "the incarnation is only truly actually real if it effects the death of the original sacred, the death of God himself" (ibid., 82–90, 113, 149–53; (*see* CHRIST, DEATH OF; RESURRECTION, EVIDENCE FOR; RESURRECTION, OBJECTIONS TO).

Death in Modern Times. Finally, God died in modern times. That is, God not only actually died in the incarnation and on the cross, but he died in our consciousness in our time as the reality of his death has worked its way out in Western culture. To understand this, one must speak of a dialectical process. "Progressively but decisively God abandons or negates his original passivity . . . becoming incarnate both *in* and *as* the actuality of world and history." Thus to cling to a belief in a transcendent God is to negate the historical reality of the incarnation. For "only the sacred that negates its own unfallen or primordial form can become incarnate in the reality of the profane." So, "dialectically, everything depends upon recognizing the meaning of God's total identification with Jesus and of the understanding that it is God who became Jesus and not Jesus who becomes God" (ibid., 46). Thus, it is the obligation of every Christian to will the death of God so that the dialectical process may continue.

Evaluation. Dialectical atheism denies the inspiration of the Bible (*see* BIBLE, EVIDENCE FOR), opting for an unfounded radical criticism (*see* BIBLICAL CRITICISM; NEW TESTAMENT, HISTORICITY OF; REDACTION CRITICISM). It denies the bodily resurrection of Christ against all the historical evidence (*see* RESURRECTION, EVIDENCE FOR).

This theology is based on a misunderstanding of the incarnation. Scripture affirms that when Christ came to earth it was not the subtraction of deity but the addition of humanity. God did not leave heaven; only the second person of the Godhead added another nature, a human one, without discarding his divine nature (*see* CHRIST, DEITY OF; TRINITY).

Philosophically it is impossible for a Necessary Being (God) to go out of existence. A Necessary Being cannot come to be or cease to be. It must always be.

The dialectical method at the basis of Altizer's view is unfounded. There is no basis for believing that reality operates through dialectical thesis, antithesis, and synthesis.

Conclusion. The "death of God" movement was short-lived, dominating the scene for only a decade or so. It was based on a dialectical theology, often attributed to Hegel. This thesis demands that every thesis, such as "God exists," calls forth its own antithesis, "God is not." This in turn becomes the basis for new synthesis. This always appears in a forward direction. Precisely what form it would take, Altizer did not know. He did believe, however, that one "must ever be open to new epiphanies of the Word or Spirit of God. . . . truly new epiphanies whose very occurrences either effects or records a new actualization or movement or the divine process" (ibid., 84, 105). In this sense, while Altizer appears to negate all forms of transcendence, in fact he negates only traditional forms which transcend backward or upward and replaces them with a forward transcendence. This has been called eschatological transcendence (see Geisler, 49–52).

Sources

T. J. Altizer, *The Gospel of Christian Atheism*
———, *Radical Theology and the Death of God*
N. L. Geisler, *Philosophy of Religion*
G. W. F. Hegel, *The Phenomenology of Spirit*
F. Nietzsche, *Joyful Wisdom*

Analogy, Principle of. Two *principles of analogy* sometimes affect Christian apologetics. One is a *rule of historicism*, laid down by historian and liberal theologian Ernst Troeltsch (1865–1923) that the only way the past can be known is by analogy in the present. The implication of this rule is that, since the kinds of miracles performed in the Bible are not taking place today, we cannot know that they took place in the past either. For a discussion of this principle and its difficulties, see the article TROELTSCH, ERNST. The other way in which this term is used is as a fundamental principle of reason (*see* FIRST PRINCIPLES). It is in this sense that the principle is considered here.

The Principle of Analogy. The principle of analogy states that an effect must be similar to its cause. Like produces like. An effect cannot be totally different from its cause. An act (or actor) communicates actuality. It affirms that the Cause of all being (God) must be like the beings he causes. It denies that God can be totally different (equivocal) from his effects, for the Being that causes all other being cannot bring into being something that does not have being like he is. Being causes being.

Likewise, analogy affirms that God cannot be totally the same as his effects, for in this case they would be identical to God. But the created cannot be identical to the uncreated, nor the finite to the Infinite. Hence, God the Creator of all being must be similar to the creatures he has made. Likewise, our judgments about God—if they are accurate—are neither totally the same nor totally different; they must be similar (analogous). Analogous religious language, then, is the only way to preserve true knowledge of God. Univocal God-talk is impossible and equivocal God-talk is unacceptable and self-defeating. Only analogy avoids the pitfalls of each and provides genuine understanding of God. As Thomas Aquinas declared "This name God . . . is taken neither univocally nor equivocally, but analogically. This is apparent from this reason—univocal names have absolutely the same meaning, while equivocal names have absolutely diverse meanings; whereas analogical, a name taken in one signification must be placed in the definition of the same name taken in other significations" (*Summa Theologica,* 1a. 13, 10).

The Basis for Analogy. Analogy preserves a true knowledge of God because it is rooted in the very nature of God's self-expressions. Of course, God can only express himself to his creatures in terms other than himself. Thus, by its very nature such expression or manifestation of God will be limited, whereas God himself is unlimited. Nonetheless, an expression about God must express God. Hence, analogy flows from the very nature of the process of God's self-revelation.

Analogy in Causality. The similarity between Creator and creature is based in the causal relation between them (*see* CAUSALITY, PRINCIPLE OF). Since God is pure existence (Being), and since he causes all other existence (beings), there must be a similarity between him as the efficient Cause and his effects. For a cause communicates itself to the effect. Being causes being. The Cause of being must be a Being. For it cannot give what it has not got; it cannot produce reality it does not possess. Therefore, even though the Cause is Infinite Being and the effect is finite being, the being of the effect is similar to the Being that caused it. Analogy is based in efficient causality. For "we can name God only from creatures. Hence, whatever is said of God and creatures is said according as there is some relation of the creature to God as to its principal cause, wherein all the perfections pre-exist excellently" (ibid., 1a. 13, 5).

The Witness of Analogy. The need for analogy is not only apparent in God's general revelation in nature; it is also essential to God's special revelation in Scripture (*see* BIBLE, EVIDENCE FOR). The Bible declares true knowledge of God (*see* BIBLE,

EVIDENCE FOR). But this knowledge is contained in a book composed of human words and sentences based in finite human experience. Thus the question is: How can finite human concepts convey an Infinite God? Aquinas's answer is that they must do so analogically. God is neither identical to nor totally different from our expressions about him. Rather, he is similar to them.

Special Revelation in Analogy. The Bible is emphatic about two things in this connection. First, God is beyond our thoughts and concepts, even the best of them (cf. Rom. 11:33). God is infinite, our concepts are finite, and no finite concept can capture the infinite. It is also clear in Scripture that God goes way beyond the puny ability of human concepts to convey his ineffable essence. Paul said, "now we see as in a mirror dimly" (1 Cor. 13:12). John said of mortal man in this life, "no one has seen God at any time" (John 1:18). Second, yet human language is adequate for expressing the attributes of God. For in spite of the infinite difference between God and creatures there is not a total lack of similarity, since the effect always resembles its efficient Cause in some way.

But if God is both adequately expressed in, and yet infinitely more than, human language—even inspired language—can express, then at best the language of Scripture is only analogous. That is, no term taken from human experience—and that is where all biblical terms come from—can do any more than tell us what God is *like*. None of them can expressive comprehensively what God really *is*. Religious language at best can make valid predications of God's essence, but it can never express his essence fully.

Language of Analogy. There are two reasons that statements made about God on the basis of general revelation (*see* REVELATION, GENERAL) are merely analogous. First is the matter of causality. The arguments for God's existence are arguments from effect to the efficient Cause of their being (ibid., 1a. 2, 3; *see* GOD, EVIDENCE FOR). Since the effects get their actuality from God (who is Pure Actuality), they must be similar to him. For Actuality communicates and produces actuality.

Second, Pure Actuality (God) cannot create another Pure Actuality. Pure Actuality is uncreated, and it is impossible to create an uncreated Being. But if uncreated Actuality cannot create another Pure Actuality, then it must create an actuality with potentiality (Aquinas, *On Being and Essence*). Thus, all created beings must be composed of actuality and potentiality. They have actual existence, and they have potential not to exist. Anything that comes into existence can pass out of existence. But if all created beings have a potential that limits their existence, then they are limited kinds of existence, and their uncreated Cause is an unlimited kind of existence.

Thus, there must be a difference between creatures and their Creator. They have limitations (potency), and he does not. It follows that, when making statements about God based on what he has revealed of himself in his creation, there is one big proviso: God is *not* like his creation in their potentialities, but only in their actuality. This negative element is called "the way of negation" (*via negative*), and all adequate God-talk must presume it. This conclusion emerges from the very nature of the proofs for God's existence.

We may state the positive and negative as two propositions:

God is a Cause.

This is the positive element of similarity in the creature-Creator analogy. Whatever actuality exists is like the Actuality that gave it.

God is an uncaused cause.

This is the negative element. The same negation must be taken into account when considering other attributes of God that emerged from the argument for his existence. As Aquinas said, "no creature being finite, can be adequate to the first agent which is infinite" (*On the Power of God,* 7.7). God is the infinite cause of all finite existence. But infinite means not-finite; it too is a negation. God is the eternal, that is not-terminal or non-temporal, Cause. Some of the negations are not immediately obvious. God is the simple Source of all complex being. But "simple" here really means noncomplex. We know creatures are contingent and God is necessary, but by "necessary" we simply mean that God is *not* contingent. We have no positive concepts in our experience that can express the transcendent dimension of God's unlimited metaphysical characteristics.

Therefore, the analogy with which we speak of God will always contain an element of negation. The creature is *like* God because Actuality communicates actuality, but *unlike* God because it has a limiting potentiality God does not have. He is Pure Actuality.

Kinds of Analogies. Two basic kinds of analogy should be distinguished: *extrinsic* and *intrinsic*. The analogy between God and the creation is based in an intrinsic analogy. Otherwise, there would be no real similarity.

Extrinsic Analogy. There is no real similarity between two parties in an *extrinsic* analogy. Only one thing possesses the characteristic; the other is *called* that characteristic by its relation to it. This can best be explained by looking at the kinds of extrinsic analogy.

Extrinsic analogy is based on efficient causality. This analogy is called "analogy by extrinsic attribution." The characteristic is only *attributed* to the cause because the cause produces the characteristic in the effect. It does not really possesses the characteristic. Some food is *called* "healthy" because it encourages health in the body, not because any food in itself really is healthy.

This analogy does not provide any real basis for knowledge of God. It simply tells us what the cause can produce, not what characteristic it actually possesses. In this kind of analogy, God might simply be *called* good because he produces good things, but not because he actually *is* good in himself. Therefore, analogy based on extrinsic attribution leaves us in a state of agnosticism about God.

Extrinsic analogy is based on similarity of relations. An analogy based on similar relationships is sometimes called "the analogy of improper proportionality." It is "improper" because the relationship exists only in the mind doing the comparing. There is no real similarity between the "analogates" (the two things being compared). This kind of analogy declares that:

$$\frac{\textit{Smile}}{\text{Face}} \text{ as } \frac{\textit{Flowers}}{\text{Meadow}}$$

A smile is not really like flowers. However, a smile brightens a face in the way flowers adorn a meadow. There is a perceived relationship between *smile* and *face* that corresponds to the perceived relationship between *flowers* and *meadow*. This is a relationship between two relationship.

$$\frac{\textit{Infinite Good}}{\text{Infinite Being}} \text{ as } \frac{\textit{Finite Good}}{\text{Finite Being}}$$

Infinite good is related to an infinite Being the way finite good is related to a finite being. This, however, is not helpful, and could be misleading, in finding a relationship (similarity) between an infinite good and finite good. This is not the kind of analogy on which Aquinas based the similarity between Creator and creature.

Intrinsic Analogy. An intrinsic analogy is one in which both things possess the same characteristic, each in accordance with its own being. There are, again, two kinds: the analogy of proper proportionality and the analogy of intrinsic attribution.

Intrinsic analogy is based on similarity of relations. By subtly changing the statement of relationship in the analogy of improper proportionality, we can develop an "analogy of proper proportionality." In the analogy of proper proportionality two like things are being compared, not two like relationships. There is a proper relationship between the attribute they each possess and their own respective natures. Applied to God this analogy would declare that:

$$\frac{\textit{Infinite Good}}{\text{Infinite Being}} \text{ as } \frac{\textit{Finite Good}}{\text{Finite Being}}$$

While this analogy does not explain a direct relationship between the attribute of goodness as it applies to both parties, it does compare the way an attribute in God relates to his essence and, by comparison, the way a similar attribute in man as a creature relate to his essence. The analogy tells us nothing directly about the similarity between God and creation. Rather, it informs us about the same relationship of goodness to being in an infinite being and in a finite being.

The analogy of intrinsic attribution. In the analogy of intrinsic attribution, the analogs possess the same attribute, and the similarity is based on a causal connection between them. For example, hot water causes the egg floating in it to become hot. The cause communicates itself to the effect. A mind communicates its intelligence to a book. The book, then, is the intelligible effect of the intelligent cause.

This is the kind of analogy on which Aquinas bases the similarity of Creator and creatures. What God creates must be like him because he communicates himself to the effect. Being communicates being. Pure Actuality creates other actualities. This kind of analogy of intrinsic attribution, where both the cause and the effect have the same attribute, is the basis for making true statements about God. These statements correspond to the way God really is because these characteristics were derived from him and communicated by him to his effects. In short, the similarity between Creator and creatures is derived from the characteristics the Creator gave to his creature.

Creatures do not possess a common characteristic (say, goodness) in the same way God does. An infinite being possesses goodness in an infinite way, and a finite being possesses goodness in a finite way. Nevertheless, they both possess goodness, because a Good Being can only communicate goodness. The extent to which the creature falls short of God's goodness is due to the finite and fallible mode of the creature's existence; it is not caused by the infinite goodness of its cause. But the degree to which a creature has *any* goodness, that goodness is like the attribute in its Creator, who *is* Goodness.

God and Creatures. All meaningfully descriptive talk about God is based on the analogy of intrinsic attribution, whereby creatures are like the Creator because of the causal relationship between them. Aquinas wrote, "Some likeness must be found between them [between effects and their cause], since it belongs to the nature of action that an agent produces its like, since each thing acts according as it is in act" (*Summa contra Gentiles,* I, 29, 2). Important features of this relationship should be understood.

A Causal Relationship. The relationship between God and the world is causal. In names given to both God and creatures "we note in the community of such names the order of cause and effect" (ibid., I, 33). Hence, "whatever is said of

God and creatures is said according as there is some relation of the creature to God as to its principal cause" (ibid., I, 13, 5). Causality is a relation of dependency, not of dualism. The creatures possess the characteristic only because they got it from the Creator. To state the matter simply, *the Cause of being shared being with the beings it brought into being*. Apart from this causal relation of dependency, there would be no common, shared attribute between the Creator and creatures.

An Intrinsic Relationship. The causal relationship between God and human beings is real. Similarity is based on the fact that both cause and effect have the same characteristic, the effect getting it from the cause. God is not called good, for example, simply because he made good things. This would be an extrinsic causal relation, like hot air making clay hard. The air is not hard; it simply made the effect hard. The same hot air makes wax soft.

Rather God *is* good, and so a human being has a source of good. Both hot air and clay become hot, because heat communicates heat. Heat producing heat is an intrinsic causal relation. This kind of causal relation exists between God and creation.

All of creation is like God insofar as it is actual, but unlike God insofar as it is limited by its potentiality to receive his likeness. A sculptor, the cause, cannot get the same effect in pudding as in stone, even though the same form is imposed on both. Pudding simply does not have the same potential as stone to receive a stable and lasting form. The similarity between God and a creature will depend on the limited potential of the creature to receive his actuality. Thus, creatures *differ* from God in their potentiality, but are *like* (though not identical to) God in their actuality.

An Essential Relationship. The causal relationship between God and the world is *per se*, not *per accidens*. That is to say, it is an essential, not an accidental relationship. God is the cause of the *being* of the world, not merely the cause of its *becoming*.

An accidental causal relationship is one where there is only nonessential relation between the cause and the effect. Musicians give birth to nonmusicians. Musical skill is not an essential element of the relationship between parent and child. So there cannot be said to be an essential relationship between two great violinists, even though they might be mother and daughter, and even if genetics and nurture did contribute to the daughter's accomplishments.

However, humans give birth to humans. Characteristics of humanness were essential to the relationship of those mother-daughter musicians. The daughter might have been born tone deaf, but she could not have been born feline. Humanity is an essential causal relation. The essential characteristics of humanness are possessed by both the cause and the effect. This is the kind of causal relation that exists between God and his creatures.

An Efficient Cause. The *efficient cause* is a cause *by which* something comes to be. An *instrumental cause* is that *through which* something comes to be. The student is the efficient cause of the completed examination paper; the student's pen is only the instrumental cause. Therefore, the exam will resemble the student's thoughts, not any ideas in the pen, even if it were fitted with a powerful microcomputer. The garage resembles the plan in the carpenter's mind, not the carpenter's hammer. Hence, there is no necessary connection between an instrumental cause and its effect, only between the efficient cause and its effect.

The same can be said of the efficient cause as opposed to the *material cause*. The material cause is that *out of which* something comes to be. The sun produces heat, which is an efficient cause of the heat absorbed by the piece of clay baking on the stone. The sun's heat is a material cause of the hardness produced as the clay bakes on a rock. But the hardness is not caused by the sun's heat. The h0ardness is not even caused "efficiently" by the material conditions of the clay. That is another sort of material cause. The efficient cause of the hardened clay is the God who designed the physics by which clay reacts to heat.

Furthermore, just because God created Adam's body out of matter (its material cause) does not mean that God is a material being. Efficient causes do not need to resemble their effects any more than Wilbur and Orville Wright's minds had wings and a fuselage. An airplane is made of matter; the mind that designed it is not. The visible, material words on this page resemble my mind (their efficient cause), but my mind is not made of paper and ink. Likewise, the invisible God (efficient cause) is not like the visible world (material cause), nor is the material world like the immaterial God (John 4:24).

Criticisms of Analogy. A number of objections have been raised against the principle of analogy (for example, Ferre, 1:94–97). Many of these were answered by Aquinas or can be inferred from what he said. The following are responses to some significant objections.

A General Theory of Analogy Does Not Work. So long as analogy is tied to the metaphysics of intrinsic causality, analogy does work. In fact, analogy seems to be the only adequate answer to the problem of religious language. All negative God-talk implies positive knowledge of God. But positive affirmations of God are possible only if univocally understood concepts can be applied to both creatures and Creator (as Duns Scotus argued).

On the other hand, since God is infinitely perfect and creatures are only finitely perfect, no perfection found in the finite world can be applied univocally to both God and creatures. But to apply them equivocally would leave us in skepticism. Hence, whatever perfections are found in creation and can be applied to God without limits are predicated analogically. The perfection is understood univocally (in the same manner), but it is predicated analogously (in a similar manner), because to affirm it univocally in a finite way of an infinite Being would not truly describe the way he is. And to affirm it equivocally in an infinite way would not describe him at all. Hence, a univocal concept, drawn from the finite world, can speak of God only analogically.

Distinctions among Univocal, Equivocal and Analogical Are Obsolete. According to Ludwig Wittgenstein, expressions receive meaning from their use in language games based in experience. Each language game is autonomous. (It sets its own rules for establishing meaning.) insofar as there are no universal criteria for meaning. Words that carry over from game to game or words with similar meanings bear family resemblance, but we can never isolate a core meaning they must share. Thus, Wittgenstein believes that the separation of meanings into categories of *univocal, analogical,* or *equivocal* breaks down in dynamic usage of language.

Is meaning so arbitrarily established at the whim of the context? Unless there is an essential, as opposed to a purely conventional, meaning to language, then all meaning (and truth) is relative (*see* CONVENTIONALISM). But it is self-defeating to claim that "No meaning is objective," since even that statement would be without objective meaning. If there were no objective meaning, then anything could mean anything to anyone, even the opposite of what the communicator intended. This would be linguistic (and social) chaos.

Also, distinctions between *univocal, equivocal,* and *analogical* are not arbitrary. In fact, they are logically exhaustive; there are no other alternatives. A term is understood or applied in entirely the same way (univocally), in an entirely different way (equivocally), or in a similar way (analogically). Wittgenstein does not offer another alternative. Rather, as applied to objective reality, his view reduces to equivocal God-talk. For although he accepts meaningful God-talk, insofar as it is based in meaningful religious experience, nonetheless, it is not really talk about God. It is really talk about religious experience. God remains part of the mystical and inexpressible, at least so far as descriptive language is concerned.

Why Only Some Qualities Apply to God. Only these characteristics (authenticity, compassion, freedom, goodness, holiness, immanence, knowledge, love, righteousness, wisdom) apply to human actuality rather than to human potentiality. So only these flow from God's efficient, essential, principal, and intrinsic causality. Other beings *have* these qualities; God *is* these qualities. Only these characteristics may be appropriately applied to an unlimited Being. Things are like God in their actuality, but not in their potentiality, since God has no potentiality. He is Pure Actuality. So, only their actuality is like God.

Applying Words to the Infinite. Words divorced from their finite condition are devoid of meaning. This means that all God-talk about analogies or anything else is meaningless, since the concepts cannot apply to an infinite, transcendent Being. Such a criticism overlooks the distinction between a concept and its predication. The concept behind a word remains the same; only the way in which it is predicated changes. The meanings of the words *goodness, being,* and *beauty* can be applied to finite reality, and they can be applied to God; when used in the divine setting, the words are merely extended without limits. Being is still being, and goodness is still goodness; in application to the essence of God they are released from any limiting mode of signification. Since the perfection denoted by some terms does not necessarily imply any limitations, there is no reason why perfection cannot be predicated of an unlimited Being. In Aquinas's terms, that which is signified is the same; only the mode of signification is different.

Analogy and Causality. It is argued that analogy rests on the questionable premise of causality. It is true that Aquinas bases analogy in the similarity that must exist between an efficient cause and its effect. This is true because Being communicates only being. The Cause of existence cannot produce perfection that it does not "possess" itself. If God causes goodness, then he must be good. If he causes existence, then he must exist. Otherwise the absurd consequence ensues that God gives what he does not have to give.

Tailoring Terms to the Infinite. An analogous predication of God fails to identify the univocal element. In drawing an analogy between the finite and the infinite, we must be able to isolate that "univocal" attribute or quality that both share. And we can identify the basic element, though we have to drop the limitations from our thinking when applying it to its Pure Actuality. For a predication of a perfection of an infinite Being cannot be done in the same way of a finite being because it does not have qualities in a finite way. The objection would hold for equivocal concepts, those that cannot be applied both to God and to creation, but it is not true of univocal concepts that have analogical predications. One must have a univocal understanding of what is being predicated. I must be careful of my definition of *love* when I say that "I love," and that "God is love." The only way to avoid equivocation when predicating the same quality to finite beings and infinite Being is to predicate it appropriately to the mode of being that each is.

Relating Creator to Creature. The real relationship between Creator and creatures is not univocally expressible. This criticism fails to distinguish between the thing signified and the mode of its expression. The concept of *being* or *existence* is understood to mean the same thing, whether we are referring to God or a human being. It is "that which is or exists." God exists and a person exists; this they have in common. So the concept *being* is univocal to both. But God exists infinitely and independently, whereas a human being exists finitely and dependently; in this they are different. That they both exist is univocally conceived; how they each exist is analogically predicated. For God exists necessarily, and creatures exist contingently.

Conclusion. Religious language does not merely evoke an experience about God that tells us nothing about who "God" is. God-talk is either univocal, equivocal, or analogical. It cannot be equivocal since we do know something about God. The claim: "We cannot make any meaningful statements about God" implies that we know what the word *God* means in the context of other words. By the same token, God-talk cannot be univocal, since we cannot predicate an attribute of an infinite Being in the *same way* that we do of a finite being. God is "good," for example, in an unlimited way. Creatures can be "good" in a limited, reflective way. Both are good, but not in the same way.

But if God-talk is neither univocal or equivocal, then it *must* be analogical. This analogy of similarity is based in the Creator/creature relations. As Cause of being, God is Being. He cannot give what he does not have to give. Being produces being; Pure Actuality actualizes other actualities. Since God cannot produce another Necessary Being like himself, he must produce contingent beings. But contingent beings, unlike a Necessary Being, have the potentiality to not be. Hence, while God is pure Actuality, everything else is a combination of actuality and the limiting potentiality not to be.

Thus, when we predicate to God things from creation, we cannot predicate any of their limitations to him. We can only ascribe the actuality the creature received from the Creator. In this sense, creatures are both like and unlike God. That opens the door to understanding by analogy.

The only alternatives to analogy are skepticism or dogmatism: Either we know nothing about God, or we assume that we know things in the same infinite way in which he knows them.

Sources

F. Ferre, "Analogy" in the *Encyclopedia of Philosophy,* Paul Edwards, ed.

N. L. Geisler, *Philosophy of Religion*

———, *Thomas Aquinas: An Evangelical Appraisal*

R. McInerny, *The Logic of Analogy*

B. Mondin, *The Principle of Analogy in Protestant and Catholic Theology*

Thomas Aquinas, *On Being and Essence*

———, *On the Power of God*

———, *Summa contra Gentiles*

———, *Summa Theologica*

Annihilationism. *Annihilationism* is the doctrine that the souls of the wicked will be snuffed out of existence rather than be sent to an everlasting, conscious hell. The existence of the unrepentant will be extinguished, while the righteous will enter into everlasting bliss.

Support from Scripture. *"The Second Death."* Annihilationists point to the Bible references to the fate of the wicked as "the second death" (Rev. 20:14) in support of their view. Since a person loses consciousness of this world at the first death (physical death), it is argued that the "second death" will involve unconsciousness in the world to come.

"Everlasting Destruction." Scripture speaks of the wicked being "destroyed." Paul said: "This will happen when the Lord Jesus is revealed from heaven in blazing fire with his powerful angels. He will punish those who do not know God and do not obey the gospel of our Lord Jesus. They will be punished with *everlasting destruction* and shut out from the presence of the Lord and from the majesty of his power" (2 Thess. 1:7b–9). Annihilationists insist that the figure of "destruction" is incompatible with a continued, conscious existence.

"Perdition." The wicked are said to go into "perdition" (KJV) or "destruction" (NIV) (2 Peter 3:7), and Judas is called the "son of perdition" (John 17:12). The word *perdition (apoleia)* means to perish. This, annihilationists argue, indicates that the lost will perish or go out of existence.

Like Not Having Been Born. Jesus said of Judas, who was sent to perdition, that "It would be better for him if he had not been born" (Mark 14:21). Before one is conceived they do not exist. Thus, for hell to be like the prebirth condition it must be a state of nonexistence.

"The Wicked Will Perish." Repeatedly, the Old Testament speaks of the wicked perishing. The psalmist wrote: "But the wicked will perish: The LORD's enemies will be like the beauty of the fields, they will vanish—vanish like smoke" (Ps. 37:20; cf. 68:2; 112:10). But to perish implies a state of nothingness.

Answering Arguments from Scripture. When examined carefully in context, none of the above passages proves annihilationism. At some points language may *permit* such a construction, but nowhere does the text demand annihilationism. In context and comparison with other Scriptures, the concept must be rejected in every case.

Separation, Not Extinction. The first death is simply the separation of the soul from the body (James 2:26), not the annihilation of the soul. Scripture presents death as conscious separation. Adam and Eve died spiritually the moment they sinned, yet they still existed and could hear God's voice (Gen. 3:10). Before one is saved, he is "dead in trespasses and sins" (Eph. 2:1), and yet he still carries God's image (Gen. 1:27; cf. Gen. 9:6; James 3:9). Though unable to come to Christ without the intervention of God, the "spiritually dead" are sufficiently aware that Scripture holds them accountable to believe (Acts 16:31), and repent (Acts 17:30). Continued awareness, but with separation from God and the inability to save oneself—these constitute Scripture's vision of the second death.

Destruction, Not Nonexistence. "Everlasting" destruction would not be annihilation, which only takes an instant and is over. If someone undergoes everlasting destruction, then they have to have everlasting existence. The cars in a junkyard have been destroyed, but they are not annihilated. They are simply beyond repair or unredeemable. So are the people in hell.

Since the word *perdition* means to die, perish, or to come to ruin, the same objections apply. In 2 Peter 3:7 *perdition* is used in the context of judgment, clearly implying consciousness. In our junkyard analogy, ruined cars have perished, but they are still junkyard cars. In this connection, Jesus spoke of hell as a dump where the fire would not cease and where a person's resurrected body would not be consumed (Mark 9:48).

In addition to comments on *death* and *perdition* above, it should be noted that the Hebrew word used to describe the wicked perishing in the Old Testament (*abad*) is also used to describe the righteous perishing (see Isa. 57:1; Micah 7:2). But even the annihilationists admit that the righteous are not snuffed out of existence. That being the case, they should not conclude that the wicked will cease to exist based on this term.

The same word (*abad*) is used to describe things that are merely lost but then later found (Deut. 22:3), which proves that lost does not mean nonexistent.

"It Would Have Been Better. . . ." When he says that it would have been better if Judas had not been born, Jesus is not comparing Judas's perdition to his nonexistence before conception but to his existence before *birth.* This hyperbolic figure of speech would almost certainly indicate the severity of his punishment, not a statement about the superiority of nonbeing over being. In a parallel condemnation on the Pharisees, Jesus said Sodom and Gomorrah would have repented had they seen his miracles (Matt. 11:23–24). This does not mean that they actually would have repented or God would surely have shown them these miracles—2 Peter 3:9. It is simply a powerful figure of speech indicating that their sin was so great that "it would be *more tolerable*" in the day of judgment for Sodom than for them (vs. 24).

Further, nothing cannot be better than something, since they have nothing in common to compare them. So nonbeing cannot be actually better than being. To assume otherwise is a category mistake.

Biblical Arguments. In addition to the lack of any definitive passages in favor of annihilationism, numerous texts support the doctrine of eternal conscious punishment. A brief summary includes:

The Rich Man in Hell. Unlike parables which have no real persons in them, Jesus told the story of an actual beggar named Lazarus who went to heaven and of a rich man who died and went to hell and was in conscious torment (Luke 16:22–28). He cried out, "'Father Abraham, have pity on me and send Lazarus to dip the tip of his finger in water and cool my tongue, because I am in agony in this fire.' But Abraham replied, 'Son, remember that in your lifetime you received your good things, while Lazarus received bad things, but now he is comforted here and you are in agony'" (vss. 24–25). The rich man then begged that his brothers be warned "so that they will not also come to this place of torment" (vs. 27). There is no hint of annihilation in this passage; he is suffering constant and conscious torment.

A Place of Weeping and Gnashing of Teeth. Jesus repeatedly said the people in hell are in continual agony. He declared that "the subjects of the kingdom will be thrown outside, into the darkness, where there will be weeping and gnashing of teeth" (Matt. 8:12; cf. 22:13; 24:51; 25:30). But a place of weeping is obviously a place of conscious sorrow. Those who are not conscious do not weep.

A Place of Unquenchable Flames. Jesus repeatedly called hell a place of unquenchable flames (Mark 9:43–48) where the very bodies of the wicked will never die (cf. Luke 12:4–5). But it would make no sense to have everlasting flames and bodies without any souls in them to experience the torment.

A Place of Everlasting Torment. John the apostle described hell as a place of eternal torment. He declared that "the devil, who deceived them, was thrown into the lake of burning sulfur, where the beast and the false prophet had been thrown. They will be tormented day and night for ever and ever" (Rev. 20:10). Eternal torment indicates that the everlasting state of woe is conscious.

A Place for the Beast and False Prophet. In a clear example of beings who were still conscious after a thousand years of conscious torment in hell, the Bible says of the beast and false prophets that "The two of them were thrown *alive* into the fiery lake of burning sulfur" (Rev. 19:20) before the "thousand years" (Rev. 20:2).

Yet after this period the devil, who deceived them, was cast into the lake of fire and brimstone where the beast and the false prophet [still] *are*" (Rev. 20:10, emphasis added). Not only were they "alive" when they entered, but they were still alive after a thousand years of conscious torment.

A Place of Conscious Punishment. The fact that the wicked are "punished with everlasting destruction" (2 Thess. 1:9) strongly implies that they must be conscious. One cannot suffer punishment without existence. It is no punishment to beat a dead corpse. An unconscious person feels no pain.

Annihilation would not be a punishment but a release from all punishment. Job can suffer something worse than annihilation in this life. The punishment of evil men in the afterlife would have to be conscious. If not, then God is not just, since he would have given less punishment to some wicked than to some righteous people. For not all wicked people suffer as much as some righteous people do in this life.

A Place That Is Everlasting. Hell is said to be of the same duration as heaven, "everlasting" (Matt. 25:41). As the saints in heaven are said to be in conscious bliss (Luke 23:43; 2 Cor. 5:8; Phil. 1:23), so the sinners in hell are in conscious woe (cf. Luke 16).

Philosophical Arguments. *For Annihilation.* In addition to biblical arguments, many annihilationists offer philosophical reasons for rejecting everlasting conscious punishment. Granting a theistic perspective, most of them, however, are a variation on the one theme of God's mercy. Arguments by those who deny theism or human immortality are covered in those respective articles.

Annihilationists reason that God is a God of mercy (Exod. 20:6), and it is merciless to allow people to suffer consciously forever. We kill trapped horses if we cannot rescue them from burning buildings. We put other suffering creatures out of their misery. Annihilationists argue that a merciful God would surely do as much for his creatures.

Against Annihilationism. The very concept of an ultimately merciful God supposes that he is the absolute standard for what is merciful and morally right. Indeed, the moral argument for God's existence demonstrates this. But if God is the ultimate standard for moral righteousness, we cannot impose our concept of justice upon him. The very idea of injustice presupposes an ultimate standard, which theists claim for God.

Annihilation would demean both the love of God and the nature of human beings as free moral creatures. It would be as if God said to them, "I will allow you to be free only if you do what I say. If you don't, then I will snuff out your very freedom and existence!" This would be like a father telling his son he wanted him to be a doctor, but when the son chose instead to be a park ranger the father shot him. Eternal suffering is eternal testimony to the freedom and dignity of humans, even unrepentant humans.

It would be contrary to the created nature of human beings to annihilate them, since they are made in God's image and likeness, which is everlasting (Gen. 1:27). Animals are often killed to alleviate their pain. But (the euthanasia movement notwithstanding) we do not do the same for humans precisely because they are not animals. They are created in the image of God and, hence, should be treated with the greatest respect for their dignity as God's image bearers. Not to allow them to continue to exist in their freely chosen destiny, painful as it may be, is to snuff out God's image in them. Since free choice is morally good, being part of the image of God, then it would be a moral evil to take it away. But this is what annihilation does: It destroys human freedom forever.

Further, to stomp out the existence of a creature in God's immortal image is to renege on what God gave them—immortality. It is to attack himself in effigy by destroying his image-bearers. But God does not act against God.

To punish the crime of telling of a half-truth with the same ferocity as the crime of genocide is unjust. Hitler should receive a greater punishment than a petty thief, though both crimes affront God's infinite holiness. Certainly not all judgment proportionate to the sin is meted out in this life. The Bible speaks of degrees of punishment in hell (Matt. 5:22; Rev. 20:12–14). But there can be no degrees of annihilation. Nonexistence is the same for all persons.

Conclusion. The doctrine of annihilation rests more on sentimental than scriptural bases. Although, there are some biblical expressions that *can* be construed to support annihilationism, there are none that *must* be understood this way. Furthermore, numerous passages clearly state that the wicked will suffer consciously and eternally in hell (*see* HELL; "HEATHEN," SALVATION OF; UNIVERSALISM).

Sources

J. Edwards, *The Works of Jonathan Edwards*

E. Fudge, *The Fire That Consumes*

L. E. Froom, *The Conditionalist's Faith of Our Father*

N. L. Geisler, "Man's Destiny: Free or Forced," *CSR*, 9.2

J. Gerstner, *Jonathan Edwards on Heaven and Hell*

C. S. Lewis, *The Great Divorce*

———, *The Problem of Pain*. Chapter 8

———, *The Screwtape Letters*

F. Nietzsche, *Toward a Genealogy of Morals*

R. A. Peterson, "A Traditionalist Response to John Stott's Arguments for Annihilationism," *JETS*, December 1994

———, *Hell on Trial: The Case for Eternal Punishment*

C. Pinnock, *A Wideness in God's Mercy*

B. Russell, *Why I Am Not a Christian*

J. P. Sartre, *No Exit*

G. T. Shed, *Eternal Punishment*

Anselm. Anselm of Canterbury (1033–1109) was born in Aosta, Piedmont (England). He became a prior in a Benedictine monastery and was later appointed archbishop of Canterbury (1093). Anselm's major works include *Proslogion, Monologion, Cur Deus Homo?,* and *Truth*.

Philosophically, Anselm's ideas were molded by Plato (428–348 B.C.). Theologically, the writings of Augustine were formative on his thought. Nonetheless, Anselm was an original thinker who originated one of the most creative, controversial, and enduring arguments for the existence of God—the *ontological argument.

Anselm's Views. Faith and Reason. Anselm's view of faith and reason was influenced by Augustine's "faith seeking understanding." Nevertheless, Anselm's establishment of reason on its own foundation had been unattained by Augustine. In fact, the late scholastic method of reasoning finds roots in Anselm's philosophical dialectic. His arguments for God are a case in point, especially the ontological argument, which began in meditation and ended with one of the most sophisticated and subtle arguments for God ever devised (*see* GOD, EVIDENCE FOR; GOD, OBJECTIONS TO PROOFS FOR).

In *Cur Deus Homo?* Anselm made it clear that reason must be used to explain and defend Christianity. He held that it is possible to disclose "in their true rationality, those things in Christian faith which seem to infidels improper or impossible" (ibid., 2.15). Even doctrines like the Trinity and the Incarnation (*see* CHRIST, DEITY OF) Anselm believed to be "reasonable and incontrovertible." He concluded that "in proving that God became man by necessity . . . you [can] convince both Jews and Pagans by the mere force of reason" (ibid., 2.22).

Anselm saw a two-fold role of reason. First, he spoke of writing the proof of a certain doctrine of our faith, "which I am accustomed to give to inquirers" (ibid., 1.1). This, he said, was "not for the sake of attaining to faith by means of reason, but that they may be gladdened by understanding and meditating on those things which they believe; and that, as far as possible, they may be always ready to convince anyone who demands of them a reason of the hope which is in us" (ibid., 1.1).

Truth. Few essays better defend the nature of truth than Anselm's work by the simple title, *Truth*. Anselm provides a strong defense of the correspondence view of truth and the absolute nature of truth (*see* TRUTH, ABSOLUTE NATURE OF; TRUTH, NATURE OF).

God. Anselm was a Christian theologian. As such, he accepted the Bible as the infallible Word of God (*see* BIBLE, EVIDENCE FOR). From this he concluded that God is one in essence (*see* GOD, NATURE OF) and three in persons—the Trinity. But Anselm believed that the existence and nature of this one God (though not his tri-unity) could be demonstrated rationally apart from supernatural revelation. Contrary to popular understanding, Anselm had many arguments for God's existence. He elaborated many forms of the cosmological argument before he ever devised the ontological argument.

Anselm's cosmological type arguments (SEE *MONOLOGION*). Anselm argued from goodness to God:

1. Good things exist.
2. The cause of this goodness is either one or many.
3. But it can't be many, for then there would be no way to compare their goodness, for all things would be equally good. But some things are better than others.
4. Therefore, one Supreme Good (God) causes the goodness in all good things.

Anselm argued from perfection to God, an argument C. S. Lewis emulated in *Mere Christianity*:

1. Some beings are more nearly perfect than are others.
2. But things cannot be more or less perfect unless there is a wholly perfect to which they can be compared.
3. Therefore, there must be a Most Perfect Being (God).

Anselm argued from being to God:

1. Something exists.
2. Whatever exists, exists either through nothing or through something.
3. But nothing cannot cause something; only something can cause something.
4. And this something is either one or many.
5. If many, they are either mutually dependent or all dependent on one for their existence.
6. They cannot be mutually dependent for their existence, for something cannot exist through a being on which it confers existence.
7. Therefore, there must be one being through which all other beings exist.
8. This one being must exist through itself, since everything else exists through it.
9. And whatever exists through itself, exists in the highest degree of all.
10. Therefore, there exists a supremely perfect Being that exists in the highest degree of all.

With the exception of the last two premises, which are distinctly platonic in speaking of degrees of being, this argument could have been expressed (and to some degree was) by Thomas Aquinas.

Anselm's ontological argument(s) (*see* PROSLOGION). Anselm's most famous contribution was his ontological argument(s), though Anselm himself never so named them. Immanuel Kant did many centuries later, believing they contained an ontological fallacy.

The first form of the ontological argument of Anselm was from the idea of an absolutely perfect being. It takes this form:

1. God is by definition that than which nothing greater can be conceived.
2. It is greater to exist in reality than to exist only in the mind.
3. Therefore God must exist in reality. If he didn't exist, he wouldn't be the greatest possible.

The second form of the ontological argument emerged from Anselm's friendly debate with another monk named Gaunilo. It argues from the idea of a Necessary Being.

1. God is by definition a Necessary Being.
2. It is logically necessary to affirm what is necessary of the concept of a Necessary Being.
3. Existence is logically necessary to the concept of a Necessary Being.
4. Therefore, a Necessary Being (God) necessarily exists.

The pros and cons of the ontological argument(s) are discussed elsewhere (*see* ONTOLOGICAL ARGUMENT). Whatever its merits, the argument has had a long and illustrious career and is still alive a millennium later.

Christ. Anselm's work *Cur Deus Homo?* (*Why the God-Man?*) is a classic in the history of Christian thought. It is a rational defense of the need for the incarnation of Christ in general and the penal view of the atonement in particular. It is a landmark treatise of rational theology.

The Influence of Anselm. Anselm's popularity, especially through his ontological argument, continues, such detractors as David Hume and Kant notwithstanding. Anselm has had a positive impact on many modern and contemporary thinkers, including Rene Descartes, Benedict Spinoza, Charles Hartshorne, Norman Malcolm, and Alvin Plantinga.

Summary. Anselm is a model of traditional or classical apologetics.* He believed in offering proofs for the existence of God. Further, he believed that historical evidence, confirmed by miracles, could be supplied to support the truth of the Christian religion (*see* MIRACLES, APOLOGETIC VALUE OF). Anselm is the antithesis of fideism and purely presuppositional apologetics.

Anselm was a child of his day, which was dominated by platonic philosophy. The idea of degrees of existence and existence as a perfection is usually rejected. But these are not crucial to his system of classical apologetics as a whole. Indeed, Anselm's cosmological argument from being compares with that of Aquinas.

Sources

Anselm, *Cur Deus Homo?*

———, *Monologion*

———, *Proslogion*

———, *Truth*

N. L. Geisler, *Philosophy of Religion*. chaps. 7–8

I. Kant, *The Critique of Pure Reason*

C. S. Lewis, *Mere Christianity*

Antedeluvians, Longevity of. ***See*** **SCIENCE AND THE BIBLE.**

Anthropic Principle. The *anthropic principle* (Greek: *anthropos,* "human being") states that the universe was fitted from the very first moment of its existence for the emergence of life in general and human life in particular (*see* BIG BANG; EVOLUTION, BIOLOGICAL; THERMODYNAMICS, LAWS OF). As agnostic astronomer, Robert Jastrow, noted, the universe is amazingly preadapted to the eventual appearance of humanity (see "A Scientist Caught"). For if there were even the slightest variation at the moment of the big bang, making conditions different, even to a small degree, no life of any kind would exist. In order for life to be present today an incredibly restrictive set of demands must have been present in the early universe—and they were.

Supporting Evidence. Not only does the scientific evidence point to a beginning of the cosmos, but it points to a very sophisticated high tuning of the universe from the very beginning that makes human life possible. For life to be present today, an incredibly restrictive set of demands must have been present in the early universe:

1. Oxygen comprises 21 percent of the atmosphere. If it were 25 percent, fires would erupt, if 15 percent, human beings would suffocate.
2. If the gravitational force were altered by 1 part in 10^{40} (that's 10 followed by forty zeroes), the sun would not exist, and the moon would crash into the earth or sheer off into space (Heeren, 196). Even a slight increase in the force of gravity would result in all the stars being much more massive than our sun, with the effect that the sun would burn too rapidly and erratically to sustain life.
3. If the centrifugal force of planetary movements did not precisely balance the gravitational forces, nothing could be held in orbit around the sun.
4. If the universe was expanding at a rate one millionth more slowly than it is, the tem-

perature on earth would be 10,000 degrees C. (ibid., 185).

5. The average distance between stars in our galaxy of 100 billion stars is 30 trillion miles. If that distance was altered slightly, orbits would become erratic, and there would be extreme temperature variations on earth. (Traveling at space shuttle speed, seventeen thousand miles an hour or five miles a second, it would take 201,450 years to travel 30 trillion miles.)
6. Any of the laws of physics can be described as a function of the velocity of light (now defined to be 186,282 miles a second). Even a slight variation in the speed of light would alter the other constants and preclude the possibility of life on earth (Ross, 126).
7. If Jupiter was not in its current orbit, we would be bombarded with space material. Jupiter's gravitational field acts as a cosmic vacuum cleaner, attracting asteroids and comets that would otherwise strike earth (ibid., 196).
8. If the thickness of the earth's crust was greater, too much oxygen would be transferred to the crust to support life. If it were thinner, volcanic and tectonic activity would make life untenable (ibid., 130).
9. If the rotation of the earth took longer than 24 hours, temperature differences would be too great between night and day. If the rotation period was shorter, atmospheric wind velocities would be too great.
10. Surface temperature differences would be too great if the axial tilt of the earth were altered slightly.
11. If the atmospheric discharge (lightning) rate were greater, there would be too much fire destruction; if it were less, there would be too little nitrogen fixing in the soil.
12. If there were more seismic activity, much life would be lost. If there was less, nutrients on the ocean floors and in river runoff would not be cycled back to the continents through tectonic uplift. Even earthquakes are necessary to sustain life as we know it.

As early as the 1960s it was explained why, on anthropic grounds, "we should expect to observe a world that possesses precisely three spatial dimensions" (Barrow, 247). Robert Dicke found "that in fact it may be necessary for the universe to have the enormous size and complexity which modern astronomy has revealed, in order for the earth to be a possible habitation for living beings" (ibid.). Likewise, the mass, the entropy level of the universe, the stability of the proton, and innumerable other things must be just right to make life possible.

Theistic Implications. Jastrow summarized the theistic implications well: "The anthropic principle . . . seems to say that science itself has proven, as a hard fact, that this universe was made, was designed, for man to live in. *It's a very theistic result*" (Jastrow, "A Scientist Caught," 17, emphasis added). That is, the incredible balance of multitudinous factors in the universe that make life possible on earth points to "fine tuning" by an intelligent Being. It leads one to believe that the universe was "providentially crafted" for our benefit. Nothing known to human beings is capable of "pretuning" the conditions of the universe to make life possible other than an intelligent Creator. Or, to put it another way, the kind of specificity and order in the universe that makes life possible on earth is just the kind of effect that is known to come from an intelligent cause.

Astronomer Alan Sandage concluded that "the world is too complicated in all of its parts to be due to chance alone. I am convinced that the existence of life with all its order in each of its organisms is simply too well put together. Each part of a living thing depends on all its other parts to function. How does each part know? How is each part specified at conception. The more one learns of biochemistry the more unbelievable it becomes unless there is some kind of organizing principle—an architect for believers . . ." (Sandage, 54). And all of the conditions were set from the moment of the universe's origin.

Stephen Hawking described how the value of many fundamental numbers in nature's laws "seem to have been very finely adjusted to make possible the development of life" and how "the initial configuration of the universe" appears to have been "very carefully chosen" (cited by Heeren, 67). In spite of the fact that only an intelligent cause can "carefully choose" anything, Hawking at this writing remains skeptical about God. He saw the evidence clearly and asked the right question when he wrote: "There may only be a small number of laws, which are self-consistent and which lead to complicated beings like ourselves who can ask the question: What is the nature of God? And even if there is only one unique set of possible laws, it is only a set of equations. What is it that breathes fire into the equations and makes a universe for them to govern? . . . Although science may solve the problem of how the universe began, it cannot answer the question: Why does the universe bother to exist?" Hawking adds, "I don't know the answer to that" (Hawking, 99).

Albert Einstein did not hesitate to answer Hawking's question when he said, "the harmony of natural law . . . reveals an intelligence of such superiority that, compared with it, all the systematic thinking and acting of human beings is an utterly insignificant reflection" (Einstein, 40). Even Nobel prize winner Steven Weinberg, an atheist, went so far as to say that "it seems to me that if the word 'God' is to be of any use, it should be taken to mean *an interested God, a creator and lawgiver who established not only the laws of nature* and the universe but also standards of good and evil, some personality that is concerned with our actions, something in short that is appropriate for us to worship" (Weinberg, 244, emphasis added). Thus, the Anthropic Principle is based on the most recent astronomical evidence for the existence of a superintelligent Creator of the cosmos. In short, it provides the evidence for an updated Teleological Argument for God's existence.

Sources

J. D. Barrow, et al., *The Anthropic Cosmological Principle*
A. Einstein, *Ideals and Opinions—The World as I See It*
S. Hawkings, *A Brief History of Time*
F. Heeren, *Show Me God*
F. Hoyle, *The Intelligent Universe*
R. Jastrow, "A Scientist Caught between Two Faiths: Interview with Robert Jastrow," *CT*, 6 August 1982
———, *God and the Astronomers*
H. R. Pagels, *Perfect Symmetry*
H. Ross, *The Fingerprints of God*
A. Sandage, "A Scientist Reflects on Religious Belief," *Truth* (1985)
S. Weinberg, *Dreams of a Final Theory—The Search for the Fundamental Laws of Nature*

Anthropology and Evolution. *See* **EVOLUTION, BIOLOGICAL; MISSING LINKS.**

Antinomy. The word *antinomy* is used two ways. Strictly, it means an *actual* contradiction, paradox, or antithesis (*see* KANT, IMMANUEL). Often used to show the absurdity or impossibility of a view, as a *Reductio Ad Absurdum*. Loosely and popularly, it is used of only *apparent* contradictions, as in the mysteries of the Christian Faith. It this sense it means something that goes beyond reason but not *against* reason (*see* FAITH AND REASON; MYSTERY).

Apocrypha, Old and New Testaments. *Apocrypha* most commonly refers to disputed books that Protestants reject and Roman Catholics and Orthodox communions accept into the Old Testament. The word *apocrypha* means "hidden" or "doubtful." So those who accept these documents prefer to call them "deuterocanonical," or books of "the second canon."

The Roman Catholic View. Catholics and Protestants agree about the inspiration of the twenty-seven books of the New Testament. They differ over eleven pieces of literature in the Old Testament (seven books and four parts of books). These disputed works became an issue in the Reformation and, in reaction to their rejection by Protestants, were "infallibly" declared to be part of the inspired canon of Scripture in 1546 at the Council of Trent (*see* BIBLE, CANONICITY OF).

The Roman Catholic Council of Trent stated: "The Synod . . . receives and venerates . . . all the books [including the *Apocrypha*] both of the Old and the New Testaments—seeing that one God is the Author of both . . . as having been dictated, either by Christ's own word of mouth or by the Holy Ghost . . . if anyone receives not as sacred and canonical the said books entire with all their parts, as they have been used to be read in the Catholic Church . . . let him be anathema" (Schaff, 2:81). Another Trent document read: "If anyone, however, should not accept the said books as sacred and canonical, entire with all their parts, . . . and if both knowingly and deliberately he should condemn the aforesaid tradition let him be anathema" (Denzinger, *Sources*, no. 784). The same language affirming the *Apocrypha* is repeated by Vatican Council II.

The *Apocrypha* Rome accepts includes eleven books or twelve, depending on whether Baruch 1–6) is split into two pieces, Baruch 1–5 and The Letter of Jeremiah (Baruch 6). The Deuterocanon includes all the fourteen (or fifteen) books in the Protestant *Apocrypha* except the Prayer of Manasseh and 1 and 2 Esdras (called 3 and 4 Esdras by Roman Catholics. Ezra and Nehemiah are called 1 and 2 Esdras by Catholics).

Although the Roman Catholic canon has eleven more pieces of literature than does the Protestant Bible, only seven extra books, or a total forty-six, appear in the table of contents (the Protestant and Jewish Old Testament has thirty-nine). As noted in the accompanying table, four other pieces of literature are incorporated within Esther and Daniel.

The Literature in Dispute

Apocryphal Books	Deuterocanonical Books
The Wisdom of Solomon	Book of Wisdom (ca. 30 B.C.)
Ecclesiasticus (Sirach)	Sirach (132 B.C.)
Tobit (ca. 200 B.C.)	Tobit
Judith (ca. 150 B.C.)	Judith
1 Esdras (ca. 150–100 B.C.)	3 Esdras
1 Maccabees (ca. 110 B.C.)	1 Maccabees
2 Maccabees (ca. 110–70 B.C.)	2 Maccabees
Baruch (ca. 150–50 B.C.)	Baruch chaps. 1–5
Letter of Jeremiah	Baruch 6 (ca. 300–100 B.C.)

2 Esdras (ca. A.D. 100)	4 Esdras
Additions to Esther	Esther 10:4–16:24 (140–130 B.C.)
Prayer of Azariah (ca. 200–0 B.C.)	Daniel 3:24–90—"Song of Three Young Men"
Susanna (ca. 200–0 B.C.)	Daniel 13
Bel and the Dragon	Daniel 14 (ca. 100 B.C.)
Prayer of Manasseh (or second Prayer of Manasseh, ca. 100–0 B.C.)	

The Apocrypha as Scripture. The larger canon is sometimes referred to as the "Alexandrian Canon," as opposed to the "Palestinian Canon" which does not contain the *Apocrypha*, because it is alleged to have been part of the Greek translation of the Old Testament (the *Septuagint*, or *LXX*) prepared at Alexandria, Egypt. Reasons generally advanced in favor of this broader Alexandrian list are:

1. The New Testament reflects the thought of the *Apocrypha*, and even refers to events described in it (cf. Heb. 11:35 with 2 Maccabees 7, 12).
2. The New Testament quotes mostly from the Greek Old Testament, the LXX, which contained the *Apocrypha*. This gives tacit approval to the whole text.
3. Some early church fathers quoted and used the *Apocrypha* as Scripture in public worship.
4. Such early fathers as Irenaeus, Tertullian, and Clement of Alexandria accepted all of the *Apocrypha* as canonical.
5. Early Christian catacomb scenes depict episodes from the *Apocrypha*, showing it was part of early Christian religious life. This at least reveals a great regard for the *Apocrypha*.
6. Important early manuscripts (*Aleph*, *A*, and *B*) interpose the *Apocrypha* among the Old Testament books as part of the Jewish-Greek Old Testament.
7. Early church councils accepted the *Apocrypha*: Rome (382), Hippo (393), and Carthage (397).
8. The Eastern Orthodox church accepts the *Apocrypha*. Their acceptance shows it to be a common Christian belief, not one unique to Catholics.
9. The Roman Catholic church proclaimed the *Apocrypha* canonical at the Council of Trent (1546) in accord with the early councils noted and the Council of Florence not long before the Reformation (1442).
10. The apocryphal books continued to be included in the Protestant Bible as late as the nineteenth century. This indicates that even Protestants accepted the *Apocrypha* until very recently.
11. Apocryphal books in Hebrew were among Old Testament canonical books in the Dead Sea community at Qumran, so they were part of the Hebrew Canon (*see* DEAD SEA SCROLLS).

Answers to the Catholic Arguments. The New Testament and the Apocrypha. There may be New Testament allusions to the *Apocrypha*, but not once is there a definite quotation from any *Apocrypha* book accepted by the Roman Catholic church. There are allusions to Pseudepigraphical books (false writings) that are rejected by Roman Catholics as well as Protestants, such as the *Bodily Assumption of Moses* (Jude 9) and the *Book of Enoch* (Jude 14–15). There are also citations from Pagan poets and philosophers (Acts 17:28; 1 Cor. 15:33; Titus 1:12). None of these sources are cited as Scripture, nor with authority.

The New Testament simply refers to a truth contained in these books which otherwise may (and do) have errors. Roman Catholic scholars agree with this assessment. The New Testament never refers to any document outside the canon as authoritative.

The Septuagint and the Apocrypha. The fact that the New Testament often quotes from other books in the Greek Old Testament in no way proves that the deuterocanonical books it contains are inspired. It is not even certain that the *Septuagint* of the first century contained the *Apocrypha*. The earliest Greek manuscripts that include them date from the fourth century A.D.

Even if these writings were in the *Septuagint* in apostolic times, Jesus and the apostles never once quoted from them, although they are supposed to have been included in the very version of the Old Testament (the *Septuagint*) that the Lord and apostles usually cited. Even notes in the currently used Roman Catholic New American Bible (NAB) make the revealing admission that the *Apocrypha* are "Religious books used by both Jews and Christians which were not included in the collection of inspired writings." Instead, they ". . . were introduced rather late into the collection of the Bible. Catholics call them 'deuterocanonical' (second canon) books" (NAB, 413).

Use by the Church Fathers. Citations of church fathers in support of the canonicity of the *Apocrypha* is selective and misleading. Some fathers did seem to accept their inspiration; other fathers used them for devotional or homiletical (preaching) purposes but did not accept them as canonical. An authority on the *Apocrypha*, Roger Beckwith, observes,

> When one examines the passages in the early Fathers which are supposed to establish the canonicity of the *Apocrypha*, one finds that

> some of them are taken from the alternative Greek text of Ezra (1 Esdras) or from additions or appendices to Daniel, Jeremiah or some other canonical book, which . . . are not really relevant; that others of them are not quotations from the *Apocrypha* at all; and that, of those which are, many do not give any indication that the book is regarded as Scripture. [Beckwith, 387]

> *Epistle of Barnabas* 6.7 and Tertullian, *Against Marcion* 3.22.5, are not quoting Wisd. 2.12 but Isa. 3:10 LXX, and Tertullian, *On the Soul* 15, is not quoting Wisd. 1.6 but Ps. 139.23, as a comparison of the passages shows. Similarly, Justin Martyr, *Dialogue with Trypho* 129, is quite clearly not quoting Wisdom but Prov. 8.21–5 LXX. The fact that he calls Proverbs "Wisdom" is in accordance with the common nomenclature of the earlier Fathers. [Beckwith, 427]

Frequently in references, the fathers were not claiming divine authority for any of the eleven books infallibly canonized by the Council of Trent. Rather, they were citing a well-known piece of Hebrew literature or an informative devotional writing to which they gave no presumption of inspiration by the Holy Spirit.

The Fathers and the Apocrypha. Some individuals in the early church held the *Apocrypha* in high esteem; others were vehemently opposed to them. J. D. N. Kelly's comment that "for the great majority [of early fathers] . . . the deuterocanonical writings ranked as scripture in the fullest sense" is out of sync with the facts. Athanasius, Cyril of Jerusalem, Origen, and the great Roman Catholic biblical scholar and translator of the Latin Vulgate, Jerome, all opposed inclusion of the *Apocrypha*. In the second century A.D. the Syrian Bible (Peshitta) did not contain the *Apocrypha* (Geisler, *General Introduction,* chaps. 27, 28).

Catacomb Art Apocrypha Themes. As many Catholic scholars admit, scenes from the catacombs do not prove the canonicity of the books whose events they depict. Such scenes indicate little more than the religious significance the portrayed events had for early Christians. At best, they show a respect for the books containing these events, not a recognition that they are inspired.

Books in the Greek Manuscripts. None of the great Greek manuscripts (*Aleph*, *A*, and *B*) contain all of the apocryphal books. Tobit, Judith, Wisdom, and Sirach (Ecclesiasticus) are found in all of them, and the oldest manuscripts (*B* or *Vaticanus*) totally exclude the Books of Maccabees. Yet Catholics appeal to this manuscript in support of their view. What is more, no Greek manuscript has the same list of apocryphal books accepted by the Council of Trent (1545–63; Beckwith, 194, 382–83).

Acceptance by Early Councils. These were only local councils and were not binding on the whole church. Local councils often erred in their decisions and were later overruled by the universal church. Some Catholic apologists argue that, even though a council was not ecumenical, its results can be binding if they were confirmed by a Pope. However, they acknowledge that there is no infallible way to know which statements by Popes are infallible. Indeed, they admit that other statements by Popes were even heretical, such as the monothelite heresy of Pope Honorius I (d. 638).

It is also important to remember that these books were not part of the Christian (New Testament period) writings. Hence, they were not under the province of the Christian church to decide. They were the province of the Jewish community which wrote them and which had, centuries before, rejected them as part of the canon.

The books accepted by these Christian Councils may not have been the same ones in each case. Hence, they cannot be used as proof of the exact canon later infallibly proclaimed by the Roman Catholic church in 1546.

Local Councils of Hippo and Carthage in North Africa were influenced by Augustine, the most significant voice of antiquity who accepted the same apocryphal books later canonized by the Council of Trent. However, Augustine's position is ill-founded: (1) Augustine himself recognized that the Jews did not accept these books as part of their canon (Augustine, 19.36–38). (2) Of Maccabees, Augustine said, "These are held to be canonical, not by the Jews but by the Church, on account of the extreme and wonderful sufferings of certain martyrs" (Augustine, 18.36). On that ground *Foxe's Book of Martyrs* should be in the canon. (3) Augustine was inconsistent, since he rejected books not written by prophets, yet he accepted a book that appears to deny being prophetic (1 Macc. 9:27). (4) Augustine's mistaken acceptance of the *Apocrypha* seems to be connected with his belief in the inspiration of the *Septuagint*, whose later Greek manuscripts contained them. Augustine later acknowledged the superiority of Jerome's Hebrew text over the Septuagint's Greek text. That should have led him to accept the superiority of Jerome's Hebrew canon as well. Jerome utterly rejected the *Apocrypha*.

The later Council of Rome (382) which accepted *Apocryphal* books did not list the same books accepted by Hippo and Carthage. It does not list Baruch, thus listing only six, not seven, of the *Apocrypha* books later pronounced canonical. Even Trent lists it as a separate book (Denzinger, no. 84).

Acceptance by the Orthodox Church. The Greek church has not always accepted the *Apocrypha*, nor is its present position unequivocal. At the synods of Constantinople (1638), Jaffa (1642), and Jerusalem (1672) these books were declared canonical. But even as late as 1839 their Larger Catechism expressly omitted the *Apocrypha* on the grounds that they did not exist in the Hebrew Bible.

Acceptance at the Councils of Florence and Trent. At the Council of Trent (1546) the infallible proclamation was made accepting the *Apocrypha* as part of the inspired Word of God. Some Catholic scholars claim that the earlier Council of Florence (1442) made the same pronouncement. However, this council claimed no infallibility and neither council's decision has any real basis in Jewish history, the New Testament, or early Christian history. Unfortunately, the decision at Trent came a millennium and a half after the books were written and was an obvious polemic against Protestantism. The Council of Florence had proclaimed the *Apocrypha* inspired to bolster the doctrine of Purgatory that had blossomed. However, the manifestations of this belief in the sale of indulgences came to full bloom in Martin Luther's day, and Trent's infallible proclamation of the *Apocrypha* was a clear polemical against Luther's teaching. The official infallible addition of books that support prayers for the dead is highly suspect, coming only a few years after Luther protested this doctrine. It has all the appearance of an attempt to provide infallible support for doctrines that lack a real biblical basis.

Apocryphal Books in Protestant Bibles. Apocryphal books appeared in Protestant Bibles prior to the Council of Trent, and were generally placed in a separate section because they were not considered of equal authority. While Anglicans and some other non-Roman Catholic groups have always held a high regard for the inspirational and historical value of the *Apocrypha*, they never consider it inspired and of equal authority with Scripture. Even Roman Catholic scholars through the Reformation period distinguished between deuterocanon and canon. Cardinal Ximenes made this distinction in his *Complutensian Polyglot* (1514–17) on the very eve of the Reformation. Cardinal Cajetan, who later opposed Luther at Augsburg in 1518, published a *Commentary on All the Authentic Historical Books of the Old Testament* (1532) after the Reformation began which did not contain the *Apocrypha*. Luther spoke against the *Apocrypha* in 1543, including its books at the back of his Bible (Metzger, 181f.).

Apocryphal Writings at Qumran. The discovery of the Dead Sea Scrolls at Qumran included not only the community's Bible (the Old Testament) but their library, with fragments of hundreds of books. Among these were some Old Testament *Apocryphal* books. The fact that no commentaries were found for an *Apocryphal* book, and only canonical books were found in the special parchment and script indicates that the *Apocryphal* books were not viewed as canonical by the Qumran community. Menahem Mansoor lists the following fragments of the *Apocrypha* and *Pseudepigrapha*: Tobit, in Hebrew and Aramaic; *Enoch* in Aramaic; *Jubilees* in Hebrew; *Testament of Levi and Naphtali*, in Aramaic; *Apocryphal* Daniel literature, in Hebrew and Aramaic, and *Psalms of Joshua* (Mansoor, 203). The noted scholar on the Dead Sea Scrolls, Millar Burroughs, concluded: "There is no reason to think that any of these works were venerated as Sacred Scripture" (Burroughs, 178).

The Catholic Arguments in Summary. At best, all that the arguments urged in favor of the canonicity of the apocryphal books prove is that various apocryphal books were given varied degrees of esteem by various persons within the Christian church, usually falling short of claims for the books' canonicity. Only after Augustine and the local councils he dominated pronounced them inspired did they gain wider usage and eventual infallible acceptance by the Roman Catholic church at Trent. This falls far short of the kind of initial, continual, and full recognition among Christian churches of the canonical books of the Protestant Old Testament and Jewish Torah (which exclude the *Apocrypha*). True canonical books were received *immediately* by the people of God into the growing canon of Scripture (see Geisler, *General Introduction*, chap. 13). Any subsequent debate was by those who were not in a position, as was the immediate audience, to know whether they were from an accredited apostle or prophet. Hence, this subsequent debate over the antilegomena was over their *authenticity*, not canonicity. They were already in the canon; some in subsequent generations questioned whether they belonged there. Eventually, all of the antilegomena (books later questioned by some) were retained in the canon. This is not true of the *Apocrypha*, for Protestants reject all of them and even Roman Catholics reject 3 Esdras, 4 Esdras and The Prayer of Manasseh.

Arguments for the Protestant Canon. Evidence indicates that the Protestant canon, consisting of the thirty-nine books of the Hebrew Bible and excluding the *Apocrypha*, is the true canon. The only difference between the Protestant and ancient Palestinian Canon lies in organization. The ancient Bible lists twenty-four books. Combined into one each are 1–2 Samuel, 1–2 Kings, 1–2 Chronicles, Ezra–Nehemiah (reducing the number by four). The twelve Minor Prophets are counted as one book (reducing the number by eleven). The Palestinian Jews represented Jewish orthodoxy. Therefore, their canon was recognized as the orthodox one. It was the canon of Jesus (Geisler, *General Introduction*, chap. 5), Josephus, and Jerome. It was the canon of many early church fathers, among them Origen, Cyril of Jerusalem, and Athanasius.

Arguments in support of the Protestant Canon can be divided into two categories: historical and doctrinal.

Historical Arguments. The test of canonicity. Contrary to the Roman Catholic argument from Christian usage, the true test of canonicity is propheticity. God determined which books would be in the Bible by giving their message to a prophet. So only books written by a prophet or accredited spokesperson for God are inspired and belong in the canon of Scripture.

Of course, while God *determined* canonicity by propheticity; the people of God had to *discover* which of these books were prophetic. The people of God to whom the prophet wrote knew what prophets fulfilled the biblical tests for God's representatives, and they authenticated them by accepting the writings as from God. Moses' books were accepted immediately and stored in a holy place (Deut. 31:26). Joshua's writing was immediately accepted and preserved along with Moses' Law (Josh. 24:26). Samuel added to the collection (1 Sam. 10:25). Daniel already had a copy of his prophetic contemporary Jeremiah (Dan. 9:2) and the law (Dan. 9:11, 13). While Jeremiah's message may have been rejected by much of his generation, the remnant must have accepted and spread it speedily. Paul encouraged the churches to circulate his inspired Epistles (Col. 4:16). Peter already had a collection of Paul's writings, equating them with the Old Testament as "Scripture" (2 Peter 3:15–16).

There were a number of ways for immediate contemporaries to confirm whether someone was a prophet of God. Some were confirmed supernaturally (Exodus 3–4; Acts 2:22; 2 Cor. 12:12; Heb. 2:3–4). Sometimes this came as immediate confirmation of their authority over nature or the accuracy of their predictive prophecy. Indeed, false prophets were weeded out if their predictions did not come true (Deut. 18:20–22). Alleged revelations that contradicted previously revealed truths were rejected as well (Deut. 13:1–3).

Evidence that each prophet's contemporaries authenticated and added his books to a growing canon comes through citations from subsequent writings. Moses' writings are cited through the Old Testament, beginning with his immediate successor, Joshua (Josh. 1:7; 1 Kings 2:3; 2 Kings 14:6; 2 Chron. 17:9; Ezra 6:18; Neh. 13:1; Jer. 8:8; Mal. 4:4). Later prophets cite earlier ones (e.g., Jer. 26:18; Ezek. 14:14, 20; Dan. 9:2; Jonah 2:2–9; Micah 4:1–3). In the New Testament, Paul cites Luke (1 Tim. 5:18); Peter recognizes Paul's Epistles (2 Peter 3:15–16), and Jude (4–12) cites 2 Peter. The Revelation is filled with images and ideas from previous Scripture, especially Daniel (see, for example, Revelation 13).

The entire Jewish/Protestant Old Testament was considered prophetic. Moses, who wrote the first five books, was a prophet (Deut. 18:15). The rest of the Old Testament books were known for centuries as "The Prophets" (Matt. 5:17; Luke 24:27). Eventually these books were divided into The Prophets and The Writings. Some believe this division was based on whether the author was a prophet by office or by gift. Others believe the separation was for topical use at Jewish festivals, or that books were arranged chronologically in descending order of size (Geisler, *General Introduction,* 244–45). Whatever the reason, it is clear that the original (cf. 7:12) and continual way to refer to the entire Old Testament up to the time of Christ was the twofold division of the "The Law and The Prophets." The "apostles and prophets" (Eph. 3:5) composed the New Testament. Hence, the whole Bible is a prophetic book, including the last book (for example, Revelation 20); this cannot be said for the *Apocryphal* books.

Nonauthenticated prophecy. There is strong evidence that the apocryphal books are not prophetic, and since propheticity is the test for canonicity, this fact alone eliminates them from the canon. No apocryphal books claim to be written by a prophet. Indeed, Maccabees disclaims being prophetic (1 Macc. 9:27). Nor is there supernatural confirmation of any of the writers of the apocryphal books, as there is for prophets who wrote canonical books. There is no predictive prophecy in the *Apocrypha*, as there is in some canonical books (e.g., Isaiah 53; Daniel 9; Micah 5:2). There is no new Messianic truth in the *Apocrypha*. Even the Jewish community, whose books these were, acknowledged that the prophetic gifts had ceased in Israel before the *Apocrypha* was written (see quotes above). Apocryphal books were never listed in the Jewish Bible with the Prophets or in any other section. Not once is an apocryphal book cited authoritatively by a prophetic book written after it. Taken together all of this provides overwhelming evidence that the *Apocrypha* was not prophetic and, therefore, should not be part of the canon of Scripture.

Jewish Rejection. In addition to the evidence for the propheticity of only the books of the Jewish and Protestant Old Testament, there is an unbroken line of rejection of the *Apocrypha* as canon by Jewish and Christian teachers.

Philo, an Alexandrian Jewish teacher (20 B.C.–A.D. 40), quoted the Old Testament prolifically from virtually every canonical book. However, he never once quoted from the *Apocrypha* as inspired.

Josephus (A.D. 30–100), a Jewish historian, explicitly excludes the *Apocrypha*, numbering the Old Testament as twenty two books (= thirty-nine books in Protestant Old Testament). Neither does he ever quote an *Apocryphal* book as Scripture, though he was familiar with them. In *Against Apion* (1.8) he wrote:

> For we have not an innumerable multitude of books among us, disagreeing from and contradicting one another [as the Greeks have,] *but only twenty-two books, which are justly believed to be divine; and of them, five belong to Moses, which contain his law, and the traditions* of the origin of mankind till his death. This interval of time was little short of three thousand years; but as to the time from the death of Moses till the reign of Artaxerxes king of Persia, who reigned at Xerxes, *the prophets*, who were after Moses, wrote down what was done in their times in *thirteen books*. The remaining *four books contain hymns to God*, and precepts for the conduct of human life. [Josephus, 1.8, emphasis added]

These correspond exactly to the Jewish and Protestant Old Testament, which excludes the *Apocrypha*.

The Jewish teachers acknowledged that their prophetic line ended in the fourth century B.C. Yet, as even Catholics acknowledge, all apocryphal books were written after this time. Josephus wrote: "From Artaxerxes until our time everything has been recorded, but has not been deemed worthy of like credit with what preceded, because the exact succession of the prophets ceased" (Josephus). Additional rabbinical statements on the cessation of prophecy support this (see Beckwith, 370). Seder Olam Rabbah 30 declares "Until then [the coming of Alexander the Great] the prophets prophesied through the Holy Spirit. From then on, 'Incline thine ear and hear the words of the wise.'" Baba Bathra 12b declares: "Since the day when the Temple was destroyed, prophecy has been taken from the prophets and given to the wise." Rabbi Samuel bar Inia said, "The Second Temple lacked five things which the First Temple possessed, namely, the fire, the ark, the Urim and Thummin, the oil of anointing and the Holy Spirit [of prophecy]." Thus, the Jewish fathers (rabbis) acknowledged that the time period during which their *Apocrypha* was written was not a time when God was giving inspired writings.

Jesus and the New Testament writers never quoted from the *Apocrypha* as Scripture, even though they were aware of these writings and alluded to them at times (e.g., Heb. 11:35 may allude to 2 Maccabees 7, 12, though this may be a reference to the canonical book of Kings; see 1 Kings 17:22). Yet hundreds of quotations in the New Testament cite the Old Testament canon. The authority with which they are cited indicates that the New Testament writers believed them to be part of the "Law and Prophets" [i.e., whole Old Testament] which was believed to be the inspired and infallible Word of God (Matt. 5:17–18; cf. John 10:35). Jesus quoted from throughout the Old Testament "Law and Prophets," which he called "all the Scriptures" (Luke 24:27).

The Jewish Scholars at Jamnia (ca. A.D. 90) did not accept the *Apocrypha* as part of the divinely inspired Jewish Canon (see Beckwith, 276–77). Since the New Testament explicitly states that Israel was entrusted with the oracles of God and was the recipient of the covenants and the law (Rom. 3:2), the Jews should be considered the custodians of the limits of their own canon. As such they have always rejected the *Apocrypha*.

Early church council rejection. No canonic list or council of the Christian church accepted the *Apocrypha* as inspired for nearly the first four centuries. This is significant, since all of the lists available and most of the fathers of this period omit the *Apocrypha*. The first councils to accept the *Apocrypha* were only local ones without ecumenical force. The Catholic contention that the Council of Rome (382), though not an ecumenical council, had ecumenical force because Pope Damasus (304–384) ratified it is without grounds. It begs the question, assuming that Damasus was a Pope with infallible authority. Second, even Catholics acknowledge this council was not an ecumenical body. Third, not all Catholic scholars agree that such affirmations by Popes are infallible. There are no infallible lists of infallible statements by Popes. Nor are there any universally agreed upon criteria for developing such lists. At best, appealing to a Pope to make infallible a statement by a local council is a double-edged sword. Even Catholic scholars admit that some Popes taught error and were even heretical.

Early fathers' rejection. Early fathers of the Christian church spoke out against the *Apocrypha*. This included Origen, Cyril of Jerusalem, Athanasius, and the great Roman Catholic Bible translator, Jerome.

Rejection by Jerome. Jerome (340–420), the greatest biblical scholar of the early Medieval period and translator of the Latin Vulgate, explicitly rejected the *Apocrypha* as part of the canon. He said the church reads them "for example and instruction of manners" but does not "apply them to establish any doctrine" ("Preface" to Vulgate *Book of Solomon*, cited in Beckwith, 343). In fact, he disputed Augustine's unjustified acceptance of these books. At first, Jerome even refused to translate the *Apocrypha* into Latin, but later made a hurried translation of a few books. After listing the exact books of the Jewish and Protestant Old Testament, Jerome concludes:

> And thus altogether there come to be 22 books of the old Law [according to the letters of the Jewish alphabet], that is, five of Moses, eight of the Prophets, and nine of the Hagiographa. Although some set down . . . Ruth

and Kinoth among the Hagiographa, and think that these books ought to be counted (separately) in their computation, and that there are thus 24 books of the old Law; which the Apocalypse of John represents as adoring the Lamb in the number of the 24 elders. . . . This prologue can fitly serve as a Helmet (i.e., equipped with a helmet, against assailants) *introduction to all the biblical books* which we have translated from Hebrew into Latin, so that we may know that *whatever is not included in these is to be placed among the apocrypha*. [ibid., emphasis added]

In his preface to Daniel, Jerome clearly rejected the apocryphal additions to Daniel (Bel and the Dragon and Susanna) and argued only for the canonicity of those books found in the Hebrew Bible. He wrote:

> The stories of Susanna and of Bel and the Dragon are not contained in the Hebrew. . . . For this same reason when I was translating Daniel many years ago, I noted these visions with a critical symbol, showing that they were not included in the Hebrew. . . . After all, both Origen, Eusebius and Appolinarius, and other outstanding churchmen and teachers of Greece acknowledge that, as I have said, these visions are not found amongst the Hebrew, *and therefore they are not obliged to answer to Porphyry for these portions which exhibit no authority as Holy Scripture*. [ibid., emphasis added]

The suggestion that Jerome really favored the apocryphal books but was only arguing that the Jews rejected them is groundless. First, he said clearly in the above quotation that they *"exhibit no authority as Holy Scripture."* Second, he never retracted his rejection of the *Apocrypha*. Third, he stated in his work *Against Rufinus*, 33 that he had "followed the judgment of the churches" on this matter. And his statement "I was not following my own personal views" appears to refer to "the remarks that they [the enemies of Christianity] are wont to make against us." In any event, he nowhere retracted his statements against the *Apocrypha*. Finally, the fact that Jerome cited apocryphal books is no proof that he accepted them. This was a common practice by many church fathers. He had stated that the church reads them "for example and instruction of manners" but does not "apply them to establish any doctrine."

Rejection by scholars. Even noted Roman Catholic scholars during the Reformation period rejected the *Apocrypha*, such as Cardinal Cajetan, who opposed Luther. As already noted, he wrote a *Commentary on All the Authentic Historical Books of the Old Testament* (1532) which excluded the *Apocrypha*. If he believed they were authentic, they certainly would have been included in a book on "all the authentic" books of the Old Testament.

Luther, John Calvin, and other Reformers rejected the canonicity of the *Apocrypha*. Lutherans and Anglicans have used it only for ethical/devotional matters but do not consider it authoritative in matters of Faith. Reformed churches followed *The Westminster Confession of Faith* (1647) which states: "The Books commonly called Apocrypha, not being of divine inspiration, are not part of the canon of the Scriptures; and therefore are of no authority in the Church of God, nor to be any otherwise approved, or made use of, than any other human writings." In short, the Christian church (including Anglicans, Lutherans, and Protestants) has rejected the deuterocanonical books as part of the canon. They do so because they lack the primary determining factor of canonicity: The apocryphal books lack evidence that they were written by accredited prophets of God. Further evidence is found in the fact that the apocryphal books are never cited as authoritative in Scripture in the New Testament, it was never part of the Jewish canon, and the early church did not accept the *Apocrypha* as inspired.

The Mistake of Trent. The infallible pronouncement by the Council of Trent that the apocryphal books are part of the inspired Word of God reveals how fallible an allegedly infallible statement can be. This article has shown that the statement is historically unfounded. It was a polemical overreaction and an arbitrary decision involving a dogmatic exclusion.

Trent's pronouncement on the *Apocrypha* was part of a polemical action against Luther. Its sponsors deemed an inspired *Apocrypha* necessary to justify teaching Luther had attacked, particularly prayers for the dead. The text of 2 Maccabees 12:46 reads "Thus he made atonement for the dead that they might be freed from his sin." Since there was an agenda for accepting certain books, the decisions were rather arbitrary. Trent accepted 2 Maccabees, which supported prayers for the dead and rejected 2 Esdras (4 Esdras in the Catholic reckoning), which had a statement that would not support the practice (cf. 7:105).

The very history of this section of 2 (4) Esdras reveals the arbitrariness of the Trent decision. It was written in Aramaic by an unknown Jewish author (ca. A.D. 100) and circulated in Old Latin versions (ca. 200). The Latin Vulgate printed it as an appendix to the New Testament (ca. 400). It disappeared from Bibles until Protestants, beginning with Johann Haug (1726–42), began to print it in the *Apocrypha* based on Aramaic texts, since it was not in Latin manuscripts of the time. However, in 1874 a long section in Latin (seventy verses of chap. 7) was found by Robert Bently in a library in Amiens, France. Bruce Metzger noted, "It is probable that the lost section was deliberately cut out of an ancestor of most extant

Latin Manuscripts, because of dogmatic reasons, for the passage contains an emphatic denial of the value of prayers for the dead."

Some Catholics argue that this exclusion is not arbitrary because this writing was not part of earlier deuterocanonical lists, it was written after the time of Christ, it was relegated to an inferior position in the Vulgate, and it was only included among the *Apocrypha* by Protestants in the eighteenth century. On the other hand, 2 [4] Esdras was part of earlier lists of books not considered fully canonical. According to the Catholic criterion, the date of writing has nothing to do with whether it should be in the Jewish *Apocrypha* but whether it was used by early Christians; it was used, alongside the other apocryphal books. It should not have been rejected because it held an inferior position in the Vulgate. Jerome relegated all these writings to an inferior position. The reason it did not reappear in Latin until the eighteenth century is apparently because some Catholic Monk cut out the section against praying for the dead.

Prayers for the dead were much on the mind of the clerics at Trent, who convened their council just twenty-nine years after Luther posted his Ninety-Five Theses against the sale of indulgences. Doctrines of indulgences, purgatory, and prayers for the dead stand or fall together.

Doctrinal Arguments. Canonicity. The true and false views of what determines canonicity can be contrasted as follows (see Geisler, *General Introduction,* 221).

Incorrect View of Canon	**Correct View of Canon**
Church Determines Canon.	Church Discovers Canon.
Church Is Mother of Canon.	Church Is Child of Canon.
Church Is Magistrate of Canon.	Church Is Minister of Canon.
Church Regulates Canon.	Church Recognizes Canon.
Church Is Judge of Canon.	Church Is Witness of Canon.
Church Is Master of Canon.	Church Is Servant of Canon.

Catholic sources can be cited to support a doctrine of canonicity that looks very much like the "correct view." The problem is that Catholic apologists often equivocate on this issue. Peter Kreeft, for example, argued that the church must be infallible if the Bible is, since the effect cannot be greater than the cause and the church caused the canon. But if the church is regulated by the canon, not ruler over it, then the church is not the cause of the canon. Other defenders of Catholicism make the same mistake, giving lip-service on the one hand to the fact that the church only discovers the canon, yet on the other hand constructing an argument that makes the church the determiner of the canon. They neglect the fact that it is God who caused (by inspiration) the canonical Scriptures, not the church.

This misunderstanding is sometimes evident in the equivocal use of the word *witness*. When we speak of the church as being a "witness" to the canon after the time it was written we do not mean in the sense of being an eyewitness (i.e., relating first-hand evidence). The proper role of the Christian church in discovering which books belong in the canon can be reduced to several precepts.

Only the people of God contemporary to the writing of the biblical books were actual eyewitnesses to the evidence. They alone were witnesses to the canon as it was developing. Only they can testify to the evidence of the propheticity of the biblical books, which is the determinative factor of canonicity.

The later church is not an evidential witness for the canon. It does not create or constitute evidence for the canon. It is only a discoverer and observer of the evidence that remains for the original confirmation of the propheticity of the canonical books. Assuming that it is evidence in and of itself is the mistake behind the Roman Catholic view.

Neither the earlier nor later church is the judge of the canon. The church is not the final arbiter for the criteria of what will be admitted as evidence. Only God can determine the criteria for our discovery of what is his Word. What is of God will have his "fingerprints" on it, and only God is the determiner of what his "fingerprints" are like.

Both the early and later church is more like a jury than a judge. The jury listens to the evidence, weighs the evidence, and renders a verdict in accord with the evidence. The contemporary (First-Century) church looked at the first-hand evidence for *propheticity* (such as miracles), and the historic church has reviewed the evidence for the *authenticity* of these prophetic books which were directly confirmed by God when they were written (*see* MIRACLES IN THE BIBLE).

In a certain sense, the church does "judge" the canon. It is called upon, as all juries are, to engage in an active sifting and weighing of the evidence as it renders a verdict. But this is not what the Roman Church practiced in its magisterial role in determining the canon. After all, this is what is meant by the "teaching magisterium" of the church. The Roman Catholic hierarchy is not merely ministerial; it is magisterial. It has a judicial role, not just an administrative one. It is not just a jury looking at evidence; it is a judge determining what counts as evidence.

Therein lies the problem. In exercising its magisterial role, the Roman Catholic church chose the wrong course in rendering its decision about the *Apocrypha*. First, it chose to follow the wrong criterion, *Christian usage* rather than *propheticity*. Second, it used *second-hand evidence* of later writers rather than the only *first-hand evidence* for canonicity (divine confirmation of the author's propheticity). Third, it did not use *immediate confirmation* by contemporaries but the *later statements* of people separated from the events by centuries. All of these mistakes arose out of a misconception of the very role of the church as judge rather than jury, as magistrate rather than minister, a sovereign over rather than servant of the canon. By contrast, the Protestant rejection of the *Apocrypha* was based on an understanding of the role of the first witnesses to propheticity and the church as custodian of that evidence for authenticity.

New Testament Apocrypha. The New Testament *Apocrypha* are disputed books that have been accepted by some into the canon of Scripture. Unlike the *Apocrypha* of the Old Testament, the New Testament *Apocrypha* has not caused a permanent or serious controversy, since the church universal agrees that only the twenty-seven books of the New Testament are inspired (*see* BIBLE, EVIDENCE FOR). Books of the *Apocrypha* have been enjoyed for their devotional value, unlike the more spurious (and usually heretical) books of the New Testament pseudepigrapha. Pseudepigraphal writings are sometimes called "*Apocrypha*," but they have been universally rejected by all traditions of the church.

The New Testament *Apocrypha* includes *The Epistle of Pseudo-Barnabas* (ca. A.D. 70–79), *The Epistle to the Corinthians* (ca. 96), *The Gospel According to the Hebrews* (ca. 65–100), *The Epistle of Polycarp to the Philippians* (ca. 108), *Didache* or *The Teaching of the Twelve* (ca. 100–20), *The Seven Epistles of Ignatius* (ca. 110), *Ancient Homily* or *The Second Epistle of Clement* (ca. 120–140), *The Shepherd of Hermas* (ca. 115–40), *The Apocalypse of Peter* (ca. 150), and *The Epistle to the Laodiceans* (fourth century [?]).

Reasons for Rejecting. None of the New Testament *Apocrypha* have experienced more than a local or temporary acceptance. Most have enjoyed at best a quasi-canonical status, merely appended to various manuscripts or listed in tables of contents. No major canon or church council accepted them as part of the inspired Word of God. Where they were accepted into the canon by groups of Christians it was because they were believed wrongly to have been written by an apostle or referred to by an inspired book (for example, Col. 4:16). Once this was known to be false they were rejected as canonical.

Conclusion. Differences over the Old Testament *Apocrypha* play a crucial role in Roman Catholic and Protestant differences over such teachings as purgatory and prayers for the dead. There is no evidence that the *Apocryphal* books are inspired and, therefore, should be part of the canon of inspired Scripture. They do not claim to be inspired, nor is inspiration credited to them by the Jewish community that produced them. They are never quoted as Scripture in the New Testament. Many early fathers, including Jerome, categorically rejected them. Adding them to the Bible with an infallible decree at the Council of Trent shows evidence of being a dogmatic and polemical pronouncement calculated to bolster support for doctrines that do not find clear support in any of the canonical books.

In view of the strong evidence against the *Apocrypha*, the decision by the Roman Catholic and Orthodox churches to pronounce them canonical is both unfounded and rejected by Protestants. It is a serious error to admit nonrevelational material to corrupt the written revelation of God and undermine the divine authority of Scripture (Ramm, 65).

Sources

H. Andrews, *An Introduction to the Apocryphal Books of the Old and New Testaments*

Augustine, *The City of God.*

R. Beckwith, *The Old Testament Canon of the New Testament Church and Its Background in Early Judaism*

M. Burroughs, *More Light on the Dead Sea Scrolls*

H. Denzinger, *Documents of Vatican II*, chapter 3

———, *The Sources of Catholic Dogma*

N. L. Geisler, "The Extent of The Old Testament Canon," in G. F. Hawthorne, ed., *Current Issues in Biblical and Patristic Interpretation*

———and W. E. Nix, *General Introduction to the Bible*, rev. ed.

Josephus, *Antiquities*, 1.8

B. Metzger, *An Introduction to the Apocrypha*

B. Ramm, *The Pattern of Religious Authority*

P. Schaff, *The Creeds of Christendom*

A. Souter, *The Text and Canon of the New Testament*

B. Westcott, *A General Survey of the Canon of the New Testament*

Apologetics, Argument of.

Apologetics, Argument of. There are many types of apologetics (*see* APOLOGETICS, TYPES OF). But according to classical apologetics, there are certain logical steps in the overall argument in defense of the Christian faith. Since each step is treated in detail in other articles, only the logic of the argument will be sketched here.

The Steps. The overall argument in defense of the Christian Faith can be put in twelve basic propositions. They flow logically one from another:

1. Truth about reality is knowable (*see* TRUTH, NATURE OF; AGNOSTICISM).
2. Opposites cannot both be true (*see* FIRST PRINCIPLES; LOGIC).

3. The theistic (*see* Theism) God exists (*see* God, Evidence for).
4. Miracles are possible (*see* Miracle).
5. Miracles performed in connection with a truth claim are acts of God to confirm the truth of God through a messenger of God (*see* Miracles as Confirmation of Truth; Miracles, Apologetic Value of).
6. The New Testament documents are reliable (*see* New Testament, Documents, Manuscripts; New Testament, Historicity of; New Testament Manuscripts).
7. As witnessed in the New Testament, Jesus claimed to be God (*see* Christ, Deity of).
8. Jesus' claim to divinity was proven by an unique convergence of miracles (*see* Miracles in the Bible).
9. Therefore, Jesus was God in human flesh.
10. Whatever Jesus (who is God) affirmed as true, is true (*see* God, Nature of).
11. Jesus affirmed that the Bible is the Word of God (*see* Bible, Evidence for; Bible, Jesus' View of).
12. Therefore, it is true that the Bible is the Word of God and whatever is opposed to any biblical truth is false (*see* World Religions and Christianity; Pluralism, Religious).

The Application. If a theistic God exists and miracles are possible and Jesus is the Son of God and the Bible is the Word of God, then it follows that orthodox Christianity is true. All other essential orthodox doctrines, such as the Trinity, Christ's atonement for sin, the physical resurrection, and Christ's second coming, are taught in the Bible. Since all these conditions are supported by good evidence, it follows that there is good evidence for concluding that orthodox Christianity is true.

And since mutually exclusive propositions cannot both be true (*see* Logic), then all opposing world religions are false religions (*see* World Religions and Christianity). That is, Buddhism, Hinduism, Islam, and other religions are false insofar as they oppose the teachings of Christianity (*see* articles related to Islam; Monism; Zen Buddhism). Therefore, only Christianity is the true religion (*see* Pluralism).

Apologetics, Classical. ***See*** **Classical Apologetics.**

Apologetics, Experiential. ***See*** **Experiential Apologetics.**

Apologetics, Historical. ***See*** **Historical Apologetics.**

Apologetics, Need for. *Apologetics* is the discipline that deals with a rational defense of Christian faith. It comes from the Greek word *apologia* which means to give a reason or defense. In spite of the objections to doing apologetics in this sense from fideists and some presuppositionalists (*see* Fideism; Presuppositional Apologetics), there are important reasons to participate in the work of apologetics.

God Commands It. The most important reason to do apologetics is that God told us to do so. The classic statement is 1 Peter 3:15, which says, "But in your hearts set apart Christ as Lord. Always be prepared to give an answer to everyone who asks you to give the reason for the hope that you have. But do this with gentleness and respect." This verse tells us to be ready. We may never run across someone who asks tough questions about our faith, but we should still be ready to respond if someone does. Being ready is not just a matter of having the right information available, it is also an attitude of readiness and eagerness to share the truth of what we believe. We are to give a reason to those who ask the questions. It is not expected that everyone needs pre-evangelism, but when they do need it, we must be able and willing to give them an answer.

This command also links the work of pre-evangelism with Christ's place as Lord in our hearts. If he is really Lord, then we should be obedient to him as "we demolish arguments and every pretension that sets itself up against the knowledge of God, and we take captive every thought to make it obedient to Christ" (2 Cor. 10:5). This means we should confront issues in our own minds and in the expressed thoughts of others that prevent us and them from knowing God. That is what apologetics is all about.

In Philippians 1:7 Paul speaks of his mission as "defending and confirming the gospel." He adds in verse 16, "I am put here for the defense of the gospel." This implies that the defender of the gospel is out where he or she can encounter others and defend truth.

Jude 3 adds, "Dear friends, although I was very eager to write to you about the salvation we share, I felt I had to write and *urge you to contend for the faith* that was once for all entrusted to the saints." The people Jude addressed had been assaulted by false teachers, and he needed to encourage them to protect (literally agonize for) the faith as it had been revealed through Christ. Jude makes a significant statement about our attitude in verse 22, that we "have mercy on some, who are doubting."

Titus 1:9 makes knowledge of Christian evidences a requirement for church leadership. An elder in the church should "hold firmly to the trustworthy message as it has been taught, so that he can encourage others by sound doctrine and *refute those who oppose it*." Paul also gives us an indication of our attitude in this work in 2 Timothy 2:24–25: "And the Lord's servant must not quarrel; instead, he must be kind to everyone, able to teach, not resentful. *Those who oppose him he must gently instruct*, in the hope that God will grant them repentance leading them to a knowledge of the truth." Anyone attempting to answer the questions of unbelievers will surely be wronged and be tempted to lose patience, but our ultimate goal is that they might come to a knowledge of the truth that Jesus has died for their sins. With so important a task at hand, we must not neglect obedience to this command.

Reason Demands It. God created humans to reason as part of his image (Gen. 1:27; cf. Col. 3:10). Indeed, it is by reasoning that humans are distinguished from "brute beasts" (Jude 10). God calls upon his people to use reason (Isa. 1:18) to discern truth from error (1 John 4:6) and right from wrong (Heb. 5:14). A fundamental principle of reason is that it should give sufficient grounds for belief. An unjustified belief is just that—unjustified (*see* FAITH AND REASON).

Socrates said, "The unexamined life is not worth living." He surely would have been willing to add that the unexamined belief is not worth believing. Therefore, it is incumbent upon Christians to give a reason for their hope. This is part of the great command to love God with all our mind, as well as our heart and soul (Matt. 22:36–37).

The World Needs It. People rightly refuse to believe without evidence. Since God created humans as rational beings, he expects them to live rationally, to look before they leap. This does not mean there is no room for faith. But God wants us to take a step of faith in the light of evidence, rather than to leap in the dark.

Evidence of truth should precede faith. No rational person steps in a elevator without some reason to believe it will hold him up. No reasonable person gets on an airplane that is missing part of one wing and smells of smoke in the cabin. People deal in two dimensions of belief: *belief that* and *belief in*. *Belief that* gives the evidence and rational basis for confidence needed to establish *belief in*. Once *belief that* is established, one can place faith *in* it. Thus, the rational person wants evidence that God exists before he places his faith in God. Rational unbelievers want evidence that Jesus is the Son of God before they place their trust in him (*see* CLASSICAL APOLOGETICS).

Objections to Apologetics. The most frequent opposition to apologetics is raised by mystics and other experientialists (*see* EXPERIENTIAL APOLOGETICS). Fideists (*see* FIDEISM) and some presuppositionalists also raise objections of two basic kinds: biblical and from outside Scripture. An apologist for apologetics can see in the Scripture texts usually quoted against the work some misunderstandings or misapplications, which do not really show apologetics to be unnecessary.

Objections to Apologetics from the Bible. The Bible does not need to be defended. One objection often made is that the Bible does not need to be defended; it simply needs to be expounded. "The Word of God is alive and powerful" (Heb. 4:12). It is said that the Bible is like a lion; it does not need to be defended but simply let loose. A lion can defend itself.

This begs the question as to whether the Bible is the Word of God. Of course, God's Word is ultimate and speaks for itself. But how do we know the Bible, as opposed to the *Qur'an* or the *Book of Mormon*, is the Word of God? One must appeal to evidence to determine this. No Christian would accept a Muslim's statement that "the *Qur'an* is alive and powerful and sharper than a two-edged sword." We would demand evidence (*see* BIBLE, EVIDENCE FOR).

The analogy of the lion is misleading. A roar of a lion "speaks for itself" with authority only because we know from previous evidence what a lion can do. Without tales of woe about a lion's ferocity, its roar would not have authority. Likewise, without evidence to establish one's claim to authority, there is no good reason to accept that authority.

God can't be known by human reason. The apostle Paul wrote, "the world by wisdom knew not God" (1 Cor. 1:21 KJV). This cannot mean that there is no evidence for God's existence, however, since Paul declared in Romans that the evidence for God's existence is so "plain" as to render "without excuse" one who has never heard the gospel (Rom. 1:19–20). Further, the context in 1 Corinthians is not God's existence but his plan of salvation through the cross. This cannot be known by mere human reason, but only by divine revelation. It is "foolish" to the depraved human mind. Finally, in this very book of 1 Corinthians Paul gives his greatest apologetic evidence for the Christian Faith—the eyewitnesses of the resurrection of Christ which his companion Luke called "many infallible proofs" (Acts 1:3 NKJV). So his reference to the world by wisdom not knowing God is not a reference to the inability of human beings to know God through the evidence he has revealed in creation (Rom. 1:19–20) and conscience (Rom. 2:12–15). Rather, it is a reference to human depravity and foolish rejection of the message of the cross. Indeed, even though humankind knows clearly through human reason that God exists, nevertheless, he "suppresses" or "holds down" this truth in unrighteousness (Rom. 1:18).

Natural humanity can't understand. Paul insisted that "the man without the Spirit does not accept the things that come from the Spirit of God" (1 Cor. 2:14). What use, then, is apologetics? In response to this argument against apologetics, it should be observed that Paul does not say that natural persons cannot *perceive* truth about God, but that they do not *receive* (Gk. *dekomai,* "welcome") it. Paul emphatically declares that the basic truths about God are "clearly seen" (Rom. 1:20). The problem is not that unbelievers are not aware of God's existence. They do not want to *accept* him because of the moral consequences this would have on their sinful lives. First Corinthians 2:14 (NKJV) says they do not "know" *(ginosko)* which can mean "to know by experience." They know God in their mind (Rom. 1:19–20), but they have not accepted him in their heart (Rom. 1:18). "The fool says *in his heart,* There is no God" (Ps. 14:1).

Without faith one cannot please God. Hebrews 11:6 insists that "without faith it is impossible to please God." This would seem to argue that asking for reasons, rather than simply believing, displeases God. But, as already noted, God does call upon us to use our reason (1 Peter 3:15). Indeed, he has given "clear" (Rom. 1:20) and "infallible proofs" (Acts 1:3 NKJV). Second, this text in Hebrews does not exclude "evidence" but actually implies it. Faith is said to be "the evidence" of things we do not see (Heb. 11:1 NKJV). Just as the evidence that a witness is reliable justifies my believing testimony of what he or she saw and I did not, even so, our faith in "things not seen" (Heb. 11:1 NKJV) is justified by the evidence that God does exist. The latter evidence is "clearly seen, being understood from what has been made" (Rom. 1:20).

Jesus refused to give signs for evil men. Jesus rebuked people who sought signs; hence, we should be content simply to believe. Indeed, Jesus did on occasion rebuke sign seekers. He said, "A wicked and adulterous generation asks for a miraculous sign!" However, this does not mean that Jesus did not desire people to look at the evidence before they believed. Even in this passage Jesus went on to offer the miracle of his resurrection as a sign of who he was, saying no signs would be given, "except the sign of the prophet Jonah" (Matt. 12:39–40; cf. Luke 16:31; *see* MIRACLES IN THE BIBLE).

Jesus offered his miracles as a proof of his messianic office (*see* MIRACLE; MIRACLES, APOLOGETIC VALUE OF). When John the Baptist inquired whether he was the Christ, Jesus offered miracles as proof, saying: "Go back and report to John what you hear and see: The blind receive sight, the lame walk, those who have leprosy are cured, the deaf hear, the dead are raised, and the good news is preached to the poor" (Matt. 11:4–5). And when replying to the Scribes, he said: "'But that you may know that the Son of Man has authority on earth to forgive sins.' He said to the paralytic, 'I tell you, get up, take your mat and go home'" (Mark 2:10–11).

Jesus was opposed to entertaining people by miracles. He refused to perform a miracle to satisfy King Herod's curiosity (Luke 23:8). On other occasions he did not do miracles because of their unbelief (Matt. 13:58), not wishing to "cast pearls before swine" (Matt. 7:6). The purpose of miracles was apologetic, viz., to confirm his message (cf. Exod. 4:1–9; John 3:2; Heb. 2:3–4). And this he did in great abundance for "Jesus of Nazareth was a man accredited by God to you by miracles, wonders and signs, which God did among you through him" (Acts 2:22).

Do not answer a fool according to his folly. It is argued that atheism is folly (Ps. 14:1), and the Bible says we should not answer a fool. We agree with Proverbs 26:4, but we also concur with Proverbs 26:5 which says, "Answer a fool according to his folly, or he will be wise in his own eyes." Either the Book of Proverbs was put together by a mad man, or the lesson of the passage is that we have to be careful in how and when we choose to confront false ideas. Don't just argue with someone who will not listen to reason, or you will be just as foolish as he is. But if you are able to show a person the error of his thinking in a way that he can understand, perhaps he will seek God's wisdom rather than relying on his own.

Apologetics is not used in the Bible. If apologetics is biblical, then why don't we see it done in the Bible? By and large the Bible was not written for unbelievers but for believers. Since they already believe in God, Christ, etc., there is no need to prove these truths to them. Apologetics is primarily for those who do not believe, so that they may have a reason to believe.

But apologetics *is used* in the Bible. Even those familiar with it don't recognize it, since they don't realize that what they are looking at is really apologetics. Moses did apologetics. The first chapter of Genesis clearly confronts the mythical accounts of creation known in his day. His miracles in Egypt were an apologetic that God was speaking through him (Exod. 4:1–9). Elijah did apologetics on Mount Carmel when he proved miraculously that Yahweh, not Baal, is the true God (1 Kings 18). Jesus constantly engaged in apologetics, proving by signs and wonders that he was the Son of God (John 3:2; Acts 2:22). The apostle Paul did apologetics at Lystra when he gave evidence from nature that the supreme God of the universe existed and that idolatry was wrong (Acts 14:6–20).

The classic case of apologetics in the New Testament is Acts 17 where Paul reasoned with the philosophers on Mars Hill. He not only presented evidence from nature that God existed but also from history that Christ was the Son of God. He cited pagan thinkers in support of his arguments. Apologetics was done in the Bible whenever the truth claims of Judaism or Christianity came in conflict with unbelief.

Objections to Apologetics from Outside the Bible. These objections against apologetics arise from assumptions of its irrationality, inadequacy, or fruitlessness. Many come from a rationalistic or skeptical point of view (*see* AGNOSTICISM). Others are fideistic (*see* FIDEISM).

Logic can't tell us anything about God. This objection is self-defeating. It says that logic doesn't apply to this issue. But the statement itself is a statement claiming logical thinking about God. It appeals to logic because it claims to be true while its opposite is false. That claim, called the law of noncontradiction (*see* FIRST PRINCIPLES; LOGIC), is the basis for all logic. A statement that logic doesn't apply to God applies logic to God. Logic is inescapable. You can't deny it with your words unless you affirm it with the very same words. It is undeniable.

Logic in itself can tell us some things about God—at least hypothetically. For instance, if God exists, then it is false that he does not exist. And if God is a Necessary Being, then he cannot not exist. Further, if God is infinite and we are finite, then we are not God. Also, if God is truth, he cannot lie (Heb. 6:18). For it is contradictory to his nature to lie. Likewise, logic informs us that if God is omnipotent, then he cannot make a stone so heavy that he cannot lift it. For whatever he can make, he can lift.

Logic cannot "prove" the existence of anything. True, mere logic shows only what is possible or impossible. We know by logic, for example, that square circles are impossible. We know also that something can exist, since no contradiction is involved in claiming something exists. But we cannot prove by mere logic that something actually exists. However, we know that something actually exists in another way. We know it intuitively and undeniably. For I cannot deny my existence unless I exist to deny it. The statement "I don't exist" is self-defeating, since I have to exist in order to be able to make the statement. So, while mere logic cannot prove the existence of anything, we have undeniable knowledge that something exists. And once we know that something exists (e.g., I do), then logic can help us determine whether it is finite or infinite. And if it is finite, logic can help us determine whether there is also an infinite being (*see* GOD, EVIDENCE FOR).

Reason is useless in religious matters. Fideism argues that reason is of no use in matters that deal with God. One must simply believe. Faith, not reason, is what God requires (Heb. 11:6).

But even in Scripture God calls on us to use reason (Isa. 1:18; Matt. 22:36–37; 1 Peter 3:15). God is a rational being, and he created us to be rational beings. God would not insult the reason he gave us by asking us to ignore it in such important matters as our beliefs about him.

Fideism* is self-defeating. Either it has a reason that we should not reason about God or it does not. If it does, then it uses reason to say we should not use reason. If fideism has no reason for not using reason, then it is without reason for its position, in which case there is no reason why one should accept fideism.

To claim reason is just optional for a fideist will not suffice. For either the fideist offers some criteria for when to be reasonable and when not, or else this timing is simply arbitrary. If a fideist offers rational criteria for when we should be rational, then he does have a rational basis for his view, in which case he is not really a fideist after all.

Reason is not the kind of thing in which a rational creature can choose not to participate. By virtue of being rational by nature one must be part of rational discourse. And rational discourse demands that one follow the laws of reason. One such principle is that one should have a sufficient reason for his beliefs. But if one must have a sufficient reason, then fideism is wrong, since it claims that one need not have a sufficient reason for what he believes.

You can't prove God by reason. According to this objection, the existence of God cannot be proven by human reason. The answer depends on what is meant by "prove." If "prove" means to demonstrate with mathematical certainty, then most theists would agree that God's existence cannot be proven. This is because mathematical certainty deals only with the abstract, and the existence of God (or anything else) is a matter of the concrete. Further, mathematical certainty is based on axioms or postulates that must be assumed in order to get a necessary conclusion. But if God's existence must be assumed to be proven, then the conclusion that God exists is only based on the assumption that he exists, in which case it is not really a proof at all.

Another way to make the point is to note that mathematical certainty is deductive in nature. It argues from given premises. But one cannot validly conclude what is not already implied in the premise(s). In this case one would have to assume God exists in the premise in order to validly infer this in the conclusion. But this begs the question.

Likewise, if by "prove" one means to reach a logically necessary conclusion, then God's existence cannot be proven either, unless the Ontological Argument is valid. But most thinkers hold that it is not. The reason one cannot prove God by logical necessity is that formal logic, like mathematics, deals with the abstract. Unless one begins with something that exists, he can never get out of the purely theoretical realm. *If* there is a triangle, we can know logically and with absolute certainty that it must have three sides and three corners. But there may not be any triangles in existence anywhere except in someone's mind. Likewise, unless we know something exists, then logic cannot help us to know whether God exists. And logic by itself cannot tell us whether anything exists.

If by "prove," however, we mean "give adequate evidence for" or "provide good reasons for," then it would seem to follow that one can prove the existence of God (*see* God, Evidence for; Cosmological Argument) and the truth of Christianity.

No one is converted through apologetics. The charge is made that no one ever comes to Christ through apologetics. If this implies that the Holy Spirit (*see* Holy Spirit, Role in Apologetics) never uses apologetic evidence to bring people to Christ, this is clearly false. C. S. Lewis noted that "nearly everyone I know who has embraced Christianity in adult life has been influenced by what seemed to him to be at least a probable argument for Theism" (Lewis, 173). Lewis is an example of an atheist who came to Christ under the influence of apologetics. The skeptic Frank Morrison was converted while attempting to write a book refuting the evidence for the resurrection of Christ (see Morrison). Augustine tells in his confessions how he was led toward Christianity by hearing a Christian debate an unbeliever. Harvard Law School professor Simon Greenleaf was led to accept the authenticity of the Gospels by applying the rules of legal evidence to the New Testament. God has used evidence and reason in some way to reach virtually all adults who come to Christ.

Sources

R. L. Bush, ed., *Classical Readings in Christian Apologetics* A.D. *100–1800*
D. Clark, *Dialogical Apologetics*
G. H. Clark, *Religion, Reason and Revelation*
W. Corduan, *Reasonable Faith*
N. L. Geisler, and R. Brooks. *When Skeptics Ask: A Handbook on Christian Evidences*
P. Kreeft, et al., *Handbook of Christian Apologetics*
G. R. Lewis, *Testing Christianity's Truth Claims*
C. S. Lewis, *God in the Dock*
J. McDowell, *Answering Tough Questions Skeptics Ask*
____, *Evidence That Demands a Verdict*
J. W. Montgomery, *Faith Founded on Fact*
J. P. Moreland, *Scaling the Secular City: A Defense of Christianity*
F. Morrison, *Who Moved the Stone?*
W. M. Smith, *Therefore Stand*

Apologetics, Objections to. ***See*** **Apologetics, Need for.**

Apologetics, Presuppositional. ***See*** **Clark, Gordon; Presuppositional Apologetics; Van Til, Cornelius.**

Apologetics, Types of. There are differing kinds of apologetics systems, and no universally-acknowledged way to categorize them. Divergent approaches seem to be determined by the perspective of the one categorizing them. Nonetheless, there are some generally understood terms one can employ to view in a meaningful way the distinctives among more popular approaches.

Categorizing Systems. It is tempting to make logically exhaustive categories of apologetic systems. Two problems preclude this. First, the category may seem to work but the corresponding category that would logically oppose it is too broad. Second, divergent systems often are lumped into one category. For example, if one uses the categories of presuppositionalism and nonpresuppositionalism, not only are there differing kinds of presuppositionalism but significant differences among nonpresuppositional systems. If one uses evidential and nonevidential the same result occurs; classical and historical apologetics and even some forms of presuppositionalism (e.g., Systematic Consistency) must be mated in the same category. The same is true if one uses classical apologetics and nonclassical apologetics as two broad categories.

Types of Systems. Despite the fact that the categories are not logically exhaustive and overlap, it seems best simply to use commonly understood titles and state the differences and similarities. Evaluation of each can be found in other articles on individual systems and their key representatives.

Three points help to understand each type: proponents will be listed; some chief characteristics will be described, and comments on overlap and/or contrast with other approaches will be made.

Classical Apologetics. Characteristics. *Classical apologetics stresses arguments for the existence of God (*see* God, Evidence for) as well as the historical evidence supporting the truth of Christianity. Classical apologetics is characterized by two basic steps: theistic and evidential arguments.

Theistic arguments are used to establish the truth of theism apart from an appeal to special revelation (e.g., the Bible). Classical apologetics accepts the validity of traditional theistic proofs for God, though some stress one over another. And some reject certain traditional proofs as invalid, often the ontological argument. But most accept some form of the cosmological argument and the teleological argument. Many also believe the moral argument is valid.

This first step of classical apologetics also involves drawing the logical inference that if a theistic God exists, miracles are possible; indeed, the greatest miracle of all, creation, is possible. The credibility of miracles (*see* Miracle) is essential to the next step in classical apologetics—the historical one—but it flows logically from the first step.

Second, confirmed historical evidence substantiates the truth. The New Testament documents are shown to be historically reliable (*see* New Testament Documents, Manuscripts; New

TESTAMENT, HISTORICITY OF; NEW TESTAMENT, NON-CHRISTIAN SOURCES). The apologist also shows that these documents reveal that Jesus claimed to be, and was miraculously proven to be, the Son of God (*see* CHRIST, DEITY OF). From this it is often argued that Jesus confirmed the Old Testament to be the Word of God and promised the same for the New Testament (*see* BIBLE, JESUS' VIEW OF).

Proponents. Classical apologetics was practiced by Augustine, Anselm, and Thomas Aquinas. Modern classical apologists include Winfried Corduan, William Lane Craig, Norman L. Geisler, John Gerstner, Stuart Hackett, Peter Kreeft, C. S. Lewis, J. P. Moreland, John Locke, William Paley, R. C. Sproul, and B. B. Warfield.

Comparison with other approaches. Sometimes classical apologists begin this second step by showing that the Bible has been proven to be the Word of God. In doing so they often use the same basic evidence used by evidential apologetics. This includes miracles (*see* MIRACLES, APOLOGETIC VALUE OF; MIRACLES IN THE BIBLE), fulfilled prophecy (*see* PROPHECY, AS PROOF OF BIBLE), the unity of the Bible, and other indications of its supernatural origin (*see* BIBLE, EVIDENCE FOR).

The difference between the classical apologists and the evidentialists on the use of historical evidence is that the classical see the need to first establish that this is a theistic universe in order to establish the possibility of and identity of miracles. Evidentialists do not see theism as a logically necessary precondition of historical apologetics. The basic argument of the classical apologists is that it makes no sense to speak about the resurrection as an act of God unless, as a logical prerequisite, it is first established that there is a God who can act. Likewise, the Bible cannot be the Word of God unless there is a God who can speak. And Christ cannot be shown to be the Son of God except on the logically prior premise there is a God who can have a Son.

Evidential Apologetics. Evidential apologetics stresses the need for evidence in support of the Christian truth claims. The evidence can be rational, historical, archaeological, and even experiential. Since it is so broad, it understandably overlaps with other types of apologetics.

Some characteristics of evidential apologetics. Since evidentialists encompass a large and diverse category, their characteristics will be delineated according to type. Evidentialists often use *rational evidence* (e.g., proofs for God) in defense of Christianity. As such, they overlap with classical apologetics. However, for an evidentialist this is just one piece of evidence. Also in contrast to classical apologists, evidentialists do not hold that rational evidence is either necessary (since it is only one piece) or logically prior to the other evidence.

In the use of *historical evidence* there is again an overlap with evidential and historical apologetics. Evidentialists do not rest their whole case on historical evidence. They are more eclectic, interweaving evidence from various fields. Evidentialists operate as attorneys who combine evidences into an overall brief in defense of their position, trusting that the combined weight will present a persuasive case.

Many evidentialists focus on *archeological evidence* in support of the Bible. They stress that both the Old and the New Testaments (*see* ARCHAEOLOGY, OLD TESTAMENT; ARCHAEOLOGY, NEW TESTAMENT) have been substantiated by thousands of discoveries. This, they believe, gives reason to accept the divine authority of the Scriptures. Other types of apologetics appeal to archaeological evidence, who use the evidence in a different way.

Some evidentialists appeal to *experiential evidence* in support of Christianity, most often from changed lives. The testimony of those converted to Christianity is offered as evidence of the truth of Christianity. How else, it is argued, can one explain the dramatic, transforming, enduring, and often radical changes? The conversion of Saul of Tarsus (Acts 9) is a classic case in point.

Prophetic evidence (*see* PROPHECY AS PROOF OF THE BIBLE) is often offered to substantiate Christianity. It is argued that only divine origin accounts for the numerous, precise biblical predictions that have been fulfilled. For the evidentialists prophetic and other evidences do not comprise a specific step in an overall logical order (as it is in classical apologetics). Rather, it is the sum total of all the interlocking evidences that offer high probability of the truth of Christianity.

Some proponents of evidential apologetics. While evidential apologetics enjoys wide popular support, it offers few clear proponents who do not fit into other categories as well. It seems best, then, to characterize evidentialism by the various kinds of evidence stressed in the particular apologetic approach. A noted evidentialist approach is offered by William Paley in his *Evidences for Christianity*, although since Paley offered proofs for God first, he can be listed as a classical apologist. Bernard Ramm's widely used *Protestant Christian Evidences* is another example of evidential apologetics, though he seemed to move way from this in his later writings. The most widely distributed of evidentialist books is Josh McDowell's *Evidence That Demands a Verdict*.

Some comparisons with other approaches. While the use of evidence is not unique to evidential apologetics, the manner in which it is used is unique. Both classical apologists and some evidentialists use theistic arguments. However, for the evidentialists, establishing the existence of God is not a logically prior and necessary step. It is simply one strand in the overall web of evidence that supports Christianity.

Unlike historical apologetics, the pure evidentialist does not appeal to historical evidence as the sole basis for his case. For the evidentialists there are certain events, such as, the healings of Jesus, raisings from the dead, and fulfilled prophecy, which in themselves, apart from prior presupposition or proof that God exists, substantiate the truth of Christianity. Since the facts "speak for themselves" there is no need, according to evidentialists, to provide an independent reason for believing in God's existence. By contrast, both classical and presuppositional apologetics insist that historical events can only be interpreted in the light of the framework of the worldview of which they are a part.

Experiential Apologetics. Some Christians appeal primarily, if not exclusively, to experience as evidence for Christian faith. Some appeal to religious experience in general. Others to special religious experiences. Within this second category are some who focus on mystical experiences and others who identify what they believe are particularly supernatural conversion experiences. There are obviously some significant differences under the broad experiential umbrella.

Types of experience. The value of general, unspecific religious experience is of limited value for a distinctly Christian apologetic. At best, *general experience* establishes credibility for belief in a supreme being of some kind (not necessarily a theistic God). Nonetheless, proofs from religious experience (*see* God, Experiential Apologetics for) have been offered by Christians and others. General religious experiences are available to all.

Special religious experiences are more limited. The mystic, for example, claims a special experience of God. *Mystical experiences* (*see* Mysticism) differ from general religious experiences in that they claim to be direct and unmediated contacts with God. Christian mystics claim such experiences are self-evidently true.

Although so-called *existential experience* encounters with God (*see* Kierkegaard, Søren) are not the same as mystical experiences, proponents claim that they too are self-authenticating. One is grasped by God in a nonrational, direct encounter that is more basic and real than a sense experience. Although not all would call such experiences apologetic evidence, they do serve, nonetheless, to vindicate Christianity among those who have them. Those who appeal to such experiences reject apologetic approaches in the traditional sense. They spurn rational arguments or factual evidence in favor of what they believe to be a self-verifying experience.

Some proponents of experiential apologetics. Among Christian mystics the name Meister Eckart stands out. Existentialists include Søren *Kierkegaard, Rudolph *Bultmann, and Karl *Barth (*see also* Fideism). Others of a more general experiential nature include Friedrich *Schleiermacher, and Paul Tillich.

Some comparisons with other approaches. Experiential arguments for God's existence are sometimes used by classical apologists and evidentialists. The difference is that, for the experiential apologist, the *only* kind of evidence is nonrational, mystical, and existential. In other apologetic approaches, the argument from religious experience is just one kind of evidence among many.

Presuppositional apologists, especially of the revelational variety, reject purely experiential arguments as unverifiable and of subjective interpretation.

Historical Apologetics. *Historical apologetics stresses historical evidence as the basis for demonstrating the truth of Christianity. These apologists believe that the truth of Christianity, including the existence of God, can be proven from the historical evidence alone. In one sense historical apologetics belongs to the broad class of evidential apologetics, but it differs in that it stresses the importance, if not necessity, of beginning with the historical record for the truth of Christianity.

Some proponents of historical apologetics. Christianity is a historical religion, so it is understandable that it would have a historical emphasis from the very beginning. The earliest apologists, including *Tertullian, *Justin Martyr, *Clement of Alexandria, and *Origen, defended the historicity of Christianity.

Since these early apologists were often unsystematic in their writing, it is difficult to tell whether they fall into the category of historical apologetics. Some did offer theistic arguments, but they probably did not all see this as a logically necessary first step in an overall apologetic. Contemporary historical apologists include John Warwick Montgomery and Gary Habermas.

Some comparisons with other approaches. Historical apologetics is distinct from evidentialism in its narrow focus, using only one kind of evidence rather than many. It also offers a sequential argument. The historical apologist only begins with historical evidence as a basic premise. With historicity established, the apologist argues that certain claims are made in Scripture from which it can be inferred that God exists, the Bible is the Word of God, and Christ is the unique Son of God. The pure evidentialist has no such logical order that begins with historical evidence alone. Rather, the evidentialist employs a whole nest of evidence from which to conclude that Christianity is true.

Both historical and classical apologetics use historical evidence. But the classical apologist believes that historical evidence is only a second step, logically preceded by theistic arguments which establish the necessary worldview evidence by which alone one can properly interpret the historical evidence.

Presuppositional Apologetics. Presuppositional apologetics affirms that one must defend Christianity from the foundation of certain basic presuppositions. Usually, a presuppositionalist presupposes the basic truth of Christianity and then proceeds to show (in any of several ways) that Christianity alone is true.

According to *revelational presuppositionalism*, one must posit that the Triune God has revealed himself in Holy Scriptures before it is possible to make any sense out of the universe, life, language, or history. This is sometimes viewed as a transcendental argument. Revelational presuppositionalists include Cornelius *Van Til, Greg Bahnsen, and John Frame.

The *rational presuppositionalist* also begins with the Trinity revealed in the written Word of God. But the test for whether this is true or not is simply the law of noncontradiction (*see* First Principles). Christianity demonstrates its own truth in that, of all religions, it alone is internally consistent. Gordon *Clark and Carl F. H. Henry are rational presuppositionalists.

Like the rational presuppositionalists, *systematic consistency* presuppositionalists believe a system must be rationally consistent. In addition, it must comprehensively take into account all facts. It must also be existentially relevant in that it meets life's basic needs. Only Christianity, they believe, offers such a consistent system. Edward John *Carnell and Gordon Lewis hold this view.

Francis *Schaeffer's apologetic approach has occasionally been listed as a separate form of presuppositionalism, a kind of *practical presuppositionalism*. Schaeffer believes that false systems are unlivable, that only Christian truth is livable.

Some comparisons with other Approaches. Presuppositional apologists reject the validity of theistic proofs. They accept the critiques of theistic argumentation by David *Hume and *Kant (*see* God, Objections to Proofs for). Or they believe there is no meaning to "facts" apart from the Christian worldview.

Conclusion. Proponents of one type of apologetic system provide critiques of opposing systems. So both evaluation and sources are listed under each type of apologetic discussed above. Only books that treat apologetic systems in general are listed below in the "Sources" section.

Sources

D. Clark, *Dialogical Apologetics*, Ch. 5
N. L. Geisler, *Christian Apologetics*, Part 1
G. Lewis, *Testing Christianity's Truth Claims*
B. Ramm, *Varieties of Apologetic Systems*

Apollonius of Tyana. Apollonius of Tyana (d. A.D. 98) is sometimes presented by critics of Christianity as an example of someone who rivaled Christ in his claim to be the Son of God and had the ability to do miracles to support his claim. Philostratus, in the *Life of Apollonius*, records post-death miracle stories, including appearances and deification (*apotheosis). Some critics use these stories to deny the uniqueness of the life, death, and resurrection of Christ.

Evaluating the Claims. The claims for Apollonius fall far short of those of Christ (*see* Christ, Deity of). Philostratus's biography of Apollonius ends with his death. Jesus' biographies do not (see Matthew 28; Mark 16; Luke 24; John 20–21). His ends in the resurrection (*see* Resurrection, Evidence for). There is nothing supernatural in Apollonius's biography, either as to claims of deity or miracles done to prove such a claim. The postresurrection miracle stories are not even part of his biography. They are simply called "stories" by his biographer, Philostratus. In fact, they are later legends.

The book by Philostratus is the only extant source of his life. Hence, the authenticity of this account is unconfirmed. In Jesus' case we have many multiple contemporary accounts of his life, death, and resurrection (*see* New Testament, Dating of; New Testament Documents, Reliability of; New Testament, Historicity of).

The alleged source for these stories, Damis, is most likely a nonexistent person used as a literary device. James Fergeson states: "Philostratus professed to have discovered an old document by one Damis as his source, but such discoveries are the stock-in-trade of historical romances, and we can place no credence upon Damis" (Fergeson, 182). Damis is alleged to have come from a city, Nineveh, that did not even exist during the time of his life. Throughout, there is no evidence for a factual basis of the stories.

By contrast, the Gospel accounts of Jesus offer various historically verifiable evidences of their accuracy. The record is filled, for example, with historical persons, among them the Herodian kings of the time, Pontius Pilate, Tiberius and Augustus, Philip Tetrarch of Iturea. Detailed information can be verified for Judea, Galilee, Samaria, Syria, Bethlehem, Nazareth, and Jerusalem (cf. Luke 1:26; 2:4; 3:1), as can times (Matt. 14:1–7; Luke 2:1–2; 3:1–2). The disciples of Jesus who wrote of him were real historical persons.

The style of writing used by Philostratus was a popular literary form of the day called "romance" or "romance fiction." It is not to be taken literally or historically. The plot unfolds through contrived situations; it involves exotic animals and formal descriptions of works of art; and it has lengthy speeches by the characters.

As a report, the account contains many geographical and historical inaccuracies. For example, Nineveh and Babylon were destroyed 300 years earlier. The Caucasus Mountains are described as a dividing point between India and Babylon, which is inaccurate. Philostratus's speeches are anachronistically put into Apollonius's mouth (from *Lives of the Sophists*).

Philostratus was not an eyewitness but was commissioned to compose his book by Julia Domna, wife of the Roman emperor Septimus, 120 years after Apollonius's death. The writers of the New Testament were contemporaries and/or eyewitnesses of the events (*see* NEW TESTAMENT, HISTORICITY OF).

A possible motive for the publication was a desire to counteract the growing influence of Jesus. One historian says, "It was she (Julia Domna) who encouraged Philostratus to put together a life of Apollonius of Tyana as a counterblast to Jesus" (ibid., 51). Another said that, since she was to become the high priestess of the Hellenistic polytheism, "Realizing the need of finding a historical figure fitted to counter the propaganda of the subversive gospels, she sought particularly to revive the memory of a hero of pagan hagiology, Apollonius of Tyana" (Cook, 613).

The miracle stories about Apollonius are contradictory. Some say he died in Ephesus, others in Lindus or Crete, and then appeared. Only one such appearance is recorded by Philostratus. This was to a man while he slept, a vision 200 years after Apollonius is to have lived (A.D. 273). Others say he did not die but was deified because he disappeared.

Finally, there is an important difference between the claims that Apollonius was deified and that Jesus was Deity (*see* CHRIST, DEITY OF). Apollonius's deification is known as apotheosis, the process by which a human becomes God. Christ's incarnation was a process by which God became human. Further, the concept of "God" differed. Christ was God in the theistic sense. The claim for Apollonius would make him God only in a polytheistic (*see* POLYTHEISM) sense.

Conclusion. There is no evidence for the historicity of Philostratus's work on Apollonius. It gives every evidence of being a work of fiction. Unlike the Gospels, it provides no eyewitnesses, no resurrection, and no confirmation. By contrast, the Gospels have abundant evidence for their authenticity and historicity. The testimony of the New Testament witnesses has been confirmed by numerous manuscripts (*see* NEW TESTAMENT MANUSCRIPTS) and other sources (*see* NEW TESTAMENT WITNESSES, RELIABILITY OF). In short, there is no real comparison between Apollonius and Christ. Jesus claimed to be the Son of the theistic God and proved it by historically verified miracles, including his own resurrection from the dead (*see* MIRACLES, APOLOGETIC VALUE OF; MIRACLES IN THE BIBLE). Apollonius made no such claims and had no such witnesses to support any alleged miracles. On the contrary, the single witness is late, unsubstantiated, and shows every sign of being myth, not history.

Sources

S. A. Cook, *The Cambridge Ancient History*
J. Fergeson, *Religions of the Roman Empire*
G. Habermas, *Ancient Evidence for the Life of Jesus*
G. Habermas, et al., "Apollonius of Tyana: First Century Miracle Worker," paper presented before Evangelical Philosophical Society

Apotheosis. Critics have used theories of apotheosis to argue that Christ's deity and resurrection are not unique beliefs to Christianity. Theories of apotheosis regarding persons who are taken to heaven and divinized have been told by other religions (*see* MITHRAISM). Among notable modern critics who have used these stories to cast doubt on the New Testament accounts are Otto Pfleiderer in *The Early Christian Conception of Christ* (1905) and W. Bousset in *Kurios Christos* (1913).

Claims of divinization are not uncommon in ancient mythology and mystery religions (Pfleiderer). Among those supposedly divinized are various Roman emperors (notably Julius and Augustus caesars) and *Apollonius of Tyana (Habermas, 168).

Claims of Apotheosis. Suetonius reported that after Julius Caesar's death "a comet appeared about an hour before sunset and shone for several days running. This was held to be Caesar's soul, elevated to heaven; hence the star, now placed above the forehead of his divine image" (Suetonius 1.88).

During the cremation of Augustus, Suetonius states that his spirit was reportedly seen "soaring up to Heaven through the flames" (ibid., 2.100). This too was taken to be a sign of apotheosis.

Antinoüs, the favorite slave of Emperor Hadrian, was also said to be divinized at death. Hadrian believed that a star was created from his soul, and so he built a city at the site and erected several statues in Antinoüs' honor. One such statue declares that Antinoüs was glorified in heaven and actually was the god Osiris (Cartlidge, 198).

Apollonius, a first-century neo-Pythagorean, was also reputed to have been transported to heaven after exhibiting miraculous powers. Later he was reported to have appeared to a young man in a dream.

Alexander the Great was said to have been born of a virgin, to have done wondrous deeds, and to have accepted accolades of being divine (Boyd, 49). He too is put in the category of divine-man legends.

Resurrection Claims. In addition to Apollonius of Tyana, there are claims that non-Christian leaders rose from the dead. Robert Price has made an extensive comparative religion study of post-death phenomena found in other religions that rival Christian claims about Christ. These stories have also been used to undercut claims of the uniqueness of Christianity (*see* CHRISTIANITY, UNIQUENESS OF; PLURALISM, RELIGIOUS).

Evaluation. The divine-man hypothesis has been debunked by such diverse theologians as Oscar Cullmann (*The Christology of the New Testament*), Reginald Fuller (*The Foundation of New Testament Christology*), Gary Habermas ("Resurrection Claims in Non-Christian Religions" in *Religious Studies 25* [1989]), and Ronald Nash (*Christianity and the Hellenistic World*).

There are difficulties if these legends are used as competitive claims to those of Christ. Sources of these stories are all far later than the events described and are questionable. Suetonius lived 150 years after Julius and nearly 100 years after Augustus. The report of Dio Cassius about Hadrian was about 100 years later. Philostratus wrote over 100 years after Apollonius died. By contrast, Christ's incarnation and divinity were attested by eyewitnesses in contemporary testimony (*see* CHRIST, DEITY OF; NEW TESTAMENT DOCUMENTS, RELIABILITY OF).

A political agenda accompanied most of these reports. Nearly one-half of Suetonius's twelve emperors were said to have been deified, and the story of Apollonius appeared at a time when some in the Empire were attempting to stimulate renewed mythological worship. They cannot be said to be historical accounts in any case, since there is no way to verify whether a spirit ascended to heaven or a soul turned into a star. Such are highly subjective testimonies. But the claim that Christ was raised physically from the dead, leaving an empty tomb and appearing in a physical body over a period of weeks to hundreds of people is historically verifiable (*see* RESURRECTION, EVIDENCE FOR).

The concept that a human being could be divinized is not the same as the Christian concept of the incarnation, wherein the second person of the Godhead became human. In Christ, the monotheistic God became human. In apotheosis a human becomes one among many gods.

The Case of Alexander. The claims about Alexander the Great illustrate the radical difference between these divine-men stories and that of Christ. Unlike the early Gospels, the earliest records of Alexander contain none of the features of the later legends about him. The stories of Alexander's miracles developed over a period of 1000 years. The miracles of Jesus were recorded within thirty years of their occurrence (*see* MIRACLES IN THE BIBLE; MIRACLES, MYTH AND). The legends of Alexander actually date from later than the time of Christ. It is likely that the stories of Alexander's super-normal feats were influenced by the Gospel accounts.

The Gospels were written within the context of Jewish monotheism, which held that human beings cannot be God. The stories of Alexander, however, were composed within a pagan, polytheistic setting where the concept of divinized humans was accepted.

Conclusion. Attempts to reduce Jesus to a Greek divine-man legend are ill-fated. The differences are too radical, and if one influenced the other the Christian record of God incarnate in human flesh came first.

Sources

B. L. Blackburn, "Miracle Working *Theioi Andres* in Hellenism (and Hellenic Judaism)," D. Wenham, *Gospel Perspectives*, Vol. 6: *The Miracles of Jesus*

W. Bousset, *Kurios Christos*

G. Boyd, *Jesus under Siege*

D. R. Cartlidge, *Documents for the Study of the Gospels*

O. Cullmann, *The Christology of the New Testament*

R. Fuller, *The Foundation of New Testament Christology*

G. Habermas, "Resurrection Claims in Non-Christian Religions," *RS* 25

R. Nash, *Christianity and the Hellenistic World*

O. Pfleiderer, *The Early Christian Conception of Christ*

R. Price, "Is There a Place for Historical Criticism?" paper presented before "Christianity Challenges the University: An International Conference of Theists and Atheists," Dallas, Texas, 7–10 February 1985

Suetonius, *The Twelve Caesars*

M. Wilkins, *Jesus under Fire*

Yamauchi, E. "Magic or Miracle? Disease, Demons and Exorcisms," D. Wenham, ed., *Gospel Perspectives*, Vol. 6: *The Miracles of Jesus*

Aquinas, Thomas. ***See*** **THOMAS AQUINAS.**

Archaeology, New Testament. The science of archaeology has brought strong confirmation to the historicity of both the Old Testament (*see* ALBRIGHT, WILLIAM F.; ARCHAEOLOGY, OLD TESTAMENT) and the New Testament. Archaeological evidence for the reliability of the New Testament is overwhelming (*see* NEW TESTAMENT, DATING OF; NEW TESTAMENT, HISTORICITY OF). This evidence will be summarized in three parts: the historical accuracy of Luke, the testimony of secular historians, and the physical evidence relating to Christ's crucifixion (*see* CHRIST, DEATH OF).

Historical Accuracy of Luke. It was once thought that Luke, writer of the most historically detailed Gospel and of Acts, had concocted his narrative from the rambling of his imagination, because he ascribed odd titles to authorities and mentioned governors that no one knew. The evidence now points in exactly the opposite direction (*see* ACTS, HISTORICITY OF).

The Census in Luke 2:1–5. Several problems are involved in the statement that Augustus conducted a census of the whole empire during the reign of both Quirinius and Herod. For one, there is no record for such a census, but we now know that regular censuses were taken in Egypt, Gaul, and Cyrene. It is quite likely that Luke's meaning is that censuses were taken throughout the empire at different times, and Augustus started this process. The present tense that Luke uses points strongly toward understanding this as a repeated event. Now Quirinius did take a census, but that was in A.D. 6, too late for Jesus' birth, and Herod died before Quirinius became governor.

Was Luke confused? No; in fact he mentions Quirinius' later census in Acts 5:37. It is most likely that Luke is distinguishing this census in Herod's time from the more well-known census of Quirinius: "This census took place before Quirinius was governor of Syria." There are several New Testament parallels for this translation.

Gallio, Proconsul of Achaia. This designation in Acts 18:12–17 was thought to be impossible. But an inscription at Delphi notes this exact title for the man and dates him to the time at which Paul was in Corinth (A.D. 51).

Lysanias, Tetrarch of Abilene. Lysanias was unknown to modern historians until an inscription was found recording a temple dedication which mentions the name, the title, and is in the right place. The inscription is dated between A.D. 14 and 29, easily compatible with the beginnings of John's ministry, which Luke dates by Lysanias' reign (Luke 3:1).

Erastus. In Acts 19:22, Erastus is named as a Corinthian who becomes a co-worker of Paul. If Luke were going to make up any names, this would seem to be the best place to do it. How would anyone know? In excavating Corinth, an inscription was found near the theater which reads, "Erastus in return for his aedileship laid the pavement at his own expense." If these are the same men, then it explains why Luke would have included the detail that a prominent and wealthy citizen of Corinth had been converted and had given his life to the ministry.

In addition to these, Luke gives correct titles for the following officials: Cyprus, *proconsul* (13:7–8); Thessalonica, *politarchs* (17:6); Ephesus, *temple wardens* (19:35); Malta, *the first man of the island* (28:7; Yamauchi, 115–19). Each of these has been confirmed by Roman usage. In all, Luke names thirty-two countries, fifty-four cities, and nine islands without an error. This led the prominent historian Sir William Ramsay to recant his critical views:

> I began with a mind unfavorable to it [Acts], for the ingenuity and apparent completeness of the Tübingen theory had at one time quite convinced me. It did not lie then in my line of life to investigate the subject minutely; but more recently I found myself often brought into contact with the book of Acts as an authority for the topography, antiquities, and society of Asia Minor. It was gradually borne in upon me that in various details the narrative showed marvelous truth. [Ramsay, 8]

In full agreement, Roman historian A. N. Sherwin-White says, "For Acts the confirmation of historicity is overwhelming. . . . Any attempt to reject its basic historicity must now appear absurd. Roman historians have long taken it for granted" (Sherwin-White, 189). The critical theories spawned in the early 1800s that persist today are left without substantiation. Archaeologist William F. Albright says, "All radical schools in New Testament criticism which have existed in the past or which exist today are pre-archaeological, and are therefore, since they were built *in der Luft* [in the air], quite antiquated today" (Albright, 29).

More recently another noted Roman historian has catalogued numerous archaeological and historical confirmations of Luke's accuracy (Hemer, 390f.). The following is a summary of his voluminous, detailed report (*see* ACTS, HISTORICITY OF; NEW TESTAMENT, NON-CHRISTIAN SOURCES):

- Geographical or other detail that may be assumed to have been generally known in the first century. It is difficult to estimate how much knowledge should be expected of an ancient writer or reader.
- Specialized details, which would not have been widely known except to a contemporary researcher such as Luke who traveled widely. These details include exact titles of officials, identification of army units, and information about major routes.
- Details archaeologists know are accurate but can't verify as to precise time period. Some of these are unlikely to have been known except to a writer who had visited the districts.
- Correlation of dates of known kings and governors with the chronology of the narrative.
- Facts appropriate to the date of Paul or his immediate contemporary in the church but not to a date earlier or later.
- "Undesigned coincidents" between Acts and the Pauline Epistles.
- Internal correlations within Acts.
- Independently attested details that help scholars separate the original Acts text from what may have been added later in the Alexandrian or the Western text families. Alleged anachronisms can now be identified as insertions referring to a later period.
- Off-hand geographical references that bespeak familiarity with common knowledge.
- Differences in formulation within Acts that indicate the different categories of sources he used.
- Peculiarities in the selection of detail, as in theology, that are explainable in the context of what is now known of first-century church life.

- Materials whose "immediacy" suggests the author was recounting a recent experience, rather than shaping or editing a text long afterward.
- Cultural or idiomatic items now known to be peculiar to the first-century atmosphere.
- Interrelated complexes of detail in which two or more kinds of correlation are combined or where related details show separate correlations. Through careful analysis of these correlations, it is possible for the historian to reconstruct quite detailed pieces of history by fitting together the interlocking pieces of fact as in a jigsaw puzzle.
- Cases where the information provided by Luke and details from other sources mesh to simply provide new background color. These do not bear significantly on historicity.
- Precise details in Luke that remain unverified or unrefuted until more is known.

Confirmation by Non-Christian Historians. One popular misconceptions about Jesus is that there is no mention of him in any ancient sources outside of the Bible. On the contrary, there are numerous references to him as an historical figure who died at the hand of Pontius Pilate. Some even noted that he was reported to have risen from the dead, and was worshiped as a god by all who followed him. Gary Habermas discusses these exhaustively. Quotations from historians and other sources are found in the article NEW TESTAMENT, NON-CHRISTIAN SOURCES.

Evidence Relating to Jesus' Death. Three fascinating discoveries illuminate the death of Christ and, to some degree, his resurrection. The first is an unusual decree; the second is the body of another crucifixion victim.

The Nazareth Decree. A slab of stone was found in Nazareth in 1878, inscribed with a decree from Emperor Claudius (A.D. 41–54) that no graves should be disturbed or bodies extracted or moved. This type of decree is not uncommon, but the startling fact is that here "the offender [shall] be sentenced to capital punishment on [the] charge of violation of [a] sepulchre" (ibid., 155). Other notices warned of a fine, but death for disturbing graves? A likely explanation is that Claudius, having heard of the Christian doctrine of resurrection and Jesus' empty tomb while investigating the riots of A.D. 49, decided not to let any such report surface again. This would make sense in light of the Jewish argument that the body had been stolen (Matt. 28:11–15). This is early testimony to the strong and persistent belief that Jesus rose from the dead.

Yohanan—A Crucifixion Victim. In 1968, an ancient burial site was uncovered in Jerusalem containing about thirty-five bodies. It was determined that most of these had suffered violent deaths in the Jewish uprising against Rome in A.D. 70. One of these was a man named Yohanan Ben Ha'galgol. He was about twenty-four to twenty-eight years old, had a cleft palate, and a seven-inch nail was still driven through both his feet. The feet had been turned outward so that the square nail could be hammered through at the heel, just inside the Achilles tendon. This would have bowed the legs outward as well so that they could not have been used for support on the cross. The nail had gone through a wedge of acacia wood, then through the heels, then into an olive wood beam. There was also evidence that similar spikes had been put between the two bones of each lower arm. These had caused the upper bones to be worn smooth as the victim repeatedly raised and lowered himself to breathe (breathing is restricted with the arms raised). Crucifixion victims had to lift themselves to free the chest muscles and, when they grew too weak to do so, died by suffocation.

Yohanan's legs were crushed by a blow, consistent with the common use of the Roman *crucifragium* (John 19:31–32). Each of these details confirms the New Testament description of crucifixion.

Much more textual and archaeological evidence supports the accuracy of the New Testament (*see* CHRIST, DEATH OF). But even these examples reveal the extent to which archaeology has confirmed the truth of the Scriptures. Archaeologist Nelson Glueck has boldly asserted that "it may be stated categorically that no archaeological discovery has ever controverted a biblical reference. Scores of archaeological findings have been made which confirm in clear outline or exact detail historical statements in the Bible" (Glueck, 31).

Sources

W. F. Albright, "Retrospect and Prospect in New Testament Archaeology," in E. J. Vardaman, ed., *The Teacher's Yoke*

F. F. Bruce, *The New Testament Documents: Are They Reliable?*

N. Glueck, *Rivers in the Desert*

G. R. Habermas, *The Verdict of History*

C. J. Hemer, *The Book of Acts in the Setting of Hellenistic History*, C. H. Gempf, ed.

J. McRay, *Archaeology and the New Testament*

W. M. Ramsay, *St. Paul the Traveller and the Roman Citizen*

J. A. T. Robinson, *Redating the New Testament*

A. N. Sherwin-White, *Roman Society and Roman Law in the New Testament*

C. A. Wilson, *Rocks, Relics and Biblical Reliability*

E. Yamauchi, *The Stones and the Scriptures*

Archaeology, Old Testament. Several things must be kept in mind when reviewing archaeological data as it relates to Christianity (*see* ARCHAEOLOGY, NEW TESTAMENT). First, meaning can only be derived from context. Archaeological evidence is dependent on the context of date, place, materials, and style. How it is understood depends on the interpreter's presuppositions.

Therefore, not all interpretations of the evidence will be friendly to Christianity.

Second, archaeology is a special kind of science. Physicists and chemists can do all kinds of experiments to recreate the processes they study and watch them over and over again. Archaeologists cannot. They have only the evidence left from the one and only time that civilization lived. They study past singularities, not present regularities. Because they can't recreate the societies that they study, their conclusions can't be tested as can other sciences. Archaeology tries to find plausible and probable explanations for the evidence it finds. It cannot make laws as can physics. For this reason, all conclusions must be subject to revision. The best interpretation is the one that best explains all the evidence.

Third, the archaeological evidence is fragmentary. It comprises only a tiny fraction of all that occurred. Hence, the discovery of more evidence can change the picture considerably. This is especially true when conclusions have been based on silence—a lack of existing evidence. Many critical views about the Bible have subsequently been overturned by archaeological discoveries (*see* BIBLE CRITICISM). For example, it was long believed that the Bible was in error when it spoke about Hittites (Gen. 23:10). But since the discovery of the Hittite library in Turkey (1906) this is no longer the case.

Archaeology Supports the Old Testament. The Creation. The opening chapters of Genesis (1–11) are typically thought to be mythological explanations derived from earlier versions of the story found in the ancient Near East. But this view chooses only to notice the similarities between Genesis and the creation stories in other ancient cultures. If we can propose derivation of the human race from one family, plus general revelation, some lingering traces of the true historical account would be expected. The differences are more important. Babylonian and Sumerian accounts describe the creation as the product of a conflict among finite gods. When one god is defeated and split in half, the River Euphrates flows from one eye and the Tigris from the other. Humanity is made of the blood of an evil god mixed with clay. These tales display the kind of distortion and embellishment to be expected when an historical account becomes mythologized.

Less likely is that the literary progression would be from this mythology to the unadorned elegance of Genesis 1. The common assumption that the Hebrew account is simply a purged and simplified version of the Babylonian legend is fallacious. In the Ancient Near East, the rule is that simple accounts or traditions give rise (by accretion and embellishment) to elaborate legends, but not the reverse. So the evidence supports the view that Genesis was not myth made into history. Rather, the extrabiblical accounts were history turned into myths (*see* CREATION AND ORIGINS; CREATION, VIEWS OF; GENESIS, DAYS OF).

The recent discoveries of creation accounts at Ebla (*see* EBLA TABLETS) add evidence of this. This library of sixteen thousand clay tablets predates the Babylonian account by about 600 years. The creation tablet is strikingly close to Genesis, speaking of one being who created the heavens, moon, stars, and earth. The people at Ebla believed in creation from nothing (*see* CREATION, VIEWS OF). The Bible contains the ancient, less embellished version of the story and transmits the facts without the corruption of the mythological renderings.

The Flood of Noah. As with the creation accounts, the flood (*see* FLOOD, NOAH'S) narrative in Genesis is more realistic and less mythological than other ancient versions, indicating its authenticity. The superficial similarities point toward an historical core of events that gave rise to all, not toward plagiarism by Moses. The names change. Noah is called Ziusudra by the Sumerians and Utnapishtim by the Babylonians. The basic story doesn't. A man is told to build a ship to specific dimensions because God(s) are going to flood the world. He does it, rides out the storm, and offers sacrifice upon exiting the boat. The Deity(-ies) respond with remorse over the destruction of life, and make a covenant with the man. These core events point to a historical basis.

Similar flood accounts are found all over the world. The flood is told of by the Greeks, the Hindus, the Chinese, the Mexicans, the Algonquins, and the Hawaiians. One list of Sumerian kings treats the flood as an historical reference point. After naming eight kings who lived extraordinarily long lives (tens of thousands of years), this sentence interrupts the list: "[Then] the Flood swept over [the earth] and when kingship was lowered [again] from heaven, kingship was [first] in Kish."

There are good reasons to believe that Genesis gives the original story. The other versions contain elaborations indicating corruption. Only in Genesis is the year of the flood given, as well as dates for the chronology relative to Noah's life. In fact, Genesis reads almost like a diary or ship's log of the events. The cubical Babylonian ship could not have saved anyone. The raging waters would have constantly turned it on every side. However, the biblical ark is rectangular—long, wide, and low—so that it would ride the rough seas well. The length of the rainfall in the pagan accounts (seven days) is not enough time for the devastation they describe. The waters would have to rise at least above most mountains, to a height of above 17,000 feet, and it is more reasonable to assume a longer rainfall to do this. The Babylonian idea that all of the flood waters subsided in one day is equally absurd. Another striking difference between Genesis and the other versions is that in these accounts the hero is granted immortality and exalted. The Bible moves on to Noah's sin. Only a version that seeks to tell the truth would include this realistic admission.

Some have suggested that this was a severe but localized flood. However, there is geological evidence to support a worldwide flood. Partial skeletons of recent animals are found in deep fissures in several parts of the world and the flood seems to be the best explanation for these. This would explain how these fissures occur even in hills of considerable height, and they extend from 140 feet to 300 feet. Since no skeleton is complete, it is safe to conclude that none of these animals (mammoths, bears, wolves, oxen, hyenas, rhinoceros, aurochs, deer, and smaller mammals) fell into these fissures alive, nor were they rolled there by streams. Yet because of the calcite cementing of these diverse bones together, they must have been deposited under water. Such fissures have been discovered in various places around the world. This is exactly the kind of evidence that a brief but violent episode of this sort would be expected to show within the short span of one year.

The Tower of Babel. There is considerable evidence now that the world did indeed have a single language at one time. Sumerian literature alludes to this several times. Linguists also find this theory helpful in categorizing languages. But what of the tower and the confusion of tongues at the tower of Babel (Genesis 11)? Archaeology has revealed that Ur-Nammu, King of Ur from about 2044 to 2007 B.C., supposedly received orders to build a great ziggurat (temple tower) as an act of worship to the moon god Nannat. A stele (monument) about five feet across and ten feet high reveals Ur-Nammu's activities. One panel has him setting out with a mortar basket to begin construction of the great tower, thus showing his allegiance to the gods by taking his place as a humble workman. Another clay tablet states that the erection of the tower offended the gods, so they threw down what the men had built, scattered them abroad, and made their speech strange. This is remarkably similar to the record in the Bible.

Conservative scholars believe Moses wrote these early chapters of Genesis (*see* PENTATEUCH, MOSAIC AUTHORSHIP OF). But how could he, since these events occurred long before his birth? There are two possibilities. First, God could have revealed the accounts to Moses supernaturally. Just as God can reveal the future by prophetic revelation, he can reveal the past by retrospective revelation too. The second possibility is more likely, namely, that Moses compiled and edited earlier records of these events. This is not contrary to biblical practice. Luke did the same in his Gospel (Luke 1:1–4). P. J. Wiseman has argued convincingly that the history of Genesis was originally written on clay tablets and passed on from one generation to the next with each "clan leader" being responsible for keeping them edited and up to date. The main clue that Wiseman found to this in the Bible is the periodic repetition of words and phrases, especially the phrase "This is the generation of" (for example, Gen. 2:4; 6:9; 10:1; 11:10). Many ancient tablets were kept in order by making the first words of a new tablet a repetition of the last words of the previous stone. A literary evaluation of Genesis compared to other ancient literature indicates that it was compiled no later than the time of Moses. It is quite possible that Genesis is a family history recorded by the patriarchs and edited into its final form by Moses.

The Patriarchs. While the narratives of the lives of Abraham, Isaac, and Jacob do not present the same kinds of difficulties as do the earlier chapters of Genesis, they were long considered legendary because they did not seem to fit with the known evidence of that period. As more has become known though, these stories are increasingly verified. Legal codes from the time of Abraham show why the patriarch would have been hesitant to throw Hagar out of his camp, for he was legally bound to support her. Only when a higher law came from God was Abraham willing to put her out.

The Mari letters reveal such names as Abamram (Abraham), Jacob-el, and Benjamites. Though these do not refer to the biblical people, they at least show that the names were in use. These letters also support the record of a war in Genesis 14 where five kings fought against four kings. The names of these kings seem to fit with the prominent nations of the day. For example, Genesis 14:1 mentions an Amorite king Arioch; the Mari documents render the king's name Ariwwuk. All of this evidence leads to the conclusion that the source material of Genesis was firsthand accounts of someone who lived during Abraham's time.

Sodom and Gomorrah. The destruction of Sodom and Gomorrah was thought to be spurious until evidence revealed that all five of the cities mentioned in the Bible were in fact centers of commerce in the area and were geographically situated as the Scriptures say. The biblical description of their demise seems to be no less accurate. Evidence points to earthquake activity, and that the various layers of the earth were disrupted and hurled high into the air. Bitumen is plentiful there, and an accurate description would be that brimstone (bituminous pitch) was hurled down on those cities that had rejected God. There is evidence that the layers of sedimentary rock have been molded together by intense heat. Evidence of such burning has been found on the top of Jebel Usdum (Mount Sodom).

This is permanent evidence of the great conflagration that took place in the long-distant past, possibly when an oil basin beneath the Dead Sea ignited and erupted. Such an explanation in no way subtracts from the miraculous quality of the event, for God controls natural forces. The timing of the event, in the context of warnings and visitation by angels, reveals its overall miraculous nature.

The Dating of the Exodus. One of the several issues about Israel's relationship with Egypt is when the Exodus into Palestine occurred (*see* PENTATEUCH, MOSAIC AUTHORSHIP OF; PHARAOH OF THE EXODUS). There is even an official "Generally Accepted Date" (GAD) for the entrance into Canaan of about 1230–1220 B.C. The Scriptures, on the other hand, teach in three different texts (1 Kings 6:1; Judg. 11:26; Acts 13:19–20) that the Exodus occurred in the 1400s B.C., with the entrance into Canaan forty years later. While the debate will rage on, there is no longer any reason to accept the 1200 date.

Assumptions have been made that the city "Rameses" in Exodus 1:11 was named after Rameses the Great, that there were no building projects in the Nile Delta before 1300, and that there was no great civilization in Canaan from the nineteenth to the thirteenth centuries. However, the name Rameses is common in Egyptian history. Rameses the Great is Ramses II. Nothing is known about Rameses I. Also, the name might not refer to a city but to an area. In Genesis 47:11, the name *Rameses* describes the Nile Delta area where Jacob and his sons settled.

Some scholars now suggest that reinterpretation of the data requires moving the date of the Middle Bronze (MB) age. If this is done, it would show that several uncovered cities of Canaan were destroyed by the Israelites. Evidence has come from recent digs that the last phase of the MB period needs more time than originally thought, so that its end is closer to 1400 B.C. than 1550 B.C. This realignment would bring together two events previously thought to be separated by centuries: the fall of Canaan's MB II cities and the conquest.

Another change may be warranted in the traditional view of Egyptian history. The chronology of the whole ancient world is based on the order and dates of the Egyptian kings, which was generally thought to have been fixed. However, Velikovsky and Courville assert that 600 extra years in that chronology throw off dates for events all around the Near East. Courville has shown that the lists of Egyptian kings should not be understood to be completely consecutive. He argues that some "kings" listed were not pharaohs, but high officials. Historians had assumed that each dynasty follows after the one before it. Instead, many dynasties list subrulers who lived at the same time as the preceding dynasty. Working out this new chronology places the Exodus about 1450 B.C. and would make the other periods of Israelite history fall in line with the Egyptian kings mentioned. The evidence is not definitive, but there is no longer any reason to demand a late-date Exodus. For more information, see the article PHARAOH OF THE EXODUS.

Saul, David, and Solomon. Saul became the first king of Israel, and his fortress at Gibeah has been excavated. One of the most noteworthy finds was that slingshots were one of the most important weapons of the day. This relates not only to David's victory over Goliath, but to the reference of Judges 20:16 that there were seven hundred expert slingers who "could sling a stone at a hair and not miss."

Upon Saul's death, Samuel tells us that his armor was put in the temple of Ashtaroth (a Canaanite fertility goddess) at Bethshan, while Chronicles says that his head was put in the temple of Dagon, the Philistine corn god. This was thought to be an error because it seemed unlikely that enemy peoples would have temples in the same place at the same time. However, excavations have found that there are two temples at this site that are separated by a hallway: one for Dagon, and the other for Ashtaroth. It appears that the Philistines had adopted the Canaanite goddess.

One of the key accomplishments of David's reign was the capture of Jerusalem. Problematic in the Scripture account was that the Israelites entered the city by way of a tunnel that led to the Pool of Siloam. However, that pool was thought to be *outside* the city walls at that time. But in the 1960s excavations it was finally determined that the wall did indeed extend well past the pool.

The psalms attributed to David are often said to have been written much later because their inscriptions suggest that there were musician's guilds (e.g., the sons of Korah). Such organization leads many to think that these hymns should be dated to about the time of the Maccabeans in the second century B.C. Following excavations at Ras Shamra it is now known that there were such guilds in Syria and Palestine in David's time.

The time of Solomon has no less corroboration. The site of Solomon's temple has not been excavated, because it is near the Muslim holy place, The Dome of the Rock. However, what is known about Philistine temples built in Solomon's time fits well with the design, decoration, and materials described in the Bible. The only piece of evidence from the temple itself is a small ornament, a pomegranate, that sat on the end of a rod and bears the inscription, "Belonging to the Temple of Yahweh." It was first seen in a shop in Jerusalem in 1979, verified in 1984, and was acquired by the Israel Museum in 1988.

The excavation of Gezer in 1969 ran across a massive layer of ash that covered most of the mound. Sifting through the ash yielded pieces of Hebrew, Egyptian, and Philistine artifacts. Apparently all 3 cultures had been there at the same time. This puzzled researchers greatly until they realized that the Bible told them exactly what they had found. "Pharaoh king of Egypt had attacked and captured Gezer. He had set it on fire. He killed its Canaanite inhabitants and then gave it as a wedding gift to his daughter, Solomon's wife" (1 Kings 9:16).

The Assyrian Invasion. Much was learned about the Assyrians when 26,000 tablets were found in the palace of Ashurbanipal, son of the Esarhaddon who took the northern kingdoms into captivity in 722 B.C. These tablets tell of the many conquests of the Assyrian empire and record with honor the cruel and violent punishments that fell to those who opposed them.

Several of these records confirm the Bible's accuracy. Every reference in the Old Testament to an Assyrian king has proven correct. Even though Sargon was unknown for some time, when his palace was found and excavated, there was a wall painting of the battle mentioned in Isaiah 20. The Black Obelisk of Shalmaneser adds to our knowledge of biblical figures by showing Jehu (or his emissary) bowing down to the king of Assyria.

Among the most interesting finds is Sennacherib's record of the siege of Jerusalem. Thousands of his men died and the rest scattered when he attempted to take the city and, as Isaiah had foretold, he was unable to conquer it. Since he could not boast about his great victory here, Sennacherib found a way to make himself sound good without admitting defeat:

> As to Hezekiah, the Jew, he did not submit to my yoke. I laid siege to 46 of his strong cities, walled forts, and to the countless small villages in their vicinity . . . I drove out of them 200,150 people, young and old, male and female, horses, mules, donkeys, camels, big and small cattle beyond counting and considered (them) booty. Himself I made a prisoner in Jerusalem, his royal residence, like a bird in a cage. [Pritchard, 288]

The Captivity. Various facets of the Old Testament history regarding the captivity have been confirmed. Records found in Babylon's famous hanging gardens have shown that Jehoiachin and his five sons were being given a monthly ration and place to live and were treated well (2 Kings 25:27–30). The name of Belshazzar caused problems, because there was not only no mention of him, but no room for him in the list of Babylonian kings; however, Nabodonius left a record that he appointed his son, Belshazzar (Daniel 5), to reign for a few years in his absence. Hence, Nabodonius was still king, but Belshazzar ruled in the capital. Also, the edict of Cyrus as recorded by Ezra seemed to fit the picture of Isaiah's prophecies too well to be real, until a cylinder was found that confirmed the decree in all the important details.

In every period of Old Testament history, we find that there is good evidence from archaeology that the Scriptures speak the truth. In many instances, the Scriptures even reflect firsthand knowledge of the times and customs it describes. While many have doubted the accuracy of the Bible, time and continued research have consistently demonstrated that the Word of God is better informed than its critics.

In fact, while thousands of finds from the ancient world support in broad outline and often in detail the biblical picture, not one incontrovertible find has ever contradicted the Bible.

Sources

W. F. Albright, *Archaeology of Palestine*

G. L. Archer, Jr., *Encyclopedia of Biblical Difficulties*

J. Bimson and D. Livingston, "Redating the Exodus," *BAR*, September–October 1987

N. Glueck, *Rivers in the Desert*

K. A. Kitchen, *Ancient Orient and Old Testament*

J. B. Pritchard, ed., *Ancient Near East Texts*

C. A. Wilson, *Rocks, Relics and Biblical Reliability*

E. Yamauchi, *The Stones and the Scriptures*

Aristotle. Aristotle (384–322 B.C.) holds immense importance for Christian apologetics. He laid down the basic principles of reason used by most apologists (*see* CAUSALITY, PRINCIPLE OF; FIRST PRINCIPLES; LOGIC). Many of the greatest apologists, especially *Thomas Aquinas, were dependent on Aristotelian principles.

Born in Stagira, Greece, as the son of a physician, Aristotle entered *Plato's academy in about 367 and remained there until Plato's death (347). He began teaching Alexander the Great (356–323) in about 342. With Alexander's conquests, Aristotle's thought spread, along with Greek language and culture, throughout the world.

Major writings of Aristotle can be categorized under logic, physical studies, psychology, and philosophy:

- Logic: *Categories*, *On Interpretation*, *Prior and Posterior Analytics*, *On Sophistical Refutations*, *Topics*
- Physical sciences: *Meteorologics*, *On Coming-to-be and Passing Away*, *On the Heavens*, *Physics*
- Psychology: *On Dreams*, *On Memory and Reminiscence*, *On Prophesying by Dreams* (*Parva Naturalia*), *On the Soul*
- Philosophy: *Art and Poetry*, *Metaphysics*, *Nicomachean Ethics*, *Politics*, *Rhetoric*

Few, if any, thinkers, before or after Aristotle, had a more analytic, encyclopedic, and productive mind.

Epistemology (Theory of Knowledge). Aristotle was an empiricist who believed all knowledge begins in the senses. Once an object is perceived by one or more of the five senses, the mind begins to act upon it with its powers of abstraction. Aristotle saw three acts of the intellect: *apprehension* (understanding), *predication* (declarations), and *syllogistic reasoning* (logic).

Apprehension. The first act of the mind is apprehension or the understanding of a thing or object. The *subject* of apprehension is a rational animal (human being). The *object* of apprehension is the essence (quiddity) or form of things. The *method* of apprehension is the intellectual process of abstraction, through which the mind obtains a universal from processing information about the particulars. In this Aristotle differed from the later nominalists, who denied universals and taught that only particulars exist.

Ten modes of apprehension are called the "predicaments" or *categories*. Categories include:

1. *Substance—what* is apprehended. This is also called the *subject* of apprehension. Primary substance is the ultimate subject of all predication. Secondary substance is the universal that is predicable for a class.
2. *Quantity* or *how much* of the subject is apprehended.
3. *Quality* is *what kind* of subject is apprehended.
4. *Relation* informs us *to what* the subject has reference.
5. *Action* speaks of *on what* the subject is acting.
6. *Passion* is *from what* the subject receives action.
7. *Place* answers *where* the subject is apprehended to be.
8. *Time* answers *when* the subject is apprehended.
9. *Position* refers to *under what circumstances* the subject is apprehended.
10. *Habit* or *state* tells *in what condition* the subject apprehended is found to be. A habit is natural but not essential to a thing, like clothes to humans.

Predication. Once an object is apprehended (understood), certain predications can be made about it. Similar to apprehension, predication can be broken down into the *subject* of predication (human being) and *object* of predication (quiddity or form of a thing). To these are added the *purpose* of predication (the definition or nature of a thing), *means* of predication, and the *mode* of predication.

The means of predication can be communicated as a proposition with a subject, predicate, and copula, a statement of what it "is" or "is not." The modes of predication are the predicables, the various kinds of reality a predicate can convey about a thing. Modes of predication include:

Genus. Humankind fits the genus "animal." This characteristic is common to many subjects.

Specific difference. Humans are "rational" animals. That is a difference specific to this subject.

Species. The subject denotes both the genus and the specific difference. Through our understanding of creation, we automatically know that *human* means "rational animal." In this particular example, the subject has been assigned a scientific species name, which says just that in Latin: *Homo sapiens*.

Property. A subject is predicated by what flows from its essence but isn't part of it. Human beings laugh. Risibility, the ability to laugh, is a property of human beings.

Accidents. The predicate describes what is in the essence of the subject but not part of it. In the sentence "He has black hair," the characteristic of black hair is not part of the human essence, but it is part of a category system that adheres to it.

Quantity/Extent. This predication can be universal, when all of the class is included, or particular, when a limitation is specified. "Human beings are rational animals, but few human beings do their thinking in Gaelic."

Quality. Predication that must be expressed by an affirmative ("is") or a negative ("is not") statement. "A human being is able to give glory to God."

Reasoning (Logic). Once something is apprehended, and propositions (declarations) are made about it, then conclusions can be drawn from combining two or more of these predications. Putting together predications and drawing conclusions from them results in a *syllogism*. There are three basic kinds of reasoning: *deductive*, *inductive*, and *fallacious*.

Deductive logic deals with the validity of deductions given to the premises in a syllogism. Aristotle developed this logic in *Prior Analytics*, and in *Posterior Analytics* he added *material logic*, which deals with the truth of such deductions or demonstrations. *Inductive logic* (called "opinion") deals with probability reasoning. This is discussed in *Topics*. *Fallacious logic* deals with incorrect reasoning and is covered in detail in *Sophistical Refutations*.

Reality and God. Aristotle's view of God grows out of his view of reality, called "metaphysics." *Metaphysics* as Aristotle understood the term can be understood most clearly in contrast to other disciplines. For Aristotle, *Physics* studies the real that can be experienced through the five senses. Metaphysics studies reality outside sensory perception. *Mathematics* is the study of the real (being) insofar as it is quantifiable (though this is not true of all modern mathematics). Metaphysics is the study of being insofar as it is real.

Actuality (Act) and Potentiality (Potency). Aristotle's understanding of reality involved what actually is (*actuality*) and what it can be (*potentiality*). Everything in creation is composed of both form (actuality) and matter (potentiality), a view called "hylomorphism." Its immutable implication is that the reality we perceive through our senses is changing.

Change is the passing from potentiality to actuality. Aristotle posited two kinds of change, *substantial* and *accidental*. Substantial changes alter substance—what something essentially is. This change happens when substance comes to be (generation) or ceases to be (corruption). Accidental change is a change in what something *has*, in its *accidents*. An accident is what inheres in a substance but is not of the essence of that substance. Dying is a substantial change. Learning is an accidental change.

The Four Causes of Things. In studying the nature of being, Aristotle posited four causes. Two intrinsic causes are inside the thing. As applied to a wooden chair, they are:

1. The formal cause—that *of which* it is made, its form or essence: chairness.
2. The material cause—that *out of which* it is made, its material: wood.

The two extrinsic causes are outside the thing. In the example of the chair they are:

3. The efficient cause—that *by which* it is made, the agent: carpenter.
4. The final cause—that *for which* it was made, the purpose: to sit in.

Aristotle's Answer to Monism. Aristotle's metaphysics can be understood as a response to the argument by Parmenides (b. 515 B.C.) for monism (*see* MONISM; ONE AND MANY, PROBLEM OF). Parmenides argued that: (1) Either everything is one or it is many. (2) If there are many beings, they must differ. (3) If they differ, they must differ by being or by nonbeing. (4) They cannot differ by nonbeing, since nonbeing is nothing (and that would mean they do not differ). (5) Neither can they differ by being, since being is what they all have in common. They cannot differ by the sense in which they are the same. (6) Hence, there can only be one being (monism).

There were four basic answers to Parmenides. (1) *Atomism said that things (atoms) differ by absolute nonbeing (the void). (2) Platonism argued (*see* PLATO) that things (forms) differ by relative nonbeing (otherness), determination by negation. (3) *Aquinas later affirmed that since being is a complex of act and potency, things differ by the kind of being they are. (4) Aristotle believed only material things were composed of form (act) and matter (potency). Pure forms, such as gods are, are simple. So the forty-seven or fifty-five forms (gods) differ in that they are simply different beings.

The Existence and Nature of God. From this answer to Parmenides, one can see that Aristotle's concept of god(s) was by no means the Creator as understood by Judaism. Like many later Christians, however, Aristotle believed that the existence of God could be proven. His proof went like this:

1. Things do change. This is established by observing movement, the most obvious form of change.
2. All change is a passing from potentiality to actuality. That is, when a potential is actualized, change has occurred.
3. No potential can actualize itself. Wood cannot make itself into a chair, although it has the capacity to become a chair.
4. There must be an actuality that actualizes everything that passes from potentiality to actuality. Otherwise, nothing would be actualized.
5. An infinite regress of actualizers is impossible, for the whole series would not be actualized unless there is a first actualizer.
6. This first actuality actualizes things by final causality, by drawing things to it the way a lover is drawn by his loved one.
7. There are forty-seven (according to the astronomer Eudoxus) or fifty-five (according to Callipus) of these pure actualities ("unmoved movers").
8. Ultimately, there is only one heaven and one God. Only material things can be numerically different, since matter is the principle of individuation.
9. This last point was either a later addition by Aristotle or by one of his editors after his death. It gives the appearance of being the latter. For Aristotle's context in the history of the cosmological argument, see COSMOLOGICAL ARGUMENT.

Several things are noteworthy about Aristotle's argument: It introduces the question of an infinite regress of causes (*see* INFINITE SERIES). It posited a plurality of first causes with a note attached (that may be by a later editor) that posits one God. Unlike Plato's demiurges, Aristotle's First Cause is a final purposing cause, not an efficient cause. Neither was the Unmoved Mover a personal God who had love or concern for creation. In fact, Aristotle's God had no religious significance or need for worship. This God was simply a logical necessity to be used to explain the cosmos and then discarded. This First Cause was not infinite as is the God of Christian theism. Aristotle followed the Greek belief that only what was formless and indefinite could be considered infinite. Aristotle's God did not create everything freely and *ex nihilo* (*see* CREATION,

VIEWS OF). The universe is eternal, and God has been forming it by drawing it to himself. So God is not the producing (efficient) cause but a pulling (final) cause.

Other views of Aristotle are of interest to Christian apologists. He believed in a literal (vs. an allegorical) hermeneutic. In contrast to Plato, Aristotle denied the immortality of the soul or the afterlife. According to Aristotle, the soul, which is the form of the body, dies with the body (*see* IMMORTALITY). Aristotle espoused a "golden mean" ethic that others have developed into a situational ethic (*see* MORALITY, ABSOLUTE NATURE OF).

Sources

Aristotle, *Aristotle's* Categories *and* De Interpretatione, W. D. Ross, trans.

———, *The Works of Aristotle Translated into English*, W. D. Ross, ed.

W. Jaeger, *Aristotle: Fundamentals of the History of His Development*, R. Robinson, trans.

J. Owen, *The Doctrine of Being in the Aristotelian Metaphysics*

W. D. Ross, *Prior and Posterior Analytics*

Athanasius. Athanasius of Alexandria (296–373) was one of the great early defenders of the Christian faith. He was educated in the catechetical school of Alexandria. As secretary to Bishop Alexander, he attended the Council of Nicea (325). He succeeded Alexander three years later. Probably before 318, while still in his twenties, he wrote *De Incarnatione* (*On the Incarnation*) and *Contra Gentes*, explaining how the Logos (Christ) became human and redeemed humanity. Later, in *Letters Concerning the Holy Spirit*, he defended the personality and deity of the third person of the Trinity.

Orthodoxy of Athanasius. Athanasius not only defended orthodox Christianity, he helped set the standard for it, particularly on the deity of Christ. From 339 to 359 he wrote a series of defenses of the faith (*Orations Against Arians*) aimed at those who denied the full deity of Christ. Grammatically, the issue centered around whether Christ was *homoiousion* (of "like substance"), or *homoousion* (of the "same substance") with the Father. Athanasius stood firm, against great odds and at great personal cost, to preserve a biblical stand when most church leaders wandered into Arianism. For this he earned the title of *contra mundum* ("against the world").

The Nicene Creed. It is uncertain what exact role Athanasius played in framing the Nicene Creed. He certainly defended it with his life. This creed reads, in part, in its original form:

> We believe in ONE GOD THE FATHER Almighty, Maker of heaven and earth, and of all things visible and invisible.
>
> And in one LORD JESUS CHRIST, the only-begotten son of God, Begotten of the Father before all worlds, Light of Light, very God of very God, begotten, not made, Being of one substance with the Father; by whom all things were made. . . .
>
> And in the HOLY GHOST, the Lord and Giver of Life; who proceeds from the Father; who with the Father and the Son together is worshiped and glorified; who spake by the Prophets.

Sources

Athanasius. *On the Incarnation*

———, *Contra Gentes*

———, *Orations Against Arians*

F. L. Cross, "Athanasius, St." in *Oxford Dictionary of the Christian Church*

———, *The Study of St. Athanasius*

J. A. Dorner, *History of the Development of the Doctrine of the Person of Christ*, vol. 2

A. Robertson, *St. Athanasius*

R. V. Sellers, *Two Ancient Christologies*

P. Schaff, *The Creeds of Christendom*, vol. 1

Atheism. While *polytheism dominated much of ancient Greek thought and theism dominated medieval Christian view, atheism has had its day in the modern world. Of course not all who lack faith in a divine being wish to be called "atheist." Some prefer the positive ascription of "Humanist" (*see* HUMANISM, SECULAR). Others are perhaps best described as "materialists." But all are nontheists, and most are antitheistic. Some prefer the more neutral term a-theists.

In distinction from a theist, (*see* THEISM) who believes God exists beyond and in the world, and a pantheist, who believes God is the world, an atheist believes there is no God either beyond or in the world. There is only a universe or cosmos and nothing more.

Since atheists share much in common with agnostics (*see* AGNOSTICISM) and skeptics, they are often confused with them (see Russell, "What Is an Agnostic?"). Technically, a skeptic says "I *doubt* that God exists" and an agnostic declares "I *don't know* (or can't know) whether God exists." But an atheist claims to *know* (or at least believe) that God does not exist. However, since atheists are all nontheists and since most atheists share with skeptics an antitheistic stand, many of their arguments are the same. It is in this sense that modern atheism rests heavily upon the skepticism of David *Hume and the agnosticism of Immanuel *Kant.

Varieties of Atheism. Broadly speaking, there are differing kinds of atheism. *Traditional* (metaphysical) atheism holds that there never was, is, or will be a God. The many with this view include Ludwig *Feuerbach, Karl *Marx, Jean-Paul *Sartre, and Antony *Flew. *Mythological* atheists, such as Friedrich *Nietzsche, believe the God-myth was never a Being, but was once a live *model* by which people lived. This myth has been killed by the advancement of man's understanding and culture. There was a short-lived form of *dialecti-*

cal atheism held by Thomas *Altizer which proposed that the once-alive, transcendent God actually died in the incarnation and crucifixion of Christ, and this death was subsequently realized in modern times. *Semantical* atheists (*see* VERIFICATION, EMPIRICAL) claim that God-talk is dead. This view was held by Paul Van Buren and others influenced by the logical positivists who had seriously challenged the meaningfulness of language about God. Of course, those who hold this latter view need not be actual atheists at all. They can admit to the existence of God and yet believe that it is not possible to talk about him in meaningful terms. This view has been called "acognosticism," since it denies that we can speak of God in cognitive or meaningful terms. *Conceptual* atheism believes that there is a God, but he is hidden from view, obscured by our conceptual constructions (*see* BUBER, MARTIN). Finally, *practical* atheists confess that God exists but believes that we should live *as if* he did not. The point is that we should not use God as a crutch for our failure to act in a spiritual and responsible way (some of Dietrich Bonhöffer's writings can be interpreted in this category).

There are other ways to designate the various kinds of atheists. One way would be by the philosophy by which they express their atheism. In this way one could speak of *existential* atheists (Sartre), *Marxist* atheists (Marx), *psychological* atheists (Sigmund *Freud), *capitalistic* atheists (Ayn *Rand), and *behavioristic* atheists (B. F. Skinner).

For apologetics purposes the most applicable way to consider atheism is in a metaphysical sense. Atheists are those who give reasons for believing that no God exists in or beyond the world. Thus we are speaking about philosophical atheism as opposed to practical atheists who simply live as though there were no God.

Arguments for Atheism. The arguments for atheism are largely negative, although some can be cast in positive terms. Negative arguments fall into two categories: (1) arguments against proofs for God's existence (*see* GOD, OBJECTIONS TO PROOFS FOR), and (2) arguments against God's existence (*see* GOD, ALLEGED DISPROOFS OF). On the first set of arguments most atheists draw heavily on the skepticism of Hume and the agnosticism of Kant.

Atheists offer what they consider to be good and sufficient reasons for believing no God exists. Four such arguments are often used by atheists: (1) the fact of evil (*see* EVIL, MORAL PROBLEM OF); (2) the apparent purposelessness of life; (3) random occurrence in the universe; and (4) the First Law of Thermodynamics*—that "energy can neither be created or destroyed" as evidence that the universe is eternal and, hence, needs no Creator.

Responses to the Arguments. *The Existence of Evil.* A detailed response to the problem of evil is given elsewhere (*see* EVIL, PROBLEM OF), so it will be treated here only in general terms. The atheist's reasoning is circular. Former atheist C. S. *Lewis argued that, in order to know there is injustice in the world one has to have a standard of justice. So, to effectively eliminate God via evil one is to posit an ultimate moral standard by which to pronounce God evil (*Mere Christianity*). But for theists God is the ultimate moral standard, since there cannot be an ultimate moral law without an Ultimate Moral Law Giver.

Atheists argue that an absolutely good God must have a good purpose for everything, but there is no good purpose for much of the evil in the world. Hence, there cannot be an absolutely perfect God.

Theists point out that just because we do not know the purpose for evil occurrences does not mean that there is no good purpose. This argument does not necessarily disprove God; it only proves our ignorance of God's plan. Along the same reasoning, just because we do not see a purpose for all evil now, does not follow that we never will. The atheist is premature in his judgment. According to theism, a day of justice is coming. If there is a God, he must have a good purpose for evil, even if we do not know it. For a theistic God is omniscient and knows everything. He is omnibenevolent and has a good reason for everything. So, by his very nature he must have a good reason for evil.

Purposelessness. In assuming that life is without purpose, the atheist is again both a presumptuous and premature judge. How does one know there is no ultimate purpose in the universe? Simply because the atheist knows no real purpose for life does not mean God does not have one. Most people have known times that made no sense for the moment but eventually seemed to have great purpose.

The Random Universe. Apparent randomness in the universe does not disprove God. Some randomness is only apparent, not real. When DNA was first discovered it was believed that it split randomly. Now the entire scientific world knows the incredible design involved in the splitting of the double helix molecule known as DNA. Even actual randomness has an intelligent purpose (*see* TELEOLOGICAL ARGUMENT). Molecules of carbon dioxide are exhaled randomly with the oxygen (and nythogine in the air), but for a good purpose. If they did not, we would inhale the same poisonous gases we have exhaled. And some of what seems to be waste may be the product of a purposeful process. Horse manure makes good fertilizer. According to the atheist's time scale the universe has been absorbing and neutralizing very well all its "waste." So far as we know, little so-called waste is really wasted. Even if there is some, it may be a necessary byproduct of a good process in a finite world like ours, just like sawdust results from logging.

The Eternality of Matter (Energy). Atheists often misstate the scientific first law of thermodynamics. It should not be rendered: "Energy *can* neither be created *nor* destroyed." Science as science should not be engaged in "can" or "cannot" statements. Operation science deals with what *is* or *is not*, based on observation. And observation simply tells us, according to the first law, that "The amount of actual energy in the universe remains constant." That is, while the amount of *usable* energy is decreasing, the amount of *actual* energy is remaining constant in the universe. The first law says absolutely nothing about the *origin* or *destruction* of energy. It is merely an observation about the continuing presence of energy in the cosmos.

Unlike the second law of thermodynamics, which tells us the universe is running out of usable energy and, hence, must have had a beginning, the first law makes no statement about whether energy is eternal. Therefore, it cannot be used to eliminate a Creator of the cosmos.

Tenets of Atheism. Atheists do not have identical beliefs, any more than do all theists. However, there is a core of beliefs common to most atheists. So while not all atheists believe all of the following, all of the following are believed by some atheists. And most atheists believe most of the following:

About God. True atheists believe that only the cosmos exists. God did not create man; people created God.

About the World. The universe is eternal. If it is not eternal, then it came into existence "out of nothing and by nothing." It is self-sustaining and self-perpetuating. As astronomer Carl *Sagan put it, "The Cosmos is all there is, all there was, and all there ever will be" (Sagan, *Cosmos,* 4). If asked "what caused the world?" most atheists would reply with Bertrand Russell that it was not caused; it is just there. Only the parts of the universe need a cause. They all depend on the whole, but the whole needs no cause. If we ask for a cause for the universe, then we must ask for a cause for God. And if we do not need a cause for God, then neither do we need one for the universe.

If one insists that *everything* needs a cause, the atheist simply suggests an infinite regress of causes that never arrives at a first cause (i.e., God). For if everything must have a cause, then so does this "first cause." In that case it really isn't first at all, nor is anything else (see Sagan, *Broca's Brain,* 287).

About Evil. Unlike pantheists (*see* PANTHEISM) who deny the reality of evil, atheists strongly affirm it. In fact, while pantheists affirm the reality of God and deny the reality of evil, atheists, on the other hand, affirm the reality of evil and deny the reality of God. They believe theists are inconsistent in trying to hold to both realities.

About Human Beings. A human being is matter in motion with no immortal soul. There is no mind apart from brain. Nor is there a soul independent of body. While not all atheists are strict materialists who identify soul and body, most do believe that the soul is dependent on the body. The soul in fact dies when the body dies. The soul (and mind) may be more than the body, the way a thought is more than words or symbols. But as the shadow of a tree ceases to exist when the tree does, so the soul does not survive the body's death.

About Ethics. No moral absolutes exist, certainly no divinely authorized absolutes. There may be some widely accepted and long enduring values. But absolutely binding laws would seem to imply an absolute Law Giver, which is not an option (*see* MORALITY, ABSOLUTE NATURE OF).

Since values are not *discovered* from some revelation of God, they must be *created*. Many atheists believe values emerge by trial and error the way traffic laws developed. Often the right action is described in terms of what will bring the greatest good in the long run (*see* UTILITARIANISM). Some frankly acknowledge that relative and changing situations determine what is right or wrong. Others speak about the expedient behavior (what "works"), and some work out their whole ethic in terms of self-interest. But virtually all atheists recognize that each person must determine personal values, since there is no God to reveal what is right and wrong. As the *Humanist Manifesto* put it, "Humanism asserts that the nature of the universe depicted by modern science makes unacceptable any supernatural or cosmic guarantees of human values" (Kurtz, 8).

About Human Destiny. Most atheists see no eternal destiny for individual persons, though some speak of a kind of collective immortality of the race. But the denial of individual immortality notwithstanding, many atheists are utopians. They believe in an earthly paradise to come. Skinner proposed a behaviorally controlled utopia in *Walden Two*. Marx believed an economic dialectic of history would inevitably produce a communist paradise. Others, such as Rand, believe that pure capitalism can produce a more perfect society. Still others believe human reason and science can produce a social utopia. Virtually all, however, recognize the ultimate mortality of the human race but console themselves in the belief that its destruction is millions of years away.

Evaluation. *Positive Contributions of Atheism.* Even from a theistic point of view, not all views expressed by atheists lack truth. Atheists have provided many insights into the nature of reality.

The reality of evil. Unlike pantheists, atheists do not close their eyes to the reality of evil. In fact, most atheists have a keen sensitivity to evil and injustice. They rightly point to the imperfection of this world and to the need for adjudication of injustice. In this regard they are surely right that an all-loving, all-powerful God would certainly do something about the situation.

Contradictory concepts of God. In contending that God is not caused by another, some have spoken of God as though he were a self-caused being *(causa sui)*. Atheists rightly point out this contradiction, for no being can cause its own existence. To do this it would have to exist and not exist at the same time. For to cause existence is to move from nonexistence to existence. But nonexistence cannot cause existence. Nothing cannot cause something (*see* CAUSALITY, PRINCIPLE OF). On this point atheists are surely right.

Positive human values. Many atheists are humanists. With others they affirm the value of humanity and human culture. They earnestly pursue both the arts and the sciences and express deep concern in ethical issues. Most atheists believe that racism, hatred, and bigotry are wrong. Most atheists commend freedom and tolerance and have other positive moral values.

The Loyal Opposition. Atheists are the loyal opposition to theists. It is difficult to see the fallacies in one's own thinking. Atheists serve as a corrective to invalid theistic reasoning. Their arguments against theism should give pause to dogmatism and temper the zeal with which many believers glibly dismiss unbelief. In fact, atheists serve a significant corrective role for theistic thinking. Monologues seldom produce refined thought. Without atheists, theists would lack significant opposition with which to dialogue and clarify their concepts of God.

A Critique of Atheism. Still, the position that God does not exist lacks adequate rational support. The atheist's arguments against God are insufficient (*see* ATHEISM). Further, there are good arguments for the existence of God (*see* GOD, EVIDENCE FOR). For many things, atheism provides no satisfactory answer.

Why is there something rather than nothing? Atheism does not provide an adequate answer as to why anything exists when it is not necessary for anything at all to exist. Nonexistence of everything in the world is possible, yet the world does exist. Why? If there is no cause for its existence, there is no reason why the world exists (*see* COSMOLOGICAL ARGUMENT).

What is the basis for morality? Atheists can believe in morality, but they cannot *justify* this belief. Why should anyone be good unless there is a Definer of goodness who holds people accountable? It is one thing to say that hate, racism, genocide, and rape are wrong. But if there is no ultimate standard of morality (i.e., God), then how can these things be wrong? A moral prescription implies a Moral Prescriber (*see* MORAL ARGUMENT FOR GOD).

What is the basis for meaning? Most atheists believe life is meaningful and worth living. But how can it be if there is no purpose for life, nor destiny after this life? Purpose implies a Purposer. But if there is no God, there is no objective or ultimate meaning. Yet most atheists live as if there were.

What is the basis for truth? Most atheists believe that atheism is true and theism is false. But to state that atheism is true implies that there is such a thing as objective truth. Most atheists do not believe that atheism is true only for them. But if atheism is true, there must be a basis for objective truth (*see* TRUTH, NATURE OF). Truth is a characteristic of a mind, and objective truth implies an objective Mind beyond our finite minds.

What is the basis for reason? Most atheists pride themselves on being rational. But why be rational if the universe is the result of irrational chance? There is no reason to be reasonable in a random universe. Hence, the very thing in which atheists most pride themselves is not possible apart from God.

What is the basis for beauty? Atheists also marvel at a beautiful sunset and are awestruck by the starry heavens. They enjoy the beauty of nature as though it were meaningful. Yet if atheism is true, it is all accidental, not purposeful. Atheists enjoy natural beauty as though it were meant for them, and yet they believe no Designer exists to mean it for them.

Sources

T. Altizer, *The Gospel of Christian Atheism*

P. Bayle, *Selections from Bayle's Dictionary*

L. Feuerbach, *The Essence of Christianity*

J. N. Findlay, "Can God's Existence Be Disproved?" A. Plantinga, *Ontological Argument*

C. Hartshorne, "The Necessarily Existent," A. Plantinga, *The Ontological Argument*

J. Hick, *The Existence of God*

B. C. Johnson, *An Atheist Debater's Handbook*

P. Kurtz, *Humanist Manifestos I* and *II*

C. S. Lewis, *Mere Christianity*

M. Martin, *Atheism: A Philosophical Justification*

K. Marx, *Marx and Engels on Religion*

G. Maurades, *Belief in God*

T. Molnar, *Theists and Atheists*

J. P. Moreland, *Does God Exist?*

F. Nietzsche, *Joyful Wisdom*

———, *Thus Spake Zarathustra*

K. Nielson, *Philosophy of Atheism*

A. Rand, *For the New Intellectual*

B. Russell, "What Is an Agnostic?" In *Look* (1953)

C. Sagan, *Broca's Brain*

———, *Cosmos*

J. P. Sartre, *Being and Nothingness*

B. F. Skinner, *About Behavioralism*

G. Smith, *The Case Against God*

R. C. Sproul, *If There is a God, Why are There Atheists?*

———, *Walden Two*

P. Van Buren, *The Secular Meaning of the Gospel*

Athenagoras. Athenagoras was a second-century Christian apologist who was called the "Christian philosopher from Athens." His famous *Apology* (ca. 177), which he called "Embassy," petitioned Marcus Aurelius on behalf of Christians. He later wrote a strong defense of the physical resurrection (*see* RESURRECTION, PHYSICAL NATURE OF), *On the Resurrection of the Dead.*

Two later writers mention Athenagoras. Methodius of Olympus (d. 311) was influenced by him in his *On the Resurrection of the Body*. Philip Sidetes (early sixth century) stated that Athenagoras had been won to Christianity while reading the Scriptures "in order to controvert them" (Pratten, 127). His English translator noted, "Both his *Apology* and his treatise on the Resurrection display a practiced pen and a richly cultured mind. He is by far the most elegant, and certainly at the same time one of the ablest, of the early Christian Apologists" (ibid.). The silence about Athenagoras by the fourth-century Church historian Eusebius, is strange in view of his work.

Apologetics. The basic elements of later apologetics were present in Athenagoras's treatises. He defended Christianity against charges of *atheism, cannibalism (eating Christ's body), and practicing incest. He focused attention on the peaceful, blameless lives of Christians and claimed that they deserved equal rights with other citizens.

Scripture. As other church Fathers, Athenagoras believed the Bible was the inspired Word of God (*see* BIBLE, EVIDENCE FOR). He claimed that "it would be irrational for us to cease to believe in the Spirit from God, who moved the mouths of the prophets like musical instruments" (ibid., vii). He spoke of "The Holy Spirit Himself also, which operates in the prophets" (ibid., ix), and "the writings either of Moses or of Isaiah and Jeremiah and the other prophets, who lifted up with ecstasy above the natural operations of their minds by the impulses of the Divine Spirit, uttered the things with which they were inspired the Spirit making use of them as a flute player breathes into a flute" (ibid.).

God. Athenagoras affirmed the existence, unity, triunity, and essential attributes of God. This he did against the challenge of *polytheism. Athenagoras first defended the existence of God against the Roman view that Christians were atheists since they did not accept the Roman pantheon nor did they worship the emperor. Christians are not atheists, Athenagoras wrote, in that they acknowledge one God. Unlike some Greeks who denied God, Christians "distinguish God from matter, and teach that matter is one thing and God another, and that they are separated by a wide interval (for that the Deity is uncreated and eternal . . . while matter is created and perishable), is it not absurd to apply the name of atheism?" (*Apology*, 4).

Against the pagan polytheistic context, Athenagoras affirmed the unity of God (ibid., 5). He chided the "absurdities of polytheism," asking, "If there were from the beginning two or more gods, they were either in one and the same place, or each of them separately in his own. In one and the same place they could not be. . . . But if, on the contrary, each of them exists separately, since He that made the world is above the things created . . . where can the other or the rest be?" (ibid., 8).

God is both unity and triunity. He is a plurality of persons within the unity of one God. Athenagoras made clear that "we acknowledge also a Son of God. . . . The Holy Spirit Himself also . . . we assert to be an effluence of God." Thus, we "speak of God the Father, and of God the Son, and of the Holy Spirit" (ibid., 10). Athenagoras stresses that, the Father and Son being one, the Son was the one through whom the universe was created. The Father had the "logos in Himself" from eternity. Hence the Logos was begotten of the Father, but "not as having been brought into existence" (ibid.).

Athenagoras affirmed the essential elements of classical theism, insisting "we acknowledge one God, uncreated, eternal, invisible, impassible, incomprehensible, illimitable . . . Who is encompassed by light, and beauty and spirit, and power ineffable, by whom the universe has been created through His Logos, and set in order, and is kept in being" (ibid., 10).

Creation. For Athenagoras, "the Deity is uncreated and eternal . . . while matter is created and perishable" (ibid., 4). And repeatedly he affirmed that the universe had been created through the Logos. He uses this radical distinction between Creator and creation to show the absurdity of polytheism. He criticized those who cannot see the distance between themselves and their Creator, and so prayed to idols made of matter (ibid., 15). Distinguishing between the Artist (God) and his art (the world), he concluded: "I admire its beauty, and adore the Artificer" (ibid., 16). He pointed out that polytheistic gods were themselves created. "Every one of them has come into existence just like ourselves" (ibid.).

The Resurrection. Athenagoras wrote a treatise *On the Resurrection of the Dead*. With all other early Fathers (except Origen who was condemned for heresy on the point), Athenagoras affirmed the physical resurrection of the same material body of flesh and bones that died (*see* GEISLER). He insisted that God's power is sufficient to raise dead bodies, since he created those bodies (*On the Resurrection*, chap. 3). As for the charge that God cannot bring together the scattered parts of a dead body, he said, "It is not possible for God to be ignorant, either of the nature of the bodies that are to be raised, as regards both the members entire and the particles of which they consist, . . . although to me it may appear quite impossible" (ibid., 2). God was quite capable, he assured the reader, of bringing together these bodies "with equal ease" (ibid., 3).

His strong teaching on the resurrection is used to refute the charge of cannibalism. He asks "Who, then, that believes in a resurrection, would make himself into a tomb for bodies that will rise again? For it is not the part of the same persons to believe that our bodies will rise again, and to eat them as if they would not" (*Apology*, 36).

One reason for the resurrection is that "Man, therefore, who consists of the two parts [body and soul], must continue forever. But it is impossible for him to continue unless he rise again. For if no resurrection were to take place, the nature of men as men would not continue." Thus, along with the interminable duration of the soul, there will be a perpetual continuance of the body according to its proper nature" (*On the Resurrection*, 15). He added that each person must have both body and soul at the judgment if it is to be just. If the body is not restored alongside the soul, there "is no longer any remembrance of past action, nor sense of what it experienced in connection with the soul" (ibid., 20). In biblical terms, a person will be judged for the things done "in the body" (2 Cor. 5:10). This is not fully possible unless the body is resurrected.

Sources

Athenagoras, *Apology: A Plea for the Christian*

———, *On the Resurrection of the Dead*

F. L. Cross, "Athenagoras," in *The Oxford Dictionary of the Christian Church*

N. L. Geisler, *The Battle for the Resurrection*, chap. 4

B. P. Pratten, "Introductory Note to the Writings of Athenagoras," in A. Roberts and J. Donaldson, eds., *The Ante-Nicene Fathers*, vol. 2

Atomism. Ancient atomists were materialists (*see* MATERIALISM) who believed that the universe was made up of pellets of reality. They believed that absolute space (the Void) was filled with these tiny, unsplittable particles. All variety in the universe was explained in terms of different combinations of atoms.

The Atomists were pluralists, as opposed to monists, believing reality is ultimately many, not one (*see* MONISM; ONE AND MANY, PROBLEM OF; PLURALISM). Ancient atomists included Greek thinkers like Democritus and Leucipus.

Since the Greek word *atom* means unsplittable, many of the atomists' hard-core materialistic views fell with the splitting of the atom. Contemporary materialists, however, still believe that all reality is comprised of physical energy which, according to the first law of thermodynamics (*see* THERMODYNAMICS, LAWS OF), is neither being created nor destroyed.

Other modern pluralists, however, have opted for a more immaterial view of atom-like entities called "monads" (*see* LEIBNIZ, GOTTFRIED) or eternal objects (*see* WHITEHEAD, ALFRED NORTH). Thus, atomism lives on in various forms, the materialistic varieties of which are still a challenge to Christianity (*see* ATHEISM).

There are several serious problems with materialistic atomism in both its ancient and modern forms. First, Atomists do not solve the problem of the one and the many. They have no adequate explanation for how simple things can differ nor how this can be a *uni*-verse when all that really exists is multiplicity, rather than unity.

Second, the ancient form of atomism has been destroyed by the splitting of the atom. These allegedly irreducibly hard pellets of reality have given way to a softer view of energy.

Third, even in its modern form, the belief in the eternality of matter (physical energy) has yielded to the second law of thermodynamics (*see* THERMODYNAMICS, LAWS OF), which reveals that the physical universe is not eternal, but is running down (*see* EVOLUTION, COSMIC).

Fourth, pure materialism is self-defeating. It is an immaterial theory about all matter that claims there is nothing immaterial. The materialist who peers into the microscope, examining all things material fails to reckon with the immaterial self conscious "I" and its mental process that are making the deductions.

Sources

J. Collins, *A History of Modern European Philosophy*

F. Copleston, *A History of Philosophy*

M. C. Nahm, *Selections from Early Greek Philosophy*

J. Owen, *A History of Ancient Western Philosophy*

J. E. Raven, et al., *The Presocratic Philosophers*

Atonement, Substitutionary. ***See* CHRIST, DEATH OF; CHRIST'S DEATH, MORAL OBJECTIONS TO; CHRIST'S DEATH, SUBSTITUTION LEGEND; RESURRECTION, EVIDENCE FOR; RESURRECTION, PHYSICAL NATURE OF.**

Augustine. Augustine, bishop of Hippo (354–430), made his spiritual pilgrimage from Greek paganism through Manichaean dualism to neoplatonism (*see* PLOTINUS) and finally to Christian theism. His great mind and immense literary output have made him one of Christianity's most influential theologians.

Faith and Reason. Like all great Christian thinkers, Augustine struggled to understand the relationship between faith and reason. Many apologists tend to stress Augustine's emphasis on faith and underplay his affirmation of reason in the proclamation and defense of the gospel (*see* FIDEISM; PRESUPPOSITIONAL APOLOGETICS). They stress passages where the Bishop of Hippo placed faith before reason, such as "I believe in order that I may understand." Indeed, Augustine said, "First believe, then understand" (*On the Creed,* 4). For "if we wished to know and then believe, we should not be able to either know or believe" (*On the Gospel of John,* 27.9).

However, these passages taken alone leave the wrong impression of Augustine's teaching on the role of reason in the Christian Faith. Augustine also held that there is a sense in which reason comes before faith. He declared that "no one indeed believes anything unless he has first thought that it is to be believed." Hence, "it is necessary that everything which is believed should be believed after thought has led the way" (*On Free Will,* 5).

He proclaimed the superiority of reason when he wrote, "God forbid that He should hate in us that faculty by which He made us superior to all other beings. Therefore, we must refuse so to believe as not to receive or seek reason for our belief, since we could not believe at all if we did not have rational souls" (*Letters,* 120.1).

Augustine even used reason to elaborate a "proof for the existence of God." In *On Free Will,* he argued that "there exists something above human reason" (2.6). Not only can reason prove God exists, but it is helpful in understanding the content of the Christian message. For "how can anyone believe him who preaches the faith if he (to say nothing of the other points) does not understand the very tongue which he speaks. . . . Our understanding therefore contributes to the belief of that which it comprehends" (cited in Przywara, 59).

Augustine also used reason to remove objections to Christian Faith. Speaking of someone who had questions prior to becoming a believer, he wrote: "It is reasonable that he inquire as to the resurrection of the dead before he is admitted to the Christian sacraments." What is more, "perhaps he ought also to be allowed to insist on preliminary discussion on the question proposed concerning Christ—why he came so late in the world's history, and of a few great questions besides, to which all others are subordinate" (*Letters 120.1,* 102.38). In short, Augustine believed that human reason was used before, during and after one exercises faith in the Gospel.

God. For Augustine, God is the self-existing I AM WHO I AM. He is uncreated substance, immutable, eternal, indivisible, and absolutely perfect (*see* GOD, NATURE OF). God is not an impersonal Force (*see* PANTHEISM) but a personal Father. In fact, he is the tripersonal Father, Son, and Holy Spirit (*see* TRINITY). In this one eternal substance there is neither confusion of persons nor division in essence.

God is omnipotent, omnipresent, and omniscient. He is eternal, existing before time and beyond time. He is absolutely transcendent over the universe and yet immanently present in every part of it as its sustaining cause. Although the world had a beginning (*see* *KALAM* COSMOLOGICAL ARGUMENT), there was never a time when God was not. He is a Necessary Being who depends on nothing, but on whom everything else depends for its existence. "Since God is supreme being, that is, since he supremely is and, therefore, is immutable, it follows that he gave being to all that he created out of nothing" (*City of God,* 12.2).

Origin and Nature of the Universe. According to Augustine the world was created *ex nihilo* (*see* CREATION, VIEWS OF), out of nothing. Creation comes *from* God but is not *out of* God. "Out of nothing didst Thou create heaven and earth—a great thing and a small—because Thou are Almighty and Good, to make all things good, even the great heaven and the small earth. Thou wast, and there was nought else from which Thou didst create heaven and earth" (*Confessions,* 12:7). Hence, the world is not eternal. It had a beginning, yet not in time but with time. For time began with the world. There was no time before time. When asked what God did before he created the world out of nothing, Augustine retorted that since God was the author of all time, there was no time before he created the world. It was not creation *in* time but the creation *of* time that God executed in his initial acts (ibid., 11.13). So God was not *doing* (acting, creating) anything before he created the world. He was simply *being* God.

The world is temporal and changing, and from it we can see that there must be an eternal and unchanging being. "Behold the heavens and the earth are; they proclaim that they were created; for they change and vary." However, "whatsoever hath not been made, and yet is, hath nothing in it, which before it had not, and this it is, to change and vary. They proclaim also, that they made not themselves" (ibid., 11.4).

Miracles. Since God made the world, he can intervene in it (*see* MIRACLE). In fact what we call Nature is simply the way God regularly works in his creation. For, "when such things happen in a continuous kind of river of ever-flowing succession, passing from the hidden to the visible, and from the visible to the hidden, by a regular and beaten track, then they are called natural." But "when, for the admonition of men, they are thrust in by an unusual changeableness, then they are called miracles" (*On the Trinity,* in *Nicene and Post-Nicene Fathers,* 3.6). But even nature's regular activities are the works of God. For,

> Who draws up the sap through the root of the vine to the bunch of grapes, and makes the wine, except God; who, while man plants and waters, himself giveth the increase? But when, at the command of the Lord, the water was turned into wine with an extraordinary quick-

ness, the divine power was made manifest, by the confession even of the foolish. Who ordinarily clothes the trees with leaves and flowers except God? Yet, when the rod of Aaron the priest blossomed, the Godhead in some way conversed with doubting humanity. [ibid., 3.5]

Human Beings. Humankind, like the rest of the world, is not eternal. Humans were created by God and are like God. They are composed of a mortal body and an immortal soul (*see* IMMORTALITY). After death the soul awaits reunion with the body in either a state of conscious bliss (heaven) or of continual torment (hell). These souls will be reunited to their bodies at the resurrection. And "after the resurrection, the body, having become wholly subject to the spirit, will live in perfect peace to all eternity" (*On Christian Doctrine,* 1.24).

For Augustine, the human soul, or spiritual dimension, is of higher value than the body. Indeed, it is in this spiritual dimension that humankind is made in God's image and likeness. Hence, sins of the soul are worse than sins of the body.

Evil. Evil is real, but it is not a substance (*see* EVIL, PROBLEM OF). The origin of evil is the rebellion of free creatures against God (*see* EVIL, PROBLEM OF). "In fact, sin is so much a voluntary evil that it is not sin at all unless it is voluntary" (*Of True Religion,* 14). Of course, God created all things good and gave to his moral creatures the good power of free choice. However, sin arose when "the will which turns from the unchangeable and common good and turns to its own private good or to anything exterior or inferior, sins" (*On Free Will,* 2.53).

By choosing the lesser good, moral creatures brought about the corruption of good substances. Evil, then, by nature is a lack or privation of the good. Evil does not exist in itself. Like a parasite, evil exists only as a corruption of good things. "For who can doubt that the whole of that which is called evil is nothing else than corruption? Different evils may, indeed, be called by different names; but that which is the evil of all things in which any evil is perceptible is corruption" (*Against the Epistle of Manachaeus,* 38).

Evil is a lack in good things. It is like rot to a tree or rust to iron. It corrupts good things while having no nature of its own. In this way Augustine answered the dualism of the Manichaean religion which pronounced evil to be a co-eternal, but opposed, reality to the good.

Ethics. Augustine believed that God is love by his very nature. Since the human obligation to the creator is to be God-like, people have an absolute moral duty (*see* MORALITY, ABSOLUTE NATURE OF) to love God and neighbor, who is made in God's image. "For this is the law of love that has been laid down by Divine authority. 'Thou shalt love thy neighbor as thyself,' but, 'Thou shalt love God with all thy heart, and with all thy soul, and with all thy mind'" (*On Christian Doctrine,* 1.22). Hence, we are to concentrate all our thoughts, our whole life, and our whole intelligence upon him from whom we derive all that we have. All the virtues are defined in terms of this love.

Augustine said, "As to virtue leading us to a happy life, I hold virtue to be nothing else than perfect love of God. For the fourfold division of virtue I regard as taken from four forms of love": "Temperance is love giving itself entirely to that which is loved; fortitude is love readily bearing all things for the sake of the loved object; justice is love serving only the loved object, and therefore ruling rightly; prudence is love distinguishing with sagacity between what hinders it and what helps it." So "temperance is love keeping itself entire and incorrupt for God; justice is love serving God only, and therefore ruling well all else, as subject to man; prudence is love making a right distinction between what helps it towards God and what might hinder it" (*On the Morals of the Catholic Church,* 15).

The object of this love is God, the chief Good. He is absolute love, and a human being's absolute obligation is to express love in every area of activity, first toward God and then toward neighbor.

History and Destiny. In his classic, *The City of God,* Augustine wrote the first great Christian philosophy of history. He said there are two "cities" (kingdoms), the city of God and the city of man. These two cities have two different origins (God and Satan), two different natures (love for God and love of oneself, pride), and two different destinies (heaven and hell).

History is headed toward a completion. At this end of time, there will be an ultimate victory of God over Satan and of good over evil. Evil will be separated from the good, and the righteous will be resurrected into a perfect body and a perfect state. The paradise lost at the beginning will be regained by God in the end.

History is *His*-story. God is working out his sovereign plan, and in the end he will defeat evil and perfect man. "Hence we have an answer to the problem why God should have created men whom he foresaw would sin. It was because both in them and by means of them he could reveal how much was deserved by their guilt and condoned by his grace, and, also, because the harmony of the whole of reality which God has created and controls cannot be marred by the perverse discordancy of those who sin" (*City of God,* 14).

Evaluation. St. Augustine has been criticized for many things, but perhaps more than anything else he is guilty of an uncritical acceptance of platonic and neoplantic (*see* PLOTINUS) thought. Even he rejected some of his own earlier platonic views in his *Retractions*, written near the end of his life. For example, he once accepted Plato's doctrine of the preexistence of the soul and the recollection of ideas from a previous existence.

Unfortunately, there were other platonic ideas that Augustine never repudiated. These include a platonic dualism of body and soul wherein human beings *are* a soul and only *have* a body. Along with this, Augustine held a very ascetic view of physical desires and sex, even within the context of marriage.

Further, Augustine's epistemology of innate ideas has been contested by modern empiricists (*see* HUME, DAVID), as has been his view of illuminationism. And even some theists question whether or not his proof for God from truth really works, asking why one needs an absolute Mind as the source of an absolute truth.

Even some who accept Augustine's classical theism point out his inconsistency in not demonstrating a unicity (oneness) of the divine ideas. This resulted from an acceptance of ideas as irreducibly simple platonic forms of which many are not possible in one simple substance (*see* ONE AND MANY, PROBLEM OF). This problem was later resolved by Thomas Aquinas with the aid of his distinction between actuality and potentiality in the order of being (*see* MONISM), which was expressed in his doctrine of analogy.

Sources

Augustine, *Against the Epistle of Manachaeus*
———, *On Christian Doctrine*
———, *City of God*
———, *Confessions*
———, *Letters*, 120.1
———, *Of True Religion*
———, *On Free Will*
———, *On Predestination*, 5
———, *On the Creed*, 4
———, *On the Gospel of John*, 27.9
———, *On the Morals of the Catholic Church*
———, *On the Trinity in Nicene and Post-Nicene Fathers*
N. L. Geisler, *What Augustine Says*
E. Przywara, *An Augustine Synthesis*

Averroes. Averroes (1126–1198) was a Spanish Muslim jurist and physician born in Cordoba. His name is a Latinization of the Arabic form of Ibn-Rushd. Averroes wrote treatises on law, astronomy, grammar, medicine, and philosophy, his most significant being a commentary on Aristotle. He was known by scholastics as "the commentator" (of Aristotle).

Philosophy and Religion. Averroes had an unappreciated influence on the Christian Middle Ages. Because he was the most widely-read commentator on Aristotle, his platonic interpretation was thought to be correct and was adopted by Christians. Actually, like many in his time, Averroes mistakenly believed Aristotle was author of a book called *Theology*, which was really a compendium of Plotinus's writings (Edwards, 221). As a result, Plotinian ideas were read into Aristotle.

The commentaries of Averroes on Aristotle were integral to the education curriculum at early Western European Universities (ibid., 223).

Emanational Pantheism. While it seems strange for an adherent of monotheistic Islam to be a pantheist (*see* PANTHEISM), this is not uncommon among Sufi Muslims. Averroes' God was entirely separated from the world, exercising no providence. Similar to the theology of Avicenna, the universe was created by emanations from God. There was a series of celestial spheres (intelligences) that descended from God until they reached humanity at the bottom. Matter and intellect are both eternal. God was a remote, impersonal Prime Mover. God's was the only actual Mind in the universe.

The individual under this schema has only a passive intellect. God does the thinking through the human mind. Averroes denied human free will and the soul's immortality.

Double-truths. Averroes has been charged with teaching a "double-truth" theory. In a double-truth, one simultaneously believes two mutually exclusive propositions to be true if one is in philosophy and the other in religion. This is a false charge. It is ironic that it has been leveled against Averroes, who composed the treatise *On the Harmony Between Religion and Philosophy* to refute this very view. Averroes did believe in alternative modes of access to truth, but he apparently did not hold that there could be incompatible truths in different domains (see Edwards, 223).

Nonetheless, later Averronians were charged with holding the double-truth view. Siger of Brabant allegedly introduced such neoplatonic teachings at the University of Paris. Bonaventure and *Thomas Aquinas reacted strongly. Aquinas is credited with destroying the popularity of Averroism in the West, particularly through his *The Unity of the Intellect Against the Averroeists* (1269).

By 1270 Stephen Tempier, bishop of Paris, condemned several of Averroes's teachings, including the eternality of the world, the denial of the universal providence of God, the unity of the human intellect, and the denial of free will. In 1277 he issued more condemnations of similar errors. In the preamble to the latter denunciation, he accused Siger and his followers of saying that "things are true according to philosophy but not according to the Catholic faith, as though there were two contradictory truths" (Cross, 116).

While there is no certainty that Siger actually held the double-truth view, this view did give rise to the Enlightenment assumption that domains of faith and reason could be separated. Forms of this view still prevail widely. Thomas Hobbes, Benedict *Spinoza, and Immanuel *Kant promoted this idea, as have New Testament critics (see BIBLE CRITICISM) who separate the Jesus of history from the Christ of faith (*see* BULTMANN, RUDOLPH; CHRIST OF FAITH VS. JESUS OF HISTORY; JESUS SEMINAR; MYTHOLOGY AND THE NEW TESTAMENT).

Allegorical Interpretation. Following Plotinus, Averroes believed the highest form of knowledge leads to a mystical experience of God (*see* MYSTICISM). This experience involves passing from a normal, rational, discursive kind of knowing to a trans-rational, intuitive, and direct experience of God. Such an approach necessitated an allegorical approach to Scripture.

Averroes interpreted the *Qur'an* allegorically and for this was accused of heresy and exiled, though he was recalled shortly before his death. Many Christians from Origen (ca. 185–ca. 254) on took this allegorical approach to Scripture.

Evaluation. Whether he actually taught it, the double-truth theory carried forward by some of his disciples is contrary to basic laws of thought (LOGIC; FIRST PRINCIPLES). Faith and reason cannot be bifurcated (*see* FAITH AND REASON).

Averroes' pantheism is contrary to the tenets of theism in general and Christian theism in particular. His views about the eternality of matter (*see* CREATION, VIEWS OF) are contrary to biblical teaching about creation (*see* *KALAM* COSMOLOGICAL ARGUMENT).

His denial of free will has serious problems and is a form of strong determinism, which most Christians reject. The same can be said for his denial of individual immortality (*see* HELL; IMMORTALITY). The form of mysticism Averroes held, in which mind and laws of reason are irrelevant, is unacceptable to thoughtful theists (*see* FAITH AND REASON; LOGIC; MYSTERY).

Sources

Averroes, *The Works of Aristotle*

———, *Averroes' Commentary on Plato's Republic*, E. I. J. Rosenthal, ed.

———, *Averroes on the Harmony of Religion and Philosophy*

P. Edwards, "Averroes," *EP*

N. L. Geisler and A. Saleeb, *Answering Islam*

E. Gilson, *History of Christian Philosophie in the Middle Ages*

A. A. Maurer, *Medieval Philosophy*

S. Munk, *Melanges de philosophie duive et arabe*

E. Renan, *Averroes et l'averroisme*. Paris

Thomas Aquinas, *The Unity of the Intellect Against the Averoeists*

Avicenna. Avicenna (980–1037) was a physician and philosopher from near Bokhara in the West Asian region of Uzbekistan. His name is a Latinized pronunciation of the Arabic form of Ibn Sinâ. Avicenna wrote about 100 books on logic, mathematics, metaphysics, and theology, and his greatest work, *The Canon,* a system of medicine. He combined Aristotelianism (*see* ARISTOTLE) and neoplatonism (*see* PLOTINUS) in his philosophy of pantheism.

Avicenna's Cosmological Argument. Following the Muslim philosopher Alfarabi, Avicenna formulated a similar cosmological argument that was emulated by later scholastics, including Thomas Aquinas. To find Avicenna's context in the history of the cosmological argument, see COSMOLOGICAL ARGUMENT.

Avicenna's proof goes like this:

1. There are possible beings (i.e., things which come into existence because they are caused to exist but would not otherwise exist on their own).
2. Whatever possible beings there are have a cause for being (since they do not explain their own existence).
3. But there cannot be an infinite series of causes of being. (a) There can be an infinite series of causes of *becoming* (father begets son, who begets son). (b) There cannot be an infinite series of causes of *being,* since the cause of being must be simultaneous with its effect. Unless there was a causal basis for the series, there would be no beings there to be caused.
4. Therefore, there must be a First Cause for all possible beings (i.e., for all beings that come into existence).
5. This First Cause must be a Necessary Being, for the cause of all possible beings cannot itself be a possible being.

Neoplatonic Influence on Avicenna. By borrowing some neoplatonic premises and a ten-sphere cosmology, Avicenna furthers his argument to prove that this necessary First Cause created a series of "Intelligences" (demiurges or angels) and ten cosmic spheres they controlled:

6. Whatever is essentially One can create immediately only one effect (called an intelligence).
7. Thinking is creating, and God necessarily thinks, since he is a Necessary Being.
8. Therefore, there is a necessary emanation from God of ten intelligences which control the various spheres of the universe. The last of these (agent intellect) forms the four elements of the cosmos. By agent intellect, the human mind (possible intellect) is formed of all truth.

Evaluation. Many criticisms of the cosmological argument have been offered by atheists, agnostics, and skepticism, most emanating from David Hume and Immanuel Kant (*see* GOD, OBJECTIONS TO PROOFS FOR).

In addition to the traditional arguments, Avicenna's form of the argument is subject to many of the criticisms of pantheism and neoplotinian thought. Emanational cosmology has been outdated by modern astronomy.

Conclusion. In common with theism, Avicenna's God was a Necessary Being. But in contrast to theism a serial creative force of ten gods emanated from God with absolute necessity.

Also, unlike the Christian theistic God who freely created *ex nihilo* and who is directly responsible for the existence of everything else, in Avicenna's cosmology the universe emanates from a chain of gods (*see* CREATION, VIEWS OF).

Sources

F. Copleston, *History of Philosophy*
N. L. Geisler, *Philosophy of Religion*
E. Gilson, "Avicenna" in *The Encyclopedia of Philosophy*
———, *History of Christian Philosophy in the Middle Ages*

Ayer, A. J. Alfred Jules Ayer (1910–1989) was a British humanist, a graduate of Oxford (1932), and a member of the Vienna Circle of logical positivism. This group, formed in 1932, was influenced by Ernst Mach (d. 1901). Their work was strongly antimetaphysical (*see* METAPHYSICS) and anti-Christian.

In *Language, Truth and Logic* (1936) Ayer tried to eliminate metaphysics via the verifiability principle. *Foundations of Empirical Knowledge* (1940) dealt with problems of private language and other minds. *Philosophical Essays* (1954) contained articles treating problems raised by his first two books. By 1956 Ayer wrote *The Problem of Knowledge* (1956), which reflects moderate antiskeptical realism. He accepts that some statements may be true even if they cannot be justified in principle. A near-death experience in the 1980s convinced Ayer of the possibility of immortality, though he continued to reject the existence of God (*see* ACOGNOSTICISM).

Ayer's Philosophy. According to Ayer and the logical positivists, meaningful statements must measure up to the criterion of verifiability. All genuine propositions must be empirically testable or else they are purely formal or definitional.

Meaningful Propositions. Following David *Hume, Ayer taught that there are three types of propositions: (1) Analytic propositions are truisms, tautologies, or true by definition. These are explicative, meaning the predicate merely states what the subject says. (2) Synthetic propositions are true by experience and/or in relation to experience. These are ampliative, since the predicate amplifies or affirms more than the subject. All other propositions are (3) nonsensical. They are meaningless, have no literal significance, and are emotive at best.

Metaphysics Is Meaningless. Ayer followed Immanuel *Kant in rejecting metaphysical or theological statements, but for different reasons. Kant used the argument that the mind cannot go beyond phenomena of the physical world. But Ayer recognized that the mind must go beyond the physical. How else would it know it cannot go beyond? Further, whereas Kant had a metaphysics, Ayer did not, reasoning that we cannot speak meaningfully of what may be beyond the empirical. As Ludwig Wittgenstein said, "That whereof you cannot speak, speak not thereof." The impossibility of metaphysics rests not in the psychology of man but in the meaning of language.

Distinctions. Ayer laid down two distinctions in the verifiability principle (*see* VERIFICATION, PRINCIPLE OF). First, there is a difference between *practical* and *principle* verification. Both are meaningful. In practical verification the means for verification are available. Principle verification, on the other hand, involves propositions that we do not have the means to verify now but we know how we could do so. For example, "There is no life on Mars" is verifiable in principle, though not yet in practice.

Second, there is a difference between *strong* and *weak verification*. Only weak verification is valid. Strong verification involves certitude, beyond doubt, or conclusive proof. Early positivists claimed to have this, but later modified their view. If there is strong verification, then there would be a general metaphysics too. And for Ayer to say that there are important types of nonsense would be hedging. Weak verification is subject to change or correction, since it is based on experience. Ayer concluded that no proposition other than tautology can be more than probable, for example, "All human beings are mortal" is either purely definitional, or else it is an empirical generalization.

Further Qualification of the Verifiability Principle. Ayer refined the verification principle in three ways. First, no proposition can be conclusively confuted by experience, any more than it can be conclusively verified by experience. Second, analytic propositions can be neither verified nor falsified by experience. Third, propositions don't have to be directly verifiable to be meaningful. They must, however, have some sense-experience relative to truth or falsity.

In the 1946 revised edition of *Language, Truth, and Logic* (1946) Ayer found it necessary to make further revisions to the verifiability principle. He reluctantly acknowledged that some definitional propositions, for example the verification principle itself, are meaningful without being either factual or purely arbitrary. Also, some empirical statements can be conclusively verified, for example a single sense experience. These qualifications, especially the first one, were to be the downfall of logical positivism.

Applying the Verification Principle. *Metaphysics and Theology.* Ayer's conclusions were severe: All metaphysical propositions are nonsensical because they are neither analytic nor empirical. All genuine philosophy is analytical, not metaphysical. Also, metaphysics arose by accident of language, a belief that nouns have real referents.

Metaphysics is not merely misplaced poetry. Poetry does not talk nonsense; there is a literal meaning behind most of what poets say. Not so for metaphysics. What is more, no meaningful propositions can be formulated about the terms *God* or *transcendent*. According to Ayer, this is neither atheism nor agnosticism, both of which hold it meaningful to speak of God. This is noncognitivism or acognosticism, which holds the very question of God to be meaningless.

Ethics. Ayer believed that ethical statements are neither formal nor factual but emotive. Such statements merely express the speaker's feeling and attempt to persuade others to feel the same way. For example, "You ought not to steal" means I dislike stealing and I want you to feel this way also. It is not a factually declarative but merely expresses the speaker's attitude. Ethical statements are not statements *about* one's feeling but statements *of* one's feelings. Ayer claims that this view is subjective but not radically subjectivistic. Ethical statements are merely ejaculative and, hence unverifiable, whereas statements about feeling are verifiable: "I am bored" is verifiable; a sigh is unverifiable.

Evaluation. Logical positivism is diametrically opposed to evangelical Christianity. If true, Ayer's logical positivism would hold disastrous consequences for orthodox Christianity. No statement about the existence or the nature of God could even be meaningful, to say nothing of whether it could be true. The Bible could not contain propositional revelation about God, nor could it be the inspired Word of God. There could be no meaningful ethical prescriptions, let alone absolute moral principles.

The Self-Defeating Nature of Empirical Verifiability. The death blow to Ayer's principle of verifiability is the self-destructive fact that it is not empirically verifiable. For according to the criterion of verifiability, all meaningful statements must be either true by definition or empirically testable. But the principle of verifiability is neither. By its own standard the principle of verifiability is meaningless.

Nor does one escape the dilemma by devising a third category intended to include the meaningfulness of the verifiability principle but to exclude all metaphysical and theological statements. For every attempt to define such a principle failed. In the end, most of the original Vienna Circle discarded their strict logical positivism, including Ayer himself.

The revised verification principles died the death-of-a-thousand-qualifications. Every attempt to push metaphysics out the front door and let verification by qualification in the back door found that metaphysics followed them in the back door. It was given new life by the broadened qualifications allowing for metaphysical statements. The narrow statements of verification inevitably eliminated their own principle of verification. The broader statements of the principle that were not self-defeating did not systematically eliminate all metaphysical and theological statements.

Legislating Meaning Without Listening. The problem with logical positivism is that it attempted to legislate what someone meant by their statements rather than to listen to what they meant. Ethical statements are a classic case in point. "Thou shalt not" statements do not mean "I do not like that action." They mean "You should not/ought not do it." It is a fallacy to reduce *ought* to *is*, the *prescriptive* to the *descriptive*. It also is a fallacy to reduce "You ought" to "I feel it is wrong."

Likewise, statements about God need not be reduced to either tautologies or empirical statements to be meaningful. Why should statements about a transempirical Being (God) be subjected to empirical criteria? Metaphysical statements are meaningful within a metaphysical context using metaphysical criteria (*see* FIRST PRINCIPLES).

Sources

A. J. Ayer, *Foundations of Empirical Knowledge*

———, *Language, Truth, and Logic*

———, *Philosophical Essays*

———, *The Problem of Knowledge*

H. Feigl, "Logical Positivism after Thirty-Five Years," *PT*, Winter 1964

F. Ferre, *Language, Logic and God*

A. Flew, et al. *New Essays in Philosophical Theology*

N. L. Geisler, *Philosophy of Religion*, chapter 12

Bb

Barnabas, Gospel of. Muslims often cite *The Gospel of Barnabas* in defense of Islamic teaching (*see* MUHAMMAD, ALLEGED DIVINE CALL OF; *QUR'AN*, ALLEGED DIVINE ORIGIN OF). In fact, it is a best-seller in many Muslim countries. Suzanne Haneef, in her annotated bibliography on Islam, highly recommends it, saying, "Within it one finds the living Jesus portrayed far more vividly and in character with the mission with which he was entrusted than any other of the four New Testament Gospels has been able to portray him." It is called "essential reading for any seeker of the truth" (Haneef, 186).

Typical of Muslim claims is that of Muhammad Ata ur-Rahim: "The Gospel of Barnabas is the only known surviving Gospel written by a disciple of Jesus. . . . [It] was accepted as a Canonical Gospel in the churches of Alexandria up until 325 A.D." (Ata ur-Rahim, 41). Another Muslim author, M. A. Yusseff, argues confidently that "in antiquity and authenticity, no other gospel can come close to *The Gospel of Barnabas*" (Yusseff, 5).

The Contents of the Gospel. It is not surprising that Muslim apologists appeal to the *Gospel of Barnabas* in that it supports a central Islamic teaching in contrast to the New Testament (*see* CHRIST, DEATH OF). It claims that Jesus did not die on the cross (cf. sura 4:157; *see* CHRIST'S DEATH, SUBSTITUTION LEGEND). Rather, it argues that Judas Iscariot died in Jesus' stead (sect. 217), having been substituted for him at the last minute. This view has been adopted by many Muslims, since the vast majority of them believe that someone else was substituted on the cross for Jesus.

Authenticity of the Gospel. Reputable scholars who have carefully examined it find absolutely no basis for this writing's authenticity. After reviewing the evidence in a scholarly article in *Islamochristiana*, J. Slomp concluded: "in my opinion scholarly research has proved absolutely that this 'gospel' is a fake. This opinion is also held by a number of Muslim scholars" (Slomp, 68). In their introduction to the Oxford edition of *The Gospel of Barnabas*, Longsdale and Ragg conclude that "the true date lies . . . nearer to the sixteenth century than to the first" (Longsdale, 37).

The evidence that this was not a first-century gospel, written by a disciple of Christ, is overwhelming:

The earliest reference to it comes from a fifth-century work, *Decretum Gelasianum* (Gelasian Decree, by Pope Gelasius, A.D. 492–495). But even this reference is in doubt (Slomp, 74). Moreover, there is no original language manuscript evidence for its existence. Slomp says flatly, "There is no text tradition whatsoever of the G.B.V. [Gospel of Barnabas Vienna manuscript]" (ibid.). By contrast, the New Testament books are verified by more than 5300 Greek manuscripts that begin over the first three centuries (*see* BIBLE, EVIDENCE FOR).

Second, L. Bevan Jones notes that "the earliest form of it known to us is in an Italian manuscript. This has been closely analyzed by scholars and is judged to belong to the fifteenth or sixteenth century, that is, 1400 years after the time of Barnabas" (Jones, 79). Even Muslim defenders of it, like Muhammad ur-Rahim, admit that they have no manuscripts from before the 1500s.

This gospel is widely used by Muslim apologists today, yet there is no reference to it by any Muslim writer before the fifteenth or sixteenth century. Surely they would have used it had it been in existence. There were many Muslim writers who wrote books who would no doubt have referred to such a work, had it been in existence. But not one of them, or anyone else, ever refers to it between the seventh and fifteenth centuries, when Muslims and Christians were in heated debate.

No father or teacher of the Christian church ever quoted it from the first to the fifteenth centuries, despite the fact that they quoted every verse of every book of the New Testament except 11 (Geisler, *General Introduction to the Bible*). If *The Gospel of Barnabas* had been considered authentic, it more surely would have been cited many times, as were all the other canonical books of Scripture. Had this gospel even been in existence, authentic or not, certainly it would have been cited by someone. But no father cited it, either pro or con, for over 1500 years.

Sometimes it is confused with the first-century *Epistle of [Pseudo] Barnabas* (ca. A.D. 70–90), which is an entirely different book (Slomp, 37–38). Because of references to this volume, Muslim scholars falsely allege support for an early date. Muhammad Ata ur-Rahim confuses the two books and so wrongly claims that the gospel was in circulation in the second and third centuries A.D. This is a strange error since he admits that they are listed as different books in the "Sixty Books" as Serial No. 18 Epistle of Barnabas and Serial No. 24 Gospel of Barnabas. Rahim even cites by name the "Epistle of Barnabas" as evidence of the existence of the *Gospel of Barnabas* (Ata ur-Rahim, 42–43).

Some have mistakenly assumed that the reference to a gospel used by Barnabas referred to in the *Apocryphal Acts of Barnabas* (pre–478) was *The Gospel of Barnabas*. However, this is clearly false, as the quotation reveals: "Barnabas, having unrolled the Gospel, *which we have received from Matthew his fellow-labourer,* began to teach the Jews" (Slomp, 110). By deliberately omitting this emphasized phrase, the impression is given that there is a *Gospel of Barnabas*.

The message of the *Gospel of Barnabas* is completely refuted by eyewitness first-century documents of the New Testament (*see* New Testament, Historicity of). For example, its teaching that Jesus did not claim to be the Messiah and that he did not die on the cross are thoroughly refuted by eyewitness first-century documents (*see* Bible Manuscripts). In fact, no Muslim should accept the authenticity of *The Gospel of Barnabas* since it clearly contradicts the *Qur'an's* claim that Jesus was the Messiah. It claims, "Jesus confessed, and said the truth; 'I am not the Messiah. . . . I am indeed sent to the house of Israel as a prophet of salvation; but after me shall come the Messiah'" (sects. 42, 48). The *Qur'an* repeatedly calls Jesus the "Messiah" [the "Christ"] (cf. suras 5:19, 75).

Even the book's Muslim promoters, such as Haneef, have to admit that "the authenticity of this book has not been unquestionably established. . . . It is believed to be an *Apocryphal* account of the life of Jesus." Haneef claims it was "lost to the world for centuries due to its suppression as a heretical document," but there is not a shred of documented evidence for this. As noted, it was not even mentioned by anyone before it in the sixth century. Other Muslim scholars doubt its authenticity too (see Slomp, 68). For the book contains anachronisms and descriptions of medieval life in western Europe that reveal that it was not written before the fourteenth century. For example, it refers to the year of Jubilee coming every 100 years, instead of fifty (*The Gospel of Barnabas*, 82). The papal declaration to change it to every 100 years was made by the church in 1343. John Gilchrist in his work titled, *Origins and Sources of the Gospel of Barnabas,* concludes that "only one solution can account for this remarkable coincidence. The author of the Gospel of Barnabas only quoted Jesus as speaking of the jubilee year as coming 'every hundred years' because he knew of the decree of Pope Boniface." He added, "but how could he know of this decree unless he lived at the same time as the Pope or sometime afterwards? This is a clear anachronism which compels us to conclude than the Gospel of Barnabas could not have been written earlier that the fourteenth century after Christ" (Gilchrist, 16–17). One significant anachronism is that *The Gospel of Barnabas* uses the text from the fourth-century Roman Catholic Latin Vulgate translation of the Bible. Other examples of anachronisms include a vassal who owes a share of his crop to his lord (*The Gospel of Barnabas,* 122), an illustration of medieval feudalism, a reference to wooden wine casks (152), rather than wine skins as were used in Palestine, and a medieval court procedure (121).

J. Jomier provides a list of mistakes and exaggerations:

The writing says that Jesus was born when Pilate was governor, though he did not become governor until A.D 26 or 27. Jesus sailed to Nazareth, though it was not on the sea shore. Likewise, *the Gospel of Barnabas* contains exaggerations, such as mention of 144,000 prophets and 10,000 prophets being slain "by Jizebel" (see Slomp).

Jomier's study shows fourteen Islamic elements throughout the text that prove that a Muslim author, probably a convert, worked on the book. The pinnacle of the temple, where Jesus is said to have preached—hardly a good place—was translated into Arabic by *dikka,* a platform used in mosques (7). Also, Jesus is represented as coming only for Israel but Muhammad "for the salvation of the whole world" (chap. 11). Finally, the denial of Jesus to be the Son of God is Qur'anic, as is the fact that Jesus' sermon is modeled after a Muslim *hutba* which begins with praising God and his holy Prophet (chap. 12).

Conclusion. Muslim use of *The Gospel of Barnabas* to support their teaching is devoid of evidence. Its teachings even contradict the *Qur'an*. This work, far from being an authentic first-century account of the facts about Jesus, is patently a late medieval fabrication. The best first-century records we have of the life of Christ are found in the New Testament, which categorically contradicts the teaching of the *Gospel of Barnabas*. Even early non-Christian references contradict the Gospel of Barnabas in key points (*see* New

Testament, Non-Christian Sources). For a further critique the reader should consult David Sox's excellent book, *The Gospel of Barnabas*.

Sources

M. Ata ur-Rahim, *Jesus: Prophet of Islam*

N. L. Geisler, *General Introduction to the Bible*

———and A. Saleeb, *Answering Islam*

S. Haneef, *What Everyone Should Know about Islam and Muslims*

J. Jomier, *Egypt: Reflexions sur la Recontre al-Azhar*

L. B. Jones, *Christianity Explained to Muslims*

J. Slomp, "The Gospel Dispute," *Islamochristiana*

D. Sox, *The Gospel of Barnabas*

M. A. Yusseff, *The Dead Sea Scrolls, the Gospel of Barnabas, and the New Testament*

Barth, Karl. Karl Barth (1886–1968) was a German theologian who studied at Berne, Berlin, Tübingen, and Marburg. He ministered at Geneva from 1901 to 1911. After a ten-year pastorate at Safenwil, Switzerland, Barth was appointed to the chair of Reformed theology at the University of Göttingen (1921). In 1925 he went to Münster and later to Bonn (1929) where his opposition to the German National Socialist movement led to his exile. He then taught theology at the University of Basel until his retirement in 1962.

Barth's most influential works include *Commentary on Romans* (1919; rev. 1922), *The Word of God and Theology* (1924; tr. 1928), *Theology and the Church* (1928), *Christian Dogmatics in Outline* (1927), *Anselm* (1931), and *Church Dogmatics* (1932–68). He also wrote a small but significant work of apologetics, *Nein* (*No*).

Influences. Barth drew on the epistemology of Immanuel *Kant by way of Albrecht Ritschl and Wilhelm Herrmann. The existentialism of Søren *Kierkegaard also had significant impact on his thinking, though he disavowed that influence later. Fyodor Dostoevsky's *The Brothers Karamazov*, a novel that portrayed the bankruptcy of human-centered philosophy, helped mold his thinking.

Barth was also influenced by the liberal theological method of Herrmann, the *atheism of Franz Overbeck, and the pietism of Jean Blumhardt, an early-nineteenth-century pastor. Barth himself would point to his reading of the Bible, especially Romans, and the Reformers as transforming influences on his life and thought (see Barth, *Romans*; unless otherwise noted, citations in this article are from Barth's writings).

Barth was also strongly influenced negatively by the human-centered atheism of Ludwig *Feuerbach. He even wrote a foreword for an edition of Feuerbach's *The Essence of Christianity*. He seemed to affirm that an anthropomorphic religion is the best human beings can do apart from divine revelation.

Elements of Barth's Thought. Barth was a student of liberalism who reacted strongly against liberal teachings. He stressed the transcendence of God and the domination of sin in the world in opposition to the modernist tendency to put humanity in the place of God. He developed a dialectical theological method that poses truth as a series of paradoxes. For example, the infinite became finite, the absolutely transcendent disclosed himself in Jesus. He also developed a theme of "crisis," describing the struggle with these paradoxes

**Fideism.* As a pastor at Safenwil, Barth became disillusioned with liberalism in the face of the practical concerns of Christian preaching. For Barth, truth in religion is based on faith rather than on reason or evidence (*Church Dogmatics*, 1.2.17). This is fideism. Barth held that transcendental truth cannot be expressed in rational categories. It needs to be made known in the clash of opposites. Theological knowledge is an internal rationality, an inner consistency within the presuppositions of faith. This knowledge is independent of the rules of thought that govern other knowledge.

The apex of Barth's fideism was reached in **Anselm* and continued in *Church Dogmatics*. Only God can make God known. Faith needs no proofs. The Word of God becomes knowable by making itself knowable (Anselm, 282). So strong was this fideism that Barth wrote *Nein* (No) to respond to another neoorthodox theologian, Emil Brunner. Barth denied that human beings even have an active capacity to receive special revelation from God (*see* Revelation, Special). Rather, God has to miraculously create the "contact point" within the person before they can communicate (*Nein*, 29). Of course, he denied the efficacy of general revelation (*see* Revelation, General) to convey truth of God (ibid., 79–85). Humanity is so totally vitiated by sin that revelation cannot be understood (*see* Faith and Reason; Noetic Effects of Sin).

*Natural theology, which seeks to establish God's existence by rational arguments (*see* God, Evidence for), is simply ruled out (*Romans*, 2.1.168). Miracles do not confirm revelation to unbelievers. They are meaningful only to those who already believe (ibid., 3.3.2; 714f.; *see* Miracles, Apologetic Value of). In his *Shorter Commentary on Romans* (1959) Barth acknowledged that there is a witness of God in nature to which all people have access, but he hastens to add that they have not profited by it (*Shorter Commentary*, 28).

Barth's View of Scripture. *Three Levels of the Word of God.* The Word of God is revealed in three forms: (1) The incarnate Word, Jesus Christ, is the ultimate level, which is identical with the second person of the Trinity. (2) The inscripturated Word is the whole canon of Scripture as a witness to revelation. (3) The proclaimed (preached) Word depends on the written Word, because it is based upon this witness to revelation.

The Bible as Record of Revelation. The Bible is not a written revelation (*Church Dogmatics*, 6.1.5–7). It merely records the revelation of God in Jesus Christ. The proclaimed Word looks forward to the fulfillment of God's Word in the future. Only that revealed Word, the incarnate Christ, has the absolute character of the Word of God. The other two are relative to the first and can only be properly labeled "Word of God" to the extent that God freely chooses to use these to confront us.

Barth was convinced that the Holy Scripture is not itself revelation, but is rather a *witness* of revelation. There is a difference between an event and its record and description. Hence, the revelation of God and the human description of it are never identical.

The Bible is fallible. The Bible is not the infallible words of God, but a thoroughly human book. The writers of the Bible were time-bound children who possessed their own perspective, which is unlike ours. They witnessed the redemptive events according to the concepts of their time. The writers erred in every word, but their work was justified and sanctified by God so that they spoke God's Word with their fallible and erring words. God's Word never coincides with the book (Bible) itself. The Word is always a free, sovereign act of God. This removes the words of the Bible from the Word of God, so that the Word of God is not subject to attacks leveled against the words of the Bible.

The Bible is a gateway. God uses this Bible for his service by taking the human text and encountering the individual through and in it. The authority of the Bible and its divine character are not subject to human demonstration. It is only when God, by the Holy Spirit, speaks through the Bible that a person hears the Word of God. The Bible consists of sixty-six canonical books recognized in the church, not because the church confers on them a special authority, but because they embody the record of those who witnessed (personal) revelation in its original form (Christ).

God's Word is always the Word of God, but it is not at our disposal. The dictum, "The Bible is the Word of God," does not refer to the book as such, but to God's being at work within the book. Inspiration does not vouchsafe the grammatical, historical, and theological character of the words on the page; it uses them as a gateway.

All likeness between God's Word and the Bible is lacking, and everything stands in opposition and in contradiction with the real Word of God. It is not an infallible revelation but a fallible record of God's revelation in Christ. It may be said that the Bible *becomes* the Word of God, if and when God is pleased to speak through it.

Religious Language. Barth strongly opposed analogous religious language. There is no *analogy of being, as in *Thomas Aquinas. There is only an analogy of faith. This means that the language of the Bible does not describe the way God really is. God so transcends our language about himself that it is equivocal as applied to him. It is evocative, but not descriptive.

*The *Resurrection.* His deviation from an orthodox view of Scripture notwithstanding, Barth held some conservative views. Inconsistently to his view of Scripture, he accepted the virgin birth, miracles, and bodily resurrection. He confessed an orthodox Trinity and a Christ who is God.

On the resurrection, Barth affirmed, "The Easter story actually speaks of . . . Christ truly, corporeally risen, and as such appearing to his disciples" (*Commentary*, 1.2.114f.). In *Credo*, his commentary on the Apostles' Creed, he added: "The miracle [of the resurrection] consists in the two facts that belong together . . .—the one, that the grave of that Jesus who died on the Cross on Good Friday was found empty on the third day, the other that Jesus Himself 'appears' . . . to His disciples as visibly, audibly, tangibly alive." Barth emphasized the "corporeally risen" and adds that "there cannot be any talk of striking out the empty grave" (*Credo*, 100).

In his work on *The Resurrection of the Dead* (tr. 1977), Barth adds, "the tomb is doubtless empty, under every conceivable circumstance empty! 'He is not here.'" Further, "It is an event which involves a definite seeing with the eyes and hearing with the ears and handling with the hands. . . . It involves real eating and drinking, speaking and answering, reasoning and doubting and then believing." The event "is fixed and characterized as something which actually happened among men like other events, and was experienced and later attested by them" (*Commentary*, 2.64.143).

Barth goes so far as to refute those who stress a "glorified corporeality" by making certain speculative inferences from the fact that Jesus was not always immediately recognized after his resurrection and that he appeared through closed doors. Barth replies, "What the Evangelists really know and say is simply that the disciples saw and heard Jesus again after His death, and that as they saw and heard Him they recognized Him, and they recognized Him on the basis of His identity with the One whom they had known before." Indeed, "in the ensuing appearances to the eleven, recognition comes when He allows them to see and touch His hands and His feet" (ibid.).

Evaluation. *Positive Features.* From the viewpoint of orthodox Christians, Barth is a mixed blessing. Among helpful dimensions of his thought are:

1. his attempt to reject modernism and liberalism;
2. his identification of the modernist's effort to put humanity in God's place;

3. his rejection of efforts to make God totally immanent;
4. his stress on a bodily resurrection;
5. his emphasis on calling the church back to the Bible, with the understanding that faith is not ultimately directed to the book, but to God alone, and
6. his support for central orthodox doctrines.

Criticisms. God is out of reach. Barth is a classic example of a fideist. In overemphasizing God's transcendence, Barth effectively makes God unknowable. He never overcame the "wholly other" form of his paradox, which will not stand alongside the revealed Son of God of the Christ (*Commentary*). Barth's God is the God of Kierkegaard. If language about God is not even analogical, all that is left is agnosticism about God's nature.

The central thesis is self-defeating. The idea that transcendental truth cannot be expressed in rational categories does the very thing it denies—it expresses transcendental truth in rational categories. To propose that "truth is a series of paradoxes" raises the question of whether this statement is true, and, if so, whether it is paradoxical.

Fideism is unfounded. To argue that there are no rational supports for the Christian faith is self-destructive. It is an argument in support of a religious position claiming that arguments cannot be given in support of religious positions. Further, fideism may be internally consistent, but there is no indication of where it touches reality, so it is impossible to distinguish from falsehood.

The denial of general revelation is unbiblical. When Barth denied the validity of general revelation he went contrary to both historical Christianity and Scripture. Romans 1:19–20 (cf. 2:12–15) declares that general revelation in nature is so clear that even fallen human beings are "without excuse." Other passages demonstrate that God can be known by general revelation, among them Psalm 119 and Acts 14 and 17.

This view of Scripture is faulty. There are serious problems with Barth's view of Scripture. In attempting to preserve God's freedom about whether to speak through Scripture, he has undermined the essential nature of Scripture and the authoritative Word of God. His view is contrary to what the Bible affirms of itself (*see* BIBLE, EVIDENCE FOR), namely, that it is not merely a witness to revelation but a revelation itself (*see* BIBLE, INSPIRATION OF).

The focus of divine revelation according to Scripture is not a self-authenticating word, but an open, public, verifiable historical event. Evidence is made known to all (Acts 17:31). Luke composed his work to show the historical foundations on which the proclamation of the gospel rests (Luke 1:1–4). Jesus offered infallible proofs (Acts 1:3).

This defective view of Scripture allows virtually no limits to picking and choosing what to believe. Barth may have accepted a literal physical resurrection, but many of those who followed him did not. He accepted such unorthodox beliefs of universalism. Following *Origen, Barth denied the existence of hell and affirmed that all will be saved.

Sources

K. Barth, *Anselm*
———, *Christian Dogmatics in Outline*
———, *Church Dogmatics*
———, *Commentary on Romans*
———, *Credo*
———, *Nein*
———, *Shorter Commentary on Romans*
———, *Theology and the Church*
———, *Word of God and Theology*
G. Bolich, *Karl Barth and Evangelicalism*
C. Pinnock, "Karl Barth and Christian Apologetics," in *Themelios* (197?)
E. Brunner, *Revelation and Reason*
S. A. Matczak, *Karl Barth on God*
B. Mondin, *Analogy in Protestant and Catholic*

Bayle, Pierre. Pierre Bayle (1647–1706) was born in Carla, France, where his father was a Calvinist clergyman. He attended the Jesuit University of Toulouse in 1669 where he converted to Catholicism. After reconsidering, he returned to Protestantism and became subject to severe penalties under French law. He thus left France for Geneva to finish his studies. He was appointed to the chair of philosophy at Sedan (1675) and later in Rotterdam (1682) where he published his *Pensees diverses sur la comete de 1680* (Diverse Thoughts on the Comet of 1680) and his *Critique generale de l'Historie du Calvinisme de M. Maimbourg* (A Critique of Maimbourg's History of Calvinism). Both his father and his brothers died in France as a result of religious persecutions. From 1684 to 1687 he published his famous journal, *Nouvelles de la republique des lettres*, an attempt to popularize literature. After being deposed from his chair in 1693, he devoted his attention to his famous *Dictionaire historique et critique* (2 vols., 1697) which was eventually expanded to sixteen volumes by the eleventh edition (1829–24). The English translation was five volumes (1734–38).

Beliefs. Since Bayle lived in a day of religious intolerance, his views were more covert than they otherwise may have been. Nevertheless, some things emerge clearly.

Skepticism. After the publication of his *Dictionary*, Bayle was charged with skepticism, Manichaeism, and disregard for Holy Scripture. Bayle was called before a Presbyterian commission and consented to change some offensive articles, which appeared in revised form in the second edition. Nonetheless, it is evident that Bayle was far from being an orthodox Protestant.

In fact, Bayle was a skeptic who strongly objected to Benedict *Spinoza's *monism and leaned toward Manichaean *dualism—the system out of which Augustine was converted. Bayle held that the realms of faith and reason are mutually exclusive. At first Protestant liberals believed Bayle was on their side, but they soon learned that he considered Christian beliefs incompatible with reason and science.

Attack on Religion. Bayle's attack on religion was relentless, though often subtle. Many of his articles in the *Dictionary* dealt with the problem of evil, immorality in the Old Testament, and the alleged irrationality of Christianity. He reveled in salacious tales about famous religious figures. Indeed, his articles were "a massive onslaught against almost any religious, philosophical, moral, scientific, or historical view that anyone held" (Edwards, 258). He considered himself "a Protestant in the true sense of the term, that he opposed everything that was said and everything that was done" (ibid.).

Religious Toleration. Bayle believed that "matters of belief should be outside the sphere of the State"—a belief that earned his work a place on the Catholic Index. In 1686 he published a *Commentaire philosphique sur ces paroles de Jesus-Christ 'Constrains-les de' enter"* (*Philosophical Commentary on the Words of Jesus "Constrain Them to Come In"*) in which he defended toleration for Jews, Muslims, Unitarians, Catholics, and even atheists.

Influence. Although he was not himself a revolutionary, his writings did pave the way for the French Revolution. Three years before John Locke (1632–1704) wrote his famous *Letters on Toleration,* Bayle penned his *Commentaire philosphique sur le Compelle Entrare* in which he argued that freedom is a natural right and that even an atheist was not necessarily a bad citizen.

Bayle had a great influence on French philosophers of the eighteenth century, especially François-Marie Voltaire (1694–1778). Bayle's *Dictionary* was the source from which they drew many of their arguments. Denis Diderot's skeptic *Encyclopedie* was based on Bayle's work. Diderot (1713–1784) wrote: "Articles dealing with respectable prejudices must expound them differentially; the edifice of clay must be shattered by referring the reader to the other articles in which the opposite truths are established on sound principles" ("Diderot, Denis," in *Encyclopedia Britannica*).

The influence of Bayle extended to figures like David Hume and Edward Gibbon. Thomas Jefferson recommended the *Dictionary* as one of the hundred basic books with which to start the Congressional Library. The famous German atheist Ludwig Feuerbach viewed Bayle as a major figure in modern thought and devoted a whole volume to him (*see* FEUERBACH).

The central theses of Bayle's skepticism are treated elsewhere, particularly in articles on Agnosticism; Apologetics; Biblical Criticism; Hume, David; Miracles; and New Testament, Reliability of.

Sources

J. Delvolve, *Religion, Critique et Philosophie Positivism chez P. Bayle*

L. Feuerbach, *Pierre Bayle*

R. Popkin, "Bayle, Pierre," *EP*

H. E. Smith, *The Literary Criticism of P. Bayle*

Berkeley, George. Bishop George Berkeley (1685–1753) was born in Kilekenny, Ireland. He studied John Locke and Rene Descartes at Trinity College, Dublin. He attempted but failed to start a college in Rhode Island. Having been ordained as an Anglican priest in 1707, he was eventually appointed bishop in 1734.

The primary philosophical writings of Berkeley include *A Treatise Concerning the Principles of Human Knowledge* (1710), *Three Dialogues Between Hylas and Philonous* (1713), and *The Analyst; or, A Discourse Addressed to an Infidel Mathematician* (1734).

The Philosophy of Berkeley. Berkeley is known for two seemingly incongruous positions. He was an epistemological empiricist in the tradition of John *Locke. He was also a metaphysical idealist who denied the existence of matter.

The Epistemology of Empiricism. According to Berkeley, the cause and cure of philosophical difficulties lies not in our senses or reason but in the philosophical principle of *abstraction*. We can imagine, compound, divide, and symbolize (generalize) and no more. General ideas are only particular ones made to stand for a group (e.g., a triangle).

The error of abstraction arises from language; we wrongly believe words have precise meanings, that every word stands for an idea or that language is primarily for communication. It also arouses passions and influences attitudes. The cure is to confine thoughts to naked ideas that are free from their traditional names, so as to avoid purely verbal controversies, to avoid the snare of abstractions, and to be clear. The result of this is that we won't look for abstract when particular is known, nor will we assume that all names represent an idea.

Berkeley believed that the *source* of all ideas is internal—sensation, perception, memory, and imagination. The *subject* of all knowledge is a perceiver (the mind or "me"). The *nature* of ideas is that they are passive objects of perception. The *results* of all this is metaphysics idealism.

The Metaphysics of Idealism. Berkeley accepted the existence of only minds and ideas. To be is either to perceive (*esse is percipere*) or to be perceived (*esse* is *percipi*). No "matter" or extramental beings exist: (1) There is no way to separate *being* from *being perceived*. (2) The arguments against existence of secondary qualities also apply to primary ones. For example, extension cannot be known apart from color and bulk. Number is based on unity, which cannot be perceived. Figure changes with perspective. Motion is relative. (3) "Things" cannot be known apart from thought; they exist only in thought. (4) Belief in "matter" charges God with a useless creation (*see* William of Ockham). It is impossible to conceive of anything existing outside of a mind. To do so is a power of mind to form an idea in the mind (not outside of it). Nothing can be conceived as existing unconceived.

Proof for God. Besides being an epistemological empiricist and a metaphysical idealist, Berkeley was a Christian theist (*see* Theism). He even offered a proof for God's existence (*see* God, Evidences for).

1. All ideas are passive objects or perception. (a) Minds perceive, but (b) Ideas are only perceived.
2. I am receiving a strong, steady succession of ideas coming from outside me, forced upon me, and over which I have no control. What I call "world" so does everyone else.
3. Therefore, there must be a Mind (God), an active Spirit causing the "world" of ideas I and others receive from outside our minds.
4. We do not directly perceive this Mind, but only its effects, the ideas it causes.

Answers to Objections. Berkeley anticipated and offered responses to many objections, though not all are plausible.

For the argument that his view does away with nature, Berkeley responds that nature is a set of rules by which God regularly excites ideas in our minds. To the assertion that substance has no meaning, he answers that it is only an idea gained from a group of sensations. Though some might insist that it sounds harsh to eat and wear ideas, this is true, but only because it goes against our customary use of words.

As for those who contend that distant objects are not in the mind, he replied that they are in our dreams if nowhere else. Further, the *sight* of a distant object is the prognostication that I may soon *feel* it hit me. Though it be objected that fire differs from the idea of fire, Berkeley reminded us that Plato did not see that difference. Even so, other universal beliefs have been false. All may *act* as if there is matter, even though it is philosophically untrue. The general objection that ideas and things differ was met with the response that this is true only because the former is a passive idea and the latter is an active idea (activated by God). Does this view destroy the concept of motion? Not so. Motion is reducible to sense phenomena (ideas). Berkeley responded to the argument that things not thought about would cease to exist. God is always thinking them. This latter response occasioned the famous response by John Knox: "A Poem on Berkeley."

> There was a young man who said, "God
> Must think it exceedingly odd
> If He finds that this tree
> Continues to be
> When there's no one about in the Quad."
> Dear Sir: Your astonishment's odd:
> I am always about in the Quad.
> And that is why the tree
> Will continue to be
> Since observed by Yours faithfully, God.

It could be argued against Berkeley that this would make everything a direct result of God or else artificial. He believed this was not true. There are secondary causes—ideas combined into regular patterns (nature) for the practical purposes of life. Fire warns of potential pain, but it doesn't cause it.

Since the Bible speaks of physical bodies, Berkeley was charged with denying the teaching of the Bible. His answer was that what we call "body" is merely a collection of sense impressions, but not really a material thing. To the insistence that his view was a denial of miracles, Berkeley responded that things are not real, but they are real perceptions. Thus the disciples really perceived they were touching the resurrected body of Christ, though it was not made of matter in the way we usually think (*see* Resurrection, Evidence for).

The Values of Idealism. Bishop Berkeley enumerated positive values of his philosophical idealism. For one, the source of skepticism (*see* Agnosticism) is gone. How can we know ideas correspond to reality? This is no problem; since ideas *are* real they do not have to correspond to anything else. The cornerstone of atheism is gone as well—matter. It is matter in motion eternally that atheists use to eliminate the idea of God.

The basis for idolatry is eliminated. Who could worship the mere idea of an object in their mind? The Socinians lose their objection to the resurrection, since there are no particulars to be resurrected (*see* Resurrection, Objections to).

Evaluation. Although Berkeley was a Christian theist in the classical tradition, his metaphysical ideas have caused great discomfort to other theists. Rather than solve problems, it seems to create them. Several criticisms should be noted:

His Basic Assumption Begs the Question. The fundamental assumption of Berkeley's idealism is that only minds and ideas exist. Once this is granted, everything else follows. But there is no compelling reason to grant it. Indeed, it begs the question by assuming that *only* minds and ideas exist. No surprise that he concludes that nothing exists beyond minds and ideas. The existence of extramental and nonmental reality is not eliminated by any of Berkeley's arguments.

His Basic Arguments Fail. Berkeley's arguments for idealism are at root based on the mistaken notion that knowing involves a sensing *of* ideas rather than sensing things *through* ideas. But this begs the question. If ideas are not the *formal* object of knowledge, but really the *instrument of* knowledge, then Berkeley's view collapses.

His Ingenious Solutions Are Contrary to Experience. To speak of bodies, matter, and nature we all experience as mere ideas that God regularly excites in us is clever but counter-intuitive. It is possible, but not credible. Indeed, it *is harsh* to speak of eating ideas. It *does undermine the resurrection* to affirm that God merely raised up a cluster of ideas.

His View Charges God with Deception. Indeed, Berkeley appears to charge God with deception (*see* God, Nature of; Moral Argument). If it is simply a matter of God's power, there is no question but that God can excite the idea of matter in our minds without matter actually existing. But it is not simply a matter of power. God is more than all powerful. He is all perfect. He cannot deceive. But exciting in us regularly the idea of an extramental world when there is no word out there is deception.

Sources

"Berkeley, George," *EP*

G. Berkeley, *A Treatise Concerning the Principles of Human Knowledge*

———, *The Analyst; or, A Discourse Addressed to an Infidel Mathematician*

———, *Three Dialogues Between Hylas and Philonous*

J. Collins, *A History of Modern European Philosophy*

Bible, Alleged Errors in. Critics claim the Bible is filled with errors. Some even speak of thousands of mistakes. However, orthodox Christians through the ages have claimed that the Bible is without error in the original text ("autographs"; see Geisler, *Decide for Yourself*). "If we are perplexed by any apparent contradiction in Scripture," *Augustine wisely noted, "it is not allowable to say, 'The author of this book is mistaken'; but either the manuscript is faulty, or the translation is wrong, or you have not understood" (Augustine, 11.5). Not one error that extends to the original text of the Bible has ever been demonstrated.

Why the Bible Cannot Err. The argument for an errorless (inerrant) Bible can be put in this logical form:

God cannot err.

The Bible is the Word of God.

Therefore, the Bible cannot err.

God Cannot Err. Logically, the argument is valid. So, if the premises are true, the conclusion is also true. If the theistic God exists (*see* God, Evidence for; Theism), then the first premise is true. For an infinitely perfect, all-knowing God cannot make a mistake. The Scriptures testify to this, declaring emphatically that "it is impossible for God to lie" (Heb. 6:18). Paul speaks of the "God who does not lie" (Titus 1:2). He is a God who, even if we are faithless, "remains faithful; he cannot deny himself" (2 Tim. 2:13). God is truth (John 14:6), and so is his word. Jesus said to the Father, "Your word is truth" (John 17:17). The psalmist exclaimed, "The entirety of Your word is truth" (Ps. 119:160).

The Bible Is the Word of God. Jesus, who is the Son of God (*see* Christ, Deity of) referred to the Old Testament as the "Word of God" which "cannot be broken" (John 10:35). He said, "until heaven and earth disappear, not the smallest letter, not the least stroke of a pen, will by any means disappear from the Law until everything is accomplished" (Matt. 5:18). Paul added, "All Scripture is God-breathed" (2 Tim. 3:16). It came "out of the mouth of God" (Matt. 4:4). Although human authors recorded the messages, "prophecy never had its origin in the will of man, but men spoke from God as they were carried along by the Holy Spirit" (2 Peter 1:20).

Jesus said to the religious leaders of his day, "You nullify the word of God by your tradition" (Mark 7:13). Jesus turned their attention to the written Word of God by affirming over and over again, "It is written" (for example, Matt. 4:4, 7, 10). This phrase occurs more than ninety times in the New Testament, a strong indication of divine authority. Stressing the unfailing nature of God's truth, the apostle Paul referred to the Scriptures as "the word of God" (Rom. 9:6). The writer of Hebrews declared that "the word of God is living and active. Sharper than any double-edged sword, it penetrates even to dividing soul and spirit, joints and marrow; it judges the thoughts and attitudes of the heart" (Heb. 4:12).

Therefore, the Bible Cannot Err. If God cannot err and if the Bible is the Word of God, then the Bible cannot err (*see* Bible, Evidence for). God has spoken, and he has not stuttered. The God of truth has given us the Word of truth, and it does not contain any untruth. The Bible is the unerring Word of God. This is not to say that there are not *difficulties* in our Bibles. There are, or such books as this would be unneeded. But God's people can approach difficult texts with confidence, knowing that they are not actual *errors*; God did not err.

Errors in Science and History? Some have suggested that Scripture can always be trusted on matters of faith and life, or moral matters, but it is not always correct on historical matters. They rely on it in the spiritual domain, but not in the sphere of science (*see* Science and the Bible). If true, this would render the Bible ineffective as a divine authority, since the historical and scientific is inextricably interwoven with the spiritual.

A close examination of Scripture reveals that the scientific (factual) and spiritual truths of Scripture are often inseparable. One cannot separate the spiritual truth of Christ's resurrection from the fact that his body permanently and physically vacated the tomb and walked among people (Matt. 28:6; 1 Cor. 15:13–19). If Jesus was not born of a biological virgin, then he is no different from the rest of the human race, on whom the stigma of Adam's sin rests (Rom. 5:12). Likewise, the death of Christ for our sins cannot be detached from the literal shedding of his blood on the cross, for "without the shedding of blood there is no remission" (Heb. 9:22). Adam's existence and fall cannot be a myth. If there were no literal Adam and no actual fall, then the spiritual teaching about inherited sin and physical and spiritual death are wrong (Rom. 5:12). Historical reality and the theological doctrine stand or fall together.

Also, the doctrine of the incarnation (*see* CHRIST, DEITY OF) is inseparable from the historical truth about Jesus of Nazareth (John 1:1, 14). Jesus' moral teaching about marriage was based on his teaching about a literal Adam and Eve who were joined by God in marriage (Matt. 19:4–5). The moral or theological teaching is devoid of meaning apart from the historical or factual event. If one denies that the literal space-time event occurred, then there is no basis for believing the scriptural doctrine built upon it, or anything else, for all is then untrustworthy (*see* MIRACLES, MYTH AND).

Jesus often directly compared Old Testament events with important spiritual truths. He related his death and resurrection to Jonah and the great fish (Matt. 12:40), his second coming to Noah and the flood (Matt. 24:37–39). Both the occasion and the manner of comparison make it clear that Jesus was affirming the historicity of those Old Testament events. Jesus asserted to Nicodemus, "If I told you earthly things and you do not believe, how shall you believe if I tell you heavenly things?" (John 3:12). The corollary to that statement is that, if the Bible does not speak truthfully about the physical world, it cannot be trusted when it speaks about the spiritual world. The two are intimately related.

Inspiration includes not only all that the Bible explicitly *teaches*, but everything the Bible *touches*. This is true of history, science, or mathematics—whatever the Bible declares is true, whether a major or a minor point. The Bible is God's Word, and God does not deviate from the truth. All the parts are as true as the whole they comprise.

If Inspired, Then Inerrant. Inerrancy is a logical result of inspiration (*see* BIBLE, EVIDENCE FOR). *Inerrancy* means "wholly true and without error." And what God breathes out (inspires) must be wholly true (inerrant). However, it is helpful to specify more clearly what is meant by "truth" and what would constitute an "error" (see Geisler, "The Concept of Truth in the Inerrancy Debate").

Truth is that which corresponds to reality (*see* TRUTH, DEFINITION OF). *Error* is what does not correspond to reality. Nothing mistaken can be true, even if the author intended the true. Otherwise, every sincere utterance ever made is true, even the grossly mistaken.

Some biblical scholars argue that the Bible cannot be inerrant through some faulty reasoning:

1. The Bible is a human book.
2. Humans err.
3. Therefore, the Bible errs.

The error of this reason can be seen from equally erroneous reasoning:

1. Jesus was a human being.
2. Human beings sin.
3. Therefore, Jesus sinned.

One can readily see that this conclusion is wrong. Jesus was "without sin" (Heb. 4:15; see also 2 Cor. 5:21; 2 Peter 1:19; 2 John 2:1; 3:3). But, if Jesus never sinned, what is wrong with the above argument that Jesus is human and humans sin, therefore, Jesus sinned? Where does the logic go astray?

The mistake is to assume that Jesus is *simply* human. Mere human beings sin. But, Jesus was not a *mere* human being. He was also God. Likewise, the Bible is not *merely* a human book; it is also the Word of God. Like Jesus, it has divine elements that negate the statement that anything human errs. They are divine and cannot err. There can no more be an error in God's written Word than there was a sin in God's living Word.

Approaching Bible Difficulties. As Augustine said above, mistakes come not in the revelation of God, but in the misinterpretations of man. Except where scribal errors and extraneous changes crept into textual families over the centuries, all the critics' allegations of error in the Bible are based on errors of their own. Most problems fall into one of the following categories.

Assuming the Unexplained Is Unexplainable. No informed person would claim to be able to fully explain all Bible difficulties. However, it is a mistake for the critic to assume that the explained cannot and will not be explained. When a scientist comes upon an anomaly in nature, he does not give up further scientific exploration. Rather, the unexplained motivates further study. Scientists once could not explain meteors, eclipses, tornadoes, hurricanes, and earthquakes. Until recently, scientists did not know how the bumblebee could fly. All of these mysteries have yielded their secrets to relentless patience. Scientists do not now know how life can grow on thermovents in the depths of the sea. But, no scientist throws in the towel and cries "contradiction!"

The true biblical scholar approaches the Bible with the same presumption that there are answers to the thus-far unexplained. When something is encountered for which no explanation is known, the student goes on with research, looking out for the means to discover an answer. There is rational reason for faith that an answer will be found, because most once-unsolvable problems have now been answered by science, textual study, archaeology, linguistics, or another discipline. Critics once proposed that Moses could not have written the first five books of the Bible, because Moses' culture was preliterate. Now we know that writing had existed thousands of years before Moses (*see* PENTATEUCH, MOSAIC AUTHORSHIP OF).

Critics once believed that Bible references to the Hittite people were totally fictional. Such a people by that name had never existed. Now that the Hittites' national library has been found in Turkey, the skeptics' once-confident assertions seem humorous. Indications from archaeological studies are that similar scoffings about the route and date of the Exodus will soon be silenced. These and many more examples inspire confidence that the biblical difficulties that have not been explained are not mistakes in the Bible.

Assuming the Bible is Guilty of Error unless Proven Innocent. Many critics assume the Bible is wrong until something proves it right. However, like an American citizen charged with an offense, the Bible should be read with at least the same presumption of accuracy given to other literature that claims to be nonfiction. This is the way we approach all human communications. If we did not, life would not be possible. If we assumed that road signs and traffic signals were not telling the truth, we would probably be dead before we could prove otherwise. If we assumed food packages mislabeled, we would have to open up all cans and packages before buying.

The Bible, like any other book, should be presumed to be telling us what the authors said, experienced, and heard. Negative critics begin with just the opposite presumption. Little wonder they conclude the Bible is riddled with error.

Confusing Interpretations with Revelation. Jesus affirmed that the "Scripture cannot be broken" (John 10:35). As an infallible book, the Bible is also irrevocable. Jesus declared, "Truly I say to you, until heaven and earth pass away, not the smallest letter or stroke shall pass away from the Law, until all is accomplished" (Matt. 5:18; cf. Luke 16:17). The Scriptures also have final authority, being the last word on all it discusses (*see* BIBLE, JESUS' VIEW OF). Jesus employed the Bible to resist the tempter (Matt. 4:4, 7, 10), to settle doctrinal disputes (Matt. 21:42), and to vindicate his authority (Mark 11:17). Sometimes a biblical teaching rests on a small historical detail (Heb. 7:4–10), a word or phrase (Acts 15:13–17), or the difference between the singular and the plural (Gal. 3:16).

But, while the Bible is infallible, human interpretations are not. Even though God's word is perfect (Ps. 19:7), as long as imperfect human beings exist, there will be misinterpretations of God's Word and false views about his world. In view of this, one should not be hasty in assuming that a currently dominant assumption in science is the final word. Some of yesterday's irrefutable laws are considered errors by today's scientists. So, contradictions between popular opinions in science and widely accepted interpretations of the Bible can be expected. But this falls short of proving there is a real contradiction.

Failure to Understand the Context. The most common mistake of all Bible interpreters, including some critical scholars, is to read a text outside its proper context. As the adage goes, "A text out of context is a pretext." One can prove anything from the Bible by this mistaken procedure. The Bible says, "there is no God" (Ps. 14:1). Of course, the context is: "The fool has said in his heart 'There is no God.'" One may claim that Jesus admonished us "not to resist evil" (Matt. 5:39), but the antiretaliatory context in which he cast this statement must not be ignored. Many read Jesus' statement to "Give to him who asks you," as though one had an obligation to give a gun to a small child. Failure to note that meaning is determined by context is a chief sin of those who find fault with the Bible.

Interpreting the Difficult by the Clear. Some passages are hard to understand or appear to contradict some other part of Scripture. James appears to be saying that salvation is by works (James 2:14–26), whereas Paul teaches that it is by grace. Paul says Christians are "saved by grace through faith, and that not of ourselves; it is a gift of God, not of works, lest anyone should boast" (Eph. 2:8–9). And, "to him who does not work but believes on him who justifies the ungodly, his faith is counted for righteousness" (Rom. 4:5). Also, it "is not by works of righteousness which we have done, but according to his mercy he saved us" (Titus 3:5–6).

A careful reading of all that James says and all that Paul says shows that Paul is speaking about justification *before God* (by faith alone), whereas James is referring to justification *before others* (who only see what we do). And James and Paul both speak of the fruitfulness that always comes in the life of one who loves God.

A similar example, this time involving Paul, is found in Philippians 2:12. Paul says, "Work out your own salvation with fear and trembling." This appears to say salvation is by works. But this is flatly contradicted by the above texts, and a host of other Scriptures. When this difficult statement about "working out our salvation" is understood in the light of clear passages, we can see that it *does not* mean we are saved by works. In fact, what it means is found in the very next verse. We are to work salvation *out* because God's grace has worked it *in* our hearts. In Paul's words, "for it is God who works in you both to will and to do for his good pleasure" (Phil. 2:13).

Teaching on an Obscure Passage. Some passages in the Bible are difficult because their meaning is obscure. This is usually because a key word in the text is used only once (or rarely), so it is difficult to know what the author is saying unless it can be inferred from the context. One of the best known passages in the Bible contains a word that appears nowhere else in all existing Greek literature up to the time the New Testament was written. This word appears in what is popularly known as the Lord's Prayer (Matt. 6:11). It is usually translated, "Give us this day our daily bread." The word in question is the one translated "daily"—*(epiousion)*. Experts in Greek still have not come to any agreement as to its origin, or its precise meaning. Different commentators try to establish links with Greek words that are known, and many suggested meanings have been proposed:

Give us this day our *continuous* bread.

Give us this day our *supersubstantial* (a supernatural gift from heaven) bread.

Give us this day bread *for our sustenance*.

Give us this day our *daily* (or, what we need for today) bread.

Each one of these proposals has its defenders, each makes sense in the context, and each is a possibility based on the limited linguistic information. There does not seem to be a compelling reason to depart from what has become the generally accepted translation, but it does add difficulty, because the meaning of some key word is obscure.

At other times, the words are clear but the meaning is not evident because we are missing some background information that the first readers had. This is surely true in 1 Corinthians 15:20 where Paul speaks of those who were "baptized for the dead." Is he referring to dead believers who were not baptized and others were being baptized for them so they could be saved (as Mormons claim)? Or, is he referring to others being baptized into the church to fill the ranks of those who have passed on? Or is he referring to a believer being baptized "for" (i.e., "with a view to") his own death and burial with Christ? Or to something else?

When we are not sure, then several things should be kept in mind. First, we should not build a doctrine on an obscure passage. The rule of thumb in the Bible is "The main things are the plain things, and the plain things are the main things." This is called the "perspicuity" (clarity) of Scripture. If something is important, it is clearly taught and probably in more than one place. Second, when a given passage is not clear, we should never conclude that it means something that is opposed to another plain teaching of Scripture.

Forgetting the Bible's Human Characteristics. With the exception of small sections such as the Ten Commandments, which were "written with the finger of God" (Exod. 31:18), the Bible was not verbally dictated (see Rice). The writers were not secretaries of the Holy Spirit. They were human composers employing their own literary styles and idiosyncrasies. These human authors sometimes used *human sources* for their material (Josh. 10:13; Acts 17:28; 1 Cor. 15:33; Titus 1:12). In fact, every book of the Bible is the composition of a *human writer*—about forty of them in all. The Bible also manifests different *human literary* styles. Writers speak from an observer's standpoint when they write of the sun rising or setting (Josh. 1:15). They also reveal *human thought patterns*, including memory lapses (1 Cor. 1:14–16), as well as *human emotions* (Gal. 4:14). The Bible discloses specific *human interests*. Hosea has a rural interest, Luke a medical concern, and James a love of nature. Biblical authors include a lawgiver (Moses), a general (Joshua), prophets (Samuel, Isaiah, et al.), kings (David and Solomon), a musician (Asaph), a herdsman (Amos), a prince and statesman (Daniel), a priest (Ezra), a tax collector (Matthew), a physician (Luke), a scholar (Paul), and fishermen (Peter and John). With such a variety of occupations represented by biblical writers, it is only natural that their personal interests and differences should be reflected in their writings.

Like Christ, the Bible is completely human, yet without error. Forgetting the humanity of Scripture can lead to falsely impugning its integrity by expecting a level of expression higher than that which is customary to a human document. This will become more obvious as we discuss the next mistakes of the critics (*see* BIBLE CRITICISM).

Assuming a Partial Report Is a False Report. Critics often jump to the conclusion that a partial report is false. However, this is not so. If it were, most of what has ever been said would be false, since seldom does time or space permit an absolutely complete report. Occasionally biblical writers express the same thing in different ways, or at least from different viewpoints, at different times, stressing different things. Hence, inspiration does not exclude a diversity of expression. The four Gospels relate the same story—often the same incidents—in different ways to different groups of people and sometimes even quotes the same saying with different words. Compare, for example, Peter's famous confession in the Gospels:

Matthew: "You are the Christ, the Son of the living God" (16:16).

Mark: "You are the Christ" (8:29).

Luke: "The Christ of God" (9:20).

Even the Ten Commandments, which were "written by the finger of God" (Deut. 9:10), are stated with variations the second time they are recorded (cf. Exod. 20:8–11 with Deut. 5:12–15). There are many differences between the books of Kings and Chronicles in their description of identical events, yet they harbor no contradiction in the events they narrate. If such important utterances can be stated in different ways, then there is no reason the rest of Scripture cannot speak truth without employing a wooden literalness of expression.

New Testament Citations of the Old Testaments. Critics often point to variations in the New Testament use of Old Testament Scriptures as a proof of error. They forget that every *citation* need not be an exact *quotation*. Sometimes we use indirect and sometimes direct quotations. It was then (and is today) perfectly acceptable literary style to give the *essence* of a statement without using precisely the *same words*. The same *meaning* can be conveyed without using the same *verbal expressions*.

Variations in the New Testament citations of the Old Testament fall into different categories. Sometimes they are because there is a change of speaker. For example, Zechariah records the Lord as saying, "they will look on *me* whom they have pierced" (12:10). When this is cited in the New Testament, John, not God, is speaking. So it is changed to "They shall look on *him* whom they have pierced" (John 19:37).

At other times, writers cite only part of the Old Testament text. Jesus did this at his home synagogue in Nazareth (Luke 4:18–19 citing Isa. 61:1–2). In fact, he stopped in the middle of a sentence. Had he gone any farther, he could not have made his central point from the text, "Today this Scripture is fulfilled in your hearing" (vs. 21). The very next phrase, "And the day of vengeance of our God," refers to his second coming.

Sometimes the New Testament paraphrases or summarizes the Old Testament text (e.g., Matt. 2:6). Others blend two texts into one (Matt. 27:9–10). Occasionally a general truth is mentioned, without citing a specific text. For example, Matthew said Jesus moved to Nazareth "that it might be fulfilled which was spoken by the prophets, 'he shall be called a Nazarene'" (Matt. 2:23). Notice, Matthew quotes no given prophet, but rather "prophets" in general. Several texts speak of the Messiah's lowliness. To be from Nazareth, a Nazarene, was a byword for low status in the Israel of Jesus' day.

There are instances where the New Testament applies a text in a different way than the Old Testament did. For example, Hosea applies "Out of Egypt have I called My Son" to the Messianic nation, and Matthew applies it to the product of that nation, the Messiah (Matt. 2:15 from Hosea 11:1). In no case does the New Testament misinterpret or misapply the Old Testament, nor draw some invalid implication from it. The New Testament makes no mistakes in citing the Old Testament, as critics do in citing the New Testament.

Assuming Divergent Accounts Are False. Because two or more accounts of the same event differ, does not mean they are mutually exclusive. Matthew 28:5 says there was one angel at the tomb after the resurrection, whereas John informs us there were two (20:12). But these are not contradictory reports. An infallible mathematical rule easily explains this problem: Where there are two, there is always one. Matthew did not say there was *only* one angel. There may also have been one angel at the tomb at one point on this confusing morning and two at another. One has to add the word "only" to Matthew's account to make it contradict John's. But if the critic comes to the texts to show they err, then the error is not in the Bible, but in the critic.

Likewise, Matthew (27:5) informs us that Judas hanged himself. But Luke says that "he burst open in the middle and all his entrails gushed out" (Acts 1:18). Once more, these accounts are not mutually exclusive. If Judas hanged himself from a tree over the edge of a cliff or gully in this rocky area, and his body fell on sharp rocks below, then his entrails would gush out just as Luke vividly describes.

Presuming That the Bible Approves of All It Records. It is a mistake to assume that everything contained in the Bible is commended by the Bible. The whole Bible is *true* (John 17:17), but it records some *lies*, for example, Satan's (Gen. 3:4; cf. John 8:44) and Rahab's (Josh. 2:4). Inspiration encompasses the Bible fully in the sense that it records accurately and truthfully even the lies and errors of sinful beings. The truth of Scripture is found in what the Bible *reveals*, not in everything it *records*. Unless this distinction is held, it may be incorrectly concluded that the Bible teaches immorality because it narrates David's sin (2 Sam. 11:4), that it promotes polygamy because it records Solomon's (1 Kings 11:3), or that it affirms atheism because it quotes the fool as saying "there is no God" (Ps. 14:1).

Forgetting That the Bible Is Nontechnical. To be true, something does not have to use scholarly, technical, or so-called "scientific" language. The Bible is written for the common person of every generation, and it therefore uses common, everyday language. The use of observational, nonscientific language is not *un*scientific, it is merely *pre*scientific. The Scriptures were written in *ancient* times by ancient standards, and it would be anachronistic to superimpose modern scientific standards upon them. However, it is no more unscientific to speak of the sun "standing still" (Josh. 10:12) than to refer to the sun "rising" (Josh. 1:16). Meteorologists still refer to the times of "sunrise" and "sunset."

Assuming Round Numbers Are False. Like ordinary speech, the Bible uses round numbers (see Josh. 3:4; cf. 4:13). It refers to the diameter as being about one-third of the circumference of something (1 Chron. 19:18; 21:5). While this technically is only an approximation (see Lindsell, 165–66); it may be imprecise from the standpoint of a technological society to speak of 3.14159265 as "3," but it is not incorrect (*see* SCIENCE AND THE BIBLE). It is sufficient for a "cast metal sea" (2 Chron. 4:2) in an ancient Hebrew temple, even though it would not suffice for a computer in a modern rocket. One should not expect to see actors referring to a wrist watch in a Shakespearean play, nor people in a prescientific age to use precise numbers.

Neglecting to Note Literary Devices. Human language is not limited to one mode of expression. So there is no reason to suppose that only one literary genre was used in a divinely inspired Book. The Bible reveals a number of literary devices: Whole books are written as *poetry* (e.g., Job, Psalms, Proverbs). The Synoptic Gospels feature *parables*. In Galatians 4, Paul utilizes an *allegory*. The New Testament abounds with *metaphors* (2 Cor. 3:2–3; James 3:6), *similes* (Matt. 20:1; James 1:6), *hyperbole* (John 21:25; 2 Cor. 3:2; Col. 1:23), and even *poetic figures* (Job 41:1). Jesus employed *satire* (Matt. 19:24; 23:24). *Figures of speech* are common throughout the Bible.

It is not a mistake for a biblical writer to use a figure of speech, but it is a mistake for a reader to take a figure of speech literally. Obviously when the Bible speaks of the believer resting under the shadow of God's "wings" (Ps. 36:7) it does not mean that God is a feathered bird. When the Bible says God "awakes" (Ps. 44:23), as though he were sleeping, it means God is roused to action.

Forgetting That Only the Original Text Is Inerrant. Genuine mistakes have been found—in copies of Bible text made hundreds of years after the autographs. God only uttered the original text of Scripture, not the copies. Therefore, only the original text is without error. Inspiration does not guarantee that every copy is without error, especially in copies made from copies made from copies made from copies (*see* NEW TESTAMENT MANUSCRIPTS; OLD TESTAMENT MANUSCRIPTS). Therefore, we are to expect that minor errors are to be found in manuscript copies.

For example, 2 Kings 8:26 gives the age of King Ahaziah as twenty-two, whereas 2 Chronicles 22:2 says forty-two. The later number cannot be correct, or he would have been older than his father. This is obviously a copyist error, but it does not alter the inerrancy of the original.

First, these are errors in the copies, not the originals. Second, they are minor errors (often in names or numbers) which do not affect any teaching. Third, these copyist errors are relatively few in number. Fourth, usually by the context, or by another Scripture, we know which is in error. For example, Ahaziah must have been twenty-two. Finally, though there is a copyist error, the entire message comes through. For example, if you received a letter with the following statement, would you assume you could collect some money?

"#OU HAVE WON $10 MILLION."

Even though there is a mistake in the first word, the entire message comes through—you are ten million dollars richer! And if you received another letter the next day that read like this, you would be even more sure:

"Y#U HAVE WON $10 MILLION."

The more mistakes of this kind there are (each in a different place), the more sure you are of the original message. This is why scribal mistakes in the biblical manuscripts do not affect the basic message of the Bible—and why studies of the ancient manuscripts are so important. A Christian can read a modern translation with confidence that it conveys the complete truth of the original Word of God.

Confusing General with Universal Statements. Critics often jump to the conclusion that unqualified statements admit no exceptions. They seize upon verses that offer general truths and then point with glee to obvious exceptions. Such statements are only intended to be generalizations.

The Book of Proverbs has many of these. Proverbial sayings, by their very nature, offer general guidance, not universal assurance. They are rules for life, but rules that admit of exceptions. Proverbs 16:7 affirms that "when a man's ways please the Lord, he makes even his enemies to be at peace with him." This obviously was not intended to be a universal truth. Paul was pleasing to the Lord and his enemies stoned him (Acts 14:19). Jesus was pleasing the Lord, and his enemies crucified him. Nonetheless, it is a general truth that one who acts in a way pleasing to God can minimize his enemies' antagonism.

Proverbs 22:6 says, "Train up a child in the way he should go, and when he is old he will not depart from it." However, other Scripture passages and experience show that this is not always true. Indeed, some godly persons in the Bible (including Job, Eli, and David) had wayward children. This proverb does not contradict experience because it is a general principle that applies in a general way, but allows for individual exceptions. Proverbs are not designed to be absolute guarantees. Rather, they express truths that provide helpful advice and guidance by which the individual should conduct his daily life.

Proverbs are *wisdom* (general guides), not *law* (universally binding imperatives). When the Bible declares "You shall therefore be holy, for I am holy" (Lev. 11:45), then there are no exceptions. Holiness, goodness, love, truth, and justice are rooted in the very nature of an unchanging God. But wisdom literature applies God's universal truths to life's changing circumstances. The results will not always be the same. Nonetheless, they are helpful guides.

Forgetting That Later Revelation Supersedes Earlier. Sometimes critics do not recognize progressive revelation. God does not reveal everything at once, nor does he lay down the same conditions for every period of history. Some of his later revelations will supersede his earlier statements. Bible critics sometimes confuse a *change* in revelation with a *mistake*. That a parent allows a very small child to eat with his fingers but demands that an older child use a fork and spoon, is not a contradiction. This is progressive revelation, with each command suited to the circumstance.

There was a time when God tested the human race by forbidding them to eat of a specific tree in the Garden of Eden (Gen. 2:16–17). This command is no longer in effect, but the later revelation does not contradict this former revelation. Also, there was a period (under the Mosaic law) when God commanded that animals be sacrificed for people's sin. However, since Christ offered the perfect sacrifice for sin (Heb. 10:11–14), this Old Testament command is no longer in effect. There is no contradiction between the later and the former commands.

Likewise, when God created the human race, he commanded that they eat only fruit and vegetables (Gen. 1:29). But later, when conditions changed after the flood, God commanded that they also eat meat (Gen. 9:3). This change from herbivorous to omnivorous status is progressive revelation, but it is not a contradiction. In fact, all these subsequent revelations were simply different commands for different people at different times in God's overall plan of redemption.

Of course, God cannot change commands that have to do with his unchangeable nature (cf. Mal. 3:6; Heb. 6:18). For example, since God is love (1 John 4:16), he cannot command that we hate him. Nor can he command what is logically impossible, for example, to both offer and not offer a sacrifice for sin at the same time and in the same sense. But these moral and logical limits notwithstanding, God can and has given noncontradictory, progressive revelations which, if taken out of its proper context and juxtaposed, can look contradictory. This is as much a mistake as to assume a parent is self-contradictory for allowing a sixteen-year-old to stay up later at night than a six-year-old.

After forty years of continual and careful study of the Bible, I can only conclude that those who have "discovered a mistake" in the Bible do not know too much about the Bible—they know too little about it. This does not mean, of course, that we understand how to resolve all the difficulties in the Scriptures. But we have seen enough problems resolved to know these also admit answers. Meanwhile, Mark Twain had a point when he concluded that it was not the parts of the Bible he did not understand that bothered him—but the parts he did understand!

Sources

G. L. Archer, Jr., *An Encyclopedia of Biblical Difficulties*

W. Arndt, *Bible Difficulties*

———, *Does the Bible Contradict Itself?*

Augustine, *Reply to Faustus the Manichaean*, in P. Schaff, ed., *A Select Library of the Nicene and Ante-Nicene Fathers of the Christian Church*

N. L. Geisler, "The Concept of Truth in the Inerrancy Debate," *Bib. Sac.*, October–December 1980

———and T. Howe, *When Critics Ask*

———and W. E. Nix, *General Introduction to the Bible*

J. W. Haley, *Alleged Discrepancies of the Bible*

H. Lindsell, *The Battle for the Bible*

J. Orr, *The Problems of the Old Testament Considered with Reference to Recent Criticism*

J. R. Rice, *Our God-Breathed Book—The Bible*

E. Thiele, *The Mysterious Numbers of the Kings of Israel*

R. Tuck, ed., *A Handbook of Biblical Difficulties*

R. D. Wilson, *A Scientific Investigation of the Old Testament*

Bible, Canonicity of. *Canonicity* (Fr. *canon,* rule or norm) refers to the normative or authoritative books inspired by God for inclusion in Holy Scripture. Canonicity is determined by God (*see* BIBLE, EVIDENCE FOR). It is not the antiquity, authenticity, or religious community that makes a book canonical or authoritative. A book is valuable because it is canonical, and not canonical because it is or was considered valuable. Its authority is *established* by God and merely *discovered* by God's people.

Definition of Canonicity. The distinction between God's determination and human discovery is essential to the correct view of canonicity, and should be drawn carefully:

The Authority Relationship Between Church and Canon

Incorrect View	Biblical View
The church is determiner of the canon.	The church is discoverer of the canon.
The church is mother of the canon.	The church is child of the canon.
The church is magistrate of the canon.	The church is minister of the canon.

The church is regulator of the canon.	The church is recognizer of the canon.
The church is judge of the canon.	The church is witness of the canon.
The church is master of the canon.	The church is servant of the canon.

In the "Incorrect View" the authority of the Scriptures is based upon the authority of the church; the correct view is that the authority of the church is to be found *in* the authority of the Scriptures. The incorrect view places the church *over* the canon, whereas the proper position views the church *under* the canon. In fact, if in the column titled "Incorrect View," the word *church* be replaced by God, then the proper view of the canon emerges clearly. It is God who *regulated* the canon; man merely *recognized* the divine authority God gave to it. God *determined* the canon, and man *discovered* it. Louis Gaussen gives an excellent summary of this position:

> In this affair, then, the Church is a servant and not a mistress; a depository and not a judge. She exercises the office of a minister, not of a magistrate. . . . She delivers a testimony, not a judicial sentence. She discerns the canon of the Scriptures, she does not make it; she has recognized their authenticity, she has not given it. . . . The authority of the Scriptures is not founded, then, on the authority of the Church: It is the church that is founded on the authority of the Scriptures. [Gaussen, 137]

Discovering Canonicity. Appropriate methods must be employed to discover which books God determined to be canonical. Otherwise, the list of canonical books might be varied and incorrectly identified. Many procedures used in the study of the Old Testament canon have been marred by the use of fallacious methods (*see* APOCRYPHA, OLD AND NEW TESTAMENTS).

Inadequate Criteria for Canonicity. Five mistaken methods have particularly troubled the church (see Beckwith, 7–8):

1. failure to distinguish a book that was "known" from a book that carried God's authority;
2. failure to distinguish disagreement about the canon between different parties from uncertainty about the canon within those parties;
3. failure to distinguish between the adding of books to the canon and the removal of books from it;
4. failure to distinguish between the canon that the community recognized and eccentric views of individuals;
5. failure to properly use Jewish evidence about the canon transmitted through Christian hands, either by denying the Jewish origins or by ignoring the Christian medium through which it has come (Beckwith, 7–8).

Principles of Canonicity. Granted that God gave authority and hence canonicity to the Bible, another question arises: How did believers become aware of what God had done? The accepted canonical books of the Bible themselves refer to other books that are no longer available, for example, the "Book of Jasher" (Josh. 10:13) and "the Book of the Wars of the Lord" (Num. 21:14). Then there are *Apocryphal* books and the so-called "lost books." How did the Fathers know those were not inspired? Did not John (21:25) and Luke (1:1) speak of a profusion of religious literature? Were there not false epistles (2 Thess. 2:2)? What marks of inspiration guided the Fathers as they identified and collected the inspired books? Perhaps the very fact that some canonical books were doubted at times, on the basis of one principle or another, argues both for the value of the principle and the caution of the Fathers in their recognition of canonicity. It provides assurance that the people of God really included the books God wanted.

Five foundational questions lie at the very heart of the discovery process:

Was the book written by a prophet of God? The basic question was whether a book was prophetic. Propheticity determined canonicity. A prophet was one who declared what God had disclosed. Thus, only the prophetic writings were canonic. Anything not written by a prophet of God was not part of the Word of God. The characteristic words "And the word of the Lord came to the prophet," or "The Lord said unto," or "God spoke" so fill the Old Testament that they have become proverbial. If substantiated these claims of inspiration are so clear that it was hardly necessary to discuss whether some books were divine in origin. In most cases it was simply a matter of establishing the authorship of the book. If it was written by a recognized apostle or prophet, its place in the canon was secured.

Historical or stylistic (external or internal) evidence that supports the genuineness of a prophetic book also argues for its canonicity. This was exactly the argument Paul used to defend his harsh words to the Galatians (Gal. 1:1–24). He argued that his message was authoritative because he was an authorized messenger of God, "an apostle not sent from men nor through the agency of man, but through Jesus Christ, and God the Father" (Gal. 1:1). He also turned the tables on his opponents who preached "a different gospel; which is really not another; only . . . to distort the gospel of Christ" (Gal. 1:6–7). His opponents' gospel could not be true because they were "false brethren" (Gal. 2:4).

It should be noted in this connection that occasionally the Bible contains true prophecies from individuals whose status as people of God is questionable, such as Balaam (Num. 24:17) and Caiaphas (John 11:49). However, granted that their prophecies were consciously given, these prophets were not writers of Bible books, but were merely quoted by the actual writer. Therefore, their utterances are in the same category as the Greek poets quoted by the apostle Paul (cf. Acts 17:28; 1 Cor. 15:33; Titus 1:12).

The arguments Paul used against the false teachers at Galatia were also used as grounds for rejecting a letter that was forged or written under false pretenses. One such letter is mentioned in 2 Thessalonians 2:2. A book cannot be canonical if it is not genuine. A book might use the device of literary impersonation without deception. One writer assumes the role of another for effect. Some scholars feel such is the case in Ecclesiastes, if *Koheleth* wrote autobiographically as though he were Solomon (see Leupold, 8f.). Such a view is not incompatible with the principle, provided it can be shown to be a literary device and not a moral deception. However, when an author pretends to be an apostle in order to gain acceptance of his ideas, as the writers of many New Testament *Apocryphal* books did, then it is moral deception.

Because of this "prophetic" principle, 2 Peter was disputed in the early church. Even Eusebius in the fourth century said, "But the so-called second Epistle we have not received as canonical, but nevertheless it has appeared useful to many, and has been studied with other Scriptures" (Eusebius 1:193). On the basis of differences in the style of writing, it was felt by some that the author of 2 Peter could not be the same as the author of 1 Peter. But 2 Peter claimed to have been written by "Simon Peter, a servant and apostle of Jesus Christ" (2 Peter 1:1). Thus, the epistle was either a forgery or there was great difficulty in explaining its different style. Those who were disturbed by such evidence doubted the genuineness of 2 Peter and it was placed among the antilegomena books for a time. It was finally admitted on the grounds that it was Peter's genuine writing. The differences in style can be accounted for by the time lapse, different occasions, and the fact that Peter verbally dictated 1 Peter to an amanuensis (or secretary; see 1 Peter 5:13).

Inspiration was so certain in many prophetic writings that their inclusion was obvious. Some were rejected because they lacked authority, particularly the pseudepigrapha. These books provided no support for their claim. In many cases the writing is fanciful and magical. This same principle of authority was the reason the book of Esther was doubted, particularly since the name of God is conspicuously absent. Upon closer examination, Esther retained its place in the canon after the Fathers were convinced that authority was present, although less observable.

Was the writer confirmed by acts of God? A miracle is an act of God to confirm the word of God given through a prophet of God to the people of God. It is the sign to substantiate his sermon; the miracle to confirm his message. Not every prophetic revelation was confirmed by a specific miracle. There were other ways to determine the authenticity of an alleged prophet. If there were questions about one's prophetic credentials it could be settled by divine confirmation, as indeed it was on numerous occasions throughout Scripture (Exodus 4; Numbers 16–17; 1 Kings 18; Mark 2; Acts 5; *see* Miracles in the Bible).

There were true and false prophets (Matt. 7:15), so it was necessary to have divine confirmation of the true ones. Moses was given miraculous powers to prove his call (Exod. 4:1–9). Elijah triumphed over the false prophets of Baal by a supernatural act (1 Kings 18). Jesus was attested to by miracles and signs God performed through him (Acts 2:22). As to the apostles' message, "God was also bearing witness with them, both by signs and wonders and by various miracles and by gifts of the Holy Spirit according to his own will" (Heb. 2:4). Paul gave testimony of his apostleship to the Corinthians, declaring, "the signs of a true apostle were performed among you with all perseverance, by signs and wonders and miracles" (2 Cor. 12:12; *see* Miracles, Apologetic Value of).

Does the message tell the truth about God? Only immediate contemporaries had access to the supernatural confirmation of the prophet's message. Other believers in distant places and subsequent times had to depend on other tests. One such test was the *authenticity* of a book. That is, does the book tell the truth about God and his world as known from previous revelations? God cannot contradict himself (2 Cor. 1:17–18), nor can he utter what is false (Heb. 6:18). No book with false claims can be the Word of God. Moses stated the principle about prophets generally that

> If a prophet or a dreamer of dreams arises among you and gives you a sign or a wonder, and the sign or wonder comes true, concerning which he spoke to you, saying, "Let us go after other gods (whom you have not known) and let us serve them," you shall not listen to the words of that prophet or that dreamer of dreams. [Deut. 13:1–3]

So any teaching about God contrary to what his people already knew to be true was to be rejected. Furthermore, any predictions made about the world which failed to come true indicated that a prophet's words should be rejected. As Moses said to Israel,

> And you may say in your heart, "How shall we know the word which the Lord has not spoken?" When a prophet speaks in the name of the Lord, if the thing does not come about or come true, that is the thing which the Lord has not spoken. The prophet has spoken it presumptuously; you shall not be afraid of him. [Deut. 18:21–22]

A prophet who made such false claims might be stoned. The Lord said, "The prophet who shall speak a word presumptuously in my name which I have not commanded him to speak, or which he shall speak in the name of other gods, that prophet shall die" (Deut. 18:20). That kind of punishment assured no repeat performance by that prophet, and it gave other prophets pause before they said, "Thus says the Lord."

Truth in itself does not make a book canonical. This is more a test of *inauthenticity* of a book, rather than canonicity. It is a negative test that could eliminate books from the canon. The Bereans used this principle when they searched the Scriptures to see whether Paul's teaching was true (Acts 17:11). If the preaching of the apostle did not accord with the teaching of the Old Testament canon, it could not be of God.

Much of the *Apocrypha* was rejected because it was not authentic. The Jewish Fathers and early Christian Fathers rejected, or considered second-rate, these books because they had historical inaccuracies and even moral incongruities. The Reformers rejected some because of what they considered to be heretical teaching, such as praying for the dead, which 2 Maccabees 12:45 supports. The apostle John strongly urged that all purported "truth" be tested by the known standard before it be received (1 John 4:1–6).

The test of authenticity was the reason James and Jude have been doubted. Some have thought Jude inauthentic because it may quote inauthentic pseudepigraphical books (Jude 9, 14; see Jerome, 4). Martin Luther questioned the canonicity of James because it lacks an obvious focus on the cross. Martin Luther thought the book appeared to teach salvation by works. Careful study has cleared James of these charges, and even Luther came to feel better about them. Historically and uniformly, Jude and James have been vindicated and their canonicity recognized after they have been harmonized with the rest of Scripture.

Did it come with the power of God? Another test for canonicity is a book's power to edify and equip believers. This requires the power of God. The Fathers believed the Word of God to be "living and active" (Heb. 4:12) and consequently ought to have a transforming force (2 Tim. 3:17; 1 Peter 1:23). If the message of a book did not effect its stated goal, if it did not have the power to change a life, then God was apparently not behind its message. A *message* of God would certainly be backed by the *might* of *God*. The Fathers believed that the Word of God accomplishes its purpose (Isa. 55:11).

Paul applied this principle to the Old Testament when he wrote to Timothy, "And that from a child thou hast known the holy scriptures, which are able to make thee wise unto salvation" (2 Tim. 3:15 KJV). If it is of God, it will work—it will come to pass. This simple test was given by Moses to try the truth of a prophet's prediction (Deut. 18:20ff.). If what was foretold did not materialize, it was not from God.

On this basis, heretical literature and good noncanonical apostolic literature was rejected from the canon. Even those books whose teaching was spiritual, but whose message was at best only devotional, were deemed noncanonical. Such is the case for most literature written in the apostolic and subapostolic periods. There is a tremendous difference between the canonical books of the New Testament and other religious writings of the apostolic period. "There is not the same freshness and originality, depth and clearness. And this is no wonder, for it means the transition from truth given by infallible inspiration to truth produced by fallible pioneers" (Berkhof, 42). The noncanonical books lacked power; they were devoid of the dynamic aspects found in inspired Scripture. They did not come with the power of God.

Books whose edifying power was questioned included Song of Solomon (or Song of Songs) and Ecclesiastes. Could a book that is erotically sensual or skeptical be from God? Obviously not; as long as these books were thought of in that manner, they could not be considered canonical. Eventually, the messages of these books were seen as spiritual, so the books themselves were accepted. The principle, nevertheless, was applied impartially. Some books passed the test; others failed. No book that lacked essential edificational or practical characteristics was considered canonical.

Was it accepted by the people of God? A prophet of God was confirmed by an act of God (miracle) and was recognized as a spokesman by the people who received the message. Thus, the seal of canonicity depended on whether the book was accepted by the people. This does not mean that everybody in the community to which the prophetic message was addressed accepted it as divinely authoritative. Prophets (1 Kings 17–19; 2 Chron. 36:11–16) and apostles (Galatians 1) were rejected by some. However, believers in the prophet's community acknowledged the prophetic nature of the message, as did other contemporary believers familiar with the prophet. This acceptance had two stages: initial acceptance and subsequent recognition.

Initial acceptance of a book by the people to whom it was addressed was crucial. Paul said of the Thessalonians, "We also constantly thank God that when you received from us the word of God's message, you accepted it not as the word of men, but for what it really is, the word of God" (1 Thess. 2:13). Whatever subsequent debate there may have been about a book's place, the people in the best position to know its prophetic credentials were those who knew the writer. The definitive evidence is that which attests acceptance by contemporary believers.

There is ample evidence that books were immediately accepted into the canon. Moses' books were immediately placed with the ark of the covenant (Deut. 31:26). Joshua's writing was added (Josh. 24:26). Following were books by Samuel and others (1 Sam. 10:25). Daniel had a copy of Moses and the Prophets, which included the book of his contemporary Jeremiah (Dan. 9:2, 10–11). Paul quoted the Gospel of Luke as "Scripture" (1 Tim. 5:18). Peter had a collection of Paul's "letter" (2 Peter 3:16). Indeed, the apostles exhorted that their letters be read and circulated among the churches (Col. 4:16; 1 Thess. 5:27; Rev. 1:3).

Some have argued that Proverbs 25:1 shows an exception. It suggests that some of Solomon's proverbs may not have been collected into the canon during his lifetime. Rather, "the men of Hezekiah . . . transcribed" more of Solomon's proverbs. It is possible that these additional proverbs (chaps. 25–29) were not officially presented to the believing community during Solomon's life, perhaps because of his later moral decline. However, since they were *authentic* Solomonic proverbs there was no reason not to later present and at that time immediately accept them as authoritative. In this case Proverbs 25–29 would not be an exception to the canonic rule of immediate acceptance.

It is also possible that these later chapters of Proverbs were presented and accepted as authoritative during Solomon's lifetime. Support for this view can be derived from the fact that the Solomonic part of the book may have been compiled in three sections, which begin at 1:1, 10:1, and 25:1. Perhaps these were preserved on separate scrolls. The word *also* in Proverbs 25:1 can refer to the fact that Hezekiah's men also copied this last section (scroll) along with the first two sections (scrolls). All three scrolls would have been immediately accepted as divinely authoritative and were only copied afresh by the scholars.

Since Scripture of every time period is referred to in later biblical writings, and each book is quoted by some early church Father or listed in some canon, there is ample evidence that there was continuing agreement within the covenant community concerning the canon. That certain books were written by prophets in biblical times and are in the canon now argues for their canonicity. Along with evidence for a continuity of belief, this argues strongly that the idea of canonicity existed from the beginning. The presence of a book in the canon down through the centuries is evidence that it was known by the contemporaries of the prophet who wrote it to be genuine and authoritative, despite the fact that succeeding generations lacked definitive knowledge of the author's prophetic credentials.

Later debate about certain books should not cloud their initial acceptance by immediate contemporaries of the prophets. True canonicity was *determined* by God when he directed the prophet to write it, and it was immediately *discovered* by the people addressed.

Technically speaking, the discussion about certain books in later centuries was not a question of *canonicity* but of *authenticity* or *genuineness*. Because later readers had neither access to the writer nor direct evidence of supernatural confirmation, they had to rely on historical testimony. Once they were convinced by the evidence that books were written by accredited spokespeople for God, the books were accepted by the church universal. But the decisions of church councils in the fourth and fifth centuries did not determine the canon, nor did they first discover or recognize it. In no sense was the authority of the canonical books contingent upon the late church councils. All the councils did was to give *later, broader,* and *final* recognition to the facts that God had inspired the books, and the people of God had accepted them.

Several centuries went by before all the books in the canon were recognized. Communication and transportation were slow, so it took longer for the believers in the West to become fully aware of the evidence for books that had circulated first in the East, and vice versa. Prior to 313 the church faced frequent persecution that did not allow leisure for research, reflection, and recognition. As soon as that was possible, it was only a short time before there was general recognition of all canonical books by the regional councils of Hippo (393) and Carthage (397). There was no great need for precision until a dispute arose. Marcion published his gnostic canon, with only Luke and ten of Paul's Epistles, in the middle of the second century. Spurious gospels and epistles appeared throughout the second and third centuries. Since those books claimed divine authority, the universal church had to define the limits of God's authentic, inspired canon that already was known.

Applying Principles of Canonicity. Lest the impression be given that these principles were explicitly and mechanically applied by some commission, some explanation is needed. Just how did the principles operate in the consciousness of the early Christian church? Although the issue of the discovery of the canon center about the Old and New Testaments alike, J. N. D. Kelly discusses these principles as they apply to the New Testament canon. He writes,

> The main point to be observed is that the fixation of the finally agreed list of books, and of the order in which they were to be arranged, was the result of a very gradual process. . . . Three features of this process should be noted. First, the criterion which ultimately came to prevail was apostolicity. Unless a book could be shown to come from the pen of an apostle, or at least to have the authority of an apostle behind it, it was peremptorily rejected, however edifying or popular with the faithful it might be. Secondly, there were certain books which hovered for a long time on the fringe of the canon, but in the end failed to secure admission to it, usually because they lacked this indisputable stamp. . . . Thirdly, some of the books which were later included had to wait a considerable time before achieving universal recognition. . . . By gradual stages, however, the Church both in East and West arrived at a common mind as to its sacred books. The first official document which prescribes the twenty-seven books of our new Testament as alone canonical is Athanasius's Easter letter for the year 367, but the process was not everywhere complete until at least a century and a half later. [Kelly, 59–60]

Some Principles Are Implicit While Others Are Explicit. All criteria of inspiration are necessary to demonstrate the canonicity of each book. The five characteristics must at least be implicitly present, though some of them are more dominant than others. For example, the dynamic equipping power of God is more obvious in the New Testament Epistles than in the Old Testament historical narratives. "Thus-says-the-Lord" authority is more apparent in the Prophets than in the poetry. That is not to say that authority isn't in the poetic sections, nor a dynamic in the redemptive history. It does mean the Fathers did not always find all of the principles explicitly operating.

Some Principles Are More Important Than Others. Some criteria of inspiration are more important than are others, in that the presence of one implies another, or is a key to others. For example, if a book is authoritatively from God, it will be dynamic—accompanied by God's transforming power. In fact, when authority was unmistakably present, the other characteristics of inspiration were automatically assumed. Among New Testament books the proof of apostolicity, its prophetic nature, was often considered a guarantee of inspiration (Warfield, 415). If propheticity could be verified, this alone established the book. Generally speaking, the church Fathers were only explicitly concerned with apostolicity and authenticity. The edifying characteristics and universal acceptance of a book were assumed unless some doubt from the latter two questions forced a reexamination of the tests. This happened with 2 Peter and 2 John. Positive evidence for the first three principles emerged victorious.

The witness of the Holy Spirit. The recognition of canonicity was not a mere mechanical matter settled by a synod or ecclesiastical council. It was a providential process directed by the Spirit of God as he witnessed to the church about the reality of the Word of God (*see* Holy Spirit, Role in Apologetics). People could not identify the Word until the Holy Spirit opened their understanding. Jesus said, "My sheep hear my voice" (John 10:27). This is not to say that the Holy Spirit mystically spoke in visions to settle questions of canonicity. The witness of the Spirit convinced them of the reality that a God-breathed canon existed, not its extent (Sproul, 337–54). Faith joined science; objective principles were used, but the Fathers knew what writings had been used in their churches to change lives and teach hearts by the Holy Spirit. This subjective testimony joined the objective evidence in confirming what was God's Word.

Tests for canonicity were not mechanical means to measure the amount of inspired literature, nor did the Holy Spirit say, "This book or passage is inspired; that one is not." That would be disclosure, not discovery. The Holy Spirit providentially guided the examination process and gave witness to the people as they read or heard.

Conclusion. It is important to distinguish between the *determination* and the *discovery* of canonicity. God is solely responsible for determining; God's people are responsible for discovery. That a book is canonical is due to divine *inspiration*. How it is known to be canonical is due to a process of human recognition. Was a book (1) written by a spokesperson for God, (2) who was confirmed by an act of God, (3) told the truth (4) in the power of God and (5) was accepted by the people of God? If a book clearly had the first mark, canonicity was often assumed. Contemporaries of a prophet or apostle made the initial confirmation. Later church Fathers sorted out the profusion of religious literature to officially recognize what books were divinely inspired in the manner of which Paul speaks in 2 Timothy 3:16.

Sources

R. Beckwith, *The Old Testament Canon of the New Testament Church and Its Background in Early Judaism*
L. Berkhof, *The History of Christian Doctrines*
Eusebius. *Ecclesiastical History*, Loeb ed.
L. Gaussen, *Theopnesustia*
N. L. Geisler and W. E. Nix, *General Introduction to the Bible*
Jerome. *Lives of Illustrious Men*
J. N. D. Kelly, *Early Christian Doctrines*
J. P. Lange, *Commentary on the Holy Scriptures*
H. C. Leupold, *Exposition of Ecclesiastes*

R. C. Sproul, "The Internal Testimony of the Holy Spirit," in N. L. Geisler, ed. *Inerrancy*
B. B. Warfield, *The Inspiration and Authority of the Bible*

Bible Criticism. *Criticism* as applied to the Bible simply means the exercise of judgment. Both conservative and nonconservative scholars engage in two forms of biblical criticism: *lower criticism* deals with the text; *higher criticism* treats the source of the text. Lower criticism attempts to determine what the original text said, and the latter asks who said it and when, where, and why it was written.

Most controversies surrounding Bible criticism involve higher criticism. Higher criticism can be divided into negative (destructive) and positive (constructive) types. Negative criticism denies the authenticity of much of the biblical record. Usually an antisupernatural presupposition (*see* MIRACLES, ARGUMENTS AGAINST; MIRACLES, MYTH AND) is employed in this critical approach. Further, negative criticism often approaches the Bible with distrust equivalent to a "guilty-until-proven-innocent" bias.

Negative New Testament Criticism. Historical, Source, Form, Tradition, and *Redaction* methods (and combinations thereof) are the approaches with the worst record for bias. Any of these, used to advance an agenda of skepticism, with little or no regard for truth, undermine the Christian apologetic.

Historical Criticism. Historical criticism is a broad term that covers techniques to date documents and traditions, to verify events reported in those documents, and to use the results in historiography to reconstruct and interpret. The French Oratorian priest Richard Simon published a series of books, beginning in 1678, in which he applied a rationalistic, critical approach to studying the Bible. This was the birth of historical-critical study of the Bible, although not until Johann Gottfried Eichhorn (1752–1827) and Johann David Michaelis (1717–1791) was the modern historical-critical pattern set. They were influenced by the secular historical research of Barthold Georg Niebuhr (1776–1831; *Romische Geschichte,* 1811–12), Leopold von Ranke (1795–1886; *Geshichte der romanischen und germanischen Volker von 1494–1535*), and others, who developed and refined the techniques. Among those influenced was Johann Christian Konrad von Hofmann (1810–1877). He combined elements of Friedrich Schelling (1775–1854), Friedrich Schleiermacher (1768–1834), and orthodox Lutheranism with historical categories and the critical methods to make a biblical-theological synthesis. This model stressed "superhistorical history," "holy history," or "salvation history" *(Heilsgeschichte)*—the sorts of history that need not be literally true. His ideas and terms influenced Karl Barth (1886–1968), Rudolf Bultmann (1884–1976), and others in the twentieth century. Toward the close of the nineteenth century, capable orthodox scholars challenged "destructive criticism" and its rationalistic theology.

Among more conservative scholars were George Salmon (1819–1904), Theodor von Zahn (1838–1933), and R. H. Lightfoot (1883–1953), who used criticism methods as the bases for a constructive criticism. This constructive criticism manifests itself most openly when it considers such matters as miracles, virgin birth of Jesus, and bodily resurrection of Christ (*see* RESURRECTION, EVIDENCE FOR). Historical criticism is today taken for granted in biblical studies. Much recent work in historical criticism manifests rationalistic theology that at the same time claims to uphold traditional Christian doctrine. As a result, it has given rise to such developments as source criticism.

Source Criticism. Source criticism, also known as literary criticism, attempts to discover and define literary sources used by the biblical writers. It seeks to uncover underlying literary sources, classify types of literature, and answer questions relating to authorship, unity, and date of Old and New Testament materials (Geisler, 436). Some literary critics tend to decimate the biblical text, pronounce certain books inauthentic, and reject the very notion of verbal inspiration. Some scholars have carried their rejection of authority to the point that they have modified the idea of the canon (e.g., with regard to pseudonymity) to accommodate their own conclusions (ibid., 436). Nevertheless, this difficult but important undertaking can be a valuable aid to biblical interpretation, since it has bearing on the historical value of biblical writings. In addition, careful literary criticism can prevent historical misinterpretations of the biblical text.

Source criticism in the New Testament over the past century has focused on the so-called "Synoptic problem," since it relates to difficulties surrounding attempts to devise a scheme of literary dependence that accounts for similarities and dissimilarities among the Synoptic Gospels of Matthew, Mark, and Luke. Theories tend to work with the idea of a now-absent *Q* or *Quelle* ("Source") used by the three evangelists, who wrote in various sequences, with the second depending on the first and the third on the other two. These theories were typical forerunners of the Two-Source theory advanced by B. H. Streeter (1874–1937), which asserted the priority of Mark and eventually gained wide acceptance among New Testament scholars. Streeter's arguments have been questioned, and his thesis has been challenged by others. Eta Linnemann, once a student of Bultmann and a critic, has written a strong critique of her former position in which she uses source analysis to conclude that no synoptic problem in fact exists. She insists that each

Gospel writer wrote an independent account based on personal experience and individual information. She wrote: "As time passes, I become more and more convinced that to a considerable degree New Testament criticism as practiced by those committed to historical-critical theology does not deserve to be called science" (Linnemann, 9). Elsewhere she writes, "The Gospels are not works of literature that creatively reshape already finished material after the manner in which Goethe reshaped the popular book about Dr. Faust" (ibid., 104). Rather, "Every Gospel presents a complete, unique testimony. It owes its existence to direct or indirect eyewitnesses" (ibid., 194).

Form Criticism. Form criticism studies literary forms, such as essays, poems, and myths, since different writings have different forms. Often the form of a piece of literature can tell a great deal about the nature of a literary piece, its writer, and its social context. Technically this is termed its "life setting" (*Sitz im Leben*). The classic liberal position is the documentary or J-E-P-D Pentateuchal source analysis theory established by Julius Wellhausen (1844–1918) and his followers (*see* PENTATEUCH, MOSAIC AUTHORSHIP OF). They actually attempted to mediate between traditionalism and skepticism, dating Old Testament books in a less supernaturalistic manner by applying the "documentary theory." These documents are identified as the "Jahwist" or Jehovistic (J), dated in the ninth century B.C., the Elohistic (E), eighth century, the Deuteronomic (D), from about the time of Josiah (640–609), and the Priestly (P), from perhaps the fifth century B.C. So attractive was the evolutionary concept in literary criticism that the source theory of Pentateuchal origins began to prevail over all opposition. A mediating position of some aspects of the theory was expressed by C. F. A. Dillman (1823–1894), Rudolph Kittle (1853–1929), and others. Opposition to the documentary theory was expressed by Franz Delitzsch (1813–1890), who rejected the hypothesis outright in his commentary on Genesis, William Henry Green (1825–1900), James Orr (1844–1913), A. H. Sayce (1845–1933), Wilhelm Möller, Eduard Naville, Robert Dick Wilson (1856–1930), and others (see Harrison, 239–41; Archer; Pfeiffer). Sometimes form-critical studies are marred by doctrinaire assumptions, including that early forms must be short and later forms longer, but, in general, form criticism has been of benefit to biblical interpretation. Form criticism has been most profitably used in the study of the Psalms (Wenham, "History and the Old Testament," 40).

These techniques were introduced into New Testament study of the Gospels as *Formgeschichte* ("form history") or *form criticism*. Following in the tradition of Heinrich Paulus and Wilhelm De Wette (1780–1849), among others, scholars at Tübingen built on the foundation of source criticism theory. They advocated the priority of Mark as the earliest Gospel and multiple written sources. William Wrede (1859–1906) and other form critics sought to eliminate the chronological-geographical framework of the Synoptic Gospels and to investigate the twenty-year period of oral traditions between the close of New Testament events and the earliest written accounts of those events. They attempted to classify this material into "forms" of oral tradition and to discover the historical situation (*Sitz im Leben*) within the early church that gave rise to these forms. These units of tradition are usually assumed to reflect more of the life and teaching of the early church than the life and teaching of the historical Jesus. Forms in which the units are cast are clues to their relative historical value.

The fundamental assumption of form criticism is typified by Martin Dibelius (1883–1947) and Bultmann. By creating new words and deeds of Jesus as the situation demanded, the evangelists arranged the units or oral tradition and created artificial contexts to serve their own purposes. In challenging the authorship, date, structure, and style of other New Testament books, destructive critics arrived at similar conclusions. To derive a fragmented New Testament theology, they rejected Pauline authorship for all Epistles traditionally ascribed to him except Romans, 1 Corinthians, 2 Corinthians, and Galatians (Hodges, 339–48).

Thoroughgoing form critics hold two basic assumptions: (1) The early Christian community had little or no genuine biographical interest or integrity, so it created and transformed oral tradition to meet its own needs. (2) The evangelists were compiler-editors of individual, isolated units of tradition that they arranged and rearranged without regard for historical reality (see Thomas and Gundry, *A Harmony of the Gospels* [281–82], who identify Dibelius, Bultmann, Burton S. Easton, R. H. Lightfoot, Vincent Taylor, and D. E. Nineham as preeminent New Testament form critics).

Tradition Criticism. Tradition criticism is primarily concerned with the history of traditions before they were recorded in writing. The stories of the patriarchs, for example, were probably passed down through generations by word of mouth until they were written as a continuous narrative. These oral traditions may have been changed over the long process of transmission. It is of great interest to the biblical scholar to know what changes were made and how the later tradition, now enshrined in a literary source, differs from the earliest oral version.

Tradition criticism is less certain or secure than literary criticism because it begins where literary criticism leaves off, with conclusions that are in themselves uncertain. It is difficult to check the hypotheses about development of an oral tradition (Wenham, ibid., 40–41). Even more tenuous is the "liturgical tradition" enunciated by S. Mowinckel and his Scandinavian associates, who argue that literary origins were related to preexilic sanctuary rituals and sociological phenomena. An offshoot of the liturgical approach is the "myth and ritual" school of S. H. Hooke, which argues that a distinctive set of rituals and myths were common to all Near Eastern peoples, including the Hebrews. Both of these approaches use Babylonian festival analogies to support their variations on the classical literary-critical and tradition-critical themes (Harrison, 241).

Form criticism is closely aligned with tradition criticism in New Testament studies. A review of many of the basic assumptions in view of the New Testament text have been made by Oscar Cullmann, *The Christology of the New Testament*, and I. Howard Marshall, *The Origins of New Testament Christology* and *I Believe in the Historical Jesus*. Also see the discussions in Brevard S. Childs, *Introduction to the Old Testament as Scripture* and *Introduction to the New Testament as Canon*, and Gerhard Hasel, *Old Testament Theology: Basic Issues in the Current Debate* and *New Testament Theology: Basic Issues in the Current Debate*.

Redaction Criticism. *Redaction criticism is more closely associated with the text than is traditional criticism. As a result, it is less open to the charge of subjective speculation. Redaction (editorial) critics can achieve absolute certainty only when all the sources are used that were at the disposal of the redactor (editor), since the task is to determine how a redactor compiled sources, what was omitted, what was added, and what particular bias was involved in the process. At best, the critic has only some of the sources available, such as the books of Kings used by the writers of Chronicles. Elsewhere, in both the Old and the New Testaments, the sources must be reconstructed out of the edited work itself. Then redaction criticism becomes much less certain as a literary device (Wenham, "Gospel Origins," 439).

Redaction critics tend to favor a view that biblical books were written much later and by different authors than the text relates. Late theological editors attached names out of history to their works for the sake of prestige and credibility. In Old and New Testament studies this view arose from historical criticism, source criticism, and form criticism. As a result, it adopts many of the same presuppositions, including the documentary hypothesis in the Old Testament, and the priority of Mark in the New Testament.

Evaluation. As already noted, higher criticism can be helpful as long as critics are content with analysis based on what can be objectively known or reasonably theorized. Real criticism doesn't begin its work with the intent to subvert the authority and teaching of Scripture.

Kinds of Criticism Contrasted. However, much of modern biblical criticism springs from unbiblical philosophical presuppositions exposed by Gerhard Maier in *The End of the Historical Critical Method*. These presuppositions incompatible with Christian faith include deism, materialism, skepticism, agnosticism, Hegelian idealism, and existentialism. Most basic is a prevailing naturalism (antisupernaturalism) that is intuitively hostile to any document containing miracle stories (*see* Miracles in the Bible; Miracles, Myth and). This naturalistic bias divides negative (destructive) from positive (constructive) higher criticism:

	Positive Criticism (Constructive)	**Negative Criticism (Destructive)**
Basis	Supernaturalistic	Naturalistic
Rule	Text is "innocent until proven guilty"	Text is "guilty until proven innocent"
Result	Bible is wholly true	Bible is partly true
Final Authority	Word of God	Mind of man
Role of Reason	To discover truth (rationality)	To determine truth (rationalism)

Some of the negative presuppositions call for scrutiny, especially as they relate to the Gospel record. This analysis is especially relevant to source criticism, form criticism, and redaction criticism, as these methods challenge the genuineness, authenticity, and consequently the divine authority of the Bible. This kind of biblical criticism is unfounded.

Unscholarly bias. It imposes its own antisupernatural bias on the documents. The originator of modern negative criticism, Benedict *Spinoza, for example, declared that Moses did not write the Pentateuch, nor Daniel the whole book of Daniel, nor did any miracle recorded actually occur. Miracles, he claimed, are scientifically and rationally impossible.

In the wake of Spinoza, negative critics concluded that Isaiah did not write the whole book of Isaiah. That would have involved supernatural predictions (including knowing the name of King Cyrus) over 100 years in advance (*see* Prophecy as Proof of the Bible). Likewise, negative critics concluded Daniel could not have been written until 165 B.C. That late authorship placed it after the fulfillment of its detailed description of world governments and rulers down to Antiochus IV Epiphanes (d. 163 B.C.). Supernatural predictions of coming events was not considered an option. The same naturalistic bias was applied to the New Testament by David Strauss (1808–1874), Albert Schweitzer (1875–1965), and Bultmann, with the same devastating results.

The foundations of this antisupernaturalism crumbled with evidence that the universe began with a big bang (*see* EVOLUTION, COSMIC). Even agnostics such as Robert Jastrow (Jastrow, 18), speak of "supernatural" forces at work (Kenny, 66; *see* AGNOSTICISM; MIRACLE; MIRACLES, ARGUMENTS AGAINST), so it is sufficient to note here that, with the demise of modern antisupernaturalism, there is no philosophical basis for destructive criticism.

Inaccurate view of authorship. Negative criticism either neglects or minimizes the role of apostles and eyewitnesses who recorded the events. Of the four Gospel writers, Matthew, Mark, and John were definitely eyewitnesses of the events they report. Luke was a contemporary and careful historian (Luke 1:1–4; see Acts). Indeed, every book of the New Testament was written by a contemporary or eyewitness of Christ. Even such critics as the "Death-of-God" theologian John A. T. Robinson admit that the Gospels were written between 40 and 65 (Robinson, 352), during the life of eyewitnesses.

But if the basic New Testament documents were composed by eyewitnesses, then much of destructive criticism fails. It assumes the passage of much time while "myths" developed. Studies have revealed that it takes two generations for a myth to develop (Sherwin-White, 190).

What Jesus really said. It wrongly assumes that the New Testament writers did not distinguish between their own words and those of Jesus. That a clear distinction was made between Jesus' words and those of the Gospel writers is evident from the ease by which a "red letter" edition of the New Testament can be made. Indeed, the apostle Paul is clear to distinguish his own words from those of Jesus (see Acts 20:35; 1 Cor. 7:10, 12, 25). So is John the apostle in the Apocalypse (see Rev. 1:8, 11, 17b–20; 2:1f.; 22:7, 12–16, 20b). In view of this care, the New Testament critic is unjustified in assuming without substantive evidence that the Gospel record does not actually report what Jesus said and did.

Myths? It incorrectly assumes that the New Testament stories are like folklore and myth. There is a vast difference between the simple New Testament accounts of miracles and the embellished myths that did arise during the second and third centuries A.D., as can be seen by comparing the accounts. New Testament writers explicitly disavow myths. Peter declared: "For we did not follow cleverly devised tales (mythos) when we made known to you the power and coming of our Lord Jesus Christ, but we were eyewitnesses of his majesty" (2 Peter 1:16). Paul also warned against belief in myths (1 Tim. 1:4; 4:7; 2 Tim. 4:4; Titus 1:14).

One of the most telling arguments against the myth view was given by C. S. Lewis:

> First then, whatever these men may be as Biblical critics, I distrust them as critics. They seem to lack literary judgment, to be imperceptive about the very quality of the texts they are reading . . . If he tells me that something in a Gospel is legend or romance, I want to know how many legends and romances he had read, how well his palate is trained in detecting them by the flavour; not how many years he has spent on that Gospel . . . I have been reading poems, romances, vision-literature, legends, myths all my life. I know what they are like. I know that not one of them is like this. [Lewis, 154–55]

Creators or recorders? Unfounded higher criticism undermines the integrity of the New Testament writers by claiming that Jesus never said (or did) what the Gospels claim. Even some who call themselves evangelical have gone so far as to claim that what "'Jesus said' or 'Jesus did' need not always mean that in history Jesus said or did what follows, but sometimes may mean that in the account at least partly constructed by Matthew himself Jesus said or did what follows" (Gundry, 630). This clearly undermines confidence in the truthfulness of the Gospels and the accuracy of the events they report. On this critical view the Gospel writers become creators of the events, not recorders.

Of course, every careful biblical scholar knows that one Gospel writer does not always use the same words in reporting what Jesus said as does another. However, they always convey the same meaning. They do select, summarize, and paraphrase, but they do not distort. A comparison of the parallel reports in the Gospels is ample evidence of this.

There is no substantiation for the claim of one New Testament scholar that Matthew created the Magi story (Matt. 2) out of the turtledove story (of Luke 2). For according to Robert Gundry, Matthew "changes the sacrificial slaying of 'a pair of turtledoves or two young pigeons,' at the presentation of the baby Jesus in the Temple (Luke 2:24; cf. Lev. 12:6–8), into Herod's slaughtering of the babies in Bethlehem" (ibid., 34–35). Such a view not only degrades the integrity of the Gospel writers but the authenticity and authority of the Gospel record. It is also silly.

Neither is there support for Paul K. Jewett, who went so far as to assert (Jewett, 134–35) that what the apostle Paul affirmed in 1 Corinthians 11:3 is wrong. If Paul is in error, then the time-honored truth that "what the Bible says, God says" is not so. Indeed, if Jewett is right, then even when one discovers what the author of Scripture is affirming, he is little closer to knowing the truth of God (cf. Gen. 3:1). If "what the Bible says, God says" (*see* BIBLE, EVIDENCE FOR) is not so, then the divine authority of all Scripture is worthless.

The early church's stake in truth. That the early church had no real biographical interest is highly improbable. The New Testament writers, impressed as they were with the belief that Jesus was the long-promised Messiah, the Son of the living God (Matt. 16:16–18), had great motivation to accurately record what he actually said and did.

To say otherwise is contrary to their own clear statements. John claimed that "Jesus did" the things recorded in his Gospel (John 21:25). Elsewhere John said "What . . . we have heard, we have seen with our eyes, we beheld and our hands handled . . . we proclaim to you also" (1 John 1:1–2).

Luke clearly manifests an intense biographical interest by the earliest Christian communities when he wrote: "Inasmuch as many have undertaken to compile an account of the things accomplished among us, just as those who from the beginning were eyewitnesses and servants of the Word have handed them down to us, it seemed fitting for me as well, having investigated everything carefully from the beginning, to write it out for you in consecutive order, most excellent Theophilus; so that you might know the exact truth about the things you have been taught" (Luke 1:1–4). To claim, as the critics do, that the New Testament writers lacked interest in recording real history is implausible.

The work of the Holy Spirit. Such assumptions also neglect or deny the role of the Holy Spirit in activating the memories of the eyewitnesses. Much of the rejection of the Gospel record is based on the assumption that the writers could not be expected to remember sayings, details, and events twenty or forty years after the events. For Jesus died in 33, and the first Gospel records probably came (at latest) between 50 and 60 (Wenham, "Gospel Origins," 112–34).

Again the critic is rejecting or neglecting the clear statement of Scripture. Jesus promised his disciples, "The Helper, the Holy Spirit, whom the Father will send in My name, he will teach you all things, and bring to your remembrance all that I said to you" (John 14:26).

So even on the unlikely assumption that no one recorded anything Jesus said during his lifetime or immediately after, the critics would have us believe that eyewitnesses whose memories were later supernaturally activated by the Holy Spirit did not accurately record what Jesus did and said. It seems far more likely that the first-century eyewitnesses were right and the twentieth-century critics are wrong, than the reverse.

Guidelines for Biblical Criticism. Of course biblical scholarship need not be destructive. But the biblical message must be understood in its theistic (supernatural) context and its actual historical and grammatical setting. Positive guidelines for evangelical scholarship are set forth in "The Chicago Statement on Biblical Hermeneutics" (see Geisler, *Summit II: Hermeneutics,* 10–13. Also Radmacher and Preus, *Hermeneutics, Inerrancy, and the Bible,* esp. 881–914). It reads in part as follows:

> Article XIII. WE AFFIRM that awareness of the literary categories, formal and stylistic, of the various parts of Scripture is essential for proper exegesis, and hence we value genre criticism as one of the many disciplines of biblical study. WE DENY that generic categories which negate the historicity may rightly be imposed on biblical narratives which present themselves as factual.
>
> Article XIV. WE AFFIRM that the biblical record of events, discourses and sayings, though presented in a variety of appropriate literary forms, corresponds to historical fact. WE DENY that any such event, discourse or saying reported in Scripture was invented by the biblical writers or by the traditions they incorporated.
>
> Article XV. WE AFFIRM the necessity of interpreting the Bible according to its literal, or normal sense. The literal sense is the grammatical-historical sense, that is, the meaning which the writer expressed. Interpretation according to the literal sense will account for all figures of speech and literary forms found in the text. WE DENY the legitimacy of any approach to Scripture that attributes to it meaning which the literal sense does not support.
>
> Article XVI. WE AFFIRM that legitimate critical techniques should be used in determining the canonical text and its meaning. WE DENY the legitimacy of allowing any method of biblical criticism to question the truth or integrity of the writer's expressed meaning, or of any other scriptural teaching.

Redaction versus Editing. There are important differences between destructive redaction and constructive editing. No knowledgeable scholars deny that a certain amount of editing occurred over the biblical text's thousands of years of history. This legitimate editing, however, must be distinguished from illegitimate redaction which the negative critics allege. The negative critics have failed to present any convincing evidence that the kind of redaction they believe in has ever happened to the biblical text.

The following chart contrasts the two views.

Legitimate Editing	Illegitimate Redacting
Changes in form	Changes in content
Scribal changes	Substantive changes
Changes in the text	Changes in the truth

The redaction model of the canon confuses legitimate scribal activity, involving grammatical form, updating of names, and arrangement of prophetic material, with illegitimate redactive changes in actual content of a prophet's message. It confuses acceptable scribal transmission with unacceptable tampering. It confuses proper discussion of which text is earlier with improper discussion of how later writers changed the truth of texts. There is no evidence that any significant illegitimate redactive changes have occurred since the Bible was first put in writing. On the contrary, all evidence supports a careful transmission in all substantial matters and in most details. No diminution of basic truth has occurred from the original writings to the Bibles in our hands today (*see* OLD TESTAMENT MANUSCRIPTS; NEW TESTAMENT MANUSCRIPTS).

Sources

O. Cullmann, *The Christology of the New Testament*
W. R. Farmer, *The Synoptic Problem*
R. Gundry, *Matthew: A Commentary on His Literary and Theological Art*
G. Hasel, *New Testament Theology: Basic Issues in the Current Debate*
R. Jastrow, "A Scientist Caught between Two Faiths" in *CT*, 6 August 1982
P. Jewett, *Man as Male and Female*
E. Krentz, *The Historical-Critical Method*
C. S. Lewis, *Christian Reflections*
E. Linnemann, *Historical Criticism of the Bible*
———, *Is There a Synoptic Problem?*
G. M. Maier, *The End of the Historical Critical Method*
Marshall, I. H., *The Origins of New Testament Christology*
A. Q. Morton, and J. McLeman, *Christianity in the Computer Age*
E. D. Radmacher and R. D. Preus, *Hermeneutics, Inerrancy, and the Bible*
J. Robinson, *Redating the New Testament*
E. P. Sanders, *The Tendencies of the Synoptic Tradition*
A. N. Sherwin-White, *Roman Society and Roman Law in the New Testament*
B. H. Streeter, *The Four Gospels: A Study of Origins*
R. L. Thomas, "An Investigation of the Agreements between Matthew and Luke against Mark," *JETS* 19, (1976)
R. L. Thomas, "The Hermeneutics of Evangelical Redaction Criticism," *JETS* 29/4 (December 1986)
J. W. Wenham, "Gospel Origins," *TJ* 7, (1978)
———, "History and The Old Testament," *Bib. Sac.*, 124, 1967

Bible, Evidence for. The Bible claims to be and proves to be the Word of God. It was written by prophets of God, under the inspiration of God.

Written by Prophets of God. The biblical authors were prophets and apostles of God (*see* MIRACLES, APOLOGETIC VALUE OF; PROPHECY AS PROOF OF BIBLE). There are many designations for prophet, and these are informative about their role in producing Scripture. They are called:

1. A *man of God* (1 Kings 12:22), meaning chosenness.
2. A *servant of the Lord* (1 Kings 14:18), indicating faithfulness.
3. A *messenger of the Lord* (Isa. 42:19), showing mission.
4. A *seer* (*ro'eh*), or *beholder* (*hozeh*) (Isa. 30:9–10), revealing insight from God.
5. A *man of the Spirit* (Hosea 9:7 KJV; cf. Micah 3:8), noting spiritual indwelling.
6. A *watchman* (Ezek. 3:17), relating alertness for God.
7. A *prophet* (most frequently), marking a spokesman for God.

The work of a biblical prophet is described in vivid terms: "The Lord has spoken; who can but prophesy" (Amos 3:8). He is one who speaks "all the words which the Lord has spoken" (Exod. 4:30). God said to Moses of a prophet, "I will put my words in his mouth, and he shall speak to them all that I command him" (Deut. 18:18). He added, "You shall not add to the word which I command you, nor take away from it" (Deut. 4:2). Jeremiah was commanded: "This is what the LORD says: Stand in the courtyard of the LORD's house and speak to all the people. . . . Tell them everything I command you; do not omit a word" (Jer. 26:2).

A prophet was someone who said what God told him to say, no more and no less.

Moved by the Spirit of God. Throughout Scripture, the authors claimed to be under the direction of the Holy Spirit. David said, "The Spirit of the Lord spoke through me; his word was on my tongue" (2 Sam. 23:2). Peter, speaking of the whole Old Testament, added, "Prophecy never had its origin in the will of man, but men spoke from God as they were carried along by the Holy Spirit" (2 Peter 1:21).

Not all prophets were known by that term. David and Solomon were kings. But they were mouthpieces of God, and David is called a "prophet" in Acts 2:29–39. Moses was a lawgiver. He too was a prophet or spokesman for God (Deut. 18:18). Amos disclaimed the term "prophet," in that he was not a professional prophet, like Samuel and his "school of the prophets" (1 Sam. 19:20). Even if Amos was not a prophet by office, he was one by gift (cf. Amos 7:14). God used him to speak. Nor did all prophets speak in an explicit "Thus says the Lord" first-person style. Those who wrote historical narrative spoke in an implied "Thus *did* the Lord" approach. Their message was about the acts of God in relation to the people and their sins. In each case God made the prophet a channel through which to convey his message to us.

Breathed Out by God. Writing about the entire Old Testament canon, the apostle Paul declared:

"All Scripture is God-breathed and is useful for teaching, rebuking, correcting and training in righteousness, so that the man of God may be thoroughly equipped for every good work" (2 Tim. 3:16–17). Jesus described the Scriptures as the very "word that comes out of the mouth of God" (Matt. 4:4, 7, 10). They were written *by* men who spoke *from* God. Paul said his writings were "words . . . which the Holy Spirit teaches" (1 Cor. 2:13). As Jesus said to the Pharisees, "How is it then that David, *speaking by the Spirit*, calls him 'Lord'?" (Matt. 22:43, emphasis added).

What the Bible Says. The basic logic of the inerrancy of Scripture is offered in the article, Bible, Alleged errors in. That the Bible is God's inerrant Word is expressed in several ways in Scripture. One is the formula, "What the Bible says, God says." An Old Testament passage claims God said something, yet when this text is cited in the New Testament, the text tells us that the Scriptures said it. Sometimes the reverse is true. In the Old Testament it is said that the Bible records something. The New Testament declares that God said it. Consider this comparison:

What God Says . . .	**the Bible Says**
Genesis 12:3	Galatians 3:8
Exodus 9:16	Romans 9:17

What the Bible Says . . .	**God Says**
Genesis 2:24	Matthew 19:4,5
Psalm 2:1	Acts 4:24, 25
Psalm 2:7	Hebrews 3:7
Psalm 16:10	Acts 13:35
Psalm 95:7	Hebrews 3:7
Psalm 97:7	Hebrews 3:7
Psalm 104:4	Hebrews 3:7
Isaiah 55:3	Acts 13:34

Scripture's Claims. *"Thus Says the Lord."* Phrases such as "thus says the Lord" (for example, Isa. 1:11, 18; Jer. 2:3, 5), "God said" (Gen. 1:3), and "the Word of the Lord came" (Jer. 34:1; Ezek. 30:1) are used hundreds of times in Scripture to stress God's direct, verbal inspiration of what was written.

"The Word of God." At some points the Bible claims, forthrightly and unequivocally, to be "the Word of God." Referring to Old Testament commands, Jesus told the Jews of his day, "Thus you nullify the word of God for the sake of your tradition" (Matt. 15:6). Paul speaks of the Scriptures as "the oracles of God" (Rom. 3:2). Peter declares, "For you have been born again, not of perishable seed, but of imperishable, through the living and enduring word of God" (1 Peter 1:23). The writer of Hebrews affirms, "For the word of God is living and active. Sharper than any double-edged sword" (Heb. 4:12).

The Claim of Divine Authority. Other words or phrases used in Scripture entail the claim of God's authority. Jesus said the Bible will never pass away and is sufficient for faith and life (Luke 16:31; cf. 2 Tim. 3:16–17). He proclaimed that the Bible possesses divine inspiration (Matt. 22:43) and authority (Matt. 4:4, 7, 10). It has unity (Luke 24:27; John 5:39) and spiritual clarity (Luke 24:25).

The Extent of Its Biblical Authority. The extent of divine authority in Scripture includes:

1. all that is written—2 Timothy 3:16;
2. even the very words—Matthew 22:43; 1 Corinthians 2:13;
3. and tenses of verbs—Matthew 22:32; Galatians 3:16;
4. including even the smallest parts of words—Matthew 5:17, 18.

Even though the Bible was not verbally dictated by God, the result is as perfectly God's thoughts as if it had been. The Bible's authors claimed that God is the source of the very words, since he supernaturally superintended the process by which each human wrote, using their vocabulary and style to record his message (2 Peter 1:20–21).

Presented in Human Terms. Although the Bible claims to be the Word of God, it is also the words of human beings. It claims to be God's communication to people, in their own language and expressions.

First, every book in the Bible was the composition of *human writers*.

Second, the Bible manifests different *human literary styles*, from the mournful meter of lamentations to the exalted poetry of Isaiah, from the simple grammar of John to the complex Greek of Hebrews. Their choices of metaphors show that different writers used their own background and interests. James is interested in nature. Jesus uses urban metaphors, and Hosea those of rural life.

Third, the Bible manifests *human perspectives and emotions;* David spoke in Psalm 23 from a shepherd's perspective; Kings is written from a prophetic vantage point, and Chronicles from a priestly point of view; Acts manifests a historical interest and 2 Timothy a pastor's heart. Paul expressed grief over the Israelites who had rejected God (Rom. 9:2).

Fourth, the Bible reveals human thought patterns and processes, including reasoning (Romans) and memory (1 Cor. 1:14–16).

Fifth, writers of the Bible used human sources for information, including historical research (Luke 1:1–4) and noncanonical writings (Josh. 10:13; Acts 17:28; 1 Cor. 15:33; Titus 1:12; Jude 9, 14).

Original Text Is Without Errors, Not the Copies. As noted in the article Bible, Alleged Errors in, this does not mean that every copy and translation of the Bible is perfect. God breathed out the originals, not the copies, so inerrancy applies to the original text, not to every copy. God in his providence preserved the copies from substantial error. In fact, the degree of accuracy is greater than that of any other book from the ancient world, exceeding 99 percent (*see* NEW TESTAMENT MANUSCRIPTS; OLD TESTAMENT MANUSCRIPTS).

The Overall Evidence. Considered as a totality, evidences for the Bible's claim to be the Word of God are overwhelming.

The Testimony of Christ. Perhaps the strongest argument that the Bible is the Word of God is the testimony of Jesus (*see* BIBLE, JESUS' VIEW OF). Even non-Christians believe he was a good teacher. Muslims believe him to be a true prophet of God (*see* MUHAMMAD, ALLEGED DIVINE CALL OF). Christians, of course, insist that he is the Son of God as he claimed to be (Matt. 16:16–18; Mark 2:5–11; John 5:22–30; 8:58; 10:30; 20:28–29) and proved to be by numerous miracles (John 3:2; Acts 2:22; *see* MIRACLES IN THE BIBLE). Even the *Qur'an* admits that Jesus did miracles (*see* MUHAMMAD, ALLEGED MIRACLES OF), and that the Bible Christians used in Muhammad's day (A.D. seventh century) was accurate, since they were challenged to consult it to verify Muhammad's claims.

Jesus affirmed the Old Testament to be the Word of God and promised to guide his disciples to know all truth. Jesus claimed for the Bible:

1. Divine authority—Matthew 4:4, 7, 10
2. Indestructibility—Matthew 5:17–18
3. Infallibility or unbreakability—John 10:35
4. Ultimate supremacy—Matthew 15:3, 6
5. Factual inerrancy—Matthew 22:29; John 17:17
6. Historical reliability—Matthew 12:40, 24:37–38
7. Scientific accuracy—Matthew 19:4–5; John 3:12

The authority of Jesus confirms the authority of the Bible. If he is the Son of God (*see* CHRIST, DEITY OF), then the Bible is the Word of God. Indeed, if Jesus were merely a prophet, then the Bible still is confirmed to be the Word of God through his prophetic office. Only if one rejects the divine authority of Christ can he consistently reject the divine authority of the Scriptures. If Jesus is telling the truth, then it is true that the Bible is God's Word.

Manuscript Evidence. New Testament manuscripts are now available from the third and fourth centuries, and fragments that may date back as far as the late first century. From these through the medieval centuries, the text remained substantially the same. There are earlier and more manuscripts for the New Testament than for any other book from the ancient world. While most books exist in ten or twenty manuscripts dating from a thousand years or more after they were composed, one nearly entire manuscript, the *Chester Beatty Papyri,* was copied in about 250. Another manuscript with the majority of the New Testament, called *Vaticanus,* is dated to about 325.

The Biblical Authors. Whatever weaknesses they may have had, the biblical authors are universally presented in Scripture as scrupulously honest, and this lends credibility to their claim, for the Bible is not shy to admit the failures of his people.

They taught the highest standard of ethics, including the obligation to always tell the truth. Moses' law commanded: "You shall not give false testimony against your neighbor" (Exod. 20:16). Indeed, only one "whose walk is blameless and who does what is righteous, who speaks the truth from his heart" (Ps. 15:2), who "has no slander on his tongue, who does his neighbor no wrong and casts no slur on his fellow-man, [and] who despises a vile man but honors those who fear the LORD, who keeps his oath even when it hurts" were considered righteous.

The New Testament also exalts integrity, commanding: "Therefore each of you must put off falsehood and speak truthfully to his neighbor" (Eph. 4:25). The person who "loves and practices falsehood" will be excluded from heaven, according to Revelation 22:15. Absolute truthfulness was extolled as a cardinal Christian virtue.

The biblical writers not only taught the highest moral standards, including truthfulness, but they exemplified them in their lives. A true prophet could not be bought off. As one prophet who was tempted confessed, "I could not go beyond the command of the Lord" (Num. 22:18). What God spoke, the prophet had to declare, regardless of the consequences. Many prophets were threatened and even martyred but never recanted the truth. Jeremiah was put into prison for his unwelcome prophecies (Jer. 32:2; 37:15) and even threatened with death (Jer. 26:8, 24). Others were killed (Matt. 23:34–36; Heb. 11:32–38). Peter and the eleven apostles (Acts 5), as well as Paul (Acts 28), were all imprisoned and most were eventually martyred for their testimony (2 Tim. 4:6–8; 2 Peter 1:14). Indeed, being "faithful unto death" was an earmark of early Christian conviction (Rev. 2:10).

People sometimes die for false causes they believe to be true, but few die for what they know to be false. Yet the biblical witnesses, who were in a position to know what was true, died for proclaiming that their message came from God. This is at least prima facie evidence that the Bible is what they claimed it to be—the Word of God.

The Miraculous Confirmation. It is always possible that someone believes he or she speaks for God and does not. There are false prophets (Matt. 7:15). This is why the Bible exhorts: "Dear friends, do not believe every spirit, but test the spirits to see whether they are from God, because many false prophets have gone out into the world" (1 John 4:1). One sure way a true prophet can be distinguished from a false one is miracles (Acts 2:22; Heb. 2:3–4). A miracle is an act of God, and God would not supernaturally confirm a false prophet to be a true one (*see* MIRACLES IN THE BIBLE; PROPHECIES AS PROOF OF THE BIBLE).

When Moses was called of God, he was given miracles to prove he spoke for God (Exodus 4). Elijah on Mount Carmel was confirmed by fire from heaven to be a true prophet of the true God (1 Kings 18). Even Nicodemus acknowledged to Jesus, "Rabbi, we know you are a teacher who has come from God. For no one could perform the miraculous signs you are doing if God were not with him" (John 3:2).

Even the *Qur'an* recognized that God confirmed his prophets (sura 7:106–8, 116–119), including Jesus, by miracles. God is said to have told Muhammad, "If they reject thee, so were rejected apostles before thee, who came with clear signs" (sura 17:103). Allah says, "Then We sent Moses and his brother Aaron, with Our signs and authority manifest" (sura 23:45). Interestingly, when Muhammad was challenged by unbelievers to perform like miracles, he refused (see sura 2:118; 3:183; 4:153; 6:8, 9, 37). In Muhammad's own words (from the *Qur'an*), "They [will] say: 'Why is not a sign sent down to him from his Lord?'" since even Muhammad admitted that "God hath certainly power to send down a sign" (sura 6:37; *see* MUHAMMAD, ALLEGED MIRACLES OF; *QUR'AN*, ALLEGED DIVINE ORIGIN OF). But miracles were a mark of Jesus' ministry, as of other prophets and apostles (Heb. 2:3–4; 2 Cor. 12:12; *see* MIRACLES, APOLOGETIC VALUE OF). When asked by John the Baptist if he was the Messiah, Jesus responded, "Go your way, and tell John what things ye have seen and heard; how that the blind see, the lame walk, the lepers are cleansed, the deaf hear, the dead are raised, to the poor the gospel is preached" (Luke 7:20–22).

Miracles, then, are a divine confirmation of a prophet's claim to be speaking for God (*see* MIRACLE). But of all the world's religious leaders, only the Judeo-Christian prophets and apostles were supernaturally confirmed by genuine miracles of nature that could not possibly have been self-delusion or trickery. Confirming miracles included the turning of water into wine (John 2), healing of those with organic sicknesses (John 5), multiplying food (John 6), walking on water (John 6), and raising the dead (John 11).

Muslims allege that Muhammad did miracles, but there is no support for this claim, even in the *Qur'an* (for his refusal to do miracles, see sura 3:181–84; *see* MUHAMMAD, CHARACTER OF). Only the Bible is supernaturally confirmed.

Predictions by Biblical Prophets. Unlike any other book, the Bible offers specific predictions that were written hundreds of years in advance of their literal fulfillment. Many of these center around the coming of Christ and others around world events. For a discussion of a number of these, *see* PROPHECY AS PROOF OF THE BIBLE. While Bible critics play with the dating of Old Testament books to claim that predictions were written after their fulfillment, these claims abuse credibility. In some cases of more recent fulfillment no such claims are even possible. These fulfillments stand as a mark of the Bible's unique, supernatural origin.

The Unity of the Bible. One supporting line of evidence for the Bible's divine origin is its unity in great diversity. Even though composed by many people of diverse backgrounds over many years, Scripture speaks from one mind.

Not taking into account unknowns in the dating for Job and sources Moses could have used, the first book was written no later than 1400 B.C. and the last shortly before A.D. 100. In all there are sixty-six different books, written by perhaps forty different authors of different backgrounds, educational levels, and occupations. Most was written originally in Hebrew or Greek, with some small portion in Aramaic.

The Bible covers hundreds of topics in literature of widely varying styles. These include history, poetry, didactic literature, parable, allegory, apocalyptic, and epic.

Yet note the amazing unity. These sixty-six books unfold one continuous drama of redemption, paradise lost to paradise regained, creation to the consummation of all things (see Sauer). There is one central theme, the person of Jesus Christ, even by implication in the Old Testament (Luke 24:27). In the Old Testament Christ is anticipated; in the New Testament he is realized (Matt. 5:17–18). There is one message: Humankind's problem is sin, and the solution is salvation through Christ (Mark 10:45; Luke 19:10).

Such incredible unity is best accounted for by the existence of a divine Mind that the writers of Scripture claimed inspired them. This Mind wove each of their pieces into one mosaic of truth.

Critics claim this is not so amazing, considering that succeeding authors were aware of preceding ones. Hence, they could build upon these texts without contradicting them. Or, later generations only accepted their book into the growing canon because it seemed to fit.

But not all writers were aware that their book would come to be in the canon (for example, Song of Solomon and the multiauthor Proverbs). They could not have slanted their writing to the way that would best fit. There was no one point when books were accepted into the canon. Even though some later generations raised questions as to how a book came to be in the canon, there is evidence that books were accepted immediately by the contemporaries of the writers. When Moses wrote, his books were placed by the ark (Deut. 31:22–26). Later, Joshua was added, and Daniel had copies of these works, plus even the scroll of his contemporary Jeremiah (Dan. 9:2). In the New Testament, Paul cites Luke (1 Tim. 5:18, cf. Luke 10:7), and Peter possessed at least some of Paul's Epistles (2 Peter 3:15–16). While not every Christian everywhere possessed every book immediately, it does seem that some writings were accepted and distributed immediately. Perhaps others were disseminated more slowly, after they were determined to be authentic.

Even if every author possessed every earlier book, there is still a unity that transcends human ability. The reader might assume that each author was an incredible literary genius who saw both the broader unity and "plan" of Scripture and just how his piece would fit in it. Could even such geniuses write so that the unforeseen end would come out, even though they could not know precisely what that end would be? It is easier to posit a superintending Mind behind the whole who devised the plot and from the beginning planned how it would unfold.

Suppose a book of family medical advice was composed by forty doctors over 1500 years in different languages on hundreds of medical topics. What kind of unity would it have, even assuming that authors knew what preceding ones had written? Due to superstitious medical practice in the past, one chapter would say that disease is caused by demons who must be exorcised. Another would claim that disease is in the blood and must be drained by blood-letting. Another would claim disease to be a function of mind over matter. At best, such a book would lack unity, continuity, and usefulness. It would hardly be a definitive source covering the causes and cures of disease. Yet the Bible, with greater diversity, is still sought by millions for its solutions to spiritual maladies. It alone, of all books known to humankind, needs a God to account for its unity in diversity.

Archaeological Confirmation. Archaeology cannot directly prove the Bible's inspiration; it can confirm its reliability as an historical document. This is an indirect confirmation of inspiration. (*See* Archaeology, New Testament, and Archaeology, Old Testament, for some of this evidence.) The conclusion of that evidence was summed up by Nelson Glueck that "no archaeological discovery has ever controverted a biblical reference. Scores of archaeological findings have been made which confirm in clear outline or exact detail historical statements in the Bible" (Glueck, 31). Millar Burroughs notes that "more than one archaeologist has found his respect for the Bible increased by the experience of excavation in Palestine" (Burroughs, 1).

Testimonies of Transforming Power. The writer of Hebrews declares that "the word of God is living and active. Sharper than any double-edged sword" (4:12). The apostle Peter added, "For you have been born again, not of perishable seed, but of imperishable, through the living and enduring word of God" (1 Peter 1:23). While not in the area of primary evidence, a subjective, supporting line of evidence is the change in life that God's Word brings. While early Islam spread by the power of the sword, early Christianity spread by the sword of the Spirit, even as Christians were being killed by the power of the Roman sword.

The great Christian apologist William *Paley summarized the differences between the growth of Christianity and Islam vividly:

> For what are we comparing? A Galilean peasant accompanied by a few fishermen with a conqueror at the head of his army. We compare Jesus, without force, without power, without support, without one external circumstance of attraction or influence, prevailing against the prejudices, the learning, the hierarchy, of his country, against the ancient religious opinions, the pompous religious rites, the philosophy, the wisdom, the authority of the Roman empire, in the most polished and enlightened period of its existence,—with Mahomet making his way amongst Arabs; collecting followers in the midst of conquests and triumphs, in the darkest ages and countries of the world, and when success in arms not only operated by that command of men's wills and persons which attend prosperous undertakings, but was considered as a sure testimony of Divine approbation. That multitudes, persuaded by this argument, should join the train of a victorious chief; that still greater multitudes should, without any argument, bow down before irresistible power—is a conduct in which we cannot see much to surprise us; in which we can see nothing that resembles the causes by which the establishment of Christianity was effected. [Paley, 257]

Despite the later misuse of military power in the Crusades and at isolated times earlier, the fact is that *early* Christianity grew by its spiritual power, not by political force. From the very beginning, as it is today around the world, it was the preaching of the Word of God which transformed lives that gave Christianity its vitality (Acts 2:41). For "Faith comes by hearing, and hearing by the word of God" (Rom. 10:17).

Conclusion. The Bible is the only book that both claims and proves to be the Word of God. It claims to be written by prophets of God who recorded in their own style and language exactly the message God wanted them to give to humankind. The writings of the prophets and apostles claim to be the unbreakable, imperishable, and inerrant words of God. The evidence that their writings are what they claimed to be is found not only in their own moral character but in the supernatural confirmation of their message, its prophetic accuracy, its amazing unity, its transforming power, and the testimony of Jesus who was confirmed to be the Son of God.

Sources

M. Burrows, *What Mean These Stones?*
F. S. R. L. Gaussen, *Theopneustia*
N. L. Geisler, ed., *Inerrancy*
———and A. Saleeb, *Answering Islam*
———and W. E. Nix, *General Introduction to the Bible*, rev. ed.
N. Glueck, *Rivers in the Desert*
R. L. Harris, *Inspiration and Canonicity of the Bible*
C. F. H. Henry, *Revelation and the Bible*
A. A. Hodge, et al., *Inspiration*
H. Lindsell, *The Battle for the Bible*
J. . Packer, *"Fundamentalism" and the Word of God*
B. B. Warfield, *Limited Inspiration*
———, *The Inspiration and Authority of the Bible*
C. Wilson, *Rocks, Relics, and Reliability*
J. D. Woodbridge, *Biblical Authority: A Critique of the Roger McKim Proposal*
E. Yamauchi, *The Stones and the Scriptures*

Bible, Islamic View of. Muslims believe that the *Qur'an* is the Word of God, superseding all previous revelations. To maintain this belief, they must sustain an attack upon the competing claims of their chief rival, the Bible.

The Attack on the Bible. Muslim accusations against the Bible fall into two basic categories: first, the text of Scripture has been changed or forged; second, doctrinal mistakes have crept into Christian teaching, such as the belief in the incarnation of Christ, the triunity of the Godhead, and the doctrine of original sin (Waardenburg, 261–63).

Praise for the Original Bible. Strangely, sometimes the *Qur'an* gives the Judeo-Christian Scriptures such noble titles as: "the Book of God," "the Word of God," "a light and guidance to man," "a decision for all matters," "a guidance and mercy," "the lucid Book," "the illumination *(al-furqan),*" "the gospel with its guidance and light, confirming the preceding Law," and "a guidance and warning to those who fear God" (Takle, 217). Christians are told to look into their own Scriptures to find God's revelation for them (5:50). And even Muhammad himself at one point is exhorted to test the truthfulness of his own message by the contents of the previous divine revelations to Jews and Christians (10:94).

The Bible Set Aside. This praise for the Bible is misleading, since Muslims hasten to claim that the *Qur'an* supersedes previous revelations, based on their concept of progressive revelation. By this they hope to show that the *Qur'an* fulfills and sets aside the less complete revelations, such as the Bible. One Islamic theologian echoes this conviction by stating that while a Muslim needs to believe in the Torah (Law of Moses), the *Zabur* (the Psalms of David), and the *Injil* (Gospels), nevertheless "according to the most eminent theologians" the books in their present state "have been tampered with." He goes on to say, "It is to be believed that the *Qur'an* is the noblest of the books. . . . It is the last of the God-given scriptures to come down, it abrogates all the books which preceded it. . . . It is impossible for it to suffer any change or alteration" (Jeffery, 126–28). Even though this is the most common view among Islamic scholars, still many Muslims claim to believe in the sacredness and truthfulness of the present-day Bible. This, however, is largely lip-service due to their firm belief in the all-sufficiency of the *Qur'an*. Very few ever study the Bible.

Against the Old Testament. Muslims often show a less favorable view of the Old Testament, which they believe has been distorted by the teachers of the law. The charges include: concealing God's Word (sura 2:42; 3:71), verbally distorting the message in their books (sura 3:78; 4:46), not believing in all the parts of their Scriptures (sura 2:85), and not knowing what their own Scriptures really teach (sura 2:78). Muslims have included Christians in these criticisms.

Due to the ambiguities in the qur'anic accounts, Muslims hold various views (that are sometimes in conflict) regarding the Bible. For instance, the well-known Muslim reformer, Muhammad Abduh writes, "The Bible, the New Testament and the *Qur'an* are three concordant books; religious men study all three and respect them equally. Thus the divine teaching is completed, and the true religion shines across the centuries" (Dermenghem, 138). Another Muslim author tries to harmonize the three great world religions in this way: "Judaism lays stress on Justice and Right; Christianity, on Love and Charity; Islam, on Brotherhood and Peace" (Waddy, 116). However, the most typical Islamic approach to this subject is characterized by comments of the Muslim apologist, Ajijola:

> The first five books of the Old Testament do not constitute the original Torah, but parts of the Torah have been mingled up with other narratives written by human beings and the original guidance of the Lord is lost in that quagmire. Similarly, the four Gospels of Christ are not the original Gospels as they came from Prophet Jesus . . . the original and the fictitious, the Divine and the human are so intermingled that the grain cannot be separated from the chaff. The fact is that the original Word of God is preserved neither with the Jews nor with the Christians. The Qur'an, on the

other hand, is fully preserved and not a jot or tittle has been changed or left out in it. [Ajijola, 79]

These charges bring us once again to the Islamic doctrine of tahrif, or corruption of the Judeo-Christian Scriptures. Based on some of the above qur'anic verses and, more important, exposure to the actual contents of other scriptures, Muslim theologians have generally formulated two responses. According to Nazir-Ali "the early Muslim commentators (e.g., Al-Tabari and Ar-Razi) believed that the alteration is tahrif bi'al ma'ni, a corruption of the meaning of the text without tampering with the text itself. Gradually, the dominant view changed to tahrif bi'al-lafz, corruption of the text itself" (Nazir-Ali, 46). The Spanish theologians Ibn-Hazm, and Al-Biruni, along with most Muslims, hold this view.

Another qur'anic scholar claims that "the biblical Torah was apparently not identical with the pure *tawrat* [law] given as a revelation to Moses, but there was considerable variation in opinion on the question to what extent the former scriptures were corrupted." On the one hand, "Ibn-Hazm, who was the first thinker to consider the problem of *tabdil* [change] systematically, contended . . . that the text itself had been changed or forged (*taghyr*), and he drew attention to immoral stories which had found a place within the corpus." On the other hand, "Ibn-Khaldun held that the text itself had not been forged but that Jews and Christians had misinterpreted their scripture, especially those texts which predicted or announced the mission of Muhammad and the coming of Islam" (Waardenburg, 257).

Whether a Muslim scholar shows more or less respect for the Bible, and whether or how he will quote from it depends on his particular interpretation of *tabdil*. Ibn-Hazm, for instance, rejects nearly the whole Old Testament as a forgery, but cheerfully quotes the *tawrat*'s bad reports of the faith and behavior of the *Banu Isra'il* as proofs against the Jews and their religion.

Against the New Testament. Noted Muslim commentator Yusuf Ali contends that "the *Injil* spoken of by the *Qur'an* is not the New Testament. It is not the four Gospels now received as canonical. It is the single Gospel which, Islam teaches, was revealed to Jesus, and which he taught. Fragments of it survive in the received canonical Gospels and in some others of which traces survive" (Ali, 287). Direct allegations against New Testament and Christian teaching are made. These include the charges that there have been a change and forgery of textual divine revelation, and that there have been doctrinal mistakes, such as the belief in the incarnation of Christ, the Trinity, the godhead, and the doctrine of original sin (Waardenburg, 261–63).

Debated among Muslim theologians is the question of the eternal destiny of the people of the Book. Although the average Muslim might consider anyone who has been a "good person" worthy of salvation, accounting for all the qur'anic evidences on this subject has created much uncertainty.

Among classical Muslim theologians, Jews and Christians were generally regarded as unbelievers (*kafar*) because of their rejection of Muhammad as a true prophet of God. For example, in the qur'anic commentary of Tabari, one of the most respected Muslim commentators of all time, we notice that, even though the author distinguishes between the people of the book and the polytheists (*mushrikun*) and expresses a higher opinion of the former, he clearly declares that the majority of Jews and Christians are in unbelief and transgression because of their refusal to acknowledge Muhammad's truthfulness (Antes, 104–5).

Added to this is the charge against Christian belief in the divinity of Christ as the Son of God (*see* Christ, Deity of), a belief that amounts to committing the unpardonable sin of *shirk*, and is emphatically condemned throughout the *Qur'an*. The condemnation of Christians is captured in 5:75: "They do blaspheme who say: 'God is Christ the son of Mary.' . . . Whoever joins other gods with God, God will forbid him the Garden, and the Fire will be his abode."

On the other hand the contemporary Muslim theologian, Falzur Rahman, goes against what he admits is "the vast majority of Muslim commentators." He champions the opinion that salvation is not acquired by formally joining the Muslim faith, but as the *Qur'an* points out, by believing in God and the last day and doing good deeds (Rahman, 166–67). The debate continues and each individual Muslim can take a different side of this issue based on his own understanding.

A Response to Islamic Charges. One evidence that these Islamic views are critically flawed is the internal inconsistency within the Muslim view of Scripture itself. Another is that it is contrary to the facts.

Tension within the Islamic View of the Bible. There is serious tension in the Islamic rejection of the authenticity of the current New Testament. This tension can be focused by the following teachings from the *Qur'an*:

The original New Testament ("Gospel") is a revelation of God (sura 5:46, 67, 69, 71).

Jesus was a prophet and his words should be believed by Muslims (sura 4:171; 5:78). As the Muslim scholar Mufassir notes, "Muslims believe all prophets to be truthful because they are commissioned in the service of humanity by Almighty God (Allah)" (Mufassir, i).

Christians were obligated to accept the New Testament of Muhammad's day (A.D. seventh century; sura 10:94).

In sura 10, Muhammad is told: "If thou wert in doubt as to what We have revealed unto thee, then ask those who have been reading the Book [the Bible] from before thee; the truth hath indeed come to thee from thy Lord; so be in no wise of those in doubt." Abdul-Haqq notes that "the learned doctors of Islam are sadly embarrassed by this verse, referring the prophet as it does to the people of the Book who would solve his doubts" (Abdul-Haqq, 23). One of the strangest interpretations is that the sura is actually addressed to those who question his claim. Others claim that "it was Muhammad himself who is addressed, but, however much they change and turn the compass, it ever points to the same celestial pole—the purity and preservation of the Scriptures." However, Abdul-Haqq adds, "If again, we take the party addressed to be those who doubted the truth of Islam, this throws open the whole foundation of the prophet's mission; regarding which they are referred to the Jews [or Christians] for an answer to their doubts; which would only strengthen the argument for the authority of the Scripture—a result the Muslim critics would hardly be prepared for" (ibid., 100).

Christians respond that Muhammad would not have asked them to accept a corrupted version of the New Testament. Also, the New Testament of Muhammad's day is substantially identical to the New Testament today, since today's New Testament is based on manuscripts that go back several centuries before Muhammad (*see* NEW TESTAMENT MANUSCRIPTS). Hence, by the logic of this verse, Muslims should accept the authenticity of today's Bible. But if they do, then they should accept the doctrines of the deity of Christ (*see* CHRIST, DEITY OF) and the *Trinity, since that is what the New Testament teaches. However, Muslims categorically reject these teachings, creating a dilemma within the Islamic view.

Another inconsistency within the qur'anic view of the Bible is that Muslims claim the Bible to be "the Word of God" (2:75). Muslims also insist that God's words cannot be altered or changed. But, as Pfander points out, "if both these statements are correct . . . then it follows that the Bible has not been changed and corrupted either before or since Muhammad's time" (Pfander, 101). However, Islamic teaching insists that the Bible has been corrupted, thus the contradiction.

As Islamic scholar Richard Bell pointed out, it is unreasonable to suppose that Jews and Christians would conspire to change the Old Testament. For "their [the Jews'] feeling towards the Christians had always been hostile" (Bell, 164–65). Why would two hostile parties (Jews and Christians), who shared a common Old Testament, conspire to change it to support the views of a common enemy, the Muslims? It does not make any sense. What is more, at the supposed time of the textual changes, Jews and Christians were spread all over the world, making the supposed collaboration to corrupt the text impossible. And the number of copies of the Old Testament in circulation were too numerous for the changes to be uniform. Also, there is no mention of any such changes by former Jews or Christians of the time who became Muslims, something that they surely would have done if it were true (see McDowell, 52–53).

Contrary to the Factual Evidence. Furthermore, Muslim's rejection of the New Testament is contrary to the overwhelming manuscript evidence. All the Gospels are preserved in the Chester Beatty Papyri, copied in about 250. And the entire New Testament exists in Vaticanus Ms. (B) which dates from about 325–50. There are more than 5300 other manuscripts of the New Testament (*see* NEW TESTAMENT MANUSCRIPTS), dating from the second century to the fifteenth century (hundreds of which are from before Muhammad) which confirm that we have substantially the same text of the whole New Testament as existed in Muhammad's day. These manuscripts also confirm that the text is the same basic New Testament text as was written in the first century. These manuscripts provide an unbroken chain of testimony. For example, the earliest fragment of the New Testament, the John Ryland Fragment, is dated about 117–38. It preserves verses from John 18 just as they are found in today's New Testament. Likewise, the Bodmer Papyri from ca. 200 preserves whole books of Peter and Jude as we have them today. Most of the New Testament, including the Gospels, is in the Beatty Papyri, and the entire New Testament is in Vaticanus from about 325. There is absolutely no evidence that the New Testament message was destroyed or distorted, as Muslims claim it was (see Geisler and Nix, chap. 22).

Finally, Muslims use liberal critics of the New Testament to show that the New Testament was corrupted, misplaced, and outdated. However, the late liberal New Testament scholar John A. T. Robinson concluded that the Gospel record was written well within the lives of the apostles, between A.D. 40 and 60 (*see* NEW TESTAMENT, HISTORICITY OF; BIBLE CRITICISM). Former Bultmannian New Testament critic Eta Linnemann has more recently concluded that the position that the New Testament as preserved in the manuscripts does not accurately preserve the words and deeds of Jesus, is no longer defensible. She writes: "As time passes, I become more and more convinced that to a considerable degree New Testament criticism as practiced by those committed to historical-critical theology does not deserve to be called science" (Linnemann, 9). She adds, "The Gospels are not works of literature that creatively reshape already finished material after the manner in which Goethe reshaped the popular book about Dr. Faust" (ibid., 104). Rather, "Every Gospel presents a complete, unique testimony. It owes its existence to direct or indirect eyewitnesses" (ibid., 194).

Further, the use of these liberal critics by Muslim apologists undermines their own view of the *Qur'an*. Muslim writers are fond of quoting the conclusions of liberal critics of the Bible without serious consideration as to their presuppositions. The antisupernaturalism that led liberal critics of the Bible to deny that Moses wrote the Pentateuch, noting the different words for God used in different passages, would likewise argue that the *Qur'an* did not come from Muhammad. For the *Qur'an* also uses different names for God in different places. *Allah* is used for God in suras 4, 9, 24, 33, but *Rab* is used in suras 18, 23 and 25 (Harrison, 517). Muslims seem blissfully unaware that the views of these critics are based on an antisupernatural bias that, if applied to the *Qur'an* and the *hadith*, would destroy basic Muslim beliefs as well. In short, Muslims cannot consistently appeal to criticism of the New Testament based on the belief that miracles do not occur, unless they wish to undermine their own faith.

Conclusion. If Christians in Muhammad's day were obligated to accept the New Testament, and if abundant manuscript evidence confirms that the New Testament of today is essentially the same, then, according to the teachings of the *Qur'an* itself, Christians are obligated to accept the teachings of the New Testament. But the New Testament today affirms that Jesus is the Son of God, who died on the cross for our sins and rose again three days later. But this is contrary to the *Qur'an*. Thus, Muslim rejection of the authenticity of the New Testament is inconsistent with their own belief in the inspiration of the *Qur'an*.

Sources

A. A. Abdul-Haqq, *Sharing Your Faith with a Muslim*
A. A. D. Ajijola, *The Essence of Faith in Islam*
A. Y. Ali, *The Holy Qur'an*
P. Antes, "Relations with the Unbelievers in Islamic Theology," in A. Shimmel and A. Falaturi, eds., *We Believe in One God*
R. Bell, *The Origin of Islam in Its Christian Environment*
M. Bucaille, *The Bible, the Qur'an and Science*
W. Campbell, *The Qur'an and the Bible in the Light of History and Science*
E. Dermenghem, *Muhammad and the Islamic Tradition*
N. L. Geisler and A. Saleeb, *Answering Islam: The Crescent in the Light of the Cross*
———and W. E. Nix, *General Introduction to the Bible*, rev. ed.
R. K. Harrison, *Introduction to the Old Testament*
A. Jeffery, ed., *Islam, Muhammad and his Religion*
E. Linnemann, *Is There a Synoptic Problem? Rethinking the Literary Dependence of the First Three Gospels*
J. McDowell, *The Islam Debate*
S. S. Mufassir, *Jesus, a Prophet of Islam*
M. Nazir-Ali, *Frontiers in Muslim-Christian Encounter*
C. G. Pfander, *The Mizanu'l Haqq*
F. Rahman, *Major Themes of the Qur'an*
J. Waardenburg, "World Religions as Seen in the Light of Islam," in *Islam: Past Influence and Present Challenge*
C. Waddy, *The Muslim Mind*

Bible, Jesus' View of. Jesus' view of the Bible is a crucial link in the chain of argument that the Bible is the Word of God (*see* BIBLE, EVIDENCE FOR). The progression (*see* APOLOGETICS, ARGUMENT OF) runs:

1. Truth about reality is knowable (*see* TRUTH, NATURE OF; AGNOSTICISM).
2. Opposites cannot both be true (*see* FIRST PRINCIPLES; LOGIC).
3. The theistic God exists (*see* GOD, EVIDENCE FOR).
4. Miracles are possible (*see* MIRACLES, ARGUMENTS AGAINST).
5. Miracles confirm truth claims of a prophet of God (*see* MIRACLES, APOLOGETIC VALUE OF).
6. New Testament documents are historically reliable (*see* NEW TESTAMENT, DATING OF; NEW TESTAMENT DOCUMENTS, RELIABILITY OF AND NEW TESTAMENT, HISTORICITY OF).
7. As witnessed by the New Testament, Jesus claimed to be God (*see* CHRIST, DEITY OF).
8. Jesus' claim to be God was confirmed by miracles (*see* MIRACLES, APOLOGETIC VALUE OF; MIRACLES IN THE BIBLE; RESURRECTION, EVIDENCE FOR).
9. Therefore, Jesus is God.
10. Whatever Jesus (who is God) affirmed is true, is true (*see* GOD, NATURE OF).
11. Jesus, who is God, affirmed the Bible is the Word of God.
12. Therefore, it is true that the Bible is the Word of God and whatever is opposed to any biblical teaching is false (*see* WORLD RELIGIONS AND CHRISTIANITY; PLURALISM, RELIGIOUS).

What Jesus Affirmed about the Bible. Step 9 is crucial to the overall argument. If Jesus is the Son of God, then what he affirmed about the Bible is true. And Jesus affirmed that the Bible is the infallible, indestructible, inerrant Word of God (*see* BIBLE, ALLEGED ERRORS IN).

What Jesus Affirmed about the Old Testament. The New Testament was not written until after Jesus ascended into heaven. Hence, his statements about the Bible refer to the Old Testament. But what Jesus confirmed for the Old Testament, he also promised for the New Testament.

Jesus affirmed the divine authority of the Old Testament. Jesus and his disciples used the phrase "it is written" more than ninety times. It is usually in the perfect tense, meaning, "it was written in the past and it still stands as the written Word of God." Often Jesus used in the sense of "this is the last word on the topic. The discussion is over." Such is the case when Jesus resisted the temptation of the Devil.

> But he answered and said, *It is written,* Man shall not live by bread alone, but by every word that proceedeth out of the mouth of God. . . . Jesus said unto him, *It is written* again, Thou shalt not tempt the Lord thy God. Jesus said to him, It is again written, Thou shalt not tempt [the] Lord thy God. . . . Then saith Jesus unto him, Get thee hence, Satan: for *it is written,* Thou shalt worship the Lord thy God, and him only shalt thou serve. [Matt. 4:4, 7, 10, emphasis added]

This use demonstrates that Jesus believed the Bible to have final and divine authority.

Jesus affirmed the Old Testament to be imperishable. "Think not that I am come to destroy the law, or the prophets: I am not come to destroy, to fulfill. Think not that I am come to make void the law or the prophets. For verily I say unto you, Till heaven and earth pass, one jot or one tittle shall in no wise pass from the law, till all be fulfilled" (Matt. 5:17–18). Jesus believed the Old Testament to be the imperishable Word of the eternal God.

Jesus affirmed the Old Testament to be inspired. Although Jesus never used the word *inspiration,* he did use its equivalent. To the Pharisees' question, he retorted: "How is it then that David, *speaking by the Spirit,* calls him 'Lord'?" (Matt. 22:43, emphasis added). Indeed, David himself said of his own words, "The Spirit of the LORD spoke through me; his word was on my tongue" (2 Sam. 23:2). This is precisely what is meant by inspiration.

Jesus affirmed that the Bible is unbreakable. The word *infallible* is not used in the New Testament, but a close cousin is—*unbreakable*. Jesus said, "If he called them gods, unto whom the word of God came, and *the scripture cannot be broken*" (John 10:35). Indeed, three powerful words describe the Old Testament in this short passage: "law" (vs. 34), "word of God," and "unbreakable." Thus, Jesus believed that the Old Testament was the unbreakable law of God.

Jesus affirmed the Old Testament is the Word of God. Jesus regarded the Bible as the "Word of God." He insisted elsewhere that it contained the "commandment of God" (Matt 15:3, 6). The same truth is implied in his reference to its indestructibility in Matthew 5:17–18. Elsewhere, Jesus' disciples call it "the oracles of God" (Rom. 3:2; Heb. 5:12).

Jesus ascribed ultimate supremacy to the Old Testament. Jesus often asserted the ultimate authority and supremacy of the Old Testament over all human teaching or "tradition." He said to the Jews: "Why do you break the command of God for the sake of your tradition? . . . Thus you nullify the word of God for the sake of your tradition" (Matt. 15:3, 6). Jesus believed that the Bible alone has supreme authority when even the most revered of all human teachings conflict with it. Scripture alone is God's supreme written authority.

Jesus affirmed the inerrancy of the Old Testament. Inerrancy means without error. That concept is found in Jesus' answer to the Sadducees, a sect who denied the divine inspiration of the Old Testament, "Ye do err, not knowing the scriptures [which do not err], nor the power of God" (Matt. 22:29 KJV). In his high priestly prayer, Jesus affirmed the total truthfulness of Scripture, saying to the Father, "Sanctify them through thy truth: *thy word is truth"* (John 17:17 KJV).

Jesus affirmed the historical reliability of the Old Testament. Jesus affirmed as historically true some of the most disputed passages of the Old Testament, including the creation of Adam and Eve (Matt. 19:4–5), the miracle about Jonah in the great fish, and destruction of the world by a flood in the days of Noah. Of the latter, Jesus declared: "As it was in the days of Noah, so it will be at the coming of the Son of Man. For in the days before the flood, people were eating and drinking, marrying and giving in marriage, up to the day Noah entered the ark" (Matt. 24:37–38). Jesus affirmed that Jonah was really swallowed by a great fish for three days and three nights: "For as Jonah was three days and three nights in the belly of a huge fish, so the Son of Man will be three days and three nights in the heart of the earth" (Matt. 12:40). Jesus also spoke of the slaying of Abel (1 John 3:12), Abraham, Isaac, and Jacob (Matt. 8:11), the miracles of Elijah (James 5:17), and many other Old Testament persons and events as historically true, including Moses, Isaiah, David, and Solomon (Matt. 12:42), and Daniel the prophet (Matt. 24:15). He affirmed the historical reliability of major disputed passages of the Old Testament. Both the manner in which these events are cited, the authority they are given, and the basis they form for major teachings Jesus gave about his life, death, and resurrection reveals that he understood these events as historical.

Jesus affirmed the scientific accuracy of the Old Testament. The most scientifically disputed chapters of the Bible are the first eleven (*see* SCIENCE AND BIBLE). Yet Jesus affirmed the account throughout this section of Genesis. He unflinchingly bases his moral teaching about marriage on the literal truth of the creation of Adam and Eve. He said to the Pharisees, "Haven't you read," he replied, "that at the beginning the Creator 'made them male and female,' and said, 'For this reason a man will leave his father and mother and be united to his wife, and the two will become one flesh'?" (Matt. 19:4–5). After speaking to Nicodemus, the ruler of the Jews, about physical earthly things like birth and wind, Jesus declared: "I have spoken to you of earthly things and you do not believe; how then will you believe if I speak of heavenly things?" (John 3:12). In short, Jesus said that, unless one could believe him when he spoke of empirical scientific matters, then they should not believe him when he speaks of heavenly matters—revealing that he considered them inseparable.

What Jesus promised about the New Testament. Jesus not only affirmed the divine authority and infallibility of the Old Testament, he also promised the same for the New Testament. And his apostles and New Testament prophets claimed for their writings what Jesus had promised them (*see* BIBLE, EVIDENCE FOR).

Jesus said the Holy Spirit would teach "all truth." Jesus promised that "the Comforter, [which is] the Holy Ghost, whom the Father will send in my name, he shall teach you *all things*, and bring *all things* to your remembrance, *whatsoever I have* said unto you." He added, "Howbeit when he, the Spirit of truth, is come, he will guide you into *all truth:* for he shall not speak of himself; but whatsoever he shall hear, [that] shall he speak" (John 14:26; 16:13, emphasis added). This promise was fulfilled when they spoke and later recorded (in the New Testament) everything Jesus had taught them.

The apostles claimed this divine authority Jesus gave them. Not only did Jesus promise his disciples divine authority in what they wrote, but the apostles claimed this authority for their writings. John said, "these are written, that ye might believe that Jesus is the Christ, the Son of God; and that believing ye might have life through his name" (John 20:31). He added, "That which was from the beginning, which we have heard, which we have seen with our eyes, which we have looked upon, and our hands have handled, of the Word of life" (1 John 1:1). Again, he said, "Beloved, believe not every spirit, but try the spirits whether they are of God: because many false prophets are gone out into the world. . . . They are of the world: therefore speak they of the world, and the world heareth them. We are of God: he that knoweth God heareth us; he that is not of God heareth not us. Hereby know we the spirit of truth, and the spirit of error" (1 John 4:1, 5–6).

Likewise, the apostle Peter acknowledged all Paul's writing as "Scripture" (2 Peter 3:15–16; cf. 2 Tim. 3:15–16), saying, "And account [that] the longsuffering of our Lord [is] salvation; even as our beloved brother Paul also according to the wisdom given unto him hath written unto you. As also in all [his] epistles, speaking in them of these things; in which are some things hard to be understood, which they that are unlearned and unstable wrest, as [they do] also the other scriptures, unto their own destruction."

The New Testament is the record of apostolic teaching. But the New Testament is the only authentic record of apostolic teachings which we have. Each book was written by an apostle or New Testament prophet (Eph. 2:20; 3:3–5).

Therefore, the New Testament is the "all truth" Jesus promised. From the fact that Jesus promised to lead his disciples into "all truth" and they both claimed this promise and recorded this truth in the New Testament, we may conclude that Jesus' promise was finally fulfilled in the inspired New Testament. In this way, Jesus directly confirmed the inspiration and divine authority of the Old Testament and promised the same, indirectly, for the New Testament. Therefore, if Christ is the Son of God, then both the Old Testament and the New Testament are the Word of God.

Jesus and the Critics. Jesus confessed the very things many modern critics deny about the Old Testament (*see* BIBLE CRITICISM). If Jesus was right, then the critics are wrong, despite the pretense of having scholarship on their side. For if Jesus is the Son of God, then it is a matter of Lordship, not a matter of scholarship.

Negative critics of the Bible claim that Daniel was not a predictive prophet, but only a historian recording the events after they happened (ca. 165 B.C.). Jesus, however, agreed with the conservative view, declaring Daniel to be a prophet (*see* DANIEL, DATING OF). Indeed, Jesus cited a prediction that Daniel made that had not yet occurred in Jesus' day. In his Mount Olivet Discourse he said, "So when you see standing in the holy place 'the abomination that causes desolation,' spoken of through *the prophet Daniel* . . ." (Matt. 24:15, emphasis added). "See, I have told you ahead of time" (Matt. 24:25).

Many critics assert that the first human beings evolved by natural processes. But, as already noted, Jesus insisted that Adam and Eve were created by God (Matt. 19:4–5; *see* ADAM, HISTORICITY OF). If Jesus is the Son of God, then the choice is between Charles Darwin and the divine; between a nineteenth-century creature and the eternal Creator.

Most negative critics of the Bible believe that the Jonah story is mythology (*see* MYTHOLOGY AND THE NEW TESTAMENT). Indeed, with strong emphasis Jesus asserted that "just as" Jonah was in the great fish three days and nights, "even so" he would be in the grave for three days and nights. Surely, Jesus would not have based the historicity of his death and resurrection on mythology about Jonah.

Bible critics often deny there was a world-wide flood in the days of Noah (*see* SCIENCE AND THE BIBLE). But, as was seen above, Jesus affirmed there was a flood in the days of Noah in which all but Noah's family perished (Matt. 24:38–39; cf. 1 Peter 3:20; 2 Peter 3:5–6).

It is common for biblical critics to teach that there were at least two Isaiahs, one of whom lived after the events described in the latter chapters (40–66) and the other of which lived earlier and wrote chapters 1 to 39. But Jesus quoted from both sections of the book as the writing of "the prophet Isaiah" (*see* ISAIAH, DEUTERO). In Luke 4:17 Jesus cited the last part of Isaiah (61:1), reading: "The Spirit of the Lord is on me, because he has anointed me to preach good news to the poor" (Luke 4:17–18). In Mark 7:6 Jesus cited from the first section of Isaiah (29:13), saying, "Isaiah was right when he prophesied about you hypocrites; as it is written: 'These people honor me with their lips, but their hearts are far from me'" (Mark 7:6). Jesus' disciple John made it unmistakably clear that there was only one Isaiah by citing from both sections of Isaiah (chapters 53 and 6) in the same passage, claiming of the second that the same "Isaiah said again" (John 12:37–41).

The negative critic of the Bible does well to ask: Who knew more about the Bible, Christ or the critics? The dilemma is this: If Jesus is the Son of God, then the Bible is the Word of God. Conversely, if the Bible is not the Word of God, then Jesus is not the Son of God (since he taught false doctrine).

In spite of the forthright proclamations of Christ about the Scriptures many critics believe that he was not really affirming but only accommodating himself to the false beliefs of the Jews of his day about the Old Testament. But this hypothesis is clearly contrary to the facts (*see* ACCOMMODATION THEORY). Others believe that since Jesus was only a human being that he made mistakes, some of which were about the origin and nature of Scripture. But this speculation too is not rooted in the facts of the matter (see ibid.). Jesus neither accommodated false beliefs (cf. Matt. 5:21–22, 27–28; 22:29; 23:1f.) nor was he limited in his authority to teach the truth of God (cf. Matt. 28:18–20; 7:29; John 12:48).

Sources

N. L. Geisler, *Christian Apologetics*, chapter 18.

———and W. E. Nix, *General Introduction of the Bible*

R. Lightner, *The Savior and the Scriptures*

J. W. Wenham, "Jesus' View of the Old Testament," N. L. Geisler, ed., *Inerrancy*

Bible and Science. ***See*** **SCIENCE AND THE BIBLE.**

Big Bang Theory. Big bang cosmology is a widely accepted theory regarding the origin of the universe (*see* EVOLUTION, COSMIC), according to which the material universe or cosmos exploded into being some 15 billion years ago. Since then the universe has been expanding and developing according to conditions set at the moment of its origin. Had these conditions been different in the slightest degree, the world and life as we know it, including human life, would never have developed. The fact that conditions necessary for and favorable to the emergence of human life were determined from the very instant of the original cosmic explosion is called the *anthropic principle*.

Evidence for the Big Bang. British astronomer Stephen Hawking stated the issue well: "So long as the universe had a beginning, we could suppose it had a creator. But if the universe is really completely self-contained, having no boundary or edge, it would have neither beginning nor end: it would simply be" (*Brief History of Time*). Robert Jastrow was one of the first to address this issue in his book, *God and the Astronomers*. This agnostic astronomer noted that "three lines of evidence—the motions of the galaxies, the laws of thermodynamics, and the life story of the stars—pointed to one conclusion: all indicated that the Universe had a beginning" (111).

The Second Law of Thermodynamics. The second law of thermodynamics is the law of entropy. It asserts that the amount of *usable* energy in any closed system is decreasing. This must be held in tension with the first law of thermodynamics (*see* THERMODYNAMICS, LAWS OF), the law of the conservation of energy, which states that the amount of *actual* energy existing within the universe changes form, yet remains constant. As energy changes to less usable forms of energy, the closed system of the universe is running down; everything tends toward disorder. Jastrow noted that "Once hydrogen has been burned within that star and converted to heavier elements, it can never be restored to its original state." Thus, "minute by minute and year by year, as hydrogen is used up in stars, the supply of this element in the universe grows smaller" ("Scientist Caught," 15–16).

Now if the overall amount of energy stays the same, but the universe is running out of usable energy, then the universe began with a finite supply of energy. This would mean that the universe could not have existed forever in the past. If the universe is getting more and more disordered, it cannot be eternal. Otherwise, it would be totally disordered by now, which it is not. So it must have had a highly ordered beginning.

The Expansion of the Galaxies. The second line of evidence is the expansion of the galaxies. Evidence reveals that the universe is not simply in a holding pattern, maintaining its movement from everlasting to everlasting. It is expanding. It now appears that all of the galaxies are moving outward as if from a central point of origin, and that all things were expanding faster in the past than they are now. As we look out into space, we are also looking back in time, for we are seeing things, not as they are now, but as they were when the light was given off many years ago. The light from a star 7 million light years away tells us what that star was like and its location 7 million years ago. The most complete study made thus far has been carried out on the 200-inch telescope by Allan Sandage. "He compiled information on 42 galaxies, ranging out in space as far as 6 billion light years from us. His measurements indicate that the Universe was expanding more rapidly in the past than it is today. This result lends further support to the belief that the Universe exploded into being" (Jastrow, *God and the Astronomers*, 95).

Another astronomer, Victor J. Stenger, used a similar phrase when he stated that "the universe exploded out of nothingness" (Stenger, 13). This explosion, called the *big bang*, was a beginning point from which the entire universe has come. Putting an expanding universe in reverse leads us back to the point where the universe gets smaller and smaller until it vanishes into nothing. By this reckoning the universe, at some point in the distant past, came into being.

The Background Radiation Echo. A third line of evidence that the universe began is the background microwave radiation "echo" that seems to come from the whole universe. It was first thought to be a malfunction or static of the instruments, or even the effect of pigeon droppings. But research has discovered that the static was coming from everywhere—the universe itself has a low-level radiation signature emanating from some past catastrophe like a giant fireball. Jastrow concludes, "No explanation other than the big bang has been found for the fireball radiation. The clincher, which has convinced almost the last doubting Thomas, is that the radiation discovered by Penzias and Wilson has exactly the pattern of wavelengths expected for the light and heat produced in a great explosion. Supporters of the Steady State theory have tried desperately to find an alternative explanation, but they have failed" (Jastrow, "A Scientist Caught," 15). Again, this evidence leads to the conclusion that there was a beginning of the universe.

The Discovery of a Large Mass of Matter. Since Jastrow wrote of three lines of evidence for the beginning of the universe a fourth has been discovered. According to the predictions of the big bang theory, there should have been a great mass of matter associated with the original explosion of the universe into being, but none was found. Then, by use of the Hubble Space Telescope (1992), astronomers were able to report that "by peering back into the beginning of time, a satellite finds the largest and oldest structure ever observed—evidence of how the universe took shape 15 billion years ago." In fact, they found the very mass of matter predicted by big bang cosmology. One scientist exclaimed, "It's like looking at God" (Lemonick, 62).

Objections to the Big Bang. Of course, not all scientists who accept an expanding universe reason that the universe was brought into existence out of nothing by God. Some have sought earnestly to find other alternatives to the theistic implications.

Cosmic Rebound Theory. Some cosmologists argue for some kind of rebound theory whereby the universe collapses and rebounds forever. They propose that there is enough matter to cause a gravitational pull that will draw together the expanding universe. They see it as part of the pulsating nature of reality in a similar way to the Hindu view that the universe moves in eternal cycles.

However, big bang proponents note that there is no evidence to support this view. It is unlikely that there is enough matter in the universe to make the expanding universe collapse even once. Even if there were enough matter to cause a rebound, there is good reason to hold that it would not rebound forever. For according to the well established second law of thermodynamics, each succeeding rebound would have less explosive energy than the previous until eventually the universe would not rebound again. Like a bouncing ball, it would finally peter out, showing that it is not eternal. The rebound hypothesis is based on the fallacious premise that the universe is 100 percent efficient, which it is not. Usable energy is lost in every process.

Logically and mathematically the evidence for the big bang suggests that originally there was no space, no time, and no matter. Hence, even if the universe were somehow going through expansion and contraction from this point on, at the beginning it came into existence from nothing. This would still call for an initial Creator.

Plasma Cosmology. Hannes Alfven proposed a plasma cosmology, according to which the universe is composed of electrically conducting gases which indirectly produce a repelling effect of galaxy superclusters, causing the observed expansion. However, the expansion does not start from a single point; it has a sort of partial big bang and then contracts to about one-third the size of the present universe. Then some unknown principle kicks in and blows it apart again, thus maintaining an eternal equilibrium. This speculation lacks scientific support. Like other expansion-contraction views, it is contrary to the second law of thermodynamics. It speculates without evidence that the universe never wears out but continually recycles old forms of energy. Nothing is ever used up.

Plasma theorists admit that they do not know any force that could be responsible for the expansion. It is simply speculation built on the presupposition of an eternal universe. Neither can the plasma theory account for the helium and light isotopes in the universe which would not have been synthesized in these quantities in stars alone. These can be explained by the big bang. It provides no good explanation for the microwave background radiation that is readily explained by the big bang view. Heavier matter should be plentiful according to the plasma theory. None has been found.

Finally, the plasma theory provides no explanation for ultimate origins. Plasma popularizer Eric Lerner proposed a "starting place" for the cosmos when it was "filled with a more or less uniform hydrogen plasma, free of electrons and protons" (Heeren, 81). When asked what brought this plasma into being, he admits that "we have no real knowledge of what such processes were" (ibid., 81).

Hawking's Infinite Time. Another speculative alternative to the big bang is Stephen Hawking's hypothesis of infinite time, according to which the universe had no beginning. However, this revisiting of Albert Einstein's view is subject to the same criticisms that led Einstein himself to discard the view (*see* *Kalam* Cosmological Argument). It is an ingenious theory destroyed by the same brutal gang of facts that demand that the universe had a beginning. Even Hawking distinguishes between his abstract mathematical time, which has no beginning, and real time in which we live and which has a beginning. And even Hawking admitted that if there was a beginning then it is reasonable to assume there was a Creator.

Hawking further admitted that, even if his proposal turned out to describe the real universe, no conclusion could be drawn about the existence of God. He wrote: "I do not believe the no-boundary proposal proves the nonexistence of God, but it may affect our ideas of the nature of God." In Hawking's words, it would simply show that "we do not need someone to light the blue torch paper of the universe" (Heeren, 83). This, however, does not mean that there would be nothing for God to do, for there is more to do in running a universe than simply igniting the initial big bang.

Scientists have no theory to show how a universe without boundaries could exist. How, for example, can the ideas of an expanding universe be combined with one or no boundaries? Alan Guth, father of the inflationary model, concluded that Hawking's proposal "suffers from the problem that it doesn't yet have a completely well-defined theory in which to embed it. That is, it really is a notion of quantum gravity, and so far we do not have a complete theory of gravity in which to embed this idea" (Heeren, 83).

Even Einstein failed to find an explanation of his general relativity equation that would not require a beginning or a Beginner for the universe. He later wrote of his desire "to know how God created the universe" (ibid., 84). Indeed, even Hawking raises the question of who put "fire into the equations" and ignited the universe (*Black Holes,* 99).

Spontaneous Eruption: No Need for a Cause. Some atheists argue that there is no need for a cause of the beginning of the universe. They insist that there is nothing incoherent about something spontaneously erupting into existence from nothing. Several points are relevant in response to this objection.

First, this contention is contrary to the established principle of causality (*see* Causality, Principle of) which affirms that everything that comes to be had a cause. Indeed, even the skeptic David Hume confessed his belief in this time-honored principle, saying, "I never asserted so absurd a proposition as that anything might arise without a cause" (Hume, 1:187).

Second, it is contrary to the scientific enterprise which seeks a causal explanation of things. Francis Bacon, the father of modern science, affirmed that true knowledge is "knowledge by causes" (Bacon, 2.2.121).

Third, it is counterintuitive to believe that things just pop into existence out of nothing, willy-nilly. Reality does not work that way in our experience.

Fourth, the idea that nothing can cause something is logically incoherent, since "nothing" has no power to do anything—it does not even exist. As the Latin axiom put it: *Ex nihilo nihil fit:* From nothing, nothing comes.

Fifth, when one examines the "nothing" from which the universe allegedly came without a supernatural cause, it is discovered that it is not really nothing. Isaac Asimov speaks of it as a state of "existence" in which there is "energy" (Asimov, 148). This is a long way from absolutely nothing. Even in physical terms it is not really nothing. Ed Tryon who originated the idea (in a 1973 *Nature* article) recognized the problem of explaining creation from pure nothingness, since the quantum effects require something more than nothing—they require *space*, something physicists now carefully distinguish from "nothing" (see Heeren, 93). As Fred Hoyle noted, "The physical properties of the vacuum [or "nothing"] would still be needed, and this would be something" (Hoyle, 144). Moreover, general relativity reveals that space in our universe is not mere nothingness. As Einstein wrote: "There is no such thing as an empty space, that is, a space without field. Space-time does not claim existence on its own, but only as a structural quality of the field" (Heeren, 93). Cosmologist Paul Davies points out that when a physicist asks how matter arose from nothing "that means not only, how did matter arise out of nothing, but 'why did space and time exist in the first place, that matter may emerge from them?'" As space scientist John Mather notes, "we have no equations whatever for creating space and time.

And the concept doesn't even make any sense, in English. . . . And I certainly don't know of any work that seriously would explain it when it can't even state the concept" (ibid., 93–94). George Smoot, principal investigator with the COBE satellite, said, "It is possible to envision the creation of the universe from almost nothing—not nothing, but practically nothing" (ibid., 94). So, the "nothing" of which some scientists suggest that the universe could spring without a supernatural cause is not really nothing—it is something. It involves at least space and time. But before the big bang there was no space, no time, and no matter. Out of this "nothing," only a supernatural cause could bring something.

The First Law of Thermodynamics. Many astronomers who propose that the universe may be eternal, including Carl Sagan, use the first law of thermodynamics to support their view. Often this law of the conservation of energy is stated: "Energy can neither be created nor destroyed." If this were so, then it would follow that the universe (i.e., the sum total of all actual energy) is eternal.

But this misunderstands the law, which should be stated: "The actual amount of energy in the universe remains constant." This formulation is based on scientific observation about what does occur and is not a dogmatic philosophical assertion about what *can* or *cannot* happen. There is really no scientific evidence that the universe is eternal.

The second law confirms that the first law cannot be stated in terms that do not allow the creation of energy. For the second law demonstrates that no energy would exist if it did not come from outside a system. Therefore, there can be no such thing as a truly closed system.

To say energy *cannot* be created begs the question. That is what is to be proven. It is victory by stipulative definition—a classic example of the logical fallacy of *petitio principii.*

Eternal Eventless Universe. Some suggest that the big bang only signals the first eruption in a previously eternal universe. That is, the universe was eternally quiet before this first event. The big bang singularity only marks the transition from primal physical stuff. Hence, there is no need for a Creator to make something out of nothing.

Theists observe that no known natural laws could account for this violent eruption out of eternal quietude. Some argue that an eternally quiet universe is physically impossible, since it would have to exist at absolute zero, which is impossible. Matter at the beginning was anything but cold, being collapsed into a fireball with temperatures in excess of billions of degrees Kelvin. In a lump of matter frozen at absolute zero, no first event could occur.

Positing eternal primordial stuff does nothing to account the incredible order that follows the moment of the big bang. Only an intelligent Creator can account for this.

The Steady-State Theory. Hoyle proposed his steady-state theory to avoid the conclusion of a Creator. It affirms that hydrogen atoms are coming into existence to keep the universe from running down. This hypothesis has fatal flaws, not the least of which is that no scientific evidence even hints at such an event. No one has ever observed energy coming into existence anywhere.

The steady-state theory contradicts the principle of causality that there must be an adequate cause for every event. Only a Creator would be an adequate cause for the creation of new hydrogen atoms out of nothing. Denying the principle of causality is a high cost for the scientist to pay.

Although Hoyle has not given up his steady-state theory, he has concluded that the incredible complexity of even the simplest forms of life necessitate a Creator. Having calculated that the chances for first life emerging without intelligent intervention at 1 in $10^{40,000}$, Hoyle acknowledges a Creator of life (Hoyle, 24, 147, 150).

Reaction to the Evidence. The combined evidence for a big bang origin of the cosmos provides a strong case for a beginning to the universe. No viable scientific alternatives have been found. But, if the universe has a beginning, then, as Hawking admitted, the evidence would point to existence of a Creator. It follows logically that whatever had a beginning had a Beginner. In the face of this powerful evidence for the beginning of the universe, it is interesting to note how some brilliant scientists reacted to this news.

Astrophysicist Arthur Eddington summed up the attitude of many naturalistic scientists when he wrote: "Philosophically, the notion of a beginning of the present order of Nature is repugnant to me. . . . I should like to find a genuine loophole" (Heeren, 81).

At first Einstein refused to admit that his own general theory of relativity leads to the conclusion that the universe had a beginning. To avoid this conclusion, Einstein added a "fudge factor" in his equations, only to be embarrassed when it became known. To his credit, he eventually admitted his error and concluded that the universe was created. Thus, he wrote of his desire "to know how God created this world." He said, "I am not interested in this or that phenomenon, in the spectrum of this of that element. I want to know his thought; the rest are details" (cited by Herbert, 177).

One has to ask just why rational beings react in irrational ways to the news the universe had a beginning. Jastrow offers an illuminating clue.

> There is a kind of religion in science. It is the religion of a person who believes there is order and harmony in the universe. . . . Every effect must have its cause: There is no first cause. . . .

This religious faith of the scientists is violated by the discovery that the world had a beginning under conditions in which the known laws of physics are not valid, and as a product of forces or circumstances we cannot discover. When that happens, *the scientist has lost control.* [Jastrow, *God and the Astronomers,* 113–14, emphasis added]

Theistic Implications. After reviewing the evidence that the cosmos had a beginning, physicist Edmund Whittaker concluded: "It is simpler to postulate creation ex nihilo—divine will constituting nature from nothingness" (cited in Jastrow, "A Scientist Caught," 111). Even Jastrow, a confirmed agnostic, said "That there are what I or anyone would call supernatural forces at work is now, I think, a scientifically proven fact" (*God and the Astronomers,* 15, 18). Jastrow adds some embarrassing words both for skeptical astronomers and liberal theologians: "Now we see how the astronomical evidence leads to a biblical view of the origin of the world. The details differ, but the essential elements in the astronomical and biblical accounts of genesis are the same: the chain of events leading to man commence suddenly and sharply at a definite moment in time, in a flash of light and energy" ("A Scientist Caught," 14). He further observed that "Astronomers now find that they have painted themselves into a corner because they have proven, by their own methods, that the world began abruptly in an act of creation. . . . And they have found that all this happened as a product of forces they cannot hope to discover" (*God and the Astronomers,* 15). Thus, he notes that "the scientists' pursuit of the past ends in the moment of creation." And "This is an exceedingly strange development, unexpected by all but theologians. They have always accepted the word of the Bible: 'In the beginning God created the heaven and the earth'" ("A Scientist Caught," 115).

Jastrow ends his book with noteworthy words: "For the scientist who has lived by faith in the power of reason, the story ends like a bad dream. He has scaled the mountain of ignorance: He is about to conquer the highest peak; as he pulls himself over the final rock, he is greeted by a band of theologians who have been sitting there for centuries" (*God and the Astronomers,* 116).

Other atheists offer similar clues that the problem with drawing a theistic conclusion from the evidence is not rational but spiritual. Julian Huxley said, "For my own part, the sense of spiritual relief which comes from rejecting the idea of God as a supernatural being is enormous" (Huxley, 32). But if one is purely objective in viewing the evidence, then why experience "spiritually relief" at the news that God does not exist?

Perhaps the famous atheist, Friedrich Nietzsche, said it most clearly: "If one were to prove this God of the Christians to us, we should be even less able to believe in him" (Nietzsche, 627). Obviously, Nietzche's problem was not rational but *moral.*

Conclusion. In view of the incredible order in the universe, it is difficult to draw any conclusion other than existence of a supernatural, superintelligent Being behind it all. As one scientist quipped, you can lead a skeptical astronomer to order but you cannot make him think. After writing what he believed were definitive critiques of any attempt to demonstrate God's existence, even the great philosophical agnostic, Immanuel Kant, wrote: "Two things fill the mind with ever new and increasing admiration and awe, the oftener and more steadily we reflect on them: the starry heavens above and the moral law within me" (Kant, 166). Modern astronomers are again faced with the evidence of God for a Creator of the cosmos. It is interesting that this is the very thing to which the apostle Paul points as the reason that all are "without excuse" (Rom. 1:19–20).

Sources

I. Asimov, *The Beginning and the End*

F. Bacon, *Novum Organum*

W. L. Craig, *Theism, Atheism, and Big Bang Cosmology*

———, *The Existence of God and the Origin of the Universe*

A. Einstein, *Ideals and Opinions—The World as I See It*

N. L. Geisler, *Origin Science*

S. Hawking, *Black Holes and Baby Universes*

———, *A Brief History of Time*

F. Heeren, *Show Me God*

N. Herbert, *Quantum Reality—Beyond the New Physics*

F. Hoyle, et al., *The Intelligent Universe*

D. Hume, *The Letters of David Hume*

J. Huxley, *Religion without Revelation*

R. Jastrow, "A Scientist Caught between Two Faiths: Interview with Robert Jastrow," *CT,* 6 August 1982

———, *God and the Astronomers*

I. Kant, *Critique of Practical Reason*

M. D. Lemonick, "Echoes of the Big Bang," *Time,* 4 May 1993

J. P. Moreland, *The Creation Hypothesis*

F. Nietzsche, *Antichrist*

C. Sagan, *The Edge of Forever*

A. Sandage, "A Scientist Reflects on Religious Belief," *Truth,* 1985

V. J. Stenger, "The Face of Chaos," *Free Inquiry,* Winter 1992–93

S. Weinberg, *Dreams of a Final Theory—The Search for the Fundamental Laws of Nature.*

Bonaventure. *See* Cosmological Argument; *Kalam* Cosmological Argument.

Bruce, F. F. Frederick Fyvie Bruce (1910–1990) was born in Elgin, Scotland and trained in the classics at Elgin Academy, the University of Aberdeen, and Cambridge University. Though he is best known for his work in biblical studies, he never took formal courses in either Bible or theology. He was awarded an honorary doctor of divinity degree from Aberdeen. He taught Greek at Edinburgh (1934–35) and Leeds (1938–47). From 1959 to 1978 he was John Rylands Professor of Biblical Criticism and exegesis at Manchester

University. Concurrently (1956–78) he was a contributing editor for *Christianity Today* Magazine.

Bruce wrote nearly fifty books and about two thousand articles, essays, and reviews. He is best known for *The New Testament Documents: Are They Reliable?* (*see* NEW TESTAMENT MANUSCRIPTS, RELIABILITY OF). His *Commentary on the Epistles to the Ephesians and Colossians* is a standard. His most explicitly apologetic work is *The Defense of the Gospel* (1959). *The Books and the Parchments* (1963) supports the authenticity and reliability of the Bible, as does *Jesus and Christian Origins Outside the New Testament* (1974). He was also known for his work on Qumran, *Second Thoughts on the Dead Sea Scrolls* (1956).

Views and Teaching. *Scripture and Apologetics.* Bruce's conclusions on the Bible did not make him a strong defender of Scripture, though he generally fell within a conservative viewpoint. He did not consider himself a conservative, nor did he believe in the "inerrancy" of the Bible, though he looked on Scripture as "truth" (Gasque, 24). "If any of my critical conclusions, for example, are conservative, they are so not because they are conservative, nor because I am conservative, but because I believe them to be the conclusions to which the evidence points" (Gasque, 24). Bruce's chief importance for apologetics was as a defender of the reliability of the biblical manuscripts.

Bruce was not a Christian apologist as such, but his works support historical apologetics (*see* APOLOGETICS, HISTORICAL). *In Defense of the Gospel* is an exposition of the apologetics practiced by the apostles in the New Testament against Judaism, paganism, and early *gnosticism. Bruce insists that "Christian apologetics is a needed part of Christian witness" (*In Defense*, 10; *see also* APOLOGETICS, NEED FOR).

Resurrection. Bruce believed in the historicity of the resurrection accounts and in the bodily resurrection itself. He distinguished the Christian view of bodily resurrection from the Greek view of the *immortality of the soul ("Paul on Immortality," 464–65). He critiques the gnostic view of a spiritual resurrection, insisting that for Paul, "This future resurrection could only be a bodily resurrection" (ibid., 466). However, his view that believers receive their spiritual resurrection body at death has helped undermine the historic evangelical view of a physical resurrection body (*see* RESURRECTION, PHYSICAL NATURE OF). Of 2 Corinthians 5:1–10 he said, "Here Paul seems to imply that for those who do not survive until the *parousia* [coming], the new body will be immediately available at death" (ibid., 470–71). This led many of his students, including Murray Harris, to affirm the unorthodox view that the believer's resurrection body will come from heaven, not the grave. Harris later retracted this view under criticism (see Geisler, *The Battle for the Resurrection*, chaps. 6, 11).

Sources

F. F. Bruce, *Commentary on the Acts of the Apostles*

———, *Commentary on the Epistles to the Ephesians and Colossians*

———, *Jesus and Christian Origins Outside the New Testament*

———, *In Defense of the Gospel*

———, "Paul on Immortality," in Scottish Journal of Theology 24.4 (November 1971)

———, *Second Thoughts on the Dead Sea Scrolls*

———, *The Books and the Parchments*

———, *The New Testament Documents: Are They Reliable?*

W. Gasque, "F. F. Bruce: A Mind for What Matters" in *Christianity Today* (7 April 1989)

N. L. Geisler, *The Battle for the Resurrection*

M. Harris, *Raised Immortal*

Buber, Martin. Jewish existentialist Martin Buber (1878–1965) was born in Vienna, Austria and studied philosophy and art at the universities of Vienna, Zurich, and Berlin. An active Zionist as a young man, he was instrumental in the revival of Hasidism, a form of Jewish *mysticism. His famous "I-Thou" philosophy was developed in 1923, though William James had used the phrase in 1897. Buber taught at the University of Frankfurt from 1923 to 1933 and fled Germany in 1938. He taught at Hebrew University from 1938 to 1951. His form of existentialism was a significant influence on neoorthodox theologian Emil *Brunner.

Buber's major works include *Good and Evil* (tr. 1953), *I And Thou* (1923; tr. 1957), *The Eclipse of God* (tr. 1952), *The Prophetic Faith* (1949; tr. 1960), and *Two Types of Faith* (that is, Jewish and Christian; 1951; Eng. 1961).

The Philosophy of Buber. *I-Thou vs. I-It.* An I-Thou relation is where others are treated as an end, rather than as a means. People should be loved and things used, not the reverse. People are the subject, not the object. But many things can hinder I-Thou relations—seeming rather than being; speechifying rather than real dialogue; imposing oneself on, rather than unfolding oneself to another.

Since Buber believed in God, and Jean-Paul Sartre did not, their existential views form an instructive contrast:

Jean-Paul Sartre	Martin Buber
Common Project	I-Thou
Others are hell.	Others are heaven.
Others are the means of objectifying myself.	Others help me discover my true subjectivity in interpersonal relations.
There is no ultimate meaning, since humanity cannot	There is ultimate meaning, since there is an ultimate personal

become God.	ground of personal relationships.

God. According to Buber, God is "wholly other," but also "wholly the same," nearer to me than I am to myself (*see* God, Nature of). God is so close he cannot be sought, since there is nowhere he is not to be found. In fact, God is not sought by the human being; the human meets God through grace as God moves to the person. All who hallow this life meet the living God as the unfathomable condition of being. To see everything in God is not to renounce the world but to establish it on its true basis. We can sense God's presence, but can never solve his mysteriousness. God is experienced in and through the world and others, but must be met alone. In union with God, we are not absorbed, but remain an individual "I." By this ontological difference, Buber avoids absolute pantheism.

Religious Language. Like *Plotinus, Buber held that God is not the Good but the Supergood; he must be loved in his concealment. God does not name himself (in the "I Am That I Am"), but reveals himself. This is a disclosure, not a definition. The idea of God is a masterpiece of human construction, an image of the Imageless. Nonetheless, the word *God* should not be given up, simply because it is the most heavily laden of all human words, and thereby the most imperishable and indispensable of words. The word *religion,* however, is vexatious and has undergone the epidemic sickening of our time. It should be replaced by the phrase *all real human dealings with God.*

The Eclipse of God. Philosophy hinders the human relation to God. The person makes selfhood supreme and thus shuts off light from heaven. The passion peculiar to philosophers is pride in which their system replaces God. Further, objective "It" language is verbal idolatry that obscures God. God does not come under the law of contradiction; we speak of him only dialectically.

Evaluation. Among positive features to Buber's thought are its stress on the need for personal relationships and for a basis in God. Buber makes a valuable critique of the way philosophy has often eclipsed God and helpful suggestions about overcoming artificial relationships.

The view, however, is subject to many of the criticisms of other forms of religious existentialism (*see* Barth, Karl; Kierkegaard, Søren). From an evangelical Christian perspective a few are particularly worthy of note.

Denial of Propositional Revelation. Buber's denial of propositional revelation (*see* Revelation, Special) had a marked influence on Brunner and neoorthodoxy (*see* Bible, Evidence for). He denies that God has revealed himself in any propositional statements. This is a strange thing to say about a theistic God. This god can act but not talk; he is not dead, but he is dumb. Therefore the creatures can do what the Creator cannot. The effect is greater than the Cause.

Equivocal God-Talk. Not only is God tongue-tied, but when he does reveal himself the language conveys to us nothing about God himself. It is equivocal, totally different from the way God is. The effect is not similar to the Cause. God gives what he does not have. There is no analogy between Creator and creatures (*see* Analogy, Principle of).

A Mystical Epistemology. Buber is subject to the same criticisms as other mystics. How does one know it is God who is being encountered in this mystical experience, rather than Satan. A totally subjective experience has no objective criteria by which it can be evaluated. The Christian mystical experience is indistinguishable from the Buddhist mystical experience (*see* Buddhism). There are no meaningful criteria by which to know truth.

Sources

M. Buber, *Good and Evil*
———, *I and Thou*
———, *The Eclipse of God*
———, *The Prophetic Faith*
———, *Two Types of Faith*
N. L. Geisler, *Philosophy of Religion*
A. Johnson, *Faith Misguided: Exposing the Dangers of Mysticism*

Buddhism. ***See*** **Zen Buddhism; Pantheism.**

Bultmann, Rudolph. ***See*** **Miracles, Myth and.**

Butler, Joseph. Joseph Butler (1692–1753) was an important eighteenth-century English apologist (*see* Apologetics, Need for). Though he came from a Presbyterian family, Butler was ordained in the Church of England in 1718, after attending Oxford University. He eventually became bishop of Durham.

Although Butler made a significant contribution to the discussion of morality in "Three Sermons on Human Nature," he is best known for *Analogy of Religion* (1736), in which he defends Christianity against *Deism, particularly that of Anthony Ashley Cooper, Earl of Shaftesbury, and Matthew Tindal. Lord Shaftesbury wrote *Characteristics of Men, Manners, Opinions, Times* (1711) and Tindal, *Christianity as Old as the Creation* (1730).

Butler's Apologetic. Butler was influenced by his older contemporary, Samuel *Clarke, a disciple of Sir Isaac Newton and defender of the Christian Faith. *Analogy of Religion* was a defense of the plausibility of Christianity in terms of the analogy between revealed and natural religion (*see* Revelation, General).

The Use of Probability. In accord with the empirical basis of knowledge and the limitations of science, Butler argued, our knowledge of nature is only probable (*see* CERTAINTY/CERTITUDE; INDUCTIVISM). Since this is the case, "one is always in the position of a potential learner, and so never can posit what one knows of nature as *the standard* to judge what is natural" (Rurak, 367). Probability, which is the guide to life, supports the belief in a supernatural revelation from God in the Bible (*see* BIBLE, EVIDENCE FOR) and the miracles of Christ.

Butler began *Analogy* by noting that "It is come, I knew not how, to be taken for granted by many persons, that Christianity is not much a subject of inquiry, but that it is, now at length, discovered to be fictitious." His response is to the point that "any reasonable man who would thoroughly consider the matter, may be as much assured, as he is of his own being, that it is not however, so clear a case that there is nothing in it. There is, I think, strong evidence of its truth" (*Analogy in Religion,* 2).

Objection to Deism. Butler directed his attack against the deist Tindal who argued that "There's a religion of nature and reason written in the hearts of everyone of us from the first creation by which mankind must judge the truth of any instituted religion whatever" (Tindal, 50).

To deists who reject Scripture as a supernatural revelation because of its difficulties, Butler responds: "He who believes the Scriptures to have proceeded from him who is the Author of nature, may well expect to find the same sort of difficulties in it, as are found in the constitution of nature" (*see* REVELATION, GENERAL). Hence, "he who denies Scripture to have been from God, upon account of these difficulties, may for the very same reason, deny the world to have been formed by him" (*Analogy in Religion,* 9–10). Since the deists admitted the latter they should not deny the former. As James Rurak notes, "both natural and revealed religion will be assessed by the same standard, the constitution and course of nature. Natural religion cannot be used as a standard to judge revelation" (Rurak, 367). There is an analogy between them.

Judging Christianity as a Whole. Another result of Butler's analogous argument is that a system of religion must be judged as a whole, not simply from attacks leveled against specific parts, as the Deists were prone to do. When this standard was applied to Christianity, Butler believed that revealed that there is an "Intelligent Author and Governor of nature." He extended this analogy to belief that:

> Mankind is appointed to live in a future state; that everyone shall be rewarded or punished; . . . that this world being in the state of apostasy and wickedness . . . gave an occasion for an additional dispensation of Providence; of the utmost importance; proved by miracles; . . . carried on by a divine person, the Messiah, in order to the recovery of the world; yet not revealed to all men, nor proved with the strongest possible evidence to all those to whom it is revealed; but only to such a part of mankind, and with such particular evidence as the wisdom of God thought fit. [*Analogy in Religion,* 16–17]

Natural and Supernatural Revelation. With the deists Butler agrees that God is the Author of nature and that Christianity contains a republication of this original revelation in creation. However, Christianity is more than a supernatural revelation. Butler explains: "the essence of natural religion may be said to consist in the religious regards to 'God the Father Almighty': and the essence of revealed religion, as distinguished from natural, to consist in religious regard to 'the Son,' and to 'the Holy Ghost.'" And "How these revelations are made known, whether by reason or revelation, makes no alteration of the case; because the duties arise out of the relations themselves, not out of the manner in which we are informed of them" (*Analogy in Religion,* 198).

The Defense of Miracles. Butler devoted a chapter to the subject "Of the supposed Presumption against a Revelation, considered as miraculous." In his own summary of the argument (in the margin) he insists that there is

> I. No presumption, from analogy, against the general Christian Scheme; for (1) although undiscoverable by reason or experience, we only know a small part of a vast whole; (2) even if it be unlike the known course of nature, (a) the unknown may not *everywhere* resemble the known; (b) we observe unlikeness sometimes in nature; (c) the alleged unlikeness is not complete. Thus no presumption lies against the general Christian scheme, whether we call it miraculous or not.
>
> II. No presumption against a primitive revelation, for (i) *miracle* is relative to a *course* of nature. (ii) Revelation may well have followed Creation, which is an admitted fact. (iii) The further miracle [is] no additional difficulty." For "(iv) Tradition declares that Religion was revealed at the first."
>
> III. No presumption from analogy against miracles in historic times, for (a) we have no parallel case of a second fallen world; (b) in particular, (i) there is a presumption against all alleged facts before testimony, not after testimony. (ii) Reasons for miraculous intervention may have arisen in 5000 years. (iii) Man's need of supernatural guidance is such a reason. (iv) Miracles [are] comparable to *extraordinary* events, against which some presumption always lies. Thus (a) Miracles [are] not incredible. In fact, (b) In some cases, [they are] *a priori* probable. (c) In no case is there a peculiar

> presumption against them. [*Analogy in Religion,* 155–61]
>
> Upon all this I conclude; that there certainly is no such presumption against miracles, as to render them in any way incredible; that on the contrary, our being able to discern reasons for them, gives a positive credibility to the history of them, in cases where those reasons hold; and that is by no means certain, that there is any peculiar presumption at all, from analogy, even in the lowest degree, against miracles, as distinguished from other extraordinary [natural] phenomena.

Therefore, by analogy with nature, miracles are both credible and even *a priori* probable (*see* MIRACLE).

Evaluation. *On the Positive Side.* Given his deist context, Butler made a significant defense of Christianity. Arguing from their premise of natural revelation, he showed that there was no probable presumption against Christianity. Further, by reducing the epistemological basis to probability he commendably avoided rational necessity for his conclusions. Regardless of how one evaluates his results, he should be commended for his rational attempt to defend Christianity against the attacks of its naturalistic critics.

On the Negative Side. From the standpoint of a classical apologists (*see* CLASSICAL, APOLOGETICS), Butler unnecessarily weakened the cosmological argument by arguing from analogy.

Some naturalists argue that Butler's argument for miracles is based on a false analogy: "The presumption against miracles is not merely a presumption against a specific event, but against that *kind* of event taking place." Further, the comparison with extraordinary events in nature is not valid. "For in the case of these forces, given the same physical antecedents, the same consequents will always follow; and the truth of this can be verified by experiment" (Bernard, 161–62).

While this critique appears valid for some of the illustrations that Butler provides (e.g., electricity and magnetism), it does not appear to work with all singularities in nature. In particular, it would not apply to the *big bang theory held by many naturalistic scientists, since the antecedent conditions were nothing or nonbeing. From these, no prediction can be made nor verified by further experiment. Further, Butler appears to be correct in the negative side of his argument that there is no *a priori* probability against miracles. Indeed, he builds a strong case for *a priori* probability (*see* MIRACLES, ARGUMENTS AGAINST).

Sources

J. Butler, *Analogy in Religion*, esp. J. H. Bernard, "Note F: The Improbability of Miracle"

———, *Fifteen Sermons*

———, *The Works of Joseph Butler,* W. E. Gladstone, ed.

E. C. Mossner, *Bishop Butler and the Age of Reason*

J. Rurak, "Butler's Analogy: A Still Interesting Synthesis of Reason and Revelation," *ATR*, October 1980

M. Tindal, *Christianity as Old as the Creation*

Cc

Calvin, John. John Calvin (1509–1564) was born in Noyon, Picardy, France, but became the Reformer of Geneva, Switzerland. A humanist scholar in Paris when he was drawn to Reformation principles, he based much of his theological thought on the writings of Augustine. In addition to his systemization of theology, *Institutes of the Christian Religion,* Reformer John Calvin was a pioneer Protestant exegete of the Bible. *Calvin's Commentaries on Holy Scripture* are still widely used commentaries. Through Geneva Academy, Calvin and his colleagues also pioneered in evangelism training, Protestant scholarship, and a full-orbed Christian living ethic.

Apologetics of John Calvin. The followers of John Calvin are not united in their interpretation of his apologetic approach. Their number includes classical apologists and presuppositionalists (*see* CLASSICAL APOLOGETICS; PRESUPPOSITIONAL APOLOGETICS).

The presuppositionalists, with roots in Herman Dooyeweerd are headed by Cornelius Van Til and such of his followers as Greg Bahnsen and John Frame. The classical apologists follow B. B. Warfield's understanding of Calvin and are represented by Kenneth Kantzer, John Gerstner, and R. C. Sproul (see Kantzer). Calvin would have identified with classical apologists.

Calvin's Roots in Classical Apologetics. Contrary to the presuppositional view, Calvin's view of the use of human reason in the proclamation of the Gospel did not differ significantly from great thinkers before him. As *Augustine and *Thomas Aquinas, Calvin believed that the general revelation of God is manifest in nature and ingrained in the hearts of all men (*see* REVELATION, GENERAL).

The Innate Sense of Deity. "That there exists in the human mind, and indeed by natural instinct, some sense of Deity, we hold to be beyond dispute," Calvin said in *Institutes of the Christian Religion,* 1.3.1. He contended that "there is no nation so barbarous, no race so brutish, as not to be imbued with the conviction that there is a God" (ibid.). This "sense of Deity is so naturally engraven on the human heart, in the fact, that the very reprobate are forced to acknowledge it" (ibid., 1.4.4).

God's Existence and the Soul's Immortality. In Part One of *Institutes,* Calvin views "the invisible and incomprehensible essence of God, to a certain extent, made visible in his works" and "proofs of the soul's *immortality" (ibid., 1.5.1–2). For "on each of his [God's] works his glory is engraven in characters so bright, so distinct, and so illustrious, that none, however dull and illiterate, can plead ignorance as their excuse" (ibid.). Calvin did not formally elaborate these, as did Aquinas, but he would likely have accepted the teleological argument, the cosmological argument, and even the moral argument. The first two can be seen in his emphasis on design and causality and the last from his belief in a natural moral law. Commenting on Romans 1:20–21, Calvin concludes that Paul "plainly testifies here, that God has presented to the minds of all the means of knowing him, having so manifested himself by his works, that they must necessarily see what of themselves they seek not to know—that there is some God" (Calvin, 2).

**Natural Law.* For Calvin this innate knowledge of God includes knowledge of his righteous law. He held that, since "the Gentiles have the righteousness of the law naturally engraved on their minds, we certainly cannot say that they are altogether blind as to the rule of life" (*Institutes,* 1.2.22). He calls this moral awareness "natural law" that is "sufficient for their righteous condemnation" but not for salvation (ibid.). By this natural law "the judgment of conscience" is able to distinguish between the just from the unjust (*New Testament Commentaries,* 48). God's righteous nature "is engraved in characters so bright, so distinct, and so illustrious, that none, however dull and illiterate, can plead ignorance as their excuse" (*Institutes,* 1.5.1).

Not only is natural law clear, but it is also specific. There "is imprinted on their hearts a discrimination and judgment, by which they distinguish between justice and injustice, honesty and dishonesty." According to Calvin, even peoples with no knowledge of God's Word "prove their knowledge . . . that adultery, theft, and murder are evils, and honesty is to be esteemed" (*New Testament Commentaries,* 48). God has left proof of himself for all people in both creation and conscience.

Since a natural moral law implies a Moral Law Giver, Calvin would have agreed with what later became known as the *moral argument for God's existence. Indeed, his acceptance of natural law places him squarely in the tradition of the classical apologetics of Augustine, Anselm, and Aquinas.

The Evidence for Inspiration of Scripture. Calvin repeatedly spoke of "proofs" of the Bible's inspiration. These included the unity of Scripture, its majesty, its prophecies, and its miraculous confirmation. Calvin wrote: "We shall see . . . that the volume of sacred Scripture very far surpasses all other writings. Nay, if we look at it with clear eyes and unbiased judgment, it will forthwith present itself with a divine majesty which will subdue our presumptuous opposition, and force us to do it homage" (*Institutes,* 1.7.4). In the light of the evidence, even unbelievers "will be compelled to confess that the Scripture exhibits clear evidence of its being spoken by God and, consequently, of its containing his heavenly doctrine (ibid.).

The Vitiating Effects of Depravity. Calvin was quick to point out that depravity obscures this natural revelation of God. Calvin wrote: "Your idea of His [God's] nature is not clear unless you acknowledge Him to be the origin and foundation of all goodness. Hence, would arise both confidence in Him and a desire of cleaving to Him, did not the depravity of the human mind lead it away from the proper course of investigation" (ibid., 1.11.2).

The Role of the Holy Spirit. Calvin believed that complete certainty of God and the truth of Scripture comes only by the Holy Spirit. He wrote: "Our faith in doctrine is not established until we have a perfect conviction that God is its author. Hence, the highest proof of Scripture is uniformly taken from the character of him whose word it is. . . . Our conviction of the truth of Scripture must be derived from a higher source than human conjecture, judgments, or reasons; namely, the secret testimony of the Spirit" (ibid., 1.7.1; cf. 1.8.1) (*see* Holy Spirit, Role in Apologetics).

But it is important to remember, as R. C. Sproul points out, that "the *testimonium* is not placed over reason as a form of mystical subjectivism. Rather, it goes beyond and transcends reason" (Sproul, 341). In Calvin's own words, "But I answer that the testimony of the Spirit is superior to reason. For God alone can properly bear witness to his own words, so these words will not obtain full credit on the hearts of men, until they are sealed by the inward testimony of the Spirit" (ibid.)

God working through the objective evidence, provides subjective certainty that the Bible is the Word of God (*see* Bible, Evidence for).

Conclusion. Although John Calvin was, by virtue of his place in history, preoccupied primarily with the disputes over authority, soteriology and ecclesiology, nevertheless, the outline of his approach to apologetics seems clear. He falls into the general category of classical apologetics. This is evident both from his belief that "proofs" for God are available to the unregenerate mind and from his stress on general revelation and natural law (*see* Law, Nature and Kinds of).

Sources

J. Calvin, *Epistles of Paul to the Romans and Thessalonians*

———, *Institutes of the Christian Religion*

K. Kantzer, *John Calvin's Theory of the Knowledge of God and the Word of God*

R. C. Sproul, "The Internal Testimony of the Holy Spirit," in N. L. Geisler, ed., *Inerrancy*

B. B. Warfield, *Calvin and Calvinism*

Camus, Albert. Albert Camus (1913–1960) was a French novelist and essayist whose primary contributions were made during and after World War II. *The Stranger*, his first novel, and *The Myth of Sisyphus* (both 1942) were followed after the war by *The Plague* (1947) and *The Rebel* (1951). His last major work, *The Fall*, appeared in 1956, and in 1957 he was awarded the Nobel Prize in literature. He died in an automobile accident.

Views of God and Life. Camus was part of a small movement of French atheists (*see* Atheism) associated with existentialism and particularly with Jean-Paul Sartre. He began as a nihilist (*see* Nihilism), believing that in view of life's absurdities, the only serious philosophical question was suicide. He gradually moved to a more humanistic position (*see* Humanism, Secular).

In view of the denial of God, Camus, like other atheists, was left with no anchor for moral absolutes. Nonetheless, he espoused a moralistic humanism, speaking out strongly about what he regarded as moral evils, including war and capital punishment. Even his moral protest against theism belies basic moral values. The freedom of the individual was paramount; the value he placed on human life left him opposed to suicide.

Camus argued forcefully that theism is antihumanitarian, in view of the intolerable suffering inflicted on humankind (*see* Evil, Problem of). In *The Plague* the dilemma he sets before theism is described through a story of a plague caused by rats. His reasoning can be stated:

> One must either join the doctor and fight the plague or join the priest and not fight the plague.

Not to join the doctor and fight the plague is antihumanitarian.

To fight the plague is to fight against God, who sent it.

Therefore, if humanitarianism is right, theism is wrong.

Evaluation. *Positives in Camus's Thought.* From the beginning in *The Myth of Sisyphus* Camus incisively penetrated the absurdity of a life lived apart from God. In his earlier nihilistic moods he saw the futility of suicide. His humanitarian philosophy demonstrated a deeply moral concern about the plight of humanity. On his journey into *existentialism, he came to see the failure of his earlier nihilism. He also moved toward an understanding of what Christians call human depravity. Throughout his life, Camus reflected a deep need for God.

Negative Dimensions. The argument from evil against theism wrongly assumes that God is the author of all evil in the world. No responsibility is assigned to human beings for their sinful actions in inflicting suffering on themselves (*see* FREE WILL). The Bible makes it clear that the rebellion of Adam and Eve and their descendants causes evil and death (Rom. 5:12). All of nature is infected by the fall (Romans 8).

Also, Camus assumes that it is inconsistent with Christian belief in the sovereignty of God for Christians to have compassion for those who suffer. Both in principle and in practice, Christianity has offered more respite to the sufferer at every level than has non-Christian philosophy. Even agnostic Bertrand *Russell acknowledged that what the world needed was Christian love and compassion (Russell, 579). Only in Christianity has something been done through the death and resurrection of Christ to stop the plague of sin (Rom. 4:25; 1 Cor. 15:1–4).

Like many other atheists, Camus revealed a longing for God (*see* GOD, EVIDENCE FOR). He wrote, "for anyone who is alone, with God and without a master, the weight of days is dreadful" (*The Fall*, 33). He added elsewhere, "Nothing can discourage the appetite for divinity in the heart of man" (*The Rebel*, 147).

The novelist's sense of moral right and wrong should have led him to posit a Moral Law Giver whose presence alone accounts for the eradicable moral conviction that some injustices are absolutely wrong (*see* MORAL ARGUMENT FOR GOD). As the former Oxford atheist, C. S. Lewis, asked himself, "Just how had I got this idea of just and unjust? A man does not call a line crooked unless he has some idea of a straight line." He adds, "What was I comparing this universe with when I called it unjust. . . . Of course I could have given up my idea of justice by saying it was nothing but a private idea of my own," he concludes. "But if I did that, then my argument against God collapsed too—for the argument depended on saying that the world was really unjust, not simply that it did not happen to please my private fancies." Thus, "in the very act of trying to prove that God did not exist—in other words, that the whole of reality was senseless—I found I was forced to assume that one part of reality—namely my idea of justice—was full of sense" (Lewis, 45, 46).

Sources

G. Bree, *Camus*

A. Camus, *The Fall*

———, *The Myth of Sisyphus*

———, *The Plague*

———, *The Rebel*

———, *The Stranger*

P. Edwards, "Camus, Albert," *EP*

C. S. Lewis, *Surprised by Joy*

B. Russell, "What Is an Agnostic?" *The Basic Writings of Bertrand Russell*, R. E. Egner, et al., eds.

Canaanites, Slaughter of the. When the Israelites reached the Canaanite city of Jericho at the beginning of their invasion of the land of promise, Joshua and his soldiers "utterly destroyed all that was in the city, both man and woman, young and old, ox and sheep and donkey, with the edge of the sword" (Josh. 6:21). Bible critics charge that such ruthless destruction of innocent life and property cannot be morally justified. It seems contrary to God's command not to kill innocent human beings (see Exod. 20:13).

Reasons for Destruction. Defenses of the actions of ancient Israel fall into three categories: (1) a challenge of the presumption of moral innocence; (2) delineation of implications from the unique theocratic nature of the command, and (3) examination of the conditions under which it was executed.

Scripture makes it very clear that Canaanites were far from "innocent." The description of their sins in Leviticus 18 is vivid: "The land is defiled; therefore I visit the punishment of its iniquity upon it, and the land vomits out its inhabitants" (vs. 25). They were cancerously immoral, "defiled" with every kind of "abomination," including child sacrifice (vss. 21, 24, 26).

God had given the people of Palestine over 400 years to repent of their wickedness. The people of that land had every opportunity to turn from their wickedness. According to Genesis 15:16, God told Abraham that his descendants would return to inherit this land, but not yet, for the iniquity of the people was not yet full. This prophetic statement indicated that God would not destroy the people of the land until their guilt merited complete destruction in judgment.

In this, Joshua and the people of Israel were not acting according to their own initiative. The destruction of Jericho was carried out by the army of Israel as the instrument of judgment upon the sins of these people by the righteous

Judge of all the earth. No other nation before or since has possessed this special relation to God or this mandate (cf. Exod. 19:5; Deut. 4:8; Ps. 147:20; Rom. 3:1–2). Consequently, anyone who would question the justification of this act is questioning God's justice.

God is sovereign over all life and has the right to take what he gives. Job declared "The LORD gave and the LORD has taken away; may the name of the LORD be praised" (Job 1:21). Moses recorded God's words: "See now that I myself am he! There is no god besides me. I put to death and I bring to life, I have wounded and I will heal, and no one can deliver out of my hand" (Deut. 32:39). Human beings do not create life, and they do not have the right to take it (Exod. 20:13), except under guidelines laid by the one who owns all human life.

God permits life taking in self-defense (Exod. 22:2), in capital punishment (Gen. 9:6), and in just war (cf. Gen. 14:14–20). And when there is a theocratic command to do so, as in the case of Israel and the Canaanites, its moral justification is vouchsafed by God's sovereignty.

As for the killing of the children as part of this command, it should be noted that, given the cancerous state of the society into which they were born, they could not avoid its fatal pollution. If children who die before the age of accountability go to heaven (*see* INFANTS, SALVATION OF), this was an act of God's mercy to take them into his holy presence from this unholy environment. Ultimately, however, the primary argument throughout Scripture is that God is sovereign over life (Deut. 32:39; Job 1:21). He can order its end according to his will, and his people can have utter confidence that God's actions are for good.

Conclusion. In the case of the Canaanites, it was necessary in establishing a holy nation and priesthood to exterminate the godlessness of the city and its people. If anything had remained, except that which was taken into the treasure house of the Lord, there would have always been the threat of heathen influence to pull the people away from the pure worship of the Lord. As the subsequent history of Israel shows, that is what happened.

Sources

G. L. Archer, Jr., *An Encyclopedia of Biblical Difficulties*

N. L. Geisler and T. Howe, *When Critics Ask*

J. Haley, *Alleged Discrepancies of the Bible*

W. Kaiser, ed., *Classical Evangelical Essays in Old Testament Interpretation*

J. Orr, *Christian View of God and the World*, appendix to Lecture 5

Canonicity. ***See*** **BIBLE, CANONICITY OF.**

Carnell, Edward John. Edward John Carnell (1919–1967) was a pioneer apologist of the evangelical renaissance after World War II. A founding faculty member at Fuller Theological Seminary in 1948, he served as president from 1955–1959. He suffered from depression and life-long insomnia which occasioned his confessed addiction to barbiturates. He tragically died of an overdose of sleeping pills, whether accidental or intentional, at the early age of forty-eight.

Carnell wrote eight books, most of which deal with apologetics: *An Introduction to Christian Apologetics* (1948); *The Theology of Reinhold Niebuhr* (1951); *A Philosophy of the Christian Religion* (1952); *Christian Commitment: An Apologetic* (1957); *The Case for Orthodox Theology* (1959); *The Kingdom of Love and the Pride of Life* (1960); and *The Burden of Søren *Kierkegaard* (1965). Articles and reviews also touch on apologetics. Of special note is the three-part article, "How Every Christian Can Defend His Faith" in *Moody Monthly* (January, February, March 1950).

The influences that molded Carnell's thought are summarized by one of his foremost disciples, Gordon Lewis: "At Wheaton College in the classes of Gordon H. *Clark, Carnell found the test of noncontradiction (*see* FIRST PRINCIPLES). The test of fitness to empirical fact was championed by Edgar S. Brightman at Boston University where Carnell earned his Ph.D." Finally, the requirement of relevance to personal experience became prominent during Carnell's Th.D. research at Harvard University in the study of Søren Kierkegaard and Reinhold Niebuhr" (Lewis, *Testing Christianity's Truth Claims*, 176).

Carnell's Apologetic. Carnell was hypothetical or presuppositional (*see* PRESUPPOSITIONAL APOLOGETICS) in his approach, in contrast to a *classical apologetic method.

Carnell defined apologetics as "that branch of Christian theology which has the task of defending the faith." He added, "There is no 'official' or 'normative' approach to apologetics." Instead, "The approach is governed by the climate of the times. This means, as it were, that an apologist must play it by ear" (*Kingdom of Love*, 6).

Looking back over his own apologetic efforts, he wrote, "In my own books on apologetics I have consistently tried to build on some useful point of contact between the gospel and culture." For example, "In *An Introduction to Christian Apologetics*, the appeal was to the law of noncontradiction; in *A Philosophy of the Christian Religion* it was to values, and in *Christian Commitment* it was to the judicial sentiment. In this book [*The Kingdom of Love and the Pride of Life*] I am appealing to the law of love" (ibid., 6).

Rejecting Classical Arguments. Like other presuppositionalists, Carnell rejected the validity of traditional theistic arguments (*see* God, EVIDENCE FOR). In this he follows many of the arguments of skeptics, such as David *Hume, and agnostics (*see* AGNOSTICISM), such as Immanuel *Kant.

The basic problems with theistic arguments. The fundamental reason Carnell rejects theistic reasoning is its starting point. It begins in experience and ends in skepticism (*An Introduction to Christian Apologetics,* 126f.). In fact, Carnell lists seven objections:

1. Empiricism ends in skepticism. "If all the mind has to work with are sense-perceptions as reports to the mind of what is going on in the external world, knowledge can never rise to the universal and the necessary, for from flux only flux can come" (ibid., 129).
2. The principle of economy eliminates the Christian God. Hume set the pace for empiricists by insisting that the cause be proportionate to the effect, but not necessarily greater. An infinite effect dictates an infinite cause, but a finite effect need not.
3. The fallacy of impartation. Even "granted that a cause *may* have more perfections than are seen in the effect, . . . the finite universe does not *require* for its explanation the existence of an infinite cause."
4. Fallacy of one God. How can we be assured that the God proved in the first argument is the same Deity as the moral Governor? Since none need be infinite, for the effect is finite, there is room for thousands of gods.
5. Fallacy of anticipation. *Thomas Aquinas used the same arguments as did Aristotle, but came out with the differing conclusion of a personal God. Was this not because Thomas *already* had heart-experience of the true God?
6. Predicament of commitment. Once we are committed to an empirical position, how can we show that what we have demonstrated is the Father of Jesus Christ? The data of nature are satisfied by Aristotle's Unmoved Mover, so why move on to the Trinity?
7. Nonempirical presuppositions. "To prove God's existence from the flux found in nature requires concepts that cannot be found in nature. . . . To know the cause one must first know the uncaused. . . . Thus empirical arguments are successful only if one begins with concepts that are significant when God is already known, for he alone is unmoved, uncaused, noncontingent, perfect, and absolute" (ibid., 133–34). Even "a chip on the statue or a flaw on the canvas makes the artist inferior. . . . In short, the universe evinces too much evil in it to bear the weight of the teleological argument" (ibid., 139).

At best, empirical theistic arguments have only "nuisance value," showing that empiricism is insufficient and pointing to something else beyond the empirical (ibid., 152).

Rejection of Other "Tests for Truth." Carnell reviews and discards other tests for truth.

1. *Instincts* "cannot be a test for truth, since they cannot distinguish between what is legitimately natural to the species and what is acquired. Only the mind can do that."
2. *Custom* is an inadequate test because "customs can be good or bad, true or false. Something beyond and outside of custom, therefore, must test the validity of customs themselves."
3. *Tradition,* a more normative body of customs handed down by a group from early times, is insufficient. "There are in existence so many traditions, so conflicting in essentials, that only in a madhouse could all be justified."
4. *Consensus gentium,* or the "consent of the nations," fails as a test for truth. All once believed that the world was the center of the universe. "A proposition must be true to be worthy of the belief of all, but it does not follow that what is believed by all is true."
5. *Feeling* is insufficient, for "without reason to guide it, feeling is irresponsible."
6. *Sense perception* is at best "a source for truth, not its definition or test. Our senses often deceive us."
7. *Intuition* cannot test truth, since we cannot detect false intuitions, of which there are many."
8. *Correspondence* of an idea to reality cannot be a test. "If reality is extra-ideational, then how can we compare our idea of the mind with it?"
9. *Pragmatism* is inadequate, for on a purely pragmatic ground there is no way to distinguish between materialism's and theism's opposing views of the highest ultimate (whether material or spiritual reality). Further, a pragmatist has no right, according to his theory, to expect his theory to be verified by future experience, since he has no basis on which to believe in the regularity of the world.

Carnell argues all deductive proofs to be inadequate, because "reality cannot be connected by formal logic alone. . . . Logical truth cannot pass into material truth until the facts of life are introduced into the picture." And inductive proofs are invalid tests for truth, for they cannot rise above probability. "A premise is demonstrated only when it is the necessary implication of a self-evident premise or when its contradiction is shown to be false" (*Introduction to Christian Apologetics,* 48–53, 105).

The Necessity of Innate Ideas. One alternative to empiricism, then, is a kind of "Christian rationalism." Augustine taught that "the mind by natural endowment from the Creator enjoys immediate apprehension of those standards which make our search for the true, the good, and the beautiful meaningful." For "to speak meaningfully of the true, the good, and the beautiful, . . . we must have criteria; but criteria that are universal and necessary must be found other than in the flux of sense perception." Otherwise, "how do we know that a thing must be coherent to be true, if the soul, by nature, is not in possession of the conviction?" And "how is it that we are able confidently to say that what is good today will be good tomorrow, unless we lodge our theory of the good in something outside the process of history?" In brief, "how can we know what the character of all reality is, so as to act wisely unless God tells us?" (ibid., 152–57).

Carnell believes the laws of logic to be innate evidence for God (*see* LOGIC). People have an inborn sense of the rules for right thinking. Therefore, the rules must be innate. Apart from the God revealed in Scripture, it would be meaningless to say that murder is wrong today, so it will be wrong tomorrow. That we can make such a statement is a verification that an Author of our moral nature exists.

There also is a knowledge of God through nature. The world is regular; it shows proof of a God who makes things that are coherent. We can make sense of our existence, and we should not be able to, except by this presupposition or hypothesis.

A Presuppositional Basis for All Knowledge. A second alternative to empiricism confirms the first. The second entails an existential analysis of what makes human life meaningful (see Lewis, "Three Sides to Every Story").

All thought involves assumptions (ibid., 91, 95). Carnell recognizes that "It may be asked why we make assumptions at all. Why not stay with the facts? The answer to this is *very easy* indeed! We make assumptions because we must make assumptions to think at all. The best assumptions are those which can account for the totality of reality" (ibid., 94). Thus, like the scientific method we must begin with a "hypothesis" and then proceed to test it (ibid., 89f.).

The Christian hypothesis is the best presupposition. "The Christian assumes both God and the Scriptures" (ibid., 101). Actually, "God is the Christian's only major premise, but this God is known through the Scriptures" (ibid.).

As to the charge of circular reasoning, Carnell answers frankly, "The Christian begs the question by assuming the truth of God's existence to establish that very existence. Indeed! This is true for establishing the validity of any ultimate. The truth of the law of [non]contradiction" must be assumed to prove the validity of that axiom (*see* FIRST PRINCIPLES). Nature must be assumed to prove nature" (ibid.). Actually, "strict demonstration of a first postulate is impossible, as Aristotle pointed out, for it leads either to infinite regress or to circular reasoning" (ibid., 102).

This is not to say that some hypotheses are not better informed than others.

The Inadequacy of Tests for Truth. "The truth is a quality of that judgment or proposition which, when followed out into the total witness of facts in our experience, does not disappoint our expectations" (*Introduction to Christian Apologetics,* 45). Truth is what corresponds to God's mind. It is thinking God's thoughts after him (ibid., 47).

The inadequacy of deductive tests for truth. Carnell rejects both strictly deductive and inductive arguments as ways to establish the truth of Christianity. In their place he favors a presuppositional approach. Deductive proofs are rejected because "When one demonstrates a proposition, he shows that it is the necessary conclusion of a premise which is already known to be true. . . . One can easily detect that pure demonstration is operative only within a system of formal symbols, as in logic and mathematics" (ibid., 104).

The inadequacy of inductive tests for truth. Inductive reasoning (*see* INDUCTIVE METHOD) is rejected as an adequate test for the truth of Christianity for "here one cannot rise above *probability" (ibid., 105). No real proof is possible with a *probability argument, since the opposite is always possible.

The inadequacy of general revelation. While some appeal is made to general revelation (*see* REVELATION, GENERAL) as a point of contact, Carnell argues that it is an inadequate basis for knowing the truth about God. Carnell agreed with Calvin that general revelation "ought not only excite us to the worship of God, but likewise to awaken and arouse us to the hope of future life. But, notwithstanding the clear representations given by God in the mirror of his works . . . such is our stupidity, that, always inattentive to these obvious testimonies we derive no advantage from them." We must then make recourse to special revelation (*Introduction to Christian Apologetics,* 159–72).

The need for special revelation. Since general revelation is inadequate, there is a need to presuppose the truth of special revelation. Therefore, the appeal to special revelation in Scripture is—like any other hypothesis—verifiable if its resulting system is horizontally self-consistent and vertically conforms to reality.

Carnell stresses that trading natural for special revelation does not divide Christian epistemology. There is a single major premise, that God who has revealed himself in Scripture exists. This premise strengthens the faith of one who believes, "for faith is a resting of the soul in the sufficiency of the evidence." The Bible is needed to give us more evidence. For "truth" is systematically constructed meaning, and if the Bible fulfills this standard, it is just as true as Lambert's law of transmission. Any hypothesis is verified when it smoothly interprets life (ibid., 175).

Carnell defends both the fact and necessity of special revelation. No philosophical argument proves revelation cannot take place, for "one can know whether God has revealed Himself or not only after examining all the facts of reality, for any one fact overlooked may be the very revelation itself. . . . To track God down, therefore, one must at least be everywhere at the same time, which is to say, he must be God Himself." In essence, "if a man says there is no God, he simply makes himself God, and thus revelation is made actual. If he says there is a God, the only way he can know this is by God's having revealed Himself." For "the fundamental reason why we need a special revelation is to answer the question, What must I do to be saved? Happiness is our first interest, but this happiness cannot be ours until we know just how God is going to dispose of us at the end of history" (ibid., 175–78).

The Systematic-Consistency Test. Two tests help us evaluate the truth of a worldview: First, it must be logically consistent; second, it must explain all the relevant facts. These join as one criteria called "systematic consistency." "Accept that revelation which, when examined, yields a system of thought which is horizontally self-consistent and which vertically fits the facts of history." The Bible is not arbitrarily accepted as the Word of God. To elect any other position would ignore the facts (ibid., 190).

The Negative Test: Noncontradiction. The basic rational test for truth is the law of noncontradiction. It is an innate necessity for human thought and life. Without the law of noncontradiction, neither sensation nor truth nor speech are possible (ibid., 161–63). This law of thought is epistemologically prior to all knowing (ibid., 164f.). Carnell's defense of the law of noncontradiction is what Cornelius Van Til called a *"transcendental argument."

The Positive Test: Factual Fit. In addition to "horizontal self-consistency," Carnell's second test for truth was that the system *vertical fits the facts* (ibid., 108–9). Self-consistency is only a starting point. Without it, truth is absent, without something more, truth is truncated (ibid., 109). As Lewis put it: "A mere formal consistency without factual adequacy is empty and irrelevant. On the other hand, an experiential relevance without consistency ends in chaos and meaninglessness" (*Testing Christianity's Truth Claims,* 206).

The "facts" included external experience, such as historical facts, and internal experience, such as personal, subjective peace of heart (Introduction, 109–13). Carnell's "facts" include ethical, existential, psychological, and value matters.

Values are part of the factual fit. Carnell was convinced that no other worldview can satisfy the human quest for personal fellowship. No other provides meaningful standards of love and forgiveness (Lewis, *Testing Christianity's Truth Claims,* 218). Carnell devotes *A Philosophy of the Christian Religion* to this thesis. Lewis noted, "Edward Carnell sought to show that Christianity is not only *true,* but most *desirable* for each individual person" (*Testing Christianity's Truth Claims,* 210, emphasis added).

Carnell wrote *Christian Commitment* and *The Kingdom of Love and the Pride of Life* to make the case that Christianity alone provides a value-satisfaction system. As stated in Francis *Schaeffer's existential authenticity, one can live by Christian principles without hypocrisy.

In *Kingdom of Love and the Pride of Life,* Carnell argued the unconventional thesis that Freudian psychotherapy provides the model for doing an apologetic of love, since it relates trust and love to happiness. He declared: "I believe that if Christian apologists would rally their wits and make better use of love as a point of contact, great things might be accomplished for the defense of the faith" (*Kingdom of Love,* 10). He added that he had not appreciated the apologetic significance of love until he read Sigmund Freud. "The more I reflected on the relationship between patient and analyst, the more convinced I became that psychotherapy has unwittingly created a new base for Christian apologetics. Christianity has always defended love as the law of life" (ibid., 6). Love is unconditional acceptance. It is always kind and truthful, and it seeks nothing but kindness and truth in return. "If man is made in the image of God (as Scripture says he is), then conservatives ought to welcome any evidence which helps establish a vital connection between the healing power of the gospel and man as a creature who is plagued by anxiety and estrangement. A divorce between common and special grace is an offense to both culture and the gospel" (ibid., 9).

Defenders of Carnell recognize that this values approach has limits. Gordon Lewis asks: "Is the psychological apologetic sufficient by itself, however, to support Christianity's truth-claims?" He answers his own question in the negative: Experientially, the truth of love answers problems, but from a theoretical viewpoint, "a religion might alleviate people's anxieties with counterfeit promises. In fact, that is what some of Christianity's cultic deviations do" (*Testing Christianity's Truth Claims,* 252).

Ethics is part of factual fit. Christianity alone can resolve the individual's moral predicament. No other religion can give a consistent answer to the question: How can a sinner be just before God? Lewis sums up Carnell's test(s) for truth: "In sum, Carnell's apologetic finds the Christian hypothesis true because, without contradiction, it accounts for more empirical evidence . . . , axiological evidence . . . , psychological evidence . . . , ethical evidence . . . , with fewer difficulties than any other hypothesis" (ibid., 282).

Probability and Moral Certainty. Carnell is aware that his method does not yield absolute rational certainty. He willingly settles for high-probability rational confidence if it accompanies a moral certainty that goes beyond reasonable doubt (*Introduction to Christian Apologetics,* 113f.).

The Point of Contact: The Image of God. Unlike Van Til, Carnell believed that the natural human was capable of understanding some truths about God. He disliked "vague homilies on the *'noetic effects of sin'" (*Christian Commitment,* 198). Among other things, the image of God provides both innate moral principles and the very idea of God. Citing John Calvin with approval, Carnell wrote, "One certainly ought not to find it strange that God, in creating me, placed this idea (God) with me to be like the mark of the workman imprinted on his work" (*Introduction to Christian Apologetics,* 160).

Evaluation. *Contributions of Carnell's Apologetics. The stress on the law of noncontradiction.* Carnell correctly emphasized the importance of the law of noncontradiction as a negative test for rationality (*see* LOGIC). He understood its transcendental importance and never wavered from using it, in spite of the fact that he added other dimensions to his overall criteria for the truth of a worldview.

The demand for factual fit. Unlike the rational presuppositionalism of Clark, Carnell's apologetic took into account the need to be comprehensive in any adequate test for truth. Logical consistency offers only a negative test for falsity. Positively, it shows only that a system *could be* true, not that it *is true.* To demonstrate truth, a worldview must touch base with reality.

The rejection of factual sufficiency. Carnell recognized that ultimate, metaphysical truth does not reside in facts as such. Facts alone are insufficient. Only fact understood in the consistent context of an entire worldview can be the basis for ultimate truth. Unless the "stuff" of experience is structured by a meaning-model, it is not possible to speak of the meaningfulness of that system. One must presuppose or hypothesize a metaphysical model of the universe before it is even possible to make ultimate truth claims. One can, of course, understand facts in an everyday sense. Believer and unbeliever may share common ground in understanding of what a dozen roses are. But that the ultimate meaning of those roses is to glorify the theistic God is known only by those who hold a theistic presupposition.

The need for a worldview framework. Carnell correctly saw the need for a world and life view, that is, with what in German is called a *Weltanschauung.* Merely one dimension of the truth question is not enough. Worldview truths must cover all that is in the world. To single out the rational element, the empirical element, or the existential element alone is inadequate. Carnell saw clearly the need to test the truth of the entire Christian system. He integrated the three basic elements in this test: the rational, the empirical, and the existential.

The contextual validity of systematic coherence. Granted a theistic framework, systematic consistency is a sufficient method for determining the truth. That is, within a theistic worldview, the position that most consistently explains all the relevant facts is true. This is why Christianity meets the test and Judaism does not, since the former accounts for all the predictive prophecy (*see* PROPHECY AS PROOF OF THE BIBLE) about the Messiah, and the latter does not. Likewise, Islam does not account for the theistic evidence that Christ died on the cross and rose from the dead three days later. Christianity does. Hence, both Judaism and Islam fail on the test of comprehensiveness.

The need for existential relevance. Carnell saw what few apologists are willing to admit, that a true *Weltanschauung* must be relevant to life. It was not fully stressed in *An Introduction to Christian Apologetics.* But by the time he wrote *Christian Commitment: An Apologetic,* existential relevance was important to Carnell's comprehensive test for the truth of his system.

Difficulties in Carnell's Apologetics. Carnell's apologetic is not without its faults, some of them crucial defects.

Innate epistemology. Carnell evidently draws on Augustine for his belief in innate ideas. While this is not a fatal criticism of his system, it is worth noting that belief in innate ideas is unfounded (*see* HUME, DAVID) and unnecessary. The same data can be accounted for by simply positing an innate *capacity* without innate *ideas.* Both *Kant and *Aquinas demonstrated how this could be done—Aquinas without ending in agnosticism.

Rejection of theistic arguments. While Carnell rejects the validity of traditional theistic arguments, he uses a theistic argument of his own. Following *Augustine and Rene *Descartes, Carnell argues that total skepticism is self-refuting. If the skeptic is doubting, then he is thinking. And if he thinks then he must exist (*cogito ergo sum*). But Carnell argues that this gives not only a knowledge of self, but "the *cogito* provides us with a knowledge of God. Knowing what truth is, we know what God is, *for God is truth.*" He adds, "Proof for God is parallel to proof for logic; logic must be used to prove logic" (ibid., 158–59). So while Carnell rejects traditional theistic arguments he offers a "proof" of his own—one that is the same as his proof for the validity of the laws of logic. Indeed, this can be put in the same form as what Van Til called a *transcendental argument. So the question is not whether one can prove God, but rather which kind of proof works. Carnell, then, is not really a presuppositionalist but a rational theist—offering a proof for God's existence.

Carnell, of course, believes that this kind of argument avoids the flux of sense experience because it has an interior starting point in the self, not an external one in nature. Yet, when commenting on Romans 1:20 he admits that "the heavens [external nature] declare the glory of God, for they constantly remind us that God exists. The limited perfection of nature is a reminder of absolute perfection; the mutability of nature is a reminder that there is absolute immutability." He even admits that his factual test for truth is the external world, for by *"fitting the facts* we mean being *true to nature"* (*Introduction to Christian Apologetics,* 109). He hastens to say, "this is not a formal demonstration of God's existence; it is simply a proof by coherence" (ibid., 169–70). But regardless of what it is called, it is still a rational "proof" for God's existence that can be made from external nature, which is what the traditional theistic arguments rejected by Carnell purport to accomplish.

Inconsistent use of probability. Carnell is also inconsistent in his use of *probability. Carnell chastises apologetic approaches that begin with empirical and historical probabilities. Empirical argumentation is rejected as an adequate test for the truth of Christianity for "here one cannot rise above probability" (ibid., 105). He insists that no real proof is possible with a probability argument, since the opposite is always possible. However, when defending against the charge that his view only yields probability on even crucial matters like the resurrection of Christ, he responds by claiming that probability is sufficient. For "No historical event, however recent, can be demonstrated beyond a degree of probability. So it would be inappropriate to expect verification of Christ's resurrection, for example, to rise to the point of logical necessity" (ibid., 198). But one cannot have it both ways. If probability is never a proof, then no matter how high the probability Carnell would have no proof of the resurrection (cf. Acts 1:3).

A methodological category mistake. Carnell explicitly treats the testing of the truth claims of Christianity like the testing of a scientific "hypothesis" (*An Introduction to Christian Apologetics,* 101). But, as Etienne Gilson has brilliantly demonstrated, this is a methodological category mistake. Borrowing a method from geometry, or mathematics, or science is not the way to do metaphysics. Each discipline has its own appropriate method. And what works in science, for example, does not necessarily work in metaphysics.

Arguing in a vicious circle. The use of facts to test the truth of the worldview, which in turn gives meaning to these facts, is a vicious circle. When testing worldviews, one cannot presuppose the truth of a given context or framework, for that is precisely what is being tested. But Carnell's apologetic method of systematic consistency cannot be a test for the context (or model) by which the very facts, to which he appeals, are given meaning.

Factual fit is inadequate to test a worldview because "fit" is determined for the facts by the overall pattern of the worldview. A fact's meaning is not found in its bare facticity but by the way it is modeled or incorporated by a worldview. Carnell says, "a fact is any unit of being which is capable of bearing meaning, but it is the meaning, not the fact, which is the knowledge" (*Introduction to Christian Apologetics,* 92). If so, then it seems clear that the same data (say, the resurrection of Christ) can be interpreted alternately as an anomaly (from a naturalistic perspective), a supernormal magical event (from a pantheistic view), or a supernatural act of God (from a theistic worldview). Incompatible worldviews inevitably color the same data to mean different things. By not using theistic arguments to establish an overall world view context for the facts of experience, Carnell is not able to avoid this criticism (*see* MIRACLES, ARGUMENTS AGAINST). For example, some ancient languages that did not divide letters into words left the reader to decide from the context. No appeal to the bare facts alone can solve the problem; only a context, model, or framework from outside can do it. And when one framework fits as well as another, then there is no way to adjudicate the problem by appealing to differing models that each in its own way accounts for all the facts. Or, differing systems may account equally well for an equal number of facts, while having difficulty with others.

Systematic coherence offers no way to know whether the model fits the facts best because the facts are prefitted to the model to give meaning to the whole from the very beginning. The fact of the resurrection of Christ is already a theistic "interprafact" and as such it will naturally fit better into a theistic scheme of things than into a naturalistic worldview. However, if one speaks merely about the anomalous or unusual event of a resuscitated corpse in the framework of a naturalistic worldview, the bare fact also fits the framework.

Conflict of multiple criteria for testing truth. A system that has many criteria for testing truth, as did Carnell's, has a problem with what to do when the criteria yield conflicting results. No criteria is offered by Carnell to adjudicate such conflicts. What happens, for example, if the love criterion conflicts with the law of noncontradiction? What happens when the facts seem to support a position that conflicts with another central tenet of one's system?

The "leaky bucket" fallacy. Systematic coherence is a form of the "leaky bucket" argument. It says, in effect, that empiricism is not an adequate test for truth, existentialism is not an adequate test for truth, and rationalism is not an adequate test for truth. However, if one leaky bucket does not hold the water, then two or three leaky buckets will not do the job either. Just adding together inadequate solutions does not make an adequate solution, unless there is some way to correct the inadequacy of one test.

But the problem with logical coherence as a test for truth is not corrected by appeal to facts. This logical argument does not fail simply because it provides no factual referents for thought, but because in its strong form it provides no rationally inescapable arguments, and in the weak form it is only a test for the possibility of a system's truth. The law of noncontradiction can show only that a system is wrong if it has contradictions in its central tenets. But several systems may be internally noncontradictory. Likewise, there may be many worldviews that account for all the data of experience as they interpret it. Pantheism, for example, has no necessary internal logical contradictions, and it can account for all the facts as interpreted through its worldview lenses. Only if one superimposes nonpantheistic lenses on it does it fail to do so. One who steps inside another worldview may find that its major tenets are consistent, that it accounts for all the facts of experience as interpreted through its framework, and that it is existentially relevant to those within that lifestyle.

Only a negative test for truth. Systematic consistency only tests for the falsity, not the truth, of a worldview. More than one view may be both consistent and adequate. However, those that are not both consistent and adequate will be determined to be false. Carnell's view would at best eliminate only false worldviews (or, aspects of worldviews). It cannot establish one worldview as uniquely true.

It is noteworthy that Frederick Ferre, who uses a similar method, recognized that even nontheistic worldviews may carry equal or even greater weight than the Christian model when tested by his criteria. If Western theists admit this, then surely the sophisticated Hindu or Buddhist could design a combinational test for truth to vindicate his worldview.

Sources

J. E. Barnhard, *The Religious Epistemology and Theodicy of Edward John Carnell and Edgar Sheffield Brightman*, unpub. diss., Boston University, 1964

E. J. Carnell, *The Burden of Søren Kierkegaard*

———, *The Case for Orthodox Theology*

———, *Christian Commitment: An Apologetic*

———, "How Every Christian Can Defend His Faith," *Moody Monthly*, January, February, March 1950

———, *An Introduction to Christian Apologetics*

———, *The Kingdom of Love and the Pride of Life*

———, *A Philosophy of the Christian Religion*

———, *The Theology of Reinhold Niebuhr*

N. L. Geisler, *Christian Apologetics*, chapter 7

E. Gilson, *The Unity of Philosophical Experience*

G. Lewis, "Edward John Carnell," W. Elwell, ed., *Handbook of Evangelical Theologians*

———, et al. *Integrative Theology*, Vol. 1

———, *Testing Christianity's Truth Claims*

———, "Three Sides to Every Story," R. L. Harris, ed., *Interpretation and History*

R. Nash, *The New Evangelicalism*

B. Ramm, *Types of Apologetic Systems*

W. S. Sailer, *The Role of Reason in the Theologies of Nels Ferre and Edward John Carnell*, unpub. S.T.D. diss., Temple University

Causality, Principle of. The principle of causality is a *first principle*. All first principles are self-evident or reducible to the self-evident. But not everything self-evident in itself appears to be self-evident to everyone. The principle of causality (*see* First Principles) fits that category and so must be unpacked.

Statement of the Principle of Causality. The principle of causality may be stated in various ways, some more easily accepted than others. For example, it may be stated:

1. Every effect has a cause.

This form is clearly self-evident, and it is analytic, in that the predicate is reducible to its subject. Other ways to state the principle are not analytic, nor so self-evident:

2. Every contingent being is caused by another.
3. Every limited being is caused by another.
4. Every thing that comes to be is caused by another.
5. Nonbeing cannot cause being.

Sometimes the principle is stated in other ways than these, but each form is reducible to one or more of these statements. For example, "Every thing that begins has a cause" is the same as "Everything that comes to be is caused by another." Also, "Every dependent being is caused by another" is the same as "Every contingent being is caused by another."

Defense of the Principle. *An Undeniable Truth.* If the principle of causality is stated, "Every effect has a cause," then it is undeniable.

In this form the principle of causality is analytically self-evident, since by an "effect" is meant what is caused and by a "cause" is meant what produces the effect. Hence, the predicate is reducible to the subject. It is like saying, "Every triangle has three sides." However, there is a difficulty with stating the principle in this way for a theist who wishes to use it to prove the existence of God (*see* God, Evidence for). It simply shifts the burden of the proof back on the theist, who must show that contingent, finite, and/or temporal beings are effects. While this can be done, it is not so useful as to use the form, "Nonbeing cannot produce being." But the question remains as to whether this form is self-evident or undeniable.

All of the ways to defend the nonanalytic forms of the principle of causality (forms 2–4) require explanation of what is meant by the terms of the statement. The following are examples:

The nature of being and nonbeing. Statement 5 can be defended by defining terms. "Nonbeing cannot cause being" because only being can cause something to exist. Nonbeing is nothing; it does not exist. And what does not exist has no power to produce anything. Only what exists can cause existence, since the very concept of "cause" implies that some existing thing has the power to effect another. From absolutely nothing comes absolutely nothing. Or it can be more popularly phrased, "Nothing comes from nothing; nothing ever could."

The nature of contingency. All contingent beings need a cause, for a contingent being is something that exists but that might, under other circumstances, not exist. Since it has the possibility not to exist, it does not account for its own existence. In itself, there is no reason why it exists. Once it was nonbeing, but nonbeing cannot cause anything. Being can only be caused by being. Only something can produce something.

Observe that both of the above defenses (being/nonbeing and contingency) depend on the principle that "Nonbeing cannot cause being" or "Nothing cannot cause something." Many philosophers hold that this principle is known to be true intuitively and is self-evident. But if someone does not accept this as self-evident, the statement can be defended in two ways:

First, inherent in the concept *produce* or *cause* is the implication that something that existed brought into being whatever is produced or caused. The alternative is to define nothing as something or a nonbeing as a being, which is nonsense. This argument should be distinguished from David *Hume's point that it is not absurd to say that *nothing can be followed by something*. Hume himself denies that *something can be caused by nothing*: "I never asserted so absurd a proposition as that something could arise without a cause" (Hume, *The Letters of David Hume,* 1:187).

Theists readily accept Hume's statement. For example, a state in which there was no world was followed by a state in which a world existed (after God created it). That is, nothing (no world) followed by something (a world). There is no inherent contradiction in saying that nothing can be followed by something. The problem arises in saying that nothing can *produce or cause* something.

The importance of its truth begins to surface when it is stated another way: *If there were ever absolutely nothing (including God), then there would always be absolutely nothing (including God).*

Second, everything that comes to be must have a cause. If it came to be, it is not a *Necessary Being,* which by its nature *must always exist.* What comes to be is a *contingent being,* which by nature is capable of either existing or not existing. Something separate from the contingent being has to determine that it comes into existence. So, everything that came to be must be caused, since there must be some efficient action which causes it to pass from a state of potentiality (potency) to a state of actuality (act). For, Aquinas noted, no potency for being can actualize itself. To actualize itself means it would have previously been in a state of actuality, and to be actualized means it would have been in a state of potentiality. It cannot be both at the same time. That would violate the principle of noncontradiction. Hence, one cannot deny the principle of causality without violating the principle of noncontradiction.

First Principles and God's Existence. Given that something exists (which is undeniable) by causality (and the principle of analogy) the existence of God can be demonstrated (*see* Cosmological Argument). In each case, of course, the burden of proof falls on the minor premise, not the premise which is the principle of causality.

Everything That Comes to Be Has a Cause. Using this statement of the principle of causality, the existence of a First Cause can be demonstrated as follows:

> Everything that comes to be is caused by another.
>
> The universe came to be.
>
> Therefore, the universe was caused by another.

Of course, one must show that the universe came to be. This the theist does by science and philosophy (*see* Big Bang; *Kalam* Cosmological Argument).

Another way to prove the existence of God uses a different statement of the principle of causality:

> Every contingent being is caused by another.
>
> The universe is contingent in its being.
>
> Therefore, the universe is caused by another.

Here too, the burden of proof is on showing that the universe as a whole is contingent. This is generally done by showing that the universe as a whole could, or did, come into being, so it is contingent. Likewise, the universe could cease to exist. It must have a cause to account for why it exists, rather than does not exist.

Of course, if one desires to show that this cause of the universe is intelligent or moral, then the principle of analogy must be used to show that effects resemble their efficient cause (*see* ANALOGY, PRINCIPLE OF; FIRST PRINCIPLES). For example:

> Effects resemble their causes in their being.
>
> The universe manifests intelligent design in its being.
>
> Therefore, the universe has an intelligent Designer.

Objections. Most answers to objections leveled against the principle of causality are implied in what has been stated.

There Is No Need for a Cause. Some atheists (*see* ATHEISM) argue that there is no need for a cause. They insist that there is nothing incoherent about something coming into existence from nothing. This is contrary to reality as it is known and lived and to the scientific enterprise, which seeks a causal explanation. It is counterintuitive to believe that things just pop into and out of existence. Those who hold such a position must also face the fact that something that does not even exist has no power to do anything.

If Everything Is Caused, So Is God. This objection is based on a misunderstanding. The principle of causality does not affirm that *everything* has a cause. It only asserts that everything *that has a beginning* (and so is finite) needs a cause. For example, if the universe had no beginning, then it does not need a cause of its beginning. Likewise, if God had no beginning, then neither does he need a cause. Only what has a beginning needs a cause. But few people argue that the universe had no beginning. Ultimately the universe needs a Cause that does not have a beginning, for the universe cannot spring into being out of nothing.

The Principle of Causality Does Not Apply to Reality. Some critics insist that the principle of causality belongs in the realm of logic but does not apply to reality (*see* REALISM). This is self-defeating. One cannot consistently affirm that the laws of thought cannot be affirmed regarding reality. It is inconsistent to think about reality that it cannot be thought about. Since the principle of causality is a fundamental principle of reason (*see* FOUNDATIONALISM), it must apply to reality. Otherwise, one ends in a self-defeating position that what is known about reality cannot be known. The principle of causality is a principle about reality. When it says "Nonbeing cannot produce being," *being* means what is real and *nonbeing* what is not real.

There Is No Need for a Here-and-Now Cause. Some critics argue that even if there may have once been a cause of the beginning of the universe, there does not need to be one now. Either such a Cause has gone out of existence, or else it may still be in existence but is not required for continually sustaining the universe.

The theistic God demonstrated by the cosmological argument cannot have caused the universe and then subsequently ceased to exist. The theistic God is a Necessary Being, and a Necessary Being cannot cease to be. If it exists, it must by its very nature exist necessarily. A Necessary Being cannot exist in a contingent mode any more than a triangle can exist in a five-sided mode.

A Necessary Being must continue to cause its contingent being(s). A contingent being must remain contingent as long as it exists, since it can never become a Necessary Being. But this is the only other alternative for a contingent being other than going out of existence or remaining a contingent being. But if a contingent being is always contingent, then it always needs a Necessary Being on which it depends for its existence. Since no contingent being holds itself in existence, it must have a Necessary Being to hold it from going into nonexistence—at all times.

The hidden assumption in positing a former Necessary Being who no longer exists is that simultaneous causality does not make sense. But there is no contradiction in saying that an effect is being effected at the very instant it is being caused. This is clearly the case in the relationship between the premises (cause) and the conclusion (effect) in a syllogism. Cause and effect are simultaneous, for the instant one takes away the premise(s) the conclusion does not follow. Likewise, the causal relation between one's face and the image in the mirror is simultaneous.

What clouds the understanding is the confusion of an *effect* with an *after-effect*. For example, when the ball is thrown, it continues to move after the thrower is no longer throwing it. The clock continues to run after it is wound. However, in these and similar examples, the after-effect is also being directly and simultaneously effected by some cause, after the original cause is gone. The force of inertia keeps the baseball moving; the forces of tension and reaction keep the spring moving the clock. If any of these forces would go out of existence, the after-effect would stop dead. If inertia ceased the very instant after the ball left my hand, the ball would instantly stop in midair. Likewise, the clock would stop ticking the instant the physical laws effecting it were no longer operative. Every so-called after-effect is only an effect of some simultaneous cause(s).

There are no existential after-effects. Whatever is, exists in the here-and-now. And whatever is being caused to exist right now must have something causing it to exist right now. A basic distinction will help illustrate the point. The artist is not the cause of the being of a painting; he is only the cause of the becoming (or coming to be) of the painting. The painting continues to be after the artist takes his hands away from the canvas. The father does not cause the *being* of the son, but only causes the son's *becoming*, for when the father dies the son continues to live.

Finite beings clearly need a cause, not only of their becoming, but also of their here-and-now being. For at every moment of their existence they are dependent for existence on another. They never cease to be limited, finite, contingent beings. And, as such, they demand a cause for every moment of their existence. It does not matter whether we are referring to John Doe at moment one, two, or three of his existence. He is still existing, he has a received existence, and therefore he is receiving existence from something outside himself.

Part of the problem would be removed if we did not talk of exist-*ence* as though the whole package were received at once, but of exist-*ing*, a moment-by-moment process. The word *being* may be even more misleading in this regard. No one receives his whole being at once, nor even the next instant of it. Each creature has a present "being." Existence comes a moment at a time. But at each moment of dependent being there must be some independent Being who gives that moment of being. In this respect, the distinction between the Latin *esse* (to be) and *ens* (being, thing) is helpful. God is pure Esse and our present esse (to-be-ness) is dependent on him. Pure Existence must existentialize our potentiality for existence; otherwise we would not exist. God as pure Actuality is actualizing everything that is actual. Hence, it is the present actuality of all that is actual that demands a causal ground.

Quantum Physics Shows that Subatomic Events Are Uncaused. Heisenberg's principle of uncertainty (*see* INDETERMINACY, PRINCIPLE OF) is a principle of quantum mechanics which states that "the position and speed of a particle cannot be simultaneously known with complete certainty. According to this view, for example, it is possible to predict accurately what fraction of uranium atoms will radioactively disintegrate over the next hour, but it is impossible to predict *which* atoms will do so" (ibid.). It is reasoned that if some events are unpredictable they must be uncaused.

However, this conclusion does not follow for several reasons discussed in the article Indeterminacy, Principle of. First, Heisenberg's principle is not a principle of *uncausality* but a principle of *unpredictability*. Second, it is only the position of a particular particle that cannot be predicted, not the overall pattern. Third, since the subatomic realm cannot be "observed" without bombarding it, the scientist cannot be sure what it is really like. Not all physicists agree with Heisenberg. Einstein's response was, "God does not play dice with the universe."

Conclusion. There are other negative arguments about the principle of causality (*see* GOD, OBJECTIONS TO PROOFS FOR), but they do not deny the principle of causality as such. For example, the argument that there may be an infinite number of causes does not deny the principle of causality; it assumes it. The principle of causality itself is as sound as any first principle. Without it neither science in particular nor rational thought in general would be possible. All natural knowledge about the external world depends on a causal connection between it and our minds.

Sources

L. Feuerbach, *The Essence of Christianity*
S. Freud, *The Future of an Illusion*
R. Garrigou-LaGrange, *God: His Existence and His Nature*
N. L. Geisler, *Christian Apologetics*
——— and W. Corduan, *Philosophy of Religion*
E. Gilson, *On Being and Some Philosophers*
D. Hume, *Dialogues Concerning Natural Religion*
———, *The Letters of David Hume*, J. Y. T. Greig, ed.
I. Kant, *A Critique of Pure Reason*
A. Lightman, *Origins*
J. Maritain, *Existence and the Existent*
E. Mascall, *Existence and Analogy*
B. Mondin, *The Principle of Analogy in Protestant and Catholic Theology*
L. M. Regis, *Epistemology*
B. Russell, *Why I Am Not a Christian*
Thomas Aquinas. *On Being and Essence*

Celsus. Celsus was a second-century pagan philosopher. His *The True Doctrine* (or *Discourse*) is the oldest known writing attacking the Christian faith (ca. 178). It is known through Origen's eight-book reply, *Contra Celsum*, which preserves most of Celsus' discourse. No other copies are extant.

Origen depicts Celsus' beliefs as a combination of a Platonic view (*see* PLATO) of God and Greek *polytheism. The result was an unknown God who set his various demons over human experience. True religion is demonstrated by concentrating on God and propitiating cultic demons. Worship is due to the emperor by celebrating public feasts, holding public office, and joining the army (see Douglas, 206).

Celsus presents himself as a detached pagan observer with no strong feelings about religion. He praises Christianity for its Logos doctrine and high morals, but he objects strongly to its exclusivity. He criticizes much of biblical history for its miracle claims and expresses repugnance to the doctrines of the incarnation and crucifixion. He also objects to Christian nonconformity, which he believed tended to undermine the Roman government. His charges boiled down to religious superstition, intolerance, and political nonconformity.

The charges were answered by Origen. Celsus failed to appreciate the historical evidence (*see* NEW TESTAMENT, HISTORICITY OF) and the philosophical justification of biblical miracles (*see*

Miracle; MIRACLES, ARGUMENTS AGAINST). He also failed to understand the evidence supporting the deity of Christ (*see* CHRIST, DEITY OF) and the uniqueness of Christianity (*see* CHRIST, UNIQUENESS OF; WORLD RELIGIONS AND CHRISTIANITY).

Sources

Celsus, *The True Doctrine*

H. Chadwick, *Origen contra Celsum*

F. L. Cross, "Celsus," in *The Oxford Dictionary of the Christian Church*

E. R. Dodds, *Pagan and Christian in an Age of Anxiety*

Origen, *Contra Celsum*

Certainty/Certitude. *Certainty* is the confidence that something is true. Sometimes certainty is distinguished from *certitude*. Certainty is objective, but certitude is subjective. A first principle or self-evident statement is objectively certain, whether a person is sure about it or not. Certitude involves a knower's assent to that which is certain; it is a subjective acceptance of what is objectively so. In common usage the terms are employed interchangeably. The difference is that certainty exists where there is objective reasons or evidence that are commensurate to the degree of certainty claimed. With certitude, however, there need not be a commensurate degree of objective reasons or evidence for the degree one possesses.

Kinds of Certainty. Certainty falls into categories of logical, moral, practical, and spiritual.

Logical Certainty. Logical certainty is found largely in mathematics and pure logic. This kind of certainty is involved where the opposite would be a contradiction. Something is certain in this sense when there is no logical possibility it could be false. Since mathematics is reducible to logic it fits into this category. It is found in statements such as 5 + 4 = 9. It is also found in tautologies or statements that are true by definition: All circles are round, and no triangle is a square.

Metaphysical Certainty. There are, however, some other things of which we can be absolutely certain that are not statements empty of content. For example, I know for certain that I exist. This is undeniably so, since I cannot deny my existence without existing to make the denial. First principles can also be known for certain, since the subject and predicate say the same thing: "Being exists"; "Nonbeing is not Being." "Nonbeing cannot produce Being" is also certain, since *produce* implies an existing producer.

Moral Certainty. Moral certainty exists where the evidence is so great that the mind lacks any reason to veto the will to believe it is so. One rests in a moral certainty with complete confidence. Of course, there is a logical possibility that things of which we are morally certain are false. However, the evidence is so great there is no reason to believe it is false. In legal terms this is what is meant by "beyond all reasonable doubt."

Practical Certainty (High Probability). Practical certainty is not as strong as moral certainty. Persons claim to be "certain" about things they believe have a high probability of truth. One may be certain she had breakfast today, without being able to prove it mathematically or metaphysically. It is true unless something changed her perception, so that she was deluded into thinking she ate breakfast. It is possible to be wrong about these matters.

Spiritual (Supernatural) Certainty. If we grant the theist God's existence, he could give supernatural assurance that something is true. Likewise, if God speaks directly to a person (for example, Abraham in Genesis 22), then that person could have a spiritual certainty that transcends other kinds of certainty, because it comes directly from God. Those *who have direct mystical experiences* of God (*see* MYSTICISM), such as Paul describes in 2 Corinthians 12, have this kind of certainty. It would be greater than any other kind of certainty, since an omniscient being is its guarantor and omniscience cannot be wrong. As to how or whether such assurance actually exists apart from a supernatural act is a moot point among theologians, although many classical apologists and others argue that it does (*see* HOLY SPIRIT, ROLE IN APOLOGETICS).

Certainty and Assent. Certainty is always accompanied by assent. That is, the mind always assents to propositions that are certain, *if it properly understands them*. However, not all assent is accompanied by certitude. In everyday life, one frequently assents to something as being only probable and not necessary. In business affairs there is usually no absolute certainty; one must assent based on varying degrees of *probability. This is virtually always the case in inductive reasoning, since the reasoner is moving from particular to general and is not sure about all the particulars. A complete induction would be an exception, since every particular is known. For instance, "There are three and only three marbles in my right hand" can be known with moral certainty. Though it is possible the person has not seen or counted correctly, the probability of correctness is high enough for the proposition to be morally certain (*see* INDUCTIVE METHOD).

A person can possess intellectual certainty about a proposition, yet lack subjective or emotional certitude. That is the common experience with doubt. There is emotional fear, despite rational verification. A person might have moral certainty that God exists and still feel his absence.

Subjective certitude often works in the opposite direction as well. A feeling of conviction so overpowers rational analysis as to move the will to assent with little or no evidence.

Certainty and Error. Subjective certitude is one way in which it is possible to have moral certainty and/or certitude about the truth of something that is objectively false. The will to believe may overpower the lack of evidence, so that one has tenacity of belief without the veracity of it. Reasons for error include defective senses or mental processes, incomplete consciousness, the drive of the will, and the need to act in the absence of compelling evidence.

One cannot be wrong about first principles or self-evident propositions. Once the mind understands them it is compelled to assent to them. There is no freedom not to assent to a self-evident truth. While this natural inclination to the truth is an unconscious drive, it would seem that, properly speaking, the assent to certitude is conscious. One can only be certain who understands that the truth is a first principle or reducible to it. This degree of analysis requires awareness. Only when one understands the principle and the truth becomes unmistakably clear is assent necessary and certitude guaranteed.

Certitude Involves a Repose. Since certitude involves a conscious assent to the certainty of the truth for which a human being has an unconscious appetite, the possession of this truth by the intellect is the reward of certitude. In the presence of such truths, nothing in the world could deprive the intellect of this possession. The reward of the hunger for truth is certitude which one consciously enjoys who perceives the certainty and necessity of the truth he or she has possessed.

Sources

Aristotle, *On Hermeneutics*

G. Habermas, *Dealing with Doubt*

J. Newman, *The Grammar of Ascent*

L. M. Regis, *Epistemology*

J. B. Sullivan, *An Examination of First Principles in Thought and Being*

Thomas Aquinas, *On Hermeneutics*

———, *Summa Theologica*

F. D. Wilhelmsen, *Man's Knowledge of Reality*

Chance. The concept of *chance* has evolved in meaning. *Chance* for Aristotle and other classical philosophers was merely the fortuitous intersection of two or more lines of causality. In modern times, however, the term has taken on two different meanings. Some regard chance as the lack of any cause. As Mortimer Adler put it, some take chance to mean "that which happens totally without cause—the absolute spontaneous or fortuitous" (cited in Sproul, xv).

Others view chance as a real cause itself, only a blind, rather than an intelligent, cause. Naturalists and materialists often speak this way. For example, since David Hume, the teleological argument has been countered with the alternative that the universe resulted from chance, not from intelligent design. Although Hume himself did not do so, some have taken this to mean that the universe was caused by chance, instead of by God.

Chance and Theism. *Chance*, conceived either as the lack of a cause or as a cause in itself, is incompatible with theism. As long as chance rules, Arthur Koestler noted, "God is an anachronism" (cited in Sproul, 3). The existence of chance tips God off his cosmic throne. God and chance are mutually exclusive. If chance exists, God is not in complete control of the universe. There cannot even exist an intelligent Designer.

The Nature of Chance. Definition of the word *chance* depends partly on the worldview agenda of the one doing the defining. Two usages are commonly confused when speaking about the origin of things: chance as a mathematical *probability and chance as a real cause. The first is merely abstract. When rolling a dice the chances are one in six that the number six will come out on top. The odds are one in thirty-six that two dice will both come up six and one in 216 that three sixes will be thrown on three dice. These are abstract mathematical probabilities. But chance did not cause those three dice to turn up sixes. What did it was the force of throwing them, their starting position in the hand, the angle of the toss, how they deflected off objects in their way, and other results of inertia. Chance had nothing to do with it. As Sproul put it, "chance has no power to do anything. It is cosmically, totally, consummately impotent" (Sproul, 6).

Lest one think we have loaded the dice by citing a theist, hear the words of Hume: "Chance, when strictly examined, is a mere negative word, and means not any real power which has anywhere a being." He added, "Though there be no such thing as *Chance* in the world; our ignorance of the real cause of any event has the same influence on the understanding, and begets a like species of belief or opinion" (Hume, Sect 6).

Attributing Causal Power to Chance. Herbert Jaki in *God and the Cosmologists* has an insightful chapter titled "Loaded Dice." He refers to Pierre Delbert who said, "Chance appears today as a law, the most general of all laws" (Delbert, 238).

This is magic, not science. Scientific laws deal with the regular, not the irregular (as chance is). Also, the laws of physics do not cause anything; they simply describe the way things happen regularly in the world as the result of physical causes. Likewise, the laws of mathematics do not cause anything. They simply insist that if I put five pennies in my empty right pocket and then put seven more, then I must have twelve pennies there. The laws of math never put one penny in anyone's pocket.

The basic fallacy of making chance into a causal power was stated well by Sproul. "1. Chance is not an entity. 2. Nonentities have no power because they have no being. 3. To say that something happens or is caused by *chance* is to suggest attributing instrumental power to nothing" (Sproul, 13). But it is absurd to claim that nothing produced something. Nothing does not even exist and, hence, has no power to cause anything (*see* CAUSALITY, PRINCIPLE OF).

Intelligent Cause(s) and "Chance" Results. Not all chance events occur from natural phenomena. Intelligent causes can juxtapose as "chance" encounters. Two scientists, working independently from different approaches, make the same discovery. One rational being buries a treasure in the earth. Another finds it by chance while digging the foundation for a house.

What appears to be a random mixture is not necessarily without rational purpose. There is a rational purpose behind the designing of a random mixture of number sequences in a lottery drawing. There is a rational purpose for the random mixture of carbon dioxide we exhale into the surrounding air; otherwise we would rebreathe it and die of oxygen deprivation. In this sense, God the designer and chance randomness are not incompatible concepts. However, to speak of a chance cause is meaningless.

Conclusion. Strictly speaking, there can be no chance cause or origin of the universe and life. Every event has an adequate cause. The choices are either intelligent causes or nonintelligent causes, either a natural cause or a non-natural cause. The only way we can know which is by the kind of effect produced (*see* ORIGINS, SCIENCE OF). Since the universe manifests intelligent design, it is reasonable to posit an intelligent cause (*see* TELEOLOGICAL ARGUMENT). The apparent chance or randomness (like the lottery or the mixture of air molecules) may be part of the overall intelligent design.

Sources

P. Delbert, *La science et la realite*
J. Gleick, *Chaos: Making a New Science*
D. Hume, *An Enquiry Concerning Human Understanding*
S. Jaki, *God and the Cosmologists*
R. C. Sproul, *Not a Chance*

Chesterton, Gilbert K. Gilbert K. Chesterton (1874–1936) was a brilliant and witty English essayist and poet, to whom C. S. Lewis acknowledged his debt. Chesterton abandoned training in art for journalism and in 1922 the Church of England for Roman Catholicism. His religious works include *Heretics* (1905), *Orthodoxy* (1908), *The Everlasting Man* (1925), and *Avowals and Denials* (1934). His *Autobiography* (1936) provides many insights into the religious scene from 1895 to 1936.

Views. God. Chesterton defended orthodox Catholicism, and his writings are filled with witty apologetic arguments for the Christian faith. In *Orthodoxy*, he declared that "There never was anything so perilous or so exciting as orthodoxy" (106). Anyone could fall into religious fads, from gnosticism to Christian Science, "but to have avoided them all has been one whirling adventure; and in my vision the heavenly chariot flies thundering through the ages, the dull heresies sprawling and prostrate, the wild truth reeling but erect" (ibid., 107).

Chesterton was critical of nontheistic worldviews. He called *atheism "the most daring of all dogmas. . . . It is the assertion of a universal negative; for a man to say there is no God in the universe is like saying that there are no insects in any of the stars" (*Five Types*, 59). He criticized pantheism for being unable to inspire moral action. "For pantheism implies in its nature that one thing is as good as another; whereas action implies in its nature that one thing is greatly preferable to another" (*Orthodoxy*, 143). Even paganism is better than pantheism, he added. "Paganism is free to imagine divinities, while pantheism is forced to pretend, in a priggish way, that all things are equally divine" (*Catholic Church and Conversion*, 89).

Chesterton distilled the difference between Christianity and *Buddhism to the insightful observation: "The Christian pities men because they are dying, and the Buddhist pities them because they are living. The Christian is sorry for what damages the life of a man; but the Buddhist is sorry for him because he is alive" (*Generally Speaking*, 115–16).

In his vivid personal testimony, Chesterton confessed: "I had always believed that the world involved magic; now I thought perhaps it involved a magician. . . . This world of ours has some purpose; and if there is a purpose, there is a person. I had always felt life first as a story; and if there is a story there is a storyteller" (*Orthodoxy*, 61).

Miracles. Chesterton held that God actively intervenes in the world. He defined *miracle* as "the swift control of matter by mind" (ibid., 137). The reality of miracles was central to Chesterton's apologetic defense. He insisted that miracles must be confirmed by evidence, just as other events of history. "My belief that miracles have happened in human history is not a mystical belief at all; I believe in them upon human evidence as I do the discovery of America" (ibid., 161). "A conspiracy of facts" forces this admission on the mind. The witnesses were not mystical dreamers, but fishermen, farmers, and others who were "coarse and cautious" (ibid., 163). Denials of miracles on the other hand, are not based on evidence at all, but on philosophical commitment. "There is only one reason an intelligent person doesn't believe in miracles. He or she believes in materialism" (*St. Francis of Assisi*, 204). Believers accept miracles because they have evidence for them. Disbelievers deny them because they have a doctrine against them.

Creation. Creation to Chesterton was the "greatest of all revolutions" (*Chaucer*, 27). He does not seem to have denied the possibility of creation through evolution (*see* EVOLUTION, THEISTIC), but he also recognized the deficiencies of evolution as a theory of origins (*see* EVOLUTION, BIOLOGICAL). Even if the theory were true, "evolution as explanation, as an ultimate philosophy of the cause of living things, is still faced with the problem of producing rabbits out of an empty hat; a process commonly involving some hint of design" (ibid., 172). Chesterton declared that the suggestion that evolution produced the human mind, "is like telling a man who asks who rolled a cab-wheel over his leg that evolution rolled it. To state the process is scarcely to state the agent" (*Handful of Authors*, 97–98). Further, "it is absurd for the evolutionist to complain that it is unthinkable for an admittedly unthinkable God to make everything out of nothing (*see* CREATION, VIEWS OF), and then pretend that it is more thinkable that nothing should turn itself into anything" (*Saint Thomas Aquinas*, 173).

Sin. Chesterton also affirmed the fall of Adam and original sin. It is bad enough that we are trapped in a bad world, he said, but we have misused a good world. Evil is the wrong use of will, and so things can be righted only through the right use of will. "Every other creed except that one is some form of surrender to fate" (*The Thing*, 226). Chesterton described the effects of the fall by saying that the doctrine of original sin is "the doctrine of the equality of men." For now all are fools (*Heretics*, 165–66).

Evaluation. Chesterton was a witty, brilliant defender of Christian Faith in general and Roman Catholic faith in particular. He is among the great intellectual Catholic apologists of the twentieth century. His approach is more literary than logical in form, but it is rational and penetrating.

Sources

G. K. Chesterton, *A Handful of Authors*

———, *Autobiography*

———, *Chaucer*

———, *Five Types*

———, *Generally Speaking*

———, *Heretics*

———, *Orthodoxy*

———, *St. Francis of Assisi*

———, *Saint Thomas Aquinas*

———, *The Catholic Church and Conversion*

———, *The Thing: Why I Am a Catholic*

C. Hollis, *The Mind of Chesterton*

A. L. Maylock, *The Man Who Was Orthodox*

J. W. Montgomery, *Myth, Allegory and Gospel* (chapter 2).

M. Ward, *Gilbert Keith Chesterton*

———, *Return to Chesterton*

Christ, Death of. The death of Christ is the necessary prerequisite to his resurrection (*see* RESURRECTION, EVIDENCE FOR), which is the crowning proof of Jesus' claim to be God (*see* APOLOGETICS, ARGUMENT OF). Further, Islam, one of the chief opponents of Christianity, denies that Jesus died on the cross (McDowell, 47f.). Many skeptics (*see* AGNOSTICISM) challenge the reality of Christ's death.

Evidence for Christ's Death. There is overwhelming historical and factual evidence that Jesus died on the cross and rose again on the third day (*see* RESURRECTION, EVIDENCE FOR). The evidence for Christ's death is greater than that for almost any other event in the ancient world. The historicity of the Gospel records has been confirmed by a multitude of New Testament Manuscripts and contemporary eyewitnesses (*see* NEW TESTAMENT, DATING OF; NEW TESTAMENT DOCUMENTS, RELIABILITY OF; NEW TESTAMENT, HISTORICITY OF).

Alternative Explanations. Skeptics and Muslims choose from among various versions of the theory that Jesus did not die on the cross. One is that a drug put Jesus in a coma-like state, so that he later revived in the tomb. The clear witness of Matthew's narrative is that he refused even the drug customarily offered to the victim before crucifixion to help deaden pain (27:34). He accepted only vinegar later (vs. 48) to quench his thirst.

If the Bible has any credibility whatsoever, its New Testament authors all say specifically or speak from the necessary implication that they believed Christ died on the cross (cf. Rom. 5:8; 1 Cor. 15:3; 1 Thess. 4:14). Neither fainting nor swooning nor being drugged would have produced the vigorous victor over death described in the resurrection appearances. The evidence that Christ actually died on the cross is overwhelming:

A Death Predicted. The Old Testament predicted (*see* PROPHECY AS PROOF OF THE BIBLE) that the Messiah would die (Ps. 22:16; Isa. 53:5–10; Dan. 9:26; Zech. 12:10). Jesus fulfilled this and nearly 100 other Old Testament prophecies about the Messiah (see, for example, Matt. 4:14; 5:17–18; 8:17; John 4:25–26; 5:39).

Jesus predicted many times during his ministry that he was going to die and rise again (Matt. 12:40; Mark 8:31; John 2:19–21; 10:10–11). One of the more explicit is Matthew 17:22–23: "The Son of Man is going to be betrayed into the hands of men. They will kill him, and on the third day he will be raised to life."

All predictions of his resurrection in the Old Testament (cf. Ps. 2:7; 16:10), and New Testament (cf. Matt. 12:40; 17:22–23; John 2:19–21) assume that he would die (*see* RESURRECTION, EVIDENCE FOR).

Death by Crucifixion. Jesus' injuries made death unavoidable. He had no sleep the night before he was crucified; he was beaten and whipped, and he collapsed while carrying his cross. This prelude to the crucifixion alone was life-draining.

The nature of the crucifixion assures death. For a description of one crucified man whose bones have been uncovered, see ARCHAEOLOGY, NEW TESTAMENT. Jesus hung on the cross from 9 in the morning until just before sunset (Mark 15:25, 33). He bled from gashes in his hands and feet and from the thorns that pierced his scalp. These wounds would have drained away much blood over more than six hours. Plus, crucifixion demands that one constantly pull up by the hands and push on the injured feet in order to breathe. This caused excruciating pain from the nails. A day of this would kill someone in good health (see Tzaferis).

Beyond these injuries, Jesus' side was pierced with a spear. From this wound flowed a mixture of blood and water (John 19:34), a proof that physical death had occurred. This detail alone, and its confirmation by modern medical experts, strongly validates the claim that this narrative is an eyewitness account. An article in the *Journal of the American Medical Association* (21 March 1986) concluded:

> Clearly, the weight of historical and medical evidence indicates that Jesus was dead before the wound to his side was inflicted and supports the traditional view that the spear, thrust between his right rib, probably perforated not only the right lung but also the pericardium and heart and thereby ensured his death. Accordingly, interpretations based on the assumption that Jesus did not die on the cross appear to be at odds with modern medical knowledge. [1463]

Jesus said he was dying when he declared on the cross, "Father, into your hands I commit my spirit" (Luke 23:46). And when "he had said this, he breathed his last" (vs. 46). John renders this, "he gave up his spirit" (John 19:30). His death cry was heard by those who stood nearby (Luke 23:47–49).

The Roman soldiers, accustomed to crucifixion and death, pronounced Jesus dead. Although it was a common practice to break the legs of the victim to speed death (so that the person could no longer breathe), they did not believe it necessary to break Jesus' legs (John 19:33).

Pilate double-checked to make sure Jesus was dead before he gave the corpse to Joseph to be buried. "Summoning the centurion, he asked him if Jesus had already died. When he learned from the centurion that it was so, he gave the body to Joseph" (Mark 15:44–45).

Jesus was wrapped in about 100 pounds of cloth and spices and placed in a sealed tomb for three days (Matt. 27:60; John 19:39–40). If he was not dead by then, the lack of food, water, and medical treatment would have finished him.

References to the Crucifixion. The article ARCHAEOLOGY, NEW TESTAMENT includes accounts by several non-Christian historians and writers from the first and second centuries who recorded the death of Christ as indisputable fact. Among these are the Talmud and Jewish historian of the time of Christ, Josephus, and the Roman historian Cornelius Tacitus (A.D. 55?–117).

According to Julius Africanus (ca. 221), the first-century Samaritan-born historian, Thallus (ca. 52), "when discussing the darkness which fell upon the land *during the crucifixion of Christ,*" spoke of it as an eclipse (Bruce, 113, emphasis added). The second-century Greek writer, Lucian, speaks of Christ as *"the man who was crucified in Palestine* because he introduced a new cult into the world." He calls him the *"crucified sophist"* (Geisler, 323). The "letter of Mara Bar-Serapion" (ca. A.D. 73), housed in the British Museum, speaks of Christ's death, asking: "What advantage did the Jews gain from *executing their wise King?*" (Bruce, 114). Finally, there was the Roman writer, Phlegon, who spoke of Christ's death and resurrection in his *Chronicles,* saying, "Jesus, while alive, was of no assistance to himself, but that *he arose after death, and exhibited the marks of his punishment, and showed how his hands had been pierced by nails*" (Phlegon, *Chronicles,* cited by Origen, 4:455). Phlegon even mentioned "the eclipse in the time of Tiberius Caesar, in whose reign Jesus appears to have been crucified, and the great earthquakes which then took place" (ibid., 445).

The earliest Christian writers after the time of Christ affirmed his death on the cross by crucifixion. Polycarp, a disciple of the apostle John, repeatedly affirmed the death of Christ, speaking, for example, of "our Lord Jesus Christ, who for our sins suffered even unto death" (Polycarp, 33). Ignatius (30–107), a friend of Polycarp, wrote, "And he really suffered and died, and rose again." Otherwise, he adds, all his apostles who suffered for this belief, died in vain. "But, (in truth) none of these sufferings were in vain; for *the Lord was really crucified* by the ungodly" (Ignatius, 107). In *Dialogue with Trypho* the Jew, Justin Martyr noted that Jews of his day believed that "Jesus [was] a Galilean deceiver, whom we crucified" (Martyr, 253).

This unbroken testimony from the Old Testament to the early Church Fathers, including believer and unbeliever, Jew and Gentile, is overwhelming evidence that Jesus suffered and died on the cross.

Sources

F. F. Bruce, *The New Testament Documents: Are They Reliable?*
N. L. Geisler, *Christian Apologetics*
G. Habermas, *Ancient Evidence for the Life of Jesus*
Journal of the American Medical Society, 21 March 1986
Justin Martyr, "Dialogue with Trypho," *The Ante-Nicene Fathers,* Vol. 1

J. McDowell, *Evidence That Demands a Verdict*
"Passover," Babylonian Talmud
Phlegon, *Chronicles*
D. Strauss, *New Life of Jesus*, Vol. 1
V. Tzaferis, "Jewish Tombs at and Near Giv'at ha-Mivtrar," *IEJ*, 20 (1970)

Christ, Deity of. Central to Christianity is the belief that Jesus Christ is the Son of God, that is, God manifest in human flesh. The evidence for this is as follows:

1. Truth about reality is knowable (*see* TRUTH, NATURE OF; AGNOSTICISM).
2. Opposites cannot both be true (*see* PLURALISM, RELIGIOUS; LOGIC).
3. God exists (*see* GOD, EVIDENCE FOR).
4. Miracles are possible (*see* MIRACLE).
5. A miracle is an act of God to confirm the truth of God claimed by a messenger of God (*see* MIRACLES, APOLOGETIC VALUE OF; MIRACLES AS CONFIRMATION OF TRUTH).
6. The New Testament documents are reliable (*see* NEW TESTAMENT DOCUMENTS, RELIABILITY OF; NEW TESTAMENT MANUSCRIPTS; NEW TESTAMENT, HISTORICITY OF).
7. In the New Testament Jesus claimed to be God.
8. Jesus proved to be God by an unprecedented convergence of miracles (*see* MIRACLES IN THE BIBLE).
9. Therefore, Jesus was God in human flesh.

Since the first six points are treated in the materials noted, this article will stress points five and six.

Jesus' Claim to Be God. Jesus claimed to be God, both directly and by necessary implication from what he said and did.

Jesus Claimed to Be Yahweh. Yahweh (*YHWH*; sometimes appearing in English translations as "Jehovah" or in small capital letters as "LORD") is the special name given by God for himself in the Old Testament. It is the name revealed to Moses in Exodus 3:14, when God said, "I AM WHO I AM." Other titles for God may be used of humans, such as *Adonai* ("Lord") in Gen. 18:12, or false gods, such as *elohim* ("gods") in Deut. 6:14. *Yahweh*, however, only refers to the one true God. No other person or thing was to be worshiped or served (Exod. 20:5), and his name and glory were not to be given to another. Isaiah wrote, "This is what the LORD says. . . . I am the first, and I am the last; apart from me there is no God" (Isa. 44:6) and, "I am the LORD; that is my name! I will not give my glory to another, or my praise to idols" (42:8).

Jesus claimed to be *Yahweh*. He prayed, "And now, O Father, glorify thou me with thine own self with the glory which I had with thee before the world was" (John 17:5). But *Yahweh* of the Old Testament said, "my glory will I not give to another" (Isa. 42:8). Jesus also declared, "I am the first and the last" (Rev. 1:17)—precisely the words used by Jehovah in Isaiah 42:8. He said, "I am the good shepherd" (John 10:11), but the Old Testament said, "*Yahweh* is my shepherd" (Ps. 23:1). Further, Jesus claimed to be the judge of all people (Matt. 25:31f.; John 5:27f.), but Joel quotes Jehovah as saying, "for there I will sit to judge all the nations on every side" (Joel 3:12). Likewise, Jesus spoke of himself as the "bridegroom" (Matt. 25:1) while the Old Testament identifies Jehovah in this way (Isa. 62:5; Hos. 2:16). While the Psalmist declares, "The LORD is my light" (Ps. 27:1), Jesus said, "I am the light of the world" (John 8:12).

Perhaps the strongest claim Jesus made to be *Yahweh* is in John 8:58, where he says, "Before Abraham was, I am." This statement claims not only existence before Abraham, but equality with the "I AM" of Exodus 3:14. The Jews around him clearly understood his meaning and picked up stones to kill him for blaspheming (cf. John 8:58 and 10:31–33). The same claim is made in Mark 14:62 and John 18:5–6.

Jesus Claimed to Be Equal with God. Jesus claimed to be equal with God in other ways. One was by claiming for himself the prerogatives of God. He said to a paralytic, "Son, your sins are forgiven" (Mark 2:5–11). The scribes correctly responded, "Who can forgive sins but God alone?" So, to prove that his claim was not an empty boast he healed the man, offering direct proof that what he had said about forgiving sins was true also.

Another prerogative Jesus claimed was the power to raise and judge the dead: "I tell you the truth, a time is coming and has now come when the dead will hear the voice of the Son of God and those who hear will live . . . and come out—those who have done good will rise to live, and those who have done evil will rise to be condemned" (John 5:25, 29). He removed all doubt about his meaning when he added, "For just as the Father raises the dead and gives them life, even so the Son gives life to whom he is pleased to give it" (John 5:21). But the Old Testament clearly taught that only God was the giver of life (Deut. 32:39; 1 Sam. 2:6) and the one to raise the dead (Ps. 2:7) and the only judge (Deut. 32:35; Joel 3:12). Jesus boldly assumed for himself powers that only God has.

Jesus also claimed that he should be honored as God. He said that all men should "honor the Son just as they honor the Father. He who does not honor the Son does not honor the Father, who sent him" (John 5:23). The Jews listening knew that no one should claim to be equal with God in this way, and again they reached for stones (John 5:18).

Jesus Claimed to Be Messiah-God. Even the *Qur'an* recognizes that Jesus was the Messiah (sura 5:17, 75). But the Old Testament teaches that the coming Messiah would be God himself. So when Jesus claimed to be that Messiah, he was also claiming to be God. For example, the prophet Isaiah (in 9:6) calls the Messiah, "Mighty God." The psalmist wrote of Messiah, "Your throne, O God, will last for ever and ever" (Ps. 45:6; cf. Heb. 1:8). Psalm 110:1 records a conversation between the Father and the Son: "The LORD (*Yahweh*) says to my Lord (*Adonai*): 'Sit at my right hand.'" Jesus applied this passage to himself in Matthew 22:43–44. In the great messianic prophecy of Daniel 7, the Son of Man is called the "Ancient of Days" (vs. 22), a phrase used twice in the same passage of God the Father (vss. 9, 13). Jesus also said he was the Messiah at his trial before the high priest. When asked, "Are you the Christ [Greek for "Messiah"], the Son of the Blessed One?" Jesus responded, "I am. . . . And you will see the Son of Man sitting at the right hand of the Mighty One and coming on the clouds of heaven." At this, the high priest tore his robe and said, "Why do we need any more witnesses? . . . You have heard the blasphemy!" (Mark 14:61–64). There was no doubt that in claiming to be Messiah, Jesus also claimed to be God (see also Matt. 26:54; Luke 24:27).

Jesus Claimed to Be God by Accepting Worship. The Old Testament forbids worshiping anyone other than God (Exod. 20:1–4; Deut. 5:6–9). The New Testament agrees, showing that humans refused worship (Acts 14:15), as did angels (Rev. 22:8–9). But Jesus accepted worship on numerous occasions, showing he claimed to be God. A healed leper worshiped him (Matt. 8:2), and a ruler knelt before him with a request (Matt. 9:18). After he stilled the storm, "those who were in the boat worshiped him saying, 'Truly you are the Son of God'" (Matt. 14:33). A group of Canaanite women (Matt. 15:25), the mother of James and John (Matt. 20:20), the Gerasene demoniac (Mark 5:6), all worshiped Jesus without one word of rebuke. The disciples worshiped him after his resurrection (Matt. 28:17). Thomas saw the risen Christ and cried out, "My Lord and my God!" (John 20:28). This could only be allowed by a person who seriously considered himself to be God. Not only did Jesus accept this worship due to God alone without rebuking those who gave it, but he even commended those who acknowledged his deity (John 20:29; Matt. 16:17).

Jesus Claimed to Have Equal Authority with God. Jesus also put his words on a par with God's. "You have heard that it was said to the people long ago. . . . But I tell you . . ." (Matt. 5:21, 22) is repeated over and over again. "All authority in heaven and on earth has been given to me. Therefore go and make disciples of all nations . . ." (Matt. 28:18–19). God had given the Ten Commandments to Moses, but Jesus said, "A new commandment I give you: Love one another" (John 13:34). Jesus said, "until heaven and earth disappear, not the smallest letter, not the least stroke of a pen, will by any means disappear from the Law" (Matt. 5:18), but later Jesus said of his words, "Heaven and earth will pass away, but my words will never pass away" (Matt. 24:35). Speaking of those who reject him, Jesus said, "that very word which I spoke will condemn him at the last day" (John 12:48). There is no question that Jesus expected his words to have equal authority with God's declarations in the Old Testament.

Jesus Claimed to Be God by Requesting Prayer in His Name. Jesus not only asked people to believe in him and obey his commandments, but he asked them to pray in his name. "And I will do whatever you ask in my name. . . . You may ask me for anything in my name, and I will do it" (John 14:13–14). "If you remain in me and my words remain in you, ask whatever you wish, and it will be given you" (John 15:7). Jesus even insisted, "No one comes to the Father except through me" (John 14:6). In response to this, the disciples not only prayed in Jesus' name (1 Cor. 5:4), but prayed to Christ (Acts 7:59). Jesus certainly intended that his name be invoked both before God and as God in prayer.

In view of these clear ways in which Jesus claimed to be God, any unbiased observer of the Gospels should recognize that Jesus of Nazareth did claim to be God in human flesh. He claimed to be identical to *Yahweh* of the Old Testament.

Alleged Counter-claims of Christ. In spite of these repeated claims to be God, some critics take certain statements of Jesus as denials of deity. Two such incidents are commonly used: In one, a rich young ruler came to Jesus and addressed him as "Good teacher." But Jesus rebuked him, saying, "Why do you call me good? No one is good—except God alone" (Mark 10:17–18; see Mark 10:17–27; cf. parallels Matt. 19:16–30; Luke 18:18–30).

Notice, however, that Jesus did not deny that he was God; he asked the young man to examine the implications of what he said. Jesus was saying, "Do you realize what you are saying when you call me good? Are you really saying that I am God?" Of course, the man did not realize the implications of either his statements or what the law was really saying, so Jesus was forcing him into a very uncomfortable dilemma. Either Jesus was good and God, or he was evil and human, for each human is evil and does not deserve eternal life.

The second supposed counter-example is found in John 14:28, where Jesus said, "My Father is greater than I." How can the Father be greater if Jesus is equal to God? The answer is that, as a man, Jesus subordinated himself to the Father and accepted limitations inherent with humanity. So, *as man* the Father was greater. Further, in the economy of salvation, the Father holds a higher office than does the Son. Jesus proceeded from the Father as a prophet who brought God's words and a high priest who interceded for his people. In nature of being as God, Jesus and the Father are equals (John 1:1; 8:58; 10:30). An earthly father is equally human with his son, but holds a higher office. So the Father and Son in the Trinity are equal *in essence* but different *in function*. In like manner, we speak of the president of a nation as being greater in dignity of office, but not in character.

Jesus cannot be said to have considered himself less than God by nature. This summary helps us understand the differences:

Jesus and the Father as God

Jesus Is Equal . . .	Jesus Is Subordinate . . .
in his divine nature.	in his human nature.
in his divine essence.	in his human function.
in his divine attributes.	in his human office.
in his divine character.	in his human position.

Jesus' Claim to Be God. In addition to Jesus' claim about himself, his disciples also acknowledged his claim to deity. This they manifested in many ways, including the following:

Disciples Attributed the Titles of Deity to Christ. In agreement with their Master, Jesus' Apostles called him "the first and the last" (Rev. 1:17; 2:8; 22:13), "the true light" (John 1:9), their "rock" or "stone" (1 Cor. 10:4; 1 Peter 2:6–8; cf. Pss. 18:2; 95:1), the "bridegroom" (Eph. 5:28–33; Rev. 21:2), "the chief shepherd" (1 Peter 5:4), and "the great shepherd" (Heb. 13:20). The Old Testament role of "redeemer" (Ps. 130:7; Hos. 13:14) is given to Jesus in the New Testament (Titus 2:13; Rev. 5:9). He is seen as the forgiver of sins (Acts 5:31; Col. 3:13; cf. Ps. 130:4; Jer. 31:34) and "savior of the world" (John 4:42; cf. Isa. 43:3). The apostles also taught of him, "Christ Jesus, who will judge the living and the dead" (2 Tim. 4:1). All of these titles are unique to Jehovah in the Old Testament but are given to Jesus in the New.

Disciples Considered Jesus the Messiah-God. The New Testament opens with a passage concluding that Jesus is Immanuel (God with us), which refers to the messianic prediction of Isaiah 7:14. The very title "Christ" carries the same meaning as the Hebrew appellation *Messiah* ("anointed"). In Zechariah 12:10, Jehovah says, "They will look on me, the one they have pierced." But the New Testament writers apply this passage to Jesus' crucifixion (John 19:37; Rev. 1:7). Paul interprets Isaiah 45:22–23 ("For I am God, and there is no other. . . . Before me every knee will bow; by me every tongue will swear") as applying to Jesus: "At the name of Jesus every knee should bow . . . and every tongue confess that Jesus Christ is Lord, to the glory of God the Father" (Phil. 2:10–11). Paul says that all created beings will call Jesus both *Messiah* (Christ) and *Yahweh* (Lord).

Disciples Attributed the Powers of God to Jesus. Works and authority that are God's alone are attributed to Jesus by his disciples. He is said to raise the dead (John 5:21; 11:38–44) and to forgive sins (Acts 5:31; 13:38). He is said to have been the primary agent in creating (John 1:2; Col. 1:16) and sustaining (Col. 1:17) the universe.

Disciples Associated Jesus' Name with God's. His followers used Jesus' name as the agent for answering and the recipient of prayer (Acts 7:59; 1 Cor. 5:4). Often in prayers or benedictions, Jesus' name is used alongside God's, as in, "Grace and peace to you from God our Father and the Lord Jesus Christ" (Gal. 1:3; Eph. 1:2). The name of Jesus appears with equal status to God's in the so-called trinitarian formulas: Jesus commanded to baptize "in the name [singular] of the Father and of the Son and of the Holy Spirit" (Matt. 28:19). This association is made at the end of 2 Corinthians (13:14): "May the grace of the Lord Jesus Christ, and the love of God, and the fellowship of the Holy Spirit be with you all."

Disciples Called Jesus God. Thomas saw Jesus' wounds and cried, "My Lord and my God!" (John 20:28). Paul calls Jesus the one in whom "all the fullness of Deity lives in bodily form" (Col. 2:9). In Titus, Jesus is "our great God and Savior" (2:13), and the writer to the Hebrews says of him, "Your throne, O God, will last for ever and ever" (Heb. 1:8). Paul says that before Christ existed in the form of man, which clearly refers to being really human, he existed in the "form of God" (Phil. 2:5–8). The parallel phrases suggest that if Jesus was fully human, then he was also fully God. A similar phrase, "the image of God," refers in Colossians 1:15 to the manifestation of God. This description is strengthened in Hebrews where it says, "The Son is the radiance of God's glory and the exact representation of his being, sustaining all things by his powerful word" (1:3).

The prologue to John's Gospel states categorically, "In the beginning was the Word, and the Word was with God, and *the Word [Jesus] was God*" (John 1:1).

Disciples Considered Jesus Superior to Angels. The disciples did not simply believe that Christ was more than a man; they believed him to be greater than any created being, including angels. Paul says Jesus is "far above all rule and authority, power and dominion, and every title that can be given, not only in the present age but also in the one to come" (Eph. 1:21). The demons submitted to his command (Matt. 8:32). Angels that refused the worship of humans are seen worshiping him (Rev. 22:8–9). The author of Hebrews presents a complete argument for Christ's superiority over angels, saying, "For to which of the angels did God ever say, 'You are my Son; today I have become your Father'? . . . And again, when God brings his firstborn into the world, he says, 'Let all God's angels worship him'" (Heb. 1:5–6).

Disciples' Alleged Counter-claims to Jesus' Deity. Critics offer texts to argue that Jesus' disciples did not believe he was God. They need to be briefly examined in context. Jehovah's Witnesses use John 1:1 to show that Jesus was "*a* god," not "*the* God," because no definite article *the* appears in the Greek. This misunderstands both the language and the verse. In Greek, the definite article is normally used to stress "the individual," and when it is not present the reference is to "the nature" of the one denoted. Thus, the verse can be rendered, "And the Word was of the nature of God." In the context of the following verses and the rest of John (for example, 1:3; 8:58; 10:30; 20:28) it is impossible that John 1:1 suggests that Jesus is anything less than divine. The rest of the New Testament joins John in forthrightly proclaiming that Jesus is God (for example, in Colossians 1:15–16 and Titus 2:13).

Further, some New Testament texts use the definite article and clearly refer to Christ as "the God." It does not matter whether John used the definite article in 1:1. He and other writers of Scripture considered Jesus as God, not "a god" (see Heb. 1:8).

Critics also use Colossians 1:15, where Paul classifies Christ as "firstborn of all creation." This seems to imply that Christ is a creature, the first creature as the universe was made. This interpretation likewise is contrary to the context, for Paul in Colossians 1:16 has just said that Christ "created all things" and he is about to say that "the fullness of the Godhead" is in him (2:9). The term *firstborn* frequently refers to a position of preeminence in the family which it clearly does in this context (cf. 1:18). Christ is heir of all things, creator and owner. He is before all things.

The same applies to Revelation 3:14, another verse used to deny Christ's deity. John refers to Christ as the "beginning of the creation of God." This sounds as if Christ was the first created being. Here, though, the meaning is that Christ is the *Beginner of* God's creation, not the *beginning in* God's creation. The same Greek word for *beginning* is used of God the Father in Revelation 21:6–7: "It is done. I am the Alpha and the Omega, *the Beginning* and the End. To him who is thirsty I will give to drink without cost from the spring of the water of life. He who overcomes will inherit all this, and *I will be his God* and he will be my son."

Force of the Testimony. There is manifold testimony from Jesus and from those who knew him best that Jesus claimed to be God and that his followers believed that he was. Whether this was the case, there can be no doubt that this is what they believed. As C. S. *Lewis observed, when confronted with the boldness of Christ's claims, we are faced with distinct alternatives.

> I am trying here to prevent anyone saying the really foolish things that people often say about Him: "I'm ready to accept Jesus as a great moral teacher, but I don't accept His claim to be God." That is the one thing we must not say. A man who was merely a man and said the sort of things Jesus said would not be a great moral teacher. He would rather be a lunatic—on a level with the man who says he is a poached egg—or else he would be the Devil of Hell. [Lewis, 55–56]

Evidence That Jesus Is God. To say that Jesus and his disciples claimed that he was God in human flesh does not in itself prove that he is God. The real question is whether there is any good reason to believe the claims. To support his claims to deity, Jesus showed supernatural power and authority that is unique in human history.

Fulfilled Messianic Prophecies. There were dozens of predictive prophecies in the Old Testament regarding the Messiah (*see* PROPHECY AS PROOF FOR BIBLE). Consider the following predictions, made centuries in advance, that Jesus would be:

1. born of a woman (Gen. 3:15; cf. Gal. 4:4).
2. born of a virgin (Isa 7:14; cf. Matt. 1:21f.) (*see* VIRGIN BIRTH).
3. cut off (would die) 483 years after the declaration to reconstruct the temple in 444 B.C. (Dan. 9:24f.; this was fulfilled to the year. See Hoehner, 115–38).
4. The seed of Abraham (Gen. 12:1–3 and 22:18; cf. Matt. 1:1 and Gal. 3:16).
5. of the tribe of Judah (Gen. 49:10; cf. Luke 3:23, 33 and Heb. 7:14).
6. a descendant of David (2 Sam. 7:12f.; cf. Matt. 1:1).
7. born in Bethlehem (Micah 5:2; cf. Matt. 2:1 and Luke 2:4–7).
8. anointed by the Holy Spirit (Isa. 11:2; cf. Matt. 3:16–17).
9. heralded by a messenger (Isa. 40:3 and Mal. 3:1; cf. Matt. 3:1–2).
10. a worker of miracles (Isa. 35:5–6; cf. Matt. 9:35; *see* MIRACLES IN THE BIBLE).
11. cleanser of the temple (Mal. 3:1; cf. Matt. 21:12f.).
12. rejected by Jews (Ps. 118:22; cf. 1 Peter 2:7).
13. die a humiliating death (Ps. 22 and Isa. 53; cf. Matt. 27:31f.). His death would involve:
    enduring rejection by his own people (Isa. 53:3; cf. John 1:10–11; 7:5, 48).
    standing silence before his accusers (Isa. 53:7; cf. Matt. 27:12–19).

being mocked (Ps. 22:7–8; cf. Matt. 27:31).
having hands and feet pierced (Ps. 22:16; cf. Luke 23:33).
being crucified with thieves (Isa. 53:12; cf. Mark 15:27–28).
praying for his persecutors (Isa. 53:12; cf. Luke 23:34).
the piercing of his side (Zech. 12:10; cf. John 19:34).
burial in a rich man's tomb (Isa. 53:9; cf. Matt. 27:57–60).
the casting of lots for his garments (Ps. 22:18; cf. John 19:23–24).

14. being raised from the dead (Ps. 2:7 and 16:10; cf. Acts 2:31 and Mark 16:6).
15. ascending into heaven (Ps. 68:18; cf. Acts 1:9).
16. sitting at the right hand of God (Ps. 110:1; cf. Heb. 1:3).

These prophecies were written hundreds of years before Christ was born. They are too precise to have been based on reading trends of the times or just intelligent guesses, like "prophecies" in a supermarket tabloid.

They are also more precise than the so-called prophecies of Muhammad in the *Qur'an* (*see* *QUR'AN* ALLEGED DIVINE ORIGIN OF). Even the most liberal critics admit that the prophetic books were completed at least 400 years before Christ and the Book of Daniel no later than 165 B.C (*see* DANIEL, DATING OF). There is good evidence to date these books much earlier (some Psalms and early prophets to the eighth and ninth centuries B.C.). But any reasonable dating places these writings long before Jesus lived. It is humanly impossible to make clear, repeated and accurate predictions 200 years in the future. The fulfillment of these prophecies in a theistic universe is miraculous and points to a divine confirmation of Jesus as the Messiah.

Some have suggested that there is a natural explanation for what only seem to be supernatural predictions here. One explanation is that the prophecies were accidentally fulfilled in Jesus. He happened to be in the right place at the right time. But what are we to say about the prophecies involving miracles? "He just happened to make the blind man see?" "He just happened to be resurrected from the dead?" These hardly seem to be chance events. If a God is in control of the universe, then chance is ruled out. Further, it is unlikely that these events would have converged in the life of one man. The probability of sixteen predictions being fulfilled in one man has been calculated at 1 in 10^{45}. If we go to forty-eight predictions, the probability is 1 in 10^{157}. It is almost impossible to conceive of a number that big (Stoner, 108).

But it is not just a logical improbability that rules out this theory; it is the moral implausibility of an all-powerful and all-knowing God letting things get out of control so that all his plans for prophetic fulfillment are ruined by someone who just happened to be in the right place at the right time. God cannot lie, nor can he break a promise (Heb. 6:18). So we must conclude that he did not allow his prophetic promises to be thwarted by chance. All the evidence points to Jesus as the divinely appointed fulfillment of the messianic prophecies. He was God's man, confirmed by God's signs. If God made the predictions to be fulfilled in the life of Christ, he would not allow them to be fulfilled in the life of any other. The God of truth would not allow a lie to be confirmed as true (*see* MIRACLES AS CONFIRMATION OF TRUTH).

A Miraculous and Sinless Life. The very nature of Christ's life demonstrates his claim to deity. To live a truly sinless life would be a momentous accomplishment, but to claim to be God and offer a sinless life as evidence is another matter. Muhammad did not (*see* MUHAMMAD, CHARACTER OF). Nor did Buddha nor any other religious leader (*see* CHRIST, UNIQUENESS OF). Some of Jesus' enemies brought false accusations against him, but the verdict of Pilate at his trial has been the verdict of history: "I find no basis for a charge against this man" (Luke 23:4). A soldier at the cross agreed, saying, "Surely this was a righteous man" (Luke 23:47), and the thief on the cross next to Jesus said, "this man has done nothing wrong" (Luke 23:41). But the real test is what those who were closest to Jesus said of his character. His disciples had lived and worked with him for three years at close range, yet their opinions of him were not diminished. Peter called Christ, "a lamb without blemish or defect" (1 Peter 1:19) and added, "no deceit was found in his mouth" (2:22). John called him, "Jesus Christ, the Righteous One" (1 John 2:1; cf. 3:7). Paul expressed the unanimous belief of the early church that Christ "had no sin" (2 Cor. 5:21), and the writer of Hebrews says that he was tempted as a man, "yet was without sin" (4:15). Jesus himself once challenged his accusers, "Can any of you prove me guilty of sin?" (John 8:46), but no one was able to find him guilty of anything. He forbid retaliation (Matt. 5:38–42). Unlike Muhammad, he never used the sword to spread his message (Matt. 26:52). This being the case, the impeccable character of Christ gives a double testimony to the truth of his claim. It provides supporting evidence as he suggested, but it also assures us that he was not lying when he said that he was God.

Beyond the moral aspects of his life, the miraculous nature of his ministry is a divine confirmation. Jesus performed an unprecedented display of miracles. He turned water to wine (John 2:7f.), walked on water (Matt. 14:25), multiplied bread

(John 6:11f.), opened the eyes of the blind (John 9:7f.), made the lame to walk (Mark 2:3f.), cast out demons (Mark 3:11f.), healed the multitudes of all kinds of sickness (Matt. 9:35), including leprosy (Mark 1:40–42), and even raised the dead to life on several occasions (John 11:43–44; Luke 7:11–15; Mark 5:35f.). When asked if he was the Messiah, he used his miracles as evidence to support the claim saying, "Go back and report to John what you hear and see: The blind receive sight, the lame walk, those who have leprosy are cured, the deaf hear, the dead are raised" (Matt. 11:4–5). This special outpouring of miracles was a special sign that Messiah had come (see Isa. 35:5–6). The Jewish leader Nicodemus even said, "Rabbi, we know you are a teacher who has come from God. For no one could perform the miraculous signs you are doing if God were not with him" (John 3:2). To a first-century Jew, miracles such as Christ performed were clear indications of God's approval of the performer's message (*see* MIRACLES AS CONFIRMATION OF TRUTH). But in Jesus' case, part of that message was that he was God in human flesh. Thus, his miracles verify his claim to be true deity.

The Resurrection. Nothing like the resurrection of Christ is claimed by any other religion, and no other miracle has as much historical confirmation. Jesus Christ rose from the dead on the third day in the same physical body, though transformed, in which he died. In this resurrected physical body he appeared to more than 500 disciples on at least one of twelve different occasions over a forty-day period and conversed with them (Acts 1:3; 1 Cor. 15:3–6; *see* RESURRECTION, ORDER OF EVENTS). The nature, extent, and times of, these appearances remove any doubt that Jesus indeed rose from the dead in the numerically same body of flesh and bones in which he died. During each appearance he was seen and heard with the natural senses of the observer. On at least four occasions he was touched or offered himself to be touched. At least twice he definitely was touched with physical hands. Four times Jesus ate physical food with his disciples. Four times they saw his empty tomb, and twice he showed them his crucifixion scars. He literally exhausted the ways it is possible to prove that he rose bodily from the grave. No event in the ancient world has more eyewitness verification than does the resurrection of Jesus (*see* RESURRECTION, EVIDENCE FOR).

What is more amazing about the resurrection is the fact that both the Old Testament and Jesus predicted that he would rise from the dead. This highlights the evidential value of the resurrection of Christ in a unique way.

Old Testament prediction of the resurrection. Jewish prophets predicted the resurrection in specific statements and by logical deduction. The apostles applied specific Old Testament texts to the resurrection of Christ (Ps. 2:7; cf. Heb. 1:5 and Acts 13:33). Peter says that, since we know that David died and was buried, he must have been speaking of the Christ when he said, "you will not abandon me to the grave, nor will you let your Holy One see decay" (Ps. 16:8–11, quoted in Acts 2:25–31). No doubt Paul used this and similar passages in the Jewish synagogues when "he reasoned with them from the Scriptures, explaining and proving that the Christ had to suffer and rise from the dead" (Acts 17:2–3).

Also, the Old Testament teaches the resurrection by logical deduction. There is clear teaching that the Messiah was to die (cf. Ps. 22; Isa. 53) and equally evident teaching that he is to have an enduring political reign from Jerusalem (Isa. 9:6; Dan. 2:44; Zech. 13:1). There is no viable way to reconcile these two teachings unless the Messiah who dies is raised from the dead to reign forever. There is no indication in the Old Testament of two Messiahs, one suffering and one reigning, as some Jewish scholars have suggested. References to the Messiah are always in the singular (cf. Isa. 9:6; 53:1f.; Dan. 9:26). No second Messiah is ever designated.

Yet Jesus had begun no reign when he died. Only by his resurrection could the prophecies of a Messianic kingdom be fulfilled.

Jesus' prediction of his resurrection. On several occasions Jesus also predicted his resurrection from the dead. In the earliest part of his ministry, he said, "Destroy this temple, [of my body] and I will raise it again in three days" (John 2:19, 21). In Matthew 12:40, he said, "as Jonah was three days and nights in the belly of a huge fish, so the Son of Man will be three days and nights in the heart of the earth." To those who had seen his miracles and stubbornly would not believe, he said, "A wicked and adulterous generation asks for a miraculous sign! But none will be given it except the sign of the prophet Jonah" (Matt. 12:39; 16:4). After Peter's confession, "he then began to teach them that the Son of Man must suffer many things . . . and that he must be killed and after three days rise again" (Mark 8:31). This became a central part of his teaching from that point until his death (Matt. 27:63; Mark 14:59). Further, Jesus taught that he would raise himself from the dead, saying of his life, "I have authority to lay it down and I have authority to take it up again" (John 10:18).

Philosopher of science Karl Popper argued that, whenever a "risky prediction" is fulfilled, it counts as confirmation of the theory that predicted it. If so, then the fulfillment of Jesus' prediction of his own resurrection is confirmation of his claim to be God. For what could be riskier than predicting your own resurrection? If a person will not accept these lines of evidence as support of Christ's truth claim, then he has a bias that will not accept anything as evidence.

Summary. Jesus claimed to be God and proved it by a convergence of three unprecedented sets of miracles: fulfilled prophecy, a miraculous life, and his resurrection from the dead. This unique convergence of supernatural events confirms his claims to be God in human flesh. It also answers David *Hume's objection that, since all miracles have similar claims, their proof claims are mutually canceling. Not all religions have like miracle claims. Only in Christianity does its leader claim to prove to be God by a convergence of unique supernatural events such as Jesus offered (*see* CHRIST, UNIQUENESS OF). Hence, only Christ is miraculously confirmed to be God and, by virtue of that, to be believed in whatever he teaches as true.

Sources

F. F. Bruce, and W. J. Martin, "Two Laymen on Christ's Deity," *CT*

J. Buell, et al., *Jesus: God, Ghost or Guru?*

N. L. Geisler, *Christian Apologetics*

——— and A. Saleeb, *Answering Islam*

C. Hodge, *Systematic Theology*, Vol. 1, chapter 8

H. W. Hoehner, *Chronological Aspects of the Life of Christ*

C. S. Lewis, *Mere Christianity*

J. McDowell and B. Larson, *Jesus: A Biblical Defense of His Deity*

R. Rhoads, *Christ Before the Manger*

P. W. Stoner, *Science Speaks*

B. . Warfield, *The Person and Work of Christ*

Christ, Humanity of. ***See*** **CHRIST, DEITY OF; DOCETISM.**

Christ, Uniqueness of. Orthodox Christians believe that Jesus is the unique Son of God in human flesh (*see* CHRIST, DEITY OF). However, some unbelievers, who may or may not believe Jesus existed, do not believe that Jesus was necessarily a wise or a particularly good man. Others, such as Muslims (*see* ISLAM), think that Jesus was a prophet, along with other prophets. *Hinduism depicts Christ as one among many great gurus. Liberal Christians and many others hold Christ as a good human being and a great moral example.

In his essay "Why I Am Not a Christian," the agnostic Bertrand Russell wrote, "Historically it is quite doubtful whether Christ ever existed at all, and if he did we know nothing about him." As to Christ's character, he said, "I cannot myself feel that either in the matter of wisdom or in the matter of virtue Christ stands quite as high as some other people known to history. I think I should put Buddha and Socrates above him in those respects" (Russell, *Why I Am Not a Christian*).

Deity and Humanity. Christianity is unique among world religions, and Christ's true uniqueness is the centerpiece of Christianity. The truth about Christ is based primarily on the New Testament documents which have been shown elsewhere to be authentic (*see* NEW TESTAMENT MANUSCRIPTS, RELIABILITY OF; NEW TESTAMENT, HISTORICITY OF). The New Testament record, especially the Gospels, is one of the most reliable documents from the ancient world. From these documents we learn that numerous facets of Christ are absolutely unique.

Jesus Christ was unique in that he alone, of all who ever lived, was both God and man. The New Testament teaches the fully unified deity and humanity of Christ. The Nicene Creed (325) states the uniform belief of all orthodox Christianity that Christ was fully God and fully man in one person. All heresies regarding Christ deny one or both of these propositions. This as a claim alone makes him unique above all other religious leaders or persons who have ever lived, and it can be backed up with factual evidence. Some of this evidence is seen in other aspects of Christ's uniqueness (*see* CHRIST, DEITY OF).

The Supernatural Nature of Christ. *Unique in Messianic Prophecies.* Jesus lived a miracle-filled and supernaturally empowered existence from his conception to his ascension. Centuries before his birth he was foretold by supernatural prophecy (*see* MIRACLES IN THE BIBLE; PROPHECY, AS PROOF OF THE BIBLE).

The Old Testament, which even the most ardent critic acknowledges was in existence centuries before Christ, predicted the *where* (Micah 5:2), the *when* (Dan. 9:26), and the *how* (Isa. 7:14) of Christ's entry into the world. He would be born of a woman (Gen. 3:15) from the line of Adam's son Seth (Gen. 4:26), through Noah's son Shem (Gen. 9:26–27), and Abraham (Gen. 12:3; 15:5). He would come through the tribe of Judah (Gen. 49:10) and would be the son of David (2 Sam. 7:12f.). The Old Testament predicted that Christ would die for our sins (Psalm 22; Isaiah 53; Dan. 9:26; Zech. 12:10) and would rise from the dead (Pss. 2:7; 16:10).

All of these supernatural prophecies were uniquely fulfilled in Jesus Christ. This is not true of any great religious leader or person who has ever lived, including Muhammad (*see* MUHAMMAD, ALLEGED MIRACLES OF).

Unique in Conception. Christ was not only supernaturally anticipated; he was also miraculously conceived. While announcing his virgin conception, Matthew (1:22–23) points to the prophecy of Isaiah (7:14). Luke, a physician, records this miraculous inception of human life (Luke 1:26f.); Paul alludes to it in Galatians 4:4. Of all human conceptions, Jesus' stands as unique and miraculous (*see* VIRGIN BIRTH).

Unique in Life. From his very first miracle in Cana of Galilee (John 2:11), Jesus' ministry was marked by its miracles (cf. John 3:2; Acts 2:22). These were not healings of delusional illnesses, nor were they explainable on natural grounds. They were unique (*see* MIRACLE) in that they were immediate, always successful, had no known relapses, and healed illnesses that were incurable by medicine, such as persons born blind (John 9). Jesus even raised several people from the dead, including Lazarus whose body was already to the point of rotting (John 11:39).

Jesus turned water to wine (John 2:7f.), walked on water (Matt. 14:25), multiplied bread (John 6:11f.), opened the eyes of the blind (John 9:7f.), made the lame to walk (Mark 2:3f.), cast out demons (Mark 3:10f.), healed all kinds of sicknesses (Matt. 9:35), including leprosy (Mark 1:40–42), and even raised the dead to life on several occasions (Mark 5:35f.; Luke 7:11–15; John 11:43–44). When asked if he was the Messiah, he used his miracles as evidence to support the claim saying, "Go back and report to John what you hear and see: The blind receive sight, the lame walk, those who have leprosy are cured, the deaf hear, the dead are raised" (Matt. 11:4–5). This outpouring of miracles was set forth ahead of time by prophets as a special sign that Messiah had come (see Isa. 35:5–6). Nicodemus even said, "Rabbi, we know you are a teacher who has come from God. For no one could perform the miraculous signs you are doing if God were not with him" (John 3:2).

Unique in Death. Events surrounding Christ's death were miraculous (*see* CHRIST, DEATH OF). This included the darkness from noon to 3 P.M. (Mark 15:33) and the earthquake that opened the tombs and rent the temple veil (Matt. 27:51–54). The manner in which he suffered the excruciating torture of crucifixion was miraculous. The attitude he maintained toward his mockers and executioners was miraculous, saying, "Father forgive them, for they do not know what they are doing" (Luke 23:34). The way in which he actually died was miraculous. As Jesus said, "I lay down my life—only to take it up again. No one takes it from me, but I lay it down of my own accord" (John 10:18). At the very moment of his departure, he was not overcome by death. Rather, he voluntarily dismissed his spirit. "Jesus said, 'It is finished.' With that, he bowed his head and gave up his spirit" (John 19:30).

Unique in the Resurrection. The crowning miracle of Jesus' earthly mission was the resurrection (*see* RESURRECTION, EVIDENCE FOR). It was not only predicted in the Old Testament (Psalms 2, 16), but Jesus himself predicted it from the very beginning of his ministry: He said, "'Destroy this temple, and I will raise it again in three days.' . . . But the temple he had spoken of was his body" (John 2:19, 21; Matt. 12:40–42; 17:9). Jesus demonstrated the reality of his resurrection in twelve appearances over forty days to more than 500 people.

Unique in the Ascension. Just like his entrance into this world, Jesus' departure was also miraculous. After commissioning his disciples, "he was taken up before their very eyes, and a cloud hid him from their sight. They were looking intently up into the sky as he was going, when suddenly two men dressed in white stood beside them" (Acts 1:10). Contrary to the view of some (see Harris, 423), this was not a "parable" but a literal bodily ascension into heaven from which he will return in the same literal body to reign in this world (Acts 1:11; Rev. 1:7, 19–20). The great Christian creeds clearly emphasize the miraculous bodily ascension of Christ.

Unique in Sinlessness. Some of Jesus' enemies brought false accusations against him, but the verdict of Pilate at his trial has been the verdict of history: "I find no basis for a charge against this man" (Luke 23:4). A soldier at the cross agreed saying, "Surely this was a righteous man" (Luke 23:47), and the thief on the cross next to Jesus said, "This man has done nothing wrong" (Luke 23:41).

For a description of what those closest to Jesus thought of his character, Hebrews says that he was tempted as a man "yet without sinning" (4:15). Jesus himself once challenged his accusers, "Which of you convicts me of sin?" (John 8:46), but no one was able to find him guilty of anything. This being the case, the impeccable character of Christ gives a double testimony to the truth of his claim. Jesus' sinlessness was unique.

The Character of Christ Is Unique. Christ's character was unique in other ways. To a perfect degree he manifested the best of virtues. He also combined seemingly opposing traits.

In Exemplifying Virtues. Even Bertrand *Russell, who fancied he saw flaws in Christ's character, confessed nonetheless that "What the world needs is love, Christian love, or compassion." But this belies a belief in what most others acknowledge, namely, that Christ was the perfect manifestation of the virtue of love.

Jesus' willing submission to the ignominious suffering and death by crucifixion, while he maintained love and forgiveness toward those killing him is proof of this virtue (Luke 23:34, 43). He alone lived perfectly what he taught in the Sermon on the Mount (Matt. 5–7). He did not retaliate against his enemies; instead, he forgave them. He rebuked his disciples for misusing the sword (Matt. 26:52), and miraculously reattached and healed the amputated ear of one of the mob who came to take him to his death (Luke 22:50).

Jesus was the perfect example of patience, kindness, and compassion. He had compassion on the multitudes (Matt. 9:36), to the point of weeping over Jerusalem (Matt. 23:37). Even though he justly condemned (in no uncertain terms) the Pharisees who misled the innocent (Matt. 23), he did not hesitate to speak with Jewish leaders who showed interest (John 3).

In Combining Seemingly Opposite Traits. One of the unique things about Christ is the way he brought together in his person characteristics that in anyone else would seem impossible. He was a perfect example of humility, to the extent of washing his disciples' feet (John 15). Yet he made bold claims to deity, such as, "I and the Father are One" (John 10:30) and "before Abraham was, I AM" (John 8:58; cf. Exod. 3:14). The claim, "I am meek and lowly in heart" (Matt. 11:29) sounds arrogant, but he backed his words among little children (Matthew 18). Yet he was so strong as to overturn the tables of those who merchandised God's house, cracking a whip to chase away their animals (John 2). Jesus was known for the virtue of kindness, yet he was severe with hypocrites who misled the innocent (Matthew 23).

Life and Teaching. As Jesus himself declared, the substance of what he taught finds its roots in the Old Testament (Matt. 5:17–18). He condemned meaningless traditions and misinterpretations of the Old Testament (Matt. 5:21f., 15:3–5; *see* ACCOMMODATION THEORY). Though the essence of what he taught was not new, the form and the manner in which he taught it was unique. The Sermon on the Mount employs a fresh teaching method.

The vivid parables, such as the good Samaritan (Luke 10), the prodigal son (Luke 15), and the lost sheep (Luke 15:4f.), are masterpieces of communication. Parables stand at the heart of Jesus' teaching style. By drawing on the lifestyles of the people to illustrate the truths he wished to convey, Jesus communicated truth and refuted error. Also, by speaking in parables he could avoid "casting pearls before swine." He could confound and confuse those who did not wish to believe (the outsider), yet illuminate those who did desire to believe (the insider). While the use of allegories and parables themselves was not unique, the manner in which Jesus employed parables was. He brought the art of teaching eternal mystery in terms of everyday experience to a new height. The "laws of teaching" identified by modern pedagogues (Shafer, *Seven Laws*), were practiced perfectly in Jesus' teaching style.

The manner in which Jesus taught was unique. The Jewish intellectuals admitted, "No one ever spoke the way this man does" (John 7:46). As he taught in parables, he was thronged by the multitudes (Matt. 13:34). As a lad, he impressed even the rabbis in the temple. For "Everyone who heard him was amazed at his understanding and his answers" (Luke 2:47). Later, he confounded those who attempted to trick him so that "No one could say a word in reply, and from that day on no one dared to ask him any more questions" (Matt. 22:46).

Christ Is Superior. Jesus Christ was unique in every way. From his complete deity to his perfect humanity; from his miraculous conception to his supernatural ascension; from his impeccable character to his incomparable teaching—Jesus stands above all other religious or moral teachers.

Christ Is Superior to Moses. As a Jew himself, Jesus had no argument with Moses, the prophet who brought the Jewish law and led the Israelites out of Egyptian bondage to freedom as an independent nation. Moses and Jesus were prophets of the same God, and Jesus said that he did not come to abolish the law (found in the writings of Moses) but to fulfill it (Matt. 5:17). Jesus implies that Moses' words are God's words (compare Matt. 19:4–5 with Gen. 2:24). However, in many respects, we find that Jesus is superior to Moses.

Christ is a superior prophet to Moses. In Deuteronomy 18:15–19, Moses predicted that God would raise up a Jewish Prophet with a special message. Anyone who did not believe this prophet would be judged by God. This passage has been traditionally interpreted as referring to Messiah. Genesis 3:15 is also understood by many to refer to Jesus as the seed of the woman who would crush the head of the serpent.

Christ's revelation is superior to that of Moses. "The Law was given through Moses; Grace and truth were realized through Jesus Christ" (John 1:17). While Moses set up the moral and social structures which guided the nation, the law could not save anyone from the penalty of their sins, which is death. As Paul says, "by the works of the law no flesh will be justified in his sight; for through the law comes the knowledge of sin" (Rom. 3:20). The revelation which came through Jesus, though, was one in which the sins which the law made known are forgiven, "being justified as a gift by his grace through the redemption which is in Christ Jesus" (Rom. 3:24). Christ's revelation builds on the foundation of Moses by solving the problem of which the law made us aware.

Christ's position is superior to that of Moses. Moses is the greatest of the Old Testament prophets, but Jesus is more than a prophet. As the Epistle to the Hebrews says, "Moses was faithful *in* all his house as a servant, for a testimony of those things which were to be spoken later; but Christ was faithful as a Son *over* his house" (Heb. 3:5–6). While Moses served God, Jesus was declared to be the Son of God with the right to rule over all servants.

Christ's miracles are superior to those of Moses. Moses performed great miracles, but Christ's miracles were greater in degree (*see* MIRACLES IN THE BIBLE). Moses lifted the bronze serpent to give healing to those who would look, but in this he was merely following instructions. He never made the blind to see, or the deaf to hear. Also, there is nothing in Moses' ministry to compare with the resurrection of Lazarus or of Christ.

Christ's claims are superior to those of Moses. Moses never made a claim to be God and did nothing other than fulfill his role as a prophet. Jesus did claim to be God and predicted his own resurrection to prove it.

Christ Is Superior to Muhammad. Muhammad, the founder of Islam agreed with Jesus and Moses that God is one (*see* ISLAM), that he created the universe, and that he is beyond the universe. There is considerable agreement over the events of the first sixteen chapters of Genesis, to the point where Hagar was cast out from Abram's house. After this, the Bible focuses on Isaac while Islam is concerned with what happened to their forefather, Ishmael. The teaching of Muhammad may be summarized in the five doctrines:

1. Allah is the one true God.
2. Allah has sent many prophets, including Moses and Jesus, but Muhammad is the last and greatest.
3. The *Qur'an* is the supreme religious book (*see* *QUR'AN*, ALLEGED DIVINE ORIGIN OF), taking priority over the Law, the Psalms, and the Injil (Gospels) of Jesus.
4. There are many intermediate beings between God and us (angels), some of whom are good and some evil.
5. Each man's deeds will be weighed to determine who will go to heaven and hell at the resurrection. The way to gain salvation includes reciting the Shahadah several times a day ("There is no God but Allah; and Muhammad is his prophet."), praying five times a day, fasting a month each year, almsgiving, and making pilgrimages to Mecca.

Christ offers a superior message. Jesus made superior claims to those made by Muhammad. Jesus claimed to be God (*see* CHRIST, DEITY OF). Muhammad claimed only to be a mere man who was a prophet (*see* MUHAMMAD, ALLEGED DIVINE CALL OF). If Jesus, then, is not God, he is certainly no prophet. Jesus offered a superior confirmation for his claims. Jesus performed numerous miracles. Muhammad performed no miracles and admitted in the *Qur'an* that Jesus did many. Only Jesus died and rose from the dead.

Christ offers a better way of salvation. Unlike the God of Islam, the God of the Bible reached out to us by sending his Son to earth to die for our sins. Muhammad offered no sure hope for salvation, only guidelines for working oneself into Allah's favor. Christ provided all that is needed to get us to heaven in his death, "For Christ also died once for all, the just for the unjust, in order that he might bring us to God" (1 Peter 3:18).

Christ offers a superior model life. Muhammad spent the last ten years of his life at war. As a polygamist he exceeding even the number of wives (four) he had prescribed for his religion. He also violated his own law by plundering caravans coming to Mecca, some of whom were on pilgrimage. He engaged in retaliation and revenge, contrary to his own teaching (*see* MUHAMMAD, CHARACTER OF).

Jesus Is Superior to Hindu Gurus. In *Hinduism (*see* HINDUISM, VEDANTA) a *guru* is a teacher. The Hindu scriptures cannot be understood by reading; they must be learned from a guru. These holy men are worshiped even after their deaths as supposed incarnations of the gods. What they teach is that humans need liberation from the endless cycle of reincarnation (*samsara*) which is brought on by *karma*, the effects of all words, deeds, and actions in the present and all former lives. Liberation (*moksha*) is obtained when the individual expands his being and consciousness to an infinite level and realizes that *atman* (the self) is the same as *Brahman* (the one absolute being from which all multiplicity comes).

In other words, each Hindu must realize personal godhood. Such a realization can only be achieved by following *Jnana Yoga*—salvation by knowledge of the ancient writings and inward meditation; *Bhakti Yoga*—salvation by devotion to one of the many deities; *Karma Yoga*—salvation by works, such as ceremonies, sacrifices, fasting, and pilgrimages, which must be done without thought of rewards. Each of these methods will to some extent include *Raja Yoga*, a meditation technique involving control over the body, breathing, and thoughts.

Hinduism as it is actually practiced consists largely of superstition, legendary stories about the gods, occult practices, and demon worship.

Christ teaches a superior worldview. Jesus teaches a theistic worldview (*see* THEISM). But pantheism, the realization of godhood, is the heart of Hinduism.

Christ's teaching is morally superior. Orthodox Hinduism insists that suffering people be left to suffer, because it is their destiny, as determined by *karma*. Jesus said, "Love your neighbor as yourself." He defined neighbor as anyone in need of help. John said, "But whoever has the world's goods, and sees his brother in need and closes his heart against him, how does the love of God abide in him?" (1 John 3:17). Also, many, if not most, gurus use their esteemed position to exploit their followers financially and sexually. The Bagwan Sri Rajneesh accumulated dozens of Rolls Royces as gifts from his followers. The Beatles became disenchanted with the Maharishi Mahesh Yogi when they learned that he was much more interested in the body of one of the women in their party than with any of their spirits. They admitted, "We made a mistake." Even the respected guru Mahatma Gandhi slept with women other than his wife.

Jesus gives a superior path to enlightenment. While the gurus are necessary to understand the sacred writings of *Bhagavad Gita* and the *Upanishads*, there is no esoteric or hidden truth in the Bible that must be explained apart from ordinary understanding. Christian meditation is not an effort to empty the mind, but rather to fill it with the truth of Scriptural principles (Psalm 1). Inward meditation is like peeling an onion; you keep tearing off layer after layer until, when you reach the middle, you find that there is nothing there. Meditation on God's Word begins with content and opens up the meaning until it yields contentment of soul.

Christ teaches a better way of salvation. The Hindu is lost in the karmic cycle of reincarnation until he reaches *moksha* and is left to work the way out of this maze alone. Jesus promised that we would be saved by faith (Eph. 2:8–9; Titus 3:5–7), and that we could know that our salvation is guaranteed (Eph. 1:13–14; 1 John 5:13).

Christ Is Superior to Buddha. Siddhartha Gautama (*Buddha* is a title meaning "enlightened one") is inferior to Christ. Buddhism began as a reformation movement within Hinduism, which had become a system of speculation and superstition. To correct this, Gautama rejected the rituals and occultism and developed an essentially atheistic religion (though later forms of Buddhism returned to the Hindu gods). His basic beliefs are summed in the Four Noble Truths:

1. Life is suffering.
2. Suffering is caused by desires for pleasure and prosperity.
3. Suffering can be overcome by eliminating desires.
4. Desire can be eliminated by the Eightfold Path.

The Eightfold Path is both a system of religious education and the moral precepts of *Buddhism. It includes (1) right knowledge ("Four Noble Truths"), (2) right intentions, (3) right speech, (4) right conduct (no killing, drinking, stealing, lying, or adultery), (5) right occupation (which causes no suffering), (6) right effort, (7) right mindfulness (denial of the finite self), and (8) right meditation (*Raja Yoga*).

The goal of all Buddhists is not heaven or being with God, for there is no God in Gautama's teaching. Rather they seek nirvana, the elimination of all suffering, desires, and the illusion of self-existence. While a liberal branch of Buddhism (Mahayana Buddhism) now has deified Gautama as a savior, Theravada Buddhism stays closer to Gautama's teachings and maintains that he never claimed divinity. As to his being a savior, it is reported that Buddha's last words were, "Buddhas do but point the way; work out your salvation with diligence." As a variant form of Hinduism, Buddhism is subject to all of the criticisms mentioned above. Jesus' teaching is superior. Further:

Christ fills life with more hope. Jesus' teaching is superior to Buddha's in that Jesus taught hope in life, while Buddhism sees life only as suffering and selfhood as something to be eradicated. Jesus taught that life is a gift of God to be enjoyed (John 10:10) and that the individual is to be honored supremely (Matt. 5:22). Furthermore, he promised hope in the life to come (John 14:6).

Christ offers a better way of salvation. The Buddhist also teaches reincarnation as the means of salvation. However, in this form the self or individuality of the soul is eradicated at the end of each life. So even though you live on, it is not you as an individual who has any hope of attaining nirvana. Jesus promised hope to each man and woman as an individual (John 14:3) and said to the thief on the cross beside him, "Today you shall be with me in paradise" (Luke 23:43).

Jesus is a better Christ. Jesus claimed and proved to be God in human flesh. Buddha was a mere mortal man who died and never rose again. Jesus, however, rose bodily from the grave. Gautama simply wanted to bring his "enlightenment" to others to help them to nirvana, where all desires and individual existence is lost.

Christ Is Superior to Socrates. Although Socrates never started a religion, he has attracted a great following. Socrates never wrote anything, but *Plato, his disciple, wrote a great deal about him, although these accounts may be as much Plato's ideas as the thought of Socrates. Plato presents Socrates as a man convinced that God has appointed him to the task of promoting truth and goodness by making humans examine their words and deeds to see if they are true and good. Vice, in his opinion, was merely ignorance, and knowledge led to virtue. He is credited as the first person to recognize a need to develop a systematic approach to discovering truth, though the system itself was finally formulated by Aristotle—a disciple of Plato's.

Like Christ, Socrates was condemned to death on the basis of false accusations from authorities who were threatened by his teaching. He could have been acquitted if he had not insisted on making his accusers and judges examine their own statements and lives, which they were unwilling to do. He was content to die, knowing that he had carried out his mission to the end, and that death, whether a dreamless sleep or a wonderful fellowship of great men, was good.

Christ has a superior basis for truth. Jesus, like Socrates, often used questions to make his hearers examine themselves, but his basis for knowing the truth about human beings and God was rooted in the fact that he was the all-knowing God. He said of himself, "I am the way, the truth, and the life." He was, in his very being, the fount from which all truth ultimately flowed. Likewise, as God, he was the absolute Goodness by which all other goodness is measured. He once asked a young man to examine his words by saying, "Why do you call me good? No one is good except God alone." Jesus was the very truth and good which Socrates wanted to understand.

Christ gives more certain knowledge. While Socrates taught some true principles, he often was left to speculate about many important issues, such as what happens at death (*see* CERTAINTY/CERTITUDE). Jesus gave a sure answer to such questions, because he had certain knowledge of the human destination (John 5:19–29; 11:25–26). Where reason (Socrates) has insufficient evidence to make a definite conclusion, revelation (Jesus) gives answers which might never be anticipated.

Christ's death was more noble. Socrates died for a cause and did so with courage, which is certainly to be commended. However, Jesus died as a substitute for others (Mark 10:45) to pay the penalty that they deserved. Not only did he die for his friends, but also for those that were, and would remain, his enemies (Rom. 5:6–7). Such a demonstration of love is unequaled by any philosopher or philanthropist.

Christ's proof of his message is superior. Rational proofs are good when there is sound evidence for their conclusions (*see* GOD, EVIDENCE FOR). But Socrates cannot support his claim to be sent by God with anything that compares to the miracles of Christ and his resurrection (*see* RESURRECTION, EVIDENCE FOR). Pagan prophets and prophetesses, such as the Oracle of Delphi, do not compare with the precise biblical prediction and miracles (*see* PROPHECY AS PROOF OF THE BIBLE). In these acts there is a superior proof that Jesus' message was authenticated by God as true (*see* MIRACLES, APOLOGETIC VALUE OF; MIRACLES AS CONFIRMATION OF TRUTH).

Christ Is Superior to Lao Tse (Taoism). Modern Taoism is a religion of witchcraft, superstition, and polytheism, but it was originally a system of philosophy, and that is how it is being presented to Western culture today. Lao Tse built this system around one principle which explained everything in the universe and guided it all. That principle is called the Tao. There is no simple way to explain the Tao (*see* ZEN BUDDHISM). The world is full of conflicting opposites—good and evil, male and female, light and dark, yes and no. All oppositions are manifestations of the conflict between *Yin* and *Yang*. But in ultimate reality *Yin* and *Yang* are completely intertwined and perfectly balanced. That balance is the mystery called the Tao. To understand the Tao is to realize that all opposites are one and that truth lies in contradiction, not in resolution (*see* LOGIC; FIRST PRINCIPLES).

Taoism goes beyond this to urge living in harmony with the Tao. A person should enter a life of complete passiveness and reflection on such questions as, "What is the sound of one hand clapping?" or "If a tree falls in the forest when no one is there to hear it, does it make a sound?" One should be at peace with nature and avoid all forms of violence. This system of philosophy has many similarities with Zen Buddhism.

Christ brings superior freedom. Jesus allows humans to use their reason. In fact, he commands them to do so (Matt. 22:37; cf. 1 Peter 3:15); Taoism does not, at least on the highest level. Taoism engages in the claim that "Reason does not apply to reality." That statement itself is self-defeating, for it is a reasonable statement about reality. It is either true or false about the way things really are, and not contradictory, yet it claims that ultimately truth lies in contradiction. Jesus commanded: "Love the Lord your God with all your heart, and with all your soul, *and with all your mind*. This is the great and foremost commandment" (Matt. 22:37–38, emphasis added). God says, "Come now, and let us reason together," (Isa. 1:18). Peter exhorts us to "give a reason for the hope that you have" (1 Peter 3:15b).

Jesus encouraged the use of freedom to choose, never imposing himself on the unwilling (Matt. 23:37). Taoism asks each follower to set will on the shelf; to give up the power to change things. Jesus says that each person has a choice and that this choice makes the difference. Each chooses to believe or not believe (John 3:18), to obey or disobey (John 15:14), to change the world or be changed by it (Matt. 5:13–16).

Jesus allows each person the freedom to be saved. Taoism offers only a way to resign oneself to the way things are. Christ offers a way to change both who we are and what we are, so that we might know the joys of life. Rather than accepting death as an inevitable end, Christ provides a way to conquer death by his resurrection. Lao Tse can make no such claim.

Conclusion. Christ is absolutely unique among all who ever lived (*see* WORLD RELIGIONS AND CHRISTIANITY). He is unique in his supernatural nature, in his superlative character, and in his life and teaching (*see* CHRIST, DEITY OF). No other world teacher has claimed to be God. Even when the followers of some prophet deified their teacher, there is no proof given for that claim that can be compared to the fulfillment of prophecy, the sinless and miraculous life, and the resurrection. No other religious leader (except some who copied Christ) offered salvation by faith, apart from works, based on acting to take away the guilt for human sin. No religious or philosophical leader has displayed the love for people that Jesus did in dying for the sins of the world (John 15:13; Rom. 5:6–8). Jesus is absolutely unique among all human beings who ever lived.

Sources

J. N. D. Anderson, *The World's Religions*
H. Bushnell, *The Supernaturalness of Christ*
N. L. Geisler, *The Battle for the Resurrection*
——— and R. Brooks, *When Skeptics Ask*
M. J. Harris, *From Grave to Glory*
C. S. Lewis, *Mere Christianity*

B. Russell, *Why I Am Not a Christian*
C. Shafer, *The Seven Laws of Teaching*

Christ, Virgin Birth of. *See* VIRGIN BIRTH.

Christ of Faith vs. Jesus of History. The distinction between the "Christ of faith" and the Jesus of history is often traced to Martin Kahler (1835–1912), though he probably did not mean by the term what most contemporary critics do. Even before Kahler, Gotthold Lessing (1729–1781) laid the ground for the separation of the Christ of faith from the Jesus of history. What happened in that separation through the "quests for the historical Jesus" is discussed in the article, Jesus, Quest for the Historical.

Lessing's "Ditch." As early as 1778, Lessing viewed the gulf between the historical and the eternal as "the ugly ditch which I cannot get across, however often and however earnestly I have tried to make the leap" (Lessing, 55). This gulf separated the contingent truths of history from the necessary truths of religion. And there is simply no way to span it from our side. Hence, he concluded that no matter how probable one finds the Gospel accounts, they can never serve as the basis for knowing eternal truths.

Kant's Gulf. In 1781, Immanuel *Kant spoke in his *Critique of Pure Reason* of a gulf between the contingent truths of our experience and the necessary truths of reason. Hence, he believed it necessary to destroy any philosophical or scientific basis for belief in God. "I have therefore found it necessary," he said, "to deny *knowledge*, in order to make room for *faith*" (Kant "Preface," 29). Kant held that one must approach the realm of religion by faith. It was the realm of practical reason, not of theoretical reason. He set up an impassable gulf between the objective, scientific, knowable realm of facts and the unknowable realm of value (morality and religion). This fact/value dichotomy is at the basis of the later disjunction between the Christ of faith and the Jesus of history.

Kahler's Historical/Historic Divide. The title of Kahler's book described the dichotomy he saw as necessary: *The So-Called Historical Jesus and the Historic, Biblical Christ* (1892). This volume is credited with originating the distinction between "historical" (*historisch*) Jesus and "historic" (*Geschichtlich*) Christ. What Kahler had in mind by "historical," though, was the reconstructed Jesus of liberal critical scholarship of his time, not the real first-century Jesus.

Kahler did ask: "Should we expect [believers] to rely on the authority of the learned men when the matter concerns the source from which they are to draw the truth for their lives?" He added, "I cannot find sure footing in probabilities or in a shifting mass of details, the reliability of which is constantly changing" (Kahler, 109, 111). While Kahler did not accept an inerrant (errorless) Bible, he did maintain that the Gospels are generally reliable. He spoke of their "comparatively remarkable trustworthiness." Kahler's confusion about how to view the Gospels led him to see even the Gospel "legends" as trustworthy, "so far as this is conceivable" (ibid., 79–90, 95, 141–42).

What "we want to make absolutely clear," said Kahler, is "that ultimately we believe in Christ, not on account of any authority, but because he himself evokes such faith from us" (ibid., 87). He asked the critical question of the church of his day, "How can Jesus Christ be the real object of faith for all Christians if what and who he really was can be ascertained only by research methodologies so elaborate that only the scholarship of our time is adequate to the task?" (see Soulen, 98).

Kierkegaard's "Leap." Also setting the stage for the latter disjunction between the Christ of faith and the historical Jesus was the Danish iconoclast, Søren *Kierkegaard. Kierkegaard asked, "How can something of an historical nature be decisive for an eternal happiness?" (*Concluding Unscientific Postscripts*, 86). Therefore, Kierkegaard downplayed the historical basis of Christianity. Real history was unimportant compared to belief "that in such and such a year the God appeared among us in the humble form of a servant, that he lived and taught in our community, and finally died" (*Philosophical Fragments*, 130). Only a "leap" of faith can place us beyond the historical into the spiritual (*see* FIDEISM).

Christ vs. Jesus. Rudolph Bultmann made the final definitive and radical disjunction between the Christ of Faith and the Jesus of History. The view can be summarized:

The Historical Jesus	The Historic Christ
Not relevant for faith	Relevant for faith
Jesus of scholars	Christ of believers
Jesus of critical history	Christ of the Gospels
Uncertain foundation	Certain foundation
Inaccessible to most Christians	Accessible to all Christians
The facticity of Jesus	The significance of Jesus
The Jesus of the past	The Christ of the present

The often-drawn implication of this disjunction is that the historical has little or no importance to the spiritual. As Kierkegaard argued, even if you could prove the historicity of the Gospels in every detail, it would not necessarily bring one closer to Christ. Conversely, if the critics could disprove the historicity of the Gospels, save that a man lived in whom people believed God dwelt, it would not destroy the foundations of true faith.

Evaluation. The whole dichotomy between the Jesus of history and the Christ of faith is based on highly dubious assumptions. The first has to do with the historicity of New Testament documents.

What Is Needed for Salvation. This concept that belief in the facts of the Gospel are historically irrelevant is contrary to the New Testament claim of what is necessary for salvation. The apostle Paul made essential the beliefs that Jesus died and rose bodily from the grave (*see* CHRIST, DEATH OF; RESURRECTION, EVIDENCE FOR). He wrote that

> if Christ has not been raised, our preaching is useless and so is your faith. More than that, we are then found to be false witnesses about God, for we have testified about God that he raised Christ from the dead. . . . And if Christ has not been raised, your faith is futile; you are still in your sins. Then those also who have fallen asleep in Christ are lost. If only for this life we have hope in Christ, we are to be pitied more than all men. [1 Cor. 15:14–19]

The Concern of the Writers. This indifference in historicity also is not shared with the New Testament writers themselves, who seem preoccupied with the details of an accurate account, not a broad-stroke myth. Luke actually tells us his research techniques and his goal as historian:

> Many have undertaken to draw up an account of the things that have been fulfilled among us, just as they were handed down to us by those who from the first were eye-witnesses and servants of the word. Therefore, since I myself have carefully investigated everything from the beginning, it seemed good also to me to write an orderly account for you, most excellent Theophilus, so that you may know the certainty of the things you have been taught. [Luke 1:1–4]

Luke expresses this historical interest by tying the story to persons and events that are part of the public record of history (*see* ACTS, HISTORICITY OF; LUKE, ALLEGED ERRORS IN), such as Herod the Great (1:5), Caesar Augustus (2:1), Quirinius (2:2), Pilate (3:1), and many others through Luke and Acts. Note his historical detail in dating John the Baptist's announcement of Christ "in the fifteenth year of the reign of Tiberius Caesar—when Pontius Pilate was governor of Judea, Herod tetrarch of Galilee, his brother Philip tetrarch of Iturea and Traconitis, and Lysanias tetrarch of Abilene—during the high priesthood of Annas and Caiaphas" (Luke 3:1–2a).

There is an unjustified assumption that the New Testament, and particularly the Gospels, lack adequate historical support. This is just not true (*see* NEW TESTAMENT ARCHAEOLOGY; NEW TESTAMENT, DATING OF; NEW TESTAMENT DOCUMENTS, RELIABILITY OF; NEW TESTAMENT, HISTORICITY OF, and other articles relating to the accuracy of the New Testament record).

A False Dichotomy. The separation of historical Jesus from historic Christ is based on a false dichotomy of fact and faith (*see* FAITH AND REASON) or of fact and value. The historic significance of Christ cannot be separated from his historicity. If he did not live, teach, die, and rise from the dead as the New Testament claims, then he has no saving significance today.

Even after a century of usage, the distinction remains ambiguous and varies in meaning from author to author. Kahler used it to defend "critical pietism." For Bultmann it meant Martin Heidegger's brand of existentialism (Meyer, 27). John Meyer observes that "the Christ of Faith exalted by Bultmann looks suspiciously like a timeless gnostic myth or a Jungian archetype" (ibid., 28). Nearer the other end of the spectrum, such scholars as Paul Althaus (1888–1966) used Kahler's distinction to defend a more conservative approach to the historicity of Jesus. Kahler would have accepted neither Bultmann's nor Althaus's conception. Albert Schweitzer (1875–1965) is more aware of what Kahler intended. He bitterly denounces those who, in the name of this distinction, have made the historic Christ responsible for every sort of trend from the destruction of ancient culture to the progress of the modern achievements. So the distinction between *historical* and *historic* has become a catch phrase and carrier of all sorts of baggage (ibid.).

Sources

G. Blomberg, *The Historical Reliability of the Gospels*

M. J. Borg, *Jesus in Contemporary Scholarship*

C. E. Braaten, "Martin Kahler on the Historic, Biblical Christ" in R. A. Harrisville, *The Historical Jesus and the Kerygmatic Christ*

G. Habermas, *The Historical Jesus*

M. Kahler *The So-Called Historical Jesus and the Historic, Biblical Christ*

I. Kant, *Critique of Pure Reason*

S. Kierkegaard, *Concluding Unscientific Postscripts*

———, *Philosophical Fragments*

J. P. Meyer, *A Marginal Jew*

G. Lessing, *Lessing's Theological Writings*, trans. H. Chadwick

R. N. Soulen, *Handbook of Biblical Criticism*, 2d ed.

R. Striple, *Modern Search for the Real Jesus*

Christ's Death, Moral Objections to. Many critics of Christianity, including Muslim and Liberal scholars, reject the doctrine of salvation through the cross on moral grounds. One reason Muslims give is that, according to Islam, the major prophets in history have always been victorious against their enemies. If the Christ of God was killed on the cross by his adversaries, then what would have become of the constant Qur'anic theme that those who did not obey God's prophet did not triumph? Isn't admission of the cross an acknowledgment that the unrighteous ultimately triumphed over the righteous? (Bell, 154).

Liberal Christian scholars object to the cross because it seems eminently unjust to punish an innocent person for the guilty. Indeed the Bible itself declares that "the son shall not bear the guilt of the father . . ." (Ezek. 18:20).

Muslim Rejection of the Crucifixion. Islamic disbelief in the crucifixion of Jesus is centered around their understanding of him as a prophet. Islamic distaste for the crucifixion of a prophet is based on their concept of the sovereignty of God and rejection of belief in human depravity.

Crucifixion Is Contrary to God's Sovereignty. All orthodox Muslims agree that God would not allow one of his prophets to suffer such an ignominious death as crucifixion (*see* CHRIST'S DEATH, SUBSTITUTION LEGEND; ISLAM). Muffasir summarized the view well when he said "Muslims believe that Jesus was not crucified. It was the intention of his enemies to put him to death on the cross, but God saved him from their plot" (Muffasir, 5).

Several passages in the *Qur'an* teach that Jesus was not crucified on the cross for our sins. Sura 4:157–58 is a key text; at face value it seems to say that Jesus did not die at all. It certainly denies that he died by crucifixion. It reads: "That they said (in boast), 'We killed Christ Jesus the son of Mary, the apostle of God';—But they killed him not, nor crucified him, but so it was made to appear to them, And those who differ therein are full of doubts, with no (certain) knowledge, but only conjecture to follow, For of a surety they killed him not:—Nay, God raised him up unto himself; and God is exalted in power, wise."

A sovereign God has control over all things, and he would not allow his servant to suffer such a death. Rather, a sovereign God, such as Allah is, would deliver his servant from his enemies. Abdalati, in a typical Muslim fashion asks, "Is it consistent with God's mercy and wisdom to believe that Jesus was humiliated and murdered the way he is said to have been?" (Abdalati, 160). The *Qur'an* states, "When Allah said: O Jesus! Lo! I am gathering thee and causing thee to ascend unto me, and am cleansing thee of those who disbelieve and am setting those who follow thee above those who disbelieve until the day of resurrection" (sura 3:55).

A Response to the Muslim View of Sovereignty. The Islamic belief in God's sovereignty defeats their own objection to the cross. If God can do anything he wants, then he can allow his own Son to die by crucifixion. The Quran declares:

> God! There is no god but he—the living, the self-subsisting, eternal. . . . Nor shall they [his creatures] compass aught his knowledge except as he willeth. His throne doth extend over the heavens and the earth, and he feeleth no fatigue in guarding and preserving them for he is the most high, the Supreme (in glory) (sura 2:255).

Many of the ninety-nine names for God express his sovereignty. *Al-Aziz,* "the Sublime," mighty in his sublime sovereignty (59:23); *Al-Ali,* "the High One," who is mighty (2:255–56); *Al-Qadir,* "the Able," who has the power to do what he pleases (17:99–101); *Al-Quddus,* "the Most Holy One," to whom all in heaven and on earth ascribe holiness (62:1); *Al-Mutaali,* "the Self-Exalted," who has set himself high above all (13:9–10); *Al-Muizz,* "the Honorer," who honors or abases whom he will (3:26); *Malik al-Mulk,* "Possessor of the Kingdom," who grants sovereignty to whom he will (3:26); *Al-Wahed,* "the One," unique in his divine sovereignty (13:16–17); *Al-Wahid,* "the Unique," who alone has created (74:11); *Al-Wakil,* "the Administrator," who has charge of everything (6:102).

Allah can do what he jolly well pleases, so he could allow his Servant to be crucified if he wished. Indeed, one passage in the *Qur'an* seems to apply this very truth to Christ: "Who then can do aught against Allah, if he had willed to destroy the Messiah son of Mary, and his mother and everyone on earth? Allah's is the sovereignty of the heavens and the earth and all that is between them. He createth what He will: And Allah is able to do all things" (sura 5:17).

Granting God is sovereign, it is utterly presumptuous to determine what he should or should not do. As the prophet Isaiah informs us, God said, "My thoughts are not your thoughts, Nor are your ways my ways" (Isa. 55:8). The prophet Isaiah instructs us that God did indeed approve of the ignominious death of his Servant:

> He had no beauty or majesty to attract us to him, nothing in his appearance that we should desire him. . . . we considered him stricken by God, smitten by him, and afflicted. . . . But, he was pierced for our transgressions, he was crushed for our iniquities; the punishment that brought us peace was upon him, and by his wounds we are healed. [Isa. 53:2–5]

So Jesus' crucifixion was not only approved by God, it was predicted (cf. Ps. 22:16; Zech. 12:10). It should be no surprise to a reader of the New Testament that the message of the crucifixion is offensive to unbelievers. Indeed, Paul even referred to the "offense of the cross" but added that "God was pleased through the foolishness of what was preached to save those who believe" (1 Cor. 1:21). For "the foolishness of God is wiser than man's wisdom" (vs. 25).

Then too, the idea of God allowing his servants to be insulted is not uncharacteristic. Muhammad's biographer, Haykai, tells of insulting experiences suffered by Muhammad. He notes, for example, that "the tribe of Thaqif, however, not only repudiated Muhammad's call but sent their servants to insult him and throw him out of their city. He ran away from them and took shelter near a wall. . . . there he sat under a vine pondering his defeat with the sight of the sons of Rabi'ah" (Haykai, 137).

What is more, even if it is assumed with Muslims that God would deliver his prophets from their enemies, it is wrong to conclude that he did not deliver Christ from his enemies. Indeed, this is precisely what the resurrection is. For "God raised him from the dead, freeing him from the agony of death, because it was impossible for death to keep its hold on him" (Acts 2:24). According to the Scriptures, God raised Christ up because, as he said: "You are my Son; today I have become your Father" (Acts 13:33). Further, the Scriptures declare that God kept his promise to his people (in Ps. 16:10) and saw to it "that he was not abandoned to the grave, nor did his body see decay." Thus, he was "exalted to the right hand of God" (Acts 2:31, 33).

Indeed, it was by Christ's death and resurrection that "death has been swallowed up in victory" (1 Cor. 15:54) and we can say, "Where, O death, is your victory? Where, O death, is your sting?" (1 Cor. 15:55).

Contrary to Islamic teaching, the death and resurrection of Christ did manifest God's mercy. Indeed, without it there would have been no mercy for a sinful world. Paul wrote: "You see, at just the right time, when we were still powerless, Christ died for the ungodly." Thus "God demonstrates his own love for us in this: While we were still sinners, Christ died for us" (Rom. 5:6, 8). He adds elsewhere that it is "not because of righteous things we had done, but because of his mercy" (Titus 3:5). As Jesus himself said, "Greater love has no one than this, that he lay down his life for his friends" (John 15:13). Yet he died for us when "we were [his] enemies" (Rom. 5:10).

Crucifixion Is Rooted in Original Sin. Another Muslim reason for rejecting the crucifixion is based on their rejection of the doctrine of depravity. Islamic scholars are quick to connect the Christian claim that Jesus died on the cross for our sins and the doctrine of depravity.

A. R. I. Doi notes that "connected with the Christian belief in crucifixion of Isa [Jesus] is the irreconcilable concept to original sin" (Doi, 19). He adds categorically that "Islam does not believe in the doctrine of the original sin. It is not Adam's sin that a child inherits and manifests at birth. Every child is born sinless and the sins of the fathers are not visited upon the children." Further, "Islam denies emphatically the concept of original sin and hereditary depravity. Every child is born pure and true; every departure in afterlife from the path of truth and rectitude is due to imperfect education." Citing the prophet Muhammad, Doi affirms that "Every child is born in a religious mold; it is his parents who make him afterward a Jew, a Christian, or a Sabaean. . . . In other words, good and evil is not created in man at birth. Infants have no positive moral character." Rather, "every human being . . . has two inclinations—one prompting him to do good and impelling him thereto, and the other prompting him to do evil and thereto impelling him; but the assistance of God is nigh" (Doi, 20).

Response to the Argument against Depravity. The orthodox Christian also connects the atoning death with human depravity. If God were not unchangeably just, and mankind not incurably depraved, the death of Christ for our sins would not have been necessary. However, contrary to Muslim belief, mankind is depraved and, hence, the suffering and death of Christ was necessary. Islamic rejection of total depravity is without foundation—as is even implied in Islamic teaching.

Even Muslims acknowledge that human beings are sinful. Otherwise, why do they need God's mercy? Indeed, why have so many (including all Christians) committed the greatest of all sins (*shirk*), attributing partners to God (sura 4:116)? Why did God need to send prophets to warn them of their sin, if they are not constant sinners? The whole prophetic ministry, which is at the heart of Islam, is occupied with a call to repentance from the sin of idolatry. But why does humankind have this insatiable appetite for false gods if people are not depraved?

What is more, why are the unbelievers sent to hell to suffer forever? This seems to imply great sinfulness to deserve such a severe penalty as eternal suffering. It is both unrealistic and un-Qur'anic to deny the inherent sinfulness of humankind.

"Some Muslim theologians have held to a doctrine of Hereditary Sin. . . . Also, there is a famous tradition that the Prophet of Islam said, 'No child is born but the devil hath touched it, except Mary and her son Jesus'" (Nazir-Ali, 165). *Qur'an* texts support the doctrine of human depravity. Humankind is sinful or unjust (sura 14:34/37; 33:72), foolish (33:72), ungrateful (14:34/37), weak (4:28/32), despairing or boastful (11:9/12–10/13), quarrelsome (16:4), and rebellious (96:6; Woodberry, 155). The *Qur'an* even declares that "If God were to punish men for their wrong-doing, He would not leave, on the (earth), A single living creature" (sura 16:61). Ayatollah Khomeini went so far as to say that "man's calamity is his carnal desires, and this exists in everybody, and is rooted in the nature of man" (Woodberry, 159).

Jesus Had to Repent for Sins. Muslim denial of Christ's death by crucifixion is based on a misunderstanding of repentance. Abdalati, for example, lists the following among his reasons for rejecting the crucifixion of Christ: "Is it just on God's part, or anybody's part for that matter, to make someone repent for the sins or wrongs of others, the sins to which the repenter is no party?" (Abdalati, 160).

Response to the Charge That Jesus Had to Repent. Nowhere in the Bible does it say that Christ repented for our sins. It simply says that he "died for our sins" (1 Cor. 15:3). *Judicially,* "God made him who had no sin to be sin for us" (2 Cor. 5:21). But at no time did he confess anyone's sins. He taught his disciples to pray, "Forgive us our debts" (Matt. 6:12), but he nowhere joins them in that petition. This is a total distortion of the concept of a substitutionary atonement.

The Bible teaches that Jesus took our place; he paid the penalty of death for us (cf. Mark 10:45; Rom. 4:25; 1 Peter 2:22; 3:18). This concept of life for life is the same principle behind Muslim belief in capital punishment. When a murder takes another's life, he must forfeit his own as a penalty. Several doctrines regarding God's justice and God's forgiveness, heaven and hell make no real sense apart from substitutionary atonement.

God Can Forgive without Punishing. Another misconception underlying the Islamic rejection of the crucifixion is that a merciful God can forgive sin without justly condemning it. This is reflected in Abdalati's question "Was God the Most Merciful, the Most Forgiving and the Most High unable to forgive men's sins except by inflicting this cruel and most humiliating alleged crucifixion on one who was not only innocent but also dedicated to his service and cause in a most remarkable way" (Abdalati, 162)?

Response to a Forgiveness Without an Atonement. Two basic mistakes are at work here. First, it is implied that what Jesus did was not voluntary, but was merely inflicted upon him. The Gospels declare that Jesus gave his life voluntarily and freely. Jesus said, "I lay down my life—only to take it up again. No one takes it from me, but I lay it down of my own accord. I have authority to lay it down and authority to take it up again" (John 10:17–18).

Muslims seem not to appreciate the basis on which the just and holy God can forgive sins. While God is sovereign, he is not arbitrary about right and wrong (see Geisler, *Christian Ethics,* 136–37). Muslims, like Christians, believe that God will punish forever in hell those who do not repent (cf. suras 14:17; 25:11–14). But if God's holy justice demands that those who do not accept him be eternally punished for their sins, then it would follow that God cannot arbitrarily forgive without a just basis for this forgiveness. In Muslim theology there is forgiveness but no basis for this forgiveness. For they reject Christ's sacrificial payment for sin to a just God by which he can then declare righteous the unrighteous who accept Christ's payment on their behalf (cf. Rom. 3:21–26).

A truly just God cannot simply close his eyes to sin. Unless someone capable of paying the debt of sin owed to God does so, then God is obligated to express his wrath, not his mercy. Lacking the Crucifixion, the Muslim system has no way to explain how Allah can be merciful when he is also just.

The theological blind spot in the Muslim system created by a rejection of Christ's atoning sacrifice leads to other unfounded statements, such as Abdalati's rhetorical question: "Does the [Christian] belief of crucifixion and blood sacrifice appear in any religion apart from pagan creeds or the early Greeks, Romans, Indians, Persians, and the like" (Abdalati, 160)?

The answer is a clear "Yes." It is the very heart of historic Judaism, as even a casual acquaintance with the Old Testament reveals. Moses told Israel: "For the life of a creature is in the blood, and I have given it to you to make atonement for yourselves on the altar; it is the blood that makes atonement for one's life" (Lev. 17:11). This is why the children of Israel were asked to sacrifice the Passover lamb, commemorating their deliverance from bondage (Exod. 12:1f.). This is why the New Testament speaks of Christ as "the Lamb of God, who takes away the sin of the world" (John 1:29). And the apostle Paul called "Christ, our Passover lamb, [who] has been sacrificed" (1 Cor. 5:7). The writer of Hebrews adds, "without the shedding of blood there is no forgiveness" (Heb. 9:22).

Of course, Muslim scholars argue that the original Old Testament was distorted too. However, like the New Testament, the ancient Dead Sea manuscripts of the Old Testament reveal that the Old Testament today is substantially the same as the one in the time of Christ, over 600 years before Muhammad (see Geisler and Nix, chap. 21). Therefore, since the *Qur'an* urges the Jews in Muhammad's day to accept God's revelation in the Law (sura 10:94), and since the Jewish Old Testament is substantially the same today as it was in Muhammad's day, then Muslims should accept that blood sacrifices for sins was a command of God.

Liberal Rejection of the Cross. With Muslims, nonorthodox "liberal" Christians reject the absolute justice of God (*see* Essentialism, Divine); the depravity of man, and substitutionary atonement. Liberals do not generally reject the historicity of the cross, but rather what they regard as its immorality. They insist that it is essentially irrational and immoral to punish an innocent person in the place of the guilty.

The Cross Is Irrational. Nothing seems more contradictory or irrational than the idea of salvation by substitution. Even the apostle Paul hinted at this when he said "For the message of the cross is foolishness to those who are perishing" (1 Cor. 1:18). In fact, did not the early church father *Tertullian (ca. 160s–ca. 215–20) say of the cross "I believe because it is absurd" (Tertullian, 5)?

Few if any past Christian scholars have ever claimed that the cross was irrational. Certainly, Tertullian never said the death of Christ was absurd, which would have been the Latin word *absurdum*. He said it was "foolish" (Lat.: *ineptum*) to those who were perishing—unbelievers—exactly as Paul said. Tertullian everywhere promotes the use of reason and rational consistency in his theology. He said, "nothing can be claimed as rational without order, much less can reason itself dispense with order in any one" (ibid.). Even when speaking of the mystery of human free choice, Tertullian declared that "it cannot even in this be ruled to be irrational" (ibid., 1.25).

Even regarding *the Trinity and incarnation of Christ, orthodox Christians have insisted that Christian teachings are rational (*see* LOGIC). The "mysteries" of faith may go beyond our reason to attain by special revelation, but never against our ability to apprehend with logical consistency (*see* MYSTERY). The Trinity, for example, is not held to be a contradiction. It does not affirm three persons in one *Person* but three persons in one *essence*.

The Cross Is Immoral. Liberals have extolled the virtues of Christ's death as an example of sacrificial love. But both Muslims and liberals loathe the idea of a substitutionary punishment for sin. This view seems to them to be essentially immoral. How can an innocent person be punished for the guilty? Does not even the Bible itself affirm "The son will not share the guilt of the father, nor will the father share the guilt of the son. The righteousness of the righteous man will be credited to him, and the wickedness of the wicked will be charged against him" (Ezek. 18:20)?

A virtually universal human practice is to consider commendable the actions of one who dies in defense of the innocent. Soldiers are honored for dying for their country. Parents are called compassionate when they die for their children. But this is precisely what Jesus did. As the apostle Paul put it, "Very rarely will anyone die for a righteous man, though for a good man someone might possibly dare to die. But God demonstrates his love for us in this: While we were still sinners, Christ died for us" (Rom. 5:7–8).

Sacrificial death is not alien to Islam. The Muslim practice of *Id Ghorban* (feat of sacrifice) features the sacrifice of a sheep in memory of Abraham's sacrifice of his son. For some this is associated with the forgiveness of sins. Muslim soldiers who sacrifice their lives for the cause of Islam are awarded Paradise (sura 3:157–58; 22:58–59). Neither is it without human precedent for one person to pay a debt for another, even by the sacrifice of his life for them.

If Allah could call upon his servants to die for Islam, why is it so strange that God could call upon his Son to die so salvation can be offered to Muslims, and the rest of the world? The *Qur'an* gives a beautiful example of a substitutionary atonement in describing Abraham's sacrifice of his son on Mount Moriah. Sura 37:102–7 reads:

> He said: "O my son! I see in vision That I offer thee in *sacrifice*. . . . So when they had both Submitted their wills (to God), And he laid him Prostrate on his forehead (For *sacrifice*), We [God] called out to him, "O Abraham! . . . And We *ransomed* him With a momentous *sacrifice*." [emphasis added]

The use of the words *sacrifice* and *ransom* are precisely what Christians mean by Christ's death on the cross. Jesus used such words of his own death (Mark 10:45). So the sacrificial death of Christ is not opposed to the Qu'ran.

As noted, the weight of this critique of the cross rests on the false premise that Jesus' death was involuntary. But it was not forced upon him. Looking forward to the Cross, he said to the Father "yet not my will, but yours be done" (Luke 22:42). Earlier in the Gospel of John Jesus referred to the giving of his life in saying, "No one takes it from me, but I lay it down of my own accord" (John 10:18). The book of Hebrews records Jesus' words "Then I said, 'Here I am—it is written about me in the scroll—I have come to do your will, O God'" (Heb. 10:7).

There is no other way for the debt of sin to be paid than for the sinless son of God to do so. As Anselm argued (in *Cur Deus Homo?*) the penalty for sin must be paid to God. God's justice demands that sin be atoned for (cf. Lev. 17:11; Heb. 9:22). So, rather than being unjust, it is justice that demands the substitutionary atonement of Christ. The *Qur'an* teaches God is just (see sura 21:47–48). Absolute justice means that God cannot simply *overlook* sin. A penalty must be paid, either by the persons themselves or by someone else for them which enables them to go to heaven.

It does not break a moral absolute to punish an innocent person for the guilty provided he is willing and a higher moral law calls for the suspension of the lower law (see Geisler, *Christian Ethics*). In the case of the cross, it is the salvation of the world for which Christ the innocent voluntarily accepted the injustice of dying on a cross.

Conclusion. The moral critique of the cross relies on circular reasoning. It makes no sense to claim that a substitutionary atonement is *essentially* im-moral unless something is essentially moral, an unchangeably moral nature of God. But the unchangeably just and holy nature of God requires that sin be punished. Unless God's justice is satisfied by someone else on behalf of lawbreakers, the essential moral and eternal principle used by liberals would demand that everyone be eternally punished for their sins in hell. But that doctrine liberals also find repugnant. So if God is loving, as liberals do happily admit, then he must find a way to pay for our debt of sin and set us free. Christ volunteered and satisfied God's justice, "the just for the unjust" (1 Peter 3:18), so as to release God's redeeming love and set us free of the guilt and consequences of our sins (John 3:16; Rom. 5:8). There was no other way.

Sources

H. Abdalati, *Islam in Focus*
A. A. Abdul-Haqq, *Sharing Your Faith with a Muslim*
M. Ali, *Religious Ideas of Sir Sayyad Ahmad Khan*
R. Bell, *The Origin of Islam in Its Christian Environment*
A. R. Doi, "The Status of Prophet Jesus in Islam-II," *MWLJ* June 1982
W. D. Edwards, et al., "On the Physical Death of Jesus Christ," *JAMA* 21 March 1986
N. L. Geisler, *Christian Ethics*
——— and A. Saleeb, *Answering Islam: The Crescent in the Light of the Cross*
——— and W. E. Nix, *General Introduction to the Bible*
G. Habermas, *Ancient Evidence for the Life of Jesus*
M. H. Haykai, *The Life of Mohammed*
Justin Martyr, *First Apology*, in *The Ante-Nicene Fathers*
S. S. Muffasir, *Jesus, A Prophet of Islam*
M. Nazir-Ali, *Frontiers in Muslim-Christian Encounter*
"Sanhedrin," *The Babylonian Talmud*
Tertullian. *On the Flesh of Christ*
J. D. Woodberry, ed., *Muslims and Christians on the Emmaus Road*
A. Z. Yamani, "Foreword," W. M. Watt, *Islam and Christianity Today: A Contribution to Dialogue*

Christ's Death, Substitution Legend. The death and resurrection of Christ are absolutely crucial to the truth of historic Christianity (1 Cor. 15:1–4). Indeed, orthodox Christianity stands or falls on whether Christ rose bodily from the dead (Rom. 10:9; 1 Cor. 15:12–19). But if Christ did not die, then he obviously did not rise from the dead. One of the ways skeptics (*see* AGNOSTICISM) and critics (*see* BIBLICAL CRITICISM) of Christianity have attempted to avoid the truth of the resurrection (*see* RESURRECTION, EVIDENCE FOR) is to posit that someone else was substituted to die on the cross for Jesus at the last moment.

Substitution Legends. Forms of the substitution legend were offered as early as the second century by opponents of Christianity as an alternative explanation to the Christian affirmation that Christ died and rose from the dead. But the factual evidence for Christ's death on the cross is substantial, and it stands on its own apart from any theological beliefs.

The substitution legend is now most commonly taught among Muslims, so their view will be answered in this article. This answer necessarily includes a rationale for the Christian position on salvation in the light of the cross. The effort to defend Christ's death as both historical and theologically intelligible is partly undertaken in the overview article, Christ, Death of, and the related article on Islamic and liberal problems with the crucifixion, Christ's Death, Moral Objections to. The following content assumes, and will avoid repeating, that content.

Reasons to Reject the Death of Christ. At one level, the Islamic reticence to accept the historical event of Christ's death is odd. Not only is there a total lack of evidence for a substitution, but Islam historically teaches that . . .

1. Jesus would die (sura 3:55; cf. 19:33).
2. Jesus would rise from the dead (19:33).
3. Jesus' disciples who witnessed the event believed that it was Jesus, not someone else in his place, who was crucified.
4. The Roman soldiers and the Jews believed that it was Jesus of Nazareth whom they had crucified.
5. Jesus performed miracles, including raising people from the dead.

If all this is accepted by Muslims, then there is no reason they should reject the fact that Jesus died on the cross, or even that he was raised from the dead three days later.

Early Substitution Legends. Substitution legends are not unique to Islam. Some early opponents of Christianity offered similar speculations. According to the second-century church father Frenacus, Basilides the Gnostic (*see* GNOSTICISM) taught that "at the Crucifixion He [Jesus] changed form with Simon of Cyrene who had carried the cross. The Jews mistaking Simon for Jesus nailed him to the cross. Jesus stood by deriding their error before ascending to heaven" (Lightfoot, 156ff.). In the third century, Mani of Persia, founder of the Manichaean religion, taught that the son of the widow of Nain, whom Jesus had raised from the dead, was put to death in his place. According to another Manichaean tradition, the devil, who was trying to crucify Jesus, was himself the victim of this switch. Photius (ca. 820–ca. 895) referred in his writings to an apocryphal book, *The Travels of Paul*, in which it was said that another was crucified in Jesus' place (Abdul-Haqq, 136).

Muslim Substitution Legends. Muslims have been drawn to the notion that Judas or Simon of Cyrene died in Jesus' place on the cross. A competing view that he swooned on the cross and was taken down while still alive, does not help their hypothesis. Al-Tabari, well-known Muslim historian and commentator on the *Qur'an*, reports that Wahab B. Munabih, who lived around 700, propagated the lore that a human form but not a person was substituted. His version is reported:

> They brought him the gibbet on which they intended to crucify him, but God raised him up to himself and a simulacrum was crucified in his place. He remained there for seven hours,

and then his mother and another woman whom He had cured of madness came to weep for him. But Jesus came to them and said, "God has raised me up to himself, and this is a mere simulacrum." [Abdul-Haqq, 135–36]

Another example of the growth of this legendary tradition is the view of Thalabi, who lived some 300 years after Munabih. "The shape of Jesus was put on Judas who had pointed him out, and they crucified him instead, supposing that he was Jesus. After three hours God took Jesus to himself and raised him up to heaven" (see Bruce, 179).

More recently, A. R. I. Doi offers the hypothesis that, when the Roman soldiers came with Judas to arrest Jesus, "the two Jews got mixed up in the dark, and the soldiers mistakenly arrested Judas instead of Jesus. Jesus was thus saved and raised up" (Doi, 21). In support, Muslims often cite the spurious *Gospel of Barnabas*.*

The Inadequate Basis. Substitution legends simply are not historically credible:

They contradict the extant record of eyewitness testimony that Jesus of Nazareth was crucified (Matthew 27; Mark 14; Luke 23; John 19).

They are contrary to the earliest extrabiblical Jewish, Roman, and Samaritan testimony (Habermas, 87–118, Bruce, 31; *see summary in* ARCHAEOLOGY, NEW TESTAMENT; CHRIST, DEATH OF). In spite of the fact that all of these writers were opponents of Christianity, they agree that Jesus of Nazareth was crucified under Pontius Pilate. There is not a shred of first-century testimony to the contrary by friend or foe of Christianity. The earliest substitution legends begin in about 150 among those heavily influenced by Gnosticism. None is based on evidence of eyewitnesses or contemporaries to the events.

They are implausible, since they demand total ignorance on the part of those closest to Jesus, his disciples, and the Romans. They suppose that Jesus told his mother and another woman that someone who looked like him was crucified and that they never informed the disciples nor corrected them as they promptly went out to preach under threat of death that Jesus had died and risen from the dead.

Since most Muslims reject the fact of Christ's crucifixion and death, they understandably have great difficulty explaining the resurrection appearances and ascension of Christ. Since they believe Christ was merely a human being, they accept the fact of Christ's mortality. They believe Jesus will eventually be resurrected with all other humans, but, after rejecting his death on the cross, they are forced to find some other place for Christ's death.

This dilemma has encouraged ingenious speculation. Many Muslim scholars believe Jesus Christ was transported into heaven alive. His death still must happen sometime in the future, when he returns to the earth before the last day. This they take from a literal understanding of sura 4:157–58: "That they said (in boast), 'We killed Christ Jesus the son of Mary, the apostle of God';—But they killed him not, nor crucified him, but so it was made to appear to them, And those who differ therein are full of doubts, with no (certain) knowledge, but only conjecture to follow, For of a surety they killed him not:—Nay, God raised him up unto himself; and God is exalted in power, wise."

Others hypothesize that Jesus died a natural death at some unknown time after the crucifixion and remained dead for three hours, or according to another tradition, seven hours—after which he was resurrected and taken to heaven (Abdul-Haqq, 131). There is no historical testimony to support such speculation.

A few Islamic writers, like Ahmad Khan of India, believe that Jesus was crucified, but did not die on the cross. Rather, he merely swooned (*see* RESURRECTION, ALTERNATE THEORIES OF) and was taken down after 3 hours (Abdul-Haqq, 132). Other Muslims in north India added the legend that Jesus visited Tibet. Abdul-Haqq notes that Ghulam Ahmad "home brew[ed] a theory that Jesus Christ took His journey to Kasmir . . . after His crucifixion. To further support his theory he conveniently found a grave in Sirinagar, Kashmir, which he declared to be the grave of Jesus." However, the Ahmadiyyas sect's "speculations have been condemned as heretical by the Muslim orthodoxy" (ibid., 133).

Abdalati notes that "whether he [Jesus] was raised alive in soul and body or in soul only after he died a natural death has not much bearing on the Islamic belief." Why? "It is no Article of Faith, because what is important and binding to a Muslim is what God reveals; and God revealed that Jesus was not crucified but was raised to Him" (see Abdalati, 159). He cites sura 4:157 (quoted above).

Most Muslims, however, believe that Jesus will be physically resurrected from the dead in the general resurrection of the last day. Nothing else is essential to the Muslim faith. Therefore, rejecting Jesus' death by crucifixion leads to a rejection of his resurrection three days later and leaves the enigma of the ascension before any death or resurrection.

The Misunderstanding. The Muslim denial of Christ's death by crucifixion is based on a theological misunderstanding. Abdalati, for example, lists the following among his reasons for rejecting the crucifixion of Christ: "Is it just on God's part, or anybody's part for that matter, to make someone repent for the sins or wrongs of others, the sins to which the repenter is no party?" (Abdalati, 160).

This, of course, is based on a complete misunderstanding of what Christians believe about the atonement of Christ. As noted in another article (CHRIST'S DEATH, MORAL OBJECTIONS TO), he did not confess or repent of our sins. He died for our sins (1 Cor. 15:3). *Judicially,* he was "made to be sin for us" (2 Cor. 5:21)—the substitution that Christians gladly admit. He paid the penalty of death in our place, so that we could stand before God without guilt (Mark 10:45; Rom. 4:25; 1 Peter 2:22; 3:18). This concept of life for life is not foreign to Islam. It is the principle behind their belief in capital punishment; a murderer who takes another's life must forfeit a life.

Another misconception beneath the Islamic rejection of the crucifixion is that a merciful God can forgive sin without justly condemning it. Actually there are two basic mistakes here. Muslim theology makes the first error when it implies that what Jesus did was not voluntary but was inflicted upon him. Jesus said, "I lay down my life—only to take it up again. No one takes it from me, but I lay it down of my own accord. I have authority to lay it down and authority to take it up again" (John 10:17–18). When Jesus died, the Bible relates, "He [freely] dismissed his spirit" (John 19:30).

The second error is that a sovereign God can be holy, yet arbitrarily change the rules about right and wrong (*see* CHRIST'S DEATH, MORAL OBJECTIONS TO). Muslims, like Christians, believe in hell for the unrepentant (sura 14:17; 25:11–14). But if holy justice demands that those who do not accept him be eternally punished, then God cannot arbitrarily forgive anyone for anything without a just basis for forgiveness. Muslim theology has none. Muslims reject Christ's sacrificial payment for sin to a just God, by which the unjust who accept Christ's payment on their behalf can be declared just (cf. Rom. 3:21–26). Unless someone capable of paying the penalty for sin does so, God is obligated to express wrath, not mercy. Lacking the crucifixion, the Muslim system has no way to explain how Allah can be merciful when he is also just.

Salvation in Christ. Superficially, it would seem that salvation by grace through faith in the death and resurrection of Christ is incomprehensible to Muslims. This, we believe, is not the case. While the unbeliever does not *receive* (Gk.: *dekomai*) God's truth (1 Cor. 2:14), nevertheless, he can *perceive* it. According to Romans 1:18–20, unbelievers are "without excuse" in view of God's revelation in nature. The very fact that unbelievers are called upon to believe the Gospel implies that they can understand it (cf. Acts 16:31; 17:30–31). Jesus rebuked unbelievers for not understanding what he was talking about, declaring, "If you were blind, you would not be guilty of sin; but now that you claim you can see, your guilt remains" (John 9:41).

An Islamic Basis for Salvation by Substitution. Even from within Islam the Christian concept of the cross makes sense. Islam has several doctrines, God's justice and God's forgiveness, heaven and hell, that make no real sense apart from a substitutionary atonement. For Islam teaches that God is just (*see* ISLAM). But absolute justice must be satisfied. God cannot simply *overlook* sin. A penalty must be paid for it which enables them to go to heaven, either by the persons or by someone else for them. In a letter to a friend explaining why he became a Christian, Daud Rahbar, argues, "the Qur'anic doctrine of God's justice demands that such a God be himself involved in suffering and be seen as involved in suffering. Only then can he be a just judge of suffering humanity." For "a God that is preserved from suffering will be an arbitrary and capricious judge" (Nazir-Ali, 28).

A Rational Basis for Salvation by Substitution. There is nothing contradictory or incredible about salvation by substitution. The Muslim mind should not have any more difficulty with this concept than any other mind. This concept is in accord with a virtually universal human practice. It is considered commendable for people to die in defense of the innocent. Warriors are hailed for dying for their tribe. Soldiers are honored for dying for their country. Parents are called compassionate when they die for their children. This is precisely what Jesus did. As the apostle Paul put it, "Very rarely will anyone die for a righteous man, though for a good man someone might possibly dare to die. But . . . While we were still sinners, Christ died for us" (Rom. 5:7–8).

Further, even in the Islamic understanding sacrificial death occurred. The Muslim practice of *id ghorban* (feat of sacrifice) features the sacrifice of a sheep in memory of Abraham's sacrifice of his son. For some this is associated with the forgiveness of sins. Furthermore, Muslim soldiers who sacrificed their lives for the cause of Islam were awarded Paradise (3:157–58; 22:58–59). If Allah could call upon his servants to die for Islam, why think it so strange that God could call upon his Son to die for salvation of Muslims, indeed of the world?

Conclusion. Much of the Islamic rejection of Christ is based on a misunderstanding of the facts about him. Since they believe in the divine inspiration of the original Old and New Testaments, Jesus' virgin birth, sinless life, divinely authoritative teaching, death, eventual resurrection (*see* RESURRECTION, EVIDENCE FOR), ascension, and second coming. It is a tragedy that the rejection of his claims to be the Son of God and Savior of the world are lost in the midst of all they do accept. The primary problem is rejection of the authenticity of the Bible. Perhaps a better understanding of the factual basis for the authenticity of the

Bible (*see* NEW TESTAMENT, HISTORICITY OF) could open a way to take more seriously the *Qur'an* when it urges doubters to go to the Scriptures:

> If thou wert in doubt As to what we have revealed unto thee, then ask those who have been reading the Book [the Bible] from before thee: The truth hath indeed come to thee from thy Lord: So be in no wise of those in doubt (10:94).

Sources

H. Abdalati, *Islam in Focus*

A. A. Abdul-Haqq, *Sharing Your Faith with a Muslim*

R. Bell, *The Origin of Islam in Its Christian Environment*

F. F. Bruce, *Jesus and Christian Origins outside the New Testament*

A. R. I. Doi, "The Status of Prophet Jesus in Islam-II," *MWLJ*

W. D. Edwards, et al., "On the Physical Death of Jesus Christ," *JAMA* 21 March 1986

Flavius Josephus, "Antiquities of the Jews," 18.3

N. L. Geisler and W. E. Nix, *General Introduction to the Bible*

G. Habermas, *Ancient Evidence for the Life of Jesus*

M. H. Haykal, *The Life of Muhammad*

Justin Martyr, *First Apology*, in *The Ante-Nicene Fathers*

J. B. Lightfoot, *The Apostolic Fathers*

S. S. Muffasir, *Jesus, A Prophet of Islam*

M. Nazir-Ali, *Frontiers in Muslim-Christian Encounter*

"Sanhedrin," *The Babylonian Talmud*

Tacitus, *Annals*

Chronology Problems in the Bible. ***See*** **GENEALOGIES, OPEN OR CLOSED.**

Clark, Gordon H. Gordon Clark (1902–1985) was born in Philadelphia and received his Ph.D. in philosophy in 1929. He taught at Wheaton College, Reformed Episcopal Seminary, and Covenant College and was chairman of the Philosophy Department at Butler University for twenty-eight years. His teaching career spanned sixty years.

Clark was a rational presuppositionalist, as differentiated from Cornelius Van Til, who was a revelational presuppositionalist (*see* PRESUPPOSITIONAL APOLOGETICS). His students included Carl F. H. Henry, John Edward Carnell, and Ronald Nash.

His thirty books covered a wide variety of philosophical, ethical, and theological topics. Some of his works of philosophy and apologetics included a complete history of philosophy, *Thales to Dewey*; *A Christian View of Men and Things*; *Religions, Reason, and Revelation*; and *Historiography, Secular and Religious*. He also wrote a logic textbook.

Clark's Reformed theology centered in the sovereignty of God, and his apologetics took the triune God as revealed in Scripture as his presuppositional starting point. His test for truth was the law of noncontradiction (*see* FIRST PRINCIPLES).

Epistemological Darkness. Empirical Skepticism. In epistemology, Clark was an empirical skeptic (*see* AGNOSTICISM), agreeing with David *Hume. The senses deceive and cannot be trusted. Universal and necessary principles go beyond the limits of empirical experience. As Hume showed, the senses never receive impressions of a necessary connection. Nothing, therefore, can be proved empirically. Clark doubted all that his senses reported about an external world. He held that, apart from divine revelation, we cannot be sure that we exist.

Clark framed three chief objections to empiricism: First, it is impossible to discover a "necessary connection" between ideas and events. This denies causality and makes all historical and scientific investigation futile. At best, knowledge can extend only so far as what is impressed on the brain at this moment, and what traces remain at this moment of memories of past impressions. Second, the ongoing task of integrating self into one's current environment inevitably influences perceptions and makes them untrustworthy. Memory is effectively annihilated in this process. Third, and most fundamentally, empiricism uses time and space surreptitiously at the beginning of the learning process. But accurate time-space perceptions can only come at the end of the learning process, so the mind is continually faced with information that it is not competent to judge accurately ("Special Divine Revelation," 33).

Historical Skepticism. Clark's historical skepticism is parallel to his empirical doubts. Thus, Clark denies the validity of historical apologetics. Even if we could know that the resurrection of Christ is a fact from empirical testimony, it would prove nothing (*see* RESURRECTION, EVIDENCE FOR). "Suppose Jesus did rise from the grave. This only proves that his body resumed its activities for a time after his crucifixion; it does not prove that he died for our sins or that he was the Son of God. . . . The resurrection, viewed purely as an isolated historical event, does not prove that Christ died for our sins." Historical and archaeological research are incompetent to deal with such questions (Clark, "Philosophy of Education," 35).

Innate Ideas. Clark considered himself Augustinian in epistemology, beginning with God-given, innate ideas (*see* AUGUSTINE). Apart from divine illumination via innate ideas, the mind would be locked in epistemological darkness. By the light of the *Logos* we can see the world. Clark boldly translated John 1:1, "In the beginning was Logic. And Logic was with God, and Logic was God" (cited in Nash, *The Philosophy of Gordon Clark*, 67, 118; *see* LOGIC). Since each human being was created by God, each person is an innate idea of God. But a person's blank mind is not able to lift itself above its sensory context to an abstract spiritual level. So unaided, no person can know God. The theories of empiricism from *Aristotle to Thomas *Aquinas to John *Locke, therefore, do not work (*Religions, Reason, and*

Revelation, 135). We cannot know God, certainly not in any saving way. God, however, revealed himself in Scripture, his infallible, inerrant Word (*see* Bible, Canonicity of). Christianity based on this revelation is the only true religion (*see* Christ, Uniqueness of; World Religions, Christianity and). Christianity is known to be true because it alone is free from internal contradictions in its truth claims. All opposing systems have contradictory beliefs in one or more central teachings.

Rejection of Theistic Proof. Like most other presuppositionalists, Clark rejected the traditional proofs for the existence of God (*see* God, Evidence for). His reasons were much the same as those of Hume and Immanuel *Kant. Since our senses cannot be trusted, we cannot begin in experience and prove anything about the world, much less about God. He referred to Thomas Aquinas's *classical apologetics as a "Christianized interpretation of Aristotelianism" (*Christian View of Men and Things*, 309). He found Aquinas's arguments for God to be circular, purely formal, invalid, and indefensible (*Religions, Reason, and Revelation*, 35).

> Thomism, Clark said, requires the concepts of *potentiality* and *actuality*, yet Aristotle never succeeded in defining precisely what is meant by those ideas ("Special Divine Revelation as Rational," 31). The reasoning is circular: *Motion* is used to define *actuality* and *potentiality*, yet *actuality* and *potentiality* are used to define *motion* (ibid., 36).
>
> Thomas traces back the causes of motion with the assumption that there is a first cause, since causes cannot go backward into infinity. But this is also the conclusion Thomas draws. Therefore, he is begging the question (ibid., 31).
>
> For Thomas there are two ways to know God. We can know by negation what God is not, and we can know what he is like by analogy (*see* Analogy, Principle of). There can be no identical meanings derived from these two methods. But unless the terms can be univocal, the argument is a fallacy (ibid.).
>
> Thomism identifies God as the Unmoved Mover. Suppose the existence of the Unmoved Mover has been demonstrated. This would not prove the Unmoved Mover to be God; it is simply a physical cause of motion. Nothing in the argument provides this force with a transcendent personality. "In fact, if the argument is valid, and if this Unmoved Mover explains the processes of nature, the God of Abraham, Isaac, and Jacob is superfluous, and indeed impossible" (ibid., 37).
>
> The argument for the existence of God is, at best, useless. It proves no more than a finite or physical God. It allows, but does not prove, the existence of a good God, but he need neither be omnipotent nor the cause of all that happens.
>
> All causal arguments involve an equivocation. This argument involves Clark's criticism of analogy (see the following section).

On these bases, Clark finds the cosmological argument "worse than useless. In fact, Christians can be pleased at its failure, for if it were valid, it would prove a conclusion inconsistent with Christianity" (*Religions, Reason, and Revelation*, 41).

Rejection of Analogy. Clark contended that the doctrine of analogy, as implied in theistic arguments, involves a logical fallacy of equivocation. Taking the propositions: "Contingent things in motion exist, which have both actuality and potentiality," and "God exists as all actuality with no potentiality," Clark questions whether the verb *exists* can be defined the same way when applied to Necessary Beings as when applied to contingent beings. He fears there is too much divergence for the argument to be valid (*Thales to Dewey*, 227, 278). *Exists* has too much of a temporal, human sense to be appropriately applied to God. "In this sense of the word *exist*, God does not exist" (ibid., 312).

"If we should arrive validly at the conclusion, God exists, this existence at which we have arrived would not be God's existence. Syllogisms [*see* Logic] and valid arguments require their terms to be used univocally" (ibid.).

The Test for Truth. Clark was an unyielding defender of the validity of the law of noncontradiction (*see* First Principles). Noncontradiction was the "inescapable" basis of all knowledge and the test for truth (*Christian View of Men and Things*, 313). Clark's defense of the law of noncontradiction was what *Van Til would call a transcendental argument. Without the forms of logic, Clark averred, no discussion on any subject would be possible (ibid., 308). Using noncontradiction, apologetics has a twofold task:

Negative Task. Apologetics must show that all non-Christian systems are contradictory within their truth claims. Clark did this in his history of philosophy, *Thales to Dewey*. He brought all the great philosophers before the bar of rationality, and found each of them wanting.

Positive Task. Clark believed that only Christianity is free from contradiction and, hence, only it can be proven true. Using a geometric method reminiscent of René Descartes, Clark reduced Christianity to its basic axioms in order to show their internal consistency. He concluded: "Christianity is a comprehensive view of all things; it takes the world, both material and spiritual, to be an ordered system" (ibid., 33).

Clark was aware that no finite system could be expected to provide answers to all problems, since no mortal is omniscient. He reasoned that "if one system can provide plausible solutions to many problems, while another leaves too many questions unanswered, if one system tends less to skepticism and gives more meaning to life, if one world view is consistent while others are self-contradictory, who can deny us, since we must choose, the right to choose the more promising first principle?" (ibid., 34).

Common Ground with Non-Christians. In opposition to his contemporary in Reformed theology, Cornelius Van Til, Clark believed that common ground could be found with unbelievers. This common ground is found in the laws of logic and "a few divine truths," which unbelievers know by virtue of the image of God in them (*Barth's Theological Method*, 96). In response to Karl *Barth, Clark affirmed that "Faith is a mental activity and by definition presupposes a rational subject. Reason, therefore, can be considered to be an element in common to believer and unbeliever" (ibid., 102).

Evaluation. *Positive Contributions.* In addition to the overall contributions Clark has made to a creative evangelical rethinking of its task, Clark has had strong influence on individual evangelicals, notably John Carnell, Carl Henry, and Ronald Nash.

Clark's system offers a comprehensive test for truth in all systems. Noncontradiction can be applied to every belief system. It is offered as a means both for discovering which are false, and in giving evidence of the true one. The law of noncontradiction is employed by all rational people, so it is something of an indisputable standard, whatever the worldview. It is both fair and universal.

Unlike some multi-step philosophical tests for truth, Clark gives only one, and it is a simple one: Truth cannot conflict with itself. Either a view is noncontradictory or it is not. Clark's criterion also is rational. It is clear and consistent, not apt to get lost in subjective, mystical experience.

As Nash correctly observes, Clark stressed "the importance of refusing to separate faith" (cited in Robbins, 89). He was an arch enemy of fideism, insisting on the need for rational religious belief.

Another positive feature is Clark's stress on objective, propositional truth (*see* TRUTH, NATURE OF). He correctly emphasizes this, not only in general, but in the propositional revelation expressed in Scripture.

Negative Critique. Empirical skepticism unjustified. Clark claimed not to trust his senses, yet he needed them to read his Bible. How could he believe what he read? Like other skeptics, Clark inconsistently trusted his senses in everyday affairs. How else could he have eaten or crossed a busy street? Also, how can one know his or her senses are unreliable unless that can be determined by senses? For example, we learn by our senses to make allowances for the appearance of a straight stick that looks crooked when thrust into the water. We could not know not to trust the bent reflection unless we could trust our senses.

And like other empirical skeptics, Clark was not skeptical about his skepticism (*see* AGNOSTICISM). He accepted it uncritically as a necessary step in his presuppositionalism. But why should skepticism have been the starting point? Why not assume we can gain knowledge by way of our senses? Many of the criticisms in the article DAVID HUME as well as in the critique of PRESUPPOSITIONAL APOLOGETICS can be leveled at Clark.

Circular reasoning. Clark commits the fallacy of *petitio principii* or begging the question (*see* LOGIC). He admits that his system involves circular reasoning, but attempts to resolve the problem, in part, by claiming that all other systems have the same problem. "Non-Christian arguments regularly assume the point in dispute before they start. The questions are so framed as to exclude the Christian answer from the beginning" (*Religions, Reason, and Revelation*, 27). He believes that he escapes the problem because skepticism is self-defeating (*Thales to Dewey*, 29–30). It hardly seems to further his cause to reduce his argument to the level of the rest, and this does not eliminate the possibility that other views are just as self-consistent.

Fallacious arguments against proof. Clark's rejection of theistic proofs (*see* GOD, ALLEGED DISPROOFS OF) was no better than that of his agnostic mentors Hume and Kant (*see* AGNOSTICISM). Clark's apologetic offers a strange rationalism. First he defended the skeptics in their arguments against God, only to argue later the need to rationally defend God by presuppositionalism. It would have been simpler to use classical arguments from the beginning.

A survey of all systems? To be fair, before Clark proves his point, he must prove every other system in history and on the contemporary scene to be inconsistent. He takes the conclusion of his argument beyond the evidence. The finiteness of the investigator limits the support for his thesis (Lewis, 119). One lifetime is simply too short to survey every other conceivable system. Clark might force the conclusion of a probability that Christianity is true by this method, but Clark reduces all probability to skepticism. By his own standard, then, his apologetic method leaves us in skepticism.

Consistency within other systems. A similar problem is that Clark uses internal consistency as the only test for the truth of a system. But he cannot know that all systems are contradictory simply using the law of noncontradiction. By Christian standards this might be possible, but many systems are self-consistency within their own view of reality. The pantheist (*see* PANTHEISM) says, "I am God." If this were an internally contradictory statement, then God himself could not say it. But he can and does. "God is all, and all is God" may be a contradictory statement to a theistic view, but to a pantheist who believes the real world is an illusion, it is perfectly self-consistent (*see* HINDUISM; MONISM).

A negative test only. At best the law of noncontradiction is a negative test for truth. It can falsify a worldview truth claim, but it cannot verify one. It cannot prove that one alone is true, since more than one view may be internally self-consistent. As Gordon Lewis put it, "Contradiction is the surest sign of error, but consistency is not a guarantee of truth" (120).

Conclusion. Clark has provided a great service to Christian apologetics by stressing the laws of logic on which all rational arguments are based. The law of noncontradiction is absolutely necessary to the affirmation and confirmation of all truth claims. However, logic is only a set of formal principles. It tells what *could be* true; not what *is* true. To know what is really true, sooner or later one must touch base with the external world. This is what classical apologetics does.

Clark's own view depends on his acceptance of the validity of sense impressions and probability (*see* INDUCTIVISM), which he denies have any validity as a test for truth. On his own principles his view could not be true. He must trust his senses, even when reading books on other views. He must confess only a probability that *all* non-Christian views are false, since he has not examined each of them. He must trust his senses even when he accepts the claim that the Bible is true. Clark's apologetic method fails to be a comprehensive positive test for the truth of Christianity.

Sources

G. H. Clark, *A Christian View of Men and Things*

———, "Apologetics," in C. F. H. Henry, ed., *Contemporary Evangelical Thought*

———, *Barth's Theological Method*

———, *Philosophy of Education*

———, *Religion, Reason, and Revelation*

———, "Special Divine Revelation as Rational," in C. F. H. Henry, ed., *Revelation and the Bible*

———, *Thales to Dewey: A History of Philosophy*

———, "The Bible as Truth," in *Sacra* 114 April 1957

———, *The Johannine Logos*

———, "Truth," in E F. Harrison, ed., *Baker's Dictionary of Theology*

N. L. Geisler, *Christian Apologetics*, chap. 2

G. Lewis, *Testing Christianity's Truth Claims*, chap. 4

R. Nash, "Gordon H. Clark," in W. Elwell, ed., *Handbook of Evangelical Theologians*

———, ed., *The Philosophy of Gordon Clark: A* Festschrift

J. W. Robbins, ed., *Gordon H. Clark: Personal Reflections*

Clarke, Samuel. Samuel Clarke (1675–1729) was an important English philosopher, physicist, and apologist of his time. Clarke studied at Cambridge and became a Newtonian in an atmosphere dominated largely by the science of René Descartes (1596–1650). He was ordained in the Church of England. His posts included rector at St. James, Westminster.

His writings are collected in *The Works of Samuel Clarke*, which include his Boyle lectures of 1704, "A Demonstration of the Being and Attributes of God," and 1705, "A Discourse Concerning the Unchangeable Obligations of Natural Religion, and The Truth and Certainty of the Christian Revelation in Answer to Mr. Hobbes, *Spinoza, the Author of the Oracles of Reason, and Other Deniers of Natural and Revealed Religion." Several volumes of sermons survive. Clarke's works exerted an influence on Joseph Butler (1692–1752) in his *Analogy in Religion* (1736).

Classical Apologetic Approach. Clarke's approach falls into the category of classical apologetics. He began with a strong cosmological argument for God's existence as expressed in natural theology. He proceeded to defend the Christian supernatural revelation (*see* MIRACLE). As the extended title of his book indicates, it is directed at Thomas Hobbes (1588–1679), Benedict Spinoza (1632–1677), and other naturalistic approaches (*see* NATURALISM).

Existence and Attributes of God. The 1704 Boyle lectures consisted of "one argument in a chain of propositions." The first three are the most important:

Proposition one. It is undeniable that something has existed from all eternity. Since something is, it is evident that something always was. Otherwise, things that are were produced out of nothing, without a cause. Something cannot be effected unless there is something that effected it. This is a "first plain and self-evident truth" ("Discourse Concerning the Being and Attributes," 1).

Proposition two. An unchangeable and independent being has existed from eternity. "Either there has always existed some one unchangeable and independent being, from which all other beings that are or ever were in the universe, have received their origin; or else, there has been an infinite succession of changeable and dependent beings produced from one another in an endless succession" (ibid., 2). There cannot be an endless succession of beings, for such a series must be caused either from within or without. It cannot be caused from without, since supposedly everything is within the series. It cannot be caused from within because no being in the series is self-existent and necessary, and such a series arose from either necessity, mere possibility, or chance. It cannot be from necessity, since the infinite regress doesn't allow anything necessary. It cannot be from chance, which is a mere word without any meaning. It cannot be explained by mere possibility, since pure potentiality for existence does not explain why anything actually exists. Therefore, "there must have existed from eternity some one immutable and independent being" (ibid.).

Proposition three. That unchangeable, independent being which existed from all eternity must be self-existent, or necessarily-existing. Whatever exists must come into being from nothing, without cause, or it must be self-existent. To arise without cause from nothing is a contradiction. "To have been produced by some external cause cannot possibly be true of everything; but something must have existed eternally and independently; as has likewise been shown already" (ibid., 3). The being must be self-existent. This eternal, necessary being cannot be the material universe (*see* MATERIALISM). The material universe is neither eternal nor necessary since many of its properties are contingent. It cannot be necessary and eternal, since its nonexistence can be conceived. And the nonexistence of a necessary being is not possible.

Morality and Christianity. The Boyle lecture of 1705 on natural religion and the truth of Christianity set out fifteen propositions. The first four are devoted to obligations of natural religion. Propositions five to fifteen are on the truth and certainty of Christian revelation. The argument is typical of the classical approach in that it defends the possibility of miracles and the historicity of supernatural events supporting Christianity (*see* APOLOGETICS, HISTORICAL; MIRACLES, ARGUMENTS AGAINST).

Evaluation. Most of the points of an evaluation of Clarke are covered in detail in the articles GOD, EVIDENCE FOR, and GOD, OBJECTIONS TO PROOFS FOR.

Positive Contributions. Clarke provided a strong classical defense of *theism and Christianity (*see* APOLOGETICS, ARGUMENT OF). His argument, especially the first part of it, is one of the most powerful ever offered for an eternal, Necessary Being. It later had a strong influence on the American apologist Jonathan *Edwards. It bears strong similarities to the "third way" of *Thomas Aquinas.

Likewise, Clarke saw what other classical theists have seen, that the defense of Christianity must come in two steps. First there must be a rational defense of the existence of God. Second there must be a historical defense of the supernatural origin of Christianity.

Negative Critique. Unfortunately, Clarke's logic in the latter part of his argument is not so tight as in the first. While it is clear that (1) something undeniably exists and (2) something must be eternal and necessary; it is not so clear from his treatment that this "something" must be (3) absolutely one. His arguments that matter cannot be eternal are dependent on Newton's physics. In the context of modern science, the evidence of a sudden, explosive origin is more compelling (*see* BIG BANG THEORY).

Sources

H. G. Alexander, ed., *The Leibniz-Clarke Correspondence*

S. Clarke, "A Discourse Concerning the Being and Attributes of God" (Boyle lecture, 1704)

———, "A Discourse Concerning the Unchangeable Obligation of Natural Religion . . ." (Boyle lecture, 1705)

———, *The Works of Samuel Clarke*

B. Peach, "Samuel Clarke," in V. Ferm, ed., *Encyclopedia of Morals*

E. Sprauge, "Clarke, Samuel," in *EP*

Classical Apologetics. *Classical apologetics* is so called because it was the apologetic method practiced by the first thinkers who studied and practiced the application of reason to the defense of Christianity. These pioneer apologists included *Augustine, *Anselm, and *Thomas Aquinas (*see* APOLOGETICS, TYPES OF). The roots of classical apologetics are found in some second- and third-century apologists as well. Modern classical apologetics is represented by William *Paley, John *Locke, C. S. *Lewis, B. B. *Warfield, John Gerstner, R. C. Sproul, William Craig, J. P. Moreland, and Norman L. Geisler.

Classical apologetics stresses rational arguments for the existence of God (*see* GOD, EVIDENCES FOR) and historical evidence supporting the truth of Christianity. Stress is placed on miracles as a confirmation of the claims of Christ and the biblical prophets and apostles.

Contrasts with Presuppositional and Evidential Apologetics. Classical apologetics differs from various forms of presuppositional apologetics in its handling of proofs for the existence of God and its use of historical evidence. Classical differs from evidential apologetics over whether there is a logically prior need to establish the existence of God before arguing for the truth of Christianity (e.g., the deity of Christ and inspiration of the Bible [*see* CHRIST, DEITY OF]).

Classical apologetics is characterized by two basic steps. Its first step is to establish valid theistic arguments for the truth of *theism apart from (but with appeal to) special revelation in Scripture. Its second step is to compile historical evidence to establish such basic truths of Christianity as the deity of Christ and the inspiration of the Bible. The use of the resurrection of Christ often plays an important role in this second step.

Validity of Theistic Proofs. Classical apologetics accepts, and presuppositionalists reject, the validity of traditional theistic proofs for God. Some presuppositionalists replace traditional proofs with transcendental arguments for God of their own (*see* PRESUPPOSITIONAL APOLOGETICS; VAN TIL, CORNELIUS). Not all classical apologists accept *all* the traditional proofs for God. For example, many reject the validity of the *Ontological Argument. But most accept some form of the *Cosmological Argument and the *Teleological Argument. Many also believe the *Moral Argument is valid.

Presuppositional apologists reject the validity of theistic proofs for God (*see* God, Evidence for). Most of them accept the validity of much of what David *Hume and Immanuel *Kant said in their critiques of theistic argumentation (*see* God, Objections to Proofs for). Some, such as Gordon *Clark, do this on the basis of empirical skepticism. Cornelius Van Til and others do it because they believe facts have no meaning apart from the presupposed trinitarian world view. Whatever the grounds, all true presuppositionalists join atheists and agnostics in rejecting the validity of traditional theistic proofs for God (*see* Agnosticism; Atheism).

Historical Evidence and Theism. One apologetic tactic is to show the historical reliability of the New Testament (*see* New Testament, Dating of; New Testament, Historicity of; New Testament Manuscripts) and argue from that credibility to the New Testament's testimony that Jesus claimed to be, and was miraculously proven to be, the Son of God (*see* Christ, Deity of). From this, Jesus' own voice is added to historical evidence that the Old Testament is the Word of God. His promise of the ministry of the Holy Spirit does the same for the New Testament (*see* Bible, Jesus' View of).

Sometimes classical apologists begin this second step by showing that the Bible claims to be, and is supernaturally proven to be, the Word of God. In doing so they often use the same basic evidence as is used by evidential apologetics. This includes miracles (*see* Miracle; Miracles, Apologetic Value of; Miracles in the Bible), fulfilled prophecy (*see* Prophecy, as Proof of the Bible), the unity of the Bible, and other indications of its supernatural origin (*see* Bible, Evidences for). The difference between the evidentialists and the classical apologists at this point is that the latter see the need to first establish a theistic universe in order to establish the possibility of miracles. Evidentialists do not see theism as a logically necessary precondition of historical apologetics.

The basic argument of the classical apologist is that it makes no sense to speak about the resurrection as an act of God unless as a logical step it is established that there is a God who can act. Likewise, the Bible cannot be the Word of God, unless there is a God who can speak. And Christ cannot be shown to be the Son of God except on the logically prior premise that there is a God who can have a Son.

While some evidentialists use theistic proofs, they do not believe it is logically necessary to do so. They believe this is simply an alternate approach. The works of John Warwick Montgomery and Gary Habermas fit this category.

At this point there is a similarity between classical apologetics and presuppositionalism. Both believe that one cannot argue legitimately from historical data unless he begins with the prior premise that a theistic God exists. They differ about how to establish this prior premise. The presuppositionalists claim that each worldview acts as a presuppositional grid to filter incoming facts and attempt to make them fit the individual's idea of how the world works. But underlying that process is a built-in, suppressed knowledge of the truth, as expressed by Romans 1 and *Augustine's dictum that every human being is "doing business" with God. The apologist is dependent on the work of the Holy Spirit to show the failure of the held worldview and to excite the innate knowledge. Classical apologists insist that the apologist takes a more active role in partnership with the Holy Spirit to reason through the truth about God and until it is established and admitted in the heart of the unbeliever.

Objections to Classical Apologetics. Other Christian views make several important objections to classical apologetics. Some of these come from evidentialists and others from presuppositionalists or fideists (*see* Fideism), who reject the validity of traditional theistic arguments.

Invalidity of Traditional Proofs. Both fideists and strict presuppositionalists reject all the classical arguments for God's existence. Their specific objections are considered elsewhere (*see* God, Objections to Proofs for).

Invalidity of Historical Arguments. Fideists and presuppositionalists contend that no appeal to any kind of evidence, including historical evidence is valid, since the same data is interpreted differently under varying worldview perspectives. There are no bare facts. All facts are interpreted, and the interpretation derives from one's worldview. If the dead body of Jesus can be agreed to have come back to life, even that information can be understood differently by different worldviews. A Christian theist (*see* Theism) sees the event as a supernatural resurrection that confirms Christ's claim to be the Son of God. But the pantheist (*see* Pantheism) views it simply as a manifestation of the One Being, of which we are all a part. It reveals Christ to be a guru, not God the Creator revealed in human flesh. The atheist or naturalist views the event as a myth or at most an anomaly that has a purely natural explanation.

In response to this objection, many classical apologists, the author included, agree with the basic point made by the presuppositionalists but note that this does not affect the approach, since classical apologetics believes it is logically necessary to establish theism first as the worldview context in which facts of history are properly understood.

Classical apologists and the presuppositionalists disagree on two matters. First, classical apologists contend that they can establish theism by traditional rational arguments, and presuppositionalists do not. Second, classical apologists argue that it is only logically necessary to establish theism before one can properly understand the historical evidence. Many presuppositionalists, following Van Til, insist that one must presuppose a Triune (*see* TRINITY) God who has revealed himself in Scripture as a necessary presupposition for any historical evidence in support of Christianity. But this, to the classical apologists, is simply arguing in a circle.

The Validity of Transcendental Arguments. Not every presuppositionalist discards *all* arguments in favor of Christianity. Some use a *transcendental argument (e.g., Greg Bahnsen). They insist that the only valid way to argue for the truth of Christianity is to show that it is transcendentally necessary to posit the basic truth of Christianity as a condition for making any sense out of our world. On no other presupposition can one even assume there is any meaning in history or science, or even attempt to communicate.

The classical apologists agree that this is true so far as theism is necessary to view life as meaningful and coherent. In a closed system there is no ultimate meaning, no ultimate values, and no "miracle" happens that cannot be accounted for by naturalistic phenomenon (cf. John 3:1–2; Acts 2:22; Heb. 2:3–4). But it is not necessary to presuppose that the God is triune, has a Son incarnated as Jesus of Nazareth, and has revealed himself in the sixty-six inspired books of Christian Scripture. One can make sense of the world by assuming less than the whole truth of Christianity.

Other differences are detailed elsewhere. It is sufficient to note here that they involve the role of faith and reason, especially the use of logic or reason to demonstrate God's existence which classical apologists use and pure presuppositionalists reject.

Sources

Anselm, *Monologion*
———, *Prologion*
R. Bush, *Readings in Classical Apologetics*
W. Corduan, *A Reasonable Faith*
W. L. Craig, *Apologetics: An Introduction*
N. L. Geisler, *Christian Apologetics*
———, *When Skeptics Ask*
J. Gerstner, *Reasons for Faith*
S. Hackett, *The Reconstruction of the Christian Revelation Claim*
C. S. Lewis, *Mere Christianity*
J. Locke, *The Reasonableness of Christianity*
J. P. Moreland, *Scaling the Secular City*
W. Paley, *Natural Theology*
R. C. Sproul, *Reasons to Believe*
Thomas Aquinas, *Summa contra Gentiles*
———, *Summa Theologica*

Clement of Alexandria. Church Fathers of the second and third centuries were apologists who defended the faith against the attacks of both Jewish and pagan thinkers. Among the first apologists was Clement of Alexandria (ca. 150–ca. 213).

The Apologetics of Clement. To some the position of some early apologists, such as Clement, seems overly rationalistic, and stresses Greek philosophy too heavily. On closer analysis, however, the first postapostolic defenders of the Faith were more Christian in apologetic than would at first appear (*see* FAITH AND REASON).

Clement affirmed that "before the advent of our Lord, philosophy was necessary to the Greeks for righteousness. . . . Perchance, too, philosophy was given to the Greeks directly and primarily, till the Lord should call the Greeks. For this was a schoolmaster to bring 'the Hellenic mind' as the law, the Hebrews, 'to Christ'" (*Stromata* 1.5). He also spoke of the inspiration of Greek poets (*Exhortation to the Heathen* 8), and went so far as to declare that "by reflection and direct vision, those among the Greeks who have philosophized accurately, saw God" (*Stomata* 1.19).

However, Clement was not so rationalistic that he did not affirm *sola Scriptura,* insisting of the Bible that "certainly we use it as a criterion in the discovery of things." For "what is subjected to criticism is not to be believed till it is so subjected; so that what needs criticism cannot be a first principle" (*Stromata* 7.16).

However, Greek philosophy at best served only a preparatory role for Christ. For "Hellenic philosophy comprehends not the whole extent of the truth, and . . . it prepares the way for the truly royal teaching . . . and fitting him who believes in providence for the reception of the truth" (*Stromata* 1.16).

There were limitations to philosophy. The Greeks had only "certain scintillations of the divine word" (*Exhortation* 7). Faith is the means of attaining the full revelation of God (*Exhortation* 8).

Like Justin *Martyr, Clement believed that the truth of philosophy was borrowed from the Hebrew Scriptures. He wrote: "I know thy teachers, even if thou woulds't conceal them. You have learned geometry from the Egyptians, astronomy from the Babylonians; . . . but for laws that are consistent with truth, and your sentiments respecting God, you are indebted to the Hebrews" (*Exhortation* 6). However, what truth philosophers possessed did have did not directly reveal Christ. He said plainly: "I do not think that Philosophy directly declared the Word, although in many instances philosophy attempts and persuasively teaches us probable arguments" (*Stromata* 1.19).

It is often overlooked that Clement believed that faith is a prerequisite of philosophy; believing is a precondition of knowing. For according to him all knowledge is based on first principles and "first principles are incapable of demonstration. . . . Accordingly, faith is something superior to knowledge and [is] its criterion" (*Stromata* 2.4).

Evaluation. Within its context, Clement's defense of the Christian faith was effective. From mastery of the prevailing philosophy, he defended the superiority of the Christian revelation. While non-Christian philosophers possessed some truth, it too came from God, either by general or special revelation. Apart from Christianity the Greeks at best had only a preparatory and partial knowledge of God. The fullness of truth is found only in Christ. Indeed, what truth the pagans possessed they borrowed from the Christian Scriptures.

Sources

Clement of Alexandria, *Exhortation to the Heathen*

______, *Stromata*, *Ante-Nicene Fathers*, Vol. 2, Philip Schaff, ed.

Coherentism. ***See*** **TRUTH, DEFINITION OF.**

Coherence as Test of Truth. ***See*** **CLARK, GORDON; TRUTH, DEFINITION OF.**

Common Ground. The question of "common ground" is largely a debate between classical apologetics and presuppositional apologetics. The issue is whether there is any area of neutral evidence or starting point at which Christian and non-Christian can meet (*see* HISTORICAL APOLOGETICS). Revelational presuppositionalists deny that there is a common ground to which both sides can connect in establishing the truth of Christianity.

Cornelius *Van Til strongly believed the noetic effects of *sin so vitiated human understanding that there is no common understanding of the facts. One cannot build an apologetic argument on the facts of experience or history apart from the supernatural work of the Holy Spirit in the heart and mind (*see* HOLY SPIRIT, ROLE IN APOLOGETICS). One's worldview must be presupposed or posited by a transcendental argument in order to give an interpretive framework to otherwise bare facts.

Both historical and classical apologists reject this view, claiming there are starting points in reason (*see* FAITH AND REASON; LOGIC) from which to build a case for a theistic and Christian worldview (*see* APOLOGETICS, ARGUMENT OF; GOD, EVIDENCE FOR).

Comte, Auguste. Auguste Comte (1797–1857) was from a rationalist (*see* RATIONALISM) French Catholic family. He studied science and was secretary of Saint-Simone at *Ecole Polytechnique*. He said he "naturally ceased believing in God" at age fourteen. Comte is the father of both positivism and sociology. He coined the latter term. He developed a mystical (*see* MYSTICISM), nontheistic, humanistic religious cult in which he installed himself as high priest (*see* HUMANISM, SECULAR).

Comte's main works were *Cours, The Positive Philosophy of Auguste Comte* (1830–42, trans. 1853) and *The Catechism of Positive Religion* (1852, trans. 1858). *The Catechism* included a calendar of secular "saints."

Comte's Positivistic Philosophy. With an epistemological starting point in Immanuel *Kant's antimetaphysical agnosticism and G. W. F. Hegel's historical developmentalism, Comte developed his "law of growth." It included three stages of human development: *theological* (child)—ancient, *metaphysical* (youth)—medieval, and *positivistic* (adulthood)—modern. The first featured primitive belief in personal gods, later replaced by the Greek idea of impersonal law, only to be superseded by the modern (positivistic) belief in the methodological unity of science. These three stages represent the mythological (mythos), metaphysical (logos), and scientific (positivistic) stages of the human race. According to Comte, human beings move forward from the personal explanation of nature, to impersonal law, and finally to an objective method. They advance from belief in supernatural beings to acceptance of natural forces, to understanding through phenomenal (empirical) descriptions. Instead of animating spirits or impersonal powers, natural laws are posited. In this three-stage growth spiritual and then rational causes are discarded for purely natural (positivistic) descriptions.

The religious stage has its own evolution. People move from polytheistic (*see* POLYTHEISM) manifestations of nature to multiple gods and finally a monotheism which consolidates all the forces that are not understood into a single godhead. The problem with the religious interpretation is that it anthropomorphizes nature. The problem with the metaphysical stage is that it makes ideas real, rather than merely describing and interrelating them, as does the positivistic stage.

Comte's goal was to find a general law by which all phenomena are related. Such a law, he believed, would be the ideal result of positivistic philosophy. However, the best likely result is a unity in scientific method.

For Comte, sociology is the final science, the science of society. Social progress is dialectical, moving from Feudalism (*see* FREUD, SIGMUND), through the French Revolution to Positivism. Freedom of thought is as out of place in society as in physics. True freedom lies in rational subjection to scientific laws. One law is that society must develop in a positivistic direction.

Comte's three stages were expressed politically as well. First, the Middle Ages society shared common religious ideas (theological stage). Second, the French Revolution society had common political ideals (metaphysical stage). Finally, the Modern (positivistic) society must share the scientific method. In this stage the Catholic priesthood was replaced by a scientific-industrial elite. Dogma is based on science and proclaimed by this elite.

Karl *Marx denied that he had read Comte before 1886, but a Comptian friend (E. S. Beesley) chaired the 1864 meeting of the Marxist International Workingmen's Association. Comte's views undoubtedly influenced the development of Marx's dialectical understanding of history.

Comte's Religious Views. Comte disliked Protestantism, pronouncing it negative and productive of intellectual anarchy. He developed his own nontheistic humanistic religion, in which Comte was the high priest of the Cult of Humanity. His mistress, Clothilde Vaux, was high priestess. Comte developed a Humanistic Religious Calendar, with such "saints" as Frederick the Great, Dante, and Shakespeare.

Evaluation. Comte's views are prey to a variety of philosophical, scientific, and historical weaknesses. Critique of some of his ideas is found elsewhere, particularly in the article, Humanism, Secular.

Comte's Atheism Is Inadequate. As other atheists (*see* God, Alleged Disproof of), Comte never succeeded in eliminating God. He provided no real rebuttal to arguments for the existence of God (*see* God, Evidence for). Instead, he tried to explain them away through his theories of historical development.

Comte's Historical Development Is Unfounded. Comte's philosophy of history is both gratuitous and unfounded. It is neither philosophically justified nor does it fit the facts. History simply does not fit into the neat stages of development his view demands. For example, there remain great modern and contemporary metaphysical views, such as *panentheism, represented by Alfred North *Whitehead, and monotheism predated polytheism, as demonstrated by the Ebla tablets (*see* Monotheism, Primitive)

Comte's Humanistic Beliefs Are Bizarre. Even other atheists and humanists are embarrassed by Comte's religious beliefs. They depict a religious and superstitious perspective that he himself characterized as primitive. If religion is outdated by the scientific, then why establish another religion, with a high priest, priestess, and holy days?

In effect, Comte deified the scientific method for studying nature. Yet Comte protested that others had deified nature. The positivist approach was not just *a* method for discovering some truth, but *the* method for discovering all truth. As such, it involved self-defeating beliefs in materialism. It was weakened as a worldview by a denial of metaphysics and absolute morality (*see* Morality, Absolute Nature of).

Sources

A. Comte, *Cours, The Positive Philosophy of Auguste Comte*
———, *The Catechism of Positive Religion*
"Comte, Auguste," *EP*
L. Levy-Bruhl, *The Philosophy of Auguste Comte*
J. . Mill, *Auguste Comte and Positivism*
T. Whittaker, *Comte and Mill*

Contradiction. ***See*** **First Principles.**

Conventionalism. *Conventionalism* is the theory that all meaning is relative. Since all truth claims are meaningful statements, this would mean that all truth is relative. But this is contrary to the Christian claim that there is absolute truth (*see* Truth, Absolute Nature of). Absolute truths are true at all times, in all places, for all people.

Conventionalism is a reaction to Platonism (*see* Plato), which contends that language has an unchanging essence or ideal forms. Conventionalists believe that meaning changes to fit each situation. Meaning is arbitrary and relative to culture and context. There are no transcultural forms. Language (meaning) has no essence of itself; linguistic meaning is derived from the relative experience on which language is based.

Some of the modern proponents of conventionalism are Ferdinand Saussure (d. 1913), Gottlob Fregge (d. 1925), and Ludwig *Wittgenstein (d. 1951). Their view is widely accepted in current linguistic philosophy.

Symbols and Meaning. An important difference separates a conventionalist theory of symbols and a conventionalist theory of meaning. Other than natural symbols (for example, smoke signifying fire) and onomatopoetic terms (for example, *crash, bang, boom*) whose sound express to the words' meanings, virtually all linguists acknowledge that symbols are conventionally relative. The word *down* has no intrinsic relation to the fluffy feathers of a duck. The word also refers to a lower position, a psychological state, a type of mountain landscape, an attempt to move the ball in American football, and the direction south. The same or similar group of sounds may carry far different meanings in other languages, and many languages will have differing sounds to refer to the feathers on a duck. This is true of most words.

This is not the same as claiming that the meaning of a sentence is culturally relative. It is only to say that the words used to convey meaning are relative. That is, individual symbols are relative, but not the significance a combination of symbols carries into a sentence.

Evaluation. As a theory of meaning, conventionalism has serious faults. First, it is a self-falsifying theory. If the theory were correct, the statement "All linguistic meaning is conventional" would be relative and ultimately meaningless. But the conventionalist who makes such statements assumes that sentences do carry objective meaning, so he makes objectively meaningful statements to argue that there are no objectively meaningful statements.

Second, if conventionalism were correct, universal statements would not translate into other languages as universal statements. But this is not the case. The sentence "All triangles have three sides." is understood to be universally true in Mongolian, Spanish, or any language with words for *triangle, three,* and *side*. The same is true of the statement "All wives are married women." If meaning were culturally relative, no such universal, transcultural statement would be possible.

There would be no universal truths in any language. One could not even say that 3 + 4 = 7. In logic there would be no law of noncontradiction. In fact, no consistent conventionalist can even deny such absolute first principles without using them. The very statement that "The meaning of all statements is relative to a culture" depends for meaning on the fact that laws of logic are not relative to a culture, but in fact transcend cultures and languages.

Third, if conventionalism were true, we would not know any truth prior to knowing the context of that truth in that language. But we can know 3 + 4 = 7 before knowing any conventions of a language. Mathematics may depend on relative symbols to express itself, but the truths of mathematics are independent of culture. Likewise, laws of logic are independent of human convention. *Logic is not arbitrary, and its rules are not created in a cultural context, but are rather discovered. They are true prior to language and cultural expression.

Fourth, a related problem is that conventionalism confuses the *source* of meaning with its ultimate *ground*. The source of a person's knowledge that "All wives are married women" may be social. One may have learned it from a parent or a teacher. But the ground for knowing that this is a true statement is not social but logical. It represents a first principle of logic in that the predicate is reducible to the subject (wife = married woman). It is true by definition, not acculturation.

Fifth, if conventionalism were correct, no meaning would be possible. If all meaning is based on changing experience, which in turn gets meaning from changing experience, there is no basis for meaning. An infinite series is impossible in finding a first cause for the universe, and it is impossible in finding the beginning of meaning if all meanings depend on other meanings. A statement without any basis for meaning is a baseless statement.

Sixth, conventionalism has only an internal criterion for meaning. But internal criteria don't help adjudicate meaning conflicts of the same statement from different worldview vantage points. Either a theist (*see* THEISM) or a pantheist (*see* PANTHEISM) can make the statement "God is a Necessary Being." The words in themselves, without objective definitions behind the words to fall back to, lack any sort of relation to truth. The theist and pantheist can talk for hours, leaving one another with the impression that they believe the same things about God. By being able to unpack firm meanings for *God* and *Necessary Being*, however, the conversants can discuss the differences in their worldviews.

It is easy to see that no truly descriptive knowledge of God is possible for a conventionalist. Language is strictly based in experience. It tells us only what God *seems to be to us in our experience*. It cannot tell us what he *really is in himself*. This reduces to self-defeating *agnosticism or the claim that we know that we cannot know anything about the nature of God (*see* ANALOGY, PRINCIPLE OF). Conventionalists reduce the meaning of *God* to a mere interpretive framework, rather than a being beyond the world. Theism shows God to be (*see* COSMOLOGICAL ARGUMENT; GOD, EVIDENCE FOR; *KALAM* COSMOLOGICAL ARGUMENT).

Seventh, conventionalism has a circular justification. It really does not justify its claims, but merely asserts them. A conventionalist asked for the basis of this belief that all meaning is conventional cannot give a nonconventional basis. If she could she would no longer be a conventionalist. But a conventional basis for conventionalism would be a relative reason for relativism. Such an argument could only be circular.

Eighth, conventionalists often distinguish between surface and depth grammar to avoid some of their dilemmas. However, such a distinction assumes that they have a vantage point independent of language and experience. Conventionalism, by its very nature, does not allow such a vantage point outside one's culture. So even this distinction is logically inconsistent with the theory.

Conclusion. The conventionalists' theory of meaning is a form of semantic relativism. Like other forms of relativism, conventionalism is self-defeating. The very theory that all meaning is relative is itself a nonrelative concept. It is a meaningful statement intended to apply to all meaningful statements. It is a nonconventional statement claiming that all statements are conventional.

Sources

G. Fregge, *Über Sinn und Bedeutung* ("On Sense and Reference") in P. Geach, ed. and trans., *Translations from the Philosophical Writings of Gottlob Fregge*

E. Gilson, *Linguistics and Philosophy*

J. Harris, *Against Relativism*

Plato, *Cratylus*

F. Saussure, *Cours de Linguistique Generale* (1916)

———, *Course in General Linguistics*

Thomas Aquinas, *Summa Theologica*, 1.84–85

Ludwig Wittgenstein, *Philosophical Investigations*

Cosmological Argument. The arguments traditionally used to prove God's existence are *the cosmological argument, the teleological argument, the moral argument*, and *the ontological argument*. Respectively, these are the arguments from the cosmos, from design, from moral law, and from the idea of an absolutely perfect (or necessary) being.

Forms of the Argument. There are two basic forms of the cosmological argument: the *horizontal* or kalam cosmological argument and the *vertical*. The horizontal cosmological argument reasons back to a Cause of the *beginning* of the universe. The vertical cosmological argument reasons from the *being* of the universe as it now exists. The former, explaining how the universe *came to be*, was championed by Bonaventure (1221–1274). The latter, explaining how it *continues to be*, flows from *Thomas Aquinas (1224–1274). The first calls for an *originating* Cause, and the latter for a *sustaining* Cause. Forms of the cosmological argument combine both dimensions.

A Survey of Cosmological Arguments. The basic idea of this argument is that, since there is a universe rather than none at all, it must have been caused by something beyond itself. This reasoning is based on the law of causality (*see* CAUSALITY, PRINCIPLE OF), which says that every finite or contingent thing is caused right now by something other than itself.

Aristotle: Unmoved Mover(s). *Plato's (428–348 B.C.) student *Aristotle (384–322 B.C.) gave further sophistication to his teacher's argument for God. In its strongest form, Aristotle's cosmological argument is unfolded in the article on Aristotle. Aristotle's argument presupposed a polytheistic (*see* POLYTHEISM) universe. He moved from the fact of change and its movements to the existence of pure actualities or unmoved movers. These necessary beings can act upon contingent beings. They move potential change so that it becomes actualized change. Aristotle's cosmology postulated dozens of unmoved movers, but ultimately one heaven and one God. For only material things can be numerically differentiated.

Noteworthy about Aristotle's argument is that it introduces the question of an infinite regress of causes (*see* INFINITE SERIES). Aristotle struggles with a view that there must have been a plurality of first causes, but unlike Plato's *"Demiurgos,"* Aristotle's First Cause is a final (purposing) cause.

This purposing cause should not, however, be confused with the efficient or producing cause of later Christian thinkers. Neither Plato's World Soul, Former, or *Demiurgos* (*see* CREATION, VIEWS OF), nor Aristotle's Unmoved Mover is identical with the absolutely perfect Being of Christian theism. Aristotle's Unmoved Mover was not a personal God and had no religious significance. No worship was due this pantheon. The First Cause was not infinite. Only what is formless or indefinite could be considered infinite to the Greeks.

Anselm: Cosmological-Type Arguments. Before *Anselm, St. *Augustine offered a "proof" for God. After him Anselm (1033–1109). He is best known for his ontological argument in the *Proslogion*, but an earlier work, the *Monologion*, offered three *a posteriori* proofs for God's existence (Anselm 1–3). A description of his arguments is given in the article on Anselm.

Anselm's first argument is from the existence of good things:

1. Good things exist.
2. The cause of this goodness is either one or many.
3. If it were many, there would be no way to compare their goodness. But some things are better than others.
4. So there is one Supreme Good who causes all goodness in all good things.

The second argument is similar but works from perfection:

1. Some beings are more nearly perfect than are others.
2. But things cannot be more or less perfect unless there is one wholly perfect standard for comparison.
3. That standard is a Most Perfect Being.

The third argument, from being, is most obviously cosmological:

1. Something exists, and
2. owes its existence either to nothing or to something.
3. Nothing cannot cause something.
4. There is, then, a something, which is either one or many.
5. If many, the beings would be mutually dependent for their own existence or dependent on another.
6. They cannot be mutually dependent for their existence. Something cannot exist through a being on which it confers existence.
7. Therefore, there must be one being through which all other beings exist.
8. This being must exist through itself.
9. Whatever exists through itself, exists in the highest degree of all.
10. Therefore, a supremely perfect Being exists in the highest degree.

These arguments, unlike Plato's but like the reasoning of *Plotinus, identify the Creator with the supreme Good. Unlike Aristotle's, the arguments view God as the *efficient*, not the *final*, Cause of the world. Unlike Plato or Aristotle, Anselm holds that this efficient Cause does not merely operate on eternally existing matter.

Rather this Cause causes everything, including matter.

These Christian theistic arguments combined at least three elements: (1) Efficient causality from Plato's *Timaeus* argument; (2) identification of this God with the Good of Plato's *Republic*, the supremely perfect Being; (3) identification of this God with the Hebrew-Christian God. This God causes the very being, not merely the forms of being, of everything that exists.

**Alfarabi: Necessary Existence Argument.* Arabian and Jewish philosophers of the Middle Ages influenced later Christian forms of the cosmological argument. The Muslim thinker Alfarabi (870?–950) provided the heart of later scholastic arguments by his distinction between *essence* and *existence*.

Aristotle distinguished between *what* a thing is and *that* it is. But Alfarabi stated this distinction as between a thing's essence and its existence. This distinction implies an argument for God's existence, the form of which is shown in the article on Alfarabi (see also Maurer, 95–97). This reasoning establishes the concept of "possible beings," whose essence is distinct from their existence. These beings do not "have" to exist. Once they did not exist, for existence is not part of their essence. It can be said that they exist *accidentally*, rather than *essentially*.

Such beings must have received existence from another being. That causing being may also have been caused. But some uncaused being had to start all the causing. This First Cause must be an essential Being, whose essence is to exist. Only existence of such a Necessary Being explains the existence of all accidental beings.

Stated philosophically, if there are beings whose essence is *not to exist*, then there must be a Being whose essence is *to exist*. Possible beings are not possible unless there is a Necessary Being from whom they can receive existence. And since a being cannot give existence to another when it is dependent for its own existence on another, there must be a Being whose existence was not given to it by another, but who gives existence to all others.

**Avicenna: First Cause Argument.* Following Alfarabi, the Muslim philosopher Avicenna formulated a similar cosmological argument that was emulated in many forms by later scholastics. For the form, see the article AVICENNA. The proof begins with Alfarabi's "possible beings," which must have a cause for their being. There cannot be an infinite series of causes of being, since the cause of being must exist at the same time as it causes another. Through this First Cause, all other beings exist. This First Cause must be a Necessary Being. The cause of all possible beings cannot itself be a possible being. It must be a Necessary Being.

By borrowing some neo-Platonic (*see* PLOTINUS) premises and a ten-sphere cosmology, Avicenna extended his argument to argue that this necessary First Cause created a series of angels or "intelligences." These control the ten cosmic spheres. He reasoned that the Necessary Being, who is essentially one, can create only one effect at a time. Since thinking is creating and God necessarily thinks, since he is a Necessary Being, there must be an emanation from God of ten beings, called "intelligences," who do the actual work. The last of these beings, called "Agent Intellect," forms the four elements of the cosmos and informs the human mind of all truth.

Avicenna's God, then, was a Necessary Being from whom a serial creative force of ten gods followed with absolute necessity. Unlike the Christian God who freely created and who is directly responsible for the existence of everything else that exists, Avicenna's chain of Gods is necessary and these Gods create all below them.

The Jewish philosopher Moses *Maimonides (1135–1204) anticipated several later Christian formulations of cosmological-type arguments. He argued for a First Mover, a First Cause, and a Necessary Being, as in Aquinas's first three arguments. He insisted that the "I AM" of the Old Testament (Exod. 3:14) meant "absolute existence" and that God alone exists absolutely and necessarily. All creatures have existence only as an "accident" superadded to their essence by their Cause.

**Thomas Aquinas: Five Arguments.* When Aquinas formulated his "Five Ways," he was not creating arguments that were substantially new. Maimonides had the first three arguments. Alfarabi and Avicenna had the first two proofs. Anselm had an argument for perfection similar to the fourth argument. And Aquinas's fifth proof was more of a teleological argument, which such scholars as Thierry of Chartes and William of Conches had adapted from Plato's *Timaeus* argument. Aquinas does, of course, state the arguments out of the context of his own philosophy, which is more Aristotelian than that of most of his Christian predecessors. The first four arguments of Aquinas may be summarized:

The Argument from Motion (Aquinas, 1.2.3).

1. Things do move. Motion is the most obvious form of change.
2. Change is a passing from *potency* to *act* (i.e., from potentiality to actuality).
3. Nothing passes from potency to act except by something that is in actuality, for it is impossible for a potentiality to actualize itself.
4. There cannot be an infinite regress of actualizers or movers. If there is no First Mover, there can be no subsequent motion, since all subsequent motion depends on prior movers for its motion.

5. Therefore, there must be a first, Unmoved Mover, a pure actualizer with no potentiality in it that is unactualized.
6. Everyone understands this to be God.

The Argument from Efficient Causality.

1. There are efficient causes in the world (i.e., producing causes).
2. Nothing can be the efficient cause of itself, for it would have to be prior to itself in order to cause itself.
3. There cannot be an infinite regress of (essentially related) efficient causes, for unless there is a first cause of the series there would be no causality in the series.
4. Therefore, there must be a first, uncaused, efficient Cause of all efficient causality in the world.
5. Everyone gives to this the name of God.

The Argument from Possibility and Necessity.

1. There are beings that begin to exist and cease to exist (i.e., possible beings).
2. But not all beings can be possible beings, because what comes to exist does so only through what already exists. Nothing cannot cause something.
3. Therefore, there must be a Being whose existence is necessary (i.e., one that never came into being and will never cease to be).
4. There cannot be an infinite regress of Necessary Beings, each of which has its necessity dependent on another because
   a. An infinite regress of dependent causes is impossible because of the reasoning in the argument for efficient causality.
   b. A Necessary Being cannot be a dependent being.
5. Therefore, there must be a first Being that is necessary in itself and not dependent on another for its existence.

The Argument from Gradation *(Perfection) in Things.*

1. There are different degrees of perfections among beings (some are more nearly perfect than others).
2. But things cannot be more or less perfect unless there is a wholly perfect.
3. Whatever is perfect is the cause of the less-than-perfect (the higher is the cause of the lower).
4. Therefore, there must be a perfect Being that is causing the perfections of the less-than-perfect beings.
5. This we call God.

The argument for a First Cause of being. There seems to be a basic form behind all of these arguments with only a different starting point. Each argument begins in some characteristic of being (change, causality, contingency, and perfection, respectively) and then argues to a First Cause:

1. Some dependent beings exist.
2. All dependent beings must have a cause for their dependent existence.
3. An infinite regress of existentially dependent causes is impossible.
4. Therefore, there must be a first, uncaused Cause of the existence of every dependent being.
5. This independent Being is identical with the "I AM" of Scripture. The implication is that it is impossible to have more than one absolutely necessary and independent being upon which everything else exists for its being.

Duns Scotus: Argument from Producibility. John Duns Scotus (1265?–1308?) modified the cosmological argument of Aquinas in two important ways. First, he began with the *producibility* of being, not merely with produced beings. Second, he amplified on the argument against an infinite regress of dependent causes. The full form of Scotus's proof (Scotus, 39–56) is:

1. Being is produced (i.e., beings come into being). This is learned through experience (by observing beings produced), but it is also true independent of experience (i.e., it would be true of beings that do not exist). It would be true, even if God had not willed to create anything.
2. What is produced is producible, either by itself, by nothing, or by something else.
3. But no being can produce itself. In order to cause its own existence, it would have to exist prior to its own existence.
4. Neither can something be caused by nothing. This is contradictory.
5. Therefore, being is producible only by some being that is productive. Only beings can produce beings.
6. There cannot be an infinite regress of productive beings, each producing the being of the one following it, because
   a. This is an essentially related, not an accidentally related, series of causes (1) where the primary cause is more nearly perfect than the secondary, (2) where the secondary cause depends on the primary for its very causality, and (3) where the cause must be simultaneous to the effect.
   b. An infinite series of essentially related causes is impossible, because, (1) if the whole series is dependent for its causality (every cause depending on a prior cause), then there must be something beyond the series that accounts for the

causality in the series. (2) If an infinite series were causing the effect, then there would have to be an infinite number of causes simultaneously causing a single effect. This is impossible. There cannot be an actual infinite number in a series, for it is always possible to add one more to any number. (3) Wherever there are prior causes, there must be a prime (first) cause. One cause would not be nearer to the beginning than any other unless there is a beginning. (4) Higher causes are more nearly perfect than lower causes, and this implies a perfect Cause at the head of all less-than-perfect causes. (5) An infinite regress of causes implies imperfection, since each cause lacks the ability to explain the succeeding causes. But an imperfect series implies something perfect beyond the series as a ground for the imperfect.

7. Therefore, there must be a first, productive Cause of all producible beings.
8. This First Cause of all producible beings must be one, because
   a. It is perfect in knowledge, and there cannot be two beings that know everything perfectly, for one would know itself more completely than would the other.
   b. It is perfect in will; hence, it loves itself more completely than it loves anything else, which means that the other infinite would be loved less than perfectly.
   c. It is infinitely good, and there cannot be two infinitely good beings, for then there would be more than an infinite good, and this is impossible since there cannot be more than the most.
   d. It is infinite in power. If there were two with infinite power, this would mean that there would be two total primary causes of the same effect, and this is impossible, since there cannot be two causes each doing all the causing.
   e. Absolute infinite cannot be excelled in perfection, since there cannot be a more perfect than the wholly Perfect.
   f. There cannot be two Necessary Beings, for to differ, one would have to have some perfection the other lacked (if there is no real difference, they do not really differ). But whatever a Necessary Being has, it must have necessarily. Hence, the one lacking what the other had necessarily would not be a Necessary Being.
   g. Omnipotent will cannot be in two beings, for then one could render impotent what the other wills omnipotently. Even if they agreed not to hinder each other, they would still be incompatible, for each would be the total primary (and direct) cause of any given thing that they agreed should exist. But an omnipotent Cause must be the total primary (and direct) Cause of what it wills. The cause agreeing to, but not directly willing, the effect would be only the indirect cause and hence not the direct (omnipotent) Cause of the effect.

**Leibniz: The Argument from Sufficient Reason.* The most influential form of the cosmological argument in modern times arose from Gottfried Wilhelm Leibniz (1646–1716), the German rationalist. The proof (Leibniz, 32–39) is stated:

1. The entire (observed) world is changing.
2. Whatever is changing lacks within itself the reason for its own existence.
3. There is a sufficient reason for everything, either in itself or else beyond itself.
4. Therefore, there must be a cause beyond this world for its existence.
5. This cause is either its own sufficient reason or else it has a cause beyond it.
6. There cannot be an infinite regress of sufficient reasons, for the failure to reach an explanation is not an explanation; but there must be an explanation.
7. Therefore, there must be a First Cause of the world that has no reason beyond it but is its own sufficient reason. The sufficient reason is in itself and not beyond itself.

Under the influence of Leibniz's disciple, Christian Wolff (1679–1754), this proof became the pattern for cosmological argument in the modern world. Wolff started the argument (Collins, 137–38) in a slightly different manner:

1. The human soul exists (i.e., we exist).
2. Nothing exists without a sufficient reason for existence.
3. The reason for our existence must be contained either in ourselves or else in another, diverse from ourselves.
4. The reason for our existence is not in ourselves. Our nonexistence is possible or conceivable.
5. So the reason for our existence must be outside of ourselves.
6. One does not arrive at a sufficient reason for existence without reaching a being that has within itself the reason for its own existence. If it did not, then there must be a sufficient reason for its existence beyond itself.
7. A being that has within itself the reason for its own existence is a Necessary Being.
8. Therefore, there must be a Necessary Being beyond us that is the sufficient reason for

our existence. If there is not a Necessary Being beyond us, we would be Necessary Beings, having the reason for own existence in ourselves.

9. It is logically impossible for a Necessary Being not to exist. Self-existence or ascetic flows necessarily from the nature of a Necessary Being.
10. Hence, this Necessary Being is identical with the self-existent God of Scripture.

The Leibniz-Wolffian formulation of the cosmological argument rests heavily on the principle of sufficient reason (*see* SUFFICIENT REASON, PRINCIPLE OF), which is usually defended as a self-evidently true analytic principle. The argument is *a posteriori* in form, but not existential. It begins with the existence of something, but then proceeds toward its conclusion, so it is based on a conceptual certainty, not an actual (existential) certainty. This is precisely the point at which modern criticism of the cosmological argument begins. Even scholastic philosophers were highly influenced by this kind of reasoning (Gurr). Their reformulation of Aquinas's cosmological argument is subject to the same criticism.

Meeting Objections to the Argument. Objections against the cosmological argument, emanating largely from Immanuel Kant and David Hume, are treated at length in biographical articles on those philosophers and in the article God, Objections to Proofs for.

Taylor: Restating the Cosmological Argument. Richard Taylor occasioned renewed interest in the cosmological argument by a restatement that evades many traditional objections. Taylor's restatement takes this shape (Taylor, 279–95).

1. The universe as a whole does not explain its own existence.
   a. No observable part explains its own existence.
   b. Nor does the whole explain its existence (its nonexistence is conceivable).
   c. Answering the questions *Where? How long? What?* or *How large?* does not answer *why* the world exists when it need not exist (e.g., a large ball found in the forest needs an explanation as to *why* it exists; expanding the ball to the size of the whole universe does not eliminate the need for an explanation).
2. Whatever does not explain its own existence calls for an explanation beyond itself.
   a. It is logically possible that the principle of sufficient reason is not true. It is not analytically true; it can be denied without contradiction.
   b. But it is implausible and unreasonable to deny its truth as applied to the world. The nonexistence of the world is conceivable, whether it includes only one grain of sand or all the stars, and we assume the principle of sufficient reason in all our thought.
3. An infinite regress of reasons is impossible, for it fails to give a sufficient reason; it just indefinitely avoids giving the reason that is demanded by existence. Therefore, there must be a first self-sufficient, (independent) cause of the whole universe.

Taylor adds that it is no less meaningful to speak of God as an independent or Necessary Being than it is to speak of square circles not existing. If it is meaningful to speak of beings that are impossible, then it is meaningful to speak of a Being that is necessary. A concept of a Being that cannot *not* exist is just as meaningful as a concept of one that *cannot* exist (i.e., one that can be nonexistent).

A few comments are in order on the state of the cosmological argument in the light of Taylor's revision. It does not provide a rationally inescapable conclusion. He admits that it is logically possible that the principle of sufficient reason is not true. Taylor's argument does appear to lend plausibility to a cosmological type of argument, since it shows that it is meaningful to ask for a cause of the whole world. It shows how the concept of a Necessary Being is meaningful and argues forcefully against infinite regress. The argument is grounded in the need for an existence-explanation for the world, not in some alleged conceptual or logical necessity, as in the ontological argument.

Despite these positive factors for theism, Taylor's argument is subject to the criticisms of the rationalistic Leibniz-Wolffian tradition. It places the success of the cosmological argument in the hands of the principle of *sufficient reason*, rather than basing it squarely on the principle of *existential causality*. The world demands a real cause and not merely an explanation or reason. This cannot be accomplished by confusing and/or equating a ground for the actual here-and-now "be-ing" of the world with an explanation of the inconceivability of its nonexistence. Conceptual problems call for conceptual solutions. Real dependent beings call for an independent Being on which they are depending for their present.

Conclusion. The vertical cosmological argument is based on the premise that something is keeping the universe in existence right now. Something has not only caused the world to *come into being* (Gen. 1:1), but is also causing it to *continue to be* (cf. Col. 1:17). The world needs both an *originating* cause and a *conserving* cause. This argument provides an answer to one of the most basic of all questions: "Why is there something (right now) rather than nothing?" Briefly, it can be put this way:

1. Every part of the universe is dependent.

2. If every part is dependent, then the whole universe must also be dependent.
3. Therefore, the whole universe is dependent right now on some independent Being beyond it for its present existence.

In response, critics argue that the second premise is the fallacy of composition. Just because every piece of a mosaic is square does not mean the whole mosaic is square. Also, putting two triangles together does not necessarily make another triangle; it may make a square. The whole may (and sometimes does) have a characteristic not possessed by the parts.

Defenders of the vertical form of the cosmological argument are quick to note that sometimes there is a necessary connection between the parts and the whole. For example, if every piece of a floor is oak, then the whole floor is oak. If every tile in the kitchen is brown, then the floor is brown. The reason for this is that it is of *the very nature of* patches of brown tile that when you put more like patches of brown tile, you still have a patch of brown. And putting two triangles together does not necessarily make another triangle. Nevertheless, putting two triangles together will necessarily make another geometric figure.

Likewise, *it is of the very nature of dependent beings that when you put more of them together, you still have a dependent being.* If one thing is dependent for its being, then another dependent being can no more hold it up than can one parachutist save another if neither of their parachutes open.

Some critics respond that the whole is greater than the parts. While the parts are dependent, the whole universe is not. However, either the sum of the parts is equal to the whole or it is more than the whole. If the whole universe is equal to its parts, then the whole must be dependent, just as the parts are. Proof of this is that, when all the parts are taken away, the whole would vanish too. Thus, it must be contingent also.

If, on the other hand, the whole universe is more than the parts and would not vanish were the parts all destroyed, then the "whole" is the equivalent of God. For it is an uncaused, independent, and eternal, and Necessary Being on which the entire universe depends for its existence.

Sources

Anselm, *Monologion*
Aristotle, *Metaphysics*
J. Collins, *God in Modern Philosophy*
J. E. Gurr, *The Principle of Sufficient Reason in Some Scholastic Systems, 1750–1900*
John Duns Scotus, *Philosophical Writings*
G. Leibniz, *Monadology and Other Philosophical Essays*
A. Mauer, *A History of Medieval Philosophy*
T. Miethe, et al., *Does God Exist? A Believer and an Atheist Debate*
J. P. Moreland, et al., *The Debate between Theists and Atheists*
R. Taylor, "Metaphysics and God," D. Burrill, ed., *The Cosmological Argument*
Thomas Aquinas, *Summa Theologica*

Creation and Origins. The Bible's Hebrew word for "creation" (*bara*) and its Greek counterpart (*ktisis*) are usually reserved for the origin or beginning of things. However, even though God has completed his work *of* creation (Gen. 2:2; Exod. 20:13), he is not finished with his work *in* creation (John 5:17). Belief in a theistic creation and continued preservation of the world are often dismissed today as unscientific (*see* ANTHROPIC PRINCIPLE; BIG BANG; ORIGINS, SCIENCE OF). This view is built partly on a misunderstanding of the biblical teaching on God's creation and providence and partly on a naturalistic bias. It is notable that most founders of modern science, who were assuredly scientific in outlook, believed that evidence from the scientific world pointed to a Creator.

This is a study of importance, both in the scientific search for truth, and in Christian faith. God's literal creation of the universe is vital to Christianity (*see* CREATION, VIEWS OF; EVOLUTION; EVOLUTION, BIOLOGICAL). In addition to its implications for theism generally, Christians find in the New Testament a direct relationship between the literal creation of Adam (*see* ADAM, HISTORICITY OF) and the most basic Christian teachings.

God's Work of Origin. There is a difference between God's work in the *origin* of the world and his work in the *operation* of it. In most biblical references, there is no doubt that the word *creation* refers to the origination of the universe. Where a process may be implied, it is not the creation of the physical universe in view but the propagation of animal or human life.

The Hebrew word *Bara* is used of God's operation of the world only rarely, as in Psalm 104:30 and Amos 4:13. It is used of the origin of the world or universe in Genesis 1:1, 21, 27; 2:3, 4; 5:1, 2; 6:7; Deuteronomy 4:32; Psalm 89:11, 12; 148:5; Isaiah 40:26; 42:5; 43:1, 7; 45:8, 12; and Malachi 2:10. The Greek *Ktisis* refers to creation in Mark 10:6; 13:19; Romans 1:20; 1 Corinthians 11:9; Ephesians 3:9; Colossians 1:16; 1 Timothy 4:3, and Revelation 3:14; 4:11, and 10:6.

The Old Testament Word Bara. Genesis 1:1 (cf. 1:21, 27). "In the beginning God created the heavens and the earth." This obviously refers, not to the functioning of the universe, but to its genesis.

Genesis 2:3. "God blessed the seventh day and made it holy, because on it he rested from all the work of creating that he had done." The fact that God *rested* (ceased the act of creating) and is still in that rest (Heb. 4:4–5) proves that the word *creation* is used here of the past, singular, unrepeated events of origin.

Genesis 2:4. "This is the account of the heavens and the earth when they were created. When the LORD God made the earth and the heavens." This places the creation event in the past.

Genesis 5:1–2. The creation of Adam and Eve is also said to be past: "When God created man, he made him in the likeness of God. He created them male and female and blessed them. And when they were created, he called them 'man.'"

Genesis 6:7. God cries out to Noah, "I will wipe mankind, whom I have created, from the face of the earth—men and animals, and creatures that move along the ground, and birds of the air—for I am grieved that I have made them." Though this seems to refer to the humans alive in Noah's time, nonetheless, their *creation as a race* in Adam (Rom. 5:12) was a past event of origin. Of course, God continues with the propagation of the race (Gen. 1:28; 4:1, 25). But the creation of Adam was an event of beginning that was not repeated.

Deuteronomy 4:32. Moses said, "Ask now about the former days, long before your time, from the day God created man on the earth; ask from one end of the heavens to the other. Has anything so great as this ever happened, or has anything like it ever been heard of?"

Job 38:4, 7; Psalm 148:5. Of the angels the psalmist says, "he commanded and they were created." Job tells us the angels were already there when God "laid the earth's foundation." So the reference to creation in this psalm returns to the very beginning.

Psalm 89:11–12. Creation is used of all things God made, which are now his and give him glory: "The heavens are yours, and yours also the earth; you founded the world and all that is in it. You created the north and the south; Tabor and Hermon sing for joy at your name."

Isaiah 40:26; 42:5; 43:1, 7. God created the stars, numbered, and named them, relates Isaiah 40:26. In 42:5 he declares that God "created the heavens . . . [and] the earth and all that comes out of it" (see also Isa. 45:8, 12). God created Jacob and "everyone who is called by my [God's] name" (Isa. 43:1, 7).

Malachi 2:10. Referring to creation of the human race, Malachi says, "Have we not all one Father? Did not one God create us?" While the race has been propagated since Adam, the Bible makes it clear that it was created in Adam (Gen. 1:27; cf. Rom. 5:12). So the creation of mankind is viewed as an event of origin. Even Jesus referred to it as an event which occurred at "the beginning the Creator 'made them male and female'" (Matt. 19:4).

The New Testament Word Ktisis. Like the Old Testament, the New Testament consistently uses the word creation (*ktisis*) only to refer to a past event of origin.

Mark 10:6. When Jesus says that "at the beginning of creation God 'made them male and female,'" he no doubt means creation as a past singularity, not a regular, observable process.

Mark 13:19. "Those will be days of distress unequaled from the beginning, when God created the world, until now—and never to be equaled again." This is an unmistakable reference to creation as the point of beginning, not a process of continuing.

Romans 1:20. Paul declared that "since the creation of the world God's invisible qualities—his eternal power and divine nature—have been clearly seen, being understood from what has been made." Paul refers both to the original work of making the world and the evidence remaining from that creation event.

1 Corinthians 11:9. Original creation of a literal Adam and Eve are in view in the acts by which God made "woman from man" and "for man."

Ephesians 3:9; Colossians 1:16. Ephesians speaks of creation as a past completed action, referring to the "God, who created all things." Paul adds in Colossians that "all things *were created* through him and for him" [Christ].

1 Timothy 4:3. First Timothy 4:3 declares that "God created [all foods] to be received with thanksgiving by those who believe and who know the truth." Now while foods are being produced in the present, the reference here is to the *original* creation of food. This is evident from the use of the aorist tense, indicating completed action. Also, the phrase "to be received" points to the original purpose of the creation of food.

Revelation 3:14. The book of Revelation refers to creation as the past work of God by which things began. John noted Christ's preeminence from the very "beginning of God's creation" (Rev. 3:14; cf. Col. 1:15, 18). The heavenly host around God's throne praise God because by him all things "were created" (4:11). And the angel swore by him "who created the heavens and all that is in them, the earth and all that is in it, and the sea and all that is in it" (10:6; cf. 14:7).

God's Ongoing Creation. Some uses of *bara* and *ktisis* do refer to God's continuing work or providence. God did not cease to relate to the world he had created. He continually operates in it. He sustains its very existence.

Psalm 104:30. "When you send your Spirit, they are created, and you renew the face of the earth." Here *create* (*bara*) is used, not of the initial *generation* of life, but of its continual *regeneration*. The context speaks of God causing "the grass [to] grow for the cattle, and plants for man to cultivate" (vs. 14). It is "He [who] makes springs pour water into the ravines; it flows between the mountains" (Ps. 104:10) and who "bring[s] darkness, [and] it becomes night" (vs. 20). It is a God who continually provides food for all living things (vs. 28). The repeated emphasis is on God's preservation of his world.

Amos 4:13. "He [God] who forms the mountains, creates the wind, and reveals his thoughts to man, he who turns dawn to darkness, and treads the high places of the earth—the LORD God Almighty is his name." *Bara* here seems to be used of God's work in his creation, not simply of his original work of creation. The word *made* which is often used interchangeably with the word *create* (cf. Gen. 1:26, 27; 2:18) is used in other texts to describe God's continual providence (cf. Ps. 104:3, 4, 10).

Other Descriptions. In numerous ways, the Bible presents God at work. In addition to creating and making, he is "doing" and "causing" the operations of nature. He *sustains* it (Heb. 1:3), *holds it together* (Col. 1:17), causes it to *have being* (Rev. 4:11), *produces* life in it (Ps. 104:14). He is the continual cause of its existence. There would be no reality of creation, past or present, were it not for God.

Comparing Creation and Providence. God's dual work of creating and preserving the world are often presented in the same passage, even the same verse. Notice these revealing contrasts.

God produced and yet produces. Genesis 1:1 says "God *created* the heavens and the earth" and later he is at work through the land *"producing* vegetation" (vs. 11). The first was an act of origin; the second was one of operation. Both are the work of God.

God rested and yet is at work. Genesis 2:3 declares that "God *rested*" from his original "work of creating." But Jesus affirmed that God *"is always at his work"* (John 5:17). The former describes the commencement of his work of creation; the latter depicts the *continuance* of his work in creation.

God laid foundations of earth and yet is making it productive. Psalm 104:5 declares that God *"set* the earth on its foundations." A few verses later God is *"bringing forth* food from the earth" (vs. 14). The first is a work of originating, the second of operating. God does both.

God brought the world into being and yet keeps it in being. In Acts 17:24 the Scriptures teach that God *"made* the world." A couple of verses later it says "in him we live and move and *have our being*" (vs. 28). God is both the past cause of its *becoming* and also the present cause of its *being*.

God created the world and yet holds it together. Colossians 1:16 expresses God's past work as one by which "all things *were created*." The very next verse explains "in him all things *hold together*." The former is an act of causing to come to be. The latter is God's act of causing to continue to be.

God made the universe and yet he still sustains it. Hebrews 1:2 declares that "through him [Christ] he [God the Father] *made* the universe." Verse 3 reveals that Christ is also *"sustaining* all things by his powerful word."

The cosmos was created by God and yet has its being through him. In Revelation 4:11, the apostle John contrasts God's works of creation and preservation. He wrote, "by your will they *were created*" and also *"have* their being." All things *got* being from God and also still *have* being from him.

The reality of creation deals with origins and present operation. The Creator is necessary, not only to make it, but also to sustain it. No picture of creation is complete that neglects either work.

Explaining God's Work. As we have seen, God's work in relation to the world's existence falls into two broad categories: creating and preserving (providential care). In each of these categories there are three areas of contrast: the actor (God), his acts, and the result of his actions. The acts of God in creation and preservation can be contrasted.

God's Acts of Creating and Preserving. Scriptures already shown declare that God's acts are necessary both for the world *coming to be* as well as for it *continuing to be*. There are several ways this may be stated that highlight nuances of the distinction:

- God brought the universe from nothing, and he keeps it from returning to nothing.
- God is the beginning cause and the conserving cause of all that exists.
- God was active in life's production, and he is active in its reproduction.
- God was operative in the generating of the world, and he actively governs it. Providence refers most specifically to God's governance of all that exists and occurs.
- God was involved in making the universe, and he is involved in caring for it.
- God is responsible for originating and operating the cosmos.

These can be summarized as a chart:

Acts of Creation	**Acts of Preservation/ Providence**
Creating the world	Preserving the world
Coming to be	Continuing to be
Bringing from nothing	Keeping from nothing
Beginning	Conserving
Producing	Reproducing
Generating	Governing
Making	Caring for
Originating	Operating

God as Actor: Primary and Secondary Causality. By focusing on God as both *Originator* and chief *Operator* of creation, one can see God as both directly and indirectly involved in his world from beginning to end. While he is the *Primary Cause* of all things, God works through *secondary causes*. What we commonly refer to as the processes of nature are, in reality, God's indirect acts through secondary (or natural) causes. In this capacity, God is the *Remote Cause,* while natural forces are *proximate* causes of events. Another way to state this is that God is the *Ultimate Cause,* while nature is the *immediate* cause of most happenings. The relation between God's two roles of *Originator* and *Operator* can be summarized:

Directly, in Creation God is:	Directly, in Providence God Is:
Originator	Operator
Source	Sustainer
Creator	Conserver
Producer	Provider

Indirectly, God Is:	As He Works Through:
Primary Cause	Secondary causes
Remote Cause	Proximate causes
Ultimate Cause	Immediate causes
Original Commander	Subauthorities in chain of command

The Results. God acts in his world in two ways: by *direct intervention* (as in creation) and by *indirect action* (as in preservation). The first is an *immediate* act of God and the other is a *mediate* action. The direct acts of God are *instantaneous;* the indirect ones involve *a process*. Also, God's acts of creation are *discontinuous* with what has gone before. They are *ex nihilo* ("out of nothing") (*see* CREATION, VIEWS OF), or *de nova* (brand new). For example, he produced something from nothing, life from nonlife, and the rational from the nonrational. These are discontinuities spanned by a direct act of God (*see* EVOLUTION, BIOLOGICAL).

Further, God's acts of creation brought about *unique* events of origin, whereas his acts of preservation involve a *repetition* of events. The one produced *singularities* and the other *regularities*. The original creation events are *unobserved* today, but God's operation of the world can be *observed* in the present. The result of God's actions can be contrasted like this:

Result of God's Action(s)

Result of Direct Intervention	Result of Indirect Action
Immediate	Mediate
Instantaneous	A process
Discontinuous with past	Continuous with past
Unique event	Repetition of events
Singularity	Regularities
Unobserved	Observed

This distinction between past singularities and present regularities, both of which are acts of God, is the basis for two kinds of science: origin science and operation science.

Scientific Importance. Until after the lifetime of Darwin, the developers of modern science were creationists, in that they believed in the supernatural origin of the universe and of life. Their number includes:

- Johann Kepler (1571–1630), celestial mechanics, physical astronomy
- Blaise Pascal (1623–1662), hydrostatics
- Robert Boyle (1627–1691), chemistry, gas dynamics
- Nicholas Steno (1638–1687), stratigraphy
- Isaac Newton (1642–1727), calculus, dynamics
- Michael Faraday (1791–1867), field theory
- Charles Babbage (1792–1871), computer science
- Louis Agassiz (1807–1873), glacial geology, ichthyology
- James Simpson (1811–1870), gynecology
- Gregor Mendel (1822–1884), genetics
- Louis Pasteur (1822–1895), bacteriology
- William Kelvin (1824–1907), energetics, thermodynamics
- Joseph Lister (1827–1912), antiseptic surgery
- James Clerk Maxwell (1831–1879), electrodynamics, statistical thermodynamics
- William Ramsay (1852–1916), isotopic chemistry

In addition to these founders of scientific and mathematical fields were their forerunners, who also held to supernatural creation. Their number included Roger Bacon, 1220–1292), Nicolaus Copernicus (1473–1543), and Galileo Galilei (1564–1642). With few exceptions, scientists before 1860 were Christians. Newton's statement is typical of what scientists believed during the first two and one-half centuries of the Enlightenment:

> This most beautiful system of the sun, planets, and comets, could only proceed from the counsel and dominion of an intelligent and powerful Being. And if the fixed stars are the centres of other like systems, these, being formed by the like wise counsel, must be all subject to the dominion of One. [Newton, 369]

Kepler clarified his motives for doing science when he wrote:

> May God make it come to pass that my delightful speculation [*The Mysterium Cosmographicum*] have everywhere among reasonable men fully the effect which I strove to obtain in the publication; namely, that the belief in the creation of the world be fortified through this external support, that thought of the Creator be recognized in nature, and that

his inexhaustible wisdom shine forth daily more brightly. [cited in Holton, 84]

Not only were founders of modern science creationists, but the very concept of creation was a significant factor in the impetus for science. M. B. Foster, writing in the prestigious English journal, *Mind*, in 1934 observed that:

> The general question arises: What is the source of the un-Greek elements which were imported into philosophy by the post-reformation philosophers, and which constitute the modernity of modern philosophy? And . . . what is the source of those un-Greek elements in the modern theory of nature by which the peculiar character of the modern science of nature was to be determined? The answer to the first question is: The Christian revelation, and the answer to the second: The Christian doctrine of creation. [Foster, 448]

The Turn to Naturalism. After Charles *Darwin (1809–1882) published *On The Origin of Species* in 1859, the scene changed radically. At first a naturalistic explanation of species became dominant (*see* NATURALISM). However, added to the last paragraph of the second edition of his bombshell book, Darwin made the disclaimer that he was not insisting on a naturalistic explanation of the origin of the first living thing(s). He wrote, "There is grandeur in this view of life, with its several powers, having been originally breathed by the Creator into a few forms or into one." Although Darwin believed life arose in a "warm little pond," he did not attempt a totally naturalistic explanation of the universe (*see* EVOLUTION, COSMIC), though his view naturally pointed in that direction. Ultimately, such naturalistic explanations gained dominance.

Fallacies of Antisupernaturalism. The naturalistic bias in science is due to the rise of antisupernaturalism following the work of Benedict *Spinoza, who argued that miracles are impossible, and David *Hume, who insisted that the miraculous is incredible. Both of these arguments have flaws, as shown in the article MIRACLES, ARGUMENTS AGAINST.

Indeed, much has happened in late-twentieth-century science to turn attention back to a supernatural Creator, especially by way of the big bang view, the anthropic principle, and developments in molecular biology.

Origin Science and Operation Science. Connected with an antisupernatural presupposition, the current scientific rejection of creationist views is based on a failure to distinguish between *operation science*, which deals with observed present regularities, and *origin science*, the speculative reconstruction of unobserved past singularities. The former is an empirical science; the later operates more like a forensic science. Neither macro-evolution nor creation is an operational science. Both operate on the principles of origin science (*see* ORIGINS, SCIENCE OF). Creation is just as much a science—an origin science—as is macro-evolution.

Theological Importance. It is the created world that manifests God's glory. "The heavens declare the glory of God; and the firmament shows his handiwork" (Ps. 19:1 KJV). The psalmist declared: "O LORD, our Lord, how majestic is your name in all the earth! You have set your glory above the heavens" (Ps. 8:1). From this statement flows the basis for theistic worship.

That creatures are to worship is evident throughout Scripture. John wrote that in heaven the glory of creation will be a theme for praise. The righteous will sing: "You are worthy, our Lord and God, to receive glory and honor and power, for you created all things, and by your will they were created and have their being" (Rev. 4:11).

Paul affirmed that this worship mandate extends to all humanity and that no one is truly ignorant of the need to worship the Creator: "Since what may be known about God is plain to them, because God has made it plain to them. For since the creation of the world God's invisible qualities—his eternal power and divine nature—have been clearly seen." However, "they neither glorified him as God nor gave thanks to him, but their thinking became futile and their foolish hearts were darkened" (Rom. 1:19–20).

Because the universe is created, and is not God, it is idolatry to worship it or any part of it. The cosmos is not made of God-stuff; it is made by God from nothing. See the section on creation *ex nihilo* in CREATION, VIEWS OF. It is a grievous sin to worship and serve the "created things rather than the Creator" (Rom. 1:25). For this reason the Bible strongly condemns idolatry. God commanded: "You shall not make for yourself an idol in the form of anything in heaven above or on the earth beneath or in the waters below" (Exod. 20:4). God is as different from the world as a potter is different from the clay pot (Rom. 9:20–21). Admiration and worship should go to the Craftsman, not the thing made.

Social/Ethical Importance. *Creation Sanctifies Marriage.* Jesus rooted the moral basis for marriage in the literal creation of Adam and Eve. Responding to the question, "Is it lawful for a man to divorce his wife for any and every reason?" (Matt. 19:3), Jesus said, "Haven't you read . . . that at the beginning the Creator 'made them male and female,' and said, 'For this reason a man will leave his father and mother and be united to his wife, and the two will become one flesh'? So they are no longer two, but one. Therefore what God has joined together, let man not separate" (vss. 4–6).

Creation Endows Humans with Dignity. Moses said that *killing* humans was wrong because "in the image of God has God made man" (Gen. 9:6). James added that *cursing* other humans is wrong for the same reason: "With the tongue we praise our Lord and Father, and with it we curse men, who have been made in God's likeness" (James 3:9).

Creation Gives Meaning to Morality. All moral principles (*see* MORALITY, ABSOLUTE NATURE OF). are rooted in the absolute perfection and unchangeable nature of God (*see* GOD, NATURE OF). Creation most particularly speaks to moral principles related to relationships among human beings as fellow image-bearers of God. For example, the prohibition against killing another human being is because only God gives and has the right to take away human life (Gen. 9:6; Job 1:21). We dare not do the same without authorization, because we did not create human life and do not own it. Our moral responsibility to protect and preserve human life springs from the fact that it is created by God.

Creation Unifies Humanity. God created Adam and Eve (Gen. 1:27), and commanded them to bear children (1:28), which they did (5:1). All human beings are their descendants (1 Chron. 1:1; Luke 3:38). On the basis of this doctrine of human unity in the first parents, Paul declares to the Greek philosophers that, from one, God made every nation (Acts 17:26–29). Malachi asked, "Have we not all one father? Did not one God create us?" (2:10). One implication of this created unity is that racism is both morally wrong before the Creator and it is incorrect. There is one race only, the Adamic race, which is divided into ethnic groups. Intermarriage among these groups is permitted. Ethnic hatred is a direct attack on God's design.

Creation Defines Sexual Equality. The doctrine of creation opposes attempts by either men or women to assert preeminence over the other. Despite charges leveled against conservative Christians to the contrary, abusive and demeaning behavior violates the teaching of Scripture. God declares that both sexes are equal in his sight: "God created them, male and female . . . in his image" (Gen. 1:27). This is equality in essence. Jesus repeated this truth in Matthew 19:4. Likewise the apostle Paul noted the interdependence of man and woman: "Neither was man created for woman, but woman for man. . . . However, woman is not independent of man, nor is man independent of woman. For as woman came from man, so also man is born of woman. But everything comes from God" (1 Cor. 11:9–12).

Creation Legitimizes Government Authority. The Bible declares that "there is no authority except that which God has established. The authorities that exist have been established by God" (Rom. 13:1). In Genesis 9:6, stated above, the image of God in created humanity is so important that murderers are to be executed. Protection of human life and punishment of those who violate it became a function of government. According to the apostle Paul, the one who governs "is God's servant to do you good. But if you do wrong, be afraid, for he does not bear the sword for nothing. He is God's servant, an agent of wrath to bring punishment on the wrongdoer" (Rom. 13:4b).

Creation Grounds Roles and Authority. Male leadership or headship is a contentious issue in churches where members hold to the biblical view of creation. It is not that conservative Christians (men and women) are misogynists, as feminist-rights advocates frequently charge. Equal value and respect of men and women and an order that stresses male headship are taught in Genesis and applied to the church in the New Testament.

Paul states the principles strongly in 1 Timothy 2:11–14: "A woman should learn in quietness and full submission. I do not permit a woman to teach or to have authority over a man; she must be silent. For Adam was formed first, then Eve. And Adam was not the one deceived; it was the woman who was deceived and became a sinner." In regard to the family authority structure, Paul wrote: "Now I want you to realize that the head of every man is Christ, and the head of the woman is man, and the head of Christ is God. . . . For man did not come from woman, but woman from man; neither was man created for woman, but woman for man" (1 Cor. 11:3, 8–9). It is evident here that the order of creation is given as one basis for the authority structure within a family.

Both by order of creation and Adam's role as head of the covenant between God and humanity, the authority structure in home and church was established through the male. Adam's was the ultimate responsibility to keep the provisions of the covenant. It was his sin that brought death to the human race (see, for example, Rom. 5:12–14).

In a brief mention of a complex issue, it must be stressed that this mandate must not be considered grounds for denying the essential equality of male and female (see above). God's plan for separate roles does not speak to relative importance or value in the spiritual body of Christ where "there is neither Jew nor Greek, slave nor free, male nor female, for you are all one in Christ Jesus" (Gal. 3:28).

Creation and Fall Are Related to Salvation. Romans 5 expressly connects redemption with the literal creation of Adam: "Therefore, just as sin entered the world through one man, and death through sin, and in this way death came to all men, because all sinned. . . . For if, by the trespass of the one man, death reigned through that one man, how much more will those who receive God's abundant provision of grace and of the gift of righteousness reign in life through the one man, Jesus Christ" (Rom. 5:12, 17). In this text, the fact of literal death, which all humans experience, is directly connected with a literal Adam and his fall. Likewise, by direct comparison, the literal death of Christ and deliverance from sin is related to this literal Adam.

Creation Is Related to the Resurrection. Citing Genesis 2:24, Paul wrote in 1 Corinthians 15:45–49:

> "The first man Adam became a living being"; the last Adam, a life-giving spirit. The spiritual did not come first, but the natural, and after that the spiritual. The first man was of the dust of the earth, the second man from heaven. As was the earthly man, so are those who are of the earth; and as is the man from heaven, so also are those who are of heaven. And just as we have borne the likeness of the earthly man, so shall we bear the likeness of the man from heaven.

Paul compares a literal Adam and a literal Christ in teaching the meaning of the literal resurrection of Christ. Since Christ is the firstfruit (1 Cor. 15:20) of the believer's physical resurrection, the doctrine of Adam's creation connects with that of Christ's resurrection and believers.

Creation Is Related to the Second Coming. The apostle Peter exhorted:

> First of all, you must understand that in the last days scoffers will come, scoffing and following their own evil desires. They will say, "Where is this 'coming' he promised? Ever since our fathers died, everything goes on as it has since the beginning of creation." But they deliberately forget that long ago by God's word the heavens existed and the earth was formed out of water and by water. By these waters also the world of that time was deluged and destroyed. By the same word the present heavens and earth are reserved for fire, being kept for the day of judgment and destruction of ungodly men. But the day of the Lord will come like a thief. The heavens will disappear with a roar; the elements will be destroyed by fire, and the earth and everything in it will be laid bare. That day will bring about the destruction of the heavens by fire, and the elements will melt in the heat. But in keeping with his promise we are looking forward to a new heaven and a new earth, the home of righteousness. [2 Peter 3:1–13]

Peter vividly compares the literal creation of the world and its eventual literal destruction and eventual salvation. The truth of one is interdependent with the other. That is, the believer's confidence in the ultimate purging and restoring of creation is based on the evidence for the creation of the universe.

Conclusion. The God of the Bible is active both in the *origination* and in the *conservation* of the universe. He is the cause of it *coming to be* as well as the cause of it *continuing to be*. The kalam cosmological argument is evidence of the first kind of God's causal relation to the universe (a *horizontal causality*). And the traditional cosmological argument is evidence of God's *vertical causality* in sustaining the universe's existence right now. This last kind of causality stands in contrariety to deism. Both kinds of causality support *ex nihilo* creation. Each corresponds to a kind of science: God's originating causality is the object of *origin science* (*see* Origins, Science of), and his conserving causality is the object of *operation science*.

Science would have developed far differently had its founders from Roger Bacon on had the atheistic outlook of much of the late-twentieth-century scientific community. Most strongly believed in a planned theistic creation, with knowable, discoverable laws set in place by a Designer. Post-Darwin prejudice against any supernatural explanation for creation is actually based on a confusion between origin and operation sciences.

Indeed, even redemption is described as a new *creation* (2 Cor. 5:17), which implies connection with the "old" one. Even the doctrine of the inspiration of Scripture (*see* Bible, Evidence for), flows from the fact that there is a God who can speak the universe into existence (for example, Gen. 1:3, 6). The apostle Paul declared that the "God, who said, 'Let light shine out of darkness,' made his light shine in our hearts to give us the light of the knowledge of the glory of God in the face of Christ" (2 Cor. 4:6). Like his creation, the Word of God comes "from the mouth of God" (Matt. 4:4).

Sources

I. Asimov, *The Beginning of the End*

Augustine, *Literary Commentary on Genesis*

———, *On the Soul and Its Origin*

F. Bacon, *Novum Organum*

P. Simon de Laplace, *The System of the World*

M. B. Foster, "The Christian Doctrine of Creation and the Rise of Modern Natural Science," *Mind*, 1934

N. L. Geisler and K. Anderson, *Origin Science*

H. Gruber, *Darwin on Man*

G. Holton, *Thematic Origins of Scientific Thought*

P. Kreeft, *Between Heaven and Hell*

C. S. Lewis, *Miracles*

K. Marx, *Marx and Engels on Religion*

I. Newton, *General Sholium* in *Mathematical Principles of Natural Philosophy*

Plato, *Timaeus*

C. Sagan, *Cosmos*

Thomas Aquinas, *On the Power of God*

A. N. Whitehead, *Science and the Modern World*

Creation and Preservation. ***See*** **Creation and Origins.**

Creation, Evidence for. ***See*** **Anthropic Principle; God, Evidence for; Cosmological**

ARGUMENT; DARWIN, CHARLES; EVOLUTION, BIOLOGICAL; EVOLUTION, COSMIC; EVOLUTION, CHEMICAL; *KALAM* COSMOLOGICAL ARGUMENT; MISSING LINKS.

Creation, Views of. Three basic views seek to explain the origin of the universe. Theists (*see* THEISM) hold that all things were created *ex nihilo*, "from nothing." Pantheists (*see* PANTHEISM) believe the material universe arose *ex Deo*, "out of God," an aspect of an impersonal God's being, rather than the work of a cognizant being who acts outside of himself. Materialism (*see* MATERIALISM) affirms creation *ex materia* (out of preexisting material).

Materialists, including atheists (*see* ATHEISM) and dualists (*see* DUALISM), think that origins do not involve creation at all, if *creation* is defined as the executed work of a being. For comparison, however, materialism and pantheism can be joined under the rubric of creation. Materialistic origin can be called Creation *ex materia*, "from matter."

Creation ex Materia. A materialistic (or dualistic) view of existing things usually asserts that matter (or physical energy) is eternal. Matter always has been, and for that matter, always will be. As the physicist claims in the first law of thermodynamics, "energy can neither be created nor destroyed."

There are two basic subdivisions in the "creation-out-of-matter" view: those that involve a God and those that do not.

God Created Out of Preexisting Matter. Many ancient Greeks (dualists) believed in creation by God out of some previously existing, eternal "lump of clay" (see Plato, 27f.). That is, both God and the "stuff" of the material universe (cosmos) were always there. "Creation" is the eternal process by which God has been continually giving shape to the stuff of the universe.

*Plato called matter the *formless* (or chaos). God was the *Former* (or *Demiurgos*). Using an eternal world of *forms* (ideas), God gave shape or structure to the formless mass of matter. The Former (God), by means of the forms (ideas which flowed from the form), formed the formless (matter) into the formed (cosmos). In Greek terms, the *Demiurgos,* by means of the *eidos* (Ideas), which flowed from the *agathos* (good), formed *chaos* into a *cosmos*. Elements of platonic dualism can be disassembled easily:

Matter is eternal. The basic stuff of the universe has always been. There never was a time when the elements of the physical universe did not exist.

"Creation" means formation, not origination. "Creation" does not mean bringing something into existence. Rather, it means formation. God organizes matter that is.

The "Creator" is a Former, not a Producer. So *Creator* does not mean *Originator*, but *Builder*. God is an Architect of the material universe, not the Source of all things.

God is not sovereign over all things. Such a God is not in ultimate control, for there is something eternal besides God. Eternal matter stands in dualistic tension with God, and he cannot do anything about it. He can shape matter within certain parameters. Just as there are limits on what can be made out of paper (it is good for making kites but not space ships), so the very nature of matter is a handicap. Both the existence and nature of matter place limits on God.

There Was No God to Do the Creating. A second view is generally called *atheism, although many agnostics (*see* AGNOSTICISM) hold nearly the same worldview. An atheist says there is no God; an agnostic claims not to know whether there is a God. But neither believes it necessary to posit God in order to explain the universe. Matter is simply there. The universe is ultimately all that exists. Even mind came from matter.

The strict materialist responds to the question of where the universe came from with the question: Where did God come from? The materialist's worldview makes the question nonsensical, because the universe fills much of the conceptual place normally reserved for the Creator (*see* CAUSALITY, PRINCIPLE OF).

That creation came out of matter has been held by thinkers since the ancient atomists (*see* ATOMISM). Karl *Marx (1818–1883) was the modern philosopher who sought to carry materialism to its ultimate conclusion in socialism (Marx, 298). A century later, astronomer Carl Sagan popularized the view on television and in popular books. Much of the Western world heard Sagan's creed: *"The Cosmos is all that is, or ever was, or ever will be"* (Sagan, 4). Humanity is simply stardust pondering stars. Human beings created God. As Marx put it, mind did not create matter; matter created mind (Marx, 231).

Granting the eternal existence of matter and motion, the atheist explains everything else by the doctrines of *natural evolution* (*see* EVOLUTION, COSMIC) and *natural laws*. Natural evolution (*see* EVOLUTION, BIOLOGICAL) works by the interaction of *matter, plus time, plus chance*. Even the complexities of human life can be explained by the purely natural laws of the physical universe. Given enough time, monkeys at a typewriter can produce the works of Shakespeare. No intelligent Creator is necessary.

The Tenets of Creation ex Materia. Nontheism's concept of origins can be summarized under four points:

Matter Is Eternal. As noted above, the central premise of materialism is that matter has always been. Or, as one atheist put it, if matter came to be, it came into existence *from* nothing and *by* nothing (Kenny, 147). The material universe is a self-sustaining and self-generating closed system. Isaac Asimov speculated that there was an equal chance that nothing would come from nothing or that something would come from nothing. As luck would have it, something emerged (Asimov, 148). So either matter is eternal or else it came from nothing spontaneously without a cause.

The original materialists, atomists (*see* ATOMISM), believed matter to be a mass of innumerable indestructible pellets of reality called atoms. With the splitting of the real atom and emergence of Albert Einstein's theory of $E = MC^2$ (Energy equals mass times the speed of light squared), materialists now speak of the indestructibility of energy (the first law of thermodynamics). Energy does not pass out of existence; it simply takes on new forms. Even at death, all the elements of our being are reabsorbed by the environment and reused by other things. So the process goes on.

No Creator Is Necessary. Strict materialism demands the premise of atheism or nontheism. There is no God, or at least there is no need for a God. The world explains itself. As *The Humanist Manifesto II* put it, "As non-theists, we begin with humans not God, nature not deity" (Kurtz, 16).

Humans Are Not Immortal. Another implication is that there is no immortal (*see* IMMORTALITY) soul or spiritual aspect to human beings. *The Humanist Manifesto I* rejected "the traditional dualism of mind and body. . . . Modern science discredits such historic concepts as the 'ghost in the machine' and the 'separable soul'" (ibid., 8, 16–17). The strict materialist does not believe in spirit or mind at all. There is no mind, only a chemical reaction in the brain. Thomas Hobbes (1588–1679) defined matter:

> The world (I mean not the earth only, that denominates the lovers of it "worldly men," but the *universe*, that is, the whole mass of all things that are) is corporeal, that is to say, body; and hath the dimensions of magnitude, namely, length, breadth, and depth: also every part of body is likewise body, and hath the like dimensions; and consequently every part of the universe is body, and that which is not body is no part of the universe: and because the universe is all, that which is no part of it is nothing, and consequently nowhere. [Hobbes, 269]

Less stringent materialists admit the existence of a soul but deny that it can exist independently of matter. For them the soul is to the body what the image in the mirror is to the one looking at it. When the body dies, so does the soul. When matter disintegrates, the mind is also destroyed.

Humans Are Not Unique. Among those holding creation out of matter there are differences regarding the nature of human beings. Most accord a special status to humans, as the highest point in the evolutionary process. However, virtually all agree that humans differ only in degree, not in kind, from lower forms of life. Human beings are simply the highest and latest animal form on the evolutionary ladder. They have more highly developed abilities than primates. Certainly humans are not unique *over* the rest of the animal kingdom, even if they are the highest *in* it.

An Evaluation of Creation ex Materia. For a critique of dualism, see FINITE GODISM. The atheist position is critiqued under ATHEISM. Further, the evidence for theism is evidence against an eternal universe (*see* COSMOLOGICAL ARGUMENT; *KALAM* COSMOLOGICAL ARGUMENT; THEISM). Contemporary science has provided powerful arguments against the eternality of matter from the big bang cosmology (*see also* EVOLUTION, COSMOLOGICAL).

Creation, ex Deo. While atheists and dualists believes in creation *ex materia*, *pantheism holds to creation *ex deo,* out of god. All pantheists fall into one of two categories: absolute and nonabsolute pantheism.

Absolute Pantheism. An absolute pantheist claims that only mind (or spirit) exists. What we call "matter" is an illusion, like a dream or mirage. It appears to exist, but it really does not. This view was defended by two classical representatives, Parmenides from the West (a Greek) and Shankara from the East (a Hindu).

Parmenides argued that all is one (*see* MONISM), because to assume more than one thing exists is absurd (Parmenides, 266–83). Two or more things would have to differ from one another. But the only ways to differ are by something (being) or nothing (nonbeing). It is impossible to differ by nothing, since to differ by nothing (or nonbeing) is just another way of saying there is no difference at all. And two things cannot differ by being because being (or existence) is the only thing they have in common. That would mean they differ in the very respect in which they are the same. Hence, it is impossible to have two or more things; there can be only one being. All is one, and one is all. Nothing else really exists.

In the terminology of creation, this means that God exists and the world does not. There is a Creator but no creation. Or at least we can only say there is a creation by reckoning that creation comes out of god the way a dream comes from a mind. The universe is only the nothing else of which god thinks. God is the totality of all reality. And the nonreal about which he thinks and which appears to us is like a zero. It is literally nothing.

Shankara described the relation of the world to God, illusion to reality, by the relation of what appears to be a snake but on closer examination turns out to be a rope (see Prabhavananda, 55). When we look at the world, what is there is not reality (Brahman). Rather, it is merely an illusion (*maya*).

Likewise, when a person looks at himself, what appears to be (body) is only an illusory manifestation of what really is (soul). And when one looks into his soul, he discovers that the depth of his soul (Atman) is really the depth of the universe (Brahman). Atman (humanity) is Brahman (God). To think we are not God is part of the illusion or dream from which we must awake. Sooner or later we must all discover that all comes from God, and all is God.

Nonabsolute Pantheism. Other pantheists hold a more flexible and elastic view of reality. While they believe all is one with god, they accept a multiplicity in the unity of God. They believe all is in the one as all radii are in the center of a circle or as all drops merge into one infinite pond. Representatives of this view include the second-century neoplatonic philosopher, *Plotinus (205–270), the modern philosopher, Benedict *Spinoza (1632–1677), and the contemporary Hindu, Radhakrishnan.

According to nonabsolute pantheism, there are many things in the world, but they all spring from the essence of the One (god). The many are in the One, but the One is not in the many. That is, all creatures are part of the Creator. They come from him the way a flower unfolds from a seed or sparks come from a fire. Creatures are simply many drops that splash up from the Infinite pond, only to eventually drop back in and blend with the All. All things come from God, are part of God, and merge back into God. Technically speaking, for the pantheist, there is no creation but only an emanation of all things from God. The universe was not made out of nothing (*ex nihilo*), nor out of something preexisting (*ex materia*). It was made out of God (*ex deo*).

Significant elements in this pantheistic view of origins can be briefly outlined:

There is no absolute distinction between Creator and creation. Creator and creation are one. They may differ in perspective, as two sides of a saucer, or relationally, as cause to effect. But creator and creation are no more different than the reflection in a pond differs from the swan swimming on it. One is a mirror image of the other, real thing. Even for those who believe the world is real, Creator and creation are simply two sides of the same coin. There is no real difference between them.

The relationship between Creator and creation is eternal. Pantheists believe that God caused the world, but they insist that he has been causing it forever, just as rays shine forever from an eternal sun. The universe is as old as God. Just as one stone could rest forever on another in an eternal world, so the world could be dependent on God forever.

The world is made of the same substance as God. Pantheists believe God and the world are of the same substance. Both are comprised of god-stuff. The creation is part of the Creator. It is one in nature with God. God is water. God is trees. As Marilyn Ferguson put it, when milk is poured into cereal, God is poured into God (Ferguson, 382)! Ultimately there is only one substance, one stuff in the universe, and it is divine. We are all made of it, so we are all God.

Humanity Is God. If all of creation is the emanation of God, then so is mankind. The pop theologian of New Age pantheism, Shirley MacLaine, believes one can say with equal truthfulness, *"I am God,"* or *"I am Christ,"* or *"I am that I am"* (MacLaine, 112). In her television special miniseries, "Out on a Limb" (January 1987), she waved to the ocean and proclaimed, "I am God. I am God!" Lord Maitreya, believed by many to be the "Christ" of the New Age, declared through Benjamin Creme, his press agent, "My purpose is to show man that he need fear no more, that all of Light and truth rests within his heart, that when this simple fact is known man will become God."

An Evaluation of Creation ex Deo. There are several ways to evaluate *ex deo* creation. Since it is part of a pantheistic worldview, the criticisms of pantheism apply to it. For example, there is a real distinction between the finite and the infinite, the contingent and the necessary, the changing and the unchanging. And since I am not a necessary or unchanging Being, then I must be a contingent being. But a contingent being is one that *can* not be. And such a being actually exists only because it was caused to exist by God where otherwise it would not have existed. In short, it exists out of nothing (*ex nihilo*).

Second, as the kalam cosmological argument shows, the universe is not eternal. Hence, it came to be. But before it existed it was nothing. Or, more properly, there was nothing (except God), and after he created the world there was something (besides God). This is what is meant by *ex nihilo* creation. Therefore, whatever comes into being (as the universe did) does so from nothing, that is, *ex nihilo*.

Creation ex Nihilo. *Ex nihilo* is from the Latin meaning "from or out of nothing." It is the theistic view of origins that affirms that God brought the universe into existence without using preexisting material. Theism declares that only God is eternal and that he brought everything else into being without the use of preexisting material and without making the universe out of "pieces" of his own substance. Rather, it was made "from nothing" (*ex nihilo*).

The Coherence of ex Nihilo Creation. Some critics contend *ex nihilo* creation is a meaningless concept. Others claim it is unbiblical, a later philosophical insertion into Christian thinking.

The argument that *ex nihilo* creation is incoherent goes like this:

1. To create "out of" implies preexisting material.
2. But *ex nihilo* creation insists there was no preexisting material.
3. Hence, *ex nihilo* creation is a contradiction in terms.

In response, theists deny the first premise, pointing out that "out of nothing" is simply a positive way to state a negative concept—"not out of something." That is, God did not create the universe out of any preexisting material. The dictum that "nothing comes from nothing" is not to be understood absolutely. It means that something cannot be caused *by nothing*, not that something cannot come *after nothing*. That is, something can be created from nothing but not by nothing. God brought the universe into existence from nonexistence. *Ex nihilo* simply denotes movement from a state of nothing to a state of something. It does not imply that nothing is a state of existence *out of which* God formed something. Nothing (other than God) is a state of nonexistence that preceded the universe coming into being. When atheists and pantheists use the preposition *ex* they mean "out of" in the sense of a material cause. By *ex* a theist means an efficient cause. Midday comes "from morning," *after* morning but not literally out of it.

The Logic of ex Nihilo Creation. The basis for *ex nihilo* creation is twofold: First, the only logical alternatives are unacceptable. Second, it is the logical conclusion from the First-Cause argument for God's existence (*see* COSMOLOGICAL ARGUMENT).

The three possibilities. That *ex deo* and *ex materia* creation are incompatible with theism has been shown. Hence, *ex nihilo* creation must be true.

First of all, a theistic God cannot create *ex deo*. Since God is a simple being (*see* GOD, NATURE OF), he cannot take a "part" of himself and make the world. Simplicity means without division or parts. Thus, there is no way the created world can be a part of God. Such a view is pantheism, not theism.

Further, a theistic God is a Necessary Being, viz., one that cannot not be. He cannot come into being or cease to be. Creation is a contingent being; creation is a being that is but can not be. So, it is impossible for creation to be a part of God, since it is contingent and he is necessary. In short, a Necessary Being has no extraneous elements of his being out of which to make something. One might say God has no *parts* with which he can *part*. If he could part with them, they would not be necessary. If they are necessary he cannot part with them. So *ex deo* creation is impossible for a theistic God.

Further, a theistic God cannot create *ex materia*. For the belief that there is something eternal outside of God is not theism but dualism. There cannot be another infinite being outside of God, since it is impossible to have two infinite beings. If there are two, they must differ, and two infinite beings cannot differ in their being, since they are the very same kind of being. Two univocal beings cannot differ in their being, since that is the very respect in which they are identical. They could only differ if they were different kinds of beings (*see* ONE AND MANY, PROBLEM OF). Hence, there cannot be two infinite beings.

And if there is one infinite and one (or more) finite being(s), then the finite being cannot be an eternal Necessary Being. It cannot be necessary since it is limited by its potentiality, and any being with the potentiality not to be is not a Necessary Being. It cannot be eternal, since what is limited in its being never reaches to eternity. Therefore, it could not have preexisted forever (*see* GOD, EVIDENCES FOR).

However, if the universe is not eternal, and if God cannot create out of himself, then he must have created *ex nihilo,* since there is no alternative. For a theist, *ex nihilo* creation is thus proven.

The Argument from the First Cause. The horizontal form of the cosmological argument (*see* *KALAM* COSMOLOGICAL ARGUMENT) argues that there is a beginning of the material, space-time universe. But if the universe has a beginning, then it has not always existed. This eliminates creation *ex materia* (out of preexisting material), since there was no material before matter came into existence. There was nothing, and then there was matter which was created by God but not from any preexisting matter. In other words, if all finite being came into existence by a First Cause who always existed, then "before" it existed there was nothing other than the eternal First Cause. Hence, all finite being came into existence out of nonexistence.

Elements of ex Nihilo Creation. *The Absolute Difference between Creator and Creation.* Christian theism holds that there is a fundamental difference between the Creator and his creation. The following contrasts will focus these differences.

Creator	**Creation**
Uncreated	Created
Infinite	Finite
Eternal	Temporal
Necessary	Contingent
Changeless	Changing

God and the world are radically different. One is Maker and the other is made. God is the Cause and the world is the effect. God is unlimited and the world is limited. The Creator is self-existing but creation is entirely dependent on him for its existence.

Some illustrations may help to further clarify the real distinction between Creator and creation. In *pantheism, God is to the world what a pond is to the drops of water in it, or what a fire is to the sparks that come from it. But in theism God is to the world what the painter is to a painting or the playwriter is to a play. While the artist is, in some sense, manifest *in* the art, he is also *beyond* it. The painter is not the painting. Its maker is beyond, over, and above it. The Creator of the world causes it to exist and is revealed in it; but God is not the world.

Creation Had a Beginning. Another crucial element of the theistic view of creation from nothing is that the universe (everything except God) had a beginning. Jesus spoke of his glory with the Father "before the world was" (John 17:5). Time is not eternal. The space-time universe was brought into existence. The world did not always exist. The world did not begin *in* time. The world was the beginning *of* time. Time was not there *before* creation and then at some moment in time God created the world. Rather, it was not a creation *in* time but a creation *of* time.

This does not mean that there was a time when the universe was not. For there was no time before time began. The only thing "prior" to time was eternity. That is, God exists forever; the universe began to exist. Hence, he is prior to the temporal world ontologically (in reality), but not chronologically (in time).

To say that creation had a beginning is to point out that it came into being out of nothing. First it did not exist, and then it did. It was not, and then it was. The cause of that coming to be was God.

Illustrating ex Nihilo Creation. There really are no perfect illustrations of *ex nihilo* creation, since it is a unique event that does not occur in our experience. We only experience something coming from something. Nonetheless, there are imperfect but helpful analogies. One is the creation of a new idea, which brings into existence something that did not exist before. We literally conceive it or conjure it up. We create it, as it were, out of nothing. Of course, unlike the physical universe, ideas are not matter. But like God's *ex nihilo* creation, they are brought into existence by a creative intelligence.

Another illustration of *ex nihilo* is an act of free will, by which a free agent initiates an action that did not before exist. Since a free choice (*see* FREE WILL) is self-determined, it did not spring from previous conditions. Hence, much like *ex nihilo,* it does not flow from previous states. Rather, a free choice is not determined by anything else; it literally creates the action itself.

Support for ex Nihilo Creation. One of the oldest extrabiblical recorded statements on creation known to archaeologists, over 4,000 years old, makes a clear statement on *ex nihilo* creation: "Lord of heaven and earth: the earth was not, you created it, the light of day was not, you created it, the morning light you had not [yet] made exist" (*Ebla Archives,* 259). Creation from nothing is clearly expressed outside the Bible in 2 Maccabees 7:28. It says, "Look at the heavens and the earth and see everything that is in them, and recognize that God did not make them out of things that existed."

While the Hebrew word for "creation," *bara*, does not necessarily mean to create from nothing (cf. Ps. 104:30), nevertheless, in certain contexts it can mean only that. Genesis 1:1 declares: "In the beginning God created the heavens and the earth." Given the context that this is speaking about the original creation, *ex nihilo* seems to be implied here. Likewise, when God commanded: "Let there be light," there was light (Gen. 1:3), *ex nihilo* creation is involved. For light literally, and apparently instantaneously, came to be where previously it was not.

Psalm 148:5 declares: "Let them [angels] praise the name of the Lord, for he commanded and they were created."

Jesus affirmed: "And now, Father, glorify Me in Your presence with the glory I had with You before the world began" (John 17:5). This phrase is repeated in 1 Corinthians 2:7 and 2 Timothy 1:9. Obviously, if the world had a beginning, then it did not always exist. It literally came into existence out of nonexistence. In this sense, every New Testament passage that speaks of the "beginning" of the universe assumes *ex nihilo* creation (cf. Matt. 19:4; Mark 13:19). Romans 4:17 asserts *ex nihilo* creation in very clear and simple terms: "God who gives life to the dead and calls things that are not as though they were." In Colossians 1:16 the apostle Paul added, "For by him all things were created: things in heaven and on earth, visible and invisible." This eliminates the view that the visible universe is simply made out of invisible matter, since even the invisible created realm was brought into existence.

In the Apocalypse John expressed the same thought, declaring, "for You created all things, and by Your will they were created and have their being" (Rev. 4:11).

From Genesis to Revelation, the Bible declares the doctrine of God's creation of everything else that exists, other than himself, out of nothing.

Criticism of Ex Nihilo Creation. There are several important implications of creation *ex nihilo*. Most of them arise out of misunderstandings of the view.

It Does Not Imply Time before Time. It is objected that the view implies that there was time before time began, since it holds that time had a beginning and yet God existed before (a temporal term) time began. This objection is answered by the theist by pointing out that *before* is not used here as a temporal term, but to indicate ontological priority. Time did not exist before time, but God did. There was no time before time, but there was eternity. For the universe, nonbeing came "before" being in a logical sense, not a chronological one. The Creator is "before all time" only by a priority of nature, not of time. God did not create in time; he executed the creation of time.

It Does Not Imply Nothing Made Something. Sometimes *ex nihilo* creation is criticized as though it affirmed that nothing made something. It is clearly absurd to assert that nonbeing produced being (*see* CAUSALITY, PRINCIPLE OF). For in order to create there must be an existing cause, but nonexistence does not exist. Hence, nothing cannot create something. Only something (or someone) can cause something. Nothing causes nothing.

In contrast to nothing producing something, *ex nihilo* creation affirms that Someone (God) made something from nothing. This is in accord with the fundamental law of causality which demands that everything that comes to be is caused. Nothing cannot bring something into existence, but Someone (God) can bring something other than himself into existence, where prior to that it did not exist. So, for theism, creation from nothing does not mean creation by nothing.

It Does Not Imply "Nothing" Is Something. When the theist declares that God created "out of nothing," he does not mean that "nothing" was some invisible, immaterial something that God used to make the material universe. Nothing *means* absolutely nothing. That is, God, and utterly nothing else, existed. God created the universe, and then alone did something else exist.

Conclusion. Ex nihilo creation is both biblically grounded and philosophically coherent. It is an essential truth of Christian theism which clearly distinguishes it from other worldviews, such as pantheism (*ex deo*) and atheism (*ex materia*). Objections to *ex nihilo* creation do not stand in the face of careful scrutiny.

Sources

Creation ex Materia

I. Asimov, *The Beginning of the End*
N. L. Geisler, *Knowing the Truth about Creation*
T. Hobbes, *Leviathan*
A. Kenny, *Five Ways*
P. Kreeft, *Between Heaven and Hell*
P. Kurtz, *Humanist Manifestos I* and *II*
K. Marx, *Marx and Engels on Religion*, R. Niebuhr, ed.
Plato, *Timaeus*
C. Sagan, *Cosmos*

Creation ex Deo

M. Ferguson, *The Aquarian Conspiracy*
N. L. Geisler, *Christian Apologetics*
———, and W. Watkins, *Worlds Apart*
S. MacLaine, *Dancing in the Light*
Parmenides, *Proem*, G. S. Kirk, et al., *The Presocratic Philosophers*
Plotinus, "The Six Enneads"
Prabhavananda, *The Upanishads: Breath of the Eternal*
S. Radhakrishnan, *The Hindu View of Life*
B. Spinoza, *A Theologico-Political Treatise*

Creation ex Nihilo

Anselm, *Prologium*
Augustine, *City of God*
Philo, *The Works of Philo*
Thomas Aquinas, *Summa Theologica*

Creationists, Early. ***See*** **CREATION AND ORIGINS.**

Crucifixion of Christ. ***See*** **CHRIST, DEATH OF.**

Dd

Daniel, Dating of. The book of Daniel contains an incredible amount of detailed predictive prophecy. It claims to speak of many of the great kingdoms in the course of human history well in advance of their times: Babylon, Medo-Persia, Greece, and Rome. If true, it is one of the great evidences of the divine origin of the Bible, and by comparison, of other books of the Bible (*see* PROPHECY, AS PROOF OF THE BIBLE).

History or Predictive Prophecy? Daniel looked ahead in time to the kingdoms of the Gentiles from the reign of Nebuchadnezzar, starting about 605 B.C., down to the Roman Empire, which began to exercise dominance as early as 241 B.C. and, under the Roman general Pompey, took over Palestine in 63 B.C. So the book of Daniel describes world events hundreds of years into the future (Dan. 2:7). Daniel 11 presents a sweeping display of detail from the reign of Cyrus the Great to the reign of antichrist, the millennial kingdom, and the end of the age.

If Daniel wrote in the sixth century B.C., as conservative scholars have maintained, then it is a powerful example of predictive prophecy. However, if Daniel is dated around 170 B.C., as many critical scholars argue, he is writing history and not prophecy. One of the great arguments for the supernatural origin of biblical prophecy is then lost.

Internal Evidence Supports an Early Writing. There is persuasive evidence that Daniel lived and wrote in the sixth century B.C. and that, therefore, his detailed descriptions of history were supernatural predictions.

These events are presented as future. Their writing is dated by specific years of the reigns of kings of Babylon and Media-Persia (for example, the opening verses of chapters 2, 7, 9, 10, and 11). They were things that the wisest men in the greatest kingdom on earth could not divine (cf. Dan. 2:1–13). The text states explicitly that they were about the future, "what will be in the later days" (Dan. 2:28; cf. 9:24–29). It even declares that "the appointed time was long" in Daniel 10:1, indicating the distant future. Hence, an attack on the predictive nature of Daniel's words is an attack on his character. Yet only Joseph among Old Testament figures shows the impeccable character of Daniel (cf. Dan. 1:4, 8; 6:3). Even his enemies recognized that they could not find fault in his character or dedication (Dan. 6:5).

The historical parts of Daniel are such clear, detailed, and accurate descriptions of his times as to lend credibility to his discourse when they speak about the future. Daniel's clear distinction of the present from the future alone is evidence that he was consciously writing prophecy, not history, in his great visions.

Before the rise of modern antisupernaturalism, the sixth-century date for Daniel (and, hence, its predictive nature) was not questioned among biblical scholars. Interestingly, it was not discovery of some archaeological or historical fact that led modern scholars after Benedict *Spinoza to attribute a second-century date to Daniel. Rather, the (unproved) philosophical presupposition of antisupernaturalism led them to assume a late date (*see* MIRACLE; MIRACLES, ALLEGED IMPOSSIBILITY OF).

That Daniel's prophecies were postdated in historical accounts shows his accuracy. Otherwise, why all the effort on the part of those who reject the supernatural origin of his prophecies to date them after the time in which events actually occurred?

Witnesses Support an Early Writing. Josephus (*see* FLAVIUS JOSEPHUS), a Jewish historian from the time of Christ, listed Daniel among *the Prophets* (the second section of the Jewish Old Testament), not among *the Writings* (the third and last section). At that date, then, Daniel was considered a prophet, not a historian. Also, the Prophets were considered to be older. Indeed, one reason for the late dating of Daniel is that it was listed among the Writings in the later Jewish Talmud (A.D. 400). However, the normal Old Testament division by later Jewish scholars was *the*

Law and *the Prophets* (see Dan. 9:2, 11–13; Zech. 7:12; Matt. 5:17; Luke 24:27). The unconventional Talmud listing may have been designed for liturgical, topical, or literary uses (see Geisler, chap. 14).

Jesus confirmed that Daniel was a prophet. In fact, Jesus used the example of a prediction made by Daniel that was yet future in Jesus' day. Looking ahead to the coming destruction of Jerusalem and the temple by the Roman army of Titus, Jesus referred to "the abomination that causes desolation," which would be standing in the holy place of the temple (Matt. 24:15). And there is strong historical evidence that the Synoptic Gospels were written before A.D. 70 (*see* ACTS, HISTORICITY OF; BIBLE CRITICISM; NEW TESTAMENT, HISTORICITY OF). The evidence supports Jesus' claim to be the Son of God. Such an intertwining of prophetic credentials means that to deny the predictive nature of Daniel's prophecies is a step toward denial of the deity of Christ (*see* CHRIST, DEITY OF).

Dead Sea manuscripts support an early Daniel. A fragment of Daniel from possibly the second century B.C. was found among the *Dead Sea scrolls at Qumran. Since this was only a copy, it would place the book earlier.

Daniel the man is mentioned in Ezekiel 14:14, 20; 28:3. Even critics recognize Ezekiel as contemporary with the sixth century. But if the only Daniel the prophet known in Old Testament times came from the sixth century, there is no reason to reject his prophecies as coming from this period as well. This is particularly true in view of the vivid, firsthand, eyewitness nature of the book.

The Jewish Talmud attributes the book of Daniel to the prophet Daniel who lived in the sixth century B.C. This lends the support of later Jewish scholars.

Even a Late Daniel Accurately Predicted. Even a late date of about 170 B.C. would make some of Daniel's predictions still future and supernaturally accurate. Some of his most sensational predictions were fulfilled at the time of Christ. Daniel 9:24–27 predicted that Christ would die, having made "reconciliation for iniquity" and having brought in "everlasting righteousness" some 483 years after 444 B.C. According to the Jewish lunar year of 360 days there are exactly 483 between 444 B.C. and 33 A.D. For added to the 477 lunar years (444 + 33) must be another six years (= 483). There are five more days (365) in an actual year than in a lunar year (360). And five days times 477 is 2385 days. That adds up to another six and one-half years (*see* HOEHNER, X).

Objections to a Predictive Daniel. *Jewish Scripture Lists Daniel as a "Writing."* Why, critics ask, if Daniel was a prophet, is his book not listed among the Prophets in the Jewish Bible but only later among the Writings? As noted above, this was a late decision, about A.D. 400 Daniel was originally listed among the Prophets. In the first century A.D., the Jewish historian Josephus listed Daniel among the prophets (*Against Apion* 1.8). In the later division of the Prophets into Prophets and Writings it was understandable that Daniel would fit in the Writings. Chapters 1 through 6 contains much history. Also, Daniel was a prophet by gift but not office, since he had a significant political role to play in the Babylonian government.

The Theology Is Too Highly Developed. Some critics assert that Daniel could not have written in the sixth century because the book's highly developed view of angels, the Messiah, the resurrection, and the final judgment are known to exist only in a later period.

This argument begs the question. If Daniel is an earlier book, then Daniel is proof that this "highly developed" theology existed at that time. Job and Isaiah are earlier books, and they refer to the resurrection (Job 19:25, 26; Isa. 26:19). Both Malachi and Zechariah were written before the second century, and they refer to the Messiah (Zech. 3:1; 6:12; Mal. 3:1; 4:2). Angels are prominent in Genesis (see chaps. 18, 19, 28) and throughout Zechariah.

Daniel Allegedly Erred. Some critics charge that the book makes historical errors. This argument shows that what is actually in dispute is not the dating of Daniel, but the divine inspiration of Scripture. It would make more sense if an early Daniel would be historically inaccurate. A later writer would know what happened.

However, none of the errors charged to Daniel has stood (see Archer, 380–93). For example, according to Daniel 5:31, the kingdom of Belshazzar fell to an invading army, and "Darius the Mede" became king. However, modern scholars have found no mention of such a person in ancient documents. Some modern scholars claim that the author of Daniel mistakenly thought that the Medes, rather than the Persians, conquered Babylon. They claim that this author confused Darius I, king of Persia (521–486 B.C.), with the conqueror of Babylon and identified this figure as Darius the Mede. This, they charged, appears to be an error in Daniel's account.

Modern archaeological evidence (*see* ARCHAEOLOGY, OLD TESTAMENT) shows that Darius the Mede could easily have been a different person than Darius I of Persia. Two men equally fit Daniel's references. Cyrus the Great, who ruled a united Medo-Persian empire, may well have been from the Median side of this alliance and could have been known outside official communications as Darius the Mede. That Daniel identifies this Darius as Median fits the Persian context where that would have been noteworthy.

A better candidate who has turned up in cuneiform texts is *Gubaru*, who was appointed by Cyrus to be governor over all of Babylonia. The common practice in Babylonian and Persian aristocracy, particularly for emigrants, was for private names to reflect an individual's background and family, while an official name represented political realities of the person's new allegiances. Daniel was known in his official capacities as Belteshazzar (Dan. 1:7). Shadrach, Meshach, and Abed-nego were Babylonian names for the Hebrew men Hananiah, Mishael, and Azariah.

In the article "Daniel in the Historians' Den," William Sierichs, Jr. affirms that Belshazzar was not the "son" of Nebuchadnezzar, and "Belshazzar was not the ruler as the Book of Daniel claims, and he was never king" (*TSR*, vol. 7.4, p. 8). But even the radical critic Dr. Philip R. Davies has admitted that both are "weak arguments" (Philip R. Davies, *Daniel* [Sheffield: JSOT Press, 1985], p. 31). He wrote:

> Critical commentaries, especially around the turn of the century, made much of the fact that Belshazzar was neither a son of Nebuchadnezzar nor king of Babylon. This is still sometimes repeated as a charge against the historicity of Daniel, and resisted by conservative scholars. But it has been clear since 1924 (J.. A. Montgomery, *Daniel,* International Critical Commentary [Edinburgh: T and T Clark/New York: C. Scribner's Sons, 1927], pp. 66–67) that although Nabonidus was the last king of the Neo-Babylonian dynasty, Belshazzar was effectively ruling Babylon. In this respect, then, Daniel is correct. The literal meaning of 'son' should not be pressed. . ." (pp. 30–31).

Daniel's Vocabulary is From a Later Period. Linguistic critics find terms in Daniel that supposedly were not in use until the second century B.C. It is alleged that such words as *harp, sackbut,* and *psaltery* originated in the later Maccabean period (second century B.C.) and not the sixth century. Old Testament scholar R. K. Harrison observes that "this argument no longer constitutes a problem in the criticism of the book, because as [William F.] Albright has shown, it is now well recognized that Greek culture had penetrated the Near East long before the Neo-Babylonian period" (Harrison, 1126). Further, this argument is logically a fallacy from ignorance. Just because a word is not *known* to have been used at any earlier period doesn't mean it was not, unless we have omniscience about language use throughout a past society. And as more is known linguistically about ancient cultures, scholars are finding evidence of earlier usage (see Archer, 380–93).

Conclusion. There is strong evidence that Daniel's predictions come from the sixth century B.C., making them amazing predictions of the course of history from Babylon through Medo-Persia, Greece and Rome to after the time of Christ. Critics gain nothing by postdating Daniel. Their latest date still demands that Daniel wrote outstanding examples of supernatural predictive prophecy (Daniel 9). If those are true prophecies, why not the others?

Sources

G. L. Archer, Jr., *A Survey of Old Testament Introduction*

———, *An Encyclopedia of Biblical Difficulties*

N. L. Geisler, *A Popular Survey of the Old Testament*

——— and T. Howe, *When Critics Ask*

H. Hoehner, *Chronological Aspects of the Life of Christ*

R. K. Harrison, *Introduction to the Old Testament*

J. McDowell, *Daniel in the Critics Den*

J. Whitecomb, *Darius the Mede*

Darius the Mede. *See* DANIEL, DATING OF.

Darrow, Clarence. Clarence Darrow (1857–1938) was a well-known attorney practicing criminal law through the early twentieth century. He is best known for his defense of a man who was charged with teaching evolution (*see* EVOLUTION, BIOLOGICAL) in public schools. Through the Scopes trial in Dayton, Tennessee (1925), Darrow was able to champion his own strongly held views as an evolutionist and agnostic (*see* AGNOSTICISM). The Christian statesman William Jennings Bryan (1860–1925) represented the state and died a few days after the verdict.

The Real Darrow. Darrow has been widely quoted as saying, "It is bigotry for public schools to teach only one theory of origins" (McIver, 1–13). Wendell Bird, whose 1978 *Yale Law Review* article has been responsible for many of the citations of this alleged quotation, has subsequently recognized that this statement probably is not authentic.

Darrow also has been misquoted to the effect that he believed creation was a scientific view. He declared at the Scopes trial that children should have "both" creation and evolution. He meant evolution should be taught as science and creation as theology. This fits his argument at the trial and his declaration a few years later: "In fact, there is no other theory to teach regarding the origin of the various animal species, including man" (Darrow, 275).

Darrow and the Charge of Bigotry. He did believe that passing and defending the Tennessee creation law was "bigotry" and used the word *bigotry* or *bigot* six times on only two pages of trial transcript (Hilleary, 75, 87). Bryan said on the witness stand, "I am perfectly willing that the world shall know that these gentlemen have no other purpose than ridiculing every Christian who believes in the Bible." Darrow snapped back, "We have the purpose of preventing *bigots* and ignoramuses from controlling the education of the United States and you know it, and that is all" (ibid., 299, emphasis added).

In another place Darrow argued that "Unless there is left enough of the spirit of freedom in the state of Tennessee, and in the United States, there is not a single line of any constitution that can withstand *bigotry* and ignorance when it seeks to destroy the rights of the individual; and bigotry and ignorance are ever active" (ibid., 75, emphasis added).

Darrow even refers to Thomas *Jefferson, asking, "Can a legislative body say, 'You cannot read a book or take a lesson, or make a talk on science until you first find out whether what you are saying [is] against Genesis. . . .' It could—except for the work of Thomas Jefferson, which has been woven into every state constitution of the Union, and has stayed there like the flaming sword to protect the rights of man against ignorance and *bigotry*" (ibid., 83).

At another point Darrow appealed to the judge, pleading, "Your honor knows that the fires that have been lighted in America to kindle religious *bigotry* and hate. . . . You know that there is no suspicion which possesses the mind of men like *bigotry* and ignorance and hatred" (ibid., 87, emphasis added). Even the lawyers opposing Darrow took note of his use of the word *bigots*, saying, "They say it is sponsored by a lot of religious *bigots*. Mr. Darrow said that, substantially that" (ibid., 197, emphasis added).

These citations leave no doubt that Darrow believed that those who produced, promoted, and defended the Tennessee anti-evolution law were bigots for denying the right to teach evolution in the public schools, even though creation was not being taught. It is interesting to observe precisely what Darrow himself was promoting to see if he himself remains above the charge of bigotry.

What Darrow Was Defending. Darrow obviously was challenging the law in order to establish the teaching of evolution. Yet, even evolutionists acknowledge that "the Dayton public schools were only teaching one view—evolution—and that was what Darrow was trying to defend" (McIver, 9). If so, then Darrow's plea, "Let them have both. Let them both be taught" rings hollow. Certainly he did not advocate that the Genesis account be taught in public schools, even as theology. Darrow was categorically opposed to teaching religion in the public schools.

Darrow's reference to Jefferson is infelicitous, since Jefferson believed that "all men were created . . ." and even refers to the "Creator" in *The Declaration of Independence*. Jefferson would be surprised to return to America and find that a new society has declared it unconstitutional to teach the truths of the *Declaration of Independence* in public schools. Jefferson himself set up a department of divinity in his state supported University of Virginia and signed into law a treaty with the Kaskaskia Indians (1803) to pay a Catholic missionary to do mission work with them.

Evaluation. The view that only evolution is scientific and only creation is religious is a form of definitional bigotry. If creation is not scientific, then most of the major scientists between 1620 and 1860 were not scientific when they said that scientific evidence points to a Creator (*see* CREATION AND ORIGINS).

As argued elsewhere (*see* ORIGINS, SCIENCE OF), creation is as scientific as is macro-evolution (Geisler, *Origin Science*, chaps. 6, 7). Neither creation nor macro-evolution represents an *empirical* science. No creature observed the origin of the universe and life, and it is not being repeated today. However, both creationist and evolutionist views are "scientific" in the sense of *forensic* science. They are simply speculative reconstructions of past unobserved events on the basis of remaining evidence. To argue that we can allow public school science teachers to teach evolution is to allow speculation about possible natural causes but not possible intelligent causes. By this same logic, archaeologists are not scientific when they posit an intelligent cause for ancient pottery. Darrow would have been more consistent in defending scientific inquiry and academic freedom if he had actually said the statement attributed to him: "It is bigotry for public schools to teach only one theory of origins!"

Sources

C. Darrow, *The Story of My Life*

N. L. Geisler, *The Creator in the Courtroom*

———, *Origin Science: A Proposal for the Creation-Evolution Controversy*, chapters 6, 7

———, "Was Clarence Darrow a Bigot?" in *C/E*, Fall 1988

W. Hilleary and W. Metzger, *The World's Most Famous Court Trial*

T. McIver, "Creationist Misquotation of Darrow," in *C/E*, Spring 1988

I. Newton, "General Scholium," *Mathematical Principles of Natural Philosophy*, Book 3, "The Systems of the World"

Darwin, Charles. Charles Robert Darwin (1809–1882) was born in Shrewsbury, England, the son of a physician. As a naturalist, he won sponsors and government backing for an expedition on the military sailing ship HMS Beagle, where he made his famous observations on the differences in finches. Later he used what he had learned on this ship as evidence for his theory of evolution (*see* CREATION AND ORIGINS; CREATION, VIEWS OF; EVOLUTION; EVOLUTION, BIOLOGICAL; EVOLUTION, CHEMICAL; MISSING LINKS).

Darwin is most famous for his *On the Origin of Species* (1859), in which he suggested in the last lines of the first edition that "whilst this planet has gone cycling on according to the fixed law of gravity," therein, "life, with its several powers, having been originally breathed [by the Creator] into a few forms or into one . . . from so simple a beginning endless forms most beautiful and most wonderful have been, and are being, evolved." The bracketed phrase was added in the second edition of *Origin*. Not until his later work, *The Descent of Man* (1871), did Darwin proclaim that humans too had evolved by natural processes from lower forms of life. This view caused a revolution in the sciences, the reverberations of which are still being felt.

It was a turning point in modern thought because, in the minds of many, Darwin gave the first plausible explanation of how evolution could have occurred. By applying the principle of natural selection (the survival of the fittest) to variations within populations, Darwin was able to argue persuasively that over long periods of time small changes added up to large ones. These large changes can account for the origin of new species without the direct intervention of a supernatural Power, except perhaps to get the whole process going.

Evolution of Darwin's God. Darwin began as a Christian theist, was baptized in the Church of England, and despite his rejection of Christianity, was buried in Westminster Abbey. Darwin's life is a microcosm of the increasing disbelief of the late eighteenth century (*Darwin's Early Religious Training*).

Although an Anglican, Darwin was sent to a school conducted by a Unitarian minister (Moore, 315). He later entered the University of Cambridge in 1828 where, his father had decided, he should prepare for the ministry (ibid.). At this early age, and with the aid of Pearson's *Exposition of the Creed* and Bishop Sumner's *Evidence of Christianity Derived from Its Nature and Reception* (1824), "Darwin abandoned whatever were his scruples about professing belief in all the doctrines of the Church" (ibid.). Nonetheless, Darwin was deeply impressed with William Paley's *A View of the Evidences of Christianity* (1794); and *Natural Theology; or, Evidences of the Existence and Attributes of the Deity* (1802).

Darwin's Original Theistic Beliefs. He accepted *Paley's design argument (*see* TELEOLOGICAL ARGUMENT). In his *Autobiography* he referred to his Journal entry "that whilst standing in the midst of the grandeur of a Brazilian forest 'it is not possible to give an adequate idea of the higher feelings of wonder, admiration, and evolution which fill and elevate the mind.'" He adds, "I remember my conviction that there is more in man than the mere breath of his body" (Darwin, *Autobiography,* 91).

Darwin recognized "the extreme difficulty or rather impossibility of conceiving this immense and wonderful universe, including man with his capacity of looking far backward and far into futurity, as the result of blind chance or necessity." Thus, "when reflecting I feel compelled to look to a First Cause having an intelligent mind in some degree analogous to that of man; and I deserve to be called a Theist." Darwin acknowledged that he once had been a creationist. He even spoke of it as a view "which most naturalists until recently entertained, and which I formerly entertained" (Darwin, 30). "This conclusion was strong in my mind about the time, as far as I can remember, when I wrote the *Origin of Species;* and it is since that time that it has very gradually become weaker" (Darwin, *Autobiography,* 92–93).

Darwin's Rejection of Christianity. By 1835, before Darwin set sail on the *Beagle* (in 1836), he was yet a creationist. Darwin describes his own religious descent in his *Autobiography*. He wrote, "Whilst on board the *Beagle* [October 1836–January 1839] I was quite orthodox, and I remember being heartily laughed at by several of the officers (though themselves orthodox) for quoting the bible as an unanswerable authority on some point of morality." However, he did not believe the Bible was an unanswerable authority on science at this time. According to Ernst Mayr, Darwin had become an evolutionist some time between 1835 and 1837 (Mayr, x). "By 1844, his views [on evolution] had reached considerable maturity, as shown by his manuscript 'Essay'" (ibid.). Charles Darwin's son and biographer, Francis Darwin said that "Although Darwin had nearly all the key ideas of the *Origin* in mind as early as 1838, he deliberated for twenty years before committing himself publicly to evolution" (F. Darwin, 3.18). Only a decade later (1848) Darwin was fully convinced of evolution, defiantly declaring to J. D. Hooker: "I don't care what you say, my species theory is all gospel" (cited by Moore, 211).

Darwin's declining Christian beliefs began with an erosion of the trustworthiness of the Bible. It is true that as late as 1848 he read Harvard's Professor Andrew Norton *(The Evidence of the Genuineness of the Gospels)* who argued that the Gospels "remain essentially the same as they were originally composed" and that "they have been ascribed to their true authors" (Moore, 212). However, his faith in the Old Testament had eroded some years before this (*see* BIBLICAL CRITICISM).

The acceptance of negative higher criticism. But "I had gradually come, by this time to see that the Old Testament from its manifestly false history of the world, with its Tower of Babel, the rainbow as a sign, etc., etc., and from its attribution to God the feelings of a revengeful tyrant, was no more to be trusted than the sacred books of the Hindoos, or the beliefs of any barbarian" (Darwin, *Autobiography,* 85).

The acceptance of antisupernaturalism. Both Benedict *Spinoza in 1670 and David *Hume a century later had attacked the basis of supernatural intervention in the world. Darwin added, "By further reflection that the clearest evidence would be requisite to make any sane man believe in miracles by which Christianity is supported—that the more we know of the fixed laws of nature the more incredible do miracles become—that the men of that time were ignorant and credulous to a degree almost incomprehensible by us—that the Gospels cannot be proved to have been written simultaneously with the events—that they differ in many important details, far too important as it seemed to me to be admitted as the usual inaccuracies of eyewitnesses—by such reflections as these . . . I gradually came to disbelieve in Christianity as a divine revelation" (*Autobiography,* 86).

Nonetheless, Darwin added, "I was very unwilling to give up my belief. . . . thus disbelief crept over me at a very slow rate, but was at last complete. The rate was so slow that I felt no distress, and have never since doubted even for a single second that my conclusion was correct" (ibid., 87).

*The "damnable doctrine" of *hell.* Darwin notes that the orthodox belief in hell was a particular influence in his rejection of Christianity. He wrote: "I can indeed hardly see how anyone ought to wish Christianity to be true; for if so plain language of the text seems to show that the men who do not believe, and this would include my Father, Brother and almost all my best friends, will be everlastingly punished. And this is a damnable doctrine" (ibid., 87).

The death of Darwin's daughter. Darwin's increased skepticism was completed by the death of his beloved daughter, Anne in 1851. Biographer James Moore notes that "Two strong emotions, anger and grief, in the *Autobiography* mark off the years from 1848 to 1851 as the period when Darwin finally renounced his faith" (Moore, 209). This, of course, was just after his view in evolution had solidified (1844–1848) and before he wrote his famous *Origins* (1859).

Although Darwin's heirs suppressed the effect this death had on Darwin, his own words betray its impact (see Moore, 220–23). Connected to the doctrine of eternal punishment, Darwin could see no reconciliation between the life of a perfect child and a vengeful God (ibid., 220). Referring to himself as a "horrid wretch," one of the condemned, in May 1856 he warned a young entomologist: "I have heard Unitarianism called a feather-bed to catch a falling Christian; & I think you are now on just such a feather bed, but I believe you will fall much lower & lower" (cited by Moore, 221). A month later, Darwin referred to himself as "the Devil's Chaplain," a satirical figure of speech of a confirmed unbeliever (Moore, 222; *see* EVIL, PROBLEM OF).

Darwin's Descent. Darwin gradually discarded theism for *deism, leaving the single act of divine intervention for the creation of the first form or forms of life. This was apparently his view at the time of *On the Origin of Species* (1859) where, in the second edition he spoke of "life, with its several powers, having been originally breathed *by the Creator* into a few forms or into one . . . from so simple a beginning endless forms most beautiful and most wonderful have been, and are being, evolved" (emphasis added).

Paley's design argument rejected. Although Darwin clung to a deistic God who created the world but let it operate by "fixed natural laws," gradually he came to reject even the cogency of the design argument. He said he was "driven" to the conclusion that "the old argument of design in nature, as given by Paley, which formerly seemed to me so conclusive, fails, now that the law of natural selection had been discovered. . . . there seems to be no more design in the variability of organic beings and in the action of natural selection, than in the course which the wind blows. Everything in nature is the result of fixed laws" (ibid., 87). Darwin wrote: "I am inclined to look at everything as resulting from designed laws, with the details, whether good or bad, left to the working out of what we may call chance" (F. Darwin, 1.279; 2.105).

With chance as his only continuing faith, the naturalist ventured so far as to call natural selection "my deity," For to believe in miraculous creations or in the "continued intervention of creative power," said Darwin, "is to make 'my deity "Natural Selection" superfluous' and to hold *the* Deity—if such there be—accountable for phenomena which are rightly attributed only to his magnificent laws" (cited by Moore, 322). Here Darwin not only stated his deism but signaled his growing agnosticism by the phrase "if such there be."

Finite Godism? Darwin seemed in the later stages of his deism to flirt with a finite god (*see* FINITE GODISM) like that John Stuart *Mill had embraced. As early as 1871 in *The Descent,* Darwin appeared to deny belief in an infinitely powerful God. He wrote: "*Belief in God—Religion.* There is no evidence that man was aboriginally endowed with the ennobling belief in the existence of an Omnipotent God" (*Descent,* 302). Here he hints at finite godism. If so, it was short-lived; Darwin definitely eventuated an agnostic (*see* AGNOSTICISM).

Agnosticism. By 1879 Darwin was an agnostic, writing: "I think that generally (and more and more as I grow older), but not always, that an Agnostic would be the more correct description of my state of mind" (cited by Moore, 204). Eventually, he wrote: "The mystery of the beginning of all things is insoluble by us; and I for one must be content to remain an Agnostic" (Darwin, *Autobiography,* 84).

His agnosticism notwithstanding, Darwin clearly denies ever being an atheist. He said, "In my most extreme fluctuations I have never been an atheist in denying the existence of God" (cited by Moore, 204). Historians reject the apocryphal story of Darwin's deathbed conversion.

As late as 1879, many years after the *Descent* (1871), Darwin declared, "It seems to me absurd to doubt that a man may be an ardent Theist and an evolutionist" (Letter 7, May 1879). Darwin himself was content to remain an agnostic.

Evaluation. In contrast to the dogmatism of many contemporary evolutionists who claim "evolution is a fact," Darwin was more reserved, at least in his published writings.

Positive Aspects of Darwin's Views. Darwin should be commended for being generally careful not to overstate his case. Certainly this is the case in *On the Origin of Species.*

Evolution is only a theory. Darwin acknowledged that his view was a theory, not a fact. He called it the "theory of evolution" as opposed to the "theory of Creation," phrases he used many times in *On the Origin of Species* (e.g., 235, 435, 437). Technically, macro-evolution is more an unconfirmed hypothesis than a theory (*see* Evolution, Biological). Many, including some evolutionists, believe it is an unfalsifiable tautology. Robert H. Peters, in *The American Naturalist,* stated that evolutionary theories "are actually tautologies and, as such, cannot make empirical testable predictions. They are not scientific theories at all" (Peters, 1). Others, like Stephen Toulmin and Langdon Gilkey have come to similar conclusions, calling it a "scientific myth" (Gilkey, 39).

Both sides should be considered. In contrast to many current evolutionists, Darwin believed that both evolution and its logical antithesis of creation should be considered, weighing the evidence carefully for both. In the "Introduction" to *Origin* Darwin stated: "For I am well aware that scarcely a single point is discussed in this volume on which facts cannot be adduced, often apparently leading to conclusions directly opposite to those at which I have arrived." He adds, "A fair result can be obtained only by fully stating and balancing the facts and arguments on both sides of each question; and this is here impossible." This seems to support a two-model theory which many creationists suggest for public schools, but the mandating of which was rejected by the Supreme Court (*Edwards,* 19 June, 1987).

Micro-evolution was confirmed. Darwin is credited, even by creationists, with confirming the existence of small changes in the natural development of species. They are even observable, as his study of the finches reveals. While creationists differ with Darwin as to whether these small changes can add up to large ones by natural selection over long periods of time, Darwin and others should be credited with the demise of the older platonic view of fixed forms on the level of what biologists call species.

The law of natural selection was explained. Darwin also correctly saw the valuable function that natural selection plays in the development of life. The survival of the fittest is a fact of animal life, as a perusal of an African nature film will reveal. Again, creationists and evolutionists differ over just how much change natural selection can make and whether it is upward. But there is agreement that natural selection can and does make some significant biological changes in the development of life.

"Missing links" were noted. Darwin was well aware of the fact that the evidence for (or against) evolution was in the fossil record and that there were gaping holes in it (see below). He, of course, hoped that future finds would fill in these gaps and confirm his "theory."

Negative Aspects. A more complete critique of biological and human evolution is found in the article Evolution, Biological. Here focus will be on the failings of Darwin's personal views.

The lack of fossil evidence. Sensing the lack of intermediate forms in the fossil record, Darwin confessed: "Geology assuredly does not reveal any such finely graduated organic change, *and this is perhaps the most obvious and serious objection which can be urged against the theory [of evolution]*" (Darwin, *Origin of Species,* 152, emphasis added). Darwin confessed that we do not find "an infinite number of those fine transitional forms which, on our theory, have connected all the past and present species of the same group into one long and branching chain of life" (ibid., 161). He attributed this to the scarcity of the "geological record as a history of the world imperfectly kept" (ibid.) and, others, to the alleged sparsity of transitional forms. But this is a virtually unfalsifiable argument from silence and begs the question in favor of transitional forms being there to begin with. The reality is that there are no missing links, but a missing chain, with only a few links here and a few there.

The fossil record is the only real evidence of what *actually did occur*, as opposed to what *could have* happened, so this is a very serious objection. And the subsequent period of about 140 years has not been friendly to Darwin. In spite of thousands of fossil finds, to borrow a term from Fred Hoyle, "the evolutionary record leaks like a sieve" (Hoyle, 77). But Harvard paleontologist Stephen Jay Gould admitted that "the extreme rarity of transitional forms in the fossil record persists as the trade secret of paleontology. The evolutionary trees that adorn our textbooks have data only at the tips and nodes of their branches; the rest is inference, however reasonable, not the evidence of fossils" (Gould, 14). Indeed, the lack of evidence for Darwin's theory has forced many contemporary evolutionists like Gould to resort to more speculative solutions such as "punctuated equilibria" where by nature takes big leaps in relatively short periods of time.

Micro-evolution does not prove macro-evolution. All that Darwin successfully showed was that small changes occur within specific forms of life, not that there is any evolution between major types. Even granting long periods of time, there is no real evidence for major changes. To cite Gould again, "The history of most fossil species includes two features particularly inconsistent with gradualism:

1. *Stasis.* Most species exhibit no directional change during their tenure on earth. They appear in the fossil record looking much the same as when they disappear; morphological change is usually limited and directionless.

2. *Sudden appearance.* In any local area, a species does not arise gradually by the steady transformation of its ancestors; it appears all at once, fully formed (Gould, ibid., 13–14).

The fossil evidence clearly gives a picture of mature, fully functional creatures suddenly appearing and staying very much the same. This is evidence of creation, not evolution.

Leaps are evidence of creation. In view of the great omissions in the fossil record, Darwin's own statements are self-incriminating. He said, "he who believes that some ancient form was transformed suddenly . . . enter[s] into the realms of miracles, and leave[s] those of science" (cited by Denton, 59). Even as a student, Darwin, commenting on Sumner's *Evidences of Christianity,* said that "when one sees a religion set up, that has no existing prototype . . . it gives great probability to its divine origin." As Howard Gruber put it, "Nature makes no jumps, but God does. Therefore, if we want to know whether something that interests us is of natural or supernatural [origin], we must ask: Did it arise gradually out of that which came before, or suddenly without any evident natural cause?" (cited ibid.). But clearly by Darwin's own premises, then, macroevolution does not follow, for he admits that there are great jumps in the fossil record, which are a sign of creation, not evolution.

Darwin made a false analogy. Much of the persuasiveness of Darwin's view came from the apparently plausible argument that if artificial selection can make significant small changes in a short time, then surely natural selection can make large changes in a long period of time. But as E. S. Russell noted, "the *action of man in selective breeding is not analogous to the action of 'natural selection,'* but *almost its direct opposite.*" For "Man has an aim or an end in view; 'natural selection' can have none. Man picks out the individuals he wishes to cross, choosing them by the characteristics he seeks to perpetuate or enhance." Rather, "He protects them and their issue by all means in his power, guarding them thus from the operation of natural selection, which would speedily eliminate many freaks; he continues his active and purposeful selection from generation to generation until he reaches, if possible, his goal." But "Nothing of this kind happens, or can happen, through the blind process of differential elimination and differential survival which we miscall natural selection (cited in Moore, 124). Thus, a central pillar of Darwin's theory is based on a false analogy (*see* EVOLUTION, BIOLOGICAL for further development of this point).

Darwin admitted to serious objections. Darwin dedicated a whole chapter of *On the Origin of Species* to what he called "a crowd of difficulties" (80). For example, "Can we believe that natural selection could produce . . . an organ so wonderful as the eye" (ibid.). How could organisms that need it survive without it while it was evolving over thousand or millions of years? Indeed, most complex organs and organisms must have all of the parts functioning together at once from the beginning. Any gradual acquiring of them would be fatal to their functioning. Further, "can instincts be acquired and modified through natural selection?" (ibid.). Darwin admits the difficulties with evolution that "some of them are so serious that to this day I can hardly reflect on them without being in some degree staggered" (ibid.).

Evidence reveals separate ancestors. Interestingly, Darwin himself acknowledged the misleading nature of analogy his view was based on. Elaborating of his oft quoted last words of the *Origin* that God created "one" or a "few" forms of life, Darwin admits two revealing things. First, he acknowledged some eight to ten created forms. He said, "I believe that animals are descended from at most four or five progenitors, and plants from an equal or lesser number" (Darwin, *Origin of Species,* 241). Beyond this, he admitted that one can only argue by analogy, adding: "Analogy would lead me one step further, namely, to the *belief* that all animals and plants are descended from some one prototype. *But analogy may be a deceitful guide*" (ibid., emphasis added). This is a very revealing admission in view of the demonstrably false analogy used between artificial and natural selection.

Darwin's theory not derived from nature. Even some evolutionists admit that Darwin did not derive his theory from the study of nature but from a naturalistic worldview. George Grinnell wrote: "I have done a great deal of work on Darwin and can say with some assurance that Darwin also did not derive his theory from nature but rather superimposed a certain philosophical world-view on nature and then spent 20 years trying to gather facts to make it stick" (Grinnell, 44). This is particularly interesting in view of the fact that the Federal Court ruled in the "Scopes II" trial (McLean, 22 January 1982) that creation is not science because, for one thing, it has a non-scientific source—the Bible. The judge ruled that creation could not be taught alongside evolution because "'creation science' . . . has as its unmentioned reference the first eleven chapters of the Book of Genesis" (cited in Geisler, 173).

One cannot help but wonder why creation is not scientific because it has a nonscientific source, whereas Darwin's view is. The truth is that a scientific theory does not need a scientific *source* but only some possible or actual scientific *support*. As the author pointed out in testimony at the "Scopes II" trial, many valid scientific views had nonscientific, even religious, sources. Nikola Tesla's idea for the AC motor came from a vision while reading a pantheistic poet. And Kekule's model of the benzene molecule was derived from a vision of a snake biting its tail (ibid., 116–17).

Darwin's View Is Tantamount to Atheism. Although Darwin, and many Darwinists, stoutly deny that Darwin's view is in principle atheistic, the charge has been laid very seriously at his door. The Princeton scholar, Charles Hodge (1797–1878), in a penetrating analysis, asked and answered his own question: "What is Darwinism? It is Atheism. This does not mean that Mr. Darwin himself and all who adopt his views are atheists; but it means that his theory is atheistic, that the exclusion of design from nature is . . . tantamount to atheism" (Hodge, 177). Hodge's logic is challenging. Evolution excludes design, and if there is no design in nature then there is no need for a Designer of nature. So, protests to the contrary, evolution is in principle an atheistic theory, since it excludes the need for an intelligent Creator (*see* COSMOLOGICAL ARGUMENT; FLEW, ANTONY).

Even many evolutionists acknowledge that Darwin's scenario of a "warm little pond" in which first life spontaneously generated excludes God entirely from the realm of biology. He wrote: "It is often said that all the conditions for the first production of a living organism are now present which could ever have been present." Thus, spontaneous generation would be possible if "we could conceive in some warm little pond with all sorts of ammonia and phosphoric salts, light, heat, electricity present that a protein was formed ready to undergo still more complex changes" (cited by F. Darwin, 3.18). Francis Darwin admitted that "Darwin never claimed his theory could explain the origin of life, but the implication was there. *Thus, not only was God banished from the creation of species but from the entire realm of biology*" (ibid.). What need for a Creator? All one need do is posit what many long believed, that the material universe was eternal and there appears to be no place for a First Cause, for God. There is, of course, mounting evidence against both spontaneous generation of first life (*see* EVOLUTION, CHEMICAL) and an eternal universe (*see* BIG BANG THEORY; *KALAM* COSMOLOGICAL ARGUMENT). And, hence, there is need for God, Darwinism not withstanding (*see* GOD, EVIDENCES FOR).

Reasons for denying Christianity were invalid. Not only were Darwin's deism and agnosticism unjustified, but so was his rejection of Christianity. For it was based on a prevailing negative higher criticism (*see* BIBLICAL CRITICISM) of his day, which was prearchaeological and has long since been discredited.

Likewise, Darwin wrongly assumed that the God of the Old Testament was vengeful and not loving, something contrary to the Old Testament statement of God's love, mercy, and forgiveness (see Exod. 20:6; Jonah 4:2). Indeed, God's love is mentioned more in the Old Testament than in the New Testament.

Further, Darwin's concept of *hell was severely truncated. The very idea that hell is unjust implies there must be an absolutely just God. And an absolutely just God must punish sin.

What is more, Darwin seemed to have no concept of hell as a consequence of a loving God not forcing free creatures to believe in him contrary to their choice.

Finally, Darwin's family downplays the fact that once Darwin had given up his Christian belief he could not cope with the death of his beloved daughter. The very time when he needed the Christian hope of the resurrection (*see* RESURRECTION, EVIDENCE FOR) and reunion with loved ones, it was not there because his increasing antisupernaturalism had eliminated any firm basis on which he could believe it. Instead, he turned on God—whatever was left of him—and blamed God for being "vengeful." Such is the condition of an ungrateful and unbelieving heart (cf. Rom. 1:18f.).

Sources

C. Darwin, *The Autobiography of Charles Darwin*
———, *The Descent of Man*
———, *On the Origin of Species*
F. Darwin, *The Life and Letters of Charles Darwin*, Vol. 3
M. Denton, *Evolution: A Theory in Crisis*
N. L. Geisler, *The Creator in the Courtroom*
L. Gilkey, *Maker of Heaven and Earth*
S. J. Gould, "Evolution's Erratic Pace," *NH*, 1972
G. Grinnell, "Reexamination of the Foundations," *Pensee*, May 1972
C. Hodge, *What Is Darwinism?*
F. Hoyle, et al., *Evolution from Space*
P. Johnson, *Darwin on Trial*
———, *Reason in the Balance*
E. Mayr, "Introduction," C. Darwin, *On the Origin of Species*, 1964 ed.
J. Moore, *The Post-Darwinian Controversies*
R. Peters, "Tautology in Evolution and Ecology," *AN*, January–February 1976

Days of Genesis. ***See*** **GENESIS, DAYS OF.**

Dead Sea Scrolls. Discovery of the Dead Sea Scrolls (hereafter DSS) at Qumran, beginning in 1949, had significant apologetic implications. These ancient texts, hidden in pots in cliff-top caves by a monastic religious community, confirm the reliability of the Old Testament text. They provide significant portions of Old Testament books—even entire books—that were copied and studied by the Essenes. These manuscripts date from as early as the third century B.C. and so give the earliest window so far found into the texts of the Old Testament books and their predictive prophecies. The Qumran texts have become an important witness for the divine origin of the Bible (*see* PROPHECY, AS PROOF OF BIBLE). They provide further evidence against the negative biblical criticism (*see* BIBLE CRITICISM) of such crucial books as Daniel and Isaiah (*see* DANIEL, DATING OF; OLD TESTAMENT MANUSCRIPTS; REDACTION CRITICISM, OLD TESTAMENT).

The DSS manuscripts date from the third century B.C. to the first century A.D. They include one complete Old Testament book, Isaiah (*see* ISAIAH, DEUTERO), and thousands of fragments, which together represent every Old Testament book except Esther. William F. *Albright called this "the greatest manuscript discovery of modern times" (see Trever, 55).

Dating the Dead Sea Scrolls. Important, though not crucial, to the apologetic value of the DSS are their dates. Dating used several lines of evidence.

Carbon 14 Dating. Carbon 14 dating is a reliable form of scientific dating when applied to uncontaminated material several thousand years old. Since it destroys a portion of the material tested, this process is used sparingly. Half of a two-ounce piece of linen wrapping from a scroll in cave 1 was tested by Dr. W. F. Libby of the University of Chicago in 1950 to give a general idea of the age of the collection. Results indicated an age of 1917 years with a 200-year (10 percent) variant, which left the date somewhere between 168 B.C. and A.D. 233.

Paleographical and Orthographical Dating. Paleography (ancient writing forms) and orthography (spelling) were more helpful, indicating that some manuscripts were inscribed before 100 B.C. Albright studied photographs of the complete Isaiah scroll and set its date at around 100 B.C. "What an absolutely incredible find!" he wrote. "And there can happily not be the slightest doubt in the world about the genuineness of the manuscript" (ibid., 55).

Archaeological Dating. Collaborative evidence for an early date came from archaeology. Pottery accompanying the manuscripts was Late Hellenistic (ca. 150–63 B.C.) and Early Roman (ca. 63 B.C. to A.D. 100). Coins found in the monastery ruins proved by their inscriptions to have been minted between 135 B.C. and A.D. 135. The weave and pattern of the cloth supported an early date. Evidence also came from the Murabba'at Discoveries south of Bethlehem, where self-dated manuscripts were discovered in 1952. Bearing dates from A.D. 132–35, these proved to be paleographically younger than the DSS (Zeitlin). In the end there was no reasonable doubt that the Qumran manuscripts came from the century before Christ and the first century A.D. Thus, they are 1000 years older than the Masoretic manuscripts of the tenth century. Before 1947, the Hebrew text was based on three partial and one complete manuscript dating from about A.D. 1000. Now, thousands of fragments are available, as well as complete books, containing large sections of the Old Testament from one millennium before the time of the Masoretic manuscripts.

Support for the Masoretic Text. The nature and number of these finds are of critical value for establishing the true text (*see* OLD TESTAMENT MANUSCRIPTS). With innumerable fragments of the entire Old Testament, there are abundant samples with which to compare the Masoretic Text. The evidence points to the following general conclusions.

Confirmation of the Hebrew Text. The scrolls give an overwhelming confirmation of the faithfulness with which the Hebrew text was copied through the centuries. By the tenth-century Masoretic copies, few errors had crept in. Millar Burrows, in *The Dead Sea Scrolls,* writes, "It is a matter of wonder that through something like a thousand years the text underwent so little alteration. As I said in my first article on the scroll, "Herein lies its chief importance, supporting the fidelity of the Masoretic tradition" (Burrows, 304). R. Laird Harris points out that "evidently the difference between the standard text of A.D. 900 and the text of 100 B.C. is not nearly so great as that between the Neutral and Western text in the New Testament study" (Harris, 99). Gleason Archer observes that the two copies of Isaiah discovered in Qumran Cave 1 "proved to be word for word identical with our standard Hebrew Bible in more than 95 percent of the text. The 5 percent of variation consisted chiefly of obvious slips of the pen and variations in spelling" (Archer, 19). To return to the original and "all important question" framed by Old Testament scholar Frederic Kenyon (1863–1952) a generation ago, it may now be more confidently asserted than ever before that the modern Hebrew text faithfully represents the Hebrew text as originally written by the authors of the Old Testament. Dead Sea discoveries have enabled us to answer this question with much greater assurance than was possible before 1948 (Bruce, 61–69).

Support for the Septuagint. Since the New Testament most often cites the Greek Septuagint (hereafter LXX) translation of the Old Testament, the reliability of this text is important, particularly where it is quoted in the New Testament. The DSS provide early support for the LXX and answers questions about variations between the Hebrew and LXX Greek:

1. A fragment containing Deuteronomy 32:8 reads, "according to the number of the sons of God," which is translated "angels of God" by the LXX, as in Genesis 6:4 (margin); Job 1:6; 2:1; and 38:7. The Masoretic Text reads, "according to the number of the children of Israel."
2. The Masoretic Text of Exodus 1:5 reads "seventy souls," whereas the LXX and its quotation in Acts 7:14 read "seventy-five souls." A DSS fragment of Exodus 1:5 reads "seventy-five souls," in agreement with the LXX.
3. Hebrews 1:6b, "Let all God's angels worship him" is a quote from the LXX of Deuteronomy 32:43. This quotation does not agree with the Masoretic Text, but DSS fragments containing this section tend to confirm the LXX.
4. Isaiah 9:6 reads, "she shall call his name" in the Masoretic Text, but the LXX and now the great Isaiah scroll read, "His name shall be called," a matter of one less consonant of the Hebrew alphabet.
5. The Greek version of Jeremiah is sixty verses (one-eighth) shorter than the Hebrew text of Jeremiah. The fragment of Jeremiah supports these omissions.
6. In Cave 11 a copy of Psalm 151 was found, which was previously unknown in the Hebrew text, although it appeared in the Septuagint. Some apocryphal books were also found among the Hebrew manuscripts in the Qumran caves that had previously been known only in the LXX (Vermes, 296).

This should by no means be construed as a uniform picture, since there are not many deviants in the DSS from the Masoretic Text to begin with. In some cases the variants do not consistently agree with the LXX; in a few cases they do not agree at all. However, even Orlinsky, who is one of the foremost defenders of the Masoretic Text against proposed emendations based on the DSS, admits, "The LXX translation, no less than the Masoretic Text itself, will have gained considerable respect as a result of the Qumran discoveries in those circles where it has long—overlong—been necessary" (cited in Wright, 121).

Light on the New Testament. Some DSS fragments have been identified as the earliest known pieces of the New Testament. Further, the messianic expectations reveal that the New Testament view of a personal messiah-God who would rise from the dead is in line with first-century Jewish thought.

The New Testament fragments? Jose *O'Callahan, a Spanish Jesuit paleographer, made headlines around the world in 1972 when he announced that he had translated a piece of the Gospel of Mark on a DSS fragment. This was the earliest known piece of Mark. Fragments from cave 7 had previously been dated between 50 B.C. and A.D. 50 and listed under "not identified" and classified as "Biblical Texts." O'Callahan eventually identified nine fragments. The center column in the following chart uses the numbering system established for manuscripts. For example, "7Q5" means fragment 5 from Qumran cave 7.

Mark 4:28	7Q6?	A.D. 50
Mark 6:48	7Q15	A.D. ?
Mark 6:52, 53	7Q5	A.D. 50
Mark 12:17	7Q7	A.D. 50
Acts 27:38	7Q6?	A.D. 60
Romans 5:11, 12	7Q9	A.D. 70+
1 Timothy 3:16; 4:1–3	7Q4	A.D. 70+
2 Peter 1:15	7Q10	A.D. 70+
James 1:23, 24	7Q8	A.D. 70+

Both friend and critic acknowledged from the beginning that, if valid, O'Callahan's conclusions would revolutionize current New Testament theories. The *New York Times* reported: "If Father O'Callahan's theory is accepted, it would prove that at least one of the gospels—that of St. Mark—was written only a few years after the death of Jesus." United Press International (UPI) noted that his conclusions meant that "the people closest to the events—Jesus' original followers—found Mark's report accurate and trustworthy, not myth but true history" (ibid., 137). *Time* magazine quoted one scholar who claimed that, if correct, "they can make a bonfire of 70 tons of indigestible German scholarship" (Estrada, 136).

Of course, O'Callahan's critics object to his identification and have tried to find other possibilities. The fragmentary nature of the ms. makes it difficult to be dogmatic about identifications. Nonetheless, O'Callahan offers a plausible, albeit revolutionary, possibility. If the identification of even one of these fragments as New Testament is valid, then the implications for Christian apologetics are enormous. It would be shown that the Gospel of Mark was written within the life time of the apostles and contemporaries of the events.

A date before A.D. 50 leaves no time for mythological embellishment of the records. They would have to be accepted as historical. It would also show Mark to be one of the earlier Gospels. Further, since these manuscripts are not originals but copies, it would reveal that the New Testament was "published"—copied and disseminated—during the life time of the writers. It would also reveal the existence of the New Testament canon during this early period, with pieces representing every major section of the New Testament: Gospels, Acts, and both Pauline and General Epistles.

The fragment of 2 Peter would argue for the authenticity of this often disputed epistle. The absence of fragments of John's writings might indicate that they were written later (A.D. 80–90) in accordance with the traditional dates. With all these revolutionary conclusions it is little wonder that their authenticity is being challenged.

First-Century Jewish Messianic Expectations. The DSS have also yielded text that, while not referring to the Christ of the New Testament, have some interesting parallels, as well as some significant differences. The similarities that confirm the New Testament picture accurately describes Jewish expectation of a personal, individual Messiah who would die and rise from the dead. A fragment called *"A Genesis Florilegorium"* (4Q252) reflects belief in an individual Messiah who would be a descendant of David. "Column 5 (1) (the) Government shall not pass from the tribe of Judah. During Israel's dominion, (2) a Davidic descendant on the throne shall [not c]ease . . . until the Messiah of Righteousness, the Branch of (4) David comes" (see Eisenman, 89).

Even the deity of the Messiah is affirmed in the fragment known as "The Son of God" (4Q246), Plate 4, columns one and two: "Oppression will be upon the earth . . . [until] the King of the people of God arises, . . . and he shall become [gre]at upon the earth. [. . . All w]ill make [peace,] and all will serve [him.] He will be called [son of the Gr]eat [God;] by His name he shall be designated. . . . He will be called the son of God; they will call him son of the Most High" (ibid., 70).

"The Messiah of Heaven and Earth" fragment (4Q521) even speaks of the Messiah raising the dead: "(12) then He will heal the sick, resurrect the dead, and to the Meek announce glad tidings" (ibid., 23; cf. 63, 95).

The Dead Sea Scrolls also confirm that Qumran was not the source of early Christianity. There are significant differences between their concept of the "Teacher of Righteousness," apparently an Essene messianic hope, and the Jesus revealed in Scripture and early Christianity. The differences are enough to show that early Christianity was not just an offshoot of the Essenes, as has been theorized (see Billington, 8–10). The Essenes emphasized hating one's enemies; Jesus stressed love. The Essenes were exclusivistic regarding women, sinners, and outsiders; Jesus was inclusive. The Essenes were legalistic sabbatarians; Jesus was not. The Essenes stressed Jewish purification laws; Jesus attacked them. The Essenes believed two messiahs would come; Christians held that Jesus was the only one (see Charlesworth).

Conclusion. The DSS provide an important apologetic contribution toward establishing the general reliability of the Old Testament Hebrew text, as well as the earliest copies of parts of Old Testament books and even whole books. This is important in showing that the predictive prophecies of the Old Testament were indeed made centuries before they were literally fulfilled. Furthermore, the DSS provide possible support for the New Testament. They may contain the earliest known fragments of the New Testament, and they definitely contain references to messianic beliefs similar to those taught in the New Testament.

Sources

W. F. Albright, *Archaeology of Palestine*

G. L. Archer, Jr., *A Survey of Old Testament Introduction*

C. Billington, "The Dead Sea Scrolls in Early Christianity," *IBA*, January–March 1996

E. M. Blaiklock, et al., *The New International Dictionary of Biblical Archaeology*

F. F. Bruce, *Second Thoughts on the Dead Sea Scrolls*

M. Burrows, *The Dead Sea Scrolls*

J. Charlesworth, et al., *Jesus and the Dead Sea Scrolls*

E. M. Cook, *Solving the Mystery of the Dead Sea Scrolls*

R. Eisenman, et al., *The Dead Sea Scrolls Uncovered*

R. L. Harris, *Inspiration and Canonicity of the Bible*

J. C. Trever, "The Discovery of the Scrolls," *BA* 11 (September 1948)

J. VanderKam, *The Dead Sea Scrolls Today*

G. Vermes, *The Dead Sea Scrolls in English*

———, *The Essene Writings of Qumran*

D. E. White and W. White, Jr., *The First New Testament*

G. E. Wright, ed. *The Bible and the Ancient Near East*

S. Zeitlin, *BA*, December 1963

———, *The Dead Sea Scrolls and Modern Scholarship*

Deconstructionism. ***See*** **DERRIDA, JACQUES.**

Deism. *Deism* is the belief in a God who made the world but who never interrupts its operations with supernatural events. It is a *theism minus miracles (*see* MIRACLE). God does not interfere with his creation. Rather, he designed it to run independent of him by immutable natural laws (*see* SPINOZA, BENEDICT). In nature, he has also provided all that his creatures need to live.

Deism flourished in the sixteenth, seventeenth, and eighteenth centuries but began to die in the nineteenth century. Today its tenets live on in antisupernatural denial of miracles (*see* MIRACLES, ARGUMENTS AGAINST), critical views of the Bible (*see* BIBLE CRITICISM), and the practice of those who believe in a supreme being who has little or nothing to do with their lives.

Deism flourished in Europe, especially France and England, and in late-eighteenth-century America (see Orr, chaps. 3–4). Some of the more prominent European deists were Herbert of Cherbury (1583–1648), the Father of English deism; Matthew Tindal (1656–1733); John Toland (1670–1722), and Thomas Woolston (1669–1731). Some of the notable American deists were Benjamin Franklin (1706–1790), Stephen Hopkins (1707–1785), Thomas Jefferson (1743–1826), and

Thomas Paine (1737–1809). The effects of views of the American deists, especially Paine and Jefferson, are more widely felt today through the United States' political foundation and heritage (see Morais, chaps. 4, 5).

Various Kinds of Deism. All deists agree that there is one God, who created the world. All deists agree that God does not intervene in the world through supernatural acts. However, not all deists agree on God's concern for the world and the existence of an afterlife for human beings (*see* IMMORTALITY). Based on these differences, four types of deism are discernible. The four range from ascribing minimal concern on the part of God to allowing his maximum concern for the world without supernaturally intervening in it (Morais, 17, 85–126).

The God of No Concern. The first type of deism was largely of French origin. According to this view, God is not concerned with governing the world he made. He created the world and set it in motion, but has no regard for what happens to it after that.

The God of No Moral Concern. In the second form of deism, God is concerned with the ongoing happenings of the world but not with the moral actions of human beings. Man can act rightly or wrongly, righteously or wickedly, morally or immorally. It is of no concern to God.

The God of Moral Concern for This Life. The third type of deism maintains that God governs the world and does care about the moral activity of human beings. Indeed God insists on obedience to the moral law that God established in nature. However, there is no future after death.

The God of Moral Concern for This Life and the Next. The fourth type of deism contends that God regulates the world, expects obedience to the moral law grounded in nature, and has arranged for a life after death, with rewards for the good and punishments for the wicked. This view was common among both English and American deists.

Basic Beliefs. Although there are points upon which deists differ, beliefs they hold in common allow an understanding of their common worldview.

God. All deists agree that there is one God (*see* THEISM). This God is eternal, unchangeable, impassable, all-knowing, all-powerful, all-good, true, just, invisible, infinite—in short, completely perfect, lacking in nothing.

God is an absolute unity, not a *trinity. God is only one person, not three persons. The Christian theistic concept of the trinity is false, if not meaningless. God does not exist as three coequal persons. Of this Jefferson scoffed that "the Trinitarian arithmetic that three are one and one is three" is "incomparable jargon." Paine believed that the trinitarian concept resulted in three Gods, and thus was polytheistic (*see* POLYTHEISM). In contrast, deists contend that God is one in nature and one in person.

The Origin of the Universe. The universe is the creation of God (*see* CREATION AND ORIGINS). Before the universe existed, there was nothing except God (*see* CREATION, VIEWS OF). He brought everything into being. Hence, unlike God, the world is finite. It had a beginning while he has no beginning or end.

The universe operates by natural laws. These laws flow from the very nature of God (*see* ESSENTIALISM, DIVINE). Like him they are eternal, perfect, and immutable, representing the orderliness and constancy of his nature. They are rules by which God measures his activity and rules he expects to be the standard for his creation.

The Relation of God and the Universe. God is as different from the universe as a painter is from a painting, a watchmaker is from a watch, and a sculptor is from a sculpture (*see* TELEOLOGICAL ARGUMENT). But, like a painting, watch, and sculpture, the universe reveals many things about God. Through its design it displays that there exists a cosmic Designer, what this Designer is like, and what he expects. The universe also reveals that it must have been caused to exist by Another and that its regularity and preservation in existence is attributable to Another. There is a God who created, regulates, and sustains the world. And this world is dependent on God, not God on the world.

God does not reveal himself in any other way but through creation. The universe is the deist's Bible. Only it reveals God. All other alleged revelations, whether verbal or written, are human inventions (*see* REVELATION, SPECIAL).

Miracles. Miracles do not occur (*see* MIRACLES, ARGUMENTS AGAINST). God either cannot intervene in nature, or he will not. Those deists who believe God cannot perform miracles often argue from the immutability of the laws of nature. A miracle would violate natural laws. But natural laws are immutable, hence cannot be violated, for a violation would involve a change in the unchangeable. Therefore, miracles are impossible. Those deists who think God could perform a miracle but would not, often argue from the proneness of humans toward superstition and deception, the lack of sufficient evidence in support of a miracle, and the unbroken human experience of nature as uniform. They insist that it magnifies the nature of the perfect Mechanic that he made the machine of nature to run without constant need of repair. For deists all miracle accounts are the result of human invention or superstition.

Human Beings. Deists agree that humanity has been created by God and is adequately suited to live happily in the world. The human being is personal, rational, and free (*see* FREE WILL), endowed with natural rights that should not be violated by any individual, group, or government. The human being has the rational ability to discover in nature all that needs to be known to live a happy and full life.

Like all other animals, *Homo sapiens* was created with strengths and weaknesses. Strengths are reason and freedom. Among weaknesses is a tendency toward superstition and a desire to dominate others of his race. Both of these innate weaknesses have led to supernatural religions and oppressive governments.

Ethics. The basis of human morality is grounded in nature (*see* LAW, NATURE AND KINDS OF; REVELATION, GENERAL). In nature each person discovers how to be self-governing, to associate with other creatures, and to relate to God. For many deists the only innate human principle is the desire for happiness. How this innate desire is satisfied is governed according to reason. A person who fails to act by reason becomes miserable and acts immorally.

Deists differ on the universality of moral laws. They agree that the basis of all value is universal, because it is grounded in nature. But they disagree as to which moral laws are absolute and which are relative. The fact that there is a right and a wrong is not in dispute. The problem is in determining exactly what is right and wrong in each case and circumstance. Some deists, such as Jefferson, conclude that specific moral rules are relative. What is considered right in one culture is wrong in another (*see* MORALITY, ABSOLUTE NATURE OF). Other deists would argue that a correct use of reason will always lead one to an absolute right and an absolute wrong, though the application of these absolutes may vary with culture and circumstance.

Human Destiny. Though some deists deny that humanity survives death in any respect, many believe that people live on. For most of these deists, the afterlife is of an immaterial nature where the morally good people will be rewarded by God and the morally bad ones will be punished.

History. In general, deists had little to say about history. They commonly held that history was linear and purposeful. They also held that God did not intervene in history through supernatural acts of revelation or signs called miracles. They differed on whether God concerned himself with what occurs in history. Many French deists in the seventeenth and eighteenth centuries believed God was utterly unconcerned. Most English deists looked to God to exercise a certain degree of providential care over the affairs of history, yet without miraculous intervention.

Many deists held that the study of history had great value. For, if nothing else, history demonstrates the human tendency toward superstition, deception, and domination, and the terrible consequences which follow when this tendency goes unchecked and unchallenged.

An Evaluation of Deism. *Contributions.* Positive things may be learned from deism. Many have agreed with the deists' insistence on the importance and use of reason in religious matters (*see* APOLOGETICS, NEED FOR; FAITH AND REASON; LOGIC). The many claims made about miracles and supernatural revelation must be verified. No reasonable person would step into an elevator if he had good reason to believe that it was unsafe. Neither should anyone trust a religious claim without good reason to believe that it is true.

Deists have been commended for their belief that the world reflects the existence of a God (*see* COSMOLOGICAL ARGUMENT). The regularity and orderliness of the world suggests a cosmic Designer. The inadequacy of the world to account for its operations and existence seems to imply an ultimate explanation beyond the world—God. The limited perfections discoverable in nature may imply that there is an unlimited perfect Being beyond nature who created and sustains all things. This natural evidence is available for all to view and respond to in a reasonable way.

Deists have also been credited with exposing much religious deception and superstition. Their relentless attacks on many beliefs and practices have helped people to evaluate their religious faith and to purge it of corruption.

Criticisms of Deism. Yet there is reason to criticize the deistic worldview. A being who could bring the universe into existence from nothing could certainly perform lesser miracles if he chose to do so. A God who created water could part it or make it possible for a person to walk on it. The immediate multiplication of loaves of bread and fish would be no problem to a God who created matter and life in the first place. A virgin birth or even a physical resurrection from the dead would be minor miracles in comparison to the miracle of creating the universe from nothing. It seems self-defeating to admit a great miracle like creation and then to deny the possibility of lesser miracles.

The deists' understanding of universal natural law is no longer valid. Scientists today consider the laws of nature to be general, not necessarily universal. Natural laws describe how nature generally behaves. They do not dictate how nature must always behave (*see* MIRACLES, ARGUMENTS AGAINST).

If God created the universe for the good of his creatures, it seems that he would miraculously intervene in their lives if their good depended on it. Surely their all-good Creator would not abandon his creation. Instead it would seem that such a God would continue to exercise the love and concern for his creatures that prompted him to create them to begin with, even if it meant providing that care through miraculous means (*see* EVIL, PROBLEM OF).

Assuming, then, that miracles are possible, then one cannot reject out of hand every claim to supernatural revelation without first examining the evidence for its support. If it lacks supporting evidence, it should be rejected. But if the evidence does substantiate the claim, then the alleged revelation should be considered authentic. It certainly should not simply be ruled out of court without further investigation.

Further, simply because many individuals and groups have invented and abused religious beliefs is not sufficient ground for rejecting supernatural religions. Scientific discoveries have been abused, but few suggest that abuse makes the discoveries false or a reason to abolish science. Also, the mutability of human language and the fact of human error does not appear to be a valid argument against supernatural revelation (*see* Bible, Alleged Errors in; Bible, Evidence for). An all-powerful, all-knowing God could conceivably overcome these problems. At least such problems should not rule out the possibility that God has revealed himself, either verbally or in written form. Again, the evidence should first be consulted.

Finally, the deists' case against Christianity and the Bible has been found wanting (*see* Bible Criticism). What antisupernaturalist has adequately answered such Christian theists as J. Gersham Machen, and C. S. Lewis (see Lewis, esp. *Miracles*; Machen)? They have built an extensive and solid case from science, philosophy, and logic against the belief that miracle stories in the Bible are necessarily mythical (*see* Mythology and the New Testament).

For example, Paine's belief that most of the books of the Bible were written by people other than the ones who claimed to write them and written very late is still proclaimed as indisputable fact by many critics. But there is not one credible shred of evidence that has not been rejected for good reason by archaeologists and biblical scholars. More than 25,000 finds have confirmed the picture of the ancient world given in the Bible (*see* Archaeology, New Testament; Archaeology, Old Testament). There is sufficient evidence to support the authorship claims and early dates for most biblical books (*see* New Testament, Dating of; New Testament Documents, Reliability of).

Further, the deistic attack against such Christian teachings as the Trinity, redemption, and deity of Christ (*see* Christ, Deity of), shows a superficial and naive understanding of these teachings.

Sources

J. Butler, *The Analogy of Religion*
R. Flint, *Anti-Theistic Theories*
N. L. Geisler, *Christian Apologetics*
———, and W. Watkins, *Worlds Apart*
I. Kant, *Religion within the Limits of Reason Alone*
J. LeLand, *A View of the Principal Deistic Writers . . .*
C. S. Lewis, *Christian Reflections*
———, *Miracles: A Preliminary Study*
J. G. Machen, *The Virgin Birth of Christ*
H. M. Morais, *Deism in Eighteenth Century America*
J. Orr, *English Deism: Its Roots and Its Fruits*
T. Paine, *Complete Works of Thomas Paine*
M. Tindal, *Christianity as Old as the Creation;* or, *The Gospel: A Republication of the Religion of Nature*

Derrida, Jacques. Jacques Derrida is usually regarded as a contemporary French "philosopher," though some challenge that he is truly a philosopher. He is the father of a movement known as "deconstructionism." He personally disavows the term's popular meaning. The movement also is called "postmodern," though Derrida again does not use the term in describing his view.

Among Derrida's influential books are *Speech and Phenomena* (1967–68, trans. 1973), *Of Grammatology* (trans. 1978), *Writing and Differance* (trans. 1978), *Positions* (1981), and *Limited Inc.* (1977, trans. 1988).

Pieces of his thinking are drawn from Immanuel Kant (metaphysics), Friedrich Nietzsche (atheism), Ludwig Wittgenstein (view of language), Friedrich Frege (conventionalism), Edmund Husserl (phenomenological method; *see* Truth, Absolute Nature of), Martin Heidegger (existentialism), and William James (pragmatism and the will to believe).

Derrida's views are difficult to understand because of the nature of the positions, his writing, and sometimes poor translations. Because of such factors, he has been often misread. He does not embrace nihilism, for example, which is the negation of all being and value (*see* Morality, Absolute Nature of). Nor is he an anarchist who negates all social structure. Despite writings which seem to negate all moral law, neither is Derrida an antinomian.

Deconstructionism is a form of hermeneutics, of interpreting a text. As such it can be distinguished from other interpretive approaches. Yet Derrida is not interested in destroying meaning, but of reconstructing it. It is not negation that dismantles a text, but criticism that remodels it. It stands against fixed rules of analysis. A deconstructionist reads and rereads a text, looking for new, deeper, forgotten meanings.

Deconstructionism embraces *conventionalism*. All meaning is relative to a culture and situation. There is no meaning prior to language.

Deconstructionism accepts *perspectivalism*. All truth is conditioned by one's perspective.

Deconstructionism holds a form of *referentialism*. There is no perfect reference or one-to-one correspondence between words and the meaning they confer. Meaning, therefore, is ultimately untransferrable between writer and reader. We constantly change the context through which we view symbols. This context is limited. We cannot know from an infinite perspective.

Deconstructionism is *differentialism*. All rational structures leave something out. The reader approaches the text with suspicion, looking for the "difference," the unknown something that is not there.

Deconstructionism embraces a form of linguistic *solipsism*. By this view we cannot escape the limits of language. We can broaden our linguistic concepts, but we cannot escape their limits.

Deconstruction holds to *semantic progressivism*. One will never exhaust all possible meanings. A text can always be deconstructed.

Derrida and Deconstructionism. Derrida is an atheist (*see* ATHEISM) regarding the existence of God and agnostic concerning the possibility of knowing absolute truth. He is antimetaphysical, claiming that no *metaphysics is possible. He believes we are locked in our own linguistic bubble. Yet he recognizes that using language to deny metaphysics is itself a form of metaphysics. This incoherence points to the need for archi-writing, a poetic protest against metaphysics.

Three factors are key to understanding Derrida's philosophy—grammar, logic, and rhetoric. Grammar expresses acceptable phrases with appropriate modifying words. Logic recognizes the absurdity of contradictory phrases. And rhetoric shows how and when to use the phrases mastered through grammar and logic.

Derrida believes that grammar is relatively superficial, having to do with keeping the signs of language in good order. *Logic and rhetoric are more profound, dealing with the use and interpretation of signs. Derrida rejects the history of Western philosophy in which language is based on logic. That would mean there is a logical underpinning of reality. He rejects that assumption.

According to Derrida, language is based on rhetoric, not logic. The sovereignty of logic is rooted in the view that signs (e.g., words) represent ideas. Ideas stand in semantical contrast to other ideas. Language differentiates ideas. We must "deconstruct" language based in logic to learn how linguistic expressions are used in human activity. Language based on logic entails a mistaken belief that there are "private languages" with "inner speech" and "private mental life." If logic is sovereign, then a private language is possible. Ideas would not vary with circumstances.

Rhetoric as Basis of Language. Derrida held that meaning is based in rhetorical force, viz., the role it plays in human activity (*see* WITTGENSTEIN, LUDWIG). Rather than an underlying formal logic, meaning comes out of the stream of life. Words express time-bound experience. So to understand what a text means one must first fully understand its actual life context. This may be seen in five central arguments of Derrida:

1. All Meaning is Complex. No pure and simple meanings stand behind the signs of language. If all language is complex, no essential meaning transcends time and place.
2. All Meaning is Contingent. Every object of language and meaning is contingent upon a changing life reality. There is no objective meaning.
3. All Meaning is Mixed. No pure experiences exist without reference to transient experience. There is no private mental life that does not presuppose an actual world. We cannot even think about a concept without contaminating it with some reference to our own past or future.
4. There is no such thing as a perception. Deconstructionists do not reject everyday experience. They reject idealized concepts disconnected from the everyday world. The nature of what is signified is not independent of the sign that signifies it.
5. Rhetoric is the basis of all meaning. All written language is dependent on spoken language. It is not dependent on the meaning of spoken signs. It is dependent on the pattern of vocalization (phonemics). Phonemes are parts of sound that can be represented by a letter. Without this difference in phonemes letters are impossible. "Differance" is the key to meaning, since all sounds must be differentiated to be distinct and form meaningful sounds.

With Derrida, many believe Western philosophy comes to an end. It literally self-destructs as it deconstructs. Derrida himself believes it goes on endlessly in continuous deconstructions or reinterpretations.

Evaluation. Derrida shows how the linguistic tradition leads to agnosticism. He makes some pointed critiques of Western thought. He reveals that, unless one's philosophy begins in reality, it will never logically end in reality. His critique of "private language," esoteric thought cut off from human experience is insightful.

Nonetheless, Derrida's deconstructionism is open to serious critique.

His difficult (highly metaphorical) expression is obscure and contradictory. This obscures his view, generates misunderstanding, and makes evaluation difficult. His view contains self-defeating claims, such as: "The history of philosophy is closed." Or, "Metaphysics has come to an end." He cannot avoid using philosophy and metaphysics in such statements. His doubt that we can really know anything is self-defeating. How does he know this unless we can know something? What sort of epistemological status should we give to his statements? If they were true, they would be false. If they are mere poetical protests, then they do not destroy objective meaning or metaphysics.

Even his denial of logic in rhetoric is highly problematic, if not self-defeating. The very language that denies logic is based in it; otherwise it would be meaningless.

Despite his rejection of (or protest against) metaphysics, Derrida has metaphysical presuppositions. The very fact he discusses "What is real?" indicates an underlying metaphysics. Also, he claims language depends on a relation to the world. That implies a metaphysical view of the world.

His view is a form of nominalism and radical empiricism ("Real" is concrete reality, immediately before me). As such it reduces to a type of solipsism and is subject to the same criticism of these views.

The primacy of difference over identity departs from common sense and makes all real communication impossible. Indeed, Derrida could not even communicate his own position to us if he is right.

Derrida's position is closely associated with logical positivism with its well-known self-defeating nature. (For a critique, see AYER, A. J.) Derrida's conventionalist view of meaning is self-defeating (*see* CONVENTIONALISM). The sentences conveying his view would have no meaning on a conventionalist theory of meaning. In short, he appears to have left himself no ground to stand on—even to express his own view.

Finally, Derrida's "speech" is no better than Kant's unknowable "noumena," Wittgenstein's "silence," or Hume's "flames." For none of them tell us anything about reality.

A faith of sorts is involved in this process, and deconstructionism is fideist (*see* FIDEISM). Faith is always necessary. Since absolute meaning is impossible, indecision is inescapable. We always live somewhere between absolute certainty and absolute doubt, between skepticism and dogmatism. Hence, faith is always necessary.

Sources

J. Derrida, *Limited Inc.*

———, *Of Grammatology*

———, *Speech and Phenomena*

———, *Writing and Differance*

R. W. Dasenboock, ed., *Redrawing the Lines*

S. Evans, *Christian Perspectives on Religious Knowledge*

Lundin, *The Culture of Interpretation*

J-F. Lyotard, *The Postmodern Condition: A Report on Knowledge*

G. B. Madison, *Working Through Derrida*

C. Norris, *Derrida*

Descartes, Rene. ***Life and Works of Descartes.*** French theist Rene Descartes was born in 1596 and died in 1650 after giving an early-morning philosophy lesson to Queen Christina of Sweden. He was called to philosophy through a dream on November 10, 1619. He was a great mathematician and learned philosophy from the Jesuits. His main works are *Meditations on First Philosophy* (1641) and *Discourse on Method* (1637).

His Philosophical Method. Descartes sought an Archimedean point at which he could begin thinking. Unlike St. *Augustine (*see*), who went through a period of actual doubt, Descartes was never a skeptic. He used doubt as a universal and methodical starting point for his philosophy.

Method Stated. Descartes' method was simple and universal. He proposed to withhold doubt only from what is indubitable. In brief, doubt everything it is consistently possible to doubt.

Method Applied. Applying his method, Descartes found that he could doubt: (1) his senses—since they sometimes deceive (e.g., a stick in water seems crooked); (2) that he was awake—since he might be dreaming he was awake; (3) that 2 + 3 = 5—since his memory may fail to remember the numbers; (4) that there is an external world—since an evil demon may be deceiving him. However, in all his doubt there was one thing Descartes found it impossible to doubt, namely, that he was doubting.

From Doubt to Existence. Descartes had found his universal starting point in doubt. He argued from doubt to thought to existence. He went from *dubito* to *cogito* to *sum* (from "I doubt" to "I think" to "I am").

Descartes reasoned thus: The one thing that I cannot doubt is that I am doubting. But if I am doubting, then I am thinking (for doubt is a form of thought). And if I am thinking, then I am a thinking thing (for only minds can think).

At this point Descartes posited that there is a difference between a thinking thing and an extended thing. My mind is a thinking thing—and I cannot doubt its existence. My body and the world are extended things—and I can doubt their existence. Hence, even though he was a theist, he could find no way to reason directly to God from the external world, such as *Aristotle, *Thomas Aquinas, Gottfried *Leibniz, and many other theists have (*see* COSMOLOGICAL ARGUMENT).

God's Existence Can Be Proven. Nevertheless, Descartes found an indirect way to demonstrate God's existence involving the external world. He would begin with his indubitable starting point in his own existence and reason from it to God and then from God to the external world.

A Cosmological Argument (A Posteriori Proof). Descartes' reasoning proceeded as follows. (1) If I doubt, then I am imperfect (for I lack in knowledge). (2) But if I know I am imperfect, then I must know the perfect (otherwise I would have no way of knowing that I am not perfect). (3) Now knowledge of the perfect cannot arise from me, since I am imperfect (an imperfect mind cannot be the source [basis] of a perfect idea). (4) Hence, there must be a perfect Mind that is the source of this perfect idea. This approach was distinctive, if not unique. Descartes had to prove God existed before he could be sure the world existed!

The Ontological Argument (A Priori Proof). Like St. *Anselm before him, Descartes believed the *ontological argument for God's existence was valid. His form of it went like this: (1)It is logically necessary to affirm of a concept what is essential to its nature (e.g., a triangle must have three sides). (2) But existence is logically necessary to the nature of a necessary Existent (i.e., Being). 3) Therefore, it is logically necessary to affirm that a necessary Existent does exist.

There were many reactions to Descartes' ontological argument. But he staunchly defended it, restating it in this form to avoid some criticism: (1) God's existence cannot be conceived as only possible but not actual (for then he would not be a necessary Existent); (2) we can conceive of God's existence (it is not contradictory); (3) therefore, God's existence must be conceived as more than possible (namely, as actual).

One objection to his argument that he never answered was that of Pierre Gassendi's insistence that Descartes did not really prove God's existence is not logically impossible. Hence, he did not prove it is logically necessary. Gottfried *Leibniz later argued that existence is a perfection and as such is a simple and irreducible quality that cannot conflict with others. Hence, God can have all perfections, including existence. But Immanuel *Kant later critiques this view, insisting that existence is not an attribute.

Descartes' Test for Truth. Descartes was a rationalist, followed by Benedict *Spinoza and Gottfried Leibniz. As such, he believed that truth was found in the realm of ideas.

Clear and Distinct Ideas. For Descartes the true idea was a clear and distinct idea. Only clear and distinct ideas are true (not mixed ones), namely, those ideas known by rational intuition as self-evident. Or, those which are (geometrically) deducible from self-evident ideas.

Four Rules of Valid Thinking. In his *Discourse on Method* Descartes set forth four rules for determining a true idea. First, the rule of certainty states that only indubitably certain (clear and distinct) ideas should be accepted as true. Second, the rule of division affirms that all problems should be reduced to their simplest parts. Third, according to the rule of order, reasoning should proceed from simple to complex. Finally, the rule of enumeration says that one should review and recheck each step in the argument.

The Source of Errors. Every epistemology must account for error, especially one like Descartes' that exalts certainty. Descartes' answer was that errors arise in judgment (the will), not in thought. For when we judge to be so what we do not clearly know to be so we fall into error.

The Proof of the Existence of an External World via God. Descartes' very method of systematic doubt brought the question of the existence of an external world in question—at least by way of the senses alone. Hence, it was necessary for him to argue for the world's existence in a more circuitous manner. This he did in the following way: (1) I am receiving a strong and steady succession of ideas of a world that are not under my control (hence, I cannot be erring about them); (2) hence, either God is making me believe them falsely or else there is a real external world causing them; (3) but God will not deceive me (nor allow me to be deceived) in what I am perceiving clearly and distinctly, since he is perfect (and deception is a sign of imperfection); (4) therefore, it is true that there is an external world; (5) since the same argument applies to my body, it is true that I have a body.

An Evaluation of Descartes' Views. Descartes is a mixed blessing to Christian *theism. On the one hand, he is a rational theist who offers arguments for God's existence. On the other hand, his form of rationalistic dualism is a significant negative factor supporting views that are contrary to biblical theism.

Some Positive Features. On the good side of the ledger, Descartes can be commended for several things. Among them several have apologetic value.

Truth is objective. For one thing, Descartes held that truth is objective (*see* Truth, Nature of). It is not subjective or mystical. Rather, truth is common to all rational minds.

Truth is knowable. In opposition to agnosticism, Descartes affirmed that truth is knowable. Unlike Immanuel *Kant or David *Hume, Descartes argued that the truth about reality is knowable by the mind. Further, he held that certitude could be gained in our knowledge. Skepticism was avoidable. Indeed, it is self-refuting.

Truth is rational. Descartes embraced *first principles of knowledge, such as the law of non-contradiction. He used them in understanding the world. He believed that without them reality could not be known.

Truth is arguable. Not only is truth knowable and rational, but one can offer rational arguments, such as arguments for the existence of God. This view is helpful for Christian apologetics, particularly for classical apologetics.

Negative Dimensions. Not everything Descartes believed is helpful for the Christian apologist. In fact, some things have proven to be a bane to orthodox Christianity.

The invalid ontological argument. Most Christian apologists do not agree with Descartes' defense of the ontological argument. Most thinkers argue that it involves an illegitimate transition from thought to reality.

His insufficient starting point. A more serious problem is Descartes' starting point. Why should one doubt what is obvious to him, namely, that he has a body and that there are other bodies around him? Why should one doubt everything that is doubtable? Why not doubt only what is necessary to doubt or what one has no good reason to believe? Or to put it another way, one can doubt whether Descartes' starting point in doubt is the best way to approach the world.

Unrealistic starting point. Descartes began his philosophy in thought (indubitable thought) and then moved to reality. He reasoned "I think, therefore, I am." In reality, however, "I am, therefore, I think." He literally got de carte before de horse!

Once one begins in the realm of thought apart from reality, he or she can never legitimately break out of the realm of pure thought. Just is the fate of any rationalism or idealism that does not begin within existence (*see* REALISM).

Unbridgeable dualism of mind and body. Descartes' particular form of rationalism set up an unbridgeable dualism between mind and matter. In fact, they are defined in such a way that they are logically separate. Mind is defined as a thinking but nonextended thing, and matter as a nonthinking extended thing. Thus, by definition "never the twain shall meet." In doing this Descartes opened himself to the criticism of holding that man is "a ghost in a machine." This Cartesian dualism has serious implications for one's view of the nature of human beings as well as the nature of Scripture. For it not only denies the unity of human nature, but sets up a dichotomy in nature between the material and spiritual that supports much of negative biblical criticism (*see* BIBLE CRITICISM; BIBLE, EVIDENCE FOR; BIBLE, ALLEGED ERRORS IN).

Other problems. Descartes has been criticized for many other things—space does not permit elaborating. Like Benedict *Spinoza, he had a questionable geometric form of deductionism. He does not justify his use of the principle of causality. Nor does Descartes prove that an imperfect mind cannot be the cause of a perfect idea. He lacks appreciation for the role of experience in the pursuit of truth. His criterion of truth is not clear. It cannot apply to concepts, since only judgments are true. And it cannot apply to judgments, since he admits some of them are false. Finally, his view reduces to mental solipsism (namely, I know only while I am thinking—right now—and not when I am not thinking).

Sources

J. Collins, *God and Modern Philosophy*
R. Descartes, *Meditations on First Philosophy*
———, *Discourse on Method*
E. Gilson, *The Unity of Philosophical Experience*

Determinism. Determinism is the belief that all events, including human choices (*see* FREE WILL), are determined or caused by another. Proponents of this view believe that human choices are the result of antecedent causes, which in turn were caused by prior causes.

Kinds of Determinism. There are two basic kinds of determinism: naturalistic and theistic. Naturalistic determinists include behavioral psychologist B. F. Skinner, author of *Beyond Freedom and Dignity* and *Beyond Behaviorism*. An atheist (*see* ATHEISM), Skinner wrote that all human behavior is determined by genetic and behavioral factors. On this view, humans are like a brush in the hands of an artist, though in his view the "artist" is a mix of societal manipulation and chance. The human being is at the mercy of these forces, simply the instrument through which they are expressed.

The theistic version of this view insists that God is the ultimate cause who determines all human actions. Martin *Luther's *Bondage of the Will* and Jonathan *Edwards' *Freedom of the Will* are examples of this theistic determinism. It is the view held by all strong Calvinists.

Arguments for Determinism. *The Argument from Alternative Possibility.* All human behavior is either uncaused, self-caused, or caused by something else. However, human behavior cannot be uncaused, since nothing occurs without a cause. Further, human actions cannot be self-caused, for no act can cause itself. To do so, it would have to be prior to itself, which is impossible. The only remaining alternative, then, is that all human behavior is caused by something external to it.

The Argument from the Nature of Causality. Edwards argued from the nature of causality. He reasoned that since the principle of causality (*see* CAUSALITY, PRINCIPLE OF; FIRST PRINCIPLES) demands that all actions are caused, then it is irrational to claim that things arise without a cause. But for Edwards a self-caused action is impossible, since a cause is prior to an effect, and one cannot be prior to himself. Therefore, all actions are ultimately caused by a First Cause (God). "Free choice" for Edwards is doing what one desires, but God gives the desires or affections that control action. Hence, all human actions ultimately are determined by God.

The Argument from Sovereignty. If God is sovereign, then all acts must be determined by him (*see* GOD, NATURE OF). For if God is in control of all, then he must ultimately be the cause of all. Otherwise, he would not be in complete control.

The Argument from Omniscience. Some determinists argue from God's omniscience. For if God knows everything, then everything he knows must occur according to his will. If it did not, then God would be wrong in what he knew. But an omniscient Mind cannot be wrong in what it knows.

A Response to Theistic Determinism. Nondeterminists, especially self-determinists (*see* FREE WILL), reject the premises of determinist arguments. It is important to distinguish two forms of determinism, hard and soft. The determinism rejected here is hard determinism:

Hard Determinism	Soft Determinism
Act is caused by God.	Act is not caused by God.
God is the only cause.	God is the primary cause; humans are the secondary cause.
Totally free human choice is eliminated.	Human free choice is compatible with sovereignty.

Soft determinism is sometimes called *compatibolism,* since it is "compatible" with free choice (self-determinism). Only hard determinism is incompatible with free choice or secondary causality of a human free agent.

Response to the Argument from Alternative Possibility. All human behavior is either uncaused, self-caused, or caused by something else. But human behavior can be self-caused, since there is nothing contradictory about a self-caused action (as there is about a self-caused being). For an action does not have to be prior to itself to be caused by oneself. Only the self (I) must be prior to the action. A self-caused action is simply one caused by my self. And my self (I) is prior to my actions.

Response to the Argument from the Nature of Causality. Jonathan Edwards rightly argued that all actions are caused, but it does not follow from this that God is the cause of all these actions. A self-caused action is not impossible, since one's self is prior to his actions. Therefore, all actions need not be attributed to the First Cause (God). Some actions can be caused by human beings to whom God gave free moral agency. Free choice is not, as Edwards contends, doing what one desires (with God giving the desires). Rather, it is doing what one decides. And one does not always do what he desires, as is the case when duty is placed above desire. Hence, it does not follow that all actions are determined by God.

Response to the Argument from Sovereignty. One need not reject God's sovereign control of the universe in order to believe determinism is wrong. For God can control by his omniscience, as well as by his causal power. As the next point reveals, God can control events by willing in accordance with his omniscient knowledge of what will occur by free choice. God need not make (or cause) the choice himself. Simply knowing for sure that a person will freely do something is enough for God to control the world.

Response to the Argument from Omniscience. It is true that everything God knows must occur according to his will. If it did not, then God would be wrong in what he knew. For an omniscient Mind cannot be wrong in what it knows. However, it does not follow from this that all events are determined (i.e., caused by God). God could simply determine that we be self-determining beings in a moral sense. The fact that he knows for certain what free creatures will do with their freedom is enough to make the event determined. But the fact that God does not force them to choose, is enough to establish that human free acts are not determined (caused) by another but by oneself. God determined the *fact* of human freedom, but free creatures perform the *acts* of human freedom.

Weaknesses of Determinism. Determinism is self-defeating. A determinist insists that both determinists and nondeterminists are determined to believe what they believe. However, determinists believe self-determinists are wrong and ought to change their view. But "ought to change" implies they are free to change, which is contrary to determinism.

Determinism is irrational. C. S. Lewis argued that naturalistic, complete determinism is irrational (see Lewis). For determinism to be true, there would have to be a rational basis for their thought. But if determinism is true, then there is no rational basis for thought, since all is determined by nonrational forces. So, if determinism claims to be true, then it must be false.

Determinism destroys human responsibility. If God is the cause of all human actions, then human beings are not morally responsible. One is only responsible for a choice if there was free will to avoid making it. All responsibility implies the ability to respond, either on one's own or by God's grace. Ought implies can. But if God caused the action, then we could not have avoided it. Hence, we are not responsible.

Determinism renders praise and blame meaningless. Similarly, if God causes all human actions, then it makes no sense to praise human beings for doing good, nor to blame them for doing evil. For if the courageous really had no choice other than to show courage, why reward it? If the evil had no choice but to commit their crime, why punish them? Rewards and punishment for moral behavior makes sense only if the actions were not caused by another.

Determinism leads to fatalism. If everything is determined beyond our control, then why do good and avoid evil? Indeed, if determinism is right, evil is unavoidable. Determinism destroys the very motive to do good and shun evil.

Determinism is unbiblical. Theistic opponents to determinism offer several objections from Scripture. Defining free choice as "doing what one desires" is contrary to experience. For people do not always do what they desire, nor do they always desire to do what they do (cf. Rom. 7:15–16).

If God must give the desire before one can perform an act, then God must have given Lucifer the desire to rebel against him. But this is impossible, for in that case God would be giving a desire against God. God would in effect be against himself, which is impossible.

Theistic determinists like Edwards have a faulty, mechanistic view of human personhood. He likens human free choice to balancing scales in need of more pressure from the outside in order to tip the scales from dead center. But humans are not machines; they are persons made in the image of God (Gen. 1:27).

Edwards wrongly assumes that self-determinism is contrary to God's sovereignty. For God could have predetermined things in accordance with free choice, rather than in contradiction to it. Even the Calvinistic *Westminster Confession of Faith* declares that "Although in relation to the foreknowledge and decree of God, the first cause, all things come to pass immutably and infallibly, yet by the same providence he ordereth them to fall out, *according to* the nature of second causes, either necessarily, freely, or contingently" (5.2 emphasis added).

Sources

Augustine, *On Free Will*
J. Edwards, *Freedom of the Will*
J. Fletcher, *Checks to Antinomianism*
D. Hume, *The Letters of David Hume*
M. Luther, *Bondage of the Will*
———, *On Grace and Free Will*
B. F. Skinner, *Beyond Behaviorism*
———, *Beyond Freedom and Dignity*
Thomas Aquinas, *Summa Theologica*

Dewey, John. John Dewey (1859–1952) has been called the father of modern American education, on which he has had immense influence. As a philosopher and writer he is closely identified with the philosophy of instrumentalism, also known as progressivism or pragmatic humanism. Through the American educational system, his views have influenced virtually every American of the twentieth century. Dewey signed the *Humanist Manifesto* and was a leader in the movement to turn education toward secular humanism (*see* HUMANISM, SECULAR).

Born and educated in Vermont, Dewey took his doctorate at Johns Hopkins University. There he studied the pragmatism of C. S. Pierce, the experimental psychology of G. S. Hall, and the philosophies of G. S. Morris (a neo-Hegelian), and T. H. Huxley. Dewey taught at the universities of Michigan and Chicago and was at Columbia University from 1904 to 1930. Dewey wrote many books and numerous articles on topics ranging from education and democracy (*Democracy and Education*, 1916), to psychology (*Human Nature and Conduct: An Introduction to Social Psychology*, 1930), logic (*Logic: The Theory of Inquiry*, 1938), and even art (*Art as Experience*, 1934). His view of God and religion is best expressed in *A Common Faith* (1934).

Religion in an Age of Science. As a secular humanist, Dewey rejected belief in a theistic God (*see* THEISM). Dewey concluded that modern science made belief in a supernatural origin of the universe untenable. "The impact of astronomy eliminated the older religious creation stories." And "geological discoveries have displaced creation myths which once bulked large." In addition, "biology has revolutionized conceptions of soul and mind, . . . and this science has made a profound impression upon ideas of sin, redemption, and immortality." Further, "anthropology, history and literary criticism have furnished a radically different version of the historic events and personages upon which Christian religions have built." Psychology "is already opening to us natural explanations of phenomena so extraordinary that once their supernatural origin was, so to say, the natural explanation" (*A Common Faith*, 31).

Science, Dewey believed, had made even *agnosticism too mild of a reaction to traditional theism. "'Agnosticism' is a shadow cast by the eclipse of the supernatural" (ibid., 86). And "generalized agnosticism is only a halfway elimination of the supernatural." As an antitheist or atheist (*see* ATHEISM), he rejected any attempt to support the existence of God. "The cause of the dissatisfaction is perhaps not so much (1) the arguments that *Kant used to show the insufficiency of these alleged proofs, as it is the growing feeling (2) that they are too formal to offer any support to religion in action" (ibid., 11). He believed the reality of evil could not be reconciled with the concept of a personal, good, and all-powerful God (*see* EVIL, PROBLEM OF).

From its infancy in the Renaissance through the eighteenth century's protest against ecclesiastical authority, Dewey believed secularism had borne fruit in the nineteenth-century "diffusion of the supernatural through secular life" (ibid., 65). Secular interests had grown independent of organized religion and had "crowded the social importance of organized religions into a corner and the area of this corner is decreasing" (ibid., 83).

Since there is no Creator, human beings were not created. For Dewey modern men and women think in scientific and secular terms, thus, they must now take a naturalistic view of origins (*see* EVOLUTION, BIOLOGICAL). Humanity is a result of naturalistic evolutionary processes, not the special creation by any kind of God.

The Elimination of Supernatural Religion. Dewey adamantly opposed any supernaturalism in religion. Since most religions pay some homage to the supernatural, he opposed religion in concept: "The claim on the part of religions to possess a monopoly of ideas and of the supernatural means by which alone, it is alleged, they can be furthered, stands in the way of the realization of distinctively religious values inherent in natural experience" (ibid., 27–28). Science calls into question the very concept of the supernatural. Many things once thought to be miraculous are now known to have natural explanations. Science will continue to explain the unusual phenomena of nature (*see* MIRACLES, ARGUMENTS AGAINST).

Not only is belief in the supernatural based on ignorance, but it hinders social intelligence. "It stifles the growth of the social intelligence by means of which the direction of social change could be taken out of the region of accident, as accident is defined" (ibid., 78).

Religions "involve specific intellectual beliefs, and they attach . . . importance to assent to these doctrines as true, true in an intellectual sense." That is, "they have developed a doctrinal apparatus it is incumbent upon 'believers' . . . to accept" (ibid., 29). Those beliefs include notions of unseen powers that control human destiny and to which obedience, reverence, and worship are due. Nothing is left in such beliefs that is worth preserving (ibid., 7).

Such beliefs hinder social progress. For "Men have never fully used the powers they possess to advance the good in life, because they have waited upon some power external to themselves and to nature to do the work they are responsible for doing. Dependence upon an external power is the counterpart of surrender of human endeavor" (ibid., 46).

The problem is religion's sacred-secular split. "The conception that 'religious' signifies a certain attitude and outlook, independent of the supernatural, necessitates no such division." For "It does not shut religious values up within a particular compartment, nor assume that a particular form of association bears a unique relation to it. Upon the social side the future of the religious function seems preeminently bound up with its emancipation from religions and a particular religion" (ibid., 66, 67).

Not only is social progress hindered by belief in the supernatural, but social values are deprecated by it. "The contention of an increasing number of persons is that depreciation of natural social values has resulted, both in principle and in actual fact, from reference of their origin and significance to supernatural sources" (ibid., 71).

Even truly religious attitudes are hampered by belief in the supernatural. Dewey wrote, "I have suggested that the religious element in life has been hampered by conceptions of the supernatural that were imbedded in those cultures wherein man had little control over outer nature and little in the way of sure method of inquiry and test" (ibid., 56).

A New Sort of Religion. Despite Dewey's rejection of religion and the supernatural, he by no means considered himself irreligious. He insisted on the need for, and preservation of, the religious. What Dewey did insist on was that religion as traditionally defined—as involving belief in the supernatural beyond this life—be discarded as a religious attitude toward all of life: "I shall develop another conception of the nature of the religious phase of experience, one that separates it from the supernatural and the things that have grown up about it." And "I shall try to show that these derivations are encumbrances and that what is genuinely religious will undergo an emancipation when it is relieved from them; that then, for the first time, the religious aspect of experience will be free to develop freely on its own account" (ibid., 2).

The most serious problem with religion is that it hinders social progress. Its belief in the supernatural hinders achievement of socially desirable goals. Therefore, nothing is lost by eliminating it. In fact, since more people are religious than have a religion, there is much to be gained by rejecting religion. For, said Dewey, "I believe that many persons are so repelled from what exists as a religion by its intellectual and moral implications, that they are not even aware of attitudes in themselves that if they came to fruition would be genuinely religious" (ibid., 9).

The Establishment of Natural Religious Attitudes. Dewey was quick to point out that he was not proposing that a new natural religion replace supernatural religion. Rather, he sought to emancipate elements and outlooks that might be called religious (ibid., 8). The difference between a religion and the religious is that a religion "always signifies a special body of beliefs and practices having some kind of institutional organization, loose or tight." By contrast, "the adjective 'religious' denotes nothing in the way of a specifiable entity, either institutional or as a system of beliefs." Rather, "it denotes an attitude that may be taken toward every object and every proposed end or ideal" (ibid., 9, 10).

Replacing traditional religion with religious attitudes would readjust and reorient life. Thus Dewey's humanistic definition of the religious is "any activity pursued in behalf of an ideal end against obstacles and in spite of threats of personal loss because of conviction of its general and enduring value is religious in quality" (ibid., 27).

Dewey acknowledges with Friedrich *Schleiermacher that a religious experience involves a feeling of dependence. But he insists it must be a dependence without traditional doctrines or fear (ibid., 25). Religious experience helps to develop a sense of unity impossible without it. For by a religious experience "the self is always directed toward something beyond itself and so its own unification depends upon the idea of the integration of the shifting scenes of the world into that imaginative totality we call the Universe" (ibid., 19).

Such experience takes place in different ways in different people. "It is sometimes brought about by devotion to a cause; sometimes by a passage of poetry that opens a new perspective; sometimes as was the case with *Spinoza . . . through philosophical reflection." So religious experiences are not necessarily unique species of their own. Rather, "they occur frequently in connection with many significant moments of living" (ibid., 14). Religious experience is a kind of unifying ideal of other experiences in life.

Dewey was willing to use the term *God*, but it meant, not a supernatural being, but " the ideal ends that at a given time and place one acknowledges as having authority over his volition and emotion, the values to which one is supremely devoted, as far as these ends, through imagination, take on unity" (ibid., 42) God represents a unification of one's essential values. For Dewey, progress and achievement were such ideal values.

He thought it essential that persons have such religious ideals. For "Neither observation, thought, nor practical activity can attain that complete unification of the self which is called a whole. The *whole* self is an ideal, an imaginative projection" (ibid., 19). Thus, self-unification can be achieved only through a religious commitment to "God" (that is, to ideal-values). Says Dewey, "I should describe this faith as the unification of the self through allegiance to inclusive ideal ends, which imagination presents to us and to which the human will responds as worthy of controlling our desires and choices" (ibid., 33).

A Common Faith. Dewey's religious form of pragmatic humanism was global. In his "common faith" he saw a religious goal for all. "Here are all the elements for a religious faith that shall not be confined to sect, class, or race. Such a faith has always been implicitly the common faith of mankind. It remains to make it explicit and militant" (ibid., 87). He saw the doctrine of the brotherhood as having the greatest religious significance. "Whether or not we are, save in some metaphorical sense, all brothers, we are at least in the same boat traversing the same turbulent ocean. The potential religious significance of this fact is infinite" (ibid., 84).

Dewey's Ultimate. For Dewey the absolute was democratic progress. Dewey opposed traditional supernatural religion because he perceived that it hindered social progress. He said "the assumption that only supernatural agencies can give control is a sure method of retarding this effort [of social betterment]" (ibid., 76).

He saw three stages in social development. "In the first stage, human relationships were thought to be so infected with the evils of corrupt human nature as to require redemption from external and supernatural sources." This must be rejected. "In the next stage, what is significant in these relations is found to be akin to values esteemed distinctively religious." This too must be surpassed. "The third stage would realize that in fact the values prized in those religions that have ideal elements are idealizations of things characteristic of natural association which have been projected into a supernatural realm for safe-keeping and sanction. . . . Unless there is a movement into what I have called the third stage, fundamental dualism and a division in life continue" (ibid., 73).

Science as the Means to Progress. Naturally, it is up to humankind to achieve social progress. This belief is neither egoistic nor optimistic. The only adequate means of achieving the goal of social progress is science. "There is but one sure road of access to truth—the road of patient, cooperative inquiry operating by means of observation, experimental record and controlled reflection" (ibid., 32). For "were we to admit that there is but one method for ascertaining fact and truth that conveyed by the word 'scientific' in its most general and generous sense—no discovery in any branch of knowledge and inquiry could then disturb the faith that is religious" (ibid., 33).

For Dewey faith in science, that is, in the critical intelligence, is more religious than faith in any revelation from God. On the other hand, "Some fixed doctrinal apparatus is necessary for *a* religion. But faith in the possibilities of continued and rigorous inquiry does not limit access to truth to any channel or scheme of things." This faith reveres intelligence as a force (ibid., 26).

Science has a decided advantage over religion as a means for human progress because it is a method, not a set of fixed beliefs. It is a way to change thinking by tested inquiry. Not only is science superior to religion, but it opposes religious dogma. "For scientific method is adverse not only to dogma but to doctrine as well, provided we take 'doctrine' in its usual meaning—a body of definite beliefs that need only to be taught and learned as true." However, "This negative attitude of science to doctrine does not indicate indifference to truth. It signifies supreme loyalty to the method by which truth is attained. The scientific-religious conflict ultimately is a conflict between allegiance to this method and allegiance to even an irreducible minimum of belief so fixed in advance that it can never be modified" (ibid., 38, 39).

Hence, science and religion are irreconcilable. But a religious dedication to science is essential to human progress.

Evaluation. **Pragmatism.* Dewey's relativism is manifest in truth and ethics. By the pragmatic view of truth, whatever works is true. But many things that "work" in the short-run are false. Truth is not what works, but what corresponds with the facts (*see* TRUTH, NATURE OF). No pragmatist would appreciate someone misrepresenting his view simply because it worked well to do so. Even pragmatist parents do not want their children to lie to them simply because it is expedient to do so from the child's perspective. Josiah Royce criticized James's pragmatism by asking whether James would take the witness stand in court and "swear to tell the expedient, the whole expedient and nothing but the expedient, so help him future experience!"

Pragmatism fares no better in the realm of ethics. Not everything that works is right. Some things that work very well are simply evil. Cheating, deceiving, and even killing undesirables have been "successful" activities. Ethical questions are not settled by obtaining desired results. All that success proves is that a given course of action *works*; it does not prove the course of action is *right*.

Progressivism. Dewey's relativism is not total. His system has the absolute of progress or achievement. Whatever works for social progress is good; what hinders it is evil. But by what standard is progress to be judged? If the standard is within society, then we cannot be sure we are *progressing*. Maybe we are only *changing*. If the standard is outside the race, this is a transcendent norm, a divine imperative, which Dewey rejects.

Another problem with progressivism is its lack of a fixed point by which one measures change. Otherwise, one could not even measure the change. If, for example, an observer of a moving car who is in a moving car cannot easily know how fast the other car is moving. If the other car is moving at the same speed in the same direction, the observer cannot even know it is moving unless something else that isn't moving can be used to measure it.

In practice progressivism is grounded in the wishes of those with the power to set the agenda. Why *social* progressivism? Why *democratic* social progressivism? One can progress toward ever-better dictatorships. Dewey's definition of "achievement" or "progress" in social and democratic terms was utterly arbitrary and philosophically unjustified. It stands on no better ground than other goals one may choose.

Relativism. Closely allied to progressivism is relativism. Dewey denies absolutes in the realm of truth (*see* TRUTH, NATURE OF) or ethics (*see* MORALITY, ABSOLUTE NATURE OF). This is inconsistent. To show that *all* is relative, one must have a nonrelative vantage point from which to view all of truth. One cannot relativize all else unless he stands on absolute ground. The statement "All is relative" either means that statement also is relative, or else that at least that statement is absolute. We have seen that Dewey believed in absolutes, but of his own choosing. Thus, his statement is self-defeating and fails according to Dewey's own worldview. He is guilty of special pleading, saying that everything is relative, except what he wants to be absolute. This is pure dogmatism.

Summary. Dewey's humanism was naturalistic, relativistic, optimistic, and even religious, despite its opposition to religion. Some characteristics of this thought are peculiar to Dewey. Dewey's form of humanism was pragmatic, militantly secular, progressive, and democratic. Also, Dewey placed great emphasis on science as the means for human achievement. His definition of *God* as the ideal, unifying goal for human progress is his own. Dewey believed in salvation by education, and the heart of education is experimentation. We learn by doing, and learning is forever incomplete. There is always room for more progress. There will not be a millennium, only a continual and relative process of seeking new goals by means of pragmatic experimentation.

Sources

R. J. Bernstein, "Dewey, John" in *EP*
J. O. Buswell, Sr., *The Philosophies of F. R. Tennant and John Dewey*
G. H. Clark, *Dewey*
J. Dewey, *A Common Faith*
N. L. Geisler, *Is Man the Measure?* Chap. 4
P. A. Schilpp, ed., *The Philosophy of John Dewey*

Divine Birth Stories. Since James *Frazer published *The Golden Bough* (1890, 1912), it has been common to charge that Christianity is not unique in its story of Christ's incarnation, but that stories of supernatural births are common to pagan gods. If true, this would appear to undermine Christianity by showing that it might have borrowed ideas from other religions.

Several lines of evidence that refute the pagan myth source theory are discussed in detail elsewhere (*see* LUKE, ALLEGED ERRORS IN; MITHRAISM; MYTHOLOGY AND THE NEW TESTAMENT; NEW TESTAMENT, HISTORICITY OF; VIRGIN BIRTH). Here the main points are summarized:

1. The New Testament was written by contemporaries and is not the result of late myth development. Legends do not develop if the stories are written while eyewitnesses are still alive to refute inaccuracies.
2. The virgin birth records do not show signs of being mythical, nor do they include borrowed elements from known pagan birth myths.
3. Persons, places, and events identified in connection with Christ's birth are accurate historically. Even details once thought to be errors have been vindicated by research.

4. No Greek myth spoke of the literal incarnation of a monotheistic God into human form. In Christianity the second person of the Godhead became human. In pagan religions gods were only disguised as humans; they were not really human. In pagan myths a god and human invariably mated sexually, which was not true in the Christian account.
5. Greek myths of gods who became human postdate the time of Christ, so the Gospel writers could not have borrowed from them.

Sources

J. Frazer, *The Golden Bough*
J. G. Machen, *The Virgin Birth of Christ*
R. Nash, *Christianity and Hellenism*
E. Yamauchi, "Easter—Myth, Hallucination, or History?" *CT* (29 March 1974; 15 April 1974)

Divine-Human Legends. ***See* APOTHEOSIS.**

Docetism. Docetism (Gk. *dokein*, "to seem") was a late-first-century heresy asserting that Jesus only seemed to be human (Kelly, 141). Docetism is "The assertion that Christ's human body was a phantasm, and that his suffering and death were mere appearances. 'If he suffered he was not God; if he was God he did not suffer'" (Bettenson, 49). They denied the humanity of Christ but affirmed his deity. This is the opposite of Arianism, which affirmed the humanity of Jesus but denied the deity of Christ (*see* CHRIST, DEITY OF). Docetism was already present in late New Testament times, as is evident by the exhortation of John the apostle about those who deny "that Jesus Christ has come *in the flesh*" (1 John 4:2; emphasis added. See also 2 John 7).

A Biblical Response. The Scriptures are replete with evidence that Jesus Christ was fully human in every respect, yet without sin (Heb. 4:15). Indeed, he is called "the man, Christ Jesus" (1 Tim. 2:5).

Jesus Had a Human Ancestry. The Gospels affirm that Jesus had an actual human genealogy all the way back to the first man, Adam. This was only possible on his mother's side, since he was born of a virgin (Matt. 1:20–25; Luke 2:1–7; *see* VIRGIN BIRTH). Matthew traces Jesus' genealogy to Abraham through his legal father, Joseph, through whom he inherited the right to the throne of David (Matt. 1:1). Luke apparently traces Jesus' genealogy through Mary, his actual mother, back to Adam, the actual head of the human race (Luke 3:23–38).

Jesus Had a Human Conception. According to Matthew, "an angel of the Lord appeared to him in a dream and said, "Joseph son of David, do not be afraid to take Mary home as your wife, because what is conceived in her is from the Holy Spirit" (Matt. 1:20). In scientific language, Jesus started the way all human beings do, by the fertilization of a human ovum. Only in his case it was supernaturally fertilized by the Holy Spirit, not by a human sperm.

Jesus Had a Human Birth. According to Dr. Luke,

> Joseph also went up from the town of Nazareth in Galilee to Judea, to Bethlehem the town of David, because he belonged to the house and line of David. He went there to register with Mary, who was pledged to be married to him and was expecting a child. While they were there, the time came for the baby to be born, and she gave birth to her firstborn, a son. She wrapped him in cloths and placed him in a manger, because there was no room for them in the inn. [Luke 2:4–7]

There was nothing unnatural, or even supernatural, about Jesus' birth. Mary had a nine-month pregnancy (Luke 1:26, 56, 57), birth pains, and Jesus was born through the birth canal as other natural children are born. Luke, citing Mosaic law, spoke of Jesus as "a male who opens the womb" (Luke 2:23 KJV), the same phrase used of all Jewish male firstborn. It was a natural birth, only in Mary's case she had no birth maid so she gave birth by herself (Luke 2:7).

Paul states Jesus' human birth more simply: "But when the time had fully come, God sent his Son, born of a woman, born under law" (Gal. 4:4). He was "born of woman," as are the rest of us (1 Cor. 11:12).

Jesus Had a Human Childhood. Although little is known of Jesus' childhood, enough is known to conclude that he grew up as did other children, learned, and developed normally. Like other Jewish boys he was circumcised when eight days old and dedicated to the Lord in the temple when he was forty days old (Luke 2:21–22). Apparently he was a precocious child (Luke 2:41–49), impressing the religious leaders with his knowledge of spiritual matters at age 12 (Luke 2:42–47). From that time, Luke reports, "Jesus grew in wisdom and stature, and in favor with God and men" (Luke 2:52). As a man, he was finite in understanding. As God, he was infinite in all things (*see* TRINITY).

Jesus Experienced Human Hunger. Luke records that Jesus went into the wilderness "where for forty days he was tempted by the devil. He ate nothing during those days, and at the end of them he was hungry" (4:2). Jesus' body needed food to sustain it.

Jesus Experienced Human Thirst. John says that "Jesus, tired as he was from the journey, sat down by the well. It was about the sixth hour. When a Samaritan woman came to draw water, Jesus said to her, 'Will you give me a drink?'" (4:6–7). Jesus needed water to sustain his body. When he did not have enough, he felt thirsty.

Jesus Experienced Human Fatigue. Jesus also got tired physically. And when he got tired, he rested. John said Jesus was "wearied with [his] journey" (John 4:6). At other times he withdrew from the crowd, "because so many people were coming and going that they did not even have a chance to eat, he said to them, 'Come with me by yourselves to a quiet place and get some rest'" (Mark 6:31).

Jesus Had Human Emotions. The shortest verse in the Bible says simply, "Jesus wept" (John 11:35) when he stood by his friend's grave. But a moment earlier, the text says, "when Jesus saw her weeping, and the Jews who had come along with her also weeping, he was deeply moved in spirit and troubled" (vs. 33). Jesus wept over Jerusalem, crying out, "O Jerusalem, Jerusalem, you who kill the prophets and stone those sent to you, how often I have longed to gather your children together, as a hen gathers her chicks under her wings, but you were not willing" (Matt. 23:37).

Jesus also experienced anger when he saw the temple being desecrated, "so he made a whip out of cords, and drove all from the temple area, both sheep and cattle; he scattered the coins of the money changers and overturned their tables" (John 2:15). Angered by religious hypocrisy he lashed out at the religious leaders,

> "Woe to you, teachers of the law and Pharisees, you hypocrites! You travel over land and sea to win a single convert, and when he becomes one, you make him twice as much a son of hell as you are.
>
> "Woe to you, blind guides! You say, 'If anyone swears by the temple, it means nothing; but if anyone swears by the gold of the temple, he is bound by his oath'" (Matt. 23:15–16).

Jesus Had a Human Sense of Humor. Contrary to some austere opinions, Jesus possessed a sense of humor. Humor is based in the sense of the incongruous. Jesus expressed this on several occasions. In the same Matthew 23 denunciation he said to the Scribes and Pharisees: "You blind guides! You strain out a gnat but swallow a camel" (vs. 24). Even after his resurrection he chided his experienced fisherman disciples that they had fished all night without catching one fish (John 21:5).

Jesus Had Human Language and Culture. Jesus was Jewish. He was the Son of Abraham and of David (Matt. 1:1). He had a Jewish mother (Matt. 1:20–25; Gal. 4:4). He had a Jewish culture and religion (John 4:5–9, 21–22). The woman of Samaria immediately recognized him as a Jew by the way he looked and talked (John 4:9).

Jesus Experienced Human Temptation. The writer of Hebrews informs us that "we do not have a high priest who is unable to sympathize with our weaknesses, but we have one who has been tempted in every way, just as we are—yet was without sin" (4:15). The temptation of Christ was real (Matthew 3). As a human being, Christ felt its full force (Matt. 26:38–42).

Jesus Was Human Flesh and Blood. Jesus, like Adam before the fall, did not possess inherent mortality. That came as a result of the fall (Rom. 5:12). Nevertheless, Jesus was capable of dying and did die. Like any other human, Jesus bled when cut. "One of the soldiers pierced Jesus' side with a spear, bringing a sudden flow of blood and water" (John 19:34). Hebrews shared the implications of that flesh and blood: "Since the children have flesh and blood, he too shared in their humanity so that by his death he might destroy him who holds the power of death—that is, the devil" (2:14).

Jesus Suffered Human Pain. Crucifixion inflicts an agonizing death, and Jesus experienced every moment of it, refusing even a drug to deaden the pain (Matt. 27:34). His pain was both physical and emotional. While on the cross he cried out in agony, "My God, my God, why have you forsaken me?" (Matt. 27:46). Before his death, he agonized in the garden, sweating as it were great drops of blood and confessing, "My soul is overwhelmed with sorrow to the point of death" (Matt. 26:38). The writer of Hebrews describes Jesus' experience vividly: "During the days of Jesus' life on earth, he offered up prayers and petitions with loud cries and tears to the one who could save him from death, and he was heard because of his reverent submission" (5:7).

Jesus Experienced Human Death. The Bible repeatedly testifies that Jesus died (for example, Matt. 16:21; Rom. 5:8; 1 Cor. 15:3; *see* CHRIST, DEATH OF). He was "put to death in the body" (1 Peter 3:18). Scriptures say repeatedly that Jesus shed his "blood" for our sins. Paul wrote, "But now in Christ Jesus you who once were far away have been brought near through the blood of Christ" (Eph. 2:13). Hebrews adds, "How much more, then, will the blood of Christ, who through the eternal Spirit offered himself unblemished to God, cleanse our consciences from acts that lead to death, so that we may serve the living God!" (9:14).

A Theological Response. The denial of Christ's humanity is as serious an error as to deny his deity. If Jesus is not both God and human, he cannot mediate between God and humans (1 Tim. 2:5). Salvation involves reconciliation of human beings to God (2 Cor. 5:18–19). This is only possible if God becomes human. *Anselm made this point in his *Cur Deus Homo?* (*Why the God Man?*) To deny Christ's true humanity is to deny the basis of our reconciliation to God. It is for this reason that the early church condemned docetism. Among those charged with teaching this false doctrine was Cerinthus, whom the apostle John opposed at Ephesus (see Cross, 413; Douglas, 305).

Sources

H. Bettenson, *Documents of the Christian Church*
F. L. Cross, *The Oxford Dictionary of the Christian Church*
J. D. Douglas, *The New International Dictionary of the Christian Church*, rev. ed.
J. N. D. Kelly, *Early Christian Doctrines*

Dooyeweerd, Herman. Herman Dooyeweerd (1894–1977) was a Dutch Reformed philosopher who attended, and later taught legal philosophy at the Free University in Amsterdam (1926–65). He is best known for his four-volume work, *A New Critique of Theoretical Thought* (1953–58). He founded the journal *Philosophia Reformata*, which was instrumental in the establishing of the Association for Calvinistic Philosophy (later called Christian Philosophy). Other works included *The Christian Idea of the State*, *In the Twilight of Western Thought*, *Roots of Western Culture*, and *Transcendental Problems*. His work followed in the Reformed tradition of Abraham Kuyper (1837–1920), although he went well beyond his predecessor in the critique of Western thought and in the development of his own system.

The Philosophy of Dooyeweerd. Although his thought springs from the Reformed thinker Kuyper, the philosophical roots of Dooyeweerd's philosophy go deeply into both Immanuel *Kant (1724–1804) and the phenomenology of Edmund Husserl (1859–1938). He begins with a critique of the foundations of Western thought, concluding that its basis in reason is ill-founded and unfruitful. It is blind to its own religious commitments, especially the pretended autonomy by which philosophy severed itself from divine revelation. Likewise, he rejected the adequacy of general revelation or common grace as a grounds for building a natural theology (*see* God, Evidence for).

The Transcendental Critique. One of Dooyeweerd's legacies is his *transcendental critique*, which was used by Cornelius *Van Til in his *presuppositional apologetics. The form of argument follows *Kant's transcendental reduction, whereby one posits the necessary conditions of thought and actions.

The transcendental critique differs from transcendent criticism. The latter is purely external, not getting at the internal root of the issue. The transcendental critique "What is it that makes science possible?" "How does Faith (the religious starting point) direct science (and philosophy)?" "How can it, unfortunately, also misdirect science?" (Klapwijk, 22). According to Jacob Klapwijk, this critique "zeroes in on the phenomena of science itself, retracing from the inside out, as it were, the train of thought which science follows, so as to finally arrive at its point of origin; the hidden religious starting point of all scientific activity" (ibid.).

The transcendental critique seeks out "antithesis," since its task is to conflict with all human-based thought structures. A law of human knowledge is that the truth is gained only in the conflict of opinion (Dooyeweerd, ix). This internal criticism opposes the absolute starting point of an unregenerate heart and "tries to open a thinker's eyes to pretheoretical presuppositions and motivations" that, according to Dooyeweerd, are religious in nature (ibid.). By it one shows "that reasoned argumentation of the human understanding is propelled (and possibly warped) by the motivation of the human heart" (ibid.). For every scientist, consciously or unconsciously, has a "cosmonomic idea" or general framework into which is fit all factual knowledge. "This framework itself, however, is erected on a (believing or unbelieving) religious foundation" (ibid.). So the transcendental method is the key to the door of the heart. Only in service of God can it be used to unlock that door.

The Heart as the Root of Reality. Dooyeweerd regarded the heart as the root of Christian existence. It is the religious center of one's being. The fallen heart is set against God; hence, there is no religiously neutral thought structure to which one can appeal in building a philosophical system (*see* Noetic Effects of Sin).

The fallacy of all non-Christian thought is that it attempts to find meaning in creation. But meaning is not found in the immanent creation but in the transcendent Creator. Hence, we must reject human autonomy (*see* Schaeffer, Francis) and live in dependence on God's revelation (see Dooyeweerd, *In the Twilight*, 67).

Sphere Sovereignty. Dooyeweerd builds a distinctively Christian system of hierarchically ordered spheres which he claims comprise the foundation of reality. His theory is known as sphere sovereignty, with each sphere of intellectual or practical activity subordinate to God's revelation.

God has set up fifteen spheres for the operation of different aspects of creation:

Succession of Sphere	Modal Moment	Science
1. numerical	discrete quantity	mathematics
2. spatial	extension	mathematics
3. kinematic	movement	mechanics
4. physical	energy	physics, chemistry
5. biological	organic life	biology, physiology, and morphology
6. psychical	feeling-sensation	empirical psychology
7. analytical	theoretical distinction	logic

8. historical	cultural process	history of the development of human society
9. linguistic	symbolic signification	philology, semantics
10. social	social intercourse	sociology
11. economic	economy	economics
12. aesthetic	harmony	aesthetics
13. juridical	retribution	jurisprudence
14. ethical	love of one's neighbor	ethics
15. pistical-faith	transcendent certainty regarding the origin	theology

(Adapted from: E. L. Hebdon Taylor: *The Christian Philosophy of Law, Politics, and the State* [Nutley, N.J.: Craig, 1969], 274.)

All meaning in created spheres points beyond itself. Dooyeweerd wrote: "*Meaning,* as we said, constantly points *without* and *beyond* itself toward an origin, which is itself no longer *meaning*. It remains within the bounds of the *relative*. *The true* Origin, *on the contrary, is* absolute and *self-sufficient!*" (*New Critique,* 10). Further, there are no isolated truths. All truth must be understood in coherence with the whole system of truth. "There exists no partial truth which is sufficient to itself. Partial *theoretical* truth is truth only in the coherence of the theoretical truths, and this coherence in its relativity pre-supposes the fullness or the totality of truth" (ibid., 116).

Only God, the Sovereign, is absolute. Each sphere is relative and subordinate to him. "The concept of an 'absolute theoretical truth' dissolves itself in inner contradiction" (ibid., 156). "This means that the dogma concerning the autonomy of theoretical thought must lead its adherents into a seemingly inescapable *impasse*. To maintain this autonomy, they are obligated to seek their starting point in theoretical thought itself" (Dooyeweerd, *In the Twilight,* 19).

Each sphere is subject to the sovereignty of God. Dooyeweerd quotes Calvin: "God is not subject to the laws [He made], but [He is] not arbitrary" (*A New Critique,* 93). This judgment is at the foundation of all speculative thought. It lays "bare the limits of human reason set for it by God in His temporal world-order" (ibid.).

Influence. Dooyeweerd's philosophy has not had wide acceptance outside Reformed circles, but has nevertheless attracted a small band of dedicated followers. Hans Rookmaaker and Van Til are perhaps his most noted disciples, although Francis *Schaeffer popularized many of his ideas.

Evaluation. *Positive Contributions.* Among the valuable aspects of Dooyeweerd's thought is his desire to preserve the sovereignty of God.

A massive critique of non-Christian thought. Few Christian philosophers have aimed more directly at the jugular of non-Christian thought. Dooyeweerd offers a massive critique of the foundations of Western thought, correctly assessing that it is blind to its own religious commitments.

Sovereignty and sphere sovereignty. Dooyeweerd keeps things in proper order. God is first, and he is sovereign. Nothing else is absolutely absolute. All else is dependent on him. With God's absolute sovereignty firmly in place, Dooyeweerd sees all other spheres as derivative. Indeed, the very idea that everything under God is only sovereign *in its sphere* is helpful. For when there are conflicts between spheres, it keeps in focus that they are not absolutely absolute.

The heart. Dooyeweerd's philosophy begins in the heart. For, as the Scriptures says, "Above all else, guard your heart, for it is the wellspring of life" (Prov. 4:23). Indeed, *atheism begins in the heart (Ps. 14:1). So, no complete understanding of humanity is possible without including the role of the heart.

The firm starting point. As a firm starting point for his philosophy the post-Kantian Dooyeweerd developed a *transcendental argument, which became characteristic of his disciple, Van Til. This approach offers firm epistemological grounds on which to build.

Negative Aspects. Dooyeweerd has critics, even among Reformed theologians. Likewise, he rejected the adequacy of general revelation (*see* REVELATION, GENERAL) or common grace as a grounds for building a natural theology (*see* GOD, EVIDENCE FOR).

The tendency toward voluntarism. Inherent in Dooyeweerd's stress on sovereignty is an implied voluntarism. While he makes a noble attempt to avoid the charge of being arbitrary, he does not seem to succeed. For unchangeable rules of reason common to God and man, but rooted in God's nature, do not seem to be what he has in mind (*see* GOD, NATURE OF).

A confusion of the autonomy and ultimacy of reason. While Dooyeweerd is right in chastising the autonomy of reason apart from God, he does not seem to appreciate that this does not mean that reason can be an ultimate standard for truth. This springs out of his voluntarism, which sees reason as springing from God's will, not as anchored in his very nature.

The lack of biblical support. There is a general failure to demonstrate that all his spheres are rooted in Scripture. From a distinctly Christian perspective, which his view claims to be, this is a serious shortcoming.

A basic inconsistency. Dooyeweerd insists that an autonomous human being cannot self-interpret creation. He must view it with the help of God from God's point of view. Yet, he claims that there is a prescientific (phenomenological) starting point at which the person can interpret creation. In this regard, Dooyeweerd is not consistent with a transcendental approach. For rather than looking for the transcendentally necessary conditions of all human thought and actions, he seems to root his epistemology in a phenomenological starting point.

A nonrational starting point. Further, this phenomenological method is self-defeating. One cannot *conceive* of the preconceptual nor *think* the prerational. The truth is that reason is inescapable. There is no prerational starting point for rational beings.

A denial of the ultimacy of the laws of logic. For Dooyeweerd, *logic as we know it applies only to the created world. But how then can we think about God without these laws of thought? Certainly, truth cannot be found in contradictory statements about God. How would this differ from a Zen Buddhist's *koan* (*see* BUDDHISM), such as one hand clapping, being a key to "understanding" ultimate reality (the Tao)?

Inadequate tests for truth. Dooyeweerd's tests for truth seem to reduce to a subjective one (the witness of the Holy Spirit) and an inadequate one (internal consistency). The latter is really only a test for falsity; all inconsistent views are false. But it is not really a test for truth, since more than one opposing view may be internally inconsistent (*see* CLARK, GORDON).

The insufficiency of general revelation. Like many other Reformed thinkers, Dooyeweerd believes that general revelation is not understandable by fallen humanity. However, this is directly contrary to the claim of the Scriptures (Rom. 1:19–20; 2:12) which affirm that general revelation is "clearly perceived" and fallen humanity stands condemned for not responding to it (*see* REVELATION, GENERAL). The fact that the unbelieving heart does not *receive* it (1 Cor 2:14) in no way means that they do not *perceive* God's general revelation (cf. Ps. 19:1–6; Acts 14:17).

Sources

V. Brummer, *Transcendental Criticism and Christian Philosophy*
A. L. Conradie, *The Neo-Calvinist Concept of Philosophy*
H. Dooyeweerd, *In the Twilight of Western Thought*
———, *A New Critique of Theoretical Thought*
L. Kalsbeeck, *Contours of a Christian Philosophy*
J. Klapwijk, "Dooyeweerd's Christian Philosophy: Antithesis and Critique," *RJ*, March 1980
R. Nash, *Dooyeweerd and the Amsterdam Philosophy*
J. M. Spier, *An Introduction to Christian Philosophy*
E. L. H. Taylor, *The Christian Philosophy of Law, Politics, and the State*

Double-Truth Theory. ***See*** **AVERROES.**

Doubt. ***See*** **CERTAINTY/CERTITUDE; FAITH AND REASON; FIRST PRINCIPLES; INDUCTIVISM; HOLY SPIRIT, ROLE IN APOLOGETICS.**

Dualism. In metaphysics dualism is the belief that there are two coeternal principles in conflict with each other, such as matter and form (or spirit) or of good and evil. Platonism is an example of the former and Zoroastrianism, *Gnosticism, and Manichaeism are examples of the latter. Dualists believe in creation *ex materia*, that is, out of preexisting matter or stuff. This is in contrast to theists, who believe in creation *ex nihilo*, out of nothing, and with pantheists (*see* PANTHEISM), who believe in creation *ex Deo*, out of God (*see* CREATION, VIEWS OF).

Difficulties with Dualism. As *Thomas Aquinas observed (see Aquinas, passim), not all first principles, such as good and evil, are eternal. Short and tall are opposites, but it does not follow that there must be eternally short and eternally tall beings. Thus, good and evil can be opposed to each other without both being eternal. He reasoned that the problem is the assumption that "because all contraries seem to be compressed under the headings of good and evil, in that one of them by comparison is always deficient, they reckon that the primary active principles are the Good and the Evil." So "there is not one first principle of evil as there is of good." One reason for this is that "the original principle of things is essentially good. [But] nothing can be essentially bad. Every being, as being, is good; evil does not exist except in a good subject" (Aquinas 1.1).

In dualism neither principle can be supreme, since each is limited by the other. But, it would seem that something must be ultimate. As C. S. *Lewis observed, "the two Powers, the good and the evil, do not explain each other. Neither . . . can claim to be the Ultimate. More ultimate than either of them is the inextricable fact of their being there together. Each of them, therefore, is *conditioned*—finds himself willy nilly in a situation; and either that situation itself, or some unknown force which produced that situation, is the real Ultimate" (Lewis, *God in the Dock,* 22). "You cannot accept two conditioned and mutually independent beings as self-grounded, self-comprehending Absolute" (ibid.).

In the moral sense, one principle cannot be pronounced "good" and the other "evil," unless they are measured by something outside either of them. But, as Lewis noted, "the moment you say that, you are putting into the universe a third thing in addition to the two Powers: some law or standard or rule of good which one of the powers conforms to and the other fails to conform to." However, since "the two powers are judged by this standard, or the Being who made this standard, then this standard, or the Being who made this standard, is farther back and higher up than either of them, and He will be the real God" (*Mere Christianity,* 49)

"Dualism gives evil a positive, substantive, self-consistent nature, like that of good." But "If evil has the same kind of reality as good, the same autonomy and completeness, our allegiance to good becomes the arbitrary chosen loyalty of a partisan." But "a sound theory of value . . . demands that good should be original and evil a mere perversion; that good should be the tree and evil the ivy; that good should be able to see all round evil (as when sane men understand lunacy) while evil cannot retaliate in kind . . ." (Lewis, *God in the Dock,* 22–23).

As *Augustine concluded, evil is the lack of good and not the reverse. For when we take all the evil out of something it is better. But when we take all the good from something there is nothing (Augustine). Hence, good is the ultimate and evil is a limitation in or privation of evil (*see* EVIL, PROBLEM OF).

Sources

Augustine, *Anti-Manichean Writings*
N. L. Geisler, *Philosophy of Religion*, chapters 14–15
———, *The Roots of Evil*
C. S. Lewis, *God in the Dock*
———, *Mere Christianity*
Thomas Aquinas, *On Evil*

Duns Scotus. ***See*** **COSMOLOGICAL ARGUMENT.**

Ee

Ebla Tablets. Sixteen thousand clay tablets from the third millennium B.C. were discovered at Ebla in modern Syria, beginning in 1974. Biovanni Pettinato dates them 2580–2450 B.C. and Paolo Matthiae suggests 2400–2250 B.C. Either period predates any other written material by hundreds of years.

Apologetic Importance of the Tablets. The importance of the Ebla tablets is that they parallel and confirm early chapters of Genesis. Although clouded by subsequent political pressure and denials, the published reports in reputable journals offer several possible lines of support for the biblical record (*see* ARCHAEOLOGY, OLD TESTAMENT).

Tablets reportedly contain names of the cities Ur, Sodom and Gomorrah, and such pagan gods mentioned in the Bible as Baal (see Ostling, 76–77).

The Ebla tablets reportedly contain references to names found in the book of Genesis, including Adam, Eve, and Noah (Dahood, 55–56).

Of great importance is discovery of the oldest known creation accounts outside the Bible. Ebla's version predates the Babylonian account by some 600 years. The creation tablet is strikingly close to that of Genesis, speaking of one being who created the heavens, moon, stars, and earth. Parallels show that the Bible contains the older, less embellished version of the story and transmits the facts without the corruption of the mythological renderings. The tablets report belief in creation from nothing, declaring: "Lord of heaven and earth: the earth was not, you created it, the light of day was not, you created it, the morning light you had not [yet] made exist" (*Ebla Archives,* 259).

There are significant implications in the Ebla archives for Christian apologetics. They destroy the critical belief in the evolution of monotheism (*see* MONOTHEISM, PRIMITIVE) from supposed earlier polytheism and henotheism. This evolution of religion hypothesis has been popular from the time of Charles *Darwin (1809–1882) and Julius *Wellhausen (1844–1918). Now monotheism is known to be earlier. Also, the force of the Ebla evidence supports the view that the earliest chapters of Genesis are history, not mythology (*see* FLOOD, NOAH'S; SCIENCE AND THE BIBLE).

Sources

S. C. Beld, et al., *The Tablets of Ebla: Concordance and Bibliography*

M. Dahood, "Are the Ebla Tablets Relevant to Biblical Research?" *BAR*, September–October 1980

H. LaFay, "Ebla," *National Geographic*, 154.6 (December 1978)

P. Matthiae, *Ebla: An Empire Rediscovered*

E. Merrill, "Ebla and Biblical Historical Inerrancy," *Bib. Sac.*, October–December 1983

R. Ostling, "New Grounding for the Bible?" *Time*, 21 September 1981

B. Pettinato, *The Archives of Ebla*

Eden, Garden of. "Now the LORD God had planted a garden in the east, in Eden; and there he put the man he had formed" relates Genesis 2:8. Since Adam and Eve are presented as real persons with real children from which the whole human race has come (Gen. 5:1; 1 Chron. 1:1; Luke 3:38; Rom. 5:12), it is also assumed that there was a literal Garden of Eden. Indeed, the Bible speaks of it as an actual place on earth that abounded with trees, plants, and animals. It had rivers and a gate (Genesis 2–3). However, critics point out that there is no archaeological (*see* ARCHAEOLOGY, OLD TESTAMENT) evidence that such a place existed. They conclude that the story of Eden is just a myth (*see* BIBLE CRITICISM).

Arguments for a Real Garden. However, strong evidence to support the literal reality of the Garden of Eden comes from various sources.

Since Scripture says that the Lord sealed off the garden in some way following the fall, this is one place where Christians would not expect to find archaeological ruins (Gen. 3:24). Nor is there any indication that Adam and Eve made pottery or built durable buildings. Whatever might have remained of a Garden of Eden would have been destroyed by the flood which covered the earth (Genesis 6–9; 2 Peter 3:5–6).

The Bible does give evidence of the location, since two of the rivers mentioned still exist—the Tigris (Hiddekel) and the Euphrates (Gen. 2:14).

Even if the rivers have a different flow since the flood, the placement of very names as rivers indicates that the writer believed this to be a literal place. The Bible even locates them in Assyria (vs. 14), which is modern Iraq.

For a discussion of the reality of Adam and Eve, see ADAM, HISTORICITY OF. There is abundant evidence that these were the first human beings and the literal progenitors of the human race. Literal people need a literal place to live. The Bible calls that place the garden God planted in Eden (Gen. 2:8).

The New Testament refers to events that took place in Eden as historical. It speaks of the creation of Adam and Eve (Matt. 19:4; 1 Tim. 2:13) and of their fall into sin (1 Tim. 2:14; Rom. 5:12). But these literal historical events need a literal geographic place in which to occur.

The Scriptures affirm that God will one day restore human beings in a literal resurrection body (*see* RESURRECTION, PHYSICAL NATURE OF) to a literal restored paradise (Rom. 8:18–23; Revelation 21–22). But what is a literal paradise regained if there was not a literal paradise lost?

Conclusion. For those who place any credibility in the biblical record, the evidence for a literal Eden is very strong. This place intertwines with central teachings of Christian faith, such as a literal Creation, Fall, and restoration which give it even more importance. To deny a literal Eden is to deny a foundation stone for basic Bible teachings for which there is strong evidence.

Edwards, Jonathan. Jonathan Edwards (1703–1758) was a significant theologian-philosopher, revivalist, and pastor in early America. Son of a Congregational minister, Edwards was a classical apologist (*see* CLASSICAL APOLOGETICS). After earning a bachelor's degree at Yale (1720), he entered the ministry in the Presbyterian church in New York in 1726. He died only a few weeks after he began his work as president of the College of New Jersey (now Princeton University) in 1758.

Edwards was heavily influenced by John *Locke (1632–1704) and Isaac Newton (1642–1727), and to a lesser extent by the British idealism of George *Berkeley (1685–1753). A child prodigy, Edwards produced his first works as a teenager. His first philosophical work "Of Being" contains a powerful cosmological argument, as does his other youthful work "The Mind." Likewise, in his *Miscellanies* he argues for the existence and necessity of God. In his unpublished "Sermon on Romans 1:20" (1743) Edwards provides a detailed cosmological and teleological argument for God. One of his greatest works, *The Freedom of the Will* (1754), is also apologetic in emphasis, as is *A Treatise Concerning Religious Affections* (1746). His great work on apologetics, *A Rational Divinity,* was never completed.

The Apologetics of Edwards. As a classical apologist in the footsteps of *Thomas Aquinas and John Locke, Edwards began with proofs for the existence of God. Edwards used both the cosmological and teleological arguments, though his emphasis was on the former.

The Relation of Faith and Reason. Edwards balanced reason and revelation. Reason had eight basic functions:

> First, reason must prove the existence of God, the Revealer. Second, reason anticipates that there will be a revelation. Third, reason alone can grasp rationally any "pretended" revelation. Fourth, only reason can demonstrate the rationality of revelation. Fifth, reason must verify any revelation as genuine. Sixth, reason argues revelation's dependability. Seventh, reason, having anticipated mysteries in any genuine divine revelation, defends them, refuting any objections to their presence. Eighth, though the "divine and supernatural light" does not come from reason, it is reason that comprehends what this light illuminates. [*Jonathan Edwards,* 22–23]

There are, however, four significant limitations to human reason.

> First, it cannot make the knowledge of God 'real' to unregenerate man. Second, it cannot yield a supernatural, salvific revelation or even 'sense' it by mere reason. Third, if it does receive a revelation, it cannot thereafter determine what that revelation may and may not contain. Fourth, it cannot even 'apprehend' divine revelation as divine revelation, though it may recognize its presence. [ibid., 27]

Proofs of the Existence of God. Edwards outlines his own approach to God's existence (*see* GOD, EVIDENCE FOR) in *Freedom of the Will* (2.3). The apologist proves *a posteriori,* or from effects, that there must be an eternal cause and then argues that this being must be necessary and perfect *a priori*. Edwards combined cosmological and teleological proofs. He even argued against an eternal universe (see "Sermon on Romans 1:20") in the mode of the *kalam* cosmological argument.

God is eternal. That God must be eternal was firm in Edwards' mind from youth. In his essay "The Mind" he concluded that "it is not strange that there should be [something eternal], for that necessity of there being something or nothing implies it." And since there is something, then there must always have been something. Why? Because nothing is an impossibility, since "we can't have any such knowledge because there is no such thing."

Edwards' firm conviction that something is eternal springs out of the law of causality (*see* CAUSALITY, PRINCIPLE OF), which he describes as a self-evident principle, a "dictate of common sense," "the mind of mankind," and "this grand principle of common sense" (*Freedom,* 2.3). In "Miscellanies" he declares that the principle that all effects have a cause is a self-evident truth (*see* FIRST PRINCIPLES). This being the case, "if we suppose a time wherein there was nothing, a body will not of its own accord begin to be." For to hold that something can arise without a cause is abhorrent to the understanding (*Freedom,* 91, p. 74).

So convinced was Edwards that something could not arise without a cause that he argued even an eternal world would need a cause. For "if we should suppose that the world is eternal, yet the beauty, contrivance, and useful disposition of the world would not less strongly conclude for the being of an intelligent author." For "if we should see such a poem as Vergil's *Aeneid,* would it be any more satisfying to us if we were told that it was from eternity. . . . Would it be at all more satisfying that if we were told that it was made by the causal falling of ink on paper?" (ibid., 312, pp. 79–80).

There must be an eternal being. So God's eternality is necessary because an eternal "nothing" is impossible, since nothing cannot produce something. Something is, so something must always have been. There are only two alternatives: Nothing or God. But as Edwards scholar John Gerstner succinctly put it, "Nothing is nothing at all. That is, we cannot form the notion of Nothing. If we think we have an idea of Nothing, then we think we know that Nothing *is*. *Nothing has become an existent entity;* Nothing then is Something" (Gerstner, "Outline of the Apologetics," 10).

Proofs of the Attributes of God. As Gerstner correctly noted, "Extraordinary theologians such as Thomas Aquinas and Jonathan Edwards find more of God in the ordinary revelation of nature than ordinary theologians find in the extraordinary revelation of Scripture" (ibid., 99).

Edwards summarizes what can be known about God by general revelation (*see* REVELATION, GENERAL): "'Tis by metaphysics only, that we can demonstrate that God is not limited to a place, or is not mutable; that He is not ignorant, or forgetful; that it is impossible for Him to lie, or be unjust; and there is one God only and not hundreds or thousands" (*Freedom,* 4.13).

God is independent. Since God is eternal and necessary, he must be independent. He is prior to the world, and the world is dependent on him, not the reverse.

God has all perfections. "To have some and not all [perfections] is to be finite. He is limited in some respects, viz., with regard to the number of virtues or perfections." But "this is . . . inconsistent with independent and necessary existence. To be limited as to the virtues and excellent qualities is a contingent being" ("Sermon on Romans 1:20").

God is infinite. Edwards asserted that "Nothing is more certain than that an unmade and unlimited Being exists" (*Works,* 97–98). For that which is necessary and independent must be infinite.

God is One. Since God is infinite he must be one. For "to be infinite is to be all and [it] would be a contradiction to suppose two alls" ("Miscellanies," no. 697). All reality is in God, either as his being or in what flows from it. In Edwards' words, "God is the sum of all being and there is no being without His being. All things are in Him, and He in all" (ibid., no. 880).

Edwards' Attack on Deism. Not only did Edwards believe that God existed but that miracles are possible (*see* MIRACLE; MIRACLES, APOLOGETIC VALUE OF). God is not deistic (*see* DEISM). In fact, Edwards' critique of deism is one of the most penetrating of the eighteenth century.

Deist, in contrast to Christian, theists believed that God created the world and has revealed himself in nature, but he never performs miracles or produces a supernatural revelation. This view was proclaimed in Matthew *Tindal's "Bible of the deists," *Christianity as Old as Creation, or the Gospel, a Republication of the Religion of Nature* (1730). For Tindal, and other deists, such as Thomas *Jefferson, Thomas Paine, and Francois *Voltaire, natural revelation was sufficient.

As Gerstner notes, Edwards "refutes the Deists not by an appeal to faith but by rational analysis" (Gerstner, "Outline of the Apologetics," 196). He demonstrates the utter insufficiency of reason as a substitute for revelation (ibid., p. 197). Contrary to Tindal, Edwards argues that, once reason has shown a revelation to be from God, it is reasonable to insist that every doctrine contained in that revelation be true (*Works,* 2.479f.). Once it is known that the Bible is the Word of God, sound reason demands that all its dictates be accepted.

Proof of the Need for Supernatural Revelation. Edwards' argument for divine revelation is threefold: "(1) Though God through nature reveals so much of himself, men do not really 'know' God from nature. (2) Even if they did know God from nature, nature does not reveal whether God will damn or save them. (3) Even if nature did reveal that fact, it would not change man's hostile attitude toward God and salvation" (Gerstner, "Outline of the Apologetics," 198–99).

People do not "know" God from nature. In one of his sermons, Edwards speaks of "Man's Natural Blindness in the Things of Religion" (Edwards, *Works,* 2.247f.). For "there is an extreme brutish blindness in things of religion, which naturally possesses the hearts of mankind" (ibid., 247). This is not the fault of the senses, but the blindness of the heart. From this "plainly appears the *necessity* of divine *revelation*" (ibid., 253).

People do not know whether they will be saved. However good natural revelation is, it is not salvific. Natural revelation brings condemnation, not salvation. It leaves people inexcusable (Rom. 1:20). If they "will not be convinced for salvation, they shall be convinced by damnation" (ibid., 255).

Natural revelation does not soften enmity. Nature leaves humanity at enmity with God. Edwards concluded, "I am of the mind that mankind would have been like a parcel of beasts, with regard to their knowledge in all important truths, if there never had been any such thing as revelation in the world, and that they never would have risen out of their brutality." Furthermore, "None ever came to tolerable notions of divine things, unless by the revelation contained in the Scriptures" ("Miscellanies," 350). As Gerstner put it, "if there is anything natural revelation reveals, it is that natural revelation is not sufficient" (Gerstner, "Outline of the Apologetics," 200).

Proof of Supernatural Revelation in the Bible. Of course, this only shows that we need special revelation, not that we have it. To establish that the Bible is the Word of God Edwards used a twofold argument: (1) It is internally consistent. (2) It is externally confirmed.

The internal test: Rationality. Stated as a negative, Christianity is not false because it has mysteries (*see* MYSTERY) but no internal contradictions (*see* "MISCELLANIES," 544). Right reason and revelation harmonize, and "the Bible does not ask [human beings] to believe things against reason" ("Sermon on Isaiah 3:10"). God's way to the heart is through the head.

The external test: Miraculous evidence. Like other classical apologists, Edwards believed that miracles follow from the existence of the theistic God. If God can create the world, he can intervene in it. This miraculous intervention takes one of four forms.

First, there is the miracle of supernatural predictive prophecy (*see* PROPHECY AS PROOF OF THE BIBLE). In "Miscellanies" he deals with the fulfillment of Old Testament predictions, both general and messianic (443, 891, 1335). Only God could make such predictions.

Second, miracles can be used to accredit a messenger of God. Edwards appeals to the miracles of Christ. Sometimes, as in the case of the raising of Lazarus, Jesus stated in advance he would perform the miracle to prove his claim. "Now can it be imagined that God would hear an impostor or so order or suffer it that so extraordinary a thing should be done immediately in consequence of the word and act of an impostor?" (ibid., 444).

Third, he appeals to the supernatural nature of the content of Moses' teaching (*see* MIRACLES AS CONFIRMATION OF TRUTH), arguing that no divine thing can come out of a purely human source. "For example, how could the Jews who were not learned in science or philosophy and were as prone to idolatry as the nations around them come forth with their refined and advanced doctrine of God" (ibid., 159, 1158).

Fourth, he argued from the supernatural results of conversion. How otherwise can a person overcome the fear of death? ("Sermon on Romans 14:7"). He went to great lengths in "A Treatise Concerning Religious Affections" to show that the joy and peace that characterize Christian conversion are not present in other religions.

The Need for Subjective Illumination. All of his stress on rational and objective evidence notwithstanding, Edwards did not believe that either general or special revelation was sufficient to open depraved hearts to God's truth. Only "the divine and supernatural light" could open the heart to receive God's revelation. Without this divine illumination, no one ever comes to accept God's revelation, regardless of how strong the evidence. A new heart is needed, not a new brain. This comes by illumination of the Holy Spirit. This divine light does not give new truth or new revelation. Rather, it provides a new heart, a new attitude of receptivity to revealed truth (see Gerstner, "Outline of the Apologetics," 295–97; *see* HOLY SPIRIT, ROLE IN APOLOGETICS).

The Reasonableness of Free Will and Predestination. As a strong predestinarian, Edwards believed that God had no obligation to save everyone. All deserve to go to *hell. So, "he might, if He had pleased, have left all to perish, or might have redeemed all" (*Jonathan Edwards,* 119). But God chose to predestine some to heaven and left others to their just deserts in hell. How can all be free and yet God irresistibly predetermine that only some will be saved? Edwards attempts to rationally reconcile these two seemingly contradictory doctrines by affirming that Liberty "is the power, opportunity, or advantage, that any one has to do as he pleases" (ibid., 311). Free choice is doing what one desires, but it is God who gives only the elect the desire to accept him. Hence, only they will be saved (*see* "HEATHEN," SALVATION OF; INFANTS, SALVATION OF; UNIVERSALISM).

Edwards' Rational Defense of Hell. Nowhere does Edwards demonstrate his belief in the rationality of Christianity any more than in his defense of the doctrine of eternal conscious punishment. He argued that even one sin deserves hell, since the eternal, holy God cannot tolerate any sin. How much more, then, does a multitude of daily sins in thought, word, and deed make one unfit for his presence? This is compounded by rejection of God's immense mercy. And add to this a readiness to find fault with God's justice and mercy, and we have abundant evidence of the need for hell. Thus, he insisted, if we had a true spiritual awareness, we would not be amazed at hell's severity but at our own depravity (*Works*, 1.109).

Edwards argued that "It is a most unreasonable thing to suppose that there should be no future punishment, to suppose that God, who had made man a rational creature, able to know his duty and sensible that he is deserving punishment when he does it not; should let man alone, and let him live as he will, and never punish him for his sins, and never make any difference between the good and the bad. . . . How unreasonable it is to suppose, that he who made the world, should leave things in such confusion, and never take any care of the governing of his creatures, and that he should never judge his reasonable creatures" (*Works*, 2.884).

Edwards answers some of the most difficult questions about hell ever posed by a rational mind:

Why do people not repent in hell? It would seem, once they get to such a horrible place, that the damned would want to leave. No so, reasoned Edwards. For how can a place devoid of God's mercy accomplish what no efforts of his grace could accomplish on earth, namely, effect a change of the heart and disposition of wicked people? If hell could reform wicked sinners, then they would be saved without Christ, who is the sole means of salvation (ibid., 2.520). Suffering has no tendency to soften a hard heart; it hardens it more. Edwards might find that the high rate of recidivism and hardened criminality in modern prisons confirms his point.

Why are temporal sins due eternal punishment? God's justice demands eternal punishment for sins because "the heinousness of any crime must be gauged according to the worth or dignity of the person it is committed against" (Davidson, 50). Thus, a murder of a President or pope is more heinous than that of a terrorist or Mafia boss. Sin against an infinite God is an infinite sin, worthy of infinite punishment (*Works*, 2.83).

Why cannot hell have redeeming value? Hell both satisfies God's justice and glorifies it by showing how great and fearful a standard it is. "The vindicative justice of God will appear strict, exact, awful, and terrible, and therefore glorious" (ibid., 2.87). The more horrible and fearful the judgment, the brighter the sheen on the sword of God's justice. Awe-inspiring punishment fits the nature of an awe-inspiring God. By a majestic display of God's wrath, God gets back the majesty he has been refused. An awful display of punishment in the afterlife will bring to God what human beings refused to give him in this life. Those who give God no glory by choice during this life will be forced to give him glory in the afterlife.

All are either actively or passively useful to God. In heaven believers will be actively useful in praising his mercy. In hell unbelievers will be passively useful in bringing majesty to his justice. Just as a barren tree is useful only for firewood, so disobedient men are only fuel for an eternal fire (ibid., 2.126). Since unbelievers prefer to keep at a distance from God in time, why should we not expect this to be their chosen state in eternity?

Would a merciful God permit suffering in hell? To suppose that God's mercy does not permit suffering in hell is contrary to fact. God allows plenty of suffering in this world. It is an empirical fact that God and creature-pain are not incompatible (Gerstner, "Outline of the Apologetics," 80). If God's mercy cannot bear eternal misery, then neither can it bear lesser amounts (*Works*, 2.84).

Further, Edwards contended that God's mercy is not a passion or emotion that overcomes his justice. Mercy so construed would constitute a defect in God. It would make him weak and inconsistent, not a fit judge.

Finally, our attitudes and feelings will be transformed and correspond more to God's. Hence, we will love only what God loves and hate what he hates. Since God is not miserable at the thought or sight of hell, neither will we be—even in the case of people we loved in this life. Edwards devoted a whole sermon to this: "The End of the Wicked Contemplated by the Righteous." In Gerstner's digest of it, "it will seem in no way cruel in God to inflict such extreme suffering on such extremely wicked creatures" (Gerstner, "Outline of the Apologetics," 90).

Evaluation. It is possible only to touch on the implications for apologetics found in Edwards' work.

Positive Evaluation. Jonathan Edwards was a noted American revivalist and a great intellectual—a rare combination. His defense of the Faith was in the tradition of the *classical apologists.

Whatever one may think of Edwards' answers to the difficult questions about hell, he attempted to confront the most difficult theological problems. He believed that God's truth is in harmony with right reason. His defense of Christianity began with one of the most rational and powerful arguments for God's existence ever offered by a theist.

Despite his stress on reasoning, Edwards was not a rationalist. He argued for the need of special revelation. He believed that reason was insufficient to bring people to Christ. Nothing short of the supernatural work of divine illumination of the human heart could do that (*see* Holy Spirit, Role in Apologetics).

Edwards saw clearly the need to give a rational defense of the existence of God before he attempted a historical defense of Christianity. However, he also perceived that the truth of Christianity cannot be justified without an appeal to external evidence. There is a factual, as well as a rational, test for the truth of Christianity.

Negative Criticism. Some justified and some unjustified criticisms have been made of Edwards. Criticisms common to Reformed theology are covered elsewhere (*see* FREE WILL). For an accurate understanding of his thought, however, two charges should be answered: that his Platonic (*see* PLATO) idealism leads him into pantheism, and that his God lacks mercy.

The charge that Edwards is a pantheist (*see* PANTHEISM) because he identified God with all Being is carefully answered in Gerstner, "An Outline of the Apologetics of Jonathan Edwards," pt. 2, 99–107. Edwards' God is only "all Being" in the sense that all being is either of his essence or flows from it. He makes clear distinctions between God and creation, Necessary Being, and contingent being. And his emphasis on individuals being eternally elect or eternally damned is incompatible with a pantheistic worldview (ibid., 104).

One of Edwards' arguments for hell is that God has no obligation to be merciful to all. Mercy, he insists, is a choice and not a duty. God only has to bestow his mercy on those he chose to do so. This argument seems to negate what Edwards says he believes: God is an all perfect being which would include omnibenevolence. But if God is all-good, then something in God obligates him to help sinners in need. Certainly, we would not think a person completely good who did not attempt to save everyone he could from a sinking ship or a burning building.

According to Edwards, no one is moved to act unless God acts upon him. Free choice is doing what one desires, but it is God alone who gives the desire to it. When applied to Lucifer's choice to rebel against God, this would mean that God gave him the desire to sin. But God cannot sin (Hab. 1:13), nor can he give free agents the desire to sin (James 1:13–14). Hence, Edwards' (and the closely connected strong Calvinist) concept of free choice would seem to be rationally incoherent.

Sources

B. W. Davidson, "Reasonable Damnation: How Jonathan Edwards Argued for the Rationality of Hell," *JETS*, 38.1 (March 95)

J. Edwards, *Freedom of the Will*

———, *Jonathan Edwards: Representative Selections . . .* , Clarence H. Faust, et al., eds.

———, "Of Being," *The Philosophy of Jonathan Edwards from His Private Notebooks*, section 12, H. G. Townsend, ed.

———, "Sermon on Isaiah 3:10," unpub. ms., Yale University Beinecke Library

———, "Sermon on Romans 1:20," unpub. ms., Yale University Beinecke Library

———, "Sermon on Romans 14:7," unpub. ms., Yale University Beinecke Library

———, "The Mind," *The Philosophy of Jonathan Edwards from His Private Notebooks*, section 12, H. G. Townsend, ed.

———, *The Works of Jonathan Edwards*, E. Hickman, ed.

J. Gerstner, *Jonathan Edwards: A Mini-Theology*

———, "An Outline of the Apologetics of Jonathan Edwards" in *Bib. Sac.*, 133 (January–March 1976; April–June 1976; July–September 1976; October–December 1976)

Enlightenment. The period of modern history known as the *Enlightenment* began in the late seventeenth century and dominated the eighteenth and much of the nineteenth centuries in Europe. It was rooted in Dutch and German rationalism, particularly Benedict Spinoza's rationalistic and antisupernatural work, *Tractatus Theologico-politicus, Tractatus Politicus* (1670). Christian Wolfe (1679–1754) set the tone for the period when he sought the way to truth through "pure reason." Immanuel *Kant later defined it in his *Religion within the Bounds of Reason Alone* (1793) as "man's emergence from a self-inflicted state of minority. A minor is one who is incapable of making use of his understanding without guidance from someone else. . . . Have the courage to make use of your understanding, is therefore the watchword of the Enlightenment" (Douglas, 345; *see* RATIONALISM).

Other writers who contributed to the Enlightenment include David *Hume, especially in his *Inquiry Concerning Human Understanding* (1748 and *Dialogue Concerning Natural Religion* (1779); Hermann S. Reimarus (1694–1768), and the deists (*see* DEISM) John Toland (1670–1722), Matthew *Tindal (1656–1733), Thomas *Paine (1737–1809), and Francois-Marie *Voltaire (1694–1778). Gottfried Lessing's work, *Nathan the Wise* (1779) argued for religious toleration, since truth was not exclusive to Christianity, but was found in many religions.

The Enlightenment stressed both reason and independence and elicited a pronounced distrust of authority. Truth is to be obtained through reason, observation, and experiment. It came to be dominated by antisupernaturalism (*see* MIRACLES, ARGUMENTS AGAINST). Religious pluralism was the result (*see* PLURALISM, RELIGIOUS). Out of this context came deism, biblical criticism, and rejection of divine revelation (*see* BIBLE CRITICISM; BIBLE, EVIDENCE FOR). Natural religion was emphasized. Its more radical forms encouraged agnosticism, skepticism, and atheism. This radicalized form lives on in secular humanism. Karl *Barth characterized the Enlightenment as "a system founded upon the omnipotence of human ability" (cited in "Enlightenment").

Sources

G. R. Craig, *Reason and Authority in the Eighteenth Century*

"Enlightenment," in F. L. Cross, ed., *The Oxford Dictionary of the Christian Church*

J. D. Douglas, *Dictionary of the Christian Church*

P. Gay, *The Party of Humanity*

Einstein, Albert. Albert Einstein was born in Ulm, Germany, in 1879. He graduated from engineering school in Zurich in 1901. In 1905 he wrote his first paper on the theory of relativity, which gained him a Ph.D. from the University of Zurich. He later gained world fame overnight in 1919 when the British Royal Society announced that his new theory of gravity had toppled the 300-year-old theory of Isaac Newton. In 1921 he won the Nobel Prize for Physics for his work in the field of theoretic physics. Rising antisemitism in Europe prompted Einstein to move to the United States in 1933 where he taught at Princeton University until his death in 1955.

Einstein embraced pacifism, liberalism, and Zionism. His life-long quest was to find a unified field theory to unite all the basic forces of nature—a goal that eluded him throughout his life. His first publication was titled "A New Determination of Molecular Dimensions" (1905). His next article, "On a Heuristic Viewpoint Concerning the Production and Transformation of Light," postulated that light is composed of quanta (later called photons) that, in addition to wave-like behavior, demonstrate certain properties unique to particles. In "On the Electrodynamics of Moving Bodies" he postulated that both time and motion are relative to the observer. His next paper, "Does the Inertia of a Body Depend upon Its Energy Content?" postulated his famous $E = MC^2$ (Energy = mass times the speed of light squared). In 1916 he wrote "The Foundation of the General Theory of Relativity," in which he contended that gravity is not a force but a curved field in the space-time continuum created by the presence of mass.

View of God and Religion. Despite his support for the Zionist movement, Einstein was not a practicing Jew. His relation to Judaism was more ethnic than religious. Judaism played little part in his life, but he insisted that a Jew can shed his faith and still be a Jew. In a war-time letter to physicist Paul Ehrenfest, Einstein expressed a sense of bitterness toward God in the face of the European holocaust: "The ancient Jehovah is still abroad. Alas, he slays the innocent along with the guilty, whom he strikes so fearsomely blind that they can feel no sense of guilt" (ibid., 156; *see* CANAANITES, SLAUGHTER OF).

As to the interaction of religion and science, Einstein believed that "To the Sphere of religion belongs the faith that the regulations valid for the world of existence are rational, that it is comprehensible to reason. I cannot conceive of a genuine scientist without that profound faith. The situation may be expressed by an image: science without religion is lame, religion without science is blind" (Frank, 286; *see* FAITH AND REASON).

The Order of the Universe. For Einstein the universe was a marvel of mathematical order:

> The more a man is imbued with the ordered regularity of all events, the firmer becomes his conviction that there is no room left by the side of this ordered regularity for causes of a different nature [than a Creator]. For him neither the rule of human nor the rule of divine will exists as an independent cause of natural events. To be sure the doctrine of a personal God interfering with natural events could never be refuted, in any real sense, by science, for this doctrine can always take refuge in those domains in which scientific knowledge has not yet been established. [ibid.; *see* TELEOLOGICAL ARGUMENT]

A biographer explained that Einstein believed that "from a mathematical standpoint the system of physical laws is very complex, and that to understand it very great mathematical capacities are required. Nevertheless, he has hope that nature actually obeys a system of mathematical laws" (cited in Herbert, 177).

The Nature of God. In a 1929 reply to a cabled inquiry from Rabbi Goldstein of New York, Einstein described his belief in a pantheistic (*see* PANTHEISM) concept of God: "I believe in Spinoza's God who reveals himself in the harmony of all that exists, not in a God who concerns himself with the fate and actions of men" (Clark, 38; *see* SPINOZA, BENEDICT). He added elsewhere, "The main source of the present-day conflicts between the spheres of religion and of science lies in the concept of a personal God" (Frank, 285). Thus, he rejected *theism in favor of pantheism.

Accordingly, he denied that there would be any day of reward or punishment after death. "What I cannot understand is how there could possibly be a God who would reward or punish his subjects or who could induce us to develop our will in our daily life" (Bucky, 85). He said, "I do not believe that a man should be restrained in his daily actions by being afraid of punishment after death or that he should do things only because in this way he will be rewarded after he dies. . . . Religion should have nothing to do with a fear of living or a fear of death, but should instead be a striving after rational knowledge" (ibid., 86).

God and Miracles. With the caveat that the existence of miracles could never be disproved, Einstein joined Spinoza in denying that they could occur: "The natural laws of science have not only been worked out theoretically but have been proven also in practice. I cannot then believe in this concept of an anthropomorphic God who has the powers of interfering with these natural laws. . . . If there is any such concept as a God, it is a subtle spirit, not an image of a man that so many have fixed in their minds. In essence, my religion consists of a humble admiration for this illimitable superior spirit that reveals itself in the slight details that we are able to perceive with our frail and feeble minds" (ibid.; *see* MIRACLES, ARGUMENTS AGAINST).

The Origin of the Universe. There is a strange irony about Einstein's view of God. His reluctant acceptance of the *big bang origin of the universe should have led him away from his pantheism to a more theistic position. For Einstein failed to find an explanation of his general relativity equation that would not require a beginning or a Beginner for the universe. Even the late twentieth-century physicist and antitheist Stephen Hawking raises the question of who put "fire into the equations" and ignited the universe (Hawking, 99).

Einstein first opposed the mounting evidence for a big bang origin, perhaps realizing its theistic implications. In order to avoid this conclusion, Einstein added a "fudge factor" in his equations, only to be embarrassed later when his maneuver was noticed. To his credit, he eventually admitted his error and concluded that the universe was created. Thus, he wrote of his desire to know how God created this world. He said, "I am not interested in this or that phenomenon, in the spectrum of this or that element. I want to know His thought, the rest are details" (see Herbert, 177).

Evaluation. Logically, after reviewing the evidence that the cosmos had a beginning, Einstein should have concluded with the British physicist Edmund Whittaker: "It is simpler to postulate creation *ex nihilo*—divine will constituting nature from nothingness" (Jastrow, "Scientist Caught," 111; *see* CREATION, VIEWS OF). Even Robert Jastrow, a confirmed agnostic, said, "that there are what I or anyone would call supernatural forces at work is now, I think, a scientifically proven fact" (*God and the Astronomers,* 15, 18). Jastrow observes that "astronomers now find that they have painted themselves into a corner because they have proven, by their own methods, that the world began abruptly in an act of creation. . . . And they have found that all this happened as a product of forces they cannot hope to discover" (ibid., 15). Unfortunately, we lack evidence that Einstein drew the conclusion that his scientific breakthroughs support (*see* ANTHROPIC PRINCIPLE; EVOLUTION, COSMIC; *KALAM* COSMOLOGICAL ARGUMENT; THERMODYNAMICS, LAWS OF).

If it is a scientific fact that the universe exploded into being by supernatural forces, Einstein should have accepted miracles. This was the biggest miracle of all.

Sources

P. A. Bucky, *The Private Albert Einstein*
R. W. Clark, *Einstein: His Life and Times*
"Einstein," *EB*, 1994 ed.
P. Frank, *Einstein: His Life and Times*
S. Hawking, *Black Holes and Baby Universes*
F. Heeren, *Show Me God*
N. Herbert, *Quantum Reality—Beyond the New Physics*
R. Jastrow, "A Scientist Caught between Two Faiths: Interview with Robert Jastrow," *CT*, 6 August 1982
———, *God and the Astronomers*

Epistemology. *Epistemology* is the discipline that deals with theory of knowledge. The term can be broken down into *epistem-ology* (Gk. *episteme,* "to know; *logos,* "study"). It is the study of how we know.

The various epistemologies include *rationalism (*see* SPINOZA, BENEDICT), empiricism (*see* HUME, DAVID), *agnosticism (*see* KANT, IMMANUEL), idealism (*see* PLATO), positivism (*see* Comte, Auguste), *existentialism (*see* SØREN KIERKEGAARD), phenomenology (*see* *HEGEL, W. F. G.; HEIDEGGER, MARTIN), and *mysticism (*see* PLOTINUS).

Epistemology considers whether ideas are innate or whether we are born a *tabula rasa,* that is, a blank slate. It also deals with tests for truth (*see* TRUTH, ABSOLUTE NATURE OF) and whether true ideas merely cohere (*see* COHERENTISM) or need an ultimate foundation (*see* FOUNDATIONALISM) in self-evident first principles.

Epistemology also treats certainty (*see* CERTAINTY/CERTITUDE) and doubt (*see* SKEPTICISM). Agnosticism claims we cannot know reality, whereas realism asserts that we can know reality. The degree of our certainty in what we know ranges from low probability (*see* INDUCTIVISM) to rational necessity (*see* FIRST PRINCIPLES; LOGIC; TAUTOLOGIES).

Eschatological Verification. *See* VERIFICATION STRATEGIES.

Essenes and Jesus. *Essenes* were a break-away Jewish sect who established a community near the Dead Sea (*see* DEAD SEA SCROLLS). Their name may derive from *Hasidim* ("loyal [or, pious] ones"). This may reflect their belief that they lived in the end times of apostasy. The evil reign of Antiochus IV Epiphanes in the second century B.C. may have been the impetus for founding such a sect. Their community lasted until the second century A.D. According to Josephus (*Jewish War,* 2.8.2), the Essenes, Pharisees, and Sadducees were the primary sects of Judaism. The elder Pliny linked them with Qumran. Their life was marked by asceticism, communism, and the rejection of animal sacrifice. In New Testament times they numbered about 4000 (Cross, 471).

Jesus and the Essenes. Some scholars, such as I. Ewing (*The Essene Christ*) have claimed that Jesus was the Essene "Teacher of Righteousness" mentioned in the Dead Sea Scrolls.

It is reasoned that John the Baptist and even Jesus were members of the Essene community. During his recorded ministry in the Gospels Jesus only opposed the Pharisees and Sadducees. Never was he critical of the Essenes. Jesus certainly thought of himself as a teacher of righteousness. When he was baptized he said, "Let it be so now: it is proper for us to do this to fulfill all righteousness." Then John consented (Matt. 3:15). Jesus was a priest. According to the New Testament, Jesus was a priest forever after the order of Melchizedek (Heb. 7:17). He fulfilled the typology of the Aaronic priesthood. Likewise, "the Teacher of Righteousness" of the Essene community was a priest. Jesus spent time in the wilderness near the Essenes. He also had a similar anti-establishment emphasis, as did the Essenes.

Evaluation. There are numerous flaws in the Essene theory. The three basic arguments in favor of the Essence view will be treated in order.

That Jesus did not criticize the Essenes is a fallacious argument from silence. He is recorded to have said nothing about them at all. Essenes were not part of official Judaism, which opposed Christ. The *Talmud* did not oppose the Essenes, either, yet it was not an Essene book. This is also an instance of the "black-and-white" fallacy. It overlooks the fact that Jesus could have been a member of no group at all. And it overlooks crucial differences between the teaching of Jesus and Essene doctrines. Jesus

- opposed ceremonial purity which they radicalized.
- opposed legalism, and they were decidedly Mosaic Law legalists.
- stressed the kingdom of God. They did not.
- preached love. They did not.
- claimed to be sinless Messiah. They placed a heavy burden of sin on each person.
- opened salvation to the Gentiles. They were Jewish nationalists.
- taught that there was one Messiah; they looked for two.
- taught the resurrection of the body; they stressed the *immortality of the soul, but not the body.

In general, Jesus' ethical teachings far more closely approximated rabbinical Judaism than Qumran austerity.

While Jesus taught righteousness, it does not follow that he was the Essene "teacher of righteousness." Such an identification overlooks crucial differences. The Essene leader

- was a priest, while Jesus was a Prophet, Priest, and King.
- was a sinner needing purification, but Jesus was sinless (*see* Christ, Deity of).
- thought of himself as a creature, not a Creator.
- atoned for no one at his death.
- was not resurrected from the dead as was Jesus.
- was not worshiped as God.
- lived long before Jesus.

There is no real evidence that Jesus ever visited the Essene community, but casual affiliation with Essenes is irrelevant, anyway. His identity remained with no one except God. In many regards, Jesus was an iconoclast of established Judaism. Though he came to fulfill, not destroy, the law (Matt. 5:17–18), he opposed official Judaism for different reasons than did the Essenes. The Jewish hierarchy rejected him as the Messiah, the Son of God. This was not true of the Essenes. Further, Jesus was not an ascetic. He was even criticized for eating with sinners (see Christ, Deity of).

Conclusion. There is no evidence that Jesus ever had contact with the Essene community. But if he did, it does not make him an Essene or disprove his unique claims. His teachings differed in important respects. Jesus alone claimed to be the Jewish Messiah (*see* Prophecy as Proof of the Bible), and Son of God (*see* Christ, Deity of).

Sources

M. Black, *The Scrolls and Christian Origins*

F. L. Cross, "Essenes," in *The Oxford Dictionary of the Christian Church*

M. Dupont-Sommer, *The Jewish Sect of Qumran and the Essenes*

I. Ewing, *The Essene Christ*

Flavius Josephus, *Jewish Wars*

C. D. Ginsburg, *The Essenes*

J. B. Lightfoot, *St. Paul's Epistles to the Colossians and to Philemon*

Essentialism, Divine. *Essentialism* (Lat. *esse*, "to be"), as it relates to moral principles and God's will, is the view that ethical principles are rooted ultimately in the unchangeable divine essence (*see* God, Nature of), not simply in God's changeable will. It is opposed to divine *voluntarism* which asserts that something is good because God wills it. Essentialism, on the contrary, holds that God wills something because it is good.

There are two basic kinds of essentialism: platonic and theistic. *Plato believed that God, the *Demiurgos*, wills all things in accordance with the Good (the *Agathos*), which is outside God and to which he is subject.

Theists (*see* Theism), on the other hand, believe that God wills things in accordance with his own unchangeably good nature (*see* God, Nature of). So the ultimate good is not outside God but inside him, his own unchanging nature. This is called divine essentialism.

Arguments for Essentialism. Christian essentialists offer three basic lines of argument in favor of their view: philosophical, biblical, and practical.

Philosophical Arguments for Essentialism. Traditional theists argue that God is unchangeable in his nature. *Thomas Aquinas offered three basic arguments for God's immutability (*see* God, Nature of).

The argument from God's pure actuality. The first argument is based on the fact that a God of pure Actuality ("I Am-ness") has no potentiality.

For everything which changes has potentiality. But there can be no potentiality in God (he is pure Actuality). Therefore, God cannot change (Exod. 3:14). For whatever changes has the potential to change. But as pure Actuality God has no potential to actualize through change.

The argument from God's perfection. The second argument for God's unchangeability argues from his absolute perfection. Whatever changes acquires something new. But God cannot acquire anything new, since he is absolutely perfect; he could not be better. Therefore, God cannot change. God is by his very nature an absolutely perfect being. If he lacked any perfection, he would not be God. However, to change one must gain something new. But to gain a new perfection is to have lacked it. A God lacking in some perfection would not be the absolutely perfect God who is.

The argument from God's simplicity. The third argument for God's immutability follows from his simplicity. Everything which changes is composed of what changes and what does not change. But there can be no composition in God (he is an absolutely simple being). Hence, God cannot change.

If everything about a being changed, it would no longer be the same being. In fact, that would not be change at all but annihilation of one thing and a recreation of something entirely new. If in every change something remains the same and something does not, the thing that changes must be composed of these two elements. Since an absolutely simple being, such as God, cannot have two elements, it follows that God cannot change.

Biblical Arguments for Divine Essentialism. Scriptures that support theistic essentialism are those that declare God to be unchangeable in his nature.

Old Testament evidence of immutability. The Old Testament psalmist declared: "In the beginning you [LORD] laid the foundations of the earth, and the heavens are the work of your hands. They will perish, but you remain; they will all wear out like a garment. Like clothing you will change them and they will be discarded. But you remain the same, and your years will never end" (Ps. 102:25–27). First Samuel 15:29 affirms that "He who is the Glory of Israel does not lie or change his mind; for he is not a man, that he should change his mind." The prophet added, "I the LORD do not change. So you, O descendants of Jacob, are not destroyed" (Mal. 3:6).

New Testament evidence of immutability. The New Testament is equally strong about God's unchangeable nature. Hebrews 1:10–12 quotes Psalm 102 with approval. A few chapters later the author of Hebrews asserts, "God did this so that, by two unchangeable things in which it is impossible for God to lie" (Heb. 6:18a). The apostle Paul adds in Titus 1:2, "God, who does not lie, promised before the beginning of time." James 1:17 points out that "Every good and perfect gift is from above, coming down from the Father of the heavenly lights, who does not change like shifting shadows."

Now if God is unchangeable in his nature, then his will is subject to his unchangeable nature. Thus, whatever God wills must be good in accordance with this nature. God cannot will contrary to his nature. He cannot lie (Heb. 6:18). He cannot be unloving, nor unjust. Divine essentialism must be correct.

Practical Arguments for God's Moral Immutability. Two practical arguments are offered in favor of divine essentialism, the need for moral stability and moral repugnance. These are supported by what we experience of God's trustworthiness and the scriptural testimony that God can be trusted not to change.

The Argument from the Need for Moral Stability. If all moral principles were based on God' changing will, then there would be no moral security. How could one be committed to a life of love, mercy, or justice only to find out that the rules had changed about whether these were the right things to do? Indeed, how could we serve God as supreme if he could will that our ultimate good was not to love him but hate him?

The Argument from Moral Repugnance. Divine essentialists insist that it is morally repugnant to assume, as voluntarists do, that God could change his will on whether love is essentially good and will instead that hate be a universal moral obligation. Likewise, it is difficult to conceive how a morally perfect being could will that rape, cruelty, and genocide would be morally good. Since it is morally repugnant for creatures made in God's image to imagine such a change in God's will, how much more must it be for the God in whose image we are made.

The Argument from God's Trustworthiness. The Bible presents God as eminently trustworthy. When he makes an unconditional promise he never fails to keep it (cf. Gen. 12:1–3; Heb. 6:16–18). Indeed, the gifts and callings of God are without change of mind on his part (Rom. 11:29). God is not a man that he should repent (1 Sam. 15:29). He can always be counted on to keep his word (Isa. 55:11). But this ultimate trustworthiness of God would not be possible if he could change his will at any time about anything. The only thing that makes God morally bound to keep his word is his unchangeable nature. Otherwise, he could decide at any moment to send all believers to hell. He could reward the wicked for murder and cruelty. Such a God would not be trustworthy. The God of the Bible is unchangeably good.

Objections to Essentialism. *Objection from God's Supremacy.* Voluntarists, such as, *William of Ockham, object to essentialism. One argument is from the supremacy of God, which can be stated:

1. Either God wills it because it is right, or else it is right because God wills it.
2. But if he wills it because it is right, then God is not supreme because there is something outside him to which he is subject.
3. Hence, it is right because God wills it.

Essentialists note two problems with this argument. Premise 1 presents a false dilemma. It need not be an either/or; it could be a both/and. That is, perhaps moral principles flow from the will of God as rooted in the nature of God. If so, then a voluntaristic conclusion does not follow. Also, premise 2 wrongly assumes that the supreme ethical standard to which God's will must be subject is "outside" of God. But if it is "inside God," namely, his own supreme moral nature, then the dilemma vanishes.

Objection from the Nature of Morality. Those opposed to essentialism argue that moral principles by their very nature flow from the will of God, not from his nature. For a moral law is a prescription, and prescriptions come only from prescribers. It is an ethical command, and commands come only from commanders. Hence, it is of the very nature of moral law that it come from a Moral Lawgiver. They insist that to claim (as essentialists do) that moral laws flow from God's essence, not his will, is to misunderstand the nature of a moral principle.

However, essentialists respond that voluntarists again wrongly assume that it is either/or, rather than both/and. The problem is resolved if one posits (as essentialism does) that moral principles flow from the will of God as rooted in the unchangeable nature of God. That is, God wills what is right in accordance with the unchangeably good character of his moral nature (*see* Morality, Absolute Nature of).

Objection from God's Sovereignty. The argument from God's sovereign will is based more on a specific interpretation of certain Scriptures than on philosophical reasoning. Did not Job declare to God: "I know that you can do all things; no plan of yours can be thwarted" (Job 42:2)? And did not the apostle Paul affirm of God: "'I will have mercy on whom I have mercy, and I will have compassion on whom I have compassion.' It does not, therefore, depend on man's desire or effort, but on God's mercy" (Rom. 9:15–16). Does not God do everything "in accordance with his pleasure and will" (Eph. 1:5)?

One need not reject the sovereignty of God to see the fallacy of this argument. These passages are not speaking of the ultimate basis of moral principles but of God's election. Even biblical texts that speak of God's will as the ultimate source of what is morally right do not prove voluntarism. Moral principles could come ultimately from God's will *as rooted in his unchangeable nature*. This is, in fact, exactly what the Bible declares of God's unchangeable character.

Objection That God Has Changed His Will. According to essentialists, there are examples in Scripture where God changed his will. Did he not "repent" of making mankind in the days of Noah (Genesis 6)? Did God not "repent" or change his mind about the destruction of Nineveh (Jonah 3)? Did not God change his mind about destroying Israel after Moses prayed (Numbers 14)?

Divine essentialists point out that God did not *actually* change in any of these cases. Human beings changed in relation to God and, hence, it only *appeared* from a human standpoint that God changed. The wind appears to change when we turn from pedaling a bike into it and ride with it at our back. A water fall has not changed its flow, simply because we right a downward-turned cup and suddenly find that it is full. As *Thomas Aquinas noted, when the person moves from one side of the pillar to the other, the pillar does not move in relation to the person. Rather, the person moves in relation to the pillar.

Conclusion. Divine essentialism is rooted in good arguments philosophically, biblically, and practically. The objections against it fail to make their points stick. Hence, while ethical principles do flow from God's will, nevertheless, they are rooted in his unchangeable nature. Thus, God cannot will anything that is contrary to his essentially good moral nature.

Sources

Augustine, *The City of God*
C. S. Lewis, *Mere Christianity*
Plato, *Protaoras*
———, *Republic*
Thomas Aquinas, *Summa Theologica*

Eusebius. Eusebius (ca. 260–340) was bishop of Caesarea and the "father of church history." His *Ecclesiastical History* is the principal source of information from the apostolic period to the fourth century. It contains an immense amount of material on the Eastern church, though little about the West. Eusebius also wrote *The Martyrs of Palestine*, an account of the Diocletian persecutions (303–310). He also wrote a biography of the emperor Constantine.

The apologetic and polemic writings of Eusebius were extensive. They include: *Against Hierocles* (answering anti-Christian rhetoric of a pagan governor of Bithynia), *The Preparation for the Gospel* (why Christians accept the Hebrew tradition and reject the Greek), and *Demonstration of the Gospel* (arguments for Christ from the Old Testament). Eusebius also wrote a work on the incarnation, *The Theophany*. *Against Marcellus, Bishop of Ancyra* is a collection of Old Testament passages foretelling the coming of Christ. To the latter he added a theological *Refutation of Mar-*

cellus. Eusebius wrote *The Defense of Origen* on *Origen's views of the *Trinity and incarnation (see Schaff, 2d series, 1.36). He wrote a book on *Problems of the Gospels*, *On Easter*, *On the Theology of the Church*, and *On the Names and Places in the Holy Scriptures*.

Eusebius is a crucial historical link between the apostles and the Middle Ages. After the apostles and earliest apologists, he is a prime example of the form taken by early Christian apologists. Further, he played a key role in the transmission of Scripture (see Geisler and Nix, 278–82) by preparing fifty copies of the Bible only 25 years after Diocletian had ordered its extinction in 302.

Other early witnesses are covered in the article NEW TESTAMENT, NON-CHRISTIAN SOURCES.

Sources

F. L. Cross, *The Oxford Dictionary of the Christian Church*
N. L. Geisler and W. Nix, *General Introduction to the Bible*
J. Stevenson, *Studies in Eusebius*
D. S. Wallis-Hadrill, *Eusebius of Caesarea*
P. Schaff, *The Nicene and Post-Nicene Fathers*

Evil, Problem of. If God is absolutely good, then why is there evil (*see* GOD, NATURE OF)? The problem of evil is a serious challenge to the defense of Christianity. Actually there are many problems relating to evil, for example, the problems about its origin, nature, purpose, and avoidability. The problems of evil can be divided among moral, metaphysical (*see* METAPHYSICS), and physical.

Worldviews and Evil. Although every worldview has to deal with the problem of evil, it is an especially acute problem for theism. Of the three major worldviews, *Atheism affirms the reality of evil and denies the reality of God. *Pantheism affirms the reality of God but denies the reality of *evil. Theism affirms the reality of both God and evil. Herein is the problem; how can an absolutely good Being (God) be compatible with evil, the opposite of good?

As compared with the other worldviews that affirm both God and evil, theism would seem to be in a more disadvantageous position. *Finite godism, for example, can claim that God desires to destroy evil but is unable to because he is limited in power. *Deism, likewise, can distance God from evil by stressing that God is not immanent in the world, at least not supernaturally. We are on our own. And for *panentheism evil is a necessary part of the ongoing progress of the interaction of God and the world (his body).

The problem for theism is that it not only believes God is all-powerful and could destroy evil, but he is all-loving and should destroy it. Further, the theistic God is all-knowing and created this world fully aware of what would happen. What is more, God created the world freely (*see* CREATION, VIEWS OF), so that he could have done otherwise.

It is in the context of this kind of theistic God that we approach problems of evil.

The Origin of Evil. Where did evil come from? An absolutely good God cannot create evil. Nor, would it seem, can a perfect creature give rise to imperfection. Whence, then, evil? The problem can be summarized:

1. God is absolutely perfect.
2. God cannot create anything imperfect.
3. But perfect creatures cannot do evil.
4. Therefore, neither God nor his perfect creatures can produce evil.

However, in a theistic universe these are the only two sources for moral evil. Therefore, there seems to be no solution for the origin of evil in a theistic universe.

The basic elements in the theistic response to this problem are found in *Augustine and *Thomas Aquinas. Theists since then have followed the contours of their thought. Both agreed on the response that can be stated as follows:

1. God is absolutely perfect.
2. God created only perfect creatures.
3. One of the perfections God gave some of his creatures was the power of free choice.
4. Some of these creatures freely chose to do evil.
5. Therefore, a perfect creature caused evil.

God is good, and he created good creatures with a good power called free will. Unfortunately, they used this good power to bring evil into the universe by rebelling against their Creator. So evil did arise from good, not directly but indirectly, by the abuse of a good power called freedom. Freedom in itself is not evil. It is good to be free. But with freedom comes the possibility of evil. So God is responsible for making evil possible, but free creatures are responsible for making it actual.

Of course, other questions attach to this free choice solution to the origin of evil. One is, what caused the first creature to choose evil?

Theists distinguish between the primary cause of a free action (God) and the secondary cause (a human being). God gave the power of choice. However, God is not responsible for the exercise of that free choice to do evil. God does not *perform* the free action for us. Human free choice is not a mere instrumental cause through which God works. Human beings are the efficient, albeit secondary, cause of their own free actions. God produces the *fact* of free choice, but each human performs the *act* of free choice. God then is responsible for the *possibility* of evil, but we must bear the responsibility for the *actuality* of it. God neither wills evil to be done, nor wills it not to be done. He wills to permit evil to be done, and this is good.

But if God cannot will evil, then what is the cause of it? No action can be uncaused, since this violates the first principle of causality (*see*

CAUSALITY, PRINCIPLE OF) that demands that every event has a cause.

To respond to this question it is necessary to unpack the nature of free choice. There are three basic views of the nature of free choice: In determinism, a free act is caused by another; in indeterminism, it is uncaused, and in self-determinism it is caused by oneself. *Determinism would eliminate human responsibility, since another caused the action, not ourselves. *Indeterminism is irrational, since a fundamental rule of reason is that every action has a cause. It follows, then, that every free choice must be self caused.

Of course, a person uses the *power* of free choice to make free choices. However, the person is not free choice. He simply *has* free choice. It is wrong to say I *am* free choice; I simply *have* free choice. So, I am the efficient cause of my own free actions, but the power of free choice is the means by which I freely act.

The Nature of Evil. There is another dimension to this difficulty. What is the *nature* of evil? That is, what is the essence or identity of evil? This too, is a particularly pesky problem for a classical theist (*see* CLASSICAL APOLOGETICS). For God alone is eternal, and everything he created was good. What, then, is evil?

Theists reject *dualism. Evil is not a coeternal principle outside of God. For not all opposites like good and evil are first principles. This wrongly assumes that just because something can be essentially good (God), something can be essentially bad. But once dualism is rejected, one has great difficulty explaining the reality of evil. If evil is not something outside of God, and it cannot be anything inside of God, then what is it? The problem can be summarized this way.

1. God is the Author of everything.
2. Evil is something.
3. Therefore, God is the Author of evil.

Rejecting the first premise leads to dualism. Likewise, denying the second leads to illusionism which denies the reality of evil (*see* PANTHEISM). Neither is acceptable to a theist. What, then, is the solution? To agree that God did not create all things is to deny his sovereignty. To say evil is nothing denies reality. However, to admit that God caused all things and evil is something is to acknowledge that God caused evil—a conclusion rejected by Aquinas. But this conclusion seems to follow logically from these premises. Unless one rejects the truth of one of the premises, he must accept the truth of the conclusion.

The theist responds that evil is not a *thing* or substance. Rather it is a *lack* or privation of a good thing that God made. Evil is a deprivation of some particular good. The essence of this position is summarized:

1. God created every substance.
2. Evil is not a substance (but a privation in a substance).
3. Therefore, God did not create evil.

Evil is not a substance but a corruption of the good substances God made. Evil is like rust to a car or rot to a tree. It is a *lack* in good things, but it is not a thing in itself. Evil is like a wound in an arm or moth-holes in a garment. It exists only in another but not in itself.

It is important to note that a privation is not the same as mere *absence*. Sight is absent in a stone as well as in a blind person. But the absence of sight in the stone is not a privation. Absence of something that *ought to be there*. Since the stone by nature ought not to see, it is not deprived of sight, as is the blind man. Evil, then is a deprivation of some good that ought to be there. It is not a mere negation.

To say that evil is not a thing, but a lack in things, is not to claim that it is not *real*. Evil is a real lack in good things, as the blind person knows only so well. Evil is not a real substance, but it is a real privation in good substances. It is not an actual entity but a real corruption in an actual entity.

Evil as privation comes in different kinds. There are physical privations, such as mutilations and there are moral privations, such as a sexual perversity. Privation can be in substance (*what* something is) or in relationships (*how* it relates to others). There are not only bad *things* but there are bad relations between things. A relationship of love is a good one; hate is an evil one. Likewise, when a creature worships its Creator, it relates well; blaspheming the Creator is an evil relationship.

From this perspective, it follows that there is no such thing as something that is totally evil. If it were totally deprived of all good, it would be nothing. A totally rusty car is no car at all. And a totally moth-eaten garment is only a hanger in a closet. Evil, like a wound, can only exist in something else. A totally wounded arm means the person is maimed.

In view of this, something cannot be totally private, at least not in a metaphysical sense. A totally corrupted being would not exist at all. And a totally incapacitated will could not make any moral actions. One must take care not to carry human depravity so far that one destroys the ability to sin. There cannot be a supreme evil, for although evil lessens good; it can never totally destroy it. Nothing can be complete, unmitigated evil. For if all good were entirely destroyed—and this would be required for evil to be complete—evil itself would vanish since its subject, namely good, would no longer be there.

The fact that evil cannot be total in a metaphysical sense by no means implies that it cannot be total in a moral sense. A being can be *totally* (or, *radically*) depraved morally in the sense that evil has invaded every part of being. But the moral total depravity can only be extensive, not intensive. It can extend to every part of a person's being, but it cannot destroy personal being. If it destroyed one's person, there would no longer be a person to do evil. Total evil in this sense would destroy a person's ability to do evil.

Classical theists described things in terms of their four causes: (1) efficient; (2) final; (3) formal, and (4) material. A human being has God as the *efficient cause*, God's glory and their good; as *final cause*, a soul as *formal cause* and a body as the *material cause*. However, since evil is not a substance, it has no formal cause, and its material cause is a good substance.

Efficient Cause—Free choice

Final Cause—None. Evil is the lack of order.

Formal Cause—None. Evil is the privation of form.

Material Cause—A good substance

The efficient cause of moral evil is free choice, not directly but indirectly. There is no purpose (final cause) of evil. It is lack of proper order to the good end. Evil has no formal cause of its own. Rather, it is the destruction of form in another. Its material cause is a good but not its own. It exists only in a good thing as the corruption of it.

The Persistence of Evil. There is another aspect of the problem of evil. Why does God allow it? Even if he did not produce it, he does permit it. Yet he is all-powerful and could destroy it. So why doesn't he do so?

The classical way to state the problem of the persistence of evil is this:

1. If God is all good, he would destroy evil.
2. If God is all powerful, he could destroy evil.
3. But evil is not destroyed.
4. Therefore, there is no such God.

Put this way, the argument leaves open the possibility of a finite god, but theists reject such a concept. For every finite or limited being has a cause (*see* COSMOLOGICAL ARGUMENT). So a finite god is only a creature that needs an infinite Creator. And since God is powerful, then he must be infinitely powerful. Likewise, since he is good, he must be infinitely good. So, a finite god is not an option for a theist. God has both the desire and ability needed to do anything possible.

Is it possible to destroy evil? The theist responds as follows:

1. God cannot do what is actually impossible.
2. It is actually impossible to destroy evil without destroying free choice.
3. But free choice is necessary to a moral universe.
4. Therefore, God cannot destroy evil without destroying this good moral universe.

It is impossible for God to do what is contradictory. He cannot make an affirmation to be true and false at the same time. He can do nothing which involve such an impossibility, such as, making a square circle or a stone so heavy he cannot lift it.

Even an omnipotent being cannot do anything. It can only do what is possible. But it is not possible to force people to freely choose the good. Forced freedom is a contradiction. Therefore, God cannot literally destroy all evil without annihilating free choice. The only way to destroy evil is to destroy the good of free choice. But when there is no moral free choice, then there is no possibility of moral good. Unless hate is possible, love is not possible. Where no creature can blaspheme, no creatures can worship either. Therefore, if God were to destroy all evil, he would have to destroy all good too.

However, theism holds that even though God could not *destroy* (annihilate) all evil without destroying all good, nevertheless, he can and will *defeat* (overcome) all evil without destroying free choice. The argument can be summarized as follows:

1. God is all good and desires to defeat evil.
2. God is all powerful and is able to defeat evil.
3. Evil is not *yet* defeated.
4. Therefore, it will one day be defeated.

The infinite power and perfection of God guarantee the eventual defeat of evil. The fact that it is not yet accomplished in no way diminishes the certainty that it will be defeated. Even though evil cannot be destroyed without destroying free choice, nonetheless, it can be *overcome*.

An all-powerful God could, for example, *separate* good persons from evil ones according to what persons freely choose. Those who love God will be separated from those who do not. Those who desire the good but are hindered by evil will no longer have their good purposes frustrated. And those who do evil and are hampered by good influences will no longer be nagged by the proddings of good. Each, whether in heaven* or hell, will have it according to their free choice. In this way God's victory over evil would not violate free choice.

Not only *can* a theistic God defeat evil, but he *will* do it. We know this because he is all good and would want to defeat evil. And because he is all-powerful and is able to defeat evil. Therefore, he will do it. The guarantee that evil will be overcome is the nature of the theistic God.

The Purpose of Evil. No evil is good, but some evil has a good purpose. Warning pains for example are painful, but there painfulness has a good purpose. Of course, not all evil seems to be of this type. What, then, of evil which seems to have no good purpose? The problem can be summarized as follows:

1. An all-good God must have a good purpose for everything.
2. There is no good purpose for some suffering.
3. Therefore, there cannot be an all-good God.

It seems evident that there is useless suffering in the world. Some people get better through suffering, but others get bitter. Broken bones are stronger when they heal, but some never heal. Many die. What about all the purposeless evil in the world?

The theistic answer to apparently purposeless evil is fourfold. First, God has a good purpose for everything. Second, we do know a good purpose for much evil. Third, some evil is a byproduct of good. Fourth, God is able to bring good out of evil.

God Has a Good Purpose for Everything. The antitheist overlooks an important distinction: God knows a good purpose for all evil, even if we do not. Simply because finite minds cannot conceive of a good purpose for some evil does not mean that there is none. Since God is omniscient, he knows everything. And since he is omnibenevolent, he has a good purpose for everything. Hence, God does know a good purpose for all evil, even if we do not know it:

1. An omnibenevolent God has a good purpose for everything.
2. There is some evil for which we see no good purpose.
3. Therefore, there is a good purpose for all evil, even if we do not see it.

The fact that finite beings don't see the purpose for some evil does not mean there is none. This inability to see the purpose for evil does not disprove God's benevolence; it merely reveals our ignorance.

The purpose for much evil is known by us. In spite of the fact that we do not know everything, we do know something. And what we do know is that there is a good purpose for much evil. Warning pains have a good purpose. In fact, the ability to have pain has a good purpose. For if we had no nervous system we could destroy ourselves without even feeling any pain. Also, physical pain can be a warning to save us from moral disaster. As C. S. *Lewis noted, pain is God's megaphone to warn a morally deaf world. And if we as finite beings know a good purpose for much evil, then surely an infinite Mind can know a good purpose for the rest.

Evil sometimes is a byproduct of a good purpose. Not every specific evil needs a good purpose. Some evil can simply be a necessary byproduct of a good purpose. The early bird gets the worm, but the early worm gets eaten. What is life for higher forms is death for lower forms. Plants and animals die so that man may have food to live. Thus, evil results indirectly from good because it is the consequence of a good purpose. Hence, the response may be put this way:

1. God has a good purpose for everything he does.
2. Some good purposes have evil byproducts.
3. Therefore, some evil is a byproduct of a good purpose.

Not every *specific* event in the world needs to have a good purpose; only the *general* purpose needs to be good. The blacksmith has a good purpose for hammering the molten iron into a horseshoe. However, not every spark that flies has a purpose for its destiny. Some sparks may ignite unintended fires. Likewise, God had a good purpose for creating water (to sustain life), but drowning is one of the evil byproducts. Thus, not every specific drowning needs to have a good purpose, even though making the water in which they drown did. So many good things would be missed if God did not permit evil to exist. Fire does not burn unless air is consumed. Neither just retribution is inflicted nor patience is achieved, but for the evil of tribulation.

God can bring good out of evil. Of course, God is all-powerful and he is able to redeem good even from evils. A drowning person may inspire acts of bravery. Although sawdust is an unintended byproduct of making lumber, it can be salvaged to make paper. Likewise, God in his providence is able to redeem much (if not all) good out of the evil byproducts in the world. God would in no wise permit evil to exist in his works unless he were so almighty and so good as to produce good even from evil.

That does not mean that this present world is the best of all possible worlds. It means that God has made it the best possible way to attain his ultimate goal of the greater good. God may not always redeem good out of every evil byproduct in a fallen world. This could be true in both the physical and the moral realm. Like radioactive waste, some evil byproducts may resist reprocessing. Indeed, in view of the second law of thermodynamics, the physical world is decaying. But God has the power to recreate it (cf. 2 Peter 3:13). Human death can be overcome by resurrection (cf. Romans 8; 1 Corinthians 15). Neither of these is any problem for an omnipotent God.

The Problem of Physical Evil. The above solution to the problem of evil do not appear to solve the problem of natural disasters. Why tornadoes, hurricanes, and earthquakes? It does not suffice to say that the free will of creatures caused all these. Further, many innocent people are killed in them. How, then, can natural evil be explained. In logical form:

1. Moral evil is explained by free choice.

2. But some natural evil does not result from free choice.
3. Natural evil cannot be explained by free choice of creatures.
4. Hence, God must be responsible for natural evil.
5. But natural evils cause innocent suffering and death.
6. Therefore, God is responsible for innocent suffering and death.

Theists question several premises of this argument. One response to premise 5, for example, is that in this fallen world no one is innocent. We sinned in Adam (Rom. 5:12) and as a consequence deserve death (Rom. 6:23). Natural disaster is a direct result of the curse on creation because of the fall of humankind (Genesis 3; Romans 8). It will not be removed until Christ returns (Revelation 21–22).

Likewise, proposition 6 is mistaken, since it implies God is morally culpable for taking the life of a creature. This is a category mistake, since it wrongly assumes that, since it is wrong for a creature to take innocent life, it is also wrong for the Creator to do so. But God gave life and alone has the right to take it (cf. Deut. 32:39; Job 1:21). We did not give life, and we do not have the right to take it.

Premise 3 is definitely untrue. For *theism can explain all natural evil by reference to free choice. In biblical language, the free choice of Adam and Eve brought natural disaster on this world. In addition the free choice of evil angels accounts for the rest of human suffering. But even putting this possibility aside, which could in itself explain all natural evil, physical suffering can be explained in reference to human free choice.

1. Some suffering is brought on directly by our own free choice. The choice to abuse my body can result in sickness.
2. Some suffering is brought on indirectly by free choice. The choice to be lazy can result in poverty.
3. Some physical evil to others can result from our free choice, as in the case of spouse or child abuse.
4. Others suffer indirectly because of our free choice. Alcoholism can lead to poverty of one's children.
5. Some physical evil may be a necessary byproduct of a good process. Rain, hot air, and cool air are all necessary for food and life, but a byproduct of these forces is a tornado.
6. Some physical evil may be a necessary condition for attaining a greater moral good. God uses pain to get our attention. Many have come to God through suffering.
7. Some physical suffering may be a necessary condition of a greater moral good. Just as diamonds are formed under pressure, even so is character.
8. Some physical evil is a necessary concomitant of a morally good physical world. For instance, it is good to have water to swim and boat in, but a necessary concomitant is that we can also drown in it. It is good to have sex for procreation and enjoyment, even though it makes rape possible. It is good to have food to eat, but this also makes dying of food poisoning possible.

At this point the critic could always ask why a physical world is necessary. Why did not God make spirits, who could not hurt their bodies or die. The answer is: God did; they are called angels. The problem is that, while no angel can die of food poisoning, neither can they enjoy a prime rib. While no angel has ever drowned, neither has any angel ever gone for a swim or went water skiing. No angel has ever been raped, but neither has any angel ever enjoyed sex or the blessing of having children (Matt. 22:30). In this kind of physical world, we simply must take the concomitant evil along with the good.

Eventually, of course, Christian theists believe God will redeem us from all physical evil too, giving us immortal and incorruptible bodies. But if we had those before we were morally ready for them, we would not have made the necessary moral progress toward being suited to them.

The Avoidability of Evil. If God knew evil would occur, why did he create it? God was free to create or not to create. Why did he choose to create a world he knew would fall? Theists believed God is all-knowing, all-good, and free. As all-knowing, God foresaw evil. As free, he could have avoided creating the world. But this conflicts with God as all-good, for such a God must have had a good purpose for creating a world he knew would fall. Why then did he create it?

There were other better alternatives open to God. He could have not created at all. He could have created a nonmoral world where no sin could occur. He could have created a free world where no one would have chosen to sin. He could have created a world where sin occurred but where everyone was ultimately saved. Any one of these worlds would have been better than the world conceived by the orthodox Christian theist, where evil occurs and where not everyone will be saved in the end (*see* HELL; ANNIHILATIONISM; UNIVERSALISM). The problem takes this form:

1. God could have chosen a better alternative by: (a) not creating at all; (b) not creating a free world; (c) creating a free world that would not sin; (d) creating a world that sinned but would all be saved.

2. But God did not choose one of these better alternatives.
3. Therefore God did not do his best.
4. But to do less than his best is an evil for God.
5. Therefore, no all-perfect God exists.

Some theists challenge the fourth premise, arguing that God does not have to do his best; he merely has to do good. And what he did in creating this world was good, even if there could have been something better. But assuming, for the argument, that God must do his best, is any other alternative really better than this world? Theists say No.

A nonworld is not better than some world. Nothing is not better than something. This is a classic category mistake. Something and nothing have nothing in common, so they cannot be compared. It is not even like comparing apples and oranges, since they both are fruit. It is like comparing apples and nonapples, insisting that nonapples taste better.

A nonfree world is not morally better than a free world. A nonfree world is a nonmoral world, since free will is necessary for morality. A nonmoral world cannot be morally better than a moral world. Since a nonfree world is not a moral world, there is no moral basis for comparison. This too is a category mistake.

A free world where no one sins or even a free world where everyone sins and then gets saved is *conceivable* but it may not be *achievable*. As long as everyone is really free, it is always possible that someone will refuse to do the good. Of course, God could force everyone to do good, but then they would not be free. Forced freedom is not freedom at all. Since God is love, he cannot force himself on anyone against their will. Forced love is not love; it is rape. And God is not a divine rapist. Love must work persuasively but not coercively. Hence, in every conceivable free world someone would choose to do evil, so a perfect evil-free world may not be possible.

A world where sin never materializes is *conceivable* but it may not be the *most desirable* morally. If evil is not permitted, then it can not be defeated. Like automobiles, a tested world is better than an untested one. Or, to put it another way, no boxer can beat an opponent without getting into the ring. God may have permitted evil in order to defeat it. If evil is not allowed, then the higher virtues cannot be attained. No pain, no gain. Tribulation works patience. There is no way to experience the joy of forgiveness without allowing the fall into sin. So, a world where evil is not defeated and the higher goods attained would not be the best world achievable. Therefore, while a world where sin does not occur is *theoretically conceivable,* it would be *morally inferior.*

Conclusion. No one has demonstrated that any alternative world is morally better than the one we have. Hence, no antitheist can show that God did not create the best world, even given the privation of good. This, of course, does not mean that the theist is committed to the belief that this present world is the best world that can be achieved. God is not finished yet, and Scripture promises that something better will be achieved. The theist's assumption is that this world is the best way *to* the best world achievable.

Sources

The Metaphysical Problem of Evil

Augustine, *Against the Epistle of the Manicheans*
———, *The City of God*
———, *On the Nature of the Good*
———, *On True Religion*
Thomas Aquinas, *Compendium Theologica*
———, *Summa Theologica*

The Moral Problem of Evil

N. L. Geisler, *Philosophy of Religion*
———, *The Roots of Evil*
G. W. Leibniz, *Theodicy*
C. S. Lewis, *The Great Divorce*
Thomas Aquinas, *On Evil*

The Physical Problem of Evil

Augustine, *The City of God*
A. Camus, *The Plague*
———, *The Roots of Evil*
C. S. Lewis, *The Problem of Pain*
A. Plantinga, *God, Freedom, and Evil*
F. M. Voltaire, *Candide*

Evolution. Evolution covers three basic areas: the origin of the universe; the origin of first life, and the origin of new life forms. Respectively, these are called cosmic evolution, chemical evolution, and biological evolution (*see* EVOLUTION, BIOLOGICAL; EVOLUTION, CHEMICAL; EVOLUTION, COSMIC). Because differing implications and arguments set apart the apologetics relating to each of these evolutionary highways, they will be discussed in separate articles.

In the broad sense, *evolution* means development, but more specifically it has come to mean the theory of common ancestry. It is the belief that all living things evolved by natural processes from earlier and more simple forms of life. *Theistic evolution posits a God who got the process going (by creating matter and/or first life) and/or has guided it. Naturalistic evolution believes the entire process is natural including the origin of the universe and first life by spontaneous generation.

For other discussions relating to a critique of evolution science, see ADAM, HISTORICITY OF; ANTHROPIC PRINCIPLE; BIG BANG THEORY; CREATION, VIEWS OF; DARWIN, CHARLES; MISSING LINKS; ORIGINS, SCIENCE OF, and TELEOLOGICAL ARGUMENT.

Evolution, Biological. Some ancient Greeks believed in evolution. However, before Charles *Darwin (1809–1882), theories of evolution tended to arise out of a pantheistic worldview (*see* PANTHEISM) and lacked scientific credibility. *Darwin theorized a mechanism, called "natural selection," to make evolution work. This placed evolution in the naturalistic framework that has been its stronghold ever since. Much of what Darwin taught has been rejected and surpassed, but his doctrine of natural selection has been maintained.

Biological evolution is divided into micro-evolution (small scale) and macro-evolution (large scale). Opponents of macro-evolution generally accept micro-evolution, since this process simply describes the ability of various forms of life to adapt to their environment. For example, there are several hundred kinds of dogs, but they are all canines. Their differences in breed "evolved" (developed) through both natural and artificial selection. Macro-evolution embraces evolution on the large scale, from microbe to man, from the first one-cell animal to human beings as the highest animal so far developed in the chain.

Most macro-evolutionists believe that life first began as a result of chemical reactions in what Darwin called a "warm little pool." Research has shown that it is possible to generate the essential proteins necessary for life using only a few basic gases and water. This has encouraged the view that life arose from nonliving matter (*see* EVOLUTION, CHEMICAL). New life forms are said to have evolved through mutations and natural selection. As conditions on earth changed, animals adapted new characteristics to meet the challenges. Those who adapted survived and those that did not passed into extinction. The great variety of extinct animals represented among fossils, and their similarities to living species are used to confirm this thesis.

Scientific Basis. Evolution, like other approaches to past events, is a *speculative*, rather than an *empirical*, science. Speculative science deals with past singularities for which there are no recurring patterns of events by which they can be tested. Theories of evolution and creation also are called theories of *origin science* (*see* ORIGINS, SCIENCE OF), rather than *operation science*. Operation science is empirical science; it deals with the way things operate now. It studies regular and repeated phenomena. Its answers can be tested by repeating the observation or experiment. Its basic principles are *observability* and *repeatability*. Micro-evolution is a legitimate study of operation science, especially as it relates to genetics.

Since origin science deals with past singularities it is more of a *forensic* science. Past events of origin were not observed and cannot be repeated. They must be reconstructed by viewing the evidence that remains. Just as a forensic scientist attempts to reconstruct how the homicide occurred from physical evidence, so the origin scientist tries to reconstruct the origin of the universe, first life, and new life forms from the evidence.

The Principles of Origin Science. Instead of observation and repetition, the origin scientist uses principles of causality and analogy. The principle of *causality* (*see* CAUSALITY, PRINCIPLE OF; FIRST PRINCIPLES), which is at the root of modern science and all rational thought, states that every event has an adequate cause. In science, the principle of *analogy* (or uniformity) states that the present is the key to the past. Or, more precisely, the kinds of causes that produced certain kinds of effects in the present are the kinds of causes that produce similar events in the past.

Two Kinds of Causes. Causality comes in two basic varieties: *natural* and *intelligent*. Intelligent causes are sometimes called *primary causes* and natural causes are called *secondary causes*. Most sciences seek natural causes in the laws of physics or chemistry. Others, however, deal with intelligent causes. Archaeology, for example, seeks an intelligent cause for the cultural remains of the past. Astronomers in the SETI (Search for Extra Terrestrial Intelligence) Program have tuned their radio telescopes into outer space, searching for a message from intelligent beings. Both of these sciences believe they can tell when they have found an effect that demands an intelligent cause by the special marks a mind leaves on what it produces. For example, there is an obvious difference between alphabet cereal spilled on the table and the arranged series of letters: "Tom, take out the garbage. Mom." Those who believe there is an intelligent cause for the origin of the universe, first life, and/or new life forms are called "creationists." Those who believe these can be explained by purely natural, nonintelligent causes are called "evolutionists." "Theistic evolutionists" try to synthesize the two views.

Three basic areas of dispute separate creationists and evolutionists on the question of *origins:* (1) the origin of the universe (*see* EVOLUTION, COSMIC), (2) the origin of first life (*see* EVOLUTION, CHEMICAL), and (3) the origin of human life. Historically, these areas have been called "cosmogony, biogony, and anthropogony" (*see* MISSING LINKS), in distinction to the operation sciences cosmology, biology, and anthropology.

Origin of New Life Forms. Naturalistic Explanation of Origins. New life forms have come either from natural or supernatural (intelligent) causes. Darwin made one of his greatest contributions to the theory of evolution with his analogy of selection by breeders to selection in nature. This principle of natural selection became the hallmark of evolution because it provided a system by which new developments of life forms could be explained without recourse to a supernatural cause.

Darwin was aware that there were serious flaws with the analogy between breeders and nature, but he hoped that what humans could do in a few generations could be done by nature in several hundred generations. However, time is not the only factor which weakens the analogy. E. S. Russell wrote:

> It is unfortunate that Darwin ever introduced the term "natural selection," for it has given rise to much confusion of thought. He did so, of course, because he arrived at his theory through studying the effects of selection as practiced by man in the breeding of domesticated animals and cultivated plants. Here the use of the word is entirely legitimate. But the *action of man in selective breeding is not analogous to the action of "natural selection,"* but *almost its direct opposite*. . . . Man has an aim or an end in view; "natural selection" can have none. Man picks out the individuals he wishes to cross, choosing them by the characteristics he seeks to perpetuate or enhance. He protects them and their issue by all means in his power, guarding them thus from the operation of natural selection, which would speedily eliminate many freaks; he continues his active and purposeful selection from generation to generation until he reaches, if possible, his goal. Nothing of this kind happens, or can happen, through the blind process of differential elimination and differential survival which we miscall "natural selection." [cited in Moore, 124]

Evidence of the Fossil Record. It is seldom fully appreciated that the only real evidence for or against evolution is in the fossil record. Every other argument for evolution is based on *what could have been*. Only the fossil record records examples of *what actually did happen*. Darwin recognized this as a problem as well and wrote in *On the Origin of Species,* "Why then is not every geological formation and every stratum full of such intermediate links? Geology assuredly does not reveal any such finely graduated organic chain, and this, perhaps, is the most obvious and gravest objection which can be urged against my theory" (Darwin, 280).

In the century and a half since Darwin wrote, the situation has only become worse for his theory. Noted Harvard paleontologist Stephen Jay Gould has written, "The extreme rarity of transitional forms in the fossil record persists as the trade secret of paleontology. The evolutionary trees that adorn our textbooks have data only at the tips and nodes of their branches; the rest is inference, however reasonable, not the evidence of fossils" (Gould, 14). Eldredge and Tattersall agree, saying, "Expectation colored perception to such an extent that the *most obvious single fact about biological evolution—non-change*—has seldom, if ever, been incorporated into anyone's scientific notions of how life actually evolves. If ever there was a myth, it is that evolution is a process of constant change" (Eldredge, 8).

What does the fossil record suggest? Evolutionists such as Gould now agree with what creationists from Louis Agassiz to Duane Gish have said all along, that the fossil record includes two features particularly inconsistent with gradualism:

Stasis. Most species appear in the fossil record looking much the same as when they disappear; morphological change is limited and directionless.

Sudden appearance. In any area, a species does not arise gradually. It appears all at once and fully formed (Gould, ibid., 13–14).

There is no real indication that one form of life transforms into a completely different form. While these two features seem to invalidate classical evolution, they are somewhat problematic to creationists also.

Some creationists say that the fossil record reflects the debris of the great flood, either because some animals were better able to escape the waters or by hydrodynamic sorting as the remains settled. These scientists are concerned with preserving evidence of a young earth because they believe creation was in seven literal twenty-four-hour-periods and that there are no large gaps in the early genealogies of Genesis.

Others, known as "old-earth creationists," hold that the earth need not be only thousands of years old. This group understands the fossil record to show that creation was accomplished in a series of stages, each new appearance in the geological strata pointing to a new moment of direct creation. Invertebrates appeared first, followed by a long period of nature balancing itself before the next burst of creation. Fish appeared next and then amphibians, until man was created. The latter view does agree with the fossil record, but there is no consensus among creationists about the age of the earth. This is a hotly debated issue, but both sides agree that the fossil evidence supports creation better than evolution.

Some evolutionists have attempted to deal with the fossil evidence by introducing the idea of punctuated equilibrium. These scientists say that the jumps in the fossil record reflect real catastrophes which induced sudden major changes in the existing species. Hence, evolution is not gradual, but punctuated by sudden leaps from one stage to the next. The theory has been criticized because no evidence has been shown for a mechanism of secondary causes needed to make these sudden advances possible. Their theory appears to be based solely on the absence of transitional fossils. This view breaks with Darwin, who understood evidence of suddenness to be evidence in favor of creation. To accept the idea of punctuation as a result of a primary cause comes dangerously close to a creationist view.

The Evidence of Vestigial Organs. Evolutionists have used the presence of "vestigial organs" in humans as a support. They argue that, since the human body has organs for which there is no known use, they are left over from an earlier animal stage in which they were useful. The fact that vestigials can be removed with no apparent harm to the body indicates that they are useless. The appendix, ear muscles, and the third eyelid are placed into this category.

However, just because functions for these organs are not known does not mean that none exist. Since scientific knowledge is finite and progressive, there may be functions of which science is not yet aware. That they can be removed without apparent harm to the body is meaningless. Other organs may compensate for their loss. Also, a loss may exist that is not readily detectable. Some organs, such as tonsils, may be more important at an earlier stage in the person's development as, for example, during early childhood to help fight off diseases. And organs such as a kidney or a lung can be removed without serious loss, yet they have a function.

It is significant that the list of vestigial organs has shrunk from around 100 when the idea was first proposed to about a half dozen today. There are hints about purposes for some of those. The appendix may aid in digestion and may be helpful in fighting off disease. Rabbits have a large appendix, and complete vegetarians may get more benefit from theirs. The muscle of the outer ear helps protect against freezing in colder climates. The "third eyelid" or *nictitating membranae* is used in humans to collect foreign material that gets in the eye. The "tail" or coccyx is necessary for sitting with comfort. The endocrine glands, once thought to be vestigial, are now known to be of great importance in the production of hormones. The thymus has been found to be involved in protecting the body against disease.

Even if some organs are truly leftovers from an earlier period in human development, this would not prove evolution. They may be left over from an earlier stage of the human race, rather than from prehuman species. One might even say that an organ has lost its function would not demonstrate that we are evolving, but devolving—losing some organs and abilities. This is the opposite of evolution.

The Evidence of the Genetic Code. Creationists reason that there are real limitations to evolutionary change that are built into the genetic code of every living being. Changes within this structure indicates design for each major category of life form. Each new life form came into being by an act of intelligent intervention that arranged genetic information to fit functions. Just as letter sequences vary to form different words, DNA patterns vary to produce different species. If it requires intelligence to create *King Lear* from a selection of the words found in a dictionary, then it also requires intelligence to select and sort genetic information to produce the variety of species which work together as a system in nature.

The sudden appearance of these life forms strengthens the case that a supernatural intelligence was at work to accomplish this organization. In accordance with the principle of uniformity, this is the most plausible solution to the problem. So, the greatest problem for evolutionists is not "missing links," but an explanation for the origin of complex new systems of genetic information.

The Evidence from Specified Complexity. Not only was the first living cell exceedingly complex, but higher forms of life are even more complex. If the genetic information in a one-cell animal exceeds that in a volume of the *Encyclopedia Britannica,* the information in the human brain is greater than that in the Library of Congress. If it takes an intelligent cause to produce the simple first life form, no less is needed for human life.

Complexity has always been a major problem for evolution. It amounts to the same problem encountered in examining the origin of first life (*see* EVOLUTION, CHEMICAL). The breeding analogy used to illustrate how natural processes did it all contains a great deal of intelligent intervention that is overlooked in the theory. Breeders manipulate according to an intelligent plan for encouraging specific developments. Informationally speaking, this is going from a state of complexity in the DNA code to a higher, or at least more specific, state of complexity. It is like changing the sentence,

> "She had brown hair."

to the more complex statement,

> "Her auburn tresses shone in the sun."

This increase in information encoded into the DNA strand requires intelligence just as surely as did the original coding to produce life. Indeed, if Darwin's analogy proves anything, it shows the need for intelligent intervention to produce new life forms. The principle of uniformity leads unhesitatingly to this conclusion once it is realized that we are working within origin science, not operation science.

The Evidence from Systemic Change. Macroevolutionary changes demand large-scale changes from one type of organism to another. Evolutionists argue that this occurred gradually over a long period. One serious objection to this view is that all functional changes from one system to another must be simultaneous (see Denton, 11). For example, one can make small changes in a car gradually over a period of time without changing its basic type. One can change the shape of the fenders, it color, and its trim gradually. But if a change is in the size of the piston, this will involve simultaneous changes in the cam shaft, block, and cooling system. Otherwise the new engine will not function.

Likewise, changing from a fish to a reptile or a reptile to a bird calls for major changes throughout the system of the animal. All these changes must occur simultaneously or blood oxygenation will not go with lung development, will not match nasal passage and throat changes, autonomic breathing reflexes in the brain, thoracic musculature, and membranes. Gradual evolution cannot account for this.

To make this same point in terms of the genetic code, one cannot go from small gradual changes in a simple genetic code to a more complex DNA molecule without major simultaneous changes, particularly not by random mutations. Small, random changes to "Mary had a little lamb. . ." will never produce *King Lear,* even if all the letters of the alphabet and punctuation are present. The first small random change might read, "Mary sad a little lamb." The next, "Mary sad a litter lamb." And the next, "Mary sad a litter lgmb." With each single change the message gets more garbled. It is a long way from *King Lear* and going in the wrong direction. Only an intelligent being can reform the same letters of the English language into *King Lear*—by simultaneous and systematic redevelopment.

The English alphabet has twenty-six letters; the genetic alphabet has only four, but the method of communicating by sequence of letters is the same. Information scientist Hubert P. Yockey insists, "It is important to understand that we are not reasoning by analogy. The sequence hypothesis applies directly to the protein and the genetic text as well as to written language and therefore the treatment is mathematically identical" (Yockey, 16). It turns out that a single strand of DNA carries the same amount of information as one volume of an encyclopedia.

Each new form of life has its own, unique code that, although it is similar in the letters used, differs vastly in the message conveyed. One can use the very same words and convey an entirely different message. Hence, the evolutionist argument from the high similarity of the words in an ape and a human being do not prove common ancestry. The two sentences "You do love me" and "Do you love me?" have the same words but convey a totally different message. With ingenuity one could construct a paragraph (or even a whole book) in which exactly the same sentences which conveyed a completely different message. A very rudimentary example might go something like this:

> John came before Mary. Mary came after John [= later than]. So John and Mary came together [= at the same place].

Compare this with the same sentences in a different order which convey a different meaning:

> Mary came after [= pursued] John. John came before Mary [= in her presence]. So John and Mary came together [= in a personal relationship].

A high degree of similarity of genetic information in an ape and a human means absolutely nothing. It is the way the pieces are put together that makes a world of difference. Hear this evolutionist's testimony: "When we get down to the business of trying to establish an evolutionary series of sequences, we cannot find the linear, primitive-to-advanced arrangement we had expected." In fact, "instead of a progression of increasing divergence, each vertebrate sequence is equally isolated [e.g.] from the cytochrome sequence for the dogfish." Thus, "in this and countless other comparisons, it has proved impossible to arrange protein sequences in a macro-evolutionary series corresponding to the expected transitions from fish > amphibian > reptile > mammal" (Thaxton, 139–40).

Conclusion. Now that we have new evidence about the nature of the universe, the information stored in DNA molecules, and further fossil confirmation, the words of Agassiz resound even more loudly than they did when first written in 1860:

> [Darwin] has lost sight of the most striking of the features, and the one which pervades the whole, namely, that there runs throughout Nature unmistakable evidence of thought, corresponding to the mental operations of our own mind, and therefore intelligible to us as thinking beings, and unaccountable on any other basis than that they own their existence to the working of intelligence; and no theory that overlooks this element can be true to nature. [Agassiz, 13]

There are two views of the origins of new life forms. One says that everything came about by natural causes; the other looks to a supernatural (intelligent) cause. The overwhelming evidence support is in favor of the latter.

Sources

L. Agassiz, "Agassiz: Review of Darwin's *Origins. . . ,*" series 2, vol. 30 (30 June 1860)

M. J. Behe, *Darwin's Black Box*

W. R. Bird, *The Origin of Species Revisited*, 2 vols.

C. Darwin, *On the Origin of Species*

R. Dawkins, *River Out of Eden*

———, *The Blind Watchmaker*

M. Denton, *Evolution: A Theory in Crisis*

N. Eldredge, *The Myths of Human Evolution*

N. L. Geisler, *Is Man the Measure?* chap. 11

———, *Origin Science*, chapter 7

D. Gish, *Evolution: The Fossils Say No*
S. J. Gould, "Evolution's Erratic Pace," *NH*, 1972
P. Johnson, *Darwinism on Trial*
———, *Reason in the Balance*
M. Lubenow, *Bones of Contention*
J. Moore, *The Post-Darwinian Controversies*
C. Thaxton, et al., eds., *Of Pandas and People*
H. P. Yockey, "Self-Organization, Origin of Life Scenarios, and Information Theory," *JTB*, 1981

Evolution, Chemical. Chemical evolutionists claim that purely natural laws can explain the origin of first life by spontaneous generation. Creationists insist that an intelligent cause is necessary to construct the basic building blocks of life. Contrary to widespread opinion, the positive evidence for an intelligent cause is not based on the statistical improbability of life arising by chance. Rather, it is because science is not based on chance; it is based on observation and repetition (*see* ORIGINS, SCIENCE OF).

In spite of the well-established fact, based on the work of Louis Pasteur (1822–1895), that life does not begin spontaneously from nonlife, all naturalistic scientists believe that it did at the beginning. The scientific basis for this conclusion is the experiments of Harold Urey and Stanley Miller. They showed that the basic building blocks of life (amino acids) can be obtained from purely chemical elements (hydrogen, nitrogen, ammonia, and carbon dioxide gases) by natural laws without any intelligent intervention. By passing an electrical discharge through these cases they produced these fundamental elements of life. Supposing lightening passing through similar cases in a primal atmosphere, first life may have arisen by a purely natural process on earth or somewhere else.

The theory is that shortly after the earth was cooled enough to allow it, the combination of hydrogen, nitrogen, ammonia, and carbon dioxide reacted to form elementary amino acids, which in time developed into the DNA chains and finally into cells. This process is said to have taken several billion years and the extra energy of the sun, volcanic activity, lightning, and cosmic rays was needed to keep the process going.

The Problems. That life could arise by purely natural causes is subject to serious objections.

It is contrary to the universal scientific experience that life never arises from nonlife. The premodern, fallacious belief that it could was based on ignorance of microscopic bacteria. Once Pasteur sterilized the container, killing the bacteria, no life emerged. The same inability is recognized by principles of causation. A fundamental causal concept demands that an effect cannot be greater than its cause (*see* CAUSALITY, PRINCIPLE OF). Just as nonbeing cannot produce being, nonlife cannot produce life. Water does not rise higher than its source on its own.

The origin-of-life experiments involve illegitimate investigator interference. For example, intelligent intervention is manifest at several levels. Why are certain gases (such as hydrogen) included and others (such as Oxygen) excluded? Is this not an intelligent choice, based on a knowledge of what will and will not work? Further, who constructed the apparatus for the experiment? Why does it not have a different design? Why did they choose to inject an electrical discharge? Obviously, intelligent choices were being made at several levels.

There is an unwarranted assumption that primal conditions on earth (or elsewhere) were similar to those in the experiment. Two crucial conditions are now known to have been different. Since the experiment will not work with oxygen present, it was assumed that the earth's early atmosphere had no oxygen. But this is now known to be false. That fact in itself is sufficient to falsify the experiment and the chemical evolution theory. Further, as even many chemical evolutionists admit, chemicals in the concentration used in the experiment are not found anywhere on earth. The whole primal soup scenario is a myth (see Thaxton, chap. 4).

The analogy between the Miller experiment and known conditions on the early earth is invalid, since it overlooks the presence of destructive forces. Oxygen would destroy the process. The energy needed from the sun and cosmic radiation damage the very substances produced. Under the conditions required for life to have arisen spontaneously, it is more likely that the elements would be destroyed faster than they could be produced. Nature is filled with destructive forces that tear down and bring disorder. This is part of the second law of thermodynamics (*see* THERMODYNAMICS, LAWS OF).

Even if the right chemicals could be produced, no satisfactory answer has been given for how they could have been arranged properly and enclosed in a cell wall. This would require another set of conditions altogether.

Further, evolutionists have never shown any mechanism that can harness the energy to do the work of selecting amino acids and sorting out which will build each gene to develop a living organism. It doesn't do any good to have a drawer full of batteries if there is no flashlight—a mechanism for harnessing energy—to contain them. The DNA molecule is very complex. See a description of this complexity in EVOLUTION, BIOLOGICAL.

Granting that there may have been enough energy available to do the work, the only systems that can harness the energy to do this kind of work are either living or intelligent. It is easy to pump a lot of energy into a system at random to make it hot, but to organize it and create information requires intelligence.

Finally, even with all the intelligent interferences in the Miller experiments, which invalidate the results for a purely natural processes, the result has not been a single living cell. An amino acid is only a chemical. However biologically interesting it may be, it is not alive. One crucial missing ingredient—the code of life or DNA—is positive evidence for a creative intelligence.

Other Naturalistic Theories. Other theories have been advanced to explain the origins of first life on earth. One is that natural laws were involved that have not yet been discovered, but scientists can only point out the need when the laws they do know about militated against creation of life. Others suggest that life may have come to earth from somewhere else in the universe, either on a meteorite or on an ancient spaceship, but both of these solutions just push the question back one step: Where did that life come from? Thermal vents in the sea floor and clay deposits are being studied as possible breeding grounds for life's beginnings, but this does not account for a way to harness energy to make specified complexity possible. The most probable cause, and the only one that the evidence supports, is an intelligent cause. The only significant debate is between pantheist and theist, both of whom insist there must be a Mind behind the specified complexity in living things, differing only on whether it is beyond the universe or only in it.

Evidence of Intelligence. Evidence is lacking for a natural cause of origin, but is there positive evidence pointing to an intelligent cause of first life?

The key to knowing which kind of cause is involved in questions of origin is the principle of analogy (uniformity). This is one of the fundamental principles in any scientific understanding of the past. Archaeology uses it to posit an intelligent cause for artifacts that might have originated with past civilizations. The SETI program sorts through radio waves from the cosmos in its search for extraterrestrial life, looking for something that breaks with uniformity.

The Principle of Analogy (Uniformity). By observing over and over what kinds of effects are produced by causes, we can determine which kind of cause is needed to produce life. We know that round stones are regularly caused by natural laws involved in the motion of water and rubbing one another. Flint and obsidian will not turn into a spear or arrow point that way. The only question, then, is whether a living cell is more like a round stone or a projectile point. Anyone viewing the faces on Mount Rushmore knows these stone shapes were formed by an intelligent cause. It is not just that natural causes never produce the kind of specified information shown on Mount Rushmore. It is also known by repeated observation that intelligent causes do produce this kind of specificity.

Specified Complexity Points to an Intelligent Cause. The kind of evidence that indicates an intelligent cause of life is called specified complexity. Carl *Sagan said that a single message from outer space would confirm his belief that there is extraterrestrial life. Such communication would be *specified complexity*. Or, to be more precise, since we know that complex messages always result from an intelligent cause, it remains only to see whether a living cell contains a complex message. With the discovery of the DNA code of life, the answer is clear. In all of nature, only living cells have complex messages known as specified complexity. A chunk of quartz has specificity but no complexity. The message in a crystal is repetitive, like the message: starstarstarstar. A chain of random polymers (called a polypeptide) is complex, but it does not give a specific message. It looks more like this: *fqpizgenyatkpvno*. Only a living cell has both specificity and complexity that is not repetitious and communicates a message or a clear function, such as: *This sentence has meaning*. Hence, a living cell calls for an intelligent cause. Science speaks of simple life and complex life. Even the simplest one-celled organism has enough information that if spelled out in English would fill a volume of the *Encyclopedia Britannica*.

A clear and distinct message—a complex design with a specified function—was caused by some form of intelligence that intervened to impose limits on the natural matter that it would not take by itself. Some natural phenomena are orderly and awe inspiring, but clearly caused by natural forces. The Grand Canyon and Niagara Falls required only the blind forces of wind and water to shape them. The same cannot be said for Mount Rushmore or a hydroelectric plant. These required intelligent intervention.

The Confirmation of Information Theory. Studies in Information Theory confirm that one can determine an intelligent cause simply by the letter frequencies. In a series of letters that carry a message (even if we do not know what the message is) there is a certain letter frequency. This is what makes unknown codes decipherable and makes it possible to remove background noise from a tape and clarify the message.

What could explain the sudden appearance of life and also provide for the informational organization of living matter? If we apply the principle of uniformity (analogy) to the question, the only cause that we know routinely does this kind of work is intelligence. The reasonable assumption is that it also required intelligence to do it in the past. Uniform experience proves this to us, and, as David *Hume said, "as a uniform experience amounts to a proof, there is here a direct and full *proof*, from the nature of the fact" (Hume, 122–23). Since it is not possible that we are speaking of human intelligence or even living beings in the natural sphere, it had to be a supernatural intelligence. This does create a disjunction in the course of nature, which irritates most scientists; however, once it is admitted that there is a radical disjunction from nothing to something at the beginning of the universe, there can be little objection to the idea of one more intervention when the evidence clearly points to it.

The Confirmation from Molecular Biology. Michael Behe's book, *Darwin's Black Box,* provides strong evidence from the nature of a living cell that it could not have originated or evolved by anything but intelligent design. The cell represents, in many cases, irreducible complexity that cannot be accounted for by small incremental changes called for by evolution.

Darwin admitted: "If it could be demonstrated that any complex organ existed which could not possibly have been formed by numerous, successive, slight modifications, my theory would absolutely break down" (*Origin of Species,* 154). Even evolutionists, such as Richard Dawkins, agree:

> Evolution is very possibly not, in actual fact, always gradual. But it must be gradual when it is being used to explain the coming into existence of complicated, apparently designed objects, like eyes. For if it is not gradual in these cases, it ceases to have any explanatory power. Without gradualness in these cases, we are back to miracle, which is a synonym for the total absence of [naturalistic] explanation. [83]

Behe provides numerous examples of irreducible complexity that cannot evolve in small steps. He concludes,

> No one at Harvard University, no one at the National Institutes of Health, no member of the National Academy of Sciences, no Nobel Prize winner—no one at all can give a detailed account of how the cilium, or vision, or blood clotting, or any complex biochemical process might have developed in a Darwinian fashion. But we are here. All these things got here somehow; if not in a Darwinian fashion, then how? [187]

Other examples of irreducible complexity that Behe points out include aspects of DNA reduplication, electron transport, telomere synthesis, photosynthesis, and transcription regulation (ibid., 160). "Life on earth at its most fundamental level, in its most critical components, is the product of intelligent activity" (ibid., 193). Behe adds, "The conclusion of intelligent design flows naturally from the data itself—not from sacred books or sectarian beliefs. Inferring that biochemical systems were designed by an intelligent agent is a humdrum process that requires no new principles of logic or science" (ibid.). Thus, "the result of these cumulative efforts to investigate the cell—to investigate life at the molecular level—is a loud, clear, piercing cry of 'design!' The result is so unambiguous and so significant that it must be ranked as one of the greatest achievements in the history of science. The discovery rivals those of Newton and Einstein" (ibid., 232–33).

Conclusion. As Hume showed, in the empirical world we posit causal connections only because we see certain events conjoined over and over. And since the present is the key to the past, the same applies to causes of origin. Hence, it is unscientific to posit anything but an intelligent cause for the first living cell, since repeated experience tells that the only kind of cause known to be able to produce specified complexity, as life has, is an intelligent cause. Chemical evolution, then, fails the scientific test. And it is beside the point to speculate that a natural cause is still possible, since science is based on evidence which points clearly in the direction of an intelligent cause by constant conjunction which David Hume called a "proof."

Sources

M. J. Behe, *Darwin's Black Box*
R. Dawkins, *The Blind Watchmaker*
M. Denton, *Evolution: A Theory in Crisis*
D. Hume, *An Inquiry Concerning Human Understanding*
A. Johnson, *Darwin on Trial*
L. Orgel, *The Origin of Life*
M. Polanyi, "Life Transcending Physics and Chemistry," *CEN*
C. Thaxton, et al., *The Mystery of Life's Origin*

Evolution, Cosmic. Either the universe had a beginning or it did not. If it did have a beginning, then it was either caused or uncaused. If it was caused, then what kind of cause could be responsible for bringing all things into being?

An Eternal Universe. Traditionally, cosmic evolutionary scientists have believed that the universe, in some form, always existed. Matter is eternal. The main scientific support is the first law of thermodynamics (*see* THERMODYNAMICS, LAWS OF) that "energy can neither be created nor destroyed."

Creationists respond that this is a misunderstanding of the first law which should be stated: "The actual amount of energy in the universe remains constant." Unlike the misstated version of the first law, this is based on scientific observation about what occurs and is not a dogmatic philosophical assertion about what can or cannot happen. There is no scientific evidence that the universe is eternal.

Fred Hoyle proposed his steady-state theory to avoid this conclusion. It affirms that hydrogen atoms are coming into existence to keep the universe from running down. This also calls for the universe to be constantly generating hydrogen atoms from nothing. This hypothesis has fatal flaws. There is no scientific evidence that such an event ever occurred. And such an occurrence would be contrary to the principle of causality (*see* CAUSALITY, PRINCIPLE OF), which affirms that there must be an adequate cause for every event. Creationists quickly note that only a Creator would be an adequate cause for the creation of new hydrogen atoms out of nothing (*see* CREATION, VIEWS OF).

Holding to such beliefs as the steady-state theory or the eternality of matter theory has a high cost for the scientist, for both violate a fundamental law of science: the principle of causality. Both views require that the scientist believe in events happening without a cause. Even the great skeptic David *Hume said, "I never asserted so absurd a proposition as that anything might arise without a cause" (Hume, 1:187). Yet this absurd proposition is accepted by scientists who make their living by the law of causality. If the whole universe is uncaused, why should we believe that the parts are caused? If the parts are all caused, then what evidence could suggest that the whole is uncaused? Nothing in the principle of causality supports this conclusion.

Some cosmic evolutionists argue for some kind of rebound theory, whereby the universe collapses and rebounds forever. But there is no evidence that enough matter exists to stop and pull back by gravitational forces the expanding universe even once. What is more, this hypothesis runs contrary to the second law of thermodynamics, which dictates that, even if the universe rebounded, it would, like a bouncing ball, eventually peter out (*see* BIG BANG THEORY).

Universe with a Beginning. Creationists can offer evidence that the universe is not eternal but had a cause. Though he is not himself a theist, Robert Jastrow, founder and former director of NASA's Goddard Institute for Space Studies, has summarized the evidence in his book *God and the Astronomers*. Jastrow points out three lines of evidence—the motions of the galaxies, the laws of thermodynamics, and the life story of the stars—indicate that the universe had a beginning (Jastrow, 111). Now if we are speaking of a movement from no matter to matter, we are clearly in the realm of unrepeatable events covered by origin science.

The Second Law of Thermodynamics. Perhaps the most significant piece of evidence is the second law of thermodynamics. According to this law, "The amount of usable energy in the universe is decreasing." Or, stated another way, "In a closed isolated system, the amount of usable energy is decreasing." Or, "Left to themselves, things tend to disorder." No matter which way it is stated, this law shows that an eternal universe would have run out of usable energy or reached a state of total disorder. Since it has not, it must have had a beginning.

The first law of thermodynamics says that the actual amount of energy in the universe remains constant—it doesn't change. The second law of thermodynamics says that the amount of *usable* energy in any closed system (which the whole universe is) is decreasing. Everything is tending toward disorder and the universe is running down. Now if the overall amount of energy stays the same, but we are running out of usable energy, then what we started with was not an infinite amount. You can't run out of an infinite amount. This means that the universe is and always has been finite. It could not have existed forever in the past. So it must have had a beginning. And, if it had a beginning, then it must have been caused, since every event has an adequate cause (*see* CAUSALITY, PRINCIPLE OF).

The Motion of the Galaxies. Scientists argue that the universe is not simply in a holding pattern, maintaining its movement from everlasting to everlasting. It now appears that all of the galaxies are moving outward, as if from a central point of origin, and that all things were expanding faster in the past than they are now. Looking out into space, we are also looking back in time. We are seeing things as they were when the light was given off by those stars many years ago. The light from a star 7 million light-years away tells us what it was like and where it was 7 million years ago. Using a 200-inch telescope, Allan Sandage compiled information on forty-two galaxies, as far as 6 billion light years away. His measurements indicate that the universe was expanding more rapidly in the past than it is today. This result lends further support to the belief that the universe exploded into being (Jastrow, *God and the Astronomers*, 95).

The Radiation Echo. A third line of evidence that the universe began is the radiation "echo" which seems to come from everything. It was first thought to be a malfunction or static on the instruments. But research has discovered that the static was coming from everywhere—the universe itself has a low-level radiation from some past catastrophe that looks like a giant fireball. Says Jastrow,

> No explanation other than the big bang has been found for the fireball radiation. The clincher, which has convinced almost the last doubting Thomas, is that the radiation discovered by Penzias and Wilson has exactly the pattern of wavelengths expected for the light and heat produced in a great explosion. Supporters of the Steady State theory have tried desperately to find an alternative explanation, but they have failed. [ibid., 5]

The Discovery of a Great Mass of Matter. Since Jastrow first recorded the three lines of evidence for the beginning of the universe a fourth has been discovered. According to the big-bang theory there should have been a great mass of matter associated with the original explosion of the universe into being, but none was known until 1992. By means of the Hubble space telescope, astronomers found the very mass of matter predicted by big-bang cosmology. Thus the combined evidence provides an overwhelming case for the fact that the universe had a beginning.

Cause of the Cosmos. If the universe is not eternal but came into existence, the law of causality tells us that it must have had a cause. For whatever comes to be is caused. Hence, the universe was caused.

Logically, if we are looking for a cause which existed before the universe (nature) began, we are looking for a supernatural cause. Even Jastrow, a confirmed agnostic, has said as much: "That there are what I or anyone would call supernatural forces at work is now, I think, a scientifically proven fact" (ibid., 15, 18). Since he is speaking from the viewpoint of operation science, he probably means that there is no secondary cause which can explain the origin of the universe. But with the recognition of origin science, we can posit a supernatural primary cause that seems to be the most plausible answer to the question.

Conclusion. Jastrow sums up the cosmic evolutionists enigma well. He concludes his book:

> For the scientist who has lived by his faith in the power of reason, the story ends like a bad dream. He has scaled the mountains of ignorance; he is about to conquer the highest peak; as he pulls himself over the final rock, he is greeted by a band of theologians who have been sitting there for centuries. [ibid., 105–6]

After being embarrassed by the evidence that the cosmos had a beginning, Albert Einstein declared his desire "to know how god created this world. I am not interested in this or that phenomenon, in the spectrum of this of that element. I want to know his thought, the rest are details" (cited in Herbert, 177).

Sources

W. L. Craig, *The Kalam Argument for the Existence of God*
F. Heeren, *Show Me God*
N. Herbert, *Quantum Reality—Beyond the New Physics*
D. Hume, *The Letters of David Hume*, Vol. 1
M. D. Lemonick, "Echoes of the Big Bang," *Time*, 4 May 1993
R. Jastrow, "A Scientist Caught between Two Faiths," *CT*, 6 August 1982
———, *God and the Astronomers*
H. Ross, *The Fingerprint of God*
E. Whittaker, *The Beginning and End of the World*

Evolution, Human. ***See*** **Darrow, Clarence; Darwin, Charles; Dewey, John; Evolution, Biological; Missing Links.**

Evolution, Theistic. *Definition.* Broadly speaking, theistic evolution is the belief that God used evolution as his means of producing the various forms of physical life on this planet, including human life. However, there are several kinds of evolution in which God is said to be involved. Indeed, there are various conceptions of God connected to evolution.

Kinds of Evolution Involving God. Not all forms of evolution involving God are technically forms of theistic evolution, since many of them do not involve a theistic concept of God. The following typology is intended as suggestive, not exhaustive.

Theistic Evolution. By "theistic" evolution is meant the belief that a theistic God used an evolutionary process he had created to produce all living species of life. In addition, "theistic" means that God performed at least one *miracle after his original creation of the universe *ex nihilo* (*see* Creation, Three Views). Otherwise, there is no difference between theism and deism on the matter of origins. Of course, a theistic evolutionist (who does not deny more than two supernatural acts of creation) could still believe in other miracles in the Bible after creation, such as the *Virgin Birth or *resurrection.

*Minimal *Theistic Evolution.* The minimal theistic evolutionist believes that God performed two supernatural acts of creation: (1) the creation of matter out of nothing, and (2) the creation of first life. After that every other living thing, including human beings, emerged by natural processes that God had ordained from the beginning.

Maximal Theistic Evolution. The maximal theistic evolutionist holds that God performed at least three supernatural acts of creation: matter, first life, and the human soul. After the initial creation of matter and life, all animal organisms, including the human body, evolved by natural laws God established from the very beginning. This is the traditional Roman Catholic view, at least for the last century.

The belief in any more supernatural acts of creation would probably be better called a minimal form of creationism (though this is an arbitrary line), since it would hold that God supernaturally intervened at least four times in creation. Most scholars who hold this, also believe that God supernaturally intervened many more times than this. They often refer to themselves as Progressive Creationists. Bernard *Ramm and Hugh Ross (*The Fingerprints of God*) fit into this category.

Deistic Evolution. *Deism does not believe in any supernatural acts or miracles after the initial act of creating the material universe out of nothing. As far as the evolutionary process and the production of life forms, including human beings, there is no real difference between deistic evolution and naturalistic evolution, which includes *atheism and *agnosticism.

Pantheistic Evolution. Another form of evolution involving a belief in God is called pantheistic evolution. *Pantheism, unlike theism and deism, believes that God is all and all is God. God is the universe or Nature. Benedict *Spinoza and Albert *Einstein held this kind of belief. Former atheist Sir Fred Hoyle adopted this view in his book *Evolution from Space* (1981). According to this view, God created first life and then many basic forms of life at various times after that, as is indicated by the great gaps in the fossil record. However, the God who intelligently intervened to form these various kinds of life did so from within the universe, not from outside it. For God is the Mind of the universe. God is Nature.

Panentheistic Evolution. Unlike pantheism, which believes God is All, *panentheism holds that God is in all. Panentheism is distinguished by its belief that God is the Vital Force within the universe and within the evolutionary force. Henri Bergson expressed this view in his book *Creative Evolution* in 1907. This seems also to be the position of the Roman Catholic evolutionist, Teilhard de Chardin. According to this position, evolution is a continuous process that moves forward, sometimes even "leaps" forward, by virtue of the immanent divine Force within the universe.

Evaluation. Since the essence of all these views are critiqued elsewhere under deism, pantheism, and panentheism, it is not necessary to do so here. It remains only to point out that its view of evolution of living organisms assumes the antisupernaturalistic presuppositions of atheism and agnosticism. Only theism truly believes in supernatural acts from a God who is beyond the universe and who occasionally intervenes in it.

Many of the same arguments used against naturalistic or materialistic evolution apply also to these other forms of evolution involving God. For it makes no difference whether the natural processes were created by a theistic God or not. The evidence shows that nonintelligent natural laws do not have the ability to bring life or new life forms into existence, to say nothing of human beings (*see* DARWIN, CHARLES; MISSING LINKS).

Sources

H. Bergson, *Creative Evolution*
C. Darwin, *On the Origin of Species*
———, *The Descent of Man*
F. Hoyle, *Evolution From Space*
G. Mills, "A Theory of Theistic Evolution as an Alternative to Naturalistic Theory," *Perspectives on Science and Christian Faith* (1995)
B. Ramm, *The Christian View of Science and Scripture*
D. Ratzsch, *Battle of Beginnings*
H. Ross, *The Fingerprints of God*
Teilhard de Chardin, *The Omega Point*
H. Van Till, *Portraits of Creation*
———, *The Fourth Day*

Existentialism. As an atheistic movement, *existentialism* flowered in the mid-twentieth century, yet its effects lingered. Existentialism has had a negative effect on evangelical Christianity.

Theological Influence. Several theological movements, broadly known as neo-orthodox, have been influenced by existentialism. Karl *Barth stressed personal encounter with God, stressing that the Bible is a fallible human record of God's Word. Emil Brunner emphasized that revelation is personal, not propositional. Rudolph *Bultmann developed the demythological method of stripping the Bible of its outdated supernatural worldview to get at the existential core (*see* MYTHOLOGY AND THE NEW TESTAMENT).

Major Proponents of Existentialism. An eclectic group of philosophers and theologians contributed to what became modern existentialism. They include Lutheran theist Søren *Kierkegaard (1813–1855), German atheist Friedrich *Nietzsche (1844–1900), French atheists Jean-Paul *Sartre (1905–1980) and Albert Camus (1913–1960), German Jewish theist Martin *Buber (1878–1965), German non-theist Martin Heidegger (1889–1976), French Roman Catholic Gabriel Marcel (1889–1964), and German Eastern Orthodox layman Karl Jaspers (1883–1969).

Emphases and Contrasts of Existentialism. Existentialism emphasizes living over knowing, willing over thinking, the concrete over the abstract, and the dynamic over the static, love over law, the personal over the propositional, the individual over society, the subjective over the objective, the non-rational over the rational, and freedom over necessity.

At the heart of existentialism is the belief that existence has precedence over essence. All existentialists hold this view in some form. They differ in other respects, but most existentialists, especially atheists, tend to accept certain other propositions:

Humans are primarily animals who have learned to choose. They are not seen as rational, political, or mechanical beings.

Humanity as an object is not free, but individuals as a subject are free.

"I" am not "myself." The "self" can be studied and described as an "it." But the "I" behind the it transcends description; it is utterly free.

Objectivity lacks being. Only the subjective really exists.

Meaning and value are found in being, living, willing, and acting. Form, essence, and structure are irrelevant and valueless.

Meaning and values are created, not discovered. Theistic existentialists such as Kierkegaard would demur at this point.

Getting from Essence to Existence. All this sounds more philosophical than practical, and existentialists struggle with the movement from the abstract to the concrete. Different existentialists describe this move in different ways. The Christian existentialist Kierkegaard depicted it as a "leap of faith" (*see* FIDEISM) in which one has a personal encounter with God. The atheist Sartre called it an attempt to move from being for itself to being in itself. He believed that to do this is, in the end, impossible, and that life is absurd. Atheistic existentialists, with Sartre and Camus, have insisted that no authentic existential experience is possible. The best one can do is to recognize one's own inauthenticity. Theistic existentialists believe that a genuine existential experience is possible but not without a personal encounter with God. Whether this is done alone as an individual (Kierkegaard), or in community (Marcel) is moot. At least it is possible. For the Jewish existentialist Martin Buber, it was a movement from I-it to I-thou relationships. Gabriel Marcel believed one can have a true existential experience only in the move from "me" (the individual) or "they" (the crowd) to "we" (the community).

Evaluation. Existentialists are so diverse that general comments inevitably fall short of accurately portraying one or more groups under the heading. There are a few generalities that can be made of the movement.

Positive Contributions. Existentialism's stress on love over legalism fits the teaching of Jesus (Mark 2:27) and is something of a corrective to the ever-present legalism within some spheres of Christian life. Emphasis on the practical as opposed to the purely theoretical fits with the Christian emphasis on a living faith (cf. James). The New Testament avoids the abstract in teaching that good works follow from true faith (Eph. 2:8–10; James 2). All evangelicals believe in human freedom, though some groups disagree about nuances of what that means (*see* DETERMINISM; FREE WILL).

In the root sense that "existence is prior to essence," *Thomas Aquinas can be classed as an existentialist. He portrayed God as Pure Existence. God who is prior in order and significance to every other being is pure Actuality with no potentiality whatsoever. God is pure "Is-ness." This is the ultimate in Christian existentialism from the perspective of realism.

Errors and Dangers. But existentialism does not adequately address the essence of existence. If existence is prior to essence then the essence of existence cannot be known. Existentialists, however, do attempt to explain, describe, and know it. They write books about it. To be consistent, the moment they acknowledge that there is an essence to existence, they cease to be existentialists in the accepted meaning of the term. Existentialism sets up a radical disjunction between essence and existence. But we never encounter pure "isness" of existence in life without some "whatness" of essence. We never know *that* something is without knowing a little of *what* something is.

Existentialism is so subjective that it tends toward the mystical (*see* MYSTICISM). Without some objective criteria, there is no way to differentiate an encounter with the real from an illusion. For theistic existentialists, there is no way to know one has encountered the true God rather than the subconscious—or even Satan (2 Cor. 11:14).

In our knowledge of other persons and God, the personal cannot be totally split from the propositional. We can say something about persons through propositions or declarations about them. Pen pals who have never met can still become intimately acquainted. Likewise, the Bible is a propositional revelation about the personal God (*see* BIBLE, EVIDENCE FOR).

The freedom espoused by atheistic existentialists is impossible. We do not have absolute freedom. And if there is a God, all other wills are subordinate to his absolute will.

Irrationality does not correspond with what life is like. God and ultimate reality are not contradictory. God is Father of all reason. Logic flows from his nature (*see* FAITH AND REASON). Existentialists do not practice irrationality. They are quite rational when expounding and defending their system. They inevitably try to make rational sense of their view of existence. The very attempt is self-defeating.

Sources

J. Collins, *The Existentialists*
W. Barrett, *Irrational Man*
J.-P. Sartre, *Existentialism and Humanism*
A. Camus, *The Myth of Sisyphus*
E. Brunner, *Revelation and Reason*
K. Barth, *Church Dogmatics*, vol. 1
M. Heidegger, *What Is Metaphysics?*
R. Bultmann, *Kerygma and Myth: A Theological Debate*, ed., H. W., trans. R. H. Fuller
G. Marcel, *The Mystery of Being*
K. Jaspers, *Reason and Existence*
S. Kierkegaard, *Fear and Trembling*

Exodus, Date of. ***See*** **ARCHAEOLOGY, OLD TESTAMENT; PHARAOH OF EXODUS.**

Experiential Apologetics. Experiential apologetics is the form of defending the Christian faith that appeals to Christian experience as evidence for the truth of Christianity. In its appeal to internal, as opposed to external, evidence, it contrasts sharply with other apologetic systems (*see* APOLOGETICS, TYPES OF).

Proponents of Experiential Apologetics. Many Christian thinkers have stressed experience, some mystical and some not. Meister Eckart in the medieval period is considered heretical in theology, but he wrote cogently on the implications of Christian mysticism. In the modern period, *existentialism (*see* KIERKEGAARD, SØREN) and neoorthodoxy (*see* BARTH, KARL) place high value on religious experience and its proofs of Christianity. Classic liberals and modernists reject objective Christian truth, so a general experiential religion is virtually the only possible foundation on which to build a Christian apologetic (*see* MIRACLES, MYTH AND; SCHLEIERMACHER, FRIEDRICH). Among evangelicals, Elton Trueblood has defended experientialism. While usually remaining outside apologetics discussions, experiential apologetics characterizes Pentecostal, charismatic, and the third-wave movement.

Types of Experiential Apologetics. Experiential Christian apologists fall into several categories. Some appeal to religious experience in general, though this is not often used to prove the unique claims of Christianity so much as the existence of teachings common to several religions. This might include the existence of a transcendent God or immortality of the soul.

Other Christian experientialists appeal to special religious experiences. Within this category are those who focus on mystical experiences and those who look to supernatural Christian conversions. Jonathan *Edwards' classic description of the nature of conversion, *A Treatise Concerning Religious Affections* argues for God from conversion experience, though Edwards generally emphasized reason.

General Religious Experience. The value of religious experience in general is limited in drawing uniquely Christian claims. Logically it is difficult to see how this argument can be used to support even a distinctively theistic God. At best it establishes some credibility for a supreme being of some kind. Proofs from religious experience have been offered by Christians and others, however.

The value of general religious experiences is that they are available to all. Even the atheist Sigmund Freud admitted having a sort of "feeling of absolute dependence" like that described by Friedrich *Schleiermacher. Paul *Tillich called this an experience of "ultimate commitment." The humanist John *Dewey believed everyone experiences a religious experience in their pursuit of goals in spite of obstacles.

Special Religious Experience. Special, in contrast to general, religious experience is not so widely shared. For those who do have such experiences, they can be a powerful demonstration of the proof of Christianity. These come in mystical and existential varieties.

Christian mystical experience. Christian mystics (*see* MYSTICISM) claim a special experience of God. Mystical experiences differ from general experiences in another way: They claim direct, unmediated contact with God. Proving such a claim is impossible, but Christian mystics often claim such evidences are unnecessary. The experience is self-evidently true, as basic to reality as the sensory experience of seeing color. For them at least, nothing needs verification.

Existential experiences. Although existential encounters with God are not mystical, their proponents claim they too are self-authenticating. There are occasions when one is grasped by God in a nonrational, direct encounter that is more basic and real than a sense experience. Although not all would consider such experiences as evidence, they do serve to vindicate the authenticity of faith for the one who experiences them. Properly speaking, those who appeal to such experiences reject apologetic approaches in their traditional sense. They spurn appeal to rational, factual evidence in favor of what they believe to be a self-verifying experience.

It should be noted that not all who experience special encounters with God regard these moments as apologetic proofs for Christianity to themselves or others. Those who focus on those experiences as a primary component of their Christian belief system, however, tend to view them as verifications of their beliefs.

Evaluating Experiential Apologetics. While some Christians seem to base their beliefs largely on experience, others totally debunk the apologetic value of such subjective arguments. However, properly seen, experience has a significant role in religion.

Positive Aspects. All religious truth should be experienced. Religious truth, in contrast to other forms of truth, is preeminently a truth to be experienced. As William *James noted, at the very heart of religious experience is the aim to have a satisfying, transcendent relationship. Religious truth, Kierkegaard said, is personal, rather than merely propositional. It is an experience that provides a living relationship with the living God. In this sense, religious truth is far more than what we know; it is what we live. It is not simply truth for believers to grasp; it grasps them.

All truth is experienced. In the most general sense, all truth must be experienced. At its root, experience means awareness—consciousness of the Ultimate. This extends from awareness of God to awareness of a mathematical truth. If it is not experienced, than one does not "know" it. So experience in this sense is not only important to religious faith; it is essential.

Conceptual truth is empty without experience. A corollary to the necessity of experiencing truth is that sterile concepts are empty because they have not been rooted in experience (*see* TAUTOLOGIES). While there are different levels and objects of experience, there is no truth about reality that is totally disjointed from experience. Unless one has an awareness of an object through experience, one cannot know it directly. Hence, experience is indispensable to knowing truth of any kind, including religious truth.

Negative Aspects. While all truth, even religious truth, should be experienced in the broad sense of an awareness of it, no religious truth claim should be based in uncritical, untestable, experience (*see* TRUTH, NATURE OF).

Experientialism confuses categories. It is a confusion of categories to speak of experiential religious truth. There are true religious *experiences* (experiences of God), but these are different from *expressions* (statements) about those experiences. Truth is found in expression about the object of our experiences, not in the experiences themselves. So, technically there are no true or false religious experiences. There are true or false statements about whether one was really experiencing God and about the God experienced. But experience itself, in its primary sense, is neither true nor false.

Reason is needed. If reason is taken in the secondary sense of reflection on our primary experience (particularly rational reflection), then it is crucial to knowing the truth about our primary experience. Primary experience, as defined by many who stress it, is unreflective and uncritical. There is allegedly no use of logic or reason. It is preconceptual. This kind of experience, if indeed it is possible, is dangerous and has no definitive function in determining truth in religion. It is "bare" experience with no way in or of itself to know whether it puts the experience in touch with divine reality. Unless so-called "secondary experience" using reason can evaluate and make judgments about this raw experience, it has no truth value. As Jonathan Edwards would say, God wants to reach the heart, but he never bypasses the head along the way.

Contrary to the claim of some, there are no self-evident religious experiences that can demonstrate the truth of Christianity. There are significant differences between a sense experience and a special religious experience. First, one is a general experience and the other is special. Second, one is continuous experience and the other only occasional. Third, one is public and the other private. Fourth, one is sensible and objective, while the other is spiritual and subjective. No comparison between the two is valid.

This leaves unsettled the claim of John *Calvin and others that all men have an innate knowledge of God. If they do, it is certainly not specific enough to establish any more than the existence of God (and perhaps immortality) but not the unique truths of Christianity, such as the deity of Christ (*see* CHRIST, DEITY OF), the *Trinity, and Christ as the only way to God (*see* CHRIST, UNIQUENESS OF; "HEATHEN," SALVATION OF; PLURALISM; WORLD RELIGIONS, CHRISTIANITY AND).

A "source of" truth is not a "support of" truth. Those who use experience in its root sense to demonstrate the truth of Christianity engage in a basic misunderstanding. Religious experience is certainly a *source* of truth about God, but it cannot be used as a *test* for that truth. Such an apologetic use of religious experience begs the question, since it appeals to the experience to prove the truth of the experience.

Religious experiences are not self-interpreting. No religious experience, certainly none of the special (mystical) variety, is self-labeled. Other interpretations are possible, which are readily given by Ludwig *Feuerbach, William James, and Freud. The fact that the religious person experienced it with a certain label on it does not mean this is the only interpretation or the proper interpretation. Hallucinations, illusions, and mental projections have occurred throughout religious experience. One needs more than a subjective experience to demonstrate objective truth.

Religious experiences lack objective value. Some objective, demonstrable criteria for determining the truth of religious experiences are needed. This is obvious from the facts that similar experiences can be interpreted in differing ways and that religious experiences conflict with one another. This is why the Bible warns against false prophets (Matt. 7:15) and teachings (1 Tim. 4:1f; 1 John 4:1f.). Indeed, it even provides objective criteria by which falsehood can be known (cf. Deut. 18:9–22).

Indescribable experiences have no truth value. Mystics often claim to have ineffable experiences. Whatever subjective value these may have to the one experiencing them, they can lay no valid truth claim on others. Subjective states are binding, if at all, only on those having them. By their very nature they are experienced by only one person. Second, an indescribable experience cannot be tested because it is not even known. One would have to know it before he could test it. If it is not rationally understood, then it cannot be rationally tested.

Conclusion. General religious experience is not specific enough to support the unique claims of Christianity. At best it can only support some vague claims about a transcendent "other," but not the unique claims of a trinitarian God who has revealed himself in Scripture. Nor are special religious experiences objective or verifiable. They afford no critical, rational scrutiny. Objective criteria are needed for all subjective experiences to be meaningful to anyone other than the person who has them. Objective testing is certainly needed before they can be used to establish a truth claim. The mind must understand and scrutinize what the heart is feeling. Otherwise, we cannot know whether it corresponds to reality (*see* TRUTH, ABSOLUTE NATURE OF).

Sources

J. Edwards, *A Treatise Concerning Religious Affections*

L. Feuerbach, *The Essence of Christianity*

S. Freud, *The Future of an Illusion*

N. L. Geisler, et al., *Philosophy of Religion*, Pt. 1

W. James, *Varieties of Religious Experience*
S. Kierkegaard, *Fear and Trembling*
R. Otto, *The Idea of the Holy*
F. Schleiermacher, *On Religion: Speeches to Its Cultured Despisers*
P. Tillich, *Ultimate Concern*
E. Trueblood, *Philosophy of Religion*

Exclusivism. *Exclusivism*, with regard to a truth claim, affirms that, if one truth proposition is true, all propositions opposed to it must be false. This is based on the logical *law of excluded middle* (either A or non-A, but not both). This law states that, if A is true, then all non-A is false (*see* LOGIC; FIRST PRINCIPLES).

Religious exclusivism affirms that only one religion can be true, and all others opposed to the one true religion must be false. Several terms related to religious pluralism must be distinguished: *pluralism*, *relativism*, *inclusivism*, and *exclusivism*. **Pluralism* is the belief that every religion is true. Each provides a genuine encounter with the Ultimate. One may be better than the others, but all are adequate. *Relativism* (*see* TRUTH, NATURE OF) is similar to pluralism, claiming that each religion is true to the one holding it. There is no objective truth in religion, so there are no criteria by which to determine which is best. *Inclusivism* claims that one religion is explicitly true, and all others are implicitly true. *Exclusivism* is the belief that only one religion is true, and the others opposed to it are false.

There are different kinds of exclusivism. Philosophical exclusivism is where one affirmation or position is exclusive of another. For example, theism is exclusive of atheism (*see* WORLDVIEW). For if the statement "God exists" is true (*see* THEISM), the statement "God does not exist" is necessarily untrue (*see* ATHEISM).

Religious exclusivism, in opposition to religious pluralism, affirms that only one religion is true (*see* CHRIST, UNIQUENESS OF), and the others opposed to it are false. If Christianity is true (*see* APOLOGETICS, ARGUMENT OF), then Islam is false, since its truth claims oppose central doctrines of Christianity, such as the death of Christ on the cross and his resurrection three days later (*see* CHRIST, DEATH OF; RESURRECTION, EVIDENCE FOR).

Ff

Faith and Reason. The relation of faith to reason is of utmost importance for the thinking believer. The problem of how to combine these aspects of personhood has existed from the earliest apologists. Justin *Martyr, *Clement of Alexandria, and Tertullian all struggled. *Augustine made the first serious attempt to relate the two, but the most comprehensive treatment came at the end of the medieval period when Christian intellectualism flowered in the work of *Thomas Aquinas.

Relation of Faith to Reason. Aquinas held that faith and reason intertwine. Faith uses reason, and reason cannot succeed in finding truth without faith.

Reason Cannot Produce Faith. Reason accompanies, but does not cause, faith. Faith is *consent without inquiry* in that faith's assent is not caused by investigation. Rather, it is produced by God. Commenting on Ephesians 2:8–9, Aquinas contended that "free will is inadequate for the act of faith since the contents of faith are above reason. . . . That a man should believe, therefore, cannot occur from himself unless God gives it" (Aquinas, *Ephesians,* 96; unless noted, all citations in this article are from works by Thomas Aquinas). Faith is a gift of God, and no one can believe without it.

Nonetheless, "this does not prevent the understanding of one who believes from having some discursive thought of comparison about those things which he believes" (*On Truth,* 14.A1.2). Such discursive thought, or reasoning from premises to conclusions, is not the *cause* of the assent of faith, but it can and should accompany it (ibid., 14.A1.6). Faith and reason are parallel. One does not cause the other because "faith involves *will* (freedom) and reason doesn't coerce the will" (ibid.). A person is free to dissent, even though there may be convincing reasons to believe.

As a matter of tactical approach in apologetics, if the authority of Scripture is accepted (faith), appeal can be made to it (reason). "Thus, against the Jews we are able to argue by means of the Old Testament, while against heretics we are able to argue by means of the New Testament. But Mohammedans [*see* ISLAM] and the pagans accept neither the one nor the other. . . . We must, therefore, have recourse to the natural reason, to which all men are forced to give their assent" (*Summa Theologica,* 1a.2.2).

However, some Christian truths are attainable by human reason, for example, that God exists and is one. "Such truths about God have been proved demonstratively by the philosophers, guided by the light of the natural reason" (ibid., 1a.3.2)

Three Uses of Reason. Reason or philosophy can be used in three ways, Aquinas says:

1. It demonstrates the "preambles of faith" (that God exists, that we are his creatures . . .; *see* COSMOLOGICAL ARGUMENT; GOD, EVIDENCE FOR).
2. It analyzes teachings of philosophers in order to reveal corresponding concepts in Christian faith. Aquinas gives the example of Augustine's *On the Trinity,* which draws on philosophy to help explain the Trinity.
3. It opposes attacks against faith from logic (*Gentiles,* 1.9).

Reason can be used to prove natural theology, which studies the existence and nature of one God. It can be used to *illustrate* supernatural theological concepts, such as the Trinity and the Incarnation (*see* CHRIST, DEITY OF). And it can be used to refute false theologies (*De Trinitate,* 2.3). The apologist directs the person to accept two kinds of truth about divine things and to destroy what is contrary to truth. The person is directed to the truths of natural theology by the investigation of the reason and to the truths of supernatural theology by faith.

So to make the first kind of divine truth known, we must proceed through demonstrative arguments. However,

> since such arguments are not available for the second kind of divine truth, our intention should not be to convince our adversary by ar-

> guments: It should be to answer his arguments against the truth; for, as we have shown, the natural reason cannot be contrary to the truth of faith. The sole way to overcome an adversary of divine truth is from the authority of Scripture—an authority divinely confirmed by miracles. For that which is above the human reason we believe only because God has revealed it. Nevertheless, there are certainly likely [probable] arguments that should be brought forth in order to make divine truth known. [*Gentiles*, 1.9; *see* MIRACLES, APOLOGETIC VALUE OF]

God's existence is self-evident absolutely (in itself) but not relatively (to us) (ibid., 1.10–11; *see* FIRST PRINCIPLES). Hence, in the final analysis, one must receive *by faith* those things that can be known by reason, as well as those things that lie above reason. Intellectual assent that lacks faith cannot have certitude, for human reason is notoriously suspect when it comes to spiritual matters. Consequently, "it was necessary for divine truth to be delivered by way of faith, being told to them as it were, by God Himself Who cannot lie" (*Summa Theologica*, 2a2ae.1, 5.4).

Divine Authority. Aquinas did not believe that reason provides the basis for believing in God. It can prove *that* God exists, but it cannot convince an unbeliever to believe *in* God.

Reason Prior to Faith. We may believe (assent without reservation) in something that is neither self-evident nor deduced from it by a movement of the will. However, this does not mean that reason plays no prior role to belief. We judge a revelation to be worthy of belief "on the basis of evident signs or something of the sort" (ibid., 2a2ae.1, 4. ad 2).

Reason inquires about what is to be believed before it believes in it. "Faith does not involve a search by natural reason to prove what is believed. But it does involve a form of inquiry unto things by which a person is led to belief, e.g. whether they are spoken by God and confirmed by miracles" (ibid., 2a2ae.2, 1, reply). Demons are not willingly convinced by the evidence that God exists but are intellectually forced by confirming signs to the fact that what the faithful believe is true. Yet they cannot truly be said to *believe* (*On Truth,* 14.9. ad 4).

The Testimony of the Spirit. In order to believe in God one must have the inner testimony of the Holy Spirit (*see* HOLY SPIRIT, ROLE IN APOLOGETICS). For "one who believes does have a sufficient motive for believing, namely the authority of God's teaching, confirmed by miracles, and—what is greater—the inner inspiration [*instinctus*] of God inviting him to believe" (*Summa Theologica,* 2a2ae.6.1). The Holy Spirit uses two causes to stimulate voluntary faith. The persuasion may be from without, for example, a miracle that is witnessed. Or persuasion may be from within. The first cause is never enough for one inwardly to assent to the things of faith. The assent of faith is caused by God as he moves the believer inwardly through grace. Belief is a matter of the will, but the will needs to be prepared by God "to be lifted up to what surpasses nature" (ibid., 2a2ae.2, 9. ad 3).

Reason in Support of Faith. Commenting on the use of *reason* in 1 Peter 3:15, Aquinas argued that "human reasoning in support of what we believe may stand in a two-fold relation to the will of the believer." First, the unbeliever may not have the will to believe unless moved by human reason. Second, the person with a will ready to believe loves the truth, thinks it out, and takes to heart its evidence. The first, unbelieving will may come to a faith of sorts, but there will be no merit in it, because belief does not extend far beyond sight. The second person also studies the human reasoning, but it is a meritorious work of faith (ibid., 2a2ae.2, 10).

Positive Evidence. Faith is supported by, though not based on, probable evidence. "Those who place their faith in this truth, however, 'for which the human reason offers no experimental evidence,' do not believe foolishly, as though 'following artificial fables'" (2 Peter 1:16). Rather, "It reveals its own presence, as well as the truth of its teaching and inspiration, by fitting arguments; and in order to confirm those truths that exceed natural knowledge, it gives visible manifestations to works that surpass the ability of all nature." The kind of positive evidence that Aquinas used included such things as raising the dead, miracles, and the conversion of the pagan world to Christianity (*On Truth,* 14.A1).

Negative Evidence. The negative evidence encompasses arguments against false religions, including things like their fleshly appeal to carnal pleasures, their teachings that contradict their promises, their many fables and falsities, the lack of miracles to witness to divine inspiration of their holy book (like the *Qur'an*), use of warfare (arms) to spread their message, the fact that wise men did not believe Muhammad, only ignorant, desert wanderers, the fact that there were no prophets to witness to him, and Muslim perversions of Old and New Testament stories (*Gentiles,* 1.6).

Faith and Fallible Testimony. How can we be sure when the support of our faith rests on many intermediary (fallible) testimonies? Aquinas responds that the intermediaries are above suspicion if they were confirmed by miracles (for example, Mark 16:20). "We believe the successors of the apostles and prophets only in so far as they tell us those things which the apostles and prophets have left in their writings" (*On Truth,* 14.10, ad 11). The Bible alone is the final and infallible authority for our faith (*see* BIBLE, EVIDENCE FOR).

Faith and Demonstrative Arguments. Aquinas distinguished between two kinds of rational arguments: demonstrative and persuasive. "Demonstrative, cogent, and intellectually convincing argument cannot lay hold of the truths of faith, though it may neutralize destructive criticism that would render faith untenable." On the other hand, "persuasive reasoning drawn from probabilities . . . does not weaken the merit of faith, for it implies no attempt to convert faith into sight by resolving what is believed into evident first principles" (*De Trinitate,* 2.1, ad 5).

Distinguishing Faith and Reason. Though faith is not separated from reason, Aquinas does formally distinguish between them. He believed they are related, but the relationship does not coerce a person to believe.

Faith in Relation to Reason. Human reason does not force faith. If it did, then faith would not be a free act. What happens is that "the mind of the one believing settles upon the one side of a question not in virtue of his reason but in virtue of his will. Therefore assent is understood in the definition [of faith] as an act of the mind in so far as the mind is brought to its decision by the will" (ibid., 2a2ae. 2, 1, ad 3).

Faith is not unreasonable. Faith is reason with assent. For "to ponder with assent is, then, distinctive of the believer: this is how his act of belief is set off from all other acts of the mind concerned with the true and the false" (*Summa Theologica,* 2a2ae.2, 1, reply). Faith, then, is defined as *"that habit of mind whereby eternal life begins in us and which brings the mind to assent to things that appear not."* Faith differs from science in that the object of faith is unseen. It also differs from doubt, suspicion and opinion in that there is evidence to support faith.

Faith is a free act. Aquinas quotes Augustine with approval that "Faith is a virtue by which things not seen are believed" (ibid., 2a2ae.4, 1, reply). He declares that

> to believe is an act of mind assenting to the divine truth by virtue of the command of the will as this is moved by God through grace; in this the act stands under control of free will and is directed toward God. The act of faith is, therefore, meritorious. That is, one is rewarded for believing in what he does not see. There is no merit (reward) in believing what can be seen, since there is no faith involved; it can be seen. The scientist [i.e., philosopher] is impelled to assent by force of a conclusive proof. Thus the assent is not meritorious. [ibid., 2a2ae. 2, 9]

Faith is an act of mind and will. Since belief is an act of the intellect under the impetus of the will, it issues from both mind and will, and both are perfectible by action. "If an act of faith is to be completely good, then, habits must necessarily be present in both mind and will" (ibid., 2a2ae. 4, 2, reply). That is, one cannot be saved without a willingness to do something with faith. Saving faith will produce good works.

Meritorious Nature of Faith. Faith is meritorious, not because one has to work for it, but because it involves the will to believe. It "depends on the will according to its very nature (ibid., ad 5). "For in science and opinion [probable arguments] there is no inclination because of the will, but only because of reason" (ibid., 14.3, reply). But "no act can be meritorious unless it is voluntary, as has been said" (ibid., 14.5, reply).

Aquinas believed that Hebrews 11:1 is a good definition of faith, for it describes not merely what faith *does* but what it *is*. He saw in it the three essentials:

> 1. It mentions the will and the object that moves the will as principles on which the nature of faith is based.
> 2. In it we can distinguish faith from those things which appear not, as opposed to science and understanding.
> 3. The whole definition reduces to the essential phrase, "the substance of things hoped for." (ibid., 14.2)

The formal difference between faith and reason is that one cannot both know and believe the same thing at the same time. For "Whatever things we know with scientific knowledge properly so called we know by reducing them to first principles which are naturally present to the understanding."

Faith and Knowledge about the Same Object. Scientific knowledge culminates in sight of the thing believed, so there is no room for faith. One cannot have faith and scientific knowledge about the same thing (ibid., 14.9, reply). The object of true faith is above senses and understanding. "Consequently, the object of faith is that which is absent from our understanding." As Augustine said, "we believe that which is absent, but we see that which is present" (ibid., 14.9, reply).

This does not mean, of course, that everyone will necessarily believe what I can see without faith (*Summa Theologica,* 2a2ae.1, 5). It does mean that the same person cannot have both faith and proof of the same object. One who sees it, does not believe it by faith on the testimony of others. One who believes it on the testimony of another does not see (know) it personally.

Probable Knowledge and Faith. Likewise, one cannot have "opinion" (probable knowledge) and "science" (certain knowledge) about the same object. As Aquinas notes, "opinion includes a fear that the other part [of the contradiction] is true, and scientific knowledge excludes such fear. However, this fear that the opposite may be true does not apply to matters of faith. For faith brings with it a greater certitude than what can be known by reason" (*On Truth,* 14.9, ad 6).

Creedal Knowledge and Faith. If the existence of God can be proved by reason, and if what is known by reason cannot also be a matter of faith, then why is belief in God proposed in the Creed? Aquinas responds that not all are capable of demonstrating God's existence. "We do not say that the proposition, God is one, in so far as it is proved by demonstration, is an article of faith, but something presupposed before the articles. For the knowledge of faith presupposes natural knowledge, just as grace presupposes nature" (ibid., 14.9, ad 8).

Perfected by Love, Produced by Grace. Reason can go only so far. Faith goes beyond reason and completes it. "Faith does not destroy reason, but goes beyond it and perfects it" (ibid., 14.10, reply, ad 7). "Love is the perfection of faith. Since charity is a perfection of the will, faith is formed by charity" (ibid., ad 1). "It is called form in so far as faith acquires some perfection from charity" (ibid., ad 7). But "the act of faith which precedes charity is an imperfect act awaiting completion from charity" (ibid., 14.A5, reply). So love perfects faith. Since believing depends on the understanding and the will, "such an act cannot be perfect unless the will is made perfect by charity and the understanding by faith. Thus formless faith cannot be a virtue" (ibid., ad 1).

However, "that which faith receives from charity is accidental to faith in its natural constitution, but essential to it with reference to its morality" (ibid., 14.6, reply).

Not only is love necessary to perfect faith, but grace is necessary to produce it. "Now, grace is the first [that is, remote] perfection of the virtues, but charity is their proximate perfection" (ibid., 14.A5, ad 6).

The Limitations of Reason. Aquinas did not believe that human reason was without limitations. In fact he offered many arguments as to why reason is insufficient and revelation is needed.

Five Reasons for Revelation. Following Jewish philosopher Moses Maimonides, Aquinas set forth five reasons why we must first believe what we may later be able to provide good evidence for (Maimonides, 1.34):

1. The object of spiritual understanding is deep and subtle, far removed from sense perception.
2. Human understanding is weak as it fights through these issues.
3. A number of things are needed for conclusive spiritual proof. It takes time to discern them.
4. Some people are disinclined to rigorous philosophical investigation.
5. It is necessary to engage in other occupations besides philosophy and science to provide the necessities of life (*On Truth,* 14.10, reply).

Aquinas said it is clear that, "if it were necessary to use a strict demonstration as the only way to reach a knowledge of the things which we must know about God, very few could ever construct such a demonstration and even these could do it only after a long time." Elsewhere, Aquinas lists only three basic reasons divine revelation is needed.

1. Few possess the knowledge of God, some do not have the disposition for philosophical study, and others do not have the time or are indolent.
2. Time is required to find the truth. This truth is very profound, and there are many things that must be presupposed. During youth the soul is distracted by "the various movements of the passions."
3. It is difficult to sort out what is false in the intellect. Our judgment is weak in sorting true from false concepts. Even in demonstrated propositions there is a mingling of false.

"That is why it was necessary that the unshakable certitude and pure truth concerning divine things should be presented to men by way of faith" (*Gentiles,* 1.4, 2–5).

*The *Noetic Effects of Sin.* Clearly, the mind falls far short when it comes to the things of God. As examples of weakness Aquinas looked at the philosophers and their errors and contradictions. "To the end, therefore, that a knowledge of God, undoubted and secure, might be present among men, it was necessary that divine things be taught by way of faith, spoken as it were by the Word of God who cannot lie" (ibid., 2a2ae. 2, 4). For "the searching of natural reason does not fill mankind's need to know even those divine realities which reason could prove" (ibid., 2a2ae.2, 4, reply).

As a result of the noetic effects of sin, grace is needed. Aquinas concluded that "If for something to be in our power means that we can do it without the help of grace, then we are bound to many things that are not within our power without healing grace—for example to love God or neighbor." The same is true of belief. But with the help of grace we do have this power (ibid., 2a2ae.2, 6, ad 1).

However, Aquinas did not believe that sin destroyed human rational ability. "Sin cannot destroy man's rationality altogether, for then he would no longer be capable of sin" (ibid., 1a2ae.85, 2).

Things above Reason. Not only is faith necessary because of human depravity, but also because some things simply go beyond the power of reason. That does not mean they are contrary to reason, but that they are not fully comprehensible. "Faith, however, is said to surpass reason, not because there is no act of reason in faith, but because reasoning about faith cannot lead to the sight of those things which are matters of faith" (ibid., 14.A2, ad 9). If one could base faith fully on reason, faith would not be a free act; it would be consent caused by the mind.

At two levels a matter of faith may be "above reason." At its highest level it can be above reason absolutely—if it exceeds the intellectual capacity of the human mind (e.g., the *Trinity). It is impossible to have scientific knowledge of this. Believers assent to it only on the testimony of God." Or, it may not absolutely exceed the intellect capacity of all, but is exceedingly difficult to comprehend, and is above the intellectual capacity of some (for example, that God exists without body). "These we may have scientific proofs of and, if not, we may believe them" (*On Truth,* 14.9, reply).

We must have faith when the light of grace is stronger than the light of nature. For "although the divinely infused light is more powerful than natural light, in our present state we do not share it perfectly, but imperfectly." Therefore, "because of this defective participation, through that infused light itself we are not brought to the vision of those things for the knowledge of which it was given us. But we will have it in heaven when we share that light perfectly and in the light of God we will see light" (*Gentiles,* 14.8, ad 2).

Faith, then, surpasses reason. For "some truths about God exceed all the ability of the human reason. Such is the truth that God is triune" (ibid., 1.3). The ineffable essence of God cannot be known by human reason. The reason for this is that the mind depends on the senses. "Now, sensible things cannot lead the human intellect to the point of seeing in them the nature of the divine substance; for sensible things are effects that fall short of the power of their cause" (ibid., 1.3, 3).

Just because we have no reasons for things that go beyond reason does not mean they are not rational. Every belief that is not self-evident can be defended as necessary. We may not know the argument, but it exists. It at least is known to God "and to the blessed who have vision and not faith about these things" (*De Trinitate,* 1.1.4; *On Truth,* 14.9, ad 1). While human reason cannot attain to the things of faith, it is the preface to them. While "philosophical truths cannot be opposed to truths of faith, they fall short indeed, yet they also admit common analogies; and some moreover are foreshadowing, for nature is the preface of grace" (*De Trinitate,* 2.3).

"Although the truth of the Christian faith which we have discussed surpasses the capacity of the reason, nevertheless that truth that the human reason is naturally endowed to know cannot be opposed to the truth of the Christian faith" (*Gentiles,* 1.7, [1]).

Summary. Aquinas's view of the relation of faith and reason blends positive elements of presuppositionalism and evidentialism, of rationalism (*see* *Descartes, Rene; *Leibniz, Gottfried) and fideism. Aquinas stresses the need for reason before, during, and after beliefs are acquired. Even the mysteries of faith are not irrational.

On the other hand, Aquinas does not believe that reason alone can bring anyone to faith. Salvation is accomplished only by the grace of God. Faith can never be *based on* reason. At best it can only be *supported by* reason. Thus, reason and evidence never coerce faith. There is always room for unbelievers not to believe *in* God, even though a believer can construct a valid proof *that* God exists. Reason can be used to demonstrate that God exists, but it can never in itself persuade someone to believe in God. Only God can do this, working in and through their free choice.

These distinctions of Aquinas are eminently relevant to the discussion between rationalists and fideists or between evidentialists and presuppositionalists. With regard to belief that God exists, Aquinas sides with the rationalists and evidentialists. But with respect to belief in God, he agrees with fideists (*see* Fideism) and presuppositionalists (*see* Apologetics, Presuppositional).

Sources

N. L. Geisler, *Thomas Aquinas: An Evangelical Appraisal*
M. Maimonides, *A Guide for the Perplexed*
Thomas Aquinas, *In Boethius, De Trinitate*
———, *Commentary on Saint Paul's Epistle to the Ephesians*
———, *Summa Contra Gentiles*
———, *Summa Theologica*
———, *On Truth*

Falsification, Principle of. *See* **Flew, Antony; Verification Strategies.**

Feuerbach, Ludwig. German atheist Ludwig Feuerbach (1804–1872) was born in Landshut, Bavaria, and educated in Heidelberg and in Berlin under G. W. F. *Hegel. He received his doctorate at Ërlangen in 1828 (White, 190). In 1830 he published an anonymous work, *Gedanken uber Tod und Unsterblichkeit*, that interpreted Christianity as an egoistic and inhumane religion. When its authorship was discovered, he was dismissed from the faculty.

Feuerbach was influenced by, and wrote a biography on, Pierre *Bayle (1838). His most influential work was *The Essence of Christianity* (1841), though he also penned *The Philosophy of the Future* (1843) and *The Essence of Religion* (1851) and *Theogonie* (1857).

The Nature of Religion. Feuerbach was influenced by Hegel's dialectic, and he influenced Karl *Marx as well as Sigmund *Freud. Feuerbach's materialism reacted to Hegel's idealism. In religion Feuerbach was influenced by David *Strauss' view that religion tells us more about the inner life of individuals than about the object of worship (White, 191).

His chief aim: "To change the friends of God into friends of man, believers into thinkers, worshipers into workers, candidates for the other world into students of this world, Christians, who on their own confession are half animal and half angel, into men—whole men" (*Essence of Christianity,* xi).

Basis of Religion: Self-Consciousness. According to Feuerbach, only a human being (not animals) has self-consciousness. Religion is an expression of that consciousness, under the guise of consciousness of God. "In the object which he contemplates, therefore, man becomes acquainted with himself" (*Essence of Christianity,* 5). But consciousness, as such, is unlimited, so, humankind must be unlimited. And consciousness is objectification. Hence, God is nothing but an objectification of the human species.

God a Projection of Human Imagination. Feuerbach believed that religion is only the dream of the human mind. He offered several arguments supporting his hypothesis that God is nothing more than a self-projection of human consciousness.

Argument from human personality. The first is from the basic elements of human personality: reason, will, and affection. Reason, will, and affection each exists for its own sake. For "to will, to love, to think, are the highest powers, are the absolute nature of man as man, and the basis of his existence" (*Essence of Christianity,* 3). But whatever exists for its own sake is God. Thus, by very nature, the person is God.

Argument from the nature of understanding. One cannot understand something without having its nature, since only like knows like. For "the measure of the nature is also the measure of the understanding." That is, it takes one to know one. But humans understand the divine. Therefore, humanity must be the divine. In Feuerbach's words, "so far as nature reaches, so far reaches thy unlimited self-consciousness, so far art thou God" (*Essence of Christianity,* 8).

Argument from the limits of one's nature. A human being can go no farther than his or her nature; one cannot get outside of self. But a person can feel (be aware of) the infinite. For, "every being is in and by itself infinite—has its God, its highest conceivable being, in itself" (*Essence of Christianity,* 7). If this is so, then human beings are infinite by nature. The infinite you feel is the infinity of yourself.

Argument from the history of religion. Feuerbach believed that historically attributes were given to God because in human reasoning those attributes were thought to be divine. They were not considered to be divine because they were given to God. This being the case, it follows that what we call "the divine" or "God" is nothing more than human characteristics that have been attributed to God.

"The object of any subject is nothing else than the subject's own nature taken objectively. Such are man's thoughts and dispositions, such is his God." Hence, "Consciousness of God is self-consciousness, knowledge of God is self-knowledge. By his God thou knowest the man, and by the man his God; the two are identical" (*Essence of Christianity,* 12).

Necessity of Religion. In spite of his pessimistic conclusions, Feuerbach believed religion to be essential. The reason is that human beings, by their very nature, must objectify; they cannot avoid doing so. And God, Feuerbach affirmed, is that objectification. However, ignorance of the fact that the object of one's objectification is really oneself is essential to religion. The child must first see herself under the form of another (the father) before she can come to see herself as herself. If this were not true in religious projections, it would be idolatry, viz., the worship of oneself. So, it is necessary to believe this projection of one's own nature is really God, even though it is not.

Progress in human understanding would not be possible without this projection. The human being grows in self-understanding as former deities become idols. Hence, the ideal course of religion is for individuals to learn to attribute more to themselves and less to God.

The attributes of God are really what people believe about themselves. God's aseity or self-existence is a desire to avoid temporality by positing an absolute beginning. The perfection of God is the human moral nature taken for absolute being. The personality of God is the effort to show that personality is the highest form of being. The providence of God is really the desire for importance. Prayer expresses the desire for self-communication. The result of a belief in miracles is the desire for immediate satisfaction of wishes without tiresome waiting.

The Irony of Religion. There is a basic irony in this process which may be seen in comparing beliefs to the body's circulatory system. Religion is a *systole action,* like the arteries, wherein people project their best on God. Goodness is transported away from the personhood like oxygen-rich blood from the heart. Without this feeling of goodness, the individual is left sinful. That sets up the diastole action, like the veins, whereby goodness is carried back to the heart in the form of grace. We send all our human goodness "upstairs" and call it God. Then feeling depraved, we call upon the God we create to send back our goodness as grace.

Feuerbach concludes, therefore, that:

1. Religion is a projection of human imagina-

tion in the act of self-consciousness.

2. God is the best that one unwittingly sees in oneself.
3. Religion is a necessary dialectic of development for human progress.
4. Religion enables indirect and involuntary self-discovery.

Feuerbach's Influence. The influence of Feuerbach on modern thought has been considerable. There was a direct and immediate impact on Karl Marx, and through him on the world communism movement. Marx and Friedrich Engels incorporated Feuerbach's arguments against God and religion into their dialectical materialism, criticizing Feuerbach for his lack of political involvement. Engels boasted that with one blow to pulverize religion, communism would place materialism back on the throne (Marx, 224).

Feuerbach also had a considerable impact on the formation of modern a-theistic existentialism through Martin Heidegger and Jean-Paul *Sartre. The father of neoorthodox theology, Karl Barth, pays tribute to Feuerbach (*see* BARTH, KARL). All in all, Feuerbach is one of the most significant and engaging atheists of modern times, anticipating even the work of Sigmund Freud.

Evaluation. *Atheism as a worldview is evaluated in other articles, but a few comments are in order on Feuerbach's unique analysis of religion.

Some Positive Contributions. Even atheists have insights into the nature of reality. Among Feuerbach's:

He saw the centrality of the question of God. Although his love affair with the divine was an unhappy one, Feuerbach identified God as the central question: "All my writings have had, strictly speaking, one purpose, one intention, one theme. This is nothing less than religion and theology and whatever is connected with them" (*Essence of Christianity,* x).

He exposed human-centered religion. Barth pointed out in the "Introductory Essay" to a reprint of *Essence of Christianity* that Feuerbach correctly analyzed any humanity-centered form of religion, including those springing from the father of modern liberalism, Friedrich Schleiermacher. *Barth observed, "Can we deny that Feuerbach himself, like a not very cunning, but slightly keen-eyed spy, lets out the esoteric secret of this whole priesthood. . . . Theology has long since become anthropology" (Barth, xxi). Once modern theology gave up the starting point of divine revelation, then human beings created God in their own image. Modern liberal theology became anthropology.

He called negative religious language useless. Feuerbach rightly said, "Only where man loses his taste for religion, and thus religion itself becomes insipid existence—does the existence of God become an insipid existence—an existence without qualities" (*Essence of Christianity,* 15). Purely negative religious language—where we can only know what God is not—is useless and inadequate. We cannot know God is not "that" unless we know what the "that" is (*see* ANALOGY, PRINCIPLE OF).

He correctly critiqued other-worldly religions. Feuerbach's condemnation of religious otherworldliness is more often accurate than most religious people admit. Some forms of Christianity tend to be more heavenly minded than earthly good. It is possible to get so caught up in the sweet-by-and-by that one forgets the wretched here-and-now. Not all believers are thinkers (*Essence of Christianity,* xi).

He exposed narcissism in much of religious experience. Feuerbach's thesis is not wrong; it is simply overextended. Many religions do make their god in human image, creating a god who is tame and harmless—one they can handle. Such a god may be whatever they demand, but such a god is not the infinite, sovereign God of the Bible (*see* GOD, NATURE OF).

Problems with Feuerbach's View. Its central thesis is self-defeating. The basic premise of Feuerbach's view is self-defeating. He contends that "God is nothing but a projection of human imagination." But all "nothing-but" statements presuppose "more-than" knowledge. How could he know that God was "nothing but" unless he knew "more than" that himself. In short, the central statement of Feuerbach's system self-destructs because it implies more knowledge than it allows.

Maybe atheism is a projection. Feuerbach does not seriously consider that his own view may be a projection of his own imagination. Maybe Feuerbach is simply imagining that there is no God. Perhaps, as Freud, Feuerbach is engaged in creating a view of God in his own image. His atheism could just as easily be an illusion—something that results from his own wishes—as the theism he rejects. Self-projection explains atheism as well, if not better, than it does theism. So, maybe we didn't create the Father; maybe atheism killed him.

He never proves infinite consciousness. Many arguments Feuerbach offers for atheism beg the question; they presuppose what is to be proven. He never really proves that human consciousness is infinite; he simply assumes it. Of course, if our consciousness is really infinite, then we are God. But this is clearly not the case, since our consciousness is changing and limited, while God is unchanging and unlimited.

One does not have to be one to know one. Another fallacious assumption is that one has to be identical to any object that is known. But he never proves this premise, and it is not the case. Like can know like. Knowledge can be by analogy (*see* ANALOGY, PRINCIPLE OF). We do not have to be a tree to know a tree, but only to take on its likeness in our mind. Likewise, we do not have to be God to know God. We simply have to be like God. Similarity is enough for knowledge; identity of subject and object is not necessary.

Such a belief would destroy human progress. Feuerbach held that positing a God who does not really exist is essential to human self-development. But one who accepts Feuerbach's analysis no longer believes self-projections are God. Then, according to Feuerbach's argument, human progress will stop. If ignorance of the fact that we are God is essential to human progress, then once one becomes a Feuerbachian, the gig is up and progress is impossible.

*Feuerbach's *materialism was inconsistent.* Although Feuerbach loathed his mentor Hegel, he never overcame the hangover of idealism. Nor did he rid himself of the nagging question of God. For someone who believes in basic materialism, this stress on consciousness is eminently unfitting. Engels noted that Feuerbach "stopped halfway; the lower half of him was materialist, the upper half idealist" (cited in White, 192).

This analysis of religious experience is shallow. Barth identified Feuerbach's problem as "shallowness." He wrote, "Feuerbach was a 'true child of his century,' a 'non-knower of death,' and a 'mis-knower of evil.' In fact, anyone who knew that we men are evil from head to foot and anyone who reflects that we must die, would recognize it to be the most illusory or all illusions to suppose that the essence of God is the essence of man" (Barth, xxviii).

Sources

K. Barth, "An Introductory Essay," Feuerbach, *The Essence of Christianity*

W. B. Chamberlain, *Heaven Wasn't His Destination: The Philosophy of Ludwig Feuerbach*

J. Collins, *God and Modern Philosophy*

———, *History of Modern European Philosophy*

F. Engels, *Feuerbach and the Outcome of Classical German Philosophy*

L. Feuerbach, *The Essence of Christianity*

———, *Pierre Bayle*

———, *The Essence of Religion*

N. L. Geisler, et al., *Philosophy of Religion*

K. Marx, *Marx and Engels on Religion*

H. White, "Feuerbach, Ludwig," *EP*

Fideism. Religious fideism argues matters of faith and religious belief are not supported by reason. Religion is a matter of faith and cannot be argued by reason. One must simply believe. Faith, not reason, is what God requires (Heb. 11:6). Fideists are skeptical with regard to the nature of evidence as applied to belief. They believe no evidence or argument applies to belief in God. God is not reached by reason, but only by faith. Søren *Kierkegaard and Karl *Barth are examples of fideists.

In epistemology, fideists are generally coherentists. They definitely reject classical foundationalism or any belief in self-evident first principles. Some presuppositionalists (*see* APOLOGETICS, PRESUPPOSITIONAL) are classed as fideists, though many believe in some form of argument to support their belief in God.

Response to Fideism. Even from a biblical point of view, God calls us to use reason (Isa. 1:18; Matt. 22:36–37; 1 Peter 3:15). God is a rational being and created us as rational beings. God would not insult the reason he gave us by asking us to ignore it in such important matters as our beliefs about him.

Fideism also is self-defeating, using reason to say we should not use reason in matters of religion. If one has no reason for not using reason, then the position is indefensible. There is no reason why one should accept fideism.

To claim reason is just optional for a fideist will not suffice. For either the fideist offers some criteria for when we should be reasonable and when we should not, or else the decision is simply arbitrary. If there are rational criteria for when we should be rational, there is a rational basis for using reason, and fideism is falsified. Reason is not the kind of thing in which a rational creature chooses to participate. By virtue of being rational by nature, one must be part of rational discourse. And rational discourse demands that one follow the laws of reason (*see* FIRST PRINCIPLES; LOGIC). One such principle is that one should have a sufficient reason for beliefs. But if one must have sufficient reason, then fideism is wrong, since it claims that one need not have a sufficient reason for belief (*see* FAITH AND REASON).

Fideists often confuse belief *in* with belief *that*. While what they claim about faith appropriately applies to belief *in* God, it does not apply to belief *that* God exists. One must have evidence *that* there is a floor in an elevator. Otherwise it is foolish to leap into it in the dark. Likewise, it is foolish to leap in the dark with an act of faith in God, unless we have evidence that he is there.

There are good reasons for belief that God exists, such as the cosmological argument, the teleological argument, and the moral argument. Further, there is good evidence to believe that miracles have occurred, including Christ's death and victory over death for us (*see* RESURRECTION, EVIDENCE FOR).

Finite Godism. *Theism believes an infinite God is both beyond and in the world. Finite godism, by contrast, posits a god who is only finite. Polytheism claims there are many such gods, but finite godists believe there is only one God.

Ancient Greek versions of a limited God included *Plato's (428–348 B.C.) philosophy (see Plato, 17–92). But in the modern Western world, most finite god views arise out of a theistic background. Generally speaking, many finite godists come to that conclusion because they cannot reconcile their theistic tradition with the pervasive presence of evil (*see* EVIL, PROBLEM OF).

Typology of Finite Godism. There are many different possibilities for a finite god position, not all of which have well-known representatives. Most finite godists hold that God is personal, though some, including Henry Wieman, posit an impersonal Being (Wieman, 6–8, 54–62). The limitations on this God could be internal, as John Stuart *Mill believed, or external to the world, as Plato believed. The limitations could be in his goodness but not his power (a minority view), or in his power but not his goodness, as in Edgar Brightman (see Brightman) and Peter Bertocci. Or, God could be limited in both power and goodness (Mill's view).

A finite god can have either one or two poles. For coverage of bipolar finite godism, see the article PANENTHEISM. Monopolar examples are discussed here. Although many finite godists believe god to be transcendent (beyond the universe), some have a finite god who is immanent (within the universe). Henri Bergson, an example of the latter view, holds that God is the Vital Force that drives the process of evolution onward (see Bergson, chap. 3).

Tenets of Finite Godism. Finite godists tend to disagree among themselves about God and the world. While this article stresses points in common, some differences will be noted.

View of God. The most fundamental characteristic of the finite god view is that this god is limited in his very nature. Some say he is limited in power and not goodness; few, if any, claim he is limited in goodness. Some claim God is limited in both power and goodness. Almost all agree that God is not infinite in power.

Properly speaking, a finite-god view holds that God is intrinsically limited in his nature. Although Plato seemed to hold that God is not intrinsically limited in his nature, most believe that the eternal world (which God did not create) places limits on God's ability to act within it (*see* DUALISM). If God did not create the world and does not sustain its existence, then he is not able to do just anything with it; for example, he cannot destroy it.

View of Evil. In contrast to pantheists, finite godists affirm that evil is real. In fact, the presence and power of evil limits God. Evil is both physical and moral. Physical evil is not always possible to avoid, but we can do something about moral evil. Cooperating with God's efforts for good, even going beyond them if necessary, is part of our moral duty in the world.

There are various explanations for the origin of evil. *Dualists* (*see* DUALISM) say it was always there in some form. Others attribute much of it to human free choices. But all agree there is no guarantee that evil will ever be totally destroyed. If God were all powerful, then he would destroy evil. But since evil is not destroyed, there must not be an all-powerful God. The argument goes like this:

1. If God were all powerful, he could destroy evil.
2. If God were all good, he would destroy evil.
3. But evil has not been destroyed.
4. Therefore, there cannot be an all-powerful, all-good God.

View of Creation. Finite godism has no uniform stand on creation. Those who come out of the dualistic Greek tradition, following Plato, hold to creation *ex materia*, that is, out of preexisting eternal matter (*see* CREATION, VIEWS OF). God did not bring the world into existence; he merely *shaped* the matter that was already there. In view of this, one limitation on God's power is external. Thus, there is something about the extent and nature of matter over which even God has no ultimate control. He simply has to work with the world and do the best he can under the limitations it places on his creative powers.

An alternative view is that God brought the universe into existence *ex nihilo*, out of nothing. In this case, God is limited by his own nature, not by something "out there" with which he has to cope and over which he has no final word.

All finite godists agree that creation was not *ex Deo* (out of God). This is not a pantheistic position, though God is limited in or by creation.

View of the World. Few statements regarding the world unite finite godists. All agree that the world exists and runs by natural laws. Beyond this there is no unanimity about whether it always existed and/or always will exist. The only other widely held view among finite godists is that the physical universe is not eternal or unlimited in energy. The universe is subject to the law of entropy (*see* THERMODYNAMICS, LAWS OF) and is running down.

View of Miracles. Most finite godists reject miracles. Some admit that supernatural interventions are possible in principle but deny they happen in practice. In this respect finite godism is similar to deism, which claims a supernatural Creator but disclaims any supernatural acts in the creation. However, deism is properly distinguished from finite godism in that the deistic God has no intrinsic limits on his power. Both views see miracles as a violation of natural law. And since they place a high emphasis on the regularity and uniformity of the world, they do not wish to concede that miracles interrupt it (*see* MIRACLE; MIRACLES, ARGUMENTS AGAINST).

View of Human Beings. Ultimately humanity is created by God. However, since Darwin, finite godists have been convinced that God used a natural evolutionary process. As noted, some finite godists even equate God with the evolutionary force in nature.

Most finite godists admit humans have a soul, and some believe persons are immortal. All reject a purely materialistic (*see* MATERIALISM) view of humanity, but not all are sure there is life after death.

View of Ethics. Few finite godists believe in ethical absolutes. Since God is not unchangeable, it follows that no value based in him would be immutable either. Many, however, believe that values are objective and enduring. Some even hold certain values are unconditional. However, for the most part, since God has revealed any unequivocal ethical norms, persons are left to decide for themselves the right course of action in each situation. The general guidance in these decisions is provided in different ways by different views.

View of History. Regarding the movement of history and humanity, some are more optimistic than others. Some point to a steady evolutionary progress of the universe as the hope for final victory. Most are less assured that good will vanquish all evil. All admit it is possible there will be no final victory at all. It is even conceivable that evil may overcome good, though most finite godists find this possibility intuitively repugnant. Nevertheless, since God is limited and (at best) is struggling with evil himself, there is no assurance. The struggle may simply go on endlessly.

Evaluation. Finite godism contains significant insights into reality. However, as a system it has serious problems.

Positive Contributions. Evil is treated realistically. Unlike such worldviews as *pantheism, finite godism cannot be blamed for attempting to avoid the reality of evil. It is in facing the problem squarely that most finite godists have come to their position.

The exercise of divine power is limited. Whatever can be said about the meaning of the word *omnipotent*, it cannot mean that God can literally do anything. Finite godists are right to point out that God is limited in his use of power. For example, God cannot use his power (limited or unlimited) to create and destroy the same thing at the same time. God cannot make square circles. God cannot give creatures free choice and at the same time force them to act contrary to their choices.

Likewise, finite godism points to a real problem in many theistic views of evil. The position recognizes that "the best possible world" may not actually be possible. Just because we can *conceive* of our present universe with less or no evil, does not mean that God can *achieve* such a universe. A world of free creatures, whether freely created by God or not, does place some limitations on the use of God's power (*see* EVIL, PROBLEM OF).

There is a need to struggle against evil. Another value that emerges from most forms of finite godism is an antidote for fatalism. The outcome of the struggle of good and evil does in a real sense depend on man. Our efforts can make a difference. Complete *determinism is fatal to the needed motivation to fight evil. Finite godists cannot be charged with a passive resignation to the inevitable. Their view calls for real involvement by persons to overcome evil.

Problems with the View. In spite of its many positive insights into the nature of things, finite godism as a system is fatally flawed.

Its view of God is inadequate. Philosophically, the concept of a finite god is contrary to the principle of causality, which affirms that every finite being needs a cause. A finite god is only a large creature, and all creatures need a Creator. A finite being is a contingent being, not a Necessary Being, which *cannot not* exist. A contingent being *can be nonexistent*. But whatever could not exist depends for its existence on what cannot not exist, a Necessary Being.

Further, those who believe God is limited in perfection as well as power do not identify what is really God, at least not God in an ultimate sense. For one could measure God's imperfection only by an ultimate standard (see Lewis, 45–46). But the ultimate standard of perfection is by definition God. So an imperfect finite god would be something less than the ultimate God. Actually, there seems to be no way to posit a finitely good god without having an infinitely good God as a standard by which to measure.

Anything incompletely good is not worthy of worship. Worship means to attribute ultimate worth to something or someone. But why should one attribute absolute worth to what is not absolutely worthy? Every finite thing is a creature, and worship of the creature, rather than the Creator, is idolatry. Or to borrow Paul *Tillich's terms, an ultimate commitment should not be given to anything less than an Ultimate. But a partially good being is not an ultimate Good. Why, then, should anyone worship a finite god?

Its view of evil is inadequate. The problem of evil does not eliminate God. In fact, we cannot even know there are ultimate injustices in the world unless we have some ultimate standard of justice, God, beyond the world. Conversely, only an all-powerful God can defeat evil, and only an all-good God desires to defeat evil. Hence, if evil will ever be defeated, then there must be an all-powerful, all-good God. A finite god will not suffice for the task.

Furthermore, there is an alternative in the argument for a finite god. Remember that the argument goes:

1. If God were all-powerful, he could destroy evil.

2. If God were all-good, he would destroy evil.
3. But evil is not destroyed.
4. Therefore, there cannot be an all-powerful, all-good God.

A theistic worldview, need only change the third premise:

3. But evil is not *yet* destroyed.

The word *yet* immediately opens up the possibility that evil will yet be destroyed (i.e., defeated) in the future. And the finite godist who insists this will never happen is presuming to know more than a finite creature is able to know.

Some finite godists even admit this point. Bertocci, for example, said there is evil "whose destructive effect, *so far as we know,* is greater than any good which may come from it." But that is precisely the problem: How can a finite man know far enough into the future to say nothing will be done to ultimately defeat evil and bring in a greater good? However improbable it may seem, the future can bring good news.

Furthermore, if there is an all-powerful and all-good God, this automatically guarantees that evil *will* be defeated in the future. The reasoning is:

1. An all good God has the desire to defeat evil.
2. An all powerful God has the ability to defeat evil.
3. But evil is not yet defeated.
4. Therefore, evil will be defeated in the future.

Put in this form, the question would not be whether evil is compatible with an infinite God; it certainly seems to be. In fact, if an infinite God exists, then it is a guarantee that evil will be defeated, since such a God would have both the desire and the power to do it. Thus it appears that finite godism has not successfully eliminated an infinite God by way of evil.

Another problem for modern forms of finite godism is that, if God is not completely good, then what is the standard for measuring his goodness? We cannot measure him by the standard of his own nature, for that he measures up to perfectly. But if we measure God by some absolute moral law beyond God, then the Legislator of this absolute law would be God. For laws come from law-givers, and moral prescriptions come from moral prescribers (*see* MORAL ARGUMENT FOR GOD). If so, would not absolutely perfect moral laws come from an absolutely perfect Moral Law-giver? If a finite god falls short of an absolute standard of goodness, then he is not God. The absolute moral Being *beyond him* would be God.

Perhaps this is why most finite godists desire to limit only God's power and not his goodness. But to an outsider this looks like an arbitrary judgment and wishful thinking. Further, how can God be an infinitely good Being when he is only a finite being? How can one be more of anything than he has the capacity to be? How can the attributes of God be extended farther than his actual nature allows? Can one's knowledge, for example, be extended farther than the brain allows?

Finite godism claims God cannot destroy all evil. Some say this is because of an intrinsic limit in his nature. Others claim it is because of an extrinsic limitation on him. But the only extrinsic limitation which the Creator could not destroy would be an eternal uncreated and Necessary Being. For a created or contingent being could be destroyed by an uncreated or Necessary Being. But if there is an eternal, uncreated, and Necessary Being beyond God, then it is the Creator, and the "finite god" turns out only to be a limited creation. If, on the other hand, the being outside God is only created and contingent, yet God is uncreated and necessary, God could destroy it. But if he can create and destroy anything, why not admit he is all powerful?

This is the dilemma: If God can destroy all else in the universe besides himself, then he is all-powerful. If there is some other indestructible being outside God, then he is not an all-powerful God; this other being can resist his power. But in either case the finite god view would seem to be wrong, for there would be an all-powerful Being who could destroy the finite god.

Finite godists admit there is no guarantee good will ultimately triumph over evil. If so, those who work for good may work for naught. Of course, in the everyday course of events our efforts are frustrated. However, a religious commitment is not an everyday commitment; it is an ultimate commitment. Can a finite god, who cannot guarantee victory, even if we put our all into it, really inspire an ultimate commitment? How many people will really make an ultimate commitment to work for what they have no assurance will ultimately win? We can be inspired to confess courageously "I would rather lose in a battle that is ultimately going to win, than to win in a battle that will ultimately lose."

Other Inadequate Views. In addition to their flawed views of God and evil, finite godists fail to adequately defend their views of annihilationism and antisupernaturalism (*see* MIRACLES, ARGUMENTS AGAINST).

Sources

H. Bergson, *Creative Evolution*
E. S. Brightman, *A Philosophy of Religion*
E. J. Carnell, *Christian Apologetics*, chapters 16, 17
J. Collins, *God and Modern Philosophy*
N. L. Geisler, et al., *Worlds Apart*, chapter 6
C. S. Lewis, *Mere Christianity*
J. S. Mill, *Three Essays on Religion: Nature, Utility of Religion, and Theism*
H. P. Owens, *Concepts of Deity*
Plato, *Timaeus*
H. N. Wieman, *The Source of Human Good*

Firmament. ***See*** **SCIENCE AND THE BIBLE.**

First Principles. First principles are the foundation of knowledge. Without them nothing could be known (*see* FOUNDATIONALISM). Even coherentism uses the first principle of noncontradiction to test the coherence of its system. *Realism affirms that first principles apply to the real world. First principles undeniably apply to reality. The very denial that first principles apply to reality uses first principles in the denial.

Principles of Reality. Without basic first principles of reality, nothing can be known. Everything we know about reality is known by them. Twelve basic first principles can be set forth.

1. Being Is (B is) = *The Principle of Existence.*
2. Being Is Being (B is B) = *The Principle of Identity.*
3. Being Is Not Nonbeing (B is Not Non-B) = *The Principle of Noncontradiction.*
4. Either Being or Nonbeing (Either B or Non-B) = *The Principle of the Excluded Middle.*
5. Nonbeing Cannot Cause Being (Non-B>B) = *The Principle of Causality.*
6. Contingent Being Cannot Cause Contingent Being (B^c>B^c) = *The Principle of Contingency* (or Dependency).
7. Only Necessary Being Can Cause a Contingent Being (B^n—>B^c) = *The Positive Principle of Modality.*
8. Necessary Being Cannot Cause a Necessary Being (B^n>B^n) = *The Negative Principle of Modality.*
9. Every Contingent Being Is Caused by a Necessary Being (B^n—>B^c) = *The Principle of Existential Causality.*
10. Necessary Being exists = *Principle of Existential Necessity* (B^n exists).
11. Contingent being exists = *Principle of Existential Contingency* (B^c exists).
12. Necessary Being is similar to similar contingent being(s) it causes = *Principle of Analogy* (B^n—similar—> B^c).

For a realist, being is the basis of knowing. The rationalist Rene *Descartes said, "I think, therefore, I am." But for a realist such as *Thomas Aquinas, "I am, therefore, I think." For one could not think unless he existed. Existence is fundamental to everything. Being is the basis for everything. Everything is (or, has) being. Hence, there is no disjunction between the rational and the real. Thought cannot be separated from things or knowing from being.

Undeniability. First principles are undeniable or reducible to the undeniable. They are either self-evident or reducible to the self-evident. And self-evident principles are either true by their nature or undeniable because the predicate is reducible to the subject. That the predicate is reducible to the subject means that one cannot deny the principle without using it. For example, the principle of noncontradiction cannot be denied without using it in the very denial. The statement: "Opposites cannot be true" assumes that the opposite of that statement cannot be true.

Not all skeptics or agnostics (*see* AGNOSTICISM) are willing to grant that the principle of causality, which is crucial in all cosmological arguments for God, is an undeniable first principle. Indeed, not every skeptic is willing to admit that something exists (the principle of existence). Thus, it is necessary to comment on their undeniability.

1. *The principle of existence*. Something exists. For example, I exist. This is undeniable, for I would have to exist in order to deny my existence. In the very attempt to explicitly deny my existence I implicitly affirm it.

2. *The principle of identity*. A thing must be identical to itself. If it were not, then it would not be itself.

With these and other principles, it is important to note the difference between *unsayable* and *undeniable*. I can say or write the words, "I do not exist." However, when I said it I implicitly affirmed that I do exist. The affirmation that I do not exist is actually unaffirmable. I must actually exist in order to grammatically say I do not exist.

Some contemporary nominalists suggest that this is a quirk of language. They insist that such statements as "I cannot speak a word in English" are only self-defeating because one is speaking in English. One could use French and avoid the difficulty. They add that one can make a metastatement in even the same language that avoids this difficulty. That is, they posit a class of statements about statements (called metastatements) which they claim are not statements about the real world. These metastatements are supposedly exempt from being self-defeating. Thus, one who says, "No statements about God are descriptive," is supposedly not making a descriptive statement about God, but rather about the statements that can be made of God.

It is true that a statement in French saying that one cannot speak in English is not self-defeating. However, a statement in French affirming that one cannot speak a word in French is self-defeating.

The metastatement maneuver does not avoid the trap of self-destruction. For statements about statements that affirm something about reality are indirectly statements about reality. For example, if one says, "I am not making a statement about reality when I say that statements cannot be made about reality" he *is* making a statement about reality. It is the most radical kind of statement that can be made about reality, since it prohibits all other statements about reality. Thus, the statement "Something exists" cannot be denied without implicitly affirming that something does exist (e.g., the maker of that statement).

3. *The principle of noncontradiction.* Being cannot be nonbeing, for they are direct opposites. And opposites cannot be the same. For the one

who affirms that "opposites can both be true" does not hold that the opposite of this statement is true.

4. *The principle of the excluded middle.* Since being and nonbeing are opposites (i.e., contradictory), and opposites cannot be the same, nothing can hide in the "cracks" between being and nonbeing. The only choices are being and nonbeing.

Any attempt to deny that all meaningful statements must be noncontradictory, by its very nature as a meaningful statement, must be noncontradictory. Likewise, any attempt to deny the law of noncontradiction applies to reality is itself a noncontradictory statement about reality—which is self-defeating. So, like other first principles, the law of noncontradiction is undeniable.

Two challenges to this conclusion have been offered, one philosophical and one scientific. The philosophical objection charges that this argument begs the question, using the law of noncontradiction to prove the law of noncontradiction. It says in effect that it is contradictory to deny the principle of noncontradiction. But the law of noncontradiction is not used as the *basis* of the argument. It is merely used in the *process* of giving an indirect argument for the validity of the law of noncontradiction. Just as the statement "I can speak a word in English" uses English in the *process* of demonstrating that I can speak a word in English, even so the law of noncontradiction is used in the process of showing the validity of the law of noncontradiction. But it is not the basis for the argument.

The direct basis for the law of noncontradiction is its self-evident nature, whereby the predicate is reducible to the subject. And the indirect proof is shown by the fact that any attempt to deny it implies it. That is, it is a necessary condition for all rational thought.

A second objection to the law of noncontradiction comes from science. Niels Bohr's principle of complementarity is used to show that subatomic reality is contradictory. For according to this principle there are contradictory ways to describe the same reality, such as, light is both particles and waves. However, this is a misunderstanding of the principle of complementarity. As Werner Heisenberg noted, these are "two complementary descriptions of the same reality . . . these descriptions can only be partially true: there must be limitations to the use of the particle concept as well as of the wave concept, else once could not avoid contradictions." Thus "if one takes into account those limitations which can be expressed by uncertainty relations, the contradictions disappear" (Heisenberg, 43).

The objection that Heisenberg's principle of uncertainty or unpredictability is contrary to the principle of causality is unfounded. At best, it does not show that events have no cause, but only that they are unpredictable as presently perceived with available technology. For a complete discussion see INDETERMINACY, PRINCIPLE OF.

5. *The principle of causality.* Only being can cause being. Nothing does not exist, and only what exists can cause existence, since the very concept of "cause" implies an existing thing that has the power to effect another. From absolutely nothing comes absolutely nothing.

The statement "Nonbeing cannot produce being" is undeniable. The very concept of "produce" or "cause" implies something exists to cause or produce the being produced. To deny that relationship of cause to effect is to say, "Nothing is something" and "Nonbeing is being," which is nonsense.

This should be distinguished from David *Hume's point that it is not absurd for nothing to be *followed by* something. Hume himself accepts, that something is always *caused by* something. And theists accept Hume's point that, as a matter of sequence, there was no world and then there was a world, which is nothing followed by something. There is no inherent contradiction in saying nothing can be followed by something. That doesn't change the fact that nothing can cause absolutely nothing.

Another way to understand why nonbeing cannot cause being is by noting that everything that "comes to be" must have a cause. If it came to be it is not a Necessary Being, which by its nature must always be. So what comes to be is, by definition, a contingent being, a being that is capable of existing or not existing. For every contingent thing that comes to be there must be some efficient action that causes it to pass from a state of potentiality (potency) to a state of actuality (act). For, Aquinas noted, no potency for being can actualize itself. To actualize itself it must be in a state of actuality, and before it is actualized it must be in a state of potentiality. But it cannot be both at the same time (a violation of the principle of noncontradiction). Hence, one cannot deny the principle of causality without violating the principle of noncontradiction.

6. *The principle of contingency (or dependency).* If something cannot be caused by nothing (5), neither can anything be caused by *what could be nothing*, namely, a contingent being. For what could be nothing does not account for its own existence. And what cannot account for even its own existence cannot account for the existence of another. Since it is contingent or dependent for its own being, it cannot be that on which something else depends for its being. Hence, one contingent being cannot cause another contingent being.

7. *The positive principle of modality.* Absolutely nothing cannot cause something (5). Neither can one contingent kind (mode) of being cause another contingent being (6). So, if anything comes to be, it must be caused by a Necessary Being.

8. *The negative principle of modality.* A Necessary Being is by definition a mode (kind) of being that cannot not be. That is, by its very mode (modality), it must be. It cannot come to be or cease to be. But to be caused means to come to be. Hence, a Necessary Being cannot be caused. For what comes to be is not necessary.

9. *The principle of existential causality.* All contingent beings need a cause. For a contingent being is something that is but could not be. But since it has the possibility not to exist, then it does not account for its own existence. That is, in itself there is no basis explaining why it exists rather than does not exist. It literally has nothing (nonbeing) to ground it. But nonbeing cannot ground or cause anything (5). Only something can produce something.

10. Necessary Being exists = *Principle of Existential Necessity* (B^n exists).

The Principle of Existential Necessity follows from two other Principles: the Principle of Existence (no. 1) and the Principle of Causality (no. 5).

Since something undeniably exists (no. 1), either it is (a) all contingent or (b) all necessary or (c) some is necessary and some is contingent. But both (b) and (c) acknowledge a Necessary Being, and (a) is logically impossible, being contrary to the self-evident principle no. 5. For if all being(s) is (are) contingent, then it is possible for all being(s) not to exist. That is, a state of total nothingness is possible. But something now undeniably exists (e.g., I do), as was demonstrated in premise no. 1. And nothing cannot cause something (no. 5). Therefore, it is not possible (i.e., it is impossible) for there to have been a state of total nothingness. But if it is impossible for nothing to exist (since something does exist), then something necessarily exists (i.e., a Necessary Being does exist).

To put it another way, if something exists and if nothing *cannot* cause something, then it follows that something *must* exist necessarily. For if something did not necessarily exist, then nothing would have caused the something that does exist. Since it is *impossible* for nothing to cause something, then it is *necessary* for something to always have been.

11. Contingent being exists = *Principle of Existential Contingency* (B^c exists).

Not everything that exists is necessary. For change is real, that is, at least some being(s) really change. And a Necessary Being cannot change in its being. (This does not mean there can be no change in external relations with another being. It simply means there can be no internal change in its being. When a person changes in relation to a pillar, the pillar does not change.) For its being is necessary, and what is necessary in its being cannot be other than it is in its being. And all change in being involves becoming something else in its being.

But it is evident that I change in my being. I change from not being to being. By "I" is meant the self-conscious individual being I call myself. (This is not to claim that all the parts or elements of my being are not eternal. There are good reasons to believe they are not because usable energy is running down and cannot be eternal [*see* Thermodynamics, Laws of], but this is not the point here.) This "I" or unifying center of consciousness around which these elemental parts of matter come and go, is not eternal. This is clear for many reasons.

First, my consciousness changes. Even those who claim they are eternal and necessary (namely, that they are a Necessary Being, God) were not always conscious of being God. Somewhere along the line they change from not being conscious they were God to being conscious they were God. But a Necessary Being cannot change. Hence, I am not a Necessary Being. Rather, I am a contingent being. Therefore, at least one contingent being exists. Everything is not necessary.

Further, there are other ways to know one is contingent. The fact that we reason to conclusions reveals that our knowledge is not eternal and necessary. We come to know (i.e., change from a state of not knowing to a state of knowing). But no necessary being can come to know anything. It either eternally and necessarily knows everything it knows, or else it knows nothing. If it is a knowing kind of being, then it necessarily knows, since it is a necessary kind of being. And a being can only know in accordance with the kind of being it is. A contingent or finite being must know contingently, and a Necessary Being must know necessarily. But I do not know all that I can know eternally and necessarily. Therefore, I am a contingent kind of being.

12. *The principle of analogy.* Since nonbeing cannot produce being (5), only being can produce being. But a contingent being cannot produce another contingent being (6). And a necessary being cannot produce another necessary being (8). So only Necessary Being can cause or produce only a contingent being. For to "cause" or "produce" being means to bring something into being. Something that comes into being, has being. A cause cannot bring nonbeing into being, since being is not nonbeing (4). The fact that Being produces being implies that there is an analogy (similarity) between the cause of being and the being it causes (8). But a contingent being is both similar and different from a Necessary Being. It is similar in that both have being. It is different in that one is necessary and the other is contingent. But whatever is both similar and different is analogous. Hence, there is an analogy between Necessary Being and the being it produces.

Two things, then, are entailed in the principle that Necessary Being causes being: First, the effect must resemble the cause, since both are being. The cause of being cannot produce what it does not possess. Second, while the effect must resemble its cause in its being (i.e., its actuality), it must also be different from it in its potentiality. For the cause (a Necessary Being), by its very nature, has no potential not to be. But the effect (a contingent being) by its very nature has the potential not to be. Hence, a contingent being must be different from its Cause. Since, the Cause of contingent beings must be both like and different from its effect, it is only similar. Hence, there is an analogical likeness between the Cause of a contingent being and the contingent being it causes to exist.

Demonstrating God's Existence. Given these principles of being, one can know many things about reality; they relate *thought* and *thing*. *Knowing* is based in *being*. By these principles, one can even prove the existence of God (*see* GOD, EVIDENCE FOR) as follows:

1. Something exists (e.g., I do) (no. 1).
2. I am a contingent being (no. 11).
3. Nothing cannot cause something (no. 5).
4. Only a Necessary Being can cause a contingent being (no. 7).
5. Therefore, I am caused to exist by a Necessary Being (follows from nos. 1–4).
6. But I am a personal, rational, and moral kind of being (since I engage in these kinds of activities).
7. Therefore, this Necessary Being must be a personal, rational, and moral kind of being, since I am similar to him by the Principle of Analogy (no. 12).
8. But a Necessary Being cannot be contingent (i.e., not-necessary) in its being which would be a contradiction (no. 3).
9. Therefore, this Necessary Being is personal, rational, and moral in a necessary way, not in a contingent way.
10. This Necessary Being is also eternal, uncaused, unchanging, unlimited, and one, since a Necessary Being cannot come to be, be caused by another, undergo change, be limited by any possibility of what it could be (a Necessary Being has no possibility to be other than it is), or to be more than one Being (since there cannot be two infinite beings).
11. Therefore, one necessary, eternal, uncaused, unlimited (= infinite), rational, personal, and moral being exists.
12. Such a Being is appropriately called "God" in the theistic sense, because he possesses all the essential characteristics of a theistic God.
13. Therefore, the theistic God exists.

Conclusion. First principles are indispensable to all knowledge. And first principles of being are a necessary prerequisite for all knowledge of being. These first principles are undeniable or reducible to the undeniable. For the very attempt to deny them affirms them. By them not only is reality known, but the existence of God can be demonstrated.

Sources

Aristotle, *On Interpretation*
———, *On Metaphysics*
W. Heisenberg, *Physics and Philosophy*
L. M. Regis, *Epistemology*
Thomas Aquinas, *Commentary on the Metaphysics of Aristotle*
———, *On Interpretation*
F. D. Wilhelmsen, *Man's Knowledge of Reality*

Flavius Josephus. Josephus (ca. A.D. 37–ca. 100) was a Pharisee of the priestly line and a Jewish historian. In addition to his autobiography he wrote two major works, *Jewish Wars* (77–78) and *Antiquities of the Jews* (ca. 94). He also wrote a minor work, *Against Apion*.

Josephus confirmed in general outline, and often in great detail, the historicity of the Old Testament and some of the New Testament (*see* NEW TESTAMENT, NON-CHRISTIAN SOURCES). Although Josephus's work is slanted so as not to offend the Romans, it has great apologetic value for Christianity—a religion also not in Roman favor. Josephus was highly appreciated and greatly used by the early church fathers in support of Christianity.

Testimony to the Canon. Josephus supports the Protestant view of the canon of the Old Testament against the Roman Catholic view, which venerates the Old Testament Apocrypha (*see* APOCRYPHA, OLD AND NEW TESTAMENTS). He even lists the names of the books, which are identical with the thirty-nine books of the Protestant Old Testament. He groups the thirty-nine into twenty-two volumes to correspond with the number of letters in the Hebrew alphabet:

> For we have not an innumerable multitude of books among us, disagreeing from and contradicting one another [as the Greeks have], but only twenty-two books, which contain the records of all the past times; which are justly believed to be divine; and of them, five belong to Moses, which contain his laws. . . . The prophets, who were after Moses, wrote down what was done in their times in thirteen books. The remaining four books contain hymns to God, and precepts for the conduct of human life. [*Against Apion* 1.8]

Another point of apologetic interest is Josephus's reference to Daniel the prophet as a sixth-century B.C. writer (*Antiquities*, 10–12). This confirms the supernatural nature of Daniel's amazing predictions about the course of history after his time (*see* PROPHECY AS PROOF OF THE BIBLE). Unlike the later Talmud, Josephus obviously lists Daniel among the prophets, since it is not in Moses or the "hymns to God" section, which would include Psalms, Proverbs, Ecclesiastes, and Song of Solomon. This helps confirm the early date of Daniel.

Testimony to the New Testament. Josephus referred to Jesus as the brother of James who was martyred. He wrote: "Festus was now dead, and Albius was but upon the raid; so he assembled the Sanhedrin of the judges, and brought before them the brother of Jesus, who was called Christ, whose name was James, and some others, [or some of his companions], and when he had formed an accusation against them as breakers of the law, he delivered them to be stoned" (*Antiquities* 20.9.1). This passage both verifies the existence of Christ by a non-Christian first-century writer and to what the central claim about him was by his immediate followers—that he was the Messiah.

Josephus also confirmed the existence and martyrdom of John the Baptist, the herald of Jesus: "Now, some of the Jews thought that the destruction of Herod's army came from God, and very justly, as a punishment of what he did against John, who was called the Baptist; for Herod slew him, who was a good man, and commanded the Jews to exercise virtue, both as to righteousness towards one another, and piety towards God, and so to come to baptism" (*Antiquities* 18.5.2). This reference confirms the existence, name, mission, and martyrdom of John the Baptist, just as the New Testament presents him.

In a disputed text, Josephus gives a brief description of Jesus and his mission:

> Now there was about this time, Jesus, a wise man, if it be lawful to call him a man, for he was a doer of wonderful works,—a teacher of such men as receive the truth with pleasure. He drew over to him both many of the Jews and many of the Gentiles. He was [the] Christ; and when Pilate, at the suggestion of the principal men amongst us, had condemned him to the cross, those that loved him at the first did not forsake him. For he appeared to them alive again the third day, as the divine prophets had foretold these and ten thousand other wonderful things concerning him; and the tribe of Christians, so named from him, are not extinct to this day. [*Antiquities* 18.3.3]

This passage was cited by Eusebius in its present form (*Ecclesiastical History* 1.11) and the manuscript evidence favors it. Yet it is widely considered to be an interpolation, since it is unlikely that Josephus, a Jew, would affirm that Jesus was the Messiah and had been proven so by fulfilled prophecy, miraculous deeds, and the resurrection from the dead. Even "Origin says that Josephus did not believe Jesus to be the Messiah, nor proclaim him as such" (*Contra Celsus* 2.47; 2.13; Bruce, 108). F. F. Bruce suggests that the phrase "if indeed we should call him a man" may indicate that the text is authentic but that Josephus is writing with tongue in cheek in sarcastic reference to Christian belief that Jesus is the Son of God (Bruce, 109).

Other scholars have suggested amending the text in ways that preserve its authenticity without the implication that Josephus personally accepted that Christ was the Messiah (see Bruce, 110–11). It may be that a tenth-century Arabic text (see McDowell, 85) reflects the original intent:

> At this time there was a wise man who was called Jesus. And his conduct was good and [he] was known to be virtuous. Many people from among the Jews and other nations became his disciples. Pilate condemned him to be crucified and to die. And those who had become his disciples did not abandon his discipleship. They reported that he had appeared to them three days after his crucifixion and that he was alive; accordingly, he was perhaps the messiah concerning whom the prophets have recounted wonders.

In this form it does not affirm that Josephus believed in the resurrection but only that his disciples "reported" it. This would at least reflect an honest report of what his immediate disciples believed. Bruce observes that there is good reason for believing that Josephus did refer to Jesus, bearing witness to his date, reputation, family connections to James, crucifixion under Pilate at the instigation of the Jewish leaders, messianic claim, founding of the church, and the conviction among his followers of the resurrection.

Sources

F. F. Bruce, *The New Testament Documents: Are They Reliable*

L. H. Feldman, *Studies on Philo and Josephus*

Josephus, *Against Apion*

———, *Antiquities of the Jews*

———, *Jewish Wars*

J. McDowell, *Evidence That Demands a Verdict*

S. Pines, *An Arabic Version of the Testimonium Flavianum and Its Implications*

R. J. H. Shutt, *Studies in Josephus*

H. St. J. Thackeray, *Josephus the Man and the Historian*

Flew, Antony. Antony Flew (b. 1923) is a prominent British atheist who lectured in philosophy at major British Universities and was professor of philosophy at the University of Keele. He has written or edited numerous books and scholarly journal articles and is well known for his works in philosophical theology. Among his most forceful work is the article "Miracles" in the *Encyclopedia of Philosophy* and his books *New Essays in Philosophical Theology* and *The Resurrection Debate*.

The Falsifiability of God. Unless some criteria exists by which one could know if something is false, asserts Flew, one cannot know it is true. If the theistic utterance, "God exists" is an assertion, "it will necessarily be equivalent to a denial of the negative of that assertion." However, "if there is nothing which a putative assertion denies then there is nothing which it asserts either; and so it is not really an assertion" (*New Essays*, 98). As this argument applies to God, Flew is saying that, unless a theist can specify conditions by which it could be proven that God does not exist, there are no conditions by which to prove that God does exist. Some event or series of events would have to be conceived which could prove that there is no God.

Other than accepting Flew's premise and admitting that no religious claim is falsifiable (*see* ACOGNOSTICISM; FIDEISM), there are two broad responses to Flew. First, one can reject the principle of falsifiability. Second, one can take up Flew's challenge and state conditions by which the existence of God could be falsified (*see* AYER, A. J.).

Rejecting Flew's Principle of Falsification. The principle of falsifiability is itself not falsifiable. There are no conditions under which one could know that this principle is false. Also, other things besides the existence of God are not falsifiable. For example, one's personal immortality can be verified if there is consciousness after death. But it cannot be falsified, since if we are annihilated at death we will not be able to falsify the claim of *immortality.

Accepting Flew's Principle of Falsification. The other response is to take Flew's bull by the horns and point out that falsification is possible in one of three ways, one past, one present, and one future.

Historical falsification. The resurrection of Jesus Christ on the third day can be falsified (*see* RESURRECTION, EVIDENCE FOR). All that ever needed to happen was to produce the body of Jesus or proof of a conspiracy to dispose of the body. Or one could find eyewitness testimony that Jesus remained in the grave longer than three days. The apostle Paul recognized this when he said, "if Christ has not been raised, our preaching is useless and so is your faith. More than that, we are then found to be false witnesses about God that he raised Christ from the dead. . . . And if Christ has not been raised, your faith is futile; you are still in your sins. Then those also who have fallen asleep in Christ are lost" (1 Cor. 15:14–18). If the resurrection can be disproven, Christianity—and Christianity's God—are false.

Falsification now. Since the apologetic evidence for the truth of Christianity is based on past events, there is no direct way to test them in the present. One can only use evidence from the past that remains in the present to argue for or against the truth of past events. Since Christianity depends on the truth of the premise "God exists (now)," this is a falsifiable premise. A theist might be willing to give up belief in God if the nontheist can present a valid disproof for the existence of God. Such disproofs have been tried, and all fail (*see* GOD, ALLEGED DISPROOFS OF). That means that falsification did not succeed, not that could not succeed in principle, if in fact no God existed.

Eschatological falsification. Eschatological falsification of some things, such as immortality, is impossible. However, many religious beliefs could be falsified. The statement "I will go to a place of bliss at death" is falsified if one remains conscious after death and goes to a place of suffering. Likewise, reincarnation can be falsified, if one dies with "bad karma" but is not reincarnated. It is more difficult to falsify the existence of God, even if one lives forever. God could choose to hide forever from view, but this is unlikely.

However it is approached, Flew's principle of falsification is far from a convincing blow to the truth of theism or of Christianity. The theist can offer many ways in which core beliefs can be falsified in principle, if not in practice.

Divine Omnipotence, Freedom, and Evil. Flew posed a difficult dilemma for theism in his article on "Divine Omnipotence and Human Freedom" (Flew, *New Essays,* chapter 8). He acknowledges the theists claim that even an omnipotent Being cannot do what is contradictory. But he challenges the view of many theists that it is contradictory to create a world where no free creature will ever do evil.

Flew insists that "omnipotence might have, could without contradiction be said to have, created people who would always as a matter of fact freely have chosen to do the right thing" (p. 152). And in response to the theist's claim that God could not have created higher-order goods without allowing lower-order goods, Flew argues that "Omnipotence could have created creatures who he could have been sure *would* respond to the appropriate challenge by a willing exercise of fortitude; without these creatures having to acquire this character by any actual exercise of fortitude" (p. 155).

Flew's arguments evoked the famous "free-will" response of Alvin Plantinga who argued that as long as one free creature chooses evil God cannot stop it without fettering their freedom—in which case they are not really free. Others note that what is logically possible is not necessarily actually achievable (*see* EVIL, PROBLEM OF). So while it is logically possible that no one would ever do evil, it is not actually achievable as long as someone freely chooses to do evil.

Miracles and Christian Apologetics. Flew alleges the unhistoricity of miracles (*see* MIRACLE; MIRACLES, APOLOGETIC VALUE OF; MIRACLES IN THE BIBLE), as well as their incredibility and their unidentifiability.

Flew's argument that miracles are unhistorical rests on the assumption that miracles are unrepeatable. Therefore they fail the test of credibility. Flew's argument follows the form developed by David Hume. As Flew sees *Hume's argument it runs something like this:

1. Every miracle is a violation of a law of nature.
2. The evidence against any violation of nature is the strongest possible evidence.
3. Therefore, the evidence against miracles is the strongest possible evidence.

Flew says that Hume was primarily concerned with the question of evidence. The problem was how the occurrence of a miracle could be proved, rather than whether such events ever occurred. However, "our sole ground for characterizing the reported occurrence as miraculous is at the same time a sufficient reason for calling it physically impossible." But why is this so? Flew responds that the critical historian, confronted with a story of a miracle, dismisses it. That is begging the question. On what grounds are miracles dismissed? "To justify his procedure he will have to appeal to precisely the principle which Hume advanced: the 'absolute impossibility or miraculous nature' of the events attested." This must be done to the satisfaction of reasonable people. So Flew believes that, even though miracles are not logically impossible, they are scientifically impossible. "It is only and precisely by presuming that the laws that hold today held in the past . . . that we can rationally interpret the detritus (fragments) of the past as evidence and from it construct our account of what actually happened ("Miracles").

To the charge that this uniformitarianism is irrationally dogmatic, Flew answers with what is at the heart of his amplification of Hume's argument. As Hume insisted, "the possibility of miracles is a matter of evidence and not of dogmatism. Further, reports of alleged occurrences of the miraculous are necessarily singular, particular, and in the past tense." Propositions of this sort cannot be tested directly. Repeatable propositions, therefore, have greater logical credibility (ibid.). This argument may be stated:

1. Miracles, by nature, are particular and unrepeatable.
2. Natural events are by nature general and repeatable.
3. In practice, the evidence for the general and repeatable is always greater than that for the particular and unrepeatable.
4. Therefore, in practice, the evidence will always be greater against miracles than for them.

From this statement it is clear that Flew regards generality and repeatability to be establishing factors for credibility.

Repeatability and Falsifiability. Most modern naturalists, such as Flew, accept some unrepeatable singularities, for example, at the formation of the universe (*see* BIG BANG THEORY). And nearly all scientists believe that the process of the origin of life has never been repeated. If Flew's argument is applied consistently, it is wrong for scientists to believe in any such singularity. Flew's argument would eliminate some basic naturalist's beliefs.

Flew's view also is subject to the very criticism Flew makes of theists, for it is not an unfalsifiable position (see above). No matter what state of affairs occurs, even a resurrection, Flew (contrary even to Hume's claims) would be obliged to deny that it was a miracle. And no event in the world would falsify naturalism. For the deck is stacked, so that the evidence always weighs more heavily for antisupernaturalism than against it. Neither would it help for Flew to claim that naturalism is falsifiable in principle, if never in practice. Then, to be fair, he would have to allow theists the same prerogative. If supernaturalism can never be established in practice, neither can naturalism. It is always possible for the theist to claim of every alleged natural event that "God is the ultimate cause." The theist may insist that all "natural" events (i.e., naturally repeatable ones) are the way God normally operates and that "miraculous" events are the way he works on occasion. By Flew's own grounds, there is no way, in practice, to falsify theistic belief.

One may object to Flew's assumption that the repeatable always evidentially outweighs the unrepeatable. If this were so, then, as Richard Whately pointed out, one could not believe in the historicity of any singular events from the past. If repeatability in practice is the true test of superior evidence, one should not believe that observed births or deaths occurred, for neither is repeatable in practice. The science of geology should be eliminated.

Scientists do not reject singularities out of hand, observes physicist professor Stanley Jaki. "Luckily for science, scientists relatively rarely brush aside reports about a really *new* case with the remark: 'It cannot be really different from the thousand other cases we have already investigated.' The brave reply of the young assistant, 'But, Sir, what if this is the thousand and first case?' which . . . is precisely the rejoinder that is to be offered in connection with facts that fall under suspicion because of their miraculous character" (Jaki, 100). So, if the naturalist pushes arguments far enough to eliminate miracles, the grounds for many other beliefs are eliminated by implication. Qualifications to include natural and scientific data reopen the door to miracles.

Identifiability. Flew's second argument is not ontological but epistemological. Miracles are not rejected because they are known not to have occurred. They are rejected because they are not or cannot be known to have occurred. Flew's argument goes beyond mere identifiability. If successful it would show that miracles have no apologetic value.

Flew claims to be willing to allow for the possibility of miracles in principle (*see* SPINOZA, BENEDICT). In practice, he argues, there is a serious, even insurmountable, problem in being unable to identify miracles. The argument may be summarized:

1. A miracle must be identifiable or distinguishable before it can be known to have occurred.
2. Miracles may only be identified in terms of nature or in terms of the supernatural.
3. To identify it by reference to the supernatural (as an act of God) begs the question.
4. To identify it in reference to natural terms takes away the necessary supernatural dimension.
5. Therefore, miracles cannot be known to have occurred, since they cannot be identified.

Flew insists against *Augustine (*City of God* 21.8), that if a miracle is merely "a portent [which] is not contrary to nature, but contrary to our knowledge of nature," then it really has no value as proof of the supernatural. It merely shows the relative knowledge of a generation. Whereas Augustine's notion of a miracle would assure the dependence of creation on God, it would do so only at the cost of subverting the apologetic value of all miracles (Flew, 348). If a miracle is not beyond the power of nature, but only beyond our *knowledge* of nature, then a miracle is nothing but a natural event. We could not know that a miracle really occurred; only that it seemed to. To truly be miraculous, a miracle must be independent of nature, but a miracle cannot be identified except as it relates to nature. There is no natural way to identify a miracle, unless it is known to be a miracle on some independent grounds. It must be considered simply an odd or inconsistent event that a broader scientific law could explain.

From this, Flew argues that no alleged miraculous event can be used to prove a religious system is true. We cannot argue that God exists because an event is an act of God. Unless there is already a God who acts, there cannot be an act of God. To argue from act of God to supernatural system begs the question. We must identify the event as supernatural from a strictly naturalistic perspective. But this is impossible, since an unusual event in the natural realm is, from a naturalistic perspective, strictly a natural perspective. Miracles, therefore, have no apologetic value.

The heart of Flew's argument is now in focus (ibid., 348–49). Miracles are not identifiable because there is no way to define them without begging the question:

1. A miracle must be identifiable before it can be identified.
2. A miracle is identified in one of two ways (a.) an unusual event in nature, or (b.) an exception to nature.
3. An unusual event in nature is simply a natural event, not a miracle.
4. An exception to nature cannot be known from within nature alone.
5. Therefore, a miracle is not identifiable and cannot be used to prove anything.

It would seem that Flew has made a penetrating point. His first premise is solid. We must know what we are looking for before we can know we have found it. We cannot discover what cannot be defined. But to define miracles in terms of natural events is to reduce them to natural events. To define them in terms of a supernatural cause is to suppose that God exists, a circular argument.

Presupposing God's Existence. One way to reply to Flew is to claim that naturalists as well as supernaturalists are arguing in a circle. Antisupernatural arguments presuppose naturalism. Thus, some theists simply claim that it is necessary to argue in a circle. All reason is circular (*Van Til, 118), for all thought ultimately is grounded in faith (*see* FIDEISM).

If a supernaturalist chooses this route the grounds (or lack of grounds) seem just as good as those of the antisupernaturalist. Naturalists who attempt to rule out miracles on the basis of a faith commitment to naturalism are in no position to forbid theists from simply believing that God exists and, hence, that miracles are identifiable. Once naturalists are granted the privilege of a mere belief basis for naturalism, with no rational or scientific proof, alternate worldviews must be allowed the same opportunity.

Evidence for God's Existence. Another avenue of approach is open, however: Theists may offer rational justification for belief in God. If successful, then they can define (show the identifiability of) miracles in terms of the supernatural realm they have *reason* to think exists. This is precisely what the cosmological argument and the teleological argument do. To the extent that one can give a rational argument for God's existence, Flew's criticism is circumvented.

Summary. Two themes of Flew are a serious threat to Christian apologetics: (1) His argument that belief in God is not falsifiable, and (2) his view that miracles are not identifiable. There are ways to meet the challenge of verifiability. Christianity can be verified from events in the past, present, and future. A more serious matter is the attack on miracles. Even though Flew does not claim that this argument eliminates the possibility of miracles, it would, if successful, seriously cripple Christian apologetics (*see* CLASSICAL APOLOGETICS; HISTORICAL APOLOGETICS). If miracles cannot be identified as supernatural events, they have no apologetic value. A mere unusual event within nature has no evidential value to prove anything beyond the existence of nature.

However, as shown above, classical apologists can evade this problem by either presupposing the existence of a supernatural realm (i.e., God) or by offering evidence for his existence. As long as there is a God who can act, special acts of God (miracles) are possible and identifiable. The only way to disprove this possibility is to disprove the possibility of God's existence. Such efforts are doomed to failure and are usually self-refuting (*see* GOD, ALLEGED DISPROOFS OF).

Historical apologists do not have this option, since they believe that the whole case for Christianity, including the existence of God, can be made from historical evidence alone. Against this view, Flew makes a telling point.

Sources

Thomas Aquinas, *Summa contra Gentiles*, Book 3

Augustine, *The City of God*

A. Flew, "Miracles," in *The Encyclopedia of Philosophy*, P. Edwards, ed.

———, "Theology and Falsification," in *New Essays in Philosophical Theology*

N. L. Geisler, *Miracles and the Modern Mind.*

S. Jaki, *Miracles and Physics*

C. S. Lewis, *Miracles*

T. Miethe, ed., *Did Jesus Rise from the Dead? The Resurrection Debate*

R. Swinburne, *Miracles*

C. Van Til, *Defense of the Faith*

Flood, Noah's. The record of Noah's flood in Genesis 6–9 has raised serious questions in the minds of Bible critics, among them:

> How could this small ark hold hundreds of thousands of species?
>
> How could a wooden ship stay afloat in such a violent storm?
>
> How could Noah's family and the animals survive so long in the ark?

Species Saved. The first problem deals with how such a small ark could hold all the animal species on earth. The consensus of ancient historians and archaeologists is that a cubit was about eighteen inches long. Translating the Bible's dimensions according to an eighteen-inch cubit, Noah's ark was only forty-five feet high, seventy-five feet wide, and four hundred and fifty feet long (Gen. 6:15). Noah was told to take two of every kind of unclean animal and seven of every kind of clean animal (6:19; 7:2). But scientists count between one-half billion and more than 1 billion animal species.

A Localized Disaster? One possible explanation is that the flood was local in geographic scope. Noah in that case would only have to repopulate the local area and have animals to eat and sacrifice.

As evidence that the flood was not universal, it is noted that the same "universal" language of Genesis 6 through 9 is used elsewhere when something less than the whole world is meant. The people on the Day of Pentecost were said to be "from every nation under heaven" (Acts 2:5) yet the nations listed are restricted to the Roman world. Paul said in Colossians 1:23 that "this is the gospel that you heard and that has been proclaimed to *every creature under heaven*." Paul's itinerary in Acts 13 to 28 shows that he went only to the Mediterranean area.

Also, the silt deposits a flood like Noah's would have left are found only in the Mesopotamian Valley, not over the entire world. There is not enough water in the world to cover the highest mountains (7:20). Some mountains are several miles high. Waters that high would have caused problems with the rotation of the earth. The mountains in the Mesopotamian area are not nearly so high.

Finally, the size of the ark would restrict the number of species. Those from a localized region would have been more manageably housed.

A Universal Flood? Other Old Testament scholars believe there is evidence of a universal flood. The language of Genesis is more intense than that of the references noted. God's commands to take animals of every kind would not have been required if only the life in a limited geographical area was to be destroyed. Animals could have migrated in to repopulate the region. And Genesis 10:32 declares that the whole world was populated after the flood from the eight who were saved. This would not have been true if those outside the local area had not drowned. Peter refers to the salvation of only eight (1 Peter 3:20).

The silt deposits in the Mesopotamian Valley were from a local flood(s), not the universal floods. The silt layers throughout the world are open to interpretation, including the possibility of a world catastrophe. There are also signs of dramatic changes in the position of earth's land masses. The mountains could have taken new, far higher, shapes because of the unparalleled forces at work during the flood.

The Ark Was Large Enough. But assuming the flood was universal, the question remains as to how Noah could get all those animals in the ark. Engineers, computer programmers, and wildlife experts have all taken a look at the problem, and their consensus is that the ark was sufficient to the task.

The ark was actually a huge structure—the size of a modern ocean liner, with three levels of deck (Gen. 6:13), which tripled its space to over 1.5

million cubic feet. This equals 569 railroad box cars.

Second, the modern concept of "species" is not the same as a "kind" in the Bible. But even if it were, there are probably only some 72,000 different kinds of land animals which the ark would have needed to contain. Since the average size of land animals is smaller than a cat, less than half of the ark would be needed to store 150,000 animals—more than there probably were. Insects take only a very small space. The sea animals stayed in the sea, and many species could have survived in egg form. There would have been plenty of room left over for eight people and food storage.

Third, Noah could have taken younger or smaller varieties of some larger animals. Given all these factors, there was plenty of room for all the animals, food for the trip, and the eight humans aboard.

Wooden Ship in a Violent Storm. The ark was made of wood and carried a heavy load of cargo. It is argued that the violent waves of a worldwide flood surely would have broken it into pieces (cf. Gen. 7:4, 11).

The ark was made of a strong and flexible material (gopher wood). Gopher wood "gives" without breaking. The heavy load gave the ark stability. Also, naval architects report that a long box-shaped, floating boxcar, such as the ark, is the most stable kind of craft in turbulent waters. One former naval architect concluded: "Noah's Ark was extremely stable, more stable in fact, than modern shipping" (see Collins, 86). Indeed, modern ocean liners follow the same basic proportions. However, their stability is lessened by the need to slice through the water with as little drag as possible. There is no reason Noah's ark could not have survived a gigantic, even worldwide, flood. Modern stability tests have shown that such a vessel could take up to 200-foot-high waves and could tip as much as 90 degrees and still right itself.

Survival Inside the Ark. How could all these animals and humans last over one year cooped up in this ark?

There is some question as to just how long the flood lasted. Genesis 7:24; 8:3 speaks of the flood waters lasting for 150 days. But other verses seem to say it was only forty days (Gen. 7:4, 12, 17). And one verse indicates that it was over a year. These numbers refer to different things. Forty days is how long it *"rained"* (7:12), and 150 days speaks of how long the flood *"waters prevailed"* (8:3; cf. 7:24). After this it was not until the fifth month after the rain began that the ark rested on Mount Ararat (8:4). About eleven months after the rain began the waters dried up (8:13). And exactly one year and ten days after the flood began, Noah and his family emerged on dry ground (8:14).

Another answer is that living things can do almost anything they must to survive, as long as they have enough food and water. Many of the animals may have gone into hibernation or semi-hibernation. And Noah had plenty of room for food on the inside and abundant water on the outside to draw on.

For notes on how nonbiblical flood reports and legends from the ancient world relate to the Bible's account, see ARCHAEOLOGY, OLD TESTAMENT; EBLA TABLETS.

Sources

G. L. Archer, Jr., *A Survey of Old Testament Introduction*
D. Collins, "Was Noah's Ark Stable?" *CRSQ*, 14 (September 1977)
A. Custance, *The Flood: Local or Global?*
G. M. Price, *The New Geology*
B. Ramm, *The Christian View of Science and Scripture*
A. Reiwinkel, *The Flood*
J. Whitcomb, *The World That Perished*
——— and H. Morris, *The Genesis Flood*
J. Woodmorappe, *Noah's Ark: A Feasibility Study*
D. A. Young, *The Biblical Flood*

Foundationalism. *Foundationalism* is the theory of knowledge (*see* EPISTEMOLOGY) that affirms the need for certain foundational principles (*see* FIRST PRINCIPLES) as the basis of all thought. By contrast, Coherentism claims that no such principles are needed but that ideas simply need to cohere like a web in a consistent way, without any ultimate foundational principles.

Argument for Foundationalism. Foundationalists argue that no knowledge, not even about ideas that cohere, would be possible unless there were first principles such as the law of noncontradiction. These principles make it possible to know if ideas are consistent and noncontradictory. They point out that no web hangs in mid air; it must be anchored somewhere. C. S. *Lewis observed,

> As such, these first principles of Practical Reason are fundamental to all knowledge and argument. To deny them is to deny knowledge itself; it is no use trying to see through first principles. If you see through everything, then everything is transparent. But a wholly transparent world is an invisible world. To "see through" all things is the same as not to see. [Lewis, 87]

The basic foundationalist argument is that there must be a basis for all truth claims and that an infinite regress never (*see* INFINITE SERIES) provides a foundation; it only delays providing one forever. Hence, ultimately there must be some first principles on which all knowledge rests. Everything not evident in itself must be made evident in terms of something that is. So, ultimately there must be some self-evident principles in terms of which everything else can be made evident.

It is unreasonable to try to get behind them. Hence, one cannot have an "open mind" about whether they are true. One cannot even have a mind without them.

Foundational Principles. Classical foundationalists generally agree that the basic laws of *logic are foundational principles. These include the law of noncontradiction—that a proposition cannot be both true and false at the same time and in the same sense. Likewise, the kindred principles of the excluded middle (either something is true or false, but not both) and identity (what is true is true and what is false is false) are foundational principles.

In metaphysics traditional foundationalists offer principles, such as: "Being is being"; "Nonbeing is not being," and "Something either is being or nonbeing."

Ethical first principles include: "Good should be sought," "Evil should be avoided," and "Either a thing is good or evil."

Criticisms. The most significant criticisms of foundationalism are:

There Is No Agreement on First Principles. Not everyone agrees on which principles are to be included in the foundational principles. In response, foundationalists point out that failure to get universal agreement on the number of foundational principles does not mean there are none, any more than failure to agree on how many ethical principles there are means there is no ultimate basis for right and wrong (*see* MORALITY, ABSOLUTE NATURE OF), or that failure to agree on how many scientific laws there are means there are none.

There Is No Basis for First Principles. But if everything needs a basis, why not seek a basis for the so-called foundational principles. What is the foundation of foundationalism?

Foundationalists do not argue that every statement needs a basis. They believe that only statements that are not self-evident need a foundation. They hold that statements that are not evident in themselves must be evident in terms of something else that is self-evident. Once one arrives at the self-evident, it need not be evident in terms of anything else (*see* REALISM).

What Is Self-evident? Some object that there is no sure way to know what is self-evident. Not everything said to be self-evident to foundationalists is self-evident to others.

To this criticism foundationalists point out that a self-evident truth is one whose predicate is reducible to its subject, either directly or indirectly. Hence, all one needs to do is analyze it clearly to find out if this is so. For example, it is self-evident that "Being exists," since whatever "exists" has "being." Likewise, it is self-evident that "Every effect has a cause," since an "effect" means that which is "caused." Further, simply because some things are not evident to everyone does not mean they are not self-evident in themselves. The reason a self-evident truth may not be evident to someone could be because the person has not analyzed it carefully. But their failure in no way invalidates the self-evident nature of the first principle.

Sources

Aristotle, *Metaphysics*

N. L. Geisler and R. M. Brooks, *Come Let Us Reason*

C. S. Lewis, *The Abolition of Man*

L. M. Regis, *Epistemology*

Thomas Aquinas. *Summa Theologica*, Pt. 1

F. D. Wilhelmsen, *Man's Knowledge of Reality*

Frazer, James. James Frazer (1854–1941) was born in Glasgow and educated at Larchfield Academy, Helensburg; Glasgow University, and Cambridge University. From 1907 to 1919 he was professor of social anthropology at the University of Liverpool. Frazer was instrumental in starting *The Cambridge Review* (1879). He delivered the first of his Gifford Lectures in 1911 on "Belief in Immortality and the Worship of the Dead." Between 1890 and 1912 he produced his monumental work, *The Golden Bough*. This and the three-volume *Folk-Lore in the Old Testament* (1918) were produced in abridged editions in 1922 and 1923, respectively. Frazer also wrote *The Worship of Nature* (1926) and *The Fear of the Dead in Primitive Religion* (1933–34).

The Golden Bough gives an evolutionary twist to the history of religions. Frazer proposed that religions evolved from magic through animism and *polytheism to *henotheism and finally to *monotheism. He alleged that Christianity copied pagan myths. In spite of its selective and anecdotal use of sources that were outdated by subsequent research, the ideas of the book are still widely believed.

Evaluation. Frazer's evolution of religion thesis is without foundation for reasons discussed in detail elsewhere. See the articles MIRACLES, MYTH AND; MITHRAISM; MYTHOLOGY AND THE NEW TESTAMENT; and RESURRECTION CLAIMS IN NON-CHRISTIAN RELIGIONS. Key reasons include:

Pagan myths most frequently cited as the models for the birth, death, and resurrection of Christ actually appeared later than did the Gospels (see Yamauchi). Therefore, the Christian writers could not have copied these stories.

There are significant differences in pagan and Christian versions. For example, pagans did not believe in the resurrection (*see* RESURRECTION, PHYSICAL NATURE OF) of the physical body that died, but in reincarnation of the soul into another body. Pagan stories were all about polytheistic (*see* POLYTHEISM) gods, not about a monotheistic (*see* THEISM) deity.

There is good evidence that monotheism was the primitive religion of the earliest known peoples, particularly in the Fertile Crescent, not animism and polytheism (*see* MONOTHEISM, PRIMITIVE). The oldest records from both Ebla (*see* EBLA TABLETS) and the Old Testament books about the earliest times, Genesis and Job, speak of monotheism. Anthropologist W. Schmidt proposes an interpretation of the data that monotheism is the most primitive view of God. Animism, polytheism, and henotheism are seen as later corruption (*Origin and Growth*; *Primitive Revelation*). William F. *Albright comments, "There can no longer be any doubt that Fr. Schmidt has successfully disproved the simple evolutionary progression . . . fetishism—polytheism—monotheism, or Tylor's animism—polytheism—monotheism. . . . The simple fact is that religious phenomena are so complex in origin and so fluid in nature that over-simplification is more misleading in the field of religion than perhaps anywhere else" (Albright, 171).

Even in the existing so-called "primitive religions" there is a widespread concept of a high god or sky god whom scholars believe closely connects with primitive monotheism. John Mbiti has described 300 traditional religions. Yet "in all these societies, without a single exception, people have a notion of God as the Supreme Being (see Mbiti, *African Religions and Philosophy*). Albright likewise acknowledges that the "high gods may be all-powerful and they may be credited with creation of the world; they are generally cosmic deities who often, perhaps usually, reside in heaven" (Albright, 170). This clearly runs counter to the animistic and polytheistic conceptions of deity.

Study of Frazer and his critics shows fairly conclusively that Frazer's thesis was not motivated by the facts, but by his evolutionary view of religion (*see* DARWIN, CHARLES). This he simply presupposed. His contribution was an ingenious presentation of existing knowledge within a particular framework.

The evolutionary view of religion was itself late, only gaining popularity in the wake of the biological evolution (*see* EVOLUTION, BIOLOGICAL; MISSING LINKS) theory popularized by Charles Darwin in *On the Origin of Species* (1859) and *Descent of Man* (1871). Frazer's evolutionary idea is based on several unproved assumptions. It assumes biological evolution to be fact, though it lacks support. It also assumes biological evolution describes events at the social and religious levels, which does not follow in any case.

Even Theodore Gaster's revision of Frazer's book states: "[The revision] eliminates, for example, Frazer's lengthy discussion of the relation between magic and Religion, because the view which is there expressed that the two things stand in genealogical succession . . . has now been shown to be a mere product of late nineteenth-century evolutionism, without adequate basis" (Frazer, *The New Golden Bough,* 1959, xv–xvi).

Frazer's theory also is based on an unsubstantiated antisupernaturalism (*see* MIRACLES, ARGUMENTS AGAINST). The Bible teaches that God revealed himself specifically to certain people and generally to all humankind through creation and the moral order (cf. Psalm 19; Rom. 1:18–20; 2:14–15). The evolutionary view makes monotheism a product of human development. God was first seen as something in nature and then as something beyond nature. He does not reveal himself to people.

In addition to these factors, it has been shown that pagan myths post-date the Christian record of the birth, death, and resurrection. Ronald Nash observes that the chronology is all wrong if pagan religions influenced Christian myth-makers. All of the sources that tell about these pagan myths are very late (Nash, 193). Christians could hardly have been the ones influenced. If anything, pagan religions borrowed from Christianity (*see* DIVINE BIRTH STORIES; MITHRAISM; MYTHOLOGY AND THE NEW TESTAMENT; RESURRECTION CLAIMS IN NON-CHRISTIAN RELIGIONS).

Significant differences between pagan and Christian versions also preclude a Christian dependence. Nash lists six differences between the death of Jesus and pagan god-death accounts: (1) No pagan deities died in the place of someone else, as did Jesus. (2) Only Jesus died to pay for sins. (3) Jesus died once for all, while Pagan deities died and came to life with the annual cycles of nature. (4) The death of Jesus was an event attested to in history; the pagan deities' stories were only mythical. (5) Jesus died voluntarily. (6) The death of Jesus was a triumph, not a defeat (Nash, 171–72). Likewise, the resurrection, the Christian concepts of new birth and redemption, and the sacraments all differ significantly from pagan religious beliefs and practices (Nash).

Sources

W. F. Albright, *From the Stone Age to Christianity*

J. Frazer, *The Golden Bough* (1890–1912)

J. Frazer, *The New Golden Bough* (1959)

E. O. James, "Frazer, James George," in *New Twentieth-Century Encyclopedia of Religious Knowledge*

S. Kim, *The Origin of Paul's Gospel*

J. S. Mbiti, *African Religion and Philosophy*

———, *Concepts of God in Africa*

J. G. Machen, *The Origin of Paul's Religion*

———, *The Virgin Birth*

R. Nash, *Christianity and the Hellenistic World*

W. Schmidt, *High Gods in North America*

———, *The Origin and Growth of Religion*

———, *Primitive Revelation*

E. Yamauchi, "Easter—Myth, Hallucination, or History?" *CT* (29 March 1974; 15 April 1974)

Free Will. Conceptions of the nature of human choice fall within three categories: determinism, indeterminism (*see* INDETERMINACY, PRINCIPLE OF), and self-determinism. A determinist looks to actions caused by another, an indeterminist to uncaused actions, and a self-determinist to self-caused actions.

Determinism. For a full discussion and the arguments for and against this viewpoint, see DETERMINISM. There are two basic kinds of determinism: naturalistic and theistic. Naturalistic determinism is most readily identified with behavioral psychologist B. F. Skinner. *Skinner held that all human behavior is determined by genetic and behavioral factors. Humans simply act according to what has been programmed into them.

All who accept strong forms of Calvinistic theology hold to some degree of theistic determinism. Jonathan *Edwards related all actions ultimately to God as First Cause. "Free choice" for Edwards is doing what one desires, and God is the Author of the heart's desires. God is sovereign, in control of all and so ultimately the cause of all. Fallen humanity is totally without freedom of the affections, so they can do whatever they want, but what they want will forever be in the control of their corrupt, world-directed heart. God's grace controls actions as God controls desires and their attendant thoughts and actions.

Response to Determinism. Nondeterminists respond that a self-caused action is not impossible, and all actions need not be attributed to the First Cause (God). Some actions can be caused by human beings to whom God gave free moral agency. Free choice is not, as Edwards contends, doing what one *desires* (with God giving the desires). Rather, it is doing what one *decides,* which is not always the same thing. One need not reject God's sovereign control to deny determinism. God can control by omniscience as well as by causal power.

Two forms of determinism may be distinguished, hard and soft. A *hard determinist* believes all acts are caused by God, that God is the only efficient Cause. A *soft determinist* holds that God as the Primary Cause is compatible with human free choice as the secondary Cause.

Indeterminism. According to the indeterminist, few if any human actions are caused. Events and action are contingent and spontaneous. Charles Pierce and William *James were indeterminists.

Arguments for Indeterminism. The arguments for indeterminism follow the nature of free actions. Since they follow no determinate pattern, it is concluded that they are indeterminate. Some contemporary indeterminists appeal to Werner Heisenberg's principle of indeterminacy (*see* Indeterminacy, Principle of) to support their position (*see* First Principles). According to this principle, events in the subatomic realm (like the specific course of a given particle) are completely unpredictable.

According to the argument from the unpredictability of free acts, an act must be predictable in order to be determinate. But free acts are not predictable. Hence, they are indeterminate.

Critique of Indeterminacy. All forms of indeterminism fall shipwreck on the principle of causality, which asserts that all events have a cause (*see* Causality, Principle of). But indeterminacy asserts that free choices are uncaused events.

Indeterminism makes the world irrational and science impossible. It is contrary to reason to affirm that things happen willy nilly without a cause. Hence, indeterminacy reduces to irrationalism. Both operation and origin sciences are dependent on the principle of causality. Simply because a free act is not caused by another does not mean that it is uncaused. It could be self-caused.

Use of Heisenberg's principle is misapplied, since it does not deal with the *causality* of an event but with *unpredictability.*

Indeterminism robs humans of their moral responsibility, since they are not the cause of these actions. If they are not, why should they be blamed for evil actions? Indeterminism, at least on a cosmic scale, is unacceptable from a biblical perspective, since God is causally related to the world as both originator (Genesis 1) and sustainer of all things (Col. 1:15–16).

Self-Determinism. According to this view, a person's moral acts are not caused by another or uncaused, but are caused by oneself. It is important to know at the outset precisely what is meant by self-determinism or free choice. Negatively, it means that a moral action is not uncaused or caused by another. It is neither indeterminate nor determined by another. Positively, it is morally self-determined, an act freely chosen, without compulsion, in which one could have done otherwise. Several arguments support this position.

Arguments for Self-determinism. Either moral actions are uncaused, caused by another, or caused by oneself. However, no action can be uncaused, since this violates the fundamental rational principle that every event has a cause. Neither can a person's actions be caused by others, for in that case they would not be *personal* actions. Further, if one's acts are caused by another, then how can he or she be held responsible for them? Both *Augustine (in *On Free Will* and *On Grace and Free Will*) and *Thomas Aquinas were self-determinists, as are moderate Calvinists and Arminians.

The denial that some actions can be free is self-defeating. A complete determinist insists that both determinists and nondeterminists are determined to believe what they believe. However, determinists believe self-determinists are wrong and ought to change their view. But "ought to change" implies freedom to change, which is contrary to determinism. If God is the cause of all human actions, then human beings are not morally responsible. And it makes no sense to praise human beings for doing good, nor to blame them for doing evil.

A dimension of this controversy has to do with how the "self" is viewed. By "self" the self-determinist believes there is an "I" (subject) that is more than the object. That is, my subjectivity transcends my objectivity. I cannot put all that I am under a microscope to analyze as an object. There is more to "me" than objectivity. This "I" that transcends being objectified is free. The scientist who attempts to study personal self always transcends the experiment. The scientist is always on the outside looking in. In fact, "I" am free to reject "me." It is not determined by objectivity, not subject to being locked into scientific analysis. As such, the "I" is free.

Objections to Self-determinism. Free will rules out sovereignty. If human beings are free, are they outside God's sovereignty? Either God determines all, or else he is not sovereign. And if he determines all, then there are no self-determined acts.

It is sufficient to note that God sovereignly delegated free choice to some of his creatures. There was no necessity for him to do so; he exercised his free will. So human freedom is a sovereignly given power to make moral choices. Only absolute freedom would be contrary to God's absolute sovereignty. But human freedom is a limited freedom. Humans are not free to become God themselves. A contingent being cannot become a Necessary Being. For a Necessary Being cannot come to be. It must always be what it is.

Free will is contrary to grace. It is objected that either free, good acts spring from God's grace, or else from our own initiative. But if the latter, they are not the result of God's grace (Eph. 2:8–9). However, this does not necessarily follow. Free will itself is a gracious gift. Further, special grace is not forced coercively onto the person. Rather, grace works persuasively. The hard determinist's position confuses the nature of faith. The ability of a person to receive God's gracious gift of salvation is not the same as working for it. To think so is to give credit for the gift to the receiver, rather than to the Giver.

A self-caused act is logically impossible. It is objected that self-determinism means to cause oneself, which is impossible. Someone cannot be prior to oneself, which is what a self-caused act entails. This objection misunderstands determinism, which does not mean that one *causes himself to exist*, but rather *causes something else to happen*. A self-determined act is one determined by oneself, not another.

Self-determinism is contrary to causality. If all acts need a cause, then so do acts of the will, which are not caused by the self but by something else. If everything needs a cause, so do the persons performing the actions (*see* CAUSALITY, PRINCIPLE OF).

There is no violation of the actual principle of causality in the exercise of free actions. The principle does not claim that every *thing* (being) needs a cause. Finite things need a cause. God is uncaused (*see* GOD, NATURE OF). The person performing free actions is caused by God. The *power* of freedom is caused by God, but the *exercise* of freedom is caused by the person. The self is the first-cause of personal actions. The principle of causality is not violated because every finite thing and every action has a cause.

Self-determinism is contrary to predestination. Others object that self-determinism is contrary to God's predestination. But self-determinists respond that God can predetermine in several ways. He can determine (1) contrary to free choice (forcing the person to do what he or she does not choose to do); (2) based on free choices already made (waiting to see what the person will do); and (3) knowing omnisciently what the person will do "in accordance with his foreknowledge" (1 Peter 1:2). "Those God foreknew he also predestined to be conformed to the likeness of his Son" (Rom. 8:29). Either positions 2 or 3 are consistent with self-determinism. Both insist that God can determine the future by free choice, since he omnisciently knows *for sure* how they will *freely* act. So, it is *determined* from the standpoint of God's infallible knowledge but *free* from the vantage point of human choice.

Connected with the argument from strong determinism is that, while Adam had free choice (Rom. 5:12), fallen human beings are in bondage to sin and not free to respond to God. But this view is contrary to both God's consistent call on people to repent (Luke 13:3; Acts 2:38) and believe (e.g., John 3:16; 3:36; Acts 16:31), as well as to direct statements that even unbelievers have the ability to respond to God's grace (Matt. 23:37; John 7:17; Rom. 7:18; 1 Cor. 9:17; Philem. 14; 1 Peter 5:2).

This argument continues that if humans have the ability to respond, then salvation is not of grace (Eph. 2:8–9) but by human effort. However, this is a confusion about the nature of faith. The ability of a person to receive God's gracious *gift* of salvation is not the same as *working* for it. To think so is to give credit for the gift to the receiver rather than to the Giver who graciously gave it.

Sources

Augustine, *On Free Will*
J. Edwards, *The Freedom of the Will*
J. Fletcher, *John Fletcher's Checks to Antinomianism*, abridged by P. Wiseman
R. T. Forster, et al., *God's Strategy in Human History*
N. L. Geisler, "Man's Destiny: Free or Forced," *CSR*, 9.2 (1979)
D. Hume, *The Letters of David Hume*
C. S. Lewis, *Miracles*
M. Luther, *On Grace and Free Will*
———, *The Bondage of the Will*
B. F. Skinner, *Beyond Behaviorism*
———, *Beyond Freedom and Dignity*
Thomas Aquinas, *Summa Theologica*

Freud, Sigmund. Sigmund Freud (1856–1939), father of psychoanalysis, was one of the most influential atheists (*see* ATHEISM) of modern times.

His views on religion have provided a widely accepted rationale for disbelief in God. As such, they bear careful scrutiny by Christian apologists.

Freud was born in 1856 in Freiberg, Moravia. When he was three years old his family moved to Vienna where he later attended university and studied medicine. He married Martha Bernays, who bore him six children.

In addition to his works on psychology, Freud was preoccupied with religion. He wrote *Totem and Taboo* and *Moses and Monotheism*, but his most influential in undermining belief in God was the 1927 work, *The Future of an Illusion*.

View of Religion. Although an atheist, Freud found some positive features in religion. He acknowledged that (1) there is definitely some truth in religion; (2) in fact, some religion may all be true, and it cannot be definitely disproved. (3) It would be of greatest significance if it were true. (4) There is a feeling of dependence from which religion arose that is shared by all. (5) Religion has provided great comfort for people, and (6) such goals of religion as brotherhood and easing suffering are good and right. (7) Historically, it has been the most important and influential part of culture. Freud even admitted that his position against religion might be entirely unjustified, but he held it strongly, nonetheless.

Despite these benefits, Freud believed that religion must be rejected as authoritarian in form, unnecessary, and inadequate. He suspected that it was founded in an illusory desire for wish-fulfillment. Religion is something we wish to be true but have no basis for trust beyond our wish. In psychoanalytic terms, God is a childhood neurosis we never outgrew, the result of a desire for a kind of heavenly security blanket. That we wish for a pot of gold at the end of a rainbow does not mean there is one. The desire for a Father to comfort us through the woes of life is just as illusory.

Freud believed religion to be harmful because:

1. It arises from the desire or wish for a Cosmic Comforter.
2. It originated during a primitive (ignorant) period of human development.
3. It drains energy from the drive to solve the world's problems.
4. It is selfish and impatient, wanting immediate, immortal reward upon death.
5. It may contribute to the passionate, irrational nature, because of early religion indoctrination and repression of sexual development.
6. It keeps people in a perpetual state of childhood and immaturity.
7. Its adherents are closed-minded; they do not willingly give it up under any circumstances.
8. It is not needed; humanity now has science to control the world and, with resignation, can live with the rest.
9. It has not brought personal and social satisfaction in thousands of years of effort.
10. It has a specious and inauthentic basis: It is alleged to be true since: (a) our primal ancestors believed it; (b) miraculous proofs have been handed down from antiquity, and it is impious to question their authenticity.

Inadequate Justifications for Religion. If one purified religion of all its contradictions, it should still be rejected because it is a wish-fulfillment. Why should we believe this one absurdity and not others? One should not simply behave "as if it were true," contrary to our sense of reality.

Spiritism and trances do not justify religion. These experiences prove only subjective mental states of the persons who have them. Religion should not be accepted by virtue of it being an ancestral belief. Our ancestor were ignorant of many things.

Nor should one accept religion by virtue of the feeling of dependence that lies inside all human beings (*see* SCHLEIERMACHER, FRIEDRICH). To dwell on this feeling alone is irreligious; it is what is done in response to this feeling of dependence that constitutes religion. Religion should not be accepted as a necessary moral restraint. A rational basis is better and is applicable to all people, not just to the religious.

Holding God to be indefinable and indescribable is inadequate. This unknowable God is of no interest to human beings.

Response to Objections. To the objection that "reason and science are too slow in providing needed comfort and answers," Freud replied that reason persists and is better in the long run. Freud admitted that there is no guarantee of reward in reason and science. Such a guarantee is sought by selfishness. Reason is less selfish than religion. He also admitted that his own view might be an illusion. He responded that the weakness of his view does not prove religion is right. If faith in reason is also intolerant and dogmatic, at least reason can be given up and no penalty for disbelief. Religion cannot.

To the charge that rejection is dangerous to the institution and work of religion, Freud comments that the truly religious person will not be moved by his view.

Are human beings too passionate to be ruled by reason? How does society know whether they are, for it has never been tried? "Moral chaos will result without religion." Not so, Freud claims. For reason is a better basis for morals. It also is untrue that we are helpless without religion, for we have science and the ability to resign ourselves to the handling of our own problems.

In general the argument to which Freud responded was that, truth or not, human beings cannot do without religious consolation. Not surprisingly, Freud insists that eventually, people must grow up.

Evaluation. It is noteworthy that Freud is not against religion, but against dogmatic, authoritarian religiosity. He admits that even the dogmatic type may be true and he may be wrong; he tends to relate most to the sort of dependence that Schleiermacher calls religion. Freud agrees with Schleiermacher that religion may be true and necessary.

These admissions make Freud's blanket rejection of religion seem prejudiced, unreasonable, and even cruel. In effect, he feigns not to care that religious tenets may be true, have altruistic goals, give comfort, and are the most significant and influential part of human culture.

The Dynamics of Religion. The assumption that the desire for satisfaction is wrong is as clearly unfounded as to say that the desire for food and water would be wrong. Freud assumes that all religion involves is a desire for comfort. But some religious obligations are not comfortable. One does them out of a sense of duty to God and others. Certainly, those who are persecuted and martyred do not find comfort.

The cultural ignorance of our ancestors does not automatically disqualify their religious judgment, any more than the lack of formal training means someone cannot have wisdom. In fact, the opposite may be true if education has a hidden agenda of instilling prejudice. One can be educated by secularist culture away from a thoughtful consideration of religious matters.

Rather than draining energy from caring about the world, religion historically has stimulated the highest help to it. Another great psychologist, William *James, showed that saints are strong, not weak. His classic *Varieties of Religious Experiences* found that those who are in touch with a higher world often have greater motivation to change this world. On the other hand, it is not selfish to desire justice or to receive a reward. What is wrong with desiring what is right? If the right is not done in this life, why not desire it in the next, assuming there is a rational hope that the next world exists? By the same token, why not reward good and punish evil? Experience teaches that this is a valuable way to learn what is worthwhile.

Regarding human passions, experience shows that true religion does not contribute to uncontrolled passion, except when religious passions are manipulated to serve an inappropriate national or racial purpose. Otherwise, religion represses and controls the human passions. Religion is a fire that motivates morality, a catalyst for commitment to values. It is the driving force behind the control of passion.

Since humans never outgrow their dependence on the Universe or All, why reject it as invalid? It is not a weakness to say that we are always dependent beings. It means we are constituted so as creatures who need to receive from the hand of the Creator. To assume that admitting a real need is a sign of psychological weakness is like saying hunger and thirst are neuroses. Everyone also has a basic need for commitment, or what Paul *Tillich called an "ultimate commitment." Freud admitted that his commitment was to the god, Reason (Logos). The question isn't whether one has an ultimate commitment but whether what he is committed to is really ultimate. Contrary to Freud, religion is needed. Human beings will never be able to control everything nor be content alone. *Augustine was right when he said the soul is restless until it finds its rest in God. Even the modern existential atheists (*see* CAMUS, ALBERT; SARTRE, JEAN-PAUL) acknowledged their need for God (*see* GOD, NEED FOR).

The failure of many to use religion properly does not invalidate it, any more than committing adultery disproves the value of marriage. The value of religion is seen better by those who accept it than those who reject it. This is seen in Freud's rejection of the Bible as unhistorical without checking the authenticity of the biblical documents. Freud's rejection of it was neither based on reason nor evidence. To borrow his own argument, Freud rejected the Bible based on his own wish, without rational evidence. Freud gives no attention to the rational or experiential arguments for the existence of God (*see* GOD, EVIDENCE FOR). He simply wishes them away.

A brief response is in order to what Freud claimed were inadequate justifications of religion. Freud is correct that wish-fulfillment, belief in the face of absurdity, belief contrary to reality, subjective mental states, and ancestral beliefs are inadequate bases for belief. Religion should not be accepted simply because it is consistent, and certainly not because it is absurd. A completely indefinable God is of little interest to man.

Freud defines religion differently than does Schleiermacher and so his rejection of absolute dependence is poorly argued. Morality need not be based solely on reason or on religious authority; it may be based on the reasonable acceptance of an ultimate authority.

Will Reason Replace Religion? Freud affirms that he is unwilling to give up science, yet he claims this is no illusion. If so, then a believer's unwillingness to give up God should not be considered an illusion either. Contrary to Freud's claim, if atheism is true then it is both dangerous and destructive of religion. For belief in God is absolutely foundational to most forms of religion. Further, Freud has an unrealistic view of human nature. Another unbeliever, Thomas Hobbes, is closer to the truth. Neither science nor resignation adequately replaces religion, as is evidenced by the existential despair of people without God. And reason is an incomplete basis for morality. We need a God to explain why there are universal reasons for doing certain things. Likewise, individual maturity and cosmic dependence are not incompatible. One can have a strong character and yet be totally dependent on God. Compare Moses, Elijah, Joan of Arc, and Oliver Cromwell.

A Response to Freud's Claim That Religion Is an Illusion. It is difficult to put Freud's position into any kind of argument that has premises to challenge. Perhaps the following is what is meant:

1. An illusion is something based only in wish, not in reality.
2. The belief in God has the characteristics of an illusion.
3. Therefore, belief in God is a wish not based in reality.

Of course, in this form the minor premise can be challenged easily. Not all who believe in God do so simply because they wish for a Cosmic Comforter. Some find God because they thirst for reality. Many find God because they are interested in truth, not simply because they are concerned about feeling good.

Further, there are many discomforting dimensions to the Christian belief in God. God is not only a Father who provides; he is also a Judge who punishes. Christians believe in hell, and yet no one really wishes this to be true.

Freud may have it backwards. Maybe our images of earthly fathers are patterned after God, rather than the reverse. Maybe this is because God has created us in his image, rather than the reverse. Perhaps the Christian's belief in God is not based on the desire to *create* a Father. Rather, maybe the atheist's belief that there is no God is based on the desire to *kill* the Father. After all, the Bible declares that rebellious human desires repress the truth about God (Rom. 1:18) because people choose to live a lifestyle contrary to his character (cf. Psalm 14).

The mere human desire for God is not the only basis for believing that God exists. There are good reasons for believing that God exists (*see* God, Evidence for). Freud's argument would, at best, only apply to those who had no other basis than their own wish that God exists. What is more, God may exist even if many (or all) people have the wrong reason for believing/wishing that he does. Just because one wishes to win the lottery does not mean that will happen. Some do win it. Just because many wish for a better way of life does not mean it is unobtainable. Many do obtain it.

Further, Freud confuses *wish* and *need*. What if, as even many atheists admit, there is a *real need* for God in the human heart. Children want candy, but they need food. If the desire for God is a need, not merely a want, then Freud's analysis of religious experience is inadequate.

It may be that Freud's belief that there is no God is itself an illusion. If one does not wish to obey God, it is much easier to believe that no God exists. Indeed, for one living in sin and rebellion against God, it is very comforting to believe that neither he nor hell exists (Ps. 14:1; Rom. 1:18f.).

Sources

S. Freud, *Moses and Monotheism*
———, *The Future of an Illusion*
———, *Totem and Taboo*
R. C. Sproul, *If There is a God, Why Are There Atheists?*
N. L. Geisler, *Philosophy of Religion*, chapter 4
P. Vitz, *The Religious Unconsciousness of Sigmund Freud*

Genealogies, Open or Closed. From an apologetic standpoint, the problem of "open" or "closed" genealogies is this: If they are open (have gaps), then why do they appear closed, especially in Genesis 5 and 11 where exact ages at which the children were born are mentioned? If they are closed, then the creation of mankind is placed somewhere around 4000 B.C., which flies in the face of all the historical and scientific evidence for a minimum date for humanity (*see* GENESIS, DAYS OF). Since they must be either open or closed, there is an apologetic problem either way with regard to the authenticity of the Genesis record.

Solutions to the Problem. *Closed Chronology View.* According to the closed chronology view, there are no gaps in the list in Genesis 5 and 11. They are both complete and provide all the numbers necessary for determining the age of the human race.

Arguments. In favor of the closed chronology view, different arguments have been offered. The strongest is the *prima facie* argument. The genealogies appear to be closed. For not only is the age given at which the son is born, and his son, and so on, but the total age of the father after he had the son is given. For example, the text says, "When Adam had lived 130 years, he had a son . . . and he named him Seth. . . . Altogether, Adam lived 930 years, and then he died. When Seth had lived 105 years, he became the father of Enos . . ." (Gen. 5:3–6). This wording appears to leave no room for gaps.

With one exception, no lists in the Bible supply missing links in this genealogy. There are only two other lists of this early period covered by Genesis 5 and 11 and both have the same names in them

Genesis 5, 11	1 Chronicles 1:1–28	Luke 3:34–38
Adam	Adam	Adam
Seth	Seth	Seth
Enosh	Enosh	Enosh
Kenan	Kenan	Kenan
Mahalalel	Mahalalel	Mahalalel
Jared	Jared	Jared
Enoch	Enoch	Enoch
Methuselah	Methuselah	Methuselah
Lamech	Lamech	Lamech
Noah	Noah	Noah
Shem	Shem	Shem
Arphaxad	Arphaxad	Arphaxad
———	———	Cainan
Shelah/Salah	Shelah/Salah	Shelah/Salah
Eber	Eber	Eber
Peleg	Peleg	Peleg
Reu	Reu	Reu
Serug	Serug	Serug
Nahor	Nahor	Nahor
Terah	Terah	Terah
Abram	Abram /Abraham	Abraham

The one exception is Cainan (in the Luke 3 list). Otherwise, disregarding the alternate spelling of Salah/Shelah and Abram's changed name to Abraham, the lists are identical and reveal no gaps. The same names appear in both, with no missing generations apparent.

It is argued that there is no solid evidence for human civilization that goes back farther than about 4000 B.C. So-called fossil "humans" are not descendants of Adam. They have been explained variously as (1) a pre-Adamic race that was wiped out between Genesis 1:1 and 1:2 (the gap theory); (2) prehuman creatures that had human-like forms but were not really human; (3) frauds (Piltdown Man) or misinterpretations (like "Nebraska Man," which turned out to be based on an extinct pig's tooth).

Finally, closed chronology proponents attempt to explain the one gap in the lists (Cainan, Luke 3:36) as either a textual problem, such as a copyist mistake, or the listing of another son of

Arphaxad in addition to Salah. According to this view, Salah and Cainan would be brothers. Hence, Cainan's name in Luke 3 would not represent a gap in the Genesis and Chronicles complete chronologies.

Objections to the Closed Chronology View. The implausible explanation of Luke 3:36. The attempt to explain away Luke 3:36 as no gap seems highly implausible. There is no real manuscript authority for omitting Cainan from Luke 3:36. That sequence is in all major, and virtually all minor, manuscripts. There is absolutely no indication in the text that Cainan should be listed as a brother of Salah. The grammatical construction is the same for all the other names in the list who were sons. Although the Greek reads "of" or "from" without the word *son,* the translators rightly supply *son* since it is what is implied in every other case in the list. Making this one an exception, when it has the same construction, is begging the question. There is no precedent in any of the genealogical lists for listing Cainan as anything but the father of Salah.

The only other explanation is that both Genesis 11 and 1 Chronicles are outlines that hit the significant points in the family tree. They have at least one known gap in their genealogies.

Other known gaps. The genealogy of Christ in Matthew 1 has at least one serious known gap, even though the text reads that Jehoram was the father of Uzziah (vs. 8), it is known from 1 Chronicles 3 that three missing generations separate Joram and Uzziah:

Matthew 1:8	1 Chronicles 3:11–12
Jehoram	Jehoram
———	Ahaziah
———	Joash
———	Amaziah
Uzziah	Azariah (more commonly Uzziah)

Now since there are known gaps in the genealogies, even from a strictly biblical point of view the genealogies cannot be considered closed.

Scientific and historical evidence. Even if one takes the most conservative interpretation of what constitutes a human remain of "modern man," the evidence is still strong that there were human beings around well before 4000 B.C. Peoples appear to have wandered North America since 10,000 B.C. Even if all fossil finds before Cro-Magnon and Neanderthal peoples were not human, there are numerous complete skeletons of these groups dated before 10,000 B.C. Even if one discounts all prehistoric precivilization fossils and speaks only of "civilized" humankind, the time extends several thousand years earlier than 4000 B.C. There was a civilization in Egypt well before this time. Scientific and historical evidence would seem to rule out a closed genealogy.

Open Genealogies. The scientific evidence. Open genealogies are a better solution to the problem.

As already discussed, even discounting the exaggerated claims of supposedly fossil human beings millions of years or even hundreds of thousands of years old, there is strong evidence for the existence for "modern" humans well beyond 4000 B.C., which a closed genealogy demands.

The biblical evidence. The biblical evidence for an open genealogy with an unknown number of missing generations is supported. First, there are those three missing generations in Matthew 1:8, even though the Greek *gennao* ("begat" KJV; "was the father of" NIV) is used. In biblical Hebrew culture being a *father* was thought in the same light as being a *forefather* or *ancestor. Begat* can mean "was the ancestor of." The word *son (ben)* can mean descendant. Jesus was the "son of David," though at least thirty-one generations separated David from the Christ (the twenty-eight named in Matt. 1:17 plus the three missing from verse 8 that are found in 1 Chron. 3:11–12).

In another example, a comparison of 1 Chronicles 6:3–14 with Ezra 7:2 reveals that Ezra omits six generations between Seraiah and Ezra:

1 Chronicles 6:6–14	Ezra 7:2
Zerahiah	Zerahiah
Meraioth	Meraioth
Amariah	———
Ahitub	———
Zadok	———
Ahimaaz	———
Azariah	———
Johnanan	———
Azariah	Azariah
Amariah	Amariah

There is at least one generation missing even in the Genesis 5 and 11 genealogy which *appears* to be closed. This demonstrates that whatever the text *seems* to say, chronology must be interpreted through an open genealogy.

If there are no gaps in the Genesis 5 and 11 genealogies, implausible examples emerge. For by adding up the numbers one can determine the following dates of birth and death A.A. (after Adam's creation):

Adam (1–930 A.A.)
Seth (130–1042 A.A.)
Enosh (235–1140)
Kenan (325–1236)
Mahalalel (395–1290)
Jared (460–1422)

Enoch (622–987)
Methuselah (687–1656)
Lamech (874–1651)
Noah (1056–2006)
Shem (1558–2158)
Arphaxad (1658–2096)
Salah (1693–2126)
Eber (1723–2187)
Peleg (1757–1996)
Reu (1787–2026)
Serug (1819–2049)
Nahor (1849–1997)
Terah (1878–2083)
Abraham (2008–2183)
Isaac (2108–2228)
Jacob (2168–2315)

First, Adam, the first man (*see* ADAM, HISTORICITY OF), would have been a contemporary of Noah's father. For Adam died in the year 930 A.A. (after Adam's creation). Lamech, Noah's father, was born in 874 A.A. This means they were contemporaries for fifty-six years. Likewise, Abraham only missed being a contemporary of Noah by two years. But there is no indication that this is the case.

It is more implausible to assume that Nahor, the grandfather of Abraham, died before his great, great, great, great, great, great, grandfather Noah. For Noah died 2006 A.A. and Nahor died in 1997 A.A.

Isaac would have been born fifty years before Noah's son Shem died.

In Genesis 10:4 a man (Javan) is said to bring forth peoples, not individuals (e.g., Kittim and Dodanim). The *im* on the end of their names is plural, indicating a plurality of people—a tribe or nation.

If there are no gaps then significant population improbabilities emerge. Numbers 3:19, 27–28 says that the four sons of Kohath gave rise to the families of the Amramites, Isharites, Hebronites, and Uzzielites, of which the males alone numbered 8600 only one year after the Exodus. Thus, the grandfather of Moses had in the lifetime of Moses 8600 male descendants alone, 2750 of whom were between the ages of thirty and fifty (Num. 4:36). This would be a very prolific family indeed.

Levi's son Kohath was born before Jacob's descent into Egypt (Gen. 46:11) where Israel stayed for 430 years (Exod. 12:40, 41). Since Moses was 80 years old at the time of the Exodus (Exod. 7:7) he must have been born more than 350 years after Kohath. Yet Kohath was Moses' grandfather (1 Chron. 6:1–3). This would make the generation between Kohath and Moses (viz., Amram) 350 years long when the life span of Moses' period had already diminished to 120. Well before Moses' time, Abraham died at 175, Isaac at 120, Jacob at 147, and Joseph at 110.

Nowhere does the Bible even suggest a summation of the numbers listed in Genesis 5 and 11. No chronological statement is deduced from these numbers either in Genesis 5 and 11 or anywhere else in Scripture. There is no total given anywhere in the biblical text of the time that elapsed between creation and Abraham, as there is for the time in Egypt (Exod. 12:40) and the time from the Exodus to Solomon (1 Kings 6:1).

The symmetry of the text argues against it being complete. Scholars have noted that their symmetrical arrangement of Genesis 5 and 11 into groups of ten argues for their compression. Noah is the tenth name from Adam and Terah the tenth from Noah. Each ends with a father who had three sons. This is certainly the case in Matthew 1 where there are three series of fourteen (double-seven, the number of completeness and perfection), for we know three generations are left out in Matthew 1:8 (cf. 1 Chron. 3:11–12).

Objection to the Open Genealogy View. Of objections to the open genealogy view not yet discussed, the most important one is based on the alleged implausible interpretation of the language of Genesis 5 and 11. It is objected that not only does it seem stretched to find gaps in Genesis 5 or 11, given the language of the text, but it seems like isogesis (reading into the text) rather than exegesis (reading out of the text). After all, the name of the father and son are given as well as their age when they had this son who became the father of the next son at a certain age. Listing the father's age at the time of the son's birth is without meaning unless he is the immediate son, and there are no gaps.

In response, some important matters must be kept in mind.

First, the Bible comes out of another culture and linguistic setting. Metaphorical imagery can mislead the reader into thinking the Bible is saying something, when it means something different. In Hebrew, as in English, one can speak of the four "corners" of the earth (Isa. 41:9; cf. Ezek. 7:2). Is the Bible saying that the world is square? Some critics say so. Yet the earth is also described as a circle or globe (Isa. 40:22). Is it possible that corners is metaphorical language that may mean the geography covered by the four "quarters" of the compass, just as it means when we say it?

Second, as noted in the implausible dates above, even within the Bible there is strong evidence of gaps in the genealogies.

Third, there are ways to understand the text of Genesis 11 that do allow for gaps. The formula phrase "and X lived so many years and begat Y" can mean "and X lived so many years and became the ancestor of Y." This is not speculation, for in Matthew 1:8 ("Jehoram begat Uzziah") it means precisely this. "Begat" must mean "became the ancestor of," since 1 Chronicles 3:11–12 fills in three missing generations between Jehoram and Uzziah. This would not have been an oversight by Matthew, for the genealogy of the line of David was known by every Jewish man.

Allusions to each father's age at the time of the son's birth is not necessarily without meaning. Just because we do not know why God included something in the text does not mean there was no purpose for doing so. It is a bit presumptuous to tell God what he should or should not have put in his inspired Word. B. B. *Warfield suggests that this information should "make a vivid impression on us of the vigor and grandeur of humanity in those old days of the world's prime" (Warfield). This detail lends credibility to the fact that people lived to enormously long ages before the flood (*see* SCIENCE AND THE BIBLE). It makes sense to know that men who lived that long did not have children at age sixteen, like men who live only three score and ten. Even discounting Noah's late age for having children (500), the average age for childbearing in Genesis 5 is over 100 years of age. This is certainly fitting for someone who lives as long as eight hundred or nine hundred years.

Conclusion. The evidence supports the view that the Bible does not give us in Genesis 5 and 11 a closed chronology but an outline genealogy. This is supported by both internal biblical evidence of missing generation(s), even in Genesis 11, but also by external evidence that humankind dates to long before 4000 B.C. This being the case, there is no real conflict on this matter between the Bible and science nor between the Bible and itself. Open genealogy provides an accurate line of descent for lineage purposes, but it does not satisfy our curiosity about the date of human creation.

Sources

M. Anstay, *Chronology of the Old Testament*
A. Custance, *The Genealogies of the Bible*
W. H. Green, "Primeval Chronology," W. Kaiser, ed., *Essays in Old Testament Interpretation*
J. Jordan, "The Biblical Chronology Question: An Analysis," *CSSHQ*, 2:2 (Winter 1979, Spring 1980)
R. Newman, et al., *Genesis One and the Origin of the Earth*
F. Schaeffer, *No Final Conflict*
B. B. Warfield, "On the Antiquity and the Unity of the Human Race," *PTR*, 1911

Genesis, Days of. The problem posed by modern science to defenders of the "literal" interpretation of Genesis 1 is legendary: How can there be six literal days of creation when scientific dating has demonstrated that life emerged gradually over many millions of years?

Six Twenty-four-Hour Days. Apologists are quick to note that this problem is acute only for those who hold to six successive, twenty-four hours (= 144 hours) of creation. It does not apply to other twenty-four-hour views nor to the view that interprets "days" to mean long periods of time.

Arguments for Solar Days. The problem is deepened by the fact that there is *prima facie* evidence to indicate that the days of Genesis 1 are indeed twenty-four-hour periods. Consider the following arguments:

The normal meaning of yom. The usual meaning of the Hebrew word *yom* ("day") is twenty-four hours unless the context indicates otherwise. But the context does not indicate anything but a twenty-four-hour day in Genesis 1.

The numbers are in series. When numbers are used in a series (1, 2, 3 . . .) in connection with days it refers to twenty-four-hour days. There is no exception to this elsewhere in the Old Testament.

"Evening and morning" is used. The phrase "and there was evening and there was morning" denotes each period. Since the literal twenty-four-hour day on the Jewish Calendar began at sunset and ended before sunset the next day, Genesis 1 must refer to literal days.

The days are compared to a work week. According to the Law of Moses (Exod. 20:11) the Jewish work week of Sunday through Friday was to be followed by rest on Saturday, just as God had done in his six-day week of creation. But we know that the Jewish work week refers to six, successive, twenty-four-hour days.

Life cannot exist without light. According to Genesis 1, the sun and stars were not made until the fourth day (1:14), but there was life on the third day (1:11–13). However, life cannot exist for long without light. Hence, the "days" must not be long periods of time.

Plants cannot live without animals. Plants were created on the third day (1:11–13) and animals were not created until the fifth day (1:20–23). But there is a symbiotic relation between plants and animals, one depending on the other for its life. For example, plants give off oxygen and take in carbon dioxide and animals do the reverse. Hence, plants and animals must have been created together, not separated by long periods of time.

A Response to the Arguments. In spite of these arguments, the case is less than definitive. Those who reject the six-solar-day view reply:

Day (yom) can mean a long period. Most often the Hebrew word *yom* means twenty-four hours. However, the meaning in Genesis 1 is determined by context, not majority vote. Even in this passage in Genesis 1–2, *yom* is used of the whole of creation. Genesis 2:4 refers to "the day (*yom*)" when they were created. The Hebrew word appears elsewhere for long periods, as in Psalm 90:4 (cited in 2 Peter 3:8): "For a thousand years in your sight are like a day (*yom*) that has just gone by, or like a watch in the night."

Numbered days need not be solar. Neither is there a rule of the Hebrew language demanding that all numbered days in a series refer to twenty-four-hour days. Even if there were no exceptions in the Old Testament, it would not mean that "day" in Genesis 1 could not refer to more than one twenty-four-hour period. But there is another example in the Old Testament. Hosea 6:1–2 reads: "Come, let us return to the LORD. He has torn us to pieces but he will heal us; he has injured us but he will bind up our wounds. After two days he will revive us; on the third day he will restore us, that we may live in his presence." Clearly the prophet is not speaking of solar "days" but of longer periods in the future. Yet he numbers the days in series.

There was a beginning and an end. That this phrase is *often* used in connection with twenty-four-hour days does not mean it is *always* used in this way. Genesis 1 is a good candidate to be an exception. Further, if one is going to take everything in Genesis 1 in a strictly literal way, then the phrase "evening and morning" does not encompass a twenty-four-hour day, but only the late afternoon and early morning. This is considerably less than twenty-four hours. Technically the text does not say the day was composed of "evening and morning" (thus making a twenty-four-hour Jewish day). Rather, it simply says "And there was evening, and there was morning—the first day" (1:5). The phrase may be a figure of speech indicating a beginning and end of a definite period of time, just as we refer to "the dawn of world history" or the "sunset years of one's life."

Finally, if every day in this series of seven is to be taken as twenty-four hours, then why is the phrase "evening and morning" not used of the seventh day? In fact, as we shall see, the seventh day is not twenty-four hours, and thus there is no necessity to take the other days as twenty-four hours either, since all of them alike use the same word *yom* and have a series of numbers with them.

The six periods are comparable to a work week. It is true that the creation week is compared with a work week (Exod. 20:11). However, it is not uncommon in the Old Testament to make unit-for-unit rather than minute-for-minute comparisons. For example, God appointed forty years of wandering for forty days of disobedience (Num. 14:34). And in Daniel 9:24–27, 490 days equal 490 years.

We know the seventh day is more than twenty-four hours, since, according to Hebrew 4, the seventh day is still going on. For Genesis says "on the seventh day he [God] rested" (2:2), but Hebrews 4:5–10 informs us that God is still in that Sabbath rest into which he entered after he created.

When did light appear? Light was not created on the fourth day, as defenders of the solar day argue. Rather, it was made on the very first day, when God said, "Let there be light" (Gen. 1:3). As to why there was light on the first day and the sun did not appear until the fourth day, there are two possibilities. Some scholars have noted a parallelism between the first three days (light, water, and land—all empty) and the second three days (light, water, and land—all filled with bodies). This may indicated a parallelism in which the first and fourth days cover the same period of time. In that case we are dealing with three periods of time, not six, and the sun existed from the beginning. Others have argued that, while the sun was created on the first day, it did not *appear* visually until the fourth day. Perhaps, this was due to a vapor cloud that allowed light through but not the distinct shape of the heavenly bodies emanating the light.

Not all plants, animals are interdependent. If Genesis 1 is a parallel outline for creation, covering three days as suggested above, then the problem of plants and animals being created separately disappears. Also, some plants and animals are interdependent, but not all. Genesis does not mention all the plants and animals but only some.

If the days are six successive periods, then those forms of plant and animal life that need each other could have been created together. In fact, the basic order of events is the order of dependence. For example, many plants and animals can exist without humans (and they were created first), but humans (who are created on the last day) cannot exist without plants and animals.

"Days" as Time Periods. Other orthodox Christians believe the days of Genesis 1 can involve long periods of time. They offer biblical and scientific evidence for this view.

The Biblical Evidence for Long Days. There are many indications in the text of Scripture to support the belief that the creation "days" were longer than twenty-four hours. The following are those most often given in support of this position.

Day (yom) often means time. Returning to word meanings, it should be noted how *yom* is used in the Bible. The word sometimes means a *prophetic day*, a significant future time as in "the day of the LORD" (Joel 2:31; cf. 2 Peter 3:10). As noted above, "A day is as a thousand years" in Psalm 90:4 and 2 Peter 3:8. And in Genesis 2:4 the word summarizes the entire creation. This indicates a broad meaning of the word *yom* in the Bible that parallels the range of meaning for the English *day*.

As also noted above, Hebrews 4:3–5 teaches that God is still in that seventh-day cessation from creating described as a day in Genesis 2:2–3. This day, then, is at least 6000 years long, even on the shortest chronologies.

The third day is longer. On the third "day" God not only created vegetation but it also grew to maturity. For the text says "The land *produced vegetation:* plants bearing seed according to their kinds and trees bearing fruit with seed in it according to their kinds. And God saw that it was good" (Gen. 1:12, emphasis added). But to grow from seeds to maturity and produce more seeds is a process that takes months or years.

The sixth day is longer. It would also appear that the sixth day was considerably longer than a solar day. Consider everything that happened during this period of time (*see* Newman, Appendix III):

God created all the many thousands of the land animals (Gen. 1:24–25).

God formed man from dust (Gen. 2:7) as a potter (cf. Jer. 18:2f.).

God planted a Garden (Gen. 2:8), suggesting activity involving time.

Adam observed and named all these thousands of animals (Gen. 2:19).

God promised "I will make him a helpmeet" (Gen. 2:18), denoting a subsequent time.

Adam searched for a help mate for himself, apparently among the creatures God had made "But for Adam no suitable helper *was found* [implying a time of searching]" (Gen. 2:20, emphasis added).

God put Adam to sleep for a time and operated on him, taking out one of his ribs and healing the flesh (Gen. 2:21).

Adam indicated he had anticipated Eve for some time (Gen. 2:23).

Eve was brought to Adam who observed her, accepted her, and was joined to her (Gen. 2:22–25).

It seems highly unlikely that all of these events, especially the second, were compressed within a twenty-four-hour period.

The Scientific Evidence for Long Days. Most scientific evidence sets the age of the world at billions of years. The age of the universe is based on the speed of light and the distance of the stars as well as the rate of expansion of the universe. Early rocks have been dated in terms of radioactivity and set at billions of years old. Simply given the rate that salt runs into the sea and the amount of salt there would suggest multimillions of years (*see* ORIGINS, SCIENCE OF).

Views of the Genesis Days. If, of course, the days of Genesis are long periods of time, then there is no conflict with modern science on the age of the earth. But even if the days of Genesis are twenty-four hours there are still ways to reconcile long periods of time with Genesis 1–2.

Revelatory Day View. Some conservative scholars have suggested that the "days" of Genesis may be days of *revelation,* not really days of *creation* (Wiseman). That is, it took God a literal solar week (of 144 hours) to reveal to Adam (or Moses) what he had done in the ages before humans were created. Even the Exodus passages (20:11) which speak of the heavens and earth being *"made" (asah)* in six days can mean "revealed."

Just as a prophet can get revelation from God looking forward to a future series of events (cf. Daniel 2, 7, 9; Revelation 6–19), even so God can reveal a past series of events to one of his servants. Indeed, Moses was on the holy mountain for forty days (Exod. 24:18). God could have taken six of these days to reveal the past creation events to him. Or after God created Adam, he could have taken six literal days to reveal to him what he had done before Adam arrived on the scene. Some scholars believe this material could have been memorized and passed on as the first "history of the heavens and the earth" (Gen. 2:4), just as the other "histories" (lit., "genealogies") were apparently recorded and passed on (for example, Gen. 5:1; 6:9; 10:1).

Alternate Day-Age View. Other evangelical scholars have suggested that the "days" of Genesis are twenty-four-hour periods of time in which God created the things mentioned, but that they are separated by long periods in between. This would account for both the indications of great lengths of time in Genesis 1 and indications that there were twenty-four-hour days involved.

Gap Theories. C. I. Scofield made popular the view that there could be a great gap of time between the first two verses of the Bible into which all of the geological ages fit. In this way the days could be twenty-four hours each and yet the world could be many millions of years old or more.

Others believe that there may be a "gap" or, better, a lapse of time before the six, twenty-four-hour days of Genesis begin. In this case, the first verse of the Bible would not necessarily refer to the original *ex nihilo* creation of God (*see* CREATION, VIEWS OF) but more recent acts of God in forming a world he had previously created (see Waltke).

So there are ways to accommodate long periods of time and still accept a basically literal understanding of Genesis 1–2. There is no necessary conflict between Genesis and the belief that the universe is millions or even billions of years old.

How Old Is the Earth? There seems to be no way to prove how old the universe really is, either from science or from the Bible. There are known and possible gaps in the biblical genealogies. And there are unprovable presuppositions in all the scientific arguments for an old earth, that is, an earth of millions or billions of years old.

Gaps in the Biblical Record. Bishop James Ussher (1581–1656), whose chronology was used in the old Scofield Bible, argued that Adam was created 4004 B.C. However, his calculations are based on the assumption that there are no gaps in the genealogical tables of Genesis 5 and 11. But we know this is false (*see* GENEALOGIES, OPEN OR CLOSED). For the Bible says "Arphaxad . . . became the father of Salah" (Gen. 11:12), but in Jesus' genealogy in Luke 3:36 "Cainan" is listed between Arphaxad and Salah (Shelah). If there is one gap there may be more. Indeed, we know there are more. For example, Matthew 1:8 says "Joram the father of Uzziah," but the parallel listing in 1 Chronicles 3:11–14 illustrates missing generations between Joram and Uzziah (Azariah), namely, Ahaziah, Joash, and Amaziah. Just how many gaps there are in biblical genealogies and how long a time gap this represents is not known. But gaps there are and, hence, complete chronologies cannot be made, only accurate genealogies (lines of descent) are given.

Presuppositions in the Scientific Arguments. There are many scientific arguments for an old universe, some of which are persuasive. However, none of these arguments is foolproof, and all of them could be wrong. A few examples will illustrate the point of why we should not be dogmatic.

The speed of light may change. In spite of the fact that Einstein considered it absolute, and modern science has held it to be unchanging, it cannot be proven that the speed of light has never changed. Yet the speed of light (ca. 186,000 miles a second) is assumed for many proofs of an old earth. However, *if* the speed of light is constant and *if* God did not also create the light rays when he created the stars, then it would appear that the universe is billions of years old. For it has apparently taken millions of years for that light to get to us. But these are big *"ifs"* that have not been proven. Indeed, they would appear to be unprovable. So, while the argument from the speed of light to an old universe may seem plausible, it is not a demonstrable proof.

Radioactive dating makes assumptions. It is well known that U235 and U238 give off lead isotopes at a known rate. By measuring the amount of their deposit one can calculate when the decay began. Many early rocks in the earth's crust have been dated in the billions of years by this method. But again, as plausible as this may be, it is not proven. For one must assume at least two things to come to the conclusion that the world is billions of years old. First, it must be assumed that there were no lead deposits at the beginning. Second, one must assume that the rate of decay has been unchanged throughout its entire history. Neither can be proven. Hence, there is no way to prove by radioactive dating that the world is billions of years old.

There is no conflict. The same is apparently true of all arguments for an old earth.

For example, the oceans have a known amount of salt and minerals in them and these go into the ocean at a fixed rate every year. By simple mathematics it can be determined how many years this has been going on. However, here too it must be assumed that there were no salts and minerals in the ocean at the start and that the rate has not changed. A worldwide flood, such as the Bible describes, would certainly have changed the rate of deposits during that period.

All of this is not to say that the universe is not billions of years old. It may be. However, the arguments in favor of great age all possess presuppositions that cannot be proven. With this in view, the following conclusions are appropriate: There is no demonstrated conflict between Genesis 1–2 and scientific fact. The real conflict is not between God's *revelation* in the Bible and scientific *fact*; it is between some Christian *interpretations* of the Bible and many scientists' *theories* about the age of the world.

Indeed, since the Bible does not say exactly how old the universe is, the age of the earth is not a test for orthodoxy. In fact, many orthodox, evangelical scholars hold the universe is millions or billions of years old, including Augustine, B. B. Warfield, John Walvoord, Francis Schaeffer, Gleason Archer, Hugh Ross, and most leaders of the movement that produced the famous "Chicago Statement" on the inerrancy of the Bible (1978).

Sources

Augustine, *The City of God*, Book 11
N. L. Geisler, *Knowing the Truth about Creation*
H. Morris, *Biblical Cosmology and Modern Science*
———, *The Genesis Record*
R. Newman, *Genesis One and the Origin of the Earth*
B. Ramm, *The Christian View of Science and Scripture*
H. Ross, *Creation and Time*
B. Waltke, *The Creation Account in Genesis 1:1–3*, 5 vols.
D. Wiseman, *Creation Revealed in Six Days*
D. Young, *Christianity and the Age of the Earth*
E. Young, *Studies in Genesis One*

Gnostic Gospels. *See* **GNOSTICISM; GOSPEL OF THOMAS; NAG HAMMADI GOSPELS.**

Gnosticism. The Gnostics followed a variety of religious movements that stressed *gnosis* or knowledge, especially of one's origins. Cosmological *dualism was also a feature of the system—opposed spiritual worlds of good and evil. The material world was aligned with the dark world of evil.

No one is certain of the origins of Gnosticism. Some believe it was rooted in a heretical group within Judaism. Supporters of this theory cite *The Apocalypse of Adam* and *The Paraphrase of Shem* as early Gnostic documents revealing Jewish origins. Others give it a Christian context. An incipient form may have infiltrated the church in Colosse. Or it may have had a totally pagan root. During the second through the fourth centuries it was addressed as a major threat by such church fathers as *Augustine, Justin *Martyr, *Irenaeus, *Clement of Alexandria, *Tertullian, and *Origen.

Early Sources. Irenaeus's book *Against Heresies* provides extensive treatment of what Gnostics believed. Three Coptic Gnostic codices were published. Two were discovered in *Nag Hammadi, Egypt in 1945. Codex Askewianus contains *Pistis Sophia* and Codex Brucianus contains *The Book of Jeu.* Best known among the Nag Hammadi documents is the **Gospel of Thomas.* A third work from this period, Codex Berolinensis, was found elsewhere and published in 1955. It contains a *Gospel of Mary* [Magdalene], a *Sophia of Jesus, Acts of Peter,* and an *Apocryphon of John.* The first translation of a tractate, *The Gospel of Truth,* appeared in 1956, and a translation of fifty-one treatises, including *Gospel of Thomas,* appeared in 1977.

Leaders. The early fathers of the church held that Gnosticism had first-century roots and that Simon the Sorcerer of Samaria (Acts 8) was the first Gnostic. According to church fathers, Simon practiced magic, claimed to be divine, and taught that his companion, a former prostitute, was reincarnated Helen of Troy. Hippolytus (d. 236) attributed the *Apophasis Megale* to Simon. Simon's disciple, a former Samaritan named Menander, who taught in Syrian Antioch near the end of the first century, taught that those who believed in him would not die. That claim was nullified when he died.

At the beginning of the second century, Saturninus (Satornilos) asserted that the incorporeal Christ was the redeemer, denying that Christ was really incarnated in human flesh. This belief is shared with *docetism. In this period Cerinthus of Asia Minor was teaching adoptionism, the heresy that Jesus was merely a man upon whom Christ descended at his baptism. Since Christ could not die, he departed from Jesus before his crucifixion. Basilides of Egypt was called both a dualist by Irenaeus and a monist by Hippolytus.

One of the more controversial, though atypical, Gnostics was *Marcion of Pontus. He believed that the God of the Old Testament was different from the God of the New Testament and that the canon of Scripture included only a truncated version of Luke and ten of Paul's Epistles (all but the pastoral Epistles). His views were severely attacked by Tertullian (ca. 160s–ca. 215). Marcion became a stimulus for the early church to officially define the limits of the canon (*see* Apocrypha, Old and New Testaments; Bible, Canonicity of).

Valentinus of Alexandria was another prominent Gnostic. He came to Rome in 140 and taught that there were a series of divine emanations. He divided humanity into three classes: (1) Hylics or unbelievers, who were immersed in material and fleshly nature; (2) psychics or common Christians, who lived by faith and pneumatics; and (3) spiritual Gnostics. His followers included Ptolemaeus, Heracleon, Theodotus, and Marcus. Heracleon's interpretation of John is the first known New Testament commentary.

Gnostic-like beliefs persisted into the fourth century. Among the late manifestations was Manichaeism, a dualistic cult that trapped Augustine in his pre-Christian life. Against it he wrote many treatises, which are collected in *The Anti-Manichaean Writings* in the *Ante-Nicene Fathers*.

Teachings. Since Gnosticism lacked a common authority, it encompassed a variety of beliefs. Central to many, if not most, were:

1. a cosmic dualism between spirit and matter, good and evil;
2. a distinction between a finite Old Testament God, *Yahweh*, who was equated with *Plato's Demiurge or Craftsman, and the transcendent God of the New Testament;
3. view of creation as resulting from the fall of Sophia (Wisdom);
4. identification of matter as evil;
5. belief that most people are ignorant of their origins and condition;
6. identification of sparks of divinity that are encapsulated in certain spiritual individuals;
7. faith in a docetic Redeemer, who was not truly human and did not die on the cross. This Redeemer brought salvation in the form of a secret *gnosis* or knowledge that was communicated by Christ after his resurrection.
8. a goal of escaping the prison of the body, traversing the planetary spheres of hostile demons, and being reunited with God;
9. a salvation based not on faith or works, but upon special knowledge or *gnosis* of one's true condition;
10. a mixed view of morality. Carpocrates urged his followers to engage in deliberate promiscuity. Epiphanes, his son, taught that licentiousness was God's law. Most Gnostics, however, took a strongly ascetic view of sexual intercourse and marriage, contending that the creation of woman was the source of evil and procreation of children simply multiplied the number of persons in bondage to the evil material world. Salvation of women depended on their one day becoming men and returning to the conditions of Eden before Eve was created. Oddly enough, women were prominent in many Gnostic sects.
11. interpretation of baptism and the Lord's supper as spiritual symbols of the *gnosis*;
12. view of the resurrection as spiritual, not physical (*see* Resurrection, Physical Nature of). In the Nag Hammadi codices *De Resurrectione* affirms that

> The Saviour swallowed up death. . . . For he laid aside the world that perishes. He changed himself into an incorruptible aeon and raised himself up, after he had swallowed up the visible by the invisible, and he gave us the way to immortality. . . . But if we are made manifest in this world wearing him, we are his beams and we are encompassed by him until our setting, which is our death in this life. We are drawn upward by him like beams by the sun, without being held back by anything. This is the spiritual resurrection which swallows up the psychic together with the fleshly. [Malinine, 45]

Gnosticism as an organized movement acknowledging its source all but died. The sole surviving remnant is in southwestern Iran. However, many Gnostic teachings live on among new agers, existentialists, and Bible critics. The revival of interest in the Gospel of Thomas by the Jesus Seminar is a case in point. There is also a tendency, even among some evangelical scholars (see Geisler), to deny the physical nature of the resurrection. However, Gnosticism lives today in the New Age Movement in an extensive way (Jones).

Evaluation. Gnosticism was thoroughly critiqued by the early church fathers, especially Irenaeus, Tertullian, Augustine, and Origin, though Origin bought into some of their views. Marcion's view of the canon is critiqued in the articles Apocrypha, New Testament, and BIBLE, CANONICITY OF. For more on Gnosticism see the articles CHRIST, DEATH OF; DOCETISM, and DUALISM.

Sources

Augustine, *The Anti-Manichaean Writings*
C. A. Evans, *Nag Hammadi Texts and the Bible*
A. Frederick, et al., *The Gnostic Gospels*
N. L. Geisler, *The Battle for the Resurrection*
R. M. Grant, *Gnosticism and Early Christianity*
P. Jones, *Spirit Wars*
M. Malinine, et al., *De Resurrection*
J. M. Robinson, *The Nag Hammadi Library in English*
F. Seigert, et al., *Nag-Hammadi-Register*
Tertullian, *Against the Valentinians*
———, *Five Books Against Marcion*
———, *On the Flesh of Christ*
———, *On the Resurrection of the Flesh*
E. Yamauchi, *Pre-Christian Gnosticism*

God, Alleged Disproofs of. Many theists offer proofs for God. Likewise, devout atheists (*see* ATHEISM) have offered what they consider to be disproofs of God corresponding to the ontological argument, the cosmological argument, the teleological argument, and the moral argument. Specific arguments by nontheists against the apologetic arguments are covered in GOD, OBJECTIONS TO PROOFS FOR.

An Ontological Disproof of God. One atheist argued as follows (see Findlay, 111f.):

1. God is by definition a necessary existence.
2. But necessity cannot apply to existence.
3. Therefore, God cannot exist.

In support of the crucial second premise he noted that necessity is a logical term, not an ontological one. That is, necessity applies to propositions, not to being or reality.

Theists point out that the second premise is self-defeating. It is a necessary statement about existence that claims that no necessary statements can be made about existence. Who said necessity cannot apply to existence? This legislates meaning rather than listens to it. In fact, the very criterion by which one concludes that necessity cannot apply to existence is arbitrary. There is no necessity to accept it.

A Cosmological Disproof of God. This argument against God can be stated:

1. God is a self-caused being (see Sartre, 758, 762).
2. But it is impossible to cause one's own being, for a cause is prior to its effect, and one can't be prior to oneself.
3. Therefore, God cannot exist.

This argument commits the straw-man fallacy in the first premise. Theists do not hold that God is a *self*-caused being. This is a contradictory concept. Rather, theists define God as an *un*caused being, which is not contradictory. Even atheists believe that the universe is uncaused, having always existed. But if God is not defined as a self-caused being, then the disproof fails.

A Teleological Disproof of God. A teleological argument against God's existence can be stated (see Hume, Part 8):

1. The universe was either designed or else it happened by chance.
2. But chance is an adequate cause of the universe.
3. Therefore, the universe was not designed.

In support of the second premise, two lines of argument have been offered. First, in an infinite amount of time every combination will occur, no matter what the odds against it. Second, no matter what the odds against something happening, it can still happen and sometimes does.

Theists note that this falls short of a disproof, since it is not logically necessary. Second, even as an argument (but not a disproof) it has serious problems. The evidence is much stronger that the universe had a beginning, since it is running out of usable energy (*see* THERMODYNAMICS, LAWS OF; BIG BANG THEORY), and since an infinite number of moments before today could not have elapsed, no infinite series can be traversed (*see KALAM* COSMOLOGICAL ARGUMENT). Further, science is not based on *chance but on observation and repetition. These principles inform us that anything as complex as life does not occur without an intelligent cause.

A Moral Disproof of God. The moral argument against God is by far the most popular (*see* EVIL, PROBLEM OF). A common version of this argument goes this way (see Bayle, 157f.):

1. An all-good God would destroy evil.
2. An all-powerful God could destroy evil.
3. But evil is not destroyed.
4. Therefore, as such God does not exist.

This argument also falls short of being a disproof because the first premise is ambiguous and the third premise fails to fully state the actual conditions. First of all, *destroy* is ambiguous. If it means "annihilate," then God cannot destroy all evil without destroying all freedom (*see* FREE WILL). But no atheist wants freedom to disbelieve in God taken away. Second, if destroy means "defeat," the third premise fails to add the important word *yet*: "Evil is not *yet* destroyed." Once this is stated, the argument does not follow, since God may yet defeat evil in the future. If the atheist (*see* ATHEISM) responds by claiming "Evil is not yet defeated *and never will be,*" there is no basis for the statement. Only God knows the future with certainty. So the atheist must be God in order to eliminate God by this kind of reasoning.

The Existential Disproof of God. Existentialist philosopher, Jean-Paul Sartre, argued:

1. If God exists, then all is determined.
2. But if all is determined, then I am not free.
3. But I am free.
4. Therefore, God does not exist.

My freedom is undeniable. For even the attempt to deny it, affirms it. But if freedom is undeniable, then God cannot exist. For an omniscient being (God) who exists knows everything that will come to pass. Thus, everything is determined, for if it did not come to pass as he knew it would, then God would have been wrong. But an omniscient being cannot be wrong. Therefore, if God exists, everything is determined. But all is not determined, because I am free. Hence, there is no God.

Theists challenge the second premise. There is no contradiction between determination and free choice. God can determine things in accordance with our free choice. They can be determined with respect to his (fore)knowledge and yet free with regard to our choice (*see* DETERMINISM). Just as every event in a video replay of a game is determined, yet it was free (*see* FREE WILL) when the game was played, every event in the world can be determined from God's perspective, yet free from ours.

Sources

P. Bayle, *Selections from Bayle's Dictionary*
W. L. Craig, *The Kalam Cosmological Argument*
J. N. Findlay, "Can God's Existence Be Disproved?" A. Plantinga, ed., *The Ontological Argument*
R. Flint, *Agnosticism*
R. Garriguou-LaGrange, *God: His Existence and His Nature*
N. L. Geisler and W. Corduan, *Philosophy of Religion*
D. Hume, *Dialogues*, Part 8
A. Kenny, *Five Ways*
J. P. Moreland, *The Existence of God Debate*
B. Russel, *Why I Am Not a Christian*
J. P. Sartre, *Being and Nothingness*

God, Coherence of. ***See*** **GOD, OBJECTIONS TO PROOFS FOR; PANENTHEISM.**

God, Evidence for. The best known arguments for God's existence are the *cosmological argument, the *teleological argument, the *moral argument, and the *ontological argument. Respectively, these are the arguments from *creation* (Gk., *cosmos*, "universe, world"), *design* (Gk., *telos*, "end, purpose"), and the idea of a perfect *being* (Gk., *ontos*, "reality, being"). In addition to these the axiological argument, the anthropological argument, and the argument from religious experience are often used. The axiological argument (Gk., *axios,* "value, worth") is the argument from making value judgments. It is closely associated with the moral argument, the argument from a moral law to a Moral Law Giver.

The Cosmological Argument. There is a universe rather than none at all, which must have been caused by something beyond itself. The law of causality (*see* CAUSALITY, PRINCIPLE OF) says that every finite thing is caused by something other than itself.

There are two basic forms of this argument. The first says that the cosmos or universe needed a cause at its *beginning,* the second form argues that it needs a cause to *continue* existing.

A Cause at the Beginning. The argument that the universe had a beginning caused by something beyond the universe can be stated this way:

1. The universe had a beginning.
2. Anything that had a beginning must have been caused by something else.
3. Therefore the universe was caused by something else (a Creator).

Scientific evidence. Both scientific and philosophical evidence can be used to support this argument. According to the second law of thermodynamics, in a closed, isolated system, such as the universe is, the amount of usable energy is decreasing. The universe is running down, hence cannot be eternal. Otherwise, it would have run out of usable energy long ago. Things left to themselves, without outside intelligent intervention, tend toward disorder. Since the universe has not reached a state of total disorder, this process has not been going on forever.

Another set of evidence comes from the widely accepted *big bang cosmology. According to this view, the universe exploded into being some 15–20 billion years ago. Evidence offered for this includes the (1) "red shift" or Doppler effect noticed in the light from stars as they move away; (2) the radiation echo from space, which has the same wavelength that would be given off by a gigantic cosmic explosion; (3) discovery of a mass of energy such as was expected from an explosion.

Agnostic Robert Jastrow, founder-director of NASA's Goddard Institute of Space Studies, said, "A sound explanation may exist for the explosive birth of our Universe; but if it does, science cannot find out what the explanation is. The scientist's pursuit of the past ends in the moment of creation." But if the universe was created, then it is reasonable to conclude there was a Creator. For everything that has a beginning needs a Beginner.

Philosophical evidence. Time cannot go back into the past forever, for it is impossible to pass through an actual infinite number of moments. A theoretically infinite number of dimensionless points exists between my thumb and first finger, but I cannot get an infinite number of sheets of paper between them no matter how thin they are. Each moment that passes uses up real time that we can never again experience. Moving your finger across an infinite number of books in a library would never get to the last book. You can never finish an infinite series of real things.

If this is so, then time must have had a beginning. If the world never had a beginning, then we could not have reached now. But we have reached now, so time must have begun at a particular point and proceeded to today. Therefore the world is a finite event after all and needs a cause for its beginning. The argument can be summarized:

1. An infinite number of moments cannot be traversed.
2. If an infinite number of moments had to elapse before today, then today would never have come.
3. But today has come.
4. Therefore, an infinite number of moments have not elapsed before today (i.e., the universe had a beginning).
5. But whatever has a beginning is caused by something else.
6. Hence, there must be a Cause (Creator) of the universe.

A Cause Right Now. The previous version of the cosmological argument has been called the "horizontal argument," since it argues in a linear fashion back to a beginning. This argument is also known as the *kalam* cosmological argument. It was formulated by the Arab philosophers of the Middle Ages and employed by Bonaventure (1217–1274). The contemporary philosopher, William Craig, has widely published on it. One problem with the argument is that it only argues that there was once a Creator at the beginning of the universe. It does not show the continuing need for a Creator. This is the point of the vertical form of the cosmological argument. The most famous proponent of this argument was *Thomas Aquinas (1225–1274).

Something is keeping us in existence right now so we don't just disappear. Something not only caused the world to come into being (Gen. 1:1), but something causes it to continue to be (cf. Col. 1:17). The world needs both an originating cause and a conserving cause. This argument answers the basic question: "Why is there something (right now) rather than nothing?" Briefly, it can be put this way:

1. Every part of the universe is dependent.
2. If every part is dependent, then the whole universe must also be dependent.
3. Therefore, the whole universe is dependent for existence right now on some Independent Being.

Critics respond that the second premise is the fallacy of composition. Just because every piece of a mosaic is square does not mean the whole mosaic is square. Also, putting two triangles together does not necessarily make another triangle; it may make a square. The whole may (and sometimes does) have a characteristic not possessed by the parts. Defenders answer that sometimes there is a necessary connection between the parts and the whole. If every piece of a floor is oak, then the whole floor is oak. And while putting two triangles together does not necessarily make another triangle, putting two triangles together will necessarily make another geometric figure. Being a geometric figure is part of a triangle's nature, just as being dependent is the nature of everything in the universe. One dependent being cannot sustain another dependent being.

Some critics argue that the whole is greater than the parts, so while the parts are dependent, the whole universe is not. However, this doesn't work in the case of the universe. If the contingent parts, which together compose the whole, vanish then the universe vanishes. Evidently the entire universe is dependent.

The Teleological Argument. There are many forms of the teleological argument, the most famous of which derives from William *Paley's watchmaker analogy. Since every watch has a watchmaker, and since the universe is exceedingly more complex in its operation than a watch, it follows that there must be a Maker of the universe. In brief, the teleological argument reasons from design to an intelligent Designer.

1. All designs imply a designer.
2. There is great design in the universe.
3. Therefore, there must be a Great Designer of the universe.

Any time we have seen a complex design, we know by previous experience that it came from the mind of a designer. Watches imply watchmakers; buildings imply architects; paintings imply artists; and coded messages imply an intelligent sender.

Also, the greater the design, the greater the designer. Beavers make log dams, but they have never constructed anything like the Golden Gate Bridge. A thousand monkeys sitting at typewriters for millions of years would never produce *Hamlet* by accident. Shakespeare did it on the first try. The more complex the design, the greater the intelligence required to produce it.

It is important to note that by "complex design" is meant *specified complexity*. A crystal, for example, has specificity but not complexity. It, like a snowflake, has the same basic patterns repeated over and over. Random polymers, on the other hand, has complexity but no specificity. A living cell, however, has both specificity and complexity. This kind of complexity is never produced by purely natural laws. It is always the result of an intelligent being. It is the same kind of complexity that is found in a human language. Letter sequence in the four-letter genetic alphabet is identical to that in a written language. And the amount of complex information in a simple one-cell animal is greater than that found in Webster's Unabridged Dictionary.

Agnostic astronomer, Carl *Sagan, unwittingly provided an even greater example. He notes that the genetic information in the human brain expressed in bits is probably comparable to the total number of connections among neurons—about 100 trillion, 10^{14} bits. If written out in English, say, that information would fill some 20 million volumes, as many as are stored in the world's largest libraries. The equivalent of 20 million books is inside the heads of every one of us. "The brain is a very big place in a very small space," Sagan said. He went on to note that "the neurochemistry of the brain is astonishingly busy, the circuitry of a machine more wonderful than any devised by humans." But if this is so, then why does the human brain not need an intelligent Creator, as does even the simplest computer?

The Ontological Argument. The ontological argument moves from the conception of a Perfect or Necessary Being to the existence of such a Being. The first philosopher known to have developed the ontological argument (though not the first to call it this) was *Anselm (1033–1109). In its simplest form it argues from the *idea* of God to the *existence* of God. There are two forms of the argument: one from the idea of a Perfect Being and the other from the idea of a Necessary Being.

The Perfect Being. According to this statement of the argument the mere concept of God as an absolutely perfect being demands that he exist. Briefly put:

1. God is by definition an absolutely perfect being.
2. But existence is a perfection.
3. Therefore, God must exist.

If God did not exist, then he would be lacking one perfection, namely, existence. But if God lacked any perfection, then he would not be absolutely perfect. But God is *by definition* an absolutely perfect being. Therefore, an absolutely perfect being (God) must exist.

Since the time of Immanuel *Kant (1724–1804), it has been widely accepted that this form of the argument is invalid because existence is not a perfection. It is argued that existence adds nothing to the concept of a thing; it merely gives a concrete instance of it. The dollar in my mind can have exactly the same properties as the one in my wallet. There is, however, a second form of the ontological argument that is not subject to this criticism.

The Necessary Being. Anselm argued that the very concept of a Necessary Being demands its existence:

1. If God exists, we must conceive of him as a Necessary Being.
2. But by definition, a Necessary Being cannot not exist.
3. Therefore, if a Necessary Being can, then it must, exist.

Since there is no contradiction in the idea of a Necessary Being, it would seem to follow that one must exist. For the very idea of a Necessary Being demands that it must exist. For if it did not exist, then it would not be a necessary *existence*.

Critics to this argument point out a problem: This is like saying: *If* there are triangles, then they must have three sides. Of course, there may not be any triangles. But the argument never really gets past that initial "if." It never gets around to proving the big question that it claims to answer. It merely *assumes*, but does not prove, the existence of a Necessary Being. It only says that, if a Necessary Being exists—and that is the open question—it must exist necessarily, since that is the only way a Necessary Being can exist, if it exists at all.

The Ontological Argument cannot prove the existence of God, but it can prove certain things about his *nature*. For example, God must necessarily exist, if he exists at all. He cannot cease to exist or exist contingently.

The Argument from Moral Law. The roots of the moral argument for God are found in Romans 2:12–15, in which humankind is said to stand unexcused since there is "a law written on their hearts." Since the time of Kant this argument has been stated in various ways. The most popular form emanates from C. S. *Lewis in *Mere*

Christianity. The heart of the argument follows this basic structure:

1. Moral laws imply a Moral Law Giver.
2. There is an objective moral law.
3. Therefore, there is a Moral Law Giver.

The first premise is self-evident. Moral laws are different from natural laws. Moral laws don't *describe what is,* they *prescribe what ought to be*. They can't be known by observing what people do. They are what all persons should do, whether or not they actually do.

The weight of the argument rests on the second premise—there is an objective moral law. That is, there is a moral law that is not just prescribed by us but also *for* us. Humans do prescribe proper behavior for other humans. The question is whether there is evidence that a universal, objective prescription binds all humans. The evidence for such a law is strong. It is implied in our judgments that "The world is getting better (or worse)." How could we know unless there were some standard beyond the world by which we could measure it. Such statements as "Hitler was wrong" have no force if this is merely an opinion or Hitler's moral judgments are right or wrong depending on the cultural norms. If he was objectively wrong, then there must be a moral law beyond all of us by which we are all bound. But if there is such a universal, objective moral law, then there must be a universal Moral Law Giver (God).

The Argument from Religious Need. Many people claim not to need God. Sigmund *Freud even considered the desire to believe in God an illusion. Is the desire for God based in reality, or is it based in unfulfillable human wishes? Is the basis for belief in God purely psychological, or is it factual? Whether humans feel a need for him, there is good evidence of God's existence. But the desire for God does exist, not as a psychological wish, but from real existential need. This need, in itself, is an evidence for the existence of God.

In skeleton form, the argument from the alleged need for God to his existence goes:

1. Human beings really need God.
2. What humans really need, probably really exists.
3. Therefore, God really exists.

For this argument to have a chance of standing, the second premise must be distinguished from the claim that what one really needs will be found. One may really need water and die of dehydration. However, that is quite different from arguing that one really needs water, and there is no water anywhere.

It would seem irrational to believe that there are real needs in the universe that are unfulfillable. There are many unfulfillable wants, but to suppose that there are unfulfillable needs is to assume an irrational universe. Likewise, it would seem reasonable to assume that, if human beings really need God, there probably is a God, even if not everyone finds him. As with other unfulfilled needs in life, it may be that some look in the wrong place or in the wrong way (cf. Prov. 14:12).

This leads us to the crux of the argument: Do human beings have a real need for God, or is it only a felt need? If there is a real need, then why do not all experience it? For example, most atheists claim that there is no real need for God.

Even Atheists Need God. Religious literature is filled with testimonies from believers who confess that they really need God. The psalmist wrote, "As the deer pants for streams of water, so my soul pants for you, O God" (Ps. 42:1). Jeremiah 29:13 declares, "You will seek me and find me when you seek me with all your heart." Jesus taught that "man does not live on bread alone, but on every word that comes from the mouth of God" (Matt. 4:4). *Augustine summarized it well when he said the heart is restless until it finds its rest in God.

What is often not appreciated by unbelievers is the fact that the felt need for God is not limited to unthinking and uncritical religious people. Some of the greatest minds, including the founders of most areas of modern science, confessed their need. Not surprisingly this list includes theologians Augustine, Anselm, and Thomas Aquinas. But it also includes Galileo Galilei, Nicolaus Copernicus, William Kelvin, Isaac Newton, Francis Bacon, Blaise *Pascal, René Descartes, Gottfried *Leibniz, John *Locke, and Søren *Kierkegaard. One can hardly claim that intellectual deficiency led to their perceived need for God.

Dealing with the feelings. But if God is a need for everyone, why does everyone not reflect this need? Surprisingly, there is evidence that they do. Take, for example, the testimony of atheists and agnostics in their more candid moments. Julian *Huxley, for example, frankly admitted a type of religious encounter:

> On Easter Sunday, early in the morning, I got up at daybreak, before anyone else was about, let myself out, ran across to a favourite copse, penetrated to where I knew the wild cherry grew, and there, in the spring dew, picked a great armful of the lovely stuff, which I brought back, with a sense of its being an acceptable offering, to the house. Three or four Easters running I remember doing this. I was fond of solitude and of nature, and had a passion for wild flowers: but this was only a general basis. . . . But when sanctity is in the air, as at Easter, then it can have free play. [70]

Friedrich *Schleiermacher defined religion as a feeling of absolute dependence on the All (Schleiermacher, 39). And even though Freud did not wish to call this feeling religious, he admits to feeling such a dependence. Paul Tillich defined religion as an ultimate commitment (Tillich, 7–8, 30). In this sense of the word *religion* most humanists have a commitment to humanism. *Humanist Manifesto II* says, "commitment to all humankind is the highest commitment of which we are capable" (Kurtz, 23). This is, to borrow Tillich's phrase, an "ultimate commitment." John *Dewey defined the religious as any ideal pursued with great conviction because of its general and enduring value. In this sense humanism certainly involves a religious experience.

Erich Fromm was even willing to use the word *God* of the feeling of ultimate commitment to all humankind. And while he wished to disassociate himself from what he called "authoritarian" beliefs, he did admit that his humanist beliefs were religious. He felt that his devotion to humanity as a whole was a religious devotion. The humanistic object of that devotion he called "God" (Fromm, 49, 54, 87). Jewish existentialist Martin *Buber said that the word *God* is the most heavily laden in our vocabulary but insisted that, by loving other persons, one has fulfilled personal religious obligations (Buber, *I and Thou,* 55).

Even the atheistic humanists (*see* HUMANISM, SECULAR) who deny having any religious experience often admit that they once did. Jean-Paul *Sartre tells of experiences as a child. He wrote, "Nevertheless, I believed. In my nightshirt, kneeling on the bed, with my hands together, I said my prayers every day, but I thought of God less and less often" (Sartre, 102). Bertrand Russell admitted to once believing in God; so did Friedrich *Nietzsche.

The secular religion. Whether past or present experience of devotion to God, to the "All" or to humankind, many humanists admit to some sort of experience that would be called "religious." And although *Humanist Manifesto I* calls for giving up the belief in any form of extraterrestrial being (see Kurtz, 14–16), many atheistic humanists do insist that they have not thereby forsaken religion. In fact, the religious urge is so great, even in humanists, that August Comte set up a humanist cult with himself as the high priest. In the sense in which the word *religious* is currently defined by dictionaries, philosophers, theologians, and humanists themselves, humanism is a religion.

Due to an interesting series of events the United States Supreme Court has come to recognize secular humanism as a religion. Their ruling in *United States v. Kauten* (1943) allowed exemption to the military draft on the basis of conscientious objection, even if the person did not believe in a deity. The Second Circuit Court stated: "[Conscientious objection] may justly be regarded as a response of the individual to an inward mentor, call it conscience or God, that is for many persons at the present time the equivalent of what has always been thought a religious impulse" (Whitehead, 10).

In 1965 the Supreme Court in *United States v. Seeger* ruled that any belief is valid if it is "sincere and meaningful [and it] occupies a place in the life of its possessor parallel to that filled by the orthodox belief in God" (ibid., 14). Having consulted the theologian Tillich, the Court defined religion to be belief "based upon a power or being or upon a faith, to which all else is subordinate or upon which all else is ultimately dependent" (ibid.).

In a very revealing article in *Humanist Magazine* (1964) the finger was placed on several weaknesses in this regard. In the article "What's Wrong with Humanism?" the indictment is made that the movement is too intellectual and almost "clinically detached from life." To reach the masses with their message, the writer suggests that an effort be undertaken to develop a humanist Bible, a humanist hymnal, ten commandments for humanists, and even confessional practices (testimonies)! In addition, "the use of hypnotic techniques—music and other psychological devices—during humanist services would give the audience that deep spiritual experience and they would emerge refreshed and inspired with their humanist faith" (cited in Kitwood, 49). Rarely do humanists speak so freely about the psychological inadequacies of their system and the need to borrow Christian practices to rectify them.

Weaknesses in the humanist religion. T. M. Kitwood has summarized the deficiencies when he observed that secular humanism "does not evoke a response from the whole person, intellect, will and emotion." Further, humanists "lack originality when making positive statements about man's life, and easily descend to the platitudinous" (Kitwood, 48).

Another weakness of humanism may be that it fails to reckon with human nature. Some humanists have reflected an incredible naiveté about life. John Stuart *Mill wrote that his father "felt as if all would be gained if the whole population were taught to read" (ibid., 50). Even Russell thought that "if we could learn to love our neighbor the world would quickly become a paradise for us all" (ibid.). Finally, Kitwood charges humanists with being "an aristocratic body, and as such insulated from some of the more terrible realities of life" (ibid., 51). One conclusion emerges clearly: Secular humanism does not measure up to the psychological realities of life. William *James pointed out in his classic treatment on religious experience that those who set this world afire are themselves set aflame from another world. They are the saints not the secularists. They believed in a supernatural world, which secular humanism denies (James, 290).

Although secular humanists often confess to having religious, even mystical, experiences, they deny that these involve a personal God. But this is inadequate, first, because their experience is strangely personal for having no personal object. They speak of "loyalty," "devotion" and "love" as basic values. But these are terms that make proper sense only when they have a personal object. Who, for example, can fall in love with the Pythagorean theorem? Or who would be religiously moved by the exhortation: "Prepare to meet thy $E = MC^2$?" As Elton *Trueblood insightfully observed, "The joy and wonder which men feel in the search for truth, including the quality of feeling of those scientists who think of themselves as materialists is the *same kind of feeling we know best when there is real communication between two finite minds*" (Trueblood, 115).

Only a personal object can really satisfy personal devotion. Perhaps this is what accounts for the lack of a satisfying religious experience among humanists. Huxley said his religious experience became dimmer over the years. He wrote, "I had been used, ever since the age of fifteen or sixteen, to have such moments come to me naturally. . . . But now . . . they were vouchsafed in diminishing measure, and (although sometimes with great intensity) more fleetingly" (Huxley, 77). Sartre confessed that his religious experiences ceased when he dismissed God from his life. He said, "I had all the more difficulty of getting rid of Him in that he had installed himself at the back of my head. . . . I collared the Holy Ghost in the cellar and threw him out; atheism is a cruel and long-range affair; I think I've carried it through" (Sartre, 252–53). Sartre's confession of the difficulty and even cruelty of the life without God should not be surprising to anyone who truly understands the human person. Satisfaction originates in the personal. Human beings are fulfilled in what Buber called an "I-Thou" experience, not an "I-it" experience. That is, persons are satisfied best by persons (subjects), not by things (objects). Hence, it is not strange that a personal religious experience is not going to be fully satisfied in anything less than a personal object.

Tillich recognized that not every ultimate commitment was to something ultimate. In fact, he believed that to be ultimately committed to what is less than ultimate is idolatry (see Tillich, 57). Buber pointed out that idols can be mental as well as metal (Buber, *Eclipse of God*, 62). Combining these two insights from their own thinkers, we may note, that when humanists make some finite ideal or goal the object of their religious commitment, they are idolaters.

Humanists recognize human life to be mortal. The race may be annihilated or become extinct. Why then do humanists treat humankind as eternal? Why an unswerving commitment to that which is changing and even perishing, the product of a blind evolutionary process? Is it not the height of humanistic arrogance for humanity to endow itself with divinity (see Geisler, chap. 15)? Such unlimited devotion humanists give to humanity is due only to the Infinite. The only thing worthy of an ultimate commitment is the Ultimate.

The confessed need of the atheist. One of the strongest indications that human beings need God is found in the very men who deny the need for God. The confessed needs of atheistic humanists is eloquent testimony to this point.

Nietzsche bemoaned his intolerable loneliness as compared to other poets who believed in God. He wrote,

> I hold up before myself the images of Dante and *Spinoza, who were better at accepting the lot of solitude. . . . and in the end, for all those who somehow still had a 'God' for company. . . . My life now consists in the wish that it might be otherwise . . . and that somebody might make *my* 'truths' appear incredible to me. [Nietzsche, 441]

Sartre admitted his own personal need for religion, saying, "I needed God." He added, "I reached out for religion, I longed for it, it was the remedy. Had it been denied me, I would have invented it myself" (Sartre, 97, 102). The French atheist Albert *Camus added, "Nothing can discourage the appetite for divinity in the heart of man" (*The Rebel*, 147). Freud undermined the reality basis for God but admitted that he too felt the Schleiermachean sense of absolute dependence. He admitted that he experienced "a sense of man's insignificance and impotence in the face of the universe" (Freud, 57). Freud further admitted that this sense of absolute dependence is inescapable and cannot be overcome by science.

The same need for the divine is dramatized in Samuel Beckett's *Waiting for Godot*, a play with a title reminiscent of Martin Heidegger's phrase "waiting for God." Franz Kafka's novels express the futility of lonely, persistent attempts to find some meaningful cosmic otherness. Walter Kaufmann reaches the point that he confesses, "Religion is rooted in man's aspiration to transcend himself. . . . Whether he worships idols or strives to perfect himself, man is the God-intoxicated ape" (Kaufmann, 354–55, 399).

Other such nonbelievers as Julian *Huxley have likewise taken a positive attitude toward man's apparently incurably religious needs. Huxley spoke of "the possibility of enjoying experiences of transcendent rapture, physical or mystical, aesthetic or religious . . . of attaining inner harmony and peace, which puts a man above the cares and worries of daily life" (cited in Kitwood, 38). What is this but another description of reaching out for a God?

If the need for God is so eradicable, even in humanists, why do so many seem capable of living without God? Some have suggested that the unbeliever is *inconsistent* at this point. The atheistic philosophy (*see* ATHEISM) of John Cage drove him to suicide when he tried to live in a purely random way. Jackson Pollock, on the other hand, chose to be inconsistent and live. His hobby was mushrooms and he wisely decided not to approach the question as to which are poisonous in a random manner, as was his view of the world.

In a frank interview with the *Chicago Sun Times* Will Durant, admits that the common man will fall to pieces morally if he thinks there is no God. But "a man like me," said Durant, "I survive morally because I retain the moral code that was taught me along with the religion, while I have discarded the religion, which was Roman Catholicism." Durant continued,

> You and I are living on a shadow . . . because we are operating on the Christian ethical code which was given us, unfused with the Christian faith. . . . But what will happen to our children . . . ? We are not giving them an ethics warmed up with a religious faith. They are living on the shadow of a shadow. [Durant, 1B:8]

It is difficult to live on a shadow and more so to dwell on a shadow's shadow. But this is precisely where humanists attempt to live without God.

Often ethics or aesthetics becomes a surrogate for God, but even this is satisfying only in so far as it rides piggyback on some belief in God. As Martin Marty noted, atheism "occurs and can occur only where belief is or has been. [This] explains why atheism . . . is itself a proof, by reason of its invariably polemical character" (Marty, 119–20). One who tries to overthrow everything—even the aesthetic and ethical shadows, finds with Camus that "for anyone who is alone, without God and without a master, the weight of days is dreadful" (Camus, *The Fall,* 133).

Sartre found atheism "cruel," Camus "dreadful," and Nietzsche "maddening." Atheists who consistently try to live without God tend to commit suicide or go insane. Those who are inconsistent live on the ethical or aesthetic shadow of Christian truth while they deny the reality that made the shadow. But believers and unbelievers evidence a definite need for God. Viktor Frankl, in *The Unconscious God,* contends that "man has always stood in an intentional relation to transcendence, even if only on an unconscious level." In this sense, he says, all men seek the "Unconscious God" (cited in Macdonald, 43).

The Argument from Joy. C. S. Lewis developed an argument from joy or the anticipation of heavenly bliss. This argument was stated by Lewis in *Mere Christianity* (12), *The Problem of Pain* (133), and *Surprised by Joy* (16–18).It was defended by Peter Kreeft in *Handbook of Christian Apologetics* and *The Heart's Deepest Longing.*

The argument from joy goes like this: Creatures are not born with desires unless satisfaction for those desires exists. A baby feels hunger; food can satisfy. A duckling wants to swim; water fills its need. Men and women feel sexual desire; sexual intercourse fulfills that desire. If I find myself with a desire that no experience in this world can satisfy, I probably was made for another world. If no earthly pleasures satisfy the need, it does not mean the universe is a fraud. Probably earthly pleasures were never meant to satisfy it, but only to arouse it (Lewis, *Surprised by Joy*, 120).

The Logic of the Argument from Joy. The logic for the argument from joy goes like this:

1. Every natural innate desire has a real object that can fulfill it.
2. Human beings have a natural, innate desire for *immortality.
3. Therefore, there must be an immortal life after death.

In defense of the first premise, it is argued that "If there is hunger, there is food; if thirst, drink; if eros, sex; if curiosity, knowledge; if loneliness, society" (Kreeft, *Handbook*, 250). Nature rushes to fill a vacuum. The second premise is supported by appeal to a mysterious longing that differs from all others in two ways: First, its object is indefinable and unobtainable in this life. Second, the mere presence of this desire in the soul is felt to be more precious and joyful than any other satisfaction. However inadequately we express it, what we long for is paradise, heaven, or eternity (ibid.). Even atheists experience this longing.

If these premises are true, then there is "more" than this life; there is a life to come. The fact that we complain about this world, pain, and death—but never about eternity—reveals a deep-seated desire for it. We may never attain it, but this no more disproves its existence than life-long singleness proves there is no marital bliss or starvation proves there is no such thing as food (ibid.).

Evaluation. This argument is not logically airtight. Few if any of the arguments are. However, it has a certain existential force to it that cannot be denied. Even great unbelievers have admitted a longing for God. The famous unbeliever, Bertrand Russell, admitted in a letter to Lady Otto: "Even when one feels nearest to other people, something in one seems obstinately to belong to God, and to refuse to enter into any earthly communion—at least that is how I should express it if I thought there was a God. It is odd, isn't it? I care passionately for this world and many things and people in it, and yet . . . what is it all for? There must be something more important, one feels, though I don't believe there is" (*Autobiography*, 125–26).

Of course, it is possible that the universe is irrational, that it is mocking our most basic needs.

But there is something in one that refuses to accept that. The desire for joy can be disbelieved, but it is harder to eradicate.

Conclusion. Few theists would rest their case for God on any one argument. Each argument seems to demonstrate a different attribute of God along with his existence. For example, the cosmological argument shows that God is infinitely powerful; the teleological argument reveals that he is intelligent; the moral argument demonstrates that he is moral and, if he exists, the ontological argument shows that he is a Necessary Being.

Some theists offer other arguments for the existence of God, such as the argument from religious need or the argument from religious experience (*see* EXPERIENTIAL APOLOGETICS). Most nontheists claim they do not need God, but their own writings and experiences betray their position. But if there is a real need for God, it is far more reasonable to believe that there is a real God who can really fill this real need.

Sources

Anselm, *Proslogion*
M. Buber, *Eclipse of God*
———, *I and Thou*
A. Camus, *The Fall*
———, *The Rebel*
W. Durant, *Chicago Sun Times*, 24 August 1975
V. Frankl, *The Unconscious God*
E. Fromm, *Psychoanalysis and Religion*
S. Hawkings, *A Brief History of Time*
F. Hoyle, *The Intelligent Universe*
J. Huxley, *Religion without Revelation*
W. James, *Varieties of Religious Experiences*
R. Jastrow, "A Scientist Caught between Two Faiths: Interview with Robert Jastrow," *CT*, 6 August 1982
———, *God and the Astronomers*
W. Kaufmann, *Critique of Religion and Philosophy*
T. M. Kitwood, *What Is Human?*
P. Kreeft, *Handbook of Christian Apologetics*
———, *The Heart's Deepest Longing*
P. Kurtz, ed. *Humanist Manifestos I* and *II*
C. S. Lewis, *Mere Christianity*
———, *Surprised by Joy*
———, *The Problem of Pain*
M. Macdonald, "The Roots of Commitment," *CT*, 19 November 1976
M. Marty, *Varieties of Unbelief*
F. Nietzsche, *The Portable Nietzsche*
H. Ross, *The Fingerprint of God*
B. Russell, *The Autobiography of Bertrand Russell*
C. Sagan, *Cosmos*
A. Sandage, "A Scientist Reflects on Religious Belief," *Truth*, 1985
J. P. Sartre, *Words*
F. Schleiermacher, *On Religion: Speeches to Its Cultural Despisers*
Thomas Aquinas, *Summa Theologica*
P. Tillich, *Ultimate Concern*
D. E. Trueblood, *Philosophy of Religion*
S. Weinberg, *Dreams of a Final Theory—The Search for the Fundamental Laws of Nature*
J. Whitehead, "The Establishment of the Religion of Secular Humanism and Its First Amendment Implications," *TTLR*

God, Moral Argument for. ***See*** **MORAL ARGUMENT FOR GOD.**

God, Nature of. *Natural theology deals with what can be known about the existence (*see* COSMOLOGICAL ARGUMENT; *KALAM* COSMOLOGICAL ARGUMENT) and nature of God by natural reason (*see* REVELATION, GENERAL), apart from any supernatural revelation (*see* REVELATION, SPECIAL). According to classical Christian theists (*see* THEISM), such as Thomas Aquinas (1225–1274), all of the essential metaphysical attributes of God can be known by natural reason. This includes God's aseity, simplicity, immutability, eternality, simplicity, unity, infinity, and morality.

Aseity (Self-Existence). Most classical theists see God's Aseity or Pure Existence as a key attribute. The early Church Fathers, as well as *Augustine (354–430), *Anselm (1033–1109), and *Aquinas, continually cite the Bible in support of this position. In defending God's self-existence (aseity) classical theists such as Aquinas are fond of citing Exodus 3:14 where God identifies himself to Moses as "I Am that I Am." This they understand to refer to God as Pure Being or Existence.

God is Pure Actuality, with no potentiality in his being whatsoever. Whatever has potentiality (potency) needs to be actualized or effected by another. And since God is the ultimate Cause, there is nothing beyond him to actualize any potential (i.e., ability) he may have. Nor can God actualize his own potential to exist, since this would mean he caused his own existence. But a self-caused being is impossible, since it cannot create itself. Something has to exist before it can do anything. Even God cannot lift himself into being by his own ontological bootstraps. Thus, God must be Pure Actuality in his Being.

Of course, God has the potential to create other things. But he cannot bring himself into being. He always was. And while God has the potential to *do* other things, he cannot *be* anything other than what he is. He has the power to *create* other things (active potency), but he does not have the power (passive potency) to *exist* in any other way than he does, namely, as an infinite, eternal, necessary, and simple Being.

God's aseity means that he *is* Being; everything else merely *has* being. God is Pure Actuality; all other things have both actuality and potentiality. Thus, God cannot not exist. All creatures can be nonexistent. That is, they have the potentiality for nonexistence. Only God is a Necessary Being. All other beings are contingent.

Simplicity (Indivisibility). Since God is not composed in his Being, but is Pure Existence, Pure Actuality with no potentiality; it follows that he is simple and indivisible. A Being that by nature is not composed cannot be decomposed. One that has no parts cannot be torn apart. Hence, God has absolute simplicity with no possibility of being divided. He is literally indivisible.

Likewise, a God of Pure Actuality with no potentiality cannot be divided. For if it were divisible, then it would have to have the potential to be divided. But Pure Actuality has no potentiality in its Being whatsoever. Hence, it must be absolutely simple or indivisible.

God's indivisibility follows also from his immutability (see below). For if God could be divided, he could change. But God is unchangeable by nature. Thus he cannot be divided. He must be absolutely simple in his nature.

Necessity (Noncontingency). God is by nature an absolutely necessary Being. That is, he cannot not exist. God is not a may-be but a must-be kind of Being. He is not contingent, since he does not have the possibility not to exist. If he has no potentiality not to exist, then he must exist.

This is not to say that the *ontological argument is valid. *Aquinas considered and rejected *Anselm's proof for God. If God (i.e., Pure Actuality) exists, then he must exist necessarily. But one cannot simply define him into existence. Aquinas offered his famous cosmological arguments for God's existence (*Summa Theologica*, 1.2.3). And once we know, from reason and revelation, that God exists, then we can be sure that he must exist necessarily. Such a Being has no potential not to exist.

Immutability (Unchangeability). In his epic *Summa Theologica* (1a.9.1), Aquinas offers three basic arguments in favor of God's unchangeability. The first argument is passed on the fact that a God of Pure Actuality ("I-Am-ness") has no potentiality. It follows, therefore, that God cannot change (Exod. 3:14). Whatever changes has to have the potential to change. But as pure Actuality, God has no potential, so he cannot change.

The second argument for God's immutability follows from his simplicity. Everything that changes is composed of what changes and what does not change. God cannot change because an absolutely simple being has no composition. If everything about a being changed, then it would be an entirely new being. In fact, it would not be change but annihilation of one thing and a creation of something entirely new. Now if, in every change in a being something remains the same and something does not, then it must be composed of these two elements. So an absolutely simple Being with no composition cannot change.

The third argument for God's unchangeability argues from his absolute perfection. Whatever changes acquires something new. But God cannot acquire anything new, since he could not be better or more complete. Therefore, God cannot change. If he did, he would not be God for he would have lacked some perfection.

Aquinas also argues that God alone is immutable (*Summa Theologica*, 1a.9.2). All creatures exist only because of the will of the Creator. His power brought them into existence, and it is his power that keeps them in existence. Therefore, if he withdrew his power they would cease to exist. Whatever can cease to exist is not immutable. Therefore, God alone is immutable; everything else could cease to exist.

Impassability (without Passions). A long-recognized attribute of God that has recently come under attack is *impassability*. God is without passions. Passion implies desire for what one does not have. But God, as an absolutely perfect Being, lacks nothing. To lack something he would have to have a potentiality to have it. But God is Pure Actuality with no potentiality whatsoever. Therefore, God is completely and infinitely satisfied in his own perfection.

However, to say that God is impassable in the sense that he has no passions or cravings for fulfillment is not to say that he has no feelings. God feels anger at sin and rejoices in righteousness. But God's feelings are unchanging. He always, unchangingly, feels the same sense of anger at sin. He never ceases to rejoice in goodness and rightness. Thus, God has no changing passions, but he does have unchanging feelings.

Eternity (Nontemporality). God is not temporal (*Summa Theologica*, 1a. 10, 1). He is beyond time. Aquinas offers several arguments in support of this conclusion. The first argument goes:

1. Whatever exists in time can be computed according to its befores and afters.
2. Changeless being, as God is, has no befores or afters; it is always the same.
3. Consequently, God must be timeless.

Time is duration characterized by substantial and accidental changes. A substantial change is a change in what something *is*. Fire changes what a piece of wood is. An accidental change is a change in what something *has*. Growing knowledge is an accidental change in a being. Aquinas sees three levels of being in relation to time and eternity:

1. God in *eternity* is Pure Actuality, without essential or accidental change.
2. Angels and saints who dwell in the spiritual world of heaven live in *aeviternity* (or *aevum*).
3. Human beings, comprising soul and body, form and matter, live in *time*.

Eternity (God) endures without any potency. Aeviternity (angels) endure with completely actualized potency. Their changes are not essential but accidental. Spiritual beings in aeviternity do not change in their essence, though they do undergo accidental changes. Angels increase in knowledge by divine infusion, and they have changeableness with regard to choice, intelligence, affections and places (ibid., 1a.10.6). But with no substantial changes in aeviternity, angels are immutable in their level of grace and charity. What is true of the angels is also true of the elect in heaven.

Time (humanity) endures with progressive actualized potency.

The second argument for God's eternity similarly follows from immutability. It begins with the premise that whatever is immutable does not change in the state of its being. Whatever is in time goes through a succession of states. So whatever is immutable is not temporal. This argument stresses another aspect of time; whatever is temporal has successive states, one after the other. God does not, so he is not temporal.

Total immutability necessarily implies eternity (ibid., 1a.10.2). For whatever changes substantially is in time and can be computed according to before and after. Whatever does not change cannot be in time, since it has no different states by which before and after can be computed. It never changes. Whatever does not change is not temporal. Not only is God eternal, but he alone is eternal (ibid., 1a.10.3), for he alone is essentially immutable.

Aquinas distinguishes eternity from endless time (ibid., 1a.10.4). First, whatever is essentially whole (eternity) is essentially different from what has parts (time). Eternity is now forever; time includes past, present, and future, now and then. The implication of this is that God's eternity is not divided; it is all present to him in his eternal now. So it must be essentially different from time in successive moments.

Second, endless time is just more an elongation of time. But eternity differs qualitatively. It differs essentially, not merely accidentally. Eternity is an essential, changeless state of being that transcends moment-by-successive-moment reality. Time measures that reality, or rather the stage on which reality plays out.

Third, an eternal being cannot change, whereas time involves change. By change can the measurements of before and after be made. Whatever can be computed according to before and after is not eternal. Endless time can be computed according to before and after. Hence, endless time is not the same as eternity. The eternal is changeless, but what can be computed by its before and after has changed. It follows, then, that the eternal now cannot live in relation to endless befores and afters.

Obviously, Aquinas saw a crucial difference between the "now" of time and the "now" of eternity (ibid.). The now of time is movable. The now of eternity is not movable in any way. The eternal now is unchanging, but the now of time is ever changing. There is only an analogy between time and eternity; they cannot be the same. God's now has no past or future; time's now does.

Some have mistakenly concluded that Aquinas did not believe in God's duration for eternity, because he rejected temporality in God. Aquinas argued that duration occurs as long as actuality exists. But eternity, aeviternity, and time endure in different ways.

It follows, therefore that the essential difference in the quality of the duration in time, aeviternity, and eternity comes from the condition of the actuality. God *is Pure Actuality*. Angels *have received total actuality* from God in their created spiritual forms. Human beings *progressively receive actuality* in both spiritual form and material body.

Since God endures without potentiality, he cannot endure progressively. He endures in a much higher way—as Pure Actuality.

Immensity. Along with eternity is the attribute of immensity (nonspatiality). God is not limited in time, nor is he limited in space. In God's immanence he fills space, but he is not spatial. Only material things exist in space and time, and God is not material. "God is spirit" (John 4:24). As spiritual, God is not material or spatial. It is part of God's transcendence that he is beyond both time and space.

Unity. Classical theists have offered three reasons for God's unity (ibid., 1a.11.3). The first argument is from the simplicity of God. An absolutely simple being cannot be more than one, since to be more than one there must be parts, but simple beings have no parts. Absolutely simple beings are not divisible. God is an absolutely simple being. Therefore, God cannot be more than one being.

God's perfection argues for his unity. If two or more gods existed, they would have to differ. In order to differ, one must have what the other lacks. But an absolutely perfect being cannot lack anything. Therefore, there can only be one absolutely perfect being. God's unity also can be inferred from the unity of the world. The world is composed of diverse things. Diverse things do not come together unless they are ordered. But the world has an ordered unity. Therefore, there must be one Orderer of the world.

Theists argue that essential unity is better explained by one Orderer than by many orderers. For one is the essential cause of oneness, but many is only the accidental cause of oneness. Therefore, it is reasonable to infer that there is only one cause of the world, not many.

Relatability (to the World). One criticism of classical theism is that an eternal, unchanging God could not relate to a changing world. Aquinas anticipated this objection and treated it extensively.

There are three kinds of relations: One where both terms are ideas; one where both terms are real; and one where one term is real and one is an idea (ibid., 1a.13.7).

Now since creatures are dependent on God but God is not dependent on them, they are related as real to an idea. That is, God *knows* about the relationship of dependence but he does not *have* it. When there is a change in the creature there is no change in God. Just as when the man changes his position from one side of the pillar to the other, the pillar does not change; only the man changes in relation to the pillar. So, while the relationship between God and creatures is real, God is in no sense dependent in that relationship.

Aquinas is only denying *dependent* relationships, not all real ones. God never changes as he relates to the world, but real changes do occur in that relation with the world. The man's relation to the pillar really changes when he moves, but the pillar does not change.

The real but unchanging relation of God to the world is made even more clear when Aquinas considers how the eternal God relates to a temporal world (ibid., 1a.13.7, ad 2). God condescends to relate to humans as if he shared time with them. He can create a temporal relation that in no way changes him. Eternity can move in time, though time cannot move in eternity. To have a relationship with the temporal world, God does not have to be temporal. It makes no more sense to say God has to be temporal in order to relate to a temporal world than to say he has to be a creature in order to create.

God is really related to creatures as their Creator. But creatures are really related to God only because he is their Creator. They are dependent on that Creator-creature bond; he is not. Therefore, the relation of God to creatures is real and not merely ideal. However, it is a real relationship of dependence on the part of the creatures but not a relation of dependence on the part of God (ibid., 1a.13.7, ad 5).

God's Knowledge. *God Knows Himself.* If God is absolutely simple, can he know himself? All knowledge involves both a knower and a known. But God has no such duality. Aquinas argues that in self-knowledge the knower and known are identical. Hence, God can only know himself through himself (ibid., 1a.14.2). Since God is simple, he knows himself simply.

God also knows himself perfectly. Something is known perfectly when its potential to be known is completely realized. And there is no unactualized potentiality to know himself. Therefore, God's self-knowledge is completely actualized (ibid., 1a.14.3).

God's knowledge is identical with his essence. For if God's acts of knowledge were really distinct from his essence, then they would be related as actuality to potentiality. But there can be no potentiality in God. Therefore, God's knowledge and essence are really identical (ibid., 1a.14.4). This does not mean that God cannot know things other than himself. For God is the efficient cause of all things.

God Knows and Does. Even though God knows other things than himself, nonetheless, he knows them through himself. For God does not know other things through himself either successively or inferentially but simultaneously and intuitively (ibid., 1a.14.7, ad 2). God's knowledge is more perfect because he does not have to know things discursively through their causes but knows them directly and intuitively (ibid., 1a.14.7 ad 3, 4). God not only knows all things in and through himself, but he also causes all things by his knowledge. God causes all things by his being, but God's being and his knowledge are identical (ibid., 1a.14.8). This does not mean that creation is eternal because he is eternal. For God causes all things as they are in his knowledge. But that creation should be eternal was not in God's knowledge (ibid., 1a.14.8, ad 2).

An effect pre-exists in the mind of its efficient cause. Hence, whatever exists must pre-exist in God, who is its efficient cause. God knows all of the various kinds of perfection in himself, as well as those which can participate in his likeness. Therefore, God knows whatever exists perfectly, insofar as it pre-exists in him (ibid., 1a.14.5).

God Knows Every Creature Ideally. God knows his own essence perfectly. And knowing his essence perfectly entails knowing it according to every mode by which it can be known, namely, in itself and as participated in by creatures. But every creature has its own proper form, in which it is like God. It follows, therefore, that God knows the form or idea of every creature as it is modeled after him. Perfect knowledge involves the ability to distinguish one thing from another. That is, he knows not only what things have in common (*esse*) but how they differ (*essence*). Therefore, God knows all things in their individual essences. But all things pre-exist in God's knowledge. Therefore, all things pre-exist in God's knowledge, not only with regard to their existence but also with regard to their individual essences.

The basis for what God knows is his own essence, but the extent of what he knows is not limited to that one essence but reaches to all things like it (ibid., 1a.15.2). God's knowledge of all things in himself does not mean that he only knows other things in general but not in particular. For God's knowledge extends as far as does his causality. And God's causality extends to singular things, since he is the cause of every individual thing. Therefore, God knows singular things (ibid., 1a.14.11). God has a perfect knowledge of everything. And to know something only in general but not in particular is improper knowledge. So, God knows everything properly. That is, he does not know the radii of circles merely by knowing the center; he knows the radii as well as the center.

God Knows Evil. For perfect knowledge of things must include knowing all that can occur to them. Evil can occur as a corruption of good things. Hence, God can know evil (*see* EVIL, PROBLEM OF). But things are knowable in the way in which they exist. Evil is a privation in good things.

Therefore, God knows evil as a privation in a good (ibid., 1a.14.10).

God Knows Changing Things. Since God is unchanging and his knowledge is identical with his essence, he knows past, present, and future in one eternal now. Therefore, when time changes, God's knowledge does not change, since he knew it in advance. God knows change, but not in the *way* we know it, in successive time frames. From eternity God knows the whole of before and after the temporal now of human history (ibid., 1a.14.15).

God knows the same things we do, but he does not know them the same way we know them. Our knowledge is discursive, moving from premises to conclusions. In human knowledge there is twofold discursiveness: One thing is known *after* another, and one thing is known *through* another. But God cannot know things sequentially, since he is timeless and knows all things eternally at once. Nor can God know things inferentially, for he is simple and knows all things through the oneness of himself. Therefore, God cannot know anything discursively (sequentially, from topic to topic), inasmuch as discursive knowledge implies a limitation to consider one thing at a time on the part of the knower (ibid., 1a.14.7).

God Knows All Possibilities. By knowing himself perfectly God knows perfectly all the different ways his perfections can be shared by others. For there is within the essence of God all the knowledge of all possible kinds of things his will could actualize. Hence, God knows all the particular things that could ever be actualized (ibid., 1a.14.6).

God's Knowledge Allows Free Will. Pulling these strands of thought about God's knowledge together shows us how God's sovereignty works alongside human free will. God's knowledge is not simply of the actual; he also knows all possible sorts of potential. He knows what is and ever could-be. For God knows whatever is in any way it can be known. Now both the actual and the potential are real. Only the impossible has no reality. Thus, whatever is potential is real. It follows that God can know what is potential as well as what is actual (ibid., 1a.14.9).

This means that God can know future contingents, that is, things that are dependent on free choice. For the future is a potential that pre-exists in God. And God knows whatever exists in himself as the cause of those things (ibid., 1a.14.13). Since God is a timeless being, he knows all of time in one eternal now. But the future is part of time. Therefore, God knows the future, including the free acts to be performed in it. Of course, whatever God knows is known infallibly, since God cannot err in his knowledge. Future contingents are known infallibly. They are contingent with regard to their immediate cause (human free choice) but necessary with regard to God's knowledge. God can do this without eliminating free choice, for an omniscient being can know whatever is not impossible to know. And it is not impossible for a timeless being to know a necessary end caused by a contingent means. God can know a *must-be* through a *may-be* but not a *can't-be*.

Therefore, an omniscient Being knows future actions as necessarily true events. If an action will occur and God knows it, then that event must occur, for an omniscient Mind cannot be wrong about what it knows. Therefore the statement "Everything known by God must necessarily be" is true if it refers to the statement of the truth of God's knowledge, but it is false if it refers to the necessity of the contingent events (ibid., 1a.14.5).

God's Will. *Will* can be defined as a being's rational inclination toward its own good. Whatever has intellect also has will, for will follows upon intellect. Further, every nature inclines to its own proper end or good. When the end is rational then the inclination is a rational inclination. God has rational inclination toward the good of his own nature. Therefore, God has will (ibid., 1a.19.1).

Having will does not mean that God changes. For the object of God's will is his divine Goodness. And whatever is in oneself necessitates no movement outside oneself to attain. Hence, God does not have to move outside himself to attain his own proper end. And will is an inclination toward one's own end. So, there is will in God, inasmuch as he inclines toward his own good. Will also involves love and delight in what is possessed. God loves and delights in the possession of his own nature. Therefore, God has will in the sense of delight but not in the sense of desire (ibid.).

God's Will Causes Things to Be. Simply because God wills things only in himself does not mean that he wills only himself. For it is in accord with the nature of being to communicate its good to others. And God is being par excellence; he is the source of all being. Hence, it is in accord with the nature of God to will other beings than himself (ibid., 1a.19.2). So God wills things other than himself in and through himself. God is not other than himself, but he can will things other than himself in himself. For will implies a relationship. Hence, although God is not other than himself, yet he wills things other than himself (ibid., 1a.19.2, ad 1).

God is not moved by anything outside himself when he wills to create through himself (ibid., 1a.19.2, ad 2). But in willing things other than himself, God is not moved by any insufficiency in himself but by the sufficiency in himself, that is, by his own goodness. Therefore, willing other things through his own sufficiency denotes no insufficiency in God (ibid., 1a.19.2, ad 3). Just as

God knows many things through the oneness of his essence, he can will many things through the oneness (good) of his will (ibid., 1a.19.2, ad 4).

God Must Will and Can Will. God wills things in two ways. Some things—his own goodness, for example—he must will. He cannot choose to will otherwise. These things he wills with *absolute* necessity. Other things God wills with *conditional* necessity—the goodness of creatures, for example. Whatever is willed by conditional necessity is not absolutely necessary. Creation is willed by conditional necessity.

Of course, God wills other things *because of* his own goodness but not as *necessitated by* it. For God can exist without willing other things. God need only will his own goodness necessarily and other things contingently. Therefore, these other things need not be willed with absolute necessity. Of course, it is necessary to God's will that he will his own nature necessarily. But God need not will anything other than himself. When God did will things other than himself, he must have willed these things voluntarily (ibid., 1a.19.3, ad 3).

It would seem that God must will things necessarily. As a Necessary Being he must know necessarily whatever he knows. It would seem then that he must will necessarily what he wills.

Aquinas responds that divine knowing is necessarily related to the created thing known, because the knowledge in the Knower is one with his essence. But divine willing is not necessarily related to the created thing willed. Willing relates to things as they exist in themselves, outside of the divine essence. God knows necessarily what he knows but does not will necessarily what he wills. Further, all things exist necessarily in God, but nothing exists necessarily outside him. But God need only will what is necessarily of his own nature. Therefore, God need only will other things as they exist in him but not as they exist in themselves outside of himself (ibid., 1a.19.3).

All Created Effects Pre-exist in God's Will. God's will is the cause of all things, so all created things pre-exist in God's knowledge. Will is the inclination to put into action what one knows. Therefore, all created effects flow from God's will (ibid., 1a.19.4). Of course, God must bestow good on all he chooses to create; God cannot create evil. But it is not necessary that God should will any other being or good than himself. Therefore, God need only bestow good on what he chooses to create (ibid., 1a.19.4, ad 1).

God's Will Is Uncaused. As to whether God's will is caused, Aquinas says that, rather, God's will *is* the cause of all things. What is the cause of all needs no cause. For in God the means and the end pre-exist in the cause as willed together. Human will looks to a desired end and what may be done to reach that goal. God's will causes both the end willed and the means to that end. And since all things pre-exist in the First Cause (God's will), there is no cause for God's will (ibid., 1a.19.5).

God's Will Can Never Fail. The will of God is the universal cause of all things. Therefore, the will of God is always fulfilled. What fails to accomplish God's will in one order does so in another order. For example, what falls from the order of his favor returns to the order of his justice. When particular causes fail, the universal cause does not fail. God cannot fail (ibid., 1a.19.6).

One may speak of an *antecedent* and *consequent* will of God. God wills antecedently that all should be saved (2 Peter 3:9). But God wills consequently that some will be lost, namely, those whom justice demands. But what is willed antecedently is not willed absolutely but conditionally. Only the consequent is willed absolutely in view of all the circumstances. Of course, God wills some things through secondary causes. And first causes are sometimes hindered through defects in secondary causes. The movement of the body is hindered by a bad leg. Likewise, God's antecedent will is sometimes hindered by a defect in a secondary cause. But his consequent will is never frustrated. For first universal causes cannot be hindered by defective secondary causes, any more than goodness, as such, can be hindered by evil. However, God is the universal first cause of being, and his will cannot be hindered in his causing of being (ibid., 1a.19.6, ad 2).

God Does Not Change His Mind. Neither can God's will be changed, for God's will is in perfect accord with his knowledge. He is omniscient, so what he knows will be will be. Therefore, God's will is unchangeable. This does not mean that God does not will that some things change. But God's will does not change, even though he does will that other things change (ibid., 1a.19.7). When the Bible speaks of God "repenting," it means that from where we stand it looks as if he has changed his mind. God knew from eternity how it would fall out. And God's will includes intermediate causes, such as human free will. So God knows what the intermediate causes will choose to do. And God's will is in accord with his unchangeable knowledge. Therefore, God's will never changes, since he wills what he knows will happen. What is willed by conditional necessity does not violate human freedom, since what is willed is conditioned on their freely choosing it. God wills the salvation of human beings conditionally. Therefore, God's will to salvation does not violate human free choice, but uses it.

Sources

Augustine, *The City of God*

S. Charnock, *Discourse upon the Existence and Attributes of God*

R. Garriguou-LaGrange, *God: His Existence and His Nature*

N. L. Geisler, *Philosophy of Religion*

Thomas Aquinas, *Summa contra Gentiles*

———, *Summa Theologica*

God, Need for. *See* God, Evidence for.

God, Objections to Proofs for. Most of the traditional objections to arguments for God's existence developed out of issues first posed by David *Hume and Immanuel *Kant. Some of these are treated more fully under the specific apologetic framework to which they are related, such as the moral argument, the ontological argument, and the teleological argument. This overview lists arguments and objections to the existence of God. These are responses to points raised by Christian apologists. Arguments against the existence of God raised by nontheists themselves are discussed in God, Alleged Disproofs of.

Finite Causes for Finite Beings. The cosmological argument reasons from a finite effect to an infinite Cause (God). This conclusion is challenged by those who insist that all one needs to account for a finite effect is a finite cause. Positing an infinite Cause is metaphysical overkill.

However, *every* finite being or effect is limited, and *every* limited being is only adequately explained if it were caused by some Being that is not limited. The first Cause is the unlimited limiter of every limited thing. If this Cause were limited (i.e., caused), it would need a cause beyond itself by which to ground its limited existence. Inescapably, *every* limited being is caused. But Pure Actuality, or Existence as such, is unlimited. And the Actuality that provides the limits for everything else that is actualized must itself be unlimited in its existence. The first Cause must be uncaused, and an Uncaused Cause must be the unlimited or infinite Cause of everything else.

No Necessary Being. It is urged that such terms as *Necessary Being* and *Uncaused Cause* are meaningless, since nothing in our experience corresponds to them. This is not a valid objection. The very sentence, "A Necessary Being has no meaning," is meaningless unless the words *necessary being* can be defined. The claim is self-defeating.

There is nothing incoherent among such terms if they are not contradictory. We know what *contingent* means, and *necessary* is the opposite, namely, "noncontingent." The meanings of these terms are derived from their relationship to what is dependent upon them. And these meanings are twofold: First, the terms *necessary* and *infinite* are negative. *Necessary* means "not contingent." *Infinite* means "not finite." We know what these limitations mean from experience, and, by contrast, we know that God does not have any of them. A negative term does not denote a negative attribute. It is not the affirmation of nothing; rather, it is the negation of all contingency and limitation in the first Cause. The positive content of what God is derives from the causal principle. He is Actuality because he causes all actuality. He is Being since he is the Cause of all being. However, as Cause of all being his being cannot be caused. As the Ground of all contingent being, he must be a Necessary (noncontingent) Being.

Unprovable Causality. Since all forms of the cosmological argument depend on the principle of causality (*see* Causality, Principle of), it would fail without the principle. But can that principle be proved? Normally we think it is obvious, based on experience. But experience may be illusion. Everything not based on experience is simply a tautology, that is, true only by definition and so not proof in itself.

This critique springs from Hume's epistemological atomism—that all empirical impressions are "entirely loose and separate." Hume believed necessary causal connection could not be established empirically from sensible experience. But causality is supported by metaphysical necessity. We need not rely solely on empirical observation. Hume himself never denied that things have a cause for their existence. He said, "I never asserted so absurd a proposition as that anything might arise without a cause" (Hume, 1:187).

It would be ontologically ill-advised to suppose that something could arise from nothing. The principle of causality used by Aquinas is that "every limited being has a cause for its existence." This principle is based in the fundamental reality that nonexistence cannot cause existence; nothing cannot produce something. It takes a producer to produce (*see* Causality, Principle of).

The need for a cause of existence is rooted in the nature of finite, changing beings as composed of *existence* (actuality or act) and *essence* (potentiality or potency). Existence as such is unlimited; all limited existence is being limited by something distinct from existence itself (this limiting factor will be called "essence"); whatever is being limited is being caused, for to be limited in being is to be caused to be in a certain finite way. A limited existence is a caused existence.

Rather, all limited beings are composed beings, composed of existence and essence. Their essence limits the kind of existence they can have. Likewise, an unlimited Being is an uncomposed Being (i.e., a Simple Being). Such a Being has no limiting essence as such. Its essence is identical to its unlimited existence. The need for causality, then, is derived from an analysis of what finite being is. Upon examination, finite being is seen to be caused being, and caused being must have a cause.

Contradictions from Causality. Many nontheists misunderstand the principle of causality. They assume the principle insists that "every *thing* has a cause." If this were true it would follow that one should never stop seeking a cause, even for God. However, the principle should not be stated: "Every *being* has a cause." Rather, it is "Every *finite, contingent being* has a cause." In this way there is no contradiction between a First Cause, which is not contingent, and the principle of causality, which holds that all finite beings need a cause. Once one arrives at an infinite and necessary being, there is no need to seek a further cause. A necessary being explains (grounds) its own existence. It exists because it must exist. It cannot not exist. Only what *can* not exist (namely, a contingent being) needs an explanation. To ask of a necessary being why it exists is like asking why necessity must be necessary, or why circles must be round.

An Infinite Series of Causes. One objection to the cosmological argument is that a First Cause is unneeded because an infinite series of causes is possible. Infinite series are common to mathematics.

The suggestion of an infinite series is only raised in the horizontal (kalam) form of the cosmological argument (*see* KALAM, COSMOLOGICAL ARGUMENT). In the vertical form of *Thomas Aquinas, the very first cause outside of a finite, contingent, changing being must be infinite and uncaused (*see* GOD, EVIDENCE FOR). This is so, because *every* finite being needs a cause. Hence, one finite being cannot cause the existence of another. There cannot be even one intermediate link between the Creator and his creatures. The very first cause outside of beings whose existence is being actualized must be the Actualizer of being.

Mathematically infinite series are possible, but not actual ones. The former are abstract; the latter are concrete. It is possible to have an infinite number of points on one line on this page. But one cannot get an infinite number of letters on this line, no matter how small they are (*see* INFINITE SERIES). Points are abstract or theoretical entities; a series of causes of existence is comprised of actual entities. An infinite number of the former are possible, but not of the latter. The reason for this is simple: No matter how many dominos one has in a line, one more could be added. The number cannot be infinite.

Furthermore, an infinite series of simultaneous and existentially dependent causes is not possible. There must be a here-and-now ground for a simultaneous series of causes, none of which would otherwise have a ground for its existence. An ungrounded infinite regress is tantamount to affirming that the existence in the series arises from nonexistence, since no cause in the series has a real ground for its existence. Or, if one cause in the series grounds the existence of the others, then it must be a First Cause, but then the series is not infinite. Otherwise the cause causes its own existence, while it is causing the existence of everything else in the series. That is impossible.

The Invalid Ontological Argument. *Kant believed that ontological sleight-of-hand imports a Necessary Being into every cosmological argument. Such a move invalidly argues from experience to necessity. This criticism is not applicable to the metaphysical form of the cosmological argument (*see* COSMOLOGICAL ARGUMENT; THOMAS AQUINAS).

Since the cosmological argument begins with existence, not thought, it does not have to smuggle existence into the equation. The first premise is, "Something exists." There is no beginning with "that from which nothing greater can be conceived," by which Anselm began his ontological argument.

The cosmological argument proceeds with principles grounded in reality, not in thought. They are ontologically grounded principles, rather than rationally inescapable ideas. It is based on metaphysical truth that "Nothing cannot cause something," rather than the rational assertion that "Everything must have a sufficient reason" (*see* SUFFICIENT REASON, PRINCIPLE OF). The argument concludes with "Pure Actuality is the cause of existence for all limited existence," rather than with "a Being which logically cannot not be."

The Concept of Necessity. One objection is that the principle of necessity applies only to logical constructs or ideas, not to real-life existence. In fact *necessary* is misapplied to the "Necessary Being" of the cosmological argument.

This argument fails because the objection is self-defeating. Either the statement "Necessity does not apply to real life" is itself a statement about existence, or else it is not. If it is a statement about existence, it is self-defeating, for it claims to be both necessary and about reality, while it is saying no necessary statements can be made about reality. If it is merely a metastatement, or statement about statements (and not really a statement about reality), then it is uninformative about what kind of statements may or may not be made about reality.

This criticism also begs the question. Critics claim to "know" that necessity does not apply to being because there is no Necessary Being. There is no valid way in advance, while looking at the argument for God's existence, to know if a Necessary Being exists. The concept is not contradictory. It simply means not-contingent, which is a coherent idea. But if there is no *a priori* way to know that a Necessary Being cannot exist, then it is possible that necessity truly *may apply* to being, namely, if a Necessary Being does, in fact, exist.

Metaphysical Contradictions. Kant offered several alleged contradictions or antinomies that he thought result from applying cosmological argumentation to reality. At least three of these antinomies apply to the cosmological argument.

The Antinomy about Time. If we assume that time applies to reality, a contradiction seems to result that the world is *both* temporal and eternal. *Thesis:* The world must have begun in time, or else an infinity of moments have elapsed before it began, and this is impossible (since an infinity of moments can never be completed). *Antithesis:* The world could not have begun in time, for that implies that there was a time before time began, and this is contradictory.

Kant's view of time is incorrect. Time is not a continuum of successive moments that exist without beginning or end. Thus, creation did not begin in time that was already there; creation *was* the beginning of time. The only thing "prior" to time is eternity, and eternity is prior in a causal, not a temporal, way.

Further, this argument overlooks the possibility of an eternal creation, which some theists, such as Aquinas, thought philosophically possible. In any event, Kant's objection, if valid, would charge only the horizontal (*kalam*) form of the cosmological argument (*see* KALAM COSMOLOGICAL ARGUMENT). It does not touch the vertical form of the argument based on a here-and-now cause of existence. This type of cosmological argument is not dependent on a specific view about the origin of creation, but only its present conservation in existence. The finite world demands a cause right now, regardless of whether it began in time or is eternal.

The Antinomy of Causality. Theists are charged with arguing that the world both has a First Cause and does not have a First Cause. *Thesis:* Not every cause has a cause or else a series of causes would not begin to cause as they in fact do. *Antithesis:* A series of causes cannot have a beginning, since everything demands a cause. Hence, the series must go on infinitely.

The antithesis of this alleged dilemma is incorrect in stating that *every* cause needs a cause. According to the principle of causality (*see* CAUSALITY, PRINCIPLE OF), only *finite*, contingent things need causes. Thus the Cause of finite being is not finite. Only finite causes need a cause; the first uncaused Cause needs no cause, because it is not finite.

The Antinomy of Contingency. Kant insists that everything must be both contingent and not be contingent, if we assume that these concepts apply to reality. *Thesis:* Not everything is contingent or else there would be no condition for contingency. The dependent must be depending on something that is not dependent. *Antithesis:* Everything must be contingent, for necessity applies only to concepts, not to things.

This objection fails because there is no way to deny that necessity can apply to reality without making a necessary statement about reality. Only an ontological disproof could establish Kant's point. And ontological disproofs (*see* GOD, ALLEGED DISPROOFS OF) are self-defeating. Further, the cosmological argument has already concluded that something necessarily exists. The validity of this argument is the refutation of Kant's contention that necessity does not apply to existence.

Cosmological God. The objection is made that the cosmological argument does not prove a theistic God. There are many other concepts of God besides theism (*see* WORLDVIEW). This First Cause may not be identified with a theistic God any more than with polytheistic gods, a pantheistic god, a panentheistic god, a deistic god, or even the material universe of *atheism* (*see* ATHEISM; DEISM; FINITE GODISM; PANENTHEISM; PANTHEISM; POLYTHEISM).

God Is Not the Gods of Polytheism. There cannot be more than one unlimited existence as such. More than the Most is not possible. Such a Cause is pure Act or Actuality, an Act that is unlimited and unique. Only actuality as conjoined with potency is limited, such as is found in contingent beings. To differ, one being would have to lack some characteristic found in the other. But any being that lacked some characteristic of existence would not be an unlimited, perfect existence. In other words, two infinite beings cannot differ in their potentiality, since they have no potentiality; they are pure actuality. And they cannot differ in their actuality, since actuality as such does not differ from actuality as such. Hence, they must be identical. There can be only one unlimited Cause of all limited existence.

God Is Not the God of Pantheism. Pantheism affirms that an unlimited and necessary Being exists but denies the reality of limited and finite beings. But change is a fundamental fact of finite existence. Pantheism is contrary to our experience of change. If all change, including that in our minds and consciousness, is unreal, then no river moves, no tree grows, and no human ages. If there is any real change, there must really be changing beings distinct from God, for God is an unchanging Being.

God Is Not the God of Panentheism. Panentheism, also known as dipolar theism or process theology, asserts that God has two poles: an *actual pole* (which is identified with the changing temporal world) and a *potential pole* (which is eternal and unchanging). Such a conception of God must be rejected. The conclusion of the cosmological argument demonstrates the need for a God of pure Actuality with no potentiality (pole) at all. Further, God cannot be subject to limitations, composition, or spatiotemporality as an unlimited being. Moreover, the theistic God cannot have poles or aspects, since he is absolutely simple (i.e., uncomposed) with no duality at all (premise 5). A partly limited unlimited existence is a contradiction.

Nor can God be subject to change. For anything that changes must be composed of actuality and potentiality for change. Change is a passing from potentiality to actuality; from what can be to what has actually become. But since existence as such has no potentiality, it cannot change. Anything that changes proves thereby that it possessed some potentiality for the change it underwent. A pure and unlimited actuality cannot change.

Finally, the God of panentheism is a confusion of the world process with the God who grounds that process. God is in the process as the unchanging basis for change, but God is not of the process. God is the cause of all finite, changing existence, but he is beyond all finitude and change. God changes relationally (by entering changing relationships with the world), but he does not change essentially. When the person moves from one side of the pillar to the other, there is a real change in relationship, but there is no change in the pillar.

God Is Not the God of Deism. A deistic God is not the here-and-now cause of the universe, as is the theistic God. Since the universe is a dependent being, it needs something Independent on which to depend—at all times. The universe never ceases to be dependent or contingent. Once contingent, always contingent. A contingent being cannot become a Necessary Being, for a Necessary Being cannot come to be or cease to be. So, if the universe ever ceased being contingent, it would become a Necessary Being, which is impossible.

God Is Not the God of Finite Godism. An uncaused cause is not finite. For every finite being needs a cause, that is, it is caused. But this cause is uncaused. Hence, it cannot be finite or limited. Rather, it is the unlimited Limiter of every limited being. In short, everything limited is caused. Thus, this uncaused Being must be unlimited.

God Is Not the God of Atheism. The uncaused Cause cannot be identical with the material universe, as many atheists believe. As ordinarily conceived, the cosmos or material universe is a limited spatiotemporal system. It is, for example, subject to the second law of thermodynamics and is running down. But an Uncaused Cause is unlimited and not running down. Further, since space and time imply limitations to a here-and-now kind of existence and an uncaused Cause is not limited, then it cannot be identical to the space-time world. The theistic God is in the temporal world as its very ground of continuing existence, but he is not of the world in that it is limited and he is not.

If, in response, one claimed that the whole of the material universe is not temporal and limited, as are the parts, this would only demonstrate what theism claims. For his conclusion is that there exists, beyond the contingent world of the limited spatiotemporality, a "whole" reality that is eternal, unlimited, and necessary. In other words, it agrees with theism that there is a God beyond the limited, changing world of experience. It is a substitute for God which admits that there is a "whole" reality that is "more" than the experienced part of reality and that has all the essential metaphysical attributes of the theistic God.

Therefore, the conclusion of the cosmological argument must be the God of theism, namely, the one, indivisible, infinite, necessary, uncaused Cause of everything that exists, both when it came to exist and right now as it continues to exist.

No Here-and-Now Cause. But much of the above reasoning comes to naught if, as some critics argue, there could be a beginning cause without the need for one now. Either such a Cause has long since gone out of existence, or at least it is not necessary to sustain the universe.

A God who caused the universe and subsequently ceased to exist could not be the theistic God demonstrated by the cosmological argument. The theistic God is a Necessary Being, and a Necessary Being cannot cease to be. If it exists, it must, by its very nature, exist necessarily. A Necessary Being cannot exist in a contingent mode any more than a triangle can exist without three sides.

A necessary being must cause a contingent being at all times. For a contingent being must always be contingent as long as it exists, since it cannot become a Necessary Being. But if a contingent being is always contingent, then it always needs a Necessary Being on which it can depend for its existence. Since no contingent being holds itself in existence, it must be held in existence at all times by a Necessary Being.

For a complete discussion of this argument, see the "objections" section of COSMOLOGICAL ARGUMENT. As is explained in that article, existing is a moment-by-moment process. No thing receives all of its being at once, nor even the next instant of it. Existence comes one moment at a time. At each moment of dependent be-ing there must be some independent Being by whom the moment of being is given. God as Pure Actuality is actualizing everything that is actual.

Arbitrary Models. This objection states that it is only because we have modeled reality as contingent or composed of actuality and potentiality that we are, therefore, forced to conclude that there is a Necessary Being or Pure Actuality. This, they insist, is an arbitrary and loaded way to view reality.

Theists point out that the contingency/necessity model is not arbitrary but is logically exhaustive. Either there is only a Necessary Being, or else there is a contingent being(s) as well as a Necessary Being. But there cannot be merely a contingent being(s). For contingent beings do not account for their own existence, since they are but might not be.

Likewise, either everything is one undifferentiated Pure Actuality or pure potentiality or a combination of actuality and potentiality. No other possibility exists. But there cannot be two Pure Actualities, since actuality as such is unlimited and unique. There cannot be two ultimates or two infinite beings. So whatever else exists must be a combination of actuality and potentiality. But since no potentiality can actualize itself, then beings composed of actuality and potentiality must be actualized by Pure Actuality.

Modal Fallacies. Modal logic is based on the distinction between the possible and the necessary. This form of reasoning has developed its own list of fallacies. Some modal logicians would argue that it is possible for all the parts of my car to break down at one time, but this does not mean that all the parts necessarily will break down at one time. Thus, though all contingent beings possibly do not exist, they do not necessarily not exist at one time and thus would need no universal cause of existence.

As far as modal logic is concerned, this objection is correct and would cast doubt on some forms of the argument from contingency. However, this objection does not apply to Aquinas's argument, since it is not concerned with showing that all things that could *not exist* needed a single cause to produce their existence, but that all things that *do exist* (though possibly could not exist) need a cause for their present existence, both individually and in toto.

A second possible charge of committing a modal fallacy is that it is illegitimate to infer from the fact that the world necessarily needs a being as First Cause that the world needs *a Necessary Being* as First Cause. Again, as it is stated, that charge would be correct, but the cosmological argument of Aquinas does not make that inference. God is not considered a Necessary Being because the argument necessarily demonstrates his being. He is called Necessary Being because ontologically he cannot not be. We learn of his Necessary Being, not from the rigor of our premises, but because the cause of all contingent being cannot be a contingent being, but must be a Necessary Being.

The mistake of many theists, especially since Gottfried *Leibniz (1646–1716), is to cast the cosmological argument in a context of *logical necessity* based on the principle of *sufficient reason*. This ultimately leads to contradictions and an invalidated argument. In contrast, other theists (including Aquinas) used the principle of existential causality to infer the existence of unlimited Cause or Actualizer of all existence. This conclusion is not rationally inescapable, but it is actually undeniable. If any contingent being exists, then a Necessary Being exists; if any being with the potentiality not to exist does exist, then a Being with no potentiality not to exist must exist.

Imperfect World, Imperfect Cause. It is also objected that, if there is a cause of the universe, it need not be perfect, since the world is imperfect. If a cause resembles its effects, then it would seem that the world must be caused by an imperfect, finite, male and female group of gods. For this is what we know as the causes of like imperfect things in our experience.

The ultimate cause, however, cannot be imperfect, since the not perfect can only be known if there is ultimately a Perfect by which it is known not to be perfect. Nor must the cause be identical to its effect. The cause cannot be less than the effect, but it can be more. The cause of finite being cannot be imperfect, since it is Being itself or Pure Actuality. Only Pure Actuality can actualize a potency (potentiality). No potency can actualize itself. Hence, the Cause of being must be perfect in its Being, since it has no potency, limitations, or privation that can constitute an imperfection.

The Explanation of Chance. Why posit an intelligent cause (designer) of the world when chance can explain the apparent design? Given enough time, any "lucky" combination will result. The universe may be a "happy accident" (*see* CHANCE).

For one thing, there has not been enough time for chance to work. One former atheist, Fred Hoyle, calculated that, given the geological time span of billions of years, the chances are still only one to $10^{30,000}$ that so complex a form as even a one-celled animal would emerge by purely natural forces (Hoyle). The chances are virtually zero that chance was responsible.

Second, chance does not "cause" anything; only forces do. And it is known that natural forces do not produce specified complexity, such as that found in living things. Chance is only an abstraction that describes the intersection of two or more lines of causes.

Finally, it is unscientific and irrational to appeal to chance. As even the skeptic David *Hume noted, science is based on observation about regularly recurring events. And the only kind of cause known to rational beings that can cause the specified complexity found in living things is an intelligent cause (*see* EVOLUTION, CHEMICAL).

A Possible Nonexistence. According to this objection, it is always possible to conceive of anything, including God, as not existing. Hence, nothing exists necessarily. Since God is said to be a Necessary Being, then even he must not exist necessarily; therefore God must not exist at all.

This is a valid objection to the ontological argument, but not against the cosmological and teleological arguments. It is possible that nothing would ever have existed, including God. So a total state of nothingness is not an impossible state of affairs. However, something does undeniably exist, and so this objection is irrelevant. For as long as something finite does exist there must be a Cause for its existence.

Only a Logical Existence. Some antitheists argue that it is logically necessary for a triangle to have three sides, but it is not necessary for any three-sided thing to exist. Even if it were logically necessary for God to exist, that does not mean he actually does exist.

At best, this is an objection only to the ontological argument. Theists need not, and most theists do not, conceive of God as a *logically* necessary being but as an *actually* necessary being.

It is logically possible that no triangle exists, but if it does exist, it actually necessarily has three sides. It is logically possible that there is no Necessary Being. But if a Necessary Being exists, then it is actually necessary for it to exist. For a Necessary Being must exist necessarily.

Inferring Cause from Experience. There is an unsurpassable gulf between the thing-to-me *(phenomena)* and the thing-in-itself (*noumena* or real), Kant said. We cannot know the noumena; we know things only as they appear to us, not as they really are. Therefore, we cannot validly infer a real cause from effects we experience.

This objection begs the question and is self-defeating. It begs the question by supposing that our senses do not provide us information about the real world. It wrongly assumes that we sense only sensation rather than sense reality. It mistakenly believes that we know only our ideas, rather than knowing reality through our ideas. Second, in claiming that one cannot know reality, one is making a statement about reality. The agnostic claims to know enough about reality to be sure that nothing can be known about reality. This is a self-defeating claim.

How can Kant know that reality causes our experiences unless there is a valid causal connection between the real (noumenal) world of the cause and the apparent (phenomenal) world of the experience? What is more, one could not even know his own ideas were the result of his mind unless there were real connections between cause (mind) and effect (ideas). Nor would he write books, as agnostics do, assuming that readers would look at the phenomenal effects (words) and be able to know something about the noumenal (real) cause (mind).

The Cause of God. Bertrand *Russell (1872–1970) argued that if everything needs a cause, then so does God. And if all things do not need a cause, then neither does the world. But in neither case do we need a First Cause.

The major premise is false. Theists do not claim that *everything* needs a cause. The principle of causality states only that everything that *begins* (or is finite) needs a cause. If something does not have a beginning, then it obviously does not need a Beginner. Nontheists such as Russell acknowledge that the universe does not need a cause—it is just "there." If the universe can just "be there" without a cause, why can't God?

Arbitrary or Not Ultimate. Russell believed that the moral law is either beyond God or else it results from his will. But if it is beyond God, then God is not ultimate, since he is subject to it (and hence, is not the Ultimate good). And if God decided what would be moral, then he is arbitrary and not essentially good, in which case he would not be worthy of our worship. So, in either case no God worthy of the name exists.

Theists respond in two ways. Voluntarists take the dilemma by the horn and agree that the moral law flows from God's will but deny that this is arbitrary. God is the source of all good. What he wills to be right, is right. And what he wills to be regarded as wrong, is wrong. God's will is the ultimate court of appeal.

Essentialists go through the horns of a dilemma, pointing out that there is a third alternative: God's will is subject to what is essentially good, but this Good is his own unchangeable nature. That is, something is not good simply because God wills it (voluntarism). Rather, God wills it because it is good. It is good because it is in accord with his unchangeably good nature. In this way God is neither arbitrary nor less than ultimate.

All-Powerful Existence. Theists claim God is all powerful. But many nontheists insist this is impossible. The logic of their argument is:

1. If God were all powerful, then he could do anything.
2. And if he could do anything, then God could make a rock so big that he can't move it.
3. But if God could not move this rock, then he could not do everything.
4. Hence, an all-powerful God that can do anything cannot exist.

Put in this form, the theist rejects the first premise as an improper definition of omnipotence. God cannot literally do anything. He can only do what is possible to do consistent with his being as God. He cannot do what is logically or actually impossible. God cannot do some things. He cannot cease being God. He cannot contradict his own nature (cf. Heb. 6:18). He cannot do what is logically impossible, for example make a square circle. Likewise, God cannot make a rock so heavy that he cannot lift for the simple reason that anything he can make is finite. Anything that is finite he can move by his infinite power. If he can make it, he can move it.

Both Good and Evil, Being and Nonbeing. Nontheists say that, if God is infinite, then he is everything, including opposites. He is both good and evil. He is both perfect and imperfect. He is also both Being and nonbeing. But these are opposites, and God cannot be opposites. Further, the theist cannot admit that God is evil or nonexistent. Therefore, no theistic God exists.

The theist rejects the premise that God is everything; he is only what he is—an absolutely perfect Being. And God is not what he is not—an imperfect being. He is the Creator and not a creature. God is pure and necessary existence. So, he cannot be nonexistent. God cannot be opposite of what he is, any more than a triangle can be a square or a circle can be a rectangle.

When we say that God is unlimited or infinite, we do not mean that he is everything. It does not mean, for example, that God is limited and finite. The unlimited cannot be limited. The uncreated Creator cannot be a created creature. The standard for all good cannot be evil.

A Projection of Imagination. Ludwig *Feuerbach (1804–1872) argued that humans made God in their image. God is only a projection of what we think of ourselves. Ideas of God come from our ideas of human beings. Hence, God is only a projection of these ideas. He does not exist beyond them.

This kind of argument makes a serious error: Who can know that God is "nothing but" a projection without "more than" knowledge? The essence of his argument can be stated this way:

1. God exists in human consciousness.
2. But humans cannot go beyond their own consciousness.
3. Therefore, God does not exist beyond our consciousness.

The problem with this argument is the second premise. Simply because we cannot go beyond our consciousness does not mean nothing exists beyond our consciousness. I cannot go beyond my mind, but I know there are other minds beyond mine with whom I converse. If we cannot go beyond our consciousness, then Feuerbach could not make the statement that no God is there. How does he know there is no God out there, unless his knowledge can go beyond his consciousness? To make "nothing-but" statements (such as, "God is nothing but a projection of our imagination") implies "more-than" knowledge.

Simply because we do not go beyond our own consciousness does not mean that our consciousness is not aware of things that are beyond us. We cannot *get* outside of ourselves, but we can *reach* outside of ourselves. This is precisely what knowledge does. Consciousness is not simply consciousness of itself. We are also conscious of others. When we read a book we are not simply conscious of our own ideas; we are conscious of another mind who wrote the words from which we got those ideas. Consciousness does reach beyond itself. That is what the senses and mind enable us to do.

An Illusion. Sigmund *Freud insisted that God is an illusion—something we wish to be true but have no basis for believing, beyond our wish. This argument is developed in the article, Freud, Sigmund. His apparent reasoning:

1. An illusion is something based only in wish but not in reality.
2. The belief in God has the characteristics of an illusion.
3. Therefore, belief in God is a wish not based in reality.

Of course, in this form the theist challenges the minor premise. Not all who believe in God do so simply because they wish for a Cosmic Comforter. Some find God because they thirst for reality; others because they are interested in truth, rather than feeling good. God is not only a comforting Father; he is also a Judge who punishes. Christians believe in hell, and yet no one really wishes this to be true. Freud, in fact, may have it backwards: perhaps our image of earthly fathers is patterned after God, rather than the reverse. Certainly the desire for God is not the only basis for believing that God exists (*see* GOD, EVIDENCE FOR). Freud's argument would, at best, apply only to those who had no other basis than their own wish that God exists.

What is more, the reality of God's existence is independent of the reasons people do or do not wish him to exist. Either God does not exist or he does. Desires cannot draw the truth an inch either way. Freud's disbelief might itself be an illusion, based on his own desire not to follow God and obey God (cf. Ps. 14:1; Rom. 1:18–32).

Chance and Origins. If chance can explain the origin of the universe (*see* EVOLUTION), there is no need for a cause. This objection to proofs for God's existence is subject to several criticisms.

An effect cannot be greater than its cause. The Cause of intelligent beings must be intelligent. It cannot give perfections it does not have to give (*see* FIRST PRINCIPLES; TELEOLOGICAL ARGUMENT).

It is unscientific to speak of chance causing the incredibly complex and intelligent patterns found in the structure of life (*see* TELEOLOGICAL ARGUMENT) and the universe (*see* BIG BANG). Only intelligent intervention adequately explains the organization of DNA in the simplest organism.

Chance is only a statistical *description* of the likelihood of events. Only forces or powers can cause events. Chance merely describes the likelihood of a force (or forces) producing a given event.

Chance cannot be a cause in terms of the cosmological argument. Chance is not a power, and a nonpower cannot cause anything.

Even the critic who proposes chance explanation of the entire universe would not agree that the very words used to express his ideas were a product of chance.

The Possibility of Nothing. Some critics object to the cosmological argument on the ground that it is logically possible that nothing ever existed, including God. If it is logically possible that God never existed, then it is not logically necessary that he does exist.

The theist can readily admit that it is possible for a Necessary Being not to exist so long as nothing else ever existed either. However, *if* there is a Necessary Being then it is not possible that he does not exist. A *logically* Necessary Being need not necessarily actually exist. But an *actually* Necessary Being must necessarily actually exist. The atheists' objection to the concept of a necessary being applies only to a logically necessary being, not to an actually necessary being.

While it is *logically* possible that nothing ever existed, including God, it is not *actually* possible. Something does exist. As long as it is not actually possible for a total state of nothingness, then something must necessarily and eternally exist (e.g., God), since nothing cannot produce something. And if there were ever a total state of nothingness, then there would always be a total state of nothingness. For nothingness cannot produce anything.

A Necessary (Uncaused) Being. But perhaps the whole idea of an uncaused Being is meaningless. It is a coherent concept in the sense of being noncontradictory. A contingent being is one that *can* not exist. A necessary being is one which *cannot* not exist. Since the latter is logically (and actually) opposite of the other, then to reject the coherence of a necessary being would involve rejecting the coherence of a contingent being. But those are the only two kinds of being there can be. Hence, to reject the meaningfulness of the concept of a necessary being would be to reject the meaningfulness of all being. But to say "all being is meaningless" is to make a statement about being which purports to be meaningful. This is self-defeating.

Another way to show the meaningfulness of the concept of an uncaused Being is to point to the atheist's concept of an uncaused universe. Most atheists believe it is meaningful to speak of a universe which had no cause. But if the concept of an uncaused universe is meaningful, so is the concept of an uncaused God.

An Uncaused Universe. Meaningful though an uncaused universe may be, pulling one together in practical terms is something else. The universe is a collection of parts, each contingent and so needing a cause. Either the whole universe is *equal* to all its parts or else it is *more* than all its parts. If it is equal to them, then it too needs a cause. The sum of many dependent parts will never equal more than a dependent whole, no matter how big it is. Adding up *effects* never yields a cause; it produces only a big pile of effects. Only if the universe is *more* than all its effects can it be uncaused and necessary. But to claim that there is a something more, uncaused and necessary on which everything in the universe is dependent is to claim exactly what the theist means by a Necessary Being on which all contingent beings depend for their existence.

The whole issue can be clarified by asking the nontheist this question: If everything in the universe (i.e., every contingent being) suddenly ceased to exist, would there be anything left in existence? If not, then the universe as a whole is contingent too, since the existence of the whole is dependent on the parts. But if something remained after every contingent part of the universe suddenly ceased to exist, then there really is a transcendent necessary uncaused Something which is not dependent on the universe for its existence. But in either case, the atheists' claim fails.

Unconvincing Arguments. Some object that theistic arguments persuade only those who already believe, and who do not need them. Therefore, they are useless. But, whether anyone is convinced by an argument depends on several factors. For one thing, even if the argument is sound, persuasiveness will depend in part on whether the argument is understood.

Once the mind understands the argument, giving assent to it is a matter of the will. No one is ever forced to believe in God simply because the mind understands that there is a God. Personal factors may lead a person to remain uncommitted to belief. Theistic arguments do not automatically convert unbelievers. But persons of good will who understand the argument ought to accept it as true. If they do not, it does not prove that the argument is wrong; rather, it shows their reluctance to accept it.

Conclusion. Many objections have been proposed against the proofs for the existence of God. They are usually based on a misunderstanding of the proofs. None succeed in falsifying the arguments. If they did they would be a proof that you cannot have a proof. That is a self-defeating argument in itself.

Sources

W. L. Craig, *The* Kalam *Cosmological Argument*
L. Feuerbach, *The Essence of Christianity*
J. N. Findlay, "Can God's Existence Be Disproved?" in A. Plantinga, ed., *The Ontological Argument*
R. Flint, *Agnosticism*
S. Freud, *The Future of an Illusion*
R. Garriguou-LaGrange, *God: His Existence and His Nature*
N. L. Geisler, *Philosophy of Religion*
F. Hoyle, et al., *Evolution from Space*
D. Hume, *Dialogues Concerning Natural Religion*
———, *The Letters of David Hume*
I. Kant, *A Critique of Pure Reason*
A. Kenny, *Five Ways*
B. Russell, *Why I Am Not a Christian*

God Talk. *See* **ANALOGY, PRINCIPLE OF.**

Gospel of Barnabas. *See* **BARNABAS, GOSPEL OF.**

Gospel of *Q*. *See* ***Q*** **DOCUMENT.**

Gospel of Thomas, The. *The Claim of the Critics.* Some radical critics of the New Testament claim that the Gnostic (*see* GNOSTICISM) Gospel of Thomas is equal or superior to the New Testament and that it does not support the resurrection of Christ. The so-called *Jesus Seminar places the Gospel of Thomas in their otherwise severely truncated Bible. Both stances are serious challenges to the historic Christian faith.

The Gospel of Thomas was discovered in Nag Hammadi, Egypt, near Cairo in 1945 and was translated into English in 1977. While some have attempted to date parts of it earlier, the Gospel of Thomas is most reliably dated no earlier than A.D. 140–170. It contains 114 secret sayings of Jesus. Defenders of the Gospel of Thomas include Walter Baur, Frederick Wisse, A. Powell Davies, and Elaine Pagels.

An Evaluation of the Credibility of the Gospel of Thomas. The best way to evaluate the credibility of the Gospel of Thomas is by way of comparison to the New Testament Gospels, which often the same critics have grave doubts about (*see* NEW TESTAMENT, HISTORICITY OF; NEW TESTAMENT DOCUMENTS, RELIABILITY OF; NEW TESTAMENT MANUSCRIPTS). When this comparison is made, the Gospel of Thomas comes up seriously short.

The Canonical Gospels Are Much Earlier. Assuming the widely accepted dates of the Synoptic Gospels (ca. A.D. 60–80), the Gospel of Thomas falls nearly a century short. Indeed, there is evidence of even earlier dates for some Gospels (*see* NEW TESTAMENT, DATING OF), as even some liberal scholars admit (see Robinson, John A., all). O. C. Edwards asserts of the Gospel of Thomas and the canonical Gospels that "As historical reconstructions there is no way the two can claim equal credentials" (27). And Joseph Fitzmyer adds, "Time and again, she is blind to the fact that she is ignoring a good century of Christian existence in which these 'gnostic Christians' were simply not around" (123).

The Gospel of Thomas Is Dependent on the Canonical Gospels. Even if the Gospel of Thomas could be shown to contain some authentic statements of Jesus, "no convincing case has been made that any given saying of Jesus in the Gospels *depends on* a saying in the Gospel of Thomas" (Boyd, 118). Rather, the reverse is true since the Gospel of Thomas presupposes truths found earlier in the canonical Gospels.

The Gospel of Thomas Portrays a Second-Century Gnosticism. The Gospel of Thomas is influenced by the kind of Gnosticism prevalent in the second century. For instance, it puts into the mouth of Jesus these unlikely and demeaning words: "Every woman who will make herself male will enter the Kingdom of Heaven" (cited by Boyd, 118).

The Gospel of Thomas's Lack of Narrative Does Not Prove Jesus Did No Miracles. The fact that the author(s) of the Gospel of Thomas did not include narratives of Jesus does not mean they disbelieved in Jesus' miracles. The book seems to be a collection of Jesus' sayings rather than his deeds.

The Canonical Gospels Are More Historically Trustworthy. There are numerous reasons why the New Testament Gospels are more trustworthy than the Gnostic ones. First, the earliest Christians were meticulous in preserving Jesus' words and deeds. Second, the Gospel writers were close to the eyewitnesses and pursued the facts (Luke 1:1–4). Third, there is good evidence that the Gospel writers were honest reporters (*see* NEW TESTAMENT, HISTORICITY OF; WITNESSES, HUME'S CRITERIA FOR). Fourth, the overall picture of Jesus presented in the Gospels is the same.

The Basic New Testament Canon Was Formed in the First Century. Contrary to claims of the critics, the basic New Testament canon was formed in the first century. The only books in dispute have no apologetic effect on the argument for the reliability of the historical material used to establish the deity of Christ.

The New Testament itself reveals that a collection of books existed in the first century. Peter speaks of having Paul's epistles (2 Peter 3:15–16). In fact, he considered them on a par with Old Testament "Scripture." Paul had access to Luke's Gospel, and quotes it in 1 Timothy 5:18. The churches were instructed to send their epistle on to other churches (Col. 4:16).

Beyond the New Testament, there are extrabiblical canonical lists that support the existence of a New Testament canon (see Geisler and Nix, 294). Indeed, all the Gospels and Paul's basic epistles are represented on these lists. Even the heretical canon of the Gnostic *Marcion (ca. A.D. 140) had the Gospel of Luke and ten of Paul's epistles, including 1 Corinthians.

The Second-Century Fathers Support the Canonical Gospels. The second-century Fathers cited a common body of books. This includes all the crucial books that support the historicity of Christ and his resurrection, namely, the Gospels, Acts, and 1 Corinthians. Clement of Roman (A.D. 95) cited the Gospels (*Corinthians*, 13, 42, 46). Ignatius (ca. 110–115) cited Luke 24:39 (*Smyrnaeans* 3). Polycarp (ca. 115) cited all the Synoptic Gospels (Philippians 2, 7). The *Didache* often cites the Synoptic Gospels (1, 3, 8, 9, 15–16). The Epistle of Barnabas (ca. 135) cites Matthew 22:14). Papias (ca. 125–140) in the *Oracles* speaks of Matthew, Mark (following Peter), and John (last) who wrote Gospels. He says three times that Mark made no errors. What is more, the Fathers considered the Gospels and Paul's epistles to be on a par with the inspired Old Testament.

Thus the Fathers vouched for the accuracy of the canonical Gospels in the early second century, well before the Gospel of Thomas was even written.

The Resurrection Account. The Gospel of Thomas does acknowledge Jesus' resurrection. In fact, the living, resurrected Christ himself speaks in it (34:25–27; 45:1–16). True, it does not stress the resurrection, but this is to be expected since it is primarily a "sayings" source rather than historical narration. Furthermore, the Gnostic theological bias against matter would downplay the bodily resurrection.

Conclusion. The evidence for the authenticity of the Gospel of Thomas does not even compare with that for the New Testament. The New Testament dates from the first century; the Gospel of Thomas, the second. The New Testament is verified by many lines of evidence, including self-references, early canonical lists, thousands of citations by the early Fathers, and the well-established dates for the Synoptic Gospels.

Sources

G. Boyd, *Jesus Under Siege*
O. C. Edwards, *New Review of Books and Religion* (May 1980)
C. A. Evans, *Nag Hammadi Texts and the Bible*
J. Fitzmyer, *America* (February 16, 1980)
A. Frederick, et al., *The Gnostic Gospels*
N. L. Geisler, and W. Nix, *General Introduction to the Bible*
R. M. Grant, *Gnosticism and Early Christianity*
E. Linneman, *Is There a Synoptic Problem?*
E. Pagels, *The Gnostic Gospels*
J. A. Robinson, *Redating the New Testament*
J. M. Robinson, *The Nag Hammadi Library in English*
F. Seigert, et al., *Nag-Hammadi Register*
M. J. Wilkins, et al., eds., *Jesus Under Fire*

Gospels, Historicity of. ***See* NEW TESTAMENT, HISTORICITY OF.**

Greenleaf, Simon. Simon Greenleaf (1783–1853) was one of the great minds in American legal history. He not only taught law at Harvard University and produced the standard three-volume study of legal evidence (*A Treatise on the Law of Evidences,* 1842–53) used to teach lawyers the rules of legal evidence and the means by which the authenticity of documents and witnesses can be tested.

When challenged to apply these rules to the New Testament documents, Greenleaf produced a volume *(The Testimony of the Evangelists)* which defends the authenticity of the New Testament. It defends an important link in the overall apologetic argument for Christianity—the trustworthiness of the New Testament witnesses.

An Authentic New Testament. Greenleaf's conclusions include strong points of evidence. The following quotations are from throughout his work:

"Every document, apparently ancient, coming from the proper repository or custody, and bearing on its face no evident marks of forgery, the law presumes to be genuine, and devolves on the opposing party the burden of proving it to be otherwise," Greenleaf wrote. According to this "Ancient Document Rule" the New Testament would qualify as authentic, since it bears no marks of forgery and has been in the proper custody of the church down through the centuries, as shown by manuscript evidence (*see* NEW TESTAMENT MANUSCRIPTS).

"In matters of public and general interest, all persons must be presumed to be conversant, on the principle that individuals are presumed to be conversant with their own affairs." Applied to the New Testament witnesses, this would mean that the books coming from them must be presumed authentic, since they were speaking of their own affairs, with which they were conversant.

"In trials of fact, by oral testimony, the proper inquiry is not whether it is possible that the testimony may be false, but whether there is sufficient probability that it is true." Since there is probable evidence that the New Testament witnesses told the truth (*see* NEW TESTAMENT, HISTORICITY OF), the possibility that they could have been lying does not outweigh the truth of their witness.

"A proposition of fact is proved, when its truth is established by competent and satisfactory evidence." There is competent and satisfactory evidence for the facticity of the New Testament record (*see* ARCHAEOLOGY, NEW TESTAMENT).

"In the absence of circumstances which generate suspicion, every witness is to be presumed credible, until the contrary is shown; the burden of impeaching his credibility lying on the objector." The New Testament, like other books, must be presumed innocent. This is just the opposite of the "presumed guilty until proven innocent" principle used by negative critics (*see* BIBLE CRITICISM).

"The credit due to the testimony of witnesses depends upon, firstly, their honesty; secondly, their ability; thirdly, their number and the consistency of their testimony; fourthly, the conformity of their testimony with experience; and fifthly, the coincidence of their testimony with collateral circumstances." In accordance with these principles the New Testament is an authentic record (*see* also RESURRECTION, EVIDENCE FOR; WITNESSES, HUME'S CRITERIA FOR).

Moral Certainty. Of the nature of moral certainty, Greenleaf wrote (24):

> But the proof of matters of fact rests upon moral evidence alone; by which is meant not merely that species of evidence which we do not obtain either from our own senses, from intuition, or from demonstration. In the ordinary affairs of life we do not require nor expect demonstrative evidence, because it is inconsistent with the nature of matters of fact, and to insist on its production would be unreasonable and absurd.

On the whole, Greenleaf found himself persuaded of a high level of probability that the accounts are true:

> Thus the force of circumstantial evidence is found to depend on the number of particulars involved in the narrative; the difficulty of fabricating them all, if false, and the great facility of detection; the nature of the circumstances to be compared, and from which the dates and other facts are to be collected; the intricacy of the comparison; the number of the intermediate steps in the process of deduction; and the circuitry of the investigation.
>
> The narratives of the sacred dwellers, both Jewish and Christian, abound in examples of this kind of evidence, the value of which is hardly capable of being properly estimated. It does not, as has been already remarked, amount to mathematical demonstration; nor is this degree of proof justly demandable in any moral conduct. In all human transactions, the highest degree of assurance to which we can arrive, short of the evidence of our own senses, is that of probability. The most that can be asserted is, that the narrative is more likely to be true than false; and it may be in the highest degree more likely, but still be short of absolute mathematical certainty. [45]

Conclusion. Greenleaf's conclusion speaks for itself:

> The narratives of the evangelists are now submitted to the reader's perusal and examination, upon the principles and by the rules already stated. . . . His business is that of a lawyer, examining the testimony of witnesses by the rules of his profession, in order to ascertain whether, if they had thus testified on oath, in a court of justice, they would be entitled to credit; and whether their narratives, as we now have them, would be received as ancient documents, coming from the proper custody. If so, then it is believed that every honest and impartial man will act consistently with that result, by receiving their testimony in all the extent of its import.

Sources

S. Greenleaf, *A Treatise on the Law of Evidences*

———, *The Testimony of the Evangelists*

Hh

Hadith, Alleged Miracles in. *See* MUHAMMAD, ALLEGED MIRACLES OF.

Healings, Psychosomatic. Healings occur in various religions. So they have no apologetic value. Furthermore, many events claimed to be supernatural are only psychosomatic. Whether something actually happens in the body, these fall into the category of false miracles (*see* MIRACLES, FALSE) and must be differentiated from true ones (*see* MIRACLES, DEFINITION OF). So it is in the interest of the apologetic enterprise to differentiate supernatural and psychological healings.

It has been demonstrated that the mind has an incredible influence on the body. Psychosomatic or "mind-body" sicknesses and cures do occur. Psychosomatic illnesses are not imaginary. Illnesses with no basis in the body are called conversion disorders or other forms of neurosis. An ulcer is a psychosomatic illness if it was caused at least in part by nervousness that disrupted the digestive process and induced overproduction of acids or other enzymes. Since they have an emotional basis, such sicknesses are prone to healing by the mind. This is used by some to argue that healings are always psycho-emotional phenomena.

Mind over Matter. People have become sick and even hospitalized simply because a group of friends (doing an experiment) have suggested to them they were ill. They have been "cured" the same way—when the friends later suggested that they looked better. This is an example of emotion-caused illness and "healing" that is only peripherally related to the body.

Physician and Christian apologist Paul Brand gives examples of the mind's power to heal the body. The mind can effectively control pain by stimulating production of endorphins, simple mental discipline, flooding the nervous system with other stimuli. Acupuncture is an example of adding sensations to disrupt pain.

In the placebo effect, faith in simple sugar pills stimulates the mind to control pain and even heal some disorders. In some experiments among those with terminal cancer, morphine was an effective painkiller in two-thirds of patients, but placebos were equally effective in half of those. The placebo tricks the mind into believing relief has come, and the body responds accordingly.

Through biofeedback, people can train themselves to direct bodily processes that previously were thought involuntary. They can control blood pressure, heart rate, brain waves, and body temperature.

Under hypnosis, 20 percent of patients can be induced to lose consciousness of pain so completely that they can undergo surgery without anesthetics. Some patients have even cured warts under hypnosis. The hypnotist suggests the idea, and the body performs a remarkable feat of skin renovation and construction, involving the cooperation of thousands of cells in a mental-directed process not otherwise attainable.

In a false pregnancy, a woman believes so strongly in her pregnant condition that her mind directs an extraordinary sequence of activities: It increases hormone flow, enlarges breasts, suspends menstruation, induces morning sickness, and even prompts labor contractions. All this without fertilization and a growing fetus (Brand, 19).

Dr. William Nolen explains that "the patient who suddenly discovers . . . that he can now move an am or leg that was previously paralyzed had that paralysis as a result of an emotional, not a physical disturbance." It is known that "Neurotics and hysterics will frequently be relieved of their symptoms by the suggestions and ministrations of charismatic healers. It is in treating patients of this sort that healers claim their most dramatic triumphs" (Nolen, 287). "There is nothing miraculous about these cures. Psychiatrists, internists, G.P.'s and M.D.'s who do psychiatric therapy, relieve thousands of such patients of their symptoms every year" (ibid.).

Christian psychiatrist Paul Meyer, revealed that he healed a young woman of blindness by merely instructing her that when she awoke from sleep in another room, she would be able to see. The cure came just as the doctor ordered. Her sight was restored by the power of suggestion. Other doctors have recorded cures of chronic diarrhea by prescribing placebos. Severe skin disease and even lameness have been cured by such means.

It is commonly known that up to 80 percent of disease is stress related (Pelletier, 8). These emotionally induced diseases can often be reversed by psychological therapy or "faith healings" where the proper mental attitude occasions a healing effect.

None of these cures are supernatural. The effect of the mind on the body is a natural process. It involves no suspension of natural laws. One can learn to do it. When performed by a person who claims to be a channel for God, it is no less natural. Faith in various kinds of gods or just faith in another person (the doctor or healer) will do the same thing.

Christians should not be surprised that natural psychosomatic cures occur. God created the mind with wonderful abilities and the body's curative powers. The Bible recognizes the effect of the mind on one's health: "A cheerful heart is good medicine, but a crushed spirit dries up the bones" (Prov. 17:22). In his book, *Anatomy of an Illness*, Norman Cousins described in detail how he literally laughed himself well from cancer. One can actually get sick when saddened by tragedy or well upon hearing good news.

Since God has created us as mind-body unities, he should get the credit when this marvelous relationship of mind affecting body is used to bring healing. However, it is a serious overclaim to call these cures supernatural.

What the Mind Cannot Do. There are some conditions "faith" alone cannot cure. The power of positive thinking cannot avoid death, raise the dead, give sight to a body without eyes, grow amputated limbs, or heal quadriplegics. Dr. Nolen observes that no paralyzing spinal cord injury has been or ever will be cured through faith-healing (Nolen, 286). Joni Earickson Tada suffered such an injury in a swimming accident and was left a quadriplegic. In spite of fervent prayers, she remains unhealed by all the faith she could muster. Joni concludes "God certainly can, and sometimes does, heal people in a miraculous way today. But the Bible does not teach that He will always heal those who come to Him in faith. He sovereignly reserves the right to heal or not to heal as He sees fit" (Tada, 132).

Supernatural Intervention. Mrs. Tada recognizes that, if God heals her spinal cord, a different kind of healing would take place, one that suspends natural processes. Miracles, in contrast to natural healings, are the way God works on special occasions. The way God usually heals is slowly. But in a miracle he works immediately. When Jesus healed the man with leprosy, the cure was instantaneous—not the result of self-rejuvenation of skin tissues (Mark 1:42).

Many of Jesus' miracles involved a speeding up of a natural process. The farmer puts grain into the ground and it slowly multiplies into more grain by harvest time. Jesus, however, took bread (grain) and immediately multiplied it to feed 5000 (John 6:10–12).

We refer to the "miracles" of birth or life. God is the one who causes both. But it confuses the issue to speak of natural, gradual, and repeatable events as "miracles." They are simply the way God works regularly. They are marvelous but not miraculous (*see* MIRACLE).

A true miracle is not a natural activity but a direct supernatural act (*see* MIRACLES IN THE BIBLE). This is why one of the biblical words for miracle is "wonder." It attracts our attention. A bush burning is not unusual, but when it burns without being consumed and the voice of God speaks from it, it is not a natural event (Exod. 3:1–14).

From an apologetic standpoint, how do we distinguish a normal cure from a miraculous one? Can we tell a psychological cure from a supernatural one? Only the latter has apologetic value (*see* MIRACLES, APOLOGETIC VALUE OF).

Faith is an essential ingredient of a psychosomatic healing, but not for a supernatural healing, though it may accompany it. Someone can be healed who does not believe healing is possible. Thirty-five miracles of Jesus are recorded in the Gospels. Of these the faith of the recipient is only mentioned in ten: (1) the lame man (John 5:1–9); (2) a leper (Matt. 8:2–4); (3) a withered hand (Matt. 9:2–8); (4) the man born blind (John 9:1–7); (5) blind Bartimaeus (Matt. 20:29–34); (6) the hemorrhaging woman (Matt. 9:20–22; Mark 5:24–34; Luke 8:43–48); (7) the ten lepers (Luke 17:11–19); (8) Peter walking on water (Matt. 14:24–33); (9) first miraculous catch of fish (Luke 5:1–11); (10) the second miraculous catch of fish (John 21:1–11).

In most of these cases faith was not explicitly demanded as a precondition. In the few cases where faith was required, it was probably faith in Christ as Messiah that was needed, not faith that the person could be healed. So even in these cases faith may not be required in order to be healed.

In at least eighteen of Jesus' miracles, faith is not present explicitly or implicitly. In some cases the faith is a result of the miracle, not a condition of it. When Jesus turned water to wine, "He thus revealed his glory, and his disciples put their faith in him" (John 2:11).

Jesus' disciples did not believe he could feed the 5000 by multiplying loaves and fishes (Luke 9:13–14; cf. Matt. 14:17). Even after they had seen Jesus feed 5000, they disbelieved he could do it again for 4000 (Matt. 15:33). In the case of the paralytic, Jesus healed him when he saw the faith of the four who carried him to Jesus, not the faith of the man himself (Mark 2:5).

In seven miracles Jesus could not have required faith. This is certainly true of the three he raised from the dead. Yet Jesus raised Lazarus (John 11), the widow's son (Luke 7), and Jairus's daughter (Matthew 9). The same is true of the cursed fig tree (Matt. 21), the miracle of the tax money in the fish (Matt. 17:24–27), the two times Jesus multiplied loaves (Matt. 14:15), and his calming of the sea (Matt. 8:18–27).

Neither can it be shown that faith of the disciples was required. In most cases the disciples lacked faith. In the miracle of raising Lazarus, Jesus prayed that those present might believe that God has sent him (John 11:42). Just before Jesus rebuked the waves, he said to the disciples, "Where is your faith?" (Luke 8:25). After he calmed the waters he asked, "Do you still have no faith?" (Mark 4:40).

Sometimes Jesus performed miracles in spite of unbelief. The disciples lacked faith to cast the demon out of the boy (Matt. 17:14–21). Even the passage most often used to show that faith is necessary for miracles proves just the opposite. Matthew 13:58 tells us that "Jesus did not do many miracles there because of their lack of faith." However, in spite of the unbelief present, Jesus laid "his hands on a few sick people and healed them" (Mark 6:5).

Distinguishing Healings. There is a clear distinction between supernatural and psychological healing. A truly miraculous cure is distinguished from a mental one by several characteristics. Only religions manifesting these characteristics can use them as a confirmation of truth claims.

Miracles Do Not Require Faith. God is in sovereign control of the universe, and he can and does perform miracles with or without our faith. Miracles are "according to his will" (Heb. 2:4). Miraculous gifts were distributed to New Testament believers "according to his will" (1 Cor. 12:11). As shown, Jesus performed miracles even where there was unbelief.

On the other hand, psychological healings require faith. Those who suffer from psychosomatic illnesses must believe, whether in God, in a physician, or in an evangelist. Their faith makes the healing possible. But there is nothing supernatural about that kind of healing. It happens to Buddhists (*see* BUDDHISM), Hindus (*see* HINDUISM), Roman Catholics, Protestants, and even atheists. Healers claiming supernatural powers can do it. So can psychologists and psychiatrists.

Miracles Do Not Require Personal Contact. Sometimes the apostle laid hands on those whom God miraculously healed (cf. Acts 8:18). However, it was not essential to the miracles. Jesus never touched many of those who were healed. Jesus raised the nobleman's son from the dead from a long distance (John 4:50–54). Jesus never touched Lazarus when he brought him back to life (John 11:43–44). The apostle laid hands on the Samaritan believers so that they could receive the Holy Spirit (Acts 8:18; 19:6). Yet the apostles themselves received the Spirit without anyone laying hands on them (Acts 2:1).

By contrast, faith healings depend on the laying on of hands or some other physical contact or personal influence. Some healers use prayer cloths. Others ask listeners to place their hands on the radio or TV as a point of contact. One evangelist asks people to stand on the Bible with their hands on the television. The personal contact or at least the psychological build up seem to be conditional to the healing itself.

Miracles Involve No Relapses. Biblical miracles last; there were no relapses. When Jesus healed a disease, it did not return. Of course, everyone eventually died, even those he raised from the dead. But this was a result of the natural process of mortality, not because the miracle was canceled. But when Jesus performed a miracle, it lasted. Whatever other eventual problems the body had, it was not because that miracle did not immediately and permanently repair that problem.

Psychological cures do not always last, whether induced by hypnotism, placebo pills, or faith healers. In fact, those "healed" and the healers eventually succumb to bad health. Radio preacher Chuck Smith relates that he knows some of the chief exponents of positive faith in the health and prosperity gospel who have spent time in the hospital for nervous exhaustion (Smith, 136–37).

Miracles Are Always Successful. Jesus never failed in a miracle he attempted. Since a miracle is an act of God, it is impossible for it to fail. It is true that Jesus did not always attempt to do a miracle. Sometimes he stated why (cf. Matt. 13:58). Since he was not in the entertainment business, Jesus did not always satisfy the fancy of his audience. God does miracles according to his will (Heb. 2:4) and purposes, not ours. But when God attempts a supernatural event, he does it.

Psychological attempts to heal are by no means all successful. As noted, some kinds of physical problems are not curable by faith. Psychological cures are most frequently successful on more suggestible personality types. Some studies show that the vast majority of people in the healing movement have these personality types.

Miracles Are on Organic Sicknesses, Not Just Functional Illness. Jesus healed people born blind (John 9), and lame (John 5). The apostles cured a man lame from birth (Acts 3:2). Jesus restored a withered hand immediately (Mark 3:1–5). Psychological healings do not take place on any of these kinds of organic healings or conditions of nature. They are usually effective only on functional diseases. Most often they only aid or speed recovery. Never do they instantaneously cure or restore the incurable.

Dr. Brand stated flatly that he has never heard an account of miraculous healing of pancreatic cancer, cystic fibrosis, a major birth defect, or amputation (interview, *Christianity Today,* 25 November 1983). George Bernard Shaw once caustically commented that the healings at Lourdes, France, left him unconvinced. He saw many crutches and wheel chairs on display "but not one glass eye, wooden leg, or toupee" (ibid.).

Miracles Are Always Immediate. As mentioned earlier, Jesus healed people "immediately" (Mark 1:42). When he spoke the sea was calmed "completely" (Matt. 18:26). When the apostle healed the man lame from birth, "instantly the man's feet and ankles became strong" (Acts 3:7). Even in the one case of a two stage miracle, each stage was accomplished immediately (Mark 8:22–25).

Summary. The mind can aid in the healing process. Positive mental attitude often hastens the natural curative process. When the sickness is psychologically caused, there can be a dramatic reversal when the person suddenly believes he can be healed. In this sense some psychosomatic cures can be immediate. But they cannot be done on all diseases, especially organic and incurable kinds. "Faith" cures of functional diseases are not supernatural. They lack the characteristics of a true miracle. It is these marks that give miracles apologetic value. Indeed, only the Judeo-Christian prophets have verified unique examples of these kinds of cures (*see* MIRACLES, AS CONFIRMATION OF TRUTH; MUHAMMAD, ALLEGED MIRACLES OF).

Sources

P. Brand, *CT* (25 November 1983)
N. L. Geisler, *Signs and Wonders*
W. Nolen, *A Doctor in Search of a Miracle*
K. Pellitier, *CMSJ* 1 (1980):8
C. Smith, *Charismatics or Charismania?*
J. E. Tada, *A Step Further*
B. B. Warfield, *Counterfeit Miracles*

"Heathen," Salvation of. The fate of those who have never heard the Gospel, traditionally called "heathen" by missiologists and apologists, poses a problem for the benevolence of God. If God is all-loving, then how can he send people to hell who have never heard about Jesus and how to be saved? Some estimate that at the end of the twentieth century about one-half of the more than 5 billion people alive had never heard the Gospel. Many more had technically "heard" the Gospel but not really been taught about Christ in any meaningful way.

Two answers to this problem have been offered. Some believe the heathen can be saved apart from the Gospel if they respond to the light of general revelation. Others believe that God provides the truth of the Gospel by special revelation to those who truly seek him.

Salvation in General Revelation. Those who believe a sinner can be saved apart from hearing that Jesus died for their sins and rose from the dead (1 Cor. 15:1–5) reason in the following manner:

The Love and Justice of God. The Bible affirms that God is just (Ps. 33:5). He is no respector of persons. For "God does not show favoritism" (Rom. 2:11). Abraham declared: "Will not the Judge of all the earth do right?" (Gen. 18:25). Further, God is all-loving. He loves the whole world and sent his only Son to die for it (John 3:16). For "The Lord is not slow in keeping his promise, as some understand slowness. He is patient with you, not wanting anyone to perish, but everyone to come to repentance" (2 Peter 3:9). Arguing from the attributes of love and justice, some Christian apologists insist that such a God would not condemn those who have never heard the Gospel of Christ. They offer some Scriptures in support for their belief:

Acts 10:35. Peter told Cornelius, the Gentile who had never heard the Gospel, that God "accepts men from every nation who fear him and do what is right" (Acts 10:35). The text indicates that he had "feared God" (vs. 2) and was accepted by him, even though he had not yet heard the Christian message.

Acts 19:2–6. Acts 19:2–6 tells of believers who were saved many years after the time of Christ, even though they had not yet received the Holy Spirit. Paul asked them, "Did you receive the Holy Spirit when you believed?" They answered, "No, we have not even heard that there is a Holy Spirit." So Paul declared the truth to them and "On hearing this, they were baptized into the name of the Lord Jesus" (Acts 19:5). But they were called "disciples" (believers) even before Paul preached to them (vs. 1).

Romans 2:6–7. Paul declared that "God 'will give to each person according to what he has done.' To those who by persistence in doing good seek glory, honor and immortality, he will give eternal life" (Rom. 2:6–7). This is in the context of "Gentiles who have not the law" (2:14), that is, heathen. But this would mean that heathen can receive "eternal life" apart from special revelation through God's law.

Galatians 3:8. According to Paul, "The Scripture foresaw that God would justify the Gentiles by faith, and announced the gospel in advance to Abraham: 'All nations will be blessed through you'" (Gal. 3:8). But the "Gospel" Abraham heard did not have the explicit content that Christ, the Son of God, died and rose from the dead. For when Abraham believed, the text simply says that, "He took him outside and said, 'Look up at the heavens and count the stars—if indeed you can count them.' Then he said to him, 'So shall your offspring be'" (Gen. 15:5).

Hebrews 11:6. According to this verse, "anyone who comes to him must believe that he exists and that he rewards those who earnestly seek him" (Heb. 11:6). This would seem to include those who have never heard the Gospel as well.

Revelation 14:6. John the apostle said: "Then I saw another angel flying in midair, and he had the *eternal gospel* to proclaim to those who live on the earth—to every nation, tribe, language and people" (Rev. 14:6). If the Gospel by which they were saved is eternal, then it was the same one proclaimed in the Old Testament. The next text indicates that this text did not have the same content as the New Testament Gospel (1 Cor. 15:1–5). Yet people were saved by believing the good news that God is gracious.

Jonah 3:1–5. The Old Testament relates an explicit story as to how the heathen were saved—at least from physical destruction. The Jewish prophet Jonah was told to go to Nineveh (Assyria) and proclaim: "Forty more days and Nineveh will be overturned." And "The Ninevites believed God. They declared a fast, and all of them, from the greatest to the least, put on sackcloth" (Jonah 3:4–5). And "When God saw what they did and how they turned from their evil ways, he had compassion and did not bring upon them the destruction he had threatened" (Jonah 3:10). Jonah later said of their conversion, "I knew that you are a gracious and compassionate God, slow to anger and abounding in love, a God who relents from sending calamity" (Jonah 4:2).

There is no indication whatsoever that the content they believed was any more than belief in a gracious God who forgives those who turn from their sins to him in faith.

Psalm 19:1–4. The very heavens proclaim the Gospel, according to Psalm 19: "The heavens declare the glory of God; the skies proclaim the work of his hands. Day after day they pour forth speech; night after night they display knowledge. There is no speech or language where their voice is not heard. Their voice goes out into all the earth, their words to the ends of the world." This passage appears to teach that everyone everywhere has heard the "Gospel" of creation by which they can be saved. Interestingly, this is the very passage referred to by the apostle Paul when he says no one can hear without a preacher (Rom. 10:14, 18).

An Important Distinction. All evangelicals believe it is necessary that Christ died and rose in order for anyone to be saved. Those who hold that salvation can be obtained through general revelation insist, however, that it is not necessary to *know* about this fact. They point out that one could receive a gift of new shoes from an unknown benefactor without knowing what animal died to provide the leather or who gave them the shoes. Hence, all verses that indicate Christ's death and resurrection were necessary for salvation are taken to refer to the *fact* of Christ's death, not to explicit *knowledge* of that fact.

Salvation through Christ. The standard orthodox position of Martin Luther and John Calvin and their disciples was that salvation is not possible apart from belief in the death and resurrection of Christ, at least not since the time of Christ.

Salvation by Knowledge of Christ. The standard orthodox position that salvation comes only through knowledge of Christ raises an even more serious problem about God's justice and benevolence with regard to the destiny of those who have never heard. Nonetheless, there are many Scriptures that point in this direction.

Acts 4:12. The apostles in Acts 4:12 declared that "Salvation is found in no one else, for there is no other name under heaven given to men by which we must be saved." Since there is explicit reference to the "name" of Christ, it is difficult to believe that explicit knowledge of Christ is not demanded as a condition of salvation. It is not simply the *fact* of Christ but the *name* of Christ that is necessary for salvation.

Romans 10:9. Paul insists that "if you confess with your mouth, 'Jesus is Lord,' and believe in your heart that God raised him from the dead, you will be saved." Romans 10:9 would seem to demand that confession of the very name of "Jesus" is necessary for salvation.

Romans 10:13–14. The apostle follows up by adding in 10:13–14: "Everyone who calls on the name of the Lord will be saved. How, then, can they call on the one they have not believed in? And how can they believe in the one of whom they have not heard? And how can they hear without someone preaching to them?" The emphasis on the fact that the unbeliever must "call" on Christ and that they must "hear" the Gospel by someone who is "preaching" to them would seem to eliminate the possibility that anyone can be saved today apart from hearing the Gospel of Christ.

John 3:18. Jesus himself said emphatically in John 3:18: "Whoever believes in him is not condemned, but whoever does not believe [in him] stands condemned already because he has not believed in the name of God's one and only Son." Explicit belief "in the name of God's one and only Son" is laid down as the condition of salvation.

John 3:36. John 3:36 makes it clear that "Whoever believes in the Son has eternal life, but whoever rejects the Son will not see life, for God's wrath remains on him." This seems to point clearly to knowledge of the "Son" (Christ) as necessary for salvation.

John 10:9, 11, 14. Jesus said in John 10:9–14, "I am the gate; whoever enters through me will be saved. . . . I am the good shepherd. The good shepherd lays down his life for the sheep. . . . I know my sheep and my sheep know me." The fact that the sheep (believers) must "know" Christ and "enter" the gate indicates that an explicit knowledge of Christ is necessary for salvation.

1 John 5:10–13. John repeats the same truth in 1 John 5:10b–13: "Anyone who does not believe God has made him out to be a liar, because he has not believed the *testimony* God has given about his Son. And this is the *testimony*: God has given us eternal life, and this life is in his Son. He who has the Son has life; he who does not have the Son of God does not have life. I write these things to you who *believe in the name of the Son of God* so that you may know that you have eternal life." The emphasized words make clear that John is teaching that explicit knowledge of Christ is necessary for salvation.

A Response to General Revelationists. Proponents of salvation only through *special revelation are well aware of proof texts used by those who believe salvation of the heathen is possible through *general revelation alone.

Acts 10:35. Two things are often mentioned about the case of Cornelius. First, Cornelius is a proof that those who seek God in view of the light they have will be given special revelation by which they can come to know Christ. After all, the whole point of the story is that God sent Peter with a special revelation and that Cornelius did not become a Christian until after he heard and believed this special revelation. Second, some point out that the book of Acts is a transitional period between the Old Testament and the New Testament, during which those who were saved on Old Testament grounds were provided with the light of Christ by which they could become Christians. Cornelius may fit this category.

Acts 19:2–6. This passage is about disciples of John the Baptist who had not yet heard about the coming of the Holy Spirit. It has nothing to do with those who have never heard the Gospel. The episode illustrates the transitional nature of the time, during which those who had not yet heard the Christian message (or the full message) were saved on the grounds of the special revelation they had received.

Hebrews 11:6. According to Hebrews 11:6, "anyone who comes to him [God] must believe that he exists and that he rewards those who earnestly seek him." While the reference is to knowledge of God, not of Christ, one includes the other. Since the context is Old Testament saints, not New Testament believers, it is understandable why the broader statement about explicit knowledge of Christ was not included. This is a statement of the minimal requirement to be saved in any age. It does not exclude belief in Christ as an explicit requirement of salvation.

Galatians 3:8. Proponents of special revelation respond in two ways to Galatians 3:8. Some hold that even in Old Testament times believers did have an explicit knowledge of the coming Christ. Paul said the "seed" of Abraham was Christ (Gal. 3:16). Jesus said to the Jews, "Your father Abraham rejoiced at the thought of seeing my day; he saw it and was glad" (John 8:56). This may indicate that Abraham knew Christ personally (perhaps as the Angel of the Lord). Other proponents simply take Galatians 3:8 to describe the more minimal content (exclusive of explicit knowledge of Christ's death and resurrection) necessary for salvation in the Old Testament. The content of what Abraham believed was clearly spelled out in the Old Testament (Gen. 15:5–6) and it said nothing about Christ's death and resurrection, only that his offspring would be as numerous as the stars of the heavens.

Revelation 14:6. John's reference to the *"eternal gospel,"* whatever it may mean, does not support the view that salvation of the "heathen" is based on only general revelation. This message came to them by special revelation. God sent an angel to preach it. Further, the content of this Gospel was about those who believed in the "lamb of God" who "redeemed" them by his blood (14:1, 4). That the Gospel is everlasting may mean no more than that Christ was "the Lamb that was slain from the creation of the world" (Rev. 13:8). There is certainly no indication John is speaking about an eternal Gospel known only by general revelation.

Jonah 3:1–5. Old Testament saints did not necessarily have the same content knowledge required for salvation in the New Testament. The doctrine of *progressive revelation indicates that God progressively unfolded his plan on earth by giving more and more revelation until the full and final revelation in Christ (Heb. 1:1–2).

Psalm 19:1–2. The psalmist is not speaking of God's special revelation but of general revelations through the "heavens" which are the "work of his [creative] hands." He is not speaking of the cross, which is the work of God's redemptive love (Rom. 10:14, 18). According to Romans, general revelation informs us about God's "eternal power and Godhead" (Rom. 1:20). It is sufficient for condemnation, since it finds all men "without excuse" (ibid.) but not for salvation.

Romans 2:6–7. This text does not affirm that heathen are saved by general revelation, but only those who "seek . . . for immortality." Later Paul said it is only Christ "who has destroyed death and has brought life and immortality to light through the gospel" (2 Tim 1:10). General revelation and other means are part of the "goodness of God that leads . . . to repentance" (vs. 4). Those who respond to the light of general revelation are given special revelation by which they can be saved.

A Vindication of God's Justice. But is it fair for God to send people to hell who have never heard the only Gospel by which they can be saved? This question is really several questions in one. They will be broken down and analyzed one by one.

Are The Heathen Lost? The biblical answer to this question is clear: All human beings are born in sin (Ps. 51:5 KJV) and are "by nature the children of wrath" (Eph. 2:3 KJV). For ". . . just as sin entered the world through one man, and death through sin, and in this way death came to all men, because all sinned [in Adam]" (Rom. 5:12). Addressing explicitly the heathen who have only general revelation, the apostle Paul declared "For since the creation of the world God's invisible qualities—his eternal power and divine nature—have been clearly seen, being understood from what has been made, *so that men are without excuse*" (Rom. 1:20). Likewise, he adds, "All who sin apart from the law will also perish apart from the law, and all who sin under the law will be judged by the law" (Rom. 2:12). Then, summing up his conclusion from the whole section, Paul pronounces that "There is no difference, for all have sinned and fall short of the glory of God" (Rom. 3:22–23). Yes, sinful rebels from God remain lost apart from knowing about Christ.

Is There Salvation Apart from Christ? All orthodox Christians agree that there is no salvation apart from Christ's redemptive work. Jesus said, "I am the way and the truth and the life. No one comes to the Father except through me" (John 14:6). The apostle Paul added "For there is one God and one mediator between God and men, the man Christ Jesus" (1 Tim. 2:5). Further, the writer of Hebrews agreed, affirming that "Christ . . . has appeared once for all at the end of the ages to do away with sin by the sacrifice of himself" (Heb. 9:26). And "this priest [Christ] had offered for all time one sacrifice for sins, he sat down at the right hand of God . . . because by one sacrifice he has made perfect forever those who are being made holy" (Heb. 10:12, 14). Literally, "Salvation is found in no one else, for there is no other name under heaven given to men by which we must be saved" (Acts 4:12).

Is It Fair to Condemn Those Who Have Not Heard? Yes, it is just to condemn those who have never received God's special revelation. First, through general revelation they know about his "eternal power and Godhead" (Rom. 1:20). They are aware that he "made heaven and earth and sea and everything in them" (Acts 14:15). They are aware that God "has not left himself without testimony: He has shown kindness by giving you rain from heaven and crops in their seasons" (Acts 14:17). Although they do not have the Law of Moses, "All who sin apart from the law will also perish apart from the law. . . . Indeed, when Gentiles, who do not have the law, do by nature things required by the law, they are a law for themselves, even though they do not have the law [of Moses], since they show that the requirements of the law are written on their hearts" (Rom. 2:12–15).

Even though God has revealed himself to the heathen in creation and in conscience, fallen humanity has universally rejected that light. Hence, God is not obligated to give them any more light, since they have turned from the light they have. In fact, although they have the truth, "the wrath of God is being revealed from heaven against all the godlessness and wickedness of men who suppress the truth by their wickedness" (Rom. 1:18). Someone lost in the darkness of a dense jungle who sees one speck of light should go toward it. If that person turns away from the little light and becomes forever lost in darkness, there is only one person to blame. The Scriptures say, "This is the verdict: Light has come into the world, but men loved darkness instead of light because their deeds were evil" (John 3:19).

If any unbeliever truly sought God through the general revelation, God would provide the special revelation sufficient for salvation. After God led Peter to the Gentile Cornelius, Peter declared: "I now realize how true it is that God does not show favoritism but accepts men from every nation who fear him and do what is right" (Acts 10:35). The writer of Hebrews tells us that those who seek, find. "He rewards those who earnestly seek him" (Heb. 11:6).

God has many ways at his disposal through which he can get the truth of the Gospel to lost souls. The normative way is through preachers of the Gospel (Rom. 10:14–15), whether in person or on radio, TV, or some recording. On one occasion God will use an angel to preach the Gospel "to every nation, tribe, language and people" (Rev. 14:6). Many people have been given a Bible, read it, and been saved. Others have been saved through Gospel literature. We have no way of knowing whether God has conveyed special revelation through visions, dreams, and in other miraculous ways. The truth is that God is more willing that all be saved than we are. For "the Lord is not slow in keeping his promise, as some understand slowness. He is patient with you, not wanting anyone to perish, but everyone to come to repentance" (2 Peter 3:9). God's justice demands that he condemns all sinners, but his love compels him to provide salvation for all who by his grace will believe. For "Everyone who calls on the name of the Lord will be saved" (Rom. 10:13).

One thing is important to keep in mind. To send people to hell who have never heard is not unjust. To think so is like claiming that it is not right for someone to die of a disease for which there is a cure of which he or she has not yet heard. The crucial question is how one got the disease, not whether he or she has heard of a cure. What is more, if one desires neither to know there is a cure or to do what is necessary to get cured, then he or she is most certainly culpable.

Will There Be People Saved from Every Nation? Those who reject the view that special revelation is necessary for salvation generally point to those in non-Christian lands. What about China, India, Africa, and many formerly Communist countries? Surely it is not fair to have so many in heaven from Western countries and so few from Eastern lands.

There is no reason why the percentage of people saved must be the same from all countries. Who is saved will depend on who believes, and that will vary from place to place. Just as in farming and fishing, some areas are more fruitful than others. The Scriptures assure us that there will be "a great multitude that no one could count, from every nation, tribe, people and language, standing before the throne and in front of the Lamb" (Rev. 7:9a). Indeed, while the percentage may understandably vary, it would seem strange if there were no one from one country that desired to be saved (just as it would if everyone from another country wanted to be saved). People have free choice, and free choice is exercised freely. Some will believe and some will not.

There are ways by which people might go to heaven, even where the Gospel has not gone out. Perhaps all (or at least some) children who die in infancy are saved (*see* Infants, Salvation of). Others may come into contact with the Gospel through Christian radio, literature, or recordings. Perhaps God reveals himself in miraculous ways. A window might be opened for the Word. Countries with a large percentage of Christians were once pagan.

Is There a Second Chance? A few Christian apologists and many cults believe that God will give a second chance after death to those who never heard the Gospel. Orthodox Christians reject this. The Bible declares that "Just as man is destined to die once, and after that to face judgment" (Heb. 9:27). The urgency with which Scripture speaks of making one's decision now in this life (Prov. 29:1; John 8:24; Heb. 3:7–13; 2 Peter 3:9) is strong evidence that there is no second chance. The fact that people immediately go to either heaven or hell (Luke 16:19–31; 2 Cor. 5:8; Rev. 19:20) indicates that a decision must be made in this life. Since God has so many ways to reveal himself to unbelievers before death, it is unnecessary that he do so after they die. Belief in a second chance undermines the missionary mandate. Why have the Great Commission (Matt. 28:18–20), if people can be saved apart from receiving Christ in this life?

Interpretations of Scripture used to support second-chance salvation are, to say the least, highly disputed (for example, 1 Peter 3:18–19). Clear texts are unambiguous in teaching that *hell awaits the unrepentant. There is no real evidence that God will give anyone a second chance to be saved after death. Jesus said, "I told you that you would die in your sins; if you do not believe that I am [the one I claim to be], you will indeed die in your sins" (John 8:24).

Sources

M. Bronson, *Destiny of the Heathen*
J. H. Gerstner, "Heathen" in *Baker's Dictionary of Theology*
M. Luther and D. Erasmus, *Free Will and Salvation*
E. D. Osburn, "Those Who Have Never Heard: Have They No Hope?" *JETS*
S. Pfurtner, *Luther and Aquinas on Salvation*
F. Pieper, *Salvation Only by Faith in Christ*
C. Pinnock, *A Wideness in God's Mercy*
I. Ramsey, "History and the Gospels: Some Philosophical Reflections," *SE*
J. O. Sanders, *How Lost Are the Heathen?*
J. Sanders, *No Other Name.*
R. Wolff, *The Final Destiny of Heathen*

Hegel, Georg Wilhelm Friedrich. ***Life and Works of Hegel.*** Hegel (1770–1831) was born in Wurtenberg, Germany, to a Lutheran family. His father was a government official. Hegel was bored by dull teachers and often cut classes. He taught at the University of Jena, where he and F. W. J. Schelling fought against the tide of skepticism. Hegel was Lutheran and apparently attended church regularly.

His main writings include *Philosophy of History, Philosophy of Nature, Encyclopedia, Logic, Philosophy of Religion,* his major work, *Phenomena of Spirit,* and *Philosophy of Aesthetics.*

Influences on Hegel. Like most other great figures, Hegel stood on the shoulders of many who had come before him. To mention a few major ones, from *Plato he learned that man's meaning is found in the state; that philosophy is the highest expression of reality, and that all determination is by negation. From *Plotinus Hegel came to understand that the world and consciousness are a manifestation of the Absolute—a form of *pantheism. From Benedict *Spinoza he learned of the inseparability of God and nature and, hence, antisupernaturalism. From Immanuel *Kant Hegel concluded that we must begin with the phenomena of experience and use the transcendental method to arrive at truth. Of course, his Judeo-Christian training provided him with a linear view of history.

Hegel's Epistemology. Hegel's theory of knowledge is not easy to spell out in a brief form. However, some aspects of it are clear.

Hegel's Dialectic. To begin, a word is necessary about what Hegel did not believe. Although he used the word "dialectic," he did not believe in a Marxist (*see* Marx, Karl) kind of dialecticalism of thesis–antithesis–synthesis. This triad does not appear once in the body of eight volumes of his published works (Mueller, 411). It appears once in the "Preface" of his *Phenomenology of Mind* where he claimed it came from Kant and rejected it calling it "a lifeless schema" (Mueller, 412). Hegelian expert Gustav Mueller asserted that "The most vexing and devastating Hegel legend is that everything is thought in 'thesis, antithesis, and synthesis'" (Mueller, 411). The legend was spread by Karl Marx's distorted understanding of Hegel.

The Law of Non-Contradiction. Hegel is not clear as to the status of the law of non-contradiction (*see* FIRST PRINCIPLES). At times he appears to deny it, claiming that "all things are themselves contradictory," that "movement is existing contradiction itself," and that "only insofar as something has contradiction in itself does it move, have impulse or activity (H. B. Acton, 443–44). Indeed, he does not even mention it as a separate category of thought in his *Science of Logic*. Some understand him as claiming only that there are contradictions on the finite level that are resolved in the Absolute. Others believe he is not using the term in its technical logical sense, but only in the practical sense in the outworking of the dialectic in history. Others take it to refer to a necessary disease of thought on its way to absolute truth. Hegel does claim that a "square circle" or a "many-sided circle" is contradictory (Acton, 444). Of course, if Hegel meant that the law of non-contradiction (see *First Principles*) did not apply to all truth-claims, then his view was *self-refuting.

The Transcendental Argument. Following Kant, Hegel argued transcendentally, though he believed it yielded absolutes in content as well as the form of knowledge. He believed there were two options; *realism and transcendentalism. That is, we can ignore Kant and return to naive realism or extend Kant and develop a transcendentalism (*see* TRANSCENDENTAL ARGUMENT). He chose the latter. Like Kant he held that a priori forms in the mind guarantee certainty. But unlike Kant, Hegel believed that even the content of our knowledge is absolute. He argued that partial (relative) knowledge is impossible because it presupposes knowledge of the whole (the absolute).

The transcendental process of knowing begins with knowledge as it appears to us (in the phenomena of our experience) and then proceeds to find the necessary conditions of it. The test for knowledge is consistency and coherence. But our knowledge cannot persist unless it is based on some higher form of knowledge. And the regress cannot be infinite (or else we would not know anything). Hence, we must eventually arrive at absolute knowledge, which is the underpinning of all other (lower knowledge).

Hegel's View of God. *Proofs for God's Existence.* Hegel believed he had overcome *Kant's objections to the existence of God (*see* GOD, OBJECTIONS TO PROOF FOR HIS EXISTENCE). In a series of lectures, he defended the *ontological argument for God's existence (see Acton, 449).

Developmental Pantheism. Hegel's metaphysics is a kind of developmental *pantheism worked out in the historical process. It may also be viewed as a form of panentheism, since there is a bipolarity of God and the world. In any event, history is the "footprints" of God in the sands of time. Better, history is God's self-unfolding in the temporal world. It is the progressive overcoming of the world by Absolute Spirit.

Dialectical Metaphysics. Hegel's *metaphysics is an example of how his dialectic worked. First, he begins with logic, which posits the eternal idea. This is emptiest of all notions, devoid of all content. It represents God as he is in his eternal essence prior to the creation of finite spirit.

Next, there is the philosophy of nature. This is creation apart from God. Yet creation must stand in relation to God. How, then, can these two be reconciled?

Hegel's answer is in the philosophy of spirit wherein there is an overcoming duality. The two poles of duality are God and world. Hegel believed that God and world must be merged and thus give up their separate identities. This is a root idea of the later panentheism of Alfred North *Whitehead. The point of contact is in man, who is the translator between nature and spirit. Thus, man has the spirituality of God and the materiality of the world.

This overcoming is in three stages: subjective spirit, objective spirit, and Absolute Spirit (God). In subjective spirit the subject–object duality is overcome. Hegel begins with man as conscious (the spiritual dimension). He then moves to man as corporeal (the material dimension). Finally, he turns to man as integrated, self-conscious being (the ethical dimension).

In objective spirit the subject–subject distinction is overcome. All are part of a greater unity—the human spirit. So in man as a whole the duality is overcome as the whole is over parts and unites them. In short, there is no God apart from nature. God is dependent on nature.

Hegel's View of Christianity. *The Incarnation.* Hegel viewed Christianity (Lutheranism) as the absolute religion, the highest manifestation of the Absolute to date. This is particularly manifest in the incarnation of God in Christ in which God appeared on earth in a particular man at a particular time. Here the Infinite is identified with the finite.

The core of religion is the incarnation. Absolute Spirit is where the God–man duality is overcome. This is done in three stages: art, religion, and philosophy. Art is only a limited manifestation (in images) of the Absolute. Religion realizes a higher manifestation of Absolute Spirit in true freedom revealed in symbols. So, the essence of religion is Christology—the God-man who died and rose. When he died both God and man died. But when he rose neither God nor man rose but Absolute Spirit unto which God and man merged.

Hegel believed that the highest manifestation of the Absolute is in philosophy. It is the eternal Idea, the epitome, the fullest and most complete of all concepts. This is only the highest "category" of all thought and existence, not the highest point of achievement. We can never "reach" Absolute Spirit, it always vanishes, leaving only the long road of argument leading to it. So, while God becomes man in religion, man becomes God in philosophy.

The Trinity. The final reconciliation of the Infinite and finite, of God and man, is found in the Trinity. For God existed before the world as Father, was manifested in his embodiment in the world as Son, and as reconciling both God and the world in the Holy Spirit. So while God cannot exist without negation and opposites, both are finally reconciled in the Trinity.

Hegel's View of the Bible. *Early Desupernaturalized Life of Christ.* In an early attempt at a life of Jesus, Hegel presented a desupernaturalized view of Jesus and formulated the teachings of Jesus in terms of a Kantian ethic, something he had learned from Kant's famous *Religion Within the Limits of Reason Alone*. Here Jesus is depicted by Hegel as narrow-minded and obscurantist as opposed to Socrates. Further, Jesus is not virgin-born (*see* VIRGIN BIRTH). All miracles mentioned are interpreted naturalistically. The prologue of John's Gospel is reinterpreted to state: "Pure Reason incapable of all limitations is the Deity itself."

Later, in *The Spirit of Christianity and Its Fate,* Hegel contrasted the Gospel ethic of love with the Jewish and Kantian ethics of law, but he never gave up either his antisupernaturalism or his moral-centered view of the Gospels. Hegel also reinterpreted the Gospel stories of the redemptive death and resurrection of Christ in terms of Greek tragedy.

In *The Positivity of the Christian Religion* Hegel affirms that in claiming to be the Messiah Jesus was merely using the language of his listener, a form of the *accommodation theory. Instead of revering him for his teaching about virtue, they revered his teaching about virtue because of the miracles he is supposed to have performed. Here Hegel argues that Greek religion was overcome by Christianity because "The despotism of the Roman emperors had chased the human spirit from the earth and spread a misery which compelled men to seek and expect happiness in heaven." Thus, "robbed of freedom, their spirit, their eternal and absolute element, was forced to take flight to deity." In this way, God's objectivity is a counterpart to the corruption and slavery of man (*Early Theological Writings,* 162–63).

*Hegel's Later Transcendentalism (*Pantheism).* Even later in his *Encyclopedia*, dominated by his transcendental idealism (i.e., developmental pantheism), Hegel was a radical revisionist of the literal, historical truth of the death and resurrection of Christ. The core of revealed religion is Christology: Jesus Christ is the God-man. As such, he died on the cross; thus both God and man died there. The resurrection was of neither God nor man. Rather, in the resurrection both God and man merge in Absolute Spirit. Thus, in Hegel's developmental pantheism is found the highest manifestation of Absolute Spirit.

Interpretation of Scripture. All Scripture must be understood in terms of Absolute Spirit which Hegel identifies as the Holy Spirit. In interpreting Scripture we must avoid both literalism and rationalism. True understanding is based on Spirit. Orthodox beliefs must be reinterpreted in the light of Hegel's (pantheistic) understanding of Spirit triumphing over all literalism. He quotes 2 Corinthians 3:6: "The letter kills, but the spirit gives life." With this theology is converted into philosophy—Hegelian philosophy.

Hegel's Influence on Others. Hegel had an immense influence on others after him. This includes the *atheism of Ludwig *Feuerbach, who argued that "God" is man's self-understanding. Professor Winfried Corduan divides these into Left, Center, and Right. On the left are those who believe that Hegel's thought leads consistently to an impersonal atheism. On the right are those who understand Hegel's philosophy in a theological sense. In the center are those who believe core belief in Absolute Spirit allows room for religion. This includes Bruno Bauer, Ludwig Feuerbach, and Karl Marx (see Corduan).

Hegel's Influence on Atheism. Hegel had a significant influence on modern atheism. Several young left-wing Hegelians were his students, including Karl Marx with his *dialectical materialism derived from his misunderstanding of Hegel's "dialectic." Friedrich *Nietzsche, Thomas *Altizer, and the "Death of God" theologians were influenced by Hegel's assertion that God and man died in the death of Christ.

*Hegel's Influence on *Existentialism.* Hegel influenced existentialists of various stripes: theistic, atheistic, pantheistic, and panentheistic. In spite of his obvious rejection of much of Hegel, Søren *Kierkegaard's theistic existentialism is dependent on Hegel's idea that the essence of consciousness is liberty; that truth is lived, not known (praxis); that existence is a concrete, dynamic process; and a realistic valuation of the individual's predicament in the process of history. Likewise, the atheistic existentialism of Jean-Paul *Sartre is also dependent on Hegel's ideas that consciousness is negativity (absolute freedom); that the self is condemned never to know itself; and that man imposes meaning on things. Husserl's phenomenology is rooted in Hegel's phenomenological (descriptive) method of analyzing human experience. And Martin Heidegger's pantheistic *existentialism is an offspring of Hegelianism.

Hegel's Influence on Modern Biblical Criticism. Of special interest to Christian apologetics is Hegel's significant influence on negative *Bible criticism. For example, following Hegel, F. C. Baur and his Tübingen school claimed that the first-century tension between Peter's Judaistic form of Christianity opposed by Paul's anti-Judaistic form found its reconciliation in John's Gospel in the second century , thus insisting on a late date for John's Gospel (*see* New Testament, Dating of). Also, David *Strauss's desupernaturalized version of the life of Christ springs from Hegel's idea that spiritual reality is higher than the historical. Thus, as Rudolph *Bultmann was to later affirm: Christianity is myth (*see* Mythology and the New Testament).

Hegel's Influence on Hermeneutics. Likewise, Martin Heidegger's mystical pantheism and hermeneutic developed by Bultmann and Gadamer are rooted in Hegel's stress on the spiritual interpretations of Scripture. This gave rise to the whole subjectivistic "new hermeneutic."

An Evaluation of Hegel's Thought. From an apologetic standpoint Hegel's system of thought has both positive and negative aspects. First, some of the positive elements will be briefly noted.

Positive Values. Without elaboration (which is done in the other articles noted), Hegel affirmed the value of metaphysics; of absolute truth (*see* Truth, Nature of); of a Christian linear view of history; of understanding humans in their concrete life situations; of human freedom (*see* Free Will); of an a priori dimension of knowledge (see *First Principles*); of a *transcendental argument; and other things.

Negative Critique. Hegel's good points notwithstanding, his overall philosophy has had a very negative effect on orthodox Christianity. Some of these include his *pantheism or *panentheism, as the case may be; his denial of realism (*see*); his foundations for Bible criticism; his antisupernaturalism (*see* Miracles), which involves the denial of the physical resurrection (*see* Resurrection, Evidence for); his idea that determination is by negation (*see* Analogy, Principle of); his "spiritual" interpretation, which anticipates postmodernism and the deconstruction of Jacques *Derrida and others (*see also* Mysticism); and his failure to ground knowledge in an unchanging God, thus undermining the absolute truth he claimed (*see* Truth, Nature of).

Sources

H. B. Acton, "Hegel, Georg Wilhelm Friedrich," in *The Encyclopedia of Philosophy* (vol. 3)
J. Collins, *A History of Modern Western Philosophy*
W. Corduan, "Transcendentalism: Hegel" in N. L. Geisler, *Biblical Errancy: Its Philosophical Roots*
G. W. F. Hegel, *Early Theological Writings*
———, *Encyclopedia*
———, *Logic*
———, *Phenomena of Spirit*
———, *Philosophy of History*
———, *Philosophy of Nature*
———, *Philosophy of Religion*
S. Kierkegaard, *Either/Or*
G. E. Meuller, "The Hegel Legend of 'Thesis, *Antithesis-Synthesis" Journal of History of Ideas* 19, no. 3 (1958)
A. V. Miller, *Hegel's Phenomenology of Spirit*
H. Sterling, *The Secrets of Hegel*

Heissenberg's Principle of Uncertainty. ***See*** **Indeterminacy, Principle of.**

Hell. Hell has been called cruel, inhuman, and barbarous. Bertrand *Russell said anyone who threatens people with eternal punishment, as Jesus did, is inhumane (Russell, 593–94). Unbelievers in general have questioned both the existence and justice of hell. Orthodox Christians, however, both Catholic and Protestant, have defended both the reality and equity of hell.

The Existence of Hell. The existence of hell has been defended by arguments both from Scripture and from human reason.

Jesus Taught the Existence of Hell. Scripture emphatically affirms the doctrine of hell. Some of the strongest assertions that there is a hell come from Jesus Christ, the Second Person of the *Trinity. He had more to say about hell than concerning Heaven. Jesus warned, "Do not be afraid of those who kill the body but cannot kill the soul. Rather, be afraid of the One who can destroy both soul and body in hell" (Matt. 10:28). He added of those who reject him, "As the weeds are pulled up and burned in the fire, so it will be at the end of the age" (Matt. 13:40).

In the Olivet Discourse our Lord said that at the final judgment God will say "to those on his left, 'Depart from me, you who are cursed, into the eternal fire prepared for the devil and his angels'" (Matt. 25:41b). Of the seriousness of the danger of hell, Jesus warned, "If your hand causes you to sin, cut it off. It is better for you to enter life maimed than with two hands to go into hell, where the fire never goes out" (Mark 9:43). The reality of hell is obvious from a vivid story told by Jesus in Luke 16. This story is unlike a parable, since in it Jesus uses the actual name of a person (Lazarus). The story concerned the fate after death of a rich man and a beggar, Lazarus:

> The rich man also died and was buried. In hell, where he was in torment, he looked up and saw Abraham far away, with Lazarus by his side. So he called to him, "Father Abraham, have pity on me and send Lazarus to dip the tip of his finger in water and cool my tongue, because I am in agony in this fire." But Abraham replied, "Son, remember that in your lifetime you received your good things, while Lazarus received bad things, but now he is comforted here and you are in agony. And besides all this, between us and you a great

chasm has been fixed, so that those who want to go from here to you cannot, nor can anyone cross over from there to us." He answered, "Then I beg you, father, send Lazarus to my father's house, for I have five brothers. Let him warn them, so that they will not also come to this place of torment." Abraham replied, "They have Moses and the Prophets; let them listen to them." "No, father Abraham," he said, "but if someone from the dead goes to them, they will repent." He said to him, "If they do not listen to Moses and the Prophets, they will not be convinced even if someone rises from the dead." [Luke 16:19–31]

The Bible Teaches That There Is a Hell. Other inspired writings of the New Testament affirm the existence of hell. Perhaps the most graphic is found in the Revelation of John:

> Then I saw a great white throne and him who was seated on it. Earth and sky fled from his presence, and there was no place for them. And I saw the dead, great and small, standing before the throne, and books were opened. Another book was opened, which is the book of life. The dead were judged according to what they had done as recorded in the books. The sea gave up the dead that were in it, and death and Hades gave up the dead that were in them, and each person was judged according to what he had done. Then death and Hades were thrown into the lake of fire. The lake of fire is the second death. If anyone's name was not found written in the book of life, he was thrown into the lake of fire. [20:11–15]

The apostle Paul spoke of everlasting separation from God, saying: "This will happen when the Lord Jesus is revealed from heaven in blazing fire with his powerful angels. He will punish those who do not know God and do not obey the gospel of our Lord Jesus. They will be punished with everlasting destruction and shut out from the presence of the Lord and from the majesty of his power" (2 Thess. 1:7b–9). The writer of Hebrews adds a note of finality: "Man is destined to die once, and after that to face judgment" (Heb. 9:27).

God's Justice Demands a Hell. In addition to direct affirmations, Scripture offers reasons for the existence of hell. One is that justice demands the existence of hell, and God is just (Romans 2). He is so pure and untainted that he cannot even look upon sin (Hab. 1:13). God is no respecter of persons, "For God does not show favoritism" (Rom. 2:11). As Abraham declared, "Will not the Judge of all the earth do right?" (Gen. 18:25). Psalm 73 is representative of passages teaching that not all justice is accomplished in this life. The wicked seem to prosper (Ps. 73:3). Thus, the existence of a place of punishment for the wicked after this life is necessary to maintain the justice of God. Surely, there would be no real justice were there no place of punishment for the demented souls of Stalin and Hitler, who initiated the merciless slaughter of multimillions. God's justice demands that there is a hell.

Jonathan *Edwards argued that even one sin deserves hell, since the eternal, holy God cannot tolerate any sin. Each person commits a multitude of sins in thought, word, and deed. This is all compounded by the fact that we reject God's immense mercy. And add to this man's readiness to find fault with God's justice and mercy, and we have abundant evidence of the need for hell. If we had a true spiritual awareness, we would not be amazed at hell's severity but at our own depravity (Edwards, 1.109).

God's Love Demands a Hell. The Bible asserts that "God is love" (1 John 4:16). But love cannot act coercively, only persuasively. A God of love cannot force people to love him. Paul spoke of things being done freely and not of compulsion (2 Cor. 9:7). Forced loved is not love; it is rape. A loving being always gives "space" to others. He does not force himself upon them against their will. As C. S. *Lewis observed, "the Irresistible and the Indisputable are the two weapons which the very nature of his scheme forbids him to use. Merely to override a human will . . . would be for Him useless. He cannot ravish. He can only woo" (Lewis, *Screwtape Letters,* 38). Hence, those who do not choose to love God must be allowed not to love him. Those who do not wish to be with him must be allowed to be separated from him. Hell allows separation from God.

Human Dignity Demands a Hell. Since God cannot force people into heaven against their free will, human free choice demands a hell. Jesus cried out, "O Jerusalem, Jerusalem, you who kill the prophets and stone those sent to you, how often I have longed to gather your children together, as a hen gathers her chicks under her wings, but you were not willing" (Matt. 23:37). As Lewis said, "There are only two kinds of people in the end: those who say to God, 'Thy will be done,' and those to whom God says, in the end, '*Thy* will be done'" (*Screwtape Letters,* 69).

God's Sovereignty Demands a Hell. Unless there is a hell there is no final victory over evil (*see* Evil, Problem of). For what frustrates good is evil. The wheat and tares cannot grow together forever. There must be an ultimate separation, or else good will not triumph over evil. As in society, punishment for evil is necessary that good might prevail. Even so, in eternity good must triumph over evil. If it does not, then God is not in ultimate control. God's sovereignty demands a hell, otherwise he would not be the ultimate victor over evil that the Bible declares him to be (cf. 1 Cor. 15:24–28; Revelation 20–22).

The Cross of Christ Implies Hell. At the center of Christianity is the cross (1 Cor. 1:17–18; 15:3). Without it there is no salvation (Rom. 4:25; Heb. 10:10–14). It is the very purpose for which Christ came into the world (Mark 10:45; Luke 19:10). Without the cross there is no salvation (John 10:1, 9–10; Acts 4:12). Only through the cross can we be delivered from our sins (Rom. 3:21–26). Jesus suffered great agony and even separation from God on the cross (Heb. 2:10–18; 5:7–9). Anticipating the cross, Jesus "sweat as it were great drops of blood" (Luke 22:44). But why the cross and all this suffering unless there is a hell? Christ's death is robbed of its eternal significance unless there is an eternal separation from God from which people need to be delivered.

The Nature and Location of Hell. The Bible describes the reality of hell in forceful figures of speech. It is said to be a place of darkness (Matt. 8:12; 22:13), which is "outside" [the gate of the heavenly city] (Rev. 22:14–15). Hell is away from the "presence of the Lord" (Matt. 25:41; 2 Thess. 1:7–9). Of course, these are relational, not necessarily spatial, terms. God is "up" and hell is "down." God is "inside" and hell is "outside." Hell is the other direction from God.

The nature of hell is a horrifying reality. It is like being left outside in the dark forever (Matt. 8:12). It is like a wandering star (Jude 13), a waterless cloud (Jude 12), a perpetually burning dump (Mark 9:43–48), a bottomless pit (Rev. 20:1, 3), a prison (1 Peter 3:19), and a place of anguish and regret (Luke 16:28).

To borrow the title of the book by Lewis, hell is the "great divorce"—an eternal separation from God (2 Thess. 1:7–9). There is, in biblical language, "a great gulf fixed" between hell and heaven (Luke 16:26) so that no one can pass from one side to the other.

Nowhere does the Bible describe it as a "torture chamber" where people are forced against their will to be tortured. This is a caricature created by unbelievers to justify their reaction that the God who sends people to hell is cruel. This does not mean that hell is not a place of torment. Jesus said it was (Luke 16:24). But unlike torture which is inflicted from without against one's will, torment is self-inflicted.

Even atheists (*see* SARTRE; ATHEISM) have suggested that the door of hell is locked from the inside. We are condemned to our own freedom from God. Heaven's presence of the divine would be the torture to one who has irretrievably rejected him. Torment is living with the consequences of our own bad choices. It is the weeping and gnashing of teeth that results from the realization that we blew it and deserve the consequences. Just as a football player may pound on the ground in agony after missing a play that loses the Super Bowl, so those in hell know that the pain they suffer is self-induced.

Hell is also depicted as a place of eternal fire. This fire is *real* but not necessarily *physical* (as we know it), because people will have imperishable physical bodies (John 5:28–29; Rev. 20:13–15), so normal fire would not affect them. Further, the figures of speech that describe hell are contradictory, if taken in a physical sense. It has *flames,* yet is outer *darkness*. It is a dump (with a *bottom*), yet a *bottomless* pit. While everything in the Bible is literally true, not everything is true literally.

The Duration of Hell. Many unbelievers would be willing to accept a temporary hell, but the Bible speaks of it as everlasting.

Hell Will Last as Long as Does God. The Bible declares that God will endure forever (Ps. 90:1–2). Indeed, he had no beginning and has no end (Rev. 1:8). He created all things (John 1:3; Col. 1:15–16), and he will abide after this world is destroyed (2 Peter 3:10–12). But God, by his very nature, cannot tolerate evil (Isaiah 6; Hab. 1:13). Hence, evil persons must be separated from God forever. As long as God is God and evil is evil, the latter must be separated from the former.

Hell Will Last as Long as Heaven Does. Heaven is described as "everlasting" in the Bible. But the same Greek word *(aionion),* used in the same context, also affirmed that hell is "everlasting" (Matt. 25:41; cf. vs. 46; 2 Thess. 1:9; Rev. 20:10). So, if heaven is forever, so is hell. There is absolutely no ground in Scripture for supposing that hell is temporal and heaven is eternal.

Nor is there a possibility of getting out of hell. A great gulf is fixed so no one can leave (Luke 16:26). Judgment begins immediately after death (John 8:21; Heb. 9:27). This is not unlike the fact that some decisions in life are irreversible. Suicide is a one-way street.

People are conscious after they die, whether they are in heaven (2 Cor. 5:8; Phil 1:23; Rev. 6:9) or in hell (Luke 16:23). The Beast was still conscious after a thousand years in hell (Rev. 19:20; 20:10). It makes no sense to resurrect unbelievers to everlasting judgment (Dan. 12:2; John 5:28–29) before the Great White Throne (Rev. 20:11–15) unless they are conscious.

Objections about Hell. Unbelievers have offered many objections to the doctrine of hell (see Lewis, *Problem of Pain,* chap. 8).

Hell Is Annihilation. The Bible clearly affirms that there is conscious suffering in hell, such as will cause "weeping and gnashing of teeth" (Matt. 8:12). Annihilated persons are not conscious of any suffering. The beast and false prophet in hell will be conscious after a thousand years of suffering (Rev. 19:20; 20:10; *see* ANNIHILATIONISM).

Annihilation would not be a punishment but a release from all punishment. Job appeared to prefer annihilation to suffering (Job 3), but God did not grant his desire. Jesus speaks of degrees of punishment (Matt. 5:22), but there can be no degrees of nonexistence.

Annihilation of the wicked is contrary to both the nature of God (*see* God, Nature of) and the nature of humans made in his image (*see* Immortality). It is not consistent with an all-loving God to snuff out those who do not do his wishes. Were God to annihilate human beings he would be attacking himself, for we are made in his image (Gen. 1:27), and God is immortal. The fact that these persons are suffering no more justifies annihilating them than it does for a parent to kill a child who is suffering. Even some atheists have insisted that annihilation is not to be preferred to conscious freedom.

Hell Is Temporal, Not Eternal. Hell could not be just a long imprisonment. Hell must exist as long as a righteous God does against whom all hell is opposed.

While the word *forever* can mean a long time in some contexts, in this context it is used of heaven as well as hell (cf. Matthew 25). Sometimes the emphatic form of "forever and forever" is used. This phrase is used to describe heaven and God himself (Rev. 14:11; 20:10). And God cannot be temporal; he is eternal (Edwards, 2.85–86).

The suggestion that temporal suffering will lead to ultimate repentance is unrealistic. People in hell are gnashing their teeth which does not indicate a more godly and reformed disposition but a more rigid and stubborn rebellion. Hence, after the people have been in hell for some time there is more justification for God's punishment of them, not less. If hell had a reformational effect on people, then Jesus would not have pronounced woe on those who reject him and are headed for hell (Matt. 11:21–24). No sin would be unforgivable if people in hell were reformable (Matt. 12:31–32). Likewise, Jesus would never have said of Judas that it would have been better if he had never been born.

How can a place devoid of God's restraining grace accomplish what no efforts of his grace could accomplish on earth, namely, a change of the heart? If hell could reform wicked sinners, then they would be saved without Christ, who is the sole means of salvation (Edwards, 2.520). Suffering has no tendency to soften a hard heart; it hardens it more (*see* Pharaoh, Hardening of). The recidivism and hardened criminality in modern prisons confirms Edwards' point.

God's justice demands eternal punishment. "The heinousness of any crime must be gauged according to the worth or dignity of the person it is committed against" (Davidson, 50). Thus, a murder of a president or pope is deemed more heinous than that of a terrorist or Mafia boss. Sin against an infinite God is an infinite sin worthy of infinite punishment (Edwards, 2.83).

Why Not Reform People? Why eternal punishment? Why doesn't God try to reform sinners? The answer is that God does try to reform people; the time of *reformation* is called life. Peter declared that "The Lord is not slow in keeping his promise, as some understand slowness. He is patient with you, not wanting anyone to perish, but everyone to come to repentance" (2 Peter 3:9; cf. 1 Tim. 2:4). However, after the time of reformation comes the time of reckoning (Heb. 9:27). Hell is only for the unreformable and unrepentant, the reprobate (cf. 2 Peter 2:1–6). It is not for anyone who is reformable. If they were reformable, they would still be alive. For God in his wisdom and goodness would not allow anyone to go to hell whom he knew would go to heaven if he gave them more opportunity. As C. S. *Lewis observed, the soul that seriously and constantly desires joy will never miss it. Those who seek find. To those who knock it is opened (Lewis, *Great Divorce,* 69).

God cannot force free creatures to be reformed. Forced reformation is worse than punishment; it is cruel and inhumane. At least punishment respects the freedom and dignity of the person. As Lewis insightfully notes, "To be 'cured' against one's will . . . is to be put on a level with those who have not yet reached the age of reason or those who never will; to be classed with infants, imbeciles, and domestic animals" (Lewis, *God in the Dock,* 226). Humans are not objects to be manipulated; they are subjects to be respected because they are made in God's image. Human beings should be punished when they do evil because they were free and knew better. They are *persons* to be punished, not *patients* to be cured.

Is Damnation for Temporal Sins Overkill? To punish a person eternally for what he did for a short time on earth seems at first like a gigantic case of overkill. However, on closer examination it turns out to be not only just but necessary. For one thing, only eternal punishment will suffice for sins against the eternal God (*see* God, Nature of). The sins may have been committed in time, but they were against the Eternal One. Furthermore, no sin can be tolerated as long as God exists, and he is eternal. Hence, punishment for sin must also be eternal.

What is more, the only alternative to eternal punishment is worse, namely, to rob human beings of freedom and dignity by forcing them into heaven against their free choice. That would be "hell" since they do not fit in a place where everyone is loving and praising the Person they want most to avoid. Or, God's other choice is to annihilate his own image within his creatures. But this would be an attack of God on himself.

Further, without eternal separation, there could be no heaven. Evil is contagious (1 Cor. 5:6) and must be quarantined. Like a deadly plague, if it is not contained it will continue to contaminate and corrupt. If God did not eventually separate the tares from the wheat, the tares would choke out the wheat. The only way to preserve an eternal place of good is to eternally separate all evil from it. The only way to have an eternal heaven is to have an eternal hell.

Finally, if Christ's temporal punishment is sufficient for our sins eternally, then there is no reason why eternal suffering cannot be appropriate for our temporal sins. It is not the *duration* of the action but the *object* that is important. Christ satisfied the eternal God by his temporal suffering, and unbelievers have offended the eternal God by their temporal sins. Hence, Christ's temporal suffering for sins satisfies God eternally (1 John 2:1), and our temporal sins offend God eternally.

Hell Has No Redeeming Value. To the objection that there is no redemptive value in the damning of souls to hell, it can be pointed out that hell satisfies God's justice and glorifies it by showing how great and fearful a standard it is. "The vindictive justice of God will appear strict, exact, awful, and terrible, and therefore glorious" (Edwards, 2.87). The more horrible and fearful the judgment, the brighter the sheen on the sword of God's justice. Awful punishment fits the nature of an awe-inspiring God. By a majestic display of wrath, God gets back the majesty he has been refused. Those who give God no glory by choice during this life will be forced to give him glory in the afterlife.

All people, thus, are either actively or passively useful to God. In heaven believers will actively praise his mercy. In hell unbelievers will be passively useful in bringing majesty to his justice. Just as a barren tree is useful only for firewood, so the disobedient are only fuel for an eternal fire (ibid., 2.126). Since unbelievers prefer to keep at a distance from God in time, why should we not expect this to be their chosen state in eternity?

Hell Is Only a Threat, Not a Reality. Some critics believe hell is only a threat that God will not carry out. But it is blasphemy to hold that a God of truth uses deliberate lies to govern human beings. Further, it implies that "those who think hell is a deception have outwitted God Himself by uncovering it" (Davidson, 53). As Edwards stated it, "They suppose that they have been so cunning as to find out that it is not certain; and so that God had not laid His design so deep, but that such cunning men as they can discern the cheat and defeat the design" (Edwards, 2.516).

Can Saints Be Happy if a Loved One Is in Hell? The presupposition of this question is that we are more merciful than is God. God is perfectly happy in heaven, and he knows that not everyone will be there. Yet he is infinitely more merciful than are we. What is more, if we could not be happy in heaven knowing anyone was in hell, then our happiness is not in our hands but someone else's. But hell cannot veto heaven. We can be happy in heaven the same way we can be happy eating knowing others are starving, if we have tried to feed them but they have refused the food. Just as we can have healing of bad memories here on earth, even so God will "wipe away all tears" in heaven (Rev. 21:4).

Edwards noted that to suppose God's mercy does not permit suffering in hell is contrary to fact. God allows plenty of suffering in this world. It is an empirical fact that God and creature-pain are not incompatible (Gerstner, 80). If God's mercy cannot bear eternal misery, then neither can it bear lesser amounts (Edwards, 2.84). God's mercy is not a passion or emotion that overcomes his justice. Mercy so construed is a defect in God. It would make him weak and inconsistent with himself, not fit to be a Judge.

The attitudes and feelings of the saints in heaven will be transformed and correspond more to God's. Hence, we will love only what God loves and hate what he hates. Since God is not miserable at the thought or sight of hell, neither will we—even if it holds people we loved in this life. Edwards devoted a sermon to this: "The End of the Wicked Contemplated by the Righteous." In Gerstner's digest of it, "it will seem in no way cruel in God to inflict such extreme suffering on such extremely wicked creatures" (Gerstner, 90).

Why Did God Create People Bound for Hell? Some critics of hell argue that if God knew that his creatures would reject him and eventuate in such a horrible place as hell, then why did he create them in the first place? Wouldn't it have been better to have never existed than to exist and go to hell?

It is important to note that nonexistence cannot be said to be a better condition than any kind of existence, since nonexistence is nothing. And to affirm that nothing can be better than something is a gigantic category mistake. In order to compare two things, they must have something in common. But there is nothing in common between being and nonbeing. They are diametrically opposed.

Some one may *feel* like being put out of a life of misery, but such a one cannot even consistently think of nonbeing as a better state of *being*. True, Jesus said it would have been better if Judas had never been born (Mark 14:21). But this is simply a strong expression indicating the severity of his sin, not a statement about the superiority of nonbeing over being. In a parallel condemnation on the Pharisees, Jesus said Sodom and Gomorrah would have repented had they seen his miracles (Matt. 11:20–24; *see* MIRACLE). This does not mean that they actually would have repented (or God would surely have shown them these miracles—2 Peter 3:9). It is simply a powerful figure of speech indicating that their sin was so great that "it would be *more tolerable*" (vs. 24) in the day of judgment for Sodom than for them.

Further, simply because some will lose in the game of life does not mean it should not be played. Before the Super Bowl ever begins both teams know that one of them will lose. Yet they all will to play. Before every driver in America takes to the road each day we know that people will be killed. Yet we will to drive. Parents know that having children could end in great tragedy for their offspring as well as for themselves. Yet the foreknowledge of evil does not negate our will to permit the possibility of good. Why? Because we deem it better to have played with the opportunity to win than not to have played at all. It is better to lose in the Super Bowl than not to be able to play in it. From God's standpoint, it is better to love the whole world (John 3:16) and lose some of its inhabitants than not to love them at all.

But People Can't Help Being Sinners. The Bible says we are born sinners (Ps. 51:5) and are "by nature the children of wrath" (Eph. 2:3). If sinners cannot avoid sinning, is it fair to send them to hell for it?

People go to hell because they are born with a bent to sin, and they choose to sin. They are born on a road that leads to hell, but they also fail to heed the warning signs along the way to turn from destruction (Luke 13:3; 2 Peter 3:9).

While human beings sin because they are sinners (by nature), their sin nature does not force them to sin. As *Augustine correctly said, "We are born with the propensity to sin and the necessity to die." Notice, he did not say we are born with the necessity to sin. While sin is *inevitable,* since we are born with a bent in that direction, sin is not *unavoidable*.

The ultimate place to which sinners are destined is also avoidable. All one needs to do is to repent (Luke 13:3; Acts 17:30; 2 Peter 3:9). All are held responsible for their decision to accept or reject God's offer of salvation. And responsibility always implies the ability to respond (if not on our own, then by God's grace). All who go to hell could have avoided going there if they had chosen to. No pagan anywhere is without clear light from God so that he is "without excuse" (Rom. 1:19–20; cf. 2:12–15; *see* "HEATHEN," SALVATION OF). As God sent a missionary to Cornelius (Acts 10:35), so he will provide the message of salvation for all who seek it. For "without faith it is impossible to please God, because anyone who comes to him must believe that he exists and that he rewards those who earnestly seek him" (Heb. 11:6).

Reasonableness of Hell. While many believe hell is unreasonable, following Jonathan *Edwards, a good argument can be made for its rationality:

> It is a most unreasonable thing to suppose that there should be no future punishment, to suppose that God, who had made man a rational creature, able to know his duty, and sensible that he is deserving punishment when he does it not; should let man alone, and let him live as he will, and never punish him for his sins, and never make any difference between the good and the bad. . . . How unreasonable it is to suppose, that he who made the world, should leave things in such confusion, and never take any care of the governing of his creatures, and that he should never judge his reasonable creatures. [Edwards, 2.884]

Reasons Hell Is Rejected. As surveys show, people are far more willing to believe in heaven than in hell. No good person wants anyone to go to hell. But, as Sigmund *Freud would say, it is an illusion to reject something simply because we *wish* not to believe in it. Indeed, as even some atheists have observed, the belief in hell eliminates the charge that it is merely an illusion. Whether there is a hell must be determined on the basis of evidence, not desire. The evidence for the existence of hell is strong.

If the evidence for hell is substantial, why then do so many people reject it? Edwards listed two main reasons for the unwillingness to accept hell: (1) It is contrary to our personal preference; (2) we have a deficient concept of evil and its deserved punishment.

Actually, a denial of hell is an indication of human depravity. Edwards draws attention to our inconsistency. We are all aware of the heinous nature of wars and acts against humanity. Why are we not equally shocked at how we regularly show contempt for the majesty of God (Edwards, 2.83). Our rejection of hell and God's mercy are an indication of our own depravity—and therefore we are deserving of hell. Edwards wrote, "Doth it seem to thee incredible, that God should be so utterly regardless of the sinner's welfare, as to sink him into an infinite abyss or misery? Is this shocking to thee? And is it not at all shocking to thee that thou shouldst be so utterly regardless as thou hast been to the honour and glory of the infinite God?" (ibid., 2.82).

Sources

Augustine, *City of God*
W. Crockett, ed., *Fours Views on Hell*
B. W. Davidson, "Reasonable Damnation: How Jonathan Edwards Argued for the Rationality of Hell," *JETS* 38.1 (March 1995)
J. Edwards, *The Works of Jonathan Edwards*
L. Dixon, *The Other Side of the Good News*
N. L. Geisler, "Man's Destiny: Free or Forced," *CSR*, 9.2 (1979)
J. Gerstner, *Jonathan Edwards on Heaven and Hell*
C. S. Lewis, *God in the Dock*
———, *The Great Divorce*
———, *The Problem of Pain*, chapter 8
———, *The Screwtape Letters*
D. Moore, *The Battle for Hell*
F. Nietzsche, *Toward a Genealogy of Morals*
R. A. Peterson, *Hell on Trial: The Case for Eternal Punishment*
B. Russell, *Why I Am Not a Christian*
J. P. Sartre, *No Exit*
W. G. T. Shed, *The Doctrine of Endless Punishment*
J. L. Walls, *Hell: The Logic of Damnation*

Hellenic Saviors. ***See*** **APOTHEOSIS; DIVINE BIRTH STORIES; MITHRAISM; RESURRECTION CLAIMS IN NON-CHRISTIAN RELIGIONS.**

Henotheism. *Henotheism* is a type of *polytheism that believes there is one supreme god among the many gods that exist, such as Zeus in Greek polytheism. It is not to be confused with theism or monotheism (*see* MONOTHEISM, PRIMITIVE) which believes there is only one supreme God and no other gods.

Hick, John. ***The Life and Works of Hick.*** John Hick is one of the most important philosophers of religion of the late twentieth century. His literary output and influence has been a strong force against orthodox Christianity at several crucial junctures. This includes the questions of the existence of God, the problem of evil, the destiny of human beings, and the deity of Christ.

The Views of Hick. Hick strongly defends *pluralism and unitarianism. His theodicy (*see* EVIL, PROBLEM OF) involves both *universalism and *reincarnationism. All of these, including Hick's views, are discussed in other articles. Hick's main works and some evaluations of these are listed below.

Sources

A. D. Clarke and B. Hunter, eds., *One God, One Lord: Christianity in a World of Religious Pluralism*

D. Geivett, *Evil and the Evidence for God: The Challenge of John Hicks's Theology*

D. Geivett, et al., in Dennis Okholm et al., *More Than One Way? Four Views on Salvation in a Pluralistic World*

K. Gnanakan, *The Pluralistic Predicament*

J. Hick, *Death and Eternal Life*

———, *An Interpretation of Religion*

———, *The Metaphor of God Incarnate: Christology in a Pluralistic Age*

———, "A Pluralist's View?" in Dennis Okholm et al., *More Than One Way? Four Views on Salvation in a Pluralistic World*

A. McGrath, "The Challenge of Pluralism for the Contemporary Christian Church," *Journal of the Evangelical Theological Society* (September 1992)

———, "Response to John Hick," in Dennis Okholm et al., *More Than One Way? Four Views on Salvation in a Pluralistic World*

R. Nash, *Is Jesus the Only Savior?*

H. Netland, *Dissonant Voices: Religious Pluralism and the Question of Truth*

D. Okholm, et al., *More Than One Way? Four Views on Salvation in a Pluralistic World*

Higher Criticism. ***See*** **BIBLE CRITICISM; REDACTION CRITICISM, OLD TESTAMENT; SPINOZA, BENEDICT; WELLHAUSEN, JULIUS.**

Hinduism, Vedanta. *Hinduism* represents a broad category of religious beliefs, most of which are pantheistic (*see* PANTHEISM) or panentheistic (*see* PANENTHEISM). One of the oldest forms of pantheism is found in the last section of the Vedas, the Hindu scriptures. This final section is called the *Upanishads*. Because the *Upanishads* came at the end of each of the four Vedas, the *Upanishads* came to be spoken of as the Vedanta, meaning end or goal of the Vedas. "Thus it is that when a modern Hindu speaks of the Vedanta he may have both senses more or less in mind, the scriptures referred to being for him that last part of the Vedas and at the same time their ultimate reason for existence, their perfect culmination—in a word, their highest wisdom" (Prabhavananda, *Spiritual Heritage,* 39).

The author and date of the *Upanishads* are unknown. They consist of the recorded experiences of Hindu sages (ibid., 39, 40). The *Upanishads,* along with the *Bhagavad-Gita,* lay the foundation for Vedanta Hinduism, which is a classic example of pantheism (*see also* MONISM; ONE AND MANY, PROBLEM OF; PARMENIDES; PLOTINUS).

Vedantic View of God. Not all forms of Hinduism believe in an impersonal God. Bhakti Hinduism does not. Nor does Hare Krishna. However Vedanta pantheism teaches that only one God (Brahman) exists. This God is at once infinite in form, immortal, imperishable, impersonal, all-pervading, supreme, changeless, absolute, and indivisibly one, and at the same time none of these. For God is beyond all thought and speech:

> Him [Brahman] the eye does not see, nor the tongue express, nor the mind grasp. Him we neither know nor are able to teach. Different is he from the known, and . . . from the unknown. He truly knows Brahman who knows him as beyond knowledge; he who thinks that he knows, knows not. The ignorant think that Brahman is known, but the wise know him to be beyond knowledge. [see *Upanishads,* 30, 31]

Brahman is inexpressible and indefinable. Nothing can be truly said or thought of Brahman. This is graphically illustrated by the Hindu philosopher Sankara in his commentary on the Upanishads: "'Sir,' said a pupil to his master, 'teach me the nature of Brahman.' The master did not reply. When a second and a third time he was importuned, he answered: 'I teach you indeed, but you do not follow. His name is silence'" (Prabhavananda, *Spiritual Heritage,* 45).

Vedantic View of the World. Vedanta pantheism also teaches that all is God and God is all. There is only one reality. The world that we see, hear, touch, taste, and smell does not actually exist. It appears to exist, but it is in fact an illusion, or *maya*. The universe we perceive is like walking through a dense forest at night and seeing what appears to be a snake. But when we return to the same spot in the light of the day, we see that the snake really was a rope. The rope looked like a snake, but it actually was not a snake. Just as the snake *appeared* to exist, so the universe *appears* to exist but it actually does not.

Instead the universe is *maya,* an illusion superimposed upon the only true reality, Brahman.

As the *Upanishads* state: "Brahman alone is—nothing else is. He who sees the manifold universe, and not the one reality, goes evermore from death to death" (Prabhavananda, *Upanishads,* 21). "Meditate, and you will realize that mind, matter, and Maya (the power which unites mind and matter) are but three aspects of Brahman the one reality" (ibid., 119).

Vedantic View of Humanity. Vedanta pantheism says that humankind is Brahman. *Maya,* or the illusory universe, has deceived us into thinking that each person is a particular in the universe. But if the person would clear the senses and mind of *maya* and meditate upon the true Self *(Atman),* then the realization would come that Atman is Brahman, the one true reality. The depth of a person's soul is identical to the depth of the universe.

Having attained to Brahman, a sage declared: "I am life. . . . I am established in the purity of Brahman. I have attained the freedom of the Self. I am Brahman, self-luminous, the brightest treasure. I am endowed with wisdom. I am immortal, imperishable" (ibid., 54).

Vedantic View of Ethics. According to Vedanta pantheism, people must transcend the world of illusion to discover the true Self (Prabhavananda, *Spiritual Heritage,* 55). This is accomplished by going beyond good and evil. "When the seer beholds the Effulgent One, the Lord, the Supreme Being, then, transcending both good and evil, and freed from impurities, he unites himself with him" (*Upanishads,* 47). When a person unites himself with Brahman, he no longer will be plagued by such thoughts as "'I have done an evil thing' or 'I have done a good thing.'" For to go beyond good and evil is to be troubled no more by what has been done (ibid., 111). It is to become unattached to personal (or anyone else's) past, present, or even future actions. Even the results of any actions will be viewed with indifference. "When your intellect has cleared itself of its delusions, you will become indifferent to the results of all action, present or future" (Prabhavananda, *Bhagavad-Gita,* 41).

This drive toward indifference to any action is explained most clearly in the *Bhagavad-Gita*. In the *Gita* a long dialogue occurs between Krishna, a manifestation of Brahman, and his friend and disciple, Arjuna. Arjuna tells Krishna of his reluctance to fight against a people among whom he has many friends. He asks Krishna how killing his friends could possibly be justified. Krishna tells Arjuna that he must detach himself from the fruits of his actions, no matter what they are. Thus states Krishna:

> He whose mind dwells
> Beyond attachment,
> Untainted by ego,
> No act shall bind him
> With any Bond:
> Though he slay these thousands
> He is no slayer. [ibid., 122]

Krishna explains to Arjuna that this state of union with Brahman can be achieved by following one or any combination of the following paths:

1. *Raga yoga*—the path of union through meditation and mind control;
2. *Karma yoga*—the path of union through work;
3. *Jnana yoga*—the path of union through knowledge; or
4. *Bhakti yoga*—the path of union through love and devotion (Prabhavananda, *Spiritual Heritage,* 98, 123–29).

But any path one follows must be accompanied by unattachment or indifference to any action. Only then will good and evil be transcended and union with Brahman attained.

Human Destiny. Realizing one's oneness with Brahman is essential in Vedanta pantheism, for apart from this realization one is doomed forever to the cycle of *samsara*. *Samsara* is the wheel of time and desire, or birth, death, and rebirth (*see* REINCARNATION). It is the wheel to which everything in the world of illusion is shackled. And *samsara* "itself is subject to and conditioned by endless cause, the *dharma* of the universe" (Corwin, 22).

One's life is also determined by the law of *karma* or action. This is the moral law of the universe. Huston Smith explains that *karma* is "the moral law of cause and effect." It is absolutely binding and allows no exceptions. *Karma* says that every decision made by an individual in the present is caused by all prior decisions in past lives and will in turn affect every future decision (Smith, 76).

A person whose *karma* is good may follow one of two possible paths. One who manages to free self from *samsara*—the cycle of birth and rebirth—will attain to higher planes of existence or consciousness until becoming one with the divine being "in his impersonal aspect and so reaches at last the end of his journey" (*Spiritual Heritage,* 70).

One who has been good, but not good enough to become free from *samsara* will go "to one or another heaven, where he enjoys the fruits of his good deeds which he has done in the body . . . and when these fruits are no more, he is born again, that is, reincarnated" on earth in "a new body appropriate to a new and higher realm of being" (ibid., 70–71). If a person's *karma* is largely evil, then he "goes to the regions of the wicked, there to eat the bitter fruits of his deeds.

These fruits once exhausted, he too returns to earth" in a reincarnated state (ibid., 71).

Concerning the law of *karma* and the cycle of *samsara*, "it is on this earth that a man determines his spiritual destiny and achieves his final realization" (ibid.). Salvation is solely of personal efforts. Higher states of existence offer rewards of happiness and lower states are punishments that each person earns on his own. "The history of a particular individual, the number of times he experiences rebirth, or reincarnation as it is called, depends entirely upon the quality of his will, upon the moral effort he puts forth" (ibid., 27) (*see* HELL).

Ultimately all humankind will achieve liberation from *samsara* and union with *Brahman*. Some people may return to earth often, but eventually they will all earn their salvation. As Prabhavananda says, "The Upanishads know no such thing as eternal damnation—and the same is true of every other Hindu scripture" (ibid., 71 [see HELL]).

Vedanta pantheism is the absolute pantheism of the East. Hinduism has found more popular expression and favor in the West through such religious groups and practices as Transcendental Meditation and the International Society for Krishna Consciousness. Vedanta pantheism is an absolute monism, declaring that God is all and all is One.

Evaluation. Like other worldviews, *monism has positive and negative dimensions. Although its view of ultimate reality is wrong, Vedantic Hinduism can be commended for its quest to know ultimate reality. There is more to reality than the world of our senses perceive. The desire to negate all limitations of ultimate reality is also good. The ultimate cannot be limited by human sensations or perceptions. Hinduism grapples with the basic problem of evil (*see* EVIL, PROBLEM OF). It acknowledges that evil must be explained and dealt with.

Since Vedantic Hinduism is a form of monism and pantheism, it is evaluated under those topics.

Its basic metaphysical error lies in a rejection of the analogy of being (*see* ANALOGY). All being is not univocal—the same thing. There is Infinite Being, and there are finite beings, and these are different kinds of beings. There is an analogy of being.

Likewise, the denial of the reality of evil is a classic form of *illusionism. But one cannot know the world is an illusion who does not know what is real. Knowing the real is a prerequisite for knowing what is not real.

In order to maintain an absolute pantheism, monists must deny the validity of sense knowledge. The senses tell us there are many things and that they are physical. The monist must deny both of these pieces of information about reality. But the denial of all sense knowledge is self-defeating. One could not know the senses were being deceptive without trusting in the senses to tell this. We see a crooked stick in the water and know that our senses are playing a trick on us. How do we know the stick is really straight? We must use our senses. The sense of sight tells what it looks like when out of the water and touch tells what it feels like in the water.

A monist expects us to trust our senses when we look at their books or listen to their lectures so that we will understand them. They fail to recognize that while knowledge is more than sensation, it begins with sensation. Everything in the mind was first in the senses except the mind itself. So, we know more than sensation, but we do not know the world without sensation. Sensation is basic to all understanding of reality.

Epistemologically, monistic Hinduism is subject to many of the same criticisms as *agnosticism. It is self-defeating, for it uses the basic laws of thought in order to express its views about what it claims is inexpressible. It uses first principles in its rejections of first principles and finite reality.

The ethics of Vedantic Hinduism is a form of relativism, since it denies that there are moral absolutes (*see* MORALITY, ABSOLUTE NATURE OF). This too is self-defeating. One cannot avoid all moral absolutes without affirming the moral absolute that there are no moral absolutes. The claim that one "ought" to avoid absolutes is a moral "ought" of its own. One cannot claim that ultimate reality goes beyond all good and evil unless there is an ultimate moral principle by which to measure good and evil. But in this case there is an ultimate moral standard.

Sources

Bhagavad-Gita. Prabhavananda, trans., with C. Usherwood

D. Clark and N. L. Geisler, *Apologetics in the New Age*

C. Corwin, *East to Eden? Religion and the Dynamics of Social Change*

N. L. Geisler and W. Watkins, *Worlds Apart: A Handbook on World Views*

H. P. Owen, *Concepts of Deity*

Prabhavananda, *The Spiritual Heritage of India*

S. Radhakrishnan, *The Hindu View of Life*

———, *The Principle Upanishads*

H. Smith, *The Religions of Man*

The Upanishads: Breath of the Eternal, Prabhavananda, F. Manchester, trans.

Historical Apologetics. Historical apologetics stresses the historical evidence as the basis for demonstrating the truth of Christianity (*see* APOLOGETICS, TYPES OF). At this point it overlaps with *classical apologetics. The crucial difference between the two is that historical apologetics does not believe that it is necessary to first establish the existence of God. Historical apologists believe that the truth of Christianity, including the existence of God, can be proven from the foundation of historical evidence alone.

This assumption places historical apologetics within the broad class of *evidential apologetics*, but it differs in that it stresses the importance, if not necessity, of beginning with the historical evidence for the truth of Christianity. Usually, the historical apologist sees the resurrection of Christ as the linchpin of apologetics. In this sense, it can be called *resurrection apologetics*.

Proponents of Historical Apologetics. Christianity is an historical religion, so it is understandable that it would have an historic emphasis from the very beginning. The earliest apologists, including *Justin Martyr, *Tertullian, *Clement of Alexandria, and *Origen, defended the historicity of Christianity. Likewise, the classical apologists (*see* CLASSICAL APOLOGETICS), such as *Augustine, *Anselm, and *Thomas Aquinas, considered historical apologetics as an important part of their overall strategy in defending the Christian faith.

However, what distinguishes historical apologetics as a discipline is its belief that one can defend the whole of the Christian faith, including the existence of God and the fact of miracles, strictly from the historical evidence, without the necessity of any prior appeal to theistic arguments (although some use theistic evidences in a supplementary way). This emphasis appears to be largely a modern phenomenon. Contemporary apologists who fall into this category include John Warwick Montgomery and Gary Habermas (*see* MIRACLES, APOLOGETIC VALUE OF; MIRACLES IN THE BIBLE).

Contrast with Other Systems. Historical apologetics differs from both presuppositional apologetics and classical apologetics, although it has things in common with them.

Historical versus Presuppositional Apologetics. Historical apologetics disagrees with the various forms of presuppositional apologetics (*see* APOLOGETICS, PRESUPPOSITIONAL) over the nature of evidence itself and the nature of historical evidence in particular.

The historical apologists, in agreement with the classical apologists, begin with evidence to demonstrate the truth of Christianity. Presuppositionalists, on the other hand, begin with the unbeliever's presuppositions. At issue is the validity of evidence to support truth. The pure (revelational) presuppositionalists insist that no evidence, historical or otherwise, makes any sense unless it is interpreted in the grid of one's overall Christian worldview. The historical apologist believes that the historical facts are self-interpreting in their historical context. Pure presuppositionalists, on the other hand, insist that no facts are self-interpreting; all facts are interpreted and require a Christian *worldview framework for proper understanding.

Historical versus Classical Apologetics. Historical apologetics has much in common with classical apologetics. Both believe in the validity of historical evidence. Both see historical evidence to be crucial to the defense of Christianity. However, they sharply disagree over the need for theistic apologetics as logically prior to historical apologetics. Classical apologetics believes it makes no sense to speak about the resurrection as an act of God unless one had first established that a God exists who can first act. The historical apologists, on the other hand, argues that one can show that God exists by demonstrating from the historical evidence alone that an act of God occurred, as in the resurrection of Jesus Christ.

The Historical Approach. The basic approach of historical apologetics is to begin with the historicity of the New Testament documents and then to use the miracles of Christ, particularly the resurrection, to demonstrate that Christ is the Son of God (thereby establishing that a theistic God exists who can work miracles).

A typical approach of historical apologetics might begin by attempting to show the historicity of the New Testament documents. This usually includes arguments for the authenticity of the New Testament documents (*see* NEW TESTAMENT, DATING OF; NEW TESTAMENT MANUSCRIPTS) and the reliability of the New Testament witnesses (*see* NEW TESTAMENT, HISTORICITY OF; NEW TESTAMENT, NON-CHRISTIAN SOURCES).

The second step would be to examine the New Testament claims of Christ to be the Son of the theistic God who offers miraculous proofs for his claims. The most important of these proofs is that Christ was resurrected from the dead (*see* MIRACLES, ARGUMENTS AGAINST).

Third, a defense of the miracles of Christ, particularly his resurrection, is given. Sometimes this is supported by historical arguments outside the New Testament, but the basic reliability of the New Testament documents is the usual (and essential) focus.

From these premises alone it is concluded that Jesus is the Son of the one, true, theistic God who alone can account for these miraculous events in Jesus' life. From the deity of Christ it can be, and often is, argued that the Bible is the Word of God, since Jesus (who is God) affirmed it to be so (*see* BIBLE, EVIDENCE FOR; BIBLE, JESUS' VIEW OF). In this way, God, miracles, the deity of Christ (*see* CHRIST, DEITY OF), and the inspiration of the Bible are all supported by way of a historical argument.

Evaluation. Critiques of historical apologetics come from two sides, the presuppositionalists and the classical apologists.

Bare Facts? Presuppositionalists, and even some classical apologists, object that historical apologetics begin with the false assumption that the historical facts "speak for themselves." The historical approach wrongly assumes that there are "bare facts" that are "self-interpreting." These are facts which any fair-minded person can see and from which draw the proper conclusions. But all "facts" gain meaning from their ultimate worldview context. A worldview is like a pair of tinted glasses that color everything seen through their lenses. All facts are interpreted facts. So-called bare facts are like dots scattered over a sheet of paper. No connecting lines are there, and the dots are meaningless unless the mind connects them. How the lines are drawn depends on one's perspective.

As noted among objections to classical apologetics, only a theist understands the resurrection of Jesus of Nazareth as a supernatural act of the theistic God and that this act demonstrates that Jesus is the unique Son of a theistic God (*see* THEISM). That only theists, or tacit theists, come to these conclusions indicates that a theistic worldview is logically prior to the identification even of a resurrection from the dead as supernatural (*see* RESURRECTION, EVIDENCE FOR). The event cannot be a special act of God unless there is a God who can perform such special acts (*see* GOD, NATURE OF).

This is not to say that *psychologically* an event like this could not trigger belief in God, were some skeptic or agnostic to come to believe it actually happened. It only means that only one who accepts at least the possibility, if not plausibility, of a theistic view would come to this conclusion. The vast majority of people who come to believe in Christianity because of the miracles of Christ and the apostles do so only because they already have an explicit or implicit theistic worldview. For example, members of preliterate people groups are often converted to Christianity after they come to believe in such miraculous events. But these people already held a tacit theism that worshiped a high god or sky God (*see* MONOTHEISM, PRIMITIVE). Even deists (*see* DEISM) believe God performed the big miracle of creating the world (*see* CREATION AND ORIGINS). Thus, a resurrection from the dead could evoke their belief that God could do other miracles as well. But the fact remains, both in principle and in practice, that belief in a miracle working God is logically prior to belief that any given event is a miracle, including the event of someone being raised from the dead.

Whose Fingerprint? Other gaps in the historical apologetic approach can only be filled if one holds a theistic worldview. For example, a crucial step in the overall apologetic is to be able to identify a given event as a miracle. But how does one know that a miracle is the "fingerprint of God" to confirm a truth claim of a prophet of God unless one already knows that there is a God and what his "fingerprints" are like? Only if one knows what God is like can he identify god-like acts. The very identifiability of an unusual act as a miracle depends on prior knowledge of such a God (*see* MIRACLES, IDENTIFIABILITY OF).

What Sort of God? Unless one assumes the existence of a theistic God (who is morally perfect and would not deceive), the historical argument does not work. Suppose there were not a morally perfect God who, nonetheless, had the ability to perform miracles. Could he not deceive people by performing miracles for an impostor? Crucial to the historical argument is the premise that *God would not perform a miracle through or for someone who is making a fraudulent claim in his Name* (*see* MIRACLES AS CONFIRMATION OF TRUTH). Unless one has prior assurance that the God who performs such miracles is an essentially perfect Being (i.e., a theistic God) who would not so deceive us, then one cannot be sure that the historical evidence for a miracle actually supports the claim of the one through whom or for whom the miracle is being performed.

Sources

G. H. Clark, *Historiography, Secular and Religious*

N. L. Geisler, *Christian Apologetics*, chapters 5, 15

G. Habermas, *The History of Jesus: Ancient Evidence for the Life of Christ*

———, *The Resurrection of Jesus: An Apologetic*

J. W. Montgomery, *Christianity and History*

———, *Evidence for Faith*

———, *The Shape of the Past*

Historical Jesus. ***See*** **CHRIST OF FAITH VS. JESUS OF HISTORY; JESUS SEMINAR.**

History, Objectivity of. The overall argument in defense of Christianity (*see* APOLOGETICS, ARGUMENT OF) is based on the historicity of the New Testament documents (*see* NEW TESTAMENT MANUSCRIPTS; NEW TESTAMENT, HISTORICITY OF). But this in turn is grounded in the assertion that history is objectively knowable. Since this is strongly challenged by contemporary historians, it is necessary to counter this claim in order to secure the defense of Christianity.

Objections to Objective History. Many arguments have been advanced against the position that history is objectively knowable. The discussion here follows generally an excellent summary found in an unpublished master's thesis by William L. Craig (see Craig). There are at least ten arguments against the objectivity of history to be examined (see Beard, 323–25).

If these arguments are valid, it will make verification of Christianity via a historical method impossible. These ten arguments fall into four broad categories: methodological, epistemological, axiological, and metaphysical.

Epistemological Objections. Epistemology deals with how one knows, and the historical relativist contends that the very conditions by which one knows history are so subjective that one cannot have an objective knowledge of history. Three main objections are offered.

The nonobservability of history. Historical subjectivists argue that the substance of history, unlike that studied by empirical science, is not directly observable. The historian does not deal with past events, but with statements about past events. This fact enables the historian to deal with facts in an imaginative way. Historical facts, they insist, exist only within the creative mind of the historian. The documents do not contain facts, but are, without the historian's understanding, mere ink lines on paper.

Further, once the event is gone it can never be fully recreated. The historian must impose meaning on the fragmentary and secondhand record. "The event itself, the facts, do not say anything, do not impose any meaning. It is the historian who speaks, who imposes a meaning" (Becker, "What Are Historical Facts?" 131).

Two reasons allow the historian only indirect access to the past. First, the historian's world is composed of records and not events. This is why the historian must contribute a "reconstructed picture" of the past. In this sense the past is really a product of the present. Second, the scientist can test his view, whereas experimentation is not possible with historical events. The empirical scientist has the advantage of repeatability; he may subject his views to falsification. The historian cannot. The unobservable historical event is no longer verifiable; it is part of the forever departed past. Hence, what one believes about the past will be no more than a reflection of imagination. It will be a subjective construction in the minds of present historians but cannot hope to be an objective representation of what really happened.

The fragmentary nature of historical accounts. At best a historian can hope for completeness of documentation, but completeness of the events themselves is never possible. Documents at best cover a small fraction of the events (Beard, 323). From only fragmentary documents one cannot validly draw full and final conclusions. The documents do not present the events but only an interpretation of the events mediated through their recorders. At best we have a fragmentary record of what someone else thought happened. So "what really happened would still have to be reconstructed in the mind of the historian" (Carr, 20). Because the documents are so fragmentary and the events so distant, objectivity becomes a will-o'-the-wisp for the historian. Too few pieces of the puzzle remain, and the partial pictures on the few pieces only suggest the mind of the one who passed the pieces down.

Historians are historically conditioned. Historical relativists insist that the historian is a product of a time and is subject to unconscious programming. It is impossible to stand back and view history objectively because the observer is part of the historical process. Historical synthesis depends on the personality of the writer as well as the social and religious milieu in which the writer lives (Pirenne, 97). In this sense one must study the historian before one can understand the historian's history.

Since the historian is part of the historical process, objectivity can never be attained. The history of one generation will be rewritten by the next, and so on. No historian can transcend historical relativity and view the world process from the outside (Collingwood, 248). At best there can be successive, less than final, historical interpretations, each viewing history from the vantage point of its own generation of historians. There is no such person as a neutral historian.

Methodological Objections. Methodological objections relate to the procedure by which historians do their work. Three major methodological objections attack the concept that history is objective enough to establish the truth of Christianity.

The selective nature of research. Not only does the historian lack access to events and must work with their fragmentary interpretations; what makes objectivity more hopeless is that the historian selects from among these fragmentary reports. Historians do not even touch some volumes in archives (Beard, 324). The actual selection among the fragmentary accounts is influenced by subjective and relative factors, including personal prejudice, availability, knowledge of languages, personal beliefs, and social conditions. The historian becomes inextricably a part of the history written. What is included and what is excluded in interpretation will always be a matter of subjective choice. No matter how objective a historian, it is practically impossible to present what really happened. A "history" is no more than an interpretation based on a subjective selection of fragmentary interpretations of past and unrepeatable events.

So, it is argued, the facts of history do not speak for themselves. "The facts speak only when the historian calls on them; it is he who decides to which facts to give the floor, and in what order or context" (Carr, 32). Indeed, when the "facts" speak, it is not the original events that are articulating, but rather later fragmentary opinions about those events. The original facts or events have perished. So, by the very nature of the project, the historian can never hope for objectivity.

The need to structure the facts. Partial knowledge of the past makes it necessary for the historian to "fill in" gaping holes with imagination. As a child draws the lines between the dots on a picture, the historian supplies the connections between events. Without the historian the dots are not numbered, nor arranged in an obvious manner. Imagination provides continuity.

Furthermore, the historian is not content to tell us simply what happened, but feels compelled to explain why it happened (Walsh, 32). This makes history fully coherent and intelligible. Good history has both theme and unity, which are provided by the historian. Facts alone do not make history any more than do disconnected dots make a picture. Herein, according to the subjectivist, lies the difference between chronicle and history. The former is merely the raw material. Without the structure provided by the historian, the "stuff" of history would be meaningless.

The study of history is a study of causes. The historian wants to know *why*, to weave a web of interconnected events into a unified whole. So subjectivity is inevitably interjected. Even if there is some semblance of objectivity in chronicle, nonetheless there is no hope for objectivity in history. History is, in principle, nonobjective because the very thing that makes it history (as opposed to mere chronicle) is the interpretive structure of framework given to it from the subjective vantage point of the historian. Hence, it is concluded, the necessity of structure inevitably makes objectivity impossible.

The need to select and arrange. The historian views fragmentary documents indirectly through the interpretation of the original source. In the process a selected amount of material from available archives is hung on an interpretive structure by the use of the historian's own value-laden language within an overall worldview. Events come to be understood from the relative vantage point of the historian's generation, and even the topics studied accord with the researcher's subjective preferences. The dice are loaded against objectivity from the start. In the actual writing an historian covers non-repeatable events from fragmentary, secondhand accounts from a personal point of view while subjectively arranging the material (Collingwood, 285–90).

The selection and arrangement will be determined by personal and social factors. The final written product will be prejudiced by what is included and by what is excluded. It will lack objectivity by how facts are arranged and emphasized. The selection in terms of the framework given will either be narrow or broad, clear or confused. Whatever its nature, the framework reflects the mind of the historian (Beard, 150–51). This moves one still further away from objectively knowing what really happened.

Subjectivists conclude that hopes of objectivity are dashed at every point in the process.

An Axiological (Value) Objection. The historian cannot avoid making value judgments (*see* TRUTH, NATURE OF). This, argue historical relativists, renders objectivity unobtainable. For even in the selection and arrangement of materials value judgments are made. Titles of chapters and sections imply values of the writer.

As one historian put it, the very subject matter of history is "value-charged" (Dray, 23). The facts of history consist of murders, oppression, and other evils that cannot be described in morally neutral words. By use of ordinary language, the historian is forced to impose values. Whether, for instance, one is called a "dictator" or a "benevolent ruler" is a value judgment. How can one describe Adolf Hitler without making value judgments? And if one were to attempt a kind of scientifically neutral description of past events without any stated or implied interpretation of human purposes, it would not be history but mere raw-boned chronicle without historical meaning.

There is no way for the historian to keep out of the history. Perspectives and prejudices will be expressed in value language by which and through which the world is viewed. In this sense objectivity is unattainable. Every writer will inevitably evaluate things from a subjective perspective and chosen words.

Metaphysical Objections. Three metaphysical objections have been leveled against the belief in objective history. Each is predicated, either theoretically or practically, on the premise that worldview colors the study of history.

The unavoidability of worldviews. Every historian interprets the past in the overall framework of a *Weltanschauung.* Every historian operates from inside one of three philosophies of history: (1) History is a *chaotic* jumble of meaningless events; (2) the events of humankind's story repeat themselves in some sort of *cycle*; and (3) events are pushing forward the story in a *linear* fashion toward an endpoint (Beard, 151). Which one of these the historian adopts will be a matter of faith or philosophy. Unless one view or another is presupposed, no interpretation is possible. The *Weltanschauungen* determine whether the historian sees the events as a meaningless maze, a series of endless repetitions, or a purposeful advance. These worldviews are both necessary and inevitably value oriented. Without a *worldview the historian cannot interpret the past; but a worldview makes objectivity impossible.

A worldview is not generated from the facts. Facts do not speak for themselves. The facts gain meaning only within the overall context of the worldview. Without the structure of the worldview framework, the "stuff" of history has no meaning. Augustine, for example, viewed history as a great theodicy, but W. F. G. Hegel saw it as an unfolding of the divine. It is not an archaeological or factual find but simply the religious or philosophical presuppositions which prompted each person to develop a view. Eastern philosophies of history are even more diverse; they involve a cyclical rather than a linear pattern.

Once one admits the relativity or perspectivity of one worldview instead of another, the historical relativists insist that all rights to claim objectivity have been waived. If there are different ways to interpret the same facts, depending on the overall perspective, then there is no single objective interpretation of history.

Miracles are suprahistorical. Even if one grants that *secular* history could be known objectively, there still remains the problem of the subjectivity of *religious* history. Some writers make a strong distinction between *Historie* and *Geschichte* (Kahler, 63; *see* KAHLER, MARTIN). The former is empirical and objectively knowable to some degree; the latter is spiritual and unknowable in a historical or objective way. But as spiritual or suprahistorical, there is no objective way to verify it. Spiritual history has no necessary connection with the spatiotemporal continuum of empirical events. It is a "myth" (*see* MIRACLES, ARGUMENTS AGAINST; MIRACLES, MYTH AND; MYTHOLOGY AND THE NEW TESTAMENT). It offers subjective religious significance to the believer but lacks objective grounding. Like the story of George Washington and the cherry tree, *Geschichte* is a story made up of events which probably never happened but which inspire men to some moral or religious good.

If this distinction is applied to the New Testament, then even granted that the life and central teachings of Jesus of Nazareth can be objectively established, there is no historical way to confirm the miraculous dimension of the New Testament (*see* MIRACLES IN THE BIBLE). Miracles do not happen as part of *Historie* and therefore are not subject to objective analysis; they are *Geschichte* events and as such cannot be analyzed by historical methodology. Many contemporary theologians have accepted this distinction. Paul *Tillich claimed that it is "a disastrous distortion of the meaning of faith to identify it with the belief in the historical validity of the Biblical stories" (Tillich, 87). Rather, with Søren *Kierkegaard, Tillich believed the important thing is that it evoke an appropriate religious response. With this Rudolf *Bultmann and Shubert Ogden would concur, as would much of contemporary theological thought.

Even such as Karl Jaspers, who oppose Bultmann's more radical demythologization view, accept the distinction between spiritual and empirical dimensions of miracles (Jaspers, 16–17). On the more conservative end of those maintaining this distinction is Ian Ramsey. According to Ramsey, "it is not enough to think of the facts of the Bible as 'brute historical facts' to which the Evangelists give distinctive 'interpretation.'" "No attempt to make the language of the Bible conform to a precise straight-forward public language—whether that language be scientific of historical—has ever succeeded." The Bible is about situations which existentialists call "authentic" or "existential-historical" (Ramsey, 118, 119, 122). There is always something "more" than the empirical in every religious or miraculous situation.

Miracles are historically unknowable. On the basis of Ernst *Troeltsch's principle of analogy, some historians have come to object to the possibility of ever establishing a miracle based on testimony about the past. As discussed more fully in Miracles, Arguments Against, Troeltsch stated the problem this way:

> On the analogy of the events known to us we seek by conjecture and sympathetic understanding to explain and reconstruct the past. . . . Since we discern the same process of phenomena in operation in the past as in the present, and see, there as here, the various historical cycles of human life influencing and intersecting one another.

Without uniformity we could know nothing about the past, for without an analogy from the present we could know nothing about the past. In accord with this principle some have argued that "no amount of testimony is ever permitted to establish as past reality a thing that cannot be found in present reality" (Becker, "Detachment," 12–13). Unless one can identify miracles in the present there is no analogy on which to base understanding of alleged miracles in the past. The historian, like the scientist, must adopt a methodological skepticism toward alleged events for which there are no contemporary parallels. The present is the foundation of our knowledge of the past. As F. H. Bradley put it:

> We have seen that history rests in the last resort upon an inference from our experience, a judgment based upon our own present state of things . . . ; when we are asked to affirm the existence in past time of events, the effects of causes which confessedly are without analogy in the world in which we live, and which we know, we are at a loss for any answer but this, that . . . we are asked to build a house without a foundation. . . . And how can we attempt this without contradicting ourselves? [Bradley, 100]

A Response to Historical Relativism. Despite these strong objections to the possibility of historical objectivity, the case is by no means closed. There are flaws in the historical relativists' position. The responses given are in the order of the above objections.

The Problem of Indirect Access. If by *objective* one means absolute knowledge, then no human historian can be objective. On the other hand, if *objective* means "a fair but revisable presentation that reasonable men and women should accept," then the door is open to the possibility of objectivity. In this latter sense, history is as objective as some sciences (Block, 50). Paleontology (historical geology) is considered one of the most objective of all sciences. It deals with physical facts and processes of the past. However, the events represented by fossil finds are no more directly accessible to the scientists or *repeatable* than are historical events to the historian. There are some differences. The fossil is a mechanically true imprint of the original event and the eyewitness of history may be less precise. But natural processes also can mar the fossil imprint. At least if one can determine the integrity and reliability of the eyewitness, one cannot slam the door on the possibility of objectivity in history any more than on objectivity in geology.

The scientist might contend that he can repeat the processes of the past by experimentation, whereas the historian cannot. But even here the situations are similar. In this sense history too can be "repeated." Similar patterns of events, by which comparisons can be made, recur today as they occurred in the past. Limited social experiments can be performed to see if human history "repeats." The historian, no less than the scientist, has the tools for determining what really happened in the past. The lack of direct access to the original facts or events does not hinder the one more than the other (*see* ORIGINS, SCIENCE OF).

Likewise, scientific facts do not "speak for themselves" any more than do historical facts. If *fact* means "original event," then neither geology nor history is in possession of any facts. *Fact* must be taken by both to mean information about the original event, and in this latter sense facts do not exist merely subjectively in the mind of the historian. What one does with data, what meaning or interpretation is given to them, can in no way eliminate the data. There remains for both science and history a hard core of objective facts. The door is thereby left open for objectivity. One may draw a valid distinction between propaganda and history. Propaganda lacks sufficient basis in objective fact but history does not. Without objective facts no protest can be raised either against poor history or propaganda. If history is entirely in the mind of the beholder, there is no reason one cannot decide to behold it any way he desires.

This brings us to the crucial question as to whether "facts speak for themselves" because they are objective. An argument might be advanced that, yes, they do. It is self-defeating to affirm that facts are without meaning, since the affirmation about the allegedly meaningless fact is a meaningful statement about fact. All facts are meaningful; there are no so-called bare facts. But this argument does not really prove that facts speak for themselves. It does show that facts can and do bear meaning. But what it must prove (and fails to prove) is that facts bear only one meaning and that they bear it evidently. The fact that no meaningful statement about facts can be made without attributing some meaning to the facts does not prove that the meaning emanated from the facts. It is possible that the meaning was assigned to the facts by the one making the meaningful statement about them. Indeed, only "mean-ers" (i.e., minds) can emanate meaning.

It is not at all clear in what sense an objective fact can mean anything in and of itself. It is a subject (e.g., a mind) that utters meaning about objects (or about other subjects), but objects as such are not subjects that are emitting meaning. This is so unless we assume that all objective facts are really little minds transmitting meaning or transmitters through which some other minds or a Mind is communicating. But to assume this would be to invoke one particular worldview over another in order to prove that "facts speak for themselves." And even then it could be argued that the facts are not speaking for themselves but for the Mind (God) who is speaking through them.

It seems best to conclude, then, that objective facts do not speak for themselves. Finite minds may give differing interpretations of them or an infinite Mind may give an absolute interpretation of them, but there is no one objective interpretation a finite mind can give to them. Of course, if there is an absolute Mind from whose vantage point the facts are given absolute or ultimate meaning, then there is an objective interpretation of the facts which all finite minds should concur is the ultimate meaning. If this is the correct worldview (*see* GOD, EVIDENCE FOR; THEISM), then there is an object meaning to all facts in the world. All facts are theistic facts, and no nontheistic way of interpreting them is objective or true. Hence, objectivity in history is possible, since in a theistic world history would be His-story. Objectivity, then, is possible within a worldview.

The Fragmentary Nature of Historical Accounts. The fact that the fossil record is fragmentary does not destroy the objectivity of paleontology. The fossil remains represent only a very tiny percentage of the living beings of the past. This does not hinder scientists from attempting to reconstruct an objective picture of what really happened in geological history. Likewise, human history is transmitted through partial records. Not every bone is necessary to make some qualified judgments about the whole animal. The reconstruction of both science and history is subject to revision. Subsequent finds may provide new facts that call for new interpretations. But at least there is an objective basis in fact for the meaning attributed to the find. Interpretations can neither create the facts nor can they ignore them, if they would approach objectivity. We may conclude, then, that history need be no less objective than geology simply because it depends on fragmentary accounts. Scientific knowledge is also partial and depends on assumptions and an overall framework which may prove to be inadequate upon the discovery of more facts (*see* SCIENCE AND THE BIBLE).

Whatever difficulty there may be, from a strictly scientific point of view, in filling in gaps between the facts, once one has assumed a philosophical stance toward the world, the problem of objectivity in general is resolved. If there is a

God, then the overall picture is already drawn; the facts of history will merely fill in the details of its meaning. If the universe is theistic, the artist's sketch is already known in advance (*see* THEISM); the detail and coloring will come only as all the facts of history are fit into the overall sketch known to be true from the theistic framework. In this sense, historical objectivity is most certainly possible within a given framework such as a theistic worldview. Objectivity resides in the view that best fits the facts consistently into an overall theistic system which is supported by good evidence (*see* GOD, EVIDENCE FOR).

Historical Conditioning. It is true that every historian is time bound. Each person occupies a relative place in the changing events of the spatiotemporal world. However, it does not follow that because the historian is a product of a time that the person's historical research is also a product of the time. Simply because a person cannot avoid a relative place in history does not preclude objectivity. The criticism confuses the content of knowledge and the process of attaining it (Mandelbaum, 94). Where one derives a hypothesis is not essentially related to how its truth is established.

Further, if relativity is unavoidable, the position of the historical relativists is self-refuting. For either their view is historically conditioned, and therefore unobjective, or else it is not relative but objective. If the latter, it thereby admits that it is possible to be objective in viewing history. On the contrary, if the position of historical relativism is itself relative, then it cannot be taken as objectively true. It is simply subjective opinion that has no basis to claim to be objectively true about all of history. If it is subjective it cannot eliminate the possibility that history is objectively knowable, and if it is an objective fact about history then objective facts can be known about history. In the first case, objectivity is not eliminated and in the second, relativity is self-defeated. In either case, objectivity is possible.

The constant rewriting of history is based on the assumption that objectivity is possible. Why strive for accuracy unless it is believed that the revision is more objectively true than the previous view? Why critically analyze unless improvement toward a more accurate view is the assumed goal? Perfect objectivity may be practically unattainable within the limited resources of the historian. But the inability to attain 100 percent objectivity is a long way from total relativity. Reaching a degree of objectivity which is subject to criticism and revision is a more realistic conclusion than the relativist's arguments. In short, there is no reason to eliminate the possibility of a sufficient degree of historical objectivity.

The Selectivity of Materials. The fact that the historian must select from among all possible materials does not automatically make history purely subjective. Jurors make judgments "beyond reasonable doubt" without having all the evidence. Availability of the relevant and crucial evidence is sufficient to attain objectivity. One need not know everything in order to know something. No scientist knows all the facts, and yet objectivity is claimed. As long as no important fact is overlooked, there is no reason to eliminate the possibility of objectivity in history, any more than in science.

The selection of facts can be objective to the degree that the facts are selected and reconstructed in the context in which the events represented actually occurred. Since it is impossible for any historian to pack into an account everything available on a subject, it is important to select the points representative of the period (Collingwood, 100). Condensation does not necessarily imply distortion. Further, the evidence for the historicity of the New Testament from which Christian apologetics draw is greater than for the truth of any other document from the ancient world (*see* NEW TESTAMENT MANUSCRIPTS; NEW TESTAMENT, HISTORICITY OF). If the events behind it cannot be known objectively, it is impossible to know anything from that time period.

There remains, however, the question of whether the real context and connections of past events are known, or, are knowable. Unless there is an accepted framework or structure for the facts, there is no way to reconstruct in miniature what really happened. The objective meaning of historical events is dependent on knowing the connection that the events really had when they occurred. But the events are subject to various combinations, depending on the structure given to them by the historian, the relative importance placed on them, and whether prior events are considered causal or merely antecedent. There is really no way to know the original connections without assuming an overall hypothesis or worldview by which the events are interpreted. Of course objectivity of bare facts and mere sequence of antecedent and consequent facts are knowable without assuming a *worldview. But objectivity of the meaning of these events is not possible apart from a meaningful structure, such as that provided by an overall hypothesis or worldview. Hence, the problem of finding objective meaning in history, like the problem of objective meaning in science, is dependent on one's *Weltanschauung*. Objective meaning is system-dependent. Only within a given system can the objective meaning of events be understood. Once that system is known, it is possible by fair and representative selection to reconstruct an objective picture of the past. Thus within an established theistic structure objectivity is possible.

Structuring the Material of History. All the historian could possibly know about past events without assuming the truth of one interpretive framework over another is the sheer facticity and sequence of the events. When the historian moves beyond bare facts and mere order of events and begins to speak of causal connections and relative importance, an interpretive framework is needed through which to understand the facts. Whether the facts are determined to have originally had the assumed causal connection and the attributed importance will depend on whether the given worldview is correct. To affirm that facts have "internal arrangement" begs the question. The real question is, How does one know the correct arrangement? Since the facts can be arranged in one of at least three ways (chaotic, cyclical, and linear), it begs the question merely to assume that one of these is the way the facts were really arranged. The same set of dots can have the lines drawn in many ways. The fact is that the lines are not known to be there apart from an interpretive framework through which one views them. Therefore, the problem of the objective meaning of history cannot be resolved apart from appeal to a worldview. Once the skeletal sketch is known, then one can know the objective placing (meaning) of the facts. However, apart from a structure the mere "stuff" means nothing.

Apart from an overall structure, there is no way to know which events in history are the most significant and, hence, there is no way to know the true significance of these and other events in their overall context. The argument that importance is determined by which events influence the most people is inadequate. It is a form of historical utilitarianism subject to the same criticisms as any utilitarian test for truth. The most does not determine the best; great influence does not mean great importance or value. Even after most people have been influenced, one can still question the truth or value of the event that influenced them. Of course, if one assumes as a framework that the most significant events are those that influence the most people in the long run, then utilitarian ideals will be determinative. But what right does one have to assume a utilitarian framework any more than a nonutilitarian one? Here again, it is a matter of justifying one's overall framework or worldview.

The argument advanced by some objectivists is that past events must be structured or else they are unknowable and faulty. All this argument proves is that it is necessary to understand facts through some structure, otherwise it makes no sense to speak of facts. The question of which structure is correct must be determined on some basis other than the mere facts themselves. If there were an objectivity of bare facts, it would provide only the mere "what" of history. But objective meaning deals with the why of these events; this is impossible apart from a meaning-structure in which facts may find their placement of significance. Objective meaning apart from a worldview is impossible.

However, granted that there is justification for adopting a theistic worldview, the objective meaning of history becomes possible (*see* THEISM; GOD, EVIDENCE FOR). Within the theistic context, each fact of history becomes a theistic fact. Granted the factual order of events and known causal connection of events, objective meaning becomes possible. The chaotic and the cyclical frameworks are eliminated in favor of the linear. And within the linear view of events, causal connections emerge as the result of their context in a theistic universe. Theism provides the sketch from which history paints the complete picture. The pigments of mere fact take on real meaning as they are blended on the theistic sketch. Objectivity means systematic consistency. That is, the most meaningful way all the facts of history blend into the whole theistic sketch is what really happened. In this way, theism can provide an objective framework for historical facts.

Selecting and Arranging Materials. The historian can rearrange data about the past without distorting it (Nagel, 208). Since the original construction of events is available to neither the historian nor the geologist, the past must be reconstructed from available evidence. But reconstruction does not require revision. The historian must arrange the material. The important thing is whether it is arranged or rearranged in accordance with the events as they really occurred. As long as the historian consistently incorporates all the significant events in accordance with an overall established worldview, objectivity is secure. Objectivity arranges facts in accordance with the way things really were. Distortion comes when facts are neglected and twisted.

The historian may desire to be selective in the compass of study, to study only the political, economic, or religious dimensions of a specific period. But such specialization does not demand total subjectivity. One can focus without losing the overall context. It is one thing to focus on specifics within an overall field but quite another to ignore or distort the overall context in which the intensified interest is occurring. As long as the specialist stays in touch with reality rather than reflecting pure subjectivity, a measurable degree of objectivity can be maintained.

Value Judgments. One may grant the point that ordinary language is value laden and that value judgments are inevitable. This by no means makes historical objectivity impossible (Butterfield, 244). Objectivity means fair dealing with the facts, to present what happened as correctly as possible. Further, objectivity means that when one interprets why these events occurred, the language of the historian should ascribe to these events the value which they had in their original context. Granting within an established worldview that certain things have a given value, then an objective account of history must reconstruct and restructure these events with the same relative value. So objectivity demands making value judgments rather than avoiding them. The question is not whether value language can be objective, but which value statements objectively portray the events. Once the worldview has been determined, value judgments are not undesirable or merely subjective; they are essential. If this is a theistic world, then it would not be objective to place anything but a theistic value on the facts of history.

The Need for an Overall Worldview. Those who argue against the objectivity of history apart from an overall worldview must be granted the point. Meaning is system-dependent. Without a worldview it makes no sense to talk about objective meaning (Popper, 150f.). Without a context meaning cannot be determined, and the context is provided by the worldview and not by the bare facts.

But granted that this is a theistic universe, it follows that objectivity is possible. In a theistic universe each fact has objective meaning; each fact is a God-fact. All events fit into the overall context of an ultimate purpose. One can determine the facts and assign them meaning in the overall context of the theistic universe by showing that they fit most consistently with a given interpretation. Then one may lay claim to having arrived at the objective truth about history.

For example, given that this is a theistic universe and that the corpse of Jesus of Nazareth returned from the grave, then the Christian can argue that this unusual event is a miracle that confirms the associated truth claims of Jesus to be the Christ. Apart from this theistic framework, it is not even meaningful to make such a claim. Overarching hypotheses are necessary to determine the meaning of events, and a theistic hypothesis is essential to claim that any historical event is a miracle.

The Historical Unknowability of Miracles. Upon examination, Ernst *Troeltsch's principle of analogy turns out to be similar to David *Hume's objection to miracles built on the uniformity of nature. No testimony about alleged miracles should be accepted if it contradicts the uniform testimony of nature. Troeltsch also rejects any particular past event for which there is no analog in the uniform experience of the present. There are at least two reasons for denying Troeltsch's argument from analogy. First, it begs the question in favor of a naturalistic interpretation of all historical events. It is a methodological exclusion of the possibility of accepting the miraculous in history. The testimony for regularity in general is in no way a testimony against an unusual event in particular. The cases are different and should not be evaluated in the same way. Empirical generalizations ("People do not rise from the dead in normal circumstance") should not be used as countertestimony to worthy eyewitness accounts that in a particular case someone did rise from the dead. The evidence for any particular historical event must be assessed on its own merits, aside from generalizations about other events.

The second objection to the Troeltsch analogy type argument is that it proves too much. As Richard *Whately convincingly argued, on this uniformitarian assumption not only miracles would be excluded, but so would any unusual event of the past. One would have to deny that the career of Napoleon Bonaparte occurred (see Whately). No one can deny that the probability against Napoleon's successes was great. His prodigious army was destroyed in Russia; yet in a few months he led another great army in Germany, which likewise was ruined at Leipzig. However, the French supplied him with yet another army sufficient to make a formidable stand in France. This was repeated five times until at last he was confined to an island. There is no doubt that the particular events of his career were highly improbable. But there is no reason on these grounds that we should doubt the historicity of the Napoleonic adventures. History, contrary to scientific hypothesis, does not depend on the universal and repeatable. Rather, it stands on the sufficiency of good testimony for particular and unrepeatable events. Were this not so, then nothing could be learned from history.

It is clearly a mistake to import uniformitarian methods from scientific experimentation into historical research. Repeatability and generality are needed to establish a scientific law or general patterns (of which miracles would be particular exceptions). But this method does not work at all in history. What is needed to establish historical events is credible testimony that these particular events did indeed occur (*see* Witnesses, Hume's Criteria for). So it is with miracles. It is an unjustifiable mistake in historical methodology to assume that no unusual and particular event can be believed, no matter how great the evidence for it. Troeltsch's principle of analogy would destroy genuine historical thinking. The honest historian must be open to the possibility of unique and particular events, regardless of whether they may be described as miraculous. One must not exclude *a priori* the possibility of establishing events like the resurrection of Christ without examining the evidence. It is a mistake to assume that the same principles by which *empirical* science works can be used in *forensic* science. Since the latter deals with unrepeated and unobserved events in the past, it operates on the principles of *origin science,* not on those of *operation science*. And these principles do not eliminate, but establish, the possibility of objective knowledge of the past—whether in science or history (*see* ORIGINS, SCIENCE OF).

The Superhistorical Nature of Miracles. A miracle is supernatural. Surely the Christian apologist does not contend that miracles are mere products of the natural process. Something is miraculous when the natural process does not account for it. There must be an injection from the realm of the supernatural into the natural, or else there is no miracle (*see* MIRACLE). This is specially true of a New Testament miracle, in which the processes by which God performed acts are unknown. This is also true to some degree of a second-class miracle, where we can describe how the miracle occurred by scientific means but not why it occurred when it did. In either case, it seems best to admit that the miraculous dimensions of a historical event are in, but not of, the natural process.

Miracles do occur within history. In accordance with the objectivity of history, there is no good reason why the Christian should yield to the radical existential theologians on the question of the objective and historical dimensions of miracles. Miracles may not be of the natural historical process but they do occur inside it. Even Karl *Barth made this distinction when he wrote, "The resurrection of Christ, or his second coming . . . is not a historical event; the historians may reassure themselves . . . that our concern here is with the event which, though it is the only real happening *in* is not a real happening *of* history" (Barth, 90, emphasis added).

Unlike many existential theologians, we must also preserve the historical context in which a miracle occurs, for without it there is no way to verify the objectivity of the miraculous. Miracles do have a historical dimension without which no objectivity of religious history is possible. And as was argued above, historical methodology can identify this objectivity just as surely as scientific objectivity can be established, within the accepted framework of a theistic world. In short, miracles may be more than historical but they cannot be less than historical. It is only if miracles do have historical dimensions that they are both objectively meaningful and apologetically valuable.

A miracle is significant in different areas. A miracle can be identified within an empirical or historical context both directly and indirectly, both objectively and subjectively. Such an event is both scientifically unusual and theologically and morally relevant. The scientific dimensions can be understood in a directly empirical way; the moral dimension is knowable only indirectly through the empirical. It is both "odd" and "evocative" of something more than its empirical data. A *virgin birth is scientifically odd, but in the case of Jesus it is represented as a "sign" to draw attention to him as something "more" than human. The theological and moral characteristics of a miracle are not empirically objective. In this sense they are experienced subjectively. This does not mean, however, that there is no objective basis for the moral dimensions of a miracle. If this is a theistic universe (*see* THEISM), then morality is objectively grounded in God. Hence, the nature and will of God are the objective grounds by which one can test whether the event is subjectively evocative of what is objectively in accord with the nature and will of God. The same thing applies to the truth dimensions of a miracle. They are subjectively evocative of a response to an associated truth claim. However, the truth claim must be in accord with what is already known of God. If its message does not correspond with what we know to be true of God, we should not believe the event is a miracle. It is axiomatic that acts by a theistic God would not be used to confirm what is not the truth of God.

So miracles happen in history but are not completely of history. They are nonetheless historically grounded. They are more than historical but not less than historical. There are both empirical and superempirical dimensions to supernatural events. The empirical dimensions are knowable objectively, and the latter make a subjective appeal to the believer. But even here there is objective ground in the known truth and goodness of God by which the believer can judge whether the empirically odd are really acts of the true and good God.

The Complete Relativity of History. In addition to the invalidity of the arguments of historical relativism there are some strong arguments against their conclusions in general. Two of these arguments are sufficient to demonstrate why the possibility of objectivity in history has not—and cannot—be systematically eliminated.

Objective Knowledge by Facts and Worldview. A careful look at the arguments of the relativists reveals that they presuppose some objective knowledge about history. This is seen in at least two ways. First, they speak of the need to select and arrange the "facts" of history. But if they are really facts, they present some objective knowledge in themselves. It is one thing to argue about the *interpretation* of the facts but quite another to deny that there are any facts to interpret. It is understandable that one's worldview framework colors understanding of the fact that Christ died on a cross in the early first century. But it is quite another to deny that this is a historical fact (*see* CHRIST, DEATH OF).

Second, if relativists believe one's worldview can distort how one views history, then there must be a correct interpretation. Otherwise, it would be meaningless to say that some views are distorted.

Total Historical Relativity Is Self-defeating. In fact, total relativity (whether historical, philosophical, or moral) is self-defeating (*see* FIRST PRINCIPLES). How could one know that history is completely unknowable unless something is known about it? It requires objective knowledge to know that all historical knowledge is subjective. Total relativists must stand on the pinnacle of their own absolute in order to relativize everything else. The claim that all history is subjective turns out to be an objective claim about history. Thus, total historical relativism cuts its own throat.

Of course, some might claim that historical knowledge is not totally relative but only partially so. Then history, at least some history, is objectively knowable, and Christian claims are at least possibly knowable. The historical claims for the central truths of Christianity are more amply supported by the evidence than are claims of facticity for almost any other event in the ancient world. Therefore, this is also an admission that partial relativity does not eliminate the historical verifiability of Christianity. In brief, total historical relativism is self-defeating, and partial historical relativism admits that historical arguments are justified in defending Christian faith.

The Objectivity of Historiography. Several general conclusions may be drawn from the subjectivity-objectivity debate: Foremost is that absolute objectivity is possible only for an infinite Mind. Finite minds must be content with systematic consistency. Humans can only devise revisable attempts to reconstruct the past based on an established framework of reference which comprehensively and consistently incorporates the facts into an overall sketch. At this level of objectivity, the historian can be as accurate as the scientist. Neither geologists nor historians have direct access to, nor complete data on, repeatable events. Both must use value judgments to select and structure the partial material available.

In reality, neither the scientist nor the historian can attain objective meaning without a worldview by which to understand the facts. Bare facts cannot even be known apart from some interpretive framework. Hence, the need for structure or a meaning-framework is crucial to the question of objectivity. Unless one can settle the question as to whether this is a theistic or nontheistic world on grounds independent of the mere facts themselves, there is no way to determine the objective meaning of history. If, on the other hand, there are good reasons to believe that this is a theistic universe, then objectivity in history is a possibility. For once the overall viewpoint is established, it is simply a matter of finding the view of history most consistent with that overall system. Systematic consistency is the test for objectivity in historical, as well as in scientific matters.

Summary. Christianity makes claims about historical events, including claims that God supernaturally intervened in it. Some historians complain, however, that there is no objective way to determine the past. And even if there were an objective basis, miracles do not fit it. The historian has fragmentary, secondhand material from which to select. These fragments cannot be objectively understood, because the historian inevitably imposes an interpretive value structure and worldview. Miracle-history is particularly unreliable, since it is neither empirical nor observable. Superhistory or myth, it is useful to evoke a subjective religious response but not to reliably describe the past.

These objections, however, fail. History can be as objective as science. The geologist also views second-hand, fragmentary, and unrepeatable evidence from a personal vantage point. Although interpretive frameworks are necessary, not every worldview must be relative and subjective.

As to the objection that miracle-history is not objectively verifiable, miracles can occur in the historical process, like any other event. The only difference is that the miracle cannot be explained by the flow of events. Christian miracles claim to be more than empirical, but they are not less than historical. Historically, miracles can be verified. Moral and theological dimensions of miracles are not totally subjective. They call for a subjective response but, there are objective standards of truth and goodness (in accordance with the theistic God) by which they can be assessed.

The door for the objectivity of history and thus the objective historicity for miracles is open. No mere question-begging, uniformitarian principle of analogy can lock it *a priori*. Evidence that supports the general nature of scientific law cannot rule out good historical evidence for unusual but particular events of history. Anti-miracle arguments are not only invincibly naturalistic in bias, but if applied consistently they rule out known and accepted secular history (*see* MIRACLES, ARGUMENTS AGAINST). The only truly honest approach is to examine carefully the evidence for an alleged miracle to determine its authenticity.

Sources

K. Barth, *The Word of God and the Word of Man*

C. Beard, "That Noble Dream," in *The Varieties of History*

C. L. Becker, "Detachment and the Writing of History," P. L. Synder, ed., *Detachment and the Writing of History,*

———, "What Are Historical Facts?" *The Philosophy of History in Our Time*

M. Block, *The Historian's Craft*

F. H. Bradley, *The Presuppositions of Critical History*

H. Butterfield, "Moral Judgments in History," H. Meyerhoff, ed., *Philosophy*

E. H. Carr, *What Is History?*

R. G. Collingwood, *The Idea of History*

W. L. Craig, "The Nature of History," unpub. master's thesis, Trinity Evangelical Divinity School

W. H. Dray, ed., *Philosophy of History*
K. Jaspers, et al., *Myth and Christianity*
M. Mandelbaum, *The Problem of Historical Knowledge*
E. Nagel, "The Logic of Historical Analysis," H. Meyerhoff, ed., *Philosophy*
H. Pirenne, "What Are Historians Trying to Do?" H. Meyerhoff, ed., *Philosophy*
K. Popper, *The Poverty of Historicism*
I. Ramsey, *Religious Language*
P. Tillich, *Dynamics of Faith*
E. Troeltsch, "Historiography," J. Hastings, ed., *Encyclopedia of Religion and Ethics*
W. H. Walsh, *Philosophy of History*
R. Whately, *Historical Doubts Relative to Napoleon Bonaparte*

Hittites, Problem of. Genesis asserts that Heth was progenitor of the Hittites, whose kingdom arose in what is now Turkey. However, according to some archaeological evidence, the Hittites did not become a prominent force in the Middle East until the reign of Mursilis I, about 1620 B.C. It was Mursilis who captured Babylon in 1600 B.C.

However, several times in Genesis 23, reference is made to Abraham's encounter with the sons of Heth, who controlled Hebron in about 2050 B.C. How could the Hittites have controlled Hebron so long before they became a significant force in the area?

Cuneiform tablets have been found describing conflicts in Anatolia (Turkey) among Hittite principalities from about 1950 to 1850. Even before this conflict there was a race of non-Indo-Europeans called Hattians. These people were subdued by invaders about 2300 to 2000. The Indo-European invaders adopted the name Hatti. In Semitic languages such as Hebrew, *Hatti* and *Hitti* would be written with the same letters. Only consonants were written, not vowels.

In the days of Ramses II in Egypt, the military strength of the Hittites was sufficient to precipitate a nonaggression pact between Egypt and the Hittite empire, setting a boundary between them. At this time the Hittite empire reached as far south as Kadesh on the Orontes River (modern Asi). However, additional evidence indicates that the Hittites actually penetrated farther south into Syria and Palestine.

Although the Hittite kingdom did not reach its zenith until the second half of the fourteenth century, there is sufficient evidence to substantiate a Hittite presence, significant enough for control, in Hebron at the time of Abraham.

Sources

C. E. A. "Hittites," in *Dictionary of Biblical Archaeology*
N. L. Geisler and T. Howe, *When Critics Ask*
G. L. Archer, Jr., *An Encyclopedia of Biblical Difficulties*
O. R. Gurney, *The Hittites*
E. Neufield, *The Hittite Laws*

Holy Spirit, Role in Apologetics. Most Christian apologists agree that the Holy Spirit witnesses to the individual with regard to their personal salvation. Romans 8:16 asserts: "The Spirit himself testifies with our spirit that we are God's children" (1 John 3:24; 4:13). Many also believe that the Holy Spirit bears witness to the truth of Christianity. One of several texts teaching that is 1 John 5:6–10:

> This is the one who came by water and blood—Jesus Christ. . . . And it is the Spirit who testifies, because the Spirit is the truth. . . . We accept man's testimony, but God's testimony is greater because it is the testimony of God, which he has given about his Son. . . . Anyone who does not believe God has made him out to be a liar, because he has not believed the testimony God has given about his Son.

Some have charged that the use of reason relating to God, as apologetic arguments do (*see* APOLOGETICS, NEED FOR), is inconsistent with the biblical emphasis on the necessity of the Holy Spirit to convince someone of the truth of Christianity. But the Christian position is that there is no contradiction between reason and evidence on one hand and the work of the Holy Spirit on the other.

The Early Church Fathers. Early Christian apologists from *Justin Martyr (100–165) to *Clement of Alexandria (ca. 155–220) used reason in their defense. They also believed in the necessity of divine revelation and the work of the Holy Spirit in bringing the truth about God to humankind. However, they provided no systematic treatment of the precise relationship between human reason and the ministry of the Holy Spirit. This was left to later theologians, especially *Augustine, *Thomas Aquinas, and the Reformers.

Augustine. Augustine (354–430) stressed the work of the Spirit to call depraved, dead-in-sin humans to new life in Christ. But he kept this work of the Spirit in tension with his belief that human reason is needed to judge and understand divine revelation. Without it we cannot know the truth of God. Each of five purposes served by reason in Augustine's thought is independent of the supernatural agency of the Holy Spirit.

Reason Comes before Faith. First, there is a sense in which reason comes before faith. Augustine declared that "no one indeed believes anything unless he has first thought that it is to be believed." Hence, "it is necessary that everything which is believed should be believed after thought has led the way" (*On Free Will*, 5).

Reason Distinguishes Human Beings. Second, reason is a distinguishing and superior faculty in human beings. "God forbid that He should hate in us that faculty by which He made us superior to all other beings. Therefore, we must refuse so to believe as not to receive or seek reason for our belief, since we could not believe at all if we did not have rational souls" (*Letters*, 120.1).

Reason Elaborates on Creation and Providence. Third, reason elaborates on the proofs God provides for his existence (*see* God, Evidence for). "It will become clear that God exists, when, with His assistance, I shall prove, as I promised, that there exists something above human reason" (*On Free Will*, 2.6).

Reason Provides Commentary on the Gospel. Fourth, reason helps people understand the content of the Christian message. How can anyone believe the preacher without understanding the words the preacher speaks? Understanding contributes to belief.

Reason Removes Objections. Fifth, reason can be used to remove objections to faith. Speaking of someone who had questions prior to becoming a believer, he wrote: "It is reasonable that he inquire as to the resurrection of the dead before he is admitted to the Christian sacraments." What is more, "Perhaps he ought also to be allowed to insist on preliminary discussion on the question proposed concerning Christ—why He came so late in the world's history, and of a few great questions besides, to which all others are subordinate" (*Letters*, 102.38).

Augustine thus taught that reason is useful before, during, and after one exercises faith in the Gospel. Nevertheless, reason has shortcomings, and without the work of the Holy Spirit, humanity would be in darkness.

The Role of the Holy Spirit. The need for and superiority of divine revelation is made abundantly clear by Augustine. His famous statement is, "First believe, then understand" (*On the Creed*, 4). "If we wished to know and then believe, we should not be able to either know or believe" (*On the Gospel of John*, 27.9). Since faith was a gift of the Spirit (*Enchiridion*, 31), there is no true understanding of the Christian faith apart from the work of the Holy Spirit.

Revelation Overcomes the Result of Sin. "Falsehood arises not because things deceive us. . . . It is sin which deceives the soul, when they seek something that is true but abandon or neglect truth" (*Of True Religion*, 36). This sin is inherited, for "the sin which they [Adam and Eve] committed was so great that it impaired all human nature—in this sense, that the nature has been transmitted to posterity with a propensity to sin and a necessity to die" (*City of God*, 14.1). Only divine revelation received by faith can overcome this. "Nor does anyone become fit to discover God unless he shall have first believed what he is later to come to know" (*On Free Will*, 2.6).

Revelation Is Superior to Reason. "What then we understand we owe to reason; what we believe to authority" (*On the Profit of Believing*, 25). Augustine made this most explicit when he confessed to God: "We were too weak by unaided reason to find out the truth, and for this reason needed the authority of the holy writings" (*Confessions* 6.5).

Not only is the Holy Spirit the means by which we receive God-written revelation (ibid., 7.21), but he is necessary for illuminating and confirming its truth. And the Spirit is truth of the presence of God in the Christian. "If in truth thou hast charity, thou hast the spirit of God in order to understand: for a very necessary thing it is" (*Homily VI*).

Thomas Aquinas. The question of the relation between the Holy Spirit and the use of human reason is really a subdivision of the broader topic of faith and reason. Aquinas (1224–1274) spoke extensively about both. He spoke of rational proofs for the existence of God and offered historical and experiential evidences in support of the truth of Christianity. Aquinas also believed that no one ever comes to faith in Christ apart from a special, gracious work of the Holy Spirit.

Philosophy Applies Reason. Aquinas saw three uses for reason in philosophy. Human reason can be used to prove natural theology (the existence and nature of one God). Also, it can be used to illustrate supernatural theology (the Trinity and incarnation), and it can be used to refute false theologies.

It demonstrates God's existence, oneness, and other propositions concerning God and creatures. "Such truths about God have been proved demonstratively by the philosophers, guided by the light of the natural reason" (*Summa Theologica*, 1a.3, 2). Philosophy uses teachings of the philosophers to explain Christian doctrines such as the Trinity. Even though demonstrative arguments are unavailable for supernatural theology, there are certain probable arguments that can make divine truth known. And philosophy can be used to oppose attacks against faith, by showing they are false or unnecessary.

Human Reason Can Support Faith. On the use of "reason" (*apologia*) in 1 Peter 3:15, Aquinas argued that human reasoning in support of what we believe stands in a two-fold relation to the will of the believer. Sometimes someone does not have the will to believe unless moved by human reason. In this sense reasoning diminishes the merit that would come with faith, since the person "ought to believe matters of faith, not because of human reasoning, but because of the divine authority." Also, "human reason may be consequent to the will of the believer." For "when a man has a will ready to believe, he loves the truth he believes, he thinks out and takes to heart whatever reasons he can find in support thereof; and in this way, human reasoning does not exclude the merit of faith, but is a sign of greater merit" (ibid., 2a2ae.2, 10).

Faith is supported by, not based on, probable evidence. "Those who place their faith in this truth, however, 'for which the human reason offers no experimental evidence,' do not believe foolishly, as though 'following artificial fables.'" Rather, "arguments confirm truths that exceed natural knowledge and manifest God's works that surpass all nature" (*Summa Contra Gentiles*, 1.6). The kind of positive evidence Aquinas used included the raising of the dead, the conversion of the world, and miracles (*see* MIRACLES, APOLOGETIC VALUE OF).

The negative evidence encompasses arguments against false religions, including their fleshly appeal to carnal pleasures, teachings that contradict their promises, fables and falsities, the lack of attesting prophets and miracles to witness to divine inspiration of their holy book (for example, the *Qur'an*), use of arms to spread the message, the testimony of wise men who refused to believe, and perversions of Scripture.

It may surprise some who know their differences to note how closely Aquinas's reasons why the Holy Spirit is needed parallel those of John Calvin." Calvin closely studied Aquinas and the medieval scholastics, though he owed the most to Augustine.

The Spirit Overcomes Effects of Sin (*see* NOETIC EFFECTS OF SIN). With the later Calvin, Aquinas believed that sin profoundly distorts the mind. This distortion makes reason unable to contemplate God, and so find the faith that brings certitude. God wants his people to have confidence, so his Spirit delivers certain knowledge of him by way of faith (*Summa Theologica*, 2a2ae.1, 5, ad 4).

The Spirit Reveals Supernatural Truth. For Aquinas the sole way to overcome an adversary of divine truth is from the authority of Scripture—an authority divinely confirmed by miracles. For that which is above the human reason we believe only because God has revealed it. It is necessary "to receive by faith not only things which are above reason, but also those which can be known by reason." Without the revelation of the Holy Spirit, we would be in darkness about such mysteries of the faith as the Trinity, salvation, and other matters revealed only in the Bible.

The Spirit Is Necessary to Give Faith. Not only are many things known only by faith, but the faith by which they are known is a gift of the Holy Spirit. Reason may accompany faith, but it does not cause faith. "Faith is called a consent without inquiry in so far as the consent of faith, or assent, is not caused by an investigation of the understanding." Faith is produced by God. Commenting on Ephesians 2:8–9, Aquinas contended that free will is inadequate for faith since the objects of faith are above reason. "That a man should believe, therefore, cannot occur from himself unless God gives it" (*Commentary on Ephesians*, 96). Faith is a gift of God, and no one can believe without it.

Reasoning accompanies the assent of faith; it does not cause it (*On Truth*, 14.A1, ad 6). One does not cause the other, but faith and reason are parallel. "Faith involves will (freedom) and reason doesn't coerce the will" (ibid.). A person is free to dissent, even in the face of convincing reasons to believe.

The Spirit Gives a Motive to Believe. In order to believe in God, one must have the inner testimony of the Holy Spirit. For "one who believes does have a sufficient motive for believing, the authority of God's teaching, confirmed by miracles, and the greater motive of the inner inspiration (*instinctus*) of God inviting him to believe" (*Summa Theologica*, 2a2ae.6, 1). As to voluntary assent in matters of faith, we can look to two types of causes. A cause that persuades *from without* is attested to by something like a miracle witnessed or a human appeal. This is sufficient if there is not a cause that persuades *from within*. "The assent of faith, which is its principal act, therefore, has as its cause God, moving us inwardly through grace." The belief is a matter of the will that has been prepared by God through his grace to receive the knowledge that surpasses nature (ibid., 2a2ae.2, 9, ad 3).

The Spirit Makes Probable Evidence Certain. How we can be sure when the support of our faith rests on intermediary (fallible) testimonies? Aquinas responds that we believe prophets and apostles because their witness has been attested by miracles (Mark 16:20; *see* MIRACLES IN THE BIBLE). We believe other teachers only as they agree with the writings of the prophets and apostles (*On Truth*, 14.10, ad 11). The Bible alone, inspired by the Holy Spirit, gives certainty and infallible authority to faith (*see* CERTAINTY/CERTITUDE).

God Is the Basis for Faith. God alone, not reason, is the basis of faith. Reason can prove *that* God exists, but it cannot convince an unbeliever to believe *in* God (*Summa Theologica*, 2a2ae.2.2, ad 3). We may believe (assent without reservation) in something which is neither self-evident nor deduced from it (where the intellect is moved) by a movement of the will.

This does not mean that reason plays no prior role. "Faith does not involve a search by natural reason to prove what is believed. But it does involve a form of inquiry unto things by which a person is led to belief, e.g., whether they are spoken by God and confirmed by miracles" (ibid., 2a2ae.2.1, reply).

Demons, for example, are convinced by the evidence that God exists, but it "is not their wills which bring assent to what they are said to believe. Rather, they are forced by the evidence of signs which convince them that what the faithful believe is true." However, "these signs do not cause the appearance of what is believed so that the demons could, on this account, be said to see those things which are believed" (*On Truth*, 14.9, ad 4).

John Calvin. John *Calvin (1509–1564) held that human reason was adequate to understand the existence of God, the immortality of the soul, and even the truth of Christianity. At the same time, he believed no one could come to certainty about these truths apart from the work of the Holy Spirit. Calvin did believe that many truths about God could be known, even apart from any special work of the Holy Spirit. These included a sense of deity, natural law, and evidence for the truth of the Bible.

The Innate Sense of Deity. Every human has a natural sense of God apart from the work of the Holy Spirit. Some sense of the person of God is built into the human mind and instincts. "There is no nation so barbarous, no race so brutish, as not to be imbued with the conviction that there is a God" (*Institutes*, 1.3.1). This *sense of deity* is so naturally engraven on the human heart that even many unbelieving philosophers are forced to acknowledge it (ibid., 1.4.4).

God's Existence and the Soul's Immortality. Calvin spoke of "the invisible and incomprehensible essence of God" that has been made visible in creation. This proof extends to the soul's immortality. "On each of his works his glory is engraven in characters so bright, so distinct, and so illustrious, that none, however dull and illiterate, can plead ignorance as their excuse" (ibid., 1.5.1–2). Regarding Romans 1:20–21, Calvin concludes that "God has presented to the minds of all the means of knowing him, having so manifested himself by his works, that they must necessarily see what of themselves they seek not to know—that there is some God" (*Commentary on Romans and Thessalonians*, 2).

Natural Knowledge of Natural Law. The innate knowledge of God includes knowledge of his righteous law. Calvin held that since "the Gentiles have the righteousness of the law naturally engraven on their minds, we certainly cannot say that they are altogether blind as to the rule of life" (*Institutes*, 1.2.22). This moral awareness is *natural law* and is enough so that no mortal has an excuse for not knowing God. By this natural law the judgment of conscience is able to distinguish between the just and the unjust. This knowledge includes a sense of justice implanted by nature in the heart. It includes a natural discrimination and judgment which distinguishes justice and injustice, honesty and dishonesty. Calvin believed that such crimes as adultery, theft, and murder are known to be evil in every society, and honesty is esteemed (*Romans and Thessalonians*, 48). It is evident that God has left proofs of himself for all in both creation and conscience.

Evidence for Inspiration of Scripture. Calvin repeatedly spoke of "proofs" of the Bible's inspiration (*see* BIBLE, EVIDENCE FOR). These include the unity of Scripture, its majesty, its prophecies, and its miraculous confirmation. Calvin wrote: "If we look at [Scripture] with clear eyes and unbiased judgment, it will forthwith present itself with a divine majesty which will subdue our presumptuous opposition, and force us to do it homage" (*Institutes*, 1.7.4). The evidence compels even unbelievers to confess (at some level of consciousness) that the Scripture exhibits clear evidence that it was spoken by God (ibid.).

The use of human reason, though not absolute, did bring a sufficient conviction about both the existence of God and the truth of Scripture. Calvin said proofs of the inspiration of Scripture may not be so strong as to produce and rivet a full conviction in the mind, but they are "most appropriate helps" (ibid., 1.8.1).

Calvin speaks of "the credibility of Scripture sufficiently proved, in so far as natural reason admits." He offers rational proofs from various areas, including the dignity, truth, simplicity, and efficacy of Scripture. To this he adds evidence from miracles, prophecy, church history, and even the martyrs (ibid.).

The Need for the Holy Spirit. At the same time, Calvin believed that no one ever came to be convinced of the certainty of truths about God, Christ, and the Bible apart from the supernatural work of the Holy Spirit. He saw no contradiction in what he said about the natural knowledge of God and Scripture.

The vitiating effects of depravity. Calvin believed human depravity obscures human ability to understand and respond to this natural revelation of God (*see* NOETIC EFFECTS OF SIN). He wrote: "Your idea of His [God's] nature is not clear unless you acknowledge Him to be the origin and foundation of all goodness. Hence, would arise both confidence in him and a desire of cleaving to him, did not the depravity of the human mind lead it away from the proper course of investigation" (ibid., 1.11.2).

The testimony of the Spirit. Complete certainty comes only by the Spirit working through the objective evidence to confirm in one's heart that the Bible is the Word of God. Calvin affirmed that "Our faith in doctrine is not established until we have a *perfect conviction* that God is its author. Hence, the *highest proof* of Scripture is uniformly taken from the character of him whose word it is." Hence, "our conviction of the truth of Scripture must be derived from *a higher source than human conjecture, judgments, or reasons*; namely, the secret testimony of the Spirit" (ibid., 1.7.1, cf. 1.8.1, 1.7.4; emphasis added). Using reason to defend Scripture is insufficient. "Although we may maintain the sacred Word of God against gainsayers, it does not follow that we shall forthwith implant the certainty which faith requires in their hearts" (ibid., 1.7.4).

Calvin insisted that the testimony of the Spirit is superior to reason. "For as God alone can properly bear witness to his own words, so these words will not obtain full credit in the hearts of men, until they are sealed by the inward testimony of the Spirit." He adds, "The same Spirit, therefore, who spoke by the mouth of the prophets, must penetrate our hearts, in order to convince us that they faithfully delivered the message with which they were divinely entrusted" (ibid., 1.7.4).

> Let it therefore be held as fixed, that those who are inwardly taught by the Holy Spirit acquiesce implicitly in Scripture; that Scripture, carrying its own evidence along with it, deigns not to submit to proofs and arguments, but owes the full conviction with which we ought to receive it to the testimony of the Spirit. . . . Enlightened by Him, we no longer believe, either on our own judgment or that of others, that the Scriptures are from God; but, in a way superior to human judgment, feel perfectly assured . . . that it came to us, by the instrumentality of men, from the very mouth of God. [ibid., 1.7.5]

Calvin went on to say that the proof the Spirit gives transcends proofs and probabilities (*see* CERTAINTY/CERTITUDE). Its assurance does not ask for reasons; in such knowledge the mind rests more firmly and securely than in any reasoning. It is a "conviction which revelation from heaven alone can produce" (ibid.). Apart from this divine confirmation, all argument and support from the church is vain. "Till this better foundation has been laid, the authority of Scripture remains in suspense" (ibid., 1.8.1).

The Testimony of the Spirit and Evidence. It is important to remember, as R C. Sproul points out, that "the *testimonium* is not placed over against reason as a form of mysticism or subjectivism. Rather, it goes beyond and transcends reason" (Sproul, "Internal Testimony of the Holy Spirit," 341). It is God working through the objective evidence, not apart from evidence, that provides the subjective certainty that the Bible is the Word of God. It is a combination of the objective and subjective, not an exclusion of the objective evidence by a subjective experience. See the comments below on B. B. *Warfield.

Jonathan Edwards. Jonathan *Edwards (1703–1758) provides further insight into the relation between apologetic evidence and the Holy Spirit. He too saw complementary relation between the two. Edwards saw eight functions in reason:

1. Reason must prove the existence of God, the Revealer.
2. Reason anticipates that there will be a revelation.
3. Reason can show that a "pretended" revelation is not from God.
4. Reason demonstrates the rationality of revelation.
5. Reason verifies a true revelation as genuine.
6. Reason argues for the dependability of revelation.
7. Reason anticipates that there will be mysteries in a genuine divine revelation, defends them, and refutes objections to their presence.
8. Reason comprehends what is illumined by revelation.

Reason Proves the Existence of God. Edwards outlines his own approach to God's existence in *Freedom of the Will* (2.3). The first proof is *a posteriori* from effects that there is an eternal cause. From arguments, such a being is shown to be necessarily existent. The necessity of this existence shows his perfections *a priori*. *Cosmological and *teleological proofs unite in this approach.

Reason Can Give Certainty. It is impossible that nothing could cause something. And since something now exists, there must be an eternal and Necessary Being. Edwards' firm conviction about this springs from the principle of causality, which he describes as a self-evident principle, a "dictate of common sense," "the mind of mankind," and "this grand principle of common sense" (ibid.). In "Miscellanies" he declares that "'Tis acknowledged by all to be self-evident that nothing can begin without a cause." Thus, "When understood 'tis a truth that irresistibly will have place in the assent." This being the case, "if we suppose a time wherein there was nothing, a body will not of its own accord begin to be." For to hold that something can arise without a cause is "what the understanding abhors" ("Miscellanies" number 91).

So convinced was Edwards that something could not arise without a cause that, like Aquinas, he argued even an eternal world would need a cause. For "if we should suppose that the world is eternal, yet the beautiful, contrivance, and useful disposition of the world would not less strongly conclude for the being of an intelligent author." He uses the example of a great work of literature. Such a work, even if it had existed from eternity, would require more explanation than that ink had fallen on paper (ibid., number 312).

We depend on metaphysics to show what that Necessary Being is like, to "demonstrate that God is not limited to a place, or is not mutable; that He is not ignorant, or forgetful; that it is impossible for Him to lie, or be unjust; and there is one God only and not hundreds or thousands" (*Freedom of the Will*, 4.13). Edwards was certain that reason demonstrates the divine attributes in their infinity (*see* GOD, NATURE OF).

Limited Reason Requires the Holy Spirit. In spite of the value placed on human reason, Edwards believed that significant limitations on human reason require the work of the Holy Spirit in the heart. Reason cannot make knowledge of God "real" to the unregenerate. It cannot yield a supernatural revelation that leads to salvation, or even sense one, because of human depravity. If it does receive a revelation, it cannot determine the full divine content of that revelation.

Nothing is more clear to Edwards than that, as valid as natural revelation is, there is an indispensable need for supernatural revelation:

> Were it not for divine revelation, I am persuaded, that there is not one doctrine of that which we call natural religion, which, notwithstanding all philosophy and learning, would not be for ever involved in darkness, doubts, endless disputes, and dreadful confusion. . . . In fact, the philosophers had the foundation of most of their truths, from the ancients, or from the Phoenicians, or what they picked up here and there of the relics of revelation. ["Miscellanies," 1.1.19]

In spite of Edwards' belief that natural reason could construct valid arguments for the existence of God, he denied that any non-Christian thinkers ever did this. "There never was a man known or heard of, who had an [right] idea of God, without being taught it" (ibid., 1.6.15).

The Spirit Breathes Life into Revelation. Christians can construct a valid natural religion where pagans fail because of the Holy Spirit's light. This is why

> the increase of learning and philosophy in the Christian world, is owing to revelation. The doctrines of revealed religion are the foundations of all useful and excellent knowledge. . . . The word of God leads barbarous nations into the way of using their understandings. It brings their minds into a way of reflecting and abstracting reasoning; and delivers from uncertainty in the first principles, such as, the being of God, the dependence of all things upon him. . . . Such principles as these are the basis of all true philosophy, as appears more and more as philosophy improves. [ibid.]

In view of this, it is unreasonable to suppose that philosophy itself could fill in the gap. Knowledge is easy, however, to those who understand by revelation.

It may seem inconsistent for Edwards to hold both that God may be proven by natural reason and that no unbelievers have really ever come to the true God in this manner. The reason, as Edwards explained it, is that reason can demonstrate a point that has been proposed by someone else far easier than it can come upon the point in the first place. Would we have known the works of creation are effects had we not been told they had a cause? The greatest minds might be led into error and contradiction were they to try to come up with a description of the cause simply by studying the effects (ibid., 1.6.16).

Edwards believed it possible for an unbeliever to construct valid proof for the existence of the true God, but the fact that none ever had done so showed him that the mind must have the illumination of the Spirit. Once the mind has knowledge of the true God from revelation, it is possible to construct a valid argument for his existence on the basis of premises drawn from nature and reason alone (*see* REVELATION, GENERAL). So special revelation is not *logically necessary* to prove the existence of the true God, but it is in practice *historically necessary*.

Edwards asserts that, when we fully understand the difficulties involved in knowing the true God, we inevitably ascribe all true religion to divine instruction and all theological error to human invention (ibid., 1.6.22).

Subjective Illumination Is Necessary. All of his stress on rational and objective evidence notwithstanding, Edwards did not believe that either general or special revelation was sufficient to make depraved people open to truth. In addition to objective special revelation there had to be a subjective divine illumination. Only the supernatural light could open the heart to receive God's revelation. Without this divine illumination no one ever comes to accept God's revelation, regardless of how strong the evidence for it is. A new heart is needed, not a new brain. This is done by the illumination of the Holy Spirit. This divine light does not give any new truth or new revelations. Rather, it provides a new heart, a new attitude of receptivity by which one is able to accept God's truth.

B. B. Warfield. Classical apologetics (*see* CLASSICAL APOLOGETICS) was carried on by Benjamin Breckinridge (B. B.) Warfield (1851–1921). He, too, saw a need for both human reason and the work of the Holy Spirit to convince people of the truth of Christianity.

The Need for Rational Apologetics. Warfield defined apologetics as "the systematically organized vindication of Christianity in all its elements and details, against all opposition" (*Works*, 9:5). Or, more technically, "Apologetics undertakes not the defense, not even the vindication, but the establishment, not, strictly speaking, of Christianity, but rather of that knowledge of God which Christianity professes to embody and seeks to make efficient in the world, and which it is the business of theology scientifically to explicate" (ibid., 3).

He divided apologetics functionally:

1. Apologetics demonstrates the being and nature of God.
2. Apologetics reveals the divine origin and authority of Christianity.
3. Apologetics shows the superiority of Christianity (ibid., 10).

The first function properly belongs to philosophical apologetics, which undertakes to establish the being of God as personal Spirit, Creator, Preserver, and Governor of all things. To it belong problems of theism with the involved discussion of antitheistic theories.

Warfield believed apologetics a necessary prolegomena to theology. He wrote:

> Apologetical Theology prepares the way for all theology by establishing its necessary presuppositions without which no theology is possible—the existence and essential nature of God, the religious nature of man which enables him to receive a revelation from God, the possibility of a revelation from God, the possibility of revelation and its actual realization in the Scriptures. [*Works*, 9.64]

Warfield held that apologetics has "a primary part" and "a conquering part" in the spreading of the Christian faith. Christianity is distinctive in its mission of reasoning its way to dominion. Other religions appeal to the sword or seek another way of propagating themselves. Christianity appeals to reason and so is "the apologetic religion" (*Selected Shorter Writings*, 2.99–100).

The Role of the Spirit. The *indicia* or demonstrations of the Bible's divine character stand side by side with the Holy Spirit to convince people of the truth of the Bible. Warfield agreed with Calvin that they are not in themselves capable of bringing people to Christ or even convincing them of the complete divine authority of Scripture. Nonetheless, Warfield believed that the Holy Spirit always exercises his convincing power through the evidence.

On the relation of apologetics and the Bible, Warfield said, "It is easy, of course, to say that a Christian man must take his standpoint not *above* the Scriptures, but *in* the Scriptures. He very certainly must. But surely he must first *have* Scriptures, authenticated to him as such, before he can take his standpoint in them" (ibid., 2.98).

In this appeal to evidence, Warfield saw common ground with unbelievers. Facts are universally available, and all can be convinced of God's existence and the truth of Scripture through them by the power of reasoning of a redeemed thinker. In his 1908 article on "Apologetics," he said that, though faith is a gift, it is still a formal conviction of the mind. All forms of conviction must have evidence on which to rest. Reason investigates the nature and validity of this ground (*Works*, 9.15).

Reasoning saves no one, not because there is no proof for Christian faith, but because the dead soul cannot respond to evidence. "The action of the Holy Spirit in giving faith is not apart from evidence, but along with evidence; and in the first instance consists in preparing the soul for the reception of the evidence." Apologetics does not make men and women Christian, but apologetics supplies the systematically organized basis on which faith must rest (ibid.).

The relationship, then, between reason and evidence on the one side and the Holy Spirit on the other is complementary. It is not *either* the Holy Spirit *or* evidence. It is the Holy Spirit working *in* and *through* evidence to convince people of the truth of Christianity. There is both an outer (objective) dimension and an inner (subjective) dimension to the process by which people come to know Christianity is true. These may be called the *rational* and the *mystical*, respectively. But the two are never separated as many Christian mystics and inner-light subjectivists tend to do (see *Biblical and Theological Studies*, chap. 16).

Bernard Ramm. According to Bernard *Ramm, there are three concentric circles of verification. These represent three stories in the confirmation of Christian truth claims.

Internal Witness. In the first circle of verification, internal witness, the sinner hears the Gospel and is convinced of its truth by the Holy Spirit. This is "a spiritual verification in that the primary verification of religion must be of this order else the case is deeded away to a method of verification alien to religion." This persuasive influence of the Holy Spirit is inward, but not subjective (*Witness of the Holy Spirit*, 44).

God's Action. The primary function of Christian evidence is to cultivate a favorable reception for the Gospel. The Gospel still must do its work, not the apologetic arguments. Proofs show that "this [biblical] God does come into our time, our history, our space, our cosmos, and make a difference. . . . Because God makes this difference, we know that we are believing truth and not fiction or mere religious philosophy" (ibid., 57). Thus, Christianity is confirmed by objective facts. The most exceptional acts of God, miracles and fulfilled prophecies, provide the best factual evidence for Christianity's truth claims (*see* MIRACLES, APOLOGETIC VALUE OF). Supernatural events validate the theological. Reason tests revelation (*see* FAITH AND REASON).

**Worldview.* Christianity is also tested by its ability to provide a vision of the whole of world, humankind, and God. Christian principles make the most sense out of life and the world. A worldview, or "synoptic vision," puts things together in the most meaningful way (ibid., 60). The choice of an appealing worldview does not make it true. Further, it must be internally coherent (ibid., 63, 67). Ramm's criteria of truth and coherence are similar to the criteria of factual fit and logical consistency proposed by John Carnell.

Ramm is convinced of the validity of the law of noncontradiction as a necessary test for truth (*see* FIRST PRINCIPLES). We cannot think without it (ibid., 68–69; *Protestant Christian Evidences*, 41, 54). However, Ramm does not put the kind of emphasis on logic as do other presuppositionalists such as Gordon *Clark.

Certainty or Probability. Ramm distinguished between *certainty* and *certitude*. Divine revelation in Scripture and the internal witness of the Holy Spirit allows a Christian full spiritual certitude. This spiritual confidence extends to the existence and attributes of God, the truth of the claims of Jesus Christ, and personal salvation. Such facts are based upon what God has done in history. No historical fact is known with "certainty," since no one can return to the physical place and time to test the event empirically. It cannot be recreated in the lab. But that doesn't mean we must use the word *probably*. Historical facts can be known with a high degree of probability. With the evidence of Scripture, the testimony of the Holy Spirit, and the changes made by the actions of the living God in the cosmos, the Christian rests faith in the high degree of probability of full certitude.

Summary. Obviously not all of the apologists surveyed above agreed on every point, but there is a general agreement in contrast with *Fideism, *Mysticism, and other forms of Subjectivism.

The Role of Reason. Human reason, apart from special revelation (*see* REVELATION, GENERAL; REVELATION, SPECIAL), can provide arguments in support of the existence of God, know many of God's essential attributes (*see* GOD, EVIDENCE FOR), offer evidence in support of Christian faith, defend Christianity against attacks, judge the truth of alleged revelations, and teach the content of a revelation from God.

There is general agreement on the limits of reason. It is marked by the effects of sin. It does not come to a proper knowledge of the true God apart from divine help. It cannot bring the highest certainty concerning truth about God. It cannot explain the mysteries of the incarnation and *Trinity. It supports faith in God, but it is not the basis for that faith. Alone it cannot move anyone to believe in God or provide saving knowledge.

The Role of the Spirit. Most classical apologists would agree that the Holy Spirit plays several needed apologetic roles: The Spirit empowered the origin of Scripture. He gives understanding of Scripture's revealed truth and its implications to individuals. The Holy Spirit is necessary for full assurance of the truths of Christianity, and he alone prompts people to believe in God's saving truth. The Holy Spirit works in and through evidence, but not separate from it. As the Spirit of a rational God, he does not bypass the head on the way to the heart. The Spirit provides supernatural evidence (miracles) to confirm Christianity.

Sources

Augustine, *Confessions*
———, *Enchiridion*
———, *Homily VI on 1 John 3:19–4:3*
———, *Letters*
———, *Of True Religion*
———, *On Free Will*
———, *On Predestination*
———, *On the Creed*
———, *On the Gospel of John*
———, *On the Morals of the Catholic Church*
———, *On the Profit of Believing*
———, *On the Trinity*, in Nicene and Post-Nicene Fathers
———, *The City of God*
J. Calvin, *Institutes of the Christian Religion*, 1559 ed.
———, *Epistles of Paul to the Romans and Thessalonians*
J. Edwards, *Freedom of the Will*
———, "Miscellanies"
———, "Of Being"
———, "The Mind"
N. L. Geisler, *Christian Apologetics*
S. Grenz, et al., eds., *Twentieth-Century Theology*
K. Kantzer, *John Calvin's Theory of the Knowledge of God and the Word of God*
G. Lewis, *Testing Christianity's Truth Claims*
B. Ramm, *Problems in Christian Apologetics*
———, *Protestant Christian Evidences*
———, *The God Who makes a Difference*
———, *The Witness of the Spirit*
R. C. Sproul, et al., *Classical Apologetics*
———, "The Internal Testimony of the Holy Spirit," in N. L. Geisler, ed., *Inerrancy*
Thomas Aquinas, *Commentary on Ephesians*
———, *On Truth*
———, *Summa Contra Gentiles*
———, *Summa Theologica*
B. B. Warfield, *Biblical and Theological Studies*
———, "Introduction," in F. R. Beattie, *Apologetics, or the Rational Vindication of Christianity*
———, *Selected Shorter Writings of Benjamin B. Warfield*. 2 vols.
———, *The Works of Benjamin B. Warfield*, 10 vols.

Hume, Criteria for Credible Witnesses. ***See*** **WITNESSES, HUME'S CRITERIA FOR.**

Humanism, Secular. Humanism focuses on the values and interests of human beings. There are Christian forms (*see* LEWIS, C. S.) and non-Christian forms. Secular humanism is the dominant form of the latter. Its confession is that "Man is the measure of all things." Rather than being *focused on* human beings, its philosophy is *based on* human values.

Secular humanists comprise a diverse group. They include *existentialists (*see* SARTRE, JEAN-PAUL), Marxists (*see* MARX, KARL), *pragmatists (*see* DEWEY, JOHN), and egocentrists (*see* RAND, AYN), and behaviorists (*see* B. F. Skinner under DETERMINISM). While all humanists believe in some form of evolution (*see* EVOLUTION, BIOLOGICAL; EVOLUTION, CHEMICAL), Julian *Huxley called his view "the religion of evolutionary humanism." Corliss Lamont could be called a "cultural humanist." Differences notwithstanding, non-Christian humanists share a core of beliefs. These have been summarized in two "humanist manifestos" and represent a coalition of various secular humanist viewpoints.

Humanist Manifesto I. In 1933, a group of thirty-four American humanists enunciated the fundamental principles of their philosophy in

Humanist Manifesto I. Signatories included Dewey, the father of American pragmatic education; Edwin A. Burtt, a philosopher of religion, and R. Lester Mondale, a Unitarian minister and brother of the later U.S. vice-president, Walter Mondale.

The Affirmations. In the preamble the authors identify themselves as "religious humanists" and affirm that "to establish such a religion is a major necessity of the present" (Kurtz, *Humanist Manifestos*). The manifesto consists of fifteen basic affirmations which read in part:

"*First: Religious humanists regard the universe as self-existing and not created*." These are nontheists (*see* THEISM) who deny existence of a Creator to bring into existence or sustain the universe.

"*Second: Humanism believes that man is a part of nature and that he has emerged as the result of a continuous process*." Naturalism and naturalistic evolution are affirmed. The supernatural is denied.

"*Third: Holding an organic view of life, humanists find that the traditional dualism of mind and body must be rejected*." Humans have no soul or immaterial aspect to their nature. Neither are they immortal (*see* IMMORTALITY). No existence extends beyond death.

"*Fourth: Humanism recognizes that man's religious culture and civilization . . . are the product of a gradual development*." Further, "the individual born into a particular culture is largely molded to that culture." This implies cultural evolution and cultural relativity. Cultural evolution means society has gradually become more sophisticated and complex; cultural relativity means that individuals are shaped largely by their respective cultures.

"*Fifth: Humanism asserts that the nature of the universe depicted by modern science makes unacceptable any supernatural or cosmic guarantee of human values*." There are no God-given values to discover; therefore values are relative and subject to change (*see* MORALITY, ABSOLUTE NATURE OF).

"*Sixth: We are convinced that the time has passed for theism, deism, modernism, and several varieties of 'new thought*.'" Framers of the first manifesto were atheists (*see* ATHEISM) or agnostics (*see* AGNOSTICISM) in the traditional senses of the terms. Even desupernaturalized beliefs are rejected (*see* MIRACLES, ARGUMENTS AGAINST).

"*Seventh: Religion consists of those actions, purposes, and experiences which are humanly significant . . . all that is in its degree expressive of intelligently satisfying human living*." The essence of this affirmation is to define religion in purely humanistic terms. Religion is anything significant, interesting, or satisfying to humans.

"*Eighth: Religious humanism considers the complete realization of human personality to be the end of man's life and seeks its development and fulfillment in the here and now*." The hope of the humanist is this-worldly. The "chief end of man" is terrestrial, not celestial (*see* MATERIALISM).

"*Ninth: In place of the old attitudes involved in worship and prayer the humanist finds his religious emotions expressed in a heightened sense of personal life and in a cooperative effort to promote social well-being*." The religious emotion is focused in the natural, personal, and social spheres, not in the spiritual or supernatural realms.

"*Tenth: It follows that there will be no uniquely religious emotions and attitudes of the kind hitherto associated with belief in the supernatural*." This point carries out the naturalistic implications of earlier statements. Religious experience must be explained in purely materialistic terms.

"*Eleventh: Man will learn to face the crises of life in terms of his knowledge of their naturalness and probability*." Humanists believe that humanistic education will promote social well-being by discouraging the wishful thinking and worry that stem from ignorance.

"*Twelfth: Believing that religion must work increasingly for joy and living, religious humanists aim to foster the creative in man and to encourage achievements that add to satisfactions in life*." This stress on humanistic values of creativity and achievement shows the influence of Dewey.

"*Thirteenth: Religious humanists maintain that all associations and institutions exist for the fulfillment of human life*." Humanists would rapidly reconstitute religious institutions, rituals, ecclesiastical organization, and communal activities around their worldview.

"*Fourteenth: The humanists are firmly convinced that existing acquisitive and profit-motivated society has shown itself to be inadequate and that radical change in methods, controls, and motives must be instituted*." In lieu of capitalism, humanists suggest "a socialized and cooperative economic order."

"*Fifteenth and last: We assert that humanism will: (a) affirm life rather than deny it; (b) seek to elicit the possibilities of life, not flee from it; and (c) endeavor to establish the conditions of a satisfactory life for all, not merely for the few*." The prosocialist tendency continues in this summary statement, which presents religious humanism in a life-affirming framework.

The humanists who framed the manifesto affirmed that "the quest for the good life is still the central task of mankind" and that each person "has within himself the power for its achievement." They were optimistic with respect to their goals and perfectionistic in their belief that humanity had the ability to achieve them.

An Evaluation of Humanist Manifesto I. Humanist Manifesto I can be summarized as:

1. atheistic (*see* ATHEISM) regarding the existence of God;
2. naturalistic regarding the possibility of miracles (*see* MIRACLES, ARGUMENTS AGAINST);
3. evolutionistic (*see* EVOLUTION) concerning human origins;
4. relativistic concerning values (*see* MORALITY, ABSOLUTE NATURE OF);
5. optimistic about the future;
6. socialistic in politico-economic policy;
7. religious in attitude toward life, and
8. humanistic with regard to the methods which it suggests to those who would achieve its goals.

The statement is not simply optimistic; it is overoptimistic about human perfectability. Even the framers of *Humanist Manifesto II* (1973) acknowledged that "events since [1933] make that earlier statement seem far too optimistic."

Manifesto I studiously avoids use of the words *ought* and *should*. It does not, however, avoid *will* (art. 15) and *must* (arts. 3, 5, 12, 13, 14). The humanists' affirmations of values they consider worthwhile implies that one "ought" to pursue those values. Hence the secular humanists are in effect offering a moral prescription they believe humans *ought to follow*.

Some moral prescriptions implied have a universal force because of the strong words used: *necessity* (preamble), *must* (arts. 3, 5, 12, 14), *insists* (art. 5), *no* or *nothing* (arts. 7, 10, conclusion), and even *demand* (art. 14) in connection with values advocated. In the preamble a universal obligation is euphemistically called an "abiding value." Likewise the values of freedom, creativity, and achievement are clearly regarded as universal and irrevocable.

It is worth noting that the religious tone of the first manifesto is very evident. The words *religion* or *religious* occur twenty-eight times. The authors consider themselves religious, wish to preserve religious experience, and even call themselves "religious humanists." Their religion, however, is without an ultimate personal object of religious experience.

Humanist Manifesto II. In 1973, forty years after the framing of *Humanist Manifesto I*, proponents of secular humanism from several countries felt an updating was necessary. "Humanist Manifesto II" was signed by Isaac Asimov, A. J. *Ayer, Brand Blanshard, Joseph Fletcher, Antony *Flew, Jacques Monod, and B. F. Skinner.

In the preface the authors deny that they "are setting forth a binding credo" but say that "for today it is our conviction." They acknowledge their continuity with earlier humanists in affirming that God, prayer, salvation, and providence are part of "an unproved and outmoded faith."

The Affirmations. The seventeen basic affirmations in *Humanist Manifesto II* appear under the headings "religion" (arts. 1–2), "ethics" (3–4), "the individual" (5–6), "democratic society" (7–11), and "world community" (12–17).

"*First: In the best sense, religion may inspire dedication to the highest ethical ideals. The cultivation of moral devotion and creative imagination is an expression of genuine 'spiritual' experience and aspiration.*" The authors quickly add "that traditional dogmatic or authoritarian religions . . . do a disservice to the human species." Moreover, they find insufficient evidence for existence of the supernatural. As "non-theists, we begin with humans not God, nature not deity." They could discover no divine providence. Hence, "no deity will save us; we must save ourselves."

"*Second: Promises of immortal salvation or fear of eternal damnation are both illusory and harmful.*" They distract from self-actualization and from concern over injustice. Science discredits belief in the soul (*see* IMMORTALITY). "Rather, science affirms that the human species is an emergence from natural evolutionary forces." Neither has science found evidence that life survives death. Humans should look after the welfare of this life, not the next.

"*Third: We affirm that moral values derive their source from human experience. Ethics is autonomous and situational, needing no theological or ideological sanction.*" Humanists base their values system on human experience, "here and now." Values have no suprahuman basis or goal (*see* MORALITY, ABSOLUTE NATURE OF).

"*Fourth: Reason and intelligence are the most effective instruments that humankind possesses.*" Neither faith nor passion will substitute. Humanists suggest that "the controlled use of scientific methods . . . must be extended further in the solution of human problems." A combination of critical intelligence and human caring is the best hope for resolving human problems.

"*Fifth: The preciousness and dignity of the individual person is a central humanist value.*" Humanists allow for as much individual autonomy as is consistent with social responsibility. Accordingly, individual freedom of choice should be increased (*see* DETERMINISM; FREE WILL).

"*Sixth: In the area of sexuality, we believe that intolerant attitudes, often cultivated by orthodox religions and puritanical cultures, unduly repress sexual conduct.*" The authors affirm rights to birth control, abortion, divorce, and any form of sexual behavior between consenting adults. "Short of harming others or compelling them to do likewise, individuals should be permitted to express their sexual proclivities and pursue their life styles as they desire."

"*Seventh: To enhance freedom and dignity the individual must experience a full range of civil liberties in all societies.*" These include freedoms of speech and press, political democracy, oppose government policies, judicial process, religion, association, artistic expression, and scientific investigation. Rights must be protected and extended to die with dignity and use euthanasia and suicide. Humanists oppose the increasing invasion of individual privacy. This detailed list is a catalog of humanist values.

"*Eighth: We are committed to an open and democratic society.*" All persons should have a voice in developing values and setting goals. "People are more important than decalogues, rules, proscriptions, or regulations." Here is manifest an opposition to divine moral law such as is found in the Ten Commandments (Decalogue).

"*Ninth: The separation of church and state and the separation of ideology and state are imperatives.*" Humanists believe that the state "should not favor any particular religious bodies through the use of public moneys, nor espouse a single ideology."

"*Tenth: . . . We need to democratize the economy and judge it by its responsiveness to human needs, testing results in terms of the common good.*" This means that the value of any economic system is to be judged on a utilitarian basis.

"*Eleventh: The principle of moral equality must be furthered through elimination of all discrimination based on race, religion, sex, age, or national origin.*" Total elimination of discrimination would result in a more equitable distribution of wealth. There would be a minimum annual income, welfare to all who need it, and the right to a university education.

"*Twelfth: We deplore the division of humankind on nationalistic grounds. We have reached a turning point in human history where the best option is to transcend the limits of national sovereignty and to move toward the building of a world community.*" This would involve a supranational political entity which allows for cultural diversity.

"*Thirteenth: This world community must renounce the resort to violence and force as a method of solving international disputes.*" This article pronounces war to be absolute, and claims a "planetary imperative" to reduce military spending.

"*Fourteenth: The world community must engage in cooperative planning concerning the use of rapidly depleting resources . . . and excessive population growth must be checked by international concord.*" For humanists, then, conservation is a moral value.

"*Fifteenth: It is the moral obligation of the developed nations to provide . . . massive technical, agricultural, medical, and economic assistance*" to underdeveloped nations. This is to be done through "an international authority that safeguards human rights."

"*Sixteenth: Technology is a vital key to human progress and development.*" This article speaks against indiscriminate condemnation of technology and its use to control, manipulate, or modify human beings without their consent.

"*Seventeenth: We must expand communication and transportation across frontiers. Travel restrictions must cease.*" This article ends with the warning: "We must learn to live openly together or we shall perish together.

The conclusion speaks out against "terror" and "hatred." It holds out the values of reason and compassion, as well as tolerance, understanding, and peaceful negotiation. It calls for "the highest commitment [i.e., to these values] of which we are capable," which "transcends . . . church, state, party, class, or race." It is clear from this that humanists are calling for an ultimate commitment to transcendent moral values—a religious commitment.

An Evaluation of Humanist Manifesto II. Humanist Manifesto II is stronger, more detailed, and less optimistic than "Humanist Manifesto I." It is less guarded in its use of moral terms such as *should* and in its call for an ultimate commitment. It is indeed a strong, urgent, moral, and religious call. Like its predecessor it is also atheistic, naturalistic, evolutionistic, socialistic, relativistic, and still optimistic that humankind can save itself. The internationalist emphasis is much stronger.

"The Secular Humanist Declaration." A third coalition voice for secular humanism has been raised. Signers of the "Secular Humanist Declaration," which appeared in the secular humanist journal *Free Inquiry*, included Asimov, Fletcher, Skinner, and some who did not sign *Manifesto II*, among them philosophers Sidney Hook and Kai Nielsen.

The Affirmations. The declaration espouses "democratic secular humanism." It is clear from the opening paragraphs that humanists see established religion as their chief enemy: "Regrettably, we are today faced with a variety of anti-secularist trends: the reappearance of dogmatic, authoritarian religions; Fundamentalist, literalist, and doctrinaire Christianity." In addition, the document complains of "a rapidly growing and uncompromising Moslem clericalism in the Middle East and Asia, the reassertion of orthodox authority by the Roman Catholic papal hierarchy, nationalistic religious Judaism; and the reversion to obscurantist religions in Asia." The platform of these humanists is:

Free inquiry. "The first principle of democratic secular humanism is its commitment to free inquiry. We oppose any tyranny over the mind of man, any efforts by ecclesiastical, political, ideological, or social institutions to shackle free thought."

Separation of church and state. "Because of their commitment to freedom, secular humanists believe in the principle of the separation of church and state." In their view "any effort to impose an exclusive conception of Truth [*see* TRUTH, NATURE OF], piety, virtue, or justice upon the whole of society is a violation of free inquiry."

The ideal of freedom. "As democratic secularists, we consistently defend the ideal of freedom." The secular humanism concept of freedom includes not only freedom of conscience and belief from repressive ecclesiastical, political, and economic powers, but also "genuine political liberty, democratic decision-making based upon majority rule, and respect for minority rights and the rule of law."

Ethics based on critical intelligence. "The secular humanist recognizes the central role of morality in human life." Ethical conduct should be judged by critical reason, and their goal is to develop "autonomous and responsible individuals, capable of making their own choices in life based upon an understanding of human behavior." Although secular humanists are ostensibly opposed to absolutist morality, they maintain that "objective standards emerge, and ethical values and principles may be discovered, in the course of ethical deliberation."

Moral education. "We believe that moral development should be cultivated in children and young adults. . . ; hence it is the duty of public education to deal with these values." Such values include "moral virtues, intelligence, and the building of character."

Religious skepticism. "As secular humanists, we are generally skeptical about supernatural claims." While it is true that "we recognize the importance of religious experience: that experience that redirects and gives meaning to the lives of human [beings, we deny] that such experiences have anything to do with the supernatural." It is maintained that there is insufficient evidence for the claim that some divine purpose exists for the universe. Men and women are free and responsible for their own destinies, and they cannot look to any transcendent being for salvation.

Reason. "We view with concern the current attack by nonsecularists on reason and science." Although secular humanists deny reason and science can solve all human problems, they affirm that they know of no better substitute than human intelligence.

Science and technology. "We believe the scientific method, though imperfect, is still the most reliable way to understand the world. Hence, we look to the natural, biological, social, and behavioral sciences for knowledge of the universe and man's place within it."

Evolution. This article laments the attack by religious fundamentalists on evolution. While denying that evolution is an "infallible principle," secular humanists believe it "is supported so strongly by the weight of evidence that it is difficult to reject it." Consequently, "we deplore the efforts by fundamentalists (especially in the United States) to invade the science classrooms, requiring that creationist theory be taught to students and requiring that it be included in biology text-books" (*see* ORIGINS, SCIENCE OF). Secular humanists consider this a serious threat both to academic freedom and educational integrity.

Education. "In our view, education should be the essential method of building humane, free, and democratic societies." The aims of education include the transmission of knowledge, occupational training, citizenship instruction and encouraging moral growth. Secular humanists also envision the broader task of embarking on "a long-term program of public education and enlightenment concerning the relevance of the secular outlook to the human condition."

The declaration concludes with the plea that "democratic secular humanism is too important for human civilization to abandon." It decries contemporary orthodox religion as "anti-science, anti-freedom, anti-human," pointing out that "secular humanism places trust in human intelligence rather than in divine guidance." It ends by deploring "the growth of intolerant sectarian creeds that foster hatred."

Evaluation of the "Secular Humanist Declaration." It may seem surprising that this declaration appeared so soon after *Humanist Manifesto II* (only eight years), especially since many of the same people signed both. Much of the content is similar to one or both manifestos. With previous humanist statements it stresses naturalism, evolution, humankind's ability for self-salvation, as well as common humanistic ethical commitments to freedom, toleration, and critical intelligence.

However, the Declaration does have distinctives. The most significant aspects of this declaration are those areas in which it differs from previous efforts. First, these secular humanists wish to be called *"democratic* secular humanists." The stress on democracy is evident throughout. Second, nowhere do they claim to be religious humanists, as do the authors of the prior documents. This is strange, since humanists have pleaded for recognition as a religious group, and the U.S. Supreme Court so defined it in *Torcasso vs. Watkins,* 1961. Indeed, the declaration could be justly characterized as antireligious, for it particularly attacks the recent trend toward conservative religious beliefs. The bulk of the declaration, in fact, seems to be a reaction against the recent trends contrary to secular humanism. Finally, one cannot help but notice a strange inconsistency in that the declaration affirms academic freedom, yet insists that scientific creationism be excluded from school science classes.

Common Elements in Secular Humanism. A study of the humanist manifestos and declaration, and other writings of prominent secular humanists, reveals a common core of at least five beliefs:

1. Nontheism is common to all forms of secular humanism. Many humanists deny the existence of God altogether, but all deny the need for a Creator of the world. Thus secular humanists join in opposing all theistic religion.
2. Naturalism is essential to humanism, following from the denial of theism. Everything in the universe must be explainable in terms of natural laws alone.
3. Evolution is the secular humanist's way to explain origins. Either the universe and living things originated by means of the intervention of a supernatural Creator, or they evolved by purely naturalistic means. Nontheists thus have no choice but to defend evolution.
4. Ethical relativism unites secular humanists, for they have a distaste for absolutes (*see* ABSOLUTES, MORAL). There are no God-given moral values; humanity decides its own values. These standards are subject to change and relative to different situations. Since there is no absolute basis for values in God, there are no absolute values to be received from God.
5. Human self-sufficiency is a central tenet. Not all secular humanists are utopian, but all believe human beings can solve their own problems without divine help. Not all believe the race is immortal, but all hold that humanity's survival depends on personal behavior and responsibility. Not all believe that science and technology are the means of saving humankind, but all do believe human reason and secular education are the only hope if the race is to endure.

Conclusion. Secular humanism is a movement consisting mostly of atheists, agnostics, and deists. All are antitheists and antisupernatural. All are strongly naturalistic. These specific doctrines are challenged in other articles, among them: GOD, ALLEGED DISPROOFS OF; GOD, EVIDENCE FOR; GOD, OBJECTIONS TO PROOFS FOR; EVOLUTION; EVOLUTION, BIOLOGICAL; EVOLUTION, CHEMICAL; EVOLUTION, COSMIC; MIRACLE, and MIRACLES, ARGUMENTS AGAINST. Morally humanists are relativists (*see* MORALITY, ABSOLUTE NATURE OF). Various kinds of nontheistic humanism are evaluated under the names of their leading proponents.

Sources

D. Ehrenfeld, *The Arrogance of Humanism*
N. L. Geisler, *Is Man the Measure?*
J. Hitchcock, *What Is Secular Humanism?*
C. S. Lewis, *The Abolition of Man*
P. Kurtz, ed., *Humanist Manifestos I* and *II*
———, ed., "A Secular Humanist Declaration," *Free Inquiry*
F. Schaeffer, *Whatever Happened to the Human Race?*
R. Webber, *Secular Humanism: Threat and Challenge*

Humanist Manifestos. ***See*** **HUMANISM, SECULAR.**

Hume, David. David *Hume (1711–1776), philosopher and historian, was born and reared in Edinburgh, Scotland and attended Edinburgh University. He earned a degree in law but soon after decided not to practice. Instead, during the height of the European Enlightenment, Hume took up a rigorous study of philosophy. This study led to skepticism (*see* AGNOSTICISM) and a disdain for the miraculous (*see* MIRACLES, ARGUMENTS AGAINST). However, unlike Benedict *Spinoza a century earlier, Hume attacked miracles from an empirical perspective, not a rationalistic one. In many ways the two men were opposites. Spinoza was dogmatic, and Hume was a skeptic. Spinoza was rationalistic, and Hume was empirical. Differences notwithstanding, they shared the conclusion that it is unreasonable to believe in miracles. For Spinoza, miracles are actually impossible; for Hume, they are merely incredible.

Hume's Empirical Skepticism. The skeptic believes in suspending judgment about metaphysical questions. Hume's skepticism was based in his epistemology. He believed that all ideas are based in sense experience. Since there were no sense experiences of concepts like *God*, Hume rejected these as meaningless.

Two Kinds of Propositions. All objects of human inquiry, Hume wrote, are either *Relations of Ideas*, or *Matters of Fact*. The first kind includes mathematical statements and definitions; the second includes everything known empirically—through one or more of the senses. So emphatic was Hume about this distinction that he concluded *Inquiry Concerning Human Understanding*:

> When we run over libraries, persuaded of these principles, what havoc must we make? If we take in our hand any volume—of divinity or school metaphysics, for instance—let us ask, *Does it contain any abstract reasoning concerning quantity or number?* No. *Does it contain any experimental reasoning concerning matter of fact and existence?* No. Commit it then to the flames, for it can contain nothing but sophistry and illusion. [12.3.173]

Causes Known by Custom. For Hume "all reasoning concerning matters of fact seems to be founded on the relation of *cause* and *effect*. By means of that relation alone we can go beyond the evidence of our memory and senses" (ibid., 4.1.41). In view of this, the mind can never find the cause for a given event. Only "after the constant conjunction of two objects, heat and flame, for instance . . . we are determined by custom alone to expect the one from the appearance of the other" (ibid., 5.1.57). That is, we use causality, but we have no empirical grounds for doing so. In short, one cannot know causal *connections* between things; one can only believe in them based on customary *conjunctions*. "All inferences from experience, therefore, are effects of custom, not of reasoning" (ibid.).

According to Hume, we cannot even be sure the sun will rise tomorrow. We believe it will because it has customarily risen in the past. Some things happen so often in conjunction with others that it is foolish not to believe they will be so conjoined in the future. Hume would even call this uniform experience a "proof," by which he means "such arguments from experience as leave no room for doubt or opposition" (ibid., 6.1.69). Nonetheless, "all events seem entirely loose and separate. One event follows another; but we never can observe any tie between them. They seem *conjoined,* but never *connected*" (ibid., 7.2.85). But conjoined events do not prove they are causally connected any more than there is a causal connection between the rooster crowing and the sun rising. All one can do is extrapolate based on oft-repeated occurrences.

An Evaluation of Hume's Skeptical Empiricism. It is self-defeating. Hume's skepticism is vulnerable to serious criticisms. Perhaps the most serious is that it is self-defeating. According to Hume, meaningful propositions are *empirical* or *analytical*. The empirical have content but tell us nothing about metaphysical reality, such as God. The *analytical* are empty and contentless. Like the principle of empirical verifiability based on Hume's two kinds of propositions, this is a self-destructive proposition (*see* LOGICAL POSITIVISM). For the statement that "only analytic or empirical propositions are meaningful" is not itself an analytic (true by definition) or empirical statement. Hence, by its own criteria, it is meaningless. If one allows that such statements are meaningful, then why cannot metaphysical statements be meaningful?

**Atomism is contrary to experience.* Another serious objection to Hume's skeptical empiricism is that it is based on an unjustified empirical atomism. Hume believed all sensations to be atomically separated. One event follows another; but we never can observe a tie between them. They seem *conjoined,* but never *connected*" (ibid., 7.2.85). But this is not how we experience them. We encounter them as a continuous flow. We do not get a staccato series of snapshots. Rather, we see a continuous flow motion picture of the external world. Only if one wrongly *assumes* that everything is atomically loose and separate is there a problem of connecting them.

Causality can be experienced internally. Hume is widely misunderstood. He did not deny the principle of causality. He denied the basis on which some people try to prove causality (*see* CAUSALITY, PRINCIPLE OF). Hume rejected intuition, dismissing causal connections we experience in our own consciousness that are not based on external events. I am the cause of this sentence as I am typing, and I experience that fact. Everyone experiences their own thoughts and actions. These are not atomically loose and separate. We experience them as a continuous flow of cause and effect.

Hume could not live his theory. Hume was not consistent with his skepticism in either the practical or the theoretical realm. In the practical area Hume admitted that he had to take a break from his depressing skeptical pursuits and play a game of backgammon. Indeed, no one can live a life of suspended judgment on all metaphysical and moral matters. Life demands certain commitments in these areas. No skeptic suspends judgment on whether the moral right exists to believe and express these views. Nor is there doubt about everything. (Hume was not skeptical of skepticism.) A complete skeptic could not eat, walk, or talk (*see* AGNOSTICISM).

More pointedly, Hume was not consistent with his own theory. When arguing that we do not know the connection between events, Hume insisted that we could not even be certain that the sun will rise tomorrow. Yet when arguing against miracles he insisted that the uniform experience to date that all men die and do not rise from the dead proves that no resurrection will occur tomorrow (*see* RESURRECTION, EVIDENCE FOR).

Hume never denied causality. What is more, Hume himself never denied that things have a cause for their existence. He wrote: "I never asserted so absurd a proposition as that anything might arise without a cause" (Hume, *Letters,* 1:187). Indeed, in the same source Hume claimed that it would be "absurd" to deny the principle of causality. What Hume denied was the way some philosophers attempt to prove the principle of causality. For Hume, customary conjunction is the basis for positing a causal connection.

Hume's Rejection of Proofs for God. Hume's skepticism concerning the existence of God was based on his empiricism and is manifest in several objections that have been often repeated since his time. They are based on his famous *Dialogues Concerning Natural Religion*.

Arguments against a Theistic God. Hume argued that all attempts to prove God, at least a theistic God (*see* THEISM), fail for any of the following reasons (*see* GOD, OBJECTIONS TO PROOFS FOR):

Finite beings need only finite causes. According to Hume, positing an infinite Cause is metaphysical overkill. A finite universe needs only a finite cause.

The principle of causality is unprovable. There is no way to prove the principle of causality. Everything based on experience could be otherwise. And everything not based on experience is simply a tautology, that is, true only by definition.

*Principle of *analogy proves nontheistic God.* Even if one grants there must be some kind of cause of the world, it would not be an infinitely perfect God. At best the argument from analogy leads us to a finite and imperfect God for a finite and imperfect world. If one insists that God must be like what he created, then is God like a cabbage or a rabbit, because he made them?

An infinite series of causes is possible. An infinite series of causes is possible. Hence, there is no need to come to a *First* Cause. Infinite series are possible in mathematics.

Necessity does not apply to existence, but only to concepts. A Necessary Being, such as the cosmological argument concludes, is a misapplication of the term "necessary." The reason is that necessity applies only to concepts or ideas, never to actual reality. Necessary statements are analytic and contentless. And statements about the real world are not necessary.

There is no need for a designer; chance can explain all (see TELEOLOGICAL ARGUMENT*).* There is no need to posit an intelligent cause (designer) of the world; chance can explain the apparent design in the world. Given enough time any "lucky" combination will result. The universe may be a "happy accident."

It is possible that nothing ever existed, including God. It is always possible to conceive of anything, including God, as not existing. Hence, nothing exists necessarily. Since God is said to be a necessary being, even he must not exist necessarily, hence God must not exist at all.

What is logically necessary does not necessarily exist. Some antitheists argue that it is logically necessary for a triangle to have three sides, but it is not necessary for any three-sided thing to exist. Hence, even if it were logically necessary for God to exist it would not mean that he actually does exist.

If all things were created, then so was God. If everything needs a cause, then so does God. And if all things do not need a cause, then neither does the world. But in neither case do we need a First Cause.

These arguments are answered and Hume's logic critiqued in the article God, Objections to Proofs for.

Conclusion. Hume was one of the most influential figures in modern philosophy. His clear and powerful presentation of skepticism and antisupernaturalism was a significant factor in molding the modern secularistic mind. However, a careful analysis of Hume's crucial positions reveals that they are both inconsistent and contrary to experience. Indeed, the heart of his skepticism is self-defeating, since he does not really suspend judgment on the many dogmatic positions he takes about God and miracles.

Sources

J. Collins, *God and Modern Philosophy*
R. Flint, *Agnosticism*
N. L. Geisler, *Philosophy of Religion*
D. Hume, *An Inquiry Concerning Human Understanding,* C. W. Hendel, ed.
———, *Dialogues Concerning Natural Religion*
———, *The Letters of David Hume*

Huxley, Julian. Julian Sorell *Huxley (1887–1975) was the grandson of Thomas Huxley, who was known for his support of Charles *Darwin. Julian received his degree from Oxford in zoology and later taught there. In 1912 he was appointed Biology Department chair at Rice University. He became professor of zoology at Kings College, London, in 1925. In 1952 he became president of the British Humanist Association. He was a signer of the 1973 Humanist Manifesto II (*see* HUMANISM, SECULAR). His books included *Principles of Experimental Embryology* (1934), *Evolution, the Modern Synthesis*, and *Religion Without Revelation* (1928, rev. 1957).

Julian is noted for his *evolutionary humanism*. This view had its most complete expression in *Religion without Revelation*. Building on the evolutionary biology of Darwin, the evolutionary philosophy of Herbert Spencer, and the evolutionary ethics of his grandfather T. H. Huxley, Julian developed a complete system of belief he called "evolutionary humanism." He expressed views on the whole gamut of topics, including God, human origins, religion, values, science, the arts, and his hopes for the future possibilities of the human race.

God and Religion. Like other humanists, Huxley did not believe in a theistic God (*see* THEISM). He believed that evolution explained all (*see* ATHEISM; EVOLUTION, BIOLOGICAL).

Huxley's Disbelief in God. Huxley was opposed to God but in favor of religion. He said, "I believe . . . that we quite assuredly at present *know* nothing beyond this world and natural experience." That is, "a personal God, be he Jehovah, or Allah, or Apollo, or Amen-Ra, or without name but simply God, I *know* nothing of." Nor did he want to know. "I am not merely agnostic on the subject. . . . I disbelieve in a personal God in any sense in which that phrase is ordinarily used" (Huxley, 17, 18).

Belief in God, Huxley held, was purely psychological. God the Father was a personification of nature; the Holy Spirit represented ideals; the Son personified ideal human nature. So "the gods are creations of man, personalized representations of the forces of destiny, with their unity projected into them by human thought and imagination" (ibid., 51).

Huxley believed that modern scientific understanding made the concept of God obsolete. "God can no longer be considered as the controller of the universe in any but a pickwickian sense. The god hypothesis is no longer of any pragmatic value," he said. Operationally, "God is beginning to resemble not a ruler, but the last fading smile of a cosmic Cheshire Cat" (ibid., 58, 59). In fact, Huxley believed "it will soon be as impossible for an intelligent, educated man or woman to believe in a god as it is now to believe that the earth is flat" (ibid., 62).

Disbelief brought Huxley great relief. "For my own part," he concluded, "the sense of spiritual relief which comes from rejecting the idea of God as a supernatural being is enormous." He passionately hoped others would join him in his belief (and relief). Then "the insufferable arrogance of those who claim to be in sole possession of religious truth would happily disappear." Along with this would go bigotry, religious war, religious persecution, the horrors of the Inquisition, attempts to suppress knowledge and learning, hastily to social and moral change (ibid., 33).

Huxley's Belief in Religion. Despite his strong disbelief in God, Huxley considered himself deeply religious. "I believe," said Huxley, "that it is necessary to believe something. Complete skepticism does not work" (ibid., 13). In the end he found that believing in the scientific method met some of his religious longing. So Huxley believed that the scientific method "is the only method which in the long run will give satisfactory foundation for beliefs" (ibid., 13).

When Huxley applied the scientific method to religious experiences, including his own, he concluded that "religion arose as a feeling of the sacred." The capacity for this feeling, he reckoned fundamental to humankind, something given in and by the construction of the normal human mind. Huxley spoke honestly and vividly of his own religious experiences;

> Another incident of the same year remains vividly with me. We were doing night exercises between Aldershot and Fleet: the warm June night was scented with broom: the monotony of exercise, enforced silence, and darkness, combined with the beauty of the hour, impelled to aimless meditation.
>
> Suddenly, for no particular reason, without apparent connection with other thoughts, a problem and its solution flashed across my mind. I had understood how it was that two views or courses of action could not only both be sincerely held as good, but both actually could *be* good—and when the two came into contact, the one could both appear and be evil. It can be so when both are aiming in the same general direction, but the one is moving so much more slowly that it becomes a drag on the other's wheel. Ideas and facts, particular examples and their general meaning, the tragedy of bitter conflict between two fine realities, two solid honesties, all jostled each other in my mind in that moment of insight, and I had made a new step towards that peaceful basis for action which is expressed by the French proverb, "Tout comprendre, c'est tout pardonner."
>
> It also had that definite quality of being thrown into consciousness, implied in the term revelation, which has been described for purely intellectual discovery by many mathematicians and men of science, notably Poincare in his essays on scientific method. It was an exaggeration of the sense that comes when one suddenly sees a point which had eluded comprehension, but without any accompanying sense of effort. The same general sense in the sphere of feeling one may have when one is suddenly transported to a complete and satisfaction by some sudden view of distant hills over plain; or by a sudden quality of light—"the light that never was on sea or land," and yet is suddenly here, transforming a familiar landscape; or by a poem or a picture, or a face. But only once before had I had such a complete sense of outside givenness in an experience—the only occasion on which I had a vision (of a non-hallucinatory but amazingly real sort: such, of a religious cast, abound in the records of mystics [*see* MYSTICISM] such as St. Theresa). [ibid., 86, 87]

Such vivid religious experiences left Huxley with passionate "beliefs in the supreme value of certain ideas and activities." He said, "these in the theological parlance are called Faith" (ibid., 76). In fact, Huxley confessed, "Life would have been intolerable but for [such] glimpses of the alternative state, occasional moments of great happiness and spiritual refreshment, coming usually through poetry or through beautiful landscape, or through people" (ibid., 77).

One day while browsing through a library in Colorado Springs, Huxley came across some essays by Lord Morley in which he found these words: "The next great task of science will be to create a religion for humanity." Huxley was challenged by this vision. He wrote, "I was fired by sharing his conviction that science would of necessity play an essential part in framing any religion of the future worthy of the name" (ibid., 82).

A Religion for Humanists. Huxley took up Morley's challenge to develop a scientific religion. He called it "evolutionary humanism." One of the foundational tenets, as the name would signify, is the theory of evolution.

Human Evolution and Destiny. The experience of the mystical led Huxley to reject a purely materialistic interpretation of the universe, such as he saw in Marxism (*see* MATERIALISM). He concluded, "the materialist hypothesis, in denying the importance of mental and spiritual factors in the cosmos, is to me as erroneous as, though more sophisticated than, the naïve notion of the magic hypothesis, which projects spiritual forces into material events." But his rejection of pure materialism notwithstanding, Huxley was a complete naturalist. He insisted that discoveries of physiology, biology, and psychology necessitated naturalism. There was no longer room for the supernatural. Both material and "spiritual" forces in the cosmos were part of nature (ibid., 187).

Evolution is, of course, the only naturalistic explanation of the origin of life. Huxley wrote, "I personally believe in the uniformity of nature, in other words, that Nature is seen to be orderly . . . and that there are not two realms of reality, one natural, the other supernatural and from time to time invading and altering the course of events in the natural" (ibid., 45). Huxley added, "I believe also in the unity of nature." Further, "I believe in unity by continuity. Matter does not appear or disappear, nor do living things arise except from previously existing things essentially like themselves" (*see* NATURALISM). Hence, "the more complex matter that is alive must at some time have originated from matter that was not alive" (ibid., 45).

As evolution moved onward it moved upward. For each new dominant type possesses improved general organization. This progressive replacement of dominant types and groups is most clearly shown in later vertebrates. "It is thus perfectly proper," said Huxley, "to use terms like *higher* and *lower* to describe different types of organism, and *progress* for certain types of trend" (ibid., 192).

The culmination of the evolutionary biological process is humankind. Huxley believed that the only avenue of advance left was the improvement of brain and mind. "It is clear that man is only at the beginning of his period of evolutionary dominance, and that vast and still undreamt-of possibilities of further advance still lie before him" (ibid., 193). Biology has revealed human destiny as the highest form produced by evolution, the latest dominant type, and the only organism capable of further major advance. Human destiny is to realize new possibilities for the world and be the instrument of further evolutionary process (ibid., 193).

The Nature of Human Beings. Huxley was not a wide-eyed optimist about the nature of man. He recognized evil urges and activities, such as greed, arrogance, fanaticism, sadism, and self-indulgence (ibid., 196–97). He believed, however, that humanity was capable of saving itself from these evils.

Further, Huxley was not a strict materialist (*see* MATERIALISM). He believed in "spiritual" and "mental" aspects to the "stuff" of the universe as well as the "material" aspect (ibid., 186–87). He rejected Marxist (*see* MARX, KARL) materialism and spoke favorably about "mystical" experience. He was nonetheless, a committed naturalist in explaining the human phenomena.

Clearly Huxley was optimistic about humankind's ability to achieve a great future. The human was the only hope for future evolution. Along with his grandfather, Huxley confessed: "My faith is in the possibilities of man" (ibid., 212). This hope was that *Homo sapiens* would continue to realize new potential through continuing evolution.

Evolution and Ethics. The evolutionary progress of the past provides guiding principles for the future. On this basis humanity should aim at those qualities that have succeeded. These principles include efficiency and control of environment, self-regulation and independence, individuation and levels of organization, harmony in work, increased awareness and knowledge, storage of experience, and mental organization (ibid., 193). Human beings would fulfill their destiny more successfully by exploiting reason, imagination and conceptual thought, and unique capacities of accumulating, organizing, and applying experience through culture and the exchange of ideas (ibid., 193). The most sacred duty, and the most glorious opportunity is to promote the maximum fulfillment of the evolutionary process and fully realize the latent human possibilities (ibid., 194).

But even though "the flowering of the individual is seen as having intrinsic value, as being an end in itself," the individual's value is limited by the need to maintain and improve society (ibid., 194, 195). The individual has duties to develop personal potential and to help others singly and collectively realize their potential. Each person must contribute at least a little to promoting the evolution of the whole (ibid., 195).

According to Huxley, "the basic postulate of evolutionary humanism is that mental and spiritual forces . . . do have operative effect, and are indeed of decisive importance in the highly practical business of working out human destiny; and that they are not supernatural, not outside man but within him" (ibid.). These forces operate not only within individuals, but also through the social process. Since the human being is the only one in conscious control of these forces, alone people are responsible for realizing life's further progress. "This applies," said Huxley, "as much to the blind urge to reproduction as to personal greed or desire for power, as much to arrogance and fanaticism, whether nationalist or religious, as to straightforward sadism or self-indulgence" (ibid., 197).

In evolutionary humanism the general duty of the individual is to realize personal potential. The right kind of individual development leaves the way permanently open for growth. Three areas of personal development are possible: specialization, cultivation of personal abilities in every area of life, and cultivating inner harmony and peace (ibid., 199, 200).

Actually, evolutionary humanism has twin goals: present personal fulfillment and long-term cosmic progress. The latter value Huxley calls "the gospel of evolutionary humanism" which is a "transcendent value" (ibid., 201).

Science and the Future. Although Huxley did not believe in individual immortality (ibid., 18), he did expect the human race to continue on. He believed that science was the best organ for accomplishing this goal—not science without religion, but a scientific religion. He wrote:

> Twentieth-century man, it is clear, needs a new organ for dealing with destiny, a new system of religious beliefs and attitudes adapted to the new situation in which his societies now have to exist. The radically new feature of the present situation may perhaps be stated thus: Earlier religions and belief-systems were largely adaptations to cope with man's ignorance and fears, with the result that they came to concern themselves primarily with stability of attitude. But the need today is for a belief-system adapted to cope with his knowledge and his creative possibilities; and this implies the capacity to meet, inspire and guide change. [ibid., 188]

Huxley's humanistic religion, then, is the organ of destiny. Even so, Huxley had no delusions of grandeur about the immediate prospects of this kind of religion. "Like all other new religions . . . it will at the outset be expressed and spread by a small minority." However, he predicted that "it will in the due course of time become universal, not only potentially and in theory, but actually and in practice." Human psychological nature makes this inevitable. "Man cannot avoid the process of convergence which makes for the integration of divergent or hostile human groups in a single organic world society and culture" (ibid., 208).

So an unavoidable evolutionary process will eventuate in a universal humanistic religion. This atheistic society will continue the evolutionary development in ever new intellectual, psychological, and social ways.

Huxley did not know what form his new religion would take, what rituals or celebrations it might practice, whether it would have a priesthood, erect buildings, or adopt symbols (ibid., 209). Whatever the form, it should be both "unified and tolerant" (ibid., 160). He was confident, however, that it would come. Since "the scientific spirit and the scientific method have proved the most effective agents for the comprehension and control of physical nature" it remains for coming generations to apply them toward controlling human destiny (ibid., 205).

Comparison and Contrast. Evolutionary humanism is much broader than Huxley's variety of it. Virtually all humanists believe in some form of evolution. What they disagree about is what mechanism made it happen. Not all agree with Huxley that natural selection (the survival of the fittest) is the means by which evolution is accomplished. What further distinguishes Huxley's variety is that he believed it should be made a universal religion and the basis for ethics. That is, whatever aids the evolutionary process is good and whatever hinders it is evil.

Evaluation. As a religion, Huxley's dream has not caught on quickly. It would seem that many secular humanists do not really desire it to catch on. More recent humanists have admitted that Huxley was too optimistic (cf. "Humanist Manifesto II," 1973). There is no good observational evidence to indicate the inevitability of the evolution of a universal humanistic religion.

The evolutionary ethic involves some serious problems. How does society preserve individual rights of those who are blocking social evolution (*see* MORALITY, ABSOLUTE NATURE OF)? How can an ethical "ought" be derived from a biological "is"? How can the assumed fact of evolution be the basis for moral value? Many bad things evolve too. If so, there must be some standard outside of the evolutionary process by which to know what is good or bad.

Huxley's confession of transcendent, supreme values, mystical experience, and a destiny of the world will be welcomed by those who claim that these are verbal indicators of a surrogate "God." They will insist that only minds can "destine" and only persons can be the object of religious commitments. They will contend that Huxley has avoided the name *God* but not his reality.

With the foundations of modern evolution crumbling (*see* EVOLUTION), the basis of Huxley's evolutionary humanism is being destroyed too. Moreover, he is inconsistent. In one breath he states that the first life arose from nonlife (ibid., 45), yet in the next he ridicules belief in spontaneous generation (ibid., 62). Huxley erroneously uses operation science to explain origins (*see* ORIGINS, SCIENCE OF). He tries to explain the unrepeatable events of the past by the repeatable events of the present. Huxley misuses the scientific method he advances as the basis of evolutionary humanism. Such naturalism also lacks philosophical justification. He offered no adequate arguments for denying the possibility of supernatural intervention (*see* MIRACLES, ARGUMENTS AGAINST).

Finally, like other nontheists, Huxley's critique of God (*see* GOD, OBJECTIONS TO ARGUMENTS FOR) is shallow and inadequate. He does not interact with the substantial evidence for the existence of a theistic God (*see* GOD, EVIDENCE FOR).

Sources

A. Desmond. *Huxley: From Devil's Disciple to Evolution's High Priest*

N. L. Geisler, *Is Man the Measure?*

J. Huxley, *Religion without Revelation*

T. M. Kitwood, *What Is Humanism?*

E. Lo, "Religion Without Revelation in J. W. Montgomery, ed., *Christianity for the Tough Minded*

E. L. Mascall, *The Secularization of Christianity*

D. A. Noebel, *Understanding the Times*

R. Seeger, "J. Huxley, Atheistic Religionist, *JASA* 39.3 (December 1987)

Ii

Illusion, Religious. *See* FREUD, SIGMUND.

Illusionism. Illusionism is the belief that the "world" only appears to be real. Our senses deceive us. The mind or spirit is the guide to true reality. Illusionism is closely associated with monism and pantheism. The Greek philosopher Parmenides is an example of a monist who believed everything other than an absolute One is an illusion (see ONE AND MANY, PROBLEM OF). Shankaristic Hinduism is an example of illusionist *pantheism. Christian Science is pantheistic and illusionist.

Illusionism, solves the problem of evil (*see* EVIL, PROBLEM OF) by denying its existence. Illusionism affirms God and denies evil, whereas atheism affirms evil and denies God. *Theism affirms the reality of both but denies that there is a contradiction.

In Hindu illusionism the illusion of the external world is call *maya*, and the illusion of diversity is called *mithya*. Ninth-century Hindu thinker, Sankara, argued that Brahman (the Hindu name for the Ultimate) is the sole reality. The external world only appears to be, the same way a rope seen at a distance appears to be a serpent. When we examine the world closely, we see that the only reality behind the illusion is Brahman. Brahman "causes" the world to appear diverse and evil only in the sense that the rope "causes" the serpent to appear.

Western illusionism has taken a number of forms. The first proponents of illusionism in the West were the Greeks Parmenides and Zeno. Parmenides (b. 515 B.C.) was one of the first philosophers to focus his attention on the metaphysical problem of whether reality was one or many. He argued that our senses could not be trusted (Parmenides, 266–67). Parmenides believed that things may appear to be many and evil, but they are ultimately one and good. The senses are easily deceived, and consequently humans falsely perceive of the world as diverse and evil.

One of Parmenides' pupils, Zeno (b. 490 B.C.), attempted to prove this through logic. His "race course argument" denied the existence of motion. A runner covering a set distance transverses a successive number of halves of the distance. To travel from A to B, one must travel past the midpoint (m1). But in order to travel from A to m1, one must travel past the midpoint (m2) of that distance. And in order to travel past midpoint m2, one must travel past midpoint (m3). Thus in order to travel in any direction, it appears that we must cross an infinite number of midpoints, which seems impossible. That means, according to Zeno, that motion is impossible and therefore an illusion.

A modern form of illusionism in the West is Christian Science. According to Mary Baker Eddy, evil is not a real entity, but is instead a false perception; it is the "error of the mortal mind." Christian Science maintains that God is truth and that "there is no pain in truth, and no truth in pain." Sin, sickness, and death, therefore, are mortal illusions that do not exist in reality (Eddy, 113, 289, 480).

Evaluation. Many of the criticisms of illusionism are the same as those covered in the article PANTHEISM.

Illusionism is self-destructive. One can only know that all is an illusion against the backdrop of reality. Illusion means not-real. There must be a real standard by which the illusion is defined.

Of course an illusionist could claim that he is not denying all reality, just the reality of this world. Brahman is real. And the world is known to be unreal by contrast with this Reality. While this solves the logical problem of illusionism, it leaves an epistemological problem. Since we are in this world and are allegedly part of the illusion, how could we know that the whole world is an illusion?

The illusionist who claims we are Ultimate Reality (God) and, hence, are not part of the world, begs the question. How do we know we are God? Illusionists admit that they were not always conscious that they were God. But the assertion "I came to realize that I was always God" is a self-defeating statement. For God (Ultimate Reality) does not change. Change is only part of the illusion. Hence, God was always aware he was God. And since we were not, then it follows that we are not God.

Further, if evil is an illusion, where did the illusion originate? And why does everyone experience it from their first moments of consciousness? How did the illusion originate, and how is it passed down to successive generation? The origin, persistence, and universality of the so-called "illusion" argues for its objectivity and reality. What is the difference between saying everyone has it all the time and cannot get rid of it and saying it is objectively real?

It seems more reasonable to assert that illusionism is an illusion. There seems to be no practical difference between viewing pain or evil as illusion and viewing it as reality. Pain or evil is part of the human experience and is encountered by all. Viewed as illusory or real, the experience is the same. This being the case, it seems more sensible to conclude that some are engaging in wishful thinking to conclude that pain or evil is not real. To rephrase Sigmund *Freud, one could ask: Why is it that we wish so desperately that evil is not real when it is so universal, persistent, and unavoidable? Could it be that our belief that evil is not real is the great illusion?

Those who believe all is an illusion do not live that way. They avoid pain like anyone else. They eat and drink like others. Those who don't soon experience the illusion of death. So, illusionism is literally an unlivable philosophy. It is denied in practice by those who affirm it.

Sources

M. B. Eddy, *Science and Health with Key to the Scriptures.*

D. Clark, *The Pantheism of Alan Watts.*

———, et al., *Apologetics in the New Age.*

N. L. Geisler, *The Roots of Evil.*

Parmenides. "The Poem," in G. S. Kirk and J. E. Raven, *The Presocratic Philosophers.*

Immortality. *Immortality* is the term commonly applied to the belief that human persons, at least in their spiritual dimension, consciously survive death and live on forever.

Greek versus Christian Concept of Immortality. Greek and Christian concepts of immortality differ (see Ladd). According to an ancient Greek concept of immortality (e.g., Plato), human beings *are* a soul and only *have* a body. The soul is to the body what a rider is to a horse. Salvation is in part deliverance *from* the body, which is the prison of the soul. There is a basic duality of soul and *soma* (body).

The Hebrew-Christian tradition, on the other hand, while acknowledging that the soul and body separate at death, holds to a unity of the spiritual and physical dimensions of human nature. The human being is a souled body. The soul is to the body what form is to matter, or shape is to a vase. Hence, salvation is not salvation *from* the body but salvation *in* the body (*see* RESURRECTION, PHYSICAL NATURE OF). Indeed, the word *immortality* is used of human beings in the New Testament exclusively in the context of the resurrection body (1 Cor. 15:53; 2 Tim. 1:10).

Biblical Evidence for Immortality. The doctrine of immortality was revealed progressively in the Bible, more explicitly in the New Testament.

Old Testament Affirmation of Immortality. As opposed to Greek thought, the Old Testament hope of life after death was definitely bodily. The Old Testament references to an immortal state are largely resurrection passages. The Jews looked toward resurrection as restoration to life on earth of the physical corpse that had been placed in the tomb. Jews not only believed that man was created "from the dust" (Gen. 2:7) and would return to dust (Eccles. 12:7), but that at the resurrection the dead would be reconstituted from the dust. This power to bring the dead back to life is expressed in many passages (see Deut. 32:39; 1 Sam. 2:6; Job 19:25–27; Ps. 49:14–15).

David spoke of the resurrection (in Psalm 16) by claiming that "the Holy One will not see decay" (vs. 10). According to the New Testament (Acts 2:25–27; 13), Peter said of David's prophecy that "seeing what was ahead, he spoke of the resurrection of Christ, that he was not abandoned to the grave, nor did his body *(sarx)* see decay" (Acts 2:31). Such a resurrection involved a physical body of "flesh" *(sarx)* (*see* RESURRECTION, PHYSICAL NATURE OF).

Jesus believed the Old Testament taught resurrection and cited it to support his position against the Sadducees who rejected it. He declared, "You are in error because you do not know the Scriptures or the power of God" (Matt. 22:29). Then he cited Exodus 3:6, 15: "I am the God of Abraham, the God of Isaac, and the God of Jacob" (Matt. 22:32), adding, "He [God] is not the God of the dead but of the living."

Isaiah spoke of the resurrection of the dead body when he wrote, "Your dead will live; their bodies will rise. You who dwell in the dust, wake up and shout for joy" (26:19). That bodies would arise from the dust makes evident the identification with physical resurrection. Daniel foretold that "Multitudes who sleep in the dust of the earth will awake: some to everlasting life, others to shame and everlasting contempt" (Dan. 12:2). The reference to "dust of the earth" again supports the idea of a physical resurrection.

Though not part of the Old Testament (*see* APOCRYPHA, OLD AND NEW TESTAMENT), the Jewish intertestamental literature also speaks of a physical resurrection. The book of *Wisdom* promises that "in the time of their visitation" the departed "souls of the righteous will be restored and "they will govern nations and rule people" (3:7–8). Second Maccabees tells of the courageous Jewish believer who suffered his tongue and hands to be cut off, saying, "I got them from Heaven, and because of his laws I disdain them, and from him I hope to get them back again [at the resurrection]" (7:11). Second (Fourth) Esdras predicts that after the time of the Messiah "the earth shall give up those who are asleep in it, and the dust those who dwell silently in it" (7:32). Death is described here as a time when "we shall be kept in rest until those times come when thou [God] wilt renew the creation" (7:75).

In the apocalyptic *2 Baruch*, God is asked, "In what shape will those live who live in Thy day?" The answer is unequivocal affirmation of belief in the material resurrection: "For the earth shall then assuredly restore the dead [which it now receives, in order to preserve them]. It shall make no change in their form, but as it has received, so shall it restore them, and as I delivered them to it, so also shall it raise them" (49:1; 50:2).

The Pharisees in New Testament times believed in the physical resurrection of the corpse from the tomb. As the Sadducees denied the resurrection (Matt. 22:23), their opponents, the Pharisees, believed in a material resurrection body (cf. Acts 23:8). They conceived of the resurrection body as being so physical that it was meaningful to ask which of her seven earthly husbands the woman would be married to in heaven (Matt. 22:28).

Mary and Martha reflected the New Testament Jewish belief in the resurrection when they implied that their brother Lazarus would be raised in the last days while his body was still in the tomb. Even Murray Harris, who rejects the Jewish view of a material resurrection, acknowledges, nonetheless, that "it was impossible, for example, for Jews to believe that Lazarus, who had been dead for four days, could be raised without the removal of the stone that lay over his burial cave and his emergence from the tomb (cf. John 11:38–44)" (Harris, 39).

New Testament Affirmation of Immortality. While the New Testament provides abundant evidence of belief in bodily immortality after the resurrection (*see* Resurrection, Evidence of), it also affirms a conscious existence of soul between death and resurrection.

Jesus promised the repentant thief on the cross conscious bliss that very day of his death, saying: "I tell you the truth, today you will be with me in paradise" (Luke 23:43). Stephen prayed, "Lord Jesus, receive my spirit" (Acts 7:59). The Apostle Paul wrote: "We are confident, I say, and would prefer to be away from the body and at home with the Lord" (2 Cor. 5:8). Contemplating death, Paul added, "I am torn between the two: I desire to depart and be with Christ, which is better by far" (Phil. 1:23).

The "souls" of those who had just been martyred were conscious in heaven, for "When he [Christ] opened the fifth seal, I saw under the altar the souls of those who had been slain because of the word of God and the testimony they had maintained" (Rev. 6:9). Even the lost beast and false prophet who where thrown alive into the lake of fire (Rev. 19:20) were still conscious "a thousand years" later (Rev. 20:10).

Moses and Elijah, who had been dead for centuries, consciously engaged in conversation about Christ's death on the mount of transfiguration (Matt. 17:3).

Objections to Immortality. Both Greek and Judeo-Christian varieties of immortal life have come under attack. Four arguments, mostly physiological, have dominated this battle: (1) the argument from self-consciousness and the brain; (2) the argument for the dependence of the conscious mind on the brain; (3) the similar argument that the brain alone gives access to the world, and (4) an argument from personhood.

The Nature of Self-Consciousness. In order for there to be immortal life, the mind must consciously survive death. But the mind cannot function without the brain. Therefore, when the brain dies, consciousness ceases. This materialistic (*see* Materialism) argument makes several false assumptions.

First, it assumes that consciousness is a physical function, that "mind" is a function of matter, a process within the brain. There is no proof behind this assumption.

Second, the argument wrongly assumes that, simply because a mind and brain function together, they must be identical. But this is not necessarily so. They could interact without being the same.

Third, the argument assumes that the self is nothing without the brain. This is a reductionist fallacy. Things that go together are not necessarily the same, any more than my ideas expressed in these words are the same as these words.

Fourth, the materialist's argument is self-defeating. "Nothing-but" statements assume "more-than" knowledge. How could I know I am nothing more than my brain unless I am more than it? I cannot put my brain in a test tube and analyze it unless I (my mind) am standing outside the test tube.

On the other hand, there are reasons to believe that the mind cannot be reduced to matter: (1) Whatever is material is limited to a particular region of space and time. If it moves, it moves in space and time. But the mind is not so limited. It roams the universe without leaving the room. (2) Even a materialist speaks of "her" thoughts. But if strict materialism is correct, I have no discrete thoughts. They are a mere stream of electrons or some other material particle. (3) Materialists claim their doctrine is true and want others to agree with their conclusions. But this implies they are *free* to consider their arguments and change their view. This is not possible if they are mere material processes and not free beings.

The Dependence on the Brain. The mind is dependent on the brain to function. Without the brain it cannot be conscious. However, at death the brain ceases to function. Hence, consciousness must cease at this time as well. This modified materialism is known as epiphenomenalism. The mind is not identical to the brain, but it is dependent on the physical brain the way a shadow is dependent on a tree.

This argument assumes, but does not prove, dependence of mind on brain. Merely because certain mental functions can be explained in physical ways does not mean they are absolutely dependent on physical processes. There may be ways for the mind to think independently of the brain. After all, God does not have a body, and there are good reasons to believe that he exists as a sentient Being (*see* GOD, EVIDENCE FOR). The science of neurobiology is an empirical study. But this does not mean everything it examines is purely physical. It cannot explain the mind in totally physical ways, any more than the mind can be confined in a test tube. There is always the "I" standing outside the experiment. Just because certain things can be quantified does not mean that there are no qualities (such as love) that cannot be quantified. Likewise, simply because we can speak in material terms about certain functions of the mind does not mean the mind is material.

Argument from Access to the World. It is also argued that, even if materialism is false, there may still be no immortality. The mind (self) gains access to the world through the brain. But death destroys the brain. Therefore, death destroys a person's means of access to the world.

The fallacies in this argument are readily detected. The argument assumes (without proof) that the person's brain is the only way of access to the world. One could lose his body and gain another body (whether temporary or permanent) and still have access to the world. It also assumes without proof that there are no other worlds to which one can have access. Perhaps there are other worlds, physical or spiritual, or other dimensions through which one can have access.

This argument further assumes that there are no other ways to be conscious than through this world. Yet no argument is offered demonstrating that one cannot be conscious without some kind of body. God is, and we have good evidence that he exists (*see* GOD, EVIDENCE FOR). Spiritual beings are conscious, yet they have no physical bodies as we know them (Luke 24:39).

Argument from the Nature of Personhood. Some insist that what we mean by "person" involves embodiment. So no person can survive without a body. Hence, death destroys what it means to be a person.

This argument begs the question by defining "person" in a way that makes it impossible to survive death. If *person* is defined as "human person," "finite person," or "personal being," no such conclusion follows. There may be other ways or other worlds through which a person can be conscious without a body.

Also, death only severs one dimension of consciousness—this-world consciousness. We could still be self-conscious, God-conscious, and/or other-world conscious (say, in a spirit world). No argument has been offered to show this to be impossible.

Argument from Self-Identity. The argument against immortality from self-identity takes the form: If Life after death is to involve individual immortality, then there must be some way of identifying an individual spirit. But spirits are not distinguishable since they have no bodies by which they can be distinguished. Therefore, there can be no individual immortality.

The assumption here is that physical characteristics are the only way to identify one person from another. This is not true, as blind acquaintances who have never touched each other know. So do pen pals who have no pictures of one another. Even if there are sound waves or Braille by which to get communications from others, these are only means of communication; they are not identifying physical characteristics.

There are things about individual human spirits (or minds) that differ from other human spirits. Each has a different history and memory. Each has a different personality or character, none of which is a physical difference. Beautiful music as understood in the mind (not the mere sounds in the air) is not physical. Yet we can distinguish one beautiful song from another, even in our mind.

Finally, one does not have to know what the identifying characteristics are to know that they do not have to be physical. It simply begs the question to say that they must be physical.

Nonbiblical Evidence for Immortality. *Plato's arguments for immortality have since been supplemented by philosophers with other kinds of evidence. Peter Kreeft lists twenty-five arguments for immortality (*Handbook*, 235f.). Most arguments for immortality have encountered significant objections.

Weak or Fallacious Arguments for Immortality. Many of the weakest arguments for immortality seemed strong to some people at some time. Most are rejected by most thinking people.

Argument from universal belief. Others have argued from universal belief in immortality. Human beings anticipate immortality. The most ancient peoples used burial rites, embalming, and other practices. However, skeptics note that this belief is not really universal, since atheists and agnostics don't practice it. Even if it were, a universal belief is not necessarily true. The vast majority once believed the sun moved around the earth.

The argument can be revised to meet at least part of the objection. Kreeft observes that what the vast majority believe is probably true. Most believe in life after death, so life after death is probably true (ibid., 236). Even in this form the first premise admits that the statement is only "probably" true. Even then this is questionable, since there are many things that the majority of people have believed.

The argument could be further qualified: What the sages believe is probably true. The sages believe in life after death. Therefore life after death is probably true (ibid.). This leaves us to ask who the "sages" are and whether sages have not also been wrong about many things.

Argument from innate knowledge. Plato pointed to the innate ability to know things one has never learned as proof that the soul existed prior to birth and would, therefore, survive after birth. In his book *Meno*, the slave boy was alleged to know geometry without ever having studied it.

Critics, however, insist that, while there may be innate capacities, there are not innate ideas (*see* HUME, DAVID). Even if there were, this does not prove that they were brought over from a preexistent state, since one could have been born with them. It is more likely that Socrates' slave boy was led along by clever questions to use his natural ability to reason to these ideas. Other so-called "memories" of previous lives have been shown to be false. In the famous Bridie Murphy case, it was later demonstrated that this young lady had not lived centuries before in Ireland, but that her grandmother had read her stories of Ireland and spoke Gaelic to her when she was a child. Under hypnosis (the power of suggestion) these childhood experiences surfaced as "memories" from a previous life (Geisler, 75).

Argument from the soul as life principle. Another argument in *Phaedo* was that since the soul is the principle of life in the body, it cannot die. Life can never admit its opposite, which is death. Hence, the soul can never die. But this proves too much, for all animals and even plants are alive too. On this ground one would have to believe in the immortality of carrots and cabbages.

Argument from the immaterial soul. Plato argued in *Phaedo* from the immateriality of the soul. Since the soul is not material, he reasoned, it is not divisible or destructible. What is indestructible is immortal. However, even his prize pupil, *Aristotle, denied the validity of this argument, denying the immortality of individual souls. After all, not every form (which is immaterial) survives death, as the form of a chair, vase, or even an animal demonstrates.

From a Christian point of view the soul is not indestructible, since whatever God creates he can also destroy. But if Plato's argument is correct, even God could not annihilate a soul. Thus, if the soul is not indestructible, then even an immaterial entity could be destroyed.

Argument from near-death experiences. Some have argued from near-death experiences to immortality. Even the British humanist and *logical positivist, A. J. Ayer, changed his mind about immortality after a near-death experience. In some of these experiences the consciousness is alleged to "pop out" of the body and observe things that could not have been observed from the body.

At best these experiences could only point to a brief survival of the soul, not an immortal existence of the person. Skeptics insist that these experiences are hallucinatory or imaginary, each person projecting personal images of the afterlife as a defense mechanism when facing possible death.

The so-called "hard-core" out-of-body experiences where the person allegedly saw or heard things it would have been impossible to witness can be explained from a Christian view as demonic. Many of these experiences are connected with occult activity and false teaching (cf. 1 Tim. 4:1f.). In any event, they do not prove immortality, since there are other explanations.

There is serious question from a Christian view whether the person was actually dead. The Christian definition of death (cf. Gen. 35:18; 2 Cor. 5:8; James 2:26) occurs when the soul leaves the body. If it did not leave the body, then the experience is not evidence of survival. If it did, then returning to the body would constitute a resurrection. Only God can raise the dead (Deut. 32:39; 1 Sam. 2:6; John 5:28–29; 11:25). But many non-Christians have had these experiences, which confirmed them in their anti-Christian beliefs. God would not perform a miracle to confirm people in error (*see* MIRACLES, APOLOGETIC VALUE OF). Further, leaving the body and returning is contrary to the Bible, which says we only die once (Heb. 9:27). By the argument that near-death experiences evidence life after death, such people would die twice.

Argument from mystical visions. Mystical (*see* MYSTICISM) experiences and visions of heaven are frequently reported in some parts of the church, which, if true, would constitute proof of an existence beyond life. Paul reported one such event in his own life (2 Corinthians 12), though he was careful not to characterize it as either vision or out-of-body experience.

If one is appealing to a revelation, proof must be offered for the reliability of that revelation (*see* BIBLE, EVIDENCE FOR). In the case of mystical experiences, there is no rational proof. If one stays in the body while having such a vision, the skeptic can argue that internal subjective experiences are just that—subjective—and have no binding evidential force on anyone else. If the person actually leaves the body and returns, this is contrary to the Bible's teaching that we only die once. Any claim that God has raised the person from the dead runs headlong into the problem that God would not raise someone so they could teach things contrary to his Word. The majority of those who claim an out-of-body experience do teach contrary to Scripture (see Abanes).

Argument from communication with the dead. Another utterly unbiblical claim is that life after death can be substantiated through communication with the dead through mediums or in trances. This is common to occult and new age circles. Elizabeth Kübler-Ross, author of *Death and Dying,* claims to have had such experiences. Skeptics, however, explain such experiences as hallucinatory or an eruption of one's subconscious mind. Christians point out that the Bible condemns contact with the dead (Deut. 18:11) and warns of deception by the demonic (1 Tim. 4:1; 1 John 4:1).

Argument from the purpose for life. Some have pointed to the meaning, purpose, or goal of life as proof of immortality. The argument has been stated: Life must have a worthwhile purpose. A life that ends in annihilation does not have a worthwhile purpose. Therefore, there must be life after death (Kreeft, *Handbook,* 248).

The answer from critics, of course, is that life need not have a worthwhile purpose (*see* Camus, Albert; Existentialism; Sartre, Jean-Paul). Others would challenge whether this worthwhile purpose cannot be the promotion of species survival in this life.

Plausible or Probable Arguments for Immortality. Apparently, the best ways to fill in this gap are to appeal to evidence which is proven in another argument. There are more plausible reasons to believe in immortality; some appear to be very strong. The strongest of all is the argument from the physical resurrection of Christ.

Argument from Christ's resurrection. Immortality is proven by the fact that Christ returned from the dead (*see* Resurrection, Evidence for). That evidence is:

The New Testament (*see* New Testament Documents, Reliability of; New Testament, Historicity of) reveals that more than 500 witnesses saw Christ after his resurrection (1 Cor. 15:6) on twelve different occasions, scattered over a forty-day period (Acts 1:3). He was seen and heard on each occasion. He was touched at least twice (Matt. 28:9; John 20:17; see also Luke 24:39; John 20:27). He ate (Luke 24:30, 42–43; John 21:12–13; Acts 1:4; cf. 10:41). His crucifixion wounds were visible (Luke 24:39; John 20:27). The disciples saw his empty tomb and the cloths with which his body had been wrapped. These experiences transformed followers of Christ from scared, scattered skeptics to the world's greatest missionary society, preaching the resurrection. Nothing else accounts for all of this evidence except the literal bodily resurrection of Christ.

Naturalistic alternatives to the resurrection have been proposed, but none are plausible. They fall into two categories. One denies that Jesus really died, though the evidence for his actual death is more than substantial (*see* Christ, Death of). The second group denies that he rose, offering a naturalistic alternative. These are all easily refuted by the evidence (*see* Resurrection, Alternative Theories).

Argument from the existence of a personal God. Granted a theistic God exists, one could argue that a created human being with a rational, moral, and immaterial dimension would not have been created to be destroyed. The argument goes:

1. There is good evidence that a personal theistic God exists.
2. Human beings are created like God, as personal, rational, and moral beings.
3. A personal theistic God would not annihilate what is like himself in these most significant ways.
4. Therefore, human beings are immortal.

The evidence for the first two premises is given in the articles Cosmological Argument; God, Evidence for; God, Moral Argument for; Kalam Cosmological Argument. The third premise is defended under Annihilationism. Critics note correctly that this is an *a priori* argument. It is based on what we would expect God would do, but there is no necessity for him to do so. While this is correct, it does not take away the force of the argument in an existential or moral sense.

The kind of beings humans are—personal, rational, and moral—wards off the criticism that even Christians believe that God annihilates the souls of animals. Why does he not destroy humans? The answer seems plausible: Humans are made in his image.

Argument from God's love. A similar argument reasons from God's love. A theistic God is a good and loving God (*see* God, Nature of). But if God is loving he would will the good of those he loves. Immortality would seem to follow: A loving being does not annihilate another; it wills the continued existence of the object of its love. God is absolutely loving. Therefore God wills the continued existence of all persons (ibid., 246).

This argument does not prove too much, as some might object. It does not insist that God *must* will an immortal creature into existence, nor even necessarily will its immortal existence. It merely affirms that, given the fact that God has chosen to will into existence other persons, it is reasonable to assume that his personal love for other persons he had made would prompt him to continue to will their existence. Of course, in this form it is not a full proof of immortality, but only a reasonable expectation.

Argument from ultimate justice. A theistic God is also absolutely just. The argument from God's justice is stated:

1. God is the ultimate standard of justice.
2. There is no ultimate justice for many things in this life.
3. Therefore, there must be another life in which ultimate justice is achieved.

Attacks on the first premise overlook the argument for God's existence (*see* MORAL ARGUMENT FOR GOD), or they boomerang when pressed. For to insist, as antitheists do, that there are ultimate injustices in this world is to posit an ultimate standard of justice by which injustice is known (*see* ATHEISM; EVIL, PROBLEM OF).

Likewise, one is hard-pressed to show that there is ultimate justice in this life. One could appeal to reincarnation by arguing that injustice will be taken care of in another incarnation. But this will not help, since reincarnationists believe in the survival of the soul and/or immortality. And without such a recourse it would seem that one must admit that there are unresolved injustices in this life. In view of this, one finds it difficult to explain why an absolutely just God would not rectify these in another life. If appeal is made to annihilationism as a punishment, then presumably at least some would receive eternal life.

Argument from moral duty. Immanuel *Kant offered an argument from practical reason: The greatest good for all persons is that they have happiness in harmony with duty. But persons are not able to realize the greatest good in this life. Nor can they find this good without God. Therefore, we must postulate a God and a future life in which the greatest good can be achieved.

Critics of Kant say he did not really prove immortality. He only proved that immortality makes sense. We also perceive that a moral duty makes sense. But we have no proof that there really is a real moral duty. These arguments have validity, but they do not really destroy the rational persuasiveness in the need to posit immortality as an explanation of morality. This ultimate reason often takes the form of the argument from ultimate justice.

Argument from the longing for heaven. C. S. Lewis (*Mere Christianity*, *Surprised by Joy*, *The Pilgrim's Regress*, *The Problem of Pain*, *The Weight of Glory*) stated an argument that runs:

1. Every natural innate desire has a real object that can fulfill it.
2. Human beings have a natural, innate desire for immortality.
3. Therefore, there must be an immortal life after death.

In defense of the first premise, it is argued that if there is hunger there is food, if thirst, drink; if *eros*, sexual fulfillment; if curiosity, knowledge; and if loneliness, society (Kreeft, *Handbook*, 250). The second premise is supported by an appeal to a strange, mysterious longing that differs from all other longings because it is undefinable and unobtainable in this life, and the mere presence of this desire is felt to be more precious and joyful than any other satisfaction. However inadvertently we express it, what we all long for is paradise, heaven, or eternity (ibid.).

If these premises are true, there is "more" than this life. The fact that we complain about this world, with its pain and death reveals a deep-seated desire for eternity. We may never attain it, but this no more disproves its existence than lifelong singleness proves there is no marital bliss or starvation proves there is no food anywhere (ibid.). This argument was a positive moral force.

The "Pascal's Wager" argument for immortality. While Blaise *Pascal's wager was used primarily as an argument for God's existence, it can also be applied to immortality. In brief, if we have everything to gain and nothing to lose by believing in immortality, then it would be foolish not to believe in it. The criticism can be offered that this is not really a proof for immortality, but an argument for believing in it with or without proof. In this respect it is like Hume's argument against miracles. At best it only shows why people should *believe* miracles do not happen. It may be that there is no immortality, even though it is foolish not to believe in it.

Conclusion. Whatever intimations, anticipations, or conclusion about the afterlife might be inferred from human consciousness and experiences, the most sure proof (Acts 1:3; 2 Tim. 1:10) of immortality comes from the resurrection of Christ and those whom he and other prophets and apostles raised from the dead in the Scriptures. Other alleged resurrections are without verification (*see* RESURRECTION, CLAIMS IN NON-CHRISTIAN RELIGIONS), usually turning out to be fraudulent or mistaken claims (see Kole). The other plausible arguments supplement the resurrection, but do not appear to be definitive without it. However, some of them have merit. Taken together they provide some evidence from general revelation (*see* REVELATION, GENERAL) apart from Scripture for the immortality of human beings.

Sources

R. Abanes, *Journey into the Light*
W. L. Craig, *Knowing the Truth about the Resurrection*
R. Geis, *Life after Death*
N. L. Geisler, *The Battle for the Resurrection*
——— and J. Y. Amano, *The Reincarnation Sensation*
M. J. Harris, *Raised Immortal*
A. Kole, *Miracle and Magic*
P. Kreeft, *Handbook of Christian Apologetics*
———, *The Heart's Deepest Longing*
G. Ladd, "The Greek Versus the Hebrew View of Man," in *The Pattern of New Testament Truth*

C. S. Lewis, *Mere Christianity*
———, *Surprised by Joy*
———, *The Pilgrim's Regress*
———, *The Problem of Pain*
———, *The Weight of Glory*
J. P. Moreland and G. Habermas, *Immortality: The Other Side of Death*
Plato, *Phaedo*
———, *Republic*

Inclusivism. *See* PLURALISM, RELIGIOUS.

Indeterminacy, Principle of. Some have mistakenly taken Werner Heisenberg's "principle of uncertainty" or indeterminacy as support for an attack on the principle of causality (*see* CAUSALITY, PRINCIPLE OF; FIRST PRINCIPLES) and thereby on the arguments for the existence of God (*see* COSMOLOGICAL ARGUMENT). It is used to show that not all events have causes, that some things happen spontaneously and unpredictably, especially on the subatomic level. Thus, the principle is also used to support the view of human freedom known as indeterminism (*see* FREE WILL; INDETERMINISM).

Understanding the Principle. Heisenberg's principle of uncertainty is a principle of quantum mechanics which states that "the position and speed of a particle cannot be simultaneously known with complete certainty. If one is known with high certainty, the other becomes very uncertain." For example, according to this theory, "it is possible to accurately predict what fraction of [uranium atoms] will radioactively disintegrate over the next hour, but it is impossible to predict *which* atoms will do so" (Lightman, 560).

However, this principle of uncertainty does not support the view that events arise without a cause or that human actions are uncaused. Heisenberg's principle of uncertainty does not say there is no cause of the events, but simply that one cannot predict the course of a given particle. Hence, it is not to be understood as the principle of *uncausality* but the principle of *unpredictability*. The principle of causality affirms that there is a cause, even if we do not know precisely what it is. Were there no cause, there would be no effect or event. In fact, modern science was built on the principle that things do not arise without a cause (*see* ORIGINS, SCIENCE OF).

Heisenberg's principle does not even deny predictability in general. It states only that "physical systems must be described in terms of probabilities" (Lightman, 553). That is, one can accurately predict what fraction of the particles will react in a certain way but not *which* atoms will do so (ibid.). Even though a particular particle's position cannot be predicted, the overall pattern can be predicted. That implies a causal connection. The point is that scientists, *with their limited instruments and observational abilities* cannot now predict the courses of individual subatomic particles.

An infinite Mind could predict both course and speed. If I empty a sack of ping-pong balls above several open bins, it is not possible for me to predict which of the falling balls will fall into which bins. *In practice* it is not possible to know and properly calculate all the physical factors involved in the falling and bouncing. We can only know that about twice as many will fall into the bins that are twice as large. This does not mean that, *in principle*, it is impossible to know which balls will fall in which bins.

Heisenberg's principle describes the subatomic realm, which is not known without investigator interference. Electron microscopes, by which the subatomic realm is observed, bombard the subatomic particles in order to "see" them. As Mortimer Adler noted, "At the same time that the Heisenberg uncertainty principles were established, quantum physics acknowledged that the intrusive experimental measurements that provided the data used in the mathematical formulations of quantum theory conferred on subatomic objects and events interdeterminate character. . . . It follows, therefore, that the indeterminacy cannot be intrinsic to subatomic reality" (Adler, 96–100). Hence, unpredictable behavior may result in part from the attempt to observe it.

Not all physicists accept quantum physics and the uncertainty theory. In response to it, Albert *Einstein complained, "God does not play dice with the universe."

Misapplication of the Principle. It is a category mistake to apply a principle from physics to metaphysical and/or moral realms without justification. Even if there is indeterminacy in physics, this would not mean indeterminacy automatically invades the *moral* realm. By definition, physics deals with what *is* (in the physical realm) and morality with what *ought to be*.

Mistakes of Indeterminacy. Neither do principles of physics automatically apply to the metaphysical. Etienne Gilson has shown the methodological fallacy of this kind of thinking in the history of Western philosophy (see Gilson). There are serious mistakes in assuming that the metaphysical (real) world operates without causality.

Presuming no causes for events makes science impossible, since both operation and origin sciences are dependent on the principle of causality. Assuming there are no causes for events makes the world irrational. It is contrary to reason to affirm that things happen without a cause. Other problems are noted in the article.

Sources

M. J. Adler, *Truth in Religion*
E. Gilson, *The Unity of Philosophical Experience*
N. L. Geisler, *Origin Science*

——— and Winfried Corduan, *Philosophy of Religion*
W. Heisenberg, *Physics and Philosophy*
S. Jaki, *Miracles and Physics*
A. Lightman, et al., *Origins*

Indeterminism. Indeterminism is a view that some or all human actions are uncaused. Actions are totally contingent and spontaneous (*see* FREE WILL). Charles Pierce and William *James were indeterminists. Some contemporary indeterminists appeal to Werner Heisenberg's principle of indeterminacy (*see* INDETERMINACY, PRINCIPLE OF) to support their position. According to this principle, events in the subatomic realm (like the specific course of a given particle) are unpredictable.

Opponents of indeterminism offer several objections. They contend

- that Heisenberg's principle is misapplied, since it does not deal with *causality* but *predictability*.
- that it would make all science impossible, since all depend on the principle of causality.
- that it makes the world irrational if things happen without a cause.
- that the principle of causality is well established and undeniable (*see* CAUSALITY, PRINCIPLE OF).
- that it robs humans of moral responsibility if they have no stake in their actions.
- that, at least on a cosmic scale, it denies God's role as Originator and Sustainer of all things (Genesis 1; Col. 1:15–16; Heb. 1:3).

Conclusion. Indeterminism asserts that actions are unconnected to free choices or any other "cause." This may be compared with the theories of Determinism, which asserts that all actions are determined by forces outside the individual and self-determinism, which affirms that all actions are self-caused, with no outside factors. Each is based on an inadequate foundation. Indeterminism violates fundamental laws of thought and, if true, would eliminate moral responsibility.

Inductive Method. Inductive and deductive *logic are quite different. Deductive logic reasons from general ideas to particular instances. Human beings are mortal. Therefore John, a human being, is mortal.

Inductive logic reasons from particular instances to general conclusions. Socrates, Aristotle, Moses, Adam, Tom, Dick, and Harry are all mortal. This is evidence that all human beings are mortal.

While deductive logic looks at the cause (or condition) and determines its effects/consequents, inductive logic observes the effects and tries to find the causes.

Deductive logic is *a priori* reasoning and inductive logic is *a posteriori*. These Latin terms mean that deductive logic draws its conclusions before, or prior to, examining experience. Inductive logic draws conclusions only *after* (posterior to) looking at experience. Of course, an inductive premise or procedure can be put in a deductive form: Humans who are born eventually die. Mary was just born. Therefore, Mary will eventually die. The form of this whole argument is deductive, but the major premise is based on an inductive survey.

The canons for deductive logic were laid down by Aristotle in the fourth century B.C. The rules were first set forth by Francis Bacon in *Novum Organum* in 1620 and later elaborated on by John Stuart Mill (1806–1873).

The Nature of Inductive Reasoning. One of the major differences between deductive and inductive logic is the kinds of conclusions reached. In contrast to the certainty of deductive reasoning, inductive reasoning provides degrees of probability.

Degrees of Probability. In deductive logic, if the premises were true, then the conclusion *must* be true (*see* CERTAINTY/CERTITUDE). The only certain induction is a *perfect induction*, such as "All the coins in my right hand are dimes." If there are only three and we can see and count all three, then we have a perfect induction and certainty. The reason inductions usually yield only probable conclusions is that they are usually argued by analogy or a generalization. An analogy is an assertion that, because there is a similarity between two things, they will be similar in other respects also. If we were to diagram such an argument it might look like this:

A, B, C, and D all have qualities p and q.

A, B, and C all have quality r.

Therefore, D has quality r also.

This seems reasonable, as long as there is some connection between qualities p and q and quality r. But this usually cannot be known for sure. For example, suppose we choose sparrows, sea gulls, and humming birds for A, B, and C above as animals having wings (p) and feathers (q). Now if D is Canadian honkers, then it follows and is true that they do also have quality r, the ability to fly. For almost all birds, this argument works fine. But what if D is a penguin? It has wings and feathers, but it can't fly. Here we see that our conclusion must remain only probable, and we can never claim it to be the absolute truth. The stronger the analogies we draw, though, the more probable our conclusions will be.

The Nature of Probability. Because induction argues from analogy, extending observations of some to the whole class, it usually involves an *inductive leap*. It must extend beyond its particular findings to make broad, general statements. Usually, inductive conclusions cannot be called universally true because they are generalizations, and exceptions are always possible. Rather than being true or false, they involve degrees of probability. Sometimes, these degrees can be measured as to their percentage of accuracy; other times, a percentage can be guessed. Inductive conclusions should be evaluated for where they stand on this scale:

99 percent—Virtually certain: overwhelming evidence. Example: the law of gravity.

90 percent—Highly probable: very good evidence. Example: No two snowflakes have identical structures.

70 percent—Probable: sufficient evidence. Example: The efficacy and safety of medicines that have been tested and approved.

50 percent—Possible: no evidence or about equal evidence pro and con. Example: Our team will win the coin toss.

30 percent—Improbable: insufficient evidence in its favor. At this point, no one believes it except the few for whom it worked.

10 percent—Highly improbable: very little evidence in its favor. The theory that Jesus spent his early years studying with a Hindu guru falls into this category.

1 percent—Virtually impossible: almost no evidence in its favor. The evidence for the existence of unicorns is at this level.

Sometimes there are real numbers to calculate the probability. This is *statistical probability*. When the numbers are not there, evidence must be weighed by *empirical probability*.

Statistical Probability. When figuring the degree of probability for a statistical problem, there are rules to follow:

Clearly define terms. One cannot meaningfully debate whether "all men are created equal" until the terms *all men*, *created* and *equal* are clarified.

Sufficient classes must be devised to cover all data. Classes *Catholic*, *Protestant*, and *Jewish* are insufficient to cover all the data of American religion. These categories leave out Muslims, Hindus, Buddhists, secular humanists, and a plethora of minor religions. The categories *monistic*, *polytheistic*, *theistic*, and *nontheistic* would likely be sufficient to cover American religions.

Only one principle of classification can be used. Only one question should be raised at a time. If the question is: "Are you Republican or Democrat?" then one should not ask as part of the same question: "Are you conservative or liberal?" This confuses the categories.

Classes cannot overlap. Republican and Democrats contain both conservatives and liberals. If two answers are possible for some people, both will be received from some, none from others, and still others will answer one or the other without letting us know that there is an overlap. Such statistics are worthless, because there is no way to know which answers give the information desired.

The most appropriate method for reporting the results must be selected. There are three ways that statistics can be stated. The *mean* (average), the *mode* (most frequent), and the *median* (the halfway number). The *mean* is the average that can be found by adding together all of the figures and dividing by the number of figures we added. (The mean of 5, 6, 7, 8, 9 is 7 [5 + 6 + 7 + 8 + 9 = 35 ÷ 5 numbers = 7].) It can be used to find out where the group as a whole stands, such as for the average score of an examination. If you want to find out what score most people earned on the exam, the *mode* is more appropriate. It is found by simply finding what number occurs most often. If the grades are 5, 6, 7, 8, 8, 8, 8, 8, 9, then 8 is the mode.

Sometimes it is helpful to know where the middle of the road is for a given question. This is the *median* of the group which represents the halfway point between the highest and lowest numbers in our data. The median of our 5, 6, 7, 8, 9 series is 7, the same as the average. Often the median will be close to the mean, but not in cases where there is one piece of data that is much higher or much lower than the other numbers. The median of 1, 2, 3, 49, 50, is 3. That may not be the best way to represent the data.

Empirical Probability. There are four basic questions that must be asked of every inductive argument where empirical data is given.

1. *How many cases were examined?* How broad is the sample?
2. *How representative is the evidence?* How well did those chosen represent the spectrum of economic, social, racial, and religious ideas found in this country? The more differences there are among cases, the stronger the conclusion. If the cases studied don't reflect what the real world is like, the conclusion will not hold true.
3. *How carefully was the evidence examined?* How were the similarities studied? How many differences were studied? Were all possible explanations accounted for? Were effected results isolated from other causes? Was all the evidence presented? Just how critically was the evidence evaluated?
4. *How does information gained correlate with preexisting knowledge?* Does it contradict any certainties? Does it help explain things better? Sometimes new evidence can rock the foundations of issues that we thought were settled, but their degree of probability and explanatory usefulness make them welcomed discoveries.

Kinds of Probability. Other than a perfect induction, inductive reasoning yields one of two kinds of probability: *a priori* or *a posteriori*.

A Priori Probability. A priori or mathematical probability has to do with working out odds and possible combinations. It offers a mathematical way to evaluate the likelihood of an event. There are various mathematical formulas for finding the odds of different kinds of events. For example, some events are simple and exclusive: Either this happens or something else happens. When you flip a coin, you get either heads or tails. Other events are more complex, like finding how many possible combinations of amino acids there are that would combine to make the proteins necessary for life (*see* CHANCE).

A priori probability for exclusive events. An exclusive event is not in combination with or dependent on other events. A single coin has two sides. So when it is flipped the chances are one in two (or one out of two) for getting heads. Likewise, there are six faces on a single die, so the odds for rolling any of the numbers are one in six. The odds of drawing the ace of spades from a deck of cards is one in fifty-two. This does not mean of course that it will actually take fifty-two draws to get it. It might show up on the first draw. It only means that the a priori probability of getting it in advance of drawing is one in fifty-two. It means that if one drew an infinite number of times, that he would get it on the average about every fifty-two times.

A priori probability for independent events. This deals with the mathematical probability in advance of the results of two or more coins, or die. These are separate and independent events and, hence, the odds must be multiplied together. This means that the probability of getting two heads from flipping two coins is 1/2 times 1/2 = 1/4 or one in four. Likewise, the probability of rolling a six on two dice is 1/6 times 1/6 = 1/36 or one in thirty-six. If one coin and one die are used then the odds are 1/2 times 1/6 or one in twelve.

A priori probability for dependent events. Sometimes one event is dependent on another, in which case we must know how many different combinations or permutations are possible. For a simple permutation, where we want to find how many combinations there are for a given number of known events, we multiply that number (n) by (n – 1) x (n – 2) x (n – 3) and so on until we reach 1. Stated another way, we multiply every whole number between 1 and n together to find out how many combinations there are. For example, to find out how many permutations there are for a string of three letters we multiply 3 x 2 x 1 = 6. For example, the possible combinations are for the letters A, B, and C. They are:

ABC	BAC	CAB
ACB	BCA	CBA

If a magician passes out four cards to four people, there are twenty-four possible combinations of what order those cards might appear (4 x 3 x 2 x 1 = 24). If a security system has ten digits on the keypad and each is to be used once, then there are 10 x 9 x 8 x 7 x 6 x 5 x 4 x 3 x 2 x 1 = 3,628,800 possible entry codes. In music there are 479,001,600 possible twelve-tone rows (a series of notes that uses each step of the chromatic scale once).

A series in which several possibilities might fit into each place is a *complex permutation*. Rather than a simple combination where each number is used only once, numbers may be repeated in a complex permutation. Instead of just punching in ten numbers in a specific order (a simple permutation), a complex permutation is more like the lock on a brief case that has three dials, each of which has the numbers 1 to 10. Any of those numbers can drop in to any position in the series. So the total number of possible combinations is 10 x 10 x 10 = 1000.

To figure the number of possible combinations for a complex permutation, you must take the number of options for each position and raise it to the power of the number of positions. For instance, in a face-making toy that has four possible noses, four chins, four mouths, four sets of eyes, four hair sets, and four foreheads, then there are four options for each position and six positions in all. We take the number of options (4) and multiply it by itself the same number of times as the number of positions (6). So we get 4 x 4 x 4 x 4 x 4 x 4 (or 4^6) = 4096 different faces.

Apologetic value of a priori probabilities. There are many applications of mathematical probability to apologetics. For example, according to Fred Hoyle (in *Evolution from Space*), a former atheist, when the possible combinations are taken into account, the chances that the first living cell could emerge without a Creator are about $1/10^{40,000}$. With odds like that how can anyone deny that the universe was created and still be called reasonable? Likewise, astronomer Hugh Ross has figured the odds for the simplest life form to have occurred by pure chance. He says that it would require a minimum of 239 protein molecules. Each of these molecules is composed of (on the average) 445 amino acids linked together. Now each one of those links must be made by a particular 1 of 20 different amino acids. So the chance that even the simplest life form came together at random is 1 in $20^{445 \times 239} - 239$ or $1/10^{137,915}$. Is it reasonable to believe that, not only the simplest life form, but all complex life forms arose from a fortunate accident?

Evolutionist Julian Huxley once calculated that the odds for the evolution of the horse were 1 in $1000^{1,000,000}$. He admitted that no one would ever bet on anything so improbable (Huxley, 45–46). Of course, many evolutionists know about these odds and say, "Well, given enough time, anything can happen." But is there enough time? Suppose the entire universe were made of amino acids (which is far from the truth). There would be 10^{77} molecules to work with. If we linked all these amino acids together at random at a rate of one per second for the widely accepted age of the universe (about 15 billion years), then the chances of that simple life form appearing shrink to $1/10^{14,999,999,905}$. That's one in ten to the fifteen billionth power. Twenty billion years is just not long enough even if the universe were packed with the building blocks to produce life.

To counter this attack, an evolutionist might respond, "But it only had to happen once. Being dealt a perfect bridge hand is a highly unlikely event too, but it has happened." This is true. It is possible; but is it probable? What is the degree of probability that the evolutionary hypothesis is true? David *Hume said, A wise man always proportions his belief to the evidence. All of the evidence says that the universe is too small and too young to permit the random assembly of life, even in a simple form. Following Hume's maxim, how can a wise man believe that life came about spontaneously and by chance when the evidence says that is virtually impossible?

On the other hand, what are the chances that Moses' record of creation just happened to put the events of creation in the right order? Suppose there are eight successive events (creation of the universe, light, water, atmosphere, seas and land, sea life, land animals, and man) which could have been put into any order. This is a simple permutation (8 x 7 x 6 x 5 x 4 x 3 x 2 x 1 = 40,320). Then the odds for Moses recording these events in the right order was only 1 in 40,320.

Further, it has been calculated that there are 191 prophecies in the Old Testament about the Messiah. These include where he would be born (Micah 5:2), how he would die (Isaiah 53), when he would die (Daniel 9), that he would rise from the dead (Psalm 16). The odds that forty-eight of these prophecies were fulfilled in one man is about $1/10^{157}$. That is a 1 with 157 zeros after it. If a gambler had managed to guess forty-eight horses right without a single mistake, it would be reasonable to suspect that he had inside information. Likewise, it is highly probable that the Old Testament prophets had some help to know so much about events that happened hundreds of years after their deaths. It is certainly the reasonable thing to believe.

A Posteriori Probability. A posteriori probability is empirical probability. Unlike *a priori* probability, it is not probability known in advance of the mathematical likelihood an event will occur. Rather, it is the actual probability after the fact that an event has occurred. Such probability is known by use of the scientific method. In origin science (*see* ORIGINS, SCIENCE OF) it is known primarily by means of the principles of causality (*see* CAUSALITY, PRINCIPLE OF) and analogy or uniformity.

Sources

F. Bacon, *Novum Organum*
N. L. Geisler, *Origin Science*
——— and R. M. Brooks, *Come Let Us Reason*
F. Hoyle, *Evolution from Space*
J. Huxley, *Evolution in Action*
J. McDowell, *Evidence That Demands a Verdict*
J. S. Mill, *System of Logic*
H. Ross, *The Fingerprint of God*
B. Russell, "On Induction," in *Basic Writings of Bertrand Russell*
P. W. Stoner, *Science Speaks*

Infants, Salvation of. Many critics have impugned the justice of God because of the status of the unborn. Belief is considered a necessary condition for salvation (John 3:18–19; Acts 16:31), and yet innocent young children have not yet reached the age at which they can believe. But it seems eminently unjust to condemn innocent infants who have not yet committed a sin nor are even old enough to believe and be saved.

Christians have struggled with the issue of the eternal status of infants. Yet nowhere does the Bible directly treat the issue. Hence, we are left to arguments based on general principle and inference from Scripture.

Baptized Infants Only. This view is held by sacramentalists, who believe that baptism is necessary for salvation. Some Roman Catholics, some Lutherans, and Anglicans espouse the position.

Statement of the View. Ambrose set forth this position: "no one ascends into the kingdom of heaven, except by means of the sacrament of baptism. . . . Moreover to this there is no exception, not the infant, nor he who is unavoidably prevented." He adds mercifully, "They have however immunity from pains" (cited by Sanders, 291). In Ambrose's notion that babies sent into damnation would at least be immune from pain is found the beginnings of a doctrine of "limbo."

*Augustine was less charitable. Born within the fall, infants inherit real depravity, so the wrath of God abides on unbaptized babies (Augustine, 1.28, 33–35). He did allow, however, that unbaptized infants must not suffer as severely as those who lived to adulthood and committed actual sins (ibid., 1.21). The argument for this position is straightforward: Baptism is essential for salvation. No unbaptized person—including infants—can be saved.

Augustine's nemesis Pelagius reacted against this harsh view on unbaptized infant damnation, saying, "where they are not, I know; where they are, I know not" (cited in Sanders, 292). Pelagius was certain infants were not in hell, although he was not certain where they were. Eventually he conceived of a middle place between heaven and hell later called limbo. *Thomas Aquinas held Augustine's view but softened it by claiming that unbaptized infants do not experience the pain of hell.

Other theologians have used the Catholic idea of "baptism of desire" to solve the problem—that is, that some can be saved who desired baptism but were prevented from obtaining it. Since it is difficult to see how infants could desire baptism, some posited that their parents' or the church's desire was sufficient. This idea goes back at least to Hincmar Rheims (A.D. 860; ibid., 293). But how can the desire of someone else be effective for infants?

Critique of the View. This entire scenario depends on a sacramental theology which demands infant baptism as a condition for salvation. The Reformed and most Anabaptists (except those in the Campbellite theological tradition) reject this in favor of the biblical exhortation that personal faith is the only condition for salvation (John 3:16, 36; 5:24; Acts 16:31; Rom. 1:17; 4:5). After all, baptism is a "work of righteousness" (Matt. 3:15), and the Bible makes it clear that we are not saved by works of righteousness (Rom. 4:5; Eph. 2:8–9; Titus 3:5–7). Those in the Campbellite theological tradition, for example, Disciples of Christ, are sacramentalists regarding adult baptism, but they do not accept infant baptism or regard it as needed for salvation.

The sacramental view of infant salvation seems harsh and cruel, whereas the Bible reveals a God of infinite mercy and grace. Some have asked how a child innocent of any personal fault can be banned from heaven? Are not people held responsible only for their personal sins and not those of others? Did not Ezekiel write: "The soul who sins is the one who will die. The son will not share the guilt of the father, nor will the father share the guilt of the son. The righteousness of the righteous man will be credited to him, and the wickedness of the wicked will be charged against him" (Ezek. 18:20). While such passages are about personal righteousness, not inherited depravity from the fall, nonetheless, many hold that the principle seems to apply.

"Elect Infants" Only. Another view asserts that among infants only "elect" babies go to heaven. Since Protestants believe in only two possible destinies, this implies that all nonelect infants go to hell. Many who hold this view are agnostic about whether some or all infants are "elect." They state the issue thus because the Bible is silent on the issue. Christians who take this view are in the covenant theology tradition.

Statement of the View. In his interaction with the Augustinian doctrine of salvation, John *Calvin rejected the idea that only baptized infants are saved. He included in his soteriology a provision that elect infants go to heaven (Calvin, 4.16.17). He contended that while salvation is ordinarily obtained through hearing the Word of God, nonetheless, God is not limited to that means. Infants who are saved are not saved because they are innocent. They are radically depraved in Adam (Rom. 5:12). Some elect die in infancy and others grow to become adults. Thus, Calvin implied that nonelect infants go to *hell.

Except among the Puritans, most Reformed writers have avoided the issue of what happens to the nonelect infants and have stressed God's ability to save infants as he elects to do so in his wisdom and mercy. The Canons of Dort reassure that "godly parents ought not to doubt the election and salvation of their children whom it pleased God to call out of this life in their infancy" (art. 17). The Westminster Confession of 1646 affirms that "elect infants, dying in infancy, are regenerated and saved by Christ" (10.3). The Westminster divines had no consensus about what extent of infants might be "elect." Some have argued that elect infants are those born to parents who are themselves inside the covenant community.

The rationale for only elect infants being saved is that since God chose the elect before they were born, even before the foundation of the world (Eph. 1:4; cf. Rom. 8:29), it is reasonable to infer that he chose at least some infants to be saved, though perhaps not all. Ultimately, salvation does not come from the will of man (Rom. 9:16). Indeed, God has to give faith to the elect (Eph. 2:8–9; Phil. 1:29). So, it is possible that, through the blood of Christ, he can impute righteousness to elect infants who are not old enough to believe for themselves.

As for the justice of God according to this view, it is argued that God justly condemns the whole human race because of Adam's sin (Rom. 5:12–21). We are all sinners by nature (Eph. 2:3), from the moment of conception (Ps. 51:5), who deserve eternal hell. God has no obligation to save anyone. Only by his grace and Christ's sacrifice can he give some the righteousness necessary to stand in his presence. Christ's death was sufficient to atone for all human beings, although it efficiently applies only to those the Holy Spirit draws to him. Among these, God is at least able and is surely willing to include infants. But just as with adults, only those who are justified can go to heaven.

Critique of the View. The elect infant view has not found a home outside of very strong Calvinistic circles. It denies universally accessible salvation. The Bible affirms that Christ did not just die for the elect but for all. And salvation is not offered only to the elect; it is offered to all. The Bible clearly affirms that Christ died for all, not just for some. John wrote that Christ "is the propitiation for our sins: and not for ours only, but also for [the sins of] the whole world" (1 John 2:2). In the same context he adds that "world" means the entire unbelieving, fallen world (vss. 15–17). Peter spoke of the apostate as being "bought" by Christ's blood (2 Peter 2:1). But if salvation is for all, then why limit its availability only to elect infants?

These passages must be taken in light of Scripture at large so as not to advance universal salvation. For adults at least, Christ's atonement saves only those who accept him as Savior and Lord.

The Bible states that God desires to save everyone. Peter wrote: God "is patient with you, not wanting anyone to perish, but everyone to come to repentance" (2 Peter 3:9). Paul speaks of God "who wants all men to be saved and to come to a knowledge of the truth" (1 Tim. 2:4). But if God really desires all to be saved, and it is possible to save some infants apart from their personal faith, then why does he not elect all of them to salvation? In other words, if there can be universal salvation for the children of the elect apart from their personal faith, then why not a universal salvation for the children of nonelect parents?

It is of no comfort to know that elect infants are saved. Limiting salvation to only infants of believing parents, as some do, would offer no hope for the heathen (*see* "HEATHEN," SALVATION OF). This problem is especially acute in view of the fact that the heathen have not heard the Gospel. It is reassuring to believe that God could still be calling out a people for his sake from "every tribe, kindred and nation" (Rev. 7:9), from among infants in nations that have not heard the Gospel.

The elect-infant-only view entails a very severe concept of God's justice. While all orthodox theologians accept that humans are born in sin, not all see this as sufficient grounds for excluding God's mercy from anyone. That is, while there is nothing in fallen humans that merits salvation, there is something in an all-loving God that prompts him to try to save all, namely, his infinite love (John 3:16; Rom. 5:6–8; 1 Tim. 2:4).

This view fails to distinguish between an inherited sin nature (on which all orthodox Christians agree) and a personal rebellion against God which only those old enough to sin can do consciously (John 9:41). That is, the natural bent toward sin is one thing but personal rebellion against God is another. Since infants have not exercised the latter, they are not in the same category as rebellious adults.

Admittedly, it is difficult to reconcile the infant election view with the seemingly universal demand that one believe in order to be saved (John 3:36; Acts 16:31; Rom. 10:17). Yet there seems to be no way a tiny infant can express conscious explicit faith in God. So-called implicit faith will sooner or later have to become explicit and conscious in heaven—otherwise they would be in eternal limbo. Further, the verses that seem to say faith is a gift of God are rejected as support of this view on two grounds. First, none of them clearly teach that faith is a gift which God gives only to some. For example, in Ephesians 2:8–9 it is not faith that is the gift but salvation. For the "it" in the phrase "It is the gift of God" is neuter in form as opposed to "faith" which is feminine. Further, it would contradict the rest of Scripture to say faith is a gift given only to some, since the Bible everywhere calls on people to believe (Rom. 10:13–14) and condemns them for not believing (John 3:18–19). This presumes they have the ability to believe.

Those God "Foreknows." According to this position, God, as an omniscient Being, foreknew which infants would have believed if they had lived long enough. God saved only those infants. The rest are lost, since they would not have believed if they had lived long enough to do so.

Statement of the View. This view has common aspects with the elect-infant-only view (above) and the evangelization-after-death view (below). It argues that the Bible declares that God is omniscient (Ps. 139:1–6). As such, he knows "the end from the beginning" (Isa. 46:10). Indeed, he "foreknew" the elect (Rom. 8:29). And there seems to be no logical reason why these could not have included persons who would die in infancy among the elect.

One advantage over the elect-infant view is that the foreknowledge approach avoids the criticism that God is unmerciful and/or unjust in not trying to save all he possibly can. It takes account of the need for faith as a condition for receiving salvation (John 3:16–19). That is, it avoids the criticism that God saves some apart from their willingness to receive salvation. Another value of the view is that it preserves God's omnibenevolence, his manifest love for all.

Critique of the View. There are some drawbacks to this position. God's foreknowledge is *based on* human *free will rather than in himself as the sovereign God. That is, it holds that God saves these infants *because of* foreseen faith. This negates the unmerited grace of God who acts solely "out of the good pleasure of his will" (Eph. 1:5) and not based on anything we do (Eph. 2:8–9).

However, since one need not hold that God's foreknowledge is *based on* anyone's free choice but simply, as the Scripture's say, *in accord with* it (cf. 1 Peter 1:2). They are simply coordinate, coeternal acts of God with no dependence of God on anything we do. God could have simply and graciously ordained that their potential free choice would be the means through which he would elect them. It is difficult to understand just how God could save people simply in view of their potential faith. If the free choice of believing is a necessary condition for receiving salvation, then it is difficult to understand how the fact that God knew that they would have believed is sufficient. This is knowledge of an alternative reality and so not knowledge in the sense of precognition. Of course, on the assumption that babies "grow up" in heaven they have a chance to actually believe. This would resolve the difficulty of how potential belief can count for actual belief. But if this is the case, it is no longer a matter of infant salvation, since they would have been actually saved after they were infants when they were old enough to believe for themselves. Also, salvation would be effected, not by potential or implicit faith, but through explicit faith.

Like the first view, this view lacks clear biblical support. It seems to be merely a theological possibility. There are no Scriptures declaring this is what God will do with infants.

Can someone be saved by potential faith? If faith is an absolute condition for salvation, then simply knowing that they could have believed is not enough. And responding that they not only would but do believe after death (when they "grow up") is to reduce the view to the view that only those infants who believe when evangelized after death are saved (see below).

Some modern Catholic theologians speak of infants as exercising "implicit faith," but it is very difficult to make sense out of the concept. How can someone whose faculties are not even developed enough to think or make moral choices possibly express any kind of faith? Certainly babies are dependent on their parents for food and other things, but they make no deliberate choice to do this. It is instinctive. But faith, at least conscious faith, is not automatic; it is voluntary. And this infants cannot do as infants.

This foreknowledge view involves the seemingly horrible injustice of condemning to eternal damnation tiny infants who have never sinned, which seems harshly unjust. A proponent of this view could argue that *all who die in infancy would have believed had they lived long enough*. Of course, one cannot deny this possibility. But then this modified position fades into the next one, that God in his mercy will save all infants.

All Infants. Since the seventeenth century the view that all infants are saved has become the most popular in varying theological traditions. Some believe that all infants will eventually believe. Others believe that God will save infants apart from the condition that they would believe.

Statement of the View. According to proponents of this teaching, there is no heaven for those who *will not believe*. Those who willingly reject God's offer of salvation will perish (John 3:18; 2 Peter 3:9). But there is no verse that says those who *cannot believe* because they are not old enough to do so will be excluded from heaven (see Lightner). They appeal to a number of verses for support.

Jesus said "little children" are part of "the kingdom of God." Mark wrote Jesus' words, "Let the little children come to me, and do not hinder them, for the kingdom of God belongs to such as these" (Mark 10:14b). Yet Jesus made it clear that "no one can see the kingdom of God unless he is born again" (John 3:3). It would follow, therefore, that these little children would all be in heaven.

Those who object point out that there is no proof that the term "children" refers to infants or those prior to an age of belief. Further, the phrase "the kingdom of God belongs to these" could refer to the fact that all must become as little children (and humble themselves) in order to enter the kingdom (Matt. 18:4).

King David prayed for his fatally ill child until the child died. Then he immediately ceased praying and said, "But now that he is dead, why should I fast? Can I bring him back again? I will go to him, but he will not return to me" (2 Sam. 12:23). King David went to heaven (Ps. 16:10–11; Heb. 11:32). And surely his hope that he would see the child again encompassed more than their bodies being in the same grave. Hence, it would follow that David's baby went to heaven.

Critics of this interpretation point out that the phrase might mean no more than "The dead do not return; we go to be with the dead." In the Old Testament, the conception of life after death was not explicit. But David clearly anticipated resurrection (Ps. 16:10–11) as did Job (cf. Job 19:25–26).

Psalm 139:13–16 speaks to God of creating and knowing him in his mother's womb. His life was recorded before it began. David refers to himself as a person, an "I" in the womb. This is taken by some to mean that God not only personally knows little embryos and infants but he covers them with his love so that they are written in his book in heaven.

Critics note that the "book" may be a figure of speech of God's omniscience or the book of his remembrance. There is no clear indication that it refers to the book of life of Revelation 20:12.

As to the age of accountability, Isaiah spoke of a little child before "he knows enough to reject the wrong and choose the right" (Isa. 7:15). This seems to imply that there is an age of moral accountability. Jesus said even of adults, "If you were blind, you would not be guilty of sin; but now that you claim you can see, your guilt remains" (John 9:41). How much more would this apply to infants who do not yet know moral right from wrong?

In response, critics observe that even if this referred to an age of accountability, it would not thereby prove all infants are saved. For there are still at least two other issues that must be settled before one can prove this, namely, that inherited depravity in itself is not enough to send one to hell and that faith is not an absolute essential to salvation. In short, Isaiah's reference to a young child not yet knowing good and evil may refer only to personal or social guilt, not to inherited sin.

Paul declared explicitly that "just as through the disobedience of the one man the many [i.e., all] were made sinners, so also through the obedience of the one man *the many [i.e., all] will be made righteous*" (Rom. 5:19, emphasis added). Since the text is clear that all are made righteous by Christ's death, it remains to ask in what sense were all saved by Christ's death.

Since *universalism is clearly excluded by the context and by other Scriptures, this can not mean they were all *actually* made righteous. Further, it does not appear to refer to declaring us righteous in the sense of justification, for that comes only by faith (Rom. 1:17; 3:21–26). It can mean, however, that original sin brought about by Adam is canceled by Christ. If so, then no human being is hell-bound because of Adam's sin. They must commit sins of their own to go there. In this case, since infants have not committed personal sins, they could all be saved even though they are not yet old enough to believe. The judicial condemnation brought by Adam (Rom. 5:12) was reversed, and God is free to save any and all. This being the case, there is no reason that God must condemn infants. Christ died for them. God can save them if he wishes to do so. But since God is long-suffering, not willing that any should perish (2 Peter 3:9), and since the infants cannot believe, God saves them through the finished work of Christ.

Critics of this view point to its novelty and deny its necessity. It is possible and traditional to interpret the verse in other ways. They also observe that this view tends toward universalism. In fact, universalists take all being "made righteous" to support their view. Most importantly, it eliminates faith as a necessary condition of salvation.

Critique of the View. The merits of this view is that it both satisfies the justice of God and magnifies God's omnibenevolence. In addition, it offers some plausible basis in Scripture. Nonetheless, it is hard to find clear scriptural justification for it and plenty of statements that faith is a necessary condition for receiving the gift of eternal life (John 3:36; Acts 16:31; Heb. 11:6). In response, it can be argued that faith is a *normative* requirement for salvation but not an *absolute* one. That is to say, faith may normally be a condition for salvation; it is the way God requires of all adults. But there may be no inherent necessity that little children must believe in order to be saved.

It is argued that, by its very nature, salvation of free creatures involves a free consent. It is not possible to force someone to be saved. Saving infants against their will is no more possible than saving adults against their will. Free creatures cannot be forced into the fold.

In response, proponents note that infants are not saved *against their will* but simply *apart from their will*—because they are too young to believe. They insist that there is a significant difference in God saving persons who *will not* believe and saving those who *cannot believe*—because they are not yet old enough to believe. The fact remains that they are saved *without believing*—which violates the belief that faith is necessary for salvation.

It is always possible that all infants are the class of those who would have believed had they been old enough to do so. And that they will be given the opportunity to do so when they "mature" in heaven. In this case, the problem of faith and freedom is resolved.

Critics point out that nowhere does the Bible spell out any age of accountability. Thus, it is purely speculative. In response, it is noteworthy that there is some evidence in Scripture that there is some point of moral responsibility in one's life. In addition, both experience and common consent inform us that tiny children are not morally responsible. This is why small children do not stand trial for wrongs they do. Psychologically, when they are infants and small children, their rational faculties have not even developed to discern good from evil. Finally, the fact that it is difficult to point to a precise age at which this occurs is not an insurmountable problem. Like self-consciousness, even if we do not know precisely when it occurs, we know that it occurs. In fact, the precise age of accountability may differ individually, depending on their moral development. Perhaps it is earlier for those who are exposed to concepts of moral right and wrong earlier. At any rate, it probably occurs sometime between ages four and twelve. The point at which it occurs is when the individual is old enough to understand the difference between moral right and wrong and the consequences of making moral choices. In biblical terms, when they are aware of the "law written in their hearts" (Rom. 2:15). They are morally accountable when they are old enough to know that what they do is against the moral law of God. Or, as Isaiah said, they are morally responsible when they are old enough to "to reject the wrong and choose the right" (Isa. 7:15).

Criticisms of this view are not definitive. It is theologically possible and biblically plausible. The most problematic issue is the need for these infants to eventually exercise conscious faith of their own. This, however, is not insurmountable, especially in view of the possibility that God foreknew that they would be among those who would eventually "grow up" and believe. At this point, of course, the view merges with both the foreknowledge view and the evangelization after death view.

In Limbo. The above views all assume there are only two possible places for infants to go. Perhaps there is a third place or condition—limbo.

Statement of the View. Some Roman Catholic theologians have posited limbo for babies who die unbaptized (= unsaved). It is possible to detach limbo from a sacramental theology and simply argue that all nonelect babies go there or all babies who would not have believed had they been old enough to exercise it.

Even proponents find it difficult to adduce Scripture in support of limbo. It is more a result of theological speculation. The argument seems to be that God cannot justly allow them into heaven nor can he mercifully send them to *hell. Hence, he sends them to a kind of neutral place, or at least a painless condition.

Critique of the View. Many contemporary Catholic theologians reject limbo as purely speculative. There is a total lack of references to any such view in the Bible. All references that can be appealed to in support speak merely about the baby having not yet reached a state of consciousness or one where they are no longer conscious of this world (cf. Job 3). And why should not God do the same for the heathen who have not heard the Gospel? After all, like infants they have not rejected Christ, since they have not even heard about him. Yet there is no evidence that God has a limbo for the heathen.

The very status of limbo is nondescript. Would it be a place of annihilation? If so, there are serious objections (*see* ANNIHILATIONISM). Are individuals alive but not conscious—as in a coma? There are more questions than answers.

Evangelization after Death. The remaining position contends that infants will mature or grow up after death, at which time they will be given an opportunity to believe. Those who believe will go to heaven. Those who do not (if there are any) will be lost.

Statement of the View. A minority view holds that young children will be allowed to "grow up" in heaven, hear the Gospel, and decide for themselves where they will spend eternity. This belief goes back at least to Gregory of Nyssa in the fourth century. Some Roman Catholic theologians now hold it (Boros, 109–11). Sanders summarizes it: "People are condemned to hell for their own willful sin. Jesus died for all people, including young children who die. All people receive sufficient grace for salvation. The act of faith is necessary for salvation" (Sanders, 298). The belief that young children who die receive an opportunity to accept Christ is one of the few positions that does justice to all four premises.

Critique of the View. Admittedly, there is an absence of any biblical text which states that infants will "grow up" in heaven, although this is not an uncommon belief as applied to the size and shape of the resurrection body. In response, proponents point out that neither are there biblical texts explicitly stating the doctrine of the Trinity, but that does not mean it has no foundation in Scripture. Doctrines can be properly deduced or inferred from other biblical teachings.

However, even if infants do mature in heaven, there is no evidence that they will be evangelized there. The only place for evangelism mentioned in the Bible is earth (Matt. 28:18–20). It is explicitly stated in Scripture that there is no hope for salvation beyond the grave. For "man is destined to die once, and after that to face judgment" (Heb. 9:27; cf. Luke 16:26–31; John 8:24). In response, it is argued that these texts apply only to those who have lived to an age of accountability and have rejected the light God has given them, not to those who have not.

Conclusion. All the views have difficulties. The foreknowledge, salvation for all, and evangelization after death views seem to be the best options, having the most merit and indirect biblical and theological support.

If faith is not absolutely essential, then a distinction must be drawn between personal innocence and conscious rejection by adults. If so it makes more sense to speak of all infants being saved. If faith is an absolute essential for salvation—and numerous Bible passages seem to affirm that it is—there is no heaven for those who cannot believe. All must believe to enter. In this case, belief that infants will mature in heaven and be given a chance to believe makes more sense.

If God does not offer a real opportunity to believe, then the views that affirm only baptized or elect infants go to heaven makes sense. But the Bible seems to say that God genuinely offers salvation to all. If so, then it would follow logically that those who would believe, if they die before they can, will be given a chance after they die. God's love and/or justice would seem to demand that this be so.

Inherited Depravity and Condemnation. If innate, radical depravity is inherited from the womb, then it would seem that only baptized infants or elect infants might go to be with God. If, however, one's own personal decision in rejecting God's message is needed before one goes to hell, then they lose plausibility. The salvation-for-all view depends on the fact that children have not had the opportunity to reject Christ, and that makes the difference.

It is worth noting that the views that allow for the possible salvation of all infants are not only compatible with God's justice and love, but they also help solve the problem of *heathen salvation. Since God is just and since one cannot be saved without the Gospel (*see* CHRIST, UNIQUENESS OF; PLURALISM, RELIGIOUS; WORLD RELIGIONS AND CHRISTIANITY) and since many heathen lands have not had the Gospel, it is reasonable to infer that God's elect will be taken from every tribe, kindred, and tongue could have been taken from the infants who die. Since it is estimated that in heathen countries one-half of the babies born die before the age of accountability, then it follows that there will be innumerable heathen in heaven who never heard the Gospel—possibly all the infants who died before they could even understand the Gospel.

Sources

J. Arminius, *The Writings of James Arminius*, Vol. 1
Augustine, *On the Merits and Forgiveness of Sins and on the Baptism of Infants*
L. Boros, *The Mystery of Death*
J. Calvin, *Institutes of the Christian Religion*, Bk. 4, chap. 16
R. Lightner, *Heaven for Those Who Cannot Believe*
M. Luther, *Luther's Works*, 54:56–58
P. Melanchthon, *On Christian Doctrine*
J. Sanders, "Limbo" in *The New Catholic Encyclopedia*
———, *No Other Name*, Appendix
B. B. Warfield, *Studies in Theology*
R. A. Webb, *The Theology of Infant Salvation*

Infinite Series. An infinite series is a beginningless or endless (or both) series of events, points, entities, or causes. It is often used of a series that has no beginning, that is, that has no beginning going backwards. In this sense it is more proper to speak of an infinite regress.

There are two kinds of infinite series: mathematical and metaphysical (actual). Mathematical infinities are abstract. The line between A and B can have an infinite number of points or dimensionless intersections of two lines. Actual infinities are concrete, and it is not possible to get an infinite number of actual entities between A and B no matter how small these entities may be.

An actual infinite series (regress) is impossible. Since an infinite series has no beginning and since a series of moments succeed one another, no matter how long the series it would always be possible to add one more. But one more cannot be added to an infinite number. Hence, one can never reach an infinite number. One can only indefinitely add one more. Infinity can never be achieved. Second, an infinite number of moments can never be traversed. But the number of moments before today has been traversed. Otherwise, today would never have come. Hence, there was not an infinite number of moments before today. Time began. This fact is used to prove the existence of a First Cause in the *kalam* cosmological argument for God's existence. Briefly stated: Everything that had a beginning had a cause. The universe had a beginning (since there could not have been an infinite number of moments before today). Therefore, the universe had a Cause.

An infinite series of causes may be actual or potential. An actual infinite series is one that is completed. A potential infinite series is one that continues to go on without end.

An infinite mathematical series can go forward or backward. A series of causes reaching backward to infinity is not possible because there needs to be a cause to get the series of causality going. However, a potential series of causes or events is possible going forward into eternity, since there is no reason why a cause cannot continue to produce a series of effects without end forever. Such a series, however, would not be actually infinite but only potentially infinite. That is, it would never be complete, always being capable of having one more added to its series.

Not only is an infinite series of moments or events impossible but so is an infinite series of causes. *Atheists sometimes argue that even if the world needs a cause there is no reason to stop positing a cause for that cause and so on infinitely. However, this is a misunderstanding of what it means to be a cause of the existence of something. For in every infinite series of causes of existence *at least one* cause must be actually causing the existence of the world. But by definition in every infinite series of causes *every* cause is being caused by a prior cause. If this is so, then the one cause that is causing existence is also causing its own existence, since every cause in the series, including itself, is being caused. But it is impossible to cause one's own existence, for a cause is ontologically prior to its effect, and something cannot actually be prior to itself. Therefore, an infinite series of causes of existence is impossible.

There are two ways to avoid this dilemma, both of which fall into the hands of the theists. First, the causality could come from outside the series so as to avoid a self-caused cause in the series. But in this case we either have another self-caused cause outside the series (which is impossible) or an uncaused Cause (which is theistic), or else we have another infinite series behind this cause (which is impossible). Or the atheist can claim that not every cause in the series is being caused. But in this case then at least one cause in the series is an uncaused Cause (which is theistic). No matter which way the atheist turns he runs either into impossibilities or into a First uncaused Cause (God).

There are other objections to the impossibility of an infinite series of events or causes. Two call for comment.

Some defenders of the possibility of an infinite series contend that they must be possible since the future is infinite, and God can know the future. If he cannot, then he is limited and theism is wrong. This objection confuses an *actual* infinite series in the future, which is not possible with an endless or *potential* infinite series, which is possible. While it is always possible to add one more event or moment to the future (a potential infinite series), it is not possible to achieve a completed number of events in the future to which one more cannot be added (i.e., an actual infinite series). Second, as has been shown, an actual infinite series of causes is impossible. And God cannot know the impossible. He can only know the actual and the possible. Hence, God cannot know an actual infinite series of causes.

Sources

Al-Ghazali, *Incoherence of the Philosophers*
Aristotle, *Metaphysics*
Bonaventure, *2 Sententiarium*
W. L. Craig, *The Existence of God and the Beginning of the Universe*
———, *The Kalam Cosmological Argument*
John Duns Scotus, *God and Creatures: The Quodlibetal Questions*
C. S. Lewis, *Miracles*
J. P. Moreland, *Scaling the Secular City*
Thomas Aquinas, *Summa Theologica*

Information Theory. *See* ANTHROPIC PRINCIPLE; EVOLUTION, CHEMICAL.

Ingersoll, Robert G. American agnostic Robert G. Ingersoll (1833–1899) was born in Dresden, New York. Ingersoll popularized higher criticism of the Bible (*see* BIBLE CRITICISM), as well as humanistic thought (*see* HUMANISM, SECULAR). With little formal education, he became an attorney in 1854 and enjoyed a prosperous profession. He was a popular national orator. Ingersoll considered himself an agnostic (*see* AGNOSTICISM). His principal popular lectures were published as *Some Mistakes of Moses (*1879) and *Why I Am an Agnostic* (1889). His complete writings are found in *The Works of Robert G. Ingersoll* (12 vols., 1902), edited by Clinton P. Farrell.

Innate. *Innate* means "inborn; natural to; possessing independent of experience." Innate ideas are those with which one is born or has prior to any sensory experience. *Plato believed in innate ideas. *Aristotle rejected them, claiming that we are born a *tabula rasa* or blank slate; all ideas are derived from our sense experience (*see* HUME, DAVID).

Isaiah, Deutero. Isaiah includes amazingly specific prophecies that came true centuries later with exact accuracy (*see* PROPHECY, AS PROOF OF THE BIBLE). The apologetic value of this prophecy, however, has been blunted by the critic's charge that there were at least two Isaiahs. They claim that the second, later Isaiah records history, rather than sets out predictive prophecy.

The traditional view of the book of Isaiah is that it was written by Isaiah, son of Amoz, between 739 and 681 B.C. However, negative critics argue that "Proto-Isaiah" encompasses chapters 1 through 39, while Deutero-Isaiah wrote chapters 40 to 66 in the fifth century B.C. If so, then the amazing prediction by Isaiah including the one that a king named Cyrus (Isa. 45:1) would be raised up by God to discipline Israel loses its prophetic punch. For if one and the same Isaiah did not write this some 150 years before Cyrus was born, but after he had lived, then there is nothing amazing about knowing his name.

A Response to the Hypothesis. The traditional view that the book of Isaiah is a single work written by the prophet Isaiah is supported by several arguments.

The critical view that separates Isaiah into two or more books is based on the assumption that there is no such thing as predictive prophecy. Modern scholars claim that the prophecies in chapters 40–55 concerning Cyrus must have been written after Cyrus ruled in Persia. This view is antisupernatural and tries to explain these sections of Isaiah as history. However, since God knows the end from the beginning (Isa. 46:10), it is not necessary to deny the supernatural element in Isaiah's prophecies (*see* MIRACLES, ARGUMENTS AGAINST).

Differences between the two halves of the book can be explained in ways other than the two-author approach. Chapters 1 through 39 prepare the reader for the prophecies contained in chapters 40 through 66. Without these preparatory chapters, the last section of the book would make little sense. Chapters 1 through 35 warn of the Assyrian menace that threatens to destroy God's people. Chapters 36–39 form a transition from the previous section to chapters 40–66, by looking forward to the invasion of Sennacherib (chaps. 36–37), and at the spiritual decline that is causing the downfall of Jerusalem (chaps. 38–39). These four intervening chapters (36–39) are not in chronological order because the author is using them to prepare the reader for what is to follow.

The difference in words and style of writing between the two sections of the book has been used by critical scholars to substantiate their claim that there are at least two different books. However, these differences are not as great as has been claimed, and the differences that do exist can be explained as a difference in subject matter and emphasis. No author writes in exactly the same style using precisely the same vocabulary when writing about different subject matter. Nevertheless, a number of phrases found in both sections attest to the unity of the book. For example, the title "the Holy one of Israel" is found twelve times in chapters 1 through 39 and fourteen times in 40 through 66.

Similar Phrases in the Two Parts of Isaiah

Chapters 1–39	Chapters 40–66
1:15b—"Your hands are full of blood."	59:3a—"For your hands are defiled with blood."
28:5—"In that day the Lord Almighty will be a glorious crown, a beautiful wreath for the remnant of his people."	62:3—"You will be a crown of splendor in the Lord's hand, a royal diadem in the hand of your God."

35:6b—"Water will gush forth in the wilderness and streams in the desert."	41:18—"I will make rivers flow on barren heights, and springs within the valleys. I will turn the desert into pools of water, and the parched ground into springs."

In Luke 4:17 Jesus rose to read in the synagogue and "was handed the book of the prophet Isaiah." The people in the synagogue and Jesus himself assumed that this book was from the prophet Isaiah. Other New Testament writers accepted Isaiah as the author of the entire book. John 12:38 states that Isaiah was the one who made the statement that is found in Isaiah 6:1f. and 53:1. Other instances where the New Testament ascribes portions of chapters 40–66 to Isaiah include Matthew 3:3; Mark 1:2–3, and John 1:23 (Isa. 40:3); Matthew 12:17–21 (Isa. 42:1–4); Acts 8:32–33 (Isa. 53:7–8); and Romans 10:16 (Isa. 53:1).

The Dead Sea Scrolls include the earliest complete copy of the book of Isaiah, and there is no gap in the scroll between chapters 39 and 40. This indicates that the Qumran community accepted the prophecy of Isaiah as a seamless book in the second century B.C. The Greek version of the Hebrew Bible, which dates from the second century B.C., treats the book of Isaiah as a single book by a single author, Isaiah the prophet.

Even if the critic could show that part or all of Isaiah was written in the fifth century or later, it would not disprove the supernatural nature of the predictions about Christ. Those were fulfilled centuries later than even the latest possible date for its appearance. Isaiah predicted the *virgin birth of the Messiah (Isa. 7:14), his ministry (Isaiah 11; 61), and his death for our sins (Isaiah 53; *see* CHRIST, DEATH OF). Isaiah 53 is so specific and so messianic that even rabbinical interpretation of it before the time of Christ viewed it as a prediction about the coming Messiah (see Driver). Indeed, even if the writing is dated to the late fifth century B.C., it is a clear and specific supernatural prediction about Christ given hundreds of years in advance. If Isaiah had a supernatural source for this prophecy, then there is no reason to believe he did not have the same supernatural source for his predictions about Cyrus.

Conclusion. The attempt by Bible critics to posit a second and later Isaiah does not negate the supernatural nature of his specific predictions. They do not even succeed in proving that there was a later Isaiah who wrote 40–66. Hence, Isaiah's predictions which mention Cyrus by name over 150 years before he was born still stand. Even were Isaiah dated later in part or in whole, the book is filled with specific predictions, especially those literally fulfilled by Christ that were made centuries in advance.

Sources

O. T. Allis, *The Old Testament: Its Claims and Its Critics*
———, *The Unity of Isaiah*
G. L. Archer, Jr., *A Survey of Old Testament Introduction*
S. R. Driver, et al., trans., *The Fifty-Third Chapter of Isaiah According to Jewish Interpreters*
N. L. Geisler and T. Howe, *When Critics Ask*
R. K. Harrison, *Introduction to the Old Testament*

Isaiah, Virgin Birth in. *See* **VIRGIN BIRTH.**

Islam. *Islam* means "submission." A follower of this religion is called a *Muslim*, "a submitted one." Muhammad, the founder of the Islamic faith, was an Arabian trader from Mecca who was born around 570 and died in 632. As Christians measure history from the birth of Christ, so Muslims set the hinge date of history at 622, the year Muhammad fled from Mecca to Medina. This *Hijra* (*hijj* means "flight" in Arabic) marked Muhammad's turning point of submission to God and his proclamation of a new revelation from God. Muslims believe Muhammad to be the last prophet of God, superseding Christ, the prophet who was before him.

Muslims believe in submitting to the one and only one God, named *Allah*. They are categorically opposed to the Christian belief in the triunity of God (*see* TRINITY). To believe that there is more than one person in God is an idolatry and blasphemy called *shirk*.

Beliefs. *The Word of God.* Although Muslims hold that God revealed himself in the Jewish Law (*tawrat*), the Psalms (*zabur*), and the Gospels (*injil*), they claim that today's Christian Bible is corrupted, or *tahrif*. They assert that the *Qur'an* is the final Word of God (*see* QUR'AN, ALLEGED DIVINE ORIGIN OF). It is divided into 114 chapters or *suras* and is about the size of the New Testament.

Doctrines. There are five basic Muslim doctrines:

1. There is one and only one God.
2. There have been many prophets, including Noah, Abraham, Moses, Jesus, and Muhammad.
3. God created angels (jinn), some of which are good and others evil.
4. The *Qur'an* is God's full and final revelation.
5. A final day of judgment is coming, followed by heaven for the faithful and hell for the lost.

Besides these five central beliefs, there are five basic pillars of Islamic practice:

1. All that is necessary to become a Muslim is to confess the *shahadah*: "There is no God but Allah, and Muhammad is his messenger."
2. One must pray the *salat*, usually five times a day.

3. One keeps an annual fast (*sawn*) through the ninth lunar month of *Ramadan*.
4. One gives alms (*sakat*) to the needy, one-fortieth of one's income.
5. Every able Muslim must make one pilgrimage during life to Mecca.

Muslims also believe in jihad or holy war, which some radical groups have exalted to the level of a pillar. While this may involve killing infidels for their faith, more moderate Muslims think of it as being a sacred struggle with the word, not necessarily with the sword.

Many doctrines are shared with Christianity, such as creation (*see* CREATION, VIEWS OF), angels, heaven, *hell, and the *resurrection of all people. As for Christ, they affirm his prophethood, *virgin birth, physical ascension, second coming, sinlessness (*see* CHRIST, UNIQUENESS OF), *miracles, and messiahship.

Muslims deny the heart of the Christian message, namely, that Christ died on the cross for our sins (*see* CHRIST, DEATH OF; CHRIST'S DEATH, MORAL OBJECTIONS TO; CHRIST'S DEATH, SUBSTITUTION LEGEND) and that he arose from the grave physically three days later (*see* RESURRECTION, EVIDENCE FOR; RESURRECTION, PHYSICAL NATURE OF).

God as Absolute One. Allah is described by Muslims in terms of several basic attributes. Fundamental to all is the attribute of absolute unity. Of all the Islamic God's attributes, the most important is his undivided unity. To deny this is blasphemous.

The Islamic God is his absolute and indivisible unity. In sura 112, Muhammad defines God in these words: "Say: He is God, The One and Only; God, the Eternal, Absolute; He begetteth not, Nor is He begotten; And there is none Like unto Him." This sura is held to be worth a third of the whole *Qur'an*. The seven heavens and the seven earths are founded upon it. Islamic tradition affirms that to confess this verse sheds one's sins "as a man might strip a tree in autumn of its leaves" (Cragg, 39).

Two words are used in the *Qur'an* to describe the oneness of God: *ahad* and *wahid*. *Ahad* is used to deny that God has any partner or companion. In Arabic, this means the negation of any other number. The word *wahid* may mean the same as the first word or it may also mean "the One, Same God for all." That is to say, there is only one God for Muslims, and he is the same God for all peoples. God is a unity and a singularity.

God's Oneness is such a fundamental aspect of Islam that, as one Muslim author put it, "Islam, like other religions before it in their original clarity and purity, is nothing other than the declaration of the Unity of God, and its message is a call to testify to this Unity" (Mahmud, 20). Another Muslim writer adds, "The Unity of Allah is the distinguishing characteristic of Islam. This is the purest form of monotheism, that is, the worship of Allah Who was neither begotten nor beget nor had any associates with Him in His Godhead. Islam teaches this in the most unequivocal terms" (Ajijola, 55).

It is because of this uncompromising emphasis on God's absolute unity that the greatest of all sins in Islam is the sin of *shirk*, or assigning partners to God. The *Qur'an* sternly declares "God forgiveth not (the sin of) joining other gods with Him; but He forgiveth whom He pleaseth other sins than this: one who joins other gods with God, hath strayed far, far away (from the Right)" (sura 4:116).

God as Absolute Ruler. In the words of the *Qur'an*,

> God—there is no god but He—the Living, The Self-subsisting, Eternal. No slumber can seize Him nor sleep. His are all things In the heavens and on the earth. Who is there that can intercede in His presence except As He permitteth? He knoweth What (appears to His creatures As) Before or After Or Behind them. Nor shall they compass Aught His knowledge Except as He willeth. His Throne doth extend Over the heavens and the earth, and He feeleth no fatigue in guarding and preserving them For He is Most High, The Supreme (in glory). [sura 2:255]

God is self-sustaining and does not need anything but everything needs him. This attribute is known as aseity, or self-existence. God is The Mighty and The Almighty. He is The Willer of existing things and the things which will exist; and nothing happens apart from his will. He is the Knower of all that can be known. His knowledge encompasses the whole universe which he has created and he alone sustains. God is completely sovereign over all his creation.

Many of God's ninety-nine Islamic names speak of his sovereignty. He is:

Al-Adl, the Just, whose word is perfect in veracity and justice (6:115);

Al-Ali, the High One, he who is high and mighty (2:225–26);

Al-Aziz, the Sublime, mighty in his sublime sovereignty (59:23);

Al-Badi, the Contriver, who contrived the whole art of creation (2:117);

Al-Hakim, the Judge, who gives judgment among his servants (40:48–51);

Al-Hasib, the Accounter, who is sufficient as a reckoner (4:6–7);

Al-Jabbar, the Mighty One, whose might and power are absolute (59:23);

Al-Jalil, the Majestic, mighty and majestic is he;

Al-Jami, the Gatherer, who gathers all men to an appointed day (3:9);

Al-Malik, the King, who is King of kings (59:23);.

Al-Muizz, the Honorer, who honors or abases whom he will (3:26);

Al-Muntaqim, the Avenger, who wreaks vengeance on sinners and succors the believers (30:47);

Al-Muqsit, the Observer of Justice, who will set up the balances with justice (21:47–48);

Al-Mutaali, the Self-Exalted, who has set himself high above all (13:9–10);

Al-Qadir, the Able, who has the power to do what he pleases (17:99–101);

Al-Quddus, the Most Holy One, to whom all in heaven and on earth ascribe holiness (62:1);

Al-Wahid, the One, unique in his divine sovereignty (13:16); the Unique, who alone has created (74:11);

Al-Wakil, the Administrator, who has charge of everything (6:102);

Malik al-Mulk, Possessor of the Kingdom, who grants sovereignty to whom he will (3:26).

God as Absolute Justice. Several of God's names bespeak his absolute justice: the Majestic, the Gatherer, the Accounter, the Judge, the Just, the Most Holy One, to whom all in heaven and on earth ascribe holiness, the Observer of Justice, and the Avenger.

God as Absolute Love. Contrary to a popular misunderstanding, Allah is a God of love. Indeed, some of God's names depict this very characteristic. For example, God is *Ar-Rahman*, the Merciful, the most merciful of those who show mercy (sura 1:3; 12:64), and *Al-Wadud*, the Loving, compassionate and loving to his servants (11:90, 92). He has imposed the law of mercy upon himself (sura 6:12). He says, "My mercy comprehends all" (7:156). Muhammad said in the *Qur'an*, "If you do love God, Follow me:, and God will love you And forgive you your sins. For God is Oft-Forgiving, Most Merciful" (sura 3:31).

God as Absolute Will. There is a certain mystery about God's names. Historian Kenneth Cragg affirms that these names "are to be understood as characteristics of the divine will, rather than laws of his nature. Action, that is arising from such descriptives, may be expected, but not as a matter of necessity." What gives unity to all God's actions is that he wills them all. As Willer he may be recognized by the descriptions given him, but he does not conform to any. The action of his will may be identified from its effects, but his will of itself is inscrutable. This accounts for the antithesis in certain of God's names (see below). For example, God is "the One Who leads astray," as well as "the One Who guides."

God as Absolutely Unknowable. Since everything is based in God's will and since his effects are sometimes contradictory and do not reflect any absolute essence, God's nature is utterly unknowable. Indeed, "the divine will is an ultimate beyond which neither reason nor revelation go. In the Unity of the single will, however, these descriptions co-exist with those that relate to mercy, compassion, and glory" (Cragg, 64) God is named from his effects, but he is not to be identified with any of them. The relation between the Ultimate Cause (God) and his creatures is extrinsic, not intrinsic. That is, God is called good because he causes good, but goodness is not part of his essence.

Evaluation. Muslim monotheism is vulnerable to many criticisms, particularly from a Christian perspective. Crucial is their rigid idea of absolute unity.

The Problem of Absolute Unity. Islamic monotheism is rigid and inflexible. Its view of God's unity is so strong that it allows for no plurality at all in God. Hence, it sees nothing between monotheism and tritheism (three gods), and Christians are placed in the latter category. There are several reasons for this misunderstanding. For one thing there appears to be a misunderstanding of the biblical text related to God (MUHAMMAD, ALLEGED BIBLICAL PREDICTIONS OF). Muslims also have a rather grossly anthropomorphic view of what it means for Christ to be a "Son" of God. This often seems to demand some kind of sexual generation, according to their thinking. But the terms "Father" and "Son" no more necessitate physical generation than the term *alma mater* implies that the school from which we were graduated was our physical womb. Paternity can be understood in more than a biological sense.

There is a deeper and more basic philosophical problem. In the final analysis God has no (knowable) essence or nature from which one can distinguish his three persons or centers of consciousness (*see* TRINITY). This position is known as *nominalism. God is absolute will, and absolute will must be absolutely one. A plurality of wills (persons) would make it impossible to have any absolute unity. And Muslims believe God is absolutely one (both from revelation and by reason). Reason informed Muhammad that unity is prior to plurality. As Plotinus put it several centuries earlier (205–70), all plurality is made up of unities. Thus unity is the most ultimate of all. Accepting this neoplatonic way of thinking leads logically to a denial of the possibility for any plurality of persons in God. Hence, by the very nature of his philosophical commitment to the kind of neo-Platonism prevalent in the Middle Ages, Islamic thought about God was solidified into an intractable singularity which allowed no form of trinitarianism.

This rigid monotheism is not entirely consistent with some of Islam's own distinctions. Muslim scholars, consistent with certain teachings in the *Qur'an*, have made distinctions within God's unity. For example, they believe the *Qur'an* is the eternal Word of God. Sura 85:21–22 declares, "Nay, this is a Glorious *Qur'an*, (Inscribed) in a Tablet Preserved! [in heaven]" And in sura 43:3–4, we read, "We have made it a *Qur'an* in Arabic, that ye may able to understand (and learn wisdom). And verily, it is in the Mother of the Book, in Our Presence, high (in dignity), full of wisdom" (cf. sura 13:39). This eternal original is the template of the earthly book we know as the *Qur'an*.

Muslims insist the true *Qur'an* in heaven is uncreated, and perfectly expresses the mind of God. Yet they acknowledge that the *Qur'an* is not identical to the essence of God. Some Muslim scholars even liken the *Qur'an* to the divine *Logos* view of Christ, held by orthodox Christians (*see* CHRIST, DEITY OF). As Professor Yusuf K. Ibish stated of the *Qur'an*, "It is not a book in the ordinary sense, nor is it comparable to the Bible, either the Old or New Testaments. It is an expression of Divine Will. If you want to compare it with anything in Christianity, you must compare it with Christ Himself." He adds, "Christ was the expression of the Divine among men, the revelation of the Divine Will. That is what the *Qur'an* is" (Waddy, 14).

Orthodox Islam describes the relation between God and the *Qur'an* by noting that speech is an eternal attribute of God, which as such is without beginning or intermission, exactly like His knowledge, His might, and other characteristics of His infinite being (see Golziher, 97). But if speech is an eternal attribute of God that is not identical to God but is somehow distinguishable from him, then does not this allow the very kind of plurality within unity which Christians claim for the Trinity? Thus, it would seem that the Islamic view of God's absolute unity is, by their own distinction, not incompatible with Christian trinitarianism. The basic Muslim logic of either monotheism or polytheism is invalid. They themselves allow that something can be an eternal expression of God without being numerically identical to him. Thus, to use their own illustration, why can't Christ be the eternal "expression of Divine Will" without being the same person as this Divine Will?

The Problem of Voluntarism. At the very basis of the Islamic view of God is a radical voluntarism (*see* ESSENTIALISM) and nominalism. For traditional Islam, properly speaking, God does not have an essence, at least not a knowable one (*see* GOD, NATURE OF). Rather, he is Will. True enough, God is said to be just and loving, but he is not essentially just or loving. And he is merciful only because "He has imposed the law of mercy upon Himself" (sura 6:12). But since God is Absolute Will, had he chosen to be otherwise he would not be merciful. There is no nature or essence in God according to which he must act.

There are two basic problems with this radical nominalism: one metaphysical and one moral.

The metaphysical problem. The orthodox Islamic view of God claims, as we have seen, that God is an absolutely Necessary Being. He is self-existent, and he cannot not exist. But if God is by nature a necessary kind of being, then it is of his nature to exist. He must have a nature. Orthodox Islam believes that there are other essential attributes of God, such as, self-existence, uncreatedness, and eternality. But if these are all essential characteristics of God, then God must have an essence. Otherwise the attributes could not be essential. This is precisely how essence is defined, namely, as the essential attributes or characteristics of a being.

The moral problem. Islamic voluntarism poses a serious moral problem. If God is only will, without an essence, then he does not do things because they are right; rather, they are right because he does them. God is arbitrary about what is right and wrong. He does not have to do good. He does not have to be loving to all; he could hate, if he chose to do so. Indeed, in sura 3:32 we read, "God will love you. . . . God is Oft-Forgiving, Most Merciful," but verse 33 says that "God loveth not those Who reject Faith." So love and mercy are not of the essence of God. God could choose not to be loving. This is why Muslim scholars have such difficulty with the question of God's predestination.

*The problems of *agnosticism.* Since God has no essence, at least not one that the names (or attributes) of God really describe, the Islamic view of God involves a form of agnosticism. Indeed, the heart of Islam is not to *know* God but to *obey* him. It is not to *meditate* on his essence but to *submit* to his will. As Pfander correctly observed of Muslims, "If they think at all deeply, they find themselves absolutely unable to know God. . . . Thus Islam leads to Agnosticism" (Pfander, 187).

Islamic agnosticism arises because Muslims believe God caused the world by extrinsic causality. Indeed, "the Divine will is an ultimate, beyond which neither reason nor revelation go. In the Unity of the single Will, however, these descriptions co-exist with those that relate to mercy, compassion, and glory" (Cragg, 42–43). God is named from his effects, but he is not to be identified with any of them. The relation between the Ultimate Cause (God) and his creatures is extrinsic, not intrinsic. That is, God is called good because he causes good, but not because goodness is part of his essence.

Among the significant weaknesses inherent in this agnosticism, a moral, a philosophical, and a religious problem stand out immediately.

First, if God is not essentially good, but only called good because he does good, why not also call God evil, since he causes evil? (*see* EVIL, PROBLEM OF) Why not call him sinful and faithless, since he causes people not to believe? It would seem consistent to do so, since God is named from his actions. If Muslims reply that something in God is the basis for calling him good, but nothing in him is the basis for calling him evil, then they admit that God's names do tell us something about his essence. In fact, they admit an intrinsic relation between the cause (Creator) and the effect (creation). This leads to a metaphysical problem with the Islamic view of God.

Second, at the root of medieval views of God, an entrenched neo-Platonism springs from Plotinus. *Plotinus' belief that the Ultimate [God] was absolutely an indivisible One heavily influenced Muslim monotheism. Further, Plotinus held that the One is so utterly transcendent (above and beyond all) that it cannot be known, except by mystical experience. This influenced both orthodox Muslim agnosticism and Sufi mysticism. The fundamental reason there can be no similarity between the One [God] and what flows from It (the universe) is because God is beyond being, and there is no similarity between being and what is beyond it.

*Thomas Aquinas provided the definitive answer to plotinian agnosticism and mysticism. Aquinas argued that an effect must resemble its cause. "You cannot give what you have not got." Hence, if God causes goodness, he must be good. If he caused being, he must be (Geisler, *Thomas Aquinas*, chap. 9).

Objections to this view generally confuse either a material or instrumental cause with an efficient cause. The efficient cause of something is that *by which* it comes to be. The instrumental cause is that *through which* it comes to be. And the material cause it that *out of which* it is made. Material and instrumental causes do not necessarily resemble their effects, but efficient causes do. The painting does not resemble the artist's paint brush, but it does resemble the artist's mind. The brush is the instrumental cause, whereas the artist is the efficient cause.

Another mistake is to confuse material and efficient causality. Hot water is soft, yet it can cause an egg to get hard, because of properties in the egg. The same hot water softens wax. The difference is the material receiving the causality. Thus an infinite God can and does cause a finite world. God is not thereby finite because he caused a finite cosmos. Nor is he contingent because he, as a Necessary Being, caused a contingent universe. Finiteness and contingency are part of the very material nature of a created being. God is unlike creation in these kinds of ways. On the other hand, everything that exists *has* being, and God *is* Being. There must be a similarity between Being and being (*see* ANALOGY, PRINCIPLE OF). God is pure actuality, with no potentiality whatsoever. Everything else that exists has the potential not to exist. So all created things have actuality, since they actually exist, and potentiality, since they could possibly not exist. God is like creatures in their actuality but unlike them in their potentiality. This is why when we name God from his effects we must negate whatever implies finitude and limitation or imperfection, and attribute to him only the pure attribute or perfection. This is the reason that evil cannot be attributed to God but good can. Evil implies imperfection or privation of some good characteristic. Good, on the other hand, does not in itself imply either limitation or imperfection (*see* EVIL, PROBLEM OF). So God is good by his very nature but he cannot be or do evil.

Third, religious experience within a monotheistic context involves the relation between two persons, the worshiper and God. It is, as Martin *Buber correctly observed, an "I-Thou" relationship. But how can a person worship someone about which he can know nothing? Even in Islam, one is supposed to love God. But how do we fall in love with someone of which we know nothing? As atheist Ludwig *Feuerbach put it, "The truly religious man can't worship a purely negative being. . . . Only when a man loses his taste for religion does the existence of God become one without qualities, an unknowable God" (Feuerbach, 15).

Some critics have suggested that the extremely transcendent Muslim view of God has led some Muslim sects to deify Muhammad. Since relationship with the transcendent God is seen to be distant, it is only through Muhammad that one even dares to approach the throne of God. In *Qawwalis* (a popular cultural event), Muhammad is praised in verse. This often takes the form of deification: "If *Muhammad* had not been, God himself would not have existed!" This is an allusion to the close relationship Muhammad is supposed to have with God. Muhammad is often given titles like "Savior of the World" and "Lord of the Universe." The popular deification of Muhammad, who so violently opposed any such idolatry, only shows the theological bankruptcy of the Muslim view of a God so distant and so unknowable that the devotee must make contact with something they can understand, even to the extent of deifying the prophet who condemned idolatry.

The problems of extreme determinism. Since in Islam the relationship between God and human beings is that of Master and slave, God is the Sovereign Monarch and humans must submit (*see* DETERMINISM; FREE WILL). This overpowering picture of God in the *Qur'an* has created its own tension in Muslim theology regarding God's absolute sovereignty and human free will. Despite protests to the contrary, Orthodox Islam teaches the absolute predestination of both good and evil, that all our thoughts, words and deeds, whether good or evil, were foreseen, foreordained, determined, and decreed from all eternity, and that everything that happens takes place according to what has been written for it. Sura 6:18 says "He is the Irresistible." Commenting on these kinds of *Qur'anic* statements, Cragg points out that God is the *Qadar,* or "determination," of all things and his *taqdir,* or "subjection," covers all people and all history. Nature, whether animate or inanimate, is subject to his command and all that comes into existence—a summer flower or a murderer's deed, a newborn child or a sinner's disbelief—is from Him and of Him." In fact if "God so willed, there need have been no creation, there need have been no idolatry, there need have been no Hell, there need have been no escape from Hell" (Cragg, 44–45).

There are four basic problems with this extreme form of predetermination: logical, moral, theological, and metaphysical. In order, it involves a contradiction; it eliminates human responsibility; it makes God the author of evil, and it gives rise to pantheism.

The logical problem with Islamic determinism is that even Muslim commentators are forced to acknowledge that God performs contradictory actions (*see* First Principles). Islamicist Ignaz Golziher summarizes the situation, "There is probably no other point of doctrine on which equally contradictory teachings can be derived from the *Qur'an* as on this one" (Golziher, 78). One Muslim scholar notes, "The *Qur'anic* doctrine of Predestination is very explicit though not very logical" (Stanton, 54–55). For example, God is "the One Who leads astray," as well as "the One Who guides." He is "the One Who brings damage," as also does Satan. He is "the Bringer-down," "the Compeller" or "Tyrant," and "the Haughty." When describing people, all these concepts have an evil sense.

Muslim scholars sometimes attempt to reconcile this by pointing out that these contradictions are not in God's nature (since he does not really have one), but are in the realm of his will. They are not in his essence but in his actions. However, this is an inadequate explanation. God does have a knowable nature or essence. Hence, Muslim scholars cannot avoid the contradiction that God has logically opposed characteristics by placing them outside his essence within the mystery of his will. Further, actions flow from nature and represent it, so there must be something in the nature that corresponds to the action. Salt water does not flow from a fresh stream.

Others attempt to downplay the harsh extremes of Muslim determinism by creating a distinction, not found in the *Qur'an*, between what God *does* and what he *allows* his creatures to do by free choice. This solves the problem, but, only through rejecting clear statements of the *Qur'an*, tradition, and creeds.

These statements can be seen in connection with the moral problem with Islamic determinism. While Muslim scholars wish to preserve human responsibility, they can only succeed in doing so by modifying what the *Qur'an* actually says. Sura 9:51 declares: "Say, Nothing will ever befall us save what Allah has written for us." Sura 7:177–79 adds, "He whom Allah guides is he who is rightly guided, but whom he leads astray, those are the losers. Indeed, We have assuredly created for Gehenna many of both jinn and men." Sura 36: 6–10 reads: "Verily the sentence comes true on most of them, so they will not believe. We, indeed, have set shackles on their necks which reach to the chins so that they perforce hold up [their heads]. And We have set a barrier in front of them, and a barrier behind them, and We have covered them over so that they do not see. Thus it is alike to them whether thou warn them or dost not warn them; they will not believe."

The *Qur'an* frankly admits that God could have saved all, but did not desire to do so. Sura 32:13 declares: "Had we so willed We should have brought every soul its guidance, but true is that saying of Mine: 'I shall assuredly fill up Gehenna with jinn and men together.'" It is extremely difficult to understand how, holding such a view, one can consistently maintain any kind of human responsibility.

There is also a theological problem with this severe view of God's sovereign determination of all events: It makes God the author of evil. In the *Hadith* traditions Muhammad declares "the decree necessarily determines all that is good and all that is sweet and all that is bitter, and that is my decision between you." According to one tradition, Muhammad slapped Abu Bakr on the shoulder and said: "O Abu Bakr, if Allah Most High had not willed that there be disobedience, he would not have created the Devil." Indeed, one of the most respected Muslim theologians of all time, Al-Ghazzali, frankly acknowledges that "He [God] willeth also the unbelief of the unbeliever and the irreligion of the wicked and, without that will, there would neither be unbelief nor irreligion. All we do we do by His will: what He willeth not does not come to pass." And if one should ask why God does not will that men should believe, Al-Ghazzali responds, "'We have no right to enquire about what God wills or does. He is perfectly free to will and to do what He pleases.' In creating unbelievers, in willing that they should remain in that state; . . . in willing, in short, all that is evil, God has wise ends in view which it is not necessary that we should know" (Haqq, 152).

In the metaphysical problem with Islamic determinism, this extreme view led some Muslim scholars to the logical conclusion that there is really only one agent in the universe—God. One

Muslim theologian wrote, "Not only can He (God) do anything, He actually is the only One Who does anything. When a man writes, it is Allah who has created in his mind the will to write. Allah at the same time gives power to write, then brings about the motion of the hand and the pen and the appearance upon paper. All other things are passive, Allah alone is active" (Nehls, 21). This pantheism is at the heart of much of medieval thought. Thomas Aquinas wrote *Summa contra Gentiles* to help Christian missionaries dealing with Islam in Spain.

This radical predeterminism is expressed in Muslim creedal statements. One reads: "God Most High is the Creator of all actions of His creatures whether of unbelief or belief, of obedience or of rebellion: all of them are by the Will of God and His sentence and His conclusion and His decreeing" (Cragg, 60–61). Another confesses:

> God's one possible quality is His power to create good or evil at any time He wishes, that is His decree. . . . Both good things and evil things are the result of God's decree. It is the duty of every Muslim to believe this. . . . It is He who causes harm and good. Rather the good works of some and the evil of others are signs that God wishes to punish some and to reward others. If God wishes to draw someone close to Himself, then He will give him the grace which will make that person do good works. If He wishes to reject someone and put that person to shame, then He will create sin in him. God creates all things, good and evil. God creates people as well as their actions: *He created you as well as what you do* (*Qur'an* 37:94). [Rippin & Knappert, 133; emphasis added]

Conclusion. The attitude of God's absolute control over every aspect of his creation profoundly influences Islamic theology and culture. Persian poet, Omar Khayyam, reflected the fatalistic strain of Muslim theology when he wrote:

> 'Tis all a chequer-board of night and days
> Where destiny with men for pieces plays;
> Hither and thither moves and mates and slays,
> And one by one back in the closet lays.

Articles related to Islam and Muslim apologetics include ALFARABI; AVICENNA; AVERROES; BIBLE, ISLAMIC VIEW OF; MAIMONIDES; NEW TESTAMENT CORRUPTION, ALLEGED; MUHAMMAD, ALLEGED BIBLE PREDICTIONS; MUHAMMAD, ALLEGED DIVINE CALL; MUHAMMAD, MIRACLES OF; MUHAMMAD, MORAL CHARACTER OF; *QUR'AN*, DIVINE ORIGIN OF, and *QUR'AN*, ALLEGED MIRACLES IN.

Sources

K. Cragg, *The Call of the Minaret*
L. Feuerbach, *The Essence of Christianity*
N. L. Geisler, *Thomas Aquinas: An Evangelical Appraisal*
———, and A. Saleeb. *Answering Islam*
I. Golziher, *Introduction to Islamic Theology*
Thomas Aquinas, *Summa contra Gentiles*
S. Zwemer, *The Moslem Doctrine of God*

Jj

James, William. William James (1842–1910) was a finite godist (*see* FINITE GODISM) in his worldview and a pragmatist (*see* PRAGMATISM) in his theory of truth and ethics (*see* MORALITY, ABSOLUTE NATURE OF; TRUTH, NATURE OF). He approached the world and God from an experiential point of view. His test for the truth of a worldview was simply "What concrete difference will its being true make in one's actual life?" Truth, then, is not inherent in an idea. "Truth happens in an idea. It becomes true, is made true, by events." The worldview that works best is true (*Essays in Pragmatism*, 160–61; all citations in this article are from the writings of James).

View of God. For James, the worldview that worked best was a form of finite godism. Such a God avoided "the hallow unreal God of scholastic theology [theism], or the unintelligible pantheistic monster" (*Pluralistic Universe*, 316). The pantheistic God swallows all individuals in the absolute unity of its consciousness (*see* MONISM; PANTHEISM). The theistic God is so transcendently distinct from his creatures that they have nothing in common (ibid., 26; *see* THEISM).

In view of these extremes, James believed that the line of least resistance was to accept a "superhuman consciousness" who was not all-embracing, who was finite in power and/or knowledge (ibid., 311). "All the evidence we have seems to me to sweep us very strongly towards the belief in some form of superhuman life with which we may, unknown to ourselves, be co-conscious" (ibid., 309). Such a God need not be infinite; for that matter there could be more than one. James readily saw *polytheism as a possible worldview for a pragmatist. The important thing was to posit a larger power that is friendly to humankind and human ideals. Such a power "should be both other and larger than our conscious selves" (*Varieties of Religious Experience*, 396).

Even to claim this much about God seemed to James an overbelief. All James knew for certain was that there is a "more" out there with which human beings feel connected as "a subconscious continuation of our conscious life." Disregarding the overbeliefs and confining ourselves to what is common and generic, there is a saving experience that comes as a positive content of religious experience. This at least, James confessed, is literally and objectively true (ibid., 386, 388).

James speculated very little about his own overbeliefs. He concluded his classic *Varieties of Religious Experience*, "Who knows whether the faithfulness of individuals here below to their own poor overbeliefs may not actually help God in turn to be more effectively faithful to his own greater tasks?" (391).

Despite the particular differences various worldviews express about God, James felt assured that the one thing all religious experience had in common was that "they all agree that the 'more' really exists; though some of them hold it to exist in the shape of a personal god or gods, while others are satisfied to conceive it as a stream of ideal tendency embedded in the eternal structure of the world." James also found generic agreement among religions that the god(s) acts, and that it is beneficial to give your life to him/them. The differences develop, he added, when religions explain what they mean by the union with the divine that comes with religious experience (ibid., 385). Anything beyond this was, to James, speculative overbelief. Christian theism, for example, would define *more* as *Yahweh* God and *union* as imputation to us of the righteousness of Christ. Such beliefs were mere speculation. This is only one way to conceptualize God (*see* PLURALISM, RELIGIOUS), and James did not regard it as the most practical way.

The Nature of the Universe. James declared himself opposed to both pantheistic and materialist/atheist conceptions of the world (*see* ATHEISM), but the distinctions between his thinking and that of the pantheist were often slight. The world is not reducible to matter, nor is it pure mind or spirit. In contrast to monism, James took a pluralistic view of the universe—that there are many diverse things. Still, such a universe is not truly distinct from God. "The theistic conception, picturing God and his creation as entities distinct from each other, still leaves the human subject outside of the deepest reality in the universe" (*Pluralistic Universe*, 25). James's distinctive views identify him as close in thought to what would later be called *"panentheism."

The theists' God is too distinct (transcendent) from what he has created.

Theists are also wrong in supposing God to be complete and sufficient unto himself.

Creation was God's free act, and he made it as a substance extraneous to himself and humankind is made of a third substance, which is other than both God and creation.

In a panentheistic view, similar to some forms of pantheism, God animates the world the way a soul does a body. This stands in contrast to naturalism, "the curdling cold and gloom and absence of all permanent meaning." Naturalism places humankind "in a position similar to that of a set of people living on a frozen lake, surrounded by cliffs over which there is no escape" (ibid., 122).

Miracles. How such a God relates to the world is a little difficult to see until James labels the Christian miracle-working God as "grotesque" in conforming nature to human wants (*see* MIRACLE). "The God whom science recognizes must be a God of universal laws exclusively, a God who does a wholesale, not a retail business" (*Varieties*, 372–74). James's God is more organically connected with the world: "The divine can mean no single quality, it must mean a group of qualities, by being champions of which in alternation, different men may all find worthy missions. Each attitude being a syllable in human nature's total message, it takes the whole of us to spell the meaning out completely" (ibid., 368).

Despite the naturalistic tone (*see* NATURALISM), James believed in the supernormal. He believed, rather, that Christianity surrendered too easily to naturalism, taking the precepts of the physical sciences at face value. As Immanuel *Kant, James believed theistic supernaturalism unnecessarily confines itself to sentiments about life as a whole, which theism views too optimistically. In this over-optimistic, universalistic way of looking at the ideal world, practicality evaporates (ibid.). Such a "crasser" supernaturalism James rejects. His more "refined" supernaturalism admits "providential leadings, and finds no intellectual difficulty in mixing the ideal and the real world together by interpolating influences from the ideal religion among the forces that causally determine the real world's details" (ibid., 392).

However he labeled it, James professed a wider view of reality than that accepted by science. He was willing to use the term *supernatural*, though not in a theistic sense. He would not, for example, accept the idea of "miraculous healings," which were prevalent in the late nineteenth century. He objected to any supernatural interruption of a natural process. Such must be dismissed by the scientist as figments of the imagination. With almost prophetic awareness of the next century, James added, "No one can foresee just how far this legitimation of occultist phenomena under newly found scientist titles may proceed—even 'prophecy,' even 'levitation,' might creep into the pale" (ibid., 378).

But another sort of everyday miraculous was more gladly received—God's subtle, even subliminal influences on us through the natural world. If "there be a wider world of being than that of our everyday consciousness, if in it there be forces whose effects on us are intermittent, if one facilitating condition of the effects be the openness of the 'subliminal' door, we have the elements of a theory to which the phenomena of religious life lend plausibility." James was so impressed by the importance of these "transmundane energies" that he believed they influenced the natural world (ibid., 394).

This denial of the miraculous, except within stringent naturalistic guidelines, amounted to a denial of a life-changing conversion experience. James skeptically claimed that "converted men as a class are indistinguishable from natural men; some natural men even excel some converted men in their fruits." Hence, "The believers in the non-natural character of sudden conversion have had practically to admit that there is no unmistakable class-mark distinctive of all true converts" (ibid., 192).

Good and Evil. James did believe that "saintliness" flowed from religious experience. He rejected Friedrich Nietzsche's view that the saint is a weak individual. James pointed to such strong figures as Joan of Arc and Oliver Cromwell as counter-examples. James lauded the holy life, saying that it gave religion its "towering place in history" even when other aspects of faith did not stand up to practical common sense and empirical testing. "Let us be saints, then, if we can, whether or not we succeed visibly and temporarily" (*Varieties*, 290).

There is, however, no absolute standard for the saintly life of good, for James was a relativist (*see* MORALITY, ABSOLUTE NATURE OF), who believed that "there is no such thing as an ethical philosophy dogmatically made up in advance" (*Essays*, 65). Each must find what works best for them. James offers only the general guideline that we should avoid "pure naturalism" on the one hand, because of its ineptness, and "pure salvationism" on the other, because of its other-worldliness (*Varieties*, 140). Between these we must find the expedient path of what works best. The human race as a whole helps in this process to determine the content of ethical philosophy so far as we contribute to the race's moral life.

Despite his relative morality and tendency toward pantheism, James sharply parted with most pantheists in that he believed that evil is real, rather than an illusion. Both pantheism and theism, he charged, made too radical a break between concepts of absolute and relative morality. In effect, he sought to give quasi-absolute force to a set of universally accepted moral guidelines, even though they could not be called "absolutes." While the system may seem to hold together by weak threads, the connecting linkage is pragmatism: "'The true,' to put it briefly, is only the expedient in the way of our thinking, just as 'the right' is only the expedient in the way of our behaving" (*Essays*, 170).

Human Beings. Human beings have a spiritual, as well as a material, dimension. Through evolution from lower forms of life, humankind has reached a point of immortality (*see* EVOLUTION, BIOLOGICAL). At this point James takes on the naturalist's assumption that the mind cannot survive death because it is merely a function of the brain. Even if thought is a function of the brain, this does not compel us to deny immortality because the spiritual aspect is undeniable. "Dependence on the brain for this natural life would in no wise make mortal life impossible—it might be quite compatible with supernatural life behind the veil hereafter" (*Human Immortality*, 24, 38–39). Science can prove only the *concomitance* in the functioning of mind and brain; the *dependence* of the mind on the brain has not been proven (ibid., 42–43).

History and Its Goal. James was opposed to both optimistic and pessimistic views of human destiny. He could not agree with those who believed the world could not be salvaged. Optimism thinks the world's salvation inevitable. Midway between the two was the doctrine of *meliorism*, which treats salvation as neither necessary nor impossible. As a pragmatist, James felt compelled to accept improvement in the world as probable but not inevitable. "Pragmatism has to postpone a dogmatic answer, for we do not yet know certainly which type of religion is going to work best in the long run" (*Pragmatism and Other Essays*, 125, 132).

James's realism led him to reject *universalism's belief that all must be saved. "When the cup is poured off, the dregs are left behind forever, but the possibility of what is poured off is sweet enough to accept" (ibid., 130). In justification of his conclusion, James offered this scenario:

> Suppose that the world's author put the case to you before creation, saying: "I am going to make a world not certain to be saved, a world the perfection of which shall be conditional merely, the condition being that each does its own 'level best.' I offer you the chance of taking part in such a world. Its safety, you see, is unwarranted. It is a real adventure, with real danger, yet it may win through. It is a social scheme of co-operative work genuinely to be done. Will you join the procession? Will you trust yourself and trust the other agents enough to face the risk?" [ibid., 127]

To such a proposal, James believed most people would prefer the risk of such an adventure to nonexistence. Such, he believes, is the world we have.

Evaluation. William James was a fascinating philosopher who fit into no mold. His views present an array of positive and negative characteristics for theists.

Positives. From a Christian perspective, James frequently appears to try to head in the direction of orthodox faith, though from a great distance.

Materialism is rejected. Theists concur with James's rejection of materialism. Humanity is more than matter. Of this immortality, James was certainly correct.

Evil is real. James had no illusions about evil (*see* ILLUSIONISM). He accepted its reality. He rejected a pantheism that affirmed God and denied evil. At the same time, he avoided the temptation of atheism to affirm evil and deny God.

The principle of the Divine is affirmed. While James was not a theist, he did believe in some sort of god and accepted that god's hand in creation. He saw the practical value of these beliefs on one's life.

Holy living is commended. James was willing to admit the significant role that religious beliefs played in his own life. He commended saintliness and its contribution to the value of religion.

Universalism is rejected. Unlike other liberal thinkers, James denied the illusory optimism of the universalist. He was willing to admit that all may not be saved and that some sort of hell exists. This is refreshing honesty from someone who rejected the divine authority of the Bible.

Negatives. Finite Godism Is Inadequate. James's finite god was limited indeed. For a discussion of the problems with this worldview, see PANENTHEISM, and WHITEHEAD, ALFRED NORTH.

Antisupernaturalism is unfounded. James's rejection of the supernatural was illogical (*see* MIRACLES, ARGUMENTS AGAINST). His claim that supernatural religion saps human impetus to advance the good in life is contrary to his own analysis. He gave religion its "towering place" in human history by virtue of the selfless love of Christian supernaturalists. He concluded that "the saintly group of qualities is indispensable to the world's welfare" (*Varieties*, 290). He admired theists whose beliefs had made considerable impact, among them Christ, Cromwell, and Stonewall Jackson. He further admitted that great educational and social institutions, including universities, hospitals, the Red Cross, the slavery abolition movement, and rescue missions, were started by people who believed in the supernatural.

His view of evil is insufficient. While James recognized the reality of evil, his finite godism left him without assurance of a final victory over evil. A finite god does not have the infinite resources necessary to assure the final triumph over evil. In this, James unwittingly offers a solution to his own problem. He admitted that "the world is all the richer for having a devil in it, so long as we can keep our foot upon his neck" (ibid., 55). That is precisely what a finite god cannot do. A limited God could lose, or at best, reach an endless draw. Only an infinitely good and powerful God of theism can guarantee the outcome of the struggle with evil (*see* EVIL, PROBLEM OF).

Pragmatism is unjustified. The most serious internal criticism against pragmatism is that, pragmatically, it doesn't work. We would have to have infinite knowledge of all possible consequences to each alternative action or philosophy. We can never be sure how things will turn out. Only a theistic God could be an effective pragmatist, and he is not one.

One of James's Harvard colleagues, Josiah Royce, penetrated to the root problem of this pragmatic view of truth when he asked James if he would take the witness stand in court and swear "to tell the expedient, the whole expedient, and nothing but the expedient, so help him future experience."

Relativism is self-defeating. James denied all moral absolutes (*see* ABSOLUTES, MORAL). For him the right was the expedient in the way of living, as the truth was the expedient in the way of knowing. But it is impossible to deny all moral absolutes without implying a moral absolute.

Sources

E. J. Carnell, *An Introduction to Christian Apologetics*, chaps. 16, 17
N. L. Geisler, *The Roots of Evil*
———, and W. Watkins, *Worlds Apart*, chapter 6
W. James, *A Pluralistic Universe*
———, *Essays in Pragmatism*
———, *Human Immortality: Two Supposed Objections to the Doctrine*
———, *Pragmatism and Other Essays*
———, *Varieties of Religious Experience*

Jefferson, Thomas. Thomas Jefferson (1743–1826), the author of the Declaration of Independence (1776) and the third President of the United States, was a deist (*see* DEISM). Some of his earliest writings earned a place for him in the hearts of historians as "the major penman of the American Revolution" (Ketcham, 4:259). His philosophical and religious views undergird his writings but are not generally made explicit, except in his letters. Chiefly from these letters can his deism be clearly discovered.

Jefferson's religious views are reflected in his abridgment of the Gospels, *The Life and Morals of Jesus of Nazareth* (1803). In an 1816 reference to it he called it "a paradigm of his doctrines, made by cutting the texts out of the book, and arranging them on the pages of a blank book, in a certain order of time or subject. . . . A more beautiful morsel of ethics I have never seen." The fifty-seventh Congress evidently agreed, ordering an edition published in 1904.

The Jeffersonian Worldview. God and the World. Jefferson believed that there is one God, the Creator, Sustainer, and Manager of the universe. He held that this God is infinitely wise, good, righteous, and powerful. Influenced by Isaac Newton, Jefferson understood the world to be harmonious, under the rule of natural law, and open to human investigation. God created it that way. That all this is true is clear from the design of the universe:

> I hold (without revelation) that when we take a view of the universe, in its parts, general or particular, it is impossible for the human mind not to perceive and feel a conviction of design, consummate skill, and indefinite power in every atom of its composition. The movements of the heavenly bodies, so exactly held in their course by the balance of centrifugal and centripetal forces; the structure of the earth itself, with its distribution of lands, waters and atmosphere; animal and vegetable bodies, examined in all their minutest particular; insects, mere atoms of life, yet as perfectly organized as man or mammoth; the mineral substances, their generation and uses; it is impossible, I say, for the human mind not to believe that there is in all this design, cause and effect up to an ultimate cause, a Fabricator of all things from matter and motion, their Preserver and Regulator. [Foote, 10]

Miracles. Jefferson also maintained that God had never broken into history through supernatural miracles or revelation (*see* MIRACLE; REVELATION, SPECIAL). Such accounts to the contrary were fabrications, superstition, or fanaticism (Fesperman, 81).

Jefferson emphatically rejected the virgin birth of Christ. "The day will come," he said, "when the account of the birth of Christ as accepted in the trinitarian churches will be classified with the fable of Minerva springing from the brain of Jupiter" (Foote, 49). He also cut the resurrection from his supernatural-sanitized "Bible," ending it: "Then took they the body of Jesus, and wound it in linen clothes with the spices, as the manner of the Jews is to bury. Now, in the place where he was crucified, there was a garden; and in the garden a new sepulcher, wherein was never man yet laid. There laid they Jesus, and rolled a great stone to the door of the sepulcher, and departed" (*Life and Morals*, 132).

Bible. Obviously Jefferson regarded the Gospels as distortions wherever they intimated supernatural action by God. He charged the writers with "forgetting often, or not understanding, what had fallen from Him, by giving their own misconceptions as His dicta, and expressing unintelligibly for others what they had not understood themselves" (ibid., vii). Jesus' teachings had been rendered "mutilated, misstated, and often unintelligible" (ibid., 49) by a band of "dupes and impostors" who corrupted the true moral teachings. Worst in this bad lot was the apostle Paul, "the great Coryphaeus, and first corrupter of the Doctrines of Jesus" (*see* BIBLE CRITICISM).

Jefferson literally cut the miracles from the Gospels and retained only the moral teachings of Jesus. His views were not as radically deistic as were Thomas *Paine's. They most closely resembled the deism of Matthew Tindal in his *Christianity as Old as the Creation; or, The Gospel: A Republication of the Religion of Nature* and those of the unitarian Joseph Priestley. Jefferson rejected all major theological teachings of Christianity, such as the deity of Christ, original sin, salvation by grace through faith alone, and the substitutionary death of Christ. He believed Jesus to be the greatest reformer and moralist in history.

It was up to those who understood the truth, such as Jefferson, to purify the truth of the errors that had been imposed upon it. He endeavored to assemble the redacted truth from various portions of the four Gospels, arranged in the order that seemed to him most natural (Fesperman, 81, 83–84).

Human Beings. As stated in the *Declaration of Independence*, Jefferson considered it "to be self-evident, that all men are created equal; that they are endowed by their Creator with certain unalienable rights; that among these are life, liberty, and the pursuit of happiness." These "unalienable rights" are grounded in nature, which is itself unchangeable. Since these rights are natural, they are universal (*see* LAW, NATURAL; MORALITY, ABSOLUTE NATURE OF). Other natural rights, in Jefferson's view, were the right of association, the right to self-government, and the right to be free in regard to religion (Padover, 89–91, 143, 148, 155, 156).

God's creation of all people as equal had logical consequences. One was that slavery as an accepted practice in the United States had to be abolished. Jefferson attempted to accomplish this end by seeking to pass a plan he drafted, the "Report of Government for the Western Territory" (1784). This provided for the abolition of slavery in all the states after 1800 (ibid., 92–93). His legislation was defeated by one vote. Two years later he wrote of this decision: "The voice of a single individual . . . would have prevented this abominable crime from spreading itself over the country. Thus we see the fate of millions unborn hanging on the tongue of one man, and Heaven was silent in that awful moment! But it is to be hoped it will not always be silent, and that the friends of the rights of human nature will in the end prevail" (Foote, 18).

The human is a "rational animal" (*see* ARISTOTLE) who has been endowed "with an innate sense of justice." Both reason and the human sense of morality could go wrong, for neither "wisdom" nor "virtue" are hereditary. However, truth will eventually prevail, and human beings can "be restrained from wrong and protected in right, by moderate powers, confided to persons of his own choice" (Padover, 143, 131–135, 178, 91).

God and Government. It is clear from the *Declaration* that Jefferson did not envision the separation of God from government. Indeed, he believed governments owed allegiance to God. Inscribed in the marble of his memorial in Washington, D. C., is the quotation: "God who gave us life, gave us liberty. Can the liberties of a nation remain secure when we have removed a conviction that these liberties are a gift of God?"

Although Jefferson was in France as ambassador when Congress ratified the First Amendment (1789), he certainly agreed that "Congress shall make no law respecting the establishment of religion; nor prohibiting the free exercise thereof." This is not the "wall of separation" he is said to have espoused. The intent of the First Amendment is clearly that the federal government was not to establish a national religion in the English manner. It is interesting that five colonies had state religions when they ratified this amendment. It was actually in a fit of pique over what the Baptist association in Danbury, Connecticut, had said about his beliefs that Jefferson wrote of the "wall of separation between Church and State." He never used the phrase outside the context of this private letter, and other statements indicate that Jeffersonian "wall" should protect the state government from federal interference with regard to religion.

Jefferson left ample evidence of his views about church and state cooperation. He established a department of religion in the University of Virginia. He even proposed that students be required to attend church and refrain from swearing. In a treaty with the Kaskaskia Indians, Jefferson and Congress paid for the services of a missionary and a church building with tax funds. Congress did this more than once, being careful not to favor one religious group over another.

The central philosophy in this was that no religious view or group should be given legal sanction at the expense of another view or group. He said, "I am for freedom of religion, and against all maneuvers to bring about a legal ascendancy of one sect over another" (Padover, 119). Besides maintaining that such action would violate the natural law right of free religion, Jefferson believed it would be disadvantageous for religion, since each sect is a check on the others.

Christ and Religion. Religion had been the cause of great evil in Jefferson's view, and it was important that one opinion be balanced by opposing opinions. Millions had been burned, tortured, fined, and imprisoned, "yet we have not advanced one inch towards uniformity." Past coercion had made half the world fools, and the other half hypocrites.

While Jefferson identified himself as a Christian, many agreed with the Danbury Baptists that he was not orthodox. He considered his redacted "Bible" proof "that I am a *real Christian*, that is to say, a disciple of the doctrines of Jesus" (*Life and Morals*, viii). Jefferson admitted he was not a Christian who accepted the historic teachings of the Bible and church. "I am a Christian in the only sense in which I believe Jesus wished anyone to be, sincerely attached to his doctrines in preference to all others; ascribing to himself every human excellence, and believing that he never claimed any other" (Foote, 4).

Evil. People have both good and evil qualities. Indeed "experience proves, that the moral and physical qualities of man, whether good or evil, are transmissible in a certain degree." A primary function of government is to protect people from injuring each other and to be attentive to the needs and desires of the masses. When a government fails to perform this function, its officers "become wolves." This is not an unusual occurrence. The tendency of people to wield abusive power over others "seems to be the law of our general nature, in spite of individual exceptions; and experience declares that man is the only animal which devours his own kind." The kind of government that tends to promote this evil is that run by kings, nobles, or priests. "There is scarcely an evil known in [Europe] which may not be traced to their king as its source" (Padover, 164, 97, 103). When governments become tyrannical, it is the *obligation* of the governed to overthrow it.

Ethics. Following John Locke's natural law tradition, Jefferson held that the natural moral law applies to nations and to individuals: "It is strangely absurd to suppose that a million human beings, collected together, are not under the same moral laws which bind each of them separately" (Foote, 42). The source of human morality is "love for others," which has been "implanted" by nature. It is this "moral instinct . . . which prompts us irresistibly to feel and to succor" the distress of others. Moral actions are relative. Actions deemed virtuous in one country are considered vicious in another. This occurs because "nature has constituted *utility* to man [as] the standard . . . of virtue" (Padover, 150–51).

Jefferson considered the greatest moral teachers to have been Epicurus and Jesus. He considered himself a follower of both, though he identified most closely with Epicurus. Concerning this he wrote, "I . . . am an Epicurean. I consider the genuine (not the imputed) doctrines of Epicurus as containing everything rational in moral philosophy which Greece and Rome have left us" (Padover, 175).

Human Destiny. The human soul does survive death. While on his deathbed Jefferson penned these words as a farewell to his surviving daughter:

> Life's visions are vanished, its dreams are no more;
> Dear friends of my bosom, why bathed in tears?
> I go to my fathers, I welcome the shore
> Which crowns all my hopes and which buries my cares.
> Then farewell, my dear, my lov'd daughter, adieu!
> The last pang of life is in parting from you.
> Two seraphs await me long shrouded in death;
> I will bear them your love on my last parting breath. [Foote, 68]

Jefferson spoke of the Judge of all humanity in the *Declaration*, but he did not define what he meant by the term. He did not omit Jesus' references to rewards in heaven for the righteous and punishment in hell for the wicked from his abbreviated Bible. Just how literally he took this is another question.

Evaluation. Since Jefferson was a deist his views fall under the same critique. This includes his denial of miracles (*see* MIRACLES, ARGUMENTS AGAINST) as well as his rejection of God's immanence (*see* THEISM). His views on the Bible were also unfounded (*see* BIBLE, ALLEGED ERRORS IN; BIBLE CRITICISM; BIBLE, EVIDENCE FOR).

Sources

J. Butler, *The Analogy of Religion Natural and Revealed to the Constitution and Course of Nature*

F. I. Fesperman, "Jefferson's Bible" in *Ohio Journal of Religious Studies*, 4:2 (October 1976)

R. Flint, *Anti-Theistic Theories*

H. W. Foote, *Thomas Jefferson: Champion of Religious Freedom, Advocate of Christian Morals*

N. L. Geisler, *Miracles and the Modern Mind*

———, and W. Watkins. *Worlds Apart*

I.. Kant, *Religion within the Limits of Reason Alone*

R. Ketcham, "Jefferson, Thomas" in *The Encyclopedia of Philosophy*, 4:259

J. LeLand, *A View of the Principal Deistic Writers . . .*

R. Nash, *Christian Faith and Historical Understanding*

J. Orr, *English Deism*

S. K. Padcver, *Thomas Jefferson and the Foundations of American Freedom*

J-E-P-D Theory. ***See*** **PENTATEUCH, MOSAIC AUTHORSHIP OF.**

Jesus, Non-Christian Sources. Negative Bible critics charge or imply that the New Testament documents are unreliable since they were written by disciples of Jesus or later Christians. They note that there is no confirmation of Jesus in any non-Christian sources. Several factors undermine the validity of this criticism (*see* BIBLE CRITICISM).

The Evidence. There is overwhelming evidence that the New Testament is a reliable record composed by contemporaries and eyewitnesses of the events (*see* BIBLE, HISTORICITY OF; NEW TESTAMENT, DATING OF; NEW TESTAMENT, HISTORICITY OF; NEW TESTAMENT MANUSCRIPTS). There are more manuscripts, earlier manuscripts, better copied manuscripts, and manuscripts written by more people who were closer to the events than for any other piece of ancient history. Archaeology is continually confirming details of their writing (*see* ARCHAEOLOGY, NEW TESTAMENT). If the New Testament record is unreliable, we have no hope for any reliable knowledge of ancient happenings.

The objection that the writings are partisan involves a significant but false implication that witnesses cannot be reliable if they were close to the one about whom they gave testimony. This is clearly false. Survivors of the Jewish holocaust were close to the events they have described to the world. That very fact puts them in the best position to know what happened. They were there, and it happened to them. The same applies to the court testimony of someone who survived a vicious attack. It applies to the survivors of the Normandy invasion during World War II or the Tet Offensive during the Vietnam War. The New Testament witnesses should not be disqualified because they were close to the events they relate.

Related to the charge that Jesus lacks testimony by unbelievers is that there is strong evidence, but a lack of weak evidence.

Suppose there were four eyewitnesses to a murder. There was also one witness who arrived on the scene after the actual killing and saw only the victim's body. Another person heard a secondhand report of the killing. In the trial the defense attorney argues: "Other than the four eyewitnesses, this is a weak case, and the charges should be dismissed for lack of evidence." Others might think that attorney was throwing out a red herring. The judge and jury were being distracted from the strongest evidence to the weakest evidence, and the reasoning was clearly faulty. Since the New Testament witnesses were the only eyewitness and contemporary testimonies to Jesus, it is a fallacy to misdirect attention to the non-Christian secular sources. Nonetheless, it is instructive to show what confirming evidence for Jesus can be gleaned outside the New Testament.

The Sources. Some excellent resources have been made available to give fuller descriptions of this testimony. Josh McDowell, *Evidence that Demands a Verdict*, devotes a chapter to the non-Christian evidence. F. F. *Bruce wrote the popular-level analysis of the evidence in *The New Testament Documents: Are They Reliable*, and Bruce's *Jesus and Christian Origins Outside the New Testament* is a more in-depth and thoroughly documented study. A recent work on the subject is by Gary Habermas in one chapter of *The Historical Jesus*.

Ancient Historians. A surprising amount of information about Jesus can be drawn from historians who were contemporary to him or lived soon after. These include:

Tacitus. The first-century Roman Tacitus is considered one of the more accurate historians of the ancient world. He gives the account of the great fire of Rome, for which some blamed the Emperor Nero:

> Consequently, to get rid of the report, Nero fastened the guilt and inflicted the most exquisite tortures of a class hated for their abominations, called Christians by the populace. Christus, from whom the name had its origin, suffered the extreme penalty during the reign of Tiberius at the hands of one of our procurators, Pontius Pilatus, and a most mischievous superstition, thus checked for the moment, again broke out not only in Judea, the first source of the evil, but even in Rome, where all things hideous and shameful from every part of the world find their center and become popular. [*Annals* 15.44]

This passage contains references to Christians, named after Christus (Latin for *Christ*), who suffered the "extreme penalty" under Pontius Pilate during the reign of Tiberius. The "superstition" which started in Judea and had made its way to Rome was most likely the resurrection of Jesus.

Suetonius. Suetonius was chief secretary to Emperor Hadrian (reign, 117–138). Two references are important:

> Because the Jews at Rome caused continuous disturbances at the instigation of Chrestus, he expelled them from the city. [*Claudius*, 25]
>
> After the great fire at Rome. . . . Punishments were also inflicted on the Christians, a sect professing a new and mischievous religious belief. [*Nero*, 16]

These brief references establish a few things. There was a man named *Chrestus* (or Christ) who lived during the first century. Certain Jews caused disturbances relating to this man. Suetonius, writing many years later, was not in a position to know whether the disturbances were instigated by Chrestus or by Jews against his followers. At any rate Claudius became annoyed enough to throw every Jew out of the city (including Paul's associates Aquila and Priscilla) in 49. Also, Christians were persecuted after the

Rome fire, and they had professed a new religious belief.

**Josephus.* Flavius Josephus (37/38–97) was a Jewish revolutionary who changed allegiance to the Romans in the Jewish revolt in time to save his life. He became a historian, working under the auspices of Emperor Vespasian. His *Antiquities* dates to the early 90s and contains two passages of interest. The first refers to James, "the brother of Jesus, who was called Christ" (20:9). This confirms the New Testament facts that there was a man named Jesus, who was known as "Christ" and had a brother named James. The second reference is much more explicit and controversial:

> Now there was about this time Jesus, a wise man, if it be lawful to call him a man. For he was one who wrought surprising feats. . . . He was [the] Christ . . . he appeared to them alive again the third day, as the divine prophets had foretold these and ten thousand other wonderful things concerning him. [*Antiquities* 18:3]

The genuineness of this passage has been questioned by scholars from all areas of belief because it seems doubtful that a Jew who lived and worked outside the Christian context would have said such things about Jesus. Even the apologist-theologian Origen (ca. 185–ca. 254) said that Josephus did not believe Jesus was the Messiah (*Contra Celsum* 1:47). Despite these concerns, there are reasons in favor of accepting most of the text as genuine. First, there is good textual evidence for the mention of Jesus, and no textual evidence against it. Second, the text is written in the style of Josephus. Third, some of the words most likely did not come from a Christian. Fourth, the passage fits its context both grammatically and historically. Fifth, the reference to Jesus in *Antiquities* 20 seems to presuppose an earlier mention. Finally, an Arabic version of the text contains the basic elements without the questionable parts:

> At this time there was a wise man named Jesus. His conduct was good and [he] was known to be virtuous. And many people from among the Jews and the other nations became his disciples. Pilate condemned him to be crucified and to die. But those who became his disciples did not abandon his discipleship. They reported that he had appeared to them three days after his crucifixion, and that he was alive; accordingly he was perhaps the Messiah, concerning whom the prophets have recounted wonders. [cited in Habermas, 186]

Even without portions that are likely Christian interpolations, this text is an extraordinary witness to the life, death, and influence of Jesus. It notes that Jesus was known as a wise and virtuous man who had Jewish and Gentile disciples. Pilate condemned him to be crucified. The disciples reported that he had risen from the dead on the third day. The idea had been attached to his proclamation that he was the Messiah.

Thallus. Thallus wrote around A.D. 52. None of his works are extant, though a few fragmented citations are preserved by other writers. One such writer is Julius Africanus in about 221, who quotes Thallus in a discussion of the darkness which followed the crucifixion of Christ:

> On the whole world there pressed a most fearful darkness; and the rocks were rent by an earthquake, and many places in Judea and other districts were thrown down. This darkness Thallus, in the third book of his *History* calls, as appears to me without reason, an eclipse of the sun. [*Extant Writings*, 18 in the *Ante-Nicene Fathers*]

Africanus identifies the darkness which Thallus explained as a solar eclipse with the darkness at the crucifixion described in Luke 23:44–45.

Government Officials. Other non-Christian sources were ancient government officials, whose occupations put them in a unique position to have official information unavailable to the public.

Pliny the Younger. Pliny the Younger was a Roman author and administrator. In a letter to the Emperor Trajan in about 112, Pliny describes the early Christian worship practices:

> They were in the habit of meeting on a certain fixed day before it was light, when they sang in alternate verses a hymn to Christ, as to a god, and bound themselves by a solemn oath, not to do any wicked deeds, but never to commit any fraud, theft or adultery, never to falsify their word, nor deny a trust when they should be called upon to deliver it up; after which it was their custom to separate, and then reassemble to partake of food—but food of an ordinary and innocent kind. [*Letters* 10:96]

This passage confirms several New Testament references. The most notable is that early Christians worshiped Jesus as God. Their practices also betray a strong ethic, probably that of Jesus. There is also a reference to the love feast and Lord's Supper. Later in the same letter, Pliny calls the teaching of Jesus and his followers "excessive superstition" and "contagious superstition," which may refer to Christian belief and proclamation of the resurrection of Jesus.

Emperor Trajan. In reply to Pliny's letter, Emperor Trajan gives the following guidelines for punishing Christians:

> No search should be made for these people; when they are denounced and found guilty they must be punished; with the restriction, however, that when the party denies himself to be a Christian, and shall give proof that he is not (that is, by adoring our gods) he shall be pardoned on the ground of repentance, even

> though he may have formerly incurred suspicion. [ibid., 10:97]

This sheds some light on how the early Roman government viewed Christianity. They were to be punished for not worshiping the Roman gods, but the persecution was not without restrictions.

Hadrian. The Christian historian Eusebius (ca. 265–339) records a letter from Emperor Hadrian to Mincius Fundanus, the Asian proconsul. Not unlike Trajan's letter to Pliny, Hadrian gives some instruction on handling Christians:

> I do not wish, therefore, that the matter should be passed by without examination, so that these men may neither be harassed, nor opportunity of malicious proceedings be offered to informers. If, therefore, the provincials can clearly evince their charges against the Christians, so as to answer before the tribunal, let them pursue this course only, but not by mere petitions, and mere outcries against the Christians. For it is far more proper, if anyone would bring an accusation, that you should examine it. [*Ecclesiastical History*, 4:9]

The passage confirms that Christians were often accused of breaking laws and were punished, but that temperance was encouraged.

Other Jewish Sources. In addition to the Jewish writers of the New Testament and Josephus, other Jewish witnesses refer to the life of Jesus.

Talmud. Talmudic writings of most value concerning the historical Jesus are those compiled between 70 and 200 during the so-called *Tannaitic Period*. The most significant text is Sanhedrin 43a:

> On the eve of Passover Yeshu was hanged. For forty days before the execution took place, a herald went forth and cried, "He is going forth to be stoned because he has practiced sorcery and enticed Israel to apostasy. Any one who can say anything in his favour, let him come forward and plead on his behalf." But since nothing was brought forward in his favour he was hanged on the eve of the Passover! [*Babylonian Talmud*]

This passage confirms the crucifixion, the timing of the event on the eve of Passover, and the accusation of sorcery and apostasy. This text also informs us of the herald who went out preceding the death of Jesus (cf. John 8:58–59; 10:31–33, 39). Another reference in this section mentions five disciples of Jesus. Most of the other references to Jesus and Christianity in *the Talmud* are much later and of questionable historical value.

Toledoth Jesu. One rather later witness is *Toledoth Jesu*, an anti-Christian document compiled in the fifth century. This document explains that the body of Jesus was secretly moved to a second grave because the disciples were planning to steal the body. When the disciples came to the tomb, Jesus' body was gone, so they concluded that he was resurrected. Meanwhile the Jewish authorities were being informed of the true location of Jesus' body. Though quite late, this document probably reflects common early opinion (cf. Matt. 18:11–15).

Other Gentile Sources. There were Gentile sources for the life of Christ other than the Romans. These include:

Lucian. Lucian of Samosata was a second-century Greek writer whose works contain sarcastic critiques of Christianity:

> The Christians, you know, worship a man to this day—the distinguished personage who introduced their novel rites, and was crucified on that account. . . . You see, these misguided creatures start with the general conviction that they are immortal for all time, which explains the contempt of death and voluntary self-devotion which are so common among them; and then it was impressed on them by their original lawgiver that they are all brothers, from the moment that they are converted, and deny the gods of Greece, and worship the crucified sage, and live after his laws. All this they take quite on faith, with the result that they despise all worldly goods alike, regarding them merely as common property. [*Death of Pelegrine*, 11–13]

Following Habermas, several things can be ascertained from this text. Jesus was worshiped by Christians. He had introduced new teachings and had been crucified for his teachings. His teachings included the brotherhood of believers, the importance of conversion, and the importance of denying other gods. Christians lived according to Jesus' laws. Further, the followers of Jesus believed themselves immortal and were characterized by contempt for death, voluntary self-devotion, and renunciation of material goods. Despite being one of the church's most vocal critics, Lucian gives one of the most informative accounts of Jesus and early Christianity outside the New Testament.

Mara Bar-Serapion. A Syrian, Mara Bar-Serapion wrote to his son Serapion sometime between the late first and early third centuries. The letter contains an apparent reference to Jesus:

> What advantage did the Athenians gain from putting Socrates to death? Famine and plague came upon them as a judgment for their crime. What advantage did the men of Samon gain from burning Pythagoras? In a moment their land was covered with sand. What advantage did the Jews gain from executing their wise King? It was just after that their kingdom was abolished. God justly avenged these three wise men: the Athenians died of hunger; the Samians were overwhelmed by the sea; the Jews, ruined and driven from their land, live in com-

> plete dispersion. But Socrates did not die for good; he lived on in the statue of Hera. Nor did the wise king die for good; he lived on in the teaching which he had given. [British Museum, Syriac ms, add. 14, 658; cited in Habermas, 200]

This passage confirms four specific teachings of the New Testament: (1) Jesus was thought to be a wise and virtuous man. (2) Jesus was considered by many to be the king of Israel. (3) The Jews put Jesus to death. (4) Jesus lived on in the teachings of his followers.

Gnostic Sources. Immediately after the time of Christ, several non-Christian groups flourished in loose connection with the church. One of the more successful was the gnostics (*see* GNOSTICISM).

The Gospel of Truth. This second-century book was perhaps written by Valentinus (135–160). It confirms that Jesus was a historical person in several passages:

> For when they had seen him and heard him, he granted them to taste him and to smell him and to touch the beloved Son. When he had appeared instructing them about the Father. . . . For he came by means of fleshly appearance. [30:27–33; 31:4–6]

In another passage we read that

> Jesus was patient in accepting sufferings . . . since he knows that his death is life for many . . . he was nailed to a tree; he published the edict of the Father on the cross. . . . He draws himself down to death through life. . . . Having stripped himself of the perishable rags, he put on imperishability, which no one can possibly take away from him. [20:11–14, 25–34]

These quotations affirm that Jesus was the Son of God and the Word, who became a man and took on a fleshly body. He taught his followers about his Father. Jesus suffered and was crucified. His death brings life for many. Jesus was raised from the dead in an imperishable body.

The Apocryphon of John was a second-century gnostic work that opens with a supposedly historical account of an encounter between Arimanius the Pharisee and John, son of Zebedee, the disciple. John is reputed to have said that Jesus "has gone to the place from which he came" (1:5–17). This was an apparent reference to the ascension. Arimanius replied that John had been deceived by Jesus. There is no evidence outside *The Apocryphon* that this event occurred.

*The *Gospel of Thomas* (140–200) is a collection of some spurious and some actual events and sayings of Jesus. It tells us several things about the identity of Jesus. Jesus identifies himself as the resurrected One, the Son of Man, the Son of his Father, and the All of the Universe. As in the Bible, the disciples fail to recognize the true identity of Jesus. *The Gospel of Thomas* refers to the death and exaltation of Jesus. It is a thoroughly gnostic document, and for this reason, as well as the late date, it has limited historical value.

The Treatise on Resurrection is a gnostic work from the late second century. Despite its heavy gnostic philosophy, *Treatise* does affirm several teachings: Jesus was truly deity. Despite this, Jesus, the Son of God, took on flesh. Jesus died, rose again, and conquered death for those who have faith in him. Its value as a source is also limited.

Other Lost Sources. Beside these non-Christian sources for the life of Christ, some documents are hinted at but have not been found.

The Acts of Pontius Pilate. Although a purportedly official document, *The Acts of Pontius Pilate* does not survive, it is referred to by *Justin Martyr in about 150 and by *Tertullian in about 200. Justin writes:

> And the expression, "They pierced my hands and my feet," was used in reference to the nails of the cross which were fixed in his hands and feet. And after he was crucified, they cast lots upon his vesture, and they that crucified him parted it among them. And that these things did happen you can ascertain from the "Acts" of Pontius Pilate. [*First Apology*, 35]

Justin also claims that the miracles of Jesus can be confirmed in this document (ibid., 48).

Phlegon. Phlegon (b. ca. 80) was a freed slave of Emperor Hadrian. None of Phlegon's writings are extant, but he is mentioned several times by later writers. He spoke of Christ's death and resurrection in his nonextant *Chronicles*, saying, "Jesus, while alive, was of no assistance to himself, but that he arose after death and exhibited the marks of his punishment, and showed how his hands had been pierced by nails" (cited in Origen, 4:455; cf. Habermas, 210; Anderson, 19). Phlegon also mentioned "the eclipse in the time of Tiberius Caesar, in whose reign Jesus appears to have been crucified, and the great earthquake which then took place" (Origen, 14). Julius Africanus confirms the same quotations (Julius Africanus, 18).

Habermas summarizes from the Phlegon references that Jesus predicted the future, that there was an eclipse at the time of the crucifixion, and that it occurred during the reign of Tiberius. After his resurrection, Jesus appeared and showed his wounds, especially the nail marks from the crucifixion (Habermas, 211).

Summary. The primary sources for the life of Christ are the four Gospels (*see* NEW TESTAMENT, HISTORICITY OF). However, there are considerable reports from non-Christian sources that supplement and confirm the Gospel accounts. These come largely from Greek, Roman, Jewish, and Samaritan sources of the first century. In brief they inform us that: (1) Jesus was from Nazareth; (2) he lived a wise and virtuous life; (3) he was crucified in Palestine under Pontius Pilate during the reign of Tiberius Caesar at Passover time, being considered the Jewish king; (4) he was believed by his disciples to have been raised from the dead three days later; (5) his enemies acknowledged that he performed unusual feats they called "sorcery"; (6) his small band of disciples multiplied rapidly, spreading even as far as Rome; (7) his disciples denied polytheism, lived moral lives, and worshiped Christ as Divine. This picture confirms the view of Christ presented in the New Testament Gospels.

Sources

J. N. D. Anderson, *The Witness of History*
F. F. Bruce, *The New Testament Documents: Are They Reliable?*
———, *Jesus and Christian Origins Outside the New Testament*
Eusebius, *Ecclesiastical History*, C. F. Cruse, trans.
Flavius Josephus, *Antiquities of the Jews*
G. Habermas, *The Historical Jesus*, chap. 9
Lucian of Samosata, *The Works of Lucian of Samosata*
J. McDowell, *Evidence that Demands a Verdict*, chap. 5
Origen, *Contra Celsus*
Pliny the Younger, *Letters*, W. Melmoth, trans.
A. Roberts and J. Donaldson, eds. *The Ante-Nicene Fathers*
Suetonius, *Life of Claudius*
———, *Life of Nero*
Tacitus, *Annals*

Jesus, Uniqueness of. *See* **CHRIST, DEITY OF; CHRIST, UNIQUENESS OF; WORLD RELIGIONS AND CHRISTIANITY.**

Jesus of History. *See* **CHRIST OF FAITH VS. JESUS OF HISTORY; JESUS, QUEST FOR THE HISTORICAL; JESUS SEMINAR.**

Jesus, Quest for the Historical. For over 100 years there has been a quest to identify the historical Jesus and differentiate this person from the Christ of Faith (*see* CHRIST OF FAITH VS. JESUS OF HISTORY). Actually, there have been several quests. All but the last have rejected the historicity of the New Testament as a whole and undermined orthodox Christianity and the Christian apologetic.

The quests for the real Jesus can be divided into four time periods: (1) the first or "old" quest, 1778–1906; (2) the "no quest" period, 1906–1953; (3) the "new" quest, 1953–1970; and (4) the third quest, from 1970 (see Holden, chap. 2).

The First-Quest Period. The quest for the historical Jesus grew out of the posthumous publication by Gotthold Lessing of Hermann Reimarus's *Fragments*. In the fragment "On the Intention of Jesus and His Disciples," Reimarus separated what the apostles said about Jesus from what Jesus actually said about himself. This partition between the Christ of Faith and the Jesus of history remains a core tenet of much of modern New Testament research (*see* JESUS SEMINAR). It is rooted in the antisupernaturalism of Benedict *Spinoza, English *Deism, and the fact/value dichotomy of Immanuel *Kant.

In 1835, David *Strauss published his desupernaturalized work, *The Life of Jesus Critically Examined*. Under the influence of David *Hume, Strauss dismissed the reliability of historical and supernatural elements in the Gospels as "outrageous" and "myths." This led to later attempts to demythologize the Gospel records (*see* MYTHOLOGY AND THE NEW TESTAMENT).

Albert Schweitzer brought this period to a close in 1906 with his *The Quest of the Historical Jesus*. He argued that Jesus' message was eschatological in nature and that the supposedly objective research into the man had produced a figure molded into the biases of the researchers. "There is nothing more negative than the result of the critical study of the life of Jesus," wrote Schweitzer. "He is a figure designed by rationalism, endowed with life by liberalism, and clothed by modern theology in historical garb" (Schweitzer, 396).

The No-Quest Period. Schweitzer severely damaged the confidence of the quest for the historical and inaugurated a time during which such research was in disrepute. Rudolph *Bultmann regarded such work as methodologically impossible and theologically illegitimate. In *Jesus and the Word* (1958), he wrote, "I do indeed think that we can know almost nothing concerning the life and personality of Jesus, since the early Christian sources show no interest in either, are moreover fragmentary and often legendary; and other sources about Jesus do not exist" (Bultmann, 8). Bultmann signaled the shift from historical quest to existential encounter. Building on Strauss, he began to demythologize the Gospels and reinterpret them in an existential way.

The New Quest. A student of Bultmann, Ernst Kasemann began the "new quest" in a 1953 lecture. He rejected Bultmann's method as docetic (*see* DOCETISM), because Bultmann disregarded the humanity of Jesus. While he kept most of the presuppositions of the former quest, Kasemann's goals differed. The old quest sought discontinuity between the Christ of Faith and the Jesus of history amid assumed continuity, the new quest was concerned with the person of Christ as the preached word of God and his relation to history. The major work of the new quest is Gunther Bornkamm's *Jesus of Nazareth* (1960).

The Third Quest. The most recent research into the historical Jesus is largely a reaction to the "new quest." It is multifaceted, including some from the radical tradition, a new perspective tradition, and conservatives. In the "conservative" category are I. Howard Marshall, D. F. D. Moule, and G. R. Beasley-Murray. They reject the idea that the picture of the New Testament Jesus was somehow painted by Hellenic Savior cults (*see* MITHRAISM; APOTHEOSIS).

The new perspective group places Jesus in his first-century Jewish setting. This group includes E. P. Sanders, Ben F. Meyer, Geza Vermes, Bruce Chilton, and James H. Charlesworth. The radical tradition is exemplified by the Jesus Seminar and their interest in the **Gospel of Thomas* and the **Q* document. More about this group can be found in the article, Jesus Seminar. The Jesus Seminar uses many of the methods of Strauss and Bultmann, but unlike the latter, the group is optimistic about recovering the historical individual. Their results to date, however, have yielded very different views, based on a small fragment of New Testament sayings they believe to be authentic.

Evaluation. *False Assumptions about Method and Premises.* With the exception of the conservative resurgence, all the quests have been built on false premises and proceed with fallacious or questionable methods. Most of these are examined in detail in other articles cited. False premises include:

Antisupernaturalism. Miracle accounts and any other references to the supernatural are immediately rejected. This is unjustified (*see* MIRACLE; MIRACLES, ARGUMENTS AGAINST; NATURALISM).

Fact/value dichotomy. *Kant's assumption that one can separate fact from value is clearly false, as is evident in the impossibility of separating the fact of Christ's death from its value. There is no spiritual significance in the virgin birth unless it is a biological fact. Nor can one separate the fact of a human life from its value; a murderer inescapably attacks the individual's value as a human by taking the person's life.

A false separation. The quests cannot substantiate the disjunction between the Christ of faith and the Jesus of fact. They assume, without proof, that the Gospels are not historical and that they do not set out the historical person of Jesus.

Denial of Historicity. At the core of the quests is a denial of the historical nature of the Gospels. But their historicity has been substantiated beyond that of other ancient books (*see* NEW TESTAMENT DOCUMENTS, RELIABILITY OF; NEW TESTAMENT, HISTORICITY OF; NEW TESTAMENT, NON-CHRISTIAN SOURCES).

Misunderstanding of "myth." Most quests have not understood the nature of "myth." Simply because an event is more than empirical does not mean it is less than historical. The miracle of the resurrection, for example, is more than a resuscitation of Jesus' body—but it is not less than that. As C. S. *Lewis noted, those who equate the New Testament with mythology have not studied too much New Testament; they have not studied enough myths (*see* MYTHOLOGY AND THE NEW TESTAMENT).

False Assumptions about Extra-Biblical Documents. In the most recent radical quest there is a misdirected effort to date the New Testament late and to place extra-biblical documents of *Q* and *The Gospel of Thomas*. But it is well-established that there are New Testament records before 70, while contemporaries and eyewitnesses were still alive. Further, there is no proof that *Q* ever existed as a written document. There are no manuscripts or citations. *The Gospel of Thomas* is a mid-second-century work too late to have figured in the writing of the Gospels.

Sources

C. Blomberg, *The Historical Reliability of the Gospels*
G. Bornkamm, *Jesus of Nazareth*
G. Boyd, *Jesus Under Siege*
R. Funk, *Five Gospels*
G. Habermas, *The Historical Jesus*
C. J. Hemer, *The Book of Acts in the Setting of Hellenic History*
J. Holden, *An Examination of the Jesus Seminar*
I. H. Marshall, *I Believe in the Historical Jesus*
D. Strauss, *The Life of Jesus Critically Examined*
A. Schweitzer, *The Quest of the Historical Jesus*
H. Reimarus, *Fragments*, ed. G. Lessing

Jesus Seminar. The Jesus Seminar is a consortium of New Testament scholars, directed by Robert W. Funk, who were organized in 1985 under the auspices of the Estar Institute of Santa Rosa, California. Seventy-plus scholars meet twice a year to make pronouncements about the authenticity of the words and deeds of Christ. The Seminar is comprised of liberal Catholics and Protestants, Jews, and *atheists. Most are male professors, though their number includes a pastor, a filmmaker, and three women. About half are graduates of Harvard, Claremont, or Vanderbilt divinity schools.

Writings. One of the intents of the organization is to publish critical books for a wider range of people than normally read such studies. So the group has a growing literary output. Among the works so far published: Marcus Borg, *Jesus in Contemporary Scholarship* and *Meeting Jesus Again for the First Time*; John Dominic Crossan, *In Fragments: The Aphorisms of Jesus*, *Jesus: A Revolutionary Biography*, *The Historical Jesus: The Life of a Mediterranean Peasant*, and *The Other Four Gospels: Shadows on the Contours of Canon*; Funk, *The Five Gospels* and *The Parables of Jesus*; and Burton Mack, *Jesus: A New Vision*, *The Myth of Innocence: Mark and Christian Origins*, *The Lost Gospel: The Book of Q and Christian Origins*, and *Who Wrote the New Testament: The Making of the Christian Myth*. The group's crowning effort has been a translation of the Gospels edited by Robert J. Miller, *The Complete Gospels: Annotated Scholars' Version*.

Aims of the Seminar's Work. While Seminar members produce critical works, from its inception the Jesus Seminar has sought to make its views available to the general public, rather than just the scholarly community: "We are going to try to carry out our work in full public view; we will not only honor the freedom of information, we will insist on the public disclosure of our work" (Funk, *Forum*, 1.1). To this end the Seminar has sought publicity from every possible source. A TV summit, many articles, interviews with the press, tapes, and even a possible movie are part of this public information campaign for anti-supernatural theology. Funk frankly confessed the radical nature of the work when he said, "We are probing what is most sacred to millions, and hence we will constantly border on blasphemy" (ibid., 8). This is an honest and accurate disclosure of what has happened.

Procedures of the Seminar. The group has used colored beads to vote on the accuracy of Jesus' sayings. A red bead means words that Jesus probably spoke. Pink indicates words that could probably be attributed to Jesus. Gray represents words probably, though not certainly, came from later sources. Black indicates words that Jesus almost certainly did not speak.

The vote was based on a variety of Christian writings other than the four canonical Gospels, including the fragmentary *Gospel of Peter*, the supposed but not extant *Q or *Quelle* ("source") document, the second-century *Gospel of Thomas, and the non-extant *Secret Mark*. *Thomas* is usually treated as a fifth Gospel, on a par with the four canonical books.

Results of the Voting. The results of their work is the conclusion that only fifteen sayings (2 percent) can absolutely be regarded as Jesus' actual words. About 82 percent of what the canonical Gospels ascribe to Jesus are not authentic. Another 16 percent of the words are of doubtful authenticity. The following chart breaks down the proportions of each Gospel in each category and the percentage of "authentic" sayings of Christ. Notice that *Thomas* had a higher percentage of authentic "red" votes than did either Mark or John.

Gospel Sayings	**Red**	**Pink**	**Gray**	**Black**	**Authentic**
Matthew (420 sayings)	11	61	114	235	2.6 %
Mark (177 sayings)	1	18	66	92	0.6 %
Luke (392 sayings)	14	65	128	185	3.6 %
John (140 sayings)	0	1	5	134	0.0 %
Thomas (202 sayings)	3	40	67	92	1.5 %

Conclusions of the Seminar. Several radical conclusions emerge from the work of the Jesus Seminar which seriously affect historic orthodox Christianity, to the extent that they are taken seriously by the public:

1. The "old" Jesus and "old Christianity" are no longer relevant.
2. There is no agreement about who Jesus was: a cynic, a sage, a Jewish reformer, a feminist, a prophet-teacher, a radical social prophet, or an eschatological prophet.
3. Jesus did not rise from the dead. One member, Crossan, theorizes that Jesus' corpse was buried in a shallow grave, dug up, and eaten by dogs.
4. The canonical Gospels are late and cannot be trusted.
5. The authentic words of Jesus can be reconstructed from the so-called "*Q document*," *The Gospel of Thomas*, *Secret Mark*, and *The Gospel of Peter*.

As Funk stated clearly, the Seminar concluded that "the narrative contexts in which the sayings of Jesus are preserved in the Gospels are the creation of the evangelists. They are fictive [fictional] and secondary" ("The Emerging Jesus," 11).

Evaluation. For a more extensive evaluation of the *Gospel of Thomas* and *Q* Document, see those articles. Most issues raised by the Seminar are covered in BIBLE, EVIDENCE FOR; BIBLE CRITICISM; CHRIST, DEATH OF; MIRACLES, ARGUMENTS AGAINST; NEW TESTAMENT, HISTORICITY OF and RESURRECTION, EVIDENCE FOR. A few other points can be made:

A Radical Fringe of Scholarship. The Jesus Seminar represents a radical fringe of New Testament scholarship, though one that unfortunately includes a large number of mainline scholars and pastors. The fact that some of their views are adopted by many contemporary scholars is not the point, for truth is not determined by majority vote. Most of the proofs they offer, in addition to the voting procedure, are uncompelling and often nonexistent except for quotations from one another and other liberal scholars as unimpeachable sources. While radical scholars are making considerable noise at the end of the twentieth century, in the broad range of Christian history they are a small minority.

Unjustified Antisupernaturalism. The radical conclusions of the group are based on radical presuppositions, one of which is an unjustified rejection of any miraculous intervention in history by God (*see* MIRACLES, ARGUMENTS AGAINST). One of the chief grounds for rejecting the authenticity of the canonical Gospels is the assumption that any reference to a miracle is not credible. This presupposition crept into biblical scholarship by way of David *Hume and David Strauss. David Hume's antisupernaturalism is without foundation.

Unfounded Acceptance of Late Dates. Flowing from the presumption of antisupernaturalism is the tendency to posit dates as late as possible for the writing of the Gospels (at earliest, 70 to 100, and in some arguments later). By doing this they can create enough time between the events and the recording for eyewitnesses to die off and a mythology to develop around the founder of Christianity. Thus they can say that 84 percent of the sayings of Jesus were invented later. However, there are problems with these late dates, and as archaeology broadens understanding of the first-century sources, the position is becoming untenable. Among problems:

Manuscript evidence from the very early second century strongly argues for an Asian origin in the first century.

Gospels are cited in other first-century works (*see* BIBLE, EVIDENCE FOR).

The Gospel of Luke was written before Acts, which has strong evidence for a date of no later than A.D. 60–62 (*see* ACTS, HISTORICITY OF). This is well within the lifetime of Jesus' contemporaries.

The writings of Paul speak of the historicity of the most crucial events in the Gospels, the death and resurrection of Christ. Even critical scholars date 1 Corinthians to ca. A.D. 55–56. This would place it within a quarter century of Jesus' death in 33.

Some critical scholars admit early dates for the basic Gospels. The late Bishop J. A. T. Robinson argued that they were written between 40 and 60. This would place the first records as close as seven years after the events they report.

Even the later dates of the 60s through the 80s do not allow time for mythological distortions to develop. It has been demonstrated that even two generations is too short a period to allow legendary tendencies to wipe out the hard core of historical fact (*see* MYTHOLOGY AND THE NEW TESTAMENT).

Uncritical Acceptance of Q. The method by which the Jesus Seminar was able to come to their radical conclusions with a flourish of scholarly activity was simple. They demoted the first-century and eyewitness contemporary accounts of Jesus' life (the four Gospels) to late works of mythology and replaced them with nonextant works, such as *Q*, and clearly apocryphal writings, such as *The Gospel of Thomas*. But *Q* is a purely hypothetical document. There are no manuscripts. No one ever quoted such a book or referred to its existence. It is a purely hypothetical literary reconstruction based on unjustified presuppositions. It stands in contradiction to the known evidence.

Use of *Thomas* is questionable on a number of accounts. It is clearly a second-century work, well out of range of contemporaries to the events. It has a heretical agenda, for its teaching is gnostic (*see* NAG HAMMADI GOSPELS). Its claim to be written by an apostle places it in the category of legend. Interestingly, its use to disprove the resurrection overlooks the fact that the work purports to be the words of the resurrected Christ.

Scholars of the Jesus Seminar also use *Secret Mark* and *The Gospel of Peter*. *Peter* is a second- or even third-century apocryphal work that is infamous for its outlandish legends. No one living in recent history has ever seen *Peter* or the copy of Clement's letter that supposedly contained it. How then can its content be used for scholarly judgment on the authenticity of the Gospels?

Circular Reasoning. The reasoning process of the Jesus Seminar is a sophisticated form of the logical fallacy known as *Petitio Princippi*, or begging the question. Its circular reasoning begins with a desupernaturalized view of a first-century religious figure and concludes at the same point.

Conclusion. Despite their desire and achievements for drawing wide publicity, nothing is new in the Jesus Seminar's radical conclusions. They offer only another example of unsubstantiated negative *Bible criticism. Their conclusions are contrary to the overwhelming evidence for the historicity of the New Testament and the reliability of the New Testament witnesses. They are based on an unsubstantiated antisupernatural bias.

Sources

C. Blomberg, *The Historical Reliability of the Gospels*

———, "The Seventy-Four 'Scholars': Who Does the Jesus Seminar Really Speak for?" in *CRJ* (Fall 1994)

G. Boyd, *Jesus Under Siege*

D. A. Carson, "Five Gospels, No Christ," *CT* (25 April 1994)

E. Ferguson, *Backgrounds of Earliest Christianity*

G. Habermas, *The Historical Jesus*

C. J. Hemer, *The Book of Acts in the Setting of Hellenic History*

I. H. Marshall, *I Believe in the Historical Jesus*

J. W. Montgomery, *History and Christianity*

A. N. Sherwin-White, *Roman Society and Roman Law in the New Testament*

M. J. Wilkins, et al., *Jesus Under Fire*

John, Gospel of. The Gospel of John is an important link in the argument for the deity of Christ and the truth of Christianity. Granting truth is knowable (*see* TRUTH, NATURE OF) the overall argument can be stated (*see* APOLOGETICS, OVERALL ARGUMENT):

1. The theistic God exists.
2. In a theistic universe, miracles are possible (*see* MIRACLE).
3. Miracles in connection with truth claims are acts of God that confirm the truth of God claimed by a messenger of God (*see* MIRACLES, APOLOGETIC VALUE OF).
4. The New Testament documents are historically reliable.
5. In the New Testament Jesus claimed to be God.

6. Jesus proved to be God by an unprecedented convergence of miracles.
7. Therefore, Jesus was God in human flesh.

John's Gospel speaks to the fifth premise, recording Jesus' explicit claims to deity:

> The Father judges no one, but has entrusted all judgment to the Son, that all may honor the Son just as they honor the Father. He who does not honor the Son does not honor the Father, who sent him. [5:22–23]
>
> I tell you the truth . . . before Abraham was born, I am! [8:58]
>
> I and the Father are one. [10:30]
>
> Father, glorify me in your presence with the glory I had with you before the world began. [17:5]

Other claims to Christ's deity claims are unrecorded in the Synoptics as they are in John (for instance, 9:35–38; 13;13–15, and 18:6). Clear statements of an eyewitness apostle about Christ's deity come from John:

> In the beginning was the Word and the Word was with God, and the Word was God. [1:1]
>
> No one has ever seen God, but God the One and Only, who is at the Father's side, has made him known. [1:18]
>
> Isaiah said this because he saw Jesus' glory and spoke about him. [12:39–41]
>
> "My Lord and my God." [The confession of Thomas to the risen Christ, 20:28]

Because these statements have no parallels in the other Gospels, negative critics have dismissed their authenticity. Apologists frequently avoid the issue by sticking to Jesus' claims to deity in the Synoptics (for example, Matt. 16:16–17; Mark 2:5–10; 14:61–65) and instances where he accepted worship (for example, Matt. 28:9; Mark 5:6; 15:19).

We cannot afford to bypass John entirely, however. If, as some critics claim, John created these sayings or does not accurately report them, the Gospel accounts are undermined, as well as the rich theological teachings found in John (*see* New Testament, Dating of; New Testament Documents, Reliability of).

Arguments against Historicity. Several arguments are used against the authenticity of John's record:

John was written in the second century, so an eyewitness could not have composed it. Allegedly, the writer put statements that attribute deity into the mouth of Jesus and his disciples.

If John had been written during the second century, that in itself would not make it unreliable. It is not uncommon for other records from antiquity—which critics accept—to be written centuries after the events about which they speak. The earliest life of Alexander the Great was written 200 years later, yet it is used by historians as a reliable source of information. But there is no evidence that John was written so late. No testimonial or documentary evidence contradicts the explicit claims to be an eyewitness of what Jesus said and did. John records: "This is the disciple who testifies to these things and who wrote them down. We know that his testimony is true" (John 21:24). In context the statement clearly identifies the author as the apostle John. There is no evidence to the contrary, so the *prima facie* case for an authentic Gospel is strong.

That case is strengthened by the freshness and vividness of the book, which is lacking in ancient accounts from many years after the events they relate. Background explanation, personal detail, and carefully related private conversation (e.g., John 3, 4, 8–10, 13–17) betray the work of an eyewitness (cf. John 2:6; 4:6; 6:10; 12:3, 5). For example, John (5:2) mentions five colonnades at the pool of Bethesda. Excavations between 1914 and 1938 uncovered this pool and found it to be just as John described it. Since that pool did not exist in the second century, it is unlikely any second-century fraud would have had access to such detail about persons, places, geography, and topography.

Another charge by critics is that John is too different, both in events and language, to be covering the same man and events as the Synoptic Gospels. Language issues will be discussed below. That the events differ proves too much. If John were written as long as a century after the Synoptics to promote a theological agenda, the tendency would be to refer to some of the same occurrences, simply filling them with new meaning. This does not happen. Yet there is overlap at the obvious points (the crucifixion and resurrection) and in other touchstone occurrences—Jesus walking on water, feeding the 5000, his triumphal entry into Jerusalem, and particularly the last supper. There is no substantial difference among these accounts.

The second-century hypothesis received a fatal blow with the discovery in Egypt of the "John Rylands fragment" of the Gospel, which can be dated as early as 114. John was written in Asia Minor. If copies were circulating in a small town the other side of the Mediterranean by 114, the original was certainly a first-century work.

Tradition has placed John as the last of the Gospels to be written, sometime during the 90s. However, recent research into the *Dead Sea Scrolls has caused a few scholars to date John before 70, because of its affinity with Qumran (Guthrie, 261–62). Evidence particularly noted is the simplicity of language and the light-darkness motif so common in Qumran thinking (John 1:4–9; cf. 8:12). Even liberal scholars, such as John A. T. Robinson, dated John as early as 40–65 (Robinson, 352). This would place it within a decade of the actual events. This may be a bit too early, but it reflects what has been learned about the author's first-hand acquaintance with the events recounted.

The first-century origin of John, while eyewitnesses were still alive, seems beyond serious dispute. This strongly suggests John's historicity.

John Does Not Use Parables. John's Gospel is distinctive in that it contains none of the parables so characteristic of the Synoptic Gospels. This is taken by some critics as evidence that John is a less trustworthy account. But given other similarities on essential events and teaching, it is difficult to see how the absence of parables proves that John's report is untrustworthy. Nonetheless, four points can be made:

This is an argument from silence. Silence at this point proves nothing logically except that John chose to confine his writing to other matters. He may have done so deliberately, particularly if his was the last Gospel to be written. There is no reason why John should repeat material already available. With three other Gospels in circulation for twenty or thirty years, John's purpose may have been largely supplementary. He was selective, noting that much more happened than could possibly be told (20:30–31; 21:24–25).

Jesus uses parabolic speech in John. Craig Blomberg observes that, although John contains no narrative parables, the book presents Jesus as fond of metaphors and figurative or proverbial language (Blomberg, 158). Jesus identifies himself as the good shepherd who seeks to rescue the errant sheep (10:1–16; cf., Matt. 18:12–14; Luke 15:3–7). Discipleship means servanthood (13:4–5, 12–17; cf., Luke 22:24–27). John introduces sowing versus reaping (4:37); the apprentice son (5:19–20a); slavery versus sonship (8:35); working and walking in the daylight (9:4; 11:9–10); the thief, the gatekeeper, and the sheepfold (10:1–3a); the growth of a grain of wheat (12:24); the vine and vinedresser (15:1–6); and the pain of a woman in childbirth (16:21; Blomberg, 158). Rather than showing that John's report is not authentic, such parabolic expression connects the Jesus in John with the Jesus of the Synoptics.

The book covers different times and places. John relates more private conversations, whereas Jesus spoke in parables to the unbelieving crowd (Matt. 13:13–15). Events recorded are not found in the Synoptics. John deals with the early and late ministries of Christ, whereas the Synoptics deal largely with the middle and Galilean ministries. It is understandable that Jesus said things a little differently at different times and places, as does any good itinerant preacher.

John was reaching a new audience. The absence of narrative parables suggests that this preacher's audience is not linguistically Semitic. John uses terms with almost universal religious appeal to minimize communication barriers (Carson, 46). This fits with a date of later than 70, when the Romans conquered Jerusalem and the Gospel was reaching a more diverse, non-Jewish audience.

Jesus' Sayings Are a Different Style. The assumption is made that any dissimilarity in style proves John creates rather than reports the words of Jesus. Logically this does not follow. There are at least three other possible explanations for dissimilarities: (1) The Synoptics may be more accurate than John. (2) John may be more accurate than the Synoptics. (3) They both may be accurately reporting largely different events, and some of the same events in different ways. Evidence supports the latter alternative.

The sayings are largely the same. If John is late and inaccurate, then why does he sometimes report Jesus' statements in the same words as the Synoptics? John and Mark report that Jesus told the paralytic: "Take up your bed and walk" (Mark 2:11; John 5:8). Jesus' words to the disciples who saw him walking on the water are, "It is I. Do not be afraid" (Mark 6:50; John 6:20). When Jesus appeared to the disciples, he said: "Peace be with you!" (Luke 24:36; John 20:19).

However, it is not necessary for reliable reporting to use the exact words, so long as the same meaning is conveyed. At numerous points the substance of what Jesus said is the same in John and in the Synoptic parallel. When feeding the five thousand, Jesus said, "Make the people sit down (cf. John 6:10) and Mark says Jesus commanded them to "make them all sit down" (6:39). In John Jesus defended the woman who anointed him with "Let her alone; she has kept this for the day of my burial" (12:7). Mark records: "She has come beforehand to anoint my body for burial" (14:8). Of Judas' betrayal Jesus said in John, "I tell you the truth, one of you is going to betray me" (13:21). Mark records, "I tell you the truth, one of you will betray me—one who is eating with me" (14:18). In John 13:38 Jesus said to Peter, "Will you really lay down your life for me? I tell you the truth, before the cock crows, you will disown me three times!" Luke reads, "I tell you, Peter, before the cock crows today, you will deny three times that you know me" (Luke 22:34). Here John agrees with one Synoptic and Mark deviates, mentioning two, rather than three, crowings (Mark 14:30). In John 18:11 Jesus said to Peter, "Put your sword away!" Matthew 26:52 reads, "Put your sword back in its place."

John records specific teachings that closely resemble the Synoptic Gospels:

Jesus is the "Son of man" (1:51; 5:27; 8:28; cf. Matt. 9:6; 16:13; 20:18; Mark 2:10; 8:31; 10:45; Luke 12:40; 19:10; 24:7, in all 80 occurrences).

Jesus taught with authority (2:18; 5:27; 10:18; cf. Matt. 7:29; 9:6; 28:18; Mark 1:22, 27; Luke 4:32, 5:24).

One must be born again to enter the kingdom of God (3:3; cf. Mark 10:15).

An abundant harvest awaits the laborers (4:35; cf. Matt. 9:37–38).

A prophet is without honor in his homeland (4:44; cf. Mark 6:4).

Jesus corrected Jewish tradition, especially about the Sabbath (5:9b–16; 7:22–23; cf. Matt. 12:1–13; Mark 2:23–3:5; Luke 13:10–17).

Unbelievers will be judged according to their works (5:29; cf. Matt. 25:46).

Jesus has unique Sonship with God, including the right to call God *Abba,* Father (5:37; 17:11; cf. Matt. 3:17; 18:10; Mark 14:36; Luke 3:22; 9:35; 23:46).

Jesus is the light of the world (8:12; cf. Matt. 5:14).

Jesus taught, in part, to harden hearts of those opposed to him (9:39; cf. 12:39–40; Mark 4:12; 8:17).

The good shepherd rescues his flock (10:1–16; cf. Matt. 18:12–14; Luke 15:3–7).

The Father reveals the Son; no one knows the Father but the Son (10:14–15; 13:3; 17:2, 25; cf. Matt. 11:25–27).

Jesus was tempted to abandon the way of the cross (12:27; cf. Mark 14:35–36).

Receiving Jesus means receiving the Father (12:44–45; cf. Matt. 10:40; Mark 9:37; Luke 10:16).

True discipleship means servanthood (13:4–5, 12–17; cf. Luke 22:24–27).

The disciple is not greater than his master (13:16; cf. Matt. 10:24; Luke 6:40).

The Holy Spirit will give the disciples their message to authorities (14:26; 15:26; cf. Matt. 10:19–20; Mark 13:11).

The disciples will be expelled from synagogues (16:1–4; cf. Matt. 10:17–18; Mark 13:9).

The disciples will be scattered over the world (16:32; cf. Mark 14:27).

Christians have authority to retain or forgive sins (20:23; cf. Matt. 18:18; Blomberg, 157–58).

"Johannine" type passages are in the Synoptics. Matthew 11:25–27 records a typical "Johannine" type passage that presents Jesus using the same straightforward, nonparabolic discourse that John attributes to him. In fact, it sounds so Johannine that, unless one knew it came from Matthew, the assumption would be that it came from John. Luke 10:21–22 also is in the Johannine style. Thus, the so-called "Johannine" style of Jesus' sayings is not unique to the Gospel of John. Rather, it could represent an actual mode of speaking Jesus often used.

The "I Am" Sayings of Jesus Are Unlike What Jesus Said in the Synoptics. Since the seven "I am" statements (4:26; 6:35; 8:12, 58; 10:9, 11; 11:25; 14:6) are exclusive to John, some claim it unlikely that Jesus said them, at least in that form.

Actually, the sword of this argument cuts both ways. One could argue equally that the Synoptic sayings cannot be trusted because they differ from the Johannine statements. But it is not accurate to say that the Synoptics have no statements of Jesus using this implied identification with *JHWH* of the Old Testament. "I am he" (Gk: *ego eimi*) is based in the Old Testament proclamation of God to be God (cf. Deut. 5:6; 32:39; Ps. 46:11; Isa. 40–45, passim). In Matthew 11:25–27 and Luke 10:21–22 the Synoptics use a similar style of expression. Most explicit is Jesus' statement to the high priest in Mark 14:62, "*I am* [the Christ]." In a demonstration of power approaching an epiphany, Jesus told the disciples, "Take courage! *I am* he. Don't be afraid" (Mark 6:50, emphasis added).

Also, where would John or the other authors get this remarkable form? Ancient apocryphal writers tried to make their style conform to a format that was accepted as genuine. No other known first-century religious leader used statements like these. The closest nonbiblical parallel comes from the Jewish Qumran *Damascus Document*. It states "Seekest thou the God of Gods? I am He," followed in the next chapter by "I am He, fear not, for I am before the days were" (cited in Stauffer, 179; note how God makes similar statements in Ps. 46:2 and Isa. 43:1).

The content of John's "I am" statements is implied in the Synoptics. Craig Blomberg has noted that all four Gospels depict a man whose words would last forever, who forgave sins, who related humanity's destiny to himself, who demanded absolute loyalty, who offered rest for the weary and salvation for the lost, who promised to be with his followers always, and who guaranteed that God would answer prayers in his name (166). The form's use by Jesus in both the Synoptics and John reveals his self-claim to deity. As Stauffer argued, "'I am He'—meant: where I am, there God is, there God lives and speaks" (Stauffer, 194–95).

Arguments for the general authenticity of John apply to the "I am" sections. There is no good reason to suspect that John and the Synoptics are not independently authentic. These sections agree in all major areas of overlap, often down to details. John also uses third-person statements like those more common in the Synoptics. In John 10:1–7 he obviously turns to first-person because his hearers don't understand the meaning of his third-person illustration.

> "I tell you the truth, the man who does not enter the sheep pen by the gate, but climbs in

> by some other way, is a thief and a robber. . . ." *Jesus used this figure of speech, but they did not understand what he was telling them. Therefore Jesus said again, "I tell you the truth, I am the gate for the sheep."* [John 10:1, 6–7, emphasis author's]

Jesus may have used the shorter, simpler style quoted by John on many occasions for emphasis or when the audience did not understand.

Since John stresses the antagonism of Jewish leaders to Jesus (see John 5:16, 18; 7:1; 10:31, etc.), it is understandable that "I am" statements would occur in John.

There is no proof John created the seven "I ams" or the seven "signs" (miracles) by which John supported Jesus' theme (cf. 20:30–31). Both were chosen for inclusion in the Gospel to make his point. It happens that there is no overlap of "sayings" in John with those in the Synoptics. Why should there be if he is consciously supplementing the already available Synoptics from the wealth of material that "even the world itself could not contain" (John 21:25)?

There is overlap between John and the Synoptics at some points, in particular the signs or miracles Jesus performed. Jesus' walking on the water and feeding the five thousand in John 6, and his resurrection in John 20 appear in the Synoptics with no significant variation from John's accounts. If the book shows no inauthentic additions or exaggerations in reporting the signs of Jesus, there is no reason to doubt John's reporting of what Jesus said.

Finally, it was John who wrote that Jesus promised divine activation of the memories of the apostles about "everything . . . [Jesus] said" (John 14:26; 16:13). If memories were supernaturally activated by the Holy Spirit, there is no real problem understanding how the writers of the Gospels could closely reproduce what Jesus said decades later.

The Brevity of Jesus' Sayings Shows That They Are the Words of John. Another charge regarding the style of Jesus' discourse is that the brevity shows the work of a writer as well as a redactor. This overlooks that not all John's accounts of Jesus' words are brief (cf. John 3:3–21; 5:19–47; 6:26–58; 10:1–18). The "Upper Room" discourse covers three chapters (John 14–16), rivaling the Sermon on the Mount of Matthew 5–7 in length. John 17 relates the longest prayer of Jesus.

On the other side, the Synoptics record brief statements of Christ. Matthew provides the pithy "Give to Caesar what is Caesar's, and to God, what is God's" (22:21). Mark records, "Everything is possible for him who believes" (9:23), and Luke, "Man shall not live by bread alone" (4:4). Note such statements as Luke 18:27; 23:34, 43, 46.

Why should brevity be a sign of inauthenticity? One could just as easily use this argument to conclude that Lincoln never gave the Gettysburg Address. Obviously there were times when Jesus spoke expansively and times when his words were crisp and succinct.

John shows careful attention to accuracy in Jesus' words. He distinguishes what Jesus said (which the disciples usually did not then understand) from what the disciples later came to understand what he had meant. Jesus said, "Destroy this temple, and I will raise it again in three days." John adds, "After he was raised from the dead, his disciples recalled what he had said. Then they believed the Scripture and the words that Jesus had spoken" (John 2:19, 22; cf. 20:9). What Jesus actually said to John is distinguished from what the other disciples mistook him to say (21:22–23). Other Gospels make the same distinction (cf. Mark 3:30). So, the brevity of statements recorded in John is no sign that Jesus did not actually say these things.

The "Verily, Verily" ("Amen, Amen") Statements Are Unique to John. Again, it is supposed by critics that John's unique use of "Verily, verily" (KJV) in the mouth of Jesus indicates that Jesus never really used this form of emphasis (John 1:51; 3:3, 5, 11; 5:19, 24, 25; 6:26, 32, 47, 53; 8:34, 51, 58; 10:1, 7; 12:24; 13:16, 20, 21, 38; 14:12; 16:20, 23; 21:18). This phrase is not used in the Synoptics, but "Verily, verily I say unto you" (John 13:38) has parallels in "Verily I say unto you" (Matt. 26:34 and Mark 14:30). The doubling may indicate emphasis (see Blomberg, 159). The NIV "I tell you the truth" and the NKJV "Most assuredly" capture the idea of emphasis in a single phrase.

There is no reason to suppose that Jesus did not speak that way on occasion. Jesus' discourses in John are generally at different times (early and late ministry) and in different places (Judea, rather than Galilee), and even to different people (e.g., the Samaritan woman would not have the same false political expectations of the Messiah as did the Jews—4:25–26 (see Carson, 58). John gives more private conversations than do the Synoptics. John records Jesus' private discourse to Nicodemus (chap. 3), to the woman at the well (chap. 4), to the adulteress (chap. 8), and to the disciples (chaps. 13–16). During his ministry Jesus avoided making explicit public claims to be the Messiah. Yet he did not hesitate to do so in private (4:25–26) and before the high priest (Mark 14:61–65). Jesus used speech appropriate to the occasion.

Some evangelical scholars suggest that John's doubling of *verily* (*"amen"*) was for homiletic reasons. Behind this view is the contention that the Gospel of John was composed as a sermon (cf. 20:30–31). Thus, D. A. Carson argues (46). Accordingly, Jesus may have actually said *"amen,"* but John doubled as a rhetorical device. While this is possible, it seems better to conclude that any doubling resulted from the writer's desire to express for a reader an emphasis that only a listener could have detected in the tone of Jesus' voice when he said it. Better yet, there is no reason why Jesus could not have actually said *"amen, amen"* on these occasions, just as John records. There are no parallel passages in the Synoptics that contradict this.

There Are Vocabulary Differences in John. Some 150 words of Jesus' mouth in John are not found in the other Gospels (Carson, 45). Many of these are so general that Jesus should have said them as part of his normal discourse, if he used them at all. This is offered as evidence that John created, not reported, what Jesus said.

Such an argument neglects to take into account that any good communicator uses words to fit the occasion. And since it is generally acknowledged that Jesus spoke in Aramaic, there is room for a different word choice in Greek by the recorder as translator. All of this brings up a point that applies to various arguments about the Gospels' quotations of Jesus. A discourse or dialogue may be reported verbatim or in a condensed version (Westcott, cxv–cxix). The style and purpose of reporting may vary. Carson notes, "At some point capturing the flavour of a discourse by including an array of verbatim phrases and quips may be important; at another, it may be far more strategic to zero in on the essential argument and outline it fairly, even if the language used is quite different from that of the original address" (46). Thus, many conservative scholars are willing to accept that not all Jesus' statements may be preserved *ipsissima verba* (in the exact words) but only *ipsissima vox* (with the same meaning).

Tense and other grammatical markers also influence word selection, as Carson points out. If the "historic present" is used relatively frequently in narrative, but infrequently in the discourses, the pattern has been shown to give no support to current source theories that attempt to assign these sections to different redactors (Carson, 45).

The argument against the authenticity of these statements is a form of the *petitio principii* fallacy, that is, begging the question. The only reason there is a problem is because these different modes of expression found in John are not taken into consideration in determining what constituted Jesus' style. But this begs the question by assuming that John's expressions are not part of the authentic way Jesus spoke.

The Record and Order of Events Differ. Another argument against the reliability of John's account is that the order of events is sometimes different. The vast majority of John 1–17 and 21 appears in none of the other Gospels, so relative sequence is not an issue.

John places the cleansing of the temple early in Jesus' ministry (2:13–22) but it is placed late in the Synoptics (cf. Mark 11:15–19). Jesus was fulfilling prophecy when he attacked the buying and selling in the Court of the Gentiles. He was making a vital point about extending the kingdom to the Gentile world. So it is entirely possible that Jesus did this object lesson twice, once near the beginning of his work, and after he arrived in the city for his final struggle. This is supported by differences in the accounts. John does not speak of the open hostility of the temple leadership, as does Mark, who intimates that this final cleansing reinforced their intention to kill him, "for they feared him, because the whole crowd was amazed at his teaching" (Mark 11:18). This antagonism from the authorities characterized Jesus' later ministry. That he used the same Old Testament text to rebuke them should be expected, since he was confronting them over the same sins (cf. Matt. 4:4, 7, 10).

None of the Gospels claim to be written in chronological sequence. Topical message, rather than sequence, orders the text. Within an overall chronology, if a pericope of the same event is placed in a different place, it may be serving a slightly different literary purpose. Matthew and Luke place the order of the three temptation events in a different order (cf. Matthew 4 and Luke 4). The argument that John's sequence shows that it is a late and unreliable record does not follow. It could be supplementary material or written with different themes in mind. Regardless of sequence, the events that John shares with the Synoptics show considerable agreement in detail as noted by Blomberg (156–57):

In both, Jesus gives sight to the blind, raises the dead, and cures an official's son at a distance (John 4:46b–54; Luke 7:1–10 par.).

In both, Jesus defies traditional Sabbath law interpretations (John 9:6–7; Mark 8:23–25).

Both tell of Jesus refusing to work miracles simply to satisfy his opponents (John 6:30–34; Mark 8:11–13 pars.).

Both report attempts to arrest Jesus that fail (John 8:59; 10:39; Luke 4:29–30).

Both describe his friendship with Mary and Martha (John 11:20; 12:2–3; Luke 10:38–42).

In both, he is accused of demon possession (John 10:19–21; Mark 3:22).

In both, John the Baptist is the voice crying in the wilderness of Isaiah 40:3 and the forerunner of the Messiah (John 1:23/Mark 1:2–3 pars.).

John's baptism with water is contrasted with the Messiah's coming baptism with the Spirit (John 1:26–27, 33/Mark 1:7–7 pars.).

The Spirit anoints Jesus, as testified by the Baptist (John 1:32/Mark 1:10 pars.).

The five thousand are fed (John 6:1–15/Mark 6:32–33 pars.).

Jesus walks on the water (John 6:16–21/Mark 6:45–52).

Gerhard Maier lists additional similarities between John and Matthew (cited in Blomberg, 159). This is particularly interesting since Matthew is usually viewed as the least similar to John by the critics.

Both use Old Testament quotations and announce their fulfillment.

Both record frequency, extent, location, and instructional nature of extended sermons of Jesus.

Both share elaborate farewell speeches (the Upper Room and Olivet Discourses).

Both emphasize the private instruction of the disciples.

Both cite an evangelistic purpose, with the Gospel being offered "first to the Jew and then to all the Gentiles."

John Has a Late Christology. An often-stated reason for rejecting John's accuracy in reporting Jesus' words is its supposed "late" and "highly developed" Christology, which stressed his full deity (for example, in John 1:1; 8:58; 10:30; 20:29). This objection is based on an unjustified dialectical view of doctrinal development. Critics, following F. C. Baur, read a Hegelian (*see* HEGEL, G. W. F.) developmental view into the Gospel record (Corduan, 90–92). They begin with the view that John must have been late, since his views were a synthesis of the earlier conflict between the thesis of Peter and the antithesis of Paul. But this thesis-antithesis view is itself indefensible.

Mark (held by most of these same critics to be the earliest Gospel) has deity claims by and about Christ. For example, when Jesus claimed to forgive sins the Pharisees saw this as a claim of deity and responded, "Why does this fellow talk like that? He's blaspheming! Who can forgive sins but God alone?" (Mark 2:7). And when Jesus was asked under oath whether he was the Messiah (whom the Old Testament said would be God—Ps. 45:8; Isa. 9:6; Zech. 12:10), Jesus responded clearly: "I am. And you will see the Son of Man sitting at the right hand of the Mighty One and coming on the clouds of heaven" (Mark 14:62). The reply clearly acknowledges his claim to be God, and the Sanhedrin used it to condemn Jesus of "blasphemy" (vs. 64). Outside the Gospels, Paul's Roman epistle (ca. 56), which is believed by many to be earlier than the Gospels, has a strong description of Christ's deity, proclaiming him "God over all" (Rom. 9:5).

Many of Jesus' strongest deity claims come in the context in which he is challenged or confronted by the crowd. While this applies to both John and the Synoptic Gospels (cf. Mark 2:7–10; 14:61–62; John 10:24, 30–33), John emphasizes the antagonism of "the Jews" (see John 5:16, 18; 7:1; 10:31). It is understandable that he would pay special attention to the clear claims to deity.

It was not the primary purpose of the Synoptics to stress the deity of Christ. Matthew's Jewish emphasis was on the long-awaited Messiah. Mark stressed Jesus as a Servant (Mark 10:45). Luke stressed Jesus' humanity. John's express purpose was to show that Jesus was God incarnate (1:1, 14; 20:31). It is no surprise that there are more claims to deity in his Gospel. At the very climax of his Gospel John reports that Thomas declared Christ's deity, proclaiming him as "My Lord and My God" (20:28). If this is not accurate, then John is misrepresenting the central point of his book, that Jesus' miracles led his disciples to recognize his true identity as God (see 20:28–31).

Conclusion. Arguments against the authenticity of the sayings of Jesus in John's Gospel seem to be based more on *a priori* philosophical grounds than on actual historical and textual evidence. There are reasonable explanations for differences based on where, when, to whom, and under what circumstances Jesus spoke. Most of these are accounted for on the reasonable premise that John wrote a later and consciously supplementary Gospel. He deliberately avoids repeating what the other Gospels have said unless it is really important to the theme. As seen in the areas of overlap, the parallels of John to the Synoptic Gospels are substantial.

There is no real evidence in any of these cases that John is creating, rather than reporting, what Jesus said. To the contrary, John's account is so fresh, vivid, private, detailed, and personal that it manifests an intimate, first-hand witness by the one writing it. There is reason to believe that John preserved the original words of Jesus or the same meaning, if not the exact words.

The reasons for accepting the authenticity of John's Gospel are as good or better than those supporting the Synoptics. All can be accepted in good conscience as historical. Matthew and Mark parallel Luke, and Luke discusses its own historiographical method and accuracy (*see* ACTS, HISTORICITY OF):

> Many have undertaken to draw up an account of the things that have been fulfilled among us, just as they were handed down to us by those who from the first were eyewitnesses and servants of the word. Therefore, since I myself have carefully investigated everything from the beginning, it seemed good also to me to write an orderly account for you, most excellent Theophilus, so that you may know the certainty of the things you have been taught. [Luke 1:1–4]

If Matthew and Mark tell substantially the same story as Luke, then they are just as historically reliable as Luke. And if John's parallel material does not deviate in substance from the Synoptics, the burden of proof is on the critics to show solid reasons why his testimony should not be taken as historically reliable (*see* NEW TESTAMENT, HISTORICITY OF).

John's differences in language use from the Synoptics can be explained largely by location (Judean), date (early and late ministry), and nature (many private conversations). The "I am" claims can be understood as shorter, simpler statements Jesus made to those who did not at first understand him. Indeed, the fact that John's account is so intimate, fresh, and detailed argues strongly for its authenticity.

John's link in the apologetic argument is one of the strongest in the chain. Indeed, it is the only Gospel that claims to be written by an eyewitness apostle (John 21:24–25). Carson concludes: "It is altogether plausible that Jesus sometimes spoke in nothing less than what we think of as 'Johannine' style, and that John's style was to some degree influenced by Jesus himself. When all the evidence is taken together, it is not hard to believe that when we listen to the voice of the Evangelist in his description of what Jesus said, we are listening to the voice of Jesus himself" (Carson, 48).

Sources

C. Blomberg, *The Historical Reliability of the Gospels*
F. F. Bruce, *The New Testament Documents: Are They Reliable?*
D. F. Carson, *The Gospel According to John*
W. Corduan, "Transcendentalism: Hegel," in *Biblical Errancy: Its Philosophical Roots*, N. L. Geisler, ed.
R. T. France, *The Evidence for Jesus*
N. L. Geisler, *Christian Apologetics*
D. Guthrie, *New Testament Introduction: The Gospels and Acts*
I. H. Marshall, *I Believe in the Historical Jesus*
J. A. T. Robinson, *Redating the New Testament*
E. Stauffer, *Jesus and His Story*
R. L. Thomas, *A Harmony of the Gospels*
B. F. Westcott, *The Gospel According to St. John*. Vol. 1

Josephus. *See* **FLAVIUS JOSEPHUS.**

Joshua's Long Day. *See* **SCIENCE AND THE BIBLE.**

Judaism. *See* **BIBLE, EVIDENCE FOR; CHRIST, DEITY OF; CHRIST, MIRACLES OF; TRINITY; PROPHECY, AS PROOF OF BIBLE.**

Justin Martyr. Justin Martyr (100[?]–164) was one of the early-second-century Christian apologists (*see* CLASSICAL APOLOGETICS). He was born of pagan parents in Samaria. He embraced Christianity in 130. Later, he taught at Ephesus, where he engaged in, and wrote, *Dialogue with Trypho the Jew* (ca. 130). Eventually, he opened a Christian school in Rome. There he wrote his *First Apology* (ca. 155). *Second Apology* (ca. 161) was addressed to the Roman Senate. His emphasis on Greek philosophy and reason has led some to wrongly conclude that he was a rationalist. Like other early church fathers, Justin believed in the inspiration and divine authority of Scripture.

Alleged Rationalism. Cited as evidence of his alleged rationalism is Justin's statement that even Greeks who "lived a reasonable and earnest life" knew Christ the Logos (2.8). He went so far as to say that Christ "is the Word of whom every race of men were partakers; and those who lived reasonably *(meta logou)* are Christians, even though they have been thought atheists" (1.46).

The Role of Reason. These citations notwithstanding, it is unwarranted to conclude that Justin believed that pagans could be philosophized into the kingdom. His critics misunderstand a subtle view of *faith and reason.

Justin stated emphatically that his faith was in Christ, not Socrates; it was in Christianity, not philosophy. He wrote: "And the right Reason [Christ], when He came, proved that not all opinions nor all doctrines are good, but that some are evil, while others are good" (ibid., 2.9). Justin believed Christianity superior to Greek philosophy, declaring, "Our doctrines, then appear to be greater than all human teaching. . . . For whatever either lawgivers or philosophers uttered well, they elaborated by finding and contemplating some part of the Word. But since they did not know the whole Word, which is Christ, they often contradicted themselves" (ibid., 2.10). Christian teachings "are more lofty than all human philosophy" (ibid., 2.15). Justin stated that no one trusted in Socrates enough to die for him, as they did for the teachings and presence of Christ (ibid., 2.10).

Like many other early Fathers, Justin believed that what truth there was in Greek philosophy was borrowed from divine revelation of Hebrew Scripture (ibid., 1.60). At best, Greek philosophy had only partial and dim truth, but Christianity had truth completely and clearly. Hence, "whatever things were rightly said among all men, are the property of us Christians" (ibid., 2.13).

View of Resurrection. Since Justin was so close in time to the apostles and since the resurrection is so crucial to Christianity, his view of the resurrection is of more than passing interest (*see* RESURRECTION, EVIDENCE OF).

Resurrection Is Possible. Against those who denied the resurrection, Justin confronted those who said they were believers yet thought it impossible that God could raise the dead. God, he said, had demonstrated his power in creating the first man, "for he was made from the earth by God. . . . But now we are demonstrating that the resurrection of the flesh is possible" (in *Ante-Nicene Fathers*, 1.294–99). Justin declares, "Let the unbelieving be silent, even though they themselves do not believe. But, in truth, He has even called the flesh to the resurrection, and promises to it everlasting life. For where he promises to save man, there He gives the promise to the flesh" (Justin., chap. 8).

A Physical Resurrection (see RESURRECTION, PHYSICAL NATURE OF). Justin admitted that there were those who maintained that Jesus had appeared only in a spiritual, with only the appearance of flesh. Such people robbed Christians of a great promise (ibid., chap. 2). "If the resurrection were only spiritual, it was requisite that He, in raising the dead, should show the body lying apart by itself, and the soul living apart by itself. But now He did not do so, but raised the body, confirming in it the promise of life." Otherwise, why did Christ rise in the body in which he had been crucified and let the disciples handle his body when they doubted? "And they were by every kind of proof persuaded that it was Himself, and in the body, they asked Him to eat with them, that they might thus still more accurately ascertain that He had in verity risen bodily" (Justin, chap. 9). Justin Martyr observed that Jesus also proved the possibility of flesh ascending to heaven, showing that the dwelling place of the physical resurrection body of Christians is in heaven.

"The resurrection is a resurrection of the flesh which died. For the spirit dies not; the soul is in the body, and without a soul it cannot live" (ibid., chap. 10).

Conclusion. The first apologists, like Justin, were not as systematic as such later apologists as *Thomas Aquinas. Nevertheless, Justin was far from a rationalist in his use of reason. He believed firmly in the superiority and necessity of divine revelation. However, there is no doubt that Justin, like classical apologists after him, used reason to explain and defend the Christian faith (*see* CLASSICAL APOLOGETICS).

Sources

H. Chadwick, "Justin Martyr's Defense of Christianity," *BJRL* 47 (1965)

F. L. Cross, *The Oxford Dictionary of the Christian Church*

Justin Martyr, "Apologia," in A. Roberts and J. Donaldson, ed., *The Ante-Nicene Fathers*, vol. 1

———, *Dialogue with Trypho the Jew*

———, *First Apology*

———, "Fragments of the Lost Work of Justin on the Resurrection," in A. Roberts and J. Donaldson, eds., *The Ante-Nicene Fathers*, vol. 1

———, *Second Apology*

Kk

Kabir (Kabirpanthis). Kabir was an Indian teacher and religious reformer who flourished in fifteenth-century North India. He revolted against the caste system of Hinduism (*see* HINDUISM, VEDANTA) and spawned a number of sects, the last of which was *Sikhism. His disciples were called Kabirpanthis and were drawn from Hinduism and Islam.

Not surprisingly, he was disliked by both Hindus and Muslims. Brahmans decried him as an associate of a woman of ill-fame. Kabir was denounced by the king of Delhi for allegedly laying claim to deity. He died at Maghar near Gorakhpur. His followers believe that he was an incarnation of deity whom his mother found floating on a lotus (*see* APOTHEOSIS; DIVINE BIRTH STORIES). There are also legends about his mother being a virgin, or that he was born from his mother's hand while she was widowed.

Kabir left no writings, but he did inspire rhyming couplets, hymns, poems, and odes (found in Khas Grantha). Some fifty years after his death many of Kabir's sayings were compiled by Bhago Das. A number of these are included in the Adi Granth of the Sikhs. He was probably a disciple of Ramanand of the Viasnava school of thought. His teaching was one of the main sources drawn on by Nanak Shah, the founder of Sikhism. He was one of the first thinkers to try to influence both Hinduism and Islam. He had some knowledge of Sufism, a mystical cult of Islam (*see* ISLAM; MYSTICISM).

It is not clear whether he believed in a distinct heaven or *hell. He did, however, believe in reincarnation. His followers believe that souls enter into heaven or hell between their incarnations (Burn, 633). Kabir was antiritualistic. He rejected the outward symbols and practices of Hinduism. He was also theistic, believing in a supreme being called Ram. His God had several names: Ram, Ali, and Karim. Polytheism is an illusion *(maya)*. Contrary to Hinduism and Islam, he believed that salvation was by faith, not by works. In the search for God a guide is necessary. However, such a teacher should not be accepted blindly without being tested. Since we all owe our existence to the same God, we should show tenderness to all that live.

An important teaching of Kabir is the doctrine of the Sabda, or the Word. Any one who wished to know the truth must turn from the many words to the Word. The Word is the gateway to truth. He said, "I am a lover of the Word, which has shown me the unseen (God)" (Burn, 633).

The Alleged Resurrection of Kabir. After his death in 1518, his Muslim and Hindu followers were divided over whether to cremate his body, a practice Hindus favor and Muslims oppose. Kabir himself is said to have appeared to stop the controversy. When he directed them to draw back the cloth placed over his body, they found only flowers. His Hindu followers burned half of the flowers and the Muslims buried the other half. There are significant problems with any attempt to verify such claims. And the differences between them and the resurrection of Christ are decisive (*see* RESURRECTION, EVIDENCE FOR; RESURRECTION CLAIMS IN NON-CHRISTIAN RELIGIONS).

Sources

R. Burn, "Kabir, Kabirpanthis," in *ERE*

———, "Sikhs, Siks, Sikhism" in *The New Schaff-Herzog Encyclopedia*

G. Habermas, "Resurrection Claims in Non-Christian Religions," *RS* 25 (1989)

———, "Did Jesus Perform Miracles?" in M. Wilkins, ed., *Jesus Under Fire*

Kahler, Martin. Martin Kahler (1835–1912) studied theology at Heidelberg, Tübingen, and Hälle and was professor at the University of Hälle. He once referred to his studies under F. C. Baur at Tübingen as a "critical cold water bath" (see Strimple, 90). His principal works in theology were *Die Wissenschaft der christlichen Lehre* (1883) and *Geschichte der protestantischen Dogmatik im 19. Jahrhundert* (pub. 1962). His most influential work, *The So-Called Historical Jesus and the Historic, Biblical Christ* (1892) was translated into English in 1964.

Kahler is credited as the impetus for the "second quest" for the historical Jesus (*see* CHRIST OF FAITH VS. JESUS OF HISTORY; QUEST FOR HISTORICAL JESUS). Kahler attacked the nineteenth-century attempt to reconstruct the Jesus of History as an exercise in speculation. He claimed the "real Christ" is the Christ of faith, not the Jesus who is the result of so-called historical research (*see* BIBLE CRITICISM). The real Christ is the Christ of the Christian *kerygma* (proclamation), who is available to all.

Kahler's views gave impetus to both conservatives and liberals. Liberal and neo-orthodox accepted his conclusion that faith cannot be dependent on historical research (*see* FIDEISM). Conservatives rejoiced when he repudiated attempts to separate the Jesus of history from the Christ of faith.

Misunderstanding Kahler. Kahler is the father of the German distinction between the "historical" (*historisch*) Jesus and the "historic" (*geschichtlich*) Christ. However, it is doubtful that he meant this distinction to be used as it has been in New Testament critical scholarship. When Kahler referred to the "so-called" historical Jesus, he had in mind the reconstructed Jesus who resulted from liberal critical scholarship, not the Jesus of the first century. As Robert Strimple put it, "Kahler's treatise and its title are misused when they are appealed to in support of the twentieth-century distinction between 'the Jesus of History' and 'the Christ of faith.'" As Carl E. Braaten said in his "Introduction" to the English translation of *The So-Called Historical Jesus*, "The 'historical Jesus' is not the earthly Jesus as such, but rather Jesus insofar as he can be made the object of historical-critical research. The term has primary reference to the problem of historical knowledge, and does not intend to deny or devalue the historicity of revelation" (Strimple, 92).

Kahler never denied the historical reliability of the New Testament. He did not reject the general picture of Christ presented in Scripture. He simply insisted that neither the Gospel sources nor the historian's naturalistic methods were adequate to produce a true biography of the real Jesus (ibid., 93). He did not deny that the Gospels present "a trustworthy picture of the Savior for believers" (ibid., 94).

Kahler emphasized that using Ernst *Troelsch's principles of analogy cannot yield the real Jesus. This requires analogies in the present through which we can understand the past (*See* ANALOGY, PRINCIPLE OF; HISTORY, OBJECTIVITY OF). "The distinction between Jesus Christ and ourselves is not one of degree, but of kind" (ibid.).

Thus the canons of naturalistic history can never discover the incarnate Son of God.

"Kahler sought to deliver the Christian believer from the tyranny of the expert, the papacy of the professor" writes Strimple (ibid., 95). He asked, "Should we expect [believers] to rely on the authority of the learned men when the matter concerns the source from which they are to draw the truth for their lives? I cannot find sure footing in probabilities or in a shifting mass of details, the reliability of which is constantly changing" (Kahler, 109, 111). This is reminiscent of Gotthold Lessing and his "ugly ditch" and the later question by Søren *Kierkegaard, "How can something of an historical nature be decisive for an eternal happiness?" (Kierkegaard, 86). However, Kahler never understood his view in the sense in which *Bultmann and later critics have taken it to pit the Christ of faith against the Jesus of history.

Reliable but Not Inerrant. Kahler did reject verbal inspiration and inerrancy of Scripture (*see* BIBLE, EVIDENCE OF), which he called an "authoritarian faith" (Kahler, 72). He derided the idea that only the inerrancy of Scripture regarding every incidental matter could guarantee its trustworthiness about the central point. He believed we should "approach the Bible without detailed theories about its nature and origin." The Gospel tradition was "inherently fallible" and the Bible as a book "contains" God's revelation (Kahler, 91, 106, 112–14).

Nevertheless he maintained that the Bible is the only fully sufficient means of coming to the "safe harbor" of faith in the living Christ. For "the more converse a person has with the Bible itself, the more he finds that the drawing power of the Savior merges with the authority of the Bible" (ibid., 76). He added, "We have been hasty in following Lessing's counsel to read the Bible as we read other books" (ibid., 123).

According to Kahler, the Bible presents a generally reliable picture of the historical Christ. "The biblical picture of Christ, so lifelike and unique beyond imagination, is not a poetic idealization originating in the human mind. The reality of Christ himself has left its ineffaceable impress upon this picture" (ibid., 79–90, 95). This impression of Christ is once again found in the "big picture" of the Bible, not the minute one:

> Nowhere in the Gospels do we detect a rigorous striving for accuracy of observation or for preservation of detail. . . . Nevertheless, from these fragmentary traditions, these half-understood recollections, these portrayals colored by the writers' individual personalities, these heartfelt confessions, these sermons proclaiming him as Savior, there gazes upon us a vivid and coherent image of a Man, an image we never fail to recognize. In his incomparable deeds and life (including his resurrection appearances) this Man has engraved his image on the mind and memory of his followers with such sharp and deeply etched features that it

could be neither obliterated nor distorted. [ibid., 141–42]

This is "a tangible human life, portrayed in a rich and concrete though brief and concise manner." Once we get past the demand for an infallible biblical record, we can appreciate even the trustworthiness of the legends, so far as this is conceivable" (ibid.). This is not a fundamentalist's view of Scripture, but it is far from the radical liberal who denies the basic historicity of the Gospels.

While Kahler upheld the general reliability of Scripture, he did not place his faith in the historical. Faith is generated in the heart by God. He wrote, "We want to make absolutely clear that ultimately we believe in Christ, not on account of any authority, but because he himself evokes such faith from us" (ibid., 87). The independent faith of the New Testament, was in Kahler's mind expressed by the Samaritans in John 4:42: "We no longer believe just because of what you said; now we have heard for ourselves, and we know that this man really is the Savior of the world" (ibid., 76–77).

Evaluation. The question of the historicity and inspiration of Scripture is dealt with in detail in such articles as ACTS, HISTORICITY OF; BIBLE CRITICISM; BIBLE, EVIDENCE FOR; LUKE, ALLEGED ERRORS IN; MIRACLE, MYTH AND, and NEW TESTAMENT, HISTORICITY OF. The attempt to separate fact and faith is treated in such articles as FIDEISM; FAITH AND REASON, and KANT, IMMANUEL. The attempt to build a wall between faith and history is discussed in the articles CHRIST OF FAITH VS. JESUS OF HISTORY and JESUS SEMINAR.

While it is true that faith is ultimately not based on the historical, but on God who evokes it, this does not mean that the Christian faith is not focused in and supported by the historical (*see* HOLY SPIRIT, ROLE IN APOLOGETICS). Neither does it mean that the revelation from God that evokes true faith is not mediated through the historical. God is the primary and remote cause, but the historical data about Christ is the secondary and mediate cause of the revelation that evokes faith.

Sources

G. Blomberg, *The Historical Reliability of the Gospels*

M. J. Borg, *Jesus in Contemporary Scholarship*

C. E. Braaten, "Martin Kahler on the Historic, Biblical Christ," in R. A. Harrisville, *The Historical Jesus and the Kerygmatic Christ*

G. Habermas, *The Historical Jesus*

M. Kahler, *The So-Called Historical Jesus and the Historic, Biblical Christ*

S. Kierkegaard, *Concluding Unscientific Postscripts*

J. P. Meyer, *A Marginal Jew*

R. N. Soulen, *Handbook of Biblical Criticism*, 2d ed.

R. Striple, *Modern Search for the Real Jesus*

***Kalam* Cosmological Argument.** The cosmological argument is the argument from creation to a Creator. It argues *a posteriori*, from effect to cause and is based on the principle of causality (*see* CAUSALITY, PRINCIPLE OF; FIRST PRINCIPLES). This states that every event has a cause, or that every thing that begins has a cause.

The *kalam* (Arabic: "eternal") argument is a horizontal (linear) form of the cosmological argument. The universe is not eternal, so it must have had a Cause. That Cause must be considered God. This argument has a long and venerable history among such Islamic philosophers as *Alfarabi, Al Ghazli, and *Avicenna. Some scholastic philosophers also used it, especially Bonaventure. The argument, however, was opposed by Thomas Aquinas, who believed it philosophically possible (though biblically untrue) that God could have caused the universe from eternity.

Essence of the Argument. The basic outline of the *kalam* argument is:

1. Everything that had a beginning had a cause.
2. The universe had a beginning.
3. Therefore, the universe had a cause.

Scientific and philosophical lines of evidence are generally given in support of the crucial second premise. The scientific evidence is based heavily on the Second Law of Thermodynamics (*see* THERMODYNAMICS, LAWS OF), which affirms that the universe is running out of usable energy and, hence, cannot be eternal. Other supportive evidence is taken from big bang cosmology, including the expanding universe and the purported radiation echo of the original explosion—all of which are taken to support the idea of a beginning of the universe.

The philosophical argument for a beginning can be summarized:

1. If an infinite number of moments occurred before today, then today would never have come, since it is impossible to traverse an infinite number of moments.
2. But today has come.
3. Hence, there was a finite number of moments before today; the universe had a beginning.

Criticisms. Criticisms have been offered against the *kalam* argument. The most significant are included here, with responses by proponents of the argument (*see also* BIG BANG THEORY).

Eternal Eventless Universe. Some suggest that big bang only signals the first eruption in a previously eternal universe. That is, the universe had eternal quiescence before this first event. The big bang singularity only marks the transition from primal physical stuff. Hence, there is no need for a Creator to make something out of nothing.

No known natural laws could account for this violent eruption out of eternal quietude. Some theists assert that an eternally quiet universe is physically impossible, since it would have to exist at absolute zero, which is impossible. Matter at the beginning was anything but cold, being collapsed into a fireball with temperatures in excess of billions of degrees Kelvin. In a lump of matter frozen to absolute zero, no first event could occur. Finally, positing eternal primordial stuff does nothing to account for the incredible order that follows the moment of the big bang (*see* ANTHROPIC PRINCIPLE). Only an intelligent Creator can account for this.

Rebounding Universe. Some scientists have suggested that the big bang may only be the most recent in an eternal process of expansion and collapse. There are several problems with this hypothesis. There is no real scientific evidence for this speculation. It contradicts the Second Law, which would demand that, even if the universe were expanding and contracting, it would still be running down, so that it would ultimately collapse anyway. Logically and mathematically, the evidence for the big bang suggests that originally there was no space, no time, and no matter. Hence, even if the universe were somehow going through expansion and contraction from this point on, at the beginning it came into existence from nothing. This would still call for an initial Creator.

Steady State Theory. Fred Hoyle devised the steady-state theory to avoid the need to posit a first cause. According to this hypothesis, hydrogen atoms are spontaneously coming into existence to keep the universe from running down. If so, then it would not need a beginning, since it is not running out of usable energy. There are, however, two serious problems with this speculation. First, there is no scientific evidence that hydrogen atoms are coming into existence. This has never been observed anywhere. Second, the belief that hydrogen atoms are coming into existence out of nothing is itself *ex nihilo* creation (*see* CREATION, VIEWS OF). It does not explain what (or Who) is creating them. Indeed, it is contrary to the fundamental principle of science (and rational thought) that everything that comes to be had a cause.

No Need for a Cause. Some *atheists argue that there is nothing incoherent about something coming into existence from nothing. They insist that the universe could come into existence "by nothing and from nothing" (Kenny, 66). Proponents of the *kalam* argument offer several points in response. First, this is contrary to the established principle of causality. It is contrary to the scientific enterprise, which seeks a causal explanation. It is counterintuitive to believe that things just pop into existence. Many argue that the idea that nothing can cause something is logically incoherent, since "nothing" has no power to do anything—it does not even exist.

An Infinite Series. Some thinkers believe an infinite number of moments is possible, since in mathematics infinite series are possible. For example, an infinite number of points exists between the ends of my ruler (*see* GOD, OBJECTIONS TO PROOFS FOR). In response to this objection, proponents of the *kalam* argument insist that there is a difference between a *mathematical* infinite series and an *actual* infinite series. Mathematical series are *abstract,* but actual series are *concrete*. In a concrete series it is impossible to have an infinite number, since no matter how long it is one more can always be added. But this would make it more than infinitely long, which is impossible. Further, that one can get an infinite number of abstract (dimensionless) points between the book ends on my desk does not mean one can get an infinite number of books (or even sheets of paper) between them, no matter how thin they are.

Others object that if God knows the future, which is endless, then he knows an infinite series of events. And if he knows it, then it must be possible no matter how contrary to our intuitions it may be. But defenders point out that the future is not an *actual* infinite series but only a *potential* one, there always being the possibility of one more event. Further, if an actual infinite series is impossible, then God cannot know it, since God cannot know the impossible, only the actual and the possible.

No Personal God. Some have objected that the *kalam* argument does not prove God is personal or intelligent. Hence, it is not helpful to Christian theism which believes in an intelligent Creator. In response, some theists argue that only a being with free choice could bring something from nothing. Also, few theists believe that the cosmological argument *alone* proves a theistic God. It must be combined with the teleological argument and/or moral argument to show that God is also intelligent and moral. Second, some proponents of the *kalam* argument offer arguments for the personality of the First Cause, apart from the teleological or moral arguments. Three have been suggested.

The argument from a First Cause can be stated:

1. The universe had a First Cause.
2. This First Cause's act to create was either determined, undetermined, or self-determined.
3. But it cannot be determined, since there is nothing before the First Cause.
4. Neither can it be undetermined, since this is contrary to the principle of causality.
5. Hence, the act to create must have been self-determined.

6. But self-determined acts are free acts, for this is what is meant by a free act (*see* FREE WILL).
7. Therefore, the act by which the First Cause created the world must have been a free act of an intelligent, personal being.

The argument from the nature of intellectual causes can be stated:

1. An intelligent cause is characterized by effects which have ordered, regular effects.
2. According to the *anthropic principle the universe was "fine tuned" or "pre-fitted" from the very moment of its big bang origin for the eventual emergence of human life. The most infinitesimal change of conditions in any way would have made life as we know it impossible.
3. Therefore, the First Cause must have been an intelligent cause.

The argument from the nature of natural causes states that natural causes have certain characteristics not present prior to the moment of the creation of the universe. The argument can be stated:

1. Natural causes have predetermined conditions.
2. But there were not predetermined conditions before the moment of the big bang origin of the space-time universe.
3. Therefore, the Cause was not a natural cause; it must have been a non-natural cause without predetermined conditions.
4. The only known cause which has these characteristics is a free cause.
5. Hence, the First Cause was a free cause.

Limits to the Argument. *The Argument and God's Continued Existence.* Three objections have more validity than others. They do not invalidate what the *kalam* argument demonstrates, but they show its severe limitations. This argument cannot prove that any God now exists. Therefore, it cannot disprove *deism. Further, its assumptions are unacceptable to a *pantheist, so it is useless against pantheism.

The *kalam* argument as such does not prove that any God now exists or necessarily exists. It is an argument about how the universe *originated,* not how it is *sustained.* It shows that a First Cause was needed to explain how the universe *came into being.* This does not mean there is no way to rectify this inadequacy. One can argue that this First Cause must now exist, since the only kind of being that can cause a contingent being (i.e., one that can come to be) is a Necessary Being. A Necessary Being cannot come to be or cease to be. However, this borrows from the vertical cosmological argument to make up the lack in the horizontal cosmological argument. It might be easier just to begin with the vertical form.

The Argument and Deism. Since the *kalam* argument as such does not prove that God is necessary to sustain the here-and-now existence of the universe, it has deistic (*see* DEISM) tones. This does not mean that this argument denies the possibility of miracles, but it denies the ontological basis for God's immanence. A God who is not, as the horizontal *cosmological argument shows he is, the here-and-now cause of the very existence of the universe, is deistically remote. The argument shows that God was needed to get the universe going, which is precisely what deists believe occurred. Again, this problem is not rectifiable unless one imports help from the vertical form of the cosmological argument, showing how a Necessary Being is necessary at all times to sustain all contingent beings at every moment of their existence.

The Argument and Pantheism. Neither does the *kalam* argument disprove pantheism. In fact, it begs the question with pantheism by assuming the reality of the finite world. No pantheist would grant the premises that a finite, space-time world really exists and is actually running down, or that time is real, involving actual discrete units that pass in succession. Hence, the *kalam* argument is not effective in combating pantheism. What value to theism is an argument that eliminates neither deism or pantheism? There appears to be no solution that does not involve appeal to the vertical form of the cosmological argument. The vertical form of the cosmological argument would appear to be necessary to sustain the *kalam* argument.

Sources

T. al-F. Al-Ghazali, *Incoherence of the Philosophers,* trans. S. A. Kamali

Al-Kindi, *On First Philosophy*

Bonaventure, *2 Sententiarium* I.I.I.2.I–6

W. Craig, *The Existence of God and the Beginning of the Universe*

———, *The* Kalam *Cosmological Argument*

A. Kenny, *Five Ways*

J. P. Moreland, "The Cosmological Argument," in *Scaling the Secular City*

Kant, Immanuel. Immanuel Kant (1724–1804) was born in Königsberg, East Prussia. He studied and later taught at Königsberg University. He never married, and lived a highly regulated life. Kant's major works were *General History of Nature and Theory of the Heavens* (1755) which propounds the nebular hypothesis; *Critique of Pure Reason* (1781); *Prolegomena to Any Future Metaphysics* (1783); *Critique of Practical Reason* (1790); *Critique of Judgment* (1790); *Religion within the Limits of Reason Alone* (1793); *Metaphysics of Morals* (1797).

Kant's Philosophical *Agnosticism. Before Kant the two dominant European streams of thought were *rationalism and *empiricism. The rationalists included René *Descartes (1596–1650), Benedict de *Spinoza (1632–1677), and Gottfried *Leibniz (1646–1716). The empiricists were led by John *Locke (1632–1704), George *Berkeley (1685–1753), and David *Hume (1711–1776). The rationalists stressed the *a priori* and the empiricists the *a posteriori*. Rationalists believed in innate ideas, but empiricists insisted we are born a *tabula rasa*. Kant was trained in the rationalist tradition, but in his own words he was "awakened from his dogmatic slumbers" by the Scottish skeptic Hume.

The genius of Kant was in synthesizing these two divergent epistemologies (*see* EPISTEMOLOGY). The empiricists, he concluded, are right that we are born blank slates, with no innate ideas. The content of all knowledge comes *a posteriori* from experience. On the other hand, the rationalists correctly stress that there is an *a priori* dimension to knowledge. While the *content* of all knowledge comes through the senses, the *form* or *structure* is provided by the *a priori* forms of sensation and categories of the mind (*Critique of Pure Reason,* 173–75, 257–75).

The price of the Kantian synthesis was high: Lost in his model of the knowing process was the ability to know reality. If Kant was right, we know how we know, but we no longer really know. For if all knowledge is formed or structured by *a priori* categories, we can only know things as they appear *to us*, not as they are *in themselves*. We can know *phenomena* but not *noumena*. Thus, the net epistemological gain was the ultimate ontological loss. Reality or the thing-in-itself, including God, is forever beyond us. What is left for us is the thing-to-me, which is appearance but not reality. Thus, Kant's view ends in philosophical agnosticism.

Kant offered a second reason for his agnosticism, the antinomies of reason (*see* ANTINOMY). When categories of understanding are applied to reality, antinomies result. Two will illustrate the point. The antinomy about time states:

Thesis: The world must have had a beginning, otherwise an infinite number of moments passed by now. But this is impossible, since an infinite cannot be traversed.

Antithesis: But the world could not begin in time, otherwise there was time before time began which is impossible.

In the antinomy of causality:

Thesis: Not every cause has a cause, otherwise the series would never begin, which it has. So, there must be a first cause.

Antithesis: But the series cannot have a beginning, since everything has a cause. So, there cannot be a first cause.

Since reason, when applied to reality, ends in contradictions, one must be content to apply reason only to the *phenomenal* world, the world to me and not to the *noumenal* world, the world in itself.

Kant's View of God. Kant believed in God, but he insisted that God's existence cannot be proven (*see* GOD, OBJECTIONS TO PROOFS FOR). All proofs for God are invalid. The cosmological argument and teleological argument are based on the ontological argument, which is invalid. Each depends on the concept of a Necessary Being. But statements about existence are not necessary. Necessity characterizes thought, not existence. A Necessary Being is not a self-clarifying concept. What is logically necessary is not actually necessary. Beside this, an infinite regress is possible. And a *noumenal* (real) cause can't be derived from a phenomenal (appearance) effect.

The ontological argument leaves experience (when speaking of the highest possible cause) and soars into the realm of pure ideas. Further, existence is not a *predicate* (attribute) but only an *instance* of something. For example, the dollar in my mind has the same attributes as the one in my wallet. The only difference is that one exists and the other does not.

Kant did not believe the existence of God could be proven by theoretical reason, but did believe it was a necessary postulate of practical reason (*see* MORAL ARGUMENT FOR GOD). A summary of his reasoning in *Critique of Practical Reason* goes like this:

1. The greatest good for all persons is that they have happiness in harmony with duty.
2. All persons should strive for the greatest good.
3. What persons ought to do, they can do.
4. But persons are not able to realize the greatest good in this life unless there is a God.
5. Therefore, we must postulate a God and a future life in which the greatest good can be achieved.

Kant's Antisupernaturalism. Kant not only synthesized rationalism and empiricism but gave impetus to modern agnosticism and deism. His impact on the history of philosophy has been felt especially in epistemology and metaphysics. In one sense, Kant's view of miracles is far more helpful to naturalism than is Hume's. Hume's attack on supernaturalism is frontal, while Kant's is subterranean (*see* MIRACLES, ARGUMENTS AGAINST). For Kant, miracles are not essential to true religion.

Morality and True Religion. Like Spinoza, Kant believed that morality is the heart of true religion, though their justifications for this conclusion differed from one another. According to Kant, theoretical reason can never reach God (see *Critique of Pure Reason*). God can only be known by practical reason (see *Critique of Practical Reason Alone*). In view of the fact that we cannot know that there is a God but must fulfill the moral imperative, we must live assuming there is a God.

Foreshadowing Friedrich *Schleiermacher (1768–1834), Kant claimed that practical or moral reason must determine what is essential to religion. This moral reason should be a guide to interpreting the Bible (*see* BIBLE CRITICISM). He even admitted that "frequently this interpretation may, in the light of the text (of the revelation), appear forced—it may often really be forced; and yet if the text can possibly support it, it must be preferred to a literal interpretation" (*Religion within the Limits,* 100–1). The Bible's moral teaching "cannot but convince him of its divine nature" (ibid., 104).

With morality as the rule for truth, miracles become an appropriate introduction to Christianity, but not strictly necessary for it. Moral religion must "in the end render superfluous the belief in miracles in general." To believe that miracles can be helpful to morality is "senseless conceit" (ibid.).

Kant affirmed that the life of Christ may be "nothing but miracles," but warned that in the use of these accounts "we do not make it a tenet of religion that the knowing, believing, and professing of them are themselves means whereby we can render ourselves well-pleasing to God" (ibid., 79–80). By this he implies that belief in miracles is not essential to Christian faith.

Naturalistic Biblical Criticism. The very nature of a miracle is unknown. "We cannot know anything at all about supernatural aid," Kant wrote (ibid., 179). One thing of which we can be sure is that, if a miracle flatly contradicts morality, it cannot be of God. What father would kill a son who is, so far as he knows, perfectly innocent (ibid., 82)? Thus the moral law disqualifies the story of Abraham's willingness to sacrifice Isaac in Genesis 22. Kant carried this moral argument to the conclusion that miracles never happen. In a revealing passage, Kant argued:

> Those whose judgment in these matters is so inclined that they suppose themselves to be helpless without miracles, believe that they soften the blow which reason suffers from them by holding that they happen but seldom. How seldom? Once in a hundred years? . . . Here we can determine nothing on the basis of knowledge of the object . . . but only on the basis of the maxims which are necessary for the use of our reason. Thus, miracles must be admitted as [occurring] daily (though indeed hidden under the guise of natural events) or else never. . . . Since the former alternative [that miracles occur daily] is not at all compatible with reason, nothing remains but to adopt the later maxim—for this principle remains ever a mere maxim for making judgments, not a theoretical assertion. [For example, with regard to the] admirable conservation of the species in the plant and animal kingdoms . . . no one, indeed, can claim to comprehend whether or not the direct influence of the Creator is required on each occasion. They are for us . . . nothing but natural effects and ought never to be adjudged otherwise. [ibid., 83–84]

One who lives by moral reason, then, "does not incorporate belief in miracles into his maxims (either of theoretical or practical reason), though, indeed, he does not impugn their possibility or reality" (ibid., 83). So, miracles may be possible, but it is never rational to believe in them, since reason is always based on universal laws.

In view of this moral naturalism, it is not surprising that Kant rejects the resurrection of Christ (*see* RESURRECTION, EVIDENCE FOR). He wrote, "The more secret records, added as a sequel, of his resurrection and ascension . . . cannot be used in the interest of religion within the limits of reason alone without doing violence to their historical valuation" (ibid., 119).

Rather than looking at the historical evidence for Scripture, he summarily dismissed it as inauthentic because it was morally unessential. Again, a forced moral hermeneutic is preferable to the "literal" understanding. Why? Not because the historical facts support it. Rather, Kant's understanding of the moral law demands it. According to Kant, historical truth is determined *a priori* by moral law, not *a posteriori* from the facts. In a moral hermeneutic, what was is understood through what ought to have been.

If the argument is sound, we should live as if miracles do not occur—even if some have. We should order our life by (practical) reason, even if it is contrary to fact. We should "reason" in practice that what is true is false.

Evaluation. This is an unreasonable use of reason, and its effects have devastated Western epistemology.

Philosophical Consequences. Philosophically, the post-Kantian world cannot know God or reality. Kant's philosophy particularly contradicts Paul that God's power and divine nature are clearly seen through nature (Rom. 1:20). Nor can Scripture tell what God is really like. Scriptures do not inform us of how God really is *in-himself*, but only the way he is *to us*. The Bible tells how God wants us to *think about him*. It merely presents God-talk which never really talks about God.

Theological Consequence. Kantian theology has followed this radical disjunction between what appears and what is. Accepting the gulf between appearance and reality, Søren *Kierkegaard (1813–1855) existentially proclaimed God to be "wholly other" and insisted that human reason played no part in the defense of the Gospel. Kierkegaard wrote, "If God does not exist it would of course be impossible to prove it; and if he does exist it would be folly to attempt it. For at the very outset, in beginning my proof, I will have presupposed it . . . otherwise I would not begin, readily understanding that the whole would be impossible if he did not exist" (*Philosophical Fragments,* 31–35).

Three of Kant's views, if true, would destroy Christian faith. First, Kant is a philosophical agnostic (*see* AGNOSTICISM). Second, he held that no arguments for God's existence are valid (*see* COSMOLOGICAL ARGUMENT). Third, he denied the right to believe in miracles.

Both of Kant's arguments for agnosticism are invalid. His antinomies fail in that one premise is false. There need not be time before time; there could be eternity. Theism does not hold to creation *in* time but to the creation *of* time with the world. Not everything needs a cause, only contingent (finite, temporal) beings. Hence a first, eternal, Necessary Being does not need a cause (*see* CAUSALITY, PRINCIPLE OF).

The argument that we cannot know the real world is self-defeating. The very statement "We cannot know reality" is a statement that presupposes knowledge about reality. The attempt to undermine theistic proofs likewise fails, as is discussed in the article God, Objections to Proofs for.

Kant implies, but does not elaborate, a crucial premise (premise three below) in his argument against miracles, that reason operates according to universal laws. From his writings, the argument can be reconstructed:

1. We cannot know the real world (the world in itself) by theoretical reason.
2. Everything in our experience (the world to us) must be determined by practical reason.
3. Practical reason operates according to universal laws.
4. Miracles must occur either daily, seldom, or never.
5. But what occurs daily is not a miracle; it occurs according to natural laws.
6. And what occurs seldom is not determined by any law.
7. But everything must be determined by practical reason that operates on universal laws.
8. Therefore, miracles never occur.

In support of the crucial third premise, Kant wrote, "In the affairs of life, therefore, it is impossible for us to count on miracles or to take them into consideration at all in our use of reason (and reason must be used in every incident of life)" (*Religion within the Limits,* 82). *Miracles are theoretically possible but practically impossible. If we live as if they occur, we overthrow practical reason and moral law, which are the essences of true religion. Therefore, admitting that miracles occur and living in their light is actually harmful to religion. Even if there are supernatural acts, we must live (and think) as if there are none.

Kant made a radical disjunction between the unknowable world of things as they are (the *noumena*) and the world of our experience (the *phenomena*). However, philosophers have noted two things about this agnosticism. First, Kant was inconsistent, since he sometimes wandered over into the *noumenal* (real) world to make statements about it. And in so doing he implied that the noumenal world *is* knowable. Second, one cannot consistently separate the two realms without some knowledge of both. A line cannot be drawn, unless one can see beyond it. To say, "I know that reality is unknowable" is to make a claim to know something about reality. Complete agnosticism is self-defeating.

Like other naturalists, Kant begs the question by laying down a uniformitarian rule, some interpretive framework by which the naturalist demands a uniformitarian understanding of the world. For Spinoza, the rule is rational, for Hume, it is empirical, for Anthony *Flew, it is methodological, and for Kant, it is moral. Kant regulates all of life by a universal moral law (practical reason). Since he allows no exceptions to a law, there are no exceptions to the rule: "Live as if there are no miracles."

But this begs the question. Why should one assume there are no exceptions to any laws? And why should we assume that everything comes under some law? Maybe there are singularities, such as the origin of the world or the history of the earth, that defy classification (*see* ORIGINS, SCIENCE OF). Kant himself originated the nebular hypothesis about a scientific singularity at the beginning of our solar system.

Science now knows more, and the model changed. Natural law is now thought of as general and statistical, but not necessarily universal and without exceptions. Immanuel Kant believed, as did others of his day, that Newton's law of gravitation was universally true, with no exceptions. If Kant is wrong in his view of scientific law—insisting that every event be subsumed under some natural law, then his moral objection to miracles fails.

Hermeneutical Consequences. According to post-Kantian fideism, the Bible is not an adaptation to human *finitude*; it is an accommodation to human *error*. It does not contain anthropomorphisms, but myths. The task of hermeneutics is not to "lead forth the truth" *(exegesis)* of the text, but to extract the truth of the text from the error surrounding it. Objective truth is out of reach anyway, so the Bible student seeks subjective "truth." Thus, post-Kantian hermeneutics is locked out of real knowledge about God from Scripture or anywhere else.

Apologetic Consequences. With this scenario, apologetics can only be fideistic or presuppositional. It is no accident that there were no presuppositionalists (*see* PRESUPPOSITIONAL APOLO-

GETICS) before Kant and fewer nonpresuppositionalists after him (*see* CLASSICAL APOLOGETICS). Those who accept Kant's conclusions are forced to forsake reason for mere faith (*see* FAITH AND REASON). They can no longer fulfill the biblical imperative to "give a reason of the hope that is within them." Karl *Barth's neo-orthodoxy denied even Emil *Brunner's limited contention that there is a capacity to receive the revelation of God. Barth forbid *natural theology and would not allow even for *analogy of God in creation. In Kierkegaard and Barth, modern Christian fideism was born, proclamation but no verification of truth claims.

Evangelistic Consequences. When Christianity is reduced to declaration without defense, its mission is seriously hampered. Among the diverse views of the intellectual marketplace, it is necessary to both declare Christ and to defend the declaration. God who created human reason in his image and who invites us to reason with him (Isa. 1:18) demands the sacrifice of sin, not reason, as a condition for entering the kingdom. Unlike Kantian agnosticism, Kierkegaardian existentialism, or pantheistic *mysticism, Christianity is not a "leap before you look." Rather, it bids all to look before they leap. *Augustine noted rightly that "no one indeed believes anything unless he has first thought that it is to be believed." Hence, "it is necessary that everything which is believed should be believed after thought has led the way" (*On Predestination* 5).

Conclusion. Kant's attack on miracles is fundamental. He sees miracles as fundamentally unnecessary to true religion. To him, true religion is to live in accord with a universal law of practical reason. However, Kant's agnosticism is self-defeating, he begs the question by assuming a moral uniformitarianism, and he assumes the nature of a scientific "law" to be a universal *sine qua non*, rather than a statistical generalization. For Kant to avoid the miraculous, he had to eliminate the miracle accounts from the basic documents of Christianity, without any historical reason for doing so.

Historic Christianity claims miracles to be a true and essential part of the religion's belief system (Rom. 10:9; 1 Cor. 15:12–32). Christianity without miracles is Christianity without Christ, whose life was (and is still) characterized by miracles (*see* MIRACLES, ARGUMENTS AGAINST).

Sources

J. Collins, *God and Modern Philosophy*
W. Craig, *The* Kalam *Cosmological Argument*
R. Flint, *Agnosticism*
N. L. Geisler, *Christian Apologetics* (chap. 1)
———, *Christian Ethics*
———, *Miracles and Modern Thought*
———, and Win Corduan, *Philosophy of Religion* (chaps. 7–9)
S. Hackett, *The Resurrection of Theism*
I. Kant, *Critique of Judgment*
———, *Critique of Practical Reason Alone*
———, *Critique of Pure Reason*, 2d ed.
———, *Prolegomena to Any Future Metaphysics*
———, *Religion within the Limits of Reason Alone*, 2d ed.
C. S. Lewis, *Miracles*

Kierkegaard, Søren. Søren Kierkegaard (1813–1855) was born in Copenhagen, the son of Michael Pederson, a poor Jutlander who amassed a fortune selling drapes, then sold his business in 1786 to study theology. Kierkegaard said he was reared with severity and piety by a melancholy old man. His mother and five of his six brothers died when he was young, the result, it was said, of a curse on the family. He referred to the deaths in the title of his first book, *From Papers of One Still Living*. He was of high intellect, but lazy, and he loved the theater, especially Mozart. A spine deformity may have colored his view of life. Hans Christian Andersen portrayed the frequently drunken young Kierkegaard as a principal character in his novel, *Shoes of Fortune*. Converted to Christianity and reconciled with his father in 1838, he studied from 1831 to 1841 before receiving a master's degree in philosophy. He became engaged to Regina Olsen after graduation, but decided not to marry.

Writings. Kierkegaard's amazing literary output began when he was twenty-one years old in 1834 and continued to 1855. His works can be categorized:

Starting with *From the Papers of One Still Living*, the writer produced many aesthetic and philosophical essays and books. These works include the discourses "The Expectation of Faith," "Every Good and Perfect Gift is from Above," "Love Shall Cover a Multitude of Sins," "Strengthened in the Inner Man," "The Lord Gave and the Lord Hath Taken Away," "To Acquire One's Soul in Patience," "To Preserve One's Soul in Patience," "Patience in Expectation," "The Thorn in the Flesh," "Against Cowardice," "The Righteous Man Strives in Prayer with God and Conquers—in that God Conquers," "A Confessional Service," "On the Occasion of a Wedding," and "At the Side of a Grave."

His books in aaesthetics include *Concluding Unscientific Postscript*, *Fear and Trembling*, *Johannes Climacus or De Omnibus Dubitandum Est*, *Philosophical Fragments*, *Prefaces*, *Repetition*, *Stages on Life's Way*, *The Concept of Dread*, and *The Concept of Irony*.

The explicitly religious writings of Kierkegaard include *Armed Neutrality*, *Attack upon "Christendom," Judge for Yourselves*, *On Authority and Revelation: The Book of Adler*, *On the Difference Between a Genius and an Apostle*, *Purity of Heart Is to Will One Thing*, *Reply to Theophilus Nicolaus (Faith and Paradox)*, *The Crisis and a Crisis in the Life of an Actress*, *The Dialectic of Ethical and Ethico-Religious Communication*, *The Gospel of Suffering*, *The High Priest—The Publican—The Woman that Was a Sinner*, *The Individual*, *The Lilies of the Field*; *The Point of View*, *The Present Age*, *The Sickness unto Death*, *The Unchangeable God*, *Training in Christianity*, *What Christ's Judgment Is about Official Christianity*, and *Works of Love*.

Other works that fit no single category include: *Meditations from Kierkegaard*, *Newspaper Articles*, *The Journals of Kierkegaard*, and *The Prayers of Kierkegaard*.

Basic Beliefs. Theologically Kierkegaard was orthodox. He wrote that he was not out to change the doctrines taught in the church but to insist that something be done with them (*Journals and Papers*, 6:362). He believed in the inspiration of Scripture (*see* BIBLE, EVIDENCE FOR), the **virgin birth*, miracles, the substitutionary atonement, the bodily resurrection, and the final judgment (*see* HELL). In "Thoughts Which Wound from Behind," he is aghast that Christendom has replaced the resurrection with platonic immortality.

Three Life Stages, One Eternal. Kierkegaard's overall beliefs are expressed in his three stages of life: the aesthetic, the ethical, and the religious. His entire purpose is to get one from the aaesthetic life of pleasure to the religious life of commitment by way of the moral life of duty. In *My Point of View for My Work as an Author*, he wrote, "I am and was a religious author, that the whole of my work as an author is related to Christianity, to the problem of becoming a Christian, with a direct or indirect polemic against the illusion that in such a land as ours all are Christians of a sort" (ibid., 5–6).

Some contrasts are helpful to summarize these three levels:

The Aesthetic Stage	The Ethical Stage	The Religious Stage
Feeling	Deciding	Existing
Self-centered	Law-centered	God-centered
Routines of Life	Rules for Life	Revelation to Life
Centered in Present	Centered in Life/Time	Centered in Eternity
Individual Is Spectator	Individual Is Participant	
Live by Personal Whims	Live by Universal Norms	
Life of Deliberation	Life of Decision	
Life of Intellect Immediate Interests	Life of Will Ultimate Concerns	
	Respect of Moral Law	Response to Moral Law Giver
	The Universal	The Individual
	Propositions about God	Person of God
	Objective Truth	Subjective Truth
	Essential Realm	Existential Realm

Kierkegaard describes the conflict between the aesthetic and ethical spheres in his work *Either/Or* (1843), an attack on the dialectical thinking of G. W. F. Hegel (1770–1831). Kierkegaard believed that passion is the culmination of existence. There is no real value in either the objective storing of knowledge, nor the blissful, mystical intuition of it. Life is not found in neutral facts nor blissful insights but in responsible choices.

Volume 1 is a dramatic presentation of the aesthetic life by a sophisticate who sees the inevitable pathos of pleasure. In this hedonism, one's own reflective experience is the object of pleasure. The refined esthete is morally indifferent, rather than defiant. The aesthetic experience is one of endless possibility, never present reality. The author despairs of ever becoming a true self and merely tinkers with his environs. He chooses, not between good or evil, but between choosing and not choosing. The ultimate for the aesthetic life is commitment to despair. The esthete has immediate interests but no ultimate concern.

Volume 2 presents the other pole—moral responsibility. A meaningful life is impossible apart from moral effort. To be ethical means to be ruled by the eternal; to be aesthetic is to be ruled by the temporal. Ethical and aesthetic are qualitatively distinct but naturally related in that the former is a prior condition to the latter. The ethical means accepting responsibilities under the sovereignty of God. Hence, self-realization is not mere self-creation but integration of the eternal and the temporal.

In this Kierkegaardian Ecclesiastes, the basic choice of the aesthetic lifestyle is ultimately to merge good and evil, while the ethical lifestyle will inevitably choose good. This is reminiscent of the Augustine maxim: "Love God and do what you will." Kierkegaard is chiefly concerned with how one lives (passion), rather than what one does (content). But the ethical person also ends in despair of finding meaning. This moves the reader toward the third stage, the religious. The ethical life leads to a failure to reach one's ideals. That leads to repentance, a precondition of faith.

Kierkegaard introduces God as the Moral Law-Giver. Ethical repentance ends in sorrow in response to one's failure. That in itself does not lead to redemption. Ethics leads to the law, with its failure, not to the Law-Giver.

This key work prepares for the religious stage without entering it. The law ends self-reliance, but it does not itself bring God-reliance. The individual in the end arrives at an "either/or"—either the religious or despair.

Kierkegaard hoped his aesthetic writings would provoke people to want to choose the religious as a way of finding eternal meaning. He wrote several "edifying discourses" to provide the answer to the despair of the aesthetic and ethical stages. Unfortunately, he found that people preferred entertainment to edification. In "Expectation of Faith," a response to the aesthetic stage, he affirmed that solace is found only in the eternal. It is a guiding star to a sailor faced with the monotonous repetition of the waves. The tedium of the temporal is overcome only by the tranquillity of the transcendent. Faith is a passion for, and response to, the eternal. Even doubt can be an instrument that helps awaken the eternal God.

In "Every Good and Perfect Gift," a response to the life of ethical duty, Kierkegaard shows how God uses the moral gloom for our good. Even denied prayer is not unjust. The one praying is changed for better, even if the answer is for worse. Even tragedies can be triumphs if received with thanksgiving. Every personal tragedy is somehow redeemed by God's sovereignty. Suffering is beneficial in destroying self-will.

The Religious vs. the Ethical. In *Fear and Trembling*, Kierkegaard reveals how the ethical is transcended by the religious. Abraham is devoted to God's law, which forbids killing. Nevertheless, God tells him to offer Isaac as a sacrifice. Unable to explain or justify his action, Abraham suspended the ethical and made a "leap of faith" to the religious. In so doing, he dethroned the ethical without destroying it.

Kierkegaard believed religious faith to be personal, something we are. We must live it, not just know it. Spiritual truth cannot be merely acknowledged; it should be appropriated by commitment.

In *Concluding Unscientific Postscripts*, a further distinction is made within the religious stage. Religion A is natural religion, while religion B is supernatural. The first is religiosity; the second is Christianity. Religion A is rational, but Religion B is paradoxical. The first focuses only in a general need; the latter is prompted by a special need for Christ.

In *Philosophical Fragments*, Kierkegaard relates faith and reason. The book is philosophical and objective. Christianity is surveyed as to its content (what), as opposed to *Concluding Unscientific Postscripts*, which stresses Christianity as an existential way of life (how). This attack on human-centered philosophy profoundly influenced Karl Barth. Human beings see God as a perplexing Unknown. God must initiate communication. Two questions are raised: First, is it possible to base eternal happiness on historical knowledge? This harkens back to Gotthold Lessing (1729–1781) and his "ditch." Second, how can the transcendent God communicate with us?

Kierkegaard uses the parable of a king who becomes a beggar to win the love of a lowly maiden to argue that one cannot get the eternal out of the purely historical, nor the spiritual out of the rational. Original sin is the elemental human fact (see *Concept of Dread*). Humanity can neither know nor find the truth unless God puts them in it through revelation. This revelation, a miraculous self-authenticating disclosure, is not part of a rational system.

Reason and Revelation. Kierkegaard compared Socrates and Christ to get at the difference between revelation and reason:

Socrates's Wisdom	**Christ's Revelation**
Backward recollection	Forward expectation
Truth aroused within	Truth given from without
Truth immanent	Truth transcendent
Truth rational	Truth paradoxical
Truth comes from wise man	Truth comes from God-Man

Christian truths are neither analytic (self-evident) nor synthetic, because even if factually correct, human knowledge lacks the certainty held in Christian claims. Christian claims are paradoxical and can be accepted only by a leap of faith. There is a real transcendent God, who can only be chosen in his self-revelation. This God is meaningful and real, but paradoxical. He is the unknown limit to knowing, and he magnetically draws reason and causes passionate collision with humanity within the paradox. Reason cannot penetrate God, nor can it avoid him. The very zeal of the positivists to eliminate God shows their preoccupation with him. The supreme paradox of all thought is its attempt to discover something that thought cannot think.

Proofs and Pointers. God is unknown to us, even in Christ. God indicates his presence only by "signs" (pointers). The paradoxical revelation of the unknown is not knowable by reason. Human response must be a leap of faith, which is given by God but not forced on us; we can accept faith or choose to live rationally (*see* FIDEISM). Faith in God cannot be either rationally or empirically grounded. Rationally we cannot even imagine how God is like or unlike himself. The most we can do is to project familiar qualities in the direction of the transcendent that never reach him. We cannot argue from the works of nature to God, for these either assume God or lead to doubt.

Those who ask for proofs for God ignore God (*see* GOD, EVIDENCE FOR). For one already possesses what he wonders about (see "On the Occasion of a Confessional Service in *Thoughts on Crucial Situations in Human Life*). Even if we could prove God's being (*in himself*) it would be irrelevant to us. It is God's existence or relatedness to us that is of religious significance. The Gospel is presented only as an existential choice, not for rational reflection (*Postscripts*, 485; *Works of Love*, 74). God is not irrational. God is suprarational, which transcends finite rationality. The real absurdity in the human situation is that people must act as though certain, even though they have no reason for certainty.

Faith and the Irrational. Concluding Unscientific Postscripts adds that objective reason can never find existential truth. Proofs can neither establish nor overthrow Christianity. To try to prove God is as shameless an insult as to ignore him. To reduce Christianity to objective probability would be to make it a treasure one could carelessly possess, like money in the bank.

Faith in religious facts, such as the incarnation or the authority of Scripture, is not true faith. True faith is the gift of God and unattainable by effort. The incarnation (*see* CHRIST, DEITY OF) and Bible are objective points of reference, but they are not reasons. True faith is a leap to God's revelation that does not rest on objectively rational or empirical evidence. Reason, however, plays the negative role of helping us distinguish nonsense from paradox. The Christian is prevented by reason from believing sheer nonsense (*Postscripts*, 504). He tells the parable of an insane man who wants to prove that he is sane. He bounces a ball, saying, "Bang, the earth is round." He points out that what the man said was true, but he nevertheless fails to prove he is sane. How he says it shows that he is not rightly related to the truth (ibid., 174).

Volitional and Rational Knowledge of God. Sin, not our mental inability, makes God seem an absolute paradox. This absolute paradox becomes absurd in the cross, the offense offered by the Gospel. The human task, therefore, is not to intellectually comprehend God but to existentially submit to him in sacrificial love. The paradox is not theoretical, but volitional. It is not metaphysical but axiological. God is folly to our mind and an offense to our heart. The objective paradox of God in Christ is to be answered by a paradoxical response of faith and love.

Scripture. Kierkegaard believed the Bible to be the inspired Word of God (*see* REVELATION, SPECIAL). He wrote, "To be alone with the Holy Scriptures! I dare not! When I turn up a passage in it, whatever comes to hand—it catches me instantly, it questions me (indeed it is as if it were God Himself that questioned me, 'Hast thou done what thou readest there?'"). He even calls it "God's Word," adding, "My hearer, how highly dost thou esteem *God's Word*" (*Self-Examination*, 51). Kierkegaard even believed the canon to be closed and that God is giving no new revelation. He severely criticized someone who claimed they had received new revelation (*see* BIBLE, CANONICITY OF).

On the other hand, Kierkegaard did not believe it necessary or important to defend the inerrancy of Scripture. This is evident in his views on the eternal and temporal, as well as his comments on *biblical criticism.

The eternal and the temporal. How can eternal salvation depend on historical (and thereby uncertain) documents? How can the historical give nonhistorical knowledge? (*see* CHRIST OF FAITH VS. JESUS OF HISTORY). Kierkegaard's answer is that, insofar as the Bible gives empirical data, it is an insufficient ground for religious belief. Only Spirit-inspired faith finds the eternal God in the temporal Christ (*see* HOLY SPIRIT, ROLE IN APOLOGETICS). The biblical writers do not primarily certify the historicity of Christ's deity (*see* CHRIST, DEITY OF); rather they testify to the deity of Christ in history. Hence biblical criticism is irrelevant. The important thing is not the historicity of Christ but his contemporaneity as a person who confronts people today by faith in the offense of the Gospel. The Jesus of history is a necessary presupposition, but history does not prove his messiahship. The only proof of his messiahship is our discipleship.

Historicity and contemporaneity. If the eternal comes as an event in history, how is it equally available to all generations? The answer is that faith does not depend on happenstance, or being in the street when Jesus walked by. This would be mere physical contemporaneity. Faith is centered in a historical event, but it is not based on it. No superficial contemporaneity can occasion faith; only spiritual contemporaneity can. For "If the contemporary generation had left nothing behind them but these words: 'We have believed that in such and such a year the God appeared among us in the humble form of a servant, that he lived and taught in our community, and finally died,' it would be more than enough" (ibid., 130). So time is immaterial to faith. There is no second-hand discipleship.

Biblical criticism. To the Bible's apologist, Kierkegaard exhorts, "Whoever defends the Bible in the interest of faith must have made it clear to himself whether, if he succeeds beyond expectations, there could from all his labor ensure anything at all with respect to faith." To the critic he warns, "Whoever attacks the bible must also have sought a clear understanding of whether, if the attack succeeds beyond all measure, anything else would follow than the philological result." If Bible defenders achieve their wildest dreams in proving what books belong to the canon, their authenticity, trustworthiness, and inspiration, so what? Has anyone who previously did not have faith been brought a step closer? Faith does not result simply from a scientific inquiry; it does not come directly at all. On the contrary, "in this objectivity one tends to lose that infinite personal interestedness in passion which is the condition of faith" (*Concluding Unscientific Postscripts*, 29–30). But what if the Bible's opponents have proven all they allege about the Bible, does that abolish Christianity? By no means. If the believer "had assumed it by virtue of any proof, he would have been on the verge of giving us his faith." Faith does not need the proof, he said. Faith, in fact, regards proof as its enemy (ibid., 31).

Elsewhere Kierkegaard affirms that, in order to make room for faith, men and women must be freed from the shackles of historical necessity. History is not an unfolding necessity, as Hegel said, but a free response to challenge and confrontation. Freedom escapes the net of scientific explanation.

Natural Theology Rejected. Natural religion is good, but it is not Christian, because it lacks transcendent disclosure. It supplements Christianity but is pathetic without Christianity to fulfill it. It arises by a collision of reason with the unknown (a concept developed in Rudolph Otto's *Numinous*), but it never goes beyond the collision. A human being is a god-maker who deifies whatever is overwhelming. But deep in the heart of natural piety lurks a caprice that knows it has produced the deity and that the deity is a fantasy. Hence, natural religion veers either to polytheism, which collects all its fantasies, or to pantheism, which is an incongruous merger of them. So Kierkegaard concludes that the nearest reason that brings God is still the farthest from us he ever is.

Kierkegaard adds an interesting observation on comparative religion. Buddhism, he says, seeks eternal outside of time—by meditation. Socrates sought eternal before time—by recollection. But Christianity seeks eternal in time—by revelation.

Evaluation. Although Kierkegaard can be taken to be a mild evidentialist with respect to objective, historical truths, when it comes to religious truth he is almost a classic example of a fideist. He, and Karl *Barth following him, are fountain heads of the Christian attack on a rational and evidential approach to Christianity in the modern world. Nonetheless, there are many values in Kierkegaardian thought, even for Christian apologetics.

Positive Contributions. Kierkegaard can be commended for his belief in the fundamentals of Christian faith. He stressed a personal encounter with authentic Christianity, the importance of individual free will vs. behavioral determinism, and a return to New Testament faith. He emphasized God's unchangeability, transcendence, and grace and human depravity. He offered creative insights into many Bible passages.

A corrective to rationalism. Some rationalists, such as Rene *Descartes, Gottfried *Leibniz, and Christian Wolfe, stressed an extreme rational approach to God. They underemphasized the role of faith and personal encounter in a genuine relationship with God. They overstated their arguments for God's existence (*see* God, Evidence for), claiming they were mathematically certain. Kierkegaard's attack on rationalism and stress on a personal encounter with the living God is a helpful corrective to sterile rationalism.

The classic distinction between reason and the truths of faith (*see* Faith and Reason) is sometimes forgotten in modern rational apologetics. There are truths that, while not going against reason, go beyond reason (*see* Mystery). Kierkegaard saw this clearly.

The real basis for belief. Some classical apologists (*see* Classical Apologetics) and evidential apologists (*see* Apologetics, Types of) tend to forget that faith is not based in evidence or reason about God but in God himself. Our belief is supported by evidence. Kierkegaard emphasized this point to a fault.

Helpful preevangelism. Few have described the despair of the aesthetic life so clearly as did Kierkegaard. *Either/Or* gives an unparalleled view of the futility of life apart from God. This can be cast into an implied argument from religious need (*see* God, Need for).

The historical and the eternal. Kierkegaard is correct in observing that there is more to a miracle than the mere historical dimensions, and the historical is insufficient to bring one into contact with the living God (*see* Miracles, Myth and). Overemphasis by historical apologists can be misconstrued to imply that one can reach God via the historical evidence alone. Pointed reminders of the gulf between the historical and the eternal are well made. He is correct in noting that, even if one had perfect historical records, that information would not in itself bring one into contact with God.

*Difficulties. *Fideism.* As other fideists, Kierkegaard offers self-defeating reasons for fideism, which claims that one cannot offer reasons for matters of faith. More on this point is discussed in the article Fideism.

Separating fact and value. Following Immanuel Kant, Kierkegaard radically separates fact and value, is and ought. This gave impetus to the separation of the Jesus of History from the Christ of Faith (*see* Christ of Faith vs. Jesus of History; Jesus Seminar; Miracles, Myth and). While the historical as such does not bring one into contact with the eternal, neither can the eternal be divorced from real history. While Kierkegaard does not deny the historical reality of miracles, he downplays the importance of that dimension. Miracles may be more than historical, but they are not less. By denying the importance of the historical, he undermines the authenticity of the New Testament and, with it, New Testament Christianity. The shift in emphasis from fact to value leads to the denial of fact and its support for faith.

Evidential support for faith. While Kierkegaard is correct that faith is based not in fact but in God, he is wrong in assuming that there is no rational and evidential support for faith. Of course, God is the basis of faith in God, but this does not mean we have no accompanying rational or evidential support for belief. Kierkegaard goes too far when he claims, "The miracle can prove nothing; for if you do not believe that he is what he says he is, you deny the miracle. A miracle can make one attentive" (*Training in Christianity*, 99).

Belief in and belief that. There is no evidence for belief *in* God. This is strictly a matter of faith. Nonetheless, there is evidence for believing *that* there is a God. Kierkegaard fails to stress the importance of having evidence that God exists. No rational person would place faith in an elevator to go to the ninth floor without evidence that the elevator could do this. Likewise, no rational person should trust in God unless it is reasonable to believe that there is a God who is trustworthy.

The role of theistic arguments. Kierkegaard offers no disproofs of arguments for God as did Kant (*see* God, Objections to Proofs for). He offers only a kind of existential complaint against theistic arguments, that they are an offense to God. But why should the God of reason be offended when we use reason. Reason is part of the very thing that makes us like him (Gen. 1:27).

A wholly other God. The concept of God as "wholly Other" is a form of *agnosticism. Like Kant's *noumenal* realm (the thing-in-itself), God can never be known. We can know only *that* he is, but not *what* he is. But it is impossible to know pure "thatness." We must know something about *what* something is or we cannot know *that* it is. Even a strange gadget we have never seen before is not "wholly other." We may not know its purpose, but we can know its size, shape, and color. The very affirmation that we know nothing about God is a claim to know something about him; hence it is self-defeating. Purely negative knowledge about something is impossible. The claim that God is not "this" implies that we know the "this." So, the view of religious language as mere pointers to God that do not really describe him leaves us in total self-defeating ignorance.

Suspension of the ethical. In his suspension of the ethical for the religious, Kierkegaard paved the way for situation ethics. Even though he believed strongly in God's moral laws, on the highest level of duty—his relation to God—there is no way to distinguish right from wrong. The existential encounter with God places one beyond rational and ethical realms. Regardless of the rational and ethical context in which one begins, the suspension of the ethical for the religious leaves one without any real guide on the highest level for right and wrong.

Subjectivity of truth. Kierkegaard did not claim that truth is subjective. He said, "Truth is subjectivity." And while he did not deny objective truth (*see* Truth, Nature of) in science or history, he did deny that religious truth is objective or testable. Not only does this leave us with a mere subjective test for religious truth, but it confuses the objective nature of religious truth with the subjective condition of receiving it. Certainly one should apply truths of Christianity to life subjectively, but this does not mean truths should be defined as subjectivity. All truth objectively corresponds to the state of affairs being described.

Minimizing the historically necessarily. When Kierkegaard spoke of the mere belief in a man named Jesus, in whom people believed God dwelt as the minimal historical facts necessary for the Christian faith, he invited the radical demythologizing of *Bultmann. It flies in the face of the New Testament claim that the fact of the bodily resurrection is absolutely necessary to Christianity. As the apostle Paul declared, "If Christ has not been raised, your faith is futile; you are still in your sins" (1 Cor. 15:17; cf. Rom. 10:9).

Personal and propositional revelation. Though he believed in the inspiration of Scripture, Kierkegaard's stress on the personal nature of religious truth and the need for an existential encounter with God tilted the axiological scales against propositional revelation. It was not only downplayed, but it was separated from what is really important, personal revelation. This led to the neo-orthodoxy of Karl *Barth and Emil *Brunner, which denied the historic, orthodox view that revelation is propositional.

There is no need for such a disjunction. Propositional revelation can be very personal, as anyone who has ever written a love letter knows. God's love letter, the Bible, is written in propositions, but it conveys a very personal message. Those who read it and respond enter into a very personal relation to God.

The terms leap, absurd, and paradox. Kierkegaard was not an irrationalist, as some have claimed, but his use of terms make him sound like one. *Absurd* and *paradox* have generally been reserved, from Zeno through Kant, to mean a logical contradiction (*see* First Principles; Logic). They are, at best, an unfortunate choice of terms and are generally misleading. Kierkegaard has been widely misunderstood, partly because he used them. Likewise, to speak of a "leap" of faith sounds irrational, as even Kierkegaard seemed later to recognize (see *Journals*, 581). Such extreme words to describe the mystery of what does not go against reason, but merely beyond it, only invite misunderstanding.

Sources

G. E. Arbaugh, *Kierkegaard's Authorship*

S. Evans, *Kierkegaard's "Fragments" and "Postscript"*

———, *Subjectivity and Religious Belief*
F. Carmical, "The Unknown and Unread Søren Kierkegaard," in *Studia Et Apologia*
J. Carnell, *The Burden of Søren Kierkegaard*
P. S. Minear, et al., *Kierkegaard and the Bible*
H. Nygeren, "Existentialism: Kierkegaard," in N. L. Geisler, ed., *Biblical Inerrancy: Its Philosophical Roots*
See also the numerous Kierkegaard works cited above.

Krishna. ***See*** **Hinduism, Vedanta; Resurrection Claims in Non-Christian Religions; World Religions, Christianity and.**

Kushner, Harold. Harold Kushner is a late-twentieth-century American Jewish rabbi whose popular version of finite godism is expressed in his best-selling books, *When Bad Things Happen to Good People* and *When All You've Wanted Isn't Enough*. Kushner challenges Christianity at several major points, particularly in his rejection of miracles and arguments for a finite God (*see* Miracles, Arguments Against).

A Limited God. According to Kushner there is one God who is limited in power and perfection. But "when we speak of one God, are we doing something more than taking a census of how many divine beings there are? Are we perhaps saying that God 'has it all together' . . . ?" (*When All You've Wanted,* 133). Further, "because He is One, He is all alone unless and until there are other people to love Him" (ibid., 56). This God "cannot monopolize all the Power and leave none for us" (ibid.). Not only is God limited because of us, but he is limited because of his nature. As Kushner put it, "I recognize His limitations. He is limited in what He can do by the laws of nature and by the evolution of human nature and human moral freedom" (*When Bad Things Happen,* 134). We must realize "that even God has a hard time keeping chaos in check and limiting the damage that evil can do" (ibid., 43).

Kushner views God's finitude as an asset to our lives, rather than a liability. For "if we can bring ourselves to acknowledge that there are some things God does not control, many good things become possible" (ibid., 45). In fact, "God, who neither causes nor prevents tragedies, helps by inspiring people to help" (ibid., 141). God cannot control the world and human beings, but he "is the divine power urging them to grow, to reach, to dare" (ibid., 132).

God, for Kushner, is a God of love, rather than power (*When All You've Wanted,* 55). He is more kind than able (ibid., 58). "God is the force that moves us to rise above selfishness and help our neighbors, even as he inspires them to transcend selfishness and help us" (ibid., 183). As to our tragic circumstances, "God may not prevent the calamity, but He gives us the strength and the perseverance to overcome it" (*When Bad Things Happen,* 141). God cannot ward off our misfortunes, but neither does he send them. "Our misfortunes are none of His doing, and so we can turn to Him for help" (ibid., 44). Even during the Jewish holocaust God "was with the victims, and not with the murderers, but . . . He does not control man's choosing between good and evil" (ibid., 84).

Good Human Beings. Humanity is an evolved result of "God's creation" (*When All You've Wanted,* 77). Each individual is made in "God's image." This is especially manifest in his ability to choose good and evil. Human beings are also rational beings. "When the opening pages of the Bible describe Adam as naming the animals, tribute is being paid to his unique ability to reason, to sort things into categories. Man alone can use his mind to make tools, . . . as well as to write books and symphonies" (ibid., 103, 104).

Humans not only have a mind and will but they have physical bodies that experience pain (ibid., 78). Nevertheless, the human body is good. For Kushner, "to view the human body and the whole natural world with disgust or mistrust is as much a heresy as to view it with unqualified reverence" (ibid., 83). God is good, and he also made mankind good. When the Bible describes Adam and Eve taking the fruit of the tree of knowledge, they did not fall downward; they "fell upward." It was a moment of progress for the human race, not of catastrophe. It was a leap forward in the evolutionary process.

Kushner refers to the human mind as "the most indisputable proof of God's hand in the evolutionary process" (ibid., 110). Elsewhere he writes of "what God had in mind when he arranged for human beings to evolve" (ibid., 135). So evolution is the means through which God expresses his creativity (*see* Evolution, Biological). The human being is the highest product of that process—the creature most like God.

A Chaotic World. Even though the world is in the process of change, there are things about the world that even God cannot change. God cannot make fatal conditions less fatal or heal an illness (*When Bad Things Happen,* 110). "The laws of nature do not make exceptions for nice people. A bullet has no conscience; neither does a malignant tumor or an automobile gone out of control" (ibid., 58).

God's hands are tied by the unfeeling laws of nature. Thus, we cannot ask God for a *miracle. When highly unusual things do occur, "we would be well advised to bow our heads in thanks at the presence of a miracle, and not to think that our prayers, contributions or abstentions are what did it" (ibid.). Prayer does not put us in touch with a supernatural God. Rather, prayer puts "us in touch with other people, people who share the same concerns, values, dreams, and pains that we do" (ibid., 119).

This world is also irrational (*When All You've Wanted,* 111). There is no ultimate meaning in anything that happens (*When Bad Things Happen,* 136). There is no reason why some people suffer and not others. "These events do not reflect God's choice. They happen at random, and randomness is another name for chaos, in those corners of the universe where God's creative light has not yet penetrated" (ibid., 53).

Forgiving God for Evil. Evil is real (*When All You've Wanted,* 89). "To be alive is to feel pain, and to hide from pain is to make yourself less alive" (ibid.). The world is unjust, and we must adjust to it. Rather than blame God, we need to forgive God. In a poignant passage, the rabbi asks:

> Are you capable of forgiving and loving God even when you have found out that He is not perfect, even when He has let you down and disappointed you by permitting bad luck and sickness and cruelty in His world, and permitting some of those things to happen to you? Can you learn to love and forgive Him despite His limitations . . . as you once learned to forgive and love your parents even though they were not as wise, as strong, or as perfect as you needed them to be? [*When Bad Things Happen,* 148]

The solution to the problem of evil (*see* Evil, Problem of) is "to forgive God for not making a better world, to reach out to the people around us, and to go on living despite it all" (ibid., 147).

Maturity in Ethics. Kushner's view of right and wrong is rooted in Jewish tradition, but blossoms in the sunlight of contemporary psychology. At times he speaks of God as Law Giver. "He commands us. He imposes on us a sense of moral obligation" (*When All You've Wanted,* 180). God "commands us. That's what we're here on earth for, to be in God's service, to do God's bidding" (*When Bad Things Happen,* 86). Obedience to God's laws, however, is a lower-level ethical activity. Following psychologist Jean Piaget, Kushner believes obedience is not necessarily the highest virtue. In fact, "a religion that defines morality as obedience to its commands is appropriate to children and immature people, and may have been appropriate to humankind as a whole when civilization was immature." Such a religion was appropriate for immature civilization, but unquestioning obedience makes perpetual children (*When All You've Wanted,* 127–28).

A higher level of ethical maturity is achieved by those who "understand that rules don't come from 'on high.' Rules are made by people like themselves, tested and perfected over the course of time, and can be changed by people like themselves." At this stage "being 'good' no longer means simply obeying rules. It now comes to mean sharing in the responsibility of evaluating and making rules which will be fair to all, so that we can all enjoy living in a fair and just society" (ibid., 123).

Hope for the Future. As to life after death, Rabbi Kushner is uncertain. Personal *immortality is only a hope. "Neither I nor any living person can know anything about the reality of that hope" (*When Bad Things Happen,* 28). He does "believe that the part of us which is not physical, the part we call soul or personality, does not and cannot die." But he adds quickly, "I am not capable of imagining what a soul without a body looks like. Will we be able to recognize disembodied souls as being the people we had known and loved?" (ibid.).

Kushner admits that belief in a world to come can help people endure the unfairness of this world. But it can excuse accepting injustice, instead of doing something about it (ibid., 29). We should live for the short run, a moment at a time. "We never solve the problem of living once and for all" (*When All You've Wanted,* 143). The important thing is to live in the now. Those who live in the present with integrity have no fear of dying (ibid., 155). "I have no fear of death because I feel that I have lived. I have loved and have been loved" (ibid., 161). Most people are not afraid of dying but of living. They fear coming to death without ever having lived (ibid., 156).

We should not seek future rewards. "When you have learned how to live, life itself is the reward" (ibid., 152). Rabbi Kushner quotes approvingly the *Talmud* which says, "One hour in this world is better than all eternity in the World to Come" (ibid., 151). When we speak of God in heaven as our hope "we trivialize religion and make it harder for thoughtful people to take it seriously and find help there" (ibid., 179). Our real immortality is to have children and to plant things that others can enjoy after we are gone (ibid., 173).

Heaven and *hell are on earth. Heaven "is having learned to do and enjoy the things that make us human, the things that only human beings can do." By contrast, "the worst kind of hell I can imagine is not fire and brimstone . . . The worst hell is the realization that you could have been a real human being . . . and now it's too late" (ibid., 157). God will not intervene someday to reward the righteous and punish the wicked. The real reward is that "he has made the human soul in such a way that only a life of goodness and honesty leaves us feeling spiritually healthy and human" (ibid., 183).

Evaluation. *Positive Contributions.* Even though his *finite godism is false, his articulation of the view contains truths:

Acknowledgment of the problem of evil. Kushner has centered his thought in a crucial area—the problem of evil. In this regard he acknowledges the reality of evil, instead of opting for a pantheism that denies it. He is right that tornadoes have no conscience; they strike both good and bad people. They hit churches and houses of prostitution. Any adequate solution to the problem of natural evil must deal with this reality (*see* Evil, Problem of). Kushner attempts to find this solution. He doesn't relegate it to the realm of the ultimately inexplicable. Although theists do not agree with the solution (see below), nonetheless, we commend his attempt to find a solution.

Insights into the problem of suffering. Having experienced physical suffering, Kushner is not a detached observer; he is sensitive to the existential impact of suffering. His perspective is the difference between C. S. *Lewis in his book, *The Problem of Pain*, when he was not experiencing it personally, and his later reflections in *A Grief Observed*, after his wife died from cancer.

Recognition of the problem in divine intervention. He also points to a problem some theists tend to overlook. Given the reality of the human condition, God cannot do everything. There are operational limits on divine intervention. God cannot violate the human freedom he gave to beings in his image. So, performing a miracle contrary to moral freedom is operationally impossible for God. Continually intervening would upset the very laws of nature that make both physical and moral life possible.

Weaknesses and Objections. Most of the objectionable aspects of Kushner's thought are critiqued in other articles. They will be noted here with references.

First, finite godism is without foundation (*see* Finite Godism).

Second, Kushner's concept of evil is inadequate (*see* Evil, Problem of).

Third, Kushner's denial of the supernatural is unfounded (*see* Miracle).

Fourth, his denial of immortality is contrary to the evidence (*see* Immortality). Without this denial his case crumbles, since it depends on the premise that wrongs of this life will not be rectified in the next life (see Geisler, *The Roots of Evil*, append. 3).

In spite of its popularity, Kushner's form of finite godism, especially as it relates to evil, does not stand up to scrutiny. It has more emotional appeal than rational justification.

Sources

H. Kushner, *When All You've Wanted Isn't Enough*

———, *When Bad Things Happen to Good People*

N. L. Geisler, *The Roots of Evil*, rev. ed.

———with H. Kushner, transcript, televised debate, "The John Ankerberg Show," 1984

Ll

Language, Religious. *See* ANALOGY, PRINCIPLE OF; LOGICAL POSITIVISM; WITTGENSTEIN, LUDWIG.

Lapide, Pinchas. Pinchas Lapide is a late-twentieth-century Jewish rabbi and biblical scholar who, without converting to Christianity, supports the Christian belief that Jesus of Nazareth rose bodily from the grave. His conclusion supports a crucial link in the Christian apologetic—that of Christ's resurrection.

In his book, *The Resurrection of Jesus,* Rabbi Lapide concluded: "In regard to the future resurrection of the dead, I am and remain a Pharisee. Concerning the resurrection of Jesus on Easter Sunday, I was for decades a Sadducee. I am no longer a Sadducee since the following deliberation has caused me to think this through anew" (125). He adds, "If God's power which was active in Elisha is great enough to resuscitate even a dead person who was thrown into the tomb of the prophet (2 Kings 13:20–21), then the bodily resurrection of a crucified Jew also would not be inconceivable" (131).

Since a miracle is an act of God that confirms the truth of a prophet of God (*see* MIRACLES, APOLOGETIC VALUE OF), it is difficult to escape the conclusion that Jesus is the Messiah (*see* CHRIST, DEITY OF). As one writer put it, "Pinchas Lapide's logic escapes me. He believes it is a possibility that Jesus was resurrected by God. At the same time he does not accept Jesus as the Messiah. But Jesus said that he was the Messiah. Why would God resurrect a liar?" (*Time*, 4 June 1979). Indeed, another rabbi said to Jesus, "Rabbi, we know you are a teacher who has come from God. For no one could perform the miraculous signs you are doing if God were not with him" (John 3:2).

Sources

P. Lapide, *The Resurrection of Jesus*

———, *Time* (4 June 1979)

Law, Nature and Kinds of. Moral law is a measure for conduct. It is a first principle (*see* FIRST PRINCIPLES) of human action. After it is proclaimed, a law is binding. Theonomists contend that the only legitimate law is divine law, insisting that human governments should be based on biblical law (Bahnsen). Situation ethicists insist that there are no moral absolutes, and all law reduces to human law. Moralists ponder the relation of divine law and human law. One of the most comprehensive and influential treatments of the topic is that of *Thomas Aquinas. Secular, Protestant, and Catholic scholars, including John *Calvin, John *Locke, and Thomas *Jefferson through the legal theorist William Blackstone, built on his analysis.

The Nature of Law. Law is a measure or rule by which we are led to act or are withheld from acting. Law is a first principle of action. It is the basic rule or principle by which actions of persons are directed. The rule and measure of human activity is reason, whose function is to direct means to ends (Aquinas, *Summa Theologica,* 1a2ae. 90, 1). Civil law is an ordinance of reason for the common good, made by public person(s) who have charge of the community. It is promulgated to them (ibid., 1a2ae. 90, 4).

Law as First Principle. Each area of human activity has *first principles. There are first principles of human thinking, such as the law of noncontradiction. Likewise, there are first principles of being, such as the principle that "Being exists." And there are first principles of human acting, such as, "Do good and shun evil." The latter is known as the natural law. The precepts of the natural law are to practical reason what first principles of thought are to philosophical thinking. The first principle of practical reason is our ultimate end or happiness. Law is primarily concerned with planning for this end. In brief, law is the rule directed toward the common good (happiness) (ibid., 1a2ae. 90, 2).

Proclamation of Law. For law to be in effect, it must be proclaimed. No one is obliged to obey a precept without first being reasonably informed of it (Aquinas, *Disputations*). This follows logically upon the nature of law as a duty of action for the common good. Thus, to lay down an obligation a law must be applied to the persons to be regulated, and it must be brought to their knowledge by promulgation (*Summa Theologica,* 1a2ae. 90, 4). Ignorance of the law is a legitimate excuse not to obey it, unless it is culpable ignorance.

Different Kinds of Law. Four kinds of law have been differentiated: eternal, natural, human, and divine. Each is the measure or rule in a different sphere.

Eternal Law. Eternal law is the idea in the mind of God, the principle of the universe that lies behind the governance of all things (ibid., 1a2ae. 91, 1). It is the source and exemplar of all other law. For all laws derive from the eternal law to the extent that they share in right reason. It is eternal because, being in the mind of God, it is the plan of things that was set up from eternity (ibid.). So eternal law is the divine reason by which the universe is ruled. All things subject to divine providence are ruled and measured by eternal law; thus they share in eternal law (ibid., 1a2ae. 91, 2). It is the eternal mind of God as it conceived and determined all that would be and how it would be run. From it flow other kinds of law.

**Natural Law.* The communication of eternal law to rational creatures is called *natural law*. Natural law is the human participation in eternal law by way of reason. It is contained in the eternal law primarily and in the natural judicial faculty of human reason secondarily (ibid., 1a2ae. 71, 6). Natural law is the light of reason by which we discern what is right and wrong (ibid., 1a2ae. 91, 2). It is the law written on human hearts (Rom. 2:15).

Natural law teaches us to do good and shun evil. Good and evil should be set in the context of what is proper to human beings as human, their rational and moral life (*Disputations,* 2). So a good act is one in accord with human rational and moral nature. An evil act is one contrary to human nature. Sadly, most people err at this point because they act according to sense rather than reason (*Summa Theologica,* 1a. 49, 3).

However, to live according to human nature does not mean that human nature is the ultimate measure. In voluntary activity the proximate measure is human reason, but the supreme measure is eternal law (ibid., 1a2ae. 71, 6). When a human act goes to its end in harmony with the order of reason and eternal law, the act is right; when it turns away from that rightness it is wrong (ibid., 1a2ae. 21, 1). Human reason is the basis for natural law only insofar as it participates in God's eternal reason. In this sense, violating the dictate of reason amounts to violating the law of God (ibid., 1a2ae. 19, 5).

Human Law. Human law, also called positive or civil law, is the attempt of human reason to make practical laws based on natural law. Human law results when the practical reason proceeds to enact concrete laws for society from the general precepts of the natural law (ibid., 1a2ae. 91, 3). It is a particularization of the general principles of natural law.

Human laws may be inferred from natural law. Some precepts are inferred from natural law as a conclusion. For example, "You should not kill" comes from "You should not harm." Other precepts are determinate embodiments of the natural law. Natural law dictates that criminals should be punished, but it does not (always) settle the character of that punishment (ibid., 1a2ae. 95, 2). Human laws may be derived from natural law, either as a conclusion or a particular application (ibid.). The first is like a demonstrative science and the second like an art. Hence, laws declared as conclusions have their force from both the natural law and the government that enacts them. Applied laws have their force from government alone.

Not everything forbidden by human law is essentially evil. Some things are commanded as good, or forbidden as evil. Others are good because they are commanded or evil because they are forbidden (ibid., 2a2ae. 57, 2). An act of vice, forbidden by a negative precept, is never to be committed. However, many factors have to conspire to make a commanded act of virtue right. A virtuous act need not be complied with in every case, "but only when the due conditions of person, time, place, and situation demand its observance" (see Gilby, 361).

Human law is imposed on imperfect people. "Therefore it does not forbid all vices, from which the virtuous keep themselves, but only the graver ones, which the majority can avoid, and chiefly those that are damaging to others and on prevention of which depends social stability" (*Summa Theologica,* 1a2ae. 96, 2). That is, "human law cannot forbid all and everything that is against virtue; it is enough that it forbid deeds against community life; the remainder it tolerates almost as if they were licit, not indeed because they are approved, but because they are not punished" (ibid., 2a2ae. 77, 1). "Every act of virtue is not commanded by human law, but only those that can be enjoined for the public good" (ibid., 2a2ae. 96, 3). For "the immediate end of human law is men's own utility" (ibid., 1a2ae. 95, 3).

Of course, not every human law is legitimate. A law has the force of law only when it benefits the community (ibid., 2ae. 90, 2). Laws contrary to common good (which is demanded by the natural law) do not have the force of law. Likewise, laws not promulgated, even if directed to the common good, are not binding (*Disputations,* 177).

Divine Law. Divine law has a different purpose from natural law. Its intent is to lead people to

God. That is, "the entire purpose of the lawgiver is that man may love God" (Aquinas, *Summa contra Gentiles,* 111–16). Divine law, therefore, is not given to unbelievers but to believers. Natural law is for unbelievers. Divine law is binding on the church, but natural law is binding on all society. Natural law is directed toward temporal good, but divine law is directed toward eternal good. Inasmuch as natural law reflects the very character of God, it cannot change. Divine law, however, is based on God's will and therefore does change. Hence, "in divine as in human law, some things are commanded because they are good. . . . Others again are good because they are commanded . . ." (*Summa Theologica,* 2a2ae. 57, 2). This is reflected in God's change in divine law from the Old Testament to the New Testament. The natural law remains the same from age to age and from person to person.

Purpose of Law. In general, God's purpose for law is to regulate human activity. Each kind of law, of course, has its own kind of regulation in mind. By eternal law God regulates the entire universe; by divine law he regulates the church, and by natural law he regulates all rational creatures. In addition to these spheres, Aquinas spells out several specific dimensions of God's purpose for giving law.

Friendship. One purpose of law is to promote friendship. "As the leading purpose of human law is to bring about friendship of men among themselves, so divine law is chiefly intended to establish men in friendship with God" (ibid., 2a2ae. 99, 2). To be civil, behavior must be regulated. Apart from laws, friendship cannot function, since it is the measure of right relationships.

Love of God. Jesus summarized all laws into two: Love God and love others. Aquinas calls love for God the "entire purpose of the lawgiver." Hence, it is not *either* law *or* love; it is the law of love. It leads humanity to God. For "love is our strongest union with God, and this above all is intended by the divine law." God is love, and the highest duty is to love him (*Summa contra Gentiles,* 111–16).

Curbing Evil. Not everyone will obey God's law, so sanctions are required, either to reform the sinner or to protect society through his punishment (*Summa Theologica,* 2a2ae. 68, 1). This is also true of divine and natural law. The primary purpose is for our good, but the secondary purpose is to penalize those who disobey.

Common Good. Human laws also have the purpose of achieving the common good. Aquinas recognized that "to make a rule fit every case is impossible." Hence, "legislators have to attend to what happens in the majority of cases and should frame their laws accordingly." For example, the law commands that things borrowed should be returned. What if a weapon has been borrowed and, if given back, it will be used for violence (ibid., 2a2ae. 120, 1)? So what is productive of the common good is not always right in a specific case. Since the law-maker cannot take every specific exception into consideration, law must be based on what usually happens (Aquinas, *Commentary, 5 Ethics,* lect. 16).

Conflicting Laws. Sometimes there is conflict among kinds of law. In such cases there is a hierarchy of priority.

Priority of Natural Law. There are exceptions even to just human laws. Human laws are only general, not universal. At times natural law overrides them. Though the law of property rights demands that we return what we have borrowed when requested, nonetheless, we should not return a weapon to someone who is in a murderous rage. In such a case, "to follow the law as it stands would be wrong; to leave it aside and follow what is demanded by fairness and the common benefit will then be right" (Aquinas, *Summa Theologica,* 2a2ae. 120, 1). The virtue of justice or equity demands this. Moral law takes precedence over human law in special cases, even if the human law is just.

Law's Based in God's Nature. Divine and human law, being based on God's will, can be changed (*see* ESSENTIALISM). The natural law, however, is based on God's nature and cannot be changed (*Summa Theologica,* 2a2ae. 57, 2; *see* GOD, NATURE OF). Hence, it would follow that, whenever there is a conflict between unchangeable law and changeable law, the former takes priority. When the disciples picked ears of corn on the Sabbath they were excused by necessity of hunger. Neither did David transgress by taking the loaves it was illegal for him to eat (ibid., 3a. 90, 4).

Letter vs. Spirit. Christian thinkers have noted that "the judgment that the letter of the law is not to be followed in certain given circumstances is not a criticism of the law, but an appreciation of a particular situation that has cropped up" (ibid., 2a2ae. 120, 1). If one does not do this, then severity takes priority over equity. For "legal-mindedness should be directed by equity, which provides a higher rule for human activity" (ibid., 2a2ae. 120, 2). There is a higher law and lower laws. When they conflict, one is obligated to obey the higher.

Sources

G. Bahnsen, *Theonomy in Christian Ethics*
N. L. Geisler, *Christian Ethics*
———, *Thomas Aquinas: An Evangelical Appraisal*
T. Gilby, *Texts of Aquinas*
Thomas Aquinas, *On the Cardinal Virtues*
———, *Commentary, V Ethics*
———, *Compendium Theologiae*
———, *Disputations*
———, *On the Perfection of Spiritual Creatures*
———, *Summa contra Gentiles*
———, *Summa Theologica*
———, *On Truth*

Leibniz, Gottfried. Gottfried Leibniz (1646–1716) was a child genius in Germany who learned both Greek and scholastic philosophy at an age so young he was denied a master's degree in law at the University of Leipzig because of his youth. He co-invented calculus with Isaac Newton in 1676. He wrote a doctoral dissertation on symbolic solutions to philosophical problems. Leibniz was greatly influenced by contemporary rationalist Benedict *Spinoza, although Spinoza was a pantheist (*see* PANTHEISM), and Leibniz remained a theist (*see* THEISM).

The most influential works of Leibniz were *Discourse on Metaphysics*, *Monadology*, and *Theodicy*. His influence on modern thought has been considerable. Immanuel *Kant was a Leibnizian rationalist before he was awakened from his "dogmatic slumbers" by reading David *Hume.

Theory of Knowledge: Rationalism. Leibniz stated three goals for his life work, which he believed stood together, the love of God, promotion of human welfare, and the perfection of reason. The Leibniz method was mathematical, yet empirically grounded. He began by analyzing scientific findings (not merely ideas, as Renĕ *Descartes). He saw everything as beginning in the senses except the mind itself. A purely logical ground for science is not possible. However, reason is necessary to complete knowledge. There is no universal collection of sense data, and sense cannot organize and relate all the data.

Metaphysical (universal) knowledge is possible only because God made all things in harmony. All ideas are innate, generated by the mind from sensory information.

First Principles. Some ideas are necessarily true. These first principles are the condition of all knowledge. As first principles, the predicate in each statement can be deduced from the subject. These include:

The Principle of Sufficient Reason. "There is a sufficient reason for everything, either in another or in itself." This principle is the ground of all true propositions and intelligibility.

The Principle of Noncontradiction. "Something cannot be both true and false at the same time and in the same sense."

The Principle of Identity. "A thing is identical to itself." I am I; A is A.

The principle of sufficient reason regulates all truth. The principles of noncontradiction and identity establish all necessary truths.

The Principle of Identity of Indiscernibles. "Where there is no discernible difference, things are identical." No separate substances (or monads) are alike. The world is filled with qualitatively different things, hierarchically graded. If two things were the same, there is no sufficient reason God would choose both of them to exist in a maximally good world (*see* EVIL, PROBLEM OF).

The Principle of Continuity. "The world is full; there are no gaps in the hierarchy of beings in the best world." Nature never acts by leaps.

The Principle of Contingency. "Every contingent thing has a cause." Possibility does not explain actuality. The basic question: Why is there something, rather than nothing?

The Principle of Perfection. "Good tends to maximize." Like the scholastic principle of finality (agents act for a good end). Good produces good in the maximal degree possible.

A corollary is that it is better to exist than not to exist. Essences have a drive *(conatus)* toward existence.

Leibniz's Proofs for God. Leibniz offered several arguments for the existence of God:

Argument from Perfection or Harmony. His argument from perfection or harmony can be stated:

1. Pure essences are eternal possibilities.
2. It is better to exist than not to exist.
3. All things have a drive toward existence (conatus). (a) Some are incompatible with others. (b) Not all can exist at a given moment. (c) But all strive to exist.
4. Yet there is harmony in the universe.
5. Hence, there must be a God who orders all things, keeping them in harmony with one another

Cosmological Argument. The *cosmological argument as formulated by Leibniz took the form:

1. The entire observed world is changing.
2. Whatever changes lacks the reason for its own existence.
3. But there is a sufficient reason for everything.
4. Hence, there must be a cause beyond the world for its existence.
5. This cause is either its own sufficient reason, or there is one beyond it.
6. But there cannot be an infinite regress of sufficient reasons, for the failure to reach an explanation is not an explanation. There must be an explanation.
7. Therefore, there must be a First Cause of the world that has no reason beyond itself but is its own sufficient reason.

This argument differs from that of Aquinas by its use of the principle of sufficient reason. *Thomas Aquinas appealed only to the principle of causality and, thus, avoided the charges of rationalism that were rightly leveled at Leibniz. The principle of sufficient reason led atheists (*see* *SARTRE, JEAN-PAUL; NIETZSCHE, FRIEDRICH) to conclude that the cosmological argument eventuated in the self-contradictory concept of God as a self-caused being.

**Ontological Argument.* Leibniz also contributed to the ontological argument debate:

1. If it is possible for an absolutely perfect being to exist, then it is necessary for it to exist. (a) By nature an absolutely perfect being cannot lack anything. (b) But if it did not exist, it would lack something. (c) Hence, an absolutely perfect being cannot lack existence.
2. It is possible (noncontradictory) for an absolutely perfect being to exist. (a) A perfection is a simple quality (= monad), since each one differs in kind. (b) But whatever is simple cannot conflict with another simple thing. (c) Hence, it is possible for one being (God) to have all perfections.
3. Therefore, it is necessary that an absolutely perfect being exists.

Metaphysics (Monadology). Leibniz developed his own theory of substance in order to bridge the physical world to metaphysical realities. His doctrine revolved around *monads*. He believed monads exist as an immaterial "particle" more elemental even than the atom, for while physical atoms can be divided, metaphysical monads cannot. Monads differ from one another in shape, size, space, and quality. They are created, they can be destroyed, but they cannot change. Each monad perceives and acts differently, at its own hierarchical level, as established by God. Together they act in total harmony with each other according to the plan of God and have an innate drive toward perfection that is built into their essence. Since body and soul are separate substances, their separate monads function together in precise harmony as ordered by God.

In the hierarchy of monads, the higher are those belonging to the spiritual realm. Soul monads are of a higher order than those of the body. The highest, uncreated Super Monad is God. God created all other monads and maximizes good among and through them.

Problem of Evil. According to Leibniz, God foreordains all things by foreknowledge, without coercing free will. Freedom is the spontaneity of an intellectual being. God has an antecedent will, which is only for good. He also has a consequent will to bring about the best world possible given the existence of evil. As best of all possible beings, God wills the best of all possible worlds. Since this world is willed by God, it must be the best possible or least defective world.

Three kinds of evil exist: metaphysical (finitude), moral (sin), and physical (suffering). Finitude underlies sin and suffering. Sin is the result of ignorance, a confused or unclarified state. Evil is part of a total picture of good, giving darkness so that the light stands out in contrast (*see* EVIL, PROBLEM OF).

God is working to perfect the universe, which can only be done by perfecting people. God aims at perfecting an immortal soul through the universal church. This view of the church borrows from *Augustine's *The City of God*.

Evaluation. Some of the ideas of Leibniz are flawed, but his positive contributions should be recognized:

Positive Contributions. Through his work in developing calculus, Leibniz did an immense service to modern math and science, and he contributed to epistemology, metaphysics, theology, and theodicy as well.

Epistemology. Leibniz was a foundationalist (*see* FOUNDATIONALISM), who correctly stressed that knowledge is impossible without first principles. Even though many disagree with his belief in innate ideas, even Kant in his *agnosticism acknowledged the necessity of an innate dimension to knowledge.

Metaphysics. As a theist (*see* THEIST), Leibniz believed in creation *ex nihilo*. He struggled with and gave modern form to theistic concepts in the tradition of *Augustine, *Anselm, and Thomas Aquinas. His cosmological argument has influenced theists.

Theodicy. Leibniz's solution to the problem of evil was classic (*see* EVIL, PROBLEM OF). It grappled with the origin, nature, and persistence of evil in a way that attempted to preserve both God's absolute perfection and human freedom. Further, in spite of justified criticisms, his concept of a "best possible world" is an essential element in theodicy.

Weaknesses. The central values notwithstanding, Leibniz is open to some criticism:

Rationalist epistemology. As Hume showed, the concept of innate ideas is contrary to experience. There is no evidence that we are born with a whole storehouse of ideas, waiting only to be activated. The *a priori* dimension to knowledge appears to be in the area of *capacity*, not *content*. That is, we are born with the capability to know truth, but not with a mind full of truths.

**Dualism.* Leibniz's dualism of mind and body leads to the unlikely views of parallelism, occasionalism, and established harmony of mind and body. There is no real interaction or unity between the two.

The principle of sufficient reason. In spite of the validity of many of Leibniz's first principles, the principle of sufficient reason leads logically to a contradictory, self-caused Being. For if the cause of God's being is within himself, then God is self-caused. Unlike the first principle of causality of Aquinas, the principle of sufficient reason is not rooted in reality (*see* REALISM) but only in the realm of ideas. Finally, the principle is not undeniable, since one can say that something does not have a reason (cause) without engaging in a self-defeating statement. Indeed, the uncreated God is the ultimate uncaused Cause.

The ontological argument. Leibniz's form of the ontological argument is based on the widely rejected premise that existence is a perfection (*see* KANT, IMMANUEL). Further, his attempt to prove that the concept is logically possible fails to reach its goal. It is subject to the same criticism leveled against other pluralisms that hold to a univocal view of being (*see* ANALOGY, PRINCIPLE OF). It is impossible to avoid monism.

Even Leibniz's form of the otherwise valid cosmological argument gives no certain starting point being based only in the observation [appearance] of change.

View of evil. This view of free will tends to reduce to a form of determinism. For if it is God who gives the drive or desire for free choices, how can it be really free (*see* FREE WILL).

Likewise, his theodicy implies that the best God can do still involves evil. This was powerfully satirized by Voltaire's *Candide*. While God must do his best, this present world is not it. This is not the best possible world, though it may very well be the best possible *way* to the best possible *world* (*see* EVIL, PROBLEM OF).

Sources

J. Collins, *God and Modern Philosophy*

N. L. Geisler and W. Corduan, *Philosophy of Religion*

J. E. Gurr, *The Principle of Sufficient Reason in Some Scholastic Systems, 1750–1900*

D. Hume, *An Enquiry of Human Understanding*

I. Kant, *The Critique of Pure Reason*

G. Leibniz, *Discourse on Metaphysics*

———, *Monadology*

———, *Theodicy*

Lessing, Gotthold Ephraim. Gotthold Ephraim Lessing (1729–1781) was the son of a scholarly German pastor who became a dramatist and critic. He studied theology at Leipzig University, where he imbibed the rationalism of the Enlightenment, whose leading spokesman was Christian Wolfe, a follower of Gottfried Leibniz. Lessing was influenced by the English deists (*see* DEISM). As a theater critic he came under the influence of the deist Hermann Reimarus, from whose book, *An Apology for Rational Worshippers of God* he published extracts in 1774 and 1777 to 1778 (*see* DEISM). Lessing finally came to be dominated by the pantheism of Benedict *Spinoza.

Lessing's influence on others was immense. It can be seen in the liberalism of Friedrich *Schleiermacher and Samuel Coleridge, as well as the existentialism of Søren *Kierkegaard and the historicism of G. W. F. *Hegel and the positivism of Auguste Comte.

Views of God. Lessing came from a trinitarian (*see* TRINITY) background, but gradually adopted deist ideas and eventually became a Spinozan pantheist. As such, his life foreshadowed much of the history of the next two centuries. By 1753 Lessing indicated in *The Christianity of Reason* that he was moving toward *pantheism, as he mixed Spinoza and *Leibniz and denied that God is a superobject beyond or behind the world (see Chadwick, 445). His 1763 work, *On the Reality of Things Outside God*, which was published posthumously in 1795, denied traditional theism. He denied that a created world exists distinct from God.

Friedrich Jacobi, in *Letters to Moses Mendelssohn on Spinoza's Doctrine* (1785), related how, seven months before Lessing's death, the critic had told him of his rejection of transcendent metaphysics in deism. He had adopted the immanentistic view of Spinoza. This was confirmed by fragments found among Lessing's papers (ibid., 446).

Lessing not only believed that nothing exists outside the divine mind, but since ideas of contingent things are necessary, believed that a contingency exists inside God. This foreshadowed the later process theologians (*see* PANENTHEISM), such as Alfred North *Whitehead.

History and the Gospels. In 1754 Lessing published a series of "Vindications," in which he defended a number of historical figures he believed had been badly treated by the church. While expressing sympathy with the Christian ethic in these leaders, he showed antipathy toward Christian doctrines.

Christ versus Jesus. The turning point for Lessing occurred in 1769. As librarian for the duke of Brunswick he began to publish fragments of a manuscript by the deist Reimarus (1766–69). The last fragment precipitated a controversy with Hamburg pastor Johann Goeze and touched off the quest for the historical Jesus (*see* CHRIST OF FAITH VS. JESUS OF HISTORY; JESUS, QUEST FOR THE HISTORICAL; JESUS SEMINAR). Not only did Lessing distinguish between the Jesus of history and the Christ of Faith; he did a critical study of the sources of the Synoptic Gospels in *New Hypotheses Concerning the Evangelists Regarded as Merely Human Historians* (1784). Lessing's views were expressed in a play, "Nathan the Wise," which pleaded for love and tolerance rather than assent to a creed. Lessing's view was the essence of Enlightenment Christianity, the view that, beneath creedal accretions, Christianity is a moral code of universal brotherhood.

Lessing's "Ditch." The legacy of Lessing was a "ditch" dug between the contingent truths of history and the necessary truths of faith. He split the revelation of timeless truths from the time-bound, contingent truths of history. It was this huge gulf with which *Kierkegaard struggled and from which he took his "leap of faith" (see *Fear and Trembling*).

Lessing affirmed that the "accidental truths of history can never become the proof of necessary truths of reason" (Chadwick, 445). There is no logical connection between historical realities and faith. Faith truths are mathematical and *a priori*, independent of experience. The former are *a posteriori*, contingent truths of experience. Therefore, historical narrative can never convey knowledge of God.

Relativism. Lessing was more a relativist than a skeptic. He immortalized his view in the aphorism, "If God held all truth in his right hand and in his left the everlasting striving after truth, so that I should always and everlastingly be mistaken and said to me, Choose, with humility I would pick on the left hand and say, Father grant me that; absolute truth is for thee alone" (Chadwick, 445).

Evaluation. Lessing's self-claimed humility aside, it is clear that the net result of his views a self-defeating form of *agnosticism, relativism (*see* TRUTH, NATURE OF), and a dichotomy of fact and value and of history and faith (*see* APOLOGETICS, ARGUMENT OF; NEW TESTAMENT, MANUSCRIPTS; NEW TESTAMENT DOCUMENTS, RELIABILITY OF). One insightful assessment is that "Lessing spent his life hoping that Christianity was true and arguing that it was not" (Chadwick, 445).

Sources

H. Chadwick, *Lessing's Theological Writings*

E. H. Gombrich, "Lessing," in *Proceedings of the British Academy*, vol. 43 (1957)

P. Hazard, *European thought in the Eighteenth Century*

F. C. A. Koelln, *The Philosophy of the Enlightenment*

G. Lessing, *Lessing's Gesammelte Werke*, ed. P. Rilla

"Lessing's Ditch." ***See*** **LESSING, GOTTHOLD EPHRAIM.**

Lewis, C. S. Because much of his work was in popular media, including radio broadcasts and children's stories, Clive Staples Lewis (1898–1963) is arguably the most influential twentieth-century Christian theist and apologist (*see* APOLOGETICS, NEED FOR). An Oxford University professor, this former atheist so expressed profound truths in simple language that he reached into the hearts of millions. Lewis disclaimed being a philosopher or theologian, but his insight into the essentials of *theism made him a significant apologist and communicator.

The Nature and Existence of God. Lewis accepted the Augustine-Anselm-Aquinas view of God as eternal, necessary, transcendent, morally perfect, and personal (*see* GOD, NATURE OF). God transcends space and time: "Almost certainly God is not in Time. His life does not consist of moments following one another. . . . Ten-thirty—and every other moment from the beginning of the world—is always the Present for Him." To put it another way, "He has all eternity in which to listen to the split second of prayer put up by a pilot as his plane crashes in flames" (*Mere Christianity,* 146).

God is, nevertheless, immanent (present and operating) in creation. Lewis wrote: "Looking for God—or Heaven—by exploring space is like reading or seeing all Shakespeare's plays in the hope that you will find Shakespeare as one of the characters or Stratford as one of the places. Shakespeare is in one sense present at every moment in every play. But he is never present in the same way as Falstaff or Lady Macbeth. Nor is he diffused through the play like a gas" (*Christian Reflections,* 167–68).

*The *Cosmological Argument.* Although he accepted a theistic form of evolution (see below), Lewis believed in creation out of nothing (*see* CREATION, VIEWS OF). For "What God creates is not God; just as what man makes is not man" (*God in the Dock,* 138). He explained that matter is not coeternal with God:

> Entropy by its very character assures us that though it may be the universal rule in the Nature we know, it cannot be universal absolutely. If a man says, "Humpty Dumpty is falling," you see at once that this is not a complete story. The bit you have been told implies both a later chapter in which Humpty Dumpty will have reached the ground, and an earlier chapter in which he was still seated on the wall. A Nature which is "running down" cannot be the whole story. A clock can't run down unless it has been wound up." [Lewis, *Miracles,* 157]

Matter is the product of a cosmic Mind (*see* DUALISM). "But to admit *that* sort of cosmic mind is to admit a God outside Nature, a transcendent and supernatural God" (ibid., 30). The universe is matter. Matter cannot produce mind; only mind can produce matter (*see* MATERIALISM). The creation of the world was not from some pre-existing matter or stuff. It was created from nothing. God created this world freely: "The freedom of God consists in the fact that no cause other than Himself produces His acts and no external obstacle impedes them—that His own goodness is the root from which they all grow and His own omnipotence the air in which they all flower." (*Problem of Pain,* 23).

God did not create the world because he had to; he created it because he wanted to. The existence of the universe is entirely contingent on the good will of the Creator.

*The *Moral Argument.* Lewis begins *Mere Christianity* with the premise that an objective moral law, such as even common disagreements presuppose, entails a Moral Law Giver. There is "something which is directing the universe, and which appears in me as a law urging me to do right and making me feel responsible and uncomfortable when I do wrong. I think we have to assume it is more like a mind than it is like anything else we know—because after all the only other thing we know is matter and you can hardly imagine a bit of matter giving instructions" (*Mere Christianity,* 34).

Lewis's argument can be summarized:

1. There must be an objective, universal moral law, or else no ethical judgments make sense (*see* MORALITY, ABSOLUTE NATURE OF). Nothing could be called evil or wrong, and there would be no reason to keep promises or treaties (*God in the Dock,* chap. 1).
2. This moral law does not originate with us. In fact, we are bound by it.
3. The source of this law is more like mind than matter, and it cannot be part of the universe any more than an architect is part of the building he designs.
4. Therefore, there exists a Moral Law Giver who is the ultimate source and standard of all right and wrong (ibid., chap. 7).

For a fuller discussion of Lewis's moral law argument and its defense, see his section in the article MORAL ARGUMENT FOR GOD.

The Nature of Human Beings. However science may show that the human body emerged, the process was divinely initiated and consummated by God in the creation of a rational human soul.

Human Beings Are Rational. Lewis would not blush at the appellation "rationalist." Repeatedly he exalts human rationality. He writes, "I couldn't get at the universe unless I could trust my reason. If we couldn't trust inference we could know nothing but our own existence" (*God in the Dock,* 277). "The heart never takes the place of the head; but can and should obey it" (*The Abolition of Man,* 30).

There also must be an ultimate reason or explanation. "You cannot go on 'explaining away' forever: you will find that you have explained explanation itself away." Moreover, "you cannot go on 'seeing through' things forever." Consequently, "it is no use trying to 'see through' first principles. If you see through everything, then everything is transparent." But "to 'see through' all things is the same as not to see" (ibid., 91).

Lewis believed rational thought is undeniable. He insists that "all arguments [against] the validity of thought make a tacit, and illegitimate, exception in favor of the bit of thought you are doing at that moment." Hence, "the validity of thought is central: all other things have to be fitted in round it as best they can" (Lewis, *Miracles,* 23).

Human Beings Are Moral. Emphasis on the rational nature does not negate human emotions. Those who put thinking above feeling are for Lewis "men without chests" (Lewis, *Abolition of Man,* 34). "The head rules the belly through the chest—the seat . . . of emotions organized by trained habit into stable sentiments." Without this middle element "man is vain: for by his intellect he is mere spirit and by his appetite mere animal" (ibid., 34). Beyond the moral nature stands an attainable moral ideal. Lewis would agree with the statement that the primary value of education is an education in primary values. Education fulfills its proper purpose as it cultivates value judgments to help perfect the moral nature. Without trained emotions, the intellect is powerless against the animal (ibid., 33, 34). Thus, Lewis observes, it is better to play cards with a skeptic who is a gentleman than a moral philosopher who was brought up among card sharks (ibid., 34). Only because we stand within God's law can we speak of having the power of self-control (ibid., 86).

Secular humanism, in a sort of ghastly simplicity, removes the moral organ and yet demands the moral function. "We make men without chests and expect of them virtue and enterprise. We laugh at honour and are shocked to find traitors in our midst" (ibid., 35).

Human Beings Are Creative. Characteristically, Lewis also affirmed the aesthetic nature within an ideal of human creatorhood. Dorothy Sayers's *Toward a Christian Aesthetic* calls the idea of art as *creation* Christianity's most important contribution to aesthetics (6). The artist or writer is not the Creator, but a sub-creator. Creative expression expresses the image of an artist's inner feelings even as the Invisible God was visibly expressed in the incarnation of his Son. He and other Christians of his Oxford University circle, called the Inklings, produced an immense literary body. Lewis himself wrote

- seven fantasy genre books of the Narnia Chronicles: *The Lion, the Witch, and the Wardrobe*; *Prince Caspian*; *The Voyage of the Dawn Treader*; *The Magician's Nephew*; *The Horse and His Boy*; *The Silver Chair*; and *The Last Battle*.
- a "space trilogy," that explored the nature of God's battle with personal and societal evil in the guise of three interlocking science fiction stories: *Out of the Silent Planet*, *Perelandra*, and *That Hideous Strength*.
- *Screwtape Letters* and *The Great Divorce*, deceptively light stories reflecting the dynamics of temptation and rebellion against God.
- a series of BBC radio lectures expanded into an apologetic classic, *Mere Christianity*, as well as deeper works in apologetics and philosophy, including *God in the Dock*, *Studies in Medieval and Renaissance Literature*, *The Abolition of Man*, and *The Problem of Pain*.

- his intellectual and spiritual autobiography, *Surprised by Joy*.
- the moving story of his crisis of faith at his wife's death, *A Grief Observed*.
- a variety of literary criticism articles and studies.
- voluminous personal correspondence, a sampling of which was published in *Letters to an American Lady*.

Human Beings Are Immortal. Lewis also affirmed humanity's eternal value (*see* IMMORTALITY). This affirmation springs from the belief that each person is made in God's image. To affirm humanity while denying the ultimate moral value does not affirm real human value at all. Secularist humanists, Lewis believed, abolish, rather than affirm, humanity (see *The Abolition of Man* and an allegorical version of its message, *That Hideous Strength*). In denying the human immortal, moral and God-like nature they deny personhood and sweep away the basis for treating the individual with ultimate respect (*The Abolition of Man,* 76, 77).

The irony, then, is that, as secular humanists elevate humanity to godhood, they sweep away all humanity, with its accompanying right to respect. By contrast, Christianity, in affirming that the basis for ultimate value comes from a transcendent God, preserves the basis for ultimate human dignity.

So secularist humanism dehumanizes what it seeks to deify. Only the Christian view retains true humanness. For Lewis holds that "either we are rational spirit obliged forever to obey the absolute values of the *Tao* [moral law], or else we are mere nature to be kneaded and cut into new shapes" (ibid., 84). The only guarantee against tyranny and slavery is to affirm immortal human worth in the context of an absolute moral law. For "the process which, if not checked, will abolish Man, goes on apace among Communists and Democrats no less than among Fascists" (ibid., 85). Only within the absolute moral law is there a concrete reality in which to be truly human (ibid., 86).

Human Beings Have Dignity. Following from rationality and moral responsibility is human dignity. There is a firm basis for this virtue in the immortal human-God-like nature: A person has rational, moral and volitional abilities. This is why punishment for wrongdoing is appropriate. The person knows better and deserves to be penalized for unlawful action (*God in the Dock,* 292). Punishment is a complement to human dignity.

Citing Martin *Buber, Lewis exhorts science not to treat the person as an "It" but to recognize the human "Thou" (Lewis, *The Abolition of Man,* 90). We must never surrender any human to science as a mere object to control. This, says Lewis, is "a 'magician's bargain' . . . whereby man surrenders object after object, and finally himself, to Nature in return for power" (ibid., 87). When science is allowed to take control, it has the same goal as magic, though its means differ (ibid., 89). He reminds us that even the father of modern science, Francis Bacon, condemned those who make scientific knowledge an end, rather than a means (ibid., 88). Lewis called science to repentance: "The regenerate science which I have in mind would not do even to minerals and vegetables what modern science threatens to do to man himself" (ibid., 89, 90).

Lewis chides the secularists for boasting in science. "As regards the powers manifested in the aeroplane or the wireless, man is as much the patient or subject as the possessor, since he is the target both for bombs and for propaganda" (ibid., 68). What we call power over nature turns out to be power by some people over others (ibid., 69). "Each new power won *by* man is a power *over* man as well. Each advance leaves him weaker as well as stronger" (ibid., 71).

Unless those in control of power are bound by an objective moral law, the power gained will be used only to bind, and not to benefit, the human race. Says Lewis, "I am very doubtful whether history shows us one example of a man who, having stepped outside traditional morality and attained power, has used that power benevolently" (ibid., 75). The final irony is that when humankind steps outside the moral law, which Lewis calls the *Tao,* the Chinese word for "way," they become no longer human, but artifacts. "Man's final conquest has proved to be the abolition of Man" (ibid., 77).

So biased against Lewis' penal view of justice were the secular humanists of his day that no academic publication would publish him on the topic. His definitive statement was first published in an Australian journal and later incorporated into *God in the Dock*. In this article Lewis attacks secular humanism's reformatory view of justice. He argues that it is tyranny to subject a human being to an undesired, compulsory cure. The reformatory view is "illusory humanitarianism," which disguises cruelty on the false premise that crime is pathological, not moral. In fact, the reformatory view dehumanizes the individual, treating him as a patient or case, rather than as a person. Lewis insists that to be 'cured' against one's will puts the man or woman in a class with those who cannot think for themselves and never will. Even severe punishment of a person as a rational human being treats the person as an image-bearer of God (*God in the Dock,* 292).

Lewis was keenly aware of the danger of replacing the objective moral law of God with subjective political laws (*see* LAW, NATURE AND KINDS OF). History shows that dictators who step outside the moral law are invariably not benevolent. The potential for evil when great power resides in a person's political grasp is horrendous. This message also figures into the social commentary of the allegorical *That Hideous Strength*.

Miracles. Naturalism claims that nature is "the whole show." So if naturalism is true, then every event in nature must be explicable in terms of the total system of nature. But human (inferential) reason, such as even naturalists assume and exercise, cannot be explained strictly in terms of nonrational natural causes. Moreover, "the Naturalist cannot condemn other people's thoughts because they have irrational causes and continue to believe his own, which have (if Naturalism is true) equally irrational causes" (*Miracles*, 22). Furthermore, argues Lewis, if naturalism is right then there is no reason that the thoughts of a lunatic or drug addict should not be valued by a naturalist as much as his or her own thoughts. This is the self-contradiction of naturalism.

There is more than nature; there is mind which cannot be reduced to matter. And there is value (ought), which cannot be reduced to nature (what is). In fact, there is an absolute moral Mind behind nature who gives the moral law.

Evil. According to Lewis, evil is not eternal, as dualism claims.

> The two Powers, the good and the evil, do not explain each other. Neither . . . can claim to be the Ultimate. More ultimate than either of them is the inexplicable fact of their being there together. Neither of them chose this *tete-a-tete*. Each of them, therefore, is *conditioned*—finds himself willy-nilly in a situation; and either that situation itself, or some unknown force which produced that situation, is the real Ultimate. Dualism has not yet reached the ground of being. You cannot accept two conditioned and mutually independent beings as the self-grounded, self-comprehending Absolute. [*God in the Dock*, 22]

Evil arose from free choice (*see* FREE WILL). This does not mean that it is evil to be free. In freedom we most resemble God and take part in eternal reality (ibid., 129). Christianity agrees with dualists that the universe is at war. But the Christian does not think this is a war between independent powers. It is, rather, a civil rebellion, and we are living in territory occupied by the rebel (*Mere Christianity*, 51). This rebellion was not at first a turning to wickedness. "Wickedness, when you examine it, turns out to be the pursuit of some good in the wrong way" (ibid., 49).

Like *Augustine and *Thomas Aquinas, C. S. Lewis believed that evil does not exist in itself but as a corruption of good (*see* EVIL, PROBLEM OF). "Goodness is, so to speak, itself: badness is only spoiled goodness. And there must be something good first before it can be spoiled" (ibid., 49). Even the devil is a fallen angel. So "evil is a parasite, not an original thing" (ibid., 50).

God does not permit evil without a good purpose. Even physical evil has a moral impact. For "God whispers to us in our pleasures, speaks in our conscience, but shouts in our pain: it is His megaphone to rouse a deaf world" (*Problem of Pain*, 81).

Human Beings. So human beings are free rational and moral beings with an immortal soul. But each is in a body in a material world with other bodies. Lewis wrote: "A creature with no environment would have no choices to make: so that freedom, like self-consciousness (if they are not, indeed, the same thing) again demands the presence to the self of something other than the self" (ibid., 17).

The human environment is called nature. But humanity is more than natural processes. Humans think rationally, and "no thought is valid if it can be fully explained as the result of irrational causes." Every worldview that makes the human mind a result of irrational causes is inadmissible. Such a view "would be a proof that there are no such things as proofs, which is nonsense" (*Miracles*, 21).

The human is both a rational and a moral being. Without a moral nature there would be no true humanity, so those who would abolish the moral law would abolish humanity in the bargain (*Abolition of Man*, 77):

> Either we are rational spirit obliged for ever to obey the absolute values of the *Tao*, or else we are mere nature to be kneaded and cut into new shapes for the pleasure of masters who must, by hypothesis, have no motive but their own "natural" impulses. Only the *Tao* provides a common human law of action which can over-arch rulers and ruled alike. A dogmatic belief in objective value is necessary to the very idea of a rule which is not tyranny or an obedience which is not slavery. [ibid., 84–85]

Ethics. The moral human creature is obligated to live by an absolute moral law (*see* MORALITY, ABSOLUTE NATURE OF) that transcends human law. Such was what the framers of the Declaration of Independence had in mind when they wrote of the "Laws of Nature and of Nature's God" and of "certain unalienable rights" with which all are "endowed by their Creator." As moral creatures, created in God's image, we have certain absolute obligations toward others.

This objective moral law is prescriptive, not descriptive. It lays down the principles by which we ought to live; it does not merely express the way we do live. It is not social convention, for it sometimes condemns society. Neither is it herd instinct, for we sometimes act out of a sense of duty against our instinct for self-preservation

(*Mere Christianity,* 22). We can progress in our understanding, but the moral law itself does not change (*Abolition of Man,* 58, 59).

History and the Goal. Life is the proving ground for eternity. During life, each rational creature makes a lifetime decision. All play the game, and "if a game is played, it must be possible to lose it." Of course, adds Lewis, "I would pay any price to be able to say truthfully 'All will be saved.' But my reason retorts, 'Without their will, or with it?' If I say 'Without their will,' I at once perceive a contradiction; how can the supreme voluntary act of self-surrender be involuntary? If I say 'With their will,' my reason replies 'How if they *will not* give in?'" (*Problem of Pain,* 106–7).

At the end of life and history, Lewis finds two kinds of people: "those who say to God, 'Thy will be done,' and those to whom God says, in the end, '*Thy* will be done.' All that are in hell, choose it." Lewis believed "without that self-choice there could be no hell. No soul that seriously and constantly desires joy will ever miss it. Those who seek, find. To those who knock it is opened" (*The Great Divorce,* 69). Thus, the doors of hell are locked on the *inside*. Even those who *wish* to come out of hell would not do so at the expense of self-abandonment through which alone the soul can reach any good (*The Great Divorce,* 127).

Evaluation. In spite of Lewis's overwhelming value to Christian apologetics, not everything in his views is compatible with evangelical Christianity. Lewis wrote one of the finest critiques of naturalism in print *(Miracles),* in which he defended literal New Testament miracles, including the resurrection of Christ. Nevertheless, Lewis inconsistently denied the literal nature of many Old Testament miracles (*see* MIRACLES IN THE BIBLE):

> The Hebrews, like other peoples, had mythology: but as they were the chosen people so their mythology was the chosen mythology—the mythology chosen by God to be the vehicle of the earliest sacred truths, the first step in that process which ends in the New Testament where truth has become completely historical. Whether we can ever say with certainty where, in this process of crystalisation, any particular Old Testament story falls, is another matter. I take it that the memoirs of David's court come at one end of the scale and are scarcely less historical than *St. Mark* or *Acts*; and that the *Book of Jonah* is at the opposite end. [*Miracles,* 139]

Lewis accepted the deity of Christ. But he did not believe in a Christ who verified the historicity and authenticity of some of the very Old Testament events Lewis rejects. Jesus verified the literal truth of Jonah (Matt. 12:40), of the nonevolutionary creation of Adam and Eve (Matt. 19:4), of the flood (Matt. 24:38–39), and of other miraculous events (see Geisler, *Inerrancy,* 3–35). Lewis seems to read into the Old Testament a non-Christian development of myth (*see* MIRACLES, MYTH AND). This is especially surprising in view of his criticism of New Testament scholars who do the same. Lewis chides them:

> A theology which denies the historicity of nearly everything in the Gospels to which Christian life and affections and thought have been fastened for nearly two millennia—which either denies the miraculous altogether or, more strangely, after swallowing the camel of the Resurrection strains at such gnats as the feeding of the multitudes—if offered to the uneducated man can produce only one or other of two effects. It will make him a Roman Catholic or an atheist. [*Christian Reflections, 153*]

Lewis does recognize that he might be wrong about Old Testament miracles. He admits that his view is tentative and liable to error, and that the subject matter is beyond his knowledge:

> A consideration of the Old Testament miracles is beyond the scope of this book and would require many kinds of knowledge which I do not possess. My present view—which is tentative and liable to any amount of correction—would be that just as, on the factual side, a long preparation culminates in God's becoming incarnate as Man, so, on the documentary side, the truth first appears in *mythical* form and then by a long process of condensing or focussing finally becomes incarnate as History. [*Miracles,* 139]

Lewis also accepted other higher critical ideas about the Old Testament (*see* BIBLE CRITICISM). He questioned the historicity of Job, "because it begins about a man quite unconnected with all history or even legend, with no genealogy, living in a country of which the Bible elsewhere has hardly anything to say" (*Mere Christianity,* 110). Lewis held this in spite of references to Job as historical in both Old (Ezek. 14:14, 20) and New Testaments (James 5:11). Uz is mentioned in Jeremiah 25:20 and Lamentations 4:21. Customs and forms of proper names connected with Job also have been verified (Archer, 438–48).

Lewis held a very negative view of many Psalms, even calling some "devilish" (*Reflections on the Psalms,* 25). He rejected the Davidic authorship of all but Psalm 18 (ibid., 114). This is especially surprising given Lewis's high view of Christ and the Gospels. Jesus verified that David wrote Psalm 110 (Matt. 22:41–46). Jesus also affirmed the divine authority of the whole Old Testament (Matt. 5:17–18; John 10:35) and especially the Psalms (cf. Luke 24:44), which was one of the books he quoted most frequently.

Although he had some later doubts (Ferngreen), his own educational background apparently led Lewis to assume an evolutionary (*see* Evolution, Biological) view of the universe's origin (see *Mere Christianity,* 52, 65). That even so pious and courageous an intellectual apologist as Lewis could be sucked into humanist and higher critical assumptions shows that each believer must continually evaluate the truth of what he or she is learning in a secular pagan environment.

Sources

G. L. Archer, Jr., *A Survey of Old Testament Introduction*
G. B. Ferngreen, et al., "C. S. Lewis on Creation and Evolution . . ."
N. L. Geisler, *Is Man the Measure?*
———, ed. *Inerrancy*
C. S. Lewis, *Christian Reflections*
———, *God in the Dock,* esp. "The Humanitarian Theory of Punishment"
———, *Mere Christianity*
———, *Miracles*
———, *The Abolition of Man*
———, *The Problem of Pain*
———, *Reflections on the Psalms*
———, *Screwtape Letters*
———, *Studies in Medieval and Renaissance Literature*
R. Purtill, *C. S. Lewis' Case for the Christian Faith*
D. Sayers, "Toward a Christian Aesthetics," in *The Whimsical Christian*
J. R. R. Tolkien, *The Lord of the Rings*

Limitation of Christ, Theory of. Bible critics have offered two theories that undermine the apologetic argument for the deity of Christ (*see* Christ, Deity of) and the authority of Scripture (*see* Bible, Evidence for). A crucial link in the overall argument for both is that Jesus taught that he was the Son of God and that the Bible is the Word of God (*see* Apologetics, Argument of). These propositions are based on the premise that the Gospels accurately tell us what Jesus taught. If Jesus intentionally accommodated his words to what his audience believed but did not disclose what he really believed, then the conclusion does not hold (*see* Accommodation Theory).

Likewise, if Jesus was so limited in his human knowledge that it did not extend to such matters as the authority and authenticity of the Old Testament, he was not really affirming these matters. Rather, his ministry was limited to spiritual and moral matters, and he affirmed nothing about historical and critical matters.

The Case for a Limited Christ. Two supporting pillars in the argument for limitation are the *humanity of Christ* and the *kenosis theory*.

Humanly Limited Knowledge. The Bible makes clear that Jesus was human (*see* Christ, Deity of). But if Jesus was truly human in every respect, why could he not experience human error? Why could Jesus not have been wrong about many of the things he believed, so long as they did not hinder his overall redemptive mission?

Emptying at the Incarnation. The Bible further teaches that Jesus "emptied himself" of his omniscience at his incarnation. That this severely limited his knowledge when he taught is called the *kenosis* theory, from the Greek word *kenoō*, to "empty." He was ignorant of the time of his second coming, for he said, "No one knows about that day and hour, not even the angels in heaven, nor the Son, but only the Father" (Mark 13:32). He did not know whether figs were on the tree in Mark 11:13. As a child he "increased in wisdom," as do other children (Luke 2:52). He had to ask questions (Mark 5:9, 30; 6:38; John 14:9). Perhaps Jesus was also ignorant of the origin of the Old Testament and of the historical truth of its record.

Response to the Limitation View. The "limitation theory" is more plausible and potentially more damaging then the accommodation theory. But both arguments in favor of the limitation of Christ's understanding ignore crucial points about who Jesus was.

Can God err or sin? In Jesus, one and the same person was both God and human at the same time. If the human person had sinned or erred, then God would have sinned or erred. This is why the Bible is careful to say, "We have one who was tempted in every way, just as we are—yet was without sin" (Heb. 4:15). He was human enough to be tired and tempted, but not to be sinful (see 2 Cor. 5:21; 1 Peter 3:18; 1 John 3:3). If a sin attributed to Christ must also be attributed to God, who cannot sin (Hab. 1:13; Heb. 6:18), then an error attributed to Christ would have been an error God made (*see* Trinity).

The *kenosis* theory that Jesus emptied himself of deity when he became human is unfounded. It is certainly not the meaning of Philippians 2. Verses 5 and 6 say that he emptied himself of his divine nature by humbling himself to become a human being. When he emptied himself he was still in the form or essence of God. If the same word, *form,* as applied to a servant means he was a servant, then applied to God it means he is God. This is what John 1:1 declares. The human Jesus claimed to be God. How he showed that to be so is covered at length in the article Christ, Deity of. The incarnation did not subtract deity; it added humanity. An error or sin would have been attributable to the second person of the godhead.

Since the orthodox doctrine of Christ acknowledges that he was fully human, there is no problem with the statement that Jesus was ignorant of many things. He had two natures, one infinite or unlimited in knowledge, the other finite or limited in knowledge. Could it be that Jesus did not really "err" in what he taught about the Old Testament but that he was simply so limited that his human knowledge and authority did not extend into those areas? The evidence in the New

Testament records demands an emphatic negative answer to that question.

Jesus had supranormal knowledge. Even in his human state, Christ possessed super-human knowledge. He saw Nathaniel under the fig tree (John 1:48). Jesus knew the private life of the Samaritan woman (John 4:18–19). He knew who would betray him (John 6:64) and all that would happen in Jerusalem (Mark 8:31; 9:31; John 18:4). He knew about Lazarus' death before he was told (John 11:14). Whatever his limitations, Jesus' knowledge was completely adequate for his mission and doctrinal teaching.

Jesus possessed final authority. Christ claimed, with absolute and final authority, that whatever he taught came from God. "Heaven and earth will pass away but my word will not pass away" (Matt. 24:35). Jesus proclaimed that "all things have been delivered to me by my Father" (Matt. 11:27). He told his disciples to teach others "to observe all that I have commanded you" (Matt. 28:18–19). Jesus claimed that the very destiny of people hung on his words (Matt. 7:24–26) and that his words would be the basis for judgment (John 12:48). The emphatic *amen, amen* or "Truly, truly" is used to preface his teachings twenty-five times in John alone. In Matthew he declared that not a single stroke would pass from the law that he had come to fulfill. Then, throughout the rest of Matthew 5, Jesus placed his own words on a par with that law. He claimed that his words bring eternal life (John 5:24), and vowed that his teaching came from the Father (John 8:26–28). Despite the fact that he was a human being on earth, Christ accepted acknowledgment as deity (for example, Matt. 28:18; John 9:38).

Conclusion. The most reasonable conclusion is that Jesus' teachings possessed divine authority. Despite the necessary limitations involved in a human incarnation, there is no error or misunderstanding in what Christ taught. Whatever limits there were in the extent of Jesus' knowledge, there were no limits to the truthfulness of his teachings. Just as Jesus was fully human, yet his *moral* character was without flaw (Heb. 4:15), likewise he was finite in human knowledge and yet without factual error in what he taught (John 8:40, 46). Whatever Jesus taught came from God and carried divine authority.

Sources

N. L. Geisler, *Christian Apologetics*, chap. 18

J. Wenham, *Christ and the Bible*, chap. 2

Locke, John. *The Life and Works of Locke.* Locke was born in Somersetshire, England, in 1632 and died in 1704. He disliked his scholastic training, but read and enjoyed Rene *Descartes and Francis Bacon. His work on tolerance strongly influenced the American Revolution—Thomas *Jefferson in particular.

Locke's main writings included *An Essay Concerning Toleration* (1667), *An Essay Concerning Human Understanding* (1690), and *The Reasonableness of Christianity* (1695).

The Empirical Epistemology of Locke. Locke was an empiricist, following the work of Aristotle (*see*). In his *Essay Concerning Human Understanding* he called his epistemology "the plain historical method," that is, treating ideas just as they appear in our minds. His goal was to discover the origin, extent, and degree of certainty in our knowledge.

The Two Sources of Ideas. Locke believed there were two sources of ideas (or, objects of thought): (1) sensation—experience of an external object (which presses on the body and produces an idea in the mind), and (2) reflection—experience of internal operations of the mind. As proof he offered four arguments. First, children are born as *tabula rasas* (blank slates) without a store of ideas. Second, where there are different experiences, there are different ideas.

Third, where there is no experience, there is no corresponding idea. For example, persons born blind have no idea of sight, nor do deaf mutes have an idea of sound. Fourth, we have only ideas that fit one or more of the five senses (or combinations thereof).

The Nature of Knowledge. For Locke all knowledge is either agreement or disagreement.

Intuition is agreement between two ideas immediately perceived (e.g., "I" and "exist" = I exist). This is the most certain kind of knowledge.

Demonstration is agreement between two ideas seen by way of a third idea (e.g., "God exists"). This is less certain to us only because the chain of argument makes it so.

Sensation is agreement between an idea and an external object (e.g., "The world exists"). This is less certain. Locke's proof of an external world went like this: (1) There must be a source of our ideas. Not all of them could have been created by us. (2) Some ideas are more lively than others, showing that they are original and not created by us. (3) We have combined testimony of several senses that these lively ideas come from the external world. (4) Pleasure and/or pain repeatedly occurs upon contact with it, even when we do not will it. Hence, there must be an external world that is the source of these lively ideas over which we have no control.

Locke's Proof for the Existence of God. Locke's proof for the existence of God follows the line of the traditional cosmological argument (*see*). (1) Something exists. For example, I exist (which is known by intuition). Further, the world exists (which is known by sensation). (2) This something that exists comes either (a) from itself, (b) from nothing, or (c) from another. But (3) only something can cause something. Something cannot be caused by nothing. (4) There cannot be an *infinite series of causes of the existence of the world. If there were, the whole world would rest on nothing. But this is impossible, for in this case (since nothing cannot cause something) the world would never have come into existence. Therefore, (5) there must be a first cause of my existence and the world. (6) This eternal being must be most powerful and most knowing. It must be most powerful because it is the source of all power, and it must be most knowing because the cognitive cannot arise from the noncognitive. Locke believed it was ridiculous to say everything else has a mind behind it except the universe.

The Defense of Christianity. Building on his rational *theism, Locke argued in the tradition of classical apologetics (*see* APOLOGETICS, CLASSICAL). In his *Reasonableness of Christianity* he defended the existence of miracles. In his two *Vindications* (1695, 1697) he defended what he said in the *Reasonableness of Christianity*.

The Defense of the Supernatural. Locke was neither a Deist (*see* DEISM) nor a Socinian who denied the resurrection (*see* RESURRECTION, EVIDENCE FOR). He defended miracles, as well as the Bible as the Word of God (*see* BIBLE, EVIDENCE FOR). He believed the Bible could be defended by reason, but that it contained mysteries of the Christian faith that go beyond reason.

The Deity of Christ. He also defended Christ's deity (*see* CHRIST, DEITY OF), claiming "we see the people justified their believing in him, i.e., their believing him to be the Messiah, because of the miracles he did" (*Reasonableness of Christianity* [58] 1). He added of Jesus, "He was sent by God: His miracles shew it" (ibid., 242). There is a conspicuous absence of discussion on the Trinity. However, absence does not necessarily mean denial. Though Locke admits in a letter to Limborch that he said some things to please the Deists (*see* DEISM), he explicitly denied Arianism.

Locke's View of Ethics and Government. Locke held that the "law of Nature" (*see* NATURAL LAW) teaches us that "being all equal and independent, no one ought to harm another in his life, health, liberty or possessions; for men being all the workmanship of one omnipotent and infinitely wise Maker" (*An Essay concerning Toleration*, 2.6).

This same view was expressed by Thomas Jefferson in the Declaration of Independence (1776) when he wrote: "we hold these truths to be self-evident, that all men are created equal, that they are endowed by their Creator with certain unalienable Rights, that among these are Life, Liberty and the pursuit of Happiness."

Sources

J. G. Clapp, "Locke, John." *In The Encyclopedia of Philosophy*, vol. 4

J. Collins, *A History of Modern European Philosophy*

J. Locke, *An Essay Concerning Toleration*

———. *An Essay Concerning Human Understanding*

——— *The Reasonableness of Christianity*

Logic. Logic deals with the methods of valid thinking. It reveals how to draw proper conclusions from premises and is a prerequisite of all thought. In fact, it builds from fundamental laws of reality and truth, the principles that make rational thought possible (*see* FIRST PRINCIPLES). Logic is such an indispensable and inescapable tool for all thought that even those who eschew it still use logical forms to argue for their rejection of it (*see* FIDEISM).

The three fundamental laws of all rational thought are:

1. the law of noncontradiction (A is not non-A),
2. the law of identity (A is A), and
3. the law of excluded middle (either A or non-A).

Each serves an important function. Without the law of noncontradiction we could say that God is God, and God is the Devil. Unless the law of identity is binding, there can be no unity or identity. Without it there is no difference in stating, "I am I" or "I am a chair." If the law of excluded middle does not hold, then opposites could both be true.

Beyond these basic principles, there are the principles of valid inference. These inferences traditionally were classed under *deductive* or *inductive* logic (*see* INDUCTIVE METHOD), or under transcendental arguments. All of these, however, use some form of the three basic laws.

Logic and God. If logic is the basis of all thought, it is the basis of all thought about God (theology). Some object that this makes God subject to logic. But God is sovereign and not subject to anything beyond himself. So, how can thought about God be subject to logic?

In one sense God is not subject to logic; rather, our *statements* about God are subservient to logic. All rational statements must be logical. Since theology purports to make rational statements, theological statements are subject to rules of rational thought, as are any other statements.

In another sense, God indeed is subject to logic, but not because there is something more ultimate than he. Since logic represents the principles of rational thought and since God is a rational Being, God is subject to his own rational nature. Insofar as logic manifests reason it flows from the very nature of God, and God is subject to his own nature. Indeed, he cannot act contrary to it, ethically or logically. For example, "It is impossible for God to lie" (Heb. 6:18). Likewise, it is impossible for God to contradict himself. Both violate his basic nature (*see* GOD, NATURE OF).

God is not only subject to his own rational self-consistency; he also is subject to logic which is derived from it. For we could not even begin to think about or talk about God without the law of noncontradiction. In this sense, logic is prior to God in that we need to use logic before we can even think about him rationally. Logic is prior to God in the *order of knowing,* but God is prior to logic in the *order of being*. Logic is prior to God *epistemologically,* but God is prior to logic *ontologically*.

To object that this makes God subject to our logic sets up a faulty dichotomy. Logic is logic; it is not "our" logic as opposed to "his." Ours is based on his. God's rational nature is the basis of our rational nature. He made it that way so we could understand something about him. The law of noncontradiction applies to God's thoughts as well as to ours. People did not *invent* it; they *discovered* it.

*Rationality versus *Rationalism.* Others protest that making truths about God subject to human reason is a form of rationalism (*see* EPISTEMOLOGY; SPINOZA, BENEDICT). However, this objection overlooks several important things. First, God is not being subjected to our reason. God is the author of reason, and he created us to be like himself. So the basic principles of reason are not arbitrarily imposed on God; rather, they come from God (*see* FAITH AND REASON).

Second, the basic laws of reason are not opposed to God's revelation; they are an essential part of God's general revelation. Human rationality, with its basic laws, is a manifestation of God's rationality. God is rational, and humans are made in his image. So using logic is not opposed to revelation; it is part of it.

Third, even special revelation (*see* REVELATION, SPECIAL) cannot be known or communicated apart from logic. We would not even be able to distinguish the revelation from God from that of the Devil unless the law of noncontradiction is valid. Furthermore, when the Bible reveals that "God so loved the world," we could not know that love is not hate unless the law of noncontradiction is valid. So logic is essential to special revelation (*see* REVELATION, SPECIAL) as well as to general revelation (*see* REVELATION, GENERAL).

Finally, there is a difference between using reason and being a rationalist. A rationalist tries to *determine* all truth by human reason. A reasonable Christian merely uses reason to *discover* truth that God has revealed, either by general revelation or by special revelation in the Bible (*see* BIBLE, EVIDENCE FOR).

Logic and Aristotle. Some critics of traditional logic object that *Aristotle invented logic, and there is no reason we must accept his Western form of logic over an "Eastern" type that does not use the law of noncontradiction. However, Aristotle did not *invent logic;* he *discovered* it. The laws of rational thought were in operation eternally in God and from the very beginning in rational creatures. Aristotle only *articulated* them.

This criticism also implies that "Eastern" thought can avoid using logic. But as we have seen, the basic laws of thought are inescapable for all rational beings, whatever their culture and worldview. No "Eastern" philosopher (*see* ZEN BUDDHISM) can even think or speak without using the law of noncontradiction. The very denial of this law employs the law in its denial. It is literally undeniable (*see* UNDENIABILITY, PRINCIPLE OF).

Many Kinds of Logic. Others object that there are many kinds of logic. Why choose just one kind and make it the norm for all kinds? In response, it need only be noted that while there are many kinds of logic (deductive, inductive, symbolic, etc.), nonetheless, all forms of logic depend on the basic rational principles of thought stated above. For example, no valid form of logic can operate apart from the principle of noncontradiction. If contradictories can be true, then thought itself is impossible. But we cannot deny thought without thinking. Hence, denying the laws of thought is literally unthinkable.

Logic and Omnipotence. The Bible says that "nothing is impossible for God" (Matt. 19:26). He is all-powerful (omnipotent), and an omnipotent Being can do anything. Therefore, it would seem that God could violate the law of noncontradiction if he wished. However, this is based on a misconception. When the Bible declares that God can do what is impossible it does not refer to what is *actually* impossible but to what is *humanly* impossible.

Further, omnipotence does not imply that God can do what is contradictory. If it did, then God could cease being God. But it is impossible for the Uncreated to decided that he wants to be created. It is impossible for a Necessary Being (which cannot cease to be) to decide it does not want to be. God cannot contradict his own nature. So omnipotence does not mean that God can do literally anything. The Bible says that "It is impossible for God to lie" (Heb. 6:18; cf. 2 Tim. 2:13). And just as God cannot contradict his moral nature, so he cannot contradict his rational nature. Indeed, omnipotence only means that God can do anything that is not actually contradictory or impossible. For example, God cannot make a square circle. Neither can he make a stone so heavy he cannot lift it. For if he can make it, then he can move it. He doesn't even have to "move" it. All he would have to do is to destroy it and recreate it wherever he wanted it to be.

Logic and Miracles. God created natural laws, yet he can transcend them by miracles (*see* MIRACLE). God engineered the law of gravity and the viscosity of liquids, but Jesus walked on water. Why can't the laws of logic be broken like the laws of physics?

First, this is an invalid analogy. Laws of nature are *descriptive,* whereas logical laws, like ethical laws, are *prescriptive*. That is, laws of logic tell us how we ought to reason in order to conform our thought to how things really are. Like moral laws, they are universal prescriptions (*see* MORALITY, AB-

SOLUTE NATURE OF). Everyone should reason that if all triangles have three sides and this figure is a triangle, then it has three sides. There are no exceptions; everyone should come to this conclusion. Laws of physics are descriptive generalizations. They merely inform us about the way things are; they do not exhort us about how something ought to be. As descriptions of the way things usually occur, they admit of exceptions. A miracle is an exception. As such it does not contradict the general law. The comparison between physical laws and laws of thought is invalid.

Further, God did not create laws of logic. They manifest his uncreated nature. God is rational, and there are certain basic principles of rationality that cannot change any more than God can change his own essential nature. The laws of physics are not so. Presumably, God could have created other kinds of worlds, with other kinds of laws. The law of gravity, for example, applies in a material universe. It does not apply to angels with no physical bodies.

Logic and the Mysteries of Faith. Some object that the great Christian mysteries, such as the Trinity, the incarnation (*see* CHRIST, DEITY OF), and predestination (*see* DETERMINISM; FREE WILL), violate laws of human reason. There is a difference between propositions that go *beyond* reason, such as mysteries of the faith, and those that go *against* reason. Those that go beyond human ability to reason do not go against reason. Human understanding unaided by special revelation cannot reach them. They can only be known by special revelation. Once these truths are known, their premises do not contradict other revealed truth.

Logic and the Trinity. The doctrine of the *Trinity affirms three persons in one Essence. It does not claim that there are three persons in one Person or three essences in one Essence. These would be logical contradictions.

Logic and the Incarnation. The Incarnation does not claim that God became human. The Infinite cannot become finite, or the Necessary contingent. Rather, it affirms that the second person of the Godhead became man. Jesus assumed a human nature without laying his deity aside. Thus the Incarnation was not the subtraction of deity but the addition of his humanity. Two natures in one person is not a contradiction. Two natures in one nature or two persons in one Person would be, but not two natures sharing one Person. It is a mystery; it is not a contradiction.

Logic and predestination. Neither is predestination and free choice a logical contradiction. It is not contradictory to assert that God has predetermined who will be saved, as long as he predetermined that it would be accomplished through their free choice. What would be contradictory is to claim that God *forced* people to *freely* accept him, since forced freedom is logically incompatible. But to claim that God knowingly determined how he would effect salvation by his grace and through our free choice is not a logical contradiction. It is a mystery, but not a logical contradiction (*see* DETERMINISM; FREE WILL).

Sources

Aristotle, *Posterior Analytics*

———, *Prior Analytics*

———, *On Sophistical Refutations*

———, *Topics*

I. Copi, Introduction *to Logic*

N. L. Geisler, *Come Let Us Reason*

Logical Positivism. Logical positivism is a school of thought that operated during the 1920s within a circle of Vienna philosophers that included Alfred J. *Ayer, Rudolf Carnap, Herbert Feigl, and Moritz Schlick. They took an antimetaphysical stand and developed a principle of empirical verification by which all but tautologies and empirical statements were considered meaningless.

This view held devastating implications for Christianity, since neither the existence nor attributes of God could be meaningfully stated. All God-talk was pronounced to be literally nonsense (*see* ANALOGY, PRINCIPLE OF; WITTGENSTEIN, LUDWIG). This view is sometimes called acognosticism or semantical atheism*.

Roots of the principle of empirical verifiability are found in David *Hume's empirical skepticism. In the last line of his *Inquiry Concerning Human Understanding* Hume wrote:

> When we run over libraries, persuaded of these principles, what havoc must we make? If we take in our hand any volume—of divinity or school of metaphysics, for instance—let us ask, *Does it contain any abstract reasoning concerning quality or number?* No. *Does it contain any experimental reasoning concerning matter of fact and existence?* No. Commit it then to the flames, for it can contain nothing but sophistry and illusion. [Hume, 173]

If Hume is correct, then there are two kinds of meaningful statements: (1) those true by definition (analytic), and (2) those known to be true through the senses (synthetic). Only definitional and sensible sensory statements are meaningful. All the rest are literally nonsense.

In the English-speaking world, Ayer was a zealous proponent of this view. He formulated Hume's conclusion into the principle of empirical verifiability, which stated in its original form that there are only two kinds of meaningful propositions.

Logical positivism died by its own sword. The principle of empirical verifiability is not empirically verifiable. Every attempt to broaden it destroys its effectiveness. Positivism cannot be used to exclude metaphysical statements (*see* METAPHYSICS).

Sources

A. J. Ayer, *Foundations of Empirical Knowledge*
———, *Language, Truth, and Logic*
———, *The Problem of Knowledge*
H. Feigl, "Logical Positivism after Thirty-Five Years," in *Philosophy Today* (Winter 1964)
F. Ferre, *Language, Logic and God*
A. Flew, et al., *New Essays in Philosophical Theology*
N. L. Geisler, *Philosophy of Religion* (chap. 12)
D. Hume, *Inquiry Concerning Human Understanding*

***Logos* Theory.** The Greek word *logos* comes from *legō* ("I say"). *Logos* means "word, speech, explanation, principle, or reason." In Greek philosophy the concept of *logos* had varying meanings. Heraclitus considered it the rational law governing the universe. Anaxagoras saw it as the principle of intelligence in the universe, though he called it *nous* ("mind"), as did *Plato. For the stoics the *logos* was the principle of all rationality in the universe. But shortly before the New Testament was written, the Jewish Philosopher *Philo (30 B.C.–A.D. 45) described the *logos* as the image of God which was distinct from God and an intermediate between God and the world (Edwards, "*Logos*"). Later, in the third century, *Plotinus made the *logos* or *nous* a lower-level emanation from the One (God).

The use of the Logos on a lower level from God led some early Fathers, such as *Origen, to assign less than full deity to Christ. This became the basis of Arianism, which was opposed by Athanasius (*see* CHRIST, DEITY OF). Some scholars have assumed that John's Gospel (1:1) borrowed from this Greek usage of *logos* and, hence, did not teach the full deity of Christ.

There is no reason, however, to suppose John is depicting something inferior to God in the *logos*. John declares clearly and emphatically that "the *Logos* was God" (John 1:1; see also 8:58; 10:30; 20:28). John's concept of the *Logos* is of a personal being (Christ), whereas the Greeks thought of it as an impersonal rational principle. The *Logos* is referred to by personal pronouns, such as *he* (1:1) and *his* (1:14). This was not true of the Greek *logos*.

According to John, the *Logos* "became flesh" (1:14). To combine *logos* (reason) or *nous* (mind) and flesh was contrary to Greek thought. Flesh was either evil, as in *Gnosticism, or nearly evil, as in Platonic, or Plotinian (*see* PLOTINUS) thought. Only in the Judeo-Christian tradition was matter or flesh thought respectable in any sense. Christians saw it as so good as to be worthy of clothing God in the incarnation.

The Old Testament, not Greek ideas, is the root of New Testament ideas. John, as all New Testament writers (except maybe Luke) were Jews. The root of their thought was in Judaism. They cite the Old Testament hundreds of times. Hence, it is contrary to the Jewish background and thought of the New Testament writers to use Greek sources for their theological ideas.

The New Testament is a theistic (*see* THEISM) book, whereas Greek thought was polytheistic and pantheistic (*see* PANTHEISM). We would not expect John to borrow from such a worldview to express his ideas. The Old Testament spoke of the coming Messiah who was God (Ps. 110:1; Isa. 9:6; 45:6; Zech. 12:10), who would come in human flesh, suffer, and rise physically from the dead (cf. Isaiah 53). Never did Greek religion or philosophy teach this doctrine. Claims that Christianity borrowed from pagan idea or gods are unsubstantiated (*see* MITHRAISM; RESURRECTION CLAIMS IN NON-CHRISTIAN RELIGIONS)

Sources

G. H. Clark, *Selections from Hellenistic Philosophy*
P. Edwards, "Logos," in *EP*
W. R. Inge, "Logos," in *ERE*
J. G. Machen, *The Origin of Paul's Religion*
R. Nash, *Christianity and the Hellenistic World*
Philo, *De Vita Contemplativa*
F. E. Walton, *Development of the Logos Doctrine in Greek and Hebrew Thought*

Luke, Alleged Errors in. Luke has been charged by the critics with containing significant historical inaccuracies in the nativity narrative of chapter 2.

The Worldwide Census. Luke 2:1–3 refers to a worldwide census under Caesar Augustus when Quirinius was governor of Syria. However, according to the annals of ancient history, no such census took place. In fact, Quirinius did not become governor in Syria until A.D. 6. It was commonly held by critics that Luke erred in his assertion about a registration under Caesar Augustus, and that the census actually took place in A.D. 6 or 7 (which is mentioned by Luke in Gamaliel's speech recorded in Acts 5:37).

A Possible Retranslation. F. F. *Bruce offers another possibility. The Greek of Luke 2:2 can be translated: "This enrollment (census) was before that made when Quirinius was governor of Syria." In this case, the Greek word translated "first" (*prōtos*) is translated as a comparative, "before." Because of the construction of the sentence, this is not an unlikely reading. In this case there is no problem, since that census of A.D. 6 is well known to historians.

Recent Archaeological Support. The lack of any extrabiblical support led some to claim this an error. However, with recent scholarship, it is now widely admitted that there was in fact an earlier registration, as Luke records.

William Ramsay discovered several inscriptions that indicated that Quirinius was governor of Syria on two occasions, the first time several years prior to A.D. 6. According to the very papers that recorded the censuses, (see Ramsay, *Was*

Christ?) there was in fact a census between 10 and 5 B.C. Periodic registrations took place every fourteen years. Because of this regular pattern of census taking, any such action was regarded as the general policy of Augustus, even though a local census may have been instigated by a local governor. Therefore, Luke recognizes the census as stemming from the decree of Augustus.

Since the people of a subjugated land were compelled to take an oath of allegiance to the Emperor, it was not unusual for the Emperor to require an imperial census as an expression of this allegiance and a means of enlisting men for military service, or, as was probably true in this case, in preparation to levy taxes. Because of the strained relations between Herod and Augustus in the later years of Herod's reign, as the Jewish historian Josephus reports, it is understandable that Augustus would begin to treat Herod's domain as a subject land, and consequently would impose such a census in order to maintain control of Herod and the people.

Third, a census was a massive project which probably took several years to complete. Such a census for the purpose of taxation begun in Gaul between 10–9 B.C. took 40 years to complete. Likely the decree to begin the census, in 8 or 7 B.C., may not have begun in Palestine until sometime later. Problems of organization and preparation may have delayed the actual census until 5 B.C. or even later.

Fourth, it was not an unusual requirement that people return to the place of their origin, or to the place where they owned property. A decree of C. Vibius Mazimus in A.D. 104 required all those absent from their home towns to return for a census. Jews were quite used to travel, making annual pilgrimage to Jerusalem.

There is simply no reason to suspect Luke's statement regarding the census. Luke's account fits the regular pattern of census taking, and its date would not be unreasonable. This may have been simply a local census taken as a result of the general policy of Augustus. Luke simply provides a reliable historical record of an event not otherwise recorded. Luke has proven himself an amazingly reliable historian (*see* ACTS, HISTORICITY OF; see Ramsay, *St. Paul the Traveler and Roman Citizen*). There is no reason to doubt him here.

Quirinius' Terms as Governor. Given Luke's statement that the census decreed by Augustus was the first one taken while Quirinius was governor of Syria, the fact that Quirinius became governor of Syria long after the death of Herod, in about 6 A.D., sounds like an error in the Gospel.

As noted, there is an alternate way to translate this verse which resolves the problem. Further, there is now evidence that Quirinius was governor of Syria on an earlier occasion that would fit with the time of Christ's birth.

Quintilius Varus was governor of Syria from about 7 to about 4 B.C. Varus was not a trustworthy leader, a fact demonstrated in A.D. 9 when he lost three legions of soldiers in the Teutoburger forest in Germany. Quirinius, on the other hand, was a noted military leader who squelched the rebellion of the Homonadensians in Asia Minor. When it came time to begin the census, in about 8 or 7 B.C., Augustus entrusted Quirinius with the delicate problem in the volatile area of Palestine, effectively superseding Varus by appointing Quirinius to a place of special authority in this matter.

Quirinius was probably governor of Syria on two separate occasions, once while prosecuting the military action against the Homonadensians between 12 and 2 B.C., and later, beginning about A.D. 6. A Latin inscription discovered in 1764 has been interpreted to the effect that Quirinius was governor of Syria on two occasions.

Gary Habermas summarizes the situation well:

> (1) A taxation-census was a fairly common procedure in the Roman Empire and it did occur in Judea, in particular. (2) Persons were required to return to their home city in order to fulfill the requirements of the process. (3) These procedures were apparently employed during the reign of Augustus (37 B.C.–14 A.D.), placing it well within the general time frame of Jesus' birth. (4) The date of the specific taxation recounted by Luke could very possibly have been 6–5 B.C., which would also be of service in attempting to find a more exact date for Jesus' birth. [*Verdict of History,* 153]

Conclusion. There are three reasons to believe Luke is accurate in his account of Jesus' birth. First, there is the general rule of "innocent until proven guilty." A document from antiquity in proper custody that purports to be giving an accurate account (cf. Luke 1:1–4) should be accepted as authentic until it is proven not to be. This is known as the *ancient document rule*. This rule is used in law courts to establish authenticity of old documents.

Second, there are, as noted, plausible explanations that harmonize the record with historical evidence (*see also* ACTS, HISTORICITY OF).

Third, Luke has proven himself to be a reliable historian even in the details. William Ramsay spent twenty years of research in the area Luke wrote about. His conclusion was that in references to thirty-two countries, fifty-four cities, and nine islands Luke made no mistakes! That is a record to be envied by historians of any era.

Sources

G. L. Archer, Jr., *An Encyclopedia of Biblical Difficulties*
F. F. Bruce, *The New Testament Documents: Are They Reliable?*
N. L. Geisler and T. Howe, *When Critics Ask*
G. Habermas, *The Verdict of History*

W. Ramsay, *St. Paul the Traveler and Roman Citizen*
———, *Was Christ Born in Bethlehem?*

J. W. Montgomery, *Christianity and History*
———, *Christianity for the Tough-Minded*
———, *Evidence for Faith*

Luther, Martin. Martin Luther (1483–1546), the great German Reformer who was not known as an apologist—he was too preoccupied with reconstructing the church. However, he said nothing, properly understood, that would negate the consistent use of reason by the *classical apologists in defending the faith.

Reason Condemned. *Luther declared that human reason is that God-given faculty by which humans are distinguished from brute beasts (*disputatio de homine*). Luther was concerned that human reason not be substituted for the Gospel, as were the other great teachers of the Church. *The Augsburg Confession* (Art. 2) condemns the belief that anyone can be justified "by his own strength and reason." Martin Chemnitz added, "reason of itself and from events cannot establish anything concerning the love of God toward us" (Chemnitz, 609). These deprecating statements about human reason must be seen in proper context (*see* FAITH AND REASON).

First, they were made in the context of someone trying to attain salvation by personal strength, rather than by the merit of Christ and grace through faith. Human reason cannot attain salvation. Only the Gospel brings salvation. However, this is not to say that reason cannot be used to defend the Gospel. Second, Luther believed the redemptive love of God cannot be established by reason. This is not to say that the existence of God cannot be established by reason (*see* COSMOLOGICAL ARGUMENT). Indeed, among the great classical apologists was *Augustine, Luther's philosophical and theological mentor.

Reason in Lutheran Theology. While Luther himself, preoccupied as he was with salvation, developed neither an apologetic nor a systematic theology, his colleague, Philipp Melancthon, did both. Melancthon and other Lutheran Reformers used classical apologetics to develop proofs for the existence of God. Chemnitz speaks of the validity of teachings derived from Scripture "by way of good, certain, firm and clear reasoning" (ibid., 249). Luther's own polemics are tightly constructed of cogently reasoned arguments.

Reason, of course, can be the "tool of the devil" when used in opposition to God. But the stand on Scripture by the Lutheran Reformers and modern Lutheran scholars reveals a tradition of reasoned theology and apologetics. One modern exemplar of the Lutheran tradition is John Warwick Montgomery in his works defending the faith. See those noted among the sources for this article.

Sources

M. Chemnitz, *Examination of the Council of Trent*, vol. 1
L. S. Keyser, *A System of Christian Evidence*
M. Luther, *Luther's Works*, vol. 34, J. Pelikan, ed.

Lying in Scripture. The Scriptures teach that God is truth (Deut. 32:4) and that it is impossible for him to lie (Heb. 6:18). God commands us not to lie (Exod. 20:16) and warns that he will severely punish liars (Rev. 21:8). However, there are many instances where God appears to bless lying. Bible critics frequently point out this seeming contradiction.

It is notable that this problem does not exist for divine voluntarists who believe that an act is good or evil only because God wills it to be such. However, according to essentialism (*see* ESSENTIALISM, DIVINE), God is essentially good and cannot do or will evil (*see* GOD, NATURE OF). In this context, the problem of divinely approved lying is acute.

Categories of Alleged Lying. The "lying passages" in the Bible do not all fall into the same category. Some are actual lies, and some are not. Some are approved by God, and some are not. But in no case does the Bible ever place divine approval on a lie as such.

Lies Reported without Approval. Actual lies are recorded in the Bible, but they are not thereby approved. The Bible relates many sins on which it places no approbation. For example, some of Satan's lies are recorded in Scripture. Satan told Eve, "You will not surely die" (Gen. 3:4) when God had said emphatically that they would (Gen. 2:17). This is a clear case of a lie that God does not approve. Many scholars place Rahab's lie (see below) in this category. If so, she was blessed *in spite of* her lie and not *because of* it.

Partial Truths That Are Not Lies. Not all partial truths are lies. In at least one case God himself told Samuel to tell only part of the truth to Saul (1 Sam. 16:1–5). Since Samuel feared for his life at the hands of King Saul when God told the prophet to anoint a new king, God instructed him to tell Saul that he had come to offer a sacrifice, which was true but a subterfuge.

Lies Approved in View of a Higher Law. Some conservative Bible scholars and Christian ethicists believe that, while lying *as such* is always wrong, lying to save a life is not. This, they argue, is based on a hierarchy or gradation of values wherein mercy (in saving a life) takes precedence over the truth that ends in murder. The Hebrew midwives in Exodus 1 appear to fall into this category, and perhaps Rahab, who lied to save the lives of the Hebrew spies.

Passages Involving Apparent Lying. Several key passages involving alleged lying with divine approval bear scrutiny. Among these is the case of Abraham's "half-truth" about his wife Sarah, who was also his half-sister.

Genesis 12:10–20. Fearing that the king of Egypt might kill him and take his wife (but under no direct threat), Abraham instructed Sarah: "Say you are my sister, so that I will be treated well for your sake and my life will be spared because of you" (Gen. 12:13). Sarah was Abraham's half-sister. Nevertheless, what Abraham instructed Sarah to do was to lie.

No divine approval of Abraham's act is shown; the opposite is implied. Abraham's increase in wealth should not be viewed as a divine reward for his lie. Pharaoh's gifts were understandable. Pharaoh may have felt obligated to pay amends for the wicked constraint that his corrupt society put on strangers who visited his land, as well as for unwittingly taking Abraham's wife into his palace. Adultery was strictly forbidden by Egyptian religion.

The years of trouble that followed may have been a direct result of Abraham's lack of faith in God's protecting power. Although some people are portrayed as men of God, they are still fallible and responsible for their sin, as was David in his adultery with Bathsheba and murder of her husband (2 Samuel 12). God blessed such leaders *in spite of,* not *because of,* their sins.

Genesis 31. Genesis 31:35 records Rachel's apparent lie about the idols she had stolen. Yet God appeared to bless Rachel, for she was not discovered and God prospered her and her husband Jacob. However, a closer look at this text reveals that God did not bless Rachel for stealing the idols or for lying about her deed. Simply because Laban did not discover that Rachel was the thief does not mean that God blessed her. It is reasonable to assume that God did not expose Rachel's theft in order to protect Jacob's life (cf. 31:31). The biblical record reveals that God allowed Rachel to fall into the background of importance until her painful death (Gen. 35:16–20).

Joshua 2:4–5. When the Hebrew spies came to Jericho, they sought refuge in the house of Rahab. When the king of Jericho commanded Rahab to bring out the men, she said that the men had already gone and that she did not know where they were. When Israel destroyed Jericho, Rahab and all her family were saved alive as a reward for her protection. How could God bless Rahab for lying?

Defenders of the biblical text fall into two groups on this issue. Some argue that it is not clear that God blessed Rahab for lying. What he blessed her for was her "faith" (Heb. 11:31), not her falsehood. God blessed Rahab *in spite of* her lie, not *because of* it. Proponents of this view insist that God saved and blessed Rahab for protecting the spies and assisting in the overthrow of Jericho. They insist that nowhere does the Bible explicitly say that God blessed Rahab for lying.

Other scholars insist that Rahab was faced with a real moral dilemma. It may have been impossible for her both to save the spies and to tell the truth to the soldiers of the king. If so, God would not hold Rahab responsible (see Geisler, chap. 7). Certainly a person cannot be held responsible for disobeying a lesser law in order to keep a higher obligation. The Bible commands obedience to the government (Rom. 13:1; Titus 3:1; 1 Peter 2:13), but civil disobedience is just when the government attempts to compel unrighteousness (Exodus 5; Dan. 3, 6; Revelation 13). The case of the Hebrew midwives (Exodus 1), who lied to save the lives of the male children, is perhaps the clearest example.

1 Samuel 16:1–5. We have seen that Abraham was judged for telling the half truth that Sarah was his sister, but in 1 Samuel 16 God actually encourages Samuel to tell that he had come to Bethlehem to offer a sacrifice, when he had also come to anoint David king as well. Did not God encourage deception here? Why did God condemn Abraham for the same thing he commanded Samuel to do?

It is important to note that the two situations are not the same. Abraham's "half-truth" was a whole lie, for the implied question was "Is Sarah your wife?" And his answer in effect was "No, she is my sister." By this answer Abraham intentionally misrepresented the facts, which is a lie.

Samuel was asked, "Why have you come to Bethlehem?" His answer was, "I have come to sacrifice to the Lord" (1 Sam. 16:2). This corresponded with the facts, namely, it was why he came and what he did. The fact that he had another purpose for coming is not directly related to the question he was asked and the answer he gave, as it was in Abraham's case. Of course, had Samuel been asked "Do you have any other purpose for coming?" then he would have had to come clean. "No" would have been a deception.

Concealment and deception are not necessarily the same. Samuel certainly concealed one of the purposes of his mission in order to save his life (1 Sam. 16:2). It is not always necessary (even possible) to tell all in order to tell the truth. The fact that God told Samuel to conceal one of the purposes of his visit in order to avoid Saul's murderous anger does not mean he was guilty of lying. Not telling part of the truth and telling a falsehood are not necessarily the same. Nor are secrecy and concealment the same as duplicity and falsehood.

2 Kings 6:19. When Elisha went out to meet his enemies, he told them "this is not the way, nor is this the city. Follow me, and I will bring you to the man whom you seek" (2 Kings 6:19). How could a man of God lie to these Syrian troops?

Very simply, what Elisha told them was not actually a lie. The Syrian troops were sent to Dothan in order to capture Elisha. The Lord blinded them, and Elisha came out of the city to meet them. What Elisha told them was "this is not the way, nor is this the city." Once Elisha came out of the city, he was no longer in Dothan. Consequently, entering Dothan was no longer the way to capture Elisha, neither was it the city. Elisha also instructed them, "follow me and I will bring you to the man whom you seek." This was also true. Elisha went before them into Samaria, and when they arrived, the Lord opened their eyes and they saw Elisha, and that they were in Samaria.

2 Chronicles 18:18–22. God is portrayed in this passage by Micaiah the prophet as enlisting lying spirits to entice wicked King Ahab to seal his own doom. The text says, "The Lord has put a lying spirit in the mouths of these prophets of yours" (vs. 22). But how can the God of all truth perpetrate such a lie?

Defenders urge that God is not promoting evil here but simply controlling evil for good. Several factors help in understanding this situation. First, this is a vision, a dramatic picture of God's sovereign authority spelled out in regal imagery.

Second, this dramatic vision represents God's sweeping authority, even over evil spirits. The God of the Bible, in contrast to some pagan religions, is in sovereign control of everything, including evil, which he uses to accomplish his good purposes (cf. Job 1–3).

Third, the Bible sometimes speaks of God "hardening" people's hearts (see Rom. 9:17–18) or even sending them strong delusions (2 Thess. 2:11). However, on closer examination, we discover that God did this to those who had hardened their own hearts (Exod. 8:15) and who "did not believe the truth" (2 Thess. 2:12). God uses even their depravity to accomplish his purposes. God *permits* lying as a judgment on evil.

God, for his own purposes of justice, allowed Ahab to be deceived by evil spirits to accomplish his sovereign and good will.

John 7:3–10. Bible critics have sometimes appealed to this text to show that Jesus lied. This is a serious charge, since it would not only be a divinely approved lie, but one told by God himself in the person of his Son. Jesus' unbelieving brothers challenged him to go up to Jerusalem and show himself openly to be the Messiah (7:3–4). Jesus refused, saying, "I am not yet going up to this feast, because for me the right time has not yet come" (vs. 8). But later Jesus did go (vs. 10). Jesus did not go openly, as the brothers had suggested, nor at the immediate time they suggested. Further, John 7:8 relates that Jesus said he was not *yet* going. "He remained in Galilee" before he went up.

Luke 24:28. When Jesus has finished his discourse to the two disciples on the road to Emmaus, "Jesus acted as if he were going farther" (Luke 24:28b). Although this is not a verbal lie, it is true that one can lie by actions. Some critics believe that this is what Jesus did here.

Calling this a lie stretches the imagination. The text goes on to say, "But they urged him strongly, 'Stay with us, for it is nearly evening.' So he went in to stay with them" (vs. 29). In other words, Jesus was going on until they persuaded him to stay with them. Rather than impose himself on his disciples, he waited for them to take the initiative, which evidently came immediately and vigorously. By showing that he could go on, he invited these hurting friends to come closer.

Exodus 1:15. Most alleged cases of divinely approved lying turn out to be either not a lie or not divinely approved. There is at least one case, however, that seems to be both.

The pharaoh (king) of Egypt directly ordered the Hebrew midwives to murder the newborn Hebrew boys. "The midwives, however, feared God and did not do what the king of Egypt had told them to do; they let the boys live" (Exod. 1:17). Not only did the midwives disobey pharaoh, but, when he questioned them about their actions, they lied saying, "Hebrew women are not like Egyptian women; they are vigorous and give birth before the midwives arrive" (Exod. 1:19). "So God was kind to the midwives," according to 1:20–21. "And because the midwives feared God, he gave them families of their own."

There is little question that the midwives both disobeyed a command of government by not murdering the newborn male children and lied to cover it up. The moral dilemma in which the midwives found themselves was unavoidable. Either they obeyed God's law not to murder, or they obeyed the lesser obligation to pharaoh. Rather than commit deliberate infanticide against the children of their own people, the midwives disobeyed the king. God commands us to obey the governmental powers, but he also commands us not to murder (Exod. 20:13).

The saving of innocent lives is a higher obligation than obedience to government. When the government commands an act against God, we should not obey. God would have held the midwives responsible had they fulfilled their duty to government. In the case of the midwives, the higher law was the preservation of the lives of the newborn male children (cf. Acts 4; Revelation 13). Further, the lie, and the larger act of disobedience, came in the context of the midwives' faith commitment to God. The midwives had to make a choice of allegiance and obedience, a choice that required courage and spiritual wisdom. A similar situation might involve obedience to parental authority. Submission is part of the moral authority. But if a parent commands a child to kill or worship an idol, the child must submit instead to the higher authority and refuse. Jesus emphasized the need to follow the higher moral law when he said, "Anyone who loves his father or mother more than me is not worthy of me" (Matt. 10:37a).

The midwives' fear of God led them to do what was necessary to save lives. Their false statement to Pharaoh was an essential part of their effort to save lives.

Conclusion. Narrative texts in which a person lies fall into one of a few categories: First, some cases were not lies but only legitimate utterance of part of the truth. Second, in most cases of clear lying, there is no indication that God approved of the falsehood. To the contrary there was usually some kind of judgment. In cases that can legitimately be called divinely approved falsification, such as the midwives in Exodus 1, there is unavoidable conflict with a higher moral law. It is when there is a rare, *unavoidable* conflict with one of God's higher moral laws that he suspends our duty to truth.

Sources

Augustine, *Against Lying*

———, *On Lying*

N. L. Geisler, *Christian Ethics: Options and Issues*, chap. 7

J. Murray, *Principles of Conduct*

"Lying Spirits," Sent by God. ***See* Lying in Scripture.**

Mm

Machen, J. Gresham. J. Gresham Machen (1881–1937) was born in Baltimore and was graduated with a degree in classics from Johns Hopkins University. He studied at Princeton Theological Seminary under B. B. *Warfield and R. D. Wilson. He also studied at Princeton University and as a fellow in Germany at Marburg and Göttingen. At Marburg he studied under Adolf Jülicher and Wilhelm Herrmann, who was a disciple of Albrecht Ritschl. At Göttingen he studied under E. Schürer and W. Bouset. In 1906 Machen became an instructor in New Testament at Princeton Seminary.

In 1912 Machen gave an address, "Christianity and Culture," which was to set a theme for his career. He identified the problem in the Christian church as the relation between knowledge and piety. There were three approaches to this relationship, he said. Liberal Protestants subordinated the gospel to science and disregarded the supernatural. Fundamentalists preserved the supernatural but rejected science. Machen's solution was to blend the pursuit of knowledge with religion.

By 1914 Machen was a full professor of New Testament at Princeton. After World War I, the Northern Presbyterian Church and Princeton Seminary both underwent a fundamental shift in theology, from historical Christianity and traditional Calvinism to a liberal or modernist following of German theological trends. In the ensuing battle, the denomination and seminary split. By 1929, Machen, Oswald T. Allis, Cornelius *Van Til, and Robert Dick Wilson, along with twenty students, left the seminary. Under Machen, these men established Westminster Seminary in Philadelphia.

In 1933, to counter the increasing liberalism in the Presbyterian Church, USA, Machen founded the Independent Board for Presbyterian Foreign Missions. This board tested and commissioned orthodox missionaries and gave conservative churches an alternative to supporting liberals sent out by their own denomination. The General Assembly demanded that Machen leave the board. He refused and was tried for violating his ordination vows. Without being given the opportunity to defend his actions he was suspended from the ministry by New Brunswick Presbytery in Trenton, New Jersey. He, along with others, was expelled from the PCUSA in 1936. Immediately a new organization was formed, the Presbyterian Church of America. Only a few months later Machen died suddenly while on a preaching tour to build support for the new denomination. Without his focused leadership, the infant church was divided by the individual agendas of its leaders. Two denominations eventually emerged, the Orthodox Presbyterian Church and the Bible Presbyterian Church.

While he rejected the label of "fundamentalist" and some of the theological emphases traditionally adopted by the fundamentalist movement, Machen was the intellectual leader of that movement during the 1920s. His scholarship and professional work were respected even by his opponents. One of his most helpful contributions for generations of students was his *New Testament Greek for Beginners* (1924). Of theological importance was his classic defense, *The *Virgin Birth of Christ* (1930). This collection of lectures given at Columbia Theological Seminary argued that the virgin birth was not a late addition to Christianity. Other significant defenses of intellectually-strong faith were *The Origin of Paul's Religion* (1921), *Christianity and Liberalism* (1923), *What Is Faith?* (1927), *The Christian Faith in the Modern World* (1938), and *The Christian View of Man* (1937).

Fervent, Thoughtful Apologetic. Machen's apologetic is closely aligned with the work of Charles Hodge, B. B. Warfield, A. A. Hodge, Caspar Wistar Hodge, and Geerhardus Vos. As the work of these men, Machen's philosophy was rooted in Thomas *Reid and Scottish *Realism. He believed that reason, which relied upon and dealt with facts, was essential for faith. He followed the classic pattern of *notitia* (cognitive knowledge), *assensus* (feeling), that leads to *fiducia* (faith). Machen pointed out that reason does not *prove* faith. This, he believed, was the fundamental error of liberalism (Lewis and Demarest, 374). Machen was ever cautious to put Christian experience in its proper context: "Christian experience is rightly used when it confirms the documentary evidence. But it can never produce a substitute for the documentary evidence. . . . Christian experience is rightly used when it helps to convince us that the events narrated in the New Testament actually did occur, but it can never enable us to be Christians, whether the events occurred or not" (*Christianity and Liberalism*, 72).

Machen's starting point for apologetics was human consciousness, which relied upon logical analysis, deduction, and common sense. He did not elaborate on theistic proofs; nonetheless, he relied upon traditional arguments. Machen went so far as to delay his ordination until he could satisfactorily answer *Kant's objections. He affirmed:

> The very basis of the religion of Jesus was a triumphant belief in the real existence of a personal God. And without that belief no type of religion can rightly appeal to Jesus today. Jesus was a theist, and a rational theism is at the basis of Christianity. Jesus did not, indeed, support His theism by argument; He did not provide in advance answers to the Kantian attack upon the theistic proofs. But that means not that He was indifferent to the belief which is the logical result of those proofs, but that the belief stood so firm, both to Him and to His hearers, that in His teaching it is always presupposed. So today it is not necessary for all Christians to analyze the logical basis of their belief in God; the human mind has a wonderful faculty for the condensation of perfectly valid arguments, and what seems like an instinctive belief may turn out to be the result of many logical steps. Or, rather, it may be that the belief in a personal God is the result of a primitive revelation, and that the theistic proofs are only the logical confirmation of what was originally arrived at by a different means. At any rate, the logical confirmation of the belief in God is a vital concern to the Christian. [ibid., 59–60]

Infallible and Inerrant. Following the old Princetonian tradition, Machen believed the Bible in its original writings (autographs) to be plenarily inspired, in that God's Word was mediated through the lives and personalities of the writers and the genre of literature through which they wrote. Thus historical narrative is not judged with the same standards as poetry. Scripture is infallibly God's truth and is without error, but it is not mechanically dictated (*see* BIBLE, EVIDENCE FOR). "In all its parts," said Machen, Scripture is "the very word of God, completely true in what it says regarding matters of fact and completely authoritative in its commands" (*Christian Faith in the Modern World*, 2, 37). He affirmed: "Only the autographs of the Biblical books, in other words—the books as they came from the pen of the sacred writers, and not any of the copies of those autographs which we now possess—were produced with that supernatural impulsion and guidance of the Holy Spirit which we call inspiration" (ibid., 39).

Defense of Christianity. Machen's apologetic for orthodoxy was mostly evidential. It began with an appeal to mostly biblical and historical facts that require an adequate explanation. Machen's defense of orthodoxy centered on two important miracles, the virgin birth and the bodily resurrection of Jesus Christ. Machen often appealed, similar to Paul, to the fact that, if Christ was not born of a virgin in history and resurrected bodily three days after his death, our faith is in vain.

Machen defended miraculous acts in Scripture (*see* MIRACLES, ARGUMENTS AGAINST), especially those of Christ, by defining a supernatural event as what "takes place by the immediate, as distinguished from the mediate, power of God" (*Christianity and Liberalism*, 99). This, he points out, presupposes the existence of a personal God and the existence of a real order of nature. Thus, miracles are supernaturally dependently joined to theism.

In defense of New Testament miracles (*see* MIRACLES IN THE BIBLE). Machen pointed out the mistake of isolating miracles from the rest of the New Testament. It is a mistake to discuss the resurrection of Jesus as though that which had to be proved was simply the resurrection of a first-century man in Palestine (ibid., 104). Rather, the resurrection is supported by the historical uniqueness of Christ in his person and claims, and the "adequate occasion" or purpose for the miracle that can be detected (ibid., 1, 104). The faith demonstrated by the early church was the most convincing argument for the resurrection (*What Is Christianity?* 6, 99). Machen further supports biblical miracles by pointing out the illegitimate naturalistic tendencies of the liberal church in rejecting them.

Evaluation. Machen defended orthodox Protestant faith at a crucial point in the first half of the twentieth century. He set a high standard of scholarship at a time when few others, liberal or conservative, were producing valuable academic studies. Many of these works are still widely used.

Machen's overall apologetic is succinctly summarized by C. Allyn Russell: "It was Machen's thesis that Christianity and liberalism were essentially two distinct and mutually exclusive religions, not two varieties of the same faith." He argued that they used similar language but proceeded from altogether different roots. "In assaulting liberalism as a non-Christian religion, Machen declared that liberal attempts to reconcile Christianity with modern science had relinquished everything distinctive of Christianity" (Russell, 50).

Sources

W. Elwell, *Evangelical Dictionary of Theology*
———, *Handbook of Evangelical Theologians*
G. Lewis and B. Demarest, *Challenges to Inerrancy: A Theological Response*
D. G. Hart, "The Princeton Mind in the Modern World and the Common Sense of J. Gresham Machen," *WTJ* 46.1 (Spring 1984): 1–25
J. G. Machen, *Christian Faith in the Modern World*
———, *Christianity and Liberalism*
———, *The Christian View of Man*
———, *The Origin of Paul's Religion*
———, *The Virgin Birth of Christ*
———, *What Is Christianity?*
———, *What Is Faith?*
G. M. Marsden, " J. Gresham Machen, History and Truth," *WTJ* 42 (Fall 1979): 157–75
C. A. Russell, "J. Gresham Machen, Scholarly Fundamentalist," *JPH* 51 (1973): 40–66
N. B. Stonehouse, *J. Gresham Machen: A Biographical Memoir*
C. I. K. Story, "J. Gresham Machen: Apologist and Exegete," *PSB* 2 (1979: 91–103

Magdalen Manuscript. ***See*** **NEW TESTAMENT MANUSCRIPTS.**

Maimonides. Moses, son of Maimon (1135–1204). latinized his name into Maimonides. He left his native Cordova, Spain, in the wake of the Muslim invasion and went to North Africa and eventually Egypt, where he died in Cairo. Though known for his legal doctrine, "Rabbi Moses," as the scholastics called him, became the most celebrated Jewish philosopher of the middle ages.

In his *Guide for the Perplexed,* he addressed the semi-intellectual Jewish thinkers who were in a state of mental confusion because they believed the principles of Greek philosophy contradicted their religious faith. It was for those who hesitated between conflicting claims of philosophy and religion. Maimonides believed one could have full knowledge of Greek philosophy without giving up the observance of the commandments. Unfortunately, the reconciliation was usually in favor of an allegorical interpretation at the expense of a literal understanding of Scripture.

In addition to his Jewish faith, especially stressing the oneness and ineffability of God, Maimonides was heavily influenced by *Alfarabi, *Aristotle, *Averroes, *Philo, *Plato, and *Plotinus. The result was his own unique synthesis of these philosophers, with preference to Plato over Aristotle and heavy influence from Plotinus. Maimonides influenced *Thomas Aquinas and other scholastic philosophers, and also the modern rationalist Benedict *Spinoza.

Philosophy. Following his Jewish training, Maimonides believed God was one. He also held that God's existence was demonstrable but that his essence was unknowable. He offered proofs for God's existence used by the later scholastics, such as God as First Cause, First Mover, and Necessary Being (three of Aquinas's five proofs for God). Unlike the Greeks, he believed God was the efficient, as well as the formal and final, cause of the world.

Greek philosophers argued for the eternality of the world, but Maimonides found these arguments inconclusive because they overlooked the omnipotence of God, who can freely create a universe of whatever duration he wishes. Aquinas followed this line of reasoning.

Following Plotinus, Maimonides held that all knowledge of God is negative. Anything positive refers only to God's actions, not to his nature, which is essentially unknowable.

The Bible reveals one positive divine name, *YHWH*. The "tetragrammaton" name means "absolute existence." God is a pure and necessary existence. All creatures are contingent. Their existence is only an "accident" added to their essence.

Evaluation. There are many positive contributions in Maimonides' views. From the perspective of classical theism and apologetics (*see* CLASSICAL APOLOGETICS), his stress on the nature of God, creation, and the proofs for God's existence are commendable.

Of concern to Christians is Maimonides' negative theology, which allows no positive analogies (*see* ANALOGY). Also, his tendency to allegorize away parts of Scripture not reconcilable with prevailing Platonic philosophy was unnecessary and unacceptable.

Sources

S. Baro, ed., *Essays on Maimonides*
Maimonides, *Guide for the Perplexed*
A. Maurer, *Medieval Philosophy*, chap. 8.
S. Pines, "Maimonides" in *EP*
H. A. Wolfson, "Maimonides on Negative Attributes" in A. Marx, ed., *Louis Ginzberg Jubilee Volume*

Manichaeism. ***See*** **DUALISM.**

Martin, Michael. Michael Martin, a late-twentieth-century Bible critic, wrote *The Case against Christianity* to argue that Jesus is not a historical figure. He contends that the earliest layer of the four Gospels is not historical, that Paul was not interested in the historical Jesus, and that Jesus, whether he existed, did not rise from the dead.

Evaluation. A critique of Martin's views begins with what Martin himself accepts regarding the earliest Epistles of Paul (*see* NEW TESTAMENT, DATING OF; NEW TESTAMENT, HISTORICITY OF; NEW TESTAMENT MANUSCRIPTS). Martin accepts the authenticity of some early Epistles, including 1 and 2 Corinthians and Galatians. In these letters, Paul affirmed that Jesus died and was raised (1 Corinthians 15). He recorded that the apostles were in Jerusalem after Jesus died (Gal. 1:17) where he had visited them twice, once after his conversion

(Gal. 1:18–19) and once fourteen years later (2:1–10). Paul also met Peter later in Antioch (Gal. 2:11–14). Paul was not only a contemporary of the apostles but on par with them (1 Cor. 9:1). Contrary to Martin, Paul knew James the "brother of our Lord" (1 Cor. 9:5; Gal. 1:18–19). This is the natural sense of these passages.

Further, Josephus called James the "brother of Jesus," not of a Jerusalem faction (Josephus 20.9.1). In fact, all four Gospels speak of Jesus' brothers in the context of his physical family (Matt. 12:46–47; Mark 3:31–32; Luke 8:19–20; John 7:5). There is no ancient evidence to the contrary.

Paul mentions other details of Jesus' life (2 Cor. 5:16, 21). So, it is simply not true that there is no support for the historicity of Jesus. Even the earliest layer of material accepted by Martin reveals details, including some basic ones about the death and resurrection of Christ.

Late Dating of the Gospels. There also are good reasons to reject Martin's late dates, from 70 to 135, for the Gospels. Once this premise is proven false, his whole case against the historicity of Jesus crumbles. Even such radical theologians as John A. T. Robinson date the Gospels between A.D. 40 to 65 (see Robinson, 352).

Several arguments for a pre–70 A.D. date can be marshaled. Most scholars date Mark in the decade 60–70, or more precisely, 65–70. Martin wrongly asserts that Mark was not mentioned until the mid-second century. Papias refers to Mark during the first quarter of the second century. Martin also errs in claiming that Luke was unknown by Clement, Ignatius, or Polycarp. All three Synoptic Gospels are cited by them, including a resurrection text from Luke 24. Martin asserts that Clement is not clear about whether disciples received instructions from Jesus while on earth. Yet Clement wrote, "The apostles received the Gospel for us from the Lord Jesus Christ: Jesus Christ was sent forth from God" (1 Clement 42). Martin's case against the earlier dates for the Gospels collapses. And once the Gospels are placed within the generation of eyewitnesses and contemporaries of the events (as pre–70 dates do), then there is good evidence for the historicity of Jesus (*see* NEW TESTAMENT, HISTORICITY OF).

Even the radical theologian John A. T. Robinson has come to believe a late date is untenable. He places the Gospels between 40 and 60. Roman historian Colin Hemer has shown that Luke wrote Acts between 60 and 62. And Luke says there that his Gospel was already finished (see Acts 1:1; cf. Luke 1:1). Most critics believe Mark and/or Matthew were written before Luke. This would place all three within the time of contemporaries and eyewitnesses (*see* NEW TESTAMENT, DATING OF).

Use of Extrabiblical Sources. Martin's use of extrabiblical sources is seriously wanting. He wrongly rejects Josephus' reference to Jesus. He even incorrectly cites two authorities as being in favor of his view, F. F. *Bruce and John Drane. Like most scholars, Bruce is skeptical of the rendering of one text from Josephus as though he believed in the resurrection of Christ. However, Bruce clearly accepts the general authenticity of *Josephus' reference to Christ as a historical figure. Drane declared: "Most scholars have no doubts about the authenticity" of most of it. So, the very people Martin uses to debunk the Josephus citations hold that these citations do show that Jesus was a historical person in the early first century.

Criticism of the Resurrection. Martin believes that Gospel discrepancies discredit the resurrection. The problem of which women were at the tomb when is a case in point. Matthew says Mary Magdalene and the other Mary. Mark adds Salome to the two Marys. Luke adds Joanna to the two Marys. John refers only to Mary Magdalene.

The answer to this problem is not difficult to find. One would expect differences between independent accounts. Were there no differences in perspective, the accounts would be highly suspect. For a fuller discussion of the women at the resurrection, see RESURRECTION OF CHRIST, EVIDENCE FOR. The discrepancies are reconcilable (*see* BIBLE, ALLEGED ERRORS; RESURRECTION, ORDER OF EVENTS). In the case of the women at the tomb, Mark and Luke indicate that other women were involved (Mark 15:40–41; Luke 23:55; 24:10). John quotes Mary as using the term "we" (20:2), showing that she was not alone, and that this was not an exhaustive report of visitors to the grave.

Martin also misapplies his analogy of evidence for Christ to that presented in a courtroom. Critics are more anxious to list inconsistencies than to give the text a fair reading. We have different standards of evidence than did the first-century witnesses. Compared with other ancient histories, the Gospels are exceptionally well attested. The purpose of the Gospels, however, was not to present depositions or present testimony from the witness stand, but to be independent narrations with a faith perspective. The resurrection can be established independent of the historicity of Gospels from facts accepted by nearly all critics (see, for example, Habermas, chap. 5).

Paul's Testimony for Resurrection. Martin and many other critics accept the authenticity of 1 Corinthians 15, along with its early date of about A.D. 55–56. This chapter alone is deadly to Martin's argument. Paul recorded eyewitness reports from as early as five years after the events and no later than twenty-five years after them, and his own eyewitness account of a post-resurrection appearance of Christ. We have other data to confirm Paul's testimony. For example, Paul's creedal material is supportive data. Martin's denial to the contrary, the Gospels were written early enough to confirm the events. And sermons in Acts confirm it (Acts 2, 10, 13; *see* ACTS, HISTORICITY OF). In these sermons, historical details are given (Jesus eating with the disciples). Indeed, the common theme of the sermons is the resurrection.

Martin's List of "Delusions." Martin claimed that the disciples were victims of a psychosis *folie a deus*. They had divine delusions. But his evidence is purely circumstantial. Furthermore, the disciples do not show accepted characteristics of deluded individuals. They were, in fact, so convinced and convincing that they were willing to die for their witness and so were their spiritual descendants. Psychosis *folie a deus* has no evidence for it and much against it.

Conclusion. Martin cannot support his contention that Jesus is not even a historical person. Even granting his own premises, one can demonstrate the historicity of Jesus. Further, there is strong reason to reject Martin's late dates for the Gospels. Once the earlier dates are acknowledged, the historicity of Jesus is a given; only the details are left for debate.

Sources

K. Aland and B. Aland, *The Text of the New Testament*
C. Blomberg, *The Historical Reliability of the Gospels*
F. F. Bruce, *The New Testament Documents: Are They Reliable?*
Clement of Alexandria, *Stromata*
Flavius Josephus, *Antiquities*
R. T. France, *I Believe in the Historical Jesus*
G. Habermas, *The Verdict of History*
I. H. Marshall, *I Believe in the Historical Jesus*
M. Martin, *The Case against Christianity*
B. Metzger, *The Text of the New Testament*
J. W. Montgomery, *Christianity and History*
———, *The Shape of the Past*
J. A. T. Robinson, *Redating the New Testament*
A. N. Sherwin-White, *Roman Society and Roman Law in the New Testament*
G. A. Wells, *Did Jesus Exist?*

Martyr, Justin. ***See*** **JUSTIN MARTYR.**

Marx, Karl. Karl Marx (1818–1883) was one of the most influential of all modern atheists (*see* ATHEISM). His German-Jewish family was converted to Lutheranism when he was six. He was influenced heavily by the idealism of G. W. F. *Hegel (1770–1831), under whom he studied, and he adopted the atheism of fellow student, Ludwig Feuerbach (1804–1872). After some radical political activity, which led to his expulsion from France (1845), he joined Friedrich Engels to produce *The Communist Manifesto* (1848). With the economic support of Engels' prosperous textile business, Marx spent years of research in the British Museum producing *Das Kapital* (1867).

God and Religion. Even as a college student, Marx was a militant atheist who believed that the "criticism of religion is the foundation of all criticism." For this criticism Marx drew heavily on the radical young Hegelian named *Feuerbach.

Engels spoke of "the influence which Feuerbach, more than any other post-Hegelian philosopher, had upon us" (*Marx and Engels on Religion*, 214). He triumphantly spoke of Feuerbach's *Essence of Christianity* which "with one blow . . . pulverized [religion] . . . in that without circumlocution it placed materialism on the throne again" (ibid., 224). Marx drew three principles from Feuerbach:

First, "man is the highest essence for man" (ibid., 50). This means there is a categorical imperative to overthrow anything—especially religion—which debases humanity. Secondly, "Man makes religion; religion does not make man" (ibid., 41). Religion is the self-consciousness of the human being who feels lost without some identification with a "God." Third, religion is "the fantastic reflection in men's minds of those external forces which control their daily life, a reflection in which the terrestrial forces assume the form of supernatural forces" (ibid., 147). God is a projection of human imagination. God did not make the human being in his image; the human being has made a god in his image (*see* SIGMUND FREUD).

Marx's *atheism, however, went well beyond that of Feuerbach. Marx agreed with the materialists that "matter is not a product of mind, but mind itself is merely the highest product of matter" (ibid., 231). Marx objected that Feuerbach did not follow the implications of his ideas into the social domain, for "he by no means wishes to abolish religion; he wants to perfect it" (ibid., 237). "Feuerbach," reasoned Marx, "does not see that the 'religious sentiment' is itself a social product" (ibid., 71). Hence, "he does not grasp the significance of 'revolutionary,' of 'practical-critical,' activity" (ibid., 69). In the words of Marxism's slogan, "Religion is the opiate of the people" (ibid., 35). People take the drug of religion "because this world is not adequate to assure man of his complete accomplishment and integrated development, [so] he compensates himself with the image of another, more perfect world" (ibid., 36).

In the Marxist evolutionary conception of the universe, there is absolutely no room for a Creator or a Ruler (*see* EVOLUTION, BIOLOGICAL). *Deism's supreme being, who is shut out from the whole existing world, is a contradiction in terms. Concluded Marx, the only service to be rendered to God is to make atheism a compulsory article of faith and prohibit religion generally (ibid., 143). Marx rejects even agnosticism: "What, indeed, is *agnosticism but, to use an expressive Lancashire term, 'shamefaced' materialism? The agnostic conception of nature is materialistic throughout" (ibid., 295).

Marx was under no delusion that religion would immediately die when socialism was adopted. Since religion is but a reflex of the real world, religion will not vanish until "the practical relations of every-day life offer to man none but perfectly intelligible and reasonable relations with regard to his fellowmen and to nature" (ibid., 136). The communist utopia must be realized before religion is no more.

Human Beings. Marxism holds a materialistic view of human origins and nature (*see* MATERIALISM). This, of course, entailed naturalistic evolution. *Das Kapital* came only eight years after Charles *Darwin's *On the Origin of Species* was published in 1859. Evolution was a helpful addition to Marx's materialistic framework. "Mind is the product of matter." That is, mind evolved from material stuff. The nonliving (matter) has always been (*see* EVOLUTION, COSMIC). The nonliving has produced the living (*see* EVOLUTION, CHEMICAL), and finally, the nonintelligent has produced the intelligent (*see* EVOLUTION, BIOLOGICAL).

Marx wrote his doctoral thesis at the University of Jena (1841) on the materialistic philosophies of the Greek philosophers Epicurus and Democritus. Adding in the support of Darwinian evolution he could explain, without God, the origin of human life as the product of evolutionary processes in a material world.

Marx dismissed pure philosophy as speculation, compared to the vital task of changing the world (Marx, *Selected Writings in Sociology and Social Philosophy,* 82). Hence, he was not particularly interested in philosophical materialism. As a materialist he did not deny mind altogether. He believed that everything about man, including the mind, was determined by material conditions. "For us, mind is a mode of energy, a function of brain; all we know is that the material world is governed by immutable laws, and so forth" (Marx, *Marx and Engels on Religion,* 298). This view would fit what philosophers call epiphenomenalism, that consciousness is nonmaterial but that it is dependent on material things for its existence. Certainly life after death was an illusion (*see* IMMORTALITY).

Karl Marx was more interested in the concrete social being. He believed "the real nature of man is the total of *social* nature" (ibid., 83). Apart from such obvious biological facts as the need for food, Marx tended to downplay individual existence. He believed that what was true of one person at one time in one society was true of all at all times in all places (ibid., 91, 92). The consciousness determines human being, but social being determines consciousness (ibid., 67). Sociology is not reducible to psychology. One central generalization was that the human is a socially active being distinguished from other animals in that people *produce* their means of subsistence (ibid., 69). They work for their living. Thus, Marx concludes, it is right to work, to have a life of productive activity.

Those who do not find fulfillment in industrial labor experience alienation. This alienation will be eliminated when private property is done away with (ibid., 250). Private property, however, is not the cause but a consequence of alienation (ibid., 176). Alienation itself consists in the fact that the worker is forced to bring fulfillment to someone else, instead of finding personal fulfillment. Even the objects produced are owned by another. The cure for this ill is the future communist society in which the individual can be fulfilled by working for the good of the whole (ibid., 177, 253).

World and History. Marx's overall view of the world is both materialistic and dialectic. Marx used the term *historical materialism* for the "view of the course of history which seeks the ultimate cause and the great moving power of all important events in the economic development of society" (*Marx and Engels on Religion,* 298). When this is applied specifically to history Marx is a *dialectical* materialist who looks for thesis, antithesis, and synthesis. History is unfolding according to a universal dialectic law that can be predicted the way an astronomer predicts an eclipse. In the preface to *Das Kapital,* Marx compared his method to that of a physicist and said, "the ultimate aim of this work is to lay bare the economic law of motion of modern society," and he also spoke of the natural laws of capitalistic production as "working with iron necessity toward inevitable results" (*Das Kapital,* "Preface").

The nature of the dialectic of modern history is that the thesis of capitalism is opposed by the antithesis of socialism, which will give way to the ultimate synthesis of communism. History is predetermined like the course of the stars, except the laws governing history are not mechanical but economic (*see* DETERMINISM). Humanity is economically determined. That is, "the mode of production of material life determines the general character of social, political, and spiritual processes of life" (ibid., 67, 70, 90, 111f.). There are other factors as well, but the economic is a primary factor of social determination. Engels emphatically proclaimed, "more than this neither Marx nor I have ever asserted. Hence if somebody twists this into saying that the economic element is the *only* determining one, he transforms that proposition into a meaningless, abstract, senseless phrase" (*Marx and Engels on Religion,* 274).

The Future. Based on his knowledge of the dialectic of history and economic determinism, Marx confidently predicted that capitalism would become increasingly unstable and that the class struggle between the bourgeois (ruling class) and the proletariat (working class) would intensify. Thus the poor would become larger and poorer until, by a major social revolution, they would seize power and institute the new communist phase of history (ibid., 79–80, 147f., 236).

The fact that these predictions did not come to pass was an embarrassment to Marxist theory. That almost the opposite has happened has been the near-demise of Marxism.

Communistic Utopia. According to Marx, capitalism has its own internal contradictions. For as the masses become more numerous and the capitalists fewer, the latter would control great concentrations of productive equipment which they would throttle for their own gain. The masses would sweep aside the capitalists as a hindrance to production and seize the industrial economy. In the emerging progressive society there would be no wages, no money, no social classes, and eventually no state. This communist utopia would simply be a free association of producers under their own conscious control. Society would move ultimately "from each according to his ability to each according to his need" (ibid., 263). There would, however, be an intermediate period of "the dictatorship of the proletariat" (ibid., 261). But in the higher stage the state would vanish and true freedom begin.

Ethics. There are several characteristic dimensions of the ethics of Marxism. Three of these are relativism (*see* MORALITY, ABSOLUTE NATURE OF), utilitarianism, and collectivism.

Relativism. Since Marxism is an atheism, and since as Nietzsche noted that when God dies all absolute value dies with him, then it is understandable that Marxism's ethic is relativistic. There are no moral absolutes. There are two reasons for this. First, there is no external, eternal realm. The only absolute is the unfolding dialectic world process. Engels wrote, "we therefore reject every attempt to impose on us any moral dogma whatever as an eternal, ultimate and forever immutable law on the pretext that the moral world has its permanent principles which transcend history" (see Hunt, 87–88).

Second, there is no foundational nature or essence for general principles of human conduct. Ideas of good and evil are determined by the socio-economic structure. Class struggle generates its own ethic.

Utilitarianism. The standard for morality is its contribution to creation of a communist society. Whatever promotes the ultimate cause of communism is good, and what hinders it is evil. Actions can be justified by their end. Lenin once defined morality as that which serves to destroy the exploiting capitalistic society and to unite workers in creating a new communist society (ibid., 89). Thus the end justifies the means. Some neo-Marxists have rejected this, insisting that means are subject to the same moral principles as the end. But they have departed from orthodox Marxism. This is the communist's equivalent of utilitarianism's "greatest good for the greatest number in the long run."

Collectivism. In the Marxist ethic, the universal transcends the individual. This is a heritage from *Hegel who believed that the perfect life is possible only when the individual is organically integrated into the ethical totality. For Marx, however, the highest ethical totality is not the state, as it was for Hegel, but "universal freedom of will." However, this "freedom" (*see* FREE WILL) is not individual but corporate and universal. The difference from Hegel is that the apex is shifted from the state to society, from the body politic to the body public.

In the perfect society private morals are eliminated and the ethical ideals of the community are achieved. This will be determined by material production. Material production determines religion, metaphysics, and morality.

Evaluation. *Positive Contributions.* Marx's concern for the condition of workers is to be commended. Working conditions are vastly improved today from those over a century ago when Marx wrote. Likewise, Marx is just in attacking the view that workers are a means to the end of capital gain. People should not be used as an end to things, even things desired by other people. Thus, Marxism has made a significant contribution to the social ethos that places the person over money.

Marxism has been a corrective on unlimited, uncontrolled capitalism. Any system which permits the rich to get richer and the poor poorer without moral limits is abusive. In ancient Jewish economy this possibility was checked by the year of Jubilee (one year every half century) when acquisitions were returned to their original owners.

The utopian aspirations of Marxism are noble. Marxism has been both a philosophy of history and a goal for overcoming perceived evils in the world. This vision has captured the imagination and dedication of many idealistic thinkers.

Negative Elements. Unfortunately, the harmful aspects of Marxism are significant. At the center of these is a militant, dogmatic atheism. It is self-defeating to insist that God is *nothing but* a projection of human imagination. "Nothing but" statements presume "more than" knowledge. One cannot know that "God" is confined only to imagination unless knowledge about God goes beyond mere imagination.

Marx's deterministic view of history is contrary to fact. Things have not worked out as Marx predicted. Marxist historical theory also is a category mistake, assuming that economic influences work like physical laws.

Materialism, as a view of humanity, ignores the rich spiritual and religious aspects of human nature, to say nothing of the evidence for human immateriality and immortality. Related to this is a view of human origins based on a flawed view of naturalistic evolution. This view has been shown to be an inadequate explanation of human origins. Marx's metaphysics is generally antisupernatural, ruling out the possibility of miracles. But this view has crucial philosophical flaws, as noted in the article MIRACLES, ARGUMENTS AGAINST.

Ethical relativism is self-destructive in its strongest form. The absolute denial of absolutes cuts its own throat, replacing one absolute with another. Socialist society has hardly avoided absolutism. Also, the fallacies of the "end justifies the means" ethic are infamous.

Marxism holds out an admirable idealism of goals (a human utopia) but demonstrates a miserable record of achievement. Reality in Marxist countries has brought millions closer to hell than paradise. While the goal of a perfect community is desirable, the revolutionary means of achieving it have resulted in mass destruction unparalleled in human history. From a Christian perspective the means of transforming humankind is not revolution but regeneration. Freedom is not by the birth of a new government but by the birth of a new inner person—that is, the new birth. Marx's view of religion was superficial. He should have heeded his father's exhortation to him at age 17: "Faith [in God] is a real [requirement] of man sooner or later, and there are moments in life when even the atheist is involuntarily drawn to worship the Almighty" ("Letter from Trier," 18 November 1835).

Marx also might have applied his own thoughts when he said, "Union with Christ bestows inner exaltation, consolation in suffering, calm assurance, and a heart which is open to love of mankind, to all that is noble, to all that is great, not out of ambition, not through the desire for fame, but only because of Christ" (written by Marx as a teenager between August 10 and 16, 1835).

Marx's own father feared it was the desire for fame which transformed Karl's Christian conscience into a demonic desire. In March 1837, he admonished his ambitious son, saying,

> At times I cannot rid myself of ideas which arouse in me sad forebodings and fear when I am struck as if by lightning by the thought: is your heart in accord with your head, your talents? Has it room for the earthly but gentler sentiments which in this vale of sorrow are so essentially consoling for a man of feeling? *And since that heart is obviously animated and governed by a demon not granted to all men, is that demon heavenly or Faustian?* [*Selected Writings*, emphasis added]

Sources

K. Blockmuehl, *The Challenge of Marxism*

N. L. Geisler, *Is Man the Measure?* (chap. 5)

R. N. C. Hunt, *The Theory and Practice of Communism*

D. Lyon, *Karl Marx: A Christian Assessment of His Life & Thought*

K. Marx, *Das Kapital*

———, *Marx and Engel on Religion*

———, *Selected Writings in Sociology and Social Philosophy*

Mary, Apparitions of. Many persons claim to see appearances of the Virgin Mary or other Roman Catholic saints. These appearances are sometimes used as verification for some doctrine or truth claim connected with the Roman Catholic Church. Are these true miracles? Do they have any apologetic value in establishing truth claims?

The Apologetic Value of Apparitions. The apparitions of Mary are not really connected with a specific truth claim (*see* MIRACLES, APOLOGETIC VALUE OF). Mary did not announce that she was God in feminine flesh and then proceed to prove it by miracles. The connections to truth claims are generally made by those who saw the apparition. It is usually not clear what the specific claim would be.

Even when specific claims are associated with the event, the alleged miraculous nature of the event is challengeable. Leading Roman Catholic authorities reject the authority of most claims that Mary has appeared. Since most of these appearances are of a basic experiential nature, it raises questions about the validity of the rest of the claims. At best the apparitions add a note of confusion to doctrinal debate, and God is never a God of confusion.

Many of the appearances have natural explanations or are a spiritualization of natural phenomena (for example, a cloud formation or reflection of light through a window). Some fit all the criteria for being hallucinations. Of the small number of hard-core events that escape purely natural explanations, some may be explained as demonic deceptions. The few apparitions with an objective basis in reality have signs of Satanic deception characteristic of false miracles (*see* MIRACLES, FALSE). The apparitions lack unique features of a true miracle, as are described in the articles Miracle and Miracles, Apologetic Value of. They tend to be associated with adoration of a statue, crucifix, or icon, which is an idolatrous form of worship (see Exod. 20:4). Some involve communication with the dead (see Deut. 18:11) and false teaching (see 1 Timothy 4), such as veneration of Mary or relics (see Geisler and MacKenzie, chap. 15).

There are also similar occurrences in other religions, so any conflicting truth claims associated with them are self-canceling, since neither of two opposing truth claims can be supported if their evidence is of the same kind. *Buddhists have visions of Buddha, *Hindus of Krishna, and many cultists of unbiblical forms of Christ. The Church of Jesus Christ of Latter-Day Saints (Mormon) is largely founded on angelic appearances to Joseph

Smith and sustained by visions seen by the "apostles" of the church, yet the Mormon Christ is the brother of Lucifer and the result of sexual union between God (who has a physical body) and Mary. There are many conflicting, self-canceling visions and appearances, but no pious visionary has been able to miraculously substantiate his or her claims as did Jesus (*see* CHRIST, UNIQUENESS OF). He performed unparalleled, objectively demonstrable miracles (*see* MIRACLES IN THE BIBLE; RESURRECTION, EVIDENCE FOR).

Conclusion. Whatever status apparitions of Mary may have as unusual events, they do not show evidence of being true miracles (*see* MIRACLE; MIRACLES, MAGIC AND). On the contrary, their association with occult practices and false teaching shows that they are not supernatural acts of God. Since they are unconnected with clear truth claims and are not unique events unparalleled in other religions, they have no apologetic value in establishing truth claims (*see* MIRACLES, APOLOGETIC VALUE OF).

Sources

N. L. Geisler, *Miracles and the Modern Mind*

———, *Signs and Wonders*

———and R. E. Mackenzie, *Roman Catholics and Evangelicals: Agreements and Differences*

A. Kole, *Miracle and Magic*

E. Miller and K. Samples, *The Cult of the Virgin: Catholic Mariology and the Apparitions of Mary*

G. Peter, *Indonesia Revival*

"Amazing" Randy, *The Healers*

B. B. Warfield, *Counterfeit Miracles*

Materialism. *Materialism* believes that all is matter or reducible to it. *Pantheism*, by contrast, holds that all is mind. Theists (*see* THEISM) hold that Mind produced matter, and materialists that matter produced mind (*see* ATHEISM). In rigid materialism "mind" does not really exist, only matter. According to soft materialism or Epiphenomenalism, mind exists but is dependent on matter the way a shadow of a tree depends on the tree.

Thomas Hobbes defined matter:

> The world (I mean not the earth only, that denominates the lovers of it "worldly men," but the *universe*, that is, the whole mass of all things that are) is corporeal, that is to say, body; and hath the dimensions of magnitude, namely, length, breadth, and depth: also every part of body is likewise body, and hath the like dimensions; and consequently every part of the universe is body, and that which is not body is no part of the universe: and because the universe is all, that which is no part of it is nothing, and consequently nowhere. [269]

Basic Tenets. All materialists hold several basic beliefs in common (such as, everything is made of matter [energy]). Most materialists share other beliefs, such as humans are not immortal (*see* IMMORTALITY).

Matter Is All There Is. As Carl *Sagan put it, the Cosmos is all that was, is, or ever will be. Everything is matter or reducible to it and dependent on it. If matter were to cease to exist, nothing would remain.

Matter Is Eternal. Most materialists believe matter has always been. Or, as one *atheist put it, if matter came to be, it came into existence from nothing and by nothing (Kenny, 66; *see* CREATION, VIEWS OF). The material universe is self-sustaining and self-generating. It is probably eternal, but if it came to be, then it came to be on its own without outside help. Isaac Asimov speculated that the probability is equally good that nothing came from nothing or that something came out of nothing. As luck would have it, something emerged (Asimov, 148). So matter is eternal, or else it came from nothing spontaneously.

Traditional materialists believed there were innumerable indestructible little hard pellets of reality called *atoms* (*see* ATOMISM). With the splitting of the atom and the emergence of *Einstein's $E=MC^2$ (energy = mass times speed of light squared), materialists now speak of the indestructibility of energy. They appeal to the first law of thermodynamics, claiming that "energy can neither be created nor destroyed." Energy does not pass out of existence; it simply takes on new forms. Even at death, all the elements of our being are reabsorbed by the environment and reused. The process goes on forever (*see* THERMODYNAMICS, LAWS OF).

There Is No Creator. Another premise of strict materialism is atheism or nontheism. That is, either there is no God or, at least, no need for a God. As the *Humanist Manifesto II* put it, "As nontheists, we begin with humans not God, nature not deity" (Kurtz, 16). According to the nontheistic view of creation out of matter, no cause is needed to bring matter into existence or to form matter already in existence. There is neither a Creator nor a Maker (Former) of the world. The world explains itself.

Humans Are Mortal. Another implication of this view is that there is no immortal, never-dying "soul" or spiritual aspect to human beings (*see* IMMORTALITY). As *Humanist Manifesto I* noted, "the traditional *dualism of mind and body must be rejected." A materialist believes modern science discredits any spiritual or soul dimension (Kurtz, 8, 16–17). There is no mind, only a chemical reaction in the brain. Less stringent materialists admit the existence of a soul but deny that it can exist independently of matter. For them the soul is to the body what the image in the mirror is to the one looking at it. When the body dies, so does the soul. When matter disintegrates, the mind is also destroyed.

Humans Are Not Unique. Materialists differ regarding the nature of human beings. Most accord a special status to humans as the highest point in the evolutionary process (*see* EVOLUTION, BIOLOGICAL). That doesn't allow a qualitative difference from animals. Humans differ only in degree, not in kind, from lower forms of life. Human beings are the highest and latest animal form on the evolutionary ladder, with more highly developed abilities than fellow primates (*see* HUMANISM, SECULAR).

Argument for Materialism. *The Nature of Self-Consciousness.* In order for there to be more than matter, the mind must consciously survive death. But the mind cannot function without the brain. Therefore, when the brain dies consciousness ceases at the same time. This argument assumes that consciousness is a physical function, that "mind" is a function of matter. Mind is only a process within the brain. There is no proof for such an assumption.

Also unwarranted is the assumption that, because the mind and brain function *together*, they must be identical. A corollary assumption is that I am nothing but my brain. This is reductionist fallacy. Things that go together are not necessarily the same, any more than ideas expressed by these words are the same as the words themselves. Mind and brain could interact without being the same.

Dependence of Consciousness. In a modified form of materialism, *epiphenominalism*, the mind is not identical to the brain, but it is dependent on the physical brain, the way a shadow is dependent on a tree. This again assumes, though it does not prove, that the mind is dependent on the brain. Certain mental functions can be explained in physical ways, but that does not mean they are dependent on physical processes. If there is a spiritual, as well as a physical, dimension to reality, the mind shows every sign of being able to function in either. Neurobiology is an empirical science, but these scientists freely admit that they have not come close to isolating the "I." They can quantify mind-brain interactions, but there has been no success in learning the qualities of emotional or self response.

Access to the World. Materialists insist that the mind or self gains access to the world through the brain. Death destroys the brain, so death closes that door. The brain is certainly one way of access, but we cannot know if it is the only way of access to this world. It may or may not be. More to the point is that there may be another world, or even multiple dimensions, with wholly different kinds of access. And there may be ways to be conscious other than through interaction with the physical world. If there are spiritual beings, God and angels, and the evidence is that there are (*see* GOD, EVIDENCE FOR), they are certainly conscious without a physical body gateway to the world. The possibility of this spiritual dimension, of course, is what the materialist wants to avoid admitting, but there is no reason to do so.

The Necessity of Embodiment. Materialists reason that no person can survive without a body, and death destroys the body. So it destroys personhood. This begs the question by defining "person" in an arbitrary way that is unwarranted by our knowledge. We do not have the information that death destroys personhood for the reasons already stated. At best we can say that death severs one dimension of consciousness—this-world consciousness. We can still be self-conscious, God-conscious, and conscious of another world.

Evaluation. Since materialists hold many beliefs in common with other atheists and agnostics, these beliefs are discussed in their respective articles. Their antisupernaturalism (*see* MIRACLE) is without philosophical grounds. Likewise, their acceptance of evolution (*see* EVOLUTION; EVOLUTION, BIOLOGICAL; EVOLUTION, COSMIC) is without scientific justification.

Materialist arguments are self-defeating. "Nothing but" statements assume "more than" knowledge. How could I know I am nothing more than my brain unless I was more than it? I cannot analyze my brain in a test tube unless I am outside the test tube.

At the heart of materialism is the rejection of the existence of mind or spirit as a separate entity that survives the dissolution of matter. Mind, rather, is really matter, or at least dependent on matter.

Strict Materialism Is Self-Defeating. The pure materialist view is clearly self-defeating (see Lewis, chap. 3). For surely the materialist *theory* is not made up of matter. That is, the *theory* about matter has no matter in it. The *idea* that all is made of molecules does not itself consist of molecules. For the *thought* about all matter must itself stand over and above matter. If the thought about matter is part of matter then it cannot be a thought about *all* matter, since being a part of matter it cannot transcend itself to make a pronouncement about *all* matter.

Mind (or its thought) only can transcend matter if it is more than matter. If it is more than matter, then matter is not all that exists. Whatever is material is limited to a region of space and time. If it moves, it moves in space and time. But the mind is not so limited. It roams the universe without leaving the room. Even the materialist speaks of personal thoughts. But if strict materialism were correct there could be no discrete thoughts. They would be a mere stream of electrons or some other material particle. Only a self-conscious being can truly make thoughts. Materialists want people to agree with their doctrine and accept their views. However, this is not possible if the views are correct. If consciousness is merely the result of a flow of electrons, persons are material processes, not free human beings.

Modified Materialism Is Self-Defeating. Some materialists admit that mind is more than matter but deny that mind can exist independent of matter. They insist that mind is more than matter the way the whole is more than the sum of its parts. And yet the whole ceases to exist when the parts do. For instance, a whole automobile engine has something more than all its individual parts spread over the floor of the garage. Nonetheless, when the parts are destroyed, the "whole" engine is destroyed too. Likewise, a mind is more than matter but it is dependent on matter and ceases to exist when man's material parts dissolve.

Although this materialistic argument is less apparently self-defeating than the first one, it is nonetheless equally wrong. It affirms that mind is ultimately dependent on matter. But the statement "mind is dependent on matter" does not claim to depend for its truth upon matter. In fact, it claims to be a truth about all mind and matter. But no truth about *all* matter can be dependent for its truth upon matter. One cannot stand outside all matter to make an affirmation about all matter and yet simultaneously claim he is really standing inside matter, being dependent upon it. If my mind is completely dependent on matter, then it can't make statements from a vantage point beyond matter. And if its statements are not from a standpoint independent of matter, then they are not really statements about *all* matter. For one must step beyond something to see it all. The whole cannot be seen from within. It claims to have transcendent knowledge with only an immanent basis of operation.

Mind Transcends Matter. While materialists attempt to reduce everything to matter rather than mind, it would appear that in an epistemological sense at least, just the opposite is true. For whatever analysis I make of matter, there is always an "I" that stands outside the object of my analysis. Indeed, even when I analyze myself, there is an "I" that transcends the "me." I can never capture my transcendental I (ego). I can only catch it, as it were, out of "the corner of my eye." Even if I attempt to put my "I" in the test-tube of analysis it becomes a me at which the elusive I is looking. There is always more than me; there is the I that is not merely me. Contrary to materialism, then, everything is reducible to (i.e., ultimately dependent on) the I.

Mind is prior to and independent of matter.

Matter Is Not Eternal. There is strong evidence for what scientists have come to call the *Big Bang origin of the universe, showing that matter had a beginning. The **kalam* cosmological argument demonstrates that the material universe has a cause. But the cause of all matter cannot itself be matter; hence something more than matter exists. As Karl *Marx put it, either matter produced mind, or mind produced matter. Since matter was produced, Mind must have produced it.

Law Giver Was Immaterial. Another way to demonstrate that all is not matter is known as the *Moral Argument for God. It can be phrased:

1. There is an objective moral law (*see* Morality, Absolute Nature of).
2. The moral law is prescriptive, not descriptive.
3. What is prescriptive is not part of the descriptive material world.
4. So there is an immaterial objective reality. More than matter exists (Lewis, *Mere Christianity*, 17–19).

Conclusions. All of the arguments in favor of materialism are essentially self-defeating. Any attempt to deny that there is a reality beyond the material implies that a nonmaterial reality, such as the mind, exists. Materialism is an untenable position.

Sources

I. Asimov, *The Beginning and the End*
N. L. Geisler, *When Skeptics Ask*
T. Hobbes, *Leviathan*
A. Kenny, *The Five Ways: St. Thomas Aquinas' Proofs of God's Existence*
P. Kurtz, ed., *Secular Humanist Manifestos I and II*
C. S. Lewis, *Mere Christianity*
———, *Miracles*
J. P. Moreland, et al., *Immortality*
C. Sagan, *Cosmos*

Metaphysics. *Metaphysics* (lit. "beyond the physical) is the study of being or reality. It is used interchangeably with *ontology* (Gk. *ontos*, "being," and *logos*, "word about").

Metaphysics is the discipline in philosophy which answers such questions as: What is real? (*see* Realism); Is reality one or many? (*see* One and Many, Problem of); Is reality material or immaterial? (*see* Materialism); Is it natural (*see* Naturalism) or supernatural? (*see* Miracles, Arguments Against). Another important metaphysical problem has to whether being is univocal or analogical (*see* Analogy, Principle of).

In the Aristotelian-Thomistic tradition, metaphysics is defined as the study of being insofar as it is being. Physics is the study of being insofar as it is physical. Mathematics is the study of being insofar as it is quantifiable.

Mill, John Stuart. John Stuart Mill (1806–1873) embraced a finite god (*see* Finite Godism) worldview, with a logical positivism that took a strong anti-metaphysical stand (*see* Ayer, A. J.). He is usually known as a pioneer in modern scientific thinking. He devised rules for inductive scientific reasoning (*see* Inductive Method) and was a fountain head of ethical utilitarianism. Mill elaborated the canons of inductive scientific thought first stated by Francis Bacon (1561–1626) in *Novum Organum* (1620).

A Small God. Mill rejected the traditional *teleological argument as expounded by William *Paley. He reasoned that Paley's argument is built on analogy, that similarity in effect implies similarity in cause. This kind of analogy weakens as dissimilarities become greater. Watches imply watchmakers only because, by previous experience, we know that watchmakers make watches. There is nothing intrinsic in the watch to demand a craftsman's hand. In like manner, footprints imply human beings and dung implies animals because previous experience informs us that this connection is appropriate. It is not that there is intrinsic design in the remains. Therefore, Mill concluded, Paley's argument is weak.

Mill went on to offer what he considered a stronger expression of the teleological argument, built on an inductive "method of agreement." This argument was the weakest of Mill's inductive methods, but he considered the teleological argument to be a strong form of this kind of induction. Mill began with the organic rather than the mechanical aspect of nature:

1. There is an amazing concurrence of diverse elements in the human eye.
2. It is not probable that random selection brought these elements together.
3. The method of agreement argues for a common cause of the eye.
4. The cause was a final (purposing) cause, not an efficient (producing) cause.

Mill said that biological evolution, if true, diminishes the strength of even this stronger form of the teleological argument. For much of what appears to be design is accounted for in evolution by the survival of the fittest (see Geisler, *Philosophy of Religion*, 177–84).

Mill's reasoning led him to posit a finite God:

> A Being of great but limited power, how or by what limited we cannot even conjecture; of great, and perhaps unlimited intelligence, but perhaps, also, more narrowly limited than his power: who desires, and pays some regard to, the happiness of his creatures, but who seems to have other motives of action which he cares more for, and who can hardly be supposed to have created the universe for that purpose alone. ["Nature," in *Three Essays on Religion*, 194; except where noted, subsequent quotations will be from this essay]

Such a description limits God in power and goodness. We can infer from nature that God has benevolent feelings toward his creatures, "but to jump from this to the inference that his sole or chief purposes are those of benevolence, and that the single end and aim of creation was the happiness of his creatures, is not only not justified by any evidence but is a conclusion in opposition to such evidence as we have" (192). Mill's deity cannot foresee the future or what will come of his acts. He is not omnipotent. The evidence shows an intelligence superior to any human being's, but the fact that God uses means to reach ends shows that he is limited. "Who would have recourse to means if to attain his end his mere word was sufficient?" (177).

While he believed there could be many creators, he favored the idea that there was only one (ibid., 133). Other than the general principles of nature's design, there is little reason to believe the Creator benevolent. Nature is not directed toward a particularly moral end, if there is a goal at all (189).

The limitations of God are in himself, not simply caused by the world or other beings. He cannot control the qualities and forces of the fabric of the universe. The materials of the universe do not allow God to more completely fulfill his purposes, or else he did not know how to accomplish it (186).

Creation. The universe was not created out of nothing, according to Mill. "The indication given by such evidence as there is, points to the creation, not indeed of the universe, but of the present order of it by an Intelligent Mind, whose power over the materials was not absolute" (243). In fact, there is from nature no reason to suppose that either matter or force were made by the Being who put them together in the ways they now appear. It is unclear that he has power to alter any of the properties of matter. Matter and energy are, therefore, eternal. Out of them God constructed a world by working with the materials and properties at hand (178).

In positing a finite God and eternal matter, Mill followed *Plato into a theistic *dualism. Creation is not *ex nihilo* (out of nothing) or *ex deo* (out of God). Rather, it is *ex materia* (out of preexisting matter; *see* CREATION, VIEWS OF).

Mill believed in a material universe he called "Nature." *Nature* is the entire system of material, with all its properties (64). It is "all facts, actual and possible" or "the mode . . . in which all things take place" (5–6). Since all things take place in a uniform way, we can speak of *laws* of nature. "All phenomena which have been sufficiently examined are found to take place with regularity, even having certain fixed conditions, positive and negative, on the occurrence of which it invariably happens" (ibid.). It is the task of science to learn those conditions.

Miracles. Mill held that the finite god is the author of Nature's laws and could intervene in the affairs of humanity, though there is no evidence that he does. Mill agrees with David *Hume that "the testimony of experience against miracles is undeviating and indubitable" (221). Mill takes another route to reach Hume's antisupernatural conclusion (*see* MIRACLE; NATURALISM). Mill believed that an unusual occurrence, even if it defeats a well established law, is merely discovery of another law, previously unknown (221).

So whatever new phenomena are discovered still depend on law and are always exactly reproduced when the same circumstances are repeated (222). A miracle claims to supersede natural laws, not just cancel out one natural law with another. Such a breaking of law cannot be accepted. How is Mill so certain that there is a natural explanation for every event? He draws proof from the absence of all experience of a supernatural cause and the frequent experience of natural causes:

> The commonest principles of sound judgment forbid us to suppose for any effect as cause of which we have absolutely no experience, unless all those of which we have experience are ascertained to be absent. Now there are few things of which we have more frequent experience than of physical facts which our knowledge does not enable us to account for. [229–30]

There is, therefore, nothing to exclude the supposition that every "miracle" has a natural cause, and as long as that supposition is possible, "no man of ordinary practical judgment, would assume of conjecture a cause which no reason existed for supposing to be real, save the necessity of accounting for something which is sufficiently accounted for without it" (231).

Miracles cannot be ruled impossible so long as there is a God. Mill believed that "If we had the direct testimony of our senses to a supernatural fact, it might be as completely authenticated and made certain as any natural one." Pending that personal contact, miracles have no historical claim, and they are invalid as evidence of revelation (239).

Evil and Ethics. One of the most convincing evidences of God's finitude was the presence of evil in the world (*see* EVIL, PROBLEM OF; FINITE GODISM; KUSHNER, HAROLD). Mill concluded that "if the maker of the world can [do] all that he will, he wills misery, and there is no escape from the conclusion" (37). Men are hanged for doing what Nature does in killing every being that lives. Much of the time that death comes with torture. Nature has total disregard for mercy and justice, treating the noblest and the worst people alike. Such evils were absolutely inconsistent with an all-powerful, all-good being. The best he could hope for was a partially good deity with limited power (29–30). In view of Nature's gross evil, it would be irrational and immoral to use natural law as the model for action. Human duty is not to imitate nature but to amend it. Some aspects of nature may be good, but "it has never been settled by any accredited doctrine, what particular departments of the order of nature shall be reputed to be designed for our moral instruction and guidance" (42). At any rate, it is impossible to decide what in nature expresses the character of God.

Since ethics cannot be based in revelation or the supernatural, there are obviously no absolute maxims of morality (99). Having rejected moral absolutes (*see* MORALITY, ABSOLUTE NATURE OF), Mill devised the utilitarian calculus by which one is obligated to do what he or she can to bring the greatest good to the greatest number in the long run.

Mill had great respect for the moral example of Jesus (253–54). But when it came to spelling what the Christian "golden rule" meant, Mill believed utilitarianism was the answer. We should so act to bring the greatest good to the greatest number. There are no ethical absolutes. There may be times when a lie brings about more good than does the truth. Our best guide is experience, through which we can develop general guidelines (*Utilitarianism*, chap. 2).

Human Destiny. A human being is mind and soul as well as material body. There is no evidence, then, that the soul could not be immortal. There simply isn't any evidence in favor of an immortal soul, either (*see* IMMORTALITY). Mill believed it certain that souls did not become "ghosts" who bothered with human affairs. Beyond that there was only a hope (201, 208–10). Of one thing he was confident: *If* there is life after death, "nothing can be more opposed to every estimate we can form of probability, than the common idea of the future life as a state of rewards and punishments (*see* HELL) in any other sense than that the consequences of our actions upon our own character and susceptibilities will follow us in the future as they have done in the past and present" (210–11). Any future life will simply continue life now. To assume a radical break at death in the change of the mode of our existence is contrary to all analogies drawn from this life. We must assume the same laws of nature will apply.

Despite the lack of evidence for immortality, life here and now is worth living, as is the effort to cultivate the improvement of character (250). There is also ground for optimism about the human race:

> The conditions of human existence are highly favorable to the growth of such a feeling inasmuch as a battle is constantly going on, in which the humblest human creature is not incapable of taking some part, between the powers of good and those of evil, and in which even the smallest help to the right side has its value in promoting the very slow and often insensible progress by which good is gradually gaining ground from evil, yet gaining it so visibly at considerable intervals as to promise the very distant but not uncertain final victory of good. [256]

Not only did Mill express optimism about the final victory over evil, but he believed that humanistic efforts in this direction were sure to become the new religion. For "to do something during life, on even the humblest scale if nothing more is within reach, towards bringing this consummation ever so little nearer, is the most animating and invigorating thought which can inspire a human creature" (257).

Evaluation. Inadequate View of God. Philosophically, a finite god is not self-explaining. Such a god is contrary to the principle of *causality that affirms a cause for every finite being. A finite god is only a large creature, who needs a Creator. A finite being is a contingent, not a necessary, being. A contingent being is one that can not exist. Whatever could not exist depends for its existence on a Necessary Being, which cannot not exist (*see* COSMOLOGICAL ARGUMENT).

Further, a god who is not absolutely perfect is not God in the ultimate sense. One could measure his imperfection only by an ultimate standard of perfection. But the ultimate perfection is, by definition, God. So if there were an imperfect finite god, he would be something less than ultimate God. Since Mill's God engages in evil, one could say that his argument best proves the existence of a Devil. At any rate, anything incompletely good is not worthy of worship. Worship attributes ultimate worth to something. Why should one attribute absolute worth to what is not absolutely worthy? Every finite being is a creature, and worship of the creature is idolatry. Or to borrow terms from Paul Tillich, *ultimate commitment* should not be given to something less than an *Ultimate*. A partially good creature is not an Ultimate.

Some finite godists attempt to avoid this criticism by positing a God limited in power but not perfection. This seems arbitrary and wishful thinking. How can God be an infinitely good Being when he is only a finite being? How can one be more of anything than he has the capacity to be? How can the attributes of God be extended further than his nature allows?

Finally, a finite god offers no assurance that evil will be defeated. Since a religious commitment is an ultimate commitment, we are ultimately committed to the cause of good, which may not ultimately succeed. Can a finite god who cannot guarantee victory really inspire ultimate commitment? How many people will really make an ultimate commitment to work for what they have no assurance will ultimately win? One can be inspired to confess courageously, "I would rather lose in a battle that is ultimately going to win, than to win in a battle that will ultimately lose." A finite god lacks the assurance to engender such motivation.

Inadequate View of Evil. The problem of evil does not eliminate God or his goodness. It calls for an infinitely powerful and perfect God to eliminate it. One cannot even know there are ultimate injustices without knowing some ultimately just Being beyond the world. Only an infinitely powerful and perfect God can defeat evil. Only an all-powerful God can defeat evil; only an all-good God desires that defeat. A finite god will not suffice (*see* EVIL, PROBLEM OF).

Mill makes a category mistake in arguing that God is not perfect because he kills in a way that would be murder among humans. God is Creator of life, and he has the right to take away what he gives (Deut. 32:39; Job 1:21). We did not create life; we do not have the right to take it. The gardener who is sovereign over the flowers and bushes in his or her own yard lacks the right to cut down those belonging to the neighbors. Those who own them are in control of them. God owns all life. He can take it if he wants without failing any moral law.

Inadequate View of Miracles. Mill's rejection of miracles, like that of Hume, begs the question. Mill bases belief in methods that preassume naturalism (*see* MIRACLE; MIRACLES, ARGUMENTS AGAINST). He assumes that every exception to a natural law will automatically have a natural explanation. If one knows in advance that every event, however unusual, has a natural explanation, miracles are ruled out in advance. Mill's approach to human immortality overlooks strong evidence favoring its existence.

Inadequate View of Ethics. Utilitarianism also is inadequate. As a form of relativism, it is subject to the criticisms against relativists (*see* MORALITY, ABSOLUTE NATURE OF). How can one know that everything is not absolute without an absolute standard by which to measure it? Further, to work properly, utilitarianism demands that finite creatures know what will bring the greatest good to the greatest number in the long run. We are seldom certain what will bring the greatest good even in the short run. Only an infinitely wise, good God could be a utilitarian. And Mill does not have such a God.

Sources

N. L. Geisler, *Christian Ethics*
———, *Philosophy of Religion*
Plato, *Timaeus*
J. S. Mill, *System of Logic*
———, *Three Essays on Religion: Nature, Utility of Religion, and Theism*
———, *Utilitarianism*

Miracle. Before a materialist, naturalistic culture, Christians believe and are called upon to defend their belief that God created and governs the universe. One theme of Christian philosophy and apologetics is to understand and explain why biblical accounts of miracles should be believed, what miracles are and are not, how they relate to natural processes, and what they reveal to us about God. Because of the importance of this subject, miracles are covered under several headings relating to the nature of miracles in general, accounts in Scripture, and attacks on the possibility of miraculous interventions by God. What Christians regard as false or occultic unexplained occurrences will be distinguished from genuine acts of God (*see* MIRACLES, FALSE).

Definition. A *miracle* is a special act of God that interrupts the natural course of events. The Christian conception of the miraculous immediately depends on the existence of a theistic God (*see* COSMOLOGICAL ARGUMENT; MORAL ARGUMENT FOR GOD; TELEOLOGICAL ARGUMENT). If the theistic God exists, miracles are possible. If there is a God who can act, then there can be acts of God. The only way to show that miracles are impossible is to disprove the existence of God.

The above statement immediately calls for clarification: What are "special acts" of God? How are they known when they occur? There must be specific distinguishing characteristics of miracles before one can analyze events that possess these characteristics. Simply to say a miracle is a singularity is insufficient. Singularities occur in nature without obvious divine intervention.

Theists (*see* THEISM) define miracles in either a weak sense or a strong sense. Following Augustine, the weaker definition describes a miracle as "a portent [which] is not contrary to nature, but contrary to our knowledge of nature" (Augustine, 21.8).

Others, following *Thomas Aquinas, define a miracle in the strong sense of an event that is outside nature's power, something only done through supernatural power. This latter, stronger sense is important to apologists. A miracle is a divine intervention, a supernatural exception to the regular course of the natural world. Atheist (*see* ATHEISM) Antony *Flew put it well: "A miracle is something which would never have happened had nature, as it were, been left to its own devices" (Flew, 346). Natural laws describe naturally caused regularities; a miracle is a supernaturally caused singularity.

To expand on this definition, we need some understanding of what is meant by *natural law*. Broadly, a natural law is a general description of the usual orderly way in which the world operates. It follows, then, that a miracle is an unusual, irregular, specific way in which God acts within the world.

Probability of Miracles. Whether we can know if miracles actually happened depends on answers to three questions: (1) "are miracles possible?" (2) "are New Testament documents reliable?" (3) "were the New Testament witnesses reliable?"

An often overlooked argument is that for the probability of miracles. It is true that philosophy (i.e., arguments for God's existence) shows miracles are *possible* but only history reveals whether they are *actual*. But it is also true that, granting existence of a theistic God, miracles are *probable*.

A theistic God has the *ability* to perform miracles since he is all-powerful or *omnipotent*. Second, he has the *desire* to perform miracles because he is all-knowing or *omniscient* and all-good or *omnibenevolent*. One who examines history to see whether God *has* performed any miracles already can know that God is the kind of God who *would* if he could, and he *can*.

Why would God perform miracles if he could? By nature and will he is the kind of God who desires to communicate with his creatures and do good for them. And a miracle by definition is an event that does this very thing. Miracles heal, restore, bring back life, communicate God's will, vindicate his attributes, and many more things that are in accord with his nature. Such things befit the nature of the One performing them (the Creator and Redeemer) and the need of the one for whom they are performed (the creature). By analogy, what good earthly father who had the ability to rescue his drowning child would not do everything in his power to do so? And if he had all power, then we know in advance that his goodness would lead him to do so. How much more our heavenly Father? So we know in advance of looking at the evidence for the actuality of miracles that if God exists they are not only possible but probable.

Further, if a miracle is an act of God to confirm the word of God through a messenger of God (*see* MIRACLES, APOLOGETIC VALUE OF), then it is reasonable that God would want to do miracles. Through miracles, God confirms his prophets (Heb. 2:3–4). This is the way God confirmed Moses (Exod. 4) and Elijah (1 Kings 18). And this is the way he confirmed Jesus (John 3:2; Acts 2:22). How better could God confirm to us who were his spokespersons. And it is a priori probably that an intelligent, personal, moral Creator would want to communicate in the most effective way with his creatures.

Reality of Miracles. While philosophy makes supernatural events possible and the nature of a theistic God shows they are probable, only history reveals whether they are actual. But "history" here includes both the history of the cosmos and the history of the human race.

Actuality of the Miraculous in Cosmic History. A fact seldom fully appreciated is that even before we look at human history, we can know that miraculous events are not only possible but *actual*. The very *cosmological argument, by which we know God exists, also proves that a supernatural event has occurred. For if the universe had a beginning and, therefore, a Beginner (*see* BIG BANG; *KALAM* COSMOLOGICAL ARGUMENT), then God brought the universe into existence out of nothing (*see* CREATION, VIEWS OF). But ex nihilo creation out of nothing is the greatest supernatural event of all. If Jesus' making much bread out of a little bread is a miracle, then how much more is making everything out of nothing? Turning water into wine pales in comparison with creating the first water molecules. So, the surprising conclusion is that, if the Creator exists, then the miraculous is not only possible but actual. The history of the cosmos, then, reveals that the miraculous has occurred in making something out of nothing; making life out of nonlife; making the rational (mind) out of the nonrational (*see* EVOLUTION and related articles). What greater miracles could occur in human history than are already known to have occurred in cosmic history?

The Miraculous in Human History. Contrary to the widely perceived misconception, if God exists then we should come to human history with the expectation of the miraculous, not with a naturalistic bias against it. For, as we have seen, if the Creator exists, then miracles are not only possible and probable, but the miraculous has already occurred in cosmic history. God has already broken through supernaturally in the history of the cosmos and life leading up to human history. In view of this, the most reasonable expectation then, is to ask not *whether* but *where* he has broken through in human history.

The reality of miracles in human history is based on the reliability of the New Testament documents (*see* NEW TESTAMENT MANUSCRIPTS) and the reliability of the New Testament witnesses (*see* NEW TESTAMENT, HISTORICITY OF; NEW TESTAMENT, NON-CHRISTIAN SOURCES). For given the trustworthiness of their combined testimony, it is beyond reasonable dispute that the New Testament records numerous miraculous events.

Dimensions of Miracles. In the Bible's pattern, a miracle has several dimensions:

First, miracles have an *unusual character*. It is an out-of-the-ordinary event in contrast to the regular pattern of events in the natural world. As a "wonder" it attracts attention by its uniqueness. A burning bush that is not consumed, fire from heaven, and a person strolling on water are not normal occurrences. Hence, they draw the interest of observers.

Second, miracles have a *theological dimension*. A miracle is an act of God that presupposes a God who acts. The view that a God beyond the universe created it, controls it, and can interfere in it is **theism*.

Third, miracles have a *moral dimension*. They bring glory to God by manifesting his moral character. Miracles are visible acts that reflect the invisible nature of God. No true miracle, then, is evil, because God is good. Miracles by nature aim to produce and/or promote good.

Fourth, miracles have a *doctrinal dimension*. Miracles in the Bible are connected directly or indirectly with "truth claims" (*see* MIRACLES IN THE BIBLE). They are ways to tell a true prophet from a false prophet (Deut. 18:22). They confirm the truth of God through the servant of God (Heb. 2:3–4). Message and miracle go hand-in-hand.

Fifth, miracles have a *teleological dimension*. Unlike magic (*see* MIRACLES, MAGIC AND), they are never performed to entertain (see Luke 23:8). Miracles have the distinctive purpose to glorify the Creator and to provide evidence for people to believe by accrediting the message of God through the prophet of God.

Theistic Context for a Miracle. An essential feature of biblical miracles is their theistic context (*see* THEISM). Only within a theistic worldview can a miracle be identified. When Moses came upon the burning bush (Exod. 3:1–6), he began to investigate it because of its unusual nature. The accompanying word from God told Moses that this event was not merely unusual, but a miracle. If Moses reported to convinced atheists (*see* ATHEISM) what had happened at the burning bush, they would have been within their rights to doubt the story. In an atheistic universe it makes no sense to speak about acts of God. A burning bush and a voice would seem to the nontheist no more miraculous than the voice from heaven did to those who took it to be thunder (John 12:29). But granting that God exists and something about his rational and moral nature, these defining characteristics give miracles their apologetic power.

Conclusion. We must know what we are looking for before we can recognize a miracle. First, miracles stand in contrast to nature, which is God's regular and naturally predictable way of working in the world. Miracles are an unusual and humanly unpredictable way in which God sometimes intervenes in the events of the world. A miracle may look like any unusual occurrence, but it has a supernatural cause. It is performed with divine power, according to the divine mind, for a divine purpose, in order to authenticate a divine message or purpose.

Sources

Augustine, *City of God*

C. Brown, "Miracle, Wonder, Sign," in *Dictionary of New Testament Theology*

A. Flew, "Miracles," in *The Encyclopedia of Philosophy*

N. L. Geisler, *Miracles and the Modern Mind*

D. Geivett and G. Habermas, *In Defense of Miracles*

C. S. Lewis, *Miracles*

R. Swinburne, *Miracles*

F. R. Tennant, *Miracle and Its Philosophical Presuppositions*

Miracles, Alleged Impossibility of. ***See*** **NATURALISM; MIRACLES, ARGUMENTS AGAINST; SPINOZA, BENEDICT.**

Miracles, Apologetic Value of. The central claims of Christianity are dependent on the apologetic value of miracles (*see* APOLOGETICS, ARGUMENT OF; MIRACLE). If miracles have no evidential value, then there is no objective, historical evidence to support the claims of historic, orthodox Christianity.

Some contemporary naturalists argue that, no matter how unusual an event is, it cannot be identified as a miracle. If true, this has serious implications for those who believe in miracles. No unusual event that lays claim to divine origin could be considered a miracle. Further, theistic religions such as Judaism and Christianity, in which miraculous claims are used apologetically, could not actually identify any of their unusual events as miraculous confirmation of their truth claims, no matter how much evidence they could produce for the authenticity of these events.

Identifiability of Miracles. There are two aspects to the case for the identifiability of miracles. First, miracles in general must be identifiable before a particular miracle can be identified. Second, one must be able to point to distinguishing marks in order to identify a specific event as a miracle. The focus here will be on the identifiability of miracles.

According to some, miracles cannot be identified because the concept of a miracle is not coherent. Alistair McKinnon, for example, claims that "the idea of a suspension of natural law is self-contradictory. This follows from the meaning of the term" (Swinburne, 49). For if natural laws are descriptive, they merely inform us about the actual course of events. But nothing, says McKinnon, can violate the actual course of events. He wrote: "This contradiction may stand out more clearly if for *natural law* we substitute the expression the *actual course of events*. Miracle would then be defined as 'an event involving the suspension of the actual course of events.'" Therefore, "someone who insisted upon describing an event as a miracle would be in a rather odd position of claiming that its occurrence was contrary to the actual course of events" (ibid., 50). McKinnon's argument can be summarized as follows:

1. Natural laws describe the actual course of events.
2. A miracle is a violation of a natural law.
3. But it is impossible to violate the actual course of events (what is, is; what happens, happens).
4. Therefore, miracles are impossible.

McKinnon's Argument. There are several problems with this argument. Three are particularly worth noting:

Begging the Question. If McKinnon is correct, miracles cannot be identified in the natural world, since whatever happens will not be a miracle. If whatever happens is *ipso facto* a natural event, then of course miracles never happen. This, however, simply begs the question; this definition of natural law is loaded against miracles. No matter what happens within the natural world, it will automatically be called a "natural event." This would eliminate in advance the possibility of any event in the world being a miracle. But this fails to recognize even the possibility that not every event *in* the world is *of* the world. For a miracle can be an effect *in* nature by a cause that is *beyond* nature. For the mind that makes a computer is *beyond* the computer, and yet the computer is *in* the world.

Misdefinition. The problem is that McKinnon has misdefined *natural laws*. Natural laws should not be defined as what *actually* happens but what *regularly* happens. As Richard Swinburne points out, "laws of nature do not just describe what happens. . . . They describe what happens in a regular and predictable way." Therefore, "when what happens is entirely irregular and unpredictable, its occurrence is not something describable by natural laws" (ibid., 78). In this way miracles can be identified as events within nature that fall into the class of the irregular and unpredictable. There may be more to a miracle than an irregular and unpredictable event in the natural world, but they are not less than this. At any rate they cannot be ruled out simply by defining a natural law as what actually occurs. Even though they occur in the natural world, miracles are distinguishable from natural occurrences.

Confusing Kinds of Events. Since natural laws deal with *regularities* and miracles with *singularities*, miracles cannot possibly be violations of natural laws. They are not even in the same class of events. A miracle is not a mini-natural law; it is a unique event with its own characteristics. Therefore, to claim that miracles don't happen (or should not be believed to have happened), because they do not fall into the class of natural events is a category mistake. By the same logic, we might as well say that no book has an intelligent cause because its origin cannot be explained by the operational laws of physics and chemistry.

Flew's Argument. A stronger attack on the apologetic value of miracles is laid out by Antony *Flew. The basic objection to miracles by contemporary naturalists is not ontological but epistemological. That is, miracles are not rejected because we know they did not occur. Rather, we do not and cannot know that they *did* occur. Flew's objection fits into this category. If successful, Flew's argument shows that miracles have no apologetic value.

Miracles Are Parasitic to Nature. Flew broadly defines a miracle as something that "would never have happened had nature, as it were, been left to its own devices" (Flew, 346). He notes that *Thomas Aquinas demonstrated that miracles are not properly a violation of natural law. Aquinas wrote that "it is not against the principle of craftsmanship . . . if a craftsman effects a change in his product, even after he has given it its first form" (Aquinas, 3.100). Not only is this *power* inherent in the idea of craftsmanship; so is the *mind* of the craftsman. A miracle bears the unmistakable mark of power and divine mind. A miracle, then, is "a striking interposition of divine power by which the operations of the ordinary course of nature are overruled, suspended, or modified" (see Flew, 346).

Accepting this theistic definition, Flew insists that "exceptions are logic dependent upon rules. Only insofar as it can be shown that there is an order does it begin to be possible to show that the order is occasionally overridden" (ibid., 347). In brief, miracles to Flew are logically parasitic to natural law. Hence, a strong view of miracles is possible without a strong view of the regularity of nature.

The Improbability of Miracles. Flew argues that miracles are *prima facie* improbable, quoting historian R. M. Grant that "credulity in antiquity varied inversely with the health of science and directly with the vigor of religion" (ibid.). David Strauss, a nineteenth-century Bible critic, was even more skeptical. He wrote, "We may summarily reject all miracles, prophecies, narratives of angels and demons, and the like, as simply impossible and irreconcilable with the known and universal laws which govern the course of events" (see ibid., 347). According to Flew, such skepticism is justified on a methodological basis.

Identifiability. Flew claims to be willing to allow in principle for the possibility of miracles. In practice, he argues that the problem of *identifying* a miracle is serious, if not insurmountable.

The argument against miracles from unidentifiability may be summarized:

1. A miracle must be identified (distinguished) before it can be known to have occurred.
2. A miracle can be distinguished in one of two ways: in terms of nature or in terms of the supernatural.
3. To identify it by reference to the supernatural as an act of God begs the question.
4. To identify it in reference to the natural event robs it of its supernatural quality.
5. Therefore, miracles cannot be known to have occurred, since there is no way to identify them.

Flew insists, against Augustine (see Augustine, 21.8), that if a miracle is merely "a portent [which] is not contrary to nature, but contrary to our knowledge of nature" (Flew, 348), then it has no real apologetic value. For, argues Flew, if an event is merely a miracle in relation *to us at present,* then it provides no proof that a revelation it alleges to support is *really* beyond the power of nature. Whereas Augustine's notion of a miracle would assure the dependence of creation on God, it does so at the cost of subverting the apologetic value of miracle (ibid.). For if a miracle is only contrary to our *knowledge* of nature, then a miracle is nothing but a natural event. In any event, we could not know that a miracle has *really* occurred, only that it *seems* to us that one did.

Flew's point can be stated another way. In order to identify a miracle within nature, the identification of that miracle must be in terms of what is independent of nature. But there is no way to identify a miracle as independent of the natural except by appealing to a supernatural realm, which begs the question. It argues in effect: "I know this is a miraculous event in the natural world, because I know (on some independent basis) that there is a supernatural cause beyond the natural world."

On the other hand, there is no natural way to identify a miracle. For unless it is already known (on independent grounds) that the event is miraculous, then it must be considered to be another natural event. From the scientific point of view, it is just "odd" or inconsistent with previously known events. Such an event should occasion *research* for a broader scientific law, not worship.

From this, it would follow that no alleged miraculous event can be used to prove that a religious system is true. That is to say, miracles can have no apologetic value. We cannot argue that God exists because an event is an act of God. For unless we know that there is a God who can act, we cannot know that an occurrence is an act of God. The latter cannot prove the former (ibid., 348–49).

If miracles are not identifiable, because there is no way to define them without begging the question, the reasoning proceeds:

1. A miracle must be identifiable before it can be identified.
2. A miracle is identified in only one of two ways—either as an unusual event in nature, or as an exception to nature.
3. But an unusual event in nature is simply a natural event, not a miracle.
4. An exception to nature cannot be known (i.e., identified) from within nature alone.
5. Therefore, a miracle is not identifiable.

And, of course, what is not identifiable has no evidential value. It cannot be used to prove the truth of Christianity.

Response to Flew's Argument. Flew's first premise is solid. We must know what we are looking for before we can know we have found it. If we cannot define it, then we cannot be sure we have discovered it. But if we can define an event in terms of nature, miracles can be reduced to natural events. However, to define them in terms of a supernatural cause (God) is to presuppose that God exists. Therefore, miracles cannot be used as an evidence of God's existence. The supernaturalist argues in a circle.

Presupposing God's Existence. One way to reply to Flew is to claim that arguing in a circle is not unique to supernaturalists. Naturalists do the same thing. Antisupernaturalist arguments presuppose naturalism. Thus, it is necessary to argue in a circle, because all reason is circular (Van Til, 118). In the final analysis, all thought is grounded in faith (*see* FAITH AND REASON; FIDEISM).

If a supernaturalist chooses to go this route, the grounds (or lack of grounds) are just as good as those of the antisupernaturalist. Certainly naturalists who rule out miracles on the basis of a faith commitment to naturalism are in no position to forbid theists from simply believing that God exists and, hence, that miracles are possible and identifiable. Once the naturalists accept the privilege of a mere belief basis for naturalism, for which they have no rational or scientific proof, they must allow alternative worldviews the same opportunity.

Evidence for God's Existence. There is, however, another avenue: Theists may first offer rational justification for belief in God through the cosmological or teleological arguments. If successful, then they can have earned the right to define (show the identifiability of) miracles in terms of the supernatural realm they have *reason* to think exists. To the degree that one can give a rational argument for God's existence, it is not difficult to circumvent Flew's criticism that miracles have no identifiable apologetic value.

Miracles as Confirmation of Truth. Christian apologetics is based in miracles. Unless miracles are possible (*see* THEISM) and actual (*see* NEW TESTAMENT, HISTORICITY OF; MIRACLES IN THE BIBLE), there is no way to verify the truth claims of Christianity. This raises the question of the relationship between a miracle and a truth claim. Are miracles an appropriate and valuable confirmation of Christianity's truth claims?

The claim of David *Hume (1711–1776) that all religious truth claims are self-canceling fails because the credibility of all alleged "miracles" is not equal. However, the question remains as to whether a miracle can confirm truth.

In both New and Old Testament contexts, people did not show naïve acceptance of every alleged word or act from God. Like moderns, they wanted proof. Miracles were assumed to confirm the message of a spokesman for God.

Miracles Confirmed the Prophetic Claim. When asked by God to lead Israel out of Egypt, Moses replied:

> "What if they do not believe me or listen to me and say, 'The LORD did not appear to you'?" Then the LORD said to him, What is that in your hand? A staff, he replied. The LORD said, "Throw it on the ground. Moses threw it on the ground and it became a snake, and he ran from it. Then the LORD said to him, Reach out your hand and take it by the tail. So Moses reached out and took hold of the snake and it turned back into a staff in his hand. This, said the LORD, is so *that they may believe that the LORD, the God of their fathers—the God of Abraham, the God of Isaac and the God of Jacob—has appeared to you.*'" [Exod. 4:1–5, emphasis added]

It is clear that the miracles were intended to confirm the message God had given him. God, in fact, offered multiple miracles. For, "If they do not believe you or pay attention to the first miraculous sign, they may believe the second. But if they do not believe these two signs or listen to you, take some water from the Nile and pour it on the dry ground. The water you take from the river will become blood on the ground" (Exod. 4:8–9).

Later, when Moses was challenged by Korah, a miracle again was Moses' vindication.

> Then [Moses] said to Korah and all his followers: "In the morning the LORD will show who belongs to him and who is holy, and he will have that person come near him. The man he chooses he will cause to come near him." . . . Then Moses said, "This is how you will know that the LORD has sent me to do all these things and that it was not my idea: If these men die a natural death and experience only what usually happens to men, then the LORD has not sent me. But if the LORD brings about something totally new, and the earth opens its mouth and swallows them, with everything that belongs to them, and they go down alive into the grave, then you will know that these men have treated the LORD with contempt." . . . They went down alive into the grave, with everything they owned; the earth closed over them, and they perished and were gone from the community. [Num. 16:5, 28–30, 33]

Few questioned Moses' divine authority from this point.

When confronted by belief in pagan deities, Elijah the prophet of Israel, challenged the people of Israel: "'How long will you waver between two opinions? If the LORD is God, follow him; but if Baal is God, follow him.' But the people said nothing" (1 Kings 18:21). To prove he was a prophet of the true God, *Yahweh*, Elijah proposed a contest in which they would invoke a supernatural confirmation. When the prophets of Baal could not bring down fire on their sacrifice from heaven, Elijah had the altar to *Yahweh* drenched with water and prayed: "O LORD, God of Abraham, Isaac and Israel, let it be known today that you are God in Israel and that I am your servant and have done all these things at your command" (1 Kings 18:36). The text adds, "Then the fire of the LORD fell and burned up the sacrifice, the wood, the stones and the soil, and also licked up the water in the trench." And "When all the people saw this, they fell prostrate and cried, 'The LORD—he is God! The LORD—he is God!'" (1 Kings 18:38–39).

Miracles Confirmed the Messianic Claim. Jesus' ministry was characterized by supernatural, confirming signs of his identity as a prophet and more. But the Gospel of Matthew records that some Pharisees and teachers of the law still demanded a confirming sign: "Teacher, we want to see a miraculous sign from you." Jesus refused on this day, not because miracles did not constitute a sign of his identity, but because the question was asked in contempt and unbelief. Instead, Jesus announced that soon they would have the greatest confirming sign of all: "A wicked and adulterous generation asks for a miraculous sign! But none will be given it except the sign of the prophet Jonah" (Matt. 12:38–39). Just as Jonah was in the fish's belly three days, so Jesus was in the grave and then returned to life. He offered the miraculous sign of his resurrection as proof that he was the Jewish Messiah.

John sent messengers to ask Jesus whether he was the Messiah. "At that very time Jesus cured many who had diseases, sicknesses and evil spirits, and gave sight to many who were blind. So he replied to the messengers, 'Go back and report to John what you have seen and heard: The blind receive sight, the lame walk, those who have leprosy are cured, the deaf hear, the dead are raised, and the good news is preached to the poor'" (Luke 7:20–22). These were just the sorts of miracles the prophets had predicted would confirm the presence of Israel's Messiah. The answer was clear: Jesus' miracles confirmed his messages.

Nicodemus, a member of the Jewish ruling council, the Sanhedrin, told Jesus, "'Rabbi, we know you are a teacher who has come from God. For no one could perform the miraculous signs you are doing if God were not with him'" (John 3:1–2).

In his great sermon on Pentecost, Peter told the crowd that Jesus had been "accredited by God to you by miracles, wonders and signs, which God did among you through him" (Acts 2:22).

Miracles Confirmed the Apostolic Claim. Hebrews 2:3–4 proclaims that God has testified to his "great salvation" in the gospel "by signs, wonders and various miracles, and gifts of the Holy Spirit distributed according to his will." (Heb. 2:3–4). Miracles were used to confirm the apostolic message. They were the supernatural sign for their sermon; the divine confirmation for their revelation.

In defense of his apostleship at Corinth, Paul wrote: "The things that mark an apostle—signs, wonders and miracles—were done among you with great perseverance" (2 Cor. 12:12). This special apostolic, miracle-working power was offered as proof of the truth he spoke to them.

Qur'an and Confirming Miracles. Judaism and Christianity are not the only religions that recognize the validity of miracles as a means of confirming a message from God. Islam does as well (*see* MUHAMMAD, ALLEGED MIRACLES OF). Muhammad recognized that prophets before him (including Jesus) were confirmed by miraculous powers. "If they reject thee, So were rejected apostles Before thee, who came With Clear Signs" (sura 3:184).

The *Qur'an* records Moses saying of his miracles, "Thou knowest Well that these things Have been sent down by none But the Lord of the heavens And the earth as eye-opening Evidence" (17:102). Allah says, "Then We sent Moses and his brother Aaron, with Our signs and Authority manifest" (23:45). So, in principle, all three great monotheistic religions agree that a truth claim can be substantiated by miracles.

Unbelievers and Confirming Miracles. Even many who reject miracles agree that unique miracles could be used to support the truth claims of the religion possessing them. Even *Hume implied that truly unique miracles would confirm the truth claims of a religion. He argued only that similar signs by conflicting religions would be self-canceling. He claimed only that "every miracle, therefore, pretended to have been wrought in any of these religions (and all of them abound in miracles) . . . so has it the same force, though more indirectly, to overthrow every other system" and "in destroying a rival system, it likewise destroys the credit of those miracles on which that system was established." Since a miracle's "direct scope is to establish the particular system to which it is attributed, so has it the same force . . . to overthrow every other system." This leaves open the possibility that a religion presenting unique miraculous confirmation would be true and all opposing claims false.

Agnostic (*see* AGNOSTICISM) Bertrand *Russell (1872–1970) admitted miracles would confirm a truth claim. In response to the question "What kind of evidence could convince you God exists?" Russell said,

> I think that if I heard a voice from the sky predicting all that was going to happen to me during the next twenty-four hours, including events that would have seemed highly improbable, and if all these events then proceed to happen, then I might perhaps be convinced at least of the existence of some superhuman in-

telligence. I can imagine other evidence of the same sort which might convince me, but as far as I know, no such evidence exists. ["What Is an Agnostic?"] To the contrary, such evidence does not exist (*see* CHRIST, DEITY OF; PROPHECY AS PROOF OF THE BIBLE).

Logical Confirmation of Miracles. The logic behind a miracle being used to confirm a religious truth claim goes like this:

1. If a theistic God exists, then miracles are possible.
2. A miracle is a special act of God.
3. God is the source and standard of all truth; he cannot err.
4. Nor would a theistic God act to confirm something as true that was false.
5. Therefore, true miracles in connection with a message confirm that message to be from God: (a) The miracle confirms the message. (b) The sign confirms the sermon. (c) An act of God confirms the Word of God. (d) New revelation needs new confirmation.

If there is an all-powerful, all-good, and all-wise God, then it follows that he would not perform a miraculous act to confirm a lie. Since miracles are by nature special acts of God, God would not act contrary to his own nature. The God of all truth would not miraculously confirm error. Hence, when a truth claim is repeatedly confirmed by miracles, such as the Old Testament prophets, Jesus, and the New Testament apostles did, then it is true and all opposing views are false.

Criteria for Confirmation. Several criteria can be established, on the basis of principles discussed above, for allowing miracles as a confirmation of a truth claim. These are criteria for apologetically valuable miracles. They all assume miracles to be possible. Confirming miracles should be:

Connected with a Truth Claim

Truly Supernatural

Unique

Multiple

Predictive

Connected with a Truth Claim. Not all supernatural events are connected with truth claims. There was no truth claim announced of which the acts of creation are evidence. Neither was there a lesson taught by the translation of Enoch to heaven (Genesis 5), the plagues on the king who took Abraham's wife (Genesis 12), the manna from heaven (Exodus 16), Samson's supernatural feats (Judges 14–16), or the resurrection of the man who touched Elisha's bones (2 Kings 13). Most miracles are connected with a person who is thereby shown to be a prophet of God. But these acts lack direct apologetic value without the specific claim of prophethood and a message from God.

Truly Supernatural. A miracle is truly supernatural, as opposed to an anomaly, magic (*see* MIRACLES, MAGIC AND), a psychosomatic cure (*see* HEALING, PSYCHOSOMATIC), or even a special act of providence. None of these involve true supernatural intervention. All can be explained by natural means, even if they are at times very unusual and though they are used by God. One characteristic of a supernatural event is that it is immediate, rather than gradual. It is an irregular and naturally unrepeatable event. It is successful every time it is attempted by God or a person he empowers.

Unique. Hume argued that an alleged supernatural event cannot support one religious claim as long as a contradictory claim is made by another who can perform the same kind of alleged miracles. Similar competing miracles are self-canceling. Logically, from a theistic standpoint, it is impossible for true miracles to confirm contradictory claims, since a true miracle is an act of God, who cannot confirm what amounts to a lie (Heb. 6:18; cf. Titus 1:2).

Multiple. As Deuteronomy 17:6 put it, "In the mouth of two or three witnesses, every word shall be established." Multiple witnesses are better than one. In fact, in crucial life-and-death legal matters multiple testimony is often mandatory. One miracle leaves room for doubt. Hence, apologetically relevant miracles should be multiple.

Predictive. Another characteristic often connected with a confirming miracle is that it is often predicted. While this is not essential, it is helpful. It eliminates charges that the miraculous event is not connected with the truth claim. Otherwise, it might be viewed as a fluke. For example, if a false teacher was teaching along the shores of the Sea of Galilee as Jesus walked by on the water, Jesus' walking should not have been taken as a confirmation of the false teacher's views.

On many occasions in the Bible, Jesus and other prophets predicted and performed miracles that confirmed their claims. Jesus predicted his resurrection from early in his ministry on (Matt. 12:40; 17:22–23; 20:18–19; John 2:19–22). He explicitly predicted the resurrection as a "sign" (miracle) of his claims (Matt. 12:39–40). Once Jesus emphatically said ahead of time that a miracle would be evidence of his claim to be the Messiah: "'But that you may know that the Son of Man has authority on earth to forgive sins,' he said to the paralytic, 'I tell you, get up, take your mat and go home'" (Mark 2:10–11).

In the Old Testament miracles were often announced in advance. Elijah predicted the fire from heaven to consume the sacrifice (1 Kings 18:22f.). Moses promised supernatural judgments of God on Egypt (Exod. 4:21–23). Moses announced that the rod would bud (Num. 17:5) and that the rebellious Korah would be judged (Num. 16:28–30).

Conclusion. Even Flew would not claim that his argument eliminates the possibility of miracles. He does believe it seriously cripples Christian apologetics (*see* CLASSICAL APOLOGETICS; HISTORICAL APOLOGETICS). If miracles cannot be identified as supernatural events, they have no real apologetic value. A merely unusual event within nature can prove nothing beyond nature. However, Christian apologists can evade this problem by either presupposing the existence of God or by offering evidence independent of miracles for his existence. For as long as there is a God who can act, then special acts of God (miracles) are possible and identifiable. The only way to disprove this possibility is to disprove the possibility of God's existence. But such attempts are notoriously unsuccessful and self-refuting (*see* GOD, ALLEGED DISPROOFS OF).

Not only can miracles confirm a truth claim, but biblical miracles (*see* MIRACLES IN THE BIBLE) fit all the criteria for such apologetically valuable miracles. As shown elsewhere, no other religion or claimants to truth contradictory to Christianity have offered verified examples of truly supernatural events (*see* CHRIST, DEITY OF). We can conclude that biblical miracles, and they alone, support the truth claims of Christ and the biblical prophets. Christianity alone is a supernaturally confirmed religion (*see* WORLD RELIGIONS AND CHRISTIANITY).

Sources

Augustine, *City of God* (21.8)
A. Flew, "Miracles," *EP*
N. L. Geisler, *Christian Apologetics*
———, *Miracles and the Modern Mind*
C. S. Lewis, *Miracles*
J. Locke, *Reasonableness of Christianity*
B. Russell, "What Is an Agnostic?" *Look*, 1953
R. Swinburne, *Miracles*
Thomas Aquinas, *Summa contra Gentiles*, Bk. 3
C. Van Til, *Defense of the Faith*
B. B. Warfield, *Counterfeit Miracles*

Miracles, Arguments Against. Most modern thinkers who reject miracles trace their reasoning to the Scottish skeptic (*see* AGNOSTICISM), David *Hume (1711–1776). Hume provided what many believe to be the most formidable of all challenges to a supernaturalist perspective: Miracles are incredible.

Hume laid out three arguments against miracles: philosophical, historical, and religious. The first argument is an argument *in principle,* based on the incredibility of claiming natural laws are ever contravened. The second is an argument *in practice,* which challenges whether miracles have ever had credible witnesses (*see* NEW TESTAMENT, HISTORICITY OF). The last is from the self-canceling nature of similar miracle claims that abound in all religions.

The Incredibility of Miracles. Building on his empirical epistemology, Hume launched his attack on miracles with the comment, "I flatter myself that I have discovered an argument . . . which, if just, will, with the wise and learned, be an everlasting check to all kinds of superstitious delusion, and consequently will be useful as long as the world endures" (Hume, *An Enquiry Concerning Human Understanding,* 10.1.18). Hume's reasoning goes like this (Inquiry, 10.1.18, 120–23):

1. A wise person proportions belief to the evidence.
2. An event that can be established on infallible experience can be, with full assurance, expected to reoccur in the future.
3. The reliability of evidence derived from witnesses and human testimony establishes proof or probability, as it is corroborated by other reports and evidence.
4. All circumstances should be considered in judging probability, and the ultimate standard is how the reports comport with personal experience and observation.
5. Where personal experience is not the same, the person should keep a contrary judgment and subject the question to thorough argument.
6. Any contradictions among witnesses should be regarded with suspicion. Suspicion should also arise if the witnesses are few in number, of "doubtful character," have a vested interest in what they affirm, hesitate in their testimony, or assert it too vigorously.
7. "But when the fact attested is such a one as has seldom fallen under our observation, here is a contest of two opposite experiences; of which the one destroys the other as far as its force goes, and the superior can only operate on the mind by the force which remains."
8. A miracle violates the laws of nature, which have, by "firm and unalterable experience" been established.
9. Therefore, "the proof against a miracle, from the very nature of the fact, is as entire as any argument from experience can possibly be imagined."
10. Experience is direct and full proof against the existence of any miracle.

Hume's argument can be abbreviated:

1. A miracle is a violation of the laws of nature.
2. Firm and unalterable experience has established these laws of nature.
3. A wise person proportions belief to evidence.
4. Therefore, the proof against miracles is overwhelming.

Hume wrote, "There must, therefore, be a uniform experience against every miraculous event. Otherwise the event would not merit that appellation." So "nothing is esteemed a miracle if it ever happened in the common course of nature" (10.1.122–23).

Alternatives in Hume's Argument. There are two basic ways to understand Hume's argument against miracles. We will call these the "hard" and "soft" interpretations. According to the "hard" interpretation, Hume would be saying:

1. Miracles, by definition, violate natural laws.
2. Natural laws are unalterably uniform.
3. Therefore, miracles cannot occur.

Now, despite the fact that Hume's argument sometimes sounds like this, it is not necessarily what he has in mind. If this is his argument, then it clearly begs the question by simply defining miracles as impossible. For if miracles are a "violation" of what cannot be "altered," then miracles are *ipso facto* impossible. Supernaturalists could easily avoid this dilemma. They could refuse to define miracles as "violations" of fixed law and simply call them "exceptions" to a general rule. Both premises are deniable. Natural law is the regular (normal) pattern of events. It is not a universal or unalterable pattern.

This would be an easy way out of the problem. Actually, Hume's position contains an argument that is much more difficult to answer, one that addresses a "softer" view of natural law. It is not an argument for the *impossibility* of miracles, but for their *incredibility*:

1. A miracle is by definition a rare occurrence.
2. Natural law is by definition a description of regular occurrence.
3. The evidence for the regular is always greater than that for the rare.
4. Wise individuals always base belief on the greater evidence.
5. Therefore, wise individuals should never believe in miracles.

Notice that this "soft" form of the argument does not rule miracles out of the question; they are held to be incredible by the nature of the evidence. Wise people do not claim that miracles cannot occur; they simply *never believe* they happen. Sufficient evidence never exists for belief.

In this "soft" interpretation of the argument, miracles are still eliminated, since by the *very nature of the case* no thoughtful person should ever hold that a miracle has indeed occurred. If this is so, Hume has seemingly avoided begging the question and yet has successfully eliminated the possibility of reasonable belief in miracles. Variations of these arguments are still held to be valid by some widely respected contemporary philosophers.

Evaluation of Hume's Argument. Since the "hard" form of Hume's argument clearly begs the question and is easily answered by redefining the terms, we will concentrate on the "soft" form. The key to unlocking this attack rests in Hume's claim for uniform experience.

Hume's "uniform" experience either begs the question or is special pleading. It begs the question if Hume presumes to know the experience is uniform *in advance* of the evidence. How can one know that all *possible* experience will confirm naturalism, without access to all possible experiences, past, present, and future? If, on the other hand, Hume simply means by "uniform" experience the select experiences of *some* persons (who have not encountered a miracle), this is special pleading. Others claim to have experienced miracles. As Stanley Jaki observes, "Insofar as he was a sensationist or empiricist philosopher he had to grant equal credibility to the recognition of any fact, usual or unusual" (Jaki, 23). As C. S. *Lewis observed,

> Now of course we must agree with Hume that if there is absolutely "uniform experience" against miracles, if in other words they have never happened, why then they never have. Unfortunately we know the experience against them to be uniform only if we know that all the reports of them are false. And we can know all the reports to be false only if we know already that miracles have never occurred. In fact, we are arguing in a circle. [Lewis, 105]

The only alternative to this circular argument is to be open to the possibility that miracles have occurred.

Further, Hume does not really *weigh* evidence objectively; he really *adds* up the evidence against miracles. Death occurs over and over; resurrection occurs rarely. Therefore we must reject the latter. In Hume's own words, "It is no miracle that a man, seemingly in good health, should die on a sudden, because such a kind of death has yet been frequently observed to happen. But it is a miracle that a dead man should come to life; because that has never been observed in any age or country." Hence, "it is more probable that all men must die" (*Enquiry*, 10.1.122).

There are other problems with Hume's concept of adding up events to determine truth. Even if a few resurrections *actually occurred,* according to Hume's principles, one should not believe them. However, truth is not determined by majority vote. Hume commits a kind of *consensus gentium* which is an informal logical fallacy of arguing that something is true because it is believed by most people.

This argument really equates "evidence" and "probability." It says in effect that one should always believe what is most probable, what has the highest "odds." One should not, therefore, believe that the rolled dice came up with three 6's on the first roll. The odds against that happening, after all, are 216 to 1. Or, one should not believe that he was dealt a perfect bridge hand (which has happened) since the odds against this happening are 1,635,013,559,600 to 1! Hume overlooks that wise people base beliefs on *facts,* not odds. Sometimes the "odds" against an event are high (based on past observation of similar events), but the evidence for the event is very good (based on current observation or testimony for this event).

Hume's concept of "adding" evidence eliminates belief in any sort of unusual or unique event. Richard *Whately satirized Hume's thesis in his pamphlet, *Historical Doubts Concerning the Existence of Napoleon Bonaparte*. Since Napoleon's exploits were so fantastic, so extraordinary, so unprecedented, no intelligent person should believe that these events ever happened. After recounting Napoleon's amazing and unparalleled military feats, Whately wrote, "Does anyone believe all this and yet refuse to believe a miracle? Or rather, what is this but a miracle? Is not this a violation of the laws of nature?" If the skeptic does not deny the existence of Napoleon, he "must at least acknowledge that they do not apply to that question the same plan of reasoning which they have made use of in others" (Whately, 274, 290).

Finally, Hume's argument proves too much. It proves that a person should not believe in a miracle *even if it happens!* For it argues, not that miracles have not occurred, but that we should not *believe* they occurred because the evidence for the regular is always greater than that for the rare. On this logic, if a miracle did occur—rare as it may be—one should still not believe in it. There is something patently absurd about claiming that an event should be disbelieved, even if one knows it happened.

Uniformitarian Denial of Miracles. Can one eliminate belief in present events based on evidence for past events? It would seem that Hume wants each wise person always to believe in advance that miracles never have, do not now, nor ever will occur. Before examining the evidence, one should be prearmed with the uniform and "unalterable" testimony of uniformitarianism. Only if one approaches the world with a kind of invincible bias against anything that has not been personally perceived in the past can all claims for the miraculous be discounted.

Hume recognized the fallacy of this reasoning when he argued that, based on past conformity, nothing can be known as true concerning the future. We cannot even know for sure that the sun will rise tomorrow morning (*An Abstract of Treatise on Human Nature,* 14–16). Hence, for Hume to deny future miracles based on past experience is inconsistent with his own principles and is a violation of his own system.

If it were true that no present exception can overthrow "laws" based on our uniform experience in the past, there could be no progress in our scientific understanding of the world. For established or repeatable exceptions to past patterns are precisely what force a change in scientific belief. When an observed exception to a past "law" is established, that "law" is revised, if possible, to account for the exception. A new "law" replaces it. This is precisely what happened when certain outer-spatial but repeatable "exceptions" to Newton's law of gravitation were found, and Einstein's theory of relativity was considered broader and more adequate. Exceptions to "laws" have a heuristic (discovery) value; they are goads to progress in our understanding of the universe. Now what is true of repeatable exceptions that call for a natural explanation is also true for unrepeatable exceptions that point to a supernatural explanation.

Lack of Credible Witnesses. Hume also argued against the testimony for miracles in practice. We have shown that the *a priori* attempts to eliminate miracles fail, so we are left with *a posteriori* arguments. Hume objects that there is not enough evidence to establish New Testament miracles. He enumerates several arguments which, if true, would exclude the credibility of the New Testament witnesses.

Hume says, "there is not to be found, in all history, any miracle attested by a sufficient number of men of such unquestioned good-sense, education, and learning as to secure us against all delusion in themselves." Nor are there enough witnesses of "such undoubted integrity, as to place them beyond all suspicion of any design to deceive others." Neither are they "of such credit and reputation in the eyes of mankind, as to have a great deal to lose in case of their being detected in any falsehood." Finally, neither have the alleged miracles been "performed in such a public manner and in so celebrated a part of the world as to render the detection unavoidable" (*Abstract of a Treatise,* 124).

"The strong propensity of mankind to the extraordinary and marvelous . . . ought reasonably to beget suspicion against all relations of this kind." And "if the spirit of religion join itself to the love of wonder, there is an end of common sense," wrote Hume (ibid., 125–26).

Miracles and the Ignorant. Hume believes the case for miracles is damaged because "they are observed chiefly to abound among ignorant and barbarous nations." Those that have found believers in civilized countries, he added, usually got them originally from "ignorant and barbarous ancestors." Further, "the advantages are so great of startling an imposture among ignorant people that . . . it has a much better chance for succeeding in remote countries than if the first scene had been laid in a city renowned for arts and knowledge" (ibid., 126–28).

"Upon the whole, then, it appears that no testimony for any kind of miracle has ever amounted to a probability, much less to a proof." Further, "even supposing it amounted to a proof, it would be opposed by another proof derived from the very nature of the fact which it would endeavor to establish" (ibid., 137).

Evaluation. Even though Hume implies that he is open to actual evidence for a miracle should it meet his standards for purity, one quickly suspects that the rules of evidence have been tampered with, so as to rule out the credibility claims for any miracle.

Hume at one point candidly admits that no number of witnesses would convince him of a miracle. Speaking of what he acknowledged to be highly attested Jansenist miracles of his day, Hume wrote: "And what have we to oppose to such a cloud of witnesses but the *absolute impossibility* or miraculous nature of the events which they relate?" Such impossibility, he adds, should be sufficient "in the eyes of all reasonable people" (ibid., 133, emphasis added). No matter how many witnesses one provides for these "absolutely impossible" events, no "reasonable person" will believe them. If this is the case, then Hume is still approaching every miraculous event, no matter how well it is attested, from an incurably *a priori* naturalistic bias. All the talk of testing the credibility of the witnesses is poorly concealed antisupernaturalism.

This bias shows that his argument cuts in two directions. Knowledge of human nature also reveals biases against accepting miracles.

Hume's position also is inconsistent. He would not allow testimony for miracles, yet he would allow testimony from those who had seen frozen water, in preference to the testimony of those who never had. But why allow testimony for one event and not the other? He cannot reply that it is because others have seen water frozen, for this begs the question. The problem is that a tropical tribe has never seen it, so why should they accept the testimony of an outsider who says he has, regardless of how often he has seen it? Miracles have happened more than once. Further, according to Hume's own principles, even if one saw water freeze only once and he walked or slid on it, that would be sufficient to know that it happened. But, the same applies to a miracle. Only an antisupernatural bias would hinder a person from honestly considering reliable testimony about its occurrence.

Hume is apparently unaware of the strong historical evidence for the reliability of the biblical documents and witnesses (*see* BIBLE, EVIDENCE FOR; NEW TESTAMENT, HISTORICITY OF). At least, he overlooks it. But biblical miracles cannot be dismissed without a closer look. For no one should rule out the possibility of these miracles in advance of looking at the evidence for them.

New Testament Witnesses and Hume's Criteria. Hume outlined the basic criteria that he believed necessary for testing the credibility of witnesses (ibid., 120). These are discussed in the article WITNESSES, HUME'S CRITERIA FOR. They can be summarized as four questions:

1. Do the witnesses contradict each other?
2. Are there a sufficient number of witnesses?
3. Were the witnesses truthful?
4. Were they prejudiced?

Witnesses do not contradict each other. Hundreds of alleged contradictions in the Gospels have been weighed and found wanting by scholars, including Gleason Archer, John Haley, William Arndt, and others (see some of these defenses in the list of sources for this article). The error is not in the Gospel but in the procedure used by the critic. For a study of sample charges, see BIBLE, ALLEGED ERRORS IN. The testimonies of the New Testament witnesses are never mutually contradictory (*see* BIBLE, ALLEGED ERRORS). Each one tells a crucial and overlapping part of the whole story.

To be sure, there are minor discrepancies. One account (Matt. 28:2–5) says there was one angel at the tomb on the morning of Jesus' resurrection; John says there were two angels (John 20:12). It should be noted about these kinds of discrepancies that they are conflicts but not irreconcilable contradictions. Matthew does not say there was *only* one angel there; that would be a contradiction. Likely at one point there was one angel, and at another a second angel was about. Conflict in details is what one would expect from authentic, independent witnesses. Any perceptive judge who heard several witnesses give identical testimony would suspect collusion (*see* GOSPELS, HISTORICITY OF).

The number of witnesses is sufficient. Twenty-seven books in the New Testament were written by some nine persons, all eyewitnesses or contemporaries of the events they recorded. Six of these books are crucial to the truth of New Testament miracles, Matthew, Mark, Luke, John, Acts, and 1 Corinthians. All of these books bear witness to the miracle of the resurrection. Even critical scholars now acknowledge that these books are first-century documents, most written before A.D. 70, while contemporaries of Christ were still alive. Virtually all scholars acknowledge that 1 Corinthians was written by the apostle Paul around A.D. 55 or 56, a little over two decades after the death of Christ. This is a powerful witness to the reality of the miracle of the resurrection: First, it is a very early document. Second, it is written by an eyewitness of the resurrected Christ (15:8, cf. Acts 9:3–8). Third, it refers to more than 500 eyewitnesses of the resurrection (15:6), stressing that most of these witnesses were still alive (vs. 6). Any immediate reader of 1 Corinthians could check out the reliability of the evidence for the resurrection.

The witnesses were truthful. Few challenge the fact that the New Testament provides a great standard of morality based on love (Matt. 22:36–37) and inner piety (Matthew 5–7). Jesus' apostles repeated this teaching in their writings (for example, Romans 13; 1 Corinthians 13; Galatians 5). Their lives exemplified their moral teaching. Most died for what they believed (2 Tim. 4:6–8; 2 Peter 1:14), an unmistakable sign of their sincerity.

In addition to teaching that truth is a divine imperative (Eph. 4:15, 25), it is evident that the New Testament writers were scrupulous about expressing it. Peter declared, "We did not follow cunningly devised fables" (2 Peter 1:16). The Apostle Paul insisted, "Do not lie one to another" (Col. 3:9).

Where the New Testament writers' statements overlap with the discoveries of historians and archaeologists, they have proven to be exactingly accurate (*see* Archaeology, New Testament). Archaeologist Nelson Glueck concludes, "It may be stated categorically that no archaeological discovery has ever controverted a Biblical reference. Scores of archaeological findings have been made which confirm in clear outline or exact detail historical statements in the Bible" (31). Millar Burrows notes that "more than one archaeologist has found his respect for the Bible increased by the experience of excavation in Palestine" (Burrows, 1). There is no hint that the New Testament writers ever falsified facts of the case. Their testimony would be accepted as valid by any unbiased jury. As the great Harvard legal expert Simon *Greenleaf concluded, their testimony shows absolutely no sign of perjury.

The witnesses were not prejudiced. There is every reason to believe that New Testament witnesses of the miracles of Christ, particularly of his resurrection, were not predisposed to believe the events to which they gave testimony. The apostles themselves did not believe the when the women reported it (Luke 24:11). Even some disciples who saw Christ were "slow of heart to believe" (Luke 24:25). Indeed, when Jesus appeared to ten apostles and showed them his crucifixion scars, "they still did not believe it because of joy and amazement" (Luke 24:41). And even after they were convinced by Jesus' eating food, their absent colleague Thomas protested that he would not believe unless he could put his finger in the scars in Jesus' hands and side (John 20:25).

Jesus also appeared to unbelievers, in particular his skeptical half-brother, James (John 7:5; 1 Cor. 15:7), and to a Jewish Pharisee named Saul of Tarsus (Acts 9). If Jesus had only appeared to those who were believers or had a propensity to believe, there might be legitimacy to the charge that the witnesses were prejudiced. But the opposite is the case.

Witnesses to the resurrection had nothing to gain personally by their witness to the resurrection. They were persecuted and threatened (cf. Acts 4, 5, 8). Most of the apostles were martyred. Yet they proclaimed and defended it in the face of death. Nor should witnesses be dismissed simply because they have an interest in what occurred. Otherwise, we should not accept testimony from the survivors of the holocaust, which we do. The question is whether there is evidence they were telling the truth.

Self-Canceling Claims. Hume claims that "every miracle, therefore, pretended to have been wrought in any of these religions (and all of them abound in miracles) . . . so has it the same force, though more indirectly, to overthrow every other system." However, Hume believes, these miracles do not accomplish their task. Rather, "in destroying a rival system, it likewise destroys the credit of those miracles on which that system was established" (Hume, 129–30). Since all religions have the same sorts of miracles, none of them establish the truth of their doctrines. They cancel one another out as witnesses to truth.

There are, however, several significant problems with Hume's argument from the self-canceling nature of miracle claims.

All Miracles Claims Are the Same? Hume wrongly assumes that all alleged miracles are created equal. This is contrary to fact. Some obviously refer to natural anomalies or psychosomatic cures. Particularly in the Eastern and New Age religions, supernatural occurrences generally can be shown to be tricks (*see* Miracles, Magic and). In the case of prophecies, their accuracy is too low to be taken seriously. There is a big difference between walking on hot coals, a feat that anyone can be taught to do, and walking on water, as Jesus did (John 6). There is a difference between healing someone of migraine headaches and healing a person born blind, as Jesus did (John 9). Faith-healers in all religions raise up the sick, but Jesus raised the dead (John 11).

All Witnesses Are Equally Reliable? Hume's reasoning assumes that the credibility of the witnesses for the miracle claims in all religions is the same. The New Testament miracles are attested by contemporary eyewitnesses. Islamic miracle stories appear generations later (*see* Muhammad, Alleged Miracles of). Some have credible witnesses; others do not. The reliability of each witness to a miracle must be evaluated on its own merits. They are decidedly not equal.

Evaluation. Rather than disproving New Testament miracles, Hume's third argument that all religion's miracle stories are equally (un)reliable, supports the authenticity of biblical miracles. For the superiority of the Christian witnesses is a sound argument against all non-Christian miracle claims. We may restate the argument this way:

1. All non-Christian religions (which claim miracles) are supported by similar "miracle" claims (in both their nature and witnesses).
2. But no such "miracles" have strong enough testimony to maintain evidential value, so they are self-canceling.
3. Therefore, no non-Christian religion is supported by miracles.

If this is so, then we can argue that only Christianity is divinely confirmed as true.

1. Only Christianity has unique miracle claims confirmed by sufficient testimony.
2. What has unique miraculous confirmation of its claims is true (as opposed to contrary views).
3. Therefore, Christianity is true (as opposed to contrary views).

Jesus' miracles were instantaneous, always successful, and unique. So-called miracle workers who claim partial success effect only psychosomatic cures, engage in trickery, perform satanic signs, or other naturally explainable events. No contemporary healer even claims to heal all diseases (including "incurable" ones) instantaneously, with 100 percent success. Jesus and his apostles did. This is unique, and it sets these miracles against all competing claims by other religions. If biblical miracles are unique, then they alone confirm the truth-claims connected with them (Exod. 4:1f.; 1 Kings 18:1f.; John 3:2; Acts 2:22; 14:3; Heb. 2:3–4). All other so-called miracles are, as Hume's argument shows, self-canceling.

Arguments from Analogy. Ernst *Troeltsch (1865–1923) laid down the rule of analogy: The only way one can know the past is by analogy in the present. That is, the unknown of the past is arrived at only through the known in the present. On the basis of this, some argue that, since no miracles occur in the present such as are alleged to exist in the past, it follows that proper historical method eliminates the miraculous.

Troeltsch used "the principle of analogy" and Antony Flew a similar principle of "critical history" against miracles. These theories are extensively examined in the article TROELTSCH, ERNST, so they will be covered only in general terms here.

Troeltsch's "Principle of Analogy." This principle of analogy, according to Troeltsch, asserts that "Without uniformity in the present, we cannot know anything from the past" (*Historicism and Its Problems*). On the basis of this principle, Troeltsch and others have insisted that no evidence or witnesses are adequate to establish miracles (Becker, 12–13).

This argument does not insist that no such miracles as are reported in the Bible occurred. The claim, rather, is that they are historically unknowable, whether they occurred or not. Most would agree that no such miracles as a virgin birth, walking on water, or raising the dead are occurring today, so by Troeltsch's analogy, such events cannot be known to have happened ever.

Flew's "Critical History." Similar is Antony *Flew's "critical history." Flew asserts that the remains of the past cannot be interpreted as historical evidence unless we presume that the same basic regularities obtained then as do today. The historian must judge the past evidence by personal knowledge of what is probable or possible (350).

Flew concluded that the critical historian dismisses stories of a miracle out of hand, ranking them with the impossible and absurd (ibid., 352). The impossibility, Flew adds, is not logical but physical. Miracles are possible in principle, but in practice they break natural laws that are simply never broken.

Evaluation of the Historical Argument. Troeltsch and Flew attempt to rule out *knowability* by what Flew calls "critical history." Further, the argument (as Flew admits) follows the basic form of Hume's antisupernaturalism, critiqued above. All of these arguments assume that to be critical and historical one must be antisupernatural. By this view, a closed mind is prerequisite to doing "critical" historical study.

The principle that the present is the key to the past, or the past is known by analogy to the present is valid. This is so since those living in the present have no direct access to the past. The kind of causes known to produce certain kinds of effects in the present can be assumed to produce similar kinds of effects in the past.

But this principle does not rule out a credible belief in miracles in the past, even if no such miracles exist in the present. Fallacies are involved in the historical argument.

Uniform or uniformitarian?. Troeltsch and Flew confused principles of *uniformity* (analogy) and *uniformitarianism.* They assumed that all past events are uniformly the same as today's. This is not only an assumption, but it doesn't fit what even naturalistic scientists believe about origins. All scientists believe that the origin of the universe and the origin of life are singular and unrepeatable events (*see* ORIGINS, SCIENCE OF). But if the past can be known only in terms of processes now at work, then there is no scientific basis for knowledge about them. Another problem with uniformitarianism is that processes change. Geological uniformitarians fail to account for catastrophes, climatic changes, landmass shifts, and other factors that might have altered geological forces.

Uniformitarianism illogically assumes that there have been no past singularities. While knowledge of the past is *based on* analogies in the present (uniformity), the *object of* this knowledge can be a singularity. Archaeologists may know on the basis of analogy that only intelligent beings can make projectile points. However, the making of one unique spear point by a particular craftsman in a particular tribe can also be studied in itself. What can be learned about this singular past event can become present knowledge—a basis for analogy when other spear points are discovered. By analogy scientists have learned that certain levels of specified complexity originate only in intelligent beings.

Analogy, properly understood, supports as credible the possibility that some past events had a supernatural intelligent cause. Even without analogy to the present, there is good evidence that the universe began (*see* BIG BANG), and that it had an intelligent supernatural cause.

Special pleading. The Historical argument against miracles makes a special pleading that evidence for individual events cannot be allowed unless the events are repeated. This weighs the evidence for all regularly occurring events, rather than for the particular event(s) at issue. This is not a standard rule of evidence. Further, it pleads that no miracle either has occurred, can, or ever will in today's world. Flew and Troeltsch are simply not omniscient enough to know this is true.

Begging the question. Flew also commits the fallacy of *petitio principii*. In practice, he begs the question when he asserts that miracles are "absolutely impossible" and that the critical thinker will dismiss them "out of hand." But why should a critical thinker be so biased against the historical actuality of a miracle? Why should one begin with a methodology loaded against certain past events, before looking at the evidence?

Hindering scientific progress. Uniformitarian views have hampered the progress of science. The big bang theory is an example. Astrophysicist Arthur Eddington spoke of this special, explosive beginning of the universe as "repugnant," "preposterous," and "incredible" (Jastrow, 112). Albert Einstein made a mathematical error, so sure was he that the big bang was "senseless" (ibid., 28).

The evidence is so compelling that many scientists now believe that the basic hydrogen atoms of the universe were created in milliseconds. Most astronomers today accept the reality of a great initial explosion. Here is a singularity, which by its nature cannot be repeated. Yet it is a viable theory of origins and the proper object of science, though scientists had to be dragged to it because it does hold definite theistic implications.

Appealing to the general to rule out the particular. A strange sort of logic works in the historical argument. One must judge all particular (special) events in the past on the basis of general (regular) events in the present. Why not use special events in the present as an analogy for special events in the past? There are unique and particular "anomalies." From a strictly scientific point of view a miracle is like an anomaly. Here the historical argument uses special pleading. Neither Troeltsch nor Flew allows evidence to count for *particular* events, in lieu of the evidence for general categories of events. There are far more regular and repeatable events than the unrepeatable kind. there is no evidence for the unrepeatable. It is like refusing to believe that someone won the lottery, because thousands more lost it. Along these same lines, the contemporary philosopher Douglas K. Erlandson argues that scientific law, as such, is concerned with general classes of events, whereas the supernaturalist is concerned with events that do not fit general classes. A belief in the latter does not upset belief in the former (Erlandson, 417–28).

Proving too much. The historicist arguments prove that much of what naturalists believe about the past cannot be true. As Richard *Whately showed in his famous satire on Hume's naturalistic skepticism (Whately, 224, 290), if one must reject unique events in the past because there is no analogy in the present, then the incredible history of Napoleon must be rejected.

Not critical enough. Actually, "critical history" is not critical enough. It does not criticize the unreasonable acceptance of presuppositions that eliminate valid historical knowledge. Far from being open to evidence, its naturalism eliminates in advance any miraculous interpretation of events in the past. It *legislates* meaning rather than *looks* for it.

Arguments from Science. Since the origin of modern science it has been common to claim that miracles are not scientific. Some critics object to miracles because they are said to be contrary to the very nature of the scientific procedure for handling irregular or exceptional events. They insist that when scientists come upon an irregular or anomalous event they do not posit a miracle. They broaden their understanding of natural processes to take in that event. To do otherwise would be to forsake the scientific method. Some individual arguments include:

Ninian Smart. Ninian Smart reasons that nothing in nature can be out of bounds for exploration. Otherwise it would stultify scientific research. But a belief that certain events are miraculous erects a bar against science. Hence, acceptance of miracles violates the proper domain of science (Smart, chap. 2). The argument can be summarized.

1. A miracle is an exception to a natural law.
2. In science, exceptions are goads to find a better explanation, not an indication to stop research.

3. Hence, accepting miracles stops scientific progress.

Therefore, a miracle cannot be identified ever as an irregular event or anomaly. Rather, it calls for further research. When one natural law does not explain an exception, scientists do not throw in the towel; they look again, more deeply. What is an exception to one scientific description (L1) can be included within a broader description (L2).

Patrick Nowell-Smith. The supernaturalist's claim that an event is a miracle because it cannot be explained in terms of scientific laws bothers Patrick Nowell-Smith. "We may believe him [the supernaturalist] when he says that no scientific method known to him will explain it. . . . But to say that it is inexplicable as a result of natural agents is already beyond his competence as a scientist, and to say that it must be ascribed to supernatural agents is to say something that no one could possibly have the right to affirm on the evidence alone (Nowell-Smith, 245–46).

However strange an event, he argues, it must not be ascribed to the supernatural, because future scientists may very well explain it. At one time the bumblebee's flight was unexplained by natural law. However, principles of this very natural occurrence have come to light in the discovery of power packs in the bee's cells called *mitochondria*, which make flight by rapid wing motion possible. The argument can be described:

1. What is scientifically unexplained is not necessarily scientifically unexplainable.
2. Miracles are scientifically unexplained.
3. Miracles are not scientifically unexplainable.

An explanation qualifies as scientific, according to Nowell-Smith, if a hypothesis from which predictions can be made can afterwards be verified (ibid., 249). Further, the explanation must describe how the event comes about.

In this definition, "lawful" miracles should be explainable by laws that can be stated. If not, the event can be explained. "If we can detect any order in God's interventions, it should be possible to extrapolate in the usual way and to predict when and how a miracle will occur" (ibid. 251). Nowell-Smith challenges supernaturalists to consider whether the notion of explanation does not necessarily include hypothesis and prediction and thought about whether the "supernatural" could play any part in it (ibid., 253).

Should it be objected that he is simply redefining the "natural" to include miracles, Nowell-Smith replies: "I will concede your supernatural, if this is all that it means. For the supernatural will be nothing but a new field for scientific inquiry, a field as different from physics as physics is from psychology, but not differing in principle or requiring any non-scientific method" (ibid.). This may be summarized:

1. Only what has predictive capabilities can qualify as an explanation of an event.
2. A miracle explanation cannot make verifiable predictions.
3. Therefore, a miracle explanation does not qualify as an explanation of the event.

The implications of this reasoning are that miracle explanations must become scientific or they cease to be explanations at all. So a miracle is methodologically unscientific. It is contrary to the scientific means of explaining events, a way that always involves the ability to predict similar events. Further, Nowell-Smith denies that rational agency is necessary to account for any anomaly in nature. Ultimately, all that happens will be shown to result from natural law.

Alistair McKinnon. Another opponent of miracles, Alistair McKinnon (see another McKinnon argument in the article Miracle.) put the scientific law argument this way:

1. A scientific law is a generalization based on past observation.
2. Any exception to a scientific law invalidates that law as such and calls for a revision of it.
3. A miracle is an exception to a scientific law.
4. Therefore, any so-called "miracle" would call for a revision of the present scientific law.

In McKinnon's view, a miracle would be assumed to be a natural event under a new law that incorporates it into its natural explanation. Laws are like maps, and maps are never violated; they are revised when found to be in error.

Malcolm Diamond. Others have attempted to argue against miracles as opposition to scientific methodology. For example, Malcolm Diamond, professor of philosophy at Princeton University, insists that it is disastrous to accept miraculous exceptions to scientific laws. If one accepts some exceptions as supernatural, "scientific development would either be stopped or else made completely capricious, because it would necessarily be a matter of whim or whether one invoked the concept of miracle" (Diamond, 317).

Diamond sees two problems with supernaturalism. First, exceptions should not stop scientific research. They are, in fact, goads to further study. Second, exceptions should not necessarily be called miracles. Does the odd prove God? If not, how does one distinguish the unusual from the supernatural?

According to Diamond, "Allowing for the possibility of supernatural explanations of naturally observable occurrences is something that would, in effect, drive working scientists to opt right out of the scientific enterprise. . . . These scientists would not be able to investigate [the miracle]. . . . As scientists they would not be able to determine whether the exception was supernatural" (ibid.,

320). Scientists must operate with autonomy. They must set their own rules and referee their own games. Therefore, although nothing logically would prevent a scientist from accepting a supernatural interpretation for an utterly extraordinary, the scientists would be selling out science.

Diamond concludes: "The answer that I shall offer on behalf of the naturalistic interpretation is pragmatic. It recommends reliance on the scientific explanations without pretending to be a conclusive refutation of supernaturalism" (ibid.).

The outline of this argument is pragmatic, based on the autonomy of the scientific method:

1. Scientists, as scientists, cannot give up looking for naturalistic explanations for every event.
2. To admit even one miracle is to give up looking for a natural explanation.
3. Therefore, to admit miracles is to give up being a scientist.

Evaluation. Unlike other arguments against miracles, the scientific objection does not try to prove that miracles are impossible or even incredible. If successful it would show that miracles are not identifiable by the scientific method. It leaves open the possibility that there are other ways to identify a miracle. If by definition the scientific method deals only with a certain class of events (the repeatable), then singular events such as miracles cannot be identified by the scientific method. But what such an argument does not prove is that miracles do not occur or that there is not some other way to identify them. Nor does it show that there is no other way to identify the scientific method by which a miracle could be identified, at least in part.

Anomalies and the scientific method. Even the scientific procedure that deals with regular repeatable events allows for exceptional events that do not call for the explanation of another natural law. A scientist who encounters an anomaly does not automatically revise previously held laws. If the exception is not repeatable, there is no right to use it as the basis for a new law. It is inappropriate to demand that *all* exceptional events be naturally caused, but only that repeatable events be explainable. So in the nonrepeatable miracle, there is no violation of a scientist's right to do science.

Science in the commonly understood sense deals with regularities, not singularities. One cannot expect a method geared to deal with regularities to eliminate the scientific viability of a miracle.

A scientific approach to the world is not limited to regular events. There are legitimate scientific approaches that deal with singular events, as even supernaturalists claim.

Even the scientific method admits exceptions or anomalies, and no scientist revises existing natural laws based on a single exception. Unless the scientist can show that it is a regular, repeatable part of nature, he has no basis on which to make a new natural law. There is no reason a miracle cannot fall into the broad category of the anomalous, even within the general sense of the scientific method.

Of course, there is more to a miracle than a mere anomaly. There are "divine" earmarks. However, even from a strictly scientific approach that deals with regularities, one cannot legitimately eliminate the possibility of identifying a miracle. To argue that every exception to a known natural law demands another natural explanation, simply begs the question. Such an argument goes beyond science and reveals a naturalistic bias (*see* MATERIALISM; NATURALISM).

As theists have long insisted, if there is a God, then he cannot be locked out of his creation. If he had the ability to create the universe, he has the power to produce occasional but naturally unrepeatable exceptional acts within his world. The only effective way to disprove miracles is to disprove God (*see* GOD, ALLEGED DISPROOFS OF).

Confusion of categories. Even some naturalists have admitted that this argument is an *a priori* argument that can be refuted by noting that a supernaturally caused exception to a scientific law would not invalidate it. Scientific laws express regularities. A miracle is a special and nonrepeatable exception (Diamond, 316–17). One nonrepeatable exception does not call for revising a natural law. More likely it would be credited to faulty observation anyway. From a strictly scientific view, a nonrepeatable exception remains just that—an exception to known scientific laws. If, under specified conditions, the anomaly recurs, then a scientist has the right to call it a natural event. In this case, anomalies would be pointers to the development of a more general natural law.

Miracles, however, are not the result of natural laws. They were caused by the willed actions of rational agents, God and his representatives. That action of will is what cannot be repeated and therefore places miracles outside the realm of scientific observation. A miracle takes place because God wants it to. One cannot arrange for God to "want it" again so that scientists can watch. Miracles do not change our view of scientific laws, they simply step outside of them.

Since miracles are unrepeatable exceptions to known laws, they leave natural laws intact and therefore are not unscientific. Smart wrote, "Miracles are not experimental, repeatable. They are particular, peculiar events. . . . They are not small-scale laws. Consequently, they do not destroy large-scale laws."

Begging the question. If scientific objections are understood to eliminate the acceptance of miracles by a rational person, they are unsuccessful.

They clearly beg the question by insisting that every event in nature must be considered a natural event. For if whatever happens—no matter how unrepeatable—must not be considered a miracle, miracles are eliminated in advance by definition. Even if a resurrection from the dead occurred, it could not be a miracle.

Despite the fact that he claims the problem must be attacked with an open mind (ibid., 243), Nowell-Smith shows an invincible bias in favor of naturalism. His standards mandate that any event will be declared to be a natural event. He is, in fact, open only to naturalistic interpretations, not to the supernatural. That he begs the question is evident. He defines "explanation" in such a narrow way as to eliminate the possibility of a supernatural explanation. He arbitrarily insists that all explanations must be naturalistic in order to be counted.

The supernaturalist does not insist that "an event no matter how strange must have been due to a supernatural agent." It does seem likely that most strange events *are* natural. But the supernaturalist does object when Nowell-Smith says that supernatural agency *cannot* be part of the report of a strange event. The supernaturalist says that one should look at the evidence on its merits.

Nowell-Smith simply assumes that all phenomena ultimately admit a natural explanation (ibid., 247). He cannot know this as a scientist. There is no empirical proof. This assumption is simply a matter of naturalistic faith. Even if he were presented with empirical evidence of a miracle, he makes it clear that he would never admit it to be supernatural. Pending discovery of a naturalistic explanation, he will persist in believing that an explanation can be found.

Neither is it necessary that all true explanations have predictive value. There are events he would call natural that no one can predict. If the naturalist replies that he cannot always predict an occurrence in practice but can in principle, the supernaturalist can make that level of prediction. In principle we know that a miracle will occur whenever God deems one necessary. If we knew all the facts, including the mind of God, we could predict precisely when the miracle would happen. Further, biblical miracles are past singularities. Like the origin of the universe, they are not currently being repeated. But no prediction can be made from any singularity; they can only be made from patterns. The past is not known by empirical science, but by forensic science. It is misdirected to ask for *predictions forward*. Rather one attempts to make *retrodictions backward*.

The supernaturalist can agree with Nowell-Smith that "the breakdown of *all* explanations in terms of present-day science does not . . . immediately force us outside the realm of the "natural"" (ibid., 248). The two part company when Nowell-Smith requires natural causes for miracles. Such a position goes beyond what is warranted by the evidence. The naturalist demonstrates a faith commitment that rivals the religious dedication of the most ardent believers in miracles.

One problem behind this kind of scientific naturalism is the confusion of naturalistic *origin* and natural *function*. Motors function in accord with physical laws, but physical laws do not produce motors; minds do. In like manner, the origin of a miracle is not the physical and chemical laws of the universe, even though the resulting event will operate in accord with natural law. While natural laws regulate the operation of things, they do not account for the origin of all things.

Methodological naturalism. Scientific arguments against miracles are a form of rigid methodological naturalism. The very method chosen does not admit the possibility that any event will ever be identified as a miracle. Explanations that cover regular events do not necessarily apply to singularities. Rounded stones in a river are produced according to describable natural forces. But no natural law can account for the faces on Mount Rushmore. Here a non-natural, intelligent cause is appropriated (*see* EVOLUTION, CHEMICAL; TELEOLOGICAL ARGUMENT).

When a singularity is not known to be attributable to natural causes and demonstrates signs of divine intervention, then there are positive reasons to accept it as a miracle. The following are discussed with more detail in the article Miracle:

1. They have an *unusual character* as an irregular event.
2. They have a *theological dimension* as an act of God.
3. They have a *moral dimension*, since God is an absolutely perfect moral Being. One moral mark of a miracle is that it brings glory to God.
4. They have a *teleological dimension*. They are purposeful events.
5. They have a *doctrinal dimension*. Miracles are connected, directly or indirectly, with "truth claims" (Heb. 2:3–4; *see* MIRACLES, APOLOGETIC VALUE OF).

When an irregular, unrepeatable event, not known to be produced by natural causes, is accompanied by other marks of intervention, there is reason to identify it as an act of a theistic God (*see* GOD, EVIDENCE FOR).

Too restrictive a definition of science. The science arguments against miracles are based on an overly restrictive definition of science, one that deals only with repeatable events. Science also deals with singularities. True, the scientific method only tests regular, repeatable events. But scientists also recognize origin science, which is largely a study of singularities. The *big bang origin of the universe is a radical singularity. The history of our planet is a singularity, yet it is the object of research. We would regard it as both strange and foolish for a geology teacher to rule out anything but a natural cause for the sculpted faces on Mount Rushmore. It would seem odd if an archaeologist were limited to natural causes for projectile points and pottery. Insisting that one who does not insist on natural causes cannot be scientific is to improperly restrict science.

Miracles and the integrity of science. We are now in a position to evaluate the charge that belief in miracles is unscientific. Diamond's comments make evident his belief in the absolute autonomy of the scientific method. He assumes as a matter of faith, with only pragmatic justification, that the scientific method is *the* method for determining all truth. Indeed, it is not just the scientific method, but one aspect of the scientific approach—the search for natural causes—that is assumed to be the only approach to truth. Diamond's arguments are vulnerable to several criticisms:

First, it is wrong to presuppose that the scientific method necessarily entails naturalism. Scientists, as scientists, need not be so narrow as to believe that nothing can ever count as a miracle. All a scientist needs to hold is the premise that every event has a cause and that the observable universe operates in an orderly way.

Second, it is wrong to assume that natural laws have dominion over every event, rather than every *regular* event. To assume that every irregular, unrepeatable event has a natural explanation is not science but metaphysics. Natural laws do not account for the origin of all events any more than the laws of physics alone explain the origin of an automobile. Natural laws account for the *operation* of these things.

Third, it is unscientific to be closed to reasonable explanations. If a God caused the universe to exist and cares for it, it is not unreasonable to expect that he can perform some regular activities and also some special events. The only way to effectively disprove this possibility is to disprove the existence of such a God, which most atheists agree is impossible to do (Geisler, *Miracles and the Modern Mind*, chap. 12). The truly scientific and open-minded person will not dismiss in advance, logically or methodologically, the possibility of identifying some miraculous events in the defense of scientific autonomy.

Fourth, when the argument against miracles reduces to its basic premises, it becomes:

1. Whatever actually occurs in the natural world is a natural event.
2. Some so-called "miracles" have occurred.
3. Therefore, these miracles are really natural events.

This formation lays bare the circular reasoning of the naturalist's argument. Whatever happens in the natural world is, *ipso facto*, a natural event. Whatever occurs *in* nature was caused *by* nature. Even Michael Polanyi seemed to fall into this trap when he wrote, "If the conversion of water into wine or the resurrection of the dead could be experimentally verified, this would strictly disprove their miraculous nature. Indeed, to the extent to which any event can be established in terms of natural science, it belongs to the natural order of things" (Jaki, 78). This, of course, assumes what is to be proven, that there is no supernatural Being who can act in nature. Just because an event occurs in the world, does not mean it was caused by the world. It may have been specially caused by a God who transcends the world.

The preservation of the scientific method. If miracles are allowed, how can one retain the integrity of the scientific method? If some events are ruled out of bounds to the scientists, then has not the supernaturalist closed the door on rational examination of some events? Positing a supernatural cause for the origin of some rare events in no way affects the domain of science, assuming science is based on a regular pattern of events. Operation science is naturalistic and has every right to demand explanatory control over all regular events. But science, as such, has no right to claim that it alone can explain singularities.

Science has unlimited authority in the classification of regular events. The scientist has a right, even an obligation, to examine all events, including anomalies. However, the singular, unrepeated event that is not part of a regular pattern must be classified among the "not yet explainable as natural events." Within this class are events that may have a supernatural cause. To assume that all not-yet-explained events are naturally explainable moves beyond science into philosophical belief in naturalism. Indeed, it rules out the possibility that there is a supernatural God who can intervene in the world he created. But this is contrary to the evidence (*see* GOD, EVIDENCE FOR).

Summary. Hume offered a forceful argument against miracles. But, strong as it may seem, the evaluation indicates that he was overly optimistic to believe that this argument could be "an everlasting check" and "useful as long as the world endures" to refute any credible claim for the miraculous. In fact, Hume's argument is not successful. In the "hard" form he begs the question by assuming that miracles are, *by definition*, impossible. In the "soft" form of the argument, Hume ignores contrary evidence, begs the question, proves too much (for example, that Napoleon did not exist), is inconsistent with his own epistemology, and makes scientific progress impossible. In brief, to eliminate miracles before looking at them seems prejudicial. A wise person does not *legislate* in advance that miracles cannot be believed to have happened; rather he *looks* at the evidence to see if they did occur. So, for the rational mind, Hume's efforts to eliminate miracles must be considered unsuccessful.

Hume was right to demand that witnesses meet criteria of trustworthiness. Indeed, courts of law depend on such criteria to determine life and death issues. However, unbeknown to Hume, his tests for the truthfulness of witnesses, which he believed would eliminate the credibility of miracles, actually verify the trustworthiness of New Testament witnesses, particularly the miracle of the resurrection.

Hume's self-canceling-witness argument fails because it is based on false presuppositions which, when corrected, boomerang into a proof for the uniqueness of Christianity. His argument is based on the premise that all alleged miracles are created equal. But this is not true, either of the nature of the alleged miracle or of the number and reliability of the witnesses.

In evaluating the historical argument against miracles it must be noted that there is a crucial difference between the principle of *uniformity* (or analogy), on which all valid inquiry is based, and the principle of *uniformitarianism*. The latter is a naturalistic dogma which rules out in advance by its very methodological principle the credibility of the miraculous. Troeltsch's principle of analogy, used to reject miracles, is an example of historical uniformitarianism. A form of historical naturalism, it assumes that all events in history are naturally explainable. This bias, however, is contrary to both rational thought in general and scientific thought in particular.

Various attempts have been made to prove that belief in miracles is contrary to scientific explanations or to scientific methods. Some argue that miracles, contrary to natural laws, are unpredictable; others contend that miracles are unrepeatable or would sacrifice the autonomy of science. Such arguments beg the question in favor of naturalism. They assume the scientific method must be defined in such a way that excludes acceptance of miracles. The central, though hidden, premise is that every event in the world must have a natural cause. If one does not now have that explanation, it must be believed to ultimately exist. The supernaturalist points out that one does not have to be incorrigibly naturalistic to be scientific. Properly speaking, the domain of scientific law is the realm of *regular*, not *all*, events.

Miracles do not destroy the integrity of the scientific method. Science is possible so long as theists believe that the world is orderly and regular and operates in accordance with the law of causality. If the origin of the world can have a supernatural cause without violating the laws by which it operates, such a God can also cause other events without violating the regular natural operation. Since empirical science deals with the way things *operate*, not how they *originate*, the origination of an event by a supernatural cause in no way violates natural law. As physicist George Stokes observed, a new effect can be introduced into the natural world without suspending the ordinary operation of the world (Stokes, 1063).

Sources

G. L. Archer, Jr., *Encyclopedia of Bible Difficulties*

W. F. Arndt, *Bible Difficulties*

———, *Does the Bible Contradict Itself?*

I. Barbour, *Issues in Science and Religion*

C. Becker, "Detachment and the Writing of History," in P. L. Snyder, ed., *Detachment and the Writing of History*

F. H. Bradley, *The Presuppositions of Critical History*

M. Burrows, *What Mean These Stones?*

M. L. Diamond, "Miracles," *Religious Studies* 9 (September 1973)

D. K. Erlandson, "A New Look" in *Religious Studies (*December 1977)

A. Flew, "Miracles," in *The Encyclopedia of Philosophy*, ed. P. Edwards

N. L. Geisler, *Answering Islam*

———, *Christian Apologetics*

———, *Miracles and the Modern Mind*

———, *When Critics Ask*

D. Geivett and G. Habermas, *In Defense of Miracles*

N. Glueck, *Rivers in the Desert: A History of the Negev*

S. Greenleaf, *The Testimony of the Evangelists*

J. W. Haley, *An Examination of the Alleged Discrepancies of the Bible*

S. Hawking, *A Brief History of Time*

D. Hume, *An Abstract of a Treatise on Human Nature*

———, *An Enquiry Concerning Human Understanding*

———, *Treatise on Human Nature*

S. Jaki, *Miracles and Physics*

R. Jastrow, *God and the Astronomers*

C. S. Lewis, *Miracles*

P. Nowell-Smith, "Miracles," in A. Flew, et al., eds., *New Essays in Philosophical Theology*

N. Smart, "Miracles and David Hume," in *Philosophers and Religious Truth*

G. Stokes, *International Standard Bible Encyclopedia*

R. Swinburne, *The Concept of Miracle*

E. Troeltsch, *Historicism and Its Problems*

———, *"Historiography" in ERE*

R. Whately, "Historical Doubts Concerning the Existence of Napoleon Bonaparte," in H. Morley, ed., *Famous Pamphlets*, 2d ed.

A. N. Whitehead, *The Concept of a Miracle*

C. Wilson, *Rocks, Relics, and Biblical Reliability*

H. P. Yockey, "Self-Organization, Origin of Life Scenarios, and Information Theory," *JTB* (1981)

Miracles, Cessation of Sign Gifts. Those who accept biblical miracles debate among one another as to whether the special gift of miracles used to confirm a revelation from God (*see* MIRACLES, APOLOGETIC VALUE OF) has ceased since the times of the apostles. The issue has significance for apologetics. First, existence of apostolic, sign gift-type miracles today raises the issue of whether the New Testament miracles uniquely confirmed the truth claims of Christ and the apostles, as recorded in Scripture. Second, if miracles that confirm divine truth claims exist today, are truth claims they accompany to be accepted on a par with those of Scripture? Has divine revelation ceased?

The select individuals known as apostles were given certain, unmistakable signs of their office (2 Cor. 12:12). These sign gifts included the ability to raise the dead on command (Matt. 10:8; Acts 20:9–10); heal diseases immediately that were naturally incurable (Matt. 10:8; John 9:1–7), instantly exorcise evil spirits (Matt. 10:8; Acts 16:16–18), speak messages in known languages they had never personally studied (Acts 2:1–8, cf. 10:44–46), and pass on supernatural gifts to others to assist them in the apostolic mission (Acts 6:6, cf. 8:5–6; 2 Tim. 1:6). On one occasion (Acts 5:1–11), apostles passed a supernatural sentence of death on two people who had "lied to the Holy Spirit."

Defense of Ongoing Miracles. Proponents of the proposition that miraculous gifts do exist in the church today defend their claims on several arguments:

God performed miracles in redemptive history. They are recorded from Genesis through Revelation (*see* MIRACLES IN THE BIBLE). There seems to be no reason to believe they would cease arbitrarily with the apostles.

God has not changed (Mal. 3:6). Jesus is "the same yesterday, today, and forever" (Heb. 13:8). If the miracle-working God has not changed, then why would miracles cease?

Jesus spoke of continuing miracles. He said, "Anyone who has faith in me will do what I have been doing. He will do even greater things than these, because I am going to the Father" (John 14:12). In his commission as recorded in Mark, Jesus said that miracles would accompany the gospel as it went out (16:17–18).

Miracles manifest God's greatness (Exod. 7:17) and glory (John 11:40), to deliver God's children in need (Exod. 14:21; Deut. 4:34; Acts 12:1–19), and to communicate God's messages to his people (Exod. 4:8; Heb. 2:3–4). These needs continue today.

There are examples of miraculous manifestations as performed through the apostles, including the gifts of tongues, special healing, and even being raised from the dead (see Wimber, *Power Evangelism*, 44).

The Position that Miracles Ceased. Both positive and negative arguments are offered for the position that the special gift of miracles ended with the time of the apostles.

Proving Present Miracles from the Past. Logically there is no connection between past and present miraculous occurrences. Even during thousands of years of Bible history miracles were clustered in three very limited periods: (1) The Mosaic period: from the exodus through the taking of the promised land (with a few occurrences in the period of the judges); (2) The prophetic period: from the late kingdom of Israel and Judah during the ministries of Elijah, Elisha, and to a lesser extent Isaiah; (3) The apostolic period: from the first-century ministries of Christ and the apostles. Occurrences of miracles were neither continuous nor without purpose. Theologically the three great periods of miracles have certain things in common: Moses needed miracles to deliver Israel and sustain the great number of people in the wilderness (Exod. 4:8). Elijah and Elisha performed miracles to deliver Israel from idolatry (see 1 Kings 18). Jesus and the apostles showed miracles to confirm establishment of the new covenant and its deliverance from sin (Heb. 2:3–4). That miracles occurred at special times for special purposes is no argument that they will exist when these conditions no longer prevail.

Changeless Attributes; Changing Acts. God never changes, but his program on earth does. There are different stages of his redemptive plan, and what is true in one stage is untrue in another. We no longer are required not to eat some forbidden fruit (Gen. 2:16–17). We need not offer a lamb as sacrifice for sins (Exodus 12). We no longer are led by the twelve apostles and Paul; rather we have God's final revelation in Scripture. Note that 2 Corinthians 12:12 calls miracles "the signs of an apostle."

Promises to Apostles. Jesus did promise that miracles would continue after he left, but he did not say they would endure until his return. It was specifically to the apostles that he made the statement of John 14:12. The antecedent of *you* in that promise is the eleven who were with him. His promise to give the Holy Spirit's baptism, with which came the gift of tongues, was only given to the apostles (Acts 1:1–2). Only the apostles received the fulfillment of this promise at Pentecost (Acts 1:26; cf. 2:1, 7, 14). Nonapostolic instances of tongues witness the salvation of the first Samaritans and Gentiles and those on whom the apostles laid hands (cf. Acts 8:17–18; 2 Tim. 1:6) or in the presence of an apostle's proclamation (Acts 10:44; cf. 11:15). The reference to special "signs of an apostle" (2 Cor. 12:12) make no sense if these gifts were possessed by anyone other than the apostles or those on whom Christ and the apostles conferred the gift.

Desire Does Not Prove Fulfillment. There is a desire for ongoing miracles, but not all felt needs are real needs. Job received no miracle cure. Nor did Epaphras. Nor did the apostle Paul, who earnestly desired to be healed (2 Corinthians 12). The moving testimony of Joni Earickson Tada includes her search for a miraculous recovery before she came to terms with the ways God had decided to use her as a quadriplegic.

When compared with the periods that prompted miracles in Bible times, there is no actual need for sign miracles today. Miracles confirmed new revelation (Exod. 4:6; John 3:2; Acts 2:22). But the Bible is so much more than the New Testament saints possessed, and it is complete and sufficient for faith and practice. Pentecost does not need to be repeated, any more than Calvary and the empty tomb.

Though miracles can manifest God's greatness, glory, and deliverance, he accomplishes these things in other ways. The heavens declare his glory and greatness (Psalm 19; Isaiah 40). Spiritual deliverance is accomplished in the power of the gospel (Rom. 1:16). God works through general and special providence without suspending natural laws (*see* MIRACLES, MAGIC AND).

Even when there is an apparent need for divine intervention, there are things for which God never performs a miracle today. He does not delay the appointed time of death (Rom. 5:12; Heb. 9:27). This does not mean God never will supernaturally intervene to solve the problem of death. A time has been appointed for it at the resurrection (1 Corinthians 15). Meanwhile we await bodily redemption (Rom. 8:23)—the miracle of the resurrection.

The Problem of Sign Gifts. The claim that apostolic sign gifts still exist fails to distinguish between the *fact* of miracles and the *gift* of miracles:

Gift of Miracles	Fact of Miracles
Limited to Bible times	Occurs any time
Temporary	Permanent
Done through humans	Done without humans
Confirms new revelation	Does not confirm revelation
Apologetic value	No apologetic value

The view that sign miracles ceased with the apostles does not demand that God has performed no miracles since the first century. It argues that the special *gift* of doing miraculous feats possessed by the apostles ceased once the divine origin of their message was confirmed. In Hebrews 2:3–4, the writer of Hebrews referred to these special sign gifts of an apostle as already past in about 69 when he spoke of the message "first announced by the Lord." "God also testified [in the past] to it by signs, wonders and various miracles, and gifts of the Holy Spirit distributed according to his will." Jude, writing later (after 70), speaks of the faith that was "once for all entrusted to the saints" (vs. 3). Jude exhorts his hearers to "remember what the apostles of our Lord Jesus Christ foretold" (vs. 17). Here also the miraculously confirmed apostolic message was spoken of as past by A.D. 70. In spite of the profusion of apostolic miracles (cf. Acts 28:1–10) up to the end of Acts, about 60–61, there is no record of apostolic miracles in Paul's Epistles after this time.

This argument from the sudden absence of miracles after their earlier abundance is not to be confused with a fallacious "argument from silence." The Bible is not silent on the nature, purpose, and function of these special apostolic miracles (see, for example, 2 Cor. 12:12; Heb. 2:3–4). This function of confirming apostolic revelation fits with their cessation, since they were not needed after the revelation was confirmed.

It is to be noted that Paul apparently could not heal some of his own trusted helpers (Phil. 2:26; 2 Tim. 4:20), asking for prayer or recommending that they take medicine (1 Tim. 5:23). Even while Paul was doing miracles he was unable to heal his own physical infirmity, Gal. 4:13. In fact, there is never a sign in Scripture of anyone performing a miracle for their own benefit. That illness may have resulted from his being blinded by God or an infliction sent to humble him. Either way, Paul regarded it as increasing his value as a servant through his weakness. Miracles were to be exercised according to God's will.

Special signs given to the apostles established their authority as representatives of Christ in founding the church. Jesus promised special "power" to them as his witnesses (Acts 1:8). In 2 Corinthians 12:12, Paul offered his miracles as confirmations of his authority. Hebrews 2:3–4 speaks of the special apostolic miracles as confirming their witnesses to Christ. It was the pattern of God from Moses on to give such special confirmation for his key servants (Exodus 4; 1 Kings 18; John 3:2; Acts 2:22).

The cessation view concludes, based on both Scripture and history, that extraordinary sign gifts, such as the apostles exercised, have not been possessed by any since their time. While special *gift* miracles have ceased, the *fact* of miracles has not necessarily vanished. There is no evidence, however, of groups or persons who possess special gifts. Given the media penchant for sensationalism, if anyone had such powers it would be a widely publicized fact. Apostolic miracles had at least three characteristics missing in the acts performed by any modern miracle worker.

The Characteristics of New Testament Miracles. First, New Testament miracles were *instantaneous.* When Jesus or the apostles performed a miracle the results were always immediate. The man with a lifelong infirmity was told to "'Get up! Pick up your mat and walk.' At once the man was cured; he picked up his mat and walked" (John 5:8–9). Peter took the hand of the beggar, and "instantly the man's feet and ankles became strong" (Acts 3:7). Even the two-stage miracle of Mark 8:22–25 took moments, and each stage had immediately intended results. There are no gradual healing over days or weeks. They were all immediate.

Second, a New Testament miracle *never failed.* A miracle is a special act of God, and God cannot fail. Further, there is no record that anyone who received one relapsed into the condition again. If there had been relapses, enemies of the gospel message would have quickly used them to discredit Christ or the apostles.

Of course those who were raised from the dead died again. Jesus alone received a permanent, immortal resurrection body (1 Cor. 15:20). Lazarus died, again, when his moment had come. The final and lasting resurrection miracle will be at Christ's second coming (1 Cor. 15:52–53).

Third, New Testament sign gifts as exercised by Jesus and the apostles were *successful on all kinds of conditions*—even incurable diseases and dead people. They healed people who were born blind (John 9) and even dead and rotting (John 11). Further, they healed all kinds of disease, not just the easier kinds (Matt. 10:8). Sometimes, they healed everyone brought to them in the entire area (Acts 28:9). It is a verifiable fact that no one today possesses the special powers of Jesus and the apostles to instantaneously cure all sicknesses and even raise the dead on command (Acts 9, 20). These special "signs of an apostle" (2 Cor. 12:12), along with the ability to give people the Holy Spirit (Acts 8:18), special gifts (2 Tim. 1:6), and smite lying Christians with death (Acts 5), have ceased.

Fourth, unlike the miracles of apostolic times, modern miracles do not confirm new revelation, nor do they establish the credentials of God's messengers. The person's fidelity in obeying and proclaiming Scripture now establishes the message. Attempts to stress the miraculous or to claim supernatural gifts has now become a *disqualifying*, rather than a *qualifying*, mark. This is especially true among those who claim to foretell the future. For those who make such claims, the biblical standard for accuracy is absolutely no false predictions (Deut. 18:22). Since new revelation ceased with the apostles, prophetic and other miraculous claims should be seriously distrusted.

Jesus the Final Revelation. Jesus was the full and final revelation of God. "In the past God spoke to our forefathers through the prophets at many times and in various ways, but in these last days he has spoken to us by his Son, whom he appointed heir of all things, and through whom he made the universe" (Heb. 1:1–2). Jesus informed the apostles that his revelation would be continued by the Holy Spirit, who "will teach you all things and will remind you of everything I have said to you" (John 14:26). Using the Scriptures, the Holy Spirit fulfills the role once taken by the prophets: "He will guide you into all truth. He will not speak on his own; he will speak only what he hears, and he will tell you what is yet to come" (John 16:13). It is clear that the apostles were the divinely authorized agents through which the Holy Spirit proclaimed the final revelation of Jesus Christ.

Indeed, the apostles claimed this revelatory power (John 20:31; 1 Cor. 2:13; 1 Thess. 4:2; 2 Thess. 2:2; 1 John 2:19; 4:6), claiming the church was "built on the foundation of the apostles and prophets" (Eph. 2:20). The early church recognized this authority and "they devoted themselves to the apostles' teaching" (Acts 2:42). The apostles were the eyewitnesses of Christ (Acts 1:22), even Paul (1 Cor. 9:1; 15:5–9). Since these divinely authorized channels of "all truth" died in the first century, it follows that divine revelation ceased with them. If revelation ceased, there was no longer a need for miracle signs of a new revelation.

Conclusion. Arguments for the continuance of gift miracles miss the mark. While God does not change, his actions differ with different times. The purpose of signs and wonders was to confirm new revelation, but revelation ceased with the apostles. This is substantiated by the fact that no one since their time has actually possessed their unique power to instantaneously heal and even raise the dead. This does not mean God cannot do miracles now. But such miracles are not connected with any truth claims, nor are they a gift possessed by an individual. Whatever truly miraculous event that may occur has no apologetic value.

Sources

T. Edgar, *Miraculous Gifts: Are They for Today?*
N. L. Geisler, *Miracles and the Modern Mind*
———, *Signs and Wonders*
W. Grudem, *Are Miraculous Gifts for Today*
J. Jividen, *Miracles: From God or Man?*
B. B. Warfield, *Counterfeit Miracles*
J. Wimber, *Power Evangelism*
———, *Power Healing*

Miracles, False. Distinguishing a true from a false miracle is important to the defense of the Christian faith. For miracles are the unique way God confirms a truth claim to be from him (see MIRACLES, APOLOGETIC VALUE OF; MIRACLES IN THE BIBLE). But the counterfeit cannot be detected unless one knows the characteristics of a genuine.

A true miracle has preconditions. A miracle is a special act of God, and there cannot be acts of God unless there is a God who can perform these special acts. Miracles can occur only within the context of a theistic worldview (*see* THEISM). A miracle is a divine intervention in the world. God cannot "intervene" unless he is in some real sense transcendent over it. Transcendence must also mean that God has *super-natural* power. A God who created the world out of nothing, *ex nihilo* (*see* CREATION, VIEWS OF), has the power to intervene.

Atheists look at the same event as a theist, for example the resurrection of Christ, and from the viewpoint of their worldview see no miracle (*see* ATHEISM; RESURRECTION, EVIDENCE FOR). Whatever happened must be an anomaly, unusual, perhaps, but someday explainable through natural processes (*see* NATURALISM). If confronted with a resurrection, pantheists do not admit a divine intervention has occurred, for they do not believe in a God who created all things (*see* PANTHEISM). Pantheists hold that God is all things. Hence, a resurrection could only be an unusual event within the world, not a supernatural event from outside it.

Description of a True Miracle. The three words Scripture uses to describe a miracle help delineate that meaning more precisely. Each of the three words for supernatural events (*sign, wonder, power*) delineates an aspect of a miracle. For a full discussion of these elements see the article MIRACLES IN THE BIBLE. From the human vantage point, a miracle is an unusual event ("wonder") that conveys and confirms an unusual message ("sign") by means of unusual power ("Power"). From the divine vantage point a miracle is an act of God ("power") that attracts the attention of the people of God ("wonder") to the Word of God (by a "sign").

According to the Bible, a miracle has five dimensions that together differentiate a true miracle from a false miracle. First, a true miracle has an *unnatural dimension*. A burning bush that is not consumed, fire from heaven, and walking on water are not normal occurrences. Their unusual character commands attention. Second, a true miracle has a *theological dimension*. It presupposes the theistic God who can perform these special acts. Third, a true miracle has a *moral dimension*. It manifests the moral character of God (*see* GOD, NATURE OF). There are no evil miracles, because God is good. A miracle that punishes or judges establishes God's nature as just.

Fourth, a miracle has a *teleological dimension*. Unlike magic (*see* MIRACLES, MAGIC AND), miracles never entertain (see Luke 23:8). Their overall purpose is to glorify the Creator. Though unnatural, they fit into creation and befit the nature of the Creator. The virgin birth, for example, was supernatural in its operation, unnatural in its properties, but purposeful in its product. It was unnatural, yet not anti-natural. Mary's virgin conception resulted in a normal nine-month pregnancy and birth (*see* DIVINE BIRTH STORIES). Fifth, miracles in the Bible, particularly the gifts of miracles, had a *doctrinal dimension*. They directly or indirectly verified truth claims. They show that a prophet is truly sent from God (Deut. 18:22). They confirm the truth of God through the servant of God (Acts 2:22; 2 Cor. 12:12; Heb. 2:3–4). Message and miracle go hand-in-hand.

Distinguishing Marks of a Miracle. In addition to its dimensions, a true miracle has distinguishing marks. The most basic is that *a true miracle is an exception to natural law*. Natural laws are regular, predictable events, but miracles are special, unpredictable events. Of course, there are some unusual natural events or anomalies that are sometimes confused with miracles. Comets, eclipses, and other natural phenomena were once thought to be miracles, but are not. Meteors pass our way infrequently, but they are purely natural and predictable. Eclipses are natural and predictable. Earthquakes are relatively unpredictable, but as scientists understand them better they know where they will occur, if not precisely when. That they are not miracles does not mean they do not belong to God's special providence. He uses them and is in control of them. We can be sure that sometimes he intervenes in their operation in dramatic ways. A fog at Normandy aided the Allied Forces' invasion of Europe on D-Day and the eventual defeat of Nazi Germany. Fog has natural causes, but the timing of this one was an evidence of God's providence. But it was no miracle. Bullets bouncing off the chests of Allied soldiers would have been a miracle.

A true miracle also produces immediate results (*see* HEALINGS, PSYCHOSOMATIC). In Matthew 8:3, Jesus touched a man and immediately he was cured of his leprosy. All of the miraculous healings by Jesus and the apostles had such immediacy. No miracle took months, or hours. Only one required a few minutes, because it was a two-stage miracle—actually two interconnected instantaneous acts of God (Mark 8:23–25). By contrast, natural events take time and process. It takes a whole season to grow, harvest, grind, and mix wheat flour for bread, but Jesus made it instantly (John 6). It takes eighteen years or longer to grow an adult human being, but God created Adam immediately (Gen. 1:27; 2:7).

A characteristic of a true miracle, is that *it always brings glory to God*. Occult "magic" brings glory to the magician, and psychosomatic "cures" to the one who performs them. Satanic delusions (see 2 Thess. 2:9; Rev. 16:14) are lies (2 Thess. 2:9) that do not glorify the God who cannot lie (Titus 1:2; Heb. 6:18).

While miracles are not natural events, *they bring good to the natural world*. The resurrection is the ultimate example. It reverses death and brings back the good of life (*see* Romans 8). Healing restores the body to the way God made it, which was "good" (Gen. 1:27–31). Even "negative" miracles are good in that it is good for God's justice to defeat sin.

True miracles never fail. They are acts of the God for whom "all things are possible" (Matt. 19:26). Since God cannot fail, neither can miracles. This does not mean that any servant of God can perform a miracle at any time. Miracles occur only according to God's will (Heb. 2:3–4; 1 Cor. 12:11). Further, true miracles have no relapses. If a person is miraculously healed, that healing is permanent. Pseudo-miracles, particularly the psychosomatic kind, often fail. They do not work on people who do not believe, and sometimes they do not work on those who do believe. When they do work, their effect is often only partial and/or temporary.

Kinds of False Miracles. As noted above, many unusual events are attributable to God that are not true miracles. God acts through natural processes. Other unusual events are acts of human beings (and/or deceiving spirits, called demons). These are not real miracles either. Satan can fool, but he cannot truly work transcendently over nature—and never intentionally for God's glory.

Magical Tricks. A true miracle is distinguishable from magic (*see* MIRACLES, MAGIC AND). Most modern magicians do not seriously pretend that the illusions they perform are anything more than entertainment that "fools" the public. Those who watch are intended to walk away mystified about how the magician did it, but assured that the magician and his assistants did "do it." This is not like occult acts unless an illusion is performed for occultic reasons. Magical tricks involve innocent deception, but miracles involve no deception. Magic has a purely natural explanation; miracles do not. A miracle is under God's control, whereas magic is under human control. Like all human actions, magic can be used for good or evil. It is not evil in itself.

Psychosomatic Curses. Mind-body interactions, psychosomatic illnesses and healing do not usually involve pretend or neurotic illnesses and charlatan faith-healers. This complex and poorly understood subject is covered with some depth in the article HEALINGS, PSYCHOSOMATIC. In this article it is sufficient to say that psycho-soma, mind-over-body cures are not miraculous. Mental cures require faith. Miracles do not. Whether using the placebo effect, touching the television as a "point of contact" with a "healer," or more directly therapeutic tools like acupuncture and biofeedback mind-training, psychosomatic healings can do good or ill. They use God's marvelous body design to work healing. But they should never be misrepresented as direct interventions or true miracles. They are human phenomena and are common to many religions.

Anomalies of Nature. As noted miracles must not be confused with a natural anomaly, like a lunar eclipse. The latter is unusual but not unnatural. Miracles are not naturally repeatable. Anomalies are predictable. The flight of a bumble bee was an anomaly for many years, but since it occurred regularly it was predictable even before it was explainable. Anomalies lack the theological, moral, and teleological dimensions.

Special Providence. Some events are caused by God indirectly, not directly. That is, God uses natural laws to accomplish them. These may be quite remarkable and may stimulate faith, but they are not supernatural. Robert Müller gathered his English orphans around the dining table and gave thanks for food they did not at that moment have to eat. At that time a wagon loaded with bread broke down in front of the orphanage, and all of it was given to Müller. That was an act of wonderful providence, but it was not a miracle.

Satanic Signs. One of the most controversial dimensions of the topic of false miracles is that of Satanic "signs." The Bible uses the same word for miracle (sign") of some unusual manifestations of Satan. Many theologians call these events "miracles." The question of whether Satan can perform miracles is made difficult because of this common usage of the same word "miracle." However, if the apologetic value of miracles is to be preserved, there must be some way to distinguish a divine miracle from a Satanic one. Most evangelical biblical scholars agree on some fundamental facts: Satan is a created being (Col. 1:15–16). He is not all-powerful (Rev. 20:10). He cannot create life (Gen. 1:21; Deut. 32:39). He cannot raise the dead (Gen. 1:21). He is a master deceiver (John 8:44).

Given these facts, there is no reason to grant that Satan can perform truly supernatural events. As a master magician and super-scientist he can deceive almost anyone he wishes (see Matt. 24:24). Indeed, "the whole world is under the control of the evil one" (1 John 5:19) who is "the prince and the power of the air" (Eph. 2:2). And "the god of this world hath blinded the minds of them which believe not" (2 Cor. 4:3–4). For "Satan himself masquerades as an angel of light" (2 Cor. 11:14).

Satan's powers, though great, are finite and God's are infinite. It thus seems best to distinguish a true miracle from a Satanic sign in both name and ability. God performs true miracles; Satan does false signs. God does genuine miracles; Satan does counterfeit miracles. This is precisely what the Bible calls them in 2 Thess. 2:9 when it speaks of "The coming of the lawless one will be in accordance with the work of Satan displayed in all kinds of *counterfeit* miracles, signs and wonders."

Just as there are marks of miracles, there are marks of a work of Satan, which are shown in the accompanying chart.

Divine Miracle	Satanic Sign
actual supernatural acts	only a supernormal act
under Creator's control	under creature's control
never associated with the occult	associated with the occult
connected with the true God	frequently connected with pantheistic or polytheistic gods
associated with truth	associated with error
associated with good	associated with evil

involves truth prophecies	involves falsehoods prophecies
glorifies the Creator	glorifies the creature

Satanic signs are not supernatural. False signs are unusual. They may be supernormal and extraordinary. But they are not miraculous. They can be recognized as false signs if they are not successful, they are not immediate or instantaneous, they are not permanent. As with Moses and the magicians of Egypt or Elijah and the prophets of Baal (Exod. 8–12; 1 Kings 18), Satan's signs lose in a contest with God.

Satanic signs are associated with error. False signs and false teaching go together. "The Spirit clearly says that in later times some will abandon the faith and follow deceiving spirits and things taught by demons" (1 Tim. 4:1). There is "a spirit of truth and a spirit of falsehood" (1 John 4:6). So false teaching will not be confirmed by a true miracle. False signs will be connected with false teachings. A true prophet does not give false prophecies. If the predicted signs do not come to pass, then it was a false sign. False teachings connected with false signs might include that: There are gods other than the one true theistic God (Deut. 6:4; 13:1–3). Worship can use images or idols (Exod. 20:3–4). Jesus is not God (Col. 2:9). Jesus did not come in human flesh (1 John 4:1–2). We should contact departed spirits (Deut. 18:11).We can predict the future (Deut. 18:21–22). Fallible or partly true revelations can come from God (Heb. 6:18). Christ does not have to be at the center of life (Rev. 19:10).

Satanic signs are associated with moral evil. Counterfeit miracles tend to accompany moral rebellion and anger with God (1 Sam. 15:23), sexual immorality (Jude 7), asceticism (1 Cor. 7:5; 1 Tim. 4:3), legalism (Col. 2:16–17), pride in alleged visions (Col. 2:18), lying and deception (1 Tim. 4:2; John 8:44), and other works of the flesh (cf. Gal. 5:19).

Satanic signs are associated with the occult. Occult practices that can accompany Satanic signs include contacts with spirits (Deut. 18:11); the use of channelers, mediums, or trances (Deut. 18:11); losing control of one's faculties (1 Cor. 14:32); disorderly conduct (1 Cor. 14:40); use of crystals, stones, rods or other means of divination (Deut. 18:11; Exod. 21:21); mind-emptying Eastern meditation, chanting or the use of repetitive phrases (Matt. 6:7); self-deification (Gen. 3:5; 2 Thess. 2:9); astrology (Deut. 4:19; Isa. 47:13–15); idolatry or the use of images in worship (Ex. 20:3–4); experiencing apparitions of dead persons (Deut. 18:11; 1 Cor. 10:18–21; 2 Cor. 11:14).

Satanic signs are limited in power. Satan can imitate God's miracles but not duplicate them. Again, the miracles of Moses and Elijah over the Egyptian magicians and Baal priests demonstrate this superiority. Some have wrongly supposed that Satan can create life and raise the dead. This is clearly contrary to Scripture. Only God is the creator of living creatures (Gen. 1:21 cf. Deut. 32:39; 1 Sam. 2:2, 6; Job 1:1). Satan himself is a created being (Col. 1:15–16), and creatures by nature do not create life. Satan's workers admitted that they could not create even lice in Exodus 8:18–19.

Raising the dead was a special sign of an apostle (Matt. 10: 8; 2 Cor. 12:12). If Satan could do it, it would hardly be a distinguishing sign of God's apostle. And if Satan could raise the dead, he could duplicate the resurrection—the crowning proof of Christ's claim to be God (Matt. 12:40; John 2:19–21; 10:18)—and thus subvert the uniqueness of the Christian apologetic. The evidence for the resurrection of Christ would not have been "infallible proofs" (Acts 1:3 NKJV). In fact, if Satan could do the same miracles God can do, then there would be no supernatural way to discern truth. For Satan could confirm lying prophets to be telling the truth. Likewise, if Satan could give infallible prophecies (*see* PROPHECY, AS PROOF OF THE BIBLE), the test that a false prophecy is a sign of a false prophet would be ineffective (Deut. 18:22).

Two texts are sometimes misapplied to support the thesis that Satan can create life or raise the dead. Upon scrutiny, neither is a legitimate example of life-giving power. One is the creating of serpents from rods by the magicians of Egypt. However, the magicians themselves admitted that they could not create life in Exod. 8:18–19. They were trained in illusion and deception. Some modern Eastern snake handlers have been seen to make certain snakes appear to go rigid.

The second instance is a prophecy about what Satan will do in the final confrontation with God (Revelation 13). The second "beast . . . was granted power to give breath to the image of the beast that it should both speak and cause as many as would not worship the [first] beast to be killed" (Rev. 13:15 NKJV). This, it claimed is proof that Satan can create life. If the power in fact was given by God, it is conceivable that the power to enliven will be granted to the beast. More likely this is speaking metaphorically, as when Jesus told Pilate, "You would have no power over me if it were not given to you from above" (John 19:11). Note also that it is not a human being who has died and is given life here. Rather, it is an "image" (we are not told what sort) of the beast that is given breath. Further, it is not given life but simply "breath." This could refer to the image being animated or made life-like. There are plenty of scenarios in which this prophetic vision would be fulfilled without Satan giving life to anything.

False Claims to Resurrection. Non-Christian religions and some fringe Christian groups have claimed great miracles, including the ability to raise the dead. No instance of an actual resurrection has been substantiated with anything like the evidence for the resurrection of Christ. Most are patently false.

Some are simply fraudulent tricks. Such is the case of the African witch doctor who claimed to have killed a man to appease the gods and then restored him to life. Illusionist Andre Kole, who has exposed many occult charades, discovered that the witch doctor had dug a tunnel by which the man he faked killing had escaped, and later returned (see Geisler, 118).

Some alleged resurrections are mystically induced "comas." Some Indian gurus are able to slow down their body processes by altering their state of consciousness. This enables them to spend hours in a grave with little oxygen. At least one modern escape artist was able to escape from a coffin buried under nine feet of dirt in an hour and a half. He made no claim to resurrection. He simply learned to conserve the oxygen from his large coffin while digging through loose soil to the surface.

Some cases are simply medical resuscitations. Medical science performs resuscitation regularly on people who are clinically but not actually dead. An actual resurrection occurs when someone was physically dead. By contrast, Jesus raised Lazarus after he had been buried for four days and his body was decomposing (John 11:39).

Some alleged resurrections are merely cases where individuals fainted or went into a coma. Evangelist and faith-healer Oral Roberts claimed to have resurrected people from the dead. When pressed for names and addresses, he declined. He finally mentioned one girl who had passed out in his service. When asked how he knew she was dead, he said her body felt cold and that both he and the girl's mother believed she was dead.

Resurrections were reported in Indonesian revivals (see Geisler, 71–72). When George Peters researched the matter first-hand, he found no evidence of real physical resurrections. He discovered, rather, that the word for "death" in the language can also refer to states of unconsciousness, such as fainting and comas (Peters, 88).

Claims of resurrections are still made, but no case has been made for a real physical resurrection from the dead (*see* RESURRECTION, PHYSICAL NATURE OF). Anyone who truly possessed this power would be thronged by crowds. Jesus had to pledge people to silence about his miracles (Matt. 8:4; 17:9). He was so besieged by miracle-seeking crowds that he often did not have time to eat (Mark 6:31; John 6:24). But no one since the time of the apostles is known to have possessed these kinds of powers.

God could raise the dead. He will raise all the dead one day (John 5:28–30; Rev. 20:4–5). Until then it is not something he is likely to do.

Conclusion. True miracles are truly supernatural; false miracles are, at best, only supernormal. Satanic signs are earmarked by association with evil and falsehood. Supernatural acts are distinguished by good and truth. Nor does Satan have the power to perform a truly supernatural act. His are always deceptions and usually obvious counterfeits to anyone who knows the signs. He is the master magician and a super scientist. But only God can create life and raise the dead. Only God can infallibly predict the future. Only God can instantaneously cure the "incurable." Satan's power is finite and evil. God's power is infinite and good, and his supernatural acts give evidence.

Sources

Augustine, *City of God*

C. Brown, "Miracle, Wonder, Sign," in *Dictionary of New Testament Theology*

N. L. Geisler, *Miracles and the Modern Mind*

———, *Signs and Wonders*

A. Kole, *Miracle and Magic*

C. S. Lewis, *Miracles*

G. Peters, *Indonesia Revival*

"Amazing" Randi, *The Healers*

M. Tari, *A Mighty Wind*

B. B. Warfield, *Counterfeit Miracles*

Miracles, Magic and. Crucial to the apologetic use of miracles is the ability to distinguish true miracles from false ones. Many religions claim to be "proven" by miraculous deeds. While Judaism claims that Moses' rod became a serpent and Christianity holds that Jesus walked on water, Islam's Muhammad is supposed to have moved a mountain, and Hindu gurus claim the power to levitate themselves.

New Age prophet Benjamin Creme offers a spirit of power and divination that "overshadowed" Jesus and is now available to followers of "the Christ": "It is this which has enabled them to perform what at that time were called miracles, which today are called spiritual or esoteric healing. Daily, all over the world, there are miracles of healing being performed. . . ."

If a miracle is properly an act of God that suspends natural laws with a purpose of confirming the source of truth in God, what are we to make of such sales pitches? Can we tell what is truly miraculous from what is not of God and could be demonic? Is it possible to define a miracle in such a way as to exclude false claims and other kinds of unusual events?

The Problem of Definition. According to theism, a miracle is a supernatural intervention by a transcendent God into the natural world. But *pantheism, like *atheism, says that there is no God beyond the universe. Hence, all events have natural causes. They disagree only on whether "natural" is limited to the physical or can include the spiritual. As the pantheistic "Jesus" of the *Aquarian Gospel of Jesus Christ* says, "All things result from natural law." Even Christian Science says that a miracle is, "that which is divinely natural, but must be learned humanly; a phenomenon of Science." Instead of saying that there are no miracles, pantheists redefine miracles as a manipulation of natural law. In a classic view of pantheism, the *Star Wars* films, Luke Skywalker learned to use "the force" (natural law) in an almost spiritual power that enabled him to do his incredible deeds. Pantheists have even tried to incorporate advanced physics into explanations of the supernormal. Fritjof Capra's book *The Tao of Physics* is an updated version of the pantheistic doctrine that all matter is at heart mystical: "The basic oneness of the universe is not only the central characteristic of the mystical experience, but is also one of the most important revelations of modern physics. It becomes apparent at the atomic level and manifests itself more and more as one penetrates deeper into matter, down into the realm of subatomic particles."

So the source of pantheistic "miracles" is not an all powerful personal God who is beyond the universe. It is an impersonal Force within the universe. Hence, these unusual events are not really supernatural; they are only *supernormal*.

Supernatural versus Supernormal. Christianity does not deny that supernormal events take place, but we deny that they are truly unique or have any apologetic value in confirming religious truth claims. The definition of a true miracle has three basic elements that are reflected in the three words associated with miracles in the Bible: *power*, *sign*, and *wonder* (for more on these elements, *see* MIRACLES IN THE BIBLE).

The *power* of miracles comes from a God who is beyond the universe. The nature of miracles are that they are *wonders,* which inspire awe because they transcend natural laws. The word *sign* tells us the purpose of miracles: They confirm God's message and messenger. The theological dimension of this definition is that miracles imply a God outside the universe who intervenes in it. Morally, because God is good, miracles produce and/or promote good. In their doctrinal dimension, miracles tell us which prophets are true and which are false. Teleologically (purposefully), miracles are never performed for entertainment. They have the purpose of glorifying God and directing people to him.

Pantheistic "miracles" don't meet this definition because their power is not from God. New Age writer David Spangler identified the source of miracles for pantheists when he wrote, "Christ is the same force as Lucifer but moving in seemingly the opposite direction. Lucifer moves in to create the light within. . . . Christ moves out to release that light." So the power for supernormal events in pantheism comes from Lucifer, or Satan, even though it is called Christ when it goes out from the individual.

From a biblical perspective, Lucifer, also called the Devil and Satan, is not the same as God or even equal to God. In the beginning, God created everything good: the earth (Gen. 1:1, 31), humanity (Gen. 1:27–28), and angels (Col. 1:15, 16). One angel was named Lucifer (Isa. 14:12). He was beautiful, but "lifted up with pride" (1 Tim. 3:6) and rebelled against God saying, "I will make myself like the Most High" (Isa. 14:14). One-third of all the angels left their home with God to follow him (Rev. 12:4). These beings are now known as Satan and his demons (Rev. 12:7 and Matt. 25:41). They do have unusual powers, in the sense that all angels have supernatural powers as part of the spiritual world. They are said to be "working in [energizing] the sons of disobedience" (Eph. 2:2). Satan is able to "disguise himself as an angel of light" (2 Cor. 11:14) even to appear to be on God's side, but it is only a disguise.

Miracles versus Magic. From a biblical perspective there are tests to distinguish miracles from New Age or occultic influences that might be called "magic." Miracles are God-ordained supernatural interventions. Magic is supernormal manipulation of natural forces. The following chart summarizes these differences:

Miracles	**Magic**
Under God's control.	Under human control.
Not available on command.	Available on command.
Supernatural power.	A supernormal power.
Associated with good.	Associated with evil.
Associated only with truth.	Associated also with error.
Can overpower evil.	Cannot overpower good.
Affirm Jesus is God in the flesh.	Denies Jesus is God in the flesh.
Prophecies always true.	Prophecies sometimes false.
Never associated with occult practices.	Often associated with occult practices.

Magic uses occult means to perform its acts. These are practices which claim to conjure powers from the spirit realm. In many cases they do just that; but it is demonic power. Some practices directly linked to demonic power in the Bible are:

Witchcraft (Deut. 18:10)
Fortune-telling (Deut. 18:10)
Communicating with spirits (Deut. 18:11)
Mediums (Deut. 18:11)
Divination (Deut. 18:10)
Astrology (Deut. 4:19; Isa. 47:13–15)

Heresy (false teaching) (1 Tim. 4:1; 1 John 4:1–3)

Immorality (Eph. 2:2–3)

Self-deification (Gen. 3:5; Isa. 14:12)

Lying (John 8:44)

Idolatry (1 Cor. 10:19–20)

Legalism and self-denial (Col. 2:16–23; 1 Tim. 4:1–4)

Many who practice and teach pantheistic "miracles" admit that they use occult practices and recommend them for others. These tests clearly show that such claims to supernatural powers are not miracles.

Test Case: Jean Dixon. Jean Dixon is one of the twentieth century's most celebrated psychics. She is alleged to have made many supernormal predictions, but her work in no sense meets the standards for the miraculous.

False Prophecies. Even her biographer, Ruth Montgomery, admits that Dixon has made false prophecies. "She predicted that Red China would plunge the world into war over Quemoy and Matsu in October of 1958; she thought that labor leader Walter Reuther would actively seek the presidency in 1964." On October 19, 1968, she assured us that Jacqueline Kennedy was not considering marriage; the next day, Mrs. Kennedy wed Aristotle Onassis! She also said that World War III would begin in 1954, the Viet Nam war would end in 1966, and Castro would be banished from Cuba in 1970.

The People's Almanac (1976) did a study of the predictions of twenty-five top psychics including Dixon. The results: "Out of the total 72 predictions, 66 (or 92 percent) were dead wrong" (Kole, 69). Of those correct to some degree, two were vague and two hardly surprising—the United States and Russia would remain leading powers and there would be no world wars. It is clear that it does not take supernatural powers to get these subnormal results.

An accuracy rate around 8 percent could be explained by chance and general knowledge of circumstances. But there may be more to it. Montgomery tells us that Dixon uses a crystal ball, astrology, and telepathy, and that her gift of prophecy was given to her by a gypsy fortuneteller when she was a little girl.

The So-called Kennedy Prediction. Even Jean Dixon's highly reputed prophecy of John F. Kennedy's death is vague, and wrong in some aspects (she says that the 1960 election would be dominated by labor, which it was not), and said at one point that Richard Nixon would win, which he did not, a prediction she contradicted elsewhere. Her assassination prophecy did not specifically name Kennedy. In contrast, Isaiah named King "Cyrus" and told what he would do a century and a half before he was born (see Isa. 45:1). Second, Dixon gave no details as to how, where, or when Kennedy would be killed. Compare this with the specificity of Old Testament prophecies concerning the birth and death of the Christ (see Isaiah 53). Third, her prediction was general. All she divined was that a Democrat President would die in office. In 1960 there was about a 50–50 chance that a Democrat would be elected and, given two four-year terms, a fair chance that he would at least be shot at. Furthermore, the early 1960s fit a century-old cycle in which every twenty years a president died in office. The 1980 President, Ronald Reagan was almost assassinated.

The Bible allows no room for such things. All forms of divination are prohibited. No error is allowed for a prophet of God. Deuteronomy 18:22 says a prophet must be 100 percent accurate: "If what a prophet proclaims in the name of the LORD does not take place or come true, that is a message the LORD has not spoken. That prophet has spoken presumptuously. Do not be afraid of him" (Deut. 18:22). That last phrase means that it is appropriate to stone such a prophet. If God has spoken, it will come about. There is no need for a second chance.

Some claims to supernormal powers have been shown to be nothing more than illusions and sleight-of-hand tricks. Danny Korem, a professional magician who has written a book to expose such frauds, says, "given the proper circumstances, anyone can be made to believe he has witnessed something which never took place."

One example of this is the "psychic" Uri Geller, who claims to have the power to bend metal objects without touching them, as well as telepathy and clairvoyance. He even received support in a Stanford Research Institute report published in a popular-level science journal. But the editors of the magazine noted that the men who had refereed the tests felt that "insufficient account had been taken of the established methodology of experimental psychology. . . . Two referees also felt that the authors had not taken into account the lessons learned in the past by parapsychologists researching this tricky and complicated area." Their skepticism proved to be well founded. *New Science* magazine recorded that "at least five people claim to have seen Geller actually cheat." One woman observing him in a television studio said that "she actually saw Geller bend—by hand, not by psychic powers—the large spoon." Another of Geller's tricks is to take his picture with a camera while the lens cap is on. But this has been duplicated by a photographer using a wide angle lens and with the cover not quite closed. Geller's success also seems to drop dramatically when the controls are tightened. On television shows, he liked to pick an object from one of ten film cans.

On the Merv Griffin show on US TV, Geller did the trick successfully, but some people thought they saw Geller jarring the table so that the cans would shake and he could tell which was heaviest. On the Johnny Carson Tonight show on 1 August 1973, therefore, special precautions were taken and Geller was not permitted to get near enough to the table to jar it or touch the cans. He failed.

It is hard to avoid the conclusion of one critic who said flatly that "the SRI paper simply does not stand up against the mass of circumstantial evidence that Uri Geller is simply a good magician." Magician Andre Kole enlightens us,

> What most people do not realize about Uri Geller—what he has tried to suppress in his publicity—is that he studied and practiced magic as a youth in Israel. But he quickly realized that he attracted a far greater following by claiming paranormal powers than he did as a conjurer. In fact, most of what he does would be rather insignificant coming from a magician.

Unique Biblical Miracles. Biblical miracles are superior and unique. The magicians of Egypt tried to reproduce Moses' works by means of illusions with some success (Exod. 7:19ff.; 8:6ff.), but when God brought forth gnats from the dust, the sorcerers failed and exclaimed, "This is the finger of God" (Exod. 8:19). Elijah silenced all claims of the prophets of Baal when he called down fire from heaven when they could not (1 Kings 18). Moses' authority was vindicated when Korah and his followers were swallowed up by the earth (Numbers 16). Aaron was shown to be God's choice as priest when his rod budded (Numbers 17).

In the New Testament, Jesus healed the sick (Matt. 8:14–17), made the blind to see (Mark 8:22–26), cleansed lepers (Mark 1:40–45), and raised people from the dead (Luke 8:49–56). His pattern continued in the apostles, as Peter healed the beggar at the Temple gate (Acts 3:1–11) and raised Dorcas from the dead (Acts 9:36–41). Hebrews 2:4 tell us the purpose of these miracles: "God also testified to it by signs, wonders and various miracles, and gifts of the Holy Spirit distributed according to his will." As far as the purposefulness, goodness, and confirmation of God's message, there is no comparison between these miracles and bending spoons.

Unique Biblical Prophecy. Biblical prophecy is also unique in that, while most predictions are vague and often wrong, the Scriptures are remarkably precise and accurate (*see* PROPHECY, AS PROOF OF THE BIBLE). God foretold not only the coming of the destruction of Jerusalem (Isa. 22:1–25), but also the name of Cyrus, the Persian ruler who would return them (Isa. 44:28; 45:1). This was 150 years before it all happened. The very place of Jesus' birth is cited in about 700 B.C. (Micah 5:2). The time of his triumphal entry into Jerusalem was predicted accurately by Daniel in 538 B.C. (Dan. 9:24–26). No fortune-teller can boast of anything like this accuracy or consistency.

Christ predicted his own death (Mark 8:31), the means of his death (Matt. 16:24), his betrayal (Matt. 26:21), and his resurrection from the dead on the third day (Matt. 12:39–40). There is nothing like this anywhere in the occult prophecies or miracles. The prediction and resurrection of Jesus stands alone as *the* unique and unrepeatable event of history.

Sources

F. Capra, *The Tao of Physics*
L. Dowling, *The Aquarian Gospel of Jesus Christ*
N. L. Geisler, *Signs and Wonders*
A. Kole, *Miracle and Magic*
D. Korem, *The Powers*
"Amazing" Randy, *Flim Flam*
B. B. Warfield, *Counterfeit Miracles*

Miracles, Myth and. Under the relentless attack from modern naturalism, many religious thinkers have retreated to the view that miracles are not events in the space-time world (*see* MIRACLE). Rather, miracles are myths or events in a spiritual world, above space and time. As a result, the religious records must be "demythologized" or divested of the mythological "husk" to get at the existential "kernel" of truth. Rudolf *Bultmann (1884–1976) was at the forefront of this view of "miracles." He adapted phenomenologist Martin Heidegger's (1889–1976) concept of existential analysis to New Testament exegesis. Using Heidegger's methods, he attempted to separate the essential gospel message from the first-century worldview.

Demythological Naturalism. Bultmann believed Scripture to be founded on a three-story universe, with the earth in the center, heaven above with God and angels, and the underworld beneath. The world "is the scene of the supernatural activity of God and his angels on the one hand, and of Satan and his demons on the other. These supernatural forces intervene in the course of nature and in all that we think and will and do" (Bultmann, 1). The New Testament documents needed to be stripped of this mythological structure. The language of mythology is incredible to moderns, for whom the mythical view of the world is obsolete. "All our thinking to-day is shaped for good or ill by modern science," so "a blind acceptance of the New Testament . . . would mean accepting a view of the world in our faith and religion which we should deny in our everyday life" (ibid., 3–4).

With confidence, Bultmann did not even open for consideration the assumption that the biblical picture of miracles is impossible. Such a view could no longer be held seriously. The only honest way of reciting the creeds was to strip the mythological framework from the truth they enshrine.

Purpose of Myth. If the biblical picture is mythological, how then are we to understand it? For Bultmann "the real purpose of myth is not to present an objective picture of the world as it is, but to express man's understanding of himself in the world in which he lives." Therefore "myth should be interpreted not cosmologically, but anthropologically, or better still, existentially."

"Myth speaks of the power or the powers which man supposes he experiences as the ground and limit of his world and of his own activity and suffering." In other words, myth speaks of a transcendent power which controls the world. It is that hope that religion shares once its dated peripheral material is cut away (ibid., 10–11).

Bultmann concludes confidently, "Obviously [the resurrection] is not an event of past history . . . An historical fact which involves a resurrection from the dead is utterly inconceivable" (ibid., 38–39). He offers several reasons for this antisupernatural conclusion. First, there is "the incredibility of a mythical event like the resuscitation of a corpse." Second, "there is the difficulty of establishing the objective historicity of the resurrection no matter how many witnesses are cited." Third, "the resurrection is an article of faith which, as such, cannot be a miraculous proof." Finally, "such a miracle is not otherwise unknown to mythology" (ibid., 39–40).

What then is the resurrection (*see* RESURRECTION, EVIDENCE FOR)? For Bultmann, it is an event of subjective history, an event of faith in the hearts of the early disciples. As such, it is not subject to historical verification or falsification, for it is not an event in the space-time world. Christ did not rise from Joseph's tomb; he arose by faith in the disciples' hearts.

It is difficult to formulate precisely the reasoning Bultmann used to support this thesis. It seems to go like this:

1. Myths are by nature more than objective truths; they are transcendent truths of faith.
2. But what is not objective cannot be part of a verifiable space-time world.
3. Therefore, miracles (myths) are not part of the objective space-time world.

Weaknesses of Demythological Naturalism. *Miracles Are Not Less Than Historical.* It does not follow that, because an event is *more* than historical, it must be *less* than historical. Gospel miracles, to be sure, have a transcendent dimension. They are more than historical events. For example, the *virgin birth involves the divine nature of Christ (*see* CHRIST, DEITY OF) and the spiritual purpose of his mission as much as biology. It is presented as a "sign" (Isa. 7:14). The *resurrection is more than the resuscitation of a corpse. Its divine dimension entails spiritual truths (Rom. 4:25; 2 Tim. 1:10).

That in no way means that these miracles are not purely objective and factual events. Even Bultmann admits that the New Testament writers believed the events they described were historical. "It cannot be denied that the resurrection of Jesus is often used in the New Testament as a miraculous proof. . . . Both the legend of the empty tomb and the appearances insist on the physical reality of the risen body of the Lord." However, "these are most certainly later embellishments of the primitive tradition" (ibid., 39). No solid reasons are given for concluding that these events could not be events in space-time history (*see* MIRACLES IN THE BIBLE).

Miracles in but not of the World. Bultmann wrongly assumes that any event *in* this world must be *of* this world. A miracle can originate in the supernatural world (its source) and yet occur in the natural world (its sphere). In this way the event can be objective and verifiable without being reducible to purely factual dimensions. One could verify directly by historical means whether the corpse of Jesus of Nazareth was raised and empirically observed (the objective dimensions of the miracle), without reducing the spiritual aspects of the event to mere scientific data. But in claiming that such miracles cannot occur in space-time history, Bultmann is merely revealing an unjustified and anti-intellectual naturalistic bias.

The basis of Bultmann's antisupernaturalism is not evidential, nor even open to discussion. It is something he holds "no matter how many witnesses are cited" (ibid.). The dogmatism of his language is revealing. Miracles are "incredible," "irrational," "no longer possible," "meaningless," "utterly inconceivable," "simply impossible," and "intolerable." Hence, the "only honest way" for modern people is to hold that miracles are spiritual and that the physical world is immune to supernatural interference.

If miracles are not objective historical events, then they are unverifiable and unfalsifiable. There is no factual way to determine if they are truth. They have been placed beyond the realm of objective truth and must be treated as purely subjective. Antony Flew's criticism (*see* VERIFICATION, KINDS OF) was to the point when he challenged, "Now it often seems to people who are not religious as if there was no conceivable event or series of events the occurrence of which would be admitted by sophisticated religious people to be a sufficient reason for conceding 'There wasn't a God after all.'" Antony *Flew asked: "What would have to occur or to have occurred to constitute for you a disproof of the love of, or of the existence of, God" (Flew, 98)?

To rephrase Flew's questions for Bultmann, "If the corpse of Jesus of Nazareth had been discovered after the first Easter, would this falsify your belief in the resurrection?" Clearly for Bultmann it would not. The apostle Paul's answer to that question, given in 1 Corinthians 15, is emphatically "Yes." For "if Christ has not been raised, your faith is futile; you are still in your sins" (1 Cor 15:17).

If miracles are not historical events, they have no evidential value (*see* FIDEISM). They prove nothing, since they have value only for those who wish to believe them. However, the New Testament writers claim evidential value for miracles. They consider them "convincing proofs" (Acts 1:3) and not "cleverly devised myths" (2 Peter 1:16 RSV). Paul declared that "God has given proof of this to all men, by raising him [Jesus] from the dead" (Acts 17:31).

Conclusion. Bultmann's demythological approach to miracles and the New Testament documents in general is unjustified. First and foremost, it is contrary to the overwhelming evidence for the authenticity of the New Testament documents and the reliability of the witnesses (*see* NEW TESTAMENT, HISTORICITY OF). Secondly, it is contrary to the New Testament claim (2 Peter 1:16, cf. John 1:1–3; 21:24). Finally, the New Testament is not the literary genre of mythology (*see* MYTHOLOGY AND THE NEW TESTAMENT). C. S. *Lewis himself a writer of myth (fairy tales) keenly noted that "Dr. Bultmann never wrote a gospel." He asks, therefore, "Has the experience of his learned . . . life really given him any power of seeing into the minds of those long dead [who have]?" As a writer of myth, Lewis found the critics usually wrong when they attempted to read his mind rather than his words. However, he adds, "the 'assured results of modern scholarship,' as to the way in which an old book was written, are 'assured,' we may conclude, only because the men who knew the facts are dead and can't blow the gaff." Bultmannian biblical critiques are unfalsifiable because, as Lewis wryly remarks, "St. Mark is dead. When they meet St. Peter there will be more pressing matters to discuss" (*Christian Reflections,* 161–63).

Sources

R. Bultmann, *Kerygma and Myth: A Theological Debate,* ed. H. W. Bartsch, trans. R. H. Fuller

A. Flew, "Theology and Falsification," in *New Essays in Philosophical Theology*

N. L. Geisler, *Miracles and the Modern Mind*

C. S. Lewis, *Christian Reflections*

———, *Miracles*

Miracles in the Bible. In the broad sense of the term *miracle*, every supernaturally caused event described in Scripture is miraculous. Scripture, however, also uses the concept in a narrower, more technical sense. In supernatural events of the past (and events predicted for the future), an unusual outward sign confirms a message from God.

Perhaps the definitive New Testament text on miracles is Hebrews 2:3–4 (KJV): "How shall we escape, if we neglect so great salvation; which at the first began to be spoken by the Lord, and was confirmed unto us by them that heard [him]; God also bearing [them] witness, both with signs and wonders, and with divers miracles, and gifts of the Holy Ghost, according to his own will?" Miracles are God's way of accrediting his spokespersons. A miracle is an act of God that confirms the message as true, substantiates the sermon, and verifies the Word of God (*see* MIRACLES, APOLOGETIC VALUE OF).

When Korah challenged Moses' divine authority, God confirmed Moses by opening up the earth to swallow Korah (Numbers 16). When Israel hesitated between the god Baal and *Yahweh*, God confirmed Elijah over the prophets of Baal by sending fire from heaven to consume the sacrifices. Elijah had prayed, "Let it be known today that you are God in Israel and that I am your servant" (1 Kings 18:36).

In miracles Jesus was both confirmed and revealed. The religious ruler Nicodemus said to Jesus, "we know you are a teacher who has come from God. For no one could perform the miraculous signs you are doing if God were not with him" (John 3:2). Many people followed him because they saw the signs he performed on those who were sick (John 6:2). John said of Jesus' first recorded miracle, "He thus revealed his glory, and his disciples put their faith in him" (John 2:11). John said he wrote about Jesus' miracles "that you may believe that Jesus is the Christ, the Son of God" (John 20:31). The apostles were confident in proclaiming, "Jesus of Nazareth was a man accredited by God to you by miracles, wonders and signs, which God did among you through him, as you yourselves know" (Acts 2:22).

Miracles were apostolic credentials in the early church. Paul claimed that the signs of a true apostle were performed among the Corinthians (2 Cor. 12:12). He and Barnabas recounted to the apostles "the miraculous signs and wonders God had done among the Gentiles through them" (Acts 15:12).

Signs, Wonders, and Power. The Bible uses three basic words to describe a miracle: *sign*, *wonder*, and *power*. Each of the words carries a connotation that clarifies the complete picture of biblical miracles (*see* MIRACLE).

"Sign." Although the Hebrew word for "sign" is sometimes used to refer to natural things such as stars (Gen. 1:14) or the Sabbath (Exod. 31:13), it usually carries supernatural significance, something appointed by God with a special message assigned to it (*see* MIRACLES, APOLOGETIC VALUE OF).

The first appearance of the concept comes in the divine prediction given to Moses that Israel would be delivered from Egypt to serve God at Horeb. God said, "I will be with you. And this will be the sign to you that it is I who have sent you" (Exod. 3:12). When Moses asked God, "What if they do not believe me or listen to me?" the Lord gave two "signs": Moses' rod turned into a serpent (Exod. 4:3) and his hand became leprous (Exod. 4:1–7). These were given "that they may believe that the Lord, the God of their fathers . . . has appeared to you" (4:5). Moses performed the signs and the people believed (4:30–31). God gave further signs, the plagues, as a witness to the Egyptians "that I am the Lord, when I stretch out My hand against Egypt and bring the Israelites out of it" (Exod. 7:3, 5; cf. 11:9).

Repeatedly the purpose of the supernatural occurrence is given as a twofold "sign": "By this you will know that I am the Lord" (Exod. 7:17; cf. 9:29–30; 10:1–2) and that these are "my people" (Exod. 3:10; cf. 5:1; 6:7; 11:7).

Several statements about signs appear in the context of God's deliverance of his people from Egypt. God complained to Moses in the wilderness, saying, "How long will they refuse to believe in me, in spite of all the miraculous signs I have performed among them?" (Num. 14:11; cf. vs. 22). Moses challenged Israel: "Has any god ever tried to take for himself one nation out of another nation, by testings, by miraculous signs and wonders?" (Deut. 4:34). Moses reminded the people, "Before our eyes the LORD sent miraculous signs and wonders—great and terrible—upon Egypt and Pharaoh and his whole household" (Deut. 6:22). "So the LORD brought us out of Egypt with a mighty hand and an outstretched arm, with great terror and with miraculous signs and wonders" (Deut. 26:8; cf. 29:2–3; Josh. 24:17; Neh. 9:10; Ps. 105:27; Jer. 32:20–21).

Throughout the Old Testament God performs miraculous "signs." Signs confirm a prophet as God's spokesman. As noted, Moses received miraculous credentials (Exodus 3 and 4). Gideon asked God, "give me a sign that it is really you talking to me" (Judg. 6:17). God responded with miraculous fire that consumed the offering (vs. 21). God confirmed himself to Eli by miraculous predictions about his sons' deaths (1 Sam. 2:34). Predictive signs confirmed God's appointment of King Saul (1 Sam. 10:7, 9). Isaiah made predictions as signs of his divine message (Isa. 7:14; 38:22). Victories over enemies were called signs (1 Sam. 14:10). Signs affirmed healing (Isa. 38:7, 22) and accompanied judgment (Jer. 44:29).

In the New Testament, *sign (semeion)* is used seventy-seven times (forty-eight times in the Gospels). It is occasionally used of ordinary events, such as circumcision (Rom. 4:11), and of a baby wrapped in swaddling clothes (Luke 2:12). These signs have special divine significance. Most often the word is reserved for what we would call a miracle. It is used when Jesus healed (John 6:2; 9:16), turned water to wine (John 2:11), and raised the dead (John 11:47). Likewise, the apostles did miracles of healing (Acts 4:16, 30), "great signs and miracles" (Acts 8:13), and "miraculous signs and wonders" (Acts 14:3; 15:12); for "many wonders and miraculous signs were done by the apostles" (Acts 2:43). Even the Jewish authorities said, "What are we going to do with these men? . . . Everybody living in Jerusalem knows they have done an outstanding miracle, and we cannot deny it" (Acts 4:16).

The word "sign" is also used of the most significant miracle in the New Testament, the resurrection of Jesus Christ from the grave. Jesus said that his unbelieving generation would see "the sign of the prophet Jonah." As Jonah had been in a fish's belly for three days, "the Son of Man will be three days and three nights in the heart of the earth" (Matt. 12:39–40). Jesus repeated this prediction of his resurrection when asked for a sign in Matthew 16:1, 4. Not only was the resurrection a miracle, but it carried with it a message from God (John 2:19).

"Wonder." Often the words *signs* and *wonders* are used together in the Old Testament of the same event(s) (Exod. 7:3; cf. Deut. 4:34; 7:19; 13:1, 2; 26:8; 28:46; 29:3; 34:11; Neh. 9:10; Ps. 135:9; Jer. 32:20–21). At other times the Bible describes as "wonders" events that are elsewhere called "signs" (Exod. 4:21; 11:9–10; Pss. 78:43; 105:27; Joel 2:30). Sometimes the word is used of a natural "wonder" (Ezek. 24:24) or a unique thing a prophet did to get his message across (Isa. 20:3). The word *wonder* usually has supernatural (divine) significance.

The Greek word *teras* means a "miraculous sign, prodigy, portent, omen, wonder" (Brown, 2:633). It carries with it the idea of that which is amazing or astonishing (ibid., 623–25). In all sixteen of its New Testament occurrences, "wonder" is used in combination with the word "sign." It describes Jesus' miracles (John 4:48; Acts 2:22), the apostles' miracles (Acts 2:43; 14:3; 15:12; Rom. 15:19; Heb. 2:3–4), Stephen's miracles (Acts 6:8), and Moses' miracles in Egypt (Acts 7:36). It connotes supernatural events before the second coming of Christ (Matt. 24:24; Mark 13:22; Acts 2:19).

"Power." "Power" is sometimes used of human power in the Old Testament (Gen. 31:6; Deut. 8:17; Nahum 2:1). But often it is used of divine power, including God's power to create: "God made the earth by his power" (Jer. 10:12; 27:5; 32:17; 51:15). The "power" of God overthrows his enemies (Exod. 15:6–7), delivers his people from Egypt (Num. 14:17; cf. vs. 13), rules the universe (1 Chron. 29:12), gives Israel their land (Ps. 111:6), and inspires the prophets (Micah 3:8). Power is often in direct connection with events called

"signs" or "wonders" or both (Exod. 9:16; 32:11; Deut. 4:37; 2 Kings 17:36; Neh. 1:10). Sometimes Hebrew words denoting power are used in the same verse with "signs and wonders." Moses speaks of the deliverance of Israel "by miraculous signs and wonders, . . . by a mighty hand" (Deut. 4:34; cf. 7:19; 26:8; 34:12).

"Power" *(dunamis)* is sometimes used in the New Testament to refer to human power (2 Cor. 1:8) or abilities (Matt. 25:15) or demonic powers (Luke 10:19; Rom. 8:38). Like its Old Testament parallel, the New Testament term is often translated "miracles." *Dunamis* is used in combination with "sign and wonder" (Heb. 2:4), of Christ's miracles (Matt. 13:58), of the virgin birth of Christ (Luke 1:35), of the outpouring of the Holy Spirit at Pentecost (Acts 1:8), of the "power" of the gospel to save sinful people (Rom. 1:16), of the special gift of miracles (1 Cor 12:10), and of the power to raise the dead (Phil. 3:10). The emphasis of the word is on the *divine energizing* aspect of a miraculous event.

Biblical Nature of a Miracle. The three words Scripture uses to describe a miracle help delineate the meaning of miracles more precisely. Each of the three words for supernatural events (*sign, wonder, power*) delineates an aspect of a miracle. From the human vantage point, a miracle is an unusual event ("wonder") that conveys and confirms an unusual message ("sign") by means of unusual power ("power"). From the divine vantage point, a miracle is an act of God ("power") that attracts the attention of the people of God ("wonder") to the Word of God (by a "sign").

The purposes of a miracle are

1. *to glorify* the nature of God (John 2:11; 11:40);
2. *to accredit* certain persons as the spokesmen for God (Acts 2:22; Heb. 2:3–4); and
3. *to provide evidence* for belief in God (John 6:2, 14; 20:30–31).

Not all witnesses to a miracle believe. In this event the miracle is a witness against those who reject this evidence. John grieved: "Even after Jesus had done all these miraculous signs in their presence, they still would not believe in him" (John 12:37). Jesus himself said of some, "They will not be convinced even if someone rises from the dead" (Luke 16:31). One result, though not the purpose, of miracles is condemnation of the unbeliever (cf. John 12:31, 37).

Biblical References to Miraculous. About 250 occurrences in Scripture fit the narrow definition of sign, wonder, or power. Since many references refer to multiple supernatural acts, the number of actual miraculous events is greater than the number of passages listed. Also, the Bible often refers to single events combining many miracles. Ten lepers were healed (Luke 17:12–14), as were all or most of the sick in one city (Matt. 9:35).

Genesis

1	Creation of all things.
5:19–24	Translation of Enoch to be with God.
7:9–12, 17–24	Noahic flood.
11:1, 5–9	Judgment at tower of Babel.
12:10–20; 17:15–19; 18:10–14	Plagues on pharaoh for taking Abraham's wife.
19:9–11	Sodomites blinded.
19:15–29	Sodom and Gomorrah destroyed.
19:24–26	Lot's wife turned to salt.
21:1–8	Sarah's conception of Isaac.

Exodus

3:1–15	The burning bush.
4:1–5	Moses' staff becomes serpent and restored.
4:6–7	Moses' hand becomes leprous and restored.
7:10–12	Aaron's staff becomes serpent, which swallows serpents of sorcerers.
7:19–24	Water turned to blood.
8:5–7; 12–13	Frogs plague Egypt.
8:16–18	Lice plague Egypt.
8:20–24	Flies plague Egypt.
9:1–7	Egyptian cattle die of disease.
9:8–11	Boils on Egyptians and their animals.
9:22–26	Storm of thunder, hail, and fire.
10:3–19	Locusts plague Egyptians.
10:21–23	Plague of darkness covers Egyptians.
12:29–30	First-born Egyptian children and animals slain.
13:21–22	Pillar of cloud and fire lead Israel.
14:19–20	Angel protects Israel from Egyptians.
14:21–29	Sea parts so Israel can pass.
15:23–25	Bitter waters of Marah sweetened.

16:12–13	Quail cover camp of Israel.
16:14–15	Manna is provided for Israel to eat.
17:5–6	Water is provided from the rock.
17:8–16	Victory over Amalek.
19:16–18	Fire and smoke engulf Mount Sinai.
19:19–25	God answers Moses at Sinai.
20:1–17	God gives law.

Leviticus

9:23–24	Fire consumes burnt offering.
10:1–7	Judgment upon Nadab and Abihu.

Numbers

11:1–2	Fire consumes murmuring Israelites.
12:10–15	Miriam is made leprous and healed.
16:28–33	Judgment on Korah and rebels.
16:35	Fire consumes rebellious who offered incense.
16:46–48	Plague stopped by offering incense.
17:8	Aaron's rod buds.
20:7–11	Moses strikes the rock for water.
21:6–9	Healing with brass serpent.
22:21–35	Balaam's donkey speaks.

Joshua

3:14–17	Waters of the Jordan divided.
5:13–15	Joshua's encounter with angelic being.
6	The fall of Jericho.
10:12–14	The sun stands still upon Gibeon.

Judges

2:1–5	Angel of Lord appears to Israel.
3:8–11	Spirit of Lord comes upon Othniel.
3:31	Shamgar slays 600 with ox goad.
6:11–24	Angel appears to Gideon.
6:36–40	The sign of Gideon's fleece.
7:15–25	God delivers Midian to Gideon.
13:3–21	Angel appears to Manoah.
14:5–6	Samson slays lion.
15:14–17	Samson slays Philistines with jawbone of a donkey.
16:3	Samson carries away a city gate.
16:27–31	Samson causes collapse of temple of Dagon.

1 Samuel

3:2–10	Voice of God calls Samuel.
5:1–5	Overturning of the god, Dagon.
5:6–12	Ashdod plagued by tumors.
6:19	God smites men of Beth-shemesh.
28:15–20	Samuel appears from dead to rebuke Saul.

2 Samuel

6:6–7	Uzzah dies after touching ark.

1 Kings

3:3–28	God gives Solomon great wisdom.
17:1	Three-year drought judges Israel.
17:2–6	Ravens feed Elijah.
17:8–16	Widow receives meal and oil.
17:17–24	Elijah raises widow's son.
18:17–38	Fire consumes Elijah's sacrifice on Carmel.
18:41–46	Elijah prays and God sends rain.
19:5–8	Elijah is fed by Angel.

2 Kings

1:9–15	Fire from heaven consumes soldiers.
2:7–8	Elijah parts Jordan.
2:11	Elijah taken to heaven in chariot of fire.
2:13–14	Elisha parts Jordan.
2:19–22	Elisha cleanses waters at Jericho.
2:24	Youths killed by bears.

3:15–20	Ditches filled with water.
4:1–7	Widow's pots are filled with oil.
4:8–17	Shunammite woman bears a son.
4:32–37	Elisha raises dead son.
4:38–41	Elisha makes poison food edible.
4:42–44	One hundred fed with loaves and corn.
5:1–14	Naaman healed of leprosy.
5:27	Gehazi judged with leprosy.
6:5–7	Iron axe head floats on water.
6:16–17	Vision of horses and chariots of fire.
6:18	Syrian army struck with blindness.
6:19–20	God opens eyes of Syrians.
13:20–21	Dead man raised by contact with Elisha's bones.
20:9–11	Ahaz's sundial turns backward.
Job	
38–42:6	God speaks from whirlwind.
Isaiah	
1:1	Isaiah's vision concerning Jerusalem.
6	Isaiah's vision of the Lord.
Ezekiel	
1	Ezekiel has a vision of God's glory.
Daniel	
2:26–45	Daniel recounts and interprets Nebuchadnezzar's dream.
3:14–30	Deliverance from fiery furnace.
5:5	Handwriting on wall.
6:16–23	Daniel saved from lions.
7:1–8:14	Daniel's visions.
9:20–27	Daniel's vision of seventy weeks.
10:1–12:13	Daniel's further visions.
Jonah	
1:4–16	Storm from God stops fleeing Jonah.
1:17	God's great fish swallows Jonah.
4:6	Gourd grows to shade Jonah.
4:7	Worm destroys gourd.
4:8	God sends east wind.

Matthew	Mark	Luke	John	Description
			2:1–11	Water becomes wine.
			4:46	Noble's son healed.
		4:30		Jesus escapes mob.
		5:6		Catch of fish.
	1:23	4:33		Unclean spirit cast out.
8:14	1:30	4:38		Peter's mother-in-law healed.
8:16	1:32	4:40		Sick healed.
8:2	1:40	5:12		Leper cleansed.
9:2	2:3	5:18		Paralytic healed.
			5:9	Infirm man healed.
12:9	3:1	6:6		Withered hand restored.
12:15	3:10			Sick healed.
8:5		7:1		Centurion's servant healed.
		7:11		Widow's son returned to life.
12:22				Demon cast from blind mute.
8:23	4:35	8:22		Storm stilled.
8:28	5:1	8:26		Demons cast out and enter herd of swine.
9:18–23	5:22–35	8:40–49		Ruler's daughter raised.

9:20	5:25	8:43		Woman with issue of blood healed.
9:27				Blind men healed.
9:32				Demon cast from deaf mute.
14:13	6:30	9:10	6:1	Five thousand fed.
14:25	6:48		6:19	Jesus walks on sea.
14:36	6:56			Sick healed at Gennesaret.
15:21	7:24			Gentile man's daughter healed.
	7:31			Deaf mute healed.
15:32	8:1			Four thousand fed.
	8:22			Blind paralytic healed.
17:1–8	9:2–8	9:28–36		Jesus' transfiguration.
17:14	9:17	9:38		Epileptic boy healed.
17:24				Coin in fish's mouth.
			9:1	Man born blind healed.
		11:14		Demon-possessed, blind mute healed.
		13:11		Infirm woman healed.
		14:1–4		Man with dropsy healed.
			11:43	Lazarus raised from dead.
		17:11		Ten lepers cleansed.
20:30	10:46	18:35		Two blind men healed.
21:18	11:12			Fig tree withers.
		22:51		Servant's ear restored.
28	16:1–8	24	20	Jesus rises from dead.
28:1–7				Angel rolls stone away, announces resurrection.
28:5–8	16:5–7	24:4–8		Angel appears at grave.
			20:11–13	Angels appear to Mary.
	16:9		20:14–17	Jesus appears to Mary Magdalene.
28:9–10				Jesus appears to women.
	16:12	24:13–35		Jesus appears on road to Emmaus.
			20:19–23	Jesus appears to ten.
	16:14–18	24:36–48	20:26–31	Jesus appears to eleven.
			21:1–25	Jesus appears to seven.
			21:6	Miraculous catch of fish.
28:16–20	16:15–18			Jesus appears to the apostles.

Acts

1:3–5	Jesus appears and addresses apostles (Luke 24:49–51).
1:6–9	Jesus ascends into heaven.
1:10–11	Angels appear to apostles.
2:1–4	Holy Spirit comes on apostles.
2:4–13	Apostles speak in foreign tongues.
3:1–11	Peter heals lame man in temple.
5:5–10	Ananias and Sapphira die.
5:12	Signs and wonders by apostles.
5:18–20	Apostles released from prison.
7:55–56	Stephen sees Jesus with God.
8:7	Unclean spirits cast out.

8:13	Philip performs miracles and signs.
8:14–17	Samaritans receive Holy Spirit.
8:39–40	Philip caught away by Holy Spirit.
9:3–7	Jesus appears to Saul (cf. 1 Cor. 15:8).
9:10–16	Jesus appears to Ananias.
9:17–19	Saul's sight is restored.
9:32–34	Peter heals Aeneas.
9:36–42	Dorcas raised from dead.
10:1–8	Cornelius receives vision.
10:9–16	Peter receives vision three times.
10:44–48	Household receives Holy Spirit.
12:7–10	Angel releases Peter from prison.
12:23	Angel kills Herod.
13:8–11	Elymas the sorcerer blinded.
14:8–10	Paul heals lame man at Lystra.
16:16–18	Paul casts demon from young woman.
16:25–26	Earthquake opens prison doors.
18:9–10	Paul receives vision.
19:6	Ephesian believers receive Holy Spirit.
19:11–12	Paul performs unusual signs.
20:9–12	Eutychus restored to life.
23:11	Paul receives vision.
28:3–6	Paul protected from viper bite.
28:7–8	Paul heals the father of Publius.

1 Corinthians

15:6	Jesus appeared to five hundred.
15:7	Jesus appeared to James.

2 Corinthians

12:1–6	Paul's vision of heaven.

Revelation

1:1–3:22	John's vision of Jesus.
4:1–22:21	John's vision of future.
6:12	Great earthquake.
6:12	Sun becomes black.
6:12	Moon becomes as blood.
6:13	Stars fall from heaven.
6:14	Mountains shaken from places.
8:7	Hail, fire, and blood fall.
8:8	Mountain is cast into the sea. Third of sea becomes blood.
8:9	Third of creatures in the sea die.
8:9	Third of ships destroyed.
8:10–11	Star falls and third of rivers and fountains become bitter.
8:12	Third of sun darkened.
8:12	Third of moon darkened.
8:12	Third of stars darkened.
9:1	Star falls from heaven.
9:2	Sun darkened by smoke from pit.
9:3–11	Plague of locusts.
9:18	Third of humanity killed.
11:5	Two witnesses destroy enemies by fire from their mouths.
11:6	Two witnesses stop rain.
11:6	Two witnesses turn water into blood.
11:6	Two witnesses call down plagues.
11:11	Two witnesses raised from dead.
11:12	Two witnesses ascend to heaven.
11:13	Earthquake destroys tenth of city.
11:19	Lightning, voices, thunder, earthquake and hail.
16:2	Sores on those who worship the beast.
16:3	Sea becomes as blood, and every soul in it dies.
16:4	Rivers, water sources become blood.
16:8	Sun scorches people.
16:10	Darkness covers kingdom of beast.
16:12	Euphrates River dries up.
16:18	Voices, thunders and earthquake.
16:20	Islands and mountains destroyed.
16:21	Stones fall on people.
18:1–24	Babylon falls.
19:11–16	Jesus Christ returns.
21:1	New heaven and earth appear.
21:10	New Jerusalem descends.

Old Testament Miracles. Negative Bible critics deny the authenticity of all miracles in the Bible. This conclusion is not based on a historical approach but on a philosophical one grounded in antisupernatural presuppositions. There are good grounds for accepting the authenticity of New Testament miracles. However, even some defenders of New Testament miracles have questioned the authenticity of some Old Testament accounts.

In a very popular book defending the possibility of miracles in general and New Testament miracles in particular, even apologist C. S. *Lewis relegates many Old Testament miracles to the realm of myth. In *Miracles* he wrote:

> My present view . . . would be that just as, on the factual side, a long preparation culminates in God's becoming incarnate as Man, so on the documentary side, the truth first appears in mythical form and then by a long process of focusing finally becomes incarnate as History. The Hebrews, like other peoples had mythology; but as they were the chosen people so their mythology was the chosen mythology. I take it that the memoirs of David's court come at one end of the scale and are scarcely less historical than St. Mark or Acts: and that the Book of Jonah is at the opposite end. [139]

There is no more reason to reject the authenticity of miracles in the Old Testament than to reject miracles in the New Testament. The evidence is of the same kind, reliable documents from contemporaries of the events. Indeed, the New Testament itself speaks of Old Testament miraculous events as historical.

General Evidence. We show, in related articles, why miracles are philosophically *possible* (*see* Cosmological Argument; Miracle; Moral Argument for God; Teleological Argument). An all-powerful, all-good personal God who created a world of personal creatures in his image can perform miracles. He will if he wishes to communicate with his finite creatures, for miracles are a crucial part of such a communication. Beginning with creation, which is the greatest miracle of all, Scripture reveals just such a God (*see* Evolution, Cosmic; *Kalam* Cosmological Argument). Historical evidence argues persuasively that miracles occurred in the New Testament (*see* Miracles, Arguments Against). Since both the God and redemptive plan of the Old Testament and New Testament are the same, there is every reason to expect that the miracles recorded in the Old Testament are authentic.

Evidence in Particular. Lewis' rejection of some Old Testament miracles is inconsistent, founded on faulty presuppositions, contrary to historical evidence, and not in accord with the New Testament use of the Old Testament.

It is based on a mistaken view of myth. Lewis' rejection of Old Testament miracles is based in an unsubstantiated view of myth (*see* Miracles, Myth and). According to Lewis, truth first appears as myth and then as history. Actually, the reverse has been the case, especially regarding pagan stories that gods appear on earth, die and then reappear in bodily form. It has been shown that these pagan myths probably copied Christ's death and resurrection rather than the reverse (*see* Divine Birth Stories; Frazer, James; Resurrection Claims in Non-Christian Religions). Further, there is no indication in the Bible that God operates in such a manner. On the contrary, the Bible condemns myths (see 1 Tim. 1:3–4; 4:7; 2 Tim. 4:4). The whole concept of myth becoming history is borrowed from an antisupernatural critical view, which Lewis himself condemns (see, for example, *God in the Dock*, chap. 16).

It is contrary to Old Testament monotheism. Old Testament miracles fit the monotheistic concept of God that permeates the entire record. A theistic God (*see* Theism) is a God beyond the world who created the world. Furthermore, since this theistic God loves what he has made, it is understandable that he would intervene on behalf of creatures in need. The fact that the Old Testament records miracles fits perfectly with its central message (*see* Miracles in the Bible).

It is inconsistent with the historical record. The Old Testament miracle stories are part of the same historical record as events known to be space-time history. There is absolutely no evidence that any manuscripts of these texts ever existed without the miracle accounts. They are present unmodified in the very oldest texts we possess. Rather, the miracles are an integral part of the history and message the Old Testament conveys. Remove miraculous events from Genesis 1–2 and the message about the Creator evaporates. The story of Noah and his faithfulness in a day of unbelief makes no sense apart from God's intervention to save him and destroy the world by flood. Israel's call of God and deliverance from Egypt are meaningless apart from the supernatural intervention to accomplish these things. The miracles of Elijah, Elisha, and Jonah are inseparable to the fabric of the history they record.

It is contrary to New Testament use of the Old Testament. New Testament references to Old Testament miracles assume their historical nature. The creation of the world is not only repeatedly cited in the New Testament but the events and persons involved are taken to be historical. Adam and Eve are referred to as historical figures many times in the New Testament (Matt. 19:4; 1 Cor. 11:8, 9; 1 Tim. 2:13–14). In Romans 5:12 the inference is unmistakable: Through one man sin and death entered the world. In Luke 3:38, Adam is listed in Jesus' genealogy. Likewise, Adam is called "the first man Adam" in direct comparison to Christ who is the "last Adam" (1 Cor. 15:45).

Supernatural events in the Old Testament are the bases for New Testament teaching. Jesus connected the truth of his resurrection with Jonah's miraculous preservation in the belly of a great fish, saying, "For *as* Jonah was three days and three nights in the belly of a huge fish, *so* the Son of Man will be three days and three nights in the heart of the earth" (Matt. 12:40). Given the context, it is inconceivable that Jesus meant: "Just as you believe that myth about Jonah, I would like to tell you about what will really happen at my death." Jesus makes a similar connection between his return and the historical flood, saying, "*That is how* it will be at the coming of the Son of Man" (Matt. 24:39).

Jesus referred to numerous miraculous Old Testament events as historical, including creation (Matt. 19:4; 24:21), the miracles of Elijah (Luke 4:26), and the prophecies of Daniel (Matt. 24:15). In view of Jesus' use of the Old Testament miracles, there is no way to challenge their authenticity without impugning his integrity. Accepting the New Testament as authentic, while rejecting Old Testament miracles, is inconsistent.

Summary. The biblical description of miracles uses three main words: *power*, *wonder*, and *sign*. These words designate the source (God's power), the nature (wonderful, unusual), and the purpose (to signify something beyond itself). A miracle is a sign to confirm a sermon; a wonder to verify the prophet's words; a miracle to help establish the message (*see* MIRACLES, APOLOGETIC VALUE OF).

There are hundreds of miracle accounts in Scripture. Those in the New Testament particularly capture our attention, because they are well-attested and reveal Jesus Christ in his power over Satan, sickness, and the grave. The New Testament shows that the ongoing power of Christ was present in the young church. However, there is nothing more incredible or unbelievable about Old Testament miracles than about those in the New Testament. In fact, once the existence of a theistic God is granted, then all miracles become possible. As *Lewis himself noted, "If we admit God must we admit miracle? Indeed, indeed, you have no security against it" (*Miracles,* 109). The greatest miracle of all—the resurrection of Christ—occurs in the New Testament. If this is historical, then there is no reason to reject the lesser miracles of Moses, Elijah, or Elisha.

Sources

G. L. Archer, Jr., *A Survey of Old Testament Introduction*
N. L. Geisler, *Miracles*
———, *Miracles and the Modern Mind*, Appendix B
C. S. Lewis, *God in the Dock*
———, *Miracles*
H. Lockyer, *All the Miracles in the Bible*

Miracles of Jesus. ***See*** **MIRACLES IN THE BIBLE.**

Missing Links, Evolutionary. Evolutionists believe in the common ancestry of all plants and animals, including humans. This theory of macro-evolution (*see* EVOLUTION; EVOLUTION, BIOLOGICAL) entails the belief that all higher forms of life evolved from lower forms by small changes over multimillions of years. However, they acknowledge that the fossil record studied by paleontology does not reveal such a finely graded series of animal forms in the proper time sequences. These transitional fossils that should be in the ground but are not are called "missing links" in the evolutionary chain.

The father of modern evolution himself, Charles Darwin, recognized this as a serious problem when he wrote in *On the Origin of Species:* "Why then is not every geological formation and every stratum full of such intermediate links? Geology assuredly does not reveal any such finely graduated organic chain, and this, perhaps, is the most obvious and gravest objection which can be urged against my theory" (152). Of course, Darwin hoped that enough of these "missing links" would eventually be found to substantiate what he called the "theory of evolution" as opposed to the "theory of creation" (235, 435, 437).

In the century and a half since Darwin wrote (1859) millions of fossils have been unearthed. But the "missing links" needed to confirm his theory have not been found. In fact, some species thought to be transitional have been found not to be real transitional fossils after all, so that the record is actually more bleak today than in Darwin's time! Harvard paleontologist Stephen Jay Gould has confessed that "The extreme rarity of transitional forms in the fossil record persists as the trade secret of paleontology. The evolutionary trees that adorn our textbooks have data only at the tips and nodes of their branches; the rest is inference, however reasonable, not the evidence of fossils" (Gould, 14).

Niles Eldredge agrees, reasoning that, "expectation colored perception to such an extent that the *most obvious single fact about biological evolution—non-change—*has seldom, if ever, been incorporated into anyone's scientific notions of how life actually evolves. If ever there was a myth, it is that evolution is a process of constant change" (Eldredge, 8).

Gould frankly acknowledged that the history of most fossil species includes two features particularly inconsistent with gradualism:

> *Stasis.* Most species exhibit no directional change during their tenure on earth. They appear in the fossil record looking much the same as when they disappear; morphological change is usually limited and directionless.
>
> *Sudden appearance.* In any local area, a species does not arise gradually by the steady transformation of its ancestors. It appears all at once, "fully formed" (Gould, 13–14). So, it is fair to say that the evolution theory, as Darwin conceived of it, has not been verified by the only source of real evidence of what actually happened, the fossil record.

Explanation of "Missing Links." Although the failure to find "missing links" has disappointed evolutionists, few have given up the theory for lack of them. Rather, they respond in various ways:

- Some transitional fossils exist to support evolution, so perhaps others will be found. Horse fossils are cited as an example of an existing fossil series.
- A tiny fraction of all the animals that ever lived have been preserved in fossils. And only a very small fraction of all fossils have been unearthed. So, we should not expect that many "missing links" will be found.
- By their nature transitional fossils were few. This adds to their rarity.
- Many species had soft parts that perished easily and would not have been preserved.
- Many evolutionists favor a view called "punctuated equilibrium," which contends that evolution occurred more rapidly than previously thought. There are leaps in the fossil record. Evolution, they claim, is more like a ball bouncing up a staircase than one rolling up a hill.
- Crucial links have been found between primates and human beings. These include Neanderthals, Peking Man, Austriapithicus, Lucie, and others.

Response to Missing-Link View. Responses of creationists to these defenses of evolutionary theory follow several lines of reasoning.

Even if a finely graded series of fossils were found, so that there were fewer missing pieces in the progression, this would not prove evolution. Similarity and progress do not necessarily prove common ancestry; they may be evidence of a common Creator. Evolutionists sometimes speak of the evolution of the airplane or of the car, from simple to later more complex models. However, neither the car nor the airplane evolved by natural forces producing small changes over a long period of time. In both cases there was intelligent interference from the outside that created a new model similar to previous ones. These illustrations actually support the creationist model of a common Designer, rather than an evolutionary common ancestor.

This leads to another problem: Different life forms can be similar outwardly or even in the basic components of their genetic code, yet be part of entirely different systems. Just as it requires intelligence to create *King Lear* from selected words of the language, so it also requires intelligence to select and sort genetic information to produce a variety of species that fit together in a biosystem.

Also, the genetic code of one form of life differs from another the way Henry Ford's Model T differs from a Mercedes. There are basic similarities, but they are quite different systems. And systemic changes must appear simultaneously for the system to work; they cannot be gradual. That is, the whole new system must come into existence as a functioning whole. But simultaneous, systematic change in an already functioning organism is consistent with creation, not evolution. One can make small changes in a car gradually over time without changing its basic type. Changes can be made in the shape of the fenders, its color, and its trim gradually. But if a change is made in the size of the pistons, this involves simultaneous changes in the cam shaft, block, cooling system, engine compartment, and other systems. Otherwise the new engine will not function (Denton, 11). Likewise, changing a fish to a reptile or a reptile to a bird involves major, simultaneous changes in every biological system of the animal. Gradual evolution cannot account for this. The same applies to the far more complex system of the genetic code.

The very concept of "missing link" begs the question in favor of evolution. The analogy envisions a chain with some breaks. The true picture can only be described as a few links with a *missing chain*. There are gigantic "gaps" between the major types of life at every "level" of the alleged evolutionary hierarchy. However, the whole analogy of a chain assumes a "chain" of evolution was there, and that there are missing "links" to be found. This superimposes an analogy in favor of evolution on the fossil record, rather than examining what is actually in the fossil record. An unbiased study of this record reveals, not sections of a chain, but different basic forms, which appear suddenly, simultaneously, fully formed and functioning, reproducing their kind, and remaining basically unchanged throughout their geological history. This evidence points to an intelligent creator.

There are fewer transitional fossils today than in Darwin's day. For many things thought to be transitional turned out not to be. The evolution of the horse is a case in point. Even evolutionists acknowledge that the alleged progression is not a continuous transformational series. There is a devolution in some cases (e.g., the number of ribs in the earlier Eohippus is 18 and the later Orohippus is 15). Likewise the number of ribs in the earlier Pliohippus is 19 while the later Equus Scotti is 18. Even most evolutionists have given this up as a proof of evolution. The smallest (dog-sized) animal in the series (Eohippus) is not a horse but a rock badger.

Among the few alleged "missing links" found, Coelacanth (a sturdy fin fish from the Devonian Period) is not half-fish and half-reptile. It is 100 percent fish. None were ever found with feet evolving on them. In fact, they have been found alive today and look identical to those in the fossil record of some 60 million years ago. Likewise, Archaeopteryx is not half bird and half reptile. Other ancient birds had teeth as it does. Some current birds, such as the ostrich, have claws in their wings. Archaeopteryx has perfectly formed feathers and wings—something necessary for flight. Neither are simple tool-making primates proof of evolution. Even some birds and seals use things as tools. Primates, however, did not make space rockets or computers.

Discovery of so-called "missing links" between primates and humans does not support macro-evolution (*see* LUBENOW).

Logically, the physical similarities among the species does not prove common ancestry. An alternative explanation is that they have a common Creator, who designed them to live in similar environments. Genetics is the only way to prove linkage. Unfortunately, there is no way to reconstruct the genetic structure of bones uncovered. It is what is "under the hood" that counts. And the gap between a primate and human brain is immense. And this gap does not refer merely to the size of the brain but to its complexity and ability to create art, human language, and highly complex mechanisms.

Further, some of the bones once widely touted as transitional species are now known not to have been, even by evolutionists. Piltdown Man, a basic form in science texts and museums for years, turned out to be a fraud. Nebraska Man was a reconstruction from one tooth, which turned out to be that of an extinct pig. Yet Nebraska Man was used as evidence in the Scopes Trial (1925) to support teaching evolution in public schools. The fossil evidence for Peking Man vanished. Some question its validity, based on studies before the pieces of bone disappeared. One serious problem is that this creature was killed by a sharp object, a highly unlikely cause of death for a prehuman. Even some evolutionists believe Australopithecine was an orangutan. Not one primate fossil find to date that has been subjected to objective scientific scrutiny is a strong candidate for the human family tree. Despite alleged genetic differences, Neanderthals had a larger brain capacity than modern man and evidence of religious ritual, characteristics normally associated with rational and moral beings. With this history, there is reason to question other fragmentary finds. The bent posture of Piltdown has been traced to a bone deformity resulting from a vitamin deficiency cave-dwellers experience from lack of sunlight.

Even if other primates *morphologically* similar to human beings are uncovered, this will not mean that they were *spiritually* the same. Behind the human form and shape is a human mind and soul (*see* IMMORTALITY). The human person has reflective self-consciousness unique to itself, and it has language, with its grammatical rule-oriented structure. What is more, humans have religious consciousness and practices; primates do not. All attempts to show physical similarities between primates and human beings as a basis for evolution overlook the gigantic gulf between the animal kingdom and a human being created in the image and likeness of God (Gen. 1:27).

Sources

W. R. Bird, *The Origin of Species Revisited*, 2 vols.
C. Darwin, *On the Origin of Species*
M. Denton, *Evolution: A Theory in Crisis*
N. Eldredge, *The Myths of Human Evolution*
N. L. Geisler, *Is Man the Measure?* chap. 11
———, *Origin Science* (chap. 7)
D. Gish, *Evolution: The Fossils Say No*
S. J. Gould, "Evolution's Erratic Pace," in *Natural History* (1972)
A. Johnson, *Darwinism on Trial*
M. Lubenow, *Bones of Contention*
J. Moore, *The Post-Darwinian Controversies*
C. Thaxton, et al., eds., *Of Pandas and People*

Mithraism. Some contemporary critics of Christianity argue that this religion is not based in divine revelation but was borrowed from mystery religions, such as Mithraism. Muslim author Yousuf Saleem Chishti attributes such doctrines as the deity of Christ and the atonement to the pagan teachings of the Apostle Paul and the doctrine of the *Trinity to pagan formulations of the church Fathers.

Pagan Source Theory. Chishti attempts to demonstrate a vast influence of mystery religions on Christianity, stating, "The Christian doctrine of atonement was greatly coloured by the influence of the mystery religions, especially Mithraism, which had its own son of God and virgin Mother, and crucifixion and resurrection after expiating for the sins of mankind and finally his ascension to the 7th heaven." He adds, "If you study the teachings of Mithraism side by side with that of Christianity, you are sure to be amazed at the close affinity which is visible between them, so much so that many critics are constrained to conclude that Christianity is the facsimile or the second edition of Mithraism" (Chishti, 87).

Chishti lists some similarities between Christ and Mithra: Mithra was considered the son of God, he was a savior, he was born of a virgin, he had twelve disciples, he was crucified, he rose from the grave the third day, he atoned for the sins of humankind, and he returned to his father in heaven (ibid., 87–88).

Evaluation. An honest reading of the New Testament data shows that Paul did not teach a new religion or draw on existing mythology. The foundation stones for Christianity are patently taken from the Old Testament, Judaism generally, and the life of a historical figure named Jesus.

Jesus and the Origin of Paul's Religion. A careful study of Epistles and Gospels reveals that the source of Paul's teachings on salvation was the Old Testament and the teachings of Jesus. A simple comparison of both Jesus' and Paul's teachings will demonstrate the point.

Both taught that Christianity fulfilled Judaism. Paul, similar to Jesus, taught that Christianity was a fulfillment of Judaism. Jesus declared: "Do not think that I have come to abolish the Law or the Prophets; I have not come to abolish them but to fulfill them" (Matt. 5:17). Jesus added, "The Law and the Prophets were proclaimed until John. Since that time, the good news of the kingdom of God is being preached, and everyone is forcing his way into it. It is easier for heaven and earth to disappear than for the least stroke of a pen to drop out of the Law" (Luke 16:16–17).

The Christ of Paul and Jesus is utterly at home in Judaism and foreign to the mystery cults. Paul wrote to the Romans: "Christ is the end of the law so that there may be righteousness for everyone who believes" (Rom. 10:4). He added in Colossians, "Therefore do not let anyone judge you by what you eat or drink, or with regard to a religious festival, a New Moon celebration or a Sabbath day. These are a shadow of the things that were to come; the reality, however, is found in Christ" (Col. 2:16–17).

Christianity taught that humans are sinful. Both Paul and Jesus taught that human beings are sinners. Jesus declared: "I tell you the truth, all the sins and blasphemies of men will be forgiven them" (Mark 3:28). He added in John, "I told you that you would die in your sins; if you do not believe that I am [the one I claim to be], you will indeed die in your sins" (John 8:24).

Paul declared that all human beings are sinful, insisting that "all have sinned and fall short of the glory of God" (Rom. 3:23). He added in Ephesians, "As for you, you were dead in your transgressions and sins" (Eph. 2:1). Indeed, part of the very definition of the Gospel was that "Christ died for our sins according to the Scriptures" (1 Cor. 15:3).

Christianity taught that blood atonement is necessary. Both Jesus and Paul insisted that the shed blood of Christ was necessary as an atonement for our sins (*see* Christ, Death of). Jesus proclaimed: "For even the Son of Man did not come to be served, but to serve, and to give his life as a ransom for many" (Mark 10:45). He added at the Last Supper, "This is my blood of the covenant, which is poured out for many for the forgiveness of sins" (Matt. 26:28).

Paul is just as emphatic. He affirmed that "In him [Christ] we have redemption through his blood, the forgiveness of sins, in accordance with the riches of God's grace" (Eph. 1:7). In Romans he added, "But God demonstrates his own love for us in this: While we were still sinners, Christ died for us" (5:8). Referring back to the Old Testament Passover, he said, "Christ, our Passover lamb, has been sacrificed" (1 Cor. 5:7).

Christianity emphasized Christ's resurrection. Jesus and Paul also taught that the death and burial of Jesus was completed by his bodily resurrection (*see* Resurrection, Evidence for; Resurrection, Physical Nature of). Jesus said, "He told them, 'This is what is written: The Christ will suffer and rise from the dead on the third day'" (Luke 24:46). Jesus challenged, "Destroy this temple, and I will raise it again in three days. . . . But the temple he had spoken of was his body" (John 2:19, 21).

After he was raised from the dead, his disciples recalled what he had said. Then they believed the Scripture and the words that Jesus had spoken (John 2:22; cf. 20:25–29).

The apostle Paul also stressed the need of the resurrection for salvation. To the Romans he wrote: "He [Jesus] was delivered over to death for our sins and was raised to life for our justification" (Rom. 4:25). Indeed, Paul insisted that belief in the resurrection was essential to salvation, writing, "That if you confess with your mouth, 'Jesus is Lord,' and believe in your heart that God raised him from the dead, you will be saved" (Rom. 10:9).

Christianity taught salvation is by grace through faith. Jesus affirmed that every person needs God's grace. Jesus' disciples said to him, "Who then can be saved?" Jesus looked at them and said, "With man this is impossible, but with God all things are possible" (Matt. 19:25–26). All through the Gospel of John Jesus presented only one way to obtain God's gracious salvation: "Whoever believes in the Son has eternal life" (3:36; cf. 3:16; 5:24; Mark 1:15).

Paul taught salvation by grace through faith, affirming, "It is by grace you have been saved, through faith—and this not from yourselves, it is the gift of God—not by works, so that no one can boast" (Eph. 2:8–9; cf. Titus 3:5–7). He added to the Romans, "To the man who does not work but trusts God who justifies the wicked, his faith is credited as righteousness" (4:5).

A comparison of the teachings of Jesus and Paul on salvation reveals clearly that there is no basis for speculating on any source of Paul's teachings other than that of Jesus. Christianity was rooted in Judaism, not in Mithraism. Indeed, Paul's message of the gospel was both checked and approved by the original apostles (Gal. 1–2), demonstrating official recognition that his message was not opposed to that of Jesus (see Habermas, 67–72). The charge that Paul corrupted Jesus' original message was long ago answered by J. Gresham *Machen in his classic work, *The Origin of Paul's Religion* and F. F. *Bruce, *Paul and Jesus*.

Origin of the Trinity. The Christian doctrine of the Trinity does not have a pagan origin. Pagan religions were *polytheistic and *pantheistic, but trinitarians are monotheists (*see* Theism). Trinitarians are not tritheists who believe in three separate gods; they are monotheists who believe in one God manifested in three distinct persons.

Though the term **Trinity* or its specific formulation does not appear in the Bible, it faithfully expresses all the biblical data. An accurate understanding of the historical and theological development of this doctrine amply illustrates that it was exactly because of the dangers of paganism that the Council of Nicea formulated the orthodox doctrine of the Trinity. For a brief treatment of the history of this doctrine see E. Calvin Beisner, *God in Three Persons*. Two classics in this field are G. L. Prestige, *God in Patristic Thought*, and J. N. D. Kelly, *Early Christian Doctrines*.

Mithraism and Christianity. From the foregoing it is evident that Judaism and the teachings of Jesus were the origin of Christianity. It is equally clear that Mithraism was not. Chishti's descriptions of this religion are baseless. In fact he gives no reference for the similarities he alleges.

Unlike Christianity (*see* NEW TESTAMENT, HISTORICITY OF), Mithraism is based in myth. Ronald Nash, the author of *Christianity and the Hellenistic World,* writes:

> We do know that Mithraism, like its mystery competitors, had a basic myth. Mithra was supposedly born when he emerged from a rock; he was carrying a knife and torch and wearing a Phrygian cap. He battled first with the sun and then with a primeval bull, thought to be the first act of creation. Mithra slew the bull, which then became the ground of life for the human race. [Nash, 144]

Christianity affirms the physical death and bodily resurrection of Christ. Mithaism, like other pagan religions, has no bodily resurrection. The Greek writer Aeschylus sums up the Greek view, "When the earth has drunk up a man's blood, once he is dead, there is no resurrection." He uses the same Greek word for "resurrection," *anastasis*, that Paul uses in 1 Corinthians 15 (Aeschylus, *Eumenides*, 647). Nash notes:

> Allegations of an early Christian dependence on Mithraism have been rejected on many grounds. Mithraism had no concept of the death and resurrection of its god and no place for any concept of rebirth—at least during its early stages. . . . During the early stages of the cult, the notion of rebirth would have been foreign to its basic outlook. . . . Moreover, Mithraism was basically a military cult. Therefore, one must be skeptical about suggestions that it appealed to nonmilitary people like the early Christians. [ibid.]

Mithraism flowered after Christianity, not before, so Christianity could not have copied from Mithraism. The timing is all wrong to have influenced the development of first-century Christianity (ibid., 147; *see* MYTHOLOGY AND THE NEW TESTAMENT).

Conclusion. All the allegations of Christian dependence on *Gnostic or mystery religions (*see* NAG HAMMADI GOSPELS) have been rejected by the scholars in biblical and classical studies (ibid., 119). The historic character of Christianity and the early date of the New Testament documents did not allow enough time for mythological developments. And there is a complete lack of *early* historical evidence to support such ideas. The British scholar Norman Anderson explains:

> The basic difference between Christianity and the mysteries is the historic basis of the one and the mythological character of the others. The deities of the mysteries were no more than "nebulous figures of an imaginary past," while the Christ whom the apostolic *kerygma* proclaimed had lived and died only a few years before the first New Testament documents were written. Even when the apostle Paul wrote his first letter to the Corinthians the majority of some five hundred witnesses to the resurrection were still alive. [Anderson, 52–53]

Sources

N. Anderson, *Christianity and World Religions*
E. C. Beisner, *God in Three Persons*
F. F. Bruce, *Paul and Jesus*
Y. S. Chishti, *What Is Christianity?*
G. Habermas, *The Verdict of History*
J. N. D. Kelly, *Early Christian Doctrines*
J. G. Machen, *The Origin of Paul's Religion*
R. Nash, *Christianity and the Hellenistic World*
G. L. Prestige, *God in Patristic Thought*
H. Ridderbos, *Paul and Jesus*

Modalism. Modalism is an unorthodox or heretical view of God that denies the orthodox trinitarian view that there are three distinct, co-eternal persons in the godhead (*see* TRINITY). Modalists claim that God simply manifests himself in different modes or forms at different times. Unfortunately, some illustrations used by trinitarians tend toward a modalistic concept of God. For example, modalists claim that God is like water, which can be manifested in one of three different modes at different times: liquid, gas, or solid.

Better illustrations are more appropriate to trinitarianism. They show that God is simultaneously a plurality within a unity, since he is three distinct persons in one eternal nature. God is like one triangle (his nature), which has three corners (his persons). In this illustration the three and one are simultaneous, not successive. Without three sides there is no triangle. Further, each corner differs from the others, yet all share in the nature of a triangle. Or God is like 1^3 ($1 \times 1 \times 1 = 1$). Here too there are three and one at the same time. It is not one manifest at three different times in three differing ways.

In modalism there is one person in the godhead. In this sense, modalism is more like the traditional monotheism of Islam, rather than trinitarian theism. In the Trinity, three distinct persons unite in one eternal nature.

Both trinitarianism and modalism are in contrast to tritheism, which affirms that there are three gods (1 + 1 + 1 = 3). This is a form of *polytheism. Like trinitarianism it has three different persons, but unlike trinitarianism, it believes three separate beings are each a god, with an individual nature. Orthodox trinitarians hold that God has only one nature, but that three distinct persons, co-eternal and co-equal, share this same nature (see bibliography under TRINITY).

Molinism. *Molinism* is a view of the relation between God's grace and human free will, emanating from the Spanish Jesuit theologian Luis de Molina (1535–1600). Molina asserted that God has a special kind of foreknowledge of human free acts, which are the basis of God's gracious gift of salvation. Molinism was widely adopted by Jesuits and opposed by Dominicans. After examination by a special congregation in Rome (1598–1607), both views were allowed in Catholic schools.

An Exposition of Molinism. According to Molinism, God has three kinds of knowledge: natural, middle, and free (Craig, *The Only Wise God,* 131).

Natural knowledge is God's knowledge of all possible worlds. This knowledge is essential to God. It is concerned with the necessary and the possible.

Free knowledge is God's knowledge of this actual world. After a free act of his will, God knows these things absolutely, but such knowledge is not essential to God.

Middle knowledge or *scientia media* is the distinctive of Molinism. God cannot know future free acts in the way he knows other things. God knows some things absolutely, but future free acts are known only contingently. "God, from a most profound and inscrutable comprehension of every free will in His essence, has intuited what each, according to its innate liberty, would do if placed in this or that condition" (Garrigou-Lagrange, *The One God*, 460; *see* FREE WILL). Unlike natural knowledge, this middle or intermediate knowledge is in some sense dependent on what free creatures choose to do. God's omniscience "waits" to see what a free creature does "before" he selects those who will be saved. Since God is eternal, the sequence is only logical, not chronological.

Arguments for Middle Knowledge. Argument from three states of affairs. One argument for *scientia media* is that there are three kinds of knowledge in God because there are three possible states of affairs. Between the merely possible and the necessary there is the contingent (free). Since God knows all future states, it follows that he must know them in the way in which they are (as three). Future free acts are contingent. God must know future free acts by way of an intermediate knowledge that is neither necessary nor merely possible, but is contingent on the way free creatures will choose.

Argument from the order of knowing. Logically, an event must occur before it can be true. It must be true before God can know it is true. God cannot know as true what is not yet true. Hence, God must wait (from a logical standpoint) the occurrence of free acts before he can know they are true.

Argument from the nature of truth. Truth corresponds to reality. God cannot know anything as true unless it actually has occurred. Since future free acts have not actually occurred, God's knowledge of them is dependent on their occurrence. Since their occurrence is contingent, God's knowledge of them is contingent.

Avoiding fatalism. A fourth argument is that middle knowledge is the only way to avoid fatalism. Theological fatalism holds that all things are predetermined necessarily, including what we call "free acts." But if we are truly free, then some things do not happen necessarily but contingently, upon free choices. But if some events are contingent, God's knowledge of them cannot be necessary. God must know what will be freely chosen to occur.

In addition, Molinists see great benefits to their view in explaining predestination, God's providence, the problems of evil (*see* EVIL, PROBLEM OF), and even *hell. "In the logical moment prior to creation, God had no idea how many would be saved and how many lost," according to one supporter (Craig, Ibid., 145–46). With regard to predestination, "the very act of selecting a world to be created is a sort of predestination. The person in that world who God knew would respond most certainly will respond and be saved. . . . Of course, if they were to reject his grace, God's middle knowledge would have been different. . . . As for the unsaved, the only reason they are not predestined is that they freely reject God's grace" (ibid., 136). The cost of having a certain number of elect is to have a certain number who will be lost. God so ordered things providentially that those who are lost would not have chosen Christ in any case (ibid., 148, 150).

Biblical Arguments for Molinism. Biblical arguments for Molinism are based on passages such as 1 Samuel 23:6–13 and Matthew 11:20–24. God knew that if David were to remain in the city, Saul would come to kill him. So if God's answers through the ephod are taken to be simple foreknowledge, his knowledge was false. What was predicted did not happen. Only if the answers are taken as what would happen under certain freely chosen circumstances were they true. This would indicate that God had contingent knowledge of them. In Matthew 11 Jesus asserts that the ancient cities he mentions would have repented if they had seen Jesus' miracles. But this makes sense only if God's knowledge is contingent on what they would have done.

Evaluation. Molinism assumes that God must "wait" to know things are true. But God is eternal, and an eternal perspective knows things "before" they occur in time. God knows things in eternity, not in time. All things preexist in their ultimate cause (God). So God knows things in himself from all eternity. He does not have to "wait" to know them.

Truth is correspondence to reality. But the reality to which God's knowledge corresponds is his own nature, by which he eternally and necessarily knows all things as they preexist in him. God's knowledge is not dependent on waiting for the effect to occur in time. The effect preexists most eminently in its Cause, so God knows all things that will happen most perfectly in himself "before" they happen in time.

God's Knowledge Is Not Contingent. God's knowledge is not dependent on the conditions of the object known. If what God knows is contingent, then he must know it contingently. But since God is a Necessary Being, he must know everything in accordance with his own nature, necessarily. Since God is eternal, all of his knowledge is intuitive, eternal, and necessary. Since his being is independent, and he must know in accord with his independent nature, it follows that God's knowledge is not dependent in any way.

Fatalism Is Not Necessary. Molinism is not the only alternative to fatalism. God can have *necessary* knowledge of *contingent* acts. He can know for sure what will happen freely. Just because he has certainty about an event does not mean that it does not occur freely. The same event can be necessary from the vantage point of God's knowledge and free from the standpoint of human choice (*see* DETERMINISM, FREE WILL). If God is omniscient, then he knows everything, including the fact that Judas would betray the Christ. If Judas had not betrayed Christ, God would have been wrong about what he knew. But that does not mean Judas was coerced. For God knew certainly that Judas would betray Christ freely. Just as prerecorded television news segments are of events that cannot be changed but were freely chosen, so God in his omniscience sees the future with the same certainty with which he sees the past.

One can hold the same solution to theological mysteries without being a Molinist. God's knowledge of the future can be necessary without any event being forced. The mysteries of predestination and providence are explained better by denying any contingency in God's knowledge of them, since fatalism does not follow from denying Molinism (*see* DETERMINISM; FREE WILL).

That God knows what people would have done under different conditions is not inconsistent with his knowledge being necessary. He simply knew with necessity what would have happened if people had chosen differently.

Evaluation. Thomists and Calvinists have strongly opposed Molinism as a denial of both the independence and grace of God.

According to Thomism, God is Pure Actuality; he has no passive potency at all (*see* ANALOGY, PRINCIPLE OF; ARISTOTLE; GOD, NATURE OF; THOMAS AQUINAS). If God had potency he would need a cause. But since he is the ultimate cause of all things, God is without potency (*see* GOD, NATURE OF). If Molinism is correct, then God is the passive recipient of the knowledge of free acts. God's "middle knowledge" is dependent on the events actually occurring. The great "I Am" becomes the "I Can Be." This implies a passivity that God as Pure Actuality cannot have. Hence, Molinism is contrary to the nature of God.

God Becomes an Effect. Another statement of the difficulty is that either God's knowledge is completely causal, determining all events, or it is determined by these events. There is no third alternative. Molinists say that God's knowledge is determined by future free acts. This sacrifices God as ultimate Cause. He is determined by events, not Determiner. This is contrary to the nature of God, for he becomes an epistemological spectator (ibid., 107).

Efficacious Grace Is Denied. Another objection is that Molinism denies God's efficacious grace in salvation. All that God wills comes to pass without our freedom being infringed upon. "He wills efficaciously that we freely consent and we do freely consent" (ibid., 401). Only in this way can God's grace be efficacious. God is the active Author of salvation (ibid., 398). As Aquinas says, "If God's intention is that this man, whose heart he is moving, shall receive sanctifying grace, then that man receives grace infallibly." God's intention cannot fail, and the saved are saved infallibly (*certissime*, says Augustine; ibid., 111).

While agreeing on the efficacious nature of grace, Thomists part company with strong Calvinists at this point. For Thomists, free creatures retain the power to choose not to follow God when God graciously and efficaciously moves them to choose according to his predetermined will. Strong Calvinists teach that this movement by the Holy Spirit in the Heart of the person choosing is irresistible. If it is God's will, that person *will* respond because the Spirit quickens the heart. Thomists insist that, "far from forcing the act, far from destroying . . . freedom, the divine motion instead actualized . . . freedom. When efficacious grace touches the free will, that touch is virginal, it does no violence, it only enriches" (ibid., 110). However, this is not essential to the anti-Molinist view. God's knowledge could be determinative of a free act without his causing the free act himself. This view was held by the early Augustine and moderate Calvinists (see Geisler).

Sources

W. Craig, *The Only Wise God*
———, *Divine Foreknowledge and Future Contingency from Aristotle to Suarez*
R. Garrigou-Lagrange, *God: His Existence and His Nature*
———, *Predestination*
———, *Reality: A Synthesis of Thomistic Thought*
———, *The One God*
N. Geisler in Basinger, *Predestination and Free Will*
L. De Molina, *On Divine Foreknowledge*
Thomas Aquinas, *Summa Contra Gentiles*
———, *Summa Theologica*

Monism. The study of reality is metaphysics. How reality is viewed is worldview. Fundamental to a person's worldview is whether they see the "one or many." This difference separates monists from pluralists and is so imbedded in the person's thought patterns that he or she seldom is aware that such a difference in viewpoint actually exists. Monism sees all as "one." God and the universe are one thing. Christianity is committed to the "many" of pluralism, holding that God differs from creation (*see* THEISM).

The Case for Monism. Monism, in contrast to all forms of pluralism, insists that all reality is one. Parmenides of Elea (b. ca. 515 B.C.) initially posed, or identified, the problem, and many philosophers since have grappled with his dilemma. Four answers have been proposed, but only one successfully solves the problem.

Parmenides argued that there cannot be more than one thing (*absolute monism*). If there were two things, they would have to differ. But for things to differ, they must differ by being or by nonbeing. Being is what which makes them identical, so they cannot differ by that. Nor can they differ by nonbeing, for nonbeing is nothing, and to differ by nothing is not to differ at all. Hence there cannot be a plurality of beings. There is only one single, indivisible being.

Alternatives to Monism. Basically, there are four alternatives to monism. Aristotelianism, Thomism, *Atomism* and *Platonism*, the latter two affirm that the many beings differ by nonbeing. Aristotelianism and Thomism hold that the many beings differ by being.

Things Differ by Absolute Nonbeing. With the generation of philosophers following Parmenides came the atomists, such as Leucippus and Democritus, who contended that the principle which separates one being (atom) from another is absolutely nothing (i.e., nonbeing). They called it the void. Being is full and nonbeing is an empty void. Atoms do not differ at all in their essence, but they are separated by different space. This difference, however, is merely extrinsic. There is no intrinsic difference in the atoms (beings). This answer was scarcely adequate. To differ by absolutely nothing is to have absolutely no difference. Whether the no difference is in one location or another makes no difference. To have absolutely no difference is to be absolutely the same. Monism wins the day over atomism.

Things Differ by Relative Nonbeing. Plato believed that things differ because differing forms or archetypes lie behind them. These ideas or forms, are the reality. All things in this world of our experience are only shadows of the real world. They have meaning because they participate in the true forms. For example, each individual human being participates in the universal form of humanness in the world of ideas.

Plato saw the weakness of his view and tried to escape by modifying it to the explanation that the forms or ideas are not indivisibly and unrelatably separated by absolute nonbeing; rather, they are related by *relative* nonbeing.

This relative nonbeing was also called the "other" (Plato, *Sophist,* 255d). Plato believed he could have many different forms (beings) and thus avoid monism. Each form differed from other forms in that it was not that other form.

All determination is by negation. A sculptor determines what the statue is in relation to the stone by chipping away what is unwanted. The finished form is other than what the sculpture would have been if different chips lay at the sculptor's feet. Likewise, each form is differentiated from every other form by what is not there. The chair is distinguished from everything else in the room in that it is *not* the table. It is *not* the floor or the wall, etc. The chair is not absolutely nothing. It has *chairness* in itself. But it is nothing in relation to other things, because it is not those other things.

Parmenides would not have been impressed by *Plato's attempt. He would have asked whether there was any difference in the beings themselves. If not, then he would have asserted that all these beings (forms) must then be identical. There are not many beings but only one.

Things Differ as Simple Beings. Both the atomist and Platonist took one horn of the Parmenidian dilemma. They tried to differentiate things by nonbeing. *Aristotle and *Thomas Aquinas sought to find a difference in the beings themselves. Both contended that beings are essentially different. Aristotle held that these beings are metaphysically simple (Aristotle, IX, 5, 1017a 35b-a). Thomas Aquinas viewed them as metaphysically composite.

See the article ARISTOTLE for the full argument that there is a plurality of forty-seven or fifty-five unmoved movers that are separate from one another in their very being. This plurality of beings causes all motion in the world, each from its own cosmic domain. Each is a pure form with no matter. Matter differentiates things in this world. This plurality of totally separated substantial forms has no commonness or community of being. The movers are completely diverse, one from another. They cannot be related (see Eslick, 152–53).

Parmenides would ask Aristotle how simple beings can differ in their very being. Things composed of form and matter can differ in that one particular matter differs from all other matter, even though they have the same form. But how do pure forms (beings) differ? Here is no principle of differentiation. If there is no difference in their beings, their being is identical. Aristotle's solution does not avoid monism.

Thomism: Things Differ as Complex Beings. The fourth pluralistic alternative to Parmenidean monism is represented by Thomas Aquinas, who with Aristotle, sought difference within beings themselves. But unlike Aristotle, who began with simple beings, Aquinas believed that all finite beings are compositions. Only God is an absolutely simple Being, and there can be only one such Being (God). However, there can be other kinds of being, namely, composed beings. Beings differ in their very being because there can be different kinds of beings (Aquinas, 1a. 4, 1, ad 3). God, for example, is an infinite kind of being. All creatures are finite kinds of beings. God is pure actuality; all creatures are composed of both actuality and potentiality. Hence, finite things differ from God in that they have a limiting potentiality; he does not. Finite things can differ from each other in whether their potentiality is completely actualized (as in angels) or whether it is being progressively actualized (as in human beings). But in all creatures their essence (whatness) is really distinct from their existence (isness). God's essence and existence are identical. Aquinas was not the first to make this distinction, but he was the first to make such extensive use of it.

Aquinas argues in his book *On Being and Essence* that existence is something other than essence except in God, whose essence is his existence. Such a being must be one and unique, since multiplication of anything is only possible where there is a difference. But in God there is no difference. It follows necessarily that in everything else, except this one unique existence, existence must be one thing and essence another.

This answered the dilemma posed by monism. Things do differ in their being because they are different kinds of beings. Parmenides was wrong because he assumed that "being" is always understood univocally (the same way). Aquinas saw that being is analogous (*see* ANALOGY, PRINCIPLE OF). This means each being can be understood in similar but different ways. All beings that exist are the same in that they are all *actual.* Finite beings differ from the one infinite Being in that they have differing potentialities to become other things, or to cease being. And they have differing actualizations of those individual potentials.

Superiority of the Thomistic Position. Aquinas' view has value both in its own rationality and in the implausibility of its alternatives. Parmenides' position does violence to our experience of a differentiated, yet interrelated, multiplicity of beings.

The *Thomistic* position on plurality is that multiplicity is possible because each thing has its own mode of *be*-ing. Essence, the principle of differentiation, is real. This is not to say that essence is independent of existence. Essence is real *because* it exists. The real distinction within being between essence *(essentia)* and existence *(esse)* seems to be the only satisfactory answer to the Parmenidian problem of unity and plurality. Without an analogy of being, there is no way to account for multiplicity.

Parmenides saw no multiplicity because he saw all being univocally. Things are either totally unrelated or totally identical. There was no middle ground. If all being is univocal, then all being is identical. There is no room for distinction; it is all one Being. This is why the monistic worldview lacks any possibility of a Creator-creature distinction. It is why monistic religions view the ultimate hope as becoming submerged into "god." Everything else is nonbeing. The only way to avoid the monistic conclusion which follows from either an equivocal or a univocal view of beings is to take an analogical view. And the only way being can be analogical is if there is within being both the principle of unification *and* the principle of differentiation. Since finite beings have different potentialities (essences), these finite beings can be differentiated in reality when these potentialities are actualized or brought into existence in different kinds of being.

Conclusion. Being is that which is. How many beings are there? Being can be either simple (pure actuality) or complex (actuality and potentiality). There cannot be two absolutely simple beings, since there is nothing in a completely simple being by which it could differ from another. A simple being must, however, differ from complex beings, since it has no potentiality and they do. This is the Creator-creature distinction. It is why there can be only one pure and simple God, but many created beings that mix actuality and potency or potentiality. Only one *is* Being; everything else *has* being. This appears to be the only adequate answer to monism.

Sources

Aristotle, *Metaphysics*

L. J. Eslick, "The Real Distinction," *Modern Schoolman* 38 (January 1961)

Parmenides, *Proem*

Plato, *Parmenides*

———, *Sophist*

R. J. Teske, "Plato's Later Dialectic," *Modern Schoolman* 38 (March 1961)

Thomas Aquinas, *On Being and Essence*

———, *Summa Theologiae*

Monotheism. *See* THEISM; ISLAM; MONOTHEISM, PRIMITIVE.

Monotheism, Primitive. The Bible teaches that monotheism was the earliest conception of God. The very first verse of Genesis is monotheistic: "In the beginning God created the heavens and the earth" (Gen. 1:1). The patriarchs Abraham, Isaac, and Jacob reflect an early monotheism. Job, the only other biblical book that is set in an ancient pre-Mosaic period, clearly has a monotheistic view of God (see, for example, Job 1:1, 6, 21). Romans 1:19–25 teaches that monotheism preceded animism and polytheism and that these forms of religion resulted as people sinfully exchanged the glory of God for "images made to look like mortal man and birds and animals and reptiles."

Monotheism, Early or Late? *Frazer's Late Monotheism.* Since James *Frazer published *The Golden Bough* (1912) it has been widely believed that religions evolved from animism through *polytheism to *henotheism and finally monotheism. Even before this Charles *Darwin set the stage for such an evolutionary scheme. Frazer alleged that Christianity copied pagan myths. In spite of its selective use of anecdotal data, that have been outdated by subsequent research, the book still holds wide influence, and its ideas are assumed true. Frazer's evolutionary thesis of religion actually is without foundation, as is noted in the article on his work.

Arguments for Early Monotheism. There is substantial evidence to support the work of Schmidt (see Schmidt) that monotheism is the primitive belief about God. Arguments for a primitive monotheism come from the earliest records and traditions that have survived. These include not only the Bible, but also the Ebla Tablets and studies of preliterate tribes. Genesis represents the oldest records of the human race, going back to the first man and woman. Archaeologist William F. *Albright has demonstrated that the Genesis patriarchal record is historical. "Thanks to modern research," he wrote, "we now recognize its [Scripture's] substantial historicity. The narratives of the patriarchs, of Moses and the exodus, of the conquest of Canaan, of the judges, the monarchy, exile and restoration, have all been confirmed and illustrated to an extent that I should have thought impossible forty years ago" (*From the Stone Age to Christianity*, 1).

Genesis is both a literary and genealogical work, tied together by a listing of family descendants (Genesis 5, 10) and the literary formula: "this is the history [or account] of." The phrase is used throughout Genesis (2:4; 5:1; 6:9; 10:1; 11:10, 27; 25:12, 19; 36:1, 9; 32:2). What is more, events from every one of the disputed first 11 chapters of Genesis are referred to by Jesus and New Testament writers as historical. This includes the existence of Adam and Eve (see Matt. 19:4–5), the temptation (1 Tim. 2:14) and fall (Rom. 5:12), the sacrifices of Cain and Abel (Heb. 11:4), the murder of Abel by Cain (1 John 3:12), the birth of Seth (Luke 3:38), the translation of Enoch to heaven (Heb. 11:5), marriage before the flood, the flood and destruction of humanity (Matt. 24:39), preservation of Noah and his family (2 Peter 2:5), the genealogy of Shem (Luke 3:35–36), and the birth of Abraham (Luke 3:34).

There is strong evidence for the historicity of Adam and Eve in particular. Yet this record reveals that these first persons were monotheists (Gen. 1:1, 27; 2:16–17; 4:26; 38:6–7).

Behind Genesis, Job is the oldest biblical book, yet this too reveals a monotheistic view of God. God is the personal (Job 1: 6, 21), moral (1:1; 8:3–4), yet sovereign (42:1–2) and almighty (5:17; 6:14; 8:3; 13:3) Creator (4:17; 9:8–9; 26:7; 38:6–7).

Aside from the Bible, the oldest relevant records come from *Ebla* in Syria. They reveal a clear monotheism, declaring, "Lord of heaven and earth, the earth was not, you created it, the light of day was not, you created it, the morning light you had not made exist" (Pettinato, *The Archives of Ebla,* 259).

Primitive religions of Africa unanimously reveal an explicit monotheism. John Mbiti studied three hundred traditional religions. "In all these societies, without a single exception, people have a notion of God as the Supreme Being" (see *African Religions and Philosophy*). This is true of primitive religions around the world. Even in polytheistic societies, a high god or sky god reflects a latent monotheism.

The idea of a late, evolved monotheism is itself late, only gaining popularity in the wake of Charles Darwin and his theory of biological evolution (see *On the Origin of Species*, 1859). The idea was stated by Darwin himself in *The Descent of Man* (1871). Frazer's evolutionary idea in religion is based on several unproven assumptions. Among them, it assumes that biological evolution is true, though it lacks support (*see* EVOLUTION, BIOLOGICAL). Even if biological evolution were true, there is no reason to believe evolution would be true of religion.

Frazer's evolution of monotheism thesis also is based on fragmentary and anecdotal evidence, not a serious historical and chronological search for origins of monotheism. It fits evidence around an evolutionary model. The evidence can be explained as well, if not better, if polytheism were a degeneration from original monotheism. Paganism is a falling away from the primitive monotheism. Albright acknowledges that "high gods may be all-powerful and they may be credited with creation of the world; they are generally cosmic deities who often, perhaps usually, reside in heaven" (*From the Stone Age*, 170). This clearly runs counter to the animistic and polytheistic conceptions.

Conclusion. There is no real reason to deny the biblical account of an early monotheism. On the contrary, there is every evidence that monotheism was the first religion, from which others devolved, just as Romans 1:19–25 declares. This better fits the evidence of the existence of a monotheistic God (*see* GOD, EVIDENCE FOR) and the proven tendency of human beings to distort the truth God reveals to them (*see* NOETIC EFFECTS OF SIN).

Sources

W. F. Albright, *From the Stone Age to Christianity*
G. W. Braswell, *Understanding World Religions*
A. Custance, *The Doorway Papers*
J. G. Frazer, *The Golden Bough*
E. O. James, "Frazer, James George," in *NTCERK*
E. Merrill, "Ebla and Biblical Historical Inerrancy," in *Sacra* (October-December, 1983)
J. Mbiti, *African Religions*
J. S. Mbiti, *African Religions and Philosophy*
———, *Concepts of God in Africa*
B. Pettinato, *The Archives of Ebla*
W. Schmidt, *High Gods in North America*
———, *The Origin and Growth of Religion*
———, *Primitive Revelation*

Moral Argument for God. Most arguments for the existence of God, such as the *cosmological argument and *teleological argument, are from the ancient world. The *ontological argument comes from medieval times. But the moral argument has modern ancestry, emanating from the works of Immanuel Kant.

Kant's Moral Postulate. Kant strongly rejected traditional arguments for God's existence (*see* GOD, OBJECTIONS TO PROOFS FOR). He did not, however, reject belief in God. Rather, he believed that God's existence is a practically (morally) necessary *postulate*, even though we cannot *prove* it.

Kant's argument from practical reason for God's existence, from his *Critique of Practical Reason*, can be stated:

1. Happiness is what all human beings desire.
2. Morality (viz., categorical imperative) is the duty of all human beings (what they ought to do).
3. The unity of happiness and duty is the greatest good (the *summum bonum*).
4. The *summum bonum* ought to be sought (since it is the greatest good).
5. But the unity of desire and duty (which is the greatest good) is not possible by finite human beings in limited time.
6. And the moral necessity of doing something implies the possibility of doing it (ought implies can).
7. Therefore, it is morally (i.e., practically) necessary to postulate: (a) a Deity to make this unity possible (i.e., a power to bring them together), and (b) immortality to make this unity achievable.

A simpler form goes:

1. The greatest good of all persons is that they have happiness in harmony with duty.
2. All persons should strive for the greatest good.
3. What persons ought to do, they can do.
4. But persons are not able to realize the greatest good in this life or without God.
5. Therefore, we must postulate a God and a future life in which the greatest good can be achieved.

Kant never offered his postulate as a *theoretical proof* for God. He did not believe such proof to be possible. Rather, he viewed God's existence as a morally necessary presupposition, not the result of a rationally necessary argument.

Kant's premises are challenged. *Existentialists, including Jean-Paul *Sartre and Albert Camus and atheists such as Friedrich *Nietzsche challenged the assumption that the greatest good is achievable. Although they lived before Kant, Martin *Luther and John *Calvin, with other Protestant Reformers, denied that ought implies can. Still others, from *Aristotle forward, believed the greatest good is achievable in this life.

Rashdall's Moral Argument. Hastings Rashdall did what Kant never attempted when he offered a rational argument for the existence of God from the moral law. Beginning with the objectivity of the moral law, he reasoned to an absolutely perfect moral Mind (see Hick, 144–52).

1. An absolutely perfect moral ideal exists (at least psychologically in our minds).
2. An absolutely perfect moral law can exist only if there is an absolutely perfect moral Mind: (a) Ideas can exist only if there are minds (thoughts depend on thinkers). (b) And absolute ideas depend on an absolute Mind (not on individual [finite] minds like ours).
3. Hence, it is rationally necessary to postulate an absolute Mind as the basis for the absolutely perfect moral idea.

In support of the objectivity of the absolute moral idea Rashdall offers this reasoning:

1. Morality is generally understood as objectively binding.
2. Mature minds understand morality as being objectively binding (i.e., binding on all, not just some).
3 Moral objectivity is a rationally necessary postulate (because something cannot be judged as better or worse unless there is an objective standard of comparison).
4. Objective moral ideals are practically necessary to postulate.

If an objective moral law exists independent of individual minds, then it must ultimately come from a Mind that exists independently of finite minds. It is rationally necessary to postulate such a Mind in order to account for the objective existence of this moral law.

The most common ways to challenge this argument are to question the existence of an objective moral law, and to deny that an absolute moral ideal would need an absolute moral Mind. Why cannot a finite mind conjure up the idea of moral perfection without there being any in the real world. After all, cannot we think of perfect triangles without there being one?

Sorley's Moral Argument. The moral argument is dependent on the objectivity of the moral law. Hence, it is necessary to offer a defense of this premise. This is precisely what W. R. Sorley does in his version of the moral argument for God's existence. Since there exists a moral ideal prior to, superior to, and independent of all finite minds, there must be a supreme moral Mind from which this moral ideal is derived:

1. There is an objective moral law that is independent of human consciousness of it and that exists in spite of human lack of conformity to it: (a) Persons are conscious of such a law beyond themselves; (b) Persons admit its validity is prior to their recognition of it; (c) Persons acknowledge its claim on them, even while not yielding to it; (d) no finite mind completely grasps its significance; (e) all finite minds together have not reached complete agreement on its meaning, nor conformity with its ideal.
2. But ideas exist only in minds.
3. Therefore, there must be a supreme Mind (beyond all finite minds) in which this objective moral law exists.

Sorley draws attention to an important difference between a natural law and this moral law. The former is descriptive of the universe, while the latter is prescriptive of human behavior. Hence, the moral law cannot be part of the natural world. It is the way humans ought to act. It is beyond the natural world and is the way we should behave in the world.

Critics of Sorley's form of the moral argument claim that simply because persons *believe* there is a moral law beyond them and independent of them, does not mean it *really* is. Following *Feuerbach, they believe that such a law is only a projection of human imagination. It is a collective ideal of human consciousness (or unconsciousness), which conjures up the best from human nature as an ideal by which we should live. Critics also point to differences in understanding of morals as an indication that there is no one universal moral law but merely a collection of different human ideals that overlap and are thereby confused as one moral law. Finally, critics challenge the premise that only a supreme, extrahuman Mind can be the basis for this universal moral ideal. Perfect ideas can be created by imperfect minds, they say.

Trueblood's Moral Argument. Evangelical philosopher Elton *Trueblood adds significantly to the moral arguments proposed by Rashdall and Sorley in his form of the argument:

1. There must be an objective moral law; otherwise: (a) There would not be such great agreement on its meaning. (b) No real moral disagreements would ever have occurred, each person being right from his own moral perspective. (c) No moral judgment would ever have been wrong, each being subjectively right. (d) No ethical question could ever be discussed, there being no objective meaning to any ethical terms. (e) Contradictory views would both be right, since opposites could be equally correct.
2. This moral law is beyond individual persons and beyond humanity as a whole: (a) It is beyond individual persons, since they often sense a conflict with it. (b) It is beyond humanity as a whole, for they collectively fall short of it and even measure the progress of the whole race by it.
3. This moral law must come from a moral Legislator because: (a) A law has no meaning unless it comes from a mind; only minds emit meaning. (b) Disloyalty makes no sense unless it is to a person, yet people die in loyalty to what is morally right. (c) Truth is meaningless unless it is a meeting of mind with mind, yet people die for the truth. (d) Hence, discovery of and duty to the moral law make sense only if there is a Mind or Person behind it.
4. Therefore, there must be a moral, personal Mind behind this moral law.

It is noteworthy that Trueblood's form of the moral argument argues its validity in terms of its rationality. It reasons, in essence, that to reject the moral law is irrational or meaningless. That is, unless we assume the universe is irrational, there must be an objective moral law and, thereby, an objective Moral Law Giver.

In addition to the things said against the other forms of the moral argument, some critics, especially existentialists and nihilists, simply point to the absurdity of the universe. They simply refuse to assume, with Trueblood, that the universe is rational. They admit that it may be meaningless to assume there is no moral law, but add quickly that this is the way things are—meaningless. Of course, the defender of the moral argument could point to the self-defeating nature of the claim that "Everything is meaningless," since that very statement is assumed to be meaningful.

Lewis' Moral Argument. The most popular modern form of the moral argument was given by C. S. *Lewis in *Mere Christianity*. He not only gives the most complete form of the argument in the most persuasive way, but he also answers major objections. The moral argument of Lewis can be summarized:

1. There must be a universal moral law, or else: (a) Moral disagreements would make no sense, as we all assume they do. (b) All moral criticisms would be meaningless (e.g., "The Nazis were wrong."). (c) It is unnecessary to keep promises or treaties, as we all assume that it is. (d) We would not make excuses for breaking the moral law, as we all do.
2. But a universal moral law requires a universal Moral Law Giver, since the Source of it: (a) Gives moral commands (as lawgivers do). (b) Is interested in our behavior (as moral persons are).
3. Further, this universal Moral Law Giver must be absolutely good: (a) Otherwise all moral effort would be futile in the long run, since we could be sacrificing our lives for what is not ultimately right. (b) The source of all good must be absolutely good, since the standard of all good must be completely good.
4. Therefore, there must be an absolutely good Moral Law Giver.

The Moral Law Is Not Herd Instinct. Lewis anticipates and persuasively answers major objections to the moral argument. Essentially, his replies are:

What we call the moral law cannot be the result of herd instinct or else the stronger impulse would always win, but it does not. We would always act *from* instinct rather than selflessly to help someone, as we sometimes do. If the moral law were just herd instinct, then instincts would always be right, but they are not. Even love and patriotism are sometimes wrong.

The Moral Law Is Not Social Convention. Neither can the moral law be mere social convention, because not everything learned *through* society is *based* on social convention. For example, math and logic are not. The same basic moral laws can be found in virtually every society, past and present. Further, judgments about social progress would not be possible if society were the basis of the judgments.

The Moral Law Differs from Laws of Nature. The moral law is not to be identified with the laws of nature. Nature's laws are descriptive (is), not prescriptive (ought) as are moral laws. Factually convenient situations (the way it *is*) can be morally wrong. Someone who tries to trip me and fails is wrong, but someone who accidentally trips me is not.

The Moral Law Is Not Human Fancy. Neither can the moral law be mere human fancy, because we cannot get rid of it even when we would like to do so. We did not create it; it is impressed on us from without. If it were fancy, then all value judgments would be meaningless, including such statements as "Hate is wrong." and "Racism is wrong." But if the moral law is not a description or a merely human prescription, then it must be a moral prescription from a Moral Prescriber beyond us. As Lewis notes, this Moral Law Giver is more like Mind than Nature. He can no more be part of Nature than an architect is identical to the building he designs.

Injustice Does Not Disprove a Moral Law Giver. The main objection to an absolutely perfect Moral Law Giver is the argument from evil or injustice in the world. No serious person can fail to recognize that all the murders, rapes, hatred, and cruelty in the world leave it far short of perfect. But if the world is imperfect, how can there be an absolutely perfect God? Lewis' answer is simple: The only way the world could possibly be imperfect is if there is an absolutely perfect standard by which it can be judged to be imperfect (*see* Morality, Absolute Nature of). For injustice makes sense only if there is a standard of justice by which something is known to be unjust. And absolute injustice is possible only if there is an absolute standard of justice. Lewis recalls the thoughts he had as an atheist:

> Just how had I got this idea of *just* and *unjust?* A man does not call a line crooked unless he has some idea of a straight line. What was I comparing this universe with when I called it unjust. . . . Of course I could have given up my idea of justice by saying it was nothing but a private idea of my own. But if I did that, then my argument against God collapsed too—for the argument depended on saying that the world was really unjust, not simply that it did not happen to please my private fancies. Thus in the very act of trying to prove that God did not exist—in other words, that the whole of reality was senseless—I found I was forced to assume that one part of reality—namely my idea of justice—was full of sense. [*Mere Christianity*, 45, 46]

Rather than disproving a morally perfect Being, the evil in the world presupposes a perfect standard. One could raise the question as to whether this Ultimate Law Giver is all powerful but not whether he is all perfect. For if anyone insists there is real imperfection in the world, then there must be a perfect standard by which this is known.

Sources

N. L. Geisler and W. Corduan, *Philosophy of Religion*
J. Hick, *The Existence of God*
I. Kant, *The Critique of Practical Reason*

C. S. Lewis, *Mere Christianity*
H. Rashdall, *The Theory of Good and Evil*
W. R. Sorley, *Moral Value and the Idea of God*
E. Trueblood, *Philosophy of Religion*

Morality, Absolute Nature of. Orthodox Christianity has always defended moral absolutes. However, most modern ethicists hold some form of relativism. Thus, it is necessary to defend the belief in moral absolutes.

Moral Absolutes. Before the absolute nature of morality can be understood, morality must be defined. Several things are meant by a moral obligation. First, a moral duty is good in itself (an *end*), not merely good as a means. Further, it is something we *ought* to pursue, a duty. Morality is *prescriptive* (an "ought"), not merely descriptive (an "is"). Morality deals with what is right, as opposed to wrong. It is an obligation, that for which a person is accountable.

An absolute moral obligation is:

- an *objective* (not subjective) moral duty—a duty for all persons.
- an *eternal* (not temporal) obligation—a duty at all times.
- a *universal* (not local) obligation—a duty for all places.

An absolute duty is one that is binding on all persons at all times in all places.

Defense of Absolutes. Moral absolutes can be defended by showing the deficiency of moral relativism. For either there is a moral absolute or else everything is morally relative. Hence, if relativism is wrong, then there must be an absolute basis for morality.

Everything is relative to an absolute. Simply by asking, "Relative to what?" it is easy to see that total relativism is inadequate. It can't be relative to the relative. In that case it could not be relative at all, ad infinitum, since there would be nothing to which it was relative, etc. Albert *Einstein did not believe everything was relative in the physical universe. He believed the speed of light is absolute.

Measurement is impossible without absolutes. Even moral relativists make such statements as, "The world is getting better (or worse)." But it is not possible to know it is getting "better" unless we know what is "Best." Less than perfect is only measurable against a Perfect. Hence, all objective moral judgments imply an absolute moral standard by which they can be measured.

Moral disagreements demand objective standards. Real moral disagreements are not possible without an absolute moral standard by which both sides can be measured. Otherwise both sides of every moral dispute are right. But opposites cannot both be right. For example, "Hitler was an evil man" vs. "Hitler was not an evil man" cannot both be true in the same sense (*see* FIRST PRINCIPLES). Unless there is an objective moral standard by which Hitler's actions can be weighed, we cannot know that he was evil.

Moral absolutes are unavoidable. Total moral relativism reduces to statements such as "You should never say never," "You should always avoid using always," or "You absolutely ought not believe in moral absolutes." "Ought" statements are moral statements, and "ought never" statements are absolute moral statements. So, there is no way to avoid moral absolutes without affirming a moral absolute. Total moral relativism is self-defeating.

Distinctions in Moral Absolutes. If there is an absolute basis for morality, then why do so many believe that all morality is relative? The reasons for this are mostly based on the failure to make proper distinctions.

Difference between Fact (Is) and Value (Ought). Relativists confuse fact and value, what is and what ought to be. What people *do* is subject to change, but what they *ought* to do is not. There is a difference between sociology and morality. Sociology is *descriptive;* morality is *prescriptive*. Relativists confuse the changing factual situation with unchanging moral duty.

Difference between Value and Instance of Value. There is confusion as well between an absolute moral value and changing attitudes regarding whether a given action violates that value. Once witches were sentenced as murderers, but now they are not. What changed was not the moral principle that murder is wrong. Rather, our understanding changed about whether witches really murder people by their curses. One's factual understanding of a moral situation is relative, but the moral values involved in the situation are not.

Difference between Values and Understandings. A similar misunderstanding is over the difference between an unchanging *value* and a changing *understanding* of that value. A couple deeply in love better understand their love after twenty years. The love itself has not changed. Their understanding of it has changed.

Difference between End (Value) and Means. Often moral relativists confuse the *end* (the value itself) with the *means* to attaining that value. Most political disputes are of this sort. Both liberal and conservative politicians agree that justice should be done (the end); they merely disagree as to whose program is the best means to attain justice. Both militarists and pacifists desire peace (the end); they simply disagree as to whether a strong military best attains this peace.

Difference between Command and Culture. Another important difference, often overlooked by moral relativists, is that between the absolute moral command and the relative way a culture can manifest it. All cultures have some concept of modesty and propriety in greeting. In some a kiss is appropriate, while in others such intimacy would horrify. *What* should be done is common, but *how* it should be done differs. Failure to make this distinction misleads many to believe that because a value differs among cultures, the value itself *(what)* differs.

Difference between Applications. A legitimate discussion to decide *which* value applies to a given situation is not the same as a discussion over *whether* there is an absolute value. For example, we err if we think that anyone who believes a pregnant woman has the right to an abortion places no value on human life. They simply do not believe that the unborn are truly human beings. This debate is vastly important, but it should not miscommunicate the notion that the absolute good of protecting life is the issue on the floor. The issue is whether the unborn are human persons (see Geisler, chapter 8).

Conclusion. Moral absolutes are unavoidable. Even those who deny them use them. The reasons for rejecting them are often based on a misunderstanding or misapplication of the moral absolute, not on a real rejection of it. That is, moral values are absolute, even if our understanding of them or the circumstances in which they should be applied are not.

Sources

M. Adler, *Six Great Ideas*, Pt. 2

A. Bloom, *The Closing of the American Mind*

N L. Geisler, *Christian Ethics: Options and Issues*

C. S. Lewis, *The Abolition of Man*

———, *Mere Christianity*

E. Lutzer, *The Necessity of Ethical Absolutes*

Muhammad, Alleged Bible Predictions of. Muhammad (570–632) claimed to be the last of the prophets of God, the culmination of God's prophetic words to humankind, the seal of the prophets (Sura 33:40). In a well-known *hadith*, Muhammad states his uniqueness this way: "I have been given permission to intercede; I have been sent to all mankind; and the prophets have been sealed with me" (Schimmel, 62). What he spoke was later written in the *Qur'an* which is considered by Muslims to be the verbally inspired and inerrant Word of God. As the last prophet, Muhammad superseded Abraham, Moses, Jesus, and others as the prophet of God.

Islamic apologetics has followed several lines of reasoning for proving the finality of Muhammad over the previous prophets. The chief of these proofs are:

1. that the Old and New Testaments contain clear prophecies about him;
2. that Muhammad's call to be a prophet was miraculous (*see* MUHAMMAD, ALLEGED DIVINE CALL OF);
3. that the language and the teaching of the *Qur'an* are without a parallel (*see* QUR'AN, ALLEGED DIVINE ORIGIN OF);
4. that Muhammad's miracles are a seal on his claims (*see* MUHAMMAD, ALLEGED MIRACLES OF), and
5. that his life and character prove him to have been the last and the greatest of prophets (*see* MUHAMMAD, CHARACTER OF).

Biblical Predictions. In a popular Muslim book, *Muhammad in the Bible,* Abdu L-Ahad Dawud argues that the Bible predicts the coming of the prophet Muhammad. He claims that "Muhammad is the real object of the Covenant, and in him alone are actually and literally fulfilled all the prophecies in the Old Testament" (11). He examines the New Testament, finding Muhammad, not Christ, to be the foretold prophet. The texts Dawud and other Muslims use to support these claims include:

Deuteronomy 18:15–18. God promised Moses, "I will raise up for them [Israel] a prophet like you from among their brothers; I will put my words in his mouth, and he will tell them everything I command him" (vs. 18). Muslims believe this prophecy is fulfilled in Muhammad, as the *Qur'an* claims when it refers to "The unlettered Prophet [Muhammad], Whom they find mentioned in their own (Scriptures), in the Law and the Gospels" (sura 7:157).

However, this prophecy could not be a reference to Muhammad. First, it is clear that the term "brothers" means fellow Israelites. The Jewish Levites were told in the same passage that "They shall have no inheritance among their brothers" (vs. 2). Since the term "brothers" refers to Israel, not to their Arab antagonists, why would God raise up for Israel a prophet from their enemies? Elsewhere in Deuteronomy the term *brothers* also means fellow Israelites, not foreigners. God told the Jews to choose a king "from among your own brothers," not a "foreigner" (Deut. 17:15). Israel never chose for herself a non-Jewish king, though the foreign Herodian kings were forced upon Israel by Rome.

So Muhammad came from Ishmael, as Muslims admit, and heirs to the Jewish throne came from Isaac. According to the Torah, when Abraham prayed "If only Ishmael might live under your blessing!" God answered emphatically, "But my covenant I will establish with Isaac" (Gen. 17:18, 21). Later God repeated, "It is through Isaac that your offspring will be reckoned" (Gen. 21:12). The *Qur'an* itself states that the prophetic line came through Isaac, not Ishmael: "And We bestowed on him Isaac and Jacob, and We established the Prophethood and the Scripture among his seed" (sura 29:27). The Muslim scholar Yusuf Ali adds the word *Abraham* and changes the meaning as follows, "We gave (Abraham) Isaac and Jacob, and ordained Among his progeny Prophethood And Revelation." By adding Abraham, the father of Ishmael, he can include

Muhammad, a descendent of Ishmael, in the prophetic line! But Abraham's name is not found in the Arabic text of the *Qur'an*, which Muslims consider to be perfectly preserved.

Jesus, not Muhammad, completely fulfilled this verse. He was from among his Jewish brethren (cf. Gal. 4:4). He fulfilled Deuteronomy 18:18 in that "he will tell them everything I command him." Jesus said, "I do nothing on my own but speak just what the Father has taught me" (John 8:28). And, "I did not speak of my own accord, but the Father who sent me commanded me what to say and how to say it" (John 12:49). He called himself a "prophet" (Luke 13:33), and the people considered him a prophet (Matt. 21:11; Luke 7:16; 24:19; John 4:19; 6:14; 7:40; 9:17). As the Son of God, Jesus was prophet (speaking to men for God), priest (Hebrews 7–10, speaking to God for men), and king (reigning over men for God, Revelation 19–20).

Other characteristics of the "Prophet" to come fit only Jesus. These include speaking with God "face to face" and performing "signs and wonders," which Muhammad admitted he did not do (see below).

Deuteronomy 33:2. Many Islamic scholars believe this verse predicts three separate visitations of God—one on "Sinai" to Moses, another in "Seir" through Jesus, and a third in "Paran" (Arabia) through Muhammad who came to Mecca with an army of "ten thousand."

This contention can be easily answered by looking at a map of the area. Paran and Seir are near Egypt in the Sinai peninsula (cf. Gen. 14:6; Num. 10:12; 12:16–13:3; Deut. 1:1), not in Palestine where Jesus ministered. Paran is hundreds of miles from Mecca in the northeastern Sinai.

More significant, this verse is speaking of the "Lord" coming, not Muhammad. And he is coming with "ten thousand *saints,*" not 10,000 *soldiers,* as Muhammad did.

This prophecy is said to be a "blessing that Moses the man of God pronounced on the Israelites before his *death*" (vs. 1). If it were a prediction about Islam, which has been a constant enemy of Israel, it could scarcely have been a blessing to Israel. In fact, the chapter goes on to pronounce a blessing on each of the tribes of Israel by God, who "will drive out the enemy" (vs. 27).

Deuteronomy 34:10. This verse claims that "Since then, no prophet has risen in Israel like Moses." Muslims argue that this proves that the predicted prophet could not be an Israelite but was Muhammad instead.

However, the "since" means since Moses' death to the time this last chapter was written, probably by Joshua. Even if Deuteronomy was written much later, as some critics believe, it was composed many centuries before the time of Christ and would not eliminate him.

As noted above, Jesus was the perfect fulfillment of this prediction of the prophet to come. One reason this could not refer to Muhammad is that the prophet to come was like Moses, who did "all those miraculous signs and wonders the Lord sent" (Deut. 34:11). Muhammad by his own confession did not perform signs and wonders, as did Moses and Jesus (see sura 2:118; 3:183). Finally, the prophet to come was like Moses who spoke to God "face to face" (Deut. 34:10). Muhammad claimed to receive his revelations through an angel (see sura 25:32; 17:105). Jesus, like Moses, was a direct mediator (1 Tim. 2:5; Heb. 9:15), who communicated directly with God (cf. John 1:18; 12:49; 17). Thus, the prediction could not have referred to Muhammad, as many Muslims claim.

Habakkuk 3:3. The text declares that "God came from Teman, the Holy One from Mount Paran. His glory covered the heavens and his praise filled the earth." Some Muslim scholars believe this refers to the prophet Muhammad coming from Paran (Arabia), and use it in connection with a similar text in Deuteronomy 33:2.

As already noted (in comments on Deut. 33:2 above), Paran is hundreds of miles from Mecca, to which Muhammad came. Further, the verse is speaking of God coming, not Muhammad, who denied being God. Finally, the "praise" could not refer to Muhammad (whose name means "the praised one"), since the subject of both "praise" and "glory" is God, and Muslims would be the first to acknowledge that Muhammad is not God and should not be praised as God.

Psalm 45:3–5. Since this verse speaks of one coming with the "sword" to subdue his enemies, Muslims sometimes cite it as a prediction of their prophet Muhammad, who was known as "the prophet of the sword." They insist it could not refer to Jesus, since he never came with a sword, as he himself admitted (in Matt. 26:52).

However, the very next verse (vs. 6) identifies the person spoken of as "God" whom, according to the New Testament, Jesus claimed to be (John 8:58; 10:30), but Muhammad repeatedly denied being anything other than a human prophet (*see* Christ, Deity of).

Further, although Jesus did not come the first time with a sword, the Bible declares that he will at his second coming, when the "armies of heaven" will follow him (Rev. 19:11–16). The first time he came to die (Mark 10:45; John 10:10–11). The second time he will come in "blazing fire with his powerful angels. He will punish those who do not know God" (2 Thess. 1:7–8). So there is no warrant in taking this as a prediction of Muhammad. Indeed Hebrews 1:8–9 explicitly identifies Christ as the subject of this passage.

Isaiah 21:7. Isaiah in vision sees chariots with teams of horses, riders on donkeys or riders on camels. Muslim commentators take the rider on the "donkeys" to be Jesus and the rider on "camels" to be Muhammad, whom they believed superseded Jesus as a prophet. But this is speculation with no basis in the text or context. Even a casual look at the passage reveals that it is speaking about the fall of Babylon several centuries before the time of Christ. Verse 9 declares: "Babylon has fallen, has fallen!" There is nothing in the text about either Christ or Muhammad. Further, the reference to horses, donkeys, and camels is speaking about the various means by which the news of Babylon's fall would spread. Again, absolutely nothing here refers to Muhammad.

Matthew 3:11. According to Dawud, this prediction of John the Baptist could not refer to Christ and must refer to Muhammad (157). John said, "after me will come one who is more powerful than I, whose sandals I am not fit to carry. He will baptize you with the Holy Spirit and with fire." Dawud argues that "the very preposition 'after' clearly excludes Jesus from being the foretold Prophet," since "they were both contemporaries and born in one and the same year." Further, "it was not Jesus Christ who could be intended by John, because if such were the case he would have followed Jesus and submitted to him like a disciple and subordinate." What is more, "if Jesus were in reality the person whom the Baptist foretold, . . . there would be no necessity nor any sense in his being baptized by his inferior in the river like an ordinary penitent Jew!" Indeed, John *"did not know* the gift of prophecy in Jesus until he heard—*while in prison*—of his miracles." Finally, since the one John proclaimed was to make Jerusalem and its temple more glorious (cf. Hag. 2:8–9; Mal. 3:1), it could not have referred to Christ; otherwise this "is to confess the absolute failure of the whole enterprise" (Dawud, 158–60).

Jesus' public ministry did not begin until "after" that of John's, precisely as John said. Jesus did not begin until after his baptism by John (Matt. 3:16–17) and temptation (Matt. 4:1–11). Second, John did defer to Jesus, saying he was unworthy even to carry his shoes (Matt. 3:11). In fact, the text says "John tried to deter him [Jesus], saying, 'I need to be baptized by you, and do you come to me?'" (Matt. 3:14). Third, Jesus stated his reason for baptism, namely, it was necessary "to fulfill all righteousness" (Matt. 3:15). Since he came not to "abolish them [Law or the Prophets] but to fulfill them" (Matt. 5:17). He had to identify with its demands. Otherwise, he would not have been, as he was, perfectly righteous (cf. Rom. 8:1–4). Fourth, John clearly knew who Christ was when he baptized him, since he proclaimed him to be "the Lamb of God who takes away the sin of the world" (John 1:29). And he, with the crowd, saw the "Spirit of God" descend on Jesus and the "voice from Heaven" proclaim, "This is my Son, whom I love; with him I am well pleased" (Matt. 3:16–17). While John did express some later questions, these were quickly answered by Christ who assured him by his miracles (Matt. 11:3–5) that he was the Messiah predicted by Isaiah (35:5–6; 40:3).

Finally, all of the Old Testament prophecies about Messiah (Christ) were not fulfilled at his first coming; some await his coming again (*see* PROPHECY, AS PROOF OF BIBLE). Jesus stated that he would not set up his kingdom until the end of the age (Matt 24:3), when they would "see the Son of Man coming on the clouds of the sky, with power and great glory" (Matt. 24:30). Only then "the Son of Man sits on his glorious throne, . . . [and his apostles] on twelve thrones, judging the twelve tribes of Israel" (Matt. 19:28).

Jesus' eyewitness contemporaries and disciples considered him to be the one predicted in the Old Testament, since that is precisely how they apply the predictions of Malachi (3:1) and Isaiah (40:3) in their writings (cf. Matt. 3:1–3; Mark 1:1–3; Luke 3:4–6).

John 14:16. Muslim scholars see in Jesus' reference to the coming of the promised "Helper" (Gk. *paraclete*) a prediction of Muhammad. They base this on the *Qur'anic* (sura 61:6) reference to Muhammad as "Ahmad" *(periclytos),* which they take to be the correct rendering of the Greek word *paraclete* here.

Of the more than 5000 Greek manuscripts of the New Testament (Geisler and Nix, chap. 22), there is absolutely no manuscript authority for placing the word *periclytos* ("praised one") in the original, as the Muslims claim it should read. Universally they read *paraclete* ("helper"). In this passage Jesus clearly identifies the "Helper" as "the Counselor, the Holy Spirit, whom the Father will send" (John 14:26).

The Helper was given to Jesus' apostles (vs. 16), namely, those who would "testify" of him because they "have been with . . . [him] from the beginning" (John 15:27; cf. Luke 1:1–2; Acts 1:22). But Muhammad was not one of Jesus' apostles, so he could not have been the one Jesus referred to as the "Helper" *(paraclete).*

The Helper Jesus promised was to abide with them "forever" (vs. 16), but Muhammad has been dead for over thirteen centuries.

Jesus said to the disciples, "You know him [the Helper]" (vs. 17), but the apostles did not know Muhammad. He would not be born for another six centuries. Also, Jesus told his apostles that the Helper will be "in you" (vs. 17). Muhammad could not have been "in" Jesus' apostles. Their teaching was not in accord with Muhammad's, so he could not have been "in" Jesus' apostles in any sort of spiritual or doctrinally compatible way.

Jesus affirmed that the Helper would be sent "in my [Jesus'] name" (John 14:26). But no Muslim believes Muhammad was sent by Jesus in Jesus' name.

The Helper Jesus was about to send would not "speak on his own" (John 16:13). But Muhammad constantly testifies to himself (for example, in sura 33:40). The Helper would "glorify" Jesus (John 16:14), but Islam declares that Muhammad supersedes Jesus. He would not be glorifying Jesus who he considered an earlier and, in that sense, inferior prophet.

Finally, Jesus asserted that the Helper would come in "not many days" (Acts 1:5), rather than after hundreds of years. The Holy Spirit came fifty days later on the Day of Pentecost (Acts 1–2).

Muslim Use of Scripture. Careful observation of all these texts in their literary setting shows that they are wrenched out of their context by Muslim apologists eager to find in Judeo-Christian Scripture something to show the superiority of Islam (*see* CHRIST, UNIQUENESS OF). Islamic scholars complain when Christians try to interpret the *Qur'an* to Christian advantage. But they are guilty of the very thing they charge.

Muslim usage of Scripture is often arbitrary and without textual warrant. Although Islamic scholars are quick to point out that the Scriptures have been corrupted (*see* NEW TESTAMENT MANUSCRIPTS), nevertheless, when they come upon a text they feel can be made to lend credence to their view, they have no problem accepting its authenticity. Their determination of which biblical texts are authentic is arbitrary and self-serving.

Conclusion. Nowhere did the Bible predict the coming of Muhammad. Attempts by Muslim apologists to claim such involved forced interpretations contrary to the context of the passage. Rather, the Old Testament prophets predicted in detail the coming of Christ. Christ, not Muhammad, is confirmed to be God's Messenger (*see* MIRACLES, APOLOGETIC VALUE OF; CHRIST, DEITY OF). Indeed, Christ is proven to be the very Son of God.

Sources

Y. Ali, *The Holy Qur'an*
A. Dawud, *Muhammad and the Bible*
N. L. Geisler and W. E. Nix, *A General Introduction to the Bible*
——— and A. Saleeb, *Answering Islam: The Crescent in the Light of the Cross*
A. Schimmel, *And Muhammad Is His Messenger*

Muhammad, Alleged Divine Call of. Muhammad claims to be called of God to be a prophet. Indeed, he claimed to be the last of God's prophets on earth, "the Seal of the Prophets" (sura 33:40). The alleged miraculous nature of his call is used by Muslims to prove that Islam is the true religion.

An examination of the facts, even from Muslim sources, reveals that the Muslim view of Muhammad suffers an acute case of overclaim. One does not find, for example, support for the claim that he was called to bring the full and final revelation from God in the circumstances that surround Muhammad's call.

Elements of the Call. *Choked by an Angel.* During his call Muhammad said he was choked by the angel—three times. Muhammad said of the angel, "he choked me with the cloth until I believed that I should die. Then he released me and said: 'Recite!' *(Iqra)*. When he hesitated, he received "twice again the repeated harsh treatment" (Andrae, 43–44). This seems an unusual form of coerced learning, uncharacteristic of the gracious and merciful God Muslims claim Allah to be, as well as contrary to the free choice they believe he has granted his creatures.

Deceived by a Demon? Muhammad himself questioned the divine origin of the experience. At first he thought he was being deceived by a *jinn* or evil spirit. In fact, Muhammad was at first deathly afraid of the source of his newly found revelation, but he was encouraged by his wife Khadijah and her cousin, Waraqah, to believe that the revelation was the same as that of Moses and that he too would be a prophet of his nation. One of the most widely respected modern Muslim biographer, Muhammad Husayn Haykal, speaks vividly of Muhammad's plaguing fear that he was demon possessed:

> Stricken with panic, Muhammad arose and asked himself, 'What did I see? *Did possession of the devil which I feared all along come to pass?*' Muhammad looked to his right and his left but saw nothing. For a while he stood there trembling with fear and stricken with awe. He feared the cave might be haunted and that he might run away still unable to explain what he saw. [74, emphasis added]

Haykal notes that Muhammad had feared demon possession before, but his wife Khadijah talked him out of it. For "as she did on earlier occasions when *Muhammad feared possession by the devil,* so now stood firm by her husband and devoid of the slightest doubt." Thus "respectfully, indeed reverently, she said to him, 'Joy to my cousin! Be firm. By him who dominates Khadijah's soul I pray and hope that you will be the Prophet of this nation. By God, he will not let you down'" (ibid., 75). Indeed, Haykal's description of Muhammad's experience of receiving a "revelation" fits that of other mediums. Haykal wrote of the revelation to remove the suspicion of guilt for one of Muhammad's wives:

> Muhammad had not moved from his spot when revelation came to him accompanied by the usual convulsions. He was stretched out in his clothes and a pillow was placed under his head. A'ishah [his wife] later reported, "Thinking that something ominous was about to happen, everyone in the room was frightened except me, for I did not fear a thing, knowing I

> was innocent . . ." Muhammad recovered, he sat up and began to wipe his forehead where beads of perspiration had gathered. [ibid., 337]

Another characteristic often associated with occult "revelations" is contact with the dead (cf. Deut. 18:9–14). The Muslim biographer, Haykal, relates an occasion when "The Muslims who overheard him [Muhammad] asked, 'Are you calling the dead?' and the Prophet answered, 'They hear me no less than you do, except that they are unable to answer me'" (ibid., 231). On another occasion Muhammad was found "praying for the dead buried in that cemetery" (ibid., 495). Haykal even frankly admits that "There is hence no reason to deny the event of the Prophet's visit to the cemetery of Baqi as out of place considering *Muhammad's spiritual and psychic power of communication with the realms of reality and his awareness of spiritual reality that surpasses that of ordinary men*" (ibid., 496, emphasis added).

Silence and Depression. Also clouding the alleged divine origin of his message is the fact that after this there was a long period of silence which, according to some accounts lasted about three years, during which time Muhammad fell into the depths of despair, feeling forsaken by God, and considering suicide. These circumstances seem uncharacteristic of a divine call.

The Satanic "Revelation." On another occasion Muhammad set forth a revelation he thought was from God, but later changed it, claiming Satan had slipped the verses into the text. God said to the prophet, "They are but names which ye have named, ye and your fathers, for which Allah hath revealed no warrant" (sura 53:23, Pickethall trans. cf. 22:51). But unfortunately human deception is always a possibility. Muslims themselves believe that all claimants to revelations opposing the *Qur'an* involve deception. In view of this, it is reasonable to ask whether Muslims have taken seriously the possibility that Muhammad's first impression was the right one, that he was being deceived by a demon. They acknowledge that Satan is real and that he is a great deceiver. Why then dismiss the possibility that Muhammad himself was being deceived, as he first thought?

Human Sources for Qur'an. Finally, some critics see nothing at all supernatural in the source of Muhammad's ideas, noting that the vast majority of ideas in the *Qur'an* have known Jewish, Christian, or pagan sources (*see* QUR'AN, ALLEGED DIVINE ORIGIN OF). Even the noted biographer, Haykal, unwittingly places his finger on a possible source of Muhammad's "revelations." He wrote,

> The Arab's imagination is by nature strong. Living as he does under the vault of heaven and moving constantly in search of pasture or trade, and being constantly forced into the excesses, exaggerations, and even lies which the life of trade usually entails, the Arab is given to the exercise of his imagination and cultivates it at all times whether for good or for ill, for peace or for war. [ibid., 319]

Conclusion. The claim that Muhammad was called of God is not supportable by the evidence. Indeed, the indication, even in Muslim sources, is just the opposite. What is more, there is no supernatural confirmation of this call (*see* MUHAMMAD, ALLEGED MIRACLES OF) such as there is in the case of Jesus (*see* CHRIST, DEITY OF; PROPHECY AS PROOF OF BIBLE; RESURRECTION, EVIDENCE FOR).

Finally, the character of Muhammad falls far short of his claim (*see* MUHAMMAD, CHARACTER OF). Compared to the impeccable character of Christ, Muhammad pales into insignificance (*see* CHRIST, UNIQUENESS OF).

Sources

A. Y Ali, *The Meaning of the Glorious Qur'an*
T. Andrae, *Muhammad: The Man and His Faith*
N. L. Geisler, and A. Saleeb, *Answering Islam*
M. H. Haykal, *The Life of Muhammad*

Muhammad, Character of. Most students of Islam acknowledge that Muhammad was generally a moral person. Many Muslims insist that he was both beyond (major) sin and was the perfect moral example. They claim that Muhammad "stands in history as the best model for man in piety and perfection. He is a living proof of what man can be and of what he can accomplish in the realm of excellence and virtue" (Abdalati, 8). This, they say, is a chief proof that Muhammad is the unique prophet from God (Pfander, 225–26).

A popular Muslim classic by Kamal ud Din ad Damiri gives us the following description of the prophet Muhammad:

> Mohammad is the most favored of mankind, the most honored of all apostles, the prophet of mercy. . . . He is the best of prophets, and his nation is the best of nations; . . . He was perfect in intellect, and was of noble origin. He had an absolutely graceful form, complete generosity, perfect bravery, excessive humility, useful knowledge . . . perfect fear of God and sublime piety. He was the most eloquent and the most perfect of mankind in every variety of perfection. . . . (Gudel, 72).

Evaluating Muhammad's Character. *Polygamy.* There are areas, however, where questions arise about the moral perfection of Muhammad. The first is the matter of his polygamy. According to the *Qur'an*, a man may have four wives (sura 4:3). This raises two questions: Is polygamy moral? Was Muhammad consistent with his own law?

In the Judeo-Christian tradition, polygamy is considered morally wrong. Although God permitted it, along with other human frailties and sins, he never approved it (*see* POLYGAMY). The *Qur'an*, however, clearly sanctions polygamy, allowing that a man may have up to four wives, if he is able to provide for them. Sura 4:3 declares, "Marry women of your choice, Two, or three, or four."

Without presupposing the truth of Christian revelation, there are arguments against polygamy from a moral point of view common to both Muslims and Christians. Monogamy should be recognized by *precedent,* since God gave the first man only one wife (Eve). It is implied by *proportion,* since the number of males and females God brings into the world are about equal. And monogamy is implied by *parity.* If men can marry several wives, it seems only fair that a wife can have several husbands.

Even biographer Muhammad Husayn Haykal tacitly acknowledged the superiority of monogamy when he affirmed that "the happiness of the family and that of the community can best be served by the limitations which monogamy imposes" (294). Muhammad's relationships with his wives are themselves an argument against polygamy. The wives went so far as to plot against him. This is understandable in that Muhammad often ignored some of his wives, and avoided others on many occasions (ibid., 436). He adds, "Indeed, favoritism for some of his wives had created such controversy and antagonism among the 'Mothers of the Believers' that Muhammad once thought of divorcing some of them" (ibid., 437). All of this falls short of an exemplary moral situation in principle and practice.

Even if polygamy, as taught in the *Qur'an*, is deemed morally right, there remains another serious problem. Muhammad received a revelation from God that a man should have no more than four wives at once, yet he had many more. A Muslim defender of Muhammad, writing in *The Prophet of Islam as the Ideal Husband,* admitted that he had fifteen wives. Yet he tells others they may have only four. How can someone be a perfect moral example and not live by one of the basic laws he laid down for others as from God?

The Muslim answer is unconvincing. Muhammad received a "revelation" that God had made an exception for him but not for anyone else. He quotes God as saying: "Prophet! We have Made lawful to thee Thy wives . . . ; And any believing women Who dedicates her soul To the Prophet if the Prophet Wishes to wed her;" but adds quickly, "—this Only for thee, and not For the Believers" (sura 33:50). What is more, Muslims believe (based on sura 4:3b and other teachings) that they may have an unlimited number of concubines, especially among those they conquer in war. This was, no doubt, a powerful motivation for success on the battlefield.

In addition, Muhammad claimed a divine exemption to another law giving each wife her conjugal rights "justly." Husbands were to observe a fixed rotation among their wives. Muhammad insists that God told him that he could have whomever he wanted when he wanted them: "Thou mayest defer (the turn Of) any of them that thou Pleasest, and thou mayest receive Any thou pleasest" (Sura 33:51). Apparently even God had to put the brakes on Muhammad's love for women. For eventually he received a revelation that said, "It is not lawful for thee [to have many more] women After this, nor to change Them for (other) wives, Even though their beauty Attract thee" (Sura 33:52). A look at the facts of Muhammad's lust and inconsistency makes one wonder how he can be considered a perfect moral example and ideal husband.

The Treatment of Women. The *Qur'an* and Hadith accord a lower status to women. The superior status of men is based directly on commands in the *Qur'an*. As noted, men can marry four wives (polygamy) but women cannot marry multiple husbands. Sura 2:228 explicitly affords men the right to divorce their wives but does not accord the equal right to women, claiming "Men have a degree of advantage over them" (sura 2:228).

Muhammad sanctioned the beating of a female servant in order to elicit the truth from her. "The servant was called in and Ali immediately seized her and struck her painfully and repeatedly as he commanded her to tell the truth to the Prophet of God" (Haykal, 336). According to the *Qur'an*, men can beat their wives. Sura 4:34 declares: "Men are in charge of women because Allah hath made the one to excel the other. . . . As for those from whom ye fear rebellion, admonish them and banish them to beds apart, and scourge them" (Pickethall trans.). Yusuf Ali attempts to soften this verse by adding "lightly," a word not found in the Arabic.

Muslim women must wear a veil, stand behind their husbands, and kneel behind them in prayer. Two women must bear witness in civil contracts as opposed to one man (Abdalati, 189–91).

In a Hadith found in the Sahih Al-Bukhari we find the following narrative describing the inferior status of women:

> Narrated [by] Ibn 'Abbas: The Prophet said: "I was shown the Hell-fire and that the majority of its dwellers were women who were ungrateful." It was asked, "Do they disbelieve in Allah?" (or are they ungrateful to Allah?) He replied, "They are ungrateful to their husbands and are ungrateful for the favors and the good (charitable deeds) done to them." [Bukhari, 1.29]

In view of these statements, it seems incredible to hear Muslim apologists say, "Evidently, Muhammad not only honored woman more than did any other man, but he raised her to the status which truly belongs to her—an accomplishment of which Muhammad alone has so far been capable" (Haykal, 298). Another Muslim writer states, "Islam has given woman rights and privileges which she has never enjoyed under other religious or constitutional systems" (Abdalati, 184).

Muhammad's Moral Imperfection. Muhammad was far from sinless. Even the *Qur'an* speaks of his need to ask God for forgiveness. In sura 40:55 God told him, "Patiently, then, persevere: For the Promise of God Is true: and *ask God* forgiveness For thy fault." On another occasion God told Muhammad, "Know, therefore, that There is no god But God, and ask Forgiveness for thy fault, and for the men And women who believe" (sura 41:19). Clearly forgiveness was to be sought for his own sins, not just for others (cf. also 48:2).

Of one occasion, Haykal said flatly, "Muhammad did in fact err when he frowned in the face of [the blind beggar] ibn Umm Maktum and sent him away. . . . in this regard he [Muhammad] was as fallible as anyone" (134). If so, then one finds it difficult to believe that Muhammad can be so eulogized. However much an improvement Muhammad's morals may have been over many others of his day, he falls short of the perfect example for all people of all times that many Muslims claim for him. Unlike the Jesus of the Gospels, he certainly would not want to challenge his foes with the question: "Which of you convicts me of sin?" (John 8:46).

Holy Wars. Muhammad believed in holy war (the *Jihad*). By divine revelation he commanded his followers: "fight in the cause Of God" (sura 2:244). He added, "fight and slay The Pagans wherever ye find them" (sura 9:5). And, "when ye meet The Unbelievers (in fight) Smite at their necks" (sura 47:4). In general, Muslims were to "fight those who believe not In God nor the Last Day" (sura 9:29). Indeed, Paradise is promised for those who fight for God. Sura 3:195 declares: "Those who have left their homes . . . Or fought or been slain,—Verily, I will blot out From them their iniquities, And admit them into Gardens With rivers flowing beneath;—A reward from the Presence Of God, and from His Presence Is the best of rewards" (cf. sura 2:244; 4:95). These "holy wars" were carried out "in the cause Of God" (cf. sura 2:244) against "unbelievers."

Sura 5:36 declares that "The punishment of those Who wage war against God [i.e., unbelievers] And His Apostle, and strive With might and main For mischief through the land Is: execution, or crucifixion, Or the cutting off of hands And feet from opposite sides, Or exile from the land." Acknowledging that these are appropriate punishments, depending on "the circumstances," Ali offers little consolation when he notes that the more cruel forms of Arabian treatment of enemies, such as, "piercing of eyes and leaving the unfortunate victim exposed to a tropical sun," were abolished! (Ali, 252, 738). Such war on, and persecution of, enemies on religious grounds—by whatever means—is seen by most critics as religious intolerance. In view of these clear commands to use the sword aggressively to spread Islam and Muslim practice down through the centuries, Muslim claims that "this fight is waged solely for the freedom to call men unto God and unto His religion" have a hollow ring (cf. Haykal, 212).

Moral Expediency. Muhammad sanctioned the raiding of commercial Meccan caravans by his followers (Haykal, 357f.). The prophet himself led three raids. Doubtless the purpose of these attacks was not only obtaining financial reward, but also to impress the Meccans with the growing power of the Muslim force. Critics of Islam question this piracy. These actions cast a dark shadow over Muhammad's alleged moral perfection.

Another time Muhammad approved of a follower lying to an enemy named Khalid in order to kill him. Then in the presence of the man's wives "he fell on him with his sword and killed him. Khalid's women were the only witnesses and they began to cry and mourn for him" (Haykal, 273).

On other occasions Muhammad had no aversion to politically expedient assassinations. When a prominent Jew, Ka'b Ibn Al-Ashraf, had stirred up discord against Muhammad and composed a satirical poem about him, the prophet asked: "Who will deliver me from Ka'b?" Immediately four persons volunteered and shortly returned to Muhammad with Ka'b's head in their hands (Gudel, 74). Haykal acknowledges many such assassinations in his book, *The Life of Muhammad.* Of one he wrote, "the Prophet ordered the execution of Uqbah ibn Abu Muayt. When Uqbah pleaded, 'Who will take care of my children, O Muhammad?' Muhammad answered, 'The fire'"(234; cf. 236, 237, 243).

The *Qur'an* itself informs us that Muhammad was not indisposed to breaking promises when he found it advantageous. He even got a "revelation" to break a long-standing pledge to avoid killing during the sacred month of pilgrimage: "They ask thee Concerning fighting In the Prohibited Month. Say: 'Fighting therein Is a grave (offense); But graver is it In the sight of God To prevent access To the path of God'" (sura 2:217). Again, "God has already ordained For you, (O men), The dissolution of your oaths (In some cases)" (sura 66:2). Rather than consistency, Muhammad's moral life was sometimes characterized by expediency.

Retaliation. On at least two occasions Muhammad ordered people assassinated for composing poems that mocked him. This extremely oversensitive overreaction to ridicule is defended by Haykal: "For a man like Muhammad, whose success depended to a large extent upon the esteem which he could win, a malicious satirical composition could be more dangerous than a lost battle" (Gudel, 74). But this is a pragmatic, end-justifies-means ethic.

Even though "the Muslims were always opposed to killing any women or children," nonetheless, Haykal says, "a Jewish woman was executed because she had killed a Muslim by dropping a millstone on his head" (314). On another occasion, two slave women who had allegedly spoken against Muhammad in song were executed with their master (410). When it was believed that one woman, Abu 'Afk, had insulted Muhammad (by a poem), one of Muhammad's followers "attacked her during the night while she was surrounded by her children, one of whom she was nursing. . . . After removing the child from his victim, he killed her" (Haykal, 243).

The zeal with which Muhammad's followers would kill for him was infamous. Haykal records the words of one devotee who would have killed his daughter at Muhammad's command. Umar ibn al Khattab declared fanatically, "By God, if he [Muhammad] were to ask me to strike off her head, I would do so without hesitation" (Haykal, 439).

Mercilessness. Muhammad attacked the last Jewish tribe of Medina on the suspicion that they had plotted with the Meccan enemies against Muslims. Unlike the previous two Jewish tribes that had been simply expelled from the city, this time all the men of the tribe were put to death and the women and children were sold into slavery. Said one who tried to justify this, "one must see Muhammad's cruelty toward the Jews against the background of the fact that their scorn and rejection was the greatest disappointment of his life, and for a time they threatened completely to destroy his prophetic authority" (Andrae, 155–56). In any case, would this justify killing the men and making slaves of the women and children? And is this kind of activity exemplary of a person who is supposed to be of flawless moral character?

In spite of this evidence against Muhammad, one defender of Islam responds that even if "their claims were true, we would still refute them with the simple argument that the great stand above the law" (Haykal, 298)!

Conclusion. Muslims make outstanding claims about the character of Muhammad, even attributing moral perfection to him. However, the record of Muhammad, even from the *Qur'an* and Muslim tradition *(Hadith)* falls far short of these claims. While being a generally moral person in his everyday dealings, Muhammad taught, approved of, and participated in morally imperfect activities. There is no evidence that he was morally superior to a typical human being. In fact, there is evidence to the contrary. By contrast, the life of Christ was impeccable (*see* CHRIST, UNIQUENESS OF).

Sources

H. Abdalati, *Islam in Focus*
S. Al-Bukhari, *The Translation of the Meanings of Sahih Al-Bukhari*
Y. Ali, *The Holy Qur'an*
T. Andrae, *Mohammed: The Man and His Faith*
A. Dawud, *Muhammad in the Bible*
N. L. Geisler and A. Saleeb. *Answering Islam*
J. P. Gudel, *To Every Muslim an Answer*
M. H. Haykal, *The Life of Muhammad*
C. G. Pfander, *The Mizanu'l Haqq [The Balance of Truth]*
M. A. Rauf, *Islam: Creed and Worship*
D. J. Sahas, *The Greek Orthodox Theological Review*, 27.2, 3
A. Schimmel and A. Falaturi, eds., *We Believe in One God*

Muhammad, Alleged Miracles of. Islam claims to be the one true religion. In support of this claim they offer the *Qur'an* as their chief miracle. However, many Muslim apologists also claim that Muhammad performed other miracles to support his claims to be a prophet of God, in spite of the fact that when asked to perform miracles to support his claims, Muhammad refused to do so (sura 3:181–84).

Muslim Definition of a Miracle. For Muslims a miracle is always an act of God (*see* MIRACLE; MIRACLES IN THE BIBLE). Nature is the way God works customarily and repeatedly and miracles are seen as *khawarik,* "the breaker of usage." There are many words for miracle in Arabic, but the only one used in the *Qur'an* is *ayah,* "sign" (cf. suras 2:118, 151, 253; 3:108; 28:86–87). The technical term used by Muslim scholars to designate a miracle that confirms one to be a prophet is *mudjiza*. To qualify it needs to be:

1. an act of God that cannot be done by any creature;
2. contrary to the customary course of things;
3. aimed at proving the authenticity of the prophet;
4. preceded by the announcement of a forthcoming miracle;
5. done in the exact manner in which it was announced;
6. done only through the hands of the prophet;
7. in no way a disavowal of his prophetic claim;
8. accompanied by a challenge to duplicate it; and
9. unduplicated by anyone present.

Muslims believe that Moses, Elijah, and Jesus performed miracles that fulfilled these criteria (see "Mudjiza"). The question is: Does the eloquence of the *Qur'an* meet these characteristics to be a miracle? A subjective answer is that it does not, in either form or content.

Miracles in the Qur'an. Miracle claims about Muhammad fall into three categories: claims recorded in the *Qur'an*; supernatural predictions of Muhammad made in the *Qur'an*; and miracle claims in the *Hadith* or Islamic tradition (Bukhari, iii–vi).

Sura 6:35 is used by many Muslims to show that Muhammad could do miracles. It reads: "If their spurning is hard On thy mind, yet if Thou wert able to seek A tunnel in the ground Or a ladder to the skies And bring them a Sign,—(What good?)."

Careful examination of the text reveals that it does not claim that Muhammad was able to perform miracles. First of all, it is hypothetical—"*If* Thou were able. . . ." It does not say he was able. Second, the passage even implies that he could not perform miracles. Otherwise, why was he being spurned for not doing so? If he could have done miracles, then he could have easily stopped the spurning that was so "hard On thy [his] mind."

The Alleged Splitting of the Moon. Many Muslims understand sura 54:1–2 to mean that upon Muhammad's command before unbelievers the moon was split in half. For it reads: "The Hour (of judgment) Is nigh, and the moon Is cleft asunder. But if they see A Sign, they turn away, And say, 'This is (But) transient magic.'"

Again there are difficulties with this understanding of the text. Muhammad is not mentioned in the passage. The *Qur'an* does not call this a miracle, though the word sign *(ayah)* is used. If it is a miracle, it contradicts other passages that claim Muhammad did not perform feats of nature like this (cf. 3:181–84).

Further, this passage is earlier than those in which unbelievers are calling for a sign. If Muhammad had pulled it off, the sign would have been universally observed and noted with wonder throughout the world. But there is no evidence that it was (Pfander, 311–12). Even Muslim scholars say this is speaking about the resurrection of the last days, not a miracle during Muhammad's day. They maintain that the phrase "the Hour (of judgment)" refers to the end times. The tense they take as the usual Arabic way of expressing a future prophetic event.

The Night Journey. One miraculous occurrence recorded in the *Qur'an* is Muhammad's *Isra* or "night journey." Many Muslims believe Muhammad, after being transported to Jerusalem, ascended into heaven on the back of a mule. Sura 17:1 declares: "Glory to (God) Who did take His Servant For a Journey by night From the Sacred Mosque To the Farthest Mosque, Whose precincts We did Bless,—in order that We Might show him some Of Our Signs." Later Muslim traditions expanded on this verse, speaking of Muhammad's escort by Gabriel through several levels of heaven. He is greeted by important people (Adam, John, Jesus, Joseph, Enoch, Aaron, Moses, and Abraham). While there he bargains God down in his command to pray fifty times to five times a day.

There is no reason to take this passage as referring to a literal trip to heaven. Many Muslim scholars do not so interpret it. The noted translator of the *Qur'an*, Abdullah Yusuf Ali, commenting on this passage, notes that "it opens with the mystic Vision of the Ascension of the Holy Prophet; he is transported from the Sacred Mosque (of Mecca) to the Farthest Mosque (of Jerusalem) in a night and shown some of the Signs of God" ("Introduction to Sura XVII," 691). Even according to one of the earliest Islamic traditions, Muhammad's wife, A'isha, reported that "The apostle's body remained where it was but God removed his spirit by night" (Ishaq, 183). Even were this to be understood as a miracle, there is no evidence presented to test its authenticity. By Islam's own definition of a confirming sign, this miracle would have no apologetic value ("Mudjiza"; *see* Miracles, Apologetic Value of).

The Victory at Badr. Another miracle claim often attributed to Muhammad is the victory at Badr (see suras 3:123; 8:17). Sura 5:12 reads: "O ye who believe! Call in remembrance The favour of God Unto you when Certain men formed the design To stretch out Their hands against you, But (God) held back Their hands from you: So fear God."

According to Islamic tradition, several miracles are said to have occurred here, the most prominent of which was that God sent 3000 angels to help in the battle (supposedly identifiable by the turbans they wore) and the miraculous rescue of Muhammad just before a Meccan was going to kill him with a sword. One tradition tells of Muhammad throwing a handful of dirt into the Meccan army to blind them and drive them into retreat.

It is questionable whether all of these passages refer to the same event. Even many Muslim scholars believe sura 8 is speaking of another event and is to be taken figuratively of God casting fear into the heart of Muhammad's enemy, Ubai ibn Khalaf (Pfander, 314). Sura 5 is taken by some to refer to another event, possibly to the attempted assassination of Muhammad at Usfan.

Only sura 3 mentions Badr, and it says nothing about a miracle. At best it would reveal only God's providential care for Muhammad, not a supernatural event. Certainly it does not speak of a miracle that confirms Muhammad's prophetic credentials, since there is no evidence that it fits the nine criteria.

If Badr's victory is a sign of divine confirmation, then why was not the subsequent defeat at Uhud a sign of divine disapproval? So humiliating was the defeat that they "pulled out two links of chain from Muhammad's wound, and two of his front teeth fell off in the process." In addition, the Muslim dead were mutilated on the battlefield by the enemy. One enemy of Muhammad "cut off a number of noses and ears [of his troops] in order to make a string and necklace of them." Even Muhammad Husayn Haykal acknowledged that "the Muslims suffered defeat" here, noting that the enemy was "intoxicated with her victory" (Haykal, 266–67). Yet he did not consider this a supernatural sign of divine disfavor. Indeed, after the battle of Badr, the *Qur'an* boasts that Muhammad's followers could overcome an army with God's help when outnumbered ten to one (sura 8:65). But here they were outnumbered only three to one, just as they were in their victory at Badr, and yet they suffered a great defeat.

Muhammad is not the first outnumbered military leader in history to win a big victory. The Israeli six-day war in 1967 was one of the quickest and most decisive battles in the annals of modern warfare. Yet no Muslim would consider it a miraculous sign of divine approval of Israel over an Arab nation.

The Splitting of Muhammad's Breast. According to Islamic tradition, at Muhammad's birth (or just before his ascension), Gabriel is said to have cut open Muhammad's chest, removed and cleansed his heart, then filled it with wisdom and replaced it. This is based in part on sura 94:1, 2, 8 which reads: "Have We not Expanded thee thy breast?—And removed from thee Thy burden . . . and to thy Lord Turn (all) thy attention?"

Most conservative Islamic scholars take this passage as a figure of speech describing the great anxiety Muhammad experienced in his early years at Mecca. The great *Qur'anic* commentator Ali said, "The breast is symbolically the seat of knowledge and of the highest feeling of love and affection" (Ali, *The Meaning of the Glorious Qur'an,* 2.1755).

Prophecies in the Qur'an. Muslims offer predictive prophesies in the *Qur'an* as a proof that Muhammad could perform miracles. But the evidence is not convincing. The suras most often cited are those in which Muhammad promised victory to his troops.

What religious military leader is there who might not say to his troops: "God is on our side; we are going to win. Fight on!"? Further, remembering that Muhammad is known as "the prophet of the Sword," with his greatest number of conversions coming after he had forsaken the peaceful but relatively unsuccessful means of spreading his message, it should be no surprise that he would predict victory.

Considering the zeal of Muslim forces, who were promised Paradise for their efforts (cf. sura 22:58–59; 3:157–58; 3:170–71), it is no surprise that they were so often victorious. Finally, it is little wonder so many "submitted," considering Muhammad commanded that "the punishment of those Who wage war against God And his Apostle, and strive With might . . . Is: execution, or crucifixion, Or the cutting off of hands And feet from opposite sides, or exile from the land" (sura 5:36).

The only substantive prediction was about the Roman victory over the Persian army at Issus. Sura 30:2–4 reads: "The Roman Empire Has been defeated—In a land close by: But they, (even) after (This) defeat of theirs, Will soon be victorious—within a few years."

This prediction is less than spectacular (see Gudel, 54). According to Ali "a few years" means three to nine years, but the real victory did not come until thirteen or fourteen years after the prophecy. The defeat of the Romans by the Persians in the capture of Jerusalem took place about 614 or 615. The counteroffensive did not begin until 622 and the victory was not complete until 625. This would be at least ten or eleven years, not "a few" spoken by Muhammad.

Uthman's edition of the *Qur'an* had no vowel points, these not being added until much later (Spencer, 21). Hence, the word *sayaghlibuna,* "they shall defeat," could have been rendered, with the change of two vowels, *sayughlabuna,* "they shall be defeated" (Tisdall, 137). Even if this ambiguity were removed, the prophecy is neither long-range nor unusual. One would have expected the defeated Romans to bounce back. It took little more than a perceptive reading of the trends of time to forecast such an event. At best, it could have been a good guess. In any event, there appears to be no sufficient proof that it is supernatural.

The only other alleged prophecy worth mentioning is found in sura 89:2 where the phrase "By the Nights twice five" is taken by some to be a prediction of the ten years of persecution early Muslims experienced (Ahmad, 374f.). But that this is a far-fetched interpretation is evident from the fact that even the translator of the *Qur'an* Ali, admitted that *By the Ten Nights* is usually understood to refer to the first ten nights of *Zul-Hajj,* the sacred season of Pilgrimage (Ali, 1731, n. 6109). There is certainly no clear prediction.

The evidence that Muhammad possessed a truly supernatural gift of prophecy is lacking. His prophecies are vague and disputable. It is far easier to read meaning back in to them after the event than it would have been to see the meaning before hand.

If Muhammad had possessed the ability to miraculously forecast the future, surely he would have used it to squelch his opponents. But he never did. Instead, he admitted that he did not do miracles as the prophets before him had and simply offered as his sign the *Qur'an*.

Finally, Muhammad never offered a prophesy as proof of his prophethood (*see* MUHAMMAD, AL-

LEGED DIVINE CALL OF). None is mentioned in this connection at all. Jesus repeatedly offered miracles as a proof that he was the Messiah, the Son of God. When about to heal the paralytic, he said to the unbelieving Jews, "that you may know that the Son of Man has power on earth to forgive sins," something the Jews asserted that only God could do (cf. vs. 7), "I say to you, arise, take up your bed and go your way to your house" (Mark 2:10–11). In view of the strong contrast in the ability to provide miraculous confirmations of their respective claims, the thinking person would have to entertain serious doubts as to whether there is sufficient evidence to support Muhammad's claims.

Miracles in the Hadith. Most miracle claims for Muhammad do not occur in the *Qur'an*, the only book in Islam for which divine inspiration is claimed (*see* MUHAMMAD, ALLEGED MIRACLES OF; *QUR'AN*, ALLEGED DIVINE ORIGIN OF). The vast majority of alleged miracles are reported in the *Hadith* (Islamic tradition), considered by Muslims to contain many authentic traditions. There are hundreds of miracle stories in the *Hadith* (*see* HADITH, ALLEGED MIRACLES IN).

Al Bukhari tells how Muhammad healed the broken leg of a companion, Addullaha ibn Atig, who was injured while attempting to assassinate one of Muhammad's enemies.

Several sources relate the story that Muhammad miraculously provided water for 10,000 of his troops at the battle of Hudaibiyah. He allegedly dipped his hand into an empty water bottle and let the water flow through his fingers. There are numerous stories of miraculous provision of water. In one, water is turned into milk.

Several stories exist of trees speaking to Muhammad, saluting him, or moving from him as he passed. Once when Muhammad could not find a private place to relieve himself, two trees are said to have come together to hide him and then returned when he was finished. Bukhari claims that a tree against which Muhammad leaned missed his company when he left. There are many stories of wolves and even mountains saluting Muhammad.

Some stories speak of Muhammad miraculously feeding large groups with little food. Anas tells that Muhammad fed eighty or ninety men with a few loaves of barley. Ibn Sa'd relates the story of a woman who invited Muhammad to a meal. He took a thousand men with him and multiplied her small meal to feed them all.

The *Hadith* often relates stories of Muhammad's miraculous dealings with his enemies. Once Muhammad cursed one of his enemies whose horse then sank up to its stomach in hard ground. Sa'd said Muhammad turned a tree branch into a steel sword.

The authenticity of these stories is questionable for many reasons:

They Are Contrary to the Qur'an. For Muslims only the *Qur'an* is divinely inspired. Yet no miracles by Muhammad are recorded in the *Qur'an*. In fact, they are in general contrary to the whole spirit of the Muhammad of the *Qur'an*, who repeatedly refused to do these very kinds of things for unbelievers who challenged him (see sura 3:181–84; 4:153; 6:8–9).

They Are Apocryphal. These alleged miracles of Islamic tradition follow the same story pattern as the apocryphal tales of Christ written a century or two after his death. They are a legendary embellishment by people who lived many years removed from the original events and not a record of contemporary eyewitnesses (*see* MIRACLES, MYTH AND).

Most of those who collected miracle stories lived 100 to 200 years later. They relied on stories passed on orally for generations with ample embellishment. Even the stories accepted by Muslims as authentic, as determined by the *isnad* (or chain of storytellers), lack credibility. These stories are not based on eyewitnesses but rely on generations of storytellers. Joseph Horowitz questioned the reliability of the *isnad:*

> The question as to who first circulated these miracle tales would be very easy to answer if we could still look upon the *isnad*, or chain of witnesses, as unquestionably as we are apparently expected to do. It is especially seductive when one and the same report appears in various essentially similar versions. . . . In general the technique of the *isnad* does not make it possible for us to decide where it is a case of taking over oral account and where of copying from the lecture books of teachers. [Horowitz, 49–58]

They Are Not Agreed Upon. Among Muslims there is no generally accepted list of authentic miracles from the *Hadith*. Indeed, the vast majority of stories from the *Hadith* are rejected by most Muslim scholars. Different groups accept different collections. This casts doubt on their authenticity.

Bukhari, considered to be the most reliable collector, admitted that of the 300,000 *Hadith* he collected, he considered only 100,000 might be true. Even these he boiled down to 7275. That means that even he admitted that more than 290,000 of them were unreliable.

No Canon Is Accepted by All. No single *Hadith* canon is accepted by all Muslims. Most Muslims rank their credibility in descending order as follows: the *Sahih* of Al Bukhari (d. 256 A.H. ["After *Hageira*," Muhammad's flight in 622 A.D.]); the *Sahih* of Muslim (d. 261 A.H.), the *Sunan* of Abu Du'ad (d. 275 A.H.), the *Jami* of Al-Tirmidhi (d. 279 A.H.), the *Suand* of Al Nasa (d. 303 A.H.), and the *Sunan* of Ibn Madja (d. 283 A.H.). Along with these *Hadith*, biographers related miracle stories. The most important are Ibn Sa'd (d. 123 A.H.), Ibn Ishaq (d. 151 A.H.), and Ibn Hisham (d. 218 A.H.). The above categories are rejected by Shia Islam, yet they, along with other Muslims, accept the *Qur'an*.

Their Origin Is Suspect. The origin of the miracle claims of Islam is suspect. It is common knowledge that Islam borrowed many of its beliefs and practices from other religions (Dashti, 55). This has been documented frequently. It is not surprising that Muslim miracle claims have arisen, then, as Christian apologists demonstrated the superiority of Jesus to Muhammad by Jesus' miracles (*see* MIRACLES IN THE BIBLE; NEW TESTAMENT, HISTORICITY OF). Islamic miracle stories began to appear after two Christian bishops, Abu Qurra from Edessa and Arethas from Caesarea, made a point of Muhammad's lack of authenticating miracles. As Sahas noted: "The implication [of the bishop's challenge] is quite clear: Muhammad's teaching is one that might have merit; but this is not enough to qualify him as a prophet, without supernatural signs. If such signs could be shown one could possibly accept him as a prophet" (312). Thus, if Muslims could invent miracles, they could respond to the Christian challenge.

Sahas notes that several miracle stories bear an amazing resemblance to miracles of Jesus found in the Gospels (ibid., 314). For example, Muhammad ascended into heaven, he changed water into milk and miraculously fed large numbers of people.

A Lack of Apologetic Value. They Do Not Fit Islamic Criteria. No miracle stories fit the nine categories accepted by Muslims for a miracle that can confirm a prophet's claim (*mudjiza*). Hence, by their own standards, none of these stories demonstrate the truth of Islam.

They do not come from the *Qur'an* (which is claimed to be inspired), so they lack divine authority by Islamic criteria. The absence of these events in the *Qur'an*, where Muhammad is constantly challenged to support his claims miraculously, is a strong argument that they are not authentic (*see* QUR'AN, ALLEGED DIVINE ORIGIN OF). Surely, if Muhammad could have silenced his critics by proving his supernatural confirmation, he would have done so.

Muhammad accepts the fact that God confirmed the prophets before him by miracles. He refers to God's confirmation of Moses' prophetic credentials (cf. sura 7:106–8, 116–19; 23:45). The *Qur'an* also refers to manifestations of God's miraculous power through other prophets (cf. sura 4:63–65; 6:84–86).

Muhammad also accepts the fact that Jesus performed miracles to prove the divine origin of his message, such as his healings and raising people from the dead (cf. sura 5:113). But if Jesus could perform miraculous feats of nature to confirm his divine commission, and Muhammad refused to do the same, Muhammad's superiority to Christ as a prophet is doubtful.

Muhammad's response to the challenge to perform miracles (cf. sura 6:8–9; 17:90–92) is illuminating: "Am I aught but a man—an apostle?" One cannot imagine Moses, Elijah, or Jesus giving such a response. Muhammad admitted that when Moses was challenged by Pharaoh he responded with miracles (cf. sura 7:106–8, 118). Knowing this was God's way to confirm his spokesperson, Muhammad refused to produce similar miracles.

Muslims offer no good explanation for Muhammad's failure to do miracles. The most familiar Islamic argument is that "it is one of the established ways of God that he gives his Prophets that kind of miracles which accord with the genius of the time so that the world may see that it is beyond human power and that the power of God manifests itself in these miracles." Thus, "During the time of Moses the art of sorcery had made the greatest development. Therefore, Moses was given miracles which dumbfounded the sorcerers and at the sight of these miracles the sorcerers accepted the leadership and prophethood of Moses." Similarly, "during the time of the Prophet of Islam, the art of eloquent speech had made great advances. Therefore, the Prophet of Islam was given the miracle of the *Qur'an* whose eloquence stilled the voices of the greatest poets of his time" (Gudel, 38–39).

But there is no evidence that this is "one of the established ways of God." To the contrary, even by the *Qur'an*'s own admission that God repeatedly gave miracles of nature through Moses and other prophets, including Jesus, it is God's established way to confirm his prophets through miracles. Further, there is nothing supernatural about eloquence.

Summary. Muhammad's unwillingness (and apparent inability) to perform miraculous feats of nature, when he knew that the prophets before him could and did perform them, sounds like a cop-out to thinking non-Muslims. They will ask, "If God confirmed other prophets by such things, then why did he not do the same for Muhammad and remove all doubt?" In Muhammad's own words (from the *Qur'an*), "They [will] say: 'Why is not A Sign sent down To him from his Lord?'" since even Muhammad admitted that "God hath certainly Power to send down a Sign" (sura 6:37).

Muhammad simply offered his own sign (the *Qur'an*) and said their reason for rejecting him was unbelief, not his inability to do miracles. In the few instances where alleged supernatural events are connected to Muhammad's life, they can be explained by natural means. For example, Muslims take Muhammad's outstanding victory at the battle of Badr in 624 as a supernatural indication of divine approval on his behalf. But exactly one year later, Muhammad's forces suffered a humiliating defeat. Yet this is not taken as a sign of divine disapproval.

Unlike the *Qur'an*, Islamic tradition (the *Hadith*) is filled with miracle claims, but they lack authenticity: They contradict the claim of Muhammad in the *Qur'an*. They were recorded a century or more after Muhammad. Most are rejected by Muslim scholars. They show evidence of embellishment. They lack criteria laid down by Muslim scholars for a supernatural confirmation of Muhammad's claims to be a prophet of God.

By contrast, Jesus performed numerous miracles. Most, if not all, of these were performed in connection with his claim to be God in human flesh (*see* CHRIST, DEITY OF; MIRACLE). The reports of these miracles are from eyewitnesses and contemporaries of Jesus. In this crucial way there is a significant difference between the supernatural confirmation of Christ to be the Son of God and the lack of credible miraculous confirmation of Muhammad to be even a prophet of God.

Sources

H. Abdalati, *Islam in Focus*

H. M. Ahmad, *Introduction to the Study of the Holy Quran*

I. R. Al Faruqi, *Islam*

A. Y. Ali, "Introduction to Sura XVII," in *The Meaning of the Glorious Qur'an*

———, "Mudjiza," in *The Encyclopedia of Islam*

M. I. Bukhari, *The Translation of the Meanings of Sahih Al-Bukhari*, M. M. Khan, trans.

A. Dashti, *Twenty-Three Years: A Study of the Prophetic Career of Mohammad*

A. Dawud, *Muhammad in the Bible*

I. R. A. Faruqi, *Islam*

N. L. Geisler and Abdul Saleeb, *Answering Islam: The Crescent in the Light of the Cross*

J. Gudel, *To Every Muslim an Answer*

M. Haykal, *The Life of Muhammad*

J. Horowitz, "The Growth of the Mohammed Legend," in *The Moslem World* 10 (1920)

I. Ishaq, *Sirat Rasul Allah* [trans. as *The Life of Muhammad*]

G. Nehls, *Christians Ask Muslims*

C. G. Pfander, *The Balance of Truth*

M. A. Rauf, *Islam: Creed and Worship*

D. J. Sahas, "The Formation of Later Islamic Doctrines as a Response to Byzantine Polemics: The Miracles of Muhammad," in *GOTR*, 1982

A. Schimmel, "The Prophet Muhammad as a Centre of Muslim Life and Thought," *We Believe in One God*

A. A. Shorrish, *Islam Revealed: A Christian Arab's View of Islam*

H. Spencer, *Islam and the Gospel of God*

W. S. C. Tisdall, *The Source of Islam*

Muslim. ***See*** **ALFARABI; AVICENNA; AVERROES; BIBLE, ISLAMIC VIEW OF; CHRIST'S DEATH, MORAL OBJECTIONS TO; CHRIST'S DEATH, SUBSTITUTION LEGEND; ISLAM; MONOTHEISM, ISLAMIC; NEW TESTAMENT CORRUPTION, ALLEGED; MUHAMMAD, ALLEGED BIBLE PREDICTIONS; MUHAMMAD, ALLEGED DIVINE CALL; MUHAMMAD, MIRACLES OF; MUHAMMAD, CHARACTER OF; *QUR'AN*, ALLEGED DIVINE ORIGIN.**

Mullins, Edgar Young. E. Y. Mullins was born on January 5, 1860, in Franklin County, Mississippi. He attended Mississippi College and Texas A & M, where he graduated in 1879. After hearing a former lawyer, Major William Evander Penn, speak at First Baptist Church, Dallas, Mullins was converted. Penn had been described as a man who used "reason and persuasion without denunciation" (Nettles, 54). Sensing a call to the ministry, he entered Southern Baptist Theological Seminary in 1881, where he graduated in 1885, having concentrated in theology and philosophy. In 1886 he married Isla May Hawley. After pastoring in Kentucky and Maryland, he was appointed president of Southern Seminary in 1899, where he remained until his death in 1928.

Mullins was both a theologian and apologist. His primary apologetic work is entitled *Why Is Christianity True?* (1905). His last work, *Christianity at the Crossroads* (1924), is strongly polemical. His other works also have apologetic overtones: *The Axioms of Religion* (1908), *The Christian Religion in Its Doctrinal Expression* (1917), and *Freedom and Authority in Religion* (1913).

Relation of Science and Scripture. Mullins was strongly influenced by the *inductive method of modern science. He also paid tribute to the pragmatist William *James. Without discarding traditional apologetics, he believed the task of the day was to "establish the Christian position by means of the principles of investigation employed by the opposition, so far as those principles are valid" (Mullins [1], 4).

Although Mullins fell short of a denunciation of *evolution, he strongly defended the direct creation of human beings. He was willing to admit that "God made the world gradually through long eras of time, that there is progress and growth in the universe" (Mullins, [4], 67). Yet his statement on science and religion attacked scientists who make "alleged discoveries in physical nature a convenient weapon of attack upon the facts of religion." Likewise, he opposed "teaching as facts what are merely hypotheses." Although he acknowledged that "evolution has long been a working hypothesis of science," he was quick to point out that "its best exponents freely admit that the causes of the origin of species have not been traced. Nor has any proof been forthcoming that man is not the direct creation of God as recorded in Genesis" (Mullins [5], 64).

Defense of Supernaturalism. Mullins declared that "The supreme issue today is between naturalism and super-naturalism (*see* MIRACLES, ARGUMENTS AGAINST). We stand unalterably for the supernatural in Christianity" (Mullins [5], 64). He spoke out strongly against its foundation in naturalism, calling the latter "an outrage against human nature, . . . a million miles away from the great struggling heart of the world" (Mullins [4], 148).

Defense of Theism. Although Mullins stressed Christian experience, he did not totally neglect the value of theist arguments for God's existence (*see* GOD, EVIDENCE FOR). In *Why Is Christianity True?* he spoke out strongly against the major alternative *worldviews of *pantheism, idealism, *materialism, *agnosticism, and naturalistic evolutionism. He did favor, however, the pragmatic verification of Christianity. Nonetheless, he attempted to extricate himself from the charges of subjectivism by stressing the factual and historical basis of Christianity as well as its rational nature. What he opposed was reducing Christianity to a philosophy. He wrote: "Christianity is primarily not a philosophy of the universe. It is a religion. . . . Christianity is a historical religion, and a religion of experience. It is grounded in facts. the Christian world-view rests upon these facts" (Mullins [4], 163)

Defense of the Historicity of the Gospels. Mullins' apologetic astuteness is captured in a tribute made by Thorton Whaling, professor of apologetics and theology at the Presbyterian Theological Seminary in Louisville who noted that "Mullins is well acquainted with the historic attacks on the Christian faith and is equally a master of the historic answers" (Nettles, 56). Even his doctrinal work, *The Christian Religion in Its Doctrinal Expression*, contains a strong defense of the facts of the historical Jesus. Based on the integrity of the New Testament witnesses (*see* NEW TESTAMENT, HISTORICITY OF), Mullins reconstructed from the historical records a supernatural Jesus who has a *virgin birth, sinless life (*see* CHRIST, UNIQUENESS OF), died a substitutionary death, and rose bodily from the dead (*see* RESURRECTION, EVIDENCE FOR).

Defense of the Inspiration of Scripture. Mullins' approach to Scripture was inductive, following that of James *Orr, Marcus Dodds, and William Sanday. He rejected what he thought of as the "scholastic" approach, which made the biblical writers "mere unintelligent instruments or pens used by the Holy Spirit" (Mullins [3], 379). However, he readily confessed his belief that the Bible is revelation from God (*see* BIBLE, EVIDENCE FOR). In it, he said, we have "an authoritative Scripture which Christian experience does not and cannot transcend" (ibid., 382). He even speaks of the biblical writers as rendering "truth unmixed with error" (Mullins [2], 144). Following James Orr, he affirms that the Bible "impartially interpreted and judged, is free from demonstrable error in its statements, and harmonious in its teachings" (Mullins [3], 381).

Stress on Christian Experience. Without neglecting the objective and rational dimensions of faith, Mullins placed a strong emphasis on the experiential elements of the Christian faith. Christianity, he said, "has to do with two great groups of facts: the facts of experience and the facts of the historical revelation of God through Christ" (Mullins [2], 18). He recorded testimonies of noted Christians from church history as well as contemporaries. He believed that he had achieved "irrefutable evidence of the objective existence of the Person [God] so moving me" (Mullins, 284). Combining all the experiential testimony of an unbroken line of Christians back to the New Testament, he concluded: "My certainty becomes absolute" (ibid.)

Sources

William E. A. Ellis, *A Man of Books and A Man of the People*

Fisher Humphreys, "E. Y. Mullins," in *Baptist Theologians*, Timothy George and David Dockery eds.

E. Y. Mullins (1), *Why Is Christianity True?*

E. Y. Mullins (2), *The Christian Religion in Its Doctrinal Expression*

E. Y. Mullins (3), *Freedom and Authority in Religion*

E. Y. Mullins (4), *Christianity at the Crossroads*

E. Y. Mullins (5), "Science and Religion," in *Review and Expositor* 22.1 (Jan. 1925)

E. Y. Mullins (6), *The Axioms of Religion*

Tom Nettles, "Edgar Young Mullins," in *Handbook of Evangelical Theologians.*

Bill Clark Thomas, *Edgar Young Mullins: A Baptist Exponent of Theological Restatement*

Mystery. St. Paul wrote: "Beyond all question, the mystery of godliness is great: He [God] appeared in a body, was vindicated by the Spirit, was seen by angels, was preached among the nations, was believed on in the world, was taken up in glory" (1 Tim. 3:16). The incarnation is a mystery (*see* CHRIST, DEITY OF). So is the *Trinity.

A mystery is not to be confused with an antinomy or paradox, which involves a logical contradiction (*see* LOGIC). A mystery goes *beyond reason* but not *against reason.* There is no contradiction, yet we lack total comprehension.

Further, a mystery is not something that can be attained by unaided human reason (*see* FAITH AND REASON). A mystery is known only by special divine revelation (*see* REVELATION, SPECIAL). Hence, mysteries are not the subject of *natural theology but only of revealed theology.

Another characteristic of a mystery is that while we know *that* both elements making up the mystery are true and ultimately fit together, nevertheless, we do not know *how* they are compatible. For example, we know *that* Christ is both God and human, but it is a mystery just *how* these two natures unite in one person.

Finally, a mystery is distinguished from a problem. A problem has a *solution;* a mystery is the object of *meditation.* A problem calls for *extensive* knowledge; a mystery for *intensive* concentration. Like a missing word in a crossword puzzle, a problem can be solved by more knowledge; a mystery cannot. If it could, it would not be a mystery. Mysteries do not call for *answers*, but for *insights.*

Sources

N. L. Geisler and R. Brooks, *When Skeptics Ask*
G. Marcel, *The Mystery of Being*
Thomas Aquinas, *Summa contra Gentiles*

Mystery Religions. ***See*** **Apocrypha, New Testament; Gnosticism; Miracle, Myth and; Mithraism; Mythology and the New Testament; Resurrection Claims in Non-Christian Religions.**

Mysticism. *Background.* The word "mysticism" is derived from the Greek word *mustikos,* meaning one initiated into the mysteries. Eventually, it was used in Christian circles as the branch of Christian theology that believes in the direct communion of the soul with God. In *pantheistic context it usually refers to one who seeks by contemplation and self-surrender to obtain absorption into the Ultimate. In philosophy it often refers to someone who believes that intuitive and immediate knowledge of ultimate reality is possible.

Kinds of Mysticism. Mysticism can be classed in many ways. In terms of worldviews (*see*) it can be divided into Christian and non-Christian or theistic and nontheistic. There are also forms of mysticism in most major world religions. Some, such as *Zen Buddhism, are mystical as such. Interest here is in whether mysticism has any apologetic value. That is, does a mystical experience help establish the truth of the belief system of the one having it?

The Nature of a Mystical Experience. Religious experiences are notoriously difficult to define. Friedrich *Schleiermacher said religion is a feeling of absolute dependence on the All. Paul *Tillich defined religion as an ultimate commitment. Our own analysis found it to be an awareness of some form of transcendent Other (*see* Geisler, *Philosophy of Religion*).

A Private Religious Experience. Religious experiences are of two basic kinds: general and specific. The first are available to all persons, and the latter are unique to only some. The former is public and the latter is private. Mystical experiences are private by nature. This does not mean that others cannot have similar experiences. It simply means that the experience is unique to the one having it. Also, the general public does not have such experiences at any time.

A Focused Religious Experience. Some forms of awareness are general and others are particular. For example, the awareness of being married is a general one that one has at all times. But the awareness of getting married is a special experience that one has only while going through the ceremony. A mystical experience is more like the latter. It is a focused and intensified awareness of an Ultimate, whereas, a general religious experience is like Schleiermacher's continual and nonspecific awareness of being dependent on the Ultimate.

An Intuitive Experience. Mystical experiences of God are noncognitive. They are not mediated through concepts or ideas. Rather, they are unmediated and intuitive. They are direct contacts with God. As such, they are not discursive. They involve no reasoning processes.

An Ineffable Experience. Although many mystics have attempted descriptions of their experience, most hasten to say that words are inadequate to express it. Many admit that they can only say what it is not. All attempts to be positive are purely metaphorical, allegorical, or symbolical. It can be experienced but not uttered (*see* Plotinus).

The Apologetic Value of Mystical Experiences. Mysticism is not without value. As William *James (*see*) noted, it points to a state beyond that of the purely empirical and rational. Indeed, Christian forms of mysticism, such as that of Meister Eckhart, have been embraced by many orthodox Christians.

However, our concern here is with the mystics' claim of the self-evident truthfulness of their mystical experiences. They insist that they are as basic as sense perceptions, being a kind of spiritual perception. Others challenge this and offer many reasons for rejecting any truth value to such experiences.

Mystical Experiences Are Not Self-Authenticating. While it is not necessary to deny that there are transcognitive mental states, it is often claimed by mystics that such experiences are self-authenticating. This appears to be a confusion of two things. They may be authenticating to the self (person) having them, but they are not self-authenticating. Self-authenticating, as in self-evident first principles (*see*), is something that can be known by examining the terms of the proposition. For example, "All triangles are three-sided figures" is self-evident because the predicate says exactly what the subject says. But there is no such parallel in a mystical experience of God.

Mystical Experience Is Not Objective. By their own admission, the experiences mystics have are not public but private. As such, then, they are subjective and not objective. But subjective experiences have validity only for the subject experiencing them. As William James noted in his landmark *Varieties of Religious Experience,* mystical experiences hold no authority over those not having them.

Mystical Experiences Are Not Testable. Since mystical experiences are without an objective basis, they are also untestable. Being subjective by nature, there is no objective test for them. Thus, they are totally relative to the individual having them. As such, there is no way that what the subject experiences can be validly applied to others.

Mystical Experiences Are Self-Cancelling. When a mystical experience is used to support the truth claim of the belief system of the one having it, it is without value for the simple reason that people with conflicting belief systems have mystical experiences. But if the same kind of evidence is used to support opposing beliefs it is self-cancelling. The evidence must be unique to one over the other for it to count for one over the other.

Mystical Experiences Can Be Misinterpreted. No attempt here is made to deny that some people have a mystical experience. Nor is it denied that they may feel that it is self-authenticating. Neither do we challenge the fact that it may appear to them to come with its own self-interpreting label.

It is simply argued that there is no evidence that this is so. Similar experiences by people from different *worldviews appear to them to vindicate their particular worldview or religious system. However, that fact in itself shows that it does not vindicate it, since opposites cannot be true. In brief, such experiences are not self-labeled and, hence, they can be mislabeled by the one having them.

Mysticism Leads to *Agnosticism. As most mystics admit, they have only a negative knowledge. That is, they know only what God is not. But they have no positive knowledge of what God is, certainly not in a cognitive sense. In short, they are religious agnostics, or *acognostics. They may believe in God and feel God, but they have no positive knowledge of what it is they are believing or feeling. They acknowledge a mystical realm, but like Ludwig *Wittgenstein they must remain silent about it. There are at least two serious problems with this position.

First, purely negative knowledge is impossible. One cannot know not-That unless he knows what That is. Likewise, one cannot know what God is not like unless he knows what he is like. Second, since religion, at least in the theistic sense, involves a personal relation with God, it is difficult to understand how one can have this if he knows none of the qualities of the Beloved. In this regard, the atheist Ludwig *Feuerbach's comment is appropriate: "Only where man loses his taste for religion, and thus religion itself becomes insipid existence—does the existence of God become an insipid existence—an existence without qualities" (Feuerbach, 15).

Sources

D. K. Clark, *The Pantheism of Alan Watts*
D. Clark and N. L. Geisler, *Apologetics in the New Age*
W. Corduan, "A Hair's Breadth from Pantheism: Meister Eckhart's God-Centered Spirituality," *JETS* 37 (1994)
M. Eckhart, Meister *Eckhart,* trans. Raymond B. Blakney
L. Feuerbach, *The Essence of Christianity*
N. L. Geisler, *Christian Apologetics* (Chap. 6)
N. L. Geisler and W. Corduan, *Philosophy of Religion* (Part One)
S. Hackett, Oriental *Philosophy*
G.W.F. Hegel, *The Phenomenology of Spirit*
D. L. Johnson, *A Reasoned Look at Asian Religions*
R. Otto, *Mysticism: East and West*
Plotinus, *Enneads*
D. T. Suzuki, *An Introduction to Zen Buddhism*
F. Schaeffer, The *God Who is There*

Myth, Mythology. ***See*** **Apocrypha; Jesus Seminar; Miracles, Myth and; Mithraism; Nag Hamadi; Q Gospel; Resurrection Claims in Non-Christian Religions.**

Mythology and the New Testament. Central to higher critical argumentation is the theory that much of the New Testament's picture of Jesus and his teachings evolved over time in the social context and theological meanderings of the early church. Jesus the man became lost in legend and myth, buried under supernatural claims of such events as the virgin birth, miracles, and the resurrection (*see* Resurrection, Evidence for). Behind these events were the patterns of Greek and Roman gods. Besides atheists and skeptics, some New Testament scholars have made such charges. Rudolf *Bultmann was in the forefront of this view of the New Testament. He insisted that the religious records must be "demythologized," or divested of their mythological "husk" to get at the existential "kernel" of truth.

Bultmann's Demythological Naturalism. At the basis of Bultmann's thought is his theory that Christianity grew from the prescientific worldview of a three-storied universe: The earth is at the center of this worldview, with God and angels in heaven above, and the underworld beneath. The material world was acted upon by supernatural forces from above and below, who intervened in human thoughts and actions (Bultmann, 1). The New Testament documents had to be stripped of this mythological structure, for science had made the supernaturalistic worldview obsolete. Blind acceptance of the New Testament would sacrifice the intellect to accept a view of the world in religion that we deny in everyday life (ibid., 3–4). The only honest way to recite the creeds is to strip the mythological framework from the truth it enshrines.

Bultmann proclaimed confidently that the resurrection is not an event of past history. "For an historical fact which involves a resurrection from the dead is utterly inconceivable" (Bultmann, 38–39). Resuscitation of a corpse is not possible. The objective historicity of the resurrection cannot be verified, no matter how many witnesses are cited. The resurrection is an article of faith. That in itself disqualifies it as a miraculous proof. Finally, similar events are known to mythology (ibid., 39–40).

Since the resurrection is not an event of objective space-time history, it is an event of subjective history. It is an event of faith in the hearts of the early disciples. As such, it is not subject to objective historical verification or falsification. Christ arose from Joseph's tomb only in the faith of the disciples' hearts.

Bultmann's argument can be summarized:

1. Myths are, by nature, more than objective truths; they are transcendent truths of faith.
2. But what is not objective cannot be part of a verifiable space-time world.
3. Therefore, miracles (myths) are not part of the objective space-time world.

Evaluation. Several objections have been offered to Bultmann's mythological naturalism.

Basically, demythologization is built on at least two unproven assumptions: First, miracles are less than historical. Second, miracles can occur in the world without being of the world. Bultmann's view is dogmatic and unverifiable. He has no evidential basis for his assertions. Yet he stands contrary to the overwhelming evidence for the authenticity of the New Testament documents and the reliability of the witnesses (*see* New Testament, Historicity of). Indeed, it is directly contrary to the New Testament writer Peter's claim that he was not preaching "cunningly devised myths" (2 Peter 1:16). Rather, he and the other apostles were eyewitnesses. John said much the same at the beginning and end of his Gospel (1:1–3; 21:24).

The New Testament is not the literary genre of mythology. C. S. *Lewis, himself a writer of fairy tales, noted that "Dr. Bultmann never wrote a gospel." Lewis asks, "Has the experience of his learned . . . life really given him any power of seeing into the minds of those long dead [who have written Gospels]?" As a living writer, Lewis found his critics usually wrong when they attempted to read his mind. He adds, "the 'assured results of modern scholarship,' as to the way in which an old book was written, are 'assured,' we may conclude, only because the men who knew the facts are dead and can't blow the gaff" (Lewis, *Christian Reflections,* 161–63).

Evidence for the New Testament. Other articles show that the New Testament was written by contemporaries and eyewitnesses of the events (cf. Luke 1:1–4) and was not the result of later legend development (*see* Bible Criticism; Mythology and the New Testament; New Testament Dating; New Testament Manuscripts). The article Miracles, Myth and, presents the following in greater detail.

New Testament books appeared within the lifetime of eyewitnesses and contemporaries. Luke was written by about 60, only twenty-seven years after Jesus' death, before Acts in 60–62 (see Hemer, all). First Corinthians was written by 55–56, only twenty-two or twenty-three years after Jesus' death (cf. 1 Cor. 15:6–8). Even radical New Testament scholar John A. T. Robinson dates basic Gospel records between 40 and 60 (see Robinson).

Given that significant parts of the Gospels and other crucial New Testament books were written before 70, there is no time or way for a legend to develop while the eyewitnesses were still alive to refute the story. A legend takes time and/or remoteness to develop, neither of which were available. Roman historian A. N. Sherwin-White calls the mythological view of the New Testament "unbelievable" (Sherwin-White, 189). Others have noted that the writings of Herodotus enable us to determine the rate at which legends develop. Two generations is too short a period for legendary tendencies to wipe out historical fact (Craig, 101). Julius Müller (1805–1898) challenged scholars of his day to produce even one example where in one generation a myth developed where the most prominent elements are myths (Müller, 29). None have been found.

New Testament stories do not show signs of being mythological. Lewis comments that the accounts are straightforward, unembellished records, written in artless, historical fashion by narrow, unattractive Jews who were blind to the mythical wealth of the pagan world around them (Lewis, *Miracles,* 236). "All I am in private life is a literary critic and historian, that's my job," said Lewis. "And I'm prepared to say on that basis if anyone thinks the Gospels are either legends or novels, then that person is simply showing his incompetence as a literary critic. I've read a great many novels and I know a fair amount about the legends that grew up among early people, and I know perfectly well the Gospels are not that kind of stuff" (*Christian Reflections,* 209).

Persons, places, and events surrounding the Gospel stories are historical. Luke goes to great pains to note that it was in the days of "Caesar Augustus" (Luke 2:1) that Jesus was born and at later baptized in "the fifteenth year of the reign of Tiberius Caesar, Pontius Pilate being governor of Judea, Herod being tetrarch of Galilee, . . . Annas and Caiaphas being high priests" (Luke 3:1–2).

Sixth, no Greek or Roman myth spoke of the literal incarnation of a monotheistic God into human form (cf. John 1:1–3, 14) by way of a literal *virgin birth (Matt. 1:18–25), followed by his death and physical resurrection. The Greeks believed in *reincarnation into a different mortal body; New Testament Christians believed in resurrection into the same physical body made immortal (cf. Luke 24:37). The Greeks were *polytheists, not monotheists as New Testament Christians were.

Stories of Greek gods becoming human via miraculous events like a virgin birth were not prior to but after the time of Christ (Yamauchi). Hence, if there is any influence of one on the other it is the influence of the historical event of the New Testament on the mythology, not the reverse.

Conclusion. The New Testament records show no signs of mythological development. Indeed, the miracle events are surrounded by historical references to real people, places, and times. The New Testament documents and witnesses are too early, too numerous, and too accurate to be charged with writing myths. Only an unjustified antisupernatural bias could ground any conclusion to the contrary (*see* MIRACLES, ARGUMENTS AGAINST).

Sources

R. Bultmann, *Kerygma and Myth: A Theological Debate*
W. Craig, *The Son Rises*
N. L. Geisler, *Miracles and the Modern Mind*, chap. 6
R. Gromacki, *The Virgin Birth: Doctrine of Deity*
C. J. Hemer, *The Book of Acts in the Setting of Hellenic History*
Justin Martyr, *Dialogue with Trypho*, chap. 84
C. S. Lewis, *Christian Reflections*
———, *Mere Christianity*
———, *Miracles*
J. G. Machen, *The Virgin Birth of Christ*
J. Muller, *The Theory of Myths, in Its Application to the Gospel History, Examined and Confuted*
R. Nash, *Christianity and the Hellenistic World*
J. A. T. Robinson, *Redating the New Testament*
A. N. Sherwin-White, *Roman Society and Roman Law in the New Testament*
E. Yamauchi, "Easter—Myth, Hallucination, or History?" *CT* (15 March 1974; 29 March 1974)

Nn

Nag Hammadi Gospels. Some radical critics of the New Testament (*see* BIBLE CRITICISM) claim that the Gnostic gospels are equal to those in the New Testament, and that they do not support the resurrection of Christ (*see* MIRACLE; RESURRECTION, EVIDENCE FOR). The Jesus Seminar places *The Gospel of Thomas* in their otherwise severely truncated Bible. Both of these conclusions are a serious challenge to the historic Christian Faith.

The *Gnostic gospels were discovered in Nag Hammadi, Egypt, near Cairo in 1945 and translated into English in 1977. *The Gospel of Thomas* (140–170) has 114 secret sayings of Jesus.

Credibility of the *Gnostic Gospels. The best way to evaluate the credibility of these gospels is by comparison to the New Testament Gospels, which the same critics have grave doubts about accepting (*see* NEW TESTAMENT, HISTORICITY OF; NEW TESTAMENT MANUSCRIPTS). Against the canonical gospels, the Gnostic gospels come up seriously short.

Late Writings. The attested dates for the canonical Gospels are no later than 60–100 (*see* NEW TESTAMENT, DATING OF). Gnostic gospels appeared nearly a century later. O. C. Edwards asserts "As historical reconstructions there is no way that the two can claim equal credentials" (Edwards, 27).

Historical Worth. The earliest Christians meticulously preserved Jesus' words and deeds. The Gospel writers were close to the eyewitnesses and pursued the facts (cf. Luke 1:1–4). There is evidence that the Gospel writers were honest reporters. They also present the same overall picture of Jesus (*see* BIBLE, ALLEGED ERRORS IN; RESURRECTION, EVIDENCE FOR).

New Testament Canon. Contrary to the critics, the New Testament canon with Gospels and most of Paul's Epistles was formed by the end of the first century. The only books in dispute, the *Antelegomena*, have no apologetic effect on the argument for the reliability of the historical material used to establish the deity of Christ.

The New Testament itself reveals a collection of books in the first century. Peter speaks of having Paul's Epistles (2 Peter 3:15–16), equating them with Old Testament Scripture. Paul had access to Luke's Gospel, quoting it (10:7) in 1 Timothy 5:18.

Beyond the New Testament, canonical lists support the existence of a New Testament canon (see Geisler and Nix, 294). Indeed, all the Gospels and Paul's basic Epistles are represented on these lists.

Even the heretical canon of Marcion (ca. 140) accepted the Gospel of Luke and ten of Paul's Epistles (*see* BIBLE, CANONICITY OF).

Support of Church Fathers. A common body of books was cited by Fathers in the second century. This includes the six books crucial to the historicity of Christ and his resurrection, the Gospels, Acts, and 1 Corinthians. Clement of Rome cited the Gospels in 95 (*Corinthians*, 13, 42, 46). Ignatius (ca. 110–115) quoted Luke 24:39 (*Smyrnaeans* 3). Polycarp (ca. 115) cites all Synoptic Gospels (*Philippians* 2, 7). The *Didache* (early second century) cites the Synoptic Gospels (1, 3, 8, 9, 15–16). The *Epistle of Barnabas* (ca. 135) cites Matthew 22:14. Papias (*Oracles*, ca. 125–140) speaks of Matthew, Mark (chronicling Peter), and John (last) who wrote Gospels. He says three times that Mark made no errors. The Fathers considered the Gospels and Paul's Epistles to be on par with the inspired Old Testament (cf. Clement's *Corinthians* [47]; Ignatius's *Ephesians* [10]; *To Polycarp* [1, 5]; and Polycarp's *Philippians* [1, 3–4, 6, 12]).

The Fathers vouched for the accuracy of canonical Gospels in early second century. This is long before gnostic gospels were written in the late second century.

Gnostic Resurrection Accounts. There is no real evidence that the so-called "Q" (*Quelle*, source) document posited by the critics ever existed (see Linneman; *see* Q DOCUMENT). It is an imaginary reconstruction, so the allegation that it has nothing about the resurrection is pointless.

The *Gospel of Thomas* does exist, even though it is from the late second century. Nonetheless, contrary to the critics who support this composition, it acknowledges Jesus' resurrection. In fact, it is the living, post-death (34:25–27; 45:1–16) Christ who allegedly speaks in it. True, it does not stress the resurrection, but this is to be expected because it is primarily a "sayings" source, rather than a historical narration. Further, the Gnostic theological bias against matter would downplay bodily resurrection.

Earliest Christian Creeds. Since the critics acknowledge the authenticity of 1 Corinthians 15, which is dated ca. 55–56 A.D., it is impossible to deny the historicity of the resurrection. This is only twenty-two or twenty-three years after Jesus died (1 Cor. 15:6). What is more, 1 Corinthians 15:1 alludes to a possible creed confessing the death and resurrection of Christ that would be even earlier. Even on the minimal assumption that the creed was ten or twelve years old, that would place it within ten or twelve years of the events themselves. Few ancient events have this immediate, contemporary verification.

Conclusion. The evidence for the authenticity of the Gnostic gospels does not compare with that for the New Testament. The New Testament is a first-century book. *The Gospel of Thomas* is a mid-second-century book. The New Testament is verified by numerous lines of evidence, including other references in the New Testament, early canonical lists, thousands of citations by the early Fathers, and the established earlier dates for the Gospels.

Sources

O. C. Edwards, *New Review of Book and Religion* (May 1980)
C. A. Evans, *Nag Hammadi Texts and the Bible*
J. Fitzmyer, *America* (16 February 1980)
A. Frederick, et al., *The Gnostic Gospels*
N. L. Geisler and W. Nix, *General Introduction to the Bible*
R. M. Grant, *Gnosticism and Early Christianity*
E. Linneman, *Is There a Synoptic Problem?*
J. P. Moreland, ed., *Jesus under Fire*
J. M. Robinson, *The Nag Hammadi Library in English*
F. Seigert, et al., *Nag-Hammadi-Resister*
C. M. Tuckett, *Nag Hammadi and the Gospel Tradition*

Natural Law. ***See*** **LAW, NATURE AND KINDS OF; REVELATION, GENERAL; MORALITY, ABSOLUTE NATURE OF.**

Natural Theology. *Theology* is the study *(logos)* of God *(theos)*. *Natural theology* (*see* LAW, NATURE AND KINDS OF) is the study of God based on what one can know from nature (*see* REVELATION, GENERAL). Natural theology is set in contrast with supernatural theology which is dependent on a supernatural revelation (*see* REVELATION, SPECIAL) from God, such as the Bible.

Natural theology depends on the rational arguments for God's existence (*see* COSMOLOGICAL ARGUMENT; MORAL ARGUMENT FOR GOD; TELEOLOGICAL ARGUMENT) and nature (*see* GOD, NATURE OF). Most natural theologians, following Thomas Aquinas, believe that one can know the existence, unity, and general nature of God from natural revelation. However, the triunity of God (*see* TRINITY), incarnation of Christ (*see* CHRIST, DEITY OF), and redemption (*see* "HEATHEN," SALVATION OF) can only be known by supernatural revelation. These are known as mysteries of the Faith (*see* MYSTERY).

Naturalism. Philosophical or metaphysical *naturalism* refers to the view that nature is the "whole show." There is no supernatural realm and/or intervention in the world (*see* MATERIALISM; MIRACLES, ARGUMENTS AGAINST). In the strict sense, all forms of nontheisms are naturalistic, including *atheism, *pantheism, *deism, and *agnosticism.

However, some theists (*see* THEISM), especially scientists, hold a form of *methodological naturalism*. That is, while acknowledging the existence of God and the possibility of miracles, they employ a method of approaching the natural world that does not admit of miracles (*see* SCIENCE OF ORIGINS). This is true of many theistic evolutionists (*see* EVOLUTION; EVOLUTION, BIOLOGICAL), such as Douglas Young (see Young) and Donald MacKay (see MacKay). They insist that to admit miracles in nature to explain the unique or anomalous is to invoke "the God of the gaps." In this sense they are bedfellows with the antisupernaturalists, who deny miracles on the grounds that they are contrary to the scientific method.

Forms of Metaphysical Naturalism. Metaphysical naturalists are of two basic kinds: materialists and pantheists. The materialist reduces all to matter (*see* MATERIALISM) and the pantheist reduces all to mind or spirit. Both deny that any supernatural realm intervenes in the natural world. They differ chiefly about whether the natural world is composed ultimately of matter or of mind (spirit). Those who hold the latter often admit the possibility of *supernormal* events by tapping into this invisible spiritual Force (*see* MIRACLE; MIRACLES, MAGIC AND). However, these are not supernatural events in the theistic sense of a *supernatural* being intervening in the natural world he created.

Bases for Naturalism. Metaphysical naturalists reject miracles outright. They vary only in the basis for their criticism of the supernatural. Benedict *Spinoza believed miracles are impossible because they are irrational. David *Hume claimed that miracles are incredible. Rudolph *Bultmann held that miracles are unhistorical and mythical (*see* MIRACLES, MYTH AND; MYTHOLOGY AND THE NEW TESTAMENT). Based on the unrepeatability of the miraculous, Antony *Flew argued that miracles are unidentifiable. Immanuel *Kant contended that miracles are not essential to religion. All of these allegations have been carefully analyzed and found to be without foundation in the articles MIRACLE and MIRACLES, ARGUMENTS AGAINST.

Evaluation. *Theistic Inadequacy of Naturalism.* Naturalistic views either admit that a deistic sort of God exists or deny or doubt existence of any divine Being. But the alleged disproofs for God are notoriously unsuccessful (*see* GOD, ALLEGED DISPROOFS OF). The evidence that God exists is strong (*see* COSMOLOGICAL ARGUMENT; MORAL ARGUMENT FOR GOD; TELEOLOGICAL ARGUMENT). As for views that admit the existence of a supernatural God but deny miracles (such as deism), many critics have pointed out their basic incoherence. For if God can and has performed the greatest supernatural act of all—creating the world out of nothing (*see* CREATION, VIEWS OF), then there is no reason to deny the possibility of lesser supernatural events (i.e., miracles). For making water out of nothing (as God did in Genesis 1) is a greater supernatural event than making water into wine (as Jesus did in John 2).

Scientific Insufficiency. Modern science has pointed to its own miracle—the origin of the material universe out of nothing. The evidence for the big bang origin of the universe is strong. This evidence includes the second law of thermodynamics (*see* THERMODYNAMICS, LAWS OF), the expanding universe, the radiation echo and the discovery of the large mass of energy predicted by the big bang theory (*see KALAM* COSMOLOGICAL ARGUMENT). If so, then matter is neither eternal nor all there is. And if there is a Creator of the whole universe from nothing, the greatest miracle of all has occurred.

Philosophical Insufficiency. Two premises common to all forms of secular humanism (*see* HUMANISM, SECULAR) are nontheism and naturalism. These can be treated together, since if there is no supernatural being (Creator) beyond the natural universe, then nature is all there is. Often naturalism means that everything can be explained in terms of chemical and physical processes. At a minimum it means that every event in the universe can be explained in terms of the whole universe (the whole system). Naturalists believe there is no need to appeal to anything (or Anyone) outside the universe to explain any event in the universe nor to explain the whole universe itself.

But the very scientific naturalists who insist on explaining *everything* in terms of physical and chemical laws cannot explain their own scientific theories or laws in terms of mere physical and chemical processes. For a "theory" or "law" about physical processes is obviously not itself a physical process. It is a nonphysical *theory* about physical things. A physics professor was once asked: "If everything is matter, then what is a scientific theory about matter?" His response was, *"It is magic!"* When asked his basis for believing that, he replied "Faith." It is interesting to note the inconsistency that a purely materialistic worldview resorts to faith in "magic" as the basis of their materialistic beliefs.

Another argument revealing the inconsistency of pure naturalism was offered by C. S. *Lewis. Quoting Haldane, Lewis wrote: "If my mental processes are determined wholly by the motion of atoms in my brain, I have no reason to suppose that my beliefs are true . . . and hence I have no reason for supposing my brain to be composed of atoms" (Lewis, 22). If naturalism is claiming to be true then there must be more than mere natural processes; there must be "reason," which is not purely a natural physical process.

Another way to state the inconsistency of naturalism is to show that a basic premise of science, which even naturalists hold, is contrary to their conclusion that every event in the universe can be explained in terms of the whole universe. This premise that "every event has a cause" is at the philosophical heart of scientific research (*see* CAUSALITY, PRINCIPLE OF). For scientists—certainly naturalistic ones—are trying to find the natural explanation or cause for all events. But if *every* event has a cause, then it follows that the *whole* universe has a cause. For the universe as conceived by modern science is the sum total of all events at a given time. But if *each* event is caused, then *every* event is caused. And if the universe is the sum total of every event, then the whole universe is caused. For instance, if each tile on the floor is brown, then the whole floor is brown. And if each part of the table is wooden, then the whole table is wooden. Likewise, if every event in the universe is an effect, then adding up all the events (effects) does not equal a cause. Rather, the sum total of all caused events needs a cause to explain it (*see* COSMOLOGICAL ARGUMENT).

It is not sufficient for the naturalist to say there is something "more" to the universe than the sum of all the events or "parts," for then he is not really explaining *everything* in terms of the physical "parts" or events but in terms of something beyond them. It is, however, perfectly consistent for the nonnaturalist to insist that all the events of the universe cannot be explained *solely* in terms of the physical universe of events. But naturalism is not able to explain either itself or the universe on a purely naturalistic premise.

Sources

N. L. Geisler, *Is Man the Measure?* chap. 5

———, *Miracles and the Modern Mind*, chap. 8

T. Hobbes, *Leviathan*

C. S. Lewis, *Miracles*

D. MacKay, *Clockwork Image*

D. A. Young, *Christianity and the Age of the Earth*

Near-Death Experiences. ***See*** **IMMORTALITY.**

Neopaganism. *Neopaganism* (lit. "New-paganism") is a revival of ancient paganism (*see* MITHRA-

ISM). It is a form of *polytheism that arose in the wake of the "death of God" movement (*see* ALTIZER, THOMAS; NIETZSCHE, FRIEDRICH). Neopaganism is also manifest in witchcraft (wicca), occultism, and other religions that fit under the New Age umbrella (see Geisler).

Mark Satin has contrasted new paganism with primitive forms of the religion. Citing Andrea Dworkin, he noted that the "old religion":

- celebrated sexuality, fertility, nature, and women's place in it.
- worshiped a hairy, merry deity who loved music and dancing and good food.
- was nature- and woman-centered, with priestesses, wise women, midwives, goddesses, and sorceresses.
- had no dogma. Each priestess interpreted the religion in her own fashion.

Not all of this could be reestablished in New Age society, writes Satin, but neopagans could adapt nature-and woman-centeredness to fit new priorities. "Nature-centeredness has an obvious parallel in our growing recognition that the quality of our connection to the environment—both natural and people-made—has a lot to do with our spiritual health and spiritual growth" (Satin, 113–14).

Roots of Neopaganism. Neopaganism is not a monolithic movement. It springs from the soil of paganism, *Hinduism, wicca, and, indirectly, atheism, and other systems. Modern *atheism fertilized the soil out of which contemporary neopaganism grew. David Miller describes it as rising from the ashes of the "death of God" heralded by Thomas *Altizer and others in the 1960s and 1970s. "The death of God gives rise to the rebirth of the gods," according to Miller. When God died in modern culture, the ancient gods rose again. Monotheism was holding back paganism.

Ancient Polytheism. Of course, the main root of Neopaganism is ancient Greek and Roman polytheism. Miller noted that ancient *polytheism remained underground or in the countercultural tradition of the West throughout the 2000-year reign of monotheistic thought. This tradition may be behind recent interest in the occult, magic, extraterrestrial life, Eastern societies and religions, communes, new forms of multiple family life, and other alternative life-style meaning systems that seem so foreign (ibid., 11). He adds that, for racial-cultural traditions, Western Europeans still draw on gods and goddesses of ancient Greece (ibid., 6, 7, 60, 81).

Hinduism. Not all modern paganism comes from Greece. The revival of *Buddhism and especially Hinduism, with its multi-millions of gods, also supports New Age religion and Neopaganism. Hinduism has infiltrated virtually every level of Western culture, tailored to fit Western humanism by teaching that each of us is a little god.

Witchcraft (Wicca) and Radical Feminism. Another stream is the religion of wicca. This movement, popularly known as witchcraft, has a strong overlap with the feminist movement. Wiccans have an abhorrence to monotheism (*see* THEISM). Feminist witch Margot Adler expresses this view. Adler refers to monotheism as one of the totalistic religious and political views that dominate society (Adler).

Occultism and Star Wars. George Lucas' *Star Wars* "religion of the Jedi" has roots in the Mexican sorcerer, Don Juan. Lucas biographer Dale Pollock notes that "Lucas' concept of the Force was heavily influenced by Carlos Castaneda's *Tales of Power*. This is an account of a supposed Mexican Indian sorcerer, Don Juan, who uses the phrase 'life force'" (Pollock, 10). The director of Lucas' movie, *The Empire Strikes Back*, Irvin Kershner, is a *Zen Buddhist. He admitted of the film: "I want to introduce some Zen here because I don't want the kids to walk away just feeling that everything is shoot-em-up, but there's also a little something to think about here in terms of yourself and your surroundings" (Kershner, 37). Whatever the source of the Force of *Star Wars*, it clearly is similar to the Force believed in by neopagan witches. Lucas himself referred to the force as a religion in the first movie of his *Star Wars* trilogy (Lucas, 37, 121, 145). The character, Luke Skywalker, was engaging in white magic when he tapped into the "light side of the Force," the Force was "God." Lucas claimed in an interview with *Time* (see source list) that "the world works better if you're on the good side" of this occult Force. Lucas' sorcery is even more evident in the hero of Lucas' subsequent film, *Willow*, whose life goal is to be a sorcerer.

Characteristics of Neopaganism. Obviously a variety of beliefs are practiced under the broad neopagan heading. There are some generally shared characteristics and beliefs that draw on polytheism, the occult, relativism, and pluralism.

Polytheism. Neopagans are free to worship any gods and goddesses, ancient or modern, from the East or West. Some worship Apollo and Diana. Author-philosopher Theodore Roszak (*Where the Wasteland Ends*) is an animist. He believes that "the statue and sacred grove were transparent windows . . . by which the witness was escorted through to sacred ground beyond and participated in the divine" (*see* Adler, 27). Most neopagans revive one of the Western forms of polytheism. The names of the gods may differ, but most often they are Celtic, Greek, or Latin.

Some neopagans debate about the ontological state of their "gods," assigning an idealistic or aesthetic role to them. But as one put it, "All these things are within the realm of possibility. It has been our nature to call these 'gods.'" God is an eternal being; so are we. Then in a sense, we, too, are god. Adler notes that there are two deities of most wicca groups: The god is the lord of animals and of death and beyond; and the goddess has three aspects: Maiden, Mother, and Crone. Each of her aspects is symbolized by a phase of the moon. The Maiden is the waxing crescent, the Mother is the full moon, and the waning crescent is like the woman who is past childbearing. Adler suggests that neopagans might be considered "duotheists," though feminist witches are often monotheists, worshiping the goddess as the one god (ibid., 35, 112). Neopagans sometimes describe themselves as monotheistic polytheists. Morgan McFarland, a Dallas witch, declared: "I see myself as monotheistic in believing in the Goddess, Creatrix, the Female Principle, but at the same time acknowledging that other gods and goddesses do exist through her as manifestations of her, facets of the whole" (ibid., 36). By her own definition, the use of *monotheistic* here is misleading. She and other neopagans look to a many-faceted (polytheistic) manifestation of pantheism. Each manifestation, of course, is finite (*see* POLYTHEISM).

The Radical Feminist Connection. Neopaganism closely connects with radical feminism. Not all neopagans are feminists, nor are all feminists neopagan. Nonetheless, neopaganism has drawn many feminists. Adler describes the dynamics this way: "Many feminist Witchcraft covens have . . . attracted women from all walks of life. But even there, most of these women have already been strengthened by the feminist movement, or by consciousness-raising groups, or by an important experience such as divorce, separation, or a homosexual encounter" (ibid., 37). One neopagan feminist said, "We have found that women working together are capable of conjuring their past and reawakening their old ascendancy. . . . This does not seem to happen when men are present . . . it seems that in mixed covens, no matter how 'feminist' the women are, a kind of competition begins to happen. Among the women alone, none of this occurs, and a great reciprocity develops, unlike anything I have seen before" (ibid., 124).

Some were witches before they were feminists. A neopagan from Los Angeles said her spiritual journey began when she observed her mother talking to the dead. "I saw her go into a trance and feel presences around her. She is an artist, and her art often reflects Sumerian influences. . . . She tells fortunes and can still the wind." But the daughter, like the mother, found herself in the traditional role of wife and mother and felt limited and enslaved. While attempting suicide she had a vision that confirmed her occult beliefs. Her awareness as a witch and feminist perspective met in the attempt to liberate her womanhood from perceived oppression (ibid. 76–77).

One draw to witchcraft for women is that their gender has equal, and often superior, status. As far back as the 1890s, a social observer named Leland wrote that in times of intellectual rebellion against conservatism and hierarchy, there is a feminist struggle for superiority. He noted that in witchcraft the female is the primitive principle. "The perception of this [tyranny] drove vast numbers of the discontent into rebellion, and as they could not prevail by open warfare, they took their hatred out in a form of secret anarchy, which was, however, intimately blended with superstition and fragments of old tradition" (ibid., 59).

Occultism. Almost inevitably neopagans are involved in the occult. They believe in an impersonal force, energy, or power, into which they can tap to do supernormal things. Luke Skywalker of *Star Wars* is the classic model for this belief. Attempts to cast spells are another example.

Pluralism and Relativism. Neopagans are strongly pluralistic. Polytheism by its nature leaves room for more gods or goddesses. All forms of worship of whatever god one may choose are legitimate. Such belief rejects absolute truth in favor of an irrationalism in which opposites can both be true. Miller denies that any system operates "according to fixed concepts and categories" and that all are controlled by either-or categories of logic. He rejects the idea that something is true or false, beautiful or ugly, good or evil (ibid., 7).

Consistently, many neopagans flatly reject the idea of *The Witches' Bible*, fuming at the word *the*. Modern pagans remain anti-authoritarian, taking pride in being "the most flexible and adaptable of religions, . . . perfectly willing to throw out dogmas" (Adler, ix, 126, 135). A neopagan "creed," therefore, is an oxymoron. They are noncreedal by definition.

Evaluation. Many criticisms of neopagan, polytheistic, and relativist (*see* TRUTH, ABSOLUTE NATURE OF) religion are treated elsewhere. See the articles DUALISM; FINITE GODISM; GNOSTICISM; GOD, NATURE OF; HINDUISM, VEDANTA; MONISM; NOSTRADAMUS; PANTHEISM; PLURALISM, RELIGIOUS; TRUTH, NATURE OF; ZEN BUDDHISM. A few central points can be briefly discussed here:

Irrationality. Neopagans claim we should discard reason as normative in life. But if this is done, then opposites could both be true. This violates the fundamental laws of thought (*see* FIRST PRINCIPLES). The person who claims that opposites can both be true does not really believe that the opposite of that statement also is true.

Relativism. Neopagans are relativists. But all truth cannot be relative. That very claim is presented as a nonrelative truth claim. There cannot be one and only one God (monotheism) and more than one god (polytheism) at the same time and in the same sense (*see* PLURALISM).

Pluralism. The pluralistic desire to embrace all forms of religion runs into the same problem. Everything cannot be true, including opposites. This violates the Law of Noncontradiction (*see* LOGIC; FIRST PRINCIPLES). Either polytheism is true or monotheism is true. Both cannot be true. Neopagans cannot use either-or statements to affirm both-and thinking. Polytheists have to deny pluralism in order to affirm it, for they do not believe the opposite of pluralism is true. But if opposites are not true, pluralism is false.

Inclusivism. The claim that we must be inclusive, holding all religions to be true, is also self-defeating. It is a non-inclusive (exclusivist) claim to assert that only inclusivism is true and all exclusivism is false. While they claim to allow total diversity of expression, the neopagan practice is quite restrictive. The very existence of *secret* covens reveals the exclusivistic nature of the group. Some refer to wicca as *the* religion. Even proponents believe in a universal element in neopaganism, insisting on universality of content but not of form (ibid., 116, 145). The existence of an initiation rite is an earmark of exclusivism. Witches claim their rite is a way to protect the institution from those who are insincere, evil, or who would give the craft a bad name (ibid., 98). But if they must protect their institution from evil or the insincere, there must be a genuine form to preserve. Adler claims that witchcraft was once the *universal religion*, which has been driven underground (ibid., 66). This is a claim to universality and implicit exclusivism to be *the* religion.

One controversy in which wiccans condemned a couple who were charging money for lessons in witchcraft, further shows exclusivity. Those who voiced disapproval insisted that "this violates Craft Law," indicating that there is a universal craft law that defines right and wrong. If it does not, witchcraft can be done in any way one wishes. Even the "Principles of Wiccan Belief" adopted by the Council of American Witches on April 11–14, 1974, has a strong statement excluding the belief that Christianity is "the only way." They frankly acknowledged this as part of "our animosity toward Christianity" (ibid., 103).

All-inclusive groups fail to realize that every truth claim is exclusive. If Christianity is true, then of necessity all non-Christian beliefs are false. If witchcraft is true, all nonwitchcraft beliefs are false. Neopaganism is just as exclusivistic as any other religion that claims to have discovered truth about reality.

Neopagans admit that "polytheism always includes monotheism. The reverse is not true" (ibid., viii). *Includes* is not the proper word here. Polytheism is willing to *absorb* or *swallow* monotheistic beliefs, but polytheism must be extremely exclusive of all orthodox forms of monotheism. These worldviews cannot share the same belief system. Under a cloak of inclusive language, neopaganism believes that the only way is to deny that there is an only way.

Failure to Explain Origins. Some pagan religions speak of origins, but few ask ultimate questions about them (*see* COSMOLOGICAL ARGUMENT). There are gods acting, but how did they get us to this point? What caused it all to be? C. S. *Lewis remarked that to bring God and nature into relation, also separates them. What makes and what is made are two, not one. "Thus the doctrine of Creation in one sense empties nature of divinity" (Lewis, 79–80). That destroys paganism.

Failure to Explain Unity. If the pagan realized that nature and God are distinct, that the one made the other; one ruled and the other obeyed, gods would not be worshiped, but rather the Creator God. C. S. Lewis observed, "The difference between believing in God and in many gods is not one of arithmetic. . . . God has no plural" (Lewis, 78, 82). Herein is revealed the depravity of polytheism, for they prefer to worship a god they make, rather than the God who made them. One neopagan concluded, "I realized it wasn't so outrageous, and that we could choose what deities to follow. . . . [for] the element of Christianity that bothered [me] . . . was its requirement to be submissive to the deity." He adds that his gods have human characteristics. They are flawed and so more approachable (*Fort Worth Star-Telegram*, 16 December 1985, 2A). In biblical language this is a vivid confession of the fact that pagans "suppress the truth in unrighteousness . . . and change the glory of the incorruptible God into an image made like corruptible man" (Rom. 1:18, 23).

Anticreedalism. Their protest notwithstanding, neopaganism has its own creeds and dogmas. Adler admits: "I've seen a lot of people in the Craft get hung up on fragments of ritual and myth. Some people accept these fragments as a dogma." While protesting creeds, Adler lays down a set of "basic beliefs" she claims "most people in this book share" (Adler, 88, ix). She seems unaware that she is thereby defining a creed.

The creed she confesses is informative: "The world is holy. Nature is holy. The body is holy. Sexuality is holy. The mind is holy. The imagination is holy. You are holy. . . . Thou art Goddess. Thou art God. Divinity is immanent in all Nature. It is as much within you as without" (ibid.). There are several standard doctrines of neopaganism in this creed, including pantheism, polytheism, animism, self-deification, and, covertly, free sexual expression. In the creed they called "Principles of Wiccan Belief," the Council of American Witches listed thirteen basic principles. These beliefs include moon worship, harmony with nature, the creative power in the universe manifest in male and female polarities, and sex as pleasure. Interestingly, they disavowed Devil worship and the belief that Christianity is "the only way" (ibid., 101–3).

Mission. Neopagans claim to seek no converts. "You don't *become* a Pagan," they insist; "You *are* a Pagan." They claim that no one converts to Wicca. Yet they admit that people are drawn into paganism by "word of mouth, a discussion between friends, a lecture, a book, or an article." Regardless of their purpose, what are these but means of evangelism. To claim that these people were always pagan and that they just "came home" (ibid., x, 14, 121) is like Christian missionaries denying that they evangelize, since those who believe have simply "come back to God." Like anyone else who believes he or she has found truth or reality, the neopagans cannot resist the urge to propagate their faith. Why else does the experience of enlightenment lead new wiccans to proclaim with the zeal of a new convert: "I was turned on to the Goddess. It was the religion" (ibid., 116)?

Sources

Adler, Margot, *Drawing Down the Moon*

———, "Neo-paganism and Feminism," in *Christian Research Journal*

N. L. Geisler and J. Amano, *The Infiltration of the New Age*

I. Kershner, Interview in *Rolling Stone* (24 July 1980)

C. S. Lewis, *Reflections on the Psalms*

G. Lucas, *Star Wars*

———, Interview in *Time* (23 May 1983), 68

D. Miller, *The New Polytheism*

D. Pollock, *Skywalking: The Life and Films of George Lucas*

M. Satin, *New Age Politics*

Neotheism. *Meaning of the Term.* Proponents of this view variously describe themselves as holding the "openness of God" view or "free will theism," by which they mean God is open to change and that humans have *free will as opposed to any divine *determinism of the future in advance. Nonetheless, "neotheism" appears to be a more appropriate, simpler, and more descriptive term. By their own confession, they see themselves as theists but have adopted some of the tenets of *panentheism or process theology (*see* WHITEHEAD, A. N.).

Some Proponents of Neotheism. Proponents of neotheism include Clark Pinnock, Richard Rice, John Sanders, William Hasker, and David Basinger (see Pinnock et al., *The Openness of God*). Others who have written in defense of the position include Greg Boyd, Stephen T. Davis, Peter Geach, Peter Lang, J. R. Lucas, Thomas V. Morris, Ronald Nash, A. N. Prior, Richard Purtill, Richard Swinburne, and Linda Zagzebski.

Some Basic Tenets of Neotheism. In their own words neotheists believe that "1. God not only created this world *ex nihilo* but can and at times does intervene unilaterally in earthly affairs. 2. God chose to create us with incompatibilist (libertarian) freedom—freedom over which he cannot exercise total control. 3. God so values freedom—the moral integrity of free creatures and a world in which such integrity is possible—that he does not normally override such freedom, even if he sees that it is producing undesirable results. 4. God always desires our highest good, both individually and corporately, and thus is affected by what happens in our lives. 5. God does not possess exhaustive knowledge of exactly how we will utilize our freedom, although he may very well at times be able to predict with great accuracy the choices we will freely make" (Pinnock, 76–77).

Neotheism can best be described by noting what it holds in common with traditional or classical theism (*see*) and also what it holds in distinction from it.

Tenets Held in Common with Theism. In accord with classical *theism, neotheists believe that God is a personal, transcendent, all-powerful Being who created the world *ex nihilo,* out of nothing (*see* CREATION, VIEWS OF), and who can and has performed supernatural acts within it. God is in charge of the universe, but he has given human beings the power to make free choices.

Tenets Held in Distinction from Theism. By way of contrast with traditional theism, neotheism holds that God does not have an infallible knowledge of future free acts. In addition, he can and does change his mind in response to our prayers. Furthermore, God is not absolutely simple nor is he nontemporal or eternal. Thus, he is not able to completely control or predict exactly the way things will turn out.

An Evaluation of Neotheism. *Positive Features.* There are many positive dimensions of neotheism. These include all the things its adherents hold in common with classical theists.

Creation ex nihilo. One of the signature beliefs of classical theism, in contrast to other *worldviews, is that God created the universe out of nothing. This clearly distinguishes the view from panentheism and places its adherents in the broad theistic camp.

Affirmation of miracles. Unlike panentheists and like theists, neotheists affirm *miracles. This places them alongside traditional theism and in contrast to *naturalism and current neoclassical theism known as process theology.

Emphasis on God's relatability with creation. Neotheists are deeply concerned, and rightly so, to preserve God's relatability with the world. A God who cannot hear and answer prayer is less than personal and is not the God described in the Bible.

Stress on Free Will. Along with classical theists, neotheists desire to defend free choice against forms of determinism that would eliminate genuine free will. This is commendable.

Along with this should be mentioned that neotheists are right in stressing that there are some things that are impossible for God to do, once he has decided to make free creatures. He cannot, for example, force them to freely choose something. Forced freedom is a contradiction in terms (*see* FREE WILL; EVIL, PROBLEM OF).

Negative Critique. On the negative side of the ledger, neotheists are to be criticized in part for creating God in their own image (see Geisler, all). They have in fact bought too deeply into panentheism and are subject to many of the same criticisms.

Neotheism is unbiblical. Since Christian neotheists claim to accept the authority of the Bible, they can be judged by its standards (Geisler, chap. 4). And the Bible, in contrast to neotheism, clearly affirms that God cannot change. The self-existent I AM (Exod. 3:14) of Scripture says "I the Lord change not" (Mal. 3:6; Heb. 1:12; James 1:17). and who "knows the end from the beginning" (Isa. 46:10). God is "infinite in understanding" (Ps. 147:5) and, hence, "foreknows" the elect (Rom. 8:29; 2 Peter 1:2). He "is not a man that he should change his mind" (1 Sam. 15:29).

When the Bible speaks of God "repenting" it is only from our perspective, as when there is a repentance on the part of man (Jonah 3). For example, when one reverses course after peddling his bike against the wind, it was not the wind that changed. Even neotheists admit there are anthropomorphisms in the Bible.

Neotheism is incoherent. For example, neotheists believe God created the temporal world out of nothing. If so, then he must be prior to time and not temporal himself. But neotheists deny that God is a nontemporal Being. This is inconsistent, for if God created time, then he cannot himself be temporal, any more than God can be a creature if he created all creatures (see Geisler, chap. 6).

Likewise, neotheists admit God is a necessary Being yet they deny he has Pure Actuality. But here again they cannot have it both ways. For a necessary Being has no potentiality for nonexistence. If it did, then it would not be necessary in its being. But if it has no potentiality not to exist, then its existence must be Pure Actuality (with no potentiality).

Finally, if God is a Necessary Being, then he cannot change in his Being. For a Necessary Being must necessarily be what it is; it cannot be other. However, neotheists claim God can change, that is, he is not immutable. But both these things held by neotheists cannot be true.

Neotheism undermines infallibility. Although many neotheists claim to believe the Bible is the infallible Word of God, this is inconsistent with their basic beliefs. If God cannot know the future infallibly, then the predictions in the Bible that involve free acts (as most do) cannot be infallible. That is, some of them may be wrong. Further, we have no way of knowing which ones. Thus, neotheism undermines the infallibility of all biblical predictions (*see* PROPHECY, AS PROOF OF THE BIBLE).

Neotheism destroys a biblical test for false prophets. The Bible declares (in Deut. 18:22) that a false prophecy is a test of a false prophet. But, as just noted, according to neotheism there may be false predictions in the Bible. If this is so, then a false prediction cannot be a test of a false prophet, since even God himself could make false predictions.

Neotheism undermines confidence in unconditional promises. If neotheism is correct, even God's unconditional promises cannot be trusted, including the answer of prayer (see Geisler, chaps. 5, 6). For as well-meaning as God may be in making the promise, if the fulfillment in any way depends on human free choices (which most do), then God may not be able to deliver on his promise.

Sources

By Neotheists

G. Boyd, *Trinity and Process*
S. T. Davis, *Logic and the Nature of God*
C. Pinnock, et al., *The Openness of God*
W. Haskers, *God, Time, and Knowledge*
N. Nash, *The Concept of God*
R. Rice, *God's Foreknowledge and Man's Free Will*
R. Swinburne, *The Coherence of Theism*

Against Neotheism

St. Augustine, *City of God.*
St. Anselm, *Proslogion.*
Thomas Aquinas, *Summa Theologica*
J. Calvin, *Institutes of the Christian Religion*
S. Charnock, *Discourse Upon the Existence and Attributes of God*
R. Garrigou-Lagrange, *God: His Existence and Nature*
N. L. Geisler, *Creating God in Man's Image*
R. Gruenler, *The Inexhaustible God*
E. Mascall, *He Who Is*
H. P. Owen, *Concepts of Deity*

New Age Religions. ***see*** **PANENTHEISM; PANTHEISM; HINDUISM; ZEN BUDDHISM; NEOPAGANISM; POLYTHEISM.**

New Testament Apologetic Concerns. The historicity of the New Testament is based on the evidence that history can be known, the reliability of the New Testament manuscripts, and the reliability of the New Testament witnesses (NEW TESTAMENT, HISTORICITY OF). The witnesses include the New Testament writers who were first-hand eyewitnesses and/or contemporaries of the events and other early secular sources.

These issues are part of a crucial link in the overall Christian apologetic (*see* APOLOGETICS, ARGUMENT OF). Without a reliable New Testament, we have no objective, historical way to know what Jesus said or did. We cannot establish whether he was God, what he taught, or what his followers did and taught. There are two basic steps in the argument for the reliability of the

New Testament documents. First, we must show that the manuscripts were written early enough and with enough attention to detail to be faithful records. A side issue, also important, is whether the New Testament books have been passed down accurately, so that we can know for sure what was written in the original copies or *autographs*. Second, we must know if the sources or witnesses used by the authors were reliable.

It may surprise those unfamiliar with the facts that there is more documentary evidence for the reliability of the New Testament than for any other book from the ancient world. Evidence will be surveyed in three articles:

NEW TESTAMENT, DATING OF discusses in general what is and is not known about when the Gospels, Epistles, Acts, Hebrews, and The Revelation of John were first penned. Further information on dating is available in the articles ACTS, HISTORICITY OF; BIBLE, EVIDENCE FOR; JESUS SEMINAR, AND Q DOCUMENT.

The articles NEW TESTAMENT, HISTORICITY OF; NEW TESTAMENT MANUSCRIPTS, and NEW TESTAMENT, NON-CHRISTIAN SOURCES cover more general concerns of the accurate transmission of documents.

New Testament, Dating of. When the New Testament was written is a significant issue as one assembles the overall apologetic argument for Christianity (*see* APOLOGETICS, ARGUMENT OF). Confidence in the historical accuracy of these documents depends partly on whether they were written by eyewitnesses and contemporaries to the events described, as the Bible claims. Negative critical scholars (*see* BIBLE CRITICISM) strengthen their own views as they separate the actual events from the writings by as much time as possible. For this reason radical scholars argue for late first century, and if possible second century, dates for the autographs (*see* JESUS SEMINAR). By these dates they argue that the New Testament documents, especially the Gospels, contain mythology (*see* MYTHOLOGY AND THE NEW TESTAMENT). The writers created the events contained, rather than reported them.

Arguments for Early Dates. *Luke and Acts.* The Gospel of Luke was written by the same author as the Acts of the Apostles, who refers to Luke as the "former account" of "all that Jesus began to do and teach" (Acts 1:1). The destiny ("Theophilus"), style, and vocabulary of the two books betray a common author. Roman historian Colin Hemer has provided powerful evidence that Acts was written between A.D. 60 and 62 (*see* ACTS, HISTORICITY OF). This evidence includes these observations:

1. There is no mention in Acts of the crucial event of the fall of Jerusalem in 70.
2. There is no hint of the outbreak of the Jewish War in 66 or of serious deterioration of relations between Romans and Jews before that time.
3. There is no hint of the deterioration of Christian relations with Rome during the Neronian persecution of the late 60s.
4. There is no hint of the death of James at the hands of the Sanhedrin in ca. 62, which is recorded by Josephus in *Antiquities of the Jews* (20.9.1.200).
5. The significance of Gallio's judgment in Acts 18:14–17 may be seen as setting a precedent to legitimize Christian teaching under the umbrella of the tolerance extended to Judaism.
6. The prominence and authority of the Sadducees in Acts reflects a pre-70 date, before the collapse of their political cooperation with Rome.
7. The relatively sympathetic attitude in Acts to Pharisees (unlike that found even in Luke's Gospel) does not fit well in the period of Pharisaic revival that led up to the council at Jamnia. At that time a new phase of conflict began with Christianity.
8. Acts seems to antedate the arrival of Peter in Rome and implies that Peter and John were alive at the time of the writing.
9. The prominence of "God-fearers" in the synagogues may point to a pre-70 date, after which there were few Gentile inquirers and converts to Judaism.
10. Luke gives insignificant details of the culture of an early, Julio-Claudian period.
11. Areas of controversy described presume that the Temple was still standing.
12. Adolf Harnack contended that Paul's prophecy in 20:25 (cf. 20:38) may have been contradicted by later events. If so, the book must have appeared before those events.
13. Christian terminology used in Acts reflects an earlier period. Harnack points to use of *Iusous* and *Ho Kurios*, while *Ho Christos* always designates "the Messiah," and is not a proper name for Jesus.
14. The confident tone of Acts seems unlikely during the Neronian persecution of Christians and the Jewish War with Rome during the late 60s.
15. The action ends very early in the 60s, yet the description in Acts 27 and 28 is written with a vivid immediacy. It is also an odd place to end the book if years have passed since the pre-62 events transpired.

For additional proofs of the accuracy and early date of Acts, see the article ACTS, HISTORICITY OF. If Acts was written in 62 or before, and Luke was written before Acts (say 60), then Luke was written less than thirty years of the death of Jesus. This is contemporary to the generation who witnessed the events of Jesus' life, death, and resurrection. This is precisely what Luke claims in the prologue to his Gospel:

> Many have undertaken to draw up an account of the things that have been fulfilled among us, just as they were handed down to us by those who from the first were eye-witnesses and servants of the word. Therefore, since I myself have carefully investigated everything from the beginning, it seemed good also to me to write an orderly account for you, most excellent Theophilus, so that you may know the certainty of the things you have been taught. [Luke 1:1–4]

Luke presents the same information about who Jesus is, what he taught, and his death and resurrection as do the other Gospels. Thus, there is not reason to reject their historical accuracy either.

First Corinthians. It is widely accepted by critical and conservative scholars that 1 Corinthians was written by 55 or 56. This is less than a quarter century after the crucifixion in 33. Further, Paul speaks of more than 250 eyewitnesses to the resurrection who were still alive when he wrote (15:6). Specifically mentioned are the twelve apostles and James the brother of Jesus. Internal evidence is strong for this early date:

1. The book repeatedly claims to be written by Paul (1:1, 12–17; 3:4, 6, 22; 16:21).
2. There are parallels with the book of Acts.
3. There is a ring of authenticity to the book from beginning to end.
4. Paul mentions 500 who had seen Christ, most of whom were still alive.
5. The contents harmonize with what has been learned about Corinth during that era.

There also is external evidence:

1. Clement of Rome refers to it in his own *Epistle to the Corinthians* (chap. 47).
2. *The Epistle of Barnabas* alludes to it (chap. 4).
3. *Shepherd of Hermas* mentions it (chap. 4).
4. There are nearly 600 quotations of 1 Corinthians in Irenaeus, Clement of Alexandria, and Tertullian alone (Theissen, 201). It is one of the best attested books of any kind from the ancient world.

Along with 1 Corinthians, 2 Corinthians and Galatians are well attested and early. All three reveal a historical interest in the events of Jesus' life and give facts that agree with the Gospels. Paul speaks of Jesus' virgin birth (Gal. 4:4), sinless life (2 Cor. 5:21), death on the cross (1 Cor. 15:3; Gal. 3:13); resurrection on the third day (1 Cor. 15:4), and post-resurrection appearances (1 Cor. 15:5–8). He mentions the hundreds of eyewitnesses who could verify the resurrection (1 Cor. 15:6). Paul rests the truth of Christianity on the historicity of the resurrection (1 Cor. 15:12–19). Paul also gives historical details about Jesus' contemporaries, the apostles (1 Cor. 15:5–8), including his private encounters with Peter and the apostles (Gal. 1:18–2:14). Surrounding persons, places, and events of Christ's birth were all historical. Luke goes to great pains to note that Jesus was born during the days of Caesar Augustus (Luke 2:1) and was baptized in the fifteenth year of Tiberius. Pontius Pilate was governor of Judea and Herod was tetrarch of Galilee. Annas and Caiaphas were high priests (Luke 3:1–2).

Acceptance of Early Dates. There is a growing acceptance of earlier New Testament dates, even among some critical scholars. Two illustrate this point, former liberal William F. *Albright and radical critic John A. T. *Robinson

William F. Albright. Albright wrote, "We can already say emphatically that there is no longer any solid basis for dating any book of the New Testament after about A.D. 80, two full generations before the date between 130 and 150 given by the more radical New Testament critics of today" (*Recent Discoveries in Bible Lands*, 136). Elsewhere Albright said, "In my opinion, every book of the New Testament was written by a baptized Jew between the forties and the eighties of the first century (very probably sometime between about A.D. 50 and 75)" ("Toward a More Conservative View," 3).

This scholar went so far as to affirm that the evidence from the Qumran community shows that the concepts, terminology, and mind set of the Gospel of John is probably early first century ("Recent Discoveries in Palestine"). "Thanks to the Qumran discoveries, the New Testament proves to be in fact what it was formerly believed to be: the teaching of Christ and his immediate followers between cir. 25 and cir. 80 A.D." (*From Stone Age to Christianity*, 23).

John A. T. Robinson. Known for his role in launching the "Death of God" movement, Robinson wrote a revolutionary book titled *Redating the New Testament*, in which he posited revised dates for the New Testament books that place them earlier than the most conservative scholars ever held. Robinson places Matthew at 40 to after 60, Mark at about 45 to 60, Luke at before 57 to after 60, and John at from before 40 to after 65. This would mean that one or two Gospels could have been written as early as seven years after the crucifixion. At the latest they were all composed within the lifetimes of eyewitnesses and contemporaries of the events. Assuming the basic integrity and reasonable accuracy of the writers, this would place the reliability of the New Testament documents beyond reasonable doubt.

Other Evidence. *Early Citations.* Of the four Gospels alone there are 19,368 citations by the church fathers from the late first century on. This includes 268 by Justin *Martyr (100–165), 1038 by Irenaeus (active in the late second century), 1017 by *Clement of Alexandria (ca. 155–ca. 220), 9231 by Origen (ca. 185–ca. 254), 3822 by Tertullian (ca. 160s–ca. 220), 734 by Hippolytus (d. ca. 236), and 3258 by Eusebius (ca. 265–ca. 339; Geisler, 431). Earlier, Clement of Rome cited Matthew, John, and 1 Corinthians in 95 to 97. Ignatius referred to six Pauline Epistles in about 110, and between 110 and 150 Polycarp quoted from all four Gospels, Acts, and most of Paul's Epistles. Shepherd of Hermas (115–140) cited Matthew, Mark, Acts, 1 Corinthians, and other books. Didache (120–150) referred to Matthew, Luke, 1 Corinthians, and other books. Papias, companion of Polycarp, who was a disciple of the apostle John, quoted John. This argues powerfully that the Gospels were in existence before the end of the first century, while some eyewitnesses (including John) were still alive.

Early Greek Manuscripts. The earliest undisputed manuscript of a New Testament book is the John Rylands papyri (P52), dated from 117 to 138. This fragment of John's Gospel survives from within a generation of composition. Since the book was composed in Asia Minor and this fragment was found in Egypt, some circulation time is demanded, surely placing composition of John within the first century. Whole books (Bodmer Papyri) are available from 200. Most of the New Testament, including all the Gospels, is available in the Chester Beatty Papyri manuscript from 150 years after the New Testament was finished (ca. 250). No other book from the ancient world has as small a time gap between composition and earliest manuscript copies as the New Testament (*see* NEW TESTAMENT MANUSCRIPTS).

Jose *O'Callahan, a Spanish Jesuit paleographer, made headlines around the world on March 18, 1972, when he identified a manuscript fragment from Qumran (*see* DEAD SEA SCROLLS) as a piece of the Gospel of Mark. The piece was from Cave 7. Fragments from this cave had previously been dated between 50 B.C. and A.D. 50, hardly within the time frame established for New Testament writings. Using the accepted methods of papyrology and paleography, O'Callahan compared sequences of letters with existing documents and eventually identified nine fragments as belonging to one Gospel, Acts, and a few Epistles. Some of these were dated slightly later than 50, but still extremely early:

text	fragment	approx. date
Mark 4:28	7Q6	A.D. 50
Mark 6:48	7Q15	A.D. ?
Mark 6:52, 53	7Q5	A.D. 50
Mark 12:17	7Q7	A.D. 50
Acts 27:38	7Q6	A.D. 60 +
Rom. 55:11, 12	7Q9	A.D. 70 +
1 Tim. 3:16; 4:1–3	7Q4	A.D. 70 +
2 Peter 1:15	7Q10	A.D. 70 +
James 1:23, 24	7Q8	A.D. 70 +

Conclusion. Both friends and critics acknowledge that, if valid, O'Callahan's conclusions will revolutionize New Testament theories. If even some of these fragments are from the New Testament, the implications for Christian apologetics are enormous. Mark and/or Acts must have been written within the lifetimes of the apostles and contemporaries of the events. There would be no time for mythological embellishment of the records (*see* MYTHOLOGY AND NEW TESTAMENT). They must be accepted as historical. Mark could be shown to be an early Gospel. There would hardly be time for a predecessor series of Q manuscripts (*see* Q DOCUMENT). And since these manuscripts are not originals but copies, parts of the New Testament would be shown to have been copied and disseminated during the lives of the writers. No first-century date allows time for myths or legends to creep into the stories about Jesus. Legend development takes at least two full generations, according to A. N. Sherwin-White (see Sherwin-White, 189). Physical remoteness from the actual events also is helpful. Neither are available here. The thought is utterly ridiculous with a ca. 50 or earlier Mark. Even putting aside O'Callahan's controversial claims, the cumulative evidence places the New Testament within the first century and the lives of eyewitnesses.

Sources

W. F. Albright, *Archaeology and the Religion of Israel*

———, *From Stone Age to Christianity*

———, *Recent Discoveries in Bible Lands*

———, "Recent Discoveries in Palestine and the Gospel of St. John," in W. D. Davies and David Daube, eds., *The Background of the New Testament and Its Eschatology*

———, " William Albright: Toward a More Conservative View," *Christianity Today* (18 January 1963)

R. Bultmann, *Kerygma and Myth: A Theological Debate*

D. Estrada and W. White, Jr., *The First New Testament*

E. Fisher, "New Testament Documents among the Dead Sea Scrolls?" *The Bible Today* 61 (1972)

P. Garnet, "O'Callahan's Fragments: Our Earliest New Testament Texts?" *Evangelical Quarterly* 45 (1972)

N. Geisler, *General Introduction to the Bible*

C. J. Hemer, *The Book of Acts in the Setting of Hellenistic History*

B. Orchard, "A Fragment of St. Mark's Gospel Dating from before A.D. 50?" *Biblical Apostolate* 6 (1972)

W. N. Pickering, *The Identification of the New Testament Text*

W. White, Jr., "O'Callahan's Identifications: Confirmation and Its Consequences," *Westminster Journal* 35 (1972)

J. A. T. Robinson, *Redating the New Testament*

A. N. Sherwin-White, *Roman Society and Roman Law in the New Testament*

H. C. Theissen, *Introduction to the New Testament*

J. Wenham, *Redating Matthew, Mark, and Luke: A Fresh Assault on the Synoptic Problem*

E. Yamauchi, "Easter—Myth, Hallucination, or History," *Christianity Today* (15 March 1974; 29 March 1974)

New Testament, Historicity of. Thomas *Paine, one of America's founding fathers and author of *Common Sense* and *The Age of Reason,* said of Jesus Christ, "There is no history written at the time Jesus Christ is said to have lived that speaks of the existence of such a person, even such a man" (Paine, 234). In his essay *Why I Am Not a Christian,* Bertrand *Russell wrote, "Historically it is quite doubtful whether Christ ever existed at all, and if he did we know nothing about him" (Russell, 16). A recent book by G. A. Wells concludes that even if there was a historical Jesus, he is not the Christ of the New Testament.

Yet Christianity depends entirely on the historical person of Jesus Christ (see 1 Corinthians 15). Since the New Testament is the primary source of information about the words and works of Christ, if it is not accurate then we do not possess a first-hand presentation of Jesus' claims, character, and credentials. The historical integrity of the New Testament is crucial to Christian apologetics.

Evidence for the historicity of the New Testament documents presupposes the knowability of history in general and the believability of miracle history in particular. There are those who believe no history can be objectively known. Their position is answered in the article History, Objectivity of. Such a radical skepticism eliminates the possibility of knowing anything about the past. Immediately, all university history and classical departments are swept away. No sources about past events could be trusted. By analogy such skepticism would eliminate all historical science, such as historical geology (paleontology), archaeology, and forensic science (*see* ORIGINS, SCIENCE OF). They too depend on examining and interpreting remains from the past.

Since everything not occurring now is history, such a view would eliminate all eyewitness testimony. Even living witnesses can only testify to what they saw at a separate point in reality. On the other hand, if their testimony can be accepted while they are living, the valid records they leave behind are just as credible.

Some critics object only to miracle history. This is discussed in detail in the article MIRACLES, ARGUMENTS AGAINST. This view clearly begs the question by assuming that no miracle story is credible in advance of looking at the evidence. No one looking for the objective truth should assume that a report of an unusual event is not to be trusted before even considering the matter. Both in science (*see* BIG BANG; EVOLUTION, CHEMICAL; EVOLUTION, COSMIC) and in history the evidence has shown that radical singularities have occurred (*see* RESURRECTION, EVIDENCE FOR; VIRGIN BIRTH).

The first step in establishing the historicity of the New Testament is to show that the New Testament documents have been accurately transmitted from the time of their original composition. This is demonstrated in the article NEW TESTAMENT MANUSCRIPTS.

The second step is to show that they were written by reliable eyewitnesses or contemporaries of the events. For this, see NEW TESTAMENT, DATING OF. Contrary to critics, there is more evidence for the historicity of the life, death, and resurrection of Christ than for any other event from the ancient world (*see* NEW TESTAMENT, NON-CHRISTIAN SOURCES).

To reject the historicity of the New Testament is to reject all history. But we cannot reject all history without engaging in some history of our own. The statement that "The past is not objectively knowable" is itself an objective statement about the past. Hence, the position against the knowability of history slits its own throat (*see* HISTORY, OBJECTIVITY OF).

Sources

K. Aland and B. Aland, *The Text of the New Testament*
C. Blomberg, *The Historical Reliability of the Gospels*
F. F. Bruce, *The New Testament Documents: Are They Reliable?*
R. T. France, *The Evidence for Jesus*
N. L. Geisler, *Christian Apologetics*, chap. 16
G. Habermas, *The Historical Jesus: Ancient Evidence for the Life of Christ*
I. H. Marshall, *I Believe in the Historical Jesus*
M. Martin, *The Case Against Christianity*
B. Metzger, *The Text of the New Testament*
J W. Montgomery, *History and Christianity*
———, *The Shape of the Past*
T. Paine, *Examination*
B. Russell, *Why I Am Not a Christian*
A. N. Sherwin-White, *Roman Society and Roman Law in the New Testament*
E. Troelsch, "Historiography," in J. Hastings, ed., *Encyclopedia of Religion and Ethics*
R. Whateley, *Historical Doubts Concerning the Existence of Napoleon Bonaparte*

New Testament Manuscripts. The fidelity of the New Testament text is an important link in the apologetic for Christianity (*see* APOLOGETICS, ARGUMENT OF; NEW TESTAMENT, HISTORICITY OF), and there is overwhelming evidence in support of the reliability of the New Testament text.

The Story of the Manuscripts. Testimony to the fidelity of the New Testament text comes primarily from three sources: Greek manuscripts, ancient translations, and quotations of Scripture by Christian writers.

Greek manuscripts are the most important and are found in four classes, *papyri, uncials, minuscules,* and *lectionaries*. These designations can be rather confusing to follow, for papyri refers to the woven material on which the writing was made. Uncials and minuscules refer to the way letters were formed in the writing style of the manuscript, and lectionaries are collections of Scripture texts bound for use in worship. What is confusing is that papyri manuscripts are written with the rounded, cursive capital letters of uncial script. More than 200 lectionaries were written in uncial letters. Still, scholars try to catalog their finds according to the most distinguishing characteristic of each. A papyrus comes from a particular era and region. The papyri Greek manuscripts tend to be compared with one another and used extensively in comparing the Greek used in the text. Those manuscripts placed in the categories of uncials and minuscules are differentiated by the style of writing and by being written on vellum or parchment. So, for example, an uncial papyri manuscript is in the *papyri* category; an uncial vellum manuscript is called an *uncial*. Minuscule script is small, plain, cursive and did not develop until medieval times. So there are far more minuscule manuscripts, but they are later, between the ninth and fifteenth centuries.

Another term frequently used in reference to ancient and medieval manuscripts is *codex*. While Jewish worship has traditionally preferred Scriptures bound as scrolls, Christians in Greek culture mostly used the bound book form that was gaining acceptance in the first century. Therefore, most Scripture manuscripts, even early ones, are bound codices.

More Manuscripts. Catalogued Greek texts include eighty-eight papyri manuscripts, 274 uncial manuscripts, and 245 uncial lectionaries. Those early uncial manuscript witnesses are extremely valuable in establishing the original text of the New Testament. The other 2795 manuscripts and 1964 lectionaries are minuscule.

This is an astounding number and variety. It is not uncommon for classics from antiquity to survive in only a handful of manuscript copies. According to F. F. *Bruce, nine or ten good copies of Julius Caesar's *Gallic War* survive, twenty copies of Livy's *Roman History,* two copies of Tacitus' *Annals*, and eight manuscripts of Thucydides' *History* (Bruce, 16). The most documented ancient secular work is Homer's *Iliad,* surviving in 643 manuscript copies. Counting Greek copies alone, the New Testament text is preserved in some 5686 partial and complete manuscript portions that were copied by hand from the second (possibly even the first) through the fifteenth centuries (see Geisler, chap. 26).

In addition to the Greek manuscripts there are numerous translations from the Greek, not to mention quotations of the New Testament. Counting major early translations in Syriac, Coptic, Arabic, Latin, and other languages, there are 9000 copies of the New Testament. This makes a total of over 14,000 copies of the New Testament. What is more, if we compile the 36,289 quotations by the early church Fathers of the second to fourth centuries we can reconstruct the entire New Testament minus 11 verses.

Earlier Manuscripts. One mark of a good manuscript is its age. Generally, the older the copy, the closer to the original composition and the fewer copyist errors. Most ancient books survive in manuscripts that were copied about 1000 years after they were composed. It is rare to have, as the *Odyssey* does, a copy made only 500 years after the original. Most of the New Testament is preserved in manuscripts less than two hundred years from the original (P^{45}, P^{46}, P^{47}), some books of the New Testament dating from little over one hundred years after their composition (P^{66}), and one fragment (P^{52}) comes within a generation of the first century. The New Testament, by contrast, survives in complete books from a little over 100 years after the New Testament was completed. Fragments are available from only decades later. One fragment, the John Ryland papyri (P^{52}), is dated 117–138. See the article NEW TESTAMENT, DATING OF.

Many critics reject the identifications, arguing that they are too fragmentary for certain identification. O'Callahan, however, is a respected paleographer and he defends his work as consistent with that by which other ancient fragments are identified. Critics have not come up with viable alternate writings from which the fragments could have come without changing the usual procedures. If they are New Testament fragments, these early dates would revolutionize New Testament critical studies.

More Accurate Manuscripts. Muslims make a point that the *Qur'an* has been accurately preserved (*see* QUR'AN, ALLEGED DIVINE ORIGIN OF). But while the *Qur'an* is a *medieval book* from the seventh century, the New Testament is the most accurately copied book from the *ancient* world. Of course, the important factor is not the precise accuracy in the copies but whether the original is the Word of God (*see* BIBLE, EVIDENCE FOR).

There is widespread misunderstanding among critics about the "errors" in the biblical manuscripts. Some have estimated there are about 200,000 of them. First of all, these are not "errors" but variant readings, the vast majority of which are strictly grammatical. Second, these readings are spread throughout more than 5300 manuscripts, so that a variant spelling of one letter of one word in one verse in 2000 manuscripts is counted as 2000 "errors." Textual scholars Westcott and Hort estimated that only one in sixty of these variants has significance. This would leave a text 98.33 percent pure. Philip Schaff calculated that, of the 150,000 variants known in his day, only 400 changed the meaning of the passage, only fifty were of real significance, and *not even one* affected "an article of faith or a precept of duty which is not abundantly sustained by other and undoubted passages, or by the whole tenor of Scripture teaching" (Schaff, 177).

Most other ancient books are not nearly so well authenticated. New Testament scholar Bruce Metzger estimated that the *Mahabharata* of *Hinduism is copied with only about 90 percent accuracy and Homer's *Iliad* with about 95 percent. By comparison, he estimated the New Testament is about 99.5 percent accurate (ibid.).

Islamic scholars recognize the textual scholar Sir Frederic Kenyon as an authority on ancient manuscripts. Yet Kenyon concluded that:

> The number of manuscripts of the New Testament, of early translations from it, and of quotations from it in the oldest writers of the Church, is so large that it is practically certain that the true reading of every doubtful passage is preserved in some one or other of these ancient authorities. This can be said of no other ancient book in the world. [55]

The Manuscript Witnesses. *Manuscripts on Papyrus.* The date of the earliest alleged New Testament manuscripts is disputed. One known as the "Magdalen" fragment contains a reference to Mary Magdalen (in Matt. 26). This bit of papyrus is found in the Oxford University library. The German papyrus expert, Carsten Thiede, argued that it could be an eyewitness account of Jesus. Other experts date it in the second century or later (see Stranton, *Gospel Truth?*).

Other Gospel fragments are dated as early as A.D. 50. These were originally found among the Dead Sea Scrolls (see). Jose O'Callahan, a Spanish Jesuit paleographer, identified a manuscript fragment from Qumran (*see* DEAD SEA SCROLLS) as the earliest known piece of the Gospel of Mark. Fragments from Cave 7 had previously been dated between 50 B.C. and A.D. 50 and listed under "not identified" and classified as "Biblical Texts?" The nine fragments from Qumran are listed as follows:

Mark 4:28	7Q6?	A.D. 50
Mark 6:48	7Q15	A.D. ?
Mark 6:52, 53	7Q5	A.D. 50
Mark 12:17	7Q7	A.D. 50
Acts 27:38	7Q6?	A.D. 60
Romans 5:11, 12	7Q9	A.D. 70+
1 Timothy 3:16; 4:1–3	7Q4	A.D. 70+
2 Peter 1:15	7Q10	A.D. 70+
James 1:23, 24	7Q8	A.D. 70+

*O'Callahan's critics object to his identification and have offered other possible sources for them. The fragmentary nature of the manuscript makes it difficult to be dogmatic about their true identification (*see* O'CALLAHAN, JOSE).

Eighty-eight undisputed papyri manuscripts have so far been found, of which the following are the most important representatives. The papyri witness to the text is invaluable, because it comes from within the first 200 years after the New Testament was written. Papyri manuscripts or fragments are identified with a "P," followed by a superscript number of 1 through 88.

John Rylands Fragment. The John Rylands Fragment (P^{52}), a two-by-three-inch papyrus fragment from a codex, is the earliest undisputed copy of a portion of the New Testament. It dates from the first half of the second century, probably 117–38. Adolf Deissmann argues that it may be even older (Metzger, *Text of the New Testament,* 39). The papyrus piece, written on both sides, contains portions of five verses from the Gospel of John (18:31–33, 37–38). Because it was found in Egypt, far from Asia Minor where John by tradition was written, this portion tends to confirm that the Gospel was written before the end of the first century. The fragment belongs to the John Rylands Library at Manchester, England.

Bodmer Papyri. The most important discovery of New Testament papyri since the Chester Beatty manuscripts was the acquisition of the Bodmer Collection by the Library of World Literature at Culagny, near Geneva, Switzerland. This also has three sections, designated P^{66}, P^{72}, P^{75}. Dating from about 200 or earlier, P^{66}, contains 104 leaves of John 1:1–6:11; 6:35b–14:26; and fragments of forty other pages from John 14–21 (Metzger, *Text of the New Testament,* 40). P^{72} is the earliest known copy of Jude, 1 Peter, and 2 Peter. Also included is a hymn fragment, Psalm 33, and Psalm 34, 1 Peter, and 2 Peter, plus several apocryphal books: *The Nativity of Mary, Correspondence of Paul to the Corinthians, Eleventh Ode of Solomon,* Melito's *Homily on the Passover,* and *The Apology of Phileas.* This third-century papyrus was apparently a private codex measuring six by five inches, prepared by some four scribes (Metzger, *Text of the New Testament,* 40–41). P^{75} is a codex of 102 pages (originally 144), measuring ten by five and one-third inches. It contains most of Luke and John in clear, carefully printed uncials, and is dated between 175 and 225. It is the earliest known copy of Luke (Metzger, *Text of the New Testament,* 42).

Chester Beatty Papyri. This papyrus dates from about 250 or later. Thirty of the leaves are owned by the University of Michigan. An important collection of New Testament papyri (P^{45}, P^{46}, P^{47}), now resides in the Beatty Museum near Dublin. The Chester Beatty Papyri consist of three codices, containing most of the New Testament. P^{45} is made up of pieces of thirty leaves of a papyrus codex: two from Matthew, six from Mark, seven from Luke, two from John, and thirteen from Acts. The original codex consisted of some 220 leaves, measuring ten by eight inches each. Several other small fragments of Matthew from those papyri have appeared in a collection at Vienna (Metzger, *Text of the New Testament,* 37). P^{46} consists of eighty-six slightly mutilated leaves (eleven by six inches), from an original that contained 104 pages of Paul's Epistles, including Romans, Hebrews, 1 Corinthians, 2 Corinthians, Ephesians, Galatians, Philippians, Colossians, 1 Thessalonians, and 2 Thessalonians. Portions of Romans and 1 Thessalonians, and all of 2 Thessalonians, are missing from the manuscripts, which were arranged in descending order according to size. Like P^{45}, P^{46} dates from about 250. P^{47} is ten slightly mutilated leaves of the book of Revelation, measuring nine by five inches. Of the original thirty-two leaves, only the middle portion, 9:10–17:2, remains.

Uncials on Vellum and Parchment. The most important manuscripts of the New Testament are generally considered to be the uncial codices that date from the fourth and following centuries. These appeared almost immediately following the conversion of Constantine and the authorization at the Council of Nicea (325) to freely copy the Bible.

There are 362 uncial manuscripts of sections of the New Testament, of which some of the more important are noted below, and 245 uncial lectionaries. The most important of the uncial manuscripts are A, B, C, and Aleph, which were not available to the King James translators. The only good Greek uncial manuscript available in 1611 was D, and it was used only slightly in the preparation of the King James Version. That fact alone indicated the need for the Revised Version, based on earlier and better manuscripts.

Codex Vaticanus. The Codex Vaticanus (designated B) is perhaps the oldest uncial on parchment or vellum (ca. 325–350), and one of the most important witnesses to the text of the New Testament. It was probably written by the middle of the fourth century, but it was not known to textual scholars until after 1475, when it was catalogued in the Vatican Library. For the next 400 years scholars were prohibited from studying it. A complete photographic facsimile was made in 1889–90, and another of the New Testament in 1904.

It includes most of the Old Testament Septuagint and the New Testament in Greek. Missing are 1 Timothy through Philemon, Hebrews 9:14 to the end of the New Testament, and the General Epistles. The Apocrypha is included with the exceptions of *1 Maccabees*, *2 Maccabees*, and the *Prayer of Manasses*. Also missing is Genesis 1:1–46:28, 2 Kings 2:5–7 and 10–13, and Psalms 106:27–138:6. Mark 16:9–20 and John 7:53–8:11 were purposely omitted from the text.

This codex was written in small and delicate uncials on fine vellum. It contains 759 leaves measuring ten inches square—617 in the Old Testament and 142 in the New. Codex Vaticanus is owned by the Roman Catholic Church, and is housed in the Vatican Library, Vatican City.

Codex Sinaiticus. Codex Sinaiticus or *Aleph*, a fourth-century Greek manuscript, is generally considered to be the most important witness to the text because of its antiquity, accuracy, and lack of omissions.

The story of the discovery of *Aleph* is one of the most fascinating in textual history. It was found in the monastery of St. Catherine on Mount Sinai by Count Lobegott Friedrich Constantine von Tischendorf (1815–1874). On his first visit (1844), he discovered forty-three leaves of vellum, containing 1 Chronicles, Jeremiah, Nehemiah, and Esther, in a basket of scraps that the monks were using to light their fires. He secured this Septuagint text and took it to the University Library at Leipzig, Germany. It remains there, known as the Codex Frederico-Augustanus. Tischendorf's second visit in 1853 proved unfruitful, but in 1859, just as he was about to return home empty-handed, the monastery steward showed him an almost complete copy of the Scriptures and some other books.

This manuscript contains over half of the Septuagint, and all of the New Testament except Mark 16:9–20 and John 7:53–8:11. The Apocrypha, with the addition of the *Epistle of Barnabas* and a large portion of the *Shepherd of Hermas,* are also included.

This codex was written in large, clear Greek uncials on 364 pages (plus the forty-three at Leipzig), measuring thirteen by fourteen inches. In 1933 the British government purchased it for the British Museum. In 1938 it was published in a volume titled *Scribes and Correctors of Codex Sinaiticus* (Metzger, *Text of the New Testament,* 42–45).

Codex Alexandrinus. Codex Alexandrinus (A) is a well-preserved manuscript that ranks second only to Sinaiticus as representative of the New Testament text. Though some have dated this manuscript in the late fourth century (Kenyon, 129), it is probably the work of fifth-century scribes of Alexandria. In 1621 it was taken to Constantinople by Patriarch Cyril Lucar. Lucar gave it to Thomas Roe, English ambassador to Turkey in 1624, to present to King James I. James died before it reached England, and the manuscript was given to Charles I in 1627, too late for use in the King James Version of 1611. In 1757, George II presented it to the National Library of the British Museum.

It contains the whole Old Testament, except for several mutilations in Genesis 14–16;, 1 Kingdoms [1 Samuel] 12–14, and Psalms 49:19–79:10. Only Matthew 1:1–25:6; John 6:50–8:52 and 2 Corinthians 4:13–12:6 are missing from the New Testament. The manuscript also contains 1 and 2 Clement and the Psalms of Solomon, with some parts missing.

The manuscript contains 773 ten-by-twelve leaves, 639 of the Old Testament and 134 of the New. The large square uncials are written on very thin vellum. Codex Alexandrinus is in the possession of the National Library of the British Museum. The text varies in quality (Metzger, *Text of the New Testament,* 47, 49).

Codex Ephraemi Rescriptus. The Ephraemi Rescriptus Codex (C) probably originated in Alexandria, Egypt, in about 345. It was brought to Italy by John Lascaris at about 1500 and later was purchased by Pietro Strozzi. Catherine de Medici, the Italian political power broker and wife and mother of French kings, acquired it about 1533. At her death, the manuscript was placed in the Bibliothèque Nationale at Paris, where it remains.

Most of the Old Testament is missing from this codex, except parts of Job, Proverbs, Ecclesiastes, Song of Solomon, and two apocryphal books, *Wisdom of Solomon*, and *Ecclesiasticus*. The New Testament lacks 2 Thessalonians, 2 John, and parts of other books (Scrivener, 1:121). The manuscript is a *palimpsest*. Because paper was so valuable, early manuscripts were often rubbed out and the material reused. With care, scholars can sometimes discern both the original text and the *rescriptus* or rewritten text. So a palimpsest can have added value.

These leaves originally contained the Old and New Testaments, but they were erased by Ephraem, who wrote his sermons on the leaves. By chemical reactivation, Tischendorf was able to decipher the almost invisible writing (Lyon, 266–72). Only 209 leaves survive: sixty-four from the Old and 145 (of an original 238) from the New Testament. The pages are nine by twelve inches, with one wide column of forty to forty-six lines (usually forty-one). C mixes all the major textual types, agreeing frequently with the inferior Byzantine family.

Codex Bezae. Written between 450 and 550, Codex Bezae (also called Codex Catabrigiensis or D) is the oldest known bilingual manuscript of the New Testament. It was written in Greek and Latin and may have originated in southern Gaul (France) or northern Italy. It was found in 1562 by Théodore de Bèze (Beza), the French theologian, at St. Irenaeus Monastery, Lyons, France. In 1581 Beza gave it to Cambridge University.

D contains the four Gospels, Acts, and 3 John 11–15, with variations from other manuscripts indicated. Missing from the Greek text are sections of Matthew 1, 6–9, and 27; John 1–3, and Acts 8–10, 21, and 22–28. In Latin, missing sections are from Matthew 1, 6–8, 26–27; Acts 8–10, 20–21; and 22–28, and 1 John 1–3. The 406 leaves are eight by ten inches, with one column of thirty-three lines to each page. The manuscript is located in the Cambridge University Library. It is remarkable for some unusual variations from the normal New Testament text (Metzger, *Text of the New Testament,* 50).

Codex Claromontanus. Codex Claromontanus is a ca. 550 text that is designated D^2 or D^{p2}. The latter stands for D^{paul} because it supplements D (Codex Bezae) for the Pauline Epistles. It contains much of the New Testament missing in Codex Bezae. Like D, D^2 is a bilingual manuscript, and it contains 533 pages, seven by nine inches. D^2 seems to have originated in Italy or Sardinia (Kenyon, *Our Bible and the Ancient Manuscripts,* 207–8; Souter, 28).

Claromontanus was named after a monastery at Clermont, France, where it was found by Beza. After Beza's death, the codex was owned by several private individuals. Finally, Louis XIV purchased it for the Bibliothèque Nationale at Paris in 1656. Tischendorf fully edited it in 1852.

It contains all of Paul's Epistles and Hebrews, although verses from Romans 1 and 1 Corinthians 14 are missing in Greek, and verses from 1 Corinthians 14 and Hebrews 13 are missing in the Latin. It was artistically written in a single column of twenty-one lines on thin, high quality vellum. The Greek is good, but the Latin is grammatically inferior in some places. The manuscript is now located in the Bibliothèque Nationale, Paris.

Other Codices. Codex Basilensis (E) is an eighth-century manuscript of the Gospels on 318 leaves. It is in the library of the University of Basel, Switzerland.

Codex Laudianus (E^2 or E^a) dates from the late sixth or early seventh century. It was edited by Tischendorf in 1870. E^2 contains Acts in Greek and Latin, arranged in very short lines of one to three words. It is the earliest known manuscript containing Acts 8:37.

Codex Sangermanensis (E^3 or E^p) is a ninth-century copy of D^2 in Greek and Latin, so it has no independent value for the textual critic.

Codex Boreelianus (F) contains the four Gospels, dates from the ninth century, and is located at Utrecht.

Codex Augiensis (F^2 or F^p) is a ninth-century manuscript of Paul's Epistles in Greek and Latin (with large omissions), but Hebrews is in Latin only. It is now at Trinity College, Cambridge.

Also called Codex Harleianus, Codex Wolfii A (G) dates to the tenth century. It contains the four Gospels with many omissions.

Dating from the ninth century, Codex Boernerianus (G^3 or G^p) contains Paul's Epistles in Greek with a literal Latin translation between the lines. Evidently it once included a copy of the apocryphal Epistle to the Laodiceans. It is possibly of Irish origin.

Codex Wolfii B (H) contains the four Gospels, but with many omissions. It dates from the ninth or tenth century and now resides in the Public Library, Hamburg.

Codex Mutinensis (H^2 or H^a) is a ninth-century copy of Acts (seven chapters missing), now in the Grand Ducal Library at Mondena, Italy. The text is Byzantine.

Codex Coislinianus (H^3 or H^p) is an important codex of Paul's Epistles, dating from the sixth century. The forty-three leaves known to exist today are divided among the libraries at Paris, Leningrad, Moscow, Kiev, Turin, and Mount Athos.

Codex Washingtonianus II (I) is a manuscript of the Pauline Epistles in the Freer Collection at the Smithsonian Institution, Washington, D.C. There are eighty-four surviving leaves of the original 210. It dates from the fifth or sixth century and has portions of Hebrews and all of Paul's letters, except Romans.

Codex Cyprius (K) is a ninth- or tenth-century complete copy of the four Gospels.

Codex Mosquensis (K^2 or K^{ap}) is a ninth- or tenth-century codex of Acts, the General Epistles, and Pauline Epistles with Hebrews.

Codex Regius (L) is an eighth-century codex of the Gospels. Its unique feature is the presence of two endings to the Gospel of Mark. The first is the shorter ending, reading as follows: "But they [the women] reported briefly to Peter and those with him all that they had been told. And after this, Jesus himself sent out by means of them, from east to west, the sacred and imperishable proclamation of eternal salvation" (Mark 16:8 RSV). The second ending is the traditional verses 9–20.

Codex Angelicus (L^2 or L^{ap}) is a ninth-century copy of Acts, the General Epistles, and the Pauline Epistles.

Codex Pampianus (M) contains the four Gospels. It dates from the ninth century.

Codex Purpureus Petropolitanus (N), written in the sixth century in silver letters on purple vellum, is a deluxe parchment of the Gospels. Of the 462 original leaves, some 230 known leaves are scattered around the world.

Codex Sinopensis (O) is another sixth-century deluxe edition of the Gospels, written with gold ink on purple vellum. It is now in Bibliothèque Nationale, Paris. It contains forty-three leaves of Matthew 13–24.

Codex Porphyrianus (P^2 or P^{apr}) is one of the few uncial manuscripts containing the book of Revelation. It also contains Acts and the General and Pauline Epistles, with omissions. It is now in St. Petersburg, Russia.

Now in the British Museum, Codex Nitriensis (R) is a palimpsest of Luke from the sixth century, over which an eighth- or ninth-century treatise of Severus of Antioch was written. It also contains four thousand lines of Homer's *Iliad.* The text is Western.

Codex Vaticanus 354 (S) is one of the earliest self-dated manuscripts of the Gospels and was prepared in 949. It resides in the Vatican Library.

Codex Borgianus (T) is a valuable fifth-century fragment of Luke 22–23 and John 6–8. The text closely resembles that of Codex Vaticanus.

Now in Moscow, Codex Mosquensis (V) is a nearly complete copy of the four Gospels from the eighth or ninth century. The manuscript is in uncials to John 8:39, where it shifts to thirteenth-century minuscules.

Codex Washingtonianus I (W) dates from the fourth or early fifth century. Professor H. A. Sanders, of the University of Michigan, edited it between 1910 and 1918. The manuscript contains Deuteronomy, Joshua, and Psalms, the Gospels, Hebrews, and portions of all the Pauline Epistles except Romans. Some psalms are missing, along with text from Deuteronomy 5–6, Joshua 3–4, Mark 15, John 14–16, and some Epistles. The Gospels manuscript has 187 leaves, 374 pages of good vellum. Each page is five and five-sixths by eight inches and has one column of thirty lines, consisting of small but clearly written, slanting uncials. The Gospels include Matthew, John, Luke, and Mark, in that order. The long ending of Mark (16:9–20) is attached, with a most noteworthy insertion after 16:14: "And they excused themselves, saying, 'This age of lawlessness and unbelief is under Satan, who does not allow the truth and power of God to prevail over the unclean things of the spirits. Therefore reveal thy righteousness now'—thus they spoke of Christ. And Christ replied to them, 'The term of years for Satan's power has been fulfilled, but other terrible things draw near. And for those who have sinned I was delivered over to death, that they may return to the incorruptible glory of righteousness which is in heaven'" (Metzger, *Text of the New Testament,* 54; *A Textual Commentary on the Greek New Testament,* 122–28). The manuscript of Deuteronomy and Joshua has 102 leaves (ten by twelve inches), with two columns on each thick vellum page. The mutilated manuscript of Psalms has portions of 107 leaves that originally measured eleven by fourteen inches, written in single columns. This codex is located in the Smithsonian Institution. The text is mysteriously mixed, as though it were compiled from manuscripts representing different textual traditions or families.

Codex Dubliensis (Z [*Zeta*]) is a palimpsest of 299 verses from Matthew. It dates from the fifth or sixth century.

Codex Sangallensis (*Delta*) is a ninth-century Greek-Latin interlinear manuscript of the four Gospels (John 19:17–35 missing).

Codex Koridethi (*Theta*) is a ninth-century copy of the Gospels. The text of John differs in tradition from that of Matthew, Mark, and Luke. It is akin to the third- or fourth-century text used by Origen and Eusebius of Caesarea.

Codex Tischendorfianus III (*Lambda*) contains the text of Luke and John. The ninth-century manuscript is located at Oxford University.

Codex Zacynthius (*Xi*) is a twelfth- or thirteenth-century palimpsest preserving most of

Luke 1:1–11:33. It is the earliest known New Testament manuscript with a marginal commentary.

Codex Petropolitanus (*Pi*) is an almost complete ninth-century copy of the Gospels.

Codex Rossanensis (*Sigma*) is a sixth-century copy of Matthew and Mark. It is the earliest known Bible adorned with watercolor pictures.

Codex Beratinus (*Phi*) is a sixth-century deluxe edition of Matthew and Mark, with large gaps.

Codex Athous Laurae (*Psi*) is an eighth- or ninth-century manuscript containing the Gospels from Mark 9 on, Acts, the General Epistles, Pauline Epistles, and Hebrews. It carries the same unusual ending of Mark as Codex Regius.

Codex Athous Dionysiou (*Omega*) dates from the eighth or ninth century and is a virtually complete copy of the four Gospels. It is one of the oldest examples of the textual tradition known as the Byzantine text.

Minuscule Manuscripts. As the dates from the ninth to the fifteenth centuries would indicate, most minuscule manuscripts do not possess the high quality of the earlier uncials. However, that is not always the case. Some minuscules are late copies of good early texts. Their main importance rests in the comparison they provide for the textual families. There are 2795 minuscule New Testament manuscripts and 1964 minuscule lectionaries. They are referred to by manuscript number.

The Alexandrian family is represented by manuscript 33, dating from the ninth or possibly the tenth century. It contains the entire New Testament except for Revelation and is now in the possession of the Bibliothèque Nationale. Although it is predominantly Alexandrian text-type, it shows traces of Byzantine in Acts and the Pauline Epistles.

Some scholars find a Caesarean family text-type in some manuscripts of the Gospels. It harks back to the Caesarean text used in the third and fourth centuries. An Italian subfamily of Caesarean is represented by about a dozen manuscripts known as family 13. These manuscripts were copied between the eleventh and fifteenth centuries. One of their interesting characteristics is that they contain the section about the adulterous woman (John 7:53–8:11) following Luke 21:38 instead of after John 7:52.

Some individual minuscules include:

Manuscript 61 consists of the entire New Testament, dating from the late fifteenth or early sixteenth century. It was the first manuscript found containing 1 John 5:7, the single basis by which Erasmus was compelled to insert that doubtful passage into his Greek New Testament in 1516.

Manuscript 69 contains the entire New Testament and dates from the fifteenth century. It is an important member of family 13.

Manuscript 81 was written in 1044 and is one of the most important of all minuscules. Its text in Acts agrees frequently with the Alexandrian text-type.

Manuscript 157 is a twelfth-century codex of the Gospels following the Caesarean type. An editorial inscription or colophon, found in this and a number of other manuscripts, states that they were copied and corrected "from ancient manuscripts at Jerusalem." For more about the "Jerusalem colophon," see *Journal of Theological Studies* 14 [1913]: 78ff., 242ff., 359ff.).

Manuscript 565 is one of the most beautiful of all known manuscripts. It has all the Gospels on purple vellum in gold letters.

Manuscript 614 is a thirteenth-century copy of Acts and the Epistles, with many pre-Byzantine readings.

Manuscript 700 is an eleventh- or twelfth-century codex remarkable for its divergent readings. It has 2724 deviations from the Received Text and 270 not found in any other manuscript.

Manuscript 892 is a ninth- or tenth-century codex of the Gospels with remarkable readings of an early (Alexandrian) type.

Manuscript 1739 is a very important codex from the tenth century that is based directly on a fourth-century Alexandrian type of manuscript. It has marginal notes from the writings of Irenaeus, *Clement, *Origen, *Eusebius, and Basil.

Manuscript 2053 is a thirteenth-century copy of Revelation. It is one of the best sources for the text of the Apocalypse.

Conclusion. Whereas there are many variant readings in New Testament manuscripts, there are a multitude of manuscripts available for comparison and correlation of those readings in order to arrive at the correct one. Through intensive comparative study of the readings in 5686 Greek manuscripts, scholars have carefully weeded out errors and additions from "helpful" copyists and discerned which early manuscripts are most accurate. Textual issues remain, but today's Bible reader, and especially those who read a recently edited Greek New Testament from the United Bible Society, can be confident that the text is extremely close to the autographs.

Sources

F. F. Bruce, *The New Testament Documents: Are They Reliable?*

P. Comfort, *The Complete Text of the Earliest New Testament Manuscripts*

A. Deissmann, *Light from the Ancient East*

D. Estrada, and W. White, Jr., *The First New Testament*

G. Fee, *The Textual Criticism of the New Testament*

N. L. Geisler and William E. Nix, *General Introduction to the Bible*

F. Kenyon, *The Bible and Archaeology*

———, *Our Bible and the Ancient Manuscripts*

R. Lyon, *Reexamination of Codex Ehp . . .*

B. Metzger, *Chapters in the History of New Testament Textual Criticism*

———, *Manuscripts of the Greek Bible*

———, *Text of the New Testament*

———, *A Textual Commentary on the Greek New Testament*

A. T. Robertson, *An Introduction to the Textual Criticism of the New Testament*
G. L. Robinson, *Where Did We Get Our Bible?*
P. Schaff, *Companion to the Greek Testament and English Version*
F. H. A. Scrivener, *Plain Introduction to the Criticism of the New Testament*
A. Souter, *The Text and Canon of the New Testament*
G. Stranton, *Gospel Truth?*
B. H. Streeter, "Codices 157, 1071 and the Caesarean Text," in *Quantulacumque: Studies Presented to Kirsopp Lake* (1937)

New Testament, Non-Christian Sources. ***See*** **JESUS, NON-CHRISTIAN SOURCES.**

Newman, John Henry. John Henry Newman (1801–1890) was born in London and ordained to the Church of England priesthood in 1825. He was the most famous English convert to Roman Catholicism and one of the great Catholic apologists of modern times. He came to Christ as a teen and was nurtured in the most Calvinistic segment of Anglicanism. He attended Oxford and remained as a fellow in Oriel College. Repelled by the theological liberalism he saw rising in his church, he launched the Oxford or Tractarian Movement. When he realized the Anglican Church as a whole would not embrace it, he took refuge in Roman Catholicism (1845), which he believed offered the best hope for overcoming the liberal onslaught. He rose to the ecclesiastical rank of cardinal.

Newman produced several works with apologetic themes. While an Anglican he wrote *Essays on Miracles* and *The Arians of the Fourth Century*. In his *University Sermons*, preached between 1826 and 1843, he developed his views on faith and reason. In *Essay on the Development of Christian Doctrine* (1845) he explained his reasons for believing the Roman Church was the true successor of the early church. His *Idea of a University* was penned in 1852. In 1864, in response to the attacks of Charles Kingsley, he composed his *Apologia pro vita sua*. His last major work was *An Essay in Aid of a Grammar of Assent* (1870).

Newman's Apologetic Views. In *Essay on the Development of Christian Doctrine*, Newman argued, against objections by liberals to all dogmatic religion, that religious assent is real. It is not a passing notion. Speculative theology, as practiced by the liberals, was about logic and abstractions, but the believer adheres with a whole heart to the living God (Dulles, 185).

Newman then addressed the problem of the degree of conviction demanded by faith and the amount of certainty on which it stands (*see* LESSING, GOTTHOLD). Newman did not believe it possible to amass a set of philosophical or historical arguments that would demonstrate Christianity beyond all possible argument. He felt that purely objective arguments would not bring true religious conviction. Because of the subjective element in all religious inquiry, Newman preferred what has been called an "existential dialect of conscience" (ibid., 186). In this he followed Joseph *Butler's use of analogies and *probabilities.

Newman counted only two consistent alternatives regarding belief in God: *atheism and Roman Catholicism. He rejected atheism because of the testimony of conscience, which he believed implied the existence of a Supreme Legislator. Nonetheless, Newman recognized that the absence of God pointed to an alienation due to sin and called for a divinely established way of salvation. This way must be accompanied by a teaching authority sufficient to withstand the arbitrary willfulness of fallen human beings. Natural religion (*see* NATURAL THEOLOGY) provides an anticipation of this revealed religion. But he held that there is only one religion in the world which tends to fulfill the aspirations, needs, and foreshadowing of natural faith and devotion (ibid., 187).

In *Grammar of Assent* (Chap. 10, part 2), Newman set forth an impressive historical argument based on the convergence of probabilities. He concluded that Christianity is more probable than other religions because of the convergence of probabilities that give rise to moral certitude (*see* CERTAINTY/CERTITUDE). First, the history of the Jews shows an example of extraordinarily strong monotheism in the face of persistent idolatry. Christianity exhibits the fulfillment of Israel's messianic expectations and agrees with Jesus' prediction that it would fill the earth and take dominion over it.

Newman argues more fully in *Apologia* for the Catholic dimension of his apologetic. He insists that, if divine revelation was delivered to the dominion of human reason, it would inevitably deteriorate and dissolve into chaos and confusion (ibid., 188). It was his opinion that only an infallible living authority could arrest this process of decline. In his *Essay on the Development of Christian Doctrine*, he sought to show how the Catholic Church has followed a line of development that manifests its continuity with the original revelation given in the Bible.

Evaluation. Newman's apologetic is valuable for both Catholics and Protestants. Some positive features include an appeal to objective and historical evidence (*see* APOLOGETICS, HISTORICAL), willingness to address the subjective and moral dimension, and focus on the moral certitude that results from converging probabilities.

On the negative side, Newman fails to make a convincing case for the uniqueness of Catholicism in holding back liberalism. Conservative Protestantism, without an infallible teaching magisterium, has more successfully held its ranks (see Geisler, chap. 11). What is more, Newman's thesis on the historical development of doctrine is without proof from either Scripture or the Fathers and is contrary to the infallible pronouncements of the Council of Trent (see Geisler, chap. 10).

Sources

A. Dulles, *A History of Apologetics*
N. L. Geisler and R. MacKenzie, *Roman Catholics and Evangelicals: Agreements and Differences*
J. H. Newman, *An Essay in Aid of a Grammar of Assent*
———, *Apologia pro vita sua*
———, *Essay on the Development of Christian Doctrine*
G. Salmon, *The Infallibility of the Church*

Nietzsche, Friedrich. Friedrich Nietzsche (1844–1900) was one of the most colorful and forceful atheists (*see* ATHEISM) of all time. His rejection of God was instinctive and incisive (*see* GOD, ALLEGED DISPROOFS OF). With the denial of God, Nietzsche denied all objective value based on God. Hence, his view is a form of nihilism. Although he was reared in a Lutheran pastor's home, Nietzsche reacted violently against his religious training. His mother, aunt, and sisters reared him from a young age after the death of his father.

God and the God Myth. Nietzsche based his belief that God never existed on several grounds (*Beyond Good and Evil,* 23). He argued that the theist's God would have to be a self-caused being, which was impossible (*see* GOD, OBJECTIONS TO PROOFS FOR). Evil in the world further ruled out a benevolent Creator (*see* EVIL, PROBLEM OF). Nietzsche thought the basis for belief in God to be purely psychological (*see* FREUD, SIGMUND). Nietzsche exhorted, "I beseech you, my brothers, remain faithful to the earth, and do not believe those who speak to you of other worldly hopes!" He added, "Once the sin against God was the greatest sin; but God died, and these sinners died with Him. To sin against the earth is now the most dreadful thing" (*Thus Spake Zarathustra,* 125).

Nietzsche did believe the God-myth was once very much alive. It had been the model by which medieval and Reformation Europe had based its life. This culture, however, was in decay. Modernity had caught up to modern humanity, who could no longer believe in God. "God is dead!" Nietzsche cried. Modern humankind must bury God and move on.

The World. Since God does not exist, the world is all there is. Matter is in motion, and life moves in cycles (*see* MATERIALISM; NATURALISM). The world is real, and God is an illusion. There is no God to which we must be faithful. Hence, each person is exhorted to "remain faithful to the earth." For Nietzsche viewed God "as the declaration of war against life, against nature . . . the deification of nothingness, the will of nothingness pronounced holy" (ibid., 92–94).

History and Destiny. Human history, as human destiny, is cyclical. Nietzsche rejected any Christian goal-oriented end or eschaton in favor of a more oriental cyclical recurrence. History is not going anywhere. There are no ultimate goals to achieve, no paradise to regain. There is simply an individual life to live by courage and creativity. Humanity creates a destiny here, and there is no hereafter—except the eternal recurrence of the same state of affairs. The supermen are the geniuses who form destiny. "They say, 'It shall be thus!' They determine the 'whether' and the 'to what end' of mankind. . . . Their knowing is creating" (*Beyond Good and Evil,* 18–19).

Ethics. The shocking realization of God's death brought Nietzsche to the conclusion that all God-based values and absolutes were also dead (*see* MORALITY, ABSOLUTE NATURE OF). Hence, Nietzsche rejected traditional Judeo-Christian values in an almost violent manner. Nietzsche questioned even general principles, such as "injure no man" (*Beyond Good and Evil,* 186–87). He ridiculed the Christian principle of love: "Why, you idiots. . . . 'How about praising the one who sacrifices himself?'" (ibid., 220). Indeed, Christianity "is the greatest of all conceivable corruptions. . . . I call it the one immortal blemish of mankind." (*Antichrist,* 230).

In place of traditional Christian values, he proposed that modern people go "beyond good and evil." He suggested a transevaluation that would reject the "soft" feminine virtues of love and humility and seize the "hard" male virtues of harshness and suspicion (*Beyond Good and Evil,* all).

Human Beings. There is no afterlife, so the best one can do to overcome the limits of personal mortality is to will the eternal recurrence of the same state of affairs (*see* IMMORTALITY). That is, he must will to come back and live the same life over and over forever. Since there is no God and there are no objective values to discover, the human race must create its own values. Meaningless and emptiness of life must be overcome. The overcomers are "supermen."

Evaluation. All atheists share the basic elements of Nietzsche's view. His contention that no God exists is refuted by strong evidence for the existence of God (*see* COSMOLOGICAL ARGUMENT; MORAL ARGUMENT FOR GOD; TELEOLOGICAL ARGUMENT). The objections to these arguments are answered elsewhere (*see* GOD, OBJECTIONS TO PROOFS FOR). Like *Freud's, Nietzsche's view that God is an illusion is without foundation. His moral relativism cannot stand against the logical strength of moral absolutism. Both the materialistic (*see* MATERIALISM) view of the universe (*see* NATURALISM) and its eternality are contrary to good scientific (*see* BIG BANG) and philosophical arguments (*see KALAM* COSMOLOGICAL ARGUMENT).

Sources

J. Collins, *A History of Modern European Philosophy*, chap. 18
N. L. Geisler and W. Watkins, *Ethics: Options and Issues*, chap. 2
———, *Worlds Apart: A Handbook on World Views*, chap. 2
R. G. Hollindale, *Nietzsche: The Man and His Philosophy*

K. Jaspers, *Nietzsche und das Christentum*, E. B. Ashton, trans.
W. Kaufmann, *The Portable Nietzsche*
F. Nietzsche, *Antichrist*
———, *Beyond Good and Evil*
———, *On the Genealogy of Morals*
———, *The Will to Power*
———, *Thus Spake Zarathustra*

Nihilism. *Nihilism* means "nothingness," the negation of all being or value (*see* NIETZSCHE, FRIEDRICH). In rejecting values, nihilism is antinomian or lawless. But even most relativists (*see* MORALITY, ABSOLUTE NATURE OF) or situationists do not deny all value, just all *absolute* value. Less stringent nihilists simply deny that any ultimate or absolute value exists. The only value that exists is what we create. There is no objective value to be discovered.

The negation of all being is self-defeating, since one has to exist in order to deny all existence. Those who do not exist do not deny anything.

Likewise, the denial of all value is self-refuting, since the very denial involves the belief that there is value in making this denial. Nihilists value their freedom to be nihilists. Thus, they cannot escape affirming value implicitly, even when they deny it explicitly.

Noah's Ark. ***See*** **FLOOD, NOAH'S.**

Noetic Effects of Sin. Some scholars object to any form of rational or evidential apologetics (*see* APOLOGETICS, TYPES OF) on the grounds that sin has so vitiated the human mind that it is neither possible for fallen humanity to understand God's revelation properly, nor to reason correctly. These objections are rooted in a certain understanding of Reformed theology and are expressed in such theologians as Søren *Kierkegaard (1813–1855), Herman Dooyeweerd (1894–1977), and Cornelius Van Til (1895–1987). Other Reformed Christians and classical apologists (*see* CLASSICAL APOLOGETICS) reject this dichotomy, claiming that, while sin effaces God's image in humankind and general revelation, it does not erase them.

Sin and the Mind. *John Calvin.* Protestant Reformers stressed the noetic effects of sin. John *Calvin (1509–1564) was quick to point out that the depravity of the human will obscures the ability to understand and respond to the natural revelation of God. He wrote: "Your idea of His [God's] nature is not clear unless you acknowledge him to be the origin and foundation of all goodness. Hence, would arise both confidence in Him and a desire of cleaving to Him, did not the depravity of the human mind lead it away from the proper course of investigation" (*Institutes*, 1.11.2).

Calvin believed that complete certainty (*see* CERTAINTY/CERTITUDE) comes only by the Holy Spirit (*see* HOLY SPIRIT, ROLE IN APOLOGETICS) working through this objective evidence to confirm in one's heart that the Bible is the Word of God. He wrote, "Our faith in doctrine is not established until we have a perfect conviction that God is its Author. Hence, the highest proof of Scripture is uniformly taken from the character of Him whose word it is." (*see* BIBLE, EVIDENCE FOR). "Our conviction of the truth of Scripture must be derived from a higher source than human conjecture, judgments, or reasons; namely, the secret testimony of the Spirit" (ibid., 1.7.1, cf. 1.8.1).

It is important to remember, however, as R. C. Sproul points out, that "the *testimonium* is not placed over against reason as a form of mysticism or subjectivism. Rather, it goes beyond and transcends reason" (Sproul, 341). In Calvin's words, "But I answer that the testimony of the Spirit is superior to reason. For God alone can properly bear witness to his own words, so these words will not obtain full credit on the hearts of men, until they are sealed by the inward testimony of the Spirit" (cited by Sproul, ibid.). It is God working through the objective evidence that provides us with subjective certainty that the Bible is the Word of God (*see* BIBLE, EVIDENCE FOR).

*Cornelius *Van Til.* One of the strongest modern expressions of the destruction of the mind by depravity is in the work of Van Til. He said that the unbeliever has within the knowledge of God by virtue of creation in the image of God. Then he hastens to say in the next sentence: "But this idea of God is suppressed by his false principle, the principle of autonomy" (*In Defense of the Faith*, 170). It is this principle that constitutes Van Til's analogy of the "jaundiced eye," by which all knowing by an unbeliever is distorted and false. The doctrine of radical depravity entails the belief that all unbelieving interpretive activity yields false conclusions.

Arguments in Scripture. The view that sin vitiates human ability to understand God's revelation or receive his redemptive grace most often appeals to certain biblical passages for support:

Dead in Sin. Paul uses the figure of speech that the unregenerate are "dead" in sins (Eph. 2:1). From this it is concluded that the dead neither hear nor see God's general revelation. They do not know it until they are regenerated by the Holy Spirit. Most often Paul is cited saying, "The man without the Spirit does not accept the things that come from the Spirit of God, for they are foolishness to him, and he cannot understand them, because they are spiritually discerned" (1 Cor. 2:14).

Wisdom Does Not Know God. Paul wrote that the world, by its wisdom, did not know God (1 Cor. 1:21). This cannot mean that there is no evidence for God's existence, since Paul declared in Romans 1:19–20 that the evidence for God's existence is so "plain" as to render the heathen "without excuse." The context of 1 Corinthians is not God's existence but his plan of salvation in the cross. This cannot be known by mere reason, but only by divine revelation. It is "foolish" to the depraved human mind. Finally, in this very book of 1 Corinthians, Paul gives his greatest apologetic evidence for the Christian faith—the eyewitness of the resurrection of Christ which his companion Luke called "many infallible proofs" (Acts 1:3 NKJV). So his reference to the world by wisdom not knowing God is not a reference to the inability of human beings to know God through the evidence he has revealed in creation (Rom. 1:19–20) and conscience (Rom. 2:12–15). Rather, it is a reference to the human depraved, foolish rejection of the message of the cross. Even though each person knows clearly through human reason that God exists, depravity "suppresses" or "holds down" this truth in unrighteousness (Rom. 1:18).

Without Faith . . . "Without faith it is impossible to please God" (Heb. 11:6) would seem to argue against the need for reason. In fact, it would appear that asking for reasons, rather than simply believing, displeases God. But God calls upon us to use our reason (1 Peter 3:15; *see* APOLOGETICS, NEED FOR). Indeed, he has given "clear" (Rom. 1:20) and "infallible proofs" (Acts 1:3). The text in Hebrews does not exclude "evidence," but actually implies it. For faith is said to be "the evidence" of things we do not see (Heb. 11:1 NKJV). Just as the evidence that someone is a reliable witness justifies my believing that person's testimony, so our faith in "things not seen" (Heb. 11:1) is justified by the evidence we have that God exists, which is clearly seen, "being understood from what has been made" (Rom. 1:20).

The One Who Can't Understand. Paul insisted that "the man without the Spirit does not accept the things that come from the Spirit of God" (1 Cor. 2:14). What use, then, is apologetics? They cannot even "know" him. But Paul does not say that natural persons cannot perceive truth about God, but that they do not receive (Gk. *dekomai*, "welcome") it. Paul emphatically declared that the basic truths about God are "clearly seen" (Rom. 1:20). The problem is not that unbelievers are not aware of God's existence but that they do not want to *accept* him because of the moral consequences this would have on their sinful lives. They do not "know" (Gk. *ginomskom*, which frequently means to "know by experience"). They *know* God in their mind (Rom. 1:19–20), but they have not accepted him in their heart (Rom. 1:18). "The fool has said *in his heart*, 'There is no God'" (Ps. 14:1).

Response. Even Van Til saw the tension in his own view. He speaks of it as a "difficult point," one which "we cannot give any wholly satisfactory account of the situation as it actually obtains" (*Introduction to Systematic Theology*, 15). Indeed, if fallen human beings really see everything with a "jaundiced eye," so that they cannot even understand the truth of general revelation or of the Gospel, they are not morally accountable.

Calvin never carried his belief in the *noetic effects of sin to the extreme of claiming no unsaved person could understand God's revelation to them. In fact, Calvin insisted "that there exists in the human mind, and indeed by natural instinct, some sense of deity" (*Institutes*, 1.3.1). He contended that there is no nation so barbarous, no race so brutish, as not to be imbued with the conviction that there is a God" (ibid.). This "sense of deity is so naturally engraven on the human heart, in the fact, that the very reprobate are forced to acknowledge it" (*Institutes*, 2.4.4). Calvin went further to claim that the invisible and incomprehensible essence of God has been made visible in God's works, along with proofs of the Soul's *immortality (*Institutes*, 1.5.1–2). For "on each of his works his glory is engraven in characters so bright, so distinct, and so illustrious, that none, however dull and illiterate, can plead ignorance as their excuse" (ibid.).

Commenting on Romans 1:20–21, Calvin concludes that Paul teaches that "God has presented to the minds of all the means of knowing him, having manifested himself by his works, that they must necessarily see what of themselves they seek not to know—that there is some God" (Commentary on Romans).

For Calvin this innate knowledge of God includes knowledge of his righteous law. He held that, since "the Gentiles have the righteousness of the law naturally engraved on their minds, we cannot say that they are altogether blind as to the rule of life" (*Institutes*, 1.2.22). He calls this moral awareness* "natural law," which is sufficient for condemnation but not for salvation (ibid.). By means of this natural law, "the judgment of conscience" is able to distinguish between what is just and unjust (Commentary on Romans, 48). Because of the bright engraving of God's glory, most people share the same basic ideas of what is right and what must be forbidden. It is evident that God has left "proof" of himself for all, in both creation and conscience (Commentary on Romans, 48).

**Van Til's Extreme View.* Even Van Til's disciples have had serious reservations about his view of the total destruction of reason by sin. John Frame responds that "To deny the restraint [of common grace], as Van Til appears to do in the present context, is to deny common grace itself" (Frame, 194). He adds that Van Til's antithesis of the mind with and without Christ requires considerable qualifying. Such an antithesis would seem to suggest that an unbeliever errs with every statement made. Depravity does not necessarily work that way. The formulation also suggests that the specifically intellectual handicap of human depravity will inevitably show up in what the unbeliever says, does, or makes, rather than in the direction of his or her life. They also fail to convey that the unbeliever's very denial of the truth is in some respects an affirmation of it (Frame, 207).

Frame adds that it is simplistic to hold that the *noetic effects of sin amount to a propositional falsification of the unbeliever's every utterance (ibid., 211).

Van Til himself offers statements that do not fit his antithesis. He urges "that we present the message and evidence for the Christian position as clearly as possible, knowing that because man is what the Christian says he is, the non-Christian will be able to understand in an intellectual sense the issues involved" ("My Credo"). But how can the non-Christian understand the issues, even in an intellectual sense, if there is no common ground, or knowledge of any kind—if he sees all with a jaundiced eye?

Scripture clearly declares unregenerate beings to be "without excuse" (Rom. 1:19–20; 2:12–15). Adam and Eve were "dead in trespasses and sin" (cf. Eph. 2:1) the very instant they took of the forbidden fruit (Gen. 3:6; Rom. 5:12). Yet they heard and understood God speaking to them (Gen. 3:9–19).

A common mistake of Reformed presuppositionalism is to misunderstand the figure of speech of "dead" to be the equivalent of spiritually "annihilated," a mistake which, fortunately, they do not make when speaking of the second death (Rev. 20:14). Death in Scripture is better understood in terms of separation, not annihilation (*see* ANNIHILATIONISM). The prophet said, "Your sins have separated you from your God" (Isa. 59:2 KJV). "Dead" is not the only figure of speech used in the Bible to describe fallen humankind. Sickness, blindness, pollution, and lameness are also used. But none of these imply a person totally unable to understand God's revelation.

Other nonpresuppositional Reformed theologians, such as Jonathan Edwards, B. B. *Warfield, John Gerstner, and Sproul believe just as firmly in total depravity without accepting this skewed view of the noetic effects of sin. Total depravity can be understood as the inability to initiate or attain salvation without the grace of God.

In this same connection, Reformed *presuppositionalists often misinterpret 1 Cor. 2:14 to mean that unbelievers cannot even understand God's truth before they are regenerated. Besides the obvious difficulty that they would have to be saved before they believe—the opposite of what Scripture says in John 3:16, 36; Acts 16:31, and Rom. 5:1—This is a misreading of the passage. Nor does it help to claim they are regenerated before they are saved (justified), since one is placed in the kingdom of God by regeneration (John 3:3; Titus 5:5). As Fred Howe noted, the Greek word for "receive," *dekomai*, means "to welcome." It does not mean they do not understand. They clearly perceive (Rom. 1:19–20), but they are not willing to receive the truths of God (Howe, 71–72). Consequently, they do not know them by experience. They know them only in their mind, not in their heart. A failure to understand these truths leads to misunderstanding of the effects of sin.

Limits of Reason. Following Jewish philosopher Moses *Maimonides (1135–1204), *Thomas Aquinas (1224–1274) set forth five reasons why we must first believe. Later we may be able to provide good evidence. We must believe,

1. because these truths are deep and subtle and far removed from the senses.
2. because the mind is weak at understanding something new.
3. because a number of facts may need to be assembled for conclusive proof to develop.
4. because some lack the scientific temperament to study philosophical concepts.
5. because we have more to do in life than just think.

It is clear that, if it required total understanding to come to God, few could put together the needed steps of knowledge, and then only after a long time. So the way of faith, which gives access to salvation at any time, is a great benefit (Aquinas, *On Truth*, 14.10, reply). Thus, for certitude in divine things, faith is necessary.

Aquinas stated that

> the mind of man falls far short when it comes to the things of God. Look at the philosophers; even in searching into questions about man they have erred in many points and held contradictory views. To the end, therefore, that a knowledge of God, undoubted and secure, might be present among men, it was necessary that divine things be taught by way of faith, spoken as it were by the Word of God who cannot lie. [Aquinas, *Summa Theologiae*, 2a2ae. 2, 4, 6]

The searching mind will not come to understand the things of God, Aquinas said. A sign of the human deficiency in understanding the divine is the fact that philosophers cannot come even to understand human affairs without error. Therefore, it was necessary for God to deliver divine truths by way of faith, told to human beings by the God who cannot lie (ibid., 2a2ae. 2, 4).

Grace, therefore, is needed to overcome the noetic effects of sin. Aquinas concluded that God must come to human aid with healing grace. We cannot love God or our neighbor without grace. Neither can we believe. But with grace we do have this power. As Augustine says, to whomever this help is given by God, it is given in mercy; to whomever it is denied, it is denied in justice, because of original and personal sin (ibid., 2a2ae. 2, 6, ad 1). Aquinas, however, did not believe that sin completely destroyed human rational ability. Rather, "sin cannot destroy man's rationality altogether, for then he would no longer be capable of sin" (ibid., 1a2ae. 85,2).

Proportionate Effects of Sin. According to Emil *Brunner (1889–1966) the noetic effects of sin are manifest on the mind in direct proportion to the distance of a discipline from religious concern. Effects of the fall are more evident, for example, in philosophy than in economics. Since the discipline of theology is the most religious, there is greater area of disagreement with unbelievers. Brunner saw religious worldview as being progressively less of an issue in ethics, psychology/sociology, physics, and the least important in mathematics. That is, in mathematics Christians and non-Christians have the least disagreement and in ethics the most.

Conclusion. Sin affects the whole person—mind, emotions, and will. Human beings are *radically depraved* in their being. Another way to say this is that they are *extensively* affected by sin. But humans are not totally depraved in an *intensive* sense, since sin does not destroy the image of God (see Gen. 9:6; James 3:9). God's image is effaced but not erased.

So revelation can be perceived, even if it is not willingly received by depraved creatures without the work of the Spirit. There is no certain, saving knowledge of God apart from God's special revelation in Scripture and the special grace of the Holy Spirit applying Scripture and convincing the person of sin and need and the truth in general and special revelation. General revelation alone (*see* REVELATION, GENERAL), however, is sufficient to reveal God, if anyone truly desired to see him, so the lost are justly condemned for not receiving what they have clearly seen (Rom. 1:20).

Sources

E. Brunner, *Revelation and Reason*
J. Calvin, *Institutes of the Christian Religion*
———, *New Testament Commentaries: Epistles of Paul to the Romans and Thessalonians*
J. Frame, *Cornelius Van Til: An Analysis of His Thought*
F. Howe, *Challenge and Response*
K. Kantzer, *John Calvin's Theory of the Knowledge of God and the Word of God*
Thomas Aquinas, *On Truth*
———, *Summa Contra Gentiles*
———, *Summa Theologiae*
Van Til, Cornelius, *In Defense of the Faith*
———, *Introduction to Systematic Theology*

Nominalism. *Nominalism* is the view that neither universals nor essences are real (*see* REALISM), that is, they have no extramental existence. Everything is particular. A universal is a general or class concept that includes all the particulars in it. The class is an abstract concept that exists only in the mind (*see* EPISTEMOLOGY; FIRST PRINCIPLES).

"Humanness" is a general concept that includes all individual human beings. But nominalists insist that humanness does not exist; only individuals really exist. "Triangleness" is a universal, but it too exists only in the mind. In reality only individual triangular shaped things exist.

Nature of Nominalism. Nominalism can be best viewed by contrast with opposing conceptions. Following *Plato, the Medieval theologian Gilbert of Porree affirmed that universals are *real things.* On the other end of the spectrum, medieval thinker Roscellinus (1050–1125) contended that universals are *a mere sign,* "a puff of the voice." Peter Abelard (1079–1142) claimed that universals are *nouns* formed by a confusion of particular ideas. *William of Ockham (1280–1349) was a true nominalist. To him, a universal is a *mere abstract concept in the mind.* John Duns Scotus (1266–1308) believed that universals are *bonds* or *common natures* that in themselves are neither universal or particular. Nature as such is neutral; it can be generalized by the mind or concretized with "thisness." *Thomas Aquinas (1224–1274) held a realistic position (*see* REALISM), declaring that a universal is *mental being.* It is a form existing in the mind but rooted in reality.

Problems with Nominalism. From a realistic perspective, nominalism has problems, some with serious consequences for important Christian beliefs.

Nominalism Leads to Skepticism. If there is no basis in reality for our general ideas, then words tell us nothing about reality. We must remain skeptical about the real world. But complete skepticism (*see* AGNOSTICISM) is self-defeating. If it suspended judgment about its own central affirmation, as it demands we do about everything else, the skeptic would have to be skeptical of skepticism. That would destroy the basis for skepticism.

Nominalism Leads to Moral Relativism. If universals have no basis in the real world, there can be no universal moral values. Everything would simply be particular or situational. There would be nothing that one ought to do in every circumstance (such as, be loving or just). However, the denial of all absolutes is self-defeating (*see* MORALITY, ABSOLUTE NATURE OF), for the claim that one absolutely *ought not* believe in moral absolutes is a moral absolute of its own.

Nominalism Leads to Heresy. All orthodox Christians believe that God has one essence or nature, and Christ has two natures (*see* TRINITY). But, if nominalists are right, then God has no nature. Likewise, Christ could not have both a human and a divine nature, as the creeds assert (*see* CHRIST, DEITY OF). Hence, nominalism is a denial of historic, creedal, orthodox Christianity.

Nominalism Overreacts to Platonism. *Plato (428–348 B.C.) believed everything that exists is part of an eternal essence or form. Nominalists deny such changeless essences, affirming that everything is particular or individual. They fail to acknowledge, however, that these are not the only two options. Aquinas showed that, while universals exist in the mind as abstractions from particulars, they are rooted in reality. There is no such entity as human nature. However, each human being shares essential characteristics (= nature or essence). So the abstraction referring to what we call humanness is not a mere name; it is a referent to a relationship that truly exists in reality.

Sources

E. Gilson, *The History of Christian Philosophy in the Middle Ages*
J. F. Harris, *Against Relativism*
J. P. Moreland, *Universals, Qualities, and Quality-Instances.*
William of Ockham, *Ockham: Philosophical Writings*
W. V. Quine, *From a Logical Point of View*
Thomas Aquinas, *Summa Theologica.*

Noncontradiction, Principle of. *See* **First Principles.**

Nostradamus. Nostradamus (1503–1566) was known by the Latin name of Michel de Notredame or Nostredame. He was graduated from University of Montpellier in France and was a physician and astrologer. He published a book of rhymed prophecies titled *Centuries* (1555). He is reputed to have predicted accurately the death of Henry II of France and many other things.

According to Andre Lamont, *Nostradamus Sees All* ("Preface," 2d. ed., v), "he was well versed in the arts of astronomy, the kabbala, astrology, alchemy, magic, mathematics and medicine."

Predictions of Nostradamus. Some critics of Christianity hold up Nostradamus as an example of someone who made predictions on the level with those in the Bible, thus canceling the claim of supernatural uniqueness made for biblical prophecy (*see* Prophecy, as Proof of the Bible). However, on examination they fall far short of this claim. The predictions of Nostradamus show signs of an occult source and may be explained according to purely natural processes.

A Great California Earthquake. Nostradamus is alleged to have predicted a great earthquake in California for May 10, 1981. This was reported on May 6, 1981, in *USA Today.* However, no such quake occurred. As a matter of fact, Nostradamus mentioned no country, city, or year. He spoke only of a "rumbling earth" in a "new city" and a "very mighty quake" on May 10 [no year].

Hitler's Rise to Power. Lamont claims that Nostradamus gave "a prophecy of the coming of Hitler and Nazism in a world divided within itself" (Lamont, 252). However, Hitler is not mentioned and the prediction gives no date and is vague. It reads: "Followers of sects, great troubles are in store for the Messenger. A beast upon the theater prepares the scenical play. The inventor of that wicked feat will be famous. By sects the world will be confused and divided" (ibid.). In this context there is a reference to "Hister" (not Hitler) by Nostradamus (C4Q68), which is obviously a place, not a person. The attempt to read back into this both his name and birthplace is stretched. What is more, Hitler grew up in Linz, Austria, not in any place called Hister.

Quatrain 2–24 reads: "Beasts mad with hunger will swim across rivers, Most of the army will be against the Lower Danube [*Hister sera*]. The great one shall be dragged in an iron cage when the child brother *[de Germain]* will observe nothing."

This is allegedly a prophecy concerning Adolf Hitler. According to followers of Nostradamus, the lower portion of the Danube is known as either *"Ister"* or *"Hister"* (Randi, 213), which seems to be close enough to "Hitler" for their purposes.

However, the substitution of "l" for "s" in *Hister*, and the inversion of "t" and "s," is totally arbitrary. In another quatrain (4–68), Nostradamus mentions the Lower Danube in conjunction with the Rhine *("De Ryn")*. But if *"Hister"* refers to Hitler, then to what does *"De Ryn"* refer? Followers of Nostradamus are inconsistent, treating one river as an anagram and taking the other literally. The Latin phrase *de Germain* should be interpreted "brother" or "near relative," not "Germany" (Randi, 214). Even if these highly questionable interpretations are allowed, the prophecy is still quite ambiguous. What are we to make of the "Beasts" and the "iron cage"? To say that Adolf Hitler ("the great one") will be "dragged in an iron cage" while Germany "will observe nothing" is so ambiguous and confusing it renders the entire prophecy meaningless.

Quatrain 4–68 is also alleged to refer to Hitler. It reads: "In the year very near, not far from Venus, The two greatest of Asia and Africa From the Rhine and Lower Danube, which will be said to have come, Cries, tears at Malta and the Ligurian coast."

As in the previous example, "Lower Danube" is here taken to mean "Hitler." "The two greatest of Asia and Africa" are taken to refer to Japan and Mussolini, respectively. Thus, the second and third lines refer to the Tripartite Pact between Japan, Italy, and Germany. The fourth is taken as a reference to the bombing of Malta and the bombardment of Genoa (Randi, 215).

In addition to the reasons given above, this prophecy claims these events would take place in a "year very near," but the Tripartite Pact (1941) came almost 400 years after the prediction. It is not clear how Asia could refer to Japan, and even more so, how Africa could refer to Mussolini or Italy. Again Nostradamus's followers are inconsistent, for they interpret Asia, Africa, and the Lower Danube figuratively while providing no corresponding interpretation for the Rhine. Finally, this prophecy is ambiguous on the whole.

It could be interpreted in various ways so as to fulfill many different events.

The Second World War. According to Lamont, Nostradamus forecast that, after the first World War, the Spanish Civil War, and other wars, a more furious one was foretold—the Second World War, with its aerial warfare and suffering. But no such details are given. It is typically vague and could be easily forecast without any supernormal powers. The passage reads simply: "After a great human exhaustion, a greater one is being prepared. As the great motor renews the centuries, a rain of blood, milk, famine, iron and pestilence [will come]. In the sky will be seen fires carrying long sparks" (Lamont, 168).

Evaluation. Nostradamus's forecasts are general, vague, and explainable on purely natural grounds. Furthermore, Nostradamus shows clear signs of demonic and occult influence (*see* MIRACLES, MAGIC AND).

False Prophecies. An evident sign of a false prophet is false prophecy (cf. Deuteronomy 18). If Nostradamus' predictions are taken literally, many are false. If they are not, then they can fit many "fulfillments." As John Ankerberg put it, "it is an undeniable fact that Nostradamus gave numerous false prophecies" (Ankerberg, 340). Noted Nostradamus scholar Erika Cheetham said flatly of his prognostications in his *Almanachs*: "Many of these predictions were wrong" (Ericka, 20). Some interpretations are so diverse that while one claims it is a reference to "Calvinist Geneva," another believes it refers to "atomic power" (*The Prophecies of Nostradamus,* 81).

Vague Predictions. The truth is that the vast majority of his prognostications are so ambiguous and vague that they could fit a great variety of events. Consider this one: "Scythe by the Pond, in conjunction with Sagittarius at the high point of its ascendant—disease, famine, death by soldiery—the century/age draws near its renewal" (*Centuries* 1. 6). The lines can be interpreted so as to fit any number of events in the future. When something is judged to be a fulfillment, Nostradamus will seem supernatural. Astrologers and fortune tellers use vague descriptions and imagery all the time. Nostradamus was a master at this art.

Contradictory Interpretations. There is no unanimity among Nostradamus' interpreters about the meaning of his predictions. This lack of agreement is further proof of their ambiguity and lack of authority. In *The Prophecies of Nostradamus* the editors note contradictory interpretations (see I, 16; I, 51; II, 41; II, 43; II, 89; III, 97, etc.).

Predictions after the Fact. Nostradamus himself acknowledged that his predictions were written in such a manner that "they could not possibly be understood until they were interpreted after the event and by it" (Randi, 31). There is nothing miraculous about reading a fulfillment back into a prophecy which could not be clearly seen there beforehand. Not a single prediction of Nostradamus has ever been proven genuine. This means that either he is a false prophet or else he was not really seriously claiming to be giving real predictions. Perhaps he was a con artist or a literary prankster.

Tongue-in-Cheek Prophecies? His prognostications were so vague and unproductive that even the encyclopedia of *Man, Myth and Magic* suggests that "Nostradamus composed them with tongue in cheek, as he was well aware that there is an enduring market for prophecies and particularly for veiled ones" (Cavendish, 2017). As James Randi put it, "The marvelous prophecies of Michel de Nostredame, upon examination, turn out to be a tiresome collection of vague, punning, seemingly badly constructed verses. . . . From a distance of more than 400 years, I fancy I can hear a bearded Frenchman laughing at the naiveté of his 20th century dupes" (36).

Confessed Demonic Source. Nostradamus admitted demonic inspiration when he wrote: "The tenth of the Calends of April roused by evil persons; the light extinguished; diabolical assembly searching for the bones of the devil (*damant*—"demon") according to Psellos" (Lamont, 71). Commenting on this, Lamont noted that "The utilization of the demons or black angels is recommended by ancient writers on magic. They claim that they have much knowledge of temporal matters and, once under control, will give much information to the operator." He adds, Nostradamus could not have avoided such a temptation" (ibid.).

Various Forms of Occult Practices. Nostradamus was associated with various occult activities. Lamont observes that "Magic—Astrology—Symbolism—Anagrams—[are a] Key to Nostradamus" (ibid., 69). In *Centuries*, Quatrain 2 is translated: "The wand in the hand seated in the midst of the Branches, He (the prophet) wets in the water both the hem (of his garment) and the foot. A fearfulness and a voice quiver through the sleeves; divine splendor, The Divine is seated near" (ibid., 70). Lamont comments that here "Nostradamus followed the rites of magic according to Iamblichus. It is night—he is seated on the stool or prophetic tripod—a little flame rises. He has the divining rod in his hand" (ibid., 70–71).

In addition to the use of the occult divining rod, Nostradamus was widely known for his knowledge of astrology—another occult practice condemned by the Bible (Deuteronomy 18). But whatever their source, these predictions in no way rival the clear, specific, and highly accurate predictions of Scripture.

Conclusion. There is no real comparison between Nostradamus' predictions and those of the Bible. His are vague, fallible, and occult. Those of the Bible are clear, infallible, and divine (*see* BIBLE, EVIDENCE FOR). The Bible made numerous clear and distinct predictions hundreds of years in advance. Nostradamus did not. There is no evidence that Nostradamus was a prophet at all; certainly he was like none in the Bible. Biblical prophecy stands unique in its claim to be supernatural (*see* PROPHECY, AS PROOF OF THE BIBLE).

Sources

J. Ankerberg, et al., *Cult Watch*

M. Cavendish, "Nostradamus" in *Man, Myth and Magic*, new ed., vol. 15

E. Cheetham, *The Final Prophecies of Nostradamus*

A. Kole, *Miracle and Magic*

A. Lamont, *Nostradamus Sees All*

M. Nostradamus, *Centuries*

J. Randi, "Nostradamus: The Prophet for All Seasons," *The Skeptical Enquirer* (Fall 1882)

[no editor named]. *The Prophecies of Nostradamus*

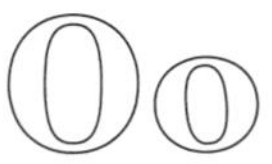

Objectivism. *See* RAND, AYN.

O'Callahan, Jose. Jose O'Callahan (b. 1922) is a Spanish Jesuit paleographer who made the astounding identification of nine fragments among Qumran's Dead Sea Scrolls as coming from multiple books of the New Testament.

The Fragments. Beginning with his first announcement in 1972, O'Callahan eventually identified the nine fragments from Cave 7 as Mark 4:28; 6:48; 6:52, 53; 12:17; Acts 27:38; Romans 5:11–12, 1 Timothy 3:16; 4:1–3; 2 Peter 1:15; and James 1:23–24. The fragments were dated: Mark, 50; Acts, 60; and Romans, 1 Timothy, 2 Peter, and James approximately 70. Fragments from Cave 7 had previously been dated between 50 B.C. and A.D. 50. For a more extensive discussion of these fragments, see the articles DEAD SEA SCROLLS; NEW TESTAMENT MANUSCRIPTS; NEW TESTAMENT, DATING OF, and NEW TESTAMENT, HISTORICITY OF.

Implications of the Identification. If valid, O'-Callahan's conclusions are correct they totally invalidate many New Testament theories. The *New York Times* reported: "If Father O'Callahan's theory is accepted it would prove that at least one of the gospels—that of St. Mark—was written only a few years after the death of Jesus." *United Press International* noted that his conclusions indicated that "the people closest to the events—Jesus' original followers—found Mark's report accurate and trustworthy, not myth but true history" (Estrada, 137). *Time* quoted one scholar who claimed that if correct, "they can make a bonfire of 70 tons of indigestible German scholarship" (ibid., 136).

Dating the Evidence. The early dates (listed above) are supported by the evidence that these pieces were not dated by O'Callahan but by other scholars prior to his identification of them; the dates have never been seriously questioned and fit with the dates determined for other manuscripts found in the same Qumran area. Archaeologists who discovered Cave 7 attested that it showed no signs of being opened since it was sealed in A.D. 70 and that its contents date from no later. The style of writing (in Greek uncials) has been identified as early first century (*see* NEW TESTAMENT MANUSCRIPTS).

O'Callahan is a reputable paleographer who has made many successful identifications of ancient texts. His identifications of these texts fit perfectly with the passages. No viable alternatives have been found. In fact, two scholars calculated the odds that these letter sequences represent some other text as about 1 in 2.25×10^{65}.

Not surprisingly, objections to O'Callahan's identification have been raised. Some have charged that O'Callahan never worked with the original mss. This is false. Others point out that the pieces are small fragments. However, other ancient texts have been identified with equal or less evidence. Some have contended that the Mark 5 manuscript is too dim or indistinct to be truly readable. Very clear photographs are now available, however.

The identification of certain letters has been disputed. If identifications are revised, the identity of the manuscript could change. But O'Callahan has mostly used the letters proposed by the original editors. Where he did not, the editors have concurred that his identification could be correct. Of the crucial Mark 5 text he used all nine whole letters and six of the ten partial letters. Where he differed, his judgment was a possible alternative based on the actual manuscript.

A few critics have offered possible non-New Testament alternatives. In order to be successful, they have had to change the number of letters on a line of ancient text from the twenties to the sixties in some cases. This many letters to a line would be highly unusual. One confirming evidence of O'Callahan's thesis is that no one has found any other non-New Testament text for these manuscripts. Using normal rules, O'Callahan has provided probable New Testament identifications.

Apologetic Relevance. If the identification of even some of these fragments as New Testament is valid, implications for Christian apologetics are enormous. The Gospel of Mark was written within the life time of the apostles and contemporaries of the events (*see* New Testament, Dating of; New Testament, Historicity of). This early date (before 50) leaves no time for mythological embellishment of the records (*see* Mythology and the New Testament). They must be accepted as historical. Mark is shown to be one of the early Gospels. The chance of there being a *Q* or series of *Q* gospel manuscripts is more remote (*see* Q Document). Since these manuscripts are not originals but copies, the New Testament was copied and disseminated quickly. The existence of a New Testament canon from the beginning is hinted at by this selection of books, representing Gospels, Acts, Pauline, and General Epistles—every major section of the New Testament. Sixth, the fragment of 2 Peter would argue for the authenticity of this often disputed Epistle. The absence of fragments of John's writings could indicate that they were written later (80–90), in accordance with the traditional dates.

Sources

D. Estrada, and W. White, Jr., *The First New Testament*

E. Fisher, "New Testament Documents among the Dead Sea Scrolls?" *The Bible Today* 61 (1972)

P. Garnet, "O'Callahan's Fragments: Our Earliest New Testament Texts?" in *Evangelical Quarterly* 45 (1972)

B. Orchard, "A Fragment of St. Mark's Gospel Dating from before A.D. 50?" in *Biblical Apostolate* 7 (1972)

W. N. Pickering, *The Identification of the New Testament Text*

W. White, Jr., "O'Callahan's Identifications: Confirmation and Its consequences," *Westminster Journal* 35 (1972)

Ockham, William. ***See*** **William of Ockham.**

Ockham's Razor. *Ockham's Razor* is the popular name for a principle laid down by William of Ockham (1285–1349). It is also called the Principle of Parsimony. In its popular form it states that the simplest explanation is the best explanation. This is often taken to mean "the fewer, the truer," and by logical extension "the fewest, the truest." However, this is not what Ockham had in mind.

In the original form given by Ockham the principle merely affirms that "causes should not be multiplied without necessity." That is, one should not posit more causes or reasons than are necessary to explain the data. The true explanation could involve many causes, and having fewer would be incorrect. But unnecessarily complicating the problem also makes reasoning incorrect.

Old Testament Manuscripts. The manuscripts of the Old Testament are not as crucial to Christian apologetics as are those of the New Testament (*see* New Testament, Historicity of; New Testament Manuscripts). However, their reliability in general is important, and the manuscripts play a crucial role in establishing the Old Testament's reliability. They also help establish the date of Old Testament prophecies (*see* Prophecy as Proof of the Bible) which play a supporting role in defending Christianity (*see* Apologetics, Argument of). Like the New Testament, the original manuscripts (*autographs*) of the Old Testament are not available, but the Hebrew text is amply represented by both pre- and post-Christian manuscripts (see Geisler, "Bible Manuscripts," 1:248–52). As a result, the reliability of the Hebrew text can be determined from available manuscript evidence. But over 2000 years of copying the text (500 B.C. to A.D. 1500) Jewish scholars performed an unbelievable preservation of the textual traditions.

History of the Old Testament Text. In Judaism a succession of scholars were charged with standardizing and preserving the biblical text:

- The *Sopherim* (from Hebrew meaning "scribes") were Jewish scholars and custodians of the text between the fifth and the third centuries B.C.
- The *Zugoth* ("pairs" of textual scholars) were assigned to this task in the second and first centuries B.C.
- The *Tannaim* ("repeaters" or "teachers") were active to 200. The work of Tannaim can be found in the *Midrash* ("textual interpretation"), *Tosefta* ("addition"), and *Talmud* ("instruction"), the latter of which is divided into *Mishnah* ("repetitions") and *Gemara* ("the matter to be learned"). The Talmud gradually was written between 100 and 500.
- Between 500 and 950 the Masoretes added the vowel pointings and pronunciation marks to the consonantal Hebrew text received from the Sopherim, on the basis of the *Masora* ("tradition") that had been handed down to them. The Masoretes were scribes who codified and wrote down the oral criticisms and remarks on the Hebrew text. There were two major schools or centers of Masoretic activity, each largely independent of the other, the Babylonian and the Palestinian. The most famous Masoretes were the Jewish scholars living in Tiberias in Galilee, Moses ben Asher (with his son Aaron), and Moses ben Naphtali, in the late ninth and tenth centuries The ben Asher text is the standard text for the Hebrew Bible today as best represented by Codex Leningradensis B19^{A} (L) and Aleppo Codex.

At issue today is the standard "Masoretic" Hebrew text—the one used in Bible translation. Frederic Kenyon posed the all-important question when he asked whether the Masoretic Text represents the Hebrew text originally written by the authors. The standard edition of the Masoretic Text was first published under the editorship of a Hebrew Christian, Jacob Ben Chayyim (ca. 1525). It was essentially a recension of the text of the Masorete Ben Asher (ca. 920) (see Geisler, *General Introduction to the Bible,* chap. 25). The answer to Kenyon's question arises from a careful examination of the number and nature of Hebrew manuscripts.

The Number of Manuscripts. The first collection of Hebrew manuscripts, made by Benjamin Kennicott (1776–1780) and published by Oxford, listed 615 manuscripts of the Old Testament. Later Giovanni de Rossi (1784–1788) published a list of 731 manuscripts. The most important manuscript discoveries in modern times are those of the Cairo Geniza (1890s) and the Dead Sea Scrolls (1947 and following years). In the Cairo synagogue attic geniza or storehouse for old manuscripts alone were discovered 200,000 manuscripts and fragments (Kahle, 13, and Würthwein, 25) some 10,000 of which are biblical (Goshen-Gottstein, 35). According to J. T. Milik, fragments of about 600 manuscripts are known from the *Dead Sea Scrolls, not all biblical. Moshe Goshen-Gottstein estimates that the total number of Old Testament Hebrew manuscript fragments throughout the world runs into the tens of thousands (ibid., 31).

Major Collections. About one-half of the 200,000 Cairo Geniza manuscript fragments are housed at Cambridge University. The rest are scattered throughout the world. Cairo Geniza authority Paul Kahle has identified more than 120 rare manuscripts prepared by the "Babylonian group" of Masoretic scribes.

The largest collection of Hebrew Old Testament manuscripts in the world is the Second Firkowitch Collection in Leningrad. It contains 1582 items of the Bible and Masora on parchment (725 on paper), plus 1200 additional Hebrew manuscript fragments in the Antonin Collection (Würthwein, 23). Kahle contends also that these Antonin Collection manuscripts and fragments are all from the Cairo Geniza (Kahle, 7). In the Firkowitch Collection are found fourteen Hebrew Old Testament manuscripts from between 929 and 1121 that originated in the Cairo Geniza.

Cairo Geniza manuscripts are scattered over the world. Some of the better ones in the United States are in the Enelow Memorial Collection at the Jewish Theological Seminary, New York (Goshen-Gottstein, 44f.).

The British Museum catalog lists 161 Hebrew Old Testament manuscripts. At Oxford University, the Bodleian Library catalog lists 146 Old Testament manuscripts, each containing a large number of fragments (Kahle, 5). Goshen-Gottstein estimates that in the United States alone there are tens of thousands of Semitic manuscript fragments, about 5 percent of which are biblical—more than 500 manuscripts (Goshen-Gottstein, 30).

Hebrew Manuscripts. The most significant Hebrew Old Testament manuscripts date from between the third century B.C. and the fourteenth century A.D. Of these the most remarkable manuscripts are those of the Dead Sea Scrolls, which date from the third century B.C. to the first century A.D. They include one complete Old Testament book (Isaiah) and thousands of fragments, which together represent every Old Testament book except Esther.

Dead Sea Scroll Discoveries. Cave 1 was discovered by the Arab shepherd boy. From it he took seven more-or-less complete scrolls and some fragments:

Isaiah A (IQIs^{a}). St. Mark's Monastery Isaiah Scroll is a popular copy with numerous corrections above the line or in the margin. It is the earliest known copy of any complete book of the Bible.

Isaiah B (IQIs^{b}). The Hebrew University Isaiah is incomplete but its text agrees more closely with the Masoretic text than does Isaiah A.

Other Cave 1 Fragments. This cave also yielded fragments of Genesis, Leviticus, Deuteronomy, Judges, Samuel, Isaiah, Ezekiel, Psalms, and some nonbiblical works, including Enoch, Sayings of Moses (previously unknown), Book of Jubilee, Book of Noah, Testament of Levi, Tobit, and the Wisdom of Solomon. An interesting fragment of Daniel, containing 2:4 (where the language changes from Hebrew to Aramaic), also comes from this cave. Fragmentary commentaries on Psalms, Micah, and Zephaniah were also found in Cave 1.

Cave 2. Cave 2 was first discovered and pilfered by the Bedouins. It was excavated in 1952. Fragments of about a hundred manuscripts, including two of Exodus, one of Leviticus, four of Numbers, two or three of Deuteronomy, one of Jeremiah, Job, Psalms, and two of Ruth, were found.

Cave 3. Cave 3 was found by the archaeologists and searched on March 14, 1952. It disclosed two halves of a copper scroll with directions to sixty or sixty-four sites containing hidden treasures. These sites were mostly in and around the Jerusalem area, ranging from north of Jericho to the Vale of Achor. Thus far, search for the treasures has been unfruitful. Various views have emerged to explain this scroll. It has been suggested that it is the work of a crank, or part of the people's folklore, or possibly a record of the deposits of the tithe money and sacred vessels dedicated to the temple service (see Allegro).

Cave 4. Partridge Cave or Cave 4, after being ransacked by Bedouins, was searched in September 1952, and it proved to be the most productive cave of all. Literally thousands of fragments were recovered by purchase from the Bedouin or by the archaeologists' sifting the dust on the floor of the cave. These scraps represent hundreds of manuscripts, nearly 400 of which have been identified. They include 100 copies of Bible books, all the Old Testament except Esther.

A fragment of Samuel from Cave 4 (4qsam[b]) is thought to be the oldest known piece of biblical Hebrew. It dates from the third century B.C. Also found were a few fragments of commentaries of the Psalms, Isaiah, and Nahum. The entire collection of Cave 4 is believed to represent the scope of the Qumran library, and judging from the relative number of books found, their favorite books seemed to be Deuteronomy, Isaiah, Psalms, the Minor Prophets, and Jeremiah, in that order. In one fragment containing some of Daniel 7:28, 8:1, the language changes from Aramaic to Hebrew.

Caves 5 and 6. Caves 5 and 6 were excavated in September 1952. Fragments of Tobit and some biblical books, all in an advanced stage of deterioration, were found in Cave 5. Cave 6 produced mostly papyrus, instead of leather fragments. Papyrus pieces of Daniel, 1 Kings, and 2 Kings were among the finds.

Caves 7–10. Caves 7–10, examined in 1955, produced no significant Old Testament manuscripts. Cave 7 did, however, yield some disputed mss. fragments that have been identified by Jose *O'Callahan as New Testament portions. If so, they would be the oldest New Testament mss. dating from as early as A.D. 50 or 60.

Cave 11. Cave 11 was excavated in early 1956. It produced a well-preserved copy of thirty-six Psalms, plus the apocryphal Psalm 151, which was previously known only in Greek texts. A very fine scroll of part of Leviticus, some large pieces of an Apocalypse of the New Jerusalem, and an Aramaic targum (paraphrase) of Job were discovered.

Several recent studies of the Dead Sea Scrolls provide detailed descriptions and inventories. Gleason L. Archer, Jr. has a good summary in an appendix to his *A Survey of Old Testament Introduction*.

Murabba'at Discoveries. Prompted by the profitable finds at Qumran, the Bedouins pursued their search and found caves southeast of Bethlehem that produced self-dated manuscripts and documents from the Second Jewish Revolt (132–135). Systematic exploration and excavation of these caves began in January 1952. The later, dated manuscripts helped establish the antiquity of the Dead Sea Scrolls. From these caves came another scroll of the Minor Prophets, the last half of Joel through Haggai, which closely supports the Masoretic Text. The oldest known Semitic papyrus (a palimpsest), inscribed the second time in the ancient Hebrew script (dating from the seventh–eighth centuries B.C.), was found here (see Barthelemy).

Another site known as Khirbet Mird has produced manuscript materials. On April 3, 1960, a parchment fragment (first century A.D.) of Psalm 15 and part of Psalm 16 was discovered at Wadi Murabba'at (see Cass, 164).

Samaritan Pentateuch. The Samaritans separated from the Jews probably during the fifth or fourth century B.C. after a long, bitter religious and cultural struggle. At the time of the schism one would suspect that the Samaritans took with them the Scriptures as they then existed, and they prepared their own, revised text of the Pentateuch. The Samaritan Pentateuch is not a version in the strict sense, but rather a manuscript portion of the Hebrew text itself. It contains the five books of Moses and is written in an ancient style of Hebrew script. Some of the older biblical manuscripts from Qumran use this script, since it was revived in the second century B.C. during the Maccabean revolt against the Greeks. Textual critic Frank M. Cross, Jr., believes that the Samaritan Pentateuch probably comes from about the Maccabean period.

A form of the Samaritan Pentateuch text seems to have been known to church Fathers Eusebius of Caesarea (ca. 265–339) and Jerome (ca. 345–ca. 419). It was not available to modern Western scholars until 1616, when Pietro della Valle discovered a manuscript of the Samaritan Pentateuch in Damascus. A great wave of excitement arose among biblical scholars. The text was regarded as superior to the Masoretic Text (MT); until Wilhelm Gesenius in 1815 judged it to be practically worthless for textual criticism. More recently the value of the Samaritan Pentateuch has been reasserted by such scholars as A. Geiger, Kahle, and Kenyon.

No extant manuscript of the Samaritan Pentateuch has been dated before the eleventh century. The Samaritan community claims that one roll was written by Abisha, the great-grandson of Moses, in the thirteenth year after the conquest of Canaan, but the authority is so spurious that the claim may be safely dismissed. The oldest codex of the Samaritan Pentateuch bears a note about its sale in 1149–50, but the manuscript itself is much older. One manuscript was copied in 1204. Another dated 1211–1212 is now in the John Rylands Library at Manchester. Another, dated ca. 1232, is in the New York Public Library.

The standard printed edition of the Samaritan Pentateuch is in five volumes by A. von Gall, *Der Hebräische Pentateuch der Samaritaner* (1914–1918). It provides an eclectic text based on eighty late medieval manuscripts and fragments. Although von Gall's text is in Hebrew characters, the Samaritans wrote in an alphabet quite different from the square Hebrew. Nevertheless, their script, like the Hebrew, descended from old Paleo-Hebrew characters.

There are about 6000 deviations of the Samaritan Pentateuch from the Masoretic Text, most trivial. In about 1900 instances the Samaritan text agrees with the Septuagint against the Masoretic Text. Some of the deviations were deliberately introduced by the Samaritans to preserve their own religious traditions and dialectic. The Masoretic Text perpetuates Judean dialect and traditions.

In the early Christian era a translation of the Samaritan Pentateuch was made into the Aramaic dialect of the Samaritans. This Samaritan Targum was also translated into Greek, called the *Samaritikon,* which was occasionally cited by Origen. After the eleventh century several translations of the Samaritan Pentateuch were made in Arabic (Kahle, 51–57).

Other Important Discoveries. Nash Papyri. Among the earliest Old Testament Hebrew manuscripts, there is extant one damaged copy of the *Shema* (from Deut. 6:4–9) and two fragments of the Decalogue (Exod. 20:2–17.; Deut. 5:6–21). The Nash Papyri are dated between the second century B.C. and the first century A.D.

Orientales 4445. Orientales 4445, a British Museum manuscript is dated by Christian D. Ginsburg at between 820 and 850, with notes added a century later. But Paul E. Kahle (see Würthwein, 18) argues that both consonantal Hebrew texts and pointing (the added vowel points or marks) are from the tenth century. Because the Hebrew alphabet consists only of consonants, Hebrew writing normally shows only those letters, with a few letters used to represent some of the vocalic sounds. Vowel marks or "points" were a medieval development. This manuscript contains Genesis 39:20—Deuteronomy 1:33, less Numbers 7:47–73 and 9:12–10:18.

Codex Cairensis. A codex is a manuscript in book form with pages. According to a colophon, or inscription at the end of the book, Codex Cairensis (C) was written and vowel-pointed in 895 by Moses ben Asher in Tiberias in Palestine (ibid., 25). It contains the Former Prophets (Joshua, Judges, 1 and 2 Samuel, 1 and 2 Kings) and the Latter Prophets (Isaiah, Jeremiah, Ezekiel, and the Minor Prophets). It is symbolized by a C in *Biblia Hebraica Stuttgartensia* and is regarded as the most authoritative Hebrew text based on the Masoretic Text tradition.

Aleppo Codex. Aleppo Codex was written by Shelomo ben Baya'a (Kenyon, 84), but according to a colophon note it was pointed (i.e., the vowel marks were added) by Moses ben Asher (ca. 930). It is a model codex, although it was not permitted to be copied for a long time and was even reported to have been destroyed (Würthwein, 25). It was smuggled from Syria to Israel. It has now been photographed and is the basis of the *New Hebrew Bible* published by Hebrew University (Goshen-Gottstein, 13). It is a sound authority for the ben Asher text.

Codex Leningradensis. According to a colophon note, Codex Leningradensis (L) was copied in Old Cairo by Samuel ben Jacob in 1008 from a manuscript (now lost) written by Aaron ben Moses ben Asher ca. 1000 (Kahle, 110). It represents one of the oldest manuscripts of the complete Hebrew Bible. Kittel adopted it as the basis for the third edition of his *Biblia Hebraica,* and it continues to be used as such in *Biblia Hebraica Stuttgartensia,* where it is represented under the symbol L.

Babylonian Codex of the Latter Prophets. The Babylonian Codex (V (ar)^P) is sometimes called the Leningrad Codex of the Prophets (Kenyon, 85) or the [St.] Petersburg Codex (Würthwein, 26). It contains Isaiah, Jeremiah, and the Twelve. It is dated 916, but its chief significance is that, through it, punctuation added by the Babylonian school of Masoretic scribes was rediscovered. It is symbolized as V (ar)^P in *Biblia Hebraica Stuttgartensia.*

Reuchlin Codex of the Prophets. Dated 1105, Reuchlin Codex is now at Karlsruhe. Like the British Museum manuscript (ca. 1150), it contains a recension of Ben Naphtali, a Tiberian Masorete. These have been of great value in establishing the fidelity of the Ben Asher text (Kenyon, 36).

Erfurt Codices. The Erfurt Codices (E1, E2, E3) are listed in the University Library in Tübingen. They represent more or less (more in E3) the text and markings of the Ben Naphtali tradition. E1 is a fourteenth-century manuscript. E2 is probably from the thirteenth century. E3, the oldest, is dated before 1100 (Würthwein, 26).

Lost Codices. There are a number of significant but now lost codices whose peculiar readings are preserved and referred to in *Biblia Hebraica Stuttgartensia.* Codex Severi is a medieval list of thirty-two variants of the Pentateuch, supposedly based on a manuscript brought to Rome in 70 that Emperor Severus (222–35) later gave to a synagogue he had built. Codex Hillel was supposedly written ca. 600 by Rabbi Hillel ben Moses ben Hillel. It is said to have been accurate and was used to revise other manuscripts. Readings from that manuscript are cited by medieval Masoretes and are noted in *Biblia Hebraica Stuttgartensia* (ibid., 27).

Nature of Manuscripts. *Types of Manuscript Errors.* Although the official text of the Old Testament was transmitted with great care, it was inevitable that certain copyist errors would creep into the texts over the hundreds of years of transmission into thousands of manuscripts. There are several kinds of copyist errors that produce textual variants (Archer, 55–57).

- *Haplography* is the writing of a word, letter, or syllable only once when it should have been written more than once.
- *Dittography* is writing twice what should have been written only once.

- *Metathesis* is reversing the proper position of letters or words.
- *Fusion* is the combining of two separate words into one.
- *Fission* is the dividing of a single word into two words.
- *Homophony* is the substitution of a word for another that is produced like it (e.g., "two" for "to"), or the misreading of similarly shaped letters.
- *Homoeoteleuton* is the omission of an intervening passage because the scribe's eye skipped from one line to a similar ending on another line.
- *Accidental omissions* occur where no repetition is involved (as "Saul was . . . year(s) old," 1 Sam. 13:1, RSV), or vowel letters are misread for consonants.

Rules for Textual Criticism. Scholars have developed certain criteria for determining which reading is correct or original. Seven rules may be suggested (ibid., 51–53).

1. An older reading is to be preferred, because it is closer to the original.
2. The more difficult reading is to be preferred, because scribes were more apt to smooth out difficult readings.
3. The shorter reading is to be preferred, because copyists were more apt to insert new material than omit part of the sacred text.
4. The reading that best explains the other variants is to be preferred.
5. The reading with the widest geographical support is to be preferred, because such manuscripts or versions are less likely to have influenced each other.
6. The reading that is most like the author's usual style is to be preferred.
7. The reading that does not reflect a doctrinal bias is to be preferred. (Würthwein, 80–81).

Quality of Manuscripts. Several reasons have been suggested for the relative scarcity of early Hebrew manuscripts. The first and most obvious reason is a combination of antiquity and destructibility; 2000 to 3000 years is a long time to expect ancient documents to last. Nonetheless, several lines of evidence support the conclusion that their quality is very good.

Variant Readings. There are very few variants in the texts available because the Masoretes systematically destroyed old manuscripts once they were carefully copied. Kenyon illustrates the paucity of variations in the Masoretic Text by contrasting the Leningrad Codex of the Prophets, from the Babylonian or Eastern tradition, with the standard Palestinian text (Western) of Ezekiel. In the Western text the Masoretic Text is sometimes corrupt. Yet there are only sixteen real conflicts between the two texts (Kenyon, 45, 70–72).

Jewish Reverence for the Bible. With respect to the Jewish Scriptures, however, it was not scribal accuracy alone that guaranteed their product. Rather, it was their almost superstitious reverence for the Bible. According to the *Talmud,* there were specifications not only for the kind of skins to be used and the size of the columns, but there was even a religious ritual necessary for the scribe to perform before writing the name of God. Rules governed the kind of ink used, dictated the spacing of words, and prohibited writing anything from memory. The lines, and even the letters, were counted methodically. If a manuscript was found to contain even one mistake, it was discarded and destroyed. This scribal formalism was responsible, at least in part, for the extreme care exercised in copying the Scriptures. It was also the reason there were only a few manuscripts (as the rules demanded the destruction of defective copies).

Comparison of Duplicate Passages. Another line of evidence for the quality of the Old Testament manuscripts is found in the comparison of the duplicate passages of the Masoretic Text itself. Several psalms occur twice (for example, 14 and 53); much of Isaiah 36–39 is also found in 2 Kings 18–20; Isaiah 2:2–4 is almost exactly parallel to Micah 4:1–3; Jeremiah 52 is a repeat of 2 Kings 25; and large portions of Chronicles are found in Samuel and Kings. An examination of those passages shows not only a substantial textual agreement but, in some cases, almost word-for-word identity. Therefore it may be concluded that the Old Testament texts have not undergone radical revisions, even if it were assumed that these parallel passages had identical sources.

Support from Archaeology. A substantial proof for the accuracy of the Old Testament text has come from archaeology. Numerous discoveries have confirmed the historical accuracy of the biblical documents, even down to the occasional use of obsolete names of foreign kings. These archaeological confirmations of the accuracy of Scripture have been recorded in numerous books (*see* ARCHAEOLOGY, NEW TESTAMENT; ARCHAEOLOGY, OLD TESTAMENT). Archaeologist Nelson Glueck asserts, "It may be stated categorically that no archaeological discovery has ever controverted a biblical reference. Scores of archaeological findings have been made which confirm in clear outline or exact detail historical statements in the Bible" (Glueck, 31).

The Septuagint and Masoretic Text. The *Septuagint* was the Bible of Jesus and the apostles. Most New Testament quotations are taken from it directly, even when it differs from the Masoretic Text. On the whole the *Septuagint* closely parallels the Masoretic Text and is a confirmation of the fidelity of the tenth-century Hebrew text.

If no other evidence were available, the case for the fidelity of the Masoretic Text could be brought to rest with confidence upon textual comparisons and understanding of the extraordinary Jewish scribal system. But with discovery of the *Dead Sea Scrolls, beginning in 1947, there is almost overwhelming substantiation of the received Hebrew text of the Masoretes. Critics of the Masoretic Text charged that the manuscripts were few and late. Through the Dead Sea Scrolls, early manuscript fragments provide a check on nearly the whole Old Testament. Those checks date about a thousand years before the Great Masoretic manuscripts of the tenth century. Before the discoveries in the Cairo Geniza and the Dead Sea caves, the Nash Papyrus (a fragment of the Ten Commandments and Shema, Deut. 6:4–9), dated between 150 and 100 B.C., was the only known scrap of the Hebrew text dating from before the Christian era.

Agreement with the Samaritan Pentateuch. Despite the many minor variants between the Samaritan Pentateuch and the Hebrew text of the Old Testament, there is substantial agreement between them. As noted above, the 6000 variants from the Masoretic Text are mostly differences in spelling and cultural word variation. Nineteen hundred variants agree with the Septuagint (for example, in the ages given for the patriarchs in Genesis 5 and 11). Some Samaritan Pentateuch variants are sectarian, such as the command to build the Temple on Mount Gerizim, not at Jerusalem (e.g., after Exod. 20:17). It should be noted, however, that most manuscripts of the Samaritan Pentateuch are late (thirteenth to fourteenth centuries), and none is before the tenth century (Archer, 44). But the Samaritan Pentateuch still confirms the general text from which it had diverged many hundreds of years earlier.

Check Against the Dead Sea Scrolls. With the discovery of the Dead Sea Scrolls, scholars have Hebrew manuscripts 1000 years earlier than the great Masoretic Text manuscripts, enabling them to check on the fidelity of the Hebrew text. There is a word-for-word identity in more than 95 percent of the cases, and the 5 percent variation consists mostly of slips of the pen and spelling (ibid., 24). The Isaiah scroll (1QIs^a) from Qumran led the Revised Standard Version translators to make only thirteen changes from the Masoretic Text; eight of those were known from ancient versions, and few of them were significant (Burrows, 305ff.). Of the 166 Hebrew words in Isaiah 53, only seventeen Hebrew letters in the Isaiah B scroll differ from the Masoretic Text. Ten letters are a matter of spelling, four are stylistic changes, and the other three compose the word for "light," (added in verse 11), which does not affect the meaning greatly (Harris, 124). Furthermore that word is also found in that verse in the Septuagint and the Isaiah A scroll.

Conclusion. The thousands of Hebrew manuscripts, with their confirmation by the Septuagint and the Samaritan Pentateuch, and the numerous other cross-checks from outside and inside the text provide overwhelming support for the reliability of the Old Testament text. Hence, it is appropriate to conclude with Kenyon's statement, "The Christian can take the whole Bible in his hand and say without fear or hesitation that he holds in it the true word of God, handed down without essential loss from generation to generation throughout the centuries."

Since the Old Testament text is related in important ways to Christian apologetics, its reliability supports the Christian faith. This is true not only in establishing the dates when supernatural predictions were made of the Messiah, but also in supporting the historicity of the Old Testament that Jesus and New Testament writers affirmed (*see* BIBLE, EVIDENCE FOR; BIBLE, JESUS' VIEW OF).

Sources

J. M. Allegro, *The Treasure of the Copper Scroll*, 2d rev. ed.

G. L. Archer, Jr., *A Survey of Old Testament Introduction*, Appen. 4

D. Barthelemy and J. T. Milik, *Ten Years of Discovery in the Judean Wilderness*

T. S. Cass, *Secrets from the Caves*

K. Elliger and W. Rudolph, eds., *Biblia Hebraica Stuttgartensia*

N. L. Geisler, "Bible Manuscripts," in *Wycliffe Bible Encyclopedia*

——— and W. E. Nix, *General Introduction to the Bible*

N. Glueck, *Rivers in the Desert: A History of the Negev*

M. Goshen-Gottstein, "Biblical Manuscripts in the United States," *Textus* 3 (1962)

R. L. Harris, *Inspiration and Canonicity*

P. E. Kahle, *The Cairo Geniza*

F. G. Kenyon, *Our Bible and the Ancient Manuscripts*

R. Kittel and P. Kahle, eds., *Biblia Hebraica*, 7th ed.

M. Mansoor, *The Dead Sea Scrolls*

J. C. Trever, "The Discovery of the Scrolls," *Biblical Archaeologist* 11 (September 1948)

G. Vermes, trans., *The Dead Sea Scrolls in English*

E. Würthwein, *The Text of the Old Testament: An Introduction to the Biblia Hebraica*

Omnipotence of God, Alleged Contradiction of.

Some critics have alleged that the theistic (*see* THEISM) view of God is incoherent, since it claims God is omnipotent or all-powerful (*see* GOD, NATURE OF). They argue:

1. An all-powerful Being can do anything.
2. An all-powerful Being can make a stone so heavy that he cannot move it.
3. Hence, an all-powerful Being cannot do everything.
4. But premises 1 and 3 are contradictory.
5. Hence, it is contradictory to hold that God is all-powerful.

No sophisticated theist really believes premise 1 in an unqualified way. What informed theists believe is that:

1a. God can do anything that is possible.

2a. It is not possible to make a stone so heavy that it cannot be moved.
3a. Therefore, it is not possible for God to make a stone so heavy that he cannot move it.

God cannot literally do any task we can imagine. He cannot contradict his own nature. Hebrews 6:18 declares. "It is impossible for God to lie." Neither can God do what is logically impossible, for example, make a square circle. He cannot make two mountains without a valley between. And he cannot deny the law of noncontradiction (*see* FIRST PRINCIPLES).

Further, God cannot do what is actually impossible. For example, he cannot will not to create a world he has willed to create. Of course, he could have willed not to create. But once he willed to create it was impossible for him to will not to create. Neither can God force free creatures (*see* FREE WILL) to believe things against their will. Forcing someone to freely do something is a contradiction in terms (*see* HELL). For if it is free, it is not forced. And if it is forced, then it is not free.

It is actually impossible to make a stone so heavy it cannot be moved. What an omnipotent Being can make, he can move. A finite creature cannot be more powerful in its resistance than the infinite Creator is in his power not to be resisted. If God brought it into existence, he can take it out of existence. Then he could recreate it somewhere else. Therefore, there is no contradiction in believing that God is omnipotent and that he can do anything that is possible to do. The critic has set up a straw-man argument and has not shown any incoherence in God's attribute of omnipotence.

One and Many, Problem of. A classic metaphysical problem asks: Is reality one or many? Or, is it both one and many? If there is an ultimate unity in reality, how is there also real diversity? Or, if there is real diversity of things, how can there be an ultimate unity? In the final analysis, the problem of the one and many boils down to monism verses pluralism.

The ancient philosopher Parmenides gave the ultimate statement of *monism, insisting that there can be only one being, since to assume there is more than one leads to absurdities and antinomies. Two different things would have to differ. And there are only two ways to differ, by being or nonbeing. But to differ by nonbeing or nothing is not to differ at all. However, to differ by being is impossible, because being is the very respect in which all things are identical. And things cannot differ in the very respect in which they are identical. Therefore, there cannot be two or more beings, only one.

Various solutions to the problem of the one and many have been posited (*see* MONISM; PLURALISM, METAPHYSICAL; ANALOGY). *Atomists suggested that things differ by absolute nonbeing (the void). But to differ by absolutely nothing is not to differ at all. *Plato argued that they differ by relative nonbeing, but this too turns out to be no real difference. Nor can they differ as *Aristotle said in their simple beings, since simple beings simply cannot differ—they are the same in their beings.

No solution has been successful for a theist (*see* THEISM) except that of *Thomas Aquinas. He showed that things can differ in their very being, since they are different kinds of being. An infinite Being differs from a finite being, and a Necessary Being differs from a contingent being. A being of pure Actuality differs from one that has actuality and potentiality. The only kind of being that cannot differ in its being is one of pure Actuality (God). That is, there can be only one such being because it is a one-of-a-kind type Being. It is Being pure and simple. All other beings are complex beings, having a mixture of actuality and potentiality. So, things differ in the kind of being they have, except the One who *is* Being and from whom all other beings *have* their being. This solves the problem of the one and many in the realm of being without going beyond being (to the Unknowable One), as did *Plotinus, which leaves one in total ignorance of God (*see* AGNOSTICISM).

Ontological Argument. The ontological argument for the existence or being (Gk. *ontos*) of God proceeds from the mere idea that God is an absolutely perfect or Necessary Being. The ontological argument was first formed by *Anselm (1033–1109), although he did not name it. It has been subject to extensive criticism by both defenders of theistic arguments (*see* THOMAS AQUINAS) and opponents (*see* HUME, DAVID; KANT, IMMANUEL). Immanuel Kant (1724–1804) was the first to call it the ontological argument because he believed it made an illicit transition from thought to being *(ontos)*.

Anselm's Form(s). The ontological argument might more accurately be called "the proof from prayer," since it came to Anselm as he meditated on the nature of God. It is widely believed that Anselm developed two forms of the ontological argument. The second emerged in his debate with another monk named Gaunilo.

The first form of the ontological argument is based on the idea of God as an absolutely perfect Being. One cannot conceive of a greater being (see Plantinga, *Ontological Argument,* 3–27). In logical form it is:

1. God is, by definition, a Being, greater than which nothing can be conceived.
2. It is greater to exist in reality than to exist only in the mind.
3. Therefore God must exist in reality. If he didn't he wouldn't be the greatest being possible.

The second form of the argument comes from the idea of a Necessary Being:

1. God is, by definition, a Necessary Being.
2. It is logically necessary to affirm what is necessary to the concept of a Necessary Being.
3. Existence is logically necessary to the concept of a Necessary Being.
4. Therefore, a Necessary Being (= God) necessarily exists.

Objections. *Anselm's Debate with Gaunilo.* The objections of Gaunilo the monk and Anselm's responses help explain the argument.

Objection 1: Necessary Existence. Gaunilo contended that the argument is built on the false premise that whatever exists in the mind must also exist in reality outside the mind. Anselm responded that this is not so. Only in the case of an absolutely perfect being, which would have to be a Necessary Being, is it true that, if it is conceivable, then it must exist outside the mind too. All contingent beings could not exist. Only a Necessary Being cannot not exist.

Objection 2: Conceiving and Doubting. Gaunilo further insisted that, if God's nonexistence were really inconceivable, no one could doubt. But people do doubt or deny it; there are skeptics and atheists. But Anselm responded that, while people can *deny* God's existence, they cannot *conceive* of the nonexistence of a Necessary Being. God's nonexistence is affirmable but not conceivable.

Objection 3: Mental Limitations. Gaunilo asserted that we cannot even form the concept of the most perfect Being possible. It is only a series of words, with no empirical reference or meaning. However, Anselm denied that, giving six reasons for his answer: (1) *God* is a common, familiar word. (2) Faith and conscience provide content for it. (3) Not all conceptions are sensible images, since abstract concepts are possible. (4) God can be understood indirectly, the way the sun is understood from its rays. (5) We can form the concept of the most perfect being by working from the less-than-perfect to the most perfect possible. (6) Even those who deny God must have some conception of what they are denying.

Objection 4: Thought and Reality. Gaunilo contended that the mere idea of a perfect Island did not guarantee its existence, nor does the idea of a perfect Being. But Anselm insisted that there is an important difference; the idea of a perfect island may lack existence, but not the idea of a perfect Being. It is possible for an island—even a perfect one—not to exist. But it is not possible for a perfect (Necessary) Being not to exist.

Objection 5: Conceiving Nonexistence. Gaunilo offered that God's nonexistence is no more inconceivable than one's own nonexistence. Yet one can conceive of personal nonexistence. However, Anselm was quick to point out that the nonexistence of everything except a Necessary Being is conceivable. For if it is possible for a Necessary Being to exist, then it is necessary for it to exist. Its nonexistence alone is inconceivable.

Objection 6: Proof of Existence. God's existence must be proved before we can discuss his essence (for example, that he is a perfect kind of Being). Hence, we cannot use his essence (as an absolutely perfect Being to prove his existence). Anselm responded that we can compare ideal characteristics before we know something is real. We can define it [for example, the mighty winged horse, Pegasus], and then ask whether it exists.

Finally, Anselm charged Gaunilo with misunderstanding his argument and, therefore, attacking a straw man. He insisted that God is not to be defined as "the greatest of all beings" (as Gaunilo thought) but as "the greatest *possible* Being." Although Gaunilo raised some good questions, none of them really refute Anselm's argument, particularly the second form of it.

Aquinas' Objection. The ontological argument did not convince *Thomas Aquinas. His objection to Anselm's argument can be seen in his restatement of Anselm's argument:

1. God is, by definition, a Being, greater than which nothing can be conceived.
2. What exists both mentally and actually is greater than that which exists only mentally.
3. Therefore, God must exist actually, for once the sentence "God exists" is understood, it is seen to be a self-evident proposition.

Aquinas offers three objections to this argument: First, not everyone understands the term "God" to mean "that than which nothing greater can be conceived." Second, even if God is understood this way it does not prove that he actually exists, but only that the conception exists mentally. This point gets to the heart of the common objection to the ontological argument. Third, the proposition, "God, a Necessary Being, exists," is self-evident *in itself,* but it is not self-evident *to us.* For we cannot know God's essence directly, but only through his effects (*see* COSMOLOGICAL ARGUMENT). Hence, we can only arrive at his existence through his effects, *a posteriori.* We cannot know it *a priori* in itself. Only God knows his own essence intuitively. This too is more to the central point of criticism.

Descartes' Form of the Argument. Not much advanced in the dialogue over the ontological argument for centuries. Then the seventeenth-century rationalist René *Descartes (1596–1650) set off a series of criticisms by reformulating and defending the argument. His statement followed Anselm's second form:

1. It is logically necessary to affirm of a concept what is essential to its nature (e.g., A triangle must have three sides.).

2. But existence is logically necessary to the nature of a necessary Existent (i.e., Being).
3. Therefore, it is logically necessary to affirm that a necessary Existent does exist.

Dialogue with Caterus. As Anselm, Descartes had his antagonists. Caterus, a priest, insisted that the argument proves only a conceptual existence of God. For the complex of words "existent lion" is conceptually necessary, but this does not prove that a lion exists. Only experience can do that. Thus, the complex "Necessary Being" does not prove that God exists.

Descartes replied that Caterus had refuted another argument, not his. His first restatement of the argument is based on his concept of truth as what is clearly perceived:

1. Whatever we clearly and distinctly perceive is true.
2. We clearly and distinctly perceive that existence must belong to a necessary Existent.
3. So, it is true that a necessary Existent does exist.

Descartes' second restatement of his argument takes another form:

1. Whatever is of the essence of something must be affirmed of it.
2. Existence is of the essence of a necessary Existent (= God).
3. Hence, existence must be affirmed of God.

The third restatement of the ontological argument takes this form:

1. God's existence cannot be conceived as only possible but not actual, for then he would not be a necessary *Existent*.
2. We can conceive of God's existence. It is not contradictory.
3. Therefore, God's existence must be conceived as more than possible (viz., as actual).

Debate with Gassendi. Pierre Gassendi's objection to Descartes' arguments took the following form:

1. God need not exist any more than must a triangle. The essence of either can be thought of apart from its existence.
2. Existence is not a necessary property for God, any more than for triangles.
3. It begs the question to list existence as part of God's essence.
4. Essence and existence are not identical, or else Plato as well as God would exist necessarily. If they are not identical, neither exists necessarily.
5. We are just as free to think of God not existing as we are of a nonexistent Pegasus.
6. We must prove triangles have three sides (not just assume it). Likewise, we must prove God exists (not merely assume it).
7. Descartes did not really prove that God's existence is not logically impossible. Hence, he did not prove it is logically necessary.

Descartes' retort took the following shape:

1. Existence is a property in the sense that it is attributable to a thing.
2. Only God has necessary existence, not Pegasus or anything else.
3. It is not begging the question to include existence among the attributes of a necessary Existent. Indeed, it is necessary to do so.
4. Existence and essence cannot be separate in a Being that is a necessary Existent. Hence, God must exist.

Descartes did not answer objection seven. Gottfried *Leibniz (1646–1716) attempted to do so by arguing that existence is a perfection and as such is a simple and irreducible quality that cannot conflict with others. Hence, God can have all perfections, including existence.

Other Reactions to Descartes' Proofs. In another negative view of Descartes' ontological argument, his view was restated:

1. If it is not contradictory that God exists, then it is certain that he exists.
2. It is not contradictory that God exists.
3. So, it is certain that God exists.

In view of this new form of the argument, critics offered two objections which, if true, would invalidate Descartes' conclusion. The first is that the minor premise can be doubted or denied. Hence, the argument does not necessarily follow. Second, Descartes admitted that his idea of God was inadequate. But if it is inadequate, then it is unclear. And if it is unclear, then, on Descartes' own definition of truth as "clear and distinct" ideas, it is untrue.

Descartes replied that God's existence is noncontradictory in whichever of the two senses one takes it. If noncontradictory means *whatever does not disagree with human thought,* it is clearly noncontradictory. For we have not attributed to him anything but what human thought necessitates that we attribute to him. If noncontradictory means *what cannot be known by the human mind,* then no one can know anything, let alone God's existence. Such a definition would overthrow all human thought, which is impossible. Even if our concept of God is inadequate, it does not follow that it is contradictory, since all contradiction arises from a lack of clarity, and we clearly see that God must be a Necessary Being. Descartes further implied that what we do not clearly see does not destroy what we do clearly see. Since we do clearly see that there is no contradiction in the concept of a Necessary Being, the argument follows. For this is all that is necessary to support the disputed minor premise of the argument.

Objections of Hume and Kant. *Hume's Critique of the Ontological Argument.* David *Hume (1711–1776) set forth what has become a standard objection to the ontological proof, as well as to other "proofs" for God's existence. It was followed by *Kant's landmark critique of the central premise of the first form of the argument.

Hume's critique of the ontological argument has this basic logical form:

1. Nothing is rationally demonstrable unless the contrary implies a contradiction, for if it leaves open any other possibility, then this position is not necessarily true.
2. Nothing that is distinctly conceivable implies a contradiction. If it were contradictory, it would not be distinctly conceivable; if it is impossible, it cannot be possible.
3. Whatever we conceive to exist we can also conceive as nonexistent. The existence or nonexistence of things cannot be ruled out conceptually.
4. There is no being, therefore, whose nonexistence implies a contradiction.
5. Consequently, there is no being whose existence is rationally demonstrable.

In essence, Hume reasons that no argument for God is rationally inescapable, because it always contains premises that logically can be denied. The conclusions always lack logical necessity, because the premises always admit of other logical possibilities. According to this, the ontological argument fails to be a rational demonstration in the strict sense.

The Critique of Kant. Kant first named the ontological argument, since he thought it made an illicit transition from the sphere of pure thought to that of reality (from *eidos* to *ontos*). Kant had several objections to the argument which he felt were fatal to the whole theistic cause (ibid., 57–64). First, he objected to the fact that we have no positive concept of a Necessary Being. God is defined only as that which cannot *not* be. Further, necessity does not apply to existence but only to propositions. Necessity is a logical, not an ontological, qualifier. There are no existentially necessary propositions. Whatever is known by experience (which is the only way existential matters are knowable) could be unknown. Next, what is logically possible is not necessarily ontologically possible. There may be no logical contradiction in the necessary existence but it still may be actually impossible. Then, there is no contradiction involved in rejecting both the idea and the existence of a Necessary Being. Likewise, there is no contradiction in rejecting the triangle along with its three-sidedness. Contradiction results in rejecting one without the other.

Finally, existence is not a predicate, as though it were a perfection or property that could be affirmed of a subject or thing. Existence is not a perfection of an essence but a positing of that perfection. Kant utilized the following argument to support this point:

1. Whatever adds nothing to the conception of an essence is not part of that essence.
2. Existence adds nothing to the conception of an essence. No characteristic is added to an essence by positing that it is real rather than imaginary. A real dollar does not have any characteristics that an imagined one lacks.
3. Therefore, existence is not part of an essence. It is not a perfection that can be predicated of something.

If Kant's third point is solid, it invalidates at least the first form of the ontological argument given by Anselm. In view of Kant, Anselm's argument would really amount to this:

1. All possible perfections must be predicated of an absolutely perfect Being.
2. Existence is a possible perfection which may be predicated of an absolutely perfect Being.
3. Therefore, existence must be predicated of an absolutely perfect Being.

An Evaluation of Kant's Critique. According to Kant's criticism, the minor premise is wrong. Existence is not a perfection that may be predicated of anything. Essence gives the definition, and existence provides an example of what was defined. The essence is given in the conceptualization of something; existence does not add to this conceptualization but merely makes it concrete. Hence, existence neither adds nor detracts from the concept of an absolutely perfect Being. This has been a standard objection to the ontological argument since Kant. It can be put in this form:

1. Anselm's argument depends on the premise that existence is a predicate—an attribute or perfection.
2. But existence is not a predicate. (a) Anselm follows a platonic concept of being. (b) Existence is not a perfection but only an instance of a perfection.
3. Hence, Anselm's argument is not valid.

The dollar in my mind has same attributes as the dollar in my pocket. The only difference is that with the one in my wallet I have an instance of one. But a concrete example of a perfection adds nothing to the perfection itself.

Modern proponents of Anselm's argument, such as Norman Malcolm and Charles Hartshorne, reply that Kant's criticism applies only to Anselm's first argument. The second form does not depend on the premise that existence is a perfection.

Leibniz's Statement. Although Gottfried *Leibniz is better known for his cosmological argument, he did set forth a form of the ontological argument. Sensing that the basic ontological argument was valid but that it was necessary to demonstrate that the concept of God was not contradictory, Leibniz restated the argument thus (ibid., 54–56).

1. If it is possible for an absolutely perfect Being to exist, then it is necessary that it exist, for (a) By definition an absolutely perfect Being cannot lack anything. (b) But if it did not exist, it would be lacking in existence. (c) Hence, an absolutely perfect Being cannot be lacking in existence.
2. It is possible (noncontradictory) for an absolutely perfect Being to exist.
3. Therefore, it is necessary that an absolutely perfect Being exist.

In support of the crucial minor premise Leibniz gave this argument:

1. A perfection is a simple and irreducible quality without any essential limits.
2. Whatever is simple cannot conflict with other simple qualities, since they differ in kind.
3. And whatever differs in kind with another cannot conflict with it, since there is no area of similarity in which they can overlap or conflict.
4. Therefore, it is possible for one Being (God) to possess all possible perfections.

Not even defenders of the ontological arguments think Leibniz really proved the compatibility of all possible attributes in God (ibid., 156ff.). Malcolm saw two problems with the argument. First, it assumes that some qualities are essentially "positive" and others "negative," whereas this may not be the case. Some qualities may be positive in one context and negative in another. Second, Leibniz wrongly assumes that some qualities are intrinsically simple, contrary to Ludwig *Wittgenstein, who showed that what is simple in one conceptual system may be complex in another. A third objection may be added. Leibniz makes an unwarranted movement from the conceptual to the actual.

Spinoza's Ontological Proof. Like Descartes, his contemporary, Benedict *Spinoza (1632–1677) held that the existence of God was mathematically demonstrable. He wrote, "We cannot be more certain of the existence of anything, than the existence of a being absolutely infinite or perfect—that is, of God." And, like Descartes, Spinoza felt that this certainty was derived from the ontological proof (ibid., 50–53). Spinoza's statement of the argument is:

1. There must be a cause for everything, either for its existence or for its nonexistence.
2. A Necessary Being (God) necessarily exists, unless there is a cause adequate to explain why he does not exist.
3. There is no cause adequate to explain why a Necessary Being does not exist, (a) for that cause would have to be either inside God's nature or outside of it. (b) But no cause outside of a necessary Existent could possibly annul it. (c) And nothing inside a necessary Existent could annul it, for nothing inside a Necessary Being can deny that it is a Necessary Being. (d) Hence, there is no cause adequate to explain why a Necessary Being does not exist.
4. Therefore, a Necessary Being necessarily exists.

The usual objection could be leveled at Spinoza's proof, that he makes being actually necessary, when it is only necessary as a concept. There is at least one other objection. The first premise affirms that "there must be a cause for nothing." Not only is this premise without proof, but it is contradictory. The law of causality demands only that "there must be a cause for something." It is unwarranted to insist on a cause for nothing. Spinoza's defense of the premise is that "the potentiality of nonexistence is a negation of power." But nonexistence is already a negative and a negation of nonexistence would be an affirmation of existence. However, this would leave the traditional basis for the ontological argument and begin with existence. This is precisely what Spinoza does in his second form of the argument:

1. Something necessarily exists. To deny this one would have to affirm that at least one thing exists, namely, himself.
2. This necessary Existence is either finite or infinite.
3. It is possible for this necessary Existence to be infinite.
4. There must be a cause as to why this is not an infinite existence.
5. No finite existence can hinder this being an infinite Existence, and to say that an infinite Existence hinders its own infinite existence is contradictory.
6. Therefore, this must be an infinite Existence (God).

Two important things must be noted about Spinoza's arguments. First, he borrows from the cosmological argument the premise, "Something exists." This leaves a strictly *a priori* proof, as he admits. Second, the conclusion of Spinoza's argument is not the theistic God of Descartes and Leibniz but a pantheistic God. There is no acknowledgment of Necessary Being and contingent beings. This infinite Existence is absolutely one; there are not, in addition to it, finite substances or creatures. What theists (*see* Theism) call creatures, Spinoza views as merely modes or moments in the one infinite Substance—God.

Findlay's Ontological Disproof. The ontological argument took a radical turn with the attempt of some atheists to turn it into a disproof for

God's existence (*see* God, Alleged Disproofs of). The ontological argument is widely rejected in modern times. Some have even turned the tables on it, making it a kind of ontological disproof of God. Such was the intention of J. N. Findlay, who argued (ibid., 111–22) that:

1. God must be thought of as a Necessary Being (i.e., as necessarily existing), for anything short of this kind of being would be unworthy of worship.
2. But existentially necessary propositions cannot be true (as Kant showed), for necessity is merely a logical characteristic of propositions, not of reality.
3. Therefore, God cannot exist.

Findlay's argument can be put in this more simple form:

1. The only way God could exist is if he exists necessarily (any kind of existence less than necessary would make him less than God).
2. But nothing can exist necessarily (for necessity does not apply to existence but only to propositions).
3. Therefore, God cannot exist (for the only way he could exist is the very way he cannot exist).

More properly, however, the argument should be stated this way:

1. The only way a Necessary Being could exist is to exist necessarily.
2. The proposition "God exists necessarily" is an existentially necessary proposition.
3. No existentially necessary proposition can be true.
4. Therefore, the proposition "God exists necessarily" cannot be true.

In the second form, the fallacies of the argument become apparent. We will pass by the objection to premise one from the vantage point of finite godism (that God does not have to be conceived as necessarily existing), since the subject here is whether or not the traditional theistic conception of an absolutely perfect Being is correct. The theist would challenge premises two and three.

Granting for the moment that there are no existentially necessary propositions, a theist could change the proposition "God exists necessarily" to "God exists." The theist could then hold that the proposition "God exists" is a logically necessary proposition to hold (see Hughes, 59). In this way, necessity applies only to the proposition and not to existence, thus invalidating the criticism.

But the theist need not grant that there are no existentially necessary propositions. Indeed, some theists have offered examples of what they consider to be existentially necessary statements. Ian T. Ramsey suggests that "I am I." is an example. Malcolm offers "There are an infinite number of prime numbers." as an example. Some feel that "Square circles do not exist." would be existentially necessary, even though it is negative in form. If there can be negative examples, why not positive examples? Negatives presuppose positives.

Still other theists, taking Anselm and Descartes literally, insist that "God necessarily exists" is a special case. It is the only existentially necessary proposition and it is not only unnecessary but impossible to give any other examples of existentially necessary propositions.

It seems, however, that the most effective way to eliminate Findlay's ontological disproof is to show that his premise is self-defeating. The statement "There are no existentially necessary propositions" is itself an existentially necessary proposition. And if it is such, then there are existentially necessary propositions. At least there is this one, and why not others? If it is not a necessary statement about existence, then it does not really eliminate the possibility that there could be an existentially necessary Existent. So either it does not accomplish its intended task of eliminating the possibility of existentially necessary propositions or else it defeats itself by offering an existentially necessary proposition in order to prove that there are no existentially necessary propositions.

Hartshorne's Restatement. After such a checkered history, this venerable argument for theism has lived to see a new day. One of the most ardent defenders of the ontological argument is the panentheist, Charles Hartshorne. His statement and defense of the argument in full view of all the traditional criticisms is instructive (see Plantinga, 123–35). Hartshorne states the argument:

1. The existence of a necessary being is either (a) impossible, and there is no example of it; (b) possible, but there is no example of it; (c) possible, and there is an example of it.
2. But premise "b" is meaningless, like saying there is a round square, for a Necessary Being cannot be merely a possible being.
3. And premise "a" is not eliminated by the ontological argument as such but the meaningfulness of the term Necessary Being is a justifiable assumption that may be defended on other grounds.

After pinpointing what he felt to be the basic logic of the ontological argument, Hartshorne proceeded to give the fuller elaboration:

1. All thought must refer to something beyond itself which is at least possible: (a) Wherever there is meaning, something must be meant. (b) Only contradictory thoughts are impossible. (c) Meaning must refer to something more than its own content and inner consistency or it is meaningless. (d) The move

from thought to reality is based on a prior reverse move from reality to thought. (e) Total illusion is impossible; illusion presupposes a backdrop of reality. (f) Confusion is possible about specific reality but not about reality in general.

2. The necessary existence of a Necessary Being is "at least possible." (a) There is nothing contradictory in the concept of a being that cannot not be. (b) The only way to reject this is to plead a special meaning to the possible. In the usual logical sense of the word possible there is no contradiction in the concept of a Necessary Being.
3. With a Necessary Being an "at-least-possible" existence is indistinguishable from a "possible and actual" existence. A Necessary Being cannot have a "merely possible" existence (if a Necessary Being can be, then it must be), for (a) God by definition is an independent Existence and hence cannot be produced by another as "merely possible" beings can be. (c) God is everlasting and so he could not have come into being as "merely possible" beings can come into existence.
4. Therefore, a Necessary Being necessarily has both a possible and an actual existence.

Hartshorne answers objections to his ontological argument:

It is not possible that God's nonexistence was always logically possible even though he actually always existed. First, this is a special pleading on the meaning of the word *possible.* In all other cases, *possible* refers to beings whose nonexistence is both logically and actually possible. Why should God be made an exception by saying that his nonexistence is actually impossible but logically possible? Further, it is not even logically possible for God to be conceived as having come into being. Indeed, by the very conception of his nature he cannot be even logically conceived as having come into existence. For it is contradictory to even think of God as being produced. By his very definition God is a Necessary Being and a being so defined cannot be merely possible.

One cannot prove a perfect island or a perfect devil on the same premises of the ontological argument. The perfect island is not indestructible, as God is. If it is made indestructible, then it becomes identical with the cosmos as the body of God. (Hartshorne's view of God is panentheistic—the material universe is viewed as the "body" of God (*see* PANENTHEISM). But there is a transcendent pole to God that is more than his cosmic "body.") A perfect demon is unequivocal nonsense, for it would be both infinitely responsible and infinitely adverse to all that exists; both infinitely loving and infinitely hateful toward all that is; it would be both intimately united and savagely opposed to all that exists. But such contradictory attitudes are impossible.

The ontological argument proves more than the mere self-consistency of the idea of a Necessary Being. For all meaning has an external referent that is either possible or actual. And God by definition cannot be merely a possible being. Therefore,

1. All meaning implicitly affirms God in reference to either (a) what he has done (called his consequent nature—God's immanence) or (b) what he can do (called his primordial nature—God's transcendence).
2. Without God as the universal ground of meaning there would be no meaning for universals. Nothing can have objective meaning unless there is a realm that is objectively meaningful.
3. We can be confused as to whether specific things exist but not as to whether God—who is the content of existence itself—exists.
4. The only way to oppose the ontological argument is to make an absolute disjunction between meaning and reality. But this disjunction is meaningless. Meaning and reality must meet at some point; that point we call God.

If existence is not a predicate, then at least the *mode* of existence is implied in every predicate. That is, when a quality is predicated of something, it is implied that something exists either contingently or necessarily. And a Necessary Being (God) cannot exist contingently.

The ontological argument does not make God an exception to general philosophical principles. That essence implies that existence in God is not an exception to philosophical principles but a result of a consistent application of philosophical principles to different kinds of beings. God's nature implies existence as does no other nature, because in God alone there is no distinction between the possible and the actual (God is the actualization of all that is possible for him to actualize). "To say a thing might not exist is not to say there might be a thing without existence. It is rather to say that there might be existence without the thing." Existence must necessarily be; this or that existence need not be.

Mere thought does not produce reality, but necessary thought does. There can be no absolute disjunction between thought and reality. Thinking is a real experience, and we do think of God as possible. Hartshorne concludes:

1. All thoughts are experiences of what is at least possible.
2. We do have thoughts about a Being which must be (a Necessary Being).
3. But a Necessary Being cannot be merely a possible being.

4. Therefore, a Necessary Being must be more than merely possible; it must be actual.

As Hartshorne put it, "We have only to exclude impossibility or meaninglessness to establish actuality." That is, "Either God is a meaningless term or there exists a divine being." Or, to restate the argument:

1. Either the existence of a Necessary Being is (a) less than an idea (i.e., contradictory and impossible), (b) merely an idea but not a reality, or (c) more than a mere idea—a reality.
2. It is not less than an idea, for it is a noncontradictory concept.
3. It is not merely an idea, for it is contradictory to speak of a Necessary Being as merely possible. If a Necessary Being exists at all, it must exist necessarily. There is no other way it can exist.
4. Therefore, the existence of a Necessary Being is more than a mere idea; it is a reality.

The ontological argument is not merely hypothetical; it does not assume existence. The ontological argument is *not* saying:

1. If there is a Necessary Being, then it exists necessarily.
2. There is a Necessary Being (thus begging the whole question).
3. Therefore, a Necessary Being exists necessarily.

This criticism contains the self-contradictory assumption that "if a Necessary Being happens to exist as a mere contingent fact, then it exists not as contingent fact but as necessary truth." This is not the meaning of the major premise. The argument, on the contrary, is not contradictory and should be stated like this:

1. If the phrase *Necessary Being* has any meaning, then what it means must actually exist (outside of the mind).
2. The phrase *Necessary Being* does have a meaning (it is not contradictory).
3. Therefore, a Necessary Being actually exists (outside of the mind).

If does not imply the possibility of nonexistence (for a necessary existence cannot possibly *not* exist). *If* means rather the possibility of meaninglessness. And even the possibility of meaninglessness vanishes, for unless there is a basis for meaning (God), there can be no meaning at all.

Hartshorne rests his case heavily on the ultimate identification of the logical with the ontological, a premise disputed by others. Second, he does not really exclude the possibility that others could show the term *God* to be meaningless. It may be that someone will yet demonstrate a contradiction in the very concept of a Necessary Being. If they do, the ontological arguments fail.

Further, the argument rests on the assumption that there must be an objective basis for meaning in order for there to be *any* meaning. This is precisely what existentialists like Jean-Paul Sartre and Albert Camus denied. They held to a subjective basis for meaning but did not deny all meaning. Their argument is that there is no meaning "out there" in the universe except the subjective meaning one puts there. Objective absurdity would still be an option unless one considers Hartshorne has given a disproof of objective absurdity.

Finally, there is an implied premise in all of the ontological arguments that, if true, would seem to vindicate the argument in the face of its standard criticism (that it makes an illicit transition from the logical to the ontological, from thought to reality). The premise is this: *The rationally inescapable is the real.* If defensible (see Geisler and Corduan, 289–96), this would prove objective absurdity to be wrong. Indeed, if the rationally inescapable is the real, and it is rationally inescapable to think of God as necessarily existing, then it would seem to follow that it is really so that God necessarily exists. But before we assume that the ontological argument has won the day we must examine another statement of it and one final criticism.

Malcolm's Restatement. Norman Malcolm is often credited with reviving the ontological argument in a more viable form, although Hartshorne's work on it said the same thing some twenty years earlier. Malcolm did occasion a popular revival of interest in the argument, at least in the area of analytic philosophy. The first form of Anselm's argument Malcolm considers invalidated by Kant's criticism that existence is not a predicate; the second form Malcolm believes is immune from this (or any other) criticism (see Plantinga, 137–59). Malcolm restates Anselm's second argument:

1. The existence of a Necessary Being must be (a) a necessary or "must-be" existence, (b) an impossible, "cannot-be" existence, or (c) a possible, "may-or-may-not-be" existence.
2. But the existence of a Necessary Being is not an impossible existence. (a) No one has ever shown the concept of a Necessary Being to be contradictory. (b) There is a basis in human experience for "a greater than which cannot be thought" (e.g., the feeling of guilt or the experience of grace). (c) Leibniz's attempt to prove that there is no contradiction fails, for there may be one. We cannot show that there cannot be one. We merely know that no one has shown that there is a contradiction. And the proof stands unless or until someone shows that there is a contradiction in the very concept of a Necessary Being.
3. And the existence of a Necessary Being cannot be merely a possible existence, for a

merely possible but not necessary existence of a Necessary Being (a) is contrary to the very nature of a Necessary Being. A "must-be" Being cannot be a "may-or-may-not-be" kind of being. (b) A possible being would be a dependent being, and this is contrary to a Necessary Being which is an independent Being by nature.
4. Therefore, a Necessary Being necessarily exists.

Malcolm's argument may also be put in hypothetical form:

1. If it is possible for a Necessary Being to exist, then it is necessary for it to exist, for the only way a Necessary Being can exist is to exist necessarily.
2. It is possible that a Necessary Being can exist. There is nothing contradictory about affirming the existence of a Necessary Being.
3. Therefore, a Necessary Being necessarily exists.

Or, to restate the heart of the argument in categorical form:

1. A Necessary Being by definition is one which cannot *not* be.
2. That which cannot *not* be, must be, for this is the logical obverse.
3. Therefore, a Necessary Being necessarily must be.

It would appear that the critical premise in the argument is the one affirming that the mere possibility of a Necessary Being is contradictory. Let us state again the argument with Malcolm's fuller defense of this premise.

1. The existence of a Necessary Being must be either (a) a necessary existence, (b) a mere possible existence, or (c) an impossible existence.
2. But it cannot be an impossible existence. There is no contradiction.
3. Nor can it be a mere possible existence, for such an existence would be: (a) A dependent existence. A dependent existence cannot, at the same time, be an independent existence, such as is a necessary existence. (b) A fortuitous existence. If God just happened to be, then he could not be a Necessary Being. (c) A temporal existence. If God came to be, then he would be dependent, which is contrary to his independent or Necessary Being.
4. Therefore, the existence of a Necessary Being is a necessary existence; that is, a Necessary Being necessarily exists.

Malcolm admits that there might be a contradiction in the concept of a Necessary Being and that he knows of no way to prove that there is not a contradiction. This admission means that his "proof" is not foolproof. It is logically possible that it is wrong. Hence, the conclusion is not rationally inescapable. Thus, even granting the validity of the rest of the argument, it is not a proof in the strongest sense of the word.

Plantinga's Critique. Plantinga assesses Malcolm's ontological argument in terms of logical schema (ibid., 160–71):

1. If God does not exist, his existence is logically impossible.
2. If God does exist, his existence is logically necessary.
3. Hence, either God's existence is logically impossible or else it is logically necessary.
4. If God's existence is logically impossible, the concept of God is contradictory.
5. The concept of God is not contradictory.
6. Therefore, God's existence is logically necessary.

Plantinga takes issue with the second premise. God could exist without his existence being logically necessary. God's existence could be logically contingent without being ontologically contingent. Or, to put it another way, Malcolm equivocates on the word *possible.* Malcolm assumes that, because it is not *possible ontologically* for God to be contingent, is it not *possible logically* for God to be contingent. Malcolm overlooks that it is logically *possible* that God is a Necessary Being but not logically *necessary*.

On the other hand, Plantinga is right only if the implied premise in the ontological argument is wrong: "The rationally inescapable is the real." If what is rationally inescapable must be ontologically so, then Hartshorne and Malcolm seem to make a good case against this criticism. They argue that it is logically necessary to think of God as real, since it is logically contradictory to conceive of a Necessary Being as not necessarily having being.

Evaluation. This does not mean that the ontological argument is valid. There is one final and possibly fatal criticism. Plantinga observes that it is also logically "possible" that God never existed at all. In fact, it is logically possible that nothing ever existed, including God. But this may be only an apparent omission in the ontological argument. Perhaps the reason that this logical possibility does not present itself as evident to the proponents of the ontological argument is that they are assuming a cosmological premise. For it seems readily apparent to anyone existing that something does exist. And if something exists, it is not true that nothing exists. And if something exists, that makes false the statement that nothing exists. But if something does exist, it is not true to affirm that nothing exists. Hence, Plantinga's criticism, that the ontological argument is unsuccessful simply because it overlooks the possible truth that nothing exists, fails.

All the proponents of the ontological argument need to do to invalidate Plantinga's criticism is to show that something exists. This is easily accomplished by insisting that no one can deny existence without existing to make the denial. For it is actually impossible to affirm that nothing exists, since there must be someone in existence to make that affirmation. In brief, the ontological arguments based merely on predictability and inconceivability are invalid, but a third argument based on undeniability appears to evade these fallacies. This seems so for the simple reason that the only apparent way to invalidate the second form of the ontological argument is on the conceivability (i.e., logical possibility) of the truth that nothing exists, but this truth is not affirmable because something does exist. Hence, it is undeniable that something exists and therefore God must necessarily exist. Therefore, it would seem that a third form of the ontological argument can successfully defend itself against Plantinga's criticism.

In this revised form, it is not really an ontological argument but a cosmological argument. For there is a difference, as Anselm recognized in his reply to Gaunilo, between the logical possibility that nothing, including God, ever existed and the reality of the statement by someone who does exist, "Nothing, including God, ever existed." Of course, it is undeniably true that something exists, but not because it is inconceivable or logically impossible that nothing exists. It is not logically contradictory to assume that there might never have been anything in existence. Nonbeing is a logical possibility. The only way one can invalidate the logical possibility that "nothing ever was, including God" is to affirm, "Something was or is." But once one affirms the premise "Something is" and argues from that to "God is," he has left the ontological argument for the cosmological argument. He has left the *a priori* realm of pure reason and entered into the *a posteriori* domain of existence. The so-called third argument from undeniability of existence is not an ontological argument but a cosmological argument. And it needs more elaboration and defense.

Plantinga's Argument. After years of studying and critiquing the ontological argument, Plantinga has proposed a version of his own, which he considers to be valid. He has provided several formulations, one of which can be summarized in ten steps (Plantinga, *The Nature of Necessity,* 214–15):

1. *Something has the property of maximal greatness if it has the property of maximal excellence in every possible world.* The *greatest* thing must be the *best* thing, not just in the world that is, but in all possible worlds. A possible world is any logically conceivable world. Any time we can close our eyes and imagine our actual world to be different in some rational way, we are conceiving a logically possible world. Obviously the actual world is a possible world. But there are many other possible worlds. They "are" in the sense that they are logical possibilities, not that they are actual. If something is not the most excellent in all possible worlds, it could not really be the greatest, for one could conceive of a greater.
2. *Maximal excellence entails omniscience, omnipotence, and moral perfection.* With this premise Plantinga defines what one would mean by saying that something is the best. He structures his argument in such a way that the being whose existence he intends to demonstrate will turn out to be God.
3. *Maximal greatness is possibly exemplified.* There is nothing self-contradictory or logically odd about positing that in a possible world we can encounter this quality. This exemplification is elaborated in premise 4, which posits a world W, and essence E, and the property of maximal greatness.
4. *There is a world (*W*) in which the essence (*E*) is such that* E *is exemplified in* W *and* E *entails maximal greatness in* W. In this hypothetical world this hypothetical essence has the property of maximal greatness. We must remember the statement of premise 1. That which is true of an essence would have to be true of an object bearing that essence.
5. *For any object (*X*), if* X *exemplifies* E, *then* X *exemplifies maximal excellence in every possible world.*
6. E *entails the property of maximal excellence in every possible world.* Plantinga argues that the same relationship that is necessarily true in W would be necessarily true in any possible world. Thus he can make such a general statement concerning this essence and the property that it would entail in any possible world.
7. *If* W *had been actual, it would have been impossible that* E *would fail to be exemplified.* This statement is a simple component of modal logic. If something holds for any possible world, it would certainly also hold if that possible world were the actual world. Thus if the possible world under consideration were actual, then this essence with maximal excellence in every possible world would have to be real. In fact, given the preceding premises, the denial of this reality would be impossible.
8. *What is impossible does not vary from world to world.* Differences among possible worlds are factual. They do not involve logical absurdities. There is no logically possible world in which circles are square or

logical deductions do not follow. Logical relationships are constant over all possible worlds. Thus logical necessity or impossibility is the same in every world. Therefore what Plantinga has said about E in W would have to apply to E in every possible world. There also it would be impossible for E not to be exemplified.

9. *There exists a being that has maximal excellence in every world.* So, it follows that
10. *The being that has maximal excellence exists in the actual world.* Thus, using modal logic, Plantinga has demonstrated that God (the Being with omniscience, omnipotence, and moral perfection) exists.

Evaluation. This tight and compelling argument avoids many criticisms traditionally brought against the ontological argument. But it puts into clear focus the critique we have brought against the argument in this context. This approach based on modal logic stipulates from the outset that *something exists.* The concept of possible worlds makes sense only in contrast to an actual world. Only if we, at least for the sake of the argument, allow that there is a reality, can the argument unfold. In short, it assumes something exists. Further, to define a maximally perfect being in theistic terms is gratuitous (premise 2). Why could not perfection be viewed in nonmoral, nonintelligent terms?

But finally, and even more to the point, the argument in premise 4 stipulates the reality of E as an essence. In Plantinga's philosophy essences are not just mental concepts or words, but they exist in a sense as real. Hence the argument is beginning to bear faint resemblance to Descartes' argument, in which he stipulates the idea of a Supreme Being and then attempts to give an account thereof (Descartes, 23–34). But that argument has also been characterized as cosmological. And the same thing may be true for Plantinga's argument. Perhaps the reason it is valid is that it has left the realm of pure ontological arguments.

Conclusion. The ontological argument has taken many forms. Each, however, seems to be invalid. The only feasible way to make it valid (if it can be made valid at all) is to assume or affirm that something exists. And once one argues, "Something exists, therefore God exists," he has really argued cosmologically. The ontological argument by itself, without borrowing the premise, "Something exists," cannot possibly prove the existence of God. For it is always logically possible that nothing ever existed and hence it is not logically necessary to affirm that God exists.

Some have suggested that our conclusion is invalid because the very concept of "nothing" is negative, and thus presupposes that something exists. If this is correct, they contend, then our contention that "it is logically possible that nothing ever existed" is wrong. This objection, however, confuses the concept of nonbeing (which does presuppose the concept of being) and a state of nonbeing that does not presuppose a state of being. We are referring to the logical possibility of the state of nothingness, not to the concept of nothingness.

It would appear that no valid ontological proof has been given that makes it rationally inescapable to conclude that there is a Necessary Being. On the other hand, neither has anyone made a successful ontological disproof of God, making it logically impossible that there is a God. Necessary to a valid theistic argument is the premise that "something exists or existed." One who argues that "something exists, therefore God exists" has left the purely *a priori* ontological approach and has moved into an *a posteriori* cosmological approach.

If one could somehow validate a theistic argument by importing the undeniable premise that "something exists" and arguing from this that "something necessarily exists," it still is a long way from this to the simple and absolutely perfect Being of Christian theism. It is interesting to note that three views of God have been concluded from the same kind of ontological argument, and others feel a fourth may be inferred. Descartes and Leibniz concluded a theistic God. Spinoza argued to a pantheistic God. Hartshorne ended with a panentheistic God (*see* PANENTHEISM). It is also suggested that, apart from importing some kind of Platonic premise, the ontological argument yields polytheistic gods (*see* POLYTHEISM). Even many atheists are willing to recognize the universe is somehow necessary, but in no way do they identify it with God. Since the positions are mutually exclusive, it follows that they cannot all be true.

In order to defend theism, one must apparently go beyond the ontological argument. For the ontological argument alone apparently does not designate which kind of God (or gods) is found at the conclusion.

Sources

R. Descartes, *Meditations on First Philosophy*

N. L. Geisler, "The Missing Premise in the Ontological Argument," in *RS* (September 1973)

——— and W. Corduan, *Philosophy of Religion*

G. E. Hughes, "Can God's Existence Be Disproved?" in A. Flew, et al., eds., *Philosophical Theology*

A. Plantinga, *The Nature of Necessity*

———, *The Ontological Argument: From Anselm to Contemporary Philosophers*

B. Spinoza, *Ethics*

Ontology. *Ontology* is the study (*logos*) of being (*ontos*). It is the study of reality. It answers the question "What is *real?*" as ethics answers the question "What is *right?*" as aesthetics answers the question, "What is *beautiful?*" and epistemology answers the question, "What is *true?*"

Ontology and metaphysics are used interchangeably. Both study being as being or the real as real. They are the disciplines that deal with ultimate reality.

Origen. Origen (185–254) was an early church Father and apologist for Christianity. He was heavily influenced by Platonic (*see* PLATO; PLOTINUS) and Gnostic (*see* GNOSTICISM) thought. As a consequence his defense of the faith tended to sacrifice important teachings. He denied the historicity of crucial sections of Scripture; he taught the preexistence of the soul and universalism (the belief that all will eventually be saved; *see* "HEATHEN," SALVATION OF THE) and denied that Jesus was raised from the dead in a physical body (*see* RESURRECTION, PHYSICAL NATURE OF). These positions were condemned as heretical by later church councils.

Origen was an early second-century Christian writer from Alexandria, Egypt. He studied eleven years with neoplatonist, Ammonius Saccas where he was a classmate of Plotinus (205–270). Origen headed up a catechetical school in Alexandria (211–232) and later founded a school in Caesarea.

His many works include the *Hexapla,* a six-column comparison of various Greek and Hebrew renditions of the Old Testament. Unfortunately, no copies of this great work survive. He also wrote *Contra Celsus,* an apologetic work answering the philosopher Celsus, and *De Principiis,* a major theological treatise.

The Bible. While Origen claimed that the Bible was divinely inspired, he did not accept the complete historicity of Scripture, nor did he interpret it all literally. Like others in the Alexandrian school of interpretation, he often allegorized crucial sections of Scripture.

Bible Only Partially Historical. Origen insisted: "We have therefore to state in answer, since we are manifestly so of opinion, that the truth of the history may and ought to be preserved in the majority of instances" (*De Principiis,* 4.19). Unfortunately, this did not include crucial sections of the Bible. He asserted that the attentive reader would find numerous passages in the Gospels in which insertions of nonhistoric events had been made. "And if we come to the legislation of Moses, many of the laws manifest the irrationality, and others the impossibility, of their literal observance" (ibid., 4.1.16–17).

Allegorical Interpretation. Accuracy was not such a concern if the message was buried in allegory. Origen sought "to discover in every expression the hidden splendour of the doctrines veiled in common and unattractive phraseology" (ibid., 4.1.7).

The story of Adam and Eve was to be taken figuratively. For "No one, I think, can doubt that the statement that God walked in the afternoon in paradise, and that Adam lay hid under a tree is related figuratively in Scripture, that some mystical meaning may be indicated by it." And "those who are not altogether blind can collect countless instances of a similar kind recorded as having occurred, but which did not literally take place? Nay, the Gospels themselves are filled with the same kind of narratives; for example, the devil leading Jesus up into a high mountain, in order to show him from thence the kingdoms of the whole world, and the glory of them" (ibid., 4.1.16).

Preexistence of the Soul. Origen's argument for the preexistence and eternality of the soul is heavily dependent on Platonism. He argues that God had made other worlds before this one, and would make more in the future (ibid., 2.5.3). In creation, "we are to suppose that God created so great a number of rational or intellectual creatures (or by whatever name they are to be called), which we have formerly termed understandings, as he foresaw would be sufficient" (ibid., 2.9.1).

To deny the eternality of the soul was to do no less than deny God's omnipotence, he believed. The soul must be preexistent and eternal because, "as no one can be a father without having a son, nor a master without possessing a servant, so even God cannot be called omnipotent unless there exist those over whom he may exercise his power; and therefore, that God may be shown to be almighty, it is necessary that all things should exist." Did he gain more power as he created more people? Rather, "He must always have had those over whom He exercised power, and which were governed by Him either as king or prince" (ibid., 1.2.10).

Finally, Origen argues that "If the soul of a man, which is certainly inferior while it remains the soul of a man, was not formed along with his body, but is proved to have been implanted strictly from without, much more must this be the case with those living beings which are called heavenly." Furthermore, "How could his soul and its images be formed along with his body, who, before he was created in the womb, is said to be known to God, and was sanctified by Him before his birth?" (ibid., 1.7.4)

****Universalism.*** Origen believed that in the end everyone would be saved. His view is explicitly universalistic:

> So then, when the end has been restored to the beginning, and the termination of things compared with their commencement, that condition of things will be re-established in which rational nature was placed, when it had no need to eat of the tree of the knowledge of good and evil; so that when all feeling of wickedness has been removed, and the individual has been purified and cleansed, He who alone is the one good God becomes to him

> "all," and that not in the case of a few individuals, or of a considerable number, but He Himself is "all in all." And when death shall no longer anywhere exist, nor the sting of death, nor any evil at all, then verily God will be "all in all." [Origen, *De Principiis,* 3.6.3]

According to Origen, this saving knowledge would come "slowly and gradually, seeing that the process of amendment and correction will take place imperceptibly in the individual instances during the lapse of countless and unmeasured ages, some outstripping others, and tending by a swifter course towards perfection, while others again follow close at hand, and some again a long way behind." Thus, "through the numerous and uncounted orders of progressive beings who are being reconciled to God from a state of enmity, the last enemy is finally reached, who is called death, so that he also may be destroyed, and no longer be an enemy. When, therefore, all rational souls shall have been restored to a condition of this kind, then the nature of this body of ours will undergo a change into the glory of a spiritual body" (ibid., 3.6.6).

The Biblical Texts. Some of Origen's arguments for universalism are based on biblical texts and others on philosophical speculation.

In the context of God's love in Christ, Origen looked to passages that spoke of God conquering and subduing his enemies. He drew on those passages which quoted Psalm 110:1, especially 1 Cor. 15:25: "The Lord said to my Lord: 'Sit at my right hand until I make your enemies a footstool for your feet.'. . . For he must reign until he has put all his enemies under his feet" (*De Principiis,* 1.6.1).

The End Like the Beginning. Origen reasoned from the neoplatonic premise that "the end is always like the beginning: and, therefore, as there is one end to all things, so ought we to understand that there was one beginning; and as there is one end to many things, so there spring from one beginning many differences and varieties, which again, through the goodness of God, and by subjection to Christ, and through the unity of the Holy Spirit, are recalled to one end, which is like unto the beginning" (ibid., 1.6.2).

Reformatory Justice. Origen rejected a penal view of justice (*see* HELL), arguing that "The fury of God's vengeance is profitable for the purgation of souls. That the punishment, also, which is said to be applied by fire, is understood to be applied with the object of healing" (ibid., 2.10.6). He added, "those who have been removed from their primal state of blessedness have not been removed irrecoverably, but have been placed under the rule of those holy and blessed orders which we have described; and by availing themselves of the aid of these, and being remoulded by salutary principles and discipline, they may recover themselves, and be restored to their condition of happiness" (ibid., 1.6.2).

God's Wisdom. Origen insisted that: "God, by the ineffable skill of his wisdom, transforming and restoring all things, in whatever manner they are made, to some useful aim, and to the common advantage of all, recalls those very creatures which differed so much from each other in mental conformation to one agreement of labour and purpose; so that, although they are under the influence of different motives, they nevertheless complete the fulness and perfection of one world, and the very variety of minds tends to one end of perfection." For "it is one power which grasps and holds together all the diversity of the world, and leads the different movements towards one work, lest so immense an undertaking as that of the world should be dissolved by the dissensions of souls." And "for this reason we think that God, the Father of all things, in order to ensure the salvation of all his creatures through the ineffable plan of his word and wisdom, so arranged each of these, that every spirit, whether soul or rational existence, however called, should not be compelled by force, against the liberty of his own will, to any other course than that to which the motives of his own mind led him (lest by so doing the power of exercising free-will should seem to be taken away, which certainly would produce a change in the nature of the being itself)" (ibid., 2.1.2).

God's Omnipotence. "For nothing is impossible to the Omnipotent, nor is anything incapable of restoration to its Creator" (ibid., 3.6.5). This, of course, implies that God desires by his goodness to do so (1 Tim. 2:1; 2 Pet. 3:9). But if God wants to save all, and he can save all (i.e., he is all-powerful), then for Origen it would seem to follow that he will save all.

Spiritualism. Origen also denied the permanent physical nature of the resurrection, for which he was condemned by the bishops of the Fifth Ecumenical Council of the Church when they wrote: "If anyone shall say that after the resurrection the body of the Lord was ethereal, . . . and that such shall be the bodies of all after the resurrection; and that after the Lord himself shall have rejected his true body and after others who rise shall have rejected theirs, the nature of their bodies shall be annihilated: let him be anathema" (Canon 10 cited by Schaff, 14:314–19). Likewise, "If any one shall say that the future judgment signifies the destruction of the body and that the end of the story will be an immaterial nature [*phusis*], and that thereafter there will no longer be any matter, but only spirit [*nous*]: let him be anathema" (ibid., Canon 11).

In about 400, the Council of Toledo declared emphatically: "We believe verily, that there shall be a resurrection of the *flesh* of mankind" (Parker, 24, 26). And the Fourth Council of Toledo (663) added, "By whose death and blood we being made clear have obtained forgiveness of (our sins) and shall be raised up again by him in the last days in the same flesh wherein we now live, (and) in the manner wherein the same (our) Lord did rise again" (ibid., 26).

Christ Inferior to the Father. Although he did not deny the deity of Christ, nonetheless, Origen did believe Jesus has a subordinate status to the Father even to the point that he forfeited his deity while on earth. Origen wrote: "The Son of God, divesting Himself of His equality with the Father, and showing to us the way to the knowledge of Him, is made the express image of His person" (*De Principiis* 1.2.8).

Even Christ's goodness is derived from the Father: "If this be fully understood, it clearly shows that the existence of the Son is derived from the Father but not in time, nor from any other beginning, except, as we have said, from God Himself" (*De Principiis* 1.2.11).

Origen spoke clearly about Christ's inferior status to the Father when he said, "Grant that there may be some individuals among the multitudes of believers who are not in entire agreement with us, and who incautiously assert that the Saviour is the Most High God; however, we do not hold with them, but rather believe Him when He says, 'The Father who sent Me is greater than I.' We would not therefore make Him whom we call Father inferior—as Celsus accuses us of doing—to the Son of God" (*Contra Celsus* 8.14).

According to Origen, although Christ is eternal, his deity is derived from the Father: "Wherefore we have always held that God is the Father of His only-begotten Son, who was born indeed of Him, and derives from Him what He is, but without any beginning" (*De Principiis* 1.2.2).

In a contorted Platonic logic, Origen even argued that somehow the existence of the Son is dependent on the Father: "For if the Son do, in like manner, all those things which the Father doth, then, in virtue of the Son doing all things like the Father, is the image of the Father formed in the Son, *who is born of Him, like an act of His will proceeding from the mind.* And I am therefore of opinion that the will of *the Father ought alone to be sufficient for the existence of that which He wishes to exist.* For in the exercise of His will He employs no other way than that which is made known by the counsel of His will. And thus also *the existence of the Son is generated by Him*" (*De Principiis* 1.2.6, emphasis added).

Evaluation. Origen was at best a mixed blessing for Christian apologetics. He did defend the basic inspiration and historicity of the Bible. He stressed the use of reason in defending early Christianity against the attacks of paganism and other false teachings. He was a textual scholar.

However, Origen's negatives seem to far outweigh the positives. He denied the inerrancy of the Bible, at least in practice (*see* BIBLE, ALLEGED ERRORS IN). He taught *universalism contrary to both Scripture and orthodox creeds. He taught the preexistence of the soul in contrast to the orthodox teaching of creation. He engaged in highly allegorical interpretation of Scripture, undermining important literal truths. He held an aberrant view on the nature of Christ, which gave rise to the later Arian heresy (*see* CHRIST, DEITY OF). He denied the tangible, physical nature of the resurrection body (*see* RESURRECTION, EVIDENCE OF; RESURRECTION, PHYSICAL NATURE OF) in contrast to the clear teaching of Scripture (Luke 24:39; Acts 2:31; 1 John 4:2) and the creeds (see Geisler, *The Battle for the Resurrection,* chap. 5, and *In Defense of the Resurrection,* chap. 9).

Sources

C. Biggs, *The Christian Platonists of Alexandria*
J. Danielou, *Origen*
W. Fairweather, *Origen and Greek Patristic Theology*
N. L. Geisler, *In Defense of the Resurrection*
———, *The Battle for the Resurrection*
Origen, *Contra Celsus*
———, *De Principiis*
T. Parker, ed., *The Decades of Henry Bullinger*
P. Schaff, ed., *A Select Library of Nicene and Post-Nicene Fathers of the Christian Church*
J. W. Trigg, *Origen: The Bible and Philosophy in the Third-Century Church*
———, *The Fifth Ecumenical Council of Constantinople* (A.D. 553)

Origins, Science of. The belief that the universe and all forms of life were created by God is not considered true science by some because science deals with theories that can be verified by testing. There is no way to test creation, since it was a unique past singularity. This objection is based in a misunderstanding of two kinds of science: *empirical* and *forensic*. *Operation science* deals with the world as it now exists and *origin science* with the *past* (Geisler, *Origin Science*, chaps. 1, 6, 7). Operation science is an *empirical* science that deals with present regularities, but origin science is a forensic science that considers past singularities—the *origin* of the universe and life forms.

Since there is no direct way to test a theory or model of origin science, it must be judged to be plausible or implausible, based on how consistently and comprehensively it reconstructs the unobserved past in conformity with the available evidence. Operation science is based on principles of *observation* and *repetition*. The laws of physics and chemistry, for example, are based on the observation of recurring patterns of events. Such observations can be made with the unaided eye or with the aid of sensitive instruments, but observation of some sort is crucial. Likewise, there must be some repetition or recurring pattern. For no scientific analysis can be made on the basis of a singular event. Operation science is based on the repetition of similar patterns of events. For operation science involves not only *present* regularities but *future* ones that can be projected. But no scientific trend or prediction can be made from a singular event.

The operation of the cosmos is studied by the operation science of *cosmology*. But the origin of the cosmos is the field of the science of *cosmogony*. The operational science of *biology* does not properly deal with the beginning of life but with its continuing functioning. How life began is for *biogeny*.

In distinguishing these two areas of investigation, it is important to note substantial differences even in the natural laws and processes they look at. Laws by which something operates today may function quite unlike how they functioned at the beginning. It is difficult to know what factors even existed to interact with one another. A simple and obvious example is that the laws operating during the *running* of a windmill are not sufficient to *produce* that windmill. A windmill functions by purely natural laws of physics—pressure, motion, and inertia. Inertia, however, cannot create the design, weld the metal, assemble the wind-powered generator, or adjust the propeller blades. Someone had to come from outside the windmill system, bringing necessary know-how, plans, and manipulation of materials. Natural laws adequately explain why electricity is generated by a windmill on a continuing basis; they are insufficient to explain the *commencement* of the system.

Only because things operate in a regular way is it possible to make observations and predictions based on them. So a whole different approach and different goals are at work in a forensic science. One normally hears of forensic science in law enforcement, where scientists may attempt to reconstruct what happened to cause an unobserved death, for example. Some elements may be repeatable, but not the essential series of events, since the person at the center of those events is dead. But the lack of empirical science principles does not totally frustrate a scientific analysis of the death. Forensic science has its own rules and principles. Using the evidence that remains (such as weapons, injury patterns, blood splatters, and finger prints), the forensic scientist can make a plausible reconstruction of the original event. In a similar way, the origin scientist attempts to reconstruct the origin of the universe and the origin of life.

Principles of Origin Science. Besides the two obvious principles that every theory or model should be consistent and comprehensive, the most crucial principles of origin science are *causality* and *uniformity* (analogy) (Geisler, *Origin Science*, 131–32).

Causality. Like the forensic scientist, the origin scientist believes that *every event has an adequate cause* (*see* CAUSALITY, PRINCIPLE OF; FIRST PRINCIPLES). This is true of unobserved as well as observed events. This principle has such universal acceptance that it scarcely needs justification. It is sufficient to note that Aristotle said, "the wise man seeks causes." Francis Bacon believed that true knowledge is "knowledge by causes" (Bacon, 2.2.121). Even the skeptic, David Hume agreed (*Letters of David Hume*, 1.187). It is self-evident to most rational beings that *everything that comes to be had a cause*. If this were not so, things would pop into and out of existence willy nilly, but they do not. Indeed, without the principle of causality, no science would be possible.

It is an important aside to note that the principle of causality does *not* claim that *everything* has a cause. With the atheist (*see* ATHEISM) we agree that *if* matter (energy) is eternal and indestructible, then it does not need a cause. Only everything that begins—or is contingent has a cause. If a Being is eternal and independent (whether it is the universe or God), then it does not need a cause. Causality applies to things that *come to be*; whatever just *is*, is uncaused.

Uniformity (Analogy). Generally stated, the scientific principle of uniformity affirms that "the present is the key to the past." Applied more specifically to the question of past unobserved causes, the principle of uniformity (analogy) asserts that the cause of certain kinds of events now would have produced like effects in the past. Past events have causes similar to the causes of the present events.

The principle of uniformity derives its name from the *uniform* experience on which it is based. Repeated observation reveals that certain kinds of causes regularly produce certain kinds of events. For example, water flowing over small rolling rocks gradually wears the rock's surface smooth and rounded. Wind on sand (or water) produces waves. Heavy rain on dirt results in erosion, and so on. These are natural, *secondary* causes. Their effects are produced by natural forces whose processes are an observable part of the ongoing *operation* of the physical universe.

However, the principle of *uniformity* should not be confused with *uniformitarianism*. That latter is a naturalistic (*see* NATURALISM) presupposition which wrongly assumes that all causes of events in the world must be natural causes. This both begs the question and is contrary to the best evidence for the origin of the universe (*see* BIG BANG; EVOLUTION, COSMIC; THERMODYNAMICS, LAWS OF). There is no reason to accept the premise that everything that happens in nature was caused by nature (*see* NATURALISM; MIRACLE). After all, the natural world did not cause itself (*see* COSMOLOGICAL ARGUMENT; *KALAM* COSMOLOGICAL ARGUMENT). Even finite minds can intervene all the time in the natural world. There is no reason an infinite Mind cannot do the same.

In addition to secondary causes, there are primary causes. Intelligence is a primary cause. And the principle of uniformity (based on constant conjunction) informs us that certain kinds of effects come only from intelligent causes: language, projectile points, pottery, portraits, and symphonies. So convinced are we by previous repeated experience that only intelligence produces these kinds of effects that when we see even a single event that resembles one of these kinds of effects we invariably posit an intelligible cause for it. When we come across the words "John loves Mary" scratched into a beach, we never assume that waves did it. The question is whether the origin of the first living organism (which we did not observe) was by a secondary (natural) cause or by a primary intelligent cause. The only scientific way to determine this is by analogy with our experience of what kind of cause regularly produces that kind of effect.

The principle of uniformity is an argument from analogy. It is an attempt to get at the unknown (past) through the known (present). Since we do not have direct access to the past, we can "know" it only by analogies with the present. This is how human history, earth history, and life history are reconstructed. Historical geology, for example, is totally dependent as a science on the principle of uniformity. Unless we can presently observe in nature or the laboratory certain kinds of causes producing certain kinds of events, we cannot validly reconstruct geological history. But since we can observe natural causes producing these kinds of effects today, we can postulate that similar natural causes produced similar effects in the geological record of the past. Archaeology as a science is possible only because we assume the principle of uniformity. Certain kinds of tools, art, or writing consistently say certain things about the intelligent beings who produced them. Even simple projectile points lead us to claim what Indians produced them and when. They can be differentiated from pieces of flint or rock shaped by wind and water. When past remains contain writing, art, poetry, or music, we immediately insist they came from intelligent beings.

So whether the evidence calls for a secondary or primary cause, the principle of uniformity is the basis. Unless we have had a constant conjunction of a certain kind of cause with a certain kind of effect in the present, we have no grounds on which to apply the principle to past events known only from their remains.

The Principle of Consistency. All theories must be consistent. Whatever scientific model one constructs of the past must be consistent or noncontradictory with all other elements of one's scientific views. Contradictory views must be rejected. One cannot hold that the universe both had a beginning and did not begin. Nor can one consistently affirm that the cosmos was both created and uncreated. The law of noncontradiction applies to all views (*see* LOGIC; FIRST PRINCIPLES).

The Principle of Comprehensiveness. Further, scientific explanations must be comprehensive. A good model comprehensively explains the known facts. Anomalies will persist, but no indisputable data can be neglected in theory construction. Thus, all other things being equal, the most comprehensive view is judged to be the best.

Various Areas of Origin Science. Now that the basic principles of origin science are set forth, they can be applied to the three main areas of origin: the beginning of the universe, the emergence of first life, and the appearance of human (rational) beings. In each case this yields a distinction between origin and operation science. Names already exist to distinguish them.

	Origin Science	**Operation Science**
Universe	Cosmogony	Cosmology
Life	Biogeny	Biology
Human Beings	Anthropogeny	Anthropology

The scientific evidence is presented elsewhere for the creationists' view of cosmogony (*see* EVOLUTION, COSMIC), biogeny (*see* EVOLUTION, CHEMICAL), and anthropogeny (*see* EVOLUTION, BIOLOGICAL). Hence, it remains here simply to ask whether creation is a science.

Creation Science. A creationist view of origins can be just as scientific as an evolutionist view. The belief that there is an intelligent Creator of the universe, first life, and new life forms is just as scientific as the naturalistic views of macroevolutionary theory. Both are origin science, not operation science. Both deal with past singularities. Both take a forensic approach by reconstructing a plausible scenario of the past unobserved event in the light of the evidence that remains in the present. Both use the principles of causality and analogy. Both seek an appropriate explanation of the data. Both sometimes appeal to a primary (intelligent) cause to explain the data. Archaeology posits an intelligent cause for pottery. Anthropologists do the same for ancient tools. Likewise, when creationists see the same kind of specified complexity in a simple one-cell animal, such as the first living thing is supposed to be, they too posit an intelligent cause for it. Their view is as scientific in procedure as the evolutionists when they offer a natural explanation for the first living thing.

Likewise, the creationists' view of the origin of the cosmos is as scientific as is the evolutionists' position. Both use scientific evidence in the present. And both use the principle of causality. The creationist points to the evidence for the Second *Law of Thermodynamics that the universe is running down as evidence that it had a beginning along with the other evidence for the *Big Bang theory. This, combined with the principle of causality, yields the conclusion that:

1. The cosmos had a beginning.
2. Everything that begins had a cause.
3. Therefore, the cosmos had a cause (*see* *KALAM* COSMOLOGICAL ARGUMENT).

Objections to Origin Science. Two basic objections to origin science surface repeatedly. The first has to do with the scientific method as such and the second with the origin of a scientific model.

Naturalism in the Scientific Approach. At this point it is often objected by the evolutionists that the creationist approach is not scientific because it appeals to a supernatural cause. Evolutionists only assume natural causes. Hence, the creationists' view is disqualified, even as an origin science. This objection is a classic case of begging the issue. Who said science can only allow natural causes for phenomena in the natural world. This move is invalid, for it eliminates creation by definition. One could, by the same move, demand that there are only supernatural causes for all events and eliminate all natural causes by definition (*see* MIRACLES, ARGUMENTS AGAINST). It is a form of methodological *naturalism. While it may admit the existence of a supernatural realm, it insists that the scientific method must permit only natural causes. While this may be true of operation science, it is not so of origin science.

Eliminating an intelligent cause of the world and life as a scientific explanation is contrary to the origin and early history of science. Most founders of modern science were creationists who believed that the scientific evidence pointed to an intelligent supernatural Creator of the universe and life. To redefine science so as to eliminate the possibility of an intelligent cause is contrary to the very commencement and character of modern science itself.

A scientific approach should go where the evidence leads, even if it leads to a supernatural cause. What is scientific about an approach that refuses to conclude that there exists the kind of cause to which the evidence points? Should an archaeologist refuse to accept anything but a natural cause for art it unearths?

The only adequate cause for the origin of life and the universe is a supernatural one. After all, if—as all the evidence indicates—the whole natural world had a beginning, then the Cause must have been beyond nature (*see* *KALAM* COSMOLOGICAL ARGUMENT). That, by definition, means supernatural. By what logic does one cease to draw the logical conclusion simply because one wishes to posit a stipulative definition of "science" so as to exclude that kind of cause from the realm of science.

Even if one stubbornly insists, for whatever reason, to exclude all but natural causes from the word *science*, that does not invalidate supernatural causes or their study. They simply move to another area of intellectual endeavor, be it "philosophy" or whatever. Science is simply impoverished in its own search for truth. There is no valid reason supernatural explanations should be excluded from an academic endeavor interested in finding and teaching the truth about our world.

The Origin of a Scientific Model. Some opponents of origin science insist that the creation model is taken from a religious document, the Bible, and religion has no place in science. While one may object that teaching the Bible in a public school science class is a religious exercise, this objection overlooks a very important distinction: The origin of a scientific theory has no relation to its validity. Some widely accepted scientific findings have had religious sources. Nikola Tesla (1856–1943) got the idea of the alternating current motor from a vision he had while reading the pantheistic poet, Goethe. The model for the benzene molecule was invented by Kekule after seeing a vision of a snake biting its tail. No scientists would reject these scientific findings simply because of their religious source. Likewise, no one should reject the idea of an intelligent Creator of the universe and life simply because it has a religious source. The question is not where the idea came from but whether it adequately explains the facts. And an intelligent Creator does adequately explain the origin of the universe and life.

A "Flat Earth" View. Many who oppose calling creation a scientific view insist that to do so is to open the door for teaching the "flat earth" view as science, too. But this is clearly not the case. Whether the earth is square or spherical is a matter of operation, not origin, science, since the shape of the earth is subject to repeated verification and observation. The ongoing shape of the earth has nothing to do with the question of its origin. There is no need to allow the flat earth view to be taught as science, since it has been scientifically disproven. This can be said of few theories, but the "Square Earth" view is factually false. And there is no reason to allow something that has been falsified to be taught as a legitimate scientific view.

This is not the case with creation, since no one has factually disproven that there could have been an intelligent cause of the universe and life (*see* GOD, ALLEGED DISPROOFS OF). Indeed, there is more plausible evidence for a Creator (*see* COSMOLOGICAL ARGUMENT) and Designer (*see* TELEOLOGICAL ARGUMENT; ANTHROPIC PRINCIPLE) of the cosmos than for naturalistic evolution (*see* EVOLUTION, BIOLOGICAL).

Creation and Other Religious Views. If one allows the biblical view of creation into science, it is said, the Islamic, Buddhist, Hindu, and other religious views must be allowed in as well. But scientific creationism is not a *religious* point of view; it is a *scientific* view which appeals only to scientific evidence to support its conclusions. Simply because the idea for a scientific view comes from a religious book does not mean that the view is religious. As noted above, the *source* of many scientific views was religious, but the *nature* of the view was not. The implication that allowing creation to be taught alongside evolution would allow an endless number of other views of origin is not the case. Basically, there are two explanations of events of origin: Either the universe had an intelligent cause or a non-intelligent cause. Either the cause is natural or supernatural. All views of origin, whether *Buddhist, *Hindu, *Islamic, or Judeo-Christian, fall into one of these two broad categories. Whether the Cause of the Universe is "God" or is to be worshiped or how to do so, are religious questions and do not come under the purview of origin science.

*Aristotle posited an Unmoved Mover (an Uncaused Cause), but he never considered it an object of religious devotion. It was simply a rational explanation for what he observed in the world.

Sources

F. Bacon, *Novum Organum*
P. Davis, et al., *Of Pandas and People*
N, L. Geisler, *Knowing the Truth about Creation*
———, et al., *Origin Science*
D. Hume, *An Enquiry Concerning Human Understanding*
———, *The Letters of David Hume*
P. Johnson, *Reason in the Balance*
J. P. Moreland, ed., *The Creation Hypothesis*
———, *Creation and the Nature of Science*
C. Thoxton, *The Mystery of Life's Origin* (Epilogue)
———, *The Soul of Science*

Orr, James. James Orr (1844–1913) was a Scottish theologian and apologist. He attended the University of Glasgow and ministered in the United Presbyterian Church in Hawick (1874–91). He taught at the United Presbyterian Theological College (1891–1901) and thereafter at the United Free Church College in Glasgow. Orr was widely read in Europe and North America. His wide knowledge, prolific pen, and penetrating analysis endeared him to embattled evangelicals during the ascendancy of classic liberalism.

Orr's early work on apologetics was his most enduring. *Christian View of God and the World* (1893) was a standard reference into the 1950s. Orr was one of the earliest British critics of liberal theologian Albrecht Ritschl (1822–1889) in his *The Ritschlian Theology and the Evangelical Faith* (1897). He defended essential Mosaic authorship of the Pentateuch (*see* PENTATEUCH, MOSAIC AUTHORSHIP OF) against the attacks of Julius Wellhausen. Although he was willing to accommodate some facets of biological evolution (*see* EVOLUTION), his work *God's Image* (1905) stressed the need to acknowledge supernatural creation of the human soul. In *God's Image in Man* (1910), he argued that moral evolution undermined the seriousness of human depravity.

Orr's apologetic approach was distinctive. In *The Progress of Dogma* (1901), he countered Adolf Harnack (1851–1930) and his attack on the history of dogma by showing the inner logic of the development of orthodoxy. *The *Virgin Birth of Christ* (1907) and *Revelation and Inspiration* (1910) were significant contributions. Another enduring work was Orr's editorship of the *International Standard Bible Encyclopedia* (1915). Orr also wrote articles for the twelve-volume defense of conservative theology, *The Fundamentals* (1910–15).

Sources

G. G. Scorgie, *A Call for Continuity: The Theological Contribution of James Orr*
———, "Orr, James," in S. B. Ferguson, et al., eds., *New Dictionary of Theology*
P. Toon, *The Development of Doctrine in the Church*

Pp

Paine, Thomas. Thomas Paine (1737–1809) was among the most militant *deists in early America. His political writings, such as *Common Sense* (1776) and *The Rights of Man* (1791–92), were greatly influenced by his deistic beliefs. Paine's thought was influential in both the American and French revolutions. But his importance does not end there. In his work *The Age of Reason* (1794–95) Paine set forth his defense of deism in such a way as to make it readable to all people. Believing that republicanism and egalitarianism were threatened by church leaders, Paine wrote *The Age of Reason* to destroy all claims to supernatural revelation and so discredit the clergy (Morias, 120–22).

View of God. "I believe in one God, and no more," wrote Paine. Like *theists, Paine believed that the one God was all-powerful, all-knowing, all-good, infinite, merciful, just, and incomprehensible (*Complete Works of Thomas Paine,* 5, 26, 27, 201). But unlike Christian theists Paine maintained that the only way to discover such a God is "by the exercise of reason." He rejected all forms of supernatural revelation, believing them to be unknowable. He claimed that "revelation when applied to religion, means something communicated *immediately* from God to man." Consequently he disavowed even revelations to other people as having prescriptive authority. What was revealed to a person was revealed to that person only. It is hearsay to anyone else, and, consequently, they are not obliged to believe it (ibid., 26, 7). Hence, although "No man will deny or dispute the power of the Almighty to make such a communication, if he pleases," such a revelation could only be knowable to the person who received it directly from God (ibid.).

Paine also argued that supernatural revelation (*see* Revelation, Special) was impossible given the inadequacy of human language to convey it. God's revelation must be absolutely "unchangeable and universal" (ibid., 25). Human language could not be the means for its communication. The changes in the meaning of words, the necessity of translation to other languages, the errors of translators, copyists, and printers, and the possibility of willful alteration all show that no human language can be the vehicle of the Word of God (ibid., 19; cf. 55, 56). Thus Paine rejected all claims to a verbal or written revelation from God. All such beliefs were "human inventions, set up to terrify and enslave mankind, and monopolize power and profit" (ibid., 6). The "revealed religion" he had the most contempt for was Christianity. He summarized his feelings:

> Of all the systems of religion that ever were invented, there is none more derogatory to the Almighty, more unedifying to man, more repugnant to reason, and more contradictory in itself, than this thing called Christianity. Too absurd for belief, too impossible to convince, and too inconsistent for practice, it renders the heart torpid, or produces only atheists and fanatics. As an engine of power, it serves the purpose of despotism; and as a means of wealth, the avarice of priests; but so far as respects the good of man in general, it leads to nothing here or hereafter. [ibid., 150]

"The only religion," added Paine, "that has not been invented, and that has in it every evidence of divine originality, is pure and simple deism." In fact, deism "must have been the first, and will probably be the last that man believes" (ibid.).

Creation. Paine believed that the universe was brought into existence by God and is sustained in existence by him. God created "millions of worlds" and they were all inhabited by intelligent creatures who "enjoy the same opportunities of knowledge as we do." One reason God created all these worlds was so that the "devotional gratitude" and "admiration" of his creatures would be called forth in their contemplation of these worlds (ibid., 46, 47).

"THE WORD OF GOD IS THE CREATION WE BEHOLD: And it is in *this word,* which no human invention can counterfeit or alter, that God speaketh universally to man." (*see* Revelation, General) The universe reveals all that is necessary to know of God. Through it we can know that God exists, what God is like, and what God expects (ibid., 24, 26, 309; emphasis Paine's).

The universe reveals the existence of God. It is evident that the things which constituted the universe could not have made themselves (*see* Cosmological Argument). There must be "a first cause eternally existing, of a nature totally different to any material existence we know of, and by the power of which all things exist; and this first cause, man calls God" (ibid., 26; cf. 28). Paine also argued from motion. Since the universe consists of matter that cannot move itself, the origin of the rotation of the planets is impossible unless there exists an external first cause which set them in motion. This First Cause must be God (Aldridge, 6:17). He also argued from design (*see* Teleological Argument). Since the "work of man's hands is a proof of the existence of man," and since a watch is "positive evidence of the existence of a watch-maker," then "in like manner the creation is evidence to our reason and our senses of the existence of a Creator" (*Complete Works*, 310). The world also reveals what God is like:

> Do we want to contemplate His power? We see it in the immensity of His creation. Do we want to contemplate His wisdom? We see it in the unchangeable order by which the incomprehensible whole is governed. Do we want to contemplate His munificence? We see it in the abundance with which He fills the earth. Do we want to contemplate His mercy? We see it in His not withholding that abundance even from the unthankful. Do we want to contemplate His will, so far as it respects man? The goodness He shows to all, is a lesson for our conduct to each other. [ibid., 201]

Whatever one needs to know, is available to the human mind by consulting "the scripture called the Creation" (ibid.).

Human Beings. According to Paine, a human being is a rational, personal, and free being. He maintained a belief in the "equality of man" and in the religious duties of each person to do justly, love mercy, and promote the happiness of fellow creatures" (ibid., 5, 41, 309). Paine adamantly denied that the human race was in rebellion against God and in need of salvation. As he stated it, humanity "stands in the same relative condition with his Maker [that] he ever did stand, since man existed, and . . . it is his greatest consolation to think so" (ibid., 24).

As for *immortality, Paine could simply say, "I hope for happiness beyond this life" (*Age of Reason*, 1.3). He added, "I trouble not myself about the manner of future existence. I content myself with believing, even to positive conviction, that the Power that gave me existence is able to continue it, in any form and manner he pleases, either with or without this body. . . . It appears more probable to me that I shall continue to exist hereafter than I should have had existence, as I now have, before that existence began" (ibid., 58).

Paine believed that morally good people would be happy in the afterlife and morally wicked people would be punished. Those who were neither particularly good or bad but indifferent would be "dropped entirely" (*Complete Works*, 5, 56).

Evil. Nowhere did Paine attempt to reconcile the presence of evil with the deistic concept of God (*see* Evil, Problem of). Indeed, the only evil he even seemed to notice was that caused by social injustice and that brought about by "revealed religion." The former could be dealt with largely on a political level. The latter, which made up the greatest class of evils, could be best prevented by not admitting "of any other revelation than that which is manifested in the book of creation," and by considering every other so-called "word of God" as "fable and imposition" (ibid., 37).

Ethics. Paine summarized the heart of his ethical beliefs as follows:

> the moral goodness and beneficence of God manifested in the creation towards all his creatures; that, seeing, as we daily do, the goodness of God to all men, it is an example calling upon all men to practice the same towards each other; and, consequently, that everything of persecution and revenge between man and man, and everything of cruelty to animals, is a violation of moral duty. [ibid., 56]

If each person was "impressed as fully and as strongly as he ought to be with the belief of a God, his moral life would be regulated by the force of that belief." Humankind "would stand in awe of God, and of himself, and would not do the thing that would not be concealed from either." On the other hand, "It is by forgetting God in his works, and running after the books of pretended revelation that man has wandered from the straight path of duty and happiness, and become by turns the victim of doubt and the dupe of delusion" (ibid., 150, 309).

The Bible and Miracles. Paine wrote no view on history or destiny. However, he was sure that the Bible was historically unreliable (*see* New Testament, Historicity of) and filled with errors (*see* Bible, Alleged Errors in). He ridiculed and considered mythical any biblical stories touching on the supernatural (*see* Mythology and the New Testament). He contended that the traditional ascriptions of authorship to practically every book in the Bible were wrong and that most were written quite later than traditionally believed. He argued that the entire New Testament was written (*see* New Testament, Dating of) "more than three hundred years after the time that Christ is said to have lived" (ibid., 9–12, 15, 19, 20, 21, 53, 61–131, 133).

Paine did not believe that supernatural acts of God had ever occurred in history (*see* MIRACLES, ARGUMENTS AGAINST). Accepting the laws of nature as prescriptions for how nature "is supposed to act," he defined a miracle as "something contrary to the operation and effect of those laws." But he added that "unless we know the whole extent of those laws, and . . . the powers of nature, we are not able to judge whether anything that may appear to us wonderful or miraculous be within, or be beyond, or be contrary to, her natural power of acting." Hence, our limited knowledge of nature leaves us with "no positive criterion to determine what a miracle is, and mankind, in giving credit to appearances under the idea of there being miracles are subject to be continually imposed upon." As a consequence of these considerations "nothing can be more inconsistent than to suppose that the Almighty would make use of means such as are called miracles." It is far more likely ("millions to one") that the reporter would lie than that nature would change. "We have never seen, in our time, nature go out of her course, but we have good reason to believe that millions of lies have been told in the same time" (ibid., 51–53).

Evaluation. The basic elements of Paine's views are evaluated elsewhere. See the articles BIBLE, ALLEGED ERRORS IN; BIBLE, EVIDENCE FOR; DEISM; HELL; MIRACLES, ARGUMENTS AGAINST, and NEW TESTAMENT, HISTORICITY OF.

Sources

A. O. Aldridge, "Paine, Thomas," in *EP*

R. Flint, *Anti-Theistic Theories*

N. L. Geisler, *Christian Apologetics*

——— and W. Watkins, *Worlds Apart: A Handbook on World Views*

I. Kant, *Religion within the Limits of Reason Alone*

J. LeLand, *A View of the Principal Deistic Writers . . .*

C. S. Lewis, *Christian Reflections*

———, *Miracles: A Preliminary Study*

J. G. Machen, *The Virgin Birth of Christ*

H. M. Morais, *Deism in Eighteenth Century America*

J. Orr, *English Deism: Its Roots and Its Fruits*

T. Paine, *Common Sense*

———, *Complete Works of Thomas Paine*

———, *The Age of Reason*, Parts 1 and 2

———, *The Rights of Man*

M. Tindal, *Christianity as Old as the Creation . . .*

Paley, William. William Paley (1743–1805), English apologist, entered Cambridge (1759) to study mathematics. After being ordained to the priesthood (1767) he taught at Cambridge for nine years. He rose to be archdeacon of Carlisle. He wrote three major books, *The Principles of Moral and Political Philosophy* (1785), *A View of the Evidences of Christianity* (1794), and *Natural Theology; or, Evidences of the Existence and Attributes of the Deity* (1802). As late as 1831, while studying for his B.A. examinations at Cambridge, Charles *Darwin studied, and was deeply impressed by, Paley's *Evidences*.

Paley's Apologetics. Paley was a classical apologist (*see* CLASSICAL APOLOGETICS). His two books in the area cover the two central areas of traditional apologetics, the existence of God *(Natural Theology)* and the truth of Christianity *(Evidences)*.

Argument for God's Existence. Paley offered what has become the classic formulation of the *teleological argument. It is based on the watch analogy: If one found a watch in an empty field, one would rightly conclude that it had a maker because of its obvious design. Likewise, when one looks at the even more complex design of the world in which we live, one cannot but conclude that there is a great Designer behind it.

In Paley's words, "In crossing a heath, suppose I pitched my foot against a *stone* and was asked how the stone came to be there, I might possibly answer that for anything I knew to the contrary it had lain there forever . . ." But "suppose I had found a *watch* upon the ground, and it should be inquired how the watch happened to be in that place, I should hardly think of the answer which I had given before, that for anything I knew the watch might have always been there." He asks, "why is it not as admissible in the second case as in the first? For this reason, and for no other, namely, that when we come to inspect the watch, we perceive—what we could not discover in the stone—that its several parts are framed and put together for a purpose . . ." (Paley, 3). Paley shows that the contrivances in nature are more incredible than those in a watch. He is careful to root his argument in observation, saying repeatedly, "We observe . . . ," "These observations . . . ," and "Our observer . . ." (Paley, *Evidences* 10, 11, 16, 17, 20, 29).

The reasoning goes: A watch shows that it was put together for an intelligent purpose (to keep time). It has a spring to give it motion. A series of wheels transmits this motion, made of brass so that they do not rust. The spring is made of resilient steel. The front cover is glass so that one can see through it. All this is evidence of intelligent design.

But the world shows greater evidence of design than a watch. It is a greater work of art than a watch. It has an endless variety of means adapted to ends. The human eye alone would suffice to demonstrate intelligent design in nature. Paley ransacked Kiell's *Anatomy* for illustrations of adaptations of means to end in nature, including the bones and muscles of human beings and their equivalents in the animal world.

Paley argued that there must be only one Designer, since there is manifest in nature a uniformity of divine purpose in all parts of the world. This intelligent (personal) Creator is also good, as evidenced from the fact that most contrivances are beneficial and by the fact that pleasure is provided as an animal sensation.

Paley added that an infinite regress of causes is not plausible (*see* INFINITE SERIES). For "a chain composed of an infinite number of links can no more support itself than a chain composed of a finite number of links." This is so "because, by increasing the number of links, from ten, for instance, to a hundred, from a hundred to a thousand, etc., we make not the smallest approach; we observe not the smallest tendency toward self-support" (Paley, 9–10).

An updated version of Paley's argument might go something like this: In crossing a valley, suppose I come upon a round stratified stone and were asked how it came to be such. I might plausibly answer that it was once laid down by water in layers which later solidified by chemical action. One day it broke from a larger section of rock and was subsequently rounded by the natural erosion processes of tumbling in water. I come upon Mount Rushmore with its granite forms of four human faces. Here are obvious signs of intelligent production, not the result of natural processes. Yet why should a natural cause serve for the stone but not for the faces? When we inspect the faces on the mountain we perceive what we could not discover in the stone—that they manifest intelligent contrivance. They convey specifically complex information. The stone, on the other hand, has redundant patterns or strata easily explainable by the observed process of sedimentation. But the faces have sharply defined, complex features. Experience leads us to conclude that such shapes only occur when made by intelligent artisans (see Geisler, *Origin Science,* 159).

Evidences for the Truth. Paley was aware that miracles (*see* MIRACLE) are essential to the certification of the Christian revelation (*see* MIRACLES, APOLOGETIC VALUE OF). He accepted David *Hume's contention that the credibility of miracles depends on the reliability of witnesses. The witnesses for Christianity, he argued, are known to be reliable since they persisted in their report even under the risk of persecution and the threat of death. He rejected other wonders that could be reduced to false perceptions, exaggeration, or that were important to the self-interest of the one claiming them.

Paley rejected Hume's contention that universal experience testified against miracles. This, he held, begged the question, since miracles by definition must be an exception to universal occurrence. The real issue is whether there are reliable witnesses.

Evaluation. Paley is one of the great apologists of the late eighteenth and early nineteenth century. Indeed, his influence continues. Paley used the core arguments. He stressed the evidence to establish the classic arguments. Two disciples, F. R. Tennant and A. E. Taylor (*see* TELEOLOGICAL ARGUMENT), carried on his version of the teleological argument. Recently Paley's thought has been the subject of a revival through the development of the anthropic principle.

Hume's Critique. It is widely believed that *Hume answered Paley's teleological argument in advance. Hume's first objection assumes design in the universe but argues by analogy that finite human designers cooperate to build great works, using trial and error or a long period of time (see Hume). Paley explicitly addressed this point in his argument that the entire world reveals one unified plan—a fact indicative of a single Intelligence.

The second argument of Hume shifted the ground by arguing that the design is only apparent. The adaptation of means to ends may result from chance. He insists that if one grants that the universe of matter in motion is eternal, then in an infinity of chance operations every combination will be realized. Thus, there is no need to posit an intelligent cause (ibid.).

Not only did Paley respond to this objection, but he used Hume's principle of uniformity to disprove Hume's contention that it is reasonable to postulate a natural cause for the manifest contrivances of nature. For Paley argued, following Hume, that "uniform experience" reveals that only an intelligent cause can produce the kinds of effects we see in nature. Paley wrote:

"Wherever we see the marks of contrivance, we are led for its cause to an *intelligent* author. And this transition of the understanding is founded upon *uniform experience.*" Intelligence, Paley said, can be distinguished by certain properties, such as an ultimate purpose, intimate relationship of the parts to one another, and complex cooperation of parts to serve a common purpose. (*Natural Theology*, 37). Uniform experiences (which Hume was even willing to call a "proof") argues against any natural causes of the kinds of effects we see throughout nature. In fact, the only kind of cause known by repeated, uniform experience (which is Hume's basis for knowing a causal connection) is an intelligent cause.

Thus, Hume's argument against design actually boomerangs into an argument for a Designer (*see* TELEOLOGICAL ARGUMENT).

Conclusion. Paley's arguments for God and for Christianity still provide the backbone for much of contemporary apologetics. The only major difference is that we now have much more "meat" to put on the skeleton. With the discovery of evidence for an origin of the universe (*see* BIG BANG), Hume's infinite time has been scientifically eliminated. With the discovery of the anthropic principle it is evident that there is only one supernatural Mind behind the universe from the moment of its inception. Microbiology, with the incredible complexity of the DNA molecule (*see* EVOLUTION, CHEMICAL) adds dimensions of specified complexity and intelligent contrivance to Paley's argument that he never could have imagined.

Sources

M. L. Clarke, *Paley: Evidence for the Man*
N. L. Geisler, et al., *Origin Science*
———, *Philosophy of Religion*
———, *When Skeptics Ask*
D. Hume, *Dialogues Concerning Natural Religion*
D. L. LeMahieu, *The Mind of William Paley*
G. W. Meadley, *Memoirs of William Paley*
W. Paley, *A View of the Evidences of Christianity*
———, *Natural Theology;* or, *Evidences of the Existence and Attributes of the Deity*
F. R. Tennant, *Philosophical Theology*

Panentheism. *Panentheism* is not to be confused with *pantheism*. Pantheism literally means all ("pan") is God ("theism"), but panentheism means "all *in* God." It is also called *process theology* (since it views God as a changing Being), *bipolar theism* (since it believes God has two poles), *organicism* (since it views all that actually is as a gigantic organism), and *neoclassical theism* (because it believes God is finite and temporal, in contrast to classical theism).

Differences between theism and panentheism can be summarized:

Theism	Panentheism
God is Creator.	God is director.
Creation is ex nihilo.	Creation is ex materia.
God is sovereign over world.	God is working with world.
God is independent of world.	God is dependent on world.
God is unchanging.	God is changing.
God is absolutely perfect.	God is growing more perfect.
God is monopolar.	God is bipolar.
God is actually infinite.	God is actually finite.

Rather than viewing God as the infinite, unchanging sovereign Creator of the world who brought it into existence, panentheists think of God as a finite, changing, director of world affairs who works in cooperation with the world in order to achieve greater perfection in his nature.

*Theism views God's relation to the world as a painter to a painting. The painter exists independently of the painting; he brought the painting into existence, and yet his mind is expressed in the painting. By contrast, the panentheist views God's relation to the world the way a mind is related to a body. Indeed, they believe the world is God's "body" (one pole) and the "mind" is the other pole. This is why the term *bipolar* is used. However, like some modern materialists who believe the mind is dependent on the brain, panentheists believe God is dependent on the world. Yet there is a reciprocal dependence, a sense in which the world is dependent on God.

Variations on Panentheism. All panentheists agree that God has two poles, an actual pole (the world) and a potential pole (beyond the world). All agree that God is changing, finite, and temporal in his actual pole. And all agree that his potential pole is unchanging and eternal.

The major difference in how they view God is whether God in his actual pole is one actual entity (event) or a society of actual entities. Alfred North *Whitehead (1861–1947) holds the former view, and Charles Hartshorne holds the latter.

Most other differences are primarily methodological. Whitehead's approach is more empirical, while Hartshorne's is more rational. Hence, Whitehead has a kind of teleological argument for God, whereas Hartshorne is famous for his ontological argument. Some panentheists, such as John Cobb, reject the disjunction between the two poles in God. He claims that God acts as a unity, not simply in one pole or the other. But all agree that God has two poles which can be diagrammed:

Primordial Nature	Consequent Nature
potential pole	actual pole
eternal	temporal
absolute	relative
unchanging	changing
imperishable	perishable
unlimited	limited
conceptual	physical
abstract	concrete
necessary	contingent
eternal objects	actual entities
unconscious drive	conscious realization

Representatives of Panentheism. There were many forerunners of a process view of God. *Plato's (428–348 B.C.) Demiurgos eternally struggled with the chaos to form it into the cosmos. This provided the dualistic (*see* DUALISM) background for God's two "poles." Even earlier (ca. 500 B.C.), Heraclitus's flux philosophy asserted that the world is a constantly changing process.

In the modern world, G. W. F. *Hegel's (1770–1831) progressive unfolding of God in the world process took a significant step toward a Panentheism. In the Cosmic Evolutionism of Herbert Spencer (1820–1903) the universe is viewed as an unfolding and developing process. Henri Bergson (1851–1941) then proposed a creative evolution (1907) of a life force *(elan vital)* which drives evolution forward in "leaps." Later he identified this Force with God (1935). Even before this, Samuel Alexander's *Space, Time and Deity* (1920) pioneered a process view of God's relation to the temporal universe. The main fountainhead of panentheism, however, is Whitehead. His influence is manifest in Hartshorne, Schubert Ogden, Cobb, and others.

Basic Beliefs of Panentheism. Although there are intramural differences among panentheists, their basic worldview has the same essential elements. Elements included are:

The Nature of God. All panentheists agree that God has two poles. The consequent or concrete pole is God in reality. It is God as he actually is in his moment-by-moment existence. It is God in the actual particulars of his becoming. In this pole God is finite, relative, dependent, contingent, and in process. God's other pole is the primordial or abstract one. This is God in abstraction, what is common and constant in God's character no matter what world exists. The divine abstract pole gives a mere outline of God's existence without filling it out with concrete or particular content. In this pole God is infinite, absolute, independent, necessary, and immutable.

Panentheists agree that God's abstract pole is included in his concrete pole. His becoming or process characterizes all of reality. But this reality of God is not to be thought of as being, which is static and uncreative. Creativity pervades all that exists. And God is supremely creative.

God is also viewed as personal. There is disagreement over whether he is one actual entity (as in Whitehead) or an ordered series of actual entities (as in Hartshorne). But almost all panentheists believe that God is personal.

Nature of the Universe. The universe is characterized by process, change, or becoming. This is so because it is constituted by a multitude of self-creative creatures that are constantly introducing change and novelty into the universe. Also, the universe is eternal. This does not necessarily mean that the present universe is eternal. Rather it could mean that there have been many universes throughout the infinite past. Some world has existed in some form always and some world in some form will always exist into the infinite future. Lastly, all panentheists reject the traditional theistic understanding of creation out of nothing, that is, *ex nihilo* (*see* CREATION, VIEWS OF). Some, including Ogden, accept the phrase *ex nihilo* but reinterpret creation to mean only that the present world or world-state once was not and was created out of a previous world. Others (like Whitehead and Hartshorne) reject even the notion of creation *ex nihilo* and affirm creation *ex materia* (out of preexistent material). Of course, since the material is really God's physical pole, so creation is also *ex deo.* In fact, the present universe is cocreated by God and man out of the preexisting "stuff." God, of course, is the prime Transformer or Shaper of each world and of each world-state.

Relation of God to Universe. In a panentheistic worldview, God's consequent pole is the world. This does not mean that God and the world are identical, for God is more than the world, and the individuals that make up the world are distinct from God. It does mean, however, that the world is God's cosmic body and that those creatures who make up the world are like cells in his body. This is why God cannot exist without some kind of physical universe. He does not need this world, but he must coexist in *some* world. Similarly, the world cannot exist without God. Hence the world and God are mutually dependent. Moreover, the creatures in the universe contribute value to God's life. The inclusive aim or goal of all creatures is to enrich God's happiness and thus help him fulfill what he lacks.

Miracles. An implication of panentheism is that supernatural acts are impossible (*see* MIRACLES, ARGUMENTS AGAINST). Since the world is the body of God there is nothing apart from God that can be broken into or interrupted. Indeed, God is largely a passive recipient of his creatures' activity rather than an active force in the world. God is a cosmic Sympathizer rather than a cosmic Activist (*see* FINITE GODISM; KUSHNER, HAROLD). Consequently miraculous intervention in the world is out of character with the nature of the panentheistic God. Many panentheists reject miracles because the contemporary scientific view of the world rules them out. Ogden takes this stance. This is one reason why he adopts Rudolph Bultmann's program to demythologize the miracle stories recorded in the Bible (*see* MYTHOLOGY AND THE NEW TESTAMENT).

Human Beings. Panentheists agree that humanity is personal and free. In fact, humanity as a whole is a co-creator with God and of God. He not only helps decide the course of human and world events but also those of God. Human identity is not found in some enduring "I" or self. Rather, like the rest of the world, identity is found only in the events or actual occasions of history in which humanity is becoming. The human being is partially creating himself or herself in every decision and act each moment. The goal is to serve God by contributing value to his ever growing experience.

Ethics. Many panentheists believe that there are no absolute values (*see* MORALITY, ABSOLUTE NATURE OF). Since God and the world are in great flux, there can be no absolute, unchanging standard of value. On the other hand, such panentheists as Hartshorne contend that there is a universal basis for ethics, namely, beauty, harmony, and intensity. Anything that promotes or builds upon or acts from this basis is good; anything that does not do so is evil. But even granting this universal aesthetic foundation, specific ethical commands or rules are not universal. Though in general one should promote beauty and not ugliness, exactly how this should be done is relative. Therefore, even though there may be an ultimate basis or ground for ethics, values themselves are not absolute but relative.

Human Destiny. The destiny of humanity is not to be looked for in an actual heaven or hell or a conscious afterlife (*see* IMMORTALITY). Rather, human beings, like all of God's creatures, will live forever only in God's cosmic memory. A person who contributes richly to God's life, will have the satisfaction of knowing that God will fondly remember him or her forever. Those who live without contributing much value to God, who, in other words, live unfaithfully, will not be remembered with much fondness by God.

In panentheism an ongoing evolutionary process helps move events forever forward. God and humanity are also seen as co-creators of history. However, unlike theism, there is no ultimate end of history. There will always be the unsurpassable deity who is constantly growing in perfection. And there will always be some world filled with self-creative creatures whose inclusive aim is to enrich the experience of God. History has no beginning and it has no end. There is no ultimate destiny, utopia, eschaton, or end. History, as everything else, has always been, is coming to be now, and will always be in process. History is not going anywhere, it is just going on.

Evaluation. *Contributions of Panentheism.* Panentheists seek a comprehensive view of reality. They recognize that a piecemeal understanding of things is inadequate. Instead they have sought to develop a coherent and reasonable view of all that exists, a complete worldview.

Panentheism manages to posit an intimate relation between God and the world without destroying that relation, as does pantheism. God is *in* the world but not identical to it. The presence of God in the universe does not destroy the multiplicity that humans experience, but rather preserves it and even bestows upon it purpose and meaning. Granting the existence of a supreme Being, panentheists show that the world must depend upon God for its origin and continuation. Unless God exists, the world could not continue to exist. They insist that there must be an adequate cause to account for the world.

Panentheists seriously relate their worldview to contemporary theories of science. Whatever worldview one holds, science cannot be ignored. Valid human discoveries in any field or discipline must be incorporated into one's worldview. If reality is truly reasonable and noncontradictory, then all of knowledge can be consistently systematized, no matter who discovers it or where it is found. Panentheists take this to heart.

Criticisms of Panentheism. Some of the more important criticisms will be noted here.

The idea of a God who is both infinite and finite, necessary and contingent, absolute and relative, is contradictory. A contradiction results when opposites are affirmed of the same thing at the same time and in the same manner or respect. For example, to say that a bucket is both filled with water and not filled with water at the same time and in the same respect is contradictory. Such a thing could never occur, for it is logically impossible.

Hartshorne has responded to the charge of contradiction by pointing out that the metaphysical contraries are not attributed to the same divine pole. Rather those attributes that belong together, such as infinity and necessity, are applied to one pole while the other attributes that belong together, such as finitude and contingency, are applied to a different pole. Infinity and finitude, necessity and contingency, though applied to the same being at the same time, are applied to the appropriate poles in God (Hartshorne, *Man's Vision of God,* 22–24). The Christian theist, H. P. Owen, has responded that there seems to be no real distinction between the two divine poles. Since the abstract pole has no concrete or actual existence, then it must be a mere idea, having mental reality but no existence (Owen, 105). Therefore God must not really be infinite, and necessary, for those attributes are in the potential pole that does not exist in reality. God in reality is only finite and contingent. Or God must be both sides of the metaphysical contraries at the same time and in the same pole. The first option makes panentheism's doctrine of God meaningless, and the second makes it contradictory. In either event the bipolar concept of God is incoherent.

The idea of God as a self-caused being is contradictory. It is difficult to see how any being could cause itself to exist. To think this could occur is to believe that potentials can actualize themselves. Cups could fill themselves with coffee and steel could make itself into a skyscraper. How could a being exist prior to itself in order to bring itself into existence? This is what a self-caused being would have to do in order to exist. A panentheist might respond that God did not bring himself into existence; he has eternally existed. Rather, the panentheistic version of a self-caused God creates his becoming. That is, God produces changes in himself. God actualizes his own potentials for growth.

But this leads to another problem. If God causes his own becoming and not his own being, then what or who sustains God in existence? How can a being change without there existing an unchanging being that grounds the changing being's existence? Everything cannot be in flux. Whatever changes passes from potentiality to actuality, from what it is not to what is. Such change could not actualize itself or be self-caused, for potentials are not yet the something they have the potential to be.

Nothing cannot produce something. Neither could such changes be uncaused, for there must be a cause for every effect or event (*see* CAUSALITY, PRINCIPLE OF). It seems, therefore, that the universe of change, which is the concrete pole of God, must be caused by something that does not change. Something outside of the changing order must sustain the entire order in existence. Therefore there must be a being other than what the process philosopher views as "God" that sustains him in existence. If this is true, then the panentheistic God is not really God, but the Being that grounds him is really God. Such a God is not an immutable-mutable being, as is the process deity, but would have to be simply immutable.

Another aspect of this problem is that the panentheist knows that everything, including God, is relative and changing. How can anyone know that something is changing when there is no stable reference point by which to measure the change? The theist has God and his absolute, unchanging character and will. The panentheist has no such standard. A panentheist could answer that his unchanging measure is the immutable primordial nature of God. But this does not seem adequate. For God's primordial pole is only an abstraction—it has no reality. It can be a conceptual measure, but not an actual one. Besides, a panentheist who says that God is immutable means that God is immutably mutable—He cannot fail to always change and always change for the better (Hartshorne, *Natural Theology,* 110, 276). Hence we seem to be back where we started, with everything changing and nothing that is being changed.

The panentheistic concept of personhood appears to conflict with our experience of ourselves. We, at least, believe ourselves to be personal beings who, to some degree, endure change. Most of us do not believe that we become new persons each moment we exist. In fact, to even say that "I become a new person each moment I exist" assumes that there is something that endures, the "I" to whom the changes occur. Otherwise, what changes? If nothing endures from moment to moment, then can it really be said that anything changes? If there is no sense in which the self is a continuous identity, then it appears that we can only speak of a series of unrelated actual "I" occasions (ibid., 58). And the only thing that can be said to change in that series of "I's" is the series itself, not each individual "I" in the series. This seems to destroy self-identity and to contradict human experience. This problem is particularly acute for Hartshorne. In accord with his view, one goes out of existence every time there is a moment with no conscious "I." That would include periods of sleep or under anesthesia or other moments of lapsed consciousness. A parent awakening a child from sleep would actually call the young one back into existence.

To say with the panentheist that some world or other must have always existed begs the question. Of course it is impossible that total nothingness could ever be experienced, for no one could be there to experience it. Otherwise it would not be *total* nothingness. But this presupposes that only what can be experienced can be true. Why should this criteria for truth be accepted? Hartshorne implies that it should be accepted because there can be no meaning without experience (ibid.). Thus a concept that cannot be experienced must be meaningless. But if this is so then Hartshorne seems to have won his case by definition. For if there can be no meaning without experience, then total nonbeing, which cannot be experienced, must be meaningless. Hartshorne has established his case by defining meaning in such a way that makes total nonbeing a meaningless concept. He has not proved the meaninglessness of "nothing exists" but only assumed it, which is question-begging.

Even if Hartshorne can establish that total nothingness is not possible, the panentheistic view does not follow. For this would simply be a way of saying that everything cannot be contingent. But this leads naturally to a theistic position (*see* THEISM) in which there must be a Necessary Being beyond the contingent world. It is not necessary to conclude that panentheism is true, simply because a total state of nothingness is not possible.

If the proposition "Nothing exists." is logically possible, then the existence of Hartshorne's and Ogden's God is tenuous. Such a God must keep the universe rolling and change universes quickly, or he poofs out of the picture. He is tied as with an umbilical cord to some world. But if it is logically possible that "some world exists" has not always been true, then it is logically possible that "God exists" has at some time been false. But, according to Hartshorne and Ogden, if God is not logically necessary, a necessary being that must always exist no matter what, then the existence of God must be logically impossible. By this rule the God of Hartshorne and Ogden is necessarily false.

Process theology faces a serious dilemma (Gruenler, 75–79). God comprehends the whole universe at one time, yet God is limited to space and time. But anything limited to space and time cannot think any faster than the speed of light, which takes billions of years to cross the universe at about 186,000 miles a second. However, there seems to be no way that a mind which takes this kind of time to think its way around the universe could simultaneously comprehend and direct the whole universe. On the other hand, if God's mind does transcend the universe of space and time and instantly and simultaneously comprehend the whole, then this is not a panentheistic view of God but a theistic view.

Sources

N. L. Geisler, "Process Theology," in *Tensions in Contemporary Theology*

——— and W. Watkins, *Worlds Apart: A Handbook on World Views*
R. G. Gruenler, *The Inexhaustible God: Biblical Faith and the Challenge of Process Theism*
C. Hartshorne, *A Natural Theology for Our Time*
———, *Man's Vision of God*
———, *The Logic of Perfection*
S. M. Ogden, *The Reality of God*
———, *Theology in Crisis: A Colloquium on The Credibility of "God"*
———, "Toward a New Theism," in *Process Philosophy and Christian Thought*
H. P. Owen, *The Christian Knowledge of God*
W. E. Stokes, "A Whiteheadian Reflection on God's Relation to the World," in *Process Theology*
Thomas Aquinas, *Summa Theologica*
A. N. Whitehead, *Adventures of Ideas*
———, *Modes of Thought*
———, *Process and Reality*

Pantheism. *Pantheism* means all ("pan") is God ("theism"). It is the worldview held by most *Hindus, many *Buddhists, and other New Age religions. It is also the worldview of Christian Science, Unity, and Scientology.

According to pantheism, God "is all in all." God pervades all things, contains all things, subsumes all things, and is found within all things. Nothing exists apart from God, and all things are in some way identified with God. The world is God, and God is the world. But more precisely, in pantheism all is God, and God is all.

Pantheism has a long history in both the East and the West. From the Eastern mysticism of Hindu sages and seers to the rationalism of such Western philosophers as Parmenides, Benedict *Spinoza, and G. W. F. *Hegel, pantheism has always had advocates.

Kinds of Pantheism. There are differing types of belief within pantheism. An *absolute* pantheism is represented by the thought of the fifth-century B.C. Greek philosopher Parmenides and the Vedanta school of Hinduism (*see* HINDUISM, VEDANTA). Absolute pantheism teaches that there is only one being in the world, God, and that all else that appears to exist actually does not. Another type is *emanational* pantheism, which was set forth by the third century A.D. philosopher, *Plotinus. According to this view, everything flows from God in the same way a flower unfolds from a seed. There is also the *developmental* pantheism of Hegel (1770–1831). Hegel viewed the events of history as the unfolding manifestations of Absolute Spirit. The *modal* pantheism of the seventeenth-century rationalist Spinoza argued that there is only one absolute substance in which all finite things are merely modes or moments. The *multilevel* pantheism is found in some forms of Hinduism, especially as expressed by Radhakrishnan. This view sees various levels of manifestation of God, with the highest level manifesting God as the Absolute One, and lower levels showing him in increasing multiplicity. *Permeational* pantheism is the view popularized by the *Star Wars* movies of George Lucas, in which the Force (Tao) penetrates all things. This belief is found in Zen Buddhism.

Basic Beliefs. There are other types of pantheism, but these lay out the worldview's commonalities. Each of these types identifies God with the world, but they vary in the conception of this identity. All pantheists believe that God and the real world are one, but they differ as to how God and the world are united. The following are basic beliefs of a pantheistic worldview.

Nature of God. God and reality are ultimately impersonal. Personality, consciousness, and intellect are characteristics of lower manifestations of God, but they are not to be confused with God in his being. In God there is the absolute simplicity of one. There are no parts. Multiplicity may flow from it, but in and of itself it is simple, not multiple.

Nature of the Universe. Those pantheists who grant any kind of reality to the universe agree that it was created *ex deo*, "out of God," not *ex nihilo*, "out of nothing," as theism maintains (*see* CREATION, VIEWS OF). There is only one "Being" or Existent in the universe; everything else is an emanation or manifestation of it (*see* ONE AND MANY, PROBLEM OF). Of course, absolute pantheists hold that the universe is not even a manifestation. We are all simply part of an elaborate illusion. Creation simply does not exist. God exists. Nothing else.

God in Relation to the Universe. In contrast to theists, who view God as beyond and separate from the universe, pantheists believe that God and the universe are one. The theist grants some reality to the universe of multiplicity, while the pantheist does not. Those who deny the existence of the universe, of course, see no real relation between God and the universe. But all pantheists agree that whatever reality exists, it is God.

Miracles. An implication of pantheism is that miracles are impossible. For if all is God, and God is all, nothing exists apart from God that could be interrupted or broken into, which is what the nature of a miracle requires. For more discussion of this, see the article on Spinoza. Since pantheists agree that God is simple (has no parts) and is all there is, then God could not perform any miracles, for a miracle implies a God who is in some sense "outside" of the world in which he "intervenes." The only sense in which God "intervenes" in the world is by a regular penetration of it in accordance with repeated higher spiritual laws, such as the law of *karma* (*see* REINCARNATION). Therefore, the pantheistic worldview rules out miracles (*see* MIRACLES, ARGUMENTS AGAINST).

Human Beings. Pantheists either believe that the human as a distinct being is absolutely unreal (absolute pantheism) or else that humanity is real but far less real than God. The primary teaching of absolute pantheism is that humans must overcome their ignorance and realize that they *are* God. Those who put a distance between God and humanity teach a dualistic view of the person—a body and a soul. The body holds the human down, keeping him or her from uniting with God. So each must purge his or her body so the soul can be released to attain oneness with the Absolute One. For all pantheists, the chief goal or end of humanity is to unite with God.

Ethics. Pantheists usually strive to live moral lives and to encourage others to do so. Often their writings are filled with exhortations to use good judgment, to be devoted to truth, and to selflessly love others.

However, these exhortations usually apply to a lower level of spiritual attainment. Once a person has achieved union with God, he has no further concern with moral laws. Nonattachment or utter unconcern for one's actions and their results are often taught as a prerequisite to achieving oneness with God. Since God is beyond good and evil, the person must transcend them to reach God. Morality is stressed as only a temporary concern, and underlying this is no absolute basis for right or wrong (*see* ABSOLUTES, MORAL). Prabhavananda and Christopher Usherwood admit as much when they say, "Every action, under certain circumstances and for certain people, may be a stepping-stone to spiritual growth—if it is done in the spirit of nonattachment. All good and all evil is relative to the individual point of growth. . . . But, in the highest sense, there can be neither good nor evil" (*Bhagavad-Gita*, 140).

Thus, for the pantheist, ethical conduct is a means, not an end in itself. It is used only to help one attain a higher level of spirituality. Ultimately reality is neither good nor evil. As Prabhavananda puts it: "If we say, 'I am good,' or 'I am bad,' we are only talking the language of *maya* [the world of illusion] (*see* ILLUSIONISM). 'I am Brahman,' is the only true statement regarding ourselves that any of us can make" (*Spiritual Heritage*, 203).

History and Human Destiny. Pantheists hardly ever talk about history, except in modified forms of pantheism usually influenced by Western theism (as in Hegel). They are not concerned with it, for either it does not exist, or it is regarded as an aspect of the world of appearances, a thing to be transcended. History has no ultimate goal or end. Whenever it is granted a kind of reality, it is always (except in Hegel's pantheism) considered to be cyclical. Like the wheel of *samsara*, history forever repeats itself. There are no unique events or final events of history. There is no millennium, utopia, or eschaton.

As to individual human destiny, most pantheists, especially Eastern varieties, believe in reincarnation. After the soul leaves the body it enters into another mortal body to work off its *karma*. Eventually the goal is to leave the body and, in the case of most pantheists, merge with God. This is called *Nirvana*, and it means the loss of individuality. Ultimate salvation in this kind of pantheistic system is *from* one's individuality, not *in* it as Christians believe (*see* IMMORTALITY).

Evaluation. *Contributions of Pantheism.* Pantheism attempts to explain all of reality, rather than parts of it. If we are part of a *uni*-verse, than any worldview must seek to embrace that unity. Pantheism does have a holistic view of things. Any comprehensive view of God must include God's immanent presence and activity in the world. A God who will not or cannot relate to humanity will not receive worship from many, nor will many think he deserves it. Pantheism rightly stresses that God is in the world and intimately related to it. He is not transcendently remote and totally removed from the universe.

Pantheism teaches that only God is absolute and necessary. Anything and everything else must be less than absolute and be utterly dependent upon God. Unless God exists, nothing else could exist either. Surely, it is necessary for a worldview to so relate everything to the ultimate.

Finally, the stress pantheism places on not ascribing limitations to God in our language about him is appropriate. If God is unlimited and transcendent, then all limitations must be negated from terms that are applied to him. Without this, verbal idolatry results. The Infinite cannot be encompassed by our finite conceptions.

Criticisms. Absolute pantheism is self-defeating. The absolute pantheist claims: "I am God." But God is the changeless Absolute. However, humanity goes through a process of change called enlightenment because he has this awareness. So how could people be God when people change but God does not?

Pantheists attempt to escape this criticism by allowing some reality to humanity, whether it be emanational, modal, or manifestational. But if we are really only modes of God, then why are we oblivious to it? H. P. Owen describes this as a "metaphysical amnesia" that pervades all our lives. If we are being deceived about the consciousness of our own individual existence, how do we know that the pantheist is not also being deceived in claiming to be conscious of reality as ultimately one?

In fact, if the world is really an illusion, how can we distinguish between reality and fantasy at all? Lao-tse puts the question well: "If, when I was asleep I was a man dreaming I was a butterfly, how do I know when I am awake I am not a butterfly dreaming I am a man?" (Guinness, 14). If what we continually perceive to be real is not, how could we ever distinguish between reality and fantasy? Maybe when we cross a busy street, with three lanes of traffic coming toward us, we should not worry, for it's all an illusion anyway. Indeed, should we even look when crossing the street, if we, the traffic, and the street do not really exist? If pantheists would live out their pantheism consistently, there would be no pantheists left.

Self-Refuting Nature of Pantheism. Pantheism is self-refuting *(see)*, at least all forms that claim individuality is an illusion caused by my mind. For according to pantheism, individual minds are themselves aspects of the illusion and can therefore provide no basis for explaining it. If the mind is part of the illusion, it cannot be the ground for explaining the illusion. Hence, if pantheism is true in asserting that my individuality is an illusion, then pantheism is false, since there is then no basis for explaining the illusion (see D.K. Clark, chapter 7).

Pantheism also fails to handle the problem of evil in a satisfactory manner (*see* EVIL, PROBLEM OF). To pronounce evil an illusion (*see* ILLUSIONISM) or as less than real is not only frustrating and hollow to those experiencing evil, but it seems philosophically inadequate. If evil is not real, then what is the origin of the illusion? Why have people experienced it for so long, and why does it seem so real? Despite the pantheist's claim to the contrary, he or she also experiences pain, suffering, and eventually will die. Even pantheists double-over in pain when they get appendicitis. They jump out of the way of an on-coming truck so as not to get hurt.

If God is all, and all is God, as pantheists maintain, then evil is an illusion and ultimately there are no rights and wrongs. For there are four possibilities regarding good and evil:

1. If God is all-good, then evil must exist apart from God. But this is impossible since God is all—nothing can exist apart from It.
2. If God is all-evil, then good must exist apart from God. This is not possible either, since God is all.
3. God is both all-good and all-evil. This cannot be, for it is self-contradictory to affirm that the same being is both all good and all evil at the same time. Further, most pantheists agree that God is beyond good and evil. Therefore God is neither good nor evil.
4. Good and evil are illusory. They are not real categories.

Option four is what most pantheists believe. But if evil is only an illusion, then ultimately there is no such thing as good and evil thoughts or actions. Hence, what difference would it make whether we praise or curse, counsel or rape, love or murder someone? If there is no final moral difference between those actions, absolute moral responsibilities do not exist. Cruelty and noncruelty are ultimately the same. One critic made the point with this illustration:

> One day I was talking to a group of people in the digs of a young South African in Cambridge. Among others, there was present a young Indian who was of *Sikh background but a *Hindu by religion. He started to speak strongly against Christianity, but did not really understand the problems of his own beliefs. So I said, "Am I not correct in saying that on the basis of your system, cruelty and non-cruelty are ultimately equal, that there is no intrinsic difference between them?" He agreed. . . . The student in whose room we met, who had clearly understood the implications of what the Sikh had admitted, picked up his kettle of boiling water with which he was about to make tea, and stood with it steaming over the Indian's head. The man looked up and asked him what he was doing and he said, with a cold yet gentle finality, "There is no difference between cruelty and non-cruelty." Thereupon the Hindu walked out into the night. [Schaeffer, *The God Who Is There*, 101]

If pantheists are correct that reality is not moral, that good and evil, right and wrong, are inapplicable to what is, then to be right is as meaningless as to be wrong (Schaeffer, *He Is There and He Is Not Silent*). The foundation for morality is destroyed. Pantheism does not take the problem of evil seriously. As C. S. *Lewis put it, "If you do not take the distinctions between good and bad seriously, then it is easy to say that anything you find in this world is a part of God. But, of course, if you think some things really bad, and God really good, then you cannot talk like that" (*Mere Christianity*, 30).

In this and other ways, the pantheistic concept of God is incoherent. To say God is infinite, yet somehow shares his being (*ex deo*) with creation, is to raise the problem of how the finite can be infinite, which is what absolute pantheists say. Otherwise, one must consider the finite world less than real, though existing. We have seen the problems with the first, absolute option. But the second option makes God both infinite and finite, for it is said to share part of its being with creatures which entails an Infinite Being becoming less than infinite. But how can the Infinite be finite, the Absolute be relative, and the Unchanging changed?

Pantheism's God also is unknowable. The very claim, "God is unknowable in an intellectual way," seems either meaningless or self-defeating. For if the claim itself cannot be understood in an intellectual way, then it is self-defeating. For what is being affirmed is that nothing can be understood about God in an intellectual way. But the pantheist expects us to intellectually know this truth that God cannot be understood in an intellectual way. In other words, the pantheist appears to be making a statement about God to the effect that no such statements can be made about God. But how can one make a positive affirmation about God which claims that only negative affirmations can be made about God? Plotinus admitted that negative knowledge presupposes some positive awareness. Otherwise, one would not know what to negate.

Critics further claim that the denial of many pantheists of the applicability of logic to reality is self-defeating. For to deny that logic applies to reality, it would seem that one must make a logical statement about reality to the effect that no logical statements can be made. For example, when *Zen Buddhist D. T. Suzuki says that to comprehend life we must abandon logic (Suzuki, 58), he uses logic in his affirmation and applies it to reality. Indeed, the law of noncontradiction (A cannot both be A and not-A) cannot be denied without using it in the very denial (*see* FIRST PRINCIPLES). Therefore, to deny that logic applies to reality, one must not make a logical statement about reality. But then how will the position be defended?

Sources

Bhagavad-Gita. Prabhavananda, trans., with C. Usherwood; see esp. Appen. 2: "The Gita and War"
D. K. Clark, *The Pantheism of Alan Watts*
D. K. Clark, *Apologetics in the New Age*
G. H. Clark, *Thales to Dewey*
W. Corduan, "Transcendentalism: Hegel," in N. L. Geisler, ed., *Biblical Errancy: An Analysis of Its Philosophical Roots*
R. Flint, *Anti-Theistic Theories*
O. Guiness, *The Dust of Death*
S. Hackett, *Oriental Philosophy*
G. W. F. Hegel, *The Phenomenology of Mind*
C. S. Lewis, *Mere Christianity*
H. P. Owen, *Concepts of Deity*
Plotinus, *Enneads*
Prabhavananda, *The Spiritual Heritage of India*
———, *The Upanishads: Breath of the Eternal*, F. Manchester, trans.
S. Radhakrishnan, *The Hindu View of Life*
J. M. Robinson, *An Introduction to Early Greek Philosophy*
F. Schaeffer, *He Is There and He Is Not Silent*
———, *The God Who Is There*
H. Smith, *The Religions of Man*
B. Spinoza, *Ethics*
D. T. Suzuki, *An Introduction to Zen Buddhism*

Pascal, Blaise. Blaise Pascal (1623–1662) was a French mathematician, scientist, and philosopher. At age sixteen, he completed an original treatise on conic sections. He contributed to the development of differential calculus, and originated the mathematical theory of probability. Several mathematical propositions and demonstrations have been named in his honor: Pascal's arithmetical triangle, Pascal's law, and Pascal's mystic hexagram.

Pascal's stress on faith brought him in contact with the Jansenists, a splinter Catholic group at odds with the Jesuits. Among the Jansenists he experienced his "first conversion" (1646). Later he experienced his "definitive conversion" when he discovered the "God of Abraham, God of Isaac, God of Jacob, not of philosophers and scholars" (Pascal, 311).

After the condemnation of the Jansenist apologist Antoine Arnuald (in 1655), Pascal wrote his eighteen *Lettres provinciales* (1656–57) which attacked the Jesuit theory of grace and morality. His most famous work is *Pensees* (Thoughts), published after his death from notes he began earlier. *Pensees* vindicated Christianity through the presentation of facts and fulfillment of prophecy and by an appeal to the heart (Cross, 1036).

Faith and Reason. Although Pascal's opposition to René Descartes and his Cartesian rationalism earned him the undeserved title of fideist (*see* FIDEISM), Pascal actually offered many evidences in support of the Christian Faith. In the tradition of *Augustine, in which he was nourished, he believed that only faith could free from sin and put him in a personal relationship with God. There is always an element of risk in faith, but it is a risk worth taking. He confessed that the "heart has its reasons of which reason knows not." However, this does exclude the use of reason in supporting the truths of the Christian Faith.

Apologetic. Pascal's rational apologetic for Christianity can be divided into three parts. First, his use of evidence; second, the appeal to fulfilled prophecies; and, third, his famous "wager."

The Use of Evidence. Pascal believed "it is a sign of weakness to prove God from nature" (Pascal, no. 466). He adds, "It is a remarkable fact that no canonical author ever used nature to prove God" (ibid., no. 463). However, he listed twelve "proofs" for Christianity:

1. the Christian religion, by the fact of being established so firmly and so gently, though so contrary to nature;
2. the holiness, sublimity, and humility of a Christian soul;
3. the miracles of holy Scripture;
4. Jesus Christ in particular;
5. the apostles in particular;
6. Moses and the prophets in particular;
7. the Jewish people;
8. prophecies;
9. perpetuity: no religion enjoys perpetuity;
10. doctrine, accounting for everything;
11. the holiness of this law, and
12. the order of the world (ibid., no. 482).

Some of these evidences Pascal discusses at great length. The proof from prophecy covers *Pensees* nos. 483–511. He notes their supernatural nature, since they "wrote down these things long before they happened" (ibid., no. 484). He points out their specificity, citing Daniel's prediction of what year the Messiah would die (ibid., no. 485). With regard to messianic prophecy he lists numerous detailed predictions, such as

Christ's precursor (Malachi 3), birth (Isaiah 9; Micah 5), and his work in Jerusalem to blind the wise and learned, Isaiah 6, 8, 29 (ibid., no. 487) (*see* PROPHECY, AS PROOF OF THE BIBLE).

Pascal's Wager. In *Pensees* he offered *Pascal's Wager*. Assuming, as Pascal does, that we cannot know for sure by reason alone whether God exists or what lies beyond this life, how then should we live in this life? What are the odds for there being a God and an afterlife? Pascal wrote:

> Either God is or he is not. But to which view shall we be inclined? Reason cannot decide this question. Infinite chaos separates us. At the far end of this infinite distance a coin is being spun which will come down heads or tails. How will you wager? Reason cannot make you choose either, reason cannot prove either wrong. . . .
>
> Yes, but you must wager. There is no choice, you are already committed. Which will you choose then? Let us see: since a choice must be made, let us see which offers you the least interest. You have two things to lose: the true and the good; and two things to stake: your reason and your will, your knowledge and your happiness; and your nature has two things to avoid: error and wretchedness. . . . Let us weigh up the gain and the loss involved in calling heads that God exists. Let us assess the two cases: if you win you win everything, if you lose you lose nothing. Do not hesitate then; wager that he does exist. . . .
>
> "I confess, I admit it, but is there really no way of seeing what the cards are?" "Yes. Scripture and the rest, etc." "Yes, but my hands are tied and my lips are sealed; I am being forced to wager and I am not free; I am being held fast and I am so made that I cannot believe. What do you want me to do then?" "That is true, but at least get it into your head that, if you are unable to believe, it is because of your passions, since reason impels you to believe and yet you cannot do so. Concentrate then not on convincing yourself by multiplying proofs of God's existence but by diminishing your passions. You want to find faith and you do not know the road. You want to be cured of unbelief and you ask for the remedy: learn from those who were once bound like you and who now wager all they have. These are people who know the road you wish to follow, who have been cured of the affliction of which they began. They behaved just as if they did believe, taking holy water, having masses said, and so on. That will make you believe quite naturally, and will make you more docile." "But that is what I am afraid of." "But why? What have you to lose? But to show you that this is the way, the fact is that this diminishes the passions which are your great obstacles. . . .
>
> I tell you that you will gain even in this life, and that at every step you take along this road you will see that your gain is so certain and your risk so negligible that in the end you will realize that you have wagered on something certain and infinite for which you have paid nothing.

According to Pascal's wager, one cannot lose by wagering that God and immortality exist. Even if one cannot prove God nor an after life, it is a good bet to believe in him. We have nothing to lose. If God does not exist, the life of the believer is a great life anyway. If he does exist, then so much the more. Not only is this life great but the one to come will be even greater. So, believing in God and a life to come is a good bet, both for this life and the one to come.

The wager cannot be avoided. We must either believe in God or not. Since we can't avoid betting, the odds overwhelmingly favor betting on God.

The game of life must be played. Even those who end their life, must play the game; they only shorten its duration. But assuming there is no God to meet beyond the grave is a big gamble—one not worth taking. But assuming there is a God is a gamble not worth missing. For believing there is a God pays in this life for sure and possibly in the next. But assuming there is no God brings unhappiness in this life and the possibility of more to come. In Pascal's own words, "That leaves no choice; wherever there is infinity, and where there are not infinite chances of losing against that of winning, there is no room for hesitation, you must give everything."

Evaluation. *His Approach Is *Fideistic.* Pascal, while emphasizing the heart and faith, is not a fideist. In *Pensees* no. 149 he puts into Jesus' mouth these words:

> I do not mean you to believe me submissively and without reason; I do not claim to subdue you by tyranny. Nor do I claim to account for everything. . . . I mean to show you by clearly, by convincing proofs, marks of divinity within me which will convince you of what I am, and establish my authority by miracles and proofs that you cannot reject, so that you will then believe the things I teach, finding no reason to reject them but your own inability to tell whether they are true or not.

This is clearly not fideism.

His Argument from Prophecy Fails. Pascal's views came in for heavy criticism in the eighteenth century. The deist Francois-Marie *Voltaire (1694–1778) is typical. As for miracles, Voltaire wrote: "not a single one of the prophecies that Pascal referred to can be honestly applied to Christ; and that his discussion of miracles was pure nonsense" (Torrey, 264). However, as seen in the article

PROPHECY, AS PROOF OF THE BIBLE, the deists' questions can be answered and Pascal's argument can be vindicated as a defense of Christianity.

His Views Were Not Enlightened. Voltaire, in his twenty-fifth philosophical letter, declared that Pascal's Christian view of the fall, redemption, divine providence, predestination, and grace was neither enlightened nor humanitarian and that he encouraged fanaticism.

As for Pascal's "Wager," Voltaire was shocked that he would resort to such a means to prove God. If "the heavens declare the glory of God," why did Pascal downplay the external evidence for God in nature (*see* GOD, EVIDENCE FOR)?

Walter Kaufmann of Harvard once quipped that maybe Pascal's God would "out-Luther Luther." That is, "God might punish those whose faith is prompted by prudence" (Kaufmann, 177). But this too is hardly a critique of the Wager. At best it would only exclude those who believe in God on such grounds. Further, the argument is based on a flawed view of God's character. No morally worthy God, to say nothing of a rational one, would punish someone who uses wisdom in thinking about his ultimate destiny.

Atheist George H. Smith argues that one loses too much by making such a wager. "What have we got to lose? Intellectual integrity, self-esteem, and a passionate, rewarding life for starters. In short, everything that makes life worth living. Far from being a safe bet, Pascal's wager requires the wager of one's life and happiness" (Smith, 184).

But it is not at all clear that this is the case. Pascal himself was a man of great intellect and great integrity, as even most of his enemies are willing to admit. And certainly it is simply false to hold that Pascal and other thinking Christians do not have a "rewarding life." Indeed, this is part of Pascal's wager, namely, that we have nothing to lose, since this life of faith alone—even if there were no God—is eminently worthwhile. Finally, Smith overlooks the major point Pascal makes: The believer anticipates eternal reward as well. "Everything to gain and really nothing to lose"; unbelief has a difficult time answering Pascal.

One could challenge the premise that believers have nothing to lose. If there is no God, Christians submit to a life of sacrifice for nothing (2 Cor. 11:22–28; 2 Tim. 3:12). They missed some fun by being a believer. But considering that the believer has true joy and peace, forgiveness, and hope, even in suffering (Romans 5, James 1), this is hardly a telling point.

However, the wager is not a proof of God, but a path of prudence. It merely shows that it is foolish not to believe in God. The question remains as to whether the "wise" path leads to truth.

Sources

D. Adamson, *Blaise Pascal: Mathematician, Physicist, and Thinker About God*

W. Kaufmann, *Critique of Religion and Philosophy*

P. Kreeft, *Christianity for Modern Pagans: Pascal's* Pensees

B. Pascal, *Pensees*

"Pascal, Blaise," in F. L. Cross, et al., eds., *The Oxford Dictionary of the Christian Church,* 2d ed.

R. H. Popkin, "Pascal," in P. Edwards, ed., *Encyclopedia of Philosophy*

G. H. Smith, *Atheism: The Case against God*

H. F. Stewart, *Pascal's Apology for Religion*

N. Torrey, "Voltaire, Francois-Marie Arouet De," in P. Edwards, ed., *Encyclopedia of Philosophy*

C. C. J. Webb, *Pascal's Philosophy of Religion*

Passover Plot. ***The Passover Plot Hypothesis.*** *The Passover Plot* is a book by radical New Testament scholar, H. J. Schonfield, who proposed that Jesus was an innocent messianic pretender who connived to "fulfill" prophecy in order to substantiate his claims (Schonfield, 35–38). According to the plot, Jesus secretly "schemed in faith" (ibid., 173), connived with a young man, Lazarus, and Joseph of Arimathea, to feign death on the cross, revive in the tomb, and demonstrate to his disciples (who were ignorant of the plot) that he was the Messiah. However, the plan went awry when the Roman soldiers pierced Jesus' side and he died. Nonetheless, the disciples mistook others as Christ some days later and believed he had risen from the dead (Schonfield, 170–72).

A Challenge to the Passover Plot. If true, the "Passover Plot" would contradict orthodox Christianity, which is built on the beliefs that Jesus was truly the Messiah who supernaturally fulfilled Old Testament prophecy, and who died on the cross and rose from the dead three days later (1 Cor. 15:1–5). Apart from these basic truths there is no historic Christianity (1 Cor. 15:12–18). Thus, it is incumbent on the evangelical apologist to refute the Passover Plot hypothesis.

At least three basic dimensions of traditional apologetics are called in question by this alleged plot: the character of Christ, the supernatural nature of messianic predictions, and the resurrection of Christ. Each will be addressed in order.

The Character of Christ. If the alleged plot is correct, then Jesus was anything but "innocent." He was a conniving, cunning, and deceptive messianic pretender. He intended to deceive his closest disciples into believing he was the Messiah when he was not. But this thesis is contrary to the character of Christ known from the Gospel records, which have been demonstrated to be reliable (*see* NEW TESTAMENT MANUSCRIPTS; NEW TESTAMENT, HISTORICITY OF; NEW TESTAMENT, DATING OF). The Jesus of the Gospels is the perfect exemplar of honesty and integrity (*see* CHRIST, UNIQUENESS OF).

The Nature of Supernatural Prophecy. Contrary to the "Passover Plot," messianic prophecy is supernatural (*see* PROPHECY, AS PROOF OF THE BIBLE). And in the case of Christ there are many reasons that he could not have manipulated events to make it look like he fulfilled all the predictions about the Old Testament Messiah.

First of all, this was contrary to his honest character as noted above. It assumes he was one of the greatest deceivers of all time. It presupposes that he was not even a good person, to say nothing of the perfect man the Gospels affirm him to be. There are several lines of evidence that combine to demonstrate that this is a completely implausible thesis.

Second, there is no way Jesus could have controlled many events necessary for the fulfillment of Old Testament prophecies about the Messiah. For example, he had no control over where he would be born (Mic. 5:2), how he would be born of a virgin (Isa. 7:14), when he would die (Dan. 9:25), what tribe (Gen. 49:10) and lineage he would be from (2 Sam. 7:12), and numerous other things.

Third, there is no way short of being supernatural that Jesus could have manipulated the events and people in his life to respond in exactly the way necessary for it to appear that he was fulfilling all these prophecies, including John's heralding him (Matt. 3), his accuser's reactions (Matt. 27:12), how the soldiers cast lots for his garments (John 19:23, 24), and how they would pierce his side with a spear (John 19:34). Indeed even Schonfield admits that the plot failed when the Romans actually pierced Christ. The fact is that anyone with all this manipulative power would have to be divine—the very thing the Passover hypothesis is attempting to avoid. In short, it takes a bigger miracle to believe the Passover Plot than to accept these prophecies as supernatural.

The Resurrection of Christ. The Passover Plot offers an implausible scenario as an alternative to the resurrection of Christ. This is true for many reasons. First, it is contrary to the Gospel records, which are demonstrably reliable (*see* NEW TESTAMENT, HISTORICITY OF), having been written by eyewitnesses and contemporaries of the events. Second, it totally overlooks the powerful testimony of the resurrection of Christ (*see* RESURRECTION, EVIDENCE FOR), including: (1) a permanently empty tomb; (2) over five hundred eyewitnesses (1 Cor. 15:5–7); (3) some twelve physical appearances of Christ in the same nail-scarred body (John 20:27); (4) which were spread over a period of forty days (Acts 1:3); (5) during which time Jesus ate with them on at least four occasions and taught them concerning the kingdom of God; (6) and transformed them from scared, skeptical, scattered disciples into the greatest missionary society the world has ever known overnight!

Conclusion. The Passover Plot is in fact an implausible scenario that is based on unjustified presuppositions and is contrary to many known facts. For example, it supposes: (1) unjustified late dates for the Gospels (*see* NEW TESTAMENT, DATING OF); (2) an antisupernatural bias (*see* MIRACLE), (3) a flawed character of Christ (*see* CHRIST, UNIQUENESS OF); (4) the incredible naivete of his disciples; (5) mass cases of mistaken identity after his death (*see* RESURRECTION, EVIDENCE FOR; RESURRECTION, ALTERNATE THEORIES OF); (6) a miraculous transformation based on a total mistake.

To put it positively, the alleged plot is contrary to (1) the early dates of the Gospels; (2) the multiplicity of the eyewitnesses' accounts; (3) the verification of history and archaeology (*see* ARCHAEOLOGY, NEW TESTAMENT); (4) the known character of Jesus' disciples; (5) the permanently empty tomb; (6) the nature of the resurrection appearances; and (7) the incredible number of eyewitnesses of the resurrected Christ—over five hundred. In short, *The Passover Plot* is just another beautiful theory ruined by a brutal gang of facts.

Sources

C. Blomberg, *The Historical Reliability of the Gospels*

G. Habermas, *The Historical Jesus*

H. J. Schonfield, *The Passover Plot*

E. Yamauchi, "Passover Plot or Easter Triumph" in John W. Montgomery, *Christianity for the Tough-Minded*

C. Wilson, *The Passover Plot Exposed*

Pascal's Wager, *see* PASCAL, BLAISE.

Paul's Religion, Alleged Contradictions with Jesus. *See* BIBLE, ALLEGED ERRORS IN; MITHRAISM.

Pentateuch, Mosaic Authorship of. The Bible attributes the first five books of the Bible, Genesis, Exodus, Leviticus, Numbers, and Deuteronomy, or the Pentateuch, to Moses in Exodus 24:4; Joshua 1:7–8; Ezra 6:18; Daniel 9:11, and Malachi 4:4. Jesus quoted from the Pentateuch, attributing the source to Moses in Mark 7:10 and Luke 20:37. Most modern critics deny Mosaic authorship and organize the writings around a much later, complex set of priestly scribes and editors. The objective has been to avoid the books' accounts of supernatural occurrences and divine authority (*see* BIBLICAL CRITICISM; REDACTION CRITICISM, OLD TESTAMENT; WELLHAUSEN, JULIUS).

As early as the late seventeenth century, Benedict *Spinoza denied that Moses wrote the Pentateuch. Many critical scholars joined him in the nineteenth century. Julius Wellhausen claimed that the first five books were written by various persons he called the Jehovist (J), Elohimist (E), Priestly (P), and Deuteronomist (D). Literary characteristics supposedly distinguished these authors.

Among arguments offered as to why Moses could not have written the first books, seven have been particularly argued:

1. Moses could not have written the account of his own death in Deuteronomy 34.
2. Certain sections are parenthetical, so must have been edited in (for example, Deut. 2:10–12; 2:20–23).
3. Moses was not yet alive when the events of Genesis were recorded.
4. Different names for God are used in different sections, reflecting a different author.
5. The style of various sections is from a later period than Moses.
6. The names of some places are not those that would have been used in Moses' day, but rather later.
7. There is reference to Israel being in the promised land, but Moses died before the people entered (Deuteronomy 34).

Responding to the Arguments. Conservative scholars have responded that none of these arguments is strong enough to warrant the extraordinary claims and theories that have arisen from them in Old Testament studies. There are stronger reasons for attributing the Pentateuch to Moses.

The Account of Moses' Death. Since Moses was a prophet (Deut. 18:15; Acts 3:22) who possessed miraculous gifts and abilities (see, for example, Exodus 4), there is no reason why he could not have written the account of his death in advance (*see* MIRACLES, APOLOGETIC VALUE OF).

However, since there are no signs in the text of this being a prophecy, it may have been written by his successor. Such scholars as R. D. Wilson, Merrill Unger, Douglas Young, R. Laird Harris, Gleason L. Archer, Jr., and R. K. Harrison easily accept that the final chapter of Deuteronomy was likely appended by Joshua or someone else in Moses' inner circle. This, in fact, supports the view of the continuity of the writing prophets, a theory that each successor prophet writes the last chapter of his predecessor's book. The addition of a chapter on Moses' funeral by another prophet in accordance with the custom of the day in no sense takes away from the belief that Moses was the author of everything up to that final chapter. This certainly doesn't conform to the J-E-P-D scenario.

Parenthetical Sections. The parenthetical sections in Deuteronomy 2 need not be later redactions. Authors often use editorial (e.g., parenthetical) material in their own writings. Such an addition was made to the previous sentence in this paragraph. No earlier manuscripts omit them. This section fits into the text. So there is no compelling evidence to suggest that they were the work of a later redactor.

But even if parenthetical comments were added into the text, this would not change anything Moses wrote in the rest of the text, nor detract from his claim to authorship of the inspired text. Many evangelical scholars are willing to admit that comments like these could have been made by later scribes to elucidate the meaning of the text. If they are additions, they are uninspired changes that are subject to the same textual debate as Mark 16:9–20 and John 8:1–11. One can argue on the basis of internal and external evidence whether they should be considered part of the inspired text of Scripture. And, like the King James Version rendering of 1 John 5:7 on the Trinity, if there is no good evidence, the text should be rejected. Lacking that kind of evidence, for this passage it seems best to consider it an editorial comment by Moses himself. In neither case is the Mosaic authorship of the inspired text of the Pentateuch brought into question.

Moses and Genesis. As to the composition of Genesis, God could have revealed the story of beginnings to Moses, as he did other supernatural revelations (for example, Exodus 20). Moses was on the Mount for 40 days, and God could have revealed to him the history up to his time.

Since there is no clear indication in the text that this is what happened, there is perhaps better reason to think that Moses compiled, rather than composed, the record of Genesis. There is indication that Genesis was a compilation of family documents and oral history that had been carefully passed down. Each section has attached to it a phrase "This is the history of . . . " (NKJV) or "account of" (NIV). These phrases occur throughout the book of Genesis (2:4; 5:1; 6:9; 10:1, 32; 11:10, 27; 25:12, 19; 36:1; 37:2), tying it together as a series of family records and genealogies. Sometimes the accounts are even called a "book" (5:1 NKJV) or "written" (NIV) account. As leader of the Jewish people, Moses would have had access to these family records of past history and could have compiled them into the form we know as the book of Genesis.

Different Names for God. Critics have argued that different names for God in different passages indicate different authors. They point to Genesis 1, where the alleged Elohist (E) author uses *Elohim* for God exclusively. Yet in Genesis 2 the phrase *Yahweh Elohim* ("Lord God") is used. The use of *Yahweh* (or Jehovah) is said to indicate the hand of the Jehovist (J).

But this argument fails. The same kind of thing occurs in the *Qur'an*, which is known to have one source, Muhammad. The name *Allah* is used for God in suras 4, 9, 24, and 33, but *Rab* is used in suras 18, 23, and 25 (Harrison, 517). In the *Qur'an* the names are used in different chapters. In Genesis they are interspersed within the same chapter or section, leading to some incredible dissections of the text. Even J-E-P-D scholars cannot agree where to draw all the lines.

The more natural explanation is that different names of God are used, depending on the subject and aspect of God being discussed. The majestic *Elohim* is an appropriate word when speaking of creation, as in Genesis 1. *Yahweh* the Covenant-maker is more appropriate when God engages people, as in Genesis 2–3.

Writing Style. J-E-P-D critics say that the Pentateuch reflects a style of writing and literary forms from a much later period. For example, the Deuteronomist (D) uses seventh-century style and structure. But this contention also cannot be grounded in fact. Archaeological discoveries show that the literary form used in Deuteronomy is, in fact, an ancient one throughout the Near East. Moses follows as a literary device the suzerainty treaties made between kings and their subjects (see Kline).

The argument makes an assumption that is not true in literary history. The critics assume that Moses could not have written in more than one style. As a well-educated Egyptian he had been exposed to suzerainty treaties and every other narrative and artistic writing form then available. Good modern authors change style and form as they change in their own craft and for effect. Sometimes they may use different forms within a single work. A notable example is C. S. *Lewis. Bible critics would go crazy if confronted with one author's name over children's stories, in-depth literary critiques, scholarly analysis, allegorical satire, science fiction, biographic narrative, and logic-driven disputations and treatises.

Late Place Names. Late names of places are easily explained as later interpolations. For example, this author's birth town was called Van Dyke, Michigan, but today one finds it on the map as Warren. Later copyists may have updated some place names so the people would better understand. In Joshua 14:15 this is almost certainly the case, since a parenthetical notation has entered the text which says "(Hebron used to be called Kiriath Arba after Arba, who was the greatest man among the Anakites)."

Possession of the Land. Deuteronomy 2:13 refers to Israel in the "land of their possession," which did not take place until after Moses died. Hence, it is argued that Moses could not have written these words.

As Old Testament commentators Kiel and Delitzsch concluded, this reference is to "the land to the east of the Jordan (Gilead and Bashan), which was conquered by the Israelites under Moses and divided among the two tribes and a half, and which is described in chap. iii.20 as the 'possession' which Jehovah had given to these tribes" (Kiel and Delitzsch, 1:293). Also, being a parenthetical reference, 2:13 could have been a later, non-Mosaic interpolation into the original text. Whatever evidence this provides for later editing, it does not support J-E-P-D authorship, nor negate Mosaic authorship of the original inspired text.

Mosaic Authorship of Exodus. There is strong evidence that Moses wrote Exodus. First, no other known person from that period had the time, interest, and ability to compose such a record. Second, Moses was an eyewitness to the events of Exodus through Deuteronomy and so was uniquely qualified. Indeed, the record is a vivid eyewitness account of spectacular events, such as the crossing of the Red Sea, the receiving of the commandments, and the wanderings.

Third, from the earliest known rabbinical records, these books have unanimously been ascribed to Moses. This is true of the Talmud, as well as the works of such Jewish writers as *Philo and *Josephus.

Fourth, the author reflects a detailed knowledge of wilderness geography (see, for example, Exodus 14). This is highly unlikely for anyone other than Moses, who spent forty years as a shepherd, as well as forty years as a national leader, in the region. The same argument can be used of the detailed reflections of customs and practices of a variety of peoples described throughout the Pentateuch.

The book's internal claim is that "Moses wrote all the words" (Exod. 24:4). If he did not, it is a forgery. Moses' successor, Joshua, claimed that Moses wrote the Law. In fact, when Joshua assumed leadership, he reported that he was exhorted by God: "Do not let this book of the Law depart from your mouth" (Josh. 1:8); he was told to "be careful to obey all the law my servant Moses gave you" (1:7). After Joshua, a long chain of Old Testament figures attributed the books of the law to Moses, among them Josiah (2 Chron. 34:14), Ezra (Ezra 6:18), Daniel (Dan. 9:11), and Malachi (Mal. 4:4). Jesus and New Testament writers also attributed the words to Moses. Scripture in other contexts refers to the Pentateuch as the books or law of Moses.

Jesus, quoting from Exodus 20:12, used the introduction, "for Moses said" (Mark 7:10; cf. Luke 20:37). The apostle Paul declared that "Moses describes in this way the righteousness that is by the law" as he cited Exodus 20:11 (Rom. 10:5). So there is confirmation of Jesus, who by miracles was attested to be the Christ, the Son of God (*see* CHRIST, DEITY OF; MIRACLES, APOLOGETIC VIEW OF). And there is apostolic authority, which was also confirmed (*see* MIRACLES IN THE BIBLE).

Sources

G. L. Archer, Jr., *A Survey of Old Testament Introduction*
Flavius Josephus, *Antiquities of the Jews*
———, *Against Apion*
N. L. Geisler and W. E. Nix, *General Introduction to the Bible*
R. K. Harrison, *Introduction to the Old Testament*
C. F. Keil and F. Delitzsch, *Commentary on the Old Testament*, vol. 1
M. Kline, *Treaty of the Great King*
M. Unger, *Introductory Guide to the Old Testament*

Pharaoh of the Exodus. The predominant view of modern biblical scholars is that the Pharaoh of the Exodus was Rameses II (*see* BIBLE CRITICISM).

If so, the Exodus took place about 1270 to 1260 B.C. However, the Bible (Judg. 11:26; 1 Kings 6:1; Acts 13:19–20), dates the Exodus to about 1447 B.C. Given the commonly accepted dating, that would make the Pharaoh of the Exodus Amenhotep II, an identification archaeologists and biblical scholars have traditionally rejected.

An Early Exodus. Modern scholarship has raised Rameses II and the mid-thirteenth century to the level of unassailable doctrine, but there is sufficient evidence to challenge conventional wisdom about the Exodus, as well as the traditional dating for many pharaohs. Alternative explanations are providing a better accounting of all the historical data, and making 1447 B.C. look like a credible departure date for the Israelites.

The Bible is very specific in 1 Kings 6:1 that 480 years passed from the Exodus to the fourth year of Solomon's reign, about 967 B.C. This would place the Exodus around 1447. This fits also with Judges 11:26, which affirms that Israel spent 300 years in the Land up to the time of Jephthah (about 1100). Likewise, Acts 13:20 speaks of 450 years of judges from Moses to Samuel, who lived around 1000. Paul said in Galatians 3:17 there were 430 years from Jacob to Moses. That would be from 1800 to 1450. The same figure is used in Exodus 12:40. If the Bible is wrong at this point, it is certainly consistent and allows for no thirteenth-century exodus.

Possible Solutions. There are at least three ways to reconcile the biblical data with the fifteenth-century date. The first posits the possibility of an early Rameses. The second offers a basis for adjusting the archaeological periods and the third reinterprets the chronology of Egyptian rulers (*see* ARCHAEOLOGY, OLD TESTAMENT). Because these changes would shake up a lot of widely held opinions about ancient history, they have faced much opposition, but the evidence is strong.

The generally accepted date was based on three assumptions:

1. "Rameses" in Exodus 1:11 was named after Rameses the Great
2. There were no building projects in the Nile Delta before 1300.
3. There was no great civilization in Canaan from the nineteenth to the thirteenth centuries.

All of these, if true, would make the conditions described in Exodus impossible before 1300. However, the name *Rameses* runs throughout Egyptian history and the city mentioned in Exodus 1 may have honored an earlier nobleman by that name. Since Rameses the Great is Rameses II, there must have been a Rameses I, about whom nothing is now known. In Genesis 47:11, the name Rameses is used to describe the area of the Nile Delta where Jacob and his sons settled. This may be the name that Moses normally used to refer to the entire geographical area. Rameses, then, need not refer to a city named after a king at all.

Second, building projects have now been found at Pi-Ramesse (Rameses) and at both possible sites for Pithom dating from the nineteenth to the seventeenth centuries, the era in which the Israelites arrived. These show strong Palestinian influence. Digging done in 1987 shows that there was building at Pi-Ramesse and one of the Pithom sites in the 1400s. So whether Exodus 1:11 refers to the building projects that were going on at the time the Israelites became slaves, or what they were working on at the time of the Exodus, there is evidence building was underway. Surface surveys yielded no signs of civilizations like the Moabites and the Edomites prior to Israel's entrance to the land, but digging deeper has found many sites that fit into the period. Even the man who did the initial research changed his position later. So all three of the arguments for dating the Exodus after 1300 have been proven false. Now if these three assumptions are wrong, then there is no reason to suppose a late date for the Exodus and we can look for evidence to support the Bible's date of about 1447.

Bimson-Livingston Revision. John Bimson and David Livingston proposed in 1987, that the date of the shift from the Middle Bronze to Late Bronze ages has been inaccurate and must be moved. At issue is evidence of destroyed cities in Canaan. Most signs of a serious invasion or conquest have been dated to about 1550 B.C.—150 years too early. This date is assigned to these ruins because it is supposed that they were destroyed when the Egyptians drove out the Hyksos, a hostile nation that dominated Egypt for several centuries. Bimson suggests moving the end of the Middle Bronze Age would show that this destruction was done by the Israelites, not the Egyptians.

Can such a change be justified? The Middle Bronze (MB) was characterized by fortified cities; the Late Bronze (LB) had mostly smaller, unwalled settlements. So whatever caused the destruction of these cities gives us our date for the period division. The evidence is sparse and unclear. Also, there is doubt that the Egyptians, just establishing a new government and armies, were in any position to carry out long sieges throughout Canaan. Positive evidence has come from recent digs which have shown that the last phase of the Middle Bronze period needs more time than originally thought, so that its end is closer to 1420.

This corresponds with the Bible, where the cities in Canaan are "great and fortified up to heaven" (Deuteronomy 1:28) just as Moses said. Also, the extent of destruction, with only a few exceptions, matches the biblical description. "Indeed, generally speaking, the area in which destruction occurred at the end of [the Middle Bronze period] corresponds with the area of Israelite settlement, while cities that survived lay outside that area."

Some archaeologists ask where the evidence is of Israelite dominance of the culture in the Late Bronze. We have always held them responsible for the shift from the Bronze Age to the Iron Age in 1200. The problem with that view is that those changes are the same all over the Mediterranean, not just in Palestine. The Hebrews could not be responsible for such widespread change. In fact, as nomads, they probably brought nothing with them, lived in tents for some time, and bought their pottery at the Canaanite markets. Besides, the book of Judges shows that after Israel entered the land, they did not dominate anybody for several hundred years. They were dominated by everyone around them.

Bimson summarizes his proposal in this way:

> We have proposed: (1) a return to the Biblical date for the conquest of Canaan (i.e., shortly before 1400 B.C.), and (2) a lowering of the date for the end of the Middle Bronze Age, from 1550 B.C. to shortly before 1400 B.C. The result is that two events previously separated by centuries are brought together: the fall of Canaan's MB II cities becomes the archaeological evidence for the conquest. These twin proposals create an almost perfect match between the archaeological evidence and the Biblical account.

Velikovsky-Courville Revision. A third possible solution sees a problem in the traditional view of Egyptian history. The chronology of the whole ancient world is based on the order and dates of the Egyptian kings. Mostly, we know this order from an ancient historian named Manetho, who is quoted by three other historians. There are also monuments that give partial lists. This order has been considered unassailable; however, the only absolutely fixed date is its end, when Alexander the Great conquered Egypt. Velikovsky and Courville assert that 600 extra years in that chronology throw off the dates for events all around the Near East.

Setting aside the idea of Egyptian history as fixed, there are three pieces of evidence where the history of Israel matches up with the history of Egypt. This kind of match, where the same event is recorded in both countries, is called a synchronism. The three places we find synchronisms are the plagues of Moses, the defeat of the Amalekites, and the reign of Ahab.

A very old papyrus written by an Egyptian priest named Ipuwer and, though various interpretations have been given, it tells of two unique events: a series of plagues and the invasion of a foreign power. The plagues match very well with the record of Moses' plagues in Exodus 7–12. It speaks of the river turning to blood (cf. Exod. 7:20), crops consumed (Exod. 9:25), fire (Exod. 9:23–24; 10:15), and darkness (Exod. 10:22). The final plague, which killed Pharaoh's son is referred to also: "Forsooth, the children of princes are dashed against the walls. . . . The prison is ruined. . . . He who places his brother in the ground is everywhere. . . . It is groaning that is throughout the land, mingled with lamentations" (Papyrus 2:13; 3:14; 4:3; 6:13). This parallels the biblical account which says, "the Lord struck all the first-born in the land of Egypt, from the first-born of the Pharaoh who sat on his throne to the firstborn of the captive that was in the dungeon . . . and there was a great cry in Egypt, for there was no home where was not someone dead" (Exod. 12:29–30). Immediately following these disasters, there was an invasion of "a foreign tribe" which came out of the desert (Papyrus 3:1). This invasion must have been the Hyksos, who dominated Egypt between the Middle Kingdom and the New Kingdom.

The monolith of el-Arish tells a similar story of darkness and suffering in the land in the days of King Thom. It also relates how the Pharaoh "went out to battle against the friends of Apopi (the god of darkness)," though the army never returned: "His majesty leapt into the so-called Place of the Whirlpool." The place of the incident is Pi-Kharoti, which may be equivalent to Pi-ha-hiroth, where the Israelites camped by the sea (Exod. 14:9). This is very interesting because the name of the city built by the Israelites is Pi-Thom, "the abode of Thom." And the king who reigned just before the Hyksos invasion was (in Greek) Timaios. But the Egyptian date for King Thom is about 600 years too early, around 2000 B.C. Either the Egyptian chronology is wrong, or history repeated itself in very unusual ways.

According to Velikovsky, the Hyksos should be identified as the Amalekites, whom the Israelites met before they even reached Sinai (Exod. 17:8–16). They might have reached Egypt within days after the Israelites left. The Egyptians referred to them as Amu and Arabian historians mention some Amalekite pharaohs. But the scriptural parallels are quite convincing. As the false prophet Baalam faced Israel, he blessed them despite his instructions, but when he turned, facing Egypt, "he looked on Amalek . . . and said, 'Amalek was the first of the nations'" (Num. 24:20). Why did he curse Amalek rather than Egypt, unless Egypt was under Amalekite domination? Also, the names of the first and last Amalekite kings in the Bible (Agag I and II, see Num. 24:7 and 1 Sam. 15:8) correspond to the first and last Hyksos kings. This would indicate that the Hyksos entered Egypt just after the Exodus and remained in power there until Saul defeated them and released the Egyptians from bondage. This would explain the genial relations that Israel had with Egypt in David and Solomon's time. In fact, Velikovsky shows striking similarities between the Queen of Sheba and the Egyptian queen Hatshepsut. She is said to have journeyed to the Divine Land and the gifts that she received there are much like those of Solomon to his visitor (see 1 Kings 10:10–22). She also built a temple in Egypt that is similar to the temple of Solomon. But according to Egyptian chronology, she lived before the Exodus. Only if this chronology is revised can this parallelism be explained. The invasion of Thutmose III into Palestine might also be equated with the attack of Shishak (2 Chron. 12:2–9).

The third synchronism is a series of letters (on clay tablets) called the el-Amarna letters. These are correspondence between the rulers in Palestine (Jerusalem, Syria, and Sumur) and the pharaohs Amenhotep III and his son Akhnaton. The Palestinians were concerned about an army approaching from the south called the Habiru, who were causing great destruction. On the basis of such a description, it has traditionally been held that these letters speak of the Israelites entering Canaan. Velikovsky shows that a closer look at these tablets reveals another picture entirely. First, Sumur can be identified as the city of Samaria, which was not built until after Solomon (1 Kings 16:24). Second, the "king of Hatti" threatens to invade from the north, which seems to be a Hittite invasion. Third, none of the names in the letters match the names of rulers given in the book of Joshua. In other words, the political situation is all wrong for these letters to have come from the time of the Exodus. If we move their date to the time when Ahab ruled from Samaria and was threatened by both the Moabites and the Hittites, then all of the names, places and events can be located in Kings and Chronicles, even to the names of the generals of armies. But this dates Amenhotep III 500 years later than the standard chronology. Either the chronology is wrong or one has to maintain that history repeated itself exactly half a millennium later.

The picture that emerges is a consistent one only if the Israelite history is used to date Egyptian events. Such an interpretation also requires a new chronology for Egyptian history. Courville has shown that the lists of Egyptian kings should not be understood as completely consecutive. He shows that some of the "kings" listed were not pharaohs, but local rulers or high officials. Among those mentioned are Joseph (Yufni) and Moses' adopted father Chenephres, who was a prince only by marriage.

Recognition that "kings" of the Thirteenth Dynasty were actually princes over local regions or subrulers provides us with insight into what Manetho regarded as comprising a dynasty. It was evidently not outside his thinking to give the names of the main line of kings as composing one dynasty and then to return on the time scale to pick up a line of secondary rulers as a distinct dynasty. By labeling these secondary rulers as kings the ancient historian caused an erroneous and grossly expanded chronology of Egypt. Working out this new chronology places the Exodus about 1440 B.C. and makes the other periods of Israelite history fall in line with the Egyptian kings mentioned.

Conclusion. The evidence is strong for a fifteenth-century date for the Exodus. This is at odds with the generally accepted date for Egyptian kings. But it may be that the conventional wisdom for Bronze Age dating, and certainly the chronology of Egyptian rulers may need to be drastically changed. More research and excavations will be needed to learn what theories come closest to describing the flow of events in Egypt and Canaan, but it appears that Bible dating is more accurate than had been suspected, even more accurate than the knowledge collected in the field of study.

Sources

G. Archer, *An Encyclopedia of Biblical Difficulties*

J. Bimson and D. Livingston, "Redating the Exodus," *Biblical Archeology Review* (September–October 1987)

Courville, D. A. *The Exodus Problem and Its Ramifications*

N. L. Geisler and R. Brooks. *When Skeptics Ask*, chap. 9

R. K. Harrison, *Introduction to the Old Testament*

Velikovsky, *Worlds in Collision*

Pharaoh, Hardening of. In Exodus 4:21 God declares: "I will harden Pharaoh's heart, so that he will not let the people go." But if God hardened Pharaoh's heart, then Pharaoh cannot be held morally responsible for his actions, since he did not do it of his own free will, but out of constraint (cf. 2 Cor. 9:7; 1 Peter 5:2). There appears to be a serious problem here for God's love and justice (*see* EVIL, PROBLEM OF). If God loves everyone, then why did he harden Pharaoh's heart so he would reject God's will? If God is just, why blame Pharaoh for his sin when it was God who hardened his heart to sin?

Proposed Solutions. There are two basic responses to this problem from differing theologies.

The Hard Determinist's Response. Calvinists or hard determinists (*see* DETERMINISM) emphasize God's sovereignty and claim he has the right to harden or soften any heart as he chooses. As for the justice of God, the answer is Paul's in Romans 9:20: "But who are you, O man, to talk back to God? Shall what is formed say to him who formed it, 'Why did you make me like this?'" God's salvific love is given to the elect. Again, citing Paul, they insist that "God has mercy on whom he wants to have mercy, and he hardens whom he wants to harden" (Rom. 9:18–19). The strong Calvinist's answer to the problem, then, is that Pharaoh was a hardened unbeliever to begin with, and God merely hardened him by withdrawing common grace that softens the effects of the fall in the unbelieving heart. He allowed Pharaoh to intensify his rebellion, as an unbeliever will do without divine restraint. God did this for the purpose of showing his power and glory. Pharaoh would not have truly repented without positive intervention from God's saving power.

This position is based on an unacceptable voluntaristic view (*see* VOLUNTARISM), wherein God can will either of two opposite actions. This seems to make God arbitrary about what is good. Contrary to the determinist, God is all-loving (John 3:16; Rom. 5:6–8; 2 Cor. 5:14–15; 1 John 2:1) and does not will that any should perish (2 Peter 3:9). Regardless of what the determinist says, God's justice is impugned if he hardens people in sin against their will. Free choice and compulsion are contradictory. As Paul noted about giving, "Each man should give what he has *decided* in his heart to give, not reluctantly or under compulsion, for God loves a cheerful giver" (2 Cor. 9:7). Peter added that leaders of the church in serving God should work, "not because you must, but because you are willing" (1 Peter 5:2).

The Response of Soft Determinists. Others respond to the problem of the hardening of Pharaoh's heart by pointing out that God did not harden Pharaoh's heart contrary to Pharaoh's free choice. The Scripture makes it clear that Pharaoh hardened his own heart. It declares that pharaoh's heart "grew hard" (Exod. 7:13), that he "hardened his heart" (Exod. 8:15), and that "Pharaoh's heart grew hard" the more God worked on it (8:19). Again, when God sent the plague of the flies, "Pharaoh hardened his heart at this time also" (8:32). This same or like phrase is repeated several times (see also 9:7, 34, 35). In fact, with the exception of God's prediction of what would happen (Exod. 4:21), the fact is that Pharaoh hardened his own heart first (7:13; 8:15, etc.), and God hardened it later (cf. 9:12; 10:1, 20, 27).

Scholars have pointed out that different Hebrew words for "harden" are used in this passage (Forster, 1555–68). *Qashah*, meaning "stubbornness" is used twice, once where God is the agent and once where Pharaoh is (7:3; 13:15). In both cases it is used of the overall process, not a particular act. *Kabed*, meaning "heavy" or "insensitive" is used many times, not only of Pharaoh's heart, but of the plagues. God sent a "heavy" swarm of flies, hailstones, and swarm of locusts. *Chazaq*, meaning "strength" or "encouragement" is used of Pharaoh's heart. When Pharaoh is the agent of hardening *kabed* is used. When God is the agent, *chazaq* is used. "Although Pharaoh is making his own moral decision, God is going to give him the strength to carry it out," writes Roger Forster (72). On this understanding there is nothing morally sinister about God "hardening," Pharaoh, and it is an understanding with which moderate Calvinists and Arminians could concur.

The sense in which God hardened his heart is similar to the way the sun hardens clay and also melts wax. If Pharaoh had been receptive to God's warnings, his heart would not have been hardened by God. But when God gave Pharaoh a reprieve from the plagues, he took advantage of the situation. "But when Pharaoh saw that there was relief, he hardened his heart and did not heed them [Moses and Aaron], as the Lord had said" (Exod. 8:15).

The question can be summarized as follows: does God harden hearts?

God does not harden hearts	God hardens hearts
initially	subsequently
directly	indirectly
against free choice	through free choice
as to their cause	as to their effect

Conclusion. If God is hardening Pharaoh's heart (or anyone else's) in accordance with their own inclination and choice, then God cannot be charged with being unjust, unloving, or acting contrary to their God-given free choice. And the Scriptures are clear that Pharaoh hardened his own heart. So, what God did was in accord with Pharaoh's own free choice (*see* FREE WILL). Events can be determined by God in his foreknowledge, yet free from the standpoint of human choice. Jesus hit this balance when he said in Matthew 18:7: "Such things must come, but woe to the man through whom they come."

Sources

Augustine, *On Free Will*

———, *On Grace and Free Will*

J. Edwards, *Freedom of the Will*

J. Fletcher, *John Fletcher's Checks to Antinomianism*, P. Wiseman, abridg.

R. T. Forster, *God's Strategy in Human History*

N. L. Geisler, *Chapters in Free Will and Predestination*, R. Basinger, et al., eds.

M. Luther, *Bondage of the Will*

Philo Judaeus. Philo Judaeus (ca. 20 B.C.–A.D. 50) was a Jewish philosopher and exegete from Alexandria, Egypt. Because of his affinity to Platonic philosophy, he is known as the Hebrew Plato. His numerous writings include *Against Flaccus, Procurator of Egypt*; *Legum Allegoriae*; *On Providence*; *On the Eternality of the World*; *Questions and Solutions in Genesis and Exodus*; *The Contemplative Life* (*De Vita Contemplativa*), and *The Life of Moses*.

Philo had a considerable influence on Christian leaders of the "Alexandrian School," such as

*Clement of Alexandria and *Justin Martyr. His allegorical method for interpreting Scripture also influenced *Origen, Ambrose, Augustine, and others. Other elements of his philosophy made an impact on later Christian thinking, including his use of proofs for God's existence, his Logos doctrine, and his views of the unknowability of God, negative language about God, *ex nihilo* creation (*see* CREATION, VIEWS OF), and particular providence.

Philo's Philosophy. Philo attempted to interpret Scripture in terms of Greek philosophy. His approach was eclectic and innovative.

Concept of God. Philo taught that human beings can know God, whether directly from divine revelation or indirectly through human reason. Various forms of proof for God included *Plato's argument for a *Demiurgos* in *Timaeus* and *Aristotle's *cosmological argument for an Unmoved Mover. Philo applies the Unmoved Mover to the existence of the world, not just motion. He even adopted the stoic argument for a Mind (God) within nature to show there was a transcendent God beyond nature.

Philo believed such arguments could only show the existence of God, not his nature. For him God was ineffable and unnamed. Only negative knowledge was possible. Positive terms can only describe God's activity, not his essence.

Mysticism and Allegorism. Since God cannot be known in a positive way, Philo, as other Platonists (*see* PLATO) and neo-Platonists (*see* Plotinus), resorted to mysticism. Even God's revelation in Scripture yielded no positive knowledge of God's nature, and could not be taken literally when it spoke of God. Only an allegorical interpretation could yield the true meaning.

Creation and Providence. As a Jewish theist (*see* THEISM), Philo believed in *ex nihilo* creation (*see* CREATION, VIEWS OF). As a Platonist he held that matter existed before creation. In a creative attempt to reconcile these views he posited that there were two creative acts of God, one by which he brought matter into existence, and the other by which he created the world out of preexisting matter.

Since God is all-powerful, he is able to intervene miraculously in the laws of nature he established. However, he does so purposefully. Contrary to Greek philosophy, God has not only general providence over the world but special and particular providence.

Logos. In interacting with Greek philosophy, Philo borrowed certain Platonic concepts to express his own theistic views. His concept of the *Logos* is a case in point. In *De Opificio* he describes the *Logos* as a cosmological principle, saying,

> God, assuming, as God would assume, that a beautiful copy could never come into existence without a beautiful model . . . when He willed to create this visible world, first blocked out the intelligible world, in order that using an incorporeal and godlike model he might make the corporeal world a younger image of the older. . . . When a city is being founded . . . sometimes there comes forward a man trained as an architect, and after surveying the favorable features of the site he first makes an outline in his mind of almost all the parts of the city that is to be built. . . . Then, receiving an impression of each of them in his soul, as if in wax, he models a city of the mind. Looking to this model he proceeds to construct the city of stone and wood, making the corporeal substance resemble each of the incorporeal ideas. In like manner we must think of God. [Dodd, 67]

The similarities and differences between Philo's *Logos* and that of John 1 are instructive (*see* LOGOS THEORY). For both the *Logos* is the image of God, the medium of creation, and the means of God's governance of creation. Only in John, however, is the *Logos* truly personal, who became a truly incarnate human being and yet is identical with God in nature (John 1:1–14). C. H. Dodd notes as a decisive difference that John "conceives of the *Logos* as incarnate, and of . . . actually living and dying on earth as a man. This means that the *Logos*, which in Philo is never personal . . . is in the gospel fully personal, standing in personal relations both with God and with men, and having a place in history." Further, "the *Logos* of Philo is not the object of faith and love. The incarnate *Logos* of the fourth Gospel is both lover and beloved" (Dodd, 73).

Evaluation. Philo is to be criticized for his purely negative theology (*see* ANALOGY, PRINCIPLE OF), his *mysticism, his allegorical method of interpretation, and his excessive attraction to Greek philosophy, which led him into errors. His Logos doctrine was wrongly applied to Christ (*see* LOGOS THEORY) by later writers.

Sources

N. Bentwich, *Philo-Judaeus of Alexandria*
C. H. Dodd, *The Interpretation of the Fourth Gospel*
J. Drummond, *Philo Judaeus*
R. Nash, *Christianity and the Hellenistic World*
Philo Judaeus, *De Vita Contemplativa*
F. E. Walton, *Development of the Logos-doctrine in Greek and Hebrew Thought*
H. A. Wolfson, *Philo: Foundations of Religious Philosophy in Judaism, Christianity and Islam*

Pi and the Bible. ***See*** **BIBLE, ALLEGED ERRORS IN.**

Plato. ***Life and Works of Plato.*** Plato was born in 428 B.C., the year of Pericles' death. He became a disciple of Socrates at the age of sixteen. Plato was twenty-nine when his mentor died.

His writing career is divided into four periods. In the first period he wrote *Apology, Crito, Pro-*

tagoras, and *Republic* (Bk I). In the second period he composed *Cratylus, Gorgias,* and *Lysis.* Between the second and third period he founded his Academy. In this third period he produced *Meno, Phaedo, Phaedrus, Symposium,* and the rest of the *Republic.* Before his last period of writing his most famous pupil, *Aristotle was born when Plato was forty-three. In his fourth and final period of literary composition Plato wrote *Parmenides, Theaetetus, Sophist, Statesman, Philebus, Timaeus, Critias,* and *Laws.*

Alexander the Great was born when Plato was seventy-two (in 347 B.C.). Just fourteen years later (in 333 B.C.) Alexander began to conquer the world and spread with it the Greek language and culture that has dominated so much of thought since that time.

Plato's Epistemology. Plato believed in innate ideas. Indeed, he believed these were the ideas the mind beheld in the world of pure Forms before birth. The ideas were irreducibly simple, eternal forms (*eidos*) that flowed from the one absolute Form, the Good (*Agathos*). Since they were beheld by the soul in a preincarnate state, all that was necessary was to recollect them. This was accomplished by a dialectical method dialogue illustrated in *Meno* when even a slave boy was able to do Euclidean geometry by simply being asked the right questions. Of course, if someone does not get it right in this life, there is another reincarnation.

When one reasoned back to the foundation of thought he found absolute first principles (*see*) of knowledge that served as the foundation of all knowledge. Skepticism, agnosticism (*see*), and relativism (*see* TRUTH, ABSOLUTE NATURE OF) are self-defeating (*see* SELF-REFUTING STATEMENTS).

Plato's Metaphysics. Plato believed the universe is eternal, an eternal process by which the Creator (*Demiurgos*) beheld the Good (the *Agathos*) and overflowed with Forms (*Eidos*) which informed the material world (*Chaos*) forever, forming it into a cosmos. Creation, then, is an eternal process of *ex materia* creation (*see* CREATION, VIEWS OF). Thus, reality is a basic *dualism of Form and matter, both being co-eternal.

As Plato set forth in the famous cave analogy in his *Republic,* the physical world is a world of shadows. The real world is the spiritual world of pure Forms. Each physical thing is structured or shaped by these Forms or universals, as opposed to nominalism (*see*), which denies the reality of universals or essences. For example, all human beings share in the one Form or Essence of humanness. And humanness exists as a pure Form in the real world, the spiritual one behind this material world. And each of these pure Forms come from the Form that contains all Forms in its absolutely perfect nature.

Plato's View of God. For Plato God was not the absolute Form (*Agathos*) but the Former (the *Demiurgos*). His argument for a Demiurgos (World Former) took the following form: (1) The cosmos would be a chaos without forms. Pure stuff without structure is shapeless. (2) Chaos (formless) is evil, and cosmos (form) is good. (3) All forms of good in the world come from a Good Former beyond the world (chaos cannot form itself into cosmos). (4) The Former cannot make good forms without a Form of Good after which to pattern them. (5) The Form after which changing forms are formed must be an unchanging Form. Only the unchanging can be basis of the changing. Only the Intelligible (Ideal) can be basis for Ideas. (6) Therefore, there is both a Former (*Demiurgos*) and the Form (Good) after which all things are formed.

To complete his Triad of ultimates, Plato offered an argument for a First Mover (or World Soul). Just as the Form is needed to explain the source of pure Forms, and the Former is necessary to account for the existence of formed things, even so a First Mover is needed to explain the existence of motion in the world. Plato's reasoning takes this shape: (1) Things move. This is known by observation. (2) But whatever moves is either moved by another or else is self-moved. (3) Self-movers (souls) are prior to non-self-movers. For what does not move itself is moved by what does. (4) Self-movers are eternal; otherwise there would be no motion, since something inert cannot move itself. Plato adds that (5) there must be two self-movers in the universe, one to account for the regular motion (good) and another to explain the irregular motion (evil). (6) The one who accounts for the good motion is the best, because it is the Supreme Mover, which he calls World Soul. (7) Hence, there is a Supreme Mover (Soul).

The Influence of Plato on Later Thought. Alfred North *Whitehead said Western philosophy is a series of footnotes on Plato. This is largely true. Specific influences are manifest in Plotinus, St. *Augustine, gnosticism, asceticism, *mysticism, innatism, dualism, allegorism, and *panentheism. Since Plato held a form of *Finite Godism, John Stewart Mill, William *James, Brightman, Peter Bertocci, Whitehead, and Charles Hartshorne were also influenced by Plato. Likewise, Friedrich *Schleiermacher, Adolph Harnack, and other liberals and humanists (*see* HUMANISM, SECULAR) who hold to man's inherent perfectibility stem from Plato, who believed that to know the good is to do the good. Salvation is by education.

An Evaluation of Plato's Views. Plato's views have numerous enduring values. An incomplete list would include at least the following:

Positive Dimensions. There are numerous positive values in Plato's thought, many of which have been helpful in expressing and defending the Christian faith. Among these are the following.

**Foundationalism.* Plato's defense of first principles has been a great help to Christian apologists in arguing against *agnosticism and *conventionalism.

Truth as correspondence. Like other classical philosophers, Plato defined truth as correspondence, thus lending support to the Christian conviction that metaphysical truth is what corresponds to reality. Truth is objective and not merely subjective (*see* TRUTH, NATURE OF).

Epistemological absolutism. Not only was truth objective for Plato, but it was absolute. Plato's arguments are still used by Christian apologists to defend their belief in absolute truth.

Moral absolutism. Plato also believed in absolute values. This too is in accord with the Christian apologetic task of defending moral absolutes (*see* ABSOLUTES, MORAL).

*Ethical *essentialism.* Not only did Plato believe in moral absolutes but he held that they are anchored in the unchanging nature of the Form (the Good).

Universals. Contrary to *nominalism, Plato argued, as do orthodox Christians, that there are universals and essences. Indeed, it is part of Christian belief that God has one essence and three persons and that Christ has two essences or natures united in one person (*see* CHRIST, DEITY OF).

Proofs for God. Plato's proofs for God were a forerunner of later Christian forms of the *cosmological argument (*see*) or the argument from perfection (*see* GOD, EVIDENCE FOR) used by *Augustine, *Anselm, and *Thomas Aquinas.

Immortality. Plato defended what all orthodox Christians believe, namely, that human beings have a spiritual dimension to their makeup that is immortal (*see* IMMORTALITY).

A life beyond this one. Another dimension of Plato's thought acceptable to Christians is his belief in a spiritual world beyond this one to which people eventually go after death. Plato posited both a heaven and a *hell.

Innate intellectual capacity. Most Christian apologists believe there is an innate, God-given, capacity of the human mind. We are not born absolutely blank but with certain rational capacities and abilities given by God. These are manifest in the universality of first principles such as the law of non-contradiction.

Negative Dimensions. Despite the many positive features of the Platonic system, many of Plato's ideas have been a continual nemesis to Christianity. A few of these are noteworthy.

Metaphysical dualism. Unlike Christianity, which holds to a monarchial creation *ex nihilo* (out of nothing), Plato affirmed a *dualism of creation *ex materia,* out of preexisting matter (*see* CREATION, VIEWS OF). Thus, for Plato the material universe is eternal, not temporal as Christians believe and offer good evidence to support (*see* *KALAM* COSMOLOGICAL ARGUMENT; BIG BANG THEORY).

**Finite Godism.* Unlike the theistic God of Christianity who is infinite in power and perfection, Plato's God was finite. But there is ample evidence to show that God is infinite.

Anthropological dualism. One of Plato's most enduring but troublesome legacies among Christians is his dualistic view of human beings. According to Plato, man is a soul and only has a body. In fact, humans are imprisoned in their bodies. From this both asceticism (denial of the body) and otherworldliness result, neither of which are endorsed by Christianity.

Allegorism. Because Plato believed that matter was less real and less good than spirit, he downplayed the literal understanding of things. In the field of interpretation this leads to looking for a deeper, more spiritual or mystical understanding of a text. From this both neoplatonism (*see* PLOTINUS) and medieval allegorism developed (*see* ORIGEN), a problem still beleaguering the Christian church.

Innatism of ideas. While Plato correctly pointed to an innate dimension of the human mind, many Christians, following Aquinas reject Plato's belief in innate ideas. Some great Christian thinkers, like Augustine, even went so far as to affirm Plato's concomitant idea of recollection of these ideas from a previous existence, only later to have to retract the view.

Reincarnation. Plato's concept of reincarnation, like that of Eastern views, has been condemned by the Christian church and is refuted by good evidence, both biblical and rational (*see* REINCARNATION).

Humanistic optimism. In some respects Plato is the father of Western humanism (*see* HUMANISM, SECULAR). His belief that human beings are perfectible by education is both contrary to the teaching of Scripture and universal human experience.

Pluralistic dilemma. Like other philosophers following Parmenides, Plato never solved the problem of the one and the many (*see* MONISM). He ended up with many irresolvably simple Forms that could not differ from one another in any real way (*see* PLURALISM, METAPHYSICAL).

Theological inadequacy. Some Christians have seen more Christian truth in Plato than there is to see. Plato's Triad of the Form, the Former, and the World Soul is by no means the Christian *Trinity, as some have claimed. For one thing, two of them (the Form and the World Soul) are not even persons in any significant sense of the term. For another thing, they do not all share one and the same nature.

Further, Plato and the other Greek philosophers never got their God and their highest metaphysical principle together, as did Christians (see Gilson). In Plato, for example, the Good is the highest metaphysical principle, but the Good is not identified with God. Rather, the Demiurgos, who is inferior to the Good, is God in Plato's system.

Sources

E. Gilson, *God and Philosophy* (chap. 1)
J. Owens, *A History of Ancient Western Philosophy*
Plato, *Republic*
———, *Apology*
———, *Timaeus*
———, *Laws*
A. E. Taylor, *Plato: The Man and His Works*

Platonic View of God. *See* COSMOLOGICAL ARGUMENT.

Plotinus. Plotinus (ca. 204–270) was born in Egypt, and in his late twenties he began to study philosophy at Alexandria. Eventually he studied under Ammonius Saccas, the teacher of *Origen, for eleven years. Plotinus did not begin to write until he had taught philosophy in Rome for ten years. His work has been extremely influential in both philosophical and religious thought. He followed the worldview of emanational pantheism.

God and the World. Contrary to vedanta *pantheism (*see* HINDUISM, VEDANTA), Plotinus held that being or reality is multiple or many. He counted three levels or planes of being. But prior to and beyond being is the One.

The One is absolutely simple, that is, it has no parts; and it is absolutely necessary, that is, it must exist. The One has not just "happened," but it exists by necessity. This absolute Unity must exist, because multiplicity presupposes a prior unity. We can only know what is many if we know the One. "Unity must precede Reality and be its author" (*Enneads*, 6.6.13; all further citations are from this source.). The One, therefore, is the absolute source of being. The One is beyond and prior to being.

The Indescribable and Unknowable. Plotinus argues that the One transcends all of which it is the source, which is everything in reality: "Certainly this Absolute is none of the things of which it is the source—its nature is that nothing can be affirmed of it—not existence, not essence, not life—since it is That which transcends all these." Even its own name, the One, it transcends: "And this name, the One, contains really no more than the negation of plurality. . . . If we are led to think positively of the One, name and thing, there would be more truth in silence" (3.8.101).

If the One is truly indescribable, why does Plotinus attempt to describe it? His writing, he says, is a call to vision, which urges on toward the One.

We can know something about the One through its offspring, *being* (6.9.5). Though we cannot speak or know the One, we can speak or know *of* the One in terms of what has come *from* the One. We must keep in mind, however, that our words and thoughts are only pointers, not truly descriptive but only evocative.

Levels of Reality. Nous. The first level of reality is *Nous* ("Mind"). *Nous* is the Divine Mind; it is God but not the highest God. It is pure Being. Of the emanations from the One, *Nous* is the first (5.1.4, 8). When the One emanates outward, and this emanant looks backward upon its source, there arises the simple duality of Knower and Known (6.7.37). This simple duality is *Nous*. *Nous* in turn gives rise to further emanations by bending inward upon itself. It produces particular intellects or forms that turn outward, producing the world soul, which in turn produces the species of individual souls (6.2.22; 6.7.15). The One, Nous, and World Soul form, not a Trinity but an emanational triad. From this tri-level God flow all other things. Creation is *ex deo*, both emanationally and necessarily (*see* CREATION, VIEWS OF).

World Soul. The second level of reality, the *World Soul*, is a middle position between *Nous* and the corporeal world. It reflects the *Nous* and organizes the corporeal. The *World Soul* is even more multiple than *Nous*, for it is further from the absolute Unity of the One. The *World Soul* emanates forth when *Nous* reflects upon itself (6.2.22). The *World Soul* animates the universe in all its multiplicity, giving it a unity or wholeness (3.1.4, 5).

Matter. The third level of reality is *matter*, the most multiple of all. Since the entire emanational process is a necessary unfolding from unity to multiplicity, it is necessary that the last stage is one step away from complete nonexistence. Plotinus describes matter as non-being, but adds that this should not be understood to mean nonexistence. Rather, matter is an image of being, or something further removed than even an image. The further removed something is from the Source of being, the One, the less unity and being it has (6.9.1). Since matter is the most multiple, it "has no residue of good in it" (1.8.7). Since the absolute Unity is absolutely good, each further degree of multiplicity is less good and capable of greater evil (1.8.5). Matter has no good in it, but it does have the capacity for good. Matter is not pure evil itself. It is simply privated of all good (1.8.3), having only the mere capacity for good left in it.

That which is beyond and prior to being, the One, eternally and necessarily unfolds itself as a seed unfolds into a flower. This produces *Nous*, or what Plotinus calls "One-Many." *Nous* is the One becoming self-conscious, that is, discovering itself. Now when *Nous* reflects inward upon itself it produces knowing beings, and when it reflects outward it produces world soul, or what Plotinus calls "One-and-Many." From World Soul all else flows, including matter or the "many."

The One flows outward from unity to multiplicity. And for Plotinus there is also a return flow back to unity. Just as there is a necessity for the many to unfold from the One, there is a need for the Many to return to the One. The process is like the stretching of a gigantic elastic band. It can be stretched so far before it snaps back to the source.

Human Beings. Plotinus believes that human beings are a soul that has a body. The true self is the eternal soul (*see* IMMORTALITY), which is temporarily coupled with a material shell. Through this attachment with matter, the soul becomes contaminated (1.2.4). If a person does not strive toward the ultimate good and unity, and instead is concerned only with matter, the self will become absolutely evil (1.8.13). To be saved and attain ultimate perfection, the person must turn from matter and toward the One. Salvation consists in overcoming the body-soul dualism. This normally requires many cycles of reincarnation. To escape the cycle, a person must turn to the inner by asceticism and meditation.

Destiny. The first step toward deliverance begins in the realm of sense, where some unity has been imposed by the Absolute above (1.6.2–3). By looking at the "beauties of the realm of sense, images and shadow-pictures, fugitives that have entered into Matter," one comes to realize that "there are earlier and loftier beauties than these" (1.6.3–4). These objects of sense point us to the source (6.9.11). We are not to stop with them but ascend beyond them. So the first step is from the sensible world to the intellectual world of *Nous*.

As the first step involved a move from the external, the second step continues the ascent from the internal, the soul, toward the eternal, *Nous*. This movement is from the lower soul to a higher soul, and then to *Nous*, which is above the soul. Human mind must identify with Mind. Knower and known must become one. This is done through meditation. Even now, however, ultimate Unity has not yet been attained.

The third and last step leads to the highest possible union—oneness with the One. It can be attained only by a mystical (*see* MYSTICISM) union that puts away all multiplicity, even intellect and reason. Says Plotinus, "One wishing to contemplate what transcends the intellectual attains by putting away all that is of the intellect." The way journeys past knowing, even the highest objects of knowledge, to the intuitional and mystical. In this last stage, everything is absolute unity again. What emanated out has returned. All that flowed from God has and must return (5.5.6; 6.9.4).

Evaluation. Despite positive features in his system (such as God's transcendence and human immortality), Plotinus' views are subject to the same criticisms as other forms of pantheism. A few of his essential premises need special evaluation.

The One and Nonbeing. For Plotinus, the Ultimate (One) is beyond being. But the one must be either in the realm of being or nonbeing. There is nothing in between something and nothing. Since the One is not in the realm of being, it must be nonbeing or nothing. But nothing cannot produce something. Yet Plotinus contends that the One produced all being. This is the ultimate metaphysical absurdity.

Effect and Cause. In the Plotinian system the effect turns out to be greater than the cause. For the one produced being but has no being. Mind emerges from the One, but the One as such has no mind. However, water cannot rise higher than its source. An effect cannot be greater than its cause (*see* CAUSALITY, PRINCIPLE OF; ANALOGY, PRINCIPLE OF).

Following from the principle of causality is the principle of analogy. Since the cause cannot produce what it does not possess, the effect must resemble its cause. Of course, it cannot be identical, since one is producer and the other the produced. One is superior. But, since only being produces being, there must be some actual similarity between cause and effect. The infinite, uncaused Cause of all other being is Being, though it is not finite, nor is it caused. For Plotinus the One does not share any characteristics with its offspring. It is totally "other." This violates the principle of *analogy (*see* FIRST PRINCIPLES).

Knowledge of the Ultimate. Plotinus could ascertain no knowledge of the One. It is beyond being and beyond description. All statements about it are negative or equivocal. However, even Plotinus admitted that we cannot know something is "not that" unless we know what "that" is. Negative knowledge presupposes positive knowledge (6.7.29; 6.9.4).

Summary. Plotinus' emanational pantheism begins in unity, which gives rise to increased multiplicity until being almost reaches the point of nonexistence. Then all returns toward increasingly greater unity, until the greatest unity is reached in the absolute unity of the One. Here one becomes one with the One and all with the All.

If words cannot express the Ultimate, Plotinus himself wrote hundreds of pages describing his view of the ultimate. Only absolute verbal and mental mutism is consistent for a mystic (*see* MYSTICISM). Even evocative language or pointers will not suffice. Unless it points to something we can understand, we still have no understanding.

Sources

A. A. Armstrong, *The Architecture of the Intelligible Universe*

E. Brehier, *The Philosophy of Plotinus*

D. Clark and N. L. Geisler, *Apologetics in the New Age*, chap. 4

G. Clark, *From Thales to Dewey*

N. L. Geisler and W. Watkins, *Worlds Apart: A Handbook on Worldviews*, chap. 3

Plotinus, *Enneads*

Pluralism, Metaphysical. Pluralism affirms that reality is found in many, as opposed to one (*see*

ONE AND MANY, PROBLEM OF). It stands in contrast to monism, which claims that reality is one. Pantheism is a form of monism, and theism is a form of pluralism. Monists hold a univocal or equivocal notion of being (*see* PLOTINUS). Theists hold an analogical view of being (*see* ANALOGY, PRINCIPLE OF).

Pluralism, Religious. To better understand religious pluralism, several terms related to religion need to be distinguished: *pluralism*, *relativism*, *inclusivism*, and *exclusivism*:

- *Religious pluralism* is the belief that every religion is true. Each provides a genuine encounter with the Ultimate. One may be better than the others, but all are adequate.
- *Relativism* (*see* TRUTH, ABSOLUTE) claims that there are no criteria by which one can tell which religion is true or best. There is no objective truth in religion, and each religion is true to the one holding it.
- *Inclusivism* claims that one religion is explicitly true, while all others are implicitly true.
- *Exclusivism* is the belief that only one religion is true, and the others opposed to it are false.

Christianity is exclusivistic; it claims to be the one and only true religion (*see* CHRIST, UNIQUENESS OF). This places Christians at odds with the modern movements to study comparative religion and work at interfaith communing. Asks Alister McGrath, "How can Christianity's claims to truth be taken seriously when there are so many rival alternatives and when 'truth' itself has become a devalued notion? No one can lay claim to possession of the truth. It is all a question of perspective. All claims to truth are equally valid. There is no universal or privileged vantage point that allows anyone to decide what is right and what is wrong" ("Challenge of Pluralism," 365).

Equality among World Religions. Pluralist John Hick argues, "I have not found that the people of the other world religions are, in general, on a different moral and spiritual level from Christians." For "The basic ideal of love and concern for others and of treating them as you would wish them to treat you is, in fact, taught by all the great religious tradition" (Hick, "A Pluralist's View," 39). Hick offers as proof the fact that statements similar to the "Golden Rule" of Christianity can be found in other religions (ibid., 39–40).

It is debatable whether practitioners in non-Christian religions can really display what Galatians 5:22–23 calls "the fruit of the Spirit": love, joy, peace, patience, kindness, goodness, faithfulness, gentleness, and self-control. Certainly non-Christians do loving things and feel the heart emotion of attachment that we call love. And others are gentle, good, kind, and self-controlled. But are they able to manifest *agape* love? One can lead a philanthropic life and even die in a stand for personal beliefs, yet not show God-founded holistic true love (see 1 Cor. 13:3). Christians are to have a qualitatively different kind of love for one another and especially for God. While God's common grace enables evil people to do good (see Matt. 7:11), only the supernatural love of God can motivate a person to express true *agape* (cf. John 15:13; Rom. 5:6–8; 1 John 4:7).

Before one conclude too quickly that William James demonstrated the equality of all forms of saintliness in *Varieties of Religious Experiences*, Jonathan Edwards' *A Treatise on Religious Affections* should be perused. Edwards argues forcefully that manifestations of Christian godliness are unique, a difference in the highest level of Christian and non-Christian piety.

Even if one could demonstrate a kind of moral equality of practice among most adherents of the great religions, this would not in itself prove moral equality among the religions. A person perfectly practicing a lesser moral code may appear to be more moral than a person imperfectly living according to a higher ethical standard. In order to make a fair comparison one must compare the highest moral teachings of the various religions. For another thing, one must compare the best examples of the adherents to each. A close comparison of the attitudes, goals, and motivations, as well as the actions, of Mother Teresa and Mohandas Gandhi would demonstrate the superiority of Christian compassion for the needy. On the modern religious scene, one must also sort out what is inherent to the moral system of another religion and what has become incorporated into it as the result of Christian missionary activity. Hinduism as a system did not generate social compassion in Gandhi. Gandhi was a student of Christianity who seriously considered conversion. He proclaimed his admiration for Jesus' teaching in the Sermon on the Mount. The social compassion found in some forms of current Hinduism is a foreign import from Christianity, the influence of those like Gandhi who had been touched by Christian principles. Even then it fell short of the full-orbed Christian compassion of Mother Teresa.

Finding a moral principle akin to the Golden Rule (cf. Matt. 7:12) is not enough to show moral equality. This is a manifestation of general revelation, the law written by God in the hearts of all (Rom. 2:12–15). When it was lived out at moments of national spirituality, Christian morality has produced dynamic social compassion, while Eastern religions have produced stagnant societies and Islam has brought intolerant ones (Pinnock in Okhlam, 61).

Hick's analysis begs the question. Only by assuming that the moral common denominator of all religions is the standard by which they should all be judged does he arrive at the not-surprising conclusion that they are all equal. But one had to negate the superior aspects of Christian morality or teaching in order to show that Christianity is not superior. Hick seems to acknowledge this tacitly when he confessed that the "Acceptance of some form of the pluralistic view prompts each to de-emphasize and eventually winnow out that aspect of its self-understanding that entails a claim to unique superiority among the religions of the world" (ibid., 51).

Further, the moral manifestation of a belief does not settle the truth question. For example, the fact that there are outwardly moral Mormons does not prove that Joseph Smith was a true prophet. Indeed, there is strong evidence that he is not a true prophet (see Tanner). Among evidence to the contrary are his demonstrably false prophecies (*see* MIRACLE; PROPHECY AS PROOF OF BIBLE). There is evidence for whether something is true other than the lifestyle of its adherents. Truth is what corresponds to reality (*see* TRUTH, NATURE OF) and, hence, a religion is true if its central tenets correspond to the real world, not merely whether its followers live a good life or even a better one than adherents of another religion.

Fifth, in the final analysis the moral superiority of Christianity does not rest on our imperfection as Christians but on Christ's unique perfection as our exemplar. It is not based on our fallible moral character but on his impeccable character (John 8:46; 2 Cor. 5:21; Heb. 4:15; 1 John 3:3). In this context, there is clearly a moral superiority of Christianity over all other religions.

Redemptive Equality of Religions. As for the Christian claim of a superior mode of salvation, Hick believes this either begs the question or is not evident in practice. "If we define salvation as being forgiven and accepted by God because of Jesus' death on the cross, then it becomes a tautology that Christianity alone knows and is able to preach the source of salvation." And "if we define salvation as an actual human change, a gradual transformation from natural self-centeredness (with all the human evils that flow from this) to a radically new orientation centered in God and manifest in the 'fruit of the Spirit,' then it seems clear that salvation is taking place within all of the world religions—and taking place, so far as we can tell, to more or less the same extent" (ibid., 43). Further, what is common to all world religions is an adequate response to the Ultimate. "But they seem to constitute more or less equally authentic human awareness of and response to the Ultimate, the Real, the final ground and source of everything" (ibid., 45). There are, of course, "a plurality of religious traditions constituting different, but apparently more or less equally salvific, human responses to the Ultimate. These are the great world faiths" (ibid., 47).

Hick's analysis of salvation beliefs is based on the assumption that all religions have a proper relation to what is really Ultimate. This begs the question. Maybe some are not connected at all to what is really Ultimate (i.e., the true God). Or, perhaps they are not properly related to what is really Ultimate (God).

Hick wrongly assumes that all religions are merely a human response to the Ultimate. But this assumes an antisupernatural view of religion. In fact, it assumes an Eastern pantheistic view of the Ultimate as what transcends all particular cultural manifestations in the various world religions.

This denial of the truth of any particular religion is itself a form of exclusivism. It favors the particular view known as pantheism in order to deny the particularity of a view known as Christian theism. To assume this kind of pantheistic position as a basis for one's analysis of all religions, including nonpantheistic ones, simply begs the question. Or to put it another way, the pluralist who denies that any particular religion is any more true than others is making a particular truth claim.

The pluralist view often degenerates to the position that whatever is sincerely believed is true. This means that it matters not whether one is a passionate nazi, satanist, or member of the Flat Earth Society. Any view would be truth. Sincerity is clearly not a test of truth. Many people have been sincerely wrong about many things.

Finally, this implies that all truth claims are a matter of "both-and," rather than either-or. By this reasoning there could be square circles, wise fools, and educated illiterates. Mutually exclusive propositions cannot both be true. Opposing truth claims of various religions cannot both be true (*see* LOGIC; FIRST PRINCIPLES). For example, Hindu pantheism and Christian theism affirm mutually exclusive worldviews. Islam denies and Christianity proclaims Jesus' death on the cross and resurrection from the dead three days later. One or the other must be wrong.

The Uniqueness of Christ. As for the Christian dogma about the uniqueness of Christ (*see* CHRIST, UNIQUENESS OF) to be God incarnate in human flesh, Hick contends that there are two main problems: First, Jesus did not teach this uniqueness himself. Second, the concept that Jesus was both God and human lacks coherence.

Hick rejects apparent statements about the uniqueness of Christ in the Gospels because he sees New Testament scholars doing the same thing. "Among mainline New Testament scholars there is today a general consensus that these are not pronouncements of the historical Jesus but words put in his mouth some sixty or seventy years later by a Christian writer expressing the theology that had developed in his part of the expanding church" (ibid., 52–53). Hick cites a list of biblical writers who allegedly agreed that "Jesus did not claim deity for himself" (ibid.).

Hick is misinformed on both points. The historical reliability of the Gospels is now beyond serious dispute (*see* ACTS, HISTORICITY OF; NEW TESTAMENT, DATING OF; NEW TESTAMENT, HISTORICITY OF). Claims that Jesus' statements were edited many years later to fit a religious program simply do not square with the facts. The Gospels were available in the forms we now know within the lifetimes of eyewitnesses and contemporaries of the events. Recent evidence seems to be pushing dates earlier. John, thought to be the last Gospel written, was by a participant of the events (John 21; 24). Luke was written by a contemporary disciple who knew the eyewitnesses (Luke 1:1–4). The Gospels are reporting, not creating, the words and deeds of Jesus. There is firm support for his unique claims to be God incarnate (*see* CHRIST, DEITY OF).

Hick's second allegation is that "it has not proved possible, after some fifteen centuries of intermittent effort, to give any clear meaning to the idea that Jesus had two complete natures, one human and the other divine?" (ibid., 55). Hick asks, "Is it really possible for infinite knowledge to be housed in a finite human brain" (ibid., 55). Again, "Do we really want to claim that Jesus was literally omnipotent but pretended not to be, as in Mark 6:5?" And "while he was good, loving, wise, just, and merciful, there is an obvious problem about how a finite human being could have these qualities in an infinite degree. . . . A finite being cannot have infinite attributes" (ibid., 56).

Hick falls short of claiming that the incarnation involves an outright logical contradiction, though his language could imply that. If it is not a logical contradiction, there is no demonstrated incoherence in the view. Indeed, Hick himself admits that "It is logically permissible to believe anything that is not self-contradictory" (*Metaphor of God Incarnate,* 104). As for the claim that it is difficult to show just how this is so, on the same grounds one would have to reject both much of our common experience as well as modern science (which has difficulty explaining just how light can be both waves and particles).

Second, Hick appears to be misinformed about the orthodox view of the two natures of Christ. His objections assume an unorthodox view known as the monophysite heresy, which confuses the two natures of Christ. His question: "is it really possible for infinite knowledge to be housed in a finite human brain?" (ibid., 55) reveals this confusion. The orthodox view does not claim that there was infinite knowledge in the finite brain of Christ. Rather, it affirms that there were two distinct natures of Christ, one infinite and the other finite. The person of Christ did not have infinite knowledge. He had infinite knowledge only in his infinite nature. As God, he knew all things. As human, Jesus grew in knowledge (Luke 2:52). The same thing applies to Jesus' other attributes. As God, He was omnipotent. As human, he was not (*see* CHRIST, DEITY OF).

Allegations of Intolerance. Another charge is that exclusivism is intolerant. This is directed at the exclusivists' view that one religious view is true and those opposed to it are false. This, to the pluralists, seems a bit of bigotry. Why should only one view have a franchise on the truth?

By this reasoning, pluralists are also "intolerant." They claim their views are true, to the exclusion of opposing views (including exclusivism). And they certainly would not tolerate the position that pluralistic and opposing nonpluralistic views are both true.

If the charge of intolerance is leveled because of the manner in which some exclusivists express their views, nonpluralists have no monopoly on rudeness, intimidation, and poorly thought-out statements. As is demonstrated in the "politically correct" movement on university campuses, pluralists can be as intolerant as anyone else. In fact, there might be more exclusivists than pluralists who act with respect and restraint. However, it should be noted that the very concept of tolerance implies a real disagreement. One does not tolerate that with which he or she agrees. Tolerance presupposes a self-confident view of truth.

Narrow-Mindedness. The tolerance issue is closely related to a favorite allegation of pluralists that nonpluralists are narrow-minded. They claim that their view is true, and everyone else is in error. This seems presumptuous. Why should only exclusivists be in possession of the truth?

The response is that pluralists (P) and exclusivists (E) make an equal claim to truth and error. Both claim that their view is true and whatever opposes it is false. For example, if E is true, then all non-E is false. Likewise, if P is true then all non-P is false. Both views are "narrow." All truth is narrow. After all, 2 plus 3 has only one true answer—5. That is the way truth is.

Intellectual Imperialism. Another charge is that exclusivists are guilty of intellectual imperialism. Exclusivists are totalitarian with regard to truth. They should be more open to input from many sources, not just to one. Some postmodern pluralists go so far as to claim that the very ideas of truth and meaning smack of fascism (cited in McGrath, "Challenge of Pluralism," 364).

This allegation has a certain appeal, especially to those of a particular political mind set, but it is without merit with regard to determining what is true. The way this allegation is often made is as a form of the *ad hominem* logical fallacy. It attacks the person rather than the position.

This objection also makes an unjustified presumption that truth should be more democratic.

But truth is not decided by majority vote. Truth is what corresponds to reality (*see* TRUTH, NATURE OF), whether the majority believe it or not. Do pluralists really believe that all views are equally true and good and should be settled on by majority rule? Is fascism or Marxism as good as democracy? Was nazism as good as any other government? Should we have tolerated the burning of widows at Hindu funerals of their husbands?

Presuppositions of Pluralism. *There Are Transreligious Moral Criteria.* To make the moral equality argument work, one must assume a set of moral criteria not unique to any particular religion by which all can be evaluated. Pluralists generally deny that there is any universally binding moral law. If there were such absolute moral laws there would need to be an absolute Moral Law Giver. But only theistic type religions accept this criteria, and some of them reject the absolute perfect nature of God (for example, Finite Godists). If there is a moral law common to all religions, then it is not unique to one, and no religion can be judged inferior for lacking it.

Finally, if there are no such universal moral laws, then there is no way to judge morally all religions from any standard beyond them. And it is not fair to take the standards of one religion and apply them to another, claiming that the other falls short.

Phenomena Can Be Explained. Beneath the pluralist's attack on exclusivism is a naturalistic presupposition. All religious phenomena can be explained naturalistically. No supernatural explanations are allowed. But this presumptive naturalism is without justification. Miracles cannot be ruled out *a priori* (*see* MIRACLES, ARGUMENTS AGAINST). Neither, as David Hume claimed, are miracles incredible. Nor are miracles without evidence. Indeed, there is substantial evidence for the greatest "miracle" of all, the *ex nihilo* creation of the world out of nothing (*see* BIG BANG and *KALAM* COSMOLOGICAL ARGUMENT). There is also abundant evidence that the resurrection of Christ occurred (*see* RESURRECTION, EVIDENCE FOR).

The World Is "Religiously Ambiguous." Hick believes that "the universe, as presently accessible to us, is capable of being interpreted intellectually and experientially in both religious and naturalistic ways" (*Interpretation of Religion,* 129; see Geivett, 77). We cannot know the truth about God; what is real cannot be differentiated from what is false.

It is a self-defeating claim that we know that we cannot know the real. Simply because we do not know reality exhaustively does not mean we cannot know it truly (*see* AGNOSTICISM; REALISM). As Geivett notes, "to the extent that God is known at all, he is known truly." The very notion of an undifferentiated Real is implausible, if not self-defeating. Hick's claim that the Real can be symbolized by the concept of *sunyata* in Buddhism is a case in point. For if the Real is so undifferentiated, then how can any symbol represent it? Neither can the Real be manifested in various traditions, as Hick claims. In order for something to be manifested, at least some of its characteristics must be revealed. But the Real, if totally undifferentiated, has no discernible characteristics. Hence, it could not be manifested in our experience in any meaningful way. There is a kind of mystical epistemology presumed in this "God is Unknowable" approach (*see* MYSTICISM). It rather imperiously decrees how God can and cannot reveal himself (Geivett, 77).

Dialogue Is the Only Way to Truth. Another seriously flawed presupposition is the position that pluralistic interreligious dialogue is the only valid way to discover truth. No genuine religious dialogue is possible if one assumes his religion is true in advance of the dialogue. This is sure proof that he is not "open" to truth. True dialogue assumes one is tolerant, open, humble, willing to listen and learn, and engage in a shared search for truth and a self-sacrificing, other-oriented love (ibid., 239).

However, true dialogue is possible without adopting a pluralistic position on truth. One can have the attitude of humility, openness, and tolerance without sacrificing convictions about truth. Even the pluralist is not willing to give up a commitment to pluralism as a condition for such dialogue. This violates the pluralist's own imperative. In fact, the call to dialogue is usually a disingenuous attempt at evangelism on behalf of the worldview of the one calling for dialogue.

Hick's View Is Religiously Neutral. Hick feigns religious neutrality, but it does not exist. His alleged pluralism is patterned after Hinduism's conception of the Transcendent. And it is antagonistic to the core principles of Christianity. It does not really encourage genuine dialogue between the traditions. Indeed, it renders virtually vacuous the concept of being "in a given religious tradition." After all, according to pluralists, every tradition is essentially the same. So, to accept pluralism is to reject one's own tradition and accept the pluralist's tradition.

A Relativistic View of Truth Is Correct. Beneath the pluralists' assertion that all major religions have equal claim to the truth is a relativistic view of truth (*see* TRUTH, NATURE OF). But the denial of absolute truth is self-defeating. It claims that relativism is true for everyone, everywhere, and always. But what is true for everyone, everywhere, and always is an absolute truth. Therefore, the relativist claims that relativism is absolutely true.

Sources

M. Adler, *Truth in Religion*

A. D. Clarke and B. Hunter, eds., *One God, One Lord: Christianity in a World of Religious Pluralism*

D. Clark and N. L. Geisler, *Apologetics in the New Age*

W. V. Crockett and J. G. Sigountos, eds., *Through No Fault of their Own? The Fate of Those Who Have Never Heard*
K. Gnanakan, *The Pluralistic Predicament*
J. Hick, *An Interpretation of Religion*
———, *The Metaphor of God Incarnate: Christology in a Pluralistic Age*
A. McGrath, "The Challenge of Pluralism for the Contemporary Christian Church," *JETS* (September 1992)
R. Nash, *Is Jesus the Only Savior?*
H. Netland, *Dissonant Voices: Religious Pluralism and the Question of Truth*
D. Okholm, et al., *More Than One Way: Four Views on Salvation in a Pluralistic World*, see esp. contributions by D. Geivett, et al., J. Hick and C. Pinnock
J. Sanders, *No Other Name: An Investigation of the Destiny of the Unevangelized*
G. Tanner and S. Tanner, *The Changing World of Mormonism*

Polygamy. First Kings 11:3 says Solomon had 700 wives and 300 concubines. Other men God highly praised in the Bible had multiple wives (and/or concubines), particularly Abraham and David. And yet the Scriptures repeatedly warn against having multiple wives (Deut. 17:17) and violating the principle of monogamy—one man for one wife (cf. 1 Cor. 7:2; 1 Tim. 2:2). This seems to many critics to be a contradiction (*see* BIBLE, ALLEGED ERRORS).

The Problem of Polygamy. Monogamy is God's ideal standard for the human race. Polygamy was never commanded by God; it was only tolerated.

From the beginning, God set the pattern by creating a monogamous marriage relationship with one man and one woman, Adam and Eve (Gen. 1:27). It is evident in the subsequent statement that "a man will leave his father and mother and be united to his wife [singular], and they will become one flesh" (Gen. 2:24). Polygamy was never established by God for any people under any circumstances.

Following from this God-established example, this was the general practice (Gen. 4:1) until interrupted by sin. The first recorded polygamist, Lamech, was a wicked man (Gen. 4:23).

Christ reaffirmed God's original intention in Matthew 19:4, noting that God created one "male and [one] female" and joined them in marriage.

The Law of Moses prohibits polygamy, commanding, "You shall not multiply wives" (Deut. 17:17).

The warning against intermarriage with unbelievers was repeated in the very passage where it numbers Solomon's wives (1 Kings 11:2). By implication, polygamy can be seen in that statement. Because of both their number and their idolatry, Solomon's wives did irreparable damage to the house of David and to Israel.

The New Testament stresses that "Each man [should] have his own wife, and let each woman have her own husband" (1 Cor. 7:2). This emphatically excludes polygamy. Paul insisted that a church leader should be "the husband of one wife" (1 Tim. 3:2, 12). Whatever else this may entail, it certainly implies a monogamous relation.

Monogamous marriage prefigures the relation between Christ and his "bride" (singular), the church (Eph. 5:31–32).

God's judgment on polygamy is evident by example and implication:

1. Polygamy is first mentioned in the context of a society in rebellion against God where the murderer "Lamech took for himself two wives" (Gen. 4:19, 23).
2. God repeatedly warned polygamists of the consequences of their actions "lest his heart turn away" from God (Deut. 17:17; cf. 1 Kings 11:2).
3. God never commanded polygamy—like divorce, he only permitted it because of the hardness of their hearts (Deut. 24:1; Matt. 19:8).
4. Every polygamist in the Bible, including David and Solomon (1 Chron. 14:3), paid dearly for his sins.
5. God hates polygamy, as he hates divorce, since it destroys his ideal for the family (cf. Mal. 2:16).

Conclusion. Though the Bible records instances of polygamy, this does not mean God approved of it. Monogamy is taught in the Bible by *precedent*, since God gave the first man only one wife; by the equal *proportion* of males and females God brings into the world; by *precept* of Old and New Testament commands; by *punishment*, since God punished those who violated his standard (1 Kings 11:2); and by the prophetic *picture* of Christ and his pure bride, the church (Eph. 5:31–32).

Sources

N. L. Geisler and T. Howe, *When Critics Ask*
S. Grenz, *Sexual Ethics: A Biblical Perspective*
R. McQuilkin, *An Introduction to Biblical Ethics*, chap. 7
"Polygamy," in R. K. Harrison, ed., *Encyclopedia of Biblical and Christian Ethics*
H. Thielicke, *The Ethics of Sex*

Polytheism. Polytheism is the worldview that many finite gods exist in the world. There are differing versions of polytheism. In some forms, all the gods are more or less equal. Each has a personal sphere or domain. In others, the gods form a hierarchy. Henotheism has a chief god, such as Zeus. In some forms, such as the Greek and Roman pantheons, the number of gods is limited. Mormonism supports an indefinite number of gods. Some forms of polytheism stand alone, unconnected with any other worldview. In Hinduism, however, polytheism and pantheism go hand-in-hand with one impersonal Brahman and 330 million-plus personal manifestations of the one impersonal ultimate Reality.

The Rise of Polytheism. The fortunes of polytheism, at least in the West, are inversely related to the health of theism (belief in one God). Greek polytheism declined with the rise of Plato and Aristotle's philosophical theism. Roman polytheism all but died with the rise of Christianity in the West. Augustine's *City of God* narrates the Christian response to Roman polytheism. Polytheism has experienced a revival with the decline of Judeo-Christian views in the broader culture. This has been accompanied with a rise in witchcraft that also embraces polytheism. Margo Adler's book, *Drawing Down the Moon*, chronicles this movement.

David L. Miller, author of *The New Polytheism: Rebirth of the Gods and Goddesses,* argues that polytheism is alive and well in contemporary society. He urges people in Western society to get in tune with the gods in order to liberate themselves to be the kind of people they really are. All citations in this article are to Miller's book.

Basic Beliefs. *Rejection of Monotheism.* The establishment of polytheism necessitates the demolition of monotheism. God must be rejected before the gods can be accepted.

Monotheism is the belief in one God above and beyond the world. Monotheistic thinking gathers all human "explanation systems, whether theological, sociological, political, historical, philosophical, or psychological" under one all-embracing system. This system operates "according to fixed concepts and categories" that are controlled by an either/or kind of logic. Something is "either true or false, either this or that, either beautiful or ugly, either good or evil." But this kind of thinking, says Miller, "fails a people in a time when experience becomes self-consciously pluralistic, radically both/and." This is what Western society is today—radically pluralistic (*see* PLURALISM, RELIGIOUS). The contemporary Westerner lives in a world where truth and morality are relative. "Life often feels anarchistic: no horizons, fences, boundaries, and no center to prove one securely close to home" (7, 9). The contemporary situation is so pluralistic that its modern interpreters "have had to rely on a strange set of words" in their attempt to explain it. Charles Baudouin speaks of *polyphonic meaning* and being. In speaking of the nature of thinking required for contemporary understanding, Philip Wheelwright points to *plurisignificative knowing* and communicating. Norman O. Brown talks about *polymorphous reality* as a key to our history, and Ray Hart names the deepest aspect of our literature articulations of reality with the phrase *polysemous functioning of imaginal discourse*. If we try to make sense of our society Michael Novak suggests it will help to think of America as a pluralistic community of radically unmeltable ethnics. Concerning government and political science, Robert Dahl speaks of "*polyarchy*" (3).

This "poly" kind of thinking betrays the fact that "we have suffered a death of God" (*see* ATHEISM). No longer is there "a single center holding things together." God is dead, as Friedrich Nietzsche so boldly declared. Western civilization has buried the monotheistic way of thinking and speaking about God, being, and reality (37). Released from the "tyrannical imperialism of monotheism," people can discover new dimensions and diversity. There is a new potential for imaginative hopes and desires, laws and pleasures (4).

Significantly, Miller avoids using references to deities in defining what he means by *polytheism*. Polytheism is "a specific religious situation, . . . characterized by plurality, and plurality that manifests itself in many forms." Socially speaking, it is a "situation" in which pluralism intermingles various values, social patterns, and moral principles. Sometimes these values and patterns work together, but more often they are incompatible and each worldview vies to dominate the "normal social order" (4).

Philosophically, polytheism is experienced when no single "truth" guides people to "a single grammar, a single logic, or a single symbol-system" (ibid.). Polytheism mediates the worldview warfare by introducing "relativism, indeterminacy, plural logic systems, irrational numbers; substances that do not have substances, such as quarks; double explanations for light; and black holes in the middle of actual realities" (5).

Behind this peace-making role, however, polytheism works by seeking to absorb other religious ideas into itself. It remains the worship of multiple gods and goddesses. In the curious popular form, these deities are not worshiped all at the same time. Rather, only one god or goddess at a time can be worshiped. In this, polytheism gives a nod to monotheism, the worship of one God. "Polytheistic religion is actually a polytheistic theology, a system of symbolizing reality in a plural way in order to account for all experience, but that the religious practice is composed of consecutive monotheisms." And this "implies that our experience of social, intellectual, and psychological worlds is religious—that is, it is so profound and far-reaching that only a theological explanation can account for it fully" (6).

At one time polytheism reigned in Western culture. But when Greek culture collapsed, polytheism died and was replaced by monotheism. Although polytheism remained "in the underground or countercultural tradition of the West" throughout the 2000-year reign of monotheistic thought, it did not have any significant effect. With the death of monotheism, says Miller, polytheism may be resurrected again to its proper place. (11).

Miller believes human beings are naturally polytheistic in consciousness, giving polytheism "advantages" over monotheism. "Only a polytheistic consciousness will account realistically for our lives" (81). People are freed from the idea that they must "get it all together"; polytheism allows an irrationalism in which one may avoid a fully constructed view. Polytheism puts people in touch with the richness and diversity of life. Monotheism encourages thought about what lies behind life, rather than thought about life itself (27, 28).

The World. Miller suggests that the new polytheism gives "a new function for the old Gods and Goddesses" (81) through three aspects. First, the new polytheism "is a modern sensibility." It is not just that "our contemporary society is pluralistic, nor that our roles are many, nor that our morality is relativistic, nor even that our political ideology is fragmented." These are manifestations of something more fundamental. "The more basic feeling is that the Gods and Goddesses are reemerging in our lives" (64).

Second, the new polytheism rethinks old religious and conceptual ways of thinking. Western thought is rooted in the early Greeks, who were largely polytheistic, so the ideas, concepts, and categories deep in the Western psyche fit the thought or logic of mythic tales (40).

Third, the new polytheism helps confused moderns put into order the "many potencies, many structures of meaning and being, all given to us in the reality of our everyday lives" (64, 65).

Given the death of monotheism and the rebirth of polytheism—even a new polytheism—who or what are the gods and goddesses of this polytheism? Miller maintains that the gods are powers or forces. These forces transcend the personal, the historical, and the social. They are not affected by events or desires. Yet they are immanent in the world as potencies in individuals, in societies, and in nature (6, 60). Miller believes these powers provide a structure of reality that informs human social, intellectual, and personal behavior. (6, 7). These powers are "the Gods and Goddesses of ancient Greece—not Egypt, not the Ancient Near East, not Hindu India, not Ancient China or Japan. Greece is the locus of our polytheism simply because, willy-nilly, we are Occidental men and women" (80, 81).

Do these many different gods act harmoniously? Miller says no. They often act in "contention." Life may even be characterized as "a war of the Powers":

> Man—his self, his society, and his natural environment—is the arena of an eternal Trojan War. Our moods, emotions, unusual behaviors, dreams, and fantasies tell us those rough moments when the war is no longer a cold war or a border skirmish, but an all-out guerilla conflict. These indicators also tell us, by feeling and intuition, when one God has absented himself and another has not yet rushed into the vacuum. We know the war well. [60]

If modern people acknowledge these gods, new life will be infused into old ways of seeing and thinking. There would be a fresh philosophical structure through which to speak and think about our "deepest experience" (62).

Miller suggests how this new function of the gods and goddesses could work. The tremendous growth in technology can be thought about and informed by the stories of Prometheus, Hephaestus and Asclepius. "Prometheus steals the fire and ends trapped on a rock, gnawed at by the power he has himself supplanted by his knowledge. Hephaestus is the divine smith, the technologist supreme, who is the bastard of his mother and at a total loss for sensuousness and feeling. . . . Asclepius is the technologist of the feelings; he is the psychotherapist whom technology and its civilization will make into the high priest of mental health culture" (66).

The story of the goddess Hera, who "tried to socialize Mount Olympus," is relived when "computers and statistical procedures come to be revered as true wisdom" and "consultants and experts must attend every decision in business and government" (67). The work of the "ever-present God Pan ("All") is seen in the irrational that is always just below the surface of the human experience, breaking out into violence or mysticism (68).

At one time the view of the world was framed around the ideas of the second-century A.D. Alexandrian astronomer Ptolemy. The earth was thought to be "an immovable sphere at the center of the universe, around which nine concentric spheres revolve." Thus, all that existed was "organized around a single center," the earth, with the end of the universe imagined to be "fixed and secure." This monotheistic view of the world collapsed with Copernicus (and subsequent scientists). Now the universe has no known center and its horizons are neither fixed nor secure. Instead, it is seen as an "infinitely expanding universe whose center is . . . unknown" (9).

Humankind. Men and women are "the playground" of the gods (55). The gods parade "through our thoughts without our control and even against our will." We do not possess the gods, but they possess us (34). They "live through our psychic structures" and "manifest themselves always in our behaviors." We do not grab the gods, but the "gods grab us, and we play out their stories" (59).

Psychologically, polytheism is experienced in the separate "selves" of personhood. Each self has an autonomy, a life of its own that comes and goes without regard to the will (5). No one can be gripped by more than one God at a time. In this sense Miller and the modern polytheists are monotheistic, or henotheistic. Each person worships one God at a time, the one in control of personhood, out of a large pantheon of gods. However, the story of the one god who is in temporary domination may involve marriages with other gods, parentage by still others, offspring and maiden goddesses. So the conception is always ultimately polytheistic. To think differently is to partake of the self-deception that has been perpetrated by monotheistic thinking (30, cf. 28).

The purpose of humankind is to incarnate the gods, to become aware of their presence, to acknowledge and celebrate them (55). This can occur only when we begin to see our world through polytheistic, mythological glasses (63, 83).

Values. All values are relative (*see* MORALITY, ABSOLUTE NATURE OF). Truth and falsehood, life and death, beauty and ugliness, good and evil, are all mixed together (29). Monotheistic thinking separates values into either/or concepts and categories (7). But this way of thinking does not adequately account for the many sides of human experience. What does is the polytheistic both/and sort of thinking, which recognizes the relativity of all values.

Evaluation. *Some Positive Values of Polytheism.* Polytheism is a reminder of separate realities, though it doesn't adequately decipher them. There is a widespread and growing recognition that humanity is not alone in the universe. Reported contacts with UFO beings or extraterrestrials persist. Even many scientists believe that there are intelligent beings in space. Even many nonpolytheistic religions recognize the existence of super human beings, such as angels and demons. If there is a divine reality, it follows that we should seek to discover our relationship to that reality and how we should respond to it. The emphasis that polytheists place on human beings getting "tuned in" to the divine reality and adjusting their behavior accordingly is commendable.

Polytheists are often praised for positing an analogy between man and the gods. If divine beings exist, and if they had something to do with the creation of humankind, then it would seem that human nature would in some way reflect deity. A cause cannot give characteristics to others it does not possess itself. As a painting displays some truths about its painter (e.g., the level of skill, the breadth of imagination, or the care taken) so human beings should display some truth about their Creator(s). Hence, if a person is a creation of some divine reality, some human characteristics should resemble the Maker(s). Thus, it would appear reasonable to conclude that there is some analogy between humanity and the gods (*see* ANALOGY, PRINCIPLE OF).

Polytheists recognize that there are various forces in the world, some uncontrollable. Many scholars today have concluded that behind most myths, be they religious or not, lie true stories of human encounters with forces that press in. These may be forces of nature (e.g., wind, rain, earthquakes, tornadoes, or floods), forces prevalent in culture (e.g., greed, hope, love, or a desire for power), or forces believed to lie behind the universe (e.g., gods, angels, demons). Polytheists, through various story forms, have managed to vividly relate human encounter to such forces (*see* SATAN, REALITY OF).

Criticisms of Polytheism. While polytheists have some insights into the nature of reality, nonetheless, their worldview is false. Ultimate reality does not consist of many finite gods. There is good evidence that there is only one God, not many (*see* COSMOLOGICAL ARGUMENT; GOD, EVIDENCE FOR; GOD, NATURE OF; THEISM). This God is Creator of all else. Hence, there are not many divine beings.

If the natural elements, say heaven and earth, had given birth to the gods, then the gods would not be ultimate beings. Whatever is derived from something else is dependent on that something, at least for its origin. How could a being that received its existence from another be above its maker? This would be like a cookie claiming to be greater than its cook, or a computer declaring itself above its creator. Similarly, if nature created the gods, then nature is ultimate. And if, as Paul Tillich thought, worship involves an ultimate commitment to an ultimate, then nature, not the gods, should be worshiped. This would be true regarding whatever was believed to have given birth to the gods or to have preceded them. If the gods are derivative beings, then they are not worthy of ultimate commitment. Why worship something that has no ultimate worth?

Also, as Plotinus noted, all plurality presupposes a prior unity. Many are just a multiple imitation of the One. Thus, many gods are not self-explanatory. What is their basis of unity? And who superintends conflict between them? This is not a polyverse but a universe. If ultimately there is a personal Power behind the universe, it must be a unity.

The anthropic principle reveals that the entire universe was one—with one purpose and Purposer—from the very beginning. From the moment of the big bang the entire universe was fine-tuned for the emergence of human life. This bespeaks of one intelligent Creator. The idea of an eternal universe posited by polytheism has other serious philosophical and scientific objections. One philosophical argument stems from the impossibility of an actual infinite series of events in time. An eternal universe would be a beginningless series of events in time. But how could such a series possibly exist? To illustrate, suppose there were a library with an infinite number of books on its shelves. Imagine that each book is numbered. Since there is an infinite number of books, every book is numbered and every possible number must be printed on the books in the library. From this it would follow that no new book could be added to the library, for there would be no number left to assign. All the numbers have been used up. But this seems absurd, for all objects in reality can be numbered. Further, it would be easy to add to the library, since one could make a new book by tearing a page out of each of the first fifty books, adding a title page, binding them together and putting the finished product on the shelf. Hence, the idea of an actual infinite series of books appears to be impossible. Therefore, the polytheistic belief in an eternal universe would appear to be impossible (see Craig, passim).

A scientific argument against the idea of an eternal universe can be derived from the modern notion that the universe is expanding. Astronomer Edwin Hubble concluded that the universe is expanding in all directions. If true, it would follow that at some point in the past the universe was only a single point from which it has been expanding. This single point would be one of "infinite density." However, no object could be infinitely dense, for if it contained any mass at all it would not be infinitely dense but finitely dense. Hence, a totally shrunken or contracted universe is really no universe at all. The concept of an expanding universe requires a point at which no universe existed. If this is so, then the universe must have begun from nothing (*see* CREATION, VIEWS OF).

Polytheistic gods are within that universe, not beyond it. But the evidence is that the universe came into existence. If the universe is not eternal but came to exist from nothing (*see* CREATION, *EX NIHILO*), then the gods posited by polytheism would not be eternal; they would have come into existence. But if they came into existence, then they are not gods but creatures made by some eternal Cause (God). But if the gods of polytheism derive their existence from another, then this other is really the supreme God of monotheism. Thus, polytheism collapses into monotheism. Therefore, if the gods exist, they would ultimately be dependent on a Cause beyond them and beyond the universe. But this conclusion coincides with the claims of theism, not those of polytheism.

The polytheistic analogy between humankind and the gods has been criticized as too anthropomorphic (interpreting what is not human on the basis of human characteristics). Certainly the creature should bear some resemblance to the Creator. But to apply human imperfections to deity renders the divine reality as less than worthy of respect and worship. Gods of polytheism appear to be made in human image, rather than we being made in their image. This tends to give credence to the view that polytheism is a human invention or superstition rather than a depiction of what actually is.

Conclusion. As a worldview, polytheism lacks rational and evidential support. The many spiritual beings that exist are limited and imperfect. Hence, they imply an unlimited and perfect Creator. Polytheism does not account for either ultimate causality or ultimate unity, which is needed to explain a diverse, changing universe.

Sources

M. Adler, *Drawing Down the Moon*
Augustine, *The City of God*
F. Beckwith, *The Mormon Concept of God*
W. Craig, *The* Kalam *Cosmological Argument*
N. L. Geisler and W. D. Watkins, *Worlds Apart: A Handbook on World Views*, chap. 8
Hesiod, *Theogony*
D. Miller, *The New Polytheism*
J. Smith, *The Pearl of Great Price*

Positivism. ***See*** **COMTE, AUGUSTE; LOGICAL POSITIVISM.**

Postmodernism. ***See*** **DERRIDA, JACQUES.**

Practical Presuppositionalism. ***See*** **PRESUPPOSITIONAL APOLOGETICS; SCHAEFFER, FRANCIS.**

Pragmatism. *Pragmatism* is an indigenous American philosophy, springing from William James (1842–1910), which stresses the practical results of a theory. John Dewey (1859–1952) is called a pragmatist, but his position might more technically be called *instrumentalism*.

For a pragmatist, an idea is said to be true if it works. A course of action is right if it brings desired results.

The roots of pragmatism are found in the ideas of Charles Sanders Pierce, who used a pragmatic method to clarify (though not to verify) ideas. There are also similarities between pragmatism and utilitarianism, which holds that the right course of action is the one that brings the greatest good. Dewey, as an instrumentalist, stressed practical results of ideas, especially in education.

The pragmatic view has been severely criticized, because something is not true simply because it works. Lying may "work" to avoid a negative result or achieve a desired objective at the expense of another person, but that doesn't make the lies true. Something can be known to be contrary to facts, yet still followed, because it seems the most practical course of action under the circumstances. Neither is something right because it works. Cheating "works," but it is not right.

The ethical philosophy also confuses cause with effect. An idea is not true because it works; it works because it is true. And how does one judge that it has "worked"? Only practical knowledge is considered true knowledge. An eternal perspective does not enter the discussion. Pragmatists recognize only the methods of science to test truth. This absolutizes the scientific method. However, for ethical concerns there are no objective criteria, as there are in science. The success of the result can only be determined by a subjective, personal, and short-sighted perspective.

A pragmatic view of truth also undermines trust. What judge would allow someone to take a courtroom oath to tell, as one philosopher quipped, "the expedient, the whole expedient, and nothing but the expedient" (*see* TRUTH, NATURE OF)?

Sources

J. O. Buswell, Jr., *The Philosophies of F. R. Tennant and John Dewey*

N. L. Geisler and P. Feinberg, *Introduction to Philosophy*, chaps. 7, 16

——— and W. D. Watkins, *Worlds Apart, A Handbook on Worldviews*

W. James, *Pragmatism and Other Essays*

H. S. Thayer, *Meaning and Action: A Critical History of Pragmatism*

Predestination. ***See*** **DETERMINISM; FREE WILL.**

Presuppositional Apologetics. Presuppositional apologetics is the apologetic system that defends Christianity from the departure point of certain basic presuppositions. The apologist presupposes the truth of Christianity and then reasons from that point. One basic presupposition is that the non-Christian also has presuppositions that color everything he or she hears about God. Another is that in some fashion the person encountered is, as Augustine said, "doing business" with God and, as Romans 1 puts it so damningly, suppressing knowledge of the truth. It is the apologist's role to present the truth of Christianity and the falsehood of any worldview opposed to Christ (*see* PLURALISM, RELIGIOUS).

Differences from Other Methods. Presuppositional apologetics is opposed to evidentialism and classical apologetics (*see* APOLOGETICS, CLASSICAL). Presuppositional apologetics differs from classical apologetics in that presuppositional apologetics rejects the validity of traditional proofs for the existence of God (*see* GOD, EVIDENCE FOR). Further, the presuppositional apologist differs with both classical and historical apologetics in its use of historical evidence. The historical apologist, in agreement with the classical apologist, argues in favor of beginning with reason and evidence to demonstrate the truth of Christianity. The presuppositionalist, on the other hand, insists that one must begin with presuppositions or worldviews. The historical apologist believes that the historical facts "speak for themselves." They are "self-interpreting" in their historical context. The pure presuppositionalist, on the other hand, insists that no facts are self-interpreting, that all facts are interpreted and can be properly understood only within the context of an overall worldview.

Several Kinds of Presuppositionalism. Depending on how one is defined, there are three or four basic kinds of presuppositionalism: (1) *revelational presuppositionalism* (*see* VAN TIL, CORNELIUS); (2) *rational presuppositionalism* (*see* CLARK, GORDON); and (3) *systematic consistency* (*see* CARNELL, EDWARD JOHN). Some view Francis Schaeffer's apologetic as an example of a fourth variation that might be called *practical presuppositionalism*. Each approach differs in the way in which a worldview is judged for truth.

Revelational Presuppositionalism. According to revelational presuppositionalism, one must begin any rational understanding of truth by presupposing the truth of the Christian faith. One must posit that the Triune God (*see* TRINITY) has revealed himself in Holy Scriptures, the divinely authoritative Word of God. Without this presupposition one cannot make any sense out of the universe, life, language, history, or anything else. This kind of argument is sometimes viewed as a transcendental argument, that is, an argument that begins by laying down the necessary conditions under which every other kind of knowledge is possible. These necessary conditions posit that the Triune God has revealed himself in Holy Scriptures.

Rational Presuppositionism. This is the apologetics system of the late Gordon Clark and his noted disciple Carl F. H. Henry. Like other presuppositionalists, the rational presuppositionalist begins with the Trinity revealed in the written Word of God. But the test for whether this is true is simply the law of noncontradiction (*see* FIRST PRINCIPLES). That is, one knows that Christianity is true and all opposing systems are false because all of them have internal contradictions and only Christianity is internally consistent. Thus, a rational principle, the law of noncontradiction, is used as the test for truth.

Systematic Consistency. John Carnell and his disciple, Gordon Lewis, developed a presuppositionalism that has two (or three) tests for the truth of the Christian presupposition. Like rational presuppositionalists, they believe a system must be rationally consistent. But in addition, they hold that the system must comprehensively include all the facts. Later in his life Carnell added a third test—existential relevance. The system must meet life's basic needs. The only system, they believe, that measures up to all three is Christianity. Thus, Christianity is true and all other opposing systems are false.

Practical Presuppositionalism. Francis Schaeffer's apologetic approach has also been listed by many as presuppositional. If so, it is a practical presuppositionalism. One of its chief features is that all non-Christian systems are unlivable. Only Christian truth is livable. In this sense, it uses unlivability as a test for the falsity of non-Christian systems and livability as a test for the truth of Christianity.

Conclusion. Presuppositional apologetics has been criticized from many quarters. Classical apologetics (*see* APOLOGETICS, CLASSICAL) has challenged its rejection of traditional proofs for the existence of God (*see* GOD, EVIDENCE FOR). Historical apologetics (*see* APOLOGETICS, HISTORICAL) has defended the neutral nature of historical facts. Others have noted the fideistic nature of revelational presuppositionalism and rejected it for this reason (*see* FIDEISM). Since each system is critiqued under the article on its chief proponent, attention is directed to the articles on Cornelius Van Til, Gordon Clark, and John Carnell.

Sources

J. Carnell, *Introduction to Christian Apologetics*
G. H. Clark, *Religion, Reason, and Revelation*
G. Lewis, *Testing Christianity's Truth Claims*
F. Schaeffer, *The God Who Is There*
C. Van Til, *The Defense of the Faith*

Princeton School of Apologetics. The Princeton School of Apologetics refers to the apologetic approach taken by "Old Princeton" scholars who flourished at the turn of the twentieth century. Broadly, it fit into the category of Classical apologetics (*see* APOLOGETICS, CLASSICAL), who believe in the validity of general revelation, classical arguments for God's existence (*see* GOD, EVIDENCE FOR), and miracles as confirmation of the truth (*see* MIRACLE).

The philosophical roots of the Princeton apologetic are found in the empirical realism of Scottish Common Sense Philosophy and Thomas Reid (1710–1796) and the rational empiricism of John Locke (1632–1704). His views were exemplified in the writings of J. Gresham Machen (1881–1937), Charles Hodge (1797–1878), and B. B. Warfield (1851–1921). Later there was a radical break in the tradition when Westminster Seminary was founded by faculty and students who broke with the modernist direction in theology being taken at Princeton Seminary. Cornelius Van Til (1895–1987), a disciple of Herman Dooyeweerd (1894–1977), led Princeton into a presuppositional apologetic (*see* APOLOGETICS, PRESUPPOSITIONAL).

The spirit, if not always the letter, of the old Princeton school has been carried on by Kenneth Hamilton, Kenneth Kantzer, John Gerstner, and R. C. Sproul. Their general epistemology and apologetic is dependent to a significant degree on the foundation laid by the old Princeton scholars.

Sources

J. Gerstner, *Reasons for Faith*
C. Hodge, *Systematic Theology*, vol. 1
J. Locke, *The Reasonableness of Christianity*
T. Reid, *An Inquiry into the Human Mind on the Principles of Common Sense*
R. C. Sproul, *Classical Apologetics*

Principle of Parsimony ("Ockham's Razor"). *See* WILLIAM OF OCKHAM.

Principle of Sufficient Reason. *See* SUFFICIENT REASON, PRINCIPLE OF.

Probability. *See* CHANCE; CERTAINTY; INDUCTIVE METHOD; LOGIC.

Process Theology. *See* PANENTHEISM; WHITEHEAD, ALFRED NORTH.

Progressive Revelation. Sometimes critics of Scripture jump to the conclusion that the Bible is in error (*see* BIBLE, ALLEGED ERRORS IN) because God commands something different for one period than for another. The classic example of that is God's command for blood sacrifices to atone for sin under the law of Moses. These are no longer in effect since Christ offered himself as the final atoning sacrifice to which the animal sacrifices looked forward (see Hebrews 7–10). Likewise, God commanded that Adam eat only plants (Gen. 1:29–30). But after the flood, Noah was told to eat meat. The Mosaic Law prohibited certain animals as "unclean" to eat (Leviticus 11). But Jesus pronounced that these animals were clean and could be eaten (Mark 7:19; Acts 10:14–15; 1 Tim. 4:4). These are not contradictions but examples of *progressive revelation*.

The principle of progressive revelation means that God does not reveal everything at once, nor does he always lay down the same conditions for every period. Later revelations will have things in them that go against earlier ones. Hence the Old Testament revealed only hints of the Trinity taught in the New Testament (for example, Matt. 3:16–17; 28:18–20). The New Testament declares explicitly what was only implicit in the Old Testament (*see* TRINITY).

God can change anything that does not involve a contradiction or that does not go against his unchangeable nature (Mal. 3:6; 2 Tim. 2:13; Titus 1:2; Heb. 6:18). God can change nonmoral things without any apparent or stated reason (*see* ESSENTIALISM, DIVINE). The change of the command for humans from being herbivorous to omnivorous (Gen. 1:29–30; 9:2–3) is one example; changes in the ceremonial laws are another. They are different commands for different times which God had different reasons for enacting, even if not fully known to us (Deut. 29:29).

Sometimes God commands change because of the changing conditions of humanity. Such is the case with permission for divorce "for any cause" in the Old Testament, and a strong prohibition in the New Testament (Matt. 19:3). Jesus said the original law "was because of the hardness of your hearts" (19:8). God sometimes overlooks certain things because of times of ignorance (Acts 17:30), but later does not.

A major reason for change is that God has an unfolding plan. This plan has stages in which some things are necessary and stages where something else is necessary. Once a prophecy "type" has been fulfilled (the blood of the lamb), when the reality comes, the type is no longer needed. Once the foundation of the church was laid in the apostles (Eph. 2:20), the apostles were no longer needed.

In view of the principle of progressive revelation, the later revelations are not contradictory, but complementary. They do not make mistakes, but reveal more truth. Later revelations do not negate the former; they simply replace them. Since they were not given for all, but only for a specified time, they do not conflict when they change. No two opposing commands are for the same people at the same time.

An example of progressive revelation can be seen in every family with growing children. When they are very small, the parent allows children to eat with their fingers. Later, the parents insist on the use of a spoon. Finally, as the child progresses, the parent commands use of a fork. These commands are temporary, progressive, and appropriate to the situation.

Proper Basicality. *Proper basicality* is a view set forth by contemporary American philosopher Alvin Plantinga, claiming that there are certain beliefs for which it is possible but foolish to require justification. These include the concepts "I exist." and "There is a past." One is entitled to hold these beliefs without giving any further account. Plantinga includes the belief "God exists." among the propositions that are "properly basic." If true, this would undercut natural theology, the need to provide any arguments for God's existence (*see* GOD, EVIDENCE FOR), and classical apologetics (*see* APOLOGETICS, CLASSICAL). Plantinga claims that belief in God is so central that it would be folly to ask for its foundation. The belief itself is the hub of the believer's worldview (*see* Plantinga, 187–98).

Plantinga replaces classic foundationalism with these "basic beliefs." His view is a kind of fideistic foundationalism (*see* FIDEISM).

The denial that there are any self-evident foundational principles of thought involves one either in an infinite regress, where no justification is ever given, or else in an arbitrary cut-off point where one simply stops giving a justification (without a justification for doing so; *see* FIRST PRINCIPLES). Plantinga offers no justification for placing belief that God exists into the category of "properly basic." An unbeliever can simply ask for his reasons for placing it in this category, at which point it is incumbent on him to provide a rational justification, or else he simply begs the question.

Like other fideists, Plantinga here failed to distinguish between belief *in* and belief *that* God exists. One needs evidence for belief *that* God exists, but not for belief *in* God. It would be an insult to one's wife to demand reasons for loving her. But it is not an insult to demand reasons that it is really she, and not the neighbor's wife, before embracing her. It is unworthy of a person's relationship with God to believe in God for the sake of evidence. If there is an Ultimate Value (i.e., God) in the universe, that Being should be believed in for his own sake. But it is not unworthy to ask for evidence that God exists and is the Ultimate Value before one place's faith in him. Reason demands that we look before we leap (Geisler, 68–69).

Sources

N. L. Geisler and W. Corduan, *Philosophy of Religion*

A. Plantinga, "The Reformed Objection to Natural Theology," *CSR* 11 (1982)

Prophecy, as Proof of the Bible. One of the strongest evidences that the Bible is inspired by God (*see* BIBLE, EVIDENCES FOR) is its predictive prophecy. Unlike any other book, the Bible offers a multitude of specific predictions—some hundreds of years in advance—that have been literally fulfilled or else point to a definite future time when they will come true. In his comprehensive catalogue of prophecies, *Encyclopedia of Biblical Prophecies*, J. Barton Payne lists 1817 predictions in the Bible, 1239 in the Old Testament and 578 in the New (674–75).

The argument from prophecy is the argument *from* omniscience. Limited human beings know the future only if it is told to them by an omniscient Being (Ramm, 81). It is important to note that this is not an argument *to* omniscience. It is sometimes wrongly argued that a forecast of unusual events is proof that there is an omniscient Being (*see* God, Nature of). This is not necessarily the case, for the odd does not prove God (*see* MIRACLES, ARGUMENTS AGAINST). No matter what the improbability, an odd event (say, a perfect hand in the card game of bridge, an extremely improbable deal) can, and sometimes does, occur. However, if an omniscient Being is known to exist (*see* GOD, EVIDENCE FOR), and highly improbable predictions are made in his name which come to pass without fail, then it is reasonable to assume that they were divinely inspired. Fulfilled prophecy does not prove the existence of God, but it does show that unusual events predicted in his Name that come to pass are evidence of his special activity.

Predictive Prophecy. If an omniscient God exists who knows the future, then predictive prophecy is possible (*see* THEISM; GOD, NATURE OF). And if the Bible contains such predictions, then they are a sign of the Bible's divine origin. Not everything called "prophecy" in the Bible is predictive. Prophets *forthtold* God's Word as well as *foretold* the future. There are several earmarks of a supernatural prediction, at least one with apologetic value. First, it is more than a vague guess or conjecture (see Ramm, 82). It cannot be a mere reading of the trends. Second, it deals with human contingencies that are normally unpredictable. Scientific predictions are not of the same order, since they deal with projections based on the regularity of nature, for example, the prediction of an eclipse. Third, it is a highly unusual event, not normally expected. Sometimes the miraculous nature of the prophecy is manifest in the length of time in advance the prediction is made, so as to reduce the probability of guessing. At other times it is revealed in the unique fulfillment itself.

Biblical Predictions. *Messianic Predictions.* There are two broad categories of biblical prophecy: messianic and nonmessianic. Payne (ibid., 665–70) lists 191 prophecies concerning the anticipated Jewish Messiah and Savior. Each was literally fulfilled in the life, death, resurrection, and ascension of Jesus of Nazareth (*see* New Testament, Historicity of; Christ, Deity of). A sampling of these prophecies includes:

Messiah's birth. God said to Satan after he had enticed Adam and Eve to fall into sin, "I will put enmity between you and the woman, and between your offspring and hers; he will crush your head, and you will strike his heel" (Gen. 3:15). The New Testament reveals that Jesus was indeed born of a woman in order to crush Satan's power. For "when the time had fully come, God sent his Son, born of a woman, born under law" (Gal. 4:4; cf. Matthew 1; Luke 2).

Isaiah 7:14 predicted that one named *Immanuel* ("God with us") would be born of a virgin (*see* Virgin Birth): "Therefore the Lord himself will give you a sign: The virgin will be with child and will give birth to a son, and will call him Immanuel." This prediction was made over 700 years in advance (*see* Isaiah, Deutero). The New Testament affirms that Christ fulfilled this prediction, saying, "All this took place to fulfill what the Lord had said through the prophet: 'The virgin will be with child and will give birth to a son, and they will call him Immanuel'—which means, 'God with us'" (Matt. 1:22–23). The objection that this is not really a prediction of Christ's birth is answered in the article, Virgin Birth of Christ.

Micah made the unambiguous prophecy, "But you, Bethlehem Ephrathah, though you are small among the clans of Judah, out of you will come for me one who will be ruler over Israel, whose origins are from of old, from ancient times" (Micah 5:2). Even the unbelieving Jewish scribes identified this as a prediction of the Messiah and directed the inquiring magi to Bethlehem (Matt. 2:1–6):

> After Jesus was born in Bethlehem in Judea, during the time of King Herod, Magi from the east came to Jerusalem and asked, "Where is the one who has been born king of the Jews? We saw his star in the east and have come to worship him." When King Herod heard this he was disturbed, and all Jerusalem with him. When he had called together all the people's chief priests and teachers of the law, he asked them where the Christ was to be born. "In Bethlehem in Judea," they replied, "for this is what the prophet has written: 'But you, Bethlehem, in the land of Judah, are by no means least among the rulers of Judah; for out of you will come a ruler who will be the shepherd of my people Israel.'"

Messiah's ancestry. God declared in Genesis 12:1–3 that the Messianic blessing for all the world would come from the offspring of Abraham: "I will make you into a great nation and I will bless you; I will make your name great, and you will be a blessing. I will bless those who bless you, and whoever curses you I will curse; and all peoples on earth will be blessed through you" (Gen. 12:2–3; cf. 22:18). Jesus was indeed the seed of Abraham. Matthew begins with "A record of the genealogy of Jesus Christ the son of David, the son of Abraham" (Matt. 1:1). Paul adds, "The promises were spoken to Abraham and to his seed. The Scripture does not say 'and to seeds,' meaning many people, but 'and to your seed,' meaning one person, who is Christ" (Gal. 3:16).

The Redeemer would come through the tribe of Judah: "The scepter will not depart from Judah, nor the ruler's staff from between his feet, until he comes to whom it belongs and the obedience of the nations is his" (Gen. 49:10). According to the New Testament genealogies this was Jesus' ancestry. Luke declares: "Now Jesus himself was about thirty years old when he began his ministry. He was the son, so it was thought, of Joseph, the son of Heli, . . . the son of Judah, the son of Jacob, the son of Isaac, the son of Abraham" (Luke 3:23, 33–34; cf. Matt. 1:1–3). Hebrews adds, "For it is clear that our Lord descended from Judah" (Heb. 7:14).

The books of Samuel record the prediction that the Messiah would be of the house of David. God said to David: "When your days are over and you rest with your fathers, I will raise up your offspring to succeed you, who will come from your own body, and I will establish his kingdom. He is the one who will build a house for my Name, and I will establish the throne of his kingdom for ever. I will be his father, and he shall be my son" (2 Sam. 7:14). The New Testament repeatedly affirms that Jesus was "the son of David" (Matt. 1:1). Jesus himself claimed to be "the son of David" (Matt. 22:42–45). The Palm Sunday crowd also hailed Christ as "the son of David" (Matt. 21:9).

Herald of Messiah's coming. Isaiah predicted that the Messiah would be heralded by a messenger of the Lord who would be "A voice of one calling: 'In the desert prepare the way for the LORD; make straight in the wilderness a highway for our God'" (40:3). Malachi (3:1) added: "'See, I will send my messenger, who will prepare the way before me. Then suddenly the Lord you are seeking will come to his temple; the messenger of the covenant, whom you desire, will come,' says the LORD Almighty." These predictions were literally fulfilled in the ministry of John the Baptist. Matthew records: "In those days John the Baptist came, preaching in the Desert of Judea and saying, 'Repent, for the kingdom of heaven is near.'" This is he who was spoken of through the prophet Isaiah: "A voice of one calling in the desert, 'Prepare the way for the Lord, make straight paths for him'" (Matt. 3:1–3).

Isaiah 11:2 foretold that the Messiah would be anointed by the Holy Spirit for his ministry: "The Spirit of the LORD will rest on him—the Spirit of wisdom and of understanding, the Spirit of counsel and of power, the Spirit of knowledge and of the fear of the LORD." This literally happened to Jesus at his baptism. Matthew 3:16–17 says, "As soon as Jesus was baptized, he went up out of the water. At that moment heaven was opened, and he saw the Spirit of God descending like a dove and lighting on him. And a voice from heaven said, 'This is my Son, whom I love; with him I am well pleased.'"

Isaiah 61 said that the Messiah would preach the gospel to the poor and brokenhearted. Jesus pointed out his fulfillment of this ministry in the Nazareth synagogue (Luke 4:17–20):

> He went to Nazareth, where he had been brought up, and on the Sabbath day he went into the synagogue, as was his custom. And he stood up to read. The scroll of the prophet Isaiah was handed to him. Unrolling it, he found the place where it is written: "The Spirit of the Lord is on me, because he has anointed me to preach good news to the poor. He has sent me to proclaim freedom for the prisoners and recovery of sight for the blind, to release the oppressed, to proclaim the year of the Lord's favor."

Jesus carefully cut off his reading in the middle of a sentence, failing to add the next phrase, "and the day of vengeance of our God." That refers to his second coming; it was not fulfilled that day in their hearing, as was the rest of the prophecy.

Isaiah 35:5–6 declared that the Messiah would perform miracles to confirm his ministry, asserting: "Then will the eyes of the blind be opened and the ears of the deaf unstopped." The Gospel record is filled with Jesus' miracles. "Jesus went through all the towns and villages, teaching in their synagogues, preaching the good news of the kingdom and healing every disease and sickness" (Matt. 9:35). Jesus even cited these very things for John the Baptist as his messianic calling card. "Jesus replied, 'Go back and report to John what you hear and see: The blind receive sight, the lame walk, those who have leprosy are cured, the deaf hear, the dead are raised, and the good news is preached to the poor'" (Matt. 11:4–5).

Messiah's work. Malachi 3:1 foretold the authority over the temple worship that Jesus showed when he twice drove out the moneychangers—at the beginning and at the end of his ministry: "'See, I will send my messenger, who will prepare the way before me. Then suddenly the Lord you are seeking will come to his temple; the messenger of the covenant, whom you desire, will come,' says the LORD Almighty."

Matthew 21:12–13 relates that: "Jesus entered the temple area and drove out all who were buying and selling there. He overturned the tables of the money changers and the benches of those selling doves. 'It is written,' he said to them, 'My house will be called a house of prayer,' but you are making it a 'den of robbers.'"

Among many psalms applicable to the ministry of Jesus is 118:22, which foretells Messiah's rejection by his people: "The stone the builders rejected has become the capstone." This very verse is cited repeatedly in the New Testament. For example, Peter wrote, "Now to you who believe, this stone is precious. But to those who do not believe, 'The stone the builders rejected has become the capstone.'" (1 Peter 2:7; cf. Matt. 21:42; Mark 12:10; Luke 20:17; Acts 4:11).

Suffering and death of Christ. One of the most amazing predictions of Christ in all of Scripture is that of Isaiah 53:2–12. This precise description of Jesus' sufferings and death of Christ was all literally fulfilled (see Matt. 26–27; Mark 15–16; Luke 22–23; John 18–19). Isaiah predicts twelve aspects of Messiah's passion, all fulfilled. Jesus . . .

1. was rejected;
2. was a man of sorrow;
3. lived a life of suffering;
4. was despised by others;
5. carried our sorrow;
6. was smitten and afflicted by God;
7. was pierced for our transgressions;
8. was wounded for our sins;
9. suffered like a lamb;
10. died with the wicked;
11. was sinless; and
12. prayed for others.

Further confirmation of the predictive nature of Isaiah 53 is that it was common for Jewish interpreters before the time of Christ to teach that Isaiah here spoke of the Jewish Messiah (see Driver). Only after early Christians began using the text apologetically with great force did it become in rabbinical teaching an expression of the suffering Jewish nation. This view is implausible in the context of Isaiah's standard references to the

Jewish people in the first-person plural ("our" or "we,") whereas he always refers to the Messiah in third-person singular, as in Isaiah 53 ("he" and "his" and "him").

Predictions elsewhere about Christ's death include:

13. the piercing of his hands and feet (Ps. 22:16; cf. Luke 23:33);
14. the piercing of his side (Zech. 12:10; cf. John 19:34); and
15. the casting of lots for his garments (Ps. 22:18; cf. John 19:23–24).

While it wasn't recognized until after the fact, one of the most precise predictions in Scripture gives the very year in which the Christ would die. Daniel was speaking of both the exile of Israel and the atonement for sin when he recorded a prayer of confession for the sins of his people (9:4–19) and a vision in response in which the angel Gabriel gave to Daniel the following foresight (9:24–26):

> Seventy "sevens" are decreed for your people and your holy city to finish transgression, to put an end to sin, to atone for wickedness, to bring in everlasting righteousness, to seal up vision and prophecy and to anoint the most holy. Know and understand this: From the issuing of the decree to restore and rebuild Jerusalem until the Anointed One [Messiah], the ruler, comes, there will be seven "sevens," and sixty-two "sevens." . . . After the sixty-two "sevens," the Anointed One will be cut off.

The context indicates that Daniel knew he was speaking of years, since he was meditating on the "number of years" that God had revealed to Jeremiah that Jerusalem would lay waste, namely, "seventy years" (vs. 2). God then told Daniel that it would be 7 x 70 (years) before the Messiah would come and be cut off (die).

Artaxerxes ordered Nehemiah "to restore and rebuild *Jerusalem*" (Dan. 9:25; cf. Nehemiah 2) in 445/444 B.C. From that year, rather than the earlier date when Cyrus approved only the rebuilding of the temple (Ezra 1:3), Daniel predicted that it would be 483 years to the time of Christ's death. Taking the widely accepted date of 33 for the crucifixion (see Hoehner), would be 483 years exactly:

Seven sevens plus sixty-two sevens is 69 x 7 = 483

444 + 33 = 477

Add six years to compensate for the five days in a solar year not in the lunar year followed by Israel (5 x 477 = 2385 days or 6+ years).

477 + 6 = 483 years

This assumes Daniel's 490 (70 x 7) is not a round number, which is possible. The Bible frequently rounds its numbers (*see* BIBLE, ALLEGED ERRORS IN; CHRONOLOGY, PROBLEMS IN THE BIBLE). In either event, Daniel's prediction takes us to the very time of Christ.

Psalm 16:10: Christ's resurrection. The Old Testament also foretold the resurrection of the Messiah from the dead. Psalm 2:7 declares: "I will proclaim the decree of the LORD: He said to me, 'You are my Son; today I have become your Father.'" In Psalm 16:10 David adds, "because you will not abandon me to the grave, nor will you let your Holy One see decay."

Both of these passages are cited in the New Testament as predictive of the resurrection of Christ. Peter said explicitly of David's prophecy in Psalm 16, "But he was a prophet and knew that God had promised him on oath that he would place one of his descendants on his throne. Seeing what was ahead, he spoke of the resurrection of the Christ, that he was not abandoned to the grave, nor did his body see decay" (Acts 2:30–31; cf. 13:35). Psalm 2 is cited as a prediction of the resurrection in Acts 13:33–34 (cf. Heb. 1:5). Indeed, using these passages, "Paul went into the synagogue, and on three Sabbath days he reasoned with them from the Scriptures, explaining and proving that the Christ had to suffer and rise from the dead. 'This Jesus I am proclaiming to you is the Christ,' he said" (Acts 17:2–3). This would scarcely have been possible unless his skeptical Jewish audience did not recognize the predictive nature of passages like Psalms 2 and 16.

The ascension of Christ. In Psalm 110:1, David even predicted the Ascension of Christ, writing, "The LORD says to my Lord: 'Sit at my right hand until I make your enemies a footstool for your feet'" (cf. Pss. 2:4–6; 68:6; used in Eph. 4:8). Jesus applied this passage to himself (Matt. 22:43–44). Peter used it as a prediction of the Ascension of Christ: "For David did not ascend to heaven, and yet he said, 'The Lord said to my Lord: "Sit at my right hand until I make your enemies a footstool for your feet"'" (Acts 2:34–45).

Prophecy and the Messiah. It is important to note unique things about biblical prophecies. Unlike many psychic predictions, many of these were *very specific,* giving, for example, the very name of the tribe, city, and time of Christ's coming. Unlike forecasts found in tabloids at the supermarket checkout counter, *none of these predictions failed.*

Since these prophecies *were written hundreds of years* before Christ was born, the prophets could have been reading the trends of the times or making intelligent guesses. Many predictions were beyond human ability to fake a fulfillment. If he were a mere human being, Christ would have had no control over when (Dan. 9:24–27), where (Micah 5:2), or how he would be born (Isa. 7:14), how he would die (Psalm 22; Isaiah 53), do miracles (Isa. 35:5–6), or rise from the dead (Psalms 2, 16).

It is unlikely that all these events would have converged in the life of one man. Mathematicians (Stoner, 108) have calculated the probability of sixteen predictions being fulfilled in one man (e.g., Jesus) at 1 in 10^{45}. That forty-eight predictions might meet in one person, the probability is 1 in 10^{157}. It is almost impossible to conceive of a number that large.

But it is not just a *logical improbability* that rules out the theory that Jesus engineered his prophecy fulfillments; it is *morally implausible* that an all-powerful and all-knowing God (*see* GOD, NATURE OF) would allow his plans for prophetic fulfillment to be ruined by someone who just happened to be in the right place at the right time. God cannot lie (Titus 1:2), nor can he break a promise (Heb. 6:18). So we must conclude that he did not allow his prophetic promises to be thwarted by chance. All the evidence points to Jesus as the divinely appointed fulfillment of the Messianic prophecies. He was God's man, confirmed by God's signs (Acts 2:22).

Nonmessianic Predictions. Other biblical prophecies are specific and predictive. The following are examples:

Daniel 2:37–42: The Succession of Great World Kingdoms. An amazing prediction in the Bible is the succession of the world empires of Babylon, Medo-Persia, Greece, and Rome by Daniel. Interpreting the metallic man in the dream of King Nebuchadnezzar of Babylon, he told Nebuchadnezzar": 'You, O king, are the king of kings. . . . You are that head of gold. After you, another kingdom will rise, inferior to yours. Next, a third kingdom, one of bronze, will rule over the whole earth. Finally, there will be a fourth kingdom, strong as iron—for iron breaks and smashes everything—and as iron breaks things to pieces, so it will crush and break all the others'" (Dan. 2:38–40).

So precise and accurate is this prophecy that even negative critics agree that Daniel spoke in order of Babylon, Medo-Persia, Greece, and Rome. Critics try to avoid the supernatural nature of the prophecy by claiming these words were written after the fact, in about 165 B.C. But there is no real substantiation for this claim.

Cyrus King of Persia. One of the most specific Old Testament predictions identifies Cyrus of Persia before he was even born. Isaiah 44:28–45:1: "The LORD . . . who says of Cyrus, 'He is my shepherd and will accomplish all that I please; he will say of Jerusalem, "Let it be rebuilt," and of the temple, "Let its foundations be laid."' This is what the LORD says to his anointed, to Cyrus, whose right hand I take hold of to subdue nations before him and to strip kings of their armor, to open doors before him so that gates will not be shut."

This prediction was made some 150 years before Cyrus was even born (*see* ISAIAH, DEUTERO). Since Isaiah lived between about 740 and 690 B.C. (2 Kings 25–21) and Cyrus did not make his proclamation for Israel to return from exile until about 536 (Ezra 1), there would have been no human way for him to know what Cyrus would be named or do. The attempt of critics to divide Isaiah and postdate the prophecy is without foundation (*see* ISAIAH, DEUTERO) and is a back-handed compliment to the detail and accuracy of the prediction.

The Return of Israel to the Land. Given their long exile of some nineteen centuries and the animosity of the occupants of Palestine against them, any prediction of the return, restoration, and rebuilding of the nation of Israel was extremely unlikely. Yet predictions made some centuries and over two and a half millennia in advance about the two restorations of the Jews to their homeland and their restoration as a nation have been literally fulfilled. Regarding the 1948 restoration of Israel, Isaiah predicted that "In that day the Lord will reach out his hand a second time to reclaim the remnant that is left of his people from Assyria, from Lower Egypt, from Upper Egypt, from Cush, from Elam, from Babylonia, from Hamath and from the islands of the sea."

The first return was under Ezra and Nehemiah in the sixth century B.C. But Israel was sent again into exile in A.D. 70 when the Roman armies destroyed Jerusalem and leveled the temple. For nearly 2000 years the Jewish people remained in exile and the nation did not exist. Then, just as the Bible foretold, they were reestablished after World War II and a bitter struggle with the Arab Palestinians. Millions have returned and rebuilt their country and in the Six-Day War in 1967 Jerusalem again became a united Jewish city. No other nation in history has managed so successfully to keep a culture, identity, and language intact over hundreds of years, let alone against the genocidal hatred repeatedly encountered by the Jews. This Bible prediction is incredible evidence of the supernatural origin of the Scriptures.

The Closing of the Golden Gate. The Golden Gate is the eastern gate of Jerusalem, through which Christ made his triumphal entry on Palm Sunday before his crucifixion (Matthew 21). Ezekiel 44:2 predicted that it would be closed one day, and not reopened until the Messiah returned: "The LORD said to me, 'This gate is to remain shut. It must not be opened; no one may enter through it. It is to remain shut because the LORD, the God of Israel, has entered through it.'"

In 1543 Sultan Suleiman the Magnificent closed the gate and walled it up as Ezekiel had predicted. He had no idea he was fulfilling prophecy. He simply sealed it because the road leading to it was no longer used for traffic. It remains sealed to this day exactly as the Bible predicted, waiting to be reopened when the King returns.

The Destruction of Tyre. Tyre, an important sea port in the Eastern Mediterranean, was one of the great cities of the ancient world. It was a heavily fortified and flourishing city. Yet Ezekiel 26:3–14 predicted her doom and entire demolition hundreds of years in advance, declaring: "This is what the Sovereign LORD says: I am against you, O Tyre, and I will bring many nations against you, like the sea casting up its waves. They will destroy the walls of Tyre and pull down her towers; I will scrape away her rubble and make her a bare rock. Out in the sea she will become a place to spread fishing nets. . . . They will plunder your wealth and loot your merchandise; they will break down your walls and demolish your fine houses and throw your stones, timber and rubble into the sea. . . . I will make you a bare rock, and you will become a place to spread fishing nets. You will never be rebuilt, for I the LORD have spoken, declares the Sovereign LORD."

This prediction was partially fulfilled when Nebuchadnezzar destroyed the city and left it in ruins. However, the stones, dust and timber were not thrown into the sea. Then Alexander the Great attacked the seemingly impregnable Island of Tyre by taking the stones, dust, and timber from the ruined mainland city and building a causeway to the Island. Not only has the city never been rebuilt; today it literally is used as a place "to spread fishing nets."

The Doom of Edom (Petra). Unlike many Old Testament predictions of doom, Edom was not promised any restoration, only "perpetual desolation." Jeremiah wrote in 49:16–17: "'The terror you inspire and the pride of your heart have deceived you, you who live in the clefts of the rocks, who occupy the heights of the hill. Though you build your nest as high as the eagle's, from there I will bring you down,' declares the Lord. 'Edom will become an object of horror; all who pass by will be appalled and will scoff because of all its wounds.'"

Given the virtually impregnable nature of the ancient city carved out of rock and protected by a narrow passage way, this was an incredible prediction. Yet, in A.D. 636 it was conquered by Muslims and stands deserted but for tourist and passers by.

Flourishing of the Desert in Palestine. For centuries Palestine lay wasted and desolate. These conditions extended throughout the land. But Ezekiel 36:33–35 predicted that "This is what the Sovereign LORD says: On the day I cleanse you from all your sins, I will resettle your towns, and the ruins will be rebuilt. The desolate land will be cultivated instead of lying desolate in the sight of all who pass through it. They will say, 'This land that was laid waste has become like the garden of Eden; the cities that were lying in ruins, desolate and destroyed, are now fortified and inhabited.'"

Today roads have been built, the land is being cultivated, and Israel's agriculture is flourishing. This renovation began before the turn of the twentieth century and continues a century later. Agricultural crops, including a large orange harvest, are part of the restoration—just as Ezekiel had predicted.

Increase of Knowledge and Communication. Another biblical prophecy being fulfilled after thousands of years is that of Daniel's forecast of the increase of knowledge and communication in the last days (12:4): God said: "But you, Daniel, close up and seal the words of the scroll until the time of the end. Many will go here and there to increase knowledge."

Never in the history of the world has there been such a burst in knowledge, transportation, and communication as in the late twentieth century. Jet aircraft propulsion and computer microcircuit have caused a transportation and information explosion.

An Important Conclusion. A fact often overlooked by critics is that only one real case of fulfilled prophecy would establish Scripture's supernatural origin (cf. Ramm, 86). Even if most biblical predictions could be explained naturally, even one clear case establishes the rest and confirms the prophetic event. Thus, if the critic is to make the case against prophecy, all instances must be naturally explainable.

Objections to Predictive Prophecy. Numerous arguments have been advanced to negate argument for the supernatural origin of biblical prophecy. The most important ones will be briefly considered:

The Language of Prophecy Is Vague. Critics insist that the language of prophecy is so indefinite that some sort of fulfillment is not difficult to find. Vague predictions are sharpened by their fulfillment.

Not all biblical prophecy is sharp. Some is vague and sharpened by its fulfillment. However, the critic must show that all prophecy is of this nature. But, as shown in the above examples, some prophecies are quite specific. The predictions of when Christ would die (Dan. 9:24f.), in what city he would be born (Micah 5:2), and how he would suffer and die (Isaiah 53) are hardly vague.

Other Religious Books Have Prophecies. It is also protested that prophecies are not unique to the Bible, but are found in other holy books. Hence, it has no value in proving the truth of Christianity over other religions. This argument is similar to David Hume's argument that similar miraculous events are claimed by all religions. Hence, alleged miracles cannot be used to establish the truth of any one religion over another.

This objection is subject to the same criticism as Hume's (*see* MIRACLES, ARGUMENTS AGAINST). First, it is not true that other religions have specific, repeated, and unfailing fulfillment of predictions many years in advance of contingent events over which the predictor had no control. These kinds of predictions are unique to the Bible. A discussion of prophecies made by Muhammad in the *Qur'an*, the Bible's closest competitor is found in the article MUHAMMAD, ALLEGED MIRACLES OF, and shows the disparity between the two books.

R. S. Foster says of other holy books and the writings of pagan religions: "No well-accredited prophecy is found in any other book or even oral tradition now extant, or that has ever been extant in the world. The oracles of heathenism are not to be classed as exceptions. There is not a single one of them that meets the tests required to prove supernatural agency, which every Scripture prophecy evinces" (Foster, 111). M'Ilvaine adds, "the history of pagan nations indeed abounds with stories of auguries and oracles and detached predictions. . . . But innumerable distance separates all the pretended oracles of paganism from the dignity of the prophecies of the Bible" (M'Ilvaine, 246–47). After making a careful examination of Hebrew and Pagan prophets, Calvin Stow concluded that there were no credible prophecies in other writings, but that each "is just what we would expect from men of this world, who have no faith in another" (cited in Newman, 17–18).

Psychics Have Made Predictions Like the Bible's. Contemporary critics of biblical prophecy nominate psychic predictions for equality with Scripture. However, there is another quantum leap between every psychic and the unerring prophets of Scripture (*see* MIRACLES, MAGIC AND). Indeed, one test of a prophet was whether they ever uttered predictions that did not come to pass (Deut. 18:22). Those whose prophecies failed were stoned (18:20)—a practice that no doubt gave pause to any who were not absolutely sure their messages were from God. Amid hundreds of prophecies, biblical prophets are not known to have made a single error. A study of prophecies made by psychics in 1975 and observed until 1981 showed that of the seventy-two predictions, only six were fulfilled in any way. Two of these were vague and two others were hardly surprising—the U.S. and Russia would remain leading powers and there would be no world wars. *The People's Almanac* (1976) did a study of the predictions of twenty-five top psychics. The results: Of the total seventy-two predictions, sixty-six (92 percent) were totally wrong (Kole, 69). An accuracy rate around 8 percent could easily be explained by chance and general knowledge of circumstances. In 1993 the psychics missed every major unexpected news story, including Michael Jordan's retirement, the Midwest flooding, and the Israel-PLO peace treaty. Among their false prophecies were that the Queen of England would become a nun, and Kathy Lee Gifford would replace Jay Leno as host of *The Tonight Show* (*Charlotte Observer* 12/30/93).

Likewise, the highly reputed "predictions" of Nostradamus were not that amazing at all. Contrary to popular belief, he never predicted either the place or the year of a great California earthquake. Most of his "famous" predictions, such as the rise of Hitler, were vague. As other psychics, he was frequently wrong, a false prophet by biblical standards. More about Nostradamus is related in the article Nostradamus.

When Were Biblical Prophecies Made? According to this objection, all biblical prophecies with enough specificity to be unexplainable were made after the events. Daniel's amazing statements were made quite late, and Isaiah's predictions about Cyrus were edited in after he arrived on the scene. They were recording history, not uttering prophecies. For discussions of the dating of these two books, see DANIEL, DATING OF, and ISAIAH, DEUTERO. Neither these nor other charges of post-dated prophecies have any foundation in fact. And many fulfillments have occurred long after the writings are known to have existed.

Alleged Fulfillments Misinterpret the Texts. Critics argue that the alleged fulfillment of Old Testament predictions are frequently misinterpretations of the Old Testament text. For example, Matthew says repeatedly "that it might be fulfilled" (cf. 1:22; 2:15, 17). However, when the Old Testament passage is examined in context, it turns out that it was not a real prediction of the event to which Matthew applied it.

A case in point is Matthew 2:15: "And so was fulfilled what the Lord had said through the prophet: 'Out of Egypt I called my son.'" When the Old Testament source passage, Hosea 11:1, is examined, it is discovered that this is not a predictive prophecy about Jesus coming out of Egypt when he was a child but a statement about the children of Israel coming out of Egypt at the exodus.

It is readily admitted that many "prophecies" are not predictive and that the New Testament *applied* certain Old Testament passages to Christ that were not directly predictive of him. Many scholars speak of these Old Testament texts being "topologically fulfilled" in Christ, without being directly predictive. That is, some truth in the passage is appropriately applied to Christ, even though it was not directly predictive of him.

Others speak of a generic meaning in the Old Testament passage which applies both to its Old Testament reference (e.g., Israel) and the New Testament reference (e.g., Christ), both of whom were God's "son." Some scholars describe this as a double-reference view of prophecy. Whatever the case, these kinds of prophetic passages are not directly predictive and have no apologetic value. There are Old Testament passages that are not merely typological but are manifestly predictive, as was shown above. For example, the time and place of Christ's birth and death were told.

What the critic cannot show is that all Old Testament "prophecies" are merely typological and nonpredictive.

Jesus Manipulated Events to Fulfill Prophecy. Another argument used by critics was popularized by Hugh Schonfield's **Passover Plot.* He argued that Jesus manipulated people and events so as to make it appear that he was the predicted Messiah. This interesting theory is destroyed by the facts. First, numerous miracles (*see* MIRACLES IN THE BIBLE) confirmed Jesus to be the Messiah. God would not confirm a fraud to appear to be his Son (*see* MIRACLES, APOLOGETIC VALUE OF). Second, there is no evidence that Jesus was a deceiver. To the contrary, his character is impeccable (*see* CHRIST, UNIQUENESS OF). Third, Jesus had no control over some predictions over which he had no control, such as, his ancestry (Gen. 12:3; 49:10; 2 Sam. 7:12–16); birthplace (Micah 5:2), time of death (Dan. 9:24–27); and conditions of his death (Isaiah 53). Fourth, in order to manipulate all the people (including his enemies) and even his disciples in order to make it appear that he was the promised Messiah, Jesus would have needed supernatural powers. But if he had such powers, he must have been the Messiah he claimed to be.

Only the Successful Prophecies Are Recorded. This objection affirms that Old Testament prophets were just as fallible as any other prophets. They got some right and some wrong. However, only the ones that succeeded were placed in the Bible. Thus, there is really nothing supernatural about them. After all, if only the successful predictions of Jean Dixon were collected into one volume long after her death, she too would look as supernatural as the biblical prophets.

This objection is based on fallacious premises. First of all, it is the fallacy of the Argument from Ignorance. It presents no evidence that there were other prophecies that failed. It merely *assumes* that there were. The burden of proof is to show that there were. Second, what it admits is sufficient to destroy its contention. If all the prophecies in the Bible are good ones, then we have numerous positive evidence, that the Bible is unfailing in its predictive power—a sure sign of their divine origin and far beyond the best psychics on their best days. Third, the argument is a false analogy, since in the case of the psychics we have numerous known examples of where they were wrong. In the case of the Bible we have none. It also assumes the prophet's contemporaries would have gone along with the misses and accepted the hits as from God. As noted, that is not how it worked.

Some Biblical Predictions Were Not Fulfilled. A number of critics have argued that not all the predictions of the Bible were fulfilled. Jonah's prediction that Nineveh would be destroyed in forty days was not (Jonah 3:4). Christ did not return in one generation, as he said he would. Indeed, Christ has not returned and set up a literal kingdom as he promised (Matthew 24–25). Neither has God destroyed the world by fire (2 Peter 3:10–13) and set up a perfect Paradise (Revelation 21–22).

The alleged unfulfilled prophecies all fall into one of the following categories (see Payne):

Some were conditional. Jonah's warning to Nineveh was conditioned on their continuing rebellion. When they repented (3:5–9), God relented of the impending doom. As Jesus said to those of his day, "Unless you repent, you too will all perish" (Luke 13:3). Likewise, there is an implied "unless you repent" in every prophet who warns of God's judgment. As Peter said, "The Lord . . . is patient with you, not wanting anyone to perish, but everyone to come to repentance" (2 Peter 3:9). The same is true of Deuteronomy 11:25 where God said to Israel, "No man will be able to stand against you. The LORD your God, as he promised you, will put the terror and fear of you on the whole land, wherever you go." Yet they did suffer defeats, for example, at Ai (Joshua 7). But when this promise is examined, it is clearly conditional—"if you carefully keep all these commandments" (vs. 22). When Israel did obey God, they were undefeatable, even against overwhelming odds (cf. Joshua 6, 8–11).

Some simply have not yet been fulfilled. Most of these relate to Jesus' second coming which has not yet occurred. It is simply fallacious to claim the Bible has false prophecies because they have not yet all been fulfilled. As Peter warned (2 Peter 3:4–5, 8–9):

> First of all, you must understand that in the last days scoffers will come, scoffing and following their own evil desires. They will say, "Where is this 'coming' he promised? Ever since our fathers died, everything goes on as it has since the beginning of creation." . . . But do not forget this one thing, dear friends: With the Lord a day is like a thousand years, and a thousand years are like a day. . . . The Lord is not slow in keeping his promise, as some understand slowness. He is patient with you, not wanting anyone to perish, but everyone to come to repentance.

The other alleged unfulfilled prophecies are not errors in the Bible but *errors in the critics'* understanding of the Bible. For example, Jesus did not say he would return to earth in the disciples' lifetime (in Matt. 24:34). He never said "I will return in your life time." What he said was, "This generation will certainly not pass away until all these things have happened." This phrase can mean one of several different things. To make their point, the critics must assume that it can mean only one thing.

Further, "generation" in Greek *(genea)* can mean "race." One interpretation of Jesus' statement is that the Jewish race would not pass away until all things are fulfilled. There were many promises to Israel, including the eternal inheritance of the land of Palestine (Genesis 12, 14, 15, 17) and the Davidic kingdom (2 Samuel 7), yet the nation was about to be destroyed by the Romans. Jesus could be promising God's preservation of the nation of Israel in order to fulfill his promises to them. Paul speaks of a future of the nation of Israel when they will be reinstated in God's covenantal promises (Rom. 11:11–26). And Jesus' response to his disciples' last question implied that there would yet be a future kingdom for Israel, when they asked: "Lord, will You at this time restore the kingdom to Israel?" Rather than rebuking them for their misunderstanding, he replied that "It is not for you to know times or seasons which the Father has put in his own authority" (Acts 1:6–7).

What is more, "generation" could also refer to a generation in its commonly understood sense of the people who will be alive at the time indicated. In this case, "generation" would refer to the group of people who are alive when these things come to pass in the future. The generation alive when these things (the abomination of desolation [vs.15], the great tribulation [vs. 21], and the sign of the Son of Man in heaven [vs. 30]) begin to come to pass will still be alive when these judgments are completed. Since it is commonly believed that the tribulation is a period of some seven years (Dan. 9:27; cf. Rev. 11:2) at the end of the age, then Jesus would be saying that "this generation" alive at the beginning of the tribulation will still be alive at the end of it.

In any event, there is no reason to assume that Jesus made the obviously false assertion that the world would come to an end within the lifetime of his contemporaries.

Summary. The Bible is filled with specific predictive prophecies that have been literally fulfilled. The *Encyclopedia of Biblical Prophecies* calculated that 27 percent of the entire Bible contains predictive prophecy (Payne, 675). This is true of no other book in the world. And it is a sure sign of its divine origin.

Sources

A. Y. Ali, *The Glorious Qur'an*
G. T. B. Davis, *Fulfilled Prophecies That Prove the Bible*
S. R. Driver, et al., trans., *The Fifty-Third Chapter of Isaiah According to Jewish Interpreters*
R. S. Foster, *The Supernatural Book*
N. L. Geisler and A. Saleeb, *Answering Islam*
H. Hoehner, *Chronological Aspects of the Life of Christ*
W. Kaiser, *The Uses of the Old Testament in the New*
A. Kole, *Miracle and Magic*
E. P. M'Ilvaine, *The Evidences of Christianity*
R. Newman, ed., *The Evidence of Prophecy*
J. B. Payne, *Encyclopedia of Biblical Prophecy*
B. Ramm, *Protestant Christian Evidences*
H. Schonfield, *The Passover Plot: New Light on the History of Jesus*
H. Spencer, *Islam and the Gospel of God*
P. W. Stoner, *Science Speaks*

Pseudepigrapha. ***See*** **Apocrypha, Old and New Testaments.**

Punctuated Equilibria. ***See*** **Evolution, Biological; Missing Links.**

Qq

Q Document. The *Gospel of Q* or *Q Document* is a hypothetical collection of Jesus' sayings that supposedly antedates the four Gospels. The *Q* hypothesis comes from the German word *Quelle*, meaning "sources." *Q* was used heavily by the Jesus Seminar to arrive at their radical conclusions. Since *Q* allegedly contains sayings, not works or miracles of Jesus, it is used as a basis for denying the resurrection. Since the earliest *Q* contained no references to Jesus' deity, this too is held to be a later mythological invention. If true, this would undermine the historic apologetic for Christianity (*see* APOLOGETICS, HISTORICAL; NEW TESTAMENT, HISTORICITY OF).

Supposed States and Dates of Q. According to *Q* proponent Burton Mack, there were really four successive states of *Q*: proto-*Q*1, *Q*1, proto-*Q*2, and *Q*2. The gospel(s) of *Q* supposedly developed between 30 and 65, before any canonical Gospels appeared. Thus, *Q* is supposed to provide, along with the **Gospel of Thomas* (*see* NAG HAMMADI GOSPELS), the earliest view of Jesus' followers.

Some scholars distinguish between *Q*1 (ca. 50), consisting of short sayings of Jesus, and *Q*2 (50–60), which may have been against the original Jesus group as evidenced by the judgmental tone of *Q*2. This includes apocalyptic pronouncements of doom on those who refused their kingdom program. After the Jewish War (70), they upgraded their mythology (*Q*3) to include statements about Jesus being divine (Mack, 53). On this breakdown, *Q*1 presents Jesus as a sage, a wise teacher; *Q*2 portrays him as prophetic and apocalyptic; and *Q*3 as superhuman, embodying the wisdom of God and divine authority (Boyd, 121).

History of the Q Hypothesis. Judging from its widespread acceptance today, one would expect that the *Q* hypothesis had been around since the early church. The truth is that Friedrich *Schleiermacher (1768–1834), the father of modern liberalism, gave impetus to the idea when he reinterpreted a statement by Papias (ca. 110) about Matthew compiling "the oracles" of Jesus (Gk. *ta logia*). This, Schleiermacher decided, was a document consisting only of Jesus' "sayings," rather than both "what the Lord said or did" (*see* Linnemann, *Is There a Synoptic Problem?* 20). Later, Christian Hermann Weisse (1801–1866) claimed that this saying-source was used by Luke in compiling his Gospel, thus giving rise to the concept of *Q*. Others added that Mark was used by both Matthew and Luke. Thus, *Q* is posited to account for the material used by Matthew and Luke that is not found in Mark, their common source.

However, in spite of its popularity, *Q* has been rejected by many biblical scholars from the time it was first proposed. B. F. Westcott (1825–1901), Theodore Zahn (1838–1933), and Adolf Schlatter (1852–1938) are examples of older scholars. Eta Linnemann, John Wenham, and William Farmer are examples of contemporary scholars.

Alleged Basis of Q. According to proponents, "the *Q* hypothesis, together with Marcan priority, is the most efficient way of accounting for the myriad details in the relationship of these three texts to one another." For "Matthew and Luke agree in their sequence of events in the life of Jesus only when they also agree with Mark." And "this peculiar pattern has led almost all scholars of the New Testament to the conclusion that Matthew and Luke must have made use of Mark as a kind of outline for their respective works, but quite independently of one another." This Marcan priority, however, doesn't account for a good deal of material shared by Matthew and Luke. "How could Matthew and Luke have included these several sayings, parables, and occasional stories—sometimes offering versions that are very close in wording—independently of one another?" In view of this, "the *Q* hypothesis arose as a way of accounting for the material common to Matthew and Luke, but not found in Mark" (Patterson, 39–40). This similarity in content and order of events is used to show literary dependence of the latter documents on the former, that is, of Matthew and Luke upon Mark and *Q*.

Evaluation. From an apologetic vantage point, the so-called "Gospel of *Q*" has serious implications for the authenticity of the Gospels and the historic apologetic for Christianity. But the evidence shows that the hypothesis in no way undermines the authenticity of the biblical Gospels.

A central consideration is that there is not one shred of documentary evidence that *Q* ever existed. No manuscript or any version of it has ever been found. No church Father ever cited any work corresponding to what current scholars mean by *Q*. From what is known of the documentary tradition of the early Christian centuries, this lacuna is improbable in the extreme if the work ever existed. Former *Q* proponent Linnemann observes the reverence with which critics regard *Q*: "This is the stuff of fairy tales" (Linnemann, "Is There a *Q*?" 19). Apologists can assume with confidence that *Q* is a modern creation and that no manuscript will turn up next week to prove them wrong.

As Gregory Boyd observes, "we could account for such similarities in other ways that don't require relying on a hypothetical document." For example, "from what we know about Jewish oral tradition and memorization, we could convincingly argue that the commonalities between Luke and Matthew simply indicate the reliability of the oral traditions that lie behind both. A number of reputable scholars take this position. Others argue that Luke used Matthew as a source document. Luke 1:1–4 indicates that he used several sources. This would account for similarity" (Boyd, 119–20).

The argument for *Q* is circular reasoning. Mack, for example, argued that "frequently the way sayings are grouped together or ordered [in *Q*] makes a point. Sometimes a saying offers a specific interpretation of a preceding unit of material" (Mack, 106). And "the order and organization of material are . . . clear signs of the coherence of a particular layer of tradition" (ibid., 108). However, the only *Q* we possess was constructed by *Q* proponents from Matthew and Luke. They decided how these sayings would be put together. So it is no surprise that they were ordered to make a point, since it is those who constructed *Q* who ordered them in this way (ibid., 125). They are begging the question.

The *Q* hypothesis is based on a reconstructionist view of history that rejects New Testament history in Acts. If the *Q* hypothesis is correct as interpreted by some modern scholars, the book of Acts must be altogether false. Yet no book in the New Testament has more authentication of its historical accuracy than Acts. Historians specializing in the Roman Empire, such as A. N. Sherwin-White and Colin Hemer, have provided overwhelming evidence of its authenticity (*see* ACTS, HISTORICITY OF). Sherwin-White wrote: "For Acts the confirmation of historicity is overwhelming. . . . Any attempt to reject its basic historicity even in matters of detail must now appear absurd. Roman historians have long taken it for granted" (Sherwin-White, 189). Before them there was the work of William Ramsay who, after decades of research, concluded that in the presentation of hundreds of historical details, Dr. Luke has not made a single mistake (see Ramsay). But if Acts is good history, the historical reconstruction of *Q* is mythology.

An important event in early Christianity was the Council of Jerusalem in 49, at which the teaching of Paul was the central focus of the controversy. As Linnemann notes, "Are we to believe that this Council was content to quibble over the interpretation of Jewish law, as Luke reports, when Paul was 'mythologizing' the gospel, claiming Jesus to be God's son, while the *Q* people believed him to be no more than a Sage?" (Linnemann, "Is There a *Q*?" 20). Surely, if the people of *Q* were Jesus people, not Christians, there would be some trace of this conflict in the New Testament. There is not (ibid.).

Neither order of events nor similarity of content is convincing grounds for positing literary dependence. The only way to show literary dependence is to prove a high percentage of identical literary construction. But this is not the case, as Linnemann has demonstrated (ibid., 21–23). "Similarity in content is in itself no proof of literary dependence. It could also be caused by different people covering the same event. A saying of Jesus should not have differed much as reported independently by two or more people who heard it. Similarity might be historically, not literarily, transmitted" (ibid., 22). Nor can the existence of a source document be demonstrated by sequence of accounts. Only twenty-four pairs of parallels, 36.9 percent, occur within one chapter of each other. Only five (7.69 percent) occur in the same point of narrative in Matthew and Luke. In view of this, Linnemann argues, "It takes a robust imagination" to suppose literary dependence (ibid.).

Literary dependence assumes identical wording. But the number of identical words in parallel verses is 1792 or 41 percent of Matthew's *Q* portion and 42 percent of Luke's. In seventeen of the sixty-five parallel pairs alleged to have come from *Q*, one-quarter of *Q*, the number of identical words is less than 25 percent. In the parable of the talents (Matt. 25:14–30), the longest *Q* passage, only sixty of 291 words are identical with Luke 19:11–27. Of these words, nine are the word *and*, seven are articles, and six are pronouns. That leaves thirty-eight of 291 words on which to establish dependence. Most of those occur in direct speech. "Thus the similarity is easily accounted for by a historically reliable memory that reached both Matthew and Luke" (ibid.). The longest passage in the high-agreement area has 78 percent identical words. That is no longer than Psalm 1, a text many know by heart. Says Linnemann, "It is not difficult to imagine accounts of this length being committed to memory in the oral culture of Jesus' day" (ibid.).

There is no reason to accept the assumption that nearly all of *Q* is contained in Matthew and Luke. The primary argument is that, since Matthew and Luke retain a large amount of Mark in their Gospels, they would do the same for *Q*. But this does not follow, since Matthew and Luke may both have valued Mark more highly.

It is also assumed that there were several versions of *Q*. Besides the subjective criteria on which this was decided, it may be a violation of "Ockham's Razor," that hypotheses should not be multiplied without necessity. There is a more simple explanation if one predicates that the Gospels were assembled by eyewitnesses and contemporaries who had access to the original sayings and deeds of Jesus.

Overlap in the Gospels can be accounted for on the premise that either (1) the writers were independent eyewitnesses whose accounts would naturally overlap; (2) the later Gospel writers used the first Gospel written, plus their independent sources, and/or a common pool of oral sayings of Jesus; or (3) an early edition of Matthew or Mark was used later by the author as well as the other Gospel writers. The sources Luke mentions (Luke 1:1–4) may be other canonical Gospels composed by eyewitnesses.

If a precanonical Gospel record of Jesus existed, there is no good reason to believe it omitted the miracle or deity claims. Indeed, since the Old Testament claimed deity for the Messiah (esp. Pss. 45:6; 110:1; Isa. 7:14; 9:6; Micah 5:2; Zech. 12:10), there is no reason why someone claiming to be the Jewish Messiah would not do so as well (*see* CHRIST, DEITY OF; VIRGIN BIRTH).

Even if there had been some miracleless deposit of original sayings of Jesus prior to the Gospels, this would not prove Jesus did not do miracles nor say many other things. It may have been an early disciple accustomed to keeping records, such as Matthew the former tax collector, recorded the sayings of Jesus because he knew they would be needed later. For example, if we had only Galatians (and not Romans, 1 Corinthians, and 1 Thessalonians), we might assume that Paul was not concerned about the resurrection. Galatians only mentions it once. Possessing an early document of sayings does not allow us to conclude that Christ did not perform miracles unless the document explicitly says so. Or, it might have been that, in view of the tremendous impact the world's greatest Teacher made on their minds and hearts for three years, there was an oral deposit of Jesus' words in the memories of the disciples before there were any written records. Indeed, according to John, Jesus promised that the Holy Spirit would bring to mind the things he had taught them (John 14:26; 16:13).

And if we take the presupposition so far as to imagine that an anti-miracle version of *Q* existed, it could have been an early revision of Jesus' words and deeds in opposition to the original disciples. After all, serious doctrinal deviations appeared even during the apostles' time (cf. Colossians 2; 1 Timothy 4; 1 John 4). Jesus warned of false prophets (Matt. 7:15).

When segments of text attributed to *Q* are examined as a whole, there is evidence of Jesus' miracles and divinity. Jesus claimed his "father" gave him authority over the whole world (*Q*s24). Jesus considered himself greater than Solomon or the prophet Jonah (*Q*s32). He believed those who disowned him would be disowned by God (*Q*s37). Jesus would determine who would be excluded from God's kingdom (*Q*s47). He predicted the future (*Q*s49). Jesus demanded that his disciples put him over all human beings, even their parents (*Q*s52). His followers would sit on thrones judging the twelve tribes of Israel (*Q*s62). Jesus even referred to his resurrection via the "sign" (miracle) of Jonah (*Q*s32). No doubt this evidence is one reason critics attempt to stratify *Q* into multiple documents, pushing the statements to as late a period as possible. However, the grounds for doing so are highly subjective, and, even so, the statements are still early enough to be authentic—during the time eyewitnesses were still alive.

In contrast to the hypothetical *Q*, the earliest known actual manuscript and documents of the Christian faith contained references to Christ's miracles and divinity. John is filled with both (*see* JOHN, GOSPEL OF) and the John Rylands Fragment is the earliest undisputed manuscript of Christian origins (*see* NEW TESTAMENT MANUSCRIPTS). First Corinthians is accepted even by critics as coming from the pen of Paul in 55 or 56, only twenty-two or twenty-three years after Jesus' death. It refers to the resurrection as having been "received" from Paul in his earlier teachings (1 Cor. 15:1, 4–8).

The Q Assumptions. Obviously, though most *Q* advocates would be reluctant to admit it, there is an antisupernatural bias behind their view. Following the naturalistic approach to the Gospels that began with David *Strauss in 1835–1836) they assume the miraculous does not occur. Thus, all records of miraculous events are categorized as later results of mythmaking (*see* MYTHOLOGY AND THE NEW TESTAMENT). The haste at which they jump to this conclusion when, even granting an early "sayings" source, betrays a desire to eliminate the supernatural. The confidence with which critics come to an antisupernatural conclusion on such speculative and hypothetical grounds supports the thesis that they really begin with a naturalistic presupposition. Compare the words of one *Q* advocate: "The narrative canonical gospels can no longer be viewed as the trustworthy accounts of unique and stupendous historical events at the foundation of the Christian faith." Instead, "the gospels must now be seen as the result of early Christian mythmaking" (Patterson, "The Lost Gospel," 40).

Beginning with a disbelief in *miracles, it comes as no surprise that their imaginary reconstruction of *Q* in the early time period is devoid of miracle stories, including the *resurrection.

The *Q* hypothesis is based on an incredible number of assumptions (see Boyd, 122–24):

1. Mark was the earliest Gospel and Matthew and Luke followed its form and content. The same data can be explained by positing an oral tradition or putting Matthew first.
2. *Q* existed as a written document. There is no proof for this.
3. A *Q* can be reconstructed from what Matthew and Luke have in common that is not found in Mark. But if *Q* existed there is no objective way to know how much of it was used.
4. *Q* was composed to express everything early Christians believed about Jesus. Why could it not have been simply a collection of sayings?
5. It is also assumed that a community of people created *Q*. There is no proof of this. One person could just as easily have collected Jesus' sayings.
6. *Q* can be accurately understood by discerning its various literary stages. No objective criteria are offered by which this can be done.
7. These alleged states reflect various stages of the thinking of Jesus' followers. The various views could as easily have been concurrent.
8. The views of Christ are incompatible with one another. Jesus could have been teacher, prophet, and divine authority. If these elements are together at the end, why could they not have all been there at the beginning?

Boyd summarizes: "We see, then, that the liberal revision of the picture of Jesus and of early church history on the basis of *Q* amounts to nothing more than a pile of arbitrary assumptions built on other arbitrary assumptions" (Boyd, 24).

Conclusion. The argument for the *Q* hypothesis, particularly in its naturalistic form, are without historical, documentary, or literary foundations. As Boyd noted, "among other things, the entire scheme is completely conjectural. These scholars ask us to trade the reliable Gospel portrait of Christ for a hypothetical reconstruction of history based on a hypothetical reconstruction of a hypothetical document" (Boyd, 121–22). There is nothing in the canonical Gospels that cannot be accounted for by positing that the authors were eyewitnesses and/or contemporaries of the events and that they provided an accurate account of what they reported just as Luke claims (Luke 1:1–4).

In the words of one former *Q* disciple, "The Gospels report the words and deeds of Jesus. They do this partly through direct eyewitnesses (Matthew and John) and partly through those who were informed by eyewitnesses (Mark and Luke). The similarities as well as the differences in the Gospel accounts are just what one expects from eyewitness reminiscence" (ibid.).

Sources

G. Boyd, *Jesus Under Siege*

W. Farmer, *The Synoptic Problem: A Critical Analysis*

E. Linnemann, "Is There a *Q*?" *BR* (October 1995)

———, *Is There a Synoptic Problem?*

B. Mack, *The Lost Gospel: The Book of Q and Christian Origins*

S. J. Patterson, "*Q*—The Lost Gospel," *BR* (October 1993)

———, "Yes, Virginia, There Is a *Q*," *BR* (October 1995)

W. Ramsay, *St. Paul, Traveler and Roman Citizen*

A. N. Sherwin-White, *Roman Society and Roman Law in the New Testament*

J. W. Wenham, *Redating Matthew, Mark, land Luke: A Fresh Assault on the Synoptic Problem*

Quantum Physics. ***See*** **INDETERMINACY, PRINCIPLE OF.**

Quest for Historical Jesus. ***See*** **JESUS, QUEST FOR HISTORICAL.**

***Qur'an*, Alleged Divine Origin of.** Orthodox Islam and historic Christianity cannot both be true. Either religion claims that its scriptures alone are the inspired Word of God. They also contain mutually exclusive claims: God is three persons. God is only one person. The Bible says Christ died on the cross and rose from the dead three days later. The *Qur'an* says that he did not (*see* CHRIST, DEATH OF; CHRIST'S DEATH, MORAL OBJECTIONS TO; CHRIST'S DEATH, SUBSTITUTION LEGEND; RESURRECTION, EVIDENCE FOR). Thus, it is necessary for the Christian apologist to challenge the divine authority claims of the *Qur'an*.

Origin of the Qur'an. The Islamic claim for the *Qur'an* is unparalleled by that in any other major religion. Is the *Qur'an* a miracle? Muhammad claimed it was—indeed it was the only miracle he offered as proof of his claims to be a prophet (sura 17:88). The evidence Muslims give for this claim includes the following points.

Argument from Unique Literary Style. Eloquence is highly questionable as a test for divine inspiration, yet a foundation stone of the Islamic position is that the *Qur'an* possesses a literary quality and style that could only have come directly from God. At best the *Qur'an*'s literary qualifications prove that Muhammad was a gifted person. But amazing artistic and intellectual gifts are hardly supernatural. Mozart wrote his first symphony at the age of six and produced his entire music corpus before age 35 when he died. Muhammad did not begin to write until age 40. But what Muslim would say that Mozart's works are miraculous? If eloquence were the test, a case could be made for the divine authority of many literary classics, from Homer's *Iliad* and *Odyssey* to Shakespeare.

Further, even some early Muslim scholars admitted that the *Qur'an* was not perfect in its literary form. The Iranian Shiite scholar Ali Dashti notes that "among the Moslem scholars of the early period, before bigotry and hyperbole prevailed, were some such as Ebrahim on-Nassam who openly acknowledged that the arrangement and syntax of the Qoran are not miraculous and that works of equal or greater value could be produced by other God-fearing persons." Although some condemned this view (based on their interpretation of sura 17:90), on-Nassam had many defenders, among them several leading exponents of the Motazelite school (Dashti, 48).

The *Qur'an* is not unrivaled, even among works in Arabic. Islamic scholar, C. G. Pfander, points out that "it is by no means the universal opinion of unprejudiced Arabic scholars that the literary style of the *Qur'an* is superior to that of all other books in the Arabic language." For example, "some doubt whether in eloquence and poetry it surpasses the Mu'allaqat, or the Magamat or Hariri, though in Muslim lands few people are courageous enough to express such an opinion" (Pfander, 264). Dashti, contends, however, that the *Qur'an* contains numerous grammatical irregularities. He notes that:

> The Qoran contains sentences which are incomplete and not fully intelligible without the air of commentaries; foreign words, unfamiliar Arabic words, and words used with other than the normal meaning; adjectives and verbs inflected without observance of the concord of gender and number; illogical and ungrammatically applied pronouns which sometimes have no referent; and predicates which in rhymed passages are often remote from the subjects.

He adds, "these and other such aberrations in the language have given scope to critics who deny the Qoran's eloquence" (Dashti, 48–49). He lists numerous examples (suras 74:1; 4:160; 20:66; 2:172, etc.), one of which is "In verse 9 of *Sura* 49 (*ol-Hojorat*), 'If two parties of believers have started to fight each other, make peace between them." The verb for "have started to fight" is in the plural, whereas it ought to be in the dual like its subject, "two parties." Anis A. Shorrosh lists other literary flaws in the *Qur'an*. For example, in sura 2:177 he points out that the word *Sabireen* in Arabic should have been *Sabiroon* because of its position in the sentence. Likewise, *Sabieen* in sura 5:69 is more correct Arabic than *Sabioon*. Also, Shorrosh notes that there is "a gross error in Arabic" in sura 3:59 (Shorrosh, 199–200). Dashti counts more than 100 aberrations from normal rules and structures of Arabic (Dashti, 50). With such problems, the *Qur'an* may be eloquent, but it is neither perfect nor unparalleled.

As Pfander observed, "even were it proved beyond the possibility of doubt that the *Qur'an* far surpassed all other books in eloquence, elegance, and poetry, that would no more prove its inspiration than a man's strength would demonstrate his wisdom or a woman's beauty her virtue" (Pfander, 267). There is no logical connection between literary eloquence and divine authority. The sovereign God (whom Muslims accept) could chose to speak in plain everyday language, if he wished. At best one might attempt to argue that if God said it, he would say it most eloquently. Even so, it would be a logical fallacy to argue that simply because it is eloquent God must have said it. Humans can speak eloquently, and God can speak in common language.

Other religions have used the beautiful literary style of their work as a sign of its divine origin. Would Muslims accept the inspiration of these works? For example, the Persian founder of the Manichaeans, Mani, "is said to have claimed that men should believe in him as the Paraclete ["Helper" Jesus promised in John 14] because he produced a book called *Artand*, full of beautiful pictures." Further, "he said that the book had been given him by God, that no living man could paint pictures equal in beauty to those contained in it, and that therefore it had evidently come from God himself" (Pfander, 264). Yet no Muslim will accept this claim. Why then should non-Muslims accept literary beauty as a valid test for the divine authority of the Qu'ran?

Argument from Muhammad's Illiteracy. In addition to its style, the human source and content of the *Qur'an* is proof of its divine origin. They insist that no book with its message could have come from an illiterate prophet, as was Muhammad.

It is questionable that Muhammad was actually illiterate. As one authority noted, the Arabic words *al umni*, translated "the unlettered" prophet in the *Qur'an* (sura 7:157), "may be [rendered] 'heathen' rather than 'illiterate.'" Pfander prefers the translation, "the Gentile Prophet," agreeing that the term does not imply illiteracy (Pfander, 254). The same word is rendered "gentiles" in sura 62:2: "He it is Who hath sent among gentiles (*al umni*)," and in suras 2:73; 3:19, 69; 7:156.

The evidence suggests that Muhammad was not illiterate. For example, "when the Treaty of Hudaibah was being signed, Muhammad took the pen from Ali, struck out the words in which Ali had designated him "the apostle of God" and wrote instead with his own hand the words, "son of Abdu'llah." And "tradition tells us too that, when he was dying, Muhammad called for pen and ink, to write a command appointing his successor, but his strength failed him before writing-materials were brought" (Pfander, 255).

W. Montgomery Watts informs us that "many Meccans were able to read and write, and there is therefore a presumption that an efficient merchant, as Muhammad was, knew something of the arts" (Watt, 40). Even Muslim scholars refer to Muhammad as being "perfect in intellect" (Gudel, 72). If Muhammad lacked formal training in earlier years, there is no reason why such an intelligent person could not have caught up on his own later.

Third, even if it were granted that Muhammad was illiterate, it does not follow that the *Qur'an* was dictated to him by God. There are other possible explanations. Even if he was not formally trained, Muhammad was a bright person possessing great skills. His scribe could have made up for deficiencies by stylizing the work. This was a common practice. Homer was blind, and so he probably did not write his epics himself. Some critics argue that it is possible that Muhammad's first impression was right, that he received the information from an evil spirit, who might have aided his ability (*see* MUHAMMAD, ALLEGED DIVINE CALL OF).

Argument from the Preservation of the Qur'an. Does perfect preservation prove divine inspiration? Muslims imply that the *Qur'an* is identical to the original, and this sets the book above the Bible. *Qur'an* critics dispute this. First, there is often a serious over-claim as to the preservation of the *Qur'an*. While it is true that the present *Qur'an* is a nearly perfect copy of its seventh-century original, it is not true that this is exactly the way it came from Muhammad.

The *Qur'an* was originally given orally by Muhammad and memorized by devout followers, most of whom where killed shortly after Muhammad's death. According to early tradition, Muhammad's scribes wrote on pieces of paper, stones, palm-leaves, shoulder-blades, ribs, and bits of leather. Muslims believe that during the lifetime of Muhammad the *Qur'an* was written down. But, according to the testimony of Zayd, a contemporary and follower of Muhammad, he was requested by Abu Bakr to "search out the [various chapters and verses of] the *Qur'an* and gather it together." He responded, "accordingly, I sought out the *Qur'an*: I gathered it together from leafless palm branches and thin white stones and men's breasts . . ." (Pfander, 258–59). In the 650s, during the reign of Uthman ibn Affan, the third Muslim Caliph, it was reported that several Muslim communities were using different versions of the *Qur'an*. Once again, Zayd was called in to prepare the official revised version. It is this version that has remained uniform and intact, not any original version that came directly from Muhammad.

In his book *Materials for the History of the Text of the Qur'an*, European archaeologist, Arthur Jeffry, revealed his discovery of one of three known copies of some early Islamic works called *Masahif*. These books related the state of the *Qur'an* text prior to its standardization under Uthman. It reveals, contrary to Muslims' claim, that there were several differing texts prior to Uthman's revision. In fact, as Dashti points out, some *Qur'anic* verses were changed due to the scribes' suggestions to Muhammad and others by the influence of Umar I, second caliph of the Muslim Empire, on Muhammad.

Jeffry concludes that Uthman's recension "was a necessary stroke of policy to establish a standard text for the whole empire." Since there were wide divergences between the *Qur'ans* of Medina, Mecca, Basra, Kufa, and Damascus, "Uthman's solution was to canonize the Medinan Codex and order all others to be destroyed." Therefore, he concludes, "there can be little doubt that the text canonized by Uthman was only one among several types of text in existence at the time" (Jeffry, 7–8).

Not all Muslims today accept the same version of the *Qur'an*. The Sunnite Muslims accept the Sahih tradition of Masud as authoritative. Masud was one of the few people authorized by Muhammad to teach the *Qur'an*. Yet the Ibn Masud Codex of the *Qur'an* has a multitude of variations from the Uthmanic recension. In the second sura alone there are nearly 150 variations. It takes Jeffry some ninety-four pages to show the variations between the two. He also demonstrates that the variant readings are not just a matter of dialect, as many Muslims claim. Some variations involved a whole clause and others omitted complete sentences. Jeffry concludes that the Uthman text that was canonized was only one out of many, and "there is grave suspicion that Uthman may have seriously edited the text he canonized" (Jeffry, ix–x).

Islamic tradition reveals certain things not found in the present *Qur'an*. One tells us that Ayishah, one of Muhammad's wives, said: "Among what was sent down of the *Qur'an* were ten well known (verses) about—Suckling, which prohibited: then they were annulled by five well known ones. Then the Apostle of God deceased, and they are what is recited of the *Qur'an*" (Pfander, 256). Another example of something not found in today's *Qur'an* is what Umar said: "Verily God sent Muhammad with the truth, and He sent down upon him the Book, accordingly the Verse of Stoning was part of what God Most High sent Down: the Apostle of God stoned, and we stoned after him, and in the Book of God stoning is the adulterer's due" (Pfander, 256). This original revelation was apparently changed and one hundred stripes replaced stoning as the punishment for adultery (sura 24:2)

The so-called "satanic verses" illustrate another change in the original text. According to one version of these verses Muhammad had an early revelation in Mecca, which allowed intercession to certain idols, which said:

> Did you consider al-hat and al-Uzza
> And al-Manat, the third, the other?
> Those are the swans exalted;
> Their intercession is expected;
> Their likes are not neglected (Watt, 60).

Sometime after this Muhammad received another revelation canceling the last three lines (verses) and substituting what we now find in sura 53 verses 21–23 which omit the part about interceding to these gods. According to Watt, both versions had been recited publicly. Muhammad's explanation was that Satan had deceived him and inserted the false verses without his knowing it!

W. St. Clair-Tisdall, who long worked among Muslims, pointed out that even in the present *Qur'an* there are some variations.

> Among various readings may be mentioned: (1) in Surah XXVIII, 48, some read "Sahirani" for "sihrani": (2) in Surah XXXII, 6, after "ummahatuhum" one reading adds the words "wa hua abun lahum": (3) in Surah XXXIV, 18, for "rabbana ba'id" some read "rabuna ba'ada": (4) in Surah XXXVIII, 22, for "tis'un" another reading is "tis'atun": (5) in Surah XIX, 35, for "tantaruna" some read "yamtaruna" (Clair-Tisdall, 60).

Although Shi'ite Muslims are in the minority, they are the second largest Islamic sect in the world, with more than 100 million followers. They claim that Caliph Uthman intentionally eliminated many verses from the *Qur'an* which spoke of Ali.

L. Bevan Jones summed up the matter well in his book, *The People of the Mosque*, when he said: "while it may be true that no other work has remained for twelve centuries with so pure a text, it is probably equally true that no other has suffered so drastic a purging" (Jones, 62).

Even were the *Qur'an* a perfect word-for-word copy of the original as given by Muhammad, it would not prove the original was inspired of God. All it would demonstrate is that today's *Qur'an* is a carbon copy of whatever Muhammad said. It would say or prove nothing about the truth of what he said. The Muslim claim that they have the true religion, because they have the only perfectly copied holy book, is as logically fallacious as someone preferring a perfectly printed counterfeit $1000 bill over a slightly imperfect genuine one. The crucial question, which Muslim apologists beg by this argument, is whether the original is God's Word, not whether they possess a perfect copy of it.

Argument from Prophecies. Does the *Qur'an* contain predictive prophesies which prove its divine origin? This is treated in detail in the article MUHAMMAD, ALLEGED MIRACLES OF. Points include:

Most of the predictions are really exhortations of a religious military leader to fight on and God will give them the victory. The one substantive prediction was about the Roman victory over the Persian army at Issus (in sura 30:2–4) did not come within the time period given by the prophecy of "within a few years" and was to be expected.

The only other notable prophecy is a reference to ten nights found in sura 89:2 that is interpreted as a veiled prediction of the ten years of persecution suffered by early Muslims. This is a doubtful interpretation, since the line apparently speaks of pilgrimage (*see* PROPHECY AS PROOF OF THE BIBLE).

Argument from Unity. Insisting that the *Qur'an* must be divine revelation because it is self-consistent and non-contradictory is also unconvincing. As noted, Muhammad's revelations were sometimes changed, including the cited "satanic verses" where the original revelation permitted a certain tribe to worship pagan gods in sura 53:21–23. This is a serious matter for a prophet who believes polytheism is the ultimate sin.

The whole concept of abrogation (*mansukh*) where previous mistakes were corrected by later verses (called *nasikh*) reveals a lack of unity in the *Qur'an*. sura 2:106 says, "Such of Our revelations as We abrogate or cause to be forgotten, We bring (in place) one better or the like thereof. Knowest thou not that Allah is Able to do all things?" For example, what is called "the sword verse" (sura 9:5) supposedly annuls 124 verses which originally encouraged tolerance (cf. sura 2:256). The *Qur'an* says emphatically "Let there be no compulsion In religions" (sura 2:256), yet in other places it urges Muslims to "Fight those who believe not" (sura 9:29) and "fight and slay The Pagans wherever ye find them" (sura 9:5). *Nasikh* is a contradiction in that the *Qur'an* claims that "No change there can be in the Words of God" (sura 10:64), which they say the *Qur'an* is. For "there is none That can alter the Words (and Decrees) of God" (sura 6:34). Yet the *Qur'an* teaches the doctrine of abrogation by which later revelations annul previous ones.

As Gerhard Nehls keenly observed, "we should like to find out how a divine revelation can be improved. We would have excepted it to have been perfect and true right from the start" (Nehls, 11). Some Muslims, like Ali, claim that abrogation is just "progressive revelation," adapting God's same message to different people living at different periods. "But Sura 2:106 [on abrogation] does not speak of culture or progressive revelation with reference to scriptures given prior to Mohammed, but to Quranic verses only!" (Nehls, 12). It makes sense that God would progressively reveal himself over 1500 years of time, as in the Bible (*see* PROGRESSIVE REVELATION). But the Bible brings to fulfillment and expands on earlier teaching, rather than making corrections, and certainly not within twenty years. This seems particularly true in view of the fact that the correction verses are often near the ones being correcited. What is more, there are verses that the Quranic abrogations apparently forgot to redact. In sura 7:54 (and 32:4) we are told that the world was made in six days. But in sura 41:9–12 it says it took God a total of eight days to create the world (two plus four plus two). How can both be correct?

The *Qur'an* also claims humans are responsible for their own choices (sura 18:29), yet it claims God has sealed the fate of all in advance, saying, "Every man's fate We have fastened On his own neck: On the Day of Judgment We shall bring out For him a scroll, Which he will see Spread open" (sura 17:13; also see 10:99–100).

Even if the *Qur'an* were consistent, unity or self-consistency is at best a negative test for truth, not a positive one. Of course, if a Book is from God who cannot err, then it won't have any contradictions in it. However, just because a book has no contradictions does not mean God is the author. As John W. Montgomery insightfully observed, Euclid's geometry is self-consistent, but this is not ground to call it divinely authoritative (Montgomery, 94).

Self-consistency is the kind of argument that others (including Christians) use for their holy books. But not all can be the inspired Word of God since they are mutually contradictory. Unity in itself does not prove divine authenticity, or all self-consistent but opposing holy books are all true. The Bible is at least as self-consistent as the *Qur'an*, but no Muslim would admit that it therefore is inspired of God.

Argument from Scientific Accuracy. This argument has gained popularity in recent times, primarily due to Maurice Bucaille's book, *The Bible, the Qur'an and Science*, in which Christianity is attacked for holding back the progress of science, and the *Qur'an* is exalted as promoting science. Indeed, he insists that the *Qur'an* marvelously fore-shadowed modern science in many of its statements, thus miraculously confirming its divine origin.

But Christianity, not Islam, was the mother of modern science. M. B. Foster, writing for the prestigious English philosophy journal *Mind* noted that the Christian doctrine of creation is the origin of modern science (see Foster, Whitehead, 13–14). The founders of almost every area of modern science were Christians working from their worldview. This includes men such as Nikolai Copernicus, Johannes Kepler, William Kelvin, Isaac Newton, Blaise *Pascal, Robert Boyle, James Clark Maxwell, and Louis Agassiz (*see* SCIENCE OF ORIGINS).

So while Islamic monotheism made many contributions to modern culture, it is an overstatement to claim credit for the origin of modern science. Muslim armies destroyed vast resources of knowledge. Pfander, for example, notes that under the Caliph Umar the Muslim soldiers destroyed the vast libraries at Alexandria and Persia. When the general asked Umar what he should do with the books, he is said to have replied: "Cast them into the rivers. For, if in these books there is guidance, then we have still better guidance in the Book of God. If, on the contrary, there is in them that which will lead astray, then may God protect us from them" (Pfander, 365).

Second, it is a mistake to assume that a book is inspired simply because it conforms with modern science (*see* SCIENCE AND THE BIBLE). Muslim and Christian apologists have made the mistake of assuming the truth of a particular scientific knowledge system. Scientific knowledge changes. Then what appeared to be "harmony" can vanish. Embarrassing mistakes have been made by defenders attempting to see modern scientific theories in their Holy Book.

Even if perfect harmony could be demonstrated between the *Qur'an* and scientific fact, this would not prove the divine inspiration of the *Qur'an*. It would simply prove that the *Qur'an* made no scientific error. At best, scientific accuracy is a negative test for truth. If error were found, it would prove that it was not the Word of God. The same applies to the Bible or any other religious book. Of course, if a book consistently and accurately anticipated by centuries what was only later discovered, then this could be used in a theistic context to indicate a supernatural source. But the *Qur'an* shows no evidence of supernatural predictions as does the Bible.

Some critics question just how scientifically accurate the *Qur'an* is. Take, for example, the *Qur'an*'s highly controversial statement that human beings are formed from a clot of blood. Surah 23:14 reads, "Then We made the sperm Into a clot of congealed blood; Then of that clot We made A (foetus) lump; then We Made out of that lump Bones and clothed the bones With flesh." This is scarcely a scientific description of embryonic development. In order to avoid the problem, Bucaille retranslates the verse, rendering the Arabia word *alaq* ("blood clot") as "the thing which clings" (Bucaille, 204). However, this is questionable. It is contrary to the work of recognized Islamic authorities who did the major English translations. And Bucaille himself recognized that "a majority of translations describe . . . man's formation from a 'blood clot' or 'adhesion'" (Bucaille, 198). This leaves the impression that his own home-made translation was generated to solve the problem, since he recognizes that "a statement of this kind is totally unacceptable to scientists specializing in this field" (ibid.).

Likewise, other critics note that the *Qur'an* in sura 18:86 speaks of one traveling west "till, when he reached the setting-place of the sun, he found it setting in a muddy spring." But even in his attempt to explain this problem, Yusuf Ali admits this has "puzzled Commentators." Nor does he really explain the problem, but simply asserts that this cannot be "the extreme west, for there is no such thing" (Ali, 754, n. 2430). Indeed, there is no extreme west, nor can anyone by traveling west come to the place eventually to the place where the sun sets. But this is what the text says, unscientific as it may be.

Others have observed that the so-called scientific foreshadowing of the *Qur'an* is highly questionable. Kenneth Cragg notes that "It has been frequently claimed by some Muslim exegetes of the *Qur'an* that modern inventions and scientific data, even nuclear fission, have been anticipated there and can now be detected in passages not hitherto appreciated for their prescience. Meanings earlier unsuspected disclose themselves as science proceeds." This conclusion, however, "is strongly repudiated by others as the kind of corroboration the *Qur'an*, as a 'spiritual' Scripture, neither needs nor approves." (Cragg, 42).

Even if the *Qur'an* were proven to be scientifically accurate, it would not thereby be divinely authoritative. All accuracy would prove is that the *Qur'an* made no scientific blunders. This would not be unparalleled. Some Jewish scholars claim the same for the Torah and many Christians claim exactly the same thing for the Bible, using very similar arguments. But Bucaille would not allow that this demonstrates that the Old and New Testaments are the Word of God.

Argument from Mathematical Structure. One popular proof for the *Qur'an*'s divine origin is its alleged miraculous basis in the number nineteen. Nineteen is the sum of the numerical value of all the letters in the word "one" (from the basic belief that God is one). Such an apologetic method does not find a great deal of acceptance in scholarly circles for good reason. No Muslim would accept a message claiming to be from God if it taught idolatry or immorality. Certainly no message containing such claims would be accepted on mathematical grounds alone. So even if the *Qur'an* were a mathematical "miracle," this would not be sufficient to prove that it was of God even to thinking Muslims.

Second, even if the odds are astronomic against the *Qur'an* having all these amazing combinations of the number 19, it proves nothing more than that there is a mathematical order behind the language of the *Qur'an*. Since language is an expression of the order of human thought and since this order can often be reduced to mathematical expression, it is not unusual that a mathematical order can be found behind the language of a document. In fact, there is nothing so unusual about sentences having nineteen letters.

Further, the same kind of argument (based on the number seven) has been used to "prove" the inspiration of the Bible. Take the first verse of the Bible "In the beginning God created the heavens and the earth." G. Nehls points out that:

> The verse consist of 7 Hebrew words and 28 letters (7x4). There are three nouns: "God, heavens, earth". their total numeric value . . . is 777 (7x11). The verb "created" has the value 203 (7x29). The object is contained in the first three words—with 14 letters (7x2). The other four words contain the subject—also with 14 letters (7x2) [and so on].

But no Muslim would allow this to count as an argument in favor of the divine inspiration of the Bible. At best the argument is esoteric and unconvincing. Even most Muslim scholars avoid using it.

Argument from Changed Lives. Apologists point to the transformation of lives and culture by the *Qur'an* as a proof of its divine origin. Such transformations should be expected. When one fervently believes something to be true they live by it. But this still leaves open the question as to whether it is the Word of God. Any set of ideas fervently believed and applied will transform believers and their culture. This is true whether the ideas are *Buddhistic, Christian, Islamic, or Judaistic. What Muslim would accept the argument that Karl *Marx's *Das Capital* is inspired because it transformed millions of lives and many cultures?

Critics find it no surprise that so many converted to Islam when it is remembered what the promised reward was for those who did and the threatened punishment for those who did not. Those who "submitted" were promised Paradise with beautiful women (sura 2:25; 4:57). But "The punishment of those Who wage war against God And His Apostle, and strive With might . . . Is: execution, or crucifixion, Or the cutting off of hands And feet from opposite sides, Or exile from the land" (sura 5:36). Islamic tradition reports that Muhammad gave the exhortation to his followers that: "The sword is the key of heaven and of hell; a drop of blood shed in the cause of God, a night spent in arms, is of more avail than two month's fasting and prayer. Whoever falls in battle, his sins are forgiven at the day of judgment" (Gibbon, 360–61).

Human greed played a part. "Arab warriors were . . . entitled to four-fifths of all the booty they gathered in the form of movable goods and captives" (Noss, 711). It was of great advantage for the enemy to submit. Polytheists had two choices: submit or die. Christians and Jews had another alternative: they could pay heavy taxes (sura 9:5, 29). Also Islamic conquests were successful because in some of the conquered lands the people were fed up with the maltreatment of their Roman rulers and willingly accepted Islam's emphasis on equality and brotherhood.

Further, a Christian or Jewish person could argue for the truth of their religions on the same ground. It should not be surprising that sincere belief in God, his moral law, and a final day of judgment would change one's life—things which all moral monotheists believe. But one cannot jump from this to prove Muhammad is the last and final prophet of God.

If it is possible to prove that changed lives in one religion are evidence of its unique divine origin, then in view of the transforming power of the Gospel (Rom. 1:16), Christianity is equal, if not superior, to Islam. In his famous *Evidences of Christianity*, William *Paley observes:

> For what are we comparing? A Galilean peasant accompanied by a few fishermen with a conqueror at the head of his army. We compare Jesus, without force, without power, without support, without one external circumstance of attraction or influence, prevailing against the prejudices, the learning, the hierarchy, of his country, against the ancient religious opinions, the pompous religious rites, the philosophy, the wisdom, the authority, of the Roman empire, in the most polished and enlightened period of its existence,—with Mahomet making his way amongst Arabs; collecting followers in the mist of conquests and triumphs, in the darkest ages and countries of the world, and when success in arms not only operated by that command of men's wills and persons which attend prosperous undertakings, but was considered as a sure testimony of Divine approbation. That multitudes, persuaded by this argument, should join the train of a victorious chief; that still greater multitudes should, without any argument, bow down before irresistible power—is a conduct in which we cannot see much to surprise us; in which we can see nothing that resembles the causes by which the establishment of Christianity was effected. [Paley, 257]

Argument from the Rapid Spread of Islam. Some Muslim scholars point to the rapid spread of Islam as proof of its divine origin. According to one Muslim apologist, "the rapid spread of Islam shows that God Most High sent it as His final revelation to men" (Pfander, 226). Islam teaches that it is destined to be the universal religion. There are several serious problems with this reasoning. First, one could question both size and rapid growth as definitive tests for truth. The majority is not always right. Indeed, history has shown they are often wrong.

Even by its own test Islam is not the true religion, since Christianity has been and still is the largest religion in the world in number of adherents—a fact that is a great embarrassment to Muslims. Further, even if rapid growth is used as a test of the truth of a system, Christianity, not Islam, would prove to be the true religion. For it grew faster at the beginning by its simple message and under heavy persecution by the Romans than did Islam by force of arms. In fact, it not only gained thousands of immediate converts from its Jewish roots within days and weeks (Acts 2:41; 4:4; 5:14), but it conquered the Roman empire by spiritual force, within its first few centuries.

To be sure, Christian crusaders (twelfth–fourteenth centuries) also engaged in the use of the sword, which Jesus forbid his disciples to do to spread his message (Matt. 26:52). But this was long after Christianity had conquered the world without it. By contrast, Islam did not grow on the mere strength of its message but only later when it used the sword. Indeed, early Christianity grew the most when the Roman government was using the sword on Christians during the first three centuries.

There are perfectly natural reasons for Islam's later rapid spread, says Shorrosh. Islam glorified Arabic people, customs, and language. It provided an incentive to conquer and plunder other lands. It utilized the ability to fight in the desert. It provided a heavenly reward for dying, and it absorbed many pre-Islamic practices in Arab culture. Even if one points to more positive reasons, such as moral, political, and cultural improvements, there seems to be no reason to posit anything but natural causes for the spread of Islam. Finally, there were natural incentives for the many converts. Soldiers were promised paradise as a reward for dying in the spread of Islam. And the people who did not submit were threatened with death, slavery, or taxation. There is no need to appeal to the supernatural to account for growth of Islam under these conditions.

Islamic scholar, Wilfred Cantwell Smith pinpoints the Muslim dilemma. Muslims believe Islam is God-willed and destined to dominate the world, so its failure to do so must be an indication that God's sovereign will is being frustrated. But Muslims deny that God's will can be frustrated. Hence, logically they should conclude that it is not God-willed. Muhammad's biographer, M. H. Haykal misses the point in his response that human beings are free, and any defeat or set-backs are to be attributed to them (Haykal, 605). If in fact God has willed the supremacy of Islam, then his sovereign will has been frustrated, through human freedom or without it. For Islam is not and has not been since the time of its inception the enduring dominant religion of the world numerically, spiritually, or culturally. Even if Islam should have a sudden burst of success and surpass all other religions, this would not prove it is of God. Logically, all that success proves is that it succeeded, not necessarily that it is true. For even after something succeeds we can still ask: Is it true or false?

Argument from God Speaking in First Person. Muslims appeal to the fact that God speaks in the first person as evidence that the *Qur'an* is the Word of God. In the Bible God is generally referred to in the second or third person, from a human point of view. However, not all the *Qur'an* speaks of God in the first person, so by this logic only those sections in the first person are inspired. No Muslim would willingly say that. Also, in much of the Bible God speaks in the first person yet Muslims do not admit that these passages *are* the words of God, especially when God blesses Israel, giving them the land of Palestine as an inheritance.

The truth is that both the *Qur'an* and the Bible have passages which speak of God in the first person and in the third person. So, Muslims can hardly use this as a unique proof of the divine origin of the *Qur'an*.

Evidence of a Human-Inspired Qur'an. Not only is evidence lacking for a divine origin of the *Qur'an*, but there is strong indications that its origin is not divine.

Fallibility. God cannot make mistakes or change his mind. Yet, as was shown above, the *Qur'an* reflects such fallibility on many occasions.

Purely Human Sources. Based on the findings of reputable scholars of Islam, the content of the *Qur'an* can be traced to either Jewish or Christian works (often from Jewish or Christian apocrypha) or pagan sources. Arthur Jeffry, in his technical and scholarly volume, *The Foreign Vocabulary of the Qur'an*, ably demonstrates that "not only the greater part of the religious vocabulary, but also most of the cultural vocabulary of the *Qur'an* is of non-Arabic origin" (Jeffry, 2). Some of the vocabulary sources include Abyssinian, Persian, Greek, Syriac, Hebrew, and Coptic (ibid., 12–32).

St. Clair-Tisdall, in *The Sources of Islam*, also reveals the direct dependence of certain *Qur'anic* stories from the Old Testament on the Jewish *Talmud*. The influence of the Talmud can be seen on the *Qur'anic* stories of Cain and Abel, Abraham and the idols, and the Queen of Sheba. The direct influence of Christian apocrypha can be seen in the story of seven sleepers and the childhood miracles of Jesus, and Zoroastrian doctrines appear in descriptions of the houris (virgins) in Paradise and the Sirat (the bridge between hell and paradise; Tisdall, 49–59, 74–91). Muslim practices of visiting the shrine of Ka'aba, and the many details of the ceremony of Hajj, including visits to the hills of Safa and Marwa, and the throwing of stones against a stone pillar symbolizing Satan, were all pre-Islamic practices of pagan Arabia (Dashti, 55, 93–94, 164).

The Genius of Muhammad. As was noted above, Muhammad may not have been illiterate, and even if he had no formal training, he was a bright and talented person. There is no reason that such a creative mind could not have been the source of teachings in the *Qur'an* that have no known human antecedents.

Muhammad biographer Haykal identifies a possible source of Muhammad's "revelations" in his description of the creative Arab imagination: "Living as he does under the vault of heaven and moving constantly in search of pasture or trade, and being constantly forced into the excesses, exaggerations, and even lies which the life of trade usually entails, the Arab is given to the exercise of his imagination and cultivates it at all times whether for good or for ill, for peace or for war" (ibid., 319).

Possible Satanic Sources of the Qur'an. It is also possible that Muhammad could have received his revelations from an evil spirit. He himself at first believed that his "revelations" were coming from a demon but he was encouraged by his wife Khadija and her cousin, Waraqah, to believe the revelation came from God. This is told more fully in the article MUHAMMAD, ALLEGED DIVINE CALL OF. Whether by his own genius, other human sources, or finite evil spirits, there is nothing in the *Qur'an* that cannot be explained without divine revelation.

Conclusion. In spite of the above evidences against any divine origin of the *Qur'an*, it is interesting that Muslim authors have been most unwilling to address the issue of the human origins of the *Qur'an*, but have simply repeated their dogmatic assertions about its divine source. In fact, seldom does one find an acknowledgment of problems, let alone a defense, among Muslim scholars.

Sources

A. A. Abdul-Haqq, *Sharing Your Faith with a Muslim*
H. Ahmad, *Introduction to the Study of the Holy Quran*
M. M. A. Ajijola, *Muhammad and Christ*
"Al-Rummani," in A. Rippin and J. Knappert, eds., *Textual Sources for the Study of Islam*
M. Ali, *The Religion of Islam*
Y. Ali, *The Holy Careen: Translation and Commentary*
M. Bucaille, *The Bible, the Careen and Science*
W. St. Clair-Tisdall, *A Manual of the Leading Muhammedan Objections to Christianity*
K. Cragg, "Contemporary Trends in Islam," in J. D. Woodberry, ed., *Muslims and Christians on the Emmaus Road*
A. Dashti, *Twenty-Three Years: A Study of the Prophetic Career of Mohammad*
M. Foreman, "An Evaluation of Islamic Miracle Claims in the Life of Muhammad," an unpublished paper (1991)
M. B. Foster, "The Christian Doctrine of Creation and the Rise of Modern Science," *Mind* (1934)
N. L. Geisler and A. Saleeb, *Answering Islam: The Crescent in the Light of the Cross*

E. Gibbon, *The History of the Decline and Fall of the Roman Empire*
J. P. Gudel, *To Every Muslim an Answer: Islamic Apologetics Compared and Contrasted with Christian Apologetics*
H. Haneef, *What Everyone Should Know about Islam and Muslims*
M. H. Haykal, *The Life of Muhammad*
A. Jeffry, ed., *Islam: Muhammad and His Religion*
L. B. Jones, *The People of the Mosque*
J. W. Montgomery, *Faith Founded on Fact*
———, "Mudjiza," in *The Encyclopedia of Islam*
G. Nehls, *Christians Ask Muslims*
J. B. Noss, *Man's Religions*
W. Paley, *Evidences of Christianity*
C. G. Pfander, *The Mizanu'l Haqq (The Balance of Truth)*
A. A. Shorrosh, *Islam Revealed: A Christian Arab's View of Islam*
H. Spencer, *Islam and the Gospel of God*
C. Waddy, *The Muslim Mind*
W. M. Watt, *Muhammad: Prophet and Statesman*
A. N. Whitehead, *Science in the Modern World*

Rr

Ramm, Bernard. Christian apologist and philosopher Bernard Ramm (1916–1992) was born in Butte, Montana. Ramm began his academic career in 1943 at the Bible Institute of Los Angeles (now Biola University). He finished his career at the American Baptist Seminary of the West (1959–74; 1978–86). Ramm was author of eighteen books and more than 100 articles and reviews. His works on apologetics include: *Problems in Christian Apologetics* (1949); *Protestant Christian Evidences* (1953); *The Christian View of Science and Scripture* (1954); "The Evidence of Prophecy and Miracle" in Carl F. H. Henry, ed., *Revelation and the Bible* (1958); *Varieties of Christian Apologetics* (1962); and *The Witness of the Spirit* (1959). *The God Who Makes a Difference* (1972) was his major apologetic work.

Ramm's Apologetic Approach. Although Ramm's earlier approach stressed the evidences for Christianity, his mature view was a form of presuppositionalism similar to that of Edward John *Carnell. His logical starting point was akin to the scientific method.

Rejection of Theistic Arguments. Like other presuppositionalists Ramm rejected traditional theistic arguments for God's existence. He offered three reasons: First, God cannot be known apart from faith (*Witness of the Spirit*, 82–83). Second, the *noetic effects of sin prevent theistic proofs from being effective (*Protestant Christian Evidences*, 29). Third, such proofs are abstract and do not reach the God of revelation (ibid., 41–42; cf. *Philosophy of the Christian Religion*, 101–4).

Ramm concluded that "The philosophical approach to the existence of God and the biblical approach to the reality of the living God are fundamentally different" (*God Who Makes a Difference*, 104). Indeed, "we can say epigrammatically that the proof of the existence of God is Holy Scripture *if* we know what we are saying." He explains: "This statement presumes an understanding of Scripture as the vicarious representative of historical events of God's action and God's word. Through the use of such events and words the Spirit of God makes God the Reality that he is to us" (ibid., 105). We know God exists, Ramm is saying, not because of any philosophical proofs, but because he acts in history as Scripture attests.

Logical Starting Point. Ramm believed one should survey the options, commit to a hypothesis, and then test it. He held that progress in knowledge is possible only if one moves from facts to some theory or hypothesis that integrates and explains the facts (*Philosophy of the Christian Religion*, 32).

The content of Ramm's choice of presuppositions was: "The Christian religion is the redemptive and revelatory work of the Holy Spirit which reaches its highest expression in revelation and redemption in the Incarnation of God in Christ; and this religion is preserved for all ages and is witnessed for all ages in the inspired Holy Scripture" (ibid., 33).

Verification of the Presupposition. According to Ramm, there are three concentric circles of verification. These represent three stages in the confirmation of the Christian truth claim.

Internal witness. In the first circle of verification the sinner hears the Gospel and is convinced of its truth by the Holy Spirit. The primary verification of religion must be internal and spiritual, or verification is by a process alien to religion (ibid., 44). This persuasive influence of the Holy Spirit is inward but not subjective (*see* Holy Spirit, Role in Apologetics).

God's action in history. Ramm affirmed that the primary function of Christian evidences is to provide a favorable reception for the Gospel. These evidences are not the Gospel and do not replace it. God's action in history, the second circle, verifies that the biblical God makes a difference and "does come into our time, our history, our space, our cosmos. . . . Because God makes this difference, we know that we are believing truth and not fiction or mere religious philosophy" (ibid., 57).

Thus, Christianity is confirmed by objective facts. *Miracles and fulfilled prophecies provide the best evidence (*see* PROPHECY, AS PROOF OF THE BIBLE). "Evidentialists believe that the evidences do establish the divine origin of the Christian faith" (*God Who Makes a Difference*, 55). Supernatural events validate the theological. Revelation is tested by reason.

Adequacy of worldview. Christianity is also tested by its ability to provide a synoptic vision of the whole of the world, humankind, and God. The third circle is that Christianity is true because its principles make the most sense out of life and the world. A *worldview is "That pattern or that picture which has the most appeal to him, that puts things together for him in the most meaningful way" (ibid., 60). "A responsible synoptic vision" must have taken into account the facts, must be testable from some kind of criteria, and must be internally coherent (ibid., 67).

These criteria are similar to factual fit and logical consistency proposed by Carnell. Carnell is convinced of the validity of the law of noncontradiction (*see* FIRST PRINCIPLES). It is a necessary test for truth. Indeed, we cannot think without it (ibid., 68–69; *Protestant Christian Evidences*, 41, 54). However, Ramm does not put the kind of emphasis on logic equal to that of such presuppositionalists as Gordon *Clark.

The Question of Certainty. Ramm distinguished between *certainty and certitude. He believed that (1) through Scripture and the internal witness of the Holy Spirit, a Christian may have full spiritual certitude that God is, that Christ is his Lord and Savior, that he is a child of God. The word *probably* is unneeded to answer these questions. Further, (2) Christian faith is a matter of history. Historical facts cannot be known with certainty, but they can be known with a high degree of probability. (3) Christians then rest their faith in full certitude, believing in the objective historical and factual basis of the Christian revelation with a high degree of *probability (Carnell, *Philosophy*, 73).

So, the Christian "is convinced of the truth of his faith by the witness of the Spirit. He is convinced of the truth of his faith by the actions of the living God in the Cosmos which make a difference. And he is a Christian because he believes that the Christian faith gives him the most adequate synoptic vision there is with reference to man, humanity, the world, and God" (ibid., 61).

Sources

E. J. Carnell, *A Philosophy of the Christian Religion*
N. L. Geisler, *Christian Apologetics*
S. Grenz, et al., eds., *Twentieth Century Theology*
G. Lewis, *Testing Christianity's Truth Claims*
B. Ramm, *A Christian Appeal to Reason*
———, *Problems in Christian Apologetics*
———, *Protestant Christian Evidences*
———, *The Christian View of Science and Scripture*
———, "The Evidence of Prophecy and Miracle," in C. F. H. Henry, ed., *Revelation and the Bible*
———, *The God Who Makes a Difference*
———, *The Witness of the Spirit*
———, *Varieties of Christian Apologetics*

Rand, Ayn. Ayn Rand (1905–1977) was an atheist (*see* ATHEISM) writer and intellectual. Born in Russia and educated at the University of Leningrad, Rand emigrated to the United States in 1926. Her most important works, written during the late 1950s and early 1960s, included *Atlas Shrugged*, *For the New Intellectual*, *Fountainhead*, and *The Virtue of Selfishness* (1961).

Influences on Rand. Rand's philosophy, called Objectivism, combined elements from Aristotelian rationalism (*see* ARISTOTLE), Nietzschean atheism (*see* NIETZSCHE, FRIEDRICH), Adam Smith's capitalism, Sigmund *Freud's illusionism, and hedonistic egoism. She populated her novels with heroic men and women who, by their courage and independence, changed the face of the earth.

Some philosophers earned Rand's scorn. She considered W. F. G.* Hegel "a witch doctor," castigated Immanuel *Kant for his deleterious influence on modern thought, and branded the pragmatism of William *James "neo-mystic." She decried the philosophy of Karl *Marx as pure *materialism which proclaimed that "mind does not exist, that everything is matter" (*For the New Intellectual*, 32–34).

Rand's Beliefs. *Atheism.* Rand created her own unique form of optimistic and egocentric atheism. She wrote: "I raise this god over the earth, this god whom men have sought since men came into being, this god who will grant them joy and peace and pride. This god, this one word: I" (ibid., 65).

With Freud she saw belief in God as an illusion: "And that is the whole of their shabby secret," she wrote. "The secret is all their esoteric philosophies, all their dialectics and super-senses, . . . is to erect upon that plastic fog a single holy absolute: their Wish" (ibid., 149). Rand chides all believers that "those irrational wishes that draw you to their creed, those emotions you worship as an idol, on whose altar you sacrifice the earth, that dark, incoherent passion within you, which you take as the voice of God or of your glands, is nothing more than the corpse of your mind" (ibid., 151).

Rand does not deny that some people feel that they experience God. She only asserts that "When a mystic (*see* MYSTICISM) declares that he feels the existence of a power superior to reason, he feels it all right, but that power is not an omniscient super-spirit of the universe. It is the consciousness of any passer-by to whom he has surrendered his own" (ibid., 161). What prompts such surrender? "A mystic is driven by the lure to impress, to cheat, to flatter, to deceive, to force that omnipotent consciousness on others" (ibid.).

"Faith in the supernatural begins as faith in the superiority of others," Rand avers (ibid.). There is no conscious, rational being other than the human. "Man is the only living species who has to perceive reality—which means to be *conscious*—by choice" (ibid., 5).

Following the First Law of Thermodynamics (*see* THERMODYNAMICS, LAWS OF), Rand declared that life spontaneously generated itself from eternal matter (*see* EVOLUTION, CHEMICAL): "Matter is indestructible; it changes its forms, but it cannot cease to exist." It is only "a living organism that faces a constant alternative: the issue of life or death" (*Virtue of Selfishness*, 15). Life was not created but was self-generated (*see* EVOLUTION, BIOLOGICAL). "Life is a process of self-sustaining and self-generated action" (ibid.).

Human Beings. According to Rand, humanity is distinguished from other living species in that the human consciousness is volitional (ibid., 19–20). Further, "to think, to feel, to judge, to act are functions of the ego" (*For the New Intellectual*, 78). Unlike animals, humankind has the ability to make "conceptions" (ibid., 14). Indeed, the mind is the only human weapon (ibid., 78). Rand adds, "Your mind is your only judge of truth—and if others dissent from your verdict, reality is the court of final appeal" (ibid., 126).

A human being, as Aristotle said, is a rational animal. But thinking is not automatic nor instinctive. The laws of *logic are needed to direct thinking (*Virtue of Selfishness*, 21–22).

The Nature of Truth. Truth is what corresponds to reality. In Rand's words, "Truth is the recognition of reality; reason, man's only means of knowledge, is his only standard of truth" (ibid.). Indeed, "moral perfection is an unbreached rationality, . . . the acceptance of reason as an absolute" (ibid., 178–79). Hence, truth is objective. It must be measured by the real world. And human reason is the only way to attain truth (*see* RATIONALISM).

The Virtue of Selfishness. Altruism demands that people live for others and place others above themselves. But no one can live for another, truly sharing the spirit (ibid., 79–80). Hence, morality should teach people, not how to suffer, but how to enjoy and live (ibid., 123). Indeed, "The creed of sacrifice is a morality for the immoral—a morality that declares its own bankruptcy by confessing that it can't impart to men any personal stake in virtue or values, and that their souls are sewers of depravity, which must be taught to sacrifice" (ibid., 141).

If we choose to love others, they must earn it. Rand wrote that she would not love someone else without reason: "I am neither foe nor friend to my brothers, but such as each of them shall deserve of me. And to earn my love, my brothers must do more than to have been born" (ibid., 65).

Based on her precept that the only god worthy of worship is one's self, Rand propounds one "ultimate value": "An organism's life is its *standard of value;* That which furthers its life is the *good;* that which threatens it is the *evil*" (ibid., 17). She opposed a *pragmatism that dismissed all absolute principles and standards (*For the New Intellectual*, 34). "The Objectivist ethics holds man's life as the *standard* of value—and *his own life* as the ethical *purpose* of every individual man" (*Virtue of Selfishness*, 25). "No value is higher than self-esteem" (*For the New Intellectual*, 176). Thus, "every '*is*' implies an '*ought*'" (ibid., 22).

Utopian Goal. As a capitalist who had fled the USSR, Rand resisted the arguments pressed by communism (*see* MARX, KARL). For when it is said "that capitalism has had its chance and has failed, let them remember that what ultimately failed was a 'mixed' economy, that the controls were the cause of the failure" (ibid., 53). If "the original American system, *Capitalism*" were practiced in its pristine purity, a kind of hedonistic utopia would emerge (*Virtue of Selfishness*, 33). The ones who were the real conquerors of life's physical realities, she said, were not those who were able to put up with their surroundings, sleeping on their bed of nails, but those who found the way to trade their bed of nails for an innerspring mattress (*For the New Intellectual*, 170).

Evaluation. *Positive Contributions.* The philosophy of objectivism has insights. Traditional theists can agree with some of her ideas.

As an objectivist, Rand defended an objectively real world. She embraced *realism and was an incisive critic of mushy forms of subjectivism, *existentialism, and *mysticism that dominate contemporary thought. Rand emphasized reason and the objectivity of truth (*see* TRUTH, ABSOLUTE NATURE OF). Truth is not putty to be shaped as we wish. It is hard reality.

Rand strongly defended the validity of the laws of logic (*see* LOGIC; FIRST PRINCIPLES). Her emphasis on reason to test the truth and know reality was a welcome corrective to the irrational strain in contemporary philosophy. Rare as an atheist, Rand does not eschew absolutes (*see* MORALITY, ABSOLUTE NATURE OF). She embraced at least the absolute value of human life. Again, this is welcomed by *theism.

Rand correctly took Marxism (*see* MARX, KARL) to task for its skewed economics and its pure materialism.

Negative Features. Some of the difficulties with Rand's philosophy can be noted in such articles as ATHEISM; EVOLUTION, BIOLOGICAL; FREUD, SIGMUND; HUMANISM, SECULAR, and MORALITY, ABSOLUTE NATURE OF. On the inadequacy of naturalism, see MIRACLES, ARGUMENTS AGAINST.

Like most atheists, Rand creates substitutes for God. She even speaks of "the grace of Reality" (God?). She argues that it is "By the grace of reality and the nature of life, [that] man—every man—is an end in himself" (ibid., 123). This is particularly ironic, since it is by the grace of the Ultimate (reality) that each individual is made ultimate.

While criticizing Marxist *materialism, she seems unaware that her own materialism is similar. She believes that only matter is eternal and indestructible. If so, then in the final analysis, mind and reason—which she treasures, must be reduced to matter. And thought has no more reality than a chemical process.

Although Rand speaks of the superiority of mind over matter, her materialistic philosophy does not really allow for such a distinction. Mind also is reducible to, and totally dependent on, matter. How then can it be superior to it? Further, the origin of mind is matter. In the beginning, matter produced mind. But how can the effect be greater than the cause. This violates everything reason tells us about reality—the very method she hails for discovering truth.

Her argument for atheism is dependent on a univocal view of being which she never defends (*see* ANALOGY). It is commendable that Rand, as an atheist, speaks of objective and ultimate truth. However, *Augustine argued that there can be no absolute truth apart from God. Truth is what is known by a mind, and absolute truth must reside ultimately in an Absolute Mind (= God). But Rand's atheism rejects any Absolute Mind.

A positive dimension of Rand's thought leads to theism, not to the atheism she professes. For she claims that one has an absolute moral obligation or duty. But absolute prescriptions are only possible if there is an Absolute Prescriber (*see* MORAL ARGUMENT FOR GOD). Absolute moral laws can come only from an Absolute Moral Law Giver (= God). The only logical conclusion for an atheist is to deny all moral absolutes, as did Nietzsche and Jean Paul Sartre.

Rand said plainly that "every *'is'* implies an *'ought'*" (ibid., 22). But as any good text on logic will inform us, this is a fallacy of reasoning. Just because something is, does not mean that it ought to be. The descriptive is not the basis of the prescriptive. Like other atheists who deny all (or all but one) absolute, Rand inevitably slips into others. For example, she insists that "no man may initiate . . . the use of physical force against others" (ibid., 134). Her stress on reason makes it clear that she also believes that "Everyone should always be rational." Indeed, her ethical egoism yields the absolute that "Everyone should always respect the rights of others." And life is such a fundamental right.

Sources

B. Branden, *The Passion of Ayn Rand*

N. L. Geisler, *Ethics: Alternatives and Issues*, chap. 8

———, and W. Corduan, *Philosophy of Religion*

A. Rand, *Atlas Shrugged*

———, *For the New Intellectual*

———, *The Virtue of Selfishness*

Rational Presuppositionalism. ***See*** **APOLOGETICS, PRESUPPOSITIONAL; CLARK, GORDON.**

Rationalism. *Rationalism* as a philosophy stresses reason as the means of determining truth. Mind is given authority over senses, the *a priori* over the *a posteriori*. Rationalists are usually foundationalists (*see* FOUNDATIONALISM), who affirm that there are first principles of knowledge, without which no knowledge is possible (see below). For a rationalist, reason arbitrates truth, and truth is objective (*see* TRUTH, NATURE OF).

Although *Aristotle (384–322 B.C.) believed that knowledge began in the senses, his stress on reason and logic made him the father of Western rationalism. René *Descartes 1596–1650), Benedict *Spinoza (1632–1677), and Gottfried *Leibniz (1646–1716) were the chief modern rationalists.

Most worldviews have at least one major rationalist proponent. Leibniz embraced *theism. Spinoza held to *pantheism. Ayn Rand (1905–1977) professed *atheism. Most deists (*see* DEISM) held some form of rationalism. Even pantheism is represented by strong rationalistic proponents, such as Charles Hartshorne (b. 1897). *Finite godism has been rationally defended by John Stuart *Mill (1806–1873) and others.

The reason that various worldviews all have forms of rationalism is that rationalism is an epistemology, whereas a worldview is an aspect of metaphysics. Rationalism is a means of discerning truth, and most worldviews have exponents who use it to determine and defend truth as they see it.

Central Premises. *Premises Shared by Rationalists.* Some ideas are common to virtually all rationalists. These include the following factors, even though some rationalists defend them, modify them, or limit them in ways others do not.

Foundationalism. Foundationalism believes that there are first principles of all knowledge, such as the principle of noncontradiction, the principle of identity, and the principle of the excluded middle (*see* LOGIC). Certain foundationalists believe there are other principles, either the principle of sufficient reason (*see* SUFFICIENT REASON, PRINCIPLE OF) or the principle of causality (*see* CAUSALITY, PRINCIPLE OF). All rationalists are foundationalists, and all foundationalists believe in some foundational principles.

Objectivism. Rationalists also believe that there is an objective reality and that it can be known by human reason. This distinguishes them from *mysticism, *existentialism, and other forms of subjectivism. For a rationalist, the real is rational, and reason is the means of determining what is real.

Exclusivism. Rationalists are also exclusivists. They believe that mutually exclusive opposites cannot both be true. According to the law of noncontradiction, if atheism is true, then all nonatheism is false. If Christianity is true, then all non-Christian systems are false. But opposite truth claims cannot both be true (*see* PLURALISM, RELIGIOUS; WORLD RELIGIONS, CHRISTIANITY AND).

A Priorism. All rationalists believe there is an *a priori* element to knowledge. Reason is in some sense independent of experience. Even rationalists who are also empiricists (for example, *Thomas Aquinas, *Aristotle, and *Leibniz), believe that there is nothing in the mind that was not first in the senses except the mind itself. Without this *a priori* (independent of experience) dimension to knowledge, nothing could be known.

Differences among Rationalists. The role of the senses. Some rationalists downplay, if not negate, any determinative role of the senses in the knowing process. They stress the rational exclusively. Spinoza is an example of this view. Others combine senses and reason, such as Aquinas and Leibniz. The former are more deductive in their approach to learning truth; the latter are more inductive and inferential.

The limits of reason. A crucial difference among rationalists is found in the scope of reason. Some rationalists, such as Spinoza, give reason an all-encompassing scope. It is the sole means of determining truth. Others, such as Aquinas, believe reason is capable of discovering some truths (for example, the existence of God), but not all truth (for example, the *Trinity). Those in the latter category believe that there are truths that are in accord with reason and some that go beyond reason. Even the latter are not *contrary* to reason. They simply are *beyond* the ability of reason to attain on its own. They can be known only from special revelation (*see* REVELATION, SPECIAL).

Evaluation. Rationalism as a whole has both positive and negative dimensions for an apologist. Unlimited rationalism that denies all special revelation, obviously is unacceptable for a theist (*see* BIBLE, EVIDENCE FOR; FAITH AND REASON). Nor is any form of rationalism that denies theism in accord with orthodox Christianity.

However, foundationalism's stress on the need for first principles, is both true and valuable. Also valuable is the belief in objective truth. The rationalist's emphasis on the exclusive nature of truth claims is also a benefit to Christian apologetics.

From a Christian perspective, the rationalist theologian Jonathan Edwards made an important distinction: All truth is given by *revelation, either general or special, and it must be received by reason. Reason is the God-given means for discovering the truth that God discloses, whether in his world or his Word. While God wants to reach the heart with truth, he does not bypass the mind along the way. In this modified sense, there is great value in Christian rationalism.

Sources

R. Descartes, *Meditations*

J. Edwards, "The Mind," in H. G. Townsend, *The Philosophy of Jonathan Edwards from His Private Notebooks*

N. L. Geisler and W. Corduan, *Philosophy of Religion*

G. Leibniz, *Metaphysics*

A. Rand, *For the New Intellectual*

B. Spinoza, *Ethics*

Thomas Aquinas, *Summa Theologica*

Realism. *Realism* is the view that there is a reality external to our minds that we can know (*see* EPISTEMOLOGY). This view is opposed by skepticism, *agnosticism, and solipsism. Christian realists believe that there is an infinite Spirit (God) and a real, finite world, comprised of both spirits (angels) and human beings. In contrast to dualism, realists believe that the all finite beings are created and not eternal. Contrary to idealists (e.g., George *Berkeley), they believe that there is a real, extra-mental, material world.

Realists also believe that there is a correspondence between thought and thing, between the mind and reality (*see* TRUTH, NATURE OF). For classical realists, such as *Aristotle and *Thomas Aquinas, this correspondence is made possible by means of first principles of knowledge. Since Immanuel *Kant it has been customary to distinguish critical realism from classical realism. The former begins with the premise that we know the real world, and the latter senses an obligation to prove we do. To state it differently, the post-Kantian realist sees a need to address Kant's *agnosticism, since the Kantians do not believe we can know reality.

Knowledge of Reality. What is at question is whether our thoughts correspond to the real world. Or, more basically, whether the principles by which we know are adapted to reality. Without such principles of knowledge, classical realists believe that our knowledge of the real world is impossible. Aristotle and Aquinas, for example, held that there are undeniable first principles by which the real world can be known.

Classical realists believe first principles are self-evident. That is, once the terms are known, it is clear to a rational mind that they are true. For example, once we know what *wife* means and what *married women* means, it is self-evident that "All wives are married women." However, for classical realists such as Aquinas, self-evident does not necessarily mean *a priori* or independent of experience. For the realists, first principles are known because the mind knows reality. In fact, these epistemological principles have an ontological basis in reality.

Without such valid principles of knowing reality, it is impossible to really know. There must be a relationship between thought and thing, between the principles of knowledge and the object of knowledge. But what is it, and how can it be established? This is the critical problem for a critical realist.

First Principles and Reality. By "reality" a realist means not only the mind, but the extra-mental realm as well. Reality is that which is. It is all that is. Reality is being, and nonreality is nonbeing. For the classical realists it was sufficient *that* we know being (or that we know that we know being) and that in reality our knowledge of first principles is based in our most fundamental knowledge of being. As Eric Mascall pointedly observed, it is as unnecessary to expound one's epistemology before beginning to talk about God as it is to understand human physiology before beginning to walk (Mascall, 45). Aristotle and Aquinas saw no need to justify this knowledge any more than one could directly demonstrate a first principle. They are self-evident. We know that they are true, even before we can explain why they are true. That something exists is known by direct intuition. It is obvious and immediate. This is not to say that there is no way to defend first principles but to note that they are self-evident, once the terms are properly known.

The Undeniability of First Principles. As was shown in the article First Principles, these precepts are undeniable or reducible to the undeniable. That is, one cannot deny them without using them. For example, the principle of noncontradiction cannot be denied without using it in the very denial. The statement, "Opposites can be true" assumes that the opposite of that statement cannot be true. While most would grant this, not all skeptics grant that the principle of causality, which is crucial in all cosmological arguments for God, is an undeniable first principle. Not every skeptic admits that something exists. Thus, it is necessary to comment on their undeniability (*see* VERIFIABILITY STRATEGIES).

The statement "I exist" is undeniable. Were I to say, "I do not exist," I would have to exist in order to say it. In explicitly denying my existence, I implicitly affirm it. Likewise, one cannot deny that reality is knowable. For the affirmation that reality is not knowable is itself an assertion of knowledge about reality. Total agnosticism is self-defeating.

Realism, then, is unavoidable. The fact that we are sometimes mistaken or deceived about reality does not negate all knowledge of it. Indeed, it requires it. For we could not know an illusion unless it was seen on the backdrop of reality.

Sources

R. Garrigou-LaGrange, *God: His Existence and His Nature*
N. L. Geisler, *Christian Apologetics*
——— and W. Corduan, *Philosophy of Religion*
E. Gilson, *On Being and Some Philosophers*
D. Hume, *The Letters of David Hume*, J. Y. T. Greig, ed.
J. Maritain, *Existent and Existence*
E. Mascall, *Existence and Analogy*
Thomas Aquinas, *On Being and Essence*

Redaction Criticism, New Testament. ***See*** **BIBLE CRITICISM.**

Redaction Criticism, Old Testament. A *redactor* edits or changes a text composed by another. Redaction criticism of the Bible claims that subsequent editors (redactors) changed the text of Scripture. If such alleged changes were substantial, it would seriously damage the credibility of Scripture (*see* BIBLE, EVIDENCE FOR). We could not be sure what was in the original text. For redaction critical views regarding the New Testament, see the article BIBLE CRITICISM.

Nature of Redaction Views. Redaction views are held by both evangelicals and non-evangelicals. The latter are more radical in their assertion of the kinds of changes they believe have occurred in the text.

Radical Views. Emanuel Tov is often quoted in support of the redacted-canon view. On the alleged redactions of Jeremiah, he argued that both minor and major details were changed. He believed these changes apparent in

1. text arrangement;
2. the addition of headings to prophecies;
3. repetition of sections;
4. addition of new verses and sections;
5. addition of new details; and
6. changes in content (Tov, 217).

Of courses, substantial changes in content would undermine the credibility of the Old Testament and particularly its apologetic value. How could one be sure that the prophecies were not tampered with later to make them fit what had actually happened.

"Inspired" Redactors. Some evangelicals have attempted to accommodate redactional models by proposing an "inspired redactor." In this way they hope both to explain the evidence for redaction while maintaining the inspiration of the Scriptures (*see* BIBLE, EVIDENCE FOR; NEW TESTAMENT MANUSCRIPTS; OLD TESTAMENT MANUSCRIPTS). For example, Bruce Waltke claims "that the books of the Bible seem to have gone through an editorial revision after coming from the mouth of an inspired spokesman." In the same passage he speaks of "later editorial activity." Waltke claims there is evidence of redaction from 1800 B.C. to A.D. 200 (Waltke, 78, 79, 92). However, respondents to Waltke's proposal strongly reject his position (ibid., 133). Even his concessions tend to undermine the biblical text.

Arguments for Redactors. Attention is focused here on the Old Testament redaction, especially as held by Waltke and some other evangelical scholars who insist that "inspired redactors" made substantial changes in the biblical writings. Along with more critical redactors, they believe that the content of biblical writers underwent continual changes until it reached its final form.

In support of this position the following arguments are sometimes offered.

1. Someone after Moses, possibly Joshua, wrote the last chapter of Deuteronomy (chap. 34), since it is not prophetic and records Moses's death.
2. Certain sections of Deuteronomy (2:10–12, 20–23) show evidence of a later redactor. They are editorial and parenthetical in nature.
3. Arrangement of the psalms into five books or sections is undoubtedly the work of compiler-editors.
4. Proverbs passed through the hands of editors after Solomon (10:1; 22:17; 25:1; 30:1; 31:1), some of whom lived in Hezekiah's day, two centuries after Solomon (25:1).
5. Some books, such as Jeremiah, survive in two substantially different versions. The longer (Hebrew) version is one-seventh larger than the Greek Septuagint version, an example of which survives in fragments from Qumran (4 QJerb).
6. The books of Chronicles present themselves as being based on prior prophetic records (1 Chron. 9:1; 27:24; 29:29; 2 Chron. 9:29; 13:22; 16:11; 20:34; 25:26; 27:7; 28:26; 32:32; 33:19; 35:27; 36:8) which were redacted by the author(s) of Chronicles.

Response to Arguments. None of the arguments advanced in support of inspired redaction are definitive. Merrill Unger granted only slight "editorial additions to the Pentateuch, regarded as *authentically* Mosaic." But he flatly rejected the notion that later non-Mosaic additions were made on the Pentateuch by redactors, inspired or not (Unger, 231–32). The response to the "inspired redactor" theory will follow the order of their arguments given above.

The Account of Moses' Death. For a full discussion of this point, see PENTATEUCH, MOSAIC AUTHORSHIP OF. That Moses might not have written Deuteronomy 34 has long been accepted by conservative scholars, even Unger. However, this is not a *redaction* in the content of anything Moses wrote. It is an *addition* of events that, humanly speaking, Moses could not have written, namely, an account of his own funeral (Deuteronomy 34). Of course, it is always possible that Moses could have written this by supernatural revelation, but there is no claim or evidence that he did. Completion of the book by another inspired prophet, Joshua in particular, would not compromise its authority.

Editorial Comments in Deuteronomy 2. This is also discussed in PENTATEUCH, MOSAIC AUTHORSHIP OF. The parenthetical sections in Deuteronomy 2 need not be later redactions. They fit into the text, and there is no reason Moses could not have included them to amplify and clarify. If these additions were made by later scribes, they are uninspired and subject to the same textual skepticism as Mark 16:9–20 and John 8:1–11. Lacking evidence to the contrary, it seems reasonable to consider these to be editorial comments by Moses.

Adding and Rearranging. Simply compiling and arranging inspired writings (individual psalms) is not proof of the redaction model. Adding psalms to the psalter as they were written fits perfectly with the prophetic model of the canon. What the redactional model would have to prove is that later inspired writers made deliberate content changes in Psalms (or other books) already in the canon, not simply rearranging what is there. There is no proof of this in the Psalms.

Small *editorial* additions to a text are not the problem. The inspired redactor view accepts *substantial* changes in content.

Proverbs Shows No Evidence of Redaction. None of the passages cited from Proverbs prove that the original author's writing (whether Solomon [1–29], Agur [30], or Lemuel [31]) were not accepted by the believing community immediately and continuously without subsequent content changes. The phrase "copied out" (25:1) does not mean "changed in content" but merely transcribed onto another manuscript. Whether this process involved a selection and rearrangement of what Solomon had previously written is irrelevant. As with Psalms, there is a big difference between *rearranging* what Solomon wrote and *redacting* (changing) its content. There is no evidence of the latter.

Two Editions by Jeremiah. Conservative scholars acknowledge that there may have been two versions (editions) of Jeremiah that originated with Jeremiah himself, possibly through Baruch his scribe (Archer, 361–62). This would account for differences found in the manuscripts. In this case there is no need to posit a *later* redactor. Jeremiah himself, while alive, could have directed a later version of his book with more prophecies in it. Jeremiah preached and prophesied as the occasion called for it. It is understandable that the collection of his writings would grow. The *Septuagint's* scholars may have had access to a preliminary version.

Citing Other Sources. The passages cited in Chronicles (1 Chron. 9:1; 27:24, etc.) do not mean that the writer of Chronicles (possibly Ezra) was *redacting* some other books. Rather he used them as sources to write his own book, just as Daniel (9) uses Jeremiah (25), and 2 Samuel 22 uses Psalm 18. Luke evidently used other records (Luke 1:1–4).

Further, it is not necessary to take all these Old Testament citations as being from inspired writings. Some were court records (e.g., 1 Chron. 9:1; 27:24; 2 Chron. 20:34). The books by "Samuel the Seer and Nathan the Prophet" (1 Chron. 29:29) may be the prophetic writing now known as

1 Samuel. Still others may have been uninspired commentaries (e.g., 1 Chron. 13:22). Paul uses uninspired sources in his works (cf. Acts 17:28; Titus 1:12). This is not making changes in an inspired book.

Problems with "Inspired" Redaction. The inspired-redactors view that editors made deliberate and substantial changes in the content of previous prophetic material is unacceptable.

It Is Contrary to God's Warning. God gave repeated warning to his prophets not to "add to the word which I [God] am commanding you" (Deut. 4:2; cf. Prov. 30:4; Rev. 22:18–19). This of course does not mean that another prophet cannot have added separate revelation to complete Deuteronomy. It does mean that no one was permitted to change (redact) the revelation God had given to another prophet, or, for that matter, to himself. No one was to add to or take way from what God had spoken (cf. Rev. 22:19).

It Confuses Textual Criticism and Canonicity. The redaction view confuses canonicity and lower textual criticism (*see* BIBLE CRITICISM). Canonicity (Gk. *canon*, rule or norm) deals with which books are inspired and belong in the Bible (*see* BIBLE, CANONICITY OF). Lower textual criticism studies the text of canonical books, attempting to get as close to the original text as possible. Now the question of scribal changes in transmitting a manuscript of an inspired book is one of lower textual criticism, not canonicity. Likewise, if material was added later, as in 1 John 5:7 (KJV) or John 8:1–11, this is a matter of textual criticism to determine whether it was in the original writing. It is not properly a question of canonicity.

Lower textual criticism is a legitimate discipline because it does not seek to change or *redact* the original text but simply to *reconstruct* it from the available manuscripts.

It Is Contrary to the Meaning of Inspired. The so-called "inspired redactor" view is contrary to the biblical use of the word *inspired* or *God-breathed* in 2 Timothy 3:16. The Bible does not speak of inspired *writers*, but only of inspired *writings* (*see* BIBLE, EVIDENCE FOR). An inspired author would be infallible and inerrant, not simply the author of an infallible and inerrant book.

It Is Contrary to Inspired Autographs. This redaction view is contrary to the evangelical view that only the autographs (original texts) are inspired. The *autograph* is the original text (or an exact replica) as it came from the prophet. Only this is believed to be inspired and, therefore, without error. Copies are inspired to the degree that they accurately reproduce the original.

But according to the "inspired redactor" view, the final redacted version is inspired. If this is so, then the original writings were not the ones breathed out by God. For God cannot err (Titus 1:2; Heb. 6:18), nor change (Mal. 3:6; Heb. 1:12; 13:8; James 1:17). If there was an "inspired redactor," God made content changes in his successive inspired editions.

Further, the "inspired redactor" view requires rejection of the evangelical view of a definite written original that God breathed out through a given prophet. Instead, the autographs would be a fluid manuscript in process, perhaps over centuries. It would in effect promote scribes to the rank of prophets. God would have to breathe out the copies (including their errors) as well as the originals.

It Eliminates Verification of a Work. Inspired redaction eliminates the means by which a prophetic utterance could be tested by those to whom it was given. According to the redaction view, the prophetic work as such was not presented to the contemporary believing community. Rather it was finished and endowed to the church by someone decades (or even centuries) later. When there was need, God confirmed his prophets by signs and wonders (cf. Exodus 3–4; 1 Kings 18; Acts 2:22; Heb. 2:3–4). Contemporaries of the prophet could test the man of God's claims (cf. Deuteronomy 18). But if the "inspired redactor" view is correct, there is no way to confirm whether that writing (in its eventual edited form) actually came from a prophet of God. Only if the original and unchanged message was confirmed by the original audience can we have assurance of its rightful place in the canon.

It Shifts Authority away from Scripture. The redaction model shifts the locus of divine authority from the original prophetic message (given by God through the prophet) to the community of believers generations later. It is contrary to the principle of canonicity that God *determines* canonicity and the people of God *discover* what God determined as inspired. In effect the redaction model locates the authority in the church rather than in the God-given prophetic message to the church.

It Involves Deception. A redaction model of canonicity entails acceptance of deception as a means of divine communication. In significant ways, a message or book which claims to come from a prophet came actually from later redactors. As applied to the Gospels, redaction criticism claims that Jesus did not necessarily say or do what the Gospel writer claims he did. Redactors literally put their own words in Jesus' mouth. But this involves intentional misrepresentation, which is deceptive (*see* NEW TESTAMENT, HISTORICITY OF). The same criticism applies if later redactors changed what a prophet wrote. That would be a deception, misleading the reader to believe that God directed what original writers had said. But God cannot lie (Heb. 6:18).

It Confuses Proper Editing with Redacting. The redaction model of the canon confuses legitimate scribal activity, involving grammatical *form*, updating of names and arrangement of prophetic material, with the illegitimate redactional changes in actual *content* of a previous prophet's message. It confuses acceptable scribal *transmission* with unacceptable redactional *tampering*. It confuses proper discussion of which is the earlier *text* with improper claims that latter prophets changed the *truth* of earlier texts?

It Is Refuted by Jewish History. The redaction theory assumes there were inspired redactors well beyond the period in which there were prophets (viz., fourth century B.C.). There can be no inspired works unless there are living prophets. And the Jews recognized no prophets after the time of Malachi (ca. 400 B.C.). Josephus, the Jewish historian, explicitly referred to revelation ceasing by "the reign of Artaxerxes king of Persia" (Josephus, 1.8). He added: "From Artaxerxes until our time everything has been recorded, but has not been deemed worthy of like credit with what preceded, because the exact succession of the prophets ceased" (ibid.).

Additional rabbinical statements on the cessation of prophecy support this (see Beckwith, 370): Seder Olam Rabbah 30 declares "Until then [the coming of Alexander the Great] the prophets prophesied through the Holy Spirit. From then on, 'Incline thine ear and hear the words of the wise.'" Baba Bathra 12b declares: "Since the day when the Temple was destroyed, prophecy has been taken from the prophets and given to the wise." Rabbi Samuel bar Inia said, "The Second Temple lacked five things which the First Temple possessed, namely, the fire, the ark, the urim and thummim, the oil of anointing and the Holy Spirit [of prophecy]."

Thus, any changes in the Old Testament text after this time could not have been inspired, since there were no prophets. Thus they are a matter of textual criticism, not canonicity.

It Is Refuted by Textual Criticism. The scholarly discipline of textual criticism refutes the claims of redaction criticism. For the history of the biblical text is well known (*see* New Testament Manuscripts). Thousands of manuscripts trace the changes. The original text can be reconstructed with a great degree of confidence. There are no redactions in the content of the prophetic message by either inspired or uninspired editors. Most changes have to do with form, not content. They are grammatical, not theological. The scribes were faithful in copying the text. This being the case, there is no reason to believe the original message of the biblical writer has been redacted. The brieftime gap and the large number of manuscripts compared to other works of antiquity vouch for the fact that the content of the biblical texts has been unchanged.

Sources

G. L. Archer, Jr., *A Survey of Old Testament Introduction*

R. Beckwith, *The Old Testament Canon of the New Testament Church and Its Background in Early Judaism*

Flavius Josephus, *Against Apion*

———, *Antiquities of the Jews*

N. L. Geisler and W. Nix, *General Introduction to the Bible*

E. Tov, "The Literary History of the Book of Jeremiah in the Light of Its Textual History," in J. Tigay, ed., *Empirical Models for Biblical Criticism*

M. Unger, *Introductory Guide to the Old Testament*

B. K. Waltke, "Historical Grammatical Problems," in E. D. Radmacher and R. D. Preus, eds., *Hermeneutics, Inerrancy and the Bible*

Reductio ad Absurdum. *Reductio ad Absurdum* refers to a logic-based argument that reduces opposing views to the absurd by showing that two or more of its central premises, or those that follow logically from them, are logically contradictory (*see* Logic). One system of Christian apologetics, the rational presuppositionalism of Gordon *Clark, depends entirely on this type of argument (*see* Apologetics, Presuppositional).

Reid, Thomas. Thomas Reid (1710–1796) was a founder of the Scottish philosophy of common sense. Born in Strachan near Aberdeen, Reid was influenced by his teacher at Marischal College, George Turnbell, who stressed the priority of sense knowledge, though under the cloak of Berkeleism. After studying David Hume's *Treatise of Human Nature* (1739), Reid renounced his Berkeleian views (*see* Berkeley, George). Reid taught at King's College, Aberdeen, until 1751. He helped form the Aberdeen Philosophical Society, which often discussed Hume. In 1764 he published his *Inquiry into the Human Mind on the Principles of Common Sense* and the same year began teaching at Old College in Glasgow. His two major works were *Essay on the Intellectual Powers* (1785) and *Essay on the Active Powers* (1788).

Philosophical Views. Unlike David *Hume, Reid believed that conceptions rise from the innate powers of conception in the mind that manifest themselves in accordance with original first principles of the mind. Evidence is the ground of belief and arises out of the use of intellect. We know these faculties are trustworthy because, however we try to refute these principles, they prevail. Further, all thinking depends on the assumption that they are reliable. In response to skeptics who distrust their faculties, Reid observes that even Hume trusted his senses in practice and is guilty of pragmatic inconsistency.

By virtue of his belief in active powers, Reid held that he was the active cause of his own acts. Free acts are not the result of antecedent causes but of will. Free actions are neither determined by another (*see* Determinism) nor fortuitous (*see* Indeterminism), but are caused by oneself (*see* Free Will).

Reid taught that common sense beliefs are "the inspiration of the Almighty." One does not have to believe in God in order to hold them, but they are imposed by our created nature. When we try to explain them we understand that God gave them to us. Indeed, we have the same evidence for God that we have for intelligence and will in another person. So those who reject God should also reject the existence of other minds.

Reid's common sense realism had an extensive influence, particularly on Old Princeton including Charles *Hodge and B. B. *Warfield (*see* Princeton School of Apologetics) in America (see Martin).

Sources

S. A. Grave, *The Scottish Philosophy of Common Sense*

C. Hodge, *Systematic Theology*, vol. 1

T. Martin, *The Instructed Vision*

J. McCosh, *The Scottish Philosophy*

T. Reid, *An Inquiry into the Human Mind on the Principles of Common Sense*

———, *Essay on the Active Powers*

———, *Essay on the Intellectual Powers*

Reimarus, Hermann. *See* **Jesus, Quest for Historical.**

Reincarnation. *Reincarnation* means literally "to come again in the flesh." This is not to be confused with Christ's "incarnation" as when he came "in the flesh" once and for all (1 John 4:1–2) (*see* Christ, Deity of). *Re*-incarnation means that after death the human soul attaches to another body and returns to live another life.

There are many forms of reincarnation. The most common spring from *Hinduism and Buddhism (*see* Zen Buddhism) and are based in the inexorable law of *karma*. Under the law of *karma*, what one sows in this life is reaped in the next. Every action in this life has a reaction or consequence in this life or in the next.

Cycles of Life. Popularity of Reincarnation. Reincarnation is not only the dominant belief in Eastern religions, but it has gained increased popularity in the Western world. About one in four Americans believe in reincarnation. Among college age young people the figure is nearly one in three. Surprisingly, about one in five who attend church regularly also believe in reincarnation, in spite of the fact that the Bible and orthodox Christian belief reject reincarnation.

Many celebrities have proclaimed their belief in reincarnation. One of the most vocal has been Shirley MacLaine. Other famous celebrities who believe in reincarnation have included Glenn Ford, Anne Francis (*Honey West*), Sylvester Stallone (*Rocky*, *Rambo*), Audry Landers (*Dallas*), Paddy Chayevsky (author of *Marty*, *The Hospital*, *Altered States*), General George S. Patton, Henry Ford, Salvador Dali, and Mark Twain. In music, ex-Beatle George Harrison, Ravi Shankar, Mahavishnu, John McLaughlin, and John Denver have been dedicated to spreading the message of their spiritual beliefs in a second chance. Even some comic books have gotten in on the act. *Camelot 3000*, *Ronin*, and *Dr. Strange* have all dealt with themes of reincarnation.

Source of the Doctrine. Reincarnation has a long history. Many believe that the original source of the doctrine appears to be the Hindu Vedas (Scriptures). Buddhist, Jainist, and *Sikh forms seem to have been derived from these, as have teachings of Transcendental Meditation and Hare Krishna. Some Western forms may have arisen from Greek philosophy without direct influence from the Hindu teaching, beginning with the Pythagoreans. Psychic Edgar Cayce and adherents of the late-eighteenth-century theosophical movement, including writer Helena Blavatsky, were influential teachers about multiple lives. Several Christian theologians have attempted to harmonize forms of reincarnation with Christianity, among them Geddes MacGregor and John *Hick.

Kinds of Reincarnation. Philosophically, reincarnation is wrapped up in Eastern religions such as Hinduism, Buddhism, and Taoism. It is strongly rejected by Islam, Judaism, and Christianity). But it was never confined to the East. Some early Western philosophers also believed that the soul lives on in different forms. Pythagoras (ca. 580–ca. 500 B.C.), *Plato (428–348 B.C.), and *Plotinus (205–270) all believed that the spirit or soul was eternal and could not be destroyed (*see* Immortality).

Plato taught that the immortal soul takes on a body only as punishment for some sin, for which suffering will be tenfold; the soul must leave the ideal realm and enter into the material world. Man is "a soul in a body, and his soul needs to grow toward the highest good, that it may no longer have to suffer continued rebirth but go into that state in which it may, like God, behold and enjoy forever the hierarchy of ideal forms, in all their truth, beauty, and goodness" (Noss, 52). Before this final blissful state is realized we may come back, even as animals.

The similarities between Plato and the Hindu doctrine are striking, especially Ramanuja's "personal" system. This school developed from the earlier "impersonal" view, but the key ingredients are the same: The soul is called *jiva* or *jivatman* and it survives death as a mental entity called the *subtle body*. This entity will enter a new embryo, bringing with it the *karma* of all its past lives. *Karma* includes both actions and the ethical consequences attached to them. You definitely reap what you sow. If you do good deeds, you are born into a "pleasant womb." If you do evil, your destiny will be proportionately less noble. You might even find yourself in a "foul and stinking womb," be it animal, vegetable, or mineral. The cycle of death and rebirth (*samsara*) is often depicted as a wheel, with death as the gateway to new life. The goal, though, is to escape from this cycle.

This escape is called *moksha*, and it is here that the difference arises between the personal and impersonal forms of the doctrine. The impersonal version says that once all karmic debt is eliminated, the soul loses all identity and simply becomes one with the One; the self merges with Brahman, a divine, impersonal force. The personal view says that the soul is simply liberated to be itself, fully devoted to *Bhagwan* (the personal God).

Other forms of the doctrine of reincarnation differ with regard to what happens at the point of death and the nature of the ultimate state of *moksha*, but the general pattern is retained. Buddhists say that the unconscious soul (*vinnana*) continues, but the self (intellect, emotions, and consciousness) is obliterated at death. Its *karma* remains in the cycle of rebirth called *samsara*. There are four interpretations of the final state in Buddhism, *nirvana,* which is attained by the grace of Buddha. Jainism and Sikhism follow the same patterns as personal and impersonal Hinduism, respectively.

Most unorthodox Christian forms of reincarnation do not differ in their basic concept, but are influenced by other factors. Most important, during human existence, a decision is made about whether to accept or reject Christ. In the simplest model, those who accept Christ go to be with God, while those who reject him are reincarnated. The cycle will continue until all recognize Christ. In this way, all will eventually be saved (*see* UNIVERSALISM). Some Christian reincarnation theories provide ultimate punishment for those who are lost causes. In MacGregor's view the punishment is annihilation (*see* ANNIHILATIONISM). Hick's theory is somewhat novel in that he supposes that humans are reincarnated to lives on other planets.

Reason for Belief. Several rationales are given to justify belief in reincarnation. Three of the most basic reasons are the belief in an immortal soul, psychological evidence of past-lives, and the argument from justice through reincarnation.

Immortality of the Soul. Plato's main reason for believing in transmigration of souls (another name for souls going to a different body) was that he considered the immaterial part of each human being to be uncreated and indestructible. It existed before we were born, and it continues to exist after we die. Nothing, either good or evil, can corrupt it. If that is the case, then reincarnationists argue that it is likely that it appears in the world in different bodies at various times. This is part of its perfecting process. In the same way, pantheistic philosophies assume that all is eternal and divine, so the soul is equally incorruptible.

Psychological Evidences. Ian Stevenson, a parapsychologist and researcher of past-life recall, has said,

> The idea of reincarnation may contribute to an improved understanding of such diverse matters as: phobias and philias of childhood; skills not learned in early life; abnormalities of child-parent relationships; vendettas and bellicose nationalism; childhood sexuality and gender identity confusion; birthmarks, congenital deformities and internal diseases; differences between members of monozygotic twin pairs; and abnormal appetites during pregnancy. [Stevenson, 305]

Past life regression, through hypnosis or other altered consciousness states, has been helpful to some to explain feelings that the patient cannot account for or overcome. By finding some experience in a past life, many have been relieved of feelings of fear, depression, or unwantedness. Though many psychologists and hypnotists who work with past-life recall do not really believe that the events recounted by their patients are real, they use it because it works. As one therapist said, "It doesn't matter if it is real or imagined if it helps someone make sense out of their lives. . . . If it works, who cares?" (Boeth, H3).

Need for Justice. To many, the idea of having more than one chance at life seems to be the most equitable solution. *Karma* is just. If you do bad things, you pay the price; if you do good, you get a reward. Punishment is in proportion to how bad your *karma* is, not all or nothing. The idea of condemning someone to an everlasting *hell for a finite amount of sin sounds too harsh. Also, suffering in this life can be justified if it is really an outworking of *karma* from past lives. This explanation eliminates the need to make God responsible for suffering. All suffering can be explained as the just outworking of bad deeds done in former incarnations.

As Quincy Howe observes, "One of the most attractive aspects of reincarnation is that it removes entirely the possibility of damnation" (Howe, 51). The doctrine of eternal punishment seems totally incompatible with the love of God to many people. Reincarnation suggests a way in which God can punish sin (through the law of *karma*), demand faith in Christ (during at least one lifetime), and still save everyone ultimately. Someone who rejects Christ gets more chances. This even protects human freedom, because God does not coerce anyone to believe; he merely gives them more time to exercise their freedom. Moral progress and spiritual growth can also occur during successive lifetimes, which will allow individuals to understand the love of God better. Some think that moral perfection cannot be attained without reincarnation.

Finally, it is argued that reincarnation is just because it makes salvation a personal matter between the individual and God. Rather than dealing with problems of imputed guilt from Adam's sin or being reckoned righteous by faith, everyone is responsible for taking care of his or her own *karma*. Howe, arguing that the atonement by a substitute is no longer valid, says, "Man himself must make his peace with God" (Howe, 107). MacGregor says, "My *karma* is particular to *me*. It is *my* problem and the triumph over it is *my* triumph." This eliminates the injustice of being punished in any way for Adam's sin and the injustice of Christ dying for sins that he did not commit. Instead, Jesus' death becomes our inspiration, "the perfect catalyst" for working out our salvation and assuring us that we stand in the unfailing light of God's love. He died as our example, not as our substitute. In these ways, reincarnation satisfies justice.

Evaluation. Response to the Arguments. The arguments for reincarnation are without real foundation. At best they show only the possibility of reincarnation, not its reality.

Immortality does not prove reincarnation. Even if one could demonstrate the *immortality of the soul on purely rational grounds, it would not thereby prove immortality. The soul could survive forever in a disembodied form. Or the soul could be reunited once with its body in a permanent immortal resurrection body, such as orthodox Jews, Muslims, and Christians believe.

Past life "memories" do not prove reincarnation. There are other ways to explain the so-called "memories" or past lives. First, they may be false memories. Many other so-called "memories" have been shown to be false. Some people have "remembered" things that were empirically proven not to have happened. Many people have recovered from the false memory syndrome. Second, these so-called "memories" of previous lives are more abundant among those who have been reared in cultures or contexts where they were exposed to the teaching of reincarnation. This suggests that they received these ideas when they were young and later revived them from their memory bank. Third, there are notable cases, such as Bridie Murphy, where the alleged "memories" of past lives turned out to be nothing more than stories her grandmother read to her when she was a little girl. Other false memories have been implanted by hypnosis (the power of suggestion) or guided imagery therapy during counseling or teaching sessions. The false memory syndrome is recognized by psychologists today.

Reincarnation does not solve the problem of justice. Rather than solving the problem of unjust suffering, reincarnation simply says that it is just after all. The innocent are not really innocent because the *karma* of their past lives is causing suffering. Reincarnationists complain that a Christian faced with the grieving mother of a dying four-month-old can only say, "I don't know." But the law of *karma* can give her an answer: "Your sweet, innocent angel is dying because in an earlier incarnation she was a scumball." This is not a *solution* to the problem, it is merely a *subversion* of it. It doesn't *deal* with the difficulty; it *dismisses* it.

Is it really fair for God to punish children for the sins they don't even remember committing? It seems morally repugnant and terribly unjust to mete out judgment on someone who does not even know what his crime was. Besides this, by putting the guilt back one lifetime, one begins an infinite regress of explanations that never really pays off with an explanation. If the suffering of each life depends on the sins of a former life, then how did it all begin? If there was a first life, where did the karmic debt come from to explain the suffering in that life? Is evil an eternal principle, right alongside God? You can't keep "back pedaling" forever to solve the problem of evil. The law of *karma* fails to resolve the conflict. It merely pushes the problem back into previous lives without ever coming to a solution.

One gets the impression, and some argue, that *karma* is the same as the biblical law—a rigid, universal moral code. However, *karma* is not a moral prescription. It is a system of retribution only; it has no content to tell us what to do. It is an impersonal, amoral law of act-consequence relations. Even comparisons with the act–consequence relationship in Proverbs fail to recognize that the Old Testament puts these forth as general principles, not absolute, unbreakable sanctions of retribution. For that matter, the law was not as unalterable as *karma*—it was part of a higher law of forgiveness and grace. The comparison is invalid.

Arguments against Reincarnation. Not only do the arguments for reincarnation fail to prove it is so, but there are arguments against reincarnation. Several of the most important can be summarized.

The moral argument. In pantheistic systems there is no source for the moral standards that *karma* enforces (*see* PANTHEISM). Why punish people for some wrong if there is no moral standard of right and wrong? For in pantheism, there is no ultimate difference between good and evil. *Karma* is not a moral law. As for morality, all is relative. Allan Watts, a spokesman for Zen Buddhism, has written, "Buddhism does not share the Western view that there is a moral law, enjoined by God or by nature, which it is man's duty to obey. The Buddha's precepts of conduct—abstinence from taking life, taking what is not given, exploitation of the passions, lying and intoxication—are voluntarily assumed rules of expediency" (Watts, 52).

This relativism poses real problems for reincarnation. Relativism is an impossible position to hold in ethics. You can't say, "Relativism is true," or even, "Relativism is better than absolutism," because these statements assume an absolute value that contradicts relativism. As C. S. *Lewis explains,

> The moment you say that one set of moral ideas can be better than another, you are, in fact, measuring them both by a standard, saying that one of them conforms to that standard more nearly than the other. But the standard that measures the two things is something different from either. . . . You are, in fact, comparing them both with some Real Morality, admitting that there is such a thing as real Right, independent of what people think, and that some people's ideas get nearer to that real Right than others. [Lewis, 25]

In order to say that relativism is right, you have to assume that some absolute Right exists, which is impossible in relativism. Unless something is absolutely right, nothing can be actually right; and if nothing is right (or wrong), then *karma* has no business punishing anyone for it (*see* Morality, Absolute Nature of).

The humanitarian argument. Reincarnation is ultimately anti-humanitarian. It generates no social compassion. Anyone who helps the thousands of poor, crippled, maimed, homeless, and starving people on the streets of India is working against the law of *karma*. People suffer to work off their karmic debt and if you helped them, then they would have to come back again and suffer even more to work off that debt. According to traditional Hindu belief, anyone who helps the suffering is not increasing their *karma* but one's own. The social compassion that exists in India is the result of non-Hindu, largely Christian, influence. Hinduism did not produce Mother Teresa.

The psychological argument. Reincarnation depends on the premise that an individual had a highly developed sense of self-consciousness before birth, so as to receive and store information for later recall. It is a scientific fact that this ability does not develop until one is about eighteen months of age. This is why we do not remember when we were one year old. To assert that every human being somehow mysteriously "forgets" his/her past highly developed consciousness and that most never regain it—unless they are trained and "enlightened" to do so—is highly implausible. The hypothesis is without foundation and is entirely *Deus ex machina*.

The scientific argument. Scientifically, we know that an individual life begins at conception, when the twenty-three chromosomes of a male sperm unite with the twenty-three chromosomes of a female ovum and form a forty-six-chromosome human zygote. At that point a unique, new human life begins. It has life (soul) and a body. It is a unique individual human being. It did not exist before. To claim that its soul (life) existed in previous body has no scientific basis. The scientific evidence points to human conception as the point of origin of an individual human being.

The social argument. If reincarnation were correct, society should be improving. After all, if we have had hundreds, even thousands, of chances to improve over millions of years, then there should be some evidence of it. There is no evidence that such moral progress is being made. All we have improved is the means by which we can manifest hate, cruelty, racism, and barbarism toward other human beings. Even a realistic optimist who hopes for a better day must acknowledge that there is no indisputable evidence that any significant moral improvement has occurred over the thousands of years we know about.

*The Problem of Evil and *Infinite Regress.* If suffering in this life always results from evil done in a previous life, then there would have to be an infinite regress of previous lives. But an infinite regress in time is not possible, since if there were an infinite number of moments before today, then today would never have come. But today has come (*see Kalam* Cosmological Argument). Therefore, there was not an infinite number of previous lives as traditional reincarnation seems to entail.

On the other hand, if there were not an infinite number of lives before this one, then there must have been a first life in which a previous incarnation was not the cause of its evil. But this is what *Theism holds, namely, that evil originated because of an individual's free choice in that first life-time (e.g., Lucifer among the angels and Adam the first human) (*see* Evil, Problem of).

Problem of Infinite Time and Lack of Perfection. Even on the reincarnationist's assumption that there has been an infinite amount of time before today, his view faces another serious problem. In an infinite amount of moments there is more than enough time to achieve the perfection of all souls which reincarnation is designed to do. In short, all souls should have received oneness with God by now, if there had been an infinite amount of time to do so. But they have not. Hence, reincarnation has failed as a solution to the problem of evil.

Biblical Arguments. Human beings are created. Fundamental to all the biblical reasons to reject reincarnation is the doctrine of creation. The Bible is the inspired Word of God (*see* Bible, Evidence for). As such, it has divine authority in whatever it teaches. According to the Bible, human beings were created (Gen. 1:27). God is eternal (1 Tim. 6:16). All other things were created by him (John 1:3; Col. 1:15–16). Everything else exists only because God brought it into existence from nothing (*see* Creation, Views of). This was not only true of Adam and Eve, the first human beings, but of all other human beings after them (Gen. 5:3; Ps. 139:13–16; Eccles. 7:29). All humans since Adam begin at conception (Ps. 51:5; Matt. 1:20). This being the case, there can be no preincarnate existence of our soul.

The intermediate state is disembodied. Scriptures teach that, upon death, the soul leaves the body and goes into the spirit world where it awaits resurrection. The apostle Paul wrote: "We are confident, I say, and would prefer to be away from the body and at home with the Lord" (2 Cor. 5:8). Second, contemplating death, Paul added, "I am torn between the two: I desire to depart and be with Christ, which is better by far" (Phil. 1:23). The "souls" of those who had just been martyred were conscious in heaven. "When he [Christ] opened the fifth seal, I saw under the altar the souls of those who had been slain because of the word of God and the testimony they had maintained" (Rev. 6:9). Jesus promised the repentant thief on the cross conscious bliss that very day of his death, saying: "I tell you the truth, today you will be with me in paradise" (Luke 23:43). Even Moses and Elijah, who had been dead for centuries, were consciously engaging in conversation about Christ's death on the Mount of Transfiguration (Matt. 17:3). Even the disembodied souls of the lost are conscious. For the beast and false prophet who where thrown alive into the Lake of Fire (Rev. 19:20) were still conscious "a thousand years" later (Rev. 20:10). There is not the slightest hint anywhere in Scripture that the soul after death goes into another body, as reincarnationists claim. It simply goes into the spirit world to await the resurrection.

The state after disembodiment is resurrection. Reincarnation is the belief that, after death, the soul passes on to another body. By contrast, the Bible declares that, after death, the same physical body is made incorruptible at the resurrection (*see* Resurrection, Evidence for). Rather than a series of bodies that die, resurrection makes alive forever the same body that died. Rather than seeing personhood as a soul in a body, resurrection sees each human being as a soul-body unity. While reincarnation is a process of perfection, resurrection is a perfected state. Reincarnation is an intermediate state, while the soul longs to be disembodied and absorbed in God; but, resurrection is an ultimate state, in which the whole person, body and soul, enjoys the goodness of God.

The differences between resurrection and reincarnation are as follows:

Resurrection	**Reincarnation**
happens once	occurs many times
into the same body	into a different body
into an immortal body	into a mortal body
a perfect state	an imperfect state
an ultimate state	an intermediate state

So there is a vast difference between the Christian doctrine of resurrection and the doctrine of reincarnation. The Bible teaching of the resurrection (for example, in John 5:28–29; 1 Corinthians 15; Rev. 20:4–15), therefore, is contrary to the doctrine of reincarnation.

Humans die only once. According to Scripture, human beings die only once, followed by the judgment. For "Just as man is destined to die once, and after that to face judgment" (Heb. 9:27). We are born once, we live once, and we die once. But according to reincarnation, we live many times. We are born and reborn over and over again. The Hindu apologist Radhakrishna recognized that this verse spelled the definitive difference between Christianity and Hinduism. He wrote: "There is a fundamental difference between Christianity and Hinduism; it is said that it consists in this: that while the Hindu to whatever school he belongs believes in a succession of lives, the Christian believes that 'it is appointed to men once to die, but after this the judgment'" (Radhakrishna, 14, 118).

Judgment is final. Not only do human beings live and die once, followed by judgment, but the judgment is final (*see* Hell). Once one goes to his destiny, there is a "great gulf fixed" that no one can cross (Luke 16:26). Indeed, the judgment is described as "eternal destruction" (2 Thess. 1:9) and "everlasting fire" (Matt. 25:41). If it lasts forever, then there is no possibility of a reincarnation into another body. There is resurrection into one's own body, which receives the final judgment of salvation or of damnation (John 5:28–29).

Jesus rejected reincarnation. When asked whether a man's sin before birth was the cause of his sin, Jesus replied: "Neither this man nor his parents sinned," said Jesus, "but this happened so that the work of God might be displayed in his life" (John 9:3). Whereas this is probably a reference to the false Jewish belief that one could sin in the womb before birth, thus producing physical deformity, Jesus' reply excludes any belief in prebirth sins and *karma*. Elsewhere, Jesus made it very emphatic that one person's unfortunate lot in life is not necessarily because of sin (Luke 13:4–5). This is true whether one is referring to early life, prenatal life, or alleged preincarnate life.

Grace is contrary to reincarnation. Reincarnation is based in the doctrine of *karma*, which dictates that, whatever one sows in this life, one reaps in the next life. *Karma* is an inexorable law, with no exceptions. Sins cannot be forgiven; they must be punished. If one does not get his due in this life, he must get it in the next life.

But, according to Christianity, forgiveness is possible. Jesus forgave his enemies who crucified him (Luke 24:34). Christians are to forgive as Christ forgave us (Col. 3:13). Forgiveness is contrary to the doctrine of *karma* and renders reincarnation entirely unnecessary. Salvation is a "gift" (John 4:10; Rom. 3:24; 5:15–17; 6:23; 2 Cor. 9:15; Eph. 2:8; Heb. 6:4) which is received by faith. Rather than working to merit God's favor, the believer is given grace or unmerited favor and pronounced righteous. God's justice is satisfied because Jesus was punished for the sins of the whole world in his death. Our sins were not simply ignored, or swept under the rug. Jesus paid (Rom. 3:25; Heb. 2:17; 1 John 2:2; 4:10) God's demand for justice by bearing our guilt as our substitute. This penalty paid by Christ is contrary to the karmic doctrine and strikes at the heart of the need for reincarnation.

Summary. The doctrine of reincarnation, based on *karma*, is without objective evidence. It is contrary to common sense, science, sound psychology of human development, and morality. Further, it is opposed by clear teaching of Scripture. Hence, in spite of its popularity, even in the West, it is without rational and evidential foundation.

Sources

M. Albrecht, *Reincarnation: A Christian Appraisal*

K. Anderson, *Life, Death and Beyond*

J. Boeth, "In Search of Past Lives: Looking at Yesterday to Find Answers for Today," *Dallas Times Herald*, 3 April 1983

W. de Arteaga, *Past Life Visions: A Christian Exploration*

L. de Silva, *Reincarnation in Buddhist and Christian Thought*

N. L. Geisler and J. Amano, *The Reincarnation Sensation*

S. Hackett, *Oriental Philosophy*

J. Hick, *Death and Eternal Life*

———, Untitled review, *Religion* (Autumn 1975)

Q. Howe, *Reincarnation for the Christian*

C. S. Lewis, *Mere Christianity*

W. Martin, *The Riddle of Reincarnation*

V. S. Naipaul, *An Area of Darkness*

J B. Noss, *Man's Religions*

S. Radhakrishna, *The Hindu View of Life*

J. Snyder, *Reincarnation vs. Resurrection*

I. Stevenson, "The Explanatory Value of the Idea of Reincarnation," in *The Journal of Nervous and Mental Disease* (September 1977)

S. Travis, *Christian Hope and the Future*

A. Watts, *The Way of Zen*

Relativism. ***See*** **TRUTH, NATURE OF; MORALITY, ABSOLUTE NATURE OF.**

Relativity, Moral. ***See*** **MORALITY, ABSOLUTE NATURE OF.**

Religious Argument for God. ***See*** **APOLOGETICS, EXPERIENTIAL; GOD, EVIDENCE FOR; TRUEBLOOD, ELTON.**

Religious Experience. ***See*** **APOLOGETICS, EXPERIENTIAL; GOD, EVIDENCE FOR; TRUEBLOOD, ELTON.**

Religious Language. ***See*** **ANALOGY, PRINCIPLE OF.**

Resurrection, Alternate Theories of. The evidence for the supernatural physical resurrection of Christ is compelling (*see* RESURRECTION, EVIDENCE FOR, AND RESURRECTION, PHYSICAL NATURE OF), and the objections can be adequately answered (*see* RESURRECTION, OBJECTIONS TO). Alternate explanations to a supernatural physical resurrection have been attempted, but a brief survey will show that they too fail.

Naturalistic Theories. In all naturalistic theories, in which the assumption is that Jesus died and did not return to life, two issues are inevitable problems: First, given the inescapable fact that Jesus actually died on the cross (*see* CHRIST, DEATH OF; SWOON THEORY), a basic problem with all naturalistic theories is to explain what happened to the body. It is necessary to explain why the earliest records speak of an empty tomb or why the dead body was never found. Second, the earliest disciples testified to seeing an empty tomb and being with Jesus in the weeks after his death. If untrue, why did these reports so motivate them to extraordinary actions?

The Authorities Moved the Body. One hypothesis proposes that the Roman or Jewish authorities took the body from the tomb to another place, leaving the tomb empty. The disciples wrongly presumed Jesus to be raised from the dead.

If the Romans or the Sanhedrin had the body, why did they accuse the disciples of stealing it (Matt. 28:11–15)? Such a charge would have been senseless. And if the opponents of Christianity had the body, why didn't they produce it to stop the resurrection story? The reaction of the authorities reveals that they did not know where the body was. They continually *resisted* the apostles' teaching, but never attempted to refute it.

This theory is contrary to the conversion of James and especially Saul. How could such a severe critic as Saul of Tarsus (cf. Acts 8–9) be so duped?

Certainly, this theory does not explain the resurrection appearances. Why did Jesus keep appearing to all these people in the same nail-scared body in which he was placed in the tomb? It is also contrary to the conversions of people from the opposition to Jesus' side. It assumes Paul was duped when he was deep in the Jewish anti-Christian camp yet unaware the body was available. And he was duped into believing in the resurrection.

The stolen body hypothesis is a fallacious argument from innocence. There is not a shred of evidence to support it.

The Tomb Was Never Visited. One theory is that in the two months after Jesus' death he appeared in some spiritual form to some of the disciples, and they preached the resurrection based on this. But no one ever checked the tomb to see if Jesus' dead body actually was there. Why should they, if they had already seen him alive?

If we can believe nothing else from the earliest record in the Gospels, we can hardly avoid the point that Jesus' tomb was a busy place on that early morning. If the issue just never came up, it certainly burned the minds of the writers of the Gospels. A harmonization of the order of events is found in the article RESURRECTION, OBJECTIONS TO. The women who came to finish burial procedures (Mark 15:1) saw the stone rolled away and the empty tomb. John reached the grave site and saw the burial clothes, followed by Peter who entered the tomb and saw the grave clothes and a headcloth (a strip wrapped around the head to keep the jaw closed) lying separately (John 20:3–8). While Paul does not mention the empty tomb explicitly, he implies it when speaking of Jesus' burial as a precondition of his resurrection (1 Cor. 15:4).

The guards were sure to have made a thorough search of the tomb before they reported to the Jewish leaders that his body had vanished (Matt. 28:11–15). Their lives were forfeited if they had been derelict in their duty. These guards would not have had to agree to the cover story that the disciples had stolen the body if they could have offered some reasonable alternative explanation. But the story of the guards does not explain the resurrection appearances, the transformation of the disciples, or the mass conversions of people only weeks later in the very city where it had happened.

The Women Went to the Wrong Tomb. Some suggest that the women went to the wrong tomb in the darkness, saw it empty and thought he had risen. This story was then spread by them through the ranks of the disciples and led to their belief in the resurrections of Christ. There are serious problems with such a simplistic story. If it was so dark, why did Mary Magdalene assume the gardener was working (John 20:15)? Why did Peter and John make the same mistake as the women when they arrived later, in daylight (John 20:4–6)? It was light enough to see the grave clothes and the rolled-up headcloth in a dim, cave-like tomb (vs. 7).

If the disciples went to the wrong tomb, the authorities had only to go to the right one and show them the body. That would have easily disproved all claims to a resurrection.

And, as with other naturalistic theories (*see* NATURALISM), this offers no explanation for the reports that Jesus appeared.

The Disciples Stole the Body. The guards spread the story that the disciples had stolen the body in the night and took it to an unknown location. This is still a popular claim, particularly in Jewish circles. It explains the story of an empty tomb and the inability of anyone to disprove the claim that Jesus rose from the dead.

Grave robbery is not in keeping with what we know of the moral character of the disciples. They were honest men. They taught and lived according to the highest moral principles of honesty and integrity. Peter specifically denied that the apostles followed cleverly devised tales (2 Peter 1:16). Furthermore, the disciples do not come off as particularly subtle or clever. If they were trying to make Christ's predictions come true, up until this time they had not understood how the prophecies fit Jesus. They had not even understood that he was going to die, let alone that he was to be raised (John 13:36).

At the grave scene we find these conspirators confused and bewildered, just as we would suspect if they had not a clue what was happening. They did not know what to think when they first saw the empty tomb (John 20:9). They scattered and hid in fear of being caught (Mark 14:50).

Perhaps the most serious objection is that the hoax was so totally successful. For that to happen the apostles had to persist in this conspiracy to the death and to die for what they knew to be false. People will sometimes die for what they believe to be true, but they have little motivation to die for what they know to be a lie. It seems unbelievable that no disciple ever recanted belief in the resurrection of Christ, in spite of suffering and persecution (cf. 2 Cor. 11:22–33; Heb. 11:32–40). Not only did they die for this "lie," but the apostles placed belief in the resurrection at the center of their faith (Rom. 10:9; 1 Cor. 15:1–5, 12–19). Indeed, it was the theme of the earliest preaching by the apostles (Acts 2:30–31; 3:15; and 4:10, 33).

It is contrary to the conversions of James and Paul (John 7:5; Acts 9, and 1 Cor. 15:7). These skeptics would certainly have learned of the plot eventually, and they would never have remained in the faith on such a basis.

Finally, if the body was stolen and still dead, then why did it keep appearing alive, both to disciples and to others who were not disciples? Jesus appeared bodily to Mary, to James (Jesus' unbelieving brother), and later to Paul, the greatest Jewish opponent of early Christianity.

Joseph of Arimathea Took the Body. A similar notion is that Joseph of Arimathea stole the body of Jesus. He was a secret believer in Jesus, and Jesus was buried in Joseph's tomb. The problems of this theory boil down to "Why?" "When?" and "Where?"

Why would he take the body? Joseph really had no reason. It could not be to prevent the disciples from stealing it, since he was a disciple (Luke 23:50–51). If he had not been a follower of Christ, he could have produced the body and squelched the whole story.

When could he (or the disciples for that matter) have taken it? Joseph was a devout Jew who would not have broken the Sabbath (see Luke 23:50–56). At night, the torches he carried would have been seen. A Roman guard was posted in front of the tomb (Matt. 27:62–66). The following morning the women came by dawn (Luke 24:1). There was simply no opportunity.

If Joseph took it, where did he put it? The body was never found, even though almost two months elapsed before the disciples began preaching. This was plenty of time to expose a fraud. There is no motive, opportunity, or method to support this theory, and it gives no explanation of the appearances of Christ in his resurrected body.

And again, there is no good explanation, other than a supernatural resurrection, for eleven appearances over the subsequent forty days to more than 500 people (*see* RESURRECTION, EVIDENCE FOR). They saw him, handled him, ate with him, talked with him, and were completely transformed overnight from scared, scattered, skeptics to the world's greatest missionary society. Much of it happened in the same city in which Jesus was crucified.

Appearances Were Mistaken Identity. One naturalistic theory made more visible by Schonfield's *The *Passover Plot* is that the post-death appearances that were the heart of the disciples' belief in the resurrection were all cases of mistaken identity. This is allegedly reinforced by the fact that the disciples themselves even believed at first that the person appearing was not Jesus. Mary thought she saw a gardener (John 20). The two disciples thought it was a stranger traveling in Jerusalem (Luke 24), and later they supposed they saw a spirit (Luke 24:38–39). Mark even admits the appearance was in "a different form" (Mark 16:12). According to Schonfield, the disciples mistook Jesus for different people at different times (Schonfield, 170–73).

This theory is beset with many difficulties. First, on none of these occasions mentioned did the disciples go away with any doubt in their minds that it was really the same Jesus they had known intimately for years who was appearing to them in physical form Their doubts were only initial and momentary. By the time the appearance was over, Jesus had convinced them by his scars, his ability to eat food, by their touching him, by his teaching, by his voice, and/or by miracles that he was the same person with whom they had spent over three years (*see* RESURRECTION, EVIDENCE FOR). Schonfield neglects all this evidence and takes their initial doubt, which is a sign of the authenticity of the account, totally out of context.

Second, the mistaken identity hypothesis does not account for the permanently empty tomb. If the disciples were seeing different persons, the Jews or Romans could have gone to Jesus' tomb and produced the body to refute their claim. But there is no evidence that they did, even though they had every reason to want to do so. The fact is that no one ever found the body. Instead, the disciples were absolutely convinced they were encountering the same Jesus in his same resurrected physical body whom they had known so closely all those years.

Third, this speculation does not account for the transformation of the disciples. Mistaken identity and a dead body rotting in some grave does not explain why the scared, scattered, and skeptical disciples were transformed into the world's greatest missionary society overnight by their mistaken encounter with several mortal beings.

Fourth, it is highly unlikely that many people could be fooled on that many occasions. After all, Jesus appeared to over five hundred people on eleven different occasions over a forty-day period. It is less miraculous to hold in the supernatural resurrection of Christ than to believe that all of these people on all of these occasions who totally deceived and yet so totally transformed. It is easier to believe in the resurrection.

Finally, it is contrary to the conversion of skeptics as James and Saul of Tarsus. How could such critics be so duped?

God Destroyed (Transformed) the Body. All of the above theories are purely naturalistic. Another group contends that some kind of miracle occurred, but it was not the miracle of a physical resurrection of the body of Jesus after he had died. Rather, this alternative to the physical resurrection contends that God destroyed (transformed) the body of Jesus so that it mysteriously and immediately disappeared from view (see Harris). The later appearances of Christ were, according to some, theophany-like appearances, and according to others, they were appearances wherein Jesus assumed bodily form(s) in which the scars he showed were replicas to convince others of his reality but not of his materiality. This view is far more sophisticated and less naturalistic. It does not fall into the typical naturalistic or liberal camp. Rather, it is more in line with the neo-orthodox error on the resurrection. Many cults, such as the Jehovah's Witnesses, hold a form of this view. But like the naturalistic views, these views too are subject to fatal flaws.

To explain away the one simple miracle of Jesus being raised immortal in the same physical body in which he died, those who seek a spiritual-body explanation posit that at least two miracles happened. First God immediately and mysteriously destroyed or transformed the physical body into a nonphysical body. Some say it was turned into gases which leaked out of the tomb (*see* BOYCE), others that it was vaporized or transmuted. God also had to miraculously enable the non-physical Jesus to assume physical form(s) on different occasions by which he could convince the apostles that he was alive.

This hypothesis uses two miracles to explain away one and in the process makes Jesus into a deceiver. For he told his disciples both before and after his resurrection that he would be raised in the same body. He even left the empty tomb and grave clothes as evidence, yet he was not raised immortal in the body that died. Speaking of his resurrection, Jesus answered them, "Destroy this temple [physical body], and I will raise *it* [the same physical body] again in three days" (John 2:19, emphasis added). This was a lie unless Jesus was raised in the numerically same physical body in which he died. Furthermore, after his resurrection Jesus presented his crucifixion wounds to his disciples as evidence that he had indeed risen in the same body in which he was crucified (cf. John 20:27). "While they were still talking about this, Jesus himself stood among them and said to them, 'Why are you troubled, and why do doubts rise in your minds? Look at my hands and my feet. It is I myself! Touch me and see; a ghost does not have flesh and bones, as you see I have'" (Luke 24:36–39). It would have been nothing short of deceptions to offer his crucifixion wounds as evidence that he had really risen unless it was in the same body that had been crucified. The whole point of the empty grave clothes (John 20:6–7; cf. Mark 16:5) was to show that the body that died was the one that had risen (cf. John 20:8). If Jesus had risen in a spiritual form there is no reason the physical body could not remain in the tomb. After all God is capable of convincing people of his presence and reality without a bodily form. he can do it with a voice from heaven and other miracles, as he did on other occasions (cf. Gen. 22:1, 11; Exod. 3:2; Matt. 3:17).

This view would make the apostles' testimony to the resurrection false, since they affirmed that Jesus was raised from the dead in the same physical body in which he died. Speaking of the *resurrection*, Peter said: "he [David] foreseeing this, spoke concerning the resurrection of the Christ, that his soul was not left in hades, nor did his flesh see corruption. This Jesus God has raised up, of which we are all witnesses" (Acts 2:31–32). If this is true, then Jesus body was not destroyed; his same body of "flesh" (*sarx*) was raised up. It was "this Jesus," the same one who was "crucified" (vs. 23), "dead and buried" (vs. 29). The apostle John shows the continuity between the preresurrection body of flesh and the one in which Jesus was raised and still has at the right hand of the Father. John wrote, "That which was from the beginning, which we have heard, which we have seen with our eyes, which we have looked at and our hands have touched—this we proclaim concerning the Word of life" (1 John 1:1). John said that "every spirit that acknowledges that Jesus Christ has come [and now remains] in the flesh is from God" (1 John 4:2). The use of the perfect participal (past action with continuing results in the present), along with the present tense (2 John 7) in a parallel passages emphasizes that Jesus was still (now in heaven) in the same flesh in which he came into this world. Thus, to deny that Jesus was raised in the same physical body in which he died makes Jesus a deceiver and his disciples false teachers.

Such a conception is strongly contrary to Jewish and biblical understanding of the resurrection, whereby the body that died is the one that comes out of the grave in the flesh. Job said, "I know that my Redeemer lives, and that in the end he will stand upon the earth. And after my skin has been destroyed, yet in my flesh I will see God" (Job 19:25–26). Daniel spoke of a physical resurrection from the grave, saying, "Multitudes who sleep in the dust of the earth will awake: some to everlasting life, others to shame and everlasting contempt" (Dan. 12:2). Jesus affirmed that what is resurrected is the physical bodies that come out from the grave: "a time is coming when all who are *in their graves will* hear his voice and *come out*—those who have done good will rise to live, and those who have done evil will rise to be condemned" (John 5:28–29). Paul held out to bereaved believers the expectation of seeing their loved ones in their resurrection bodies (1 Thess. 4:13–18), noting that we will have bodies like Christ's (Phil. 3:21).

Conclusion. There are various attempts to explain away the physical resurrection of Christ. Besides the overwhelming evidence for the physical resurrection of Christ in the same body in which he lived and died (*see* RESURRECTION, EVIDENCE FOR), there is no basis in fact for any of these theories. None of them explain the data. Most are purely naturalistic, which is contrary to the fact that God exists (*see* COSMOLOGICAL ARGUMENT; MORAL ARGUMENT FOR GOD; TELEOLOGICAL ARGUMENT) and that he can do and has done miracles (*see* MIRACLE; MIRACLES, ARGUMENTS AGAINST). Others allow some kind of mysterious divine intervention to produce an empty tomb, but at the same time unnecessarily demean both the biblical data and the character of Christ (*see* CHRIST, UNIQUENESS OF).

Sources

J. Boice, *Foundations of the Christian Faith*

W. Craig, *Knowing the Truth about the Resurrection*

N. L. Geisler, *The Battle for the Resurrection*

———, *In Defense of the Resurrection*

R. Gundry, Soma *in Biblical Theology with Emphasis on Pauline Anthropology*

G. Habermas, *The Resurrection of Jesus: An Apologetic*

M. Harris, *From Grave to Glory*

G. Ladd. *I Believe in the Resurrection of Jesus*

J. A. Schep, *The Nature of the Resurrection Body*

Resurrection Apologetics. ***See*** **Apologetics, Types of; Apologetics, Historical; Resurrection, Evidence for.**

Resurrection of Christ. *Order of Events. Background.* Critics often object that the Gospel record, especially that of the resurrection, is not credible because of the contradictions in the accounts. For example, the order of events appears to be different in the various accounts. For example, the Gospels list Mary as the first person who saw Jesus after his resurrection whereas 1 Corinthians 15:5 lists Peter as first. Likewise Matthew 28:2 lists Mary Magdalene and the other Mary as the first at the tomb whereas John 20:1 names only Mary Magdalene as being there.

Nonetheless, despite these differences, closer scrutiny of the resurrection accounts reveals a hidden harmony. Indeed, it demonstrates the kinds of unity in differences one would expect from independent, reliable witnesses who were not in collusion. Hence, the contention that the Gospels contradict each other fails for many reasons.

The Harmony of the Resurrection Accounts. There is a discernible overall order of postresurrection events in the New Testament accounts. All the other events can be fit into this overall list as follows.

	Matt	Mark†	Luke	John	Acts	1 Cor.
1. Mary Magdalene		X		X		
2. Mary & Women	X	X				
3. Peter				X		X
4. Two Disciples		X		X		
5. Ten Apostles			X	X		
6. Eleven Apostles				X		
7. Seven Apostles				X		
8. All Apostles (Gt. Commission)	X	X				X
9. 500 Brethren						X
10. James						X
11. All Apostles (Ascension)	X					
12. Paul					X	X

Peter saw the empty tomb, not Christ

†These verses in Mark are not in some of the earliest mss. of the NT

Other scholars (cf. Wenham, 139) reverse numbers 3 and 4 (but see Luke 24:34) and some combine 8 and 9. But this is of no consequence in reconciling all the data. There is no demonstrable contradiction either way.

Once several factors are noted, there is no major problem in fitting the various appearances together.

First, because Paul is defending the resurrection, he provides an official list that includes only men (women at that time were not allowed to give testimony in court).

Second, it is understandable that Christ's appearance to Paul would not be listed in the Gospels, since their narration ends by the time of Christ's ascension and Paul saw Christ many years later (Acts 9:3f.; 1 Cor. 15:7).

Third, since Paul's point is to provide proof of the resurrection it was fitting that he singled out the appearance to the five hundred witnesses, most of whom were still alive when he wrote (ca. A.D. 55).

Fourth, the rest of the appearances, such as those to James (1 Cor. 15:7) and the two disciples on the road to Emmaus (Luke 24:13f.) fit in as supplementary information that does not contradict the other appearances.

Fifth, even the difficulty in discerning the exact order of events of the first appearances to the women is not insurmountable. The following order of events appears to account for all the data consistently:

1. "Mary Magdalene" visited Jesus' tomb early Sunday morning "while it was still dark" (John 20:1). (It is possible that someone else was with her, since she refers to "we" [John 20:2].)
2. Seeing that the stone had been rolled away (John 20:1), she ran back to Peter and John in Jerusalem and said, "We do not know where they have laid him" (v. 2).
3. Peter and John ran to the tomb and saw the empty graveclothes (John 20:3–9) and then "the disciples" (Peter and John) "returned to their homes" (v. 11).
4. Mary Magdalene had followed Peter and John to the tomb. After Peter and John left, Mary Magdalene, lingering at the tomb, saw two angels "where the body of Jesus had lain" (John 20:12). Then Jesus appeared to her (Mark 16:9) and told her to return to the disciples (John 20:14–17).
5. As Mary Magdalene was leaving, the "other women" arrived at the tomb with spices to anoint the body of Jesus (Mark 16:1). By this time, it "began to dawn" (Matt. 28:1). The group including the "other Mary" (Matt.

28:1), the mother of James (Luke 24:10), Salome (Mark 16:1), and Johanna (Luke 24:1, 10) also saw that the stone had been rolled away (Matt. 28:2; Mark 16:4; Luke 24:2; John 20:1). Entering the tomb, they saw "two men" (Luke 24:4), one of whom spoke to them (Mark 16:5) and told them to return to Galilee, where they would see Jesus (Matt. 28:5–7; Mark 16:5–7). These two young "men" were actually angels (John 20:12).

6. As Mary Magdalene and the women left to go tell the disciples, Jesus appeared to them and told them to go to Galilee to his "brethren" (Matt. 28:9–10). Meanwhile, the "eleven disciples went to Galilee, to the mountain which Jesus had appointed for them" (Matt. 28:16; Mark 16:7).
7. Mary Magdalene with the "other women" (Luke 24:10) returned that evening to the eleven (Luke 24:9) and "all the rest" (v. 11) now reassembled in Galilee behind closed doors "for fear of the Jews" (John 20:19). Mary Magdalene told them she had seen the Lord (v. 18). But the disciples did not believe her (Mark 16:11). Neither did they believe the story of the other women (Luke 24:11).
8. Upon hearing this news, Peter got up and ran again to the tomb. Seeing the empty graveclothes (Luke 24:12), he marveled. There are noticeable differences between this visit and his first one. Here Peter is alone, whereas John was with him the first time (John 20:3–8). Here, Peter is definitely impressed; the first time, only John "saw and believed" (John 20:8).

Conflict in Independent Testimony. The fact that various accounts do not fit together with perfect ease is to be expected of independent authentic testimony. Indeed, were the accounts perfectly harmonious on the surface, we would have to suspect collusion. But the fact that the many events and general order are clear is exactly what we should expect of a credible account (verified by great legal minds who have scrutinized the Gospel accounts and pronounced them so). Simon *Greenleaf, the famous Harvard lawyer who wrote a textbook on legal evidence, was converted to Christianity based on his careful examination of the Gospel witnesses from a legal perspective. He concluded that "Copies which had been as universally received and acted upon as the Four Gospels, would have been received in evidence in any court of justice, without the slightest hesitation" (Greenleaf, 9–10).

Positive Evidence for Authenticity. There is overwhelming positive evidence that the Gospel records are authentic. There are a greater number of manuscripts for the New Testament than for any other book from the ancient world (*see* New Testament Manuscripts). Indeed, even taking the criteria for credibility of the great skeptic, David Hume, the New Testament passes with flying colors (*see* New Testament Witnesses, Tests for Credibility of). There is no reason, then, to reject the authenticity of the New Testament accounts based on their alleged disorder. Given the fact that there are five major accounts of Jesus' postresurrection appearances (Matt. 28; Mark 16; Luke 24; John 20–21; Acts 9; 1 Cor. 15) filled with eyewitness accounts, there is no reasonable doubt about the reality of his resurrection.

Sources

W. L. Craig, *Knowing the Truth about the Resurrection*
N. L. Geisler, *The Battle for the Resurrection*
S. Greenleaf, *The Testimony of the Evangelists*
G. Habermas, *Ancient Evidence on the Life of Jesus*
A. T. Robertson, *Harmony of the Gospels*
J. Wenham, *Easter Enigma*

Resurrection Claims in Non-Christian Religions. Some critics of Christ's resurrection point to claims that many non-Christian leaders also rose from the dead. If true, the resurrection of Jesus would not be a unique confirmation of his claim to deity (*see* Christ, Deity of). In particular, Robert Price claims that the many post-death phenomena found in other religions rival Christian claims about Christ (Price, 2–3, 14–25). If so, then the resurrection of Christ cannot be used to support the truth of Christianity over other religions (*see* Pluralism, Religious; World Religions and Christianity).

Apollonius of Tyana. Apollonius of Tyana (d. A.D. 98) is said to rival Christ's claim to be the son of God, and his biographer Philostratus is supposed to have reported post-death appearances. Actually, stories about Apollonius fit more under the apotheosis category than as resurrection accounts. In an apotheosis legend, a human is deified.

These claims are questionable (see Habermas, "Resurrection Claims"). The biography ends with the death of Apollonius. There is nothing about any resurrection. The after-death record comes from what Philostratus called "stories." They are later legends that were appended to the biography after it was written. The biography is the primary source for his life, along with one other minor one. There is no other confirmation.

The source for Philostratus's stories is said to be "Damis," which many scholars think was a nonexistent person used as a literary device. There is no other evidence. Damis's credibility is not helped by the fact that his birth place is given as Nineveh, a city that had not existed for 300 years. The writing style also was a popular literary form of the day called "romance" or "romance fiction." It is not to be taken literally or historically. The plot unfolds through contrived situations, it involves exotic animals and formal descriptions of works of art; it has lengthy speeches, and it has frequent historical inaccuracies. More about these is given in the article Apollonius of Tyana.

It is also notable that Philostratus was commissioned to compose this biography by Julia Domna, the wife of the emperor Septimus, 120 years after Apollonius's death. Since the author's patroness was to become a high priestess of Hellenistic polytheism, there may have been an anti-Christian polemic agenda in adding a resurrection-like ending. Those writing about Jesus clearly had a very different set of motives. They wanted to show that he was the long-awaited Messiah, the Savior of the world (John 20:31).

The one reported "resurrection" appearance that Philostratus adds in the appendix was a vision to a sleeping man in the year 273, nearly two centuries after his death. The story also was given that Apollonius might not have actually died, but instead been deified. This is in the context of Greek polytheism. Greeks and Romans did not believe in a resurrection in the same physical body. They followed a reincarnation model. The philosophers mocked the apostle Paul when he proclaimed a bodily resurrection on Mar's Hill (Acts 17:19, 32). For the Greeks who believed in immortality, salvation involved deliverance from their body, not resurrection in their body.

Sabbatai Sevi. Sabbatai Sevi was a seventeenth-century Jewish teacher who claimed to be the Messiah and was heralded by a contemporary named Nathan. It was reported many years later that, after Sevi's death in 1676, his brother found his tomb empty but full of light (see Scholem).

Actually, there were two conjectures about Sevi. Many of his followers refused to believe he had really died, so they refused to believe he had risen from the dead. Whatever happened to him, no one ever reported seeing him again. His disappearance, like that of Apollonius, has characteristics of an apotheosis legend. Such legends lack historical support. The story of Sabbatai Sevi itself lacks any kind of evidence. If the story of Jesus grew from such fragmentary reports it would be rejected by any credible scholar. The role of Nathan is conflicting. One letter reported that Nathan taught that Sevi had never died. Another source reported that Nathan had died one month before Sevi, and that they had never actually met one another (Habermas, "Resurrection Claims," 175).

Rabbi Judah. Rabbi Judah was a major figure in Judaism and was involved in the completion of the *Mishnah* in about 200. According to the *Talmud*, after Rabbi Judah died, "he used to come home again at twilight every Sabbath Eve." Allegedly, when a neighbor approached the rabbi's door to greet him they were turned away by his maid. When the rabbi heard of this he stopped coming, so as not to upstage other good persons who returned to their homes after their deaths (*Talmud*, 3.12.103a).

While the rabbi died in 220, the first reference to his appearances came in the fifth century ("Resurrection Claims," 173). This gap is too large to support credibility. No reputable scholar would accept the claims about Jesus if they came from one witness two centuries after he died. In addition, the testimony is too scant. There is only one witness to the event—the maid. Nor is there any attempt to provide substantiation. The only possible confirmatory testimony was the neighbor, who was turned away.

The immediate cessation of the appearances after others inquired about him casts suspicion on whether he had appeared at all. The reason given for his failure to return seems disingenuous. No evidence of an empty tomb or a physical appearance were ever presented. At best there seemed to be only one person with a vested interest who had some kind of subjective experienced regarding a person she no doubt missed very much. If it happened at all, this event seems more a candidate for a psychological than a supernatural explanation.

Kabir. Kabir was a fifteenth-century religious leader who combined facets of the Muslim and *Hindu religions. After his death in 1518, his followers were divided over whether to cremate his body, which Hindus favor but Muslims oppose. Kabir himself is said to have appeared to stop the controversy. When he directed them to draw back the cloth placed over his body, they found only flowers underneath. His Hindu followers burned half of the flowers, and the Muslims buried the other half.

Little or nothing is extant from contemporaries of Kabir. Some of his teachings may have been written down about fifty years after his death, but these contain nothing about a resurrection (Archer, 50–53).

There is evidence of a growing set of legends that grew up among his followers. These include a miraculous birth, miracles performed during his life, and appearances to his disciples after his death. As Habermas notes, "It was found that this is a very natural and expected process in the formation of Indian legend" ("Resurrection Claims," 174).

Since *resurrection of the same physical body is contrary to Hindu belief in soul transmigration to another body, it is unlikely that his Hindu followers, dedicated as they were to Hindu practices, would have come to believe that their leader was raised bodily from the dead.

The scant evidence suggests a contrived plan to pacify both sets of followers and keep the movement together. It looks like a clever plot to satisfy both religious burial practices without offending either.

Conclusion. There is no real comparison between these stories and the accounts of Christ's resurrection. The non-Christian resurrections set the Bible's quality of truth in sharp relief. Consider the significant differences in most, if not all, cases:

Christ's Resurrection	Non-Christian Resurrections
numerous credible witnesses	no credible eyewitnesses
numerous contemporary records	no contemporary records
abundant physical evidence	no physical evidence given
claims to deity made	some claims to deification only
other confirming miracles	no corroborating miracles

"Non-Christian resurrection claims have not been proven by evidence," notes Habermas. "Any of several naturalistic hypotheses is certainly possible and, in some cases, one or more can specifically be postulated as a probable cause. . . . Simply to report a miracle is not sufficient to establish it, especially if that miracle is going to be used to support a religious system" (ibid., 177).

Sources

J. C. Archer, *The Sikhs*

S. A. Cook, *The Cambridge Ancient History*

J. Ferguson, *Religions of the Roman Empire*

G. Habermas, *Ancient Evidence for the Life of Jesus*

———, "Did Jesus Perform Miracles?" in M. Wilkins, ed., *Jesus under Fire*

———, "Resurrection Claims in Non-Christian Religions," *Religious Studies* 25 (1989)

L. McKenzie, *Pagan Resurrection Myths and the Resurrection of Jesus*.

R. Price, "Is There a Place for Historical Criticism?" in *Christianity Challenges the University*

G. Scholem, *Sabbati Sevi: The Mystical Messiah*

I. Slotki, ed., *The Babylonian Talmud*

Resurrection, Evidence for. The bodily resurrection of Christ is the crowning proof that Jesus was who he claimed to be, God manifested in human flesh (*see* CHRIST, DEITY OF). Indeed, the resurrection of Christ in flesh is of such importance to the Christian faith that the New Testament insists that no one can be saved without it (Rom. 10:9; 1 Cor. 15:1–7).

Direct Evidence. Some have opted for a spiritual or immaterial resurrection body (*see* RESURRECTION, PHYSICAL NATURE OF), but the New Testament is emphatic that Jesus rose in the same physical body of flesh and bones in which he died. The evidence for this consists in the New Testament testimony of numerous appearances of Christ to his disciples for a period of forty days, in the same physical, nail-scarred body in which he died, now immortal.

Of course, the evidence for the resurrection of Christ depends on the fact of his death. For arguments that Jesus actually died physically on the cross, see the article CHRIST, DEATH OF; SWOON THEORY. It remains here only to show that the same body that permanently vacated his tomb was seen alive after that time. The evidence for this is found in his twelve appearances, the first eleven of which cover the immediate forty days after his crucifixion (*see* RESURRECTION, EVIDENCE FOR).

Appearances. To Mary Magdalene (John 20:10–18). It is an unmistakable sign of the authenticity of the record that, in a male dominated culture, Jesus first appeared to a woman. In the first-century Jewish culture, a writer inventing a resurrection account would never have taken this approach. A woman's testimony was not even accepted in court. Anyone faking the record would have Jesus appear first to one or more of his twelve disciples, probably a prominent one such as Peter. Instead, Jesus' first postresurrection appearance was to Mary Magdalene. During this appearance there were unmistakable proofs of the visibility, materiality, and identity of the resurrection body.

She *saw* Christ with her natural eyes. The text says, "she turned around and saw Jesus standing there" (vs. 14). The word "saw" (*theoreo*) is a normal word for seeing with the naked eye. It is used elsewhere in the New Testament for seeing human beings in their physical bodies (Mark 3:11; 5:15; Acts 3:16) and even for seeing Jesus in his preresurrection body (Matt. 27:55; John 6:19).

Mary *heard* Jesus. "Woman, why are you crying? Who is it you are looking for?" (vs. 15). Then again, she heard Jesus say "Mary" and she recognized his voice (vs. 16). Of course, hearing alone is not a sufficient evidence of materiality. God is immaterial, and yet his voice was heard in John 12:28. Nevertheless, physical hearing connected with physical seeing *is* significant supportive evidence of the material nature of what was seen and heard. Mary's familiarity with Jesus' voice is evidence of the identity of the resurrected Christ.

Mary *touched* Christ's resurrection body. Jesus replied, "Do not hold on to me, for I have not yet returned to the Father" (vs. 17). The word "hold" (*aptomai*) is a normal word for physical touching of a material body. It too is used of physical touching of other human bodies (Matt. 8:3; 9:29) and of Christ's pre-resurrection body (Mark 6:56; Luke 6:19). The context indicates that Mary was grasping on to him so as not to lose him again. In a parallel experience the women "clasped his feet" (Matt. 28:9).

Mary "went to the tomb and saw that the stone had been removed from the entrance." So she ran to Peter and announced that the body was gone (vs. 2).

The parallel account in Matthew informs us that the angels said to her, "Come and see the place where he lay" (Matt. 28:6). Both texts imply that she saw that the tomb was empty. Later, Peter and John also went into the tomb. John "bent over and looked in at the strips of linen lying there" and Peter "went into the tomb. He saw the strips of linen lying there, as well as the *burial cloth* that had been around Jesus' head" (vss. 5–7). But seeing the same physical body that once laid there is proof of the numerical identity of the pre- and postresurrection body.

In this one account Jesus was seen, heard, and touched. In addition, Mary witnessed both the empty tomb and Jesus' grave clothes. All the evidence for an unmistakable identity of the same visible, physical body that was raised immortal are present in this first appearance.

To the Women (Matt. 28:1–10). Jesus not only appeared to Mary Magdalene but also to the other women with her (Matt. 28:1–10), including Mary the mother of James and Salome (Mark 16:1). During this appearance there were four evidences presented that Jesus rose in the same tangible, physical body in which he was crucified.

First, the women *saw* Jesus. They were told by the angel at the empty tomb, "He has risen from the dead and is going ahead of you into Galilee. There you will see him." And as they hurried away from the tomb, "suddenly Jesus met them. 'Greetings,' he said" (vs. 9). So they received visual confirmation of his physical resurrection.

Second, the women *clasped his feet* and worshiped him. That is, they not only saw his physical body but they felt it as well. Since spiritual entities cannot be sensed with any of the five senses, the fact that the women actually handled Jesus' physical body is a convincing proof of the tangible, physical nature of the resurrection body.

Third, the women also *heard* Jesus speak. After giving greetings (vs. 9), Jesus said to them, "Do not be afraid. Go and tell my brothers to go to Galilee; there they will see me" (vs. 10). Thus the women saw, touched, and heard Jesus with their physical senses, a three-fold confirmation of the physical nature of his body.

Fourth, the women *saw the empty tomb* where that body had lain. The angel said to them at the tomb, "He is not here; he has risen, just as he said. Come and see the place where he lay" (vs. 6). The "he" who had been dead is now alive, demonstrated by the fact that the same body that once lay there is now alive forevermore. So in both the case of Mary Magdalene and the other women, all four evidences of the visible, physical resurrection of the numerically identical body were present. They saw the empty tomb where his physical body once lay and they saw, heard and touched that same body after it came out of the tomb.

To Peter (1 Cor. 15:5; cf. John 20:3–9). First Corinthians 15:5 declares that Jesus "was seen of Cephas (Peter)." There is no narration of this event, but the text says he was *seen* (Gk. *ōphthē*) and implies that he was *heard* as well. Certainly Peter was not speechless. Jesus definitely spoke with Peter in a later appearance when he asked Peter to feed his sheep (John 21:15, 16, 17). Mark confirms that Peter (and the disciples) would *"see* him, just as he told you" (Mark 16:7). Peter, of course saw the *empty tomb* and the *grave clothes* just before this appearance (John 20:6–7). So Peter experienced at least three evidences of the physical resurrection; he saw and heard Jesus, and he observed the empty tomb and grave clothes. These are definite pieces of evidence that the body that rose is the same, visible, tangible, material body he had before the resurrection.

On the Emmaus Road (Mark 16:12; Luke 24:13–35). During this appearance three evidences of the physical resurrection were presented. They not only saw and heard Jesus but they also ate with Jesus. Combined they provide clear proof of the tangible, physical nature of the resurrection body.

There were two disciples, one of which was named Cleopas (vs. 18). As they were walking toward Emmaus, "Jesus himself came up and walked along with them" (vs. 16). At first they did not recognize who he was; they nevertheless clearly *saw* him. When they finally realized who it was, the text says "he disappeared out of their *sight"* (vs. 31). Jesus' resurrection body was as visible as any other material object.

They *heard* Jesus with their physical ears (vss. 17, 19, 25–26). In fact, Jesus carried on a lengthy conversation with them. For "beginning at Moses and all the Prophets, he explained to them what was said in all the Scriptures concerning himself" (vs. 27). Of course, they were not the only ones Jesus taught after the resurrection. Luke informs us elsewhere that "he appeared to them [the apostles] over a period of forty days and spoke about the kingdom of God" (Acts 1:3). During these times he "gave many convincing proofs that he was alive" (vs. 3).

They *ate* with him. Luke says, "when he was at the table with them, he took bread, gave thanks, broke it and began to give it to them" (vs. 30).

Although the text does not say specifically that Jesus also ate, it is implied by being "at table with them." And later in the chapter it is explicitly stated that he ate with the ten apostles (vs. 43). In two other places Luke states that Jesus did eat with the disciples (Acts 1:4; 10:41). So on this appearance of Christ the eyewitnesses saw him, heard him, and ate with him over a considerable period of time one evening. It is difficult to image how Jesus could have done anything more to demonstrate the physical nature of the resurrection body.

To the Ten (Luke 24:36–49; John 20:19–23). When Jesus appeared to ten disciples, Thomas being absent, he was seen, heard, touched, and they saw him eat fish. Thus four major evidences of the visible, physical nature of the resurrection body were present on this occasion.

"While they were still talking about this, Jesus himself stood among them and said to them, 'Peace be with you.'" In fact, Jesus carried on a conversation with them also about how "everything must be fulfilled that is written about me in the Law of Moses, the Prophets and the Psalms" (vs. 44). So Jesus was obviously *heard* by the disciples.

The disciples also *saw* Jesus on this occasion. In fact, they thought at first that he was a "spirit" (vs. 37). But Jesus *"showed* them his hands and his feet." So they clearly saw him as well as heard him. In the parallel account, John records that "the disciples were overjoyed when they *saw* the Lord" (John 20:20; cf. vs. 25).

It may be inferred from the fact that they were at first unconvinced of his tangible materiality when Jesus presented his wounds to them that they *touched* him as well. In fact, Jesus clearly said to them, "Touch me and see; a ghost does not have flesh and bones, as you see I have" (vs. 39). Jesus' use of "I" and "me" in connection with his physical resurrection body expresses his claim that he is numerically identical with his preresurrection body. Jesus also *"showed them his hands and feet,"* confirming to his disciples that his resurrection body was the very same nail-scared body of flesh and bones that was crucified.

On this occasion Jesus *ate* physical food to convince the disciples that he was resurrected in a literal, physical body. "They gave him a piece of broiled fish, and he took it and ate it in their presence" (vs. 43). What makes this passage such a powerful proof is that Jesus offered his ability to eat physical food as a proof of the material nature of his body of flesh and bones. Jesus literally exhausted the ways in which he could prove the corporeal, material nature of his resurrection body. Thus, if Jesus' resurrection body was not the same material body of flesh and bones in which he died, he was being deceptive.

To the Eleven (John 20:24–31). Thomas was not present when Jesus appeared to his disciples (John 20:24). Even after his fellow apostles reported who they had seen, Jesus, Thomas refused to believe unless he could see and touch Christ for himself. A week later his wish was granted: "A week later his disciples were in the house again, and Thomas was with them. Though the doors were locked, Jesus came and stood among them and said, 'Peace be with you!'" (John 20:26). When Jesus appeared to Thomas he saw, heard, and touched the resurrected Lord.

Thomas *saw* the Lord. Jesus was clearly visible to Thomas who later said to him, "you have *seen* me" (vs. 29).

Thomas also *heard* the Lord say, "Put your finger here; see my hands. Reach out your hand and put it into my side. Stop doubting and believe" (vs. 27). To this unquestionably convincing display of physical evidence Thomas replied, "My Lord and my God!" (vs. 28).

It can be inferred that Thomas also *touched* the Lord. Certainly this is what Thomas said he wanted to do (vs. 25). And Jesus told him to (vs. 27). Although the text only says Thomas saw and believed (vs. 29), it is natural to infer that he also touched Jesus. Jesus was touched on at least two other occasions (John 20:9, 17). So it may very well be that Thomas also touched him on this occasion also. At any rate, Thomas certainly encountered a visible, physical resurrection body with his natural senses. Whether Thomas touched Christ, he certainly *saw his crucifixion wounds* (John 20:27–29). The fact that Jesus still had these physical wounds from his crucifixion is an unmistakable proof that he was resurrected in the material body in which he was crucified. This was the second time that Jesus exhibited his wounds. It is difficult to imagine that he could have offered greater proof that the resurrection body is the same body of flesh that was crucified and now glorified.

To the Seven Disciples (John 21). John records Jesus' appearance to the seven disciples who went fishing in Galilee. During this appearance the disciples saw Jesus, heard him, and ate breakfast with him.

The Bible says that "Jesus *appeared* again to his disciples, by the Sea of Tiberias" (John 21:1). Early in the morning they saw him standing on the shore (vs. 4). After he talked and ate with them, the text says, "this is now the third time Jesus appeared to his disciples after he was raised from the dead" (vs. 14).

The disciples also *heard* Jesus speak (vss. 5, 6, 10, 12). Jesus carried on an extended conversation with Peter in which he was asked three times whether he loved Jesus (vss. 15, 16, 17). Since Peter had denied Jesus three times, not only did Peter hear Jesus speak but Jesus' words no doubt rang in his ears. Jesus also told Peter how he would die (vss. 18, 19).

Jesus apparently also *ate* with the disciples during this appearance. He asked them, "Friends, haven't you any fish?" (vs. 5). After telling them where to catch some (vs. 6), Jesus told them to "Bring some of the fish you have just caught" (vs. 10). Then he said to the disciples, "Come and have breakfast" (vs. 12). As they did, "Jesus came, took the bread and gave it to them, and did the same with the fish" (vs. 14). Although the text does not explicitly state that Jesus ate, nevertheless, as host of the meal it would have been noteworthy had he not. It is safe to say that, in addition to seeing and hearing Jesus, the disciples shared a physical meal with him.

To Commission Apostles (Matt. 28:16–20; Mark 16:14–18). The next appearance of Christ was at the Great Commission (Matt. 28:16–20). As Jesus commissioned them to disciple all nations, he was both seen and clearly heard by all the apostles.

The text says that the disciples went to Galilee where Jesus had told them to go (vs. 16). And "when they *saw* him, they worshiped him" (vs. 17). Mark adds that they were eating (Mark 16:14), although this version is in the questionably authentic final section of Mark. However, it was not simply what they saw but what they heard that left a lasting impression.

Jesus said, "All authority in heaven and earth has been given to me. Therefore go and make disciples of all nations, baptizing them in the name of the Father and of the Son and of the Holy Spirit" (Matt. 28:19). The fact that this small band shortly became the world's greatest missionary society is ample testimony for how powerfully what the apostles *heard* Jesus speak impressed them.

To Five Hundred (1 Cor. 15:6). There is no narration of this appearance. It is simply noted by Paul in 1 Corinthians 15:6 where he says: After that, he *appeared* to more than five hundred of the brothers at the same time, most of whom are still alive.

Since Jesus was *seen* on this occasion and since he left such a lasting impression on them, it can be assumed that they *heard* him speak. Why else would Paul imply their readiness to testify on behalf of the resurrection, saying in essence, "If you do not believe me, just go and ask them?"

Despite its brevity, this one verse is a powerful testimony to the bodily resurrection of Christ. It has the ring of truth about it. Paul is writing in 55 or 56, only twenty-two or twenty-three years after the resurrection (33). Most of these eye witnesses were still alive. And Paul challenges his reader to check out what he is saying with this multitude of witness who saw and probably heard Christ after his resurrection.

To James (1 Cor. 15:7). Jesus' brothers were unbelievers before his resurrection. The Gospel of John informs us that "even his own brothers did not believe in him" (John 7:5). But after his resurrection at least James and Jude, the half-brothers of Jesus, became believers (cf. Mark 6:3). However, the Scriptures say explicitly that Jesus "*appeared* to James" (1 Cor. 15:7). No doubt Jesus also *spoke* to James. At least as a result of his experience James became a pillar of the early church and played a prominent part in the first church council (Acts 15:13).

James also wrote one of the books of the New Testament in which he spoke of "the crown of life" (James 1:12) and of the "Lord's coming" (5:8) which was made possible only through the resurrection of Christ (2 Tim 1:10). So whatever James saw or heard during this resurrection appearance of Christ not only converted him but made him into a prominent figure in the apostolic church.

At the Ascension (Acts 1:4–8). Jesus' last appearance before his ascension was again to all the apostles. During this time they saw him, heard him, and ate with him. These three lines of evidence are the final confirmation of the literal, material nature of his resurrection body.

Jesus was *seen* by his apostles on this occasion. Luke says, "after his suffering, he *showed* himself to these men and gave many convincing proofs that he was alive" (Acts 1:3). He adds, Jesus *"appeared* to them over a period of forty days."

They also *heard* Jesus, since on this occasion he *"spoke* about the kingdom of God" (Acts 1:3). And during this specific appearance Jesus commanded them: "Do not leave Jerusalem, but wait for the gift my Father promised, which you have *heard* me speak about" (vs. 4). So it was not only a familiar voice but a familiar teaching that confirmed that this was the Jesus who had taught them before the crucifixion.

Luke also says in this passage that Jesus *ate* with the disciples, as he had done on many occasions. For this last appearance before the ascension was "on one occasion, while he was eating with them" (Acts 1:4). This is the fourth recorded instance of Jesus eating after the resurrection. It was apparently something he did rather often, since even the short summary of his ministry by Peter in Acts 10 declares that the apostles "ate and drank with him after he rose from the dead" (vs. 41). Surely, both the intimate fellowship and the physical ability to eat food was more than sufficient proof that Jesus was appearing in the same tangible, physical body he possessed before his resurrection.

To Paul (Acts 9:1–9; 1 Cor. 15:8). Jesus' last appearance was to Paul (see 1 Cor. 15:8). It is important to note that this appearance was no vision that occurred only within the mind of Paul. Rather, it was an objective, external event observable to all who were within visual distance.

- Paul called this an "appearance" (Gk. *ōphthē*), the same word used of Christ's literal appearances to the other apostles (1 Cor. 15:5–7). Indeed, Paul calls it the "last" appearance of Christ to the apostles.
- Seeing the resurrected Christ was a condition for being an apostle (Acts 1:22). Yet Paul claimed to be an apostle, saying, "Am I not an apostle? Have I not seen Jesus our Lord?" (1 Cor. 9:1).
- Visions are not accompanied by physical manifestations, such as light and a voice.

The resurrection experiences, including Paul's, are never called "visions" (*optasia*) anywhere in the Gospels or Epistles. During the appearance to Paul, Jesus was both seen and heard. The Gospels do speak of a "vision" of angels (Luke 24:23), and Acts refers to Paul's "heavenly vision" (Acts 26:19) which may be a reference to the vision(s) he and Ananias received later (Acts 9:11–12; cf. 22:8; 26:19). As for the actual appearance to Paul, Christ was both seen and heard with the physical senses of those present. In 1 Corinthians 15 Paul said Jesus "*appeared* to me also" (vs. 8). In the detailed account of it in Acts 26, Paul said "I *saw* a light from heaven" (vs. 13). That Paul is referring to a physical light is clear from the fact that it was so bright that it blinded the physical eyes (Acts 22:6, 8). Paul not only saw the light but he saw Jesus.

Paul also *heard* the voice of Jesus speaking distinctly to him "in Aramaic" (Acts 26:14). The physical voice Paul heard said, "Saul, Saul, why do you persecute me?" (Acts 9:4). Paul carried on a conversation with Jesus (vss. 5–6) and was obedient to the command to go into the city of Damascus (9:6). Paul's miraculous conversion, his tireless efforts for Christ, and his strong emphasis on the physical resurrection of Christ (Rom. 4:25; 10:9; 1 Corinthians 15) all show what an indelible impression the physical resurrection made upon him (*see* RESURRECTION, PHYSICAL NATURE OF).

Not only did Paul see the light and hear the voice but those who were with him did as well (Acts 22:8). This shows that the experience was not private to Paul. It was not purely subjective but had an objective referent. It happened "out there" in the real physical world, not merely in the world of his private spiritual experience. Anyone who had been there could also have seen and heard the physical manifestation.

A Summary of the Direct Evidence. The witness evidence for the physical resurrection of Christ is massive. Compared to the evidence for other events from the ancient world, it is overwhelming:

	Saw	Heard	Touched	Other Evidence
1. Mary Magdalene John 20:10–18	X	X	X	empty tomb
2. Mary /women Matt. 28:1–10	X	X	X	empty tomb
3. Peter 1 Cor. 15:5	X	X		empty tomb, clothes
4. Two disciples Luke 24:13–35	X	X		*ate with him
5. Ten disciples Luke 24:36–49; John 20:19–23	X	X	**X	saw wounds ate food
6. Eleven disciples John 20:24–31	X	X	**X	saw wounds
7. Seven disciples John 21	X	X		*ate food
8. All disciples —commissioning Matt. 28:16–20; Mark 16:14–18	X	X		
9. 500 brethren 1 Cor. 15:6	X	X		
10. James 1 Cor. 15:7	X	X		
11. All apostles —Ascension Acts 1:4–8	X	X		ate food
12. Paul Acts 9:1–9; 1 Cor. 15:8	X	X		

*Implied
**Offered himself to be touched

During the first eleven appearances alone Jesus appeared to more than 500 people over a forty-day period of time (Acts 1:3). On all twelve occasions Jesus was seen and probably heard. Four times he offered himself to be touched. He was definitely touched twice. Jesus revealed his crucifixion scars on two occasions. In four testimonies the empty tomb was seen, and twice the empty grave clothes were viewed. On another four occasions almost certainly Jesus ate food. The sum total of this evidence is overwhelming confirmation that Jesus arose and lived in the same visible, tangible, physical body of flesh and bones he had possessed before his resurrection body.

Indirect Evidence. In addition to all the direct evidence for the bodily resurrection of Christ, there are lines of corroboration. These include the immediate transformation of the men who became the apostles, the reaction of those who rejected Christ, the existence of the early church, and the immediate, amazingly rapid spread of Christianity.

The Transformed Disciples. After Jesus' death his apostles were scared, scattered, and skeptical. Only one, John, was at the crucifixion (John 19:26–27). The rest fled (Matt. 27:58). They also were skeptical. Mary, the first one to whom Jesus appeared, doubted, thinking she had seen a gardener (John 20:15). The disciples doubted the reports of the women (Luke 24:11). Some doubted until they saw Christ for themselves (John 20:25). One would not even believe when all the other apostles told them Christ had appeared to them. Two disciples on the road to Emmaus even doubted as they talked with Jesus, thinking he was a stranger (Luke 24:18).

A few weeks these very same men and women who had huddled in secret (John 20:19) were fearlessly and openly proclaiming the resurrection of Christ—even before the Sanhedrin that was responsible for Christ's death (Acts 4–5). The only thing that can account for this immediate and miraculous change is that they were absolutely convinced they had encountered the bodily resurrected Christ.

The Theme of Apostolic Preaching. Of all the wonderful things Jesus taught the disciples about love (Matt. 22:36–37), non-retaliation (Matthew 5), and the kingdom of God (cf. Matthew 13), the dominant theme of apostolic preaching was none of these themes. Above all else, they proclaimed the resurrection of Christ. It was the subject of Peter's first sermon at Pentecost (Acts 2:22–40) and his next sermon at the temple (Acts 3:14, 26). It was the content of his message before the Sanhedrin (Acts 4:10). Indeed, everywhere and "with great power the apostles gave witness to the resurrection of the Lord Jesus" (Acts 4:33; cf. 4:2). Being a witness to the resurrection was a condition for being an apostle (Acts 1:22; cf. 1 Cor. 9:1). The best explanation of why this theme was their immediate preoccupation within weeks of his death was that they had, as the Gospels tell us, repeatedly encountered him alive in the days after his crucifixion.

The Reaction of Those Who Rejected Christ. The reaction of the Jewish authorities is also testimony to the fact of Christ's resurrection. They did not produce the body, nor even organize a search. Instead, they bribed the soldiers who had guarded the tomb to lie (Matt. 28:11–15), and they *fought* the disciples who testified they had seen the body alive. The fact that they *resisted*, rather than *refuted*, the disciples' claims speaks for the reality of the resurrection.

The Existence of the Early Church. Another indirect proof of the resurrection is the very existence of the early church. There are good reasons why the church should not have been born:

The first church consisted largely of Jews who believed there was only one God (Deut. 6:4), and yet they proclaimed that Jesus was God (*see* CHRIST, DEITY OF). They prayed to Jesus (Acts 7:59), baptized in his name (Acts 2:38), claimed he was exalted to God's right hand (Acts 2:33; 7:55), and called him Lord and Christ (2:34–36), the very title which earned Jesus the charge of blasphemy from the Jewish High Priest at his trial (Matt. 26:63–65).

The first Christians had insufficient time to establish themselves before they were persecuted, beaten, threatened with death, and even martyred (Acts 7:57–60). Yet they not only maintained their belief but quickly grew in number. If what they testified to was not real, they had every reason and opportunity to give it up. But they did not. Only a real encounter with the resurrected Christ can adequately account for their existence as a Jewish sect that came to be known as Christians (Acts 11:26).

The Growth of Christianity. By contrast to other religions, like *Islam which grew slowly at first, Christianity experienced an immediate and rapid growth. Three thousand were saved the very first day (Acts 2:41). Many others were added to their ranks daily (Acts 2:47). Within days 2000 more became believers (Acts 4:4). The "number of the disciples was multiplying" so rapidly that deacons had to be appointed to care for the widows (Acts 6:1). Surely nothing other than the bodily resurrection of Christ and his sending of the Holy Spirit (Acts 1:8) can sufficiently account for this immediate and amazing growth.

Summary of the Evidence. Evidence for the resurrection of Christ is compelling. There are more documents, more eyewitnesses, and more corroborative evidence than for any other historical event of ancient history. The secondary, supplementary evidence is convincing; when combined with the direct evidence, it presents a towering case for the physical resurrection of Christ. In legal terminology, it is "beyond all reasonable doubt."

Objections to the Resurrection. Many objections have been leveled against the physical resurrection of Christ. Some claim that this would qualify as a miracle, and miracles are not believable (*see* MIRACLES, ARGUMENTS AGAINST). Others claim that the documents and witnesses recording these events were not reliable (*see* NEW TESTAMENT DOCUMENTS, RELIABILITY OF; NEW TESTAMENT, HISTORICITY OF). Still others have devised alternative theories opposing the resurrection (*see* CHRIST'S DEATH, SUBSTITUTION LEGEND; RESURRECTION, ALTERNATE THEORIES). But those who try to get around the resurrection walk against the gale-force winds of the full evidence. The facts are that Jesus of Nazareth really died (*see* CHRIST, DEATH OF) and actually came back from the dead in the same physical body.

Sources

W. Craig, *Knowing the Truth about the Resurrection*
N. L. Geisler, *The Battle for the Resurrection*
G. Habermas, *Ancient Evidence on the Life of Jesus*
———, *The Resurrection of Jesus: An Apologetic*
R. Kittel, *The Theological Dictionary of the New Testament*
T. Miethe, *Did Jesus Rise from the Dead? The Resurrection Debate*
J. W. Montgomery, *Christianity and History*
F. Morrison, *Who Moved the Stone?*

Resurrection, Objections to. Among standard objections raised against the physical resurrection of Christ, some aver that miracles in general, including the resurrection miracle, are not credible (*see* MIRACLES, ARGUMENTS AGAINST). These are specifically answered in the article Miracles, Arguments Against. Others insist that we cannot know the true happenings surrounding the death and resurrection of Christ because the New Testament documents are flawed. Regarding this uncertainty, see ACTS, HISTORICITY OF; ARCHAEOLOGY, NEW TESTAMENT; BIBLE CRITICISM; JESUS SEMINAR; NEW TESTAMENT MANUSCRIPS; and NEW TESTAMENT, HISTORICITY OF.

In the late twentieth century, two other objections have arisen. One is that the Gospel sequences of events cannot be harmonized. A second theory that has gained some following even in evangelical New Testament scholarship argues that the resurrection body of Christ was a spiritual, not a physical, body. Murray Harris was at the forefront of this view until he quietly modified his view. However, a number of other New Testament scholars, including George Ladd, held the same view. Because several facets of this view need to be considered, objections to the resurrection will be answered here, and the overall consideration of the resurrection body—Christ's and ours—is discussed at some length in RESURRECTION, PHYSICAL NATURE OF.

Harmony of the Accounts. It is often objected by critics that the resurrection record is self-contradictory. The order of events appears to differ among the accounts. For example, the Gospels list Mary of Magdala as the first to see Jesus after the resurrection (cf. Matt. 28:1f.), whereas 1 Corinthians 15:5 lists Peter as the first to see the resurrected Christ. Likewise, Matthew (28:2) lists "Mary Magdalene and the other Mary" as first at the tomb, whereas John (20:1) names only Mary Magdalene.

Closer scrutiny reveals that the descriptions are saying the same things from different perspectives; they do harmonize when closely compared.

There is a discernible overall order of postresurrection events in the New Testament accounts. The other events fit around this overall schema (*see* RESURRECTION, EVIDENCE FOR):

	Matt	Mark	Luke	John	Acts	1 Cor.
1. Mary Magdalene			X		X	
2. Mary /women	X	X				
3. Peter			X		X	
4. Two disciples		X	X			
5. Ten disciples			X	X		
6. Eleven disciples		X				
7. Seven disciples				X		
8. Commission of apostles	X		X		X	
9. 500 brethren					X	
10. James					X	
11. Ascension	X					
12. Paul					X	X

Earliest and most reliable manuscripts do not have Mark 16:9–20.

Peter saw the empty tomb; he did not immediately encounter Christ.

Other scholars (cf. Wenham, 139) reverse numbers 3 and 4 (but see Luke 24:34), and some combine 8 and 9. These differences are of no consequence in reconciling the events (*see* RESURRECTION OF CHRIST).

Some factors help in understanding why some writers approached the subject as they did:

- Paul in 1 Corinthians is summarizing the defense of the resurrection from a legal and official viewpoint, not giving a blow-by-blow account. Therefore, he presents an official list of witnesses, which would never have included women in a Greco-Roman setting like Corinth. A woman's testimony was not allowed in court.
- Christ's appearance to Paul was not listed in the Gospels, since Paul saw Christ years after the ascension (Acts 9; cf. 1 Cor. 15:7).
- As an apologist, Paul would highlight the impressive appearance to the 500 witnesses, most of whom were still alive when he wrote 1 Corinthians (ca. 55).
- Other appearances, as to James (1 Cor. 15:7) and on the road to Emmaus (Luke 24:13–34), fit as supplementary information. They do not come up in the harmonizing debate.

The Women's Story. Even the confusing events of the first morning involving the women are not too difficult to sort out (*see* RESURRECTION OF CHRIST).

Conflict in Independent Testimony. The fact that various accounts do not fit together with perfect ease should be expected of authentic testimony from independent witnesses. Were the accounts perfectly harmonious on the surface, there would be suspicion of collusion. That the events and order are described from differing perspectives that depend on personal involvement of the participants and some confusion of detail at an intense and bewildering moment is exactly what one would expect of credible accounts. Indeed, many legal minds, trained in sleuthing out false witnesses, have scrutinized the Gospel accounts and pronounced them credible. Simon Greenleaf, the Harvard law professor who wrote the standard study of legal evidence, counted his own conversion to Christianity from his careful examination of the Gospel witnesses. He concluded that "copies which had been as universally received and acted upon as the Four Gospels, would have been received in evidence in any court of justice, without the slightest hesitation" (Greenleaf, 9–10).

The Essentially Physical Nature of the Resurrection Body. Several passages are used by critics to argue that Jesus' resurrection body was not continuously and essentially physical (Harris, *From Grave to Glory*, 373). However, none state that Jesus' body was ever nonphysical.

Paul and the "Spiritual Body." Proponents of the view that the postresurrection body is immaterial cite 1 Corinthians 15:44. Paul refers to the resurrection body as a "spiritual body," in contrast to the preresurrection "natural body" (1 Cor. 15:44). But a study of the context does not support this conclusion.

A "spiritual" body denotes an immortal one, not an immaterial one. A "spiritual" body is one dominated by the spirit, not one devoid of matter. The Greek word *pneumatikos* (translated "spiritual" here) means a body directed by the spirit, as opposed to one under the dominion of the flesh. It is not ruled by flesh that perishes but by the spirit that endures (vss. 50–58) So "spiritual body" here does not mean immaterial and invisible but immortal and imperishable.

"Spiritual" also denotes a supernatural body, not a nonphysical one. The resurrection body Paul refers to is supernatural. The series of contrasts used by Paul in this passage reveals that the resurrection body was a supernatural body. Notice the parallels:

Preresurrection Body—Earthly	Postresurrection Body—Heavenly
perishable (vs. 42)	imperishable
weak (vs. 43)	powerful
mortal (vs. 53)	immortal
natural (vs. 44)	[supernatural]

The complete context indicates that "spiritual" (*pneumatikos*) could be translated "supernatural" in contrast to "natural." This is made clear by the parallels of perishable and imperishable, corruptible and incorruptible. In fact, *pneumatikos* is translated "supernatural" in 1 Corinthians 10:4 when it speaks of the "supernatural rock that followed them in the wilderness" (RSV). The *Greek-English Lexicon of the New Testament* explains, "That which belongs to the supernatural order of being is described as *pneumatikos:* accordingly, the resurrection body is a *sōma pneumatikos* [supernatural body]."

"Spiritual" refers to physical objects. A study of Paul's use of the same word in other passages reveals that it does not refer to something that is purely immaterial. First, Paul spoke of the "spiritual rock" that followed Israel in the wilderness, from which they got "spiritual drink" (1 Cor. 10:4). But the Old Testament story (Exodus 17; Numbers 20) reveals that it was a physical rock from which they got literal water to drink. But the actual water they drank from that material rock was produced supernaturally. Hence, the Revised Standard Version properly translates it as follows: "All ate the same supernatural food and all drank the same supernatural drink. For they drank from the supernatural Rock which followed them, and the Rock was Christ" (1 Cor. 10:3–4).

That is to say, the supernatural Christ was the source of these supernatural manifestations of natural food and water. But just because the physical provisions came from a spiritual (i.e., supernatural) source did not make them immaterial. When Jesus supernaturally made bread for the 5000 (John 6), he made literal bread. However, this literal, material bread could have been called "spiritual" bread because of its supernatural source. In the same way, the literal manna given to Israel is called "spiritual food" (1 Cor. 10:4).

Further, when Paul spoke about a "spiritual man" (1 Cor. 2:15) he obviously did not mean an invisible, immaterial man with no corporeal body. He was speaking of a flesh-and-blood human being whose life was lived by the supernatural power of God. He was referring to a literal person whose life had spiritual direction. A spiritual man or woman is one who is "taught by the Spirit" and who "accepts the things that come from the Spirit of God" (1 Cor. 2:13–14). The resurrection body can be called a "spiritual body" in much the same way we speak of the Bible as a "spiritual book." Regardless of the spiritual source and power, both the resurrection body and the Bible are material objects.

The New International Dictionary of New Testament Theology says that *spiritual* is used "in contrast to the *merely* material or to those activities, and attitudes that derive from the flesh and draw their significance from the *merely* physical, human and worldly" (Brown, 3.707). So "spiritual" does not mean something purely immaterial or intangible. The spiritual man, like the spiritual rock and spiritual food, was a physical being that received spiritual or supernatural help.

Christ's Ability to Appear. It is argued that the resurrection body was essentially invisible and, therefore, not an object observable in our history. The New Testament says that it could "appear"

(Harris, *Raised Immortal*, 46–47). Therefore, it must have been invisible before it appeared (see Luke 24:34; Acts 9:17; 13:31; 26:16; 1 Cor. 15:5–8). Each of these times it says, "he appeared" or "he let himself be seen" (in the Greek's aorist passive). Grammatically, the action rests on the one who appears, not on the one who sees him appear. This, it is argued, implies that Jesus took the initiative to make himself visible at his resurrection appearances.

However, Christ's resurrection body could be seen with the eye. Appearance accounts use the word *horaō* ("to see"). Although this word is sometimes used of seeing invisible realities (cf. Luke 1:22; 24:23), it often means to see by the eye. The usual word meaning "vision" is *orama*, not *horaō* (see Matt. 17:9; Acts 9:10; 16:9). In the New Testament a vision usually, if not always, refers to something that is essentially invisible, such as, God or angels. For example, John uses *horaō* of seeing Jesus in his earthly body before the resurrection (6:36; 14:9; 19:35) and also of seeing him in his resurrection body (20:18, 25, 29). Since the same word for *body* (*sōma*) is used of Jesus before and after the resurrection (cf. 1 Cor. 15:44; Phil. 3:21), and since the same word for its appearing (*horaō*) is used of both, there is no reason to believe the resurrection body is not the same physical body now immortal.

Even the phrase "he let himself be seen" (aorist passive, *ōphthē*), simply means that Jesus took the initiative to disclose himself, not that he was essentially invisible until he did so. The same form ("He/they appeared") is used in the Greek Old Testament (2 Chron. 25:21), in the Apocrypha (1 Macc. 4:6), and in the New Testament (Acts 7:26) of human beings appearing in physical bodies (Hatch, 2.105–7). In further references *ōphthē* is used of ocular vision.

In its passive form *ōphthē* means "to initiate an appearance for public view, to move from a place where one is not seen to a place where one is seen." It does not mean that what is by nature invisible becomes visible. When the expression "he let himself be seen" (*ōphthē*) is used of God or angels (cf. Luke 1:11; Acts 7:2), who are invisible realities, then *in that context* it refers to an invisible entity becoming visible. But since the same expression is used of other humans with physical bodies and since Christ is said to have had a body (*sōma*), there is no reason to take the expression to refer to anything but a literal, physical body, unless the context demands otherwise. To say otherwise contradicts the emphatic declaration of John that the body of Jesus, even after the resurrection (when John wrote) was continuously physical (1 John 4:2; 2 John 7).

The same event that is described by "he appeared" or "let himself be seen" (aorist passive), such as the appearance of Christ to Paul (1 Cor. 15:8), is also found in the active mood. Paul wrote of this experience in the same book, "Have I not seen Jesus our Lord?" (1 Cor. 9:1). But if the resurrection body can be seen by the eye, then it is not invisible until it makes itself visible by some kind of "materialization."

Christ's "appearances" were natural. The word "appeared" (*ōphthē*) refers to a natural event. Arndt and Gingrich's *Greek-English Lexicon of the New Testament* points out that the word is used "of persons who appear in a natural way." *The Theological Dictionary of the New Testament* notes that appearances "occur in a reality which can be perceived by the natural senses." In his *Linguistic Key to the New Testament*, Fritz Rienecker notes that *appeared* means "He could be seen by human eyes, the appearances were not just visions" (Rienecker, 439).

This is not to neglect texts which at least may be interpreted to suggest a miraculous appearance or disappearance. Christ was God and did work miracles. So a distinction must be drawn between Christ's essential resurrection body and the power of Christ as God incarnate. *That* Jesus could be seen was not a miracle, but the *way* in which he appeared was miraculous. The texts are simply ambiguous about what these sudden appearances involved, and some believe Jesus came and went quickly in a normal human manner. But there is a strong suggestion that he appeared *suddenly*. And the texts also speak of sudden disappearances. Luke writes of the two disciples on the road to Emmaus, "Then their eyes were opened and they recognized him, and he disappeared from their sight" (Luke 24:31; cf. Luke 24:51; Acts 1:9). This would indicate an act of power, a sign of his identity.

The text nowhere states that Jesus became nonphysical when the disciples could no longer see him. Just because he was out of their sight does not mean he was out of his physical body. God has the power to miraculously transport persons in their preresurrection physical bodies from one place to another. Although the precise meaning of the text is unclear, it would seem that this happened to Philip the evangelist when he was "caught up by the spirit" to journey to a city miles away (Acts 8).

The writers may stress Christ's self-initiated "appearances" precisely because of their apologetic value as signs. The appearances proved that he had conquered death (Acts 13:30–31; 17:31; Rom. 1:4; cf. John 10:18; Rev. 1:18). The translation, "He let himself be seen," is a perfectly fitting expression of self-initiated triumph. Christ was sovereign over death and in his resurrection appearances.

The reason for the stress on the many appearances of Christ is not because the resurrection body was essentially invisible and immaterial, but rather it was material and immortal. Without an empty tomb and repeated appearances of the same body that was once buried in it raised immortal, there would be no proof of the resurrection. So it is not surprising at all that the Bible strongly stresses the many appearances of Christ. They are the real proof of the physical resurrection.

Resurrection Appearances as "Visions." The contention that resurrection appearances are called "visions" is also used to support the nonphysical view of the resurrection body. Luke records that women at the tomb "had seen a vision of angels, who said he was alive" (Luke 24:23). But visions are always of invisible, unseen realities, not of physical, material objects. The miracle is that these spiritual realities can be seen. Hence. it is argued that a spiritual body is angel-like and, therefore, cannot be seen. Some point to the fact that those who were with Paul during his Damascus road experience did not see Christ (Pannenberg, 93). Hence, the experience of the resurrected Christ is called a vision. But this reasoning is flawed.

Luke 24:23 does not say that seeing the resurrected Christ was a vision; it refers only to the vision of seeing angels at the tomb. The Gospels never refer to a resurrection appearance of Christ as a vision, nor does Paul in his list in 1 Corinthians 15. The only possible reference to a resurrection appearance as a vision is in Acts 26:19 where Paul says: "I was not disobedient to the heavenly vision." But even if this is a reference to the Damascus appearance of Christ, it is merely an overlap in usage of the words. For Paul clearly calls this event an "appearance" (1 Cor. 15:8) in which he saw Jesus and was given apostolic credentials (1 Cor. 9:1; cf. Acts 1:22).

It is possible that even in Acts 26:19 the word "vision" refers to the subsequent revelation to Ananias, through whom God gave Paul's commission to minister to the Gentiles (Acts 9:10–19). Paul says nothing about seeing the Lord, as he does when referring to his Damascus experience (cf. Acts 22:8; 26:15). When having a "vision" (*optasia*), Paul clearly designates it as such (2 Cor. 12:1), in distinction from a real appearance.

Most significant, however, is that when Paul referred to the vision he was not relaying the content of the experience on the road but what he learned later. Paul did not received his specific missionary mandate immediately (Acts 9:1–9). Rather, he was told "to go into the city, and you will be told what you must do" (vs. 5). It was there in the city through a "vision" (vs. 10) to Ananias that Paul was given his missionary mandate "to carry my [Christ's] name before the Gentiles" (9:15). Paul may have had a supplementary vision to that of Ananias while "praying in the house of Judas on Strait Street in Damascus" (Acts 9:11, 12). It was here that he was told specifically that Ananias would lay hands on him (vs. 12). So when Paul said "I was not disobedient to the heavenly vision" in Acts 26:19, it was probably to the mandate through Ananias's vision that he refers.

The word *vision* (*optasia*) is never used of a resurrection appearance anywhere else in the New Testament. It is always used of a purely visionary experience (Luke 1:22; 24:23; 2 Cor. 12:1). Whatever the case, the *Theological Dictionary of the New Testament* correctly notes that the New Testament distinguishes visions from the Damascus experience.

Appearances differ from visions. The postresurrection encounters with Christ are usually described as literal "appearances" (1 Cor. 15:5–8), and never as visions. The difference between a mere vision and a physical appearance is significant. Visions are of invisible, spiritual realities, such as God and angels. Appearances are of physical objects that can be seen with the naked eye. Visions have no physical manifestations associated with them; appearances do.

People sometimes "see" or "hear" things in visions (Luke 1:11–20; Acts 10:9–16) but not with their physical eyes. When someone truly saw or had physical contact with angels (Gen. 18:8; 32:24; Dan. 8:18), it was not a vision but an appearance of the angel in the physical world. During these appearances the angels assumed a visible form, then returned to their normal invisible state. However, the resurrection appearances of Christ were experiences of seeing Christ in his continued visible, physical form with the natural eye.

The contention that Paul's experience must have been a vision because those with him did not see Christ also is unfounded. Paul's companions on the way to Damascus did not see or understand everything, but they did share in the sound and light phenomena. The Bible says, "they heard the sound" (Acts 9:7) and "saw the light" (Acts 22:9). They heard, but did not understand, the meaning of what was said. That they "did not see anyone" (Acts 9:7) is not surprising. Paul was physically blinded by the brightness of the light (Acts 9:8–9). Apparently only Paul looked straight into the blaze of divine glory. Hence, only he actually saw Christ, and only he was literally stricken blind by it (cf. Acts 22:11; 26:13). But it was, nonetheless, an experience of a real physical reality, for those who were with Paul also saw and heard it with their natural eyes and ears.

Appearances Only for Believers. It is argued that Jesus' sovereignty over his appearances indicates that he was essentially invisible, making himself visible only when he wished to do so. In this connection they note that Jesus did not appear to unbelievers, supposedly indicating that he was not naturally visible.

But Scripture never says Jesus did not appear to unbelievers. He appeared to his unbelieving brother (1 Cor. 15:7; James), and Matthew 28:17 indicates that not all believed who saw him. He appeared to the most hostile unbeliever of all, Saul of Tarsus (Acts 9). As far as his resurrection is concerned, even his disciples were at first unbelievers. When Mary Magdalene and others reported that Jesus was resurrected "they did not believe the women, because their words seemed to them like nonsense" (Luke 24:11). Later Jesus had to chide the two disciples on the road to Emmaus about disbelief in his resurrection, "How foolish you are, and how slow to believe all that the prophets have spoken!" (Luke 24:17). Even after Jesus had appeared to the women, to Peter, to the two disciples and to the ten apostles, still Thomas said, "Unless I see the nail marks in his hands and put my finger where the nails were, and put my hand into his side, I will not believe it" (John 20:25).

Selectivity does not prove invisibility. The fact that Jesus was selective about those he wanted to see him does not indicate that he was essentially invisible. Jesus was also in control of those who wanted to lay hands on him before the resurrection. On one occasion an unbelieving crowd tried to take Jesus and "throw him down a cliff. But he walked right through the crowd and went on his way" (Luke 4:30; cf. John 8:59; 10:39).

Jesus was also selective about those for whom he performed miracles. He refused to perform miracles in his own home area "because of their lack of faith" (Matt. 13:58). Jesus even disappointed Herod, who had hoped to see him perform a miracle (Luke 23:8). The truth is that Jesus refused "to cast pearls before swine" (Matt. 7:6). In submission to the Father's will (John 5:30) he was sovereign over his activity both before and after his resurrection. But this in no way proves that he was essentially invisible and immaterial either before or after his resurrection.

Passing Through Closed Doors. It is inferred by some that, since the resurrected Christ could appear in a room with closed doors (John 20:19, 26), his body must have been essentially immaterial. Others suggest that he dematerialized on this occasion. But these conclusions are not warranted.

The text does not actually say Jesus passed through a closed door. It simply says that "when the disciples were together with closed doors for fear of the Jews, Jesus came and stood among them" (John 20:19). The text does not say how he got into the room. Since the text does not explicitly say how Jesus got in behind closed doors, any suggestion is only speculation. We do know that angels used their special powers to unlock prison doors to release Peter (Acts 12:10). The supernatural Christ certainly possessed this power. Although physical, the resurrection body is by its very nature a supernatural body. Hence, it should be expected that it can do supernatural things like appearing in a room with closed doors.

If he chose to do so, Jesus could have performed this same feat before his resurrection with his physical body. As the Son of God, his miraculous powers were just as great before the resurrection. Even before his resurrection Jesus performed miracles with his physical body that transcended natural laws, such as walking on water (John 6:16–20). But walking on water did not prove that his preresurrection body was not physical or even that it could dematerialize.

According to modern physics it is not impossible for a material object to pass through a door. It is only statistically improbable. Physical objects are mostly empty space. All that is necessary for one physical object to pass through another is for the right alignment of the particles in the two physical objects. This is no problem for the One who created the body to begin with.

The Decaying Physical Body. Another argument given in favor of an immaterial resurrection body is that a physical resurrection body would imply "a crassly materialistic view of resurrection according to which the scattered fragments of decomposed corpses were to be reassembled" (Harris, *Raised Immortal*, 126).

It is unnecessary to the orthodox view to believe that the same particles will be restored in the resurrection body. Even common sense dictates that a body can be the same physical body without having the same physical particles. The observable fact that bodies eat food and give off waste products, as well as get fatter and skinnier, is sufficient evidence of this. Certainly, we do not say a body is not material or not the same body because someone loses ten pounds—or even fifty.

If necessary it would be no problem for an omnipotent God to bring all of the exact particles of one's body together again at the resurrection. Certainly he who created every particle in the universe could reconstitute the relatively few particles in a human body. The God who created the world out of *nothing* is surely able to fashion a resurrection body out of *something*. But, as already noted, this is not necessary, for the resurrection body does not need the same particles in order to be the same body.

In the light of modern science it is unnecessary to believe that God will reconstitute the exact particles one had from the preresurrection body. For the physical body remains physical and retains its genetic identity, even though the exact physical molecules in it change every seven years or so. The resurrection body can be just as material as our present bodies and still have new molecules in it.

Unlike our bodies, Jesus' body did not become corrupted while in the tomb. Quoting the psalmist, Peter said emphatically of Jesus, "he was not abandoned to the grave, nor did his body decay" (Acts 2:31). Paul adds by contrast that the prophet could not have spoken about David since "his body decayed" (Acts 13:36). So in Jesus' case most (if not all) of the material particles in his preresurrection body were in his resurrection body. Some say there may have been some dissolution involved in Jesus' body, since death itself involves some breaking down of organic molecules. Then again, this may apply only to mortal humans. In any event there was no *eventual* dissolution, since his resurrection reversed the process of decay (Schep, 139).

The Body Destroyed. Paul said, "'Food for the stomach and the stomach for food'—but God will destroy them both" (1 Cor. 6:13). From this text some have argued that "the resurrection body will not have the anatomy or physiology of the earthly body" (Harris, *Raised Immortal*, 124). However, this inference is unjustified.

Study of the context here reveals that when Paul says God will destroy both food and the stomach he is referring to the *process* of death, not to the *nature* of the resurrection body. For he refers to the process of death by which "God will destroy them both" (vs. 13).

As already noted, while the resurrection body may not have the necessity to eat, it does have the ability to eat. Eating in heaven will be a joy without being a need. Jesus ate at least four times in his resurrection body (Luke 24:30, 42; John 21:12; Acts 1:4). Hence, his resurrected body was capable of assimilating physical food. To argue that there will be no resurrection body because the stomach will be "destroyed" is tantamount to claiming that the rest of the body—head, arms, legs, and torso—will not be resurrected because death will also turn them into dust.

"Flesh and Blood" and the Kingdom. Paul said "flesh and blood cannot inherit the kingdom of God" (1 Cor. 15:50). As early as the second century Irenaeus noted that this passage was used by heretics in support of their "very great error" (Irenaeus, 30.13), that the resurrection body will not be a body of physical flesh.

The very next phrase omitted from 1 Corinthians 15:50 shows clearly that Paul is speaking not of flesh as such but of corruptible flesh, for he adds, "nor does the perishable inherit the imperishable." So Paul is not affirming that the resurrection body will not have flesh; rather it will not have *perishable* flesh.

In order to convince the frightened disciples he was not an immaterial spirit (Luke 24:37), Jesus emphatically told them that his resurrection body had flesh. He declared: "Look at my hands and my feet. It is I myself! Touch me and see; a ghost does not have flesh and bones, as you see I have" (Luke 24:39).

Peter said that Jesus' resurrection body is the same body of flesh, now immortal, that went into the tomb and never saw corruption (Acts 2:31). Paul reaffirmed this truth in Acts 13:35. And John implies that it is against Christ to deny that he remains "in the *flesh*" even after his resurrection (1 John 4:2; 2 John 7).

This conclusion cannot be avoided by claiming that Jesus' resurrection body had flesh and bones but not flesh and blood. For if it had flesh and bones, then it was a literal, material body, whether or not it had blood. Flesh and bones stress the solidity of Jesus' physical post-resurrection body. They are more obvious signs of tangibility than blood, which cannot be as easily seen or touched.

The phrase "flesh and blood" in this context apparently means *mortal* flesh and blood, that is, a mere human being. This is supported by parallel uses in the New Testament. When Jesus said to Peter, "Flesh and blood has not revealed this to you" (Matt. 16:17), he could not have been referring to the mere substances of the body. Obviously those could not reveal that he was the Son of God. Rather, as J. A. Schep concludes, "the only correct and natural interpretation [of 1 Cor. 15:50] seems to be that *man, as he now is, a frail, earth-bound, perishable creature,* cannot have a place in God's glorious, heavenly kingdom" (Schep, 204).

Biblical scholar Joachim Jeremias observes that a misunderstanding of this text "has played a disastrous role in the New Testament theology of the last sixty years." After careful exegesis of the passage, he concludes that the sentence "flesh and blood cannot inherit the kingdom of God" refers not to the resurrection, but to the changes that will take place in the living at Christ's coming (Jeremias, 154).

Resurrection and Resuscitation. Jesus' resurrection was more than the resuscitation of a physical corpse, argue those who say the resurrection was spiritual. But this is insufficient grounds to deny the physical nature of the resurrection body. Jesus' resurrection assuredly was more than a resuscitation, but it was not less than one. Resuscitated corpses die again, but Jesus' resurrection body was immortal. He conquered death (1 Cor. 15:54–55; Heb. 2:14), whereas merely resuscitated bodies will eventually be conquered by death. For example, Jesus raised Lazarus from the dead (John 11), but Lazarus eventually died again. Jesus was the first to be raised in an immortal body, one that will never die again (1 Cor. 15:20). However, simply because Jesus was the first to be raised in an immortal body does not mean it was an immaterial body. It was more than a reanimation of a physical corpse, but it was not less than that.

It does not follow that, because Jesus' resurrection body could not die, therefore, it could not be seen. What is immortal is not necessarily invisible. The recreated physical universe will last forever (Rev. 21:1–4), yet it will be visible. Here again, the resurrection body differs from resuscitation, not because it is immaterial but because it is immortal (1 Cor. 15:42, 53).

Jesus' "Different Form." Harris wrote, "We cannot rule out the possibility that the visible form of Jesus had been altered in some mysterious way, delaying recognition of him." This suggests that "the expression 'he appeared in another form' in the Marcan appendix (Mark 16:12) encapsulates this" (Harris, *From Grave to Glory*, 56). However, this conclusion is unnecessary.

There are serious questions about the authenticity of this text. Mark 16:9–20 is not found in some of the oldest and best manuscripts. And in reconstructing the original texts from the existing manuscripts, many scholars believe that the older texts are more reliable.

Even granting its authenticity, the event of which it is a summary (cf. Luke 24:13–32) says simply "they were kept from recognizing him" (Luke 24:16). This makes it clear that the miraculous element was not in Jesus' body but *in the eyes of the disciples* (Luke 24:16, 31). Recognition of Jesus was kept from them until their eyes were opened. At best it is an obscure and isolated reference upon which it is unwise to base any significant doctrinal pronouncement. Whatever *another form* means, it certainly does not mean a form other than a real physical body. On this very occasion Jesus ate physical food (Luke 24:30). Later in Luke 24 he said that his ability to eat was a proof that he was not an immaterial spirit (vss. 38–43).

One authority on the meaning of New Testament Greek says that *another form* simply means that, just as Jesus appeared in the form of a gardener to Mary, so here, he appeared in the form of a traveler (Friedrich, *Theological Dictionary*).

Raised "In the Spirit" (1 Pet. 3:18). According to Peter, Jesus was "put to death in the flesh, but made alive in the spirit" (KJV). This has been taken to prove that the resurrection body was "spirit" or immaterial. This interpretation, however, is neither necessary nor consistent with the context of this passage and the rest of Scripture.

The passage can be translated "He was put to death in the body but made alive by the [Holy] Spirit" (NIV). The passage is translated with this same understanding by the New King James Version and others. The parallel between death and being made alive normally refers in the New Testament to the resurrection of the body. For example, Paul declared that "Christ died and returned to life" (Rom. 14:9) and "He was crucified in weakness, yet he lives by God's power" (2 Cor. 13:4).

Even if *spirit* refers to Jesus' human spirit, not to the Holy Spirit, it cannot mean Jesus had no resurrection body. Otherwise, the reference to his "body" (flesh) before the resurrection would mean he had no human spirit then. It seems better to take *flesh* in this context as a reference to his whole condition of humiliation before the resurrection and *spirit* to refer to his unlimited power and imperishable life after the resurrection (Schep, 77).

Like Angels in the Resurrection. Jesus said that in the resurrection we "will be like the angels" (Matt. 22:30). But angels have no physical bodies; they are spirits (Heb. 1:14). Thus, it is argued, we will have no physical resurrection bodies.

This misinterprets the passage. The context is not the nature of the resurrection body but whether there will be marriage in heaven. Jesus' reply was that there will no more be human marriages than there are angelic ones. Jesus said nothing here about having immaterial bodies. He did not say they would be like angels in that humans would be immaterial but because they will be immortal (cf. Luke 20:36).

A Life-Giving Spirit. According to 1 Corinthians 15:45 Christ was made a "life-giving spirit" after his resurrection. This passage is used to prove that Jesus had no physical resurrection body.

Life-giving spirit does not speak of the *nature* of the resurrection body, but of the divine *origin* of the resurrection. Jesus' physical body came back to life only by the power of God (cf. Rom. 1:4). So Paul is speaking about its spiritual *source*, not its physical *substance* as a material body.

If *spirit* describes the nature of Christ's resurrection body, then Adam (with whom he is contrasted) must not have had a soul, since he is described as "of the dust of the earth" (vs. 47). But the Bible says clearly that Adam was "a living being [soul]" (Gen. 2:7).

Christ's resurrection body is called a "spiritual body" (vs. 44). We have seen that Paul uses this terminology to describe material food and a literal rock (1 Cor. 10:4). It is called a "body" (*sōma*), which always means a physical body in the context of an individual human being (Gundry, 168).

The resurrection body is called "spiritual" and a "life-giving spirit" because its source is the spiritual realm, not because its substance is immaterial. Christ's supernatural resurrection body is "from heaven," as Adam's natural body was "of the earth" (vs. 47). But just as the one from "earth" also has an immaterial soul, so the One from "heaven" has a material body.

What We Shall Be. First John 3:2 has been used to argue that the resurrection body will differ from a physical body. John said, "Dear friends, now we are children of God, and what we will be has not yet been made known. But we know that when he appears, we shall be like him, for we shall see him as he is" (1 John 3:2).

When John speaks of not knowing what we shall be he is referring to our *status* in heaven, not the *nature* of the resurrection body. For he is contrasting it with our status now as "sons of God," claiming he does not know what higher status we may have in heaven. He does know that we shall be like Christ. Paul said the same thing in Philippians 3:21: God will use his power to "transform our lowly bodies so that they will be like his glorious body [*sōma*]" (Phil. 3:21).

Also in 1 John the apostle affirms that Jesus now has a body of "flesh" (*sarx*) in heaven. "Every spirit that acknowledges that Jesus Christ has come in the flesh is from God" (1 John 4:2). The use of the perfect tense ("has come") indicates past action with continuing results in the present. That is, Jesus came in the past in the flesh and he is still in the flesh after the resurrection. The same is affirmed in the present tense in 2 John 7. Jesus is in the flesh in heaven.

Indeed, Jesus will return in the same physical body in which he left (Acts 1:10–11), physical scars and all (Rev. 1:7).

Confusion Regarding Christ's Body. There are two common areas of confusion in the use of biblical material to prove that Jesus did not rise in an essentially physical body. One is that the resurrection body's *attributes* are confused with its *activities*. In none of the clear passages about the physical nature of the resurrection body is it stated that Jesus ceased to have a physical body at any point (Harris, *From Grave to Glory*, 390). None of these verses even addresses *what* the resurrection body *is*. At issue is what it can *do*. For example, it can pass through solid objects, suddenly appear, or suddenly disappear. But the fact that Jesus' body could pass through a solid object no more proves it was immaterial than his walking on water proves his feet were made of balsa wood.

A second blunder is to assume that, because some passages speak of Jesus as *unseen* by the disciples at certain times, he was therefore *invisible* during these periods. However, this is a confusion of *perception* and *reality*. It fails to distinguish *epistemology* (the study of what we know) from *metaphysics* (the study of what really is). Common sense informs us that, even if we cannot see something, it may not be invisible and immaterial. The summit of Mount McKinley is hidden in clouds most of the time, but it still is material all of the time.

Conclusion. The evidence for the physical resurrection is compelling, and its importance to Christianity can scarcely be overestimated.

The New Testament passes the criteria for credibility. There is every reason to accept the authenticity of the New Testament accounts, with all their supposed disorder (*see* New Testament, Historicity of). Six accounts of the post resurrection appearances, Matthew 28; Mark 16; Luke 24; John 20–21; Acts, 9; and 1 Corinthians 15, cover a forty-day period in which Jesus was seen alive by more than 500 persons on eleven occasions. Given that some of these witnesses saw the empty tomb and grave clothes, touched Jesus' scars, and saw him eat, there is no reasonable doubt about the reality of his resurrection.

There is no biblical basis for believing that Jesus was not raised in the same physical body of "flesh and bones" in which he died. There is no indication in any New Testament text that our bodies or Jesus' body will be anything less than physical in heaven. As biblical scholar Joachim Jeremias put it: "look at the transfiguration of the Lord on the mountain of transfiguration, then you will have the answer to the question how we shall imagine the event of the resurrection" (Jeremias, 157). Jesus' material body was manifested in its glory. Similarly, his resurrection body will do the same.

All the arguments used to show that Jesus was raised in a numerically different, invisible, immaterial body are unbiblical and unconvincing. To be sure, the resurrection body was imperishable and immortal, but the contention that it was not visible and material is unfounded. At best it is a speculative inference from isolated references using questionable interpretations. Often, arguments against the material resurrection are clear misinterpretations of the text. They always run contrary to the overwhelming evidence that the resurrection body was the real physical body of "flesh and bones" Jesus said it was (in Luke 24:39).

Historic Christianity stands or falls on the historicity, tangibility, and materiality of the bodily resurrection of Christ (1 Cor. 15:12f.; Luke 24:37).

Sources

W. F. Arndt and F. W. Gingrich, *A Greek-English Lexicon of the New Testament*

C. Brown, *The New International Dictionary of New Testament Theology*

W. Craig, *Knowing the Truth about the Resurrection*

G. Friedrich, *The Theological Dictionary of the New Testament*

N. L. Geisler, *The Battle for the Resurrection*

———, *In Defense of the Resurrection*

——— and W. E. Nix, *General Introduction to the Bible: Revised and Expanded*

S. Greenleaf, *The Testimony of the Evangelists*

R. Gundry, *Sōma in Biblical Theology with Emphasis on Pauline Anthropology*

G. Habermas, *The Resurrection of Jesus: An Apologetic*

———, *Ancient Evidence on the Life of Jesus*

M. Harris, *From Grave to Glory*

———, *Raised Immortal*

E. Hatch and H. Redpath, *A Concordance to the Septuagint and Other Greek Versions of the Old Testament*

Irenaeus, *Against Heresies*, in A. Roberts, et al., eds., *The Ante-Nicene Fathers*, vol. 1

J. Jeremias, "Flesh and Blood Cannot Inherit the Kingdom of God," in *New Testament Studies II* (1955–56)

W. Pannenberg, *Jesus—God and Man*

F. Rienecker, *A Linguistic Key to the Greek New Testament*

A. T. Robertson, *Harmony of the Gospels*

J. A. Schep, *The Nature of the Resurrection Body*

J. Wenham, *Easter Enigma*

Resurrection, Physical Nature of. Even some who acknowledge that Jesus' body mysteriously vanished from the tomb and that he appeared in bodily form on several occasions thereafter deny the essential physical nature of the resurrection body. That is, they deny the orthodox belief that

Jesus was raised in the same physical body—crucifixion scars and all—in which he died.

The resurrection of Christ loses its apologetic value unless it is a physical resurrection of the same body that died. Indeed, the apostle Paul is willing to say that Christianity is false if Christ was not raised bodily from the grave. Hence, the defense of the resurrection as a physical event involving a reanimation of the physical body of Christ that died is crucial to Christian apologetics. Denial of the physical resurrection of Christ is tantamount to a denial of the resurrection itself, since it is only the physical body, not the soul, that dies. And if that physical body does not come back to life, then there was no *bodily* resurrection.

The Importance of a Body. The significance of the physical resurrection of Christ is far-reaching, and the implications of its denial are fundamental to orthodox Christianity. In fact, a denial of it affects both Christian apologetics and our very salvation (Rom. 10:9; 1 Cor. 15:12f.).

Apologetic Considerations. Why is it so important to Christ's claim to deity that his resurrection body be the same physical body that was laid in the tomb? The answer is twofold.

Verification of the real God. First, this is the only way to know for sure that the resurrection occurred. The empty tomb in itself does not prove the resurrection of Christ any more than does the report that a body has turned up missing at a morgue. Neither does an empty tomb plus a series of appearances prove the resurrection. The original body could have disappeared and the appearances could be by someone else or by the same person in another body—which is reincarnation, not resurrection. But in a theistic (*see* THEISM) context where miracles are possible, an empty tomb plus appearances of the *same physical body*, once dead but now alive, are proof of a miraculous resurrection.

Without this physical identity connecting the pre- and postresurrection body, the apologetic value of the resurrection is destroyed. If Christ did not rise in the same physical body that was placed in the tomb, then the resurrection proves nothing of his claim to be God (John 8:58; 10:30). The resurrection only substantiates Jesus' claim to be God if he was resurrected in the same literal body in which he was crucified.

The truth of Christianity is based squarely on the bodily resurrection of Christ. Jesus offered the resurrection as a proof of his deity throughout his ministry (Matt. 12:38–40; John 2:19–22; 10:18). In one passage he presented his resurrection as the unique evidence of his identity. Jesus said to those seeking a "sign," "None will be given it except the sign of the prophet Jonah. For as Jonah was three days and three nights in the belly of a huge fish, so the Son of Man will be three days and three nights in the heart of the earth" (Matt. 12:40).

Not only did Jesus present his resurrection as the proof of his deity, but for the apostles his resurrection appearances were "many convincing proofs" (Acts 1:3). When presenting the claims of Christ they continually used the fact of Christ's bodily resurrection as the basis of their argument (cf. Acts 2:22–36; 4:2, 10; 13:32–41; 17:1–4, 22–31). Paul concluded that God "has given proof . . . to all men by raising him from the dead" (Acts 17:31).

The physical continuity between the pre- and postresurrection body of Christ is made repeatedly in apostolic preaching. Peter's first sermon declared that the Jews "put him to death by nailing *him* to the cross. But God raised *him* from the dead . . ." (Acts 2:23–24). He adds, "he was not abandoned to the grave, nor did *his body* see decay. God has raised *this Jesus* to life, and we are witnesses of the fact" (vss. 31–32). Paul is equally specific in making the connection between the actual body that was put in the grave and the one that was resurrected. He says, "they took him down from the tree and laid *him* in a tomb. But God raised *him* from the dead" (Acts 13:29–31).

Verification of the real event. Second, unless Christ rose in a physical, material body the resurrection is unverifiable. There is no way to verify that he was really resurrected unless he was resurrected in the same tangible, physical body in which he died and was buried. If the resurrected body was essentially immaterial and "angel-like" (Harris, *Raised Immortal*, 53, 124, 126), then, there is no way to verify that the resurrection occurred. A manifestation in an angel-like form does not prove a bodily resurrection. At best, an angelic-like manifestation proves that there is a spirit with the power to materialize after it has departed from the body.

Even angels who are pure spirits (Heb. 1:14) had the power to "materialize" (Genesis 18). The angels that appeared to Abraham assumed a visible form (Gen. 18:8; 19:3). But this was not proof that by nature they possessed physical bodies. In fact, they do not; they are spirits (Matt. 22:30; Luke 24:39; Heb. 1:14). Nor were their manifestations in physical continuity with a previous earthly body, as is the case in the resurrection body of Christ. The angelic manifestations were merely temporarily assumed forms to facilitate communication with human beings. To place Jesus' appearances in this category is to reduce the resurrection to a theophany.

It not only demeans the nature of the resurrection body of Christ to call it "angel-like," but it destroys its evidential value. For there is a real difference between an angelic manifestation and a literal physical body. Resurrection in an immaterial body is no proof that Christ conquered the death of his material body (cf. 1 Cor. 15:54–56). An immaterial resurrection body does not differ substantively from no resurrection body at all.

Theological Considerations. The problem of creation. God created a material world and pronounced it "very good" (Gen. 1:31; cf. Rom. 14:14 and 1 Tim. 4:4). Sin disrupted the world and brought decay and death (Gen. 2:17; Rom. 5:12). The whole of material creation was subjected to bondage because of sin (Rom. 8:18–25). However, through redemption decay and death will be reversed. For "creation itself will be liberated from its bondage to decay" (vs. 21). Indeed, "the whole [material] creation has been groaning . . . as we wait eagerly for our adoption as sons, the redemption of our bodies" (vss. 22–23). God will reverse the curse upon material creation by a material resurrection. Anything less than the resurrection of the physical body would not restore God's perfect creation as a material creation. Hence, an immaterial resurrection is contrary to God's creative purposes. Just as God will recreate the physical universe (2 Pet. 3:10–13; Rev. 21:1–4), even so he will reconstitute the material human body in redeeming the one that died.

Anything short of a material recreation of the world and a material reconstruction of the body would spell failure for God's creative purpose. New Testament scholar Robert Gundry notes, "Anything less than that undercuts Paul's ultimate intention that redeemed man possess physical means of concrete activity for eternal service and worship of God in a restored creation." So "to dematerialize resurrection, by any means, is to emasculate the sovereignty of God in both creative purpose and redemptive grace" (Gundry, 182).

The problem of salvation. There are serious *salvation* problems with denying the physical nature of the resurrection of Christ. The New Testament teaches that belief in the bodily resurrection of Christ is a condition for salvation (Rom. 10:9, 10; 1 Thess. 4:14). It is part of the essence of the Gospel itself (1 Cor 15:1–5). The New Testament understanding of *body* (*sōma*) was of a literal, physical body. Hence, a denial of the physical resurrection of Christ undercuts the Gospel.

Further, without a physical resurrection there is no material continuity between the pre- and postresurrection body. Indeed, they would be two different bodies (Harris, *From Grave to Glory*, 54–56, 126). However, as Gundry observes, "A physical continuity is also needed. If a human spirit—a sort of third party—be the only connection between the mortal and resurrected bodies, the relationship of the two bodies to each other is extrinsic and to that decree unimpressive as a demonstration of Christ's victory over death" (Gundry, 176).

In stronger terms Gundry concludes that "the resurrection of Christ was and the resurrection of Christians will be physical in nature" (Gundry, 182). Without a physical resurrection there is no grounds for celebrating victory over physical death.

The problem of the incarnation. The denial of the physical nature of the resurrection body is a serious *doctrinal* error. It is a kind of neodocetism (*see* DOCETISM). The docetists were a second-century unorthodox group who denied that Jesus was truly human (Cross, 413). They believed that Jesus was really God but that he only appeared to be human. They denied that he had real human flesh.

A similar doctrinal error existed in the first century. John warns against those who deny that "Jesus Christ has come in the *flesh*" (1 John 4:2; cf. 2 John 7). In fact, when John said "has come" (perfect participle) he implies that Christ came in the flesh and still remains (after his resurrection) in the flesh. In 1 John 4:2 the perfect participle (*eleluthota*) means "not only that Jesus Christ came in the fullness of time clothed with flesh, but that thus he is *still present* . . . He is a Christ who is come, who came and who abides in the flesh" (Schep, 71, 72). Commenting on the parallel passage in 2 John 7, Greek scholar, A. T. Robertson, observes that it is the (present middle participle) construction treats the incarnation as a continuing fact. That is what docetic Gnostics (*see* GNOSTICISM) denied (Robertson, 6:253). Denying that Christ had a material body either before or after his resurrection is false doctrine. The current postresurrection *docetism denies that the one who came in the flesh was also raised in the flesh (Harris, *From Grave to Glory*, 124–26).

Having human flesh is essential to the full humanity of Christ and is used repeatedly to describe it (John 1:14; 1 Tim. 3:16; 1 John 4:2; 2 John 7). If this is so, then unless Christ arose immortal in the flesh, he was not fully human. This is particularly acute, since Christ's ministry for our salvation did not end at the cross. According to Hebrews, Christ "ever lives to make intercession for us" (Heb. 7:24). Indeed, it is because Jesus is fully human that he is able "to sympathize with our weakness" in his high priestly ministry (Heb. 4:15). Therefore, Christ's full humanity is necessary for our salvation. But according to Scripture, human *flesh* was a necessary part of his full humanity. Hence, unless Christ rose in that human flesh, then he is not fully human and cannot be effective in achieving our salvation.

The problem of human immortality. Further, denying the physical resurrection leaves a serious problem about Christian immortality. If Christ did not rise in the same physical body in which he was crucified, then we have no hope that we will be victorious over physical death either. It is only through the physical resurrection of Christ that the believer can triumphantly proclaim: "Where, O death, is your victory? Where, O death, is your sting?" (1 Cor. 15:55). For it is only through the physical resurrection that God has "destroyed death and has brought life and immortality to light through the gospel" (2 Tim. 1:10). As Paul told the Corinthians, "if Christ has not been raised . . . those who have fallen asleep in Christ are lost" (1 Cor. 15:18).

The problem of moral deception. There is a serious *moral* problem of deception with denying the physical resurrection. No one can look squarely at the Gospel record of Christ's postresurrection appearances and deny that Jesus tried to convince the skeptical disciples that he had a real physical body. He said, "Look at my hands and my feet. It is I myself! Touch me and see; a spirit does not have flesh and bones, as you see I have" (Luke 24:27). He ate in their presence (vss. 41–43). He challenged Thomas: "Put your finger here; see my hands. Reach out your hand and put it into my side. Stop doubting and believe" (John 20:27; *see* RESURRECTION, EVIDENCE FOR).

Given the context of Jesus' claim and of the Jewish belief in the physical resurrection (cf. John 11:24; Acts 23:8), there is no other reasonable impression these statements could have left on the disciples' minds than that Jesus was trying to convince them that he arose in the same physical body in which he died. If Jesus' resurrection body was only an immaterial body, then Jesus misled his disciples. If Jesus' resurrection body was not a tangible, physical body, then he was lying.

Evidence of a Physical Resurrection. As shown in the article Resurrection, Objections to, arguments against the resurrection are groundless. What is more, the evidences in favor of the physical nature of the resurrection are also overwhelming. While some of the following are also evidences for the historicity of the resurrection, they also verify that Jesus was not "angel-like" in his appearances. Rather he displayed a very real body—the same body in which he was crucified.

Jesus Was Touched by Human Hands. Jesus challenged Thomas, "Put your finger here; see my hands. Reach out your hand and put it in my side" (John 20:27). Thomas responded, "My Lord and My God!" (vs. 28). Likewise, when Mary clung to Jesus after his resurrection he commanded, "Do not hold on to me, for I have not yet returned to the Father" (John 20:17). Matthew adds that the women clasped Jesus' feet and worshiped him (Matt. 28:9). Later, when Jesus appeared to the ten disciples he said, "look at my hands and my feet. It is I myself! *Touch me* and see" (Luke 24:39). Jesus' resurrection body was a physical body that could be touched, including the nail and spear prints.

Jesus' Body Had Flesh and Bones. Perhaps the strongest evidence of the physical nature of the resurrection body is that Jesus said emphatically "Touch me and see; a spirit does not have flesh and bones, as you see I have" (Luke 24:39). Then to prove his point he asked for something to eat and "They gave him a piece of broiled fish, and he took it and ate it in their presence" (vss. 41–42).

Paul correctly noted that corruptible "flesh and blood cannot inherit the kingdom of God" (1 Cor. 15:50), but Jesus did not have corruptible flesh; he was sinless (2 Cor. 5:21; Heb. 4:15). He was fleshy but not fleshly. He did not have *sinful* human flesh (Heb. 4:15); nevertheless, he died and rose from the dead in actual human flesh (*sarx*, Acts 2:31). John stressed Jesus' continuing incarnation in flesh, when he warned: "Many deceivers, who do not acknowledge Jesus Christ as coming [and remaining] in the flesh, have gone out into the world" (2 John 7). The use of the present participle in Greek means Christ remained in the flesh even while this was written. The claim that it was physical flesh before the resurrection but non-physical flesh after is a form of Gnosticism or docetism.

Jesus Ate Physical Food. Another evidence Jesus offered of the physical, tangible nature of his resurrection body was the ability to eat, which he did on at least four occasions (Luke 24:30, 41–43; John 21:12–13; Acts 1:4). Acts 10:40 indicates that Jesus ate often with the disciples after his resurrection, speaking of the apostles who "ate and drank with him after he arose from the dead."

Unlike angels, Jesus' resurrection body was material by nature (Luke 24:39). Given this context, it would have been sheer deception by Jesus to have shown his flesh and bones and offered his ability to eat physical food as proof of his physical body, if he had not been resurrected in a physical body.

Jesus' Body Has His Wounds. Another unmistakable evidence of the physical nature of the resurrection body was that it possessed the physical wounds from Jesus' crucifixion. No so-called "spiritual" or immaterial body would have physical scars (John 20:27). Indeed, in this same physical body Jesus ascended into heaven where he is still seen as "a Lamb, looking as if it had been slain" (Rev. 5:6). And when Christ returns, it will be *"this same Jesus*, who has been taken away from you into heaven" (Acts 1:11). These same physical scars of his crucifixion will be visible at his second coming, for John declared: "Look, he is coming with the clouds, and *every eye will see him, even those who pierced him"* (Rev. 1:7).

Jesus' Body Was Recognized. The usual words for "seeing" (*horao, theoreo*) and "recognizing" (*epiginosko*) physical objects were used over and over again of Christ in his resurrection state (see Matt. 28:7, 17; Mark 16:7; Luke 24:24; John 20:14; 1 Cor. 9:1). Occasionally Jesus was not initially recognized by some of the disciples, some perhaps supernatural. Luke says of one occasion that "their eyes were prevented from recognizing him" (24:16) and later "their eyes were opened and they recognized him" (vs. 31). However, often there were purely natural factors, such as their perplexity (Luke 24:17–21), sorrow (John 20:11–15), the dimness of the light (John 20:14–15), the visual distance (John 21:4), the suddenness of Jesus' appearance (Luke 24:36–37), the different clothes he had on (John 19:23–24; 20:6–8), or their spiritual dullness (Luke 24:25–26) and disbelief (John 20:24–25). In every case the difficulty was temporary. Before the appearances were over there remained absolutely no doubts in their minds that Christ had arisen in a literal, material body.

Jesus' Body Could Be Seen and Heard. Jesus' resurrection body could not only be touched and handled, it could also be seen and heard. Matthew says that "when they *saw* him, they worshiped him" (Matt. 28:17). The Emmaus disciples recognized him while eating together (Luke 24:31), perhaps from his bodily movements (cf. vs. 35). The Greek term for recognize (*epiginosko*) means "to know, to understand, or to recognize." It is a normal term for recognizing a physical object (Mark 6:33, 54; Acts 3:10). Mary may have recognized Jesus from the tone of his voice (John 20:15–16). Thomas recognized him, probably even before he touched the crucifixion scars (John 20:27–28). During the forty-day period, all the disciples saw and heard him, and experienced the "convincing proofs" that he was alive (Acts 1:3; cf. 4:2, 20).

Resurrection Is Out from among Dead. Resurrection in the New Testament is often described as "from (*ek*) the dead" (cf. Mark 9:9; Luke 24:46; John 2:22; Acts 3:15; Rom. 4:24; 1 Cor. 15:12). Literally, this Greek word *ek* means Jesus was resurrected "out from among" the dead bodies, that is, from the grave where corpses are buried (Acts 13:29–30). These same words are used to describe Lazarus's being raised "from the dead" (John 12:1). In this case there is no doubt that he came out of the grave in the same body in which he was buried. Thus, resurrection was of a physical corpse out of a tomb or graveyard. As Gundry correctly noted, "for one who had been a Pharisee, such phraseology could carry only one meaning—physical resurrection" (Gundry, 177).

Sōma Always Means a Physical Body. When used of an individual human being, the word *body* (*sōma*) always means a physical body in the New Testament. There are no exceptions to this usage in the New Testament. Paul uses *sōma* of the resurrection body of Christ (1 Cor. 15:42–44), thus indicating his belief that it was a physical body. The definitive exegetical work on *sōma* was done by Gundry (ibid.). As evidence of the physical nature of the resurrection body, he points to "Paul's exceptionless use of *sōma* for a physical body" (Gundry, 168). Thus he concludes that "the consistent and exclusive use of *sōma* for the physical body in anthropological contexts resists dematerialization of the resurrection, whether by idealism or by existentialism" (ibid.).

For those who think Paul should have used another word to express physical resurrection, Robert Gundry responds: "Paul uses *sōma* precisely because the physicality of the resurrection is central to his soteriology" (Gundry, 169). This consistent use of the word *sōma* for a physical body is one more confirmation that the resurrection body of Christ was a literal, material body.

The Tomb Was Vacated. Joined with the appearances of the same crucified Jesus, the empty tomb provides strong support of the physical nature of the resurrection body of Christ. The angels declared, "he is not here; he has risen, just as he said. Come and see the place where he lay" (Matt. 28:6). Since it was a literal, material body that was placed there, and since *that same physical body* had come alive, it follows that the resurrection body was that same material body that died.

The Grave Clothes Were Unwrapped. When Peter entered the tomb he "saw strips of linen lying there, as well as the burial cloth that had been around Jesus' head. The cloth was folded up by itself, separate from the linen" (John 20:6–7). Certainly, if thieves had stolen it, they would not have taken time to take off and fold the head cloth. Nor if Jesus had vaporized through the grave clothes would the head cloth have been in a separate place all folded up by itself. These details reveal the truth that the material body of Jesus that had once laid there had been restored to life (Acts 13:29–30). John was so convinced by this evidence of a physical resurrection that when he saw it he believed Jesus had risen, though he had not yet seen him (John 20:8).

The Body That Died Is the Same One Raised. If the resurrection body is numerically identical to the post-resurrection body and the pre resurrection body is unquestionably material, then it follows that the resurrection body is also material. This, of course, does not mean every particle is the same. Even our pre resurrection body changes its particles continually, yet it is the same material body. It means that the resurrection body is one and the same substantial and continuous material body, whatever accidental changes there may be in its given molecules. In addition to the empty tomb, the empty grave clothes, the seed analogy, and the crucifixion scars there are other lines of evidence that the resurrection of Christ was in the same physical body that died.

First, Jesus said in advance that the same temple, his body, would be destroyed raised again. He said "destroy this temple, and in three days I will raise *it* up" (John 2:21–22). The *it* manifests that the body raised is one and the same as the body destroyed by death.

Second, the same identity is implied in the strong comparison between Jesus' death and resurrection and Jonah's experience in the great fish (Matt. 12:39; 16:4). He said, "*As* Jonah was three days and three nights inside the belly of a huge fish, *so* the Son of Man will be three days and three nights in the heart of the earth" (Matt. 12:40). Obviously, in both cases the same physical body that went in was the same one that came out. Thus, the inseparable identity between the pre- and postresurrection body of Jesus by Paul, the converted Pharisee, is strong confirmation that he is affirming the physical nature of the resurrection body.

Third, Paul added, "The perishable must clothe itself with the imperishable, and the mortal with immortality" (1 Cor. 15:53). It is noteworthy that Paul does not say that this corruptible body will be *replaced* by an incorruptible model. Rather, this physical body which is now corruptible will "clothe itself" with the additional element of incorruptibility. If a material body was buried and a spiritual or immaterial body were raised, it would not be the same body. But in this text Paul affirms the numerical identity between the pre- and postresurrection body.

Fourth, Paul's sermon in Antioch reveals the identity between the body that was killed on the cross and the one that was raised from the dead. He said, "When they had carried out all that was written about *him*, they took *him* down from the tree and laid *him* in a tomb. But God raised *him* from the dead " (Acts 13:29–30).

Finally, the close connection between the death and resurrection points to numerical identity *of the resurrection body*. Paul considered it of first importance that "Christ died for our sins, . . . that he was buried, that he was raised on the third day" (1 Cor. 15:3, 4). Elsewhere, Paul declares that what was "buried" was "raised from death" (Rom 6:3–5; cf. Acts 2:23–24; 3:15; 4:10; 5:30; 10:39–40; 13:29–30; Col. 2:12). It is noteworthy that, "as an ex-Pharisee, Paul could not have used such traditional language without recognizing its intent to portray the raising of a corpse" (Gundry, 176).

In view of the evidence, there is no justification for the claim that the pre- and postresurrection body has no "material identity" and "the resurrection body will not have the anatomy or physiology of the earthly body" (Harris, *Raised Immortal*, 124, 126). And since believers will have bodies like his (Phil. 3:21), it follows that theirs will also be material. Indeed, many of the above arguments can be directly applied to believers. For example, the Bible says they will rise out of "the dust of the earth" (Dan. 12:2) and "come forth" from being "in the graves" (John 5:28, 29), thus indicating the material nature of their resurrected bodies.

Conclusion. Murray Harris claimed that the resurrection body is "spiritual" and not really a physical body of flesh and bones. He wrote: "Consequently the material 'flesh and bones' that Jesus had during this encounter with his disciples were not integral to his 'spiritual body' but had been assumed temporarily, but none the less really, for evidential reasons, as accommodations to the understanding of his disciples" (Harris, *From Grave to Glory*, 392). But if the crucifixion scars were not in the actual "spiritual" resurrection body, but only in the one temporarily assumed for evidential reasons, then Jesus deceived his disciples when he said of this temporary body of flesh and bones "Look at my hands and my feet. It is I myself!" (Luke 24:39). According to Harris, this temporary body was neither the physical body in which Jesus was crucified nor his real ("spiritual") resurrection body. If Harris's assertion is correct, Jesus flatly deceived his disciples.

The only body that actually had the crucifixion scars in it was the physical body of flesh and bones in which Jesus died. But, according to Harris, the temporarily assumed material body in which Jesus appeared was not the same body of flesh which had the actual crucifixion scars in it. It follows, then, that the temporarily assumed physical body which Jesus showed his disciples was only a replica of the crucifixion body. If Harris is right, then Jesus flatly lied; this seems a serious objection to Harris's view.

The Bible is very clear about the nature of the resurrection body. It is the same physical, material body of flesh and bones that dies. There are, in fact, numerous lines of evidence to support this. The evidence for the physical nature of the resurrection body is overwhelming (*see* Resurrection, Evidence for). And its importance to Christianity can scarcely be overestimated. Any denial of the physical bodily resurrection of Christ is a serious matter. Denials by evangelicals are even more serious, including some who use the traditional term *bodily resurrection* to affirm their view. For "bodily" resurrection has always meant that Jesus was resurrected in the same physical, material body in which he died. As the poet John Updike put it,

> Make no mistake; if He rose at all
> it was as His body,
> if the cells' dissolution did not reverse, the
>   molecules
> reknit, the amino acids rekindle,
> the Church will fall.

That Jesus rose from the dead in the essentially same physical body of flesh and bones in which he was crucified is a linchpin of orthodox theology and apologetics. Historic Christianity stands of falls on the historicity and materiality of the bodily resurrection of Christ.

Sources

W. F. Arndt and F. W. Gingrich, *A Greek-English Lexicon of the New Testament*

W. Craig, *Knowing the Truth about the Resurrection*

F. L. Cross, ed., *The Oxford Dictionary of the Christian Church*

G. Friedrich, *The Theological Dictionary of the New Testament*

N. L. Geisler, *The Battle for the Resurrection*

———, *In Defense of the Resurrection*

R. Gundry, Soma *in Biblical Theology*

M. Harris, *From Grave to Glory*

———, *Raised Immortal*

A. T. Robertson, *Word Pictures in the New Testament*

J. A. Schep, *The Nature of the Resurrection Body*

Revelation, General. *General revelation* refers to God's revelation in nature as opposed to his revelation in Scripture (*see* NATURAL THEOLOGY). More specifically, general revelation is manifest in physical nature, human nature, and history. In each case God has disclosed something specific about himself and his relation to his creation. General revelation is important to Christian apologetics, since it is the data with which the theist constructs arguments from the existence of God (*see* COSMOLOGICAL ARGUMENT; TELEOLOGICAL ARGUMENT). Without it there would be no basis for apologetics (*see* CLASSICAL APOLOGETICS).

God's Revelation in Nature. "The heavens declare the glory of God; the skies proclaim the work of his hands" (Ps. 19:1), the psalmist wrote. "The heavens proclaim his righteousness, and all the peoples see his glory" (Ps. 97:6). Job added, "Ask the animals, and they will teach you, or the birds of the air, and they will tell you; or speak to the earth, and it will teach you, or let the fish of the sea inform you. Which of all these does not know that the hand of the Lord had done this?" (Job 12:7–9).

Paul spoke of "the living God, who made heaven and earth and sea and everything in them. In the past, he let all nations go their own way. Yet he has not left himself without testimony: He has shown kindness by giving you rain from heaven and crops in their seasons; he provides you with plenty of food and fills your hearts with joy" (Acts 14:15–17). He reminded the Greek philosophers that "The God who made the world and everything in it is the Lord of heaven and earth and does not live in temples built by hands. And he is not served by human hands, as if he needed anything, because he himself gives all men life and breath and everything else" (Acts 17:24–25).

Paul instructed the Romans that even the heathen stand guilty before God, "since what may be known about God is plain to them, because God has made it plain to them. For since the creation of the world God's invisible qualities—his eternal power and divine nature—have been clearly seen, being understood from what has been made, so that men are without excuse" (Rom. 1:18–20). In view of this the psalmist concluded, "The fool says in his heart, 'There is no God'" (Ps. 14:1).

God is revealed in nature in two basic ways: as *Creator* and as *Sustainer* (*see* CREATION AND ORIGINS; ORIGINS, SCIENCE OF). He is both the cause of the *origin* as well as the *operation* of the universe. The first speaks of God as the originator of all things. "By him all *were created*" and "in him all things *hold together*" (Col. 1:16–17); God "*made* the universe" and he also "*sustains* all things by his powerful word" (Heb. 1:2–3); he "*created* all things" and by him "all things *have their being*" (Rev. 4:11).

In addition to *Originator*, God is also the *Sustainer* of all things. He is active not only in the universe *coming to be* but also in its *continuing to be*. The psalmist referred to this latter function when he said of God: "He makes springs pour water into the ravines. . . . He makes grass to grow for the cattle, and plants for man to cultivate—bringing forth food from the earth" (Ps. 104:10, 14).

God's Revelation in Human Nature. God created human beings in his image and likeness (Gen. 1:27). Something about God, therefore, can be learned from studying human beings (cf. Psalm 8). Since humans are like God, it is wrong to murder them (Gen. 9:6) and even to curse them (James 3:9). The redeemed human self is "renewed in knowledge in the image of its Creator" (Col. 3:10). Paul affirmed that God created:

> From one man he made every nation of men, that they should inhabit the whole earth; and he determined the times set for them and the exact places where they should live. God did this so that men would seek him and perhaps reach out for him and find him, though he is not far from each one of us. "For in him we live and move and have our being." As some of your own poets have said, "We are his offspring." Therefore since we are God's offspring, we should not think that the divine being is like gold or silver or stone—an image made by man's design and skill. [Acts 17:26–29]

By looking at the creature we can learn something about the Creator (*see* ANALOGY, PRINCIPLE OF). For "Does he who implanted the ear not hear? Does he who formed the eye not see? Does he who disciplines nations not punish? Does he who teaches man lack knowledge?" (Ps. 94:9–10). Even Christ in the flesh is said to be an "image" of the invisible God (John 1:14; Heb. 1:3).

God is manifested not only in the intellectual nature of human beings, but also in their moral nature (*see* MORALITY, ABSOLUTE NATURE OF). God's moral law is written in human hearts. For "when Gentiles, who do not have the law, do by nature things required by the law, they are a law for themselves, even though they do not have the law, their conscience also bearing witness" (Rom. 2:12–15). Since moral responsibility entails the ability to respond, man in God's image is also a free moral creature (Gen. 1:27; cf. 2:16–17).

God's Revelation in Human History. History has been called "His-story." It is the footprints of God in the sands of time. Paul declared that God "determined the times set for them [the nations] and the exact places they should live" (Acts 17:26). God disclosed to Daniel that "the Most High is sovereign over the kingdoms of men and gives them anyone he wishes and sets over them the lowliest of men" (Dan. 4:17). God also revealed to Daniel that human history is moving toward the ultimate goal of the kingdom of God on earth (Daniel 2, 7). So a proper understanding of history informs us about the plan and purpose of God.

God Is Revealed in Human Art. The Bible declares that God is beautiful, and so is his creation. The psalmist wrote: "O LORD, our Lord, how majestic is your name in all the earth!" (Ps. 8:1). Isaiah beheld a marvelous display of God's beauty when he "saw the Lord seated on a throne, high and exalted, and the train of his robe filled the temple" (Isa. 6:1). Scriptures encourage us to "worship the LORD in the beauty of holiness" (Ps. 29:2; cf. 27:4).

Solomon pointed out that God has made everything "beautiful in its time" (Eccles. 3:11). The psalmist speaks of his city of Zion as "perfect in beauty" (Ps. 50:2). What God created is good like himself (Gen. 1:31; 1 Tim. 4:4), and the goodness of God is beautiful. So, insofar as creation reflects God, it is also beautiful. Not only is God beautiful and has made a beautiful world, but he has created beings who can appreciate beauty. Like him, they can also make beautiful things. Human beings are, as it were "sub-creators." God endows certain humans with special creative gifts which reveal something of his marvelous nature.

God Is Revealed in Music. God apparently loves music, since he orchestrated the angelic choir at creation when "the morning stars sang together and all the angels shouted for joy" (Job 38:7). Angels also continually chant the *tersanctus* in his presence, "Holy, holy, holy" (Isa. 4:7; 6:3). Furthermore, angels gather around God's throne and "in a loud voice they sing: Worthy is the Lamb, who was slain" (Rev. 5:12).

Moses' sister, Miriam, led the triumphant Israelites in singing after God delivered them through the Red Sea (Exod. 15). David, the "sweet psalmist of Israel," set up a choir for the temple and wrote many songs (psalms) to be sung in it. Paul admonished the church to "Speak to one another with psalms, hymns and spiritual songs. Sing and make music in your heart to the Lord" (Eph. 5:19).

We learn something more about God's nature through the human voice, a God-ordained instrument of music. Even the Jewish high priest entered within the holy of holies with bells on his garment. And the psalmist commanded that God be praised with trumpet, harp, lyre, tambourine, and cymbals (Ps. 150:3–5). In heaven the angels play trumpets (Rev. 8:2) and others play harps (Rev. 14:2). Music too is a gift and manifestation of God. Like the rest of his creation, it is a manifestation of his glory.

So even apart from God's special revelation in Scripture, he has manifested himself in general revelation in nature.

General and Special Revelation. While the Bible is God's only *written* revelation (*see* BIBLE, EVIDENCE FOR), it is not God's only revelation. God has more to say to us than is in the Bible. His general revelation in nature, man, history, art and music offers vast opportunities for continual exploration. The following chart summarizes this relationship:

Special Revelation	**General Revelation**
God as Redeemer	God as Creator
norm for church	norm for society
means of salvation	means of condemnation

The Role of Special Revelation. Special revelation contributes uniquely to Christian theology. The Bible alone is infallible and inerrant (*see* BIBLE, ALLEGED ERRORS IN). Further, the Bible is the only source of both God's revelation as Redeemer and his plan of salvation. Thus Scripture is normative for all (*see* REVELATION, SPECIAL).

The Bible alone is infallible and inerrant. The Bible is normative for all Christian thought. It is a revelation of Christ (Matt. 5:17; Luke 24:27, 44; John 5:39; Heb. 10:7). The task of the Christian, then, is "to bring every thought captive to Christ" (2 Cor. 10:5) as revealed in Scripture. We must think as well as live Christocentric lives (Gal. 2:20; Phil. 1:21).

The Bible alone reveals God as Redeemer. While general revelation manifests God as Creator, it does not reveal him as Redeemer. The universe speaks of God's greatness (Ps. 8:1; Isa. 40:12–17), but only special revelation reveals his redeeming grace (John 1:14). The heavens declare the glory of God (Ps. 19:1), but only Christ declared his saving grace (Titus 2:11–13).

The Bible alone has the message of salvation. In view of God's general revelation all are "without excuse" (Rom. 1:20). For all who sin apart from the [written] law will also perish apart from the law" (Rom. 2:12). General revelation is a sufficient ground for condemnation. However, it is not sufficient for salvation. One can tell how the heavens move by studying general revelation, but not how to go to heaven (*see* HEATHEN, SALVATION OF). For "there is no other name under heaven [except Christ's] given to men by which men must be saved" (Acts 4:12). To be saved, one must confess "Jesus is Lord" and believe that God has raised him from the dead (Rom. 10:9). But they cannot call upon someone of whom they have not heard, "and how can they hear without someone preaching to them?" (Rom. 10:14). Thus, preaching the Gospel in all the world is the Christian's great commission (Matt. 28:18–20).

The Bible is the written norm. Without the truth of Scripture there would be no Church, for "the church is built on the foundation of the apostles and prophets" (Eph. 2:20). The revealed Word of God is the norm for faith and practice. Paul said "all Scripture is God-breathed and is useful for teaching, training, rebuking, correcting and training in righteousness" (2 Tim. 3:16). However, not all unbelievers have access to a Bible. Nonetheless, God holds them responsible to his general revelation. For "all who sin apart from the [written] law will also perish apart from the law," since they have a law in their hearts (Rom. 2:12, 14).

The Role of General Revelation. While the Bible is all true, God has not revealed all truth in the Bible. Whereas the Bible is only truth, it is not the only truth. All truth is God's truth, but all God's truth is not in the Bible (*see* TRUTH, NATURE OF). General revelation, then, plays an important role in God's plan, and as such it has several unique roles.

General is broader than special revelation. General revelation encompasses much more than special revelation. Most of the truths of science, history, mathematics, and the arts are not in the Bible. The bulk of truth in all these areas is found only in God's general revelation. While the Bible is everywhere scientifically accurate, it is not a textbook on science. The mandate to do science is not a redemption mandate; it is a creation mandate. Right after God created Adam he commanded him to "fill the earth and subdue it" (Gen. 1:28). Likewise, there are no mathematical errors in God's inerrant Word, but then again there is very little geometry or algebra and no calculus in it either (*see* SCIENCE AND THE BIBLE). Similarly, the Bible records accurately much of the history of Israel, but has little on the history of the world, except as it bears on Israel. The same is true of every area of the arts and science. Whenever the Bible speaks in these areas, it speaks authoritatively, but God has largely left the discoveries of his truths in these areas to a study of general revelation.

General revelation is essential to human reason. Not even an unbeliever thinks apart from God's general revelation in human reason (*see* FAITH AND REASON). God is a rational being, and humanity is made in his image (Gen. 1:27). Just as God thinks rationally, so human beings were given that capacity. Brute beasts, by contrast, are called "irrational" (Jude 10). Indeed, the highest use of human reason is to love the Lord with "all our mind . . ." (Matt. 22:37).

The basic laws of human reason are common to believer and unbeliever (*see* LOGIC; FIRST PRINCIPLES). Without them no writing, thinking, or rational inferences would be possible. But nowhere are these laws of thought spelled out in the Bible. Rather, they are part of God's general revelation and the special object of philosophical thought.

General revelation is essential to government. God has ordained that believers live by his written law, but he has written his law in the hearts of unbelievers (Rom. 2:12–15). Divine law in Scripture is the norm for Christians, but natural law is binding on all. Nowhere in Scripture does God judge the nations by either the law of Moses he gave to Israel (Exod. 19–20) or by the law of Christ he enjoins on Christians. To think otherwise is the central error of theonomists. Nowhere, for example, were non-Jewish nations ever condemned in the Old Testament for not observing the Sabbath or sacrificing a lamb. Strangers and sojourners in Israel were, of course, required to respect the civil and moral laws of Israel as long as they were in the country. But this no more means the Jewish law was intended for them than that Christians are under the *Quranic* law because they must abide by it when in Muslim lands.

The law of Moses was not given to the Gentiles. Paul said clearly, "the Gentiles who have not the law" (Rom. 2:14). The psalmist said "He has revealed his word to Jacob, his laws and decrees to Israel. He has done this for no other nation: they do not know his laws" (Ps. 147:19–20). This is confirmed by the fact that, in spite of the many condemnations of Gentiles' sins in the Old Testament, never once were they condemned for not worshiping on the Sabbath or not making pilgrimages or bringing tithes to Jerusalem. This does not mean that there is no law of God for non-believers; they are bound by the law "written in their hearts" (Rom. 2:2–15). While they have no special revelation in holy Scripture, they are responsible to general revelation in human nature.

General revelation is essential to apologetics. Without general revelation there would be no basis for Christian apologetics (*see* CLASSICAL APOLOGETICS). For if God had not revealed himself in nature, there would be no way to argue from the design evident in it to the existence of a Designer, known as the *teleological argument for God's existence. Nor would there be any way to argue from the beginning or contingency of the world to the existence of a First Cause, known as the cosmological argument. Likewise, unless God had revealed himself in the very moral nature of human beings it would not be possible to argue to a Moral Lawgiver (*see* MORAL ARGUMENT FOR GOD). And, of course, without a God who can act in creating the world, there could be no special acts of God (miracles) in the world (*see* MIRACLE).

Interaction Between Revelations. Since it is the task of a systematic thinker to organize all truth about God and his relation to his creation, both general and special revelation are needed. However, since special revelation overlaps with general revelation, it is necessary to discuss the interaction between general and special revelation. God has revealed himself in his Word and in his world. His truth is found both in Scripture and in science. The problem arises when they seem to conflict. It is too simplistic to conclude that the Bible is always right and science wrong.

When dealing with conflicts between Christianity and culture we must be careful to distinguish between *God's Word,* which is infallible, and *our interpretation* of it which is not. We must further distinguish between *God's revelation* in his world, which is always true, and current *understanding* of it, which is not always correct and is likely to change. In the past, Christians have frequently given up claims to biblical truth for scientific theories that are no longer held to be so.

Two important things follow from these distinctions. First, God's revelations in his Word and his world never contradict each other. God is consistent; he never talks out of both sides of his mouth. Second, whenever there is a real conflict, it is between a human interpretation of God's Word and a human understanding of his world. Either one or both of these are wrong, but God has not erred.

Which gets the priority? When conflicts in understanding God's general and special revelations occur, which one gets the priority? The temptation might be to give precedent to the biblical interpretation because the Bible is infallible, but this overlooks the crucial distinction just made. The Bible is inerrant, but interpretations of it are prone to error. The history of interpretation reveals that God's infallible Word is as capable of being misunderstood as is anything else, including the arts and science.

This does not leave one at an impasse. Whenever there is a conflict between an interpretation of the Bible and a current understanding of God's general revelation, priority should generally be given to the interpretation that seems more certain. Sometimes this is our understanding of special revelation, and sometimes it is our understanding of general revelation, depending on which one is more thoroughly proven. A few examples will help illuminate the point.

Some interpreters have wrongly concluded on the basis of Biblical references to "the four corners of the earth" (Rev. 7:1) that the earth is flat. However, science has proven with *certainty* that this is wrong. Therefore, in this case the certainty in interpreting God's general revelation takes precedence over whatever uncertainty there may be in interpreting these biblical references. "Four corners" can be understood as a figure of speech.

Others have claimed that the sun moves around the earth on the basis of Bible references to "sun set" (Josh 1:15) or the sun "standing still" (Josh. 10:13). However, this interpretation is not necessary. It could be only the language of appearance from an observer's point of view on the face of the earth (*see* SCIENCE AND THE BIBLE). Furthermore, since Copernicus there is good reason to believe that the sun does not move around the earth. Hence, we assign a higher *probability* to the heliocentric interpretation of God's world at this point than to a geocentric interpretation of his Word.

Unfortunately some are willing to believe in a given interpretation of God's Word, even if it involves a logical contradiction. But general revelation demands (by way of the law of noncontradiction) that opposites cannot both be true (*see* FIRST PRINCIPLES). Hence, we cannot believe that God is both one person and also three persons at the same time and in the same sense. Thus, both monotheism, so defined, and Trinitarianism (*see* TRINITY) cannot be true. We can, and do, believe that God is three Persons in one Essence. For even though this is a mystery, it is not a contradiction. Therefore, we can be *absolutely certain* that any interpretation of Scripture that involves a contradiction is false. However, there are times when an interpretation of Scripture should take precedence over even highly popular views in science.

Macroevolution is a good example (*see* EVOLUTION, BIOLOGICAL; EVOLUTION, CHEMICAL). It is *virtually certain* that the Bible cannot be properly interpreted to accommodate macroevolution (see Geisler). The Bible teaches that God brought the universe into existence out of nothing (Gen. 1:1), that he created every basic kind of animal and plant (Gen. 1:21), and that he specially and directly created man and woman in his image (Gen. 1:27). Hence, in spite of the prevailing and popular (though not highly probable) evolutionary views to the contrary, the Christian must give priority to this highly probable interpretation of Scripture over the improbable theory of macroevolution.

Mutual Enrichment. Often there is no serious conflict between widely accepted Bible interpretation and the general understanding of the scientific world. Rather, there is mutual enrichment. For example, a knowledge of the content of the Bible is essential for much of western Art and Literature. Further, biblical history and world history overlap significantly, so that neither should be ignorant of the other. More neglected is the connection between modern science and the biblical idea of creation. In this connection it is important to note that the biblical concept of creation helped give rise to modern science. Of course, in the study of origins there is a direct overlap and mutual enrichment of the scientific and biblical data.

Conclusion. The Bible is essential to both systematic thinking and to apologetics. It is the only infallible writing we have. It speaks with unerring authority on every topic it covers, whether spiritual or scientific, whether heavenly or earthly. However, the Bible is not God's only revelation to mankind. God has spoken in his world as well as in his Word. It is the task of the Christian thinker to appropriate the information from both and to form a *worldview that includes a theocentric interpretation of science, history, human beings, and the arts. However, without God's revelation (both general and special) as the basis, this task is as impossible as it would be to move the world with no place to put one's fulcrum.

In theology the interaction between biblical studies and other disciplines should always be a two-way street. No one provides a monologue for the other; all engage in a continual dialogue. Although the Bible is infallible in whatever it addresses, it does not speak to every issue. And while the Bible is infallible, our interpretations of it are not. Thus, those in biblical studies must listen to as well as speak to the other disciplines so that a complete and correct systematic view can be constructed.

Sources

G. C. Berkouwer, *General Revelation*
E. Brunner, *Revelation and Reason*
J. Butler, *The Analogy of Religion*
J. Calvin, *Institutes of the Christian Religion*
B. Demerest, *General Revelation*
N. L. Geisler, "God's Revelation in Scripture and Nature," in D. Beck, ed., *The Opening of the American Mind*
———, *Origin Science*
C. Hodge, *Systematic Theology*, vol. 1
J. Locke, *The Reasonableness of Christianity*
W. Paley, *Natural Theology*
Thomas Aquinas, *Summa Theologica*

Revelation, Progressive. *See* PROGRESSIVE REVELATION.

Revelation, Special. *Special revelation* (*see* BIBLE, EVIDENCE FOR) is God's revelation in his Word (Scripture), as opposed to God's revelation in his world (*see* REVELATION, GENERAL). Special revelation may have originally been given orally or some other way (cf. Heb. 1:1) but has subsequently been written down and is now found only in God's written Word, the Bible (2 Tim. 3:16–17).

God's special revelation has been confirmed by miracles (*see* MIRACLE; MIRACLES, APOLOGETIC VALUE OF; MIRACLES IN THE BIBLE). This is how the canon of Scripture was determined (*see* APOCRYPHA, OLD AND NEW TESTAMENT; BIBLE, CANONICITY OF).

Revelational Presuppositionalism. *See* VAN TIL, CORNELIUS; PRESUPPOSITIONAL APOLOGETICS.

Russell, Bertrand. Bertrand Russell (1872–1970) was born in Ravenscroft, England, to freethinking parents who were friends of John Stuart Mill. After the death of his parents, he was reared by austere grandparents who changed from being Presbyterians to Unitarians. He began questioning the immortality of the soul by the time he was fourteen and abandoned his belief in God by eighteen (in 1890) after reading Mill's *Autobiography*.

He studied philosophy at Cambridge and later taught at its Trinity College, from which he was eventually dismissed because of his pacifistic activism (1916). He said, "when the war came I felt as if I heard the voice of God. I knew that it was my business to protest." Russell lectured in the United States several times (1896, 1927, 1929, 1931, 1938f.). He was married and divorced many times, spent six months in prison for antigovernment activity (1918) where he wrote *Introduction to Mathematical Philosophy*, and in 1940 he was ruled morally unfit to teach in New York. Yet Russell was eventually awarded a Nobel Prize for literature (in 1950) for championing freedom of thought.

The writings of Russell are voluminous, including everything from co-authoring the weighty *Principia Mathematica* (1910) with Alfred North *Whitehead to his more popular *Why I Am Not a Christian* (based on a 1927 series of lectures). Other works include *A Critical Exposition of the Philosophy of *Leibniz* (1900), "Free Man's Worship" (1903), "The Essence of Religion" (1912), *Religion and Science* (1935), "The Existence of God Debate" with Father Copleston (1948), "What Is An Agnostic?" (a 1953 interview), and "Can Religion Cure Our Troubles?" (based on 1954 articles). His primary works on philosophy express a linguistic atomism. He was a mentor to Ludwig *Wittgenstein, wrote the introduction to Wittgenstein's *Tractatus*, and acknowledged Wittgenstein's influence on his own logical atomism.

Russell's Religion. Bertrand Russell's religious view evolved considerably over his ninety-eight-year life. For the first fourteen years of his life he was a theist (*see* THEISM). Between fourteen and eighteen he adopted a deistic (*see* DEISM) position. At eighteen he became a-theistic (i.e., nontheistic). At thirty-one he embraced a kind of fatalistic Stoic naturalism expressed in "Free Man's Worship." By age forty he had a kind of experiential pantheism that Friedrich *Schleiermacher (1768–1834) might have approved (see Russell, "The Essence of Religion"). Later, he became a militantly antitheistic and anti-Christian. At age

76, he described himself as an "agnostic" (*see* AGNOSTICISM) in his interview with *Look* magazine (1953).

Agnosticism and Antireligion. Whatever one calls Russell's metaphysical wanderings, he was consistently anti-Christian and antireligious, though he did not consider himself an atheist. "My position is agnostic," he said (Russell, "The Existence of God Debate," 144). In his *Look* magazine interview he claimed that "An agnostic thinks it is impossible to know the truth in matters such as God and the future life with which Christianity and other religions are concerned." After this strong statement, he then hedges his bet, adding: "Or, if not impossible, at least impossible at the present time" ("What Is an Agnostic?" 577).

Russell distinguishes agnosticism from atheism, claiming that "An atheist, like a Christian, holds that we *can* know whether or not there is a God; the atheist, that we can know there is not (*see* ATHEISM). The agnostic suspends judgment, saying that there are not sufficient grounds either for affirmation or for denial. . . . An Agnostic may hold that the existence of God, though not impossible, is very improbable" (ibid.).

From Russell's pen came a relentless attack, not only on Christianity, but on religion in general. He wrote, "I am as firmly convinced that religions do harm as I am that they are untrue" (*Why I Am Not a Christian*, xi). The basic reason is that they are based on a belief that is generated through fear, which in essence is bad. Organized religion retards progress in the world. In particular, "I say quite deliberately that the Christian religion, as organized in its Churches, has been and still is the principal enemy of moral progress in the world" (ibid., 15).

No Authority Accepted. Russell claimed to reject all authority. The agnostic, he said, holds that a man should think out personal conduct, listening to the wisdom of others. "No one but a fool indulges every impulse, but what holds a desire in check is always some other desire" ("What Is an Agnostic?" 578).

He denied having "faith in reason alone," insisting that there is more than facts and reason. He saw himself guided by his thought-through purposes or ends. "The Agnostic will find his ends in his own heart and not in an external command" (ibid., 583). For example, reason can tell how to get to New York, but only the individual can come up with the reason (purpose) for going there.

Sin is not a useful notion, though some kinds of conduct are desirable and some are undesirable (ibid., 578). But he hastens to add that punishment for undesirable conduct should only be a deterrent or reformatory and not penal.

Problems with Christianity. The Bible is rejected with all other authority. Russell considered it legendary history on a level with Homer. Some of its moral teaching is good, but much of it is very bad (ibid., 579).

Russell doubted whether Christ ever lived. "Historically," he claimed, "it is quite doubtful whether Christ ever existed at all, and if he did we do not know anything about him" (*Why I Am Not a Christian*, 11). Nonetheless, he claims that "Most [which does not necessarily include himself] agnostics admire the life and moral teachings of Jesus as told in the Gospels [which he does not accept], but not necessarily more that those of certain other men. Some [not Russell] would place him on the level with Buddha, . . . Socrates and some with Abraham Lincoln" ("What Is an Agnostic?" 579). Unlike many unbelievers, Russell declared: "I do not think that Christ was the best and wisest of men" ("Can Religion Cure Our Troubles?" 2). Russell's estimation of the Jesus of the Bible was that he was unwise, unmerciful, inhumane, and cruel (see below). He presented Socrates in a better light. He wrote, "There is one very serious defect to my mind in Christ's moral character, and that is that he believed in hell. I do not myself feel that any person who is really profoundly humane can believe in everlasting punishment" (*Why I Am Not a Christian*, 12).

No Immortality. Russell disbelieved in any afterlife, whether heaven or hell. Speaking of agnostics in general, he said: "An Agnostic, as such, does not take a view about survival unless he thinks that there is evidence one way or the other." For himself, Russell adds, "I do not think there is any good reason to believe that we survive death" ("What Is an Agnostic?" 580). For "it is rational to suppose that mental life ceases when bodily life ceases" ("What I Believe," 40). He adds, "I believe that when I die I shall rot, and that nothing of my ego will survive" (*Why I Am Not a Christian*, 43).

While somewhat uncertain about an afterlife in general, he was absolutely certain that there is no hell. For "Belief in hell is bound up with the belief that the vindictive punishment of sin is a good thing. . . . There might conceivably someday be evidence of its [heaven's] existence through spiritualism, but most Agnostics do not think there is such evidence, and therefore do not believe in heaven" ("What Is an Agnostic?" 580–81). As to whether he fears God's judgment, Russell responded: "Most certainly not. I also deny Zeus and Jupiter and Odin and Brahma, but these cause no qualms. . . . If there were a God, I think it is very unlikely that He would have such an uneasy vanity as to be offended by those who doubt his existence" (ibid., 581).

*Naturalistic Denial of *Miracles.* As for the supernatural, Russell asserted that "Agnostics do not think there is any evidence of 'miracles' in the sense of happenings contrary to natural law." Indeed, "it is possible to dispense with miracles, since Providence has decreed that the operation of natural laws shall produce the best possible results" (*Why I Am Not a Christian*, 42). He admits there are unusual events, but these are not miraculous. "We know that faith healing occurs and is in no sense miraculous." He saw as much miraculous evidence for the Greek gods in Homer as for the Christian God in the Bible" ("What Is an Agnostic?" 581).

Along the same line, he regarded the virgin birth as a vestige of pagan mythology (*see* MITHRAISM; MYTHOLOGY AND THE NEW TESTAMENT). He pointed to a *virgin birth story attached to Zoroaster and the fact that Ishtar, the Babylonian goddess, is called "the holy virgin" (ibid., 579).

Russell also rejected the idea of a purpose for life. "I do not think that life in general has any purpose. It just happened. But individual human beings have purposes, and there is nothing in Agnosticism to cause them to abandon these purposes" (ibid., 582).

Early Buddhism the Best Religion. Asked which religions he most respected, Russell responded that he preferred Buddhism, "especially in its earliest forms, because it has had the smallest element of persecution." He admired Confucianism and liberal Christians who reduced dogma to a minimum. But that there is actually a God behind any religion, he said the only evidence he would accept would be a voice from the sky accurately predicting all that would happen in the next twenty-four hours. However, even that would only convince him of a superhuman intelligence. He could, in fact, think of no evidence that would convince him of a God's existence (ibid., 583–84).

Evaluation. Such antagonism even to the possibility of proof for God's existence calls into question Russell's definition of *agnosticism*. His attitude differs little from that of most atheists who claim to know (on "very probable" grounds) that God does not exist. What is the difference? Few atheists claim to be absolutely certain that there is no God (*see* GOD, ALLEGED DISPROOFS OF). At one point in his *Look* interview, Russell admitted that, for all practical purposes he was "at one with the atheists" (ibid., 577). Such reluctance to admit atheism brings to mind Karl *Marx's quip that "an agnostic is nothing but a gutless atheist."

Self-Defeating Agnosticism. If Russell was an "agnostic," he was a hard-core one, claiming it "impossible" to know if there is a God. This boils down to the statement: "I know for sure about God's existence that you cannot know anything for sure about God's existence." Adding the caveat "at the present time" does not mitigate the problem. The statement is still self-defeating "at the present time."

Russell's evaluation of religion is shallow and faulty. His claim that all religions are based on fear is a "sociological fallacy." That is, it uses descriptive statements as though they were prescriptive. Fear is a factor in bringing some to religion, but it is insufficient to give a genuine or enduring faith. People seek religion also for happiness, security, freedom from guilt, and other factors. Russell seemed to have a pathological fear of fear. Not all fear is bad. There is a wholesome fear that warns one of possible danger or negative consequences. The fear of failing an exam can be a helpful motivation to study. The fear of being hit by a drunk driver can make one more watchful on the road. Also, psychological reasons do not explain the origin of a belief. They help to show *why* people believe, but do not account for *what* they believe (see Woods, 23). Finally, the origin does not determine the value of a thing. Most people fear fire, but this says nothing about the value of a fire.

The Need for God. Though Russell did not believe, a need for God is occasionally implicit. At one of his more candid moments he wrote: "Even when one feels nearest to other people, *something in one seems obstinately to belong to God, and to refuse to enter into any earthly communion*—at least that is how I should express it if I thought there was a God. It is odd, isn't it? I care passionately for this world and many things and people in it, and yet . . . what is it all? *There must be something more important, one feels,* though I don't believe there is" (*Autobiography*, 125–26, emphasis added).

Authority of Reason. Russell claimed to reject all authority, yet he acknowledged the final authority of human reason. He denied having "faith in reason alone," only in the sense that human purposes helped determine his actions. But one does not have faith in purposes but in some source of, and test for, truth. Reason alone suffices here. Hence, it is fair to say that Russell rejects any authority except that of human reason (*see* RATIONALISM). Of course, "reason is concerned with matters of fact, some observed, some inferred" ("What Is an Agnostic?" 583). So, Russell did have a final authority.

Like other agnostics and atheists, Russell had an inconsistent view of sin. He denied its validity, reducing everything to the "desirable" or "undesirable." Yet, when it came to issues of free speech and life style he expressed unmovable moral convictions. Russell seem to have no doubt that belief in hell was really and truly "cruel," "unmerciful," and "inhumane." These are moral absolutist positions. If morality is merely the "desirable" or "undesirable," then there is no real moral grounds to say anything is cruel or wrong. To be consistent, he should have said only that the concept of hell was contrary to his desires. He had no moral grounds to make any value judgment (*see* MORALITY, ABSOLUTE NATURE OF).

Further, there is a basic ambivalence in Russell's view of humanity. R. E. D. Clark observed that Russell based his code of morality on essential human goodness, then elsewhere urges that a good God could never have created such a revolting biped.

Authority and Christianity. Russell's dislike for all things Christian rises with the sensitivity of a Geiger counter when he approaches anything smacking of authority or a claim on his own life and freedom. He rejects the Bible along with all other authority. He likes some of its moral teachings, but those that bother him are "very bad" (ibid., 579). His attacks against Jesus, besides his basic unbelief in Jesus' existence, seem to stem from the fact that Christ in Scripture is an authority figure. Buddha, who he likes better, makes few commands and offers a personally-tailored road of wisdom. Socrates is even less directive.

Why Russell Rejected Christ. The militant anti-Christianity in *Why I Am Not a Christian* leaves the impression of one strongly atheistic. But he seemed more intent in setting up a straw-man argument against the Christian authoritarian personality and lifestyle. His ideal of the Christian religious person is one who does good and does not follow creeds. Christians must be more than do-gooders, however, or nothing would distinguish them from other religionists, such as Muslims. Minimally a Christian believes certain things about the existence of God, immortality, and the character and person of Christ. None of these can Russell accept. In particular, Russell came to the following positions:

The Fallacy of the First-Cause Argument. Russell rejected the traditional arguments for God's existence (*see* GOD, EVIDENCE FOR), in particular the cosmological argument for a First Cause. He reasoned that if something can exist without a cause, then it could be the world, just as it could be God. He attributed belief that the world had a beginning to the poverty of human imagination.

According to Russell, the very concept of a "cause," on which the *Cosmological Argument depends, had lost its vitality in current philosophy. But even granting causality, he posed this dilemma:

1. Either all things are caused or else they are not.
2. If all beings are caused, then so is God since he is a being.
3. If all things are not caused, then neither is the world since it is something.
4. So either God is caused by another (and is not the First Cause) or else the world is not caused by any God (and no God exists).
5. In either event there is no First Cause.

Logically it does not follow that, just because God can be without a cause, the world can too. God and the world are in two different categories. Since one is Creator and the other created, only the world needs a cause, not God. Also, there are good scientific and philosophical reasons for believing that the world had a beginning, something Russell brushes aside without due consideration (*see* BIG BANG; *KALAM* COSMOLOGICAL ARGUMENT). Hence, Russell's anti-first-cause argument fails.

Russell's question "Who caused God?" is based on a misstatement of the principle of causality (*see* CAUSALITY, PRINCIPLE OF). *Thomas Aquinas did not argument that *everything* needs a cause. Rather, *contingent* or *dependent* beings need a cause. For example, beings that have a beginning need a cause. For whatever comes to be needs a cause to bring it to be. But an eternal independent Being, such as God is, does not need a cause. Hence, to ask "Who made God?" is absurd. It is asking who made the unmade? It should not be difficult for Russell to understand this. He believed that the world did not need a cause; it was simply "there" ("Existence of God Debate"). But if the universe can be uncaused, so can God.

The Argument from Natural Law. The argument from natural law is rejected by Russell because it depends on understanding laws in a prescriptive sense (arguing that every prescription has a prescriber). But the laws of nature are only descriptive, not prescriptive. Hence, he insisted, the natural law argument fails. Further,

1. If God created law, then it was either for a reason or not for a reason.
2. It could not have been for a reason, since in that case God would be subject to it and not ultimate.
3. It could not have been for no reason, for in that case a rational God would not have done it. For God has a reason for everything.
4. Therefore, God could not have created law (i.e., there is no need for a Creator of law).

Russell is correct in pointing out that the laws of nature are only descriptive, not prescriptive. But it does not follow from this that the regular patterns and order of nature need no Orderer (*see* TELEOLOGICAL ARGUMENT; ANTHROPIC PRINCIPLE; EVOLUTION, CHEMICAL). Indeed, many modern agnostics and atheists contemplating the anthropic principle have had serious second thoughts. For who ordered the universe by specifying from the very beginning the precise conditions that would make human being possible?

Further, Russell poses a false dilemma about whether God had a reason for creating law. The reason does not have to be beyond himself, or it can be totally absent. God's reason for doing things is in himself: He is the ultimate Reason, for he is the ultimate rational Being in the universe.

The Argument from Design. Following David *Hume and Charles *Darwin, Russell rejected the concept of design in nature that leads to positing a Designer of nature. His reasoning can be put in this form:

1. Either living things are adapted to their environment because of design or because of evolution.
2. Science has demonstrated via natural selection that they are adapted to their environs because of evolution.
3. Hence, they were not designed by a Designer.

Russell's argument against design is a classic fallacy in logic. He sets up alternatives and then he selects which he wishes to deny. The inevitable result is begging the question. He also ignores evidence. He argues fallaciously that adaptation results from *either* design *or* evolution and then that it results only from evolution (affirming one alternate). The implication: It does not result from design. But in order for there to be a valid conclusion, one must deny one of the two alternates. He overlooks the possibility that adaptation might result from both design and evolution. After all, the Creator could have designed evolution as the means to accomplish his purpose (*see* EVOLUTION). Further, Russell assumes that the evidence for evolution is greater than that for creation. But this is not the case (*see* EVOLUTION, BIOLOGICAL).

The Moral Argument. Russell chided Immanuel *Kant for his moral argument for God. He insists that one does not easily get rid of what was learned at a mother's knee, and this is where *Kant learned to believe in God. This *ad hominem* argument aside, Russell posed this logical dilemma for those who argue from a moral law to a Moral Law Giver:

1. If there is a moral law, it either comes from God's fiat (will) or it does not.
2. But it cannot be from God's fiat or else he would not be essentially moral but arbitrary.
3. Neither can it not be by God's will, for in that case God would be subject to a moral standard beyond himself and would not be God (i.e., the Ultimate).
4. In either event there is no reason to posit a God as the source of moral law.

Putting Russell's *ad hominem* fallacy aside as unworthy of comment, his argument is another false dilemma. For the moral law does not have to be either arbitrary or outside of God (*see* ESSENTIALISM, DIVINE); it can be inside (viz., his own unchangeable moral nature). Hence, God can be ultimate without being arbitrary.

The Argument from Remedial Justice. Theists have sometimes argued that there must be a next life and a morally perfect God to remediate the injustice of this life. But Russell responds that whatever we find true here is probably true elsewhere. And we find that injustice rules in this life. There is no reason to believe it would not also rule in all other possible worlds.

It is not necessarily the case that what is true here is also true elsewhere. A desert in Arizona does not mean there is one in Florida or Alaska. Even if it were true that human behavior in one place is indicative of human behavior elsewhere under similar conditions, Russell's argument would fail. After all, heaven is an entirely different condition—one of perfection. If this is so, then one would expect human behavior to be different there. Russell also overlooks the prescriptive nature of the moral law. If there is an absolutely perfect God, then he cannot allow injustice to rule forever. He must rectify it. And Russell cannot assume that no morally perfect God exists as a basis for proving that no such God exists.

The Character of Christ. Not only did Russell reject the arguments for God's existence and immortality, but he also denied that Christ was a person of high moral character. He believed that Jesus' character had serious moral flaws.

Russell's belief about Jesus' character has flaws of its own. First, he entirely overlooks all the positive evidence for Christ's impeccable character (*see* CHRIST, UNIQUENESS OF). Second, his negative arguments all fall short of being actual proofs of flaws in Christ's character..

Jesus lacked wisdom. A very wise man cannot be wrong about important things. Yet Jesus was wrong about one of his important teachings, namely, that he would return immediately to earth after his death (Matt. 24:34). Hence, Jesus was not a very wise man. On another occasion, he manifested his lack of wisdom by cursing a fig tree for not having fruit before it was the season for bearing fruit (Matt. 21:19; cf. Mark 11:14). No truly wise person would do such a thing.

Russell wrongly assumes that Jesus claimed he would return within the life-time of his disciples (*Why I Am Not a Christian*, 11). The evidence is to the contrary. Jesus did not say he would return immediately but only immanently (cf. Acts 1:7). The reference to "this generation" (Matt. 24:34) could refer to the Jewish nation not passing away before he returns, since the word for generation (*genea*) can refer to a race or nation (cf. Matt. 23:36). Or, it may refer to the fact that he would come before the end of the generation in the future when the events predicted in this passage begin to come to pass (Matt. 24:33). Jesus explicitly said no one knew the time of his coming (Matt. 24:36; Acts 1:7). Thus, it is contrary to his very teaching in this same passage to understand him as telling them when he would return.

As to whether it was unwise to curse the fig tree, Russell misses an important point. It was the time of year (Passover) in which early figs do appear. This is why the text says: "and seeing from afar a fig tree *having leaves*, he went to find out if it had any fruit" (vs. 13). He certainly would not have done this unless figs sometimes appeared, as they do, under new leaves at this time of year.

Further, if Jesus is the Creator, then simply because a finite being does not see a reason for some event does not mean that an infinite Mind has none. As it turns out, Jesus' purpose here is expressed: The fig true illustrated Israel's fruitless rejection of the Messiah, and it would lead to disaster. Immediately following this he was accosted in the temple by the Jewish leaders (Mark 11:15f.) who soon thereafter called for his crucifixion.

Jesus was not profoundly humane. According to the Gospels, Jesus believed in hell—the eternal suffering of the lost (Matt. 5:22; 10:28). Russell insisted that no one who is profoundly human would believe in a place like hell.

The fact that Jesus believed in hell does not make him any more inhumane than someone who believes in the Jewish holocaust. Certainly, if the holocaust happened, then is not inhumane to believe in it. Likewise, if hell is real, then one is not inhumane for believing it is real. The question is one of truth, not of humanity.

Jesus was vindictive. Russell believes that Jesus was vindictive toward his enemies, pronouncing woes and judgments on them (cf. Matt. 23). But vindictiveness toward one's enemies is a moral flaw. Therefore, Jesus' character was morally flawed.

Contrary to Russell's claim, there is no evidence that Jesus was vindictive. He retaliated against no one. He warned them of the destructive end of their life, unless they turned around. And that is a merciful thing to do. Jesus exercised one of the greatest acts of non-vindictive mercy known to many when he look at those who torturously crucified him and said, "Father, forgive them for they do not know what they are doing" (Luke 23:34). Jesus explicitly taught that we should not be vindictive, insisting that: "If someone strikes you on the right cheek, turn to him the other also." He added, "Love you enemies, bless those who hate you, and pray for those who spitefully use you and persecute you" (Matt. 5:39, 44).

Jesus lacked proper kindness. Russell argued that any one who threatened people with eternal unforgiveness was not properly kind. Yet Jesus did this on occasion (Matt. 5:22; 23:35–36; John 5:24–29; 12:48).

That Jesus warned people about hell does not prove he lacked proper kindness. In fact, if there is a hell—and who is in a better position to know than is the Son of God (*see* CHRIST, DEITY OF)—then Jesus would have been unkind not to warn people about it. What would Russell think about someone who failed to warn him that there was a gaping fault in the road ahead of him in which he would perish if he did not turn around?

Jesus promoted cruelty. Another flaw in the character of Christ, according to Russell, was that he unnecessarily drowned a herd of pigs. Such an act is unkind to animals, unnecessarily destroying them in a lake. This reveals another flaw in Jesus' character.

There was no moral imperfection in the act of drowning a herd of pigs (Matt. 8:32). As God, Jesus was sovereign over all life. He created it, and he had the right to take it (Deut. 32:39; Job 1:21). All animals eventually die at the Creator's fiat anyway. That it happens earlier or later is irrelevant. The purpose of this herd of swine was not to give swine milk. The owners were going to take their lives anyway. Jesus did not directly kill the pigs anyway; the demons did. Jesus simply cast the demons out of the man and the demons entered the pigs and drove them over the cliff. Jesus was more concerned about saving the person, and Russell is more interested in the pigs.

Summary. Russell argued that there is no real basis to believe in either the existence of God or the high moral character of Christ (*see* CHRIST, UNIQUENESS OF). And since both of these beliefs are essential to being a Christian, he did not wish to call himself a Christian. But Russell's arguments fail to take way the Christian arguments for the existence of God and the moral superiority of Christ. They lack both a logical and a factual basis to do the job he desired. They indicate more about what he wanted to be the case, rather than an honest search for truth.

Sources

N. L. Geisler, *When Critics Ask*

B. Russell, *A Critical Exposition of the Philosophy of Leibniz*

———, "Can Religion Cure Our Troubles?"

———, "The Essence of Religion"

———, "The Existence of God Debate" with Father Copleston, BBC radio broadcasts, 1948

———, "Free Man's Worship"

———, *Introduction to Mathematical Philosophy*

———, *Religion and Science*

———, "What I Believe"

———, "What Is an Agnostic?" in *Look* magazine (1953)

———, *Why I Am Not a Christian*

A. D. Weigel, "A Critique of Bertrand Russell's Religious Position," *Bulletin of the Evangelical Theological Society* 8.4 (Autumn 1965).

H. G. Woods, *Why Mr. Bertrand Russell Is Not Christian*

Ss

Sagan, Carl. Carl Sagan (d. 1996) was a popular television personality, author of science and science fiction and an agnostic astronomer who strongly defended naturalistic evolution (*see* Evolution, Biological). He wrote numerous books, including *Cosmos*, *Cosmic Connection*, *Life in the Universe*, and *Broca's Brain*.

Although a confessed agnostic (*see* Agnosticism), Sagan made a surrogate religious experience of celebrating the cosmos. The universe, in his system of belief, functioned like a god. The cosmos is ultimate, eternal, creator, and object of worship. The set for his popular-level Public Broadcasting Service series, "Cosmos," was consciously decorated to give the feeling of both a space ship and a cathedral. The theme statement of those programs, Sagan's books, and much of his life's work was *"THE COSMOS IS ALL THAT IS OR EVER WAS OR EVER WILL BE"* (*Cosmos*, 4). The cosmos is supreme and all-encompassing. It is COSMOS, with all capitals.

In the Image of the COSMOS. Sagan believed that human beings are "created" in the image of the cosmos. He writes: "The ocean calls. Some part of our being knows this is from where we came. We long to return. These aspirations are not, I think, irreverent, although they may trouble whatever gods may be" (ibid., 5). Everything in the universe employs the same patterns over and over. Conservatively and ingenuously. This is true of plants and animals, oak trees and humans. Humanity is the product of a long series of biological accidents (*Cosmic Connection*, 52). As to human origins, Sagan states plainly, "Evolution is a fact, not a theory" (*Cosmos*, 27). Humans emerged by a powerful but random process (ibid., 282).

A Moral Duty to the COSMOS. Since humankind is created in the image of the cosmos, people have a moral obligation to their creator. "Our obligation to survive is owed, not just to ourselves but also to the COSMOS, ancient and vast, from which we spring" (ibid., 345). Since we have received our existence, we have a duty to perpetuate its existence. Indeed, "the very key to our survival is the cosmos, on which we float like a speck of dust in a beam of light" (ibid., 4). In such a universe, present and future well-being depends upon scientific knowledge (*UFO's—A Scientific Debate*, xv).

Salvation from the COSMOS. An openness to the cosmos is necessary to advance our knowledge (*Broca's Brain*, 58). Since humans evolved on earth, Sagan reasoned that life evolved elsewhere as well. Every star may be a sun to someone (*Cosmos*, 5). Contact with these extraterrestrials could be the salvation of the human race. So we must tune in to outer space by way of radio telescopes to receive possible messages. "Receipt of a single message from space would show that it is possible to live through such technological adolescence" (*Broca's Brain*, 275). After all, the transmitting civilization survived. Sagan believed such knowledge might be worth a great deal. Such a message might strengthen the bonds that join all beings on this planet. Since the cosmos is our creator and may be our savior, we have a moral duty to it. Scientists, and particularly astronomers, are priests who remind us of our ethical obligations and show us the way of cosmic salvation.

Evaluation. While Sagan presented his views as scientific, they really are religious. He goes way beyond science into the realm of speculative philosophy and religion. He deifies the cosmos (notice the capital letters, "COSMOS"). It replaces God as Creator and Object of moral duty and religious worship. Sagan even looks to it as the source of our salvation as a race.

Sagan either overlooks or downplays the vast scientific evidence for the existence of God and the creation of life (*see* God, Evidence for). He admitted that the second law of thermodynamics (*see* Thermodynamics, Laws of) would imply a Creator but countered that the first law of thermodynamics shows that the cosmos is eternal and needs no creator. This, however, misunderstands the first law, which does not in its scientific form say anything about whether energy can or cannot be created, but merely that the existing amount of actual energy in the universe remains constant.

By contrast with Sagan, another agnostic astronomer is more fair with the scientific evidence from which one can infer a Creator. Robert Jastrow, founder and director of the Goddard Institute for Space Research, notes that the evidence for a beginning of the universe has mounted. "For the scientist who has lived by his faith in the power of reason, the story sounds like a bad dream. He has scaled the mountains of ignorance; he is about to conquer the highest peak; as he pulls himself over the final rock, he is greeted by a band of theologians who have been sitting there for centuries" (Jastrow, 15).

Inconsistent References to Design. Sagan is inconsistent in his inferences from complex design (specified complexity). He admits that one short message from outer space implies an intelligent being(s) as its source (*see* EVOLUTION, CHEMICAL). Yet he denies the human brain, with some 20 million volumes of the same kind of specified complexity needs an intelligent Creator (*see* TELEOLOGICAL ARGUMENT; ANTHROPIC PRINCIPLE). Sagan wrote that "the neurochemistry of the brain is astonishingly busy, the circuitry of a machine more wonderful than any devised by humans" (*Cosmos* 278).

If a single message from space requires an intelligent creator, how about 20 million volumes of information? If ordinary machines need an intelligent cause, how about one more wonderful than any devised by humans? Another unbelieving astronomer, Fred Hoyle, was converted to *theism when he discovered that the chances of a one-celled organism emerging by purely natural process was 1 in $10^{40,000}$ (see Hoyle).

Sources

N. L. Geisler, *Carl Sagan's Religion for the Scientific Mind*
F. Hoyle, *Evolution from Space*
C. Sagan, *Broca's Brain*
———, *Cosmic Connection*
———, *Cosmos*
———, *UFO's—A Scientific Debate*

Salvation of Infants. *See* INFANTS, SALVATION OF.

Sartre, Jean Paul. Jean Paul Sartre (1905–1980), a popular French atheist (*see* ATHEISM) of the mid twentieth century, approached philosophy from an existential perspective. He, along with Albert Camus, stressed the absurdity of life. Sartre was born in Paris to nominal Christians (Catholic-Protestant mix), educated in Germany, and taught philosophy in France. His first work of note was *La Nausea* (*Nausea*). In 1938, Sartre was captured by Germany (1940), returned to France, and taught philosophy until 1944. He attempted an abortive leftist political movement (1951), and later cooperated with French Communists, trying to reconcile *Existentialism and *Marxism.

Becoming an Atheist. In his autobiography, *Words*, Sartre wrote of his training, "I was taught . . . the Gospel, and catechism without being given the means for believing" (*Words*, 249). He added, "My family had been affected by the slow movement of dechristianization that started among the Voltairian upper bourgeoisie and took a century to spread to all levels. . . . Good Society believed in God in order to speak of Him. How tolerant religion seemed! How comfortable it was" (ibid., 97, 98).

Sartre said he was sickened by the *mysticism and indifference of his grandparents. Outwardly he continued to believe, but he thought of God less and less (ibid., 100–101). As for the origin of his atheism, Sartre wrote: "Only once did I have the feeling that He existed. I had been playing with the matches and burned a small rug. I was in the process of covering up my crime when suddenly God saw me. I felt his gaze inside my head and on my hand. . . . I flew into a rage against so crude an indiscretion, I blasphemed. . . . He never looked at me again" (ibid., 102).

His conversion was confirmed one day, at age 12, when he tried to think about God and could not. From that moment he thought the matter settled, but it wasn't entirely. "Never have I had the slightest temptation to bring Him back to life. But the other One remained, the Invisible One, the Holy Ghost. . . . I had all the more difficulty getting rid of Him in that he had installed himself at the back of my head. . . . I collared the Holy Ghost in the cellar and threw him out; atheism is a cruel and long-range affair: I think I've carried it through. I see clearly, I've lost my illusions" (ibid., 252–53).

There were many philosophical influences on Sartre. From German philosopher Edmund Husserl (1859–1938) he learned the *phenomenological. Dialectical* negations (freedom is negativity) came from G. W. F. *Hegel (1770–1831). *Atheism* he learned from Friedrich *Nietzsche (1844–1900). His *metaphysics* was influenced by Martin Heidegger (1889–1976), though Heidegger disowned Sartre's "Existentialism."

Important Writings. Sartre's majors works follow the development of his thought. The early period of his career was dominated by phenomenological psychology under the influence of Husserl. Here he produces *Transcendence of the Ego* (1936 French, 1937 English), *The Emotions: Outline of a Theory* (1939, 1948), and *The Psychology of Imaginations* (1940, 1948). The middle period focused on ontology of human existence from Heidegger. Here he produced *Being and Nothingness* (1943, 1956) and *Existentialism and Humanism* (1946, 1948). In a latter period his concerns turned toward Marxism. He wrote

Questions de methode (1960) and *Critique de la raison dialectique* (1960).

The Atheism of Sartre. *View of God.* Like other atheists Sartre believed God's existence was impossible because God is by his very nature a self-caused being (*see* GOD, ALLEGED DISPROOFS OF). But one would have to be ontologically prior to himself in order to cause himself, which is impossible. In Sartre's terms, the "being-for-itself" can never become the "being-in-itself" (*Being and Nothingness*, 755–68). That is, the contingent cannot become the necessary. Nothing cannot become something. So God, a self-caused being, cannot exist.

View of Human Beings. Sartre viewed humanity as an empty bubble on the sea of nothingness. The basic human project is to become God. But it is impossible for the contingent to become a necessary being, for the subjective to become objective, or for freedom to become determined. The individual is, in fact, condemned to freedom (*see* FREE WILL). If one were to attempt to escape his destiny he would still be freely fleeing it. Even suicide is an act of freedom by which one would vainly attempt to avoid his freedom. So the human "essence" is absolute freedom, but absolute freedom has no objective or definable nature. The "I" (subject) always transcends the "me" or "it" (object).

View of Ethics. There are no absolute or objective moral prescriptions. For "no sooner had you [Zeus] created me than I ceased to be yours," wrote Sartre. "I was like a man who's lost his shadow. And there was nothing left in heaven, no right or wrong, nor anyone to give me orders. . . . For I, Zeus, am a man, and every man must find out his own way" (*No Exit*, 121–23).

Not only are there no divine imperatives or moral prescriptions, but there are no objective values. In the last lines of *Being and Nothingness*, Sartre wrote, "it amounts to the same thing whether one gets drunk alone or is a leader of nations." For all human activities are equivalent. We must, in fact, repudiate this "spirit of seriousness" which assumes there are absolute or objective values and accept the basic absurdity and subjectivity of life (see de Beavoir, 10, 16–18, 156).

What then should one do? Literally, "his own thing." Since there are no ultimate and objective values, we must create them. A person can act for personal good or for the good of all humanity. But there is no ethical obligation to think about others. In the final analysis, each is responsible only for the use of personal, unavoidable freedom.

View of the World and Destiny. The world for Sartre is real but contingent. It is simply there. It, like human life, is a given. Philosophically, it is uncaused. It is the field in which subjective choices are performed. It has no objective meaning. Each person creates personal meaning. The fact that several people may choose the same subjective projects (like Marxism for Sartre) makes no difference. Each person still is objectively the result only of the personal choices he or she has made. For example, Sartre said, "I am my books." Yet each transcends the world that has been personally created. The author is more than the words. He or she is the "Nothing" (freedom) out of which it was created.

Evaluation. Beside the general case for *theism (*see* APOLOGETICS, ARGUMENT FOR; COSMOLOGICAL ARGUMENT; MORAL ARGUMENT FOR GOD; TELEOLOGICAL ARGUMENT) and the answers to atheists' objections (*see* GOD, OBJECTIONS TO PROOF FOR), there are things that can be said of Sartre's form of atheism.

First, God is not a *self-caused* Being, which is impossible; he is an *uncaused* Being. By creating a false definition of God, Sartre was able to dismiss God too easily. But this was only a straw man, not the real God.

Second, God is not a contradiction to human freedom and creativity. God is the supreme creator and man is sub- and co-creator of good and value. God is the primary cause, and human freedom is the secondary cause. Free will and determinism are not logically contradictory, for God can predetermine that a person is free.

Third, Sartre makes an unjustified, radical disjunction between subject and object, fact and value. But in an individual human being this is a distinction without a real difference. I am me. An attack upon my objectivity (say, my body) is an attack upon me. When one kills a body the person leaves too. Someone cannot cut off my arm in anger without attacking me. My objectivity and subjectivity are not separable in this life.

Fourth, if there are no objective values and each is fully responsible only for self, then there is no meaningfully ethical sense in which one ought to choose responsibly for others. Indeed, there is no moral obligation to do anything. Atheistic existentialists do what they do only because they choose to do it. Atheistic *existentialism reduces to antinomianism (*see* MORALITY, ABSOLUTE NATURE OF).

Fifth, despite his autobiographical comments, Sartre was unable to dismiss God so easily. Before he died, he turned back to the God who created him. As reported in a French magazine, Sartre embraced Christian theism before he died. In his own words (Spring 1980): "I do not feel that I am the product of chance, a speck of dust in the universe, but someone who was expected, prepared, prefigured. In short, a being whom only a Creator could put here; and this idea of a creating hand refers to God." Sartre's mistress, Simone de Beavoir, reacted to Sartre's apparent recantation, complaining, "How should one explain this senile act of a turncoat?" She adds: "All my friends, all the Sartrians, and the editorial team of *Les Temps Modernes* supported me in my consternation" (cited in *National Review*, 677).

If view of this conversion, it was little wonder that his existential colleagues reacted as they did, for it is a tacit self-condemnation of Sartrian Humanism by Sartre himself. Two men, Alain Larrey and Michael Viguier, who lived in Paris in 1980, report that two months before his death, Sartre complained to his Catholic doctor that he "regretted the impact his writings had on youth," that so many had "taken them so seriously."

Sources

S. de Beavoir, *The Ethics of Ambiguity*
N. L. Geisler, *Christian Ethics*, chap. 2
———, *Is Man the Measure?* chap. 3
——— and W. Watkins, *Worlds Apart*, chap. 3
J. P. Sartre, *Being and Nothingness*
———, *Existentialism and Humanism*
———, *Nausea*
———, *No Exit*
———, *Nouvel Observateur*, as reported in *National Review* (11 June 1982) by T. Molnor
———, *Words*

Satan, Reality of. A good deal of skepticism has been expressed about Satan. Those who take the Bible seriously are obliged to believe in Satan's existence, since the Bible unmistakably refers to the demonic. Nonetheless, it is objected by skeptics and atheists (*see* ATHEISM) that belief in a sinister evil power in the universe is outmoded and superstitious.

In Defense of Satanic. A real personal Devil is given distinctive traits of personality, including intellect (2 Cor. 11:3; Luke 4:1f.). Ascribed to him are the emotions of desire (1 Tim. 3:6; cf. Isa. 14:12f.), jealousy (Job 1:8, 9), hatred (1 Peter 4:8), anger (Rev. 12:12), and will. The Devil commands (Luke 4:3, 9) and leads rebellions (Rev. 12:1–3).

Some evidence for the personality and reality of Satan is direct. In total, it is sufficient to establish existence of a personal Devil.

The Authority of Bible. Once the authenticity and Divine origin of the Bible are established (see BIBLE, EVIDENCE FOR; NEW TESTAMENT, HISTORICITY OF), the existence of Satan follows.

Genesis 3:1 describes Satan as a personal enemy of God and humans who deceives: "Indeed, has God said, 'You shall not eat from any tree of the garden?'" The historicity of this passage is confirmed by New Testament references to the historicity of Adam and Eve (see ADAM, HISTORICITY OF; EDEN, GARDEN OF) and their fall (cf. Rom. 5:12; 1 Tim. 2:13–14).

First Chronicles 21:1 and Psalm 109:6 describe Satan as standing against God's people. Job 1–2 records that Satan has access to God's presence and accuses people: "Now there was a day when the sons of God came to present themselves before the Lord, and Satan also came among them" (1:6). Satan is the real cause of Job's otherwise unexplainable suffering.

Nineteen of the twenty-seven New Testament books refer to Satan (and four more to demons). We gain a lot more informed understanding of this sphere of rebellion against God. The personal encounters and conversations of Christ with Satan and demons made it evident that Jesus believed in a real, personal Satan. Jesus made twenty-five of the twenty-nine references to Satan found in the Gospels. Indeed, Jesus carried on an extended conversation with Satan during his temptation. Matthew 4 and Luke 4 describe a personal encounter between Satan and Jesus. Mark 1:12 and Hebrews 4:13 refer to this confrontation. To deny the reality of a personal Satan in this passages is to impugn the integrity or sanity of Christ (*see* CHRIST, DEITY OF). In Revelation 12:9 several names describing Satan are mentioned in one passage: "And the great dragon was thrown down, the serpent of old who is called the devil and Satan, who deceives the whole world; he was thrown down to the earth, and his angels were thrown down with him." Rev. 20:2 speaks of an angel of God who "laid hold of the dragon, the serpent of old, who is the devil and Satan, and bound him for a thousand years."

The events surrounding the temptation are all historical—the ministry of John the Baptist and baptism of Jesus (cf. Matthew 3). The nature and reality of the account is too vivid to be merely symbolic. The Gospels accord considerable significance to the event as a watershed point in the life of Christ and salvation history. He declared himself to be the Son of God; he conquered temptation. He passed the test the first Adam had failed.

The Enemy of God's People. The history of both Israel and the church are difficult to understand apart from a personal Satan who seeks to thwart God's plan for history. At the fall it was announced that human salvation would come through the promised seed of the woman (Gen. 3:15). This covenant promise was eventually narrowed to the offspring of Abraham through Isaac and Jacob (Gen. 12:1–3; 36; 46). The covenant came to be centered in twelve tribes of Israel (Genesis 49). Satan relentlessly attacked that bloodline (cf. Num. 24:10; Zech 3:1).

Considering the relative insignificance of Israel in the history of the world, they have been the continual, repeated victims of programs of genocide, starting with the Persians (cf. Esther). The Greek conquest of Palestine was a studied attempt to destroy the Jewish culture with few parallels. From Haman through medieval pogroms to Hitler, Stalinization, and Sadam Hussain, this tiny people have been targeted. This conspiracy of hatred against the Jews is best explained as emanating from one sinister evil mind. This is to say nothing of the two millennia of attacks on Christian identity, purity, and community. On numerous occasions these attacks have seemed perilously close to demolishing God's new covenant people.

The Reality of Demons. Another argument in support of the reality of the Devil is that of demons who express a unified conspiracy against God, his plan, and his people. Without a leader the demonic forces would not manifest such an organized show of force against God. Indeed, the Bible describes Satan as their "prince" (Luke 11:15) and "king" (Rev. 9:11). The increasing evidence for true demonic possession is an extrabiblical source of support for the reality of demons.

The Universality of Temptation and Evil. Another evidence of the reality of a personal Devil is the universal, powerful and persistent nature of the temptation to do evil. What else accounts for heinous crimes committed by seemingly decent people, from David to the present. Even law-abiding people (who pass for what we call "good") show that they are not good by feeling the urge to do things totally out of keeping with their character. And this includes Christians. The universal temptation to sin, even by godly people, is best explained by a sustained, personal attack. Evil does not fit the impersonal force category under which it is often placed. Gravity and magnetism are impersonal forces, but they do not personally allure. Evil by its very nature interacts with intellect and will.

The Proliferation of Deception. The existence of thousands of false religions and cults testifies to the existence of a great Deceiver. Paul wrote: "The Spirit clearly says that in latter times some will abandon the faith and follow deceiving spirits and things taught by demons. Such teachings come through hypocritical liars, whose consciences have been seared as with a hot iron" (1 Tim. 4:1–2).

Considered as a whole the direct and indirect evidence for the existence of a personal evil power behind this world is substantial. It is based both in history and in personal experience.

Objections to the Devil. A common objection to the existence of the demonic is that there are natural explanations for what is sometimes called "demonic" or evil. A common argument is that sicknesses once attributed to the demonic, even by the Bible, are now known to have natural causes. This objection overlooks that the Bible distinguishes between sickness and demonic possession. Jesus differentiated between them when he listed them as separate miracles the apostles were given power to do: "Heal the sick, raise the dead, cleanse those who have leprosy, drive out demons" (Matt. 10:8). The Bible does not claim that all sickness is demonically caused. The Bible recommends the use of medicine in treating natural sickness (cf. 1 Tim. 5:23).

Similar symptoms may be present in sicknesses and some demon possessions, but that does not prove there is a natural explanation for both. The young man from whom a demon was cast in Matthew 17:14-17 had symptoms similar to those of an epileptic seizure, but that doesn't mean he had epilepsy. Similar effects do not prove identical causes (*see* MIRACLES, FALSE). Both God and the magicians of Egypt turned water blood-red. Even a demon-caused illness might respond to medicine. Many induced sicknesses can be treated. Because a mind caused it (whether human or demonic) does not mean medicine cannot relieve symptoms.

At least some demonic activity manifests distinctive spiritual characteristics not present with natural sickness. These symptoms could include such things as opposition to God, violent reaction to Christ, and the manifestation of supernormal strength (cf. Mark 5:1–4). These do no respond to any purely natural treatment.

Another argument is that belief in satanic activity is characteristic among the uneducated. These beliefs diminish as a society moves to a modern culture. However, this may partly be due to different strategies Satan uses among different peoples. He can adapt to the culture he is deceiving. What better way to deceive the sophisticated anti-supernaturalists than to lead them to believe he does not exist. The Bible declares that Satan disguises himself as an angel of light (2 Cor. 11:14). But it is not true that demonic manifestations occur only among "primitive" people. With the "post-Christian age" the Western world has seen far more occultic activity and reports of demonic manifestations.

Some of the greatest Western minds have believed in Satan and the demons. This includes Augustine, Anselm, Thomas Aquinas, Blaise Pascal, Søren Kierkegaard, and C. S. Lewis. It is not the degree of intelligence or education that determines whether one believes in a personal Satan. Rather, it depends on whether one has rejected the supernatural revelation of Scripture (*see* BIBLE, EVIDENCE FOR).

Sources

N. L. Geisler, *Miracles and the Modern Mind*

———, *Signs and Wonders*

C. S. Lewis, *Screwtape Letters*

Thomas Aquinas. *Summa Theologica* 1a, 50–64

M. Unger, *Demonology*

Schaeffer, Francis. Francis Schaeffer (1912–1984) was born in Germantown, Pennsylvania. After being graduated from Hampden-Sydney College, he came under the teaching of Cornelius Van Til at Westminster Seminary and the biblical/historical evidence focus of Allan MacRae at Faith Seminary. After ten years in the pastorate in the United States, he and his wife Edith went to Switzerland as child evangelism missionaries in 1948. After a personal spiritual and ecclesiastical crisis in 1955, during which he was abandoned by his mission board, he began L'Abri Fellowship there as an outreach primarily to U.K. and American college students wandering Europe. L'Abri became an intellectual center that critiqued culture and challenged those influenced by *existentialism and modernist European theologies.

Many of Schaeffer's works are related to apologetics, but three in particular spell out his views: *The God Who Is There* (written first but published 1968), *Escape from Reason* (1968), and *He Is There and He Is Not Silent* (1972). *Genesis in Space and Time* (1972) and *No Final Conflict* (1975) engage in biblical apologetics. While *How Shall We Then Live?* (1976), *Whatever Happened to the Human Race?* (1979), and *A Christian Manifesto* (1981) can be viewed as cultural apologetics. *Back to Freedom and Dignity* (1972) defended human free choice (*see* FREE WILL) and the image of God against the determinism of B. F. Skinner. Schaeffer also wrote many books on the spiritual life including *The Mark of a Christian* (1970) and *True Spirituality* (1971).

Schaeffer's Apologetic Approach. Schaeffer was neither a professional philosopher nor an apologist. He considered himself an evangelist, though more properly he was a pre-evangelist or popular apologist. As such, he did not employ terms in a precise or technical sense. Nor did he write systematically. His early apologetic works first were given as lectures (Duriez, 252). The result is that his precise apologetic method is difficult to reconstruct; elements in his approach, however can be distinguished.

Presuppositional Starting Point. Thomas V. Morris points to presuppositional elements in Schaeffer's approach (*see* PRESUPPOSITIONAL APOLOGETICS). Schaeffer refused to be pigeonholed as either a presuppositionalist or an evidentialist (cited by Ruegsegger, 64). Nonetheless, he was influenced by *Van Til and considered presuppositions "crucial" (Duriez, 256). He went so far as to say that presuppositional apologetics would have stopped the decay of modern culture. "So now for us, more than ever before, a presuppositional apologetic is imperative" (*The God Who Is There*, 15). Schaeffer even speaks of "necessity" for his arguments (Morris, 31), though Gordon Lewis insists that this is a "descriptive necessity" (Lewis, 88) of a popular evangelist, not a philosophical necessity of a technical apologist. Schaeffer biographer Colin Duriez describes Schaeffer's theme of the "'necessity' of historic Christianity," that "without God's existence and communication there are no answers to the fundamental human questions" (Duriez, 256). This is a *transcendental argument. Schaeffer, like other presuppositionalists, begins with the Christian starting point of the triune God revealed in Scripture.

Schaeffer's presuppositional starting point, like Van Til's, was the "infinite-personal God" of the Bible (Schaeffer, *The God Who Is There*, 94). Schaeffer noted that "every person we speak to, whether the shop girl or university student, has a set of presuppositions, whether they have analyzed them or not" (ibid., 109). Presuppositions provide a starting point for spiritual journey (ibid., 126). One must go on to provide a rational verification of beliefs. In this context, Kenneth Harper views Schaeffer as an "inconsistent presuppositionalist," for, unlike Van Til, Schaeffer believed in common ground with unbelievers (Harper, 138). However, even Van Til recognized common ground in a formal sense as well as verification by means of a transcendental argument.

Logical Coherence. Over against the radical existentialism, irrationalism, and growing mysticism of culture, Schaeffer stressed the principle of noncontradiction (*The God Who Is There*, 109). He believed that modern people were engaged in an "escape from reason." All non-Christian views are inconsistent. Christianity by contrast, "constitutes a non-self-contradictory answer" (ibid., 156). *Logic is part of God's image in man by which truth claims are to be tested. Without logical coherence there is no truth. Schaeffer refers often to this theme.

Pragmatic Element. Since the thrust of Schaeffer's apologetic strategy was to show that the non-Christian view was *unlivable*, there is a pragmatic dimension to it (see Geisler, *Christian Apologetics*, chap. 6). Only Christian presuppositions can be lived out consistently, according to Schaeffer. He insists that "we must be able to live consistently with our theory" if it is true (*The God Who Is There*, 109). The materialistic (*see* MATERIALISM) view is false because "man simply cannot live as though he were a machine." The Christian view "can be lived with, both in life and in scholarly pursuits." Furthermore, the Christian "has years of experimental evidence" in support of his belief. Thus, livability is a test for the truth of a view and unlivability is a test for its falsity (ibid., 109–11).

Verification Aspect. Gordon Lewis sees his own from of presuppositionalism in Schaeffer, which is patterned after that of John *Carnell. He prefers to call it a verification apologetic that is neither deductive nor inductive but an abductive approach (Lewis, "Schaeffer's Apologetic Method"). Indeed, Schaeffer does say rationality is gained "on the basis of what is open to verification and discussion" (*Escape from Reason*, 82). He even defines *verification* as "the procedure required for the establishment of the truth or falsity of a statement" (*The God Who Is There*, 180). He lists a two-fold form of verification, though the first one contains two elements:

1. The theory must be non-contradictory, and it must give an answer to the phenomenon in question.

2. We must be able to live it out consistently (ibid., 109).

So Schaeffer's definition of *verification* is more broad than that of science. As noted above, at times he seem to engage in a kind of transcendental argument, setting forth the necessity of God's being there and not being silent in order for us to make sense out of the world.

Evaluation. *Positive Contributions.* There are many commendable things about Francis Schaeffer's approach to apologetics. Among these the following should be noted.

The propositional authority of Scripture. Schaeffer, like other presuppositionalists, began with the triune God (*see* TRINITY) who has revealed himself in Scripture. He stressed the need for propositional revelation (ibid., 109; *see* BIBLE, EVIDENCE FOR). Schaeffer never wavered on his belief that the inerrancy of Scripture is a "watershed" issue. It is God's objective, propositional revelation to mankind. He encouraged the formation of the International Council of Biblical Inerrancy (ICBI), 1978–1988, which produced the "Chicago Statement" on inerrancy and the book *Inerrancy*. Schaeffer attended one of its early formation meetings of the ICBI. His book *No Final Conflict* drew a line in the sand for evangelicals on this issue.

The rational character of belief. He constantly stressed the objective, rational character of belief. In *Escape from Reason* he critiques the irrationalism, subjectivism, and *existentialism that had permeated so much of the twentieth century. In this context, Schaeffer had a greater appreciation for human reason than did Van Til.

Schaeffer was adamant about the objective nature of truth (*see* TRUTH, NATURE OF). Truth "open to verification [and] can also be communicated verbally in writing" (ibid., 141). There are no special tests for religious truth, for "scientific proof, philosophical proof and religious proof follow the same rules" (ibid., 109). Truth is truth. Although since the term has been diluted to mean subjective truth, Schaeffer sometimes refers to objective truth by the deliberately redundant phrase, "true truth."

The need for common ground. Another positive dimension of Schaeffer's approach was his stress on the need for common ground in discussions with unbelievers. This he believed was rooted in the fact that "we are made in the image of God" (*Escape from Reason*, 83). The fall does not mean we cease to be human or rational (*The God Who Is There*, 178). Nonbelievers share with believers both moral and rational absolutes. Both a moral framework and moral guilt is experienced by unbelievers (ibid., 102). Further, humans have the "power to reason consistently" (ibid., 179). The law of noncontradiction is not from *Aristotle but is part of being created in the image of God (*see* FIRST PRINCIPLES). While these factors are shared with unbelievers, they deny the adequate ground for them in God (*He Is There and He Is Not Silent*, 65).

Negative Aspects of Schaeffer's Apologetic. Much of the negative reaction to Schaeffer's approach is generated by his imprecise use of terms. Most of this can be explained by his lack of scholarly background in philosophy or apologetics. By his own confession he was an evangelist who developed a practical method for doing evangelism, or better, pre-evangelism. Nonetheless, Schaeffer must take responsibility for the inaccuracies and insufficiencies in his system.

Misunderstanding of modern thinkers. While Schaeffer generally intuited correctly the major flow of modern thought, nonetheless, he often misunderstood the actual sources. Most experts on Søren *Kierkegaard believe that Schaeffer wrongly understood him to be an irrationalist. Schaeffer also misunderstood *Thomas Aquinas, characterizing him as someone who separated faith and reason, thus giving rise to modern Humanism (*see* FAITH AND REASON). In an unmistakable distortion of Aquinas, Schaeffer contended that, as a result of Aquinas, philosophers "were making the particulars autonomous and thus losing the universal that gave rise to the particulars meaning." Thus, "if nature or the particulars are autonomous from God, then nature begins to eat up grace. Or, we could put it this way: all we are left with are particulars, and universals are lost, not only in the area of morals, which would be bad enough, but in the area of knowing" (Schaeffer, *He Is There and He Is Not Silent*, 41–42). As detailed analysis of the writings of Aquinas reveal (see Geisler, *Inerrancy*, all), nothing could be farther from the truth. Aquinas was one of the greatest defenders of universals in knowledge and moral absolutes of all time.

Duriez attempts in vain to exonerate Schaeffer of this charge by citing obscure references and secondary sources but fails to produce any text from Aquinas to support his misunderstanding (Duriez, 252–54). His effort to show indirect causal relations only manifests misuse (not proper use) of Aquinas (see Geisler, *Inerrancy*, chaps. 1, 5).

Lack of appreciation for classical apologetics. Although some of his own reasoning can be construed in the form of a *teleological argument or *cosmological argument for God's existence, Schaeffer makes these no formal part of his apologetic system. In fact, he explicitly rejects *classical apologetics (*The God Who Is There*, 15). He does not seem to appreciate the need expressed by the great Christian apologists from earliest times to offer theistic arguments to establish the existence of God—the linchpin of theistic apologetics.

Ironically, while Schaeffer rejects classical apologetics, he nonetheless at times emulates what would be arguments for the existence of God. For example, employing a transcendental form of argument, he concludes that *"everyone has to explain the fact that the universe and he, the individual exist; thus, something has 'been there'!"* (*He Is There and He Is Not Silent*, 92, emphasis added). He even uses the basic premises of the cosmological argument, namely, that 1) something exists, and 2) nothing cannot produce something. For he rejects the view that "everything that exists has come out of absolutely nothing" (ibid., 7).

Invalid reasoning processes. From a philosophical or apologetic standpoint Schaeffer's logic is often loose and lacking. As Lewis notes, "Schaeffer would have done well to define the law of noncontradiction more carefully. His popular purposes actually led him to inaccuracy, since not every 'opposite' is a contradictory" ("Schaeffer's Apologetic Method," 81).

Others have seen a logical fallacy of affirming the consequent in his presuppositional approach. It argues if "P" is true, then "Q" is true. "Q" is true. Therefore, "P" is true. This is the same difficulty faced by scientific forms of reasoning. Some contend that it can be overcome by divergent lines of evidence (ibid., 99). Others conclude that this is why the scientific method can falsify views but not verify any. Of course this can be overcome if one's argument is put in a valid transcendental form. But there seems to be no valid way to do this—at least not with all that Schaeffer and other presuppositionalists wish to pack into their presuppositions, namely, the Trinity and inspiration of the Bible (see Van Til).

Insufficient pragmatic element. While Schaeffer has more than a pragmatic dimension to his apologetic (there being rational and evidential elements as well), nonetheless, he places great emphasis on the "unlivability" of the non-Christian views. This no doubt arose out of his use of apologetics as a practical aid to evangelism. However, even "practical" approaches should involve valid thinking. And it is not sufficient to test a view on the basis of its "livability" or "unlivability." First, it is a pragmatic test subject to all the criticism of that test for truth (*see* TRUTH, NATURE OF; PRAGMATISM). Second, "livability" will be defined differently by different worldviews. And it begs the question to use a Christian view to test whether a Hindu or some other view is livable.

Third, of course, if a view is true it should be livable. But this does not mean that if something is livable then it must be true. In fact, simply because some people find Christianity unlivable does not mean it is false. They may not be living it correctly, namely, by the power of God.

Insufficient systematic coherence. If Schaeffer's view is considered substantially the same as that of John Carnell's, as Lewis suggests, then it is subject to the same criticism discussed in the articles on Carnell and Presuppositionalism. More than one worldview may be systematically consistent with the facts as they are interpreted. However, each worldview interprets the facts differently. By systematic coherence alone one cannot properly adjudicate between conflicting worldviews. *Hinduism and *Zen Buddhism are internally consistent and account for all the data of experience as they understand it (though they fall on other grounds). So the Christian worldview cannot be proven unique by this method.

Overstating his conclusions. Even some defenders of Schaeffer's method admit that he overdraws his conclusions. Lewis observes that "Schaeffer often thinks he has examined all possible hypothesis when he has examined few" (ibid., 100). One cannot know that all non-Christian views are incoherent and/or unlivable unless he has carefully examined all of them. Schaeffer nowhere even attempts to do this in his writings.

Sources

L. T. Dennis, *Francis Schaeffer: Portraits of the Man and His Work*

———, *Letters of Francis A. Schaeffer*

C. Duriez, "Francis Schaeffer," in W. Elwell, ed., *Handbook of Evangelical Theologians*

N. L. Geisler, *Christian Apologetics*, chap. 6

———, *Thomas Aquinas*

———, ed., *Inerrancy*

K. C. Harper, "Francis Schaeffer: An Evaluation," *Bibliotheca Sacra* 133 (1976)

G. Lewis, "Schaeffer's Apologetic Method," in R. W. Ruegsegger, ed., *Reflections on Francis Schaeffer*

———, *Testing Christianity's Truth Claims*

T. V. Morris, *Francis Schaeffer's Apologetics: A Critique*

R. Raymond, *The Justification of Knowledge*

R. W. Ruegsegger, *Reflections on Francis Schaeffer*

F. Schaeffer, *Escape from Reason*

———, *He Is There and He Is Not Silent*

———, *The Complete Works of Francis Schaeffer*

———, *The God Who Is There*

C. Van Til, *The Apologetic Method of Francis Schaeffer*

Schleiermacher, Friedrich. Friedrich Schleiermacher (1768–1834) was a German theologian educated in Moravian pietism. He was ordained and preached in Berlin (1796) before teaching theology at Halle (1804) and Berlin (1810). His two major works are *On Religion* (1799), which is experiential in its orientation, and *The Christian Faith* (1821–22), which is doctrinal in approach. He also wrote a *Brief Outline on the Study of Theology* and a posthumously published book *Hermeneutics*.

Schleiermacher was influenced by pietism, which stressed the devotional over the doctrinal; romanticism, which included a belief in *pantheism in contrast to theism, and agnosticism, following Immanuel Kant that emphasized the practical over the theoretical.

Schleiermacher himself exerted a tremendous influence on his followers. As the father of modern liberalism, he influenced most major liberals after him, among them Albrecht Ritschl (1822-

1889), *Critical History of the Christian Doctrine of Justification and Reconciliation*; Adolf von Harnack (1851–1930), *What is Christianity?*, and Julius *Wellhausen (1844–1918), who wrote *Introduction to the History of Israel* in which he defended the J-E-P-D hypothesis of authorship/redaction of the Pentateuch (*see* PENTATEUCH, MOSAIC AUTHORSHIP OF).

Elements of Religion. For Schleiermacher, the basis of religion is human experience, rather than divine existence. We must *have* it before we can *utter* it. The locus of religion is in the self. The inner is key to the outer. The object of religion is the "All," which many call "God." And the nature of religion is found in a feeling (sense) of absolute dependence, which is described as a sense of creaturehood, an awareness that one is dependent on the All, or a sense of existential contingency.

Schleiermacher distinguished religion from ethics and science in the following manner:

Ethics	**Science**	**Religion**
way of living	way of thinking	way of feeling
way of acting	way of knowing	way of being (sensing)
practical	contemplative rationalization	attitudinal intuition
self-control		self-surrender

The relation of religion to doctrine is that of a sound to its echo or experience to an expression of that experience. Religion is found in feeling, and doctrine is only a form of the feeling. Religion is the "stuff" and doctrine the structure. Doctrine is not essential to religious experience and is scarcely necessary to expressing it, since it can be expressed in symbol as well.

As to the universality of religion, Schleiermacher believed that all have a religious feeling of dependence on the All. In this sense there are no atheists (*see* ATHEISM). In this he foreshadowed Paul *Tillich.

Being primarily a feeling, religion is best communicated by personal example. It is better caught than taught. Religion can also be communicated through symbols and doctrines. But doctrines are accounts of religious feeling. They are statements about our feeling, not about God, his attributes, or his nature. So there is an endless variety of religious expression, due largely to personality differences. The pantheistic expression results from those who delight in the obscure. Theists (*see* THEISM) by propensity are those who delight in the definite.

The aim of religion is the love of the All, the World-Spirit. This is achieved through loving other human beings. The result of religion is unity of life. And its influence is manifest in morals. Religion produces a wholeness of life, but it has no specific influence on individual acts. We act *with* religion, not *from* it.

Likewise, the influence of religion on science is not direct. One cannot be scientific without piety. For the feeling of dependence on the All removes presumption to knowledge, which is ignorance. The true goal of science cannot be realized without a vision arising from religion.

The Test for Truth. Religions are neither true nor false, as such. Truth categories do not apply to a feeling of absolute dependence. Truth and falsity relate to ideas (*see* TRUTH, NATURE OF). And the truth of an idea is determined by two sets of criteria, scientific and ecclesiastical. Scientific criteria include clarity, consistency, coherence, and fit with other doctrines into a system. The ecclesiastical criteria apply to the life of the church. Indeed the knowledge of God is mediated through the corporate experience of redemption, rather than in a body of doctrine. It is for this reason that Schleiermacher relegated his treatment of the Trinity to an appendix. He believed it a speculation divorced from piety.

For example, Schleiermacher's evaluation of the doctrine of God's timelessness (*see* GOD, NATURE OF) yielded these results:

1. Timelessness does not fit well with the incarnation. How can the eternal become temporal?
2. Timelessness conflicts with the doctrine of creation. How can the eternal act in time?
3. Timelessness conflicts with foreknowledge, or even with knowledge. Why does the Bible speak of God as foreknowing? How could a timeless God know anything in time?
4. Timelessness conflicts with God's personality. How can God plot his purpose and respond to happenings in time if eternal?
5. Timelessness conflicts with God's worship-appropriateness. It necessitates God's immutability. Who can worship a God who cannot be moved to change in an way?

Hence, timelessness is rejected as a true doctrine.

Schleiermacher's concept of salvation was not orthodox. He understood redemption to be the impression made by Jesus. This unclouded God-consciousness transformed the Christian community when an impoverished God-consciousness was replaced with that of Jesus. His view of *miracles and providence was ambivalent. And his almost complete stress on God's immanence made him liable to the charge of *pantheism.

Evaluation. Christian apologists take note of a number of Schleiermacher's views, particularly his views of God, religion, truth, and *biblical criticism.

Schleiermacher offered insight into religion with his stress on the contingent and dependent nature of all creatures; his emphasis on the importance of religious experience; his distinctions between religion, science, and ethics; his belief that truth needs to be tested; his stress on community; and his belief in systematic theology.

But this doesn't mitigate some serious problems: his experimental form of pantheism; his acceptance of Kantian epistemology (*see* KANT; AGNOSTICISM); his disjunction of experience and doctrine; his contention that truth does not apply to religion (*see* TRUTH, NATURE OF); his reduction of theology to anthropology (see Barth); and his acceptance of negative higher criticism of the Bible (*see* BIBLE CRITICISM).

Sources

G. L. Archer, Jr., *A Survey of Old Testament Introduction*
K. Barth, *From Rousseau to Ritschl*
———, *The Theology of Schleiermacher*
R. Brandt, *The Philosophy of Friedrich Schleiermacher*
R. K. Harrison, *Introduction to the Old Testament*
R. Niebuhr, *Schleiermacher on Christ and Religion*
F. Schleiermacher, *On Religion*
———, *The Christian Faith*

Schopenhauer, Arthur. Arthur Schopenhauer (1788–1860) was born in Danzig, Germany. He was educated in France, England, and India. He came from a mentally unstable family. His father probably committed suicide. He became completely estranged from his mother and had unfortunate relationships with women in general. His academic career was cut short for lack of students; he deliberately scheduled classes to compete with W. F. G. *Hegel at the peak of Hegel's career. After years of solitude and resentment in which his work was never widely accepted, he died in 1860.

Schopenhauer's books include his published dissertation, *On the Fourfold Root of the Principle of Sufficient Reason* (1813) and *The World as Will and Representation [or Idea]* (1818/1819). In 1844 the latter volume was enlarged by fifty chapters. He also produced *On the Will in Nature* (1836) and *The Basis of Morality* (1841).

Philosophy. Although he studied under Friedrich Schleiermacher (1768–1834) and Johann Fichte (1762–1814), they disappointed him. *Plato (428–348 B.C.) and Immanuel *Kant impressed him. He also acknowledged Hindu influences and the idealism of George *Berkeley. Through his mother, a novelist, he learned the ideas of poet and dramatist Johann Goethe (1749–1832).

Epistemology. Schopenhauer was an archenemy of both rationalism and empiricism (*see* HUME, DAVID). The senses offer us only impressions of the phenomenal world (appearance), as David Hume informed us. And the mind cannot know reality as Kant demonstrated.

He severely criticized the principle of sufficient reason used by Gottfried *Leibniz and the rationalists. He noted their confusion between real cause and a sufficient reason. Sufficient reason is an *a priori* structure of consciousness; it can't be proven. It applies only to objects of thought, that is, to phenomena and not to the noumena or real world. The four roots of sufficient reason are being, becoming, acting, and knowing.

There is disagreement over whether Schopenhauer was a true atheist (*see* ATHEISM), or perhaps adopted some kind of *pantheism. He was clearly opposed to theism. He contended that the ontological argument is based on a confusion by René *Descartes between cause and reason. A cause demands something beyond it *ad infinitum*. But reason needs no cause beyond it; reason can be itself (*see* CAUSALITY, PRINCIPLE OF). So, the principle of sufficient reason does not lead to a First Cause (God).

The *ontological argument is a "charming joke," a sleight of hand, according to Schopenhauer. It assumes existence of God by definition, and then pretends to arrive at the proof for God in the conclusion (*see* GOD, EVIDENCE FOR). *Aristotle showed that defining (*what* it is) differs from existing (*that* it is). Hence, existence can never belong to the essence of a thing, as the ontological argument affirms.

World as Representation (or Idea). Central to Schopenhauer's system is the premise of the world as representation, that is, that which directly confronts the one who perceives it.

The world is the individual's presentation (or Idea). It appears phenomenally as a mental presentation, and noumenally (really) as thing-in-itself or will. He cites *Berkeley that "to be is to be perceived" in support of this. He rejects Fichte's reduction of object to subject and Friedrich Schelling's subject to object. He reduces Kant's forms and categories to space, time, and cause. Reason is the tool of will in opposition to Hegel's concept of the rule of reason.

There are distinctive elements in Schopenhauer's view of reality (metaphysics). Reality is not rational; it is volitional. The thing-in-itself is "cosmic will." Appearance manifests reality (phenomena reveals the noumena). Humanity carries the answer to metaphysical puzzles in his own breast in the principle of freedom.

Cosmic Pessimism. Schopenhauer's cosmic pessimism stood against both the "enlightenment" and "mechanism" of his day. He viewed reality as a universal will, that is, a single whole, omnipresent in nature as opposed to many individual wills. Will is the nonrational and irrational ground of every sufficient reason. It is a blind cosmic force, incessantly striving to embody itself in space and time. Its operations are without ultimate purpose of design. Nature is a vast phenomenological field for the multitudinous projects of will.

This cosmic dynamism is essentially a will-to-live. The subjective will-to-live is manifest in various degrees of objectification. In fact, these function like Platonic forms (*see* PLATO). There are higher and lower forms that are more or less adequate expressions for will. These forms are engaged in an incessant strife to provide a place in the world for will. This strife leads to optimism in *Leibniz where God is needed to order them. But it leads to pessimism in Schopenhauer, since there is no such God and will is essentially at variance with itself.

Will has essential and internal hostilities so that moments of happiness (accord) are accidental. Pain is the positive essence of life. Will is based in need, deficiency, and pain. It is constantly striving because it hurts. Reason is only a byproduct of this vital force (will). And the human being is worse off with reason, since it anticipates future pain and meditates on the certainty of approaching death. It only enables man to outdo the animals in evil. Freedom is the strongest motive in man, and it alone provides a sufficient reason for action.

Human Nature. Human beings are the embodiment of will, a microcosm of the universe. Will and the body are the same thing, only under different aspects. The mind is the servant of will, not its master. "Schopenhauer utterly rejected such ideas as the inevitability of human progress and the perfectibility of man and replaced them with a picture of mankind in general as doomed to an eternal round of torment and misery," relates biographer Patrick Gardner (*Schopenhauer*, 329). He denied that even radical changes in the social order would solve anything, since "the evil condition of life as we find it is merely the reflection of the aggressive and libidinous urges rooted in our own natures" (ibid.).

Art and Morality. Schopenhauer's pessimism led him to contemplate suicide as the remedy for misery. But he rejected suicide and suggested art as a temporary release from the tensions of life. Suicide yields to irrational will which should be resisted.

Art provides a way of escape. A person should lose himself in quiet contemplation of ideal nature—looking for the perfect forms within the natural world. Art draws one out of self into a painless and timeless knowledge. It is a kind of knowledge vastly superior to that found in natural sciences, which provide only knowledge of the phenomenal world. Art, however, provides insight into the very archetypal (Platonic) forms of which this world is at best an inadequate expression. Creative genius possesses surplus energy of the will, enabling one to concentrate on these ideas.

Morality is an even better release than art. Its sympathy delivers us from egoism and its denunciation delivers us from suffering. The moral worth of an individual is found in his ability to liberate himself from the pressures and urges of irrational will. But ultimate salvation (from suffering) is found in nothingness (*see* HINDUISM, VEDANTA; ZEN BUDDHISM).

Music, of all human expressions, stands closest to ultimate reality. It is not concerned with the representation of reality in ideas or with the fundamental ideas (forms) that underlie them. Rather, it speaks in "the universal imageless language of the heart" (ibid.). This idea was expressed by Richard Wagner in his opera *Tristan und Isolde*, though Schopenhauer actually disliked the opera.

Evaluation. *Positive Dimensions. Realistic view of human nature.* In stark contrast to the perfectibility of humankind held by so many of his contemporaries, Schopenhauer saw more clearly the true human nature. Self-made progress and perfectibility are an illusion. Humankind of itself is doomed to a perpetual suffering and misery.

Emphasis on pessimism. Likewise, he correctly affirmed that pain is the essence of life. Apart from any transcendent hope, a legitimate pessimism emerges. Given the history of human terror, there is no realistic reason to believe that changing social structures will change human nature.

*Insufficiency of *sufficient reason.* Schopenhauer accurately assessed the rationalistic principle of sufficient reason. If everything has a reason, so does God. This observation has been made by theists (see Gurr). If, on the other hand, God is his own reason (ground), then he is a self-caused Being. But this is impossible, since one cannot be ontologically prior to oneself.

*Invalidity of the *ontological argument.* Like *Kant and most philosophers since, Schopenhauer saw that the ontological argument is invalid. It does smuggle existence into its premises. For only *if* one assumes that a Necessary Being exists, does it follow that it must in reality exist necessarily. In like manner, only *if* a triangle really exists, does it in really have to have three sides.

The volitional nature of reality. Although Schopenhauer carried it to an irrational extreme, he was certainly correct in observing that ultimate reality has a volitional element. This factor was largely neglected by the rationalists and idealists of this day.

Criticisms. Schopenhauer's atheism as such is subject to the same criticisms as other forms of atheism, which are described in the articles ATHEISM and GOD, ALLEGED DISPROOF OF. A few of his crucial premises are worthy of particular note.

Self-defeating nature. Like others who follow Kant, Schopenhauer's denial of knowledge of God was self-defeating. Indeed, his whole system is a description of ultimate reality as he sees it—the very thing that is not possible on Kantian premises. He is claiming to know with his mind that reality cannot be known with the mind.

Unjustified dismissal of the law of causality. He was correct in dismissing the principle of sufficient reason, but not the principle of causality (*see* CAUSALITY, PRINCIPLE OF). He chided Kant for applying causality to the real (noumenal) world, but he did the same implicitly. He believed that cosmic will was the *cause* of phenomena we observe. But how could he know this unless the principle of causality applied. It does not help to claim that there no Cosmic Mind out there. To argue from what we observe to a real Cause of any kind is to use the principle of causality.

Self-destructive nature of denying rationality. To claim that ultimate reality is not rational is self-defeating. The assertion that all reality is irrational is to deny the reality of the very mind asserting this (*see* REALISM; FIRST PRINCIPLES). Further, how can the effect be greater than the cause. How can nonrational will be the cause of rational mind (*see* CAUSALITY, PRINCIPLE OF).

Sources

W. Caldwell, *Schopenhauer's System in Its Philosophical Significance*

F. C. Copleston, *Schopenhauer, Philosopher of Pessimism*

P. Gardner, *Schopenhauer*

———, "Schopenhauer, Arthur," in P. Edwards, *The Encyclopedia of Philosophy*

J. E. Gurr, *The Principle of Sufficient Reason in Some Scholastic Systems 1750–1900*

D. J. O'Connor, *A Critical History of Western Philosophy*

A. Schopenhauer, *The Basis of Morality*

———, *On the Fourfold Root of the Principle of Sufficient Reason*

———, *On the Will in Nature*

———, *The World as Will and Representation*

Science and the Bible. The conflict between science and the Bible has been bitter, especially in the last 150 years. Most reasons for this hostility relate to what one perceives to be the nature and procedure of either domain. For many, the alleged conflict is resolved by separating the two spheres entirely. This is sometimes done by limiting the role of religion or the Bible to matters of faith and science to matters of fact. Specifically, some Christians in science argue that the Bible tells us "Who and Why" (God), and science deals with "How."

However, this neat separation of the domains of science and the Bible is unsatisfactory since the Bible does not so limit itself to questions of Who and Why. It often makes assertions of fact about the scientific world. Neither does science limit itself merely to questions of How. It also deals with origins (*see* ORIGINS, SCIENCE OF).

From a Christian perspective the relation between the Bible and Nature is the relation between two revelations of God, special revelation and general revelation (*see* REVELATION, GENERAL and REVELATION, SPECIAL). The first is found in God's revelation in Scripture (*see* BIBLE, EVIDENCE FOR) and the latter in his revelation in Nature. Between these two, when properly understood, there are no conflicts, since God is the Author of both, and he cannot contradict himself.

However, since scientific understanding is merely a fallible human understanding of Nature and since Bible scholars have only a fallible interpretation of infallible Scripture, it is understandable that there will be contradictions in these areas. The situation can be diagrammed as follows:

Scripture ◄—	**no conflict**	—► Nature
Theology ◄—	**some conflict**	—► Science

Biblical theology involves human understanding of the biblical text. As such, it is subject to misunderstanding and error. Likewise, science is fallible human attempts at understanding the universe. So conflict is inevitable. For example, most scientists believe the universe is billions of years old. Some Bible scholars hold that it is only thousands of years old. Obviously, both cannot be right.

Principles of Reconciliation. Before areas of specific conflicts are noticed, several guidelines are useful to the nature and procedure of both disciplines.

Either Group Is Subject to Error. Informed persons from both sides, both Bible interpreters and scientists, have made mistakes. Many Bible scholars once believed the sun revolved around the earth (as did many scientists); some believed the earth to be square. But they were wrong. Likewise, the model of an eternal cosmos has been discarded in favor of the big bang model. Evolutionary theories about inheriting acquired characteristics have been overthrown (*see* EVOLUTION, BIOLOGICAL; EVOLUTION, CHEMICAL).

Either Group Is Subject to Correction. Another important principle is that both areas are subject to correction by the other. For example, scientific fact has refuted the flat-earth theory. Hence, any interpretation that takes verses about the "four corners of the earth" as literal depictions of geography are wrong. Science has proven them wrong.

Likewise, scientists who insist that the universe is eternal hold a theory that has been proven false, both by science and in critiques by Christians (*see* CREATION, VIEWS OF; EVOLUTION, COSMIC; BIG BANG THEORY).

Not all conflicts are so easily resolved. Very few things are proven with certainty in science. Some things are only probable or highly probable. For example, that the earth moves around the sun is not absolutely proven. This theory fits the facts as they are known and is a highly probable scientific interpretation of Nature that conflicts with a disputable interpretation of Scripture, then we should assume the latter is wrong. And vice versa.

For example, macro-evolution is disputable and the creation of the universe, first life, and new life forms is highly probable. Hence, creation should be accepted as true and macro-evolution rejected (*see* EVOLUTION).

The Bible Is Not a Science Textbook. One principle that some overzealous Christian apologists sometimes forget is that, while the Bible makes no scientific mistakes (*see* BIBLE, ALLEGED ERRORS IN), neither is it a science textbook. It does not speak in technical scientific terms nor with precision. It uses round numbers. It employs observational, rather than astronomical, language (*see* BIBLE, ALLEGED ERRORS). The Bible only affirms partial truths in the various areas of science. It does not teach much geometry, any algebra, or trigonometry. One cannot assume conflicts without taking these factors into consideration.

Science Is Constantly Changing. Science understandings change continually. That means an apologist of years ago who succeeded in reconciling the Bible to some view of science might have been absolutely wrong since there wasn't a real conflict to reconcile. Perfect conformity may be wrong today as well, since science may change tomorrow. Given that science is a tentative and progressive discipline, never reaching a final conclusion on everything, it behooves us not to assume that there are scientific errors in the Bible unless

1. something is known for certain to be a scientific fact, and
2. it conflicts with an interpretation of Scripture that is beyond all doubt.

For example, it is beyond any reasonable doubt that the Bible teaches that a theistic God exists (*see* THEISM). Hence, one would have to prove that it was a scientific fact beyond all uncertainty that God did not exist in order to show a real conflict. It is unlikely that *real* conflicts between science and the Bible will ever be demonstrated. Some apparent conflicts deserve note, along with some probable and even highly probable views of modern science that find an amazing parallel in the Bible. It is to these that we first turn.

Bible and Science Converge. Given that not much scientific information was known in Bible times, the Bible speaks with considerable scientific credibility, an evidence of its supernatural nature.

Origins. Universe had a beginning. The very first verse of the Bible proclaims that "in the beginning God created the heavens and the earth." It was common in ancient views to consider the universe eternal, yet the Bible taught that it had a beginning. This is precisely what most scientists now believe in accepting the *Big Bang theory. Agnostic astrophysicist Robert Jastrow wrote that "three lines of evidence—the motions of the galaxies, the laws of thermodynamics, and the life story of the stars—pointed to one conclusion: All indicated that the Universe had a beginning" (*God and the Astronomers*, 111).

Order of events. Genesis 1 also indicates a progressive creation, universe, followed by formless earth, followed by what happened to give form to the earth. This is a much more scientifically sophisticated conception than held by the common ancient creation story. The Bible affirms that God said in the beginning, "Let there be light. And there was light" (Gen. 1:3). Jastrow wrote of the parallel of this statement with modern science, "the details differ, but the essential elements in the astronomical and biblical accounts of Genesis are the same: the chain of events leading to man commence suddenly and sharply at a definite moment in time, in a flash of light and energy" (ibid., 14).

No new matter is being created. The Bible declared from the beginning that creation is complete. God rested from his work (Gen. 2:2) and is still at rest (Heb. 4:4f.). In short, no new matter (energy) is coming into existence. This is precisely what the First Law of Thermodynamics declares, namely, that the amount of actual energy in the universe remains constant (*see* THERMODYNAMICS, LAWS OF).

Universe is running down. According to the second law of *thermodynamics, the universe is running out of useable energy. It is literally growing old. This is precisely what the Psalmist said: "In the beginning you laid the foundations of the earth, and the heavens are the work of your hands. They will perish, but you remain; like clothing you will change them and they will be discarded" (Ps. 102:25–27).

Genesis declares that life first appeared in the sea (Gen. 1:21), and only later on land (1:26–27). This accords with the view that multicellular life teamed in the Cambrian waters before it multiplied on land.

Life produces after its kind. In Genesis 1:24 God said, "Let the land produce living creatures according to their kinds: livestock, creatures that move along the ground, and wild animals, each according to its kind." According to agnostic paleontologist Stephen Jay Gould, "Most species exhibit no directional change during their tenure on earth. They appear in the fossil record looking much the same as when they disappear; morphological change is usually limited and directionless" (Gould, "Evolution's Erratic Pace," 13–14). In that fossil record, as in Genesis, human beings were the last to appear.

Humans made from the earth. Unlike ancient myths or the Qur'an, which claims that humans were made from a "clot of congealed blood" (see Sura 23:14), the Bible states that "the LORD God formed the man from the dust of the ground and breathed into his nostrils the breath of life, and the man became a living being" (Gen. 2:7). Further, it adds, "By the sweat of your brow you will eat your food until you return to the ground, since from it you were taken; for dust you are and to dust you will return" (Gen. 3:19). According to science, the constituent elements of the human body are the same as those found in the earth.

Earth Sciences. Water returns to its source. Scripture affirms that "All streams flow into the sea, yet the sea is never full. To the place the streams come from, there they return again" (Eccles. 1:7; cf. Job 37:16). While the author may not have been aware of the exact process of evaporation, condensation, and precipitation, his description is in perfect harmony with these processes.

The earth is round. Isaiah spoke of God who "sits enthroned above the circle of the earth" (40:22). This is a remarkably accurate description for an eighth-century B.C. prophet (*see* ISAIAH, DEUTERO). And Solomon had given the same truth in the tenth-century B.C. (Prov. 8:27).

The earth hangs in space. In an era when it was common to believe the sky was a solid dome, the Bible accurately speaks of God spreading out the northern skies over empty space and suspending the earth over nothing (Job 26:7).

The Bible is not only compatible with true scientific findings, but it anticipated many of them. Scientific knowledge is compatible with the truths of Scripture.

Other scientific findings. Many other things discovered by modern science were stated in the Bible hundreds and even thousands of years in advance. These include the fact that: (1) the sea has paths and channels (2 Sam. 22:16; Ps. 8:8; Prov. 8:28); (2) the sea has boundaries (Prov. 8:29); (3) life is in the blood (Lev. 17:11); (4) disease can be spread by physical contact (Lev. 13).

Alleged Conflicts. *Genesis 1–2.* The most frequently cited example of conflict between science and the Bible is over the doctrine of creation. There is conflict over the origin of the universe (*see* ORIGINS, SCIENCE OF); conflict over the origin of first life, and the conflict over human origins. A forceful attack against the Bible from the scientific standpoint is found in the book *The Bible, the Qur'an and Science* by Muslim author Maurice Bucaille. Some of the following specific examples of alleged conflict are cataloged by Bucaille. A strong Christian response to this work appeared in William Campbell, *The Qur'an and the Bible in the Light of History and Science*.

Days of Genesis. It is argued by critics that, since the "days" of Genesis are obviously twenty-four hours long, the Bible is in conflict with modern scientific dating which has proven that the origin of the world and life took a much longer period of time. But it has been shown in the article GENESIS, DAYS OF, that the Hebrew word for "day" can mean era or eon, and that if "solar days" are in view they need not have been successive twenty-four-hour periods. Also, scientific dating methods are built around two unprovable presuppositions: (1) that the original conditions were pure and uncontaminated and (2) that the rate of change has not fluctuated since the original conditions.

Genesis 1:2. Genesis 1:2 has been called "a masterpiece of inaccuracy from a scientific point of view" (Bucaille, 40). Bucaille cites the fact that Genesis 1:2 mentions water in an early stage of the earth's history, yet he insists, "to mention the existence of water at this period is however simply pure allegory" (Bucaille, 41).

This is a strange charge, for Bucaille himself admits that "there is every indication that at the initial stage of the formation of the universe a gaseous mass existed" (ibid.). Yet water itself has a gaseous state known as vapor. Further, scientific views change. The theories of today are often discarded tomorrow. So, even if there were some theory today that holds there was no water in the initial states of the universe, it remains highly theoretical. Further, there was water in the early stages of earth's history, at least in the form of vapor. This is one reason life as we know it is possible on earth, but not on other planets in our solar system. So in his haste to find errors in the Bible Bucaille has made one of his own.

Genesis 1:3–5. About Genesis 1:3–5 Muslim critic Bucaille affirms, "it is illogical, however, to mention the result (light) on the first day, when the cause of this light [the sun] was created three days later" (ibid., 41).

But the sun is not the only source of light in the universe. Further, it is not necessary to understand the text as saying the sun was created on the fourth day. It may have been only *made to appear* on the fourth day, after the mist of water vapor had cleared away so that its outline became visible. (The Hebrew word for *made, asah,* occurs about 1200 times in the Old Testament. It has a wide range of meanings, including: did, made, show, appear, reveal, and made to appear.) Before this its light may have been shining through, as on a misty day, without observers on earth being able to see the outline of the sun.

Genesis 1:14–19. Many would agree with Bucaille that "to place the creation of the Sun and Moon after the creation of the Earth is contrary to the most firmly established ideas on the formation of the elements of the Solar System" (Bucaille, 42).

Again, there are two problems. One is to assume that even the most prevailing scientific ideas are to be taken as absolute fact. Indeed, it is strange that Muslims use this argument, since they too point to the mistake of theologians who once assumed that the almost universally prevailing scientific view of a geocentric (earth-centered) universe was a scientific fact. In like manner, prevailing scientific ideas about the origin of the sun and moon *could* be wrong.

But, as we have seen above in comments on Genesis 1:3–5, it is not necessary to believe that the sun and moon were created on the fourth day. Rather, for whatever reason (perhaps as the original vapor disappeared), their form may have only become visible from the face of the earth on the fourth day.

Genesis 1:19–23. Critical scholars find two things unacceptable in Gen. 1:19–23: "the fact that continents emerged at the period in earth's history, when it was still covered with water" and "that a highly organized vegetable kingdom with reproduction by seed could have appeared before the existence of the sun" (Bucaille, 42).

The first point is unsubstantiated, and the second one was answered under Genesis 1:3–5. Who finds it acceptable that God created seed-bearing plants early in earth's history? Nontheistic evolutionists who reject God and his special work of creation might find it difficult. It should not be unacceptable to a Muslim, such as Bucaille, who claims to believe the *Qur'an*. The *Qur'an* affirms that God created the world and all that is in it in a few days. The contradiction here is between the Bible and a prevalent scientific hypothesis (see Denton; Johnson; Geisler, chaps. 5–7).

Genesis 1:20–30. Bucaille insists that this passage contains unacceptable assertions that the animal kingdom began with creatures of the sea and winged birds. However, birds did not appear until after reptiles and other land animals (ibid., 42–43).

The Bible does not actually say that God created feathered birds before reptiles. It refers to winged creatures (Gen. 1:21). This is often translated "birds" (i.e., flying animals) but is never rendered "*feathered* creatures." And, according to science, winged creatures did exist before feathered birds. Their mention with the "great sea creatures" is an indication that the reference is to winged dinosaurs. Bucaille here assumes an evolutionary scenario. But evolution is an unsubstantiated hypothesis. To offer as scientific proof that "numerous biological characteristics common to both species makes this deduction possible" is to make a fallacious deduction. For common characteristics do not prove common ancestry; it may indicate a common Creator. After all, there is a progressive similarity in automobiles from the first ones to current ones. No one, however, believes that one evolved from another by natural processes.

Finally, some contemporary scientists are questioning the long-held assumption that all winged creatures appeared after reptiles. Some fossils of flying marine animals have been found in earlier strata that were commonly assigned to the origin of reptiles. In any event, there is no contradiction, except between theories of science and some misinterpretations of Genesis.

Genesis 2:1–3. Commenting on the biblical teaching that God created in six days (Gen. 2:1–3), Bucaille contends that "today we are perfectly aware that the formation of the Universe and the Earth took place in stages that lasted for very long periods." This was shown above to be without grounds in the article Genesis, Days of.

Genesis 2:4–25. Bucaille adopts the outdated view that Genesis 2 contradicts the account given in Genesis 1. The charge here is that Genesis 1 declares that animals were created before humans, while Genesis 2:19 seems to reverse this, saying, "the LORD God had formed out of the ground all the beasts of the field . . . He brought them to the man to see what he would name them," implying Adam was created before they were (*see* ADAM, HISTORICITY OF; GARDEN OF EDEN).

The solution to this problem, however, becomes apparent when we take a closer look at the two texts. The differences appear from the fact that Genesis 1 gives the *order* of events; Genesis 2 provides more *content* about them. Genesis 2 does not contradict chapter 1, since it does not affirm exactly when God created the animals. He simply says he brought the animals (which he had previously created) to Adam in order that he might name them. The focus in chapter 2 is on the naming of the animals, not on creating them. Thus, Genesis 2:19, stressing the naming (not the creating) of animals, simply says: "Now the LORD God [who] had [previously] formed out of the ground all the beasts of the field . . . He brought them to the man to see what he would name them."

Genesis 1 provides the outline of events, and chapter 2 gives details. Taken together, the two chaps. provide a harmonious and more complete picture of the creation events. The differences, then, can be summarized as follows:

Genesis 1	**Genesis 2**
chronological order	topical order
outline	details
creating animals	naming animals

Once this is understood, the two texts are perfectly complementary.

Genesis 2–3. Many Bible critics have charged that there is no scientific evidence that the Garden of Eden ever existed, as the Bible maintains. But besides being an argument from silence which is a form of the fallacy of the argument from ignorance, this is not true. There is ample historical and geographical evidence for the existence of a literal Garden of Eden.

Genesis 4. The problem here is that the Bible says Cain married when there was apparently no one to marry. Cain and Abel were the first children born to Adam: There were no women for Cain to marry. There was only Adam, Eve (Gen. 4:1), and his dead brother Abel (4:8). Yet the Bible says Cain married and had children.

Although this is a favorite of Bible critics, the solution is rather simple. Cain married his sister (or possibly a niece). The Bible says Adam "begot sons and *daughters*" (Gen. 5:4). In fact, since Adam lived 930 years (Gen. 5:5), he had plenty of time to produce plenty of children. Cain could have married one of his many sisters, or even a niece, if he married after his brothers or sisters had grown daughters.

As to the subsidiary problem of forbidden and genetically dangerous incest (Levit. 18:6) if Cain married his sister, the solution is not difficult either. First of all, there were no genetic imperfections at the beginning of the human race. God created a genetically perfect Adam (Gen. 1:27). Genetic defects resulted from the Fall and only occurred gradually over long periods of time. Further, there was no command in Cain's day not to marry a close relative. This command (Leviticus 18) came thousands of years later in Moses' day (ca. 1500 B.C.). Finally, since the human race began with a single pair (Adam and Eve), Cain had no one else to marry except a close female relative (sister or niece).

Genesis 5. The problem of the long lives of people before the flood is obvious: Adam lived 930 years (Gen. 5:5); Methuselah lived 969 years (Gen. 5:27), and the average age of those who lived out their normal life-span was over 900 years old. Yet even the Bible recognizes what scientific fact shows, namely, that most people live only seventy or eighty years before natural death (Ps. 90:10).

It is a fact that people do not live that long today. But this is merely a descriptive statement, not a prescriptive one. No scientist has shown that it is impossible for someone to live that long. In fact, biologically there is no reason humans could not live hundreds of years. Scientists are more baffled by aging and death than by longevity.

Second, the reference in Psalm 90 is to Moses' time (1400s B.C.) and later, when longevity had decreased to seventy or eighty years for most, though Moses himself lived 120 years (Deut. 34:7).

Third, some have suggested that these "years" are really only months, which would reduce nine hundred years to the normal life span of eighty years. However, this is implausible. There is no precedent in the Hebrew Old Testament for taking the word *year* to mean "month." And Mahalalel had children when he was "only" sixty-five (Gen. 5:15), and Cainan had children when he was seventy (Gen. 5:12); this would mean they were less than six years old—which is not biologically possible.

Fourth, others suggest that these names represent family lines or clans that went on for generations before they died out. However, this does not make sense. For one thing, some of these names (e.g., Adam, Seth, Enoch, Noah) are definitely individuals whose lives are narrated in the text (Gen. 1–9). For another, family lines do not "beget" family lines by different names. Neither do family lines "die," as each of these individuals did (cf. 5:5, 8, 11). Furthermore, the reference to having "sons and daughters" (5:4) does not fit the clan theory.

Fifth, it seems best to take these as years (though they were lunar years of 12 x 30 = 360 days).

The Bible is not alone in speaking of hundreds of years life spans among ancients. There are also Greek and Egyptian records of humans living hundreds of years.

A related problem noted is that in Genesis (6:3) God decided just before the Flood to limit man's life span to 120 years. In Genesis 11:10–32, however, the ten descendants of Noah had life spans from 148 to 600 years (Bucaille, 39–40).

Even on the assumption that 6:3 refers to the life span of Noah's descendants, it does not say that this shortening of life would take place *immediately*. It may refer only to the eventual life span of the postdiluvians. Indeed, Moses, who wrote these words, lived to exactly 120 years (Deut. 34:7).

Furthermore, there is no need to take it as a reference to the life span of individuals after the flood at all. It likely refers to the length of time humankind then had left before God would send his fatal judgment. This fits better with the immediate context that speaks of how long God would exhort humankind to repent before he sent a flood.

Genesis 5, 11. Critics claim that the Bible makes a scientific error when it dates humankind around 4000 B.C. But the Bible nowhere gives any such total of years. In fact, there are demonstrable gaps in the biblical genealogies. Hence, it is impossible to obtain a total of years from Adam to Abraham. The Bible has *accurate outline genealogies* in which there are demonstrable gaps (*see* GENEALOGIES, OPEN OR CLOSED).

Genesis 6–9. The flood story has been charged with scientific improbabilities, including the fact that there is no geological evidence, and it would be impossible to get all the animal species in the world in such a small boat. But it has been shown (*see* FLOOD, NOAH'S) that there is evidence for a flood, and that the size of the ark was huge, sufficient to house the kinds of animals that could not survive the flood.

Genesis 30. According to Genesis 30, Jacob seemed to accept the unscientific view of his time that prenatal influence on a mother affects the physical characteristics of the unborn. For he got streaked, speckled, and spotted kids by placing stripped rods before the parent goats while they mated (Gen. 30:37).

While the spotted kids were not born because of Jacob's scheme with the rods, there is a scientific basis for his results. "[T]o the casual observer they were of solid color, for all the spotted goats had been removed; but their hereditary factors or genes for color were mixed, the condition which the geneticist calls heterozygous." For "breeding tests have shown that spotting is recessive to solid color in goats, making it possible for a goat to have spots that can be transmitted, although they do not appear to the eye" (ASA, 71).

God blessed Jacob, in spite of his scheme to get his crooked uncle's livestock. The Lord revealed to Jacob in a dream the real reason the kids were born that way: "Look up and see that all the male goats mating with the flock are streaked, speckled or spotted, *for I have seen all that Laban has been doing to you*" (Gen. 31:12, emphasis added).

Exodus 14. According to this account of the crossing of the Red Sea, the massive group of fleeing Israelites must have had no more than twenty-four hours to cross through the portion of the Red Sea which God had prepared. However, according to the numbers given, there were some 2 million of them (see Num. 1:45–46). But, for a multitude of this size, a twenty-four-hour period is just not enough time to make such a crossing.

It should be noted that, although the passage may give the idea that the time that the nation of Israel had to make the crossing was short, this is not a necessary conclusion. The text states that God brought forth an east wind which drove back the waters "all that night" (Exod. 14:21). Verse 22 seems to indicate that it was the very next morning when the multitude of Israelites began their journey across the sea bed. Verse 24 then states, "Now it came to pass, in the morning watch, that the Lord looked down upon the army of the Egyptians." Finally, according to verse 26 God told Moses to "stretch out your hand over the sea, that the waters may come back upon the Egyptians." There is no time reference to this command, however, and it is not necessary to conclude that Israel had completed their crossing that very morning.

A twenty-four-hour crossing is not as impossible as it may seem. The passage never states that the people crossed in single file, or that they crossed over on a section of ground the width of a modern superhighway. In fact, it is much more likely that God prepared a section several miles wide. This would certainly fit the situation, since the camp of Israel on the bank of the Red Sea probably stretched out for three or four miles along the shoreline. When the time came for the people to cross on dry ground, they probably moved as one magnificent throng, moving as a great army advancing upon the enemy lines. The Red Sea stretches some 1450 miles, and averages 180 miles wide. If this great multitude crossed in such a manner as described, to cross a distance of 180 miles in a twenty-four-hour period they would have had to move at about eight miles an hour. This would have been a reasonable pace and sufficient time to cross over the long and narrow body of water.

Leviticus 11. In Leviticus 11:5–6, two animals, the rock hyrax and the rabbit, were designated as unclean by Leviticus because, although they chew the cud, they do not divide the hoof. But, modern science has discovered that these two animals do not chew the cud. Thus, the Bible would appear to be in error at this point.

It is unfair to impose a modern scientific understanding on the ancient phrase "chew the cud." Rabbits do not chew the cud in the technical sense, they engage in a chewing action called "refection," which looks the same to an observer. This is known as "observational language," and we use it all the time, especially when speaking with people who are unfamiliar with the technical aspects of a subject. For example, we use observational language to talk about the sun rising and setting. The description is not technically correct by modern scientific standards, but it is functionally useful for the level of understanding of the pre-scientific common person. The biblical phrase should be taken as a broad, practical observation that includes both the modern technical definition of cud chewing or *rumination*, as well as other animals, including rabbits, that appear to chew the cud. They are listed with animals that chew the cud so that the common person could make the distinction in everyday observation.

This is a good example of why the Bible has no factual errors, but it is not a scientific textbook in the modern sense. The distinctions being made in Leviticus were practical, not scientific. They were to help people select food. Animals which chew the cud are identified as ruminants from "to ruminate," which is the action of regurgitating food into the mouth to be chewed again. Ruminants normally have four stomachs. They were normally "clean," acceptable food for the Israelites. Neither the rock hyrax (translated "rock badger" in the NASB) nor the rabbit are ruminants and technically do not chew the cud. However, both move their jaws in such a manner as to appear to be chewing the cud. Even the Swedish scientist Linnaeus originally classified them as ruminants.

Refection is a process in which indigestible vegetable matter absorbs certain bacteria and is passed as droppings and then eaten again. This process enables the rabbit to better digest it. The process is similar to rumination.

Leviticus 13. Leviticus 13 lists "leprosy" as an infectious disease that can contaminate clothing. However, leprosy is a disease caused by a bacterium and does not affect inanimate objects such as garments.

Bible scholars have observed in response that this is simply a matter of the use of a word changing over time. What in modern times is called leprosy is known as Hansen's Disease. This is not the same type of infection that is described as "leprosy" in the Old Testament. The bacterial disease now identified as leprosy does not produce the symptoms described in various Old Testament passages. The Hebrew term *tsarath*, translated "leprosy," is a more general term for any serious skin disease or sign of infection or defilement on the surface of inanimate objects. The defilement on garments, or walls as in Leviticus 14:33–57, was probably some type of fungus or mold. Garments found to be infected were burned (Lev. 13:52). Infected houses were cleansed. If the infection could not be eradicated, the houses were demolished and the ruins were taken outside the city (Lev. 14:45).

Numbers 5. Here Moses allegedly commanded the practice of a superstition that has no basis in science. The accused wife was found guilty after drinking bitter water only if her stomach swelled. But, both the innocent and guilty wives drank the same bitter water, which shows that there was no chemical or biological basis for one swelling and the other not.

In response, several things are of importance. First, the text does not say that the difference in the guilty woman's condition had a *chemical* or *physical* cause. In fact, it indicates that the cause was *spiritual* and *psychological*. "Guilt" is not a physical cause. The reason the belly of a guilty woman might swell can be easily explained by what is known scientifically about psychosomatic (mind over matter) conditions. Many women have experienced "false pregnancies" where their stomach and breasts enlarge without actually having any baby growing in their uterus. Some people have even experienced blindness from psychological causes. Experiments with placebo pills (sugar pills) indicate that many people with terminal illnesses get the same relief from them as from morphine. So, it is a scientific fact that the mind can have a great effect on bodily processes.

The text says the woman was placed under an "oath" before God and under the threat of a "curse" (vs. 21). If she was guilty, the bitter water would have worked like a psychosomatic lie detector. A woman who really believed she would be cursed and knew she was guilty would be affected. But those who knew they were innocent would not.

Finally, the text does not say anyone actually drank the water and experienced an enlarged stomach. It simply says "if" (cf. vss. 14, 28) she does, then this will result. No doubt just the *belief* that this would happen and that one would be found guilty would have convinced the woman who knew she was guilty not to subject herself to the process.

Joshua 6. Joshua 6 records the conquest and destruction of the city of Jericho. If this account is accurate, it would seem that modern archaeological excavations would have turned up evidence of this monumental event. However, no such evidence from Joshua's time has been unearthed.

For many years the prevailing view of critical scholars has been that there was no city of Jericho at the time Joshua was supposed to have entered Canaan. Although earlier investigations by the notable British archaeologist Kathleen Kenyon confirmed the existence of ancient Jericho and its sudden destruction, her findings led her to conclude that the city could have existed no later than ca. 1550 B.C. This date is much too early for Joshua and the children of Israel to have been party to its demise.

However, recent reexamination of these earlier findings, and a closer look at current evidence indicates that not only was there a city that fits the biblical chronology, but that its remains coincide with the biblical account of the destruction of this walled fortress. In a paper published in *Biblical Archaeology Review* (March/April 1990), Bryant G. Wood, visiting professor to the department of Near Eastern Studies at the University of Toronto, has presented evidence that the biblical report is accurate. His detailed investigation has yielded the following conclusions:

> First, the city which once existed on this site was strongly fortified, corresponding to the biblical record in Joshua 2:5, 7, 15; 6:5, 20.
>
> Second, the ruins give evidence that the city was attacked after harvest time in the spring, corresponding to Joshua 2:6; 3:15; 5:10.
>
> Third, the inhabitants did not have the opportunity to flee with their foodstuffs from the invading army, as reported in Joshua 6:1.
>
> Fourth, the siege was short, not allowing the inhabitants to consume the food which was stored in the city, as Joshua 6:15 indicates.
>
> Fifth, the walls were leveled in such a way to provide access into the city for the invaders, as Joshua 6:20 records.
>
> Sixth, the city was *not* plundered by the invaders, according to God's instructions in Joshua 6:17–18.
>
> Seventh, the city was burned after the walls had been destroyed, just as Joshua 6:24 says.

Although some dispute that these are from the right time period, there is evidence that they are (see Wood). At any rate, the possibility that this is indeed the remains of Joshua's Jericho has not been disproved. Hence, no scientific disproof of the biblical story of Jericho has been made. What is more, even if there were no present or remaining evidence does not prove that it did not occur. It is possible that the evidence may have been destroyed or be in another place. The argument that "No evidence exists, therefore, there is none" is tenuous at best. It involves the argument from ignorance fallacy.

Joshua 10. During the battle with the kings of the land, God gave Israel the power to overcome their enemies. As the armies of the people of the land fled from before Israel, Joshua sought the Lord to cause the sun to stand still so that they might have sufficient daylight to complete the destruction of their enemies. But critics insist that there are at least two scientific errors here. First, Joshua is affirming wrongly a geocentric (earth-centered) view of the solar system. Second, even if one accepts that this occurred by the earth halting in its spin on its axis as it moves around the sun, this would only cause greater problems. For example, such slowing would cause things on earth to fly off into space.

This argument is based on the unproven assumption that miracles are not possible (*see* MIRACLE; MIRACLES, ARGUMENTS AGAINST). The God who made the sun and the earth can certainly make the sun to shine on it longer in one day if he wishes to do so. Some orthodox scholars (e.g., Robert Dick Wilson of Princeton) held that the Hebrew word *dom* (trans. "stand still") can be translated "be silent," "cease," or "leave off." Thus, they take it to mean the sun ceased to pour down its intense heat so the troops were able to do the work of two days in one. This view would involve no slowing down of the earth on its axis. However, it is hard to reconcile with verse 13 which states that "the sun stopped in the middle of the sky and did not hasten to go down for about a whole day."

Further, even if the earth did slow down in its rotation, it is not necessary to conclude that the earth's rotation was completely halted. Verse 13 states that the sun "did not hasten to go down for about a whole day." This could indicate that the earth's rotation was not completely halted, but that it was retarded to such a degree that the sun did not set for about a whole day. Or, it is possible that God caused the light of the sun to refract through some cosmic "mirror" so that it could be seen a day longer. If the earth's rotation was completely stopped, we must remember that God is not only capable of halting the rotation of the earth for a whole day, but he is also able to prevent any possible catastrophic effects that might result from the cessation of the earth's rotation. Although we do not necessarily know *how* God brought about this miraculous event, this does not mean we cannot know *that* he did it.

The phrase "the sun stood still" is no more unscientific that the phrases "sun rise" and "sun set" used by scientists (meteorologist) every day as they report the weather. It is simply an observational statement from the vantage point of a person on the face of the earth which is, after all, where we are. In short, there is no scientific proof that Joshua did not get about an extra day of light to finish his battle.

1 Kings 7:23. Some critics have alleged a scientific error in Scripture since according to 1 Kings 7:23, Hiram constructed a "Sea of cast bronze ten cubits from one brim to the other; it was completely round. Its height was five cubits, and a line of thirty cubits measured its circumference." From this report we learn that the ratio of the circumference to the diameter is three to one. However, this is an inaccurate value of *pi* which is actually 3.14158, etc.

Apologists have offered two possible solutions to this problem. Harold Lindsell writes that 1 Kings did not error in the use of *pi*. For if the ten cubits width of the bronze container is measured from outside brim to brim and the circumference is only of the water which is the inside of the container, then *pi* would be 3.14. In this way the inside measurement of the container would be less than 10, thus accounting for how the circumference of the water (or the inside of the container) would be only 30 and still be 3.14 times the diameter of 9.58 (= 30.0).

There are two difficulties with this view. First, one has to assume a width of the bronze container of .21 cubits, which is not stated in the text. Second, one must assume that the diameter is measured from the outside but the circumference from the outside. But this seems unusual and is not mentioned in the text.

Round Number View. According to this view, it is characteristic of the Bible to speak in round numbers (*see* BIBLE, ALLEGED ERRORS IN), and 3 is the rounded number for 3.14. The biblical record of the various measurements of the different parts of the temple are not necessarily designed to provide precise scientific or mathematical calculations. Scripture simply provides an approximation. The evidence seems to support this view. The rounding of numbers or the reporting of approximate values or measurements was a common practice in ancient times when exact scientific calculations were not used. The Bible uses round numbers elsewhere (cf. Josh. 3:4; cf. 4:13; 2 Chron. 9:25; 13:17). Even 3.14 is not precise. Nor is 3.1415, since pi goes on indefinitely without coming out even. So even "scientific precision" is a relative term with pi. But 3 is relatively correct, since that is what pi is for all practical purposes. And that was sufficient to make a pool by the ancient temple. To get a man on the moon takes more precision. But it is anachronistic to superimpose this kind of mathematical precision on the Bible.

2 Kings 20. In response to Hezekiah's prayer, God instructed Isaiah to prophesy to Hezekiah that God would add fifteen years to Hezekiah's life (2 Kings 20:11). When he heard this, Hezekiah asked for a sign to confirm God's promise. The sign was that the shadow would retreat ten degrees. This would involve making the shadow go backwards instead of forward as the sun set. But critics insist that it is not scientifically possible for shadows to retreat. In order to do so, the earth would have to suddenly reverse its spin.

This objection has the same problems as does critics' complaints about the sun standing still in Joshua's time. In a theistic (*see* THEISM) universe there is no reason that a miracle like this could not happen. It is credible to believe that some miraculous events have occurred (*see* MIRACLES, ARGUMENTS AGAINST), including creation out of nothing (*see* CREATION, VIEWS OF).

The retreat of Ahaz's sun dial was undoubtedly a miracle. Things like this do not occur naturally. Indeed, Hezekiah realized that it would not be a miraculous confirmation of God's promise if the sign involved some phenomenon that could be explained (2 Kings 20:10). It was the miraculous nature of the event that qualified it as a sign from God. Any attempt at an explanation of how this was accomplished would be pure speculation. Although God can employ the forces of nature to accomplish his purposes, he can also accomplish his will in a way that transcends natural law. The Bible does not indicate precisely how God did this, but this is not uncommon for miracles which involve the direct intervention of God. As to whether God miraculously reversed the earth's spin on its axis or the shadow of the sun (say, by refraction) need not concern us. It is sufficient to note that God can perform miracles, and this was clearly a miracle.

Job 38:7. Many Bible critics believe that the Old Testament errs when it speaks of the firmament as a solid dome. Job speaks of God who "spread out the skies" like "a cast metal mirror" (37:18). Indeed, the Hebrew word for the "firmament" (*raqia*) which God created (cf. Gen. 1:6) is defined in the Hebrew lexicon as a solid object. But this is in clear conflict with the modern scientific understanding of space as nonsolid and largely empty.

It is true that the origin of the Hebrew word *raqia* meant a solid object. However, meaning is not determined by *origin* (etymology), but by *usage*. Originally, the English word "board" referred to a wooden plank. But when we speak of a board of directors, the word no longer has that meaning. When used of the atmosphere above the earth, "firmament" clearly does not mean something solid (see Newman).

The related word *raqa* ("beat out, spread out") is correctly rendered "expanse" by recent translations. Just as metal spreads out when beaten (cf. Exod. 39:3; Isa. 40:19), so the firmament is a thinned out area. The root meaning "spread out" can be used independently of "beat out," as it is in several passages (cf. Ps. 136:6; Isa. 42:5; 44:24). Isaiah wrote, "So says Jehovah God, he who created the heavens and *stretched them out*, spreading out the earth and its offspring" (Isa. 42:5 NKJV). This same verb is used of extending curtains or tents in which to dwell, which would make no sense if there was no empty space there in which to live. Isaiah, for example, spoke of the Lord "who sits on the circle of the earth, and its people are like grasshoppers; who *stretches out the heavens like a curtain, and spreads them out like a tent to dwell in*" (Isa. 40:22 NKJV).

The Bible speaks of rain falling through the sky (Job 36:27–28). But this makes no sense if the sky is a metal dome. Nowhere does the Bible refer to little holes in a metal dome through which the drops fall. It does speak figuratively of the "windows of heaven" opening for the Flood (Gen. 7:11). But this should probably not be taken any more literally than our idiom, "It is raining cats and dogs."

The creation account speaks of birds that "fly above the earth across the face of the firmament" (Gen. 1:20). But this would be impossible if the sky was solid. Thus, it is more appropriate to translate *raqia* by the word "expanse" (as the NASB and NIV). And in this sense there is no conflict with the concept of space in modern science.

Even if taken literally, Job's statement (37:18) does not affirm that the "skies" *are* a "metal mirror," but simply that they are *as* [or like] a mirror. It is a poetic comparison that need not be taken literally, any more does the statement in Proverbs 18:10 that God is a "strong tower." Further, the point of comparison in Job is not the solidity of the "skies" and a mirror, but their respective durability (*strong* [*chazaq*]).

Jonah 1. Many people have difficulty believing that a person could live inside a whale for three days and nights. The problem of breathing, to say nothing of the gastronomical processes would surely have been fatal well before three days.

Again, the event is presented as a miracle (Jonah 1:17; cf. Matt. 12:40). The God who created Jonah and the whale could preserve Jonah's life in the whale. Second, Jonah and his prophetic ministry are mentioned in the historical book of 2 Kings (14:25). There is archaeological confirmation of a prophet named Jonah whose grave is found in northern Israel, from which Jonah comes. There are even credible stories from modern history of persons who have survived in whales without any special divine intervention.

A strong argument for the historical accuracy of Jonah is that it was attested by Jesus, the Son of God (*see* CHRIST, DEITY OF). In Matthew 12:40, Jesus predicts his own burial and resurrection as a sign to the doubting scribes and Pharisees on the order of the sign of Jonah. Jesus says, "For as

Jonah was three days and three nights in the belly of the great fish, so will the Son of Man be three days and three nights in the heart of the earth." If the tale of Jonah's experience in the belly of the great fish was fiction, then this provided no prophetic support for Jesus' claim. As far as Jesus was concerned, the historical fact of his own death, burial, and resurrection was on the same historical ground as Jonah in the belly of the fish. To reject one is to cast doubt on the other (cf. John 3:12).

Jesus went on to mention the significant historical detail. His own death, burial, and resurrection was the supreme sign that verified his claims. When Jonah preached to the unbelieving Gentiles, they repented. But, here was Jesus in the presence of the very people of God, yet they refused to believe. Therefore, those of Nineveh would stand up to give testimony against them at the judgment, because the Ninevites repented at the preaching of Jonah (Matt. 12:41). If the events of the book of Jonah were merely parable or fiction, and not literal history, then the men of Nineveh did not really repent, and any judgment upon the unrepentant Pharisees would be unjust and unfair. Because of the testimony of Jesus, we can be sure that Jonah records literal history.

Conclusion. All attempts to convict the Bible of a scientific error fail. Both Nature and Scripture are revelations of God, and God cannot contradict himself (*see* God, Nature of; Truth, Nature of). Conflicts that exist are not between Nature and Scripture but between fallible understandings of one or the other of them, or both.

Sources

G. L. Archer, Jr., *An Encyclopedia of Biblical Difficulties*

ASA authors. *Modern Science and the Christian Faith*

M. Bucaille, *The Bible, the Qur'an and Science*

W. Campbell, *The Qur'an and the Bible in the Light of History and Science*

N. L. Geisler, and T. Howe, *When Critics Ask*

S. J. Gould, "Evolution's Erratic Pace," *Natural History* (1972)

J. Haley, *An Examination of the Alleged Discrepancies of the Bible*

R. Jastrow, *God and the Astronomers*

———, "A Scientist Caught Between Two Faiths: Interview with Robert Jastrow," *CT* (6 August 1982)

H. Lindsell, *The Battle for the Bible*

M. Nahn, *Selections from Early Greek Philosophy*

R. Newman, *The Biblical Teaching on the Firmament*

B. Ramm, *The Christian View of Science and the Bible*

H. Ross, *Joshua's Long Day and Other Mysterious Events* (video)

Science of Origins. ***See* Origins, Science of.**

Scientific Dating. *The Problem.* The generally accepted dating (GAD) in the scientific community poses several problems for Christian apologetics, since it posits 10 to 20 billion years for the universe and hundreds of thousands of years for human life. This is contrary to a widely assumed dating of 10,000 to 20,000 years for the universe and human life by many evangelical Christians.

Actually, there are four separate problem with GAD for the defense of historic Christianity: (1) Does GAD support evolution? (2) Does GAD contradict the biblical view of the age of the universe? (3) Does GAD conflict with the biblical view of the age of the human race? (4) Does GAD conflict with the biblical view of creation in "six days"? Since the last one is discussed in detail elsewhere (*see* Genesis, Days of), only the first three will be discussed here.

Scientific Dating and Evolution. Even assuming GAD's conclusion that the universe is billions of years old and that life is at least a half billion years old, macroevolution does not follow (*see* Evolution, Biological). For billions of years are only a *necessary* condition for the truth of evolution but not a *sufficient* condition for it. A longer period of time is simply not sufficient to explain how gradual changes by natural processes could produce a man from a microbe. Multi-millions of years are a necessary condition for all living things to evolve. However, long periods of time are not sufficient to prove that macroevolution is true for two basic reasons: (1) long time periods do not produce specified complexity; and (2) a natural mechanism is needed to explain macroevolution.

Long Time Periods Do Not Produce Specified Complexity. There is no empirical or experimental evidence that long periods of time produce the kind of incredible specified complexity and irreducible complexity found in living things (*see* Evolution, Chemical). Simple observation reveals that if one drops bags of red, white, and blue confetti from an airplane a thousand feet above the ground it will not form an American flag on someone's lawn. The laws of nature, apart from intelligent intervention, will randomize the colors; they will not form fifty stars and thirteen stripes out of them. And both observation and experimentation demonstrate that dropping the colored paper fragments from ten thousand feet will not provide the necessary time for them to organize. There is only one cause known to human beings that can organize these tiny pieces of paper into an American flag, and that is intelligence. But intelligent intervention is not naturalistic evolution; it is creation.

The Need for a Natural Mechanism. If naturalistic evolution is to occur, there must be more than long periods of time. There must also be some natural causes that can account for the increased complexity in living things from the original one-celled organism all the way up to a human being. No such mechanism has ever been found. Natural selection does not do it. It is only a principle of survival of existing types of life, not the arrival of brand-new types (*see* Darwin, Charles). Natural mutations do not do it either. They are generally not helpful and are often lethal. Variation with populations are only sufficient to account for small changes within specific types of life and not for the macroevolutionary changes needed between all the various forms of life from simpler to more complex. So, long time periods do not explain how macroevolution could occur. What is needed are natural causes that can be shown to produce increased specified complexity apart from any intelligent cause. But in fact the evidence is to the contrary (*see* TELEOLOGICAL ARGUMENT; ANTHROPIC PRINCIPLE). Natural laws do not specify; they randomize. They do not cause greater specified order; they cause disorder. They do not create life; they cause decay.

Short Time Is Fatal to Macroevolution. One reason that naturalistic evolutionists are so vehemently opposed to dating schemes that posit a young universe (of 10,000 to 20,000 years of age) is that this is fatal to evolutionary theory. Evolution simply must have longer periods of time than just several thousand years. Thus, while long periods of time posited by the GAD scheme do not eliminate creation, short periods of time do eliminate evolution.

Scientific Dating and the Age of the Universe. The GAD view does not pose a problem for all orthodox Christians—only for those who hold to a young universe (of thousands of years). Young-universe apologists, such as Henry Morris (see Morris, all) and followers, must object to GAD. This they do in two ways.

Negative Scientific Arguments Against an Old Universe. The minimal essential element of a young-universe apologetic is to find loopholes in the currently accepted scientific dating scheme. This is attempted in several ways.

Unprovable Presuppositions. Young-universe proponents point out that there are unprovable presuppositions of old-universe dating methods. For example, radiometric dating methods assume an original condition of the substance that was "pure." They also assume that there has been a constant rate of change since that time. For example, to argue from the amount of salt in the sea to an old earth one must assume there was no salt there to begin with and that salt has been deposited in it by rivers and streams at a relatively constant rate since the beginning. But both of these premises are questionable, especially if there was a universal flood (*see* NOAH, FLOOD OF). Likewise, to argue to an old-universe of billions of years from the lead isotopes in uranium one must assume that there were none there at the beginning and that the rate of decay has been constant ever since. This too has been challenged.

Furthermore, there is always the problem of a contaminated sample or some other factor to throw off the rate of decay or deposit. That is, to maintain the old-universe argument one must show that the sample used has not been contaminated with material from a later time. This is particularly true of carbon dating. Otherwise, the date one gets is not the original date of the material.

Positive Arguments for a Young Universe. Another tactic open to young-universe apologists is to provide scientific evidence that the universe is young. Many such arguments have been offered. The problem with this method is that it too must accept some unproven (or unprovable) presuppositions like an original condition and a constant process since then. But these are the very things they challenge in the old-universe view. For example, some young-universe proponents have argued from the shallow depth of moon dust that the moon is only thousands of years old. But to do this they must assume that the moon had no dust to begin with and that the rate of buildup since has been relatively constant per year. These too are unproven, if not practically unprovable. Nonetheless, young-universe proponents have every right to offer positive scientific evidence for their view, whether it is by the nature of a universal flood, or the faster rate of decay or deposits. And if the weight of the evidence favors their view, then the weight of the evidence goes against macroevolution, which demands long time periods.

The Other Alternative: An Old Universe. Other orthodox Christians defend their stance by accepting the possibility of an old universe of billions of years and pointing to the fact that the Bible nowhere commits them to a young universe. They usually point to several factors. First, Genesis 1:1 only says there was a "beginning" but not exactly when that was. Second, the "days" of Genesis may represent long periods of time. Third, there may be a time gap before the days of Genesis begin (as in some form of Gap Theory). Fourth, there are known gaps in the genealogical record (*see* GENEALOGIES, OPEN).

Scientific Dating and the Age of the Human Race. Another problem that both young-earth Christians and even many old-earthers have is reconciling the GAD of the age of the human race with the biblical record. Since this is discussed in more detail elsewhere (*see* MISSING LINKS), it will only be touched on here. There are several ways this problem may be resolved.

Rejecting the Dating Methods for the Human Race. The dating methods for the antiquity of the human race are subject to even more debate than those for the date of the universe—and for the same reasons, only to a higher degree in some cases. First, there is the problem of assuming the original state was pure. Second, there is also the problem of demonstrating a constant, uninterrupted rate of decay. Third, there is the question of contamination of the sample or influence of other forces. In addition, some dating methods (like Carbon 14) are only accurate for thousands, not hundreds of thousands or millions of years.

Other dating methods like the interglacial periods are even less accurate.

Challenging the Human Status of the Fossils. Another problem is the assumption that humanlike anthropoids or Hominids of great age were really human beings created in the image and likeness of God rather than just highly developed apelike creatures. After all, morphology (bone structure) and even skull size does not prove true humanness. Nor does simple tool-making prove humanness, since some animals today are known to use simple tools (like seals using stones to open shells). Most scholars admit, civilized man is not hundreds of thousands of years old. And human beings with evidence of religion and God-consciousness are not much earlier. These much later forms point to the time of origin of true human beings made in God's image, that is, beings with rational, moral, and religious capacity.

Demonstrating Gaps in the Biblical Genealogies. It is true that if one assumes there are no gaps in the biblical genealogies, then the human race must be little more than six thousand years old. However, there are demonstrable gaps in the ancestral records in the Bible (cf. Matt. 1:8 and 1 Chron 3:11–14), even in the early tables in Genesis (cf. Luke 3:36 with Gen. 11:12). This is discussed in more detail elsewhere (*see* GENEALOGIES, OPEN). Many noted evangelical scholars have held this view, from B. B. *Warfield to Gleason Archer.

Conclusion. While there are conflicts between certain interpretations of the biblical record and prevailing theories of the age of the earth and humankind, there are no real contradictions. This is true for two basic reasons. First, no one has proven with absolute certainty that the universe is a given age, young or old. Second, there are different ways to interpret the biblical record so as to avoid conflict with the GAD of billions of years. Hence, while there is conflict with prevailing scientific theory and favored interpretations of the biblical record, there is no irresolvable contradiction.

Sources

G. Archer, *Introductory Survey of the Old Testament*
A. Custance, *The Genealogies of the Bible*
R. Gentry, *Creation's Tiny Mystery*
W. H. Green, "Primeval Chronology" in Walter Kaiser ed, *Essays in Old Testament Interpretation*
H. Morris, et al., *What is Creation Science?*
J. D. Morris, *The Young Earth*
R. Newman et al., *Genesis One and the Origin of the Earth*
B. Ramm, *The Christian View of Science and Scripture*
H. Ross, *Creation and Time*
B. B. Warfield, "On the Antiquity and the Unity of the Human Race," *The Princeton Theological Review* (1911)
J. Whitcomb, et al., *The Genesis Flood*
D. E. Wonderly, *God's Time-Records in Ancient Sediments*
D. A. Young, *Christianity and the Age of the Earth*

Scientism. *Scientism* is the belief that the scientific method is the only method for discovering truth. The father of modern scientism was the atheist (*see* ATHEISM) Auguste *Comte (1798–1857), who also began a religion of secular humanism (*see* HUMANISM, SECULAR). Comte's view is also known as positivism, an ancestor to the logical positivism of A. J. Ayer.

Since scientism often embraces many individual beliefs, including atheism, evolution theories (*see* EVOLUTION BIOLOGICAL), antisupernaturalism (*see* MIRACLES, ARGUMENTS AGAINST), and *materialism, it is evaluated in those articles. Those who reject God fail to seriously appreciate the weight of evidence (*see* GOD, EVIDENCE FOR). This misuse of the scientific method is restricted and truncated (*see* FAITH AND REASON; ORIGINS, SCIENCE OF), being a form of naturalism and often materialism.

The methods of scientism are questionable, even if there is one universally agreed-upon scientific method. There is no reason to believe the scientific method is the only way to acquire truth.

This dependence on the scientific method also leaves out differences that most scientists see between operation sciences, which are empirically studied, and the equally legitimate forensic sciences, for which a strict scientific methodology is impossible (*see* ORIGINS, SCIENCE OF). The forensic sciences are not religion-based, though one of them, Origin science, has religious implications. But origin science is the only way to look at some key questions about humanity and its significance. Unlike scientism, it does draw on evidence to back up its assumptions. Those assumptions do lead toward a beginning point and the existence of an intelligent Designer (*see* ANTHROPIC PRINCIPLE; BIG BANG; EVOLUTION, CHEMICAL; TELEOLOGICAL ARGUMENT). The findings of origin science directly contradict scientism.

Even empirical scientists recognize the limitations of the scientific method (see Sullivan), since it can only deal with observable phenomena. It begs the question in favor of *materialism to assume that there is nothing beyond the observable. Other aspects of reality cannot be captured by the scientific method (see Gilson). Some are known intuitively (*see* FIRST PRINCIPLES), others inferentially (*see* CAUSALITY, PRINCIPLE OF) or transcendentally (*see* TRANSCENDENTAL ARGUMENT), and some only by special revelation (*see* REVELATION, SPECIAL).

Sources

A. J. Ayer, *Language, Truth, and Logic*
J. Collins, *A History of Modern European Philosophy* (chapter 16).
A. Comte, *Cours, The Positive Philosophy of Auguste Comte*
E. Gilson, *The Unity of Philosophical Experience*
J. N. D. Sullivan, *The Limitations of Science*
T. Whittaker, *Comte and Mill*

Scotus, John Duns. ***See*** **COSMOLOGICAL ARGUMENT.**

Secular Humanism. ***See*** **HUMANISM, SECULAR.**

Self-Evident Truths. As applied to propositions, self-evident means that once the terms are known the truth of the proposition is evident in itself, needing no elucidation or confirmation from anything outside it. For example, "All wives are married women" is self-evident, since the terms *wives* and *married women* mean the same thing. This kind of self-evident statement is said to be a tautology since it is empty of all meaning, not really stating that there are any wives. It simply means, "*If* there is a wife, then she is a married woman."

Self-Evident First Principles. First principles are said to be self-evident since they are the foundation (*see* FOUNDATIONALISM) on which all other true statements. Though there seems to be an order of priority among some first principles.

In contrast to foundationalism, coherentism rejects all first principles and self-evident truths, except tautologies which they claim are vacuous and useless in knowing reality. They insist that there need be no ultimate foundation for truth but merely consistency among its statements.

"I am I" is a self-evident statement. One needs no further information to know it is true. Once the terms are understood, it is evident within itself that it is true. Also, the basic laws of logic are held to be self-evident. For example, the law of noncontradiction states that a proposition cannot be both true and false at the same time and in the same sense. This is an irreducible truth in terms of which all other truths are known to be true. Without the law of noncontradiction, nothing else can be known to be true. It is a self-evident first principle.

Defense of Self-Evident Statements. There is no *direct* proof of a self-evident proposition in terms of anything but itself. It is known to be true simply by examining its terms. If the predicate is reducible to the subject, then it is self-evident. Self-evident statements cannot be proven in terms of anything else. If they could, then they would not be *self*-evident. That is, they would not be evident within themselves.

There is, however, an indirect "proof" of self-evident statements. For a self-evident truth cannot be denied without affirming it. For example, I cannot deny "I exist" unless I exist to deny it. Likewise, the law of noncontradiction cannot be denied without implying that it is true. The statement: "A statement can be both true and false at the same time and in the same sense"—must be true or false. But it can only be accepted as true or opposed as false if the law of noncontradiction is valid. One has to assume the law is valid before affirming that it is not.

In this way there is an indirect "proof" of self-evident truths: They cannot be denied without employing them. This kind of proof is sometimes put in the form of a *transcendental argument.

Self-Refuting Statements. *Various Names.* Self-refuting statements are those which fail to satisfy their own criteria of validity or acceptability. They are also called self-referential, self-stultifying, self-destructive, and self-falsifying.

Some Examples. Statements such as "I cannot express a word in English" are self-refuting because that very statement is an expression in English. Likewise, the statement "I do not exist" is self-defeating, since the statement implies that I do exist in order to make the statement.

The principle of self-stultification is a handy apologetic tool, since most, if not all, non-Christian views involve self-defeating statements. Take, for example, the following self-refuting statements:

1. "Be skeptical about all truth claims."
2. "No truth can be known."
3. "No statements are meaningful."

The problem with (1) is that it is a truth-claim about which it is not skeptical. But this is inconsistent with its own claim. Likewise, (2) is itself a truth-claim that can be known which is contradictory to what it affirms (namely, no truth can be known). The same point can be made about (3), which is offered as a meaningful statement that no meaningful statement can be made.

Defense of Principle of Self-Falsification. The principle of self-falsification is not a *first principle, such as the law of non-contradiction. Rather, it is based in the law of non-contradiction. For a statement is self-refuting when it entails two statements that are contradictory, one that it makes explicitly and a contradictory one implied in the very act or process of making the first one. Hence, self-refuting statements are contradictory. And the law of non-contradiction is a self-evident first principle that is known to be such by examining the statement to see if the predicate is reducible to the subject.

Undeniability Principle. The principle of undeniability is also known as the principle of self-stultification, or of self-referentiality. The flip side of undeniability is unaffirmability. Certain things are undeniable because any attempt to deny them affirms them in the very process. So, they are literally unaffirmable without denying what they affirm or affirming what they deny. For example, the statement "I cannot utter a word in English" is obviously not true, because it is the utterance of a sentence in English, claiming not to be able to utter a sentence in English. As such, it cuts its own throat.

Value of the Undeniability Principle. The principle of undeniability is used by many *theists to establish a starting point for its argument for God's existence (*see* GOD, EVIDENCE FOR). It begins with "Something exists" (e.g., I do). This must be true since any attempt to deny my existence affirms it in the process. For I must exist in order to deny that I exist. Hence, my existence is undeniable.

Comparison and Contrast with Other Principles. However, the principle of undeniability is not to be confused with the first principle of logical thought, such as the law of non-contradiction.

Difference from The Laws of Logic. The laws of logic are self-evident and rationally necessary. And logical necessity affirms that the opposite cannot possibly be true. For example, it is logically necessary for a triangle to have three sides. And a square circle is logically impossible. It is also logically necessary—if there is a Necessary Being—for it to exist necessarily. However, it is not logically necessary for there to be a Necessary Being. It is logically possible that there could have been a total state of nothingness forever (*see* ONTOLOGICAL ARGUMENT). This is not to say that there cannot be an undeniable argument for God's existence (*see* GOD, EVIDENCE FOR); it is only to note that there is a difference between *logical necessity* (which some allege for invalidating the ontological argument) and *actual undeniability* (which other theists claim for the *cosmological argument).

Likewise, my nonexistence is *logically possible*. But it is not *actually affirmable*. Indeed, it is actually undeniable, since I have to exist in order to deny that I do not exist.

There is, however, an important connection between the laws of logic and the principle of undeniability. The law of non-contradiction, for example, can be defended by showing that it is self-evident in that its predicate is either identical or reducible to its subject. So, self-refuting statements are false because they are contradictory. And contradictions are false because they violate the self-evident principle of noncontradiction.

Difference from a Transcendental Argument. The principle of undeniability bears resemblance to a *transcendental argument. Both claim that certain conditions are necessary preconditions of other things. For example, I cannot deny truth (*see* TRUTH, ABSOLUTE) unless I affirm it by claiming that the statement "There is no truth" is true. A transcendentally necessary truth is an undeniable truth. But a transcendental argument posits something beyond what is being affirmed. For instance, it is a transcendentally necessary precondition of meaning that there is a mind behind meaning. In this sense, a transcendental argument is a kind of indirect form of undeniability. For its posits that certain things could not be true unless other preconditions prevailed.

However, the statement "No sentence is meaningful including this one" is directly self-defeating because it pulls the rug out from under itself without appealing to the necessity of any other conditions. Thus, a transcendental argument involves an indirect form of undeniability.

Status of the Principle of Undeniability. The principle of undeniability is not self-evident the way the traditional first principles are said to be. Some claim it is a metaprinciple, that is, a principle about principles. If so, it is neither arbitrary nor noninformative. It is applicable to reality (*see* REALISM). It is a principle that grows out of the very project of futile attempts to deny first principles or other statements that cannot be denied without affirming them. It is a principle that emerges from the impossible attempts to escape certain things without affirming them (either directly or indirectly) in the very process. It is not deduced or induced but adduced. It is not prescriptive but is descriptive of a process of thought that boomerangs and is self-destructive.

Undeniability is not a new rule for the game of truth but more of a referee. Using the rules of logic (such as the law of non-contradiction), it simply calls attention to the fact that certain statements have eliminated themselves from the game of truth by being self-contradictory or self-destructive. In this sense the principle of undeniability indirectly "referees" the truth game by pointing out which kinds of statements are allowed into the game. It points to certain "statements" that do not really belong in the truth game because they imply opposite statements in the very process of making them. They have eliminated themselves (*see also* FIRST PRINCIPLES; REALISM; AGNOSTICISM).

Sevi, Sabbatai. Sabbatai Sevi was a seventeenth-century Jewish teacher who claimed to be the Messiah and was apparently heralded by a contemporary named Nathan. After Sevi's death in 1676, it was reported that his brother Elijah went to the tomb and found it empty but full of light. Many of his followers believed he had not really died and that he would soon reveal himself (see Scholem).

Critics of the resurrection use Sabbatai Sevi as one reason for claiming that the claims concerning the resurrection are not unique to Christianity. A close look at the facts, however, shows that the reports about this teacher place them solidly in the category of legend (*see* RESURRECTION CLAIMS IN NON-CHRISTIAN RELIGIONS).

Jesus started on a higher footing from Sevi. Dozens of Old Testament predictions were fulfilled in Jesus of Nazareth before his death. He then fulfilled prophetic prediction about how he would die (Isaiah 53) and even the approximate year of his death (ca. A.D. 33, Daniel 9:24–26). For more on the prophecies regarding Jesus, see PROPHECY AS PROOF OF THE BIBLE.

Another difference is that many of Sabbatai Sevi's followers refused to believe he had died and arisen because they believed he could not die at all. His general disappearance theme fits more under apotheosis legends, in which a human being achieves divinity.

Using the group's documents, researcher Gershom Scholem is able to trace the development of the story that Sabbatai's brother found the empty tomb. While critics of Christianity theorize about the Christ legend changing and growing over time, there is no proof of the existence of protogospels, and at least one or two of the four Gospels we have apparently can be dated within the first three decades after the resurrection (*see* RESURRECTION, EVIDENCE FOR). Despite this the accounts of Jesus' life, death, and resurrection have neither changed nor been embellished in the orthodox church since those original documents.

In the case of Sabbatai Sevi, there is conflicting evidence even about whether Nathan taught that the teacher was still alive. One letter that has been found relates that Nathan actually preceded Sevi in death by one month, and the two never actually had met one another.

Sources

G. Scholem, *Sabbatai Sevi: The Mystical Messiah*

G. Habermas, "Resurrection Claims in Non-Christian Religions," *Religious Studies* 25 (1989)

Sherlock, Thomas. Thomas Sherlock (1678–1761) wrote against *deism in the early eighteenth century. He penned *The Use and Interest of Prophecy in the Several Ages of the World* (1725) against deist (*see* DEISM) Anthony Collins, author of *Grounds of the Christian Religion*. Sherlock is best known for *The Tryal of the Witnesses of the Resurrection of Jesus* (1729), which is a reply to Thomas Woolston's *Discourses on the Miracles*. *The Tryal* went through fourteen editions and is a model of the early use of courtroom procedure to defend Christianity:

> The judge and the rest of the company were for bringing on the cause a week sooner; but counsel for Woolston took the matter up, and said, Consider sir, the gentleman is not to argue out of Littleton, Plowden, or Coke, authors to him well known; but he must have his authorities from Matthew, Mark, Luke, and John; and a fortnight is time little enough of all conscience to gain familiarity with a new acquaintance; and turning to the gentleman, he said, I will call on you before the fortnight is out, to see how reverend an appearance you make behind Hammond on the New Testament, a Concordance on one hand and a folio Bible with references on the other.

Following a legal procedure model, others have come to vindicate the truth of Christianity. Evidential specialist Simon *Greenleaf took that approach, as did John Warwick Montgomery and others.

Sources

S. Greenleaf, *The Testimony of the Evangelists*

J. W. Montgomery, *The Law above the Law*

T. Sherlock, *The Tryal of the Witnesses of the Resurrection of Jesus*

Shroud of Turin. *Description.* The Shroud of Turin is a linen cloth that measures 14.25 feet by 3.58 feet (*Biblical Archaeology Review* [1986]: 26) and is housed in Turin, Italy. There is a double, head-to-head image of a man on the material, revealing the front and back of his body.

The Shroud has been known to exist since 1354, but many believe it is much older. In 1978, the Shroud was subjected to extensive scientific investigation. No sign of paint or dye that could account for the image was on it. The image was thought to be three-dimensional and was found only on the surface of the cloth.

However, in 1988, three independent laboratories made carbon-dating tests of threads of the Shroud. They all gave it a late medieval date. Proponents of the Shroud objected that the sample was too fragmentary and was from a contaminated section of the Shroud that reflected a medieval church fire.

Authenticity. The authenticity of the Shroud is hotly debated. Those favoring it stress its unique features. Those against it point to the lack of historical evidence and the scientific dating evidence against it.

Arguments for Authenticity. Those who believe the Shroud is authentic (see Habermas) argue that (1) there is no known naturalistic way to explain the unique images on it; (2) there is no other explanation for the pollen unique to Palestine found on it; (3) the weave is compatible with first-century cloth; (4) the coin over the eye is quite possibly that of Pontius Pilate, minted around A.D. 29–32; (5) it fits with first-century crucifixion procedure and burial rights; (6) the lack of composition marks on the cloth reveals that the body exited quickly; (7) in 1982, a "secret" dating reportedly dated a thread to the first or second century A.D.

Arguments Against Authenticity. Those who reject its authenticity (see Mueller) note that none of the above arguments is definitive. For (1) there are some possible natural explanations, and there may be as yet an unknown natural explanation of the images; (2) the pollen may represent a time it spent in the Holy Land during the Middle Ages or pollen carried from there; (3) the weave is not necessarily unique to the first century or it could be a later reduplication of it or even a medieval image put on a first-century cloth; (4) the alleged coin is not clear enough to be beyond dispute, and if the Shroud is a fraud, then the coin is not real but only an artificially produced image; (5) detailed knowledge of first-century crucifixion and burial may have been known to some in the late Middle Ages; (6) the lack of composition marks could also be part of a knowledgeable artist's reconstruction; (7) this "secret" dating is unconfirmed and contradicted by the three independent medieval scientific datings done in 1988.

Further, opponents of the Shroud argue that: (1) the lack of any early history of the Shroud places it in doubt; (2) the Bible speaks of many pieces of cloth, not just one (John 19:40); (3) independent carbon tests all point to a late medieval date, not to the first century (*Time*, 81). Even defenders of the Shroud admit that "It is still possible that the shroud is a fake" (Habermas, "Turin, Shroud of," 1116). The Roman Catholic Church never officially pronounced it authentic. Indeed, "Shortly after the earliest known exhibit of the shroud, in 1354, a French bishop declared it to be a fraud" (*Time*, 81). And when the scientific dating proved negative, Pope John Paul ordered "Publish it" (ibid.).

Apologetic Value. As far as the apologetic value of the Shroud, the matter of its authenticity is not really relevant. All the essential evidence to defend Christianity is in fact apart from the Shroud. If it is authentic, it provides no essential evidence for Christ's death or resurrection that we do not already possess elsewhere. And if it is not authentic, then we risk using a bad argument for a good cause and lose credibility for Christian apologetics.

Essential Value. There is no essential apologetic value in the Shroud. The evidence for Christianity is more than sufficient without it. The miracles of Jesus confirm that he is the Son of God. Both Jesus and supernatural prophecy are sufficient to support the claim that the Bible is the Word of God. No other evidence is needed. Christianity does not stand or fall in any sense on the question of the authenticity of the Shroud of Turin.

Theoretical Value. Theoretically, the Shroud has some factual apologetic value. If authentic, it would tend to confirm both the death and resurrection of Christ. Certainly the former, and possibly the latter, since resurrection would be a plausible explanation for the image on the Shroud.

Tactical Value. Given the dispute about the Shroud and the possibility that it may be a fraud, the tactical value of using it apologetically is negative. Since it is both unnecessary to the Christian apologetic and highly disputed, it is tactically wiser not to use it as evidence for the truth of Christianity.

Sources

G. Habermas, *Verdict on the Shroud*

M. E. Mueller, "The Shroud of Turin: A Critical Appraisal," *Skeptical Inquirer*, Spring, 1982

D. Sox, *Is the Turin Shroud a Forgery?*

K. F. Weaver, "The Mystery of the Shroud," *National Geographic*, June 1980

R. A. Wild, "The Shroud: Probably the Work of a 14th Century Artist or Forger," *Biblical Archaeology Review*, March–April 1984

Time, 24 October 24 1998

Sikhism. ***The Roots of Sikhism.*** Sikhism is one of the youngest world religions, stemming from only the fifteenth century. Its founder, Nanak, was a Hindu who desired to cleanse *Hinduism by way of Islam. He claimed a revelation from a monotheistic God ("The true Name"), who charged him with this redemptive mission.

Early Reformers of Hinduism. By the tenth century there were militant forms of Islam in India pressing for a purification of decadent *Hinduism. By the eleventh century Islam dominated northwest India. In the twelfth century a reformer-poet called Jaidev, taught a key idea of future Sikhism, namely, that religious ceremonies and asceticism were of no value compared to the pious repetition of God's Name. By the fourteenth century another reformer named Ramananda established a Vishnuite sect that sought to purge Hinduism of certain Hindu beliefs and practices such as the caste system and prohibitions against eating meat.

Kabir (1440–1518): Forerunner of Sikhism. Ramandanda's chief claim to fame was that he had a follower who was greater than himself. A contemporary of the Protestant Reformer, Martin *Luther, who tacked up his 95 theses the year before Kabir died, Kabir caught his hatred of idols from Muslims (*see* ISLAM). As a monotheist he declared that the God of mercy was able to free anyone from the law of karma (*see* REINCARNATION). He denied the special authority of the Hindu Vedas (*see* HINDUISM) and attacked both Brahmins and Muslims for their barren ritualism (see Noss, 311–12).

After his death in A.D. 1518, his Muslim and Hindu followers were divided over whether or not to cremate his body (which Hindus favor and Muslims oppose). Kabir himself is said to have appeared to stop the controversy. When he directed them to draw back the cloth placed over his body, they found only flowers there. His Hindu followers burned half of the flowers and the Muslims buried the other half. Although some claim this is proof of his resurrection, there are substantial grounds for rejecting this claim (*see* RESURRECTION, NON-CHRISTIAN CLAIMS FOR).

Nanak: Founder of Sikhism. Nanak was born in 1469 in the village of Talwandi near Lahore, the capital of Punjab. His parents were Hindus, and his town ruler, Rai Bular, converted to Islam and encouraged reconciliation of the two religions.

Nanak is said to have been a precocious youth and a poet by nature. However, he was a failure as a husband and father, eventually leaving his wife and two children. Then "One day after bathing in the river Nanak disappeared into the forest, and was taken in a vision to God's presence." After accepting a cup of nectar, it is claimed that God said to him: "I am with thee. I have made thee happy, and so those who shall take thy name. Go and repeat Mine, and cause others to do likewise. Abide uncontaminated by the world. Practice the repetition of My name, charity, ablutions, worship, and meditation. I have given thee this cup of nectar, a pledge of My reward" (see Noss, 313).

Nanak is said to have uttered the preamble of the Japji, which is repeated silently each morning by Sikhs: "There is but one God whose name is True, the Creator, devoid of fear and enmity, immortal, unborn, self-existent, great and bountiful. The True One was in the beginning, the True One was in the primal age. The True One is, was, O Nanak, and the True One also shall be" (ibid.).

After three days Nanak is said to have left the forest and after remaining silent for one day he uttered: "There is no Hindu and no Musalman." This was the beginning of his evangelistic campaign to convert all India, Persia, and Arabia. He wandered through cities, singing his hymns on a small stringed instrument.

The Ten Gurus. Nanak appointed his successor and so on through the Ten Gurus: Nanak (1469–1538); Angad (1538–52); Amar Das (1552–74); Ram Das Sodhi (1574–81); Arjun Mal (1581–1606); Hargobind (1606–44); Har Raj (1644–61); Hari Krishen (1661–64); Tegh Bahadur (1664–75); and Gobind Rai (1675–1708). The succession ended when Gobind Rai had no sons left and appointed no successor.

The Sikh Bible. Guru Arjun, the fifth Guru, gathered many of the hymns and writings to that point. This collecting process continued until it was completed by the tenth Guru, Gobind Rai. These volumes containing the doctrines of Sikhism are known as the *Siri Guru Granth Sahib* (also called *Adi Granth*).

Sikh Doctrines and Practices. The teachings of Sikhism include monotheism, meditation, *Reincarnation with its samsara and karma (see Mather, 257–58). Stricker Sikhs, called Khalsa, practice the five K's: (1) *kesa*—long hair kept uncut; (2) *kangha*—comb; (3) *kacha*—short pants; (4) *kacku*—metal bracelet; and (5) *kirpan*—weapon or sword.

Sikhs are forbidden to worship icons, though the *Adi Granth* has become an object of devotion. Their temples are called *Gurdwaras*. Sacred times, usually in the mornings, are reserved for prayers.

Sikhism gained a considerable influence in the West through Yogi Bhajan, who established a unique form of Sikhism known as Sikh Dharma. In 1968 he founded the Healthy, Happy, Holy Organization (3HO), beginning his first ashram in Los Angeles. Many young Americans of the counterculture movement joined him. From there he moved to a forty-acre ranch in New Mexico, where his follows practice methods of awakening Kundalini by staring into the eyes of fellow practitioners or at pictures of their Guru and uttering a mantra. They are strict vegetarians and live a drug-free life, egalitarian life.

Evaluation. Sikhism is certainly to be commended for its stress on monotheism and its iconoclastic crusade against idolatry, empty ritualism, and asceticism. Likewise, its emphasis on the nature of God and ethical life rank it among the other ethical monotheisms of the world such as Judaism, Christianity, and *Islam.

However, its belief in *reincarnation has been severely criticized by Christian theists. And the lack of any verified supernatural confirmations of his claims to be a prophet (*see* MIRACLES AS CONFIRMATION OF TRUTH) disqualify Sikhism as being the true religion such as Christianity claims. Its origins can be explained in terms of its roots, a natural reaction against decadent Hinduism in favor of a more Muslim form of monotheism without buying into the Islamic rituals. This kind of syncretism is typical of the Indian mind-set.

Sources

Sir Norman Anderson, *Christianity and World Religions*

W. Corduan, *Neighboring Faiths*

J. B. Noss, *Man's Religions*

G. A. Mather, et al., *Dictionary of Cults, Sects, Religions and the Occult*

H. Smith, *The Religions of Man*

Sin, Noetic Effects of. ***See*** **NOETIC EFFECTS OF SIN; Skepticism;** ***See*** **AGNOSTICISM; APOLOGETICS NEED FOR; APOLOGETICS, OBJECTIONS TO; BIBLE CRITICISM; CERTAINTY/CERTITUDE; FAITH AND REASON; GOD, OBJECTIONS TO PROOFS FOR; HUME, DAVID; KANT, IMMANUEL; MIRACLES, APOLOGETIC VALUE OF.**

Skinner, B. F. ***See*** **DETERMINISM**

Smith, Wilbur M. Although Wilbur Smith (1894–1977) never earned a formal degree, he taught for many years at major evangelical institutions. Smith was a Bible teacher at Moody Bible Institute (1939–47), a member of the founding faculty at Fuller Theological Seminary (1947–63), and professor emeritus of English Bible at Trinity Evangelical Divinity School (1963–68). His major apologetic works include *The Supernaturalness of Christ* (1940) and *Therefore Stand* (1945).

Smith's most comprehensive case for Christianity is found in *Therefore Stand*. The book studies Paul's three points as he spoke in the Areopagus (Acts 17:24–31): creation, resurrection, and judgment. Around these themes, the first two of which are discussed below, Smith constructed his apologetic.

Existence of God. Smith argues for the Christian view of creation by appealing to science. All scientific inquiry is founded on the principles of causality and uniformity (*see* ORIGINS, SCIENCE OF). The former states that whatever has a beginning has a cause, the latter that whatever causes a certain effect in the present probably caused the same effect in the past. From these principles Smith developed a pair of *cosmological arguments. The first shows that there must be a first cause of the universe because of the impossibility of an infinite series of past events (*see* KALAM COSMOLOGICAL ARGUMENT). This first cause, furthermore, must be a Mind, because the order and unity of the universe betray a certain intelligence (*see* TELEOLOGICAL ARGUMENT).

The second argument attempts to show that the universe needs a cause, not only to get started, but for its continual existence. For if the universe consists wholly of contingent things, the universe itself must be contingent. But if the universe as a whole is contingent, it must require a Cause beyond the universe. This Cause is God.

Resurrection. Smith held the resurrection of Christ to be the very citadel of faith (*see* RESURRECTION, EVIDENCE FOR). "If this goes, so must almost everything else that is vital and unique in the Gospel" ("Scientists and the Resurrection," 22). Fortunately, the most evidence is found where evidence is needed the most. Smith proceeds to give historical evidence in support of the burial of Jesus, the empty tomb, and the resurrection of Jesus, along the way refuting various naturalistic explanations (*see* MIRACLES, ARGUMENTS AGAINST; NATURALISM) of the data (*see* RESURRECTION, ALTERNATIVE THEORIES). He concludes that evidence for the resurrection "is so overwhelming that by no honorable intellectual device can the evidence be set aside" (*Therefore Stand*, 406).

Sources

W. Elwell, "Smith, Wilbur," in *Handbook of Evangelical Theologians*

W. M. Smith, *Before I Forget*

———, "Scientists and the Resurrection," *CT* (15 April 1957)

———, *The Supernaturalness of Christ*

———, *Therefore Stand*

Son of Man, Jesus as. The phrase *Son of Man* is used more frequently to denote Jesus than is any other name, except the word *Jesus* itself. *Son of Man* occurs in all four Gospels; it appears thirty times in Matthew, fourteen in Mark, twenty-five in Luke, and thirteen in John (Marshall, 777). It is also found in Acts 7:56. Hebrews 2:6 and Revelation 14:14 refer to "a son of man."

The problem posed is why Jesus refers to himself almost exclusively as "the Son of Man," when Christians claim he is the Son of God. Is this a tacit denial of his deity? Beyond the literal meaning of the words, Scriptures are used to argue this view: Psalms 8:4; 80:17, and Ezekiel 2:1; 3:1; 4:1, and others.

The literal meaning of the words does not necessarily convey the literal meaning of the expression. A lot of projects are "in the bag" that would not literally fit into a grocery sack or duffel bag. An organization's "board" is not a wood plank, the original meaning of the word. Context has to help us understand these expressions. Ezekiel is responsible for ninety-three Old Testament appearances of the term. In most God is speaking, and they seem to express special intimacy toward Ezekiel, the servant. Daniel uses the term only twice but raises the stakes, for Daniel 7:13 is displaying a king Messiah in all his glory in the very presence of God. This is the One Daniel said looked "like a man" in 8:15, with the implication that he was far more than flesh and blood. Interestingly, in 8:17 the Messiah passes on his name. Daniel is called by the name of the Messiah: "Son of man." There are, obviously, some complex and subtle nuances at work in the Old Testament use of this term.

Whether Jesus uses the self-identification "Son of Man" to stress his own humanity and servanthood as in Ezekiel, or to announce his Messiahship as in Daniel, or both, the phrase certainly isn't a denial of deity.

New Testament scholar I. Howard Marshall points out, that Jesus often employed the phrase when he was highlighting his divinity (ibid.; *see* CHRIST, DEITY OF). Jesus said to the crowd that he had forgiven the sins of the paralytic, "that you may know that the Son of Man has authority on earth to forgive sins" (Mark 2:10). Rather than figuring that he was denying divinity, the crowd was ready to stone him for his blasphemy.

Jesus repeatedly said that the Son of Man would die and rise from the dead, events that gave his messianic credentials. Mark wrote: "He then began to teach them that the Son of Man must suffer many things and be rejected by the elders, chief priests and teachers of the law, and that he must be killed and after three days rise again" (8:31; cf. Mark 9:9, 12, 31; 10:33; 14:21). Jesus also used the phrase in connection with his second coming in power and glory. When asked by the high priest, "Are you the Christ, the Son of the Blessed One?" Jesus replied: "I am, and you will see the Son of Man sitting at the right hand of the Mighty One and coming on the clouds of heaven." It was on the basis of these words that the Sanhedrin condemned Jesus to death for blasphemy (Mark 14:62–64). They recognized that the Son of Man in view was clearly the mighty man in Daniel's vision:

> "In my vision at night I looked, and there before me was one like a son of man, coming with the clouds of heaven. He approached the Ancient of Days and was led into his presence. He was given authority, glory and sovereign power; all peoples, nations and men of every language worshiped him. His dominion is an everlasting dominion that will not pass away, and his kingdom is one that will never be destroyed." [7:13–14]

In the Matthew account of Jesus' trial (27:63), Jesus described himself as the "Son of Man sitting at the right hand of the Power [God]." Who else but the Christ, the Son of God, could sit in the honored position at the right hand of God?

Further, when a voice from heaven confirmed Christ's deity and glory, Jesus spoke of the Son of Man being "lifted up" in death (John 12:28–32). Then the crowd replied, "We have heard from the Law that the Christ will remain for ever, so how can you say, 'The Son of Man must be lifted up'?" The crowd obviously understood the meaning of the phrase. It is used interchangeably with *Messiah* and the concept from Isaiah 48:11 of the Messiah's "glory of the Father," which God declared he would not share with another.

Even if the phrase were only a reference to humanity, that would not be a denial of his deity. Jesus clearly claimed to be God in various ways and on multiple occasions, as is shown in the article, Christ, Deity of. He also accepted acclaim as God on other occasions (see, for example, Matt. 16:16–18; John 20:28–29).

Sources

D. Guthrie, *Introduction to New Testament Theology*

T. Miethe and G. Habermas, *Why I Believe God Exists*

O. Cullmann, *Christology in the New Testament*

I. H. Marshall, "Son of Man," in *Dictionary of Christ and the Gospels*

Soul, Immortality of. ***See*** **IMMORTALITY.**

Spinoza, Benedict. Benedict Spinoza (1632–1677) was born to Portuguese Jewish refugee parents in Amsterdam. Although a lens grinder by trade who never taught philosophy at university, he exerted a strong influence on modern philosophy. He has particularly made a negative impact on orthodox Christianity. Spinoza was even excommunicated from his synagogue in 1656 for believing that God is "extended," a form of *pantheism, that angels are imaginary, and that there is no *immortality of the soul.

The Medieval philosopher Moses *Maimonides (1135–1204), through his *A Guide for the Perplexed*, helped Spinoza conceptualize God as a Necessary Being and to employ human reason independent of divine revelation. *Anselm's (ca. 1034–1109) idea of God as an absolutely perfect and necessary being was also formative on Spinoza's thought. The French rationalist René *Descartes (1596–1650), who penned the *Meditations*, taught Spinoza the use of mathematical methods in philosophy. The first-century Jewish philosopher Philo (13 B.C.–A.D. 45) influenced Spinoza to believe that God is ground of all being and that the Bible should be understood allegorically. Euclid's (ca. 300 B.C.) geometry taught Spinoza his deductive rationalism. From his Jewish background he brought a strong stress on the unity of God. All these and other factors contributed to a unique form of rationalistic pantheism.

The two primary works of Spinoza are *Tractatus Theologico-politicus, Tractatus Politicus* (1670), and *Ethics* (1674).

Philosophy. As Euclid, Spinoza begins by defining his axioms and then proceeds to make deductions from them. In this way alone, he writes, can one find certainty in his conclusions. Truth is known only through a true idea. Perfect truth is known only through the perfect idea. Error has four causes: (1) Our minds provide only fragmentary expression of ideas. (2) Imagination is affected by the physical senses and confuses us. (3) Reasoning is too abstract and general. (4) We fail to begin with the perfect idea. The remedy for error is to return to the perfect Idea of God. The more one feeds on the perfect Idea, the more perfect one becomes. Sensations are confused and blurred.

Spinoza's philosophy begins with the perfect Idea of God as an absolutely necessary and perfect being. God must be conceived as a being existing through himself—that is, self-caused. But there can only be one absolutely independent Being. All other beings are modally dependent on God. These "modes" are aspects or moments of God, God's attributes in himself and properties to us. The only two attributes of God we know are thought and the *extension* of God infinitely in space.

Proofs for God. Spinoza believed the existence of God could be proven with mathematical certainty. The first form of his proof can be stated:

1. There must be a cause for everything, both existing and nonexistent.
2. A Necessary Being must necessarily exist, unless there is a cause adequate to explain its nonexistence.
3. But there is no cause adequate to explain why a Necessary Being does not exist: (a.) Such a cause would have to be either inside God's nature or outside of it. (b.) No cause outside a necessary existence could possibly annul its existence, (c.) and nothing inside a Necessary Being denies it is a necessary Being. (d.) So there is no cause adequate to explain why a Necessary Being does not exist.
4. Therefore, a Necessary Being necessarily exists.

The second form of Spinoza's argument is this:

1. Something necessarily exists.
2. This Necessary Existence is either finite or infinite.
3. But no finite cause can hinder infinite existence,
4. and it is contradictory to say that an infinite Cause hindered infinite Existence.

5. Therefore, there must be an infinite Existence.

Creation differs from God only as a mode differs from its substance or a thought from the mind that thought it. All modes flow necessarily from God as 180 degrees flows from a triangle. This is creation *ex Deo*, not creation *ex nihilo* (*see* CREATION, VIEWS OF). The effect must be as infinite as the Cause. Will is not an attribute of God but only a mode (hence, it is not a source of creation).

This world is the most perfect world possible. Evil is necessary. Natural world operates by natural (scientific) law (*see* NATURALISM). Newton's law of gravity is universal and is the model for all scientific laws. There are no exceptions to a true law.

The Impossibility of *Miracles. Spinoza believed that there could be only one infinite substance, and that, therefore, the universe was uncreated. God is identical with the universe. He could not have created it, for it is of his substance (*see* MIRACLES, IMPOSSIBILITY OF). For Spinoza, God is not transcendent; he is not beyond or "other" than creation. This means God's creativity is no more than nature's activity. If Spinoza's supposition is true, miracles are impossible. If God (the supernatural) is identical with nature (the natural), there is no supernatural intervention into nature from outside it. With this general framework in mind, we can examine Spinoza's arguments against miracles.

Spinoza declared that "nothing then, comes to pass in nature in contravention to her universal laws, nay, everything agrees with them and follows from them, for . . . she keeps a fixed and immutable order." In fact, "a miracle, whether in contravention to, or beyond, nature, is a mere absurdity." Spinoza was dogmatic about the impossibility of miracles. He proclaimed, "We may, then, be absolutely certain that every event which is truly described in Scripture necessarily happened, like everything else, according to natural laws" (*Tractatus*, 1:83, 87, 92).

Spinoza's argument against miracles goes something like this:

1. Miracles are violations of natural laws.
2. Natural laws are immutable.
3. It is impossible to violate immutable laws.
4. Therefore, miracles are impossible.

The second premise is the key to Spinoza's argument. Nature "keeps a fixed and immutable order" (ibid., 83). Everything "necessarily happens . . . according to natural laws" (ibid., 92, emphasis added). If it is true that "nothing comes to pass in nature in contravention to her universal laws," then Spinoza is right in believing a miracle "is a mere absurdity" (ibid., 83, 87).

To appreciate the implications, one must be aware that Spinoza was a rationalist who tried to construct his philosophy around Euclidean geometry (*Ethics*, 1.1–42). He believed that one should accept as true only what is self-evident or what is reducible to the self-evident. Like *Descartes, Spinoza argued in a geometric way from axioms to conclusions contained in these axioms. Spinoza lived in an age that was impressed by the orderliness of a physical universe. This is why it was axiomatic that natural laws are immutable.

****Biblical Criticism.*** Spinoza's rationalism and naturalism have far-reaching consequences for anyone who believes in either miraculous events or supernatural revelations. Spinoza became one of the first modern intellectuals to engage in systematic higher criticism of the Bible (*see* BIBLE CRITICISM; WELLHAUSEN, JULIUS). His book, *A Theologico-Political Treatise*, widely circulated in the late seventeenth century, was chiefly a critical commentary of the Bible. He came to some radical conclusions that, if true, falsifies supernaturally inspired Scriptures.

Spinoza's *naturalism led him to conclude that Moses could not have written many passages in the Pentateuch (*see* PENTATEUCH, MOSAIC AUTHORSHIP OF), so the view that Moses was its author is unfounded (*Tractatus*, 126). He believed that Ezra the scribe wrote the first five books of the Old Testament, as he wrote the rest of the Old Testament (ibid., 129–30).

Not surprisingly, Spinoza rejected the Gospel accounts of the resurrection. The apostles, he said, preached a universal religion based only in the crucifixion (ibid., 170). Christianity was a mystical, nonpropositional religion without foundations. Essentially, Spinoza agreed with Paul in 1 Corinthians 15 that, without the resurrection of Christ, Christianity is a religion without hope. Not believing the resurrection happened, that was his conception of it. All other miracles are likewise condemned. He commends "anyone who seeks for the true causes of miracles and strives to understand natural phenomena as an intelligent being" (*Ethics*, Appendix, pt. 1, proposition 36). Not only did everything happen according to natural laws, but Scripture itself "makes the general assertion in several passages that nature's course is fixed and unchangeable" (*Ethics*, 92, 96).

For Spinoza, Scripture merely "*contains* the word of God" (*Tractatus*, 165, emphasis added). This position was characteristic of later liberal Christianity from Friedrich *Schleiermacher (1768–1834). It is false to say that the Bible *is* the Word of God (*see* BIBLE, EVIDENCE FOR). Parts of the Bible that *contain* the word are known to be such because the morality conforms to a natural law known by human reason (ibid., 172, 196–97).

The prophets did not speak from supernatural "revelation" and "the modes of expression and discourse adopted by the *apostles in the Epistles, show very clearly that the latter were not written by revelation and divine command, but merely by the natural powers and judgment of the authors" (ibid., 159). Spinoza occasionally says the prophets spoke by "revelation," but he understands this as the extraordinary power of the imagination (ibid., 24).

The general concepts and antisupernaturalism of Spinoza's biblical criticism is still widely held by both secular and liberal Christian scholars.

Evaluation. Three elements in Spinoza's thought are of interest to Christian apologetics, his *pantheism, his antisupernaturalism (*see* MIRACLES, ARGUMENTS AGAINST), and his *biblical criticism. The three are related. Since pantheism and biblical criticism are critiqued in those respective articles, the focus here will be on naturalistic presuppositions and their consequences on belief in the inspiration of Scripture.

Spinoza's attack on miracles rests on the foundations of Euclidean geometry or deduction, rationalism, natural determinism, and his view of the nature of God.

A Stacked Deductive Deck. Spinoza's deductive, rationalistic pantheism suffers from an acute case of *petitio principii* or begging the question. This is true both of his pantheism and the antisupernaturalism that flows from it. As David *Hume noted, anything validly deducible from premises must have already been present in those premises from the beginning. If God is defined as an absolutely necessary being, of which all else is nothing but a mode, then of course pantheism follows. For this builds a pantheistic definition of God into the axiom. If a pantheistic conception is stuffed into the hat, it is no surprise that it later can be pulled out.

Likewise, if *materialism is already presupposed in Spinoza's rationalistic premises, it is no surprise that he attacks the miracles of the Bible. The question is whether his rationalistic premises are defensible. He provides no convincing argument. But once one defines natural laws as "fixed," "immutable," and "unchangeable," there is no great leap to the position that miracle reports are irrational. Nothing can break the unbreakable.

Spinoza's God and Science. Spinoza's God was of one substance with the universe. Miracles as supernatural interventions are possible only in a theistic universe. Hence, scientists will want reason to believe that a theistic God (*see* THEISM) exists before they are likely to believe there is any evidence for miracles. In a Nature = God universe, miracles simply do not happen.

Albert *Einstein's belief in Spinoza's God gave rise to one of the fascinating stories in modern science. Astrophysicist Robert Jastrow tells of the reluctance of scientists to conclude that the universe came into existence through a "big bang" billions of years ago. Jastrow offers several lines of scientific evidence that support a beginning to the universe: the fact that the universe is running down, Einstein's theory of relativity, and the expansion pattern and radiation echo that can be detected. The radiation echo "has convinced almost the last doubting Thomas" (Jastrow, 15). Einstein developed the general theory of relativity but failed to observe that an expanding universe followed as a conclusion from his own theory. The Russian mathematician Alexander Friedmann pointed out the reason for Einstein's omission, a schoolboy's error in algebra. In effect, he had divided by zero. Einstein responded by defending his original thesis, only he made another mistake in this proof.

Eventually Einstein recognized his error and wrote, "My objection rested on an error in calculation. I consider Mr. Friedmann's results to be correct and illuminating." However, "this circumstance [of an expanding universe] irritated me." Elsewhere he said, "To admit such possibilities seems senseless" (ibid., 16, 25–28).

Why would the view that the universe had a beginning seem "senseless" and so irritating that it caused Einstein to make a mathematical error? The answer, writes Jastrow, came when Einstein described his own religion as belief "in Spinoza's God, who reveals himself in the orderly harmony of what exists" (ibid., 28).

Conclusion. Spinoza was a rationalist (*see* RATIONALISM) for whom God's essence was equated with the universe, and for whom the universe is eternal and operates according to the uniformity of natural law. He led the philosophical attack against miracles and the Bible's testimony about a personal God and Savior. But as shown, this faith presupposition begs the question when defended logically, because his definition of miracles, without foundation, assumes them to be unbreakable (*see* MIRACLES, ARGUMENTS AGAINST).

What Spinoza needed to do, but did not, was to provide a sound argument for his rationalistic presuppositions. His reasoning is geometric, but he spun his axioms out of thin air rather than empirical observation.

Spinoza's concept of natural law as a deterministic system is self-defeating. If everything is determined, then so is the view of any that determinism is wrong. But determinism cannot be both true and false. Thus, Spinoza's basis for antisupernaturalism is unfounded. Therefore, miracles cannot be pronounced as impossible.

Finally, the evidence has mounted for a unique beginning of the space-time universe (*see* BIG BANG THEORY; EVOLUTION, COSMIC). If this is so, then there is an irrefutable example of a miracle, and the Spinozan hypothesis is falsified. Further, concluding that the universe had a beginning strikes a devastating blow to Spinoza's concept of God, who does not exist beyond the universe.

Sources

B. de Spinoza, *Tractatus Theologico-Politicus, Tractatus Politicus*
R. Jastrow, *God and the Astronomers*
W. James, *Some Problems of Philosophy*
C. F. von Weizsacker, *The Relevance of Science*
W. Craig, *The* Kalam *Cosmological Argument*
S. Hawking, *A Brief History of Time*

Strauss, David. David Strauss (1808–1874) was a German native of Ludwigsburg, who launched the quest for the historical Jesus with his naturalistic biography of the life of Christ.

Strauss studied under F. C. Baur (1792–1860) and came under the influences of Friedrich *Schleiermacher (1768–1834) and G. W. F. *Hegel (1770–1831) at Tübingen. After studying at Berlin he was appointed lecturer on Hegel at Tübingen (1832). His demythologized *Life of Jesus* (2 vols.) appeared in 1835–36, and in the resulting uproar Strauss was dismissed. In 1840–41 he published *History of Christian Doctrine*, a polemical history from the development of the New Testament to its dissolution in Hegel. In 1862 he wrote on biblical critic Herman Samuel Reimarus, whose *Fragments* in 1778 gave rise to the first quest for the historical Jesus (*see* Jesus, Quest for the Historical). Late works included *The Life of Jesus for the German People* (1864), *The Life of Christ and the History of Jesus* (1865) and *The Old Faith and the New* (1872/1873). The latter called for a new humanist religion that traded belief in theism and immortality for scientific materialism. It promoted Darwinian evolution (*see* Darwin, Charles; Evolution, Biological).

Strauss moved from an earlier form of Hegelian developmental pantheism to materialistic evolutionism. Following David Hume, he rejected all miracles as myths. He eventually denied all belief in God and immortality of the soul. Since he rejected miracles, he viewed the Gospels as unintentional myths created by the piety of the early second century (*see* Mythology and the New Testament). They were steeped in the messianic anticipation of the Old Testament and an eagerness to prove that Jesus was the Messiah (*see* Christ of Faith vs. Jesus of History). Strauss was the first to consistently apply this thesis throughout the New Testament.

Sources

R. S. Cromwell, *David Friedrich Strauss and His Place in Modern Thought*
H. Harris, *David Friedrich Strauss and His Theology*
D. Strauss, *The Life of Jesus Critically Examined*
T. Ziegler, *David Friedrich Strauss*

Sufficient Reason, Principle of. The principle of sufficient reason arises out of modern *rationalism, particularly as developed by Gottfried *Leibniz (1646–1716). It was developed by Christian Wolfe and originally accepted by Immanuel *Kant (1724–1804), though Kant subsequently rejected its metaphysical value, since he believed it led to contradictions and *agnosticism.

The principle claims that "Everything has a sufficient reason, either in another or in itself." That is, there is either a sufficient reason outside of everything, or else it is its own sufficient reason. Leibniz believed that since the world was contingent, it had a sufficient reason outside of itself (in God). And the sufficient reason for God is inside himself.

Since "reason" for the world means "ground" or "cause," then the principle of sufficient reason means that everything that exists has a cause, either outside itself or inside itself. It did not take philosophical agnostics (*see* Agnosticism), such as Kant, or atheists, such as Arthur *Schopenhauer (1788–1860), long to figure out that this either leads to an infinite regress (*see* Infinite Series), or else to a self-caused being, which is impossible. If literally *everything* has a cause, either the series of causes never ends, or it ends in a being who caused its own being. Since nothing can lift itself from ontological nonbeing, then the very concept of God is contradictory. God could not exist.

Many critics of rational *theism believe the principle of sufficient reason spells the end of all theistic arguments (*see* God, Evidence for; God, Objections to Proofs for) that use any causal premise (*see* Cosmological Argument). This is not the case. There is a great difference between the principles of sufficient reason and cause. Criticisms of sufficient reason do not apply to the principle of causality (*see* Causality, Principle of). The latter was held by *Thomas Aquinas, who never referred to any principle of sufficient reason, though some scholastic philosophers after Leibniz did mistakenly buy into it (see Gurr). The two principles are:

Principle of Sufficient Reason:	**Principle of Causality:**
1. All things need a cause.	1. Contingent things need a cause.
2. God is the Ultimate Reason.	2. God is the only Ultimate Being.
3. God is a Self-Caused Being.	3. God is an Uncaused Being.

The principle of sufficient reason leads to a contradiction. The principle of causality does not. Leibniz's principle leads logically to modern atheism. Aquinas's principle leads to theism. The God of the principle of sufficient reason is a God of reason, not reality. The God of the existential principle of causality leads to a God who exists and, in fact, is existence itself (*see* God, Nature of). It is no more incoherent to have an uncaused God than for atheists to claim there is an uncaused universe. Nor is there an inherent logical contradiction in the concept of a Being who just *is* and ever has been.

Sources

N. L. Geisler and W. Corduan, *Philosophy of Religion*
J. E. Gurr, *The Principle of Sufficient Reason in Some Scholastic Systems, 1750–1900*
I. Kant, *The Critique of Pure Reason*
G. Leibniz, *Monadology*
———, *Discourse on Metaphysics*
Thomas Aquinas, *Summa Theologica*

Sun Dial of Ahaz. ***See*** **SCIENCE AND THE BIBLE.**

Suzuki, Daisetz Teitaro. ***See*** **ZEN BUDDHISM.**

Swietzer, Albert. ***See*** **JESUS, QUEST FOR HISTORICAL**

Swoon Theory. *The swoon theory* is the naturalistic (*see* Naturalism) view that Christ was not dead when taken from the cross and placed in the tomb. Therefore, he was not raised from the dead (*see* RESURRECTION, EVIDENCE FOR). It was proposed by H. E. G. Paulus in *The Life of Jesus* (1828).

This theory has serious failings as an alternate explanation of the resurrection (*see* RESURRECTION, ALTERNATE THEORIES), since there is strong evidence that Jesus experienced an actual physical death on the cross (*see* CHRIST, DEATH OF), and hundreds of witnesses who saw him in a fully whole and transformed resurrection body (*see* RESURRECTION, EVIDENCE FOR). Even the naturalistic work, *A New Life of Jesus* (1879) by David Strauss debunked the swoon theory:

> It is impossible that a being who had stolen half-dead out of the sepulchre, who crept about weak and ill, wanting medical treatment, who required bandaging, strengthening and indulgence, and who still at last yielded to his sufferings, could have given to his disciples the impression that he was a Conqueror over death and the grave, the Prince of Life, an impression which lay at the bottom of their future ministry. . . . Such a resuscitation could only have weakened the impression which he had made upon them in life and in death, at the most could only have given it an elegiac voice, but could by no possibility have changed their sorrow into enthusiasm, have elevated their reverence into worship. [Strauss, 1.412]

Sources

W. Craig, *Knowing the Truth about the Resurrection*
G. Habermas, *The Resurrection of Jesus: An Apologetic*
H. E. G. Paulus, *The Life of Jesus*
D. Strauss, *A New Life of Jesus*

Systematic Presuppositionalism. ***See*** **APOLOGETICS, ARGUMENT OF; CARNELL, EDWARD JOHN; PRESUPPOSITIONAL APOLOGETICS.**

Tt

Tautology. A *tautology* is a contentless statement; something true by definition and uninformative of the real world. "All bachelors are unmarried men" is a tautology, as is "All triangles have three sides." Neither statement informs us that the subject exists. They only mean, "If X exists, then it is X." If there are any bachelors in the universe, they are unmarried. The tautology does not tell us that a bachelor really exists. David *Hume called this kind of statement the "relation of ideas." Immanuel *Kant called them "analytic."

Tautologies and Empirical Statements. Tautologies are usually contrasted with empirical statements that have content: "The tree outside my window is an oak." "The car in my yard is black." While empirical statements have content, they are not logically necessary. That is, they may be false. Tautologies, on the other hand, are logically necessary, since they are true by definition. They do not say a thing, but they are necessarily true.

An analytic statement is simply expletive because the predicate explains the idea present in the subject. Unlike empirical statements, analytic statements are not ampliative. The predicate doesn't add to what is known from the subject. "The house is brown" is ampliative, since the predicate amplifies on the subject. We learn the color of the house, which we would not have known simply from examining the concept "house."

While all tautologies are absolutely certain, not everything that is absolutely certain is a tautology. "I exist." is certain. I cannot deny it unless I actually exist to deny it. Likewise the assertion about my existence, "I am I" is not a mere tautology, since it asserts something about existence. Also, "Being exists" is not an empty statement, since it affirms existence (*see* First Principles; Metaphysics; Realism).

While tautologies or statements true by definition are empty in themselves, they can be filled with content and used to prove something is true. The statement, "If this is an effect, it must have a cause" is an empty statement. But once it is combined with a statement about the real world, such as "The existing world is an effect," then it can be used to assert that the world has a Cause (*see* God, Evidence for). So simply because a statement is analytic (true by definition) does not mean it cannot be used to demonstrate something about the real world.

Teleological Argument. Four kinds of "classical" arguments have attempted to establish the existence of God, the **ontological argument*, the **moral argument*, the **cosmological argument*, and the **teleological argument*. The ontological argument argues from the concept of a Necessary Being to that Being's existence. Since the time of Immanuel *Kant, the ontological argument has been widely believed to be invalid. The moral argument is the argument from a moral law to a Moral Law Giver. The cosmological argument reasons from the existence of the cosmos to a Creator. The teleological argument moves from design to a Designer. Forms of the teleological argument can be found in early Greek philosophy. It can be found in Socrates (Xenophon's *Memorabilia* 1.4.4ff.); *Plato (*Phaedo*), and *Philo (*Works, of Philo* 3.182, 183.33). But it came to fruition later in the middle ages and modern world (*see* Paley, William).

Design Arguments. **Thomas Aquinas's World Governor.* While Thomas Aquinas is better known for his cosmological argument, the last of his "Five Ways" to prove the existence of God is a teleological argument. Aquinas calls it the argument from *"the governance of the world"* (Aquinas 1.2.3):

1. Every agent acts for an end, even natural agents.
2. Now what acts for an end manifests intelligence.
3. But natural agents have no intelligence of their own.
4. Therefore, they are directed to their end by some Intelligence.

The first premise is simply the self-evident *principle of teleology* or finality (*see* FIRST PRINCIPLES). Between the first and second premise exists an unstated assumption that all or most things in nature can be called "agents." They do move toward an end, be it staying alive or reproducing, and they move toward secondary purposes that have nothing to do with themselves. In the big picture their existence and actions make the world habitable, or beautiful, or enjoyable, or meaningful. These agents act in predictable, purposeful ways that seem to work toward the best results. If one accepts the assumption and the reasonable first two premises, the trap is sprung in the third premise, whatever lacks knowledge must be directed toward an end, as an arrow is directed by the archer. Whatever intelligence is directing it all fits the concept *God* (Burrill, 165–70).

Paley's Watchmaker. One of the most popular forms of the argument was given by William *Paley (1743–1805), the archdeacon of Carlisle. Paley insisted that if one found a watch in an empty field, one would rightly conclude that it had a watchmaker because of its obvious design. Likewise, when one looks at the even more complex design of the world in which we live, one cannot but conclude that there is a great Designer behind it. Let us put the argument in summary form (ibid.).

1. A watch shows that it was put together for an intelligent purpose (to keep time): (a) It has a spring to give it motion. (b) It has a series of wheels to transmit this motion. (c) The wheels are made of brass so that they do not rust. (d) The spring is made of steel because of the resilience of that metal. (e) The front cover is of glass so that one can see through it.
2. The world shows an even greater evidence of design than a watch: (a) The world is a greater work of art than a watch. (b) The world has more subtle and complex design than a watch. (c) The world has an endless variety of means adapted to ends.
3. Therefore, if the existence of a watch implies a watchmaker, the existence of the world implies an even greater intelligent Designer (God).

Cleanthes's Machine Maker. In David Hume's *Dialogues Concerning Natural Religion*, the fictional theist Cleanthes offers a similar form (171–76):

1. All design implies a designer.
2. Great design implies a great designer.
3. There is great design in the world (like that of a great machine).
4. Therefore, there must be a great Designer of the world.

The argument extends beyond Paley's. Cleanthes uses illustrations of design other than a watch or a machine. The human eye, male-female relations, a book, and a voice from heaven are all used to illustrate design. He also makes it clear that the teleological argument is an *argument from analogy*, insisting that like effects have like causes. Cleanthes alludes to chance as an improbable explanation that a distinct voice from heaven could have been an accidental whistling of the wind. Finally, he insists that irregularities in nature do not effect the argument. Rather, these are the exceptions that establish the rule.

Hume used this argument to anticipate some of his own criticisms, thus making his final case all the stronger. However, Hume did not do justice to Paley's argument (*see* PALEY, WILLIAM).

Mill's Objection. John Stuart *Mill (1806–73) objected to Paley's form of the argument from analogy and then offered what he thought was a better one. His objection does not destroy the argument, but it does weaken it (ibid., 177–84):

1. Paley's argument is built on analogy—similarity in effect implies similarity in cause.
2. This kind of analogy is weaker when the dissimilarities are greater.
3. There is a significant dissimilarity that weakens this argument. (a) Watches imply watchmakers only because, by previous experiences, we know that watches are made by watchmakers. (b) In like manner, footprints imply human beings, and dung implies animals only because previous experience informs us that this is so, not because of any intrinsic design in the remains.
4. Therefore, Paley's argument is weaker than he thought.

After criticizing Paley's form of the teleological argument, Mill offered what he considered to be a stronger expression of it. It is built on Mill's inductive "method of agreement." This argument was the weakest of Mill's inductive methods but he considered the teleological argument to be a strong form of this kind of induction. Mill began with the organic rather than the mechanical aspect of nature.

1. There is an amazing concurrence of many diverse elements in a human eye.
2. It is not probable that random selection brought these elements together.
3. The method of agreement argues for a common cause of the eye.
4. The cause was a final (purposing) cause, not an efficient (producing) cause.

But Mill admitted that the alternative explanation of evolution diminishes the strength of this form. Much of what appears to be design is accounted for in evolution by the survival of the fittest (*see* EVOLUTION, BIOLOGICAL).

Hackett's Rejoinder. Stuart C. Hackett takes issue with Mill on the question of whether the method of analogy inherently weakens the argument (Hackett, 106):

1. All composites that involve the relation of complex means so as to produce a significant result are composites of whose cause purposive intelligence is an indispensable aspect.
2. The space-time universe is a composite in which complex means are so related as to produce significant results (*see* ANTHROPIC PRINCIPLE).
3. Therefore, the space-time universe is a composite of whose cause purposive intelligence is an indispensable aspect.

Certainly this argument proceeds by analogy, since the space-time universe is placed alongside all other apparently similar composites. But Hackett asserts that this feature can hardly be considered a flaw. He states, "Granted that the reasoning involves analogy; nevertheless it should be pointed out that virtually all reasoning about matters of fact involves analogy, . . . so that the rejection of the analogical principle would be virtually tantamount to rendering all factual reasoning spurious" (ibid., 104).

The weakness of dissimilarity shown in Mill's third premise has been attacked by others. As Hackett also points out, however, the similarity for the analogy does not lie in the production of the artifact, but in its features that lead us to draw conclusions regarding its production.

Alvin Plantinga, though not himself a proponent of the teleological argument, also showed that this criticism is not as forceful as it appears. The universe is unique in many ways, but in crucial ways it surely bears sufficient resemblance to other things so that we cannot immediately rule out inductive analogies (Plantinga, 97–107).

Still, Mill leaves us with the possibility that apparent design is only the result of natural selection. That point is examined more closely by Russell.

Russell's Evolutionary Disproof. Bertrand *Russell (1872–1970) attempted a disproof of the teleological argument from evolution. The logic can be put in this form (Russell, 589):

1. The adaptation of means to end in the world is either the result of evolution or else the result of design.
2. This adaptation is the result of evolution.
3. Therefore, this adaptation is not the result of design.

Russell's point is that, if adaptation can be accounted for by the survival of the fittest, there is no need to invoke design to explain it. Of course, Russell's argument does not follow logically, for there is no logical reason why adaptation cannot be the result of both evolution and design (*see* EVOLUTION, BIOLOGICAL). Further, one need not grant that natural selection can explain all adaptation (Geisler, *Origin Science*). And if natural selection cannot explain all apparent design, it gives some force to the design argument. Hence, Russell's argument does not disprove the teleological argument; at best it only forces a modification in the argument.

**Hume's Alternatives to Teleology.* The most famous critique of the teleological argument comes from Hume. Although many scholars believe it is Hume's own view, he placed two responses to the teleological argument in the mouth of a skeptic, Philo.

Hume's argument assuming design. The first argument is based on the assumption that there is design in nature (Burrill, 184–91). It rather considers what this reasoning might prove about God. At best, the God indicated by this design would be:

1. different from human intelligence, since human inventions differ from those of nature.
2. finite, since the effect is finite (and the cause is like the effect).
3. imperfect, for there are imperfections in nature.
4. multiple, for the creation of the world is more like the cooperative building of a ship.
5. male and female, for this is the way humans generate.
6. anthropomorphic, for his creatures have eyes, ears, noses, and other physical traits.

According to Hume, the best one could conclude from assuming there is design in the world is that the world arose from something like design. At worst, the world may be the crude product of some infantile god(s) or the inferior result of some senile deity(ies).

Hume's argument not assuming design. The second argument of Hume (through the literary figure "Philo") does not assume that there is design in the world (ibid., 191–98). It insists it is possible that the world arose by chance:

1. The apparent order in the world resulted from either design or from chance (but not both, for they are mutually exclusive).
2. It is entirely plausible that the world resulted from chance. (a) It is possible that the universe of matter in motion is eternal. (b) In an infinity of chance operations every combination will be realized. (c) Combinations that best fit will tend to perpetuate themselves once they happen. (d) What does not fit tends to move around until it, too, settles down. (e) Hence, the present "ordered" arrangement of the universe may be the result of pure chance.

Philo adds the argument of evolutionary adaptation: Animal adaptation cannot be used to prove design, for they could not survive unless they adapt to their environs. If things could not have been otherwise, that is not an evidence of intelligent planning. However, Philo admits that it is difficult to explain organs not needed for survival. Why two eyes and two ears? Noting that the design theories have problems and absurdities, Philo suggests suspending judgment on the whole question of whether there is a God. The groundwork for this shift in method was laid by Hume in the argument by Philo. From this point, any argument on either side needs to reckon with the choice between a cosmic Designer and chance. And to make this kind of argument work, it is not enough to simply endorse one's own view. It becomes necessary to show that the argument of the other side is insufficient. The teleological theist must show both that the existence of God explains design, and that the world did not come about by chance.

Taylor's Anticipatory Design. With the rise of evolution, it seemed to some theists that the survival of the teleological argument hinged upon its ability to handle both the evolutionary and chance alternatives. This is precisely what A. E. Taylor hoped to accomplish with his argument based on the apparent advanced planning within nature (Burrill, 209–32). It can be summarized:

1. Nature reveals an anticipatory order; it plans for its preservation. (a) Bodily need for oxygen is anticipated by membranes that provide it. (b) Many insects deposit eggs where food is available for their babies. (c) A cat's movements are prospectively adapted to capture prey.
2. Nature's advanced planning cannot be accounted for by physical laws alone. There are countless ways electrons could run, but they move in accord with the advanced planning needed to preserve the organism. (a) This is true in healthy and unhealthy organisms (e.g., antibodies). (b) On the basis of physical laws alone, misadaptations would be as probable as adaptations. (c) Unless we retreat to the absurd, something more than physical laws must account for overcoming the high improbabilities.
3. Mind or intelligence is the only known condition that can remove these improbabilities against life's emergence. (a) The human mind is direct evidence of anticipatory adaptation. Humans plan ahead. Aged people make wills. No jury considers a man guilty of first-degree murder unless he anticipated the result of his actions. (b) Even scientists who reduce anticipation to complicated reflex action do not live that way. They write books in hope that others will read them. They vote in hope that it will provide a better future.
4. The mind or intelligence that explains anticipatory adaptations cannot be explained as a result of evolution. (a) Mind is not a life-force that resulted from evolution and then took over and captured lifeless matter, since the advanced planning which gave rise to mind can only be explained as a result of Mind. We use tools that other minds make, but some mind had to make the tool to begin with. Likewise, the fact that mind can use nature as a tool assumes that the process of nature that produced mind is itself intelligently directed. (b) The very appearance and persistence of species is impossible without preparatory adaptation of the environment. Without the right chemicals and under different conditions, life would not be possible. (c) Therefore, either prospective adaptation is meaningless or else a Mind guides the whole process.
5. Darwinian (*see* DARWIN, CHARLES) natural selection cannot explain the advance planning evident in nature, for: (a) The fittest are not necessarily the best; the most stupid sometimes survive (e.g., a drunk in an accident). (b) Even mutations imply design, since to make evolution work, mutations must not be random and impartial but occur in trends, implying design. Also mutations must not be small and gradual but large and sudden. This indicates design. (c) Darwinism does not explain, but merely presupposes, life with a preparatory environment. (d) The human mind cannot be explained by survival of the fit or adaptation, for there is no reason these adjustments should produce foresight, and the human mind does not adapt to the environment but transforms it. (e) Therefore, if Mind was not totally produced by nature, it must have been active in the producing of nature, since nature indicates advanced planning accountable only by intelligence.

Taylor's advanced planning argument is further discovery of what is known as the anthropic principle. According to this principle, the possibility of human life and all that leads up to it was set from the very moment of the big bang origin of the material universe. For had the conditions which were set then have been off in the most infinitesimal way, neither life nor human life could have arisen. This is strong evidence for anticipatory design from the moment of the inception of the universe (see Ross).

Taylor admits that objections can be leveled against the teleological argument. He contends, however, that they do not affect the basic argument but are applicable only to certain unjustifiable assumptions that have sometimes been connected with the argument. The teleological argument itself, at least as based on the design apparent in the anticipatory adaptations of nature, is valid.

The Argument's New Form. Hume's second critique of the teleological argument succeeded in shifting the form of the argument itself. In essence the reasoning took on this form:

1. The universe resulted either from design or from chance.
2. It is highly improbable that it resulted from chance.
3. Hence, it is highly probable that the universe was designed.

The high improbability of a chance happening is due to the fact that there is not, as Hume's Philo assumed, an eternity of time in which to realize the ordered arrangement in which things now find themselves. There are only so many billions of geological years for things to take their present arrangement. Hackett said, "I conclude that the notion of chance simply does not provide any rationally plausible explanation of the significant order in the universe, and that therefore the principle of purposively directed activity provides an overwhelmingly more reasonable explanation" (Hackett, 106).

Attempting to Plug the Loophole. The chances for chance are slim. Defenders of the teleological argument attempted to fill the loopholes created by Hume's chance argument. Some took the bull by the horn and argued simply that the chances for a chance explanation are not very good.

Theists (*see* THEISM) argued that the chances that one will get two sixes on a roll of two dice is one in thirty-six, but this does not mean that it will actually take thirty-six rolls to get two sixes. They may come on the first roll. Likewise, the *a priori* odds against the universe happening by chance alone are immense. Nonetheless, in actual fact (*a posteriori*) the universe does exist, and it could have happened that way, however remote the odds.

Julian *Huxley, an arch-defender of evolution, estimated that at the known rate of helpful mutations over the known time scale, the odds against evolution happening by pure chance are 1 followed by 3 million zeros (fifteen hundred pages of zeros) to one (Huxley, 46). Huxley felt, however, that natural selection was the process that overcame these stupendous odds. But from the teleologist's point of view, natural selection functions as a kind of supreme intelligence, deciding with apparent foresight at thousands of points against thousand-to-one odds. What but intelligent advance planning could possibly make the right selection so consistently, against such overwhelming odds?

Perhaps the gravest objection to the teleological argument comes from the chance hypothesis: that the design in the knowable universe may be only a temporary and fragmentary episode in the history of the whole universe (a kind of oasis of design in the much wider desert of chance). F. R. Tennant replies to this alternative (in Hick, 120–36) by pointing out that it is conceivable but highly improbable because.

1. The mere possibilities of the unknowable (or unknown) world cannot be used to refute the probabilities within the knowable world.
2. There is no evidence to support the thesis that the knowable world is a lie to the unknowable world.
3. The knowable universe is not isolated from the unknowable, but is interwoven and interdependent with it.
4. *Thermodynamics makes completely random development unlikely.
5. Chance reshuffling of matter by mechanical forces cannot explain the origin of mind and personality.
6. The qualitative greatness of human values in the oasis of the knowable world outweigh the quantitative immensity of the unknowable world.

After attempting to plug the alleged loophole in the teleological argument, Tennant offers his own revised form. It is based on what he calls a wider teleology: Innumerable cases of design have conspired to produce and maintain, by united and reciprocal action, a general order. The value in arguing that nature as a whole is designed is, according to Tennant, that such an argument is not susceptible to many of the criticisms to which the "narrow" teleology is open.

For instance, a wider teleology does not demand that every detail of the process be foreordained. A purposeful process may produce as a by-product some inevitable evils. (For example, a by-product of lakes to enjoy is that some persons will drown in them.) Tennant sees six areas in which the world reflects its wider teleology:

1. adaptation of thought to thing (the thinkability of the world),
2. adaptation of the internal parts of organic beings,
3. adaptation of inorganic nature to purposeful ends,
4. adaptation of nature to human aesthetic needs,
5. adaptation of the world to human moral goals, and
6. adaptation of world processes to culminate in the rational and moral status of a human being.

All the parts and processes of the world contrived to produce the human. This places beyond any reasonable doubt the fact that the world was planned. William Lane Craig agrees that "the cosmic considerations have also breathed new life into the argument from design" (Craig, 73).

Hume's Uniformity Principle. Another alternative to Hume's chance argument is to use his own principle of uniformity. That is precisely what Paley did. Indeed, when Hume is arguing against miracles (*see* MIRACLES, ARGUMENTS AGAINST) he bases his reasoning on what he called "uniform experience." This amounts to a practical "proof" because a conjunction of events is repeated without exception so often that one cannot help but posit a causal connection. Using the information from modern microbiology to state Hume's principle, the teleological argument can be restated as follows:

1. Living cells are characterized by their specified complexity. (a) Crystals are specified but not complex. (b) Random polymers are complex but not specified. (c) Living cells are both specified and complex.
2. A written language has specified complexity (Yockey, 13–31). (a) A single word repeated over and over is specified. (b) A long series of random letters has complexity. (c) A sentence has specified complexity.
3. Uniform experience informs us that only intelligence is capable of regularly producing specified complexity.
4. Therefore, it is reasonable to assume that living organisms were produced by intelligence (*see* EVOLUTION, CHEMICAL).

The same is true of recent biological considerations which show a strong analogy (actually, mathematical identity) between the genetic code in living organisms and that of a human language produced by intelligence. Leslie Orgel noted that "living organisms are distinguished by their *specified complexity*. Crystals . . . fail to qualify as living because they lack *complexity;* random mixtures of polymers fail to qualify because they lack *specificity*" (Orgel, 189, emphasis added). Michael Behe has further shown that this specified complexity is irreducible, demonstrating that it could not have evolved in steps (*see* Behe). All basic elements must be present simultaneously from the beginning in order for it to function. In this light, Paley's argument can be restated:

1. A living being, from the simplest one-celled organism to a human being, displays many structures that are both complex and specified. These structures are like those in all other organisms at the same level of being.
2. Human bodies are complex systems of complex systems and fit into a larger natural ecosystem context. At each level, immense complexity is organized in a very specific way and fits the need of all the higher levels of organization.
3. Therefore, the uniformity of specified design at all levels intensely implies an intelligent Designer (God).

Two things should be noted about the teleological argument in this form. First, it is based on the scientific principle of regularity. The cause of an event is that which can regularly produce that event. Second, as applied to the origin of life, this argument is based on the Humean principle of uniformity: A constant conjunction of antecedent and consequent factors is the basis for attributing causal connection (*see* SCIENCE OF ORIGINS). Paley clearly accepted this Humean principle and used it in his argument:

> Wherever we see marks of contrivance, we are led for its cause to an *intelligent* author. And this transition of the understanding is founded upon uniform experience. We see intelligence constantly contriving; that is, we see intelligence constantly producing effects, marked and distinguished by certain properties . . . We see, wherever we are witnesses to the actual formation of things, nothing except intelligence producing effects so marked and distinguished in the same manner. We wish to account for their origin. Our experience suggests a cause perfectly adequate to this account . . . because it agrees with that which in all cases is the foundation of knowledge—the undeviating course of their experience. [Paley, 37]

Therefore, Hume did not answer Paley in advance. Rather, Paley based his argument on the principle of uniformity (constant conjunction) that he borrowed from Hume. Thus, he argued that since intelligence is the only cause constantly joined with design (such as in a watch), then intelligence is the most reasonable cause to postulate for nature that manifests this same kind of design. Paley was, of course, unaware of microbiology, so he did not foresee how his argument would be strengthened by the discovery of specified complexity in DNA.

In view of the rediscovered principle of uniformity (constant conjunction) as a basis for the teleological argument, a new critique to the chance alternative suggested by Hume emerges: It is contrary to the principle of constant conjunction laid down by Hume himself. That is, chance is not a rational explanation on Hume's own grounds, since a rational person should posit as a cause only that which is constantly conjoined to the effect. But the only cause constantly conjoined to specified complexity (such as is found in living things) is intelligence. Hence, only intelligence (not chance) should be posited as the cause of life.

Rational or scientific thinking is not based on chance occurrences but on constant conjunction. Hence, to posit a nonintelligent natural force as a cause of specified complexity, one must show how it constantly conjoined to a purely natural nonintelligent cause. This has not been done. In fact, purely naturalistic explanations of the origin of life have been demonstrated to be implausible (see Thaxton). Even biologically interesting chemicals (such as amino acids), which are as far from a living cell as a few words are from a volume of an encyclopedia, result only when there is illegitimate intelligent intervention (as in Urey's and Miller's experiments). Hackett makes a strong case for the teleological argument, but only after he has argued that the world is an effect with God for its cause. Serious questions, such as those brought up by Kant and C. J. Ducasse, will ultimately lead us to look for an argument behind the teleological argument. Kant says it is the ontological, whereas Ducasse looks for the cosmological argument.

Other Objections. *Ontological Defects in the Teleological Argument.* Those opposed to the teleological argument offer still other objections. Kant neither offered a disproof of God nor suggested a complete disregard of the teleological argument (*see* God, Objections to Proofs for). He did, however, insist that the teleological argument is inconclusive:

1. The teleological argument is based on experience of design and order in the world.
2. But experience never provides us with the idea of an absolutely perfect and necessary Being. For, (a) If God is only the highest in an actual chain of experienced beings, then a higher is possible. (b) And if God is separate from this chain, then he is not being based in experience. And we have thereby left the experiential basis for the argument and imported an invalid ontological argument from pure thought (Burrill, 199–207).
3. Hence, a Necessary Being cannot be proved from design in the world.

This is not to say, however, that there is no force to the teleological argument. Kant, too, was impressed when he looked at the stars. When he put this experience in logical summary it took this form:

1. There is everywhere in the world clear indication of intentional arrangement.
2. The fitness of this arrangement is foreign to the things themselves. They possess this order contingently, not spontaneously.
3. Hence, there is a sublime and wise cause (or causes) that arranged the world.
4. That this cause is one may be inferred from the reciprocal relation of the parts to the whole universe in a mutual fit, forming a unified whole.

Kant concluded that the teleological argument, while not conclusive, does have value. Even though it does not prove a Creator, it does indicate an Architect. Since the cause can only be proportioned to the effect, the Architect is only a very great being and not an all-sufficient being. The argument at best yields only the highest cause which is not a sufficient basis of religion. The step from the highest actual cause indicated by experience to the highest possible cause demanded by pure reason is an unjustifiable ontological leap. Kant concluded that theists using the teleological argument to prove the existence of God made a desperate leap from the soil of experience to fly in the thin air of pure possibility without even admitting that they left the ground.

Most theists readily admit that the teleological argument alone does not prove an infinite, Necessary Being who created the universe out of nothing (*see* Creation, Views of). The *cosmological argument is intended to do that. However, when combined with the cosmological argument the teleological argument does show that the infinite Cause of all finite being is an intelligent one, was evidenced by the extremely complex design manifested in the universe. The cosmological argument does not "fly in the thin air of pure possibility." Rather, it begins in the actual existing finite world and moves to an actual existing infinite God. There is no more ontological sleight of hand in it than to conclude that a person with a real navel had a real mother.

The Perfection Problem. According to Ducasse, the teleological argument suffers from other defects (ibid., 234–39). He lists three basic defects.

1. It does not prove a perfect Creator. (a) Design in the world is not perfect, and it needs only an imperfect cause to explain it. Human beings are just as capable of judging what is not purposeful as what is purposeful. (b) Evil, waste, and disease all show lack of purpose (*see* Evil, Problem of).
2. Designers can be inferior to what they design. Microscopes, steam shovels, and computers all have powers their inventors do not.
3. The teleological argument has the same defects as the cosmological argument: (a) If the world needs a designer then so does that designer, ad infinitum. (b) But if everything is caused (according to the principle of sufficient reason), then there can be no first cause.

Then, Ducasse offers what he considers a more plausible alternative to the teleological argument. It involves no creator of any kind.

1. The most economical explanation is probably the correct one.

2. The world is more economically explained by a purposeless craving within human beings (*Schopenhauer) than by some intelligence beyond the world. (a) It is simpler, since it is located in humanity and not dependent on causes beyond the world. (b) It explains things as well as God does. For example, the eye is a purposeless craving for sight which is never satisfied.
3. Therefore, it is more probable that the world is the result of a purposeless craving, than that it has arisen through intelligent design.

This argument is far from definitive. It is open to challenge at several points. First, is the principle of economy or simplicity appropriately applied to the question of the cause of the universe? Hume's skeptic argued against applying it, and skepticism cannot have it both ways. It appears to beg the question by assuming that the best cause will come from within the universe but not beyond it. Second, even granting that the simplest explanation is best, is a purposeless craving really the simplest explanation? It appears far more obscure and complicated in some respects. Third, how can a purposeless craving result in purposeful activity? How can the effect be greater than the cause?

Conclusion. The teleological argument, as such, is a highly probable but not absolutely certain argument for intelligent design manifested in the world. *Chance is possible though not probable. The teleological evidence favors the unity of this cause since this world is really a universe, not a multiverse. This is especially evident in view of the anthropic principle which reveals that the world, life, and humankind were anticipated from the very moment of the origin of the material universe (*see* EVOLUTION, COSMIC).

The teleological argument as such does not demand that this cause be absolutely perfect. Nor does it *ipso facto* explain the presence of evil and disorder in the world. The teleological argument is dependent on the cosmological and moral arguments to establish these other aspects of a theistic God.

It is really a causal argument from effect to cause, only it argues from the intelligent nature of the effect to an intelligent cause. This last point is important. For if the principle of causality (*see* CAUSALITY, PRINCIPLE OF) cannot be supported, then admittedly one cannot insist that there must be a cause or ground of the design in the world. Design might just be there without a cause. Only if there is a purpose for everything can it follow that the world must have a Purposer. The teleological argument depends on the cosmological argument in this important sense that it borrows from it the principle of causality. As can be readily seen from every form of the design argument, the underlying assumption is that there needs to be a cause for the order in the world. Deny this and the argument fails, for the alleged design (if uncaused) would be merely gratuitous.

Sources

M. Behe, *Darwin's Black Box.*
D. R. Burrill, ed., *The Cosmological Arguments: A Spectrum of Opinion*
W. Craig, *Apologetics: An Introduction*
N. L. Geisler, *Origin Science*
———, and W. Corduan. *Philosophy of Religion*
S. C. Hackett, *The Reconstruction of the Christian Revelation Claim*
J. Huxley, *Evolution in Action*
L. Orgel, *The Origins of Life*
W. Paley, *Natural Theology*
A. Plantinga, *God and Other Minds*
H. Ross, *The Fingerprint of God*
B. Russell, *The Basic Writings of Bertrand Russell*
F. R. Tennant. *The Existence of God*
W. Thaxton, et al., *The Mystery of Life's Origin*
Thomas Aquinas, *Summa Theologica*
H. P. Yockey, "Self Organization Origin of Life Scenarios and Information Theory," *Journal of Theoretical Biology* (7 July 1981)

Tertullian. Quintus Septimius Florens Tertullianus (160/70–215/20) was an early Christian apologist from Carthage, North Africa. He was educated in law and converted to Christianity in about 190. He devoted himself to the study of the Scriptures. He broke from the mainline church and became head of a small Montanist group. His interaction with the unbelievers of his day is illustrative of an early Christian interaction view of faith and reason.

Among Tertullian's many works were *Apologeticus*, *On Baptism*, *The Prescription Against Heretics*, *Against Hermogones*, *On the Flesh of Christ*, *The Treatise on the Soul*, *To Scapula*, and *Against Marcion*. While Justin *Martyr and *Clement of Alexandria are wrongly considered rationalists, Tertullian is often falsely accused of fideism.

Tertullian's alleged *fideism is based on several passages. He wrote: "With our faith, we desire no further belief" (Tertullian, *The Prescription against Heretics*, 7). He also asked: "What indeed has Athens to do with Jerusalem? What concord is there between the Academy and the Church?" (ibid.). He even called philosophers "those patriarchs of all heresy" (Tertullian, *Against Hermogones*, 8). In his most famous passage Tertullian went so far as to declare of the crucifixion of Christ "it is by all means to be believed, because it is absurd." He added, "And He [Christ] was buried, and rose again, the fact is certain, because it is impossible" (Tertullian, *On the Flesh of Christ*, 5).

Tertullian was neither an irrationalist, nor a fideist. Contrary to popular belief, Tertullian never said *"Credo ad absurdum."* He did not use the Latin word *absurdum* here, meaning a rational contradiction. Rather, he used the word *ineptum* or "foolish" in this quote. Like the apostle Paul (in 1 Cor. 1:18) he was simply noting that the Gospel seems "foolish" to unbelievers, but he never affirmed that it was logically contradictory in itself. Likewise, the resurrection is only "impossible" in a human way but not divinely or actually impossible.

Tertullian's Stress on Reason. As a lawyer and defender of the Christian Faith, Tertullian knew well the value of human reason in the declaration and defense of the Christian Faith. He spoke of the rationality of all goodness (*Against Marcion*, 1.23). He said, "nothing can be claimed as rational without order, much less can reason itself dispense with order in any one" (ibid.). Even when speaking of the mystery of human free choice (*see* FREE WILL), Tertullian declared that "It cannot even in this be ruled to be irrational" (ibid., 1.25). He also speaks of applying "the rule of reason" as the guiding principle in the interpretation of Scripture (*The Prescription against Heretics*, 9). Tertullian also declared that "all the properties of God ought to be as rational as they are natural." For "nothing else can properly be accounted good than that which is rationally good; much less can goodness itself be defected in any irrationality" (*Against Marcion*, 1.23). He was even against someone being baptized into the Christian Faith if he is "content with having simply believed, without full examination of the grounds or the tradition" (*On Baptism*, 1).

Occasionally, Tertullian even spoke favorably of philosophers, admitting, "Of course we shall not deny that philosophers have sometimes thought the same things as ourselves." This is because of God's revelation in "nature," that is, "by the common intelligence wherewith God has been pleased to endow the soul of man" (*Treatise on the Soul*, 2). His highest praise for human reason was reserved for the testimony of God in the human soul. "These testimonies of the soul are as simple as true, commonplace as simple, universal as commonplace, natural as universal, divine as natural. . . . And if you have faith in God and Nature, have faith in the soul; thus you will believe yourself" (*Treatise on the Soul*, 5). This is not to say that Tertullian rejected general revelation in the external world. In fact he said, "We are worshippers of one God, of whose existence and character Nature teaches all men" (*To Scapula*, 2).

Conclusion. Despite his strong emphasis on faith, Tertullian, like Justin and Clement, believed there was a significant role for human reason in defense of the truth of the Christian religion (*see* FAITH AND REASON). He believed in general *revelation in both the external and internal world of the soul, though he stressed the latter.

Sources

Tertullian, *Against Hermogones*
———, *Against Marcion*
———, *Apologeticus*
———, *On Baptism*
———, *On the Flesh of Christ*
———, *The Prescription against Heretics*
———, *To Scapula*
———, *Treatise on the Soul*

Theism. *Theism* is the worldview that an infinite, personal God created the universe and miraculously intervenes in it from time to time (*see* MIRACLE). God is both transcendent over the universe and immanent in it. The three great theistic religions are Judaism, *Islam, and Christianity.

*Finite godism, *deism, and, to some extent, even Western *panentheism, grew out of the theistic (*see* THEISM) worldview. The central difference between theism and finite godism is the question of whether God is infinite or finite. Deism is primarily a theistic view minus supernatural intervention in the world (*see* MIRACLE). Panentheism modifies theism to posit a finite God with two poles, one being theoretical infinitude. It is sometimes called "neoclassical theism."

Different Kinds of Theism. One of the most helpful ways to distinguish among theist systems is to note the perspective from which each approaches God. There are *rational* theists such as René *Descartes and Gottfried *Leibniz, *existential* theists such as Søren *Kierkegaard, *phenomenological* theists such as Peter Koestenbaum, *analytic* theists such as Alvin Plantinga, *empirical* theists such as Thomas *Reid, *idealistic* theists such as George *Berkeley, and *pragmatic* theists such as Charles Sanders Pierce. Each of these uses a somewhat distinct philosophical method to approach belief in God.

Theists can also be distinguished by what they believe about God and his relation to the world. Most believe the material world is real, but some believe it exists only in minds and ideas (Berkeley). Most theists believe God is unchangeable, but some (generally influenced by panentheism) believe God can and does change. Some theists believe it is possible that the created universe is eternal (*Thomas Aquinas), while most believe the universe must be temporal (Bonaventure). Perhaps the most important difference among theists is that many believe God is only one person (monotheism), such as Judaism and Islam. Others, notably orthodox Christians, believe in a *trinitarian* form of monotheism: God has three centers of personhood within one perfect monotheistic unity.

Among the leading defenders of classical theism were *Augustine (354–430), *Anselm (1033–1109), and Thomas Aquinas (1224–1274). In the modern world *Descartes (1596–1650) *Leibniz (1646–1716), and William *Paley (1743–1805) are some the more noted defenders of theism. Perhaps the most popular exponent of theism in the twentieth century was C. S. *Lewis (1898–1963).

Since theism is described in detail in articles for these representatives, only a summary of theistic views will be included here.

Outline of a Theistic Worldview. Those who hold a theistic worldview have a common core of beliefs. To the degree theists are consistent, their thoughts and actions are shaped from this core:

God Exists beyond and in the World. Theism holds to both the *transcendence* and *immanence* of God. God exists beyond and independently of the world, yet governs all parts of the world as the sustaining Cause. The world was *originated* by God and it is *conserved* by him (*see* CREATION AND ORIGINS).

The World Was Created Ex Nihilo. The world is not eternal. It came into existence by God's fiat (decree). Its existence is totally contingent and dependent. The universe was not created from pre-existing material (*ex materia*), as in *dualism or *materialism, nor was it made out of God's essence (*ex Deo*), as in *pantheism. It was brought into existence by God, but from nothing (*ex nihilo*; *see* CREATION, VIEWS OF).

Miracles Are Possible. Although God operates his universe in a regular and orderly way by the laws of nature, nevertheless, God does transcend those laws. Nature is not the "whole show." There is a supernatural realm (*see* NATURALISM). This supernatural can invade the natural realm. The sovereign Creator cannot be locked outside his creation. Although God normally works in a regular way, on occasion he directly intervenes. This occasional invasion of nature by the supernatural is called a "miracle."

Most theists not only believe that miracles can happen; they believe some actually *have* happened (*see* MIRACLES, ARGUMENTS AGAINST). Jewish theists point to the miracles surrounding the exodus, Muslims to God's revelations to Muhammed, and Christian theists point to the birth and resurrection of Christ as chief examples of miracles.

People Are Made in God's Image. Theism believes in the creation of humankind in God's image. This means man has both freedom (*see* FREE WILL) and dignity that ought to be treated with utmost respect. Humans are God's representatives on earth. Human life is sacred. Humans should be loved as persons, not used as things.

As creatures of God, men and women are not sovereign over their own lives. No one has the right to take his or her own life nor end the life of another, except as killing is directly sanctioned. Only God gives life, and only God can take it or command that it be taken.

Humanity had a beginning in time. There was no preexistent soul, so no eternality, but the soul was created to be immortal (*see* IMMORTALITY). Nor is there annihilation of the soul (*see* ANNIHILATIONISM), as is the belief of atheism and some theists. Each person is immortal, not by his essence, but because God will sustain us forever.

There Is a Moral Law. Since the theist God is a moral being and since humankind is created in God's image, a moral corollary of theism is that the ultimate duty of people is to obey the moral law. This law is absolutely binding since it comes from God (*see* MORALITY, ABSOLUTE NATURE OF). It is over and above any human laws. It is prescriptive, not merely descriptive, as are laws of nature.

Rewards and Punishment Await. Each individual life, like all of history, is pointed toward an end or goal. Human moral actions will be rewarded or punished. There will be no reincarnated nor post-death second chance. Each person will be rewarded or punished according to the individual's relation to God during life (*see* HELL). This has to do with what the person has "done," or on God's grace. Some modern theists minimized (or negate) the punishment aspect of human destiny in hope that all might be saved (*see* UNIVERSALISM) or at least annihilated if unsaved. But traditional theists believe this is wishful thinking. All theists, however, acknowledge a day that will bring about justice.

Evaluation. Many nontheists literally believe that theism is too good to be true. Sigmund Freud wrote, "We say to ourselves: it would indeed be very nice if there were a God, who was both creator of the world and a benevolent providence, if there were a moral world order and a future life, but at the same time it is very odd that this is all just as we should wish it ourselves" (*Freud, 57–58).

The real question, of course, is not how satisfying a view is, but whether it is true. Many nontheists believe it is not true (*see* GOD, ALLEGED DISPROOFS OF). Other are content with simply attempting to show that arguments for the existence of God fail (*see* GOD, OBJECTIONS TO PROOFS FOR). Both are unsuccessful, and there are good arguments that a theistic God exists (*see* COSMOLOGICAL ARGUMENT; MORAL ARGUMENT; TELEOLOGICAL ARGUMENT), that there are moral absolutes, and that there is a life after death—all of which are essential parts of a theistic worldview.

Sources

Augustine, *On Free Will*

———, *On the Nature of the Good*

———, *The City of God*

S. Freud, *The Future of an Illusion*

N. L. Geisler and W. Watkins, *Worlds Apart: A Handbook on World Views*, chap. 2

——— and W. Corduan, *Philosophy of Religion*

G. Leibniz, *Theodicy*

C. S. Lewis, *Mere Christianity*

Thomas Aquinas, *Summa contra Gentiles*

———, *On Evil*

Theistic Evolution. ***See*** **EVOLUTION, THEISTIC.**

Thermodynamics, Laws of. Thermodynamics is a field of physical science that relates matter to energy. The principles of thermodynamics are regarded as inviolable and are applied constantly to engineering and the sciences, including origin science (*see* ORIGINS, SCIENCE OF). Thermodynamic principles work within what are called macroscopic systems, mass or energy that can be isolated and studied in its properties, such as Temperature, density, volume, compressibility, expansion and contraction with temperature changes. Macroscopic systems are studied in equilibrium with their surroundings, including their ultimate context—the entire universe. Changes in context—temperature for example—produce reactions in the system that compensate and bring toward a new equilibrium. The move from one equilibrium to another is called a "thermodynamic process." The limitations on thermodynamic processes that have been discovered led to the formation of the *laws* of thermodynamics.

Two laws of thermodynamics, the first and second, hold important implications for creationists and materialists (*see* MATERIALISM) in their debate over origins. Both sides invoke the laws with surprising frequency, and varying degrees of comprehension of what they truly mean. Other laws also have occasional roles to play in apologetics.

Zeroth Law. The first law is not truly the "first" listed law of thermodynamics, for there is a zeroth law which states that when each of two systems is in equilibrium with a third, the first two systems must be in equilibrium with each other. This shared property of equilibrium is the temperature. Basically that means that any object will eventually reach the temperature of its surroundings. This law occasionally is referred to in planetary physics and theories of how the earth, with its internal molten core furnace precious heat from the sun and exposure to frigid space came to establish a atmosphere-insulated thermal equilibrium conducive for life (*see* ORIGINS, SCIENCE OF).

First Law. The first law of thermodynamics is sometimes stated: "Energy can be neither created nor destroyed." In this form the law is often used by nontheists to show that the universe is eternal and that there is no need for God. Certainly there can be no God who created a temporal world *ex nihilo* (*see* CREATION, VIEWS OF).

The first law is a law of energy conservation. Heat is measured in calories of energy. Calories can drift from one object to another, can be converted into mechanical work, and can be stored, even though energy is not a material substance. But not one calorie of energy actually goes out of existence. It merely changes form.

Another, more accurate, way to state this law of conservation is that "The amount of *actual* energy in the universe remains constant." This says nothing about how the energy came to be in the universe. It also has no power to theorize about whether God could bring new energy into the system if he so wished. It is a statement of observation that the energy does not just disappear, and no more has been seen popping into existence from nonexistence.

The statement "Energy can neither be created nor destroyed" expresses philosophical dogmatism. This is a metaphysical pronouncement not supported by observation. As far as we can observe, no new energy is coming into existence, and no actual energy is going out of existence.

As such, the First Law supports neither a theistic or nontheistic worldview. It does not claim that energy is eternal, so God is unnecessary. But neither does it claim that God has endowed the system with energy at any point. It simply affirms that right now the actual amount of energy—however long it has been here—is not changing.

Second Law. The second law of thermodynamics is a whole other story. It can be stated: "In a closed, isolated system, the amount of usable energy in the universe is decreasing." It is being changed, the *dynamics* part of *thermodynamics*, into unusable heat energy, the *thermo* part. Notice that this law does not infringe on the First Law; it amplifies on it. If energy is constant, why do we keep needing more electricity? The answer is that *entropy* happens. The second law states that "overall, things left to themselves tend to disorder." Overall, the amount of disorder is increasing. The entropy—that is, the disorder—of an isolated system can never decrease. When an isolated system achieves maximum entropy, it can no longer undergo change: It has reached equilibrium. We would say it has "run down."

The second law is supportive of one form of cosmological argument for God's existence. If the universe is running down it cannot be eternal (*see* *KALAM* COSMOLOGICAL ARGUMENT; BIG BANG THEORY; EVOLUTION, CHEMICAL). If there was a beginning, there had to be a cause (*see* CAUSALITY, PRINCIPLE OF). Therefore, the universe had a Cause.

The Second Law is also used by creationists to argue against macro-evolution (*see* EVOLUTION, BIOLOGICAL). Evolutionists object, noting that the second law only applies to closed systems, such as the whole universe, rather than to open systems, like living organisms. True, an organism can take in energy from outside, so in that respect the second law does not apply. On the other hand, the second law does say that this undirected natural energy of food, water, and sunshine cannot increase in specified complexity. Calories of sun energy do not help a creature grow new eyes with which to see the sun's light. It does not even charge a creature's batteries so that it can live indefinitely. Entropy happens in both the individual organism's life cycle and in species' life.

The second law assures that a perpetual motion machine (or universe) will not work either. All engines expend some fraction of its heat input to entropy, or exhaust. The second law of thermodynamics places an upper limit on the efficiency of a system. It is always less than 100 percent.

Third Law. There is a third law of thermodynamics which seldom if ever comes up in apologetic considerations. This law basically says that a system never completely reaches "zero" in energy. There is an absolute temperature scale, with an absolute zero temperature. The third law of thermodynamics states that absolute zero can be approached very closely, but it can never be reached.

Sources

J. Collins, *A History of Modern European Philosophy*

W. L. Craig, *The Existence of God and the Origin of the Universe*

N. L. Geisler, *Origin Science*

R. Jastrow, "A Scientist Caught between Two Faiths: Interview with Robert Jastrow," *CT*, 6 August 1982

———, *God and the Astronomers*

M. D. Lemonick, "Echoes of the Big Bang," *Time*, 4 May 1993

A. Sandage, "A Scientists Reflects on Religious Belief," *Truth*, 1985

V. J. Stenger, "The Face of Chaos," *Free Inquiry*, Winter 1992–93

Thomas Aquinas. Thomas Aquinas (1224–1274) was a theologian, philosopher, and the consummate apologist of the medieval church. Born in Italy, he joined the Dominican order. He studied at Naples and Paris. He started a school at Cologne and taught at Paris throughout his career except for eight years at the papal Curiae at Rome. He was canonized by the Roman church in 1326. Aquinas wrote *De anima* (*On the Soul*), *De Ente et Essentia* (*On Being and Essence*), *De veritate* (*On Truth*), *On the Power of God*, *Summa contra Gentiles*, and *The Unity of the Intellect Against the Averoeists*. By far his most important and influential writing went into his *magnum opus* systematic theology, *Summa Theologica*, which was still unfinished at his death.

The thought of Aquinas is rich and varied. He wrote on many topics, including faith and reason, revelation, knowledge, reality, God (*see* God, Evidence for; God, Nature of), analogy (*see* Analogy, Principle of), creation (*see* Creation and Origins; Creation, Views of), human beings, government, and ethics (*see* Morality, Absolute Nature of). His mind was intensely analytical, making his arguments difficult for the modern reader to follow. His writing style is sometimes dialectical and highly complex, especially in *Summa Theologica*. This is less true in *Summa contra Gentiles*.

Theology and Apologetics. *Revelation.* God has revealed himself in both nature and Scripture. His natural revelation (Rom. 1:19–20) is available to all and is the basis for natural theology (*see* Revelation, General). The creation reveals one God and his essential attributes, but not the *Trinity or the unique doctrines of the Christian faith, such as the incarnation of Christ (*see* Christ, Deity of) or the way of salvation. This revelation in nature also includes a moral law that is binding on all people (Rom. 2:12–15). God's divine law is for believers; it is revealed in Scripture (*see* Revelation, Special). Although written by humans with differing literary styles (*Summa Theologica*, 2a2ae. 173,3,ad1), the Bible is the only divinely authoritative writing (ibid., 1a.1, 2, ad2). The Bible is inspired and inerrant (*see* Bible, Inspiration of), even in matters that are not essential to redemption (ibid., 1a.1, 10, ad3). No other Christian writing, neither the Fathers nor the creeds, are inspired or revelatory. They are only human interpretations of God's revelation in Scripture (ibid., 2a2ae. 1, 9).

**Faith and Reason.* Following *Augustine, Aquinas believes faith is based on God's revelation in Scripture. Support for faith, however, is found in miracles (*see* Miracles, Apologetic Value of) and probable arguments (Aquinas, *De Veritate* [*On Truth*], 10, 2). Although God's existence is provable by reason (*see* Cosmological Argument), sin obscures our ability to know (*Summa Theologica*, 2a2ae. 2, 4) and so belief (not proof) *that* God exists is necessary for most persons (*Summa Contra Gentiles*, 1.4, 3–5). Human reason, however, is never the basis for faith *in* God. Demanding reasons for belief in God actually lessens the merit of faith (*Summa Theologica*, 2a2ae. 2, 10). Believers, nonetheless, should reason about and for their faith (*see* Apologetics, Classical).

According to Aquinas, there are five ways we can demonstrate God's existence. We can argue: (1) from motion to an Unmoved Mover; (2) from effects to a First Cause; (3) from contingent being to a Necessary Being; (4) from degrees of perfection to a Most Perfect Being; and (5) from design in nature to a Designer of nature (ibid., 1a, 2, 3). Behind these arguments is the premise that all finite, changing beings need a cause outside themselves.

There are mysteries of the Christian faith, however, such as the *Trinity and the incarnation (*see* Christ, Deity of), which can be known only by faith in God's revelation in Scripture (*Summa Contra Gentiles*, 1.3, 2). These go beyond reason, but are not contrary to reason.

Knowledge. Aquinas believes that knowledge comes either by supernatural revelation (in Scripture) or by natural means (*see* Epistemology). All natural knowledge begins in experience (Aquinas, *De Anima* [*On the Soul*], 3.4). We are born, however, with an *a priori*, natural, innate capacity to know (*Summa Theologica*, 1a2ae. 17, 7). Everything that is in our mind was first in the senses, except the mind itself. Knowing something for certain is possible by means of first principles. *First principles are known by way of inclination before they are known by cognition. These include: (1) the principle of identity (being is being); (2) the principle of noncontradiction (being is not nonbeing); (3) the principle of excluded middle (either being or nonbeing); (4) the principle of causality (nonbeing cannot cause being; *see* CAUSALITY, PRINCIPLE OF); and (5) the principle of finality (every being acts for an end). By these and other first principles, the mind can attain knowledge of reality—even some certain knowledge. Once the terms are properly understood, these first principles are self-evident and, thus, undeniable (Aquinas, *Summa Theologica*, 1a. 17, 3, ad2).

Reality. Like *Aristotle, Aquinas believes it is the function of the wise person to know order. The order that reason produces in its own ideas is called logic. The order that reason produces through acts of the will is ethics. The order that reason produces in external things is art. The order that reason contemplates (but does not produce) is nature. Nature, when it is contemplated insofar as it is sensible, is physical science. Nature, when it is studied insofar as it is quantifiable, is mathematics. The modern concept of mathematics is much broader, and includes more abstract and nonquantifiable dimensions. Aquinas would have considered this philosophy, not mathematics. Nature or reality, when studied insofar as it is real, is metaphysics. Metaphysics, then, is the study of the real as real or being, insofar as it is being.

The heart of Aquinas's metaphysics is the real distinction between *essence* (*what* something is) and *existence* (*that* which is) in all finite beings (*De Ente et Essentia* [*On Being and Essence*]). Aristotle had distinguished between actuality and potentiality, but applied this only to things composed of form and matter, not to the order of being. Aquinas takes Aristotle's distinction between act and potency and applies it to form (being). Aquinas argues that only God is Pure Being, Pure Actuality, with no potentiality whatsoever (*see* GOD, NATURE OF). Hence, the central premise of the Thomistic view of reality is that actuality in the order in which it is actuality is unlimited and unique, unless it is conjoined with passive potency. God alone is pure act (or actuality) with no potentiality or form. Angels are completely actualized potentialities (pure forms). Humankind is a composition of form (soul) and matter (body) which is progressively actualized.

God. God alone *is* Being (I am-ness). Everything else merely *has* being. God's essence is identical to his existence. It is of his essence to exist. God is a Necessary Being. He cannot not exist. Neither can God change, since he has no potentiality to be anything other than what he is. Likewise, God is eternal, since time implies a change from a before to an after. But as the "I AM," God has no befores and afters. God also is simple (indivisible) since he has no potential for division. And he is infinite, since pure act as such is unlimited, having no potentiality to limit it (Aquinas, *Summa Theologica*, 1a. 3; 1a. 7–11). Besides these metaphysical attributes, God is also morally perfect and infinitely wise (ibid., 1a. 4, 5).

Analogy. Natural knowledge of God is derived from his creation, as an efficient cause is known from its effects. Since God made the world, his creation resembles him. It is not the same as him (univocal), but it is like him. Our natural knowledge of God is based on that resemblance or analogy. Neither can it be totally different from him (equivocal), since the cause communicates something of itself to its effects. Univocal (totally the same) knowledge of God is impossible, since our knowledge is limited and God is unlimited. Equivocal (totally different) knowledge of God is impossible, since creation resembles the Creator; the effect resembles its efficient cause. Of course, there are great differences between God and creatures. Hence, the *via negativa* (the way of negation) is necessary. That is, we must negate all limitations from our concepts before we apply them to God. We must apply to God only the perfection signified (such as goodness or truth), but not the finite mode of signification (*see* ANALOGY, PRINCIPLE OF).

So the same attribute will have the same definition for creatures and Creator but a different application or extension. Like God, I can know that 2 + 2 = 4. But the mathematical facts I know, and the other attributes I share with God, are limited and contingent. And I cannot do with that knowledge what God can. The reason for this is that creatures are only finitely good while God is infinitely Good. So before we can appropriately apply the term "good" to God, we must negate the finite mode (how) in which we find good among creatures and apply the meaning (what) to God in an unlimited way (*Summa Contra Gentiles*, I, 29–34; *Summa Theologica*, 1a. 13).

Creation. God did not create the world out of himself (*ex Deo*) or out of preexisting matter (*ex materia*). Rather, he created it out of nothing *ex nihilo* (*see* CREATION, VIEWS OF). Although an eternal creation is theoretically possible, since there is no logical reason why an eternal Cause cannot keep causing eternally. Nevertheless, divine revelation teaches that the universe had a beginning. So God created a temporal universe. There was literally no time before God created—only eternity. God did not create *in* time; rather, with the world there was the creation *of* time. So there was no time before time began (*Summa Theologica*, 1a. 44–46).

Further, the universe is dependent on God for its existence. He not only caused it to come to be, but he also causes it to continue to be. God is both the Cause of the origination of the whole of creation and the Cause of its continuation. The universe is absolutely dependent on God; it is contingent. Only God is necessary.

Human Beings. A human being is a matter/form unity of soul and body. Despite this unity, there is no identity between soul and body. The soul survives death and awaits reunion with the physical body at the final *resurrection (Aquinas, *Summa Theologica*, 1a. 75–76). The human soul is the formal cause while the body is the material cause of a human being. God, of course, is the efficient cause. Parents are only the instrumental cause of the body. The final cause (purpose) is to glorify God, who created us. Adam was directly created by God at the beginning, and God directly creates each new soul in the womb of its mother (ibid., 1a. 90–93).

Ethics. Just as there are first principles of thought, so there are first principles of action, called laws. Aquinas distinguishes four kinds of law (*see* LAW, NATURE AND KINDS OF):

Eternal law is the plan by which God governs creation.

Natural law (*see* MORALITY, ABSOLUTE NATURE OF) is the participation of rational creatures in this eternal law.

Human law is a particular application of natural law to local communities.

Divine law (*see* REVELATION, SPECIAL) is the revelation of God's law through Scripture to believers (ibid., 1a2ae. 91).

Aquinas divides virtues into two classes: natural and supernatural. Prudence, justice, courage, and temperance are natural virtues. These are revealed through natural revelation and are applicable to all human beings. Supernatural virtues consist of faith, hope, and love. They are known from supernatural revelation in Scripture and are binding on believers (ibid., 1a. 60–61).

Evaluation. Criticisms have been leveled at Aquinas's views by atheists and agnostics, and are covered in those articles. Relativists' arguments with his thought are covered in MORALITY, ABSOLUTE NATURE OF. Some have objected that his proofs for God are invalid (*see* GOD, OBJECTIONS TO PROOFS FOR). Others have denied his doctrine of analogy (*see* ANALOGY, PRINCIPLE OF). Still others attack his epistemology and use of first principles. Likewise, his dependence on Aristotelian logic has been critiqued. Nonetheless, the philosophy of Aquinas has undergone a renaissance in recent years, particularly among evangelicals.

Sources

R. J. Deferrari, *A Complete Index of the Summa Theologica of St. Thomas Aquinas*

———, *A Lexicon of St. Thomas Aquinas Based on Summa Theologica and Select Passages of His Other Work*

———, *Latin-English Dictionary of Thomas Aquinas*

N. L. Geisler, *Thomas Aquinas: An Evangelical Appraisal*

A. Kenny, *Five Ways*

T. Miethe, and V. Bourke, *Thomistic Bibliography*

M. Stockhammer, *Thomas Aquinas Dictionary*

Thomas Aquinas, *De anima* (*On the Soul*)

———, *De Ente et Essentia* (*On Being and Essence*)

———, *Summa Contra Gentiles*

———, *Summa Theologica*

———, *De veritate* (*On Truth*)

Tindal, Matthew. Matthew Tindal (1656–1733), an English lawyer, was one of the best known and most respected deists (*see* DEISM) of his time. His most important deistic work, *Christianity as Old as the Creation: or, the Gospel, a Republication of the Religion of Nature* (1730), was not published until he was about seventy-four years of age. Because of its influence and completeness, it has been called the "Deistic Bible" and its author "The great Apostle of Deism." This major work prompted more than 150 replies, including the classic critique of deism, Joseph *Butler's *Analogy of Religion* (1872).

Existence and Nature of God. Tindal's view of the existence and nature of God was very similar to that of theists. He believed God to be completely perfect, infinitely loving, eternal, just, merciful, immutable, omnipresent, omniscient, true, omnibenevolent, wise, without parts, and invisible (Tindal, 39, 41, 42, 44, 45, 65, 66, 87). He also held God to be impassable, that is, without passions. As he argued,

> If we dare consult our Reason, it will tell us that Jealousy in point of Honour and Power, Love of Fame and Glory can only belong to limited Creatures; but are as necessarily excluded from an unlimited, absolutely perfect Being, as Anger, Revenge, and such like Passions; which would make the Deity resemble the weak, womanish, and impotent part of our Nature, rather than the manly, noble, and generous. [ibid., 39]

Likewise, God is not moved by man's actions. For "Cou'd God strictly speaking, be made angry, provok'd, or griev'd by the Conduct of us wretched Mortals, he wou'd not enjoy a Moment's Quiet; but must be much more miserable than the most unhappy of his Creatures." Or, "Had God any Comfort, or Satisfaction to gain from the Thoughts and Actions of his Creatures, he wou'd never have been without an Infinity of them jointly contributing to this End" (ibid.).

Creation and Humanity. According to Tindal, the universe was created by God *ex nihilo* (out of nothing). Human beings were also brought into existence by a direct creative act of God: "'tis God, who from Nothing brings us into Being, frames us after the Manner that best pleases him, imprints on us what Faculties, inclinations, Desires and Passions he thinks fit" (ibid., 29, 30, 106).

As to why God created all things, Tindal states that it was not because of any lack or need in

God, since he is absolutely perfect. Rather God's motive for creating was solely for the good of his creatures (ibid., 30).

God's Relation to the World. According to Tindal, God not only created all things, but he constantly preserves or sustains all things as well. Hence everything is dependent on God for its existence and preservation, whereas God is dependent on nothing for his existence or character. Indeed, God needs nothing from his creatures since he is totally perfect and all-sufficient in himself (ibid., 30, 44–46).

God is also the cosmic Governor of the world. His divine laws are those of nature which govern the activities of his creatures. These natural laws are perfect, immutable, and eternal, for these laws govern God's own actions. Consequently, these laws are the same ones by which God "expects all the rational world should govern" their actions. To insure this, God "continues daily to implant" his law "in the Minds of all Men, Christians as well as Others" (ibid., 59, 114).

God has established the end or goal of all actions—the honor of God and the good of man—but not the means:

> It not only commands that *Evil Doers should be punish'd*, but that Men, according to the different Circumstances they are under, should take the most proper Methods for doing it, and vary as Exigencies require; so it not only requires that Justice should be done Men as to their several Claims, but that the readiest, and most effectual Way of doing it should be taken; and the same may be said of all other Instances of this Nature (ibid., 115).

Natural law reveals *what* people should work toward, but it does not reveal exactly *how* to attain that end (ibid., 70, 107). This is only proper. "If God interposes further, and prescribes a particular Way of doing these Things, from which Men at no Time, or upon no Account ought to vary; he not only interposes unnecessarily, but to the Prejudice of the End for which he thus interposes" (ibid., 115). Therefore God does not need to intercede in the affairs of his creation, nor should he. The natural laws that he has established are sufficient for the continued governance of the world. Miracles do not occur (*see* MIRACLES, ARGUMENTS AGAINST).

Human Beings. Humans are personal, rational, and free, but it is reason "which makes us the Image of God himself, and is the common Bond which unites Heaven and Earth." By reason we can prove the existence of God, demonstrate God's attributes, and discover and work out the whole of natural religion. Tindal defined *natural religion* as "the Belief of the Existence of a God, and the Sense and Practice of those Duties, which result from the Knowledge, we, by our Reason, have of him, and his Perfections; and of ourselves, and our own Imperfections; and of the Relation we stand in to him, and to our Fellow-Creatures" (ibid., 13).

Every person is capable of arriving at the basic articles of natural religion: (1) belief in God; (2) worship of God, and (3) doing what is for one's personal good or happiness, and promoting the common happiness (ibid., 11–18).

Tindal readily acknowledged that not all people accepted the natural religion revealed in nature. The reason for this, he thought, was because of an "innate weakness" to believe in superstition. From this weakness came most of the problems of humankind (ibid., 165, 169).

Although many people have strayed from natural religion, God has made human nature to act in conformity with the rest of nature. Those who do not act this way are contradicting their own rational nature, thus acting irrationally (ibid., 26).

Origin and Nature of Evil. Tindal believed that evil came about because people succumb to superstition and act against the natural order of things (*see* EVIL, PROBLEM OF). He did believe that some people were in need of a savior for their wicked ways. Jesus Christ came to "teach" these people "to repent of the Breach of known Duties." As Tindal points out, Jesus said, "I am not come to call the righteous, but sinners to repentance" (Matt. 9:13). There are two types of people, Tindal said, the '"whole or righteous," and the "sick or Sinners." Jesus did business entirely with the latter, for "there is but one universal Remedy for all sick Persons, *Repentance* and *Amendment*." This has been revealed in nature since creation (ibid., 48, 49). Further, if God, who is no respecter of persons, will judge the world in righteousness and will accept the righteous, the righteous need no physician. They are already living in a way that pleases God. Christ came to reform those who do not have a good enough level of morality (ibid., 49).

Nature of Ethics. "The Principle from which all human Actions flow is the Desire of Happiness," wrote Tindal. This central principle is the "only innate Principle in Mankind" and so it must be implanted by God. Since human beings are rational creatures, their happiness is found when they govern all their "Actions by the Rules of right Reason." These rules of self-discipline are grounded in the moral perfections of God discoverable in nature. When people live "according to the Rules of right Reason, we more and more implant in us the moral Perfections of God, from which his Happiness [and ours] is inseparable" (ibid., 23, 24, 30).

"From these Premises," said Tindal, "we may conclude, that Men, according as they do, or do not partake of the Nature of God, must unavoidably be either happy, or miserable." In the wisdom of God, the consequences of both good and evil actions are found in happiness and unhappiness in this life. Hence, "there's no Virtue, but what has some Good inseparably annex'd to it; and no Vice, but what as necessarily carries with it some Evil" (ibid., 25).

Tindal rejected the idea that any book or books could have been used by God to reveal what is right and wrong . One book could not cover every case. However, the light of nature teaches us our duty in most cases (ibid., 27).

History and Destiny. Tindal had little to say about history. He does think that history shows how people have been duped by greedy, dishonest religious leaders who have taken advantage of man's proneness to believe in superstition (ibid., 169).

He also attempted to discredit the historicity of the Bible (*see* Bible Criticism). He ridiculed many Bible stories, such as the accounts of the garden of Eden, the Fall of man, Jacob's wrestling with God, and Balaam's talking donkey. He also argued that many of the miracles recorded in the Bible had parallels in pagan mythical stories and thus were mythical as well (ibid., 170, 192, 229, 340, 349).

Tindal did believe in an afterlife. Humanity's rational nature will survive death and pass on to another life where there are no "sensual things to divert his Thoughts." There will also be a "last Day" wherein God will judge every human being, not for what was said or believed, "but what you have done more than others." God's judgment will be impartial and fair since "God, at all Times, has given Mankind sufficient Means of knowing whatever he requires of them; and what those Means are" (ibid., 1, 25, 26, 51).

Evaluation. The antisupernaturalism of deism is critiqued in articles on deism, such deists as Thomas *Jefferson and Thomas *Paine, and in articles on such particular miracles as the *Virgin Birth and Resurrection of Christ. See also Miracle and Miracles, Arguments Against. Historically, two of the best critiques of Tindal were by Butler (*Analogy of Religion*) and Jonathan *Edwards in various of his critiques on deism, rationalism, and universalism.

Sources

J. Butler, *Analogy of Religion*
J. Edwards, *The Works of Jonathan Edwards*
N. L. Geisler, *Worlds Apart: A Handbook on Worldviews*, chap. 5
H. M. Morais, *Deism in Eighteenth Century America*
J. Orr, *English Deism: Its Roots and Its Fruits*
M. Tindal, *Christianity as Old as the Creation: or, the Gospel, a Republication of the Religion of Nature*

Transcendental Argument. *The transcendental argument* is used by some presuppositional apologists (*see* Presuppositional Apologetics) to demonstrate the truth of Christianity. It is patterned after Immanuel *Kant's reasoning in *Critique of Pure Reason*. A transcendental argument is neither deductive nor inductive. It is more reductive, arguing back to the necessary preconditions of something being the case.

As used by presuppositional apologetics, the transcendental argument affirms that, in order to make sense of the world, it is necessary to postulate the existence of the triune God as revealed in the Bible. This argument is employed by Cornelius *Van Til and a modified form is used by Francis *Schaeffer.

Van Til's thought is rooted in Herman Dooyeweerd, who got it from Kant. Once Kant's agnosticism is accepted, first principles, such as the principle of causality cannot be applied to the real world. This occasions the necessity of finding some other way to get at reality. The transcendental realist (*see* Realism) argues that this can be done in the same way that Kant posited the existence of *a priori* forms and categories of sense and the mind. Using this kind of reduction, they seek to find the necessary conditions for something being so. Kant himself concluded that it was necessary to posit God and immortality in order to make sense out of moral obligations (*see* Moral Argument).

Some apologists have made a minimal use of the transcendental argument. John *Carnell, for example, seemed to use it to defend the principle of causality (*see* Causality, Principle of). Van Til made maximal use of it, claiming that the whole Christian system is based on it. Others are in-between, asserting that it is necessary to posit the existence of the basic laws of reason (*see* Logic; First Principles), a theistic God, and perhaps some other things in order to make sense out of the world.

Transcendental and First Principles. Classical apologetics is based on such first principles, as *noncontradiction*, *causality*, and *analogy* (*see* Cosmological Argument). Presuppositionalists reject traditional proofs for God's existence (*see* God, Evidences for) in favor of many of the atheistic and agnostic arguments (*see* Agnosticism; Atheism). They seem to replace the traditional first principles of knowing the real world with a new *transcendental principle*. This raises the question of the relationship between the transcendental principle and the traditional first principles.

Similarities and Differences. There are similarities and differences in the use of the transcendental principle and of first principles by evangelical apologists. In general, the following comparison will represent the thinking of representatives of the positions of *Thomas Aquinas and Van Til. Other viewpoints differ but generally follow one of these two lines of thinking (*see* Apologetics, Types of).

Similarities. In both systems the principles operate like a first principle. There is nothing more basic than either in terms of which it can be proven to be true. It is interesting that transcendentalists give a status to their principle that they deny to traditional first principles. This appears to be a valid criticism of transcendental apologetics.

Both believe their respective principle(s) can be used to prove the existence of God.

Both hold that their principle(s) apply to the real world. Unlike Kant, however, they believe one can know reality (*see* REALISM; AGNOSTICISM) by means of their principle(s).

Both hold that their principle(s) can be understood in a meaningful way, even by finite human beings. They do not have equivocal meaning as understood by God and by us (*see* ANALOGY).

Both believe their arguments are valid, even if rejected by others.

Differences. Transcendentalists have only one principle—the transcendental principle. Traditionalists look to many first principles, including noncontradiction, causality, and analogy.

Transcendentalists presuppose their first principle with no attempt to demonstrate it. Traditionalists offer proof of the first principles by showing that they are self-evident or reducible to the self-evident. This can be seen in the article on First Principles.

While both imply a causal connection between the world and God, transcendentalists deny the ontological validity of the principle of causality. The transcendentalists insist that it is transcendentally necessary to posit a First Cause (i.e., God) of the finite world in order for it to make sense. But how does this differ from saying that every finite, contingent existence needs a First Cause, which is precisely what the first principle of causality demands?

The transcendental principle formally speaks of the necessary condition, but not the sufficient condition, of something. The principle of causality gives both. Thus, the transcendental principle does give only a necessary condition, not an actual cause, of the finite world. For a necessary condition (e.g., dry leaves) only explains how a fire is possible. It still takes ignition (a sufficient condition) to explain how it is actual.

Conclusion. The transcendental principle is neither self-evident, nor can it, by definition, be justified in terms of something more basic than itself. As such, it is without foundation. However, first principles, such as noncontradiction and causality, are self-evident or reducible to the self-evident. Hence, they serve better as a basis for apologetics.

Sources

J. Frame, *Cornelius Van Til: An Analysis of His Thought*
I. Kant, *Critique of Pure Reason*
Thomas Aquinas, *Summa contra Gentiles*
Van Til, Cornelius, *In Defense of the Faith*

Trinity. *Trinity* simply means "triunity." God is not a simple unity; there is plurality in his unity. The Trinity is one of the great mysteries (*see* MYSTERY) of the Christian Faith. Unlike an antinomy (see Kant) or paradox, which is a logical contradiction (*see* LOGIC), the Trinity goes beyond reason but not against reason. It is known only by divine revelation, so the Trinity is not the subject of *natural theology but of revelation (*see* REVELATION, SPECIAL).

The Basis for the Trinity. While the word *Trinity* does not occur there, the concept is clearly taught in the Bible. The logic of the doctrine of the Trinity is simple. Two biblical truths are evident in Scripture, the logical conclusion of which is the Trinity:

1. There is one God.
2. There are three distinct persons who are God: Father, Son, and Holy Spirit.

One God. The central teaching of Judaism called the *Shema* proclaims: "Hear, O Israel: The LORD our God, the LORD is one" (Deut. 6:4). When Jesus was asked the question, "What is the greatest commandment?" he prefaced the answer by quoting the *Shema* (Mark 12:29). In spite of his strong teaching on the deity of Christ (cf. Col. 2:9), the apostle Paul said emphatically, "there is but one God, the Father, from whom all things came and for whom we live" (1 Cor. 8:6a). From beginning to end, the Scriptures speak of one God and label all other gods as false (Exod. 20:3; 1 Cor. 8:5–6).

The Bible also recognizes a plurality of persons in God. Although the doctrine of the Trinity is not as explicit in the Old Testament as the New Testament, nonetheless, there are passages where members of the Godhead are distinguished. At times they even speak to one another (see Ps. 110:1).

The Father Is God. Throughout Scripture God is said to be a Father. Jesus taught his disciples to pray, "Our Father in heaven" (Matt. 6:9). God is not only "our heavenly Father" (Matt. 6:32) but the "Father of our spirits" (Heb. 12:9). As God, he is the object of worship. Jesus told the woman of Samaria, "Yet a time is coming and has now come when the true worshippers will worship the Father in spirit and truth, for they are the kind of worshippers the Father seeks" (John 4:23). God is not only called "our Father" (Rom. 1:7) many times but also "the Father" (John 5:45; 6:27). He is also called "God and Father" (2 Cor. 1:3). Paul proclaimed that "there is but one God, the Father" (1 Cor. 8:6). Additionally, God is referred to as the "Father of our Lord Jesus Christ" (Rom. 15:6). Indeed, the Father and the Son are often related by these very names in the same verse (Matt. 11:27; 1 John 2:22).

The Son Is God. The deity of Christ is treated below in the section on attacks on the Trinity and most extensively in the article Christ, Deity of. As a broad overview it should be noted that:

Jesus claimed to be *Yahweh* God. *YHWH;* translated in some versions *Jehovah,* was the special name of God revealed to Moses in Exodus 3:14, when God said, "I AM WHO I AM." In John 8:58, Jesus declares: "Before Abraham was, I am." This statement claims not only existence before Abraham, but equality with the "I AM" of Exodus 3:14. The Jews around him clearly understood his meaning and picked up stones to kill him for blaspheming (see Mark 14:62; John 8:58; 10:31–33; 18:5–6). Jesus also said, "I am the first and the last (Rev. 2:8).

Jesus took the glory of God. Isaiah wrote, "I am the LORD [*Yahweh*], that is my name; I will not give to another, or my praise to idols" (42:8) and, "This is what the LORD [*Yahweh*] says . . . I am the first, and I am the last; apart from me there is no God" (44:6). Likewise, Jesus prayed, "Father, glorify me in your presence with the glory I had with you before the world began" (John 17:5). But *Yahweh* had said he would not give his glory to another.

While the Old Testament forbids giving worship to anyone other than God (Exod. 20:1–4; Deut. 5:6–9), Jesus accepted worship (Matt. 8:2; 14:33; 15:25; 20:20; 28:17; Mark 5:6). The disciples attributed to him titles the Old Testament reserved for God, such as, "the first and the last" (Rev. 1:17; 2:8; 22:13), "the true light" (John 1:9), the "rock" or "stone" (1 Cor. 10:4; 1 Peter 2:6–8; cf. Ps. 18:2; 95:1), the "bridegroom" (Eph. 5:28–33; Rev. 21:2), "the chief Shepherd" (1 Peter 5:40), and "the great shepherd" (Heb. 13:20). They attributed to Jesus the divine activities of creating (John 1:3; Col. 1:15–16), redeeming (Hosea 13:14; Ps. 130:7), forgiving (Acts 5:31; Col. 3:13; cf. Ps. 130:4; Jer. 31:34), and judging (John 5:26). They used titles of deity for Jesus. Thomas declared: "My Lord and my God!" (John 20:28). Paul calls Jesus, "the one in whom the fullness of deity dwells bodily" (Col. 2:9). In Titus, Jesus is called, "our great God and savior" (2:13), and the writer to the Hebrews says of him, "Thy throne, O God, is forever" (Heb. 1:8). Paul says that, before Christ existed as a human being, he existed as God" (Phil. 2:5–8). Hebrews 1:5 says that Christ reflects God's glory of God, bears the stamp of his nature, and upholds the universe. The prologue to John's Gospel also minces no words, stating, "In the beginning was the Word, and the Word was with God, and the Word [Jesus] was God' (John 1:1).

Jesus claimed equality with God in other ways. He claimed the prerogatives of God. He claimed to be Judge of all (Matt. 25:31–46; John 5:27–30), but Joel quotes *Yahweh* as saying, "for there I will sit to judge all the nations on every side" (Joel 3:12). He said to a paralytic, "Son, your sins are forgiven" (Mark 2:5b). The scribes correctly responded, "Who can forgive sins but God alone?" (vs. 7b). Jesus claimed the power to raise and judge the dead, a power which only God possesses (John 5:21, 29). But the Old Testament clearly taught that only God was the giver of life (Deut. 32:39; 1 Sam. 2:6) and the one to raise the dead (Ps. 2:7).

Jesus claimed the honor due God, saying, "He who does not honor the Son does not honor the father, who sent him" (John 5:23b). The Jews listening knew that no one should claim to be equal with God in this way and again they reached for stones (John 5:18). When asked at his Jewish trial, "Are you the Christ (Messiah), the Son of the Blessed One?" Jesus responded, "I am, and you will see the Son of Man sitting at the right hand of the Mighty One and coming on the clouds of heaven" (Mark 14:61b–62).

The Holy Spirit Is God. The same revelation from God that declares Christ to be the Son of God also mentions another member of the triunity of God called the Spirit of God, or Holy Spirit. He too is equally God with the Father and the Son, and he too is a distinct person.

The Holy Spirit is called "God" (Acts 5:3–4). He possesses the attributes of deity, such as omnipresence (cf. Ps. 139:7–12) and omniscience (1 Cor. 2:10, 11). He is associated with God the Father in creation (Gen. 1:2). He is involved with other members of the Godhead in the work of redemption (John 3:5–6; Rom. 8:9–17, 27–27; Titus 3:5–7). He is associated with other members of the Trinity under the "name" of God (Matt. 28:18–20). Finally, the Holy Spirit appears, along with the Father and Son, in New Testament benedictions (for example, 2 Cor. 13:14).

Not only does the Holy Spirit possess deity but he also has a differentiated personality. That he is a distinct person is clear in that Scripture refers to "him" with personal pronouns (John 14:26; 16:13). Second, he does things only persons can do, such as teach (John 14:26; 1 John 2:27), convict of sin (John 16:7–7), and be grieved by sin (Eph. 4:30). Finally, the Holy Spirit has intellect (1 Cor. 2:10, 11), will (1 Cor. 12:11), and feeling (Eph. 4:30).

That the three members of the Trinity are distinct persons is clear in that each is mentioned in distinction form the others. The Son prayed to the Father (cf. John 17). The Father spoke from heaven about the Son at his baptism (Matt. 3:15–17). Indeed, the Holy Spirit was present at the same time, revealing that they coexist. Further, the fact that they have separate titles (Father, Son, and Spirit) indicate they are not one person. Also, each member of the Trinity has special functions that help us to identify them. For example, the Father planned salvation (John 3:16; Eph. 1:4); the Son accomplished it on the cross (John 17:4; 19:30; Heb. 1:1–2) and at the resurrection (Rom. 4:25; 1 Cor. 15:1–6), and the Holy Spirit applies it to the lives of the believers (John 3:5; Eph. 4:30; Titus 3:5–7). The Son submits to the Father (1 Cor. 11:3; 15:28), and the Holy Spirit glorifies the Son (John 16:14).

A Philosophical Defense of the Trinity. The doctrine of the Trinity cannot be proven by human reason; it is only known because it is revealed by special revelation (in the Bible). However, just because it is beyond reason does not mean that it goes against reason (*see* MYSTERY). It is not irrational or contradictory, as many critics believe.

The Logic of the Trinity. The philosophical law of non-contradiction informs us that something cannot be both true and false at the same time and in the same sense. This is the fundamental law of all rational thought. And the doctrine of the Trinity does not violate it. This can be shown by stating first of all what the Trinity is not. The Trinity is not the belief that God is three persons and only one person at the same time and in the same sense. That would be a contradiction. Rather, it is the belief that there are three persons in one *nature*. This may be a mystery, but it is not a contradiction. That is, it may go beyond reason's ability to comprehend completely, but it does not go against reason's ability to apprehend consistently.

Further, the Trinity is not the belief that there are three natures in one nature or three essences in one essence. That would be a contradiction. Rather, Christians affirm that there are three *persons* in one essence. This is not contradictory because it makes a distinction between person and essence. Or, to put it in terms of the law of non-contradiction, while God is one and many at the same time, he is not one and many in the *same sense*. He is one in the sense of his essence but many in the sense of his persons. So there is no violation of the law of non-contradiction in the doctrine of the Trinity.

A Model of the Trinity. By saying God has one essence and three persons it is meant that he has one "What" and three "Whos." The three Whos (persons) each share the same What (essence). So God is a unity of essence with a plurality of persons. Each person is different, yet they share a common nature.

God is one in his substance. The unity is in his essence (what God is), and the plurality is in God's persons (how he relates within himself). This plurality of relationships is both internal and external. Within the Trinity each member relates to the others in certain ways. These are somewhat analogous to human relationships. The Bible's descriptions of *Yahweh* as Father and Jesus as Son says something of how the Son relates to the Father. Also, the Father sends the Spirit as a Messenger, and the Spirit is a Witness of the Son (John 14:26). These descriptions help us understand the functions within the unity of the Godhead. Each is fully God, and each has his own work and interrelational theme with the other two. But it is vital to remember that the three share the same essence, so that they unify as one Being..

Some Illustrations of the Trinity. No analogy of the Trinity is perfect, but some are better than others. First, some bad illustrations should be repudiated. The Trinity is *not* like a chain with three links. For these are three separate and separable parts. But God is neither separated nor separable. Neither is God like the same actor playing three different parts in a play. For God is simultaneously three persons, not one person playing three successive roles. Nor is God like the three states of water: solid, liquid, and gaseous. For normally water is not in all three of these states at the same time, but God is always three persons at the same time. Unlike other bad analogies, this one does not imply tritheism. However, it does reflect another heresy known as modalism.

Most erroneous illustration of the Trinity tend to support the charge that trinitarianism is really tritheism, since they contain separable parts. The more helpful analogies retain the unity of God while they show a simultaneous plurality. There are several that fit this description.

A Mathematical Illustration. One aspect of the problem can be expressed in mathematical terms. Critics make a point of computing the mathematical impossibility of believing there is a Father, Son and Holy Spirit in the Godhead, without holding that there are three gods. Does not $1 + 1 + 1 = 3$? It certainly does if you *add* them, but Christians insist that the triunity of God is more like $1 \times 1 \times 1 = 1$. God is triune, not triplex. His one essence has multiple centers of personhood. Thus, there is no more mathematical problem in conceiving the Trinity than there is in understanding 1 cubed (1^3).

A Geometric Illustration. Perhaps the most widely used illustration of the Trinity is the triangle. One triangle has three corners, which are inseparable from, and simultaneous to, one another. In this sense it is a good illustration of the Trinity. Of course, the triangle is finite and God is infinite, so it is not an imperfect illustration.

Another aspect of the Godhead is that Christ is one person (shown as one corner of the triangle), yet he has two natures, a divine nature and a human nature. Some show this aspect graphically by symbolizing Christ's divinity by the corner of the triangle and using another geometric figure, a circle for instance, to illustrate the human nature. At the point of the person of Jesus Christ, the circle is welded onto the triangle, human nature touching, but not mixed with, divine. Human and divine natures exist side-by-side without confusion in the Son. His two natures are conjoined in one person. Or, in Christ there are two *Whats* and one *Who*, whereas, in God there are three *Whos* and one *What*.

A Moral Illustration. *Augustine suggested an illustration of how God is both three and one at the same time. The Bible informs us that "God is love" (1 John 4:16). Love involves a lover, a beloved, and a spirit of love between lover and loved. The Father might be likened to the Lover; the Son to the One loved, and the Holy Spirit is the Spirit of love. Yet love does not exist unless these three are united as one. This illustration has the advantage of being personal, since it involves love, a characteristic that flows only from persons.

An Anthropological Illustration. Since humankind is made in the image of God (Gen. 1:27), it would seem reasonable that men and women bear some snapshot of the Trinity within their being. One that causes more problems than it solves is to visualize the human being as a "trichotomy" of body, soul, and spirit. Whether the trichotomist position is accurate, this is not a helpful illustration. Body and soul are not an indivisible unity. They can be (and are) separated at death (cf. 2 Cor. 5:8; Phil 1:23; Rev. 6:9). The nature and persons of the Trinity cannot be separated.

A better illustration based in human nature is the relation between the human *mind,* to its *ideas,* and the expression of these ideas in *words.* There is obviously a unity among all three of these without there being an identity. In this sense, they illustrate the Trinity.

An Islamic Illustration of Plurality in God. When talking with Muslims, the best illustration of a plurality is the relation between the Islamic conception of the Qur'an and God. Yusuf K. Ibish in an article entitled, "The Muslim Lives by the Qur'an," cited by Charis Waddy, *The Muslim Mind,* described it this way: The Qur'an "is an expression of Divine Will. If you want to compare it with anything in Christianity, you must compare it with Christ himself. Christ was the expression of the Divine among men, the revelation of the Divine Will. That is what the Qur'an is."

Orthodox Muslims believe the Qur'an is eternal and uncreated. It is not the same as God but is an expression of God's mind as imperishable as God himself. Surely, there is here a plurality within unity, something that is other than God but is nonetheless one with God in essential characteristics.

Attacks on the Trinity. The Trinity is at the heart of orthodox Christianity. But many critics—Jews and Muslims in particular—contend that it is incoherent and contradictory. Orthodox Christians insist that the teaching that God is one in essence but three in personhood is complex, but not contradictory.

The central issue is the deity of Christ (*see* CHRIST, DEITY OF), a doctrine inseparable from the Trinity. If one accepts the biblical teaching about the deity of Christ, then a plurality in the Godhead has been acknowledged. Conversely, if the doctrine of the Trinity is received, the deity of Christ is part of the package. Of course, strict monotheists (*see* ISLAM), such as Muslims and Orthodox Jews, reject both the deity of Christ and the Trinity as a denial of the absolute unity of God.

Muslim Misunderstanding. Obstacles in the Muslim mind hinder acceptance of the triunity of God. Some are philosophical; some biblical. Islamic scholars often engage in an arbitrary and selective use of the biblical texts as it suits their purposes (*see* BIBLE, ISLAMIC VIEW OF). However, even the texts they pronounce "authentic" are twisted or misinterpreted to support their teachings (*see* NEW TESTAMENT, HISTORICITY OF).

Christ as "begotten" of God. Perhaps no Christian concept draws so violent a reaction among Muslims than that of Jesus as the "only begotten Son of God." This raises red flags immediately, because Muslims understand the words in a grossly anthropomorphic way. Evangelical Christians likewise would be offended to hear what Muslims think they hear in this term. Clearing away this misunderstanding is necessary.

The King James Version Bible refers to Christ as the "only begotten" Son of God (John 1:18; cf. 3:16). However, Muslim scholars often misconstrue this in a fleshly, carnal sense of someone who literally begets children. To "beget" implies the physical act of sexual intercourse. This they believe, and Christians agree, is absurd. God is a Spirit with no body. As the Islamic scholar Anis Shorrosh contents, "He [God] does not beget because begetting is an animal act. It belongs to the lower animal act of sex. We do not attribute such an act to God" (Shorrosh, 254). But only a few cults, notably the Latter-Day Saints (Mormons) have a teaching that approaches this view of "begetting."

Further, to the Islamic mind, *begetting* is "creating." "God cannot create another God. . . . He cannot create another uncreated" (ibid., 259). Once again, Christians would agree fully. The foregoing statements reveal the degree to which the biblical concept of Christ's Sonship is misunderstood by Muslim scholars. For no orthodox Christian equates the King James Version translation of "begat" with "made" or "create." Arianism taught that and was strenuously fought wherever it has appeared in church history. Its primary adherents today belong to another cult, the Jehovah's Witnesses. No wonder 'Abdu 'L-Ahad Dawud concludes that from a "Muslim point of belief the Christian dogma concerning the eternal birth or generation of the Son is blasphemy" (205).

New, more accurate English translations have been more careful to say in English what was originally meant in Greek. *Only begotten* does not refer to any physical generation but to a special relationship between the Son and the Father. It means a unique relationship, or could be translated, as the New International Version, "one and only Son." It does not imply creation by the Father or any other sort of generation. Just as an earthly father and son have a special filial relationship, so the eternal Father and his eternal Son are uniquely and intimately working in concert with one another. It does not refer to physical generation but to an eternal *procession* from the Father. Just as for Muslims the Word of God (Qur'an) is not identical to God but eternally proceeds from him, even so for Christians, Christ, God's "Word" (sura 4:171) eternally proceeds from him (*see* QUR'AN, ALLEGED DIVINE ORIGIN OF). Words like *generation* and *procession* are used of Christ in a filial and relational sense, not in a carnal and physical sense.

Some Muslim scholars confuse Christ's Sonship with his *virgin birth. Michael Nazir-Ali noted that "in the Muslim mind the generation of the Son often means his birth of the Virgin Mary" (Nazir-Ali, 29). As Shorrosh notes, many Muslims believe Christians have made Mary a goddess, Jesus her son, and God the Father her husband (114). With such a carnal misrepresentation of a spiritual reality, there is little wonder Muslims reject the Christian concept of eternal Father and Son.

Islamic misunderstanding of the Trinity is encouraged by the misunderstanding of Muhammad, who said, "O Jesus, son of Mary! didst thou say unto mankind: Take me and my mother for two gods beside Allah?" (sura 5:119). Hundreds of years before Muhammad Christians condemned such a gross misunderstanding of the sonship of Christ. The Christian writer Lactantius (240–320), writing in about 306, said, "He who hears the words 'Son of God' spoken must not conceive in his mind such great wickedness as to fancy that God procreated through marriage and union with any female,—a thing which is not done except by an animal possessed of a body and subject to death." Furthermore, "since God is alone, with whom could he unite? or [sic], since He was of such great might as to be able to accomplish whatever He wished, He certainly had no need of the comradeship of another for the purpose of creating" (Pfander, 164).

Distortion of John 1:1. If rejection of the eternal Sonship of Christ is based on a serious misunderstanding of the Christian concept of Christ as God's Son, another text proclaiming Christ's deity is often distorted: "In the beginning was the Word, and the Word was with God, and the Word was God" (John 1:1). Without textual support from even one of the 5300 plus Greek manuscripts, Muslims render the last phrase, "and the Word was *God's*." Dawud declares, without any warrant, "the Greek form of the genitive case '*Theou*,' i.e., 'God's' was corrupted into '*Theos*'; that is, 'God,' in the nominative form of the name!" (16–17).

This translation is not only arbitrary, but it is contrary to the rest of the message of John's Gospel where the claims that Christ is God are made multiple times (cf. John 8:59; 10:30; 12:41; John 20:28).

Misconstruing Thomas's confession. When Jesus challenged Thomas to believe after seeing him in his physical resurrection body (*see* RESURRECTION, EVIDENCE FOR), Thomas confessed Jesus' deity, declaring, "My Lord and My God" (John 20:28). Many Muslim writers diminish this proclamation of Christ's deity by reducing it to an ejaculatory exclamation, "My God!" Deedat declares, "What? He was calling Jesus his Lord and his God? No. This is an exclamation people call out. . . . This is a particular expression" (Shorrosh, 278).

Deedat's alternative reading is not viable. First, in an obvious reference to the content of Thomas's confession of Jesus as "my Lord and my God," Jesus blessed him for what he had correctly "seen" and "believed" (John 20:29). Thomas's confession of Christ's deity comes in the context of a miraculous appearance by the risen Christ, not to mention at the climax of the post-resurrection ministry, when Jesus' disciples were gaining increasing belief in Christ, based on his miraculous signs (cf. John 2:11; 12:37). Thomas's confession of Christ's deity fits with the stated theme of the Gospel of John "that you may believe that Jesus is the Christ, the Son of God, and that believing you may have life in his Name" (John 20:31). Even putting all this aside, Thomas was a devout Jew who revered the name of God. He simply would not have used God's name in so profane an ejaculation.

No doubt there was an amazed note in Thomas's voice as he pronounced Christ's deity, but to reduce it to an emotional ejaculation is to claim that Jesus blessed Thomas for breaking the commandment against using God's name in vain.

David's Son and David's Lord. In Matthew 22:43, citing Psalm 110, Jesus said, "How is it then that David, speaking by the Spirit, calls him 'Lord' [Messiah]?" According to Dawud, "By his expression that the 'Lord,' or the 'Adon,' could not be a son of David, Jesus excludes himself from that title" (89).

However, a careful look at the context shows that Jesus is saying just the opposite. Jesus stumped his skeptical Jewish questioners by presenting them with a dilemma that blew their own neat calculations about the Messiah out of the sky. How could David call the Messiah "Lord" (as he did in Ps. 110:1), when the Scriptures also say the Messiah would be the "Son of David" (which they do in 2 Sam. 7:12f.)? The only answer is that the Messiah must be both a man (David's son or offspring) *and* God (David's Lord.) Jesus is claiming to be both God and human. The Islamic mind should have no more difficulty understanding how Jesus can unite in one person both divine and human natures than their own belief that human beings combine both spirit and flesh, the enduring and the transient in one person (sura 89:27–30; cf. 3:185). Even according to Muslim belief, whatever Almighty God, the Creator and Ruler of all things, wills in his infinite wisdom he is also able to accomplish for "He is the irresistible" (sura 6:61).

God only good. Many Islamic scholars claim that Jesus denied being God when he rebuked the rich young ruler, saying, "Why do you call me good? No one is good—except God alone" (Mark 10:18). A careful look at this text in its context reveals that Jesus was not denying his deity. He was rather warning the young man to consider the implications of his careless appellation. Jesus does not say, "I am not God, as you claim" or "I am not good." Indeed, both the Bible and *Qur'an* teach that Jesus is sinless (cf. John 8:46; Heb. 4:14). Rather, Jesus challenged him to examine what he was really saying when he called Jesus "Good Master." In essence, Jesus was saying, "Do you realize what you are saying when you call Me 'Good Master'? Only God is good. Are you calling me God?" The fact that the young ruler refused to do what Jesus said, proves that he did not really consider Jesus his Master. But nowhere did Jesus deny that he was either the Master or God of the rich young ruler. Indeed, elsewhere Jesus freely claimed to be both Lord and Master of all (Matt. 7:21–27; 28:18; John 12:40).

The greater Father. Jesus' assertion that "My Father is greater than I" (John 14:28) is also misunderstood by Muslims. It is taken out of its actual context to mean that the Father is greater in *nature*, but Jesus meant only that the Father is greater in *office*. This is evident from the fact that in this same Gospel (of John) Jesus claimed to be the "I Am" or Yahweh of the Old Testament (Exod. 3:14). He also claimed to be "equal with God" (John 10:30, 33). In addition, he received worship on numerous occasions (John 9:38; cf. Matt. 2:11; 8:2; 9:18; 14:33; 15:25; 28:9, 17; Luke 24:52). He also said, "He who does not honor the Son does not honor the Father who sent him" (John 5:23).

Further, when Jesus spoke of the Father being "greater" it was in the context of his "going to the Father" (John 14:28). Only a few chapters later Jesus speaks to the Father, saying, "I have completed the work you gave me to do" (John 17:4). But this functional difference of his role as Son in the very next verse reveals that it was not to be used to diminish the fact that Jesus was equal to the Father in nature and glory. For Jesus said, "And now, Father, glorify me in your presence with the glory which I had with you before the world began" (John 17:5).

Misunderstood Philosophical Concepts. Islamic scholars also offer philosophical objections to the doctrine of the Trinity. These too must be cleared away before they will be able to understand the biblical teaching about a plurality of persons within the unity of God.

Emphasis on the Oneness of God is fundamental to Islam. One Muslim scholar said, "In fact, *Islam, like other religions before it in their original clarity and purity, is nothing other than the declaration of the Unity of God, and its message is a call to testify to this Unity" (Mahud, 20). Another author adds, "The Unity of Allah is the distinguishing characteristic of Islam. This is the purest form of monotheism, i.e., the worship of Allah Who was neither begotten nor beget nor had any associates with Him in his Godhead. Islam teaches this in the most unequivocal terms" (Ajijola, 55).

Because of this uncompromising emphasis on God's absolute unity, in Islam the greatest of all sins is the sin of *shirk*, or assigning partners to God. The *Qur'an* sternly declares "God forgiveth not (The sin of) joining other gods With Him; but He forgiveth Whom He pleaseth other sins Than this: one who joins Other gods with God, Hath strayed far, far away (From the Right)" (sura 4:116). However, this misunderstands the unity of God.

The Trinity and heresy. There are two primary heresies from which the Trinity is to be distinguished: modalism and tritheism. The heresy of modalism, also called Sabellianism, denies there are three distinct eternal persons in the Godhead. It believes that the so-called "persons" of the Trinity are modes of God substance, not distinct persons. Like water with its three states (liquid, solid, and gaseous), the Trinity is said to be only three different modes of the same essence. Unlike modalists, trinitarians believe there are three distinct persons (not just modes) in the one substance of God.

Both Islam and Christianity proclaim that God is one in essence. What is in dispute is whether there can be any plurality of persons in this unity of nature. The inadequacies in the Muslims' view of God arise in part out of their misunderstanding of Christian monotheism (*see* THEISM). Many Muslims misconstrue the Christian view of God as tritheism rather than as monotheism. The opposite error of tritheism affirms that there are three separate gods. Few, if any, Christian theologians or philosophers have held this view, but it often has been attributed to trinitarians. Unlike tritheists, trinitarians do not affirm a god with three different substances; they confess that God is three distinct persons in one substance.

The Bible declares emphatically: "The LORD our God, the LORD is one" (Deut. 6:4). Both Jesus (Mark 12:29) and the apostles repeat this formula in the New Testament (1 Cor. 8:4, 6). And early

Christian creeds speak of Christ being one in "substance" or "essence" with God. The Athanasian Creed, reads: "We worship one God in Trinity, and Trinity in Unity; Neither confounding the Persons; nor dividing the Substance (Essence)." So Christianity is a form of monotheism, believing in one and only one God.

The Trinity and complexity. Many Muslims complain that the Christian concept of the Trinity is too complex. They forget, however, that truth is not always simple. As C. S. *Lewis aptly puts it, "If Christianity was something we were making up, of course we could make it easier. But it is not. We cannot compete, in simplicity, with people who are inventing religions. How could we? We are dealing with fact. Of course anyone can be simple if he has no facts to bother about" (Lewis, 145).

The fact confronting Christians which led to their formulating this complex truth was, of course, the claims and credentials of Jesus of Nazareth to be God (*see* CHRIST, DEITY OF). This led them of necessity to posit a plurality within deity and thus the doctrine of the Trinity, since this Jesus was not the same as the one whom he addressed as Father. So Christians believe and Muslims deny that there are three persons in this one God. At this point the problem gets philosophical.

The Neoplatonic concept of unity. At the heart of the Muslim inability to understand the Trinity is the neoplatonic concept of oneness. The second-century A.D. philosopher *Plotinus, who heavily influenced the thinking of the middle ages, viewed God (the Ultimate) as the One, an absolute unity in which is no multiplicity at all. This One was so absolutely simple that it could not even know itself, since self-knowledge implies a distinction between knower and known. It was not until it emanated one level down, in the *Nous* or Mind, that it could reflect back on itself and therefore know itself. For Plotinus, the One itself was beyond knowing, beyond consciousness, and even beyond being. It was so undividedly simple that in itself it had no mind, thoughts, personality, or consciousness. It was void of everything, even being. Thus, it could not be known, except by its effects which, however, did not resemble itself (Plotinus, 1.6; 3.8–9; 5.1, 8; 6.8, 18).

It is not difficult to see strong similarities between the Plotinian and Muslim views of God. Nor is it hard to see the difficulty with this view. It preserves a rigid unity in God at the expense of real personality. It clings to a rigid simplicity by sacrificing relationship. It leaves us with an empty and barren concept of deity. By reducing God to a bare unity, they are left with a barren unity. As Joseph Ratsinger insightfully noted,

> The unrelated, unrelatable, absolutely one could not be a person. There is no such thing as a person in the categorical singular. This is already apparent in the words in which the concept of person grew up; the Greek word *"prosopon"* means literally "(a) look towards"; with the prefix *'pros'* (toward). It includes the notion of relatedness as an integral part of itself. . . . To this extent the overstepping of the singular is implicit in the concept of person. [Ratsinger, 128–29]

Confusion Regarding the Trinity. Confusing unity with singularity. The Muslim God has unity and singularity. But these are not the same. It is possible to have unity without singularity. For there could be plurality within the unity. Indeed, the Trinity is precisely a plurality of persons within the unity of one essence. Human analogies help to illustrate the point in a superficial way. My mind, my thoughts, and my words have a unity, but they are not a singularity, since they are all different. Likewise, Christ can express the same nature as God without being the same person as the Father.

In this connection, Muslim monotheism sacrifices plurality in an attempt to avoid duality. In avoiding the extreme of admitting any partners to God, Islam goes to the other extreme and denies any personal plurality in God. But, as Joseph Ratsinger observed, "belief in the Trinity, which recognizes the plurality in the unity of God, is the only way to the final elimination of dualism as a means of expanding plurality alongside unity; only through this belief is the positive validation of plurality given a definite base. God stands above singular and plural. He bursts both categories" (Ratsinger, 128).

Confusing person (who) and nature (what). That Christ "bursts the categories" explains why Christian and non-Christian alike, have struggled to understand the two natures of Christ. One of the better explanations of what Christians believe, though it doesn't go far toward explaining it, is found in one of the sixteenth-century Reformation statements of faith, the Belgic Confession, chapter 19:

> We believe that by this conception [of two natures], the person of the Son is inseparably united and connected with the human nature; so that there are not two Sons of God, nor two persons, but two natures united in one single person; yet each nature retains its own distinct properties. As, then, the divine nature has always remained uncreated, without beginning of days or end of life, filling heaven and earth, so also has the human nature not lost its properties but remained a creature, having beginning of days, being a finite nature, and retaining all the properties of a real body . . . . But these two natures are so closely united in one

person that they were not separated even by his death. . . . Wherefore we confess that he is *very God* and *very man*: very God by His power to conquer death; and very man that He might die for us according to the infirmity of His flesh.

Orthodox Christianity does not believe Jesus Christ was like a milkshake, the two natures blended together in an indistinguishable mass. Neither do Christians believe Jesus had a schizophrenically split identity in which divine and human natures were so distinct they would have had to call one another long-distance. These views and other equally wrong ideas have muddied Christian theology throughout its history. A popular modern theory, which misses the whole point of Philippians 2 and the reason God had to take on a human nature states that Jesus emptied himself of all his divine attributes of power and authority and kept only his moral perfection.

So how is it conceivable? The orthodox view is that God the Son took off nothing of his godhood, but rather added to it the human nature. He accepted limitations. As a human being, Jesus had to grow up and learn. He felt want and sorrow and there were things the human nature of Jesus did not know, such as the date of his return (Matt. 24:36).

One theologian, Charles *Hodge, wondered if God did not draw the clearest analogy of the two natures in the design of Israel's temple at Jerusalem. The inner court where the daily work of worship and the sacrifice happened was the court of Israel or the holy place. But within this space was another room that represented the presence of God in the midst of his people. This central room, the "holy of holies" was only entered by the high priest once a year. A curtain separated the two sections of the sanctuary so that the room was hidden. But symbolically it empowered the priests in their daily life in temple worship. The two were unmixed but united and inseparable.

The orthodox view of the two natures of Christ is that one person is both God and human. The two natures commune intimately but do not overlap. Christ possesses two natures united. Hence, when Jesus died on the cross for our sin he died as the God-man. It is not going too far, said John *Calvin, to say that at the moment Jesus was hanging on the cross his power as Creator God was holding together the hill on which the cross stood. Unless Jesus is God and human he cannot reconcile God and humanity. But the Bible says clearly, "there is one God and one mediator between God and men, the man Christ Jesus" (1 Tim. 2:5).

Since Christ is one *Who* (person) with two *Whats* (natures), whenever one question is asked about him it must be separated into two questions, one applying to each nature. For example, did he get tired? As God, no; as human, yes. Did Christ get hungry? In his divine nature, no; in his human nature, yes. Did Christ die? In his human nature, he did die. His divine nature is eternally alive. He died as the God-man, but his Godness did not die.

When this same logic is applied to other theological questions raised by Muslims it yields the same kind of answer. Did Jesus know everything? As God he did, since God is omniscient. But as man Jesus did not know the time of his second coming (Matt. 24:36), and as a child he "increased in wisdom" (Luke 2:52).

Could Jesus sin? The answer is the same: as God, no; as man yes (but he didn't). God cannot sin. For example, the Bible says "it is impossible for God to lie" (Heb. 6:18; cf. Titus 1:2). Yet Jesus was "in all points tempted as we are, yet without sin" (Heb. 4:15). While he never sinned (cf. 2 Cor. 5:21; 1 Peter 1:19; 1 John 3:3), he was really tempted and it was possible for him to sin. Otherwise, his temptation would have been a charade. Jesus possessed the power of free choice which means that when he chose not to sin it was a meaningful choice. He could have done otherwise.

Dividing every question of Christ into two and referring them to each nature unlocks a lot of theological puzzles that otherwise remain shrouded in ambiguity. And it makes it possible to avoid logical contradictions which are urged upon Christians by Muslims and by other nonbelievers.

Conclusion. The doctrine of the Trinity is one of the great mysteries of the Christian Faith. That is, it transcends reason without being contrary to reason (*see* FAITH AND REASON). It is not known by reason (*see* REVELATION, GENERAL) but only by special revelation (*see* REVELATION, SPECIAL). God is one in essence but three in persons. He is a plurality within unity. God is a triunity, not a rigid singularity.

Once those conceptions are understood, many of the barriers that separate even such radical monotheists as Orthodox Jews and Muslims fall.

Sources

A. Ajijola, *The Essence of Faith in Islam*
Augustine, *On the Trinity*
S. Balic, "The Image of Jesus in Contemporary Islamic Theology," in A. Shimmel and A. Falaturi, eds., *We Believe in One God*
C. Beisner, *God in Three Persons*
A. Dawud, *Muhammad in the Bible*
J. N. D. Kelly, *Early Christian Doctrines*
C. S. Lewis, *Mere Christianity*
A. H. Mahud, *The Creed of Islam*
M. Nazir-Ali, *Frontiers in Muslim-Christian Encounter*
C. G. Pfander, *The Mizanu'l Haqq* (*The Balance of Truth*)
Plotinus. *The Enneads*
G. L. Prestige, *God in Patristic Thought*.
J. Ratsinger, *Introduction to Christianity*, J. R. Foster, trans.
A. Shorrosh, *Islam Revealed*
Thomas Aquinas, *On the Trinity*

Troeltsch, Ernst. Ernst Peter Wilhelm Troeltsch (1865–1923) was born in Haunstetten and educated at Göttingen, Berlin, and Erlängen. Troeltsch was minister of education for Germany before World War I and taught, primarily at Berlin and Heidelberg, from 1894 until his death. He was a liberal theologian who was intensely involved in social and political issues, as well as a historian and philosopher. His work dismissed the Bible and regarded all religion as culturally conditioned, yet he detested the relativism his ideas promoted. Troeltsch believed Christianity to be the religion best suited for the Western world, and he sought to legitimize it through social action in modern history rather than supernatural action in the ancient world. Among his works were *Christian Thought in History and Application* (1924/trans. 1923), and *The Social Teaching of the Christian Church* (1912/1931).

Troeltsch laid down the rule of analogy: The only way one can know the past is by analogies in the present. The unknown of the past is arrived at only through what is known. On this principle, some argue that the miracles of the Bible should not be believed, since they do not relate to anything happening now (*see* MIRACLES, ARGUMENTS AGAINST). A proper historical method, thus, eliminates the miraculous. Antony *Flew added his own twist to the "critical historical argument."

Troeltsch used the *principle of analogy* and Flew the *principle of critical history* against miracles. Both have the same naturalistic basis (*see* NATURALISM).

It should be noted that the term *principle of analogy* is used in two entirely differing senses. For a discussion on the principle of analogy related to reason and knowledge of God, see the article ANALOGY, PRINCIPLE OF.

The Principle of Analogy. This principle of analogy, according to Troeltsch, asserts that "on the analogy of the events known to us we seek by conjecture and sympathetic understanding to explain and reconstruct the past." Without uniformity of the past and present, we could not know anything from the past. For without analogies from the present we cannot understand the past (Troeltsch, *Historicism and Its Problems*).

On the basis of this principle, some have insisted that "no amount of testimony is ever permitted to establish as past reality a thing that cannot be found in present reality." Even if the witness has a perfect character, the testimony has no power as proof (Becker, "Detachment and the Writing of History," 12–13). This means that, unless one can identify in today's world such miracles as are found in the New Testament, we have no reason to believe they occurred in the past either. The philosopher F. H. Bradley (1846–1924) stated the problem this way:

> We have seen that history rests in the last resort upon an inference from our experience, a judgment based upon our own present state of things; . . . when we are asked to affirm the existence in past time of events, the effects of causes which confessedly are without analogy in the world in which we live, and which we know—we are at a loss for any answer but this, that . . . we are asked to build a house without a foundation. . . . And how can we attempt this without contradicting ourselves? [Bradley, 100]

It is widely admitted on all sides of the issue that no *virgin births, no raising the dead and no walking on water are occurring today, then it follows by the principle of analogy that such events cannot be known to have happened in history. So biblical miracles are historically unknowable.

Similar to Troeltsch's "Principle of Analogy" is Flew's "critical history." Critical history owes its existence partly to two principles stated by David Hume, which attempt to undermine the credibility of miracles (Hume, *Treaties on Human Nature*, 2.3.1; *Inquiry Concerning Human Understanding*, 8; *see* MIRACLES, ARGUMENTS AGAINST). Flew comments:

1. "The present detritus [remains] of the past cannot be interpreted as historical evidence at all, unless we presume that the same basic regularities obtained then as today."
2. "The historian must employ as criteria all his present knowledge, or presumed knowledge, of what is probable or improbable, possible or impossible" (Flew, 350).

Only by presuming that the laws of today also governed reality in the past can the historian rationally interpret evidence and construct an account of what actually happened (ibid., 351).

Flew concludes that the critical historian dismisses a story of a miracle. With Hume, he argues that reasonable people regard the "absolute impossibility or a miraculous nature" as sufficient to refute reported occurrences (ibid., 352). Miracles are possible in principle, but in practice the historian must always reject them. The very nature of the historical method demands that the past be interpreted in accordance with the (naturalistic) regularities of the present. In logical structure, this argument against miracles can be summarized:

1. All critical history depends on the validity of two principles: (a) The remains of the past can be used as evidence for reconstructing history only if we presume the same basic regularities of nature held then as now. (b) The critical historian must use today's knowledge of the possible and probable as criteria for knowing the past.
2. Belief in miracles is contrary to both these principles.

3. Therefore, belief in miracles is contrary to critical history.

Conversely, only the naïve and uncritical can believe in miracles. The past can be known only in terms of the regular patterns of the present. And these patterns of nature in the present rule out any knowledge of miracles in the past.

Evaluation. It should be noted first that this argument does not claim to eliminate the possibility of miracles (*see* SPINOZA, BENEDICT). It simply attempts to rule out their *knowability* by what Flew calls "critical history." Further, the argument (as Flew admits) follows the basic form of *Hume's antisupernaturalism, which has been critiqued in the article MIRACLES, ARGUMENTS AGAINST. That is to say, it assumes that to be truly critical and historical, one must be antisupernatural. Anyone who allows for the supernatural is automatically naïve (incidentally, an *ad hominem* attack). However, one would think that closed-mindedness would not be lauded as a prerequisite for evaluating evidence and compiling history.

It is a valid principle that "the present is the key to the past," or that "the past is known by analogy with the present." This is so since those living in the present have no direct access to the past. We were not there and cannot go back. We must depend, therefore, on comparing remains of the past with events in the present. This is precisely how origin science works (*see* ORIGINS, SCIENCE OF), whether applied to archaeology, biology, or geology. In geology the principle of analogy is known as the principle of uniformity or uniformitarianism. However, the two should be distinguished. For uniformitarianism is loaded with an extraneous antisupernatural bias. Whereas, in sciences about the past, the principle of uniformity (analogy) is legitimate. When an archaeologist finds a piece of pottery, it helps to know what pottery is used for in the present, how different materials, forms, and glazes apply to different functions, and how the potter performs the craft. The archaeologist postulates from that what the origin of this potsherd might have been.

A valid application of the principle that "the present is the key to the past" is that "the kinds of causes known to produce certain kinds of effects in the present can be assumed to produce similar kinds of effects in the past." But, contrary to Troeltsch and Flew, this principle does not rule out a credible belief in past miracles, even if no such miracles exist in the present. This use misapplies the principle.

Problems with the Arguments. Several difficulties involved in the arguments against miracles are discussed in the section on arguments against miracles from analogy in the article MIRACLES, ARGUMENTS AGAINST. In abbreviated form those arguments are:

Both Troeltsch and Flew adopt historical uniformitarianism. They assume all past events are uniformly the same as all present ones. By uniformitarian logic, geology long overlooked the fact that many past processes were catastrophic and caused change faster than what can be observed. By the uniformitarian argument, scientists should not study the singular, unrepeatable events surrounding the origins of the universe and life on earth.

The historical argument confuses uniformity with uniformitarianism. It does not follow that the object in the past cannot be a singularity. Unique finds by archaeologists can be studied by analogy to other finds. They may not be uniformly the same, perhaps nothing like, but that does not disqualify their study. The SETI (Search for Extra-Terrestrial Intelligence) program is not unscientific in believing that receipt of a unique message from space will reveal the existence of intelligent life (*see* SAGAN, CARL). The *basis* for knowing that a singular group of radio waves is produced by intelligence is their organized complexity, not receipt of more messages. Historical evidence provides ample grounds for affirming that the miracles of Christ occurred, even if none occur today.

It is special pleading to assume that no miracles are occurring. God may or may not still work in this way. Troeltsch and Flew do not demonstrate that miracles never happen today. If there are miracles, an analogy for knowing the past does exist.

In practice, Flew says that miracles are "absolutely impossible" and must be dismissed out of hand. This is the fallacy of *petitio principii* or question begging. Why should a critical thinker be so biased against the historical actuality of a miracle as to begin with a mind closed to all other evidence?

By closing off discussion and mocking those who disagree with their assumptions, uniformitarians are actually betraying the foundations of science. A recent example is the time and energy wasted in avoiding the evidence that the universe had a beginning, though the explosive eruption of mass in the big bang is readily accepted today.

Why should exceptional events of the past be judged against normal events of today's world? The healing of a man born blind seemed as incredible in Jesus' day as it would if it happened now (see Matthew 9). The only legitimate comparison of a past anomaly is comparison with today's anomalous happenings, rather than the general run of life.

The uniformitarian argument proves that much of what uniformitarians believe about the past cannot be true. Many historical events they do accept were exceptional or unique.

"Critical history" does not criticize the uncritical, unreasonable acceptance of presuppositions that eliminate valid historical knowledge. It legislates, rather than seeks, truth.

Conclusion. Troeltsch sought to synthesize religion and social culture, but he seldom could come to a final conclusion about where the synthesis was headed, so he made a sometimes helpful but incomplete theology of Christian action in the world. Part of the problem was his theological liberal skepticism, which left unanswered the question of the foundations of Christianity and where this religion itself fit in the world of reality. Much of the problem with his historical philosophy related to his "Principle of Analogy," a uniformitarian dogma that dismissed the uniqueness of Christ's life and miracles. Who Christ was and what he did could not even be considered without similar occurrences repeating now. This historical *naturalism assumes that all events can be naturally explained. This, however, is contrary to rational thought in general and scientific thought in particular (*see* ORIGINS, SCIENCE OF).

Sources

C. Becker, "Detachment and the Writing of History," in *Detachment and the Writing of History,* ed. P. L. Snyder

F. H. Bradley, *The Presuppositions of Critical History*

D. K. Erlandson, "A New Look," *Religious Studies (*December 1977)

A. Flew, "Miracles," in *The Encyclopedia of Philosophy,* ed. P. Edwards

N. L. Geisler, *Christian Apologetics*

———, *Miracles and the Modern Mind*

S. Hawking, *A Brief History of Time*

D. Hume, *An Enquiry Concerning Human Understanding*

———, *Treatise on Human Nature*

R. Jastrow, *God and the Astronomers*

C. S. Lewis, *Miracles*

E. Troeltsch, *Historicism and Its Problems*

———. "Historiography," *in Encyclopedia of Religion and Ethics*

R. Whately, "Historical Doubts Concerning the Existence of Napoleon Bonaparte," in H. Morley, ed., *Famous Pamphlets,* 2d ed.

H. P. Yockey, "Self-Organization, Origin of Life Scenarios, and Information Theory," in *Journal of Theoretical Biology* (1981)

Trueblood, Elton. Elton Trueblood (1900–1994) was an American Quaker theologian and philosopher. After serving as Stanford University chaplain, he became a philosophy professor at Earlham College. He retired from Earlham in 1966 to become professor at large.

Trueblood published thirty-seven books, including *The Essence of Spiritual Religion* (1937), *The Predicament of Modern Man* (1944), *The Company of the Committed* (1961), *The Incendiary Fellowship* (1967), and *While It Is Day: An Autobiography* (1974). Of special interest to apologists is his *Philosophy of Religion* (1957).

While remaining true to his Quaker beliefs in the "inner light," pacifism, and civil rights, Trueblood moved into the mainstream of evangelicalism. His work on the *Philosophy of Religion* went beyond traditional Quaker *mysticism.

Trueblood argued that "revelation must be tested by reason for the simple reason that there are false claims to revelation (*Philosophy of Religion,* 32). While he acknowledged the need for authority, he insisted that it should be a reasonable authority, one that can be trusted (ibid., 67). He believed there is ample evidence to support the truth of Christianity as such an authority. With Joseph *Butler, he believed that "probable proofs, by being added, not only *increase* the evidence but *multiply* it" (ibid., 74).

Evidence for God. Trueblood drew his defense for God from the classical sources of evidence:

Cosmological Argument. Speaking of the Second Law of Thermodynamics (*see* THERMODYNAMICS, LAWS OF), Trueblood said, "If the universe is running down like a clock, . . . the clock must have been wound up. . . . The world, if it is to have an end of time, must have had a beginning of time." He summarized that the evidence suggests that "the world is not self-explanatory. . . . Nature points beyond nature for an explanation of nature" (ibid., 104). See article on BIG BANG THEORY.

Moral Argument. One of the best statements of the *moral argument for God's existence is found in Trueblood. He reasoned that there must be an objective moral law (*see* MORALITY, ABSOLUTE NATURE OF). Otherwise, there would be no such agreement on morality. Without a moral law, every person would be right, whatever he or she did, nor could there be any disagreements over ethical standards. No ethical question could even be discussed, for the concept of ethics would be meaningless. Contradictory views would both be right, since opposites could be equally correct. The moral law that does exist must be beyond individual persons and beyond humanity as a whole, for each person and the whole race are measured for moral progress.

This moral law must come from a moral Legislator, because a law has no meaning unless it comes from a mind to give it meaning. Disloyalty makes no sense unless loyalty is owed to a person, yet people die in loyalty to what is morally right. Truth is meaningless except in the context of a meeting of mind with mind, yet people die for the truth. Hence, discovery of, and duty to, the moral law makes sense only if there is a Mind or Person behind it.

Therefore, a moral, personal Mind that is outside humanity stands behind this moral law. Otherwise, the universe would be irrational. Unless we assume the universe is irrational, there must be an objective moral law and an objective moral Law Giver.

Religious Argument. Trueblood also presents a good summary of the argument from religious experience (*see* APOLOGETICS, EXPERIENTIAL). He notes that not only have the masses claimed to have experienced God, but if even one person is right about a religious experience, there must be a God. In view of this, there are two alternatives: "Either God is, or all of those who have claimed to know Him have been deluded" (ibid., 146). But since, among those who claim to have experienced God are some of the most brilliant and critical minds in the history of humankind, it seems unlikely that they all are wrong. It is more likely that God exists. Of course, it is always possible that everyone is deluded (*see* FREUD, SIGMUND; FEUERBACH, LUDWIG), but this is not to say there is good reason for believing they are. In fact, there are good reasons for believing that God exists (*see* GOD, EVIDENCE FOR).

Source

E. Trueblood, *Philosophy of Religion*

Truth, Absolute. ***See*** **TRUTH, NATURE OF**

Truth, Nature of. Pilate asked: What is truth? Philosophers from Socrates to the last century answered: Is it *absolute?* Is it *knowable* (*see* AGNOSTICISM)? And does it correspond to a referent or, in the case of metaphysical truth, does it correspond to reality?

The Importance of the Nature of Truth. The nature of truth is crucial to the Christian faith. Not only does Christianity claim there is absolute truth (truth for everyone, everywhere, at all times), but it insists that truth about the world (reality) is that which corresponds to the way things really are. For example, the statement "God exists" means that there really is a God outside the universe, an extracosmic Being (*see* GOD, EVIDENCE OF). Likewise, the claim that "God raised Christ from the dead" means that the dead corpse of Jesus of Nazareth supernaturally vacated its tomb alive a few days after its burial (*see* RESURRECTION, EVIDENCE OF). Christian truth claims really correspond to the state of affairs about which they claim to inform us.

The Nature of Truth. *What Truth Is Not . . .* Truth can be understood both from what it is and from what it is not. There are many inadequate views of the nature of truth. Most of these result from a confusion between the nature (definition) of truth and a test (defense) of truth, or from not distinguishing the result from the rule.

Truth is not "what works." One popular theory is the pragmatic view of William James and his followers that truth is what works. According to James, "Truth is the expedient in the way of knowing. A statement is known to be true if it brings the right results. It is the expedient as confirmed by future experience." That this is inadequate is evident from its confusion of cause and effect. If something is true it will work, at least in the long run. But simply because something works does not make it true. This is not how truth is understood in court. Judges tend to regard the expedient as perjury. Finally, the results do not settle the truth question. Even when results are in, one can still ask whether the initial statement corresponded to the facts. If it did not, it was not true, regardless of the results.

Truth is not "that which coheres." Some thinkers have suggested that truth is what is internally consistent; it is coherent and self-consistent. But this too is an inadequate definition. Empty statements hang together, even though they are devoid of truth content. "All wives are married women" is internally consistent, but it is empty. It tells us nothing about reality. The statement would be so, even if there were no wives. It really means, "*If* there is a wife, then she must be married." But it does not inform us that there is a wife anywhere in the universe. A set of false statements also can be internally consistent. If several witnesses conspire to misrepresent the facts, their story may cohere better than if they were honestly trying to reconstruct the truth. But it still is a lie. At best, coherence is a negative test of truth. Statements are wrong if they are inconsistent, but not necessarily true if they are.

Truth is not "that which was intended." Some find truth in intentions, rather than affirmations. A statement is true if the author intends it to be true and false if he does not intend it to be true. But many statements agree with the intention of the author, even when the author is mistaken. "Slips of the tongue" occur, communicating a falsehood or misleading idea the communicator did not intend. If something is true because someone intended it to be true, then all sincere statements ever uttered are true—even those that are patently absurd. Sincere people are often sincerely wrong.

Truth is not "what is comprehensive." Another idea is that the view that explains the most data is true. And those that are not as comprehensive are not true—or not *as true*. Comprehensiveness is one test for truth, but not the definition of truth. Certainly a good theory will explain all relevant data. And a true worldview will be comprehensive. However, this is only a negative test of whether it is true. The affirmations of that view must still correspond with the real state of affairs. If a view was true simply because it was more encyclopedic, then a comprehensive statement of error would be true and a digested presentation of truth automatically would be in error. Not all long-winded presentations are true and concise ones are not all false. One can have a comprehensive view of what is false or a superficial or incomplete view of what is true.

Truth is not "what is existentially relevant." Following Søren *Kierkegaard and other existential philosophers, some have insisted that truth is what is relevant to our existence or life and false if it is not. Truth is subjectivity, Kierkegaard said; truth is livable. As Martin *Buber stated, truth is found in persons, not in propositions.

However, even if truth is existential in some sense, not all truth fits into the existential category. There are many kinds of truth, physical, mathematical, historical, and theoretical. But if truth by its very nature is found only subjectively in existential relevance, then none of these could be true. What is true will be relevant, but not everything relevant is true. A pen is relevant to an atheist writer. And a gun is relevant to a murderer. But this does not make the former true nor the latter good. A truth about life will be relevant to life. But not everything relevant to one's life will be true.

Truth is not "what feels good." The popular subjective view is that truth gives a satisfying feeling, and error feels bad. Truth is found in our subjective feelings. Many mystics (*see* MYSTICISM) and new age enthusiasts hold versions of this faulty view, though it also has a strong influence among some experientially oriented Christian groups.

It is evident that bad news can be true. But if what feels good is always true, then we would not have to believe anything unpleasant. Bad report cards do not make a student feel good, but the student refuses to believe them at his or her academic peril. They are true. Feelings are also relative to individual personalities. What feels good to one may feel bad to another. If so, then truth would be highly relative. But, as will be seen in some detail below, truth cannot be relative.

Even if truth makes us feel good—at least in the long run—this does not mean that what feels good is true. The nature of truth does not depend on the result of truth.

What Truth Is. *Correspondence with Reality.* Now that the inadequate views of the nature of truth have been examined, it remains to state an adequate view. Truth is what corresponds to its referent. Truth about reality is what corresponds to the way things really are. Truth is "telling it like it is." This correspondence applies to abstract realities as well as actual ones. There are mathematical truths. There are also truths about ideas. In each case there is a reality, and truth accurately expresses it.

Falsehood, then, is what does not correspond. It tells it like it is not, misrepresenting the way things are. The intent behind the statement is irrelevant. If it lacks proper correspondence, it is false.

Arguments for Correspondence. All noncorrespondence views of truth imply correspondence, even as they attempt to deny it. The claim: "Truth does not correspond with what is" implies that this view corresponds to reality. Then the noncorrespondence view cannot express itself without using a correspondence frame of reference.

If one's factual statements need not correspond to the facts in order to be true, then any factually incorrect statement is acceptable. It becomes impossible to lie. Any statement is compatible with any given state of affairs.

In order to know something is true or false, there must be a real difference between things and statements about the things. But correspondence is the comparison of words to their referents. Hence, a correspondence view is necessary to make sense of factual statements.

Communication depends on informative statements. But correspondence to facts is what makes statements informative. All communication ultimately depends on something being literally or factually true. We cannot even use a metaphor unless we understand that there is a literal meaning over against which the figurative sense is not literal. So, it would follow that all communication depends in the final analysis on a correspondence to truth.

The intentionalist theory claims that something is true only if what is accomplished corresponds fulfils what is intended by the statement. Without correspondence of intentions and accomplished facts there is no truth.

Objections to Correspondence. Objections to the correspondence view of truth come from Christian and non-Christian sources.

When Jesus said "I am the truth" (John 14:6), it is argued that he demonstrated that truth is personal, not propositional. This falsifies the correspondence view of truth, in which truth is a characteristic of propositions (or expressions) which correspond to its referent. But a person, as well as a proposition, can correspond to reality. As the "exact image" of the invisible God (Heb. 1:3), Jesus perfectly corresponds to the Father (John 1:18). He said to Philip, "when you have seen me, you have seen the Father" (John 14:9). So, a person can correspond to another in his character and actions. In this sense, persons can be said to be true, or express the truth.

God is truth, yet there is nothing outside of himself to which he corresponds. Yet according to the correspondence view, truth is that which correctly represents reality. Since God lacks correspondence, this argument goes, the correspondence theory denies that God is true, as the Bible says he is (Rom. 3:4). However, truth as correspondence does relate strongly to God. God's words correspond to his thoughts. So God is true in the sense that his word can be trusted. God's thoughts are identical to themselves, a kind of perfect "correspondence." In this sense, God is true to himself. If truth is understood as what corresponds to another, then in this sense God is not "true." Rather, he is the ultimate reality and so the standard for truth. Other things must correspond to him in a limited way in order to be called true, not he to them.

The basic fallacy in this objection that God is truth yet not correspondent is that it equivocates in its definitions. If correspondence relates only to something *outside* oneself, then God cannot be truth, but the ultimate reality to which truth corresponds. If correspondence can also be *inside oneself*, God corresponds to himself in the most perfect way. He is perfect truth by perfect self-identity. Consider the following fallacious thinking:

1. All who submit to the authority of the Pope are Roman Catholic.
2. But the Pope cannot submit to himself.
3. Therefore, the Pope is not Roman Catholic.

The mistake is in the second premise. Contrary to the claim, the Pope can submit to himself. He simply has to follow the rules he lays down for Roman Catholics. Likewise, God can and does live in accord with his own authority. In this sense he is true to himself.

The Absolute Nature of Truth. The relativity of truth is commonly a premise of current thought. Yet orthodox Christianity is predicated on the position that truth is absolute. Thus, the defense of the possibility of absolute truth is crucial to the defense of the historic Christian faith. According to theories of relative truth, something may be true for one person, but not for all people. Or, it may be true at one time, but not at another. According to the absolutist view, what is true for one person is true for all persons, times, and places.

As argued above, there is only one adequate view of the nature of truth—the correspondence view. Other views, such as coherence and pragmatism, describe tests for truth, not an explanation of the nature of truth itself. *Factual truth is that which corresponds to the facts.* It is that which corresponds to the actual state of affairs being described.

Relative Truth. The relativity of truth is a popular contemporary view. However, truth is not determined by majority vote. Let's take a look at the reasons people give for belief that truth is relative.

Of all, some things appear only to be true at some times and not at others. For example, many people once believed the world to be flat. Now we know that truth statement was wrong. It would seem that this truth has changed with the times. Or has it? Did the truth change, or did beliefs about what is true change? Well, certainly the world did not change from a box to a sphere. What changed in this regard is our belief, not our earth. It changed from a false belief to a true one.

Within a statement's universe of discourse, every truth is an absolute truth. Some statements really apply only to some people, but the truth of those statements is just as absolute for all people everywhere at all times as a statement that applies to all people generally. "Daily injections of insulin are essential for continued life" is true of persons with some life-threatening forms of diabetes. This statement has an applied universe of discourse. It isn't purporting to be a truth that applies to everyone. But if it applies to Fred, then it is true of Fred for everyone. The caveat that this statement is false for people with a normally functioning pancreas does not detract from the statement's truth within its universe of discourse—diabetics to whom it is properly addressed.

Some statements appear to be true only for some. The statement, "I feel warm" may be true for me but not for another person, who may feel cold. I am the only one within the statement's universe of discourse. The statement, "I [Norman Geisler] feel warm" (on July 1, 1998, at 3:37 P.M.) is true for everyone everywhere that Norman Geisler did feel warm at that moment in history. It corresponds to facts and so is an absolute truth.

A teacher facing a class says: "The door to this room is on my right." But it is on the left for the students. Relativists argue that surely this truth is relative to the teacher since it is false for the class. But on the contrary it is equally true for everyone that the door is on the professor's right. This is an absolute truth. It will never be true for anyone, anywhere at any time that the door was on the professor's left during this class on this day in this room. The truth is equally absolute that the door was on the student's left.

It seems obvious that the temperature frequently is relatively high in Arizona and relatively cold at the North Pole. So, apparently some things are true for some places but not for other places. Right?

Not so. Some things are true concerning some places, but not true in other places where the conditions are different. But that isn't the point. Within the Arizona weather report's universe of discourse, the statement corresponds to the facts. So it is true everywhere. The statement: "It is relatively cold for earth at the North Pole" is true for people in Arizona in the summer, or on Pluto where it is colder than on the North Pole. Truth is what corresponds to the facts, and the fact is that it feels cold at the North Pole.

All truth is absolute. There are no relative truths. For if something is really true, then it is really true for everyone everywhere, and for all time. The truth statement 7 + 3 = 10 is not just true for mathematics majors, nor is it true only in a mathematics classroom. It is true for everyone everywhere.

Evaluation. Like an old apple, relativism may look good on the surface but it is rotten at the core. Among its problems:

Absolutely Relative? Most relativists really believe relativism is true for everybody, not just for them. But that is the one thing they cannot hold if they are really relativists. For a relative truth is just true for me but not necessarily for anyone else. So, the relativist who thinks relativism is true for everyone is an absolutist. Such a person believes in at least one absolute truth. The dilemma is this: a consistent relativist cannot say "It is an absolute truth for everyone that truth this is only relatively true." Nor can the person say, "It is only relatively true that relativism is true." If it is only relatively true, then relativism may be false for some or all others. Why then should I accept it as true? Either the claim that truth is relative is an absolute claim, which would falsify the relativist position, or it is an assertion that can never really be made, because every time you make it you have to add another "relatively." This begins an *infinite regress that will never pay off in a real statement.

The only way the relativist can avoid the painful dilemma of relativism is to admit that there are at least some absolute truths. As noted, most relativists believe that relativism is absolutely true and that everyone should be a relativist. Therein lies the self-destructive nature of relativism. The relativist stands on the pinnacle of an absolute truth and wants to relativize everything else.

A World of Contradictions. If relativism were true, then the world would be full of contradictory conditions. For if something is true for me but false for you, then opposite conditions exist. For if I say "There is milk in the refrigerator" and you say "there is not any milk in the refrigerator"—and we both are right, then there must both be and not be milk in the refrigerator at the same time and in the same sense. But that is impossible. So, if truth were relative, then an impossible would be actual.

In the religious realm it would mean that Billy Graham is telling the truth when he says, "God exists," and Madalyn Murray O'Hare is also right when she claims, "God does not exist." But these two statements cannot both be true. If one is true, then the other is false. And since they exhaust the only possibilities, one of them must be true.

No Wrongs and No Rights. If truth is relative, then no one is ever wrong—even when they are. As long as something is true to me, then I'm right even when I'm wrong. The drawback is that I could never learn anything either, because learning is moving from a false belief to a true one—that is, from an absolutely false belief to an absolutely true one. The truth is that absolutes are inescapable.

Answering Objections. Relativists have leveled several objections to the view of truth as absolute. The following are the most important:

No Absolute Knowledge. It is objected that truth cannot be absolute since we do not have an absolute knowledge of truths. Even most absolutists admit that most things are known only in terms of degrees of probability. How, then, can all truth be absolute?

We can be absolutely sure of some things. I am absolutely sure that I exist. In fact, my existence is undeniable. For I would have to exist in order to make the statement, "I do not exist." I am also absolutely sure that I cannot exist and not exist at the same time. And that there are no square circles. And that $3 + 2 = 5$.

There are many more things of which I am not absolutely certain. But even here the relativist is misguided in rejecting absolute truth simply because we lack absolute *evidence* that some things are true. The truth can be absolute no matter what our grounds for believing it. For example, if it is true that Sidney, Australia, is on the Pacific Ocean, then it is absolutely true no matter what my evidence or lack of evidence may be. An absolute truth is absolutely true in itself, no matter what evidence there is. Evidence, or the lack thereof, does not change a fact. And truth is what corresponds to the facts. The truth doesn't change just because we learn something more about it.

In-between Truths. Another objection is that many things are comparative—like relative sizes such as shorter and taller. As such they cannot be absolute truths, since they change depending on the object to which they relate. For example, some people are good compared to Hitler but evil as compared to Mother Teresa. Contrary to the claim of relativists, in-between things do not disprove absolutism. For the facts that "John is short in relation to an NBA (National Basketball Association) player," and "John is tall compared to a jockey" are absolutely true for all times and all people. John is in-between in size, and it depends on which one to whom he is compared whether he is shorter or taller. Nonetheless, it is absolutely true that John (being five feet ten inches) is short compared to most basketball players and tall compared to the majority of jockeys. The same thing is true of other in-between things, such as, warmer or colder, and better or worse.

No New Truth (or Progress). If truth never changes, then there can't be any new truth. This would mean that no progress is possible. But we do come to know new truths. That is what scientific discovery is all about. In response to this, "new truth" can be understood in two ways. It might mean "new to us," like a new discovery in science. But that is only a matter of us discovering an "old" truth. After all, the law of gravity was there long before Isaac Newton. Many truths have always been there, but we are just finding out about them. The other way we might understand "new truth" is that something new has come into existence that makes it possible to make a new statement about it that is only then true for the first time. That's no problem either. When January 1, 2020, arrives, a new truth will be born. Until that day it will not be true to say,

"This is January 1, 2020." But when that happens it will be true for all people and places forever more. So "old" truths don't change and neither do "new" truths when they come to pass. Once it is true, it is always true—for everyone.

Truth and Growth in Knowledge. It is also objected that knowledge of truth is not absolute, since we grow in truth. What is true today may be false tomorrow. The progress of science is proof that truth is constantly changing. This objection fails to note that it is not the truth that is changing but our understanding of it. When science truly progresses, it does not move from an old truth to a new truth, but from error to truth. When Copernicus argued that the earth moves around the sun and not the reverse, truth did not change. What changed was the scientific understanding about what moves around what.

Narrow Absolutes. Of course truth is narrow. There is only one answer for what is 4 + 4. It is not 1. It is not 2, 3, 4, 5, 6, 7, 9, 10 or any other number. It is 8 and only 8. That's narrow, but it is correct.

Non-Christians often claim that Christians are narrow-minded, because they claim that Christianity is true and all non-Christian systems are false. However, the same is true of non-Christians who claim that what they view as truth is true, and all opposing beliefs are false. That is equally narrow. The fact of the matter is that if C (Christianity) is true, then it follows that all non-C is false. Likewise, if H (say, Humanism) is true, then all non-H is false. Both views are equally narrow. That's the way truth is. Each truth claim excludes contradictory truth claims. Christianity is no more narrow than is any other set of beliefs, whether *atheism, *agnosticism, skepticism, or *pantheism.

Dogmatic Absolutes. The claim that those who believe in absolute truth are dogmatic misses the point. If all truth is absolute—true for all people, times, and places—everyone who claims anything is true is "dogmatic." Even the relativist who claims relativism is true is dogmatic. For the person who claims that relativism is absolutely true is particularly dogmatic. This person claims to own the only absolute truth that can be uttered, namely, that everything else is relative.

Something important is overlooked in this charge of dogmatism. There is a big difference between the pejorative charge that belief in absolute truth is dogmatic and the manner in which someone may hold to this belief. No doubt the manner with which many absolutists have held to and conveyed their beliefs has been less than humble. However, no agnostic would consider it a telling argument against agnosticism that some agnostics communicate their beliefs in a dogmatic manner.

Nonetheless, there is an important distinction to keep in mind: Truth is absolute, but our grasp of it is not. Just because there is absolute truth does not mean that our *understanding* of it is absolute. This fact in itself should cause the absolutists to temper convictions with humility. For while truth is absolute, our understanding of absolute truth is not absolute. As finite creatures, we grow in our understanding of truth.

Summary. Truth may be tested in many ways but it should be understood in only one way. There is one reality, to which statements or ideas must conform in order to be regarded as true. There may be many different ways to *defend* different truth claims, but there is really only one proper way to *define* truth, namely, as correspondence. The confusion between the nature of truth and the verification of truth is at the heart of the rejection of a correspondence view of truth.

Likewise, there is a difference between what truth *is* and what truth *does*. Truth is *correspondence*, but truth has certain *consequences*. Truth itself should not be confused with its results or with its application. The failure to make this distinction leads to wrong views of the nature of truth. Truth is that which corresponds to reality or to the state of affairs it purports to describe. And falsehood is what does not correspond.

Sources

Anselm, *Truth, Freedom, and Evil*
Aristotle. *Posterior Analytics*
Augustine, *Against the Academics*
A. Bloom, *The Closing of the American Mind*
N. L. Geisler, *Thomas Aquinas*, chap. 6
J. F. Harris, *Against Relativism*
C. S. Lewis, *The Abolition of Man*
Plato, *Protagoras*
———, *Theaetetus*
Thomas Aquinas, *On Truth*
D. Wells, *God in the Wastelands: No Place for Truth*

Turin, Shroud of. ***See*** **SHROUD OF TURIN.**

Uu

Uncertainty, Principle of. *See* INDETERMINACY, PRINCIPLE OF.

Undeniability, Principle of. *See* SELF-REFUTING STATEMENTS.

Universalism. Universalism is the belief that everyone eventually will be saved. It was first proposed by the unorthodox church Father, *Origen (ca. 185–ca. 254). Origen and universalism in general were condemned as unorthodox at the Fifth Ecumenical Council of Constantinople (A.D. 553). The theology of universalism should be distinguished from the Universalist Church, an extreme anticreedal movement born in colonial America whose rejection of historic Christianity extended far beyond the doctrine of universalism itself. This group was a force in the liberal theologies of nineteenth-century North America and continues to the present.

One of the most influential twentieth-century theologians to embrace universalism was Karl *Barth (1886–1968). Philosopher John *Hick is a contemporary proponent of the view (see Hick). A small number of otherwise evangelical theologians, such as Clark Pinnock and John Stott, have embraced forms of universalism and/or *annihilationism. Most liberal theologians and cults hold to some form of universalism or its cousin, annihilationism, the view that persons who cannot qualify for heaven simply go out of existence. The common principle throughout universalist and annihilationist theologies is that there is no eternal punishment.

Basis for Universalism. Universalists generally appeal to arguments from God's love in support of their positions. They cite several passages of Scripture to substantiate their views.

God's Omnibenevolence. Universalism is usually based on the notion that a God of love would never allow any of his creatures to perish. But, as C. S. *Lewis demonstrated (see, for example, his book, *The Great Divorce*), just the opposite is the case. For while God "so loved the world that he gave his only begotten Son" (John 3:16) and "does not desire that any should perish" (2 Peter 3:9), he does not force his love on anyone. Forced love is a self-contradictory concept (*see* FREE WILL). Jesus said, "O Jerusalem, Jerusalem, you who kill the prophets and stone those sent to you, how often I have longed to gather your children together, as a hen gathers her chicks under her wings, but you were not willing" (Matt. 23:37). Lewis noted that "There are only two kinds of people in the end: those who say to God, 'Thy will be done,' and those to whom God says, in the end. '*Thy* will be done'" (Lewis, *The Great Divorce*, 69).

Further, the Bible unmistakably teaches that there is an eternal *hell and that human beings will go into it (see, for example, Matt. 25:41; 2 Thess. 1:7–9; Rev. 20:11–15). Jesus had more to say about hell than he did about heaven. He warned, "Do not be afraid of those who kill the body but cannot kill the soul. Rather, be afraid of the One who can destroy both soul and body in hell" (Matt. 10:28). He added of those who reject him, "As the weeds are pulled up and burned in the fire, so it will be at the end of the age" (Matt. 13:40). In what is sometimes called his Mount Olivet Discourse, Jesus declared, "Then he will say to those on his left, 'Depart from me, you who are cursed, into the eternal fire prepared for the devil and his angels'" (Matt. 25:41). Elsewhere he stressed the horror of hell with the statement: "If your hand causes you to sin, cut it off. It is better for you to enter life maimed than with two hands to go into hell, where the fire never goes out" (Mark 9:43). One of his most vivid stories was of the rich man and a beggar named Lazarus. Since this story uses an actual name, most Bible teachers distinguish this from a parable and believe it refers to people who really lived. The description of hell speaks for itself:

> In hell, where he was in torment, he looked up and saw Abraham far away, with Lazarus by his side. So he called to him, "Father Abraham, have pity on me and send Lazarus to dip the tip of his finger in water and cool my

tongue, because I am in agony in this fire." But Abraham replied, "Son, remember that in your lifetime you received your good things, while Lazarus received bad things, but now he is comforted here and you are in agony. And besides all this, between us and you a great chasm has been fixed, so that those who want to go from here to you cannot, nor can anyone cross over from there to us." He answered, "Then I beg you, father, send Lazarus to my father's house, for I have five brothers. Let him warn them, so that they will not also come to this place of torment." Abraham replied, "They have Moses and the Prophets; let them listen to them." [Luke 16:23–31]

God's Omnipotence. Others have argued for universalism from God's omnipotence. Origen, declared: "For nothing is impossible to the Omnipotent, nor is anything incapable of restoration to its Creator" (*On First Principles*, 3.6.5). This, of course, implies that God desires by his goodness to do so, a position easily supported by many Scriptures (1 Tim. 2:4; 2 Peter 3:9). But if God wants to save all, and he can save all (i.e., he is all-powerful), then it seemed to follow for Origen that he will save all.

Two points should be made in response. First, God's attributes do not operate in contradiction to each other. God is internally consistent in his nature. This is why the Bible insists that "It is impossible for God to lie" (Heb. 6:18). This is also the reason that God's power must be exercised in accordance with his love. That is, God cannot do what is unloving. Second, as already demonstrated (above), it is unloving to force people to love him. Forced love is a contradiction, and God cannot do what is contradictory. Love cannot work coercively but only persuasively. And if some refuse to be persuaded, as the Bible says some will, then God will not coerce them into his kingdom.

Reformatory View of Justice. Origen argued that God's justice has reformation in view, not punishment (*see* Hell). He claimed, "The fury of God's vengeance is profitable for the purgation of souls. That the punishment, also, which is said to be applied by fire, is understood to be applied with the object of healing" (2.10.6). He added, "those who have been removed from their primal state of blessedness have not been removed irrecoverably, but have been placed under the rule of those holy and blessed orders which we have described; and by availing themselves of the aid of these, and being remoulded by salutary principles and discipline, they may recover themselves, and be restored to their condition of happiness" (1.6.2).

One cannot apply God's obvious desire that persons reform their lives to prove that all will be saved in the end. Nor can one assume, contrary to both Scripture and fact, that all persons choose to be reformed (Matt. 23:37; Rev. 20:10–15), or that no decision is final. In this life suicide is both one-way and final. Likewise, the Bible declares that each person "is destined to die once, and after that to face judgment" (Heb. 9:27). It is contrary to the proper concept of justice, which is penal, rather than reformatory. God's absolute justice and holiness demand that a penalty be paid for sin (see Levit. 17:11; Ezek. 18:20).

The reformatory view of justice also is contrary to the substitutionary death of Christ. "Christ died for sins once for all, the righteous for the unrighteous, to bring you to God" (1 Peter 3:18; cf., 1 Cor. 15:3; 2 Cor. 5:21). "God made him who had no sin to be sin for us, so that in him we might become the righteousness of God." Why did Christ have to pay the awful price for sin if sin is not an infinite crime and does not have to be punished?

God is indeed interested in reformation. That is what this life is all about. Those who refuse to accept what Christ did in the atonement cannot be reformed in this life. And then they must stand without the righteousness of Christ before an infinitely holy God who cannot abide in the presence of sin's corruption. Separation from God is the necessary punishment for those who cannot exist in God's presence and are rightly the objects of his anger. This is why God is so long-suffering with those who live. He does not wish that any should perish (2 Peter 3:9).

Origen offered an argument for universalism from God's wisdom:

> God, by the ineffable skill of his wisdom, transforming and restoring all things, in whatever manner they are made, to some useful aim, and to the common advantage of all, recalls those very creatures which differed so much from each other in mental conformation to one agreement of labour and purpose; so that, although they are under the influence of different motives, they nevertheless complete the fullness and perfection of one world, and the very variety of minds tends to one end of perfection. For it is . . . is one power which grasps and holds together all the diversity of the world, and leads the different movements towards one work, lest so immense an undertaking as that of the world should be dissolved by the dissensions of souls.

This again misses the point that God's wisdom does not act contrary to his love. And love cannot force anyone to do something.

The fact that God is infinitely wise (omniscient) allows him to know that not everyone will freely choose to serve him. The attempt to save people God knows will never accept him would be contrary to God's wisdom. Still, all are invited, even those God knows will reject him.

Many, with Origen, respond "that God, the Father of all things, in order to *ensure the salvation of all* his creatures through the ineffable plan of his word and wisdom, so arranged each of these, that every spirit, whether soul or rational existence, however called, should *not be compelled by force*, against the liberty of his own will, to any other course than that to which the motives of his own mind led him (lest by so doing the power of exercising free-will should seem to be taken away, which certainly would produce a change in the nature of the being itself)" (Origen, 2.1.2, emphasis added). But God cannot "ensure the salvation of all" without compelling them by force. As long as someone refuses to freely accept God's love, a loving God cannot ensure they will be saved.

Biblical Support for Universalism. A number of biblical texts have been used to support the claim of universalists. It should be noted at the start of this survey that the Bible does not contradict itself (*see* BIBLE, ALLEGED ERRORS IN). Texts that can be interpreted in more than one way must be understood in the light of those that cannot:

Psalm 110:1. David said and Christ repeated (Ps. 110:1; Matt. 22:44): "The LORD says to my Lord: 'Sit at my right hand until I make your enemies a footstool for your feet.'" The enemies, literally of the Christ, are here referred to as subjugated, not saved. They are called the Lord's "footstool"—hardly an appropriate description of saints who are joint heirs with Christ (Rom. 8:17; Eph. 1:3). In Psalm 110, David is speaking of the visitation of God's wrath on his enemies, not of blessings on his people.

Acts 3:21. Peter speaks of Jesus who "must remain in heaven until the time comes for God to restore everything, as he promised long ago through his holy prophets." This reference to the "restoration of all things" is taken by universalists to mean the restoration of all to God. However, the context does not support such a conclusion. Acts 3:20–21 does not even remotely hint that there will be a total salvation. Other passages totally refute such an idea. Jesus said the gates of hell would not prevail against the church (Matt. 16:18). He also promised his followers, "Surely I am with you always, to the very end of the age" (Matt. 28:20). Jesus could not be with his followers to the end of the age if the entire church had gone into complete apostasy soon after its founding. In Ephesians 3:21, the apostle Paul says, "To him be the glory in the church and in Christ Jesus to all generations forever and ever." How could God be glorified in the church throughout all ages if there was no church for many centuries? Ephesians 4:11–16 speaks of the church growing to spiritual maturity, not degeneracy.

What then does "the restoration of all things" mean? Peter is speaking to the Jews and refers to the "restoration of all things, which God has spoken by the mouth of all his holy prophets since the world began" (Acts 3:21). Here is the "covenant which God made with our [Jewish] fathers, saying to Abraham, 'And in your seed all the families of the earth shall be blessed'" (vs. 25). This Abrahamic covenant was unconditional and included the promises of possessing the land of Palestine "forever" (Gen. 13:15). Peter refers to the future fulfillment of this Abrahamic covenant, the restoration of all *things* to Israel. Paul affirms the same in Romans 11 (see vss. 23–26).

Romans 5:18–19. Paul wrote: "Consequently, just as the result of one trespass was condemnation for all men, so also the result of one act of righteousness was justification that brings life for all men. For just as through the disobedience of the one man the many were made sinners, so also through the obedience of the one man the many will be made righteous" (Rom. 5:18–19). From these verses universalists infer that Christ's death for all guarantees salvation for all. This conclusion, however, is contrary to the context and certainly to the message of Romans as a whole. This is explicitly in the context of being justified *by faith* (5:1), not automatically. In the preceding verse he declares that salvation comes to those "who receive . . . the gift of righteousness" (5:17).

The rest of Romans makes it unmistakably clear that not everyone will be saved. Romans 1–2 speaks of the heathen, who are "without excuse" (Rom. 1:19). Upon them the wrath of God falls (1:18). It declares that "as many as have sinned without the law will also perish without law " (Rom. 2:12). At the heart of his argument, Paul concludes that, apart from justification by faith, the world is "guilty before God" (Rom. 3:19). Speaking of the destiny of both saved and lost, Paul affirms that "the wages of sin is death, but the gift of God is eternal life in Christ Jesus our Lord" (Rom. 6:23). Likewise, Paul recognized that, in spite of his prayers, not all of his kinsmen would be saved (Romans 11) but would be "accursed" (Rom. 9:3). The whole point of Romans is to show that only those who believe will be justified (Rom. 1:17; cf. 3:21–26). Romans 9 leaves no doubt that only the elect not everyone will be saved. The rest are "vessels of wrath prepared for destruction" (Rom. 9:22).

Outside of Romans are numerous passages that speak of the eternal destiny of lost people, including the vivid passage at the end of Revelation when John said:

> Then I saw a great white throne and him who was seated on it. Earth and sky fled from his presence, and there was no place for them. And I saw the dead, great and small, standing before the throne, and books were opened. Another book was opened, which is the book of

life. The dead were judged according to what they had done as recorded in the books. The sea gave up the dead that were in it, and death and Hades gave up the dead that were in them, and each person was judged according to what he had done. Then death and Hades were thrown into the lake of fire. The lake of fire is the second death. If anyone's name was not found written in the book of life, he was thrown into the lake of fire. [Rev. 20:11–15]

2 Corinthians 5:19. Universalists also use 2 Corinthians 5:19, in which Paul told the Corinthians "that God was reconciling the world to himself in Christ, not counting men's sins against them. And he has committed to us the message of reconciliation." It is argued that "the world" was reconciled to God by Christ's work. Thus, all are saved on the basis of Jesus' work on the Cross.

The context clarifies the meaning of "the world." First, reconciliation is regarded as a process according to God's purpose, not an accomplished universal fact. God desires to save all (2 Peter 3:9), but all will not be saved (Matt. 7:13–14; Rev. 20:11–15). Second, the context indicates that actual reconciliation is only for those "in Christ," not for all (vs. 17). If all were already saved, then Paul's exhortation to be "ambassadors for Christ" and to "plead" with the world to "be reconciled to God" is senseless. They already are reconciled. All are made savable by Christ's reconciliation, but not all are thereby saved.

Ephesians 1:10. Also misconstrued by universalists is Paul's statement that in "the fullness of the times he might gather together in one all things in Christ, both which are in heaven and which are under the earth—in Him" (Eph. 1:10 NKJV). A careful examination of this text reveals that Paul is speaking only of believers. First, the context is those "he chose in Him before the foundation of the world" (1:4). Second, the phrase "in Christ" is never used in Scripture of anyone but believers. That unbelievers are excluded is further clarified by the omission of those "under the earth," which Paul elsewhere uses to speak of the lost (Phil 2:10).

Philippians 2:10–11. Paul predicts that one day "at the name of Jesus every knee should bow, of those in heaven, and of those on earth, and of those under the earth, and the every tongue should confess that Jesus Christ is Lord to the glory of God the Father" (Phil. 2:10–11). Here, the universalists insist, unbelievers are clearly in view in the phrase "under the earth."

No one denies that unbelievers will eventually confess Jesus is Lord, but that does not mean they will be saved. Even demons believe *that* Jesus is Lord, but they refuse to submit to him (cf. James 2:19). Believing *that* Jesus is Lord will not save anyone. Only belief *in* Christ (James 2:21–26) saves. "Those under the earth" (= the lost) in this text, make a confession from their mouth, but this acknowledgment will not be from the heart. For salvation, Paul insisted, one must both confess and "believe in your heart" (Rom. 10:9).

1 Corinthians 15:25–28. Of the eschaton or culmination of history, Paul affirmed in 1 Corinthians 15:25–28 that "then the end will come, when he hands over the kingdom to God the Father after he has destroyed all dominion, authority and power. He must reign, till he hath put all enemies under his feet. . . . And when all things shall be subdued unto him, then shall the Son also himself be subject unto him that put all things under him, that God may be all in all." On this text Origen wrote, "But if even that unreserved declaration of the apostle do not sufficiently inform us what is meant by 'enemies being placed under his feet,' listen to what he says in the following words, 'For all things must be put under Him.' What, then, is this 'putting under' by which all things must be made subject to Christ?" He added, "I am of opinion that it is this very subjection by which we also wish to be subject to Him, by which the apostles also were subject, and all the saints who have been followers of Christ" (Origen, 1.6.1)

This interpretation ignores both the content and context of this passage. Paul is not speaking of the salvation of the lost but, rather their condemnation. This is evident in such phrases as *destroy*, *put under his feet*, and *put an end to all rule*. This is the language of subjugation (see vss. 24, 27, 28). Those in view are spoken of as God's "enemies," not his friends or children. They are subjugated enemies, not saved friends. That God will be "all in all" (vs. 28) does not mean that all will be in God. He will reign supreme in all the universe after ending the rebellion against him. The phrase *all things* must be understood in its context. All things are made subject to Christ (vs. 28). But these "all things" are enemies (vs. 25). The phrase is used in parallel with *enemies* in successive verses (vss. 26–27).

Heaven is not a place where God overpowers the will of his enemies and forces them into the fold. So, there is not a hint in such passages of salvation for all unbelievers.

Conclusion. Not only is there a lack of support for universalism, but there are decisive arguments against it.

Universalism is contrary to the implications of being created in the image of God. God made humankind in his image (Gen. 1:27) which included freedom. For everyone to be saved, those who refuse to love God would be forced to love him against their will. Forced "freedom" is not freedom. A corollary to this is that universalism is contrary to God's love. Forced love is not love, but a kind of rape. No truly loving being forces himself on another.

Universalism is contrary to God's perfection and justice. God is absolutely holy. And as such he must separate himself from and punish sin. Hence, as long as there is someone living in sin and rebellion against God, God must punish them. The Bible identifies this place of separation and punishment as *hell (see Matthew 5, 10, 25).

Universalism is based on Scriptures wrenched out of context, and it ignores other clear passages.

Universalism is based on a kind of Freudian illusion. Sigmund Freud called any belief based on a mere wish to be an illusion. We do not *wish* anyone to suffer in hell forever, and this strong wish seems to be a primary impulse in the universalist thinking. But it is an illusion to believe that all wishes will be fulfilled.

Sources

K. Barth, *Church Dogmatics*

J. D. Bettis, "A Critique of the Doctrine of Universal Salvation," *RS* 6 (December 1970): 329–44

W. V. Crockett, "Will God Save Everyone in the End?" in W. V. Crockett and J. G. Sigountos, eds., *Through No Fault of Their Own?* The Fate of Those Who Have Never Heard

J. Danielou, *Origen*

J. Gerstner, *Jonathan Edwards on Heaven and Hell*

J. Hick, *Evil and the God of Love*

C. S. Lewis, *The Great Divorce*

———, *The Problem of Pain*

D. Moore, *The Battle for Hell*

Origen, *On First Principles*

R. A. Peterson, *The Fifth Ecumenical Council of Constantinople*

———, *Hell on Trial: The Case for Eternal Punishment*

B. Russell, *Why I Am Not a Christian*

J. Sanders, *No Other Name*, part 2

J. P. Sartre, *No Exit*

W. G. T. Shed, *The Doctrine of Endless Punishment*

J. L. Walls, *Hell: The Logic of Damnation*

Vv

Van Til, Cornelius. Cornelius Van Til (1895–1987) was born in Holland, emigrated to the United States as a child, and grew up on a farm in Indiana. He attended Calvin College and Princeton Seminary. After pastoring a Michigan church, he was professor of apologetics at Westminster Theological Seminary from its founding in 1929 till his retirement in 1972. Francis *Schaeffer was among students who adopted a form of presuppositionalism under his influence.

His views on apologetics are expressed in *The Defense of the Faith* (1955; rev. 1963); *The Protestant Doctrine of Scripture* (1967); *A Survey of Christian Epistemology* (1969); *A Christian Theory of Knowledge* (1969); *Introduction to Systematic Theology* (1969); *The Great Debate Today* (1971); *The Defense of Christianity and My Credo* (1971); *Common Grace and the Gospel* (1972); *Introduction to Systematic Theology* (1974); *Christian Apologetics* (1975); *Christian-Theistic Evidences* (1976); and two undated works, *Why I Believe in God,* which is Van Til's summary of his own view. Other significant writings include an introduction to an edition of B. B. Warfield's *The Inspiration and Authority of the Bible*, and an essay, "My Credo" in E. R. Geehan, ed., *Jerusalem and Athens* (1971).

Philosophy of Apologetics. In a succinct statement of his own views, Van Til divided his philosophy of apologetics into three major areas: "My problem with the 'traditional method,'" "my understanding of the relationship between Christian and non-Christian, philosophically speaking," and "my proposal for a consistently Christian methodology of apologetics."

"Traditional" Apologetics. Van Til found seven problems in classical apologetics:

1. It compromises God by maintaining that his existence is only "possible," albeit "highly probable," rather than ontologically and "rationally" necessary.
2. It compromises the counsel of God by not understanding it as the only all-inclusive, ultimate "cause" of whatsoever comes to pass.
3. It compromises the revelation of God in its necessity, its clarity, its sufficiency, and its authority.
4. It compromises human creation as the image-bearer of God by conceptualizing human creation and knowledge as independent of the Being and knowledge of God. Human beings need not "think God's thoughts after him."
5. It compromises humanity's covenantal relationship with God by not understanding Adam's representative action as absolutely determinative of the future.
6. It compromises the sinfulness resulting from the sin of Adam by not understanding ethical depravity as extending to the whole of life, even to thoughts and attitudes.
7. It compromises the grace of God by not understanding it as the necessary prerequisite for "renewal unto knowledge." On the traditional view men and women must renew themselves unto knowledge by the "right use of reason."

Christian and Non-Christian Together. Van Til makes four basic points about the relationship of faith and reason. Each reveals something about the nature of his apologetic approach.

1. Both have presuppositions about the nature of reality: (a) The Christian presupposes a triune God and his redemptive plan for the universe as set forth once for all in Scripture. (b) The non-Christian presupposes a dialectic between "chance" and "regularity," the former accounting for the origin of matter and life, the latter accounting for the current success of the scientific enterprise.

2. Neither Christian nor unbeliever can, as finite beings, use logic to say what reality *must* or *cannot* be. (a) The Christian attempts to understand the world through observation and logically ordering facts. This is done in self-conscious subjection to the plan of the self-attesting Christ of Scripture. (b) The non-Christian, while attempting to understand through observation, at-

tempts to use *logic to destroy the Christian position. Appealing to the *nonrationality* of "matter," the unbeliever says that the chance-character of "facts" witnesses conclusively against the Christian worldview. Then the non-Christian maintains that the Christian story cannot possibly be true. Each human being must be autonomous. "Logic" must legislate what is "possible" and possibility must exclude God.

3. Both claim that their position is "in accordance with the facts": (a) The Christian claims this on the basis of experience in the light of the revelation of the self-attesting Christ in Scripture. Both the uniformity and the diversity of facts have at their foundation the all-embracing plan of God. (b) The non-Christian claims this after interpreting the facts and personal experience in the light of human autonomy. The unbeliever rests upon the ultimate "givenness" of the world and the amenability of matter to mind. No fact can deny human autonomy or attest to a divine origin of the world and humanity.

4. Both claim that their position is "rational." (a) The Christian claims the faith position is self-consistent. The seemingly inexplicable can be explained through rational logic and the information available in Scripture. (b) The non-Christian may or may not claim that facts are totally self-consistent and in accord with the ultimate rationality of the cosmos. One who does claim total self-consistency will be crippled when it comes to explaining naturalistic "evolution." If rational beings and a rational world sprang from pure chance and ultimate irrationality, such an explanation is in fact no explanation. A basis in irrational chance destroys predication.

A Consistently Apologetic Method. Van Til's own positive view proposes:

1. that we use the same principle in apologetics that we use in theology—the self-attesting, self-explanatory Christ of Scripture.
2. that we no longer appeal to "common notions" on which Christian and non-Christian can agree. Their "common ground" is that each person and each person's world are what Scripture says they are.
3. that we appeal to human beings as God's image-bearer. To do so we set the non-Christian's rational autonomy against Christian dependence. Human knowledge depends on God's knowledge, as revealed in the person and by the Spirit of Christ.
4. that we claim, therefore, that Christianity alone is reasonable. It is wholly irrational to hold any other position than that of Christianity. Christianity alone does not slay reason on the altar of "chance."
5. that we argue, therefore, by "presupposition." The Christian, as did Tertullian, must contest the very principles of an opponent's position. The only "proof" of the Christian position is that, unless its truth is presupposed, there is no possibility of "proving" anything. The state of affairs proclaimed by Christianity is the necessary foundation for "proof" itself.
6. that we preach with the understanding that acceptance of the Christ of Scripture comes about only as the Holy Spirit uses inescapably clear evidence to open a fleeing sinner's eyes to see things as they truly are.
7. that we present the message and evidence for the Christian position as clearly as possible. Because a human being is what the Christian says he or she is, the non-Christian can understand intellectually the issues involved. To an extent, the Christian message tells what the unbeliever already knows but seeks to suppress. This reminder provides a fertile ground for the Holy Spirit. According to God's sovereign grace the Spirit may grant the non-Christian repentance and knowledge of him who is life eternal.

*Revelational Presuppositionalism. Rejection of *Classical Apologetics.* Van Til rejects classical apologetics, which he calls the "traditional" method. In its place he substitutes a presuppositional apologetics. He believes the classical apologetics of *Thomas Aquinas is based on human autonomy. "There is on this basis no genuine point of contact with the mind of the natural man at all. . . . The revelation of a self-sufficient God can have no meaning for a mind that thinks of itself as ultimately autonomous." The problem is "how it may be known that the God of reason and the God of faith are the same" (*In Defense of the Faith*, 73, 94, 127). He described the Thomistic method as "a position half way between that of Christianity and that of paganism." Theistic arguments are invalid and, at any rate, they do not lead to the "self-contained ontological trinity of Scripture." Thomistic apologetics reduces the Gospel through rationalism as to make it acceptable to the natural man" (*Great Debate Today*, 91).

He insisted that unless the God of the Bible is the foundation of human experience, experience operates in a void (*Common Grace and the Gospel*, 192). So Van Til begins with the Triune God and his self-revelation in Holy Scripture. Thus, his position has been called *revelational* presuppositionalism.

Van Til's Apologetic Method. The method of implication. Early in his career, Van Til called his apologetic a "method of implication" (*A Survey of Christian Epistemology*, 6–10; 201–2). John Frame said the phrase suggested to Van Til a combination inductive and deductive approach. The general has priority over the particular (*Cornelius Van Til*, 311).

Reasoning by presupposition. In his later writings Van Til typically calls his method "reasoning by presupposition" (ibid., 312). He asserted that "To argue by presupposition is to indicate what are the epistemological and metaphysical principles that underlie and control one's method." The issues cannot be settled by appealing to mutually-agreed-upon "facts" or "laws." The worldviews are too far apart for that. What must be searched out on both sides is a final reference-point that can make the facts and laws intelligible (*In Defense of the Faith*, 99, 100).

Van Til's reference point is so Scripture-dependent that it has been called *"revelational* presuppositionalism." He rejects the *rational* presuppositionalism of Gordon *Clark, believing that his stress on the law of noncontradiction is not subservient to God's sovereignty. Likewise, Van Til disagreed with Edward J. *Carnell's presuppositionalism, known as *systematic coherency*. Systematic coherency combines the law of noncontradiction, factual evidence, and existential adequacy as tests for truth.

Indirect method. Van Til described the method as "indirect" to distinguish it from "direct" classical evidential arguments. It was indirect because it showed the truth of Christianity by showing the contradiction in opposing views. An opponent's position is reduced to an absurdity. Frame adds that this suggests "a model like that of the indirect argument in mathematics. In that model, one proves a proposition by assuming the opposite" (*Cornelius Van Til*, 313–14).

External and internal method. Van Til's apologetic method is both external and internal. He argues:

> We should address the unbeliever always from our own presuppositional commitment. From that commitment, however, we may legitimately examine the unbeliever's presuppositions and tell him our evaluation of them, how they look from our point of view. . . . this criticism is "external" in the sense of being based on criteria outside the unbeliever's own system of thought. . . . But it can become "internal" in another sense, when we ask the unbeliever how, even from his own point of view, he is able to account for the intelligibility of the world. . . . Our criticism will never be purely internal, purely from the unbeliever's point of view; it will always be external in the sense that it is determined by the Christian point of view. Otherwise, we would be . . . drowning with the one we would rescue." [ibid., 322]

Transcendental. Those familiar with Immanuel *Kant understand a *transcendental argument. Van Til also affirmed that "the method of implication may also be called a *transcendental method*. . . . A truly transcendental argument takes any fact of experience which it wishes to investigate, and tries to determine what the presuppositions of such a fact must be, in order to make it what it is." The transcendental argument seeks a foundational epistemology for knowledge. Van Til observes that this always presupposes that a foundation does, in fact, exist (*Survey of Christian Epistemology*, 10, 11).

Robert Knudsen, in his essay "Progressive and Regressive Tendencies in Christian Apologetics" (in *Jerusalem and Athens*), noted that the transcendental method gained ascendancy after David *Hume undermined the traditional methodology. Greg Bahnsen defended the transcendental method in his essay "the Reformation of Christian Apologetics" (in North, 191–239). However, Van Til never really spelled out how his transcendental argument actually works. Nonetheless, he claimed that "the only argument for an absolute God that holds water is a transcendental argument" (*In Defense of the Faith*, 11; *see* SCHAEFFER, FRANCIS on his use of the transcendental argument).

Van Til said that both inductive and deductive arguments are bound to the universe. "In either case there is no more than an infinite regression." It is always possible to ask, "If God made the universe, who made God?" Yet unless there were an absolute God the very questions and doubts of the skeptic would have no meaning. At some point every epistemological base depends on the existence of God. The transcendental argument seeks to discover that presupposed foundation (*Survey of Christian Epistemology*, 11). Thus, transcendentalism and presuppositionalism are one. For, according to Van Til, it is transcendentally necessary to presuppose that a triune God (*see* TRINITY) revealed in Holy Scripture in order to make any sense of the world. Without this necessary presupposition, no thought or meaning is possible.

The reductio ad absurdum method. Frame recognized three elements in this method: First, it seeks to show that all intelligibility depends on, or presupposes, Christian theism. Second, it is indirect rather than direct, negative rather than positive, essentially a *reductio ad absurdum*. Third, each participant in the discussion must be able to put on the opposing position for the sake of argument to see how it works (*Cornelius Van Til*, 314–15). According to Frame, "The unbeliever supplies the premises of the indirect argument, the premises which the believer then reduces to absurdity" (ibid., 315). Once the unbeliever supplies the premise of the indirect argument, the believer shows that it entails the rational-irrationalist dialectic. The unbeliever's system inevitably applies purely abstract laws to irrational facts. Rational thought is impossible.

Two things happen in the use of the method: The Christian assumes the correctness of the opposing method, then runs it to its final implications to show that its "facts" are not facts and "laws" are not laws. The non-Christian is asked to assume the Christian position for argument's sake and is shown that only these "facts" and "laws" appear intelligible" (*In Defense of the Faith*, 100–101). It is pointed out that "the non-Christian himself refutes his own irrationalism, for despite his philosophy he continues to live as if the world were a rational place. Thus, the unbeliever's own mind is part of God's revelation, witnessing against his irrationalist defense" (*Cornelius Van Til*, 322).

Key Concepts. An understanding of Van Til's approach depends on the meaning of certain key concepts:

God's Sovereignty. Van Til is first and foremost a Reformed theologian. Apart from God's sovereign control of the universe and his revelation to us we would know absolutely nothing. Facts and laws are what they are because of God's plan. God's decree "is the final and exclusively determining power of whatsoever comes to pass." It is the source (*In Defense of the Faith*, 11; *Christian Apologetics*, 11; *Introduction to Systematic Theology*, 247).

Common Ground. Since all truth is God's and nothing makes sense apart from him, there is no common intellectual epistemological foundation to share with unbelievers. In place of that foundation we set the self-attesting, self-explanatory Christ of Scripture. We no longer appeal to common ground, but to the real common ground that every human being is an image-bearer who is doing business with God at some level.

Brute Facts. A "brute fact" is a fact that is meaningless because it is uninterpreted by God. It represents a universe of pure chance. Brute facts assume human autonomy and take their starting point outside God's sovereign revelation of himself. Van Til affirms that Christians should appeal to *God-interpreted* facts, but never to brute facts (Van Til, *Christian-Theist Evidences*, 51, 57; Frame, *Cornelius Van Til*, 180).

Because of his presuppositional starting point, it is sometimes wrongly assumed that Van Til does not believe in the validity of traditional *historical apologetics (*see* HISTORICAL APOLOGETICS). He says, "I would engage in historical apologetics." Historical investigation sooner or later will vindicate the truth of the Christian position. "But I would not talk endlessly about the facts and more facts without ever challenging the unbeliever's philosophy of fact. A really fruitful historical apologetic argues that every fact *is* and *must be* such as proves the truth of the truth of the Christian position" (*Christian Theory of Knowledge*, 293). All facts must be interpreted within the framework of the presupposed Christian worldview revealed in the Bible or they are tainted by their rejection of God's revelation.

Human Depravity. As a result of Adam's sin the human race is radically depraved and so sees everything with a twisted perspective, a "jaundiced eye." Being "dead" in sins, fallen human beings are unable to accurately "know" anything in its context of reality until the Holy Spirit opens their eyes in the process of salvation. With John *Calvin, Van Til balances a recognition of God's common grace to the unbeliever with a view that sin vitiates the unbeliever's mind. Even the most learned non-Christian scientist cannot truly understand reality (*In Defense of the Faith*, chap. 15). "The natural man cannot will to do God's will. He cannot even know what is good" (ibid., 54). The *noetic effects of sin are total and devastating.

Analogy and Paradox. Even a regenerate mind only knows God's knowledge by analogy. At no point is our knowledge univocal with God's. Whenever the creature attempts to understand divine reality it runs into "paradoxes" or apparent contradictions. Van Til argues that "since God is not fully comprehensible to us we are bound to come into what seems to be contradiction in all our knowledge. Our knowledge is analogical and therefore must be paradoxical" (*In Defense of the Faith*, 61). God is so sovereignly transcendent above human understanding that it would be blasphemous for us to suppose that we can know the way God knows. Even our supernaturally enlightened knowledge is only analogous to God's. This view of the mind constantly keeps two ideas to the front, the distinction between Creator and creature and (2) the sovereignty of Creator over creature (*Cornelius Van Til*, 89). For these reasons our knowledge must be analogical. Our knowledge is derived from the original knowledge in God's thinking. The human must attempt to think God's thoughts after him. "But this means that he must, in seeking to form his own system, constantly be subject to the authority of God's system *to the extent* that this is revealed to him" (*Christian Theory of Knowledge*, 16).

Evaluation. *Positive Contributions.* Few apologists have more forthrightly and courageously stressed the sovereignty of God than has Van Til. Unless God sovereignly wills to reveal himself, we would be in complete ignorance. Revelation, whether general or special, is the source of all truth.

While some apologetic systems give begrudging recognition to man's finitude, few give explicit acknowledgment to human depravity and the inability associated with depravity. Sin does have an effect on the whole person, including the mind. Van Til saw this as clearly as has any apologist.

Van Til defended the formal laws of *logic in principle and practice. He believed the laws of logic were the same for both the Creator and creatures. However, formally because of sin they are not understood or applied in the same way. He was not an irrationalist.

Van Til offered a strong argument for Christianity. He regarded it as "proof" and chided other views for weakening their defense to mere "probable" arguments.

It seems proper to acknowledge that there is validity to a transcendental approach. What is often described as a self-defeating argument is strikingly similar to Van Til's approach. There are certain rationally necessary preconditions for meaning, and they do, as Van Til argued, demand that we posit the existence of a theistic God.

Van Til believed in historical evidence, and even devoted a book, *Christian-Theist Evidences*, to it. Unlike fellow Reformed apologist (but personal antagonist), Gordon Clark, Van Til was not an empirical skeptic. He believed in the validity of historic evidence for Christianity. But only as understood from the presupposition of biblical revelation.

Also, unlike Clark, Van Til correctly saw that our knowledge of God is only analogous (*see* ANALOGY, PRINCIPLE OF). To believe otherwise is presumptuous, if not blasphemous. For finite beings can know only in a finite way. To affirm that they know infinitely, as does God, is to deify our knowledge.

Often overlooked by nonpresuppositionalists is the practical value of a presuppositional approach. Non-Christians do implicitly (and even unconsciously) presuppose the basic principles of a theistic worldview in order to make sense out of the world. Pointing this out debunks their world view and invites them to consider the positive value of the Christian worldview. No doubt Schaeffer's effectiveness in doing this is a result of his study under Van Til.

Negatives in Van Til's Apologetics. Some criticisms of Van Til seem to be based on misunderstanding, but others appear to be valid.

Even staunch defenders such as John Frame, while defending the general validity of Van Til's method, admit that he goes too far in demanding that all apologetic argument fit the one pattern (*Cornelius Van Til*, 315). Frame correctly points out that one may need more traditional arguments to make Van Til's overall argument work. "To show that a non-Christian view of motion and rest is unintelligible, we may find it necessary to use a theistic proof from motion like that of Aquinas. We would argue that if motion is to be intelligibly explained, God must exist" (ibid., 318).

Proving Van Til's conclusion, writes Frame, requires a complex argument to show that intelligible communication presupposes biblical theism. "A Van Tillian apologist would have to go into some detail in showing that intelligibility requires an equal ultimacy of one and many, and that such equal ultimacy in turn presupposes the ontological Trinity. . . . I believe that Van Til's conclusion is better described as a *goal* of apologetics. . . . It is unrealistic to expect that all of Christian theism can be established in a single encounter, let alone in a single argument of syllogism" (ibid.).

Van Til wrongly assumes his view is a purely indirect (negative) approach. There is no clear demarcation between indirect and direct arguments. Most arguments can be put in either form. Frame summarizes Van Til's apologetic:

1. If God does not exist, the world is unintelligible.
2. God does not exist.
3. Therefore, the world is unintelligible (ibid., 318).

Since it is agreed that the world is intelligible, then God must exist. However, Frame points out that the same argument can be stated in a positive form:

1. If the world is intelligible, God exists.
2. The world is intelligible.
3. Therefore, God exists (ibid.).

Van Til's protests to the contrary, he cannot avoid giving a positive apologetic argument. This being the case, much of Van Til's steam against classical apologetics evaporates.

Van Til misunderstands the traditional method of apologetics, so wrongly criticizes it for views very similar to his own. Frame says he questions whether transcendental reasoning is so very different from traditional reasoning, especially since traditional arguments may be needed to flesh out this approach (ibid., 45). Frame is insightful in noting that revelational presuppositionalism is strikingly similar to Thomistic approaches. Aquinas would agree with Van Til:

1. that in the realm of being (metaphysics), logic is dependent on God and not God on logic (*Summa Contra Gentiles*, 1.7; 3.47; 1a. 105, 3).
2. that the existence of God is ontologically necessary (ibid., 1a. 2, 3).
3. that without God nothing could be either known or proven true (ibid., 1a. 16, 1–8; 1a2ae. 109, 1).
4. that the basis for Christian truth is neither reason nor experience but the authority of God expressed in Scripture (*On Truth*, 14.8–9; *Summa Contra Gentiles*, 2a2ae. 2, 10; *On the Trinity*, 2.1, ad).
5. that depraved natural humanity willfully represses the revelation of God in Nature (*Summa Contra Gentiles*, 1a2ae. 77, 4: 83, 3; 84, 2; cf. 1a2ae. 109, 1–10).

Van Til complains that traditional apologetic compromises certainty about God. He seeks absolutely certain proof for Christian theism (*In Defense of the Faith*, 103, 104). Yet "Van Til himself admits that our apologetic *argument* may not be adequate to establish that certain conclusion," writes Frame. "If the argument is never stated adequately enough to justify the certainty of its conclusions, then on what basis may the apologists claim certainty for his argument?" (*Cornelius Van Til*, 277). Van Til overstates the case when he appears to insist that every argument should be certain (*see* CERTAINTY/CERTITUDE). The evidence is no less cogent in an argument for high probability (ibid., 279).

Van Til was no Thomist in disguise, but he knew less about Aquinas and was far closer to Thomist thought than he realized. The basic difference between Van Til and Aquinas is that, while they both agree *ontologically* that all truth depends on God, Van Til fails to fully appreciate that finite man must ask *epistemologically* how we knows this. In this he confuses the order of *being* and the order of *knowing*.

Either there is a rational basis for knowing or there is not. But one cannot beg the question and merely presuppose the theistic God. Presuppositions cannot be arbitrary. If we argue, as Van Til implied that we should, that Christian theism is a rationally necessary position, it is difficult to see on what rational grounds one could criticize Aquinas for providing rational support for it. How does Van Til know the Christian position is true? If Van Til answered, as he seems to in his writings, "Because it is the only truly rational view," perhaps Aquinas would reply, "That is what I believe. Welcome, dear brother, to the bimillennial club of rational theists."

Van Til goes further than most Reformed theologians, who themselves take a stronger stance than other Protestant theologies, regarding the *noetic effects of radical depravity. Even some of Van Til's strongest defenders admit an overstatement in his formulation. Speaking of Van Til's assertion that "all unbeliever's interpretive activity results in false conclusions," Frame responds that by implication Van Til denies common grace itself (*Cornelius Van Til*, 194). He adds, "the extreme antithetical formulations [of Van Til] are inadequate without considerable qualification." This understanding asserts that the unbeliever literally never makes a correct statement. Even the answer to a mathematical problem is incorrect in that it represents a false view of how the universe works mathematically. Frame finds it simplistic to hold that the noetic effects of sin amount to a propositional falsification of the unbeliever's every utterance (ibid., 211).

Van Til also suggests that human depravity shows itself as much or more in the discrete statements the unbeliever makes, than in life direction. And there is a failure to convey that the unbeliever's very denial of truth in some respects affirms truth (ibid., 207).

Indeed, Van Til himself offers statements inconsistent with his own antithesis between the knowledge of believers and unbelievers. He urges "that we present the message and evidence for the Christian position as clearly as possible, knowing that because man is what the Christian says he is, the non-Christian will be able to understand in an intellectual sense the issues involved" ("My Credo"). Van Til even says of unbelievers: "He has within himself the knowledge of God by virtue of his creation in the image of God." But Van Til hastens to say in the very next sentence: "But this idea of God is suppressed by his false principle, the principle of autonomy" (*In Defense of the Faith*, 170). This principle is the "jaundiced eye" by which all knowing is distorted and false. But how can he understand the issues even in an intellectual sense if there is no common facts, ground, or knowledge of any kind—if he sees all with a jaundiced eye?

Van Til saw this tension in his own view. He speaks of it as a "difficult point." "We cannot give any wholly satisfactory account of the situation as it actually obtains" (*Introduction to Systematic Theology*, 15). If fallen human beings really see everything with a "jaundiced eye," so that they cannot even understand the truth of general revelation or of the gospel, they are not morally accountable. But Scriptures says they are "without excuse" (Rom. 1:19–20; 2:12–15). Indeed, Adam and Eve were "dead in trespasses and sin" (cf. Eph. 2:1) the instant they took of the forbidden fruit (Gen. 3:6; Rom. 5:12). Yet they heard and understood God when he spoke (Gen. 3:9–19).

A common mistake of Reformed presuppositionalism is to equate the figure of speech *dead* with the concept *annihilated*, a mistake which, fortunately, they do not make when speaking of the "second death" (Rev. 20:14). Death in Scripture is better understood in terms of separation, not annihilation. The prophet said, "your sins have separated you from your God" (Isa. 59:2 KJV). Indeed, "dead" is not the only figure of speech used in the Bible to describe fallen humankind. Sickness, blindness, pollution, and lameness are also used. But none of these imply a person totally unable to understand God's revelation. Many nonpresuppositional Reformed theologians, among whom are Jonathan *Edwards, B. B. *Warfield, John Gerstner, and R. C. Sproul, believe just as firmly in radical depravity without accepting this skewed view of the noetic effects of sin. Depravity can be understood as an inability to initiate or attain salvation without the grace of God.

In this same connection, Reformed presuppositionalists often misinterpret 1 Corinthians 2:14 to mean that unbelievers cannot even understand God's truth before they are regenerated. Besides the obvious difficulty that they would have to be saved before they believe (just the opposite of what the Bible says in such texts as John 3:16, 36; Acts 16:31, and Rom. 5:1, this misreads the passage. Nor does it help to set up an order of events in salvation to claim the person being saved is regenerated before being justified, since one is placed in the kingdom of God by regeneration (John 3:3; Titus 5:5). The Greek word for "receive" (*dekomai*) means "to welcome." It does not mean they do not understand. They clearly *perceive* them, but do not willingly *receive* (Rom. 1:19–20). As a consequence, they do not know them by experience. A failure to understand these truths leads to a misunderstanding of the effects of sin on the unregenerate mind.

It is supposed by Van Til that a transcendental argument avoids the effects of depravity to which the traditional apologetic arguments are subject. But why should not sin lead the unbeliever to repress the force of a *transcendental argument as much as any evidence (*Cornelius Van Til*, 200)? Here the transcendental approach loses a touted advantage over classical apologetics.

This same point applies to Van Til's rejection of a content-filled general *revelation, on which traditional theistic arguments are based. It is often alleged that the effects of sin on general revelation make a supernatural revelation necessary. But sin has equally vitiating effects on supernatural revelation as well, as is evidenced by all the Christian denominations, sects, and cults who claim the same supernatural revelation but interpret it in radically different ways. Thus, presupposing a starting point in Holy Scripture does not in itself offer any advantage over beginning in general revelation, as classical apologetics do. The noetic effects of sin do not vanish simply because one turns his head from nature to the Bible.

Van Til's view of the Trinity involved two apparently opposing propositions: God is one person; God is three persons. He never clearly differentiates between the two senses of the term *person*. Van Til's doctrine of the Trinity "begins with an affirmation or the ancient creeds and the Reformed confessions" (*Cornelius Van Til*, 63). However, it goes on to say that "We therefore claim that we have not asserted unity and trinity of exactly the same thing. Yet this is not the whole truth of the matter. We do assert that God, that is, the whole Godhead is one person" (*Introduction to Systematic Theology*, 229). So, "God is not simply a unity of persons; he is *a* person" (*Cornelius Van Til*, 65).

This is a theological move that no orthodox creed, confession, or major church Father ever took before. Gordon Clark's disciple, John Robbins, went so far as to call it "a radical new heresy" (Robbins, 20). The more common objection, however, is that it violates the law of noncontradiction. Defenders point out that Van Til never calls the doctrine of the Trinity "contradictory," but rather finds it "apparently contradictory" (*Common Grace and the Gospel*, 9). Nor does he deny the traditional view that God is one in essence and three in person; he says it "is not the whole truth of the matter." He tries to supplement the traditional doctrine, not replace it (*Cornelius Van Til*, 67). It still seems a bit presumptuous to hold that he discovered what nineteen centuries of theologians, creeds and councils had failed to see. The question is not whether Van Til affirms the orthodox formula that God is one is essence and three in persons (with a distinct difference between *person* and *essence*). The controversy is that he also affirms God to be both three persons and yet also only one person (without offering a difference between *person* and *persons*).

His defenders claim that Clark and Robbins do not answer Van Til's argument. "He is one 'being,' not three; the three partake of one 'essence.' Now the question becomes, is this one being personal or impersonal?" Van Til believed the historic formulation made the Father, Son, and Spirit, individuals, but the divine essence, God, could only be regarded as an abstraction. This model could only be inadequate, for God is not an abstraction (ibid., 68).

However, the argument offered is a false dilemma. God is not either personal (in a singular sense) or impersonal. He is tripersonal. Hence, it is not necessary to conclude that the essence of God is impersonal because there are three persons in it. Being tripersonal is being personal. Frame asks the appropriate question: "How, then, do we relate the 'one person' to the 'three persons'? Van Til asserts that 'this is a mystery that is beyond our comprehension.'" Van Til does not say the two assertions are contradictory, but he does not appear to leave any options to contradiction.

The heart of Frame's defense is that something can be both A and not-A if the two A's have different senses. "The traditional language, 'one in essence, three in person' (which, again, Van Til does not reject) brings out more clearly, of course, that the oneness and the threeness are in different respects. But the formulation 'one person and three persons' does not deny that difference of respect" (ibid., 69).

This leads to Frame's last connected point. Obviously, there is a difference between the sense of *person* as applied to the oneness of God and the sense of *persons* as applied to the three members of the Trinity. For one thing, the Father is the begetter, the Son is begotten, and the Spirit is the one who proceeds from both Father and Son. The Godhead as a unity is not any of those three roles.

> Neither Van Til nor I would claim to be able to state, precisely and exhaustively, the differences between God's essence and the individual persons of the Godhead. Doubtless the Clarkite critics of Van Til will find this a damaging admission, for they insist that all theological statements be perfectly precise. Never mind that Scripture itself often fails to be precise about the mysteries of the faith. But the creedal tradition, too, fails to give a "precise" account of the relations between God's "essence" and his "persons." [ibid., 71]

Frame at this point argues, regarding the confessions, which sort out the biblical conception of the Trinity, that "*ousia* and *hypostasis* can be interchangeable. They can mean one substance and three substances."

While Van Til is willing to admit that he cannot really specify any difference in meaning between the two usages of the term "person," yet he criticizes non-Christian views for their contradictions. He says one view "will not lead to greater knowledge, but only to skepticism about the very possibility of truth" (ibid. 77). That very thing could be said of Van Til's view.

Van Til does not overlook the fact that he has not provided a real difference in the definition of the term "person" as used of "one person" and "three persons." He admits that "We may not always be able to show how two concepts can logically coexist" (*Cornelius Van Til,* 71). But unless a difference can be shown, Van Til has not avoided the charge of contradiction. For one cannot have both three and only one of the same subject (person).

Van Til denies "that we can prove to men that we are not asserting anything that they ought to consider irrational, inasmuch as we say that God is one in essence and three in persons." But if we cannot do this, what grounds do we have for objecting when unbelievers cannot do the same for their view? Indeed, the whole transcendental method depends on being able to show that the unbeliever's view is reducible to the logically contradictory.

Van Til claims: "I do not maintain that Christians operate according to new laws of thought any more than that they have new eyes or noses" (*In Defense of the Faith,* 296). This claim notwithstanding, Van Til's "laws of thought" are not really the same for believers. There is only a formal identity. There is no real point of contact that is the same for God and humanity. But this leads to skepticism about God, since there is no point of actual identity between our knowledge and his. It is transcendentally necessary to affirm such a content-filled point of identity.

Granting that a transcendental argument is valid, it does not follow that Van Til's form of it is valid. Certainly, as Van Til argues, it is necessary to posit a God to make sense out of the world. However, he has not shown that it is necessary to postulate a triune God. This is true whether or not one accepts his argument that only the Trinity solves the problem of the one and many. Even granting for the sake of argument that there must be more than one person in the Godhead if the world is to make sense, this does not mandate that there are three persons. This they simply believe from Scripture. The same is true of other aspects of Christianity, such as the plan of salvation. Nowhere does Van Til demonstrate this is a transcendentally necessary precondition for making sense out of our world. Thus, there are fideistic elements in Van Til's form of presuppositionalism. It is interesting to note that even Van Til's defenders admit: "I believe that much of Van Til's presuppositionalism should be understood as an appeal to the heart rather than as a straightforward apologetic method" (Frame, *Cornelius Van Til,* 320).

Sources

G. Bahnsen, *By This Standard*

J. DeBoer, et al., "Professor Van Til's Apologetics," in *The Calvin Forum* (August–September, December 1953; March–April 1955)

J. Frame, *Cornelius Van Til: An Analysis of His Thought*

———, "The Problem of Theological Paradox," in G. North, ed., *Foundations of Christian Scholarship*

N. L. Geisler, *Christian Apologetics*

S. Hackett, *The Resurrection of Theism*

F. Howe, *Challenge and Response*

R. Knudsen, "Progressive and Regressive Tendencies in Christian Apologetics," in E. R. Geehan, *Jerusalem and Athens*

D. E. Kucharsky "At the Beginning, God: An Interview with Cornelius Van Til," *Christianity Today* (30 December 1977)

G. Lewis, *Testing Christianity's Truth Claims*

S. Oliphint, *The Consistency of Van Til's Methodology*

J. Robbins, *Cornelius Van Til: The Man and the Myth*

N. Stonehouse, ed. *Nature and Scripture*

Thomas Aquinas, *Summa Contra Gentiles*

———, *On the Trinity*

———, *On Truth*

C. Van Til, *A Survey of Christian Epistemology*

———, *Christian Apologetics*

———, *Christian Theory of Knowledge*

———, *Christian-Theist Evidences*

———, *Common Grace and the Gospel*

———, *In Defense of the Faith*

———, interview, in *Christianity Today* (3 December 1977)

———, Introduction, in B. B. Warfield, *The Inspiration and Authority of the Bible*

———, *Introduction to Systematic Theology*

———, "My Credo," in *Jerusalem and Athens*

———, *The Great Debate Today*

———, *The Inspiration and Authority of the Bible*

White, William. *Van Til, Defender of the Faith: An Authorized Biography*

Vedanta. *See* HINDUISM, VEDANTA.

Verifiability, Principle of. *See* AYER, A. J.

Verification, Kinds of. *Eschatology* (Gk. *eschatos,* "last things") deals with what will happen in the end. *Verification* has to do with how to test the meaning or truth of a claim. Out of the school of *logical positivism grew the verification principle. Such proponents as A. J. *Ayer, following David *Hume, originally claimed that for a statement to be meaningful it had to be either true by definition or else empirically verifiable through one or more of the senses. This proved too narrow, since on this ground the principle of empirical verifiability was not itself empirically verifiable. It too was meaningless.

In the wake of the death of strict verifiability grew a broadening of the principle to include other kinds of verification—experiential, historical, and eschatological. Most philosophers agreed that there had to be specific conditions under which one could know if a statement was meaningful or true. Antony *Flew, following John Wisdom's "invisible gardener" parable, argued that, unless there are criteria by which one could know if something is false, one cannot know it is true. Unless one can specify some condition(s) by which a claim could be falsified, there is no way to verify it either. Something has to be able to count against a proposition if evidence is to count for it. This means that, unless a theist can specify conditions under which we could know that God does not exist, there is no ground on which to claim that he does exist.

Types of Verification. Attempts to meet the challenge of verification of a truth claim fall into three categories, past, present, and future. Those that offer criteria for the present can be divided into *theistic proofs* and *experiential tests*.

Historical. Among Christian apologists, John W. Montgomery and Gary Habermas argue that the Christian truth claims can be verified from history by way of the resurrection of Christ (*see* RESURRECTION, EVIDENCE FOR). This view is called historical apologetics or historical verification.

Present Verification. Those who seek some sort of verification in the present fall into the broad categories of rational and experiential. The former offer traditional theistic proofs as verification. Traditional theists note that this is precisely what arguments for and against God's existence do (*see* GOD, EVIDENCE FOR). If one could offer a disproof of God, then they could falsify the claim of theism (*see* GOD, ALLEGED DISPROOFS OF). Likewise, a proof for God can verify his existence. Anything short of a full proof still tends to verify or falsify.

Experiential tests can be special or general. The special ones are often called mystical and deal with unique religious experiences. The latter deal with experiences available to all. Some apologists offer nonmystical experiential tests for the truthfulness of religious statements. Ian Ramsey spoke of the empirical fit of statements that evoke an experience of God (see Ramsey). Friedrich *Schleiermacher spoke of a feeling of absolute dependence. Paul Tillich's sense of ultimate commitment fits this category. Some have developed an argument from religious experience as a test for their claims about God. Elton *Trueblood is an evangelical who has tried this.

Eschatological Tests. Those coming from the empirical traditions tried other kinds of verification-falsification. John *Hick offered the principle of eschatological verification (Hick, 252–74). Claims for immortality can be verified if, for example, we consciously observe our own funerals. We can know God exists after death if we have an experience of transcendent rapture and bliss that brings ultimate fulfillment.

Evaluation. Since other forms of verification are discussed as noted above, eschatological verification will be treated here. On the positive side, future verification does seem to meet the minimal criteria for meaning and truth. It does provide specific conditions under which we could know if certain religious claims are true.

On the other hand, the knowledge will be too late to do anything with it. Atheists (*see* ATHEISM) bank on the nonexistence of God and hell. If the atheist wakes up after death to find that he or she was in error on both counts it will be too late. That was the point of Pascal's Wager (*see* PASCAL, BLAISE). Even for the theist it could be too late. We want to know *now* whether it is worth sacrificing all for God, and which God is the true one. Why suffer for Christ, even to the point of death without evidence that Christianity is true (cf. 2 Cor. 11:22–28; 2 Tim. 3:12)? It might be deemed better to avoid all the misery and have a fun-filled life now.

Sources

A. J. Ayer, *Language, Truth and Logic*
A. Flew, *New Essays in Philosophical Theology*
G. R. Habermas, *The Resurrection of Jesus: An Apologetic*
J. Hick, *The Existence of God*
J. W. Montgomery, *The Shape of the Past*
———, *Christianity and History*
I. Ramsey, *Religious Language*
E. Trueblood, *Philosophy of Religion*

Vestigial Organs. ***See*** **EVOLUTION, BIOLOGICAL.**

Virgin Birth in Isaiah 7:14. ***See*** **VIRGIN BIRTH OF CHRIST.**

Virgin Birth of Christ. The virgin birth of Christ is the perennial target of naturalistic Bible critics, who tend to regard it as the result of pagan influence on Christian writers of the second century. These Christians developed the myth in an emulation of stories from Greek mythology (*see* MIRACLES, MYTH AND; MYTHOLOGY AND THE NEW TESTAMENT). One reason for the vehemence of these pronouncements is that, if true, the virgin birth establishes beyond question the life of Jesus as a supernatural intervention of God. If antisupernaturalists concede at this point, they have no case left.

Evidence for the Virgin Birth. Credibility of Miracle. At the root of the rejection of the virgin birth of Christ is the rejection of miracles (*see* MIRACLE; MIRACLES, ARGUMENTS AGAINST; MIRACLES IN THE BIBLE). A virgin birth is a miracle. If a theistic God exists, and there is evidence that he does (*see* COSMOLOGICAL ARGUMENT; MIRACLES, APOLOGETIC VALUE OF), then miracles are automatically possible. For if there is a God who can act, then there can be acts of God. Indeed, there is every reason to believe that miracles have occurred from the instant of the founding of the universe (*see* BIG BANG; EVOLUTION, COSMIC). Hence, the record of Jesus' virgin birth cannot be ruled as mythological in advance of looking at the evidence.

Anticipation of the Virgin Birth. Genesis 3:15. Long before the New Testament recorded the virgin birth, the Old Testament anticipated it. In fact, the earliest messianic prediction in the Bible (*see* PROPHECY, AS PROOF OF THE BIBLE) implies the virgin birth. Speaking to the Tempter (Serpent), "God said 'And I will put enmity between you and the woman, and between your offspring and hers; he will crush your head, and you will strike his heel.'" (Gen. 3:15).

That the coming Redeemer was to be the "offspring" or "seed" of the woman is important in a patriarchal culture. Why of a woman? Normally, descendants were traced through their father (cf. Gen. 5, 11). Even the official genealogy of the Messiah in Matthew 1 is traced through Jesus' legal father Joseph. In the unique term, *seed of the woman*, there is implied that the messiah would come by a woman but not a natural father.

Jeremiah 22 (cf. 2 Samuel 7). Another possible intimation of the virgin birth in the Old Testament is found in the curse placed on Jeconiah which said: "Record this man as if childless, a man who will not prosper in his lifetime, for none of his offspring will prosper, none will sit on the throne of David or rule any more in Judah" (Jer. 22:30). The problem with this prediction is that Jesus was the descendant of the throne of David through Jeconiah (cf. Matt. 1:12).

However, since Joseph was only Jesus' *legal* father (by virtue of being engaged to Mary when she became pregnant), Jesus did not inherit the curse on Jeconiah's *actual* descendants. And since Jesus was the actual son of David through Mary according to Luke's matriarchal genealogy (Luke 3), he fulfilled the conditions of coming "from the loins of David" (2 Sam. 7:12–16) without losing legal rights to the throne of David by falling under the curse on Jeconiah. Thus, the virgin birth is implied in the consistent understanding of these Old Testament passages.

Isaiah 7:14. Both the New Testament (Matt. 1:23) and many Christian apologists use Isaiah 7:14 as a predictive prophecy to prove the Bible (*see* PROPHECY, AS PROOF OF THE BIBLE) makes specific supernatural predictions centuries in advance. However, critics (*see* BIBLE CRITICISM), following the interpretation of many Bible scholars, say verse 16 refers to the birth of Isaiah's own child shortly before the fall of Samaria in 722 B.C. If so, this is not a prophecy about the virgin birth of Jesus and, it has no apologetic value.

Of the three interpretations of Isaiah 7:14, only one is incompatible with a supernatural predictive understanding in reference to Christ's birth. That is that this prophecy referred only to Isaiah's day and was fulfilled in the natural birth of Maher-Shalal-Hash-Baz (Isa. 8:3). Of the other two possibilities, the prophecy could have had a double fulfillment—a preliminary one in Isaiah's child and the final one in Christ's birth. Or this prophecy refers only to the supernatural birth of Christ (Matt. 1:23).

Single Reference to a Natural Birth. Liberal scholars and some conservatives view Isaiah 7:14 as having reference only to the natural conception and birth of the son of the prophetess. They argue that the Hebrew *'almâ*, sometimes translated "virgin" (KJV, ASV, NIV), refers to a young woman, whether married or unmarried, and should be translated "young maiden" (RSV). If the prophet had intended someone who was a virgin, he would have used *bethulah* (cf. Gen. 24:16; Levit. 21:3; Judg. 21:12). Further, the context reveals that the prophecy had a near-view fulfillment. Verse 16 declares that "before the boy knows enough to reject the wrong and choose the right, the land of the two kings you dread will be laid waste" (Isa. 7:16). This was literally fulfilled in the invasion of the Assyrian Tiglath Pileser.

Even in the broader context, only the birth of Maher-Shalal-Hash-Baz fit the prophecy. Isaiah 8:3 reads: "Then I went to the prophetess, and she conceived and gave birth to a son. And the LORD said to me, 'Name him Maher-Shalal-Hash-Baz'" (Isa. 8:3). The "sign" was promised to Ahaz (7:10) and would have made no sense if its fulfillment was after his time (7:14).

Therefore, the argument concludes that no prediction of Christ's virgin birth should be found here. The use by Matthew was either faulty or purely typological, with no predictive or apologetic value. Matthew uses the phrase "that it might be fulfilled" typologically in other cases (for example, 2:15, 23). Matthew *applied* to Christ texts that were not messianic in their contexts.

There is a difficulty with the claim that *'almâ* refers to someone who is married. Not once does the Old Testament use *'almâ* to refer to a married person. *Bethulah*, on the other hand, is used for a married women (see Joel 1:8). Among texts using *'almâ* to refer to a virgin are Genesis. 24:43, Exodus 2:8, Psalms 68:25, Proverbs 30:19, and Song of Solomon 1:3; 6:8.

Some critics use and 1 Chronicles 15:20 and Psalm 46 as examples of *'almâ* (or *alamoth*) referring to a married person. In Psalm 46 it is simply part of the title of the Psalm, "A Song for *Alamoth*." Nothing in the title or psalm text helps us understand what *Alamoth* means, let alone whether it refers to a married person. It may be a musical notation, as one for the young women's choir to sing, or it could refer to some kind of musical accompaniment. The reference in 1 Chronicles 15:20 is similar. Music is being sung "with strings according to *Alamoth*." Whatever this may mean, it does not prove that *'almâ* means a married woman.

It can be argued that some features of the passage could not possibly refer only to the immediate circumstances: the supernatural nature of the "sign"; the reference to the one born as *Immanuel*, "God with us," and the reference to the whole "house of David" (vs. 13). The birth of Maher-Shalal-Hash-Baz in the next chapter cannot fulfill 7:14, since the one born was to be named "Immanuel."

While the "sign" was for Ahaz, it also was for the whole "house of David" (vs. 13). A distant sign can be for someone who lives long before the event, provided the benefits of the sign extend to the one for whom it is given. Since the "sign" was the birth of Messiah, the hope of salvation for Ahaz and everyone else, the sign was certainly for him.

But what of 7:16? The only meaningful way to understand this verse is that it refers to a child born in Isaiah's day. It should be kept in mind that 7:16's reference to the Assyrian invasion is itself a supernatural predictive prophecy. The issue is not, then, whether 7:14 is predictive and was fulfilled. The question is whether it was fulfilled in three years or 700. There is a possibility that Isaiah 7:16 can be understood in terms of the virgin-birth-only view. Commentator William Hendriksen suggests this possible interpretation: "Behold, the virgin conceives and gives birth to a son. . . . Before this child, *who before my prophetic eye has already arrived*, shall know to refuse the evil and chose the good—i.e., *within a very short time*—the land whose two kings you abhor shall be deserted" (Hendriksen, 139). Or, if one wants to be more literal, the Assyrians did invade *before* the child Jesus grew up—long before.

It is generally acknowledged that not all usages of the phrase "that it might be fulfilled" entail a truly predictive prophecy, Isaiah 7:14 need not be one of them. Matthew cites Micah 5:2, a clear prediction that the Christ would be born in Bethlehem (Matt. 2:5; see also Matt 3:3; 21:5; 22:43).

Double Reference. Even if the immediate context reveals that the prophecy had a near-view fulfillment in mind, this does not mean that there is not also a fuller fulfillment in a far-view reference to Christ. According to this view, many Old Testament prophecies have both a partial fulfillment in their day and a complete fulfillment in the distant future. Because of their desperate situation, God promised to give to Ahaz a sign that would assure the people that God would ultimately deliver them from bondage. This was a sign of the physical deliverance of Israel from the bondage of their enemies. It ultimately was a sign of the spiritual deliverance of spiritual Israel from bondage to Satan. The first aspect of the sign was fulfilled in the birth of Maher-Shalal-Hash-Baz, the second aspect in the birth of Jesus to the true virgin, Mary. Such double fulfillments are clear in other prophecies. Zechariah 12:10 can be applied both to Christ's first (John 19:37) and second comings (Rev. 1:7). Part of Isaiah 61 was fulfilled in Jesus (Isa. 61:1–2a; cf. Luke 4:18–19). Part remains for the second coming (Isa. 61:2b–11).

According to the double-reference view, *'almâ* refers to a young maiden who has never had sexual intercourse. The wife of Isaiah who bore the son in fulfillment of the first aspect of the prophecy was a virgin until she conceived by Isaiah. However, Mary, the mother of Jesus, was a complete fulfillment—a virgin when she conceived Jesus (Matthew 1:24–25).

Other arguments for this position also fit the supernatural birth-only view. Both of these views reject the idea that the significance of Isaiah 7:14 is exhausted in the natural birth of the prophetess's son.

Single Reference to a Supernatural Birth. Some scholars defend the position that Isa. 7:14 refers only to the supernatural virgin birth of Christ. Contrary to the first option, *'almâ* is only translated "virgin" in the Old Testament and has no other options. The prophetess, therefore, does not qualify. The Greek Old Testament (*Septuagint*) translated *'almâ* by the unambiguous word *parthenos* which can only mean "virgin." These translators, working before the advent, evidently believed that this was a prediction of the virgin birth of the Messiah. The inspired New Testament sanctioned this work by quoting from the *Septuagint* in Matt. 1:23. Further, to translate *'almâ* as a young girl who is not yet married, but would soon marry Isaiah means that it would be no longer a *virgin* who is conceiving, but a married woman. Isaiah 7:14 regards both the conception and birth as by a virgin.

Proponents of the supernatural-birth-only view point out that the prediction obviously goes beyond Ahaz to the whole "house of David" (Isa. 7:13). That hardly would apply to a natural birth by the prophetess in Isaiah's day. Also, the emphasis is on some wonderful, unheard of "sign" (Isa. 7:11–14). Why should an ordinary birth be understood as an extraordinary sign?

The whole context of Isaiah 7–11 (cf. Micah 5:2f.) forms an unbreakable chain of messianic prophecy:

> "Therefore the Lord himself will give you a sign: The virgin will be with child and will give birth to a son, and will call him Immanuel." [7:14]
>
> "Its outspread wings will cover the breadth of your land, O Immanuel!" [8:8b]
>
> For to us a child is born, to us a son is given, and the government will be on his shoulders. And he will be called Wonderful Counselor, Mighty God, Everlasting Father, Prince of Peace. [9:6]
>
> A shoot will come up from the stump of Jesse; from his roots a Branch will bear fruit. The Spirit of the LORD will rest on him—the Spirit of wisdom and of understanding, the Spirit of counsel and of power, the Spirit of knowledge and of the fear of the LORD—and he will delight in the fear of the LORD. He will not

> judge by what he sees with his eyes, or decide by what he hears with his ears; but with righteousness he will judge the needy, with justice he will give decisions for the poor of the earth. He will strike the earth with the rod of his mouth; with the breath of his lips he will slay the wicked. Righteousness will be his belt and faithfulness the sash round his waist. [11:1–5]

Matthew 1:22 both interprets Isaiah 7:14 as prophetic with the phrase "that it might be fulfilled" and adds an intensifying phrase, *"now all this was done* that it might be fulfilled . . ." (emphasis added). The manner of the quotation emphasizes the supernatural quality of the birth and the deity of Christ. Most scholars on both sides of the issue acknowledge that the phrase "that it might be fulfilled" does not necessarily refer to a predicative prophecy. However, indications are that Matthew 1:23 is an example of one that is predictive.

Finally, the same verse cannot refer to the birth of Maher-Shalal-Hash-Baz, for the same verse cannot mean two different (opposing things). If both the *Septuagint* and the inspired New Testament affirm that this refers to an actual virgin, it must refer to Christ alone.

Translating the Name Immanuel. A final issue that arises in this debate regards whether the name *Immanuel* mandates that Isaiah was referring to God incarnate. It does not. *Immanuel* can mean "God *is* with us." While the translation "God with us" seems to mean the name-bearer has deity, it is linguistically possible to translate "Immanuel" as "God is with us," which does not denote deity for the name-bearer. The name of a child can refer to a situation meaningful to the giver of the name. Thus Sarah named her son *Isaac*, meaning "laughter."

However, overall evidence indicates that the traditional translation is correct. When a point is made of a biblical name, it most often refers to the one who bears it: *Eve*, mother of the "living" (Gen. 3:20); *Noah*, related to the Hebrew for "comfort" (Gen. 5:29); *Abram*, "father" and *Abraham*, "father of many" (Gen. 17:5); *Sarai*, "princess," and *Sarah*, "princess of God" (Gen. 17:15); *Esau*, "hairy" (Gen. 25:25); *Jacob*, "He grasps the heel" or "deceiver," and *Israel*, "He struggles with God" (Gen. 27:36; 32:28); *Naomi*, "pleasant," and *Mara*, "bitter" (Ruth 1:20); *Nabal*, "fool" (1 Sam. 25:3, 25); *Jesus*, *"Yahweh* saves" (Matt. 1:21); Peter, "rock" (Matt. 16:18); and Barnabas, "son of encouragement" (Acts 4:36).

Both the immediate and broad contexts show that *Immanuel* refers to the character of the one bearing the name. The event is a supernatural sign. The whole "house of David," is in view, especially within the "messianic chain" of Isaiah 7–11. The New Testament interprets it as referring to Christ. All these factors support the view that it is a reference to Christ.

The Reliability of the New Testament Record. The evidence that Jesus was conceived of a virgin is based in the reliability of the New Testament documents and the New Testament witnesses. Both of these have been established with strong evidence. In fact, as is shown elsewhere, the evidence for the authenticity of the New Testament is greater than for that of any book from the ancient world (*see* Acts, Historicity of; New Testament, Dating of; New Testament Manuscripts; New Testament, Historicity of; New Testament Manuscripts; New Testament, Non-Christian Sources). It remains only to show that these records do testify to the virgin birth of Christ.

There can be no doubt that the New Testament clearly affirms that Christ was born of a virgin.

Matthew 1:18–23. Matthew wrote:

> This is how the birth of Jesus Christ came about: His mother Mary was pledged to be married to Joseph, but *before they came together*, she was found to be with child through the Holy Spirit. Because Joseph her husband was a righteous man and did not want to expose her to public disgrace, *he had in mind to divorce her quietly*. But after he had considered this, an angel of the Lord appeared to him in a dream and said, "Joseph son of David, do not be afraid to take Mary home as your wife, because *what is conceived in her is from the Holy Spirit*. She will give birth to a son, and you are to give him the name Jesus, because he will save his people from their sins." *All this took place to fulfil what the Lord had said through the prophet: "The virgin will be with child and will give birth to a son, and they will call him Immanuel"*—which means, "God with us." [1:18–23]

The emphasized sections point to four factors which demonstrate that Christ was virgin born: First, Mary conceived *"before they came together,"* thus revealing that it was not a natural conception. Second, Joseph's initial reaction reveals that he had not had sexual intercourse with Mary, since when he found that she was pregnant *"he had in mind to divorce her quietly."* Third, the phrase *"what is conceived in her is from the Holy Spirit"* reveals the supernatural nature of the event. Finally, the citation from the *Septuagint* translation of Isaiah 7:14 about a *parthenos*, "virgin," giving "birth" to a child indicates that Mary had not had sexual relations with anyone. She was not simply a virgin before the baby was conceived, but after it was conceived and even when it was born.

Luke 1:26–35. Mark begins immediately with Jesus' ministry, in accord with his stress on Christ as "Servant" (cf. 10:45). But we would expect a physician, Dr. Luke, to give attention to the circumstances of the birth. He begins with the announcement of Christ birth of a virgin:

In the sixth month, God sent the angel Gabriel to Nazareth, a town in Galilee, to a *virgin pledged to be married* to a man named Joseph, a descendant of David. The *virgin's* name was Mary. The angel went to her and said, "Greetings, you who are *highly favored!* The Lord is with you." Mary was *greatly troubled* at his words and wondered what kind of greeting this might be. But the angel said to her, "Do not be afraid, Mary, you have found favor with God. You will be with child and give birth to a son, and you are to give him the name Jesus." . . . "How will this be," Mary asked the angel, "since I am a virgin?" The angel answered, *"The Holy Spirit will come upon you, and the power of the Most High will overshadow you.* So the holy one to be born will be called the Son of God." [1:26–35]

The emphasized text again demonstrates that the conception of Christ was supernatural: Mary was a "virgin" (*parthenos*), "pledged to be married." Mary's reaction of being "greatly troubled" and being "afraid," as well as her astonished question, "How will this be?" reveals that she was a virgin. The angel gave some description of how the conception would happen through the Holy Spirit and "the power of the Most High."

Luke 2:1–19. When Luke records the birth he again stresses that Mary was only "pledged to be married," which in that culture meant she had not yet had sexual intercourse with Joseph. The supernatural appearance of the angel and the heavenly choir demonstrate that something extraordinary had happened. Mary's reaction was to contemplate in awe the mystery of it all. Obviously she knew something supernatural and holy had occurred (vs. 19).

John 2:2–11. John stresses the overall divinity of Christ (*see* CHRIST, DEITY OF), and doesn't dwell on particulars. Nevertheless, there are a couple of strong intimations in John's Gospel that Jesus was virgin born. When Jesus performed his first miracle at Cana of Galilee his mother was obviously aware of his supernatural origin and confident that he could do the supernatural. John wrote: "On the third day a wedding took place at Cana in Galilee. Jesus' mother was there, and Jesus and his disciples had also been invited to the wedding. When the wine was gone, Jesus' mother said to him, *'They have no more wine.'* 'Dear woman, why do you involve me?' Jesus replied. *'My time has not yet come.'* His mother said to the servants, *'Do whatever he tells you.'*" Indeed, the emphasized text reveals that Mary seems not only to believe that Jesus could do a miracle but to be requesting one, even though she had never seen him do one since this was Jesus' "first miracle" (vs. 11). Her understanding of his supernatural ability came from her past relationship with Jesus, including his birth.

John 8:41. Even the insult of Jesus' enemies shows that the circumstances of his birth had stirred general gossip, as might be expected if the story spread. Jesus said to them, "'You are doing the things your own father [Satan] does.' 'We are not illegitimate children,' they protested. 'The only Father we have is God himself." The Jews may have simply been responding defensively to Jesus' attack on their misplaced confidence in the fatherhood of Abraham. If so, it is an odd rejoinder. But it makes perfect sense if they were turning the argument back on Jesus' own legitimacy. Even Joseph had needed an angelic visitation to be convinced Mary's purity (Matt. 1:20). He and Mary likely faced a continuing shadow on their reputations. But Jesus faced the matter boldly in responding to his sniggering accusers, "Can any of you prove me guilty of sin?" (John 8:46).

Galatians 4:4. The Epistles are filled with references to Jesus' sinlessness. In the context of teaching about the innate sinfulness that adheres to each descendant of Adam (for example, Romans 5), these teachings themselves indicate that God had done something different in Jesus (2 Cor. 5:21; Heb. 4:15; 1 John 3:3). Paul's reference to Jesus as "born of a woman" is relatively explicit. He wrote, "But when the time had fully come, God sent his Son, born of a woman, born under law" (Gal. 4:4). This refers to Genesis 3:15. In a Jewish patriarchal culture one is begotten of a male (the father). To bring attention to being "born of a woman" is to show that something unusual is occurring—in Jesus' case a virgin birth.

The Charge of Mythology. It is difficult to deny that the New Testament teaches the virgin birth of Christ. The easier attack is to say that it is a myth patterned after Greek and Roman gods and was not really a historical event. For a full refutation of the charge that the Gospels evolved over a few generations into a myth-filled legend of Jesus' life, see in particular articles on the New Testament, plus see MITHRAISM, DIVINE BIRTH STORIES, BIBLE CRITICISM, JESUS SEMINAR, and Q DOCUMENT. In brief:

- Evidence is unassailable that the New Testament was written by contemporaries and eyewitnesses (cf. Luke 1:1–4). Second-century dating theories have now been thoroughly discredited by archaeological and manuscript evidence, allowing no time for legend development (*see* NEW TESTAMENT MANUSCRIPTS; NEW TESTAMENT WITNESSES, RELIABILITY OF, and NEW TESTAMENT, HISTORICITY OF).
- Virgin birth records do not show any of the standard literary marks of the myth genre (*see* MITHRAISM; DIVINE BIRTH STORIES; MYTHOLOGY AND THE NEW TESTAMENT).
- Persons, places, and events of Christ's birth precise and historically substantiated. Luke in particular goes to great pains to note his-

torical detail (Luke 3:1–2; for Luke's credentials as historian see ACTS, HISTORICITY OF).

- No Greek myth even remotely corresponds to the literal incarnation of a monotheistic God in human form (cf. John 1:1–3, 14) by way of a literal virgin birth (Matt. 1:18–25). The Greeks were polytheists, not monotheists.
- Stories of Greek gods become human via miraculous events like a virgin birth postdated the time of Christ. Hence, if there is any influence it is from Christianity on mythology, not the reverse.

Conclusion. Historical evidence that Jesus was supernaturally conceived of a virgin is more than substantial. Indeed, there are more eyewitness contemporary records of the virgin birth than for most events from the ancient world. The records show no signs of myth development. Indeed, they are surrounded by historical references to real people, places, and times. Thus, there is no reason to believe Jesus was not literally, biologically born of a virgin just as the Bible claims he was. Only an unjustified antisupernatural bias is ground for any conclusion to the contrary.

A particular battleground text is Isaiah 7:14, which is cited by Matthew. Critics argue that it has no predictive value. At worst the text refers to events in Isaiah's time only, which were applied typologically to Christ but have no predictive value. There is reason to believe the text refers, in part or whole, to a prediction of the virgin birth. In any case, there are other clear predictive texts in the Old Testament (*see* PROPHECY, AS PROOF OF THE BIBLE).

Sources

F. E. Gaeberlein, *The Expositor's Bible Commentary*, vol. 6
R. Gromacki, *The Virgin Birth: Doctrine of Deity*
W. Hendriksen, *New Testament Commentary: Exposition of the Gospel According to Matthew*
C. S. Lewis, *Mere Christianity*
———, *Surprised by Joy*
J. G. Machen, *The Virgin Birth of Christ*
Justin Martyr, *Dialogue with Trypho*, chap. 84
J. Orr, *The Virgin Birth of Christ*
R. D. Wilson, *Princeton Theological Review*, no. 24 (1926)
E. Yamauchi, "Easter—Myth, Hallucination, or History?" (2 parts), *Christianity Today* (29 March 1974; 15 April 1974)
E. J. Young, "The Virgin Birth" in *The Banner* (15 April 1955)

Voltaire, François-Marie. François-Marie Voltaire (1694–1778) was born in Paris to a well-to-do French family. He received a classical education under the Jesuits at Louis-le-Grand. He abandoned the study of law for literary pursuits. His strongly satirical penchant resulted in banishment to Holland in 1713 and imprisonment in the Bastille (1717–1718). Beginning with his epic poem, *La Henriade* (1723) on Henry IV (1366–1413), the last tolerant English king, Voltaire dominated the French stage for a half century.

Voltaire wrote *Letters Concerning the English Nation*, where there was more religious toleration at the time than in France. In the French edition, he included a critique of Blaise Pascal's (1623–1662) *Pensees*. *Lettres philosphiques* (1734) was an inspiration for liberal thinkers in the eighteenth century. *Essai sur les moeurs* (1756) was published while he lived in Geneva, and *Candide*, a satire on Gottfried *Leibniz's "best of all possible worlds" theodicy, was published in 1756. The themes of his earlier *Lettres* were developed more fully later in *Dictionare philosophique* (1764).

Voltaire's Deistic God. Although he used the term "theist" (*see* THEISM) to describe his philosophy, Voltaire was a deist (*see* DEISM). He believed in a Creator who did not supernaturally intervene in the world. His strong belief in the design of nature kept Voltaire from *atheism, a view that was later attacked by Charles *Darwin (1809–1882).

Voltaire did not believe that the existence of God is inborn. He observed that some nations have no knowledge of a creating Deity. "Every man comes into the world with a nose and five fingers, but not one possesses at birth any knowledge of God" (*Philosophical Letters*, 39–40). Like consciousness of a moral law, the sense of deity develops gradually, though inevitably as one contemplates the evidence God placed in the natural world.

Evidence for the Existence of God. He accepted many of *Thomas Aquinas's arguments for the existence of God. His *cosmological argument is tight and persuasive:

1. I exist; so something exists.
2. If something exists, something has existed from all eternity; for what exists either is self-existent or has had its existence communicated to it by another being.
3. If what exists is self-existent, it exists *necessarily*; it always has existed necessarily: and it is God.
4. If what exists has had existence communicated to it from another being, and that other being has derived *its* existence from a third, who must necessarily be God (*Voltaire and Rousseau against the Atheists*, 42–43).

His *teleological argument followed the form of William *Paley's (1743–1805): "I shall always be of the opinion that a clock proves a clock-maker, and that the universe proves a God." He adds, "For my part, in nature as an art, I see nothing but final causes; and I as much believe that apple-trees were made for the purpose of bearing apples, as the watches are made for the purpose of showing the time of day" (ibid., 35). "Can it be that these *copies* imply an intelligent maker, and the *originals* do nothing of the kind? . . . "This of itself appears to me the most convincing demonstration of the existence of a God, and I cannot conceive in what way it can be answered" (ibid., 9).

The Attributes of God. Voltaire believed, with Aquinas, that the essential attributes of God, the First Mover, could be inferred from nature. "This one mover is very *powerful*, otherwise he could not regulate so vast and complicated a machine [as the universe]." Likewise, "He is very *intelligent*, since we, who are intelligent, can produce nothing equal to the least of the springs of this machine." Further, "He is a *necessary* being, inasmuch as the machine could not exist, but for him. . . . He is *eternal*, for he cannot have sprung from nonentity, which being nothing can produce nothing" (ibid., 9–10). Voltaire seemed to accept God's *simplicity* or indivisibility. For he speaks of the "feat to convey a false idea of God, by appearing to consider him as composed of parts—and those, too, unconnected parts—parts hostile to each other" (ibid., 24).

However, Voltaire equivocates on God's *infinity*. He said, "I am forced to admit eternity, but I am not forced to admit that there is any such thing as infinity" (ibid., 12). "I perceive only that there is something which is more powerful than myself, but nothing further" (ibid., 42). "I know no reason why God should be infinite" (ibid., 11). However, while God is not infinite in his being, Voltaire seems to acknowledge God's infinite in duration (eternity) power (omnipotent), "for what restraint is there upon him?" (ibid., 44). Voltaire appears to foreshadow the later finite God views of John Stuart *Mill.

What God wills, he wills with necessity. For he is a Necessary Being. This necessity does not nullify free will. "I necessarily will that I may be happy. I do not will this the less because I *necessarily* will it; on the contrary, I will it only the more forcibly from the fact that my will is invincible" (ibid., 16).

God expects his creatures to live by the natural moral law. In a very frank passage, he wrote: "What other restraint could be laid on cupidity and on secret and unpunished transgressions than the idea of an eternal master who sees us, and will judge even our most hidden thoughts?" (ibid., 35). It is not clear how Voltaire reconciled this with his doubts about immortality, unless all the judgment was to come in this life, something not apparent to most people.

Other Beliefs of Voltaire. Ethics. Ethics was Voltaire's chief concern. Dogmas divide, but ethics unite. All civil law should be based on the moral law common to all men rooted in a common human nature. Justice was the underlying principle. He hated injustice, cruelty, and oppression. Happiness of the individual and society were the chief goal of ethical behavior.

Voltaire had a naturalistic view of both religion and ethics. People are born with a moral capacity, if not with moral instincts. However derived, they are the foundation of society. Without them, there is no possibility to operate a humane world.

*Special Providence and *Miracles.* God was necessary to get the world going, but he has not manifested any special providential care toward it since then. Indeed, the general theme of Voltaire's *Zadig* seem to have been to question God's justice. Voltaire distinguished between God's general and special providence. He allowed for the former in the deistic sense that God endowed human beings with reason and feelings of benevolence, but he denies the latter. The evil in the world stood between him and an omnibenevolent God (*see* EVIL, PROBLEM OF).

As for miracles, "not a single one of the prophecies that Pascal referred to can be honestly applied to Christ; . . . his discussion of miracles was pure nonsense" (Torrey, *Voltaire and the English Deists*, 264).

Immortality of the Soul. Voltaire's view on the existence of mind and soul gave rise to later materialism, though he remained skeptical. Rooted in English empiricism, Voltaire eventually concluded: "I cannot doubt that God has not granted sensations, memory, and consequently ideas, to organized matter" (ibid., 264). Throughout his life he maintained a skeptical view of the soul, his expression in the last chapter of *Micromegas* (1752) humorously sums up his view: "May God, if there is one, save my soul, if I have one." Others developed Voltaire's skepticism about the soul into a complete atheistic *materialism.

Inhumane Christianity. His anonymous poem *Epitre a Uranie* (1722) was a diatribe against Christian belief in a jealous, tyrannical deity of the Old Testament and the inhumane condemnation of all pagans to eternal punishment. Addressing the benevolent, merciful deity he adored, Voltaire prayed: "I am not a Christian that I may love thee more" (ibid., 266). Voltaire denounced all revealed religions (*see* REVELATION, SPECIAL).

Voltaire's attack on Christianity fired on one of its most noted defenders of his time, *Pascal. In Voltaire's twenty-fifth philosophical letter, he focused on Pascal's Christian view of the Fall, redemption, divine providence, predestination, and grace. He believed Pascal was neither enlightened nor humanitarian and that he encouraged fanaticism. As for *Pascal's "wager," Voltaire was shocked that he would resort to such a means to prove God. Voltaire replied "the heavens declare the glory of God."

Other than this anonymous work, Voltaire reserved his strongest criticism of Christianity until after his retirement in the early 1760s. In his account of the renegade priest, Jean Meslier (1762), he wrote:

> What then are the vain resources of Christians? Their moral principles? These are basi-

> cally the same in all religions. Their distinctives are in cruel dogmas [that] have arisen from them and have preached persecution and dissension. Should we believe their miracles? But what people have not theirs and what philosophic minds do not despise these fables? . . . Their prophecies? Has not their falsity been demonstrated? . . . Their morals? Are they not often infamous? The establishment of their religion? But did it not begin with fanaticism, was it not fostered by intrigue, and the edifice visibly maintained by force? Its doctrine? But is not that the height of absurdity? [ibid., 266]

For Voltaire "the establishment of Christianity [was] a grievous aberration of the human mind, a halt in the progress of humanity" (ibid., 267).

Voltaire found arguments against miracles (*see* MIRACLES, ARGUMENTS AGAINST) from David *Hume and English deists. In Anthony Collins he discovered arguments against predictive prophecy. And from French rationalists he was convinced of countless contradictions and inconsistencies in the Bible.

As for Christ, he was accepted as his master over other religious leaders, such as Confucius (551–479 B.C.), whom he admired. However, he depicted Christ as a deist or humanist. Voltaire rejected the Christ of the Gospels, though, as Thomas *Jefferson (1743–1826), he accepted Christ's essential moral teachings as reported there. The only sense in which Voltaire's views can be called Christian is in the deistic sense. The core Christian theistic and moral teachings of the fatherhood of God and the brotherhood of humankind are common to all religions as revealed in nature (see his *Traite sur la tolerance* [1763]).

Evil. Citing Epicurus (341–270 B.C.), Voltaire agreed that: "Either God can remove evil from the world and will not; or being willing to do so, cannot; or he neither can or will; or he is both able and willing." But "if he is willing and cannot, he is not omnipotent. If he can but will not, he is not benevolent. If he is neither willing nor able, he is neither omnipotent nor benevolent. . . . if he both wants to and can, whence comes evil over the face of the earth?" (cited in *Voltaire and the English Deists*, 265).

Voltaire's writings on evil were directed against the optimism of Leibniz and Alexander Pope (1688–1744). His classic satire *Candide* was directed against this "best of all possible worlds" in the most cutting way. He rejected the optimistic "whatever is, is good" or "partial ill is universal good" for a stoic acceptance of fate and a desire to make life endurable in spite of it (*see* EVIL, PROBLEMS OF).

Religious Attitude. Despite his antipathy to Christianity and supernatural religion, Voltaire had a deep religious experience of his own and strongly defended natural religion. As Norman Torrey put it, "he felt a genuine sense of awe and veneration, expressed far too often to be ignored, that could have come only from the personal mystical experience of cosmic grandeur" (*Voltaire and the English Deists*, 265).

Evaluation. *Positive Aspects.* Voltaire ardently defended many of the same things that theists, moralists, and freedom lovers have cherished. He defended God's existence, exposed superstition, maintained a deeply religious attitude, valued human reason in the pursuit of truth, and had a high sense of morality and justice.

With theists Voltaire spoke against atheism. He wrote: "I have always been convinced that atheism cannot do any good, and may do very great harm. I have pointed to the infinite difference between the sages who have written against superstition and the madmen who have written against God. There is neither philosophy nor morality in any system of atheism" (*Philosophical Letters*, 33). He adds, "it would not be difficult to prove from history that atheism may sometimes produce as much evil as the most barbarous superstitions" (ibid., 29). Indeed, "it is altogether probable that all the powerful men who have passed their lives in that round of crimes which fools denominate *strokes of policy, revolutionary remedies, art of governing, & c.*, have been atheists" (ibid., 33).

Having long admired the English, Voltaire was influenced by John Locke (1632–1704) and Isaac Newton (1642–1727). Newton's law of gravitation inspired in Voltaire a deep sense of awe for nature and its supremely intelligent Cause. He wrote: "The same gravitation penetrates into all the heavenly bodies, and impels them toward each other . . . and this let me remark in passing, establishes what *Plato had divined (I know not how), that the world is the work of the *Everlasting Geometer*" (ibid., 7).

Voltaire correctly perceived that evil is one of the great problems for a theist. He also saw clearly the form of the objection, namely, the seeming impossibility of God being both all-good and all-powerful without defeating evil. What he did not see was that there is a way between the horns of the dilemma (*see* EVIL, PROBLEM OF).

Those who believe in rational religion can be grateful for Voltaire's exposure of superstition and ignorance in religion. This emphasis aids greatly the pursuit of the truth. It is an objective check on what would otherwise be unbridled passion and irrationality.

Voltaire learned well from *Locke and English deists the need for religious freedom and tolerance. Locke's influence on Jefferson was a significant influence on the American Revolution. Forced religion, involving as it does a free expression of the soul, is a contradiction in terms. It is the obligation of government to protect freedom of religion, not to enforce a State religion.

Negative Critiques. As a form of *deism, Voltaire's theology is vulnerable to the inconsistency inherent in deism. As noted in the article DEISM, it admits the big miracle (creation of the universe) but denies smaller ones. It was common for desists to follow the arguments against miracles laid down by Benedict *Spinoza (1632–1677) and *Hume. These arguments have been shown to be without foundation, begging the question, and designed to favor naturalism (*see* MIRACLES, ARGUMENTS AGAINST).

From a purely natural point of view, one might sympathize with Voltaire's doubts about immortality. However, in view of the overwhelming evidence for the resurrection of Christ (*see* RESURRECTION, EVIDENCE FOR), there is every reason to believe in life after death. Indeed, Voltaire does not appear to be consistent with his own belief in a God who judges all men, for he knows that not all evils are justly punished in this life. As many other deists, skeptics, and atheists, Voltaire presses the dilemma of evil. But in so doing he undermines his own view. For how can we know there are ultimate injustices unless we posit an ultimate standard of justice? But if God is ultimately just, then the problem of evil is resolved. For the unpunished evils we see are only immediately unjust. If God is perfectly just, he will take care of them at the time he decides (*see* EVIL, PROBLEM OF).

Voltaire's dilemma is a false one. For the fact that evil is *not yet* defeated does not mean it will not be. If God is all-good, he wants to defeat it. If he is all-powerful, he can defeat it. And if he is both of those things and evil is *not yet* defeated, it *will be*.

It was common for *"enlightenment" thinkers to take pot-shots at the injustice of hell. But their presupposed standard of ultimate justice demands it. Otherwise, there is no ultimate justice and God is not ultimately just, which he must be since the very concept of an ultimate injustice implies an ultimate Justice.

Also typical of this period was negative Bible criticism. But these criticisms were built on an unjustified antisupernaturalism and they were pre-archaeological. The biblical texts have since been overwhelmingly substantiated (*see* ACTS, HISTORICITY OF; ARCHAEOLOGY, OLD TESTAMENT; ARCHAEOLOGY, NEW TESTAMENT; NEW TESTAMENT, HISTORICITY OF).

Like others who adopted the history-of-religion theory's unjustified evolutionary hypothesis of animism to henotheism to polytheism to monotheism, Voltaire bought into the notion that the Old Testament God was a vengeful tribal deity in contrast to the New Testament's God of love. As a matter of fact, God is described as loving and merciful much more in the Old Testament (see, for example, Gen. 43:14; Exod. 20:6; Num. 14:19; Deut. 7:9; Psalm 136; Jonah 4:2). The most severe passages on eternal judgment are found in the New Testament (for example, Matt. 25:41; Luke 16:19–31; Rev. 20:11–15).

Sources

G. Lanson, *Voltaire*

N. Torrey, *Voltaire and the English Deists*

———, "Voltaire, Francois-Marie Arouet De," in Edwards, *Encyclopedia of Philosophy*

Voltaire, Francois-Marie. *Candide, Zadig, and Selected Stories*, D. M. Frame, trans.

———, *Philosophical Dictionary*, P. Gay, trans., 2 vols.

———, *Philosophical Letters*, E. Dilworth trans.

———, *Selected Letters*

———, *Voltaire and Rousseau against the Atheists, Or, Essays and Detached Passages from Those Writers in Relation to the Being and Attributes of God* (1845), J. Akerly, trans.

Voltarism. ***See*** **ESSENTIALISM, DIVINE.**

Warfield, B. B. Benjamin Breckinridge Warfield (1851–1921) was born near Lexington, Kentucky. He was graduated from the College of New Jersey (later Princeton University) in 1871 and Princeton Theological Seminary in 1876. After studying at the University of Leipzig (1876–1877), he supplied at the First Presbyterian Church in Baltimore, Maryland (1877–1878). He taught at Western Theological Seminary, Allegheny, Pennsylvania (1878–1887), before being called to teach theology at Princeton Theological Seminary, where he taught from 1887 until his death.

In addition to his biblical and theological writings, Warfield wrote apologetically related books and articles, including *An Introduction to the Textual Criticism of the New Testament* (1886), *The Gospel of the Incarnation* (1893), *The Lord of Glory* (1907), *Counterfeit Miracles* (1918), *Revelation and Inspiration* (1927), *Christology and Criticism* (1929), and *Studies in Tertullian and Augustine* (1930). His articles with an apologetic theme included "Revelation" in the *International Standard Bible Encyclopedia* (1915),"On the Antiquity and the Unity of the Human Race," and "The Idea of Systematic Theology."

Warfield's View of Apologetics. John *Calvin and the Scottish Presbyterian Westminster Confession tradition were anchoring theological influences on Warfield. He greatly respected his predecessor at Princeton, Charles Hodge. James McCosh implanted the Scottish *realism of Thomas *Reid (1710–1796) in Warfield's thinking. He also was heavily influenced by Augustine and, to a lesser degree, by *Thomas Aquinas.

Warfield was preeminently an apologetical theologian. He stressed the need for apologetics and a rational faith founded on evidence.

Definition of Apologetics. Warfield defined apologetics as "the systematically organized vindication of Christianity in all its elements and details, against all opposition . . ." (*Works*, 9:5). "What apologetics undertakes to establish is just this Christianity itself—including all its 'details' and involving its 'essence'—in its unexplicated and uncompressed entirety, as the absolute religion" (ibid., 9).

Relation of Apologetics and Theology. In his "Idea of Systematic Theology" Warfield spelled out the relation of apologetics to theology: "philosophical apologetics is . . . presupposed in and underlies the structure of scientific theology. . . . Apologetical Theology prepares the way for all theology by establishing its necessary presuppositions without which no theology is possible—the existence and essential nature of God (*see* GOD, NATURE OF), the religious nature of man which enables him to receive a revelation from God, the possibility of a revelation from God, the possibility of a revelation and its actual realization in the Scriptures" (ibid., 9:55, 64). It is "the function of apologetics to investigate, expiate, and establish the grounds on which a theology—a science, or systematized knowledge of God—is possible" (ibid., 9:4).

The Importance of Apologetics. Few apologists have ever envisioned a greater role for apologetics than did Warfield. The 1887 inaugural address of his professorship at Princeton, "The Idea of Systematic Theology Considered as a Science," emphasized apologetics as "a primary part, . . . a conquering part" in the spread of Christian faith. "It is the distinction of Christianity that it has come into the world clothed with the mission to *reason* its way to dominion. Other religions may appeal to the sword, or seek some other way to propagate themselves. Christianity makes its appeal to right reason, and stands out among all religions, therefore, as distinctively the 'Apologetic religion.' It is solely by reasoning that it has come thus far on its way to kingship" (*Selected Shorter Writings*, 2:99–100).

On the relation of apologetics to the Bible he said, "It is easy, of course, to say that a Christian man must take his standpoint not *above* the Scriptures, but *in* the Scriptures. He very certainly must. But surely he must first *have* Scriptures, authenticated to him as such, before he can take his standpoint in them" (ibid., 2:98).

Faith and Reason. Warfield believed that the *indicia* (demonstrations of the Bible's divine character) work side by side with the Holy Spirit to convince people of the truth of the Bible. Warfield agreed with Calvin that proofs cannot bring people to Christ or even convince them of the divine authority of Scripture. Nonetheless, Warfield believed that the Holy Spirit exercises his convincing power through them.

Contrary to presuppositional apologetics (*see* PRESUPPOSITIONAL APOLOGETICS), there is common ground with unbelievers. "The world of facts is open to all people and all can be convinced of God's existence and the truth of Scripture through them by the power of reasoning of a redeemed thinker." In his 1908 article on "Apologetics" he affirmed that faith is a moral act and a gift of God. However, it is also a matter of conviction become confidence. And all forms of conviction must have a reasonable ground. "It is not faith but reason which investigates the nature and validity of this ground. . . . We believe in Christ because it is rational to believe in him, not even though it be irrational" (*Works*, 9:15).

As a Calvinist, Warfield said that mere reasoning cannot make a Christian because of the inability for sinners to come to God under the curse of the fall. The problem is not that faith does not terminate on evidence, but that a dead soul cannot respond to evidence. However, on the other hand, the Holy Spirit does not bring anyone to salvation apart from evidence. The Spirit works to prepare the soul to receive the evidence. Therefore, men and women do not become Christians by apologetics, but apologetics supplies "the systematically organized basis on which the faith of Christian men must rest" (ibid.).

To be sure, not every Christian can do apologetics, nor are many even aware of the rational justification of their faith. However, the systematic proof that is implicit in every act of Christian faith is a product of apologetics. It is not necessary for salvation to be conscious of these proofs or to explicitly understand them. Nonetheless, such understanding is necessary for the vindication of faith (ibid., 16).

The Various Steps of Apologetics. As a proponent of classical apologetics (*see* CLASSICAL APOLOGETICS), Warfield believed apologetics could be divided into demonstrations of the being and nature of God (*see* GOD, EVIDENCE FOR), the divine origin and authority of Christianity, and the superiority of Christianity over other systems (ibid., 10). He carved up the field by functions and which arguments meet which opponents in battle:

Philosophical apologetics establishes that God exists as a personal Spirit, as Creator, Preserver, and Governor. Philosophical apologetics tackles antitheistic theories.

Psychological apologetics establishes the religious nature of humankind and the validity of human religious sensitivities. It involves the psychology, philosophy, and phenomena of religion. It faces naturalist attacks from "comparative religion" or "history of religions" movements.

An unnamed form might be called *revelational apologetics*, for it reveals the reality of divine governance of history and the actual relationship in which God stands to his world and the ways he makes himself known.

Historical apologetics presents the case for the divine origin of Christianity as God's revealed religion. It discusses all the topics that fall under the popular category heading of the "evidences for Christianity."

Biblical apologetics establishes the trustworthiness of the Bible as a God-revealed document for the redemption of sinners (ibid., 13).

Inspiration of the Bible. Warfield may be best known for his strong defense of the inspiration (*see* BIBLE, EVIDENCE FOR) and inerrancy (*see* BIBLE, ALLEGED ERRORS IN) of the Bible in the originally written texts or "autographs." Warfield produced two major works: *Revelation and Inspiration* and *Limited Inspiration* [*Inerrancy*] and coauthored *Inspiration* with A. A. Hodge.

Legacy. Warfield's views on apologetics have made a lasting impact on the American scene. The works defending an inspired Scripture had a strong influence on the inerrancy movement many years later among evangelicals known as the International Council on Biblical Inerrancy (see Geisler, *Inerrancy*). In general, Warfield is a spiritual ancestor of most classical apologists of the late twentieth century, such leaders as John Gerstner, Kenneth Kantzer, Arthur Lindsley, and R. C. Sproul (see Sproul).

Sources

A. A. Hodge and B. B. Warfield, *Inspiration*

M. Noll, "B. B. Warfield," in Walter Elwell, *Handbook of Evangelical Theologians*

R. C. Sproul, et al., *Classical Apologetics*

B. B. Warfield, *An Introduction to the Textual Criticism of the New Testament*

———, "Introduction," in F. R. Beattie, *Apologetics, or the Rational Vindication of Christianity*

———, "Revelation" in *International Standard Bible Encyclopedia*, 1915 ed.

———, *Christology and Criticism*

———, *Counterfeit Miracles*

———, *Limited Inspiration* [*Inerrancy*]

———, *Revelation and Inspiration*

———, *Selected Shorter Writings of Benjamin B. Warfield*, 2 vols.

———, *Studies in Tertullian and Augustine*

———, *The Gospel of the Incarnation*

———, *The Lord of Glory*

———, *Works of Benjamin B. Warfield*, 10 vols.

Wellhausen, Julius. Julius Wellhausen (1844–1918) was a German Bible scholar known as the father of modern biblical criticism (*see* BIBLE CRITICISM). He studied at Göttingen and taught at Göttingen, Greifswald, Halle, Marburg and finally returned to Göttingen as historian, philologist, and master of Hebrew, Aramaic, Syriac, and Arabic.

Wellhausen's most significant work, which presented a mature development of the historical critical method, was *Introduction to the History of Israel*, 1878, 6th ed., 1905. He also wrote "Israel" in the 9th ed. of *Encyclopedia Britannica*, 1878, and *Die Komposition des Hexateuchs* (*The Composition of the Hexateuch*), 1877.

Wellhausen was influenced by W. F. G. *Hegel and Wilhelm Vatke, who applied the Hegelian dialectic of historical development to the development of the religion of Israel. From this platform Wellhausen developed the documentary hypothesis.

Documentary Hypothesis. Wellhausen sought to show that the Old Testament as it is possessed by the church is a postexilic product of Judaism with its priestly hierarchy. Religion among the Hebrews has actually developed by a natural evolution, as it had among all other peoples, from fetishism (belief in or worship of objects which are held by superstitious people to possess magical power), to *polytheism, to henotheism which is the belief in or worship of one God without denying the existence of other gods), to ethical monotheism. The last stage was achieved by the writings of the prophets of the eighth century B.C. culminating in the preaching of the Deuteronomists. The final development was the institutionalization of this religion in the legislation of the priestly code and the rewriting of Israel's history in the light of this latest religious perspective (*see* ARCHAEOLOGY, OLD TESTAMENT; BIBLE, EVIDENCE FOR; OLD TESTAMENT MANUSCRIPTS; PENTATEUCH, MOSAIC AUTHORSHIP OF; REDACTION CRITICISM, OLD TESTAMENT; SPINOZA, BENEDICT; STRAUSS, DAVID).

The result is the famous J-E-P-D theory of the authorship of the Pentateuch. According to this theory, Moses did not write the Pentateuch (Genesis–Deuteronomy), as both Jewish and Christian scholars have held through the centuries. Rather, it was written by a number of persons over a long period. These documents are identified as:

1. the *Jehovist* or *Yahwist* (*J*), ninth century B.C.;
2. the *Elohist* (*E*), eighth century B.C.;
3. the *Deuteronomist* (*D*), ca. the time of Josiah, 640–609 B.C., and
4. the *Priestly* (*P*), ca. fifth century B.C.

The Pentateuch was a mosaic put together from different authors who can be identified partly by their various uses of *Jehovah* (*Yahweh*), or *Elohim* for God or by references to the work of the priests (*P*) or to laws (*D*).

One or more "redactors" or editor/compilers brought together all of this evolutionary development within the religious history of Israel. Wellhausen assumes that there is a "popular religion" of Israel which must be discovered among the many impositions by later redactors, and when this religion is discovered it reveals its form at each stage in the evolutionary development.

Evaluation. Wellhausen's work is critiqued in the article BIBLE CRITICISM, PENTATEUCH, MOSAIC AUTHORSHIP OF, J-E-P-D THEORY, and related entries. In general, Wellhausen's thought has guided the work of "negative" historical-critical efforts to undermine the authority of Scripture. The theory is still widely believed, though archaeological and other research has undermined its assumptions.

The Collapse of the J-E-P-D Theory. Deuteronomy provides one example of arguments refuting the theories first developed by Wellhausen: Textually, Deuteronomy claims that "these are the words of Moses (1:1; 4:44; 29:1). To deny this is to claim the book of the law is a total fraud. Joshua, Moses' immediate successor, attributed the book of Deuteronomy to Moses (Josh. 1:7), as does the rest of the Old Testament (Judg. 3:4; 1 Kings 2:3; 2 Kings 14:6; Ezra 3:2; Neh. 1:7; Ps. 103:7; Dan. 9:11; Mal. 4:4). Deuteronomy is the book of the Law most quoted in the New Testament, with attribution to Moses (Acts 3:22; Rom. 10:19; 1 Cor. 9:9). Jesus quoted Deuteronomy 6:13, 16 in resisting the Devil (Matt. 4:7, 10), and he also directly attributed it to the hand of Moses (Mark 7:10; Luke 20:28).

Geographical and historical details of the book display a firsthand acquaintance with sites Moses would have known; its covenantal forms also place it at the period of Moses (Kline, all).

Apparent references within the book to a later period are easily explained. Deuteronomy 34, with its description of Moses' death, was probably written by his successor Joshua, in accordance with the custom of the day.

Moses and the Entire Pentateuch. The evidence that Moses wrote Deuteronomy destroys the J-E-P-D theory as such. Variations of the theory still deny Moses is the author of all five books.

Four of the five books (excepting Genesis) claim to be written by Moses (see Exod. 24:4; Levit. 1:1; 4:1; 5:14; Numbers 1:1; 33:2, and as noted above in Deuteronomy. The lack of a direct claim in Genesis is understandable since the events occurred before Moses' birth. In this book, Moses apparently acted something as an editor and compiler himself, basing his work on records preserved from the patriarchs. This is indicated by the frequent formula "this is the history of" (as in 5:1; 10:1, and 25:19). There is considerable evidence that Moses composed what we know as Genesis:

1. Moses had access to the family histories which traced their ancestry to Abraham and the beginning. As leader Moses was familiar with God's promises to give them Palestine (Gen. 12:1–3; 13:15–1; 15:18–21; 17:8; 26:3) after delivering them from Egypt (46:3–4; cf. Exod. 2:24).
2. Citations of Genesis identify it as part of the "law of Moses" (Luke 24:44; cf. 2 Chron. 25:4). These are found in Moses' own Deuteronomy 1:8; 2 Kings 13:23; 1 Chronicles 1, and Matt. 19:8. It is lumped with the other four as books of Moses in Luke 24:27, 44.
3. From earliest times, Jewish teaching has attributed Genesis to Moses. References are found throughout the Jewish Talmud and in other Jewish writers, such as Philo and Josephus.
4. Exodus through Deuteronomy are incomplete without the background of Genesis. Together they form a narrative unit.

With the possible exception of some parenthetical explanatory material and updating of place names that changed, the language and culture of the entire Pentateuch reflects that of Moses' day (*see* ALBRIGHT, WILLIAM F.).

Other evidence against Wellhausen's hypothesis. Virtually the whole corpus of archaeological evidence has tended to prove Wellhausen's evolutionary theory wrong. Most significant is the earliest findings at Ebla, Syria. The *Ebla tablets confirm monotheism extremely early, as opposed to Wellhausen's supposition that it was a late evolutionary development from earlier polytheism and henotheism.

Sources

O. T. Allis, *The Five Books of Moses*
———, *The Old Testament: Its Claims and Its Critics*
G. L. Archer, Jr., *A Survey of Old Testament Introduction*
F. Delitzsch, *Commentary on Genesis*
N. L. Geisler, and W. E. Nix, *General Introduction to the Bible*
R. K. Harrison, "Historical and Literary Criticism of the Old Testament," in F. Gaberlein, *The Expositor's Bible Commentary*, vol. 1
———, *Old Testament Introduction*
M. Kline, *Treaty of the Great King*
E. Krentz, *The Historical-Critical Method*
R. H. Pfeiffer, *Introduction to the Old Testament*
J. Wellhausen, *Die Komposition des Hexateuchs [The Composition of the Hexateuch]*
———, *Prolegomena to the History of Ancient Israel*
———, "Israel," in *Encyclopedia Britannica*, 9th ed.
J. Wenham, "History and The Old Testament," *Sacra* 124 (1967)
R. D. Wilson, *A Scientific Investigation of the Old Testament*

Wells, G. A. Modern scholars have denied that Jesus did and said the things attributed to him by the Gospels (*see* BIBLE CRITICISM; JESUS SEMINAR). Few, however, have joined with G. A. Wells in denying that the man Jesus of Nazareth ever existed. It is, perhaps, the curious nature of his ideas that has earned him some interest in theological circles. Wells believes that, if Jesus did exist, he was an obscure person whose story became patterned after mystery religions (*see* MITHRAISM) and Jewish wisdom literature.

In his books, *Did Jesus Exist?* and *The Historical Evidence for Jesus*, Wells sees four stages in the development of the early ideas about Christ:

- Stage one—Paul's Epistles, written by 60. This "Jesus" was viewed as a supernatural being who spent a brief but obscure time on earth, perhaps centuries earlier (*Did Jesus Exist?* chap. 5).
- Stage two—non-Pauline canonical Epistles, completed in the 70s. Jesus is now said to have lived on earth recently.
- Stage three—the Pastoral Epistles and Ignatius, ca. 80s. Jesus is linked with historical figures such as Pilate and is said to have died at the hands of the romans.
- Stage four—the Gospels (ca. 90, Mark to ca. 120, John). The Gospels are more or less fabricated. They were accepted by the early church uncritically, since they did not conflict with established beliefs (see Habermas, chap. 2).

In view of these stages, Wells believes that historical facts about Jesus came late. He contends that Paul was uninterested in historical details, only a divine Christ. Jesus' concept of wisdom, plus mystery religions, influenced the early picture. Early Christianity began without any contact with a historical Jesus. Thus, nothing can be known about such a man, since there is no first-hand information. The Gospels simply guessed about Jesus' life, accepting what fit with their general views. If Jesus existed, he was probably an obscure peasant.

Difficulties with Wells's Thesis. Problems with this type of argument are covered in articles on the historicity of the New Testament and Jesus. See, in particular, ACTS, HISTORICITY OF; ARCHAEOLOGY, NEW TESTAMENT; BIBLE, EVIDENCE FOR; CHRIST, UNIQUENESS OF; CHRIST OF FAITH VS. JESUS OF HISTORY; JESUS, NON-CHRISTIAN SOURCES; JESUS SEMINAR; NEW TESTAMENT, DATING THE; NEW TESTAMENT, HISTORICITY OF, and SON OF MAN, JESUS AS.

The first problem is that Wells, with most other critics, accepts Paul's basic writings as in circulation by 60. But this damages his thesis. Even in these books, written while eyewitnesses were still alive, there is ample evidence of historical interest. Paul speaks of Jesus' virgin birth (Gal. 4:4), sinless life (2 Cor. 5:21), death on the cross (1 Cor. 15:3; Gal. 3:13), resurrection (1 Cor. 15:4, 12–20), and postresurrection appearances (1 Cor. 15:3–8). He appealed to the fact that literally hundreds of eyewitnesses could verify his words. Paul also gives historical details about Jesus' immediate followers, the apostles (1 Cor. 15:5–8; Gal. 1:18–19; 2).

Another pillar of Wells's argument crumbles in his dating of the Gospels. Even some critical scholars place Mark at 65 and Matthew and Luke prior to 90. As noted in the article NEW TESTAMENT, HISTORICITY OF, that is about as late as is reasonable, given the evidence. Actual dates may be quite a bit earlier. Certainly the dating cannot fit the "stage four" scenario. Paleographers speak for most legitimate recent scholarship when he concludes that "every book of the New Testament was written by a baptized Jew between the forties and the eighties of the first century A.D. (very probably sometime between 50 and 75 A.D." ("Toward a More Conservative View," 359). Carl Hemer provides powerful evidence that Acts was written between 60–62. Luke was written before Acts (see Acts 1:1), placing it no later than 62 (*see* ACTS, HISTORICITY OF). Rather than being later additions as Wells suggests, the interwoven detail and accuracy of the historical data—especially in Luke and Acts strongly present an early date.

Finally, the John Rylands papyri fragment (*see* NEW TESTAMENT MANUSCRIPTS) is good evidence that John was written before the end of the first century. The possibility of New Testament fragments from the mid-first-century at Qumran, if substantiated, will definitively put to rest any talk of late Gospels.

Christianity and Mystery Religions. Contrary to Wells, accounts of Christ's life was not based on the mystery religions (*see* MITHRAISM). According to a contemporary account by Paul (1 Corinthians 15), the Gospels were based on eyewitness testimony. In view of this, Wolfhart Pannenberg concludes, "Under such circumstances it is an idle venture to make parallels in the history of religions responsible for the *emergence* of the primitive Christian message about Jesus' resurrection" (Pannenberg, 91).

Christianity was monotheistic, and the mystery religions by nature were polytheistic (*see* POLYTHEISM). The gods of the mystery religions were not incarnated as human beings (see John 1:1, 14). The stories of gods coming back from the dead are not resurrections in the Christian sense, but rather examples of reincarnation (*see* MITHRAISM).

And the final, fatal flaw is that these stories postdate the time of Christ and the Gospels (*see* NEW TESTAMENT, DATING OF).

Historical Methodology. Wells's contention that the Gospels were guesswork or fabrications about Jesus is without foundation. It is based on the disproven assumption that they were late books, and it neglects the overlap in Paul's writings and the presence of eyewitnesses who could set the record straight. Also, the Gospels and Paul present the same basic picture of Jesus.

If the same criteria are applied to the life of Christ as are generally used to evaluate ancient writings, the historicity of Jesus must be accepted. Evaluated by these standards, critical historian Michael Grant noted, "we can no more reject Jesus' existence than we can reject the existence of a mass of pagan personages whose reality as historical figures is never questioned" (Grant, 199–200).

Sources

W. F. Albright, "William Albright: Toward a More Conservative View," in *Christianity Today* (18 January, 1963)
M. Grant, *Jesus: An Historian's Review of the Gospels*
G. Habermas, *The Historical Jesus*
R. Nash, *Christianity and the Hellenistic World*
W. Pannenberg, *Jesus—God and Man*
J. A. T. Robinson, *Redating the New Testament*
G. A. Wells, *Did Jesus Exist?*
———, *The Historical Evidence for Jesus*
E. Yamauchi, "Easter—Myth, Hallucination, or History?" *Christianity Today* (29 March, 1974; 15 April, 1974)

Wells, H. G. ***Life and Works.*** Herbert George Wells (1866–1946) was a scientific humanist who affirmed a new religious faith, a faith in man. He was an admirerer of Auguste *Comte and Herbert Spencer. Wells was an English journalist, secondary-level science teacher, and co-author with Julian *Huxley of a popularized work, the *Science of Life*.

He "grew up in Victorian England; but he reacted violently, even as a child, against the evangelical faith of his mother" Indeed, "He especially despised the doctrine of the *Trinity" (Glover, 121). Nonetheless, Wells' writings reflect many Christian truths, including that of original sin seen in his belief in the "persistent wickedness" of human beings.

H. G. Wells wrote a series of science romances and other works including *The Time Machine* (1895), *The Food of the Gods* (1904), *First and Last Things* (1908), *God The Invisible King* (1917), *The Secret Places of the Heart* (1922), *The Fate of Man* (1939), *You Can't Be Too Careful* (1941), *New World Order* (194?), and *Mind at the End of Its Tether* (194?).

Wells' Views. There are many words that describe the beliefs of Wells: evolutionism, antipessimism, *mysticism, *dualism, *finite godism, *agnosticism and even *fideism were all embraced by Wells. What is consistent throughout his work is humanistic evolutionism (*see* HUMANISM, SECULAR).

Reacting to his early pessimism, Wells wrote: "I dismiss the idea that life is chaotic because it leaves my life ineffectual, and I cannot contemplate an ineffectual life patiently." Further, "I assert . . . that I am important in a scheme, that we are all important in a scheme. . . . What the scheme as a whole is I do not know; with my limited mind I cannot know. There I become a Mystic." He adds, "And this unfounded and arbitrary declaration of the ultimate righteousness and significance of things I call the Act of Faith. It is my fundamental religious confession. It is a voluntary and deliberate determination to believe, it is a choice made" (*First and Last Things*, 66–67).

In 1917, he professed to have found salvation from the purposelessness of life described in a book entitled *God the Invisible King*. William Archer charged that here Wells saw himself as the apostle of a new religious faith (Archer, 32).

God was finite and had come into existence in time but outside space. God was the personal Captain of Mankind who grows as mankind grows. Nonetheless, God was not the collective Mind of mankind but a being with a character of his own.

God's Enemy was Nature or, more specifically, Death. Thus God's aim was to overcome death. God stands over the Veiled Being or Life Force which is "Nature red in tooth and claw."

In the end Wells turned pessimistic (*Mind at the End of Its Tether*). He despairs that man will be able to adapt and fears he will go the way of the dinosaur. Nevertheless, he believes evolution will go on through some other organism.

Evaluation. For an evaluation of Wells' views, see the articles mentioned above under "Wells' Views."

Sources

W. Archer, *God the Invisible King*

W. B. Glover, "Religious Orientations of H. G. Wells . . .," *Harvard Theological Review* 65 (1972)

H. G. Wells, *First and Last Things*

———, *God the Invisible King*

———, *Mind at the End of Its Tether*

Whateley, Richard. Richard Whateley (1786–1863) was an English logician and theologian and archbishop of Dublin (1831–1863). His book *Logic* (1826) set forth the essence of his understanding of the use of reason. He left behind his own memoir, which was published posthumously by his daughter, *Life and Correspondence . . .* (1866). Whateley also edited William *Paley's *Evidences and Moral Philosophy*. But his most enduring legacy from an apologetics standpoint is *Historic Doubts Relative to Napoleon Bonaparte* (1819). In this short work he satirized skepticism by reducing to the absurd the logic used to deny the authenticity of the Bible.

Using the still-living historical figure Napoleon I (1769–1821) as an example, Whateley applied David *Hume's (1711–1776) principles of skepticism. He said it was no wonder the public was still occupied with recounting the exploits of Napoleon, given their extraordinary character. But no one seemed to be asking the crucial question of whether Napoleon even existed. Whateley noted that the unquestioned is not necessary unquestionable. People admit hastily what they are accustomed to take for granted. Hume had pointed out the readiness with which people believe on slight evidence the stories that please their imagination.

Upon examining the evidence, Whateley concludes that, aside from the rare first-hand witness, the newspaper had become the authority for truth. But using Hume's three principles of credibility (*see* NEW TESTAMENT, HISTORICITY OF), the authority of the newspaper fails on all points. Hume asked of witnesses:

1. whether they have the means of gaining correct information.
2. whether they are interested in concealing truth or propagating falsehood.
3. whether they agree in their testimony.

"It appears then that those on whose testimony the existence and actions of Bonaparte are generally believed, fail in all the most essential points on which the credibility of witnesses depends; first, we have no assurance that they have access to correct information; second, they have an apparent interest in propagating falsehood; and, thirdly, they palpably contradict each other in the most important points" (266). Whateley challenges the free thinker to weigh all the evidence, "and if he then finds it amounts to anything more than a probability," Whateley said he would congratulate him for his easy faith (271).

Whateley insists that the story becomes even more doubtful when it partakes of the extraordinary. Tracing the incredible nature of Napoleon's military exploits, Whateley asked whether anyone would believe this, yet not believe in miracles. For it seemed to him that Napoleon had violated the laws of nature (274). Hence, every skeptic who follows his own principles should reject such stories about Napoleon as highly improbable.

In addressing the question of motive, Whateley pointed out that, while the story about Napoleon *may* be true, a more ingenious one could not have been fabricated for the amusement of the British people. He speculates, as well, on how the name *Napoleon Bonaparte* could have mistakenly arisen, as had others in history. He called free thinkers to listen to no testimony that runs contrary to their experience but to follow their principles consistently. "If, after all that has been said, they cannot bring themselves to doubt the existence of Napoleon Bonaparte, they must at least acknowledge that they do not apply to that question the same plan of reasoning which they have made use of in others" (290).

Whether any skeptics announced their doubt about Napoleon, a few of the more open minded should have been encouraged to check their biases regarding biblical accounts of miracles in general, and the New Testament's record of Jesus in particular.

Sources

D. Hume, *An Inquiry Concerning Human Understanding*, book 10

R. Whateley, *Historic Doubts Relative to Napoleon Bonaparte*, in H. Morley, ed., *Famous Pamphlets*

Whitehead, Alfred North. Alfred North Whitehead (1861–1947) is the father of the contemporary worldview known as *panentheism (not to be confused with pantheism), or Process Theology. He was born on the Isle of Thanet, the son of an Anglican minister. He attended Sherborne public school in Dorset, learning classics, history, and mathematics. He attended Trinity College, Cambridge, on a mathematics scholarship (1880–84) and was awarded a fellowship at Trinity in 1884.

The first period of writing (1898–1910) was focused on the philosophy of mathematics. He produced *A Treatise on Universal Algebra* (1898) and *Principia Mathematica* (with Bertrand Russell, 1910–13).

The second period of writing (1910–24) concentrated on the philosophy of science. While teaching at the University of London (1910–14) he wrote *Introduction to Mathematics* (1911).

Later, at Imperial College of Science and Technology (1914–24) he produced "Space, Time, and Relativity" (1915), *The Organization of Thought* (1917), *An Enquiry Concerning the Principles of Natural Knowledge* (1919), *The Concept of Nature* (1920), and *The Principle of Relativity* (1922).

A third period of writing (1924–47) stressed the philosophy of history and reality as well as cosmology and metaphysics. The transitional period (1925–27) brought forth *Science and the Modern World* (1925), *Religion in the Making* (1926), and *Symbolism, Its Meaning and Effect* (1927). His mature works in this field came from 1927 to 1947 and produced the epic *Process and Reality* (1929), *Adventures of Ideas* (1933), *Modes of Thought* (1938), and *Essays in Science and Philosophy* (1947).

Religion in the Making. Whitehead's understanding of religion is a landmark in modern thought. His understanding of dogma or propositional religious statements, if valid, would negate the orthodox Christian belief in an inspired and infallible Scripture (*see* BIBLE, EVIDENCE FOR). Whitehead's complex thought is sometimes called *process theology*, since its bottom-line reality is that all things are in process of becoming, including God.

Definition of Religion. Religion is defined as "A system of general truths which have the effect of transforming character when they are sincerely held and vividly apprehended." Religion emerged in *ritual*—habitual performances of acts irrelevant to physical preservation. It then manifested itself in *emotion*—definite types of expressing ones religious feelings, following ritual. Belief (*myth*) followed, giving definite explanations for the ritual. Finally came *rationalization*; the organization and clarification of beliefs and application to conduct. As rituals encouraged emotions (cf. holy-day and holiday), so myths begot thought.

Religion and Dogma. Religious experiences relate to dogma in that dogmas are attempts at precise formulations of religions experience. Rational religions have expressed their experience in three main concepts, first, the value of the individual, second, the value of diverse individuals for each other, and third, the value of the objective world for the existence of a community of individuals. "Religion is world-loyalty," though it begins with consciousness of value within the individual.

According to Whitehead, rational religion is an attempt to find a permanent, intelligible interpretation of experience. Buddhism and Christianity differ in that the latter is metaphysics seeking a religion, whereas the latter is religion seeking a metaphysics. In Buddhism (*see* ZEN BUDDHISM), evil is necessary, but in Christianity it is only contingent. While Buddhists seek relief from the world, Christians seek to change the world. Buddha gave doctrine to enlighten, but Christ gave his life to save. Buddhism begins from general principles, but Christianity begins with facts and generalizes on them.

****Metaphysics.*** According to Whitehead, both *process* and *permanence* interplay as aspects of reality. Permanence is a *potential element* of reality. Temporal (time) permanence is found in eternal objects. Nontemporal permanence is found in God (or at least in God's primordial nature, as noted below).

A bit of reality is the *actual element* or entity. Being *is* the potential for becoming. This is the *principle of relativity*. How a thing becomes is what a thing is. This is the *principle of progress*. Actual entities are real occasions, events, or drops of experience. As in *Plato's *Sophist*, they are becoming but never really finish the journey. With each passing moment of process, old dies and new is born. They pass from subjectivity to objectivity (immortality). This they do by final causality—namely, by their subjective aim. Once they are objectified, then they can act by efficient causality on others from past to present.

So how does one move along this pole-to-pole progression, objectifying and becoming? It is a mental process of seizing and incorporating into self an apprehension of the surrounding world. Actually it goes beyond "apprehending" or "comprehending" knowledge to uniting with the world being apprehended, so Whitehead dusts off the seldom-used term *prehension*.

Prehension is a process of feeling, so it goes beyond objective handling of objective realities. It absorbs what is prehended into the unity and satisfaction of the actual entity that is prehending. There are two kinds of prehension, negative or exclusive and positive or inclusive. There are three factors of prehension:

1. the occasion of experience (the subject, actual entity);

2. the data prehended (the object prehended);
3. the subjective form (how the datum is prehended).

All actual entities are bipolar by nature. The *conceptual pole* (potential aspect) is simple and can be negatively prehended in total. What is conceptual or potential is not now. The *physical pole* (actual aspect) is complex and can be prehended partly negatively and partly positively. It is some things; it is not other things. The ontological principle is that the only real causes of anything come from the physical pole. Only actual entities become real causes, final facts.

View of God. The God Options. Whitehead's view of God is bipolar. His actual pole is the universe, the cosmos. This pole is in constant change as God prehends more experiences or entities. God's potential pole is beyond the actual world. It is the infinite world of eternal and unchanging potential.

It may be helpful to see how Whitehead contrasted his view of God to other conceptions:

1. The Eastern Asiatic concept of an impersonal order to which the world conforms. This order is the self-ordering of the world; it is not the world obeying an imposed rule.
2. The Semitic concept of a definite personal. individual entity, whose existence is the one ultimate metaphysical fact. God is absolute and underived. This God decreed and ordered the derivative existence we call the actual world.
3. The pantheistic concept has connections to the Semitic concept, except that the actual world is a *phase* within the complete fact of the being of God. The complete fact is the ultimate individual entity of God. The actual world, conceived apart from God, is unreal. Its only reality is God's reality. The actual world is real only to the extent that it is a partial description of what God is. But in itself it is merely a certain mutuality of "appearance." This appearance is a phase of the being of God. This is the extreme doctrine of monism as held by Parmenides and Shankara (*see* Hinduism, Vedanta) in India (*Religion in the Making*, 66, 67).

Whitehead rejects these views. Christianity is a form of the "Semitic" view, though Christian doctrine has attempted to add some immanence to the utterly transcendent simple Semitic Being. It is the radical transcendence (otherness) of the Semitic God to which Whitehead objects. He also rejects the all-sufficiency of this conception of God,. "There is no entity, not even God, 'which requires nothing but itself in order to exist'" (ibid., 71).

The Existence and Nature of God. Following Immanuel Kant, Whitehead rejects the ontological argument as invalid. The cosmological argument can get us only so far as to postulate a God immanent in the world. Whitehead opts for an "aesthetic argument" from the order of the world. God is posited to account for the creative order in world process.

That is, God is dependent on the world, and the world is dependent on God. Apart from God, there would be no actual world. Apart from the dynamic creativity of the actual world, there would be "no rational explanation of the ideal vision which constitutes God."

In his actual pole, God is finite and limited. "To be an actual thing is to be limited." God cannot be infinite in his actual pole or he would be all things that actually are—evil as well as good (ibid., 144).

Note that this argument is interacting primarily with, and recasting the pantheistic worldview. Pantheism is denied, for its being is too immanent, yet it is the alternative that Whitehead's thought takes most seriously. To reduce God to an impersonal Force, as the Asiatic concept does, is to demean God's religious significance. God is personal, intimately related to the world. But likewise rejected is a transcendent God who is independent and self-existent. God is either finite, or he *is* the universe, including its evil (*see* Evil, Problem of). God is not *beyond* the world nor is he *identical* with it. God is *in* the world. "God is that function in the world by reason of which our purposes are directed to ends which in our own consciousness are impartial as to our own interests. Further, God is the actual realization (in the world) of the ideal world. 'The kingdom of heaven is God'" (ibid., 148, 151).

There is a God in the world, because "The order of the world is no accident. There is nothing actual which could be actual without some measure of order. . . . this creativity and these forms are together impotent to achieve actuality apart from the completed ideal harmony, which is God" (ibid., 115). God functions as the ground for creativity necessary for the attainment of value in the world. "God, as conditioning the creativity with his harmony of apprehension, issues into the mental creature as moral judgment according to a perfection of ideals." Thus, "the purpose of God in the attainment of value is in a sense a creative purpose. Apart from God, the remaining formative elements would fail in their functions" (ibid., 110, 114).

According to Whitehead, God has both a *primordial nature* and a *consequent nature*. The latter is the being which is being continually enriched by God prehends. Whitehead also calls it God's *superject nature*.

The primordial nature of God was to be the orderer of eternal objects. Eternal objects are pure potentials which, like Gottfried *Leibniz's monads, cannot relate themselves. The ontological principle demands that there be an actual entity behind them, since only actual entities are real causes.

God also is the orderer of actual entities. It is necessary for God to have a consequent nature. All actual entities are bipolar. The physical pole is needed to realize the vision of the conceptual pole. Also, the primordial nature relates only to eternal objects. And the principle of relativity demands that something relate to actual entities. Without God the actual world would fall into chaos.

The superject nature of God is merely the consequent nature as enriched by God's prehensions and as available for prehension by other actual entities—a never-ending process. Evil is incompatibility. What is evil does not fit into a given order of the world process. Creativity is the principle of conjunction and continuity that fills in the gaps between the atoms, that grounds the world process, that makes manyness into oneness. It is the "substance" of which all actual entities (even God) are the "accidents."

View of the World. God and the world are not actually different. God *is* the order (and value) in the actual world. The world is God's consequent nature. It is the sum total of all actual entities (events) as ordered by God. But the world is in process. It is constantly changing. Hence, God in his consequent nature is constantly in flux.

Creation. The universe is eternal. God does not create eternal objects. He is dependent on them as they are on him. Thus, God "is not *before* all creation, but *with* all creation" (ibid., 392, 521). He does not bring the universe into existence; he directs its progress.

As another process theologian put it, creation from nothing is too coercive. The temptation is great to interpret God's role by means of coercive power. "If the entire created order is dependent for its existence upon his will, then it must be subject to his full control. . . . Insofar as God controls the world, he is responsible for evil: directly in terms of the natural order, and indirectly in the case of man" (Ford, 201).

God is more of a cosmic persuader who lures the actual out of potential by final causality the way one is drawn by an object of their love.

In one sense the origin or "creation" of the universe is *ex materia* (out of preexisting matter). But the eternal "stuff" is not material but the realm of eternal forms or potentials which are there available for God to order and to urge into the world process as various aspects of actual entities. But since the realm of eternal objects is God's primordial nature, the movement of creation is also *ex deo*, that is, out of God's potential pole into his actual pole (the world). Reality moves from the unconscious to the conscious, from potential to actual, from abstract to concrete, from forms to facts.

What prompts this movement? What actualizes it? The answer is *creativity*. "'Creativity' is the principle of *novelty*." Creativity introduces novelty into the actual world. "The 'creative advance' is the application of this ultimate principle of creativity to each novel situation which it originates." Even God is grounded in creativity. "Every actual entity, including God, is a creature transcended by the creativity which it qualifies." Hence, "all actual entities share with God this character of self-causation" (*Process and Reality*, 31, 32, 135, 339).

There is a self-caused movement in God from his potential pole to his actual pole. God is a self-caused 'being' who is constantly becoming. Thus the process of creation is an eternal ongoing process of God's self-realization.

The World. The world is pluralistic (*see* PLURALISM). As a whole it is God's "body." It is made up of many "actual entities," what Whitehead calls "final facts," "drops of experience," or "actual occasions" (*Primordial Nature of God*, 95). The world is an atomistic series of events (*see* ATOMISM).

A process metaphysics of the world abandons the concept of actual entities that are the unchanging subjects of change. All things are rather constantly perishing and being reborn as different things. The idea that "no one crosses the same river twice" is extended to the person doing the crossing, as well as the water flowing in the stream. No thinker thinks twice. No subject experiences twice. There are no unchanging beings (ibid., 43, 122). There is no concrete being, all is becoming. "It belongs to the nature of every 'being' that it is a potential for every becoming. There is a becoming of continuity, but no continuity of becoming" (ibid., 53, 71).

Despite the atomic distinctness and continual change in the universe, there is order. This order is given by God. In his primordial nature God gives order to all eternal objects (forms) and the "consequent nature" of "God is the physical prehension by God of the actualities of the evolving universe" (ibid., 134).

Evil. God's self-realization is never perfect, nor is it totally incomplete. The actual world is neither purely orderly, nor purely chaotic. The immanence of an ordering God makes pure chaos impossible (ibid., 169). God is doing all he can to achieve the most possible out of every moment in world history. "The image under which this operative growth of God's nature is best conceived, is that of a tender care that nothing be lost" (ibid., 525). Evil can be defined as whatever is incompatible with these divine efforts at any given moment. Since God does not force the world, but only persuades it, he cannot destroy evil. He must simply work with it and do the best he can to overcome it (*see* FINITE GODISM; KUSHNER, HAROLD). "[The theory of] divine persuasion responds to the problem of evil radically, simply denying that God exercises full control over the world. Plato sought to express this by saying that

God does the best job he can in trying to persuade a recalcitrant matter to receive the impress of the divine forms" (Ford, 202).

What a finite God cannot persuade to fit into the overall unity of the actual world is evil. Evil is incompatibility. It is incongruence. Evil is like the left-over pieces of glass that did not fit into the stain glass window. Only this "picture" or order changes every split second. What does not fit one moment may fit later. Evil, then, must be conceived of as relative.

Human Beings. The human is a personal being with a free will. Each person has "subjective aims," for which ends are purposed and final causality is achieved. God gives overall aim—the initial direction, but where the creature goes from there is his or her own responsibility (Ford, 202–3).

In the mind-body relationship described by Whitehead, the living body is a coordination of actual occasions. Each person (God included) is a society of actual entities that constantly change. There is no changeless, enduring "I." An individual's unity is not found in any unchanging essence or being. It is self-caused becoming. Whitehead wrote:

> I find myself as essentially a unity of emotions, enjoyments, hopes, fears, regrets, valuations of alternatives, decisions—all of them subjective reactions to the environment as active in my nature. My unity—which is Descartes' *"I am"*—is my process of shaping this welter of material into a consistent pattern of feelings. I shape the activities of the environment into a new creation, which is myself at this moment; and yet, as being myself, it is a continuation of the antecedent world. [*Modes of Thought*, 228]

A person's identity is produced moment by moment within the community of actual events. As in the broader world, there is no continuity in becoming; there is only this becoming in continuity (*Religion in the Making*, 112).

Personal immortality was not an essential part of Whitehead's view. He saw no scientific evidence for it, but neither did he oppose it. He simply noted that at present it is generally held that a purely spiritual being is necessarily immortal. His doctrine is entirely neutral on the question of immortality, or on the existence of purely spiritual beings other than God (ibid., 107–8).

Ethics and Values. In this ever-changing kaleidoscope, there is no absolute evil, so there are no absolute values (*see* MORALITY, ABSOLUTE NATURE OF). Value is changing and subjective. "There are many species of subjective forms, such as emotions, valuations, purposes, adversions, aversions, consciousness, etc." (*Process and Reality*, 35). God is the measure of all value, but God is no more stable than is anything else. Nothing is not changing.

On the other hand, value is specific and concrete. God wants to attain value, and the search is creative. "The actual world is the outcome of the aesthetic order [of value], and the aesthetic is derived from the immanence of God" (*Religion in the Making*, 97, 100–1). The problem with the theistic Christian ethic is that it looks to an end of the world—definite goals and an absolute way to go. Christians give free rein "to their absolute ethical intuitions respecting ideal possibilities without a thought of the preservation of society" (*Adventures of Ideas*, 16).

For Whitehead, good and evil "solely concern inter-relations within the real world. The real world is good when it is beautiful" (ibid., 269). Goodness always comes in comparative degrees, just as things are more or less beautiful. But nothing is either most beautiful or most perfect. "Morality consists in the aim at the ideal.... Thus stagnation is the deadly foe of morality" (ibid., 269–70). There is at best, for both God and human beings, only a relative achievement of more good.

History and Destiny. There is an ongoing evolutionary (*see* EVOLUTION, COSMIC; EVOLUTION, BIOLOGICAL) process. God is achieving more and more value. It is being stored in his consequent nature, which, as enriched, is called God's "superject nature." However, "neither God, nor the world, reaches static completion" (ibid., 135, 529). Evil is recalcitrant, and no final victory over it is possible. Hence, Whitehead concludes, "In our cosmological construction we are, therefore left with the final opposites, joy and sorrow, good and evil, disjunction and conjunction—that is to say, the many in one—flux and permanence, greatness and triviality, freedom and necessity, God and the World" (ibid., 518).

Since God is neither omniscient nor omnipotent, even God does not know how the world process will eventuate (*see* GOD, NATURE OF). For "during that process God, as it were, has to wait with bated breath until the decision is made, not simply to find out what the decision was, but perhaps even to have the situation clarified by virtue of the decision of that concrete occasion" (Loomer, 365).

Evaluation. The complexity and vastness of Whitehead's thought makes it difficult to offer a comprehensive evaluation of his ideas in a short space. Much of this is evaluated elsewhere. His underlying epistemology of relative truth and morality is covered in TRUTH, ABSOLUTE NATURE OF; MORALITY, NATURE OF). On the process view of God and reality, see PANENTHEISM. The process concept of evil is exposed in EVIL, PROBLEM OF.

Sources

Ford, L. "Biblical Recital and Process Philosophy" in *Interpretation*

Geisler, N. L. "Process Theology," in S. Gundry et al., eds., *Tensions in Contemporary Theology*

———, et al., *Worlds Apart: A Handbook of World Views*, chap. 4
D. F. Lindsey, "An Evangelical Overview of Process Theology," *Sacra* 134 (January–March 1977)
B. Loomer, "A Response to David Griffin," *Encounter* 36:4 (Autumn 1975)
A. N. Whitehead, *Process and Reality*
———, *Religion in the Making*

William of Ockham. Modern skepticism (*see* AGNOSTICISM) did not begin with David *Hume. It began in the late Middle Ages with William of Ockham (1285–1349). Ockham was the younger contemporary of Duns Scotus (1266–1308) and Thomas Aquinas (1224–1274). He stood at the end of the middle ages, and contributed to the rise of the modern age. Whereas skepticism flowered in David Hume (1711–1776), its roots were in William of Ockham.

Ockham's thought had a significant influence on the radical empiricism and skepticism of Hume, the ethical situationalism of Joseph Fletcher (*see* MORALITY, ABSOLUTE NATURE OF), the idealism of George *Berkeley (1685–1753), the antitransubstantiation of Martin Luther (1483–1546), as well as ethical voluntarism, nominalism, and the univocity of religious language (*see* ANALOGY, PRINCIPLE OF).

Epistemological Skepticism. His skepticism was manifest on three levels: epistemological, methodological, and apologetic. In his epistemology he was a nominalist and a skeptical empiricist.

Ockham distrusted the senses. He stressed intuition. He held that essences or universals were mental abstractions that were based in real things (*see* REALISM). But Ockham believed that an essence was merely a mental construct with no root in reality. Such things as human nature were not real. Only individual humans exist.

*Nominalism has serious implications when applied to the fall of humanity and its redemption. How can a sinful being inherit a single nature if there is no such thing as a nature? How can Christ assume human nature and die for all people, unless there is a human nature? How can one hold an orthodox belief in the Trinity, which affirms that God is three persons in one essence if there are no essences?

Ockham argued that since God was omnipotent that he could do anything. He could create the idea of a tree in our mind, even without the presence of a tree (*see* GOD, NATURE OF). This, of course, undercut trust in the process of "knowing" something. One could "know" something to be true that did not really exist. Could not God create the idea of a world in our minds when there was no world? To apply Ockham to a later skeptic, could not the "demon" conceived by René *Descartes (1596–1650) deceive us into believing a nonexistent world existed?

Even without malevolent deception, why could not a benevolent God create impressions he desired without there being any external object corresponding to them?

Methodological Skepticism. Ockham also posited the principle of economy of causes, known as *Ockham's razor*. This tool also proved useful to later skeptics, with its principle of simplicity or economy of causes. Although Ockham's statement was "Do not multiply causes without necessity," this has been popularized (corrupted) into the idea, "The simplest cause is the best explanation," or "The fewer the truer." This leads to "The fewest the truest." When this is combined with the principle of omnipotence, the consequences can be devastating. For example, God could create the impression there is a physical world when there is none. This simpler explanation would, then, be the true one. This, indeed, is the conclusion at which Bishop Berkeley later arrived.

Apologetic Skepticism. Ockham was not a skeptic about the existence of God. He was a theist. However, his skepticism undermined the apologetic defense of theism. His objections to the cosmological argument anticipated Hume and Immanuel Kant. Ockham raised at least three questions about the cosmological argument (Ockham, 129ff; *see* GOD, OBJECTIONS TO ARGUMENTS FOR).

*The Possibility of an *Infinite Series.* Ockham denied that an essentially related infinite regress of causes was impossible (*see KALAM* COSMOLOGICAL ARGUMENTS). Since essentially related causes (for example, father begetting son) need not be simultaneous, they could be originating causes and not conserving causes. The father is not the continued cause of the son's existence. Only if this simultaneity of the here-and-now conserving cause is added to the concept of an essentially related series of causes, argued Ockham, is an infinite regress impossible.

It is contradictory to affirm that there is no First Cause for what is right now being conserved in existence. So the cosmological argument is valid in reference to what now exists, but not for any original creation.

Knowledge of Efficient Causes. Anticipating Hume, Ockham based knowledge of efficient causes on experience (*see* CAUSALITY, PRINCIPLE OF). Causality is defined as "that whose existence or presence is followed by something" (Maurer, 270). The distinction anticipates Hume's criticism that there is no basis in experience for making a necessary connection between cause and effect. But the inescapability of the conclusion of the cosmological argument depends on the necessity of the connection between cause and effect. Ockham thus placed his razor on the central cord binding the cosmological argument.

Inability to Prove One God. Ockham also held that one could not prove in an absolute sense the existence of only one God (*see* THEISM; GOD, NATURE OF). Only if the unity of God is taken to mean "the most perfect Being that actually exists" can it be said that the unity of God has been proven. If, however, as Christian theists insist, the unity of God refers to the "most perfect" Being possible, then the unity of God cannot be proven. The proposition "God exists." is not a self-evident proposition. Many doubt it, and a self-evident proposition cannot be doubted. Nor is the absolute unity of God known through other propositions, which can also be doubted, nor by experience, for experience can provide one only with the actual, not with the possible.

Therefore, there is no way to demonstrate that God is absolutely one.

Univocal Religious Language. In one area Ockham held the line against skepticism. He spoke strongly against any equivocal or analogical concepts as applied to God. Ockham argues convincingly that no concept can have a totally different or equivocal meaning as applied to God. For if it did, then we would have no idea what it meant. Likewise, an analogous concept must have an element of sameness, otherwise it would be totally different. This element of sameness is really univocal. Hence, without univocal concepts we can know nothing about God.

While the point is well taken when speaking about univocal concepts, Ockham seemed not to understand the need for analogical predication, such as was posited by Aquinas. That is, we must define terms used of God and creatures in the same way, but they are applied in a different way. God is infinitely good, while creatures can strive only for finite goodness. Goodness cannot be applied univocally or in entirely the same way to the infinite and the finite (*see* ANALOGY, PRINCIPLE OF).

Evaluation. Ockham's epistemological skepticism is discussed in the articles CAUSALITY, PRINCIPLE OF; FIRST PRINCIPLES; HUME, DAVID, and REALISM. Apologetic skepticism is treated in COSMOLOGICAL ARGUMENT; GOD, OBJECTIONS TO PROOFS FOR; HUME, DAVID, and KANT, IMMANUEL.

As for Ockham's methodological skepticism, even granting his premises, "Ockham's Razor" does not work in discussions of God, since it presupposes the existence of an omnipotent God as a premise. Even granting that God *could* create ideas in us without external objects does not mean God *would* do this. The theistic God of Ockham is not only all-powerful but also all-good. And a omnibenevolent God will not deceive (*see* ESSENTIALISM, DIVINE). Ockham's skepticism does not work without the questionable principle of parsimony. But how can one prove that the positing the fewest causes possible is the way to determine what is true. This is not a first principle. At best, it is only a general guide in scientific matters. It is no universal rule in metaphysical issues.

Why assume an external world is redundant? God may have very good purposes for it. Using Ockham's own Razor, it can be viewed as a simpler explanation that an objectively real world is sending impressions to every one than that God must create impressions in every human being individually. Ockham's explanation that God could be directly creating ideas of an external world in every human being is *Deus ex Machina* (the God-out-of-the-machine). It invokes the supernatural to save its conclusion from collapse. God must pop out of the machine and save it. Again, it is simpler in this case to take the natural explanation than to invoke a supernatural one.

Sources

O. F. M. Boehner, "Introduction," in William of Ockham, *Philosophical Writings*
N. L. Geisler and W. Corduan, *Philosophy of Religion*
E. Gilson, *History of Christian Philosophy in the Middle Ages*
A. Maurer, *Medieval Philosophy*
William of Ockham, *Expositio super librum Perihermenias*
———, *Ordinatio* (D. II, Q. viii, prima redactio)
———, *Philosophical Writings*
———, *Summa totius logicae* (I, c.xiv)

Witnesses, Hume's Criteria for. David *Hume (1711–1776), is the skeptic exemplar for modern times (*see* AGNOSTICISM). He outlines the basic criteria that he believed necessary for testing the credibility of witnesses. In his own words: "We entertain suspicion concerning any matter of fact when the witnesses contradict each other, when they are but few or of a doubtful character, when they have an interest in what they affirm, when they deliver their testimony with hesitation, or with too violent asseverations [declarations]" (Hume, 120).

These concerns can be framed as four questions:

1. Do the witnesses contradict each other?
2. Are there a sufficient number of witnesses?
3. Were the witnesses truthful?
4. Were they nonprejudicial?

Hume's tests can be readily applied to the New Testament witnesses for the resurrection of Christ.

No Contradiction of Witnesses. The evidence is that the testimony of the witnesses does not contradict (*see* NEW TESTAMENT, HISTORICITY OF). Each New Testament writer tells a crucial and overlapping part of the whole story.

- Christ was crucified [around A.D. 30] under Pontius Pilate in Jerusalem.
- He claimed to be the Son of God and offered miracles in support of his claim.
- He was crucified, confirmed to be dead and buried, and yet three days later the tomb was empty (*see* CHRIST, DEITY OF).
- Jesus physically appeared to a number of groups of people over the next weeks, in the same nail-scarred body that had died.

- He proved his physical reality to them so convincingly that these skeptical men boldly preached the Resurrection a little over a month later in the same city, whereupon thousands of Jews were converted to Christianity.

There are minor discrepancies in the Gospel accounts. One account (Matt. 28:5) says there was one angel at the tomb; John says there were two angels (John 20:12). Such conflicts are not contradictions in that they are not irreconcilable. Matthew does not say there was *only* one angel there; that would be a contradiction. We are uncertain of whether the two texts are speaking of the same moments (*see* BIBLE, ALLEGED ERRORS IN). Also, minor differences in testimony are not what Hume had in mind in his first rule. One would not expect authentic, independent witnesses to give identical testimony. If they did we might discount their testimony, assuming they were in collusion.

Number of Witnesses. There are twenty-seven books in the New Testament written by about nine different persons, all eyewitnesses or contemporaries of the events they recorded.

When threatened by the authorities the apostles said, "We cannot but speak of what we have seen and heard" (Acts 4:20). Peter claimed to be a witness of Jesus (1 Peter 5:1). In 2 Peter 1:16 he wrote, "For we have not followed cunningly devised fables, when we made known unto you the power and coming of our Lord Jesus Christ, but were eyewitnesses of his majesty" (KJV). The author of the Fourth Gospel said, "And he that saw [it] bare record, and his record is true: and he knoweth that he saith true, that ye might believe" (John 19:35 KJV). He adds, "This is the disciple which testifieth of these things, and wrote these things: and we know that his testimony is true" (John 21:24 KJV). Indeed, John claimed about Christ: "That which was from the beginning, which we have heard, which we have seen with our eyes, which we have looked upon, and our hands have handled, of the Word of life. . . . That which we have seen and heard declare we unto you . . ." (1 John 1:1, 3 KJV). And Luke said, "Forasmuch as many have taken in hand to set forth in order a declaration of those things which are most surely believed among us, Even as they delivered them unto us, which from the beginning were eyewitnesses, and ministers of the word" (Luke 1:1–2 KJV).

Six witnesses are crucial to the topic of New Testament miracles (Matthew, Mark, Luke, John, Acts, and 1 Corinthians). These six books by five writers bear witness to the miracle of the resurrection. Even critical scholars now acknowledge that these books were written before A.D. 70, while contemporaries of Christ remained alive. There is little argument that 1 Corinthians was written by the apostle Paul around A.D. 55 or 56, only about two decades after the death of Christ. This is a powerful witness to the reality of the miracle of the resurrection. It is a very early document. It is written by an eyewitness of the resurrected Christ (1 Cor. 15:8; cf. Acts 9). Paul refers to more than 500 who had seen and heard the resurrected Christ directly (1 Cor. 15:6). Fourth). At the time, most of these witnesses were alive, available for cross-examination (*see* RESURRECTION, EVIDENCE FOR).

Truthfulness. Few challenge the fact that the New Testament provides a high standard for morality, particularly in Jesus' emphasis on love (Matt. 5–7; 22:36–37). His apostles repeated this teaching in their writings (for example, Romans 13; 1 Corinthians 13; Galatians 5). They lived, and even died for what they taught about Christ (2 Tim. 4:6–8; 2 Peter 1:14), an unmistakable sign of their sincerity.

In addition to teaching that truth is a divine imperative (Rom. 12:9), it is evident that the New Testament writers were scrupulous about truth in their writings. Peter declared, "We did not follow cunningly devised fables" (2 Peter 1:16). The Apostle Paul insisted, "Do not lie one to another" (Col. 3:9). The New Testament writers were honest men, willing to die for the truth of what they had written. Further, where the New Testament writers' statements overlap with the discovery of historians and archaeologists, they have proven to be accurate (*see* ACTS, HISTORICITY OF; ARCHAEOLOGY, NEW TESTAMENT). Archaeologist Nelson Glueck concludes, "It may be stated categorically that no archaeological discovery has ever controverted a Biblical reference. Scores of archaeological findings have been made which confirm in clear outline or exact detail historical statements in the Bible" (Glueck, 31). There is no proof that the New Testament writers ever lied in their writings or deliberately falsified the facts. As Harvard legal expert Simon Greenleaf concluded, their testimony shows absolutely no sign of perjury (see Greenleaf).

Finally, the New Testament record has received strong and significant support from historians of this Roman period. Noted Roman historian Sherwin-White chided scholars for not recognizing the historical value of the New Testament documents compared to the sources of Roman history (Sherwin-White, 188–91). Another noted historian of the period, Colin Hemer, presented strong evidence that supports the historical nature of the Book of Acts and its Lucan authorship (by A.D. 62) placing it "unequivocally in the lifetime of many eyewitnesses and surviving contemporaries of Jesus, Peter, and Paul, as prospective readers who could object to the presence of material falsification" (Hemer, 409–10).

Unprejudiced Witnesses. Nor were witnesses of the miracles of Christ, particularly his resurrection, predisposed to believe the events to which they gave testimony.

The apostles themselves disbelieved the first reports that Christ had risen from the dead (*see* RESURRECTION, EVIDENCE FOR). The story of the women "seemed to them like idle tales, and they did not believe them" (Luke 24:11). Even when some of the disciples saw Christ themselves they were "slow of heart to believe" (Luke 24:25). When Jesus appeared to ten apostles and showed them his crucifixion scars, "they still did not believe for joy, and marveled" (Luke 24:41). Thomas protested that he would not believe unless he could put his finger in the scars in Jesus' hand (John 20:25).

Jesus also appeared to unbelievers, at least his unbelieving half-brother, James (John 7:5; 1 Cor. 15:7), and the greatest unbeliever of the day—Saul of Tarsus (Acts 9).

Witnesses to the resurrection had nothing to gain personally from their testimony. They were persecuted and threatened with death for their stand (cf. Acts 4, 5, 8). As a matter of fact, most of the apostles were martyred. Certainly, it would have been much more profitable to deny the resurrection.

To discount their testimonies of those who believed in the resurrected Christ is like discounting an eye-witness of a murder because he actually saw it occur. The prejudice in this case is not with the witnesses but with those who reject their testimony.

Finally, to reject a witness simply because they have some kind of bias is groundless. Everyone has a bias or set of beliefs. No one's testimony could be accepted on anything if every bias were a disqualification. Doctors are biased in favor of a patient's survival. Yet they can still be trusted to give an objective analysis of the patient's condition. Richard Whateley argued satirically that we cannot believe the military exploits about Napoleon, since the British practically demonized him and the French virtually worshiped him. But in fact people do not discard their testimony since they have a bias. Rather, they examine carefully their testimony in order to determine the facts.

Conclusion. Hume was one of the great skeptics of modern times. He devised criteria by which he believed one could eliminate all belief in miracles. However, when his criteria are applied to witnesses to the resurrection of Christ they pass as credible. This confirms the Christian contention that the New Testament witnesses were reliable and, therefore, that the New Testament accurately reports what Jesus said and did (*see* NEW TESTAMENT, HISTORICITY OF).

Sources

M. Burrows, *What Mean These Stones?*
N. L. Geisler and R. Brooks, *When Critics Ask*
N. Glueck, *Rivers in the Desert: A History of the Negev*
S. Greenleaf, *The Testimony of the Evangelists*
C. Hemer, *The Book of Acts in the Setting of Hellenic History*
D. Hume, *An Enquiry Concerning Human Understanding*
A. N. Sherwin-White, *Roman Society and Roman Law in the New Testament*
C. Wilson, *Rocks, Relics, and Biblical Reliability*

Wittgenstein, Ludwig. Ludwig Wittgenstein (1889–1951) was the son of a wealthy Viennese steel magnate. His father was a Jewish Protestant. His mother was Roman Catholic, and Ludwig was baptized a Catholic. He studied engineering in Berlin and Manchester, England. He also studied at Cambridge under Bertrand Russell. Wittgenstein wrote what became an influential work in philosophy, *Tractatus Logico-Philosophicus* (1921, Eng., 1961) while in an internment camp as a captured prisoner of war. Wittgenstein believed he had solved all the problems of philosophy with *Tractatus*, so he retired from the field to teach school. He also gave away his inherited fortune. In the late 1920s, Wittgenstein met frequently with the Vienna circle of logical positivists (*see* LOGICAL POSITIVISM), including A. J. Ayer. He taught at Cambridge until 1947 and then took a job as a hospital porter. In 1948 he went into seclusion and soon learned he had cancer.

In addition to *Tractatus*, Wittgenstein's works included *Notebooks: 1914–1916* (1914–16, Eng. 1961), *Prototractatus* (1914–18, 1971), *Lectures and Conversations on Aesthetics, Psychology, and Religious Belief* (1930–38, 1966); *The Blue and Brown Books* (1933–35, 1958), *Remarks on the Foundations of Mathematics* (1937–44, 1956), *Zettell* (1945–48, 1966), *On Certainty* (1949–. 1969), and *Philosophical Investigations* (part 1, 1945; part 2, 1947–49, Eng. 1953).

Wittgenstein also continued to do research as an engineer and patented several inventions, including a jet reaction propeller for aircraft.

Three influences stand out among several on his philosophical thinking, Immanuel *Kant, Arthur *Schoppenauer, and Bertrand *Russell. Leo Tolstoy and Fyodor Dostoyevsky guided his lifestyle, and *Augustine and Søren *Kierkegaard were his favorite authors in religion.

Philosophical Thought. Wittgenstein knew two great periods of work. The early period was expressed by *Tractatus Logico-Philosophicus*. Wittgenstein himself said the point of the book was ethical. In the preface he explained that he hoped to set limits on the expression of thoughts. There can be no limits on thought, he declared. "We should have to be able to think what cannot be thought." However, to set limits on language is to differentiate between meaningful ideas and nonsense. "What we cannot speak about we must pass over in silence," he said. That reflected his own work on the book. He said, "My work consists of two parts: The one presented here plus all that I have not written and it is precisely this second part that is the important one."

The project in *Tractatus* is Kantian. The method is that of logical atomism in that Wittgenstein assumes there is a convergence between language and reality. Language mirrors the world. This convergence has serious implications for ethics and philosophy in his thinking. All that can be expressed in language are propositions of natural science (*Tractatus*, 6:42). No transcendental propositions about ethics, aesthetics, or God can be expressed.

The second period of Wittgenstein's work was expressed in *Philosophical Investigations*. Wittgenstein presents and then tries to refute statements of Augustine on the "picture theory of meaning" as the essence of human language. He regards as an oversimplification the ideas that the function of language is to state facts and that all words are names, referring to something. He strikes down as mistaken Augustine's idea that meaning is taught by examples in definition. Example definitions can be variously interpreted (ibid., 1.1:28). The statement of Augustine that the meaning of a name is the object that the name denotes he regarded as absurd.

He also rejected the ideas that meaning is a matter of producing mental images, that one clarifies propositions by analyzing them, and that words have a determinate sense. He rejected both univocal and analogical language (*see* ANALOGY, PRINCIPLE OF). On the positive side, Wittgenstein was a strong proponent of *conventionalism.

The central point is that religious language is meaningless. It belongs to the realm of the inexpressible because there is an unbridgeable gulf between fact and value. As discussed in the article on analogy, this view is that all "God-talk" is nonsense. That does not mean that the person cannot feel or know anything about God. It is clear from *Notebooks* that there is a feeling of dependence and a belief in God because "the facts of the world are not the end of the matter." But what Wittgenstein knows he cannot really talk about. Such things are outside the limits of language, and ultimately thought.

Because the higher and transcendent are inexpressible is not to say they are totally incommunicable. They can be shown if not said. An apparent contradiction in *Tractatus* is that although propositions about language are employed they are not propositions of natural science. By Wittgenstein's own reasoning they must be nonsense. He acknowledges this, saying that they can only serve as elucidations—an example of showing and saying (6:45).

In *Investigations*, Wittgenstein does not directly speak about religious discourse, but he seems to assume that prayer and theology are meaningful linguistic activities. Praying in particular is mentioned as a language game. Since stating facts is only one of many linguistic activities, there is no *a priori* bar against the meaningfulness of religious language. Since language games have intrinsic criteria of meaning, and religious language is a language game, it must be judged by its own standards and not by standards imposed upon it. This is a form of fideism.

In *Lectures and Conversations*, Wittgenstein portrays religious language as possibly being meaningful (as a language game). But it is clear that he remains an acognostic. He rejects any cognitive knowledge in religious language. For example, it is legitimate to utter a belief in a last judgment. But no one could say whether the belief is possibly true or false (58). Such beliefs are purely a matter of blind faith (*see* FIDEISM). There is no evidence for them. He would not, however, ridicule those who claim to base their beliefs on evidence, for example, historical apologetics.

"It has been said that Christianity rests on an historical basis. It has been said a thousand times by intelligent people that indubitability is not enough in this case, even if there is as much evidence as for Napoleon (*see* WHATELY, RICHARD). Because the indubitability wouldn't be enough to make me change my whole life" (57).

Religious beliefs help orient our lives, but they do not inform us about reality. Wittgenstein believes we are locked in a linguistic bubble. Religious language is fine as a language game, but it tells us nothing about God or ultimate reality.

Evaluation. Unlike the logical positivists (*see* AYER, A. J.), Wittgenstein did not utterly deny the meaningfulness of religious language. It remained a legitimate form of language and was based in a meaningful experience. Also, Wittgenstein did not join the Vienna Circle in affirming empirical verifiability. They insisted that only empty tautologies (*see* TAUTOLOGY), which are true by definition or know through the senses, could be meaningful. Wittgenstein rejected this form of positivism, realizing that meaning should be listened to, not legislated.

Therefore, he did not embrace atheism. He was a fideistic theist. He read both the New Testament and Søren *Kierkegaard. He acknowledged the validity of prayer and belief in last things. He even recognized that religious language has value. Though it was not descriptive to him, it did aid the religious life in a practical way. It was a meaningful expression of religious experience and helped one live.

Wittgenstein was the archenemy of the Platonic (*see* PLATO) view that there is a one-to-one univocal correspondence between our ideas and those of God. This Augustinian view he rejected outright. There is no correspondence between our thought and God's (*see* TRUTH, NATURE OF).

However, his view is open to serious criticism. All forms of *fideism are untenable. If one takes his writings as a rational justification of the nonrational fideistic faith, they are self-defeating. If he offers no rational justification for his beliefs, they are simply unproven propositions that no reasonable person should accept.

He also follows Kant into a false dichotomy between fact and value. They saw the two in totally separate domains. But this is not the case. Human beings combine both. One cannot attack human facticity (the physical presence of the body) without attacking the value of life and personhood. One cannot separate rape or genocide from the value of the object that is at the center of those actions. In theology, the fact of the death of Christ cannot be separated from its redemptive value.

Wittgenstein believed we are locked inside a language that tells us nothing about the realm of value beyond language itself. This is self-defeating. Any attempt to forbid statements about the mystical realm beyond language transgresses that prohibition. Like Kant's *agnosticism, one cannot know that he cannot know, and he cannot say that he cannot say. In claiming that the mystical cannot be spoken, one speaks about it.

Among Wittgenstein's legacies, none is more deadly than the conventionalist view of meaning. All meaning cannot be relative. If it were the statement "All meaning is relative." would be meaningless. Like other attempts to deny objective meaning, Wittgenstein had to assume the objective meaning of his statements (*see* CONVENTIONALISM).

Sources

N. L. Geisler and W. Corduan, *Philosophy of Religion*
E. Gilson, *Linguistics and Philosophy*
Plato, *Cratylus*
Thomas Aquinas, *Summa Theologica*
L. Wittgenstein, *Tractatus Logico-Philosophicus*
———, *Philosophical Investigations*

Wolfe, Christian. ***See*** **COSMOLOGICAL ARGUMENT.**

World Religions and Christianity. Orthodox Christianity claims to be the true religion. So does Islam and other religions. Even *Hinduism and Buddhism (*see* ZEN BUDDHISM), in spite of their eclectic veneer, claim to be true. Since there are mutually exclusive truth claims among these religions, it is obvious that they cannot all be correct. For example, some religions are monotheistic, such as, traditional Judaism, Christianity, and Islam. Others are pantheistic, such as, Hinduism, Zen Buddhism, and Christian Science. Paganism, Neopaganism, and Mormonism are polytheistic (*see* POLYTHEISM). These have incompatible views of God. In the final analysis, only one can be true, and the others must be false.

Uniqueness of Christianity. The uniqueness of Christianity is found in its singular claims about God, Christ, the Bible, and the way of salvation. While there are other monotheistic religions, Christianity claims to have the true view of God—Trinitarianism (*see* TRINITY).

A Unique View of God. No other religion in human history is explicitly trinitarian. *Plato had a triad in ultimate reality of the Good, the Demiurgos, and the World Soul (see Plato). But the Good was neither personal nor God. The World Soul was not personal. The three did not share one nature. Neoplatonism had a One, a Nous, and a World Soul (see Plotinus). But this series of emanations is not three distinct persons in one essence. Neither the One nor the World Soul is personal. The One has no essence or being. Only in the Christian *Trinity is there one God in essence who is expressed eternally in three distinct persons—Father, Son, and Holy Spirit (Matt. 28:18).

Christians claim that this view of God is the true view of God and that there is no other God (1 Cor. 8:4, 6). Other views are either false views of the true God (as Judaism) or false gods (as in Hinduism). The Islamic view of God is false because it insists that there is only one person in the godhead.

The Jewish (i.e., Old Testament) view of God is of the true God, but it is incomplete. It rightly insisted that there is only one God (Exod. 20:2–3; Deut. 6:4). The Old Testament allowed for a plurality within the unity of God (Ps. 110:1) and sometimes spoke of God's Son (Prov. 30:4). Once all three members of the Trinity are mentioned in one passage (Isa. 63:7–10). But the Old Testament never explicitly delineates the members of the Trinity as three persons in One God. The Old Testament Jewish God is the true God revealed explicitly in his unity. It is revelation in progress. The God represented in all other religions is false. These gods are incompatible with the Bible's view of God. It is the exclusivity of Christianity that this view alone is true.

A Unique View of Christ. No other world religion believes that Christ is the unique Son of God, God himself manifested in human flesh (*see* CHRIST, DEITY OF). Orthodox Christianity alone confesses that Jesus is fully God and fully human, two natures in one person. Other religions pay homage to Christ. But none considers him to be God incarnate. To Buddhism and Hinduism he is a Guru showing a path to ultimate reality (Brahman). Islam acknowledges him as one of several prophets (*see* MUHAMMAD, ALLEGED DIVINE CALL OF). To Hinduism the incarnation is really a *reincarnation) of Krishna. But there are significant differences between Krishna and Christ. Krishna is only a temporary incarnation. He is not an incarnation of a monotheistic God but of a pantheistic God. There is no real comparison between the Christian concept of Christ and that of any other religion. Some religious movements and cults have adopted a view of Christ's deity. But each has added its own unorthodox beliefs to destroy the truth claims made in Scripture. One form of Buddhism even has

Buddha dying for our sins. But this is far from Christianity and is foreign even to the nature of indigenous Buddhism (*see* Christ, Uniqueness of).

Speaking of the mystery religions, British scholar Norman Anderson explains,

> The basic difference between Christianity and the mysteries is the historic basis of the one and the mythological character of the others. The deities of the mysteries were no more than "nebulous figures of an imaginary past," while the Christ whom the apostolic *kerygma* proclaimed had lived and died only a few years before the first New Testament documents were written. Even when the apostle Paul wrote his first letter to the Corinthians the majority of some five hundred witnesses to the resurrection were still alive. [Anderson, 52–53]

A Unique View of the Written Word of God. Most religions have holy or wisdom books, including all the major world religions. Judaism has the Torah, *Islam the *Qur'an*, and Hinduism the *Bhagavad-gita*. In comparison with these and other writings, the Christian Bible is unique.

- Only the Bible claims to come by the unique process of divine inspiration (*see* Bible, Inspiration of). The *Qur'an* claims to have come by verbal dictation from the angel Gabriel to Muhammad.
- Only the Bible has supernatural predictive prophecy (*see* Prophecy, As Proof of the Bible). Other religions claim predictive prophecy but fail to provide examples of clear predictions hundreds of years in advance that have been literally fulfilled, such as the Bible has. Muslims, for example, claim that Muhammad made predictions in the *Qur'an*. But upon closer examination they fail to measure up to their billing (*see* Muhammad, Alleged Miracles of; *Qur'an*, Alleged Divine Origin of).
- Only the Bible has been supernaturally confirmed (*see* Bible, Evidence for; Christ, Deity of). For only the Bible was written by men of God who were confirmed by special acts of God (cf. Exod. 4:1f.; Heb. 2:3–4) to be telling the truth about God (*see* Miracles, Apologetic Value of; Miracles in the Bible).

Uniqueness of the Way of Salvation. While some other religions (e.g., "Cat" School of Bhakti Hinduism) employ grace (see Otto), Christianity is unique in its plan of salvation:

- It declares humankind sinful and alienated from a holy God (Gen. 6:5; Psalm 14.; Eccles. 7:28; Luke 13:3; Rom. 3:23).
- It insists that no amount of good works can get a human being into heaven (Isa. 64:6; Rom. 4:5; Eph. 2:8–9; Titus 3:5–7).
- It declares that there is only one way to God—through the death and resurrection of Jesus Christ for our sins (John 10:1, 9; 14:6; 1 Cor. 15:1–6). One must believe from his heart and confess with his mouth to be saved (Rom. 10:9). There is no other way. Jesus said, "I am the way and the truth and the life. No-one comes to the Father except through me" (John 14:6; cf. John 10:1; Acts 4:12).

Salvation and Other Religions. Christianity, therefore, admits salvation through no other cult or religion. For Christ is not considered to be the Son of God who died for our sins and rose again in any non-Christian religion (*see* Resurrection, Evidence for).

It is important not to draw false implications from this exclusivity:

It does not follow that God does not love the unbelievers in the world. "For God so loved the world that he gave his one and only Son, that whoever believes in him shall not perish but have eternal life" (John 3:16). Paul said that God wants all to know the truth (1 Tim. 2:4).

It does not follow that God did not provide salvation for all. John informs us that Christ is the atoning sacrifice for both our sins and "the sins of the whole world" (1 John 2:2). Christ died not only for the elect but for all the "ungodly" (Rom. 5:6). He even died for those who "deny" him (2 Peter 2:1).

It does not follow that only a few select nations will be evangelized. John declared: "After this I looked and there before me was a great multitude that no one could count, from every nation, tribe, people and language, standing before the throne and in front of the Lamb. They were wearing white robes and were holding palm branches in their hands" (Rev. 7:9).

It does not follow that no salvation is available to those who have never heard of Christ (Acts 10:35; Heb. 11:6; *see* "Heathen," Salvation of). Anyone anywhere who seeks God will find him. Peter insisted that God "accepts men from every nation who fear him and do what is right" (Acts 10:35). The writer of Hebrews says "he rewards those who earnestly seek him" (Heb. 11:6).

All have the light of creation (Rom. 1:19) and conscience (Rom. 2:12–15), which is sufficient for condemnation but not salvation. There are many ways by which God could get the gospel to those who will to be saved. The normal way is through a missionary (Rom. 10:14–15). But God can save through his word (Heb. 4:12) which he can convey through a vision, a dream, a voice from heaven, or an angel (Rev. 14:6). God is not limited in the ways in which he can get the saving message to those who seek him (cf. Heb. 1:1). But if men turn from the light they have, God is not responsible to give more light (John 3:19).

Truth and Other Religions. Many Christians are willing to accept that there is truth or value in other religions (*see* TRUTH, NATURE OF). All humanity receives general revelation (Psalm 19; Acts 17; Rom. 1:19–29; 2:12–15). God has revealed truth to them, so it is no surprise that their beliefs express both good and truth.

There is, however, an important difference between truth as Christians hold it and truth as embraced by non-Christians. The Christian system is a system of truth with some error in it. All non-Christian religions are systems of error with some truths (*see* PLURALISM). The only system of truth is the Christian system. Since Christians are finite, our understanding of this system of truth will have some error in it. This is why we must continue to grow in the truth (2 Peter 3:18), knowing that now we understand imperfectly (1 Cor 13:9, 12). By contrast, no non-Christian system is true as a system, although there are truths within the system. However, the system itself obscures and taints these truths so that even they are distorted. And no non-Christian system provides the light of salvation.

Some Objections Answered. The unique claims of Christianity are offensive to the unbelieving mind. "The message of the cross is foolishness to those who are perishing, but to us who are being saved it is the power of God" (1 Cor 1:18). Nonetheless, the offended critic deserves an answer (Col. 4:5–6; 1 Pet. 3:15).

The Charge of Narrowness and Exclusivity. It is objected that Christianity is narrow and exclusivistic. Nothing sounds worse to the contemporary mind than narrow-mindedness. But this argument is more emotional than rational:

Only one worldview can be true. If the various worldviews have mutually exclusive truth claims, only one can be true (*see* PLURALISM). A true system of thought must be comprehensive of thought and life. It must possess consistency and coherence in its overall claims. But most important, the system must correspond to reality, past, present, and future, natural and supernatural. And all major systems of thought contain key truth claims which are contrary to those of all other systems. Either Christianity teaches true precepts about the *Trinity, the deity of Christ (*see* CHRIST, DEITY OF), and the one way of salvation, or else another system is true, and Christianity is false.

Truth by nature is narrow. It is narrow to claim that 3 + 3 = 6 is the only answer, but every other answer is wrong. The unbeliever's viewpoint is just as narrow. The claim "Christianity is true and all non-Christian systems are false" is no more narrow than to claim *"Hinduism is true and all non-Hindu systems are false." No truth claim is all-inclusive.

This does not mean that minor truths within opposing systems of thought cannot both be true. Non-Christians hold that murder is wrong and that the earth is spherical. But only Christians (and Judaism from which it emerged) believe that the world was created *ex nihilo* by a triune God. Christians and non-Christians can believe that Jesus was a good man. But only Christians believe that he was the God-man. So while here can be agreement between truths, there is no agreement on the major truths unique to the Christian system.

All religions claim to have the truth. As noted, the claim to unique truth is shared by every religious system that makes truth claims. This is true even of "broad," "eclectic" religions. Hindus claim that it is true that "There are many ways to God." This appears open-minded, but it is just as narrow as the Christian claim. It excludes all opposing views.

The Charge of Injustice. Is it unfair and unjust to claim that there is salvation in no other religion? This objection is without merit for reasons detailed in the article HEATHEN, SALVATION OF. It suffices to mention that God had provided salvation for everyone (John 3:16; 1 John 2:2). Everyone who really wants it will get it (Acts 10:35; Heb. 11:6).

Conclusion. Any truth claim is exclusive. A system that is all-inclusive makes no truth claim. And every proposition that affirms something denies something else by logical implication. Statements such as, "God is all" are opposed by statements such as, "God is not all." They cannot both be true. All truth claims exclude their contradictory. Indeed, all religions claim to have *the truth*—even if that truth is that they believe other noncontradictory religious systems are true also. But if two or more religions embrace the same truths, then they are really one. And that one basic religious system behind them claims to be the true religion to the exclusion of all opposed religious systems. So, Christianity's claim to be the true religion is no more narrow than the claim of any other religion (*see* PLURALISM, RELIGIOUS).

Sources

N. Anderson, *Christianity and World Religions*
E. C. Beisner, *God in Three Persons*
F. F. Bruce, *Paul and Jesus*
Y. S. Chishti, *What Is Christianity?*
W. Corduan, *Neighboring Faiths*
G. Habermas, *The Verdict of History*
J. N. D. Kelly, *Early Christian Doctrines*
J. G. Machen, *The Origin of Paul's Religion*
R. Nash, *Christianity and the Hellenistic World*
R. Otto, *India's Religion of Grace and Christianity Compared and Contrasted*
Plato, *The Republic*
Plotinus, *Enneads*
G. L. Prestige, *God in Patristic Thought*
H. Ridderbos, *Paul and Jesus*
H. Smith, *The Religions of Man*

Worldview. A *worldview* is how one views or interprets reality. The German word is *Weltanschauung*, meaning a "world and life view," or "a paradigm." It is the framework through which or by which one makes sense of the data of life. A worldview makes a world of difference in one's view of God, origins, evil, human nature, values, and destiny.

There are seven major worldviews. Each is unique. With one exception, *pantheism/*polytheism, no one can consistently believe in more than one worldview, because the central premises are mutually exclusive (*see* Truth, Nature of; Pluralism, Religious; World Religions, Christianity and). Logically, only one worldview can be true. The seven major worldviews are theism, deism, atheism, pantheism, panentheism, finite godism, and polytheism.

Looking Through the Views. *Theism. An infinite, personal God exists beyond and in the universe.* Theism says that the physical universe is not all there is. There is an infinite, personal God beyond the universe who created it, sustains it, and who acts within it in a supernatural way. He is transcendently "out there" and immanently "in here." This is the view represented by traditional Judaism, Christianity, and Islam.

Deism. God is beyond the universe, but not in it. Deism is theism minus miracles. It says God is transcendent over the universe but not immanent in it, certainly not supernaturally. It holds a naturalistic view of the operation of the world. In common with theism, it believes the originator of the world is a Creator. God made the world but does not work with it. He wound up creation and lets it run on its own. In contrast to pantheism, which negates God's transcendence in favor of his immanence, deism negates God's immanence in favor of his transcendence. Deists have included Francois-Marie *Voltaire, Thomas *Jefferson, and Thomas *Paine.

Atheism. No God exists beyond or in the universe. Atheism claims that the physical universe is all there is. No God exists anywhere, either in the universe or beyond it. The universe or cosmos is all there is and all there will be. All is matter. It is self-sustaining. A few of the more famous atheists were Karl *Marx, Friedrich *Nietzsche, and Jean-Paul *Sartre.

Pantheism. God is the All/Universe. For a pantheist, there is no transcendent Creator beyond the universe. Creator and creation are two ways of denoting one reality. God is the universe or All, and the universe is God. There is ultimately one reality, not many different ones. All is mind. Pantheism is represented by certain forms of Hinduism, *Zen Buddhism, and Christian Science.

Panentheism. God is in the universe, as a mind is in a body. The universe is God's "body." It is his actual pole. But there is another "pole" to God other than the physical universe. He has infinite potential to become. This view is represented by Alfred North *Whitehead, Charles *Hartshorne, and Shubert Ogden.

**Finite Godism. A finite God exists beyond and in the universe.* Finite godism is like theism, only the god beyond the universe and active in it is limited in nature and power. Like deists, finite godists generally accept creation but deny miraculous intervention. Often God's inability to overcome evil is given as a reason for believing God is limited in power. John Stuart *Mill, William *James, and Peter Bertocci hold this worldview.

**Polytheism. Many gods exist beyond the world and in it.* Polytheism is the belief in many finite gods, who influence the world. They deny any infinite God stands beyond the world. They hold that the gods are active, often believing that each has its own domain. When one finite god is considered chief over others, the religion is called henotheism. Chief representatives of polytheism include the ancient Greeks, Mormons, and neopagans (for example, wiccans).

Importance of a Worldview. Worldviews influence personal meaning and values, the way people act and think. The most important question a worldview answers is "Where did we come from?" The answer to this question is crucial to how other questions are answered. *Theism declares that God created us. Creation was from nothing, *ex nihilo*. *Atheism believes we evolved by chance. *Atheism holds to creation out of matter, *ex materia*. *Pantheism holds that we emanated from God like rays from the sun or sparks from a fire. Creation is out of God himself, *ex Deo* (*see* Creation, Views of). The others play on some form of these understandings, with nuances of difference.

That understanding would influence a person's view of death, for example. A theist believes in personal immortality; an atheist generally does not. For the theist, death is a beginning, for the atheist an ending of existence. For the pantheist, death is the cessation of one life and the beginning of another, leading toward ultimate merging with God.

Theists believe we were created by God with the purpose to eternally fellowship with and worship him. Pantheists believe we will eventually lose all individual identity in God. Atheists generally see *immortality only as the ongoing of the species. We live on in memories (for awhile) and in the influence we have on future generations.

Obviously, what one believes about the future will influence how he or she lives now. In classical theism, "We only come this way once" (cf. Heb. 9:27), so life takes on a certain sobriety and urgency it would not have for one who believes in *reincarnation. The urgency there is to deal with bad *karma* so the next life will be a step up. But there are always more chances in future lives to try, try again. For the atheist, the old beer commercial said it well: We have to "grab the gusto, because we only go around once."

A virtuous act is given different meanings by various worldviews. A theist views an act of compassion as an absolute obligation imposed by God (*see* Morality, Absolute Nature of), which has intrinsic value regardless of the consequences. An atheist views virtue as a self-imposed obligation that the human race has placed upon its members.

An act has no intrinsic value apart from that assigned to it by society.

There is also a gulf between worldviews with regard to the nature of values. For a theist, God has endowed certain things, human life for example, with ultimate value. It is sacred because God made it in his image. So there are divine obligations to respect life and absolute prohibitions against murder. For an atheist, life has the value the human race and its various societies have assigned to it. It is relatively valuable, as compared with other things. Usually an atheist believes an act is good if it brings good results and evil if it does not. A Christian believes that certain acts are good, whatever their results.

The differences in worldviews can be summarized in the accompanying chart. In some cases the words represent only the dominant or characteristic form of the view, not that of everyone who accepts the system.

Summary. Reality is either the universe only, God only, or the universe and God(s). If the universe is all that exists then atheism is right. If God is all that exists then pantheism is right. If God and the universe exists then either there is one God or many gods. If there are many gods, polytheism is right. If there is only one God then this God is either finite or infinite. If there is one finite god then finite godism is correct. If this finite god has two poles (one beyond and one in the world), then panentheism is right. If there is one infinite God then either there is intervention of this God in the universe or there is not. If there is intervention, then theism is true. If there is not, then deism is true.

Sources

N. L. Geisler, *Worlds Apart: A Handbook on World Views*

J. Sire, *The Universe Next Door*

D. Noebel, *Understanding the Times*

	Theism	Atheism	Deism	Finite Godism	Panentheism	Pantheism	Polytheism
God	One Infinite Personal	None	One Infinite Personal	One Finite Personal	One Potentially infinite Actually finite	One Infinite Impersonal or personal	Multiple Finite Personal
World	Created *ex nihilo* Finite	Eternal (material) Created *ex materia*	Finite Created *ex nihilo*	Created *ex materia* or *ex nihilo*	Created *ex Materia* and *ex deo* Eternal	Created *ex deo* immaterial	Created *ex materia* Eternal
God and World	God beyond and in world	World only	God beyond, but not in, world	God in world and beyond world	God beyond world potentially and in it actually	God is world (all)	Gods in world
Miracles	Possible and actual	Impossible	May be possible, but not actual	May be possible, but not actual	Impossible	Impossible	Possible and actual
Human nature	Soul and body immortal	Body Mortal	Body mortal/soul immortal	Body mortal/soul immortal	Body mortal/soul immortal (some)	Body mortal/soul immortal	Body mortal/soul immortal
Human destiny	Resurrection to reward or punishment	Annihilation	Reward or punishment of the soul	Rewards and/or punishment	In God's memory	Reincarnation, merging with God	Divine reward and punishment
Origin of evil	Free choice	Human ignorance	Free choice and/or ignorance	God's inner struggle, or man's choice	Necessary aspect of God	An illusion	In struggles between gods
End of evil	Will be defeated by God	Can be defeated by human beings	Can be defeated by human beings or God	Can be defeated by human beings or God	Cannot be defeated by human beings or God	Will be absorbed by God	Will not be defeated by gods
Basis of ethics	Grounded in God	Grounded in humanity	Grounded in nature	Grounded in God or in humanity	Grounded in changing God	Grounded in lower manifestations of God	Grounded in gods
Nature of ethics	Absolute	Relative	Absolute	Relative	Relative	Relative	Relative
History and goal	Linear Purposeful God-appointed end	Chaotic, Purposeless Eternal	Linear Purposeful Eternal	Linear Purposeful Eternal	Linear Purposeful Eternal	Circular Illusory Eternal	Linear or circular Purposeful Eternal

Zz

Zen Buddhism. *Forms of Buddhism.* Like *Hinduism from which it sprang, Buddhism is not a monolithic religion. It too encompasses many beliefs, and even different worldviews (see). All, of course, claim Gautama Buddha (563–483 B.C.). Buddha, who was raised in India, left his home and family in search for enlightenment, which he is said to have found while meditating under a Bo tree. Buddhists look to him as their source of enlightenment.

The two main branches of Buddhism are called Mahayana ("the greater vehicle") and Hinayana ("the lesser vehicle"). The former claimed enlightenment is available to all and the latter to only a few of the committed. Being aware of the negative connotation of the term, Hinayana Buddhists began to call themselves Theravada ("the teaching of the elders").

Basic Beliefs of Buddhists. Both groups of Buddhist accept the "Four Noble Truths" and the "Eightfold Path" to enlightenment.

The Four Noble Truths. The First Noble Truth is that life consists of suffering *(dukkha)* which entails pain, misery, sorrow, and the lack of fulfillment.

The Second Noble Truth is that nothing is permanent or unchanging in the world (the doctrine of *anicca*). And we suffer because we desire what is not permanent.

The Third Noble Truth is that the way to liberate oneself is by eliminating all desire or craving for what is temporal.

The Fourth Noble Truth is that desire can be eliminated by following the Eightfold Path:

The Eightfold Path is divided as follows:

WISDOM:

1. Right Speech
2. Right Thought

ETHICAL CONDUCT:

3. Right Speech
4. Right Action
5. Right Livelihood

MENTAL DISCIPLINE

6. Right Effort
7. Right Awareness
8. Right Meditation

These are not steps to be taken in sequential order, but attitudes and actions to be developed simultaneously.

In addition to these teachings, Buddhists believe in *reincarnation and Nirvana (Buddhist "heaven") which is the final state of "Nothingness" where is no more desire or frustration.

By far and away, however, the most influential form of Buddhism is known as Zen Buddhism. Its origins are found in Tao-sheng (A.D. 360–434), a Mahayana Buddhist and in Bodhi-dharma (d. A.D. 534). He migrated from China to Japan, where his form of Buddhism combined with Taoism emphasis on oneness with Nature. This eclectic blend is known as Zen ("meditation"). Since Zen has made the deepest inroads into Christianity, it is of the greatest interest to the Christian apologists.

One of the most influential advocates of *pantheism in the West was Daisetz Teitaro Suzuki. Through his long-term activity as a professor at Columbia University and at various other American universities, as well as his lectures throughout the Western world, Suzuki furthered the cause of Zen in its Western interpretation. D. T. Suzuki has influenced and convinced such Westerners as Christmas Humphreys and Alan Watts.

Nature of Zen. In order to understand Suzuki's form of pantheism, one must seek to grasp the nature of Zen. First, we shall note what Suzuki believes Zen is not, and then what he believes Zen is.

What Zen Is Not. According to Suzuki, Zen is not a system or philosophy "founded upon *logic and analysis." Zen is opposed to any form of dualistic thinking—that is, making any kind of subject-object distinction (*Introduction to Zen Buddhism*, 38). Instead Suzuki calls us to "Hush the dualism of subject and object, forget both, transcend the intellect, sever yourself from the understanding, and directly penetrate deep into the identity of the Buddha-mind; outside of this there are no realities."

Neither is Zen a set of teachings. Says Suzuki: "Zen has nothing to teach us in the way of intellectual analysis; nor has it any set doctrines which are imposed on its followers for acceptance." As such Zen has "no sacred books or dogmatic tenets." Indeed, "Zen teaches nothing." It is we who "teach ourselves; Zen merely points the way" (ibid., 38, 46).

Nor is Zen a religion as "popularly understood." It has no god to worship, no ceremonial rites, no afterlife, and no soul. When Suzuki says that there is no god in Zen, he neither denies nor affirms existence of some deity. "In Zen, God is neither denied nor insisted upon; only there is in Zen no such God as has been conceived by Jewish and Christian minds" (ibid., 39).

Zen claims not to be theistic or pantheistic as such, denying such metaphysical designations. Unlike the God of Christian theism or Vedanta Hinduism, "there is no object in Zen upon which to fix the thought" of the disciple. "Zen just feels fire warm and ice cold, because when it freezes we shiver and welcome fire. The feeling is all in all . . . ; all our theorization fails to touch reality" (ibid., 41).

What Zen Is. So what may we say Zen is? According to Suzuki, "Zen is the ocean, Zen is the air, Zen is the mountain, Zen is thunder and lightening, the spring flower, summer heat, and winter snow; nay, more than that, Zen is the man." Suzuki recounted a story that a Zen master defined Zen as, "Your everyday thought" (ibid., 45). Suzuki puts it another way:

"When a hungry monk at work heard the dinner-gong he immediately dropped his work and showed himself in the dining room. The master, seeing him, laughed heartily, for the monk had been acting Zen to its fullest extent" (ibid., 85). In other words, Zen is life. "I raise my hand; I take a book from the other side of this desk; I hear the boys playing ball outside my window; I see the clouds blown away beyond the neighboring woods:—in all these I am practicing Zen, I am living Zen. No wordy discussion is necessary, nor any explanation" (ibid., 75). Zen is the personal experience of life, unencumbered by any abstractions or conceptualizations (ibid., 45, 132).

God and the World. In Zen Buddhism God is man, and man is God. Citing the Western mystic (*see* MYSTICISM) Meister Eckhart with approval, Suzuki states: "'Simple people conceive that we are to see God as if he stood on that side and we on this. It is not so; God and I are one in the act of my perceiving Him.' In this absolute oneness of things Zen establishes the foundations of its philosophy" (*Zen Buddhism*, 113). Not only is a human being God, but all is God and God is all. Everything and everyone are really One. "Buddhas [i.e., enlightened Ones] and sentient beings [i.e., those still ignorant] both grow out of One Mind, and there is no other reality than this Mind" (*Manual of Zen Buddhism*, 112).

What this all-embracing Mind is, is no-mindedness which is the human spiritual nature. Says Suzuki: "This Nature [i.e., the human spiritual nature] is the Mind, and the Mind is the Buddha, and the Buddha is the Way, and the Way is Zen" (*Zen Buddhism*, 88). The Mind may be described as having "been in existence since the beginningless past." Mind is not born and does not die; it is beyond the categories of age or being (*Manual of Zen Buddhism*, 112). Mind is all and all is Mind.

Suzuki is quick to point out that this form of monism is not a denial of the world we perceive and feel around us. However the world we do sense which is outside of us is a "relative world," which has no final reality." Individual beings exist, but they are real "only in so far as they are considered a partial realization of Suchness." Indeed Suchness "exists immanently *in* them. Things are empty and illusory so long as they are particular things and are not thought of in reference to the All that is Suchness and Reality" (*Outlines of Mahayana Buddhism*, 140, 141).

Ordinary experience, then takes the world for something that exists in itself, but it is an illusion. What really exists is Mind (*Manual of Zen Buddhism*, 51).

Buddhists do not like to call Suchness or Mind by the word *God*. The very term is offensive to most Buddhists, "especially when it is intimately associated in vulgar minds with the idea of a Creator who produced the world out of nothing (*see* CREATION, VIEWS OF), caused the downfall of mankind, and, touched by the pang or remorse, sent down his only son to save the depraved." The variety of ways Buddhists describe this Ultimate reality is partly an effort to avoid speaking of Deity (*Outlines of Mahayana Buddhism*, 219, 220).

Further, Absolute Suchness or Reality cannot be grasped "as it truly is." It goes beyond categories, even of existence. Suzuki states: "We cannot even say that it is, for everything that is presupposes that which is not: existence and non-existence are relative terms as much as subject and object, mind and matter, this and that, one and other: one cannot be conceived without the other. 'It is not so (*na iti*),' therefore may be the only way our imperfect human tongue can express it. So the Mayahanists generally designate absolute Suchness as *Cunyata* or void."

This indefinable and unthinkable "void" may be more fully interpreted in this way: Suchness is neither existence or non-existence; it is neither unity nor plurality (ibid., 101–2). This is God, and God is All, and All is Mind, and Mind is Buddha, and Buddha is the Way, and the Way is Zen.

View of Human Beings. Individual human beings then are simply a manifestation of this All or

Mind or God. Individuals are not isolated entities anyway, as we imagine. By themselves people are no more meaningful than soap bubbles. Particular existence acquires meaning only when thought of in terms of the whole oneness (ibid., 46–47). This is not precisely a denial of materiality. Human beings have both materiality and immateriality, and more (ibid., 149). It is a denial of individuality in any ultimate sense. People only appear to be individual beings, but in reality they are all one in the One. The goal of Zen is to help people go beyond egoism to realize their oneness in God and so become immortal (ibid., 47).

Ethics. Zen is primarily fundamentally a "practical discipline of life" (*An Introduction to Zen Buddhism*, 37). From an ethical perspective, Zen is a discipline aimed "at the reconstruction of character" (*Zen Buddhism*, 16). This rebuilding of character is necessary to do battle with egoism, "the source of all evils and sufferings." Buddhism "concentrates its entire ethical force upon the destruction of the ego-centric notions and desires" (*Outlines of Mahayana Buddhism*, 124).

Basically, Zen's answer to egoism is to learn. This ignorance is the clinging "Man needs to detach himself from Ignorance (i.e., *dualism), thus transcending all duality. When this is accomplished one "is said to be in harmony and even one with Suchness" (ibid., 122, 124, 146). This goal can only be met through selfless labor and devotion to others, which requires the prior destruction of all selfish desires. The realization of this goal is called *nirvana*. Destruction of self-orientation brings enlightenment, hence the ability to love others as ourselves (ibid., 52–55).

Involved in this process toward enlightenment and within enlightenment for a Zen monk is "a great deal of manual labour, such as sweeping, cleaning, cooking, fuel-gathering, tilling the farm, or going about begging in the villages far and near." The central principle by which the Zen monk is to live his life "is not to waste but to make the best possible use of things as they are given us" (*Introduction to Zen Buddhism*, 118, 121). The ethical teaching of Zen is succinctly summarized in "The Teaching of the Seven Buddhas":

> Not to commit evils
> But to do all that is good,
> And to keep one's thought pure—
> This is the teaching of all the Buddhas.
> [*Manual of Zen Buddhism*, 15]

Nature of History. Since the world is viewed as illusory (*see* ILLUSIONISM), history is considered illusory as well. Past, present, and future are "unborn." They have no reality beyond being manifestations of Mind (ibid., 53).

Granting this illusory existence of history in no way rules out its role as part of Maya or Ignorance. Suzuki states that history is "a grand drama visualizing the Buddhist doctrine of karmic immortality." Just as in many forms of Hindu pantheism, so Zen Buddhism holds to the belief in *karma*. The Buddhist concept of *karma* is that "any act, good or evil, once committed and conceived, never vanishes like a bubble in water, but lives, potentially or actively as the case may be, in the world of minds and deeds." Suzuki likens the doctrine of *karma* to "the theory of evolution and heredity as working in our moral field" (*Outlines of Mahayana Buddhism*, 183, 200, 207).

As everything else in the world of duality, history must be transcended. This is done in the following way:

> Events past are already past; therefore have no thoughts of them, and your mind is disconnected from the past. Thus past events are done away with. Present events are already here before you; then have no attachment to them. Not to have attachment means no to rouse any feeling of hate or love. Your mind is then disconnected from the present, and the events before your eyes are done away with. When the past, present, and future are thus in no way taken in, they are completely done away with. . . . If you have a thoroughly clear perception as to the mind having no abiding place anywhere, this is known as having a thoroughly clear perception of one's own being. This very Mind . . . is the Buddha-Mind itself; it is called Emancipation-Mind, Enlightenment-Mind, the Unborn Mind, and Emptiness of Materiality and Ideality. [*Zen Buddhism*, 196, 197]

Human Destiny. Human destiny is the achievement of *nirvana*—that is, "the annihilation of the notion of ego-substance and of all the desires that arise from this erroneous conception" and the practical expression of "universal love or sympathy (*karuna*) for all beings" (*Outlines of Mahayana Buddhism*, 50, 51). *Nirvana* is sometimes spoken of as possessing four attributes: Nirvana "is eternal because it is immaterial; it is blissful because it is above all sufferings; it is self-acting because it knows no compulsion; it is pure because it is not defiled by passion and error" (ibid., 348; cf. 399). Nirvana also is God and to achieve it is to realize one's essential oneness with the absolute One.

Nirvana is not achieved easily. However it does not involve asceticism, knowledge of certain books or doctrines, or even meditation divorced from life. Instead the realization of *nirvana* begins and ends in life itself. "Salvation [i.e., the attainment of *nirvana*] must be sought in the finite itself, there is nothing infinite apart from finite things; if you seek something transcendental, that will cut you off from this world of relativity, which is the same as the annihilation of yourself. You do not want salvation at the cost of your own existence."

"Nirvana is to be sought in the midst of Samsara (birth-and-death)." No one can escape Samsara. It is one's subjective perception of life. If a person will but change his inner awareness, he will see that reality is "absolutely one" (*Zen Buddhism*, 14, 15). The awareness of this in the inner life is Nirvana.

The road to Nirvana involves many things. However the most fundamental aspect is the ridding of all dualistic thinking. And the root of all such thinking is logic. Suzuki acknowledges that "we generally think that 'A is A' is absolute, and that the proposition 'A is not-A' or 'A is B' is unthinkable." But such thinking only keeps us in bondage so that we cannot comprehend the truth. We must therefore shed the shackles of logic, and approach life from a new point of view. In this new experience there "is no logic, no philosophizing; here is no twisting of facts to suit our artificial measures; here is no murdering of human nature in order to submit it to intellectual dissections; the one spirit stands face to face with the other spirit like two mirrors facing each other, and there is nothing to intervene between their mutual reflections" (*An Introduction to Zen Buddhism*, 58, 59, 61).

In order to help the Zen disciple beyond the logical interpretation of reality, the Zen masters created a whole approach to reality which included illogical sayings and questions as well as responses to questions—called the *koan*. For example, a very familiar question is "If you have heard the sound of one hand [clapping], can you make me hear it too?" (ibid., 59). A famous saying from Fudaishi graphically illustrates the irrationality of Zen:

Empty-handed I go, and behold the spade is in my hands;
I walk on foot, and yet on the back of an ox I am riding;
When I pass over the bridge, Lo, the water floweth not, but the bridge doth flow.
[ibid., 58]

For the attainment of nirvana, one must transcend all the things that keep one from seeing life in its fullness. This step toward nirvana is called *satori*. *Satori* is achieved through the *koan*. It is this process from the *koan* to *satori* and then to nirvana that is the road to spiritual happiness (ibid., 60).

The essence of Suzuki's absolute pantheism is that the world of particulars is both finite and infinite, relative and absolute, illusory and real. What one needs to do in order to see reality in all its fullness, is to free oneself from logic, words, concepts, abstractions—anything that keeps one from personally experiencing what is neither being nor non-being. When this occurs Nirvana is attained—one becomes one with the One.

Evaluation. For a critique of Zen, see articles on PANTHEISM; FIRST PRINCIPLES; EVIL, PROBLEM OF.

Sources

D. Clark, *The Pantheism of Alan Watts*
D. Clark, and N. L. Geisler, *Apologetics in the New Age*
N. L. Geisler, and W. Watkins, *Worlds Apart: A Handbook on World Views*
S. Hackett, *Oriental Philosophy*
D. Johnson, *A Reasonable Look at Asian Religions*
D. T. Suzuki, *An Introduction to Zen Buddhism*
———, *Manual of Zen Buddhism*
———, *Outlines of Mahayana Buddhism*
———, *Zen Buddhism*
A. W. Watts, *The Spirit of Zen*
———, *The Way of Zen*
J. I. Yamamoto, *Beyond Buddhism*

Bibliography

Abanes, Richard. *Journey into the Light*. Grand Rapids: Baker, 1996.

Abdalati, Hammudah. *Islam in Focus*. Indianapolis: American Trust, 1975.

Abdul-Haqq, Abdiyah Akbar. *Sharing Your Faith with a Muslem*. Minneapolis: Bethany, 1980.

Acton, H. B. "Hegel, Georg Wilhelm Friedrich." In *The Encyclopedia of Philosophy*, ed. Paul Edwards. Vol. 3. New York: Macmillan and the Free Press, 1967.

Adamson, Donald. *Blaise Pascal: Mathematician, Physicist and Thinker about God.* New York: St. Martin's, 1995.

Adler, Margo. *Drawing Down the Moon*. New York: Viking, 1979.

Adler, Mortimer Jerome. *Saint Thomas and the Gentiles.* Milwaukee: Marquette University Press, 1938.

Adler, Mortimer Jerome. *Six Great Ideas.* New York: Thirteen, 1982.

Adler, Mortimer Jerome.*Truth in Religion: The Plurality of Religions and the Unity of Truth.* New York: Macmillan, 1990.

Afnan, S. M. *Avicenna: His Life and Works*. London: George Allen & Unwin, 1958.

Agassiz, Louis. *Prof. Agassiz on the Origin of Species.* 2nd series. Vol. 30. Cambridge, Massachusetts: June 30, 1860.

Ahmad, Mirza Bashiruddin Mahmud. *Introduction to the Study of the Holy Quran.* Islam International, 1989.

Ajijola, Alhaj A. D., *The Essence of Faith in Islam.* Lahore, Pakistan: Islamic Publications, Ltd., 1978.

Akin, James. "Material and Formal Sufficiency." *This Rock* 4, no. 10. (October, 1993).

Aland, Kurt. *The Text of the New Testament : an Introduction to the Critical Editions and to the Theory and Practice of Modern Textual Criticism* . Grand Rapids: Eerdmans 1988.

Al-Bagillani, (ed.) Richard J. McCarthy. *Miracle and Magic*. Place de l'Etoile: Librairie Orientale, n.d.

Albrecht, Mark. *Reincarnation: A Christian Appraisal.* Downers Grove, Ill.: InterVarsity, 1982.

Albright, William F. *The Archaeology of Palestine.* Baltimore: Penguin, 1949.

Albright, William F. *Archaeology and the Religion of Israel.* Baltimore: The Johns Hopkins Press, 1953.

Albright, William F. *From Stone Age to Christianity.* Garden City, N.Y.: Doubleday, Anchor, 1957.

Albright, William F. *History, Archaeology, and Christian Humanism.* New York: McGraw-Hill, 1964.

Albright, William F. *Recent Discoveries in Bible Lands.* New York: Funk & Wagnalls, 1956.

Albright, William F. "Recent Discoveries in Palestine and the Gospel of St. John." In *The Background of the New Testament and Its Eschatology*, ed. W. D. Davies and David Daube. Cambridge: Cambridge University Press, 1954.

Albright, William F. "Retrospect and Prospect in New Testament Archaeology." In *The Teacher's Yoke*, ed. E. Jerry Vardaman. Waco, Tex.: Baylor University, 1971.

Albright, William F. "William Albright: Toward a More Conservative View." *Christianity Today,* 18 January 1963.

Aldridge, Alfred O. *Man of Reason: The Life of Thomas Paine.* Philadelphia: Lippincott, 1959.

Aldridge, Alfred O. "Paine, Thomas." In *The Encyclopedia of Philosophy*. vol. 6. Reprinted. Editor in chief, Paul Edwards. 5.v. 6:17–18. New York: Macmillan and the Free Press, 1967.

Alhaj, A. D. Ajijola. *The Essence of Faith in Islam.* Lahore, Pakistan: Islamic Publications, Ltd., 1978.

Ali, A. Yusaf. *The Holy Qur'an: Translation and Commentary*. Damascus: Ouloom Alqur'an, 1934.

Ali, A. Yusaf. *The Meaning of the Glorious Qur'an*. Vol. 2. Cairo, Egypt: Dar Al-Kitab Al-Masri, n.d..

Ali, Maulu: Muhammad. *Muhammad and Christ.* Uahore: The Ahmadiyya Anjuman-i-Ishaa-i-Islam, 1921.

Ali, Muhammad. *The Religion of Islam.* 6th ed., rev. Lahore: Ahmadiyya anjuman ishaat Islam, 1990.

Ali, Yusuf. "Mudjiza." In *Shorter Encyclopedia of Islam,* ed. H.A. R. Gibb and J. H. Kramers. Ithaca, N.Y.: Cornell University Press, 1953.

Allegro, John M. *The Treasure of the Copper Scroll.* 2nd rev. ed. Garden City, N.Y.: Doubleday, 1965.

Allis, O. R. *The OT: Its Claims and Its Critics.* Grand Rapids: Baker, 1972.

Allis, Oswald Thompson. *The Five Books of Moses.* 2nd ed. Philadelphia: Presbyterian & Reformed, 1949.

Altizer, Thomas J. J., and William Hamilton. *Radical Theology and The Death of God*. Indianapolis: Bobbs-Merrill, 1966.

Altizer, Thomas. *The Gospel of Christian Atheism*. Philadelphia: Westminster, 1966.

Anderson, J. N. D. *A Lawyer Among the Theologians*. Grand Rapids: Eerdmans, 1973.

Anderson, J. N. D. *The World's Religions*. London: Inter-Varsity Fellowship, 1950.

Anderson, John. *Psychic Phenomena-Confessions of a New Age Warlock*. Lafayette, La.: Huntington House, 1991.

Anderson, Kerby. *Life, Death and Beyond*. Grand Rapids: Zondervan, 1980.

Anderson, Norman. *Christianity and World Religions*. Downers Grove, Ill.: InterVarsity, 1984.

Anderson, Norman. *Islam in the Modern World*. Leicester: Apollos, 1990.

Andrae, Tor. *Mohammed: The Man and His Faith*. Rev. ed. New York: Harper & Row, 1955.

Ankerberg, John, and John Weldon. *Cult Watch*. Eugene, Ore.: Harvest House 1991.

Anselm, St. *Basic Writings: Proslogium, Monologium, Gaunilon's: On Behalf of the Fool, Cur Deus Homo*. Translated by S.W. Deane. 2nd ed. LaSalle, Ill: Open Court, 1962.

Anselm, St. *Truth, Freedom, and Evil: Three Philosophical Dialogues*. Edited and translated by Jasper Hopkins and Herbert Richardson. New York: Harper & Row, 1967.

Anstey, Martin. *Chronology of the OT: Complete in One Volume*. Grand Rapids: Kregel, 1973.

Antes, Peter. "Relations with the Unbelievers in Islami Theology." In *We Believe in One God*, ed. Annemarie Schimmel and Abdoldjavad Falaturi. New York: Seabury, 1979.

Aquinas, St. Thomas. *Commentary on the Metaphysics of Aristotle*. Translated by John P. Rowan. Chicago: H. Regnery, 1961.

Aquinas, St. Thomas. *Commentary on the Posterior Analytics of Aristotle*. Albany, N.Y.: Magi, 1970.

Aquinas, St. Thomas. *Commentary on Saint Paul's Epistle to the Ephesians by St. Thomas Aquinas*. Translated by Matthew L. Lamb. Albany, N.Y.: Magi, 1966.

Aquinas, St. Thomas. *Compendium of Theology*. Translated by Cyril Vollert. St. Louis: B. Herder, 1949.

Aquinas, St. Thomas. *De Ente*. Translated by Joseph Bobik. Notre Dame, Ind.: University of Notre Dame Press, 1965.

Aquinas, St. Thomas. *On Being and Essence*. Translated by Armand Maurer, C.S.B., 2nd ed. Toronto, Canada: The Pontifical Institute of Mediaeval Studies, 1968.

Aquinas, St. Thomas. *On Evil*. Edited by Jean Oesterle. Notre Dame, Ind.: University of Notre Dame Press, 1995.

Aquinas, St. *On the Power of God*. 3 vols. Edited and translated by Lawrence Shapcote. London: Burns, Oates & Washbourne, 1932.

Aquinas, St. Thomas. *On Truth*. Translated by J. V. McGlynn. Chicago: H. Regnery, 1952–54.

Aquinas, St.Thomas. *Summa Contra Gentiles*. In *On the Truth of the Catholic Faith: Book One: God*. Translated by Anton C. Pegis. New York: Image, 1955.

Aquinas, St. Thomas. *Summa Theologica*. 60 vols. Edited by O. P. Gilby. New York: McGraw-Hill, 1966.

Aquinas, St. Thomas. *Summa Theologica*. Translated by Thomas Gilby. New York: McGraw Hill Book Co., 1968. Also in *The Basic Writings of Aquinas*. Translated by Anton C. Pegis. New York: Random House, 1944.

Aquinas, St.Thomas. *Summa Theologica*, vol. 1, trans. Fathers of the English Dominican Province, vol. 19 of *Great Books of the Western World*, ed. Robert Maynard. Hutchins. Chicago: William Benton, 1952.

Arbaugh, G. E. and G. B. *Kierkegaard's Authorship*. London: George Allen & Unwin, 1968.

Arberry, A. J. *Avicenna on Theology*. London: John Murray, 1951.

Archer, Gleason. *Encyclopedia of Biblical Difficulties*. Grand Rapids: Zondervan, 1982.

Archer, Gleason . *A Survey of Old Testament Introduction*. Rev. ed. Chicago: Moody, 1974.

Archer, John Clark. *The Sikhs*. Princeton, N.J.: Princeton University Press, 1946.

Aristotle. *Metaphysics*. Edited and trans. by John Warrington. N.Y.: Denton, 1966.

Aristotle. *Posterior Analytics*. 2nd ed. by Jonathan Barnes. Oxford: Oxford University Press, 1994.

Aristotle. *Topics*. Edited by Robin Smith. New York: Oxford University Press, 1996.

Aristotle. *The Works of Aristotle Translated Into English*. Edited by W. D. Ross. Oxford: Oxford University Press, 1961.

Arminius, James. *The Writings of Arminius*. 3 vols. Translated from the Latin by James Nichols and W. R. Bagnall. Grand Rapids: Baker, 1956.

Armstrong, A. H. *The Architecture of the Intelligible Universe in the Philosophyof Plotinus; An Analytical and Historical Study*. Cambridge, Eng.: The University Press, 1967.

Arndt, W. *Bible Difficulties: An Examination of Passages of the Bible Alleged to Be Irreconcilable with Inspiration*. St. Louis: Concordia, 1971.

Arndt, W. *Does the Bible Contradict Itself? A Discussion of Alleged Contradictions in the Bible*. 5th rev. ed. St. Louis: Concordia, 1955.

Arndt, William F. and F. Wilbur Gingrich, *A Greek-English Lexicon of the New Testament and Other Early Christian Literature*. Translation and adaption of the 4th rev. and augmented of Walter Bauer, Chicago: University of Chicago, 1957. 2nd rev. ed., 1979.

Asimov, Isaac. *The Beginning and the End*. Garden City, N.Y.: Doubleday, 1977.

'Ata ur-Rahim, Muhammad. *Jesus: Prophet of Islam*. New York: Diwan, n.d.

"Athenagoras." In *The Ante-Nicene Fathers*, ed. Alexander Roberts and James Donaldson. Vol. 2. Grand Rapids: Eerdmans, 1989.

Athenagoras. *Apologia pro Christianis*. Edited and translated by William R. Schoedel. Oxford: Clarendon, 1972.

Athenagoras. *De resurrectione*. Edited and translated by William R. Schoedel. Oxford: Clarendon, 1972.

Bibliography

Augustine, St. "Against the Epistle of the Manichaeans." In *Nicene and Post-Nicene Fathers*, ed. Philip Schaff. 14 vols. 1st series. 1886–94. Reprint, Grand Rapids: Eerdmans, 1952.

Augustine, St. "Against Lying." In *Nicene and Post-Nicene Fathers*., Augustine, St. "AntiManichaean Writings." In *Nicene and Post-Nicene Fathers*, ed. Philip Schaff. 14 vols. 1st series. 1886–94. Reprint, Grand Rapids: Eerdmans, 1952.

Augustine, St. "*City of God*." In *Nicene and Post-Nicene Fathers*, ed. Philip Schaff. 14 vols. 1st series. 1886–94. Reprint, Grand Rapids: Eerdmans, 1952.

Augustine, St. *The City of God*. Translated by Marcus Dods. New York: Random House, 1950.

Augustine, St. "Confessions and Enchiridon" In *Nicene and Post-Nicene Fathers*, ed. Philip Schaff. 14 vols. 1st series. 1886–94. Reprint, Grand Rapids: Eerdmans, 1952.

Augustine, St. "Letters" 82,3. In *The Nicene and Post-Nicene Fathers of the Christian Church*, ed. Philip Schaff, 1st series, vols. 1–7 (1886–1888) Reprint, Grand Rapids: Eerdmans, 1979.

Augustine, St. *The Literal Meaning of Genesis*. Edited by John Taylor. New York: Newman, 1982.

Augustine, St. "Of True Religion." In *Augustine: Earlier Writings*. Edited by J. H. S. Burleigh Philadelphia: Westminster, 1953.

Augustine, St. "On the Creed." In *Nicene and Post-Nicene Fathers*,. ed. Philip Schaff. 14 vols. 1st series. 1886–94. Reprint, Grand Rapids: Eerdmans, 1952.

Augustine, St. "On Christian Doctrine." In *Nicene and Post-Nicene Fathers*, ed. Philip Schaff. 14 vols. 1st series. 1886–94. Reprint, Grand Rapids: Eerdmans, 1952.

Augustine, St. "On Free Will." In *Augustine: Earlier Writings*, ed. J. H. S. Burleigh. Philadelphia: Westminster, 1953.

Augustine, St. "On the Gospel of John" Tractate 12435. In *The Nicene and Post-Nicene Fathers of the Christian Church*, ed. Philip Schaff. 1st series, Vols. 1–7. 1886–88. Reprint, Grand Rapids: Eerdmans, 1979.

Augustine, St. "On the Gospel of John 27:9." In *Nicene and Post-Nicene Fathers*, ed. Philip Schaff. 14 vols. 1st series. 1886–94. Reprint, Grand Rapids: Eerdmans, 1952.

Augustine, St. "On Grace and Free Will." In *The Ante-Nicene Fathers*, ed. Alexander Roberts and James Donaldson. Vol. 2. Grand Rapids: Eerdmans, 1885.

Augustine, St. "On Lying." In *Nicene and Post-Nicene Fathers*, ed. Philip Schaff. 14 vols. 1st series. 1886–94. Reprint, Grand Rapids: Eerdmans, 1952.

Augustine, St. "On the Morals of the Catholic Church." In *Nicene and Post-Nicene Fathers*, ed. Philip Schaff. 14 vols. 1st series. 1886–94. Reprint, Grand Rapids: Eerdmans, 1952.

Augustine, St. "On the Nature of Good." In *Nicene and Post-Nicene Fathers*, ed. Philip Schaff. 14 vols. 1st series. 1886–94. Reprint, Grand Rapids: Eerdmans, 1952.

Augustine, St. "On Predestination 5." In *Nicene and Post-Nicene Fathers*, ed. Philip Schaff. 14 vols. 1st series. 1886–94. Reprint, Grand Rapids: Eerdmans, 1952.

Augustine, St. "On the Soul and Its Origin." In *Nicene and Post-Nicene Fathers*, ed. Philip Schaff. 14 vols. 1st series. 1886–94. Reprint, Grand Rapids: Eerdmans, 1952.

Augustine, St. "On the Trinity." In *Nicene and Post-Nicene Fathers*, ed. Philip Schaff. 14 vols. 1st series. 1886–94. Reprint, Grand Rapids: Eerdmans, 1952.

Augustine, St. "Reply to Faustus the Manichaean." In *Nicene and Post-Nicene Fathers*, ed. Philip Schaff. 14 vols. 1st series. 1886–94. Reprint, Grand Rapids: Eerdmans, 1952.

Avicenna. *Metaphysica sive Prima Philosophia*. Louvain: Edition de la bibliotheque, 1961.

Ayer, A. J. *Foundations of Empirical Knowledge*. London: Macmillan, 1964.

Ayer, A. J. *Language, Truth and Logic*. New York: Dover, 1952.

Ayer, A. J. *Philosophical Essays*. New York: St. Martin's, 1969.

Ayer, A. J. *The Problem of Knowledge*. London: Macmillan, 1956.

Bacon, Francis. *The New Organon and Related Writings*. Edited by Fulton H. Anderson. New York: Bobbs-Merrill, 1960.

Baldwin, Lindley. *Samuel Morris: The March of Faith*. Minneapolis: Dimension, 1942.

Balic, Smail. "The Image of Jesus in Contemporary Islamic Theology." In *We Believe in One God*, edited by Annemarie Shimmel and Abdoldjavad Falaturi. New York: Seabury, 1979.

Barbet, Pierre. *A Doctor at Calvary*. Garden City, N.Y.: Doubleday, 1953.

Barbet, Pierre. *A Doctor at Calvary; the Passion of Our Lord Jesus Christ as Described by a Surgeon*. New York: Image, 1963.

Barbour, Ian G. *Issues in Science and Religion*. Englewood Cliffs, N.J.: Prentice-Hall, 1966.

Baron, Salo, ed. *Essays on Maimonides*. New York: AMS, 1966.

Barrett, William. *Irrational Man: A Study in Existential Philosophy* New York: Doubleday, 1958.

Barrow, John D. *The Anthropic Cosmological Principle*. New York: Oxford University Press, 1986.

Barth, Karl. *Church Dogmatics*. With an introduction by Helmut Gollwitzer. Translated and edited by G. W. Bromiley. New York: Harper Torchbooks, 1961.

Barth, Karl. "An Introductory Essay" In *The Essence of Christianity*, ed. Ludwig Feuerbach. New York: Harper & Brothers, 1957.

Barth, Karl. *From Rousseau to Ritschl*. London: SCM, 1959.

Barth, Karl. *The Resurrection of the Dead*. Translated by H. J. Stenning. New York: Arno, 1977.

Barth, Karl. *The Theology of Schleiermacher*. Edited by Deitrich Ritschl. Translated by Geoffrey W. Bromiley. Grand Rapids: Eerdmans, 1982.

Barthelemy, D., and J. T. Milik. *Ten Years of Discovery in the Judaean Desert*. London: Oxford University Press, 1955.

Bayle, Pierre. *Selections from Bayle's Dictionary*. Translated by R. H. Popkin. Indianapolis: Bobbs-Merrill, 1965.

Beauvoir, Simone de. *The Ethics of Ambiguity.* Translated by Bernard Frechtman. NewYork: Philosophical Press, 1948.

Beck, William David. *Opening the American Mind: The Integration of Biblical Truth in the Curriculum of the University.* Grand Rapids: Baker, 1991.

Becker, Carl. "Detachment and the Writing of History." In *Detachment and the Writing of History*, ed. Phil L. Snyder. Westport, Conn.: Greenwood, 1972.

Beckwith, Roger. *The Old Testament Canon of the New Testament Church and Its Background in Early Judaism.* Grand Rapids: Eerdmans, 1986.

Behe, Michael J. *Darwin's Black Box.* New York: The Free Press, 1996.

Beisner, E. Calvin. *God in Three Persons.* Wheaton, Ill. : Tyndale House, 1984.

Beld, Scott C. et al. *The Tablets of Ebla: Concordance and Bibliography.* Winona Lake, Ind.: Eisenbrauns, 1984.

Bell, Richard. *The Origin of Islam in Its Christian Environment.* Frank Cass, 1968.

Bergson, Henri. *Creative Evolution.* 1911. Reprint Translated by Arthur Mitchell. Westport, Conn.: Greenwood, 1977.

Berkouwer, G. C. *General Revelation.* Grand Rapids: Eerdmans, 1955.

Berkouwer, G. C. *Man: The Image of God.* Translated by Dirk W. Jellema. Grand Rapids: Eerdmans, 1962.

Bernard, J. H. "Note F: The Improbability of Miracle" In *Analogy of Religion,* ed. Joseph Butler. London: Macmillan, 1900.

Bettenson, Henry, ed. *Documents of the Christian Church.* New York & London: Oxford University Press, 1961.

Bettis, Joseph Dabney. "A Critique of the Doctrine of Universal Salvation." *Religious Studies* 6 (1970).

Bhagavad-Gita. Translated by Swami Prabhavananda and Christopher Isherwood. Bergerfield: The New American Library, 1972.

Bimson, John, and David Livingston. "Redating the Exodus." *Biblical Archeology Review* (September–October 1987).

Bird, Wendel. R. *The Origin of Species Revisited.* 2 vols. New York: Philosophical Library, 1987–89.

Black, M. *The Scrolls and Christian Origins.* New York: Scribner, 1961.

Blakney, Raymond Bernard. *Meister Eckhart: A Modern Translation.* New York: Harper & Row, 1941.

Blockmuehl, Klaus. *The Challenge of Marxism.* Colorado Springs: Helmers & Howard, 1986.

Blomberg, Craig. *The Historical Reliability of the Gospels.* Downers Grove, Ill.: InterVarsity, 1987.

Bloom, Alan. *The Closing of the American Mind.* New York: Simon & Schuster, Inc., 1987.

Blum, Harold F. *Time's Arrow and Evolution.* Princeton, N.J.: Princeton University Press, 1955.

Boehner, Philotheus, ed. *Ockham: Philosophical Writings.* Selections with translations. Edinburgh, 1957.

Boeth, Jennifer. "In Search of Past Lives: Looking at Yesterday to Find Answers for Today." *Dallas Times Herald.* 3 April 1983.

Boice, James. M. *Foundations of the Christian Faith.* Downers Grove, Ill.: InterVarsity, 1986.

Bolich, Gregory G. *Karl Barth and Evangelicalism.* Downers Grove, Ill.: InterVarsity, 1980.

Borg, Marcus. *Jesus in Contemporary Scholarship.* Valley Forge, Pa.: Trinity Free Press, 1994.

Borg, Marcus. *Meeting Jesus Again for the First Time.* San Francisco: Harper San Francisco, 1993.

Boudreau, Albert H. *The Born-Again Catholic.* Locust Valley: Living Flame, 1983.

Bouquet, A. C. *Sacred Books of the World.* Baltimore: Penguin, 1959.

Bowle, J. *Hobbes and His Critics: A Study of Seventeenth-Century Constitutionalism.* London: Cape, 1951.

Boyd, Gregory A. *Jesus Under Siege.* Wheaton, Ill.: Victor, 1995.

Boyer, Louis. *The Spirit and Forms of Protestantism.* Westminster, Md.: The Newman, 1961.

Braaten, C. E. "Martin Kahler on the Historic, Biblical Christ." In *The Historical Jesus and the Kerygmatic Christ*, ed. R. A. Harrisville. New York: Abingdon, 1964.

Bradley, F. H. *The Presuppositions of Critical History.* Chicago: Quadrangle, 1968.

Brand, Paul. With Philip Yancey. "A Surgeon's View of Divine Healing." *Christianity Today.* 25 November 1983.

Branden, Barbara. *The Passion of Ayn Rand.* Garden City, N.Y.: Doubleday, 1986.

Brandt, Richard. *The Philosophy of Friedrich Schleiermacher.* New York: Harper & Brothers, 1941.

Braswell, George, W., Jr. *Understanding World Religions.* Nashville, Tenn.: Broadman & Holman, 1994.

Bree, Germaine. *Camus.* New Brunswick, N.J.: Rutgers University Press, 1972.

Brehier, Emily. *The Philosophy of Plotinus.* Translated by Joseph Thomas. Chicago: University of Chicago Press, 1958.

Brightman, Edgar S. *A Philosophy of Religion.* New York: Prentice-Hall, 1940.

Brooks, J., and Gordon Shaw. *Origin and Development of Living Systems.* New York: Academic, 1973.

Brown, C. *Miracles and the Critical Mind.* Grand Rapids: Eerdmans, 1984.

Brown, Colin, ed. *The New International Dictionary of New Testament Theology.* 3 vols. Translated from Lothar Coenen, Erich Beyreuther, and Hans Beitenhard, eds. *Theologisches Begriffslexikon zum Neuen Testament* (1967–71). Grand Rapids: Zondervan, 1975–78.

Brown, Colin. "Sign, Wonder, Miracle." In *The New International Dictionary of New Testament Theology,* ed. Colin Brown. Vol. 2 Translated from Lothar Coenen, Erich Beyreuther, and Hans Beitenhard, eds. *Theologisches Begriffslexikon zum Neuen Testament* (1967–71). Grand Rapids: Zondervan, 1975–78.

Brown, Harold O. J. *The Protest of a Troubled Protestant.* Grand Rapids: Zondervan, 1969.

Bruce, F. F. *The Books and the Parchments.* Old Tappan, N.J.: Revell, 1984.

Bruce, F. F. *Commentary on the Acts of the Apostles.* Grand Rapids: Eerdmans, 1954.

Bruce, F. F. *Commentary on the Epistles to the Ephesians and Colossians.* Grand Rapids: Eerdmans, 1957.

Bruce, F. F. *In Defense of the Gospel.* Grand Rapids: Eerdmans, 1977.

Bruce, F.F. *Jesus and Christian Origins Outside the New Testament.* Grand Rapids: Eerdmans, 1974.

Bruce, F. F. *The New Testament Documents: Are They Reliable.* Downers Grove, Ill.: InterVarsity, 1960.

Bruce, F. F. *Paul and Jesus.* Grand Rapids: Baker, 1974.

Bruce, F. F. *Peter, Stephen, James and John.* Grand Rapids: Eerdmans, 1979.

Bruce, F. F. *Second Thoughts on the Dead Sea Scrolls.* Grand Rapids: Eerdmans, 1956.

Bruce, F. F., and William J. Martin. "Two Laymen on Christ's Deity." *Christianity Today,* 18 December1964.

Brummer, Vincent. *Transcendental Criticism and Christian Philosophy.* Franeker, Netherlands: T. Wever, 1961.

Brunner, Emil. *The Christian Doctrine of God.* Vol. 1, *Dogmatics.* Translated by Olive Wyon. London: Lutterworth, 1949.

Brunner, Emil. *The Divine-Human Encounter.* Translated by Amandus W. Loos. Philadelphia: Westminster, 1943.

Brunner, Emil. *The Mediator: A Study of the Central Doctrine of the Christian Faith.* Translanted by Olive Wyon. Philadelphia: Westminster, 1947.

Brunner, Emil. *The Philosophy of Religion from the Standpoint of Protestant Theology.* Translated by A. J. D. Farrer and Bertram Lee Woolf. London: James Clarke, 1937. Reprint, 1958.

Brunner, Emil. *Revelation and Reason.* Philadelphia: Westminster, 1946.

Buber, Martin. *Eclipse of God: Studies in the Relation Between Religion and Philosophy.* New York: Harper Torchbooks, 1957.

Buber, Martin. *I and Thou.* Translated by Ronald Gregor Smith. 2nd ed. New York: Charles Scribner's Sons, 1958.

Bucaille, Maurice. *The Bible, the Qur'an and Science.* Translated by Alastair D. Pannell and the author. Delhi, India: Taj, 1988.

Buckley, William F. A transcript of "Firing Line." 17 October 1971.

Bucklin, Robert. "The Legal and Medical Aspects of the Trial and Death of Christ." *Medicine, Science and the Law* (January, 1970).

Buell, Jon A., and Quentin O. Hyder. *Jesus: God, Ghost or Guru.* Grand Rapids: Zondervan, 1978.

Bukhari. *The Translation of the Meanings of Sahih Al-Bukhari.* Translated by Muhammad Musin Kham. 10 vols. Al-Medina: Islamic University.

Bultmann, Rudolf. *Kerygma and Myth: A Theological Debate.* Edited by Hans Werner Bartsch. Translated by Reginald H. Fuller. London: Billing & Sons, 1954.

Burrill, Donald R., ed., *The Cosmological Arguments: A Spectrum of Opinion.* Garden City, N.Y.: Doubleday, 1967.

Burrows, Millar. *More Light on the Dead Sea Scrolls.* New York: Viking, 1958.

Burrows, Millar. *What Mean These Stones?* New Haven, Conn.: American Schools of Oriental Research, 1941.

Bush, Russ L., ed. *Classical Readings in Christian Apologetics, A.D. 100–1800.* Grand Rapids: Academie , 1983.

Buswell, James O. *The Philosophies of F. R. Tennant and John Dewey.* New York: Philosophical Library, 1950.

Buswell, James O. *A Systematic Theology of the Christian Religion.* Grand Rapids: Zondervan, 1972.

Butler, Joseph. *The Analogy of Religion Natural and Revealed to the Constitution and Course of Nature.* 3rd ed. London: George Routledge and Sons, 1887; first published, 1872.

Butler, Joseph. *Fifteen Sermons.* Charlottesville, Va.: Lincoln-Rembrandt, 1993.

Butler, Joseph. *The Works of Joseph Butler.* Edited by W. E. Gladstone. Oxford, 1897.

Caldwell, William. *Schopenhauer's System in Its Philosophical Significance.* 1896 Reprint, Bristol, England: Thoemmes, 1993.

Calvin, John. *Calvin's Commentaries: Epistles of Paul to the Romans and Thessalonicians.* 22 vols. Edited by David W. Torrance and Thomas F. Torrance. Grand Rapids: Eerdmans, 1972.

Calvin, John. *Institutes of the Christian Religion.* 2 vols. Edited by John T. McNeill. Translated by Ford Lewis Battles. In Library of Christian Classics, vols. 20–21, edited by John Baillie, John T. McNeill, and Henry P. Van Dusen. Philadelphia: Westminster, 1960.

Campbell, William. *The Qur'an and the Bible in the Light of History and Science.* Middle Eastern SIM Resources, n.d.

Camus, Albert *The Myth of Sisyphus and Other Essays.* Translated by Justin O'Brien New York: Random House, 1955.

Camus, Albert. *The Plague.* Translated by S. Gilbert. New York: Modern Library, 1948.

Capra, Fritjof. *The Tao of Physics : An Exploration of the Parallels Between Modern Physics and Eastern Mysticism.* London: Fontana, 1975.

Carmical, Frank. "The Unknown and Unread Soren Kierkegaard: An Orthodox, Evangelical Christian." *Studia Theologica Et Apologia* 1, no. 3 (1985): 1–29.

Carnell, Edward John. *An Introduction to Christian Apologetics: A Philosophic Defense of the Trinitarian-theistic Faith.* 5th ed. Grand Rapids : Eerdmans, 1956.

Carson, D. A. *The Gagging of God.* Grand Rapids: Zondervan, 1996.

Carson, D. A. *The Gospel According to John.* Grand Rapids: Eerdmans, 1991.

Carson, D. A. "Redaction Criticism: On the Legitimacy and Illegitimacy of a Literary Tool." In *Scripture and Truth,* ed. D. A. Carson and John D. Woodbridge, 119–42. Grand Rapids: Baker, 1992.

Carver, W. O. "Edgar Young Mullins—Leader and Builder." *Review and Expositor* (April, 1929).

Cassius, Dio. *Roman History.* 69.11.2. See *Documents for the Study of the Gospels*, ed. David R. Cartlidge and David L. Dungan. Cleveland: William Collins, 1980.

Castaneda, Carlos. *Tales of Power*. New York: Pocket Books, 1974.

Castaneda, Carlos. *The Teachings of Don Juan*. Berkeley: University of California Press, 1968.

Cavendish, Marshall. "Nostradamus." In *Man, Myth and Magic: The Illustrated Encyclopedia of Mythology, Religion, and the Unknown*. New ed. Edited and compiled by Yvonee Deutc. New York: Marshall Cavendish, 1983.

Celsus. *On the True Doctrine (or Discourse)*. Translated by R. Joseph Hoffman. New York: Oxford University Press, 1987.

Chadwick, H. "Justin Martyr's Defense of Christianity." *Bulletin of the John Ryland Library* 47 (1965).

Chamberlain, W. B. *Heaven Wasn't His Destination: The Philosophy of Ludwig Feuerbach*. London: Allen & Unwin, 1941.

Charlesworth, James H., ed. *The Dead Sea Scrolls*. Vol. 4, *Angelic Liturgy, Prayers, and Psalms*. Louisville, Ky.: Westminster/John Knox, 1997.

Charlesworth, James, et al. *Jesus and the Dead Sea Scrolls*. New York: Doubleday, 1992.

Charnock, Stephen. *Discourses upon the Existence and Attributes of God*. 2 vols. Reprint, Grand Rapids: Baker, 1979.

Chemnitz, Martin. *Examination of the Council of Trent*. St. Louis: Concordia, 1971.

Chesterton, G. K. *The Autobiography of G. K. Chesterton*. New York: Sheed & Ward, 1936.

Chesterton, G. K. *The Catholic Church and Conversion*. New York: Macmillan, 1951.

Chesterton, G. K. *Chaucer*. New York: Sheed & Ward, 1956.

Chesterton, G. K. *Five Types*. London: Henry Holt, 1911.

Chesterton, G. K. *Generally Speaking*. New York: Dodd, Mead, 1929.

Chesterton, G. K. *A Handful of Authors: Essays on Books and Writers*. New York: Sheed & Ward, 1953.

Chesterton, G. K. *Heretics*. New York: Devin Adair, 1950.

Chesterton, G. K. *Orthodoxy*. New York: Dodd, Mead, 1954.

Chesterton, G. K. *Saint Thomas Aquinas*. Garden City, N.Y.: Doubleday, 1956.

Chesterton, G. K. *St. Francis of Assisi*. Garden City, N.Y.: Doubleday, 1954.

Chesterton, G. K. *The Thing: Why I Am a Catholic*. New York: Dodd, Mead, 1946.

Childs, Brevard S. *Introduction to the Old Testament as Scripture*. London: SCM, 1983.

Childs, Brevard. S. *The New Testament as Canon: An Introduction*. Valley Forge, Pa.: Trinity Press International, 1985.

Chishti, Yousuf, Saleem. *What is Christianity: Being A Critical Examination of Fundamental Doctrines of the Christian Faith*. Karachi, Pakistan: World Federation of Islamic Missions, 1970.

Clapp, James Gordon. "Locke, John." In *Encyclopedia of Philosophy*, ed. Paul Edwards. Vol. 4. New York: Macmillan and The Free Press, 1967.

Chryssides, George D. "Miracles and Agents." *Religious Studies*, 11. September 1975.

Clark, David. *Dialogical Apologetics*. Grand Rapids: Baker, 1993.

Clark, David K. *The Pantheism of Alan Watts*. Downers Grove, Ill.: InterVarsity, 1978.

Clark, David, and Norman L. Geisler. *Apologetics in the New Age*. Grand Rapids: Baker, 1990.

Clark, Gordon. "Apologetics." In *Contemporary Evangelical Thought*, ed. Carl F. H. Henry. Grand Rapids: Baker, 1968.

Clark, Gordon. "The Bible as Truth." *Bibliotheca Sacra* 114 (April, 1957).

Clark, Gordon . *A Christian Philosophy of Education*. 2nd rev. ed. Jefferson, Md.: Trinity Foundation, 1988.

Clark, Gordon. *A Christian View of Men and Things*. Grand Rapids: Eerdmans, 1952.

Clark, Gordon. *Dewey*. Philadelphia: Presbyterian & Reformed, 1960.

Clark, Gordon. *Historiography: Secular and Religious*. Grand Rapids: Baker, 1971.

Clark, Gordon. *The Johannine Logos*. Nutley, N.J.: Presbyterian & Reformed, 1972.

Clark, Gordon. *Karl Barth's Theological Method*. Philadelphia: Presbyterian & Reformed, 1963.

Clark, Gordon. *Religion, Reason and Revelation*. Philadephia: Presbyterian & Reformed, 1961.

Clark, Gordon. *Selections from Hellenistic Philosophy*. New York: Irvington, 1978.

Clark, Gordon. "Special Divine Revelation as Rational." In *Revelation and the Bible*, ed. Carl Henry. Grand Rapids: Baker, 1969.

Clark, Gordon. *Thales to Dewey: A History of Philosophy*. 1957. Reprint, Grand Rapids: Baker, 1980.

Clark, Gordon. "Truth." In *Baker's Dictionary of Theology*, ed. Everett F. Harrison. Grand Rapids: Baker, 1960.

Clark, Ronald W. *Einstein: His Life and Times*. New York: Avon, 1984.

Clarke, Andrew D., and Bruce W. Winter, eds. *One God, One Lord: Christianity in a World of Religious Pluralism*. Grand Rapids: Baker, 1993.

Clement of Alexandria. "Exhortation to the Heathen." In *Ante-Nicene Fathers*, ed. Alexander Roberts and James Donaldson. Grand Rapids: Eerdmans, 1989.

Clement of Alexandria. *Stromata* In *Ante-Nicene Fathers*, ed. Alexander Roberts and James Donaldson. Grand Rapids: Eerdmans, 1989.

Cloud, Preston. "Pseudofossils: A Plea for Caution." *Geology* (November, 1973.

Cobb, John B., Jr. *A Christian Natural Theology*. Philadelphia: Westminster, 1965.

Cobb, John B., Jr., and David Ray Griffin. *Process Theology: An Introductory Exposition*. Philadelphia: Westminster, 1976.

Collins, David. "Was Noah's Ark Stable?" *Creation Research Society Quarterly* 14 (1977).

Collins, James. *The Existentialists*. Chicago: H. Regnery, 1952.

Collins, James. *God in Modern Philosophy*. Westport, Conn.: Greenwood, 1978.

Collins, James. *A History of Modern European Philosophy.* Milwaukee: Bruce, 1954.

Comfort, Philip W., and David P. Barrett. *The Complete Text of the Earliest New Testament Manuscripts.* Grand Rapids: Baker, 1998.

Comte, Auguste. *The Catechism of Positive Religion.* Translated by Richard Congreve. 3rd ed. London: Kegan Paul, Trench, Trubner, 1858.

Comte, Auguste. *Cours: The Positive Philosophy of Auguste Comte.* Translated by Harriet Martineau. 2 vols. London, 1853.

Comte, Auguste. *The Positive Philosophy of Auguste Comte.* New York: D. Appleton, 1853.

Conradie, A. L. *The Neo-Calvinistic Concept of Philosophy.* Natal: University Press, 1960.

Cook, Edward M. *Solving the Mysteries of the Dead Sea Scrolls: New Light on the Bible.* Grand Rapids: Zondervan, 1994.

Cook, Stanley Arthur. *The Cambridge Ancient History.* London: Cambridge University Press, 1965.

Copi, Irving M. *Introduction to Logic.* 7th ed. New York: Macmillan, 1986.

Copleston, Frederick C. *Arthur Schopenhauer: Philosopher of Pessimism.* S. I. Burn, Oates and Wahbourne, 1947.

Copleston, Frederick. *The History of Philosophy.* Vol. 1, *Greece and Rome.* Garden City, N.Y.: Image, 1962.

Corduan, Winfried. "A Hair's Breadth from Pantheism: Meister Eckhart's God-Centered Spirituality." *Journal of the Evangelical Theological Society* 37 (1994): 263–74.

Corduan, Winfried. *Neighboring Faiths: A Christian Introduction to World Religions.* Downers Grove, Ill.: InterVarsity, 1998.

Corduan, Winfried. *Reasonable Faith: Basic Christian Apologetics.* Nashville, Tenn.: Broadman & Holman, 1993.

Corduan, Winfried. "Transcendentalism: Hegel." In *Biblical Errancy: An Analysis of its Philosophical Roots,* ed. Norman L. Geisler, 81–101. Grand Rapids: Zondervan, 1981.

Corwin, Charles. *East to Eden? Religion and the Dynamics of Social Change.* Grand Rapids: Eerdmans, 1972.

Courville, Donovan A. *The Exodus Problem and Its Ramifications.* Loma Linda, Calif.: Challenge, 1971.

Cousins, Ewert H., ed. *Process Theology: Basic Writings.* New York: Newman, 1971.

Cragg, Kenneth. *The Call of the Minaret.* New York: Oxford University Press, 1964.

Cragg, Kenneth. "Contemporary Trends in Islam." In *Muslims and Christians on the Emmaus Road,* ed. J. Dudley Woodberry. Monrovia, 1989.

Cragg, Kenneth. *Jesus and the Muslim: An Exploration.* London: George Allen & Unwin, 1985.

Craig, William. *Apologetics: An Introduction.* Chicago: Moody, 1989.

Craig, William Lane. *Assessing the New Testament Evidence for the Historicity of the Resurrection of Jesus.* Lewiston: Mellen, 1989.

Craig, William Lane. *Divine Foreknowledge and Human Freedom: the Coherence of Theism : Omniscience.* New York : E. J. Brill, 1990.

Craig, William Lane. *The Existence of God and the Beginning of the Universe.* San Bernardino: Here's Life, 1979.

Craig, William Lane. *The Kalam Cosmological Argument.* London: Macmillan, 1979.

Craig, William Lane. *Knowing the Truth About the Resurrection.* Rev. ed. Ann Arbor: Servant, 1981.

Craig, William Lane. *The Only Wise God: the Compatibility of Divine Foreknowledge and Human Freedom.* Grand Rapids: Baker, 1987.

Craig, William Lane, and Quentin Smith. *Theism, Atheism, and Big Bang Cosmology.* Oxford: Clarendon, 1993.

Craighead, Houston. "Non-Being and Hartshorne's Concept of God." *Process Studies* 1 (1971):9–24.

Craighead, Houston. "Response." *The Southwestern Journal of Philosophy* 5 (1974).

Creme, Benjamin. *Message from Maitreya the Christ and the Masters of Wisdom.* North Hollywood, Calif.: Tara Center, 1980.

Crockett, William V., ed. *Fours Views on Hell.* Grand Rapids: Zondervan, 1992.

Crockett, William V. "Will God Save Everyone in the End?" In *Through No Fault of Their Own: The Fate of Those Who Have Never Heard,* ed. William V. Crockett and James G. Sigountos. Grand Rapids: Baker, 1991.

Crockett, William V., and James G. Sigountos, eds. *Through No Fault of Their Own? The Fate of Those Who Have Never Heard.* Grand Rapids" Baker, 1991.

Cromwell, R. S. *David Friedrich Strauss and His Place in Modern Thought.* Fair Lawn, N.J.: R. E. Burdick, 1974.

Cross, F. L. "Athenagoras." In *The Oxford Dictionary of the Christian Church,* ed. F. L. Cross. 2nd ed. London: Oxford University Press, 1974.

Cross, F. L. "Celsus." In *The Oxford Dictionary of the Christian Church,* ed. F. L. Cross. 2nd ed. London: Oxford University Press, 1974.

Cross, F. L. "Essenes." In *The Oxford Dictionary of the Christian Church,* ed. F. L. Cross. 2nd ed. London: Oxford University Press, 1974.

Cross, F. L. "Eusebius." In *The Oxford Dictionary of the Christian Church,* ed. F. L. Cross. 2nd ed. London: Oxford University Press, 1974.

Cross, F. L. "Marcion." In *The Oxford Dictionary of the Christian Church,* ed. F. L. Cross. 2nd ed. London: Oxford University Press, 1974.

Cross, F. L., et al. eds. "Pascal, Blaise." In *The Oxford Dictionary of the Christian Church.* 2nd ed. London: Oxford University Press, 1974.

Cross, F. L., and E. A. Livingstone, eds. *The Oxford Dictionary of the Christian Church.* 2nd ed. London: Oxford University Press, 1974.

Crossan, John Dominic. *The Historical Jesus: The Life of a Mediterranean Peasant.* San Francisco: Harper San Francisco, 1991.

Cullmann, Oscar. *The Christology of the New Testament.* London: SCM, 1959.

Custance, Arthur. *The Doorway Papers.* Vol. 2, *Genesis and Early Man.* Grand Rapids: Zondervan, 1975.

Custance, Arthur. *The Doorway Papers*. Vol. 9, *The Flood: Local or Global?* Grand Rapids: Zondervan, 1979.

Custance, Arthur. *The Doorway Papers*. Vol. 1, *Noah's Three Sons*. Grand Rapids: Zondervan, 1975.

Custance, Arthur. *The Genealogies of the Bible: A Study of the Names in Genesis 10*. Ottawa: N.p., 1964.

Custance, Arthur. *Genesis and Early Man*. Grand Rapids: Zondervan, 1975.

Dahood, Michael. "Are the Ebla Tablets Relevant to Biblical Research?" *Biblical Archaeology Review* (September–October, 1980).

Danielou, Jean. *Origen*. New York: Sheed & Ward, 1983.

Darrow, Clarence. *The Story of My Life*. New York: Charles Scribner's Sons, 1932.

Darwin, Charles. *The Autobiography of Charles Darwin, with original omissions restored*. Edited by Nora Darwin Barlow N.Y.: W. W. Norton, 1993.

Darwin, Charles. *The Descent of Man and Selection in Relation to Sex*. New York: D. Appleton, 1896.

Darwin, Charles. *On The Origin of Species*. New York: New American Library. 1958: Reprint from 1859.

Darwin, Francis. *The Life and Letters of Charles Darwin*. Vol. 3. London: John Murray, 1888.

Dashti, Ali. *Twenty Three Years: A Study of the Prophetic Career of Mohammad*. London: George Allen & Unwin, 1985.

Davidson, Bruce W. "Reasonable Damnation: How Jonathan Edwards Argued for the Rationality of Hell." *Journal of the Evangelical Theological Society* 38, no. 1 (1995).

Davies, Philip R. *Daniel*. Sheffield: JSOT, 1985.

Davis, C. Truman. "The Crucifixion of Jesus: The Passion of Christ from a Medical Point of View." *Arizona Medicine* (March 1965): 183–87.

David, George T. B. *Fulfilled Prophecies That Prove the Bible*. Philadelphia: Million Testaments Campaign, 1931.

Davis, John J. *Foundations of Evangelical Theology*. Grand Rapids: Baker, 1994.

Davis, Percival, and Dean H. Kenyon. *Of Pandas and People: The Central Question of Biological Origins*. Edited by Charles B. Thaxton. Dallas, Tex.: Haughton, 1993.

Dawud, Abdu L-Ahad. *Muhammad in the Bible*. 2nd ed. Kuala Lumpur: Pustaka Antara, 1979.

De Arteaga, William. *Past Life Visions: A Christian Exploration*. New York: Seabury, 1983.

De Beauvoir, Simone. *The Ethics of Ambiguity*. Translated by Bernard Frechtman Secaucus, N.J.: Citadel, 1948.

De Boer, T. J. *The History of Philosophy in Islam*. Translated by Edward R. Jones. New Delhi: Cosmo, 1983.

De Mille, Richard, ed. *The Don Juan Papers*. Santa Barbara, Calif.: Ross Erickson, 1980.

De Saussure, Ferdinand. *Cours de Linguistique Generale*. Edited by Charles Bally and Albert Sechebaye with the collaboration of Albert Riedilinger. Translated and annotated by Roy Harris. LaSalle, Ill.: Open Court, 1986.

De Silva, Lynn. *Reincarnation in Buddhist and Christian Thought*. Colombo: Christian Literature Society of Ceylon, 1968.

Deedat, Ahmed. *Is the Bible God's Word?*. South Africa: N.p., 1987.

Deferrari, R. J. *A Complete Index of the Summa Theologiae of St. Thomas Aquinas*. Catholic University of America Press, 1956.

Deferrari, R. J. A. *A Lexicon of St. Thomas Aquinas Based on Summa Theologiae and Select Passages of His Other Work*. Catholic University of America Press, 1960.

Deferrari, R. J. A. *Latin-English Dictionary of Thomas Aquinas*. Daughters of St. Paul, 1960.

Deissmann, Adolf. *Light from the Ancient East*. Translated by L. R. M. Strachan. New York: Harper, 1923.

Delaney, John J., and James Edward Tobin. *Dictionary of Catholic Biography*. Garden City, N.Y.: Doubleday, 1961.

Delbert, Pierre, and Louis Ernest. *La science et la realite*. Paris: Flammarion, 1920.

Delvolve, Jean. *Religion, Critique et Philosophie Positive chez Pierre Bayle*. Paris: Felix Alcan, 1906.

Demarest, Bruce A. *General Revelation: Historical Views and Contemporary Issues*. Grand Rapids: Zondervan, 1983.

Demarest, Bruce A. "Process Theology and the Pauline Doctrines of the Incarnation." In *Pauline Studies: Essays Presented to F. F. Bruce on His 70th Birthday*, ed. by Donald A. Hagner and Murray J. Harris. Exeter" Paternoster., 1980.

Denton, Michael *Evolution: A Theory in Crisis*. Bethesda, Md: Adler & Adler, 1985.

Denzinger, Henry. *The Sources of Catholic Dogma*. Translated by Roy J. Deferrari. London: B. Herder, 1957.

Dermenghem, Emile. *Muhammad and the Islamic Tradition*. Translated by Jean M. Watt. Westport, Conn.: Greenwood, 1974.

Derrida, Jacques. *The Ear of the Other*. New York: Schocken, 1985.

Derrida, Jacques. *Edmund Husserl's Origin of Geometry: An Introduction*. Lincoln: University of Nebraska, 1989.

Derrida, Jacques. *Of Grammatology*. Baltimore: John Hopkins University Press, 1976.

Derrida, Jacques. *Limited Inc*. Evanston, Ill.: Northwestern University Press, 1988.

Derrida, Jacques. *Positions*. Chicago: University of Chicago Press, 1981.

Derrida, Jacques. *Specters of Marx*. New York: Routledge, 1994.

Derrida, Jacques. *Speech and Phenomena*. Evanston, Ill.: Northwestern University Press, 1973.

Derrida, Jacques. *Writing and Difference*. Chicago: University of Chicago, 1978.

Descartes, Rene. *Discourse on Method*. Indianapolis: Hackett, 1980.

Descartes, Rene. *Meditations*. Translated by L. Lafleur. New York: Liberal Arts, 1951.

Dewey, John *A Common Faith*. London:Yale University Press, 1934.

Dewey, John *Recontruction and Philosophy*. London: University of London Press, 1921.

Diamond, Malcolm L. "Miracles," *Religious Studies.* 9 (1973).

Dickason, C. Fred. *Angels: Elect and Evil.* Chicago: Moody, 1995.

Dixon, Larry. *The Other Side of the Good News: Confronting the Contemporary Challenges to Jesus' Teaching on Hell.* Wheaton, Ill.: Bridgepoint, 1992.

Dodd, C. H. *The Interpretation of the Fourth Gospel.* Cambridge: Cambridge University Press, 1968.

Dodds, E. R. *Pagan and Christian in an Age of Anxiety.* Cambridge: Cambridge University Press, 1965.

Doi, A.R.I. "The Status of Prophet Jesus in Islam." *Muslim Magazine World League Journal.* (June 1982).

Doi, A. R. I. "The Status of Prophet Jesus in Islam—II." *Muslim Magazine World League Journal.* (June 1982).

Dooyeweerd, Herman. *A New Critique of Theoretical Thought.* 4 vols. Ontario: Paideia, 1984.

Dooyeweerd, Herman. *In The Twilight of Western Thought: Studies in the Pretended Autonomy of Philosophical Thought.* Nuttley, N.J.: Craig, 1972.

Douglas, J. D., ed. *The New International Dictionary of the Christian Church.* Grand Rapids: Zondervan, 1974.

Douillet, Jacques. *What Is a Saint.* New York, 1960.

Dowling, Levi H. *The Aquarian Gospel of Jesus the Christ; the Philosophic and Practical Basis of the Religion of the Aquarian Age of the World.* Santa Monica, Calif.: DeVorss, 1972.

Dulles, Avery. *A History of Apologetics.* New York: Westminster, 1971.

Dulles, Avery. "Infallibility: The Terminology." In *Teaching Authority and Infallibility in the Church,* ed. Paul C. Empie, T. Austin Murphy, and Joseph A. Burgess. Minneapolis: Augsburg, 1980.

Dupont-Sommer, A. *The Jewish Sect of Aumran and the Essenes.* London: Vallentine, Mitchell, 1954.

Eareckson, Joni and Steve Estes. *A Step Further.* Grand Rapids: Zondervan, 1978.

Eddy, Mary Baker. *Science and Health with Key to the Scriptures.* Boston: The First Church of Christ Scientist, 1971.

Edgar, Thomas. *Miraculous Gifts: Are They for Today?* Neptune, N.J.: Loizeaux Brothers, 1983.

Edwards, Jonathan. "Freedom of the Will." In *The Works of Jonathan Edwards.* 2 vols. Carlisle, Pa.: Banner of Truth, 1974.

Edwards, Jonathan. *Jonathan Edwards: Representative Selections . . .* Edited by Clarence H. Faust et al. New York: Hill & Wang, 1962.

Edwards, Jonathan. "The Mind." In *The Philosophy of Jonathan Edwards from His Private Notebooks,* ed. Harvey G. Townsend. Eugene: University of Oregon, 1955.

Edwards, Jonathan. "Miscellanies." In *The Works of Jonathan Edwards.* 2 vols. Carlisle, Pa.: Banner of Truth, 1974.

Edwards, Jonathan. "Of Being." In *Jonathan Edwards: Representative Selections,* ed. Clarence H. Faust et al. New York: Hill & Wang, 1962.

Edwards, Jonathan. "Religious Affections." In *The Works of Jonathan Edwards.* 2 vols. Carlisle, Pa.: Banner of Truth, 1974.

Edwards, Jonathan. *The Works of Jonathan Edwards.* 2 vols. Carlisle, Pa.: Banner of Truth, 1974.

Edwards, Paul, ed. *Encyclopedia of Philosophy.* 8 vols. New York: Macmillan and The Free Press, 1967.

Edwards, William D., Wesley J. Gabel, and Floyd E. Hosmer. "On the Physical Death of Jesus Christ." *Journal of the American Medical Association* 255, no. 11 (1986).

Eerdman's Handbook of the World Religions. Grand Rapids: Eerdmans, 1982.

Ehrenfeld, David. *The Arrogance of Humanism.* N.ew York: Oxford University Press, 1981.

Einstein, Albert. *Ideas and Opinions—The World as I See It.* 3rd ed. New York: Crown, 1982.

Eisenman, Robert H., and Michael Wise. *The Dead Sea Scrolls Uncovered.* New York: Barnes & Nobel, 1992.

Eisley, Loren. *The Immense Journey.* New York: Vintage, 1957.

Elderedge, Niles. *The Myths of Human Evolution.* New York: Columbia University Press, 1982.

Elliger, K., and W. Rudolph, eds. *Biblia Hebraica Stuttgartensia.* 2nd ed. Stuttgart: Deutsche Bibelstiftung, 1967–77, 1983: Editio minor, 1984.

Elwell, Walter, ed. *Evangelical Dictionary of Theology.* Grand Rapids: Baker, 1984.

Elwell, Walter, ed. *Handbook of Evangelical Theologians.* Grand Rapids: Baker, 1993.

Encyclopedia Britannica. ed. S. v. "Einstein."

Engels, Friedrich. *Ludwig Feuerbach and the Outcome of Classical German Philosophy.* New York: International Publishers, 1934.

Erlandson, Douglas K. "A New Look." *Religious Studies* (December, 1977).

Estrada, David, and William White, Jr. *The First New Testament.* Nashville, Tenn.: Thomas Nelson, 1978.

Evans, Craig A., et al. *Nag Hammadi Texts and the Bible.* New York: E. J. Brill, 1993.

Evans, C. Stephen. *Existentialism: The Philosophy of Despair and the Quest for Hope.* Dallas: Probe/Word, 1989.

Evans, C. Stephen. *Passionate Reason: Making Sense of Kierkegaard's Philosophical Fragments.* Bloomington: Indiana University Press, 1992.

Evans, C. Stephen, and Merold Westphal, eds. *Christian Perspectives on Religious Knowledge.* Grand Rapids: Eerdmans, 1993.

"Eve of Passover." In *Babylonian Talmud Sanhedrin* 43a, ed. Israel W. Slotki. Translated by S. Daiches. Vol. 3. Rebecca Bennett Publications, 1959.

Ewing, I. *The Essene Christ.* New York: Philosophical Library, 1961.

Farmer, William R. *The Synoptic Problem.* New York: Macmillan, 1964.

Farmer, William. *The Synoptic Problem: A Critical Analysis.* Dillsboro:: Western North Carolina Press, 1976.

Faruqi, Isma'il R. Al. *Islam.* Argus Communications, 1984.

Feigel, Herbert. "Logical Positivism after Thirty Five Years." *Philosophy Today* (Winter, 1964).

Feldman, L. H. *Scholarship on Philo and Josephus 1937–1962.* New York: Yeshiva University, 1963.

Ferguson, Everett. *Background of Early Christianity.* Grand Rapids: Eerdmans, 1993.

Ferguson, John. *The Religions of the Roman Empire*. London : Thames & Hudson, 1982.

Ferguson, Marilyn, *The Aquarian Conspiracy: Personal and Social Transformation in the 1980's*. Los Angeles: J. P. Tarcher, 1980.

Ferngren, Gary B., and Ronald L. Numbers. "C. S. Lewis on Creation and Evolution: The Acworth Letters, 1944–1960." *Journal of American Scientific Affiliation* 48, no. 1 (1996).

Ferre, Frederick. "Analogy." In the *Encyclopedia of Philosophy*, ed. Paul Edwards. Vol. 1. New York: Macmillan and The Free Press, 1967.

Ferre, Frederick. *Language, Logic and God.* New York: Harper, 1961.

Ferrin, Howard W. "Manipulation or Motivation? Skinner's Utopia vs. Jesus' Kingdom." *Christianity Today,* September 29, 1972.

Fesperman, Francis I. "Jefferson's Bible." *Ohio Journal of Religious Studies* 4 (1976):78–88.

Feuerbach, Ludwig. *The Essence of Christianity.* Translated by George Eliot. New York: Harper Torchbooks, 1957.

Fifty-Third Chapter of Isaiah according to the Jewish Interpreters. Translated by S. R. Driver and A. Neubauer. New York: KTAV, 1969.

Findlay, J. N. "Can God's Existence Be Disproved?" In the *Ontological Argument,* ed. Alvin Plantinga. Garden City, N.Y.: Doubleday, 1965.

Fisher, E. "NT Documents Among the Dead Sera Scrolls?" *The Bible Today,* Collegeville, Minn., 1972.

Fletcher, John. *Checks to Antinomianism.* Kansas City: Beacon Hill. 1948.

Fletcher, Joseph *Situation Ethics: The New Morality.* Philadelphia: Westminster, 1966.

Flew, Antony. *New Essays in Philosophical Theology*. New York: Macmillan, 1955.

Flew, Antony. "Miracles." In *The Encyclopedia of Philosophy,* ed. Paul Edwards. Vol. 5. New York: Macmillan and The Free Press, 1967.

Flew, Antony. "Theology and Falsification." In *New Essays in Philosophical Theology*. London: SCM, 1963.

Flint, Robert. *Agnosticism.* New York: Charles Scribner's Sons, 1903.

Flint, Robert. *Anti-Theistic Theories*. 3rd ed. Edinburgh and London: Wm. Blackwood & Sons, 1885.

Foote, Henry Wilder. *Thomas Jefferson: Champion of Religious Freedom, Advocate of Christian Morals*. Boston: Beacon, 1947.

Ford, Lewis. "Biblical Recital and Process Philosophy." *Interpretation* 26, no. 2 (1972).

Foreman, Mark. "An Evaluation of Islamic Miracle Claims in the Life of Muhammad." Unpublished paper, 1991.

Forster, T. Roger. and V. Paul Marston. *God's Strategy in Human History.* Wheaton, Ill.: Tyndale House, 1973.

Foster, M. B. "The Christian Doctrine of Creation and the Rise of Modern Natural Science." *Mind* 43 (1934).

Foster, R. S. *The Supernatural Book: Evidence of Christianity.* New York: Cranston & Curts, 1893.

Foxe, John. *Acts and Monuments of Matters Most Special and Memorable, Happening in the Church, with an universal historie of the same.* 4th ed. London: John Daye, 1583.

France, R. T. *The Evidence for Jesus.* Downers Grove, Ill..: InterVarsity, 1986.

Frank, Philipp. *Einstein: His Life and Times.* New York: Alfred A. Knopf, 1953.

Frazer, James G. *The Golden Bough.* London: Macmillan, 1890. One-volume abridged edition. New York: Crown , 1981.

Frazer, Sir George. *The New Golden Bough.* Revised by Theodore Gaster. New York: Phillips, 1959.

Frege, Gottlob. *Uber Sinn und Bedeutung.* In *Translations from the Philosophical Writings of Gottlob Frege,* ed. Peter Geach and Max Black. Oxford: Blackwell, 1980.

Freud, Sigmund. *The Future of an Illusion*. Translated by W. D. Robson-Scott. New York: Doubleday, 1957.

Freud, Sigmund. *Moses and Monotheism*. Translated by Katherine Jones. New York: Vintage, 1939.

Freud, Sigmund. *Totem and Taboo: Some Points of Agreement Between the Mental Lives of Savages and Neurotics.* London: Routledge & K. Paul, 1960.

Funk, Robert et al. *The Parables of Jesus: Red Letter Edition.* Sonoma, Calif.: Polebridge, 1988.

Furlong, William R., and Byron McCandless. *So Proudly We Hail: The History of the United States Flag.* Washington, D.C.: Smithsonian Institution Press, 1981.

Gaeberlein, Frank E., ed. *The Expositor's Bible Commentary.* 12 vols. Grand Rapids: Zondervan, 1979.

Gangel, Kenneth. "John Dewey: An Evangelical Evaluation Part II." In *Bibliotheca Sacra* 124 (1967).

Gardner, Patrick. "Schopenhauer, Arthur." In the *Encyclopedia of Philosophy,* ed. Paul Edwards. New York: Macmillan and The Free Press, 1967.

Garnet, P. "O'Callahan's Fragments: Our Earliest New Testrment Texts? *Evangelical Quarterly* 45 (1972).

Garrigou-Lagrange, Reginald. *God: His Existence and His Nature*. 2 vols. St. Louis: B. Herder, 1934–36.

Garrigou-Lagrange, Reginald. *The One God.* Translated by Bede Rose. St. Louis: B. Herder, 1943.

Garrigou-Lagrange, Reginald. *Predestination*. Translated by Dom Bede Rose. St. Louis: B. Herder, 1939.

Garrigou-Lagrange, Reginald. *Reality: A Synthesis of Thomistic Thought*. Translated by Patrick Cummins St. Louis: B. Herder, 1950.

Gasque, Ward. "F. F. Bruce: A Mind for What Matters." *Christianity Today,* 7 April 1989.

Gaussen, S. R. L. *Theopneustia: The Bible, Its Divine Origin and Inspiration, Deduced from Internal Evidence and the Testimonies of Nature, History, and Science.* Rev. ed. New York: Jennings & Pye, 1867.

Geach, Peter, and Max Black, eds. *Translations From the Philosophical Writings of Gottlob Frege.* Oxford: Blackwell, 1980.

Geisler, Norman L. *The Battle for the Resurrection*. Updated edition. Nashville, Tenn.: Thomas Nelson, 1992.

Geisler, Norman L. "Bible Manuscripts." In *Wycliffe Bible Encyclopedia,* ed. Charles F. Pfeiffer, Howard F. Vos, and John Rea. 2 vols. Chicago: Moody, 1975.

Geisler, Norman L. "Biblical Studies." In *The Opening of the American Mind,* ed. W. David Beck, 25–45. Grand Rapids: Baker, 1991.

Geisler, Norman L. *Carl Sagan's Religion for the Scientific Mind.* Dallas: Quest, 1983.

Geisler, Norman L. *Christian Apologetics.* Grand Rapids: Baker, 1976.

Geisler, Norman L. *Christian Ethics: Options and Issues.* Grand Rapids: Baker, 1989.

Geisler, Norman L. "The Concept of Truth in the Inerrancy Debate." *Bibliotheca Sacra* (October–December, 1980.

Geisler, Norman. *The Creator in the Courtroom: Scopes II.* Milford, Mich.: Mott Media, 1982.

Geisler, Norman L. "The Extent of the Old Testament Canon." In *Current Issues in Biblical and Patristic Interpretation,* ed. Gerald F. Hawthorne. Grand Rapids: Eerdmans, 1975.

Geisler, Norman L. "God's Revelation in Scripture and Nature." In *The Opening of the American Mind,* ed. David Beck. Grand Rapids: Baker, 1991.

Geisler, Norman L. *In Defense of the Resurrection.* Lynchburg, Va.: Quest, 1991.

Geisler, Norman L. *Is Man the Measure?: An Evaluation of Contemporary Humanism.* Grand Rapids: Baker, 1983.

Geisler, Norman L. *Knowing the Truth About Creation: How It Happened and What It Means to Us.* Ann Arbor, Mich.: Servant, 1989.

Geisler, Norman. L. "Man's Destiny: Free or Forced." *Christian Scholar's Review* 9, no. 2 (1979).

Geisler, Norman L. *Miracles and the Modern Mind.* Grand Rapids: Baker, 1992.

Geisler, Norman L. *Miracles and Modern Thought.* Grand Rapids: Zondervan, 1982.

Geisler, Norman L. "The Missing Premise in the Ontological Argument." *Religious Studies* (September, 1973).

Geisler, Norman L. "The Natural Right." In *In Search of a National Morality,* ed. William Bentley Ball, 112–28. Grand Rapids: Baker, 1992.

Geisler, Norman L. "Neopaganism, Feminism, and the New Polytheism." *Christian Research Journal* (Fall, 1991): 8.

Geisler, Norman L. "Of Pandas and People: The Central Questions of Biological Origins." *Perspectives on Science & Christian Faith* 42, no. 4 (1990): 246–49.

Geisler, Norman L. *A Popular Survey of the Old Testament.* Grand Rapids: Baker, 1977.

Geisler, Norman L. "Process Theology." In *Tensions in Contemporary Theology,* ed. Stanley N. Gundry and Alan F. Johnson. Chicago: Moody, 1976.

Geisler, Norman L. "Purpose and Meaning: The Cart and the Horse." *Grace Theological Journal* 5 (1984).

Geisler, Norman L. *The Roots of Evil.* 2nd rev. ed. Dallas: Probe, 1989.

Geisler, Norman L. *Signs and Wonders.* Wheaton, Ill.: Tyndale House, 1988.

Geisler, Norman L. *Thomas Aquinas: An Evangelical Appraisal.* Grand Rapids: Baker, 1991.

Geisler, Norman L. "Was Clarence Darrow a Bigot?" *Creation/Evolution* (Fall, 1988).

Geisler, Norman L. *What Augustine Says.* Grand Rapids: Baker, 1982.

Geisler, Norman L. "When Did I Begin?: A Review Article." *Evangelical Theological Society* 33, no. 4 (1990): 509–12.

Geisler, Norman L., ed. *Inerrancy.* Grand Rapids: Zondervan, 1979.

Geisler, Norman L., and J. Yutaka Amano. *The Infiltration of the New Age.* Wheaton, Ill.: Tyndale House, 1989.

Geisler, Norman L., and J. Yutaka Amano. *The Reincarnation Sensation.* Wheaton, Ill.: Tyndale House, 1986.

Geisler, Norman L., and Ronald M. Brooks. *Come Let Us Reason: An Introduction to Logical Thinking.* Grand Rapids: Baker, 1990.

Geisler, Norman L., and Ronald M. Brooks. *When Skeptics Ask.* Wheaton, Ill.: Victor, 1990.

Geisler, Norman L., and Winfried Corduan. *Philosophy of Religion.* 2nd ed. Grand Rapids: Baker, 1988.

Geisler, Norman L., and Paul D. Feinberg. *Introduction to Philosophy: A Christian Perspective.* Grand Rapids: Baker, 1980.

Geisler, Norman L., and Thomas Howe. *When Critics Ask.* Wheaton, Ill.: Victor, 1992.

Geisler, Norman L., and J. Kerby. *Origin Science: A Proposal for the Creation-Evolution Controversy.* Grand Rapids: Baker, 1987.

Geisler, Norman L., and Harold Kushner. *Why Do Good Things Happen to Bad People?* Video Debate on "John Ankerberg TV Show," Chattanooga, Tenn., 1984.

Geisler, Norman L., and Ralph McKenzie. *Roman Catholics and Evangelicals: Agreements and Differences.* Grand Rapids: Baker, 1995.

Geisler, Norman L., and William E. Nix. *A General Introduction to the Bible.* Rev. ed. Chicago: Moody, 1986.

Geisler, Norman L., and Abdul Saleeb. *Answering Islam: The Crescent in the Light of the Cross.* Grand Rapids: Baker, 1993.

Geisler, Norman L., and William D. Watkins. *Perspectives: Understanding and Evaluating Today's World Views.* San Bernardino, Calif: Here's Life, 1984.

Geisler, Norman L., and William D. Watkins. *World's Apart: A Handbook on World Views.* Grand Rapids: Baker, 1989.

Geivett, Douglas R. *Evil and the Evidence for God: The Challenge of John Hick's Theodicy.* Philadelphia: Temple University Press, 1993.

Geivett, Douglas R., and Gary R. Habermas, eds. *In Defense of Miracles: A Comprehensive Case for God's Action in History.* Downers Grove, Ill.: InterVarsity, 1997.

Gentry, Robert. *Creation's Tiny Mystery.* Knoxville, Tenn.: Earth Science Association, 1988.

George, Timothy, and David S. Dockery, eds. *Baptist Theologians.* Nashville, Tenn.: Broadman, 1990.

Gerstner, John H. "Heathen." In *Baker's Dictionary of Theology,* ed. Everett F. Harrison. Grand Rapids: Baker, 1960.

Gerstner, John. *Jonathan Edwards on Heaven and Hell.* Grand Rapids: Baker, 1980.

Gerstner, John. *Jonathan Edwards: A Mini-Theology.* Wheaton, Ill..: Tyndale House, 1987.

Gerstner, John . "An Outline of the Apologetics of Jonathan Edwards." *Bibliotheca Sacra*, 133, no.4 (January–March, 1976); (April–June, 1976); (July–September, 1976); (October–December, 1976).

Gerstner, John. *Reasons for Faith.* New York: Harper, 1960. Reprint, Morgan, Pa.: Soli Deo Gloria, 1995.

Gibb, H. A. R., and J. H. Kramers. *Shorter Encyclopedia of Islam.* Ithaca, N.Y.: Cornell University Press, 1953.

Gibbon, Edward. *The History of the Decline and Fall of the Roman Empire*. vol. 5. Edited by J. B. Bury. London: Methuen, 1898.

Gilby, Thomas. *St. Thomas Aquinas: Philosophical Texts*. New York: Oxford University Press, 1964.

Gilchrist, John. *The Texual History of the Qur'an and the Bible*. Villach, Australia: Light of Life, 1988 reprint.

Gilkey, Landgon. *Maker of Heaven and Earth: A Study of the Christian Doctrine of Creation.* Garden City, N.Y.: Doubleday, 1959.

Gilson, Etienne. *Being and Some Philosophers.* Toronto: Pontifical Institute of Medieval Studies, 1949.

Gilson, Etienne. *God and Philosophy.* New Haven, Conn.: Yale University Press, 1992.

Gilson, Etienne. *History of Christian Philosophy in the Middle Ages.* New York: Random House, 1955.

Gilson, Etienne. *Linguistics and Philosophy.* Notre Dame, Ind.: University of Notre Dame, 1988.

Gilson, Etienne. *The Unity of Philosophical Experience*. New York: Charles Scribner's Sons, 1937.

Ginsburg, C. D. *The Essenes.* London: Routledge & Kegan Paul, 1955.

Gish, Duane T. *Evolution The Fossils Say No!* San Diego: Creation-Life, 1979.

Gleick, James. *Chaos: Making a New Science.* New York: Penguin, 1988.

Glover, Willis B. "Religious Orientations of H. G. Wells: A Case Study in Scientific Humanism." *Harvard Theological Review* 65 (1972): 117–35.

Glueck, Nelson. *Rivers in the Desert: A History of the Negev.* Philadelphia: Jewish Publication Society, 1969.

Glut, Donald F. *The Empire Strikes Back*. New York: Ballantine, 1980.

Gnanakan, Ken. *The Pluralistic Predicament.* Bangalore, India: Theological Book Trust, 1992.

Goetz, Stewart C. Review of *The Kalam Cosmological Argument*, by William Lane Craig. *Faith and Philosophy* 9 (1989): 99–102.

Goldziher, Ignaz. *Introduction to Islamic Theology*. Princeton, N.J.: Princeton University Press, 1981.

Gombridh, E. H. "Lessing." *Proceedings of the British Academy* 43 (1957).

Gooch, George Peabody. *History and Historians in the Nineteenth Century.* New York: Longmans, Green, 1913.

Goshen-Gottstein, Moshe. "Biblical Manuscripts in the United States" *Textus* 3 (1962).

Gould, Stephen J. "Evolution's Erratic Pace" *Natural History* 86 (1977).

Govier, Gordon. "Celebration Underway: Jerusalem 3000." *Institute for Biblical Archeology* (January–March 1996).

Grant, Michael. *Jesus: An Historian's Review of the Gospels.* New York: Collier, 1992.

Grant, R. M. *Gnosticism and Early Christianity.* New York: Columbia University, 1996.

Grave, S. A. *The Scottish Philosophy of Common Sense.* Westport, Conn.: Greenwood, 1973.

Green, J. B., S. McKnight, and I. H. Marshall, eds. *Dictionary of Jesus and the Gospels.* Downers Grove, Ill.: InterVaristy, 1992.

Green, William H. "Primeval Chronology." In *Classical Evangelical Essays in Old Testament Interpretation*, ed. Walter Kaiser. Grand Rapids: Baker, 1972.

Greenleaf, Simon. *The Testimony of the Evangelists.* Grand Rapids: Baker,1984; 1874 reprint.

Greenleaf, Simon. *A Treatise on the Law of Evidence.* Boston: C. C. Little & J. Brown, 1842.

Gregory, John, and Carl. Shafer. *Excellence in Teaching with the Seven Laws:Aa Contemporary Abridgment of Gregory's Seven Laws of Teaching*. Grand Rapids: Baker, 1985.

Gromacki, Robert. *The Virgin Birth: Doctrine of Deity*. Grand Rapids: Baker, 1981.

Groothuis, Douglas R. *Confronting the New Age : How to Resist a Growing Religious Movement*. Downers Grove, Ill. : InterVarsity, 1988.

Groothuis, Douglas R. *Unmasking the New Age*. Downers Grove, Ill.: InterVarsity, 1986.

Gruber, Howard. *Darwin on Man*. London: Wildwood House, 1974.

Grudem, Wayne A., ed. *Are Miraculous Gifts for Today?* Grand Rapids: Zondervan, 1996.

Gruenler, Gordon R. *The Inexhaustible God: Biblical Faith and the Challenge of Process Theism*. Grand Rapids: Baker, 1983.

Gudel, Joseph P. *To Every Muslim An Answer.* Unpublished thesis at Simon Greenleaf School of Law, 1982.

Guiness, Os. *The Dust of Death*. Downers Grove, Ill.: InterVarsity, 1973.

Gundry, Robert. *Matthew: A Commentary on His Literary and Theological Art*. Grand Rapids: Eerdmans, 1982.

Gundry, Robert. *Soma in Biblical Theology: with Emphasis on Pauline Anthropology*. Cambridge: Cambridge University Press, 1976.

Gurney, O. R. *The Hittites.* Baltimore: Penguin, 1952.

Gurr, John E. *The Principle of Sufficient Reason in Some Scholastic Systems, 1750–1900*. Milwaukee: Marquette University Press, 1959.

Guthrie, Donald. *New Testament Introduction: The Gospels and Acts.* London: Tyndale House, 1965.

Haas, N. "Anthropological Observations of the Skeletal Remains from Giv'at ha-Mivtar." *Israel Exploration Journal* 20 (1970).

Habermas, Gary . *Ancient Evidence for the Life of Jesus*. Nashville, Tenn.: Thomas Nelson 1984.

Habermas, Gary. *Dealing with Doubt.* Chicago: Moody, 1990.

Habermas, Gary. "Did Jesus Perform Miracles?" In *Jesus Under Fire*, ed. Michael Wilkins and J. P. Moreland. Grand Rapids: Zondervan, 1995.

Habermas, Gary. *The Historical Jesus: Ancient Evidence for the Life of Christ.* Joplin, Mo.: College Press, 1996.

Habermas, Gary. "Resurrection Claims in Non-Christian Religions." *Religious Studies* (1989).

Habermas, Gary. *The Resurrection of Jesus: An Apologetic*. Grand Rapids: Baker, 1980.

Habermas, Gary. *The Verdict of History.* Nashville, Tenn.: Thomas Nelson, 1988.

Habermas, Gary, and Antony G. N. Flew. *Did Jesus Rise from the Dead?: The Resurrection Debate.* Edited by Terry L. Miethe. Sn Francisco: Harper & Row, 1987.

Habermas, Gary, and James Porter Moreland. *Immortality: The Other Side of Death.* Nashville, Tenn. : Thomas Nelson, 1992.

Hackett, Stuart. *Oriental Philosophy: A Westerner's Guide to Eastern Thought.* Madison: University of Wisconsin Press, 1979.

Hackett, Stuart. *The Resurrection of Theism*. Chicago: Moody, 1957.

Haley, John W. *An Examination of the Alleged Discrepancies of the Bible.* Grand Rapids: Baker, 1951.

Hamilton, Floyd E. *The Basis of Christian Faithy: A Modern Defense of the Christian Religion,* 3rd rev. ed. New York: Harper & Brothers, 1965.

Haneef, Suzanne. *What Everyone Should Know about Islam and Muslims.* Chicago: Kazi, 1979.

Hannah, John D., ed. *Inerrancy and the Church.* Chicago: Moody, 1984.

Haqq, Abdul *Sharing Your Faith with a Muslim.* Minnesota: Bethany, 1980.

Harbin, Michael. *To Serve Other Gods: An Evangelical History of Religion.* New York: University Press of America, 1994.

Hardon, John A. *The Catholic Catechism: A Contemporary Catechism of the Teachings of the Catholic Church.* New York: Doubleday, Image, 1966.

Harris, H. *David Friedrich Strauss and His Theology.* Cambridge: Cambridge University Press, 1973.

Harris, Murray. *From Grave to Glory.* Grand Rapids: Zondervan, 1990.

Harris, Murray. *Raised Immortal: Resurrection and Immortality in the New Testament*. Grand Rapids: Eerdmans, 1983.

Harris, R. Laird. *Inspiration and Canonicity of the Bible.* Grand Rapids: Zondervan, 1957.

Harris, R. Laird, Swee Hwa Quek, and J. Robert Vannoy, eds. *Inspiration and History: Essay in Honour of Alan A. MacRae.* Singapore: Christian Life, 1986.

Harrison, Everett F., ed. *Baker's Dictionary of Theology*. Grand Rapids: Baker, 1960.

Harrison, R. K. "Historical and Literary Criticism of the Old Testament." In *The Expositor's Bible Commentary,* ed. Frank E. Gaebelein. Vol. 1. Grand Rapids: Zondervan, 1979.

Harrison, R. K., *An Introduction to the Old Testament*. Grand Rapids: Eerdmans, 1969.

Hart, Daryl G. "The Princeton Mind in the Modern World and the Common Sense of J. Gresham Machen. *Westminster Theological Journal* 46, no. 1 (1984): 1–25.

Hartshorne, Charles. "Abstract and Concrete Approaches to Deity." *Union Seminary Quarterly Review*. 20 (1965).

Hartshorne, Charles. *Aquinas to Whitehead: Seven Centuries of Metaphysics of Religion. The Aquinas Lecture, 1976.* Milwaukee: Marquette University Publications, 1976.

Hartshorne, Charles. "Beyond Enlightened Self-Interest: A Metaphysics of Ethics." *Ethics* 84 (1974).

Hartshorne, Charles. *Creative Synthesis and Philosophic Method*. LaSalle: Open Court, 1970.

Hartshorne, Charles. "The Dipolar Conception of Deity." *The Review of Metaphysics.* 21 (1967).

Hartshorne, Charles. *The Divine Relativity: A Social Conception of God*. New Haven and London: Yale University Press, 1948.

Hartshorne, Charles. "Efficient Causality in Aristotle and St. Thomas: A Review Article." *The Journal of Religion.* 25 (1945).

Hartshorne, Charles. "The Idea of God—Literal or Analogical?" *The Christian Scholar* 34 (1956).

Hartshorne, Charles. "Idealism and Our Experience of Nature." In *Philosophy, Religion, and the Coming World Civilization: Essays in Honor of William Ernest Hocking,* ed. Leroy S. Rouner, 70–80. The Hague: Martinus Nijhoff, 1966.

Hartshorne, Charles. "Is God's Existence a State of Affairs?" In *Faith and the Philosophers,* ed. John Hick, 26–33. New York: St. Martin's, 1966.

Hartshorne, Charles. *The Logic of Perfection*. LaSalle: Open Court, 1962.

Hartshorne, Charles. "Love and Dual Transcendance." *Union Seminary Quarterly Review*. 30 (1975): 97.

Hartshorne, Charles. *Man's Vision of God and the Logic of Theism*. Hamden: Archon, 1964; first published 1941.

Hartshorne, Charles. *A Natural Theology for Our Time*. LaSalle: Open Court, 1967.

Hartshorne, Charles. "The Necessarily Existent." In *The Ontological Argument from St. Anselm to Contemporary Philosophers*, ed. Alvin Plantinga. New York: Doubleday, 1965.

Hartshorne, Charles. "Personal Identity from A to Z." *Process Studies*. 2 (1972).

Hartshorne, Charles. "Two Levels of Faith and Reason." *The Journal of Bible and Religion*. 16 (1948).

Hartshorne, Charles. *Whitehead's Philosophy: Selected Essays.* Lincoln: University of Nebraska Press, 1972.

Hartshorne, Charles, and William L. Reese. *Philosophers Speak of God*. Reprinted. Chicago and London: University of Chicago Press, 1976; first published, 1953.

Hasel, Gerhard. *New Testament Theology: Basic Issues in the Current Debate.* Grand Rapids: Eerdmans, 1978.

Hastings, James. et al., eds. *Encyclopedia of Religion and Ethics.* 13 vols. New York: Scribner's, 1908–26.

Hastings, Rashdal. *The Theory of Good and Evil.* Vol. 2. Oxford: Clarendon and New York: Oxford University Press, 1907.

Hatch, Edwin, and Henry Redpath, *A Concordance to the Septuagint and Other Greek Versions of the Old Testament*. Oxford: Claredon, 1900.

Hawking, Stephen. *A Brief History of Time: From the Big Bang to Black Holes*. New York : Bantam, 1988.

Hawking, Stephen. *Black Holes and Baby Universes and Other Essays*. London: Bantam, 1994.

Haykal, Muhammad Husayn. *The Life of Muhammad*. Indianapolis: North America Trust, 1976.

Hazard, Paul. *European Thought in the Eighteenth Century*. New Haven, Conn.: Yale University Press, 1954.

Heeren, Fred. *Show Me God: What the Message from Space Is Telling Us About God*. Wheeling, Ill..: Search Light, 1995.

Hegel, G. W. F. *Early Theological Writings*. Philadelphia: University of Pennsylvania Press, 1988.

Hegel, G. W. F. *Encyclopedia of Philosophy*. New York: Philosophical Library, 1959.

Hegel, G. W. F. *Lectures on the Philosophy of Religion*. Berkeley: University of California Press, 1984–87.

Hegel, G. W. F. *Logic*. Oxford: Clarendon, 1975.

Hegel, G. W. F. *The Phenomenology of Mind*. Translated by J. B. Baillie. New York: Macmillan, 1931.

Hegel, G. W. F. *Phenomenology of Spirit*. University Park: Pennsylvania State University, 1994.

Hegel, G. W. F. *Philosophy of History*. New York: Wiley, 1944.

Hegel, G. W. F. *Philosophy of Nature*. Oxford: Clarendon, 1970.

Heidegger, Martin. *Was Ist Metaphysics?* Bonn: F. Cohen, 1949.

Heisenberg, Werner. *Physics and Philosophy: The Revolution in Modern Science*. New York: Harper Torchbooks, 1958.

Hemer, Colin J. *The Book of Acts in the Setting of Hellenistic History*. Winona Lake, Ind.: Eisenbrauns, 1990.

Hendriksen, William. *New Testament Commentary: Exposition of the Gospel According to Matthew*. Grand Rapids: Baker, 1973.

Hengel, Martin. *Crucifixion*. Philadelphia: Fortress, 1977.

Herbert, Nick. *Quantum Reality: Beyond the New Physics*. Garden City, N.Y.: Anchor, 1987.

Hick, John. *Death and Eternal Life*. Lousiville, Ky.: Westminster, 1994.

Hick, John. *Evil and the God of Love*. New York: Harper & Row, 1966.

Hick, John. *An Interpretation of Religion: Human Responses to the Transcendent*. London: Macmillan, 1989.

Hick, John. *The Metaphor of God Incarnate: Christology in a Pluralistic Age*. Louisville: Westminster/John Knox, 1993.

Hick, John. "A Pluralist's View." In *More Than One Way? Four Views on Salvation in a Pluralistic World*, ed. Dennis L. Okholm and Timothy R. Phillips. Grand Rapids, Zondervan, 1995.

Hick, John, ed. *The Existence of God*. New York: Macmillan 1964.

Hick, John, Clark H. Pinnock, Alister E. McGrath, R. Douglas Geivett, and W. Gary Phillips. *More Than One Way? Four Views on Salvation in a Pluralistic World* ed. Dennis L. Okholm and Timothy R. Phillips. Grand Rapids: Zondervan, 1995.

Hilleary, William, and W. Metzger. *The World's Most Famous Court Trial*. Cincinnati: National Book Company, 1925.

Hitchcock, James. *What Is Secular Humanism? Why Humanism Became Secular and How It Is Changing Our World*. Ann Arbor: Servant, 1982.

Hitching, Francis. *The Neck of the Giraffe*. New Haven, Conn.: Ticknor & Fields, 1982.

Hitler, Adolf. *Mein Kampf*. London: Gurst & Blackett, 1939.

Hobbes, Thomas. *Leviathan*. *Great Books of the Western World*. Edited by Robert M. Hutchins. Vol. 23. Chicago: Encyclopaedia Britannica, 1952.

Hodge, Archibald A., and Benjamin B. Warfield. *Inspiration*. Philadelphia: Presbyterian Board of Publication, 1881. Reprint, Grand Rapids: Baker, 1979.

Hodge, Charles. *Systematic Theology*. 3 vols. New York: Scribner's, 1872. Reprint, Grand Rapids: Eerdmans, 1940.

Hodge, Charles. *What Is Darwinism?* Edited by Mark A. Noll and David N. Livingstone..Grand Rapids: Baker, 1994; 1874 reprint.

Hodges, Zane C. "Form-Criticism and the Resurrection Accounts." *Bibliotheca Sacra* 124 (1967).

Hoehner, Harold, *Chronological Aspects of the Life of Christ*. Grand Rapids: Zondervan, 1978.

Holden, Joseph. *An Examination of the Jesus Seminar*. Unpublished Master's thesis, Southern Evangelical Seminary, 1996.

Holis, C. *The Mind of Chesterton*. Coral Gables, Fla.: University of Miami, 1970.

Hollingdale, R. G. *Nietzsche: The Man and His Philosophy*. London: Routledge & K. Paul, 1965.

Holton, Gerald. *Thematic Origins of Scientific Thought*. Cambridge, Mass.: Harvard University Press, 1973.

Horowitz, Joseph. "The Growth of the Mohammed Legend." *The Moslem World* 10 (1920).

Howe, Quincy. *Reincarnation for the Christian*. Philadelphia: Westminster Press,1974.

Hoyle, Fred. *The Intelligent Universe*. London: Joseph, 1985.

Hoyle, Fred, and N. C. Wickramasinghe, *Evolution From Space*, London: J. M. Dent & Sons, 1981.

Hoyt, Karen,. and J. Isamu.Yamamoto. *The New Age Rage*. Old Tappan, N.J.: Power Books, 1987.

Hughes, G. E. "Can God's Existence Be Disproved?" In *New Essays in Philosophical Theology*, ed. Antony Flew et al. New York: Macmillan, 1955.

Hume, David. *An Abstract of a Treatise on Human Nature*. 1740 ed. Cambridge: Cambridge University Press, 1938.

Hume, David. *Dialogues Concerning Natural Religion*. Indianapolis: Bobbs-Merrill, 1962.

Hume, David. *Enquiry Concerning Human Understanding*. Edited by Chas. W. Hendel. New York: Liberal Arts, 1955.

Hume, David. *The Letters of David Hume*. 2 vols. Edited by J. Y. T. Greig. Oxford: Clarendon, 1932.

Hummel, Charles E. *The Galileo Connection*. Downers Grove, Ill.: InterVarsity, 1986.

Humphrey, J. Edward. *Emil Brunner.* Peabody, Mass.: Hendrickson, 1991.

Humphreys, Fisher. "E. Y. Mullins." In *Baptist Theologians*, ed. Timothy George and David S. Dockery, 330–50. Nashville, Tenn.: Broadman, 1990.

Hunt, Robert Nigel Carew. *The Theory and Practice of Communism, an Introduction*. Baltimore: Penguin, 1963.

Hutchins, Robert Maynard, ed. *Great Books of the Western World*. Vol. 15, *The Annals and The Histories* by Cornelius Tacitus. Chicago: William Benton, 1952.

Huxley, Julian. *Evolution in Action*. New York: Penguin, 1953.

Huxley, Julian *Religion Without Revelation*. New York: The New American Library, 1957.

Huxley, T. H. "Agnosticism and Christianity." In *Collected Essays*, ed. Frederick Barry. New York: Macmillan, 1929.

Ibish, Yusuf. "The Muslim Lives by the Qur'an." In *The Muslim Mind*, ed. Charis Waddy. London/New York: Longman, 1976.

Ibn Ishaq. *Sirat Rasul Allah. The Life of Muhammad.* Translated by A. Guillaume. New York: Oxford University Press, 1980.

Ibn Taymiyya. *A Muslim Theologian's Response to Christianity*. Delmar, New York: Caravan, 1984.

Ingersoll, Robert G. *The Works of Robert Ingersoll.* Edited by Clinton P. Farrell. 12 vols. New York: AMS, 1978.

Ingersoll, Robert G. *Some Mistakes of Moses*. Reprint, Buffalo, N.Y.: Prometheus, 1986.

Irenaeus. "Against Heresies" In *The Ante-Nicene Fathers*, ed. Rev. Alexander Roberts and James Donaldson. Grand Rapids: Eerdmans, 1885.

Ishaq, Ibn. Sirat Rasul Allah. *The Life of Muhammad.* Translated by A. Guillaume. New York: Oxford University Press, 1980.

Jaeger, Werner. *Aristotle, Fundamentals of the History of His Development*. Translated by Richard Robinson. Oxford, 1948.

Jaki, Stanley L. *Miracles and Physics*. Front Royal, Va.: Christendom, 1989.

Jaki, Stanley L. *The Absolute Beneath the Relative and Other Essays*. Lanham, Md.: University Press of America, 1988.

Jaki, Stanley L. *God and the Cosmologists*. Edinburgh: Scottish Academy Press, 1989.

Jaki, Stanley L. *Miracles and Physics.* Front Royal, Va.: Christendom, 1989.

James, Edwin O. "Frazer, James George." In *New 20th Century Encyclopedia of Religious Knowledge*, ed. J. D. Douglas. Grand Rapids: Baker, 1991.

James, William. *Essays in Pragmatism*, ed. New York: Hafner, 1968.

James, William. *Human Immortality: Two Supposed Objections to the Doctrine.* London: Archibald Constable, 1906.

James, William. *A Pluralistic Universe.* London: Longmans, Green, 1909.

James, William. *Pragmatism and Other Essays*. New York: Washington Square, 1963.

James, William. *Some Problems of Philosophy: A Beginning of an Introduction to Philosophy.* New York : Longmans, Green, 1948.

James, William. *The Varieties of Religious Experience*. New York: The New American Library of World Literature, 1958, first published, 1902.

Jaspers, Karl. *Nietzsche: An Introduction to the Understanding of His Philosophical Activity.* Tucson: University of Arizona, 1965.

Jaspers, Karl. *Nietzsche and das Christentum*. Translated by E. B. Ashton. Chicago, 1961.

Jaspers, Karl. *Reason and Existence.* Milwaukee: Marquette University, 1997.

Jastrow, Robert. "A Scientist Caught Between Two Faiths: Interview with Robert Jastrow." *Christianity Today*, 6 August 1982.

Jastrow, Robert. *God and the Astronomers*. New York: W. W. Norton, 1978.

Jeffery, Arthur. ed. *Islam, Muhammad andHhis Religion.* Indianapolis/New York: Bobbs-Merrill, 1958.

Jeremias, Joachim. "'Flesh and Blood Cannot Inherit the Kingdom of God." *New Testament Studies II* 1955–56.

Jerome, St. "Preface" to *Jerome's Commentary on Daniel.* Translated by Geason Archer, Grand Rapids: Baker, 1958.

Jewell, James H., and Patricia A. Didden. "A Surgeon Looks at the Cross." *Voice* 58 (1979): 3–5.

Jewett, Paul K. *Emil Brunner's Concept of Revelation.* London: J. Clarke, 1954.

Jewett, Paul K. *Emil Brunner: An Introduction to the Man and His Thought.* Chicago: InterVarsity, 1961.

Jewett, Paul K. *Man as Male and Female.* Grand Rapids: Eerdmans, 1975.

Jividen, Jimmy. *Miracles: From God or Man?* Abilene, Tex.: ACU, 1987.

Johnson, B. C. *An Atheist Debater's Handbook.* Buffalo, N.Y.: Prometheus, 1983.

Johnson, David L. *A Reasoned Look at Asian Religions.* Minneapolis: Bethany, 1985.

Johnson, Phillip E. *Darwin on Trial.* Washington, D.C.: Regnery Gateway, 1991.

Johnson, Phillip. *Reason in the Balance: The Case Against Naturalism in Science, Law and Education.* Downers Grove, Ill.: InterVarsity, 1995.

Jones, Bevan. L. *Christianity Explained to Muslims: A Manual for Christian Workers.* Calcutta: Y.M.C.A. Publishing House, 1938.

Jones, Bevan L. *The People of the Mosque.* London: Student Christian Movement Press, 1932.

Jordan, James. "The Biblical Chronology Question: An Analysis." *Creation Social Science and Humanity Quarterly* 2, no. 2 (Winter 1979 and Spring 1980).

Josephus, Flavius. *The Antiquities of the Jews.* New York: Ward, Lock, Bowden, 1900.

Josephus, Flavius. *Complete Works.* Translated by William Whiston, Grand Rapids: Kregel, 1963.

Josephus, Flavius. *Jewish Wars.* Baltimore: Penguin, 1959.

Kahle, Paul E. *The Cairo Geniza.* 2nd ed. Oxford: Oxford University Press, 1959.

Kahler, Martin. *The So-Called Historical Jesus and the Historic, Biblical Christ.* Philadelphia: Fortress, 1988.

Kahn, James. *Return of the Jedi.* New York: Ballantine, 1983.

Kaiser, Walter. *The Uses of the Old Testament in the New.* Chicago: Moody, 1985.

Kaiser, Walter, ed. *Classical Evangelical Essays in OT Interpretation.* Grand Rapids: Baker, 1972.

Kalsbeek, L. *Contours of a Christian Philosophy: An Introduction to Herman Dooyeweerd's Thought.* Toronto: Wedge, 1981.

Kant, Immanuel. *Critique of Judgment.* Indianapolis, Ind.: Hackett, 1987.

Kant, Immanuel. *Critique of Practical Reason.* New York: Liberal Arts, 1956.

Kant, Immanuel. *Critique of Pure Reason.* Translated by Norman Kemp Smith. New York: St. Martin's, 1965.

Kant, Immanuel. *Prolegomena to Any Future Metaphysics.* New York: Bobbs-Merrill, 1950.

Kant, Immanuel. *Religion Within the Limits of Reason Alone.* New York: Harper & Row, 1960.

Kantzer, Kenneth. *John Calvin's Theory of the Knowledge of God and the Word of God.* Harvard University Thesis, Cambridge, 1950.

Kantzer, Kenneth S., and Stanley N. Gundry, eds. *Perspectives on Evangelical Theology.* Grand Rapids: Baker, 1979.

Kateregga, Badru D. *Islam and Christianity: A Muslem and a Christian in Dialogue.* Grand Rapids: Eerdmans, 1981.

Kaufmann, Walter. *Critique of Religion and Philosophy.* New York: Doubleday, 1961.

Kaufmann, Walter. *Nietzsche: Philosopher, Psychologist, Antichrist.* 4th ed. Princeton, N.J.: Princeton University Press, 1974.

Keating, Karl. *Catholicism and Fundamentalism.* San Francisco: Ignatius, 1988.

Keil, C. F., and F. Delitzsch *Commentary on the Old Testament: The Pentateuch.* Translated by James Martin. Grand Rapids: Eerdmans, 1983.

Kelly, J. N. D. *Early Christian Doctrines.* New York: Harper & Row, 1960.

Kenny, Anthony. *The Five Ways: St. Thomas Aquinas' Proofs of God's Existence.* New York: Schocken, 1969.

Kenyon, Fredric. *Our Bible and the Ancient Manuscripts.* 4th ed., revised by A. W. Adams. New York: Harper, 1958.

Kenyon, Sir Frederick. *The Bible and Archaeology.* New York: Harper, 1940.

Ketcham, Ralph. "Jefferson, Thomas." In *The Encyclopedia of Philosophy,* ed. Paul Edwards, 4:259 New York: Macmillan, 1967.

Keyser, Leander S. *A System of Christian Evidence,* 5th rev. ed. Burlington, Iowa: The Lutheran Literary Board, 1930.

Kierkegaard, Søren. *Fear and Trembling and The Sickness Unto Death.* Translated with introduction and notes by Walter Lowrie. New York: Doubleday, 1954.

Kierkegaard, Søren. *For Self-Examination and Judge for Yourselves and Three Discourses.* Translated by Walter Lowrie. Princeton, N.J.: Princeton University Press, 1941.

Kim, Seyoon. *The Origin of Paul's Gospel.* Grand Rapids: Eerdmans, 1982.

Kirk, G. S., and J. E. Raven. *The Presocratic Philosophers.* Cambridge: Cambridge University Press, 1964.

Kitchen, K. A. *Ancient Orient and the Old Testament.* Downers Grove, Ill.: InterVarsity, 1966.

Kittel, Gerhard, ed. *Theological Dictionary of the New Testament.* Translated and edited by Geoffrey William Bromiley. Grand Rapids: Eerdmans, 1964–76.

Kittel, R., and P. Kahle, eds. *Biblia Hebraica,* 7th ed. Stuttgart: Deutsche Bibelstiflung, 1951.

Kitwood, T. M. *What Is Human?* Downers Grove, Ill.: InterVarsity, 1970.

Klapwijk, Jacob. "Dooyeweerd's Christian Philosophy: Antithesis and Critique." *Reformed Journal* (March, 1980).

Kline, Leonard R. "Lutherans in Sexual Commotion" *First Things* (May, 1994).

Kline, Meredith G. *Treaty of the Great King: The Covenant Structure of Deuteronomy: Studies and Commentary.* Grand Rapids : Eerdmans, 1963.

Kloppenborg, J. *Q Parallels: Synopsis, Critical Notes and Concordance.* Sonoma, Calif.: Polebridge, 1988.

Koelin, F. C. A. *The Philosophy of the Enlightenment.* Princeton, N.J.: Princeton University Press, 1951.

Kole, Andre, and Al Janssen. *Miracles or Magic?* Eugene, Ore.: Harvest House, 1984.

Korem, Danny. *Powers: Testing the Psychic and Supernatural.* Downers Grove, Ill: InterVarsity, 1988.

Korem, Danny, and Paul Meier. *The Fakers.* Rev. ed. Grand Rapids: Baker, 1981.

Kreeft, Peter. *Between Heaven and Hell: A Dialog Somewhere Beyond Death with John F. Kennedy, C. S. Lewis, and Aldous Huxley.* Downers Grove, Ill: InterVarsity, 1982.

Kreeft, Peter. *Christianity for Modern Pagans.* Pascal's Pensees. San Francisco: Ignatius, 1993.

Kreeft, Peter. *Fundamentals of the Faith.* San Francisco: Ignatius, 1988.

Kreeft, Peter, ed. *Summa of the Summa.* San Francisco: Ignatius, 1990.

Kreeft, Peter, and Ronald K. Tacelli. *Handbook of Christian Apologetics.* Downers Grove, Ill.: InterVarsity, 1994.

Krentz, Edgar. *The Historical-Critical Method.* Philadelphia: Fortress, 1975.

Kung, Hans. *Infallible: An Inquiry* Translated by Edwards Quinn. Garden City, N.Y.: Doubleday, 1971.

Kurtz, Paul, ed. *Humanist Manifestos I & II.* Buffalo: Prometheus, 1973.

Kurtz, Paul, ed. "A Secular Humanist Declaration" *Free Inquiry* (Winter, 1980–81).

Kushner, Harold S. *When All You've Ever Wanted Isn't Enough.* New York : Summit, 1986.

Kushner, Harold S. *When Bad Things Happen to Good People.* New York: Avon, 1981.

Ladd, George Eldon. *I Believe in the Resurrection of Jesus.* Grand Rapids: Eerdmans, 1975.

LaFay, Howard. "Ebla." *National Geographic* 154, no. 6 (1978).

Lamont, Corliss. "The Affirmative Ethics of Humanism." *The Humanist* 40. (1980).

Lamont, Corliss. *The Philosophy of Humanism*. New York: Frederick Ungar, 1979.

Lange, John Peter. *Commentary on the Holy Scriptures*. Translated and edited by Philip Schaff. Grand Rapids: Zondervan, 1864.

Lanson, Gustave. *Voltaire*. Paris: Hachette, 1910.

Lapide, Pinchas. "The Resurrection of Jesus." *Time*, 7 May 1979.

Laplace, Pierre Simon. *The System of the World*. Vols. 1–2. London: Longman, Rees, Orme, Brown, & Green, 1830.

Larue, Gerald A. "Committee for the Scientific Examination of Religion." (CSER's investigation) *Free Inquiry* (Fall, 1986).

Leibniz, Gottfried. *The Monadology*. Translated by Robert Latta. London: Oxford University Press, 1925.

Leibniz, Gottfried. *Theodicy: Essays on the Goodness of God, the Freedom of Man, and the Origin of Evil*. New Haven: Yale University Press, 1952.

LeLand, John. *A View of the Principal Deistic Writers . . .* London: B. Dod, 1754.

Lemonick, Michael D. "Echoes of the Big Bang." *Time*, 4 May 1993.

Lessing, Gotthold. *Lessing's Theological Writings*. Translated by Henry Chadwick. London: Adam & Charles Black, 1956.

Lessing, Gotthold. *Selected Prose Works of G. E. Lessing*. Translated by E. C. Beasley and Helen Zimmern. Edited by Edward Bell. London: George Bell, 1885. Rev. ed., 1905.

Levy-Bruhl, Lucien. *The Philosophy of Auguste Comte*. London: S. Sonnenschein, 1903.

Lewis, C. S. *The Abolition of Man*. New York: Macmillan, 1947.

Lewis, C. S. *Christian Reflections*. Edited by Walter Hooper. Grand Rapids: Eerdmans, 1967.

Lewis, C. S. *God in the Dock: Essays on Theology and Ethics*. Edited by Walter Hooper. Grand Rapids: Eerdmans, 1970.

Lewis, C. S. *The Great Divorce*. New York: Macmillan, 1946.

Lewis, C. S. *Mere Christianity*. New York: Macmillan, 1953.

Lewis, C. S. *Miracles: A Preliminary Study*. New York: Macmillan, 1947.

Lewis, C. S. *The Problem of Pain*. New York: Macmillan, 1940.

Lewis, C. S. *Reflections on the Psalms*. New York: Harcourt, Brace, 1958.

Lewis, C. S. *The Screwtape Letters*. New York: Macmillan, 1961.

Lewis, C. S. *Studies in Medieval and Renaissance Literature*. New York: Cambridge University Press, 1966.

Lewis, C.S. *Surprised by Joy: The Shape of My Early Life*. Rev. ed. New York: Harcourt Brace, 1995.

Lewis, Gordon R. *Testing Christianity's Truth Claims*. Chicago: Moody, 1976.

Lewis, G., and B. Demarest. *Challenges to Inerrancy: A Theological Response*. Chicago: Moody, 1984.

Lewis, James F., and William G. Travis. *Religious Traditions of the World*. Grand Rapids: Zondervan, 1991.

Lightfoot, J. B. *The Apostolic Fathers*. London: Macmillan, 1891.

Lightfoot, J. B. *Colossians and Philemon*. Wheaton, Ill.: Crossway, 1997.

Lightman, Alan, and Roberta Brawer. *Origins: The Lives and Worlds of Modern Cosmologists*. Cambridge, Mass.: Harvard University Press, 1990.

Lightner, Robert. *Heaven for Those Who Can't Believe*. Schaumburg, Ill.: Regular Baptist Press, 1977.

Lightner, Robert. *The Savior and the Scriptures*. Philadelphia: Presbyterian & Reformed, 1966.

Lindsell, Harold *The Battle for the Bible*. Grand Rapids: Zondervan, 1976.

Lindsey, Duane F. "An Evangelical Overview of Process Theology." *Bibliotheca Sacra* 134 (1977).

Linnemann, Eta. *Historical Criticsm of the Bible: Methodology or Idealogy?* Grand Rapids: Baker, 1990.

Linnemann, Eta. *Is There A Synoptic Problem? Rethinking the Literary Dependence of the First Three Gospels*. Grand Rapids,: Baker , 1992.

Locke, John *The Reasonableness of Christianity with A Discourse of Miracles and Part of A Third Letter Concerning Toleration*. Stanford: Stanford University Press, 1974.

Lockyer, Herbert. *All the Miracles of the Bible; The Supernatural in Scripture, Its Scope and Significance*. Grand Rapids: Zondervan, 1978.

Longenecker, Richard N. *The Christology of Early Jewish Christianity*. London: SCM, 1970.

Loomer, Bernard. "A Response to David Griffin." *Encounter* 36, no. 4 (1975).

Lubenow, Marvin. *Bones of Contention: a Creationist Assessment of the Human Fossils*. Grand Rapids: Baker, 1992.

Lucas, George. *Star Wars*. New York: Ballantine 1976.

Lundin, Roger. *The Culture of Interpretation*. Grand Rapids: Eerdmans, 1993.

Luther and Erasmus. *Free Will and Salvation*. Translated and edited by E. Gordon Rupp et al. London: SCM, 1969.

Luther, Martin. *Bondage of the Will*. Translated by Henry Cole. Grand Rapids: Baker, 1976.

Lutzer, Erwin. *The Necessity of Ethical Absolutes*. Grand Rapids: Zondervan, 1981.

Lyon, David. *Karl Marx: A Christian Assessment of His Life and Thought*. Downers Grove, Ill.: InterVarsity, 1981.

Lyotard, Jean-Francois. *The Postmodern Condition: A Report on Knowledge*. Minneapolis: University of Minneapolis, 1984.

MacGregor, Geddes. *The Christening of Karma*. Wheaton, Ill.: Theosophical Publishing House, 1984.

Machen, J. Gresham. *Christian Faith in the Modern World*. New York: Macmillan, 1936.

Machen, J. Gresham. *The Christian View of Man*. New York: Macmillan, 1937.

Machen, J. Gresham. *Christianity and Liberalism*. Grand Rapids: Eerdmans, 1923.

Machen, J. Gresham. *The Origin of Paul's Religion.* Grand Rapids: Eerdmans, 1947.

Machen, J. Gresham. *The Virgin Birth of Christ*. Reprint, Grand Rapids: Baker, 1977; first pub., 1930.

Machen, J. Gresham. *What Is Christianity?* Grand Rapids: Eerdmans, 1951.

Machen, J. Gresham. *What Is Faith?* Carlisle, Pa.: Banner of Truth, 1991.

Mack, Burton. *The Lost Gospel: The Book of Q and Christian Origins.* San Francisco: Harper San Francisco, 1993.

MacKay, Donald M. *The Clock Work Image*. Downers Grove, Ill.: InterVarsity, 1974.

MacLaine, Shirley. "Out on a limb." From TV Program aired in January, 1987.

MacLaine, Shirley. *Dancing in the Light.* New York: Bantam, 1985.

MacPherson, John. *The Westminster Confession of Faith.* 2nd ed. Edinburgh: T. & T. Clark, 1911.

Madison, Gary B. *Working Through Derrida.* Evanston, Ill.: Northwestern University, 1993.

Maharaj, Rabindranath R. *Death of a Guru.* With Dave Hunt. ed. Russell Hitt. Nashville, Tenn.: Holman, 1977.

Mahud, Abdel Haleem. *The Creed of Islam.* World of Islam Festival Trust, 1978.

Maier, Gerhard. *The End of the Historical Critical Method.* Translated by Edwin W. Leverenz and Rudolph F. Norden. St. Louis: Concordia, 1974.

Maimonides. *Guide of the Perplexed.* Indianapolis: Hackett, 1995.

Malinine, M., ed. and trans. *De Resurrectione epistula ad Rheginum.* Zurich: Rascher, 1963.

Mandonnet, P., and J. Destrez. *Bibliographie Thomiste.* Paris, 1921.

Mansoor, Menahem. "The Dead Sea Scrolls." In *New Catholic Encyclopedia,* 2:390. Washington, D.C.: Catholic University Press of America, 1967, 1974, 1979.

Marcel, Gabriel. *Le Mystere de l'etre.* 2 vols. Paris, 1951. Translated by G. S. Fraser and Rene Hauge as *The Mystery of Being.* 2 vols. Chicago, 1950.

Maritain, Jacques. *Existence and the Existent.* Garden City, N.Y.: Doubleday, 1956.

Marsden, George M. "J. Gresham Machen, History and Truth." *Westminster Theological Journal* 42 (1979): 157–75.

Marshall, I. Howard. *I Believe in the Historical Jesus.* Grand Rapids: Eerdmans, 1977.

Marshall, I. Howard. *The Origins of New Testament Christology.* Downers Grove, Ill.: InterVarsity, 1976.

Martin, Michael. *Atheism: A Philosophical Justification.* Philadelphia: Temple University Press, 1990.

Martin, Michael. *The Case Against Christianity.* Philadelphia: Temple University Press, 1991.

Martin, T. *The Instructed Vision.* Bloomington: Indiana University Press, 1961.

Martin, Walter. *The New Age Cult.* Minneapolis: Bethany, 1989.

Martin, Walter. *The Riddle of Reincarnation.* San Juan Capistrano, Calif.: Christian Research Institute, 1980.

Martyr, Justin. "Apology." In *Ante-Nicene Fathers.* Vol. 1. Edited by Alexander Roberts and James Donaldson. Grand Rapids: Eerdmans, 1952.

Martyr, Justin, "Dialogue with Trypho." In *The Ante-Nicene Fathers,* ed. Alexander Roberts and James Donaldson. Grand Rapids: Eerdmans, 1989.

Marx, Karl. *Das Kapital.* Edited by Friedrich Engels. Translated by Samuel Moore and Edward Aveling. In *Great Books of the Western World*, Vol. 50, ed. Robert Maynard Hutchins. Chicago: Encyclopedia Britannica, 1952.

Marx, Karl. *Selected Writings in Sociology and Social Philosophy.* New York: McGraw-Hill, 1956.

Marx, Karl, and Friedrich Engels. *On Religion.* New York: Schocken, 1964.

Mascall, E. L. *Existence and Analogy.* London: Longmans, Green, 1949.

Mascall, E. L.. *The Secularization of Christianity.* New York: Holt, Rinehart, Winston, 1966.

Mather, George A., and Larry A. Nichols. *Dictionary of Cults, Sects, Religions and the Occult.* Grand Rapids: Zondervan, 1993.

Matrisciana, Caryl. *Gods of the New Age.* Eugene, Ore.: Harvest House, 1985.

Matthews, L. Harrison. 1971. "Introduction." In *On the Origin of Species,* Charles Darwin. London: Dent, 1971.

Matthiae, Paolo. *Ebla: An Empire Rediscovered.* Translated by Christopher Holme. Garden City, N.Y.: Doubleday, 1981.

Mauer, Armand. *A History of Medieval Philosophy.* New York: Random House, 1962.

Mauer, Armand. "St. Thomas and the Analogy of Genus." *New Scholasticism* 29 (1955).

Mavrodes, George. *Belief in God: a Study in the Epistemology of Religion.* Washington, D.C.: University Press of America, 1981.

Mavrodes, George I. "Some Puzzles Concerning Omnipotence." *Philosophical Review* 72 (1963): 221–23.

Maylock, A. I. *The Man Who Was Orthodox.* London: D. Dobson, 1963.

Mayr, Ernst. "Introduction" in *Darwin's On the Origin of Species.* Cambridge, Mass.: Harvard University Press, 1964.

Mazlish, Bruce. "Comte, Auguste." In *The Encyclopedia of Philosophy*, ed/ Paul Edwards. New York: Macmillan and The Free Press, 1967.

Mbiti, John S. *African Religions and Philosoophy.* New York: Praeger, 1969. Reprint, Anchor, 1970.

Mbiti, John S. *Concepts of God in Africa.* New York: Praeger, 1970.

McCallum, Dennis, ed. *The Death of Truth.* Minneapolis: Bethany, 1996.

McCormick, Charles Tilford. *McCormick's Handbook of the Law of Evidence.* 2nd ed. by Edward W. Cleary St. Paul: West, 1972.

McCosh, J. *The Scottish Philosophy.* New York: AMS, 1980.

McDonald, H. D. *Theories of Revelation: An Historical Study 1700–1960.* 2 vols. Twin Books Series. Grand Rapids: Baker, 1979.

McDowell, Josh. *Answers to Tough Questions Skeptics Ask about the Christian Faith.* San Bernardino, Calif.: Here's Life, 1980.
McDowell, Josh. *Daniel in the Critics Den.* San Bernardino, Calif.: Campus Crusade for Christ International, 1979.
McDowell, Josh. *Evidence That Demands A Verdict.* Vol. 1. Rev. ed. San Bernadino, Calif.: Here's Life, 1979.
McDowell, Josh. *Jesus: AA Biblical Defence of His Deity.* Eastbourne: Crossway, 1991.
McDowell, Josh, and John Gilchirst. *The Islam Debate.* San Bernardino, Calif.: Here's Life, 1983.
McGrath, Alister. "The Challenge of Pluralism for the Contemporary Christian Church." *Journal of the Evangelical Theological Society* (September, 1992): 361–73.
McGrath, Alister. "Response to John Hick." In *More Than One Way? Four Views on Salvation in a Pluralistic World,* ed. Dennis L. Okholm and Timothy R. Phillips. Grand Rapids: Zondervan, 1995.
McIlvaine, C.P. *The Evidences of Christianity.* 6th ed. C. & H. Carvill, 1857.
McInerny, Ralph. *The Logic of Analogy.* The Hague: Nijhoff, 1961.
McIver, Tom. "Creationist Misquotations of Darrow." *Creation/Evolution.* 8, no. 2 (1988).
McKeon, Richard, ed. and trans. *Selections from Medieval Philosophers.* Vol. 2. New York: Scribner, 1957.
McRay, John. *Archaeology and the New Testament.* Grand Rapids: Baker, 1991.
Meier, John P. *A Marginal Jew: Rethinking the Historical Jesus.* Vol. 1, *The Roots of the Problem and the Person.* New York: Doubleday, 1991.
Mercati, A. "The New List of the Popes." *Medieval Studies.* 1947.
Merill, Eugene. "Ebla and Biblical Historical Inerrancy." *Bibliotheca Sacra* 140 (1983).
Metzger, Bruce. *Chapters in the History of New Testament Textual Criticism.* Grand Rapids: Eerdmans, 1963.
Metzger, Bruce. *An Introduction to the Apocrypha.* New York: Oxford University Press, 1957.
Metzger, Bruce. *Manuscripts of the Greek Bible: An Introduction to Greek Paleography.* New York: Oxford University Press, 1981.
Metzger, Bruce. *The Text of the New Testament.* New York: Oxford University Press, 1964.
Metzger, Bruce. *A Textual Commentary on the Greek New Testament: A Companion Volume to the United Bible Societies' Greek New Testament. Third edition.* London; New York: United Bible Societies, 1975.
Meuller, G. E. "The Hegel Legend of 'Thesis, Antithesis–Synthesis." *Journal of the History of Ideas* 19, no. 3 (1958).
Miceli,Vincent P. *The Gods of Atheism.* Harrison, N.Y.: Roman Catholic Books, 1971.
Miethe, Terry, ed. *Did Jesus Rise fom the Dead? The Resurrection Debate.* San Francisco: Harper & Row, 1987.
Miethe, Terry, and Vernon Bourke. *Thomistic Bibliography, 1940–1978,* Westport, Conn.: Greenwood, 1980.
Miethe, Terry, and Anthony Flew. *Does God Exist? A Believer and an Atheist Debate.* San Francisco: Harper San Francisco, 1991.
Miles, T. R. *Religion and the Scientific Outlook.* London: George Allen & Unwin, 1959.
Mill, John Stuart. *Auguste Comte and Positivism.* Bristol, England: Thoemmes, 1993; 1865 reprint.
Mill, John Stuart. *A System of Logic: Ratiocinative and Inductive.* 8th ed. New York: Harper, 1874.
Mill, John Stuart. *Three Essays on Religion: Nature, Utility of Religion, and Theism.* London: Longmans, Green, 1885.
Mill, John Stuart. *Utilitarianism.* New York: Meridian, 1962.
Miller, David. *The New Polytheism.* New York: Harper & Row, 1974.
Miller, Elliot. *A Crash Course on the New Age.* Grand Rapids: Baker, 1989.
Miller, Elliot, and Kenneth R. Samples. *The Cult of the Virgin: Catholic Mariology and the Apparitions of Mary.* Grand Rapids: Baker, 1992.
Miller, Robert J., ed. *The Complete Gospels.* Sonoma, Calif.: Polebridge, 1992.
Milne, Bruce. *Know the Truth.* Downers Grove, Ill.: InterVarsity, 1982.
Mitchell, Basil, ed. *Faith and Logic.* London: Allen & Unwin, 1957.
Molina, Luis de, and Alfred J.Freddoso. *On Divine Foreknowledge: Part IV of the Concordia.* Ithaca, N.Y.: Cornell University Press, 1988.
Molnar, Thomas. *Theists and Atheists: A Typology of Non-Belief.* New York: Mouton, 1980.
Momen, Moojan. *An Introduction to Shii Islam : The History and Doctrines of Twelver. Shiism.* New Haven, Conn.: Yale University Press, 1987.
Mondin, B. *The Principle of Analogy in Protestant and Catholic Theology.* The Hague: Nijhoff, 1963.
Montgomery, John W. *Christianity and History.* Downer's Grove, Ill.: InterVarsity, 1964.
Montgomery, John W. *Christianity for the Tough-Minded.* Minneapolis: Bethany, 1973.
Montgomery, John W. *Evidence for Faith.* Dallas: Probe, 1991.
Montgomery, John W. *Faith Founded on Fact.* Nashville, Tenn.: Thomas Nelson, 1978.
Montgomery, John W. *The Law Above the Law.* Minneapolis: Bethany, 1975.
Montgomery, John W. *The Shape of the Past: An Introduction to Philosophical Historiography.* Ann Arbor, Mich.: Edwards Bros., 1962.
Montgomery, John W., ed. *Myth, Allegory and Gospel: An Interpretation of J. R. R. Tolkien/C. S. Lewis/G. K. Chesterton/Charles Williams.* Minneapolis: Bethany, 1974.
Montgomery, John W., and Thomas Altizer. *The Altizer-Montgomery Dialogue.* Downers Grove, Ill.: InterVarsity, 1967.
Moore, David. *The Battle for Hell: A Survey and Evaluation of Evangelicals' Growing Attraction to the Doctrine of Annihilationsim.* Lanham, Md.: University Press of America, 1995.

Moore, James R. *The Post-Darwinian Controversies.* New York: Cambridge University Press, 1979.

Morais, Herbert M. *Deism in Eighteenth Century America*. 1934. Reprint. New York: Russell & Russell, 1960.

Moreland, J. P. *Christianity and the Nature of Science.* Grand Rapids: Baker, 1989.

Moreland, J. P. *Scaling The Secular City: A Defense of Christianity.* Grand Rapids: Baker,1987.

Moreland, J. P. *Universals, Qualities, and Quality-Instances*. New York: University Press of America, 1985.

Moreland, J. P., ed. *The Creation Hypothesis: Scentific Evidence for an Intelligent Designer.* Downers Grove, Ill.: InterVarsity, 1994.

Moreland, J. P., and Kai Nielsen. *Does God Exist? The Great Debate.* Nashville, Tenn.: Thomas Nelson, 1990.

Morris, Henry. *Biblical Cosmology and Modern Science.* Phillipsburg, N.J.: Presbyterian & Reformed, 1970.

Morris, Henry. *The Genesis Record.* Welwyn: Evangelical Press, 1977.

Morris, Henry , ed. *Scientific Creationism*. San Diego: Creation-Life, 1974.

Morris, Henry, and Gary E. Parker. *What Is Creation Science?* El Cajon, Calif.: Master Books, 1987.

Morris, John D. *The Young Earth*. Colorado Springs: Master Books, 1994.

Morris, Thomas. *Our Idea of God.* Downers Grove, Ill.: InterVarsity, 1991.

Morrison, Frank. *Who Moved the Stone?* London: Faber & Faber, 1958.

Morton, A. Q. and James McLeman. *Christianity in the Computer Age.* New York: Harper & Row, 1964.

Mossner, E. C. *Bishop Butler and the Age of Reason.* New York: Macmillan, 1936.

Most, G. *Catholic Apologetics Today: Answers to Modern Critics*. Rockford, Ill.: Tan, 1986.

Mueller, Marvin E. "The Shroud of Turin: A Critical Appraisal." *Skeptical Inquirer* (Spring, 1982).

Mufassir,Sulaiman Shahid. *Jesus, a Prophet of Islam.* American Trust Publications, 1980.

Muller, Julius. *The Theory of Myths, in Its Application to the Gospel History, Examined and Confuted.* London: John Chapman, 1844.

Mullins, Edgar Young. *The Axioms of Religion.* Philadelphia: American Baptist Publication Society, 1908.

Mullins, Edgar Young. *The Christian Religion in Its Doctrinal Expression*. Philadelphia: Roger Williams, 1917.

Mullins, Edgar Young. *Christianity at the Cross Roads.* Nashville, Tenn.: Sunday School Board of the S.B.C., 1924.

Mullins, Edgar Young. *Freedom and Authority in Religion.* Philadelphia: Griffith & Rowland, 1913.

Mullins, Edgar Young. *Why Is Christianity True?* Philadelphia: Judson, 1905.

Murray, John. *Principles of Conduct.* Grand Rapids: Eerdmans, 1957.

Nahm, Milton C. *Selections from Early Greek Philosophy.* 4th ed. New York: Appleton-Century-Crofts, 1964.

Naipaul, V. S. *An Area of Darkness.* London: Picador, 1995.

Nash, Ronald. *Christian Faith and Historical Understanding*. Probe Ministries International, 1984.

Nash, Ronald. *Christianity and the Hellenistic World.* Grand Rapids: Zondervan, 1984.

Nash, Ronald. *Dooyeweerd and the Amsterdam.* Grand Rapids: Zondervan, 1962.

Nash, Ronald. "Gordon H. Clark" In *Handbook of Evangelical Theologians.*. ed. Walter Elwell. Grand Rapids: Baker, 1993.

Nash, Ronald. *The Gospel and the Greeks.* Dallas:Probe, 1992.

Nash, Ronald. *Is Jesus the Only Savior?* Grand Rapids: Zondervan, 1994.

Nash, Ronald. *The Word of God and the Mind of Man.* Phillipsburg, N.J.: Presbyterian & Reformed, 1992.

Nash, Ronald ed. *The Philosophy of Gordon Clark.* Philadelphia: Presbyterian & Reformed, 1968.

Nash, Ronald, ed. *Process Theology.* Grand Rapids: Baker, 1987.

Nehls, Gerhard. *Christians Ask Muslims.* SIM International Life Challenge, 1987.

Netland, Harold A. *Dissonant Voices: Religious Pluralism and the Question of Truth.* Grand Rapids: Eerdmans, 1991.

Nettles, Thomas J. "Edgar Young Mullins." In *Handbook of Evangelical Theologians.* Grand Rapids: Baker, 1993.

Neufeld, E. *The Hittite Laws.* London: Luzac, 1951.

Neuner, S. J., and J. Dupuis, "Discourse to Scientists on the 350th Anniversary of the Publication of Galileo's 'Dialoghi." In *The Christian Faith: Doctrinal Documents of the Catholic Church.* 5th rev.ed. New York: Alba House, 1990.

New Catholic Encyclopedia, 17 vols. New York: McGraw-Hill, 1979.

Newman, John H. *Apologia pro vita sua.* New York: W. W. Norton, 1968.

Newman, John H. *An Essay in Aid of a Grammar of Assent.* Notre Dame, Ind.: University of Notre Dame, 1979.

Newman, John H. *Essay on the Development of Christian Doctrine.*Notre Dame, Ind.: University of Notre Dame, 1989.

Newman, John H. *A Grammar of Assent.* London: Burns & Oates, 1881.

Newman, Robert. *The Biblical Teaching on the Firmament*. Unpublished Masters Thesis, Biblical Theological Seminary, 1972.

Newman, Robert, ed. *The Evidence of Prophecy: Fulfilled Prediction as a Testimony to the Truth of Christianity.* Hatfield, Pa.: Interdisciplinary Biblical Research Institute, 1988.

Newman, Robert Chapman, and Herman J. Eckelmann. *Genesis One & the Origin of the Earth.* Downers Grove, Ill.: InterVarsity Press, 1977. Reprint, Grand Rapids: Baker, 1981.

Newton, Sir Isaac. "General Scholium". In *Mathematical Principles of Natural Philosophy*. *Great Books of the Western World*, ed. Robert M. Hutchins. Vol. 34. Chicago: Encyclopedia Britannica, n.d.

Niebuhr, Reinhold, ed. *Marx and Engels on Religion*. New York: Schocken, 1964.

Niebuhr, Richard R. *Schleiermacher on Christ and Religion*. New York: Scribner, 1964.

Nielsen, Kai. *Philosophy and Atheism: A Defense of Atheism*. Buffalo, N.Y.: Prometheus, 1985.

Nietzsche, Friedrich. *Anti-Christ*. Translated by H. L. Mencken. New York: Knopf, 1920

Nietzsche, Friedrich. *Beyond Good and Evil: Prelude to a Philosophy of the Future*. Translated and edited by Walter Kaufmann. New York: Vintage, 1966.

Nietzsche, Friedrich. *The Birth of Tragedy and the Genealogy of Morals*. Translated by Francis Golffing. Garden City, N.Y.: Doubleday, 1956.

Nietzsche, Friedrich. *Joyful Wisdom*. Translated by Thomas Common. Frederick Unger, 1960.

Nietzsche, Friedrich. *Thus Spoke Zarathustra*. Translated by Walter Kaufmann. New York: Viking, 1966.

Noebel, David A. *Understanding the Times*. Manitou Springs, Colo.: Summit, 1991.

Nolen, William A. *Healing: A Doctor in Search of a Miracle*. New York: Random House, 1974.

Noss, John B. *Man's Religions*. New York: Macmillan, 1956.

Nowell-Smith, Patrick. "Miracles." In *New Essays in Philosophical Theology*, ed. Antony Flew and Alasdair MacIntyre. New York: Macmillan, 1955.

Nygren, E. Herbert. "Existentialism: Kierkegaard." In *Biblical Errancy*. Grand Rapids: Zondervan, 1981.

O'Connor, D.J. *A Critical History of Western Philosophy*. New York: Free Press of Glencoe, 1965.

Ogden, Schubert M. "Bultmann's Demythologizing and Hartshorne's Dipolar Theism." In *Process and Divinity: Philosophical Essays Presented to Charles Hartshorne*, ed. William L. Reese, 493–513. LaSalle: Open Court, 1964.

Ogden, Schubert M. "The Meaning of Christian Hope." *Union Seminary Quarterly Review* 30 (1975).

Ogden, Schubert M. "Toward a New Theism." In *Process Philosophy and Christian Thought*, ed. Delwin Brown, Ralph E. James Jr., and Gene Reeves. Indianapolis: Bobbs-Merrill, 1971.

Ogden, Schubert M. *Faith and Freedom: Toward a Theology of Liberation*. Nashville: Abingdon, 1979.

Ogden, Schubert M. *The Reality of God and Other Essays*. 1963. Reprint. San Francisco: Harper & Row, 1977.

Ogden, Schubert M. *Theology in Crisis: A Colloquim on the Credibility of "God."* New Concord: Muskingum College, March 20–21, 1967.

Ogletree, Thomas W. *The Death of God Controversy*. Nashville: Abingdon, 1966.

Okholm, Dennis L., and Timothy R. Phillips, eds. *More Than One Way? Four Views on Salvation in a Pluralistic World*. Grand Rapids: Zondervan, 1995.

Orchard, B. "A Fragment of St. Mark's Gospel Dating from Before A. D. 50?" *Biblical Apostolate*, Rome, 6, 1972.

Orgel, Leslie. *The Origins of Life*. New York: Wiley, 1973.

Origen. "Contra Celsus." In *The Ante-Nicene Fathers*, ed. Alexander Roberts and James Donaldson. Grand Rapids: Eerdmans, 1989.

Origen. "On First Principles." In *The Ante-Nicene Fathers*, ed. Alexander Roberts and James Donaldson. Grand Rapids: Eerdmans, 1989.

Orr James. "The Old Testament Doctrine of Immortality." In *The Christian View of God and the World*. Grand Rapids: Eerdmans, 1948.

Orr, James. *The Problems of the Old Testament*. London: Nisbet, 1906.

Orr, James. *The Virgin Birth of Christ*. New York: C. Scribner's Sons, 1907.

Orr, John. *English Deism: Its Roots and Its Fruits*. Grand Rapids: Eerdmans, 1934.

Osburn, Evert D. "Those Who Have Never Heard: Have They No Hope?" *Journal of the Evangelical Theological Society*. 32, no. 3 (1989).

Ostling, Richard. "New Grounding for the Bible?" *Time*, September 21, 1981.

Ott, Ludwig. *Fundamentals of Catholic Dogma*. Edited by James Canon Bastible. Translated by Patrick Lynch. Rockford, Ill.: Tan, 1960.

Otto, Rudolf. *India's Religion of Grace and Christianity Compared and Contrasted*. New York: Macmillan, 1930.

Otto, Rudolf. *Mysticism East and West*. Translated by Bertha L. Bracey and Richenda C. Payne. New York: Meridian, 1957.

Owen, H. P. *The Christian Knowledge of God*. University of London: Athlone, 1969.

Owen, H. P. *Concepts of Deity*. London: Macmillan, 1971.

Owen, Joseph. *The Doctrine of Being in the Aristotelian Metaphysics*. Toronto: Pontifical Institute of Medieval Studies, 1978.

Owens, Joseph. *A History of Ancient Western Philosophy*. New York: Appleton-Century-Crofts, 1959.

Pache, Rene. *The Inspiration and Authority of Scripture*. Salen, Wis: Sheffield, 1969.

Pache, Rene. *The Inspiration and Authority of Scripture*. Translated by Helen I. Needham. Chicago: Moody, 1969.

Packer, J. I. *The Apostles' Creed*.Wheaton, Ill. : Tyndale House, 1988, 1977.

Packer, J. I. *"Fundamentalism" and the Word of God*. Grand Rapids: Eerdmans, 1958.

Packer, J. I. "Sola Scriptura: Crucial to Evangelicalism." In *The Foundations of Biblical Authority*, ed. James Montgomery Boice. Grand Rapids: Zondervan, 1978.

Padover, Saul K. *Thomas Jefferson and the Foundations of American Freedom*. New York: Van Nostrand Reinhold, 1965.

Pagels, Heinz R. *Perfect Symmetry: The Search for the Beginning of Time*. London: Penguin, 1992.

Paine, Thomas. *The Age of Reason*. New York: G. P. Putnam's Sons, 1907.

Paine, Thomas. *Complete Works of Thomas Paine*. Edited by Calvin Blanchard. Chicago and New York: Belford, Clarke, 1885.

Paley, William. *Evidence of Christianity*. London, 1851.

Pannenberg, Wolfhart. *Jesus, God and Man*. Philadelphia: Westminster Press, 1968.

Parker, Barry. *Creation—The Story of the Origin and Evolution of the Universe*. New York: Plenum, 1988.

Parmenides. "Proem" in G. S. Kirk et al., *The Presocratic Philosophers*. Cambridge: Cambridge University Press, 1964.

Parrinder, Geoffrey. *Jesus in the Qur'an*. New York: Oxford University Press, 1977.

Parshall, Phil. *Bridges to Islam*. Grand Rapids: Baker, 1983.

Pascal, Blaise. *Pensees*. Translated by A.J. Krailsheimer. New York: Penguin, 1966.

Patterson, Colin. In the "Plaintiff's Pre-Trail Brief," William J. Guste Jr., Attorney General, June 3, 1982. Appendix A.

Payne, Barton. *Encyclopedia of Biblical Prophecy*. London: Hodder & Stoughton, 1973.

Pearcey, Nancy R., and Charles Thaxton. *The Soul of Science: A Christian Map to the Scientific Landscape*. Wheaton, Ill.: Crossway, 1994.

Pelikan, Jaroslav. *The Riddle of Roman Catholicism*. New York: Abingdon, 1960.

Pelletier, Kenneth. *Christian Medical Society Journal* 11, no.1 (1980).

Peters, George W. *Indonesia Revival*. Grand Rapids: Zondervan, 1973.

Peters, Richard. *Hobbes*. Baltimore: Penguin, 1956.

Peters, Robert. "Tautology in Evolution and Ecology" *The American Naturalist*, January–February, 1976.

Peterson, Robert A. *Hell on Trial: The Case for Eternal Punishment*. Phillipsburg, N.J.: Presbyterian & Reformed, 1995.

Peterson, Robert A. "A Traditionalist Response to John Stott's Arguments for Annihilationism." *Journal of the Evangelical Theological Society* (December 1994).

Pettinato, Giovanni. *The Archives of Ebla: An Empire Inscribed in Clay*. New York: Doubleday, 1981.

Pfander, C. G. *The Mizanu'l Haqq: The Balance of Truth*. Austria: Light of Life, 1986.

Pfeiffer, Robert Henry. *Introduction to the Old Testament*. London: Adam & Charles Black, 1948.

Pfleiderer. *The Early Christian Conception of Christ: Its Significance and Value in the History of Religion*. London: Williams & Norgate, 1905.

Pfurtner, Stephan. *Luther and Aquinas on Salvation*. New York: Sheed & Ward, 1965.

Philips, Timothy R., and Dennis L. Okholm, eds. *Christian Apologetics in the Postmodern World*. Downers Grove, Ill.: InterVarsity, 1995.

Phillips, W. Gary, and William E. Brown. *Making Sense of Your World from a Biblical Viewpoint*. Chicago: Moody, 1991.

Philo (of Alexandria). *De Vita Contemplativa*. Translated with introduction by David Winston. New York: Paulist, 1981.

Philostratus. *The Life of Apollonius of Tyana*. Translated by F. C. Conybeare. 2 vols. Loeb Classical Library. Cambridge, Mass.: Harvard University Press, 1969.

Phlegon. "Chronicles" as cited by Origen, *Against Celsus*. In *The Ante-Nicene Fathers*, ed. Alexander Roberts and James Donaldson. Grand Rapids: Eerdmans, 1989.

Pickering, Wilbur N. *The Identity of the New Testament Text*. Nashville: Thomas Nelson, 1977.

Pines, S. *An Arabic Version of the Testimonium Flavianum and its Implications*. Jerusalem: Israel Academy of Sciences and Humanities, 1971.

Pines, S. "Maimonides." In *Encyclopedia of Philosophy*, ed. Paul Edwards. 8 vols. New York: Macmillan and The Free Press, 1967.

Pinnock, Clark. *Grace Unlimited*. Minneapolis: Bethany, 1975.

Pinnock, Clark. "Response to John Hick." In *More Than One Way? Four Views on Salvation in a Pluralistic World*, ed. Dennis L. Okholm and Timothy R. Phillips. Grand Rapids: Zondervan, 1995.

Pinnock, Clark. *A Wideness in God's Mercy*. Grand Rapids: Zondervan, 1992.

Plantinga, Alvin. *God and Other Minds*. Ithaca, N.Y.: Cornell University Press, 1970.

Plantinga, Alvin. *God, Freedom, and Evil*. Grand Rapids: Eerdmans, 1977.

Plantinga, Alvin. *The Nature of Necessity: From St. Anslem to Contemporary Philosophers*. Oxford: Clarendon, 1992.

Plantinga, Alvin. "Reason and Belief in God." In *Faith and Rationality*, ed. Alvin Plantinga and Nicholas Wolterstorff. Notre Dame, Ind.: University of Notre Dame, 1983.

Plantinga, Alvin. "The Reformed Objection to Natural Theology." *Christian Scholars Review* 11 (1982): 187–98.

Plantinga, Alvin, ed. *The Ontological Argument*. Garden City, N.Y.: Doubleday, 1965.

Plato. *The Collected Dialogues of Plato*. Edited by Edith Hamilton and Huntington Cairns. New York: Pantheon, 1964.

Plato. "Parmenides." In *The Collected Dialogues of Plato*.

Plato. "Protagoras." In *The Collected Dialogues of Plato*.

Plato. *The Republic of Plato*. Translated with introduction and notes by Francis MacDonald Cornford. New York: Oxford University Press, 1945.

Plato. "Sophist." In *The Collected Dialogues of Plato*

Plato. "*Timaeus*." In *The Collected Dialogues of Plato*.

Plotinus, *The Six Enneads*, Chicago: Encylopedia Britannica, 1952.

Polanyi, Michael. "Life Transcending Physics and Chemistry." *Chemical Engineering News*, August 21, 1967.

Pollock, Dale. *Skywalking: The Life and Films of George Lucas*. New York: Harmony, 1983.

Popkin, Richard. "Bayle, Pierre." In *The Encyclopedia of Philosophy*, ed. Paul Edwards. New York: Macmillan and The Free Press, 1967.

Popkin, Richard. "Pascal." In the *Encyclopedia of Philosophy*, ed. Paul Edwards. Vol 6. New York: Macmillan and The Free Press, 1967.

Popper, Karl. *Unending Quest*. LaSalle, Ill.: Open Court, 1976.

Prabhavananda, Swami. *The Spiritual Heritage of India*. Hollywood: Vedanta, 1963.

Prabhavananda, Swami, trans. "Appendix II: The Gita and War." *The Song of God: Bhagavad-gita*. New York: Harper, 1951.

Prabhavananda, Swami, and Frederick Manchester, trans. *The Upanishads: Breath of the Eternal*. New York: Mentor, 1957.

Prestige, G. L. *God in Patristic Thought*. London: S.P.C.L., 1952.

Preus, Robert. *The Inspiration of Scripture*. Edinburgh: Oliver & Boyd, 1955.

Price, George M. *The New Geology*. Mountain View, Calif.: Pacific Press. Publishing Association, 1923.

Price, Robert M. "Is There a Place for Historical Criticism?" *Religious Studies* 27, no. 3 (1991): 2, 3, 14, 25.

Pritchard, James B., ed. *The Ancient Near East*, vol. 2, *A New Anthology of Texts and Pictures*. Princeton N.J.: Princeton University Press, 1975.

Przywara, Erich. *An Augustine Synthesis*. Glouster, Mass.: Peter Smith, 1970.

Purtill, Richard L. *C. S. Lewis' Case for the Christian Faith*. San Francisco: Harper & Row, 1981.

Quine, Willard Van Orman. "Two Dogmas of Empiricism." In *From a Logical Point of View*, 2nd ed. New York: Harper & Row, 1953.

Radhakrishnan, Sarvepail. *The Hindu View of Life*. London: Allen & Unwin, 1927.

Radhakrishnan, Sarvepail. *The Principal Upanishads*. London: Allen & Unwin, 1958.

Rahman, Fazlur, *Islam*. Chicago: University of Chicago Press, 1979.

Rahman, Fazlur, *Major Themes of the Qur'an*. Minneapolis: Bibliotheca Islamica 1980.

Ramm, Bernard. *A Christian Appeal to Reason*. Waco, Tex.: Word, 1977.

Ramm., Bernard. *The Christian View of Science and Scripture*. Grand Rapids: Eerdmans, 1954.

Ramm, Bernard. *The Pattern of Religious Authority*. Grand Rapids: Eerdmans, 1959.

Ramm, Bernard. *Protestant Biblical Interpretation: A Textbook of Hermeneutics for Conservative Protestants*. Boston: W. A. Wilde, 1950.

Ramm, Bernard. *Protestant Christian Evidences*. Chicago: Moody, 1953

Ramm, Bernard. *Varieties of Christian Apologetics*. Grand Rapids: Baker, 1973.

Ramsay, Sir William. *St. Paul the Traveller and the Roman Citizen*. New York: G. P. Putnam's Sons, 1896.

Ramsay, Sir William. *Was Christ Born at Bethlehem?* New York: Putnam, 1898. Reprint, 1960.

Ramsey, Ian T. *Religious Language: An Empirical Placing of Theological Phrases*. New York: Macmillan, 1957.

Rand, Ayn. *Atlas Shrugged*. New York: Dutton, 1992.

Rand, Ayn. *For the New Intellectual*. New York: New American Library, 1961.

Rand, Ayn. *The Virtue of Selfishness*. New York: New American Library, 1964.

Randi, James. *The Faith Healers*. With a foreword by Carl Sagan. Buffalo, N.Y.: Prometheus, 1987.

Randi, James. *Flim-Flam*. Buffalo, N.Y.: Prometheus, 1982.

Randi, James. "Nostradamus: The Prophet for all Seasons." *Skeptical Enquirer* (Fall 1982).

Ratzinger. Joseph. *Introduction to Christianity*. New York: Seabury, 1979.

Rauf, Muhammad Abdul. *Islam: Creed and Worship*. Washington, D.C.: The Islamic Center, 1974.

Regis, Louis Marie. *Epistemology*. New York: Macmillan, 1959.

Rehwinkel, Alfred. *The Flood*. St. Louis: Concordia, 1951.

Reid, Thomas. *Essay on the Active Powers of Man*. New York: Garland, 1977.

Reid, Thomas. *Essay on the Intellectual Powers of Man*. New York: Garland, 1971.

Reid, Thomas. *An Inquiry into the Human Mind: On the Principles of Common Sense*. Edited by Derek R. Brookes. University Park: Pennsylvania State University, 1997.

Reimarus, Hermann. *Fragments*. Edited by Charles H. Talbert. Philadelphia: Fortress, 1970.

Reisser, Paul C., Teri K. Reisser, and John Weldon *The Holistic Healers: a Christian Perspective on New-age Health Care*. Downers Grove, Ill. : InterVarsity, 1983.

Renan, Ernest. *The Life of Jesus*. New York: A. L. Burt, 1897.

"Revelation." *Anglican Theological Review* (October, 1980).

Rhodes, Ron. *Christ Before the Manger*. Grand Rapids: Baker, 1992.

Rice, John R. *Our God-Breathed Book—The Bible*. Murfreesboro, Tenn.: Sword of the Lord, 1969.

Rickaby, J. *Free Will and Four English Philosophers*. London: Burns, Oates, 1906.

Ridderbos, Herman N. *Paul and Jesus; Origin and General Character of Paul's Preaching of Christ*. Grand Rapids: Baker, 1958.

Rienecker, Fritz. *A Linguistic Key to the Greek New Testament*. Edited by Cleon L. Rogers Jr. Grand Rapids: Zondervan, 1980.

Rippin, Andrew, and Jan Knappert. eds. and trans. *Texual Sources for the Study of Islam*. Manchester: Manchester University Press, 1986.

Robbins, John W. *Cornelius Van Til: The Man and the Myth*. Jefferson, Md.: Trinity Foundation, 1986.

Robbins, John W., ed. *Gordon H. Clark: Personal Recollections*. Jefferson, Md.: Trinity Foundation, 1989.

Robert, Lyon. "Re-examination of Codex Ephraemi Rescriptus." *New Testament Studies* 5 (1959).

Robertson, A. T. *A Harmony of the Gospels for Students of the Life of Christ: Based on the Broadus Harmony in the Revised Version*. New York : Harper & Row, 1950.

Robertson, A. T. *An Introduction to the Textual Criticsim of the New Testament*. Nashville, Tenn.: Broadman, 1925.

Robertson, A. T. *Word Pictures in The New Testament*. 6 vols. Nashville, Tenn.: Broadman, 1930.

Robinson, G. L. *Where Did We Get Our Bible?* New York: Doubleday, Doran, 1928.

Robinson, James M., and Robert J. Miller, eds. *The Nag Hammadi Library in English.* San Francisco: Harper & Row, 1988.

Robinson, John A. T. *Honest to God.* Philadelphia: Westminster, 1963.

Robinson, John A. T. *The Human Face of God.* Philadelphia: Westminster, 1973.

Robinson, John A. T. *Redating the New Testament.* Philadelphia: Westminster, 1976.

Robinson, John Mansley. *An Introduction to Early Greek Philosophy.* Boston: Houghton Mifflin, 1968.

Ross, Hugh. *Creation and Time.* Colorado Springs, Colo.: NavPress, 1994.

Ross, Hugh. *The Creator and the Cosmos: How the Greatest Scientific Discoveries of the Century Reveal God.* Colorado Springs, Colo.: NavPress, 1993.

Ross, Hugh. *The Fingerprint of God: Recent Scientific Discoveries Reveal the Unmistakable Identity of the Creator.* Orange, Calif.: Promise, 1989.

Ross, Hugh. *Joshua's Long Day and Other Mysterious Events.* 120 min. Pasadena, Calif.: Reasons to Believe, n.d. Videocassette.

Ross, W. D. *Aristotle's Categories and De Interpretatione.* Translated with Notes. Oxford, 1961.

Ross, W. D. *Prior and Posterior Analytics.* Oxford, 1949.

Rurak, James. "Butler's Analogy: A Still Interesting Synthesis of Reason and Revelation." *Anglican Theological Review* 62 (1980): 365–81.

Russell, Bertrand. *The Autobiography of Bertrand Russell.* Boston: Little, Brown, 1968.

Russell, Bertrand. *The Basic Writings of Bertrand Russell.* Edited by Robert E. Egner and Lester E. Denonn. New York: Simon & Schuster, 1961.

Russell, Bertrand. "Can Religion Cure Our Troubles." In *Why I Am Not a Christian,* ed. Paul Edwards. New York: Simon & Schuster, 1957.

Russell, Bertrand. *A Critical Exposition of the Philosophy of Leibniz.* 2nd ed. London: Routledge, 1992.

Russell, Bertrand. "The Essence of Religion." In *The Basic Writings of Bertrand Russell,* ed. Robert E. Egner and Lester E. Denonn. New York: Simon & Schuster, 1961.

Russell, Bertrand. "The Existence of God Debate" with Father Copleston. *The Existence of God,* ed. John Hick. New York: Macmillan, 1964.

Russell, Bertrand. *A Free Man's Worship.* Portland, Maine: T. B. Mosher, 1923.

Russell, Bertrand. *Introduction to Mathematical Philosophy.* New York: Dover, 1919.

Russell, Bertrand. "On Induction." In *The Basic Writings of Bertrand Russell,* ed. Robert E. Egner and Lester E. Denonn. New York: Simon & Schuster, 1961.

Russell, Bertrand. *Religion and Science.* New York: Oxford University Press, 1961.

Russell, Bertrand. *What I Believe.* New York: Dutton, 1925.

Russell, Bertrand. "What is An Agnostic." In *The Basic Writings of Bertrand Russell,* ed. Robert E. Egner and Lester E. Denonn. New York: Simon & Schuster, 1961.

Russell, Bertrand. *Why I Am Not a Christian.* New York: Simon & Shuster, 1957.

Russell, C. Allyn. "J. Gresham Machen, Scholarly Fundamentalist." *Journal of Presbyterian History* 51 (1973): 40–66.

Russell, Edward S. *The Diversity of Animals: An Evolutionary Study.* Leiden: Brill, 1962.

Sachedina, Abdulaziz Abdulhussein. *Islamic Messianism: The Idea of Mahdi in Twelver Shiism.* Albany: State University of New York Press, 1981.

Sagan, Carl. *Broca's Brain.* New York: Random House, 1979.

Sagan, Carl. *The Cosmic Connection.* New York: Anchor, 1973.

Sagan, Carl. *Cosmos.* New York: Random House, 1980.

Sagan, Carl. *The Edge of Forever.* New York: Turner Home Entertainment, 1989.

Sagan, Carl. *UFO'S—A Scientific Debate.* Ithaca, N.Y.: Cornell University Press, 1972.

Sahas, Daniel J. "The Formation of Later Islamic Doctrines as a Response to Byzantine Polemics: The Miracles of Muhammad." *The Greek Orthodox Theological Review*27, nos. 2 & 3 (1982).

Salmon, George. *The Infallibility of the Church.* London: John Murray, 1914.

Sandage, Alan. "A Scientist Reflects on Religious Belief." *Truth.* Vol. 1. Dallas: Truth Incorporated, 1985.

Sanders, E. P. *The Tendencies of the Synoptic Tradition.* Cambridge: Cambridge University Press, 1969.

Sanders, J. Oswald. *How Lost Are the Heathen?* Chicago: Moody, 1988.

Sanders, John. *No Other Name: An Investigation into the Destiny of the Unevangelized.* Grand Rapids: Eerdmans, 1992.

Sartre, Jean-Paul. *Being and Nothingness.* Translated by Hazel Barner. New York: Philosophical Library, 1956.

Sartre, Jean-Paul. *Existentialism and Humanism.* Translated by Philip Mairet. London: Methuen, 1948.

Sartre, Jean Paul. *Nausea.* Norfolk, Conn: New Directions, 1953.

Sartre, Jean Paul. *No Exit and Three Other Plays.* New York: Vintage, 1955.

Sartre, Jean-Paul. *The Words.* Translated by B. Frechtman. New York: George Braziller, 1964.

Satin, Mark. *New Age Politics.* New York: Dell, 1979.

Savage, C. Wade. "The Paradox of the Stone." *Philosophical Review* 76 (1967): 74–79.

Sayers, Dorothy Leigh. "Towards a Christian Esthetic." In *The Whimsical Christian.* New York: Macmillan, 1978.

Schacht, Richard. *Making Sense of Nietzsche: Reflections Timely and Untimely.* Urbana: University of Illinois Press, 1995.

Schaeffer, Francis. *Back to Freedom and Dignity.* Downers Grove, Ill.: InterVarsity, 1972.

Schaeffer, Francis. *The God Who is There.* Downers Grove, Ill.: InterVarsity, 1973.

Schaeffer, Francis. *He Is There and He Is Not Silent.* Wheaton, Ill.: Tyndale House, 1972.

Schaeffer, Francis. *No Final Conflict.: The Bible Without Errror in All That It Affirms.* Downers Grove, Ill.: InterVarsity, 1975.

Schaeffer, Francis. *Whatever Happened to the Human Race?* Old Tappan, N.J.: Revell, 1979.

Schaff, Philip. *A Companion to the Greek Testament and the English Version.* 3rd ed. New York : Harper, 1883.

Schaff, Philip, ed. *The Creeds of Christendom.* 3 vols. 6th rev. ed. New York: Harper, 1919.

Schaff, Philip, ed. *Nicene and Post-Nicene Fathers of the Christian Church.* 14 vols. 1st series. 1886–94. Reprint. first series. Grand Rapids: Eerdmans, 1952.

Schep, J. A., *The Nature of the Resurrection Body*. Grand Rapids: Eerdmans, 1964.

Schilpp, Paul Arthur, and Lewis Edwin Hahn, eds.*The Philosophy of John Dewey.* LaSalle, Ill.: Open Court, 1989.

Schimmel, Annemarie. "The Prophet Muhammad as a Centre of Muslim Life and Thought." In *We Believe in One God,* ed. Annemarie Schimmel and Abdoldjavad Falaturi. New York: Seabury, 1979.

Schimmel, Annemarie, and Abdoldjavad Falaturi. *We Believe In One God.* New York: Seabury , 1979.

Schipper, Reinier. "Paul and the Computer." *Christianity Today,* 4 December 1964.

Scheiermacher, Friedrich. *The Christian Faith.* Philadelphia: Fortress, 1976.

Schleiermacher, Friedrich. *On Religion.* New York: Cambridge University Press, 1996.

Schmidt, W. *High Gods in North America.* Oxford: Clarendon, 1933.

Schmidt, W. *The Origin and Growth of Religion: Facts and Theories.* Reprint, New York: Cooper Square, 1972.

Schmidt, W. *Private Revelation.* St. Louis: B. Herder, 1939.

Scholem, Gershom. *Sabbatai Sevi: The Mystical Messiah.* Princeton, N.J.: Princeton University Press, 1973.

Schonfield, Hugh J. *The Passover Plot: New Light on the History of Jesus.* New York: Bantam, 1967.

Schopenhauer, Arthur. *The Basis of Morality.* 2nd ed. London: G. Allen & Unwin, 1915.

Schopenhauer, Arthur. *On the Fourfold Root of the Principle of Sufficient Reason.* Translated by E. F. J. Payne. La Salle, Ill.: Open Court, 1974.

Schopenhauer, Arthur. *On the Will in Nature.* New York: Berg, 1992.

Schopenhauer, Arthur. *The World as Will and Representation.* Glouster, Mass.: Peter Smith, 1980.

Schroeder, Henry J., ed. *Canons of the Council of Trent. Canon 30, Session t, 1547.* Rockford, Ill.: Tan, 1978.

Scorgie, Glen G. *A Call for Continuity: The Theological Contribution of James Orr.* Macon, Ga.: Mercer University Press, 1988.

Scorgie, Glen G. "Orr, James." In *New Dictionary of Theology,* ed. Sinclair B. Ferguson and David F. Wright. Downers Grove, Ill.: InterVarsity, 1988.

Scotus, John Duns. *Philosphical Writings*. Translated with an introduction by Allan Wolter. Indianapolis: Bobbs-Merrill, 1962.

Scrivener, F. H. A. *Plain Introduction to the Criticism of the New Testament.* 2 vols. 4th ed. Edited by Edward Miller. London: Bell, 1894.

Sell, Alan P. F. *Defending and Declaring the Faith: Some Scottish Examples, 1860–1920.* Colorado Springs: Helmers & Howard, 1987.

Shanks, Hershel, James Vanderkam, and P. K. Carter Jr. *The Dead Sea Scrolls after Forty Years.* Washington, D.C.: Biblical Archaeology Society, 1992.

Sharot, Stephen. *Messianism, Mysticism and Magic: A Sociological Analysis of Jewish Religious Movements.* Chapel Hill: University of North Carolina Press, 1982.

Shedd, W. G. T. *The Doctrine of Endless Punishment.* New York: Scribner, 1886.

Shedd, W. G. T. *Dogmatic Theology.* Vol 1. New York: Charles Scribner & Sons, 1868–94.

Sherwin-White, A. N. *Roman Society and Roman Law in the New Testament.* Oxford: Clarendon, 1963.

Shorrosh, Anis A. *Islam Revealed: A Christian Arab's View of Islam.* Nashville: Thomas Nelson, 1988.

Short, Robert. *The Gospel from Outer Space*. San Francisco: Harper & Row, 1983.

Shutt, R. J. H. *Studies in Josephus.* London: S.P.C.K., 1961.

Sire, James W. *The Universe Next Door*. Downers Grove, Ill.: InterVarsity, 1988.

Skinner, B. F. *About Behaviorism*. New York: Alfred A. Knopf, 1974.

Skinner, B. F. *Beyond Freedom and Dignity.* New York: Bantam, 1971.

Skinner, B. F. "The Problem of Consciousness—A Debate." *Philosophy and Phenomenological Research* 27, no. 3 (1967).

Skinner, B. F. *Walden Two*. New York: Macmillan, 1976.

Slomp, J. "The Gospel in Dispute." *Islamo Christiana* (journal). Rome: Pontificio Instituto de Saudi Arabia, 1978.

Slotki, Israel W, ed. *The Babylonian Talmud.* Translated by S. Daiches. Vol. 3. Rebecca Bennett Publications, 1959.

Smart, Ninian. *Philosophers and Religious Truth*. London: SCM, 1964.

Smith, Chuck. *Charisma vs. Charismania.* Eugene, Ore.: Harvest House, 1983.

Smith, George H. *Atheism: The Case Against God.* Los Angeles: Nash, 1974.

Smith, H. E. *The Literary Criticism of Pierre Bayle.* Albany, N.Y.: Brandow, 1912.

Smith, Huston. *The Religions of Man*. New York: Harper & Row, 1965.

Smith, Whitney. *The Flag Book of the United States.* New York: William Morrow, 1970.

Smith, Wilbur M. *Before I Forget.* Chicago: Moody, 1971.

Smith, Wilbur M. "Scientists and the Resurrection." *Christianity Today,,* 15 April 1957.

Smith, Wilbur M. *The Supernaturalness of Christ.* Boston: W.A. Wilde, 1944.

Smith, Wilbur M. *Therefore Stand: a Plea for a Vigorous Apologetic in the Present Crisis of Evangelical Christianity.* Boston: W. A. Wilde, 1945.

Snyder, John. *Reincarnation vs. Resurrection.* Chicago: Moody, 1984.

Sorley, W. R. *Moral Values and the Idea of God.* 3rd ed. Cambridge: Cambridge University Press, 1919.

Soulen, Richard N. *Handbook of Biblical Criticism.* 2nd ed. Atlanta: John Knox, 1981.

Souter, Alexander. *The Text and Canon of the New Testament.* London: Duckworth, 1913. Reprint. Edited by C. S. C. Williams. Naperville, Ill.: Allenson, 1954.

Sox, David. *The Gospel of Barnabas.* London: George Allen & Unwin, 1984.

Spencer, Harold. *Islam and the Gospel of God: A Comparison of the Central Doctrines of Christianity and Islam, Prepared for the Use of Christian Workers among Muslims.* Delhi : I.S.P.C.K., 1956.

Spier, J. M. *An Introduction to Christian Philosophy.* 2nd ed. Nutley, N.J.: Craig, 1973.

Spinoza, Benedict. *Ethics.* Translated by A. Boyle. New York: Dutton, 1910.

Spinoza, Benedict De. *A Theologico-Political Treatise and a Political Treatise.* Translated with introduction by R. H. M. Elwes. New York: Dover, 1951.

Sproul, R. C. "The Internal Testimony of the Holy Spirit." In *Inerrancy,* ed. N. L. Geisler. Grand Rapids: Zondervan, 1979.

Sproul, R. C. *Not a Chance: The Myth of Chance in Modern Science and Cosmology.* Grand Rapids: Baker, 1994.

Sproul, R. C. *Reason to Believe: A Response to Common Objections to Christianity.* Grand Rapids: Zondervan, 1978.

Stanley, Jake. *Miracles and Physics.* Front Royal, Va.: Christendom, 1989.

Stanton, Graham. *Gospel Truth?* Valley Forge, Pa.: Trinity, 1995.

Stauffer, Ethelbert. *Jesus and His Story.* London: SCM, 1960.

Stenger, Victor J. "The Face of Chaos" *Free Inquiry* (Winter, 1992–93).

Stephen, Leslie. *An Agnostic's Apology.* New York: G. P. Putnam's Sons, 1893.

Stevenson, Ian. "The Explanatory Value of the Idea of Reincarnation." *The Journal of Nervous and Mental Disease* (September, 1977).

Stevenson, J. *Studies in Eusebius.* Cambridge: Cambridge University Press, 1929.

Stevenson, Kenneth E., and Gary Habermas. *Verdict on the Shroud.* Ann Arbor, Mich.: Servant, 1981.

Stevenson, Leslie. *Seven Theories of Human Nature.* Oxford: Clarendon, 1974.

Stewart, H. F. *Pascal's Apology for Religion.* Cambridge: Cambridge University Press, 1942.

Stockhammer, Morris. ed. *Thomas Aquinas Dictionary.* London: Vision, 1965.

Stokes, Walter E. "A Whiteheadian Reflection on God's Relation to the World." In *Process Theology: Basic Writings,* ed. Ewert H. Cousins, 137–52. New York: Newman, 1971.

Stonehouse, Ned B. *J. Gresham Machen: A Biographical Memoir.* Grand Rapids: Eerdmans, 1954.

Stoner, Peter, *Science Speaks.* Wheaton, Ill.: Van Kampen, 1952.

Strauss, David. *The Life of Jesus.* New York: C. Blanchard, 1900.

Strauss, David Friedrich. *The Life of Jesus Critically Examined.* Lives of Jesus Series. Translated and edited by George Eliot. With an introduction by Peter C. Hodgson. London: SCM , 1973.

Strauss, David Friedrich. *A New Life of Jesus.* 2nd ed. 2 vols. London: Williams & Norgate, 1879.

Streeter, B. H. "Codices 157, 1071 and the Caesarean Text." *Quantulacumque,* Studies Presented to Kirsopp Lake 1937.

Streeter, B. H. *The Four Gospels: A Study of Origins.* London: Macmillan, 1936.

Strimple, B. *Modern Search for the Real Jesus.* Phillipsburg: Presbyterian & Reformed, 1995.

Strong, A. H. *Systematic Theology.* 3 vols. in one. Revell, 1907.

Stroud, William. *The Physical Cause of the Death of Christ and its Relation to the Principles and Practice of Christianity.* New York: Appleton, 1871.

Stroud, William. *Treatise on the Physical Cause of the Death of Christ and Its Relation to the Principles and Practice of Christianity.* London: Hamilton, Adams, 1847.

Sullivan, J. W. N. *The Limitations of Science.* New York: New American Library, 933.

Sullivan, James B. *An Examination of First Principles in Thought and Being in the Light of Aristotle and Aquinas.* Washington D.C.: The Catholic University of America Press, 1939.

Suzuki, D. T. *An Introduction to Zen Buddhism.* New York: Grove , 1964.

Swanson, Guy E. *The Birth of the Gods.* Ann Arbor: University of Michigan Press, 1968.

Sweitzer, Albert. *Quest of the Historical Jesus.* New York: Macmillan, 1968.

Swinburne, Richard. *The Christian God.* London: Oxford University Press, 1994.

Swinburne, Richard. *The Coherence of Theism.* London: Oxford University Press, 1977.

Swinburne, Richard. *Miracles.* New York: Macmillan, 1989.

Swinburne, Richard, ed. *The Concept of Miracle.* London: Macmillan, 1989.

Takle, John. "Islam and Christianity." In *Studies in Islamic Law, Religion and Society,* ed. H. S. Bhatia. New Delhi, India: Deep & Deep, 1989.

Tanner, Gerald and Sandra. *The Changing World of Mormonism.* Chicago: Moody, 1981.

Tari, Mel. *Like a Mighty Wind.* Carol Stream, Ill.: Creation House, 1971.

Taylor, A. E. *Plato: The Man and His Works.* Freeport, N.Y.: Books for Libraries, 1971.

Taylor, Richard. "Metaphysics and God." In *The Cosmological Arguments,* ed. Donald Burrill. Garden City, N.Y.: Anchor, 1967.

Tennant, F. R. *Miracle and Its Philosophical Presuppositions.* Cambridge: Cambridge University Press, 1925.

Tennant. F. R. *Philosophical Theology.* 2 vols. Cambridge, 1928–30.

Teske, R. J. "Plato's Later Dialectic." *The Modern Schoolman* 38 (1961).

Thackeray, H. St. J. *Josephus: The Man and the Historian.* New York: Jewish Institute of Religion, 1929.

Thaxton, Charles B., Walter L. Bradley, and Roger Olsen. *The Mystery of Life's Origin: Reassessing Current Theories.* New York: Philosophical Library, 1984.

Thiele, E. R. *The Mysterious Numbers of the Hebrew Kings.* Rev. ed. Grand Rapids: Eerdmans, 1965.

Thomas, Heywood J. *Philosophy of Religion in Kierkegaard's Writings.* Lewiston, N.Y.: Edwin Mellen, 1994.

Thomas, Robert L. "The Hermeneutics of Evangelical Redaction." *Journal of the Evangelical Theological Society* 29, no. 4 (1986): 447–59.

Thomas, Robert L. "An Investigation of the Agreements Between Matthew and Luke Against Mark." *Journal of the Evangelical Theological Society* 19 (1976).

Thomas, Robert L., and Stanley N. Gundry. "Form Criticism." In *A Harmony of the Gospels with Explanations and Essays: Using the Text of the New American Standard Bible,* ed. Robert L. Thomas and Stanley N. Gundry. Chicago: Moody, 1978; San Francisco: Harper & Row, 1985.

Thomas, Robert L., and Stanley N. Gundry. "Source Criticism." In *A Harmony of the Gospels with Explanations and Essays: Using the Text of the New American Standard Bible,* ed. Robert L. Thomas and Stanley N. Gundry. Chicago: Moody, 1978; San Francisco: Harper & Row, 1985.

Tindal, Matthew. *Christianity as Old as the Creation: or, the Gospel, a Republication of the Religion of Nature.* New York & London: Garland , 1978; first published, 1730.

Tisdall, W. St. Clair. *A Manual of the Leading Muhammadan Objections to Christianity.* London: S.P.C.K., 1904.

Tisdall, W. St. Clair. *The Source of Islam.* Edinburgh: T & T. Clark, n.d.

Tolkein, J. R. R., *The Lord of the Rings.* Boston: Houghton Mifflin, 1979.

Toon, Peter. *The Development of Doctrine in the Church.* Grand Rapids: Eerdmans, 1979.

Torrey, Norman. "Voltaire, Francois-Marie Arouet De." In *Encyclopedia of Philosophy* ed. Paul Edwards. (see).

Torrey, Norman. *Voltaire and the English Deists.* Oxford: Marston, 1963.

Torrey, Norman. "Voltaire, Francois-Marie Arouet de." In *Encyclopedia of Philosophy,* ed. Paul Edwards. New York: Macmillan and The Free Press, 1967.

Tov, Emanuel. "The Literary History of the Book of Jeremiah in the Light of its Textual History." In *Empirical Models for Biblical Criticism,* ed. J. Tigay. Philadelphia: University of Pennsylvania Press, 1985.

Townsend, Harvey G., ed. *Jonathan Edwards from His Private Notebooks.* Eugene: University of Oregon, 1955.

Travis, Stephen. *Christian Hope and the Future.* Downers Grove, Ill.: InterVarsity, 1980.

Trever, J. C. "The Discovery of the Scrolls." *Biblical Archaeologist* 11 (1948).

Troeltsch, Ernst. "Historiography" In *Encyclopedia of Religion and Ethics,* ed. James Hastings et al. 13 vols. New York: Scribner's, 1908–26.

Trueblood, David Elton. *Philosophy of Religion.* New York: Harper & Brothers, 1957.

Tuck, Robert. ed. *A Handbook of Biblical Difficulties.* New York: Revell, 1914.

Tuckett, C. M. *Nag Hammadi and the Gospel Tradition.* London: T. & T. Clark, 1986.

Tertullian. *Against Marcion.* In *The Ante-Nicene Fathers,* ed. Alexander Roberts and James Donaldson. Vol. 3. Grand Rapids: Eerdmans, 1989.

Tertullian. *Against the Valentinians.* In *The Ante-Nicene Fathers.*

Tertullian. *Five Books Against Marcion.* In *The Ante-Nicene Fathers.*

Tertullian. *On the Flesh of Christ.* In *The Ante-Nicene Fathers.*

Tertullian. *On the Resurrection of the Flesh.* London: S.P.C.K., 1960.

Tzaferis, Vasilius. "Jewish Tombs at and Near Giv'at ha-Mitvar." *Israel Exploration Journal* 20 (1970): 38–59.

Unger, Merrill. *Biblical Demonology.* Grand Rapids: Kregel, 1994.

Unger, Merrill. *Introductory Guide to the Old Testament.* 2nd ed. Grand Rapids: Zondervan, 1956.

Van Buren, Paul. *The Secular Meaning of the Gospel.* New York: Macmillan, 1963.

Van Til, Cornelius. *The Defense of the Faith.* Philadelphia: The Presbyterian & Reformed, 1955.

VanderKam, James. *The Dead Sea Scrolls Today.* Grand Rapids: Eerdmans, 1994.

Van Till, Howard J. *The Fourth Day: What the Bible and the Heavens Are Telling Us about the Creation.* Grand Rapids: Eerdmans, 1986.

Van Till, Howard. *Portraits of Creation.* Grand Rapids: Eerdmans, 1990.

Velikovsky, Immanuel. *Worlds in Collision.* Cutchogue, N.Y.: Buccaneer, 1950.

Vermes, Geza. *The Dead Sea Scrolls in English.* New York: Penguin, 1987.

Vitz, Paul. *Sigmund Freud's Christian Unconscious.* Grand Rapids: Eerdmans, 1993.

Voltaire, Francois-Marie. *Candide, Zadig, and Selected Stories.* New York: New American Library, 1961.

Voltaire, Francois-Marie. *Philosophical Dictionary.* 2 vols. Translated by Peter Gay. N.Y.: Basic, 1962.

Voltaire, Francois-Marie. *Philosophical Letters.* Translated by Ernest Dilworth. New York: Macmillan, 1961.

Voltaire, Francois-Marie. *Selected Letters of Voltaire,* ed. L. C. Syms. New York: New York University Press, 1973.

Voltaire, Francois-Marie. *Voltaire and Rousseau Against the Atheists.* New York: Wiley & Putnam, 1845.

Von Weizsacker, C. F. *The Relevance of Science.* New York: Harper & Row, 1964.

Vos, Howard H. "Albright, William Foxwell." In *Evangelical Dictionary of Theology.* Grand Rapids: Baker, 1984.

Waardenburg, Jacques "World Religions as Seen in the Light of Islam." In *Islam: Present Influence and Past Challenge,* ed. Alford T. Welch and Pierre Cachia. New York State: University of New York Press, 1979.

Waddy, Charis. *The Muslim Mind*. London and New York: Longman, 1976.

Wald, George. "The Origin of Life." In *Life: Origin and Evolution*. Reprinted from *Scientific American*, August, 1954.

Wallis-Hadrill, D. S. *Eusebius of Caesaria*. London: A. R. Mowbray, 1960.

Walls, Jerry L. *Hell: The Logic of Damnation*. Notre Dame, Ind.: University of Notre Dame Press, 1992.

Waltke, Bruce K., "Historical Grammatical Problems." In *Hermeneutics, Inerrancy and the Bible*, ed Earl D. Radmacher and Robert D. Preus. Grand Rapids: Zondervan, 1984.

Walton, F. E. *Development of the Logos-Doctrine in Greek and Hebrew Thought*. London: Simkin, Marshall, Hamilton, Kent, 1911.

Ward, James. *Naturalism and Agnosticism*. New York: Charles Scribner's Sons, 1903.

Ward, Maisie. *Gilbert Keith Chesterton*. New York: Sheed & Ward, 1943.

Ward, Maisie. *Return to Chesterton*. New York: Sheed & Ward, 1952.

Warfield, B. B. "On the Antiquity and the Unity of the Human Race." *The Princeton Theological Review* 1911.

Warfield, B. B. *Biblical and Theological Studies*. Edited by Samuel G. Craig. Philadelphia: Presbyterian & Reformed, 1968.

Warfield, B. B. *Calvin and Calvinism*. Grand Rapids: Baker, 1991.

Warfield, B. B. *Counterfeit Miracles*. London: Banner of Truth Trust, 1972.

Warfield, B. B. *The Inspiration and Authority of the Bible*. Philadelphia: Presbyterian & Reformed, 1948.

Warfield, B. B. *Limited Inspiration*. Reprint, Grand Rapids: Baker, 1947.

Warfield, B.B. *The Person and Work of Christ*. Grand Rapids: Baker, 1980.

Warfield, Benjamin. *Calvin and Calvinism*. Grand Rapids: Baker Book House, 1991.

Wassenar, Robert. "A Physician Looks at the Suffering of Christ." *Moody Monthly* 79, no. 7 (1979): 41–42.

Watt, W. Montgomery. *Islam and Christianity Today: A Contribution to Dialogue*. Routledge & Kegan Paul, 1983.

Watt, W. Montgomery. *Muhammad: Prophet and Statesman*. Reprint ed. London: Oxford University Press, 1967.

Watts, Alan W. *The Spirit of Zen*. New York: Grove, 1958.

Watts, Alan W. *The Way of Zen*. New York: Vintage, 1957.

Weaver, K. F. "The Mystery of the Shroud." *National Geographic*, June, 1980.

Webb, C. C. J. *Pascal's Philosophy of Religion*. New York: Kraus Reprint, 1929.

Webber, Robert. *Secular Humanism: Threat and Challenge*. Grand Rapids: Zondervan, 1982.

Weigel, Arnold D. "A Critique of Bertrand Russell's Religious Position." *Bulletin of the Evangelical Theological Society* 8, no. 4 (1965).

Weinberg, Steven. *Dreams of a Final Theory—The Search for the Fundamental Laws of Nature*. New York: Pantheon, 1992.

Weizsacker, C. F. *The Relevance of Science*. New York: Harper & Row, 1964.

Wellhausen, Julius. *Die Composition des Hexateuchs und der Historischen Bucher des Alten Testament*. Berlin: G. Reimer, 1889.

Wellhausen, Julius. "Israel." *Encyclopedia Britannica*, 9th ed. New York: H. G. Allen, 1875.

Wellhausen, Julius. *Prolegomena to the History of Ancient Israel*. Reprint edition. Goucester, Mass.: Peter Smith, 1973.

Wells, David. "Tradition: A Meeting Place for Catholic and Evangelical Theology?" *The Christian Scholar's Review* 5, no. 1 (1975).

Wells, David F. *No Place for Truth*. Grand Rapids: Eerdmans, 1993.

Wells, G. A. *Did Jesus Exist?* Buffalo, N.Y.: Prometheus, 1975.

Wells, G. A. *The Biblical Evidence for Jesus*. Buffalo, N.Y.: Prometheus, 1982.

Wenham, D., and C. Blomberg, eds. *Gospel Perspectives 6: The Miracles of Jesus*. Sheffield: JSOT, 1986.

Wenham, Gordon J. et al. "History and the Old Testament." In *History, Criticism and Faith*, ed. Colin Brown, 13–73. Downers Grove: InterVarsity, 1976.

Wenham, John William. *Christ and the Bible*. Downers Grove, Ill: InterVarsity, 1972.

Wenham, John William. *Easter Enigma*. Grand Rapids.: Academie, 1984.

Wenham, John William. "Gospel Origins." *Trinity Journal* 7 (1978).

Wenham, John William. "History and The Old Testament." *Bibliotheca Sacra* 124 (1967).

Wenham, John. *Redating Matthew, Mark and Luke: A Fresh Assault on the Synoptic Problem*. Downer's Grove, Ill.: InterVarsity, 1992.

Westcott, B. F. *The Gospel According to St John: The Authorized Version*. Reprint of 1882 ed. Grand Rapids: Eerdmans, 1954.

Whately, Richard. *Histroic Doubts Relative to Napoleon Bonaparte*. In *Famous Pamphlets*, ed. H. Morley. New York: Routledge, 1890.

Whitcomb, John. *Chart of Old Testament Kings and Propehts*. Rev. ed. Winona Lake, Ind.: Bible Charts, 1976.

Whitcomb, John. *The World that Perished*. Winona Lake, Ind.: BMH, 1978.

Whitcomb, John, and Henry Morris. *The Genesis Flood: The Biblical Record and Its Scientific Implications*. Philadelphia: Presbyterian & Reformed, 1961.

White, Hayden. "Feuerbach, Ludwig." In the *Encyclopedia of Philosophy*, ed. Paul Edwards. New York: Macmillan and The Free Press, 1967.

White, James R. *Answers to Catholic Claims*. Southbridge, Mass.: Crowne, 1990.

White, Mel. *Deceived*. Old Tappan, N.J.: Revell, 1979.

White, W., Jr. "O'Callahan's Identifications: Confirmation and Its Consequences" *The Westminster Journal* 35 (1972).

Whitehead, Alfred North. *Adventures of Ideas*. 1933. Reprint, New York: The Free Press, 1967.

Whitehead, Alfred North. *Modes of Thought*. New York: The Free Press, 1968.

Whitehead, Alfred North. *Process and Reality*. 1929. Reprint, New York: Harper Torchbooks, 1960.

Whitehead, Alfred North. *Religion in the Making*. 1926. Reprint. New York: Meridian, 1967.

Whitehead, Alfred North. *Science and the Modern World*. New York: Macmillian, 1967.

Whittaker, Edmund. *The Beginning and End of the World*. London: Oxford University Press, 1942.

Whittaker, Thomas. *Comte and Mill*. Bristol: Thoemmes, 1908.

Wieman, Henry N. *The Source of Human Good*. Chicago: University of Chicago Press, 1946.

Wild, Robert A. "The Shroud: Probably the Work of a 14th Century Artist or Forger." *Biblical Archaeology Review* (March/April, 1984).

Wilder-Smith, A. E. *Man's Origin, Man's Destiny*. Minneapolis: Bethany, 1968.

Wilhelmsen, Frederick D. *Man's Knowledge of Reality: An Introduction to Thomistic Epistemology*. Englewood Clifffs, N.J.: Prentice-Hall, 1956.

Wilkins, Michael J., and J. P. Moreland, eds. *Jesus Under Fire*. Grand Rapids: Zondervan, 1995.

Williams, John Alden. *Islam*. New York: George Braziller, 1962.

Wilson, Clifford A. *The Passover Plot Exposed*. San Diego, Calif.: Master, 1977.

Wilson, Clifford A. *Rocks, Relics and Biblical Reliability*. Grand Rapids: Zondervan, 1977.

Wilson, Robert Dick. "The Meaning of Almah in Isaiah 7:14." *Princeton Theological Review* 24 (1926).

Wilson, Robert Dick. *A Scientific Investigation of the Old Testament*. Chicago: Moody, 1959.

Wimber, John, and Kevin Springer. *Power Evangelism*. San Francisco: Harper San Francisco, 1992.

Wimber, John, and Kevin Springer. *Power Healing*. San Francisco: Harper San Francisco, 1991.

Wisdom, John. "Gods." In *Logic and Language*, ed. Antony Flew. Oxford: Blackwell, 1955.

Wiseman, D. J. *Chronicles of the Chaldean Kings in the British Museum*. British Museum, 1956.

Wiseman, Donald. *Creation Revealed in Six Days: The Evidence of Scripture Confirmed by Archaeology*. 3rd ed. London: Marshall, 1958.

Wittgenstein, Ludwig. *Philosophical Investigations*. New York: Macmillan, 1953.

Wittgenstein, Ludwig. *Tractatus Logico-Philosophicus*. Translated by D.F. Pears and B. F. McGuinness. London: Routledge & Kegan Paul, 1961.

Wolff, Richard. *The Final Destiny of Heathen*. Ridge Field Park, N.J.: Interdenominational Foreign Mission Association, 1961.

Wolff, Richard. *Is God Dead?* Wheaton, Ill.: Tyndale House, 1966.

Wolfson, H. A. "Maimonides on Negative Attributes." In *Louis Ginzberg: Jubilee Volume*, ed. A. Marx. New York: The New American Academy for Jewish Research, 1945.

Wolterstorff, Nicholas. *Divine Discourse*. New York: Cambridge University Press, 1995.

Wonderly, Daniel E. *God's Time-Records in Ancient Sediments*. Flint, Mich.: Crystal, 1977.

Woodberry, J. Dudley, ed. *Muslims and Christians on the Emmaus Road*. Monrovia: March, 1989.

Woodbridge, John D. *Biblical Authority: A Critique of the Roger/McKim Proposal*. Grand Rapids: Zondervan, 1982.

Woodmorappe, John. *Noah's Ark: A Feasibility Study*. Impact: March 1996.

Woods, Herbert G. *Why Mr. Bertrand Russell Is Not Christian: An Essay in Controversy*. London: Student Christian Movement, 1928.

Wright, G. E. ed. *The Bible and the Ancient Near East*. Garden City, N.Y.: Doubleday, 1961.

Wurthwein, Ernst. *The Text of the Old Testament: An Introduction to the Biblia Hebraica*. Translated by Erroll F. Rhodes. Grand Rapids: Eerdmans, 1979.

Yamani, Amed Zaki. "Foreword." In W. Watt, Montgomery. *Islam and Christianity Today: A Contribution to Dialogue*. Routledge & Kegan Paul, 1983.

Yamauchi, Edwin. "Easter—Myth, Hallucination, or History?" (2 parts) *Christianity Today* , 29 March 1974; 15 April 1974.

Yamauchi, Edwin. "Passover Plot or Easter Triumph." In *Christianity for the Tough-Minded*, ed. John W. Montgomery. Minneapolis: Bethany, 1973.

Yamauchi, Edwin. *Pre-Christian Gnosticism*. Grand Rapids: Eerdmans, 1973.

Yamauchi, Edwin. *The Stones and the Scriptures* Philadelphia: J. B. Lippincott, 1972.

Yockey, Herbert. "Self Organization, Origin of Life Scenarios and Information Theory." *The Journal of Theoretical Biology* 91 (1981).

Young, David A. *The Biblical Flood: a Case Study of the Church's Response to Extra Biblical Evidence*. Grand Rapids: Eerdmans, 1995.

Young, Davis. *Christianity and the Age of the Earth*. Thousand Oaks, Ca.: Artisan Sales, 1988.

Young, Edward J. "The Virgin Birth." *The Banner*, 15 April 1955.

Yusseff, M.A. *The Dead Sea Scrolls, The Gospel of Barnabas, and the New Testament*. Indianapolis: American Trust, 1985.

Zaleckas, Eva. "Letter to the Editor." *Time*, 4 June 4 1979.

Zeitlin, Solomon. *The Dead Sea Scrolls and Modern Scholarship*. Philadelphia: Dropsie College, 1956.

Zias, J., and E. Sekeles. "The Crucified Man from Giv'at Ha-Mivtar: A Reappraisal." *Israel Exploration Journal* 35 (1985): 22–27.

Zwemer, Samuel M. *The Moslem Doctrine of God*. American Tract Society,1905.

Article Index

Index of Scripture and Apocrypha

Genesis

Mark

Luke

Romans

2 Timothy

Titus

Hebrews

1 Peter